D0208217

DISCOVERING

LITERATURE

STORIES, POEMS, PLAYS

Third Edition

Hans P. Guth
Santa Clara University

Gabriele Rico
San Jose State University

Prentice
Hall

Upper Saddle River, New Jersey 07458

Library of Congress Cataloging-in-Publication Data

GUTH, HANS PAUL (date)
   Discovering literature : stories, poems, plays / Hans P. Guth, Gabriele Rico.—3rd ed.
     p. cm.
   Includes index.
   ISBN 0-13-048230-7
    1. English language—Rhetoric.   2. Literature—Collections.   3. College readers.   I. Rico,
Gabriele L.   II. Title.

PE1417 .G866 2002
808—dc21
                                                      2002021827

VP, Editor in Chief: Leah Jewell
Senior Acquisitions Editor: Carrie Brandon
Editorial Assistant: Jennifer Migueis
Production Assistant: Elizabeth Best
Copyeditor: Ann Lesser
Permissions Researcher: Mary Dalton-Hoffman
Prepress and Manufacturing Buyer: Sherry Lewis
Director of Marketing: Beth Mejia
Marketing Manager: Rachel Falk
Marketing Assistant: Christine Moodie
Image Resource Center Director: Melinda Reo
Image Permissions Coordinator: Valerie H. Gold
Rights and Permissions Manager: Zina Arabia
Interior Image Specialist: Beth Boyd-Brenzel
Image Researcher: Clare Maxwell
Cover and Insert Designer: Robert Farrar-Wagner
Cover Art: Costel Iarca
Interior Cover Line Art: Christopher Hawthorne

This book was set in 10.5/12 Garamond Light by Lithokraft II
and was printed and bound by Courier Companies, Inc.
Covers were printed by Phoenix Color Corp.

For permission to use copyrighted material, grateful
acknowlegment is made to the copyright holders
on pages 1976–1994, which are considered an extension
of this copyright page.

Printed in the United States of America
10 9 8 7 6 5 4 3 2

ISBN 0-13-048230-7

Pearson Education LTD., London
Pearson Education Australia PTY, Limited, Sydney
Pearson Education Singapore, Pte. Ltd
Pearson Education North Asia Ltd, Hong Kong
Pearson Education Canada, Ltd., Toronto
Pearson Educación de Mexico, S.A. de C.V.
Pearson Education—Japan, Tokyo
Pearson Education Malaysia, Pte. Ltd
Pearson Education, Upper Saddle River, New Jersey

BRIEF CONTENTS

CONTENTS

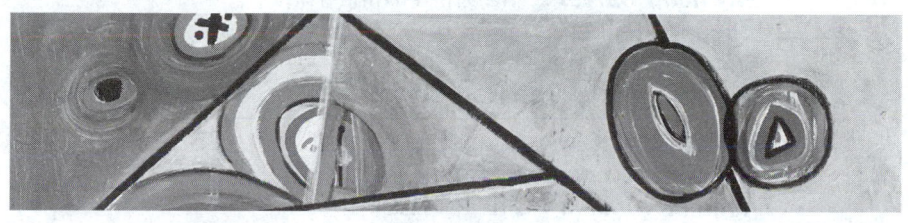

Fiction

9 A WRITER IN DEPTH   *Flannery O'Connor*   *352*

10 CRITICAL PERSPECTIVES
The Reader's Response   *398*

11 OTHER VOICES/OTHER VISIONS   *435*

Poetry

13 PATTERN   *The Whole Poem*   *650*

19 PERSONA   *Masks and Faces*   *847*

JUXTAPOSITIONS: IMAGE AND WORD

INSERT III

23 THREE POETS IN DEPTH

25 OTHER VOICES/OTHER VISIONS

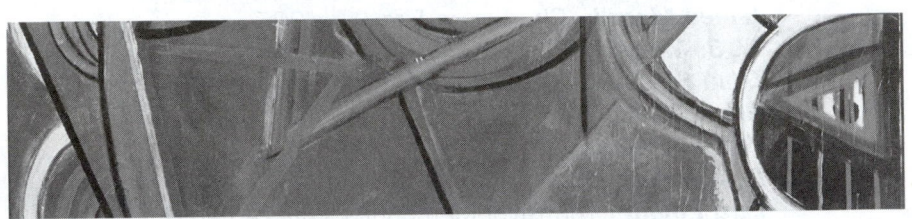

Drama

WRITING ABOUT LITERATURE
Writing Workshops

Note **boldface** for documented papers requiring library work, parenthetical documentation, and a list of Works Cited.

Fiction

Poetry

Drama

PREFACE
To the Instructor

Everything is new under the sun.
CZESLAW MILOSZ

Silence is the real crime against humanity.
NADYEZHDA MANDELSHTAM

In this new edition of *Discovering Literature*, we have aimed at building on the strengths of the earlier editions of the book. Our aim is to give students of literature a textbook for reading and writing that will be

✗ unexcelled in selections that work well in today's classrooms and help teachers turn reluctant readers into readers

✗ unexcelled in showing students the contemporary relevance of the classics, revitalizing our shared literary heritage for a new generation

✗ unexcelled in showing how the elements of literature serve its human meaning

✗ unexcelled in honoring the rich diversity of the literary experience, integrating multicultural authors and women authors in a new synthesis

✗ unexcelled in making literary terms and concepts meaningful for a new generation of students, with a wide range of background and motivation

✗ unexcelled in validating student writing with hands-on writing instructions and student models for writing about literature

✗ unexcelled in bringing the students' own creative imagination into play, with interactive activities encouraging students to become active participants

FEATURES OF THE NEW THIRD EDITION

New features give teachers an expanded range of options and alternative perspectives for reaching and motivating today's students:

✗ New full-color "Word and Image" sections

  pair paintings and poetry
  bring the students's visual imagination into play
  correlate imaginative literature and the sister arts

xxxiii

- New <<<Find-It-on-the-Web>> feature

  provides guidelines and caveats for Internet searches

  guides students to online background and criticism

- New Web link icon placed in the margin throughout the text alerts students to additional resources on the web site to support the instruction in the text 👁

  - New expanded "Promise of Literature" introduction

    contains interactive student responses to literature

    has new writing process overview

    includes new introduction to searching online sources

  - New "Festival of Classic Stories"

    presents classic stories by Edgar Allan Poe, Sarah Orne Jewett, Upton Sinclair, Ambrose Bierce, Joseph Conrad, Willa Cather, Edith Wharton, and D. H. Lawrence

  - New "Festival of Nature Poems"

    groups of poems renewing communion with nature thematically

  - New expanded writing workshops

    have a new "Questions for Peer Review" strand

    update guidelines for citation of online sources

Teaching literature is a rich and challenging undertaking. As teachers of literature we share a basic commitment to the students in our classes. Whatever our theoretical disagreements, we believe in the power of imaginative literature to open windows on the world. We have faith that literature will enrich the imagination, educate the emotions, and nourish the spiritual growth of our students.

Many teachers today share the following concerns:

Discovering the Literary Heritage   We aim at helping students discover the richness and diversity of their literary heritage. Classics speak beyond time and distance to succeeding generations. We try to give students a "way in" to the reading of Sophocles, Shakespeare, Emily Dickinson, John Steinbeck, John Donne, Gwendolyn Brooks, or Flannery O'Connor. Stressing the presence of the the past, this book integrates treatment of the classics with the best current writing. "Juxtapositions" frequently show the treatment of the same theme by authors of different times, cultures, or genders.

Close Reading and the Personal Response   The apparatus in this book encourages close attentive reading. What kind of window does the story or the poem open on the world? What question or concern comes into focus? What image or what symbol comes to play a central role? What kind of pattern takes shape as we follow the poem or the story to its conclusion? How does a central conflict take shape in a play, and how is it resolved? At the same time, we encourage students to see the personal connection that gives a widely read and loved story its resonance in people's lives. Some of the stories that are most popular with young readers are stories like Alice Munro's "Boys and Girls" or Bobbie Ann Mason's "Shiloh"—stories of initiation that explore turning points that untold readers have experienced in their own way in their lives.

Redefining the Canon   Each generation rediscovers the classics, discovers tomorrow's classics, and rethinks its list of canonical works. Among today's classics included in this edition are stories by Louise Erdrich, Toni Morrison, Tim O'Brien, Sandra Cisneros, Alice Walker, Gabriel García Márquez, and Yukio Mishima. New voices in poetry are represented by poems from Maurya Simon, Alberto Ríos, Rita Dove, Kathleen Lynch, Yusef Komunyakaa, Bethlyn Madison Webster, and Alison Hawthorne Deming. Strong new entries in the drama section include plays by Luis Valdez, David Henry Hwang, David Mamet, and Marsha Norman.

Gender and Ethnic Balance   Imaginative literature transcends boundaries of gender, ethnicity, race, or sexual orientation. Among the poets in this volume, women from earlier periods include Juana Inés de la Cruz, the Countess of Dia, Marie de Pisan, and Aphra Behn. Selections include fiction by Laurence Dunbar, Frank Chin, Guadalupe Valdéz, and new poems by Janice Mirikitani, Chitra Divakaruni, Maya Angelou, and Martín Espada. Women writing poetry with a strong personal dimensions include Sharon Olds, Anne Sexton, May Swenson, Sylvia Plath, and Denise Levertov.

The Creative Dimension   If students are to enter into the spirit of a poem or play, our teaching needs to honor the students' own imagination. *Discovering Literature* encourages students to cease being passive readers and instead to bring their own imagination into play. The "Creative Dimension" strand encourages students to discover their own creativity as they write a sequel or update a story whose ending left them dissatified, write a letter from the future from the later life of a character in a story or play, assume the identity of a character in a play to tell his or her first-person story, or write a lovingly-crafted reply to a traditional poem.

The Uses of Criticism   *Discovering Literature* examines the currents of contemporary literary theory for their relevance to the student reader's response to literature. "Perspectives" sections introduce the student to the range of critical approaches to fiction, poetry, and drama. Critical perspectives covered include reader response, author biography, literary history, the New Criticism (or formalism), myth criticism, psychoanalytic criticism, political (often neo-Marxist) criticism, structuralism and post-structuralism, deconstructionism, and feminist criticism. Critical revaluations make us see writers in a new light, as current critics bring new criteria and expectations to bear—for instance, making us see Ibsen's or Steinbeck's strong women with a new awareness. Resisting the proliferation of critical terminology, we introduce and clarify key critical terms to help illuminate the literature—rather than making imaginative literature serve the purposes of literary theory.

Validating Student Writing   Writing about literature makes students more intelligent and more responsive readers. *Discovering Literature* provides guidelines for writing and model papers with each chapter. Writing workshops repeatedly take students through major stages in the writing process, from preliminary exploration and note-taking through shaping and drafting to rethinking and revising in response to feedback from instructor and peers. A wealth of motivated, well-developed student writing provides model papers for class discussion of writing strategies and for peer review.

Inviting Shakespeare Editions   We offer students a more inviting, accessible, and motivating introduction to Shakespeare than competing books. We include two glossed (rather than footnoted) student editions—*Hamlet* and *A Midsummer Night's Dream*. Specially prepared for this book, the marginal glosses replace the thicket of conventional footnotes at the bottom of the page. Close at hand and available at a glance, the glosses illuminate difficult passages and provide the closest modern meaning in the context of a line.

Demystifying Research and Documentation   *Discovering Literature* initiates students into library research and sets up an ample choice of research paper projects on literary topics. The text provides guidelines and models of documented papers for each genre—short story, poetry, and drama. Pointed instructions demystify for students the current MLA documentation style, clarifying the rationale while giving an expanded range of sample entries.

A SUPPORT SYSTEM FOR *DISCOVERING LITERATURE*   www.prenhall.com/guth

A range of resources for teaching and testing is available to teachers of *Discovering Literature*. The *Discovering Literature* Web site will offer

- more juxtapositions of poetry and art with interactive questions

- multiple-choice and essay questions for the majority of selections in the text
- many author links for independent student research
- an interactive timeline
- literary walking tours of four cities: San Francisco, London, New York, and Paris
- a "Writers on Writing" section with video clips of authors talking about writing
- a "library" of additional readings from the public domain

The online Instructor's Resource area will offer teaching tips and discussion strategies with additional test banks.

A free audio CD for Literature will be available in 2003.

ACKNOWLEDGMENTS

We owe a large debt to our own teachers who guided and inspired us and introduced us to the world of imaginative literature. We cherish the friendship and good example of colleagues who believe in the potential of their students and know how to make the printed page come to life in the classroom. We have enjoyed joining in the dialogue with critics and theorists who have in recent decades made the teaching of literature a heady intellectual undertaking.

We are thankful to reviewers and to users of our book who shared with us their reactions, questions, and concerns. We want to thank Barbara A. Farrelly, University of Dayton, Dayton, OH; Shearle Furnish, West Texas A&M University, Canyon, TX; Myrna A. Goldberg, Montgomery College, Rockville, MD; Kelley L. Logan, Southwestern Oklahoma State University, Weatherford, OK; Troy D. Nordman, Butler County Community College, El Dorado, KS; Anita Obermeier, Arizona State University, Tempe, AZ; William Provost, University of Georgia, Athens, GA; and Valerie A. Reimers, Southwestern Oklahoma State University, Weatherford, OK.

As always, our largest debt of gratitude is to our students, whose intelligence, curiosity, and imagination have kept alive our faith in the power of literature and in the human enterprise. Of the many students who have allowed us to use or adapt their work, we want to thank especially Debbie Nishimura, Andrea Sandke, Olivia Nunez, Francia Stephens, Mike deAngelis, Dea Nelson, Kam Chieu, Greg Grewell, Joanna Wright, Merritt Ireland, Linda Spencer, Elizabeth Kerns, Conrad Mangrum, Joyce Halenar, Marilyn Johnson, Michael Guth, John Newman, Judith Gardner, Pamela Cox, Rita Frakas, Barbara Hill, Melody Brune, Paul Francois, Ruth Randall, Katheryn Crayton-Shay, Dorothy Overstreet, Bill Irwin, Ruth Veerkamp, Martha Kell, Kevin McCabe,

Thomas Perez-Jewell, Janelle Ciraulo, Irina Raicu, Joyce Sandoval, Catherine Hooper, Gail Bowman, Todd Marvin, Catherine Russell, and Simone Rico, Danny Smith, Juanita Wilson. Cynthis Ortiz, and Michael Helms.

Hans P. Guth

Gabriele L. Rico

INTRODUCTION

The Promise of Literature

The person who writes out of an inner need
is trying to order his corner of the universe;
very often the meaning of an experience or
an emotion becomes clear only in this way.

MAXINE KUMIN

Reading and writing aren't sacred yet people
have been killed as if they were.

ADRIENNE RICH

Why read literature? Imaginative literature invites you to share in human experience. It makes you more fully aware of how other human beings think and feel. Literature "holds the mirror" up to life, but it is more active than a mirror. Unlike a mirror, it selects what is important. It finds a pattern in what it sees; it finds a meaning. Readers who love imaginative literature know that it enriches their lives. It helps them understand what it means to be human.

Each poem is different. Each story or play creates its own world. Nevertheless, guidelines like the following should help make your reading more rewarding:

Becoming a Receptive Reader   The English novelist Virginia Woolf defined the ideal reader as the "author's fellow-worker and accomplice." She wanted us to be on the writer's side—trying to respond to whatever the author was trying to say. We shut ourselves off from what literature has to offer if we fend off what is different or new. If we stop listening to characters we dislike, we may miss the chance to discover that in some ways they are like us or like people we care about. A receptive reader is ready to try out new visions, new ways of looking at life.

Using Your Imagination   Poets say that it takes two poets to make a poem. First, the poet-author writes the poem. Then the poet-reader recreates the poem in the theater of the mind, seeing its sights with the mind's eye. To help a poem come to life, you have to develop your gift for vivid imagining. Let a story or poem create for you its own world of shapes, colors, textures, or sounds. Let it call up the sights, sounds, and smells of an apple market in Michigan. Imagine yourself watching a father building a fire to fight the bitter morning cold on a winter Sunday.

Bringing Your Feelings into Play   Literature invites you to see, and to think about what you see, but it also invites you to feel. It activates the empathy, or imaginative sympathy, that makes you share in the range of human emotions. Responsive readers do not merely register sights and sounds and events, like a camcorder. They share in some way in the emotions an event triggers. They get into the spirit of a poem or a story, reliving in some way the tensions or anxieties a situation brings into play. Like a good audience in the theater, they gasp, sigh, look grave, sob, or burst into laughter as the script prompts.

Crossing Boundaries   Literature crosses the borders. The Greek playwright Sophocles wrote his *Antigone* 2,500 years ago. In the play, a young woman has to choose between what the law commands and what her own conscience tells her to do. (You might say this is an old familiar story.) In Yukio Mishima's "Swaddling Clothes," a story set in modern Japan, the wife cares about a baby born into poverty, with no family or hope of a decent education. Her callous husband jokes about the mother and the child with his friends. If we subtract from the story the Japanese setting—with its Imperial Palace and cherry blossoms—the basic contrast could be played out in Glendale, California, or Buffalo, New York. Some people there, as in Tokyo, feel a personal responsibility toward children born into poverty, and others don't.

Reading the Language of Literature   The language of poetry is not the language of business or the language of science. Poets and short-story writers and playwrights have their own ways of reaching their audience. As you become a more expert reader, you respond to the way the language, the form, and the patterns of imaginative literature convey meaning. You read the clues to character, to plot, and to meanings only suggested or implied. You see how a storyteller's point of view opens a window upon the world. You respond to how the poet's image-making takes you beyond pale general ideas. You see how a conflict between worthy opponents organizes true drama.

Finding the Personal Connection   Readers go back to literature that has something to say to them personally. A poem or a story has a strong hold on them when it speaks to something in their own experience or personality. Many readers, for instance, are fascinated by stories about growing up, about being initiated into the adult world. When they read a story like Alice Munro's "Boys and Girls," they identify at some level with a character caught between conflicting role models or rival influences—whether father or mother, school as against church, or traditional gender roles versus the individual's true potential. Many young people reach a stage where they have to make choices, chart their own course. Many at some point try to break free—trying to be themselves rather than what the family, religion, the team, or the gang wants them to be.

Literature and Creativity   Creativity is everyone's birthright. There is a poet buried in every one of us. (How else could people respond to song and poem and story?) You will often make a story, poem, or play truly your own if you try an imaginative or creative response. You may choose to re-create in your own way a key image in a poem, following the train of associations it sets in motion. Or you may want to re-create a haunting overall impression that a story imprinted on your mind. You are likely to get more fully into the spirit of a play if you look at its world through the eyes of a character—perhaps starting an imaginary monologue with "I, Antigone, . . ." or "I, Hamlet, . . ." or "I, Ophelia, . . ." You may want to join a group in a mini-production or adaptation of a scene from a play.

Writing about Literature   When you write about literature, you write to share your impressions with others—but you write first of all to find out what *you* think and feel as you read. You write to *learn* as much as to enlighten others. When you keep a reading log or journal, you have a chance to record revealing details, striking quotations, first impressions, tentative conclusions, or personal reactions. When you prepare for a formal paper, you reread, you take notes, you reconsider. You sort out and organize your responses. Just as people who read well become better writers, people who write about what they read become better readers.

Don't be discouraged when a challenging short story or poem seems baffling at first reading. Think about it. Come back to it again. Listen to what others have to say about it. One definition of a classic is that it has rich meanings that unfold on second or third reading. Remember that the selections you read in this book are here because they have given pleasure to readers before you—stimulating their imagination, making them think and feel, and giving them joy.

INTERACTING WITH LITERATURE

Writers have always known that what they create is not entered on a blank page in a reader's or spectator's mind. They know that who you are and what your previous experience with literature has been will shape or color your responses. Your encounter with literature and art is a two-way interaction: You don't experience a poem or a play until you re-create it in the theater of the mind.

What do you bring to your reading of fiction, poems, and plays? Look back over your previous encounters with imaginative literature. Choose one poem, short story or novel, play, or live theatrical performance that made a special impression on you. Why do you remember it? What do you remember? Or write about a creative effort of your own. Write about a poem or story you wrote, or tell your readers about a performance you helped script or stage.

Each of the following sample student responses shows something about the power, the outreach, or the human meaning of imaginative literature.

The Language of the Emotions   We read the poets' words, but the poets read our minds. They know our thoughts and feelings, sometimes better than we do. They have a language of the emotions. A student wrote about Robert Frost's "Stopping by Woods on a Snowy Evening," one of the most universally known and loved American poems. On the way home on a winter evening, the speaker stops to take in the beckoning calm and peace of the snowed-in dark woods. There is a powerful temptation to rest here and not go on to the tasks and obligations of the speaker's life. Untold readers have recognized the feeling: The stresses and the frustrations of modern life make us long for a way to find peace.

Robert Frost became the best-known American poet of modern times, late in his career packing auditoriums with student audiences and reading a poem at a presidential inauguration. His "Stopping by Woods on a Snowy Evening" shows us a traveler passing by woods and a frozen lake "the darkest evening of the year." He seems to be on an ordinary errand in a familiar setting. He says "Whose woods these are I think I know." However, as he pauses to take notice of the "frozen lake," "the easy wind" and "downy snowflake," he reveals to us the thoughts and feelings running through his mind. The traveler seems to be exhausted from his journey as he points out his desire to rest and "sleep." The conditions of the environment he is in—deep and dark woods, easy wind, and the lazy descent of the snow—make it hard for him to resist his desire to "sleep." The horse, more practical or commonsensical than its master, must think it odd to "stop without a farmhouse near." The only reason that keeps the traveler continuing on his journey is to keep the promises he has made.

The poem is symbolically referring to an individual traveling through the journey of life. The individual has been burdened by responsibilities and promises for a significant length of time. The world has finally eased up on him a bit with the "easy wind" and "downy flake" and provided him with a little comfort. In the moment of peace and comfort, a thought runs through his head about falling into the eternal sleep. For some of us, the burden is heavy and the journey long, but like all of us, the traveler has people who love him and people who depend on him. That alone is all the reason he needs in the world to keep going the extra mile in spite of his fatigue. He says he has "miles to go before I sleep" twice at the end of the poem to reassure himself that he cannot just give up. He has to keep going.

The Definition of a Classic   A classic reaches across distances in time and place. A young woman challenging the state in an ancient Greek play can speak to us across a gulf of 2,500 years and have the audience understand and share her defiance. William Blake was a little-known poet and engraver in eighteenth-century England in a society of status and privilege that many American immigrants had left behind. However, his poem "Tyger, Tyger" may be the best-known and most widely recited poem in the English-speaking world, asking questions that have disturbed many deeply religious people. Why did God, who created the lamb as a symbol of meekness and innocence, also create the fiery tiger? Why is the tiger, "burning bright / In the forests of the night," overwhelmingly powerful and beautiful?

There are few people who have not heard the opening lines of William Blake's poem—"Tyger, Tyger / burning bright." Today when we try to preserve nature's creatures, we may think of whales, dolphins, or spotted owls who are not threatening to us. However, the tiger is a ferocious frightening man-killing animal, and yet it is strangely beautiful at the same time. Blake wrote at a time when Romantic nature poets were beginning to tell people to escape from the grime and noise of cities to find peace and harmony in the unspoiled natural world. Blake reminds us that the tiger is also one of God's creatures. If we want to commune with the vital powers of nature, we cannot just limit ourselves to what is mild and pleasant. We cannot filter out what is powerful and threatening and destructive.

The Relevance of Literature   George Orwell was one of the great masters of political satire of the twentieth century. In some of the most widely read books of our time, he used ridicule as a powerful tool against the callousness, hypocrisy, and disloyalty of those usurping power in the name of the people. In *Animal Farm,* a piggish leadership, headed by Comrade Napoleon and kept in power by bleating sheep, hogs all privilege. It suppresses all dissent and delivers faithful followers to the slaughter. The disillusionment as the utopia of a new just society and a new dawn for humanity turned into the nightmare of twentieth-century totalitarianism was a traumatic experience shaping the outlook of a generation.

When I checked a list of the "100 Best Books of All-Time," I found that I had never read George Orwell's *Animal Farm,* which combines simplicity with a powerful message. Using animals as people was an ingenious idea because many traditional stories have talking animals and I see people everyday talking to their pets as if they were able to talk back. Most of the animals in *Animal Farm* can read, but the pigs in power are the ones who write the rules all must abide by and lead the group because of their intelligence. The animals in *Animal Farm* rebel against exploitation by humans and form a coalition against the farmer whom they live under. They eventually overrun and operate the farm. They organize rallies to celebrate the triumph of the revolution, and the head pig becomes worshiped as Comrade Napoleon.

Orwell was an English socialist who became a leading critic of the Soviet system. He shows how the new leadership usurped and abused power. The oppressed and persecuted turn into the new oppressors. In the end, the pigs are running the farm as if the human owner had never left. There are smaller rations of food, longer working hours, and less favorable conditions for the other animals of *Animal Farm.*

Opposition is brutally suppressed. Greed and power are a part of nature—be it human or animal—and the main vision can easily be lost. In the end, the pigs enter into an alliance with neighboring humans. During the last scene in the book, a poker game brings together both humans and pigs—the leaders of their respective farms. One of the animals looking in through the window can no longer tell the difference between pig and man.

The Personal Connection   Many readers look in the mirror of imaginative literature and see their own face. They see a reflection of some vital part of their own experience. Someone has lived through and thought through what they have lived, and they may come away from the encounter with a new understanding of who and what they are. This does not mean that for a reader to be personally moved by a story by an Irish or Jewish writer that reader has to be Irish or have close ties with the Jewish tradition.

The Bluest Eye by Toni Morrison is one of my favorite American novels. The reader is able to see the characters as more than just victims of circumstance in the violent and racist world they occupy. The characters possess cultural wisdom and values that aid them in their daily survival. The specific things in African American culture that were used by the characters in their survival and healing include music, singing the blues, "griot" tales (storytelling), family bonds, the extended family or "village" that helps raise the children, and strong religious beliefs.

This novel is a deeply personal one for me. I have feelings and experiences in common with the central character of Pecola McTeer. As a child I wanted to be an idealized pretty, little white girl so that people would accept me and think that I was smart, instead of a "dumb Mexican" who didn't really belong here. To pretend that I was an ideal white girl, I cut long cloth strips from retired white bedsheets, fashioned them into braids, and wore them like a wig reminiscent of Rapunzel's beautiful, long locks. It occurs to me just now that Rapunzel's hair was used as a method of escape to freedom from the tower that imprisoned her. Just as I felt trapped in my family's home, defined by our poverty, and cursed with so much violence, so did Pecola feel trapped by her environment, her skin and eye color. Pecola believed that if her eyes turned blue, she would finally be loved.

Literature and Popular Culture   American popular culture—music, film, musicals—has shaped much of the youth culture around the world. The best in popular culture is not an opposite of traditional "high culture" but part of a continuum with it. Working as an actor and scriptwriter, Shakespeare helped fill a large popular theater several times a week. (He did admonish comic characters in his plays not to ad-lib crude popular humor to cater to customers with cheap tickets.)

This past July, I went with family and friends to see the musical *Rent*. I had listened to all of the songs over the computer, to see what the show was all about and to see if I had any interest in it. This musical is based in New York City and focuses on a group of struggling young adults who can't afford—rent. The characters represent all races and all walks of life. The show takes us into their lives; the audience sees good and bad, the forming of new and breaking of old relationships, and life and death. One example of this is when the audience first meets Mimi, a "dancer" and drug user, and Roger, a struggling musician whose ex-girlfriend, April, had committed suicide after finding out that both she and Roger had AIDS. The new relationship first forms when Mimi asks Roger if he'll "Light her candle." She has no heat, no food, barely anything, and a candle is all she has for warmth. Throughout the play they break up and get back together again. But during the finale, part of the cast finds Mimi in Central Park, huddled, shivering, hungry, suffering from withdrawal symptoms, and begging to be brought to Roger. Roger was determined to write one song that meant something, and by the end of the play, he found his song: It was about Mimi's eyes. Before I had ever known about this show, I was struggling through some tough times, and this show really helped me cope and see the brighter side of life. By the end of the night, I was unbelievably touched with the theme of "No day but today," meaning living life to the fullest and not regretting anything you've done in your lifetime.

> There's only now . . .
> There's only here . . .
> Give in to love . . .
> Or live in fear . . .
> No other path . . .
> No other way. . .
> No day but today.

The Creative Dimension   Readers who love literature often do not think of themselves as passive consumers. As children, they may have made up jingles and taunts. As adolescents, they may have written love notes or poems for Valentine's Day. They may be part of a group of friends who read poems to one another on special occasions (or recite them from memory), keeping alive the tradition of poetry as a performance art. They may have grown up in a setting where people still delighted in telling stories—sad and funny and making you want to cry.

In the following sample entry, a student writes about her early introduction to the storyteller's art.

I want to write about my early, unique encounter with storytelling that began as a family pastime and has evolved into a collection of stories I hope to have published one day. When I was a young girl, my father, who worked for the government, moved our family from the Chicago area to a town in New Mexico. Besides the cultural shock of moving to a place that my grandmother called "a one-horse town," we no longer had easy access to the cultural pursuits Chicago offered, like movies, concerts, the opera and plays, or fun activities like shopping in fine stores and visiting extended family. To assuage our boredom, my eldest sister, Leslie, began telling us stories that she made up as she went along, with each listener adding an idea here and there. One such story is entitled "Johnny and the Liver." Johnny is a little Black boy that is sent to the store by his mother to buy liver for dinner. Instead, he buys candy and ice cream. He finds a comfortable spot under an old oak tree and eats his fill. Suddenly he remembers: the money! the liver! His mother had already admonished him not to take all day to bring back the food. He is left with the dilemma of having to get the liver or face sure punishment. We also made up another version named Sandra and the Neck Bones because we wanted a story about a little girl, and there were not many children's books about Black children. These stories provided entertainment for us on Sunday afternoons when we sat in our bedroom with a roasting pan full of popcorn that we dipped our individual bowls into. I believe this experience fostered my love of reading and writing and is responsible for my hope to publish my work.

WRITING ABOUT LITERATURE

The writing strand in this book is designed to build on your previous instruction in writing. It aims at helping you become a more confident, more resourceful, and more effective writer. Improved competence in written work boosts your performance in academic work—both in general education classes and in your vocational or professional specialty.

Writing in Today's World
Competence in written communication is a crucial asset to you as an educated person, as a job seeker, and as a fully functioning citizen in today's society. Many college instructors use written exams and term papers to test what you know and how you think. Much work in today's workplace involves letters, memos, scripted presentations, well-worked-out proposals, background studies, written evaluations, briefs, and reports. Much public opinion is shaped by newspaper columns, magazine articles, brochures, and publicity releases. News-magazines and magazines of opinion include extensive reviews of both fiction and nonfiction books and of theatrical and musical performances. National magazines like the *New Yorker* and the *Atlantic* and many limited-circulation periodicals publish current fiction and poetry.

Reviewing the Writing Process   Writing is a creative process. The finished piece on the printed page is deceptive. It does not tell the reader about the process that produced the final document. It does not chronicle the search for promising leads, the trial hypotheses revised in the light of new facts, and late-at-night sessions when things do not seem to jell—until the pieces of the puzzle finally fall into place.

Different writing teachers chart the dimensions of the writing process in slightly different ways. You might want to think of your writing as a seven-step process. Always remember that the different stages of the process overlap and are often in progress concurrently.

✖ Purpose—What sets writing in motion; what brings it on? What are you trying to accomplish? Are you trying to explain a difficult concept or bring the reader up to date on new research? Are you trying to help your readers understand and enjoy a difficult poem or story? Are you trying to correct a misunderstanding or a stereotype? Are you trying to change the reader's mind about an author you admire or fend off censorship initiatives?

✖ Audience—What does it take to bring the subject to life for your audience? What background or specialized information may your readers need? What key terms may you have to explain? What assumptions or possibly hostile reactions do you have to take into account? What does it take to persuade an educated audience?

✖ Input—How careful a reader are you? How good are you at close reading? Do you take in revealing details? Do you highlight key quotations? Do you go back over a reading selection to track how its major outlines take shape? In reading background material or critical reviews, can you tell apart biased or superficial accounts and carefully thought-out or well-researched ones? Do you draw on informal consultation or formal interviews with insiders or people in the know? How resourceful are you in tracking down needed data in printed and electronic sources?

✖ Structure—How do you turn miscellaneous or unsorted materials into a coherent piece of writing—writing that "hangs together"? What kind of thinking goes into writing? Do you push toward a tentative major idea or thesis and then refine or adjust it as you review the evidence? What generalizations are justified by your data? What balanced conclusion can you reach after exploring the play of pro and con on a controversial issue? How do you structure your writing so that the reader can see the major stages in your line of thought or the steps in your argument?

✖ Revision—Revision and rethinking loom large in the work of professional writers. How do writers rework a rough draft to help an ugly small bird turn into a beautiful swan? How are you going to respond to feedback and second thoughts? Do you welcome criticism or feel threatened by it? How good are you at reshuffling material for a better flow and at feeding in missing links?

✖ Editing—What are professional, businesslike ways of editing your work to meet the standards of written English? What is the right middle ground between an awkward hyperformal style and a disrespectful slangy style? What special formats or guidelines for style are you expected to observe?

✖ Publication—A diary may be for our own eyes only, but generally we write to be read. In the real world, writers meet deadlines. They deal with editorial second-guessing; they hope for a warm favorable reception and steel themselves for hostile criticism. If at all possible, publish your writing—in a class publication, in a departmental or schoolwide publication, in the newsletter of a special-interest group. Send your letters to the editor, your poems, or your humorous pieces to the campus daily or the local press.

Today's Writing Classroom   Writing instruction over the years has changed with the aim of making it more positively oriented, more productive, and more dynamic. You may encounter a range of teaching styles or pedagogy—from traditional classroom instruction to emphasis on work in small groups and to distance learning over the Internet.

✗ The Workshop Format—Much writing instruction today shares features of a writing workshop. With members of a small group or with your class, you may discuss readings that can serve as both material and as models for your writing. You may explore and develop possible topics with your fellow students. You may explore promising sources together. You will provide feedback to others and serve as a trial audience for finished papers. You will often revise your own work in response to input from your instructor and from classmates. Writing grows and develops in interaction with other people—friends, editors, peers.

✗ Collaboration—You may be asked to help organize and participate in **group projects**. For instance, you may join in scripting oral class presentations or group readings. You may join in collaborative writing of studies or reports, for instance on the life and work of a major author. You learn how to contribute to group work by making good use of your special skills or background. At the same time, you learn how to deal with others' needs and adjust to both their strengths and limitations. You learn how to assure fair credit for your contribution to the group effort.

✗ Protocols and Portfolios—In many writing classes today, students are asked to save all notes, drafts, and revised papers. The collected material can then serve as a record of work accomplished and of progress toward course goals. A **portfolio** is a complete file or a selection that can be available at the end of a term for evaluation, helping determine a course grade.

✗ Research and Documentation—Informal research goes into most meaningful writing. However, when working on an investigative paper or a formal research paper, you will be paying special attention to how writers research a topic. You will profit from instruction in library research, data retrieval, and search strategies for Internet sources. You will learn how to integrate material from a range of different sources—working it smoothly into your text in the proverbial seamless web. You will have to follow a documentation style appropriate to your subject and your field. Where and how are you expected to identify author, publication, and publisher? What other publishing data will you need to include?

A Warning on Plagiarism

When you draw on other writers' work, you need to respect other people's intellectual property. Authors who plagiarize pass off someone else's writing as their own. Plagiarism can ruin a grade. At worst, it gets people expelled from institutions or taken to court. The best insurance against plagiarism is a full disclosure policy like the following:

✗ When in doubt, credit the source. Acknowledge the original source when you incorporate in your paper statements, ideas, and perspectives developed by someone else.

✗ Put all direct quotation—all material you copy word for word— in quotation marks. Use quotation marks for all quoted phrases, whole sentences, and short passages. Use specially indented block quotations (no quotation marks) for selected longer key passages.

✗ Identify your source also when using indirect quotation or paraphrase—putting source material into your own words. Show the source of statistics, graphs, and visual materials.

✗ Talk freely with others about what materials you found, what is right or wrong with them, and how you are going to use them. Make sure your instructor and your peers can see how your paper took shape.

✗ Keep your prewriting notes, first drafts, and copies of subsequent revisions. This way no one can suspect you of having obtained a ready-made paper from a research paper mill or fraternity file.

✗ Do not try to outsmart sophisticated modern software that can track thinly disguised copied passages or repeated phrases to a wide range of original publications.

Participating in Peer Review   In writing classes today, you are likely to participate in **peer review**. You help provide fellow students with feedback for work in progress or near-finished work. You try to offer constructive criticism, sizing up the author's intention and overall effort. You try to do justice to a paper as a whole while not overlooking minor points that affect the effectiveness of the writing. In turn, other students will respond to your own writing, raising questions and making suggestions for improvement. Especially in responding to early drafts, you will ask: What is promising here? What should the writer build on and develop? What needs to be strengthened or reconsidered? Where are examples missing or not clearly enough explained? Does the organizing strategy have to be rethought or more clearly spelled out? Will anything here alienate the intended audience?

No two papers are the same. Each paper presents its own challenge. We judge the writing by how well the writer has done what she or he set out to do. However, questions like the following come up again and again in feedback from instructor, editors, or peer reviewers.

Questions for Peer Review   **A Checklist**

Student Writer _____   Peer Reviewer _____

Study the student paper, highlighting and annotating as you wish as you go along. Then answer questions like the following, concentrating on those that seem most important for the paper you are reviewing. Be prepared to compare and discuss your answers with members of your class or small group.

✘ *How effective is the introduction?* How does the writer get the reader's attention? Does the introduction bring a central question into focus? What is the core issue, and does the author bring it to life for you?

✘ *Does the introduction lead up to a central unifying thesis?* What is it? Where is it most clearly or most directly stated? Is it echoed or reinforced later in the paper? Is it clarified or developed further as the paper takes shape?

✘ *Does the paper have a workable plan?* Is it easy or hard to chart? Can you prepare an informal outline that shows the flow of topics? What are the main points? Are there major stages? Is there a turning point or are there key steps in an argument? Are major signposts or transitions clearly marked, or do they need to be strengthened or more fully spelled out?

✘ *Are key terms clearly explained or defined?* Are there key concepts and related terms that strengthen coherence or continuity of thought?

✘ *How well has the writer used supporting material?* Are general points backed up with well-chosen examples, revealing details, and quotations? Is there a good mix of short quotations, more extended quotations, and summarized or paraphrased material—material put into the writer's own words? Has the writer turned for evidence or support to critics, authorities, or insiders? Where is supporting material strongest? Where may it need to be built up?

> ✗ *Does the author have a personal connection with the topic?* Is this a dutiful or routine paper, or does the author have a special commitment or agenda? Does the author share a special enthusiasm or excitement with the readers?
>
> ✗ *Are you part of the ideal audience for this paper?* Why or why not? Does the issue have a special personal meaning for you? Where do you most strongly agree or disagree with the author?
>
> ✗ *What would you say in a brief personal communication to the student writer?* Columnists and reviewers now often provide e-mail addresses for responses from their readers. What would you say in an e-mail to the student author?

From Feedback to Revision   In many writing classes today, the student writer takes a paper through several drafts in response to feedback from the instructor and from peers. The following is a draft of a student paper about Yukio Mishima's "Swaddling Clothes," a story reprinted early in this book (Chapter 2). After class discussion and after receiving comments from the instructor, the student writer will have the opportunity to prepare one or more revisions. The student author revises and rethinks the early draft for a near final draft.

Your instructor may write brief comments or questions in the margin of your paper. Or you may find longer comments covering major sections. Often a general comment will sum up the instructor's editorial suggestions or overall evaluation of a paper. Comments like the following may appear on a paper, emerge from class discussion, or come up during a conference.

Early Draft

A Child Scorned

Yukio Mishima's "Swaddling Clothes" is a short story that takes place in Japan—a land that is rich in culture and tradition, but is being tested by Westernization. It is a story where the three central figures' roles in regards to traditional Japanese culture are reflected in their qualities and traits. The author uses the setting and the traditional values within it to contrast these three characters' physical appearances to the roles that they assume. The baby born out of wedlock to the maid symbolizes shame and dishonor because of these traditional values. Although he seems very much Westernized, the husband's following of traditional roles is very much alive. However, for Toshiko, as fragile as she is, these roles are slowly dying.

> **Instructor's Comment:**   Your introduction brings your subject into focus. It sets up the tension between the traditional culture and Western influences that pervades the story. However, you talk about "qualities," "traits," and "values" in fairly colorless general terms—nothing to make us visualize the setting and the people in the mind's eye? And you talk about the contrast between physical appearances and underlying values when your paper really shows that both appearances and behavior are deceptive. Start with a more dramatic opening and push toward a thesis that spells out the basic contrast more clearly?

Toshiko's husband is an actor and has sent for her to meet him and their friends at a jazz club. The husband's choice of venue indicates that he is living a modern lifestyle, because jazz is something that comes from the United States and is not consistent with Japanese tradition. His occupation, by Japanese standards, is a nontraditional one. His Westernization is also evidenced by his choice of attire and his attitude. He is "sitting there in his American-style suit" and "gesturing flamboyantly as if in an attempt to outweigh the attractions of the dance band." He even drives an American car and has even provided her with a house that is "unhomely with its Western-style furniture."

However nontraditional his lifestyle seems, Toshiko's husband remains true to Japanese customs. He assumes the traditional role of the domineering breadwinner who, since he is the sole provider, can do as he pleases—even control what his own wife does. He treats her as his possession, flagging down a taxi to send Toshiko home as he dashes "off to an appointment." He does this even though "He must have known how she dreaded going back to their house."

> **Instructor's Comment:**   Your graphic description of the superficially Westernized husband is the best and most fully developed part of your paper. You use revealing details from the story (the suit, the gesturing, the jazz, the American car, the Western-style furniture) and contrast them with his traditional domineering male behavior, lording it over a traditional nonassertive wife. You use short quotations well here to anchor your points to the actual text of the story.

It is these same traditional roles and values that the baby is born into. He is born out of wedlock, which, by traditional standards, is a very disgraceful act. This is clearly what the doctor who handles the baby thinks. "As if to emphasize his scorn for this mother who had given birth to a bastard under such sordid conditions, he had told his assistant to wrap the baby in some loose newspapers, rather than proper swaddling." These conventional standards dictate that, through the illegitimacy of his birth, the child will grow up to be scorned by society. This view is consistent with how Toshiko feels. She feels that "even if that baby should grow up in ignorance of the secret of his birth, he can never become a respectable citizen, reflected Toshiko, pursuing the same train of thoughts. Those soiled newspaper swaddling clothes will be the symbol of his entire life."

> **Instructor's Comment:** You show well the contemptuous treatment of the newborn "illegitimate" child by both the husband and the doctor. The husband's attitude here is really the strongest example of his roots in harsh traditional attitudes. You need a strong link and tradition at the beginning of this paragraph to show this connection and tie things together? Then, however, the turning point needs to be marked (new paragraph!) as we go on to Toshiko, the wife, and the contrast she offers with her husband.

Toshiko is cast in the role of the traditional Japanese wife. She is passive and soft. "Toshiko had been oversensitive since girlhood: that was her nature." "Her delicacy of spirit was evident to her most casual acquaintance." She does not tell her husband of the baby in newspapers "fearing that he would think her oversoft, oversentimental." Toward the end of the story, however, she moves away from this role and gains her independence. This is evidenced by her taking a walk to the dark Chidorigafuchi park by herself. It is this independence that finally leads her to take control and "take her son's place." Ultimately, Toshiko's feeling of guilt and shame for the child lead her to expose herself to terrible danger. She seems to believe that it was her destiny to sacrifice herself. In the process, she gains her independence from her husband and the roles of traditional Japanese society.

> **Instructor's Comment:** You really show that the wife, like the husband, presents a deceptive surface appearance until we get to know her underlying character. However, in her case we go in the opposite direction—from a traditional appearance to a strange rebellion. Bring this out more clearly as your thesis early in your paper? This would sum up well what your paper really shows. And then you could rewrite your title so it shows this focus. Finally, the story takes a jump from the neglected newborn to the homeless man in the park who apparently destroys Toshiko. Can you relate him in some way to the central "clash of cultures" or "blending of cultures" theme?

Peer responses to this paper agreed on the good use of evidence and the effective use of key quotations. However, several student readers looked for a clearer thesis or overall framework. They felt the structure and transitions were not strong enough or not clearly enough worked out. They felt a lack of a personal connection or of a tie-in with the concerns of the reader's own world.

Sample Peer Response

Your introduction did not really grab my attention. (I would have liked a little more of a "hook" in the opening lines.) You state several ideas in the introduction without a clear enough indication for me of the main focus of the paper. You use evidence from the story well. Good description of the husband. He's Americanized, but deep down he has traditional attitudes. Great quotes! (Especially the one about the newborn child never having a chance to "become a respectable citizen.") You need a better transition from talking about the husband to talking about the wife. I see at the end how she sides with the illegitimate child and finally gains independence from her husband, but I wasn't clear on this or prepared for it earlier in the paper. I wrote "well said" in the margin when you called the husband "the domineering breadwinner who, since he is the sole provider, can do as he pleases." Once in a while the word choice seems awkward: "This was evidenced by . . ." just doesn't sound right. Wouldn't it be simpler to say "this was shown by . . ."?

Study the following revision. How well does it incorporate suggestions from the instructor or from peer responses? Pay special attention to three dimensions of this rewrite:

▮ a strengthened introduction and unifying thesis;

▮ key transitions accentuating the structure of the paper;

▮ a new conclusion that does not merely repeat points but makes readers look at the central issue of the paper from a thought-provoking perspective.

Mishima's Japan: A Culture in Transition

In Yukio Mishima's "Swaddling Clothes," we see white spots that we expect to be the traditional Japanese cherry blossoms but that turn out to be dirty pieces of newspaper. In much of the story appearances are deceptive; things are not what they seem. Mishima's Japan is a land that is rich in culture and tradition, but is being tested by Westernization. The central characters in the story move between the two influences, but they seem to be headed in opposite directions. Although he seems very much Westernized, the husband's following of traditional roles is very much alive. The wife Toshiko seems fragile and meek in the traditional manner but in the end breaks out of the traditional role. The baby born out of wedlock to the couple's maid provides the test of each character's attitudes and values.

Toshiko's husband is an actor and has sent for her to meet him and their friends at a jazz club. The husband's choice of venue indicates that he is living a modern lifestyle, because jazz is something that comes from the United States and is not consistent with Japanese tradition. His occupation, by Japanese standards, is a nontraditional one. His Westernization is also evidenced by his choice of attire and his attitude. He is "sitting there in his American-style suit" and "gesturing flamboyantly as if in an attempt to outweigh the attractions of the dance band." He even drives an American car and has even provided her with a house that is "unhomely with its Western-style furniture."

However nontraditional his lifestyle seems, Toshiko's husband remains true to Japanese customs. He assumes the traditional role of the domineering breadwinner who, since he is the sole provider, can do as he pleases—even control what his own wife does. He treats her as his possession, flagging down a taxi to send

Toshiko home as he dashes "off to an appointment." He does this even though "he must have known how she dreaded going back to their house."

The newborn baby in the story provides the best test of the husband's traditional attitudes. The maid's child is born out of wedlock, which, by traditional standards, is very disgraceful. This is clearly what the doctor who handles the baby thinks. "As if to emphasize his scorn for this mother who had given birth to a bastard under such sordid conditions, he had told his assistant to wrap the baby in some loose newspapers, rather than proper swaddling." These conventional standards dictate that, through the illegitimacy of his birth, the child will grow up to be scorned by society.

Toshiko, the wife, knows the traditional standards well. "Even if that baby should grow up in ignorance of the secret of his birth, he can never become a respectable citizen, reflected Toshiko, pursuing the same train of thoughts. Those soiled newspaper swaddling clothes will be the symbol of his entire life." Toshiko is cast in the role of the traditional Japanese wife. She is passive and soft. "Toshiko had been oversensitive since girlhood: that was her nature." "Her delicacy of spirit was evident to her most casual acquaintance." She does not tell her husband of the baby in newspapers "fearing that he would think her oversoft, oversentimental."

Toward the end of the story, however, she moves away from this role and gains her independence. This is evidenced by her taking a walk to the dark threatening Chidorigafuchi park by herself. It is this independence that finally leads her to take control and "take her son's place." Ultimately, Toshiko's feeling of guilt and shame for the child lead her to expose herself to terrible danger. She believes that it is her destiny to sacrifice herself. In the process, she gains her independence from her husband and the roles of traditional Japanese society.

The homeless man who is lying on the bench in the dark park and who makes Toshiko meet her fate may actually provide a bridge between tradition and the Westernized modern world. He is a symbol of what Toshiko, along with traditional society, thinks will happen to the child in the future. He is wrapped in newspapers, just as the baby was. However, in spite of this link with the past, this man's homelessness represents a condition widespread in modern industrialized society. Neglect and mistreatment of the unfortunate survive from the traditional into the modern world.

The Range of Writing Assignments Many of the questions following selections in this book suggest writing options. They suggest possible topics for papers—ranging from short papers focused on a single selection to longer papers tracing connections among several selections or papers integrating material from critics and reviewers. Often these writing assignments will ask you to think about how the means of expression that writers of imaginative literature use serve its human purposes.

✘ How does the **setting** of a story shape the outlook or the personality of its people?

✘ How does a central **symbol**—an object or event acquiring a larger meaning beyond itself—focus our attention on a key concern or traumatic challenge in people's lives?

✘ How does the **point of view** of a narrator (telling the story) or a **persona** (the assumed identity of a speaker in a poem) channel or guide our vision of the world?

✗ Does a **conflict** between strong opposites in a play result in the
defeat of one of the contenders—or does it lead toward a more comprehensive new vision?

Some writing assignments will ask you to focus on larger questions
raised by a selection or group of selections. For instance, you may be
asked to consider questions about society and the individual, about idealism and disillusionment, or about differing visions of good and evil.
The following is a sample assignment:

Sample Writing Assignment

Culture and Individual

Select one of the following four stories. Or
select two of the stories for a comparison and
contrast.

BOBBIE ANN MASON *Shiloh*

ALICE MUNRO *Boys and Girls*

LOUISE ERDRICH *The Red Convertible*

BERNARD MALAMUD *The Magic Barrel*

Write a paper focused on the following question:
Current cultural studies stress the role culture plays in shaping us as people—our personalities, our behavior patterns, our thoughts and
feelings. Strong movements in current sociology
see much of what we are as socially constructed—
a product of our social environment. How much is
our character or our identity as a person shaped
by the culture or society in which we grew up?
Traditionally, Western civilization has encouraged people to think of themselves as individuals, developing their own personal identity. How
much are the characters in the fiction we are
reading shaped by their society or their
culture—often in ways they are not consciously
aware of? How much are they individuals in their
own right? What makes people dissenters, rebels,

```
or nonconformists—people marching to the beat of
a different drummer?
    Bring your paper into focus in a brief lively
introduction and push toward a central question
of unifying your thesis early in your paper.
Work out an organizing strategy. Use details and
quotations from the story to support your
points. Prepare a brief progress report for
class discussion.
```

SEARCHING ONLINE SOURCES

The **Internet** today gives you instant access to background material for your reading and to source material for your writing. A wealth of critical and background material is at your fingertips as you work at your computer keyboard. A quick search can take you to recent critical studies, reevaluations of well-known authors, or biographical background incorporating new research. It can take you to reviews of experimental modern drama or of spectacular revivals of classics of the stage.

In the *New York Times Online,* you may find a review of two new author biographies that dramatize the impact of the poetry of Edna St. Vincent Millay as an icon of the Jazz Age—and that then chronicle the fading of her influence with the rise of modernism. In *Atlantic Online,* you may find interviews with the Nigerian novelist Chinua Achebe and with Louise Erdrich, author of fiction and poetry on the tension between Native American tradition and the white mainstream culture. You may find a scholarly journal devoted to Emily Dickinson, America's greatest poet, in the opinion of many. You may find a **website** devoted to Franz Kafka, prophet of alienation and the traumas of the modern world, with links to publications and organizations monitoring Kakfa's astonishing continuing influence in our times.

Internet researchers try out and come to trust **search engines** that best help them navigate the world of web resources. Many rely on the most widely used Yahoo! Many convert to newer ambitious search engines, from Lycos to Google, that promise faster or better targeted searches. Keep concerns like the following in mind when sifting Net resources:

✘ Authorship—Are authors and sources clearly identified? Do their **credentials** inspire confidence? Or are you looking at near-anonymous material, with no one assuming responsibility for accuracy of facts or validity of accusations? Are you looking at an authentic verified document—or are you looking at a document that may have been excerpted, massaged, or pirated?

▮ Permanence—When was a document posted? How long is it likely to be available on the Net? Is it likely to be saved in **archives** maintained by a major publication or organization? (The American Psychological Association—APA—warns researchers against using Internet resources that may no longer be available when readers or other researchers try to consult them.)

▮ Audience—The intended audience for Internet sources ranges widely in educational level or scholarly commitment. Does a site seem to cater to audiences that relish amusing sidelights or insider's gossip? Does a source draw on the work of other researchers and support its claims with impressive evidence? Does a source aim at a specialized constituency—like business groups wary of what they consider an antibusiness bias in some modern literature?

▮ Commercialism—When a search generates a large number of promising entries, these may be ranked according to frequency of hits—how many users have previously visited the site? Or entries may actually have been sifted by human moderators making a judgment about their quality or importance. However, increasingly today entries may be ranked high because they serve the interest of commercial sponsors, who pay for favorable placement.

Guidelines for giving source information for online sources are still evolving. The following shows the current Modern Language Association (MLA) style for documented papers requiring full publishing information. You may encounter variations from the style shown in the following sample entries.

<<<Find It on the Web>>>

Your online exploration of material on a work or an author you are studying may produce a full range of items. The following sample entries show how you would feed publishing data on online material and other nonprint sources into a final source list or alphabetical list of Works Cited. Two dates for an item show first the date it was posted and then the day it was accessed. The **URL,** or retrieval code for online material, appears in *angled brackets.*

NEWSLETTER ONLINE:
McCalla, John. "Kafka's Hot and He's Also Funny." <u>Penn News</u> 2 Apr. 1998.
18 Oct. 1999.
<http://www.upenn.edu/pennnews/current/1998/040298/Kafka.html>

BOOK REVIEW ONLINE:
Smith, Dinitia. "Two Portraits of Edna St. Vincent Millay as Poet and Free
    Spirit." <u>New York Times Online</u>. 30 Aug. 2001. 19 Sept. 2001.
    <http://www.nytimes.com/2001/08/30/books/30MILL.html>

LITERARY OR SCHOLARLY JOURNAL ONLINE:
<u>The Emily Dickinson Journal</u>. U of Colorado Dept. of English: 1998. 24 Sept.
    2001.
    <http://www.colorado.edu/EDIS/journal/index.html>

SPECIAL INTEREST WEBSITE:
Nervi, Mauro. <u>The Kafka Project Website</u>. Updated 6 Sept. 2001. 24 Sept.
    2001.
    <http://www.kafka.org>

REFERENCE WORK ONLINE, WITH VERSION NUMBER AND DATE:
"Kafka." <u>Britannica Online</u>. Vers. 97.1.1. Mar. 1997. Encyclopaedia Britan-
    nica. 17 Oct. 2001.
    <http://www.eb.com/>

SPECIALIZED DATABASE:
Miller-Schultz, Chantal. <u>Shakespeare's Globe Research Database</u>. 12 Jan.
    2001. 24 Sept. 2001.
    <http://www.rdg.ac.uk./globe/>

PHOTOGRAPHS AND OTHER VISUALS ONLINE:
Eckel, Yacov. <u>Franz Kafka Photo Album</u>. 6 Sept. 2000. 24 Sept. 2001.
    <http://www.cs.technion.ac.il/eckel/Kafka/main.htm>

COLLECTION OF MATERIALS ON CD-ROM:
Fresca, Dolores. "Kafka and Patriarchy." <u>The World of Kafka</u>. CD-ROM. New
    York: Klamm Publications, 1999.

Preview assignment: Explore **online** materials on an author of fiction featured in this volume. Select a writer whose work or life has in recent years
attracted attention from critics, reviewers, biographers, or film critics. For instance, prepare a source list of currently available online material or
archived material on Tobias Wolff, Chinua Achebe, Louise Erdrich, John
Steinbeck, Toni Morrison, Alice Walker, Flannery O'Connor, Amy Tan, or
Tim O'Brien. Include a brief annotation if you can.

Fiction

A story really isn't any good unless it successfully hangs on and expands in the mind.

JOYCE CAROL OATES

1 PREVIEW

The World of Fiction

Truth may be stranger than fiction, but fiction is truer.

FREDERIC RAPHAEL

Fiction…is like a spider's web, attached ever so lightly perhaps, but still attached to life at all four corners.

VIRGINIA WOOLF

Catching the very note and trick, the strange irregular rhythm of life, that is the attempt whose strenuous force keeps fiction upon her feet.

HENRY JAMES

FOCUS ON FICTION

What is the appeal of a good story? The Greek writer Nikos Kazant-zakis tells a brief story that has in it essential elements of the story-teller's art:

> There was a smell of fig trees in the air. A little old woman who was walking past stopped next to me. She lifted up some leaves covering a basket she was carrying. She picked out two of the figs in the bas-ket and offered them to me. "Do you know me from somewhere, granny?" I asked. She looked at me, surprised. "No, my lad. Do I have to know you to give you something? You are a human being. So am I. Isn't that enough?"

This story does in miniature what other stories take longer to do for their readers. It takes us on a flight of the imagination to a setting; it takes us to a time and a place. We come to know two characters, who become real to us as human beings. Something happens that is worth remembering, worth telling. As we imagine ourselves in the traveler's place, we are likely to be moved by what the old woman said. The figs become a symbol—they represent the nourishment that sustains life, but they are also a token of the fellow feeling or bonding that helps us sur-vive. In the hurry of everyday life, this incident stands out. It is complete and self-contained, with a meaning of its own. It makes a good story.

The storyteller's art has enchanted listeners since time immemorial. The people who painted bison and horses on cave walls very likely gath-ered around the fire to listen to the storyteller of the clan or tribe. The gift of storying, of weaving stories, enabled human beings to find the con-necting thread in the events of the past. It helped them find continuity and meaning in their lives. Through the centuries, people have told and listened to stories—on winter evenings on a farm, in a country retreat while waiting out an epidemic ravaging the city, on the dusty road while on a pilgrimage to a shrine.

In the last hundred years, the writing of short stories has become a craft. The authors may also write novels, but they approach the shorter form as a challenge, where they make every detail count. A good reader in turn is prepared to take in all the story has to offer. Storytelling is a cooperative enterprise—the writer provides the script, but the readers bring it to life by using their imagination. What can you do to get out of a story what the writer put in? Consider guidelines like the following:

✗ *Read with an open mind.* A story takes you into a world of its own, with values that may be different from yours. Try to be a receptive reader. Some readers are wary of what is new and unfamiliar. They are quick to judge writing that looks at the world through a lens different from their own. If you are quick to judge, to reject, you may cut yourself off from much that good reading has to offer.

✗ *Read a story more than once.* The editor of a recent collection of stories said, "These stories can be read once, twice, many times, slowly. I found that the best ones haunted me for days after the reading" (Louise Erdrich). The stories in this book offer rewards for readers who linger over them, who go back to them for a closer look. Look for significant details that may have passed by too quickly. Be alert for revealing words, telling gestures.

✗ *Use your imagination.* Try to visualize the scenes, the people, the events. Learn to hear the dialogue with the mind's ear as if it were being read aloud. Try to see the world from the vantage point of the narrator, the person telling the story.

✗ *Allow your emotions to come into play.* Respond with your feelings as well as your analytical mind. A short story does not present a case history for diagnosis. Try to relate to the characters as people. Develop your capacity for empathy—for entering imaginatively into what others think and feel.

✗ *Try to get a sense of the story as a whole.* As you look back over your notes, try to see whether an overall pattern has taken shape. Try to see what role details play in the larger context of the story.

✗ *Think about your reactions.* Were you charmed? puzzled? appalled? Were you frustrated when the story took a turn you did not expect? What standards and expectations did you bring to the story?

✗ *Talk with other readers.* Learn from their reactions, questions, and confusions. Explore your reading with others—one on one or in small groups. What did they see that you had missed? What triggered reactions different from yours?

THE ART OF THE STORY

*We are story-telling animals. As our primitive
ancestors sat around the fire carving spearheads
and eating blackberries, they told stories which
in time were woven into a tapestry of myth and
legend. These tales were the first encyclopedia of
human knowledge.*

SAM KEEN

*Writing a story is one way of discovering se-
quence in experience. Connections slowly emerge.
Like distant landmarks you are approaching,
cause and effect begin to align themselves.*

EUDORA WELTY

*A writer out of loneliness is trying to communi-
cate like a distant star sending signals. ... We are
lonely animals. We spend all life trying to be less
lonesome. One of our ancient methods is to tell a
story, begging the listener to say—and to feel—
"Yes, that's the way it is, or at least the way I feel
it. You're not as alone as you thought."*

JOHN STEINBECK

Every story is different. It makes its own rules; it creates its own world.
Nevertheless, as readers, we become aware of questions that arise in our
minds again and again. We expect the storyteller to answer them in one
way or another—not in so many words; rather, we expect the story as a
whole to provide the answers. A preview of key questions that readers
and critics may ask about a story might look like this:

SETTING
: Where are we? Where is the story taking us? What
kind of world, what kind of reality, does it create for
us? What difference do the time and the place make
to the story as a whole?

CHARACTER
: Who are these people? What is their history or their
current situation? What are their real motives, needs,
or desires? What explains the way they act?

PLOT
: What happens in the story, and why? What pattern,
or story line, gives shape to the story as a whole? Is
there a central conflict or a central problem, and how
is it going to be resolved? Is there a turning point, a
turning of the tide?

POINT OF VIEW	Who is telling the story? Through whose eyes do you see the people and events? Through what window are you looking at the world?
SYMBOL	What in the story has a meaning beyond itself? Do objects, people, or incidents acquire a symbolic meaning—the way a handshake might symbolize brotherhood, or the way a new shoot on a tree might stand for rebirth or renewal?
THEME	Does the story make you think? What issues does it raise; what ideas does it explore? Does it act out a view of human nature that you can try to spell out?
STYLE	How does the author use language? Is the language rich in striking images? Does the story play down or play up emotion? Is the tone mournful, bitter, happy, or ironic—making us look at events with a wry smile?

Look at the following *short* short stories (or short shorts), in which one or another of these elements plays a major role.

Setting   *Where are we?* Storytellers take us to a world of their creation. The story takes us to a place, a time, a situation. Often the place becomes so vivid that we forget we are not in a real place but merely in an imagined setting, a country of the mind. Ask yourself: Could this story be happening anywhere? You will be reading a different story depending on whether you watch white officials in a colonial situation in Africa, or tenant farmers scraping together a living in the backwoods, or a young woman growing up in an old-fashioned patriarchal family. Setting, in fiction as in reality, is a major player in the drama of life. It helps make people what they are. It sets boundaries, limiting what people can strive for or aspire to. It sets up challenges, creating or limiting opportunities.

Sandra Cisneros   *(born 1954)*

Sandra Cisneros is a widely published Chicana, or Mexican American, writer, born of a Mexican father and a Mexican American mother in Chicago. Her stories re-create in loving detail the environment where many working-class Americans live. In the following story, she uses a few more or less self-explanatory Spanish phrases and references to Mexican history. *La Virgen de Guadalupe* is the Virgin Mary of Guadalupe. The first PRI elections, which brought Mexico's traditional ruling party to power, disillusioned many of the more radical supporters of the Mexican Revolution. The story takes us to a setting and asks us to imagine what it would be like to be there, to live there. How does the setting come to life for the reader?

Mericans   *1991*

We're waiting for the awful grandmother who is inside dropping pesos into *la ofrenda* box before the altar to La Divina Providencia. Lighting votive candles and genuflecting. Blessing herself and kissing her thumb. Running a crystal rosary between her fingers. Mumbling, mumbling, mumbling.

There are so many prayers and promises and thanks-be-to-God to be given in the name of the husband and the sons and the only daughter who never attend mass. It doesn't matter. Like La Virgen de Guadalupe, the awful grandmother intercedes on their behalf. For the grandfather who hasn't believed in anything since the first PRI elections. For my father, El Periquín, so skinny he needs his sleep. For Auntie Light-skin, who only a few hours before was breakfasting on brain and goat tacos after dancing all night in the pink zone. For Uncle Fat-face, the blackest of the black sheep—*Always remember your Uncle Fat-face in your prayers.* And Uncle Baby—*You go for me, Mamá—God listens to you.*

The awful grandmother has been gone a long time. She disappeared behind the heavy leather outer curtain and the dusty velvet inner. We may stay near the church entrance. We must not wander over to the balloon and punch-ball vendors. We cannot spend our allowance on fried cookies or Familia Burrón comic books or those clear cone-shaped suckers that make everything look like a rainbow when you look through them. We cannot run off and have our picture taken on the wooden ponies. We must not climb the steps up the hill behind the church and chase each other through the cemetery. We have promised to stay right where the awful grandmother left us until she returns.

There are those walking to church on their knees. Some with fat rags tied around their legs and others with pillows, one to kneel on, and one to flop ahead. There are women with black shawls crossing and uncrossing themselves. There are armies of penitents carrying banners and flowered arches while musicians play tinny trumpets and tinny drums.

La Virgen de Guadalupe is waiting inside behind a plate of thick glass.   5 There's also a gold crucifix bent crooked as a mesquite tree when someone once threw a bomb. La Virgen de Guadalupe on the main altar because she's a big miracle, the crooked crucifix on a side altar because that's a little miracle.

But we're outside in the sun. My big brother Junior hunkered against the wall with his eyes shut. My little brother Keeks running around in circles.

Maybe and most probably my little brother is imagining he's a flying feather dancer, like the ones we saw swinging high up from a pole on the Virgin's birthday. I want to be a flying feather dancer too, but when he circles past me he shouts, "I'm a B-Fifty-two bomber, you're a German," and shoots me with an invisible machine gun. I'd rather play flying feather dancers, but if I tell my brother this, he might not play with me at all.

"*Girl*. We can't play with a *girl*." *Girl*. It's my brothers' favorite insult now instead of "sissy." "You *girl*," they yell at each other. "You throw that ball like a *girl*."

I've already made up my mind to be a German when Keeks swoops past again, this time yelling, "I'm Flash Gordon. You're Ming the Merciless and the Mud People." I don't mind being Ming the Merciless, but I don't like being the Mud People. Something wants to come out of the corners of my eyes, but I don't let it. Crying is what *girls* do.

I leave Keeks running around in circles—"I'm the Lone Ranger, you're   10
Tonto." I leave Junior squatting on his ankles and go look for the awful grandmother.

Why do churches smell like the inside of an ear? Like incense and the dark and candles in blue glass? And why does holy water smell of tears? The awful grandmother makes me kneel and fold my hands. The ceiling high and everyone's prayers bumping up there like balloons.

If I stare at the eyes of the saints long enough, they move and wink at me, which makes me a sort of saint too. When I get tired of winking saints, I count the awful grandmother's mustache hairs while she prays for Uncle Old, sick from the worm, and Auntie Cuca, suffering from a life of troubles that left half her face crooked and the other half sad.

There must be a long, long list of relatives who haven't gone to church. The awful grandmother knits the names of the dead and the living into one long prayer fringed with the grandchildren born in that barbaric country with its barbarian ways.

I put my weight on one knee, then the other, and when they both grow fat as a mattress of pins, I slap them each awake. *Micaela, you may wait outside with Alfredito and Enrique.* The awful grandmother says it all in Spanish, which I understand when I'm paying attention. "What?" I say, though it's neither proper nor polite. "What?" which the awful grandmother hears as "¿Guat?" But she only gives me a look and shoves me toward the door.

After all that dust and dark, the light from the plaza makes me squinch   15
my eyes like if I just came out of the movies. My brother Keeks is drawing squiggly lines on the concrete with a wedge of glass and the heel of his shoe. My brother Junior squatting against the entrance, talking to a lady and man.

They're not from here. Ladies don't come to church dressed in pants. And everybody knows men aren't supposed to wear shorts.

"*¿Quieres chicle?*" the lady asks in a Spanish too big for her mouth.

"*Gracias.*" The lady gives him a whole handful of gum for free, little cellophane cubes of Chiclets, cinnamon and aqua and the white ones that don't taste like anything but are good for pretend buck teeth.

"*Por favor,*" says the lady. "*¿Un foto?*" pointing to her camera.

"*Sí.*"   20

She's so busy taking Junior's picture, she doesn't notice me and Keeks.

"Hey, Michele, Keeks. You guys want gum?"

"But you speak English!"

"Yeah," my brother says, "we're Mericans."

We're Mericans, we're Mericans, and inside the awful grandmother prays.   25

The Receptive Reader

1. Where are we? What details does the writer use to help you visualize the place, to bring it to life?

2. Like many Americans, the people in this story live in a place between two languages or two cultures. Which people and which details in the story best represent the two poles?

3. How do the young people in the story relate to their bilingual or cultural context? Are they "Americanized"?

The Personal Response

Do you recognize the place? (Does it resemble any setting familiar to you?) Does the place become real for you? Why, or why not?

Character   *Who are the people?* In a traditional story, the storyteller places believable characters in a vividly imagined setting and then puts them in motion. How well do you get to know them? What is their history? What goes on behind the subdued public surface? What are their true needs, their true motives?

You come to know characters in fiction by reading a range of clues. You may know them from what the author says about them—or, more exactly, from what the **narrator** says, the person telling the story. You learn about them through what *other* characters in the story tell you. You watch characters in action—reaching conclusions about their motives, their problems, their ambitions, their desires. But above all, you know them from listening to them. The following short short story by Grace Paley consists mostly of **dialogue**. The verbal exchange in the story is like a tennis match—except that instead of our eyes following the ball from one side of the net to the other, our ears keep turning from one speaker to the other. At the same time, we listen in to the narrator mentally talking to herself, thinking to herself.

Grace Paley   *(born 1922)*

Grace Paley grew up as the daughter of Russian Jewish immigrants in the Bronx and was educated at Hunter College and New York University. She is known for stories that are mostly talk, with little plot or action. Readers and critics have loved her stories about ordinary New Yorkers, whose Jewish, black, or Irish ways of talking she reproduces with uncanny accuracy. How much do you learn about the two people in her story? How much can you infer about these characters from listening to what one critic has called their "loud, energetic, quirky voices full of Paley's humor" (Kathleen A. Coppula)?

Wants   *1974*

I saw my ex-husband in the street. I was sitting on the steps of the new library.

Hello, my life, I said. We had once been married for twenty-seven years, so I felt justified.

He said, What? What life? No life of mine.

I said, O.K. I don't argue when there's real disagreement. I got up and went into the library to see how much I owed them.

The librarian said $32 even and you've owed it for eighteen years. I didn't   5
deny anything. Because I don't understand how time passes. I have had those books. I have often thought of them. The library is only two blocks away.

My ex-husband followed me to the Books Returned desk. He interrupted the librarian, who had more to tell. In many ways, he said, as I look back, I attribute the dissolution of our marriage to the fact that you never invited the Bertrams to dinner.

That's possible, I said. But really, if you remember: first, my father was sick that Friday, then the children were born, then I had those Tuesday-night meetings, then the war began. Then we didn't seem to know them any more. But you're right. I should have had them to dinner.

I gave the librarian a check for $32. Immediately she trusted me, put my past behind her, wiped the record clean, which is just what most other municipal and/or state bureaucracies will *not* do.

I checked out the two Edith Wharton books I had just returned because I'd read them so long ago and they are more apropos now than ever. They were *The House of Mirth* and *The Children,* which is about how life in the United States in New York changed in twenty-seven years fifty years ago.

A nice thing I do remember is breakfast, my ex-husband said. I was sur-   10
prised. All we ever had was coffee. Then I remembered there was a hole in the back of the kitchen closet which opened into the apartment next door. There, they always ate sugar-cured smoked bacon. It gave us a very grand feeling about breakfast, but we never got stuffed and sluggish.

That was when we were poor, I said.

When were we ever rich? he asked.

Oh, as time went on, as our responsibilities increased, we didn't go in need. You took adequate financial care, I reminded him. The children went to camp four weeks a year and in decent ponchos with sleeping bags and boots, just like everyone else. They looked very nice. Our place was warm in winter, and we had nice red pillows and things.

I wanted a sailboat, he said. But you didn't want anything.

Don't be bitter, I said. It's never too late.   15

No, he said with a great deal of bitterness. I may get a sailboat. As a matter of fact I have money down on an eighteen-foot two-rigger. I'm doing well this year and can look forward to better. But as for you, it's too late. You'll always want nothing.

He had had a habit throughout the twenty-seven years of making a narrow remark which, like a plumber's snake, could work its way through the ear down the throat, halfway to my heart. He would then disappear, leaving me choking with equipment. What I mean is, I sat down on the library steps and he went away.

I looked through *The House of Mirth,* but lost interest. I felt extremely accused. Now, it's true, I'm short of requests and absolute requirements. But I do want *something.*

I want, for instance, to be a different person. I want to be the woman who brings these two books back in two weeks. I want to be the effective citizen who changes the school system and addresses the Board of Estimate on the troubles of this dear urban center.

I *had* promised my children to end the war before they grew up.   20

I wanted to have been married forever to one person, my ex-husband or my present one. Either has enough character for a whole life, which as it turns out is really not such a long time. You couldn't exhaust either man's qualities or get under the rock of his reasons in one short life.

Just this morning I looked out the window to watch the street for a while and saw that the little sycamores the city had dreamily planted a couple of years before the kids were born had come that day to the prime of their lives.

Well! I decided to bring those two books back to the library. Which proves that when a person or an event comes along to jolt or appraise me I *can* take some appropriate action, although I am better known for my hospitable remarks.

The Receptive Reader

1. What would you include in a brief *capsule portrait* of the narrator—the character doing most of the talking in this story? What do you think are her outstanding traits, and how are they shown? (Do they go together to make up a believable personality?)

2. What kind of person is the ex-husband? How does he serve as a *foil*—a character who brings out traits in the other character that otherwise might have lain dormant?

3. Do you think readers will care about these people? Why, or why not?

Plot   *What is happening, and why?* What is the situation? What needs or wants create an unfinished agenda? What conflicts are coming to a head? What resentments are waiting to be acted out? Stories vary greatly in how much overt action they incorporate. In fact, whatever development unfolds in a story may be taking place in a character's mind. The following African folktale shows the power of a good story line to create **suspense**, to hold the reader's attention. The tale is one of many retold by Chinua Achebe, a famous Nigerian novelist, in his novel *Things Fall Apart* (1958).

Chinua Achebe   *(born 1930)*   ◉

Chinua Achebe, whose father was a Christian minister, was educated in Nigeria, studied at London University and with the BBC, and has taught at universities in Nigeria and the United States. He has been active in broadcasting, publishing, and Nigerian politics. His re-creating of a traditional tale shows how a storyteller hooks us into a story. We need to know: How will it come out? In this story, as we see Tortoise best his friends, their—and our?—resentment builds. We are waiting for his comeuppance, and we are not disappointed. A good storyteller creates expectations and then fulfills them—or sometimes disappoints them on purpose.

Why the Tortoise's Shell Is Not Smooth   *1958*

Low voices, broken now and again by singing, reached Okonkwo from his wives' huts as each woman and her children told folk stories. Ekwefi and her daughter, Ezinma, sat on a mat on the floor. It was Ekwefi's turn to tell a story.

"Once upon a time," she began, "all the birds were invited to a feast in the sky. They were very happy and began to prepare themselves for the great day. They painted their bodies with red cam wood and drew beautiful patterns on them with dye.

"Tortoise saw all these preparations and soon discovered what it all meant. Nothing that happened in the world of the animals ever escaped his notice; he was full of cunning. As soon as he heard of the great feast in the sky his throat began to itch at the very thought. There was a famine in those days and Tortoise had not eaten a good meal for two moons. His body rattled like a piece of dry stick in his empty shell. So he began to plan how he would go to the sky."

"But he had no wings," said Ezinma.

"Be patient," replied her mother. "That is the story. Tortoise had no   5 wings, but he went to the birds and asked to be allowed to go with them.

" 'We know you too well,' said the birds when they had heard him. 'You are full of cunning and you are ungrateful. If we allow you to come with us you will soon begin your mischief.'

" 'You do not know me,' said Tortoise. 'I am a changed man. I have learned that a man who makes trouble for others is also making it for himself.'

"Tortoise had a sweet tongue, and within a short time all the birds agreed that he was a changed man, and they each gave him a feather, with which he made two wings.

"At last the great day came and Tortoise was the first to arrive at the meeting place. When all the birds had gathered together, they set off in a body. Tortoise was very happy as he flew among the birds, and he was soon chosen as the man to speak for the party because he was a great orator.

" 'There is one important thing which we must not forget,' he said as they   10 flew on their way. 'When people are invited to a great feast like this, they take new names for the occasion. Our hosts in the sky will expect us to honor this age-old custom.'

"None of the birds had heard of this custom but they knew that Tortoise, in spite of his failings in other directions, was a widely traveled man who knew the customs of different peoples. And so they each took a new name. When they had all taken, Tortoise also took one. He was to be called *All of you.*

"At last the party arrived in the sky and their hosts were very happy to see them. Tortoise stood up in his many-colored plumage and thanked them for their invitation. His speech was so eloquent that all the birds were glad they had brought him, and nodded their heads in approval of all he said. Their hosts took him as the king of the birds, especially as he looked somewhat different from the others.

"After kola nuts had been presented and eaten, the people of the sky set before their guests the most delectable dishes Tortoise had even seen or dreamed of. The soup was brought out hot from the fire and in the very pot in which it had been cooked. It was full of meat and fish. Tortoise began to sniff aloud. There was pounded yam and also yam pottage cooked with palm oil and fresh fish. There were also pots of palm wine. When everything had been set before the guests, one of the people of the sky came forward and tasted a little from each pot. He then invited the birds to eat. But Tortoise jumped to his feet and asked: 'For whom have you prepared this feast?'

" 'For all of you,' replied the man.

"Tortoise turned to the birds and said: 'You remember that my name is   15 *All of you.* The custom here is to serve the spokesman first and the others later. They will serve you when I have eaten.'

"He began to eat and the birds grumbled angrily. The people of the sky thought it must be their custom to leave all the food for their king. And so Tortoise ate the best part of the food and then drank two pots of palm wine, so that he was full of food and drink and his body grew fat enough to fill out his shell.

"The birds gathered round to eat what was left and to peck at the bones he had thrown all about the floor. Some of them were too angry to eat. They chose to fly home on an empty stomach. But before they left each took back the feather he had lent to Tortoise. And there he stood in his hard shell full of food and wine but without any wings to fly home. He asked the birds to take a message for his wife, but they all refused. In the end Parrot, who had felt more angry than the others, suddenly changed his mind and agreed to take the message.

" 'Tell my wife,' said Tortoise, 'to bring out all the soft things in my house and cover the compound with them so that I can jump down from the sky without very great danger.'

"Parrot promised to deliver the message, and then flew away. But when he reached Tortoise's house he told his wife to bring out all the hard things in the house. And so she brought out her husband's hoes, machetes, spears, guns, and even his cannon. Tortoise looked down from the sky and saw his wife bringing things out, but it was too far to see what they were. When all seemed ready he let himself go. He fell and fell and fell until he began to

fear that he would never stop falling. And then like the sound of his cannon he crashed on the compound."

"Did he die?" asked Ezinma.   20

"No," replied Ekwefi. "His shell broke into pieces. But there was a great
medicine man in the neighborhood. Tortoise's wife sent for him and he
gathered all the bits of shell and stuck them together. That is why Tortoise's
shell is not smooth."

The Receptive Reader

1. What makes the characters and the story *believable?* (Do you think modern readers would be too sophisticated to be charmed by animals talking and
acting like people?)

2. Do you feel a sneaking admiration for the cleverness of the turtle? Or do
you mainly sympathize with his victims?

3. How did you expect the story to come out? When did you first guess
what the ending would be?

4. Many traditional stories follow the pattern of a journey. How does this one?

The Creative Dimension

Modern readers have often felt the urge to update proverbs or to rewrite
folktales to bring them into harmony with the modern temper. Try your hand at
a rewrite of this traditional tale or of a folktale likely to be familiar to your readers. (In rewriting this story, would you choose different and more familiar animals? Would you change the way the animals behave and the way readers—or
listeners—are expected to react?)

Point of View   *Through whose eyes are we looking at the world?* From
what point of view? What is included, what left out? What special insights or privileged information are we able to share? What biases may
cloud our vision? What blind spots do we need to take into account?

Tobias Wolff   *(born 1945)*

Tobias Wolff became known when he published a collection of his
stories, *In the Garden of the North American Martyrs,* in 1981. He was
born in Birmingham, Alabama; he went to the Pacific Northwest with
his mother after her divorce; and he was expelled from the prep school
he attended. He served in the U.S. Army in Vietnam and wrote about his
army experience in his short novel, or novella, *The Barracks Thief*
(1984) and in his memoir *In Pharao's Army* (1994). In his story "Hunters in the Snow," he takes the reader into a world of buddies—of outdoor pursuits, rough kidding, half-meant insults, and sometimes deadly

horseplay. In the story that follows, Wolff looks at a relationship between man and woman from the point of view of a white male. What difference does it make?

Say Yes   *1985*

They were doing the dishes, his wife washing while he dried. He'd washed the night before. Unlike most men he knew, he really pitched in on the housework. A few months earlier he'd overheard a friend of his wife's congratulate her on having such a considerate husband, and he thought, *I try.* Helping out with the dishes was a way he had of showing how considerate he was.

They talked about different things and somehow got on the subject of whether white people should marry black people. He said that all things considered, he thought it was a bad idea.

"Why?" she asked.

Sometimes his wife got this look where she pinched her brows together and bit her lower lip and stared down at something. When he saw her like this he knew he should keep his mouth shut, but he never did. Actually it made him talk more. She had that look now.

"Why?" she asked again, and stood there with her hand inside a bowl,   5 not washing it but just holding it above the water.

"Listen," he said, "I went to school with blacks, and I've worked with blacks and lived on the same street with blacks, and we've always gotten along just fine. I don't need you coming along now and implying that I'm a racist."

"I didn't imply anything," she said, and began washing the bowl again, turning it around in her hand as though she were shaping it. "I just don't see what's wrong with a white person marrying a black person, that's all."

"They don't come from the same culture as we do. Listen to them sometime—they even have their own language. That's okay with me, I *like* hearing them talk"—he did; for some reason it always made him feel happy—"but it's different. A person from their culture and a person from our culture could never really *know* each other."

"Like you know me?" his wife asked.

"Yes. Like I know you."   10

"But if they love each other," she said. She was washing faster now, not looking at him.

Oh boy, he thought. He said, "Don't take my word for it. Look at the statistics. Most of those marriages break up."

"Statistics." She was piling dishes on the drainboard at a terrific rate, just swiping at them with the cloth. Many of them were greasy, and there were flecks of food between the tines of the forks. "All right," she said, "what about foreigners? I suppose you think the same thing about two foreigners getting married."

"Yes," he said, "as a matter of fact I do. How can you understand someone who comes from a completely different background?"

"Different," said his wife. "Not the same, like us."   15

"Yes, different," he snapped, angry with her for resorting to this trick of repeating his words so that they sounded crass, or hypocritical. "These are dirty," he said, and dumped all the silverware back into the sink.

The water had gone flat and gray. She stared down at it, her lips pressed tight together, then plunged her hands under the surface. "Oh!" she cried, and jumped back. She took her right hand by the wrist and held it up. Her thumb was bleeding.

"Ann, don't move," he said. "Stay right there." He ran upstairs to the bathroom and rummaged in the medicine chest for alcohol, cotton, and a Band-Aid. When he came back down she was leaning against the refrigerator with her eyes closed, still holding her hand. He took the hand and dabbed at her thumb with the cotton. The bleeding had stopped. He squeezed it to see how deep the wound was and a single drop of blood welled up, trembling and bright, and fell to the floor. Over the thumb she stared at him accusingly. "It's shallow," he said. "Tomorrow you won't even know it's there." He hoped that she appreciated how quickly he had come to her aid. He'd acted out of concern for her, with no thought of getting anything in return, but now the thought occurred to him that it would be a nice gesture on her part not to start up that conversation again, as he was tired of it. "I'll finish up here," he said. "You go and relax."

"That's okay," she said. "I'll dry."

He began to wash the silverware again, giving a lot of attention to the   20 forks.

"So," she said, "you wouldn't have married me if I'd been black."

"For Christ's sake, Ann!"

"Well, that's what you said, didn't you?"

"No, I did not. The whole question is ridiculous. If you had been black we probably wouldn't even have met. You would have had your friends and I would have had mine. The only black girl I ever really knew was my partner in the debating club, and I was already going out with you by then."

"But if we had met, and I'd been black?"   25

"Then you probably would have been going out with a black guy." He picked up the rinsing nozzle and sprayed the silverware. The water was so hot that the metal darkened to pale blue, then turned silver again.

"Let's say I wasn't," she said. "Let's say I am black and unattached and we meet and fall in love."

He glanced over at her. She was watching him and her eyes were bright. "Look," he said, taking a reasonable tone, "this is stupid. If you were black you wouldn't be you." As he said this he realized it was absolutely true. There was no possible way of arguing with the fact that she would not be herself if she were black. So he said it again: "If you were black you wouldn't be you."

"I know," she said, "but let's just say."

He took a deep breath. He had won the argument but he still felt cor-   30 nered. "Say what?" he asked.

"That I'm black, but still me, and we fall in love. Will you marry me?"

He thought about it.

"Well?" she said, and stepped close to him. Her eyes were even brighter. "Will you marry me?"

"I'm thinking," he said.

"You won't, I can tell. You're going to say no." 35

"Let's not move too fast on this," he said. "There are lots of things to consider. We don't want to do something we would regret for the rest of our lives."

"No more considering. Yes or no."

"Since you put it that way—"

"Yes or no."

"Jesus, Ann. All right. No." 40

She said, "Thank you," and walked from the kitchen into the living room. A moment later he heard her turning the pages of a magazine. He knew that she was too angry to be actually reading it, but she didn't snap through the pages the way he would have done. She turned them slowly, as if she were studying every word. She was demonstrating her indifference to him, and it had the effect he knew she wanted it to have. It hurt him.

He had no choice but to demonstrate his indifference to her. Quietly, thoroughly, he washed the rest of the dishes. Then he dried them and put them away. He wiped the counters and the stove and scoured the linoleum where the drop of blood had fallen. While he was at it, he decided, he might as well mop the whole floor. When he was done the kitchen looked new, the way it looked when they were first shown the house, before they had ever lived here.

He picked up the garbage pail and went outside. The night was clear and he could see a few stars to the west, where the light of the town didn't blur them out. On El Camino the traffic was steady and light, peaceful as a river. He felt ashamed that he had let his wife get him into a fight. In another thirty years or so they would both be dead. What would all that stuff matter then? He thought of the years they had spent together, and how close they were, and how well they knew each other, and his throat tightened so that he could hardly breathe. His face and neck began to tingle. Warmth flooded his chest. He stood there for a while, enjoying these sensations, then picked up the pail and went out the back gate.

The two mutts from down the street had pulled over the garbage can again. One of them was rolling around on his back and the other had something in her mouth. Growling, she tossed it into the air, leaped up and caught it, growled again and whipped her head from side to side. When they saw him coming they trotted away with short, mincing steps. Normally he would heave rocks at them, but this time he let them go.

The house was dark when he came back inside. She was in the bath- 45 room. He stood outside the door and called her name. He heard bottles clinking, but she didn't answer him. "Ann, I'm really sorry," he said. "I'll make it up to you, I promise."

"How?" she asked.

He wasn't expecting this. But from a sound in her voice, a level and definite note that was strange to him, he knew that he had come up with the right answer. He leaned against the door. "I'll marry you," he whispered.

"We'll see," she said. "Go on to bed. I'll be out in a minute."

He undressed and got under the covers. Finally he heard the bathroom door open and close.

"Turn off the light," she said from the hallway.   50
"What?"
"Turn off the light."
He reached over and pulled the chain on the bedside lamp. The room went dark. "All right," he said. He lay there, but nothing happened. "All right," he said again. Then he heard a movement across the room. He sat up, but he couldn't see a thing. The room was silent. His heart pounded the way it had on their first night together, the way it still did when he woke at a noise in the darkness and waited to hear it again—the sound of someone moving through the house, a stranger.

The Receptive Reader

1. How does the world look as we see it through the eyes of the white male narrator?

2. Do you find yourself taking sides in the argument between him and the woman? Would you call him a biased or prejudiced person? (How do you think he looks to readers who are not male or not white?)

3. How do you react to the way the story ends?

The Creative Dimension

How might the story read if it were retold from the point of view of the woman? Write a short alternative story as told by her; or write a part of her story.

Symbol   *What in the story might have a meaning beyond itself?* What objects, people, or incidents seem to have a special significance beyond their literal meaning? A river, for instance, might begin to suggest the steady, slow flow of time, which can never be stopped or reversed. How do such symbolic elements acquire a meaning beyond themselves?

Mary Robison   *(born 1949)*

Mary Robison, the author of the following short short, has been described as a runaway at sixteen, another child of the sixties dropping out from a society that seemed to have lost its meaning. In the story that follows, we focus on a single significant day in the life of a couple. We learn something about the setting of their lives, about them as people, about their relationship. But details of setting, character, and plot are almost crowded out by something the wife had brought home from the store: Halloween pumpkins. They are the first and last things we see in the story. The people work on them and talk about them for most of the story. They loom large. What do they mean? What role do they play? For what do they serve as symbols?

Yours   *1983*

Allison struggled away from her white Renault, limping with the weight of the last of the pumpkins. She found Clark in the twilight on the twig-and-leaf-littered porch behind the house.

He wore a wool shawl. He was moving up and back in a padded glider, pushed by the ball of his slippered foot.

Allison lowered a big pumpkin, let it rest on the wide floorboards.

Clark was much older—seventy-eight to Allison's thirty-five. They were married. They were both quite tall and looked something alike in their facial features. Allison wore a natural-hair wig. It was a thick blond hood around her face. She was dressed in bright-dyed denims today. She wore durable clothes, usually, for she volunteered afternoons at a children's day-care center.

She put one of the smaller pumpkins on Clark's long lap. "Now, nothing surreal," she told him. "Carve just a *regular* face. These are for kids."   5

In the foyer, on the Hepplewhite desk, Allison found the maid's chore list with its cross-offs, which included Clark's supper. Allison went quickly through the day's mail: a garish coupon packet, a bill from Jamestown Liquors, November's pay-TV program guide, and the worst thing, the funniest, an already opened, extremely unkind letter from Clark's relations up North. "You're an old fool," Allison read, and, "You're being cruelly deceived." There was a gift check for Clark enclosed, but it was uncashable, signed, as it was, "Jesus H. Christ."

Late, late into this night, Allison and Clark gutted and carved the pumpkins together, at an old table set on the back porch, over newspaper after soggy newspaper, with paring knives and with spoons and with a Swiss Army knife Clark used for exact shaping of tooth and eye and nostril. Clark had been a doctor, an internist, but also a Sunday watercolorist. His four pumpkins were expressive and artful. Their carved features were suited to the sizes and shapes of the pumpkins. Two looked ferocious and jagged. One registered surprise. The last was serene and beaming.

Allison's four faces were less deftly drawn, with slits and areas of distortion. She had cut triangles for noses and eyes. The mouths she had made were just wedges—two turned up and two turned down.

By one in the morning they were finished. Clark, who had bent his long torso forward to work, moved back over to the glider and looked out sleepily at nothing. All the lights were out across the ravine.   10

Clark stayed. For the season and time, the Virginia night was warm. Most leaves had been blown away already, and the trees stood unbothered. The moon was round above them.

Allison cleaned up the mess.

"Your jack-o'-lanterns are much, much better than mine," Clark said to her.

"Like hell," Allison said.

"Look at me," Clark said, and Allison did.   15

She was holding a squishy bundle of newspapers. The papers reeked sweetly with the smell of pumpkin guts.

"Yours are *far* better," he said.

"You're wrong. You'll see when they're lit," Allison said.

She went inside, came back with yellow vigil candles. It took her a while to get each candle settled, and then to line up the results in a row on the porch railing. She went along and lit each candle and fixed the pumpkin lids over the little flames.

"See?" she said.

They sat together a moment and looked at the orange faces.   20

"We're exhausted. It's good night time," Allison said. "Don't blow out the candles. I'll put in new ones tomorrow."

That night, in their bedroom, a few weeks earlier in her life than had been predicted, Allison began to die. "Don't look at me if my wig comes off," she told Clark. "Please."

Her pulse cords were fluttering under his fingers. She raised her knees and kicked away the comforter. She said something to Clark about the garage being locked.

At the telephone, Clark had a clear view out back and down to the porch. He wanted to get drunk with his wife once more. He wanted to tell her, from the greater perspective he had, that to own only a little talent, like his, was an awful, plaguing thing; that being only a little special meant you expected too much, most of the time, and liked yourself too little. He wanted to assure her that she had missed nothing.   25

He was speaking into the phone now. He watched the jack-o'-lanterns. The jack-o'-lanterns watched him.

The Receptive Reader

1. How do you learn about the situation in which the two characters find themselves? What clues are especially important?

2. What role does the age difference between the two people play in the story? Is it treated differently from what you might have expected? How?

3. When do you first suspect that the pumpkins have a special significance? (What kind of fruit are they; what associations with them do you bring to the story?) What role do they play in the story as a whole? Does it matter that they are carved differently? What do you think they symbolize?

The Personal Response

1. This story deals with age, illness, and death. How does it treat these topics? Do you think the story as a whole is affirmative toward life or disillusioned or depressing?

Theme   *What is the meaning of the story as a whole?* A good story-teller makes us think. Even a lighthearted story may say something about human nature; it may offer some comment on life. It is likely to have a point, although that point may not be spelled out in so many words. We call the implied point, the implied comment, the **theme** of the story. Most writers today are wary of spelling out the theme of a story too directly—afraid that it would sound like a secondhand sentiment, a cliché. They refuse to preach, to editorialize. They want us to live through the experience of the story to discover what it has to say.

What we witness raises questions to which the story as a whole suggests possible answers. Old-fashioned storytelling was often less shy about pointing the moral of the tale. A case in point is the traditional **fable**, going back thousands of years to ancient Greece.

Aesop   *(sixth century B.C.)*

Many familiar traditional fables are attributed to Aesop. Traditionally, the fable ends by spelling out the advice the story was written to drive home. Even so, many of the fables would make their point even if the moral had been lost. Often, the story speaks for itself. The following is a modern rendering of a fable that William Caxton in the fifteenth century had included in one of the first books printed in England. In this retelling, the moral has been left out. What, to you, is the idea acted out in the story?

The Wolf and the Lamb   *about 570 B.C.*

The wolf and the lamb were both thirsty and went to the river to drink. It happened that the wolf drank a ways up the river and the lamb drank farther down. And as the wolf saw and perceived the lamb, he said in a loud voice: "Hah, knave, why hast thou troubled and befouled my water that I should now drink?" "Alas, My Lord, God save Your Grace," said the lamb, "the water flows down the river from you towards me!" Then said the wolf to the lamb: "Hast thou no shame or dread to curse me?" And the lamb said: "My Lord, I am sorry." And the wolf said again: "It is only six months ago that thy father wronged me in the same manner." And the lamb answered: "I was then not even born." And the wolf said again to him: "Thou hast killed and devoured my father!" And the lamb said: "But I have no teeth to eat meat!" Then said the wolf: "Thou art like your father, and for that sin and misdeed thou shalt die!" The wolf then seized the lamb and devoured him.

The Receptive Reader

1. What is the *moral?* What statement does the fable seem to make about human nature? Is it out-of-date, obsolete—or does the fable have a meaning for you as a modern reader?

2. Does this fable give us a *realistic* view of human nature? Or would you call it pessimistic? Would you call it cynical?

Style   *What is the author's personal manner of telling a story?* Is the language factual and low key, or is it passionate and rich in imagery? Is it cheerful or perhaps half teasing, or is it bitter? Does the story follow a conventional story line, building up suspense and leading perhaps to an expected conclusion or else to a surprise ending? Or does the story perhaps proceed in dreamlike fashion, with strange shifts that leave the reader to fill in the connections?

Margaret Atwood   *(born 1939)*

*Put yourself in a different room, that's what the
mind is for.*

MARGARET ATWOOD

In the following story, Margaret Atwood does not follow a conventional story line. Instead she focuses on a central symbol and at each
stage of her story makes us see it in a different light. Atwood is a
widely published Canadian novelist, short story writer, poet, and critic
who has been called "a national icon." In her best-selling guide *Survival* (1972), she wrote about major recurrent themes in Canadian
literature, including the struggle for survival in an inhospitable environment, such as Canada's arctic North. Born in Ottawa, Atwood grew up
in the bush country of northern Ontario and Quebec, where her father
worked as an entomologist. With no formal schooling until she was
twelve, she later studied at the University of Toronto and at Radcliffe
College in Massachusetts. In 1967, the year of Canada's centennial, she
at age twenty-seven won the Governor General's Award for *The Circle
Game.*

Atwood's work has often focused on oppression and exploitation in
the patriarchal societies of the West. She first became widely known for
her book of feminist poems titled *Power Politics* (1971). A recurrent
theme in her poetry has been the spiritual journey taking us back beyond our decaying cities and "civilized distinctions" to the primordial
forces of the wilderness. "I need wolf's eyes to see / the truth" says the
speaker in one of her poems. Her novel *The Handmaid's Tale* (1985)
was made into a chilling movie set in a future where the trappings of
affluent suburban living hide a nightmare of sexist domination and exploitation. In the following short short, Atwood lives up to her reputation for raising disturbing questions and shaking up her readers.

Bread   *1981*

Imagine a piece of bread. You don't have to imagine it, it's right here in
the kitchen, on the breadboard, in its plastic bag, lying beside the bread
knife. The bread knife is an old one you picked up at an auction; it has the
word BREAD carved into the wooden handle. You open the bag, pull back
the wrapper, cut yourself a slice. You put butter on it, then peanut butter,
then honey, and you fold it over. Some of the honey runs out onto your
fingers and you lick it off. It takes you about a minute to eat the bread. This
bread happens to be brown, but there is also white bread, in the refrigerator, and a heel of rye you got last week, round as a full stomach then, now
going moldy. Occasionally you make bread. You think of it as something
relaxing to do with your hands.

Imagine a famine. Now imagine a piece of bread. Both of these things are real but you happen to be in the same room with only one of them. Put yourself into a different room, that's what the mind is for. You are now lying on a thin mattress in a hot room. The walls are made of dried earth, and your sister, who is younger than you, is in the room with you. She is starving, her belly is bloated, flies land on her eyes; you brush them off with your hand. You have a cloth too, filthy but damp, and you press it to her lips and forehead. The piece of bread is the bread you've been saving, for days it seems. You are as hungry as she is, but not yet as weak. How long does this take? When will someone come with more bread? You think of going out to see if you might find something that could be eaten, but outside the streets are infested with scavengers and the stink of corpses is everywhere.

Should you share the bread or give the whole piece to your sister? Should you eat the piece of bread yourself? After all, you have a better chance of living, you're stronger. How long does it take to decide?

Imagine a prison. There is something you know that you have not yet told. Those in control of the prison know that you know. So do those not in control. If you tell, thirty or forty or a hundred of your friends, your comrades, will be caught and will die. If you refuse to tell, tonight will be like last night. They always choose the night. You don't think about the night however, but about the piece of bread they offered you. How long does it take? The piece of bread was brown and fresh and reminded you of sunlight falling across a wooden floor. It reminded you of a bowl, a yellow bowl that was once in your home. It held apples and pears; it stood on a table you can also remember. It's not the hunger or the pain that is killing you but the absence of the yellow bowl. If you could only hold the bowl in your hands, right here, you could withstand anything, you tell yourself. The bread they offered you is subversive, it's treacherous, it does not mean life.

There were once two sisters. One was rich and had no children, the   5
other had five children and was a widow, so poor that she no longer had any food left. She went to her sister and asked her for a mouthful of bread. "My children are dying," she said. The rich sister said, "I do not have enough for myself," and drove her away from the door. Then the husband of the rich sister came home and wanted to cut himself a piece of bread; but when he made the first cut, out flowed red blood.

Everyone knew what that meant.

This is a traditional German fairy tale.

The loaf of bread I have conjured for you floats about a foot above your kitchen table. The table is normal, there are no trap doors in it. A blue tea towel floats beneath the bread, and there are no strings attaching the cloth to the bread or the bread to the ceiling or the table to the cloth, you've proved it by passing your hand above and below. You didn't touch the bread though. What stopped you? You don't want to know whether the bread is real or whether it's just a hallucination I've somehow duped you into seeing. There's no doubt that you can see the bread, you can even smell it, it smells like yeast, and it looks solid enough, solid as your own arm. But can you trust it? Can you eat it? You don't want to know, imagine that.

The Receptive Reader

1. In the opening paragraph, what is the meaning of bread for the person telling the story? What images and associations does the word bring into play? How does the opening of the story make you feel about bread?

2. How did the author get from the bread in her kitchen to the place ravaged by famine? What is the connection? How has the meaning of bread changed? What moral question does it now raise?

3. Is there any connection between the land of famine and the prison? How has the meaning of bread changed now?

4. What is the meaning of bread in the fairy tale that is part of the story? Do the moral issues raised by each successive segment of the story begin to fall into a pattern?

5. For you, does the final paragraph wrap up the story in a satisfactory fashion? Why, or why not?

The Personal Response

How would you respond to the moral challenges you encounter in the different parts of this story? Which is most meaningful or challenging for you as a person?

The Creative Dimension

Did you like the fairy tale that was part of Atwood's story? Why, or why not? Write a modern fairy tale in which a basic symbol from human experience—bread, water, a flower, the heart—plays a major role.

CLOSE READING AND THE PERSONAL RESPONSE

My writing expects, demands participatory reading, and that is what I think literature is supposed to do. It's not just about telling the story; it's about involving the reader. The reader supplies the emotions. The reader supplies even some of the color, some of the sound. My language has to have holes and spaces so that the reader can come into it.

TONI MORRISON

Reading imaginative literature is different from recording data or crunching numbers. It is more multidimensional. It brings not only our intelligence but also our imagination and our emotions into play. It involves us as complete human beings. When we respond fully to a story or a poem, we are living more alertly in the world. We are broadening our sympathies. We are educating the emotions.

You may want to think of your reading as involving three major dimensions:

The Receptive Reader   A receptive reader is on the writer's side. As a receptive reader, you make an extra effort of understanding; you give a difficult story the benefit of the doubt. You develop the habit of close, attentive reading (rather than skimming the page to get a "general idea"). In a well-crafted short story, details are not just there to fill the page. You are likely to notice striking details that make the author's world real for the reader. You should be alert to gestures or actions that provide a clue to a character's motives. You will need an eye for objects with symbolic overtones, an ear for revealing comments and shades of meaning. You will need to respond to patterns that give shape to the story as a whole.

The Personal Response   The stories and the writers we return to have some special personal meaning for us. The stories that move us powerfully do in some way touch our own lives, though the connection may not always be obvious. At some level, they engage with our own needs, desires, or apprehensions. The writer does not really expect us to read the story the way an electronic scanner would, retrieving data to be analyzed later. Our emotions as well as our intellect must be engaged if we are to understand what mattered to the author.

The following is one student's reaction to a short story classic. How did she make the personal connection? What mattered to her most in the story, and why?

"The Open Boat" by Stephen Crane is a story about men who were shipwrecked and forced to brave the open sea with very little protection and with little hope of survival. While I read this story, I felt much concern about the men who were trying to survive in a contest with nature that seemed bent on defeating them and had the power to destroy them. What struck me most in this story was the spirit of teamwork, of working together. They helped each other out in order to survive; they knew that was the only way to beat the sea. The cook bailed the water out of their tiny boat; the journalist and the engineer took turns rowing the boat ("Will you spell me for a little while?"), never complaining or saying they were dead tired when they were all on the brink of exhaustion. The captain, although he was injured and unable to do physical work, gave directions and moral support to the "crew." What if they had not been able to work as a team? What if they had started bickering, using abusive language, as many people would today? What if they had let the short fuse set off an explosion of stupid hostility and pride? They would all have drowned. At the end of the story, I found myself cheering them all on, and I was full of grief when one of the crew drowned. The surprising thing to me was that the one who drowned was the strongest of the four. It may not always be the "fittest" who survives.

The Creative Dimension   Fiction stimulates the reader's imagination. For instance, you may want to re-create an impression that lingered in your memory. You may want to evoke a haunting image that in some way seems to sum up the story. Look at the following student-written response to Mary Robison's "Yours." How does it add to or enhance your own reading of the story?

              Harvest
      Pumpkins in orange October—
           their sweet soggy smell
           rises from carved insides
           on wet news.
      Their fierce pumpkin faces, lit by candles,
           glow till morning,
           the live flame softening their shells.
      Pumpkin, a child's toy,
           not for May or December,
           but for late October, ushering in
           November and a Thanksgiving of sorts.
      Pumpkins from the brittle vine:
           the last sweet
           harvest.

WRITING ABOUT LITERATURE

1 Starting a Short Story Journal
WRITING FOCUS: Preparing for Writing

The Writing Workshop   Writing is more than a way of communicating what you already know. It is a way of learning, of thinking through what you have learned. Writing about literature can make you a more attentive, more thoughtful reader. When you keep a short story **journal**, you record your impressions and reactions as you read. You have a chance to register your questions, to record tentative conclusions, and to do some preliminary sorting out of your thinking. You try to formulate your personal responses, puzzling over contradictory or unexpected reactions on your part. You experiment with creative responses to what you have read, such as quickly sketched re-creations of a haunting image, a prevailing mood, a turning point in a story.

Writing weekly or biweekly entries in a reading journal or reading log gives you a chance to do some extensive prewriting for more structured papers, to accumulate a rich fund of materials for more formal writing tasks. Here are some possible kinds of entries for your journal:

Thinking about Previous Reading   In one of your first journal entries, you may want to look back over your previous experiences as a reader. What kind of reading has shaped your expectations? For instance, what kind of story made a lasting impression on you, and why? You may write about a story you loved or admired but also about a story that upset or disturbed you. Perhaps you will choose a work of literature that did not mean much at the time but that in retrospect has acquired a special meaning.

First Impressions   You will often find it helpful to record your initial impressions after your first reading. You may want to sort out and put into words your first reactions and your preliminary understanding of a story. Take time to gather your thoughts, to pull together what seems most significant. Include any questions the story may have raised in your mind. Here is one reader's first reaction to a story by the Canadian author Alice Munro:

Alice Munro's "Boys and Girls" takes place in Canada where the head of a small family raises silver foxes for furs. Of the two children, the girl tells the story, making pertinent observations on life on the fox farm and on the other members of the family. Life is seen entirely through her eyes. Foxes are slaughtered and their skins prepared for sale. Old injured horses are killed for food for the foxes. What it means to be a boy and what it means to be a girl become major issues in the story. (Is it significant that both the foxes and the horses are given male and female names?) Gender roles flip-flop in the story as the narrator prides herself on doing "man's work" as her father's helper while her mother grumbles about not getting enough help from her in the kitchen. Stereotypes are constantly challenged, but in the end they seem to triumph as the girl realizes she is "only a girl."

Running Commentary   An excellent way to make the most of your reading is to prepare a running commentary. You jot down your observations, queries, and comments as you read along. You include striking details, quotable quotations, and puzzlers to be checked out later. What at first was a puzzling detail may acquire fuller meaning as the author sounds the same note again or follows up an earlier hint.

Your entry will be your record of how your understanding of a story took shape. Doing such a running commentary will alert you to the clues the author provides to the intention, overall pattern, or overall meaning of a story. However, it will also make sure you get involved in the detail of the story before you interpret, speculate, or editorialize. It will make you realize how much of the **texture** of a story—its web of revealing details, significant dialogue—can be missed in a quick reading.

Running Commentary on "Say Yes"
The setting is in the house of the two main characters. It is in the first few lines that the husband does his portion of the housework. Why is it such a big deal in

the first few sentences? Has something happened between him and his wife regarding this issue?

They are having a conversation that turns to interracial marriages and relationships. She asks her husband if white people should marry black people. He thinks it is a bad idea. He knows her looks well enough to know when she's upset. He knew that he should keep his mouth shut when, "she pinched her brows together and bit her lower lip and stared down at something." But he doesn't. If they are having a fight, or disagreement about something, is this his way to fuel it?

This initial disagreement over relationships feeds into whether he knows her as well as he thinks he does. She asks him this by saying, "Like you know me?" and he says yes. This is where the story becomes about their relationship and how well they know each other for who they really are.

She turns the interracial comments on their marriage and asks him if he would have married her if she were black. His reply is, "Look, if you were black you wouldn't be you." As he is saying it, he realizes the truth, and repeats it again, "if you were black, you wouldn't be you." His wife keeps pushing the issue, and finally he tells her, "Jesus, Ann. All right. No." It is the final moment in that discussion.

This is the point where they both realize that they don't know each other as well as they thought before. It strikes them both that one simple topic could turn each of them. However, one point that was brought up in our small group was the possibility that maybe the wife was getting too emotional. The husband wasn't letting this get in the way of how he felt about his wife. She was, though, and it was bothering her more that he wasn't this emotionally involved in their discussion. Does she have a right to get this emotional over this topic?

The husband knows his wife's movements, and when she is very angry, she is trying to make a point to him. She is reading a magazine in another room, and turning the pages so that he will think that she is actually reading. He notes that if he were in her position, he would be furiously turning the pages to show that he was mad. It's her way to spite him.

The fight continues into the evening where they are getting ready for bed together. She tells him, "Turn off the light." He's not sure why and so questions her. She repeats herself, "Turn off the light." He does so, and comments to himself that he feels a stranger in the house. It is like their first night together. This is symbolic because in the actions from the evening, the couple has realized that they do not know each other as well as they thought. They are once again strangers. This is providing the husband with some new excitement in their relationship. Does the wife have this same feeling?

The Personal Response

Much effective writing about literature offers the results of close reading (what does the story have to offer?) but goes beyond careful interpretation to the personal response (why should the reader care?). In a journal entry, you may focus on your personal connection with a story. In the following example, the student writer is beginning to take sides with one of the characters; he interprets the issue raised in the story in the light of his own personal experience.

The husband in Tobias Wolff's "Say Yes" thinks white people should not marry black people. He defends his argument by comparing the two different cultures of black and white people and stating they are incompatible. The wife has the exact opposite mentality, and defends her opinion by asking the question of why, to almost everything he has to say. As the two are talking about the question at hand, the wife mentions love: "But if they love each other." As I read on, I side with the wife more and more. I'm starting to think the husband is not as considerate as he seemed to be in the beginning when he shared in the chores. The bickering goes on and on until a turning point comes. The wife proposes the idea that "if she was black, would he have still married her." That is a double-sided question if I ever heard one. If he says yes, his argument would be destroyed and he will have lost the argument. If he says no, she will have every right to be angry because this would mean he never completely loved her for who she is. Much of his love would be based on what she looks like. The way I see it, based on six years of dating experience, he needs to cut his losses and admit he was wrong. The whole time she is pushing for a "yes" or "no."

Clustering   Many writers use clustering to start and organize the flow of ideas. For a story to work, it has to engage with what we already know. What images and feelings does a story activate in the reader's mind? What associations with a central term does the reader bring to the story? **Clustering** is a prewriting technique that lets you explore a network of images, memories, or associations. With strands of ideas branching out from a central stimulus word, you can follow the different chains of associations the central idea brings into play. The idea is to sketch freely, spontaneously, what a key word or key term brings to mind.

Clustering is a stimulus technique of double value to you if you are the kind of writer who might otherwise be staring at a blank sheet or screen. First, you call up from the memory bank of your mind much material that might potentially be relevant to a topic. You access thoughts and feelings; you map graphically what you are inclined to think and feel on a topic. At the same time, however, a pattern takes shape. You begin to see possible connections and relations. Some sorting, some shaping is going on at the same time that you are taking stock of relevant memories, associations, and overtones.

In a story like Bernard Malamud's "The Magic Barrel" or Shirley Jackson's "The Lottery," tradition plays a central role—tradition and the way the characters in the story live up to it, fight it, or make it suit their purposes. A cluster like the one on the next page might map the network of associations that a reader brings to the story. Notice that in this cluster a pattern is taking shape: The cluster graphically shows thinking in progress. It shows the writer thinking about the two-sided nature of tradition, a force for good and evil.

The following passage lays out the material and traces the pattern that the cluster has generated:

Tradition to many of us means first of all nostalgic memories of Christmas or Easter or Passover, happy hours spent with family and friends, birthday celebrations with balloons and ice cream, cake, and candles. In the traditional family, there is a sense of security—of knowing what to do, of relying on the tried and true. However, we also feel the weight of tradition—feeling guilty about not going to mass, feeling fear of retribution for our sins and backslidings. The inherent danger

Sample Cluster

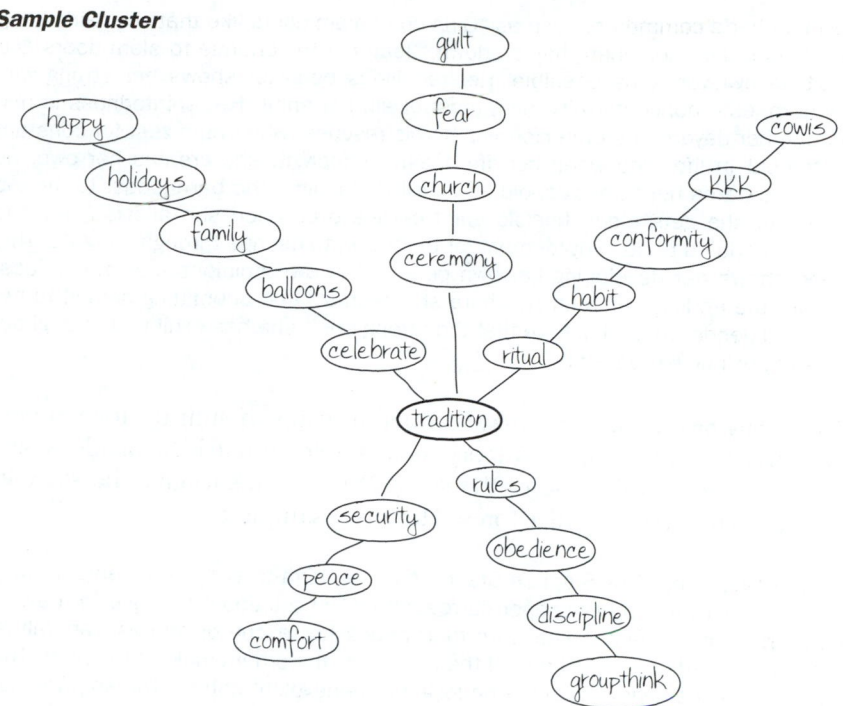

in tradition is the reliance on groupthink. Blind obedience to traditional rules and regulations can lead to unquestioned acceptance of cruel or idiotic practices. When we look at the dual nature of tradition, we see interlocking elements that can suddenly cover the face of love with a cowl of enmity and violence.

Focusing on Character   In other journal entries, you may go beyond note taking to start to organize your thinking. For instance, in a **capsule portrait** of a character, you pull together traits illustrated in the incidents of the story. You integrate crucial hints about the character that may be scattered over quite a few pages. What kind of person does the author show you? What are key traits, and how are they related? Is there a trait that provides the clue to the character as a whole? Does the character change or grow in the course of the story? Here is a sample of such a character portrait:

The central character in Alice Munro's story "Boys and Girls" is struggling to adjust to the fact that she is slowly changing from a girl to a young woman. In the beginning, she is her daddy's helper around the fox farm where her father raises foxes for their pelts. Oblivious to the stereotypical female gender role, she helps her father care for the animals, rakes up the grass or weeds he has cut, and does other traditional "male" chores. However, she begins to realize that as a female she is expected to do some things and not others; in particular, she is expected to help her mother in the kitchen, a place she detests. She rebels against her expected role, trying to stay out of the kitchen and close to the outdoors she loves. Her grandmother's comments, such as "Girls don't slam doors like that" or "Girls keep their knees together when they sit down," lead her to continue to slam doors and to sit as awkwardly as possible. Her rebellious behavior shows her strong will, stubbornness, nonconformity, and, most of all, her spirit. Her spiritedness is mirrored in her daydreams of performing heroic rescues. She has a zest for constant excitement in life, and when her life doesn't supply it, she creates her own, as when she dares her three-year-old little brother to climb the barn ladder to the top beam. As she gets older, her old spirit carries over when she allows Flora, the horse scheduled to be shot for meat for the foxes, to escape through the gate. This scene shows her developing her own person, her own opinions, her own values. Despite the ending of the story, where she seems to be submitting herself to her expected gender roles, I believe that the strong spirit she has exhibited throughout the story will never leave her.

Focusing on Theme   You may frequently want to sum up for yourself the impact or meaning of a story as a whole. What idea or ideas stay with the reader at the end of the story? What seems to give the story its special quality or particular force? Here is a sample entry:

"The Open Boat," by Stephen Crane, is a late 19th to early 20th century story. Crew members and a newspaper correspondent in a lifeboat struggle for days in the stormy shark-infested sea, with their hopes for rescue or an easy landfall repeatedly dashed. In the end one of them drowns; the others make it to shore. This is an early modern view: There is no loving or benevolent nature. The shipwrecked sailors undergo a terrible ordeal, but they do not conclude that nature was out to punish them, nor do they feel that nature is loving or maternal. Birds were made to survive on the ocean; they are part of nature. The only way for human beings to survive is to work together—practice brotherhood. Since they are not at home in nature, they must make their home within it with the help of others. They need solidarity. Nature is alien and inhospitable; it couldn't care less.

For Class Interaction   You may want to share one or more early journal entries with your classmates. For instance, you might want to discuss with them what made a story especially meaningful to you, or what expectations you brought to it, or what made it difficult for you to read or enjoy.

2   SETTING

Landscapes of the Mind

Courtesy Richard B. Ressman

*Here I am, where I ought to be. A writer must
have a place where he or she feels this, a place to
love and be irritated with.*

LOUISE ERDRICH

*Once in their lives people ought to concentrate their
minds upon the remembered earth. They ought to
give themselves up to a particular landscape in
their experience, looking at it from as many angles
as they can, to wonder upon it, to dwell upon it.*

N. SCOTT MOMADAY

FOCUS ON SETTING

A story creates its own world. It takes us to a **setting** in space and in time. In a successful story, that place becomes a small universe of its own, consistent in itself. The author creates a context whose assumptions we accept for the duration of the story. We enter into the world of the story the way we might honor customs, closing hours, and curfews when we spend time in another country. Some writers sketch times and locations only in rough outline, leaving much to our imagination. But other writers painstakingly re-create a setting or reenact a scene. They use the setting to create the illusion of reality, so that we will accept characters and events as real also.

One of the first questions we ask of a story is, "Where is the story taking us?" By establishing the setting, a writer lets us know where we are, makes us realize what time it is. Often the setting plays a major role in shaping the characters, the action, or the theme of a story. A *New York Times* reviewer said about the stories in Bobbie Ann Mason's *Shiloh and Other Stories* (1982):

> Mason's setting was Kentucky—not the old Kentucky of small towns and gracious farms, but that proud territory of the new South speckled with shopping malls and subdivisions, fast-food franchises and drive-in movies, a shiny new place, vacuumed clean of history and tradition. Reeling from the swiftness of the transition, Mason's characters all seemed to wander about in a fog, either spacing out in front of the television or passively drifting away from their families and friends, aware, however dimly, that they had misplaced something important along the way.

Here are ways the setting may help give shape to a story as a whole.

The Setting as Mirror   The setting may mirror a prevailing mood. It may signal or reinforce prevailing emotions. An arid landscape, for instance, may mirror despair, spiritual desolation. Barren hills, scrubby vegetation, and dusty dirt roads may provide a fitting setting for emotionally dried-up characters. However, you cannot always expect a direct connection between the setting and the people who play their roles in it. The setting may be ironic, as when a character feels depressed in a springtime setting. Our sense of **irony** makes us respond with a grim smile when things do not turn out the way we would like or expect.

The Setting as Mold   The setting of a story often shapes character. It helps make people what they are. Someone growing up on a farm, with its chores, dependence on rain and sun, and closeness to living things, is likely to have a different outlook, a different definition of life, than someone growing up in a neighborhood where the only open spaces are parking lots. A story may show its characters as creatures of the setting, reflecting its mood, living out its mores or approved ways of acting and thinking. A familiar theme in serious modern fiction is that of invisible walls: Characters may find themselves trapped in the spiritual wasteland of suburbia, or in a small decaying town that becomes for them the graveyard of hope. On the other hand, a story may show a character rebelling against a stifling environment, struggling to break free.

The Setting as Escape   Escape literature takes us to imaginary settings where we act out daydreams. The story may take us to a mansion in the pre–Civil War South to make us witness scenes of flaming passion. It may take us to ancient Rome to appall us with scenes of treachery and depravity. However, a faraway setting may not really provide an escape; it may be the destination of a journey of discovery. In a strange setting, we may encounter facets of our own personality denied an outlet in our ordinary world.

The Alien Setting   Much modern literature circles back to the loss of roots, the loss of home. You may find yourself in a setting that is inhospitable, like an alien planet. You may identify with the exile, the undesirable, the refugee. In much early-twentieth-century fiction, you encounter the eternal tourist, the expatriate—the person in exile from his or her own country. In the fiction of Franz Kafka, you find yourself in a nightmare setting. As in a bad dream, you may struggle with an environment that defies your best efforts to get control of the situation, to understand what is going on.

FIRST READING

Responding to a Place

Have you ever come to a place where you felt instantly at home? Try bringing back to mind the sights and sounds that made you feel at home and at ease. Or have you ever been in a place where you felt like a stranger? Try bringing back to mind the sights and sounds that made you feel alien or unwanted. Then read the following short short by Larry Fondation, paying special attention to the setting. The story has appeared in several collections of short stories and *very* short stories—stories that, in the words of one editor, can be "apprehended all at once."

Larry Fondation   *(born 1957)*

Deportation at Breakfast   *1991*

The signs on the windows lured me inside. For a dollar I could get two eggs, toast, and potatoes. The place looked better than most—family-run and clean. The signs were hand-lettered and neat. The paper had yellowed some, but the black letters remained bold. A green-and-white awning was perched over the door, where the name "Clara's" was stenciled.

Inside, the place had an appealing and old-fashioned look. The air smelled fresh and homey, not greasy. The menu was printed on a chalk-board. It was short and to the point. It listed the kinds of toast you could choose from. One entry was erased from the middle of the list. By deduction, I figured it was rye. I didn't want rye toast anyway.

Because I was alone, I sat at the counter, leaving the empty tables free for other customers that might come in. At the time, business was quiet. Only two tables were occupied; and I was alone at the counter. But it was still early—not yet seven-thirty.

Behind the counter was a short man with dark black hair, a mustache, and a youthful beard, one that never grew much past stubble. He was dressed immaculately, all in chef's white—pants, shirt, and apron, but no hat. He had a thick accent. The name "Javier" was stitched on his shirt.

I ordered coffee, and asked for a minute to choose between the break-   5
fast special for a dollar and the cheese omelette for $1.59. I selected the omelette.

The coffee was hot, strong, and fresh. I spread my newspaper on the counter and sipped at the mug as Javier went to the grill to cook my meal.

The eggs were spread out on the griddle, the bread plunged inside the toaster, when the authorities came in. They grabbed Javier quickly and with-out a word, forcing his hands behind his back. He, too, said nothing. He did not resist, and they shoved him out the door and into their waiting car.

On the grill, my eggs bubbled. I looked around for another employee—maybe out back somewhere, or in the washroom. I leaned over the counter and called for someone. No one answered. I looked behind me toward the tables. Two elderly men sat at one; two elderly women at the other. The two women were talking. The men were reading the paper. They seemed not to have noticed Javier's exit.

I could smell my eggs starting to burn. I wasn't quite sure what to do about it. I thought about Javier and stared at my eggs. After some hesitation, I got up from my red swivel stool and went behind the counter. I grabbed a spare apron, then picked up the spatula and turned my eggs. My toast had popped up, but it was not browned, so I put it down again. While I was cooking, the two elderly women came to the counter and asked to pay. I asked what they had had. They seemed surprised that I didn't remember. I checked the prices on the chalkboard and rang up their order. They paid slowly, fishing through large purses, and went out, leaving me a dollar tip. I took my eggs off the grill and slid them onto a clean plate. My toast had come up. I buttered it and put it on my plate beside my eggs. I put the plate at my spot at the counter, right next to my newspaper.

As I began to come back from behind the counter to my stool, six new   10
customers came through the door. "Can we pull some tables together?" they asked. "We're all one party." I told them yes. Then they ordered six coffees, two decaffeinated.

I thought of telling them I didn't work there. But perhaps they were hungry. I poured their coffee. Their order was simple: six breakfast specials, all with scrambled eggs and wheat toast. I got busy at the grill.

Then the elderly men came to pay. More new customers began arriving. By eight-thirty, I had my hands full. With this kind of business, I couldn't understand why Javier hadn't hired a waitress. Maybe I'd take out a help-wanted ad in the paper tomorrow. I had never been in the restaurant business. There was no way I could run this place alone.

The Receptive Reader

Do you recognize the setting in this story? Can you put yourself in this setting—why, or why not? Which details do most to make this setting real for you? Would you feel strange or at home here? Did the fate of the cook seem possible or fantastic to you? Could you have taken over the way the narrator—the person telling the story—did?

SETTINGS: THE SENSE OF PLACE

Some writers are especially effective at creating a compelling environment—a world that we can imaginatively enter and re-enter. In reading the following stories, pay special attention to the role the setting plays in the story as a whole.

James Joyce   *(1882–1941)*

"This race and this country and this life produced me," he said. "I shall express myself as I am."
JAMES JOYCE, *A Portrait of the Artist as a Young Man*

James Joyce was one of the Irish writers that helped shape twentieth-century literature. Like other artists and intellectuals of his time, Joyce worked most of his life in self-imposed exile from his native country.

Born in a suburb of Dublin, he left Dublin at the age of twenty-two, and he returned only twice for brief visits. However, the city of his birth and its people are in almost everything he wrote.

Joyce was the son of an outgoing but spendthrift father and a devoutly Catholic mother. At the age of six, he entered a school run by Jesuit priests; he later enrolled at the Jesuit order's Belvedere College in Dublin. (His mother wanted him, as the oldest of her ten children, to become a priest in the Roman Catholic Church.) However, he decided against entering the priesthood, refusing to commit to a traditional creed. He similarly distanced himself from the passionate, intolerant nationalism that was the legacy of Ireland's struggle against British colonial rule. Family, church, and country came to seem to him like nets thrown to restrain the free exercise of the creative spirit. As he said in his largely autobiographical first novel, *A Portrait of the Artist as a Young Man* (1916), "I will not serve that in which I no longer believe."

Joyce barely survived by teaching English and doing clerical work, first in Zurich (Switzerland) and later in Trieste (Italy) and Paris. He wrote constantly, developing the **stream-of-consciousness** technique that was to revolutionize much of modern fiction. Human beings do not think in complete sentences, carry on coherent logical conversations with themselves, or make rational decisions after lining up the pros and cons. Instead, their mental world is a shifting sequence of sensations, thoughts, and feelings—a kaleidoscopic mix of fleeting images, bodily sensations, memories, half-finished trends of thought. In Joyce's masterpiece, *Ulysses* (1922), a thread of external events alternates with stretches of **interior monologue,** immersing the reader in a stream of impressions, reminiscences, and half-formulated thoughts. At the same time, the novel uses complex allusions to Greek mythology, with the daily rounds of Leopold Bloom, a Dublin salesman, paralleling the mythical journey of Ulysses. In his *Finnegan's Wake* (1939), Joyce developed a rich private language exploiting multileveled puns, allusions, and associations.

We call a work of literature a classic when readers and critics return to it again and again, when it survives changes in fashion. The following classic short story is from an early collection, *Dubliners* (1914), intended by Joyce as "a chapter of the moral history of Ireland." Compared with Joyce's later work, these stories have a straightforward, conventional story line. However, like his later work, they focus on the private thoughts, emotions, and daydreams of his characters. A few references in this story might puzzle today's reader. One of the books mentioned early told the life story of Vidocq, a legendary French detective. The Freemasons, members of private fraternal organizations, were viewed with suspicion by people with traditional religious views. The florin was a British silver coin worth two shillings. A *café chantant* was a French coffeehouse with musical entertainment.

Araby *1914*

North Richmond Street, being blind, was a quiet street except at the hour when the Christian Brothers' School set the boys free. An uninhabited house of two stories stood at the blind end, detached from its neighbors in a square ground. The other houses of the street, conscious of decent lives within them, gazed at one another with brown imperturbable faces.

The former tenant of our house, a priest, had died in the back drawing-room. Air, musty from having been long enclosed, hung in all the rooms, and the waste room behind the kitchen was littered with old useless papers. Among these I found a few paper-covered books, the pages of which were curled and damp: *The Abbot,* by Walter Scott, *The Devout Communicant* and *The Memoirs of Vidocq.* I liked the last best because its leaves were yellow. The wild garden behind the house contained a central apple-tree and a few straggling bushes under one of which I found the late tenant's rusty bicycle-pump. He had been a very charitable priest; in his will he had left all his money to institutions and the furniture of his house to his sister.

When the short days of winter came dusk fell before we had well eaten our dinners. When we met in the street the houses had grown somber. The space of sky above us was the color of ever-changing violet and toward it the lamps of the street lifted their feeble lanterns. The cold air stung us and we played till our bodies glowed. Our shouts echoed in the silent street. The career of our play brought us through the dark muddy lanes behind the houses where we ran the gauntlet of the rough tribes from the cottages, to the back doors of the dark dripping gardens where odors arose from the ashpits, to the dark odorous stables where a coachman smoothed and combed the horse or shook music from the buckled harness. When we returned to the street light from the kitchen windows had filled the areas. If my uncle was seen turning the corner we hid in the shadow until we had seen him safely housed. Or if Mangan's sister came out on the doorstep to call her brother in to his tea we watched her from our shadow peer up and down the street. We waited to see whether she would remain or go in and, if she remained, we left our shadow and walked up to Mangan's steps resignedly. She was waiting for us, her figure defined by the light from the half-opened door. Her brother always teased her before he obeyed and I stood by the railings looking at her. Her dress swung as she moved her body, and the soft rope of her hair tossed from side to side.

Every morning I lay on the floor in the front parlor watching her door. The blind was pulled down to within an inch of the sash so that I could not be seen. When she came out on the doorstep my heart leaped. I ran to the hall, seized my books and followed her. I kept her brown figure always in my eye and, when we came near the point at which our ways diverged, I quickened my pace and passed her. This happened morning after morning. I had never spoken to her, except for a few casual words, and yet her name was like a summons to all my foolish blood.

Her image accompanied me even in places the most hostile to romance. 5
On Saturday evenings when my aunt went marketing I had to go to carry some of the parcels. We walked through the flaring streets, jostled by

drunken men and bargaining women, amid the curses of laborers, the shrill litanies of shop-boys who stood on guard by the barrels of pigs' cheeks, the nasal chanting of street-singers, who sang a *come-all-you* about O'Donovan Rossa, or a ballad about the troubles in our native land. These noises converged in a single sensation of life for me: I imagined that I bore my chalice safely through a throng of foes. Her name sprang to my lips at moments in strange prayers and praises which I myself did not understand. My eyes were often full of tears (I could not tell why) and at times a flood from my heart seemed to pour itself out into my bosom. I thought little of the future. I did not know whether I would ever speak to her or not or, if I spoke to her, how I could tell her of my confused adoration. But my body was like a harp and her words and gestures were like fingers running upon the wires.

One evening I went into the back drawing-room in which the priest had died. It was a dark rainy evening and there was no sound in the house. Through one of the broken panes I heard the rain impinge upon the earth, the fine incessant needles of water playing in the sodden beds. Some distant lamp or lighted window gleamed below me. I was thankful that I could see so little. All my senses seemed to desire to veil themselves and, feeling that I was about to slip from them, I pressed the palms of my hands together until they trembled, murmuring: *"O love! O love!"* many times.

At last she spoke to me. When she addressed the first words to me I was so confused that I did not know what to answer. She asked me was I going to *Araby*. I forgot whether I answered yes or no. It would be a splendid bazaar, she said she would love to go.

"And why can't you?" I asked.

While she spoke she turned a silver bracelet round and round her wrist. She could not go, she said, because there would be a retreat that week in her convent. Her brother and two other boys were fighting for their caps and I was alone at the railings. She held one of the spikes, bowing her head towards me. The light from the lamp opposite our door caught the white curve of her neck, lit up her hair that rested there and, falling, lit up the hand upon the railing. It fell over one side of her dress and caught the white border of a petticoat, just visible as she stood at ease.

"It's well for you," she said.

"If I go," I said, "I will bring you something."

What innumerable follies laid waste my waking and sleeping thoughts after that evening! I wished to annihilate the tedious intervening days. I chafed against the work of school. At night in my bedroom and by day in the classroom her image came between me and the page I strove to read. The syllables of the word *Araby* were called to me through the silence in which my soul luxuriated and cast an Eastern enchantment over me. I asked for leave to go to the bazaar on Saturday night. My aunt was surprised and hoped it was not some Freemason affair. I answered few questions in class. I watched my master's face pass from amiability to sternness; he hoped I was not beginning to idle. I could not call my wandering thoughts together. I had hardly any patience with the serious work of life which, now that it stood between me and my desire, seemed to me child's play, ugly monotonous child's play.

10

On Saturday morning I reminded my uncle that I wished to go to the bazaar in the evening. He was fussing at the hallstand, looking for the hat-brush, and answered me curtly:

"Yes, boy, I know."

As he was in the hall I could not go into the front parlor and lie at the window. I left the house in bad humor and walked slowly toward the school. The air was pitilessly raw and already my heart misgave me.

When I came home to dinner my uncle had not yet been home. Still it was early. I sat staring at the clock for some time and, when its ticking began to irritate me, I left the room. I mounted the staircase and gained the upper part of the house. The high cold empty gloomy rooms liberated me and I went from room to room singing. From the front window I saw my companions playing below in the street. Their cries reached me weakened and indistinct and, leaning my forehead against the cool glass, I looked over at the dark house where she lived. I may have stood there for an hour, see-ing nothing but the brown-clad figure cast by my imagination, touched dis-creetly by the lamplight at the curved neck, at the hand upon the railings and at the border below the dress.

When I came downstairs again I found Mrs. Mercer sitting at the fire. She was an old garrulous woman, a pawn-broker's widow, who collected used stamps for some pious purpose. I had to endure the gossip of the tea-table. The meal was prolonged beyond an hour and still my uncle did not come. Mrs. Mercer stood up to go: she was sorry she couldn't wait any longer, but it was after eight o'clock and she did not like to be out late, as the night air was bad for her. When she had gone I began to walk up and down the room, clenching my fists. My aunt said:

"I'm afraid you may put off your bazaar for this night of Our Lord."

At nine o'clock I heard my uncle's latchkey in the halldoor. I heard him talking to himself and heard the hallstand rocking when it had received the weight of his overcoat. I could interpret these signs. When he was midway through his dinner I asked him to give me the money to go to the bazaar. He had forgotten.

"The people are in bed and after their first sleep now," he said.

I did not smile. My aunt said to him energetically:

"Can't you give him the money and let him go? You've kept him late enough as it is."

My uncle said he was very sorry he had forgotten. He said he believed in the old saying: "All work and no play makes Jack a dull boy." He asked me where I was going and, when I had told him a second time he asked me did I know *The Arab's Farewell to his Steed*. When I left the kitchen he was about to recite the opening lines of the piece to my aunt.

I held a florin tightly in my hand as I strode down Buckingham Street to-ward the station. The sight of the streets thronged with buyers and glaring with gas recalled to me the purpose of my journey. I took my seat in a third-class carriage of a deserted train. After an intolerable delay the train moved out of the station slowly. It crept onward among ruinous houses and over the twinkling river. At Westland Row Station a crowd of people pressed to the carriage doors; but the porters moved them back, saying that it was a special train for the bazaar. I remained alone in the bare carriage. In a few minutes the train drew up beside an improvised wooden platform. I passed out on to the road and saw by the lighted dial of a clock that it was ten minutes to ten. In front of me was a large building which displayed the magical name.

I could not find any sixpenny entrance and, fearing that the bazaar would   25 be closed, I passed in quickly through a turnstile, handing a shilling to a weary-looking man. I found myself in a big hall girdled at half its height by a gallery. Nearly all the stalls were closed and the greater part of the hall was in darkness. I recognized a silence like that which pervades a church after a service. I walked into the center of the bazaar timidly. A few people were gathered about the stalls which were still open. Before a curtain, over which the words *Café Chantant* were written in colored lamps, two men were counting money on a salver. I listened to the fall of the coins.

Remembering with difficulty why I had come I went over to one of the stalls and examined porcelain vases and flowered tea-sets. At the door of the stall a young lady was talking and laughing with two young gentlemen. I remarked their English accents and listened vaguely to their conversation.

"O, I never said such a thing!"

"O, but you did!"

"O, but I didn't!"

"Didn't she say that?"   30

"Yes. I heard her."

"O, there's a . . . fib!"

Observing me the young lady came over and asked me did I wish to buy anything. The tone of her voice was not encouraging; she seemed to have spoken to me out of a sense of duty. I looked humbly at the great jars that stood like eastern guards at either side of the dark entrance to the stall and murmured:

"No, thank you."

The young lady changed the position of one of the vases and went back   35 to the two young men. They began to talk of the same subject. Once or twice the young lady glanced at me over her shoulder.

I lingered before her stall, though I knew my stay was useless, to make my interest in her wares seem the more real. Then I turned away slowly and walked down the middle of the bazaar. I allowed the two pennies to fall against the sixpence in my pocket. I heard a voice call from one end of the gallery that the light was out. The upper part of the hall was now completely dark.

Gazing up into the darkness I saw myself as a creature driven and derided by vanity; and my eyes burned with anguish and anger.

The Receptive Reader

1. What striking details help the setting come to life for you? Which seem to set the tone or point forward to the rest of the story?

2. What striking images help you understand the boy's feelings? What images give his devotion a quasi-religious quality? (What are the associations of the word *chalice?* What feelings does it bring into play?)

3. Is the boy able to share his feelings with anyone? If not, why not?

4. What is the role of the uncle in the story?

5. Is it a coincidence that the climactic high point of the story takes place in a bazaar—a special annual event?

6. As we watch crucial scenes in the story, we at times have to sense the boy's feelings rather than having them explained in so many words by the author. What are some examples?

The Personal Response

Is the boy merely infatuated? Should he have known better? Is he acting "immature"?

The Creative Dimension

Writers sometimes describe how a short story took shape from a striking, teasing image in the writer's mind. Sometimes after we finish reading, what stays with us is a haunting image that seems to sum up something essential in the story. The following student-written passage re-creates a key moment in Joyce's "Araby." What does it capture in the story? Write your own re-creation of a haunting image or key moment in Joyce's story or in another story in this chapter.

> We played in
>   the cold, short winter evenings
>   colored violet with dusk.
>   We made a career
>   of playing long in
>   the streets
>   and alleys with shadows
>   our bodies small and cold
>   and glowing.
>   In the street the lamps
>   lined up,
>   illuminating
>   a playmate's sister strolling
>   towards us,
>   soft smooth hair,
>   swinging skirt.

Making Connections—For Discussion or Writing

Another story in which the world is seen through the prism of youth and innocence is Anton Chekhov's "Vanka" (see Chapter 5). How might the two central characters in these stories appear when seen through the eyes of an adult observer?

Bobbie Ann Mason   *(born 1940)*

Mason was part of a group of writers (informally called the literary "brat pack") who became known in the eighties. Their trademark was studied understatement and a determination to be true to the trivial, undramatic realities of ordinary life. The stories in her collection *Shiloh and Other Stories* (1982) are set in Paducah, in rural Kentucky, where she grew up. She takes her readers to a New South, where the struggles with the North are ancient history. Her characters are part of a new working class of truck drivers, retail clerks, and Tupperware sales representatives, who bake zucchini bread and make casseroles from potatoes and mushroom soup, and who pass their free time building model log cabins from Lincoln Logs or making wall hangings of an Arizona sunset. These characters are steeped in American popular culture—talk shows, shopping malls, made-for-TV movies.

Against this setting, Mason plays off plots where, "with no decisive snap of the thread, human relationships become unraveled" (Francis King); where "restless women strain again the confines of marriage" (Robert Towers); and where the men are sometimes "silent and transient" (Anatole Broyard). As David Quammen said in the *New York Times Book Review,* Mason "examines in her various truck drivers and sales clerks the dawning recognition—in some cases only a vague worry—of having missed something, something important, some alternate life more fruitful than the life that's been led." What has struck reviewers of her stories is that she does not treat these "unremarkable" people with condescension but with "complete respect." They are capable of moments of insight or self-understanding; they try "so hard, and with such optimism, to keep up with change" (Anne Tyler).

Shiloh   1982

Leroy Moffitt's wife, Norma Jean, is working on her pectorals. She lifts three-pound dumbbells to warm up, then progresses to a twenty-pound barbell. Standing with her legs apart, she reminds Leroy of Wonder Woman.

"I'd give anything if I could just get these muscles to where they're real hard," says Norma Jean. "Feel this arm. It's not as hard as the other one."

"That's 'cause you're right-handed," says Leroy, dodging as she swings the barbell in an arc.

"Do you think so?"

"Sure."

Leroy is a truckdriver. He injured his leg in a highway accident four months ago, and his physical therapy, which involves weights and a pulley, prompted Norma Jean to try building herself up. Now she is attending a body-building class. Leroy has been collecting temporary disability since his tractor-trailer jackknifed in Missouri, badly twisting his left leg in its socket. He has a steel pin in his hip. He will probably not be able to drive his rig

5

again. It sits in the backyard, like a gigantic bird that has flown home to roost. Leroy has been home in Kentucky for three months, and his leg is almost healed, but the accident frightened him and he does not want to drive any more long hauls. He is not sure what to do next. In the meantime, he makes things from craft kits. He started by building a miniature log cabin from notched Popsicle sticks. He varnished it and placed it on the TV set, where it remains. It reminds him of a rustic Nativity scene. Then he tried string art (sailing ships on black velvet), a macramé owl kit, a snap-together B-17 Flying Fortress, and a lamp made out of a model truck, with a light fixture screwed in the top of the cab. At first the kits were diversions, something to kill time, but now he is thinking about building a full-scale log house from a kit. It would be considerably cheaper than building a regular house, and besides, Leroy has grown to appreciate how things are put together. He has begun to realize that in all the years he was on the road he never took time to examine anything. He was always flying past scenery.

"They won't let you build a log cabin in any of the new subdivisions," Norma Jean tells him.

"They will if I tell them it's for you," he says, teasing her. Ever since they were married, he has promised Norma Jean he would build her a new home one day. They have always rented, and the house they live in is small and nondescript. It does not even feel like a home, Leroy realizes now.

Norma Jean works at the Rexall drugstore, and she has acquired an amazing amount of information about cosmetics. When she explains to Leroy the three stages of complexion care, involving creams, toners, and moisturizers, he thinks happily of other petroleum products—axle grease, diesel fuel. This is a connection between him and Norma Jean. Since he has been home, he has felt unusually tender about his wife and guilty over his long absences. But he can't tell what she feels about him. Norma Jean has never complained about his traveling; she has never made hurt remarks, like calling his truck a "widow-maker." He is reasonably certain she has been faithful to him, but he wishes she would celebrate his permanent homecoming more happily. Norma Jean is often startled to find Leroy at home, and he thinks she seems a little disappointed about it. Perhaps he reminds her too much of the early days of their marriage, before he went on the road. They had a child who died as an infant, years ago. They never speak about their memories of Randy, which have almost faded, but now that Leroy is home all the time, they sometimes feel awkward around each other, and Leroy wonders if one of them should mention the child. He has the feeling that they are waking up out of a dream together—that they must create a new marriage, start afresh. They are lucky they are still married. Leroy has read that for most people losing a child destroys the marriage—or else he heard this on *Donahue*. He can't always remember where he learns things anymore.

At Christmas, Leroy bought an electric organ for Norma Jean. She used to   10
play the piano when she was in high school. "It don't leave you," she told him once. "It's like riding a bicycle."

The new instrument had so many keys and buttons that she was bewildered by it at first. She touched the keys tentatively, pushed some buttons, then pecked out "Chopsticks." It came out in an amplified fox-trot rhythm, with marimba sounds.

"It's an orchestra!" she cried.

The organ had a pecan-look finish and eighteen preset chords, with optional flute, violin, trumpet, clarinet, and banjo accompaniments. Norma Jean mastered the organ almost immediately. At first she played Christmas songs. Then she bought *The Sixties Songbook* and learned every tune in it, adding variations to each with the rows of brightly colored buttons.

"I didn't like these old songs back then," she said. "But I have this crazy feeling I missed something."

"You didn't miss a thing," said Leroy.   15

Leroy likes to lie on the couch and smoke a joint and listen to Norma Jean play "Can't Take My Eyes Off You" and "I'll Be Back." He is back again. After fifteen years on the road, he is finally settling down with the woman he loves. She is still pretty. Her skin is flawless. Her frosted curls resemble pencil trimmings.

Now that Leroy has come home to stay, he notices how much the town has changed. Subdivisions are spreading across western Kentucky like an oil slick. The sign at the edge of town says "Pop: 11,500"—only seven hundred more than it said twenty years before. Leroy can't figure out who is living in all the new houses. The farmers who used to gather around the courthouse square on Saturday afternoons to play checkers and spit tobacco juice have gone. It has been years since Leroy has thought about the farmers, and they have disappeared without his noticing.

Leroy meets a kid named Stevie Hamilton in the parking lot at the new shopping center. While they pretend to be strangers meeting over a stalled car, Stevie tosses an ounce of marijuana under the front seat of Leroy's car. Stevie is wearing orange jogging shoes and a T-shirt that says CHATTAHOOCHEE SUPER-RAT. His father is a prominent doctor who lives in one of the expensive subdivisions in a new white-columned brick house that looks like a funeral parlor. In the phone book under his name there is a separate number, with the listing "Teenagers."

"Where do you get this stuff?" asks Leroy. "From your pappy?"

"That's for me to know and you to find out," Stevie says. He is slit-eyed   20 and skinny.

"What else you got?"

"What you interested in?"

"Nothing special. Just wondered."

Leroy used to take speed on the road. Now he has to go slowly. He needs to be mellow. He leans back against the car and says, "I'm aiming to build me a log house, soon as I get time. My wife, though, I don't think she likes the idea."

"Well, let me know when you want me again," Stevie says. He has a cig-   25 arette in his cupped palm, as though sheltering it from the wind. He takes a long drag, then stomps it on the asphalt and slouches away.

Stevie's father was two years ahead of Leroy in high school. Leroy is thirty-four. He married Norma Jean when they were both eighteen, and their child Randy was born a few months later, but he died at the age of four months and three days. He would be about Stevie's age now. Norma Jean and Leroy were at the drive-in, watching a double feature (*Dr. Strangelove* and *Lover Come Back*), and the baby was sleeping in the back seat. When the first movie ended, the baby was dead. It was the sudden infant death syndrome. Leroy remembers handing Randy to a nurse at the emergency room, as though he were offering her a large doll as a present. A dead baby feels like a sack of flour. "It just happens sometimes," said the doctor, in what Leroy always recalls as a nonchalant tone. Leroy can hardly remember the child anymore, but he still sees vividly a scene from *Dr. Strangelove* in which the President of the United States was talking in a folksy voice on the hot line to the Soviet premier about the bomber accidentally headed toward Russia. He was in the War Room, and the world map was lit up. Leroy remembers Norma Jean standing catatonically beside him in the hospital and himself thinking: Who is this strange girl? He had forgotten who she was. Now scientists are saying that crib death is caused by a virus. Nobody knows anything, Leroy thinks. The answers are always changing.

When Leroy gets home from the shopping center, Norma Jean's mother, Mabel Beasley, is there. Until this year, Leroy has not realized how much time she spends with Norma Jean. When she visits, she inspects the closets and then the plants, informing Norma Jean when a plant is droopy or yellow. Mabel calls the plants "flowers," although there are never any blooms. She always notices if Norma Jean's laundry is piling up. Mabel is a short, overweight woman whose tight, brown-dyed curls look more like a wig than the actual wig she sometimes wears. Today she has brought Norma Jean an off-white dust ruffle she made for the bed; Mabel works in a custom-upholstery shop.

"This is the tenth one I made this year," Mabel says. "I got started and couldn't stop."

"It's real pretty," says Norma Jean.

"Now we can hide things under the bed," says Leroy, who gets along   30
with his mother-in-law primarily by joking with her. Mabel has never really forgiven him for disgracing her by getting Norma Jean pregnant. When the baby died, she said that fate was mocking her.

"What's that thing?" Mabel says to Leroy in a loud voice, pointing to a tangle of yarn on a piece of canvas.

Leroy holds it up for Mabel to see. "It's my needlepoint," he explains. "This is a *Star Trek* pillow cover."

"That's what a woman would do," says Mabel. "Great day in the morning!"

"All the big football players on TV do it," he says.

"Why, Leroy, you're always trying to fool me. I don't believe you for one   35
minute. You don't know what to do with yourself—that's the whole trouble. Sewing!"

"I'm aiming to build a log house," says Leroy. "Soon as my plans come."

"Like *heck* you are," says Norma Jean. She takes Leroy's needlepoint and shoves it into a drawer. "You have to find a job first. Nobody can afford to build now anyway."

Mabel straightens her girdle and says, "I still think before you get tied down y'all ought to take a little run to Shiloh."

"One of these days, Mama," Norma Jean says impatiently.

Mabel is talking about Shiloh, Tennessee. For the past few years, she has   40
been urging Leroy and Norma Jean to visit the Civil War battleground there.

Mabel went there on her honeymoon—the only real trip she ever took. Her husband died of a perforated ulcer when Norma Jean was ten, but Mabel, who was accepted into the United Daughters of the Confederacy in 1975, is still preoccupied with going back to Shiloh.

"I've been to kingdom come and back in that truck out yonder," Leroy says to Mabel, "but we never yet set foot in that battleground. Ain't that something? How did I miss it?"

"It's not even that far," Mabel says.

After Mabel leaves, Norma Jean reads to Leroy from a list she has made. "Things you could do," she announces. "You could get a job as a guard at Union Carbide, where they'd let you set on a stool. You could get on at the lumberyard. You could do a little carpenter work, if you want to build so bad. You could—"

"I can't do something where I'd have to stand up all day."

"You ought to try standing up all day behind a cosmetics counter. It's   45 amazing that I have strong feet, coming from two parents that never had strong feet at all." At the moment Norma Jean is holding on to the kitchen counter, raising her knees one at a time as she talks. She is wearing two-pound ankle weights.

"Don't worry," says Leroy. "I'll do something."

"You could truck calves to slaughter for somebody. You wouldn't have to drive any big old truck for that."

"I'm going to build you this house," says Leroy. "I want to make you a real home."

"I don't want to live in any log cabin."

"It's not a cabin. It's a house."   50

"I don't care. It looks like a cabin."

"You and me together could lift those logs. It's just like lifting weights."

Norma Jean doesn't answer. Under her breath, she is counting. Now she is marching through the kitchen. She is doing goose steps.

*   *   *

Before his accident, when Leroy came home he used to stay in the house with Norma Jean, watching TV in bed and playing cards. She would cook fried chicken, picnic ham, chocolate pie—all his favorites. Now he is home alone much of the time. In the mornings, Norma Jean disappears, leaving a cooling place in the bed. She eats a cereal called Body Buddies, and she leaves the bowl on the table, with the soggy tan balls floating in a milk puddle. He sees things about Norma Jean that he never realized before. When she chops onions, she stares off into a corner, as if she can't bear to look. She puts on her house slippers almost precisely at nine o'clock every evening and nudges her jogging shoes under the couch. She saves bread heels for the birds. Leroy watches the birds at the feeder. He notices the peculiar way goldfinches fly past the window. They close their wings, then fall, then spread their wings to catch and lift themselves. He wonders if they close their eyes when they fall. Norma Jean closes her eyes when they are in bed. She wants the lights turned out. Even then, he is sure she closes her eyes.

He goes for long drives around town. He tends to drive a car rather care- 55
lessly. Power steering and an automatic shift make a car feel so small and
inconsequential that his body is hardly involved in the driving process. His
injured leg stretches out comfortably. Once or twice he has almost hit something, but even the prospect of an accident seems minor in a car. He cruises
the new subdivisions, feeling like a criminal rehearsing for a robbery. Norma
Jean is probably right about a log house being inappropriate here in the new
subdivisions. All the houses look grand and complicated. They depress him.

One day when Leroy comes home from a drive he finds Norma Jean in
tears. She is in the kitchen making a potato and mushroom-soup casserole,
with grated-cheese topping. She is crying because her mother caught her
smoking.

"I didn't hear her coming. I was standing here puffing away pretty as you
please," Norma Jean says, wiping her eyes.

"I knew it would happen sooner or later," says Leroy, putting his arm
around her.

"She don't know the meaning of the word 'knock,'" says Norma Jean.
"It's a wonder she hadn't caught me years ago."

"Think of it this way," Leroy says. "What if she caught me with a joint?"   60

"You better not let her!" Norma Jean shrieks. "I'm warning you, Leroy
Moffitt!"

"I'm just kidding. Here, play me a tune. That'll help you relax."

Norma Jean puts the casserole in the oven and sets the timer. Then she
plays a ragtime tune, with horns and banjo, as Leroy lights up a joint and
lies on the couch, laughing to himself about Mabel's catching him at it. He
thinks of Stevie Hamilton—a doctor's son pushing grass. Everything is funny.
The whole town seems crazy and small. He is reminded of Virgil Mathis, a
boastful policeman Leroy used to shoot pool with. Virgil recently led a drug
bust in a back room at a bowling alley, where he seized ten thousand dollars' worth of marijuana. The newspaper had a picture of him holding up the
bags of grass and grinning widely. Right now, Leroy can imagine Virgil breaking down the door and arresting him with a lungful of smoke. Virgil would
probably have been alerted to the scene because of all the racket Norma
Jean is making. Now she sounds like a hard-rock band. Norma Jean is terrific. When she switches to a Latin-rhythm version of "Sunshine Superman,"
Leroy hums along. Norma Jean's foot goes up and down, up and down.

"Well, what do you think?" Leroy says, when Norma Jean pauses to
search through her music.

"What do I think about what?"   65

His mind has gone blank. Then he says, "I'll sell my rig and build a
house." That wasn't what he wanted to say. He wanted to know what she
thought—what she *really* thought—about them.

"Don't start in on that again," says Norma Jean. She begins playing
"Who'll Be the Next in Line?"

Leroy used to tell hitchhikers his whole life story—about his travels, his
hometown, the baby. He would end with a question: "Well, what do you
think?" It was just a rhetorical question. In time, he had the feeling that he'd
been telling the same story over and over to the same hitchhikers. He quit
talking to hitchhikers when he realized how his voice sounded—whining

and self-pitying, like some teenage-tragedy song. Now Leroy has the sudden impulse to tell Norma Jean about himself, as if he had just met her. They have known each other so long they have forgotten a lot about each other. They could become reacquainted. But when the oven timer goes off and she runs to the kitchen, he forgets why he wants to do this.

The next day, Mabel drops by. It is Saturday and Norma Jean is cleaning. Leroy is studying the plans of his log house, which have finally come in the mail. He has them spread out on the table—big sheets of stiff blue paper, with diagrams and numbers printed in white. While Norma Jean runs the vacuum, Mabel drinks coffee. She sets her coffee cup on a blueprint.

"I'm just waiting for time to pass," she says to Leroy, drumming her fin- 70
gers on the table.

As soon as Norma Jean switches off the vacuum, Mabel says in a loud voice, "Did you hear about the datsun dog that killed the baby?"

Norma Jean says, "The word is 'dachshund.' "

"They put the dog on trial. It chewed the baby's legs off. The mother was in the next room all the time." She raises her voice. "They thought it was neglect."

Norma Jean is holding her ears. Leroy manages to open the refrigerator and get some Diet Pepsi to offer Mabel. Mabel still has some coffee and she waves away the Pepsi.

"Datsuns are like that," Mabel says. "They're jealous dogs. They'll tear a 75
place to pieces if you don't keep an eye on them."

"You better watch out what you're saying, Mabel," says Leroy.

"Well, facts is facts."

Leroy looks out the window at his rig. It is like a huge piece of furniture gathering dust in the backyard. Pretty soon it will be an antique. He hears the vacuum cleaner. Norma Jean seems to be cleaning the living room rug again.

Later, she says to Leroy, "She just said that about the baby because she caught me smoking. She's trying to pay me back."

"What are you talking about?" Leroy says, nervously shuffling blueprints. 80

"You know good and well," Norma Jean says. She is sitting in a kitchen chair with her feet up and her arms wrapped around her knees. She looks small and helpless. She says, "The very idea, her bringing up a subject like that! Saying it was neglect."

"She didn't mean that," Leroy says.

"She might not have *thought* she meant it. She always says things like that. You don't know how she goes on."

"But she didn't really mean it. She was just talking."

Leroy opens a king-sized bottle of beer and pours it into two glasses, di- 85
viding it carefully. He hands a glass to Norma Jean and she takes it from him mechanically. For a long time, they sit by the kitchen window watching the birds at the feeder.

Something is happening. Norma Jean is going to night school. She has graduated from her six-week body-building course and now she is taking an adult-education course in composition at Paducah Community College. She spends her evenings outlining paragraphs.

"First you have a topic sentence," she explains to Leroy. "Then you divide it up. Your secondary topic has to be connected to your primary topic."

To Leroy, this sounds intimidating. "I never was any good in English," he says.

"It makes a lot of sense."

"What are you doing this for, anyhow?"   90

She shrugs. "It's something to do." She stands up and lifts her dumbbells a few times.

"Driving a rig, nobody cared about my English."

"I'm not criticizing your English."

Norma Jean used to say, "If I lose ten minutes' sleep, I just drag all day." Now she stays up late, writing compositions. She got a B on her first paper—a how-to theme on soup-based casseroles. Recently Norma Jean has been cooking unusual foods—tacos, lasagna, Bombay chicken. She doesn't play the organ anymore, though her second paper was called "Why Music Is Important to Me." She sits at the kitchen table, concentrating on her outlines, while Leroy plays with his log house plans, practicing with a set of Lincoln Logs. The thought of getting a truckload of notched, numbered logs scares him, and he wants to be prepared. As he and Norma Jean work together at the kitchen table, Leroy has the hopeful thought that they are sharing something, but he knows he is a fool to think this. Norma Jean is miles away. He knows he is going to lose her. Like Mabel, he is just waiting for time to pass.

One day, Mabel is there before Norma Jean gets home from work, and   95
Leroy finds himself confiding in her. Mabel, he realizes, must know Norma Jean better than he does.

"I don't know what's got into that girl," Mabel says. "She used to go to bed with the chickens. Now you say she's up all hours. Plus her a-smoking. I like to died."

"I want to make her this beautiful home," Leroy says, indicating the Lincoln Logs. "I don't thinks she even wants it. Maybe she was happier with me gone."

"She don't know what to make of you, coming home like this."

"Is that it?"

Mabel takes the roof off his Lincoln Log cabin. "You couldn't get *me* in a   100
log cabin," she says. "I was raised in one. It's no picnic, let me tell you."

"They're different now," says Leroy.

"I tell you what," Mabel says, smiling oddly at Leroy.

"What?"

"Take her on down to Shiloh. Y'all need to get out together, stir a little. Her brain's all balled up over them books."

Leroy can see traces of Norma Jean's features in her mother's face.   105
Mabel's worn face has the texture of crinkled cotton, but suddenly she looks pretty. It occurs to Leroy that Mabel has been hinting all along that she wants them to take her with them to Shiloh.

"Let's all go to Shiloh," he says. "You and me and her. Some Sunday."

Mabel throws up her hands in protest. "Oh, no, not me. Young folks want to be by theirselves."

When Norma Jean comes in with groceries, Leroy says excitedly, "Your mama here's been dying to go to Shiloh for forty-five years. It's about time we went, don't you think?"

"I'm not going to butt in on anybody's second honeymoon," Mabel says.

"Who's going on a honeymoon, for Christ's sake?" Norma Jean says loudly. 110

"I never raised no daughter of mine to talk that-a-way," Mabel says.

"You ain't seen nothing yet," says Norma Jean. She starts putting away boxes and cans, slamming cabinet doors.

"There's a log cabin at Shiloh," Mabel says. "It was there during the battle. There's bullet holes in it."

"When are you going to *shut up* about Shiloh, Mama?" asks Norma Jean.

"I always thought Shiloh was the prettiest place, so full of history," Mabel 115 goes on. "I just hoped y'all could see it once before I die, so you could tell me about it." Later, she whispers to Leroy, "You do what I said. A little change is what she needs."

"Your name means 'the king,'" Norma Jean says to Leroy that evening. He is trying to get her to go to Shiloh, and she is reading a book about another century.

"Well, I reckon I ought to be right proud."

"I guess so."

"Am I still king around here?"

Norma Jean flexes her biceps and feels them for hardness. "I'm not fool- 120 ing around with anybody, if that's what you mean," she says.

"Would you tell me if you were?"

"I don't know."

"What does *your* name mean?"

"It was Marilyn Monroe's real name."

"No kidding!"   125

"Norma comes from the Normans. They were invaders," she says. She closes her book and looks hard at Leroy. "I'll go to Shiloh with you if you'll stop staring at me."

On Sunday, Norma Jean packs a picnic and they go to Shiloh. To Leroy's relief, Mabel says she does not want to come with them. Norma Jean drives, and Leroy, sitting beside her, feels like some boring hitchhiker she has picked up. He tries some conversation, but she answers him in monosyllables. At Shiloh, she drives aimlessly through the park, past bluffs and trails and steep ravines. Shiloh is an immense place, and Leroy cannot see it as a battleground. It is not what he expected. He thought it would look like a golf course. Monuments are everywhere, showing through the thick clusters of trees. Norma Jean passes the log cabin Mabel mentioned. It is surrounded by tourists looking for bullet holes.

"That's not the kind of log house I've got in mind," says Leroy apologetically.

"I know *that*."

"This is a pretty place. Your mama was right."   130

"It's O.K.," says Norma Jean. "Well, we've seen it. I hope she's satisfied."

They burst out laughing together.

At the park museum, a movie on Shiloh is shown every half hour, but they decide that they don't want to see it. They buy a souvenir Confederate flag for Mabel, and then they find a picnic spot near the cemetery. Norma Jean has brought a picnic cooler, with pimiento sandwiches, soft drinks, and Yodels. Leroy eats a sandwich and then smokes a joint, hiding it behind the picnic cooler. Norma Jean has quit smoking altogether. She is picking cake crumbs from the cellophane wrapper, like a fussy bird.

Leroy says, "So the boys in gray ended up in Corinth. The Union soldiers zapped 'em finally, April 7, 1862."

They both know that he doesn't know any history. He is just talking 135 about some of the historical plaques they have read. He feels awkward, like a boy on a date with an older girl. They are still just making conversation.

"Corinth is where Mama eloped to," says Norma Jean.

They sit in silence and stare at the cemetery for the Union dead and, beyond, at a tall cluster of trees. Campers are parked nearby, bumper to bumper, and small children in bright clothing are cavorting and squealing. Norma Jean wads up the cake wrapper and squeezes it tightly in her hand. Without looking at Leroy, she says, "I want to leave you."

Leroy takes a bottle of Coke out of the cooler and flips off the cap. He holds the bottle poised near his mouth but cannot remember to take a drink. Finally he says, "No, you don't."

"Yes, I do."

"I won't let you."   140

"You can't stop me."

"Don't do me that way."

Leroy knows Norma Jean will have her own way. "Didn't I promise to be home from now on?" he says.

"In some ways, a woman prefers a man who wanders," says Norma Jean. "That sounds crazy, I know."

"You're not crazy."   145

Leroy remembers to drink from his Coke. Then he says, "Yes, you *are* crazy. You and me could start all over again. Right back at the beginning."

"We *have* started all over again," says Norma Jean. "And this is how it turned out."

"What did I do wrong?"

"Nothing."

"Is this one of those women's lib things?" Leroy asks.   150

"Don't be funny."

The cemetery, a green slope dotted with white markers, looks like a subdivision site. Leroy is trying to comprehend that his marriage is breaking up, but for some reason he is wondering about white slabs in a graveyard.

"Everything was fine till Mama caught me smoking," says Norma Jean, standing up. "That set something off."

"What are you talking about?"

"She won't leave me alone—*you* won't leave me alone." Norma Jean 155 seems to be crying, but she is looking away from him. "I feel eighteen again. I can't face that all over again." She starts walking away. "No, it *wasn't* fine. I don't know what I'm saying. Forget it."

Leroy takes a lungful of smoke and closes his eyes as Norma Jean's words sink in. He tries to focus on the fact that thirty-five hundred soldiers died on the grounds around him. He can only think of that war as a board game with plastic soldiers. Leroy almost smiles, as he compares the Confederates' daring attack on the Union camps and Virgil Mathis's raid on the bowling alley. General Grant, drunk and furious, shoved the Southerners back to Corinth, where Mabel and Jet Beasley were married years later, when Mabel was still thin and good-looking. The next day, Mabel and Jet visited the battleground, and then Norma Jean was born, and then she married Leroy and they had a baby, which they lost, and now Leroy and Norma Jean are here at the same battleground. Leroy knows he is leaving out a lot. He is leaving out the insides of history. History was always just names and dates to him. It occurs to him that building a house out of logs is similarly empty—too simple. And the real inner workings of a marriage, like most of history, have escaped him. Now he sees that building a log house is the dumbest idea he could have had. It was clumsy of him to think Norma Jean would want a log house. It was a crazy idea. He'll have to think of something else, quickly. He will wad the blueprints into tight balls and fling them into the lake. Then he'll get moving again. He opens his eyes. Norma Jean has moved away and is walking through the cemetery, following a serpentine brick path.

Leroy gets up to follow his wife, but his good leg is asleep and his bad leg still hurts him. Norma Jean is far away, walking rapidly toward the bluff by the river, and he tries to hobble toward her. Some children run past him, screaming noisily. Norma Jean has reached the bluff, and she is looking out over the Tennessee River. Now she turns toward Leroy and waves her arms. Is she beckoning to him? She seems to be doing an exercise for her chest muscles. The sky is unusually pale—the color of the dust ruffle Mabel made for their bed.

The Receptive Reader

1. This story takes us to a working-class *setting,* with such class markers as the characters' working-class language. Where does their language become most noticeable, or where does it become an issue, in the story? Attitudes toward the working class have traditionally ranged from snobbish contempt to solidarity for the aspirations of common people. What is the attitude of the author?

2. Some Southern readers feel particularly at home in this story. To you, what if anything is Southern about the setting and about this story as a whole?

3. Mason is a fanatic for apparently trivial *realistic detail*—about Leroy's job, his accident, his therapy; about Norma Jean's job at the drugstore, her body-building exercises, her classes at the college; about their trip to Shiloh, and so forth. What to you are striking examples of these apparent trivia? What do they do for the story as a whole?

4. Mason makes the setting real by striking uses of *figurative language*—language using imaginative comparisons. What images and feelings does she bring into play when she says that Leroy's rig parked in the back was like a big bird come home to roost? What are other striking examples of imaginative comparisons?

5. How ordinary are the lives of these people? What are some of the ordinary, everyday things that make their lives average? Do extraordinary things happen to them?

6. The *dialogue* in this story is very sparse. What are occasions in the story where you expect the characters to say more about their lives or their feelings than they do? Are their feelings "frozen," as one student reader said?

7. What role does Mabel, Leroy's mother-in-law, play as a *minor character* in the story? What is her relationship with Leroy? with her daughter? How does the author use her to develop or round out the setting of the story?

8. Readers are likely to detect symbolic meanings or overtones in details and incidents in this story. What are the possible symbolic meanings of the parked rig, the "nondescript" rented home, the electronic organ, the change in the cooking, Mabel's hair, the log cabin Leroy wants to build, the trip to the battlefield?

9. When did you first decide that the marriage was going to break up? For you, was the breakup a foregone conclusion? Who or what is to blame?

10. Both *major characters,* Leroy and Norma Jean, change or develop in the course of this story. How do they change or grow? Do they develop in the same direction or along parallel lines? Do they understand what is happening to them? (How much self-realization is there in this story?)

The Personal Response

Anne Tyler, a fellow writer reviewing Mason's stories for *The New Republic,* said that it was "heartening to find male characters portrayed sympathetically, with an appreciation for the fact that they can feel as confused and hurt and lonely as the female characters." What are your personal feelings toward the two major characters in "Shiloh"? Do you feel closer to Leroy or to Norma Jean? Why?

Yukio Mishima   *(1925–1970)*

Yukio Mishima (pen name of Kimitake Hiraoka) was a prolific writer of novels, plays, and stories. He was a flamboyant media personality who became a cult figure in Japan and a legend in the West. He was alienated from Westernized, materialistic modern Japan and became obsessed with Japanese history and traditional Japanese values. He set out to revive and reenact the code and ritual of the samurai warriors of Japan's feudal, aristocratic past, with traditions akin to the code of chivalry of the European Middle Ages. He studied the martial arts—boxing, karate, and sword fighting; he created the Shield Society, a private army of a hundred dedicated followers. In a final spectacular rejection of the decadent present, he committed *seppuku,* or public ritual suicide, in 1970.

Translations of Mishima's best-known works include *Confessions of a Mask* (1958), *The Sailor Who Fell from Grace with the Sea* (1965), and *Sun and Steel* (1970). In *The Sailor Who Fell from Grace,* a boy who disapproves of the lover of his widowed mother joins with a band of his fellows in an effort to terminate the love affair and the lover. Mishima's short stories were collected in *Death and Midsummer and Other Stories* (1966). Some of his best-known stories celebrate the ecstasy of married love, loyalty to the empire, and ceremonial suicide. He once spoke of "my heart's leaning toward Death, Night, and Blood." The following story will take you to a different world—not merely a different geographical setting but a different world of thought and feeling.

Swaddling Clothes   *1966*

TRANSLATED BY IVAN MORRIS

He was always busy, Toshiko's husband. Even tonight he had to dash off to an appointment, leaving her to go home alone by taxi. But what else could a woman expect when she married an actor—an attractive one? No doubt she had been foolish to hope that he would spend the evening with her. And yet he must have known how she dreaded going back to their house, unhomely with its Western-style furniture and with the bloodstains still showing on the floor.

Toshiko had been oversensitive since girlhood: that was her nature. As the result of constant worrying she never put on weight, and now, an adult woman, she looked more like a transparent picture than a creature of flesh and blood. Her delicacy of spirit was evident to her most casual acquaintance.

Earlier that evening, when she had joined her husband at a night club, she had been shocked to find him entertaining friends with an account of "the incident." Sitting there in his American-style suit, puffing at a cigarette, he had seemed to her almost a stranger.

"It's a fantastic story," he was saying, gesturing flamboyantly as if in an attempt to outweigh the attractions of the dance band. "Here this new nurse for our baby arrives from the employment agency, and the very first thing I notice about her is her stomach. It's enormous—as if she had a pillow stuck under her kimono! No wonder, I thought, for I soon saw that she could eat more than the rest of us put together. She polished off the contents of our rice bin like that. . . . " He snapped his fingers. " 'Gastric dilation'—that's how she explained her girth and her appetite. Well, the day before yesterday we heard groans and moans coming from the nursery. We rushed in and found her squatting on the floor, holding her stomach in her two hands, and moaning like a cow. Next to her our baby lay in his cot, scared out of his wits and crying at the top of his lungs. A pretty scene, I can tell you!"

"So the cat was out of the bag?" suggested one of their friends, a film actor like Toshiko's husband.   5

"Indeed it was! And it gave me the shock of my life. You see, I'd completely swallowed that story about 'gastric dilation.' Well, I didn't waste any time. I rescued our good rug from the floor and spread a blanket for her to lie on. The whole time the girl was yelling like a stuck pig. By the time the doctor from the maternity clinic arrived, the baby had already been born. But our sitting room was a pretty shambles!"

"Oh, that I'm sure of!" said another of their friends, and the whole company burst into laughter.

Toshiko was dumbfounded to hear her husband discussing the horrifying happening as though it were no more than an amusing incident which they chanced to have witnessed. She shut her eyes for a moment and all at once she saw the newborn baby lying before her: on the parquet floor the infant lay, and his frail body was wrapped in bloodstained newspapers.

Toshiko was sure that the doctor had done the whole thing out of spite. As if to emphasize his scorn for this mother who had given birth to a bastard under such sordid conditions, he had told his assistant to wrap the baby in some loose newspapers, rather than proper swaddling. This callous treatment of the newborn child had offended Toshiko. Overcoming her disgust at the entire scene, she had fetched a brand-new piece of flannel from her cupboard and, having swaddled the baby in it, had lain him carefully in an armchair.

This all had taken place in the evening after her husband had left the house. Toshiko had told him nothing of it, fearing that he would think her oversoft, oversentimental; yet the scene had engraved itself deeply in her mind. Tonight she sat silently thinking back on it, while the jazz orchestra brayed and her husband chatted cheerfully with his friends. She knew that she would never forget the sight of the baby, wrapped in stained newspapers and lying on the floor—it was a scene fit for a butchershop. Toshiko, whose own life had been spent in solid comfort, poignantly felt the wretchedness of the illegitimate baby.

I am the only person to have witnessed its shame, the thought occurred to her. The mother never saw her child lying there in its newspaper wrappings, and the baby itself of course didn't know. I alone shall have to preserve that terrible scene in my memory. When the baby grows up and wants to find out about his birth, there will be no one to tell him, so long as I preserve silence. How strange that I should have this feeling of guilt! After all, it was I who took him up from the floor, swathed him properly in flannel, and laid him down to sleep in the armchair.

They left the night club and Toshiko stepped into the taxi that her husband had called for her. "Take this lady to Ushigomé," he told the driver and shut the door from the outside. Toshiko gazed through the window at her husband's smiling face and noticed his strong, white teeth. Then she leaned back in the seat, oppressed by the knowledge that their life together was in some way too easy, too painless. It would have been difficult for her to put her thoughts into words. Through the rear window of the taxi she took a last look at her husband. He was striding along the street toward his Nash car, and soon the back of his rather garish tweed coat had blended with the figures of the passers-by.

The taxi drove off, passed down a street dotted with bars and then by a theater, in front of which the throngs of people jostled each other on the pavement. Although the performance had only just ended, the lights had already been turned out and in the half dark outside it was depressingly obvious that the cherry blossoms decorating the front of the theater were merely scraps of white paper.

Even if that baby should grow up in ignorance of the secret of his birth, he can never become a respectable citizen, reflected Toshiko, pursuing the same train of thoughts. Those soiled newspaper swaddling clothes will be the symbol of his entire life. But why should I keep worrying about him so much? Is it because I feel uneasy about the future of my own child? Say twenty years from now, when our boy will have grown up into a fine, carefully educated young man, one day by a quirk of fate he meets the other boy, who then will also have turned twenty. And say that the other boy, who has been sinned against, savagely stabs him with a knife. . . .

It was a warm, overcast April night, but thoughts of the future made   15 Toshiko feel cold and miserable. She shivered on the back seat of the car.

No, when the time comes I shall take my son's place, she told herself suddenly. Twenty years from now I shall be forty-three. I shall go to that young man and tell him straight out about everything—about his newspaper swaddling clothes, and about how I went and wrapped him in flannel.

The taxi ran along the dark wide road that was bordered by the park and by the Imperial Palace moat. In the distance Toshiko noticed the pinpricks of light which came from the blocks of tall office buildings.

Twenty years from now that wretched child will be in utter misery. He will be living a desolate, hopeless, poverty-stricken existence—a lonely rat. What else could happen to a baby who has had such a birth? He'll be wandering through the streets by himself, cursing his father, loathing his mother.

No doubt Toshiko derived a certain satisfaction from her somber thoughts: she tortured herself with them without cease. The taxi approached Hanzomon and drove past the compound of the British Embassy. At that point the famous rows of cherry trees were spread out before Toshiko in all their purity. On the spur of the moment she decided to go and view the blossoms by herself in the dark night. It was a strange decision for a timid and unadventurous young woman, but then she was in a strange state of mind and she dreaded the return home. That evening all sorts of unsettling fancies had burst open in her mind.

She crossed the wide street—a slim, solitary figure in the darkness. As a   20 rule when she walked in the traffic Toshiko used to cling fearfully to her companion, but tonight she darted alone between the cars and a moment later had reached the long narrow park that borders the Palace moat. Chidorigafuchi, it is called—the Abyss of the Thousand Birds.

Tonight the whole park had become a grove of blossoming cherry trees. Under the calm cloudy sky the blossoms formed a mass of solid whiteness. The paper lanterns that hung from wires between the trees had been put out; in their place electric light bulbs, red, yellow, and green, shone dully beneath the blossoms. It was well past ten o'clock and most of the flower-viewers had gone home. As the occasional passers-by strolled through the park, they would automatically kick aside the empty bottles or crush the waste paper beneath their feet.

Newspapers, thought Toshiko, her mind going back once again to those happenings. Bloodstained newspapers. If a man were ever to hear of that piteous birth and know that it was he who had lain there, it would ruin his entire life. To think that I, a perfect stranger, should from now on have to keep such a secret—the secret of a man's whole existence. . . .

Lost in these thoughts, Toshiko walked on through the park. Most of the people still remaining there were quiet couples; no one paid her any attention. She noticed two people sitting on a stone bench beside the moat, not looking at the blossoms, but gazing silently at the water. Pitch black it was, and swathed in heavy shadows. Beyond the moat the somber forest of the Imperial Palace blocked her view. The trees reached up, to form a solid dark mass against the night sky. Toshiko walked slowly along the path beneath the blossoms hanging heavily overhead.

On a stone bench, slightly apart from the others, she noticed a pale object—not, as she had at first imagined, a pile of cherry blossoms, nor a garment forgotten by one of the visitors to the park. Only when she came closer did she see that it was a human form lying on the bench. Was it, she wondered, one of those miserable drunks often to be seen sleeping in public places? Obviously not, for the body had been systematically covered with newspapers, and it was the whiteness of those papers that had attracted Toshiko's attention. Standing by the bench, she gazed down at the sleeping figure.

It was a man in a brown jersey who lay there, curled up on layers of news-   25 papers, other newspapers covering him. No doubt this had become his normal night residence now that spring had arrived. Toshiko gazed down at the man's dirty, unkempt hair, which in places had become hopelessly matted. As she observed the sleeping figure wrapped in its newspapers, she was inevitably reminded of the baby who had lain on the floor in its wretched swaddling clothes. The shoulder of the man's jersey rose and fell in the darkness in time with his heavy breathing.

It seemed to Toshiko that all her fears and premonitions had suddenly taken concrete form. In the darkness the man's pale forehead stood out, and it was a young forehead, though carved with the wrinkles of long poverty and hardship. His khaki trousers had been slightly pulled up; on his sockless feet he wore a pair of battered gym shoes. She could not see his face and suddenly had an overmastering desire to get one glimpse of it.

She walked to the head of the bench and looked down. The man's head was half buried in his arms, but Toshiko could see that he was surprisingly young. She noticed the thick eyebrows and the fine bridge of his nose. His slightly open mouth was alive with youth.

But Toshiko had approached too close. In the silent night the newspaper bedding rustled, and abruptly the man opened his eyes. Seeing the young woman standing directly beside him, he raised himself with a jerk, and his eyes lit up. A second later a powerful hand reached out and seized Toshiko by her slender wrist.

She did not feel in the least afraid and made no effort to free herself. In a flash the thought had struck her. Ah, so the twenty years have already gone by! The forest of the Imperial Palace was pitch dark and utterly silent.

The Receptive Reader

1. What is strange and what is familiar about the *setting*? What expectations (or what stereotypes) do you bring to the Japanese setting of the story? How much of an effort of the imagination is necessary for you to get into the spirit of this story?

2. The author makes a point of the Westernized or Americanized ways of Toshiko's husband. What are revealing details? What contrast is Mishima setting up between the husband and the wife as *key characters?* What role does that contrast play in the story as a whole? What is the author's attitude toward the husband?

3. What are Toshiko's feelings about the illegitimate child? Does she reflect the expected attitudes of her culture? Are there parallels in American culture or social mores to the attitude toward unwed mothers and children born out of wedlock that play a strong role in this story? (Are our attitudes more enlightened or just different?)

4. Is the ending a **surprise ending**, or has the author prepared you for it? Does the story as a whole lead up to it? How? Do you react to it as something that really happened or as a dream, a nightmare?

5. Some of the details in this story are not just mentioned in passing. They come up again, providing a kind of link or a continuing strand. What is the role of recurrent details like the cherry blossoms or newspapers in this story?

6. One editor said that "this fiercely condensed" story, focused on a "single, overpowering incident," "explodes in a burst of revelation or illumination" (Irving Howe). For you, what is that revelation? Does this story have a point? Does it have a *theme*—some key idea acted out or implied in the story as a whole?

The Personal Response

Does the story as a whole remain strange or alien for you? How do you relate to Toshiko as the central character? How do you relate to the story as a whole?

The Range of Interpretation

Mishima's story invites a wide range of reactions. In your judgment, which of the following student responses best gets into the spirit of the story? How or why does the student writer seem to do justice to the author's intention? How are these responses different from your own interpretation of the story?

1. This story is very disturbing. Although it is set in Japan, the story reflects stereotypical sex roles reminding me of many couples I know. The husband is domineering and shallow, and Toshiko is the stereotypically passive, dependent, "oversensitive" wife. Under the quiet stereotypical surface, Toshiko is a warm, caring person. But whereas she is a keen observer of her culture (her gloomy prediction for the baby reveals this), she lives her whole life in her fears and feelings. While the husband is vain and self-absorbed, Toshiko spends her life alone in the private world of her fears. She feels great warmth toward the child, but she knows that it will suffer greatly as the result of its dishonorable beginnings. What we see in Toshiko is the constant battle waged between the traditional role and the emergence of the more modern woman. She is alienated from her callous, self-centered husband, and she assumes responsibility for the harsh treatment that society has in store for the newborn child.

2. This story is very fatalistic. The child, because of its illegitimate birth, is doomed to "utter misery." I expected Toshiko to come to a tragic end. I could

empathize with Toshiko somewhat because of her culture and beliefs, but I wanted to stop her from feeling so guilty and destroying her life. It is as if Toshiko created the ending in the park. She is determined to sacrifice herself. At times I wanted to reach into the story and stop her from being so guilt-ridden and oversensitive. As a woman, it made me angry that she would destroy herself.

3. On the literal level, this story leaves many questions unresolved. The abrupt, surprising ending leaves me wondering whether it is real—is it a dream? a nightmare? If the derelict in the park literally attacked the woman, was the result death? rape? Symbolically, in the context of the story as a whole, Toshiko is taking the place of her own son. She is sacrificing herself in his stead, so that she, rather than he, will be the target of the dispossessed child's anger and resentment when it returns to exact vengeance. In spite of the difference in cultures, the story made me hear echoes of my own Catholic upbringing. The incident where Toshiko wrapped the child in swaddling clothes mirrored the birth of Christ in a manger where Mary wrapped him in swaddling clothes. The ending where Toshiko is willing to give up her life so that her son may live parallels Christ's willingness to give up his life so that his people may have eternal life.

Making Connections: For Discussion or Writing

Other stories in which setting plays a major role include Eudora Welty's "A Visit of Charity," set in a soulless institution (Chapter 11); Toni Morrison's "1920," set in the Old South (Chapter 11); Alice Munro's "Boys and Girls," set on a fox farm in Canada (Chapter 3); Joyce Carol Oates' "Stalking," set in a sterile suburban landscape (Chapter 5); and Nathaniel Hawthorne's "Young Goodman Brown," set in Puritan New England (Chapter 7).

WRITING ABOUT LITERATURE

2 Exploring the Setting
WRITING FOCUS: Writing the Critical Paper

It still comes as a shock to me to realize that I don't write about what I know: I write in order to find out what I know.

PATRICIA HAMPL

The Writing Workshop   As you develop a paper focused on setting, you will go through many of the same basic steps as in writing papers focused on other facets of the storyteller's art. The first step toward real writing is to build up a rich backlog of material. No one can write a full paper from an empty mind. To write good papers about literary topics, try to operate on the computer principle of "Good input makes for good output." Build the habit of scribbling comments in the margins of what you read (not in library copies!). Make it a habit to take ample reading notes. Compare notes and impressions with classmates or friends.

However, the second major step is to bring your material under control. Early in the process of gathering the material, you will start thinking through the issues it raises. You may begin to focus on a key question you will want to answer, a key issue that you may want to explore. You will start formulating a strategy for presenting your findings to your reader. You will think about laying out your evidence in a pattern that makes sense. Early in your reading, you will start pulling together quotations that bear on the same point; you will begin collating details that help you answer the same question. This process of sorting out, of pulling your material into shape, will provide the ground plan or working outline for your first draft. You then refine or adjust your plan as necessary as you revise your paper.

What are some basic requirements for the finished paper that will result from this process of focusing, shaping, and revising? Remember: Each paper is different. The following guidelines are meant to alert you to needs that arise again and again in student papers. In considering these guidelines, try not to look at them as a formula that fits all topics. Change or adapt what needs to be changed to suit your purpose.

▮ *Avoid generic titles.* Although you may not hit on the right title until late in the process of writing your paper, remember that the title will be the first thing to strike your reader. Titles should not be perfunctory and interchangeable—good perhaps for filing the paper under the author's name or the name of the story, but not enough to hook the reader into reading your essay. A good title is informative (it helps map the territory), but it should also be beckoning. Your title should be specific and attractive enough to invite the reader. It need not be a "grabber," but it should be alive: It should suggest a topic but also a point of view, a program, or a style.

TOO INTERCHANGEABLE:	Joyce's "Araby"
TOO INFORMAL?	A Boy and His Bubble
FORMAL:	The Dark Infatuation of Joyce's "Araby"

▮ *Take your reader into the world of the story.* Help your reader get into the spirit by starting with a revealing quotation or a crucial incident:

"Your name means 'the king,' " Norma Jean informs her husband Leroy in Bobbie Ann Mason's "Shiloh," but Leroy, a disabled truck driver, model-kit hobbyist, and occasional joint smoker, is more like the palace groundkeeper than the king.

▮ *Bring your paper into focus.* The first page is crucial. What is your central focus? What is your overall plan? After a brief pointed introduction, use your opening paragraphs to set directions. Try to provide a preview or program. Sketch out or hint at your overall scheme. Avoid a program that is too general—too open and interchangeable:

WEAK: In this story, certain elements of the setting underscore and highlight the problems of the main characters.

(What certain elements? This is too vague: No one is going to say "I am all excited—I am going to be told about certain elements!")

Instead, for a short paper, try to sketch out a three-point or four-point program that provides a road map for your reader. Create expectations that your paper as a whole is going to fulfill. For instance, in writing about Mason's "Shiloh," you might plan to show how three main characters relate differently to their setting:

> The characters in Mason's story relate differently to their Southern setting: Leroy, the husband, is stranded in the present; Mabel, the mother-in-law, is living in the past; Norma Jean, the wife, has a future.

This statement provides a **thesis**, summing up the central idea of the paper. However, it also implies an itinerary. It alerts the reader to how the thesis is going to be followed up as the writer looks at each of the major characters in turn.

⧗ *Wean yourself from a mere plot summary.* Follow a logical rather than mere chronological order. Sometimes, especially for a story with a complicated plot, an initial tracing of the story line can help writer and reader get their bearings. But avoid a mere "read-along-with-me" effect—make sure your readers do not think your paper as a whole will merely retell the story. Show that you have tied things together, that you can bring together evidence from different parts of the story. Show that you can pull out relevant quotations or incidents that bear on a key question or key point. (If you follow the order of the story, look at each segment from the angle that is the issue. Use each stage in the story to make a point that is part of your overall argument.)

⧗ *Weave in rich authentic detail.* Follow up general points with detailed examples and support. Look for revealing details—details that alert you to what is important in a story. The student author of the following passage tracked a wealth of telling details that all point in the same direction:

> **The influence of the Catholic church is everywhere in James Joyce's "Araby."** The physical surroundings constantly remind us of the church, and the boy's language of thought and feeling is borrowed from the world of religious devotion. The boy lives on a street that is uneventful and quiet except when the school sets the boys "free" from their religious upbringing and its

restrictions. This may be a first implied criticism of the Catholic church and hints at the desire for freedom in the story. The boys see the detached, uninhabited house of a dead priest and can feel the suffocating effect in the room of long-trapped musty air. The author calls the priest "charitable" because he left all his money to institutions. (How did the priest, who represents the Church and must have taken a vow of poverty, accumulate wealth?) The boy finds a trilogy or trinity of discarded books. One is romantic, another religious, and the third is adventurous. This represents the boy's inner conflict of beliefs versus desires, the romantic and sensual mind versus the religious obligation of a devout communicant. The boy reveals an almost religious devotion when he speaks the name of his friend's sister as a prayer. His thought of her is a sacred "chalice" as he walks through the crowd of "foes" who could never understand his "confused adoration" for her. With "pressed palms," he repeats his prayer of "O love! O love!"

✖ *Early in your paper, start weaving in telling, revealing short quotations.* Let your readers hear the voices of the characters in a story, so your readers can listen not just to the message but to the tone that often reveals personality.

In Erdrich's story, Lyman felt the only hope for the older brother was the red convertible. It was a way the brother might be able to escape and remember who he once was. Lyman said, **"I thought the car might bring him back somehow. So I bided my time and waited for my chance to interest him in the vehicle."** Lyman ruined the car to give Henry something positive and constructive to do. When Henry fixed it, it would make him feel accomplished. He could feel like the old Henry. This worked temporarily. **"He was better than he was before."**

✖ *Strengthen logical connections.* A link or transition like *and* or *another* may make your readers move on, but it may not show them where they are headed. Are you really just saying: "More of same—I am giving an additional example"? Or are you moving an explanation or an argument an important step forward? Transitions like *however* or *on the other hand* can alert the reader to an important turn in the argument. *Therefore* or *as a result* will prepare the reader for a conclusion you are drawing from what came before. *Granted that* or *it is true that* can show your reader that you are aware of an important objection and are prepared to deal with it.

In discussing Bobbie Ann Mason's "Shiloh," you may have made a point of Leroy's inability to communicate. He wants to talk about their marriage—but instead he just lamely repeats that he wants to build his wife a house. You now want to move on to a second point: "Leroy's fixation on the past is *another problem* in the Moffitt household." His playing with the plans for a model log house points to the past, not the future. What is the logical connection between the two points? That he can only talk about things he can do with his hands is already a limitation. But that he seems fixed on the log cabin past makes matters worse. Look at the *however* that provides the logical link:

TRANSITION: Having no way to voice his feelings articulately with words, he builds model log houses because he has no other way to express himself. However, this preoccupation with symbols of the past only serves to widen the gap between him and his wife. . . .

✗ *Aim at a strong conclusion*. Revise a conclusion that is merely a lame recapitulation of points already clear. Try bringing your paper full circle by picking up an image, incident, or keynote from the beginning of the paper. Use the opportunity to drive home a key point. Or use the opportunity to branch out, showing larger implications, showing a personal connection. One student paper started: " 'Shiloh' by Bobbie Ann Mason presents a dull yet strikingly real vision of America." The following conclusion drives home the central point and highlights the connection between the story and our own lives:

"Shiloh" is a perfect portrayal of life in the 1990s. It is realistic, poignant, and depressing. It is ordinary, sometimes dismal, but rarely extravagant. That is left for Oprah and Geraldo to display on television. We see ourselves in the couple—our drive to succeed and prosper in Norma Jean and our love of the couch in Leroy.

Study the following sample paper. What role does the setting of the story play in the paper? How well does the paper live up to the requirements sketched above?

Sample Student Paper

Muscle Building in the New South

Bobbie Ann Mason's short story "Shiloh" is a bleak portrait of a marriage at the point of dissolution—a picture of two people poised at the brink of what for the woman is a new life of personal growth and freedom but what is for the man the loss of most in his life that he thought secure. Mason uses physical detail—the way the characters relate to their bodies and to their physical setting—to mirror the wife's upward spiral and the husband's decline. They both find themselves in a new world that is different from the Old South represented by Leroy's mother-in-law. But for one of them this new world means disillusionment and stagnation; for the other it means opportunity.

Leroy Moffitt is a truck driver from Kentucky, who is at home recovering from an accident in which his leg was badly injured. It is the first time since the early days of his marriage that he has been at home for any length of time, and he begins to feel that he has missed much of his married life. He realizes "that in all the years he was on the road he never took time to examine anything. He was always flying past scenery." Now his years of flying past the scenery of his life are over, and he for the first time is experiencing what it is like to stay in one place. Having a chance to watch his wife for more than hurried intervals, he finds that she is a different person from the woman he married.

His injured leg symbolizes Leroy's new slowing down, his new lack of mobility. It was badly twisted in its socket when his truck jackknifed in the road, and he now has a steel pin in his hip. Although he is healing, he is scared to go back on the road; he has moved from an extremely fast-paced, always-moving lifestyle to one in which he can walk only with difficulty. His career and his marriage have shuddered painfully to a standstill. He finds himself in a setting where much of what he does merely helps to pass the time: building small-scale model log houses, expecting his wife to play old favorites on a state-of-the-art electronic piano.

Leroy's new immobility is reflected even in Leroy's drug of choice. Whereas before he took drugs that were suited to his fast, mobile lifestyle, he now uses drugs of a more mellow nature: "Leroy used to take speed on the road. Now he has to go slowly. He needs to be mellow." The weed he buys allows him to dull and slow down his perception of his surroundings. He buys his joints from a source who represents the downside of the New South—a son of a doctor, whose drug-dealing symbolizes the rejection of his goal-oriented doctor father.

While Leroy is slowing down, however, his wife Norma Jean is speeding up. After fifteen years of staying home while her husband traveled, she is physically and symbolically stepping out into a new world. She is trying to move beyond the drugstore job—beyond the feeling of going nowhere experienced by people who are trapped in an average existence. She is taking steps toward personal improvement and intellectual growth—steps which are reflected in her new attention to her body. Early in the story, we see her working out with dumbbells, improving her muscle tone and physical appearance: "I'd give anything if I could just get these muscles to where they're real hard," she says impatiently. Leroy, with some foreboding, sees the potential for improvement in her, thinking that as she stood with her legs apart she reminded him of "Wonder Woman." Norma Jean wears ankle weights, lifts barbells, and flexes her arm to test the size of her biceps—testing, symbolically, her emotional and intellectual strength as she nears the point of breaking away from Leroy.

As she is improving herself physically, she improves herself intellectually with night classes and reading. As Leroy notes, "She stays up late, writing compositions." Norma Jean breaks out of confining old habits: She quits smoking; she cooks unusual foods, walking around the kitchen with ankle weights attached. Although she is still living in their house, her mind and body are already in a different place.

The differences in Leroy's and Norma Jean's emotional and intellectual needs lead to the final breakup in a setting full of hints of forgotten conflicts, the Civil War battleground at Shiloh. When Norma Jean walks away from Leroy, he is physically unable to follow her, for "his good leg is asleep and his bad leg still hurts him." She moves quickly, widening the chasm where their marriage used to be. In our last glimpse of Leroy and Norma Jean, she is waving her arms in some sort of "exercise for her chest muscles," testing her wings, perhaps, before moving upward and away from her old life.

Questions for Peer Review

1. Some *introductions* dispense with lead-in or background and head straight for the point. In the introduction, this student writer several times paints a dramatic contrast between the two major characters in the Mason story. What key terms or labels characterize the one character? What terms or labels does

she use to characterize the other? How well does this introduction sum up the meaning of the story for you?

2. Throughout this paper, the student writer goes beyond a mere *plot out-line* to spell out the meaning of events. What are the bare-facts events in Leroy's life that are summarized in the second paragraph? How did they change Leroy's life?

3. The injured leg and Leroy's drug use again are not merely mentioned as plot developments but become *symbols* of what is happening to Leroy's life. What role do they play?

4. Where is the key transition or *turning point* in this paper? What *key details* from the story does the student author select to show that Norma Jean is "already in a different place"? Which details are most revealing?

5. Where and how does the student author keep reminding you of the contrast between the Old South and the New South that provides the backdrop and *setting* for what happens in this story? According to this paper, does Leroy represent the Old South and Norma Jean the New South?

6. How does the *conclusion* hark back to earlier parts of the paper? What does it add to conclude the paper on a strong note?

7. Do you think this student author is taking sides? Is the paper *biased* against the male character in the story? Does this paper change your mind about the two characters or change your response to the story?

3   CHARACTER

The Buried Self

I don't invent characters because the Almighty
has already invented millions, just as experts at
fingerprints do not create fingerprints but learn
how to read them.

ISAAC BASHEVIS SINGER

I am enormously interested in other people, other
lives, and with the least provocation I could "go
into" your personality and try to imagine it, try
to find a way of dramatizing it. I am fascinated
by people I meet, or don't meet, people I only cor-
respond with, or read about. . . . It seems to me
that there are so many people who are inarticu-
late but who suffer and doubt and love, nobly,
who need to be explained.

JOYCE CAROL OATES

I live with the people I create, and it has always
made my essential loneliness less keen.

CARSON MCCULLERS

FOCUS ON CHARACTER

Storytellers create characters and set them in motion. The writers appeal to an ancient curiosity: We are fascinated with the variety of people in our world. We are willing to hear about their hopes and fears, their goals and self-doubts, their quirks and ploys, their clever and dense ways. The more we learn about them, the harder it is for us to stay aloof. We begin to care; we take sides; we become involved.

In the following passage from Bobbie Ann Mason's "Shiloh," we begin to see character traits of the husband who was a truck driver but has been in a bad accident. What kind of a person is beginning to emerge?

> . . . Leroy has been home in Kentucky for three months, and his leg is almost healed, but the accident frightened him, and he does not want to drive any more long hauls. He is not sure what to do next. In the meantime, he makes things from craft kits. He started by building a miniature log cabin from notched Popsicle sticks. He varnished it and placed it on the TV set, where it remains. It reminds him of a rustic nativity scene. Then he tried string art (sailing ships on black velvet), a macramé owl kit, a snap-together B-17 Flying Fortress, and a lamp made out of a model truck, with a light fixture in the top of the cab. At first, the kits were diversions, something to kill time, but now he is thinking about building a full-scale log house from a kit. It would be considerably cheaper than building a regular house, and besides, Leroy has come to appreciate how things are put together.

What clues to the character does this description furnish the reader?

The person that emerges does not seem to feel the need to act macho, to prove something by going back to the dangerous job. Instead, he was spooked by the accident, as many ordinary people might have been. He is not making any grandiose plans but has the patience for tasks that require careful plodding work—and not a great deal of imagination. Like many average people, he seems to have a liking for tradition—the nativity scene, the log cabin. He likes the idea of saving money and doing something with his hands by building an actual log cabin to live in. Notice that the author here does not take shortcuts but lets the character build as you read. The author does not put labels on Leroy but lets you reach your own conclusions. The character is not static, set in cement. He is changing or developing in response to what he experiences (he has come to appreciate how things are put together).

How do you come to understand the characters in a short story you read? An author may give you a capsule portrait as advance notice of what you may expect. However, in much modern fiction, you read to see character *unfold*. You see people act out (and hear them talk out) who they are. The author may choose to make you watch a character from outside, letting you draw your own conclusions. Or the author may take you inside the character's mind, letting you overhear private thoughts and share in feelings masked to the outside world.

As you study character in fiction, bear in mind features like the following:

Action and Motivation   When you pay close attention to character, you will find yourself going from the *what* to the *why*—from people's words and actions to their motives. Why do people talk and act the way they do? Be prepared to think about a character's **motivation**. Look for clues to behavior that may seem puzzling on the surface. For instance, characters who act spiteful or hostile may not be by temperament spiteful or hostile people. They may be venting pent-up frustrations. They may have been driven to the edge by a series of adverse events. Also, apparent hostility may be a way to fend off unwanted sympathy.

Flat and Round Characters   **Flat characters** have a one-track personality: The miser is always a Scrooge; the whiner always finds fault. Such one-dimensional characters are common in popular fiction and make for easy recognition (and, sometimes, the easy laugh). **Round characters** have the combination of traits that make real people complicated and at times infuriating. They may be loyal to a person or a cause—with their loyalty tempered by private doubts. They may have been raised in an atmosphere of rah-rah patriotism but discover unsuspected sympathies for a prisoner of war—the enemy. Be prepared to recognize divided loyalties and mixed emotions.

Static and Growing Characters   In serious fiction, characters may prove capable of growth, of development. Stories like Alice Munro's "Boys and Girls" are stories of **initiation**. They reenact rites of passage—from childhood to adolescence, from the happy protected childhood world to a realization of the limitations of the adult world. A story may chronicle a stage in a character's spiritual journey. It may focus on an important turn in the road of a character's life.

Person and Persona   Many writers of modern fiction go beyond the surface, beyond the stereotype. They probe for the hidden personality, the buried self, beneath the public **persona**. They explore the contrast between the image, the face we present to the outside world (perfect hostess, Mr. Personality), and our private insecurities, hang-ups, or vendettas.

The Interplay of Characters   Sometimes, only a single character emerges from the background—giving a solo performance. More typically, a character's personality is revealed in the interaction with others. We see characters as part of a web of relationships. In the Alice Munro story, the girl who is at the center of the story is influenced by two conflicting role models, her father and her mother.

FIRST READING
Encountering People

Do you remember an encounter with a person who was very different from people you knew? Does the central character in the following short short seem strange to you, or do you feel that you understand him? Tim O'Brien was drafted when in college in 1968 and sent to Vietnam. In *If I Die in a Combat Zone, Box Me Up and Ship Me Home* (1973) and *Going after Cacciato* (1976), he has told the story of GIs dying or being ground down in a losing war.

Tim O'Brien   *(born 1946)*   ◉

Stockings   *1990*

Henry Dobbins was a good man, and a superb soldier, but sophistication was not his strong suit. The ironies went beyond him. In many ways he was like America itself, big and strong, full of good intentions, a roll of fat jiggling at his belly, slow of foot but always plodding along, always there when you needed him, a believer in the virtues of simplicity and directness and hard labor. Like his country, too, Dobbins was drawn toward sentimentality.

Even now, twenty years later, I can see him wrapping his girlfriend's pantyhose around his neck before heading out on ambush.

It was his one eccentricity. The pantyhose, he said, had the properties of a good-luck charm. He liked putting his nose into the nylon and breathing in the scent of his girlfriend's body; he liked the memories this inspired; he sometimes slept with the stockings up against his face, the way an infant sleeps with a magic blanket, secure and peaceful. More than anything, though, the stockings were a talisman for him. They kept him safe. They gave access to a spiritual world, where things were soft and intimate, a place where he might someday take his girlfriend to live. Like many of us in Vietnam, Dobbins felt the pull of superstition, and he believed firmly and absolutely in the protective power of the stockings. They were like body armor, he thought. Whenever we saddled up for a late-night ambush, putting on our helmets and flak jackets, Henry Dobbins would make a ritual out of arranging the nylons around his neck, carefully tying a knot, draping the two leg sections over his left shoulder. There were some jokes, of course, but we came to appreciate the mystery of it all. Dobbins was invulnerable. Never wounded, never a scratch. In August, he tripped a Bouncing Betty, which failed to detonate. And a week later he got caught in the open during a fierce little firefight, no cover at all, but he just slipped the pantyhose over his nose and breathed deep and let the magic do its work.

It turned us into a platoon of believers. You don't dispute facts.

But then, near the end of October, his girlfriend dumped him. It was a hard blow. Dobbins went quiet for a while, staring down at her letter, then after a time he took out the stockings and tied them around his neck as a comforter.   5

"No sweat," he said. "I still love her. The magic doesn't go away."

It was a relief for all of us.

The Receptive Reader

Does Henry Dobbins become a real person for you? Does he seem weird to you? Why or why not? Would you agree that Henry Dobbins "was like America itself"? In what ways? Would you call him sentimental? Were you surprised by how he acted at the end of the story? How do you think you would act or react if you had to deal with a person like Henry—for example, on the job or as one of your fellow students?

THE RANGE OF CHARACTERIZATION

You would have me, when I describe horse
thieves, say: "Stealing horses is evil." But that has
been known for ages without my saying so. Let
the jury judge them; it's my job simply to show
what sort of people they are.

ANTON CHEKHOV

*Unlike social scientists, who make descriptive
statements about the varying divorce rates
between, say, middle-class blacks and blue-collar
whites, short-story writers seek to strip away these
labels and create characters whose lives are contradictory and unfinished and do not possess the
coherence of a psychological theory. Writers
reveal instead the unpredictability of human
beings, caught between the lack of consciousness
or conviction or certainty and the need to make
decisions and get on with their lives.*

MICHAEL NAGLER AND WILLIAM SWANSON

In some stories, the characters stay pale. They may seem interchangeable with others of their time or their setting. They may seem representative of their stage in life or of their class. In other stories,
however, the mystery of personality is at the center of the story. The
story tries to make us understand a complex human being. It probes a
character's motives, explores surface contradictions, or ponders a
change of heart. To a large extent, the character is the story. In the stories that follow, character plays a central role.

Raymond Carver   *(1939–1988)*

*Carver has an acute sense of the singularity, the
endearing oddity, of each human being; to each
person he grants a measure of dignity because, if
nothing else at all, this person has the sure distinction that no one else is exactly like him—no
human life can be replicated; therefore each,
however flawed, is precious.*

JONATHAN YARDLEY

*No one's brevity is as rich, as complete, as
Raymond Carver's.*

PATRICIA HAMPL

Raymond Carver has been praised for his intentional "blue-collar realism and unsophistication" (John Barth). Carver had himself worked at
blue-collar jobs in the towns of the Pacific Northwest that is the setting
of many of his stories. He himself, like some of his characters, had done
battle against alcoholism. His characters are often unskilled, unemployed, and unremarkable, yet of sufficient human interest to the author.

He often gives a voice to the feelings or point of view of people of few words, "speaking the thoughts of those who cannot themselves speak" (John Clute). One reviewer thought of him as the kind of writer "who turned banality's pockets out and found all their contents beautiful" (Marilynne Robinson).

Carver is one of a group of contemporary writers tending toward a **minimalist** stance (though he himself disliked the fashionable label). Like other minimalist writers, he kept his stories to the essential minimum, writing on the theory that "less is more," being suspicious of all showy effects. He once said, "I cut my work to the marrow, not just the bone." Carver seems to enjoy teasing the reader with the puzzle of personality. His narrator, as in the following story, may be someone listening to another character, piecing together the pieces of the puzzle, wanting to say (as does Carver's reader) "Tell me more."

The Third Thing That Killed My Father Off   1977

I'll tell you what did my father in. The third thing was Dummy, that Dummy died. The first thing was Pearl Harbor. And the second thing was moving to my grandfather's farm near Wenatchee. That's where my father finished out his days, except they were probably finished before that.

My father blamed Dummy's death on Dummy's wife. Then he blamed it on the fish. And finally he blamed himself—because he was the one that showed Dummy the ad in the back of *Field and Stream* for live black bass shipped anywhere in the U.S.

It was after he got the fish that Dummy started acting peculiar. The fish changed Dummy's whole personality. That's what my father said.

I never knew Dummy's real name. If anyone did, I never heard it. Dummy it was then, and it's Dummy I remember him by now. He was a little wrinkled man, baldheaded, short but very powerful in the arms and legs. If he grinned, which was seldom, his lips folded back over brown, broken teeth. It gave him a crafty expression. His watery eyes stayed fastened on your mouth when you were talking—and if you weren't, they'd go to someplace queer on your body.

I don't think he was really deaf. At least not as deaf as he made out. But he sure couldn't talk. That was for certain.   5

Deaf or no, Dummy'd been on as a common laborer out at the sawmill since the 1920s. This was the Cascade Lumber Company in Yakima, Washington. The years I knew him, Dummy was working as a cleanup man. And all those years I never saw him with anything different on. Meaning a felt hat, a khaki workshirt, a denim jacket over a pair of coveralls. In his top pockets he carried rolls of toilet paper, as one of his jobs was to clean and supply the toilets. It kept him busy, seeing as how the men on nights used to walk off after their tours with a roll or two in their lunchboxes.

Dummy carried a flashlight, even though he worked days. He also carried wrenches, pliers, screwdrivers, friction tape, all the same things the millwrights carried. Well, it made them kid Dummy, the way he was, always carrying everything. Carl Lowe, Ted Slade, Johnny Wait, they were the worst kidders of the ones that kidded Dummy. But Dummy took it all in stride. I think he'd gotten used to it.

My father never kidded Dummy. Not to my knowledge, anyway. Dad was a big, heavy-shouldered man with a crew-haircut, double chin, and a belly of real size. Dummy was always staring at that belly. He'd come to the filing room where my father worked, and he'd sit on a stool and watch my dad's belly while he used the big emery wheels on the saws.

Dummy had a house as good as anyone's.

It was a tarpaper-covered affair near the river, five or six miles from town.   10
Half a mile behind the house, at the end of a pasture, there lay a big gravel pit that the state had dug when they were paving the roads around there. Three good-sized holes had been scooped out, and over the years they'd filled with water. By and by, the three ponds came together to make one.

It was deep. It had a darkish look to it.

Dummy had a wife as well as a house. She was a woman years younger and said to go around with Mexicans. Father said it was busybodies that said that, men like Lowe and Wait and Slade.

She was a small stout woman with glittery little eyes. The first time I saw her, I saw those eyes. It was when I was with Pete Jensen and we were on our bicycles and we stopped at Dummy's to get a glass of water.

When she opened the door, I told her I was Del Fraser's son. I said, "He works with—" And then I realized. "You know, your husband. We were on our bicycles and thought we could get a drink."

"Wait here," she said.   15

She came back with a little tin cup of water in each hand. I downed mine in a single gulp.

But she didn't offer us more. She watched us without saying anything. When we started to get on our bicycles, she came over to the edge of the porch.

"You little fellas had a car now, I might catch a ride with you."

She grinned. Her teeth looked too big for her mouth.

"Let's go," Pete said, and we went.   20

There weren't many places you could fish for bass in our part of the state. There was rainbow mostly, a few brook and Dolly Varden in some of the high mountain streams, and silvers in Blue Lake and Lake Rimrock. That was mostly it, except for the runs of steelhead and salmon in some of the fresh-water rivers in late fall. But if you were a fisherman, it was enough to keep you busy. No one fished for bass. A lot of people I knew had never seen a bass except for pictures. But my father had seen plenty of them when he was growing up in Arkansas and Georgia, and he had high hopes to do with Dummy's bass, Dummy being a friend.

The day the fish arrived, I'd gone swimming at the city pool. I remember coming home and going out again to get them since Dad was going to give Dummy a hand—three tanks Parcel Post from Baton Rouge, Louisiana.

We went in Dummy's pickup, Dad and Dummy and me.

These tanks turned out to be barrels, really, the three of them crated in pine lath. They were standing in the shade out back of the train depot, and it took my dad and Dummy both to lift each crate into the truck.

Dummy drove very carefully through town and just as carefully all the   25 way to his house. He went right through his yard without stopping. He went on down to within feet of the pond. By that time it was nearly dark, so he kept his headlights on and took out a hammer and a tire iron from under the seat, and then the two of them lugged the crates up close to the water and started tearing open the first one.

The barrel inside was wrapped in burlap, and there were these nickel-sized holes in the lid. They raised it off and Dummy aimed his flashlight in.

It looked like a million bass fingerlings were finning inside. It was the strangest sight, all those live things busy in there, like a little ocean that had come on the train.

Dummy scooted the barrel to the edge of the water and poured it out. He took his flashlight and shined it into the pond. But there was nothing to be seen anymore. You could hear the frogs going, but you could hear them going anytime it newly got dark.

"Let me get the other crates," my father said, and he reached over as if to take the hammer from Dummy's coveralls. But Dummy pulled back and shook his head.

He undid the other two crates himself, leaving dark drops of blood on   30 the lath where he ripped his hand doing it.

From that night on, Dummy was different.

Dummy wouldn't let anyone come around now anymore. He put up fencing all around the pasture, and then he fenced off the pond with electrical barbed wire. They said it cost him all his savings for that fence.

Of course, my father wouldn't have anything to do with Dummy after that. Not since Dummy ran him off. Not from fishing, mind you, because the bass were just babies still. But even from trying to get a look.

One evening two years after, when Dad was working late and I took him his food and a jar of iced tea, I found him standing talking with Syd Glover, the millwright. Just as I came in, I heard Dad saying, "You'd reckon the fool was married to them fish, the way he acts."

"From what I hear," Syd said, "he'd do better to put that fence round his   35 house."

My father saw me then, and I saw him signal Syd Glover with his eyes.

But a month later my dad finally made Dummy do it. What he did was, he told Dummy how you had to thin out the weak ones on account of keeping things fit for the rest of them. Dummy stood there pulling at his ear and staring at the floor. Dad said, Yeah, he'd be down to do it tomorrow because it had to be done. Dummy never said yes, actually. He just never said no, is all. All he did was pull on his ear some more.

When Dad got home that day, I was ready and waiting. I had his old bass plugs out and was testing the treble hooks with my finger.

"You set?" he called to me, jumping out of the car. "I'll go to the toilet, you put the stuff in. You can drive us out there if you want."

I'd stowed everything in the back seat and was trying out the wheel when   40
he came back out wearing his fishing hat and eating a wedge of cake with
both hands.

Mother was standing in the door watching. She was a fair-skinned
woman, her blonde hair pulled back in a tight bun and fastened down with
a rhinestone clip. I wonder if she ever went around back in those happy
days, or what she ever really did.

I let out the handbrake. Mother watched until I'd shifted gears, and then,
still unsmiling, she went back inside.

It was a fine afternoon. We had all the windows down to let the air in.
We crossed the Moxee Bridge and swung west onto Slater Road. Alfalfa
fields stood off to either side, and farther on it was cornfields.

Dad had his hand out the window. He was letting the wind carry it back.
He was restless, I could see.

It wasn't long before we pulled up at Dummy's. He came out of the   45
house wearing his hat. His wife was looking out the window.

"You got your frying pan ready?" Dad hollered out to Dummy, but
Dummy just stood there eyeing the car. "Hey, Dummy!" Dad yelled. "Hey,
Dummy, where's your pole, Dummy?"

Dummy jerked his head back and forth. He moved his weight from one
leg to the other and looked at the ground and then at us. His tongue rested
on his lower lip, and he began working his foot into the dirt.

I shouldered the creel. I handed Dad his pole and picked up my own.

"We set to go?" Dad said. "Hey, Dummy, we set to go?"

Dummy took off his hat and, with the same hand, he wiped his wrist over   50
his head. He turned abruptly, and we followed him across the spongy pasture. Every twenty feet or so a snipe sprang up from the clumps of grass at
the edge of the old furrows.

At the end of the pasture, the ground sloped gently and became dry and
rocky, nettle bushes and scrub oaks scattered here and there. We cut to the
right, following an old set of car tracks, going through a field of milkweed
that came up to our waists, the dry pods at the tops of the stalks rattling angrily as we pushed through. Presently, I saw the sheen of water over
Dummy's shoulder, and I heard Dad shout, "Oh, Lord, look at that!"

But Dummy slowed down and kept bringing his hand up and moving his
hat back and forth over his head, and then he just stopped flat.

Dad said, "Well, what do you think, Dummy? One place good as another?
Where do you say we should come onto it?"

Dummy wet his lower lip.

"What's the matter with you, Dummy?" Dad said. "This your pond,   55
ain't it?"

Dummy looked down and picked an ant off his coveralls.

"Well, hell," Dad said, letting out his breath. He took out his watch. "If
it's all right with you, we'll get to it before it gets too dark."

Dummy stuck his hands in his pockets and turned back to the pond. He
started walking again. We trailed along behind. We could see the whole
pond now, the water dimpled with rising fish. Every so often a bass would
leap clear and come down in a splash.

"Great God," I heard my father say.

We came up to the pond at an open place, a gravel beach kind of.   60

Dad motioned to me and dropped into a crouch. I dropped too. He was peering into the water in front of us, and when I looked, I saw what had taken him so.

"Honest to God," he whispered.

A school of bass was cruising, twenty, thirty, not one of them under two pounds. They veered off, and then they shifted and came back, so densely spaced they looked like they were bumping up against each other. I could see their big, heavy-lidded eyes watching us as they went by. They flashed away again, and again they came back.

They were asking for it. It didn't make any difference if we stayed squatted or stood up. The fish just didn't think a thing about us. I tell you, it was a sight to behold.

We sat there for quite a while, watching that school of bass go so inno-   65
cently about their business, Dummy the whole time pulling at his fingers and looking around as if he expected someone to show up. All over the pond the bass were coming up to nuzzle the water, or jumping clear and falling back, or coming up to the surface to swim along with their dorsals sticking out.

Dad signaled, and we got up to cast. I tell you, I was shaky with excitement. I could hardly get the plug loose from the cork handle of my pole. It was while I was trying to get the hooks out that I felt Dummy seize my shoulder with his big fingers. I looked, and in answer Dummy worked his chin in Dad's direction. What he wanted was clear enough, no more than one pole.

Dad took off his hat and then put it back on and then he moved over to where I stood.

"You go on, Jack," he said. "That's all right, son—you do it now."

I looked at Dummy just before I laid out my cast. His face had gone rigid, and there was a thin line of drool on his chin.

"Come back stout on the sucker when he strikes," Dad said. "Sons of   70
bitches got mouths hard as doorknobs."

I flipped off the drag lever and threw back my arm. I sent her out a good forty feet. The water was boiling even before I had time to take up the slack.

"Hit him!" Dad yelled. "Hit the son of a bitch! Hit him good!"

I came back hard, twice. I had him, all right. The rod bowed over and jerked back and forth. Dad kept yelling what to do.

"Let him go, let him go! Let him run! Give him more line! Now wind in! Wind in! No, let him run! Woo-ee! Will you look at that!"

The bass danced around the pond. Every time it came up out of the   75
water, it shook its head so hard you could hear the plug rattle. And then he'd take off again. But by and by I wore him out and had him in up close. He looked enormous, six or seven pounds maybe. He lay on his side, whipped, mouth open, gills working. My knees felt so weak I could hardly stand. But I held the rod up, the line tight.

Dad waded out over his shoes. But when he reached for the fish, Dummy started sputtering, shaking his head, waving his arms.

"Now what the hell's the matter with you, Dummy? The boy's got hold of the biggest bass I ever seen, and he ain't going to throw him back, by God!"

Dummy kept carrying on and gesturing toward the pond.

"I ain't about to let this boy's fish go. You hear me, Dummy? You got another thing coming if you think I'm going to do that."

Dummy reached for my line. Meanwhile, the bass had gained some   80 strength back. He turned himself over and started swimming again. I yelled and then I lost my head and slammed down the brake on the reel and started winding. The bass made a last, furious run.

That was that. The line broke. I almost fell over on my back.

"Come on, Jack," Dad said, and I saw him grabbing up his pole. "Come on, goddamn the fool, before I knock the man down."

That February the river flooded.

It had snowed pretty heavy the first weeks of December, and turned real cold before Christmas. The ground froze. The snow stayed where it was. But toward the end of January, the Chinook wind struck. I woke up one morning to hear the house getting buffeted and the steady drizzle of water running off the roof.

It blew for five days, and on the third day the river began to rise.   85

"She's up to fifteen feet," my father said one evening, looking over his newspaper. "Which is three feet over what you need to flood. Old Dummy going to lose his darlings."

I wanted to go down to the Moxee Bridge to see how high the water was running. But my dad wouldn't let me. He said a flood was nothing to see.

Two days later the river crested, and after that the water began to subside.

Orin Marshall and Danny Owens and I bicycled out to Dummy's one morning a week after. We parked our bicycles and walked across the pasture that bordered Dummy's property.

It was a wet, blustery day, the clouds dark and broken, moving fast   90 across the sky. The ground was soppy wet and we kept coming to puddles in the thick grass. Danny was just learning how to cuss, and he filled the air with the best he had every time he stepped in over his shoes. We could see the swollen river at the end of the pasture. The water was still high and out of its channel, surging around the trunks of trees and eating away at the edge of the land. Out toward the middle, the current moved heavy and swift, and now and then a bush floated by, or a tree with its branches sticking up.

We came to Dummy's fence and found a cow wedged in up against the wire. She was bloated and her skin was shiny-looking and gray. It was the first dead thing of any size I'd ever seen. I remember Orin took a stick and touched the open eyes.

We moved on down the fence, toward the river. We were afraid to go near the wire because we thought it might still have electricity in it. But at the edge of what looked like a deep canal, the fence came to an end. The ground had simply dropped into the water here, and the fence along with it.

We crossed over and followed the new channel that cut directly into Dummy's land and headed straight for his pond, going into it lengthwise and forcing an outlet for itself at the other end, then twisting off until it joined up with the river farther on.

You didn't doubt that most of Dummy's fish had been carried off. But those that hadn't been were free to come and go.

Then I caught sight of Dummy. It scared me, seeing him. I motioned to   95
the other fellows, and we all got down.

Dummy was standing at the far side of the pond near where the water was rushing out. He was just standing there, the saddest man I ever saw.

"I sure do feel sorry for old Dummy, though," my father said at supper a few weeks after. "Mind, the poor devil brought it on himself. But you can't help but be troubled for him."

Dad went on to say George Laycock saw Dummy's wife sitting in the Sportsman's Club with a big Mexican fellow.

"And that ain't the half of it—"

Mother looked up at him sharply and then at me. But I just went on eat-   100
ing like I hadn't heard a thing.

Dad said, "Damn it to hell, Bea, the boy's old enough!"

He'd changed a lot, Dummy had. He was never around any of the men anymore, not if he could help it. No one felt like joking with him either, not since he'd chased Carl Lowe with a two-by-four stud after Carl tipped Dummy's hat off. But the worst of it was that Dummy was missing from work a day or two a week on the average now, and there was some talk of his being laid off.

"The man's going off the deep end," Dad said. "Clear crazy if he don't watch out."

Then on a Sunday afternoon just before my birthday, Dad and I were cleaning the garage. It was a warm, drifty day. You could see the dust hanging in the air. Mother came to the back door and said, "Del, it's for you. I think it's Vern."

I followed Dad in to wash up. When he was through talking, he put the   105
phone down and turned to us.

"It's Dummy," he said. "Did in his wife with a hammer and drowned himself. Vern just heard it in town."

When we got out there, cars were parked all around. The gate to the pasture stood open, and I could see tire marks that led on to the pond.

The screen door was propped ajar with a box, and there was this lean, pock-faced man in slacks and sports shirt and wearing a shoulder holster. He watched Dad and me get out of the car.

"I was his friend," Dad said to the man.

The man shook his head. "Don't care who you are. Clear off unless you   110
got business here."

"Did they find him?" Dad said.

"They're dragging," the man said, and adjusted the fit of his gun.

"All right if we walk down? I knew him pretty well."

The man said, "Take your chances. They chase you off, don't say you wasn't warned."

We went on across the pasture, taking pretty much the same route we had the day we tried fishing. There were motorboats going on the pond, dirty fluffs of exhaust hanging over it. You could see where the high water had cut away the ground and carried off trees and rocks. The two boats had uniformed men in them, and they were going back and forth, one man steering and the other man handling the rope and hooks.

An ambulance waited on the gravel beach where we'd set ourselves to cast for Dummy's bass. Two men in white lounged against the back, smoking cigarettes.

One of the motorboats cut off. We all looked up. The man in back stood up and started heaving on his rope. After a time, an arm came out of the water. It looked like the hooks had gotten Dummy in the side. The arm went back down and then it came out again, along with a bundle of something.

It's not him, I thought. It's something else that has been in there for years.

The man in the front of the boat moved to the back, and together the two men hauled the dripping thing over the side.

I looked at Dad. His face was funny the way it was set.

"Women," he said. He said, "That's what the wrong kind of woman can do to you, Jack."

But I don't think Dad really believed it. I think he just didn't know who to blame or what to say.

It seemed to me everything took a bad turn for my father after that. Just like Dummy, he wasn't the same man anymore. That arm coming up and going back down in the water, it was like so long to good times and hello to bad. Because it was nothing but that all the years after Dummy drowned himself in that dark water.

Is that what happens when a friend dies? Bad luck for the pals he left behind?

But as I said, Pearl Harbor and having to move back to his dad's place didn't do my dad one bit of good, either.

The Receptive Reader

1. How do we learn what we come to know about Dummy? Who is the *narrator*—what kind of person tells us the story? What is his role in the story? Is he a major or a minor character? What is his vantage point? What are his limitations?

2. How does the author make Dummy come to life in the early sections of the story? What is Dummy's problem? Can you visualize his physical appearance? How much and what kind of *descriptive detail* do you get?

3. How do Dummy's coworkers treat him, and how are we expected to feel about them?

4. What is the relationship between the narrator's father and Dummy? Who is the true *central character* in the story? Does the story have a hero?

5. As the story unfolds, how much insight do we get into Dummy's personality or character? Do you understand the way Dummy acts about the fish, the pond, the flood? (How important are the fish in the story as a whole?)

6. What role does Dummy's wife play in the story? Is she playing a bit part? Is she expendable?

7. A central *irony* in the story is that Dummy is the character who seems to have urgent things to say to the others, but he is unable to communicate through language. How *does* he communicate? What is he trying to tell the others?

8. What is the role of humor in the story? What is the tone of the references to the father's death in the title, at the beginning, and in the conclusion? Do they color the story as a whole?

The Personal Response

For you, is Dummy an eccentric—an isolated individual, a person with special personal problems all of his own? Is he someone "acting peculiar"? Or does his story have a more general human meaning?

The Creative Dimension

Assume Dummy could have been a more articulate or eloquent character. Write an extended suicide note that he might have written to explain himself to his friends.

Alice Munro   *(born 1931)*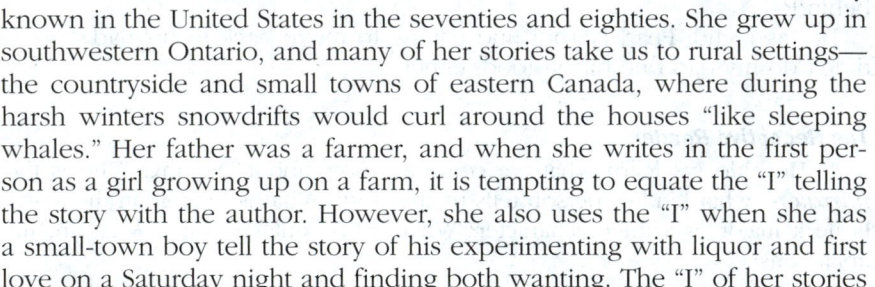

Alice Munro is one of several Canadian writers who became widely known in the United States in the seventies and eighties. She grew up in southwestern Ontario, and many of her stories take us to rural settings— the countryside and small towns of eastern Canada, where during the harsh winters snowdrifts would curl around the houses "like sleeping whales." Her father was a farmer, and when she writes in the first person as a girl growing up on a farm, it is tempting to equate the "I" telling the story with the author. However, she also uses the "I" when she has a small-town boy tell the story of his experimenting with liquor and first love on a Saturday night and finding both wanting. The "I" of her stories is fictitious—it is part of a vividly imagined world that blends autobiographical materials and sharp-eyed observation of fellow humanity.

Her first collection of short stories, *Dance of the Happy Shades,* was published in 1968 and received the Canadian Governor General's Literary Award. She published her second collection of stories, *Something I've Been Meaning to Tell You,* in 1972. Her novel *Lives of Girls and Women* appeared in 1971.

Munro has a special gift for creating a sense of place. In her story "Thanks for the Ride," she takes us to a town where the signs in Pop's Café (between fly-speckled and slightly yellowed cutouts of strawberry sundaes and tomato sandwiches) say things like "Don't ask for information—if we knew anything, we wouldn't be here." One of the boys in the story has a habit of reading signs out loud—"Mission Creek. Population 1700. Gateway to the Bruce. We love our children." The houses are likely to have linoleum on the floor; there is likely to be a glossy sofa "with a Niagara Falls and 'To Mother' cushion on it."

In such settings, she places characters who are often undergoing a rite of passage. (One editor said about Munro's stories that her "characters' lives and landscapes are inextricably intertwined.") They may be at a turning point in their lives, moving from childhood to adolescence, or from the confused passions of adolescence to the world of adult responsibilities. Her characters are often people who are still spontaneous and innocent but who encounter people more knowing and perhaps more defeated than they are. Such a story may become a story of **initiation**, as the hero or heroine discovers the limitations, the invisible walls, that mark off his or her world.

In the following story, there is much nostalgic re-creation of the golden world of childhood. But at the center of the story is a young woman at the crossroads. Who is this young woman? What are the contradictory influences that help shape her identity? Viewed as a rite of passage, her story is a passage from what to what? Where is she headed at the end of the story?

The Ave referred to in a song mentioned early in the story is short for the Catholic prayer Ave Maria, or Hail Mary. Orangemen's Day (July 12) is a Protestant holiday dedicated to the memory of William of Orange, who replaced the Catholic James II as king of England in 1689. Judy Canova was a popular entertainer of the thirties and forties.

Boys and Girls   *1968*

It is difficult to stand forth in one's growing if one
is not permitted to live through the states of one's
unripeness, clumsiness, unreadiness, as well as
one's grace and aptitude.

M. C. RICHARDS

My father was a fox farmer. That is, he raised silver foxes, in pens; and in the fall and early winter, when their fur was prime, he killed them and skinned them and sold their pelts to the Hudson's Bay Company or the Montreal Fur Traders. These companies supplied us with heroic calendars to hang, one on each side of the kitchen door. Against a background of cold blue sky and black pine forests and treacherous northern rivers, plumed adventurers planted the flags of England or of France; magnificent savages bent their backs to the portage.

For several weeks before Christmas, my father worked after supper in the cellar of our house. The cellar was whitewashed, and lit by a hundred-watt bulb over the worktable. My brother Laird and I sat on the top step and watched. My father removed the pelt inside-out from the body of the fox, which looked surprisingly small, mean and ratlike, deprived of its arrogant weight of fur. The naked, slippery bodies were collected in a sack and buried at the dump. One time the hired man, Henry Bailey, had taken a swipe at me with this sack, saying, "Christmas present!" My mother thought that was not funny. In fact she disliked the whole pelting operation—that was what the killing, skinning, and preparation of the furs was called—and wished it did not have to take place in the house. There was the smell. After the pelt had been stretched inside-out on a long board my father scraped away delicately, removing the little clotted webs of blood vessels, the bubbles of fat; the smell of blood and animal fat, with the strong primitive odor of the fox itself, penetrated all parts of the house. I found it reassuringly seasonal, like the smell of oranges and pine needles.

Henry Bailey suffered from bronchial troubles. He would cough and cough until his narrow face turned scarlet, and his light blue, derisive eyes filled up with tears; then he took the lid off the stove, and, standing well back, shot out a great clot of phlegm—hsss—straight into the heart of the flames. We admired him for this performance and for his ability to make his stomach growl at will, and for his laughter, which was full of high whistlings and gurglings and involved the whole faulty machinery of his chest. It was sometimes hard to tell what he was laughing at, and always possible that it might be us.

After we had been sent to bed we could still smell fox and still hear Henry's laugh, but these things, reminders of the warm, safe, brightly lit downstairs world, seemed lost and diminished, floating on the stale cold air upstairs. We were afraid at night in the winter. We were not afraid of *outside* though this was the time of year when snowdrifts curled around our house like sleeping whales and the wind harassed us all night, coming up from the buried fields, the frozen swamp, with its old bugbear chorus of threats and misery. We were afraid of *inside,* the room where we slept. At this time the upstairs of our house was not finished. A brick chimney went up one wall. In the middle of the floor was a square hole, with a wooden railing around it; that was where the stairs came up. On the other side of the stairwell were the things that nobody had any use for any more—a soldiery roll of linoleum, standing on end, a wicker baby carriage, a fern basket, china jugs and basins with cracks in them, a picture of the Battle of Balaclava, very sad to look at. I had told Laird, as soon as he was old enough to understand such things, that bats and skeletons lived over there; whenever a man escaped from the county jail, twenty miles away, I imagined that he had somehow let himself in the window and was hiding behind the linoleum. But we had rules to keep us safe. When the light was on, we were safe as long as we did not step off the square of worn carpet which defined our bedroom-space; when the light was off no place was safe but the beds themselves. I had to turn out the light kneeling on the end of my bed, and stretching as far as I could to reach the cord.

In the dark we lay on our beds, our narrow life rafts, and fixed our eyes   5 on the faint light coming up the stairwell, and sang songs. Laird sang "Jingle Bells," which he would sing any time, whether it was Christmas or not, and I sang "Danny Boy." I loved the sound of my own voice, frail and supplicating, rising in the dark. We could make out the tall frosted shapes of the windows now, gloomy and white. When I came to the part, *When I am dead, as dead I well may be*—a fit of shivering caused not by the cold sheets but by pleasurable emotion almost silenced me. *You'll kneel and say, and Ave there above me*—What was an Ave? Every day I forgot to find out.

Laird went straight from singing to sleep. I could hear his long, satisfied, bubbly breaths. Now for the time that remained to me, the most perfectly private and perhaps the best time of the whole day, I arranged myself tightly under the covers and went on with one of the stories I was telling myself from night to night. These stories were about myself, when I had grown a little older; they took place in a world that was recognizably mine, yet one that presented opportunities for courage, boldness and self-sacrifice, as mine never did. I rescued people from a bombed building (it discouraged me that the real war had gone on so far away from Jubilee). I shot two rabid wolves who were menacing the schoolyard (the teachers cowered terrified at my back). I rode a fine horse spiritedly down the main street of Jubilee, acknowledging the townspeople's gratitude for some yet-to-be-worked-out piece of heroism (nobody ever rode a horse there, except King Billy in the Orangemen's Day parade). There was always riding and shooting in these stories, though I had only been on a horse twice—bareback because we did not own a saddle—and the second time I had slid right around and dropped under the horse's feet; it had stepped placidly over me. I really was learning to shoot, but I could not hit anything yet, not even tin cans on fence posts.

Alive, the foxes inhabited a world my father made for them. It was surrounded by a high guard fence, like a medieval town, with a gate that was padlocked at night. Along the streets of this town were ranged large, sturdy pens. Each of them had a real door that a man could go through, a wooden ramp along the wire, for the foxes to run up and down on, and a kennel—something like a clothes chest with airholes—where they slept and stayed in winter and had their young. There were feeding and watering dishes attached to the wire in such a way that they could be emptied and cleaned from the outside. The dishes were made of old tin cans, and the ramps and kennels of odds and ends of old lumber. Everything was tidy and ingenious; my father was tirelessly inventive and his favorite book in the world was *Robinson Crusoe*. He had fitted a tin drum on a wheelbarrow, for bringing water down to the pens. This was my job in summer, when the foxes had to have water twice a day. Between nine and ten o'clock in the morning, and again after supper, I filled the drum at the pump and trundled it down through the barnyard to the pens, where I parked it, and filled my watering can and went along the streets. Laird came too, with his little cream and green gardening can, filled too full and knocking against his legs and slopping water on his canvas shoes. I had the real watering can, my father's, though I could only carry it three-quarters full.

The foxes all had names, which were printed on a tin plate and hung beside their doors. They were not named when they were born, but when they survived the first year's pelting and were added to the breeding stock. Those my father had named were called names like Prince, Bob, Wally and Betty. Those I had named were called Star or Turk, or Maureen or Diana. Laird named one Maud after a hired girl we had when he was little, one Harold after a boy at school, and one Mexico, he did not say why.

Naming them did not make pets out of them, or anything like it. Nobody but my father ever went into the pens, and he had twice had blood-poisoning from bites. When I was bringing them their water they prowled up and down on the paths they had made inside their pens, barking seldom—they saved that for nighttime, when they might get up a chorus of community frenzy—but always watching me, their eyes burning, clear gold, in their pointed, malevolent faces. They were beautiful for their delicate legs and heavy, aristocratic tails and the bright fur sprinkled on dark down their backs—which gave them their name—but especially for their faces, drawn exquisitely sharp in pure hostility, and their golden eyes.

Besides carrying water I helped my father when he cut the long grass, and the lamb's quarter and flowering money-musk, that grew between the pens. He cut with the scythe and I raked into piles. Then he took a pitchfork and threw fresh-cut grass all over the top of the pens, to keep the foxes cooler and shade their coats, which were browned by too much sun. My father did not talk to me unless it was about the job we were doing. In this he was quite different from my mother, who, if she was feeling cheerful, would tell me all sorts of things—the name of a dog she had had when she was a little girl, the names of boys she had gone out with later on when she was grown up, and what certain dresses of hers had looked like—she could not imagine now what had become of them. Whatever thoughts and stories my father had were private, and I was shy of him and would never ask him questions. Nevertheless I worked willingly under his eyes, and with a feeling of pride. One time a feed salesman came down into the pens to talk to him and my father said, "Like to have you meet my new hired man." I turned away and raked furiously, red in the face with pleasure.

"Could of fooled me," said the salesman. "I thought it was only a girl."

After the grass was cut, it seemed suddenly much later in the year. I walked on stubble in the earlier evening, aware of the reddening skies, the entering silences, of fall. When I wheeled the tank out of the gate and put the padlock on, it was almost dark. One night at this time I saw my mother and father standing talking on the little rise of ground we called the gangway, in front of the barn. My father had just come from the meathouse; he had his stiff bloody apron on, and a pail of cut-up meat in his hand.

It was an odd thing to see my mother down at the barn. She did not often come out of the house unless it was to do something—hang out the wash or dig potatoes in the garden. She looked out of place, with her bare lumpy legs, not touched by the sun, her apron still on and damp across the stomach from the supper dishes. Her hair was tied up in a kerchief, wisps of it falling out. She would tie her hair up like this in the morning, saying she did not have time to do it properly, and it would stay tied up all day. It was true, too; she really did not have time. These days our back porch was piled with baskets of peaches and grapes and pears, bought in town, and onions and tomatoes and cucumbers grown at home, all waiting to be made into jelly and jam and preserves, pickles and chili sauce. In the kitchen there was a fire in the stove all day, jars clinked in boiling water, sometimes a cheese-cloth bag was strung on a pole between two chairs straining blue-black grape pulp for jelly. I was given jobs to do and I would sit at the table peel-ing peaches that had been soaked in the hot water, or cutting up onions, my eyes smarting and streaming. As soon as I was done I ran out of the house, trying to get out of earshot before my mother thought of what she wanted me to do next. I hated the hot dark kitchen in summer, the green blinds and the flypapers, the same old oilcloth table and wavy mirror and bumpy linoleum. My mother was too tired and preoccupied to talk to me, she had no heart to tell about the Normal School Graduation Dance; sweat trickled over her face and she was always counting under her breath, point-ing at jars, dumping cups of sugar. It seemed to me that work in the house was endless, dreary and peculiarly depressing; work done out of doors, and in my father's service, was ritualistically important.

I wheeled the tank up to the barn, where it was kept, and I heard my mother saying, "Wait till Laird gets a little bigger, then you'll have a real help."

What my father said I did not hear. I was pleased by the way he stood   15 listening, politely as he would to a salesman or a stranger, but with an air of wanting to get on with his real work. I felt my mother had no business down here and I wanted him to feel the same way. What did she mean about Laird? He was no help to anybody. Where was he now? Swinging himself sick on the swing, going around in circles, or trying to catch cater-pillars. He never once stayed with me till I was finished.

"And then I can use her more in the house," I heard my mother say. She had a dead-quiet, regretful way of talking about me that always made me uneasy. "I just get my back turned and she runs off. It's not like I had a girl in the family at all."

I went and sat on a feed bag in the corner of the barn, not wanting to appear when this conversation was going on. My mother, I felt, was not to be trusted. She was kinder than my father and more easily fooled, but you could not depend on her, and the real reasons for the things she said and did were not to be known. She loved me, and she sat up late at night mak-ing a dress of the difficult style I wanted, for me to wear when school started, but she was also my enemy. She was always plotting. She was plot-ting now to get me to stay in the house more, although she knew I hated it (*because* she knew I hated it) and keep me from working for my father. It seemed to me she would do this simply out of perversity, and to try her power. It did not occur to me that she could be lonely, or jealous. No grown-up could be; they were too fortunate. I sat and kicked my heels mo-notonously against a feed bag, raising dust, and did not come out till she was gone.

At any rate, I did not expect my father to pay any attention to what she said. Who could imagine Laird doing my work—Laird remembering the padlock and cleaning out the watering dishes with a leaf on the end of a stick, or even wheeling the tank without it tumbling over? It showed how little my mother knew about the way things really were.

I have forgotten to say what the foxes were fed. My father's bloody apron reminded me. They were fed horsemeat. At this time most farmers still kept horses, and when a horse got too old to work, or broke a leg or got down and would not get up, as they sometimes did, the owner would call my father, and he and Henry went out to the farm in the truck. Usually they shot and butchered the horse there, paying the farmer from five to twelve dollars. If they had already too much meat on hand, they would bring the horse back alive, and keep it for a few days or weeks in our stable, until the meat was needed. After the war the farmers were buying tractors and gradually getting rid of horses altogether, so it sometimes happened that we got a good healthy horse, that there was just no use for any more. If this happened in the winter we might keep the horse in our stable till spring, for we had plenty of hay and if there was a lot of snow—and the plow did not always get our road cleared—it was convenient to be able to go to town with a horse and cutter.

The winter I was eleven years old we had two horses in the stable. We did not know what names they had had before, so we called them Mack and Flora. Mack was an old black workhorse, sooty and indifferent. Flora was a sorrel mare, a driver. We took them both out in the cutter. Mack was slow and easy to handle. Flora was given to fits of violent alarm, veering at cars and even at other horses, but we loved her speed and high-stepping, her general air of gallantry and abandon. On Saturdays we went down to the stable and as soon as we opened the door on its cosy, animal-smelling darkness Flora threw up her head, rolled her eyes, whinnied despairingly and pulled herself through a crisis of nerves on the spot. It was not safe to go into her stall; she would kick.

This winter also I began to hear a great deal more on the theme my mother had sounded when she had been talking in front of the barn. I no longer felt safe. It seemed that in the minds of the people around me there was a steady undercurrent of thought, not to be deflected, on this one subject. The word *girl* had formerly seemed to be innocent and unburdened, like the word *child;* now it appeared that it was no such thing. A girl was not, as I had supposed, simply what I was; it was what I had to become. It was a definition, always touched with emphasis, with reproach and disappointment. Also it was a joke on me. Once Laird and I were fighting, and for the first time ever I had to use all my strength against him; even so, he caught and pinned my arm for a moment, really hurting me. Henry saw this, and laughed, saying, "Oh, that there Laird's gonna show you, one of these days!" Laird was getting a lot bigger. But I was getting bigger too.

My grandmother came to stay with us for a few weeks and I heard other things. "Girls don't slam doors like that." "Girls keep their knees together when they sit down." And worse still, when I asked some questions, "That's none of girls' business." I continued to slam the doors and sit as awkwardly as possible, thinking that by such measures I kept myself free.

When spring came, the horses were let out in the barnyard. Mack stood against the barn wall trying to scratch his neck and haunches, but Flora trotted up and down and reared at the fences, clattering her hooves against the rails. Snow drifts dwindled quickly, revealing the hard gray and brown earth, the familiar rise and fall of the ground, plain and bare after the fantastic

20

landscape of winter. There was a great feeling of opening-out, of release. We just wore rubbers now, over our shoes; our feet felt ridiculously light. One Saturday we went out to the stable and found all the doors open, letting in the unaccustomed sunlight and fresh air. Henry was there, just idling around looking at his collection of calendars which were tacked up behind the stalls in a part of the stable my mother had probably never seen.

"Come to say goodbye to your old friend Mack?" Henry said. "Here, you give him a taste of oats." He poured some oats into Laird's cupped hands and Laird went to feed Mack. Mack's teeth were in bad shape. He ate very slowly, patiently shifting the oats around in his mouth, trying to find a stump of a molar to grind it on. "Poor old Mack," said Henry mournfully. "When a horse's teeth's gone, he's gone. That's about the way."

"Are you going to shoot him today?" I said. Mack and Flora had been in   25 the stable so long I had almost forgotten they were going to be shot.

Henry didn't answer me. Instead he started to sing in a high, trembly, mocking-sorrowful voice, *Oh, there's no more work, for poor Uncle Ned, he's gone where the good darkies go.* Mack's thick, blackish tongue worked diligently at Laird's hand. I went out before the song was ended and sat down on the gangway.

I had never seen them shoot a horse, but I knew where it was done. Last summer Laird and I had come upon a horse's entrails before they were buried. We had thought it was a big black snake, coiled up in the sun. That was around in the field that ran up beside the barn. I thought that if we went inside the barn, and found a wide crack or a knothole to look through, we would be able to see them do it. It was not something I wanted to see; just the same, if a thing really happened, it was better to see it, and know.

My father came down from the house, carrying the gun.

"What are you doing here?" he said.

"Nothing."   30

"Go on up and play around the house."

He sent Laird out of the stable. I said to Laird, "Do you want to see them shoot Mack?" and without waiting for an answer led him around to the front door of the barn, opened it carefully, and went in. "Be quiet or they'll hear us," I said. We could hear Henry and my father talking in the stable, then the heavy, shuffling steps of Mack being backed out of his stall.

In the loft it was cold and dark. Thin, crisscrossed beams of sunlight fell through the cracks. The hay was low. It was a rolling country, hills and hollows, slipping under our feet. About four feet up was a beam going around the walls. We piled hay up in one corner and I boosted Laird up and hoisted myself. The beam was not very wide; we crept along it with our hands flat on the barn walls. There were plenty of knotholes, and I found one that gave me the view I wanted—a corner of the barnyard, the gate, part of the field. Laird did not have a knothole and began to complain.

I showed him a widened crack between two boards. "Be quiet and wait. If they hear you you'll get us in trouble."

My father came in sight carrying the gun. Henry was leading Mack by the   35 halter. He dropped it and took out his cigarette papers and tobacco; he rolled cigarettes for my father and himself. While this was going on Mack nosed around in the old, dead grass along the fence. Then my father opened the gate and they took Mack through. Henry led Mack way from the path to a patch of ground and they talked together, not loud enough for us to hear. Mack again began searching for a mouthful of fresh grass, which was not to be found. My father walked away in a straight line, and stopped short at a distance which seemed to suit him. Henry was walking away from Mack too, but sideways, still negligently holding on to the halter. My father raised the gun and Mack looked up as if he had noticed something and my father shot him.

Mack did not collapse at once but swayed, lurched sideways and fell, first on his side; then he rolled over on his back and, amazingly, kicked his legs for a few seconds in the air. At this Henry laughed, as if Mack had done a trick for him. Laird, who had drawn a long, groaning breath of surprise when the shot was fired, said out loud, "He's not dead." And it seemed to me it might be true. But his legs stopped, he rolled on his side again, his muscles quivered and sank. The two men walked over and looked at him in a business-like way; they bent down and examined his forehead where the bullet had gone in, and now I saw his blood on the brown grass.

"Now they just skin him and cut him up," I said. "Let's go." My legs were a little shaky and I jumped gratefully down into the hay. "Now you've seen how they shoot a horse," I said in a congratulatory way, as if I had seen it many times before. "Let's see if any barn cat's had kittens in the hay." Laird jumped. He seemed young and obedient again. Suddenly I remembered how, when he was little, I had brought him into the barn and told him to climb the ladder to the top beam. That was in the spring, too, when the hay was low. I had done it out of a need for excitement, a desire for something to happen so that I could tell about it. He was wearing a little bulky brown and white checked coat, made down from one of mine. He went all the way up just as I told him, and sat down on the top beam with the hay far below him on one side, and the barn floor and some old machinery on the other. Then I ran screaming to my father, "Laird's up on the top beam!" My father came, my mother came, my father went up the ladder talking very quietly and brought Laird down under his arm, at which my mother leaned against the ladder and began to cry. They said to me, "Why weren't you watching him?" but nobody ever knew the truth. Laird did not know enough to tell. But whenever I saw the brown and white checked coat hanging in the closet, or at the bottom of the rag bag, which was where it ended up, I felt a weight in my stomach, the sadness of unexorcised guilt.

I looked at Laird, who did not even remember this, and I did not like the look on this thin, winter-pale face. His expression was not frightened or upset, but remote, concentrating. "Listen," I said, in an unusually bright and friendly voice, "you aren't going to tell, are you?"

"No," he said absently.

"Promise."

"Promise," he said. I grabbed the hand behind his back to make sure he was not crossing his fingers. Even so, he might have a nightmare; it might come out that way. I decided I had better work hard to get all thoughts of what he had seen out of his mind—which, it seemed to me, could not hold very many things at a time. I got some money I had saved and that afternoon we went into Jubilee and saw a show, with Judy Canova, at which we both laughed a great deal. After that I thought it would be all right.

Two weeks later I knew they were going to shoot Flora. I knew from the night before, when I heard my mother ask if the hay was holding out all right, and my father said, "Well, after tomorrow there'll just be the cow, and we should be able to put her out to grass in another week." So I knew it was Flora's turn in the morning.

This time I didn't think of watching it. That was something to see just one time. I had not thought about it very often since, but sometimes when I was busy, working at school, or standing in front of the mirror combing my hair and wondering if I would be pretty when I grew up, the whole scene would flash into my mind: I would see the easy, practiced way my father raised the gun, and hear Henry laughing when Mack kicked his legs in the air. I did not have any great feeling of horror and opposition, such as a city child might have had; I was too used to seeing the death of animals as a necessity by which we lived. Yet I felt a little ashamed, and there was a new wariness, a sense of holding-off, in my attitude to my father and his work.

It was a fine day, and we were going around the yard picking up tree branches that had been torn off in winter storms. This was something we had been told to do, and also we wanted to use them to make a teepee. We heard Flora whinny, and then my father's voice and Henry's shouting, and we ran down to the barnyard to see what was going on.

The stable door was open. Henry had just brought Flora out, and she had broken away from him. She was running free in the barnyard, from one end to the other. We climbed up on the fence. It was exciting to see her running, whinnying, going up on her hind legs, prancing and threatening like a horse in a Western movie, an unbroken ranch horse, though she was just an old driver, an old sorrel mare. My father and Henry ran after her and tried to grab the dangling halter. They tried to work her into a corner, and they had almost succeeded when she made a run between them, wild-eyed, and disappeared around the corner of the barn. We heard the rails clatter down as she got over the fence, and Henry yelled, "She's into the field now!"

That meant she was in the long L-shaped field that ran up by the house. If she got around the center, heading towards the lane, the gate was open; the truck had been driven into the field this morning. My father shouted to me, because I was on the other side of the fence, nearest the lane, "Go shut the gate!"

I could run very fast. I ran across the garden, past the tree where our swing was hung, and jumped across a ditch into the lane. There was the open gate. She had not got out, I could not see her up on the road; she must have run to the other end of the field. The gate was heavy. I lifted it out of the gravel and carried it across the roadway. I had it halfway across when she came in sight, galloping straight toward me. There was just time to get the chain on. Laird came scrambling through the ditch to help me.

Instead of shutting the gate, I opened it as wide as I could. I did not make any decision to do this, it was just what I did. Flora never slowed down; she galloped straight past me, and Laird jumped up and down, yelling, "Shut it, shut it!" even after it was too late. My father and Henry appeared in the field a moment too late to see what I had done. They only saw Flora heading for the township road. They would think I had not got there in time.

They did not waste any time asking about it. They went back to the barn and got the gun and the knives they used, and put these in the truck; then they turned the truck around and came bouncing up the field toward us. Laird called to them, "Let me go too, let me go too!" and Henry stopped the truck and they took him in. I shut the gate after they were all gone.

I supposed Laird would tell. I wondered what would happen to me. I had never disobeyed my father before, and I could not understand why I had done it. Flora would not really get away. They would catch up with her in the truck. Or if they did not catch her this morning somebody would see her and telephone us this afternoon or tomorrow. There was no wild country here for her to run to, only farms. What was more, my father had paid for her, we needed the meat to feed the foxes, we needed the foxes to make our living. All I had done was make more work for my father who worked hard enough already. And when my father found out about it he was not going to trust me any more; he would know that I was not entirely on his side. I was on Flora's side, and that made me no use to anybody, not even to her. Just the same, I did not regret it; when she came running at me and I held the gate open, that was the only thing I could do.

I went back to the house, and my mother said, "What's all the commotion?" I told her that Flora had kicked down the fence and got away. "Your poor father," she said, "now he'll have to go chasing over the countryside. Well, there isn't any use planning dinner before one." She put up the ironing board. I wanted to tell her, but thought better of it and went upstairs and sat on my bed.

Lately I had been trying to make my part of the room fancy, spreading the bed with old lace curtains, and fixing myself a dressing table with some leftovers of cretonne for a skirt. I planned to put up some kind of barricade between my bed and Laird's, to keep my section separate from his. In the sunlight, the lace curtains were just dusty rags. We did not sing at night any more. One night when I was singing Laird said, "You sound silly," and I went right on but the next night I did not start. There was not so much need to anyway, we were no longer afraid. We knew it was just old furniture over there, old jumble and confusion. We did not keep to the rules. I still stayed awake after Laird was asleep and told myself stories, but even in these stories something different was happening, mysterious alterations took place. A story might start off in the old way, with a spectacular danger, a fire or wild animals, and for a while I might rescue people; then things would change around, and instead, somebody would be rescuing me. It might be a boy from our class at school, or even Mr. Campbell, our teacher, who tickled girls under the arms. And at this point the story concerned itself at great length with what I looked like—how long my hair was, and what kind of dress I had on; by the time I had these details worked out the real excitement of the story was lost.

It was later than one o'clock when the truck came back. The tarpaulin was over the back, which meant there was meat in it. My mother had to heat dinner up all over again. Henry and my father had changed from their bloody overalls into ordinary working overalls in the barn, and they washed

50

their arms and necks and faces at the sink, and splashed water on their hair and combed it. Laird lifted his arm to show off a streak of blood. "We shot old Flora," he said, "and cut her up in fifty pieces."

"Well I don't want to hear about it," my mother said. "And don't come to my table like that."

My father made him go and wash the blood off.   55

We sat down and my father said grace and Henry pasted his chewing gum on the end of his fork, the way he always did; when he took it off he would have us admire the pattern. We began to pass the bowls of steaming, overcooked vegetables. Laird looked across the table at me and said proudly, distinctly, "Anyway it was her fault Flora got away."

"What?" my father said.

"She could of shut the gate and she didn't. She just open' it up and Flora run out."

"Is that right?" my father said.

Everybody at the table was looking at me. I nodded, swallowing food   60 with great difficulty. To my shame, tears flooded my eyes.

My father made a curt sound of disgust. "What did you do that for?"

I did not answer. I put down my fork and waited to be sent from the table, still not looking up.

But this did not happen. For some time nobody said anything, then Laird said matter-of-factly, "She's crying."

"Never mind," my father said. He spoke with resignation, even good humor, the words which absolved and dismissed me for good. "She's only a girl," he said.

I didn't protest that, even in my heart. Maybe it was true.   65

The Receptive Reader

1. What about the physical *setting* of this story is most real? What striking images or imaginative comparisons help bring the setting to life? How would you expect the physical world of the story to influence a person's character? How do you think watching the work with the foxes and horses would affect a person's outlook?

2. Like many adolescents, the girl in this story faces a *conflict* between different models that she might choose to follow. What kind of role model is her father? How would you describe the kind of person or temperament? How does she feel about his work? What scenes or incidents do most to illuminate her relationship with her father?

3. What kind of role model is the mother? What is the girl's relationship with the mother and what she stands for? What makes the father and the mother in this story *polar opposites?* What details for you most strikingly bring the opposition between the father's and the mother's influence into focus?

4. The setting in which people grow up often set limits to what they can be or become. What are these limits in this story? How do we become aware of them? Can you point to a key phrase or to a *thematic passage*—spelling out a key idea acted out in the story as a whole?

5. The story reaches its *climax*, or high point, when Flora, the horse about to be shot, gets away. Why does the girl relate to Flora differently than she did

to Mack, the other horse in the story? What is the girl's role in the climactic episode? Why does she do what she does? How does her behavior here change the way she thinks of her father and of herself?

6. What is the role of the *minor characters* in this story? What are the roles of Henry and of the grandmother? In this story of growing up, how does the role of Laird, the girl's younger brother, change? What facets of the girl's character are shown in her relationship with her brother?

7. If you read this story as a story of *initiation,* of passing from one stage to another, how would you sum up the girl's starting point and the stage she reaches at the end of the story?

The Personal Response

Do you think of the girl as defeated by the end of the story? What do you think are her prospects for the future? What facets of her character would you consider in making a prediction?

The Creative Dimension

In a **monologue,** one person is talking without interruption by others. Write a monologue in which you imagine yourself in the place of one of the characters in the story. From that person's point of view, look at one of the *other* characters in the story. For instance, look at

- the younger brother as seen through the eyes of the girl (or vice versa);
- the father as seen through the eyes of the girl;
- the girl as seen through the eyes of her mother;
- the mother as seen through the eyes of her daughter.

Making Connections—For Discussion or Writing

Compare and contrast Joyce's "Araby" and Munro's "Boys and Girls" as stories of initiation. How do the two authors treat the theme of growing up?

Louise Erdrich   *(born 1954)*

History has a way of intruding upon the present.

DEE BROWN

Louise Erdrich ranks high among widely published Native American writers who in recent decades have introduced a new generation of readers to the world of American Indian life. She has been praised for "conveying unflinchingly the funkiness, humor, and great unspoken sadness of the Indian reservations, and a people exiled to a no-man's-land between two worlds" (Peter Matthiessen). In her prize-winning poems and stories, she writes with great empathy about the people who were stripped of their way of life, their religion, and self-respect and who experienced the failures of forced assimilation.

Erdrich was born in Little Falls, Minnesota, of Chippewa and German American descent. She grew up on a reservation in North Dakota where her grandfather had been tribal chair and where her father was a teacher. She studied at Dartmouth College and Johns Hopkins University. She has been actively involved in Native American issues, ranging from the litigation of land claims to the effects of alcoholism on the unborn.

In her widely read *Love Medicine* (1984), Erdrich wove together stories about the lives of two reservation families. In the following selection from the book, she tells the story of two brothers, with the younger brother trying to understand and help an older brother who went to Vietnam and was never the same after his return. Erdrich continued writing the history of the fictional families in these stories in *Beet Queen* (1986) and *Tracks* (1988).

The Red Convertible   *1984*

Lyman Lamartine

I was the first one to drive a convertible on my reservation. And of course it was red, a red Olds. I owned that car along with my brother Henry Junior. We owned it together until his boots filled with water on a windy night and he bought out my share. Now Henry owns the whole car, and his younger brother Lyman (that's myself), Lyman walks everywhere he goes.

How did I earn enough money to buy my share in the first place? My one talent was I could always make money. I had a touch for it, unusual in a Chippewa. From the first I was different that way, and everyone recognized it. I was the only kid they let in the American Legion Hall to shine shoes, for example, and one Christmas I sold spiritual bouquets for the mission door to door. The nuns let me keep a percentage. Once I started, it seemed the more money I made the easier the money came. Everyone encouraged it. When I was fifteen I got a job washing dishes at the Joliet Café, and that was where my first big break happened.

It wasn't long before I was promoted to busing tables, and then the short-order cook quit and I was hired to take her place. No sooner than you know it I was managing the Joliet. The rest is history. I went on managing. I soon became part owner, and of course there was no stopping me then. It wasn't long before the whole thing was mine.

After I'd owned the Joliet for one year, it blew over in the worst tornado ever seen around here. The whole operation was smashed to bits. A total loss. The fryalator was up in a tree, the grill torn in half like it was paper. I was only sixteen. I had it all in my mother's name, and I lost it quick, but before I lost it I had every one of my relatives, and their relatives, to dinner, and I also bought that red Olds I mentioned, along with Henry.

The first time we saw it! I'll tell you when we first saw it. We had gotten   5
a ride up to Winnipeg, and both of us had money. Don't ask me why, because we never mentioned a car or anything, we just had all our money.
Mine was cash, a big bankroll from the Joliet's insurance. Henry had two
checks—a week's extra pay for being laid off, and his regular check from
the Jewel Bearing Plant.

We were walking down Portage anyway, seeing the sights, when we saw
it. There it was, parked, large as life. Really as *if* it was alive. I thought of
the word *repose,* because the car wasn't simply stopped, parked, or whatever. That car reposed, calm and gleaming, a FOR SALE sign in its left front
window. Then, before we had thought it over at all, the car belonged to us
and our pockets were empty. We had just enough money for gas back
home.

We went places in that car, me and Henry. We took off driving all one
whole summer. We started off toward the Little Knife River and Mandaree
in Fort Berthold and then we found ourselves down in Wakpala somehow,
and then suddenly we were over in Montana on the Rocky Boy, and yet the
summer was not even half over. Some people hang on to details when they
travel, but we didn't let them bother us and just lived our everyday lives
here to there.

I do remember this one place with willows. I remember I laid under
those trees and it was comfortable. So comfortable. The branches bent down
all around me like a tent or a stable. And quiet, it was quiet, even though
there was a powwow close enough so I could see it going on. The air was
not too still, not too windy either. When the dust rises up and hangs in the
air around the dancers like that, I feel good. Henry was asleep with his arms
thrown wide. Later on, he woke up and we started driving again. We were
somewhere in Montana, or maybe on the Blood Reserve—it could have
been anywhere. Anyway it was where we met the girl.

All her hair was in buns around her ears, that's the first thing I noticed
about her. She was posed alongside the road with her arm out, so we
stopped. That girl was short, so short her lumber shirt looked comical on
her, like a nightgown. She had jeans on and fancy moccasins and she carried a little suitcase.

"Hop on in," says Henry. So she climbs in between us.   10

"We'll take you home," I says. "Where do you live?"

"Chicken," she says.

"Where the hell's that?" I ask her.

"Alaska."

"Okay," says Henry, and we drive.   15

We got up there and never wanted to leave. The sun doesn't truly set
there in summer, and the night is more a soft dusk. You might doze off,
sometimes, but before you know it you're up again, like an animal in nature. You never feel like you have to sleep hard or put away the world. And
things would grow up there. One day just dirt or moss, the next day flowers and long grass. The girl's name was Susy. Her family really took to us.
They fed us and put us up. We had our own tent to live in by their house,
and the kids would be in and out of there all day and night. They couldn't

get over me and Henry being brothers, we looked so different. We told them we knew we had the same mother, anyway.

One night Susy came in to visit us. We sat around in the tent talking of this and that. The season was changing. It was getting darker by that time, and the cold was even getting just a little mean. I told her it was time for us to go. She stood up on a chair.

"You never seen my hair," Susy said.

That was true. She was standing on a chair, but still, when she unclipped her buns the hair reached all the way to the ground. Our eyes opened. You couldn't tell how much hair she had when it was rolled up so neatly. Then my brother Henry did something funny. He went up to the chair and said, "Jump on my shoulders." So she did that, and her hair reached down past his waist, and he started twirling, this way and that, so her hair was flung out from side to side.

"I always wondered what it was like to have long pretty hair," Henry says.   20 Well we laughed. It was a funny sight, the way he did it. The next morning we got up and took leave of those people.

On to greener pastures, as they say. It was down through Spokane and across Idaho then Montana and very soon we were racing the weather right along under the Canadian border through Columbus, Des Lacs, and then we were in Bottineau County and soon home. We'd made most of the trip, that summer, without putting up the car hood at all. We got home just in time, it turned out, for the army to remember Henry had signed up to join it.

I don't wonder that the army was so glad to get my brother that they turned him into a Marine. He was built like a brick outhouse anyway. We liked to tease him that they really wanted him for his Indian nose. He had a nose big and sharp as a hatchet, like the nose on Red Tomahawk, the Indian who killed Sitting Bull, whose profile is on signs all along the North Dakota highways. Henry went off to training camp, came home once during Christmas, then the next thing you know we got an overseas letter from him. It was 1970, and he said he was stationed up in the northern hill country. Whereabouts I did not know. He wasn't such a hot letter writer, and only got off two before the enemy caught him. I could never keep it straight, which direction those good Vietnam soldiers were from.

I wrote him back several times, even though I didn't know if those letters would get through. I kept him informed all about the car. Most of the time I had it up on blocks in the yard or half taken apart, because that long trip did a hard job on it under the hood.

I always had good luck with numbers, and never worried about the draft myself. I never even had to think about what my number was. But Henry was never lucky in the same way as me. It was at least three years before Henry came home. By then I guess the whole war was solved in the government's mind, but for him it would keep on going. In those years I'd put his car into almost perfect shape. I always thought of it as his car while he was gone, even though when he left he said, "Now it's yours," and threw me his key.

"Thanks for the extra key," I'd said. "I'll put it up in your drawer just in   25 case I need it." He laughed.

* * *

When he came home, though, Henry was very different, and I'll say this: the change was no good. You could hardly expect him to change for the better, I know. But he was quiet, so quiet, and never comfortable sitting still anywhere but always up and moving around. I thought back to times we'd sat still for whole afternoons, never moving a muscle, just shifting our weight along the ground, talking to whoever sat with us, watching things. He'd always had a joke, then, too, and now you couldn't get him to laugh, or when he did it was more the sound of a man choking, a sound that stopped up the throats of other people around him. They got to leaving him alone most of the time, and I didn't blame them. It was a fact: Henry was jumpy and mean.

I'd bought a color TV set for my mom and the rest of us while Henry was away. Money still came very easy. I was sorry I'd ever bought it though, because of Henry. I was also sorry I'd bought color, because with black-and-white the pictures seem older and farther away. But what are you going to do? He sat in front of it, watching it, and that was the only time he was completely still. But it was the kind of stillness that you see in a rabbit when it freezes and before it will bolt. He was not easy. He sat in his chair gripping the armrests with all his might, as if the chair itself was moving at a high speed and if he let go at all he would rocket forward and maybe crash right through the set.

Once I was in the room watching TV with Henry and I heard his teeth click at something. I looked over, and he'd bitten through his lip. Blood was going down his chin. I tell you right then I wanted to smash that tube to pieces. I went over to it but Henry must have known what I was up to. He rushed from his chair and shoved me out of the way, against the wall. I told myself he didn't know what he was doing.

My mom came in, turned the set off real quiet, and told us she had made something for supper. So we went and sat down. There was still blood going down Henry's chin, but he didn't notice it and no one said anything, even though every time he took a bite of his bread his blood fell onto it until he was eating his own blood mixed in with the food.

While Henry was not around we talked about what was going to happen   30
to him. There were no Indian doctors on the reservation, and my mom couldn't come around to trusting the old man, Moses Pillager, because he courted her long ago and was jealous of her husbands. He might take revenge through her son. We were afraid that if we brought Henry to a regular hospital they would keep him.

"They don't fix them in those places," Mom said; "they just give them drugs."

"We wouldn't get him there in the first place," I agreed, "so let's just forget about it."

Then I thought about the car.

Henry had not even looked at the car since he'd gotten home, though like I said, it was in tip-top condition and ready to drive. I thought the car might bring the old Henry back somehow. So I bided my time and waited for my chance to interest him in the vehicle.

One night Henry was off somewhere. I took myself a hammer. I went out   35 to that car and I did a number on its underside. Whacked it up. Bent the tail pipe double. Ripped the muffler loose. By the time I was done with the car it looked worse than any typical Indian car that has been driven all its life on reservation roads, which they always say are like government prom- ises—full of holes. It just about hurt me, I'll tell you that! I threw dirt in the carburetor and I ripped all the electric tape off the seats. I made it look just as beat up as I could. Then I sat back and waited for Henry to find it.

Still, it took him over a month. That was all right, because it was just get- ting warm enough, not melting, but warm enough to work outside.

"Lyman," he says, walking in one day, "that red car looks like shit."

"Well it's old," I says. "You got to expect that."

"No way!" says Henry. "That car's a classic! But you went and ran the piss right out of it, Lyman, and you know it don't deserve that. I kept that car in A-one shape. You don't remember. You're too young. But when I left, that car was running like a watch. Now I don't even know if I can get it to start again, let alone get it anywhere near its old condition."

"Well you try," I said, like I was getting mad, "but I say it's a piece of   40 junk."

Then I walked out before he could realize I knew he'd strung together more than six words at once.

After that I thought he'd freeze himself to death working on that car. He was out there all day, and at night he rigged up a little lamp, ran a cord out the window, and had himself some light to see by while he worked. He was better than he had been before, but that's still not saying much. It was easier for him to do the things the rest of us did. He ate more slowly and didn't jump up and down during the meal to get this or that or look out the win- dow. I put my hand in the back of the TV set, I admit, and fiddled around with it good, so that it was almost impossible now to get a clear picture. He didn't look at it very often anyway. He was always out with that car or going off to get parts for it. By the time it was really melting outside, he had it fixed.

I had been feeling down in the dumps about Henry around this time. We had always been together before. Henry and Lyman. But he was such a loner now that I didn't know how to take it. So I jumped at the chance one day when Henry seemed friendly. It's not that he smiled or anything. He just said, "Let's take that old shitbox for a spin." Just the way he said it made me think he could be coming around.

We went out to the car. It was spring. The sun was shining very bright. My only sister, Bonita, who was just eleven years old, came out and made us stand together for a picture. Henry leaned his elbow on the red car's windshield, and he took his other arm and put it over my shoulder, very carefully, as though it was heavy for him to lift and he didn't want to bring the weight down all at once.

"Smile." Bonita said, and he did.   45

That picture. I never look at it anymore. A few months ago, I don't know why, I got his picture out and tacked it on the wall. I felt good about Henry at the time, close to him. I felt good having his picture on the wall, until one night when I was looking at television. I was a little drunk and stoned. I looked up at the wall and Henry was staring at me. I don't know what it was, but his smile had changed, or maybe it was gone. All I know is I couldn't stay in the same room with that picture. I was shaking. I got up, closed the door, and went into the kitchen. A little later my friend Ray came over and we both went back into that room. We put the picture in a brown bag, folded the bag over and over tightly, then put it way back in a closet.

I still see that picture now, as if it tugs at me, whenever I pass that closet door. The picture is very clear in my mind. It was so sunny that day Henry had to squint against the glare. Or maybe the camera Bonita held flashed like a mirror, blinding him, before she snapped the picture. My face is right out in the sun, big and round. But he might have drawn back, because the shadows on his face are deep as holes. There are two shadows curved like little hooks around the ends of his smile, as if to frame it and try to keep it there—that one, first smile that looked like it might have hurt his face. He has his field jacket on and the worn-in clothes he'd come back in and kept wearing ever since. After Bonita took the picture, she went into the house and we got into the car. There was a full cooler in the trunk. We started off, east, toward Pembina and the Red River because Henry said he wanted to see the high water.

The trip over there was beautiful. When everything starts changing, drying up, clearing off, you feel like your whole life is starting. Henry felt it, too. The top was down and the car hummed like a top. He'd really put it back in shape, even the tape on the seats was very carefully put down and glued back in layers. It's not that he smiled again or even joked, but his face looked to me as if it was clear, more peaceful. It looked as though he wasn't thinking of anything in particular except the bare fields and windbreaks and houses we were passing.

The river was high and full of winter trash when we got there. The sun was still out, but it was colder by the river. There were still little clumps of dirty snow here and there on the banks. The water hadn't gone over the banks yet, but it would, you could tell. It was just at its limit, hard swollen, glossy like an old gray scar. We made ourselves a fire, and we sat down and watched the current go. As I watched it I felt something squeezing inside me and tightening and trying to let go all at the same time. I knew I was not just feeling it myself; I knew I was feeling what Henry was going through at that moment. Except that I couldn't stand it, the closing and opening. I jumped to my feet. I took Henry by the shoulders and I started shaking him. "Wake up," I says, "wake up, wake up, wake up!" I didn't know what had come over me. I sat down beside him again.

His face was totally white and hard. Then it broke, like stones break all 50 of a sudden when water boils up inside them.

"I know it," he says. "I know it. I can't help it. It's no use."

We start talking. He said he knew what I'd done with the car. It was obvious it had been whacked out of shape and not just neglected. He said he wanted to give the car to me for good now, it was no use. He said he'd fixed it just to give it back and I should take it.

"No way," I says. "I don't want it."

"That's okay," he says, "you take it."

"I don't want it, though," I says back to him, and then to emphasize, just   55
to emphasize, you understand, I touch his shoulder. He slaps my hand off.

"Take that car," he says.

"No," I say. "Make me," I say, and then he grabs my jacket and rips the arm loose. That jacket is a class act, suede with tags and zippers. I push Henry backwards, off the log. He jumps up and bowls me over. We go down in a clinch and come up swinging hard, for all we're worth, with our fists. He socks my jaw so hard I feel like it swings loose. Then I'm at his rib cage and land a good one under his chin so his head snaps back. He's dazzled. He looks at me and I look at him and then his eyes are full of tears and blood and at first I think he's crying. But no, he's laughing. "Ha! Ha!" he says. "Ha! Ha! Take good care of it."

"Okay," I says. "Okay, no problem. Ha! Ha!"

I can't help it, and I start laughing, too. My face feels fat and strange, and after a while I get a beer from the cooler in the trunk, and when I hand it to Henry he takes his shirt and wipes my germs off. "Hoof-and-mouth disease," he says. For some reason this cracks me up, and so we're really laughing for a while, and then we drink all the rest of the beers one by one and throw them in the river and see how far, how fast, the current takes them before they fill up and sink.

"You want to go on back?" I ask after a while. "Maybe we could snag a   60
couple nice Kashpaw girls."

He says nothing. But I can tell his mood is turning again.

"They're all crazy, the girls up here, every damn one of them."

"You're crazy too," I say, to jolly him up. "Crazy Lamartine boys!"

He looks as though he will take this wrong at first. His face twists, then clears, and he jumps up on his feet. "That's right!" he says. "Crazier 'n hell. Crazy Indians!"

I think it's the old Henry again. He throws off his jacket and starts springing his legs up from the knees like a fancy dancer. He's down doing something between a grass dance and a bunny hop, no kind of dance I ever saw before, but neither has anyone else on all this green growing earth. He's wild. He wants to pitch whoopee! He's up and at me and all over. All this time I'm laughing so hard, so hard my belly is getting tied up in a knot.   65

"Got to cool me off!" he shouts all of a sudden. Then he runs over to the river and jumps in.

There's boards and other things in the current. It's so high. No sound comes from the river after the splash he makes, so I run right over. I look around. It's getting dark. I see he's halfway across the water already, and I know he didn't swim there but the current took him. It's far. I hear his voice, though, very clearly across it.

"My boots are filling," he says.

He says this in a normal voice, like he just noticed and he doesn't know what to think of it. Then he's gone. A branch comes by. Another branch. And I go in.

* * *

By the time I get out of the river, off the snag I pulled myself onto, the sun is down. I walk back to the car, turn on the high beams, and drive it up the bank. I put it in first gear and then I take my foot off the clutch. I get out, close the door, and watch it plow softly into the water. The headlights reach in as they go down, searching, still lighted even after the water swirls over the back end. I wait. The wires short out. It is all finally dark. And then there is only the water, the sound of it going and running and going and running and running. 70

The Receptive Reader

1. What kind of person is the brother telling the story? What is his relationship to his older brother? What details or incidents do most to help you imagine or understand the narrator?

2. What happened to Henry in the army? How do you find out? Why do you think you get the clues to what happened to him in bits and pieces?

3. How does the car come to play a central role in the story? Does it have a symbolic meaning?

4. What contribution, if any, do minor characters make to this story?

5. What is happening at the end of the story? Were you puzzled by the way the two brothers act? Why do the two brothers fight? What are their motives?

6. Does this story tend to confirm or to counteract prejudices or preconceptions about reservation life?

The Personal Response

Would you have acted differently than the younger brother in the story? Do you think he understood his older brother?

The Creative Dimension

This is a story in which much that is important remains unsaid. Imagine that a counselor or close friend could have gotten the older brother to talk more freely about his thoughts and feelings. What might he have said?

Making Connections—For Discussion or Writing

Do you find the central characters in the stories by Carver, Munro, and Erdrich puzzling or easy to understand? Do they seem complicated or relatively simple to you? Is one of them more complex than the others?

JUXTAPOSITIONS

Capsule Portraits

The world is a mine of good stories that haven't been told.

CARLOS FUENTES

In both of the following short shorts, a character takes shape before our eyes in a brief space. The first story was written by a writer who for a time was one of the most authentic voices of heartland America. The second was written by an immigrant from the West Indies whose candor and commitment gained her a large audience in her adopted country. What would you include in a capsule portrait of the central character in each story? Do you recognize or understand these people?

Sherwood Anderson   *(1876–1941)*

Sherwood Anderson grew up in the small country towns and factory towns of Ohio. He worked on farms, in livery stables, and on race tracks; and he eventually left his family and a job as a factory manager to become a full-time writer in Chicago. His *Winesburg, Ohio* (1919) went beyond the polite social surface to probe the emotional drives and frustrations of his characters. Anderson inspired critics and writers searching for a more vigorous, more experimental American literature, including H. L. Mencken, Ernest Hemingway, and William Faulkner. A fellow writer said of him that in his fiction "the uneventful and imprisoned life he saw around him became moving and tragic as though another dimension had been added when it passed through his passionate survey—like the same river flowing between deeper walls."

Paper Pills   *1919*

He was an old man with a white beard and huge nose and hands. Long before the time during which we will know him, he was a doctor and drove a jaded white horse from house to house through the streets of Winesburg. Later he married a girl who had money. She had been left a large fertile farm when her father died. The girl was quiet, tall, and dark, and to many people she seemed very beautiful. Everyone in Winesburg wondered why she married the doctor. Within a year after the marriage she died.

The knuckles of the doctor's hands were extraordinarily large. When the hands were closed they looked like clusters of unpainted wooden balls as large as walnuts fastened together by steel rods. He smoked a cob pipe and after his wife's death sat all day in his empty office close by a window that was covered with cobwebs. He never opened the window. Once on a hot day in August he tried but found it stuck fast and after that he forgot all about it.

Winesburg had forgotten the old man, but in Doctor Reefy there were the seeds of something very fine. Alone in his musty office in the Heffner Block above the Paris Dry Goods Company's store, he worked ceaselessly, building up something that he himself destroyed. Little pyramids of truth he erected and after erecting knocked them down again that he might have the truths to erect other pyramids.

Doctor Reefy was a tall man who had worn one suit of clothes for ten years. It was frayed at the sleeves and little holes had appeared at the knees and elbows. In the office he wore also a linen duster with huge pockets into which he continually stuffed scraps of paper. After some weeks the scraps of paper became little hard round balls, and when the pockets were filled he dumped them out upon the floor. For ten years he had but one friend, another old man named John Spaniard who owned a tree nursery. Sometimes, in a playful mood, old Doctor Reefy took from his pockets a handful of the paper balls and threw them at the nursery man. "That is to confound you, you blithering old sentimentalist," he cried, shaking with laughter.

The story of Doctor Reefy and his courtship of the tall dark girl who be- 5
came his wife and left her money to him was a very curious story. It is delicious, like the twisted little apples that grow in the orchards of Winesburg. In the fall one walks in the orchards and the ground is hard with frost underfoot. The apples have been taken from the trees by the pickers. They have been put in barrels and shipped to the cities where they will be eaten in apartments that are filled with books, magazines, furniture, and people. On the trees are only a few gnarled apples that the pickers have rejected. They look like the knuckles of Doctor Reefy's hands. One nibbles at them and they are delicious. Into a little round place at the side of the apple has been gathered all of its sweetness. One runs from tree to tree over the frosted ground picking the gnarled, twisted apples and filling his pockets with them. Only the few know the sweetness of the twisted apples.

The girl and Doctor Reefy began their courtship on a summer afternoon. He was forty-five then and already he had begun the practice of filling his pockets with the scraps of paper that became hard balls and were thrown away. The habit had been formed as he sat in his buggy behind the jaded white horse and went slowly along country roads. On the papers were written thoughts, ends of thoughts, beginnings of thoughts.

One by one the mind of Doctor Reefy had made the thoughts. Out of many of them he formed a truth that arose gigantic in his mind. The truth clouded the world. It became terrible and then faded away and the little thoughts began again.

The tall dark girl came to see Doctor Reefy because she was in the family way and had become frightened. She was in that condition because of a series of circumstances also curious.

The death of her father and mother and the rich acres of land that had come down to her had set a train of suitors on her heels. For two years she saw suitors almost every evening. Except two they were all alike. They talked to her of passion and there was a strained eager quality in their voices and in their eyes when they looked at her. The two who were different were much unlike each other. One of them, a slender young man with white hands, the son of a jeweler in Winesburg, talked continually of virginity. When he was with her he was never off the subject. The other, a black-haired boy with large ears, said nothing at all but always managed to get her into the darkness, where he began to kiss her.

For a time the tall dark girl thought she would marry the jeweler's son.   10 For hours she sat in silence listening as he talked to her and then she began to be afraid of something. Beneath his talk of virginity she began to think there was a lust greater than in all the others. At times it seemed to her that as he talked he was holding her body in his hands. She imagined him turning it slowly about in the white hands and staring at it. At night she dreamed that he had bitten into her body and that his jaws were dripping. She had the dream three times, then she became in the family way to the one who said nothing at all but who in the moment of his passion actually did bite her shoulder so that for days the marks of his teeth showed.

After the tall dark girl came to know Doctor Reefy it seemed to her that she never wanted to leave him again. She went into his office one morning and without her saying anything he seemed to know what had happened to her.

In the office of the doctor there was a woman, the wife of the man who kept the bookstore in Winesburg. Like all old-fashioned country practitioners, Doctor Reefy pulled teeth, and the woman who waited held a handkerchief to her teeth and groaned. Her husband was with her and when the tooth was taken out they both screamed and blood ran down on the woman's white dress. The tall dark girl did not pay any attention. When the woman and the man had gone the doctor smiled. "I will take you driving into the country with me," he said.

For several weeks the tall dark girl and the doctor were together almost every day. The condition that had brought her to him passed in an illness, but she was like one who has discovered the sweetness of the twisted apples, she could not get her mind fixed again upon the round perfect fruit that is eaten in the city apartments. In the fall after the beginning of her acquaintanceship with him she married Doctor Reefy and in the following spring she died. During the winter he read to her all of the odds and ends of thoughts he had scribbled on the bits of paper. After he had read them he laughed and stuffed them away in his pockets to become round hard balls.

The Receptive Reader

1. Like other characters in Anderson's stories, the doctor as the *central character* is likely to seem an eccentric or outsider to the people around him. Do *you* think he is strange? What makes him seem strange or understandable to you? What is the author's attitude toward him, and how can you know?

2. What kind of person is the woman in the story? What picture do you form of the two men who are courting her? What determines her choices?

3. What might be the *symbolic* significance of the "twisted apples"?

The Personal Response

Would you call this story a love story? How is it different from what you might expect in a love story? How do you react to it?

Jamaica Kincaid   *(born 1941)*   ◉

*When people say you're charming you are in
deep trouble.*

JAMAICA KINCAID

Jamaica Kincaid was born in Antigua in the West Indies and left home to come to the United States when she was sixteen. An interviewer said of her that she grew up "in the shadow of a loving but domineering mother while learning proper British etiquette at colonial schools" (Donna Perry). After she came to New York and shed her original name (Elaine Potter Richardson), she worked at odd jobs, took photography classes, and was eventually discovered by the *New Yorker*. Two novels, *Annie John* (1983) and *Lucy* (1990), grew out of her *New Yorker* stories. She says that she felt like an outsider even when she lived at home among people who were mostly black like her and many of whom were women like her. She has been praised for her honesty and criticized for her anger, which she directs both at the suffering brought by colonialism and at the shortsightedness of the new rulers of the Third World.

A few words in her story go back to the local dialect of her childhood: *benna* is Calypso-inspired popular music; *doukona* is a spicy pudding.

Girl   *1978*

Wash the white clothes on Monday and put them on the stone heap; wash the color clothes on Tuesday and put them on the clothesline to dry; don't walk barehead in the hot sun; cook pumpkin fritters in very hot sweet oil; soak your little cloths right after you take them off; when buying cotton to make yourself a nice blouse, be sure that it doesn't have gum on it, because that way it won't hold up well after a wash; soak salt fish overnight before you cook it; is it true that you sing benna in Sunday school?; always eat your food in such a way that it won't turn someone else's stomach; on Sundays try to walk like a lady and not like the slut you are so bent on becoming; don't sing benna in Sunday school; you mustn't speak to wharf-rat boys, not even to give directions; don't eat fruits on the street—flies will follow you; *but I don't sing benna on Sundays at all and never in Sunday school;* this is how to sew on a button; this is how to make a buttonhole for the button you have just sewed on; this is how to hem a dress when you see the hem coming down and so to prevent yourself from looking like the slut I know you are so bent on becoming; this is how you iron your father's khaki shirt so that it doesn't have a crease; this is how you iron your father's khaki pants so that they don't have a crease; this is how you grow okra—far from the house, because okra tree harbors red ants; when you are growing dasheen, make sure it gets plenty of water or else it makes your throat itch when you are eating it; this is how you sweep a corner; this is how you sweep a whole house; this is how you sweep a yard; this is how you smile to someone you don't like too much; this is how you smile to someone you don't like at all; this is how you smile to someone you like completely; this is how you set a table for tea; this is how you set a table for dinner; this is how you set a table for dinner with an important guest; this is how you set a table for lunch; this is how you set a table for break-fast; this is how to behave in the presence of men who don't know you very well, and this way they won't recognize immediately the slut I have warned you against becoming; be sure to wash every day, even if it is with your own spit; don't squat down to play marbles—you are not a boy, you know; don't pick people's flowers—you might catch something; don't throw stones at blackbirds, because it might not be a blackbird at all; this is how to make a bread pudding; this is how to make doukona; this is how to make pep-per pot; this is how to make a good medicine for a cold; this is how to make a good medicine to throw away a child before it even becomes a child; this is how to catch a fish; this is how to throw back a fish you don't like, and that way something bad won't fall on you; this is how to bully a man; this is how a man bullies you; this is how to love a man, and if this doesn't work there are other ways, and if they don't work don't feel too bad about giv-ing up; this is how to spit up in the air if you feel like it, and this is how to move quick so that it doesn't fall on you; this is how to make ends meet; always squeeze bread to make sure it's fresh; *but what if the baker won't let me feel the bread?;* you mean to say that after all you are really going to be the kind of woman who the baker won't let near the bread?

The Receptive Reader

1. The central character in this short short takes shape entirely through *dia-logue*. What kind of person do you hear talking? What is her range of favorite topics? (*Benna* in the story is a dialect word for popular music—calypso, rock-and-roll—that the speaker considers a bad influence.) What expressions or ways of talking do you recognize, and why?

2. As in many one-way conversations, the listener in this story does not have a chance to have her say. Do you nevertheless hear her thinking? What would she say if she had a chance?

The Personal Response

Do you find yourself siding with the girl? Does the older woman have a point?

The Creative Dimension

Write a last letter from Anderson's doctor to his wife, or from the wife to her husband. Or write a letter from the girl in Kincaid's story to the person lectur-ing her.

WRITING ABOUT LITERATURE

3 Tracing Character
WRITING FOCUS: From Prewriting to Draft

The Writing Workshop   A paper about a central character may trace vital contradictions that make a character a complex human being. Or a paper may trace the growth of a character in flux, still subject to formative influences. It may center on the interaction of two or more characters in a story. In working on this and on other papers, imagine yourself in a writing workshop situation. In a workshop format, no one expects a full-blown paper to materialize overnight. Instead, there is time for preliminaries, for tentative first attempts, for feedback, for revision and fine-tuning. In writing your paper on characterization, your basic task will be the same as in writing papers on other dimensions of fiction. You will need to immerse yourself in the story first—and then push toward general conclusions that you can present and support in a well-developed paper. You will need to take your paper through major (overlapping) stages in the writing process.

In particular, make time for three important **prewriting** activities that should precede your writing of your first draft: note taking—pushing toward a thesis—structuring your paper.

Running Commentary   The following is part of a running commentary—on the Munro story—prepared by a reader with open eyes and alert ears, keeping an open mind about the possible general drift of the story. These reading notes seize on possibly meaningful striking details; they record verbatim quotations that could be useful in helping get a reader into the prevailing mood of the story. These notes already include much material related to the girl narrator's search for identity:

Senses predominate. Penetrating smell of foxes, dead flesh, blood. Beauty of live foxes contrasts with scraping particles of fat and blood from the inside of the dead skin. Naked slippery dead carcasses look "surprisingly small, mean, and rat-like." When alive, foxes have faces "drawn exquisitely sharp in pure hostility" and "golden eyes."

Death and blood are taken rather casually by the men. There is something alarming about the coldness of the term "fox farm." There is a hierarchy of value? Horses are killed to feed foxes, who provide furs and money.

Children's unfinished bedroom in the loft is a place of childhood fears. Brother and sister sing "Jingle Bells" and "Danny Boy" to ward off fear of the dark.

Life is seen entirely through the eyes of the young girl telling the story. Naturally inclined toward "male activities." The work done "in her father's service" was important like a ritual. Her little brother tags timidly along, obeying her.

The narrator is treated like a boy and acts like one, and she is introduced by her father as "the new hired man." The salesman responds that he thought it was "only a girl." The girl wants to possess the characteristic masculine strengths and virtues.

The mother is constantly invoking the female stereotype, implying that when her daughter helps the father with "male" duties, the help is not real. She is eager to get her daughter into the house to help with girl work. ("It is not like I had a girl in the family at all.") The girl "hated the hot dark kitchen in summer"; "work in the house was endless, dreary and peculiarly depressing."

The horses give an interesting twist to the gender issue, because there is a male and a female. The male, Mack, is slow and docile, while the female, Flora, is spirited, temperamental, and rebellious . . .

Pushing toward a Thesis   Early in your note taking, the central question is likely to emerge: In the world of Munro's story, what does it mean to be a girl? What does it mean to be a boy? In your paper, you may want to focus on the key issue: Some people easily take to the role society has sketched out for them. They fit the mold. But the girl in this story is an independent, adventurous, imaginative spirit.

In the following paragraph, the student who prepared the reading notes sums up what might become the unifying overall idea of a paper:

Children search for their identities and constantly run up against the wall of gender stereotypes to which they are made to conform. *The girl in the story reluctantly conforms to the stereotypes that will deny a part of her personality.* In her innocence, the girl in the story identifies with the outdoor work of her father, "red in the face with pleasure" when her father seems to praise and accept her as a coworker. Her daydreams are about heroic rescues in which she plays the hero's part. However, her mother and grandmother conspire to drive home what is expected of a girl. It seems that after a last act of futile rebellion the invisible walls of the predestined gender roles will close in on her.

Structuring the Paper   How will your paper be laid out? Since this is a story of initiation, your paper as a whole might follow the pattern of a spiritual journey. In addition, a contrast of polar opposites (light/dark, male/female) may help structure the paper. For instance, in writing about the Munro story, you may move from the girl's innocent identification with the father's work and *male* values to the weight of traditional stereotypes about the *female* role. Early in your work with the paper, prepare a **scratch outline** like the one that guided the author of the reading notes in her first draft:

—spirited imaginative character—the prank played on kid brother, leadership etc. daydreams: "courage, boldness, and self-sacrifice"
   —the lure of the father's job
   —the mother and grandmother as voices of the stereotype
   —the climactic rebellion
   —pivotal role of younger brother—he will overtake her by virtue of the mere fact of being born male; he has the advantage

Look at the way the student's prewriting fed into a first draft of a paper. What use did the student make of her prewriting? How nearly finished is this paper? What suggestions or advice would you give the student writer when she is ready to prepare a final draft?

Sample First Draft

A Story of Initiation

Alice Munro's story "Boys and Girls" introduces us to a spirited, imaginative young girl. She plays scary pranks on her kid brother, making him climb to the top beam of the barn. She also experiences the fears of childhood, as she and the brother try to mark off a "safe" zone among the scary shadows of the unfinished loft where they sleep, singing "Jingle Bells" and "Danny Boy" to ward off fear of the dark. Above all, she admires her father, who runs a fox farm for the pelts of the animals. As her father's helper and Girl Friday, she is used to the penetrating smell of the foxes. She responds to the beauty of the live foxes who have faces "drawn exquisitely sharp in pure hostility" and "golden eyes." She is just as used to the naked slippery dead carcasses that look "surprisingly small, mean, and rat-like." However, in the course of the story, the girl has to leave this world of her childhood behind, growing up to discover her true destined role in a "man's world."

Children search for their identities and constantly run up against the wall of gender stereotypes to which they are made to conform. The girl in the story reluctantly conforms to the stereotypes that will deny a part of her personality. In her innocence, the girl in the story identifies with the outdoor work of her father, "red in the face with pleasure" when her father seems to praise and accept her as a coworker. Her daydreams are about heroic rescues in which she plays the hero's part. However, her mother and grandmother conspire to drive home what is expected of a girl. It seems that after a last act of futile rebellion the invisible walls of the pre-destined gender roles will close in on her.

Life is seen entirely through the eyes of the young girl telling the story. As a child, she seems naturally inclined toward "male activities." The work done "in her father's service" is important to her like a ritual. (Her little brother tags timidly along, obeying her.) The narrator is treated like a boy and acts like one, and she is introduced by her father as "the new hired man." The salesman he is talking to responds that he thought it was "only a girl," a hint of the disillusionment that lies ahead. In her innocence, the narrator values and espouses those traditionally male qualities admired by the world, and she strives to cultivate those strengths within herself, as yet unburdened by the weight of stereotypes.

However, the mother increasingly represents the weight of the adult world, invoking the female stereotype, implying that when her daughter helps the father with "male" duties, the help is not real. The mother is eager to get her daughter into the house to help with girl work. ("It is not like I had a girl in the family at all.") The girl "hated the hot dark kitchen in summer"; "work in the house was endless, dreary and peculiarly depressing."

The horses that are kept to provide meat for the foxes give an interesting twist to the gender issue, because there are a male and a female. The male, Mack, is slow and docile, while the female, Flora, is spirited, temperamental, and rebellious. When Flora's turn comes to be killed and butchered to feed the foxes, the narrator, in a dramatic act of rebellion against the way things are, lets her escape through the open gate that her father asks her to close. In trying to free the horse, she is making a last symbolic attempt to free herself. But she fails, both literally and symbolically. Flora is free for only a few hours longer. And the narrator, who is "only a girl," cannot free herself from the stereotype society has imposed on her, except for a few brief childhood years.

Questions for Peer Review

1. What key facets of the girl's character does the student writer include in the *capsule portrait* that opens this paper? For you, which of the details included do most to bring the character to life or make her real for the reader?

2. This paper leads up to its central idea in a *thesis statement* at the end of a brief introduction. How well does the thesis add up what the paper as a whole says about the story? What other sentences later in the paper sum up well for you what the story as a whole says about what is happening to the central character?

3. How clear is the overall pattern of the paper? Where is the *turning point* in this student paper? What "hints" in the paper lead up to it?

4. In a final draft, what *details* do you think the student writer should add or develop further to round out the central character? What *key quotations* would you recommend the writer should weave into the paper?

5. How does the *conclusion* tie in the girl's involvement with the horses with the rest of the paper?

4 PLOT

The Chain of Events

Courtesy Richard B. Ressman

*There has to be a tension, a sense that something
is imminent, that certain things are in relentless
motion, or else, most often, there simply won't be
a story.*

RAYMOND CARVER

*A narrative line is in its deeper sense the tracing
out of a meaning, and the real continuity of a
story lies in this probing forward.*

EUDORA WELTY

Writing prose is like laying a mosaic.

KURT TUCHOLSKY

FOCUS ON PLOT

A traditional short story puts characters in a setting and then sets them
in motion. You focus on **plot** when you trace what happens as a result.
The plot is the story line, the sequence of actions or events that gives direction to the story as a whole. When you study plot, you focus on what
drives, motivates, or shapes the story. Plot maps out the itinerary that
takes the reader to the conclusion.

An effective plot pulls us into the story. Frank O'Connor's classic
"Guests of the Nation" takes us to the war between the Irish and the
English that led to the founding of the Irish Free State in 1922, after centuries of English rule. We spend our time with two young soldiers in the
Irish Republican Army who are guarding two English prisoners. Security
is lax, since with their English accents and khaki tunics the prisoners
would not get far, even if they had a mind to escape. The foursome pass
the time playing cards, arguing about capitalism and communism, about
priests and love of country. The Englishmen join in the occasional
dances with the local young women; one of the Englishmen becomes a
helpmate to the lady of the house, doing chores and running errands for
her. However, the grim realities of the war catch up with us: The English have executed Irish rebels, and the two English hostages will be shot
in retaliation.

Where are we as readers in this story? Maybe we can keep cool and
refuse to become involved. It's not *our* war; the hostages have long been
dead and buried. More likely, however, we will be drawn into the story.
We will be saying when word comes down from headquarters to execute the hostages: "No, you cannot do that!" We are likely to argue and
agonize and prevaricate. The chances are we will finally do as told; and,
like the narrator in the story, we will never again be quite the same. We
will not know what to say when the lady of the house asks: "What did
ye do with them?"

When tracing the plot of a story, you ask yourself: "How does the story take shape? What sets it in motion? What keeps it going? What brings it to a satisfying close?" Look for features like the following when thinking about plot:

✗ *Look for a situation that has in it the seeds of a story.* Are there signs of an agenda to be attended to, a score to be settled? The initial setting up or **exposition** creates a situation that has the seed of further developments in it. Think about where the story might be headed. Perhaps a new element disturbs the status quo: A stranger arrives; an outsider marries into the family; a distant relative comes close.

✗ *Size up characters for what they might do.* What actions do they seem capable of; what events might they precipitate? Their motives—their motivation—is their potential for action: "what sets them in motion." An accident-prone character is "an accident waiting to happen." A character with seething resentment is a time bomb waiting to go off. A lonely character may take desperate steps to make human contact.

✗ *Look for sources of conflict.* Are rivals in love or ambition likely to face off like the **protagonist** (the first or chief contender) and the **antagonist** (the worthy opponent) in ancient Greek drama? Or is a conflict simmering that will be treated in a lower key? People may find themselves at cross-purposes without articulating loud grievances. Mason's "Shiloh" develops a conflict between the opposed, diverging needs of a couple; the conflict plays itself out without fireworks or fanfare.

✗ *Keep your eye on the central action or progression of events.* Does the story line focus on **external** physical action—quarrels, journeys, acts of defiance, suicides? The characters may have mountains to scale or pursuers to evade. Or is the action of the story mainly **internal,** psychological? A character may experience a change in perspective, learning something about others. A character may reach a moment of self-realization, facing up to something important about himself or herself.

✗ *Do not expect stories to follow a standard formula.* There may be a **loose narrative structure,** with events coming to pass in leisurely fashion, in chronological order. Things just seem to happen—"and then this," "and then that." In Carver's "The Third Thing That Killed My Father Off," we see the central character develop an interest in a hobby that interferes with his performance at work. An apparent misunderstanding leads to the alienation of old friends. Unexpected natural events intervene. In other stories, there may be a **tight narrative structure,** with events marching on from cause to effect. In John Steinbeck's story "Flight," a proud young boy is provoked into a fatal brawl and then is hunted down methodically by the friends of the man he killed. The result is a compact, tightly plotted story. **Flashbacks** may break up the chronological sequence of events. In a Faulkner story like "A Rose for Emily," you may have to reconstruct the actual chain of events from partial clues, gradually filling in the missing pieces of the puzzle.

The plot gives shape to a story as a whole. Bobbie Ann Mason's "Shiloh" takes us from first signs of estrangement, through the husband's ineffectual yearning for a return to their happier past, to a last attempt at picking up the pieces during the trip to the battlefield at Shiloh. At the end of the story, something has been settled; a chapter in their lives has been written. The story leaves us with a satisfying sense of completion. It achieves **closure**—a satisfying wrapping up or pulling together.

FIRST READING
The Unifying Thread

Doris Lessing was born in Persia (now Iran), grew up in British Rhodesia in Africa before it became Zimbabwe, and went to live and write in England. After World War II, she was involved in radical left-wing politics at the time of the Stalinist purges in East Bloc countries, an experience she described with searing candor in *The Golden Notebook* (1962). The Isaac Babel mentioned in the title of the following story was a Jewish writer who wrote about Jewish life in Russia. Do we need to know who he is or how he writes for the story to work? What happens in the story?

Doris Lessing   *(born 1919)*

Homage for Isaac Babel   1958

The day I had promised to take Catherine down to visit my young friend Philip at his school in the country, we were to leave at eleven, but she arrived at nine. Her blue dress was new, and so were her fashionable shoes. Her hair had just been done. She looked more than ever like a pink-and-gold Renoir girl who expects everything from life.

Catherine lives in a white house overlooking the sweeping brown tides of the river. She helped me clean up my flat with a devotion which said that she felt small flats were altogether more romantic than large houses. We drank tea, and talked mainly about Philip, who, being fifteen, has pure stern tastes in everything from food to music. Catherine looked at the books lying around his room, and asked if she might borrow the stories of Isaac Babel to read on the train. Catherine is thirteen. I suggested she might find them difficult, but she said: "Philip reads them, doesn't he?"

During the journey I read newspapers and watched her pretty frowning face as she turned the pages of Babel, for she was determined to let nothing get between her and her ambition to be worthy of Philip.

At the school, which is charming, civilized, and expensive, the two children walked together across green fields, and I followed, seeing how the sun gilded their bright friendly heads turned toward each other as they talked. In Catherine's left hand she carried the stories of Isaac Babel.

After lunch we went to the pictures. Philip allowed it to be seen that he thought going to the pictures just for the fun of it was not worthy of intelligent people, but he made the concession, for our sakes. For his sake we chose the more serious of the two films that were showing in the little town. It was about a good priest who helped criminals in New York. His goodness, however, was not enough to prevent one of them from being sent to the gas chamber; and Philip and I waited with Catherine in the dark until she had stopped crying and could face the light of a golden evening. 5

At the entrance of the cinema the doorman was lying in wait for anyone who had red eyes. Grasping Catherine by her suffering arm, he said bitterly: "Yes, why are you crying? He had to be punished for his crime, didn't he?" Catherine stared at him, incredulous. Philip rescued her by saying with disdain: "Some people don't know right from wrong even when it's *demonstrated* to them." The doorman turned his attention to the next red-eyed emerger from the dark; and we went on together to the station, the children silent because of the cruelty of the world.

Finally Catherine said, her eyes wet again: "I think it's all absolutely beastly, and I can't bear to think about it." And Philip said: "But we've got to think about it, don't you see, because if we don't it'll just go on and *on,* don't you see?"

In the train going back to London I sat beside Catherine. She had the stories open in front of her, but she said: "Philip's awfully lucky. I wish I went to that school. Did you notice that girl who said hullo to him in the garden? They must be great friends. I wish my mother would let me have a dress like that, it's *not* fair."

"I thought it was too old for her."

"Oh, *did* you?" 10

Soon she bent her head again over the book, but almost at once lifted it to say: "Is he a very famous writer?"

"He's a marvellous writer, brilliant, one of the very best."

"Why?"

"Well, for one thing he's so simple. Look how few words he uses, and how strong his stories are."

"I see. Do you know him? Does he live in London?" 15

"Oh no, he's dead."

"Oh. Then why did you—I thought he was alive, the way you talked."

"I'm sorry, I suppose I wasn't thinking of him as dead."

"When did he die?"

"He was murdered. About twenty years ago, I suppose." 20

"*Twenty years.*" Her hands began the movement of pushing the book over to me, but then relaxed. "I'll be fourteen in November," she stated, sounding threatened, while her eyes challenged me.

I found it hard to express my need to apologize, but before I could speak, she said, patiently attentive again: "You said he was murdered?"

"Yes."

"I expect the person who murdered him felt sorry when he discovered he had murdered a famous writer."

"Yes, I expect so."   25

"Was he old when he was murdered?"

"No, quite young really."

"Well, that was bad luck, wasn't it?"

"Yes, I suppose it was bad luck."

"Which do you think is the very best story here? I mean, in your honest   30
opinion, the very very best one."

I chose the story about killing the goose. She read it slowly, while I sat waiting, wishing to take it from her, wishing to protect this charming little person from Isaac Babel.

When she had finished, she said: "Well, some of it I don't understand. He's got a funny way of looking at things. Why should a man's legs in boots look like *girls?*" She finally pushed the book over at me, and said: "I think it's all morbid."

"But you have to understand the kind of life he had. First, he was a Jew in Russia. That was bad enough. Then his experience was all revolution and civil war and.. . . "

But I could see these words bounding off the clear glass of her fiercely denying gaze; and I said: "Look, Catherine, why don't you try again when you're older? Perhaps you'll like him better then?"

She said gratefully: "Yes, perhaps that would be best. After all, Philip is   35
two years older than me, isn't he?"

A week later I got a letter from Catherine.

Thank you very much for being kind enough to take me to visit Philip at his school. It was the most lovely day in my whole life. I am extremely grateful to you for taking me. I have been thinking about the Hoodlum Priest. That was a film which demonstrated to me beyond any shadow of doubt that Capital Punishment is a Wicked Thing, and I shall never forget what I learned that afternoon, and the lessons of it will be with me all my life. I have been meditating about what you said about Isaac Babel, the famed Russian short story writer, and I now see that the conscious simplicity of his style is what makes him, beyond the shadow of a doubt, the great writer that he is, and now in my school compositions I am endeavoring to emulate him so as to learn a conscious simplicity which is the only basis for a really brilliant writing style. Love, Catherine. P.S. Has Philip said anything about my party? I wrote but he hasn't answered. Please find out if he is coming or if he just forgot to answer my letter. I hope he comes, because sometimes I feel I shall die if he doesn't. P.P.S. Please don't tell him I said anything, because I should die if he knew. Love, Catherine.

The Receptive Reader

What happens in the story? What is the unifying thread? How do its characters interact? What leaves the reader with a gratifying sense of completion?

PLOTTING THE STORY

A plot is a narrative of events, the emphasis
falling on causality. "The king died and then the
queen died" is a story. "The king died, and then
the queen died of grief" is a plot.

E. M. FORSTER

Order and form no more spring out of order
and form than they come riding in to us upon
seashells through the spray. In fiction they have
to be made out of their very antithesis, life.

EUDORA WELTY

The following three selections are by authors who write gripping stories. They entice readers into a story and then lock in their interest until the story reaches its satisfying conclusion. However, these writers use very different techniques, ranging from the more traditional to the more modern. Try to chart the plot, the story line, as you read.

Bernard Malamud   *(1914–1986)*

A bad reading of my work would indicate that
I'm writing about losers. That would be a very
bad reading. One of my most important themes is
a man's hidden strength.

BERNARD MALAMUD

Bernard Malamud was born and went to school in Brooklyn, and to college at the College of the City of New York and Columbia University. He taught high school evening classes for years before he could make a living as a writer and university teacher. He knew the cultural heritage of the American Jewish community, and he wrote about Jewish everyday life and Jewish history in novels like *The Assistant* (1956), about a struggling neighborhood grocer and the down-and-out stranger he befriends. *The Fixer* (1966) told the story of a Jew accused of ritual murder in czarist Russia. Malamud's fiction is colored by the tragic view of life of a people who underwent centuries of persecution. In the depths of loneliness and bitterness, Leo Finkle, the rabbinical student in Malamud's story "The Magic Barrel," reminds himself "that he was yet a Jew and that a Jew suffered." However, intermeshing with this mournful strand is a zany sense of humor, as likely to target one's own shortcomings as those of others.

What is the plot? Malamud's "The Magic Barrel" has the kind of straightforward surface plot that delights lovers of spontaneous storytelling. A young rabbinical student, shy and lonely, enlists the services of a traditional matchmaker or marriage broker in his search for a suitable wife. The young man's quest for happiness leads him through a series of tragicomic adventures that seem to doom him to disappointment. The story leads up to a surprise ending that is a happy ending or not depending on the beholder's point of view.

However, while the official plot is played out toward its conclusion, much of what the characters publicly say and do plays to a counterpoint of private thoughts and feelings. These are often betrayed by revealing gestures, hesitations, or slips of the tongue. The role each character plays—the matchmaker, the serious theology student, the teacher looking for a spouse—is a public **persona**; it is the personality they exhibit to the outside world, the face they wear in public. Once you focus on the private feelings of the characters, you are likely to observe that, parallel to the overt action, a spiritual journey takes place—a journey toward self-discovery. Leo learns things about himself that before he did not care to admit. He reexamines his life, his history, his vocation. What does he learn? How does his character develop or grow in the course of the story?

The Magic Barrel   *1958*

Not long ago there lived in uptown New York, in a small, almost meager room, though crowded with books, Leon Finkle, a rabbinical student in the Yeshivah University. Finkle, after six years of study, was to be ordained in June and had been advised by an acquaintance that he might find it easier to win himself a congregation if he were married. Since he had no present prospects of marriage, after two tormented days of turning it over in his mind, he called in Pinye Salzman, a marriage broker, whose two-line advertisement he had read in the *Forward*.

The matchmaker appeared one night out of the dark fourth-floor hallway of the graystone rooming house, grasping a black, strapped portfolio that had been worn thin with use. Salzman, who had been long in the business, was of slight but dignified build, wearing an old hat and an overcoat too short and tight for him. He smelled frankly of fish, which he loved to eat, and although he was missing a few teeth, his presence was not displeasing, because of an amiable manner curiously contrasted by mournful eyes. His voice, his lips, his wisp of beard, his bony fingers were animated, but give him a moment of repose, and his mild blue eyes soon revealed a depth of sadness, a characteristic that put Leo a little at ease although the situation, for him, was inherently tense.

He at once informed Salzman why he had asked him to come, explaining that his home was in Cleveland, and that but for his parents, who had married comparatively late in life, he was alone in the world. He had for six years devoted himself entirely to his studies, as a result of which, quite understandably, he had found himself without time for a social life and the company of young women. Therefore he thought it the better part of trial and error—of embarrassing fumbling—to call in an experienced person to advise him in these matters. He remarked in passing that the function of the marriage broker was ancient and honorable, highly approved in the Jewish community, because it made practical the necessary without hindering joy. Moreover, his own parents had been brought together by a matchmaker. They had made, if not a financially profitable marriage—since neither had possessed any worldly goods to speak of—at least a successful one in the sense of their everlasting devotion to one another. Salzman listened in embarrassed surprise, sensing a sort of apology. Later, however, he experienced a glow of pride in his work, an emotion that had left him years ago, and he heartily approved of Finkle.

The two men went to their business. Leo had led Salzman to the only clear place in the room, a table near a window that overlooked the lamplit city. He seated himself at the matchmaker's side but facing him, attempting by an act of will to suppress the unpleasant tickle in his throat. Salzman eagerly unstrapped his portfolio and removed a loose rubber band from a thin packet of much-handled cards. As he flipped through them, a gesture and sound that physically hurt Leo, the student pretended not to see and gazed steadfastly out the window. Although it was still February, winter was on its last legs, signs of which he had for the first time in years begun to notice. He now observed the round white moon, moving high in the sky through a cloud-menagerie, and watched with half-open mouth as it penetrated a huge hen and dropped out of her like an egg laying itself. Salzman, though pretending through eyeglasses he had just slipped on, to be engaged in scanning the writing on the cards, stole occasional glances at the young man's distinguished face, noting with pleasure the long, severe scholar's nose, brown eyes heavy with learning, sensitive yet ascetic lips, and a certain almost hollow quality of the dark cheeks. He gazed around at shelves upon shelves of books and let out a soft but happy sigh.

When Leo's eyes fell upon the cards, he counted six spread out in Salzman's hand.   5

"So few?" he said in disappointment.

"You wouldn't believe me how much cards I got in my office," Salzman replied. "The drawers are already filled to the top, so I keep them now in a barrel, but is every girl good for a new rabbi?"

Leo blushed at this, regretting all he had revealed of himself in a curriculum vitae he had sent to Salzman. He had thought it best to acquaint him with his strict standards and specifications, but in having done so now felt he had told the marriage broker more than was absolutely necessary.

He hesitantly inquired, "Do you keep photographs of your clients on file?"

"First comes family, amount of dowry, also what kind promises," Salzman   10
replied, unbuttoning his tight coat and settling himself in the chair. "After comes pictures, rabbi."

"Call me Mr. Finkle. I'm not a rabbi yet."

Salzman said he would, but instead called him doctor, which he changed to rabbi when Leo was not listening too attentively.

Salzman adjusted his horn-rimmed spectacles, gently cleared his throat and read in an eager voice the contents on the top card:

"Sophie P. Twenty-four years. Widow for one year. No children. Educated high school and two years college. Father promises eight thousand dollars. Has a wonderful wholesale business. Also real estate. On mother's side comes teachers, also one actor. Well known on Second Avenue."

Leo gazed up in surprise. "Did you say a widow?"   15

"A widow don't mean spoiled, rabbi. She lived with her husband maybe four months. He was a sick boy, she made a mistake to marry him."

"Marrying a widow has never entered my mind."

"This is because you have no experience. A widow, specially if she is young and healthy like this girl, is a wonderful person to marry. She will be thankful to you the rest of her life. Believe me, if I was looking now for a bride, I would marry a widow."

Leo reflected, then shook his head.

Salzman hunched his shoulders in an almost imperceptible gesture of dis-   20
appointment. He placed the card down on the wooden table and began to read another:

"Lily H. High-school teacher. Regular. Not a substitute. Has savings and new Dodge car. Lived in Paris one year. Father is successful dentist thirty-five years. Interested in professional man. Well Americanized family. Wonderful opportunity.

"I know her personally," said Salzman. "I wish you could see this girl. She is a doll. Also very intelligent. All day you could talk to her about books and theater and what not. She also knows current events."

"I don't believe you mentioned her age?"

"Her age?" Salzman said, raising his brows in surprise. "Her age is thirty-two years."

Leo said after a while, "I'm afraid that seems a little too old."   25

Salzman let out a laugh. "So how old are you, rabbi?"

"Twenty-seven."

"So what is the difference, tell me, between twenty-seven and thirty-two? My own wife is seven years older than me. So what did I suffer?—Nothing. If Rothschild's daughter wants to marry you, would you say on account of her age, no?"

"Yes," Leo said dryly.

Salzman shook off the no in the yes. "Five years don't mean a thing. I   30
give you my word that when you will live with her for one week, you will forget her age. What does it mean five years—that she lived more and knows more than somebody who is younger? On this girl, God bless her, years are not wasted. Each one that it comes makes better the bargain."

"What subject does she teach in high school?"

"Languages. If you heard the way she reads French, you will think it is music. I am in the business twenty-five years, and I recommend her with my whole heart. Believe me, I know what I'm talking, rabbi."

"What's on the next card?" Leo said abruptly.

Salzman reluctantly turned up the third card:

"Ruth K. Nineteen years. Honor student. Father offers thirteen thousand   35
dollars cash to the right bridegroom. He is a medical doctor. Stomach specialist with marvelous practice. Brother-in-law owns own garment business. Particular people."

Salzman looked up as if he had read his trump card.

"Did you say nineteen?" Leo asked with interest.

"On the dot."

"Is she attractive?" He blushed. "Pretty?"

Salzman kissed his fingertips. "A little doll. On this I give you my word. 40 Let me call the father tonight and you will see what means pretty."

But Leo was troubled. "You're sure she's that young?"

"This I am positive. The father will show you the birth certificate."

"Are you positive there isn't something wrong with her?" Leo insisted.

"Who says there is wrong?"

"I don't understand why an American girl her age should go to a mar- 45 riage broker."

A smile spread over Salzman's face.

"So for the same reason you went, she comes."

Leo flushed. "I am pressed for time."

Salzman, realizing he had been tactless, quickly explained. "The father came, not her. He wants she should have the best, so he looks around himself. When we will locate the right boy, he will introduce him and encourage. This makes a better marriage than if a young girl without experience takes for herself. I don't have to tell you this."

"But don't you think this young girl believes in love?" Leo spoke uneasily. 50

Salzman was about to guffaw, but caught himself and said soberly, "Love comes with the right person, not before."

Leo parted dry lips but did not speak. Noticing that Salzman had snatched a quick glance at the next card, he cleverly asked, "How is her health?"

"Perfect," Salzman said, breathing with difficulty. "Of course, she is a little lame on her right foot from an auto accident that it happened to her when she was twelve years, but nobody notices on account she is so brilliant and also beautiful."

Leo got up heavily and went to the window. He felt curiously bitter and upbraided himself for having called in the marriage broker. Finally, he shook his head.

"Why not?" Salzman persisted, the pitch of his voice rising. 55

"Because I hate stomach specialists."

"So what do you care what is his business? After you marry her, do you need him? Who says he must come every Friday night to your house?"

Ashamed of the way the talk was going, Leo dismissed Salzman, who went home with melancholy eyes.

Though he had felt only relief at the marriage broker's departure, Leo was in low spirits the next day. He explained it as arising from Salzman's failure to produce a suitable bride for him. He did not care for his type of clientele. But when Leo found himself hesitating over whether to seek out another matchmaker, one more polished than Pinye, he wondered if it could be—his protestations to the contrary, and although he honored his father and mother—that he did not, in essence, care for the matchmaking institution? This thought he quickly put out of his mind yet found himself still upset. All day he ran around in a fog—missed an important appointment, forgot to give out his laundry, walked out of a Broadway cafeteria without paying and had to run back with the ticket in his hand; had even not recognized his landlady in the street when she passed with a friend and courteously called out, "A good evening to you, Doctor Finkle." By nightfall, however, he had regained sufficient calm to sink his nose into a book and there found peace from his thoughts.

Almost at once there came a knock on the door. Before Leo could say   60
enter, Salzman, commercial cupid, was standing in the room. His face was gray and meager, his expression hungry, and he looked as if he would expire on his feet. Yet the marriage broker managed, by some trick of the muscles, to display a broad smile.

"So good evening. I am invited?"

Leo nodded, disturbed to see him again, yet unwilling to ask him to leave.

Beaming still, Salzman laid his portfolio on the table. "Rabbi, I got for you tonight good news."

"I've asked you not to call me rabbi. I'm still a student."

"Your worries are finished. I have for you a first-class bride."   65

"Leave me in peace concerning this subject." Leo pretended lack of interest.

"The world will dance at your wedding."

"Please, Mr. Salzman, no more."

"But first must come back my strength," Salzman said weakly. He fumbled with the portfolio straps and took out of the leather case an oily paper bag, from which he extracted a hard seeded roll and a small smoked whitefish. With one motion of his hand he stripped the fish out of its skin and began ravenously to chew. "All day in a rush," he muttered.

Leo watched him eat.   70

"A sliced tomato you have maybe?" Salzman hesitantly inquired.

"No."

The marriage broker shut his eyes and ate. When he had finished, he carefully cleaned up the crumbs and rolled up the remains of the fish in the paper bag. His spectacled eyes roamed the room until he discovered, amid some piles of books, a one-burner gas stove. Lifting his hat, he humbly asked, "A glass of tea you got, rabbi?"

Conscience-stricken, Leo rose and brewed the tea. He served it with a chunk of lemon and two cubes of lump sugar, delighting Salzman.

After he had drunk his tea, Salzman's strength and good spirits were   75
restored.

"So tell me, rabbi," he said amiably, "you considered any more the three clients I mentioned yesterday?"

"There was no need to consider."

"Why not?"

"None of them suits me."

"What, then, suits you?"   80

Leo let it pass because he could give only a confused answer.

Without waiting for a reply, Salzman asked, "You remember this girl I talked to you—the high-school teacher?"

"Age thirty-two?"

But, surprisingly, Salzman's face lit in a smile. "Age twenty-nine."

Leo shot him a look. "Reduced from thirty-two?"   85

"A mistake," Salzman avowed. "I talked today with the dentist. He took me to his safety deposit box and showed me the birth certificate. She was twenty-nine last August. They made her a party in the mountains where she went for her vacation. When her father spoke to me the first time, I forgot to write the age and I told you thirty-two, but now I remember this was a different client, a widow."

"The same one you told me about? I thought she was twenty-four?"

"A different. Am I responsible that the world is filled with widows?"

"No, but I'm not interested in them, nor for that matter, in schoolteachers."

Salzman passionately pulled his clasped hands to his breast. Looking at   90
the ceiling he exclaimed, "Jewish children, what can I say to somebody that he is not interested in high-school teachers? So what then you are interested?"

Leo flushed but controlled himself.

"In who else you will be interested," Salzman went on, "if you not interested in this fine girl that she speaks four languages and has personally in the bank ten thousand dollars? Also her father guarantees further twelve thousand. Also she has a new car, wonderful clothes, talks on all subjects, and she will give you a first-class home and children. How near do we come in our life to paradise?"

"If she's so wonderful, why wasn't she married ten years ago?"

"Why," said Salzman with a heavy laugh. "—Why? Because she is *partikler*. This is why. She wants only the *best*."

Leo was silent, amused at how he had trapped himself. But Salzman had   95
aroused his interest in Lily H., and he began seriously to consider calling on her. When the marriage broker observed how intently Leo's mind was at work on the facts he had supplied, he felt positive they would soon come to an agreement.

Late Saturday afternoon, conscious of Salzman, Leo Finkle walked with Lily Hirschorn along Riverside Drive. He walked briskly and erectly, wearing with distinction the black fedora he had that morning taken with trepidation out of the dusty hatbox on his closet shelf, and the heavy black Saturday coat he had thoroughly whisked clean. Leo also owned a walking stick, a present from a distant relative, but had decided not to use it. Lily, petite and not unpretty, had on something signifying the approach of spring. She was *au courant,* animatedly, with all subjects, and he weighed her words and found her surprisingly sound—score another for Salzman, whom he uneasily sensed to be somewhere around, hiding perhaps high in a tree along the street, flashing the lady signals; or perhaps a cloven-hoofed Pan, piping nuptial ditties as he danced his invisible way before them, strewing wild buds on the walk and purple summer grapes in their path, symbolizing fruit of a union, of which there was yet none.

Lily startled Leo by remarking, "I was thinking of Mr. Salzman, a curious figure, wouldn't you say?"

Not certain what to answer, he nodded.

She bravely went on, blushing, "I for one am grateful for his introducing us. Aren't you?"

He courteously replied, "I am." 100

"I mean," she said with a little laugh—and it was all in good taste, or at least gave the effect of being not in bad—"do you mind that we came together so?"

He was not afraid of her honesty, recognizing that she meant to set the relationship aright, and understanding that it took a certain amount of experience in life, and courage, to want to do it quite that way. One had to have some sort of past to make that kind of beginning.

He said that he did not mind. Salzman's function was traditional and honorable—valuable for what it might achieve, which, he pointed out, was frequently nothing.

Lily agreed with a sigh. They walked on for a while, and she said after a long silence, again with a nervous laugh, "Would you mind if I asked you something a little bit personal? Frankly, I find the subject fascinating." Although Leo shrugged, she went on half embarrassedly, "How was it that you came to your calling? I mean, was it a sudden passionate inspiration?"

Leo, after a time, slowly replied, "I was always interested in the Law." 105

"You saw revealed in it the presence of the Highest?"

He nodded and changed the subject. "I understand you spent a little time in Paris, Miss Hirschorn?"

"Oh, did Mr. Salzman tell you, Rabbi Finkle?" Leo winced, but she went on, "It was ages and ages ago and almost forgotten. I remember I had to return for my sister's wedding."

But Lily would not be put off. "When," she asked in a trembly voice, "did you become enamored of God?"

He stared at her. Then it came to him that she was talking not about Leo 110 Finkle, but a total stranger, some mystical figure, perhaps even passionate prophet that Salzman had conjured up for her—no relation to the living or dead. Leo trembled with rage and weakness. The trickster had obviously sold her a bill of goods, just as he had him, who'd expected to become acquainted with a young lady of twenty-nine, only to behold, the moment he laid eyes upon her strained and anxious face, a woman past thirty-five and aging very rapidly. Only his self-control, he thought, had kept him this long in her presence.

"I am not," he said gravely, "a talented religious person," and in seeking words to go on, found himself possessed by fear and shame. "I think," he said in a strained manner, "that I came to God not because I love Him, but because I did not."

This confession he spoke harshly because its unexpectedness shook him.

Lily wilted. Leo saw a profusion of loaves of bread sailing like ducks high over his head, not unlike the loaves by which he had counted himself to sleep last night. Mercifully, then, it snowed, which he would not put past Salzman's machinations.

He was infuriated with the marriage broker and swore he would throw him out of the room the moment he reappeared. But Salzman did not come that night, and when Leo's anger had subsided, an unaccountable despair grew in its place. At first he thought this was caused by his disappointment in Lily, but before long it became evident that he had involved himself with Salzman without a true knowledge of his own intent. He gradually realized—with an emptiness that seized him with six hands—that he had called in the broker to find him a bride because he was incapable of doing it himself. This terrifying insight he had derived as a result of his meeting and conversation with Lily Hirschorn. Her probing questions had somehow irritated him into revealing—to himself more than her—the true nature of his relationship with God, and from that it had come upon him, with shocking force, that apart from his parents, he had never loved anyone. Or perhaps it went the other way, that he did not love God so well as he might, because he had not loved man. It seemed to Leo that his whole life stood starkly revealed and he saw himself, for the first time, as he truly was—unloved and loveless. This bitter but somehow not fully unexpected revelation brought him to a point of panic controlled only by extraordinary effort. He covered his face with his hands and wept.

The week that followed was the worst of his life. He did not eat, and lost 115 weight. His beard darkened and grew ragged. He stopped attending lectures and seminars and almost never opened a book. He seriously considered leaving the Yeshivah, although he was deeply troubled at the thought of the loss of all his years of study—saw them like pages from a book strewn over the city—and at the devastating effect of this decision upon his parents. But he had lived without knowledge of himself, and never in the Five Books and all the Commentaries—*mea culpa*—had the truth been revealed to him. He did not know where to turn, and in all this desolating loneliness there was no *to whom,* although he often thought of Lily but not once could bring himself to go downstairs and make the call. He became touchy and irritable, especially with his landlady, who asked him all manner of questions; on the other hand, sensing his own disagreeableness, he waylaid her on the stairs and apologized abjectly, until mortified, she ran from him. Out of this, however, he drew the consolation that he was yet a Jew and that a Jew suffered. But gradually, as the long and terrible week drew to a close, he regained his composure and some idea of purpose in life: to go on as planned. Although he was imperfect, the ideal was not. As for his quest of a bride, the thought of continuing afflicted him with anxiety and heartburn, yet perhaps with this new knowledge of himself he would be more successful than in the past. Perhaps love would now come to him and a bride to that love. And for this sanctified seeking who needed a Salzman?

The marriage broker, a skeleton with haunted eyes, returned that very night. He looked, withal, the picture of frustrated expectancy—as if he had steadfastly waited the week at Miss Lily Hirschorn's side for a telephone call that never came.

Casually coughing, Salzman came immediately to the point: "So how did you like her?"

Leo's anger rose and he could not refrain from chiding the matchmaker: "Why did you lie to me, Salzman?"

Salzman's pale face went dead white, as if the world had snowed on him.

"Did you not state that she was twenty-nine?" Leo insisted.   120

"I give you my word—"

"She was thirty-five. At *least* thirty-five."

"Of this I would not be too sure. Her father told me—"

"Never mind. The worst of it was that you lied to her."

"How did I lie to her, tell me?"   125

"You told her things about me that weren't true. You made me out to be more, consequently less than I am. She had in mind a totally different person, a sort of semimystical Wonder Rabbi."

"All I said, you was a religious man."

"I can imagine."

Salzman sighed. "This is my weakness that I have," he confessed. "My wife says to me I shouldn't be a salesman, but when I have two fine people that they would be wonderful to be married, I am so happy that I talk too much." He smiled wanly. "This is why Salzman is a poor man."

Leo's anger went. "Well, Salzman, I'm afraid that's all."   130

The marriage broker fastened hungry eyes on him.

"You don't want any more a bride?"

"I do," said Leo, "but I have decided to seek her in a different way. I am no longer interested in an arranged marriage. To be frank, I now admit the necessity of premarital love. That is, I want to be in love with the one I marry."

"Love?" said Salzman, astounded. After a moment he said, "For us, our love is our life, not for the ladies. In the ghetto they—"

"I know, I know," said Leo. "I've thought of it often. Love, I have said to 135
myself, should be a by-product of living and worship rather than its own end. Yet for myself I find it necessary to establish the level of my need and to fulfill it."

Salzman shrugged but answered, "Listen, rabbi, if you want love, this I can find for you also. I have such beautiful clients that you will love them the minute your eyes will see them."

Leo smiled unhappily. "I'm afraid you don't understand."

But Salzman hastily unstrapped his portfolio and withdrew a manila packet from it.

"Pictures," he said, quickly laying the envelope on the table.

Leo called after him to take the pictures away, but as if on the wings of 140
the wind, Salzman had disappeared.

March came. Leo had returned to his regular routine. Although he felt not quite himself yet—lacked energy—he was making plans for a more active social life. Of course it would cost something, but he was an expert in cutting corners; and when there were no corners left he could make circles rounder. All the while Salzman's pictures had lain on the table, gathering dust. Occasionally as Leo sat studying, or enjoying a cup of tea, his eyes fell on the manila envelope, but he never opened it.

The days went by, and no social life to speak of developed with a member of the opposite sex—it was difficult, given the circumstances of his situation. One morning Leo toiled up the stairs to his room and stared out the window at the city. Although the day was bright, his view of it was dark. For some time he watched the people in the street below hurrying along and then turned with a heavy heart to his little room. On the table was the packet. With a sudden relentless gesture he tore it open. For a half-hour he stood there, in a state of excitement, examining the photographs of the ladies Salzman had included. Finally, with a deep sigh he put them down. There were six, of varying degrees of attractiveness, but look at them long enough and they all became Lily Hirschorn: all past their prime, all starved behind bright smiles, not a true personality in the lot. Life, despite their anguished struggles and frantic yoohooings, had passed them by; they were photographs in a briefcase that stank of fish. After a while, however, as Leo attempted to return the pictures into the envelope, he found another in it, a small snapshot of the type taken by a machine for a quarter. He gazed at it a moment and let out a cry.

Her face deeply moved him. Why, he could at first not say. It gave him the impression of youth—all spring flowers—yet age—a sense of having been used to the bone, wasted; this all came from the eyes, which were hauntingly familiar, yet absolutely strange. He had a strong impression that he had met her before, but try as he might he could not place her, although he could almost recall her name, as if he had read it written in her own handwriting. No, this couldn't be; he would have remembered her. It was not, he affirmed, that she had an extraordinary beauty—no, although her face was attractive enough; it was that *something* about her moved him. Feature for feature, even some of the ladies of the photographs could do better; but she leaped forth to the heart—had lived, or wanted to—more than just wanted, perhaps regretted it—had somehow deeply suffered: it could be seen in the depths of those reluctant eyes, and from the way the light enclosed and shone from her, and within her, opening whole realms of possibility: this was her own. Her he desired. His head ached and eyes narrowed with the intensity of his gazing, then, as if a black fog had blown up in the mind, he experienced fear of her and was aware that he had received an impression, somehow, of filth. He shuddered, saying softly, it is thus with us all. Leo brewed some tea in a small pot and sat sipping it, without sugar, to calm himself. But before he had finished drinking, again with excitement he examined the face and found it good: good for him. Only such a one could truly understand Leo Finkle and help him to seek whatever he was seeking. How she had come to be among the discards in Salzman's barrel he could never guess, but he knew he must urgently go find her.

Leo rushed downstairs, grabbed up the Bronx telephone book, and searched for Salzman's home address. He was not listed, nor was his office. Neither was he in the Manhattan book. But Leo remembered having written down the address on a slip of paper after he had read Salzman's advertisement in the "personals" column of the *Forward*. He ran up to his room and tore through his papers, without luck. It was exasperating. Just when he needed the matchmaker he was nowhere to be found. Fortunately Leo remembered to look in his wallet. There on a card he found his name written and a Bronx address. No phone number was listed, which, Leo now recalled, was the reason he had originally communicated with Salzman by letter. He got on his coat, put a hat on over his skull cap and hurried to the subway station. All the way to the far end of the Bronx he sat on the edge of his seat. He was more than once tempted to take out the picture and

see if the girl's face was as he remembered it, but he refrained, allowing
the snapshot to remain in his inside coat pocket, content to have her so
close. When the train pulled into the station, he was waiting at the door
and bolted out. He quickly located the street Salzman had advertised.

The building he sought was less than a block from the subway, but it was   145
not an office building, nor even a loft, nor a store in which one could rent
office space. It was an old and grimy tenement. Leo found Salzman's name
in pencil on a soiled tag under the bell and climbed three dark flights to his
apartment. When he knocked, the door was opened by a thin, asthmatic,
gray-haired woman, in felt slippers.

"Yes?" she said, expecting nothing. She listened without listening. He could
have sworn he had seen her somewhere before but knew it was illusion.

"Salzman—does he live here? Pinye Salzman," he said, "the matchmaker?"

She stared at him a long time. "Of course."

He felt embarrassed. "Is he in?"

"No." Her mouth was open, but she offered nothing more.   150

"This is urgent. Can you tell me where his office is?"

"In the air." She pointed upward.

"You mean he has no office?" Leo said.

"In his socks."

He peered into the apartment. It was sunless and dingy, one large room   155
divided by a half-open curtain, beyond which he could see a sagging metal
bed. The nearer side of the room was crowded with rickety chairs, old bu-
reaus, a three-legged table, racks of cooking utensils, and all the apparatus
of a kitchen. But there was no sign of Salzman or his magic barrel, probably also a figment of his imagination. An odor of frying fish made Leo weak
to the knees.

"Where is he?" he insisted, "I've got to see your husband."

At length she answered, "So who knows where he is? Every time he thinks
a new thought he runs to a different place. Go home, he will find you."

"Tell him Leo Finkle."

She gave no sign that she had heard.

He went downstairs, deeply depressed.   160

But Salzman, breathless, stood waiting at his door.

Leo was overjoyed and astounded. "How did you get here before me?"

"I rushed."

"Come inside."

They entered. Leo fixed tea and a sardine sandwich for Salzman.   165

As they were drinking, he reached behind him for the packet of pictures
and handed them to the marriage broker.

Salzman put down his glass and said expectantly, "You found maybe
somebody you like?"

"Not among these."

The marriage broker turned sad eyes away.

"Here's the one I like." Leo held forth the snapshot.   170

Salzman slipped on his glasses and took the picture into his trembling
hand. He turned ghastly and let out a miserable groan.

"What's the matter?" cried Leo.

"Excuse me. Was an accident this picture. She is not for you."

Salzman frantically shoved the manila packet into his portfolio. He thrust the snapshot into his pocket and fled down the stairs.

Leo, after momentary paralysis, gave chase and cornered the marriage 175 broker in the vestibule. The landlady made hysterical outcries, but neither of them listened.

"Give me back the picture, Salzman."

"No." The pain in his eyes was terrible.

"Tell me where she is then."

"This I can't tell you. Excuse me."

He made to depart, but Leo, forgetting himself, seized the matchmaker 180 by his tight coat and shook him frenziedly.

"Please," sighed Salzman. "*Please.*"

Leo ashamedly let him go. "Tell me who she is," he begged. "It's very important for me to know."

"She is not for you. She is a wild one—wild, without shame. This is not a bride for a rabbi."

"What do you mean wild?"

"Like an animal. Like a dog. For her to be poor was a sin. This is why 185 she is dead now."

"In God's name, what do you mean?"

"Her I can't introduce to you," Salzman cried.

"Why are you so excited?"

"Why he asks," Salzman said, bursting into tears. "This is my baby, my Stella, she should burn in hell."

Leo hurried up to bed and hid under the covers. Under the covers he 190 thought his whole life through. Although he soon fell asleep he could not sleep her out of his mind. He woke, beating his breast. Though he prayed to be rid of her, his prayers went unanswered. Through days of torment he struggled endlessly not to love her; fearing success, he escaped it. He then concluded to convert her to goodness, himself to God. The idea alternately nauseated and exalted him.

He perhaps did not know that he had come to a final decision until he encountered Salzman in a Broadway cafeteria. He was sitting alone at a rear table sucking the bony remains of a fish. The marriage broker appeared haggard, and transparent to the point of vanishing.

Salzman looked up at first without recognizing him. Leo had grown a pointed beard, and his eyes were weighted with wisdom.

"Salzman," he said, "love has at last come to my heart."

"Who can love from a picture?" mocked the marriage broker.

"It is not impossible."   195

"If you can love her, then you can love anybody. Let me show you some new clients that they just sent me their photographs. One is a little doll."

"Just her I want," Leo murmured.

"Don't be a fool, doctor. Don't bother with her."

"Put me in touch with her, Salzman," Leo said humbly. "Perhaps I can do her a service."

Salzman had stopped chewing, and Leo understood with emotion that it 200 was now arranged.

Leaving the cafeteria, he was, however, afflicted by a tormenting suspicion that Salzman had planned it all to happen this way.

Leo was informed by letter that she would meet him on a certain corner, and she was there one spring night, waiting under a street lamp. He appeared, carrying a small bouquet of violets and rosebuds. Stella stood by the lamppost, smoking. She wore white with red shoes, which fitted his expectations, although in a troubled moment he had imagined the dress red, and only the shoes white. She waited uneasily and shyly. From afar he saw that her eyes—clearly her father's—were filled with desperate innocence. He pictured, in hers, his own redemption. Violins and lit candles revolved in the sky. Leo ran forward with the flowers outthrust.

Around the corner, Salzman, leaning against a wall, chanted prayers for the dead.

The Receptive Reader

1. What kind of story is this? What kind of story do the title and the *beginning* lead you to expect? Are your expectations fulfilled or disappointed by the rest of the story?

2. What is the *conflict* between the traditional view of love and romantic love in this story? How central is this conflict to the plot? How is the conflict resolved?

3. What are hints or touches that require you to read between the lines? Where are you most aware of the comic contrast between what the characters say and what they really think or know? What are striking examples of the contrast between make-believe and reality?

4. What role does Salzman play in the story as a whole? How essential is he to the plot? What are Finkle's mixed feelings about the "commercial cupid"?

5. What makes Salzman a *comic* figure? (What features do you recognize in his use of English?) How would you describe the kind of humor that pervades this story? What are striking examples?

6. Where in this story does Finkle experience *self-discovery* or self-revelation? What does he discover about himself? What role does this self-examination play in the story as a whole?

7. How believable is the *ending?*

The Personal Response

How essential is an understanding of Jewish culture or tradition to the reader's appreciation of this story? For you, does the author's ethnic background limit or enhance the appeal of the story? Why (or why not)?

The Creative Response

Critics and reviewers at times remind us that the characters in a play or in a story are creations of the author. They are fictional—not full three-dimensional living beings. However, a writer's ideal audience are often readers or spectators who become fully absorbed in a story. They begin to think of the fictional characters as real people—second-guessing or judging them, speculating about their past, or wondering about their real motives. The "illusion of reality" works so well for such readers or playgoers that they may wonder what will happen to the characters after the story ends.

Write an imaginary "Letter from the Future" from a character that became exceptionally real to you. In the letter, have your character tell a close friend or relative what became of the character or what happened to the character in the five or ten years after the story came to a close. For instance, your letter from the future might come from one of the following:

❚ Norma Jean in Bobbie Ann Mason's "Shiloh," after she set out in search of a new life;
❚ the young girl in Alice Munro's "Boys and Girls," now grown up;
❚ younger brother Lyman in Louise Erdrich's "The Red Convertible";
❚ the former rabbinical student in Bernard Malamud's "The Magic Barrel."

Sample Student Response:

Dear J.:
I haven't spoken with you for quite some time so I thought I would write to you in order to catch up. How are you? How is your job? family? everything? Things with me have been quite good recently. I went through sort of a dry period after my brother died, but it has worked itself out. There were times when I was angry with him for leaving me the way he did, and I began to resent him for it. However, one day I got that old photograph of us with the convertible out of the closet and confronted the anger and fear that made me put it there in the first place. I began to reminisce about our trip to Alaska and the days we spent lying under the willow trees, and something from inside of me was set free. I truly realized why my brother went into the river that time, and I reached a level of understanding I hadn't known before. The picture of us is now framed and hanging on the wall in my living room.
Since then, I have gone back into the restaurant business, and with my luck I now own my own restaurant again. I named it Henry's. I met a young woman and got married. Every once in a while I'll pass by a car dealership and see a red convertible and am very tempted to buy it. But then, in my mind Henry speaks to me and tells me to keep moving forward, and I will just pass on by. I hope to hear from you soon and hope that all is well.
Your friend, Lyman

Making Connections—For Discussion or Writing

Compare and contrast the plot of Malamud's story with the plot or narrative line of one or more of the stories by Joyce, Erdrich, or Mason printed earlier in this volume.

Shirley Jackson   *(1919–1965)*

This story is about you—de te fabula.

FRANK O'CONNOR

I hoped, by setting a particularly brutal ancient
rite in the present and in my own village, to
shock the story's readers with a graphic dramati-
zation of the pointless violence and general inhu-
manity in their own lives.

SHIRLEY JACKSON

Shirley Jackson, a native of San Francisco, attended Syracuse University and settled in Vermont. She is a master of the modern horror story in which evil surfaces in ordinary everyday surroundings. Her story "The Lottery" is one of the great controversial stories of modern times. When first published in the *New Yorker* on June 28, 1948, it raised a tempest of protest. The story takes you to a village where you watch the preparations for a traditional ritual, in which one of the villagers is going to meet a terrible fate. The proceedings might remind you of accounts of ceremonial sacrifices to a vegetation god to ensure a rich harvest. ("Lottery in June, corn be heavy soon" is a folk saying in the village.)

Many of its original readers hated this story. It generated "great batches" of mail, much of it abusive, making the author feel grateful that many in her own town did not know she was a writer. Apparently two facets of the story were particularly disturbing: First, the people in the story were not a prehistoric tribe whose primitive rituals they could have watched with detachment. This was a village that had a post office, a bank, and a school; the villagers talked about tractors and taxes. (Jackson once said she had in mind North Bennington, the town where she lived with her husband, who taught at Bennington College.) Second, the people selected to play the central role in the ritual were selected by lot—without the benefit of due process or trial by jury.

What explains the climate of fear in Jackson's story? We might try to see the story in its historical context: Totalitarian regimes in Hitler's Germany and in Stalin's Russia had been persecuting artists, intellectuals, dissidents—a whole range of supposed "antisocial elements" and "enemies of the people." People whose families had lived in Germany for centuries discovered—because their grandparents held the Jewish faith—that they were denied the right to live. In Stalinist Russia, young people whose family had owned a farm or a store were of the wrong social class—they had no right to go to school, to join the army, to make a living. Closer to home, during the Great Depression, families had been losing their farms or businesses and turned into hoboes. They were the random victims of an economic tailspin that threw millions out of work.

What happens in Jackson's story is irrational, but it seems inevitable. We see it coming but find it impossible to stop, like a freight train. The story has a concentrated impact created by a tightly crafted, linear plot. She once said about the writing of short stories, "no scene and no character can be allowed to wander off by itself; there must be some furthering of the story in every sentence." The characters in this story are part of the group, and they do what the community expects them to do. As the Irish writer Frank O'Connor said about the secret of a powerful story, "*De te fabula*"—this fable, this story, is not about somebody else; it is about you.

The Lottery   *1948*

The morning of June 27th was clear and sunny, with the fresh warmth of a full-summer day; the flowers were blossoming profusely and the grass was richly green. The people of the village began to gather in the square, between the post office and the bank, around ten o'clock; in some towns there were so many people that the lottery took two days and had to be started on June 26th, but in this village, where there were only about three hundred people, the whole lottery took less than two hours, so it could begin at ten o'clock in the morning and still be through in time to allow the villagers to get home for noon dinner.

The children assembled first, of course. School was recently over for the summer, and the feeling of liberty sat uneasily on most of them; they tended to gather together quietly for a while before they broke into boisterous play, and their talk was still of the classroom and the teacher, of books and reprimands. Bobby Martin had already stuffed his pockets full of stones, and the other boys soon followed his example, selecting the smoothest and roundest stones; Bobby and Harry Jones and Dickie Delacroix—the villagers pronounced this name "Dellacroy"—eventually made a great pile of stones in one corner of the square and guarded it against the raids of the other boys. The girls stood aside, talking among themselves, looking over their shoulders at the boys, and the very small children rolled in the dust or clung to the hands of their older brothers or sisters.

Soon the men began to gather, surveying their own children, speaking of planting and rain, tractors and taxes. They stood together, away from the pile of stones in the corner, and their jokes were quiet and they smiled rather than laughed. The women, wearing faded house dresses and sweaters, came shortly after their menfolk. They greeted one another and exchanged bits of gossip as they went to join their husbands. Soon the women, standing by their husbands, began to call to their children, and the children came reluctantly, having to be called four or five times. Bobby Martin ducked under his mother's grasping hand and ran, laughing, back to the pile of stones. His father spoke up sharply, and Bobby came quickly and took his place between his father and his oldest brother.

The lottery was conducted—as were the square dances, the teenage club, the Halloween program—by Mr. Summers, who had time and energy to devote to civic activities. He was a round-faced, jovial man and he ran the coal business, and people were sorry for him, because he had no children and his wife was a scold. When he arrived in the square, carrying the black wooden box, there was a murmur of conversation among the villagers, and he waved and called, "Little late today, folks." The postmaster, Mr. Graves, followed him, carrying a three-legged stool, and the stool was put in the center of the square and Mr. Summers set the black box down on it. The villagers kept their distance, leaving a space between themselves and the stool, and when Mr. Summers said, "Some of you fellows want to give me a hand?" there was a hesitation before two men, Mr. Martin and his oldest son, Baxter, came forward to hold the box steady on the stool while Mr. Summers stirred up the papers inside it.

    The original paraphernalia for the lottery had been lost long ago, and the   5
black box now resting on the stool had been put into use even before Old Man Warner, the oldest man in town, was born. Mr. Summers spoke frequently to the villagers about making a new box, but no one liked to upset even as much tradition as was represented by the black box. There was a story that the present box had been made with some pieces of the box that had preceded it, the one that had been constructed when the first people settled down to make a village here. Every year, after the lottery, Mr. Summers began talking again about a new box, but every year the subject was allowed to fade off without anything's being done. The black box grew shabbier each year; by now it was no longer completely black but splintered badly along one side to show the original wood color, and in some places faded or stained.

    Mr. Martin and his oldest son, Baxter, held the black box securely on the stool until Mr. Summers had stirred the papers thoroughly with his hand. Because so much of the ritual had been forgotten or discarded, Mr. Summers had been successful in having slips of paper substituted for the chips of wood that had been used for generations. Chips of wood, Mr. Summers had argued, had been all very well when the village was tiny, but now that the population was more than three hundred and likely to keep on growing, it was necessary to use something that would fit more easily into the black box. The night before the lottery, Mr. Summers and Mr. Graves made up the slips of paper and put them in the box, and it was then taken to the safe of Mr. Summers' coal company and locked up until Mr. Summers was ready to take it to the square next morning. The rest of the year, the box was put away, sometimes one place, sometimes another; it had spent one year in Mr. Graves's barn and another year underfoot in the post office, and sometimes it was set on a shelf in the Martin grocery and left there.

    There was a great deal of fussing to be done before Mr. Summers declared the lottery open. There were the lists to make up—of heads of families, heads of households in each family, members of each household in each family. There was the proper swearing-in of Mr. Summers by the postmaster, as the official of the lottery; at one time, some people remembered, there had been a recital of some sort, performed by the official of the lottery, a perfunctory, tuneless chant that had been rattled off duly each year; some people believed that the official of the lottery used to stand just so when he said or sang it, others believed that he was supposed to walk among the people, but years and years ago this part of the ritual had been allowed to lapse. There had been, also, a ritual salute, which the official of the lottery had had to use in addressing each person who came up to draw from the box, but this also had changed with time, until now it was felt necessary only for the official to speak to each person approaching. Mr. Summers was very good at all this; in his clean white shirt and blue jeans, with one hand resting carelessly on the black box, he seemed very proper and important as he talked interminably to Mr. Graves and the Martins.

Just as Mr. Summers finally left off talking and turned to the assembled villagers, Mrs. Hutchinson came hurriedly along the path to the square, her sweater thrown over her shoulders, and slid into place in the back of the crowd. "Clean forgot what day it was," she said to Mrs. Delacroix, who stood next to her, and they both laughed softly. "Thought my old man was out back stacking wood," Mrs. Hutchinson went on, "and then I looked out the window and the kids was gone, and then I remembered it was the twenty-seventh and came a-running." She dried her hands on her apron, and Mrs. Delacroix said, "You're in time, though. They're still talking away up there."

Mrs. Hutchinson craned her neck to see through the crowd and found her husband and children standing near the front. She tapped Mrs. Delacroix on the arm as a farewell and began to make her way through the crowd. The people separated good-humoredly to let her through; two or three people said, in voices just loud enough to be heard across the crowd, "Here comes your Missus, Hutchinson," and "Bill, she made it after all." Mrs. Hutchinson reached her husband, and Mr. Summers, who had been waiting, said cheerfully, "Thought we were going to have to get on without you, Tessie." Mrs. Hutchinson said, grinning, "Wouldn't have me leave m'dishes in the sink, now, would you, Joe?" and soft laughter ran through the crowd as the people stirred back into position after Mrs. Hutchinson's arrival.

"Well, now," Mr. Summers said soberly, "guess we better get started, get   10 this over with, so's we can go back to work. Anybody ain't here?"

"Dunbar," several people said, "Dunbar, Dunbar."

Mr. Summers consulted his list. "Clyde Dunbar," he said. "That's right. He's broke his leg, hasn't he? Who's drawing for him?"

"Me, I guess," a woman said, and Mr. Summers turned to look at her. "Wife draws for her husband," Mr. Summers said. "Don't you have a grown boy to do it for you, Janey?" Although Mr. Summers and everyone else in the village knew the answer perfectly well, it was the business of the official of the lottery to ask such questions formally. Mr. Summers waited with an expression of polite interest while Mrs. Dunbar answered.

"Horace's not but sixteen yet," Mrs. Dunbar said regretfully. "Guess I gotta fill in for the old man this year."

"Right," Mr. Summers said. He made a note on the list he was holding.   15 Then he asked, "Watson boy drawing this year?"

A tall boy in the crowd raised his hand. "Here," he said. "I'm drawing for m'mother and me." He blinked his eyes nervously and ducked his head as several voices in the crowd said things like "Good fellow, Jack," and "Glad to see your mother's got a man to do it."

"Well," Mr. Summers said, "guess that's everyone. Old Man Warner make it?"

"Here," a voice said, and Mr. Summers nodded.

A sudden hush fell on the crowd as Mr. Summers cleared his throat and looked at the list. "All ready?" he called. "Now, I'll read the names—heads of families first—and the men come up and take a paper out of the box. Keep the paper folded in your hand without looking at it until everyone has had a turn. Everything clear?"

The people had done it so many times that they only half listened to the directions; most of them were quiet, wetting their lips, not looking around. Then Mr. Summers raised one hand high and said, "Adams." A man disengaged himself from the crowd and came forward. "Hi, Steve," Mr. Summers said, and Mr. Adams said, "Hi, Joe." They grinned at one another humorlessly and nervously. Then Mr. Adams reached into the black box and took out a folded paper. He held it firmly by one corner as he turned and went hastily back to his place in the crowd, where he stood a little apart from his family, not looking down at his hand.

"Allen," Mr. Summers said. "Anderson. . . . Bentham."

"Seems like there's no time at all between lotteries any more," Mrs. Delacroix said to Mrs. Graves in the back row. "Seems like we got through with the last one only last week."

"Time sure goes fast," Mrs. Graves said.

"Clark.. . . Delacroix."

"There goes my old man," Mrs. Delacroix said. She held her breath while her husband went forward.

"Dunbar," Mr. Summers said, and Mrs. Dunbar went steadily to the box while one of the women said, "Go on, Janey," and another said, "There she goes."

"We're next," Mrs. Graves said. She watched while Mr. Graves came around from the side of the box, greeted Mr. Summers gravely, and selected a slip of paper from the box. By now, all through the crowd there were men holding the small folded papers in their large hands, turning them over and over nervously. Mrs. Dunbar and her two sons stood together, Mrs. Dunbar holding the slip of paper.

"Harburt.. . . Hutchinson."

"Get up there, Bill," Mrs. Hutchinson said, and the people near her laughed.

"Jones."

"They do say," Mrs. Adams said to Old Man Warner, who stood next to him, "that over in the north village they're talking of giving up the lottery."

Old Man Warner snorted. "Pack of crazy fools," he said. "Listening to the young folks, nothing's good enough for *them*. Next thing you know, they'll be wanting to go back to living in caves, nobody work any more, live *that* way for a while. Used to be a saying about 'Lottery in June, corn be heavy soon.' First thing you know, we'd all be eating stewed chickweed and acorns. There's *always* been a lottery," he added petulantly. "Bad enough to see young Joe Summers up there joking with everybody."

"Some places have already quit lotteries," Mrs. Adams said.

"Nothing but trouble in *that*," Old Man Warner said stoutly. "Pack of young fools."

"Martin." And Bobby Martin watched his father go forward. "Overdyke 35
. . . Percy."

"I wish they'd hurry," Mrs. Dunbar said to her older son. "I wish they'd
hurry."

"They're almost through," her son said.

"You get ready to run tell Dad," Mrs. Dunbar said.

Mr. Summers called his own name and then stepped forward precisely
and selected a slip from the box. Then he called, "Warner."

"Seventy-seventh year I been in the lottery," Old Man Warner said as he 40
went through the crowd. "Seventy-seventh time."

"Watson." The tall boy came awkwardly through the crowd. Someone
said, "Don't be nervous, Jack," and Mr. Summers said, "Take your time, son."

"Zanini."

After that, there was a long pause, a breathless pause, until Mr. Summers,
holding his slip of paper in the air, said, "All right, fellows." For a minute,
no one moved, and then all the slips of paper were opened. Suddenly, all
the women began to speak at once, saying, "Who is it?," "Who's got it?," "Is
it the Dunbars?," "Is it the Watsons?" Then the voices began to say, "It's
Hutchinson. It's Bill," "Bill Hutchinson's got it."

"Go tell your father," Mrs. Dunbar said to her older son.

People began to look around to see the Hutchinsons. Bill Hutchinson 45
was standing quiet staring down at the paper in his hand. Suddenly, Tessie
Hutchinson shouted to Mr. Summers, "You didn't give him time enough to
take any paper he wanted. I saw you. It wasn't fair."

"Be a good sport, Tessie," Mrs. Delacroix called, and Mrs. Graves said,
"All of us took the same chance."

"Shut up, Tessie," Bill Hutchinson said.

"Well, everyone," Mr. Summers said, "that was done pretty fast, and now
we've got to be hurrying a little more to get done in time." He consulted his
next list. "Bill," he said, "you draw for the Hutchinson family. You got any
other households in the Hutchinsons?"

"There's Don and Eva," Mrs. Hutchinson yelled. "Make *them* take their
chance!"

"Daughters draw for their husbands' families, Tessie," Mr. Summers said 50
gently. "You know that as well as anyone else."

"It wasn't *fair*," Tessie said.

"I guess not, Joe," Bill Hutchinson said regretfully. "My daughter draws
with her husband's family, that's only fair. And I've got no other family except the kids."

"Then, as far as drawing for families is concerned, it's you," Mr. Summers
said in explanation, "and as far as drawing for households is concerned,
that's you, too. Right?"

"Right," Bill Hutchinson said.

"How many kids, Bill?" Mr. Summers asked formally.   55

"Three," Bill Hutchinson said. "There's Bill, Jr., and Nancy, and little Dave.
And Tessie and me."

"All right, then," Mr. Summers said. "Harry, you got their tickets back?"

Mr. Graves nodded and held up the slips of paper. "Put them in the box, then," Mr. Summers directed. "Take Bill's and put it in."

"I think we ought to start over," Mrs. Hutchinson said, as quietly as she could, "I tell you it wasn't *fair.* You didn't give him time enough to choose. *Every*body saw that."

Mr. Graves had selected the five slips and put them in the box, and he   60
dropped all the papers but those onto the ground, where the breeze caught them and lifted them off.

"Listen, everybody," Mrs. Hutchinson was saying to the people around her.

"Ready, Bill?" Mr. Summers asked, and Bill Hutchinson, with one quick glance around at his wife and children, nodded.

"Remember," Mr. Summers said, "take the slips and keep them folded until each person has taken one. Harry, you help little Dave." Mr. Graves took the hand of the little boy, who came willingly with him up to the box. "Take a paper out of the box, Davy," Mr. Summers said. Davy put his hand into the box and laughed. "Take just *one* paper," Mr. Summers said. "Harry, you hold it for him." Mr. Graves took the child's hand and removed the folded paper from the tight fist and held it while little Dave stood next to him and looked up at him wonderingly.

"Nancy next," Mr. Summers said. Nancy was twelve, and her school friends breathed heavily as she went forward, switching her skirt, and took a slip daintily from the box. "Bill, Jr.," Mr. Summers said, and Billy, his face red and his feet over-large, nearly knocked the box over as he got a paper out. "Tessie," Mr. Summers said. She hesitated for a minute, looking around defiantly, and then set her lips and went up to the box. She snatched a paper out and held it behind her.

"Bill," Mr. Summers said, and Bill Hutchinson reached into the box and   65
felt around, bringing his hand out at last with the slip of paper in it.

The crowd was quiet. A girl whispered, "I hope it's not Nancy," and the sound of the whisper reached the edges of the crowd.

"It's not the way it used to be," Old Man Warner said clearly. "People ain't the way they used to be."

"All right," Mr. Summers said. "Open the papers. Harry, you open little Dave's."

Mr. Graves opened the slip of paper and there was a general sigh through the crowd as he held it up and everyone could see that it was blank. Nancy and Bill, Jr. opened theirs at the same time, and both beamed and laughed, turning around to the crowd and holding their slips of paper above their heads.

"Tessie," Mr. Summers said. There was a pause, and then Mr. Summers   70
looked at Bill Hutchinson, and Bill unfolded his paper and showed it. It was blank.

"It's Tessie," Mr. Summers said, and his voice was hushed. "Show us her paper, Bill."

Bill Hutchinson went over to his wife and forced the slip of paper out of her hand. It had a black spot on it, the black spot Mr. Summers had made the night before with the heavy pencil in the coal-company office. Bill Hutchinson held it up, and there was a stir in the crowd.

"All right, folks," Mr. Summers said. "Let's finish quickly."

Although the villagers had forgotten the ritual and lost the original black box, they still remembered to use stones. The pile of stones the boys had made earlier was ready; there were stones on the ground with the blowing scraps of paper that had come out of the box. Mrs. Delacroix selected a stone so large she had to pick it up with both hands and turned to Mrs. Dunbar. "Come on," she said. "Hurry up."

Mrs. Dunbar had small stones in both hands, and she said, gasping for 75 breath, "I can't run at all. You'll have to go ahead and I'll catch up with you."

The children had stones already, and someone gave little Davy Hutchinson a few pebbles.

Tessie Hutchinson was in the center of a cleared space by now, and she held her hands out desperately as the villagers moved in on her. "It isn't fair," she said. A stone hit her on the side of the head.

Old Man Warner was saying, "Come on, come on, everyone." Steve Adams was in the front of the crowd of villagers, with Mrs. Graves beside him.

"It isn't fair, it isn't right," Mrs. Hutchinson screamed, and then they were upon her.

The Receptive Reader

1. The story is told in straightforward *chronological* fashion. As you read along, do you feel nevertheless that essential information is missing? What is being withheld and why? Why does the author tell the story the way she does?

2. Why do you think the author goes into such detail about the procedure, the preparations, the box used and its history? What details stand out?

3. How did you expect the story to come out? When were you sure of the outcome? Does the author provide any *foreshadowing* or early hints of what is to come?

4. *Tradition* becomes a key force in this story. What role does it play in the story as a whole? What is its influence, its power? Who speaks up for it? Does anyone question it?

5. Jackson is a master of *irony*—of contradictions between what we might innocently expect and what happens in grim reality. What is ironic about the organizer, Mr. Summers—his other activities, his behavior during the ritual? Is there any humor in the way the author portrays him, and if so, what kind?

6. How does the author lead up the *climactic* event? How does she first introduce the victim, and why? Why do you think the author puts in a second drawing—somewhat like a run-off election?

7. This story is often read as a study in mass psychology. What are the reactions of the crowd as the story approaches its climactic ending? Do they provide a comment on or insights into mob psychology?

8. How does the victim react? Is she right when she says the drawing was not fair? What are your feelings as you watch her reaction?

9. Where are you in this story? Do you identify with the victims? the instigators? the bystanders? Or do you stay aloof, like an observer from a distant planet? (How do your reactions compare with those of your classmates?)

The Personal Response

Do you object to or resent the story? How do you explain the reactions of hostile readers? Does our society today have similar rituals? Can you think of any parallel situation from your own observation, experience, reading, or viewing?

The Range of Interpretation

The following passage is from Lenemaja Friedman's book *Shirley Jackson* (1975). What evidence from the story would you cite when supporting or taking issue with her view?

> Jackson views man's nature as basically evil, and she indicates that, in his relationship with his fellow beings, man does not hesitate to lie, cheat, and steal—even to kill when it suits his purposes to do so. As in "The Lottery," he may be persuaded that the evil committed is for the common good; but he nevertheless has the herd instinct and does not oppose the harmful mores of his community. And, sadly enough, man does not improve with age; the grandmothers are as guilty of hypocrisy and wrongdoing as the younger members of society.

The Creative Dimension

Have you ever felt unsatisfied at the end of a story? Have you felt unwilling to let the matter rest where the author concluded the story? Or have you felt the need for a modern update? Use your imagination—write a sequel or update to a story you have read. Study the following update as an example. How well does it get into the spirit of the original?

Winning the Lottery

Over the years, many of the old buildings have been torn down to make room for Seven Elevens and a large SUPER-mart with a cafeteria. Young women come in for the latest cosmetic or fashion magazine. There's even an aisle for the devout; it has Bibles and plastic Virgins that customers can attach to the dashboards of their cars. People are remodeling, improving, and accessorizing their homes, their bodies, and their televisions. The annual lottery has been moved to the large SUPER-mart parking lot. This year, it's—Mr. Stanfield! He was a pretty good man, and he watched television regularly too. The crowd moves to his home and dismantles it piece by piece. Pictures of his family are distributed, clothing passed around, and patterned dishes lovingly packed in bubble wrap. He wanders slowly down the road, past the store where he used to rent movies and the station where he used to put gas in his car. He ambles slowly in the single pair of sneakers he was allowed to keep; of course it's taboo for anyone to give him a ride. He dejectedly holds on to a hand-lettered sign that says he'll work for food, but he knows it's against the rules for anyone to help him. Every morning he leaves the old cardboard that's his cover during the nights under the overpass and stands in line at the Bureau with the other lottery winners of years past. The lone window opens for a short span at ten. The person working the window tells the waiting line of winners that the forms they need to get sustenance stamps were delayed at the printers but that they can expect them any day.

William Faulkner   *(1897–1962)*   👁

INTERVIEWER: Some people say they can't under-stand your writing, even after they read it two or three times. What approach would you suggest to them?

FAULKNER: Read it four times.

William Faulkner was one of the great experimenters in early-twentieth-century fiction. In spite of many-layered sentences that sprawl across paragraph breaks and in spite of the broken-mirror effects of his narrative technique, he became one of the most widely read, translated, and discussed writers of modern times. His best-known novels—*As I Lay Dying* (1931), *Sanctuary* (1931), *Absalom! Absalom!* (1936), *Intruder in the Dust* (1948), *Requiem for a Nun* (1951)—have been read around the world. His first major critical success, *The Sound and the Fury* (1929), told the story of the same events as seen in turn by four different characters. He made readers look at characters and events as though seen through the different facets of a prism, with his readers left to form their own perception of the underlying story.

Faulkner's fiction takes us to a setting rich in the memories and traumas of the Old South. Many of his stories and novels were part of an ongoing saga of the people of his fictitious Yoknapatawpha County, modeled on Lafayette County in northern Mississippi, where he lived in Oxford, home of the University of Mississippi. As a child, Faulkner lived with a kindly but determined Scottish great-grandfather who made each child in the house recite a memorized Bible verse before breakfast. Faulkner served briefly in the Royal Canadian Flying Corps in World War I and lived in New Orleans for a time, working for a newspaper and trying to make a living as a writer. He returned to Mississippi in 1926 and eventually became a writer in residence at the university. He received the Nobel Prize for literature in 1950 and gave a much-reprinted acceptance speech in which he spoke of "the writer's duty" to champion personal values in an age of mass culture.

Faulkner's characters are often embittered by seeing their values threatened in an uprooted modern world. They are often country people trying to live "off here to themselves"—to keep their distance from a new world of neon lights, easy quick money, and shiny automobiles traded in for a new model before the old one is paid for. Often the characters in his stories are fiercely, stubbornly independent—a thorn in the side to state officials, tax collectors, and government agents trying to "interfere with how a man farmed his own land, raised his own cotton."

At the same time, Faulkner's characters are often caught in the traditional class structure of the South. His own great-grandfather had become wealthy and famous in the Mississippi of before the Civil War. He became a colonel in the Confederate army and was killed years later in a duel. Many of Faulkner's characters belong to clans—the Sartoris, the Compsons, the Sutpens, the McCaslins—that represent the old social aristocracy of the South, often still living in the antebellum, prewar mansions with their columned porticoes. However, often the offspring of the old families are beset by debts and social upstarts, such as Flem Snopes, one of the "litter" of a family of poor white tenant farmers—pushy, unscrupulous, advancing his fortunes with dubious money-making schemes. And always, there are the black people of the Old South—often as observers, but at other times caught up in the whirlpool of racial hatred and bigotry.

Faulkner broke up traditional plot structure. He told his stories in indirect, or oblique, ways, forcing us to puzzle out what is happening (the way we are often forced to in real life). He frequently uses **flashbacks**, in which glimpses of the past slowly begin to explain or illuminate the present. The stories often lead up to a **climax**—a climactic event or revelation.

A Rose for Emily   *1931*

I

When Miss Emily Grierson died, our whole town went to her funeral: the men through a sort of respectful affection for a fallen monument, the women mostly out of curiosity to see the inside of her house, which no one save an old manservant—a combined gardener and cook—had seen in at least ten years.

It was a big, squarish frame house that had once been white, decorated with cupolas and spires and scrolled balconies in the heavily lightsome style of the seventies, set on what had once been our most select street. But garages and cotton gins had encroached and obliterated even the august names of that neighborhood; only Miss Emily's house was left, lifting its stubborn and coquettish decay above the cotton wagons and the gasoline pumps—an eyesore among eyesores. And now Miss Emily had gone to join the representatives of those august names where they lay in the cedar-bemused cemetery among the ranked and anonymous graves of Union and Confederate soldiers who fell at the battle of Jefferson.

Alive, Miss Emily had been a tradition, a duty, and a care; a sort of hereditary obligation upon the town, dating from that day in 1894 when Colonel Sartoris, the mayor—he who fathered the edict that no Negro woman should appear on the streets without an apron—remitted her taxes, the dispensa-tion dating from the death of her father on into perpetuity. Not that Miss Emily would have accepted charity. Colonel Sartoris invented an involved tale to the effect that Miss Emily's father had loaned money to the town, which the town, as a matter of business, preferred this way of repaying. Only a man of Colonel Sartoris' generation and thought could have invented it, and only a woman could have believed it.

When the next generation, with its more modern ideas, became mayors and aldermen, this arrangement created some little dissatisfaction. On the first of the year they mailed her a tax notice. February came, and there was no reply. They wrote her a formal letter, asking her to call at the sheriff's of-fice at her convenience. A week later the mayor wrote her himself, offering to call or to send his car for her, and received in reply a note on paper of an archaic shape, in a thin, flowing calligraphy in faded ink, to the effect that she no longer went out at all. The tax notice was also enclosed, with-out comment.

They called a special meeting of the Board of Aldermen. A deputation   5
waited upon her, knocked at the door through which no visitor had passed since she ceased giving china-painting lessons eight or ten years earlier. They were admitted by the old Negro into a dim hall from which a stairway mounted into still more shadow. It smelled of dust and disuse—a close, dank smell. The Negro led them into the parlor. It was furnished in heavy, leather-covered furniture. When the Negro opened the blinds of one win-dow, they could see that the leather was cracked; and when they sat down, a faint dust rose sluggishly about their thighs, spinning with slow motes in the single sun-ray. On a tarnished gilt easel before the fireplace stood a crayon portrait of Miss Emily's father.

They rose when she entered—a small, fat woman in black, with a thin gold chain descending to her waist and vanishing into her belt, leaning on an ebony cane with a tarnished gold head. Her skeleton was small and spare; perhaps that was why what would have been merely plumpness in another was obesity in her. She looked bloated, like a body long submerged in motionless water, and of that pallid hue. Her eyes, lost in the fatty ridges of her face, looked like two small pieces of coal pressed into a lump of dough as they moved from one face to another while the visitors stated their errand.

She did not ask them to sit. She just stood in the door and listened qui-etly until the spokesman came to a stumbling halt. Then they could hear the invisible watch ticking at the end of the gold chain.

Her voice was dry and cold. "I have no taxes in Jefferson. Colonel Sar-toris explained it to me. Perhaps one of you can gain access to the city records and satisfy yourselves."

"But we have. We are the city authorities, Miss Emily. Didn't you get a notice from the sheriff, signed by him?"

"I received a paper, yes," Miss Emily said. "Perhaps he considers himself   10
the sheriff. . . . I have no taxes in Jefferson."

"But there is nothing on the books to show that, you see. We must go by the—"

"See Colonel Sartoris. I have no taxes in Jefferson."

"But, Miss Emily—"

"See Colonel Sartoris." (Colonel Sartoris had been dead almost ten years.) "I have no taxes in Jefferson. Tobe!" The Negro appeared. "Show these gentlemen out."

II

So she vanquished them, horse and foot, just as she had vanquished their   15 fathers thirty years before about the smell. That was two years after her father's death and a short time after her sweetheart—the one we believed would marry her—had deserted her. After her father's death she went out very little; after her sweetheart went away, people hardly saw her at all. A few of the ladies had the temerity to call, but were not received, and the only sign of life about the place was the Negro man—a young man then— going in and out with a market basket.

"Just as if a man—any man—could keep a kitchen properly," the ladies said; so they were not surprised when the smell developed. It was another link between the gross, teeming world and the high and mighty Griersons.

A neighbor, a woman, complained to the mayor, Judge Stevens, eighty years old.

"But what will you have me do about it, madam?" he said.

"Why, send her word to stop it," the woman said. "Isn't there a law?"

"I'm sure that won't be necessary," Judge Stevens said. "It's probably   20 just a snake or a rat that nigger of hers killed in the yard. I'll speak to him about it."

The next day he received two more complaints, one from a man who came in diffident deprecation. "We really must do something about it, Judge. I'd be the last one in the world to bother Miss Emily, but we've got to do something." That night the Board of Aldermen met—three graybeards and one younger man, a member of the rising generation.

"It's simple enough," he said. "Send her word to have her place cleaned up. Give her a certain time to do it in, and if she don't . . . "

"Dammit, sir," Judge Stevens said, "will you accuse a lady to her face of smelling bad?"

So the next night, after midnight, four men crossed Miss Emily's lawn and slunk about the house like burglars, sniffing along the base of the brickwork and at the cellar openings while one of them performed a regular sowing motion with his hand out of a sack slung from his shoulder. They broke open the cellar door and sprinkled lime there, and in all the outbuildings. As they recrossed the lawn, a window that had been dark was lighted and Miss Emily sat in it, the light behind her, and her upright torso motionless as that of an idol. They crept quietly across the lawn and into the shadow of the locusts that lined the street. After a week or two the smell went away.

That was when people had begun to feel really sorry for her. People in   25 our town, remembering how old lady Wyatt, her great-aunt, had gone completely crazy at last, believed that the Griersons held themselves a little too high for what they really were. None of the young men were quite good enough for Miss Emily and such. We had long thought of them as a tableau, Miss Emily a slender figure in white in the background, her father a spraddled silhouette in the foreground, his back to her and clutching a horsewhip, the two of them framed by the back-flung front door. So when she got to be thirty and was still single, we were not pleased exactly, but vindicated; even with insanity in the family she wouldn't have turned down all of her chances if they had really materialized.

When her father died, it got about that the house was all that was left to her; and in a way, people were glad. At last they could pity Miss Emily. Being left alone, and a pauper, she had become humanized. Now she too would know the old thrill and the old despair of a penny more or less.

The day after his death all the ladies prepared to call at the house and offer condolence and aid, as is our custom. Miss Emily met them at the door, dressed as usual and with no trace of grief on her face. She told them that her father was not dead. She did that for three days, with the ministers calling on her, and the doctors, trying to persuade her to let them dispose of the body. Just as they were about to resort to law and force, she broke down, and they buried her father quickly.

We did not say she was crazy then. We believed she had to do that. We remembered all the young men her father had driven away, and we knew that with nothing left, she would have to cling to that which had robbed her, as people will.

III

She was sick for a long time. When we saw her again, her hair was cut short, making her look like a girl, with a vague resemblance to those angels in colored church windows—sort of tragic and serene.

The town had just let the contracts for paving the sidewalks, and in the summer after her father's death they began the work. The construction company came with niggers and mules and machinery, and a foreman named Homer Barron, a Yankee—a big, dark, ready man, with a big voice and eyes lighter than his face. The little boys would follow in groups to hear him cuss the niggers, and the niggers singing in time to the rise and fall of picks. Pretty soon he knew everybody in town. Whenever you heard a lot of laughing anywhere about the square, Homer Barron would be in the center of the group. Presently we began to see him and Miss Emily on Sunday afternoons driving in the yellow-wheeled buggy and the matched team of bays from the livery stable.

At first we were glad that Miss Emily would have an interest, because the ladies all said, "Of course a Grierson would not think seriously of a Northerner, a day laborer." But there were still others, older people, who said that even grief could not cause a real lady to forget *noblesse oblige*—without calling it *noblesse oblige*. They just said, "Poor Emily. Her kinsfolk should come to her." She had some kin in Alabama; but years ago her father had fallen out with them over the estate of old lady Wyatt, the crazy woman, and there was no communication between the two families. They had not even been represented at the funeral.

30

And as soon as the old people said, "Poor Emily," the whispering began. "Do you suppose it's really so?" they said to one another. "Of course it is. What else could . . . " This behind their hands; rustling of craned silk and satin behind jalousies closed upon the sun of Sunday afternoon as the thin, swift clop-clop-clop of the matched team passed: "Poor Emily."

She carried her head high enough—even when we believed that she was fallen. It was as if she demanded more than ever the recognition of her dignity as the last Grierson; as if it had wanted that touch of earthiness to reaffirm her imperviousness. Like when she bought the rat poison, the arsenic. That was over a year after they had begun to say "Poor Emily," and while the two female cousins were visiting her.

"I want some poison," she said to the druggist. She was over thirty then, still a slight woman, though thinner than usual, with cold, haughty black eyes in a face the flesh of which was strained across the temples and about the eyesockets as you imagine a lighthouse-keeper's face ought to look. "I want some poison," she said.

"Yes, Miss Emily. What kind? For rats and such? I'd recom—"   35

"I want the best you have. I don't care what kind."

The druggist named several. "They'll kill anything up to an elephant. But what you want is—"

"Arsenic," Miss Emily said. "Is that a good one?"

"Is . . . arsenic? Yes, ma'am. But what you want—"

"I want arsenic."   40

The druggist looked down at her. She looked back at him, erect, her face like a strained flag. "Why, of course," the druggist said. "If that's what you want. But the law requires you to tell what you are going to use it for."

Miss Emily just stared at him, her head tilted back in order to look him eye for eye, until he looked away and went and got the arsenic and wrapped it up. The Negro delivery boy brought her the package; the druggist didn't come back. When she opened the package at home there was written on the box, under the skull and bones: "For rats."

IV

So the next day we all said, "She will kill herself"; and we said it would be the best thing. When she had first begun to be seen with Homer Barron, we had said, "She will marry him." Then we said, "She will persuade him yet," because Homer himself had remarked—he liked men, and it was known that he drank with the younger men in the Elks' Club—that he was not a marrying man. Later we said, "Poor Emily" behind the jalousies as they passed on Sunday afternoon in the glittering buggy, Miss Emily with her head high and Homer Barron with his hat cocked and a cigar in his teeth, reins and whip in a yellow glove.

Then some of the ladies began to say that it was a disgrace to the town and a bad example to the young people. The men did not want to interfere, but at last the ladies forced the Baptist minister—Miss Emily's people were Episcopal—to call upon her. He would never divulge what happened during that interview, but he refused to go back again. The next Sunday they again drove about the streets, and the following day the minister's wife wrote to Miss Emily's relations in Alabama.

So she had blood-kin under her roof again and we sat back to watch de- 45 velopments. At first nothing happened. Then we were sure that they were to be married. We learned that Miss Emily had been to the jeweler's and ordered a man's toilet set in silver, with the letters H.B. on each piece. Two days later we learned that she had bought a complete outfit of men's clothing, including a nightshirt, and we said, "They are married." We were really glad. We were glad because the two female cousins were even more Grierson than Miss Emily had ever been.

So we were not surprised when Homer Barron—the streets had been finished some time since—was gone. We were a little disappointed that there was not a public blowing-off, but we believed that he had gone on to prepare for Miss Emily's coming, or to give her a chance to get rid of the cousins. (By that time it was a cabal, and we were all Miss Emily's allies to help circumvent the cousins.) Sure enough, after another week they departed. And, as we had expected all along, within three days Homer Barron was back in town. A neighbor saw the Negro man admit him at the kitchen door at dusk one evening.

And that was the last we saw of Homer Barron. And of Miss Emily for some time. The Negro man went in and out with the market basket, but the front door remained closed. Now and then we would see her at a window for a moment, as the men did that night when they sprinkled the lime, but for almost six months she did not appear on the streets. Then we knew that this was to be expected too; as if that quality of her father which had thwarted her woman's life so many times had been too virulent and too furious to die.

When we next saw Miss Emily, she had grown fat and her hair was turning gray. During the next few years it grew grayer and grayer until it attained an even pepper-and-salt iron-gray, when it ceased turning. Up to the day of her death at seventy-four it was still that vigorous iron-gray, like the hair of an active man.

From that time on her front door remained closed, save for a period of six or seven years, when she was about forty, during which she gave lessons in china-painting. She fitted up a studio in one of the downstairs rooms, where the daughters and granddaughters of Colonel Sartoris' contemporaries were sent to her with the same regularity and in the same spirit that they were sent on Sundays with a twenty-five-cent piece for the collection plate. Meanwhile her taxes had been remitted.

The newer generation became the backbone and the spirit of the town, 50 and the painting pupils grew up and fell away and did not send their children to her with boxes of color and tedious brushes and pictures cut from the ladies' magazines. The front door closed upon the last one and remained closed for good. When the town got free postal delivery, Miss Emily alone refused to let them fasten the metal numbers above her door and attach a mailbox to it. She would not listen to them.

Daily, monthly, yearly we watched the Negro grow grayer and more stooped, going in and out with the market basket. Each December we sent her a tax notice, which would be returned by the post office a week later, unclaimed. Now and then we would see her in one of the downstairs windows—she had evidently shut up the top floor of the house—like the carven torso of an idol in a niche, looking or not looking at us, we could never tell which. Thus she passed from generation to generation—dear, inescapable, impervious, tranquil, and perverse.

And so she died. Fell ill in the house filled with dust and shadows, with only a doddering Negro man to wait on her. We did not even know she was sick; we had long since given up trying to get any information from the Negro. He talked to no one, probably not even to her, for his voice had grown harsh and rusty, as if from disuse.

She died in one of the downstairs rooms, in a heavy walnut bed with a curtain, her gray head propped on a pillow yellow and moldy with age and lack of sunlight.

V

The Negro met the first of the ladies at the front door and let them in, with their hushed, sibilant voices and their quick, curious glances, and then he disappeared. He walked right through the house and out the back and was not seen again.

The two female cousins came at once. They held the funeral on the second day, with the town coming to look at Miss Emily beneath a mass of bought flowers, with the crayon face of her father musing profoundly above the bier and the ladies sibilant and macabre; and the very old men—some in their brushed Confederate uniforms—on the porch and the lawn, talking of Miss Emily as if she had been a contemporary of theirs, believing that they had danced with her and courted her perhaps, confusing time with its mathematical progression, as the old do, to whom all the past is not a diminishing road, but, instead, a huge meadow which no winter ever quite touches, divided from them now by the narrow bottleneck of the most recent decade of years. 55

Already we knew that there was one room in that region above stairs which no one had seen in forty years, and which would have to be forced. They waited until Miss Emily was decently in the ground before they opened it.

The violence of breaking down the door seemed to fill this room with pervading dust. A thin, acrid pall as of the tomb seemed to lie everywhere upon this room decked and furnished as for a bridal: upon the valance curtains of faded rose color, upon the rose-shaded lights, upon the dressing table, upon the delicate array of crystal and the man's toilet things backed with tarnished silver, silver so tarnished that the monogram was obscured. Among them lay a collar and tie, as if they had just been removed, which, lifted, left upon the surface a pale crescent in the dust. Upon the chair hung the suit, carefully folded; beneath it the two mute shoes and the discarded socks.

The man himself lay in the bed.

For a long while we just stood there, looking down at the profound and fleshless grin. The body had apparently once lain in the attitude of an embrace, but now the long sleep that outlasts love, that conquers even the grimace of love, had cuckolded him. What was left of him, rotted beneath what was left of the nightshirt, had become inextricable from the bed in which he lay; and upon him and upon the pillow beside him lay that even coating of the patient and biding dust.

Then we noticed that in the second pillow was the indentation of a head. 60 One of us lifted something from it, and leaning forward, that faint and invisible dust dry and acrid in the nostrils, we saw a long strand of iron-gray hair.

The Receptive Reader

1. Faulkner said that the seed of this story was a picture in his mind "of the strand of hair on the pillow. . . . Simply a picture of a strand of hair on the pillow in the abandoned house." How does the strand of hair sum up what happened in this story or what is important in this story?

2. How and why does Faulkner's story depart from straightforward chronological storytelling? Where and how does Faulkner introduce the plot elements most essential to your understanding of the story? Can you reconstruct from the author's *flashbacks* a chronological sequence of events?

3. What is the keynote in Faulkner's treatment of the *setting*—Miss Emily's house, her street, the town?

4. How essential to the story is Faulkner's treatment of tradition and the Old South? What is Faulkner's attitude toward Colonel Sartoris' generation and the "next generation with its more modern ideas"? What is the meaning of *noblesse oblige,* and what is the role of this concept in the story?

5. What picture emerges of Miss Emily as the *main character?* Is there a central clue to her personality? Is she a creature of her environment? What explains the attitude of the townspeople toward her?

6. Faulkner is known for a style rich in unusual words, provocative images, and emotional overtones. What is the meaning of *coquettish, macabre, impervious, perverse?* How are these words related to the prevailing mood of the story? What is the effect on the reader of comparing Emily to a "carven torso of an idol in a niche"? What other striking imaginative comparisons play a role in the story?

7. One student wrote: "Time does not pass in linear chronological fashion in this story; the plot does not move forward through the traditional buildup of tension to climax and denouement. However, in its indirect and apparently meandering way, the story leads to a much more startling climax than could have been possible in a classic short-story format." Can you show whether the student was right?

The Personal Response

As you read the story, do you feel you are expected to admire Miss Emily, condemn her, or write her off as an eccentric? What are your feelings about her? Poetic justice is meted out to a character in poetry or fiction when he or she is

<<<Find It on the Web>>>

Millions of readers around the world have read Faulkner's novels and short stories. Much criticism and scholarship continue to be published on topics like his relationship to the Old South, his treatment of African Americans and poor whites, or his defense of values he saw threatened in our modern world. Working alone or with a group you may conduct an Internet search of critical or biographical material showing current concerns and issues in Faulkner scholarship. Which of the following sample items are still available online? Prepare a report with a selected listing of currently available online materials.

Powell, Janice A. "Changing Portraits in 'A Rose for Emily.' " <u>Teaching Faulkner Newsletter</u> 24 Sept. 2001.
<http://www2.semo.edu/cfs/powell.html>

Srikanth, Rajini. "Why I, a Woman of Color from India, Enjoy Teaching William Faulkner." <u>The Mississippi Quarterly</u> 1999. 24 Sept. 2001.
<http://library.northernlight.com/PN19991222010001162.html>

Urgo, Joseph R. Rev. of <u>Reading Faulkner's Best Short Stories</u> and <u>Percyscapes: The Fugue State in Twentieth-Century Southern Fiction</u>. <u>American Literature</u> Mar. 2000. 24 Sept. 2001.
<muse.jhu.edu/journals/american_literature/v072/72.1urgo.html>

Kinney, Arthur F. "Faulkner's Racism." <u>Connotations</u> 1993–1994. 24 Sept. 2001.
<http://www.anglistik.uni.muenster.de/connotations/kinney33.htm>

justly punished for an offense, whether or not it was punishable according to law. Is Homer Barron the victim of poetic justice?

Making Connections—For Discussion or Writing

✘ Compare and contrast the Old South of Faulkner's "A Rose for Emily" with the New South of Mason's "Shiloh." What is the relationship between the setting and the characters in each story?

✘ Compare and contrast plot structure in this story and in a more traditional story like Welty's "A Visit of Charity" or Malamud's "The Magic Barrel." How do differences in the story line affect the overall impact of each story?

✘ Compare and contrast Jackson's "The Lottery" and Faulkner's "A Rose for Emily" as modern horror stories. How does their use of horror differ from its use in popular entertainment? What use do the two authors make of the grotesque—a mixture of terror and dark humor?

WRITING ABOUT LITERATURE

4 Charting the Plot
WRITING FOCUS: Revising and Rethinking

The Writing Workshop   In writing about a story, you will often focus on how the parts serve the story as a whole. In writing about plot, do not just retell the story. Ask yourself: What am I going to do with this story? In the sequence of miscellaneous events, try to find a ground plan. Look for the pattern—the design in the carpet. (When you start writing in the "and-then," "and-then" mode, your paper is likely to be in trouble.) Consider guidelines like the following:

❚ *Avoid mere plot summaries.* Use them only if they are needed to help the readers find their bearings. Summaries can be useful for giving an initial overview—they can make the reader see the overall line of development in a complex or multilayered story.

❚ *Look at what sets a story in motion.* Look at key characters and their unmet needs, unfulfilled desires, or hidden agendas. Look at a situation that has in it potential sources of conflict: festering resentments, fatal misunderstandings.

❚ *Identify major stages.* Make sure your readers get a sense of the overall development of the story. Highlight turning points. Show how a story builds to a climactic event. Show how a conflict plays itself out and reaches a resolution.

❚ *Disentangle major threads.* Look for **polarities**—the possible play of polar opposites, such as the romantic and the realistic strands in Malamud's "The Magic Barrel."

❚ *Look for features that reinforce the overall pattern.* Look for examples of **foreshadowing**—for early hints of what is to come. Look for **recurrence** of key elements, for passages that echo earlier issues or concerns.

❚ *Take a second look at apparent detours or digressions.* See if you can relate apparently minor details to the larger pattern.

Instructor's Comments and Revision   Much revision of student writing used to be little more than retyping with a few cosmetic touches. With the coming of computers, changes in a previous draft have become much easier to make. Take seriously editorial suggestions that ask you to do some real rewriting, some real rethinking.

Learn to respond to feedback from an instructor or editor as you revise a first draft. Study the samples of instructors' comments in the material that follows. Look at rewrites of passages in response to an instructor's comments.

✘ *Pay special attention to comments on your opening paragraphs.* Does the focus of your paper become clear enough? Does your reader get a preview of your overall approach? Should you spell out your main point or thesis more fully or more clearly early in your paper? (Remember that in real life many readers don't go on beyond the opening of an essay if they find it unfocused, murky, or confusing.)

✘ *Respond to suggestions for strengthening your overall plan.* Consider if reshuffling material might make for a stronger progression—for instance, moving from the fairly obvious to the controversial or new.

✘ *Respond to advice for improving the flow of material.* Respond to suggestions for building up a rich texture of comment, quotation, and interpretation.

ORIGINAL: After his first meeting with Salzman, the strange little matchmaker, Leo expresses doubts about the wisdom of having a bride chosen by someone else. Malamud writes,

Leo was in low spirits. . . . He explained it as arising from Salzman's failure to produce a suitable bride for him. He did not care for his type of clientele. But when Leo found himself hesitating over whether to seek out another matchmaker, one more polished than Pinye, he wondered if it could be—his protestations to the contrary, and although he honored his father and mother—that he did not, in essence, care for the matchmaking institution? This thought he quickly put out of his mind.

COMMENT: You are probably using too many block quotations ("chunk quotations"—because they can make your paper seem chunky or lumpy). Save them to clinch an argument or highlight a major turning point. Try to work short, apt quotations into the flow of your argument.

REVISED: The first meeting with Salzman, the strange little matchmaker, does not go well. Leo is disheartened and expresses doubts about the wisdom of having a bride chosen by someone else. He entertains notions of hiring another matchmaker, someone "more polished than Pinye." But when Leo examines his deeper feelings, he wonders "if it could be—his protestations to the contrary, and although he honored his father and mother—that he did not, in essence, care for the matchmaking institution?" Although Leo has not yet realized it, this question is the beginning of the conflict between his traditional upbringing and his romantic nature. Although he "quickly put this thought out of his mind," it has planted a niggling suspicion that reaches full bloom as the story progresses.

✘ *Pay special attention to comments on weak transitions.* Where did the reader fail to see a logical connection that you thought was there? Be sure to respond to questions like "Why is this in here at this point?

How are these two sections of your paper *related?* How does this fit into your overall plan?"

▮ *Respond to suggestions for strengthening your conclusion.*

ORIGINAL: . . . Jackson's "The Lottery" showed how people will do all kinds of crazy things, even things they don't really want to do, in the name of tradition.

COMMENT: Perfunctory or lame conclusion? What is the force of tradition? Why does it seem to carry such weight?

REVISED: . . . Jackson's "The Lottery" shows how tradition is like a subliminal force—because of it, people will do all kinds of crazy things, even things they don't really want to. We witness the peer pressure involved in tradition, forcing people to do something just because everyone else is doing it, and no one else is questioning it. As the story shows, human beings have a strong need to belong and be accepted by their society. This need causes them to want to conform, blindly and almost unconsciously, to the rules that their society has set up. Even stronger than tradition itself are the peer pressure and the human need for acceptance that fuels it.

Study the following sample student paper. Does it make you more conscious of the role of plot in giving shape to a story as a whole?

Sample Student Paper

Magic and Reality

"The Magic Barrel." In its very title, Bernard Malamud hints at the paradoxical nature of his short story. "The Magic Barrel" prepares us, the readers, to expect a fairy tale; it asks us to enter imaginatively into a world where miracles are possible. On the other hand, "The Magic Barrel" also gives us pause. "The Magic Barrel?" A rounded wooden vessel used to store wine or fish, magical? Had Malamud chosen "The Magic Well" or "The Magic Chalice" as his title, we would have been less puzzled, less intrigued. Adept at creating dualities and contrasts, Malamud invests his plot with "magic" elements as well as with sobering, realistic ones, just as he does his title. Malamud's plot introduces us to the lonely young scholar and the eccentric, enigmatic matchmaker, both likely inhabitants of a fairy-tale world. However, it also reveals conditions all too familiar to many in their everyday reality: the desperate lovelessness of the scholar and the harsh poverty of the matchmaker. As the plot is unveiled, Bernard Malamud's story is both like and unlike a fairy tale, ultimately a story in which fantasy and reality blend.

As "The Magic Barrel" begins, we are introduced to a person who is well suited to the world of the fairy tale: Leo Finkle, a rabbinical student, lives in a room which is "small, almost meager . . . though crowded with books." Leo has been studying for six years and is about to be ordained. From the first words of the story, Leo appears to be the stereotypical poor, lonely scholar, possessing little in the way of worldly goods but rich in spirituality, a kind of inner prosperity. We would wish a devoted companion for such a worthy, lonely fellow, and we are not disappointed. Leo, the author tells us, has decided to enlist the services of Pinye Salzman, a professional matchmaker, or "commercial cupid" as Malamud calls him. Malamud prepares the reader for a traditional romantic story, and he does not disappoint. The plot follows Leo as he listens without satisfaction to the descriptions of Salzman's clients, and as he meets, without enthusiasm, one of the eligible women. It follows Leo after he decides he must have romantic love before marriage, and after he finds a small, displaced photograph in an envelope of snapshots loaned to him by Salzman to help him in his quest. In true romantic style, Leo chases around the city attempting to locate the matchmaker (and so the woman) as frantically as Prince Charming's courtiers tried to locate the owner of the lone glass slipper. In true romantic style, Leo finds he has fallen for the one woman he should not have, Stella, the "shameless" daughter Salzman considers dead, a woman whose picture found its way into the matchmaker's envelope only by mistake (a marvelous, unlikely coincidence). In true romantic style, Leo pursues her anyway, and, with the power of wishful thinking triumphing over probability fairy-tale style, he finds her. Leo's discovery of his need for romantic love and the actions he takes to fulfill that need are suited to the world of fairy tales.

However, Malamud's plot not only explores the romantic occurrences in Leo's life, it also explores the more mundane, realistic ones. If Leo is not Prince Charming, he is at least a close relative. He is, however, also very human. The plot takes him through experiences that belong in the potentially painful real world rather than in the fairy-tale world. Leo has been studying diligently to become a rabbi for six years, but we also learn that his motives were not particularly admirable. "I think," Leo confesses to Lily Hirschorn, startling himself as much as the reader, "that I came to God not because I love Him, but because I did not." After this revelation, Leo experiences the worst week of his life. "With shocking force," he realizes that apart from his parents, he had never loved anyone. "It seemed to Leo that his whole life stood starkly revealed and he saw himself, for the first time, as he truly was—unloved and loveless." This young student stops eating and begins to lose weight. As his health suffers, he stops attending class. Malamud eventually allows Leo to "regain his composure," but this section of the plot takes the student about as far down as a human can go. The romantic events in Leo's life may predominate in the story, but they do not create an unrealistic story. Leo earns his romance the hardest way possible.

Malamud's most ambiguous scene occurs at the end of "The Magic Barrel." On one hand, it is the most romantic moment. On the other, it is curious and ambiguous. In this scene, after he has extracted some cooperation from Salzman, Leo succeeds in meeting Stella, the love of his life. She seems a bit wild, but not in an incorrigible way. She stands by a lamppost, smoking, but she waits "uneasily and shyly," her eyes filled with "desperate innocence." Experiencing "violins and lit candles" revolving in the sky, Leo rushes toward her, a bouquet of flowers outstretched in his hands. This moment, the most romantic in the story, is love found. However, its ambiguity lies in Salzman's presence and actions. The matchmaker stands "around the corner . . . leaning against a wall," chanting "prayers for the dead." Salzman could be blessing the union in the only way he knows how while steadfastly opposing Stella's earlier lifestyle, thus contributing to a romantic ending. Conversely, he could be offering his last prayers to a daughter whom he is deserting. He could be saying a farewell to one who he thinks is making her biggest and final error in an already "wicked" life, contributing to a modern, realistic ending. Malamud's plot follows the fairy-tale romantic events in Leo's life as well as the soberingly realistic ones. In his ambiguous ending, the author illustrates both views in one stroke.

Bernard Malamud's "The Magic Barrel" navigates between fantasy and reality. Some of Leo's acts, such as finding the woman of his dreams in a displaced photograph, desperately searching for her, then finding her, are very romantic, befitting a fairy tale. Other events in Leo's life, such as his realization that he is "unloved and loveless" and his ensuing crisis, belong in the realm of reality, not the fairy tale. In choosing to craft his plot to encompass both realms, Malamud creates a story that satisfies both the romantic and the pragmatist in us, the readers. He reminds us that fairy tales were created by real people; they are based on real life, not separate from it. Romantic happenings and happy endings can be and should be a part of everyday reality.

Questions for Peer Review

How successfully does this student paper take you into the world of Malamud's storytelling? Does it help you follow the story line? Compare your answers to the following questions with those of fellow students or members of a small group.

1. How does the word *paradoxical* sum up the student writer's major point about the story? How and where does the student writer for you best spell out the two sides of the paradox? Is this the kind of paradox that begins to make sense on second thought? Why, or why not?

2. The student writer devotes a long paragraph to the "romantic" *fairy tale* element that to him predominates in much of the story. What "stereotypical" fairy tale elements does the student writer trace? Are they all what you would expect, or are any surprising or thought provoking? How many phrases in the paragraph echo and reinforce the idea of fairy tale and "wishful thinking"— keeping the reader "on track"?

3. Where is the turning point in this paper from the romantic to the *anti-romantic* side of the story? At the end of a long paragraph, the student writer says, "this section of the plot takes the student about as far down as a human can go. . . . Leo earns his romance the hardest way possible." How does the paragraph build up to this statement? What details and quotations from the story does the writer trace to show the "mundane, realistic" side of the story? (What does the word *mundane* mean?)

4. How well does the student writer trace the role of Salzman and other supporting characters in the story line? (How is Salzman a "commercial cupid"?)

5. For you, does the *conclusion* merely repeat what the student writer said earlier? Or does it add to or drive home the basic point? (What is a *pragmatist?*)

6. Does this paper add something to your understanding of the story? Does it change your personal response to the story? Why, or why not?

7. Is the world of fairy tale and wishful thinking dead in today's realistic and often cynical world? How would you sum up the student writer's answer to this question? How would you sum up your own answer?

5 POINT OF VIEW

Windows on the World

Courtesy Richard B. Ressman

*The deepest quality of a work of art will always
be the quality of the mind of the producer.*

HENRY JAMES

*The effect of compactness and instantaneity
sought in the short story is attained mainly by the
observance of two "unities"—the old traditional
one of time, and that other, more modern and
complex, which requires that any rapidly
enacted episode shall be seen through only one
pair of eyes.*

EDITH WHARTON

*The author is the central intelligence through
whose eyes and mind we see the story.*

MARTHA COX

FOCUS ON POINT OF VIEW

When reading a short story, we look at the world through the eyes of the writer. Whatever reality the story creates for us is a selection. We attend to what the author has brought into focus; we look at it from his or her angle of vision. No objective reality exists "out there" that is the same for everyone. What we call reality is our *perception* of reality—a picture we have constructed in our minds from input that is biased or incomplete. We read a story in part to share imaginatively in a writer's perception of reality. We share in a writer's vision of the world.

Much modern fiction takes this awareness of the angle of vision a step further. Apart from the author who is writing the story, who is telling the story *in the story?* Who is the **narrator** observing the events—observing them from what angle? In much nineteenth-century fiction, the author could pretend to be God—to know everything. The all-knowing author seemed to be able to read the minds of all the different characters in a story, to be in several places at once to observe dispersed events. But this all-knowingness is not the way we take in reality in our own lives. We perceive reality according to our limited lights. We try to piece together the truth from partial and contradictory information.

Much modern fiction opts for a **limited** point of view. In Faulkner's "A Rose for Emily," we know of Miss Emily only what the townspeople had a chance to observe. We share in what they had the opportunity to hear and to suspect. In a modern story, we are often aware of the person through whose eyes and ears we register details and events. We may take in only what a participant or an observer at the scene would actually have witnessed. We then become more conscious of the window that a story opens on the world.

When you study point of view, you ask: From what vantage point does the person telling the story look at the world? Here are possible variations of narrative point of view:

The Omniscient Author   The traditional **omniscient,** all-knowing author had access to the private thoughts and feelings of everyone in a novel or a story. A nineteenth-century novelist like George Eliot (pen name of Marian Evans) knew what went on in the minds and hearts of her several characters. Of course, what the omniscient author chose to tell the readers was a limited selection—the author merely *acted* as if she "knew all." The typical objection of her twentieth-century successors was that in our own reality we see the world from our particular window. A story should limit itself to what can be taken in by "one pair of eyes."

The Intruding Author   Some authors serve the reader as guides to their fictional world. The **intruding** author feels free to comment, to chat with us as the readers, to take us into his or her confidence. We are very much aware of the author's presence as the narrator. Every so often the author steps into the story from the outside, interrupting it to turn to us and offer asides, philosophical reflections, a personal view of life.

Third Person Objective   In many stories, there is no "I, the storyteller" and no "You, the reader." The story talks about its characters in the third person: *She* did so-and-so; *he* did such-and-such. What the characters think and feel is seen from the outside. In much early modern fiction, the stance of the author was: We are not mind readers; we can never enter totally into someone else's world of thinking and feeling. We *can* try to be impartial observers, faithful to what we see and hear. In a Hemingway story, for instance, the author often assumes the stance of the honest witness, the incorruptible reporter. In such an **objective** narrative, there is little comment—a minimum of editorializing, judging, or preaching.

First Person Autobiographical   In many stories that seem deeply felt, we sense that the authors are speaking in thinly disguised form about their own childhood, their own families, their own conflicts or alienation. The "I" speaking in the story is talking about scenes and people from personal experience—perhaps with names and dates altered. Such writing may have a **confessional tone;** the writer may be unburdening his or her heart. However, we have to remember that the autobiographical material is fictionalized—shaped by the creative imagination. The "I" speaking to us in the story then becomes a **persona**—an assumed identity. (A *persona* was originally the mask actors wore on the classical Greek stage. Through it the sound of their voices came forth to reach the spectator—it "sounded through.") The distance between person and persona varies greatly from story to story, or from writer to writer. The persona of the narrator may have much in common with the author. Or else it may represent the author in disguise, as if wearing a mask. Finally, it may be an imaginary identity incorporating some elements or traits from the author's personality or experience.

First Person Observer   The fictionalized "I" will play different roles in different stories. We may see the story through the eyes of someone at the center of the action. However, we may also see events through the eyes of someone on the sidelines, who is not a major player. This person then becomes our scout, our reliable source, our "chosen interpreter." The person becomes our **reflector**—anything that happens in the story will reach us by way of his or her perceptions. Edith Wharton, in *The Writing of Fiction* (1925), spelled out the modern credo that to create the "effect of probability" it was necessary

> never to let the character who serves as a reflector record anything not naturally within his register. It should be the storyteller's first care to choose this reflecting mind deliberately, as one would choose a building site, or decide upon the orientation of one's house, and when this is done, to live inside the mind chosen, trying to feel, see, and react exactly as the latter would, no more, no less, and, above all, no otherwise.

A special **irony** may make us smile at the naive narrator who seems to know less than an alert reader. Mark Twain's Huckleberry Finn in the classic of the same name watches the world with wide-open innocent eyes—recognizing human duplicity or vindictiveness long after the more knowing reader.

Third Person Observer   While limiting the point of view to that of one person, the author may tell us *about* that person's observations and reactions rather than letting the character speak in his or her own voice to us as readers.

Interior Monologue   James Joyce and other early moderns experimented with the **stream-of-consciousness** technique. We enter into the mind of the narrator, sharing in a flow of thought and feeling. We listen in on the **interior monologue.** The narrative is not linear or logical but moves by leaps and bounds of association. We may be distracted by bodily sensations (like the feel of a wet bar of soap in a trouser pocket). We may be sent off on a tangent by a scent, or by a remark that rekindles a long-forgotten memory. Like our own private thoughts and feelings, the narrator's flow of thought is likely to circle back sooner or later to the hopes, anxieties, or traumas that really matter. In a story like Tillie Olsen's "I Stand Here Ironing," we follow a more focused, *edited* interior monologue. We share in the private thoughts of the narrator. However, her memories, thoughts, and feelings are focused on the hardships, struggles, and regrets related to the bringing up of her oldest child. No current distractions interfere with the stock taking, the weighing of responsibilities, at the heart of the story.

FIRST READING
The World of Youth

Stories of youth and adolescence often adopt a distinctive, limited point of view. They see the world through the eyes of people less experienced, less knowing than we are. The following story is by Anton Chekhov, a nineteenth-century Russian writer whose grandfather had been a serf and who became famous as a playwright and as a writer of short stories. Chekhov's plays—*The Seagull, The Cherry Orchard, Three Sisters*—are still part of the modern repertory. The story that follows looks at the world from the perspective of youth. How, and how well, does the author control the point of view? What does the reader gain, and what does the reader lose, by looking at the world from a limited perspective?

Anton Chekhov   *(1860–1904)*

Vanka   *1886*

Vanka Zhukov, a nine-year-old boy, who had been apprenticed to Alyahin the shoemaker these three months, did not go to bed on Christmas Eve. After his master and mistress and the journeymen had gone to midnight Mass, he got an inkpot and a penholder with a rusty nib out of the master's cupboard and, having spread out a crumpled sheet of paper, began writing. Before he formed the first letter he looked fearfully at the doors and windows several times, shot a glance at the dark icon, at either side of which stretched shelves filled with lasts, and heaved a broken sigh. He was kneeling before a bench on which his paper lay.

"Dear Granddaddy, Konstantin Makarych," he wrote. "And I am writing you a letter. I wish you a merry Christmas and everything good from the Lord God. I have neither father nor mother, you alone are left me."

Vanka shifted his glance to the dark window on which flickered the reflection of his candle and vividly pictured his grandfather to himself. Employed as a watchman by the Zhivaryovs, he was a short, thin, but extraordinarily lively and nimble old man of about sixty-five whose face was always crinkled with laughter and who had a toper's eyes. By day he slept in the servants' kitchen or cracked jokes with the cook; at night, wrapped in an ample sheepskin coat, he made the rounds of the estate, shaking his clapper. The old bitch, Brownie, and the dog called Wriggles, who had a black coat and a long body like a weasel's, followed him with hanging heads. This Wriggles was extraordinarily deferential and demonstrative, looked with equally friendly eyes both at his masters and at strangers, but did not enjoy a good reputation. His deference and meekness concealed the most Jesuitical spite. No one knew better than he how to creep up behind you and suddenly snap at your leg, how to slip into the icehouse, or how to steal a hen from a peasant. More than once his hind legs had been all but broken, twice he had been hanged, every week he was whipped till he was half dead, but he always managed to revive.

At the moment Grandfather was sure to be standing at the gates, screwing up his eyes at the bright-red windows of the church, stamping his felt boots, and cracking jokes with the servants. His clapper was tied to his belt. He was clapping his hands, shrugging with the cold, and, with a senile titter, pinching now the housemaid, now the cook.

"Shall we have a pinch of snuff?" he was saying, offering the women his   5
snuffbox.

They each took a pinch and sneezed. Grandfather, indescribably delighted, went off into merry peals of laughter and shouted:

"Peel it off, it has frozen on!"

The dogs too are given a pinch of snuff. Brownie sneezes, wags her head, and walks away offended. Wriggles is too polite to sneeze and only wags his tail. And the weather is glorious. The air is still, clear, and fresh. The night is dark, but one can see the whole village with its white roofs and smoke streaming out of the chimneys, the trees silvery with hoarfrost, the snowdrifts. The entire sky is studded with gaily twinkling stars and the Milky Way is as distinctly visible as though it had been washed and rubbed with snow for the holiday. . . .

Vanka sighed, dipped his pen into the ink and went on writing:

"And yesterday I got it hot. The master pulled me out into the courtyard   10
by the hair and gave me a hiding with a knee-strap because I was rocking the baby in its cradle and happened to fall asleep. And last week the mistress ordered me to clean a herring and I began with the tail, and she took the herring and jabbed me in the mug with it. The helpers make fun of me, send me to the pothouse for vodka and tell me to steal pickles for them from the master, and the master hits me with anything that comes handy. And there is nothing to eat. In the morning they give me bread, for dinner porridge, and in the evening bread again. As for tea or cabbage soup, the master and mistress bolt it all themselves. And they tell me to sleep in the entry, and when the baby cries I don't sleep at all, but rock the cradle. Dear Granddaddy, for God's sake have pity on me, take me away from here, take me home to the village, it's more than I can bear. I bow down at your feet and I will pray to God for you forever, take me away from here or I'll die."

Vanka puckered his mouth, rubbed his eyes with his black fist, and gave a sob.

"I will grind your snuff for you," he continued, "I will pray to God for you, and if anything happens, you may thrash me all you like. And if you think there's no situation for me, I will beg the manager for Christ's sake to let me clean boots, or I will take Fedka's place as a shepherd boy. Dear Granddaddy, it's more than I can bear, it will simply be the death of me. I thought of running away to the village, but I have no boots and I am afraid of the frost. And in return for this when I grow big, I will feed you and won't let anybody do you any harm, and when you die I will pray for the repose of your soul, just as for my Mom's.

"Moscow is a big city. The houses are all the kind the gentry live in, and there are lots of horses, but no sheep, and the dogs are not fierce. The boys here don't go caroling, carrying the star at Christmas, and they don't let anyone sing in the choir, and once in a shop window I saw fishing-hooks for sale all fitted up with a line, for every kind of fish, very fine ones, there was even one hook that will hold a forty-pound sheatfish. And I saw shops where there are all sorts of guns, like the master's at home, so maybe each one of them is a hundred rubles. And in butchers' shops there are woodcocks and partridge and hares, but where they shoot them the clerks won't tell.

"Dear Granddaddy, when they have a Christmas tree with presents at the master's, do get a gilt walnut and put it away in the little green chest. Ask the young lady, Olga Ignatyevna, for it, say it's for Vanka."

Vanka heaved a broken sigh and again stared at the window. He recalled that it was his grandfather who always went to the forest to get the Christmas tree for the master's family and that he would take his grandson with him. It was a jolly time! Grandfather grunted, the frost crackled, and, not to be outdone, Vanka too made a cheerful noise in his throat. Before chopping down the Christmas tree, Grandfather would smoke a pipe, slowly take a pinch of snuff, and poke fun at Vanka who looked chilled to the bone. The young firs draped in hoarfrost stood still, waiting to see which of them was to die. Suddenly, coming out of nowhere, a hare would dart across the snowdrifts like an arrow. Grandfather could not keep from shouting: "Hold him, hold him, hold him! Ah, the bob-tailed devil!"

When he had cut down the fir tree, Grandfather would drag it to the master's house, and there they would set to work decorating it. The young lady, Olga Ignatyevna, Vanka's favorite, was the busiest of all. When Vanka's mother, Pelageya, was alive and a chambermaid in the master's house, the young lady used to give him goodies, and, having nothing with which to occupy herself, taught him to read and write, to count up to a hundred, and even to dance the quadrille. When Pelageya died, Vanka had been relegated to the servants' kitchen to stay with his grandfather, and from the kitchen to the shoemaker's.

"Do come, dear Granddaddy," Vanka went on. "For Christ's sake, I beg you, take me away from here. Have pity on me, an unhappy orphan, here everyone beats me, and I am terribly hungry, and I am so blue, I can't tell you how, I keep crying. And the other day the master hit me on the head with a last, so that I fell down and it was a long time before I came to. My life is miserable, worse than a dog's—I also send greetings to Alyona, one-eyed Yegorka and the coachman, and don't give my harmonica to anyone. I remain, your grandson, Ivan Zhukov, dear Granddaddy, do come."

15

Vanka twice folded the sheet covered with writing and put it into an envelope he had bought for a kopeck the previous day. He reflected a while, then dipped the pen into the ink and wrote the address:

To Grandfather in the village

Then he scratched himself, thought a little, and added: *Konstantin Makarych*. Glad that no one had interrupted him at his writing, he put on his cap and, without slipping on his coat, ran out into the street with nothing over his shirt.

The clerks at the butchers' whom he had questioned the day before had told him that letters were dropped into letter boxes and from the boxes they were carried all over the world in troikas with ringing bells and drunken drivers. Vanka ran to the nearest letter box and thrust the precious letter into the slit.

An hour later, lulled by sweet hopes, he was fast asleep. In his dream he   20 saw the stove. On the stove sat grandfather, his bare legs hanging down, and read the letter to the cooks. Near the stove was Wriggles, wagging his tail.

The Receptive Reader

1. What would you include in a *capsule portrait* of Vanka?

2. Why do you think Chekhov does not include any specific reference to the boy's mistreatment until we have read one third of the story?

3. What details in the story keep reminding us of Vanka's limited *point of view?* (Does anything get into the story that should really be beyond the central character's ken?)

4. Where is the author in this story, and why does he adopt this limited perspective? What is the appeal for the reader—what do you gain (or lose) from looking at the world through Vanka's eyes?

The Creative Dimension

Write a letter that you might have written when you were nearer Vanka's age. Write about a topic that seemed important at the time; address your letter to someone who was then important in your life.

WORLDS OF THOUGHT AND FEELING

There are both outer space and inner space to be explored.

NIKKI GIOVANNI

The following stories take us into a central character's personal world. They make us look at the world as seen through one character's eyes.

Since the central characters in these stories are very different people, each takes us into a different universe of thought and feeling. However, in addition, the point of view from which the author chooses to tell the story varies, with the later stories taking us a step closer to sharing in the character's personal, private thoughts and emotions.

Joyce Carol Oates   *(born 1938)*

Writers are always under attack, usually for not being "moral" enough. . . . There is insufficient recognition of the fact that one of the traditional roles of the writer is to bear witness—not simply to the presumably good things in life, the uplifting, life-enhancing, happy things, but to their polar opposites as well.

JOYCE CAROL OATES

Joyce Carol Oates' disturbing stories often make the reader look at familiar reality from a startling new perspective. Oates was thirty-one and one of the youngest writers so honored when she received the National Book Award for fiction in 1970. In the course of her career, she has published over twenty novels and over fifteen collections of short stories, not counting books of poems, essays, and literary criticism as well as plays and countless articles and reviews. Her best-known novel, *Them* (1961), is set in Detroit, where she taught. It takes place in a violent urban landscape that many Americans would prefer to ignore or block out. Her method is to activate a "brimming" memory not merely of images but also of the emotions connected with them—and to combine the results with systematic research of a topic (like boxing) or a period in history.

Oates has a gift for taking us into a reality that at first we may accept only reluctantly as part of our world. Her characters are often defined by what they are not; they often upset or annoy the reader by their failure to fit the reader's assumptions about what is normal, comforting, reassuring. Her characters tend to be "opaque, ungiving, uncharming; they have the taciturn qualities that come with the kind of people they are—heavy, hallucinated, outside the chatty middle class" (Alfred Kazin).

Oates' stories often call for a change in our usual perspective, making us try out a new and different point of view. Her story "Stalking" focuses on Gretchen, the central character, and takes us into her own private world. For the duration of the story, like it or not, we live in Gretchen's universe. We see what is in her field of vision. (What do we see?) We are tuned in to her continuing daydream or fantasy. (What role does it play in the story?) We return with her to her suburban home. (What is her connection with home and family?)

Stalking   1972

The Invisible Adversary is fleeing across a field.

Gretchen, walking slowly, deliberately, watches with her keen unblinking eyes the figure of the Invisible Adversary some distance ahead. The Adversary has run boldly in front of all the traffic—on long spiky legs brisk as colts' legs—and jumped up onto a curb of new concrete, and now is running across a vacant field. The Adversary glances over his shoulder at Gretchen.

Saturday afternoon. November. A cold gritty day. Gretchen is out stalking. She has hours for her game. Hours. She is dressed for the hunt, her solid legs crammed into old blue jeans, her big, square, strong feet jammed into white leather boots that cost her mother forty dollars not long ago, but are now scuffed and filthy with mud. Hopeless to get them clean again, Gretchen doesn't care. She is wearing a dark-green corduroy jacket that is worn out at the elbows and the rear, with a zipper that can be zipped up or down, attached to a fringed leather strip. On her head nothing, though it is windy today.

She has hours ahead.

Cars and trucks and buses from the city and enormous interstate trucks   5
hauling automobiles pass by on the highway; Gretchen waits until the way is nearly clear, then starts out. A single car is approaching. *Slow down,* Gretchen thinks; and like magic he does.

Following the footprints of the Invisible Adversary. There is no sidewalk here yet, so she might as well cut right across the field. A gigantic sign announces the site of the new Pace & Fischbach Building, an office building of fifteen floors to be completed the following year. The land around here is all dug up and muddy; she can see the Adversary's footsteps leading right past the gouged-up area . . . and there he is, smirking back at her, pretending panic.

I'll get you. Don't worry. Gretchen thinks carefully.

Because the Adversary is so light-footed and invisible, Gretchen doesn't make any effort to be that way. She plods along as she does at school, passing from classroom to classroom, unhurried and not even sullen, just unhurried. She knows she is very visible. She is thirteen years old and weighs one hundred and thirty-five pounds. She's only five feet three—stocky, muscular, squat in the torso and shoulders, with good strong legs and thighs. She could be good at gym, if she bothered; instead, she just stands around, her face empty, her arms crossed and her shoulders a little slumped. If forced, she takes part in the games of volleyball and basketball, but she runs heavily, without spirit, and sometimes bumps into other girls, hurting them. *Out of my way,* she thinks; at such times her face shows no expression.

And now? . . . The Adversary is peeking out at her from around the corner of a gas station. Something flickers in her brain. *I see you,* she thinks, with quiet excitement. The Adversary ducks back out of sight. Gretchen heads in the direction, plodding through a jumbled, bulldozed field of mud and thistles and debris that is mainly rocks and chunks of glass. The gas station is brand-new and not yet opened for business. It is all white tile, white concrete, perfect plate-glass windows with whitewashed X's on them, a large driveway and eight gasoline pumps, all proudly erect and ready for business. But the gas station has not opened since Gretchen and her family moved here—about six months ago. Something must have gone wrong. Gretchen fixes her eyes on the corner where the Adversary was last seen. He can't escape.

One wall of the gas station's white tile has been smeared with something   10 like tar. Dreamy, snakelike, thick twistings of black. Black tar. Several windows have been broken. Gretchen stands in the empty driveway, her hands jammed into her pockets. Traffic is moving slowly over here. A barricade has been set up that directs traffic out onto the shoulder of the highway, on a narrow, bumpy, muddy lane that loops out and back again onto the pavement. Cars move slowly, carefully. Their bottoms scrape against the road. The detour signs are great rectangular things, bright yellow with black zigzag lines. SLOW DETOUR. In the two center lanes of the highway are bulldozers not being used today, and gigantic concrete pipes to be used for storm sewers. Eight pipes. They are really enormous; Gretchen's eyes crinkle with awe, just to see them.

She remembers the Adversary.

There he is—headed for the shopping plaza. *He won't get away in the crowds,* Gretchen promises herself. She follows. Now she is approaching an area that is more completed, though there are still no sidewalks and some of the buildings are brand-new and yet unoccupied, vacant. She jumps over a concrete ditch that is stained with rust-colored water and heads up a slight incline to the service drive of the Federal Savings Bank. The drive-in tellers' windows are all dark today, behind their green-tinted glass. The whole bank is dark, closed. Is this the bank her parents go to now? It takes Gretchen a minute to recognize it.

Now a steady line of traffic, a single lane, turns onto the service drive that leads to the shopping plaza. BUCKINGHAM MALL. 101 STORES. Gretchen notices a few kids her own age, boys or girls, trudging in jeans and jackets ahead of her, through the mud. They might be classmates of hers. Her attention is captured again by the Invisible Adversary, who has run all the way up to the Mall and is hanging around the entrance of the Cunningham Drug Store, teasing her.

You'll be sorry for that, Gretchen thinks with a smile.

Automobiles pass her slowly. The parking lot for the Mall is enormous,   15 many acres. A city of cars on a Saturday afternoon. Gretchen sees a car that might be her mother's, but she isn't sure. Cars are parked slanted here, in lanes marked LOT K, LANE 15; LOT K, LANE 16. The signs are spheres, bubbles, perched up on long slender poles. At night they are illuminated.

Ten or twelve older kids are hanging around the drugstore entrance. One of them is sitting on top of a mailbox, rocking it back and forth. Gretchen pushes past them—they are kidding around, trying to block people—and inside the store her eye darts rapidly up and down the aisles, looking for the Invisible Adversary.

Hiding here? Hiding?

She strolls along, cunning and patient. At the cosmetics counter a girl is showing an older woman some liquid makeup. She smears a small oval onto the back of the woman's hand, rubs it in gently. "That's Peach Pride," the girl says. She has shimmering blond hair and eyes that are penciled to show a permanent exclamatory interest. She does not notice Gretchen, who lets a hand drift idly over a display of marked-down lipsticks, each only $1.59.

Gretchen slips the tube of lipstick into her pocket. Neatly. Nimbly. Ignoring the Invisible Adversary, who is shaking a finger at her, she drifts over to the newsstand, looks at the magazine covers without reading them, and edges over to another display. Packages in a cardboard barrel, out in the aisle. Big bargains. Gretchen doesn't even glance in the barrel to see what is being offered . . . she just slips one of the packages in her pocket. No trouble.

She leaves by the other door, the side exit. A small smile tugs at her   20
mouth.

The Adversary is trotting ahead of her. The Mall is divided into geometric areas, each colored differently; the Adversary leaves the blue pavement and is now on the green. Gretchen follows. She notices the Adversary going into a Franklin Joseph store.

Gretchen enters the store, sniffs in the perfumy, overheated smell, sees nothing that interests her on the counters or at the dress racks, and so walks right to the back of the store, to the ladies' room. No one inside. She takes the tube of lipstick out of her pocket, opens it, examines the lipstick. It has a tart, sweet smell. A very light pink: *Spring Blossom*. Gretchen goes to the mirror and smears the lipstick onto it, at first lightly, then coarsely; part of the lipstick breaks and falls into a sink littered with hair. Gretchen goes into one of the toilet stalls and tosses the tube into the toilet bowl. She takes handfuls of toilet paper and crumbles them into a ball and throws them into the toilet. Remembering the package from the drugstore, she takes it out of her pocket—just toothpaste. She throws it, cardboard package and all, into the toilet bowl, then, her mind glimmering with an idea, she goes to the apparatus that holds the towel—a single cloth towel on a roll—and tugs at it until it comes loose, then pulls it out hand over hand, patiently, until the entire towel is out. She scoops it up and carries it to the toilet. She pushes it in and flushes the toilet.

The stuff doesn't go down, so she tries again. This time it goes partway down before it gets stuck.

Gretchen leaves the rest room and strolls unhurried through the store. The Adversary is waiting for her outside—peeking through the window— wagging a finger at her. *Don't you wag no finger at me,* she thinks, with a small tight smile. Outside, she follows him at a distance. Loud music is blaring around her head. It is rock music, piped out onto the colored squares and rectangles of the Mall, blown everywhere by the November wind, but Gretchen hardly hears it.

Some boys are fooling around in front of the record store. One of them   25
bumps into Gretchen and they all laugh as she is pushed against a trash can.

"Watch it, babe!" the boy sings out. Her leg hurts. Gretchen doesn't look at them but, with a cold, swift anger, her face averted, she knocks the trash can over onto the sidewalk. Junk falls out. The can rolls. Some women shoppers scurry to get out of the way and the boys laugh.

Gretchen walks away without looking back.

She wanders through Sampson Furniture, which has two entrances. In one door and out the other, as always, it is a ritual with her. Again she notices the sofa that is like the sofa in their family room at home—covered with black and white fur, real goatskin. All over the store there are sofas, chairs, tables, beds. A jumble of furnishings. People stroll around them, in and out of little displays, displays meant to be living rooms, dining rooms, bedrooms, family rooms. . . . It makes Gretchen's eyes squint to see so many displays: like seeing the inside of a hundred houses. She slows down, almost comes to a stop. Gazing at a living-room display on a raised platform. Only after a moment does she remember why she is here—whom she is following—and she turns to see the Adversary beckoning to her.

She follows him outside again. He goes into Dodi's Boutique and, with her head lowered so that her eyes seem to move to the bottom of her eyebrows, pressing up against her forehead, Gretchen follows him. *You'll regret this,* she thinks. Dodi's Boutique is decorated in silver and black. Metallic strips hang down from a dark ceiling, quivering. Salesgirls dressed in pants suits stand around with nothing to do except giggle with one another and nod their head in time to the music amplified throughout the store. It is music from a local radio station. Gretchen wanders over to the dress rack, for the hell of it. Size 14. "The time is now 2:35," a radio announcer says cheerfully. "The weather is 32 degrees with a chance of showers and possible sleet tonight. You're listening to WCKK, Radio Wonderful. . . ." Gretchen selects several dresses and a salesgirl shows her to a dressing room.

"Need any help?" the girl asks. She has long swinging hair and a high-shouldered, indifferent, bright manner.

"No," Gretchen mutters.

Alone, Gretchen takes off her jacket. She is wearing a navy blue sweater. She zips one of the dresses open and it falls off the flimsy plastic hanger before she can catch it. She steps on it, smearing mud onto the white wool. She lets it lie there and holds up another dress, gazing at herself in the mirror.

She has untidy, curly hair that looks like a wig set loosely on her head. Light brown curls spill out everywhere, bouncy, a little frizzy, a cascade, a tumbling of curls. Her eyes are deep set, her eyebrows heavy and dark. She has a stern, staring look, like an adult man. Her nose is perfectly formed, neat and noble. Her upper lip is long, as if it were stretched to close with difficulty over the front teeth. She wears no makeup, her lips are perfectly colorless, pale, a little chapped, and they are usually held tight, pursed tightly shut. She has a firm, rounded chin. Her facial structure is strong, pensive, its features stern and symmetrical as a statue's, blank, neutral, withdrawn. Her face is attractive. But there is a blunt, neutral stillness to it, as if she were detached from it and somewhere else, uninterested.

30

She holds the dress up to her body, smooths it down over her chest, staring at herself.

After a moment she hangs the dress up again, and runs down the zipper so roughly that it breaks. The other dress she doesn't bother with. She leaves the dressing room, putting on her jacket.

At the front of the store the salesgirl glances at her . . . "—Didn't fit?—"   35
"No," says Gretchen.

She wanders around for a while, in and out of Carmichael's, the Mall's big famous store, where she catches sight of her mother on an escalator going up. Her mother doesn't notice her. She pauses by a display of "winter homes." Her family owns a home like this, in the Upper Peninsula, except theirs is larger. This one comes complete for only $5330: PACKAGE ERECTED ON YOUR LOT—YEAR-ROUND HOME FIBER GLASS INSULATION—BEAUTIFUL ROUGH-SAWN VERTICAL B. C. CEDAR SIDING WITH DEEP SIMULATED SHADOW LINES FOR A RUGGED EXTERIOR.

Only 3:15. Gretchen goes into the Big Boy restaurant and orders a ground-round hamburger with French fries. Also a Coke. She sits at the crowded counter and eats slowly, her jaws grinding slowly, as she glances at her reflection in the mirror directly in front of her—her mop of hair moving almost imperceptibly with the grinding of her jaws—and occasionally she sees the Adversary waiting outside, coyly. *You'll get yours,* she thinks.

She leaves the Big Boy and wanders out into the parking lot, eating from a bag of potato chips. She wipes her greasy hands on her thighs. The afternoon has turned dark and cold. Shivering a little, she scans the maze of cars for the Adversary—yes, there he is—and starts after him. He runs ahead of her. He runs through the parking lot, waits teasingly at the edge of a field, and as she approaches he runs across the field, trotting along with a noisy crowd of four or five loose dogs that don't seem to notice him.

Gretchen follows him through that field, trudging in the mud, and   40
through another muddy field, her eyes fixed on him. Now he is at the highway—hesitating there—now he is about to run across in front of traffic—now, now—now he darts out—

Now! He is struck by a car. His body knocked backward, spinning backward. Ah, now, *now how does it feel?* Gretchen asks.

He picks himself up. Gets to his feet. Is he bleeding? Yes, bleeding! He stumbles across the highway to the other side, where there is a sidewalk. Gretchen follows him as soon as the traffic lets up. He is staggering now, like a drunken man. *How does it feel? Do you like it now?*

The Adversary staggers along the sidewalk. He turns onto a side street, beneath an archway, *Piney Woods.* He is leading Gretchen into the Piney Woods subdivision. Here the homes are quite large, on artificial hills that show them to good advantage. Most of the homes are white colonials with attached garages. There are no sidewalks here, so the Adversary has to walk in the street, limping like an old man, and Gretchen follows him in the street, with her eyes fixed on him.

Are you happy now? Does it hurt? Does it?

She giggles at the way he walks. He looks like a drunken man. He   45
glances back at her, white-faced, and turns up a flagstone walk . . . goes right up to a big white colonial house. . . .

Gretchen follows him inside. She inspects the simulated brick of the foyer: yes, there are blood spots. He is dripping blood. Entranced, she follows the splashes of blood into the hall, to the stairs . . . forgets her own boots, which are muddy . . . but she doesn't feel like going back to wipe her feet.

Nobody seems to be home. Her mother is probably still shopping, her father is out of town for the weekend. The house empty. Gretchen goes into the kitchen, opens the refrigerator, takes out a Coke, and wanders to the rear of the house, to the family room. It is two steps down from the rest of the house. She takes off her jacket and tosses it somewhere. Turns on the television set. Sits on the goatskin sofa and stares at the screen: a return of a Shotgun Steve show, which she has already seen.

If the Adversary comes crawling behind her, groaning in pain, weeping, she won't even bother to glance at him.

The Receptive Reader

1. Oates is a master at noting in passing apparently random, mindless *detail* that we later suspect was planted deliberately in the story. What is the point of telling us about Gretchen's white leather boots—or about the car approaching when she crosses the highway? (What other details early in the story stuck in your mind?)

2. Gretchen is the kind of person who has an "attitude." What is her attitude toward school and gym? What is her attitude toward the schoolmates she meets at the mall?

3. What are striking details about the suburban landscape through which Gretchen wanders? As you follow her through this *setting,* do you notice any connecting thread? Is there a keynote—a recurrent note struck more than once?

4. What kind of shoplifter is Gretchen? How does she do it? What are her *motives*—why does she do it? Do you feel you are getting an inside look at teenage vandalism in this story? How does she operate, and why?

5. Late in the story, Oates furnishes a fairly complete physical description of Gretchen. Do you learn anything from it? Does it include any clues to her character?

6. At a few points earlier in the story, we are reminded that Gretchen has a mother, a family, a home. What impression do these hints create? What kind of home, what kind of family, awaits Gretchen at the end of her excursion?

7. What is the role of the imaginary adversary in the story?

The Personal Response

The story presents Gretchen strictly on her own terms—with no comment. There is no editorializing, moralizing, or preaching by the author. For you, what is the point of the story? Is there a key to the central character—a unifying thread to her behavior and attitudes? How do you relate to her?

The Range of Interpretation

How much depends on what you as a reader bring to Gretchen's story? Which of the following student-written responses is closest to your own? Why? Which to you seems least responsive to the story, and why?

1. Gretchen seems to me to be a very angry adolescent. Her anger is directed against her absent parents, her schoolmates who probably don't even notice her, but mostly against herself. Gretchen is an overweight, unattractive thirteen-year-old. She is a loner. She can only express her anger through her game of stalking "the adversary." This make-believe character represents to Gretchen all the anger she hides inside herself. These stalking games are ritualistic to Gretchen; through them she can release her anger and best her adversary for a period of time.

2. I was able to feel empathy toward the character of Gretchen in Oates' story, despite her unpleasant personality. I thought both she and her surroundings epitomized the sterility and alienation of much modern suburban life; there is a rootlessness inherent in the setting that manifests itself in Gretchen's utter lack of interest or engagement. This lack of engagement with the world around her is central to explaining many of the things she does, such as her aimless shoplifting and careless muddying of her parents' home. She was not raised in an environment that would give her any cause for enthusiasm for anything. It is perhaps because Gretchen had no positive interests to draw her attention and enthusiasm outward that she became so carelessly destructive of herself and her environment.

3. Gretchen is pure isolation. She is an imaginative, creative person trapped in a suburban theater where the only stimuli are shopping malls and television. Her mother and father are not shown as bad people; they are just kept out of the picture. Her companion instead is the invisible adversary—playmate, lover, villain, whipping boy who never says no to any adventure she devises. Her relentless pursuit of him gives her day a purpose and a victory. In her conventional reality, the frustration and pain of failure in a social arena where only pretty girls are admitted would be too much to bear. Her destructive behavior is an acting out of her frustrated need to belong. If a lipstick or dress is not going to improve the problem, then they should be destroyed. And if there is no place to go, why hurry?

The Creative Dimension

What do you think you would see if you could be a mind reader looking into Gretchen's mind? Write a passage in which you change the point of view of the story. Imagine you can share in Gretchen's private thoughts and feelings instead of watching her much of the time from the outside. Write in the first person, as if she were talking confidentially to the reader.

Tillie Olsen   *(born 1912)*

We must not speak of women writers in our century (as we cannot speak of women in any area of recognized human achievement) without speaking also of the invisible, the as-innately-capable: the born to wrong circumstances—diminished, excluded, foundered, silenced.

TILLIE OLSEN

Tillie Olsen came to be widely admired for giving voice to the story of the unheard, the silenced, in American society. Writing about the

Great Depression of the thirties, she wrote with bitter eloquence about the working-class experience—poverty, illness, hunger, unemployment, soul-deadening jobs. Her novel *Yonnondio: From the Thirties* (1974) paid tribute to people thwarted, deprived of their chance to develop into full human beings "so that a few may languidly lie on couches and trill 'how exquisite' to paid dreamers." A native of Omaha, Nebraska, with only a high school education, she herself lived through gray poverty to write powerful stories shaking up our complacency, our euphemisms and alibis. Her story "Tell Me a Riddle" won the O. Henry Award as the best short story of the year in 1961. She has since received prestigious grants and honors and lectured at universities including Amherst and Stanford.

Women readers and women writers made her a revered figure in the women's movement. They identified with the heroic struggle of a "family wage earner at dull and time-sapping menial jobs" (Nolan Miller)—a woman who "held down a job, raised four children, and still somehow managed to become and remain a writer," surviving a "grueling obstacle race" that cost her "twenty years of her writing life" (Margaret Atwood). In her collection *Silences* (1978), Olsen collected and reprinted the testimony of writers, and especially women from Virginia Woolf to Katherine Mansfield, about the social and psychological forces that hobble the creative spirit, forcing many who are not white, male, or affluent into silence.

The following story is the kind of personally committed writing that stays close to personal experience but turns it into art by focusing it and interpreting it. We look through the eyes of a mother at a daughter who was "the child of anxious, not proud love." What world do we see through the narrator's eyes? (The WPA referred to in the story is the Works Progress Administration, begun in 1935 to provide federally funded jobs for the unemployed during the Great Depression.)

I Stand Here Ironing   *1961*

I stand here ironing, and what you asked me moves tormented back and forth with the iron.

"I wish you would manage the time to come in and talk with me about your daughter. I'm sure you can help me understand her. She's a youngster who needs help and whom I'm deeply interested in helping."

"Who needs help." . . . Even if I came, what good would it do? You think because I am her mother I have a key, or that in some way you could use me as a key? She has lived for nineteen years. There is all that life that has happened outside of me, beyond me.

And when is there time to remember, to sift, to weigh, to estimate, to total? I will start and there will be an interruption and I will have to gather it all together again. Or I will become engulfed with all I did or did not do, with what should have been and what cannot be helped.

She was a beautiful baby. The first and only one of our five that was   5
beautiful at birth. You do not guess how new and uneasy her tenancy in her
now-loveliness. You did not know her all those years she was thought
homely, or see her poring over her baby pictures, making me tell her over
and over how beautiful she had been—and would be, I would tell her—and
was now, to the seeing eye. But the seeing eyes were few or nonexistent.
Including mine.

I nursed her. They feel that's important nowadays. I nursed all the children, but with her, with all the fierce rigidity of first motherhood, I did like
the books then said. Though her cries battered me to trembling and my
breasts ached with swollenness, I waited till the clock decreed.

Why do I put that first? I do not even know if it matters, or if it explains
anything.

She was a beautiful baby. She blew shining bubbles of sound. She loved
motion, loved light, loved color and music and textures. She would lie on
the floor in her blue overalls patting the surface so hard in ecstasy her hands
and feet would blur. She was a miracle to me, but when she was eight
months old I had to leave her daytimes with the woman downstairs to
whom she was no miracle at all, for I worked or looked for work and for
Emily's father, who "could no longer endure" (he wrote in his good-bye
note) "sharing want with us."

I was nineteen. It was the pre-relief, pre-WPA world of the depression. I
would start running as soon as I got off the streetcar, running up the stairs,
the place smelling sour, and awake or asleep to startle awake, when she saw
me she would break into a clogged weeping that could not be comforted,
a weeping I can hear yet.

After a while I found a job hashing at night so I could be with her days,   10
and it was better. But it came to where I had to bring her to his family and
leave her.

It took a long time to raise the money for her fare back. Then she got
chicken pox and I had to wait longer. When she finally came, I hardly knew
her, walking quick and nervous like her father, looking like her father, thin,
and dressed in a shoddy red that yellowed her skin and glared at the pock-
marks. All the baby loveliness gone.

She was two. Old enough for nursery school they said, and I did not
know then what I know now—the fatigue of the long day, and the lacerations of group life in the kinds of nurseries that are only parking places for
children.

Except that it would have made no difference if I had known. It was the
only place there was. It was the only way we could be together, the only
way I could hold a job.

And even without knowing, I knew. I knew the teacher that was evil because all these years it has curdled into my memory, the little boy hunched
in the corner, her rasp, "why aren't you outside, because Alvin hits you?
that's no reason, go out, scaredy." I knew Emily hated it even if she did not
clutch and implore "don't go Mommy" like the other children, mornings.

She always had a reason why we should stay home. Momma, you look   15
sick. Momma, I feel sick. Momma, the teachers aren't there today, they're

sick. Momma, we can't go, there was a fire there last night. Momma, it's a holiday today, no school, they told me.

But never a direct protest, never rebellion. I think of our others in their three-, four-year-oldness—the explosions, the tempers, the denunciations, the demands—and I feel suddenly ill. I put the iron down. What in me demanded that goodness in her? And what was the cost, the cost to her of such goodness?

The old man living in the back once said in his gentle way: "You should smile at Emily more when you look at her." What *was* in my face when I looked at her? I loved her. There were all the acts of love.

It was only with the others I remembered what he said, and it was the face of joy, and not of care or tightness or worry I turned to them—too late for Emily. She does not smile easily, let alone almost always as her brothers and sisters do. Her face is closed and sombre, but when she wants, how fluid. You must have seen it in her pantomimes, you spoke of her rare gift for comedy on the stage that rouses laughter out of the audience so dear they applaud and applaud and do not want to let her go.

Where does it come from, that comedy? There was none of it in her when she came back to me that second time, after I had had to send her away again. She had a new daddy now to learn to love, and I think perhaps it was a better time.

Except when we left her alone nights, telling ourselves she was old 20
enough.

"Can't you go some other time, Mommy, like tomorrow?" she would ask. "Will it be just a little while you'll be gone? Do you promise?"

The time we came back, the front door open, the clock on the floor in the hall. She rigid awake. "It wasn't just a little while. I didn't cry. Three times I called you, just three times, and then I ran downstairs to open the door so you could come faster. The clock talked loud. I threw it away, it scared me what it talked."

She said the clock talked loud again that night I went to the hospital to have Susan. She was delirious with the fever that comes before red measles, but she was fully conscious all the week I was gone and the week after we were home when she could not come near the new baby or me.

She did not get well. She stayed skeleton thin, not wanting to eat, and night after night she had nightmares. She would call for me, and I would rouse from exhaustion to sleepily call back: "You're all right, darling, go to sleep, it's just a dream," and if she still called, in a sterner voice, "now go to sleep, Emily, there's nothing to hurt you." Twice, only twice, when I had to get up for Susan anyhow, I went in to sit with her.

Now when it is too late (as if she would let me hold and comfort her like 25
I do the others) I get up and go to her at once at her moan or restless stirring. "Are you awake, Emily? Can I get you something?" And the answer is always the same: "No, I'm all right, go back to sleep, Mother."

They persuaded me at the clinic to send her away to a convalescent home in the country where "she can have the kind of food and care you can't manage for her, and you'll be free to concentrate on the new baby." They still send children to that place. I see pictures on the society page of sleek young women planning affairs to raise money for it, or dancing at the affairs, or decorating Easter eggs or filling Christmas stockings for the children.

They never have a picture of the children so I do not know if the girls still wear those gigantic red bows and the ravaged looks on the every other Sunday when parents can come to visit "unless otherwise notified"—as we were notified the first six weeks.

Oh it is a handsome place, green lawns and tall trees and fluted flower beds. High up on the balconies of each cottage the children stand, the girls in their red bows and white dresses, the boys in white suits and giant red ties. The parents stand below shrieking up to be heard and the children shriek down to be heard, and between them the invisible wall: "Not to Be Contaminated by Parental Germs or Physical Affection."

There was a tiny girl who always stood hand in hand with Emily. Her parents never came. One visit she was gone. "They moved her to Rose Cottage," Emily shouted in explanation. "They don't like you to love anybody here."

She wrote once a week, the labored writing of a seven-year-old. "I am fine. How is the baby. If I write my leter nicly I will have a star. Love." There never was a star. We wrote every other day, letters she could never hold or keep but only hear read—once. "We simply do not have room for children to keep any personal possessions," they patiently explained when we pieced one Sunday's shrieking together to plead how much it would mean to Emily, who loved so to keep things, to be allowed to keep her letters and cards.   30

Each visit she looked frailer. "She isn't eating," they told us.

(They had runny eggs for breakfast or mush with lumps, Emily said later, I'd hold it in my mouth and not swallow. Nothing ever tasted good, just when they had chicken.)

It took us eight months to get her released home, and only the fact that she gained back so little of her seven lost pounds convinced the social worker.

I used to try to hold and love her after she came back, but her body would stay stiff, and after a while she'd push away. She ate little. Food sickened her, and I think much of life too. Oh she had physical lightness and brightness, twinkling by on skates, bouncing like a ball up and down up and down over the jump rope, skimming over the hill; but these were momentary.

She fretted about her appearance, thin and dark and foreign-looking at a time when every little girl was supposed to look or thought she should look a chubby blonde replica of Shirley Temple. The doorbell sometimes rang for her, but no one seemed to come and play in the house or be a best friend. Maybe because we moved so much.   35

There was a boy she loved painfully through two school semesters. Months later she told me how she had taken pennies from my purse to buy him candy. "Licorice was his favorite and I brought him some every day, but he still liked Jennifer better'n me. Why, Mommy?" The kind of question for which there is no answer.

School was a worry to her. She was not glib or quick in a world where glibness and quickness were easily confused with ability to learn. To her overworked and exasperated teachers she was an overconscientious "slow learner" who kept trying to catch up and was absent entirely too often.

I let her be absent, though sometimes the illness was imaginary. How different from my now-strictness about attendance with the others. I wasn't working. We had a new baby, I was home anyhow. Sometimes, after Susan grew old enough, I would keep her home from school, too, to have them all together.

Mostly Emily had asthma, and her breathing, harsh and labored, would fill the house with a curiously tranquil sound. I would bring the two old dresser mirrors and her boxes of collections to her bed. She would select beads and single earrings, bottle tops and shells, dried flowers and pebbles, old postcards and scraps, all sorts of oddments; then she and Susan would play Kingdom, setting up landscapes and furniture, peopling them with action.

Those were the only times of peaceful companionship between her and   40 Susan. I have edged away from it, that poisonous feeling between them, that terrible balancing of hurts and needs I had to do between the two, and did so badly, those earlier years.

Oh there are conflicts between the others too, each one human, needing, demanding, hurting, taking—but only between Emily and Susan, no, Emily toward Susan that corroding resentment. It seems so obvious on the surface, yet it is not obvious. Susan, the second child, Susan, golden- and curly-haired and chubby, quick and articulate and assured, everything in appearance and manner Emily was not; Susan, not able to resist Emily's precious things, losing or sometimes clumsily breaking them; Susan telling jokes and riddles to company for applause while Emily sat silent (to say to me later: that was *my* riddle, Mother, I told it to Susan); Susan, who for all the five years' difference in age was just a year behind Emily in developing physically.

I am glad for that slow physical development that widened the difference between her and her contemporaries, though she suffered over it. She was too vulnerable for that terrible world of youthful competition, of preening and parading, of constant measuring of yourself against every other, of envy, "If I had that copper hair," "If I had that skin. . . ." She tormented herself enough about not looking like the others, there was enough of the unsureness, the having to be conscious of words before you speak, the constant caring—what are they thinking of me? without having it all magnified by the merciless physical drives.

Ronnie is calling. He is wet and I change him. It is rare there is such a cry now. That time of motherhood is almost behind me when the ear is not one's own but must always be racked and listening for the child cry, the child call. We sit for a while and I hold him, looking out over the city spread in charcoal with its soft aisles of light. "*Shoogily,*" he breathes and curls closer. I carry him back to bed, asleep. *Shoogily.* A funny word, a family word, inherited from Emily, invented by her to say: *comfort.*

In this and other ways she leaves her seal, I say aloud. And startle at my saying it. What do I mean? What did I start to gather together, to try and make coherent? I was at the terrible, growing years. War years. I do not remember them well. I was working, there were four smaller ones now, there was not time for her. She had to help be a mother, and housekeeper, and shopper. She had to set her seal. Mornings of crisis and near hysteria trying to get lunches packed, hair combed, coats and shoes found, everyone to school or Child Care on time, the baby ready for transportation. And always the paper scribbled on by a smaller one, the book looked at by Susan then mislaid, the homework not done. Running out to that huge school where she was one, she was lost, she was a drop; suffering over the unprepared-ness, stammering and unsure in her classes.

There was so little time left at night after the kids were bedded down.   45
She would struggle over books, always eating (it was in those years she de-veloped her enormous appetite that is legendary in our family) and I would be ironing, or preparing food for the next day, or writing V-mail to Bill, or tending the baby. Sometimes, to make me laugh, or out of her despair, she would imitate happenings or types at school.

I think I said once: "Why don't you do something like this in the school amateur show?" One morning she phoned me at work, hardly understand-able through the weeping: "Mother, I did it. I won, I won; they gave me first prize; they clapped and clapped and wouldn't let me go."

Now suddenly she was Somebody, and as imprisoned in her difference as she had been in anonymity.

She began to be asked to perform at other high schools, even in colleges, then at city and statewide affairs. The first one we went to, I only recog-nized her that first moment when thin, shy, she almost drowned herself into the curtains. Then: Was this Emily? The control, the command, the convuls-ing and deadly clowning, the spell, then the roaring, stamping audience, un-willing to let this rare and precious laughter out of their lives.

Afterwards: You ought to do something about her with a gift like that—but without money or knowing how, what does one do? We have left it all to her, and the gift has as often eddied inside, clogged and clotted, as been used and growing.

She is coming. She runs up the stairs two at a time with her light grace-   50
ful step, and I know she is happy tonight. Whatever it was that occasioned your call did not happen today.

"Aren't you ever going to finish the ironing, Mother? Whistler painted his mother in a rocker. I'd have to paint mine standing over an ironing board." This is one of her communicative nights and she tells me everything and nothing as she fixes herself a plate of food out of the icebox.

She is so lovely. Why did you want me to come in at all? Why were you concerned? She will find her way.

She starts up the stairs to bed. "Don't get me up with the rest in the morn-ing." "But I thought you were having midterms." "Oh, those," she comes back in, kisses me, and says quite lightly, "in a couple of years when we'll all be atom-dead they won't matter a bit."

She has said it before. She *believes* it. But because I have been dredging the past, and all that compounds a human being is so heavy and meaning-ful in me, I cannot endure it tonight.

I will never total it all. I will never come in to say: She was a child seldom   55
smiled at. Her father left me before she was a year old. I had to work her first six years when there was work, or I sent her home and to his relatives.

There were years she had care she hated. She was dark and thin and foreign-looking in a world where the prestige went to blondeness and curly hair and dimples, she was slow where glibness was prized. She was a child of anxious, not proud, love. We were poor and could not afford for her the soil of easy growth. I was a young mother, I was a distracted mother. There were other children pushing up, demanding. Her younger sister seemed all that she was not. There were years she did not want me to touch her. She kept too much in herself, her life was such she had to keep too much in herself. My wisdom came too late. She has much to her and probably little will come of it. She is a child of her age, of depression, of war, of fear.

Let her be. So all that is in her will not bloom—but in how many does it? There is still enough left to live by. Only help her to know—help make it so there is cause for her to know—that she is more than this dress on the ironing board, helpless before the iron.

The Receptive Reader

1. Who is the *you* addressed in the story?

2. How do the physical conditions, the circumstances of her life, shape the narrator's outlook? What physical details are especially telling or have a possible symbolic meaning?

3. Early in the story, we catch glimpses of the teacher, of Emily's father, and of the old man who lives in the back. What role do these people on the periphery of the story play in the narrator's world and her view of the world?

4. What is the narrator's attitude toward *institutions?* Why do they loom so large in the story? What are striking details? Is the narrator's attitude one-sided?

5. What picture of Emily as the oldest child emerges in this story? What are key points the narrator wants us to see or understand about Emily as a person? What makes the child—and the mother's relationship with her—*complex* rather than simple?

6. Although it is told in a low key, without melodrama or eloquent indictments, there are powerful undercurrents of *emotion* running in this story. What are they? Where are they harshest—or most frankly described?

7. What kind of summing up does the *ending* of the story provide? What attitude toward life or view of the world emerges here? Is it of one piece with the story as a whole?

8. How do you think the situation or the child might have looked when seen from a *different* point of view? For instance, what might have been the perspective of a teacher or social worker? Does the narrator acknowledge different points of view?

The Personal Response

How do you relate to the narrator in the story? Do you think of her as a bitter person? an angry person? a defeated person? How do you relate to the daughter in the story? What do you think the future holds for her?

Making Connections—For Discussion or Writing

Critics reading literature from a Marxist perspective emphasize the role of social class in shaping people's lives. Compare the perspectives on American working-class life in Bobbie Ann Mason's "Shiloh," in Raymond Carver's "The Third Thing That Killed My Father Off," and Tillie Olsen's "I Stand Here Ironing."

Katherine Anne Porter   *(1890–1980)*

The truth is, I have never written a story in my life that didn't have a very firm foundation in actual human experience—somebody else's experience quite often, but an experience that became my own by hearing the story, by witnessing the thing, by hearing just a word perhaps. It doesn't matter, it just takes a little—a tiny seed. Then it takes root, and it grows.

KATHERINE ANNE PORTER

Katherine Anne Porter became known as a writer more interested in a character's state of mind than in external action. She published *Flowering Judas,* her first collection of short stories, in 1930. Born in Texas, she drew on her experiences as a young girl growing up in the South and as an observer of revolutionary turmoil in Mexico. She is best known for her novellas (long short stories or short novels) "Noon Wine" (1937) and "Pale Horse, Pale Rider" (1939). She traveled widely, and she drew on her observations of Europe in the thirties and forties in her novel *Ship of Fools* (1962). This novel, made into a movie with José Ferrer, Oskar Werner, and Simone Signoret, followed a group of travelers on a voyage to Germany in 1931, when anti-Semitism was on the rise and ominous signs pointed toward the Nazi takeover in 1933.

"The Jilting of Granny Weatherall" is a short story that takes us inside the consciousness of the main character. We follow the stream of observations, memories, and rationalizations as they pass through the character's mind. Instead of following external action from cause to effect, or from action to reaction, we follow the **stream of consciousness.** In most of the story, we hear the main character thinking to herself; we listen to the **interior monologue.** Eudora Welty has said in *The Eye of the Story* (1965) that Porter is contemplating "the inner, secret faces" of her characters:

> Often the revelation that pierces a character's mind and heart and shows him his life or his death comes in a dream, in retrospect, in illness or in utter defeat, the moment of vanishing hope, the moment of dying. What

Porter makes us see are those subjective worlds of hallucination, obsession, fever, guilt. The presence of death hovering about Granny Weatherall she makes as real and brings as near as Granny's own familiar room that stands about her bed.

In this story, we move on two levels: We get glimpses of the outer, or surface, reality of the sickroom. But we also participate in the inner reality of the central character's observations, thoughts, and feelings. As often with the stream-of-consciousness technique, some of the stream of thoughts and emotions seems trivial or routine. But eventually the character's thinking circles back to what really matters.

The Jilting of Granny Weatherall   1929

She flicked her wrist neatly out of Doctor Harry's pudgy careful fingers and pulled the sheet up to her chin. The brat ought to be in knee breeches. Doctoring around the country with spectacles on his nose! "Get along now, take your schoolbooks and go. There's nothing wrong with me."

Doctor Harry spread a warm paw like a cushion on her forehead where the forked green vein danced and made her eyelids twitch. "Now, now, be a good girl, and we'll have you up in no time."

"That's no way to speak to a woman nearly eighty years old just because she's down. I'd have you respect your elders, young man."

"Well, Missy, excuse me." Doctor Harry patted her cheek. "But I've got to warn you, haven't I? You're a marvel, but you must be careful or you're going to be good and sorry."

"Don't tell me what I'm going to be. I'm on my feet now, morally speak-   5
ing. It's Cornelia. I had to go to bed to get rid of her."

Her bones felt loose, and floated around in her skin, and Doctor Harry floated like a balloon around the foot of the bed. He floated and pulled down his waistcoat and swung his glasses on a cord. "Well, stay where you are, it certainly can't hurt you."

"Get along and doctor your sick," said Granny Weatherall. "Leave a well woman alone. I'll call for you when I want you. . . . Where were you forty years ago when I pulled through milk-leg and double pneumonia? You weren't even born. Don't let Cornelia lead you on," she shouted, because Doctor Harry appeared to float up to the ceiling and out. "I pay my own bills, and I don't throw my money away on nonsense!"

She meant to wave good-by, but it was too much trouble. Her eyes closed of themselves, it was like a dark curtain drawn around the bed. The pillow rose and floated under her, pleasant as a hammock in a light wind. She listened to the leaves rustling outside the window. No, somebody was swishing newspapers: no, Cornelia and Doctor Harry were whispering together. She leaped broad awake, thinking they whispered in her ear.

"She was never like this, *never* like this!" "Well, what can we expect?" "Yes, eighty years old. . . ."

Well, and what if she was? She still had ears. It was like Cornelia to whis-   10
per around doors. She always kept things secret in such a public way. She

was always being tactful and kind. Cornelia was dutiful; that was the trouble with her. Dutiful and good: "So good and dutiful," said Granny, "that I'd like to spank her." She saw herself spanking Cornelia and making a fine job of it.

"What'd you say, Mother?"

Granny felt her face tying up in hard knots.

"Can't a body think, I'd like to know?"

"I thought you might want something."

"I do. I want a lot of things. First off, go away and don't whisper."   15

She lay and drowsed, hoping in her sleep that the children would keep out and let her rest a minute. It had been a long day. Not that she was tired. It was always pleasant to snatch a minute now and then. There was always so much to be done, let me see: tomorrow.

Tomorrow was far away and there was nothing to trouble about. Things were finished somehow when the time came; thank God there was always a little margin over for peace: then a person could spread out the plan of life and tuck in the edges orderly. It was good to have everything clean and folded away, with the hair brushes and tonic bottles sitting straight on the white embroidered linen: the day started without fuss and the pantry shelves laid out with rows of jelly glasses and brown jugs and white stone-china jars with blue whirligigs and words painted on them: coffee, tea, sugar, ginger, cinnamon, allspice: and the bronze clock with the lion on top nicely dusted off. The dust that lion could collect in twenty-four hours! The box in the attic with all those letters tied up, well, she'd have to go through that tomorrow. All those letters—George's letters and John's letters and her letters to them both—lying around for the children to find afterwards made her uneasy. Yes, that would be tomorrow's business. No use to let them know how silly she had been once.

While she was rummaging around she found death in her mind and it felt clammy and unfamiliar. She had spent so much time preparing for death there was no need for bringing it up again. Let it take care of itself now. When she was sixty she had felt very old, finished, and went around making farewell trips to see her children and grandchildren, with a secret in her mind: This is the very last of your mother, children! Then she made her will and came down with a long fever. That was all just a notion like a lot of other things, but it was lucky too, for she had once for all got over the idea of dying for a long time. Now she couldn't be worried. She hoped she had better sense now. Her father had lived to be one hundred and two years old and had drunk a noggin of strong hot toddy on his last birthday. He told reporters it was his daily habit, and he owed his long life to that. He had made quite a scandal and was very pleased about it. She believed she'd just plague Cornelia a little.

"Cornelia! Cornelia!" No footsteps, but a sudden hand on her cheek. "Bless you, where have you been?"

"Here, Mother."   20

"Well, Cornelia, I want a noggin of hot toddy."

"Are you cold, darling?"

"I'm chilly, Cornelia. Lying in bed stops the circulation. I must have told you that a thousand times."

Well, she could just hear Cornelia telling her husband that Mother was getting a little childish and they'd have to humor her. The thing that most annoyed her was that Cornelia thought she was deaf, dumb, and blind. Little hasty glances and tiny gestures tossed around her and over her head saying, "Don't cross her, let her have her way, she's eighty years old," and she sitting there as if she lived in a thin glass cage. Sometimes Granny almost made up her mind to pack up and move back to her own house where nobody could remind her every minute that she was old. Wait, wait, Cornelia, till your own children whisper behind your back!

In her day she had kept a better house and had got more work done. She wasn't too old yet for Lydia to be driving eighty miles for advice when one of the children jumped the track, and Jimmy still dropped in and talked things over: "Now, Mammy, you've a good business head, I want to know what you think of this? . . . " Old. Cornelia couldn't change the furniture around without asking. Little things, little things! They had been so sweet when they were little. Granny wished the old days were back again with the children young and everything to be done over. It had been a hard pull, but not too much for her. When she thought of all the food she had cooked, and all the clothes she had cut and sewed, and all the gardens she had made —well, the children showed it. There they were, made out of her, and they couldn't get away from that. Sometimes she wanted to see John again and point to them and say, Well, I didn't do so badly, did I? But that would have to wait. That was for tomorrow. She used to think of him as a man, but now all the children were older than their father, and he would be a child beside her if she saw him now. It seemed strange and there was something wrong in the idea. Why, he couldn't possibly recognize her. She had fenced in a hundred acres once, digging the post holes herself and clamping the wires with just a negro boy to help. That changed a woman. John would be looking for a young woman with the peaked Spanish comb in her hair and the painted fan. Digging post holes changed a woman. Riding country roads in the winter when women had their babies was another thing: sitting up nights with sick horses and sick negroes and sick children and hardly ever losing one. John, I hardly ever lost one of them! John would see that in a minute, that would be something he could understand, she wouldn't have to explain anything!

It made her feel like rolling up her sleeves and putting the whole place to rights again. No matter if Cornelia was determined to be everywhere at once, there were a great many things left undone on this place. She would start tomorrow and do them. It was good to be strong enough for everything, even if all you made melted and changed and slipped under your hands, so that by the time you finished you almost forgot what you were working for. What was it I set out to do? she asked herself intently, but she could not remember. A fog rose over the valley, she saw it marching across the creek swallowing the trees and moving up the hill like an army of ghosts. Soon it would be at the near edge of the orchard, and then it was time to go in and light the lamps. Come in, children, don't stay out in the night air.

Lighting the lamps had been beautiful. The children huddled up to her and breathed like little calves waiting at the bars in the twilight. Their eyes followed the match and watched the flame rise and settle in a blue curve, then they moved away from her. The lamp was lit, they didn't have to be scared and hang on to mother any more. Never, never, never more. God, for all my life I thank Thee. Without Thee, my God, I could never have done it. Hail, Mary, full of grace.

I want you to pick all the fruit this year and see that nothing is wasted. There's always someone who can use it. Don't let good things rot for want of using. You waste life when you waste good food. Don't let things get lost. It's bitter to lose things. Now, don't let me get to thinking, not when I am tired and taking a little nap before supper. . . .

The pillow rose about her shoulders and pressed against her heart and the memory was being squeezed out of it: oh, push down the pillow, some-body: it would smother her if she tried to hold it. Such a fresh breeze blow-ing and such a green day with no threats in it. But he had not come, just the same. What does a woman do when she has put on the white veil and set out the white cake for a man and he doesn't come? She tried to re-member. No, I swear he never harmed me but in that. He never harmed me but in that . . . and what if he did? There was the day, the day, but a whirl of dark smoke rose and covered it, crept up and over into the bright field where everything was planted so carefully in orderly rows. That was hell, she knew hell when she saw it. For sixty years she had prayed against re-membering him and against losing her soul in the deep pit of hell, and now the two things were mingled in one and the thought of him was a smoky cloud from hell that moved and crept in her head when she had just got rid of Doctor Harry and was trying to rest a minute. Wounded vanity, Ellen, said a sharp voice in the top of her mind. Don't let your wounded vanity get the upper hand of you. Plenty of girls get jilted. You were jilted, weren't you? Then stand up to it. Her eyelids wavered and let in streamers of blue-gray light like tissue paper over her eyes. She must get up and pull the shades down or she'd never sleep. She was in bed again and the shades were not down. How could that happen? Better turn over, hide from the light, sleep-ing in the light gave you nightmares. "Mother, how do you feel now?" and a stinging wetness on her forehead. But I don't like having my face washed in cold water!

Hapsy? George? Lydia? Jimmy? No, Cornelia, and her features were   30
swollen and full of little puddles. "They're coming, darling, they'll all be here soon." Go wash your face, child, you look funny.

Instead of obeying, Cornelia knelt down and put her head on the pillow. She seemed to be talking but there was no sound. "Well, are you tongue-tied? Whose birthday is it? Are you going to give a party?"

Cornelia's mouth moved urgently in strange shapes. "Don't do that, you bother me, daughter."

"Oh, no, Mother. Oh, no. . . ."

Nonsense. It was strange about children. They disputed your every word. "No what, Cornelia?"

"Here's Doctor Harry."   35

"I won't see that boy again. He just left five minutes ago."

"That was this morning, Mother. It's night now. Here's the nurse."

"This is Doctor Harry, Mrs. Weatherall. I never saw you look so young and happy!"

"Ah, I'll never be young again—but I'd be happy if they'd let me lie in peace and get rested."

She thought she spoke up loudly, but no one answered. A warm weight on her forehead, a warm bracelet on her wrist, and a breeze went on whispering, trying to tell her something. A shuffle of leaves in the everlasting hand of God, He blew on them and they danced and rattled. "Mother, don't mind, we're going to give you a little hypodermic." "Look here, daughter, how do ants get in this bed? I saw sugar ants yesterday." Did you send for Hapsy too?

It was Hapsy she really wanted. She had to go a long way back through a great many rooms to find Hapsy standing with a baby on her arm. She seemed to herself to be Hapsy also, and the baby on Hapsy's arm was Hapsy and himself and herself, all at once, and there was no surprise in the meeting. Then Hapsy melted from within and turned flimsy as gray gauze and the baby was a gauzy shadow, and Hapsy came up close and said, "I thought you'd never come," and looked at her very searchingly and said, "You haven't changed a bit!" They leaned forward to kiss, when Cornelia began whispering from a long way off, "Oh, is there anything you want to tell me? Is there anything I can do for you?"

Yes, she had changed her mind after sixty years and she would like to see George. I want you to find George. Find him and be sure to tell him I forgot him. I want him to know I had my husband just the same and my children and my house like any other woman. A good house too and a good husband that I loved and fine children out of him. Better than I hoped for even. Tell him I was given back everything he took away and more. Oh, no, oh, God, no, there was something else besides the house and the man and the children. Oh, surely they were not all? What was it? Something not given back. . . . Her breath crowded down under her ribs and grew into a monstrous frightening shape with cutting edges; it bored up into her head, and the agony was unbelievable: Yes, John, get the doctor now, no more talk, my time has come.

When this one was born it should be the last. The last. It should have been born first, for it was the one she had truly wanted. Everything came in good time. Nothing left out, left over. She was strong, in three days she would be as well as ever. Better. A woman needed milk in her to have her full health.

"Mother, do you hear me?"

"I've been telling you—"

"Mother, Father Connolly's here."

"I went to Holy Communion only last week. Tell him I'm not so sinful as all that."

"Father just wants to speak to you."

He could speak as much as he pleased. It was like him to drop in and inquire about her soul as if it were a teething baby, and then stay on for a cup of tea and a round of cards and gossip. He always had a funny story of some sort, usually about an Irishman who made his little mistakes and confessed them, and the point lay in some absurd thing he would blurt out in the confessional showing his struggles between native piety and original sin. Granny felt easy about her soul. Cornelia, where are your manners? Give Father Connolly a chair. She had her secret comfortable understanding with a few favorite saints who cleared a straight road to God for her. All as surely signed and sealed as the papers for the new Forty Acres. Forever heirs and assigns forever. Since the day the wedding cake was not cut, but thrown out and wasted. The whole bottom dropped out of the world, and there she was blind and sweating with nothing under her feet and the walls falling away. His hand had caught her under the breast, she had not fallen, there was the freshly polished floor with the green rug on it, just as before. He had cursed like a sailor's parrot and said, "I'll kill him for you." Don't lay a hand on him, for my sake leave something to God. "Now, Ellen, you must believe what I tell you. . . ."

So there was nothing, nothing to worry about any more, except some-   50
times in the night one of the children screamed in a nightmare, and they both hustled out shaking and hunting for the matches and calling, "There, wait a minute, here we are!" John, get the doctor now, Hapsy's time has come. But there was Hapsy standing by the bed in a white cap. "Cornelia, tell Hapsy to take off her cap. I can't see her plain."

Her eyes opened very wide and the room stood out like a picture she had seen somewhere. Dark colors with the shadows rising toward the ceiling in long angles. The tall black dresser gleamed with nothing on it but John's picture, enlarged from a little one, with John's eyes very black when they should have been blue. You never saw him, so how do you know how he looked? But the man insisted the copy was perfect, it was very rich and handsome. For a picture, yes, but it's not my husband. The table by the bed had a linen cover and a candle and a crucifix. The light was blue from Cornelia's silk lampshades. No sort of light at all, just frippery. You had to live forty years with kerosene lamps to appreciate honest electricity. She felt very strong and she saw Doctor Harry with a rosy nimbus around him.

"You look like a saint, Doctor Harry, and I vow that's as near as you'll ever come to it."

"She's saying something."

"I heard you, Cornelia. What's all this carrying-on?"

"Father Connolly's saying—"   55

Cornelia's voice staggered and bumped like a cart in a bad road. It rounded corners and turned back again and arrived nowhere. Granny stepped up in the cart very lightly and reached for the reins, but a man sat beside her and she knew him by his hands, driving the cart. She did not look in his face, for she knew without seeing, but looked instead down the road where the trees leaned over and bowed to each other and a thousand birds were singing a Mass. She felt like singing too, but she put her hand in the bosom of her dress and pulled out a rosary, and Father Connolly murmured Latin in a very solemn voice and tickled her feet. My God, will you stop that nonsense? I'm a married woman. What if he did run away and leave me to face the priest by myself? I found another a whole world better. I wouldn't have exchanged my husband for anybody except Saint

Michael himself, and you may tell him that for me with a thank you in the bargain.

Light flashed on her closed eyelids, and a deep roaring shook her. Cornelia, is that lightning? I hear thunder. . . . There's going to be a storm. Close all the windows. Call the children in. . . . "Mother, here we are, all of us." "Is that you, Hapsy?" "Oh, no, I'm Lydia. We drove as fast as we could." Their faces drifted above her, drifted away. The rosary fell out of her hands and Lydia put it back. Jimmy tried to help, their hands fumbled together, and Granny closed two fingers around Jimmy's thumb. Beads wouldn't do, it must be something alive. She was so amazed her thoughts ran round and round. So, my dear Lord, this is my death and I wasn't even thinking about it. My children have come to see me die. But I can't, it's not time. Oh, I always hated surprises. I wanted to give Cornelia the amethyst set— Cornelia, you're to have the amethyst set, but Hapsy's to wear it when she wants, and, Doctor Harry, do shut up. Nobody sent for you. Oh, my dear Lord, do wait a minute. I meant to do something about the Forty Acres, Jimmy doesn't need it and Lydia will later on, with that worthless husband of hers. I meant to finish the altar cloth and send six bottles of wine to Sister Borgia for her dyspepsia. I want to send six bottles of wine to Sister Borgia, Father Connolly, now don't let me forget.

Cornelia's voice made short turns and tilted over and crashed. "Oh, Mother, oh, Mother, oh, Mother. . . ."

"I'm not going, Cornelia. I'm taken by surprise. I can't go."

You'll see Hapsy again. What about her? "I thought you'd never come."   60 Granny made a long journey outward, looking for Hapsy. What if I don't find her? What then? Her heart sank down and down, there was no bottom to death, she couldn't come to the end of it. The blue light from Cornelia's lampshade drew into a tiny point in the center of her brain, it flickered and winked like an eye, quietly it fluttered and dwindled. Granny lay curled down within herself, amazed and watchful, staring at the point of light that was herself; her body was now only a deeper mass of shadow in an endless darkness and this darkness would curl around the light and swallow it up. God, give a sign!

For the second time there was no sign. Again no bridegroom and the priest in the house. She could not remember any other sorrow because this grief wiped them all away. Oh, no, there's nothing more cruel than this— I'll never forgive it. She stretched herself with a deep breath and blew out the light.

The Receptive Reader

1. In how much of this story do we look at the world from Granny Weatherall's *point of view?* How much is inner reality, or stream-of-consciousness? What is the alternative strand of things happening that the main character does not fully take in? How much of the story is the outer reality of the sickroom?

2. What kinds of memories and concerns take up the early pages of the story? What are striking examples of the blending of present and past?

3. When does the narrative begin to close in on the events alluded to in the title? How are you able to piece together the story of what happened sixty years earlier? What is the central character's attitude toward those events? What role did the jilting play in her life as a whole? Why do you think the author approaches this central topic in such a roundabout way?

4. Look at the *minor characters:* What role does Cornelia play in the story? What role do Granny's husband and family play in the story as a whole? What role does Hapsy play in Granny's thoughts and feelings as the end approaches?

5. Does this story have a *plot?* Does any action or development take place parallel to the physical events of the sickroom? How does the ending tie major concerns of the story together?

6. How would you sum up in one sentence the attitude toward life implied in this story?

The Personal Response

How would you describe the central character in the story? What kind of person emerges from the story as a whole? What kind of life has she had? How do you relate to her as the reader? How do you think the author *expected* you to feel toward the central character? (Does she seem to steer the reader's feelings or reactions?)

Making Connections—For Discussion or Writing

✖ The technique of the interior monologue is designed to give you an inside view of a character's thoughts and feelings. Does this story give you a fuller understanding of its central character than other stories you have read so far? Compare what and how you learn about the central character in this story and in a story like Alice Munro's "Boys and Girls."

✖ Feminist critics have praised in Porter's writing "the splendid portraits of women which fill her work"; her sympathy with "frustrated, maligned, unvalued, struggling, emotionally blocked, and intellectually undernourished women"; and her exasperation with "conventional social patterns, especially male-dominated marriage and the creed of domesticity" (Jane Flanders). How much of this description fits "The Jilting of Granny Weatherall"?

WRITING ABOUT LITERATURE

5 Sharing a Point of View
WRITING FOCUS: Responding to Peer Reviews

The Writing Workshop   What window does a story open on the world? Through whose eyes do we see the people and events, and what difference does it make? In writing a paper about point of view, ask yourself questions like the following:

✗ What is the narrator's relation to the events of the story? Are we listening to a casual observer? to a reliable impartial witness? to a person with an ax to grind? Does the story read like self-justification? like nostalgic reenactment of the past?

✗ How does the point of view limit your vision as the reader? (What is left out that you might want to know?) How does it steer your reactions? (Do you anywhere resist what the narrator apparently expects you to think or feel?)

✗ How might the events of the story look if seen from a different point of view? Try to imagine what the story would be like if told from the perspective of someone else in the story.

✗ Does the narrator take in more of what happens than someone else might—or less? Do you at times feel that you know (or suspect) more than the narrator does? Are you expected to question the perceptions of the narrator?

✗ Are there deliberate shifts in perspective or changes in point of view? Is part of the story seen through one pair of eyes, and another part through another? Does a more comprehensive overall view emerge from such a double perspective?

Focus on Peer Response   When you work on papers about the stories you read, bringing the topic into focus, gathering material, and pulling it into shape will absorb much of your attention. But sooner or later, you will begin to focus on what happens when your writing reaches the reader. In many writing classes, student writers have a chance to learn from **peer response.** When your writing is critiqued by your peers, you become more audience-conscious. You become more aware of how readers react. You become more conscious of what will help and what may hinder your reader.

When you in turn participate in peer response, you formulate your reactions to the writing of fellow students, trying to help them revise and strengthen their papers. Remember the golden rule of peer criticism: Respond unto others as you would have them respond unto you. Try to avoid mere fault-finding. Respond to both strengths and weaknesses, showing that you are basically on the writer's side. In responding to the paper of a fellow student, try to see details in the context of the paper as a whole. How do they affect the overall effectiveness of the paper? What can the writer do to make the paper more effective? Try to answer questions like the following:

✗ *What is the writer trying to do?* What seems to be the general purpose? How well has it been achieved?

✗ *Does the paper get off to a good start?* Do the title and the opening lines capture the attention of the reader? Do they channel it in the right direction?

✗ *Does the paper have a strong central idea or thesis?* Is it spelled out clearly enough—at the beginning or, sometimes, toward the end of the paper? Does the writer keep it in view or lose sight of it as the paper develops?

✗ *What is the general strategy or master plan?* Does it become clear enough to the reader? Or does the reader need more of a preview or program early in the paper? Does the reader run into apparent detours or digressions? Should the organization be streamlined? Should major sections of the paper be reshuffled?

✗ *Are key points well developed?* Is there a rich supporting texture of short quotable quotes and striking authentic detail? Where do you feel a lack of support or follow-through? Are any points merely mentioned in passing and then dropped?

✗ *How effective are the transitions from one point to the next?* Does the paper show the connection between major parts? Does it signal turning points or steps in an argument? Does the paper need stronger logical links?

✗ *Does the conclusion merely rehash points already made?* Or does it do a needed job of pulling together different parts of an argument? Does it add anything to show the larger meaning or implications of the author's points? Does it leave readers with a striking quotation or telling incident to remember?

✗ *How well does the paper communicate its points?* Where would you put in the margin "well put" or "well said" or "good touch"? Where are readers likely to stumble over garbled or incomplete sentences or over missing commas? Where are they likely to be confused by words that are near misses or just plain wrong? Where are big words or shifting, confusing terms used without definition? Where is the wording too disrespectful or slangy—and where too stiff or pretentious? Where do you hear clichés rather than the writer's own voice?

✗ *Does the paper show any personal involvement or commitment?* Does it sound too much like an "assignment"? Is there a personal connection?

Peer Responses to a Draft   Study the following sample student paper and the excerpts from peer responses that follow it. How carefully have the authors of the peer responses read the paper? How do these readers compare with your own vision of an ideal responsive reader for your own writing?

Sample Student Paper

Creating an Empathetic Audience: A Skillful Use of Point of View

Point of view is a useful author's tool. If used skillfully, it can allow the reader to learn much about a character from a few carefully placed clues. This type of storytelling avoids preachy didacticism and allows the reader to form personal opinions about the character that are not influenced by other characters' thoughts or actions. Tillie Olsen's "I Stand Here Ironing" is an example of a first-person narrative in which the main character is speaking mostly about her nineteen-year-old daughter Emily, but the reader still learns much about the narrator herself. Also, by telling the story from the mother's point of view, Olsen allows the reader to feel empathy for a character who might otherwise inspire anger or disgust.

If this story were told from the troubled Emily's point of view, one can only imagine the vision of the mother that would emerge. A fly on the wall in the counselor's office who confronts Emily's mother at the beginning of the story might have heard Emily describe her mother in a negative light. Emily might tell the counselor, "My mother never smiled at me; she only smiled at my younger sister, Susan, who was prettier. She sent me away all the time—first to my father's family, then to a day school, then to an awful convalescent hospital. She never had time for me; she always worked. She was never there when I needed her." And so on, until all the mother's evils were categorized and the reader feels nothing but anger at the seemingly heartless mother and sympathy for Emily. But by telling the story from the mother's point of view, Olsen uncovers the flip side of the situation, allowing the woman to respond to her daughter's allegations and explain her actions, thus letting the reader empathize with her and gain a better understanding of her. In this way, Olsen also makes a point about the difficulties a single woman can face raising a child and how, oftentimes, innocent lives can be sacrificed and lost in the daily struggle to survive.

The narrator begins the story by describing how difficult it was for her in the early years after her husband left her, describing the hectic pace of her life as she tried to scrape up the daily necessities. "I would start running as soon as I got off the streetcars, running up the stairs, . . ." She describes how she had to send her daughter away to her husband's family, and then later, once she was finally able to bring her back, how she had to send her to nursery school during the day. The narrator guiltily admits that she knew the nursery was evil, but "it was the only place there was." It was the only way we could be together, the only way I could hold a job. The first-person narrative of the story allows her readers this insight into the woman's actions. It allows them to learn that such actions, although they may seem cruel, were the only alternative the woman had as she desperately tried to support herself and her child.

Later in the story, the narrator explains how she had to send Emily away again— this time because she did not get well after a bout with the red measles. "They persuaded me at the clinic to send her away to a convalescent home in the country," she says. They told her Emily would receive "the kind of food and care you can't manage for her." The narrator discusses with heartwrenching guilt the "ravaged looks" of the girls in the home and how she desperately tried to get Emily back. If her readers did not have this insight into the woman's feelings, they might believe she was a careless or apathetic mother who found it easier to stick her child into a gruesome home rather than take proper care of her.

The narrator does admit, however, that she made many mistakes with Emily. She rarely smiled at Emily when she was a child, she never held and loved Emily as she did the other children, and she denied Emily the affection she showered on Susan, the second child. She knows these and other things made life harder on Emily than it was on the other children. The narrator admits her error, but knows in her heart that sometimes such happenings are inevitable. "I was at the terrible, growing years. War years. I do not remember them well. I was working, there were four smaller ones now, there was not time for her. She had to help be a mother, and housekeeper, and shopper." Through comments such as these, the reader learns that the narrator, very young herself, was also having a rough time making ends meet. And although it does seem a heavy burden to fall on Emily's small shoulders, placed in the context of an impoverished woman struggling to feed six mouths with one paycheck, Emily's burden becomes one of necessity, not of cruelty. The story's first-person point of view allows the reader the indulgence of pity for Emily and her difficult youth, yet also allows empathy for the mother. Because the reader is privy to the narrator's side of the situation, Emily's hardship is lessened in the face of the family's fierce struggle to survive.

Tillie Olsen's use of first-person narrative in "I Stand Here Ironing" permits the reader to step into the shoes of a poor working-class mother and her daily fight for survival. It permits those of us who have never experienced such hardship to ask ourselves, "What would I do if? . . ." The answer might shock us: We might do the exact thing the narrator was forced to do, which was to rely on a child to perform chores beyond her, in essence robbing that child of the playtime essential to healthy growth. The narrator Olsen creates is universal: a character struggling to survive despite overwhelming odds. And, although that character makes mistakes, these are forgiven in the face of the struggle. The situation Olsen creates is also universal, telling the often unavoidable fate of the children born into such conditions, whose own personalities are lost in the cycle of poverty and the fight for survival.

Peer Responses

1. While reading this essay, I started on a very negative slant, but the author won me over. The paper starts slowly and actually somewhat awkwardly. To begin with, the title, for me, is too long and general. It gives no hint of what the major focus of the story is. Then the first three sentences are solely generalizations about point of view in general. Then, finally, the writer introduces the story that will be the major subject of the essay. So I stop to wonder—is the author writing about point of view, using this story as a convenient example, or is she writing about how point of view makes this story what it is? It is a subtle difference, but it significantly affects how one approaches the story. Both the title and the beginning talk about point of view in very general terms, and that hardly draws the reader in. However, once the author starts writing about Tillie Olsen and her story, she does an excellent job of following up and using quotes effectively to support her thesis: In this story, point of view creates a receptive, empathetic reader. She keeps this central idea in focus well throughout her essay.

2. The writer hints at her thesis in the title and then spells it out at the end of her first paragraph. The main point is that the first-person narrative—the point of view used in "I Stand Here Ironing"—lets the reader get inside the skin of the character and helps readers understand and empathize with her. The paper shows good use of counterpoint in the second paragraph: One key element that works well in this paper is that the writer balances the narrator's point of view with the projected point of view of the daughter. The reader is made to see how the story might have been completely different if told from the perspective of the daughter. The paper leads up effectively to an awareness of the universal nature of the narrator's predicament and her guilt. The ending shows great strength, making up for some of the mechanical quality of the beginning. As for the title, something more imaginative, perhaps drawn from the inner core of the story, would be better.

3. We get a good idea of the importance of point of view in this paper. The author gets right to the point and stays there. The purpose of the paper is to justify the mother's actions and decisions. I feel more attention could have been paid to how the mother actually felt about Emily. She may have resented ever having her. Often a parent will like one child and dislike another. Some phrases slip into clichés: "making ends meet"; "despite overwhelming odds."

Questions for Peer Review

Writers vary greatly in how much they profit from feedback from their readers. How useful or instructive are the peer responses to the student paper on the Olsen story?

1. Authors are wary of reviewers who seize on a few isolated points and do not do justice to what a paper or an article is trying to accomplish as a whole. What details in the student responses would help convince you that the peer reviewers gave the paper a careful *responsive reading?*

2. Studying feedback from a range of sources, writers look for areas of agreement or even a true meeting of minds, or *consensus.* Where are the peer responses in substantial agreement on the strengths and weaknesses of the paper?

3. How do the peer responses *differ?* (And can you try to explain why?) If you were the student author of the paper, whose judgment would you be inclined to trust, and why?

4. What revised *title* would you suggest that would be more pointed and more informative at the same time?

5. What *opening quotation* from the story might get the reader's attention and lead up effectively to the writer's thesis?

6. How would you sum up what you learned from the student paper and the peer responses about the role of *point of view* in short fiction?

6 SYMBOL
The Eloquent Image

Courtesy Richard B. Ressman

*A symbol assumes two planes, two worlds of ideas
and sensations, and a dictionary of correspondences between them.*

ALBERT CAMUS

*Symbolism adds a new value to an object or an
act, without thereby violating its immediate or
"historical" validity. . . . Seen in this light the
universe is no longer sealed off, nothing is
isolated inside its own existence: everything is
linked by a system of correspondences and
assimilations.*

MIRCEA ELIADE

FOCUS ON SYMBOLS

Symbols are images that have a meaning beyond themselves. In a short story, a symbol is a detail, a character, or an incident that has a meaning beyond its literal role in the narrative. As we read, the mind's eye takes in images—vividly imagined details, shapes, textures. But often we sense that there is more than meets the eye. Something tells us: The sun in this story is not just a physical fact. It leaves the landscape parched; it dries up the sources of life-giving water. It becomes over-powering, threatening. It means something—it tells us something, if only we knew how to read between the lines. To respond fully to a story, you have to become sensitive to symbolic overtones and implications. As you interpret the language of symbols, keep points like the following in mind:

✗ *Some symbols come into a story from a shared language of symbols.* Much in human experience has traditional symbolic associations: the dawn with hope, the dark forest with evil, clay with death, water with fertility. Light is often the symbol for knowledge, for "enlightenment"— *fiat lux* ("let there be light") is the rallying cry of those fighting the dark-ness of ignorance.

✗ *Some symbols have a special personal meaning for the writer.* Their meaning may come into focus as they return again and again in the writer's work. Speaking of the Irish poet Seamus Heaney, a critic said that the source of his imaginative power lay in his rural childhood ex-perience "that is centered and staked in the image of the pump. The pump, like his poetry, taps hidden springs to conduct what is sustain-ing and life-giving. The pump is a symbol of the nourishment which comes from knowing and belonging to a certain place and a certain mode of life" (Elmer Andrews).

❚ *Literary symbols are rich in associations.* They have more resonance, more reverberations than simple signs. The skull and bones that say "poison" have a clear, unequivocal message. But literary symbols do not simply signal "Danger" or "All Clear." An ancient symbol in Western culture is the garden. It brings with it a wealth of associations: The Garden of Eden was a scene of innocence and happiness, before the fall of Adam. The garden is a symbol of nature seen as fruitful and life-sustaining. Like the garden of Eden, it may be the cultivated spot in the surrounding wilderness. It may suggest the oasis in the desert. It may suggest a retreat from the intrigues of office or business—we retreat there to "cultivate our own garden."

❚ *Symbols may be ambiguous.* In Herman Melville's great American classic *Moby Dick,* the mythic white whale seems paradoxically double-faced. To the obsessed Captain Ahab, the whale stands for everything that is destructive in nature—and the whale does in the end send his ship and his crew to the bottom of the sea. But at other times, the whale seems to stand for everything that is most serenely beautiful in nature—as it floats through the becalmed sea, shedding "enticings."

❚ *Symbols acquire their full meaning in the context of a story.* In Nathaniel Hawthorne's novel *The Scarlet Letter,* the letter *A* for adultery, embroidered on the sinner's gown, may at first seem a matter of historical interest. We can say, "This is how the Puritans identified an adulteress." But as we watch her and her innocent child, the scarlet letter begins to haunt us; it makes us think. The author used it as the title of the whole novel: *The Scarlet Letter.* As we finish the novel, that scarlet letter is likely to have been burned into our consciousness. It becomes a symbol of our consciousness of guilt, of our doubts about who is truly guilty. We begin to imagine it carried by others (like the Puritan minister Dimmesdale), who are implicated but not literally stigmatized.

FIRST READING

Responding to Symbols

Before you read the following short short story, take a few minutes for freewriting about snow. What images, thoughts, or associations does it bring to mind? Write freely without sorting or second thoughts. Jot down any ideas or memories that the word triggers in your mind. Then read the story and answer the questions that follow it. Ann Beattie often writes about urban Americans who remember the euphoria of the anti-war demonstrations, the rock festivals, and the counterculture of their

youth and who feel a vague sense of being let down, "by not having in-volved themselves enough" or "by having involved themselves to no avail."

Ann Beattie   *(born 1947)*

Snow   *1986*

I remember the cold night you brought in a pile of logs and a chipmunk jumped off as you lowered your arms. "What do you think *you're* doing in here?" you said, as it ran through the living room. It went through the library and stopped at the front door as though it knew the house well. This would be difficult for anyone to believe, except perhaps as the subject of a poem. Our first week in the house was spent scraping, finding some of the house's secrets, like wallpaper underneath wallpaper. In the kitchen, a pattern of white-gold trellises supported purple grapes as big and round as Ping-Pong balls. When we painted the walls yellow, I thought of the bits of grape that remained underneath and imagined the vine popping through, the way some plants can tenaciously push through anything. The day of the big snow, when you had to shovel the walk and couldn't find your cap and asked me how to wind a towel so that it would stay on your head—you, in the white towel turban, like a crazy king of snow. People liked the idea of our being together, leaving the city for the country. So many people visited, and the fireplace made all of them want to tell amazing stories: the child who happened to be standing on the right corner when the door of the ice-cream truck came open and hundreds of Popsicles crashed out; the man standing on the beach, sand sparkling in the sun, one bit glinting more than the rest, stooping to find a diamond ring. Did they talk about amazing things because they thought we'd turn into one of them? Now I think they proba-bly guessed it wouldn't work. It was as hopeless as giving a child a matched cup and saucer. Remember the night, out on the lawn, knee-deep in snow, chins pointed at the sky as the wind whirled down all that whiteness? It seemed that the world had been turned upside down, and we were look-ing into an enormous field of Queen Anne's lace. Later, headlights off, our car was the first to ride through the newly fallen snow. The world outside the car looked solarized.

You remember it differently. You remember that the cold settled in stages, that a small curve of light was shaved from the moon night after night, until you were no longer surprised the sky was black, that the chipmunk ran to hide in the dark, not simply to a door that led to its escape. Our visitors told the same stories people always tell. One night, giving me a lesson in story-telling, you said, "Any life will seem dramatic if you omit mention of most of it."

This, then, for drama: I drove back to that house not long ago. It was April, and Allen had died. In spite of all the visitors, Allen, next door, had been the good friend in bad times. I sat with his wife in their living room, looking out the glass doors to the backyard, and there was Allen's pool, still

covered with black plastic that had been stretched across it for winter. It had rained, and as the rain fell, the cover collected more and more water until it finally spilled onto the concrete. When I left that day, I drove past what had been our house. Three or four crocuses were blooming in the front— just a few dots of white, no field of snow. I felt embarrassed for them. They couldn't compete.

This is a story, told the way you say stories should be told: Somebody grew up, fell in love, and spent a winter with her lover in the country. This, of course, is the barest outline, and futile to discuss. It's as pointless as throwing birdseed on the ground while snow still falls fast. Who expects small things to survive when even the largest get lost? People forget years and remember moments. Seconds and symbols are left to sum things up: the black shroud over the pool. Love, in its shortest form, becomes a word. What I remember about all that time is one winter. The snow. Even now, saying "snow," my lips move so that they kiss the air.

No mention has been made of the snowplow that seemed always to be   5 there, scraping snow off our narrow road—an artery cleared, though neither of us could have said where the heart was.

The Receptive Reader

Beattie says in this story, "Seconds and symbols are left to sum things up." What symbols do you see in this story? What do they sum up? For example, is the snow a symbol? What does it symbolize for you? (Do your classmates agree with your interpretation?) What does the cover of the pool symbolize? Could the chipmunk be a symbol? For what?

THE CENTRAL SYMBOL

In the short story the action is usually small,
while the meanings are large.

THOMAS A. GULLERSON

Often a **central symbol** becomes the focal point of a story. A central symbol focuses our attention. It provides a tangible object for our emotions—since we find it hard to anchor our feelings to disembodied ideas. A central symbol becomes the hub for meanings and associations. It may slowly evolve, acquiring its full meaning only as the story as a whole takes shape. In each of the following stories, a rich central symbol helps give shape to the story as a whole.

John Steinbeck   *(1902–1968)*

Much of Steinbeck's fiction takes us to Steinbeck Country—California's agricultural Salinas Valley and scenic Monterey Bay, stretching south to the rugged coast of Big Sur. This area, where Steinbeck grew

up and went to school, sets the scene for books like *Tortilla Flat* (1935), *Of Mice and Men* (1937), *Cannery Row* (1945), and *East of Eden* (1952). Many characters he places in this setting are social outcasts, poor people, derelicts, migrant workers, and the people who befriend them.

Steinbeck's work was part of the tradition of naturalistic fiction, represented earlier by Americans like Stephen Crane and Jack London. After decades of Victorian high-mindedness, **naturalism** late in the nineteenth century had set out to correct the balance—to recognize the physical and instinctual nature of people. It tried to be more honest about their suppressed (or repressed) physical and emotional needs. Writers stripped life of its genteel pretenses, looking at it, if necessary, in the raw. Steinbeck represents the native tradition of naturalistic fiction in his special sympathy for unglamorous, unfashionable characters and his affectionate rendering of the coarse texture of common life.

Some of Steinbeck's best-known work was part of the literature of **social protest** of the thirties and forties. In the depths of the Great Depression, Steinbeck became famous with his novel *The Grapes of Wrath* (1939). Made into a movie starring Henry Fonda, Steinbeck's mythical novel proved to have a powerful hold on the imagination of millions around the world. Steinbeck told the story of the "Okies" (rural Americans from Oklahoma and other parts of the dust bowl of the thirties) who were driven from their farms by dust storms and *laissez-faire* (let-market-forces-do-their-work) economics.

Feminist critics have in recent years taken a fresh look at the "strong women" in Steinbeck's fiction. These range from Ma Joad and Rose of Sharon, the "earth mother" figures in *Grapes of Wrath,* to women like Elisa Allen in his short story "The Chrysanthemums." They may be women who have a strength of will missing in their husbands; they seem to have more energy and vitality than is needed for their tasks. They "must somehow express themselves meaningfully within the narrow possibilities open to women in a man's world" (Marilyn H. Mitchell).

The Chrysanthemums   *1937*

The high grey-flannel fog of winter closed off the Salinas Valley from the sky and from all the rest of the world. On every side it sat like a lid on the mountains and made of the great valley a closed pot. On the broad, level land floor the gang plows bit deep and left the black earth shining like metal where the shares had cut. On the foothill ranches across the Salinas River, the yellow stubble fields seemed to be bathed in pale cold sunshine, but there was no sunshine in the valley now in December. The thick willow scrub along the river flamed with sharp and positive yellow leaves.

It was a time of quiet and of waiting. The air was cold and tender. A light wind blew up from the southwest so that the farmers were mildly hopeful of a good rain before long; but fog and rain do not go together.

Across the river, on Henry Allen's foothill ranch there was little work to be done, for the hay was cut and stored and the orchards were plowed up to receive the rain deeply when it should come. The cattle on the higher slopes were becoming shaggy and rough-coated.

Elisa Allen, working in her flower garden, looked down across the yard and saw Henry, her husband, talking to two men in business suits. The three of them stood by the tractor shed, each man with one foot on the side of the little Fordson. They smoked cigarettes and studied the machine as they talked.

Elisa watched them for a moment and then went back to her work. She   5
was thirty-five. Her face was lean and strong and her eyes were as clear as water. Her figure looked blocked and heavy in her gardening costume, a man's black hat pulled low down over her eyes, clodhopper shoes, a figured print dress almost completely covered by a big corduroy apron with four big pockets to hold the snips, the trowel and scratcher, the seeds and the knife she worked with. She wore heavy leather gloves to protect her hands while she worked.

She was cutting down the old year's chrysanthemum stalks with a pair of short and powerful scissors. She looked down toward the men by the tractor shed now and then. Her face was eager and mature and handsome; even her work with the scissors was over-eager, over-powerful. The chrysanthemum stems seemed too small and easy for her energy.

She brushed a cloud of hair out of her eyes with the back of her glove, and left a smudge of earth on her cheek in doing it. Behind her stood the neat white farm house with red geraniums close-banked around it as high as the windows. It was a hard-swept looking little house, with hard-polished windows, and a clean mud-mat on the front steps.

Elisa cast another glance toward the tractor shed. The strangers were getting into their Ford coupe. She took off a glove and put her strong fingers down into the forest of new green chrysanthemum sprouts that were growing around the old roots. She spread the leaves and looked down among the close-growing stems. No aphids were there, no sowbugs or snails or cutworms. Her terrier fingers destroyed such pests before they could get started.

Elisa started at the sound of her husband's voice. He had come near quietly, and he leaned over the wire fence that protected her flower garden from cattle and dogs and chickens.

"At it again," he said. "You've got a strong new crop coming."   10

Elisa straightened her back and pulled on the gardening glove again. "Yes. They'll be strong this coming year." In her tone and on her face there was a little smugness.

"You've got a gift with things," Henry observed. "Some of those yellow chrysanthemums you had this year were ten inches across. I wish you'd work out in the orchard and raise some apples that big."

Her eyes sharpened. "Maybe I could do it, too. I've a gift with things, all right. My mother had it. She could stick anything in the ground and make it grow. She said it was having planters' hands that knew how to do it."

"Well, it sure works with flowers," he said.

"Henry, who were those men you were talking to?"   15

"Why, sure, that's what I came to tell you. They were from the Western Meat Company. I sold those thirty head of three-year-old steers. Got nearly my own price, too."

"Good," she said. "Good for you."

"And I thought," he continued, "I thought how it's Saturday afternoon, and we might go into Salinas for dinner at a restaurant, and then to a picture show—to celebrate, you see."

"Good," she repeated. "Oh, yes. That will be good."

Henry put on his joking tone. "There's fights tonight. How'd you like to   20 go to the fights?"

"Oh, no," she said breathlessly. "No, I wouldn't like fights."

"Just fooling, Elisa. We'll go to a movie. Let's see. It's two now. I'm going to take Scotty and bring down those steers from the hill. It'll take us maybe two hours. We'll go in town about five and have dinner at the Cominos Hotel. Like that?"

"Of course I'll like it. It's good to eat away from home."

"All right, then. I'll go get up a couple of horses."

She said, "I'll have plenty of time to transplant some of these sets, I guess."   25

She heard her husband calling Scotty down by the barn. And a little later she saw the two men ride up the pale yellow hillside in search of the steers.

There was a little square sandy bed kept for rooting the chrysanthemums. With her trowel she turned the soil over and over, and smoothed it and patted it firm. Then she dug ten parallel trenches to receive the sets. Back at the chrysanthemum bed she pulled out the little crisp shoots, trimmed off the leaves of each one with her scissors and laid it on a small orderly pile.

A squeak of wheels and plod of hoofs came from the road. Elisa looked up. The country road ran along the dense bank of willows and cottonwoods that bordered the river, and up this road came a curious vehicle, curiously drawn. It was an old springwagon, with a round canvas top on it like the cover of a prairie schooner. It was drawn by an old bay horse and a little grey-and-white burro. A big stubble-bearded man sat between the cover flaps and drove the crawling team. Underneath the wagon, between the hind wheels, a lean and rangy mongrel dog walked sedately. Words were painted on the canvas, in clumsy, crooked letters. "Pots, pans, knives, sisors, lawn mores, Fixed." Two rows of articles, and the triumphantly definitive "Fixed" below. The black paint had run down in little sharp points beneath each letter.

Elisa, squatting on the ground, watched to see the crazy, loose-jointed wagon pass by. But it didn't pass. It turned into the farm road in front of her house, crooked old wheels skirling and squeaking. The rangy dog darted from between the wheels and ran ahead. Instantly the two ranch shepherds flew out at him. Then all three stopped, and with stiff and quivering tails, with taut straight legs, with ambassadorial dignity, they slowly circled, sniffing daintily. The caravan pulled up to Elisa's wire fence and stopped. Now the newcomer dog, feeling out-numbered, lowered his tail and retired under the wagon with raised hackles and bared teeth.

The man on the wagon seat called out, "That's a bad dog in a fight when   30
he gets started."

Elisa laughed. "I see he is. How soon does he generally get started?"

The man caught up her laughter and echoed it heartily. "Sometimes not
for weeks and weeks," he said. He climbed stiffly down, over the wheel.
The horse and the donkey drooped like unwatered flowers.

Elisa saw that he was a very big man. Although his hair and beard were
greying, he did not look old. His worn black suit was wrinkled and spotted
with grease. The laughter had disappeared from his face and eyes the moment his laughing voice ceased. His eyes were dark, and they were full of
the brooding that gets in the eyes of teamsters and of sailors. The calloused
hands he rested on the wire fence were cracked, and every crack was a
black line. He took off his battered hat.

"I'm off my general road, ma'am," he said. "Does this dirt road cut over
across the river to the Los Angeles highway?"

Elisa stood up and shoved the thick scissors in her apron pocket. "Well,   35
yes, it does, but it winds around and then fords the river. I don't think your
team could pull through the sand."

He replied with some asperity, "It might surprise you what them beasts
can pull through."

"When they get started?" she asked.

He smiled for a second. "Yes. When they get started."

"Well," said Elisa, "I think you'll save time if you go back to the Salinas
road and pick up the highway there."

He drew a big finger down the chicken wire and made it sing. "I ain't   40
in any hurry, ma'am. I go from Seattle to San Diego and back every year.
Takes all my time. About six months each way. I aim to follow nice
weather."

Elisa took off her gloves and stuffed them in the apron pocket with the
scissors. She touched the under edge of her man's hat, searching for fugitive hairs. "That sounds like a nice kind of a way to live," she said.

He leaned confidentially over the fence. "Maybe you noticed the writing
on my wagon. I mend pots and sharpen knives and scissors. You got any
of them things to do?"

"Oh, no," she said quickly. "Nothing like that." Her eyes hardened with
resistance.

"Scissors is the worst thing," he explained. "Most people just ruin scissors
trying to sharpen 'em, but I know how. I got a special tool. It's a little bob-
bit kind of thing, and patented. But it sure does the trick."

"No. My scissors are all sharp."   45

"All right, then. Take a pot," he continued earnestly, "a bent pot, or a pot
with a hole. I can make it like new so you don't have to buy no new ones.
That's a saving for you."

"No," she said shortly. "I tell you I have nothing like that for you to do."

His face fell to an exaggerated sadness. His voice took on a whining undertone. "I ain't had a thing to do today. Maybe I won't have no supper tonight.
You see I'm off my regular road. I know folks on the highway clear from
Seattle to San Diego. They save their things for me to sharpen up because
they know I do it so good and save them money."

"I'm sorry," Elisa said irritably. "I haven't anything for you to do."

His eyes left her face and fell to searching the ground. They roamed about until they came to the chrysanthemum bed where she had been working. "What's them plants, ma'am?"

The irritation and resistance melted from Elisa's face. "Oh, those are chrysanthemums, giant whites and yellows. I raise them every year, bigger than anybody around here."

"Kind of a long-stemmed flower? Looks like a quick puff of colored smoke?" he asked.

"That's it. What a nice way to describe them."

"They smell kind of nasty till you get used to them," he said.

"It's a good bitter smell," she retorted, "not nasty at all."

He changed his tone quickly. "I like the smell myself."

"I had ten-inch blooms this year," she said.

The man leaned farther over the fence. "Look. I know a lady down the road a piece, has got the nicest garden you ever seen. Got nearly every kind of flower but no chrysantheums. Last time I was mending a copper-bottom washtub for her (that's a hard job but I do it good), she said to me, 'If you ever run acrost some nice chrysantheums I wish you'd try to get me a few seeds.' That's what she told me."

Elisa's eyes grew alert and eager. "She couldn't have known much about chrysanthemums. You *can* raise them from seed, but it's much easier to root the little sprouts you see there."

"Oh," he said. "I s'pose I can't take none to her, then."

"Why yes you can," Elisa cried. "I can put some in damp sand, and you can carry them right along with you. They'll take root in the pot if you keep them damp. And then she can transplant them."

"She'd sure like to have some, ma'am. You say they're nice ones?"

"Beautiful," she said. "Oh, beautiful." Her eyes shone. She tore off the battered hat and shook out her dark pretty hair. "I'll put them in a flower pot, and you can take them right with you. Come into the yard."

While the man came through the picket gate Elisa ran excitedly along the geranium-bordered path to the back of the house. And she returned carrying a big red flower pot. The gloves were forgotten now. She kneeled on the ground by the starting bed and dug up the sandy soil with her fingers and scooped it into the bright new flower pot. Then she picked up the little pile of shoots she had prepared. With her strong fingers she pressed them into the sand and tamped around them with her knuckles. The man stood over her. "I'll tell you what to do," she said. "You remember so you can tell the lady."

"Yes, I'll try to remember."

"Well, look. These will take root in about a month. Then she must set them out, about a foot apart in good rich earth like this, see?" She lifted a handful of dark soil for him to look at. "They'll grow fast and tall. Now remember this: In July tell her to cut them down, about eight inches from the ground."

"Before they bloom?" he asked.

"Yes, before they bloom." Her face was tight with eagerness. "They'll grow right up again. About the last of September the buds will start."

She stopped and seemed perplexed. "It's the budding that takes the most care," she said hesitantly. "I don't know how to tell you." She looked deep into his eyes, searchingly. Her mouth opened a little, and she seemed to be listening. "I'll try to tell you," she said. "Did you ever hear of planting hands?"

"Can't say I have, ma'am."   70

"Well, I can only tell you what it feels like. It's when you're picking off the buds you don't want. Everything goes right down into your fingertips. You watch your fingers work. They do it themselves. You can feel how it is. They pick and pick the buds. They never make a mistake. They're with the plant. Do you see? Your fingers and the plant. You can feel that, right up your arm. They know. They never make a mistake. You can feel it. When you're like that you can't do anything wrong. Do you see that? Can you understand that?"

She was kneeling on the ground looking up at him. Her breast swelled passionately.

The man's eyes narrowed. He looked away self-consciously. "Maybe I know," he said. "Sometimes in the night in the wagon there—"

Elisa's voice grew husky. She broke in on him, "I've never lived as you do, but I know what you mean. When the night is dark—why, the stars are sharp-pointed, and there's quiet. Why, you rise up and up! Every pointed star gets driven into your body. It's like that. Hot and sharp and—lovely."

Kneeling there, her hand went out toward his legs in the greasy black   75
trousers. Her hesitant fingers almost touched the cloth. Then her hand dropped to the ground. She crouched low like a fawning dog.

He said, "It's nice, just like you say. Only when you don't have no dinner, it ain't."

She stood up then, very straight, and her face was ashamed. She held the flower pot out to him and placed it gently in his arms. "Here. Put it in your wagon, on the seat, where you can watch it. Maybe I can find something for you to do."

At the back of the house she dug in the can pile and found two old and battered aluminum saucepans. She carried them back and gave them to him. "Here, maybe you can fix these."

His manner changed. He became professional. "Good as new I can fix them." At the back of his wagon he set a little anvil, and out of an oily tool box dug a small machine hammer. Elisa came through the gate to watch him while he pounded out the dents in the kettles. His mouth grew sure and knowing. At a difficult part of the work he sucked his under-lip.

"You sleep right in the wagon?" Elisa asked.   80

"Right in the wagon, ma'am. Rain or shine I'm dry as a cow in there."

"It must be nice," she said. "It must be very nice. I wish women could do such things."

"It ain't the right kind of a life for a woman."

Her upper lip raised a little, showing her teeth. "How do you know? How can you tell?" she said.

"I don't know, ma'am," he protested. "Of course I don't know. Now   85
here's your kettles, done. You don't have to buy no new ones."

"How much?"

"Oh, fifty cents'll do. I keep my prices down and my work good. That's why I have all them satisfied customers up and down the highway."

Elisa brought him a fifty-cent piece from the house and dropped it in his hand. "You might be surprised to have a rival some time. I can sharpen scissors, too. And I can beat the dents out of little pots. I could show you what a woman might do."

He put his hammer back in the oily box and shoved the little anvil out of sight. "It would be a lonely life for a woman, ma'am, and a scarey life, too, with animals creeping under the wagon all night." He climbed over the singletree, steadying himself with a hand on the burro's white rump. He settled himself in the seat, picked up the lines. "Thank you kindly, ma'am," he said. "I'll do like you told me; I'll go back and catch the Salinas road."

"Mind," she called, "if you're long in getting there, keep the sand damp."   90

"Sand, ma'am?. . . . Sand? Oh, sure. You mean around the chrysantheums. Sure I will." He clucked his tongue. The beasts leaned luxuriously into their collars. The mongrel dog took his place between the back wheels. The wagon turned and crawled out the entrance road and back the way it had come, along the river.

Elisa stood in front of her wire fence watching the slow progress of the caravan. Her shoulders were straight, her head thrown back, her eyes half-closed, so that the scene came vaguely into them. Her lips moved silently, forming the words "Good-bye—good-bye." Then she whispered, "That's a bright direction. There's a glowing there." The sound of her whisper startled her. She shook herself free and looked about to see whether anyone had been listening. Only the dogs had heard. They lifted their heads toward her from their sleeping in the dust, and then stretched out their chins and settled asleep again. Elisa turned and ran hurriedly into the house.

In the kitchen she reached behind the stove and felt the water tank. It was full of hot water from the noonday cooking. In the bathroom she tore off her soiled clothes and flung them into the corner. And then she scrubbed herself with a little block of pumice, legs and thighs, loins and chest and arms, until her skin was scratched and red. When she had dried herself she stood in front of a mirror in her bedroom and looked at her body. She tightened her stomach and threw out her chest. She turned and looked over her shoulder at her back.

After a while she began to dress, slowly. She put on her newest underclothing and her nicest stockings and the dress which was the symbol of her prettiness. She worked carefully on her hair, penciled her eyebrows and rouged her lips.

Before she was finished she heard the little thunder of hoofs and the   95
shouts of Henry and his helper as they drove the red steers into the corral. She heard the gate bang shut and set herself for Henry's arrival.

His step sounded on the porch. He entered the house calling, "Elisa, where are you?"

"In my room, dressing. I'm not ready. There's hot water for your bath. Hurry up. It's getting late."

When she heard him splashing in the tub, Elisa laid his dark suit on the bed, and shirt and socks and tie beside it. She stood his polished shoes on the floor beside the bed. Then she went to the porch and sat primly and stiffly down. She looked toward the river road where the willow-line was still yellow with frosted leaves so that under the high grey fog they seemed a thin band of sunshine. This was the only color in the grey afternoon. She sat unmoving for a long time. Her eyes blinked rarely.

Henry came banging out of the door, shoving his tie inside his vest as he came. Elisa stiffened and her face grew tight. Henry stopped short and looked at her. "Why—why, Elisa. You look so nice!"

"Nice? You think I look nice? What do you mean by 'nice'?"   100

Henry blundered on. "I don't know. I mean you look different, strong and happy."

"I am strong? Yes, strong. What do you mean 'strong'?"

He looked bewildered. "You're playing some kind of a game," he said helplessly. "It's a kind of a play. You look strong enough to break a calf over your knee, happy enough to eat it like a watermelon."

For a second she lost her rigidity. "Henry! Don't talk like that. You didn't know what you said." She grew complete again. "I'm strong," she boasted. "I never knew before how strong."

Henry looked down toward the tractor shed, and when he brought his   105 eyes back to her, they were his own again. "I'll get out the car. You can put on your coat while I'm starting."

Elisa went into the house. She heard him drive to the gate and idle down his motor, and then she took a long time to put on her hat. She pulled it here and pressed it there. When Henry turned the motor off she slipped into her coat and went out.

The little roadster bounced along on the dirt road by the river, raising the birds and driving the rabbits into the brush. Two cranes flapped heavily over the willow-line and dropped into the river-bed.

Far ahead on the road Elisa saw a dark speck. She knew.

She tried not to look as they passed it, but her eyes would not obey. She whispered to herself sadly, "He might have thrown them off the road. That wouldn't have been much trouble, not very much. But he kept the pot," she explained. "He had to keep the pot. That's why he couldn't get them off the road."

The roadster turned a bend and she saw the caravan ahead. She swung   110 full around toward her husband so she could not see the little covered wagon and the mismatched team as the car passed them.

In a moment it was over. The thing was done. She did not look back.

She said loudly, to be heard above the motor, "It will be good, tonight, a good dinner."

"Now you're changed again," Henry complained. He took one hand from the wheel and patted her knee. "I ought to take you in to dinner oftener. It would be good for both of us. We get so heavy out on the ranch."

"Henry," she asked, "could we have wine at dinner?"

"Sure we could. Say! That will be fine."   115

She was silent for a while; then she said, "Henry, those prize fights, do the men hurt each other very much?"

"Sometimes a little, not often. Why?"

"Well, I've read how they break noses, and blood runs down their chests. I've read how the fighting gloves get heavy and soggy with blood."

He looked around at her. "What's the matter, Elisa? I didn't know you read things like that." He brought the car to a stop, then turned to the right over the Salinas River bridge.

"Do any women ever go to the fights?" she asked.   120

"Oh, sure, some. What's the matter, Elisa? Do you want to go? I don't think you'd like it, but I'll take you if you really want to go."

She relaxed limply in the seat. "Oh, no. No. I don't want to go. I'm sure I don't." Her face was turned away from him. "It will be enough if we can have wine. It will be plenty." She turned up her coat collar so he could not see that she was crying weakly—like an old woman.

The Receptive Reader

1. What is the meaning of the chrysanthemums as the central, gradually evolving *symbol* in the story? How much of a continuing thread do they provide for the story as a whole? What role do they play at the high point of the story? Were you surprised when you saw the flowers in the road?

2. When flowers are used as symbols, they activate a whole range of memories, associations, *connotations*. Cluster the word *flower*. What chains of association and patterns of thought does it bring to mind? Which of these do you think are especially relevant to this story?

3. What telling or revealing *details*—dress, the weather, features of the physical setting, the boxing, the wine—might be charged with symbolic significance?

4. Critics have found much sexual imagery, symbolism, or allusion in the encounter between Elisa and the tinker. What are striking examples? What is significant in the description of his arrival? What is strange or paradoxical about their relationship?

5. What is the role of the husband in this story? What kind of person is he? What kind of marriage do he and Elisa have? What are striking details or images that bring the nature of their relationship into focus?

6. What is the role of traditional assumptions about men's work and women's work, or about men's interests and women's interests, in this story? Do you see in the heroine an "ambiguous combination of feminine and masculine traits" (Marilyn Mitchell)?

7. Would you call the sight of the discarded flowers in the road the *climax*, or high point, of the story? Where does the story go afterward? What impact have the developments of the story had on Elisa? How does the story end?

8. Critics have singled out Steinbeck as one of the few male authors of his time who went beyond stereotypical portraits of women. Do you think they are right? How might this story have been different if it had been written by a woman?

The Personal Response

How do you relate to Elisa as the *central character*? Do you find her sympathetic? strong? weak? strange? (Support your answer in detail.)

<<<Find It on the Web>>>

John Steinbeck continues to be one of the most popular and most widely read American authors around the world. A new Steinbeck Center recently opened its doors in Salinas in the heart of Steinbeck country in Northern California. Scholars from Japan and Europe travel to Steinbeck conferences. The following is a sampling of results of one student's search for Internet materials related to Steinbeck's life and work.

San Jose State University. Center for Steinbeck Studies.
    Last Updated Nov. 1999. 5 Oct. 2001.
    Home page for the Center of Steinbeck Studies located at San Jose State University. The center preserves Steinbeck memorabilia and hosts conferences devoted to Steinbeck's life and work. The site guides visitors to archived information on Steinbeck's life and writings with links to other archives.
    <http://www.sjsu.edu/depths/steinbec/srchome.html>

The Nobel Association. *The Nobel Prize in Literature 1962.* Nobel e-Museum.
    Updated 16 June 2000. 9 Oct. 2001.
    Steinbeck won the Nobel Prize for literature in 1962. The official site for the Nobel Prize provides biographies, acceptance speeches, press coverage, and other resources for winners in all categories of the Nobel Prize.
    <http://www.nobel.se/literature/laureates/1962>

The National Steinbeck Center. Updated Sept. 2001. 9 Oct. 2001.
    This site uses colorful graphics and much animation to motivate the learner. The website includes a visitor's guide, information about John Steinbeck, information for members and donors, and a guide to exhibits or programs and educational resources.
    <http://www.steinbeck.org>

Simkins, Scott. *John Steinbeck Page.* Updated 14 Aug. 2001. 5 Oct. 2001.
    This site guides readers to critical responses, essays, and articles on Steinbeck's works. It also provides detailed biographical information and photos.
    <http://www.ocean.st.usm.edu/Ÿwsimkins/steinb.htm>

Trosow, Esther. *John Steinbeck's Pacific Grove.*
    Updated 22 Apr. 2000. 5 Oct. 2001.
    This website features information on the true-life history of John Steinbeck's days in California's Pacific Grove, with a biography of the author.
    <http://www.93950.com/steinbeck/index.htm>

Nale, David. *Steinbeck's Cannery Row and Sweet Thursday.*
    Updated 27 Aug. 2001. 5 Oct. 2001.
    Photo essay of many of the locations that provided the settings of Stein-
beck's novels in Northern California's Salinas Valley. Includes pictures and
descriptions of the sites and their significance in Steinbeck's works.
    <http://www.kelvin.org/nale.html>

"Steinbeck, John Ernst." *Microsoft Encarta Online Encyclopedia.*
    2001. 5 Oct. 2001.
    Encyclopedia article on the life of John Steinbeck and brief descriptions
of his works and accomplishments.
    <http://encarta.msn.com>

JUXTAPOSITIONS

The Range of Interpretation

In the following two critical excerpts, compare a traditional reading of
the story by a male critic with a rereading of this and another story from
a feminist point of view.

Stanley Renner

Stanley Renner, in "The Real Woman inside the Fence in 'The
Chrysanthemums,' " claims that "the story's evidence does not support
the view that Elisa is a woman kept from fulfillment by male domination." For him, the story is shaped by traditional male complaints
"against the sexual unresponsiveness of the female, against an ambivalent female sexuality that both invites and repels male admiration,
against the sexual delicacy of the female, who, repelled by sexual reality, holds out for indulgences of her emotional and spiritual yearnings":

The Real Woman in "The Chrysanthemums"

Unlike men, women incline more toward romantic fantasies of sex than
the act of love itself. Clearly Elisa romanticizes the tinker. In ironic mockery
of Elisa's great and perverse capacity for romanticizing reality, Steinbeck
makes everything about the tinker the utter antithesis of her fastidious tidi-
ness, which symbolizes her delicate sexual sensibility. Unshaven, unwashed,
his clothes "wrinkled and spotted with grease," he represents everything she
furiously purges from her garden and scrubs out of her house. Yet she fan-
tasizes sexual intercourse with him when he gratifies her hunger for romance because it is only a fantasy: he will presently climb back into his
slovenly wagon and ride away into the romantic sunset. Henry, clean and

reliable if a bit stodgy and clumsy, is reality pressing against Elisa's fence seeking an actual sexual relationship. But in rejecting reality, albeit unideal, as reality always is, for a patently falsified romantic fantasy, she defeats her own impulses toward a fuller life.

From *Modern Fiction Studies,* Summer 1985

Marilyn H. Mitchell

Contrasting with Renner's perspective focusing on male dissatisfaction and complaints, Marilyn H. Mitchell, in "Steinbeck's Strong Women: Feminine Identity in the Short Stories," claims that Steinbeck shows women who "are trapped between society's definition of the masculine and the feminine and are struggling against the limitations of the feminine." Steinbeck is using them "to refute outmoded conceptions of what a woman should be" and aims to show "the real human beauty beneath Elisa's rough and somewhat masculine exterior":

Steinbeck's Strong Women and "The Chrysanthemums"

Two of John Steinbeck's more intricate and memorable stories are "The Chrysanthemums" and "The White Quail." Both examine the psychology and sexuality of strong women who must somehow express themselves meaningfully within the narrow possibilities open to women in a man's world. In each case the woman chooses a traditional feminine activity, gardening, as a creative outlet. . . . Steinbeck reveals fundamental differences between the way women see themselves and the way they are viewed by men. For example, both husbands relate primarily to the physical attributes of their wives, making only meager attempts to comprehend their personalities. Consequently, a gulf of misunderstanding exists between the marriage partners, which creates verbal as well as sexual blocks to communication. In each marriage, at least one of the spouses is aware of some degree of sexual frustration, although dissatisfaction is never overtly articulated. Furthermore, the propensity of the men to see their wives as dependent inferiors, while the women perceive themselves as being equal if not superior partners, creates a strain within the marriage which is partially responsible for the isolation of each of the characters.

Both Elisa Allen of "The Chrysanthemums" and Mary Teller in "The White Quail" display a strength of will usually identified with the male but which, in these cases, the husbands are not shown to have. . . . Elisa Allen demonstrates a very earthly sensuality in "The Chrysanthemums," though not in the presence of her husband, indicating that their failure as a couple may be as much his fault as hers.

From *Southwest Review,* Summer 1976

The Receptive Reader

Is there any common basis for these two approaches to the story? How and why do they disagree? Who do you think is more nearly right, and why?

Making Connections—For Discussion or Writing

Compare and contrast the treatment of unfulfilled desire in Katherine Anne Porter's "The Jilting of Granny Weatherall" and in John Steinbeck's "The Chrysanthemums." Does it make a difference that one of the stories is by a female author and the other by a male author?

Charlotte Perkins Gilman   *(1860–1935)*

Gilman was a leading feminist and social activist at the turn of the century. She grew up in a family that included prominent suffragists (advocates of a woman's right to vote); one of her great-aunts was the abolitionist Harriet Beecher Stowe, author of *Uncle Tom's Cabin*. In her *Women and Economics* (1898) and other nonfiction works, Gilman argued that the traditional conception of women's roles was the result of social custom; it was culturally conditioned rather than anchored in biology. She proposed revolutionary rearrangements of domestic life to free women for work outside the home.

Born and raised in Connecticut, Gilman moved to California after separating from her first husband, and she edited and published feminist publications there. She helped organize the California Women's Congresses of 1894 and 1895 and was one of the founders of the Women's Peace Party. Besides writing nonfiction, she wrote novels and short stories that dramatized her belief in women's capacity for independence and self-realization.

Gilman's much-anthologized "The Yellow Wallpaper" chronicles a young woman's descent into insanity. The story has been read as a clinical study of the escalation of mental illness—as if we were watching the patient from the *outside,* somewhat the way the husband-physician does in the story. However, the author makes us see everything in her story from the *inside.* We see everything from the point of view of the patient. Gilman herself had suffered from severe postpartum depression after the birth of a daughter in 1884. She was treated by a specialist who prescribed a "rest cure"—bed rest and no physical exertion or intellectual stimulation. (This is the Weir Mitchell mentioned by the patient's husband in the story.) The treatment, Gilman said later, drove her "so near the borderline of mental ruin" that she "could see over."

The Yellow Wallpaper   *1892*

It is very seldom that mere ordinary people like John and myself secure ancestral halls for the summer.

A colonial mansion, a hereditary estate, I would say a haunted house, and reach the height of romantic felicity—but that would be asking too much of fate!

Still I will proudly declare that there is something queer about it.

Else, why should it be let so cheaply? And why have stood so long untenanted?

John laughs at me, of course, but one expects that in marriage.

John is practical in the extreme. He has no patience with faith, an intense horror of superstition, and he scoffs openly at any talk of things not to be felt and seen and put down in figures.

John is a physician, and *perhaps*—(I would not say it to a living soul, of course, but this is dead paper and a great relief to my mind—) *perhaps* that is one reason I do not get well faster.

You see he does not believe I am sick!

And what can one do?

If a physician of high standing, and one's own husband, assures friends and relatives that there is really nothing the matter with one but temporary nervous depression—a slight hysterical tendency—what is one to do?

My brother is also a physician, and also of high standing, and he says the same thing.

So I take phosphates or phosphites—whichever it is, and tonics, and journeys, and air, and exercise, and am absolutely forbidden to "work" until I am well again.

Personally, I disagree with their ideas.

Personally, I believe that congenial work, with excitement and change, would do me good.

But what is one to do?

I did write for a while in spite of them; but it *does* exhaust me a good deal—having to be so sly about it, or else meet with heavy opposition.

I sometimes fancy that in my condition if I had less opposition and more society and stimulus—but John says the very worst thing I can do is to think about my condition, and I confess it always makes me feel bad.

So I will let it alone and talk about the house.

The most beautiful place! It is quite alone, standing well back from the road, quite three miles from the village. It makes me think of English places that you read about, for there are hedges and walls and gates that lock, and lots of separate little houses for the gardeners and people.

There is a *delicious* garden! I never saw such a garden—large and shady, full of box-bordered paths, and lined with long grape-covered arbors with seats under them.

There were greenhouses, too, but they are all broken now.

There was some legal trouble, I believe, something about the heirs and coheirs; anyhow, the place has been empty for years.

That spoils my ghostliness, I am afraid, but I don't care—there is something strange about the house—I can feel it.

I even said so to John one moonlight evening, but he said what I felt was a *draught,* and shut the window.

I get unreasonably angry with John sometimes. I'm sure I never used to be so sensitive. I think it is due to this nervous condition.

But John says if I feel so, I shall neglect proper self-control; so I take pains to control myself—before him, at least, and that makes me very tired.

I don't like our room a bit. I wanted one downstairs that opened on the piazza and had roses all over the window, and such pretty old-fashioned chintz hangings! but John would not hear of it.

He said there was only one window and not room for two beds, and no near room for him if he took another.

He is very careful and loving, and hardly lets me stir without special direction.

I have a schedule prescription for each hour in the day; he takes all care   30 from me, and so I feel basely ungrateful not to value it more.

He said we came here solely on my account, that I was to have perfect rest and all the air I could get. "Your exercise depends on your strength, my dear," said he, "and your food somewhat on your appetite; but air you can absorb all the time." So we took the nursery at the top of the house.

It is a big, airy room, the whole floor nearly, with windows that look all ways, and air and sunshine galore. It was nursery first and then playroom and gymnasium, I should judge; for the windows are barred for little children, and there are rings and things in the walls.

The paint and paper look as if a boys' school had used it. It is stripped off—the paper—in great patches all around the head of my bed, about as far as I can reach, and in a great place on the other side of the room low down. I never saw a worse paper in my life.

One of those sprawling flamboyant patterns committing every artistic sin.

It is dull enough to confuse the eye in following, pronounced enough to   35 constantly irritate and provoke study, and when you follow the lame uncertain curves for a little distance they suddenly commit suicide—plunge off at outrageous angles, destroy themselves in unheard of contradictions.

The color is repellent, almost revolting; a smouldering unclean yellow, strangely faded by the slow-turning sunlight.

It is a dull yet lurid orange in some places, a sickly sulphur tint in others.

No wonder the children hated it! I should hate it myself if I had to live in this room long.

There comes John, and I must put this away,—he hates to have me write a word.

I

We have been here two weeks, and I haven't felt like writing before,   40 since that first day.

I am sitting by the window now, up in this atrocious nursery, and there is nothing to hinder my writing as much as I please, save lack of strength.

John is away all day, and even some nights when his cases are serious.

I am glad my case is not serious!

But these nervous troubles are dreadfully depressing.

John does not know how much I really suffer. He knows there is no   45 *reason* to suffer, and that satisfies him.

Of course it is only nervousness. It does weigh on me so not to do my duty in any way!

I meant to be such a help to John, such a real rest and comfort, and here I am a comparative burden already!

Nobody would believe what an effort it is to do what little I am able,—
to dress and entertain, and order things.

It is fortunate Mary is so good with the baby. Such a dear baby!

And yet I *cannot* be with him, it makes me so nervous.   50

I suppose John never was nervous in his life. He laughs at me so about
this wallpaper!

At first he meant to repaper the room, but afterwards he said that I was
letting it get the better of me, and that nothing was worse for a nervous patient than to give way to such fancies.

He said that after the wallpaper was changed it would be the heavy bedstead, and then the barred windows, and then that gate at the head of the
stairs, and so on.

"You know the place is doing you good," he said, "and really, dear, I
don't care to renovate the house just for a three months' rental."

"Then do let us go downstairs," I said, "there are such pretty rooms   55
there."

Then he took me in his arms and called me a blessed little goose, and
said he would go down cellar, if I wished, and have it whitewashed into the
bargain.

But he is right enough about the beds and windows and things.

It is as airy and comfortable room as any one need wish, and, of course,
I would not be so silly as to make him uncomfortable just for a whim.

I'm really getting quite fond of the big room, all but that horrid paper.

Out of one window I can see the garden, those mysterious deep-shaded   60
arbors, the riotous old-fashioned flowers, and bushes and gnarly trees.

Out of another I get a lovely view of the bay and a little private wharf
belonging to the estate. There is a beautiful shaded lane that runs down
there from the house. I always fancy I see people walking in these numerous paths and arbors, but John has cautioned me not to give way to fancy
in the least. He says that with my imaginative power and habit of story-
making, a nervous weakness like mine is sure to lead to all manner of excited fancies, and that I ought to use my will and good sense to check the
tendency. So I try.

I think sometimes that if I were only well enough to write a little it would
relieve the press of ideas and rest me.

But I find I get pretty tired when I try.

It is so discouraging not to have any advice and companionship about
my work. When I get really well, John says we will ask Cousin Henry and
Julia down for a long visit; but he says he would as soon put fireworks in
my pillow-case as to let me have those stimulating people about now.

I wish I could get well faster.   65

But I must not think about that. This paper looks to me as if it *knew* what
a vicious influence it had!

There is a recurrent spot where the pattern lolls like a broken neck and
two bulbous eyes stare at you upside down.

I get positively angry with the impertinence of it and the everlastingness.
Up and down and sideways they crawl, and those absurd, unblinking eyes
are everywhere. There is one place where two breadths didn't match, and
the eyes go all up and down the line, one a little higher than the other.

I never saw so much expression in an inanimate thing before, and we all know how much expression they have! I used to lie awake as a child and get more entertainment and terror out of blank walls and plain furniture than most children could find in a toy-store.

I remember what a kindly wink the knobs of our big, old bureau used to   70
have, and there was one chair that always seemed like a strong friend.

I used to feel that if any of the other things looked too fierce I could always hop into that chair and be safe.

The furniture in this room is no worse than inharmonious, however, for we had to bring it all from downstairs. I suppose when this was used as a playroom they had to take the nursery things out, and no wonder! I never saw such ravages as the children have made here.

The wallpaper, as I said before, is torn off in spots, and it sticketh closer than a brother—they must have had perseverance as well as hatred.

Then the floor is scratched and gouged and splintered, the plaster itself is dug out here and there, and this great heavy bed which is all we found in the room, looks as if it had been through the wars.

But I don't mind it a bit—only the paper.   75

There comes John's sister. Such a dear girl as she is, and so careful of me! I must not let her find me writing.

She is a perfect and enthusiastic housekeeper, and hopes for no better profession. I verily believe she thinks it is the writing which made me sick!

But I can write when she is out, and see her a long way off from these windows.

There is one that commands the road, a lovely shaded winding road, and one that just looks off over the country. A lovely country, too, full of great elms and velvet meadows.

This wallpaper has a kind of subpattern in a different shade, a particu-   80
larly irritating one, for you can only see it in certain lights, and not clearly then.

But in the places where it isn't faded and where the sun is just so—I can see a strange, provoking, formless sort of figure, that seems to skulk about behind that silly and conspicuous front design.

There's sister on the stairs!

II

Well, the Fourth of July is over! The people are all gone and I am tired out. John thought it might do me good to see a little company, so we just had mother and Nellie and the children down for a week.

Of course I didn't do a thing. Jennie sees to everything now.

But it tired me all the same.   85

John says if I don't pick up faster he shall send me to Weir Mitchell in the fall.

But I don't want to go there at all. I had a friend who was in his hands once, and she says he is just like John and my brother, only more so!

Besides, it is such an undertaking to go so far.

I don't feel as if it was worth while to turn my hand over for anything, and I'm getting dreadfully fretful and querulous.

I cry at nothing, and cry most of the time.   90

Of course I don't when John is here, or anybody else, but when I am alone.

And I am alone a good deal just now. John is kept in town very often by serious cases, and Jennie is good and lets me alone when I want her to.

So I walk a little in the garden or down that lovely lane, sit on the porch under the roses, and lie down up here a good deal.

I'm getting really fond of the room in spite of the wallpaper. Perhaps *because* of the wallpaper.

It dwells in my mind so!   95

I lie here on this great immovable bed—it is nailed down, I believe—and follow that pattern about by the hour. It is as good as gymnastics, I assure you. I start, we'll say, at the bottom, down in the corner over there where it has not been touched, and I determine for the thousandth time that I *will* follow that pointless pattern to some sort of a conclusion.

I know a little of the principle of design, and I know this thing was not arranged on any laws of radiation, or alternation, or repetition, or symmetry, or anything else that I ever heard of.

It is repeated, of course, by the breadths, but not otherwise.

Looked at in one way each breadth stands alone, the bloated curves and flourishes—a kind of "debased Romanesque" with *delirium tremens* go waddling up and down in isolated columns of fatuity.

But, on the other hand, they connect diagonally, and the sprawling out- 100
lines run off in great slanting waves of optic horror, like a lot of wallowing seaweeds in full chase.

The whole thing goes horizontally, too, at least it seems so, and I exhaust myself in trying to distinguish the order of its going in that direction.

They have used a horizontal breadth for a frieze, and that adds wonderfully to the confusion.

There is one end of the room where it is almost intact, and there, when the crosslights fade and the low sun shines directly upon it, I can almost fancy radiation after all,—the interminable grotesques seem to form around a common center and rush off in headlong plunges of equal distraction.

It makes me tired to follow it. I will take a nap I guess.

III

I don't know why I should write this.   105

I don't want to.

I don't feel able.

And I know John would think it absurd. But I *must* say what I feel and think in some way—it is such a relief!

But the effort is getting to be greater than the relief.

Half the time now I am awfully lazy, and lie down ever so much.   110

John says I mustn't lose my strength, and has me take cod liver oil and lots of tonics and things, to say nothing of ale and wine and rare meat.

Dear John! He loves me very dearly, and hates to have me sick. I tried to have a real earnest reasonable talk with him the other day, and tell him how I wish he would let me go and make a visit to Cousin Henry and Julia.

But he said I wasn't able to go, nor able to stand it after I got there; and I did not make out a very good case for myself, for I was crying before I had finished.

It is getting to be a great effort for me to think straight. Just this nervous weakness I suppose.

And dear John gathered me up in his arms, and just carried me upstairs 115 and laid me on the bed, and sat by me and read to me till it tired my head.

He said I was his darling and his comfort and all he had, and that I must take care of myself for his sake, and keep well.

He says no one but myself can help me out of it, that I must use my will and self-control and not let any silly fancies run away with me.

There's one comfort, the baby is well and happy, and does not have to occupy this nursery with the horrid wallpaper.

If we had not used it, that blessed child would have! What a fortunate escape! Why, I wouldn't have a child of mine, an impressionable little thing, live in such a room for worlds.

I never thought of it before, but it is lucky that John kept me here after 120 all, I can stand it so much easier than a baby, you see.

Of course I never mention it to them any more—I am too wise,—but I keep watch of it all the same.

There are things in that paper that nobody knows but me, or ever will.

Behind that outside pattern the dim shapes get clearer every day.

It is always the same shape, only very numerous.

And it is like a woman stooping down and creeping about behind that 125 pattern. I don't like it a bit. I wonder—I begin to think—I wish John would take me away from here!

IV

It is so hard to talk with John about my case, because he is so wise, and because he loves me so.

But I tried it last night.

It was moonlight. The moon shines in all around just as the sun does.

I hate to see it sometimes, it creeps so slowly, and always comes in by one window or another.

John was asleep and I hated to waken him, so I kept still and watched 130 the moonlight on that undulating wallpaper till I felt creepy.

The faint figure behind seemed to shake the pattern, just as if she wanted to get out.

I got up softly and went to feel and see if the paper *did* move, and when I came back John was awake.

"What is it, little girl?" he said. "Don't go walking about like that—you'll get cold."

I thought it was a good time to talk, so I told him that I really was not gaining here, and that I wished he would take me away.

"Why, darling!" said he, "our lease will be up in three weeks, and I can't 135 see how to leave before.

"The repairs are not done at home, and I cannot possibly leave town just now. Of course if you were in any danger, I could and would, but you really are better, dear, whether you can see it or not. I am a doctor, dear, and I know. You are gaining flesh and color, your appetite is better, I feel really much easier about you."

"I don't weigh a bit more," said I, "nor as much; and my appetite may be better in the evening when you are here, but it is worse in the morning when you are away!"

"Bless her little heart!" said he with a big hug, "she shall be as sick as she pleases! But now let's improve the shining hours by going to sleep, and talk about it in the morning!"

"And you won't go away?" I asked gloomily.

"Why, how can I, dear? It is only three weeks more and then we will take 140 a nice little trip of a few days while Jennie is getting the house ready. Really dear you are better!"

"Better in body perhaps—" I began, and stopped short, for he sat up straight and looked at me with such a stern, reproachful look that I could not say another word.

"My darling," said he, "I beg of you, for my sake and for our child's sake, as well as for your own, that you will never for one instant let that idea enter your mind! There is nothing so dangerous, so fascinating, to a temperament like yours. It is a false and foolish fancy. Can you not trust me as a physician when I tell you so?"

So of course I said no more on that score, and we went to sleep before long. He thought I was asleep first, but I wasn't, and lay there for hours trying to decide whether that front pattern and the back pattern really did move together or separately.

V

On a pattern like this, by daylight, there is a lack of sequence, a defiance of law, that is a constant irritant to a normal mind.

The color is hideous enough, and unreliable enough, and infuriating 145 enough, but the pattern is torturing.

You think you have mastered it, but just as you get well underway in following, it turns a back-somersault and there you are. It slaps you in the face, knocks you down, and tramples upon you. It is like a bad dream.

The outside pattern is a florid arabesque, reminding one of a fungus. If you can imagine a toadstool in joints, an interminable string of toadstools, budding and sprouting in endless convolutions—why, that is something like it.

That is, sometimes!

There is one marked peculiarity about this paper, a thing nobody seems to notice but myself, and that is that it changes as the light changes.

When the sun shoots in through the east window—I always watch for 150 that first long, straight ray—it changes so quickly that I never can quite believe it.

That is why I watch it always.

By moonlight—the moon shines in all night when there is a moon—I wouldn't know it was the same paper.

At night in any kind of light, in twilight, candlelight, lamplight, and worst of all by moonlight, it becomes bars! The outside pattern I mean, and the woman behind it is as plain as can be.

I didn't realize for a long time what the thing was that showed behind, that dim subpattern, but now I am quite sure it is a woman.

By daylight she is subdued, quiet. I fancy it is the pattern that keeps her 155 so still. It is so puzzling. It keeps me quiet by the hour.

I lie down ever so much now. John says it is good for me, and to sleep all I can.

Indeed he started the habit by making me lie down for an hour after each meal.

It is a very bad habit I am convinced, for you see I don't sleep.

And that cultivates deceit, for I don't tell them I'm awake—O no!

The fact is I am getting a little afraid of John. 160

He seems very queer sometimes, and even Jennie has an inexplicable look.

It strikes me occasionally, just as a scientific hypothesis,—that perhaps it is the paper!

I have watched John when he did not know I was looking, and come into the room suddenly on the most innocent excuses, and I've caught him several times *looking at the paper!* And Jennie too. I caught Jennie with her hand on it once.

She didn't know I was in the room, and when I asked her in a quiet, a very quiet voice, with the most restrained manner possible, what she was doing with the paper—she turned around as if she had been caught stealing, and looked quite angry—asked me why I should frighten her so!

Then she said that the paper stained everything it touched, that she had 165 found yellow smooches on all my clothes and John's, and she wished we would be more careful!

Did not that sound innocent? But I know she was studying that pattern, and I am determined that nobody shall find it out but myself!

VI

Life is very much more exciting now than it used to be. You see I have something more to expect, to look forward to, to watch. I really do eat better, and am more quiet than I was.

John is so pleased to see me improve! He laughed a little the other day, and said I seemed to be flourishing in spite of my wallpaper.

I turned it off with a laugh. I had no intention of telling him it was *because* of the wallpaper—he would make fun of me. He might even want to take me away.

I don't want to leave now until I have found it out. There is a week more, 170 and I think that will be enough.

VII

I'm feeling ever so much better! I don't sleep much at night, for it is so interesting to watch developments; but I sleep a good deal in the daytime.

In the daytime it is tiresome and perplexing.

There are always new shoots on the fungus, and new shades of yellow all over it. I cannot keep count of them, though I have tried conscientiously.

It is the strangest yellow, that wallpaper! It makes me think of all the yellow things I ever saw—not beautiful ones like buttercups, but old foul, bad yellow things.

But there is something else about that paper—the smell! I noticed it the 175 moment we came into the room, but with so much air and sun it was not bad. Now we have had a week of fog and rain, and whether the windows are open or not, the smell is here.

It creeps all over the house.

I find it hovering in the dining-room, skulking in the parlor, hiding in the hall, lying in wait for me on the stairs.

It gets into my hair.

Even when I go to ride, if I turn my head suddenly and surprise it—there is that smell!

Such a peculiar odor, too! I have spent hours in trying to analyze it, to 180 find what it smelled like.

It is not bad—at first, and very gentle, but quite the subtlest, most enduring odor I ever met.

In this damp weather it is awful, I wake up in the night and find it hanging over me.

It used to disturb me at first. I thought seriously of burning the house—to reach the smell.

But now I am used to it. The only thing I can think of that it is like is the *color* of the paper! A yellow smell.

There is a very funny mark on this wall, low down, near the mopboard. 185 A streak that runs round the room. It goes behind every piece of furniture, except the bed, a long, straight, even *smooch,* as if it had been rubbed over and over.

I wonder how it was done and who did it, and what they did it for. Round and round and round—round and round and round!—it makes me *dizzy!*

VIII

I really have discovered something at last.

Through watching so much at night, when it changes so, I have finally found out.

The front pattern *does* move—and no wonder! The woman behind shakes it!

Sometimes I think there are a great many women behind, and sometimes 190 only one, and she crawls around fast, and her crawling shakes it all over.

Then in the very bright spots she keeps still, and in the very shady spots she just takes hold of the bars and shakes them hard.

And she is all the time trying to climb through. But nobody could climb through that pattern—it strangles so; I think that is why it has so many heads.

They get through, and then the pattern strangles them off and turns them upside down, and makes their eyes white!

If those heads were covered or taken off it would not be half so bad.

IX

I think that woman gets out in the daytime!   195

And I'll tell you why—privately—I've seen her!

I can see her out of every one of my windows!

It is the same woman, I know, for she is always creeping, and most women do not creep by daylight.

I see her in that long shaded lane, creeping up and down. I see her in those dark grape arbors, creeping all around the garden.

I see her on that long road under the trees, creeping along, and when a 200 carriage comes she hides under the blackberry vines.

I don't blame her a bit. It must be very humiliating to be caught creeping by daylight!

I always lock the door when I creep by daylight. I can't do it at night, for I know John would suspect something at once.

And John is so queer now, that I don't want to irritate him. I wish he would take another room! Besides, I don't want anybody to get that woman out at night but myself.

I often wonder if I could see her out of all the windows at once.

But, turn as fast as I can, I can only see out of one at one time.   205

And though I always see her, she *may* be able to creep faster than I can turn!

I have watched her sometimes away off in the open country, creeping as fast as a cloud shadow in a high wind.

X

If only that top pattern could be gotten off from the under one! I mean to try it, little by little.

I have found out another funny thing, but I shan't tell it this time! It does not do to trust people too much.

There are only two more days to get this paper off, and I believe John is 210 beginning to notice. I don't like the look in his eyes.

And I heard him ask Jennie a lot of professional questions about me. She had a very good report to give.

She said I slept a good deal in the daytime.

John knows I don't sleep very well at night, for all I'm so quiet!

He asked me all sorts of questions, too, and pretended to be very loving and kind.

As if I couldn't see through him!   215

Still, I don't wonder he acts so, sleeping under this paper for three months.

It only interests me, but I feel sure John and Jennie are secretly affected by it.

XI

Hurrah! This is the last day, but it is enough. John to stay in town over night, and won't be out until this evening.

Jennie wanted to sleep with me—the sly thing! but I told her I should undoubtedly rest better for a night all alone.

That was clever, for really I wasn't alone a bit! As soon as it was moon- 220
light and that poor thing began to crawl and shake the pattern, I got up and
ran to help her.

I pulled and she shook, I shook and she pulled, and before morning we
had peeled off yards of that paper.

A strip about as high as my head and half around the room.

And then when the sun came and that awful pattern began to laugh at
me, I declared I would finish it today!

We go away tomorrow, and they are moving all my furniture down again
to leave things as they were before.

Jennie looked at the wall in amazement, but I told her merrily that I did 225
it out of pure spite at the vicious thing.

She laughed and said she wouldn't mind doing it herself, but I must not
get tired.

How she betrayed herself that time!

But I am here, and no person touches this paper but me,—not *alive!*

She tried to get me out of the room—it was too patent! But I said it was
so quiet and empty and clean now that I believed I would lie down again
and sleep all I could; and not to wake me even for dinner—I would call
when I woke.

So now she is gone, and the servants are gone, and the things are gone, 230
and there is nothing left but that great bedstead nailed down, with the canvas mattress we found on it.

We shall sleep downstairs tonight, and take the boat home tomorrow.

I quite enjoy the room, now it is bare again.

How those children did tear about here!

This bedstead is fairly gnawed!

But I must get to work. 235

I have locked the door and thrown the key down into the front path.

I don't want to go out, and I don't want to have anybody come in, till
John comes.

I want to astonish him.

I've got a rope up here that even Jennie did not find. If that woman does
get out, and tries to get away, I can tie her!

But I forgot I could not reach far without anything to stand on! 240

This bed will *not* move!

I tried to lift and push it until I was lame, and then I got so angry I bit
off a little piece at one corner—but it hurt my teeth.

Then I peeled off all the paper I could reach standing on the floor. It
sticks horribly and the pattern just enjoys it! All those strangled heads and
bulbous eyes and waddling fungus growths just shriek with derision!

I am getting angry enough to do something desperate. To jump out of
the window would be admirable exercise, but the bars are too strong even
to try.

Besides I wouldn't do it. Of course not. I know well enough that a step 245
like that is improper and might be misconstrued.

I don't like to *look* out of the windows even—there are so many of those creeping women, and they creep so fast.

I wonder if they all come out of that wallpaper as I did?

But I am securely fastened now by my well-hidden rope—you don't get *me* out in the road there!

I suppose I shall have to get back behind the pattern when it comes night, and that is hard!

It is so pleasant to be out in this great room and creep around as I please! 250

I don't want to go outside. I won't, even if Jennie asks me to.

For outside you have to creep on the ground, and everything is green instead of yellow.

But here I can creep smoothly on the floor, and my shoulder just fits in that long smooch around the wall, so I cannot lose my way.

Why there's John at the door!

It is no use, young man, you can't open it! 255

How he does call and pound!

Now he's crying for an axe.

It would be a shame to break down that beautiful door!

"John dear!" said I in the gentlest voice, "the key is down by the front steps, under a plantain leaf!"

That silenced him for a few moments. 260

Then he said—very quietly indeed, "Open the door, my darling!"

"I can't," said I. "The key is down by the front door under a plantain leaf!"

And then I said it again, several times, very gently and slowly, and said it so often that he had to go and see, and he got it of course, and came in. He stopped short by the door.

"What is the matter?" he cried. "For God's sake, what are you doing!"

I kept on creeping just the same, but I looked at him over my shoulder. 265

"I've got out at last," said I, "in spite of you and Jennie! And I've pulled off most of the paper, so you can't put me back!"

Now why should that man have fainted? But he did, and right across my path by the wall, so that I had to creep over him every time!

The Receptive Reader

1. At the beginning, the narrator refers to her husband John and herself as "ordinary people." What makes the setting and the people at the beginning of the story seem ordinary? What kind of ordinary person does the narrator seem to be? When do you notice the first hints of something extraordinary?

2. What and how do you learn about the narrator's illness? What and how do you learn about the treatment proposed by the doctor-husband?

3. What is the husband-physician's attitude toward his wife? What is her attitude toward him? How does it change in the course of the story?

4. How does the wallpaper become an obsessive preoccupation in this story? How does its appearance slowly change and shift? How does its meaning change or evolve as the *central symbol* in the story? What are some major stages?

5. Who is the woman behind the wallpaper? How does your perception of her change and evolve? What is the significance of the smudge (running the length of the wallpaper) that the woman begins to perceive?

6. What is the symbolic contrast between the garden and the enclosed, confined room? (Why does the woman herself throw the key away?)

7. What, for you, is the symbolic meaning of the way the story ends? Can the ending be read as a kind of liberation?

8. Feminist critics have found a special significance in the fact that the narrator has to do her writing secretly, against the wishes of her husband. What symbolic significance do you think they find in his prohibition?

The Personal Response

For you, what does the story as a whole say about the author's view of mental illness and her view of the relation between women and male physicians? Is the story still thought-provoking to current readers, or have changes in the modern world made the questions it raises obsolete?

Gabriel García Márquez   *(born 1928)*

In García Márquez's world, love is the primordial power that reigns as an obscure, impersonal, and all-powerful presence.

OCTAVIO PAZ

It always amuses me that the biggest praise for my work comes for the imagination, while the truth is that there's not a single line in all my work that does not have a basis in reality. The problem is that Caribbean reality resembles the wildest imagination.

GABRIEL GARCÍA MÁRQUEZ

García Márquez is a Colombian writer who became internationally famous with his novel *One Hundred Years of Solitude* (1967). His work became part of a Latin American renaissance that made the writings of Octavio Paz, Pablo Neruda, Jorge Luis Borges, and Carlos Fuentes known around the world. García Márquez' stories are often marked by a mixture of grim reality and the surreal that has been called "magic realism." His "A Very Old Man with Enormous Wings" (1968) is about a very old, moth-eaten angel—"a dirty, muttering, helpless old man with bedraggled wings" (John Updike)—who falls out of the sky and confounds the inhabitants of the town. García Márquez is a master at evoking mixed emotions. His tales mix wit and horror; his voice is "able to praise and curse, laugh and cry, fabulate and sing" (Thomas Pynchon).

García Márquez moved from Colombia to Mexico in 1954 and later went to live in Spain. He has written plays and film scripts as well as novels and stories; he was awarded the Nobel Prize in literature in 1982. He became famous when he was almost forty after years of struggle that made him feel "like an extra," thinking that "I did not count anywhere." In an interview, he said that he sees both his books and his work with films as helping "to create a Latin American identity," helping "Latin Americans to become more aware of their own culture." His novel *Love in the Time of Cholera*—about a man who maintains his unanswered, unfulfilled passion for the love of his youth for fifty-one years—appeared in 1987.

Esteban is Spanish for *Stephen*. The Sir Walter Raleigh alluded to in the story lived from 1552 to 1618 and was an English explorer and pirate of the Elizabethan age.

The Handsomest Drowned Man in the World   1970

A Tale for Children

TRANSLATED BY GREGORY RABASSA

The first children who saw the dark and slinky bulge approaching through the sea let themselves think it was an empty ship. Then they saw it had no flags or masts and they thought it was a whale. But when it washed up on the beach, they removed the clumps of seaweed, the jellyfish tentacles, and the remains of fish and flotsam, and only then did they see that it was a drowned man.

They had been playing with him all afternoon, burying him in the sand and digging him up again, when someone chanced to see them and spread the alarm in the village. The men who carried him to the nearest house noticed that he weighed more than any dead man they had ever known, almost as much as a horse, and they said to each other that maybe he'd been floating too long and the water had got into his bones. When they laid him on the floor they said he'd been taller than all other men because there was barely enough room for him in the house, but they thought that maybe the ability to keep on growing after death was part of the nature of certain drowned men. He had the smell of the sea about him and only his shape gave one to suppose that it was the corpse of a human being, because the skin was covered with a crust of mud and scales.

They did not even have to clean off his face to know that the dead man was a stranger. The village was made up of only twenty-odd wooden houses that had stone courtyards with no flowers and which were spread about on the end of a desertlike cape. There was so little land that mothers always went about with the fear that the wind would carry off their children and the few dead that the years had caused among them had to be thrown off the cliffs. But the sea was calm and bountiful and all the men fit into seven boats. So when they found the drowned man they simply had to look at one another to see that they were all there. That night they did not go out to work at sea. While the men went to find out if anyone was missing in neighboring villages, the women stayed behind to care for the drowned man.

They took the mud off with grass swabs, they removed the underwater stones entangled in his hair, and they scraped the crust off with tools used for scaling fish. As they were doing that they noticed that the vegetation on him came from faraway oceans and deep water and that his clothes were in tatters, as if he had sailed through labyrinths of coral. They noticed too that he bore his death with pride, for he did not have the lonely look of other drowned men who came out of the sea or that haggard, needy look of men who drowned in rivers. But only when they finished cleaning him off did they become aware of the kind of man he was and it left them breathless. Not only was he the tallest, strongest, most virile, and best built man they had ever seen, but even though they were looking at him there was no room for him in their imagination.

They could not find a bed in the village large enough to lay him on nor was there a table solid enough to use for his wake. The tallest men's holiday pants would not fit him, nor the fattest ones' Sunday shirts, nor the shoes of the one with the biggest feet. Fascinated by his huge size and his beauty, the women then decided to make him some pants from a large piece of sail and a shirt from some bridal brabant linen so that he could continue through his death with dignity. As they sewed, sitting in a circle and gazing at the corpse between stitches, it seemed to them that the wind had never been so steady nor the sea so restless as on that night and they supposed that the change had something to do with the dead man. They thought that if that magnificent man had lived in the village, his house would have had the widest doors, the highest ceiling, and the strongest floor, his bedstead would have been made from a midship frame held together by iron bolts, and his wife would have been the happiest woman. They thought that he would have had so much authority that he could have drawn fish out of the sea simply by calling their names and that he would have put so much work into his land that springs would have burst forth from among the rocks so that he would have been able to plant flowers on the cliffs. They secretly compared him to their own men, thinking that for all their lives theirs were incapable of doing what he could do in one night, and they ended up dismissing them deep in their hearts as the weakest, meanest, and most useless creatures on earth. They were wandering through that maze of fantasy when the oldest woman, who as the oldest had looked upon the drowned man with more compassion than passion, sighed:

"He has the face of someone called Esteban."   5

It was true. Most of them had only to take another look at him to see that he could not have any other name. The more stubborn among them, who were the youngest, still lived for a few hours with the illusion that when they put his clothes on and he lay among the flowers in patent leather shoes his name might be Lautaro. But it was a vain illusion. There had not been enough canvas, the poorly cut and worse sewn pants were too tight, and the hidden strength of his heart popped the buttons on his shirt. After midnight the whistling of the wind died down and the sea fell into its Wednesday drowsiness. The silence put an end to any last doubts: he was Esteban. The women who had dressed him, who had combed his hair, had cut his nails and shaved him were unable to hold back a shudder of pity when they had to resign themselves to his being dragged along the ground. It was then that they understood how unhappy he must have been with that huge body since it bothered him even after death. They could see him in life, condemned to going through doors sideways, cracking his head on crossbeams, remaining on his feet during visits, not knowing what to do with his soft, pink, sea lion hands while the lady of the house looked for her most resistant chair and begged him, frightened to death, sit here, Esteban, please, and he, leaning against the wall, smiling, don't bother, ma'am, I'm fine where I am, his heels raw and his back roasted from having done the same thing so many times whenever he paid a visit, don't bother, ma'am, I'm fine where I am, just to avoid the embarrassment of breaking up the chair, and never knowing perhaps that the ones who said don't go, Esteban, at least wait till the coffee's ready, were the ones who later on would whisper the big boob finally left, how nice, the handsome fool has gone. That was what the women were thinking beside the body a little before dawn. Later, when they covered his face with a handkerchief so that the light would not bother him, he looked so forever dead, so defenseless, so much like their men that the first furrows of tears opened in their hearts. It was one of the younger ones who began the weeping. The others, coming to, went from sighs to wails, and the more they sobbed the more they felt like weeping, because the drowned man was becoming all the more Esteban for them, and so they wept so much, for he was the most destitute, most peaceful, and most obliging man on earth, poor Esteban. So when the men returned with the news that the drowned man was not from the neighboring villages either, the women felt an opening of jubilation in the midst of their tears.

"Praise the Lord," they sighed, "he's ours!"

The men thought the fuss was only womanish frivolity. Fatigued because of the difficult nighttime inquiries, all they wanted was to get rid of the bother of the newcomer once and for all before the sun grew strong on that arid, windless day. They improvised a litter with the remains of foremasts and gaffs, tying it together with rigging so that it would bear the weight of the body until they reached the cliffs. They wanted to tie the anchor from a cargo ship to him so that he would sink easily into the deepest waves, where fish are blind and divers die of nostalgia, and bad currents would not bring him back to shore, as had happened with other bodies. But the more they hurried, the more the women thought of ways to waste time. They walked about like startled hens, pecking with the sea charms on their breasts, some interfering on one side to put a scapular of the good wind on the drowned man, some on the other side to put a wrist compass on him, and after a great deal of *get away from there, woman, stay out of the way, look, you almost made me fall on top of the dead man,* the men began to feel mistrust in their livers and started grumbling about why so many main-altar decorations for a stranger, because no matter how many nails and holy-water jars he had on him, the sharks would chew him all the same, but the women kept piling on their junk relics, running back and forth, stumbling, while they released in sighs what they did not in tears, so that the men finally exploded with *since when has there ever been such a fuss over a drifting corpse, a drowned nobody, a piece of cold Wednesday meat.* One of the women, mortified by so much lack of care, then removed the handkerchief from the dead man's face and the men were left breathless too.

He was Esteban. It was not necessary to repeat it for them to recognize him. If they had been told Sir Walter Raleigh, even they might have been impressed with his gringo accent, the macaw on his shoulder, his cannibal-killing blunderbuss, but there could be only one Esteban in the world and there he was, stretched out like a sperm whale, shoeless, wearing the pants of an undersized child, and with those stony nails that had to be cut with a knife. They only had to take the handkerchief off his face to see that he was ashamed, that it was not his fault that he was so big or so heavy or so hand-some, and if he had known that this was going to happen, he would have looked for a more discreet place to drown in, seriously, I even would have tied the anchor off a galleon around my neck and staggered off a cliff like someone who doesn't like things in order not to be upsetting people now with this Wednesday dead body, as you people say, in order not to be bothering anyone with this filthy piece of cold meat that doesn't have any-thing to do with me. There was so much truth in his manner that even the most mistrustful men, the ones who felt the bitterness of endless nights at sea fearing that their women would tire of dreaming about them and begin to dream of drowned men, even they and others who were harder still shud-dered in the marrow of their bones at Esteban's sincerity.

That was how they came to hold the most splendid funeral they could   10 conceive of for an abandoned drowned man. Some women who had gone to get flowers in the neighboring villages returned with other women who could not believe what they had been told, and those women went back for more flowers when they saw the dead man, and they brought more and more until there were so many flowers and so many people that it was hard to walk about. At the final moment it pained them to return him to the wa-ters as an orphan and they chose a father and mother from among the best people, and aunts and uncles and cousins, so that through him all the in-habitants of the village became kinsmen. Some sailors who heard weeping from a distance went off course and people heard of one who had himself tied to the mainmast, remembering ancient fables about sirens. While they fought for the privilege of carrying him on their shoulders along the steep escarpment by the cliffs, men and women became aware for the first time of the desolation of their streets, the dryness of their courtyards, the nar-rowness of their dreams as they faced the splendor and beauty of their drowned man. They let him go without an anchor so that he could come back if he wished and whenever he wished, and they all held their breath for the fraction of centuries the body took to fall into the abyss. They did not need to look at one another to realize that they were no longer all pres-ent, that they would never be. But they also knew that everything would be different from then on, that their houses would have wider doors, higher ceilings, and stronger floors so that Esteban's memory could go everywhere without bumping into beams and so that no one in the future would dare whisper the big boob finally died, too bad, the handsome fool has finally died, because they were going to paint their house fronts gay colors to make Esteban's memory eternal and they were going to break their backs digging for springs among the stones and planting flowers on the cliffs so that in fu-ture years at dawn the passengers on great liners would awaken, suffocated by the smell of gardens on the high seas, and the captain would have to come down from the bridge in his dress uniform, with his astrolabe, his pole star, and his row of war medals and, pointing to the promontory of roses on the horizon, he would say in fourteen languages, look there, where the wind is so peaceful now that it's gone to sleep beneath the beds, over there, where the sun's so bright that the sunflowers don't know which way to turn, yes, that's Esteban's village.

The Receptive Reader

1. What are your reactions as the story develops in the opening paragraphs? What are striking or puzzling details that linger in the reader's mind?

2. Is it a coincidence that the corpse washed up on the beach is discovered by children? (What is it about children that makes them the right—or the wrong—audience for this tale?)

3. A reviewer said of García Márquez' stories that the "arid, unyielding rock" on which the tales are built is a reality of "poverty, hopelessness, exploitation, despotic and demonic rulers" from which the tales "are an escape" (Charles Champlin). What harsh realities provide the "rock" on which this story is built?

4. The same reviewer said that the wellsprings of García Márquez' stories "are in the legends, folk tales, superstition, and indeed in the prevalence of miracles in the orthodox faith of Latin America." What miracle happens in this story? Does the reader have to believe in miracles to respond to the story?

5. What does the corpse of the drowned man symbolize? Do other supporting *symbols* play a role in this story?

6. What is the significance of the way the story ends?

7. What is paradoxical about the role death plays in this story?

The Personal Response

The following is the conclusion of a student paper titled "The Most Vibrant Corpse in the World." How do you react to this reader's search for a real-life application of the symbolism in the story? What real-life parallel or application would *you* suggest? How would you explain it or defend it?

> All that is beautiful, enriching, animating, and ultimately effective in life is symbolized—with no lack of strangeness or irony—by a corpse in "The Handsomest Drowned Man in the World." García Márquez' attractive cadaver is dead, yet he is far from lifeless. This corpse named Esteban is so full of life, he transmits it to anyone who looks upon him. After finishing the story, the slightly startled reader may wonder, what in real life is inanimate and yet so stimulating? The author may be suggesting that the answer is his own medium, literature. A story is alive and vibrant when it is being written down, fresh from the imagination of the writer, but it is only a dead thing when lying between the covers of a book; it is only flat, black print on a page. When it finds its way into the hands of an inhabitant of the village of Earth, however, and is gazed upon and absorbed by this inhabitant, it lives again, in a completely new way. No reader is exactly the same after such an encounter. She too may be inspired to paint her "house front gay colors"; she too may be inspired to break her back "digging for springs among the stones and planting flowers on the cliffs."

Making Connections—For Discussion or Writing

Examine the role of the imagination in the stories by Steinbeck, Gilman, and García Márquez. How does it mirror or reflect reality? How does it change or transform it?

WRITING ABOUT LITERATURE

6 Decoding Symbols
WRITING FOCUS: Two Readings of a Story

The Writing Workshop Writing about symbols tests your ability to be a responsive reader—to respond fully to the way imaginative literature acts out or embodies meanings. You cannot be literal-minded if strong, richly charged symbols are to bring into play the emotions and attitudes they are likely to carry. Here is the kind of advice a writing teacher might give you after studying papers focused on the role symbols play in short fiction:

✘ *Explore the full range of possible associations of a symbol.* Literary symbols tend not to be one-track, one-dimensional signals that simply say "danger" or "evil lurks here." A serpent may symbolize danger. It may symbolize guile (the snake in the grass). It may stand for the alien or otherness (since reptiles represent a very different life from our own mammalian existence). It may represent danger that has a strange paradoxical attraction or beauty.

The following cluster traces some of the possible associations of flowers as familiar recurrent symbols carrying rich traditional freight. Many of these associations may be activated by a story like Steinbeck's "The Chrysanthemums," where flowers play a central role at turning points in the story. (Which of these associations do you think are relevant to Steinbeck's story?)

✘ *Trace the full meaning of a gradually evolving central symbol.* A symbol is not likely to come into a story with its symbolic value ready-made, like the monetary value of a dollar bill. In Gilman's "The Yellow Wallpaper," we at first look at the twisted pattern of the paper the way an interior designer might wonder at its strange design. But gradually we—or rather the narrator through whose eyes we see everything in the story—read more and more human meaning into its strange shapes. They come to life, making the narrator participate in the struggle of whatever seems imprisoned behind its bars. It is as if each time we look at the paper we discover a new and frightening dimension, leading to an escalation of apprehension and terror. We have to read and ponder

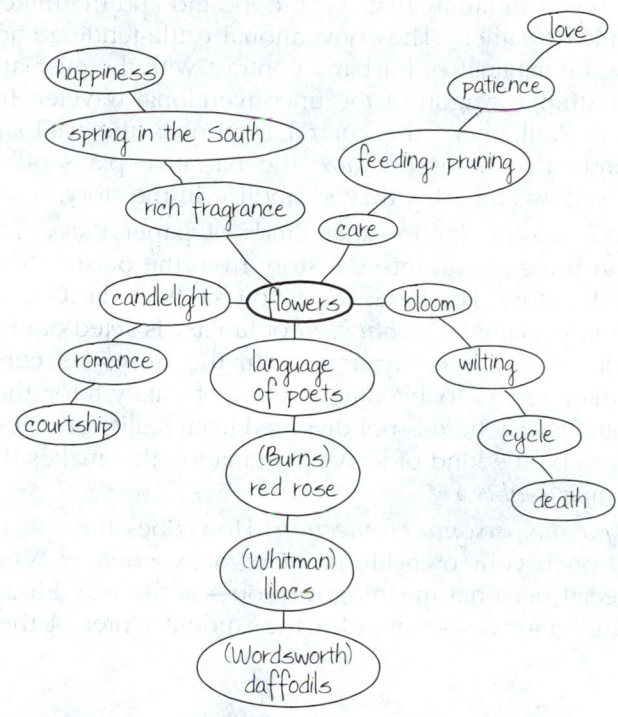

the story as a whole to sense what the wallpaper comes to stand for as the story heads for its frightening conclusion.

✘ *Look for secondary symbols that echo the major theme of a story.* In addition to the chrysanthemums in Steinbeck's story, readers have scrutinized the pots and pans in need of mending as a possible symbol; they have wondered about the symbolic meaning of the fog that closes off the valley:

> "The high grey-flannel fog of winter closed off the Salinas Valley from the sky and from all the rest of the world," Steinbeck begins. This introductory sentence points to one of the basic themes of the story. Something (in this case, the fog) is keeping something or someone "closed off"—held in, cut off. The fog covers the valley. Similarly, Elisa's situation closes in on her, keeps her trapped, holds her back. Neither her husband nor the itinerant tinker understands the energy and care she puts into the chrysanthemums, and her ability and potential go unrecognized and unappreciated; they are kept under wraps, "closed off." The fog is the lid that keeps the sun from penetrating; Elisa's circumstances put the "lid" on her vital energy and desires.

✘ *Look for contrasts or polarities.* Often the play of opposites helps organize a story. In Steinbeck's "The Chrysanthemums," a key contrast juxtaposes the farm family that stays fogbound and the tinker who follows "the nice weather." The conventional cattle-tending chores of the predictable, unimaginative husband contrast with the mismatched team pulling the strange wagon of the unconventional traveler. In Gilman's "The Yellow Wallpaper," the central symbol is the wallpaper, but a major polarity that helps organize the narrative plays off the colors green and yellow and what they symbolize in the story.

✘ *Relate key terms* (as in other kinds of papers) *specifically to the story*. If you bring a term into the story from the outside, show how it applies to the story. For instance, if you say that the García Márquez story "is simply a fantasy," *what kind* of fantasy is acted out in the story? What are its workings or dynamics? (In the story, the corpse of the drowned man seems to become a kind of catalyst for the villagers' imagination. Fantasy here is not divorced from reality or an escape from it; it seems to be the kind of active imagination that makes the villagers transform their *reality*.)

✘ *Look for the personal connection*. How does the use of symbols in a story touch your own life, your own experience? What symbols have a special personal meaning for you—as the way Elisa dresses in the chrysanthemums story had for the student writer of the following passage?

> Steinbeck's story dealt with feminine emotions that can be very hard to understand. I was struck by the contrast between Elisa's mannish "working clothes" (her shapeless outfit, her heavy gloves) and the makeup and dress she puts on after her encounter with the tinker. Much of her thinking revolved around whether the men in her world would respect her work and desire her at the same time. Her change of clothes symbolizes the fact that in the male world the woman has to play a dual role. She has to be a man's equal to survive in the world of work, yet on the other hand she is expected to be feminine and seductive. Today a woman has to look more like a man by wearing a dark "power" suit and practically no makeup to compete with men, or she may not be taken seriously. In a recent sitcom episode, I watched a sterile-looking businesswoman teaching a fashionable female how to dress for business success. Her pupil donned a blue suit, a buttoned white shirt, and a bandage-type thing to hide her breasts. Steinbeck's story points up this unresolved conflict: It is a sad but honest account of how women are taken advantage of when they expose their feminine selves.

Two Readings of a Story   The language of symbols may be universal, but it also by its very nature fosters a range of interpretation. Writers relying heavily on symbols are the least likely to spell out the meaning or the moral of a story in so many words. Where do the two following readings of "The Yellow Wall-paper" seem to agree? Where do they differ in emphasis or interpretation? Which is closer to your own reading of the story? Which do you learn from the most?

Sample Student Paper 1

"The Yellow Wallpaper": A Woman's Struggle with Madness

"I've got out at last . . . and I've pulled off most of the paper, so you can't put me back!" declares the narrator of "The Yellow Wallpaper" at the end of her futile struggle with madness. By peeling off the yellow wallpaper and releasing the woman the narrator sees trapped behind its "conspicuous front design," the narrator peels off the façade of normalcy she is trapped behind and releases her own madness. This façade is created by a "very careful and loving" husband, who refuses to believe his wife is ill, and is perpetuated by the medical conventions of the time that dismiss her mental illness as "a slight hysterical tendency."

In his effort to help his wife get over her "temporary nervous depression," John takes her to a house in the country which is "quite alone, standing well back from the road, quite three miles from the village." He feels that this quiet atmosphere along with "perfect rest" is just what she needs. In fact, she is "absolutely forbidden to work" and has "a scheduled prescription for each hour of the day." The narrator, on the other hand, feels "that congenial work, with excitement and change, would do me good." However, because her husband is "a physician of high standing," she feels he must know what is best for her. When they first move into the house, she wants a room "downstairs that opened on the piazza and had roses all over the window, and such pretty old-fashioned chintz hangings" but "John would not hear of it." He insists they take "the nursery at the top of the house" even though "the windows are barred, . . . the floor is scratched and gouged and splintered, the plaster itself is dug out here and there," and the room is covered in a "horrid paper"—"one of those sprawling flamboyant patterns committing every artistic sin" and colored "repellent, almost revolting . . . unclean yellow." He also insists that she stop writing, which she feels would "relieve the press of ideas and rest me." She does manage to write a bit "in spite of them," but it is too exhausting "having to be so sly about it."

Consequently, with no outlet for her "imaginative power and habit of story-making," she develops a grotesque fascination with the yellow wallpaper. At first the paper is just irritating, "dull enough to confuse the eye in following, pronounced enough to constantly irritate and provoke study." But, as the narrator studies the wallpaper more and more, she begins to see hideous images in the pattern. "The pattern lolls like a broken neck and two bulbous eyes . . . those absurd, unblinking eyes are everywhere." She dwells on this pattern and soon sees "a kind of subpattern in a different shade . . . that seems to sulk behind" the front design. The wallpaper so disturbs the narrator that she tries to have "a real earnest and reasonable talk" with her husband about her condition. He tells her that she is getting better, but she replies, "Better in body, perhaps." He dismisses her concern for her mental state as "a false and foolish fancy." He tells her that she must not give in to her feelings, and that only she can help herself get better. She must use her "will and self-control and not let any silly fancies run away with her."

It is at this point in the story, after the narrator tries, unsuccessfully, to share her fears for her sanity, that she can no longer control the madness she has been struggling to contain. This madness takes the form of the woman behind the wallpaper. "I didn't realize for a long time what the thing was that showed behind, that dim subpattern, but now I am quite sure it is a woman." The narrator describes the woman as "subdued, quiet," and the narrator believes "it is the pattern that keeps her so still." The narrator is, in fact, describing herself, so quiet and subdued, and the pattern keeping her that way is her life.

As the narrator's illness progresses, she begins to identify more and more with the woman behind the wallpaper. She sees the woman creeping around everywhere: "in that long shaded lane . . . in those dark grape arbors . . . on that long road under the trees, creeping along, and when a carriage comes she hides." The narrator sympathizes with this woman for she, too, is creeping around. "I always lock the door when I creep by daylight," the narrator writes.

Ultimately, her madness takes complete control and her one purpose in life is to help the woman escape from the wallpaper. Piece by piece, the narrator peels off the wallpaper as she peels away at her own sanity, until the woman is able to escape from behind the paper, and the narrator is able to escape into her own madness. The narrator wonders "if they all come out of the wallpaper as I did?"

No less obvious than the symbolism of the yellow wallpaper is the irony of the story. A loving husband, a physician no less, prescribes a treatment of rest and relaxation he feels will improve his wife's slightly depressed condition; however, instead of helping her, he unwittingly drives her to insanity. His mistake was in not taking her condition seriously, not accepting that she was, indeed, very ill. We want to say, "Poor woman, if she existed today, she could have been helped." Maybe, and maybe not. Situations similar to the narrator's do exist today. The modern term for John is "enabler." Just as John, by pretending nothing was seriously wrong, enabled his wife to succumb to her illness, many spouses and families of alcoholics enable them to continue being alcoholics by not admitting they have a problem. They, too, are trapped behind the façades of normalcy they create. This is only one example. We are all "enablers" in one way or another. By ignoring the problems that exist all around us, and refusing to admit they are real problems, we perpetuate those problems. Only by admitting a problem exists, whether in the family or in society, can we truly begin to find a solution.

Sample Student Paper 2

Yellow Women

Gilman's "The Yellow Wallpaper" is a tragic story of a woman's attempt to recover from postpartum depression. This story represents through symbolism the characteristic attitude towards women and of women during the late 1800s and early 1900s. Gilman writes honestly of the isolated and confused feelings women were feeling. The woman in "The Yellow Wallpaper" goes through three periods of change throughout the story. The story begins with the description of the woman as being sick, but there are no signs of mental illness, and she is aware of her environment and even believes she is not really sick. Then there is a curious change in her character, and she appears to be disillusioned and on the verge of becoming mentally insane. And in the end she does go over the edge, and her character is literally lost. There are factors which cause these changes; I will explore these three major changes in her life as well as the use of powerful symbolism.

The woman in this story is taken to a summer house to rest and recuperate. Her husband, John, who is also her doctor, treats her as a child, and she says that "perhaps that is one reason I do not get well faster." She is apparently suffering from the baby blues, which is a depression some women experience after giving birth to a child. However, her husband sticks her in an atrocious nursery with barred windows and a wallpaper that she describes as

dull enough to confuse the eye in following, pronounced enough to constantly irritate and provoke study, and when you follow the lame uncertain
curves for a little distance they suddenly commit suicide—plunge off at
outrageous angles, destroy themselves in unheard of contradictions.

Her description of the wallpaper represents her feelings about the paper, but it
also symbolizes the feelings she has about herself. This confusing pattern could
be a typical categorization of women, whereas a typical pattern for men might be
straight and neat lines that meet at edges and appear to have an overall meaning.
I say this because, in the story, John apparently knows all and has prescribed his
wife's life as he sees fit. In a description of John's sister, the woman says she is
"a perfect and enthusiastic housekeeper, and hopes for no better profession."
This heartless description lacks praise for her sister-in-law's profession; it also
symbolizes the status of women in the time the story was written.

Her husband, who calls her "his little girl" and his "blessed goose," forbids her
to work until she is well; she disagrees, believing "congenial work, with excitement
and change," would do her good. She believes she could recover from her baby
blues if only she were able to keep active and do other things than sit alone in a
nursery and stare at the wallpaper. She even asks her husband to have company
for companionship, but he tells her, "he would as soon put fireworks in my pillow-
case as to let me have those stimulating people about now." She might not even
have progressed to her second stage if it were not for her husband, brother, and
sister-in-law constantly reminding her of how tired and sick she is.

Her second stage begins when she becomes "fond" of the wallpaper. She is losing contact with the outside world, instead spending her time trying, in a painstak-
ing effort, to understand the overall pattern of the wallpaper. She sees a figure
that looks like a "woman stooping down and creeping about behind that pattern."
She also goes on to say, "I don't like it a bit. . . . I wish John would take me away
from here." She is herself the woman "creeping" through the wallpaper. The woman
creeping symbolizes women who are not allowed to stand tall and free and speak
their minds. She "creeps" at night when her husband is asleep and, when she is
caught "creeping," her husband tells her to get back in bed. Her husband, who has
good intentions, keeps on assuring her that she is getting better, and when she
disagrees with him by saying, "Better in body perhaps," he looks at her with such
a "stern, reproachful" stare that she does not dare say another word.

She is alone in her own little world with no real support from anyone. She cannot be blamed for her condition and eventually insanity takes over her body. Here
is another example of how the wallpaper symbolizes women:

> The front pattern does move—and no wonder! The woman behind shakes
> it! Sometimes I think there are a great many women behind, And she is all
> the time trying to climb through. But nobody could climb through that pat-
> tern—it strangles so; I think that is why it has so many heads.

She realizes she is not the only woman who is lost but also many other women.
This realization pushes her to her mental limit, and she tries to peel all of the wallpaper off so that the "strangled heads" can be free. She feels secure and safe in
the room "creeping" and she says, "I don't want to go outside. For outside you
have to creep on the ground, and everything is green instead of yellow." She has
no desire to live in the "green" world, and she chooses the "yellow" familiar world

instead. She even locks herself in the room and throws away the key. This act symbolizes an instance of control over her own life. Comfortable in her "creeping" role, she does not want anyone to bother her. She is now mentally insane.

The woman in "The Yellow Wallpaper" represents many women, even today, in the late 20th century. There are many women who do not take advantage of their freedom, many who are also servants in life. I have seen this to be so in my grandmother's as well as in my mother's marriage. However, the wallpaper women are hiding behind is slowly being peeled off by both men and women.

Questions for Peer Review

Much current writing about literature stresses that *reader response* is shaped by what readers bring to their reading: their background, their expectations, or their previous experience with an author or kind of literature. Do you think it is true that no story is the same for two different readers?

1. Many discussions of this story focus on the *relationship* between the woman and her physician husband. Do the two papers agree or differ in their description of the relationship?

2. Discussions of the story find symbolic meaning in many key elements of the story. How do the two papers compare in their interpretation of key *symbols?* How do they read the symbolic meaning of the wallpaper pattern, the woman behind the paper, the creeping, the peeling of the paper?

3. Critics have probed the symbolic meaning of the *colors* green and yellow that play a major role in the story. Do the student writers agree in their reading of the color symbolism in the story?

4. Like the writing of other earlier woman authors, Gilman's story is read by today's readers with a new awareness of traditional *gender roles* and women's issues. How do the two student papers compare in their estimate of what the story means to today's women?

5. After reading the second paper, one student reader wrote the following *personal response.* Where do you agree or disagree with it, and why?

I remember that when first reading the story I was totally overpowered by it. This is a fascinating, disturbing paper that has made me see this terrible story in a new way. The "yellow women" designated by this student writer are not just victims to her; they are also "yellow," i.e. chicken, afraid, able only to escape via insanity. There's a strange implication—and judgment of—learned helplessness. Without quite saying it, this writer attempts to say that the flight into insanity is as much a cop-out as it is the oppressor's unknowing way of forcing insanity on the female. I get an ambiguous picture: the male isn't being deliberately patronizing; he is just as much a victim of the cultural norm as the female is. Conversely, the female plays as big a part in her insanity as the male. She could "choose" the green way—partly because she knows where the "green way" is: downstairs, near the roses and the entrance to the garden—and in her writing. A key word in this paper is "choose." The implication is that she can't buck convention enough to stand up for herself, so she retreats into the "yellow" room on the second floor, giving up the organic living greenness and groundedness in earth and reality of the first floor where she could heal naturally from a natural disequilibrium. If this writer does what I think she's doing, she has become aware of a double tragedy often missed:

the pathetic ignorance of men as well as women in roles they wear because they know no other.

7 THEME

The Search for Meaning

Courtesy Richard B. Ressman

*Invention, not preaching, enchants the modern
reader and sustains the illusion of
reality.*

ANN CHARTERS

*Instead of placing one body of knowledge against
another, storytellers invite us to return from
knowledge to thinking, from a bounded way of
looking to an unbounded way of seeing.*

JAMES P. CARSE

*The truth about any subject only comes when all
the sides of the story are put together, and all
their different meanings make one new one.*

ALICE WALKER

FOCUS ON THEME

Imaginative literature has the power to make you think. A story that has a strong impact is likely to raise questions to which the story as a whole suggests answers. It is likely to make you reexamine or rethink some facet of human life. When you try to put the human meaning of a story into your own words, you formulate its **theme.** You try to state the idea or ideas that the story as a whole seems to act out.

Writers of earlier generations felt free to spell out the meaning of a story in thematic passages. They might put these in the mouth (or in the mind) of an observer or of a key character. In his "The Blue Hotel" (1898), a story set in Nebraska in the Old West, Stephen Crane traces the events leading up to a barroom brawl in which a man is killed. From the beginning, our attention centers on the strange behavior of a recent arrival, the Swede. He is subject to neurotic fears, he covers up his apprehensions with bluster and bravado, and he is a constant source of irritation to the small group of men spending the night in the hotel. A long evening of drinking and random quarreling comes to a head when the Swede accuses a loudmouthed local boy of cheating at poker and batters him in a bloody fight. Flushed with liquor and his sense of victory, the Swede checks out of the hotel and stumbles on to a saloon. He there picks a fight with a gambler who refuses to drink with him, and the trouble-making Swede is killed in the ensuing brawl.

Crane has a grim sense of **irony.** The Swede's paranoid fears were unjustified. No one was out to destroy him. The irony is that he was destroyed anyway. The locals feel that the Swede only got what he deserved; he had it coming. However, Crane wants us to learn something else from this story, and he puts it in the mouth of one of his characters. The "Easterner" has been mostly a silent observer and at times a calming influence in the story. He finally says to a local cowboy who accuses the Swede of acting like a jackass:

> You're a bigger jackass than the Swede by a million majority. Now let me tell you one thing. . . . Johnnie *was* cheating. I saw him . . . And I refused to stand up and be a man. I let the Swede fight it out alone. And you—you were simply puffing around the place and wanting to fight. . . . We are all in it! . . . Every sin is the result of collaboration. We, five of us, have collaborated in the murder of this Swede . . . that fool of an unfortunate gambler came merely as the culmination . . . and gets all the punishment.

Evil is the result of collaboration. Crane's theme in this story is a general statement, but it is not a glib generalization. It is an earned generalization—not brought into the story from the outside. It is fully anchored in the lived experience of the story.

Most twentieth-century writers have gone a step beyond Crane. Rather than have the gambler sum up the theme in so many words, they would have preferred to have the reader *think* about the role collaboration plays in causing evil. Because of the writers' reluctance to editorialize, the themes of modern fiction tend to be implied rather than spelled out. They are ideas organically embedded in image, action, and emotion. When reading for theme, remember cautions like the following:

✘ *Beware of large abstractions.* Part of the modern temper has been a suspicion of big words, hasty generalizations, and premature abstractions. **Abstractions** (from a Latin word meaning "pulling away") draw us away from the nitty-gritty of unsorted detail to the larger labels and categories that we need to find our way in a multilayered world. But abstract terms cover much; they are "umbrella" terms. They easily become foggy or misleading. Be prepared to ask: "freedom"—to do what? "love of humanity"—what part or what features of it?

✘ *Beware of oversimplification.* Often the meaning of a story takes shape in the interplay of conflicting human commitments and emotions. If you were to look for a common denominator for stories by Faulkner, Jackson, and Hawthorne in this volume, you might start by saying their authors agree that "evil lurks in the human heart." However, the questions each story raises and the possible answers it leads us to explore are more complex than that. Like other writers who have wrestled with the problem of how to explain evil, how to think of evil in our world, each of these authors has arrived at a somewhat different answer.

✘ *Beware of clichés.* "All You Need Is Love" makes a marvelous Beatles song. But it is too sweeping and inspirational (and too obviously untrue) to serve as an insight that we carry away from a gripping story. If you bring a ready-made phrase to a story from outside, it may not carry the authentic stamp of honest feeling, of lived experience. Be wary of greeting-card phrases—phrases we take down ready-made from the rack when we find it hard to put our own honest feeling and thinking into words.

You may encounter two related meanings of the term *theme.* It may mean simply a focus of attention, an area of concern. In this sense, one great modern theme is alienation—the feeling of uprootedness, the loss of a sense of home. However, as used in this chapter and in many critical discussions, the theme is what a story as a whole says *about* alienation. The story as a whole may be making a statement about the roots of alienation. Or it may say something about our ways of coping with it. It may make us think about how alienation explains the people we are or the people we encounter.

FIRST READING
A Story with a Twist

The following short short is by a writer known for the surreal quality and dark humor of her stories. Luisa Valenzuela was born in Argentina and worked with Jorge Luis Borges at the National Library in Buenos Aires before she was twenty. She went to live in Paris for a time, working for Argentine publications, writing for French television and radio, and becoming part of a circle of avant-garde writers and critics. She later came to the United States, where she has participated in programs for writers at the University of Iowa and Columbia University. Her collection titled *Strange Things Happen Here* was published in 1975; *The Lizard's Tail,* a later volume, in 1983. The story that follows creates suspense and ends with a shuddery surprise twist. Does it have a larger meaning? What is its theme?

Luisa Valenzuela   *(born 1938)*

The Censors   1988

TRANSLATED BY DAVID UNGER

Poor Juan! One day they caught him with his guard down before he could even realize that what he had taken as a stroke of luck was really one of fate's dirty tricks. These things happen the minute you're careless and you let down your guard, as one often does. Juancito let happiness—a feeling you can't trust—get the better of him when he received from a confidential source Mariana's new address in Paris and he knew that she hadn't forgotten him. Without thinking twice, he sat down at his table and wrote her a letter. *The* letter that keeps his mind off his job during the day and won't let him sleep at night (what had he scrawled, what had he put on that sheet of paper he sent to Mariana?).

Juan knows there won't be a problem with the letter's contents, that it's irreproachable, harmless. But what about the rest? He knows that they examine, sniff, feel, and read between the lines of each and every letter, and check its tiniest comma and most accidental stain. He knows that all letters pass from hand to hand and go through all sorts of tests in the huge censorship offices and that, in the end, very few continue on their way. Usually it takes months, even years, if there aren't any snags; all this time the freedom, maybe even the life, of both sender and receiver is in jeopardy. And that's why Juan's so down in the dumps: thinking that something might happen to Mariana because of his letters. Of all people, Mariana, who must finally feel safe there where she always dreamed she'd live. But he knows that the *Censor's Secret Command* operates all over the world and cashes in on the discount in air rates; there's nothing to stop them from going as far as that hidden Paris neighborhood, kidnapping Mariana, and returning to their cozy homes, certain of having fulfilled their noble mission.

Well, you've got to beat them to the punch, do what everyone tries to do: sabotage the machinery, throw sand in its gears, get to the bottom of the problem so as to stop it.

This was Juan's sound plan when he, like many others, applied for a censor's job—not because he had a calling or needed a job: no, he applied simply to intercept his own letter, a consoling but unoriginal idea. He was hired immediately, for each day more and more censors are needed and no one would bother to check on his references.

Ulterior motives couldn't be overlooked by the *Censorship Division,* but they needn't be too strict with those who applied. They knew how hard it would be for those poor guys to find the letter they wanted and even if they did, what's a letter or two when the new censor would snap up so many others? That's how Juan managed to join the *Post Office's Censorship Division,* with a certain goal in mind.

The building had a festive air on the outside which contrasted with its inner staidness. Little by little, Juan was absorbed by his job and he felt at peace since he was doing everything he could to get his letter for Mariana. He didn't even worry when, in his first month, he was sent to *Section K* where envelopes are very carefully screened for explosives.

It's true that on the third day, a fellow worker had his right hand blown off by a letter, but the division chief claimed it was sheer negligence on the victim's part. Juan and the other employees were allowed to go back to their work, albeit feeling less secure. After work, one of them tried to organize a strike to demand higher wages for unhealthy work, but Juan didn't join in; after thinking it over, he reported him to his superiors and thus got promoted.

You don't form a habit by doing something once, he told himself as he left his boss's office. And when he was transferred to *Section J,* where letters are carefully checked for poison dust, he felt he had climbed a rung in the ladder.

By working hard, he quickly reached *Section E* where the work was more interesting, for he could now read and analyze the letters' contents. Here he could even hope to get hold of his letter which, judging by the time that had elapsed, had gone through the other sections and was probably floating around in this one.

Soon his work became so absorbing that his noble mission blurred in his   10 mind. Day after day he crossed out whole paragraphs in red ink, pitilessly chucking many letters into the censored basket. These were horrible days when he was shocked by the subtle and conniving ways employed by people to pass on subversive messages; his instincts were so sharp that he found behind a simple "the weather's unsettled" or "prices continue to soar" the wavering hand of someone secretly scheming to overthrow the Government.

His zeal brought him swift promotion. We don't know if this made him happy. Very few letters reached him in *Section B*—only a handful passed the other hurdles—so he read them over and over again, passed them under a magnifying glass, searched for microprint with an electronic microscope, and tuned his sense of smell so that he was beat by the time he made it home. He'd barely manage to warm up his soup, eat some fruit, and fall into bed, satisfied with having done his duty. Only his darling mother worried, but she couldn't get him back on the right road. She'd say, though it wasn't always true: Lola called, she's at the bar with the girls, they miss you, they're waiting for you. Or else she'd leave a bottle of red wine on the table. But Juan wouldn't overdo it: any distraction could make him lose his edge and the perfect censor had to be alert, keen, attentive, and sharp to nab cheats. He had a truly patriotic task, both self-denying and uplifting.

His basket for censored letters became the best fed as well as the most cunning basket in the whole *Censorship Division*. He was about to congratulate himself for having finally discovered his true mission, when his letter to Mariana reached his hands. Naturally, he censored it without regret. And just as naturally, he couldn't stop them from executing him the following morning, another victim of his devotion to his work.

The Receptive Reader

Does this story make a statement about censorship? about human nature? What does it say? Does it act out ideas about life? about society? How?

THE THINKING READER

Art shrinks from . . . every abstract thing, from all that is of the brain only, from all that is not a fountain jetting from the entire hopes, memories, and sensations of the body.

WILLIAM BUTLER YEATS

The concepts of beauty and ugliness are mysterious to me. Many people write about them.

*In mulling over them, I try to get underneath
them and see what they mean, understand the
impact they have on what people do. I also write
about love and death. The problem I face as a
writer is to make my stories mean something.
You can have wonderful, interesting people, a
fascinating story, but it's not about anything. It
has no real substance.*

TONI MORRISON

Thinking readers have always looked in literature for an interpretation of experience. They listen to writers who help them make sense of life— or of some corner of it. They remember writers who were guideposts or beacons in times of bewilderment, of confusion. Each of the following stories puts its characters into situations that confront them with searching questions. What are these questions in each story? What answers does the story as a whole suggest? What ideas—about people, about human nature, about evil—are at the heart of each story?

Alice Walker   *(born 1944)*

*Her deepest concern is with individuals and
how their relationships are affected by their
confrontations with wider political and moral
issues.*

CAROL RUMENS

Alice Walker's novel *The Color Purple* (1982) established her as a dominant voice in the quest for a new black identity. In her Pulitzer Prize–winning novel, as in some of her short stories, her heroines are women in the African American community struggling to emerge from a history of oppression and abuse. They find strength in bonding with other women, and they turn to the African past in the search for alternatives to our rapacious technological civilization. A recurrent feature in her fiction are black males representing a generation of men who "had failed women—and themselves." Walker's more recent novel, *The Temple of My Familiar* (1989), has been called a book of "amazing, overwhelming" richness, with characters "pushing one another towards self-knowledge, honesty, engagement" (Ursula K. Le Guin).

Born in Eatonton, Georgia, Walker knew poverty and racism at close quarters as the child of sharecroppers in the Deep South. While a student at Spelman College in Atlanta, she joined in the rallies, sit-ins, and freedom marches of the civil rights movement, which, she said later, "broke the pattern of black servitude in this country." She worked as a caseworker for the New York City Welfare Department and as an editor for *Ms.* magazine. She has written and lectured widely on the relationship between black men and women, between black and white women, and between her writing and the work of African American writers—Jean Toomer, Zora Neale Hurston—who were her inspiration. She has taught creative writing and black literature at colleges including Jackson State College, Wellesley, and Yale.

Many of Walker's essays, articles, and reviews were collected in her *In Search of Our Mothers' Gardens* (1983). In the title essay, she paid tribute to women of her mother's and grandmother's generations, who channeled the creative and spiritual energies that were denied other outlets into their rich gardens and into the "fanciful, inspired, and yet simple" quilts they fashioned from "bits and pieces of worthless rags." In the following story, the older generation tries to hold on to its hard-won pride, while members of a younger generation assert their independence from the past by adopting Muslim names and African greetings.

Everyday Use   *1973*

For Your Grandmamma

I will wait for her in the yard that Maggie and I made so clean and wavy yesterday afternoon. A yard like this is more comfortable than most people know. It is not just a yard. It is like an extended living room. When the hard clay is swept clean as a floor and the fine sand around the edges lined with tiny, irregular grooves, anyone can come and sit and look up into the elm tree and wait for the breezes that never come inside the house.

Maggie will be nervous until after her sister goes: she will stand hopelessly in corners, homely and ashamed of the burn scars down her arms and legs, eyeing her sister with a mixture of envy and awe. She thinks her sister has held life always in the palm of one hand, that "no" is a word the world never learned to say to her.

You've no doubt seen those TV shows where the child who has "made it" is confronted, as a surprise, by her own mother and father, tottering in weakly from backstage. (A pleasant surprise, of course: What would they do if parent and child came on the show only to curse out and insult each other?) On TV mother and child embrace and smile into each other's faces. Sometimes the mother and father weep, the child wraps them in her arms and leans across the table to tell how she would not have made it without their help. I have seen these programs.

Sometimes I dream a dream in which Dee and I are suddenly brought together on a TV program of this sort. Out of a dark and soft-seated limousine I am ushered into a bright room filled with many people. There I meet a smiling, gray, sporty man like Johnny Carson who shakes my hand and tells me what a fine girl I have. Then we are on the stage and Dee is embracing me with tears in her eyes. She pins on my dress a large orchid, even though she has told me once that she thinks orchids are tacky flowers.

In real life I am a large, big-boned woman with rough, man-working 5
hands. In the winter I wear flannel nightgowns to bed and overalls during
the day. I can kill and clean a hog as mercilessly as a man. My fat keeps me
hot in zero weather. I can work outside all day, breaking ice to get water
for washing; I can eat pork liver cooked over the open fire minutes after it
comes steaming from the hog. One winter I knocked a bull calf straight in
the brain between the eyes with a sledge hammer and had the meat hung
up to chill before nightfall. But of course all this does not show on television. I am the way my daughter would want me to be: a hundred pounds
lighter, my skin like an uncooked barley pancake. My hair glistens in the hot
bright lights. Johnny Carson has much to do to keep up with my quick and
witty tongue.

But that is a mistake. I know even before I wake up. Who ever knew a
Johnson with a quick tongue? Who can even imagine me looking a strange
white man in the eye? It seems to me I have talked to them always with one
foot raised in flight, with my head turned in whichever way is farthest from
them. Dee, though. She would always look anyone in the eye. Hesitation
was no part of her nature.

"How do I look, Mama?" Maggie says, showing just enough of her thin
body enveloped in pink skirt and red blouse for me to know she's there,
almost hidden by the door.

"Come out into the yard," I say.

Have you ever seen a lame animal, perhaps a dog run over by some careless person rich enough to own a car, sidle up to someone who is ignorant
enough to be kind to them? That is the way my Maggie walks. She has been
like this, chin on chest, eyes on ground, feet in shuffle, ever since the fire
that burned the other house to the ground.

Dee is lighter than Maggie, with nicer hair and a fuller figure. She's a 10
woman now, though sometimes I forget. How long ago was it that the other
house burned? Ten, twelve years? Sometimes I can still hear the flames and
feel Maggie's arms sticking to me, her hair smoking and her dress falling off
her in little black papery flakes. Her eyes seemed stretched open, blazed
open by the flames reflected in them. And Dee. I see her standing off under
the sweet gum tree she used to dig gum out of; a look of concentration on
her face as she watched the last dingy gray board of the house fall in toward the red-hot brick chimney. Why don't you do a dance around the
ashes? I'd wanted to ask her. She had hated the house that much.

I used to think she hated Maggie, too. But that was before we raised the
money, the church and me, to send her to Augusta to school. She used to
read to us without pity; forcing words, lies, other folks' habits, whole lives
upon us two, sitting trapped and ignorant underneath her voice. She
washed us in a river of make-believe, burned us with a lot of knowledge
we didn't necessarily need to know. Pressed us to her with the serious way
she read, to shove us away at just the moment, like dimwits, we seemed
about to understand.

Dee wanted nice things. A yellow organdy dress to wear to her graduation from high school; black pumps to match a green suit she'd made from

an old suit somebody gave me. She was determined to stare down any disaster in her efforts. Her eyelids would not flicker for minutes at a time. Often I fought off the temptation to shake her. At sixteen she had a style of her own: and knew what style was.

I never had an education myself. After second grade the school was closed down. Don't ask me why: in 1927 colored asked fewer questions than they do now. Sometimes Maggie reads to me. She stumbles along good naturedly but can't see well. She knows she is not bright. Like good looks and money, quickness passed her by. She will marry John Thomas (who has mossy teeth in an earnest face) and then I'll be free to sit here and I guess just sing church songs to myself. Although I never was a good singer. Never could carry a tune. I was always better at a man's job. I used to love to milk till I was hooked in the side in '49. Cows are soothing and slow and don't bother you, unless you try to milk them the wrong way.

I have deliberately turned my back on the house. It is three rooms, just like the one that burned, except the roof is tin; they don't make shingle roofs any more. There are no real windows, just some holes cut in the sides, like the portholes in a ship, but not round and not square, with rawhide holding the shutters up on the outside. This house is in a pasture, too, like the other one. No doubt when Dee sees it she will want to tear it down. She wrote me once that no matter where we "choose" to live, she will manage to come see us. But she will never bring her friends. Maggie and I thought about this and Maggie asked me, "Mama, when did Dee ever *have* any friends?"

She had a few. Furtive boys in pink shirts hanging about on washday 15 after school. Nervous girls who never laughed. Impressed with her they worshiped the well-turned phrase, the cute shape, the scalding humor that erupted like bubbles in lye. She read to them.

When she was courting Jimmy T she didn't have much time to pay to us, but turned all her faultfinding power on him. He *flew* to marry a cheap city girl from a family of ignorant flashy people. She hardly had time to recompose herself.

When she comes I will meet—but there they are!

Maggie attempts to make a dash for the house, in her shuffling way, but I stay her with my hand. "Come back here," I say. And she stops and tries to dig a well in the sand with her toe.

It is hard to see them clearly through the strong sun. But even the first glimpse of leg out of the car tells me it is Dee. Her feet were always neat-looking, as if God himself had shaped them with a certain style. From the other side of the car comes a short, stocky man. Hair is all over his head a foot long and hanging from his chin like a kinky mule tail. I hear Maggie suck in her breath. "Uhnnnh," is what it sounds like. Like when you see the wriggling end of a snake just in front of your foot on the road. "Uhnnnh."

Dee next. A dress down to the ground, in this hot weather. A dress so 20 loud it hurts my eyes. There are yellows and oranges enough to throw back the light of the sun. I feel my whole face warming from the heat waves it throws out. Earrings gold, too, and hanging down to her shoulders. Bracelets dangling and making noises when she moves her arm up to shake the folds of the dress out of her armpits. The dress is loose and flows, and as she walks closer, I like it. I hear Maggie go "Uhnnnh" again. It is her sister's hair. It stands straight up like the wool on a sheep. It is black as night and around the edges are two long pigtails that rope about like small lizards disappearing behind her ears.

"Wa-su-zo-Tean-o!" she says, coming on in that gliding way the dress makes her move. The short stocky fellow with the hair to his navel is all grinning and he follows up with "Asalamalakim, my mother and sister!" He moves to hug Maggie but she falls back, right up against the back of my chair. I feel her trembling there and when I look up I see the perspiration falling off her chin.

"Don't get up," says Dee. Since I am stout it takes something of a push. You can see me trying to move a second or two before I make it. She turns, showing white heels through her sandals, and goes back to the car. Out she peeks next with a Polaroid. She stoops down quickly and lines up picture after picture of me sitting there in front of the house with Maggie cowering behind me. She never takes a shot without making sure the house is included. When a cow comes nibbling around the edge of the yard she snaps it and me and Maggie *and* the house. Then she puts the Polaroid in the back seat of the car, and comes up and kisses me on the forehead.

Meanwhile Asalamalakim is going through motions with Maggie's hand. Maggie's hand is as limp as a fish, and probably as cold, despite the sweat, and she keeps trying to pull it back. It looks like Asalamalakim wants to shake hands but wants to do it fancy. Or maybe he don't know how people shake hands. Anyhow, he soon gives up on Maggie.

"Well," I say. "Dee."

"No, Mama," she says. "Not 'Dee,' Wangero Leewanika Kemanjo!"   25

"What happened to 'Dee'?" I wanted to know.

"She's dead," Wangero said. "I couldn't bear it any longer, being named after the people who oppress me."

"You know as well as me you was named after your aunt Dicie," I said. Dicie is my sister. She named Dee. We called her "Big Dee" after Dee was born.

"But who was *she* named after?" asked Wangero.

"I guess after Grandma Dee," I said.   30

"And who was she named after?" asked Wangero.

"Her mother," I said, and saw Wangero was getting tired. "That's about as far back as I can trace it," I said. Though, in fact, I probably could have carried it back beyond the Civil War through the branches.

"Well," said Asalamalakim, "there you are."

"Uhnnnh," I heard Maggie say.

"There I was not," I said, "before 'Dicie' cropped up in our family, so why   35
should I try to trace it that far back?"

He just stood there grinning, looking down on me like somebody inspecting a Model A car. Every once in a while he and Wangero sent eye signals over my head.

"How do you pronounce this name?" I asked.

"You don't have to call me by it if you don't want to," said Wangero.

"Why shouldn't I?" I asked. "If that's what you want us to call you, we'll call you."

"I know it might sound awkward at first," said Wangero.   40

"I'll get used to it," I said. "Ream it out again."

Well, soon we got the name out of the way. Asalamalakim had a name twice as long and three times as hard. After I tripped over it two or three times he told me to just call him Hakim-a-barber. I wanted to ask him was he a barber, but I didn't really think he was, so I didn't ask.

"You must belong to those beef-cattle peoples down the road," I said. They said "Asalamalakim" when they met you, too, but they didn't shake hands. Always too busy: feeding the cattle, fixing the fences, putting up salt-lick shelters, throwing down hay. When the white folks poisoned some of the herd the men stayed up all night with rifles in their hands. I walked a mile and a half just to see the sight.

Hakim-a-barber said, "I accept some of their doctrines, but farming and raising cattle is not my style." (They didn't tell me, and I didn't ask, whether Wangero (Dee) had really gone and married him.)

We sat down to eat and right away he said he didn't eat collards and pork   45 was unclean. Wangero, though, went on through the chitlins and corn bread, the greens and everything else. She talked a blue streak over the sweet potatoes. Everything delighted her. Even the fact that we still used the benches her daddy made for the table when we couldn't afford to buy chairs.

"Oh, Mama!" she cried. Then turned to Hakim-a-barber. "I never knew how lovely these benches are. You can feel the rump prints," she said, running her hands underneath her and along the bench. Then she gave a sigh and her hand closed over Grandma Dee's butter dish. "That's it!" she said. "I knew there was something I wanted to ask you if I could have." She jumped up from the table and went over in the corner where the churn stood, the milk in it clabber by now. She looked at the churn and looked at it.

"This churn top is what I need," she said. "Didn't Uncle Buddy whittle it out of a tree you all used to have?"

"Yes," I said.

"Uh huh," she said happily. "And I want the dasher, too."

"Uncle Buddy whittle that, too?" asked the barber.   50

Dee (Wangero) looked up at me.

"Aunt Dee's first husband whittled the dash," said Maggie so low you almost couldn't hear her. "His name was Henry, but they called him Stash."

"Maggie's brain is like an elephant's," Wangero said, laughing. "I can use the churn top as a centerpiece for the alcove table," she said, sliding a plate over the churn, "and I'll think of something artistic to do with the dasher."

When she finished wrapping the dasher the handle stuck out. I took it for a moment in my hands. You didn't even have to look close to see where hands pushing the dasher up and down to make butter had left a kind of sink in the wood. In fact, there were a lot of small sinks; you could see where thumbs and fingers had sunk into the wood. It was beautiful light yellow wood, from a tree that grew in the yard where Big Dee and Stash had lived.

After dinner Dee (Wangero) went to the trunk at the foot of my bed and started rifling through it. Maggie hung back in the kitchen over the dishpan. Out came Wangero with two quilts. They had been pieced by Grandma Dee and then Big Dee and me had hung them on the quilt frames on the front porch and quilted them. One was in the Lone Star pattern. The other was Walk Around the Mountain. In both of them were scraps of dresses Grandma Dee had worn fifty and more years ago. Bits and pieces of Grandpa Jarrell's Paisley shirts. And one teeny faded blue piece, about the size of a penny matchbox, that was from Great Grandpa Ezra's uniform that he wore in the Civil War.

"Mama," Wangero said sweet as a bird. "Can I have these old quilts?"

I heard something fall in the kitchen, and a minute later the kitchen door slammed.

"Why don't you take one or two of the others?" I asked. "These old things was just done by me and Big Dee from some tops your grandma pieced before she died."

"No," said Wangero. "I don't want those. They are stitched around the borders by machine."

"That'll make them last better," I said.

"That's not the point," said Wangero. "These are all pieces of dresses Grandma used to wear. She did all this stitching by hand. Imagine!" She held the quilts securely in her arms, stroking them.

"Some of the pieces, like those lavender ones, come from old clothes her mother handed down to her," I said, moving up to touch the quilts. Dee (Wangero) moved back just enough so that I couldn't reach the quilts. They already belonged to her.

"Imagine!" she breathed again, clutching them closely to her bosom.

"The truth is," I said, "I promised to give them quilts to Maggie, for when she marries John Thomas."

She gasped like a bee had stung her.

"Maggie can't appreciate these quilts!" she said. "She'd probably be backward enough to put them to everyday use."

"I reckon she would," I said. "God knows I been saving 'em for long enough with nobody using 'em. I hope she will!" I didn't want to bring up how I had offered Dee (Wangero) a quilt when she went away to college. Then she had told me they were old-fashioned, out of style.

"But they're *priceless!*" she was saying now, furiously; for she has a temper. "Maggie would put them on the bed and in five years they'd be in rags. Less than that!"

"She can always make some more," I said. "Maggie knows how to quilt."

Dee (Wangero) looked at me with hatred. "You just will not understand. The point is these quilts, *these* quilts!"

"Well," I said, stumped. "What would *you* do with them?"

"Hang them," she said. As if that was the only thing you *could* do with quilts.

Maggie by now was standing in the door. I could almost hear the sound her feet made as they scraped over each other.

"She can have them, Mama," she said, like somebody used to never winning anything, or having anything reserved for her. "I can 'member Grandma Dee without the quilts."

I looked at her hard. She had filled her bottom lip with checkerberry   75
snuff and it gave her face a kind of dopey, hangdog look. It was Grandma Dee and Big Dee who taught her how to quilt herself. She stood there with her scarred hands hidden in the folds of her skirt. She looked at her sister with something like fear but she wasn't mad at her. This was Maggie's portion. This was the way she knew God to work.

When I looked at her like that something hit me in the top of my head and ran down to the soles of my feet. Just like when I'm in church and the spirit of God touches me and I get happy and shout. I did something I never had done before: hugged Maggie to me, then dragged her on into the room, snatched the quilts out of Miss Wangero's hands and dumped them into Maggie's lap. Maggie just sat there on my bed with her mouth open.

"Take one or two of the others," I said to Dee.

But she turned without a word and went out to Hakim-a-barber.

"You just don't understand," she said, as Maggie and I came out to the car.

"What don't I understand?" I wanted to know.   80

"Your heritage," she said. And then she turned to Maggie, kissed her, and said, "You ought to try to make something of yourself, too, Maggie. It's really a new day for us. But from the way you and Mama still live you'd never know it."

She put on some sunglasses that hid everything above the tip of her nose and her chin.

Maggie smiled; maybe at the sunglasses. But a real smile, not scared. After we watched the car dust settle I asked Maggie to bring me a dip of snuff. And then the two of us sat there just enjoying, until it was time to go in the house and go to bed.

The Receptive Reader

1. What is the self-image of the mother? How does her sense of her real self contrast with her daydreams? How does her initial self-portrait as the *narrator* and central character point forward to what happens later in the story?

2. What is the contrasting history of the two siblings? How does one serve as a *foil* to the other? What is most significant in their earlier history?

3. What is the mother's view of Dee and her companion? How would you spell out the mother's attitude implied at various points in the story? What touches seem satirical, and why? Is everything in the story seen from the mother's *point of view*?

4. How does the confrontation over the quilts bring things to a head? What do the quilts symbolize? How does the climactic ending resolve the central conflict in this story? How does it turn the tables on Dee's use of terms like *backward* and *heritage*?

5. How would you spell out in so many words the *theme* of this story? (How does the title hint at the central theme?)

6. What in the story helps especially to bring the theme to life for you and keep it from becoming an abstract idea?

The Personal Response

Do you identify with the narrator in this story? Is there another side to the story? Could you say something in defense of Dee?

The Creative Dimension

Write a passage in which one or the other of the daughters tells her side of the story. Or rewrite the ending the way you would have preferred the story to come out.

Stephen Crane   *(1871–1900)*

Stephen Crane is an outstanding early representative of **naturalism** in American fiction. Naturalist writers were not squeamish about looking at nature in the raw or confronting unembellished human nature. Like other writers in that tradition, Crane preferred not to preach or editorialize but to let the grim facts speak for themselves. He was born in Newark, New Jersey, the fourteenth child in the home of a Methodist minister. After his college years at Lafayette and Syracuse, he scraped together a living as a freelance journalist, and much of his fiction looks at harsh realities with the impartial honesty of the reporter. His first novel, *Maggie: A Girl of the Streets* (1893), took an uncompromising look at a subject then not considered a fit topic for polite conversation. He became famous with *The Red Badge of Courage* (1895), a novel about the Civil War. Anticipating modern war novels, Crane went beyond the flag-waving and heroic oratory of stay-at-home patriots to probe the psychological realities of war: the fear of death, the horror of mass destruction, the sense of solidarity with one's doomed comrades.

Crane had the strongly developed sense of **irony** that was to become the hallmark of much twentieth-century literature. His stories and poems highlight the sad and laughable contrast between our naive hopes or rosy daydreams and the world in which we live. Driven into exile by gossip about his irregular personal life, enmeshed in what one editor has called "a malignant tangle of debts," he died of tuberculosis after publishing fourteen books in his short lifetime.

The following short story classic, which he called a tale "after the fact," is based on his personal experience as the survivor of the shipwreck of the steamer *Commodore*. He had earlier written a factual account of the experience for the New York *Press*, published on January 7, 1887. What is the theme—or are the themes—of this story? What does it say about the relationship between human beings and nature? What does it say about male bonding? What does it say about the survival of the fittest—or, for that matter, the survival of the unfit?

The Open Boat   1897

I

None of them knew the color of the sky. Their eyes glanced level, and were fastened upon the waves that swept toward them. These waves were of the hue of slate, save for the tops, which were of foaming white, and all of the men knew the colors of the sea. The horizon narrowed and widened, and dipped and rose, and at all times its edge was jagged with waves that seemed thrust up in points like rocks.

Many a man ought to have a bathtub larger than the boat which here rode upon the sea. These waves were most wrongfully and barbarously abrupt and tall, and each froth-top was a problem in small-boat navigation.

The cook squatted in the bottom, and looked with both eyes at the six inches of gunwale which separated him from the ocean. His sleeves were rolled over his fat forearms, and the two flaps of his unbuttoned vest dangled as he bent to bail out the boat. Often he said, "Gawd! that was a narrow clip." As he remarked it he invariably gazed eastward over the broken sea.

The oiler, steering with one of the two oars in the boat, sometimes raised himself suddenly to keep clear of water that swirled in over the stern. It was a thin little oar, and it seemed often ready to snap.

The correspondent, pulling at the other oar, watched the waves and wondered why he was there. 5

The injured captain, lying in the bow, was at this time buried in that profound dejection and indifference which comes, temporarily at least, to even the bravest and most enduring when, willy-nilly, the firm fails, the army loses, the ship goes down. The mind of the master of a vessel is rooted deep in the timbers of her, though he command for a day or a decade; and this captain had on him the stern impression of a scene in the greys of dawn of seven turned faces, and later a stump of a topmast with a white ball on it, that slashed to and fro at the waves, went low and lower, and down. Thereafter there was something strange in his voice. Although steady, it was deep with mourning, and of a quality beyond oration or tears.

"Keep 'er a little more south, Billie," said he.

"A little more south, sir," said the oiler in the stern.

A seat in his boat was not unlike a seat upon a bucking broncho, and by the same token a broncho is not much smaller. The craft pranced and reared and plunged like an animal. As each wave came, and she rose for it, she seemed like a horse making at a fence outrageously high. The manner of her scramble over these walls of water is a mystic thing, and, moreover, at the top of them were ordinarily these problems in white water, the foam racing down from the summit of each wave requiring a new leap, and a leap from the air. Then, after scornfully bumping a crest, she would slide and race and splash down a long incline, and arrive bobbing and nodding in front of the next menace.

A singular disadvantage of the sea lies in the fact that after successfully surmounting one wave you discover that there is another behind it just as important and just as nervously anxious to do something effective in the way of swamping boats. In a ten-foot dinghy one can get an idea of the resources of the sea in the line of waves that is not probable to the average experience which is never at sea in a dinghy. As each salty wall of water approached, it shut all else from the view of the men in the boat, and it was not difficult to imagine that this particular wave was the final outburst of the ocean, the last effort of the grim water. There was a terrible grace in the move of the waves, and they came in silence, save for the snarling of the crests.

In the wan light the faces of the men must have been grey. Their eyes must have glinted in strange ways as they gazed steadily astern. Viewed from a balcony, the whole thing would doubtless have been weirdly picturesque. But the men in the boat had no time to see it, and if they had had leisure, there were other things to occupy their minds. The sun swung steadily up the sky, and they knew it was broad day because the color of the sea changed from slate to emerald green streaked with amber lights, and the foam was like tumbling snow. The process of the breaking day was unknown to them. They were aware only of this effect upon the color of the waves that rolled toward them.

In disjointed sentences the cook and the correspondent argued as to the difference between a life-saving station and a house of refuge. The cook had said: "There's a house of refuge just north of the Mosquito Inlet Light, and as soon as they see us they'll come off in their boat and pick us up."

"As soon as who see us?" said the correspondent.

"The crew," said the cook.

"Houses of refuge don't have crews," said the correspondent. "As I understand them, they are only places where clothes and grub are stored for the benefit of shipwrecked people. They don't carry crews."

"Oh, yes, they do," said the cook.

"No, they don't," said the correspondent.

"Well, we're not there yet, anyhow," said the oiler, in the stern.

"Well," said the cook, "perhaps it's not a house of refuge that I'm thinking of as being near Mosquito Inlet Light; perhaps it's a life-saving station."

"We're not there yet," said the oiler in the stern.

II

As the boat bounced from the top of each wave the wind tore through the hair of the hatless men, and as the craft plopped her stern down again the spray slashed past them. The crest of each of these waves was a hill, from the top of which the men surveyed for a moment a broad tumultuous expanse, shining and wind-riven. It was probably splendid, it was probably glorious, this play of the free sea, wild with lights of emerald and white and amber.

10

15

20

"Bully good thing it's an on-shore wind," said the cook. "If not, where would we be? Wouldn't have a show."

"That's right," said the correspondent.

The busy oiler nodded his assent.

Then the captain, in the bow, chuckled in a way that expressed humor, 25 contempt, tragedy, all in one. "Do you think we've got much of a show now, boys?" said he.

Whereupon the three were silent, save for a trifle of hemming and hawing. To express any particular optimism at this time they felt to be childish and stupid, but they all doubtless possessed this sense of the situation in their minds. A young man thinks doggedly at such times. On the other hand, the ethics of their condition was decidedly against any open suggestion of hopelessness. So they were silent.

"Oh, well," said the captain, soothing his children, "we'll get ashore all right."

But there was that in his tone which made them think; so the oiler quoth, "Yes! if this wind holds."

The cook was bailing. "Yes! if we don't catch hell in the surf."

Canton-flannel gulls flew near and far. Sometimes they sat down on the 30 sea, near patches of brown seaweed that rolled over the waves with a movement like carpets on a line in a gale. The birds sat comfortably in groups, and they were envied by some in the dinghy, for the wrath of the sea was no more to them than it was to a covey of prairie chickens a thousand miles inland. Often they came very close and stared at the men with black bead-like eyes. At these times they were uncanny and sinister in their unblinking scrutiny, and the men hooted angrily at them, telling them to be gone. One came, and evidently decided to alight on the top of the captain's head. The bird flew parallel to the boat and did not circle, but made short sidelong jumps in the air in chicken-fashion. His black eyes were wistfully fixed upon the captain's head. "Ugly brute," said the oiler to the bird. "You look as if you were made with a jackknife." The cook and the correspondent swore darkly at the creature. The captain naturally wished to knock it away with the end of the heavy painter, but he did not dare do it, because anything resembling an emphatic gesture would have capsized this freighted boat; and so, with his open hand, the captain gently and carefully waved the gull away. After it had been discouraged from the pursuit the captain breathed easier on account of his hair, and others breathed easier because the bird struck their minds at this time as being somehow gruesome and ominous.

In the meantime the oiler and the correspondent rowed. And also they rowed. They sat together in the same seat, and each rowed an oar. Then the oiler took both oars; then the correspondent took both oars; then the oiler; then the correspondent. They rowed and they rowed. The very ticklish part of the business was when the time came for the reclining one in the stern to take his turn at the oars. By the very last star of truth, it is easier to steal eggs from under a hen than it was to change seats in the dinghy. First the man in the stern slid his hand along the thwart and moved with care, as if he were of Sèvres. Then the man in the rowing-seat slid his hand along the other thwart. It was all done with the most extraordinary care. As the two sidled past each other, the whole party kept watchful eyes on the coming wave, and the captain cried: "Look out, now! Steady, there!"

The brown mats of seaweed that appeared from time to time were like islands, bits of earth. They were travelling, apparently, neither one way nor the other. They were, to all intents, stationary. They informed the men in the boat that it was making progress slowly toward the land.

The captain, rearing cautiously in the bow after the dinghy soared on a great swell, said that he had seen the lighthouse at Mosquito Inlet. Presently the cook remarked that he had seen it. The correspondent was at the oars then, and for some reason he too wished to look at the lighthouse; but his back was toward the far shore, and the waves were important, and for some time he could not seize an opportunity to turn his head. But at last there came a wave more gentle than the others, and when at the crest of it he swiftly scoured the western horizon.

"See it?" said the captain.

"No," said the correspondent, slowly; "I didn't see anything."   35

"Look again," said the captain. He pointed. "It's exactly in that direction."

At the top of another wave the correspondent did as he was bid, and this time his eyes chanced on a small, still thing on the edge of the swaying horizon. It was precisely like the point of a pin. It took an anxious eye to find a lighthouse so tiny.

"Think we'll make it, Captain?"

"If this wind holds and the boat don't swamp, we can't do much else," said the captain.

The little boat, lifted by each towering sea and splashed viciously by the   40 crests, made progress that in the absence of seaweed was not apparent to those in her. She seemed just a wee thing wallowing, miraculously top up, at the mercy of five oceans. Occasionally a great spread of water, like white flames, swarmed into her.

"Bail her, cook," said the captain, serenely.

"All right, Captain," said the cheerful cook.

III

It would be difficult to describe the subtle brotherhood of men that was here established on the seas. No one said that it was so. No one mentioned it. But it dwelt in the boat, and each man felt it warm him. They were a captain, an oiler, a cook, and a correspondent, and they were friends—friends in a more curiously iron-bound degree than may be common. The hurt captain, lying against the water-jar in the bow, spoke always in a low voice and calmly; but he could never command a more ready and swiftly obedient crew than the motley three of the dinghy. It was more than a mere recognition of what was best for the common safety. There was surely in it a quality that was personal and heart-felt. And after this devotion to the commander of the boat, there was this comradeship, that the correspondent, for instance, who had been taught to be cynical of men, knew even at the time was the best experience of his life. But no one said that it was so. No one mentioned it.

"I wish we had a sail," remarked the captain. "We might try my overcoat on the end of an oar, and give you two boys a chance to rest." So the cook and the correspondent held the mast and spread wide the overcoat; the oiler steered; and the little boat made good way with her new rig. Sometimes the oiler had to scull sharply to keep a sea from breaking into the boat, but otherwise sailing was a success.

Meanwhile the lighthouse had been growing slowly larger. It had now al-   45 most assumed color, and appeared like a little grey shadow on the sky. The man at the oars could not be prevented from turning his head rather often to try for a glimpse of this little grey shadow.

At last, from the top of each wave, the men in the tossing boat could see land. Even as the lighthouse was an upright shadow on the sky, this land seemed but a long black shadow on the sea. It certainly was thinner than paper. "We must be about opposite New Smyrna," said the cook, who had coasted this shore often in schooners. "Captain, by the way, I believe they abandoned that life-saving station there about a year ago."

"Did they?" said the captain.

The wind slowly died away. The cook and the correspondent were not now obliged to slave in order to hold high the oar. But the waves continued their old impetuous swooping at the dinghy, and the little craft, no longer under way, struggled woundily over them. The oiler or the correspondent took the oars again.

Shipwrecks are apropos of nothing. If men could only train for them and have them occur when the men had reached pink condition, there would be less drowning at sea. Of the four in the dinghy none had slept any time worth mentioning for two days and two nights previous to embarking in the dinghy, and in the excitement of clambering about the deck of a foundering ship they had also forgotten to eat heartily.

For these reasons, and for others, neither the oiler nor the correspondent   50 was fond of rowing at this time. The correspondent wondered ingenuously how in the name of all that was sane could there be people who thought it amusing to row a boat. It was not an amusement; it was a diabolical punishment, and even a genius of mental aberrations could never conclude that it was anything but a horror to the muscles and a crime against the back. He mentioned to the boat in general how the amusement of rowing struck him, and the weary-faced oiler smiled in full sympathy. Previously to the foundering, by the way, the oiler had worked a double watch in the engine-room of the ship.

"Take her easy now, boys," said the captain. "Don't spend yourselves. If we have to run a surf you'll need all your strength, because we'll sure have to swim for it. Take your time."

Slowly the land arose from the sea. From a black line it became a line of black and a line of white—trees and sand. Finally the captain said that he could make out a house on the shore. "That's the house of refuge, sure," said the cook. "They'll see us before long, and come out after us."

The distant lighthouse reared high. "The keeper ought to be able to make us out now, if he's looking through a glass," said the captain. "He'll notify the life-saving people."

"None of those other boats could have got ashore to give word of this wreck," said the oiler, in a low voice, "else the life-boat would be out hunting us."

Slowly and beautifully the land loomed out of the sea. The wind came   55
again. It had veered from the north-east to the south-east. Finally a new
sound struck the ears of the men in the boat. It was the low thunder of the
surf on the shore. "We'll never be able to make the lighthouse now," said
the captain. "Swing her head a little more north, Billie."

"A little more north, sir," said the oiler.

Whereupon the little boat turned her nose once more down the wind,
and all but the oarsman watched the shore grow. Under the influence of this
expansion doubt and direful apprehension were leaving the minds of the
men. The management of the boat was still most absorbing, but it could not
prevent a quiet cheerfulness. In an hour, perhaps, they would be ashore.

Their backbones had become thoroughly used to balancing in the boat,
and they now rode this wild colt of a dinghy like circus men. The correspondent thought that he had been drenched to the skin, but happening to
feel in the top pocket of his coat, he found therein eight cigars. Four of them
were soaked with sea-water; four were perfectly scatheless. After a search,
somebody produced three dry matches; and thereupon the four waifs rode
impudently in their little boat and, with an assurance of an impending rescue shining in their eyes, puffed at the big cigars, and judged well and ill of
all men. Everybody took a drink of water.

IV

"Cook," remarked the captain, "there don't seem to be any signs of life
about your house of refuge."

"No," replied the cook. "Funny they don't see us!"   60

A broad stretch of lowly coast lay before the eyes of the men. It was of
low dunes topped with dark vegetation. The roar of the surf was plain, and
sometimes they could see the white lip of a wave as it spun up the beach.
A tiny house was blocked out black upon the sky. Southward, the slim lighthouse lifted its little grey length.

Tide, wind, and waves were swinging the dinghy northward. "Funny they
don't see us," said the men.

The surf's roar was here dulled, but its tone was nevertheless thunderous
and mighty. As the boat swam over the great rollers the men sat listening to
this roar. "We'll swamp sure," said everybody.

It is fair to say here that there was not a life-saving station within twenty
miles in either direction; but the men did not know this fact, and in consequence they made dark and opprobrious remarks concerning the eyesight
of the nation's life-savers. Four scowling men sat in the dinghy and sur-
passed records in the invention of epithets.

"Funny they don't see us."   65

The light-heartedness of a former time had completely faded. To their
sharpened minds it was easy to conjure pictures of all kinds of incompe-
tency and blindness and, indeed, cowardice. There was the shore of the
populous land, and it was bitter and bitter to them that from it came no sign.

"Well," said the captain, ultimately, "I suppose we'll have to make a try
for ourselves. If we stay out here too long, we'll none of us have strength
left to swim after the boat swamps."

And so the oiler, who was at the oars, turned the boat straight for the shore. There was a sudden tightening of muscles. There was some thinking.

"If we don't all get ashore," said the captain—"if we don't all get ashore, I suppose you fellows know where to send news of my finish?"

They then briefly exchanged some addresses and admonitions. As for the   70 reflections of the men, there was a great deal of rage in them. Perchance they might be formulated thus: "If I am going to be drowned—if I am going to be drowned—if I am going to be drowned, why, in the name of the seven mad gods who rule the sea, was I allowed to come thus far and contemplate sand and trees? Was I brought here merely to have my nose dragged away as I was about to nibble the sacred cheese of life? It is preposterous. If this old ninny-woman, Fate, cannot do better than this, she should be deprived of the management of men's fortunes. She is an old hen who knows not her intention. If she has decided to drown me, why did she not do it in the beginning and save me all this trouble? The whole affair is absurd.—But no; she cannot mean to drown me. She dare not drown me. She cannot drown me. Not after all this work." Afterward the man might have had an impulse to shake his fist at the clouds. "Just you drown me, now, and then hear what I call you!"

The billows that came at this time were more formidable. They seemed always just about to break and roll over the little boat in a turmoil of foam. There was a preparatory and long growl in the speech of them. No mind unused to the sea would have concluded that the dinghy could ascend these sheer heights in time. The shore was still afar. The oiler was a wily surfman. "Boys," he said swiftly, "she won't live three minutes more, and we're too far out to swim. Shall I take her to sea again, Captain?"

"Yes; go ahead!" said the captain.

This oiler, by a series of quick miracles and fast and steady oarsmanship, turned the boat in the middle of the surf and took her safely to sea again.

There was a considerable silence as the boat bumped over the furrowed sea to deeper water. Then somebody in gloom spoke: "Well, anyhow, they must have seen us from the shore by now."

The gulls went in slanting flight up the wind toward the grey, desolate   75 east. A squall, marked by dingy clouds and clouds brick-red like smoke from a burning building, appeared from the southeast.

"What do you think of those life-saving people? Ain't they peaches?"

"Funny they haven't seen us."

"Maybe they think we're out here for sport! Maybe they think we're fishin'. Maybe they think we're damned fools."

It was a long afternoon. A changed tide tried to force them southward, but wind and wave said northward. Far ahead, where coast-line, sea, and sky formed their mighty angle, there were little dots which seemed to indicate a city on the shore.

"St. Augustine?"   80

The captain shook his head. "Too near Mosquito Inlet."

And the oiler rowed, and then the correspondent rowed; then the oiler rowed. It was a weary business. The human back can become the seat of more aches and pains than are registered in books for the composite anatomy of a regiment. It is a limited area, but it can become the theatre of innumerable muscular conflicts, tangles, wrenches, knots, and other comforts.

"Did you ever like to row, Billie?" asked the correspondent.

"No," said the oiler; "hang it!"

When one exchanged the rowing-seat for a place in the bottom of the 85 boat, he suffered a bodily depression that caused him to be careless of everything save an obligation to wiggle one finger. There was cold sea-water swashing to and fro in the boat, and he lay in it. His head, pillowed on a thwart, was within an inch of the swirl of a wave-crest, and sometimes a particularly obstreperous sea came inboard and drenched him once more. But these matters did not annoy him. It is almost certain that if the boat had capsized he would have tumbled comfortably out upon the ocean as if he felt sure that it was a great soft mattress.

"Look! There's a man on the shore!"

"Where?"

"There! See 'im? See 'im?"

"Yes, sure! He's walking along."

"Now he's stopped. Look! He's facing us!"   90

"He's waving at us!"

"So he is! By thunder!"

"Ah, now we're all right! Now we're all right! There'll be a boat out here for us in half an hour."

"He's going on. He's running. He's going up to that house there."

The remote beach seemed lower than the sea, and it required a search- 95 ing glance to discern the little black figure. The captain saw a floating stick, and they rowed to it. A bath towel was by some weird chance in the boat, and, tying this on the stick, the captain waved it. The oarsman did not dare turn his head, so he was obliged to ask questions.

"What's he doing now?"

"He's standing still again. He's looking, I think.—There he goes again— toward the house.—Now he's stopped again."

"Is he waving at us?"

"No, not now; he was, though."

"Look! There comes another man!"   100

"He's running."

"Look at him go, would you!"

"Why, he's on a bicycle. Now he's met the other man. They're both wav-ing at us. Look!"

"There comes something up the beach."

"What the devil is that thing?"   105

"Why, it looks like a boat."

"Why, certainly, it's a boat."

"No; it's on wheels."

"Yes, so it is. Well, that must be the life-boat. They drag them along shore on a wagon."

"That's the life-boat, sure."   110

"No, by God, it's—it's an omnibus."

"I tell you it's a life-boat."

"It is not! It's an omnibus. I can see it plain. See? One of these big hotel omnibuses."

"By thunder, you're right. It's an omnibus, sure as fate. What do you suppose they are doing with an omnibus? Maybe they are going around collecting the life-crew, hey?"

"That's it, likely. Look! There's a fellow waving a little black flag. He's 115 standing on the steps of the omnibus. There come those other two fellows. Now they're all talking together. Look at the fellow with the flag. Maybe he ain't waving it!"

"That ain't a flag, is it? That's his coat. Why, certainly, that's his coat."

"So it is; it's his coat. He's taken it off and is waving it around his head. But would you look at him swing it!"

"Oh, say, there isn't any life-saving station there. That's just a winter-resort hotel omnibus that has brought over some of the boarders to see us drown."

"What's that idiot with the coat mean? What's he signalling, anyhow?"

"It looks as if he were trying to tell us to go north. There must be a life- 120 saving station up there."

"No; he thinks we're fishing. Just giving us a merry hand. See? Ah, there, Willie!"

"Well, I wish I could make something out of those signals. What do you suppose he means?"

"He don't mean anything; he's just playing."

"Well, if he'd just signal us to try the surf again, or to go to sea and wait, or go north, or go south, or go to hell, there would be some reason in it. But look at him! He just stands there and keeps his coat revolving like a wheel. The ass!"

"There come more people."   125

"Now there's quite a mob. Look! Isn't that a boat?"

"Where? Oh, I see where you mean. No, that's no boat."

"That fellow is still waving his coat."

"He must think we like to see him do that. Why don't he quit it? It don't mean anything."

"I don't know. I think he is trying to make us go north. It must be that 130 there's a life-saving station there somewhere."

"Say, he ain't tired yet. Look at 'im wave!"

"Wonder how long he can keep that up. He's been revolving his coat ever since he caught sight of us. He's an idiot. Why aren't they getting men to bring a boat out? A fishing-boat—one of those big yawls—could come out here all right. Why don't he do something?"

"Oh, it's all right now."

"They'll have a boat out here for us in less than no time, now that they've seen us."

A faint yellow tone came into the sky over the low land. The shadows 135 on the sea slowly deepened. The wind bore coldness with it, and the men began to shiver.

"Holy smoke!" said one, allowing his voice to express his impious mood, "if we keep on monkeying out here! If we've got to flounder out here all night!"

"Oh, we'll never have to stay here all night! Don't you worry. They've seen us now, and it won't be long before they'll come chasing out after us."

The shore grew dusky. The man waving a coat blended gradually into this gloom, and it swallowed in the same manner the omnibus and the group of people. The spray, when it dashed uproariously over the side, made the voyagers shrink and swear like men who were being branded.

"I'd like to catch the chump who waved the coat. I feel like socking him one, just for luck."

"Why? What did he do?"   140

"Oh, nothing, but then he seemed so damned cheerful."

In the meantime the oiler rowed, and then the correspondent rowed, and then the oiler rowed. Grey-faced and bowed forward, they mechanically, turn by turn, plied the leaden oars. The form of the lighthouse had vanished from the southern horizon, but finally a pale star appeared, just lifting from the sea. The streaked saffron in the west passed before the all-merging darkness, and the sea to the east was black. The land had vanished, and was expressed only by the low and drear thunder of the surf.

"If I am going to be drowned—if I am going to be drowned—if I am going to be drowned, why, in the name of the seven mad gods who rule the sea, was I allowed to come thus far and contemplate sand and trees? Was I brought here merely to have my nose dragged away as I was about to nibble the sacred cheese of life?"

The patient captain, drooped over the water-jar, was sometimes obliged to speak to the oarsman.

"Keep her head up! Keep her head up!"   145

"Keep her head up, sir." The voices were weary and low.

This was surely a quiet evening. All save the oarsman lay heavily and listlessly in the boat's bottom. As for him, his eyes were just capable of noting the tall black waves that swept forward in a most sinister silence, save for an occasional subdued growl of a crest.

The cook's head was on a thwart, and he looked without interest at the water under his nose. He was deep in other scenes. Finally he spoke. "Billie," he murmured, dreamfully, "what kind of pie do you like best?"

V

"Pie!" said the oiler and the correspondent, agitatedly. "Don't talk about those things, blast you!"

"Well," said the cook, "I was just thinking about ham sandwiches and—"   150

A night on the sea in an open boat is a long night. As darkness settled finally, the shine of the light, lifting from the sea in the south, changed to full gold. On the northern horizon a new light appeared, a small bluish gleam on the edge of the waters. These two lights were the furniture of the world. Otherwise there was nothing but waves.

Two men huddled in the stern, and distances were so magnificent in the dinghy that the rower was enabled to keep his feet partly warm by thrusting them under his companions. Their legs indeed extended far under the rowing-seat until they touched the feet of the captain forward. Sometimes, despite the efforts of the tired oarsman, a wave came piling into the boat, an icy wave of the night, and the chilling water soaked them anew. They would twist their bodies for a moment and groan, and sleep the dead sleep once more, while the water in the boat gurgled about them as the craft rocked.

The plan of the oiler and the correspondent was for one to row until he lost the ability, and then arouse the other from his sea-water couch in the bottom of the boat.

The oiler plied the oars until his head drooped forward and the over-powering sleep blinded him; and he rowed yet afterward. Then he touched a man in the bottom of the boat, and called his name. "Will you spell me for a little while?" he said, meekly.

"Sure, Billie," said the correspondent, awaking and dragging himself to a 155 sitting position. They exchanged places carefully, and the oiler, cuddling down in the seawater at the cook's side, seemed to go to sleep instantly.

The particular violence of the sea had ceased. The waves came without snarling. The obligation of the man at the oars was to keep the boat headed so that the tilt of the rollers would not capsize her, and to preserve her from filling when the crests rushed past. The black waves were silent and hard to be seen in the darkness. Often one was almost upon the boat before the oarsman was aware.

In a low voice the correspondent addressed the captain. He was not sure that the captain was awake, although this iron man seemed to be always awake. "Captain, shall I keep her making for that light north, sir?"

The same steady voice answered him. "Yes. Keep it about two points off the port bow."

The cook had tied a life-belt around himself in order to get even the warmth which this clumsy cork contrivance could donate, and he seemed almost stove-like when a rower, whose teeth invariably chattered wildly as soon as he ceased his labor, dropped down to sleep.

The correspondent, as he rowed, looked down at the two men sleeping 160 underfoot. The cook's arm was around the oiler's shoulders, and, with their fragmentary clothing and haggard faces, they were the babes of the sea—a grotesque rendering of the old babes in the wood.

Later he must have grown stupid at his work, for suddenly there was a growling of water, and a crest came with a roar and a swash into the boat, and it was a wonder that it did not set the cook afloat in his life-belt. The cook continued to sleep, but the oiler sat up, blinking his eyes and shaking with the new cold.

"Oh, I'm awful sorry, Billie," said the correspondent, contritely.

"That's all right, old boy," said the oiler, and lay down again and was asleep.

Presently it seemed that even the captain dozed, and the correspondent thought that he was the one man afloat on all the oceans. The wind had a voice as it came over the waves, and it was sadder than the end.

There was a long, loud swishing astern of the boat, and a gleaming trail 165 of phosphorescence, like blue flame, was furrowed on the black waters. It might have been made by a monstrous knife.

Then there came a stillness, while the correspondent breathed with open mouth and looked at the sea.

Suddenly there was another swish and another long flash of bluish light, and this time it was alongside the boat, and might almost been reached with an oar. The correspondent saw an enormous fin speed like a shadow through the water, hurling the crystalline spray and leaving the long glowing trail.

The correspondent looked over his shoulder at the captain. His face was hidden, and he seemed to be asleep. He looked at the babes of the sea. They certainly were asleep. So, being bereft of sympathy, he leaned a little way to one side and swore softly into the sea.

But the thing did not then leave the vicinity of the boat. Ahead or astern, on one side or the other, at intervals long or short, fled the long sparkling streak, and there was to be heard the *whirroo* of the dark fin. The speed and power of the thing was greatly to be admired. It cut the water like a gigantic and keen projectile.

The presence of this biding thing did not affect the man with the same 170 horror that it would if he had been a picnicker. He simply looked at the sea dully and swore in an undertone.

Nevertheless, it is true that he did not wish to be alone with the thing. He wished one of his companions to awake by chance and keep him company with it. But the captain hung motionless over the water-jar, and the oiler and the cook in the bottom of the boat were plunged in slumber.

VI

"If I am going to be drowned—if I am going to be drowned—if I am going to be drowned, why, in the name of the seven mad gods who rule the sea, was I allowed to come thus far and contemplate sand and trees?"

During this dismal night, it may be remarked that a man would conclude that it was really the intention of the seven mad gods to drown him, despite the abominable injustice of it. For it was certainly an abominable injustice to drown a man who had worked so hard, so hard. The man felt it would be a crime most unnatural. Other people had drowned at sea since galleys swarmed with painted sails, but still—

When it occurs to a man that nature does not regard him as important, and that she feels she would not maim the universe by disposing of him, he at first wishes to throw bricks at the temple, and he hates deeply the fact that there are no bricks and no temples. Any visible expression of nature would surely be pelleted with his jeers.

Then, if there be no tangible thing to hoot, he feels, perhaps, the desire 175 to confront a personification and indulge in pleas, bowed to one knee, and with hands supplicant, saying, "Yes, but I love myself."

A high cold star on a winter's night is the word he feels that she says to him. Thereafter he knows the pathos of his situation.

The men in the dinghy had not discussed these matters, but each had, no doubt, reflected upon them in silence and according to his mind. There was seldom any expression upon their faces save the general one of complete weariness. Speech was devoted to the business of the boat.

To chime the notes of his emotion, a verse mysteriously entered the correspondent's head. He had even forgotten that he had forgotten this verse, but it suddenly was in his mind.

A soldier of the Legion lay dying in Algiers;
There was lack of woman's nursing, there was dearth of woman's tears;
But a comrade stood beside him, and he took that comrade's hand,
And he said, "I never more shall see my own, my native land."

In his childhood the correspondent had been made acquainted with the fact that a soldier of the Legion lay dying in Algiers, but he had never regarded the fact as important. Myriads of his schoolfellows had informed him of the soldier's plight, but the dinning had naturally ended by making him perfectly indifferent. He had never considered it his affair that a soldier of the Legion lay dying in Algiers, nor had it appeared to him as a matter for sorrow. It was less to him than the breaking of a pencil's point.

Now, however, it quaintly came to him as a human, living thing. It was 180 no longer merely a picture of a few throes in the breast of a poet, meanwhile drinking tea and warming his feet at the grate; it was an actuality— stern, mournful, and fine.

The correspondent plainly saw the soldier. He lay on the sand with his feet out straight and still. While his pale left hand was upon his chest in an attempt to thwart the going of his life, the blood came between his fingers. In the far Algerian distance, a city of low square forms was set against a sky that was faint with the last sunset hues. The correspondent, plying the oars and dreaming of the slow and slower movements of the lips of the soldier, was moved by a profound and perfectly impersonal comprehension. He was sorry for the soldier of the Legion who lay dying in Algiers.

The thing which had followed the boat and waited had evidently grown bored at the delay. There was no longer to be heard the slash of the cutwater, and there was no longer the flame of the long trail. The light in the north still glimmered, but it was apparently no nearer to the boat. Sometimes the boom of the surf rang in the correspondent's ears, and he turned the craft seaward then and rowed harder. Southward, some one had evidently built a watch-fire on the beach. It was too low and too far to be seen, but it made a shimmering, roseate reflection upon the bluff in back of it, and this could be discerned from the boat. The wind came stronger, and sometimes a wave suddenly raged out like a mountain cat, and there was to be seen the sheen and sparkle of a broken crest.

The captain, in the bow, moved on his water-jar and sat erect. "Pretty long night," he observed to the correspondent. He looked at the shore. "Those life-saving people take their time."

"Did you see that shark playing around?"

"Yes, I saw him. He was a big fellow, all right."   185

"Wish I had known you were awake."

Later the correspondent spoke into the bottom of the boat. "Billie!" There was a slow and gradual disentanglement. "Billie, will you spell me?"

"Sure," said the oiler.

As soon as the correspondent touched the cold, comfortable sea-water in the bottom of the boat and had huddled close to the cook's life-belt he was deep in sleep, despite the fact that his teeth played all the popular airs. This sleep was so good to him that it was but a moment before he heard a voice call his name in a tone that demonstrated the last stages of exhaustion. "Will you spell me?"

"Sure, Billie."   190

The light in the north had mysteriously vanished, but the correspondent took his course from the wide-awake captain.

Later in the night they took the boat farther out to sea, and the captain directed the cook to take one oar at the stern and keep the boat facing the seas. He was to call out if he should hear the thunder of the surf. This plan enabled the oiler and the correspondent to get respite together. "We'll give those boys a chance to get into shape again," said the captain. They curled down and, after a few preliminary chatterings and trembles, slept once more the dead sleep. Neither knew they had bequeathed to the cook the company of another shark, or perhaps the same shark.

As the boat caroused on the waves, spray occasionally bumped over the side and gave them a fresh soaking, but this had no power to break their repose. The ominous slash of the wind and the water affected them as it would have affected mummies.

"Boys," said the cook, with the notes of every reluctance in his voice, "she's drifted in pretty close. I guess one of you had better take her to sea again." The correspondent, aroused, heard the crash of the toppled crests.

As he was rowing, the captain gave him some whisky-and-water, and this   195
steadied the chills out of him. "If I ever get ashore and anybody shows me even a photograph of an oar—"

At last there was a short conversation.

"Billie!—Billie, will you spell me?"

"Sure," said the oiler.

VII

When the correspondent again opened his eyes, the sea and the sky were each of the grey hue of the dawning. Later, carmine and gold was painted upon the waters. The morning appeared finally, in its splendor, with a sky of pure blue, and the sunlight flamed on the tips of the waves.

On the distant dunes were set many little black cottages, and a tall white   200
windmill reared above them. No man, nor dog, nor bicycle appeared on the beach. The cottages might have formed a deserted village.

The voyagers scanned the shore. A conference was held in the boat. "Well," said the captain, "if no help is coming, we might better try a run through the surf right away. If we stay out here much longer we will be too weak to do anything for ourselves at all." The others silently acquiesced in this reasoning. The boat was headed for the beach. The correspondent wondered if none ever ascended the tall wind-tower, and if then they never looked seaward. This tower was a giant, standing with its back to the plight of the ants. It represented in a degree, to the correspondent, the serenity of nature amid the struggles of the individual—nature in the wind, and nature in the vision of men. She did not seem cruel to him then, nor beneficent, nor treacherous, nor wise. But she was indifferent, flatly indifferent. It is, perhaps, plausible that a man in this situation, impressed with the unconcern of the universe, should see the innumerable flaws of his life, and have them taste wickedly in his mind, and wish for another chance. A distinction between right and wrong seems absurdly clear to him, then, in this new ignorance of the grave-edge, and he understands that if he were given another opportunity he would mend his conduct and his words, and be better and brighter during an introduction or at a tea.

"Now, boys," said the captain, "she is going to swamp sure. All we can do is to work her in as far as possible, and then when she swamps, pile out and scramble for the beach. Keep cool now, and don't jump until she swamps sure."

The oiler took the oars. Over his shoulders he scanned the surf. "Captain," he said, "I think I'd better bring her about and keep her head-on to the seas and back her in."

"All right, Billie," said the captain. "Back her in." The oiler swung the boat then, and, seated in the stern, the cook and the correspondent were obliged to look over their shoulders to contemplate the lonely and indifferent shore.

The monstrous inshore rollers heaved the boat high until the men were 205 again enabled to see the white sheets of water scudding up the slanted beach. "We won't get in very close," said the captain. Each time a man could wrest his attention from the rollers, he turned his glance toward the shore, and in the expression of the eyes during this contemplation there was a singular quality. The correspondent, observing the others, knew that they were not afraid, but the full meaning of their glances were shrouded.

As for himself, he was too tired to grapple fundamentally with the fact. He tried to coerce his mind into thinking of it, but the mind was dominated at this time by the muscles, and the muscles said they did not care. It merely occurred to him that if he should drown it would be a shame.

There were no hurried words, no pallor, no plain agitation. The men simply looked at the shore. "Now, remember to get well clear of the boat when you jump," said the captain.

Seaward the crest of a roller suddenly fell with a thunderous crash, and the long white comber came roaring down upon the boat.

"Steady now," said the captain. The men were silent. They turned their eyes from the shore to the comber and waited. The boat slid up the incline, leaped at the furious top, bounced over it, and swung down the long back of the wave. Some water had been shipped, and the cook bailed it out.

But the next crest crashed also. The tumbling, boiling flood of white 210 water caught the boat and whirled it almost perpendicular. Water swarmed in from all sides. The correspondent had his hands on the gunwale at this time, and when the water entered at that place he swiftly withdrew his fingers, as if he objected to wetting them.

The little boat, drunken with this weight of water, reeled and snuggled deeper into the sea.

"Bail her out, cook! Bail her out!" said the captain.

"All right, Captain," said the cook.

"Now, boys, the next one will do for us sure," said the oiler. "Mind to jump clear of the boat."

The third wave moved forward, huge, furious, implacable. It fairly swal- 215 lowed the dinghy, and almost simultaneously the men tumbled into the sea. A piece of life-belt had lain in the bottom of the boat, and as the correspondent went overboard he held this to his chest with his left hand.

The January water was icy, and he reflected immediately that it was colder than he had expected to find it off the coast of Florida. This appeared to his dazed mind as a fact important enough to be noted at the time. The coldness of the water was sad; it was tragic. This fact was somehow mixed and confused with his opinion of his own situation, so that it seemed almost a proper reason for tears. The water was cold.

When he came to the surface he was conscious of little but the noisy water. Afterward he saw his companions in the sea. The oiler was ahead in the race. He was swimming strongly and rapidly. Off to the correspondent's left, the cook's great white and corked back bulged out of the water; and in the rear the captain was hanging with his one good hand to the keel of the overturned dinghy.

There is a certain immovable quality to a shore, and the correspondent wondered at it amid the confusion of the sea.

It seemed also very attractive; but the correspondent knew that it was a long journey, and he paddled leisurely. The piece of life-preserver lay under him, and sometimes he whirled down the incline of a wave as if he were on a hand-sled.

But finally he arrived at a place in the sea where travel was beset with 220 difficulty. He did not pause swimming to inquire what manner of current had caught him, but there his progress ceased. The shore was set before him like a bit of scenery on a stage, and he looked at it and understood with his eyes each detail of it.

As the cook passed, much farther to the left, the captain was calling to him, "Turn over on your back, cook! Turn over on your back and use the oar."

"All right, sir." The cook turned on his back, and, paddling with an oar, went ahead as if he were a canoe.

Presently the boat also passed to the left of the correspondent, with the captain clinging with one hand to the keel. He would have appeared like a man raising himself to look over a board fence if it were not for the extraordinary gymnastics of the boat. The correspondent marvelled that the captain could still hold to it.

They passed on nearer to shore—the oiler, the cook, the captain—and following them went the water-jar, bouncing gaily over the seas.

The correspondent remained in the grip of this strange new enemy—a 225 current. The shore, with its white slope of sand and its green bluff topped with little silent cottages, was spread like a picture before him. It was very near to him then, but he was impressed as one who, in a gallery, looks at a scene from Brittany or Algiers.

He thought: "I am going to drown? Can it be possible? Can it be possible? Can it be possible?" Perhaps an individual must consider his own death to be the final phenomenon of nature.

But later a wave perhaps whirled him out of this small deadly current, for he found suddenly that he could again make progress toward the shore. Later still he was aware that the captain, clinging with one hand to the keel of the dinghy, had his face turned away from the shore and toward him, and was calling his name. "Come to the boat! Come to the boat!"

In his struggle to reach the captain and the boat, he reflected that when one gets properly wearied drowning must really be a comfortable arrangement—a cessation of hostilities accompanied by a large degree of relief; and he was glad of it, for the main thing in his mind for some moments had been horror of the temporary agony. He did not wish to be hurt.

Presently he saw a man running along the shore. He was undressing with most remarkable speed. Coat, trousers, shirt, everything flew magically off him.

"Come to the boat!" called the captain.   230

"All right, Captain." As the correspondent paddled, he saw the captain let himself down to bottom and leave the boat. Then the correspondent performed his one little marvel of the voyage. A large wave caught him and flung him with ease and supreme speed completely over the boat and far beyond it. It struck him even then as an event in gymnastics and a true miracle of the sea. An overturned boat in the surf is not a plaything to a swimming man.

The correspondent arrived in water that reached only to his waist, but his condition did not enable him to stand for more than a moment. Each wave knocked him into a heap, and the undertow pulled at him.

Then he saw the man who had been running and undressing, and undressing and running, come bounding into the water. He dragged ashore the cook, and then waded toward the captain; but the captain waved him away and sent him to the correspondent. He was naked—naked as a tree in winter; but a halo was about his head, and he shone like a saint. He gave a strong pull, and a long drag, and a bully heave at the correspondent's hand. The correspondent, schooled in the minor formulae, said "Thanks, old man." But suddenly the man cried, "What's that?" He pointed a swift finger. The correspondent said, "Go."

In the shallows, face downward, lay the oiler. His forehead touched sand that was periodically, between each wave, clear of the sea.

The correspondent did not know all that transpired afterward. When he 235 achieved safe ground he fell, striking the sand with each particular part of his body. It was as if he had dropped from a roof, but the thud was grateful to him.

It seemed that instantly the beach was populated with men with blankets, clothes, and flasks, and women with coffee-pots and all the remedies sacred to their minds. The welcome of the land to the men from the sea was warm and generous; but a still and dripping shape was carried slowly up the beach; and the land's welcome for it could only be the different and sinister hospitality of the grave.

When it came night, the white waves paced to and fro in the moonlight, and the wind brought the sound of the great sea's voice to the men on the shore, and they felt that they could then be interpreters.

The Receptive Reader

1. In the naturalistic manner, Crane traces in patient *detail* the physical dimension of the men's ordeal. How does he make the grueling experience real for the reader? What are striking details? What are recurrent notes, struck again and again?

2. The *dialogue* of the men in the boat may at first seem trivial or inane (like many other conversations). Does it nevertheless circle back to major issues or concerns? What is the subject matter of these conversations? What is their tone?

3. When do you first conclude that there is something representative and symbolic about the men's experience? What *symbols* do you recognize? What do you think might be the symbolic meaning of the sea? of the boat? of the seabirds? of the shark? of the unmanned life-saving station? of the lighthouse? of the tourists on the beach?

4. How much commentary is there by the *intruding author?* What does Crane have to say about the captain of the ship? about the relationship developing among the men in the boat?

5. Much of the story centers on the men's reactions to their fate. Are there different *stages?* Do individuals react differently?

6. How did you expect the story to *end?* Does the ending seem unexpected? Does it make you think?

7. What is the *theme* of the story? What does the story as a whole say about human beings and nature? about male bonding? about survival? How are these three topics related in the story as a whole?

8. What are striking examples of *irony* in the story—of the sad and comical discrepancy between what should be and what is? What are some striking examples of the author's ironic tone?

The Personal Response

Much literature through the centuries has celebrated the beauty of nature. What role does the beauty of nature play in this story? What is your own personal view of the relationship between nature and humankind? How is it different from the view that seems to be dominant in this story?

Nathaniel Hawthorne   *(1804–1864)*

*A dreamer may dwell so long among fantasies
that the things without him will seem as real as
those within.*

                    NATHANIEL HAWTHORNE

*The mere doubt of the existence of good and the
thought that other human beings are evil can
become such a corrosive force that it can eat out
the life of the heart.*

                    STUDENT PAPER

Nathaniel Hawthorne was born in Salem in Massachusetts and lived there for many years at his mother's house after finishing college. An ancestor had been a member of the court that sentenced the witches at the Salem trials in 1692. As a student and at first little-read writer, Hawthorne immersed himself in the history of colonial New England. When he married after a brief stint at a socialistic commune (Brook Farm), he settled at Concord, in the heart of historical New England.

Until he went to Liverpool in England as an American consul, Hawthorne lived in the heartland of American Puritanism. Here ministers like Cotton Mather and Jonathan Edwards had preached the Puritan dogma of the depravity of humankind. They had painted in vivid colors the ever-powerful temptation of sin, the fear and trembling of sinners in the hands of an angry God, and the ever-lurking presence of the devil. Hawthorne's puritanical ancestors had left England to escape persecution as dissenters from the established Anglican church. In the New World, they set up a religious commonwealth where prayer and attendance at church services were rigidly enforced and where Quakers and other independent spirits were persecuted in turn.

Much of Hawthorne's fiction made his readers rethink and reexamine the Puritan past. His novel *The Scarlet Letter* (1850) has left readers around the world with unforgettable images of Hester Prynne, wearing the scarlet *A* branding her as an adulteress; her love child Pearl at play in the forest; and the child's father, the Puritan minister Dimmesdale, in the spiritual agonies of guilt.

The following much-analyzed story is set in Puritan New England at the time of King William III, who ruled in England from 1689 to 1702. Salem Village, established only forty years before, was on the edge of the wilderness, with heathen natives in the forests. The King Philip mentioned in the story was Metacomet, leader of the last organized Native American resistance in southern New England. The people in the story, too humble to be called gentlemen and ladies, are called Goodman Brown and Goody (short for Goodwife) Cloyse or Goody Cory. These women were among the victims of the Salem witch-hunt that took the lives of twenty men and women. Much of the learning of the Puritan divines had been concerned with witchcraft and with the devil's power to create delusions and apparitions. At a Witches' Sabbath, the devil himself would preside at rituals that were a blasphemous perversion of the rites of the church.

Young Goodman Brown   *1835*

Young Goodman Brown came forth at sunset into the street at Salem village; but put his head back, after crossing the threshold, to exchange a parting kiss with his young wife. And Faith, as the wife was aptly named, thrust her own pretty head into the street, letting the wind play with the pink ribbons of her cap while she called to Goodman Brown.

"Dearest heart," whispered she, softly and rather sadly, when her lips were close to his ear, "prithee put off your journey until sunrise and sleep in your own bed tonight. A lone woman is troubled with such dreams and such thoughts that she's afeard of herself sometimes. Pray tarry with me this night, dear husband, of all nights in the year."

"My love and my Faith," replied Goodman Brown, "of all nights in the year, this one night must I tarry away from thee. My journey, as thou callest it, forth and back again, must needs be done 'twixt now and sunrise. What, my sweet, pretty wife, dost thou doubt me already, and we but three months married?"

"Then God bless you!" said Faith, with the pink ribbons; "and may you find all well when you come back."

"Amen!" cried Goodman Brown. "Say thy prayers, dear Faith, and go to   5
bed at dusk, and no harm will come to thee."

So they parted; and the young man pursued his way until, being about to turn the corner by the meeting-house, he looked back and saw the head of Faith still peeping after him with a melancholy air, in spite of her pink ribbons.

"Poor little Faith!" thought he, for his heart smote him. "What a wretch am I to leave her on such an errand! She talks of dreams, too. Methought as she spoke there was trouble in her face, as if a dream had warned her what work is to be done tonight. But no, no; 'twould kill her to think it. Well, she's a blessed angel on earth; and after this one night I'll cling to her skirts and follow her to heaven."

With this excellent resolve for the future, Goodman Brown felt himself justified in making more haste on his present evil purpose. He had taken a dreary road, darkened by all the gloomiest trees of the forest, which barely stood aside to let the narrow path creep through, and closed immediately behind. It was all as lonely as could be; and there is this peculiarity in such a solitude, that the traveller knows not who may be concealed by the innumerable trunks and the thick boughs overhead; so that with lonely footsteps he may yet be passing through an unseen multitude.

"There may be a devilish Indian behind every tree," said Goodman Brown to himself; and he glanced fearfully behind him as he added, "What if the devil himself should be at my very elbow!"

His head being turned back, he passed a crook of the road, and, looking   10
forward again, beheld the figure of a man, in grave and decent attire, seated at the foot of an old tree. He arose at Goodman Brown's approach and walked onward side by side with him.

"You are late, Goodman Brown," said he. "The clock of the Old South was striking as I came through Boston, and that is full fifteen minutes agone."

"Faith kept me back a while," replied the young man, with a tremor in his voice, caused by the sudden appearance of his companion, though not wholly unexpected.

It was now deep dusk in the forest, and deepest in that part of it where these two were journeying. As nearly as could be discerned, the second traveller was about fifty years old, apparently in the same rank of life as Goodman Brown, and bearing a considerable resemblance to him, though perhaps more in expression than features. Still they might have been taken for father and son. And yet, though the elder person was as simply clad as the younger, and as simple in manner too, he had an indescribable air of one who knew the world, and who would not have felt abashed at the governor's dinner table or in King William's court, were it possible that his affairs should call him thither. But the only thing about him that could be fixed upon as remarkable was his staff, which bore the likeness of a great black snake, so curiously wrought that it might almost be seen to twist and wriggle itself like a living serpent. This, of course, must have been an ocular deception, assisted by the uncertain light.

"Come, Goodman Brown," cried his fellow-traveller, "this is a dull place for the beginning of a journey. Take my staff, if you are so soon weary."

"Friend," said the other, exchanging his slow pace for a full stop, "having   15
kept covenant by meeting thee here, it is my purpose now to return whence I came. I have scruples touching the matter thou wot'st of."

"Sayest thou so?" replied he of the serpent, smiling apart. "Let us walk on, nevertheless, reasoning as we go; and if I convince thee not thou shalt turn back. We are but a little way in the forest yet."

"Too far! too far!" exclaimed the goodman, unconsciously resuming his walk. "My father never went into the woods on such an errand, nor his father before him. We have been a race of honest men and good Christians since the days of the martyrs; and shall I be the first of the name of Brown that ever took this path and kept—"

"Such company, thou wouldst say," observed the elder person, interpreting his pause. "Well said, Goodman Brown! I have been as well acquainted with your family as with ever a one among the Puritans; and that's no trifle to say. I helped your grandfather, the constable, when he lashed the Quaker woman so smartly through the streets of Salem; and it was I that brought your father a pitch-pine knot, kindled at my own hearth, to set fire to an Indian village, in King Philip's war. They were my good friends, both; and many a pleasant walk have we had along this path, and returned merrily after midnight. I would fain be friends with you for their sake."

"If it be as thou sayest," replied Goodman Brown, "I marvel they never spoke of these matters; or, verily, I marvel not, seeing that the least rumor of the sort would have driven them from New England. We are a people of prayer, and good works to boot, and abide no such wickedness."

"Wickedness or not," said the traveller with the twisted staff, "I have a   20
very general acquaintance here in New England. The deacons of many a church have drunk the communion wine with me; the selectmen of divers towns make me their chairman; and a majority of the Great and General Court are firm supporters of my interest. The governor and I, too—But these are state secrets."

"Can this be so?" cried Goodman Brown, with a stare of amazement at his undisturbed companion. "Howbeit, I have nothing to do with the governor and council; they have their own ways, and are no rule for a simple husbandman like me. But, were I to go on with thee, how should I meet the eye of that good old man, our minister, at Salem village? Oh, his voice would make me tremble both Sabbath day and lecture day."

Thus far the elder traveller had listened with due gravity; but now burst into a fit of irrepressible mirth, shaking himself so violently that his snake like staff actually seemed to wriggle in sympathy.

"Ha! ha! ha!" shouted he again and again; then composing himself, "Well, go on, Goodman Brown, go on; but, prithee, don't kill me with laughing."

"Well, then, to end the matter at once," said Goodman Brown, considerably nettled, "there is my wife, Faith. It would break her dear little heart; and I'd rather break my own."

"Nay, if that be the case," answered the other, "e'en go thy ways, Goodman Brown. I would not for twenty old women like the one hobbling before us that Faith should come to any harm." 25

As he spoke he pointed his staff at a female figure on the path, in whom Goodman Brown recognized a very pious and exemplary dame, who had taught him his catechism in youth, and was still his moral and spiritual adviser, jointly with the minister and Deacon Gookin.

"A marvel, truly, that Goody Cloyse should be so far in the wilderness at nightfall," said he. "But with your leave, friend, I shall take a cut through the woods until we have left this Christian woman behind. Being a stranger to you, she might ask whom I was consorting with and whither I was going."

"Be it so," said his fellow-traveller. "Betake you to the woods, and let me keep the path."

Accordingly the young man turned aside, but took care to watch his companion, who advanced softly along the road until he had come within a staff's length of the old dame. She, meanwhile, was making the best of her way, with singular speed for so aged a woman, and mumbling some indistinct words—a prayer, doubtless—as she went. The traveller put forth his staff and touched her withered neck with what seemed the serpent's tail.

"The devil!" screamed the pious old lady. 30

"Then Goody Cloyse knows her old friend?" observed the traveller, confronting her and leaning on his writhing stick.

"Ah, forsooth, and is it your worship indeed?" cried the good dame. "Yea, truly it is, and in the very image of my old gossip, Goodman Brown, the grandfather of the silly fellow that now is. But—would your worship believe it?—my broomstick hath strangely disappeared, stolen, as I suspect, by that unhanged witch, Goody Cory, and that, too, when I was all anointed with the juice of smallage, and cinquefoil, and wolf's bane—"

"Mingled with fine wheat and the fat of a new-born babe," said the shape of old Goodman Brown.

"Ah, your worship knows the recipe," cried the old lady, cackling aloud. "So, as I was saying, being all ready for the meeting, and no horse to ride on, I made up my mind to foot it; for they tell me there is a nice young man to be taken into communion tonight. But now your good worship will lend me your arm, and we shall be there in a twinkling."

"That can hardly be," answered her friend. "I may not spare you my arm, 35 Goody Cloyse; but here is my staff, if you will."

So saying, he threw it down at her feet, where, perhaps, it assumed life, being one of the rods which its owner had formerly lent to the Egyptian magi. Of this fact, however, Goodman Brown could not take cognizance. He had cast up his eyes in astonishment, and, looking down again, beheld neither Goody Cloyse nor the serpentine staff, but his fellow-traveller alone, who waited for him as calmly as if nothing had happened.

"That old woman taught me my catechism," said the young man; and there was a world of meaning in this simple comment.

They continued to walk onward, while the elder traveller exhorted his companion to make good speed and persevere in the path, discoursing so aptly that his arguments seemed rather to spring up in the bosom of his auditor than to be suggested by himself. As they went, he plucked a branch of maple to serve for a walking stick, and began to strip it of the twigs and little boughs, which were wet with evening dew. The moment his fingers touched them they became strangely withered and dried up as with a week's sunshine. Thus the pair proceeded, at a good free pace, until suddenly, in a gloomy hollow of the road, Goodman Brown sat himself down on the stump of a tree and refused to go any farther.

"Friend," said he, stubbornly, "my mind is made up. Not another step will I budge on this errand. What if a wretched old woman do choose to go to the devil when I thought she was going to heaven: is that any reason why I should quit my dear Faith and go after her?"

"You will think better of this by and by," said his acquaintance, composedly. "Sit here and rest yourself a while; and when you feel like moving again, there is my staff to help you along."   40

Without more words, he threw his companion the maple stick, and was as speedily out of sight as if he had vanished into the deepening gloom. The young man sat a few moments by the roadside, applauding himself greatly, and thinking with how clear a conscience he should meet the minister in his morning walk, nor shrink from the eye of good old Deacon Gookin. And what calm sleep would be his that very night, which was to have been spent so wickedly, but so purely and sweetly now, in the arms of Faith! Amidst these pleasant and praiseworthy meditations, Goodman Brown heard the tramp of horses along the road, and deemed it advisable to conceal himself within the verge of the forest, conscious of the guilty purpose that had brought him thither, though now so happily turned from it.

On came the hoof tramps and the voices of the riders, two grave old voices, conversing soberly as they drew near. These mingled sounds appeared to pass along the road, within a few yards of the young man's hiding-place; but, owing doubtless to the depth of the gloom at that particular spot, neither the travellers nor their steeds were visible. Though their figures brushed the small boughs by the wayside, it could not be seen that they intercepted, even for a moment, the faint gleam from the strip of bright sky athwart which they must have passed. Goodman Brown alternately crouched and stood on tiptoe, pulling aside the branches and thrusting forth his head as far as he durst without discerning so much as a shadow. It vexed him the more, because he could have sworn, were such a thing possible, that he recognized the voices of the minister and Deacon Gookin, jogging along quietly, as they were wont to do, when bound to some ordination or ecclesiastical council. While yet within hearing, one of the riders stopped to pluck a switch.

"Of the two, reverend sir," said the voice like the deacon's, "I had rather miss an ordination dinner than tonight's meeting. They tell me that some of our community are to be here from Falmouth and beyond, and others from

Connecticut and Rhode Island, besides several of the Indian powwows, who, after their fashion, know almost as much deviltry as the best of us. Moreover, there is a goodly young woman to be taken into communion."

"Mighty well, Deacon Gookin!" replied the solemn old tones of the minister. "Spur up, or we shall be late. Nothing can be done, you know, until I get on the ground."

The hoofs clattered again; and the voices, talking so strangely in the empty air, passed on through the forest, where no church had ever been gathered or solitary Christian prayed. Whither, then, could these holy men be journeying so deep into the heathen wilderness? Young Goodman Brown caught hold of a tree for support, being ready to sink down on the ground, faint and overburdened with the heavy sickness of his heart. He looked up to the sky, doubting whether there really was a heaven above him. Yet there was the blue arch, and the stars brightening in it.

"With heaven above and Faith below, I will yet stand firm against the devil!" cried Goodman Brown.

While he still gazed upward into the deep arch of the firmament and had lifted his hands to pray, a cloud, though no wind was stirring, hurried across the zenith and hid the brightening stars. The blue sky was still visible, except directly overhead, where this black mass of cloud was sweeping swiftly northward. Aloft in the air, as if from the depths of the cloud, came a confused and doubtful sound of voices. Once the listener fancied that he could distinguish the accents of townspeople of his own, men, and women, both pious and ungodly, many of whom he had met at the communion table, and had seen others rioting at the tavern. The next moment, so indistinct were the sounds, he doubted whether he had heard aught but the murmur of the old forest, whispering without a wind. Then came a stronger swell of those familiar tones, heard daily in the sunshine at Salem village, but never until now from a cloud of night. There was one voice, of a young woman, uttering lamentations, yet with an uncertain sorrow, and entreating for some favor, which, perhaps, it would grieve her to obtain; and all the unseen multitude, both saints and sinners, seemed to encourage her onward.

"Faith!" shouted Goodman Brown, in a voice of agony and desperation; and the echoes of the forest mocked him, crying, "Faith! Faith!" as if bewildered wretches were seeking her all through the wilderness.

The cry of grief, rage, and terror was yet piercing the night, when the unhappy husband held his breath for a response. There was a scream, drowned immediately in a louder murmur of voices, fading into far-off laughter, as the dark cloud swept away, leaving the clear and silent sky above Goodman Brown. But something fluttered lightly down through the air and caught on the branch of a tree. The young man seized it, and beheld a pink ribbon.

"My Faith is gone!" cried he, after one stupefied moment. "There is no good on earth; and sin is but a name. Come, devil; for to thee is this world given."

And, maddened with despair, so that he laughed loud and long, did Goodman Brown grasp his staff and set forth again, at such a rate that he seemed to fly along the forest path rather than to walk or run. The road grew wilder and drearier and more faintly traced, and vanished at length, leaving him in the heart of the dark wilderness, still rushing onward with the instinct that guides mortal man to evil. The whole forest was peopled with frightful sounds—the creaking of the trees, the howling of wild beasts, and the yell of Indians; while sometimes the wind tolled like a distant church bell, and sometimes gave a broad roar around the traveller, as if all Nature were laughing him to scorn. But he was himself the chief horror of the scene, and shrank not from its other horrors.

"Ha! ha! ha!" roared Goodman Brown when the wind laughed at him. "Let us hear which will laugh loudest. Think not to frighten me with your deviltry. Come witch, come wizard, come Indian powwow, come devil himself, and here comes Goodman Brown. You may as well fear him as he fear you."

In truth, all through the haunted forest there could be nothing more frightful than the figure of Goodman Brown. On he flew among the black pines, brandishing his staff with frenzied gestures, now giving vent to an inspiration of horrid blasphemy, and now shouting forth such laughter as set all the echoes of the forest laughing like demons around him. The fiend in his own shape is less hideous than when he rages in the breast of man. Thus sped the demoniac on his course, until, quivering among the trees, he saw a red light before him, as when the felled trunks and branches of a clearing have been set on fire, and throw up their lurid blaze against the sky, at the hour of midnight. He paused, in a lull of the tempest that had driven him onward, and heard the swell of what seemed a hymn, rolling solemnly from a distance with the weight of many voices. He knew the tune; it was a familiar one in the choir of the village meeting-house. The verse died heavily away, and was lengthened by a chorus, not of human voices, but of all the sounds of the benighted wilderness pealing in awful harmony together. Goodman Brown cried out, and his cry was lost to his own ear by its unison with the cry of the desert.

In the interval of silence he stole forward until the light glared full upon his eyes. At one extremity of an open space, hemmed in by the dark wall of the forest, arose a rock, bearing some rude, natural resemblance either to an altar or a pulpit, and surrounded by four blazing pines, their tops aflame, their stems untouched, like candles at an evening meeting. The mass of foliage that had overgrown the summit of the rock was all on fire, blazing high into the night and fitfully illuminating the whole field. Each pendent twig and leafy festoon was in a blaze. As the red light arose and fell, a numerous congregation alternately shone forth, then disappeared in shadow, and again grew, as it were, out of the darkness, peopling the heart of the solitary woods at once.

"A grave and dark-clad company," quoth Goodman Brown.

55

In truth they were such. Among them, quivering to and fro between gloom and splendor, appeared faces that would be seen next day at the council board of the province, and others which, Sabbath after Sabbath, looked devoutly heavenward, and benignantly over the crowded pews, from the holiest pulpits in the land. Some affirm that the lady of the governor was there. At least there were high dames well known to her, and wives of honored husbands, and widows, a great multitude, and ancient maidens, all of excellent repute, and fair young girls, who trembled lest their mothers should espy them. Either the sudden gleams of light flashing over the obscure field bedazzled Goodman Brown, or he recognized a score of the church members of Salem village famous for their especial sanctity. Good old Deacon Gookin had arrived, and waited at the skirts of that venerable saint, his revered pastor. But, irreverently consorting with these grave, reputable, and pious people, these elders of the church, these chaste dames and dewy virgins, there were men of dissolute lives and women of spotted fame, wretches given over to all mean and filthy vice, and suspected even of horrid crimes. It was strange to see that the good shrank not from the wicked, nor were the sinners abashed by the saints. Scattered also among their pale-faced enemies were the Indian priests, or powwows, who had often scared their native forest with more hideous incantations than any known to English witchcraft.

"But where is Faith?" thought Goodman Brown; and, as hope came into his heart, he trembled.

Another verse of the hymn arose, a slow and mournful strain, such as the pious love, but joined to words which expressed all that our nature can conceive of sin, and darkly hinted at far more. Unfathomable to mere mortals is the lore of fiends. Verse after verse was sung; and still the chorus of the desert swelled between like the deepest tone of a mighty organ; and with the final peal of that dreadful anthem there came a sound, as if the roaring wind, the rushing streams, the howling beasts, and every other voice of the unconverted wilderness were mingling and according with the voice of guilty man in homage to the prince of all. The four blazing pines threw up a loftier flame, and obscurely discovered shapes and visages of horror on the smoke wreaths above the impious assembly. At the same moment the fire on the rock shot redly forth and formed a glowing arch above its base, where now appeared a figure. With reverence be it spoken, the figure bore no slight similitude, both in garb and manner, to some grave divine of the New England churches.

"Bring forth the converts!" cried a voice that echoed through the field and rolled into the forest.

At the word, Goodman Brown stepped forth from the shadow of the trees 60 and approached the congregation, with whom he felt a loathful brotherhood by the sympathy of all that was wicked in his heart. He could have well-nigh sworn that the shape of his own dead father beckoned him to advance, looking downward from a smoke wreath, while a woman, with dim features of despair, threw out her hand to warn him back. Was it his mother? But he had no power to retreat one step, nor to resist, even in thought, when the minister and good old Deacon Gookin seized his arms and led him to the blazing rock. Thither came also the slender form of a veiled female, led between Goody Cloyse, that pious teacher of the catechism, and Martha Carrier, who had received the devil's promise to be queen of hell. A rampant hag was she. And there stood the proselytes beneath the canopy of fire.

"Welcome, my children," said the dark figure, "to the communion of your race. Ye have found thus young your nature and your destiny. My children, look behind you!"

They turned; and flashing forth, as it were, in a sheet of flame, the fiend worshippers were seen; the smile of welcome gleamed darkly on every visage.

"There," resumed the sable form, "are all whom ye have reverenced from youth. Ye deemed them holier than yourselves, and shrank from your own sin, contrasting it with their lives of righteousness and prayerful aspirations heavenward. Yet here are they all in my worshipping assembly. This night it shall be granted you to know their secret deeds: how hoary-bearded elders of the church have whispered wanton words to the young maids of their households; how many a woman, eager for widows' weeds, has given her husband a drink at bedtime and let him sleep his last sleep in her bosom; how beardless youths have made haste to inherit their fathers' wealth; and how fair damsels—blush not, sweet ones—have dug little graves in the garden, and bidden me, the sole guest, to an infant's funeral. By the sympathy of your human hearts for sin ye shall scent out all the places—whether in church, bedchamber, street, field, or forest—where crime has been committed, and shall exult to behold the whole earth one stain of guilt, one mighty blood spot. Far more than this. It shall be yours to penetrate, in every bosom, the deep mystery of sin, the fountain of all wicked arts, and which inexhaustibly supplies more evil impulses than human power—than my power at its utmost—can make manifest in deeds. And now, my children, look upon each other."

They did so; and, by the blaze of the hell-kindled torches, the wretched man beheld his Faith, and the wife her husband, trembling before that unhallowed altar.

"Lo, there ye stand, my children," said the figure, in a deep and solemn   65
tone, almost sad with its despairing awfulness, as if his once angelic nature could yet mourn for our miserable race. "Depending upon one another's hearts, ye had still hoped that virtue were not all a dream. Now are ye undeceived. Evil is the nature of mankind. Evil must be your only happiness. Welcome again, my children, to the communion of your race."

"Welcome," repeated the fiend worshippers, in one cry of despair and triumph.

And there they stood, the only pair, as it seemed, who were yet hesitating on the verge of wickedness in this dark world. A basin was hollowed, naturally, in the rock. Did it contain water, reddened by the lurid light? or was it blood? or, perchance, a liquid flame? Herein did the shape of evil dip his hand and prepare to lay the mark of baptism upon their foreheads, that they might be partakers of the mystery of sin, more conscious of the secret guilt of others, both in deed and thought, than they could now be of their own. The husband cast one look at his pale wife, and Faith at him. What polluted wretches would the next glance show them to each other, shuddering alike at what they disclosed and what they saw!

"Faith! Faith!" cried the husband, "look up to heaven, and resist the wicked one."

Whether Faith obeyed he knew not. Hardly had he spoken when he found himself amid calm night and solitude, listening to a roar of the wind which died heavily away through the forest. He staggered against the rock, and felt it chill and damp; while a hanging twig, that had been all on fire, besprinkled his cheek with the coldest dew.

The next morning young Goodman Brown came slowly into the street of   70 Salem village, staring around him like a bewildered man. The good old minister was taking a walk along the graveyard to get an appetite for breakfast and meditate his sermon, and bestowed a blessing, as he passed, on Goodman Brown. He shrank from the venerable saint as if to avoid an anathema. Old Deacon Gookin was at domestic worship, and the holy words of his prayer were heard through the open window. "What God doth the wizard pray to?" quoth Goodman Brown. Goody Cloyse, that excellent old Christian, stood in the early sunshine at her own lattice, catechizing a little girl who had brought her a pint of morning's milk. Goodman Brown snatched away the child as from the grasp of the fiend himself. Turning the corner by the meeting-house, he spied the head of Faith, with the pink ribbons, gazing anxiously forth, and bursting into such joy at the sight of him that she skipped along the street and almost kissed her husband before the whole village. But Goodman Brown looked sternly and sadly into her face, and passed on without a greeting.

Had Goodman Brown fallen asleep in the forest and only dreamed a wild dream of a witch-meeting?

Be it so if you will; but, alas! it was a dream of evil omen for young Goodman Brown. A stern, a sad, a darkly meditative, a distrustful, if not a desperate man did he become from the night of that fearful dream. On the Sabbath day, when the congregation were singing a holy psalm, he could not listen because an anthem of sin rushed loudly upon his ear and drowned all the blessed strain. When the minister spoke from the pulpit with power and fervid eloquence, and, with his hand on the open Bible, of the sacred truths of our religion, and of saint-like lives and triumphant deaths, and of future bliss or misery unutterable, then did Goodman Brown turn pale, dreading lest the roof should thunder down upon the gray blasphemer and his hearers. Often, waking suddenly at midnight, he shrank from the bosom of Faith; and at morning or eventide, when the family knelt down at prayer, he scowled and muttered to himself, and gazed sternly at his wife, and turned away. And when he had lived long, and was borne to his grave a hoary corpse, followed by Faith, an aged woman, and children and grandchildren, a goodly procession, besides neighbors not a few, they carved no hopeful verse upon his tombstone, for his dying hour was gloom.

The Receptive Reader

1. As the story opens, what are major steps and key details in Young Goodman Brown's journey into the forest? What is strange, what is frightening, and what is funny about the journey? Where does it go counter to our naive expectations, creating the effect of *irony?*

2. Much critical discussion of this story has focused on the role of Brown's "aptly named" wife, Faith. What is her role in the story? When is she real? When is she a *symbol?* Could she be both? (What is the role of the pink ribbon?)

3. What happens at the Witches' Sabbath? How does it end? What question or questions does it leave open?

4. How are we as readers expected to react to Brown's transformation after his experience in the forest?

5. How would you sum up in a sentence or two what the story as a whole says about sin or about evil? How does your statement of the *theme* compare with statements of the theme by your classmates?

The Range of Interpretation

Hawthorne has a reputation for **ambiguity,** intentionally leaving his stories ambiguous and open-ended. Critics have read widely differing meanings into "Young Goodman Brown." Which of the following interpretations is to you most convincing? What evidence from the story would support it?

✗ Is Young Goodman Brown's journey into the forest an evil dream (perhaps inspired by the devil)?

✗ Is his journey a dream vision telling him the truth about human nature?

✗ Is his journey a symbolic acting out of his own paranoid fears and suspicions about others?

✗ Is his journey a symbolic acting out of his own sinful nature, his secret inclination toward evil?

✗ Is Hawthorne's vision of evil in this story a re-creation of a historical cycle that his generation had left behind? Or is it his own view?

Making Connections—For Discussion or Writing

Two other stories about evil lurking behind a genteel or reassuring surface are Shirley Jackson's "The Lottery" and William Faulkner's "A Rose for Emily." What is similar, or what is different, about the vision of evil in these three stories? Which do you find most persuasive, which least?

WRITING ABOUT LITERATURE

7 Tracing a Recurrent Theme
WRITING FOCUS: Comparing Two Stories

The Writing Workshop   A crucial part of your task as a writer is to make connections. When you compare stories by two different writers, you become more aware of each author's distinct way of looking at the world. You may want to try your hand at tracing the same or a similar theme in two stories by different authors. See what you can learn from such a paper about comparison and contrast as a major organizational strategy.

When you try to show the connections between several stories, the overall plan of your paper will be more complex than usual. (You won't be able to follow the developments of a single story from beginning to end.) How will you make your readers' eyes travel between the two stories to make them see the connections you want them to see? How will you go about highlighting similarities and differences? How are you going to lay out your material?

However you proceed, try not to let your paper break up into two mini-essays (one on each story)—with your readers left to establish the cross-references themselves.

Let us assume you are writing about the vision of evil in Hawthorne's "Young Goodman Brown" and Jackson's "The Lottery." You have tentatively mapped out three areas where the stories seem to converge in their vision of how evil enters our world. Both stories take us into a world that is superficially benign—people seem superficially dignified, harmless, friendly, or virtuous. But these apparently harmless or well-meaning people are observed to engage in strange rituals—puzzling, disturbing observances that seem like part of an ancient tribal religion. Finally, the community as a whole seems implicated—*all* seem in some way involved in evil.

What plan of organization will allow you to show these three features in both of the stories? Here are organizing strategies you might consider:

✗ You might try a **point-by-point** comparison. The first third of your paper might show that in both stories there is a reassuring facade of normalcy that hides evil from the casual observer (Point A). Then the second third of your paper might show that in both stories we witness strange quasi-religious rituals—as if evil were not something that happens casually or almost by accident. It is built into the traditions of the community (Point B). Finally, the last third of your paper might show that evil does not seem the work of isolated individuals—a "criminal element." The whole community seems implicated in one way or another (Point C). With a point-by-point comparison there is little danger that your readers will miss the connections.

✗ You might feel that in a point-by-point comparison your readers would not get enough of a sense of the characteristic atmosphere of each story as a whole. You might then try a **parallel-order** comparison. You discuss each story separately, but each time you run through the three key points in the same order: first the reassuring benign surface, then the strange traditional rituals, and finally the involvement in evil of the whole community. As you go through the second story, you might nudge your reader into realizing that you are in fact lining up the major points in the same order for easy cross-reference.

✗ You might decide to start by showing *similarities* between the two stories first—especially if they are likely to be readily noticed by the reader. You might then go on to show a crucial *difference* your readers might have overlooked. (Conversely, you might point out differences first but then go on to important features that two superficially very different stories have in common.)

The following student paper compares and contrasts two short stories treating a similar or related theme. What is the writer's organizing strategy? Does it become clear to the reader? How successful is the writer in carrying it out?

Sample Student Paper

Two Women's Passions

John Steinbeck's "The Chrysanthemums" and Alice Walker's "Everyday Use" explore obstacles that women, both white and black, have had to face. Women often find that they are taken for granted; their intelligence, creative abilities, even the hard labor that they do often go unappreciated. Facing this reality, women find themselves pulled in conflicting directions. On the one hand, there is the strong desire to be attractive to men. Yet by pursuing the traditional ideal of femininity, they may be stifling their true being: their true passions about independence and their struggle toward their own reality.

Elisa in "The Chrysanthemums" is a housewife who has a particular talent in working with flowers. Because this is normally considered "women's work," there is no one restricting her from becoming passionate about it, so she does. Perhaps she puts her energy into her garden only because of her discontent with the rest of her life, where there is little outlet for her energy and strength. Like Elisa's chrysanthemums, the handmade quilts in "Everyday Use" also represent a passion in a woman's life. These quilts were pieced together by the woman and other women in her family from scraps of old dresses, shirts, and even a "teeny faded blue piece . . . that was from Great Grandpa Ezra's uniform that he wore in the Civil War." More than Elisa's flowers, however, these quilts were objects of everyday life, in "everyday use" as bed covers and sources of warmth. They represent a tradition of making do with limited resources, making the best of what you have, in a setting where there is little room for waste or extravagance.

In both stories, the women struggle with the desire to be attractive to men and the harsh realities these longings produce. Elisa finds herself spilling her passions to an old, dirty tinker who shows some false interest in her flowers. She begins by telling him of the budding process and of how to plant the seeds, and his encouraging nods and grunts lead her to continue. She talks passionately of nighttime and the stars—"driven into your body. . . . Hot and sharp—and lovely." Apparently even this poor excuse for a man holds her attention enough for Elisa to reach out to him, hoping to find some connection to make her less isolated and trapped in her restricted existence. Unfortunately, the encounter turns into a humbling experience for her, as in the end the tinker is only looking for some pots to mend and cares little for the passions of a sexually frustrated housewife.

The black woman in "Everyday Use" wishes to be attractive as well, although for her this attractiveness would be a way of gaining her daughter's approval. Ideally, she would be "the way my daughter would want me to be: a hundred pounds lighter, my skin like an uncooked barley pancake," giving the quick-witted Johnny Carson "much to do to keep up with my quick and witty tongue." She realizes, however, that this image is far from reality:

> In real life I am a large, big-boned woman with rough, man-working hands.
> In the winter I wear flannel nightgowns to bed and overalls during the day.
> I can kill and clean a hog as mercilessly as a man.

She knows too that in reality she has trouble looking white men (let alone a famous white comedian) in the eye; instead she has "talked to them always with one foot raised in flight." This fear or lack of confidence is part of her nature even though this woman is surviving on her own, feeding and educating her children with no help from a man.

Both women are patronized by others who care little for their passions and want to use them only for their own ends. The tinker in Steinbeck's story seems to listen with strong interest when Elisa goes on about the stars while he is actually waiting for the appropriate moment to ask for work. The mother in Walker's story is patronized by her daughter Dee, who goes through her mother's house looking for black artifacts that would be interesting objects to exhibit in her own home.

Today's reader is waiting for these women to leave their humiliation behind or to express their anger, to turn on those who condescend to them. Elisa's rebellion is weak and indirect at best. After seeing the chrysanthemums the tinker has discarded lying in the road, Elisa turns to her husband and asks him about some boxing matches, imagining them bloody and gory. Her interest in going to one surprises her husband, but he invites her to go. But she almost immediately draws back:

> She relaxed limply in the seat. "Oh, no. No. I don't want to go. I'm sure I don't." Her face was turned away from him. "It will be enough if we can have wine. It will be plenty." She turned up her coat collar so he could not see that she was crying weakly—like an old woman.

The mother in "Everyday Use" is more assertive in regaining her pride. Despite her daughter Dee's claim that the mother knew nothing of her heritage, she did not give in to her daughter's request for the quilts. The mother had promised the quilts to Maggie, Dee's younger sister, and despite Dee's protest that Maggie would ruin them by using them every day, their mother "dragged" Maggie into the room, "snatched the quilts" out of Dee's hand, and "dumped them into Maggie's lap." In this seemingly insignificant incident, the mother stood up for what she believed in.

In these stories, we get glimpses of women's needs and passions but also of the strength and wisdom women have. Perhaps in the future they will be able to channel their passion into science, politics, art, and our changing world rather than into 10-inch chrysanthemums and patchwork quilts.

Questions for Peer Review

We usually try to read each story on its own terms. Does the writer of the student paper make a judgment about which of the two stories being compared is stronger? Answer the following questions, and compare your answers with those of classmates or members of a small group.

1. Like other writers from a minority background, Alice Walker is often read in courses with a special multicultural or minority emphasis. How does the student writer's *introduction* from the beginning cross the divide and move beyond the mainstream/minority distinction?

2. Prepare an *informal outline* of the key points the student writer has chosen for comparison. On which of these does the writer trace a connection that you yourself had seen in the story? On which of these does the writer show a connection that you and maybe other readers might have missed?

3. What are the key *similarities* that the student writer sees between the two stories? What are the key *differences?*

4. What *key quotations* has the student writer woven into the paper? Where do they help the writer to dramatize feeling and attitudes that might seem less strong or too bland in a paraphrase or indirect quotation?

5. How do the concluding paragraphs bring to bear the *expectations* that today's readers bring to these two stories? What did the student writer expect of the two women who are the main characters? How did they live up to or disappoint the student's expectations?

6. What seems more important in the paper as a whole—what the characters have in common or how they are different? Does the introduction or the thesis give a hint of the key difference between the two women that is stressed later in the paper? Do you think the paper would have been stronger or weaker if the thesis were more of a *preview*—spelling out the key difference early in the paper?

8 STYLE
The Writer's Voice

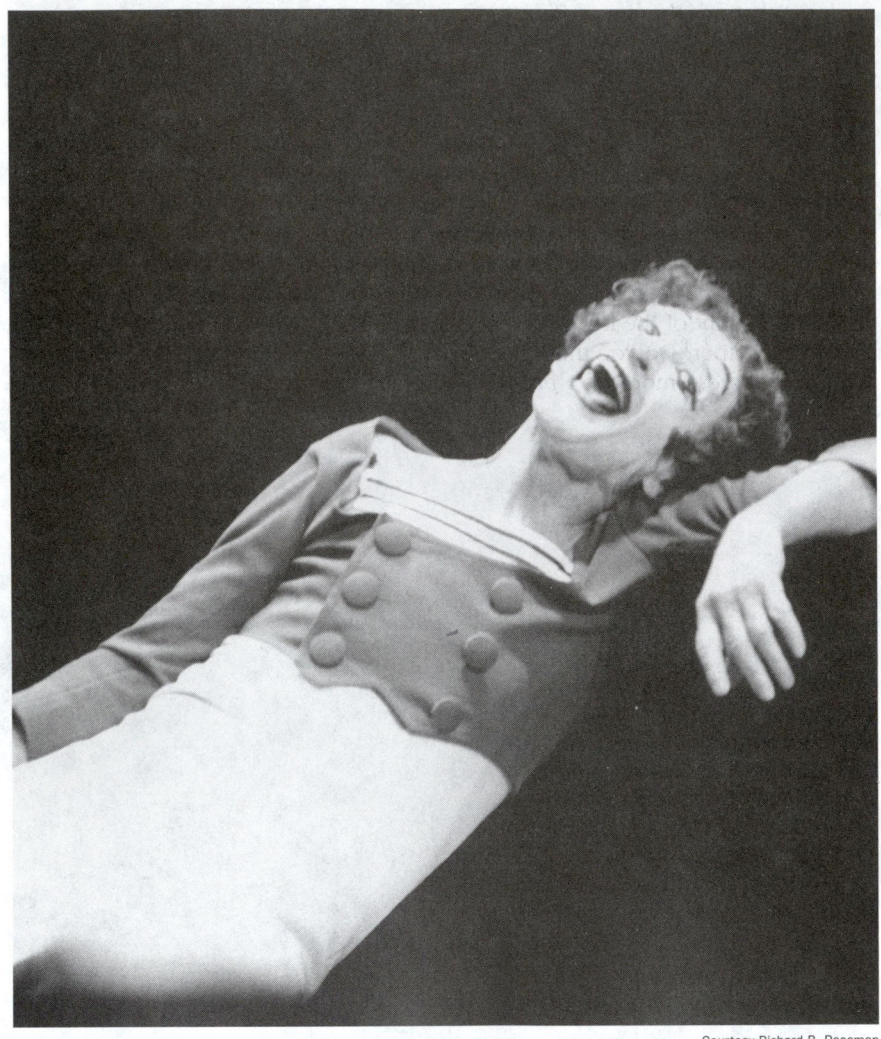

Courtesy Richard B. Ressman

Great writers leave their mark by the originality
of their style, stamping it with an imprint that
imposes a new face on the coins of language.
JEAN-JOSEPH GOUX

Writing is a struggle against silence.
CARLOS FUENTES

FOCUS ON STYLE

What is style? **Style** is the writer's personal way of using language to create his or her reality. It is a distinctive manner of choosing words and putting sentences together. It is a writer's own way of moving from one idea to another. A discussion of style may take a close look at the texture of sentences or paragraphs. However, just as often stylistic analysis will focus on the larger elements of style, tracing the writer's way of weaving images and events into a larger pattern.

Style is more than a matter of style. It makes a statement of its own. The following two passages come from short stories at opposite poles of the spectrum of prose style. The first is from Ernest Hemingway's "Big Two-Hearted River," a story about a camping trip to Michigan's Upper Peninsula, a trout fisher's paradise.

> He came down a hillside covered with stumps into a meadow. At the edge of the meadow flowed the river. Nick was glad to get to the river. He walked upstream through the meadow. His trousers were soaked with the dew as he walked. After the hot day, the dew had come quickly and heavily. The river made no sound. It was too fast and smooth. At the edge of the meadow, before he mounted to a piece of high ground to make camp, Nick looked down the river at the trout rising. They were rising to insects come from the swamp on the other side of the stream when the sun went down. The trout jumped out of water to take them. While Nick walked through the little stretch of meadow alongside the stream, trout had jumped high out of the water. Now as he looked down the river, the insects must be settling on the surface, for the trout were feeding steadily all down the stream. As far down the long stretch as he could see, the trout were rising, making circles all down the surface of the water, as though it were starting to rain.

This passage shows an unadorned modern style that aims at doing justice to reality. It does without embellishment, without grand gestures, without emoting. There are the bare-fact sentences that for many readers became the hallmark of the Hemingway style: "At the edge of the meadow flowed the river. . . . The river made no sound. It was too fast and smooth." The words are simple, direct—and make the scene real for us: *soaked, dew, mist, jumped, feeding, stream*. The author does not come between us and the outdoor setting. The sentences that tell us about his state of mind are like minimal bulletins: "Nick was glad to get to the river." However, this style of deliberate **understatement** does not keep us from responding to the fresh, startling beauty of the unspoilt natural scene. It does not keep us from responding to the lovely image of the trout rising from below to feed on the insects settled on the surface of the water and making circles everywhere "as though it were starting to rain."

Fifty or a hundred years before Hemingway, the dominant style expressed emotion much more freely. A master at arousing the emotions of the audience was Edgar Allan Poe, who wrote the following passage in his short story "The Black Cat":

> With my aversion to this cat, however, its partiality for myself seemed to increase. It followed my footsteps with a pertinacity which it would be difficult to make the reader comprehend. Whenever I sat, it would crouch beneath my chair or spring upon my knees, covering me with its loathsome caresses. If I arose to walk, it would get between my feet and thus nearly throw me down, or, fastening its long and sharp claws in my dress, clamber in this manner to my breast. At such time, although I longed to destroy it with a blow, I was yet withheld from so doing, partly by a memory of my former crime, but chiefly—let me confess it at once—by absolute *dread* of the beast.

There are no bare-bones sentences here. Several sentences start with preambles like "If I . . ." or "Whenever I . . ." and then work their way through layers of mixed or complicated emotions. (The narrator would love to strangle the cat but is held back by his guilt feelings about having done the same to an earlier specimen.) The language is elevated, **formal**—deliberately above the trivial talk of everyday: *partiality* for *kindness, pertinacity* for *stubbornness, comprehend* for *understand*. Does the language signal that the events of this story are more important, more momentous, more ominous than what ordinary cat fanciers are likely to experience? The whole passage builds up to a climax of "absolute *dread*." No reluctance here to use superlatives! (or to italicize for emphasis). Poe's style thrives on **hyperbole**—he is willing to exaggerate, to enhance, to pull the stops. If Poe continues to be read, it may be because readers have a capacity for strong feeling that an understated modern style leaves unused.

How do you become more sensitive to the texture of what you read? You can try to place elements of a writer's style on a spectrum, or on a scale, ranging from one extreme to the other. The two poles do not necessarily represent good and bad, although writers and critics often have strong preferences one way or the other.

Abstract and Concrete   Some prose remains general or **abstract,** whereas other prose becomes **concrete:** It engages in rich specific detail with the sensory surface of life—with what we can see, hear, smell, touch, feel. Hemingway was a stickler for detail (like many of his characters, who are often perfectionists, sticklers for doing something exactly the right way). In his story about the camping trip, he makes us see the water *swirl* (rather than wash) around the logs of the bridge; he makes us see and hear the wings of grasshoppers *whirr.* The camper breaks off *sprigs* of the heathery fern; with his ax he cuts off a *slab* of pine; the current raises a mist of sand in *spurts* from the bottom of the creek.

Denotation and Connotation   Some words point and identify. The word *glass* simply points to an object that holds liquid for drinking. The word in itself says nothing about whether the person who used it was thirsty, or likes to drink, or prefers a glass to a mug or a stein. Other words, however, bring into play attitudes or emotions. When James Joyce in "Araby" uses the word *chalice,* it calls up a range of feelings associated with religious ritual: otherworldliness, devotion, religious exaltation. The objective, emotionally neutral meaning of a word is its **denotation.** The denotation of *knife* is simply an instrument for cutting. The range of attitudes or emotions a word brings into play is its **connotation.** The word *knife* may suggest menace, threat, treachery, as when someone is knifed in the back.

Literal and Figurative   Figurative language uses imaginative comparisons to carry meanings that otherwise might be hard to put into words. In the following passage from a story by Sandra Cisneros, her characters use exuberant imaginative comparisons to convey the feeling of being in love:

> Rachel says love is like a big black piano being pushed off the top of a three-story building and you're waiting on the bottom to catch it. But Lourdes says it's not that way at all. It's like a top, like all the colors in the world are spinning so fast they're not colors anymore and all that's left is a white hum.
>
> From "One Holy Night"

Metaphors are imaginative comparisons that do not come with a sign that says: "This is a comparison!" There is no word such as *like* or *as if* to alert us that someone is speaking on an as-if basis. **Similes** are figurative expressions that *do* provide the *like* or *as if* that signals the comparison. (In Bobbie Ann Mason's "Shiloh," Norma Jean picks up "cake crumbs from the cellophane wrapper, *like a fussy bird.*") In imaginative writing, metaphors are often rich and provocative. Patricia Hampl, talking about her own writing, said, "Our most ancient metaphor says life is a journey." Writing about her experience, she "is the traveler who goes on foot, living the journey, taking in mountains, enduring deserts, marveling at the lush green places." As she writes, she moves "through it all faithfully, not so much a survivor with a harrowing tale to tell as a pilgrim, seeking, wondering." The journey metaphor here is rich in meaning and visual content: It makes us think of life as something that is not disjointed but has continuity, a destination. The journey will be on foot; we will have a chance to take things in, responding to sights and sounds missed by the traveler in a speeding car or on a plane. It will be a journey like a pilgrimage, undertaken with a solemn purpose.

Formal and Informal Formal language can make events seem important and characters dignified. (When overdone, it can make characters seem pompous.) Informal language can put the reader at ease, but when it shades over into slang it easily becomes disrespectful or insulting. If the formal or informal way of talking appears in **dialogue**, it helps create character—dignified, stodgy, tough, or laid-back. If it is used by the narrator, it will color the tone of the story as a whole. ("Ain't nobody gonna beat me at nuthin," says the tough city-kid narrator at the end of Toni Cade Bambara's "The Lesson.")

Simple and Complex Varied sentence length (the short and the long of it) is a major source of sentence variety: An arresting short sentence after a series of long and involved sentences, full of ifs and buts, may focus our attention and highlight an important thought or detail. It catches us up short. Sentences with elaborate **parallelism**—repetition of grammatically similar elements—can create a strong rhythm, building up emotion, hammering home a point, leading up to climactic finale. The following is the climactic final sentence of a story in a florid nineteenth-century style, ending the story with a last rhetorical flourish:

> And pulseless and cold,
>> with a Derringer by his side and
>> a bullet in his heart.
> though still calm as in life,
>> beneath the snow lay he who was
>>> at once the strongest and
>>> yet the weakest
> of the outcasts of Poker Flat.
>
>> Bret Harte

Sentimental and Ironic Popular fiction has often catered to the readers' love of **sentimentality,** making them cry at the undeserved sufferings of the innocent and at unsuspected evidence of goodness in the guilty. Serious modern prose has tended to deny the reader the warm gush of self-approving feelings. A pervasive feature of much modern fiction is a lively sense of **irony**—a refusal to be taken in. Irony heightens the sad and comic contrast between expectation and event, between ideal and reality. The ironic tone may range from amused tolerance and indulgence of human foibles to cutting, sardonic exposure of stupidity and greed.

FIRST READING
Adopting a Style

In your fiction journal, write for a few minutes to verbalize your honest feelings *about* a parent, family member, or other person close to you. Then write for a few minutes to express your feelings directly *to* that person. Did you change your style in the second version? Why, or how? Then read the following short short, and discuss the questions after it with your classmates. David Michael Kaplan, who lives and teaches in Chicago, has published stories in *The Atlantic, Redbook,* and other publications; his stories were collected in *Comfort* (1987). He has said about short shorts, "when we feel we understand so little of our lives," a well-written story "allows us to glimpse, for a moment, their possible mystery and meaning."

David Michael Kaplan   *(born 1946)*

Love, Your Only Mother   1987

I received another postcard from you today, Mother, and I see by the blurred postmark that you're in Manning, North Dakota now and that you've dated the card 1961. In your last card you were in Nebraska, and it was 1962; you've lost some time, I see. I was a little girl, nine years old, in 1961. You'd left my father and me only two years before. Four months after leaving, you sent me—always me, never him—your first postcard, of a turnpike in the Midwest, postmarked Enid, Oklahoma. You called me "My little angel" and said that the sunflowers by the side of the road were tall and very pretty. You signed it, as you always have, "Your only mother." My father thought, of course, that you were in Enid, and he called the police there. But we quickly learned that postmarks meant nothing: you were never where you had been, had already passed through in the wanderings only you understand.

A postcard from my mother, I tell my husband, and he grunts.

Well, at least you know she's still alive, he says.

Yes.

This postcard shows a wheat field bending in the wind. The colors are   5
badly printed: the wheat's too red, the sky too blue—except for where it touches the wheat, there becoming aquamarine, as if sky and field could

somehow combine to form water. There's a farmhouse in the distance. People must live there, and for a moment I imagine you do, and I could walk through the red wheat field, knock on the door, and find you. It's a game I've always played, imagining you were hiding somewhere in the postcards you've sent. Your scrawled message, as always, is brief: "The beetles are so much larger this year. I know you must be enjoying them. Love, your only mother."

What craziness is it this time? my husband asks. I don't reply.

Instead, I think about your message, measure it against others. In the last postcard seven months ago, you said you'd left something for me in a safety deposit box in Ferndale. The postmark was Nebraska, and there's no Ferndale in Nebraska. In the card before that, you said you were making me a birthday cake that you'd send. Even though I've vowed I'd never do it again, I try to understand what you are telling me.

"Your only mother." I've mulled that signature over and over, wondering what you meant. Are you worried I'd forget *you*, my only mother? In favor of some other? My father, you know, never divorced you. It wouldn't be fair to her, he told me, since she might come back.

Yes, I said.

Or maybe you mean singularity: out of all the mothers I might have had, I have you. You exist for me alone. Distances, you imply, mean nothing. You might come back.   10

And it's true: somehow, you've always found me. When I was a child, the postcards came to the house, of course; but later, when I went to college, and then to the first of several apartments, and finally to this house of my own, with husband and daughter of my own, they still kept coming. How you did this I don't know, but you did. You pursued me, and no matter how far away, you always found me. In your way, I guess, you've been faithful.

I put this postcard in a box with all the others you've sent over the years—postcards from Sioux City, Jackson Falls, Horseshoe Bend, Truckee, Elm City, Spivey. Then I pull out the same atlas I've had since a child and look up Manning, North Dakota, and yes, there you are, between Dickinson and Killdeer, a blip on the red highway line.

She's in Manning, North Dakota, I tell my husband, just as I used to tell my friends, as if that were explanation enough for your absence. I'd point out where you were in the atlas, and they'd nod.

But in all those postcards, Mother, I imagined you: you were down among the trees in the mountain panorama, or just out of frame on that street in downtown Tupelo, or already through the door to The World's Greatest Reptile Farm. And I was there, too, hoping to find you and say to you, Come back, come back, there's only one street, one door, we didn't mean it, we didn't know, whatever was wrong will be different.

Several times I decided you were dead, even wished you were dead, but then another postcard would come, with another message to ponder. And I've always read them, even when my husband said not to, even if they've driven me to tears or rage or a blankness when I've no longer cared if you were dead or anyone were dead, including myself. I've been faithful, too, you see. I've always looked up where you were in the atlas, and put your   15 postcards in the box. Sixty-three postcards, four hundred–odd lines of scrawl: our life together.

Why are you standing there like that? my daughter asks me.

I must have been away somewhere, I say. But I'm back.

Yes.

You see, Mother, I always come back. That's the distance that separates us.

But on summer evenings, when the windows are open to the dusk, I   20
sometimes smell cities . . . wheat fields . . . oceans—strange smells from far away—all the places you've been to that I never will. I smell them as if they weren't pictures on a postcard, but real, as close as my outstretched hand. And sometimes in the middle of the night, I'll sit bolt upright, my husband instantly awake and frightened, asking, What is it? What is it? And I'll say, She's here, she's here, and I am terrified that you are. And he'll say, No, no, she's not, she'll never come back, and he'll hold me until my terror passes. She's not here, he says gently, stroking my hair, she's not—except you are, my strange and only mother: like a buoy in a fog, your voice, dear Mother, seems to come from everywhere.

The Receptive Reader

What difference does it make that the speaker in the story is not talking *about* her mother but *to* her mother? What is her attitude toward her mother? Where or how do the speaker's mixed feelings or contradictory emotions show? Does the speaker analyze or try to understand her feelings? How and how much do you learn about the mother? Are you annoyed or are you intrigued by the incomplete information about her? Does this short short tell a story? What is the story?

THE CHALLENGE TO CONVENTION

We are what we imagine.

    N. SCOTT MOMADAY

We most easily notice a writer's style when it is different. Much modern fiction has experimented with new ways of storytelling. It has bypassed surface realism and conventional cause-and-effect thinking. It has journeyed in the inner space of private obsessions and hidden feelings. The three writers represented in this section each abandon linear storytelling—narration that moves ahead in a straight line from understandable motives to plausible consequences. Ernest Hemingway writes in an understated early modern style, making the readers listen to the undertones and overtones of a conversation in which nothing much really seems to happen. John Cheever writes in an ironic **postmodern** style—allusive, detached, and wryly amused. Franz Kafka takes us into a surreal dream world of haunting images and nameless anxieties.

Ernest Hemingway   *(1899–1961)*

Ernest Hemingway is one of the two or three most widely read American authors around the world. Like many of his generation, he witnessed the butchery of World War I (1914–1918), when seven million died on the battlefields and in the trenches. He served as an American volunteer driving an ambulance on the Italian front, and the experience left him radically disillusioned with the windbag oratory of politicians. It left him and many of his generation distrustful of language, disgusted with big words. His short stories and novels—including *The Sun Also Rises* (1926), *A Farewell to Arms* (1929), *For Whom the Bell Tolls* (1940), and *The Old Man and the Sea* (1953)—often focus on shell-shocked survivors searching for a definition of manhood without "all that talking."

For later readers, the Hemingway legend began to overshadow his work as a writer. The public remembered his life as an expatriate in France and Cuba—deep-sea fisherman, great white hunter, bullfight aficionado. However, far from being strutting macho males, the men in his fiction are often emotionally impaired characters who have lost their bearings in a cynical, violent modern world.

Hemingway set the direction for the style of much early modern fiction with his suspicion of cheap words or stylistic embellishments. Most of what is important in the following story we have to read between the lines. Many of Hemingway's stories are set in Italy or Spain. In the following story, the Ebro is a river in Spain, and *reales* are Spanish coins.

Hills like White Elephants   1927

The hills across the valley of the Ebro were long and white. On this side there was no shade and no trees and the station was between two lines of rails in the sun. Close against the side of the station there was the warm shadow of the building and a curtain, made of strings of bamboo beads, hung across the open door into the bar, to keep out flies. The American and the girl with him sat at a table in the shade, outside the building. It was very hot and the express from Barcelona would come in forty minutes. It stopped at this junction for two minutes and went on to Madrid.

"What should we drink?" the girl asked. She had taken off her hat and put it on the table.

"It's pretty hot," the man said.

"Let's drink beer."

"Dos cervezas," the man said into the curtain.

"Big ones?" a woman asked from the doorway.

"Yes. Two big ones."

The woman brought two glasses of beer and two felt pads. She put the felt pads and the beer glasses on the table and looked at the man and the girl. The girl was looking off at the line of hills. They were white in the sun and the country was brown and dry.

5

"They look like white elephants," she said.

"I've never seen one," the man drank his beer. 10

"No, you wouldn't have."

"I might have," the man said. "Just because you say I wouldn't have doesn't prove anything."

The girl looked at the bead curtain. "They've painted something on it," she said. "What does it say?"

"Anis del Toro. It's a drink."

"Could we try it?" 15

The man called "Listen" through the curtain. The woman came out from the bar.

"Four reales."

"We want two Anis del Toro."

"With water?"

"Do you want it with water?" 20

"I don't know," the girl said. "Is it good with water?"

"It's all right."

"You want them with water?" asked the woman.

"Yes, with water."

"It tastes like licorice," the girl said and put the glass down. 25

"That's the way with everything."

"Yes," said the girl. "Everything tastes of licorice. Especially all the things you've waited so long for, like absinthe."

"Oh, cut it out."

"You started it," the girl said. "I was being amused. I was having a fine time."

"Well, let's try and have a fine time." 30

"All right. I was trying. I said the mountains looked like white elephants. Wasn't that bright?"

"That was bright."

"I wanted to try this new drink. That's all we do, isn't it—look at things and try new drinks?"

"I guess so."

The girl looked across at the hills. 35

"They're lovely hills," she said. "They don't really look like white elephants. I just meant the coloring of their skin through the trees."

"Should we have another drink?"

"All right."

The warm wind blew the bead curtain against the table.

"The beer's nice and cool," the man said. 40

"It's lovely," the girl said.

"It's really an awfully simple operation, Jig," the man said. "It's not really an operation at all."

The girl looked at the ground the table legs rested on.

"I know you wouldn't mind it, Jig. It's really not anything. It's just to let the air in."

The girl did not say anything. 45

"I'll go with you and I'll stay with you all the time. They just let the air in and then it's all perfectly natural."

"Then what will we do afterward?"

"We'll be fine afterward. Just like we were before."

"What makes you think so?"

"That's the only thing that bothers us. It's the only thing that's made us   50
unhappy."

The girl looked at the bead curtain, put her hand out and took hold of
two of the strings of beads.

"And you think then we'll be all right and be happy."

"I know we will. You don't have to be afraid. I've known lots of people
that have done it."

"So have I," said the girl. "And afterward they were all so happy."

"Well," the man said, "if you don't want to you don't have to. I wouldn't   55
have you do it if you didn't want to. But I know it's perfectly simple."

"And you really want to?"

"I think it's the best thing to do. But I don't want you to do it if you don't
really want to."

"And if I do it you'll be happy and things will be like they were and you'll
love me?"

"I love you now. You know I love you."

"I know. But if I do it, then it will be nice again if I say things are like   60
white elephants, and you'll like it?"

"I'll love it. I love it now but I just can't think about it. You know how I
get when I worry."

"If I do it you won't ever worry?"

"I won't worry about that because it's perfectly simple."

"Then I'll do it. Because I don't care about me."

"What do you mean?"   65

"I don't care about me."

"Well, I care about you."

"Oh, yes. But I don't care about me. And I'll do it and then everything
will be fine."

"I don't want you to do it if you feel that way."

The girl stood up and walked to the end of the station. Across on the   70
other side, were fields of grain and trees along the banks of the Ebro. Far
away, beyond the river, were mountains. The shadow of a cloud moved
across the field of grain and she saw the river through the trees.

"And we could have all this," she said. "And we could have everything
and every day we make it more impossible."

"What did you say?"

"I said we could have everything."

"We can have everything."

"No, we can't."   75

"We can have the whole world."

"No, we can't."

"We can go everywhere."

"No, we can't. It isn't ours any more."

"It's ours."   80

"No, it isn't. And once they take it away, you never get it back."

"But they haven't taken it away."

"We'll wait and see."

"Come on back in the shade," he said. "You mustn't feel that way."

"I don't feel any way," the girl said. "I just know things."   85

"I don't want you to do anything that you don't want to do—"

"Nor that isn't good for me," she said. "I know. Could we have another beer?"

"All right. But you've got to realize—"

"I realize," the girl said. "Can't we maybe stop talking?"

They sat down at the table and the girl looked across at the hills on the   90
dry side of the valley and the man looked at her and at the table.

"You've got to realize," he said, "that I don't want you to do it if you don't want to. I'm perfectly willing to go through with it if it means anything to you."

"Doesn't it mean anything to you? We could get along."

"Of course it does. But I don't want anybody but you. I don't want any one else. And I know it's perfectly simple."

"Yes, you know it's perfectly simple."

"It's all right for you to say that, but I do know it."   95

"Would you do something for me now?"

"I'd do anything for you."

"Would you please please please please please please please stop talking?"

He did not say anything but looked at the bags against the wall of the station. There were labels on them from all the hotels where they had spent nights.

"But I don't want you to," he said, "I don't care anything about it."   100

"I'll scream," the girl said.

The woman came out through the curtains with two glasses of beer and put them down on the damp felt pads. "The train comes in five minutes," she said.

"What did she say?" asked the girl.

"That the train is coming in five minutes."

The girl smiled brightly at the woman, to thank her.   105

"I'd better take the bags over to the other side of the station," the man said. She smiled at him.

"All right. Then come back and we'll finish the beer."

He picked up the two heavy bags and carried them around the station to the other tracks. He looked up the tracks but could not see the train. Coming back, he walked through the barroom, where people waiting for the train were drinking. He drank an Anis at the bar and looked at the people. They were all waiting reasonably for the train. He went out through the bead curtain. She was sitting at the table and smiled at him.

"Do you feel better?" he asked.

"I feel fine," she said. "There's nothing wrong with me. I feel fine."   110

The Receptive Reader

1. As you first listen to the conversation of the two characters in this story, what makes the *dialogue* seem trivial or empty? (How does their style of talking echo their lifestyle?)

2. The woman's comparing the hills to white elephants is touched on several times in the story. (And it gave the story its title.) Do the hills or other elements of the story have a *symbolic* significance?

3. When do you first realize that these two people are talking about an important *choice?* How does the man talk about it? (What does it mean to him?) How does the woman talk about it? (What does it mean to her?) How does the woman react to the man's attitude?

4. Hemingway, as one of the first great moderns, was wary of emotionalism and melodrama. Where in the story are you most aware of the emotions and tensions beneath the understated, "cool" surface?

5. Does this story reach a *conclusion?* Has anything changed or been accomplished by the end? (Where do you think these two people are headed? What is ahead for them?)

The Personal Response

Eloquent pleas for sympathy are not part of the Hemingway style. Do you find yourself taking sides? If so, how and why?

<<<Find It on the Web>>>   *Hemingway on Film*

Hemingway reached millions around the world with his short stories and novels about a generation of young Americans who were left shell-shocked or uprooted by the upheavals of World War I and who looked in Italy, in Spain, in Africa, or in Cuba for values to fill the void in their lives. Although Hemingway's commitment as a truth teller made him suspicious of the Hollywood dream factory, many of its most outstanding directors and acting talent took a hand in bringing Hemingway's stories to the screen. The many film versions range from faithful adaptations (some of them the work of William Faulkner working as a Hollywood scriptwriter) to films using a Hemingway story as a springboard only. Working alone or with a group, you may want to check availability of films from the Facets organization or other film archives.

Facets Multi-Media publishes one of the most complete and reliable video catalogs available.
    <http://www.facets.org>
The Internet Movie Database lists Hemingway films currently available.
    <http://imdb.com>
The Hemingway Filmography catalogs videos.
    <http://www.hemingway.org/catalog/videos.html>
Amazon.com has a listing of videos based on Hemingway's books.
    <http://www.amazon.com>

SELECTED MOVIE TITLES:

The Killers   In a 1946 version, a young Burt Lancaster plays the role of the doomed boxer called the Swede. In a 1964 version with Lee Marvin and Angie Dickinson, the story is told from the point of view of the two professional killers.

A Farewell to Arms   Idealism gives way to brutal disillusionment as an American volunteer and a nurse try to make their separate peace during the carnage of World War I. Gary Cooper and Helen Hayes star in a 1932 film, recently released in a new black and white DVD version. Rock Hudson is Lieutenant Frederich Henry in a 1957 version directed by Charles Vidor.

The Sun also Rises   In the 1957 version, Ava Gardner and Tyrone Power play Lady Brett Ashley and the physically and emotionally impaired Jake Barnes whose war wound becomes a symbol of the alienation and impotence that is legacy of the Great War.

For Whom the Bell Tolls   An Oscar-winning cast with Gary Cooper, Ingrid Bergman, and Katina Patinou performs in this 1943 filming of Hemingway's novel about foreigners caught in the Spanish Civil War of the thirties. Fascist Germany and Italy on the one side and Stalinist Russia and international communism on the other support the opposing factions fighting it out over the dead body of Spanish democracy.

The Old Man and the Sea   Spencer Tracy, who was Hemingway's personal friend, played the old man in the 1958 film. Anthony Quinn portrays the old man's "extraordinary dignity" (*Chicago Tribune*) in the 1990 version. A short 1999 Imax film won an Academy Award.

OTHER RELATED INTERNET SOURCES:

Palin, Michael <u>A Hemingway Adventure</u>. April 1999. 4 Oct. 2001.
   <http://www.pbs.org/hemingwayadventure>

Ernest Hemingway: <u>Wrestling with Life</u>. A&E video biography. 1999.
   4 Oct. 2001.
   <http://www.AandE.com>

John Cheever   *(1912–1982)*

*Fiction is art and art is the triumph over chaos
(no less) and we can accomplish this only by the
most vigilant exercise of choice, but in a world
that changes more swiftly than we can perceive
there is always the danger that our powers of
selection will be mistaken and that the vision
we serve will come to nothing.*

JOHN CHEEVER

John Cheever was expelled from a private New England academy at seventeen. He returned to academic life only for brief teaching stints and was much honored by the academic establishment later in his life. He published more than two hundred stories in the *New Yorker* magazine, an ideal outlet for him. He played to the self-image of the *New Yorker* reader—tolerant of eccentricity, politically liberal, and disdainful of sensationalism and popular enthusiasm. A key to Cheever's style is **irony**—the witty exposure of the discrepancy between what people should be and what they are. His stories often reach a turning point where the sunny, reassuring surface wears thin and a chilling note is heard, similar to "that hour of a spring day . . . when the dark of the woods and the cold and damp from any nearby pond or brook are suddenly felt, when you realize that the world was lighted, until a minute ago. . ., and that your clothes are thin" ("Just Tell Me Who It Was").

Cheever often regards his characters with wry amusement—rather than getting embroiled in their inner turmoil, sharing in their confusions and frustrations. After his death, his own journals and his daughter's book about her parents' unhappy marriage (*Home before Dark,* 1984) gave readers a glimpse of the writer's own traumas, which he had masked by the defensive armor of his witty, ironic style. His son, Benjamin Cheever, said about him, "He showed the world what he thought it wanted to see. The picture he presented was sharp, witty, cogent, and often false." Many of Cheever's journal entries focus on his gay lifestyle (his "contested sexuality") and his struggles with alcoholism.

Cheever's "The Enormous Radio" revolves around strange fragmentary messages heard on a radio. The story is thus an ideal vehicle for the **allusions** and name-dropping that became a feature of a late-twentieth-century postmodern style. An allusion is a brief mention that activates our memory. It brings to mind a range of associations; it reminds us of a story. Reading about the upwardly mobile couple in this story, we are expected to recognize that Andover is a tony private boarding school on the New England preppie circuit (the husband is an alumnus). Westchester, where the couple eventually hope to live, is a suburban sanctuary for well-shod commuters to New York City. The couple love classical composers like Mozart, Schubert, and Chopin—great composers, but part of a safe, well-worn repertory.

The Enormous Radio   1947

Jim and Irene Westcott were the kind of people who seem to strike that satisfactory average of income, endeavor, and respectability that is reached by the statistical reports in college alumni bulletins. They were the parents of two young children, they had been married nine years, they lived on the twelfth floor of an apartment house near Sutton Place, they went to the theatre on an average of 10.3 times a year, and they hoped someday to live in Westchester. Irene Westcott was a pleasant, rather plain girl with soft brown hair and a wide, fine forehead upon which nothing at all had been written, and in the cold weather she wore a coat of fitch skins dyed to resemble mink. You could not say that Jim Westcott looked younger than he was, but you could at least say of him that he seemed to feel younger. He wore his graying hair cut very short, he dressed in the kind of clothes his class had worn at Andover, and his manner was earnest, vehement, and intentionally naïve. The Westcotts differed from their friends, their classmates, and their neighbors only in an interest they shared in serious music. They went to a great many concerts—although they seldom mentioned this to anyone—and they spent a good deal of time listening to music on the radio.

Their radio was an old instrument, sensitive, unpredictable, and beyond repair. Neither of them understood the mechanics of radio—or of any of the other appliances that surrounded them—and when the instrument faltered, Jim would strike the side of the cabinet with his hand. This sometimes helped. One Sunday afternoon, in the middle of a Schubert quartet, the music faded away altogether. Jim struck the cabinet repeatedly, but there was no response; the Schubert was lost to them forever. He promised to buy Irene a new radio, and on Monday when he came home from work he told her that he had got one. He refused to describe it, and said it would be a surprise for her when it came.

The radio was delivered at the kitchen door the following afternoon, and with the assistance of her maid and the handyman Irene uncrated it and brought it into the living room. She was struck at once with the physical ugliness of the large gumwood cabinet. Irene was proud of her living room, she had chosen its furnishings and colors as carefully as she chose her clothes, and now it seemed to her that the new radio stood among her intimate possessions like an aggressive intruder. She was confounded by the number of dials and switches on the instrument panel, and she studied them thoroughly before she put the plug into a wall socket and turned the radio on. The dials flooded with a malevolent green light, and in the distance she heard the music of a piano quintet. The quintet was in the distance for only an instant; it bore down upon her with a speed greater than light and filled the apartment with the noise of music amplified so mightily that it knocked a china ornament from a table to the floor. She rushed to the instrument and reduced the volume. The violent forces that were snared in the ugly gumwood cabinet made her uneasy. Her children came home from school then, and she took them to the Park. It was not until later in the afternoon that she was able to return to the radio.

The maid had given the children their suppers and was supervising their baths when Irene turned on the radio, reduced the volume, and sat down to listen to a Mozart quintet that she knew and enjoyed. The music came through clearly. The new instrument had a much purer tone, she thought, than the old one. She decided that tone was most important and that she could conceal the cabinet behind a sofa. But as soon as she had made her peace with the radio, the interference began. A crackling sound like the noise of a burning powder fuse began to accompany the singing of the strings. Beyond the music, there was a rustling that reminded Irene un-pleasantly of the sea, and as the quintet progressed, these noises were joined by many others. She tried all the dials and switches but nothing dimmed the interference, and she sat down, disappointed and bewildered, and tried to trace the flight of the melody. The elevator shaft in her build-ing ran beside the living-room wall, and it was the noise of the elevator that gave her a clue to the character of the static. The rattling of the elevator ca-bles and the opening and closing of the elevator doors were reproduced in her loudspeaker, and, realizing that the radio was sensitive to electrical cur-rents of all sorts, she began to discern through the Mozart the ringing of tele-phone bells, the dialing of phones, and the lamentation of a vacuum cleaner. By listening more carefully, she was able to distinguish doorbells, elevator bells, electric razors, and Waring mixers, whose sounds had been picked up from the apartments that surrounded hers and transmitted through her loudspeaker. The powerful and ugly instrument, with its mis-taken sensitivity to discord, was more than she could hope to master, so she turned the thing off and went into the nursery to see her children.

When Jim Westcott came home that night, he went to the radio confi- 5
dently and worked the controls. He had the same sort of experience Irene had had. A man was speaking on the station Jim had chosen, and his voice swung instantly from the distance into a force so powerful that it shook the apartment. Jim turned the volume control and reduced the voice. Then, a minute or two later, the interference began. The ringing of telephones and doorbells set in, joined by the rasp of the elevator doors and the whir of cooking appliances. The character of the noise had changed since Irene had tried the radio earlier; the last of the electric razors was being unplugged, the vacuum cleaners had all been returned to their closets, and the static re-flected that change in pace that overtakes the city after the sun goes down. He fiddled with the knobs but couldn't get rid of the noises, so he turned the radio off and told Irene that in the morning he'd call the people who had sold it to him and give them hell.

The following afternoon, when Irene returned to the apartment from a luncheon date, the maid told her that a man had come and fixed the radio. Irene went into the living room before she took off her hat or her furs and tried the instrument. From the loudspeaker came a recording of the "Missouri Waltz." It reminded her of the thin, scratchy music from an old-fashioned phonograph that she sometimes heard across the lake where she spent her summers. She waited until the waltz had finished, expecting an explanation of the recording, but there was none. The music was followed by silence, and then the plaintive and scratchy record was repeated. She turned the dial and got a satisfactory burst of Caucasian music—the thump of bare feet in the dust and the rattle of coin jewelry—but in the background she could hear the ringing of bells and a confusion of voices. Her children came home from school then, and she turned off the radio and went to the nursery.

When Jim came home that night, he was tired, and he took a bath and changed his clothes. Then he joined Irene in the living room. He had just turned on the radio when the maid announced dinner, so he left it on, and he and Irene went to the table.

Jim was too tired to make even pretense of sociability, and there was nothing about the dinner to hold Irene's interest, so her attention wandered from the food to the deposits of silver polish on the candlesticks and from there to the music in the other room. She listened for a few minutes to a Chopin prelude and then was surprised to hear a man's voice break in. "For Christ's sake, Kathy," he said, "do you always have to play the piano when I get home?" The music stopped abruptly. "It's the only chance I have," a woman said. "I'm at the office all day." "So am I," the man said. He added something obscene about an upright piano, and slammed a door. The passionate and melancholy music began again.

"Did you hear that?" Irene asked.

"What?" Jim was eating his dessert.   10

"The radio. A man said something while the music was still going on—something dirty."

"It's probably a play."

"I don't think it *is* a play," Irene said.

They left the table and took their coffee into the living room. Irene asked Jim to try another station. He turned the knob. "Have you seen my garters?" a man asked. "Button me up," a woman said. "Have you seen my garters?" the man said again. "Just button me up and I'll find your garters," the woman said. Jim shifted to another station. "I wish you wouldn't leave apple cores in the ashtrays," a man said. "I hate the smell."

"This is strange," Jim said.   15

"Isn't it?" Irene said.

Jim turned the knob again. " 'On the coast of Coromandel where the early pumpkins blow,' " a woman with a pronounced English accent said, " 'in the middle of the woods lived the Yonghy-Bonghy-Bò. Two old chairs, and half a candle, one old jug without a handle . . .' "

"My God!" Irene cried. "That's the Sweeneys' nurse."

" 'These were all his worldly goods,' " the British voice continued.

"Turn that thing off," Irene said. "Maybe they can hear *us*." Jim switched   20
the radio off. "That was Miss Armstrong, the Sweeneys' nurse," Irene said. "She must be reading to the little girl. They live in 17-B. I've talked with Miss Armstrong in the Park. I know her voice very well. We must be getting other people's apartments."

"That's impossible," Jim said.

"Well, that was the Sweeneys' nurse," Irene said hotly. "I know her voice. I know it very well. I'm wondering if they can hear us."

Jim turned the switch. First from a distance and then nearer, nearer, as if borne on the wind, came the pure accents of the Sweeneys' nurse again: " *'Lady Jingly! Lady Jingly!'* " she said, " *'sitting where the pumpkins blow, will you come and be my wife? said the Yonghy-Bonghy-Bò . . .'* "

Jim went over to the radio and said "Hello" loudly into the speaker.

" *'I am tired of living singly,'* " the nurse went on, " *'on this coast so wild*   25 *and shingly, I'm a-weary of my life; if you'll come and be my wife, quite serene would be my life . . .'* "

"I guess she can't hear us," Irene said. "Try something else."

Jim turned to another station, and the living room was filled with the up- roar of a cocktail party that had overshot its mark. Someone was playing the piano and singing the "Whiffenpoof Song," and the voices that surrounded the piano were vehement and happy. "Eat some more sandwiches," a woman shrieked. There were screams of laughter and a dish of some sort crashed to the floor.

"Those must be the Fullers, in 11-E," Irene said. "I knew they were giv- ing a party this afternoon. I saw her in the liquor store. Isn't this too divine? Try something else. See if you can get those people in 18-C."

The Westcotts overheard that evening a monologue on salmon fishing in Canada, a bridge game, running comments on home movies of what had apparently been a fortnight at Sea Island, and a bitter family quarrel about an overdraft at the bank. They turned off their radio at midnight and went to bed, weak with laughter. Sometime in the night, their son began to call for a glass of water and Irene got one and took it to his room. It was very early. All the lights in the neighborhood were extinguished, and from the boy's window she could see the empty street. She went into the living room and tried the radio. There was some faint coughing, a moan, and then a man spoke. "Are you all right, darling?" he asked. "Yes," a woman said wearily. "Yes, I'm all right, I guess," and then she added with great feeling, "But, you know, Charlie, I don't feel like myself anymore. Sometimes there are about fifteen or twenty minutes in the week when I feel like myself. I don't like to go to another doctor, because the doctor's bills are so awful already, but I just don't feel like myself, Charlie. I just never feel like myself." They were not young, Irene thought. She guessed from the timbre of their voices that they were middle-aged. The restrained melancholy of the dialogue and the draft from the bedroom window made her shiver, and she went back to bed.

The following morning, Irene cooked breakfast for the family—the maid   30 didn't come up from her room in the basement until ten—braided her daughter's hair, and waited at the door until her children and her husband had been carried away in the elevator. Then she went into the living room and tried the radio. "I don't want to go to school," a child screamed. "I hate school. I won't go to school. I hate school." "You will go to school," an en- raged woman said. "We paid eight hundred dollars to get you into that school and you'll go if it kills you." The next number on the dial produced the worn record of the "Missouri Waltz." Irene shifted the control and in- vaded the privacy of several breakfast tables. She overheard demonstrations of indigestion, carnal love, abysmal vanity, faith, and despair. Irene's life was nearly as simple and sheltered as it appeared to be, and the forthright and sometimes brutal language that came from the loudspeaker that morning astonished and troubled her. She continued to listen until her maid came in. Then she turned off the radio quickly, since this insight, she realized, was a furtive one.

Irene had a luncheon date with a friend that day, and she left her apartment at a little after twelve. There were a number of women in the elevator when it stopped at her floor. She stared at their handsome and impassive faces, their furs, and the cloth flowers in their hats. Which one of them had been to Sea Island? she wondered. Which one had overdrawn her bank account? The elevator stopped at the tenth floor and a woman with a pair of Skye terriers joined them. Her hair was rigged high on her head and she wore a mink cape. She was humming the "Missouri Waltz."

Irene had two Martinis at lunch, and she looked searchingly at her friend and wondered what her secrets were. They had intended to go shopping after lunch, but Irene excused herself and went home. She told the maid that she was not to be disturbed; then she went into the living room, closed the doors, and switched on the radio. She heard, in the course of the afternoon, the halting conversation of a woman entertaining her aunt, the hysterical conclusion of a luncheon party, and a hostess briefing her maid about some cocktail guests. "Don't give the best Scotch to anyone who hasn't white hair," the hostess said. "See if you can get rid of that liver paste before you pass those hot things, and could you lend me five dollars? I want to tip the elevator man."

As the afternoon waned, the conversations increased in intensity. From where Irene sat, she could see the open sky above the East River. There were hundreds of clouds in the sky, as though the south wind had broken the winter into pieces and were blowing it north, and on her radio she could hear the arrival of cocktail guests and the return of children and businessmen from their schools and offices. "I found a good-sized diamond on the bathroom floor this morning," a woman said. "It must have fallen out of that bracelet Mrs. Dunston was wearing last night." "We'll sell it," a man said. "Take it down to the jeweler on Madison Avenue and sell it. Mrs. Dunston won't know the difference, and we could use a couple of hundred bucks . . ." "'Oranges and lemons, say the bells of St. Clement's,'" the Sweeneys' nurse sang. " 'Halfpence and farthings, say the bells of St. Martin's. When will you pay me? say the bells at old Bailey . . .'" "It's not a hat," a woman cried, and at her back roared a cocktail party. "It's not a hat, it's a love affair. That's what Walter Florell said. He said it's not a hat, it's a love affair," and then, in a lower voice, the same woman added, "Talk to somebody, for Christ's sake, honey, talk to somebody. If she catches you standing here not talking to anybody, she'll take us off her invitation list, and I love these parties."

The Westcotts were going out for dinner that night, and when Jim came home, Irene was dressing. She seemed sad and vague, and he brought her a drink. They were dining with friends in the neighborhood, and they walked to where they were going. The sky was broad and filled with light. It was one of those splendid spring evenings that excite memory and desire, and the air that touched their hands and faces felt very soft. A Salvation Army band was on the corner playing "Jesus Is Sweeter." Irene drew on her husband's arm and held him there for a minute, to hear the music. "They're really such nice people, aren't they?" she said. "They have such nice faces. Actually, they're so much nicer than a lot of the people we know." She took a bill from her purse and walked over and dropped it into the tambourine. There was in her face, when she returned to her husband, a look of radiant melancholy that he was not familiar with. And her conduct at the dinner party that night seemed strange to him, too. She interrupted her hostess rudely and stared at the people across the table from her with an intensity for which she would have punished her children.

It was still mild when they walked home from the party, and Irene looked   35
up at the spring stars. " 'How far that little candle throws its beams,' " she exclaimed. " 'So shines a good deed in a naughty world.' " She waited that night until Jim had fallen asleep, and then went into the living room and turned on the radio.

Jim came home at about six the next night. Emma, the maid, let him in, and he had taken off his hat and was taking off his coat when Irene ran into the hall. Her face was shining with tears and her hair was disordered. "Go up to 16-C, Jim!" she screamed. "Don't take off your coat. Go up to 16-C. Mr. Osborn's beating his wife. They've been quarreling since four o'clock, and now he's hitting her. Go up there and stop him."

From the radio in the living room, Jim heard screams, obscenities, and thuds. "You know you don't have to listen to this sort of thing," he said. He strode into the living room and turned the switch. "It's indecent," he said. "It's like looking in windows. You know you don't have to listen to this sort of thing. You can turn it off."

"Oh, it's so horrible, it's so dreadful," Irene was sobbing. "I've been listening all day, and it's so depressing."

"Well, if it's so depressing, why do you listen to it? I bought this damned radio to give you some pleasure," he said. "I paid a great deal of money for it. I thought it might make you happy. I wanted to make you happy."

"Don't, don't, don't, don't quarrel with me," she moaned, and laid her   40
head on his shoulder. "All the others have been quarreling all day. Everybody's been quarreling. They're all worried about money. Mrs. Hutchinson's mother is dying of cancer in Florida and they don't have enough money to send her to the Mayo Clinic. At least, Mr. Hutchinson says they don't have enough money. And some woman in this building is having an affair with the handyman—with that hideous handyman. It's too disgusting. And Mrs. Melville has heart trouble, and Mr. Hendricks is going to lose his job in April and Mrs. Hendricks is horrid about the whole thing and that girl who plays the 'Missouri Waltz' is a whore, a common whore, and the elevator man has tuberculosis and Mr. Osborn has been beating Mrs. Osborn." She wailed, she trembled with grief and checked the stream of tears down her face with the heel of her palm.

"Well, why do you have to listen?" Jim asked again. "Why do you have to listen to this stuff if it makes you so miserable?"

"Oh, don't, don't, don't," she cried. "Life is too terrible, too sordid and awful. But we've never been like that, have we, darling? Have we? I mean, we've always been good and decent and loving to one another, haven't we? And we have two children, two beautiful children. Our lives aren't sordid, are they, darling? Are they?" She flung her arms around his neck and drew his face down to hers. "We're happy, aren't we, darling? We are happy, aren't we?"

"Of course we're happy," he said tiredly. He began to surrender his resentment. "Of course we're happy. I'll have that damned radio fixed or taken away tomorrow." He stroked her soft hair. "My poor girl," he said.

"You love me, don't you?" she asked. "And we're not hypercritical or worried about money or dishonest, are we?"

"No, darling," he said.   45

A man came in the morning and fixed the radio. Irene turned it on cautiously and was happy to hear a California-wine commercial and a recording of Beethoven's Ninth Symphony, including Schiller's "Ode to Joy." She kept the radio on all day and nothing untoward came from the speaker.

A Spanish suite was being played when Jim came home. "Is everything all right?" he asked. His face was pale, she thought. They had some cocktails and went in to dinner to the "Anvil Chorus" from *Il Trovatore*. This was followed by Debussy's "La Mer."

"I paid the bill for the radio today," Jim said. "It cost four hundred dollars. I hope you'll get some enjoyment out of it."

"Oh, I'm sure I will," Irene said.

"Four hundred dollars is a good deal more than I can afford," he went   50
on. "I wanted to get something that you'd enjoy. It's the last extravagance we'll be able to indulge in this year. I see that you haven't paid your clothing bills yet. I saw them on your dressing table." He looked directly at her. "Why did you tell me you'd paid them? Why did you lie to me?"

"I just didn't want you to worry, Jim," she said. She drank some water. "I'll be able to pay my bills out of this month's allowance. There were the slipcovers last month, and that party."

"You've got to learn to handle the money I give you a little more intelligently, Irene," he said. "You've got to understand that we don't have as much money this year as we had last. I had a very sobering talk with Mitchell today. No one is buying anything. We're spending all our time promoting new issues, and you know how long that takes. I'm not getting any younger, you know. I'm thirty-seven. My hair will be gray next year. I haven't done as well as I'd hoped to do. And I don't suppose things will get any better."

"Yes, dear," she said.

"We've got to start cutting down," Jim said. "We've got to think of the children. To be perfectly frank with you, I worry about money a great deal. I'm not at all sure of the future. No one is. If anything should happen to me, there's the insurance, but that wouldn't go very far today. I've worked awfully hard to give you and the children a comfortable life," he said bitterly. "I don't like to see all my energies, all of my youth, wasted in fur coats and radios and slipcovers and—"

"Please, Jim," she said. "Please. They'll hear us."   55

"*Who'll hear us?* Emma can't hear us."

"The radio."

"Oh, I'm sick!" he shouted. "I'm sick to death of your apprehensiveness. The radio can't hear us. Nobody can hear us. And what if they can hear us? Who cares?"

Irene got up from the table and went into the living room. Jim went to the door and shouted at her from there. "Why are you so Christly all of a sudden? What's turned you overnight into a convent girl? You stole your mother's jewelry before they probated her will. You never gave your sister a cent of that money that was intended for her—not even when she needed it. You made Grace Howland's life miserable, and where was all your piety and your virtue when you went to that abortionist? I'll never forget how cool you were. You packed your bag and went off to have that child murdered as if you were going to Nassau. If you'd had any reasons, if you'd had any good reasons—"

Irene stood for a minute before the hideous cabinet, disgraced and sick-   60 ened, but she held her hand on the switch before she extinguished the music and the voices, hoping that the instrument might speak to her kindly, that she might hear the Sweeneys' nurse. Jim continued to shout at her from the door. The voice on the radio was suave and noncommittal. "An early-morning railroad disaster in Tokyo," the loudspeaker said, "killed twenty-nine people. A fire in a Catholic hospital near Buffalo for the care of blind children was extinguished early this morning by nuns. The temperature is forty-seven. The humidity is eighty-nine."

The Receptive Reader

1. What is the *keynote* in Cheever's description of his suburban couple? What are telling details? What is his attitude toward these people—how does it show?

2. Is there a *pattern*—a thread that connects the snatches of conversation or the fragments of people's lives that are heard on the strange radio?

3. On the subject of *allusions:* What is funny about the "Whiffenpoof Song" picked up by the radio being a college drinking song, or about the "Missouri Waltz" being a sentimental favorite that President Truman used to play on the piano? The snatches of humorous verse read by the "woman with the pronounced English accent" are from the work of Edward Lear, a cherished author of nonsense verse and a contemporary and kindred spirit of Lewis Carroll, the author of *Alice in Wonderland.* What touch do they lend to the story?

4. What has happened to the couple at the end? Why is what has happened to them *ironic* in the light of how the author described them at the beginning?

The Personal Response

For you, is the story as a whole amusing or serious, or both?

Franz Kafka   *(1883–1924)*

We need the books that affect us like a disaster,
that grieve us deeply, like the death of someone
we loved more than ourselves, like being

*banished into forests far from everyone, like a
suicide. A book must be the axe for the frozen
sea within.*

FRANZ KAFKA

*Kafka's fictions all seem to be awakenings into
an incomprehensible world, which he truly
wants to understand.*

FREDERICK R. KARL

Franz Kafka's strange dreamlike stories and novels make us ponder the great twentieth-century themes. According to one recent critic, Kafka "has been the dominant influence in the shaping of our postmodern sensibility since World War II" (Alan Thiher). Kafka was the prophet of alienation—homelessness, rootlessness—and the anxiety it generates. He foresaw a totalitarian future in which the individual is helpless when struggling against a faceless all-pervading bureaucratic authority. Kafka made *angst*—a feverish, all-pervading anxiety—a household word.

Kafka was the first great prophet of the **absurd.** Although we are forever anxiously trying to make sense of the world, we come to suspect that we are living in an irrational universe. We find ourselves in a reality that we cannot really understand or bring under control. Depending on our perspective, we may respond with madcap absurdist humor or with a pervading feeling of loss and alienation. Kafka was one of the first great masters of the **surreal:** He shifted from surface realism to a hallucinatory dreamlike reality mirroring our hidden or buried feelings. In his stories, as in a dream, logical connections are missing. Haunting images pull us into a world in which our yearnings, traumas, and anxieties are acted out.

Kafka grew up as a German-speaking Jew in Prague, a Czech city that was still part of the Austrian empire. Acutely aware of the anti-Semitic society around him, Kafka hated the feeling of needing police protection from hate-filled thugs. At the same time, many Jews, including Kafka, felt that their people had a special mission to point the way for humanity—to help humanize our species. Though surrounded by people speaking Czech, Kafka and his friends spoke German; he studied first German literature and then law at the German university in Prague.

Kafka wrote his best-known works—*The Judgment, Metamorphosis, The Trial, The Castle, Amerika*—between 1912 and his death from tuberculosis in 1924. He worked in an insurance office, dealing with workers' compensation. However, he was channeling his vital energies into writing, which he pursued with intense seriousness and bouts of paralyzing self-doubt. Kafka published only his short stories during his lifetime, and even these only reluctantly. He instructed his friend Max Brod to burn all unpublished work (including the great novels) in case of Kafka's death. These instructions Brod decided he could not in good conscience carry out, thus saving for posterity what Thomas Mann called some of the "great mysterious fictions" of the twentieth century.

Kafka's narratives have been called "anti–fairy tales." In a fairy tale, the hero often sets out alone on a quest and overcomes obstacles in his search for good fortune. In a Kafka story, the hero is likely to get bogged down in the struggle. Critics have differed widely on what these stories say about the human condition.

The Country Doctor   *1919*

TRANSLATED BY WILLA MUIR AND EDWIN MUIR

I was in great perplexity; I had to start on an urgent journey; a seriously ill patient was waiting for me in a village ten miles off; a thick blizzard of snow filled all the wide spaces between him and me; I had a gig, a light gig with big wheels, exactly right for our country roads; muffled in furs, my bag of instruments in my hand, I was in the courtyard all ready for the journey; but there was no horse to be had, no horse. My own horse had died in the night, worn out by the fatigues of this icy winter; my servant girl was now running round the village trying to borrow a horse; but it was hopeless, I knew it, and I stood there forlornly, with the snow gathering more and more thickly upon me, more and more unable to move. In the gateway the girl appeared, alone, and waved the lantern; of course, who would lend a horse at this time for such a journey? I strode through the courtway once more; I could see no way out; in my confused distress I kicked at the dilapidated door of the yearlong uninhabited pigsty. It flew open and flapped to and fro on its hinges. A steam and smell as of horses came out of it. A dim stable lantern was swinging inside from a rope. A man, crouching on his hams in that low space, showed an open blue-eyed face. "Shall I yoke up?" he asked, crawling out on all fours. I did not know what to say and merely stooped down to see what else was in the sty. The servant girl was standing beside me. "You never know what you're going to find in your own house," she said, and we both laughed. "Hey there, Brother, hey there, Sister!" called the groom, and two horses, enormous creatures with powerful flanks, one after the other, their legs tucked close to their bodies, each well-shaped head lowered like a camel's, by sheer strength of buttocking squeezed out through the door hole which they filled entirely. But at once they were standing up, their legs long and their bodies steaming thickly. "Give him a hand," I said, and the willing girl hurried to help the groom with the harnessing. Yet hardly was she beside him when the groom clipped hold of her and pushed his face against hers. She screamed and fled back to me; on her cheek stood out in red the marks of two rows of teeth. "You brute," I yelled in fury, "do you want a whipping?" but in the same moment reflected that the man was a stranger; that I did not know where he came from, and that of his own free will he was helping me out when everyone else had failed me. As if he knew my thoughts he took no offense at my threat but, still busied with the horses, only turned round once toward me. "Get in," he said then, and indeed everything was ready. A magnificent pair of horses, I observed, such as I had never sat behind, and I climbed in hap-pily. "But I'll drive, you don't know the way," I said. "Of course," said he, "I'm not coming with you anyway, I'm staying with Rose." "No," shrieked Rose, fleeing into the house with a justified presentiment that her fate was inescapable; I heard the door chain rattle as she put it up; I heard the key turn in the lock; I could see, moreover, how she put out the lights in the en-trance hall and in further flight all through the rooms to keep herself from being discovered. "You're coming with me," I said to the groom, "or I won't go, urgent as my journey is. I'm not thinking of paying for it by handing the girl over to you." "Gee up!" he said; clapped his hands; the gig whirled off like a log in a freshet; I could just hear the door of my house splitting and bursting as the groom charged at it and then I was deafened and blinded by a storming rush that steadily buffeted all my senses. But this only for a mo-ment, since, as if my patient's farmyard had opened out just before my courtyard gate, I was already there; the horses had come quietly to a stand-still; the blizzard had stopped; moonlight all around; my patient's parents hurried out of the house, his sister behind them; I was almost lifted out of the gig; from their confused ejaculations I gathered not a word; in the sick-room the air was almost unbreathable; the neglected stove was smoking; I wanted to push open a window; but first I had to look at my patient. Gaunt, without any fever, not cold, not warm, with vacant eyes, without a shirt, the youngster heaved himself up from under the feather bedding, threw his arms around my neck, and whispered in my ear: "Doctor, let me die." I glanced round the room; no one had heard it; the parents were leaning for-ward in silence waiting for my verdict; the sister had set a chair for my hand-bag; I opened the bag and hunted among my instruments; the boy kept clutching at me from his bed to remind me of his entreaty; I picked up a pair of tweezers, examined them in the candlelight and laid them down again. "Yes," I thought blasphemously, "in cases like this the gods are help-ful, send the missing horse, add to it a second because of the urgency, and to crown everything bestow even a groom—" And only now did I remem-ber Rose again; what was I to do, how could I rescue her, how could I pull her away from under that groom at ten miles' distance, with a team of horses I couldn't control. These horses, now, they had somehow slipped the reins loose, pushed the windows open from outside, I did not know how; each of them had stuck a head in at a window and, quite unmoved by the star-tled cries of the family, stood eyeing the patient. "Better go back at once," I thought, as if the horses were summoning me to the return journey, yet I permitted the patient's sister, who fancied that I was dazed by the heat, to take my fur coat from me. A glass of rum was poured out for me, the old man clapped me on the shoulder, a familiarity justified by this offer of his treasure. I shook my head; in the narrow confines of the old man's thoughts I felt ill; that was my only reason for refusing the drink. The mother stood by the bedside and cajoled me toward it; I yielded, and, while one of the horses whinnied loudly to the ceiling, laid my head to the boy's breast, which shivered under my wet beard. I confirmed what I already knew; the boy was quite sound, something a little wrong with his circulation, saturated with coffee by his solicitous mother, but sound and best turned out of bed with one shove. I am no world reformer and so I let him lie. I was the district doctor and did my duty to the uttermost, to the point where it became almost too much. I was badly paid and yet generous and helpful to the poor. I had still to see that Rose was all right, and then the boy might have his way and I wanted to die too. What was I doing there in that endless winter! My horse was dead, and not a single person in the village would lend me another. I had to get my team out of the pigsty; if they hadn't chanced to be horses I should have had to travel with swine. That was how it was. And I nodded to the family. They knew nothing about it, and, had they known, would not have believed it. To write prescriptions is easy, but to come to an understanding with people is hard. Well, this should be the end of my visit, I had once more been called out needlessly, I was used to that, the whole district made my life a torment with my night bell, but that I should have to sacrifice Rose this time as well, the pretty girl who had lived in my house for years almost without my noticing her—that sacrifice was too much to ask, and I had somehow to get it reasoned out in my head with the help of what craft I could muster, in order not to let fly at this family, which with the best will in the world could not restore Rose to me. But as I shut my bag and put an arm out for my fur coat, the family meanwhile standing together, the father sniffing at the glass of rum in his hand, the mother, apparently disappointed in me—why, what do people expect?—biting her lips with tears in her eyes, the sister fluttering a blood-soaked towel, I was somehow ready to admit conditionally that the boy might be ill after all. I went toward him, he welcomed me smiling as if I were bringing him the most nourishing invalid broth—ah, now both horses were whinnying together; the noise, I suppose, was ordained by heaven to assist my examination of the patient—and this time I discovered that the boy was indeed ill. In his right side, near the hip, was an open wound as big as the palm of my hand. Rose-red, in many variations of shade, dark in the hollows, lighter at the edges, softly granulated, with irregular clots of blood, open as a surface mine to the daylight. That was how it looked from a distance. But on a closer inspection there was another complication. I could not help a low whistle of surprise. Worms, as thick and as long as my little finger, themselves rose-red and blood-spotted as well, were wriggling from their fastness in the interior of the wound toward the light, with small white heads and many little legs. Poor boy, you were past helping. I had discovered your great wound; this blossom in your side was destroying you. The family was pleased; they saw me busying myself; the sister told the mother, the mother the father, the father told several guests who were coming in, through the moonlight at the open door, walking on tiptoe, keeping their balance with outstretched arms. "Will you save me?" whispered the boy with a sob, quite blinded by the life within his wound. That is what people are like in my district. Always expecting the impossible from the doctor. They have lost their ancient beliefs; the parson sits at home and unravels his vestments, one after another; but the doctor is supposed to be omnipotent with his merciful surgeon's hand. Well, as it pleases them; I have not thrust my services on them; if they misuse me for sacred ends, I let that happen to me too; what better do I want, old country doctor that I am, bereft of my servant girl! And so they came, the family and the village elders, and stripped my clothes off me;

a school choir with the teacher at the head of it stood before the house and sang these words to an utterly simple tune:

> Strip his clothes off, then he'll heal us,
> If he doesn't, kill him dead!
> Only a doctor, only a doctor.

Then my clothes were off and I looked at the people quietly, my fingers in my beard and my head cocked to one side. I was altogether composed and equal to the situation and remained so, although it was no help to me, since they now took me by the head and feet and carried me to the bed. They laid me down in it next to the wall, on the side of the wound. Then they all left the room; the door was shut; the singing stopped; clouds covered the moon; the bedding was warm around me; the horses' heads in the opened windows wavered like shadows. "Do you know," said a voice in my ear, "I have very little confidence in you. Why, you were only blown in here, you didn't come on your own feet. Instead of helping me, you're cramping me on my deathbed. What I'd like best is to scratch your eyes out." "Right," I said, "it is a shame. And yet I am a doctor. What am I to do? Believe me, it is not too easy for me either." "Am I supposed to be content with this apology? Oh, I must be, I can't help it. I always have to put up with things. A fine wound is all I brought into the world; that was my sole endowment." "My young friend," said I, "your mistake is: you have not a wide enough view. I have been in all the sickrooms, far and wide, and I tell you: your wound is not so bad. Done in a tight corner with two strokes of the ax. Many a one proffers his side and can hardly hear the ax in the forest, far less that it is coming nearer to him." "Is that really so, or are you deluding me in my fever?" "It is really so, take the word of honor of an official doctor." And he took it and lay still. But now it was time for me to think of escaping. The horses were still standing faithfully in their places. My clothes, my fur coat, my bag were quickly collected; I didn't want to waste time dressing; if the horses raced home as they had come, I should only be springing, as it were, out of this bed into my own. Obediently a horse backed away from the window; I threw my bundle into the gig; the fur coat missed its mark and was caught on a hook only by the sleeve. Good enough. I swung myself onto the horse. With the reins loosely trailing, one horse barely fastened to the other, the gig swaying behind, my fur coat last of all in the snow. "Gee up!" I said, but there was no galloping; slowly, like old men, we crawled through the snowy wastes; a long time echoed behind us the new but faulty song of the children:

> O be joyful, all you patients,
> The doctor's laid in bed beside you!

Never shall I reach home at this rate; my flourishing practice is done for; my successor is robbing me, but in vain, for he cannot take my place; in my house the disgusting groom is raging; Rose is the victim; I do not want to think about it any more. Naked, exposed to the frost of this most unhappy of ages, with an earthly vehicle, unearthly horses, old man that I am, I wander astray. My fur coat is hanging from the back of the gig, but I cannot reach it, and none of my limber pack of patients lifts a finger. Betrayed! Betrayed! A false alarm on the night bell once answered—it cannot be made good, not ever.

The Receptive Reader

1. How far into the story can you read while assuming it to be a realistic narrative of events? What are your first clues that this story is going to be *surreal,* like a dream?

2. What is the role of the *groom?* How is he different from the doctor, who is supposedly his employer? What is the doctor's attitude toward him?

3. What is the possible *symbolism* of the horses? the pigsty?

4. What is the role of *Rose?* (Could she be a "mother figure"? Could she be for the doctor an object of unacknowledged sexual desire?)

5. What do you make of the doctor's first declaring the patient healthy and then finding the incurable wound? (Could the wound be the wound in the side of Christ on the cross?)

6. What is the doctor's interaction with the patient's family? How do they treat him?

7. The doctor seems very inadequate as the modern physician-healer who is supposed to perform the miracles of modern medicine. Could he be a *satirical* portrait of the overreaching pride—or hubris—of modern science?

8. Why is the *priest* sitting at home "unraveling his vestments"?

9. Although the events of the story are surreal, the doctor often uses *trite sayings* that sound as if things were normal. Why? What are striking examples?

The Personal Response

Although many critics approach Kafka with deadly earnestness, other readers have marveled at the mixture of the sad and comic in his fiction. Kafka read some of his stories to his friends with tears of laughter streaming down his face. Does anything about this story strike you as comical?

Making Connections—For Discussion or Writing

✗ Look at one or more stories that have been called Kafkaesque, such as Luisa Valenzuela's "The Censors" or Shirley Jackson's "The Lottery." What is Kafka-like about these stories?

✗ Compare the dream element in "Young Goodman Brown" and "The Country Doctor." In what ways are the two stories like dreams?

JUXTAPOSITIONS

Playing the Role

Each of the two stories that follow was written by a writer with a sharp eye for how people act and a quick ear for how people talk. Both authors are alert observers of someone's personal *style*. In both stories, young people without money come downtown to the pricey avenues of Manhattan. They come into stores that they know are not for them. The focus is on their manner: their style of behavior, their style of talking. What is similar, what is different, about the point of view from which we see the events of each story? What do the young people in the stories have in common? What is similar or different about the way they act and talk? Do the stories differ in theme—in what each story as a whole has to say?

Dorothy Parker   *(1893–1967)*

Dorothy Parker, who got her start in the publishing world by working for *Vogue* and *Vanity Fair,* became legendary in the twenties and thirties for her devastating wit. One interviewer said about her, "Her sentences are punctuated with observations phrased with lethal force." Parker was an early regular contributor to the *New Yorker.* She wrote plays for the New York stage and worked on screenplays in Hollywood. She was for a time one of the most widely quoted, praised, and criticized women in the United States.

The Standard of Living   *1926*

Annabel and Midge came out of the tea room with the arrogant slow gait of the leisured, for their Saturday afternoon stretched ahead of them. They had lunched, as was their wont, on sugar, starches, oils, and butter-fats. Usually they ate sandwiches of spongy new white bread greased with butter and mayonnaise; they ate thick wedges of cake lying wet beneath ice cream and whipped cream and melted chocolate gritty with nuts. As alternates, they ate patties, sweating beads of inferior oil, containing bits of bland meat bogged in pale, stiffening sauce; they ate pastries, limber under rigid icing, filled with an indeterminate yellow sweet stuff, not still solid, not yet liquid, like salve that has been left in the sun. They chose no other sort of food, nor did they consider it. And their skin was like the petals of wood anemones, and their bellies were as flat and their flanks as lean as those of young Indian braves.

Annabel and Midge had been best friends almost from the day that Midge had found a job as stenographer with the firm that employed Annabel. By now, Annabel, two years longer in the stenographic department, had worked up to the wages of eighteen dollars and fifty cents a week; Midge was still at sixteen dollars. Each girl lived at home with her family and paid half her salary to its support.

The girls sat side by side at their desks, they lunched together every noon, together they set out for home at the end of the day's work. Many of their evenings and most of their Sundays were passed in each other's company. Often they were joined by two young men, but there was no steadiness to any such quartet; the two young men would give place, un-lamented, to two other young men, and lament would have been inappropriate, really, since the newcomers were scarcely distinguishable from their predecessors. Invariably the girls spent the fine idle hours of their hot-weather Saturday afternoons together. Constant use had not worn ragged the fabric of their friendship.

They looked alike, though the resemblance did not lie in their features. It was in the shape of their bodies, their movements, their style, and their adornments. Annabel and Midge did, and completely, all that young office workers are besought not to do. They painted their lips and their nails, they darkened their lashes and lightened their hair, and scent seemed to shimmer from them. They wore thin, bright dresses, tight over their breasts and high on their legs, and tilted slippers, fancifully strapped. They looked conspicuous and cheap and charming.

Now, as they walked across to Fifth Avenue with their skirts swirled by   5
the hot wind, they received audible admiration. Young men grouped lethargically about newsstands awarded them murmurs, exclamations, even—the ultimate tribute—whistles. Annabel and Midge passed without the condescension of hurrying their pace; they held their heads higher and set their feet with exquisite precision, as if they stepped over the necks of peasants.

Always the girls went to walk on Fifth Avenue on their free afternoons, for it was the ideal ground for their favorite game. The game could be played anywhere, and, indeed, was, but the great shop windows stimulated the two players to their best form.

Annabel had invented the game; or rather she had evolved it from an old one. Basically, it was no more than the ancient sport of what-would-you-do-if-you-had-a-million dollars? But Annabel had drawn a new set of rules for it, had narrowed it, pointed it, made it stricter. Like all games, it was the more absorbing for being more difficult.

Annabel's version went like this: You must suppose that somebody dies and leaves you a million dollars, cool. But there is a condition to the bequest. It is stated in the will that you must spend every nickel of the money on yourself.

There lay the hazard of the game. If, when playing it, you forgot, and listed among your expenditures the rental of a new apartment for your family, for example, you lost your turn to the other player. It was astonishing how many—and some of them among the experts, too—would forfeit all their innings by such slips.

It was essential, of course, that it be played in passionate seriousness.   10
Each purchase must be carefully considered and, if necessary, supported by argument. There was no zest to playing wildly. Once Annabel had introduced the game to Sylvia, another girl who worked in the office. She explained the rules to Sylvia and then offered her the gambit "What would be the first thing you'd do?" Sylvia had not shown the decency of even a second of hesitation. "Well," she said, "the first thing I'd do, I'd go out and hire somebody to shoot Mrs. Gary Cooper, and then . . ." So it is to be seen that she was no fun.

But Annabel and Midge were surely born to be comrades, for Midge played the game like a master from the moment she learned it. It was she who added the touches that made the whole thing cozier. According to Midge's innovations, the eccentric who died and left you the money was not anybody you loved, or, for the matter of that, anybody you even knew. It was somebody who had seen you somewhere and had thought, "That girl ought to have lots of nice things. I'm going to leave her a million dollars when I die." And the death was to be neither untimely nor painful. Your benefactor, full of years and comfortably ready to depart, was to slip softly away during sleep and go right to heaven. These embroideries permitted Annabel and Midge to play their game in the luxury of peaceful consciences.

Midge played with a seriousness that was not only proper but extreme. The single strain on the girls' friendship had followed an announcement once made by Annabel that the first thing she would buy with her million dollars would be a silver-fox coat. It was as if she had struck Midge across the mouth. When Midge recovered her breath, she cried that she couldn't imagine how Annabel could do such a thing—silver-fox coats were common! Annabel defended her taste with the retort that they were not common, either. Midge then said that they were so. She added that everybody had a silver-fox coat. She went on, with perhaps a slight loss of head, to declare that she herself wouldn't be caught dead in silver fox.

For the next few days, though the girls saw each other as constantly, their conversation was careful and infrequent, and they did not once play their game. Then one morning, as soon as Annabel entered the office, she came to Midge and said that she had changed her mind. She would not buy a silver-fox coat with any part of her million dollars. Immediately on receiving the legacy, she would select a coat of mink.

Midge smiled and her eyes shone. "I think," she said, "you're doing absolutely the right thing."

Now, as they walked along Fifth Avenue, they played the game anew. It   15
was one of those days with which September is repeatedly cursed; hot and glaring, with slivers of dust in the wind. People drooped and shambled, but the girls carried themselves tall and walked a straight line, as befitted young heiresses on their afternoon promenade. There was no longer need for them to start the game at its formal opening. Annabel went direct to the heart of it.

"All right," she said. "So you've got this million dollars. So what would be the first thing you'd do?"

"Well, the first thing I'd do," Midge said, "I'd get a mink coat." But she said it mechanically, as if she were giving the memorized answer to an expected question.

"Yes," Annabel said, "I think you ought to. The terribly dark kind of mink." But she, too, spoke as if by rote. It was too hot; fur, no matter how dark and sleek and supple, was horrid to the thoughts.

They stepped along in silence for a while. Then Midge's eye was caught by a shop window. Cool, lovely gleamings were there set off by chaste and elegant darkness.

"No," Midge said, "I take it back. I wouldn't get a mink coat the first thing.   20
Know what I'd do? I'd get a string of pearls. Real pearls."

Annabel's eyes turned to follow Midge's.

"Yes," she said, slowly. "I think that's kind of a good idea. And it would make sense, too. Because you can wear pearls with anything."

Together they went over to the shop window and stood pressed against it. It contained but one object—a double row of great, even pearls clasped by a deep emerald around a little pink velvet throat.

"What do you suppose they cost?" Annabel said.

"Gee, I don't know." Midge said. "Plenty, I guess."   25

"Like a thousand dollars?" Annabel said.

"Oh, I guess like more," Midge said. "On account of the emerald."

"Well, like ten thousand dollars?" Annabel said.

"Gee, I wouldn't even know," Midge said.

The devil nudged Annabel in the ribs. "Dare you to go in and price   30
them," she said.

"Like fun!" Midge said.

"Dare you," Annabel said.

"Why, a store like this wouldn't even be open this afternoon," Midge said.

"Yes, it is so, too," Annabel said. "People just came out. And there's a doorman on. Dare you."

"Well," Midge said. "But you've got to come too."   35

They tendered thanks, icily, to the doorman for ushering them into the shop. It was cool and quiet, a broad, gracious room with paneled walls and soft carpet. But the girls wore expressions of bitter disdain, as if they stood in a sty.

A slim, immaculate clerk came to them and bowed. His neat face showed no astonishment at their appearance.

"Good afternoon," he said. He implied that he would never forget it if they would grant him the favor of accepting his soft-spoken greeting.

"Good afternoon," Annabel and Midge said together, and in like freezing accents.

"Is there something—?" the clerk said.   40

"Oh, we're just looking," Annabel said. It was as if she flung the words down from a dais.

The clerk bowed.

"My friend and myself merely happened to be passing," Midge said, and stopped, seeming to listen to the phrase. "My friend here and myself," she went on, "merely happened to be wondering how much are those pearls you've got in your window."

"Ah, yes," the clerk said. "The double rope. That is two hundred and fifty thousand dollars, Madam."

"I see," Midge said.   45

The clerk bowed. "An exceptionally beautiful necklace," he said. "Would you care to look at it?"

"No, thank you," Annabel said.

"My friend and myself merely happened to be passing," Midge said.

They turned to go; to go, from their manner, where the tumbrel awaited them. The clerk sprang ahead and opened the door. He bowed as they swept by him.

The girls went on along the Avenue and disdain was still on their faces.   50

"Honestly!" Annabel said. "Can you imagine a thing like that?"

"Two hundred and fifty thousand dollars!" Midge said. "That's a quarter of a million dollars right there!"

"He's got his nerve!" Annabel said.

They walked on. Slowly the disdain went, slowly and completely as if drained from them, and with it went the regal carriage and tread. Their shoulders dropped and they dragged their feet; they bumped against each other, without notice or apology, and caromed away again. They were silent and their eyes were cloudy.

Suddenly Midge straightened her back, flung her head high, and spoke,   55
clear and strong.

"Listen, Annabel," she said. "Look. Suppose there was this terribly rich person, see? You don't know this person, but this person has seen you somewhere and wants to do something for you. Well, it's a terribly old person, see? And so this person dies, just like going to sleep, and leaves you ten million dollars. Now, what would be the first thing you'd do?"

The Receptive Reader

1. How well do you come to know the young women? What is their style? How do they dress, act, and talk?

2. What does the game the two young women play tell you about them?

3. Parker was known for her sharp tongue and malicious *wit*. Do these show in the style of this story?

4. What is the author's attitude toward the two young women? How do you think she expects you to react to them?

The Personal Response

Does this story strike you as being based on real life? Do you think this story is out of date?

Toni Cade Bambara   *(born 1939)*   👁

Toni Cade Bambara became known for the stories collected in *Gorilla, My Love* (1972) and *The Sea Birds Are Still Alive* (1977). Her novel *If Blessing Comes* was published in 1987. Born in New York City, with degrees from Queens and City College, she has had an active career as a dancer, teacher, critic, editor, lecturer, civil rights activist, and writer. Anne Tyler has said about the echoes of street talk in Bambara's fiction, "Everything these people say, you feel, ordinary, real-life people are saying right now on any street corner. It's only that the rest of us didn't realize it was sheer poetry they were speaking."

The Lesson   *1972*

Back in the days when everyone was old and stupid or young and fool-ish and me and Sugar were the only ones just right, this lady moved on our block with nappy hair and proper speech and no makeup. And quite natu-rally we laughed at her, and laughed the way we did at the junk man who went about his business like he was some big-time president and his sorry-ass horse his secretary. And we kinda hated her too, hated the way we did the winos who cluttered up our parks and pissed on our handball walls and stank up our hallways and stairs so you couldn't halfway play hide-and-seek without a goddamn gas mask. Miss Moore was her name. The only woman on the block with no first name. And she was black as hell, cept for her feet, which were fish-white and spooky. And she was always planning these boring-ass things for us to do, us being my cousin, mostly, who lived on the block cause we all moved North the same time and to the same apartment then spread out gradual to breathe. And our parents would yank our heads into some kinda shape and crisp up our clothes so we'd be presentable for travel with Miss Moore, who always looked like she was going to church, though she never did. Which is just one of the things the grownups talked about when they talked behind her back like a dog. But when she came calling with some sachet she'd sewed up or some gingerbread she'd made or some book, why then they'd all be too embarrassed to turn her down and we'd get handed over all spruced up. She'd been to college and said it was only right that she should take responsibility for the young ones' edu-cation, and she not even related by marriage or blood. So they'd go for it. Specially Aunt Gretchen. She was the main gofer in the family. You got some ole dumb shit foolishness you want somebody to go for, you send for Aunt Gretchen. She been screwed into the go-along for so long, it's a blood-deep natural thing with her. Which is how she got saddled with me and Sugar and Junior in the first place while our mothers were in a la-de-da apartment up the block having a good ole time.

So this one day Miss Moore rounds us all up at the mailbox and it's puredee hot and she's knockin herself out about arithmetic. And school sup-pose to let up in summer I heard, but she don't never let up. And the starch in my pinafore scratching the shit outta me and I'm really hating this nappy-head bitch and her goddamn college degree. I'd much rather go to the pool or to the show where it's cool. So me and Sugar leaning on the mailbox being surly, which is a Miss Moore word. And Flyboy checking out what everybody brought for lunch. And Fat Butt already wasting his peanut-butter-and-jelly sandwich like the pig he is. And Junebug punchin on Q.T.'s arm for potato chips. And Rosie Giraffe shifting from one hip to the other wait-ing for somebody to step on her foot or ask her if she from Georgia so she can kick ass, preferably Mercedes'. And Miss Moore asking us do we know what money is, like we a bunch of retards. I mean real money, she say, like it's only poker chips or monopoly papers we lay on the grocer. So right away I'm tired of this and say so. And would much rather snatch Sugar and go to the Sunset and terrorize the West Indian kids and take their hair rib-bons and their money too. And Miss Moore files that remark away for next week's lesson on brotherhood, I can tell. And finally I say we oughta get to the subway cause it's cooler and besides we might meet some cute boys. Sugar done swiped her mama's lipstick, so we ready.

So we heading down the street and she's boring us silly about what things cost and what our parents make and how much goes for rent and how money ain't divided up right in this country. And then she gets to the part about we all poor and live in the slums, which I don't feature. And I'm ready to speak on that, but she steps out in the street and hails two cabs just like that. Then she hustles half the crew in with her and hands me a five-dollar bill and tells me to calculate 10 percent tip for the driver. And we're off. Me and Sugar and Junebug and Flyboy hangin out the window and hollering to everybody, putting lipstick on each other cause Flyboy a faggot anyway, and making farts with our sweaty armpits. But I'm mostly trying to figure how to spend this money. But they all fascinated with the meter ticking and Junebug starts laying bets as to how much it'll read when Flyboy can't hold his breath no more. Then Sugar lays bets as to how much it'll be when we get there. So I'm stuck. Don't nobody want to go for my plan, which is to jump out at the next light and run off to the first bar-b-que we can find. Then the driver tells us to get the hell out cause we there already. And the meter reads eighty-five cents. And I'm stalling to figure out the tip and Sugar say give him a dime. And I decide he don't need it bad as I do, so later for him. But then he tries to take off with Junebug foot still in the door so we talk about his mama something ferocious. Then we check out that we on Fifth Avenue and everybody dressed up in stockings. One lady in a fur coat, hot as it is. White folks crazy.

"This is the place," Miss Moore say, presenting it to us in the voice she uses at the museum. "Let's look in the windows before we go in."

"Can we steal?" Sugar asks very serious like she's getting the ground rules   5
squared away before she plays. "I beg your pardon," say Miss Moore, and we fall out. So she leads us around the windows of the toy store and me and Sugar screamin, "This is mine, that's mine, I gotta have that, that was made for me, I was born for that," till Big Butt drowns us out.

"Hey, I'm goin to buy that there."

"That there? You don't even know what it is, stupid."

"I do so," he say punchin on Rosie Giraffe. "It's a microscope."

"Whatcha gonna do with a microscope, fool?"

"Look at things."   10

"Like what, Ronald?" ask Miss Moore. And Big Butt ain't got the first notion. So here go Miss Moore gabbing about the thousands of bacteria in a drop of water and the somethinorother in a speck of blood and the million and one living things in the air around us is invisible to the naked eye. And what she say that for? Junebug go to town on that "naked" and we rolling. Then Miss Moore ask what it cost. So we all jam into the window smudgin it up and the price tag say $300. So then she ask how long'd take for Big Butt and Junebug to save up their allowances. "Too long," I say. "Yeh," adds Sugar, "outgrown it by that time." And Miss Moore say no, you never outgrow learning instruments. "Why, even medical students and interns and," blah, blah, blah. And we ready to choke Big Butt for bringing it up in the first damn place.

"This here costs four hundred eighty dollars," says Rosie Giraffe. So we pile up all over her to see what she pointin out. My eyes tell me it's a chunk of glass cracked with something heavy, and different-color inks dripped into the splits, then the whole thing put into a oven or something. But for $480 it don't make sense.

"That's a paperweight made of semi-precious stones fused together under tremendous pressure," she explains slowly, with her hands doing the mining and all the factory work.

"So what's a paperweight?" asks Rosie Giraffe.

"To weigh paper with, dumbbell," say Flyboy, the wise man from the   15
East.

"Not exactly," say Miss Moore, which is what she say when you warm or way off too. "It's to weigh paper down so it won't scatter and make your desk untidy." So right away me and Sugar curtsy to each other and then to Mercedes who is more the tidy type.

"We don't keep paper on top of the desk in my class," say Junebug, figuring Miss Moore crazy or lyin one.

"At home, then," she say. "Don't you have a calendar and pencil case and a blotter and a letter-opener on your desk at home where you do your homework?" And she know damn well what our homes look like cause she nosys around in them every chance she gets.

"I don't even have a desk," say Junebug. "Do we?"

"No. And I don't get no homework neither," says Big Butt.   20

"And I don't even have a home," say Flyboy like he do at school to keep the white folks off his back and sorry for him. Send this poor kid to camp posters, is his specialty.

"I do," says Mercedes. "I have a box of stationery on my desk and a picture of my cat. My godmother bought the stationery and the desk. There's a big rose on each sheet and the envelopes smell like roses."

"Who wants to know about your smelly-ass stationery," say Rosie Giraffe fore I can get my two cents in.

"It's important to have a work area all your own so that . . ."

"Will you look at this sailboat, please," say Flyboy, cuttin her off and   25
pointin to the thing like it was his. So once again we tumble all over each other to gaze at this magnificent thing in the toy store which is just big enough to maybe sail two kittens across the pond if you strap them to the posts tight. We all start reciting the price tag like we in assembly. "Handcrafted sailboat of fiberglass at one thousand one hundred ninety-five dollars."

"Unbelievable," I hear myself say and am really stunned. I read it again for myself just in case the group recitation put me in a trance. Same thing. For some reason this pisses me off. We look at Miss Moore and she lookin at us, waiting for I dunno what.

"Who'd pay all that when you can buy a sailboat set for a quarter at Pop's, a tube of glue for a dime, and a ball of string for eight cents? It must have a motor and a whole lot else besides," I say. "My sailboat cost me about fifty cents."

"But will it take water?" say Mercedes with her smart ass.

"Took mine to Alley Pond Park once," say Flyboy. "String broke. Lost it. Pity."

"Sailed mine in Central Park and it keeled over and sank. Had to ask my   30
father for another dollar."

"And you got the strap," laugh Big Butt. "The jerk didn't even have a
string on it. My old man wailed on his behind."

Little Q.T. was staring hard at the sailboat and you could see he wanted
it bad. But he too little and somebody'd just take it from him. So what the
hell. "This boat for kids, Miss Moore?"

"Parents silly to buy something like that just to get all broke up," say
Rosie Giraffe.

"That much money it should last forever," I figure.

"My father'd buy it for me if I wanted it."   35

"Your father, my ass," say Rosie Giraffe getting a chance to finally push
Mercedes.

"Must be rich people shop here," say Q.T.

"You are a very bright boy," say Flyboy. "What was your first clue?" And
he rap him on the head with the back of his knuckles, since Q.T. the only
one he could get away with. Though Q.T. liable to come up behind you
years later and get his licks in when you half expect it.

"What I want to know is," I says to Miss Moore though I never talk to
her, I wouldn't give the bitch that satisfaction, "is how much a real boat
costs? I figure a thousand'd get you a yacht any day."

"Why don't you check that out," she says, "and report back to the group?"   40
Which really pains my ass. If you gonna mess up a perfectly good swim day
least you could do is have some answers. "Let's go in," she say like she got
something up her sleeve. Only she don't lead the way. So me and Sugar turn
the corner to where the entrance is, but when we get there I kinda hang
back. Not that I'm scared, what's there to be afraid of, just a toy store. But
I feel funny, shame. But what I got to be shamed about? Got as much right
to go in as anybody. But somehow I can't seem to get hold of the door, so
I step away from Sugar to lead. But she hangs back too. And I look at her
and she looks at me and this is ridiculous. I mean, damn, I have never ever
been shy about doing nothing or going nowhere. But then Mercedes steps
up and then Rosie Giraffe and Big Butt crowd in behind and shove, and
next thing we all stuffed into the doorway with only Mercedes squeezing
past us, smoothing out her jumper and walking right down the aisle. Then
the rest of us tumble in like a glued-together jigsaw done all wrong. And
people lookin at us. And it's like the time me and Sugar crashed into the
Catholic church on a dare. But once we got in there and everything so
hushed and holy and the candles and the bowin and the handkerchiefs on
all the drooping heads, I just couldn't go through with the plan. Which was
for me to run up to the altar and do a tap dance while Sugar played the
nose flute and messed around in the holy water. And Sugar kept givin me
the elbow. Then later teased me so bad I tied her up in the shower and
turned it on and locked her in. And she'd be there till this day if Aunt
Gretchen hadn't finally figured I was lyin about the boarder takin a shower.

Same thing in the store. We all walkin on tiptoe and hardly touchin the
games and puzzles and things. And I watched Miss Moore who is steady
watchin us like she waitin for a sign. Like Mama Drewery watches the sky
and sniffs the air and takes note of just how much slant is in the bird

formation. Then me and Sugar bump smack into each other, so busy gazing at the toys, specially the sailboat. But we don't laugh and go into our fat-lady bump-stomach routine. We just stare at that price tag. Then Sugar run a finger over the whole boat. And I'm jealous and want to hit her. Maybe not her, but I sure want to punch somebody in the mouth.

"Watcha bring us here for, Miss Moore?"

"You sound angry, Sylvia. Are you mad about something?" Givin me one of them grins like she tellin a grown-up joke that never turns out to be funny. And she's lookin very closely at me like maybe she planning to do my portrait from memory. I'm mad, but I won't give her that satisfaction. So I slouch around the store bein very bored and say, "Let's go."

Me and Sugar at the back of the train watchin the tracks whizzin by large then small then getting gobbled up in the dark. I'm thinkin about this tricky toy I saw in the store. A clown that somersaults on a bar then does chin-ups just cause you yank lightly at his leg. Cost $35. I could see me askin my mother for a $35 birthday clown. "You wanna who that costs what?" she'd say, cocking her head to the side to get a better view of the hole in my head. Thirty-five dollars could buy new bunk beds for Junior and Gretchen's boy. Thirty-five dollars and the whole household could go visit Granddaddy Nelson in the country. Thirty-five dollars would pay for the rent and the piano bill too. Who are these people that spend that much for performing clowns and $1000 for toy sailboats? What kinda work they do and how they live and how come we ain't in on it? Where we are is who we are, Miss Moore always pointin out. But it don't necessarily have to be that way, she always adds then waits for somebody to say that poor people have to wake up and demand their share of the pie and don't none of us know what kind of pie she talking about in the first damn place. But she ain't so smart cause I still got her four dollars from the taxi and she sure ain't gettin it. Messin up my day with this shit. Sugar nudges me in my pocket and winks.

Miss Moore lines us up in front of the mailbox where we started from, seem like years ago, and I got a headache for thinkin so hard. And we lean all over each other so we can hold up under the draggy-ass lecture she always finishes us off with at the end before we thank her for borin us to tears. But she just looks at us like she readin tea leaves. Finally she say, "Well, what did you think of F.A.O. Schwarz?"

Rosie Giraffe mumbles, "White folks crazy."

"I'd like to go there again when I get my birthday money," says Mercedes, and we shove her out the pack so she has to lean on the mailbox by herself.

"I'd like a shower. Tiring day," say Flyboy.

Then Sugar surprises me by sayin, "You know, Miss Moore, I don't think all of us here put together eat in a year what that sailboat costs." And Miss Moore lights up like somebody goosed her. "And?" she say, urging Sugar on. Only I'm standin on her foot so she don't continue.

"Imagine for a minute what kind of society it is in which some people can spend on a toy what it would cost to feed a family of six or seven. What do you think?"

"I think," say Sugar pushing me off her feet like she never done before, cause I whip her ass in a minute, "that this is not much of a democracy if you ask me. Equal chance to pursue happiness means an equal crack at the dough, don't it?" Miss Moore is besides herself and I am disgusted with Sugar's treachery. So I stand on her foot one more time to see if she'll shove me. She shuts up, and Miss Moore looks at me, sorrowfully I'm thinkin. And somethin weird is goin on, I can feel it in my chest.

"Anybody else learn anything today?" lookin dead at me. I walk away and Sugar has to run to catch up and don't even seem to notice when I shrug her arm off my shoulder.

"Well, we got four dollars anyway," she says.

"Uh hunh."

"We could go to Hascombs and get half a chocolate layer and then go to the Sunset and still have plenty money for potato chips and ice cream sodas." 55

"Un hunh."

"Race you to Hascombs," she say.

We start down the block and she gets ahead which is O.K. by me cause I'm going to the West End and then over to the Drive to think this day through. She can run if she want to and even run faster. But ain't nobody gonna beat me at nuthin.

The Receptive Reader

1. In this story we see the children from uptown through the eyes of one of their own. How does this *point of view* shape the story as a whole? What do we take in of their behavior, their thinking, their sense of humor? Do you recognize a pattern or a type?

2. How does the tough street language the narrator and her friends speak differ from the genteel middle-class language used by other authors? What distinctive features do you recognize? Do you find the language offensive? Why, or why not?

3. How is Miss Moore introduced to the reader? How do you feel about her at the beginning? How does her role change in the story? Does your estimate of her change?

4. The story reaches a *turning point* when the group comes to the store. What theme becomes overt at this point? (What is "the lesson" promised in the title?) Does the story get too preachy for you?

5. Where does the story go after the climactic episode in the toy store? How does it *end*? What does the ending do for the story as a whole?

6. What do you think is the relationship between the author and the first-person narrator in the story? (What do you think is the distance between the author as a person and the *persona* speaking in the story?)

The Personal Response

People who talk tough may be playing a role. Do you think there is a different personality behind the narrator's public persona?

The Creative Dimension

Write about a situation, real or imagined, in which a central character plays a public role—different from what he or she is when not observed by strangers or outsiders. The central character could be an imaginary third party (as in the Parker story), or *you* could be speaking in the first person as the narrator (as in the Bambara story). Re-create for your readers a manner of behaving, a style of talking. You may want to try your hand at an episode or vignette in which the punch line is "Ain't nobody gonna beat me at nuthin."

WRITING ABOUT LITERATURE

8 Responding to Style
WRITING FOCUS: Reviewing the Writing Process

The Writing Workshop When your writing focuses on an author's style, you pay close attention to detail. You look at word choice—solemn or lighthearted, formal or casual, easily accessible or challenging for the ordinary reader. You look at images that may be ordinary and familiar or that may be striking and provocative. You listen to sentence rhythms with the mind's ear or listen to sample sentences read out loud. Are the sentences sparse and matter-of-fact? Or, at the other extreme, do they have the passionate rhythm or the flourishes that were dear to nineteenth-century readers?

At the same time, you try to see how features of style shape the world of thought and feeling of the story as a whole. You try to trace how a writer's style reflects a personal way of looking at the world.

A Paper from Start to Finish Do you ever suffer from **writer's block?** Do you look too long at a blank screen or crumple up a sheet of paper with notes that did not lead anywhere? Review the steps other writers take to start the flow. Review prewriting and note-taking techniques that help a substantial paper take shape. Review how student writers of sample papers have sorted out and laid out their material, developing an organizing strategy that makes sense to the reader and that the reader can follow.

Brainstorming **Brainstorming** allows you to bring up from hidden corners of your memory material that might prove relevant to your topic. Let us assume you have read Bret Harte's much-anthologized "The Outcasts of Poker Flat." You want to write about it as an example of the sentimentality that is a staple of American popular culture. You start by trying to call up and jot down any phrases, catch words, quotations, images, or incidents connected with your key word. Leave sifting and editing for later. Sample:

> Sentimentality: The word brings to mind true love and romance, life lovingly and beautifully portrayed, with death only a momentary transition to a better place. Every cloud has a silver lining. Life may be harsh and cruel, but redemption and salvation are the eventual outcome. Everything is loaded with sympathy, empathy, compassion, caring. There is some good in everyone. "Life is real; life is earnest." Life is invigorating, challenging.
>
> Death is softened, described almost tenderly. Mother holds the hand of darling child dying of tuberculosis. Dying soldier props himself up on elbow to remember loved ones. The gentle easing from sleep to death. Nothing gory, bloody, sickening.
>
> Hearts, flowers, sunsets, baby shoes. Make the reader feel good. Life may be cruel, but there is justice and beauty. Hallmark greeting cards.

Reading Notes   Focus your reading notes on questions of tone or style. Look for possible connections; try to be open to a possible pattern that might emerge. Sample notes:

appeal to our sympathy: the heartless, self-righteous townspeople turn out the band of sinners in the dead of winter

(Holman and Harmon on sentimentality in *A Handbook of Literature:* "an optimistic overemphasis on the goodness of humanity")

finding goodness in unexpected places: Oakhurst, the gambler, gives up his horse to the Duchess, trading for her "sorry mule"; later, Oakhurst decides to stay with his "weaker and more pitiable companions"

the naive young "innocents": "they unaffectedly exchanged a kiss, so honest and sincere that it might have been heard above the swaying pines"; note: the naive purity of the innocents softens the hardened sinners

Mother Shipton, notorious for her coarse language and violent oaths, becomes the hooker with the heart of gold who starves herself so that the virginal Piney may eat an additional portion of the rations and so have a chance to live

final good deed: Oakhurst piles firewood by the cabin before he dies with a flourish, "handing in his checks"

softening of death: the Duchess and Piney (sin and innocence) die "locked in each other's arms," with the "younger and purer pillowing the head of her soiled sister upon her virgin breast"; they "fall asleep"; the fatal blizzard becomes a flurry of soft flakes—"feathery drifts of snow" cover the dead

saving touches of grim realism: Uncle Billy is a true rascal and hard-bitten cynic (and he survives when the others die); the hypocritical citizens of Poker Flat are satirized for their self-righteousness

Structuring Your Paper   Look at the way the following paper plays off two different facets of an author's style in an "on-the-one-hand" and "on-the-other-hand" pattern:

The Sentimental Sinners of Poker Flat

(Introduction: defining the key term)

Driven out of town by the moral majority, "The Outcasts of Poker Flat" perish (with one exception) in an early snowstorm that traps them in the mountains. Two prostitutes, a gambler, and a drunk—these, along with two innocents, are the main characters of Bret Harte's sentimental tale. In sentimental writing, the tender emotions, such as love and pity, are superabundant, and evil exists mainly to stimulate our pity for the victims and our moral indignation. We feel tender pity for the innocent victims and we feel a warm glow of emotion when evildoers repent or show an unexpected noble side.

(Thesis: a sentimental story saved from mawkishness)

Bret Harte's characters do indeed act their parts in a story that has most of the elements of nineteenth-century sentimentality. Nevertheless, somehow the story does not leave us with that sickeningly sweet, cloying sensation that a truly sentimental narrative often produces. Harte's skillful use of humor rescues "The Outcasts" from complete mawkishness.

(First major point: the sentimental side of the story)

The story is indeed sentimental. A group of characters who are extremely unlikely candidates for sainthood nevertheless exhibit heroic virtue and selflessness. Their ordeal, rather than demonstrating the baseness of human nature, shows humanity's basic goodness. The only appearance of anything less than virtuous is in Uncle Billy, the drunk. He steals away in the night with the mules, stranding the others in the snowstorm. The rest of the group are inspired to attain a saintly goodness. There is no fighting over food or shelter; each individual is concerned only for the others.. . .

(Further follow-up of first point: clinching examples)

The real heroics, though, come from the greatest "sinners," in true sentimental fashion. The gambler, Oakhurst, although he is known to be "a coolly desperate man," never "thought of deserting his weaker and more pitiable companions." Mother Shipton, the legendary prostitute with a heart of gold, starves herself to save the young virgin.

(Turning point of the essay: Harte's saving humor)

However, Harte's story as a whole is more successful and more enjoyable than this description would suggest. Humor is the key to Harte's success. Harte's wry humor—a Western, often ironic brand—runs throughout the story, setting it apart from other sentimental writing and allowing a modern reader to appreciate it. The beginning of the story sets the tone: The community of Poker Flat, having lately suffered the loss of "several thousand dollars, two valuable horses," and (almost as an afterthought) "a prominent citizen," is experiencing "a spasm of virtuous reaction." The real reason the townspeople are after Oakhurst is not simply that he is a gambler but that he is a better one than they are—and they want their money back. Oakhurst himself is presented as a worldly-wise character who looks at life with dry ironic humor: "With him life was at best an uncertain game, and he rec- ognized the usual percentage in favor of the dealer."

(Conclusion: sentimental ending with a final humorous touch)

The ending of the story is the closest approach to cloying sentimentality. The vir- gin and the prostitute huddle together in the snow and freeze to death in each other's arms. However, the story does not end there but with a final touch of humor. Oakhurst has left his own epitaph, scribbled on the deuce of clubs and pinned to a tree with a knife. In keeping with his character, it reads: "Beneath this tree lies the body of John Oakhurst, who struck a streak of bad luck . . . and handed in his checks on the 7th December, 1850."

Questions for Peer Review

How does the student paper go beyond the material collected in the reading notes? How does it go beyond the trial definition of sentimen- tality? Do you wish the paper could have included more of the striking details and quoted phrases from the reading notes? Which would you like to see included? Answer the following questions, and compare your answers with those of classmates or members of a small group.

1. How would you sum up the opening *definition* of sentimentality in the first paragraph? Are you familiar with the concept as presented here? Or is it in some way different or new? Does it remind you of examples of sentimentality that you yourself have observed?

2. Where does the writer first state the *thesis* of the paper? Is it echoed again later in the paper?

3. What is the student writer's *follow-up* for the initial definition of senti- mentality? Does the student writer show that all or most parts of the definition apply to this story? How and where? What are the most striking examples?

4. Do the examples in the paper show you that Harte has a wry sense of *humor?* What is humorous about the solid citizens of Poker Flat? Does Uncle Billy seem to have a humorous side?

5. *Irony* becomes the counterpoint to sentimentality in this student writer's discussion of Harte's story. What is irony, and in how many ways can you see it at work in the story? The gambler becomes a central character in the story. What is ironic about his role?

6. In his time, Harte found a large appreciative *audience.* Do you think readers of your generation could relate to the sentimental side of the story? (Do you think they would consider it "mawkish"?) Do you think readers of your generation could relate to the ironic side of the story? (Would they consider it cynical?) Do you think they could relate to Harte's blend of the two? Why, or why not?

> *"Art transcends its limitations only by staying within them."*

Flannery O'Connor

*No writer is a pessimist; the very act of writing is
an optimistic act.*

                              FLANNERY O'CONNOR

FOCUS ON THE WRITER

To do justice to a story, we need to read it on its own terms. We should let it create its own world, its own version of reality. In practice, however, we often do not read an anonymous story. We read James Joyce or Alice Walker or Flannery O'Connor. Reading an unfamiliar story by a familiar writer, we may feel like a traveler recognizing landmarks. We find our bearings more easily than in reading an unknown author. We recognize the writer's voice: a familiar solemn or ironic tone; a familiar mood of foreboding or expectation; a way of looking at places and people.

Critics try to help you understand an individual work of literature by placing it in a larger **context.** They help you see it in relation to the author's life and work. As you read Kafka, an awareness of his Jewish roots may help you relate to his sense of living in a world that threatens to spin out of control, of coping with developments that are absurd and should never have happened. As you come to know the life and work of an author, you bring expectations to a story, and you can take pleasure in seeing them fulfilled. At the same time, you need to expect the unexpected. You need to remain flexible enough to see a side of the author that you did not notice before.

FLANNERY O'CONNOR:
AUTHOR AND WORK

*The creator of our nature has also imparted to us
the character of love. . . . If love is absent, all the
elements of the image are deformed.*

                              GREGORY OF NYSSA

*With the serious writer, violence is never an end
in itself. It is the extreme situation that best reveals what we are essentially, and I believe these
are the times when writers are more interested in
what we are essentially than in the tenor of our
daily lives.*

                              FLANNERY O'CONNOR

When Flannery O'Connor (1924–1964) was asked to name the most important influences on her life, she replied they were probably "being a Catholic and a Southerner and a writer." O'Connor was a devout Catholic in the Baptist South; she attended Catholic schools before she went to Georgia Women's College. Readers of her fiction encounter two sides of a central paradox: Her characters live in a violent world in which evil seems to triumph. But her stories are written by an author who believes in redemption, in divine grace, in the supremacy of God's mercy. She once said that a writer of fiction is "concerned with ultimate mystery as we find it embodied in the concrete world of sense experience."

O'Connor grew up in Savannah and Milledgeville, Georgia, in the segregated South, in a landscape dotted with sharecroppers' shacks. When a Southern novelist was asked why the South had produced so many of America's best writers, he pointed to the lost war that made the Southern experience different from that of the North. O'Connor commented on his reply that he

> didn't mean by that simply that a lost war makes good subject matter. What he was saying was that we had our Fall. We have gone into the modern world with an inburnt knowledge of human limitations and with a sense of mystery which could not have developed in our first state of innocence—as it has not sufficiently developed in the rest of the country.

O'Connor was a master of the **grotesque**—the freakish mixture of the frightening and the comic. She had a sharp eye for the laughable, for the absurd. ("It is not surprising that she first wanted to be a cartoonist, and sent off cartoons, week after week, to *The New Yorker,* where they were invariably rejected"—Joyce Carol Oates.) But in her fiction, horror and comedy mingle, and laughter is muted by our sense of unease, fear, and puzzlement as we watch her parables of antagonism and violence unfold. It is as if she had some implied vision of humankind in harmony with God's purposes by which our imperfect, sinful human reality is judged and found wanting—and laughable. She said:

> Whenever I am asked why Southern writers particularly have a penchant for writing about freaks, I say it is because we are still able to recognize one. To be able to recognize a freak, you have to have some conception of the whole man, and in the South the general conception of man is still, in the main, theological.

Even the good, in O'Connor's view, had traits of the freakish, the grotesque, because "in us the good is something under construction."

O'Connor suffered from a debilitating hereditary illness (lupus), and she was on crutches during most of her writing life. Some of her best work was not published until after her early death at age thirty-nine. Joyce Carol Oates said of her, "we measure an artist by the quality and depth of interior vision, and by the magnitude of achievement, and by these standards Flannery O'Connor is one of our finest writers." Her work "is a deeply moving, deeply disturbing, and ultimately a very beautiful record of a highly complex woman artist whose art was, perhaps, too profound for even the critic in her to grasp."

The following widely read story may be the first O'Connor story you encounter. As you start reading it, what about it seems familiar, reassuring, or easy to understand? Where or how does it become strange or perturbing? Overall, how do you react to the story?

A Good Man Is Hard to Find   1955 👁

The grandmother didn't want to go to Florida. She wanted to visit some of her connections in east Tennessee and she was seizing every chance to change Bailey's mind. Bailey was the son she lived with, her only boy. He was sitting on the edge of his chair at the table, bent over the orange sports section of the *Journal*. "Now look here, Bailey," she said, "see here, read this," and she stood with one hand on her thin hip and the other rattling the newspaper at his bald head. "Here this fellow that calls himself The Misfit is aloose from the Federal Pen and headed toward Florida and you read here what it says he did to these people. Just you read it. I wouldn't take my children in any direction with a criminal like that aloose in it. I couldn't answer to my conscience if I did."

Bailey didn't look up from his reading so she wheeled around then and faced the children's mother, a young woman in slacks, whose face was as broad and innocent as a cabbage and was tied around with a green headkerchief that had two points on the top like rabbit's ears. She was sitting on the sofa, feeding the baby his apricots out of a jar. "The children have been to Florida before," the old lady said. "You all ought to take them somewhere else for a change so they would see different parts of the world and be broad. They never have been to east Tennessee."

The children's mother didn't seem to hear her, but the eight-year-old boy, John Wesley, a stocky child with glasses, said, "If you don't want to go to Florida, why dontcha stay at home?" He and the little girl, June Star, were reading the funny papers on the floor.

"She wouldn't stay at home to be queen for a day," June Star said without raising her yellow head.

"Yes, and what would you do if this fellow, The Misfit, caught you?" the   5
grandmother asked.

"I'd smack his face," John Wesley said.

"She wouldn't stay at home for a million bucks," June Star said. "Afraid she'd miss something. She has to go everywhere we go."

"All right, Miss," the grandmother said. "Just remember that the next time you want me to curl your hair."

June Star said her hair was naturally curly.

The next morning the grandmother was the first one in the car, ready to   10
go. She had her big black valise that looked like the head of a hippopotamus in one corner, and underneath it she was hiding a basket with Pitty Sing, the cat, in it. She didn't intend for the cat to be left alone in the house for three days because he would miss her too much and she was afraid he might brush against one of the gas burners and accidentally asphyxiate himself. Her son, Bailey, didn't like to arrive at a motel with a cat.

She sat in the middle of the back seat with John Wesley and June Star on either side of her. Bailey and the children's mother and the baby sat in the front and they left Atlanta at eight forty-five with the mileage on the car at 55890. The grandmother wrote this down because she thought it would be interesting to say how many miles they had been when they got back. It took them twenty minutes to reach the outskirts of the city.

The old lady settled herself comfortably, removing her white cotton gloves and putting them up with her purse on the shelf in front of the back window. The children's mother still had on slacks and still had her head tied up in a green kerchief, but the grandmother had on a navy blue straw sailor hat with a bunch of white violets on the brim and a navy blue dress with a small white dot in the print. Her collar and cuffs were white organdy trimmed with lace and at her neckline she had pinned a purple spray of cloth violets containing a sachet. In case of an accident, anyone seeing her dead on the highway would know at once that she was a lady.

She said she thought it was going to be a good day for driving, neither too hot nor too cold, and she cautioned Bailey that the speed limit was fifty-five miles an hour and that the patrolmen hid themselves behind bill-boards and small clumps of trees and sped out after you before you had a chance to slow down. She pointed out interesting details of the scenery: Stone Mountain; the blue granite that in some places came up to both sides of the highway; the brilliant red clay banks slightly streaked with purple; and the various crops that made rows of green lace-work on the ground. The trees were full of silver-white sunlights and the meanest of them sparkled. The children were reading comic magazines and their mother had gone back to sleep.

"Let's go through Georgia fast so we won't have to look at it much," John Wesley said.

"If I were a little boy," said the grandmother, "I wouldn't talk about my   15
native state that way. Tennessee has the mountains and Georgia has the hills."

"Tennessee is just a hillbilly dumping ground," John Wesley said, "and Georgia is a lousy state too."

"You said it," June Star said.

"In my time," said the grandmother, folding her thin veined fingers, "children were more respectful of their native states and their parents and everything else. People did right then. Oh look at the cute little pickaninny!" she said and pointed to a Negro child standing in the door of a shack. "Wouldn't that make a picture, now?" she asked and they all turned and looked at the little Negro out of the back window. He waved.

"He didn't have any britches on," June Star said.

"He probably didn't have any," the grandmother explained. "Little niggers   20
in the country don't have things like we do. If I could paint, I'd paint that picture," she said.

The children exchanged comic books.

The grandmother offered to hold the baby and the children's mother passed him over the front seat to her. She set him on her knee and bounced him and told him about the things they were passing. She rolled her eyes and screwed up her mouth and stuck her leathery thin face into his smooth bland one. Occasionally he gave her a faraway smile. They passed a large cotton field with five or six graves fenced in the middle of it, like a small island. "Look at the graveyard!" the grandmother said, pointing it out. "That was the old family burying ground. That belonged to the plantation."

"Where's the plantation?" John Wesley asked.

"Gone With the Wind," said the grandmother. "Ha. Ha."

When the children finished all the comic books they had brought, they   25
opened the lunch and ate it. The grandmother ate a peanut butter sandwich and an olive and would not let the children throw the box and the paper napkins out the window. When there was nothing else to do they played a game by choosing a cloud and making the other two guess what shape it suggested. John Wesley took one the shape of a cow and June Star guessed a cow and John Wesley said, no, an automobile, and June Star said he didn't play fair, and they began to slap each other over the grandmother.

The grandmother said she would tell them a story if they would keep quiet. When she told a story, she rolled her eyes and waved her head and was very dramatic. She said once when she was a maiden lady she had been courted by a Mr. Edgar Atkins Teagarden from Jasper, Georgia. She said he was a very good-looking man and a gentleman and that he brought her a watermelon every Saturday afternoon with his initials cut in it, E.A.T. Well, one Saturday, she said, Mr. Teagarden brought the watermelon and there was nobody at home and he left it on the front porch and returned in his buggy to Jasper, but she never got the watermelon, she said, because a nigger boy ate it when he saw the initials, E.A.T.! This story tickled John Wesley's funny bone and he giggled and giggled but June Star didn't think it was any good. She said she wouldn't marry a man that just brought her a watermelon on Saturday. The grandmother said she would have done well to marry Mr. Teagarden because he was a gentleman and had bought Coca-Cola stock when it first came out and that he had died only a few years ago, a very wealthy man.

They stopped at The Tower for barbecued sandwiches. The Tower was a part-stucco and part-wood filling station and dance hall set in a clearing outside of Timothy. A fat man named Red Sammy Butts ran it and there were signs stuck here and there on the building and for miles up and down the highway saying, TRY RED SAMMY'S FAMOUS BARBECUE. NONE LIKE FAMOUS RED SAMMY'S! RED SAM! THE FAT BOY WITH THE HAPPY LAUGH. A VETERAN! RED SAMMY'S YOUR MAN!

Red Sammy was lying on the bare ground outside The Tower with his head under a truck while a gray monkey about a foot high, chained to a small chinaberry tree, chattered nearby. The monkey sprang back into the tree and got on the highest limb as soon as he saw the children jump out of the car and run toward him.

Inside, The Tower was a long dark room with a counter at one end and tables at the other and dancing space in the middle. They all sat down at a broad table next to the nickelodeon and Red Sam's wife, a tall burnt-brown woman with hair and eyes lighter than her skin, came and took their order. The children's mother put a dime in the machine and played "The Tennessee Waltz," and the grandmother said that tune always made her want to dance. She asked Bailey if he would like to dance but he only glared at her. He didn't have a naturally sunny disposition like she did and trips made him nervous. The grandmother's brown eyes were very bright. She swayed her head from side to side and pretended she was dancing in her chair. June Star said play something she could tap to so the children's mother put in another dime and played a fast number and June Star stepped out onto the dance floor and did her tap routine.

"Ain't she cute?" Red Sam's wife said, leaning over the counter. "Would   30 you like to come be my little girl?"

"No, I certainly wouldn't," June Star said. "I wouldn't live in a broken-down place like this for a million bucks!" and she ran back to the table.

"Ain't she cute?" the woman repeated, stretching her mouth politely.

"Aren't you ashamed?" hissed the grandmother.

Red Sam came in and told his wife to quit lounging on the counter and hurry up with these people's order. His khaki trousers reached just to his hip bones and his stomach hung over them like a sack of meal swaying under his shirt. He came over and sat down at a table nearby and let out a combination sigh and yodel. "You can't win," he said. "You can't win," and he wiped his sweating red face off with a gray handkerchief. "These days you don't know who to trust," he said. "Ain't that the truth?"

"People are certainly not nice like they used to be," said the grandmother.   35

"Two fellers come in here last week," Red Sammy said, "driving a Chrysler. It was an old beat-up car but it was a good one and these boys looked all right to me. Said they worked at the mill and you know I let them fellers charge the gas they bought? Now why did I do that?"

"Because you're a good man!" the grandmother said at once.

"Yes'm, I suppose so," Red Sam said as if he were struck with this answer.

His wife brought the orders, carrying the five plates all at once without a tray, two in each hand and one balanced on her arm. "It isn't a soul in this green world of God's that you can trust," she said. "And I don't count nobody out of that, not nobody," she repeated, looking at Red Sammy.

"Did you read about that criminal, The Misfit, that's escaped?" asked the   40 grandmother.

"I wouldn't be a bit surprised if he didn't attack this place right here," said the woman. "If he hears about it being here, I wouldn't be none surprised to see him. If he hears it's two cent in the cash register, I wouldn't be a tall surprised if he . . ."

"That'll do," Red Sam said. "Go bring these people their Co'-Colas," and the woman went off to get the rest of the order.

"A good man is hard to find," Red Sammy said. "Everything is getting terrible. I remember the day you could go off and leave your screen door unlatched. Not no more."

He and the grandmother discussed better times. The old lady said that in her opinion Europe was entirely to blame for the way things were now. She said the way Europe acted you would think we were made of money and Red Sam said it was no use talking about it, she was exactly right. The children ran outside into the white sunlight and looked at the monkey in the lacy chinaberry tree. He was busy catching fleas on himself and biting each one carefully between his teeth as if it were a delicacy.

They drove off again into the hot afternoon. The grandmother took cat   45 naps and woke up every few minutes with her own snoring. Outside of Toombsboro she woke up and recalled an old plantation that she had visited in this neighborhood once when she was a young lady. She said the house had six white columns across the front and that there was an avenue of oaks leading up to it and two little wooden trellis arbors on either side in front where you sat down with your suitor after a stroll in the garden. She recalled exactly which road to turn off to get to it. She knew that Bailey would not be willing to lose any time looking at an old house, but the more she talked about it, the more she wanted to see it once again and find out if the little twin arbors were still standing. "There was a secret panel in this house," she said craftily, not telling the truth but wishing that she were, "and the story went that all the family silver was hidden in it when Sherman came through but it was never found . . ."

"Hey!" John Wesley said. "Let's go see it! We'll find it! We'll poke all the woodwork and find it! Who lives there? Where do you turn off at? Hey Pop, can't we turn off there?"

"We never have seen a house with a secret panel!" June Star shrieked. "Let's go to the house with the secret panel! Hey, Pop, can't we go see the house with the secret panel!"

"It's not far from here, I know," the grandmother said. "It wouldn't take over twenty minutes."

Bailey was looking straight ahead. His jaw was as rigid as a horseshoe. "No," he said.

The children began to yell and scream that they wanted to see the house   50
with the secret panel. John Wesley kicked the back of the front seat and June Star hung over her mother's shoulder and whined desperately into her ear that they never had any fun even on their vacation, that they could never do what THEY wanted to do. The baby began to scream and John Wesley kicked the back of the seat so hard that his father could feel the blows in his kidney.

"All right!" he shouted and drew the car to a stop at the side of the road. "Will you all shut up? Will you all just shut up for one second? If you don't shut up, we won't go anywhere."

"It would be very educational for them," the grandmother murmured.

"All right," Bailey said, "but get this. This is the only time we're going to stop for anything like this. This is the one and only time."

"The dirt road that you have to turn down is about a mile back," the grandmother directed. "I marked it when we passed."

"A dirt road," Bailey groaned.   55

After they had turned around and were headed toward the dirt road, the grandmother recalled other points about the house, the beautiful glass over the front doorway and the candle lamp in the hall. John Wesley said that the secret panel was probably in the fireplace.

"You can't go inside this house," Bailey said. "You don't know who lives there."

"While you all talk to the people in front, I'll run around behind and get in a window," John Wesley suggested.

"We'll all stay in the car," his mother said.

They turned onto the dirt road and the car raced roughly along in a swirl   60
of pink dust. The grandmother recalled the times when there were no paved roads and thirty miles was a day's journey. The dirt road was hilly and there were sudden washes in it and sharp curves on dangerous embankments. All

at once they would be on a hill, looking down over the blue tops of trees for miles around, then the next minute, they would be in a red depression with the dust-coated trees looking down on them.

"This place had better turn up in a minute," Bailey said, "or I'm going to turn around."

The road looked as if no one had traveled on it in months.

"It's not much farther," the grandmother said and just as she said it, a horrible thought came to her. The thought was so embarrassing that she turned red in the face and her eyes dilated and her feet jumped up, upsetting her valise in the corner. The instant the valise moved, the newspaper top she had over the basket under it rose with a snarl and Pitty Sing, the cat, sprang onto Bailey's shoulder.

The children were thrown to the floor and their mother, clutching the baby, was thrown out the door onto the ground; the old lady was thrown into the front seat. The car turned over once and landed right-side-up in a gulch on the side of the road. Bailey remained in the driver's seat with the cat—gray-striped with a broad white face and an orange nose—clinging to his neck like a caterpillar.

As soon as the children saw they could move their arms and legs, they   65 scrambled out of the car, shouting, "We've had an ACCIDENT!" The grandmother was curled up under the dashboard, hoping she was injured so that Bailey's wrath would not come down on her all at once. The horrible thought she had had before the accident was that the house she had remembered so vividly was not in Georgia but in Tennessee.

Bailey removed the cat from his neck with both hands and flung it out the window against the side of a pine tree. Then he got out of the car and started looking for the children's mother. She was sitting against the side of the red gutted ditch, holding the screaming baby, but she only had a cut down her face and a broken shoulder. "We've had an ACCIDENT!" the children screamed in a frenzy of delight.

"But nobody's killed," June Star said with disappointment as the grandmother limped out of the car, her hat still pinned to her head but the broken front brim standing up at a jaunty angle and the violet spray hanging off the side. They all sat down in the ditch, except the children, to recover from the shock. They were all shaking.

"Maybe a car will come along," said the children's mother hoarsely.

"I believe I have injured an organ," said the grandmother, pressing her side, but no one answered her. Bailey's teeth were clattering. He had on a yellow sport shirt with bright blue parrots designed in it and his face was as yellow as the shirt. The grandmother decided that she would not mention that the house was in Tennessee.

The road was about ten feet above and they could see only the tops of   70 the trees on the other side of it. Behind the ditch they were sitting in there were more woods, tall and dark and deep. In a few minutes they saw a car some distance away on top of a hill, coming slowly as if the occupants were watching them. The grandmother stood up and waved both arms dramatically to attract their attention. The car continued to come on slowly, disappeared around a bend and appeared again, moving even slower, on top of the hill they had gone over. It was a big black battered hearselike automobile. There were three men in it.

It came to a stop over them and for some minutes, the driver looked down with a steady expressionless gaze to where they were sitting, and didn't speak. Then he turned his head and muttered something to the other two and they got out. One was a fat boy in black trousers and a red sweat shirt with a silver stallion embossed on the front of it. He moved around on the right side of them and stood staring, his mouth partly open in a kind of loose grin. The other had on khaki pants and a blue striped coat and a gray hat pulled down very low, hiding most of his face. He came around slowly on the left side. Neither spoke.

The driver got out of the car and stood by the side of it, looking down at them. He was an older man than the other two. His hair was just beginning to gray and he wore silver-rimmed spectacles that gave him a scholarly look. He had a long creased face and didn't have on any shirt or undershirt. He had on blue jeans that were too tight for him and was holding a black hat and a gun. The two boys also had guns.

"We've had an ACCIDENT!" the children screamed.

The grandmother had the peculiar feeling that the bespectacled man was someone she knew. His face was as familiar to her as if she had known him all her life but she could not recall who he was. He moved away from the car and began to come down the embankment, placing his feet carefully so that he wouldn't slip. He had on tan and white shoes and no socks, and his ankles were red and thin. "Good afternoon," he said. "I see you all had you a little spill."

"We turned over twice!" said the grandmother.   75

"Oncet," he corrected. "We seen it happen. Try their car and see will it run, Hiram," he said quietly to the boy with the gray hat.

"What you got that gun for?" John Wesley asked. "Whatcha gonna do with that gun?"

"Lady," the man said to the children's mother, "would you mind calling them children to sit down by you? Children make me nervous. I want all you all to sit down right together there where you're at."

"What are you telling us what to do for?" June Star asked.

Behind them the line of woods gaped like a dark open mouth. "Come   80 here," said their mother.

"Look here now," Bailey began suddenly, "we're in a predicament! We're in . . ."

The grandmother shrieked. She scrambled to her feet and stood staring. "You're The Misfit!" she said. "I recognized you at once!"

"Yes'm," the man said, smiling slightly as if he were pleased in spite of himself to be known, "but it would have been better for all of you, lady, if you hadn't of reckernized me."

Bailey turned his head sharply and said something to his mother that   85 shocked even the children. The old lady began to cry and The Misfit reddened.

"Lady," he said, "don't you get upset. Sometimes a man says things he don't mean. I don't reckon he meant to talk to you thataway."

"You wouldn't shoot a lady, would you?" the grandmother said and removed a clean handkerchief from her cuff and began to slap at her eyes
with it.

The Misfit pointed the toe of his shoe into the ground and made a little
hole and then covered it up again. "I would hate to have to," he said.

"Listen," the grandmother almost screamed, "I know you're a good man.
You don't look a bit like you have common blood. I know you must come
from nice people!"

"Yes mam," he said, "finest people in the world." When he smiled he   90
showed a row of strong white teeth. "God never made a finer woman than
my mother and my daddy's heart was pure gold," he said. The boy with the
red sweat shirt had come around behind them and was standing with his
gun at his hip. The Misfit squatted down on the ground. "Watch them children, Bobby Lee," he said. "You know they make me nervous." He looked
at the six of them huddled together in front of him and he seemed to be
embarrassed as if he couldn't think of anything to say. "Ain't a cloud in the
sky," he remarked, looking up at it. "Don't see no sun but don't see no
cloud neither."

"Yes, it's a beautiful day," said the grandmother. "Listen," she said, "you
shouldn't call yourself The Misfit because I know you're a good man at
heart. I can just look at you and tell."

"Hush!" Bailey yelled. "Hush! Everybody shut up and let me handle this!"
He was squatting in the position of a runner about to spring forward but he
didn't move.

"I pre-chate that, lady," The Misfit said and drew a little circle in the
ground with the butt of his gun.

"It'll take a half a hour to fix this here car," Hiram called, looking over
the raised hood of it.

"Well, first you and Bobby Lee get him and that little boy to step over   95
yonder with you," The Misfit said, pointing to Bailey and John Wesley. "The
boys want to ask you something," he said to Bailey. "Would you mind stepping back in them woods there with them?"

"Listen," Bailey began, "we're in a terrible predicament! Nobody realizes
what this is," and his voice cracked. His eyes were as blue and intense as
the parrots in his shirt and he remained perfectly still.

The grandmother reached up to adjust her hat brim as if she were going
to the woods with him but it came off in her hand. She stood staring at it
and after a second she let it fall on the ground. Hiram pulled Bailey up by
the arm as if he were assisting an old man. John Wesley caught hold of his
father's hand and Bobby Lee followed. They went off toward the woods and
just as they reached the dark edge, Bailey turned and supporting himself
against a gray naked pine trunk, he shouted, "I'll be back in a minute,
Mamma, wait on me!"

"Come back this instant!" his mother shrilled but they all disappeared into
the woods.

"Bailey Boy!" the grandmother called in a tragic voice but she found she
was looking at The Misfit squatting on the ground in front of her. "I just
know you're a good man," she said desperately. "You're not a bit common!"

"Nome, I ain't a good man," The Misfit said after a second as if he had 100 considered her statement carefully, "but I ain't the worst in the world neither. My daddy said I was a different breed of dog from my brothers and sisters. 'You know,' Daddy said, 'it's some that can live their whole life out without asking about it and it's others has to know why it is, and this boy is one of the latters. He's going to be into everything!' " He put on his black hat and looked up suddenly and then away deep into the woods as if he were embarrassed again. "I'm sorry I don't have on a shirt before you ladies," he said, hunching his shoulders slightly. "We buried our clothes that we had on when we escaped and we're just making do until we can get better. We borrowed these from some folks we met," he explained.

"That's perfectly all right," the grandmother said. "Maybe Bailey has an extra shirt in his suitcase."

"I'll look and see terrectly," The Misfit said.

"Where are they taking him?" the children's mother screamed.

"Daddy was a card himself," The Misfit said. "You couldn't put anything over on him. He never got in trouble with the Authorities though. Just had the knack of handling them."

"You could be honest too if you'd only try," said the grandmother. "Think 105 how wonderful it would be to settle down and live a comfortable life and not have to think about somebody chasing you all the time."

The Misfit kept scratching in the ground with the butt of his gun as if he were thinking about it. "Yes'm, somebody is always after you," he murmured.

The grandmother noticed how thin his shoulder blades were just behind his hat because she was standing up looking down on him. "Do you ever pray?" she asked.

He shook his head. All she saw was the black hat wiggle between his shoulder blades. "Nome," he said.

There was a pistol shot from the woods, followed closely by another. Then silence. The old lady's head jerked around. She could hear the wind move through the tree tops like a long satisfied insuck of breath. "Bailey Boy!" she called.

"I was a gospel singer for a while," The Misfit said. "I been most every- 110 thing. Been in the arm service, both land and sea, at home and abroad, been twict married, been an undertaker, been with the railroads, plowed Mother Earth, been in a tornado, seen a man burnt alive oncet," and he looked up at the children's mother and the little girl who were sitting close together, their faces white and their eyes glassy; "I even seen a woman flogged," he said.

"Pray, pray," the grandmother began, "pray, pray . . ."

"I never was a bad boy that I remember of," The Misfit said in an almost dreamy voice, "but somewheres along the line I done something wrong and got sent to the penitentiary. I was buried alive," and he looked up and held her attention to him by a steady stare.

"That's when you should have started to pray," she said. "What did you do to get sent to the penitentiary that first time?"

"Turn to the right, it was a wall," The Misfit said, looking up again at the cloudless sky. "Turn to the left, it was a wall. Look up it was a ceiling, look

down it was a floor. I forget what I done, lady. I set there and set there, trying to remember what it was I done and I ain't recalled it to this day. Oncet
in a while, I would think it was coming to me, but it never come."

"Maybe they put you in by mistake," the old lady said vaguely.   115

"Nome," he said. "It wasn't no mistake. They had the papers on me."

"You must have stolen something," she said.

The Misfit sneered slightly. "Nobody had nothing I wanted," he said. "It
was a head-doctor at the penitentiary said what I had done was kill my
daddy but I known that for a lie. My daddy died in nineteen ought nineteen
of the epidemic flu and I never had a thing to do with it. He was buried in
the Mount Hopewell Baptist churchyard and you can go there and see for
yourself."

"If you would pray," the old lady said, "Jesus would help you."

"That's right," The Misfit said.   120

"Well then, why don't you pray?" she asked trembling with delight
suddenly.

"I don't want no hep," he said. "I'm doing all right by myself."

Bobby Lee and Hiram came ambling back from the woods. Bobby Lee
was dragging a yellow shirt with bright blue parrots in it.

"Throw me that shirt, Bobby Lee," The Misfit said. The shirt came flying
at him and landed on his shoulder and he put it on. The grandmother
couldn't name what the shirt reminded her of. "No, lady," The Misfit said
while he was buttoning up, "I found out the crime don't matter. You can do
one thing or you can do another, kill a man or take a tire off his car, because sooner or later you're going to forget what it was you done and just
be punished for it."

The children's mother had begun to make heaving noises as if she couldn't   125
get her breath. "Lady," he asked, "would you and that little girl like to step
off yonder with Bobby Lee and Hiram and join your husband?"

"Yes, thank you," the mother said faintly. Her left arm dangled helplessly
and she was holding the baby, who had gone to sleep, in the other. "Hep
that lady up, Hiram," The Misfit said as she struggled to climb out of the
ditch, "and Bobby Lee, you hold onto that little girl's hand."

"I don't want to hold hands with him," June Star said. "He reminds me of
a pig."

The fat boy blushed and laughed and caught her by the arm and pulled
her off into the woods after Hiram and her mother.

Alone with The Misfit, the grandmother found that she had lost her voice.
There was not a cloud in the sky nor any sun. There was nothing around
her but woods. She wanted to tell him that he must pray. She opened
and closed her mouth several times before anything came out. Finally she
found herself saying, "Jesus, Jesus," meaning, Jesus will help you, but the
way she was saying it, it sounded as if she might be cursing.

"Yes'm," The Misfit said as if he agreed. "Jesus thrown everything off bal-   130
ance. It was the same case with Him as with me except He hadn't committed any crime and they could prove I had committed one because they had
the papers on me. Of course," he said, "they never shown me my papers.
That's why I sign myself now. I said long ago, you get you a signature and
sign everything you do and keep a copy of it. Then you'll know what you

done and you can hold up the crime to the punishment and see do they match and in the end you'll have something to prove you ain't been treated right. I call myself The Misfit," he said, "because I can't make what all I done wrong fit what all I gone through in punishment."

There was a piercing scream from the woods, followed closely by a pistol report. "Does it seem right to you, lady, that one is punished a heap and another ain't punished at all?"

"Jesus!" the old lady cried. "You've got good blood! I know you wouldn't shoot a lady! I know you come from nice people! Pray! Jesus, you ought not to shoot a lady. I'll give you all the money I've got!"

"Lady," The Misfit said, looking beyond her far into the woods, "there never was a body that give the undertaker a tip."

There were two more pistol reports and the grandmother raised her head like a parched old turkey hen crying for water and called, "Bailey Boy, Bailey Boy!" as if her heart would break.

"Jesus was the only One that ever raised the dead," The Misfit continued, 135 "and He shouldn't have done it. He thrown everything off balance. If He did what He said, then it's nothing for you to do but throw away everything and follow Him, and if He didn't then it's nothing for you to do but enjoy the few minutes you got left the best way you can—by killing somebody or burning down his house or doing some other meanness to him. No pleasure but meanness," he said and his voice had become almost a snarl.

"Maybe He didn't raise the dead," the old lady mumbled, not knowing what she was saying and feeling so dizzy that she sank down in the ditch with her legs twisted under her.

"I wasn't there so I can't say He didn't," The Misfit said. "I wisht I had of been there," he said, hitting the ground with his fist. "It ain't right I wasn't there because if I had of been there I would of known. Listen lady," he said in a high voice, "if I had of been there I would of known and I wouldn't be like I am now." His voice seemed about to crack and the grandmother's head cleared for an instant. She saw the man's face twisted close to her own as if he were going to cry and she murmured, "Why, you're one of my babies. You're one of my own children!" She reached out and touched him on the shoulder. The Misfit sprang back as if a snake had bitten him and shot her three times through the chest. Then he put his gun down on the ground and took off his glasses and began to clean them.

Hiram and Bobby Lee returned from the woods and stood over the ditch, looking down at the grandmother who half sat and half lay in a puddle of blood with her legs crossed under her like a child's and her face smiling up at the cloudless sky.

Without his glasses, The Misfit's eyes were red-rimmed and pale and defenseless-looking. "Take her off and throw her where you thrown the others," he said, picking up the cat that was rubbing itself against his leg.

"She was a talker, wasn't she?" Bobby Lee said, sliding down the ditch 140 with a yodel.

"She would of been a good woman," The Misfit said, "if it had been somebody there to shoot her every minute of her life."

"Some fun!" Bobby Lee said.

"Shut up, Bobby Lee," The Misfit said. "It's no real pleasure in life."

The Receptive Reader

1. What kind of person is the grandmother? What roles (or how many roles) does she play as a *central character* in the development of the story? At how many points in the story does she play a major or minor part? Does she symbolically represent the past—the "old South"? Is there a conflict between the generations?

2. What is your reaction to the other members of the family as *minor characters* in the story? Are they comical? strange? ordinary? repellent?

3. What role does the *episode,* or interlude, at the "fat man's" barbecue play in the story?

4. How or why did these characters meet their fate? How would you summarize the *plot* or story line?

5. Is there anything representative or *symbolic* about what happens to these people?

6. What is the Misfit's story (and how much of it do you believe)? What are his manners? (Do you find them surprising or *ironic?*) What is the gist of the climactic conversation between the Misfit and the grandmother? Does it suggest a *theme;* does it have thematic implications?

7. Where would you draw the line between the comic and the tragic in this story? How does it illustrate the mixed genre critics call the *grotesque?*

8. Does this story change your idea about "senseless violence"? How?

The Personal Response

How true to the spirit of the story, or how far off, is the personal reaction in the following journal entry?

> Maybe the Misfit was like Lucifer, the misfit Angel. Lucifer didn't see things God's way, so God cast him out of heaven and punished him. Did Lucifer become evil because of the punishment not fitting the crime? Or was Lucifer just inherently evil? If he was inherently evil, he wouldn't have been an angel in the first place. I think those who jailed the Misfit turned him from just different to bad. I wasn't terribly sorry to see that family go, especially those rancid children. The mother was harmless, but I had real sympathy only for the Misfit, the baby, and the cat, Pitty Sing. Maybe O'Connor made the family so nasty and annoying to act as a foil for the Misfit, who really was a pitiful man.

The Creative Dimension

O'Connor's stories leave readers with haunting images or the memory of striking incidents. Critics puzzle over key phrases ("good country people"), provocative sentences ("a good man is hard to find"), symbolic gestures, climactic exchanges, violent confrontations. Focus on a haunting image, incident, gesture, or saying in O'Connor's stories. Re-create it, following the train of ideas, images, or associations it calls up in your mind.

As you start reading the following story by the same author, do you find yourself in familiar territory? Do its characters seem in some way akin to those in the preceding story? Does this second story raise issues or explore questions that seem related to those in the first?

Everything That Rises Must Converge   1965 👁

Her doctor had told Julian's mother that she must lose twenty pounds on account of her blood pressure, so on Wednesday nights Julian had to take her downtown on the bus for a reducing class at the Y. The reducing class was designed for working girls over fifty, who weighed from 165 to 200 pounds. His mother was one of the slimmer ones, but she said ladies did not tell their age or weight. She would not ride the buses by herself at night since they had been integrated, and because the reducing class was one of her few pleasures, necessary for her health, and *free,* she said Julian could at least put himself out to take her, considering all she did for him. Julian did not like to consider all she did for him, but every Wednesday night he braced himself and took her.

She was almost ready to go, standing before the hall mirror, putting on her hat, while he, his hands behind him, appeared pinned to the door frame, waiting like Saint Sebastian for the arrows to begin piercing him. The hat was new and had cost her seven dollars and a half. She kept saying, "Maybe I shouldn't have paid that for it. No, I shouldn't have. I'll take it off and return it tomorrow. I shouldn't have bought it."

Julian raised his eyes to heaven. "Yes, you should have bought it," he said. "Put it on and let's go." It was a hideous hat. A purple velvet flap came down on one side of it and stood up on the other; the rest of it was green and looked like a cushion with the stuffing out. He decided it was less comical than jaunty and pathetic. Everything that gave her pleasure was small and depressed him.

She lifted the hat one more time and set it down slowly on top of her head. Two wings of gray hair protruded on either side of her florid face, but her eyes, sky-blue, were as innocent and untouched by experience as they must have been when she was ten. Were it not that she was a widow who had struggled fiercely to feed and clothe and put him through school and who was supporting him still, "until he got on his feet," she might have been a little girl that he had to take to town.

"It's all right, it's all right," he said. "Let's go." He opened the door himself and started down the walk to get her going. The sky was a dying violet and the houses stood out darkly against it, bulbous liver-colored monstrosities of a uniform ugliness though no two were alike. Since this had been a fashionable neighborhood forty years ago, his mother persisted in thinking they did well to have an apartment in it. Each house had a narrow collar of dirt around it in which sat, usually, a grubby child. Julian walked with his hands in his pockets, his head down and thrust forward and his eyes glazed with the determination to make himself completely numb during the time he would be sacrificed to her pleasure.

The door closed and he turned to find the dumpy figure, surmounted by the atrocious hat, coming toward him. "Well," she said, "you only live once and paying a little more for it, I at least won't meet myself coming and going."

5

"Some day I'll start making money," Julian said gloomily—he knew he never would—"and you can have one of those jokes whenever you take the fit." But first they would move. He visualized a place where the nearest neighbors would be three miles away on either side.

"I think you're doing fine," she said, drawing on her gloves. "You've only been out of school a year. Rome wasn't built in a day."

She was one of the few members of the Y reducing class who arrived in hat and gloves and who had a son who had been to college. "It takes time," she said, "and the world is in such a mess. This hat looked better on me than any of the others, though when she brought it out I said, 'Take that thing back. I wouldn't have it on my head,' and she said, 'Now wait till you see it on,' and when she put it on me, I said, 'We-ull,' and she said, 'If you ask me, that hat does something for you and you do something for the hat, and besides,' she said, 'with that hat, you won't meet yourself coming and going.' "

Julian thought he could have stood his lot better if she had been selfish, 10 if she had been an old hag who drank and screamed at him. He walked along, saturated in depression, as if in the midst of his martyrdom he had lost his faith. Catching sight of his long, hopeless, irritated face, she stopped suddenly with a grief-stricken look, and pulled back on his arm. "Wait on me," she said. "I'm going back to the house and take this thing off and tomorrow I'm going to return it. I was out of my head. I can pay the gas bill with that seven-fifty."

He caught her arm in a vicious grip. "You are not going to take it back," he said. "I like it."

"Well," she said, "I don't think I ought . . ."

"Shut up and enjoy it," he muttered, more depressed than ever.

"With the world in the mess it's in," she said, "it's a wonder we can enjoy anything. I tell you, the bottom rail is on the top."

Julian sighed.   15

"Of course," she said, "if you know who you are, you can go anywhere." She said this every time he took her to the reducing class. "Most of them in it are not our kind of people," she said, "but I can be gracious to anybody. I know who I am."

"They don't give a damn for your graciousness," Julian said savagely. "Knowing who you are is good for one generation only. You haven't the foggiest idea where you stand now or who you are."

She stopped and allowed her eyes to flash at him. "I most certainly do know who I am," she said, "and if you don't know who you are, I'm ashamed of you."

"Oh hell," Julian said.

"Your great-grandfather was a former governor of this state," she said. 20 "Your grandfather was a prosperous land-owner. Your grandmother was a Godhigh."

"Will you look around you," he said tensely, "and see where you are now?" and he swept his arm jerkily out to indicate the neighborhood, which the growing darkness at least made less dingy.

"You remain what you are," she said. "Your great-grandfather had a plantation and two hundred slaves."

"There are no more slaves," he said irritably.

"They were better off when they were," she said. He groaned to see that she was off on that topic. She rolled onto it every few days like a train on an open track. He knew every stop, every junction, every swamp along the way, and knew the exact point at which her conclusion would roll majestically into the station: "It's ridiculous. It's simply not realistic. They should rise, yes, but on their own side of the fence."

"Let's skip it," Julian said.   25

"The ones I feel sorry for," she said, "are the ones that are half white. They're tragic."

"Will you skip it?"

"Suppose we were half white. We would certainly have mixed feelings."

"I have mixed feelings now," he groaned.

"Well let's talk about something pleasant," she said. "I remember going to   30
Grandpa's when I was a little girl. Then the house had double stairways that went up to what was really the second floor—all the cooking was done on the first. I used to like to stay down in the kitchen on account of the way the walls smelled. I would sit with my nose pressed against the plaster and take deep breaths. Actually the place belonged to the Godhighs but your grandfather Chestny paid the mortgage and saved it for them. They were in reduced circumstances," she said, "but reduced or not, they never forgot who they were."

"Doubtless that decayed mansion reminded them," Julian muttered. He never spoke of it without contempt or thought of it without longing. He had seen it once when he was a child before it had been sold. The double stairways had rotted and been torn down. Negroes were living in it. But it remained in his mind as his mother had known it. It appeared in his dreams regularly. He would stand on the wide porch, listening to the rustle of oak leaves, then wander through the high-ceilinged hall into the parlor that opened onto it and gaze at the worn rugs and faded draperies. It occurred to him that it was he, not she, who could have appreciated it. He preferred its threadbare elegance to anything he could name and it was because of it that all the neighborhoods they had lived in had been a torment to him— whereas she had hardly known the difference. She called her insensitivity "being adjustable."

"And I remember the old darky who was my nurse, Caroline. There was no better person in the world. I've always had a great respect for my colored friends," she said. "I'd do anything in the world for them and they'd . . ."

"Will you for God's sake get off that subject?" Julian said. When he got on a bus by himself, he made it a point to sit down beside a Negro, in reparation as it were for his mother's sins.

"You're mighty touchy tonight," she said. "Do you feel all right?"

"Yes I feel all right," he said. "Now lay off."   35

She pursed her lips. "Well, you certainly are in a vile humor," she observed. "I just won't speak to you at all."

They had reached the bus stop. There was no bus in sight and Julian, his hands still jammed in his pockets and his head thrust forward, scowled down the empty street. The frustration of having to wait on the bus as well as ride on it began to creep up his neck like a hot hand. The presence of his mother was borne in upon him as she gave a pained sigh. He looked at her bleakly. She was holding herself very erect under the preposterous hat, wearing it like a banner of her imaginary dignity. There was in him an evil urge to break her spirit. He suddenly unloosened his tie and pulled it off and put it in his pocket.

She stiffened. "Why must you look like *that* when you take me to town?" she said. "Why must you deliberately embarrass me?"

"If you'll never learn where you are," he said, "you can at least learn where I am."

"You look like a—thug," she said.   40

"Then I must be one," he murmured.

"I'll just go home," she said. "I will not bother you. If you can't do a little thing like that for me . . ."

Rolling his eyes upward, he put his tie back on. "Restored to my class," he muttered. He thrust his face toward her and hissed, "True culture is in the mind, the *mind,*" he said, and tapped his head, "the mind."

"It's in the heart," she said, "and in how you do things and how you do things is because of who you *are.*"

"Nobody in the damn bus cares who you are."   45

"I care who I am," she said icily.

The lighted bus appeared on top of the next hill and as it approached, they moved out into the street to meet it. He put his hand under her elbow and hoisted her up on the creaking step. She entered with a little smile, as if she were going into a drawing room where everyone had been waiting for her. While he put in the tokens, she sat down on one of the broad front seats for three which faced the aisle. A thin woman with protruding teeth and long yellow hair was sitting on the end of it. His mother moved up beside her and left room for Julian beside herself. He sat down and looked at the floor across the aisle where a pair of thin feet in red and white canvas sandals were planted.

His mother immediately began a general conversation meant to attract anyone who felt like talking. "Can it get any hotter?" she said and removed from her purse a folding fan, black with a Japanese scene on it, which she began to flutter before her.

"I reckon it might could," the woman with the protruding teeth said, "but I know for a fact my apartment couldn't get no hotter."

"It must get the afternoon sun," his mother said. She sat forward and   50
looked up and down the bus. It was half filled. Everybody was white. "I see we have the bus to ourselves," she said. Julian cringed.

"For a change," said the woman across the aisle, the owner of the red and white canvas sandals. "I come on one the other day and they were thick as fleas—up front and all through."

"The world is in a mess everywhere," his mother said. "I don't know how we've let it get in this fix."

"What gets my goat is all those boys from good families stealing automobile tires," the woman with the protruding teeth said. "I told my boy, I said you may not be rich but you been raised right and if I ever catch you in any such mess, they can send you on to the reformatory. Be exactly where you belong."

"Training tells," his mother said. "Is your boy in high school?"

"Ninth grade," the woman said.

"My son just finished college last year. He wants to write but he's selling typewriters until he gets started," his mother said.

The woman leaned forward and peered at Julian. He threw her such a malevolent look that she subsided against the seat. On the floor across the aisle there was an abandoned newspaper. He got up and got it and opened it out in front of him. His mother discreetly continued the conversation in a lower tone but the woman across the aisle said in a loud voice, "Well that's nice. Selling typewriters is close to writing. He can go right from one to the other."

"I tell him," his mother said, "that Rome wasn't built in a day."

Behind the newspaper Julian was withdrawing into the inner compartment of his mind where he spent most of his time. This was a kind of mental bubble in which he established himself when he could not bear to be a part of what was going on around him. From it he could see out and judge but in it he was safe from any kind of penetration from without. It was the only place where he felt free of the general idiocy of his fellows. His mother had never entered it but from it he could see her with absolute clarity.

The old lady was clever enough and he thought that if she had started from any of the right premises, more might have been expected of her. She lived according to the laws of her own fantasy world, outside of which he had never seen her set foot. The law of it was to sacrifice herself for him after she had first created the necessity to do so by making a mess of things. If he had permitted her sacrifices, it was only because her lack of foresight had made them necessary. All of her life had been a struggle to act like a Chestny without the Chestny goods, and to give him everything she thought a Chestny ought to have; but since, said she, it was fun to struggle, why complain? And when you had won, as she had won, what fun to look back on the hard times! He could not forgive her that she had enjoyed the struggle and that she thought *she* had won.

What she meant when she said she had won was that she had brought him up successfully and had sent him to college and that he had turned out so well—good looking (her teeth had gone unfilled so that his could be straightened), intelligent (he realized he was too intelligent to be a success), and with a future ahead of him (there was of course no future ahead of him). She excused his gloominess on the grounds that he was still growing up and his radical ideas on his lack of practical experience. She said he didn't yet know a thing about "life," that he hadn't even entered the real world—when already he was as disenchanted with it as a man of fifty.

The further irony of all this was that in spite of her, he had turned out so well. In spite of going to only a third-rate college, he had, on his own initiative, come out with a first-rate education; in spite of growing up dominated by a small mind, he had ended up with a large one; in spite of all her foolish views, he was free of prejudice and unafraid to face facts. Most miraculous of all, instead of being blinded by love for her as she was for

55

60

him, he had cut himself emotionally free of her and could see her with complete objectivity. He was not dominated by his mother.

The bus stopped with a sudden jerk and shook him from his meditation. A woman from the back lurched forward with little steps and barely escaped falling in his newspaper as she righted herself. She got off and a large Negro got on. Julian kept his paper lowered to watch. It gave him a certain satisfaction to see injustice in daily operation. It confirmed his view that with a few exceptions there was no one worth knowing within a radius of three hundred miles. The Negro was well dressed and carried a briefcase. He looked around and then sat down on the other end of the seat where the woman with the red and white canvas sandals was sitting. He immediately unfolded a newspaper and obscured himself behind it. Julian's mother's elbow at once prodded insistently into his ribs. "Now you see why I won't ride on these buses by myself," she whispered.

The woman with the red and white canvas sandals had risen at the same time the Negro sat down and had gone further back in the bus and taken the seat of the woman who had got off. His mother leaned forward and cast her an approving look.

Julian rose, crossed the aisle, and sat down in the place of the woman   65 with the canvas sandals. From this position, he looked serenely across at his mother. Her face had turned an angry red. He stared at her, making his eyes the eyes of a stranger. He felt his tension suddenly lift as if he had openly declared war on her.

He would have liked to get in conversation with the Negro and to talk with him about art or politics or any subject that would be above the comprehension of those around them, but the man remained entrenched behind his paper. He was either ignoring the change of seating or had never noticed it. There was no way for Julian to convey his sympathy.

His mother kept her eyes fixed reproachfully on his face. The woman with the protruding teeth was looking at him avidly as if he were a type of monster new to her.

"Do you have a light?" he asked the Negro.

Without looking away from his paper, the man reached in his pocket and handed him a packet of matches.

"Thanks," Julian said. For a moment he held the matches foolishly. A NO   70 SMOKING sign looked down upon him from over the door. This alone would not have deterred him; he had no cigarettes. He had quit smoking some months before because he could not afford it. "Sorry," he muttered and handed back the matches. The Negro lowered the paper and gave him an annoyed look. He took the matches and raised the paper again.

His mother continued to gaze at him but she did not take advantage of his momentary discomfort. Her eyes retained their battered look. Her face seemed to be unnaturally red, as if her blood pressure had risen. Julian allowed no glimmer of sympathy to show on his face. Having got the advantage, he wanted desperately to keep it and carry it through. He would have liked to teach her a lesson that would last her a while, but there seemed no way to continue the point. The Negro refused to come out from behind his paper.

Julian folded his arms and looked stolidly before him, facing her but as if he did not see her, as if he had ceased to recognize her existence. He visualized a scene in which, the bus having reached their stop, he would remain in his seat and when she said, "Aren't you going to get off?" he would look at her as a stranger who had rashly addressed him. The corner they got off on was usually deserted, but it was well lighted and it would not hurt her to walk by herself the four blocks to the Y. He decided to wait until the time came and then decide whether or not he would let her get off by herself. He would have to be at the Y at ten to bring her back, but he could leave her wondering if he was going to show up. There was no reason for her to think she could always depend on him.

He retired again into the high-ceilinged room sparsely settled with large pieces of antique furniture. His soul expanded momentarily but then he became aware of his mother across from him and the vision shriveled. He studied her coldly. Her feet in little pumps dangled like a child's and did not quite reach the floor. She was training on him an exaggerated look of reproach. He felt completely detached from her. At that moment he could with pleasure have slapped her as he would have slapped a particularly obnoxious child in his charge.

He began to imagine various unlikely ways by which he could teach her a lesson. He might make friends with some distinguished Negro professor or lawyer and bring him home to spend the evening. He would be entirely justified but her blood pressure would rise to 300. He could not push her to the extent of making her have a stroke, and moreover, he had never been successful at making any Negro friends. He had tried to strike up an acquaintance on the bus with some of the better types, with ones that looked like professors or ministers or lawyers. One morning he had sat down next to a distinguished-looking dark brown man who had answered his questions with a sonorous solemnity but who had turned out to be an undertaker. Another day he had sat down beside a cigar-smoking Negro with a diamond ring on his finger, but after a few stilted pleasantries, the Negro had rung the buzzer and risen, slipping two lottery tickets into Julian's hand as he climbed over him to leave.

He imagined his mother lying desperately ill and his being able to secure only a Negro doctor for her. He toyed with that idea for a few minutes and then dropped it for a momentary vision of himself participating as a sympathizer in a sit-in demonstration. This was possible but he did not linger with it. Instead, he approached the ultimate horror. He brought home a beautiful suspiciously Negroid woman. Prepare yourself, he said. There is nothing you can do about it. This is the woman I've chosen. She's intelligent, dignified, even good, and she's suffered and she hasn't thought it *fun*. Now persecute us, go ahead and persecute us. Drive her out of here, but remember, you're driving me too. His eyes were narrowed and through the indignation he had generated, he saw his mother across the aisle, purple-faced, shrunken to the dwarf-like proportions of her moral nature, sitting like a mummy beneath the ridiculous banner of her hat.

He was tilted out of his fantasy again as the bus stopped. The door opened with a sucking hiss and out of the dark a large, gaily dressed, sullen-looking colored woman got on with a little boy. The child, who might have been four, had on a short plaid suit and a Tyrolean hat with a blue feather in it. Julian hoped that he would sit down beside him and that the woman would push in beside his mother. He could think of no better arrangement.

As she waited for her tokens, the woman was surveying the seating possibilities—he hoped with the idea of sitting where she was least wanted. There was something familiar-looking about her but Julian could not place what it was. She was a giant of a woman. Her face was set not only to meet opposition but to seek it out. The downward tilt of her large lower lip was like a warning sign: DON'T TAMPER WITH ME. Her bulging figure was encased in a green crepe dress and her feet overflowed in red shoes. She had on a hideous hat. A purple velvet flap came down on one side of it and stood up on the other; the rest of it was green and looked like a cushion with the stuffing out. She carried a mammoth red pocketbook that bulged throughout as if it were stuffed with rocks.

To Julian's disappointment, the little boy climbed up on the empty seat beside his mother. His mother lumped all children, black and white, into the common category, "cute," and she thought little Negroes were on the whole cuter than little white children. She smiled at the little boy as he climbed on the seat.

Meanwhile the woman was bearing down upon the empty seat beside Julian. To his annoyance, she squeezed herself into it. He saw his mother's face change as the woman settled herself next to him and he realized with satisfaction that this was more objectionable to her than it was to him. Her face seemed almost gray and there was a look of dull recognition in her eyes, as if suddenly she had sickened at some awful confrontation. Julian saw that it was because she and the woman had, in a sense, swapped sons. Though his mother would not realize the symbolic significance of this, she would feel it. His amusement showed plainly on his face.

The woman next to him muttered something unintelligible to herself. He was conscious of a kind of bristling next to him, a muted growling like that of an angry cat. He could not see anything but the red pocketbook upright on the bulging green thighs. He visualized the woman as she had stood waiting for her tokens—the ponderous figure, rising from the red shoes upward over the solid hips, the mammoth bosom, the haughty face, to the green and purple hat.

His eyes widened.

The vision of the two hats, identical, broke upon him with the radiance of a brilliant sunrise. His face was suddenly lit with joy. He could not believe that Fate had thrust upon his mother such a lesson. He gave a loud chuckle so that she would look at him and see that he saw. She turned her eyes on him slowly. The blue in them seemed to have turned a bruised purple. For a moment he had an uncomfortable sense of her innocence, but it lasted only a second before principle rescued him. Justice entitled him to laugh. His grin hardened until it said to her as plainly as if he were saying aloud: Your punishment exactly fits your pettiness. This should teach you a permanent lesson.

80

Her eyes shifted to the woman. She seemed unable to bear looking at him and to find the woman preferable. He became conscious again of the bristling presence at his side. The woman was rumbling like a volcano about to become active. His mother's mouth began to twitch slightly at one corner. With a sinking heart, he saw incipient signs of recovery on her face and realized that this was going to strike her suddenly as funny and was going to be no lesson at all. She kept her eyes on the woman and an amused smile came over her face. The little Negro was looking up at her with large fascinated eyes. He had been trying to attract her attention for some time.

"Carver!" the woman said suddenly. "Come heah!"

When he saw that the spotlight was on him at last, Carver drew his feet   85
up and turned himself toward Julian's mother and giggled.

"Carver!" the woman said. "You heah me? Come heah!"

Carver slid down from the seat but remained squatting with his back against the base of it, his head turned slyly around toward Julian's mother, who was smiling at him. The woman reached a hand across the aisle and snatched him to her. He righted himself and hung backwards on her knees, grinning at Julian's mother. "Isn't he cute?" Julian's mother said to the woman with the protruding teeth.

"I reckon he is," the woman said without conviction.

His mother yanked him upright but he eased out of her grip and shot across the aisle and scrambled, giggling wildly, onto the seat beside his love.

"I think he likes me," Julian's mother said, and smiled at the woman. It was   90
the smile she used when she was being particularly gracious to an inferior. Julian saw everything lost. The lesson had rolled off her like rain on a roof.

The woman stood up and yanked the little boy off the seat as if she were snatching him from contagion. Julian could feel the rage in her at having no weapon like his mother's smile. She gave the child a sharp slap across his leg. He howled once and then thrust his head into her stomach and kicked his feet against her shins. "Behave," she said vehemently.

The bus stopped and the Negro who had been reading the newspaper got off. The woman moved over and set the little boy down with a thump between herself and Julian. She held him firmly by the knee. In a moment he put his hands in front of his face and peeped at Julian's mother through his fingers.

"I see yoooooooo!" she said and put her hand in front of her face and peeped at him.

The woman slapped his hand down. "Quit yo' foolishness," she said, "before I knock the living Jesus out of you!"

Julian was thankful that the next stop was theirs. He reached up and   95
pulled the cord. The woman reached up and pulled it at the same time. Oh my God, he thought. He had the terrible intuition that when they got off the bus together, his mother would open her purse and give the little boy a nickel. The gesture would be as natural to her as breathing. The bus stopped and the woman got up and lunged to the front, dragging the child, who wished to stay on, after her. Julian and his mother got up and followed. As they neared the door, Julian tried to relieve her of her pocketbook.

"No," she murmured, "I want to give the little boy a nickel."

"No!" Julian hissed. "No!"

She smiled down at the child and opened her bag. The bus door opened and the woman picked him up by the arm and descended with him, hanging at her hip. Once in the street she set him down and shook him.

Julian's mother had to close her purse while she got down the bus step but as soon as her feet were on the ground, she opened it again and began to rummage inside. "I can't find but a penny," she whispered, "but it looks like a new one."

"Don't do it!" Julian said fiercely between his teeth. There was a street-   100
light on the corner and she hurried to get under it so that she could better see into her pocketbook. The woman was heading off rapidly down the street with the child still hanging backward on her hand.

"Oh little boy!" Julian's mother called and took a few quick steps and caught up with them just beyond the lamppost. "Here's a bright new penny for you," and she held out the coin, which shone bronze in the dim light.

The huge woman turned and for a moment stood, her shoulders lifted and her face frozen with frustrated rage, and stared at Julian's mother. Then all at once she seemed to explode like a piece of machinery that had been given one ounce of pressure too much. Julian saw the black fist swing out with the red pocketbook. He shut his eyes and cringed as he heard the woman shout, "He don't take nobody's pennies!" When he opened his eyes, the woman was disappearing down the street with the little boy staring wide-eyed over her shoulder. Julian's mother was sitting on the sidewalk.

"I told you not to do that," Julian said angrily. "I told you not to do that!"

He stood over her for a minute, gritting his teeth. Her legs were stretched out in front of her and her hat was on her lap. He squatted down and looked her in the face. It was totally expressionless. "You got exactly what you deserved," he said. "Now get up."

He picked up her pocketbook and put what had fallen out back in it. He   105
picked the hat up off her lap. The penny caught his eye on the sidewalk and he picked that up and let it drop before her eyes into the purse. Then he stood up and leaned over and held his hands out to pull her up. She remained immobile. He sighed. Rising above them on either side were black apartment buildings, marked with irregular rectangles of light. At the end of the block a man came out of a door and walked off in the opposite direction. "All right," he said, "suppose somebody happens by and wants to know why you're sitting on the sidewalk?"

She took the hand and, breathing hard, pulled heavily up on it and then stood for a moment, swaying slightly as if the spots of light in the darkness were circling around her. Her eyes, shadowed and confused, finally settled on his face. He did not try to conceal his irritation. "I hope this teaches you a lesson," he said. She leaned forward and her eyes raked his face. She seemed trying to determine his identity. Then, as if she found nothing familiar about him, she started off with a headlong movement in the wrong direction.

"Aren't you going on to the Y?" he asked.

"Home," she muttered.

"Well, are we walking?"

For answer she kept going. Julian followed along, his hands behind him. 110
He saw no reason to let the lesson she had had go without backing it up
with an explanation of its meaning. She might as well be made to understand what had happened to her. "Don't think that was just an uppity Negro
woman," he said. "That was the whole colored race which will no longer
take your condescending pennies. That was your black double. She can
wear the same hat as you, and to be sure," he added gratuitously (because
he thought it was funny), "it looked better on her than it did on you. What
all this means," he said, "is that the old world is gone. The old manners are
obsolete and your graciousness is not worth a damn." He thought bitterly of
the house that had been lost for him. "You aren't who you think you are,"
he said.

She continued to plow ahead, paying no attention to him. Her hair had
come undone on one side. She dropped her pocketbook and took no
notice. He stooped and picked it up and handed it to her but she did not
take it.

"You needn't act as if the world had come to an end," he said, "because
it hasn't. From now on you've got to live in a new world and face a few realities for a change. Buck up," he said, "it won't kill you."

She was breathing fast.

"Let's wait on the bus," he said.

"Home," she said thickly.   115

"I hate to see you behave like this," he said. "Just like a child. I should
be able to expect more of you." He decided to stop where he was and make
her stop and wait for a bus. "I'm not going any farther," he said, stopping.
"We're going on the bus."

She continued to go on as if she had not heard him. He took a few steps
and caught her arm and stopped her. He looked into her face and caught
his breath. He was looking into a face he had never seen before. "Tell
Grandpa to come get me," she said.

He stared, stricken.

"Tell Caroline to come get me," she said.

Stunned, he let her go and she lurched forward again, walking as if one 120
leg were shorter than the other. A tide of darkness seemed to be sweeping
her from him. "Mother!" he cried. "Darling, sweetheart, wait!" Crumpling,
she fell to the pavement. He dashed forward and fell at her side, crying,
"Mamma, Mamma!" He turned her over. Her face was fiercely distorted. One
eye, large and staring, moved slightly to the left as if it had become unmoored. The other remained fixed on him, raked his face again, found nothing and closed.

"Wait here, wait here!" he cried and jumped up and began to run for help
toward a cluster of lights he saw in the distance ahead of him. "Help, help!"
he shouted, but his voice was thin, scarcely a thread of sound. The lights
drifted farther away the faster he ran and his feet moved numbly as if they
carried him nowhere. The tide of darkness seemed to sweep him back to
her, postponing from moment to moment his entry into the world of guilt
and sorrow.

The Receptive Reader

1. What kind of person is Julian's mother? What kind of attitudes and mental habits shape her personality? (How are they revealed in such telling details as the hat, the to-do about the seating in the bus, the coin for the black child?) What are her true feelings about her son? Is there any one dominant trait that provides a clue to her character?

2. O'Connor is a master of mixed feelings and contradictory emotions. What kind of person is Julian? What is his basic conflict with his mother? What are the central themes of his mental monologues? Which incidents are most revealing of his character? What would you identify as his most characteristic trait or problem? Are there any contradictions in his personality? (Are we supposed to like him or identify with his point of view?)

3. This story takes us to the South in a period of *transition*. Blacks or African Americans are still called Negroes (or, more politely, "colored"). Buses have recently been integrated, with no more relegation of colored people to the back of the bus. What is the role of black people in this story? What kind of person is the mother of the little boy? Is the author's portrait of her unflattering or favorable?

4. Can you find any passages that would serve as *capsule portraits* of the major characters?

5. What is the significance of the *ending?*

6. Does this story reinforce or does it counteract stereotypes about Southerners and African Americans?

The Personal Response

In this story, do you find yourself taking sides between Julian's mother and her son? What side are you on, and why? Do you think the author expects you to like Julian or identify with his point of view?

The Creative Dimension

Flannery O'Connor is a writer who keeps very tight control over her characters, with every detail meaningful and very little left to chance. Suppose one or more of the characters—Julian's mother, Julian, or the black woman (or maybe the child)—had a chance to have a last word, talking freely about what they felt deep down. Choose one of these, and write what you think they might say.

The following is a lesser-known story by O'Connor. Do you recognize in it her characteristic way of looking at the world? Do you recognize features of the O'Connor style?

Enoch and the Gorilla   1952👁

Enoch Emery had borrowed his landlady's umbrella and he discovered as he stood in the entrance of the drugstore, trying to open it, that it was at least as old as she was. When he finally got it hoisted, he pushed his dark glasses back on his eyes and reentered the downpour.

The umbrella was one his landlady had stopped using fifteen years before (which was the only reason she had lent it to him) and as soon as the rain touched the top of it, it came down with a shriek and stabbed him in the back of the neck. He ran a few feet with it over his head and then backed into another store entrance and removed it. Then to get it up again, he had to place the tip of it on the ground and ram it open with his foot. He ran out again, holding his hand up near the spokes to keep them open and this allowed the handle, which was carved to represent the head of a fox terrier, to jab him every few seconds in the stomach. He proceeded for another quarter of a block this way before the back half of the silk stood up off the spokes and allowed the storm to sweep down his collar. Then he ducked under the marquee of a movie house. It was Saturday and a lot of children were standing more or less in a line in front of the ticket box.

Enoch was not very fond of children, but children always seemed to like to look at him. The line turned and twenty or thirty eyes began to observe him with a steady interest. The umbrella had assumed an ugly position, half up and half down, and the half that was up was about to come down and spill more water under his collar. When this happened the children laughed and jumped up and down. Enoch glared at them and turned his back and lowered his dark glasses. He found himself facing a life-size four-color picture of a gorilla. Over the gorilla's head, written in red letters was "GONGA! Giant Jungle Monarch and a Great Star! HERE IN PERSON!!!" At the level of the gorilla's knee, there was more that said, "Gonga will appear in person in front of this theater at 12 A.M. *TODAY!* A free pass to the first ten brave enough to step up and shake his hand!"

Enoch was usually thinking of something else at the moment that Fate began drawing back her leg to kick him. When he was four years old, his father had brought him home a tin box from the penitentiary. It was orange and had a picture of some peanut brittle on the outside of it and green letters that said, "A NUTTY SURPRISE!" When Enoch had opened it, a coiled piece of steel had sprung out at him and broken off the ends of his two front teeth. His life was full of so many happenings like that that it would seem he should have been more sensitive to his times of danger. He stood there and read the poster twice through carefully. To his mind, an opportunity to insult a successful ape came from the hand of Providence.

He turned around and asked the nearest child what time it was. The child said it was twelve-ten and that Gonga was already ten minutes late. Another child said that maybe the rain had delayed him. Another said, no, not the rain, his director was taking a plane from Hollywood. Enoch gritted his teeth. The first child said that if he wanted to shake the star's hand, he would have to get in line like the rest of them and wait his turn. Enoch got into line. A child asked him how old he was. Another observed that he had funny-looking teeth. He ignored all this as best he could and began to straighten out the umbrella.

In a few minutes a black truck turned around the corner and came slowly up the street in the heavy rain. Enoch pushed the umbrella under his arm and began to squint through his dark glasses. As the truck approached, a phonograph inside it began to play "Tarara Boom Di Aye," but the music

5

was almost drowned out by the rain. There was a large illustration of a blonde on the outside of the truck, advertising some picture other than the one with the gorilla.

The children held their line carefully as the truck stopped in front of the movie house. The back door of it was constructed like a paddy wagon, with a grate, but the ape was not at it. Two men in raincoats got out of the cab part, cursing, and ran around to the back and opened the door. One of them stuck his head in and said, "Okay, make it snappy, willya?" The other jerked his thumb at the children and said, "Get back willya, willya get back?"

A voice on the record inside the truck said, "Here's Gonga, folks, Roaring Gonga and a Great Star! Give Gonga a big hand, folks!" The voice was barely a mumble in the rain.

The man who was waiting by the door of the truck stuck his head in again. "Okay, willya get out?" he said.   10

There was a faint thump somewhere inside the van. After a second a dark furry arm emerged just enough for the rain to touch it and then drew back inside.

The man who was under the marquee took off his raincoat and threw it to the man by the door, who threw it into the wagon. After two or three minutes more, the gorilla appeared at the door, with the raincoat buttoned up to his chin and the collar turned up. There was an iron chain hanging from around his neck; the man grabbed it and pulled him down and the two of them bounded under the marquee together. A motherly-looking woman was in the glass ticket box, getting the passes ready for the first ten children brave enough to step up and shake hands.

The gorilla ignored the children entirely and followed the man over to the other side of the entrance where there was a small platform raised about a foot off the ground. He stepped up on it and turned facing the children and began to growl. His growls were not so much loud as poisonous; they appeared to issue from a black heart. Enoch was terrified and if he had not been surrounded by the children, he would have run away.

"Who'll step up first?" the man said. "Come on, come on, who'll step up first? A free pass to the first kid stepping up."

There was no movement from the group of children. The man glared at them. "What's the matter with you kids?" he barked. "You yellow? He won't hurt you as long as I got him by this chain." He tightened his grip on the chain and jangled it at them to show he was holding it securely.   15

After a minute a little girl separated herself from the group. She had long wood-shaving curls and a fierce triangular face. She moved up to within four feet of the star.

"Okay okay," the man said, rattling the chain, "make it snappy."

The ape reached out and gave her hand a quick shake. By this time there was another little girl ready and then two boys. The line re-formed and began to move up.

The gorilla kept his hand extended and turned his head away with a bored look at the rain. Enoch had got over his fear and was trying frantically to think of a remark that would be suitable to insult him with. Usually he didn't have any trouble with this kind of composition but nothing came to him now. His brain, both parts, was completely empty. He couldn't think even of the insulting phrase he used every day.

There were only two children in front of him by now. The first one shook hands and stepped aside. Enoch's heart was beating violently. The child in front of him finished and stepped aside and left him facing the ape, who took his hand with an automatic motion.   20

It was the first hand that had been extended to Enoch since he had come to the city. It was warm and soft.

For a second he only stood there, clasping it. Then he began to stammer. "My name is Enoch Emery," he mumbled. "I attended the Rodemill Boys' Bible Academy. I work at the city zoo. I seen two of your pictures. I'm only eighteen years old but I already work for the city. My daddy made me come. . ." and his voice cracked.

The star leaned slightly forward and a change came in his eyes: an ugly pair of human ones moved closer and squinted at Enoch from behind the celluloid pair. "You go take a jump," a surly voice inside the ape-suit said, low but distinctly, and the hand was jerked away.

Enoch's humiliation was so sharp and painful that he turned around three times before he realized which direction he wanted to go in. Then he ran off into the rain as fast as he could.

In spite of himself, Enoch couldn't get over the expectation that something was going to happen to him. The virtue of hope, in Enoch, was made up of two parts suspicion and one part desire. It operated on him all the rest of the day. He had only a vague idea what he wanted, but he was not a boy without ambition: he wanted to become something. He wanted to better his condition. He wanted, some day, to see a line of people waiting to shake his hand.

All afternoon he fidgeted and fooled in his room, biting his nails and   25 shredding what was left of the silk off the landlady's umbrella. Finally he denuded it entirely and broke off the spokes. What was left was a black stick with a sharp steel point at one end and a dog's head at the other. It might have been an instrument for some specialized kind of torture that had gone out of fashion. Enoch walked up and down his room with it under his arm and realized that it would distinguish him on the sidewalk.

About seven o'clock in the evening he put on his coat and took the stick and headed for a little restaurant two blocks away. He had the sense that he was setting off to get some honor, but he was very nervous, as if he were afraid he might have to snatch it instead of receive it.

He never set out for anything without eating first. The restaurant was called the Paris Diner; it was a tunnel about six feet wide, located between a shoeshine parlor and a dry-cleaning establishment. Enoch slid in and climbed up on the far stool at the counter and said he would have a bowl of split-pea soup and a chocolate malted milkshake.

The waitress was a tall woman with a big yellow dental plate and the same color hair done up in a black hairnet. One hand never left her hip;

she filled orders with the other one. Although Enoch came in nightly, she had never learned to like him.

Instead of filling his order, she began to fry bacon; there was only one other customer in the place and he had finished his meal and was reading a newspaper; there was no one to eat the bacon but her. Enoch reached over the counter and prodded her hip with the stick. "Listen here," he said, "I got to go. I'm in a hurry."

"Go then," she said. Her jaw began to work and she stared into the skil-   30
let with a fixed attention.

"Lemme just have a piece of theter cake yonder," he said, pointing to a half of pink and yellow cake on a round glass stand. "I think I got something to do. I got to be going. Set it up there next to him," he said, indicating the customer reading the newspaper. He slid over the stools and began reading the outside sheet of the man's paper.

The man lowered the paper and looked at him. Enoch smiled. The man raised the paper again. "Could I borrow some part of your paper that you ain't studying?" Enoch asked. The man lowered it again and stared at him; he had muddy unflinching eyes. He leafed deliberately through the paper and shook out the sheet with the comic strips and handed it to Enoch. It was Enoch's favorite part. He read it every evening like an office. While he ate the cake that the waitress had torpedoed down the counter at him, he read and felt himself surge with kindness and courage and strength.

When he finished one side, he turned the sheet over and began to scan the advertisements for movies that filled the other side. His eye went over three columns without stopping; then it came to a box that advertised Gonga, Giant Jungle Monarch, and listed the theaters he would visit on his tour and the hours he would be at each one. In thirty minutes he would arrive at the Victory on 57th Street and that would be his last appearance in the city.

If anyone had watched Enoch read this, he would have seen a certain transformation in his countenance. It still shone with the inspiration he had absorbed from the comic strips, but something else had come over it: a look of awakening.

The waitress happened to turn around to see if he hadn't gone. "What's   35
the matter with you?" she said. "Did you swallow a seed?"

"I know what I want," Enoch murmured.

"I know what I want too," she said with a dark look.

Enoch felt for his stick and laid his change on the counter. "I got to be going now."

"Don't let me keep you," she said.

"You may not see me again," he said, "—the way I am."   40

"Any way I don't see you will be all right with me," she said.

Enoch left. It was a pleasant damp evening. The puddles on the sidewalk shone and the store windows were steamy and bright with junk. He disappeared down a side street and made his way rapidly along the darker passages of the city, pausing only once or twice at the end of an alley to dart a glance in each direction before he ran on. The Victory was a small theater, suited to the needs of the family, in one of the closer subdivisions; he passed through a succession of lighted areas and then on through more alleys and back streets until he came to the business section that surrounded it. Then he slowed up. He saw it about a block away, glittering in its darker setting. He didn't cross the street to the side it was on but kept on the far side, moving forward with his squint fixed on the glary spot. He stopped when he was directly across from it and hid himself in a narrow stair cavity dividing a building.

The truck that carried Gonga was parked across the street and the star was standing under the marquee, shaking hands with an elderly woman. She moved aside and a gentleman in a polo shirt stepped up and shook hands vigorously, like a sportsman. He was followed by a boy of about three who wore a tall Western hat that nearly covered his face; he had to be pushed ahead by the line. Enoch watched for some time, his face working with envy. The small boy was followed by a lady in shorts, she by an old man who tried to draw extra attention to himself by dancing up instead of walking in a dignified way. Enoch suddenly darted across the street and slipped noiselessly into the open back door of the truck.

The handshaking went on until the feature picture was ready to begin. Then the star got back in the van and the people filed into the theater. The driver and the man who was master of ceremonies climbed in the cab part and the truck rumbled off. It crossed the city rapidly and continued on the highway, going very fast.

There came from the van certain thumping noises, not those of the nor-   45
mal gorilla, but they were drowned out by the drone of the motor and the steady sound of wheels against the road. The night was pale and quiet, with nothing to stir it but an occasional complaint from a hoot owl and the distant muted jarring of a freight train. The truck sped on until it slowed for a crossing, and as the van rattled over the tracks, a figure slipped from the door and almost fell, and then limped hurriedly off toward the woods.

Once in the darkness of a pine thicket, he laid down a pointed stick he had been clutching and something bulky and loose that he had been carrying under his arm, and began to undress. He folded each garment neatly after he had taken it off and then stacked it on top of the last thing he had removed. When all his clothes were in the pile, he took up the stick and carefully began making a hole in the ground with it.

The darkness of the pine grove was broken by paler moonlit spots that moved over him now and again and showed him to be Enoch. His natural appearance was marred by a gash that ran from the corner of his lip to his collarbone and by a lump under his eye that gave him a dulled insensitive look. Nothing could have been more deceptive for he was burning with the intensest kind of happiness.

He dug rapidly until he had made a trench about a foot long and a foot deep. Then he placed the stack of clothes in it and stood aside to rest a second. Burying his clothes was not a symbol to him of burying his former self; he only knew he wouldn't need them any more. As soon as he got his breath, he pushed the displaced dirt over the hole and stamped it down with his foot. He discovered while he did this that he still had his shoes on, and when he finished, he removed them and threw them from him. Then he picked up the loose bulky object and shook it vigorously.

In the uncertain light, one of his lean white legs could be seen to disappear and then the other, one arm and then the other: a black heavier shaggier figure replaced his. For an instant, it had two heads, one light and one dark, but after a second, it pulled the dark black head over the other and corrected this. It busied itself with certain hidden fastenings and what appeared to be minor adjustments of its hide.

For a time after this, it stood very still and didn't do anything. Then it 50 began to growl and beat its chest; it jumped up and down and flung its arms and thrust its head forward. The growls were thin and uncertain at first but they grew louder after a second. They became low and poisonous, louder again, low and poisonous again; they stopped altogether. The figure extended its hand, clutched nothing, and shook its arm vigorously; it withdrew the arm, extended it again, clutched nothing, and shook. It repeated this four or five times. Then it picked up the pointed stick and placed it at a cocky angle under its arm and left the woods for the highway. No gorilla anywhere, Africa or California or New York, was happier than he.

A man and woman sitting close together on a rock just off the highway were looking across an open stretch of valley at a view of the city in the distance and they didn't see the shaggy figure approaching. The smokestacks and square tops of buildings made a black uneven wall against the lighter sky and here and there a steeple cut a sharp wedge out of a cloud. The young man turned his neck just in time to see the gorilla standing a few feet away, hideous and black, with its hand extended. He eased his arm from around the woman and disappeared silently into the woods. She, as soon as she turned her eyes, fled screaming down the highway. The gorilla stood as though surprised and presently its arm fell to its side. It sat down on the rock where they had been sitting and stared over the valley at the uneven skyline of the city.

The Receptive Reader

1. What features of this story might make a reader recognize it as the work of Flannery O'Connor? For instance, what makes Enoch an outsider or misfit?

2. What details introduce *grotesque* overtones—or undertones? (What, for instance, makes the umbrella a very nonordinary umbrella?) Where does the author's wicked sense of humor show, and what is its relation to the more serious aspects of the story?

3. What is the role of *violence?* Is it similar to or different from its role in other O'Connor stories?

4. What is the meaning or *theme* of Enoch's story? Does the story as a whole have a redeeming or humanizing quality?

The Personal Response

How do you personally react to the story? Does it seem too far removed from your own concerns or from the concerns of ordinary people?

<<<Find It on the Web>>>   *Rereadings of Flannery O'Connor*

Flannery O'Connor's disturbing paradoxical tales of evil and redemption continue to receive much critical attention. Critics, teachers, and students often disagree strongly on the meaning of a story or an incident. Working with a group, you may want to explore Internet sources like the following. What are current questions or new directions in these or other recent materials?

ARTICLES AND REVIEWS:

Gilbert, Susanna. "Blood Don't Lie: The Diseased Family in Flannery O'Connor's 'Everything that Rises Must Converge.'"
Literature and Medicine Mar. 1999. 24 Sept. 2001.
<http://muse.jhu.edu/journals/literature_and_medicine/v018/18.1gilbert.html>

Schaum, Melita. "Erasing Angel: The Lucifer-Trickster Figure in Flannery O'Connor's Short Fiction." The Southern Literary Journal. 2000.
24 Sept. 2001.
<http://muse.jhu.edu/demo/slj/33.1schaum.html>

Caron, Timothy Paul. Rev. of Writing against God: Language as Message in the Literature of Flannery O'Connor. American Literature Mar. 2000.
24 Sept. 2001.
<http://muse.jhu//journals/american_literature/v072/72.1caron.html>

Bieber, Christina. Rev. of Flannery O'Connor, Hermit Novelist. American Literature Mar. 2001. 24 Sept. 2001.
<http://muse.jhu.edu//journals/american_literature/v073/73.1bieber.html>

Chapman, C. Stuart. Rev. of Flannery O'Connor and the Mystery of Love.
Modern Fiction Studies Winter 2001. 24 Sept. 2001.
<http://muse.jhu.edu//journals/modern_fiction_studies/v046/46.4.chapman.html>

BOOKS:

Gordon, Sarah. Flannery O'Connor: The Obedient Imagination. Athens:
U of Georgia P, 2000.
<http://www.uga.edu/ugapress/books/shelf/0820322032.html>

Rath, Sura and Mary Neff Shaw, eds. Flannery O'Connor: New Perspectives.
Athens: U of Georgia P, 1996.
<http://www.uga.edu/ugapress/books/shelf/0820318043.html>

JUXTAPOSITIONS

A Range of Sources

However we interpret the ending of "A Good Man," it seems to go on resonating in the imagination, perhaps the single story that most compellingly captured that condition of American life where . . . "the safety net drops away" and we are suddenly confronted with an overwhelming violence, a violence that apparently chooses its victims at random and before which they are helpless.

FREDERICK ASALS

With a puzzling, provocative author like Flannery O'Connor, readers may turn for help to a range of **secondary sources.** They may look for guidance in the author's own comments in conversations, lectures, or letters. They may look for helpful hints in tributes by fellow writers or in expert testimony by literary critics.

Author Testimony   O'Connor herself lectured and wrote extensively about the writing and teaching of literature. (She did, however, once say, "Asking me to lecture about story-writing is like asking a fish to lecture on swimming.") The following is her interpretation of one of her stories from a reading she presented to a college audience.

Flannery O'Connor

On "A Good Man Is Hard to Find"

This is the story of a family of six which, on its way driving to Florida, gets wiped out by an escaped convict who calls himself the Misfit. The family is made up of the Grandmother and her son, Bailey, and his children, John Wesley and June Star and the baby, and there is also the cat and the children's mother. The cat is named Pitty Sing, and the Grandmother is taking him with them, hidden in a basket.

Now I think it behooves me to try to establish with you the basis on which reason operates in this story. Much of my fiction takes its character from a reasonable use of the unreasonable, though the reasonableness of my use of it may not always be apparent. The assumptions that underlie this use of it, however, are those of the central Christian mysteries. These are assumptions to which a large part of the modern audience takes exception. About this I can only say that there are perhaps other ways than my own in which this story could be read, but none other by which it could have been written. Belief, in my own case anyway, is the engine that makes perception operate.

The heroine of this story, the Grandmother, is in the most significant position life offers the Christian. She is facing death. And to all appearances she, like the rest of us, is not too well prepared for it. She would like to see the event postponed. Indefinitely.

I've talked to a number of teachers who use this story in class and who tell their students that the Grandmother is evil, that in fact, she's a witch, even down to the cat. One of these teachers told me that his students, and particularly his Southern students, resisted this interpretation with a certain bemused vigor, and he didn't understand why. I had to tell him that they resisted it because they all had grandmothers or great-aunts just like her at home, and they knew, from personal experience, that the old lady lacked comprehension, but that she had a good heart. The Southerner is usually tolerant of those weaknesses that proceed from innocence, and he knows that a taste for self-preservation can be readily combined with the missionary spirit.

This same teacher was telling his students that morally the Misfit was several cuts above the Grandmother. He had a really sentimental attachment to the Misfit. But then a prophet gone wrong is almost always more interesting than your grandmother, and you have to let people take their pleasures where they find them.

It is true that the old lady is a hypocritical old soul; her wits are no match for the Misfit's, nor is her capacity for grace equal to his; yet I think the unprejudiced reader will feel that the Grandmother has a special kind of triumph in this story which instinctively we do not allow to someone altogether bad.

I often ask myself what makes a story work, and what makes it hold up as a story, and I have decided that it is probably some action, some gesture of a character that is unlike any other in the story, one which indicates where the real heart of the story lies. This would have to be an action or a gesture which was both totally right and totally unexpected; it would have to be one that was both in character and beyond character; it would have to suggest both the world and eternity. The action or gesture I'm talking about would have to be on . . . the level which has to do with the Divine life and our participation in it. It would be a gesture that transcended any neat allegory that might have been intended or any pat moral categories a reader could make. It would be a gesture which somehow made contact with mystery.

There is a point in this story where such a gesture occurs. The Grandmother is at last alone, facing the Misfit. Her head clears for an instant and she realizes, even in her limited way, that she is responsible for the man before her and joined to him by ties of kinship which have their roots deep in the mystery she has been merely prattling about so far. And at this point, she does the right thing, she makes the right gesture. . .

I don't want to equate the Misfit with the devil. I prefer to think that, however unlikely this may seem, the old lady's gesture, like the mustard seed, will grow to be a great crow-filled tree in the Misfit's heart, and will be enough of a pain to him there to turn him into the prophet he was meant to become. But that's another story.

From *Mystery and Manners,* edited by Sally and Robert Fitzgerald, 1969

The Receptive Reader

Does this account by the author change your understanding of the story?

Author Correspondence   Readers often turn to an author's published **letters** for insights into the writer's personality and work. The following is an excerpt from a review by Joyce Carol Oates of a volume of O'Connor's letters. Oates said, "It will be no surprise to admirers of Flannery O'Connor's enigmatic, troubling, and highly idiosyncratic fiction to learn that there were, behind the near-perfect little rituals of violence and redemption she created, not one but several Flannery O'Connors."

Joyce Carol Oates

A Self-Portrait in Letters

It must be said of the letters that they give life to a wonderfully warm, witty, generous, and complex personality, surely one of the most gifted of contemporary writers. At the same time they reveal a curiously girlish, child-like, touchingly timid personality. . . . The letters give voice, on one side, to a hilariously witty observer of the grotesque, the vulgar, and the merely silly in this society, and in the rather limited world of the Catholic imagination; and then they reveal a Catholic intellectual so conservative and docile that she will write to a priest-friend for permission to read Gide and Sartre (at that time on the Church's Index of forbidden writers). . . .

The first letter in the collection was written in 1948, when Flannery was "up north" at Yaddo, the writers' colony in Saratoga Springs. The last letter, a heartbreaking one, was written just before her death on August 3, 1964, when she knew she was dying of complications following an operation for the removal of a tumor. The years between 1948 and 1964 were rich, full ones, despite the fact that Flannery's debilitating condition (lupus) kept her at home, and frequently bedridden, for long periods of time. She was not at all a solitary, reclusive person; she had a wide circle of friends, and clearly loved seeing them, and writing to them often. . . .

She always knew that the process of creation was subjected to no rules, and that, as an artist, she "discovered" the truth of her stories in the writing of them. She enjoyed writing—perhaps it is not an exaggeration to say that she lived for it, and in it. Easily exhausted, she forced herself to work two or three hours every day, in the morning, and managed by this discipline to write about one story a year during the worst periods. During the final year of her life, 1964, when everything seemed to go wrong she was completing the volume that would be her finest achievement, "Everything That Rises Must Converge," which would be published, to wide critical acclaim, after her death. One cannot imagine an ailing person less given to self-pity. When, as a fairly young woman, she learned she would probably be on crutches the rest of her life, she says merely, "So, so much for that. I will henceforth be a structure with flying buttresses. . . . " Writing to a friend in

1964, she says she must submit to an operation because "I have a large tumor and if they don't make haste and get rid of it, they will have to remove me and leave it." It is only near the very end of her life that she says, briefly, to the same friend: "Prayers requested. I am sick of being sick."

From "Flannery O'Connor: A Self-Portrait in Letters," in *Antaeus,* Autumn 1987

The Receptive Reader
Which details or comments in this review do most to round out your mental picture of O'Connor? Which are most enlightening or thought-provoking?

Tribute by a Fellow Writer   Alice Walker, author of *The Color Purple,* grew up in a sharecropper's shack a few miles from where O'Connor lived for a time in a house built by slaves. Walker discovered the "dazzling perfection" of O'Connor's writing while taking a course on Southern writers up North. Walker appreciated O'Connor's work because she wrote about Southern white women with "not a whiff of magnolia" hovering in the air and about "black folks without melons and superior racial patience." Walker says, "as a college student in the sixties I read her books endlessly, scarcely conscious of the difference between her racial and economic background and my own, but put them away in anger when I discovered that, while I was reading O'Connor—Southern, Catholic, and white—there were other women writers—some Southern, some religious, all black—I had not been allowed to know." Later, after discovering black writers like Zora Neale Hurston and Jean Toomer, Walker came to look at O'Connor's fiction from a new perspective.

Alice Walker

Beyond the Peacock

Whether one "understands" her stories or not, one knows her characters are new and wondrous creations in the world and that none of her stories— not even the earliest ones in which her consciousness of racial matters had not evolved sufficiently to be interesting or to differ much from the insulting and ignorant racial stereotyping that preceded it—could have been written by anyone else. As one can tell . . . a Picasso from a Hallmark card, one can tell an O'Connor story from any story laid next to it. Her Catholicism did not in any way limit (by defining it) her art. After her great stories of sin, damnation, prophecy and revelation, the stories one reads casually in the average magazine seem to be about love and roast beef. . . .

She destroyed the last vestiges of sentimentality in white Southern writing; she caused white women to look ridiculous on pedestals, and she approached her black characters—as a mature artist—with unusual humility and restraint. She also cast spells and worked magic with the written word.

From *In Search of Our Mothers' Gardens,* 1975

The Receptive Reader

How did you react to the references to black people in O'Connor's stories? Can you relate Walker's comments to the stories you have read?

The Critic's Voice   Many critics take their clue from O'Connor's Catholicism in looking in her "startling dramas" for hints of divine love or redemption—for religious overtones that are implied rather than spelled out. The critic who wrote the following excerpt said that love is "at the very core of Flannery O'Connor's fiction."

Richard Giannone

The Mystery of Love

There is no reason to contest the fact that human dereliction sets O'Connor's narratives in motion and directs their course and outcome. What we need to look for is the gift of grace, the exultant salute to the eternal that she avows in her lectures and correspondence and that brings her anguished conflicts to a higher resolution. "It is a sign of maturity not to be scandalized and to try to find explanations in charity." O'Connor candidly challenges us to take a charitable view of her work, and scarcely anyone has met that challenge.

A shift in the locus of inquiry will bring about a change in our perception of O'Connor. She will emerge as more than an astute recorder of casual disasters. A quiet, patient smile of controlled abandonment to love shines through all of her fictional violence. And an unexpected contour will emerge from her art. . . . To the undiscerning or the psychologically oriented, O'Connor's unrelenting exposure of human fault might seem like obsession or preacherly harangue; for O'Connor, however, the sight of inner wretchedness precedes the experience of love. . . . The guilt and punishment that her characters bring upon themselves have no independent reality of their own, but are the dark shadows of the grace and life that O'Connor finds in existence. . . .

Her strange choices for heroes—nihilists, petty tyrants, and killers—turn out to be wanderers in love. Their encounter with the mystery of their existence, the adventurer of love whom O'Connor calls God, brings the quest to a close. All the endings take both protagonist and reader by surprise. O'Connor believes, and in powerful action shows, unfathomable reality to suggest the overwhelming boldness of divine love invading human life. Her fundamental understanding of this mysterious incursion is that love is not a human right or a mental deduction but a divine revelation, a gift of plenitude found within the human heart. "I believe love to be efficacious in the loooong run" she writes to a friend. O'Connor's fiction enacts her belief.

From *Flannery O'Connor and the Mystery of Love,* 1989

The Receptive Reader

Does this critic make you reexamine the role of the author's religious convictions in her stories? How?

WRITING ABOUT LITERATURE

9 One Author in Depth
WRITING FOCUS: Integrating Your Sources

*The role autobiography plays in fiction is
precisely the role that reality plays in a dream.*
JOHN CHEEVER

The Writing Workshop When you are puzzled, intrigued, or provoked by your reading, you may turn to other work by the same author to see if you can find a pattern. You try to see if you can detect clues to familiar preoccupations or a recurrent theme. In addition, you may want to turn to personal testimony by the author—in letters, in lectures, in conversations with friends. You may be able to get ideas or help from biographers and critics who focus on the relationship between the author and the work. Your exploration may lead to a paper in which you look for the common thread or a recurrent issue in several works by the same author.

In a paper drawing on a variety of sources, your task will be to write a unified paper while integrating diverse materials. It will be especially important to develop an agenda—an overall purpose or direction. Ask yourself: "What am I trying to do in this paper?" Here are accounts of what gave purpose and direction to some sample projects:

✘ A student writer was intrigued by the fact that both the talkative grandmother in "A Good Man Is Hard to Find" and the mother in "Everything That Rises Must Converge" seem to live in the past, holding on to genteel traditions and to concepts of good breeding that no longer fit the realities of the South. The student found a third O'Connor story that spells out the same underlying theme even more directly: In "A Late Encounter with the Enemy," a teacher has been taking summer classes for years to earn a belated teaching credential. She plans to have her grandfather present at her graduation. He is a Confederate general, 104 years old, and she wants him to shame the upstarts by having him there to represent the "old traditions! Dignity! Honor! Courage! My kin!" The irony of the story is that the supposed general was actually a foot soldier in the war, who was given his general's uniform by a movie company promoting *Gone with the Wind*.

✘ One student wrote about a recurrent pattern in three stories by John Cheever: We start out with people in a comfortable middle-class or upper-middle-class existence, but something happens to show that these people "are not quite who they appear to be at first, and by the end of the story, their true natures are revealed." The "fragile veneer of the characters' happy lives begins to crack." Their weaknesses, disguised by a smug façade, are shown. By the end of the story, they may, like the main character in "The Swimmer," find themselves "miserable, cold, tired, and bewildered"; exposed to the ridicule of passing motorists. Drawing on revealing comments by both Cheever himself and by his son, the student writer showed that this fear of exposure was a haunting preoccupation in Cheever's own private life.

✘ In a paper discussing several stories by Flannery O'Connor, a student writer focused on the "moment of revelation" (the *epiphany*) when a character "suddenly accepts into his or her consciousness key facts or conditions of his or her life." For instance, at the end of "A Good Man Is Hard to Find," the Misfit rejects the grandmother's last frantic appeal to spare her life because "I know you come from nice people." She urges him to pray and reaches out to touch him: "Why, you're one of my babies. You're one of my own children!" The student writer quoted O'Connor as explaining the ending to an audience to whom she was reading this story: The grandmother realizes, "even in her limited way, that she is responsible for the man before her and joined to him by ties of kinship which have their roots deep in the mystery she has been merely prattling about so far." The paper found a similar pattern of a climactic final insight or realization in two other stories.

Writing an Integrated Paper   A paper tracing a common thread in several stories by the same author tests your ability to integrate material. Keep your paper from seeming stitched together—with too many of the seams showing. Consider guidelines like the following:

✘ *Push toward a unifying thesis.* Note the weak *also* in the following opening paragraph of a first draft. (How are the two points raised there related?)

FIRST DRAFT: O'Connor's stories shock the reader because, as she herself says, "No matter how well we are able to soften the grotesque by humor or compassion, there is always an intensity about it that creates a general discomfort." O'Connor writes about the mixture of the frightening and the comical that we call the grotesque. The conflict between good and evil is also central to O'Connor's themes. These themes are evident in several of her stories. . .

A more integrated trial thesis might read like this:

SECOND DRAFT: O'Connor's stories shock the reader because, as she herself says, "No matter how well we are able to soften the grotesque by humor or compassion, there is always an intensity about it that creates a general discomfort." O'Connor's preoccupation with the grotesque is rooted in one of her most basic themes: the struggle between good and evil. *When evil erupts in our ordinary world, it is frightening, but it is also comical because it is so different from what we expect or what should be.*

❚ *Chart your overall strategy.* For instance, you may decide to explore the role of violence in each of three stories, tracing important continuities and key differences as you examine *each story* in turn. You then have to make sure to keep important connections in view as you leave one story behind and move on to the next. Instead, you might plot your essay to move not from story to story but from point to point. You may set up three or four key features of the archetypal Southern lady found in many of O'Connor's stories and take up *each feature* in turn. You might identify such common character traits as nostalgia for a more genteel past, outdated condescending views on race, and unrealistic expectations of the current crop of white people merely because they are white. You would then take each of these up in turn and show that each can be found in all three or four major characters you are examining.

❚ *Use brief characteristic quotations to take your reader into the author's world.* Suppose you are trying to show in a lesser-known story by O'Connor the familiar blend of the threatening and strange with the zany and comical. A web of specific references and short apt quotations will create the familiar atmosphere:

> Enoch in "Enoch and the Gorilla" is isolated from others. When he had opened "a nutty surprise" that his father had brought for him from the penitentiary, a "coiled piece of steel had sprung out at him and broken off the ends of his two front teeth." The waitress who instead of filling his order begins to fry bacon for herself bids him farewell by saying "Any way I don't see you will be all right with me." When Enoch lines up with the children waiting to shake hands with a man in a gorilla suit promoting a gorilla movie, the gorilla's hand is "the first hand that had been extended to Enoch since he had come to the city." This handshake changes Enoch's life; he attacks the hapless gorilla to take over the suit so that he can "see people waiting to shake his hand."

❚ *Test a critic's opinion against your own firsthand reading.* Do not just accept the critic's say-so as gospel. Show why the critic's comment is helpful; show why you agree or disagree. The following passage does a good job of working a critical quotation into the student writer's own text:

Susanne M. Paulson, in *Flannery O'Connor: A Study of the Short Fiction*, says, "both the Misfit and the grandmother derive from the same human family tainted by sin and suffering in the material world." O'Connor is indeed showing the reader that the Misfit is not an alien being but might be one of our neighbors or our own family. The Misfit himself says, "I been most everything. Been in the arm service . . . twict married, been an undertaker, been with the railroads." He says, "I was a gospel singer for a while." We could have encountered him anywhere in familiar everyday reality.

▌ *Pay special attention to transitions.* You will need strong ties and cross references between the several different stories you are discussing. Suppose you are moving on from the story about the Misfit to the story about Enoch and the gorilla. Avoid a lame transition like "We see similar themes in another O'Connor story." Provide the missing link between the two sections of your paper. Show a strong thematic connection by highlighting a major shared element:

TRANSITION: Like the Misfit in "A Good Man Is Hard to Find," Enoch in "Enoch and the Gorilla" is also a "misfit" in his world.

What is the focus of the following student paper? How successful is it in integrating material from several different stories? How successful is it in defining and making meaningful a key term in critical discussions of O'Connor's work?

Sample Student Paper

Flannery O'Connor's Grotesques
The grotesque: absurdly incongruous; departing markedly from the natural, the expected, or the typical . . . a combination of horror and humor.

This definition of the word *grotesque* perfectly describes the life of Flannery O'Connor. After all, isn't it absurd and unexpected that, as a young woman of twenty-five, her bones were so weak from lupus that she was forced to hobble around on crutches like a woman of eighty? Or ironic that she would eventually die from complications of an abdominal operation that was supposed to help improve her condition? And despite the horror O'Connor undoubtedly had to deal with during her illness, she still held a positive outlook on life, writing shortly before her relapse and death in 1964, "I intend to survive this." This absurdity, this incongruity, this grotesqueness that seemed to dominate the path of her life has carried over into O'Connor's writing, as can be seen in the short stories "A Good Man Is Hard to Find," "Everything That Rises Must Converge," and "Enoch and the Gorilla." In each of these stories lurk characteristics of the grotesque—descriptions and comparisons that seem unnatural or incongruous, ideas that are absurd or unexpected, and that same ironic combination of horror and positive humor that haunted O'Connor throughout her illness.

Perhaps it was her own physical illness that caused O'Connor's fascination with physical deformity. Many brief descriptions in her stories reflect this fascination, such as in "Everything That Rises Must Converge," when Julian turned his stricken mother over and saw that "her face was fiercely distorted. One eye, large and staring, moved slightly to the left as if it had become unmoored." This sense of grotesque distortion is also evident in the description of Enoch putting on the gorilla suit in "Enoch and the Gorilla." O'Connor portrays the act as a weird metamorphosis, as if the boy were actually turning into a gorilla:

> In the uncertain light, one of his lean white legs could be seen to disappear and then the other, one arm and then the other: a black heavier shaggier figure replaced his. For an instant, it had two heads, one light and one dark . . .

Likewise, the comparisons O'Connor draws between two objects often seem unnatural or incongruous. In "A Good Man Is Hard to Find," the mother's face is described as "broad and innocent as a cabbage," which I found to be a peculiar comparison. Similarly, in "Enoch and the Gorilla," Enoch's broken umbrella is compared to "an instrument for some specialized kind of torture that had gone out of fashion," which I thought was a warped, distorted way of viewing a common household object.

The descriptions and comparisons were not the only hints of distortion or unnaturalness. In fact, some of O'Connor's main story ideas contain elements of the unnatural or the unexpected, sometimes to the point of absurdity. In "A Good Man Is Hard to Find," the whole idea of the grandmother trying to talk a hardened criminal out of killing her on the basis that she is "a good lady" and of "good blood" is absurd. The situation becomes even more ridiculous when the grandmother and the Misfit begin very nonchalantly to discuss the weather, or when the grandmother, showing her good breeding and southern hospitality, kindly offers him one of her own son's shirts to wear, despite the fact that he is just about to have her son killed and is planning to own the shirt the son had been wearing.

Also unexpected and absurd is the Misfit's exceedingly calm and polite manner. In fact, when he notices that the mother is getting very uneasy and anxious, he politely asks her, "Lady, would you and that little girl like to step off yonder with Bobby Lee and Hiram and join your husband?" to which the mother answers in obvious relief, "Yes, thank you." Ever the gentleman, he orders his men to "Hep that lady up."

Although the Misfit's gentlemanly mannerisms are very surprising, perhaps the most unexpected part of the story occurs when the grandmother has been talking to the Misfit for a while. Suddenly feeling as if she were beginning to understand him, she declares, "Why, you're one of my babies. You're one of my own children!" Ironically it is at this moment of understanding and intimacy that the Misfit chooses to kill her.

Despite the grim ending of this and the other two stories, there is evidence of an ironic blending of humor with horror. In "A Good Man Is Hard to Find," the images of the cat jumping onto Bailey's shoulder, "clinging like a caterpillar" and the children scrambling out of the overturned car shouting, " 'We've had an ACCIDENT!' " are humorous. In fact, even after we realize the mother has suffered serious injury, the accident still seems funny in a sick sort of way.

Similarly, in "Enoch and the Gorilla," Enoch's nervous introduction to Gonga the Gorilla is hilarious, although we know how hurt and humiliated Enoch must have felt afterwards:

> "My name is Enoch Emery," he mumbled. "I attended the Rodemill Boys' Bible Academy. I work at the city zoo. I seen two of your pictures. I'm only

eighteen years old but I already work for the city. My daddy made me come . . ." and his voice cracked. . . . "You go take a jump," a surly voice inside the ape-suit said.

In "Everything That Rises Must Converge," the humor found in Julian's rebellious fantasies in which he "brought home a beautiful suspiciously Negroid woman" or "imagined his mother lying desperately ill and his being able to secure only a Negro doctor for her" lies on the surface of a pain that lurks underneath, the pain of his and his mother's strained relationship. The humor is there, but the underlying pain and horror make it feel warped and distorted.

This warping of reality, this distortion of common things, this grotesqueness, is something O'Connor shows an affinity for and a talent in using. Through her manipulation of unnatural comparisons, unexpected and absurd ideas, and humor laced with horror, she shows how even her most self-righteous characters are not clean of the grotesque. Despite the grandmother's "good blood," she too was grotesque in her absurd conversation with The Misfit. Even bright, young, nonprejudiced, socially aware Julian was tainted with the grotesque because of the delight he took in destroying his mother's comfortable little dreamworld in which she and her ancestors had a special identity. O'Connor has a knack for using distortion to create a confusing environment for her characters in which the line between the "good" and "evil" characters is very finely drawn. As one critic put it, "the real grotesques are the self-justified, the apparent grotesques may be the blessed."

Questions for Peer Review

How successfully does this student paper take you into the world of O'Connor's stories? How well does it help you understand the stories better or respond to them more fully? Compare your answers to the following questions with those of fellow students or members of a small group.

1. How would you sum up in your own words the student writer's *definition* of the key term *grotesque?* What is the student's main point or central statement about the role of the grotesque in O'Connor's fiction? Is the central idea spelled out in a central unifying *thesis?* Where? Is it restated or driven home again elsewhere in the paper—for instance, in a strong conclusion?

2. *Synonyms* and near-synonyms of the key term *grotesque* appear throughout this paper—including *distortion, absurd,* and *weird.* What other similar related terms can you trace that together form a *semantic web*—a network of terms closely related in meaning? How does each of these synonyms or related terms echo or reinforce the central term or central idea?

3. This student paper moves systematically from point to related point. Often the connection is established by *transitions* like *likewise, not the only . . ., also, similarly.* These transitions signal to the reader that the student author is staying focused on the same key issue. Prepare an informal outline listing the key points. You may want to identify one key point or subtopic of the paper for each paragraph.

4. Study the writer's selection and weaving in of details and quotations from the stories. Which are especially revealing or helpful *key quotations?* What is the mix of short quoted phrases, sentence-length quotations, and block quotations?

5. *Humor* is often very subjective and risky. The student writer calls various incidents or details in O'Connor's stories "humorous" or "hilarious." How do you or your fellow students personally react to the *dark humor* of the story?

6. Is the term *grotesque* familiar to you, or is it new and difficult for you? Where have you or fellow students encountered it? Flannery O'Connor is a Southern American writer. Some cultures—the culture of the Old South or the traditional culture of Mexico—have traditions of cultivating dark humor centered on the morbid and on death. Have you or your fellow students encountered evidence of such traditions?

10 CRITICAL PERSPECTIVES

The Reader's Response

Courtesy Richard B. Ressman

Writing disappears unless there is a response to it.
                                        BARBARA CHRISTIAN

Art, the art that matters, is not cement. It is
mobile, complex, elusive, disturbing. A love of
literature may help to forge community, but it is
a community founded on imaginative freedom,
the play of language, and scholarly honesty, not
on flag waving, boosterism, and conformity.
                                        STEPHEN GREENBLATT

FOCUS ON CRITICAL PERSPECTIVES

Literature is not dead letters on a page. It is not really a self-contained text that is the same for all. Living literature is created by a human being and re-created in the mind of the reader, listener, or spectator. Critical discussions of literature may focus our attention on different facets of this interaction:

✘ *We may focus on the work itself.* Much of the time we encounter literature as **text** on the printed page. (We may also be listening to it— at readings or on tape, sometimes with stories or poems read by the original author.) We try to do justice to "what is there"—to respond to what the author has put in the story, the poem, the play.

✘ *We may focus on the writer.* For the **author**, the crucial experience is in the joy and challenge of creation. The excitement is in making the story, the poem, or the play take shape. At the same time, we need to see the work in context: The writer is a human being enmeshed in the needs, passions, and loyalties of human existence. The writer's perspective is influenced by race or ethnic background, gender, and social class. In the process of creation, writers are influenced by tradition, by their reading of other authors. The way writers write reflects how they observe or rebel against the conventions of their craft. It reflects how they exploit the opportunities and deal with the limitations of language.

✘ *We may focus on the reader.* For the reader, literature comes to life in the interaction between the text and its audience. What readers bring to a story or a poem shapes what they see. Readers do not come to their reading with an idling, empty mind. Critics stressing **reader response** focus on how the experience, expectations, and needs that readers bring to a story shape their reading of the text. A story is words on a page until the reader's imagination brings it to life in the theater of the mind. Readers experience and reconstruct a story or a poem in accordance with their own vital concerns and interests. They provide the "missing bridges" between the world of the story and their own personal experience (Wolfgang Iser).

Here are some of the agendas that help explain how a critic responds to a work of literature:

Author Biography   Much traditional criticism focused on the author. **Author biography** aimed at a full accounting of the author's life and times. It studied the setting of the artist's work. It would place John Steinbeck, for instance, in the context of the California fishing and farming region that was his home. It would see his sympathy with the down-and-out against the background of the Great Depression of the thirties, when millions lost their jobs, their homes, and their sense of self-worth. The historical situation would help explain his ties with the Communist party, "in dubious battle" (the title of one of his books) against the capitalist system that had failed a generation of American farmers and workers.

Today's biographers often go beyond an author's public image—the warm-hearted storyteller, the loving parent. Schooled in the art of the exposé, they probe the personal problems behind the public persona. Best-selling author biographies dwell on childhood traumas or failed personal relationships. Biographers today often probe the writers' complex ways of revealing, transforming, or hiding their personal experience.

Formalist Criticism   Reacting against the traditional focus on the author's life and times, the **New Criticism** (originally new in the forties and fifties) focused on the work itself. It focused on a story or poem as a finished artifact—self-contained, complete in itself. It saw a successful story or poem as a finely crafted text, repaying close study of its verbal texture, imagery, or pattern. Critics paying close attention to form and technique are sometimes called **formalists**, a label implying that *too much* attention is being paid to form (rather than to the larger meanings).

Rather than studying the background, the author, or the times, critics in this tradition let the work speak for itself. Instead of bringing preconceptions to a story from the outside, readers read *out of* the story what it had to say about contemporary politics, contemporary religion, or whatever. In practice, this approach meant above all **close reading** of the text itself. It meant close study of matters of form and technique that could be studied directly in the text. In a New Critical reading of a short story or poem, every word or every detail counts. Critics paid detailed attention to image, symbol, irony, and point of view. They disliked fiction with a simpleminded message, steering readers instead to fiction that was challenging, subtle, and complex. Critical favorites were authors like William Faulkner, whose "A Rose for Emily" is an early example of his reliance on multilayered symbols, weighty hints and allusions, intermeshing flashbacks, and sudden revelations.

Psychoanalytic Criticism   As formalism came to dominate the study and teaching of literature, critics began to charge that overemphasis on close formal analysis tends to slight the connection between literature and life. In the words of the poet Adrienne Rich, it puts a layer of asbestos between literature and the "fiery passions of the human heart." Literature that moves us powerfully speaks to our needs, desires, and traumas as thinking, feeling human beings. **Psychoanalytic** critics, or critics influenced by psychoanalysis, early claimed that a story grips the readers' imagination when it engages with deep-seated concerns, agendas, or traumas in their own personal experience. The **symbolic action** of the story takes them through a process of recognizing their own psychological burdens and trying to cope with them. Often these are rooted in traumatic early childhood experiences or family conflicts—repressed or thwarted love for the mother, rebellion against a domineering father, or sibling rivalry. Seen from the perspective of Freudian psychology, the neuroses or maladjustments of adult life are rooted in what happened to people in their earliest formative childhood years.

In the tradition of the depth psychology of the Austrian neurologist Sigmund Freud (1856–1939) and his followers, psychoanalytic critics assume a basic similarity between the world of dreams and the world created by the imagination of a great artist. In both, according to Freud, repressed material beyond the grasp of the conscious intellect rises from the unconscious. It lets us know things about ourselves that we did not suspect. With a writer like Kafka, the psychoanalytic critic has a head start: Many of Kafka's stories have the feverish, oppressive quality of an anxiety dream, a nightmare that we find hard to shake off. For a psychoanalytic critic, "the Country Doctor's fantastic adventure points to an unrecognized, unadmitted sexual crisis on the part of a middle-aged bachelor professional" (James M. McGlathery). On the unconscious level, the doctor is likely to identify with the brutish groom whose crude impulse is to pursue and violate the doctor's maid. On the conscious level, however, the doctor sees himself as the opposite, trying to protect the young woman against rape.

Myth Criticism   Myth critics looked for the echoes of myths and archetypes anchored in the collective racial memory of the human species. Stories that have a powerful hold on the reader activate unconscious memories of basic patterns of human life. Archetypes are "the psychic residue" of numberless experiences "deeply implanted in the memory of the race." Although they may seem strange on the surface, there is "that within us which leaps at the sight of them, a cry of the blood which tells us we have known them always" (Gilbert Murray). In much imaginative literature, followers of the Swiss psychologist Carl Jung (1875–1961) trace patterns of initiation into adulthood or rituals of death and rebirth that find a profound echo in our "racial memory."

In a story like Gabriel García Márquez' "The Handsomest Drowned Man in the World," there are many clues that we cannot just read the story on a surface level. There is more to this story than a corpse washed up on the shore and buried by the villagers. The solemn attention paid to the body and the extraordinary effect it has on the villagers may remind us of the way the appearance of a god in ancient Greek myth transfigures the lives of mortals.

Marxist Criticism   Critics who claim imaginative literature as a world of its own, with its own laws and its own language, have often been challenged by others who insist on the social responsibilities of writers and artists. **Marxist** critics focus on how literature mirrors, distorts, or tries to change social and economic reality. They look at the way a writer's assumptions and loyalties are shaped by social class and economic status. They study the way the power structure of a society tries to use (and at times suppress) literature for its own purposes. Much current criticism indebted to a Marxist perspective examines the way literary works deal with patterns of power and powerlessness, domination and oppression, wealth and exploitation.

The German Jewish political scientist Karl Marx (1818–1883), coauthor of the *Communist Manifesto,* had made economic relations and social class the key to his analysis of bourgeois society. Marxist critics look for the social and political implications of a writer's work. To what social class does the author belong? Does a writer accept or attack the existing class structure? Much traditional literature mirrors or serves a society of wealth and status. Openly or by implication, it endorses the privileged status of a feudal aristocracy or of the bourgeois middle class. Some writers show their political commitments openly, others by implication. A writer who keeps quiet about the injustices of his society endorses and supports them by implication. Artists and writers often allow themselves to be used to lend the prestige of culture to unjust social systems.

In a story like Tillie Olsen's "I Stand Here Ironing," the grinding poverty and the impersonality of the institutions shape the mother's and the daughter's lives. Although the story has a stark, documentary quality, like other working-class literature it appeals to our social conscience; it indicts a system that rewards time-servers and grinds honest working people into the dust.

Feminist Criticism   Inevitably, as women have become more critical of their traditional status in society, they have challenged the literary and critical establishment as part of a male-dominated, patriarchal culture. **Feminist** critics take a special interest in how literature mirrors, perpetuates, or challenges the condition of women. They heighten our awareness of how literature reflects or questions traditional gender roles. In the words of Adrienne Rich, "A radical critique of literature, feminist in its impulse, would take the work first of all as a clue to how we live, how we have been living." It would probe how women have been led to imagine themselves and their lives.

Feminist critics have made readers more conscious of the way male authors have traditionally shaped our assumptions about men and women. For example, a feminist critic reading Kafka may start by questioning his alleged "universality." Male critics finding universal themes in Kafka's prose were not necessarily speaking for women. "Kafka's fictional world is male." Kafka's women are pawns in the power struggles of a male world.

Feminist critics have asked readers to reread literary classics from the perspective of the woman reader. How have traditional assumptions about what it means to be male or female shaped the literature of the past? How have these assumptions shaped the way scholars or critics have interpreted the classics of our literary heritage? Today many readers *re*read traditional texts with a heightened awareness of how they mirror traditional patterns of disenfranchisement or oppression. They reread the novels of some of the great women novelists of the past, like Charlotte Brontë's *Jane Eyre*, with an eye on how they anticipate the struggle of later generations for equality and liberation.

Feminist critics have a special interest in female authors and their neglect or recognition in a male-dominated culture. They have championed or rediscovered writers like Edith Wharton, Kate Chopin, and Zora Neale Hurston, who were slighted by critics putting a premium on stylistic experiment or technical sophistication. Feminists find special relevance in a story like Charlotte Perkins Gilman's "The Yellow Wallpaper," which chronicles the experience of a woman driven to the brink of madness by a domineering, insensitive male medical establishment.

Structuralism **Structuralists** focus on the way language structures our reality—the way our language system organizes our perception of the world. For example, many polar opposites (hot/cold, light/dark, good/evil) are built into our language—where in a world prior to language there might be infinite gradations. Focusing on such major organizing principles embedded in language, structuralists try to construct a grammar of meaning that does on a larger scale what the grammar of sentences does for our understanding of sentence structure.

Examining the narrative structure of Kate Chopin's "The Story of an Hour," a reader following the lead of structuralist critics may highlight three key stages: In the early stage, a woman happily married in the eyes of friends or acquaintances actually feels confined or oppressed. News of her husband's death in a train accident initiates a deceptive second stage of freedom or liberation. However, the final twist of the story has the supposedly dead husband reappear (the report was erroneous), leading to the collapse and death of the wife. The bystanders see a pattern of happy marriage—tragic loss—fatal excitement at the reunion. The reader, knowing the truth as an insider, sees a different structure: oppression—a brief euphoric interval of freedom—closing in of oppression.

Poststructuralism In recent years, **poststructuralist** critics have shifted emphasis from the overt surface structures of literary works to more basic theoretical questions. They have shown a special interest in writers who seem to be self-conscious or "self-reflexive" about their creative process or use of language. They have focused on how works of literature reveal or act out their authors' probing of the language system that is their medium. Much critical discussion has dwelt on the limitations of language and on the perspectives it imposes on its users. Critics have stressed the difficulties in assuming "impersonal" knowledge or an "objective" reality that is independent of the way our language shapes our perception of the world.

A critical discussion of Hawthorne's fiction, for instance, may shift attention from the apparent thematic content or human meaning of a story—its exploration of the Puritan sense of sin or of the evil that lurks in the human heart. It may concentrate instead on the story's implied comment on the signaling system or sign system of language and the role it played in Hawthorne's society. It may focus on such topics as the ambiguities in the relationship between author and narrator or between the author and the assumed reader. It may probe Hawthorne's ambivalent relationship to his role as a writer.

Deconstructionism **Deconstructionists** are often included under the larger heading of poststructuralism. Deconstruction (like modern literary theory generally) shows the strong influence of French intellectuals of the sixties and seventies and their radical critique of traditional society and culture. Jacques Derrida, generally credited as the originator of deconstructionism, made it his declared aim to "disrupt," to undermine traditional notions of structure and of objective truth. He insisted on the inherent, insoluble contradictions of our available think schemes, including his own. All systems of concepts are suspect; they can be used at best in a provisional, experimental way to see what they will yield in a given situation.

Deconstructionist critics probe beyond the finished surface of a story. Having been written by a human being with unresolved conflicts and contradictory emotions, a story may disguise rather than reveal the underlying anxieties or perplexities of the author. Below the surface, unresolved tensions or contradictions may account for the true dynamics of the story. A story may have one message for the ordinary unsophisticated reader and another for a reader who responds to its subtext, its subsurface ironies. Readers who deconstruct a text will be "resistant" readers. They will not be taken in by what a story says on the surface but will try "to penetrate the disguises" of the text. They may be especially attracted to works that used to be considered flawed because they seemed unfinished or contradictory. They may engage in radical rereadings of familiar classics.

Multicultural Perspectives   As late as 1970, the African American poet Ishmael Reed could say that "in this country art is what white people do." However, he also said, "it may turn out that the great restive underground language arising from the American slums and fringe communities is the real American poetry and prose, that can tell you the way things are happening now." In the years since, publishers, teachers, and critics have recognized a wide range of authors from minority backgrounds. They have tried to honor the true diversity of America's rich multicultural tradition. Among writers widely published and discussed are African American writers like Alice Walker, Toni Morrison, Terry McMillan, and August Wilson; Spanish American (Latino/Latina) authors like Victor Villaseñor, Sandra Cisneros, and Gary Soto; Asian American authors like Tam Lin, Maxine Hong Kingston, Frank Chin, and David Henry Whang; and Native American authors like Louise Erdrich, Joy Harjo, and Leslie Marmon Silko.

Critics responding to the full multicultural range of imaginative literature have broadened their assumptions and criteria to reckon with the influence of nonwhite, non-Western traditions. They probe the way current fiction or poetry reflects minority experience. For instance, studying the fiction of Morrison or Walker, they may deal with the legacy of racism, the rediscovery of African roots, antagonism between black women and black men, or the role of the Black Muslim movement in the African American community. Critics have had to reexamine the relationship between literature and militancy, or between mainstream culture and cultural separatism.

JUXTAPOSITIONS

The Range of Interpretation

A challenging, complex short story may attract a wide range of critics who approach it as a test case for their critical theories. For instance, Franz Kafka's "The Country Doctor" has attracted critics of every persuasion trying to find a key to its meaning. From the perspective of the psychoanalytic critic, the disorientation, the confusion, that we experience in the story mirrors the tension that results when the conscious mind is at war with the repressed instinctual self. From the perspective of the Marxist critic, the pervasive fear, the paralyzing anxiety of Kafka's fiction is the result of living among the insecurities and injustices of a capitalistic, bourgeois society. From the perspective of the feminist critic, Kafka's fiction seems centered on the power struggles of the male world, in which woman is "seen as purely instrumental." These perspectives need not be mutually exclusive: They remind us that human beings are social and political animals and at the same time physical sexual beings.

James M. McGlathery

The Psychoanalytic Kafka

The Country Doctor's experiences in answering a sick call in the middle of the night are best read as fantasy on the central figure's part. Also, just because it happens first, one should not assume that the night call brings on the crisis in the physician's relationship with his maid Rosa. On the contrary, the imaginary call to duty likely is the product of a developing crisis in his feelings about the live-in maid. And most important, his experiences with his patient cannot be divorced from his feelings—conscious and unconscious—regarding Rosa.

To some extent, at least, the physician must identify in his fantasy with the demonic figure of the stable boy, Rosa's would-be and presumably successful ravisher. Yet, on the conscious level, the doctor sees himself as quite the opposite, as Rosa's angel of rescue, as her only hope of escape from the rape attempt. This state of affairs suggests that his emotional crisis stemmed from unadmitted, unconscious sexual guilt. . . . Thus he blames his professional calling for the loss of his maid and of the opportunity to prove himself a hero in her eyes. Up to this time, however, he has not allowed himself to notice Rosa, much less to think of possessing her—a thought which even in his fantasy he cannot attribute to himself, and thus projects onto the stable boy.

The young man to whom the doctor is called to minister likely represents the latter's image of himself as a youth, when he was first reaching an age to marry. The patient's wish to die would then be a projection of the doctor's middle-aged bachelor guilt over his having fled as a young man from marriage into devotion to his calling. The doctor's failure at first to discover the wound may project his guilt over having suppressed awareness regarding the motivation for his complete dedication to his calling. And his subsequent discovery of the wound may reflect his dawning awareness of this guilt, even though he still cannot admit these feelings to himself.

The doctor's unadmitted shame and remorse over having escaped from the challenges of Desire into a career of healing may likewise express itself in the conclusion of his nightmarish fantasy, where he has given up the patient—that is, himself as a youth—for dead, and then finds himself condemned to be carried endlessly through the snowy wastes by an uncontrollable horse, bereft of his maid, his clothing, and likely also his practice. Read this way, the Country Doctor's fantastic adventure points to an unrecognized, unadmitted sexual crisis on the part of a middle-aged bachelor professional. His adventure is a dream of anxiety, produced by unconscious grief over lost youth and over a life that has been based on a lie, in particular, on self-deceit regarding the reason for his complete devotion of himself to medicine.

From "Desire's Persecutions in Kafka's 'Judgement,' 'Metamorphosis,' and 'The Country Doctor,' " in *Perspectives on Contemporary Literature,* vol. 7, 1981

The Receptive Reader

According to McGlathery, how do psychological mechanisms of projection and identification work in the story? How or why does the doctor identify with the groom, with the patient? Do you see a conflict between the doctor's professional calling and his sexual needs in the story?

Ernst Fischer

The Marxist Kafka

Kafka's hero, always the same . . . is not a romantic hero, but a desperate petty bourgeois in the world of late capitalism. He would like to conform to society and applaud its everyday phenomena such as family, marriage, and job—but it doesn't work. The breach is unbridgeable: business success and private happiness, social career and humane personality have become irreconcilable. . . . In contrast to most writers of his generation, Kafka constantly dealt with the problem of work and profession, that is, with the great problems of the mechanized, industrialized, commercialized world. Horrified by the specialization, Taylorization [dehumanizing and speedup of labor], and fragmentation of work, Kafka senses the growing divergence between occupation and personality.

His heroes fail because of this division: they are not satisfied with an occupation they feel to be senseless; they are alienated by it; they are overwhelmed by the vanity of their efforts.

The country doctor, by nature an isolated person, is vulnerable to the tragicomic contradiction between the idea of being the helper in a wide area and the poverty of his means. He clings to the idea of being a helper, wards off resignation, is ready to sacrifice his private life for his professional ethics, and is forced in the most cruel way to recognize the vanity of his efforts. . . . [O]ne can recognize in the "unearthly horses" which emerge from the pigpen a fantastic and melancholy satire on ideals which have become ghosts, which are no longer appropriate to social conditions: . . . the bourgeois sense of duty, unconditional obedience when the signal sounds. Everything begins with a "false ringing of the night bell." . . . Not one word says: "Defend yourself, country doctor! You need a living horse, not ideological ghosts!" But when the ghost horses . . . so unwillingly drag themselves through the infinite snow after the death of the patient, we hear the lament, the protest:

> Naked, prey to the frost of this most unfortunate age, I, an old man, am driven around with an earthly coach and unearthly horses. My fur coat is hanging in the back of the coach; I can't reach it, and not one of the active churls among the patients lifts his finger. Deceived! Deceived!

It is the lament, the protest of him who has been cheated out of the dignity of his occupation; the sense of his life, the echo of a false alarm from the very beginning—not a call to revolution, but also not a recognition of the historically determined as an eternal *condition humaine* [human condition]; rather, a rebellion against the coldness, the frost of "this most unfortunate age."

In Kenneth Hughes, *Franz Kafka: An Anthology of Marxist Criticism,*
1981

The Receptive Reader

How much direct evidence is there in the story of the doctor's view of his vocation or profession? How crucial is his inadequacy as a healer to the story as a whole?

Evelyn Torton Beck

Kafka: A Feminist Perspective

The essential power struggles in Kafka's texts are between the males. . . . Nowhere in Kafka does woman speak for herself. . . . Because it is his male heroes who organize the text's way of seeing, the angle of vision in Kafka's texts is necessarily androcentric—i.e., male centered. . . .

Throughout, Kafka's male characters think of women in the language of ownership. "I'm not thinking of handing the girl over to you," says the country doctor to his groom. . . . Woman exists only on the margins, entrapped in a power system in which she is never an actor, only acted upon. . . .

For women have been taught to see through an androcentric lens, it is a way of seeing we all have to un-learn. Such a paradigm shift is both exhilarating and disorienting, since it forces us to rethink our received truths about literary study and about the world. It challenges our codified values, especially about "old masters" and "eternal truths." It forces us to rethink and reconceptualize the values systems by which we live. Such disruptions are never comfortable, but to paraphrase a Kafka aphorism, a book should act on us like a sharp blow—it should serve as an ax for "frozen sea within us." Though I would prefer less violent language, this perception well describes the kind of awakening a feminist analysis of literature can catalyze. We ought to welcome it.

From "Kafka's Traffic in Women: Gender, Power, and Sexuality," in *The*
Literary Review, 1983

The Receptive Reader

How stereotypical is the treatment of Rose in the story? Do you think female readers can identify with the anxieties of the doctor? How, or why?

CONTEXTS FOR READING

Critics present differing personal readings of a story or poem. They may build their interpretation on a close analysis of details that other readers may have overlooked. In interviews and critical biographies, they probe an author's intentions and the relation between the author's life and work. In recent years especially, critics have placed works of literature in the context of the larger culture. They may involve the reader in sexual politics, the class struggle, or theories about the workings of language.

Shirley Jackson

One of the most terrifying aspects of publishing stories and books is the realization that they are going to be read, and read by strangers.

How do writers respond to critical reactions to their work? Many writers have a love-hate relationship with the audience. Like Shirley Jackson in the following excerpt, they may have thought with pleasurable anticipation of the "millions and millions of people who were going to be uplifted and enriched and delighted" by the author's work. However, Jackson here tells the story of one author's discovery of her audience not as anonymous, passive readers but as human beings with agendas and resentments of their own.

Biography of a Story

On the morning of June 28, 1948, I walked down to the post office in our little Vermont town to pick up the mail. I was quite casual about it, as I recall—I opened the box, took out a couple of bills and a letter or two, talked to the postmaster for a few minutes, and left, never supposing that it was the last time for months that I was to pick up the mail without an active feeling of panic. By the next week I had had to change my mailbox to the largest one in the post office, and casual conversation with the postmaster was out of the question, because he wasn't speaking to me. June 28, 1948, was the day *The New Yorker* came out with a story of mine in it. It was not my first published story, nor my last, but I have been assured over and over that if it had been the only story I ever wrote or published, there would be people who would not forget my name.

I had written the story three weeks before, on a bright June morning when summer seemed to have come at last, with blue skies and warm sun and no heavenly signs to warn me that my morning's work was anything but just another story. The idea had come to me while I was pushing my daughter up the hill in her stroller—it was, as I say, a warm morning, and the hill was steep, and beside my daughter the stroller held the day's groceries—and perhaps the effort of that last fifty yards up the hill put an edge to the story; at any rate, I had the idea fairly clearly in my mind when I put my daughter in her playpen and the frozen vegetables in the refrigerator, and, writing the story, I found that it went quickly and easily, moving from beginning to end without pause. As a matter of fact, when I read it over later I decided that except for one or two minor corrections, it needed no changes, and the story I finally typed up and sent off to my agent the next day was almost word for word the original draft. This, as any writer of stories can tell you, is not a usual thing. All I know is that when I came to read the story over I felt strongly that I didn't want to fuss with it. I didn't think it was perfect, but I didn't want to fuss with it. It was, I thought, a serious, straightforward story, and I was pleased and a little surprised at the ease with which it had been written; I was reasonably proud of it, and hoped that my agent would sell it to some magazine and I would have the gratification of seeing it in print.

My agent did not care for the story, but—as she said in her note at the time—her job was to sell it, not to like it. She sent it at once to *The New Yorker,* and about a week after the story had been written I received a telephone call from the fiction editor of *The New Yorker;* it was quite clear that he did not really care for the story, either, but *The New Yorker* was going to buy it. He asked for one change—that the date mentioned in the story be changed to coincide with the date of the issue of the magazine in which the story would appear, and I said of course. He then asked, hesitantly, if I had any particular interpretation of my own for the story; Mr. Harold Ross, then the editor of *The New Yorker,* was not altogether sure that he understood the story, and wondered if I cared to enlarge upon its meaning. I said no. Mr. Ross, he said, thought that the story might be puzzling to some people, and in case anyone telephoned the magazine, as sometimes happened, or wrote in asking about the story, was there anything in particular I wanted them to say? No, I said, nothing in particular; it was just a story I wrote.

I had no more preparation than that. I went on picking up the mail every morning, pushing my daughter up and down the hill in her stroller, anticipating pleasurably the check from *The New Yorker,* and shopping for groceries. The weather stayed nice and it looked as though it was going to be a good summer. Then, on June 28, *The New Yorker* came out with my story.

Things began mildly enough with a note from a friend at *The New Yorker:* "Your story has kicked up quite a fuss around the office," he wrote. I was flattered; it's nice to think that your friends notice what you write. Later that day there was a call from one of the magazine's editors; they had had a couple of people phone in about my story, he said, and was there anything I particularly wanted him to say if there were any more calls? No, I said, nothing particular; anything he chose to say was perfectly all right with me; it was just a story.

I was further puzzled by a cryptic note from another friend: "Heard a man talking about a story of yours on the bus this morning," she wrote. "Very exciting. I wanted to tell him I knew the author, but after I heard what he was saying I decided I'd better not."

One of the most terrifying aspects of publishing stories and books is the realization that they are going to be read, and read by strangers. I had never fully realized this before, although I had of course in my imagination dwelt lovingly upon the thought of the millions and millions of people who were going to be uplifted and enriched and delighted by the stories I wrote. It had simply never occurred to me that these millions and millions of people might be so far from being uplifted that they would sit down and write me letters I was downright scared to open; of the three-hundred-odd letters that I received that summer I can count only thirteen that spoke kindly to me, and they were mostly from friends. Even my mother scolded me: "Dad and I did not care at all for your story in *The New Yorker,*" she wrote sternly, "it does seem, dear, that this gloomy kind of story is what all you young people think about these days. Why don't you write something to cheer people up?"

By mid-July I had begun to perceive that I was very lucky indeed to be safely in Vermont, where no one in our small town had ever heard of *The New Yorker,* much less read my story. Millions of people, and my mother, had taken a pronounced dislike to me.

The magazine kept no track of telephone calls, but all letters addressed to me care of the magazine were forwarded directly to me for answering, and all letters addressed to the magazine—some of them addressed to Harold Ross personally; these were the most vehement—were answered at the magazine and then the letters were sent me in great batches, along with carbons of the answers written at the magazine. I have all the letters still, and if they could be considered to give any accurate cross section of the reading public, or the reading public of *The New Yorker,* or even the reading public of one issue of *The New Yorker,* I would stop writing now.

Judging from these letters, people who read stories are gullible, rude, frequently illiterate, and horribly afraid of being laughed at. Many of the writers were positive that *The New Yorker* was going to ridicule them in print, and the most cautious letters were headed, in capital letters: NOT FOR PUBLICATION or PLEASE DO NOT PRINT THIS LETTER, or, at best, THIS LETTER MAY BE PUBLISHED AT YOUR USUAL RATES OF PAYMENT. Anonymous letters, of which there were a few, were destroyed. *The New Yorker* never published any comment of any kind about the story in the magazine, but did issue one publicity release saying that the story had received more mail than any piece of fiction they had ever published; this was after the newspapers had gotten into the act, in midsummer, with a front-page story in the San Francisco *Chronicle* begging to know what the story meant, and a series of columns in New York and Chicago papers pointing out that *New Yorker* subscriptions were being canceled right and left.

Curiously, there are three main themes which dominate the letters of that first summer—three themes which might be identified as bewilderment, speculation, and plain old-fashioned abuse. In the years since then, during which the story has been anthologized, dramatized, televised, and even—in one completely mystifying transformation—made into a ballet, the tenor of letters I receive has changed. I am addressed more politely, as a rule, and the letters largely confine themselves to questions like what does this story mean? The general tone of the early letters, however, was a kind of wide-eyed, shocked innocence. People at first were not so much concerned with what the story meant; what they wanted to know was where these lotteries were held, and whether they could go there and watch.

The Receptive Reader

What is ironic about the mood and the setting in which Jackson wrote her story? What did she discover about her audience—how does she describe and classify the letter writers? What would you include in a capsule portrait of Shirley Jackson's ideal reader? Do you think that an anthology like this one should print fewer "gloomy" and instead more cheerful pieces?

Toni Cade Bambara

Interviewers have extensively questioned well-known current writers. The following excerpts are from a long interview Claudia Tate conducted with Toni Cade Bambara and included in the book *Black Women Writers at Work*. In this part of the interview, Bambara talks to the interviewer about being a woman and a writer, being a black writer in a white-dominated society, and balancing the personal motives and political challenges of being a writer.

Trying to Stay Centered

C.T.: How does being black and female constitute a particular perspective in your work?

BAMBARA: As black and woman in a society systematically orchestrated to oppress each and both, we have a very particular vantage point and, therefore, have a special contribution to make to the collective intelligence, to the literatures of this historical moment. I'm clumsy and incoherent when it comes to defining that perspective in specific and concrete terms, worse at assessing the value of my own particular pitch and voice in the overall chorus. I leave that to our critics, to our teachers and students of literature. I'm a nationalist; I'm a feminist, at least that. That's clear, I'm sure, in the work. My story "Medley" could not have been written by a brother, nor could "A Tender Man" have been written by a white woman. Those two stories are very much cut on the bias, so to speak, by a seamstress on the inside of the cloth. I am about the empowerment and development of our sisters and of our community. That sense of caring and celebration is certainly reflected in the body of my work and has been consistently picked up by other writers, reviewers, critics, teachers, students. But as I said, I leave that hard task of analysis to the analysts. I do my work and I try not to blunder.

C.T.: How do you fit writing into your life?

BAMBARA: Up until recently, I had never fully appreciated the sheer anguish of that issue. I never knew what the hell people were talking about when they asked, "How do you manage to juggle the demands of motherhood, teaching, community work, writing and the rest?" Writing had never been a central activity in my life. It was one of the things I did when I got around to it or when the compulsion seized me and sat me down. The short story, the article, the book review, after all, are short-term pieces. I would simply commandeer time, space, paper and pen, close the door, unplug the phone, get ugly with would-be intruders and get to work for a few days. Recently, however, working on a novel and a few movie scripts—phew! I now know what that question means and I despair. I had to renegotiate a great many relationships that fell apart around me; the novel took me out of action for nearly a year. I was unfit to work—couldn't draft a simple office memo, couldn't keep track of time, blew meetings, refused to answer the door, wasn't interested in hanging out in any way, shape, or form. My daughter hung in there, screened calls, learned to iron her own clothes and generally kept out of my sight. My mama would look at me funny every now and then, finding that days had gone by and I hadn't gotten around to combing my hair or calling her to check in and just chat. Short stories are a piece of time. The novel is a way of life.

I have no shrewd advice to offer developing writers about this business of snatching time and space to work. I do not have anything profound to offer mother-writers or worker-writers except to say that it will cost you something. Anything of value is going to cost you something. I'm not much of a caretaker, for example, in relationships. I am not consistent about giving vibrancy and other kinds of input to a relationship. I don't always remember the birthdays, the anniversaries. There are periods when I am the most attentive and thoughtful lover in the world, and periods, too, when I am just unavailable. I have never learned, not yet anyway, to apologize for or continually give reassurance about what I'm doing. I'm not terribly accountable or very sensitive to other people's sense of being beat back, cut out, blocked, shunted off.

I've had occasion, as you can well imagine, to talk about just this thing with sister writers. How do the children handle your "absence"—standing at the stove flipping them buckwheats but being totally elsewhere? How does your man deal with the fact that you are just not there and it's nothing personal? Atrocity tales, honey, and sad. I've known playwrights, artists, filmmakers—brothers I'm talking about—who just do not understand, or maybe pretend not to understand, that mad fit that gets hold of me and makes me prefer working all night and morning at the typewriter to playing poker or going dancing. It's a trip. But some years ago, I promised myself a period of five years to tackle this writing business in a serious manner. It's a priority item now—to master the craft, to produce, to stick to it no matter how many committee meetings get missed.

My situation isn't nearly as chary as others I know. I'm not a wife, and my daughter couldn't care less what the house looks like so long as the hamper isn't overflowing. I'm not a husband; I do not have the responsibility of trying to live up to "provider." I'm not committed to any notion of "career." Also, I'm not addicted to anything—furniture, cars, wardrobe, etc.—so there's no sense of sacrifice or foolishness about how I spend my time in non-money-making pursuits. Furthermore, I don't feel obliged to structure my life in respectably routine ways; that is to say, I do not mind being perceived as a "weirdo" or whatever. My situation is, perhaps, not very characteristic; I don't know. But to answer the question—I just flat out announce I'm working, leave me alone and get out of my face. When

I "surface" again, I try to apply the poultices and patch up the holes I've left in relationships around me. That's as much as I know how to do . . . so far.

C.T.: What determines your responsibility to yourself and to your audience?

BAMBARA: I start with the recognition that we are at war, and that war is not simply a hot debate between the capitalist camp and the socialist camp over which economic/political/social arrangement will have hegemony in the world. It's not just the battle over turf and who has the right to utilize resources for whomsoever's benefit. The war is also being fought over the truth: what is the truth about human nature, about the human potential? My responsibility to myself, my neighbors, my family and the human family is to try to tell the truth. That ain't easy. There are so few truth-speaking traditions in this society in which the myth of "Western civilization" has claimed the allegiance of so many. We have rarely been encouraged and equipped to appreciate the fact that the truth works, that it releases the Spirit and that it is a joyous thing. We live in a part of the world, for example, that equates criticism with assault, that equates social responsibility with naive idealism, that defines the unrelenting pursuit of knowledge and wisdom as fanaticism.

I do not think that literature is *the* primary instrument for social transformation, but I do think it has potency. So I work to tell the truth about people's lives; I work to celebrate struggle, to applaud the tradition of struggle in our community, to bring to center stage all those characters, just ordinary folks on the block, who've been waiting in the wings, characters we thought we had to ignore because they weren't pimp-flashy or hustler-slick or because they didn't fit easily into previously acceptable modes or stock types. I want to lift up some usable truths—like the fact that the simple act of corn-rowing one's hair is radical in a society that defines beauty as blonde tresses blowing in the wind; that staying centered in the best of one's own cultural tradition is hip, is sane, is perfectly fine despite all claims to universality-through-Anglo-Saxonizing and other madnesses.

It would be dishonest, though, to end my comments there. First and foremost I write for myself. Writing has been for a long time my major tool for self-instruction and self-development. I try to stay honest through pencil and paper. I run off at the mouth a lot. I've a penchant for flamboyant performance. I exaggerate to the point of hysteria. I cannot always be trusted with my mouth open. But when I sit down with the notebooks, I am absolutely serious about what I see, sense, know. I write for the same reason I keep track of my dreams, for the same reason I meditate and practice being still— to stay in touch with me and not let too much slip by me. We're about building a nation; the inner nation needs building, too. I would be writing whether there were a publishing industry or not, whether there were presses or not, whether there were markets or not.

The Receptive Reader

What is Bambara's attitude toward critics? What for her is the connection between being black and a woman? What for her are the special challenges and demands of being a woman and a writer? How does she cope with them? What is her view of the political responsibilities or potential of literature? What is the personal meaning her writing has for her?

Stanley Kozikowski

The New Criticism, or formalism, that became influential in the forties and fifties dominated the teaching of literature for decades. It asked readers to concentrate on the literary text in front of them and give it an intense close reading. In a New Critical reading of a short story or poem, every detail is potentially significant, contributing to the meaning of the whole. Like the author of the following critical analysis, critics influenced by this tradition find symbolic significance, unsuspected double meanings, and thematic echoes in words and objects that the casual reader might overlook.

Symbolism in "Hills like White Elephants"

Recent observations about the bamboo curtain in Hemingway's "Hills like White Elephants," particularly those of Sherlyn Abdoo, draw suggestive reference to the richly and immensely detailed pattern of Hemingway's story. The pivotal image of the curtained doorway, I would add, is even more powerfully implicated in the story's highly imaginative structure of contrasting meanings than is already assumed to be the case. The image, as it is signaled in the figural consciousness of "the girl" and in the literal awareness of "the man" helps the reader to reformulate the events of the story into a new coherence.

Hills are like white elephants for Jig because they carry ambivalent evocations of the child within her—like a white elephant, an unwanted gift, a seemingly remote but immense problem. They ominously suggest the pallid skin tone of a stillborn infant, but they also evoke that which is "bright," "lovely," beautiful with the promise of life, and intrinsically of value, as was the highly esteemed Siamese white elephant. Stirring Jig's acute apprehension and her cherished affections, the apparently distant hills attract to the "very hot" and "dry" Ebro plain and the train station an uncomfortable but refreshing "warm wind" that blows through the bamboo curtain. To this bimodal breeze, the American man and Jig respond differently: He feels it as a simple, quick remedy to a removable annoyance. She experiences it, in her ambivalence, as a "lovely" invigoration, at the very moment that she has looked upon the "lovely hills," which are like white elephants—fearfully unwanted but precious.

To the American man, as distant from metaphor as he is from the hills, the "wind" of the hills simply defines casually and literally what an abortion is: As "the warm wind blew the bead curtain against the table," he is quick to say, "I know you wouldn't mind it, Jig. It's really not anything. It's just to let the air in. . . . I'll go with you. . . . They just let the air in and then it's perfectly natural."

Jig's reaction, delayed but deliberate, and consistent with her sense of what the hills are like, is signaled in the doorway. The wind through the bamboo curtain illustrates for her the sweet past and the bitter present. The curtain, painted with the words "Anis del Toro," signifies the sweet-now-bitter anise-seed of the bull. In the very drinks that both have, it conveys to the man, with doltish literalism, "a drink," but to Jig, a licorice taste grown as bitter as wormwood—the very taste evoking "all the things you've waited so long for, like absinthe." Jig, again figuratively, thus experiences what life—precious and unwanted—is "like." The breeze, the moving beaded curtain, and the evocative drink—like hills like white elephants—connote to Jig the sweet promise of seeding and the bitter termination of birthing. The same objects convey to the man an easy sense of exit, excision, and getting on with other things. Ever opposite, his ironic and brutal, but now figurative, words, "Oh, cut it out," are answered by Jig's sharp but now literal, "You started it"—a remarkable counterpoint of clauses, playing off his dour, unimaginative indelicacy against her superb delicacy of self-awareness.

Just as Jig holds the two strings of bamboo beads blown into her hand, she maintains full literal possession of her self and her child, as we see in the story's culminating design. But Jig nevertheless has an abortion of sorts, one precisely like hills like white elephants: Having taken "the [not their] two bags"—"Two heavy bags" to the other side of the station, symbolically the mother and child, the man then goes into the bar from that other side, drinks "an Anis at the bar," and finally, with an astonishing irony to which he is oblivious, struts "out through the bead curtain" to the table outside, where Jig and he had sat previously, and where Jig, now smiling, remains seated. Conveyed out from the barroom, through the breezy doorway, through which the "air" gets "let in" from the other side, "the man" (appropriately nameless, mere reiterated "seed" from "bull"—Anis del Toro—but now like an aerated fetus himself) is ironically terminated, expelled—in her (now triumphantly ironic figural) consciousness—from any further relationship with Jig. Clearly, Jig and her child have now come out literally "fine" after this "awfully simple operation." He, metaphorically, goes "out through the bead curtain" and out of their lives.

Reasonably, Jig's name, which among its various meanings denotes a device that separates waste from precious ore (*OED*), symbolizes her excision of the identityless "man"—his bull and seed—from her and her precious child's lives. Moreover, Jig's literally precise "nothing wrong with me" addresses numerous ambivalent references to "things" in the story—the man's naming the child within as an "only thing" and Jig's perception of the child as "everything." With splendid verbal and situational irony, Hemingway's American man, aborted from Jig's world, becomes the very "nothing"—the white elephant—that he had urged Jig to renounce and remove from their lives moments before. We may now fathom Jig's "smile" as she grasps how indeed things can be like other things—hills can be like white elephants, and lovers, too—in Hemingway's bravely and imaginatively affecting tale.

From *The Explicator,* 1994

The Receptive Reader

According to this reading, how do details of the setting and the words and movements of the characters mirror the major symbolic action of the story? For instance, what does this reader make of the white elephants, the breeze, the moving beaded curtain, the drink? How does he show that the man and the woman in the story read their setting and their situation in very different ways? What for this reader is the heart of the story?

Sandra M. Gilbert and Susan Gubar

They shut me up in prose—
As when a little Girl
They put me in the closet—
Because they liked me "still"—
                        EMILY DICKINSON

In 1985, Sandra M. Gilbert and Susan Gubar published a comprehensive anthology of literature in English by women. Their book was designed to help rediscover women writers neglected or ignored in the patriarchal, male-dominated literary tradition. In an earlier book, *The Madwoman in the Attic* (1979), they had traced images of imprisonment and escape in the work of the great English and American women writers of the nineteenth century. They discussed recurrent symbolic uses of madness as an escape from the intolerable restrictions society imposed on women and women writers. In the following excerpt, the two authors read Charlotte Perkins Gilman's "The Yellow Wallpaper" from a feminist perspective. The story becomes a "paradigmatic" tale that "seems to tell *the* story" that all literary women could tell if they were to give voice to their experience as women and writers.

Enclosure and Escape: Gilman's "The Yellow Wallpaper"

As if to comment on the unity of all these points—on, that is, the anxiety-inducing connections between what women writers tend to see as their parallel confinements in texts, houses, and maternal female bodies—Charlotte Perkins Gilman brought them all together in 1890 in a striking story of female confinement and escape, a paradigmatic tale which (like *Jane Eyre*) seems to tell *the* story that all literary women would tell if they could speak their "speechless woe." "The Yellow Wallpaper," which Gilman herself called "a description of a case of nervous breakdown," recounts in the first person the experiences of a woman who is evidently suffering from a severe postpartum psychosis. Her husband, a censorious and paternalistic physician, is treating her according to methods by which S. Weir Mitchell, a famous "nerve specialist," treated Gilman herself for a similar problem. He has confined her to a large garret room in an "ancestral hall" he has rented, and he has forbidden her to touch pen to paper until she is well again, for he feels, says the narrator, "that with my imaginative power and habit of story-making, a nervous weakness like mine is sure to lead to all manner of excited fancies, and that I ought to use my will and good sense to check the tendency."

The cure, of course, is worse than the disease, for the sick woman's mental condition deteriorates rapidly. "I think sometimes that if I were only well enough to write a little it would relieve the press of ideas and rest me," she remarks, but literally confined in a room she thinks is a one-time nursery because it has "rings and things" in the walls, she is literally locked away from creativity. The "rings and things," although reminiscent of children's gymnastic equipment, are really the paraphernalia of confinement, like the gate at the head of the stairs, instruments that definitively indicate her imprisonment. Even more tormenting, however, is the room's wallpaper: a sulphurous yellow paper, torn off in spots, and patterned with "lame uncertain curves" that "plunge off at outrageous angles" and "destroy themselves in unheard of contradictions." Ancient, smoldering, "unclean" as the oppressive structures of the society in which she finds herself, this paper surrounds the narrator like an inexplicable text, censorious and overwhelming as her physician husband, haunting as the "hereditary estate" in which she is trying to survive. Inevitably she studies its suicidal implications—and inevitably, because of her "imaginative power and habit of story-making," she revises it, projecting her own passion for escape into its otherwise incomprehensible hieroglyphics. "This wallpaper," she decides, at a key point in her story,

> has a kind of subpattern in a different shade, a particularly irritating one, for you can only see it in certain lights, and not clearly then.
>
> But in the places where it isn't faded and where the sun is just so—I can see a strange, provoking, formless sort of figure, that seems to skulk about behind that silly and conspicuous front design.

As time passes, this figure concealed behind what corresponds (in terms of what we have been discussing) to the facade of the patriarchal text becomes clearer and clearer. By moonlight the pattern of the wallpaper "becomes bars! The outside pattern I mean, and the woman behind it is as plain as can be." And eventually, as the narrator sinks more deeply into what the world calls madness, the terrifying implications of both the paper and the figure imprisoned behind the paper begin to permeate—that is, to *haunt*—the rented ancestral mansion in which she and her husband are immured. The "yellow smell" of the paper "creeps all over the house," drenching every room in its subtle aroma of decay. And the woman creeps too—through the house, in the house, and out of the house, in the garden and "on that long road under the trees." Sometimes, indeed, the narrator confesses, "I think there are a great many women" both behind the paper and creeping in the garden, "and sometimes only one, and she crawls around fast, and her crawling shakes [the paper] all over. . . . And she is all the time trying to climb through. But nobody could climb through that pattern—it strangles so; I think that is why it has so many heads."

Eventually it becomes obvious to both reader and narrator that the figure creeping through and behind the wallpaper is both the narrator and the narrator's double. By the end of the story, moreover, the narrator has enabled this double to escape from her textual/architectural confinement: "I pulled and she shook, I shook and she pulled, and before morning we had peeled off yards of that paper." Is the message of the tale's conclusion mere madness? Certainly the righteous Doctor John—whose name links him to the anti-hero of Charlotte Brontë's *Villette*—has been temporarily defeated, or at least momentarily stunned. "Now why should that man have fainted?" the narrator ironically asks as she creeps around her attic. But John's unmasculine swoon of surprise is the least of the triumphs Gilman imagines for her madwoman. More significant are the madwoman's own imaginings and creations, mirages of health and freedom with which her author endows her like a fairy godmother showering gold on a sleeping heroine. The woman from behind the wallpaper creeps away, for instance, creeps fast and far on the long road, in broad daylight. "I have watched her sometimes away off in the open country," says the narrator, "creeping as fast as a cloud shadow in a high wind."

Indistinct and yet rapid, barely perceptible but inexorable, the progress of that cloud shadow is not unlike the progress of nineteenth-century literary women out of the texts defined by patriarchal poetics into the open spaces of their own authority. That such an escape from the numb world behind the patterned walls of the text was a flight from disease into health was quite clear to Gilman herself. When "The Yellow Wallpaper" was published she sent it to Weir Mitchell whose strictures had kept her from attempting the pen during her own breakdown, thereby aggravating her illness, and she was delighted to learn, years later, that "he had changed his treatment of nervous prostration since reading" her story. "If that is a fact," she declared, "I have not lived in vain." Because she was a rebellious feminist besides being a medical iconoclast, we can be sure that Gilman did not think of this triumph of hers in narrowly therapeutic terms. Because she knew, with Emily Dickinson, that "Infection in the sentence breeds," she knew that the cure for female despair must be spiritual as well as physical, aesthetic as well as social. What "The Yellow Wallpaper" shows she knew, too, is that even when a supposedly "mad" woman has been sentenced to imprisonment in the "infected" house of her own body, she may discover that, as Sylvia Plath was to put it seventy years later, she has "a self to recover, a queen."

The Receptive Reader

1. What is the connection between *patriarchal* and *paternalistic?*

2. What is the parallel Gilbert and Gubar trace between the way women are treated traditionally in literary texts by male authors, between the way women are treated literally in the home, and between the way their lives are traditionally defined by "maternal female bodies"?

3. How do the two critics trace the theme of imprisonment and escape in Gilman's story? What parts of the story does this discussion make you see in a new light?

Making Connections—For Discussion and Writing
    How do Bambara in the interview and Gilbert and Gubar in this excerpt see
the connection between literature and life?

Wilfred L. Guerin

Freud, the pioneering Austrian psychoanalyst, helped shape the thinking and vocabulary of many modern readers. He influenced the way
they think and talk about human psychology—even if they disagree with
major points of his theory, such as his making sexual energy (or libido)
an all-pervasive human motive, or his tracing mental illness to traumatic
childhood events, or his skepticism about women's memories of sexual
abuse. Freud himself had looked to art and imaginative literature for evidence of the workings of the unconscious. Critics draw on the Freudian
perspective especially when dealing with the literature that moves in the
border country between waking and dream, reality and fantasy, or the
conscious intellect and buried unconscious motives.

"Young Goodman Brown": Id versus Superego

The theme of innocence betrayed is central to Nathaniel Hawthorne's
"Young Goodman Brown," the tale of the young bridegroom who leaves his
wife Faith to spend a night with Satan in the forest. The events of that terrifying night are a classic traumatic experience for the youth. At the center
of the dark wilderness he discovers a witches' Sabbath involving all the
honored teachers, preachers, and friends of his village. The climax is
reached when his own immaculate bride is brought forth to stand by his
side and pledge eternal allegiance to the Fiend of Hell. Following this climactic moment in which the hero resists the diabolical urge to join the fraternity of evil, he wakes to find himself in the deserted forest wondering if
what has happened was dream or reality. Regardless of the answer, he is a
changed man. He returns in the morning to the village and to his Faith, but
he is never at peace with himself again. Henceforth he can never hear the
singing of a holy hymn without also hearing the echoes of the anthem of
sin from that terrible night in the forest. He shrinks even from the side of
Faith. His dying hour is gloom, and no hopeful epitaph is engraved upon
his tombstone.
    Aside from the clearly intended allegorical meanings discussed elsewhere
in this book, it is the story's underlying psychological implications that concern us here. We start with the assumption that, through symbolism and
technique, "Young Goodman Brown" means more than it says. In this respect our task is one of extrapolation, an inferring of the unknown from the
known. Our first premise is that Brown's journey is more than a physical
one; it is a psychological one as well. To see what this journey means in
psychological terms, we need to examine the setting, the time and place.
Impelled by unmistakably libidinal force, the hero moves from the village of

Salem into the forest. The village is a place of light and order, both social and spiritual order. Brown leaves Faith behind in the town at sunset and returns to Faith in the morning. The journey into the wilderness is taken in the night: "My journey . . . forth and back again," explains the young man to his wife, "must needs be done 'twixt now and sunrise." It is in the forest, a place of darkness and unknown terrors, that Brown meets the Devil. On one level, then, the village may be equated with consciousness, the forest with the dark recesses of the unconscious. But, more precisely, the village, as a place of social and moral order (and inhibition) is analogous to Freud's superego, conscience, the morally inhibiting agent of the psyche; the forest, as a place of wild, untamed passions and terrors, has the attributes of the Freudian id. As mediator between these opposing forces, Brown himself resembles the poor ego, which tries to effect a healthy balance and is shattered because it is unable to do so.

Why can't he reconcile these forces? Is his predicament that of all human beings, as is indicated by his common, nondistinctive surname? If so, are we all destined to die in gloom? Certainly, Hawthorne implies, we cannot remain always in the village, outside the forest. And sooner or later, we must all confront Satan. Let us examine this diabolical figure for a moment. When we first see him (after being prepared by Brown's expressed fear, "What if the devil himself should be at my very elbow!"), he is "seated at the foot of an old tree"—an allusion to the "old tree" of forbidden fruit and the knowledge of sin. He is described as "bearing a considerable resemblance" to the hero himself. He is, in short, Brown's own alter ego, the dramatic projection of a part of Brown's psyche, just as Faith is the projection of another part of his psyche. The staff Satan is carrying, similar to the maple stick he later gives to Brown, is like a "great black snake . . . a living serpent"—a standard Freudian symbol for the uncontrollable phallus. As he moves on through the forest, Brown encounters other figures, the most respected of his moral tutors: old Goody Cloyse, Deacon Gookin, and, at last, even Faith herself, her pink ribbon reflecting the ambiguity that Brown is unable to resolve, for pink is the mixture of white (for purity) and red (for passion). Thoroughly unnerved—then maddened—by disillusionment, Brown capitulates to the wild evil in this heart of darkness and becomes "himself the chief horror of the scene, [shrinking] not from its other horrors." That the whole lurid scene may be interpreted as the projection of Brown's formerly repressed impulses is indicated in Hawthorne's description of the transformed protagonist:

> In truth, all through the haunted forest there could be nothing more frightful than the figure of Goodman Brown. On he flew among the black pines, brandishing his staff with frenzied gestures, now giving vent to an inspiration of horrid blasphemy, and now shouting forth such laughter as set all the echoes of the forest laughing like demons around him. *The fiend in his own shape is less hideous than when he rages in the breast of man.* (italics added)

Though Hawthorne implies that Brown's problem is that of Everyman, he does not suggest that all humans share Brown's gloomy destiny. Like Freud,

Hawthorne saw the dangers of an overactive suppression of libido and the consequent development of a tyrannous superego, though he thought of the problem in his own terms as an imbalance of head versus heart. Goodman Brown is the tragic victim of a society that has shut its eyes to the inevitable "naturalness" of sex as a part of humankind's physical and mental constitution, a society whose moral system would suppress too severely natural human impulses.

Among Puritans the word "nature" was virtually synonymous with "sin." In Hawthorne's *The Scarlet Letter,* little Pearl, illegitimate daughter of Hester Prynne and the Reverend Mr. Arthur Dimmesdale, is identified throughout as the "child of nature." In his speech to the General Court in 1645, Governor John Winthrop defined "natural liberty"—as distinguished from "civil liberty"—as a "liberty to do evil as well as good . . . the exercise and maintaining of [which] makes men grow more evil, and in time to be worse than brute beasts. . . . " Hawthorne, himself a descendant of Puritan witch hunters and a member of New England society, the moral standards of which had been strongly conditioned by its Puritan heritage, was obsessed with the nature of sin and with the psychological results of violating the taboos imposed by this system. Young Goodman Brown dramatizes the neurosis resulting from such a violation.

After his night in the forest he becomes a walking guilt complex, burdened with anxiety and doubt. Why? Because he has not been properly educated to confront the realities of the external world or of the inner world, because from the cradle on he has been indoctrinated with admonitions against tasting the forbidden fruit, and because sin and Satan have been inadvertently glamorized by prohibition, he has developed a morbid compulsion to taste of them. He is not necessarily evil; he is, like most young people, curious. But because of the severity of Puritan taboos about natural impulses, his curiosity has become an obsession. His dramatic reactions in the forest are typical of what happens in actual cases of extreme repression. Furthermore, the very nature of his wilderness fantasy substantiates Freud's theory that our repressed desires express themselves in our dreams, that dreams are symbolic forms of wish fulfillment. Hawthorne, writing more than a generation before Freud, was a keen enough psychologist to be aware of many of the same phenomena Freud was to systematize through clinical evidence.

In *Handbook of Critical Approaches to Literature,* third edition, 1992

The Receptive Reader

Does Guerin's synopsis, or brief overview of the story, include the most important points? What clues does Guerin find in the story to its symbolic, nonliteral meanings? How does Guerin show the role in the story of two key terms of Freudian psychology: the Freudian superego and the Freudian id? What does the critic mean when he says, "sooner or later, we must all confront Satan"? (How is the devil "Brown's own alter ego"?) What is the role of Brown's wife Faith in this Freudian analysis? What, according to Guerin, is Hawthorne's comment on a repressive society?

WRITING ABOUT LITERATURE

10 Examining Critical Perspectives
WRITING FOCUS: Documenting Your Critical Paper

The Writing Workshop For a paper based on library research, you may be asked to study in depth one important critical approach to a much-discussed story. Or, instead of studying one critical perspective in depth, you may be asked to compare two or more different critical approaches. Some sample projects:

- Hundreds of critical articles (and chapters in books) have been written on Nathaniel Hawthorne's richly symbolic and ambiguous "Young Goodman Brown." You might want to focus on critics' differing views of the relationship between Hawthorne's story and the role of sin and guilt in the Puritan tradition of New England. Was Hawthorne himself profoundly influenced by that tradition? Or was he critical of it, distancing himself from it?

- A classic short story like John Steinbeck's "The Chrysanthemums" or Charlotte Perkins Gilman's "The Yellow Wallpaper" will reveal new or unexpected depth when a new generation of critics looks at it from a fresh perspective. You might want to contrast a more traditional approach to such a story with a recent rereading from a feminist perspective.

- You may want to choose a Kafka story—like "The Country Doctor," "Metamorphosis," or "The Judgement." Your paper might focus on the definition of a key term. For example, you might focus on the "Jewish" Kafka; or on Kafka as the prophet of totalitarianism; or on the Freudian Kafka.

Finding Promising Leads To work up material for your paper, you are likely to begin by checking in electronic or printed indexes for books, collections of critical articles, and individual articles in periodicals. For a writer like Kafka, Hawthorne, or O'Connor, most college libraries will have a wide range of critical and scholarly sources.

For instance, although Kafka's work was banned in Nazi Germany after 1935 and by the communists in his native Prague after 1945, he became one of the most widely known and discussed authors of the twentieth century. (In the words of the critic Susan Sontag, he attracted "armies of interpreters.") Beginning with Angel Flores' *The Kafka Problem* (1946), there have been over fifty collections of critical articles on Kafka, including critical anthologies like the following:

Ronald Gray, *Kafka: A Collection of Critical Essays*
Heinz Politzer, *Franz Kafka*
Angel Flores, *The Kafka Debate*

J. P. Stern, *The World of Franz Kafka*

Kenneth Hughes, *Kafka: An Anthology of Marxist Criticism*

Ruth V. Gross, *Critical Essays on Franz Kafka*

In addition, by searching for sources with Kafka's name in the title, you might be able to locate books like Anthony Northey's *Kafka's Relatives* (with background material for a biographical perspective on Kafka's fiction) or recent articles like John Felstiner's "Looking for Kafka" (in *Stanford,* December 1991).

Taking Notes   During your exploratory reading, you need to look sources over quickly, deciding whether they will be helpful. But you also have to slow down and close in when you hit upon promising materials. Remember:

✘ *Be a stickler for accuracy.* Copy direct quotations accurately, word for word. Enclose all quoted material in quotation marks to show material copied verbatim. (Include the *closing* quotation mark to show where the quotation ends.)

✘ *Tag your notes.* Start your notes with a tag or **descriptor**. (Indicate the subtopic or section of your paper where a quotation or piece of information will be useful.)

✘ *Look ahead.* Include all the publishing information you will need later when you identify your sources in a documented paper. Include exact page numbers for your quotations. (Also note *inclusive* page numbers for a whole article or story.) Sample notes might look like this:

Self-contained quotation

KAFKA THE WRITER

" 'The Country Doctor' reveals much about Kafka's attitude toward being a writer . . . what qualifies him to be a writer, what people expected of him as a writer, what he could accomplish, what would be his ultimate fate."

Peter Mailloux, *A Hesitation before Birth: The Life of Franz Kafka*
Newark: U of Delaware P, 1989), 392.

Partial quotation

SYMBOLS—HORSES

Critic John Hibberd believes Kafka's "unearthly" horses "represent the power of inspiration that promised Kafka fulfillment but carried him away to a devastating reminder of his helplessness."

John Hibberd, *Kafka in Context* (New York: Studio Vista, 1975), 84.

Distinguish clearly between **paraphrase** and direct firsthand quotation. When you paraphrase, you put someone else's ideas in your own words. You can thus highlight what seems most important to you and condense other parts. Even when you paraphrase, be sure to use quotation marks for striking phrases that you keep in the exact wording of the author. (For instance, in summing up briefly a critic's view of Kafka's doctor, put in quotation marks a striking reference to the doctor himself as "the patient, the smitten victim.")

Note finer points: Use **single quotation marks** for a phrase that appears as a quote-within-a-quote: "Freudian critics are fascinated by Kafka's 'unearthly horses.' " Use the **ellipsis**—three spaced periods—to show an omission (see Mailloux quotation above). Use four periods when the periods include the period at the end of a sentence. **Square brackets** show that you have inserted material into the original quotation: "He became engaged [to Felice Bauer], broke off the engagement, became engaged again."

Pushing toward a Thesis   Your note taking becomes truly productive when you begin to follow up tentative patterns and promising connections that you discover in your reading. Even during your preliminary reading and note taking, you will be looking for a unifying thread, for a figure in the carpet. Avoid a stitched-together pattern that goes from "one critic said this" to "another critic said that." Look for recurrent issues; look for a note that in your materials is struck again and again.

The following might be a tentative thesis:

TRIAL THESIS: Critics again and again find a connection between the hesitations and ineffectualness of the country doctor and Kafka's own hesitations and doubts as a writer.

Using a Working Outline   To give direction to your reading and writing, sketch out a **working outline** as soon as you have a rough idea of how your material is shaping up. At first, your plan might be very tentative. A working outline is not a final blueprint; its purpose is to help you visualize a possible pattern and to help you refine it as you go along. Suppose you are moving toward a paper showing how different critical approaches make the reader notice and concentrate on different key images in a story. At an intermediate stage, your working outline might look like this:

WORKING OUTLINE: —Freudian emphasis on sexual overtones
　　　　　the buttocking horses
　　　　　the animalistic groom
　　　　　Rose as victim
　　　　—Marxist emphasis on the doctor's social role
　　　　　ineffectualness of the doctor
　　　　　doctor vs. priest
　　　　　immobilized doctor at the end

—Religious critic's emphasis on religious symbols
    wound in the side of the boy (allusion to Christ on
    the cross?)
    jeering, hostile patients (Christ reviled?)

Drafting and Revising   In your first draft, you are likely to concentrate on feeding into your paper the evidence you have collected. As always, feel free to work on later sections of the paper first—perhaps concentrating on key segments and filling in the connecting threads later. In your first draft, quotations are likely to be chunky, to be woven into the paper more tightly or more smoothly during revision. Often you will need to read a first draft back to yourself to see where major changes in strategy would be advisable. A reordering of major sections might be necessary to correct awkward backtrackings. You might need to strengthen the evidence for major points and play down material that tends to distract from your major arguments.

Documenting the Paper   When you draw on a range of sources—for instance, a range of critical interpretations of a story—you may be asked to provide **documentation**. In a documented paper, you fully identify your sources, furnishing complete publishing information and exact page numbers. Accurate documentation shows that your readers are welcome to go to the sources you have drawn on—to check your use of them and to get further information from them if they wish. Unless instructed otherwise, follow the current style of documentation of the Modern Language Association (MLA). This current style no longer uses the traditional **footnotes**. It still provides for optional explanatory notes (headed **Endnotes**) at the end of a paper—before the final source list.

✘ *Identify your sources briefly in your text.* Provide a **credit tag** naming the author (sometimes briefly weaving in the author's credentials). Briefly identify or describe the publication. You will typically introduce a quotation by saying something like "Lucy M. Freibert says in her article on Margaret Atwood's *The Handmaid's Tale*, . . ."

✘ *Give page references in parentheses in your text.* At the end of a sentence or passage containing quoted material, type parenthetical **page numbers** such as (89) or (280–82). If you have not mentioned the author, this is the place to include his or her last name: (Freibert 280–82). If you are using more than one source by the same author, you may also have to specify briefly which one (Freibert, "Control" 280–82). Remember: Tag author or title in parentheses only if you have not already given the information in your running text.

✘ *Describe each source fully in a final alphabetical listing.* This will be your **Works Cited**. This listing used to be the bibliography (literally the "book list"), but it now often includes nonprint sources—online articles, personal interviews, lectures, PBS broadcasts, CD-ROMS. Here is a typical entry for an article in a critical journal. This entry includes volume number (a volume usually covers all issues for one year), date, and the complete page numbers for the whole article (not just the material you have quoted):

Shumaker, Conrad. " 'Too Terribly Good to Be Printed': Charlotte Gilman's 'The Yellow Wallpaper.' " <u>American Literature</u> 57 (1985): 588–99.

Works Cited Format   **A Checklist**

Study sample entries for your alphabetical listing of Works Cited. Remember the following guidelines:

✗ Type the first line of the entry flush left (no indentation.) *Indent* the second and following lines of each entry five spaces.

✗ Use *italics* or <u>underlining</u> as required by your instructor for the title of a *whole* publication. (The current MLA style still requires underlining instead of italics for submissions to scholarly publications.) For instance, underline or italicize the title of a book-length study, a collection or anthology of stories or essays, a periodical that prints critical articles, or a newspaper that prints reviews.

✗ Use **quotation marks** for titles of short stories or critical articles that are *part* of a collection. Remember: Underlining or italics for the whole; quotation marks for a part.

✗ Leave one space after periods marking off **blocks** of data in the entry.

✗ Use *ed.* for editor; *trans.* for a translator.

✗ Abbreviate the names of publishing houses (Prentice for Prentice Hall Inc; Southern Illinois UP for Southern Illinois University Press). Abbreviate the names of the months: Dec., Apr., Mar.)

Primary sources: Listing of Short Stories, Letters, Interviews

Cheever, John. <u>The Stories of John Cheever</u>. New York: Knopf, 1978.
   Collected stories of the author. The publisher's name is short for Alfred A. Knopf.]

O'Connor, Flannery. <u>Everything That Rises Must Converge</u>. New York: Farrar, 1965.
   [A selection of the author's stories, named after the title story. Name of publisher is short for Farrar, Straus and Giroux.]

Achebe, Chinua. "Dead Men's Path." <u>The Story and Its Writer: An Introduction to Short Fiction</u>. Ed. Ann Charters. 3rd ed. Boston: Bedford, 1991. 10–12.
   [a story reprinted in an anthology, with editor's name and number of edition and with inclusive page numbers for the story]

Cheever, Benjamin, ed. <u>The Letters of John Cheever</u>. New York: Simon, 1988.

[author's correspondence, edited by his son]

Faulkner, William. Interview. <u>Writers at Work: The Paris Review Interviews</u>. Ed. Malcolm Cowley. New York: Viking-Compass, 1959. 122–41.

[Compass was an imprint, or special line of books, of Viking Press. The title of the *Paris Review* is roman—straight type—to set it off from the underlined book title.]

Tan, Amy. Lecture. Visiting Author Series. Santa Clara, 23 Oct. 1999.

[talk by an author as part of a lecture series]

Secondary Sources: Listing of Critical Studies, Articles, or Reviews

Abel, Darrel. <u>The Moral Picturesque: Studies in Hawthorne's Fiction</u>. West Lafayette: Purdue UP, 1988.

[Book with subtitle, published by a university press]

Emrich, Wilhelm. <u>Franz Kafka: A Critical Study of His Writings</u>. Trans. Sheema Zeben Buehne. New York: Ungar, 1968.

[Book with translator's name]

Cady, Edwin H., and Louis J. Budd, ed. Introduction. <u>On Hawthorne: The Best from</u> American Literature. Durham: Duke UP. vi–x.

[Introduction to a collection with two editors—only the first typed with last name first. Page number for prefaces and the like are given in small Roman numerals. Use roman type (straight type—not underlining or italics) for title within title.]

Freibert, Lucy M. "Control and Creativity: The Politics of Risk in Margaret Atwood's <u>The Handmaid's Tale</u>." <u>Critical Essays on Margaret Atwood</u>. Ed. Judith McCombs. Boston: Hall, 1988. 280–91.

[Article in a collection, with inclusive page numbers. Note "Ed." for the editor who assembled the collection.]

Davenport, Mary. "Today's Minimalist Fiction." <u>New York Times</u> 15 May 1991, late ed., sec. 2: 1+.

[Newspaper article, with edition and section specified. Article starts on page 1 and continues later in the newspaper.]

Shumaker, Conrad. " 'Too Terribly Good to Be Printed': Charlotte Gilman's 'The Yellow Wallpaper.' " <u>American Literature</u> 57 (1985): 588–99.

[Journal article, with volume number and inclusive page numbers. Note quotation in title—single quotation marks; note that title of story is quoted in title of article—single quotation marks. Sometimes number of volume *and* issue may be needed when pages are not numbered consecutively throughout a single volume: <u>Fiction Review</u> 14. 3 (1992): 17–21.]

The World of the Writer. Narr. Leah Melas. Writ. and prod. Kenneth Simmons.
  KCDB, Santa Maria. 12 Aug. 2000.
  [A television program with names of narrator and writer-producer. To be listed alphabetically under "World."]

Documenting Online Sources

Guidelines for documenting online sources are still evolving, and you may encounter variations from the style shown in the sample entries here.

<<<Find It on the Web>>>

In the late 1990s, a new translation of Franz Kafka's novel *The Castle,* which helped make alienation a household word, became a major publishing event. One student's online exploration of the subsequent Kafka revival produced items like the following. These sample entries show how you feed publishing data on online material and other nonprint sources into your alphabetical list of Works Cited. Two dates for an item show first the date it was posted and then the day it was accessed. The *URL,* or retrieval code for online material, appears in *angled brackets.* You may want to work alone or with a group to explore online materials like these testifying to Kafka's astonishing continuing influence as a modern cultural icon.

NEWSLETTER ONLINE:
McCalla, John. "Kafka's Hot and He's Also Funny." Penn News 2 Apr. 1998.
  18 Oct. 1999.
    <http://www.upenn.edu/pennnews/current/1998/040298/Kafka.html>

BOOK REVIEW ONLINE:
L., Harold. Rev. of The Castle: A New Translation, by Franz Kafka. Trans.
  Mark Harman. Philadelphia Inquirer 26 Apr. 1998. 18 Oct. 1999.
    <http://www.phillynews.com/inquirer/98/Apr/26/books/KAFKA26.tml>

SPECIAL INTEREST WEBSITE:
Nervi, Mauro. The Kafka Project Website. Updated 6 Sept. 2001.
  24 Sept. 2001.
    <http://www.kafka.org>

REFERENCE WORK ONLINE, WITH VERSION NUMBER AND DATE:
"Kafka." Britannica Online. Vers. 97.1.1. Mar. 1997.
  Encyclopaedia Britannica. 17 Oct. 2001.
    <http://www.eb.com/>

PHOTOGRAPHS AND OTHER VISUALS ONLINE:
Eckel, Yacov. <u>Franz Kafka Photo Album</u>. 6 Sept. 2000. 24 Sept. 2001.
    <http://www.cs.technion.ac.il/~eckel/Kafka/main.htm

COLLECTION OF MATERIALS ON CD-ROM:
Fresca, Dolores. "Kafka and Patriarchy." <u>The World of Kafka</u>. CD-ROM. New
    York: Klamm Publications, 1999.

Research paper format   Study the example of a documented paper that concludes this chapter. The sample typewritten page is the opening page of the paper formatted according to the instruction in the *MLA Handbook for Writers of Research Papers,* fifth edition (1999).

✗ **Double-space** your typescript throughout, including your title and your final list of Works Cited.

✗ Leave **standard margins**—an inch on each side, half an inch at the top and bottom.

✗ Use **running heads** (your last name and page number) at the top of each page, flush right.

✗ Use half an inch for paragraph indentation, an additional half inch for **block quotations**.

Sample Documented Page

                                                 Nansen 1

Pat L. Nansen

Professor Holton

English 2

12 September 2001

    The Psychoanalytic Kafka: Dream and Reality

    What explains the fascination of readers with

an author who worked as an obscure insurance

clerk and who obsessively guarded future clas-

sics of world literature against publication?

Mauro Nervi's <u>Kafka Project</u> website lists new

current translations from the original German

into English, Italian, and Russian. It lists new

critical discussions in English, Italian, Spanish,

and German. It announces the current winner of the Kafka Prize and the meeting of a Kafka Society. It includes a link to a Kafka filmography, directing the reader to films that include the Kafka movie starring the Kafkaesque Jeremy Irons.

Kafka served a generation of readers as an early guide to the dream world of the subconscious that was just like a strange frightening new mysterious continent being explored by students of human psychology. Once, when Kafka was visiting his good friend Max Brod, he accidentally woke up Brod's father, who was sleeping on the couch. Instead of just simply apologizing, Kafka slowly tiptoed out of the room, whispering, "Please consider me a dream" (Baumer 2). When we look at Kafka the writer, this incident acquires symbolic meaning. Dreams fascinated Kafka, and he was obsessed with chronicling "his dreamlike inner existence," which threatened to crowd out ordinary daylight reality. He said in a diary entry for August 6, 1914:

> The taste for describing my dreamlike inner existence has pushed everything else in the background, where it has atrophied in a terrifying way and does not cease to atrophy. Nothing else can satisfy me. (qtd. in Baumer 3)

Sample Documented Paper

The Psychoanalytic Kafka: Dream and Reality

What explains the fascination of readers with an author who worked as an obscure insurance clerk and who obsessively guarded future classics of world literature against publication? Mauro Nervi's Kafka Project website lists new current translations from the original German into English, Italian, and Russian. It lists new critical discussions in English, Italian, Spanish, and German. It announces the current winner of the Kafka Prize and the meeting of a Kafka Society. It includes a link to a Kafka filmography, directing the reader to films that include the Kafka movie starring the Kafkaesque Jeremy Irons.

Kafka served a generation of readers as an early guide to the dream world of the subconscious that was just like a strange frightening new mysterious continent being explored by students of human psychology. Once, when Kafka was visiting his good friend Max Brod, he accidentally woke up Brod's father, who was sleeping on the couch. Instead of just simply apologizing, Kafka slowly tiptoed out of the room, whispering, "Please consider me a dream" (Baumer 2). When we look at Kafka the writer, this incident acquires symbolic meaning. Dreams fascinated Kafka, and he was obsessed with chronicling "his dreamlike inner existence," which threatened to crowd out ordinary daylight reality. He said in a diary entry for August 6, 1914:

> The taste for describing my dreamlike inner existence has pushed everything else in the background, where it has atrophied in a terrifying way and does not cease to atrophy. Nothing else can satisfy me. (qtd. in Baumer 3)

In a letter to Max Brod in 1922, Kafka called this exploration of the inner self "this descent to the dark powers, this unleashing . . . of dubious embraces and everything else that may be happening below." He said that a writer who "writes stories in the sunlight" above "no longer knows anything" about this hidden subconscious reality (qtd. in Baumer 7). For Kafka, "the dream reveals the reality" while "conception"—our ability to understand—"lags behind" (qtd. in Hamalian 12). It is this search for a deeper truth buried in our subconscious and revealed in dreams that made Franz Kafka, in the words of Peter Dow Webster, "the psychologist's perfect dreamer" (118). The psychoanalytical theory concerning dreams, first introduced by Freud, assumes that dreams tell us the real truth about ourselves, especially about our subconscious fears and desires. Our dreams keep coming back to our innermost preoccupations and dilemmas. In Kafka's case, in the words of Ruth Gross, these include "power and impotence," "marriage versus bachelorhood," and "success versus failure" (577).

Kafka's "A Country Doctor" has a typical dreamlike sequence of events, with time and space distorted in such a way that the events cannot be literally happening. The story reveals Kafka's innermost struggle with a choice he made in his own life and the subconscious feelings surrounding that choice. In a letter to Brod, Kafka wrote that "in order to devote himself to literature, the writer must sacrifice fulfillment in life" (qtd. in Sokel 1158). Kafka had a strong desire for marriage and family, but because of his fears and hesitancies—and because of his exclusive devotion to his mission as a writer—his various engagements and romantic involvements ended in failure. In his own words, "The price to pay for this 'life as a writer' is rigid, uncompromising aloneness, a radical isolation from the outside world, from other people and—most painfully—from his beloved" (qtd. in Beug 125).

The dreamlike images and plot of "A Country Doctor" encourage us to see the story as an explanation of Kafka's own ambivalent feelings toward major choices in his own life. As suggested in one critical interpretation, when the country doctor heeds "the call of the 'nightbell' summoning him to the bedside of a patient," the call of the bell "can be understood as a translation into sensory terms of Kafka's call to literature, which he understood as an art of healing and self-preservation, a 'doctor's' art" (Sokel 1158).

However, when the doctor tries to respond to the call, he finds out his horse has died from overexertion. Rose, the servant girl he has just begun to notice, is unable to borrow a horse—"no horse to be had, no horse." In his dilemma, the doctor turns "absentmindedly" to his forgotten pigsty and in doing so releases the animal-like groom and a team of unearthly horses (Kafka 137). He allows the groom to take Rose; contrary to what the doctor says, he does in fact leave Rose behind. She is the price for the groom's aid. "The 'unearthly horses' transport the doctor away from life, woman, and home" (Sokel 1158). This scene seems to mirror Kafka's continual withdrawal from the various women in his life when they would press him for a commitment. Whenever a relationship became too serious, he would back away, claiming that his fanatical dedication to his writing "would condemn his spouse to monastic loneliness" (Sokel 1153).

As Kafka writes about the journey between the two houses, the doctor's and the patient's, he mirrors his own ambivalence toward his writer's art and the sacrifices he has made on behalf of that art. In the story, the two houses graphically represent the two poles of the doctor's existence. In his own house, the doctor abandons the possibility of fulfillment through love; in the other house, the house of the patient, he dedicates himself to his art, exploring "the congenital wound of mortality"—the wound in the young patient's side (Sokel 1158).

The doctor's ambivalence is such that he cannot be content at either pole. At home, he sacrifices the young woman to his mission, but at his destination he regrets the price he has paid and wants to return. Thoughts of Rose begin to haunt him: "And only now did I remember Rose again: what was I to do, how could I rescue her, how could I pull her away from under that groom at ten miles distance, with a team of horses I couldn't control" (Kafka 139). This pull in contradictory directions mirrors Kafka's own problem. He would make every effort to discourage a woman's hope for the future. However, in the case of Felice Bauer, for instance, the moment she showed signs of heeding his warning, he would return to the role of ardent wooer. As much as Kafka desired marriage and family, he was also fearful and would become "oppressed by the actual prospect of marriage" (Sokel 1154).

At the end of the story, the doctor is seen escaping the patient's house. While it took the doctor only seconds to arrive at the house of the sick boy, now it is taking him forever to get home: "Never shall I reach home at this rate; my flourishing practice is done for; my successor is robbing me . . . " (Kafka 143). The doctor is shown riding aimlessly between the houses—the distance between them has become immeasurable, and he cannot stay at either place.

Kafka's tendency to explore the subconscious in a dreamlike fashion is strongly evident in "The Country Doctor." As readers, we cannot be quite sure whether, in fact, his story is an actual dream (where the subconscious is revealed and dominates) or whether it is based on actual events with subconscious thoughts quickly intruding on the conscious mind. Kafka has chosen a country doctor to portray his own inner struggles as an author who must deal with the choices he has made. In this sense, we are all country doctors and have to deal with our own internal voices speaking to our consciousness. Kafka is not alone. What career mother leaving home and a sick child does not experience a twinge of guilt as her guilt feelings about her choices rise to the surface? What student working late into the night does not have visions of responsibilities denied or postponed—the dinner not cooked, the phone calls not returned?

Works Cited

Baumer, Franz. <u>Franz Kafka</u>. New York: Unger, 1971.

Beug, Joachim. "The Cunning of a Writer." <u>The World of Franz Kafka</u>. Ed. J. P. Stern. New York: Holt, 1980. 122–33.

Gross, Ruth V. "Fallen Bridge, Fallen Women, Fallen Text." <u>The Literary Review</u>

26.4 (1983): 577–87.

Hamalian, Leo. Introduction. <u>Franz Kafka: A Collection of Criticism</u>. Ed. Leo Hamalian. New York: McGraw, 1981. 1–17.

Kafka, Franz. <u>The Metamorphosis, the Penal Colony, and Other Stories</u>. Trans. Willa and Edwin Muir. New York: Schocken, 1975.

Nervi, Mauro. <u>The Kafka Project Website</u>. Updated 6 Aug. 2001. 24 Aug. 2001. <http://www.kafka.org>

Sokel, Walter H. "Franz Kafka." <u>European Writers: The Twentieth Century</u>. Ed. George Stade. Vol. 9. New York: Scribner's, 1989. 1151–77.

Webster, Peter Dow. " 'Dies Irae' in the Unconscious, or the Significance of Franz Kafka." <u>Franz Kafka: A Collection of Criticism</u>. Ed. Leo Hamalian. New York: McGraw, 1981. 118–25.

Questions for Peer Review

How effectively does the student writer integrate material from the sources—weaving it into the text of the paper without awkward breaks?

1. Where does the student writer best explain the role that the interpretation of *dreams* plays in psychoanalytic criticism and especially in critical discussions of Kafka's work? How much do you know about Freud—his work and influence? Would a reader have to be familiar with Freudian psychology to understand this student paper?

2. The term *ambivalence* became a key concept and often repeated buzzword in twentieth-century literary criticism. How would you sum up the meaning of the term? Can you trace the role it plays in this student paper? How does the student's following up of the term help shape the organization of the paper?

3. Can you explain the *parallel* between the doctor as healer and the writer who provides spiritual comfort?

4. Where and how effectively does the student author turn to *sources*? Do you think any of the quotations are particularly useful, helping the student writer clarify or support main points?

5. How clear or adequate are parenthetical *documentation* and the entries in the Works Cited? Are there unusual situations or entries?

6. The *Kafka Project* website offers "Help for a Paper" ranging from listings of new or recent criticism to links to newsgroups as well as mention of poetry or film projects related to Kafka. Working alone or with a group, you may want to explore the help this *website* offers to a student researcher working on Kafka or the help a similar source offers to a student researcher working on another major author.

11 OTHER VOICES/ OTHER VISIONS

Courtesy Richard B. Ressman

A FESTIVAL OF CLASSIC STORIES

The short story developed as a hugely popular form of entertainment for a large reading public before the age of radio and television. Edgar Allan Poe created the genre of the horror story, tapping into a vast reservoir of buried fears and nameless terrors in his readers. Storytellers from Mark Twain to Bret Harte and O. Henry spun their yarns of the West and of city life for a large loyal audience. However, from the beginning writers took readers beyond melodramatic thrills and surprise endings to probings of human nature and the mysteries of the human heart.

Edgar Allan Poe   *(1809–1849)*

INVITATION TO READING: Edgar Allan Poe may be the most universally known storyteller of our world. Millions of readers and moviegoers have shuddered and groaned at his scenarios of horror: People presumed dead come back gibbering from the crypt. A mad-scientist machinery of torture and destruction moves in on a prisoner paralyzed with fear and apprehension. A gloating arrogant homicidal criminal gets away with murder until at the very end he is tripped up by a stupid mistake. Losing early his actress mother and his alcoholic father, Poe was befriended for a time by a rich foster parent. He fought a losing battle against poverty, gambling, alcoholism, low-end publishing jobs, and a callous self-righteous establishment. Millions around the world have read stories like "The Murders of the Rue Morgue," "The Pit and the Pendulum," and "The Black Cat." His poem "The Raven" is an all-time classic of spooky nighttime thoughts and futile regrets for irreparable loss. Do Poe's scare-you-out-of-your-wits effects still work for the modern reader?

The Black Cat   *1843*

For the most wild yet most homely narrative which I am about to pen, I neither expect nor solicit belief. Mad indeed would I be to expect it, in a case where my very senses reject their own evidence. Yet, mad am I not—and very surely do I not dream. But tomorrow I die, and today I would unburden my soul. My immediate purpose is to place before the world, plainly, succinctly, and without comment, a series of mere household events. In their consequences, these events have terrified—have tortured—have destroyed me. Yet I will not attempt to expound them. To me, they have presented little but horror—to many they will seem less terrible than *baroques*. Hereafter, perhaps, some intellect may be found which will reduce my phantasm to the commonplace—some intellect more calm, more logical, and far less excitable than my own, which will perceive, in the circumstances I detail with awe, nothing more than an ordinary succession of very natural causes and effects.

From my infancy I was noted for the docility and humanity of my disposition. My tenderness of heart was even so conspicuous as to make me the jest of my companions. I was especially fond of animals, and was indulged by my parents with a great variety of pets. With these I spent most of my time, and never was so happy as when feeding and caressing them. This peculiarity of character grew with my growth, and, in my manhood, I derived from it one of my principal sources of pleasure. To those who have cherished an affection for a faithful and sagacious dog, I need hardly be at the trouble of explaining the nature or the intensity of the gratification thus derivable. There is something in the unselfish and self-sacrificing love of a brute, which goes directly to the heart of him who has had frequent occasion to test the paltry friendship and gossamer fidelity of mere *Man*.

I married early, and was happy to find in my wife a disposition not uncongenial with my own. Observing my partiality for domestic pets, she lost no opportunity of procuring those of the most agreeable kind. We had birds, gold-fish, a fine dog, rabbits, a small monkey, and a *cat*.

This latter was a remarkably large and beautiful animal, entirely black, and sagacious to an astonishing degree. In speaking of his intelligence, my wife, who at heart was not a little tinctured with superstition, made frequent allusion to the ancient popular notion, which regarded all black cats as witches in disguise. Not that she was ever *serious* upon this point—and I mention the matter at all for no better reason than that it happens, just now, to be remembered.

Pluto—this was the cat's name—was my favorite pet and playmate. I alone fed him, and he attended me wherever I went about the house. It was even with difficulty that I could prevent him from following me through the streets.

Our friendship lasted, in this manner, for several years, during which my general temperament and character—through the instrumentality of the Fiend Intemperance—had (I blush to confess it) experienced a radical alteration for the worse. I grew, day by day, more moody, more irritable, more regardless of the feelings of others. I suffered myself to use intemperate language to my wife. At length, I even offered her personal violence. My pets, of course, were made to feel the change in my disposition. I not only neglected, but ill-used them. For Pluto, however, I still retained sufficient regard to restrain me from maltreating him, as I made no scruple of maltreating the rabbits, the monkey, or even the dog, when, by accident, or through affection, they came in my way. But my disease grew upon me—for what disease is like Alcohol!—and at length even Pluto, who was now becoming old, and consequently somewhat peevish—even Pluto began to experience the effects of my ill temper.

One night, returning home, much intoxicated, from one of my haunts about town, I fancied that the cat avoided my presence. I seized him; when, in his fright at my violence, he inflicted a slight wound upon my hand with his teeth. The fury of a demon instantly possessed me. I knew myself no longer. My original soul seemed, at once, to take its flight from my body; and a more than fiendish malevolence, gin-nurtured, thrilled every fibre of my frame. I took from my waistcoat-pocket a penknife, opened it, grasped the poor beast by the throat, and deliberately cut one of its eyes from the socket! I blush, I burn, I shudder, while I pen the damnable atrocity.

5

When reason returned with the morning—when I had slept off the fumes of the night's debauch—I experienced a sentiment half of horror, half of remorse, for the crime of which I had been guilty; but it was, at best, a feeble and equivocal feeling, and the soul remained untouched. I again plunged into excess, and soon drowned in wine all memory of the deed.

In the meantime the cat slowly recovered. The socket of the lost eye presented, it is true, a frightful appearance, but he no longer appeared to suffer any pain. He went about the house as usual, but, as might be expected, fled in extreme terror at my approach. I had so much of my old heart left, as to be at first grieved by this evident dislike on the part of a creature which had once so loved me. But this feeling soon gave place to irritation. And then came, as if to my final and irrevocable overthrow, the spirit of PERVERSENESS. Of this spirit philosophy takes no account. Yet I am not more sure that my soul lives, than I am that perverseness is one of the primitive impulses of the human heart—one of the indivisible primary faculties, or sentiments, which give direction to the character of Man. Who has not, a hundred times, found himself committing a vile or a stupid action, for no other reason than because he knows he should *not?* Have we not a perpetual inclination, in the teeth of our best judgment, to violate that which is *Law,* merely because we understand it to be such? This spirit of perverseness, I say, came to my final overthrow. It was this unfathomable longing of the soul *to vex itself*—to offer violence to its own nature—to do wrong for the wrong's sake only—that urged me to continue and finally to consummate the injury I had inflicted upon the unoffending brute. One morning, in cold blood, I slipped a noose about its neck and hung it to the limb of a tree;—hung it with the tears streaming from my eyes, and with the bitterest remorse at my heart;—hung it *because* I knew that it had loved me, and *because* I felt it had given me no reason of offence;—hung it *because* I knew that in so doing I was committing a sin—a deadly sin that would so jeopardize my immortal soul as to place it—if such a thing were possible—even beyond the reach of the infinite mercy of the Most Merciful and Most Terrible God.

On the night of the day on which this most cruel deed was done, I was 10 aroused from sleep by the cry of fire. The curtains of my bed were in flames. The whole house was blazing. It was with great difficulty that my wife, a servant, and myself, made our escape from the conflagration. The destruction was complete. My entire worldly wealth was swallowed up, and I resigned myself thenceforward to despair.

I am above the weakness of seeking to establish a sequence of cause and effect, between the disaster and the atrocity. But I am detailing a chain of facts—and wish not to leave even a possible link imperfect. On the day succeeding the fire, I visited the ruins. The walls, with one exception, had fallen in. This exception was found in a compartment wall, not very thick, which stood about the middle of the house, and against which had rested the head of my bed. The plastering had here, in great measure, resisted the action of the fire—a fact which I attributed to its having been recently spread. About this wall a dense crowd were collected, and many persons seemed to be examining a particular portion of it with very minute and eager attention. The words "strange!" "singular!" and other similar expressions, excited my curiosity. I approached and saw, as if graven in *bas-relief* upon the white surface, the figure of a gigantic *cat*. The impression was given with an accuracy truly marvellous. There was a rope about the animal's neck.

When I first beheld this apparition—for I could scarcely regard it as less—my wonder and my terror were extreme. But at length reflection came to my aid. The cat, I remembered, had been hung in a garden adjacent to the house. Upon the alarm of fire, this garden had been immediately filled by the crowd—by some one of whom the animal must have been cut from the tree and thrown, through an open window, into my chamber. This had probably been done with the view of arousing me from sleep. The falling of other walls had compressed the victim of my cruelty into the substance of the freshly-spread plaster; the lime of which, with the flames, and the *ammonia* from the carcass, had then accomplished the portraiture as I saw it.

Although I thus readily accounted to my reason, if not altogether to my conscience, for the startling fact just detailed, it did not the less fail to make a deep impression upon my fancy. For months I could not rid myself of the phantasm of the cat; and, during this period, there came back into my spirit a half-sentiment that seemed, but was not, remorse. I went so far as to regret the loss of the animal, and to look about me, among the vile haunts which I now habitually frequented, for another pet of the same species, and of somewhat similar appearance, with which to supply its place.

One night as I sat, half stupefied, in a den of more than infamy, my attention was suddenly drawn to some black object, reposing upon the head of one of the immense hogsheads of gin, or of rum, which constituted the chief furniture of the apartment. I had been looking steadily at the top of this hogshead for some minutes, and what now caused me surprise was the fact that I had not sooner perceived the object thereupon. I approached it, and touched it with my hand. It was a black cat—a very large one—fully as large as Pluto, and closely resembling him in every respect but one. Pluto had not a white hair upon any portion of his body; but this cat had a large, although indefinite splotch of white, covering nearly the whole region of the breast.

Upon my touching him, he immediately arose, purred loudly, rubbed against my hand, and appeared delighted with my notice. This, then, was the very creature of which I was in search. I at once offered to purchase it of the landlord; but this person made no claim to it—knew nothing of it—had never seen it before.

I continued my caresses, and when I prepared to go home, the animal evinced a disposition to accompany me. I permitted it to do so; occasionally stooping and patting it as I proceeded. When it reached the house it domesticated itself at once, and became immediately a great favorite with my wife.

For my own part, I soon found a dislike to it arising within me. This was just the reverse of what I had anticipated; but—I know not how or why it was—its evident fondness for myself rather disgusted and annoyed me. By slow degrees these feelings of disgust and annoyance rose into the bitterness of hatred. I avoided the creature; a certain sense of shame, and the remembrance of my former deed of cruelty, preventing me from physically abusing it. I did not, for some weeks, strike, or otherwise violently ill use it; but gradually—very gradually—I came to look upon it with unutterable loathing, and to flee silently from its odious presence, as from the breath of a pestilence.

What added, no doubt, to my hatred of the beast, was the discovery, on the morning after I brought it home, that, like Pluto, it also had been deprived of one of its eyes. This circumstance, however, only endeared it to my wife, who, as I have already said, possessed, in a high degree, that humanity of feeling which had once been my distinguishing trait, and the source of many of my simplest and purest pleasures.

With my aversion to this cat, however, its partiality for myself seemed to increase. It followed my footsteps with a pertinacity which it would be difficult to make the reader comprehend. Whenever I sat, it would crouch beneath my chair, or spring upon my knees, covering me with its loathsome caresses. If I arose to walk it would get between my feet and thus nearly throw me down, or, fastening its long and sharp claws in my dress, clamber, in this manner, to my breast. At such times, although I longed to destroy it with a blow, I was yet withheld from so doing, partly by a memory of my former crime, but chiefly—let me confess it at once—by absolute *dread* of the beast.

This dread was not exactly a dread of physical evil—and yet I should be   20
at a loss how otherwise to define it. I am almost ashamed to own—yes, even in this felon's cell, I am almost ashamed to own—that the terror and horror with which the animal inspired me, had been heightened by one of the merest chimeras it would be possible to conceive. My wife had called my attention, more than once, to the character of the mark of white hair, of which I have spoken, and which constituted the sole visible difference between the strange beast and the one I had destroyed. The reader will remember that this mark, although large, had been originally very indefinite; but, by slow degrees—degrees nearly imperceptible, and which for a long time my reason struggled to reject as fanciful—it had, at length, assumed a rigorous distinction of outline. It was now the representation of an object that I shudder to name—and for this, above all, I loathed, and dreaded, and would have rid myself of the monster *had I dared*—it was now, I say, the image of a hideous—of a ghastly thing—of the GALLOWS!—oh, mournful and terrible engine of Horror and of Crime—of Agony and of Death!

And now was I indeed wretched beyond the wretchedness of mere Humanity. And *a brute beast*—whose fellow I had contemptuously destroyed— *a brute beast* to work out for *me*—for me, a man fashioned in the image of the High God—so much of insufferable woe! Alas! neither by day nor by night knew I the blessing of rest any more! During the former the creature left me no moment alone, and in the latter I started hourly from dreams of unutterable fear to find the hot breath of *the thing* upon my face, and its vast weight—an incarnate nightmare that I had no power to shake off— incumbent eternally upon my *heart!*

Beneath the pressure of torments such as these the feeble remnant of the good within me succumbed. Evil thoughts became my sole intimates—the darkest and most evil of thoughts. The moodiness of my usual temper increased to hatred of all things and of all mankind; while from the sudden, frequent, and ungovernable outbursts of a fury to which I now blindly abandoned myself, my uncomplaining wife, alas, was the most usual and the most patient of sufferers.

One day she accompanied me, upon some household errand, into the cellar of the old building which our poverty compelled us to inhabit. The cat followed me down the steep stairs, and, nearly throwing me headlong, exasperated me to madness. Uplifting an axe, and forgetting in my wrath the childish dread which had hitherto stayed my hand, I aimed a blow at the animal, which, of course, would have proved instantly fatal had it descended as I wished. But this blow was arrested by the hand of my wife. Goaded by the interference into a rage more than demoniacal, I withdrew my arm from her grasp and buried the axe in her brain. She fell dead upon the spot without a groan.

This hideous murder accomplished, I set myself forthwith, and with entire deliberation, to the task of concealing the body. I knew that I could not remove it from the house, either by day or by night, without the risk of being observed by the neighbors. Many projects entered my mind. At one period I thought of cutting the corpse into minute fragments, and destroying them by fire. At another, I resolved to dig a grave for it in the floor of the cellar. Again, I deliberated about casting it in the well in the yard—about packing it in a box, as if merchandise, with the usual arrangements, and so getting a porter to take it from the house. Finally I hit upon what I considered a far better expedient than either of these. I determined to wall it up in the cellar, as the monks of the Middle Ages are recorded to have walled up their victims.

For a purpose such as this the cellar was well adapted. Its walls were loosely constructed, and had lately been plastered throughout with a rough plaster, which the dampness of the atmosphere had prevented from hardening. Moreover, in one of the walls was a projection, caused by a false chimney, or fireplace, that had been filled up and made to resemble the rest of the cellar. I made no doubt that I could readily displace the bricks at this point, insert the corpse, and wall the whole up as before, so that no eye could detect any thing suspicious.

And in this calculation I was not deceived. By means of a crowbar I easily dislodged the bricks, and, having carefully deposited the body against the inner wall, I propped it in that position, while with little trouble I relaid the whole structure as it originally stood. Having procured mortar, sand, and hair, with every possible precaution, I prepared a plaster which could not be distinguished from the old, and with this I very carefully went over the new brick-work. When I had finished, I felt satisfied that all was right. The wall did not present the slightest appearance of having been disturbed. The rubbish on the floor was picked up with the minutest care. I looked around triumphantly, and said to myself: "Here at least, then, my labor has not been in vain."

My next step was to look for the beast which had been the cause of so much wretchedness; for I had, at length, firmly resolved to put it to death. Had I been able to meet with it at the moment, there could have been no

25

doubt of its fate; but it appeared that the crafty animal had been alarmed at the violence of my previous anger, and forbore to present itself in my present mood. It is impossible to describe or to imagine the deep, the blissful sense of relief which the absence of the detested creature occasioned in my bosom. It did not make its appearance during the night; and thus for one night, at least, since its introduction into the house, I soundly and tranquilly slept; aye, *slept* even with the burden of murder upon my soul.

The second and the third day passed, and still my tormentor came not. Once again I breathed as a free man. The monster, in terror, had fled the premises for ever! I should behold it no more! My happiness was supreme! The guilt of my dark deed disturbed me but little. Some few inquiries had been made, but these had been readily answered. Even a search had been instituted—but of course nothing was to be discovered. I looked upon my future felicity as secured.

Upon the fourth day of the assassination, a party of the police came, very unexpectedly, into the house, and proceeded again to make rigorous investigation of the premises. Secure, however, in the inscrutability of my place of concealment, I felt no embarrassment whatever. The officers bade me accompany them in their search. They left no nook or corner unexplored. At length, for the third or fourth time, they descended into the cellar. I quivered not in a muscle. My heart beat calmly as that of one who slumbers in innocence. I walked the cellar from end to end. I folded my arms upon my bosom, and roamed easily to and fro. The police were thoroughly satisfied and prepared to depart. The glee at my heart was too strong to be restrained. I burned to say if but one word, by way of triumph, and to render doubly sure their assurance of my guiltlessness.

"Gentlemen," I said at last, as the party ascended the steps, "I delight to have allayed your suspicions. I wish you all health and a little more courtesy. By the bye, gentlemen, this—this is a very well-constructed house," (in the rabid desire to say something easily, I scarcely knew what I uttered at all),—"I may say an *excellently* well-constructed house. These walls—are you going, gentlemen?—these walls are solidly put together"; and here, through the mere frenzy of bravado, I rapped heavily with a cane which I held in my hand, upon that very portion of the brick-work behind which stood the corpse of the wife of my bosom.

But may God shield and deliver me from the fangs of the Arch-Fiend! No sooner had the reverberation of my blows sunk into silence, than I was answered by a voice from within the tomb!—by a cry, at first muffled and broken, like the sobbing of a child, and then quickly swelling into one long, loud, and continuous scream, utterly anomalous and inhuman—a howl—a wailing shriek, half of horror and half of triumph, such as might have arisen only out of hell, conjointly from the throats of the damned in their agony and of the demons that exult in the damnation.

Of my own thoughts it is folly to speak. Swooning, I staggered to the opposite wall. For one instant the party on the stairs remained motionless, through extremity of terror and awe. In the next a dozen stout arms were toiling at the wall. It fell bodily. The corpse, already greatly decayed and clotted with gore, stood erect before the eyes of the spectators. Upon its head, with red extended mouth and solitary eye of fire, sat the hideous beast whose craft had seduced me into murder, and whose informing voice had consigned me to the hangman. I had walled the monster up within the tomb.

Guy de Maupassant   *(1850–1893)*

INVITATION TO READING: The Frenchman Guy de Maupassant was a pioneering widely read writer of the short story. His "Tallow Ball" (1880) and "The Necklace" (1884) made him famous, and he published two hundred stories in his lifetime. He helped establish the fashion of the story with a surprise ending or cruel twist: A woman loses a very valuable borrowed necklace and scrimps and sacrifices much of her life to pay off the replacement—only to find out that the lost necklace had been a cheap imitation of the real thing. However, in his strongest stories, Maupassant expertly draws his readers into the inner world or mental life of characters they would have avoided as weird or dismissed as eccentrics in real life. One of his characters tells the readers that not the great catastrophes but the intimate personal disillusionments or losses of faith are truly shattering. Do you come to know and understand the loner who tells his story in the following classic Maupassant tale?

Looking Back

TRANSLATED BY H.P.N. SLOMEN

"Now, darlings," said the Comtesse, "it's bed-time."

The three children, two girls and a boy, got up and went across to kiss their grandmother.

After that they went to say good-night to the Curé, who had been dining at the castle, as he always did on Thursdays.

The Abbé Mauduit took the two girls on his knee, put his long arms in the black-sleeved cassock round their necks and, drawing their heads towards him with a fatherly gesture, he pressed a long affectionate kiss on each forehead.

Then he put them down and the little things left the room, the boy in   5 front and the girls behind.

"You are fond of children, M. le Curé?" said the Comtesse.

"Very fond, Madame."

The old lady raised her eyes to the priest's face:

"And don't you ever find it hard living alone?"

"Yes, sometimes."   10

He fell silent and after a pause he went on: "But I was never made for everyday life."

"What do you know about it?"

"Oh! I know well enough. I was made to be a priest. I have followed my vocation."

The Comtesse was still looking at him.

"Come, M. le Curé, tell me about it; tell me how you made up your mind   15
to renounce all that makes the rest of us love life, all that comforts and con-
soles us. What decided you not to follow the normal path of marriage and
family life? You are neither a mystic nor a fanatic, neither a kill-joy nor a pessimist. Was it something that happened, a great sorrow, that made you take
life vows?"

The Abbé Mauduit got up and went to the fire, holding out the heavy
shoes of a country priest to the flames. He still seemed to hesitate about answering.

He was a tall, white-haired old man, who had been the parish priest of
Saint-Antoine-du-Rocher and the neighbourhood for twenty years. The peasants always said of him: "He's a real good sort."

He was a good man, kindly, good-tempered, accessible and, above all,
generous. He would have divided his cloak like Saint Martin. He was ready
to laugh and equally ready to cry, like a woman, which lowered his reputation a little in the eyes of the dour peasants.

The old Comtesse de Saville, who had retired to her castle at Rocher to
bring up her grandchildren after the deaths in close succession of her son
and daughter-in-law, was very fond of her curé and used to say of him:
"He's got a good heart."

He came every Thursday and spent the evening at the castle, and he and   20
the Comtesse had become close friends with the genuine, open-hearted
friendship possible only to the old. They were so much of a mind that they
hardly needed to put their thoughts into words, being both good souls with
the simple goodness of unsophisticated kindly folk.

She insisted: "Now, M. le Curé, it's time for *you* to make your confession
to *me*."

He repeated: "I was not born for ordinary life. Fortunately I discovered it
in time and I have very often had cause to know how right I was.

"My parents, who were wholesale haberdashers at Verdiers and quite
well off, were very ambitious for me. They sent me to a boarding-school
very young. People do not realize how unhappy a boy can be at school simply from loneliness and being away from home. The routine life without affection is good for some but disastrous for others. Children are often more
sensitive than people think, and, if they are shut up in this way too early
away from those they love, excessive sensitiveness, which plays havoc with
their nerves, may develop and become pathological and dangerous.

"I hardly played any games; I made no friends and was violently home-
sick all the time; I cried in bed at night and was always trying to recall memories of home, trivial memories of little insignificant things and happenings.
I could not get out of my mind all I had left behind me. I gradually became
a nervous wreck, for whom trifling difficulties assumed the proportions of
acute misery.

"The result was that I remained morose and self-centred, inhibited and   25
friendless. The process of increasing mental strain went on subconsciously
but surely. Children's nerves are easily affected; great care ought to be taken
to avoid any disturbance in their lives, until they are practically mature. But
who realizes that for some boys at school an undeserved imposition may

cause as much mental anguish as the death of a friend will later on? Who really appreciates that something quite trivial may cause in certain immature minds an emotional upset which may in a very short time inflict incurable damage?

"This is what happened in my case; home-sickness developed in me to such an extent that my whole life became one long agony.

"I told no one and said nothing about it. My natural sensitiveness gradually increased till it became pathological and my mind was one open wound. The slightest touch produced twinges of pain and agonizing repercussions which did me permanent harm. Happy indeed are those to whom nature has given a thick skin and the armour of stoicism!

"I reached the age of sixteen. The fact that everything hurt me made me abnormally shy. Knowing that I had no defence against the blows of chance or fate, I shrank from all contacts, all advances, all the activities of school life. I was continually on the defensive, as if constantly threatened by some unknown but always anticipated misfortune. I dared not speak or act in public. I was obsessed with the idea that life was a battle, a frightful struggle, in which one received terrible blows and wounds not only painful but mortal.

"Instead of hopes of happiness for the morrow, such as normal people have, I was conscious only of an undefined terror and I wanted to hide and avoid the struggle, in which I was bound to be defeated and killed.

"When I had finished my studies, I was given six months' holiday in which to choose my career. A very simple incident suddenly enabled me to understand myself and revealed to me my unhealthy psychological condition; I realized my danger and made up my mind to avoid it.

"Verdiers is a small town in flat country with woods all round it. My parents' house was in the main street. I now spent my time away from the home I had missed and longed for so much. I wandered over the countryside, day-dreaming, by myself, so that my dreams could develop without interruption.

"My father and mother, wrapped up in their business and anxious about my future, could talk of nothing but their sales and the careers open to me. They loved me like hard-headed practical people with their head rather than their heart. I lived in the prison of my own thoughts, never free from the terrors of anxiety.

"Well, one evening after a long day out, as I was walking fast in order not to be late home, I saw a dog running at full speed towards me. He was a sort of red spaniel, very thin, with long curly ears.

"He halted ten yards from me; I stopped too. He began to wag his tail and came slowly towards me with timid movements of his whole body, cowering down as if begging and moving his head gently from side to side. I spoke to him. Then he began to crawl towards me on his belly, looking so humble, so miserable, so appealing that tears came into my eyes. I went towards him but he ran away; he soon came back and I knelt down on one knee and spoke kindly to him, enticing him to come closer. At last he was within reach of my hand and I stroked him very gently, taking great care not to frighten him.

"He became bolder, gradually stood upright, put his paws on my shoul- 35
der and began to lick my face. He followed me home.

"This was the first living creature I had ever loved passionately, because
he returned my affection. My love for the animal was, no doubt, exaggerated and ridiculous. I had a vague idea that in some way we were brothers,
both lost in life, both lonely and defenseless. He never left me, slept at the
foot of my bed, was fed in the dining-room in spite of my parents' protests
and he came with me on my solitary walks.

"I often stopped on the edge of a ditch and sat down on the grass. Sam
immediately ran to me and lay down by my side or on my knee, nosing at
my hand to make me stroke him.

"One day towards the end of June, as we were on the road to Saint-
Pierre-de-Chavrol, I saw the bus from Ravereau coming. It was travelling fast
with the four horses at full gallop; it had a yellow body and a black leather
tilt over the seats on the top like a cap. The driver was cracking his whip
and a cloud of dust rose under the wheels of the heavy vehicle and drifted
away behind.

"Suddenly, just as it reached me, Sam, perhaps frightened by the noise
and wanting to get to me, dashed in front of it. The hoof of one of the
horses knocked him over; I saw him roll, summersault, get up and fall again
amid the forest of legs; the whole bus gave two great bumps and I saw behind it something writhing in the dust. He was almost severed in two; his
belly was torn open and his entrails were hanging out, spouting blood. He
tried to get up and walk, but he could only move his fore legs, which scrab-
bled at the ground; his hind quarters were already dead. And he was howling pitiably, mad with pain.

"In a minute or two he was dead. I cannot describe my feelings and how 40
much I was affected. I could not leave my room for a month.

"One evening my father, who was furious with me for making such a fuss
over such a little thing, cried: 'What will you do when you have a real sorrow, if you lose a wife or children?'

"In a flash I began to understand myself. I realized why little everyday
troubles assumed catastrophic proportions in my eyes; I saw that I was so
constituted that I felt everything over-keenly and was hyper-susceptible to
painful impressions, which were intensified by my abnormal sensitiveness;
and a paralyzing fear of life gripped me.

"I was without physical desires or ambition; so I decided to sacrifice the
possibility of happiness to the certainty of suffering. 'Life is short; I will devote myself to the service of others; I will soothe their sorrows and rejoice
in their happiness,' I said to myself. 'As I shall not feel either myself directly,
I shall experience these emotions only with diminished intensity.'

"And if you only knew how suffering still tortures me and wrings my
heart! But what would have been intolerable agony in my own case has
been sublimated into sympathy and pity.

"I could never have endured the sorrow with which I come into contact 45
every day had it been my own. I could not have seen a child of my own
die without dying myself. And, in spite of everything I still have such an undefined, subconscious fear of something happening, that the sight of the

postman coming to my door sends a shiver down my spine, though now I have nothing to fear."

The Abbé Mauduit fell silent. He was looking into the fire in the great fireplace, as if seeking to read there all the mysteries and secrets of the life he might have lived, if he had faced suffering more bravely. He went on in a lower voice:

"I was right; I am not made to live in this world."

The Comtesse said nothing; at last, after a long silence, she commented:

"As for me, if I had not got my grandchildren, I don't think I should have the courage to go on living."

The Curé got up without another word.   50

As the servants in the kitchen were asleep, she took him herself to the door into the garden and watched his tall, slow-moving shadow in the light of his lantern plunge into the darkness.

Then she went back and sat down by the fire, and thought of many things that do not occur to the young.

Bret Harte   *(1836–1902)*

INVITATION TO READING: Bret Harte was born in Albany, New York, and moved to the California of Gold Rush days at age sixteen. He worked as a printer, teacher, typesetter, and magazine editor. He first acquired local fame with humorous sketches and stories but became nationally known with stories like "The Luck of Roaring Camp." His immensely popular stories helped create the folklore of the American West. He wrote about a rugged outdoor world where many disregarded or skirted the law and others took the law into their own hands. Lionized for a time, Harte returned to the East, but like the gambler in the following story he struck a streak of bad luck and left wife and children behind to work in Europe as a consular official. Harte gave his readers staples of sentimental popular fiction: innocent young love, the cool unflappable cynical gambler, a no-account sneaky villain, and the prostitute with a heart of gold. However, he also, like his contemporary Mark Twain, painted with deft strokes the smug callousness of the righteous.

The Outcasts of Poker Flat   *1869*

As Mr. John Oakhurst, gambler, stepped into the main street of Poker Flat on the morning of the 23d of November, 1850, he was conscious of a change in its moral atmosphere since the preceding night. Two or three men, conversing earnestly together, ceased as he approached, and exchanged significant glances. There was a Sabbath lull in the air, which, in a settlement unused to Sabbath influences, looked ominous.

Mr. Oakhurst's calm, handsome face betrayed small concern in these indications. Whether he was conscious of any predisposing cause was another question. "I reckon they're after somebody," he reflected; "likely it's me." He returned to his pocket the handkerchief with which he had been whipping away the red dust of Poker Flat from his neat boots, and quietly discharged his mind of any further conjecture.

In point of fact, Poker Flat was "after somebody." It had lately suffered the loss of several thousand dollars, two valuable horses, and a prominent citizen. It was experiencing a spasm of virtuous reaction, quite as lawless and ungovernable as any of the acts that had provoked it. A secret committee had determined to rid the town of all improper persons. This was done permanently in regard of two men who were then hanging from the boughs of a sycamore in the gulch, and temporarily in the banishment of certain other objectionable characters. I regret to say that some of these were ladies. It is but due to the sex, however, to state that their impropriety was professional, and it was only in such easily established standards of evil that Poker Flat ventured to sit in judgment.

Mr. Oakhurst was right in supposing that he was included in this category. A few of the committee had urged hanging him as a possible example and a sure method of reimbursing themselves from his pockets of the sums he had won from them. "It's agin justice," said Jim Wheeler, "to let this yer young man from Roaring Camp—an entire stranger—carry away our money." But a crude sentiment of equity residing in the breasts of those who had been fortunate enough to win from Mr. Oakhurst overruled this narrower local prejudice.

Mr. Oakhurst received his sentence with philosophic calmness, none the   5
less coolly that he was aware of the hesitation of his judges. He was too much of a gambler not to accept fate. With him life was at best an uncertain game, and he recognized the usual percentage in favor of the dealer.

A body of armed men accompanied the deported wickedness of Poker Flat to the outskirts of the settlement. Besides Mr. Oakhurst, who was known to be a coolly desperate man, and for whose intimidation the armed escort was intended, the expatriated party consisted of a young woman familiarly known as "The Duchess"; another who had won the title of "Mother Shipton"; and "Uncle Billy," a suspected sluice-robber and confirmed drunkard. The cavalcade provoked no comments from the spectators, nor was any word uttered by the escort. Only when the gulch which marked the uttermost limit of Poker Flat was reached, the leader spoke briefly and to the point. The exiles were forbidden to return at the peril of their lives.

As the escort disappeared, their pent-up feelings found vent in a few hysterical tears from the Duchess, some bad language from Mother Shipton, and a Parthian volley of expletives from Uncle Billy. The philosophic Oakhurst alone remained silent. He listened calmly to Mother Shipton's desire to cut somebody's heart out, to the repeated statements of the Duchess that she would die in the road, and to the alarming oaths that seemed to be bumped out of Uncle Billy as he rode forward. With the easy good humor characteristic of his class, he insisted upon exchanging his own riding-horse, "Five-Spot," for the sorry mule which the Duchess rode. But even this act did not draw the party into any closer sympathy. The young woman readjusted her somewhat draggled plumes with a feeble, faded coquetry; Mother Shipton eyed the possessor of "Five-Spot" with malevolence, and Uncle Billy included the whole party in one sweeping anathema.

The road to Sandy Bar—a camp that, not having as yet experienced the regenerating influences of Poker Flat, consequently seemed to offer some invitation to the emigrants—lay over a steep mountain range. It was distant a day's severe travel. In that advanced season the party soon passed out of the moist, temperate regions of the foothills into the dry, cold, bracing air of the Sierras. The trail was narrow and difficult. At noon the Duchess, rolling out of her saddle upon the ground, declared her intention of going no farther, and the party halted.

The spot was singularly wild and impressive. A wooded amphitheatre, surrounded on three sides by precipitous cliffs of naked granite, sloped gently toward the crest of another precipice that overlooked the valley. It was, undoubtedly, the most suitable spot for a camp, had camping been advisable. But Mr. Oakhurst knew that scarcely half the journey to Sandy Bar was accomplished, and the party were not equipped or provisioned for delay. This fact he pointed out to his companions curtly, with a philosophic commentary on the folly of "throwing up their hand before the game was played out." But they were furnished with liquor, which in this emergency stood them in place of food, fuel, rest, and prescience. In spite of his remonstrances, it was not long before they were more or less under its influence. Uncle Billy passed rapidly from a bellicose state into one of stupor, the Duchess became maudlin, and Mother Shipton snored. Mr. Oakhurst alone remained erect, leaning against a rock, calmly surveying them.

Mr. Oakhurst did not drink. It interfered with a profession which required   10
coolness, impassiveness, and presence of mind, and in his own language, he "couldn't afford it." As he gazed at his recumbent fellow exiles, the loneliness begotten of his pariah trade, his habits of life, his very vices, for the first time seriously oppressed him. He bestirred himself in dusting his black clothes, washing his hands and face, and other acts characteristic of his studiously neat habits, and for a moment forgot his annoyance. The thought of deserting his weaker and more pitiable companions never perhaps occurred to him. Yet he could not help feeling the want of that excitement which, singularly enough, was most conducive to that calm equanimity for which he was notorious. He looked at the gloomy walls that rose a thousand feet sheer above the circling pines around him, at the sky ominously clouded, at the valley below, already deepening into shadow; and doing so, suddenly he heard his own name called.

A horseman slowly ascended the trail. In the fresh, open face of the newcomer Mr. Oakhurst recognized Tom Simson, otherwise known as "The Innocent," of Sandy Bar. He had met him some months before over a "little game," and had, with perfect equanimity, won the entire fortune—amounting to some forty dollars—of that guileless youth. After the game was finished, Mr. Oakhurst drew the youthful speculator behind the door and thus addressed him: "Tommy, you're a good little man, but you can't gamble worth a cent. Don't try it over again." He then handed him his money back, pushed him gently from the room, and so made a devoted slave of Tom Simson.

There was a remembrance of this in his boyish and enthusiastic greeting of Mr. Oakhurst. He had started, he said, to go to Poker Flat to seek his fortune. "Alone?" No, not exactly alone; in fact (a giggle), he had run away with Piney Woods. Didn't Mr. Oakhurst remember Piney? She that used to wait on the table at the Temperance House? They had been engaged a long time, but old Jake Woods had objected, and so they had run away, and were going to Poker Flat to be married, and here they were. And they were tired out, and how lucky it was they had found a place to camp, and company. All this the Innocent delivered rapidly, while Piney, a stout, comely damsel of fifteen, emerged from behind the pine tree, where she had been blushing unseen, and rode to the side of her lover.

Mr. Oakhurst seldom troubled himself with sentiment, still less with propriety; but he had a vague idea that the situation was not fortunate. He retained, however, his presence of mind sufficiently to kick Uncle Billy, who was about to say something, and Uncle Billy was sober enough to recognize in Mr. Oakhurst's kick a superior power that would not bear trifling. He then endeavored to dissuade Tom Simson from delaying further, but in vain. He even pointed out the fact that there was no provision, nor means of making a camp. But, unluckily, the Innocent met this objection by assuring the party that he was provided with an extra mule loaded with provisions, and by the discovery of a rude attempt at a log house near the trail. "Piney can stay with Mrs. Oakhurst," said the Innocent, pointing to the Duchess, "and I can shift for myself."

Nothing but Mr. Oakhurst's admonishing foot saved Uncle Billy from bursting into a roar of laughter. As it was, he felt compelled to retire up the canyon until he could recover his gravity. There he confided the joke to the tall pine trees, with many slaps of his leg, contortions of his face, and the usual profanity. But when he returned to the party, he found them seated by a fire—for the air had grown strangely chill and the sky overcast—in apparently amicable conversation. Piney was actually talking in an impulsive girlish fashion to the Duchess, who was listening with an interest and animation she had not shown for many days. The Innocent was holding forth, apparently with equal effect, to Mr. Oakhurst and Mother Shipton, who was actually relaxing into amiability. "Is this yer a d—d picnic?" said Uncle Billy, with inward scorn, as he surveyed the sylvan group, the glancing firelight, and the tethered animals in the foreground. Suddenly an idea mingled with the alcoholic fumes that disturbed his brain. It was apparently of a jocular nature, for he felt impelled to slap his leg again and cram his fist into his mouth.

As the shadows crept slowly up the mountain, a slight breeze rocked the   15 tops of the pine trees and moaned through their long and gloomy aisles. The ruined cabin, patched and covered with pine boughs, was set apart for the ladies. As the lovers parted, they unaffectedly exchanged a kiss, so honest and sincere that it might have been heard above the swaying pines.

The frail Duchess and the malevolent Mother Shipton were probably too stunned to remark upon this last evidence of simplicity, and so turned without a word to the hut. The fire was replenished, the men lay down before the door, and in a few minutes were asleep.

Mr. Oakhurst was a light sleeper. Toward morning he awoke benumbed and cold. As he stirred the dying fire, the wind, which was now blowing strongly, brought to his cheek that which caused the blood to leave it—snow!

He started to his feet with the intention of awakening the sleepers, for there was no time to lose. But turning to where Uncle Billy had been lying, he found him gone. A suspicion leaped to his brain, and a curse to his lips. He ran to the spot where the mules had been tethered—they were no longer there. The tracks were already rapidly disappearing in the snow.

The momentary excitement brought Mr. Oakhurst back to the fire with his usual calm. He did not waken the sleepers. The Innocent slumbered peacefully, with a smile on his good-humored, freckled face; the virgin Piney slept beside her frailer sisters as sweetly as though attended by celestial guardians; and Mr. Oakhurst, drawing his blanket over his shoulders, stroked his mustaches and waited for the dawn. It came slowly in a whirling mist of snowflakes that dazzled and confused the eye. What could be seen of the landscape appeared magically changed. He looked over the valley, and summed up the present and future in two words, "Snowed in!"

A careful inventory of the provisions, which, fortunately for the party, had been stored within the hut, and so escaped the felonious fingers of Uncle Billy, disclosed the fact that with care and prudence they might last ten days longer. "That is," said Mr. Oakhurst *sotto voce* to the Innocent, "if you're willing to board us. If you ain't—and perhaps you'd better not—you can wait till Uncle Billy gets back with provisions." For some occult reason, Mr. Oakhurst could not bring himself to disclose Uncle Billy's rascality, and so offered the hypothesis that he had wandered from the camp and had accidentally stampeded the animals. He dropped a warning to the Duchess and Mother Shipton, who of course knew the facts of their associate's defection. "They'll find out the truth about us *all* when they find out anything," he added significantly, "and there's no good frightening them now."

Tom Simson not only put all his worldly store at the disposal of Mr. 20 Oakhurst, but seemed to enjoy the prospect of their enforced seclusion. "We'll have a good camp for a week, and then the snow'll melt, and we'll all go back together." The cheerful gayety of the young man and Mr. Oakhurst's calm infected the others. The Innocent, with the aid of pine boughs, extemporized a thatch for the roofless cabin, and the Duchess directed Piney in the rearrangement of the interior with a taste and tact that opened the blue eyes of that provincial maiden to their fullest extent. "I reckon now you're used to fine things at Poker Flat," said Piney. The Duchess turned away sharply to conceal something that reddened her cheeks through their professional tint, and Mother Shipton requested Piney not to "chatter." But when Mr. Oakhurst returned from a weary search for the trail, he heard the sound of happy laughter echoed from the rocks. He stopped in some alarm, and his thoughts first naturally reverted to the whiskey, which he had prudently cached. "And yet it don't somehow sound like whiskey," said the gambler. It was not until he caught sight of the blazing fire through the still blinding storm, and the group around it, that he settled to the conviction that it was "square fun."

Whether Mr. Oakhurst had cached his cards with the whiskey as something debarred the free access of the community, I cannot say. It was certain that, in Mother Shipton's words, he "didn't say 'cards' once" during that evening. Haply the time was beguiled by an accordion, produced somewhat ostentatiously by Tom Simson from his pack. Notwithstanding some difficulties attending the manipulation of this instrument, Piney Woods managed to pluck several reluctant melodies from its keys to an accompaniment by the Innocent on a pair of bone castanets. But the crowning festivity of the evening was reached in a rude camp-meeting hymn, which the lovers, joining hands, sang with great earnestness and vociferation. I fear that a certain defiant tone and covenanter's swing to its chorus, rather than any devotional quality, caused it speedily to infect the others, who at last joined in the refrain:

"I'm proud to live in the service of the Lord,
And I'm bound to die in His army."

The pines rocked, the storm eddied and whirled above the miserable group, and the flames of their altar leaped heavenward, as if in token of the vow.

At midnight the storm abated, the rolling clouds parted, and the stars glittered keenly above the sleeping camp. Mr. Oakhurst, whose professional habits had enabled him to live on the smallest possible amount of sleep, in dividing the watch with Tom Simson somehow managed to take upon himself the greater part of that duty. He excused himself to the Innocent by saying that he had "often been a week without sleep." "Doing what?" asked Tom. "Poker!" replied Oakhurst sententiously. "When a man gets a streak of luck—nigger-luck—he don't get tired. The luck gives in first. Luck," continued the gambler reflectively, "is a mighty queer thing. All you know about it for certain is that it's bound to change. And it's finding out when it's going to change that makes you. We've had a streak of bad luck since we left Poker Flat—you come along, and slap you get into it, too. If you can hold your cards right along you're all right. For," added the gambler, with cheerful irrelevance—

" 'I'm proud to live in the service of the Lord,
And I'm bound to die in His army.' "

The third day came, and the sun, looking through the white-curtained valley, saw the outcasts divide their slowly decreasing store of provisions for the morning meal. It was one of the peculiarities of that mountain climate that its rays diffused a kindly warmth over the wintry landscape, as if in regretful commiseration of the past. But it revealed drift on drift of snow piled high around the hut—a hopeless, uncharted, trackless sea of white lying below the rocky shores to which the castaways still clung. Through the marvelously clear air the smoke of the pastoral village of Poker Flat rose miles away. Mother Shipton saw it, and from a remote pinnacle of her rocky fastness hurled in that direction a final malediction. It was her last vituperative attempt, and perhaps for that reason was invested with a certain degree of sublimity. It did her good, she privately informed the Duchess. "Just you go out there and cuss, and see." She then set herself to the task of amusing "the child," as she and the Duchess were pleased to call Piney. Piney was no chicken, but it was a soothing and original theory of the pair thus to account for the fact that she didn't swear and wasn't improper.

When night crept up again through the gorges, the reedy notes of the accordion rose and fell in fitful spasms and long-drawn gasps by the flickering campfire. But music failed to fill entirely the aching void left by insufficient food, and a new diversion was proposed by Piney—storytelling. Neither Mr. Oakhurst nor his female companions caring to relate their personal experiences, this plan would have failed too, but for the Innocent. Some months before he had chanced upon a stray copy of Mr. Pope's ingenious translation of the Iliad. He now proposed to narrate the principal incidents of that poem—having thoroughly mastered the argument and fairly forgotten the words—in the current vernacular of Sandy Bar. And so for the rest of that night the Homeric demigods again walked the earth. Trojan bully and wily Greek wrestled in the winds, and the great pines in the canyon seemed to bow to the wrath of the son of Peleus. Mr. Oakhurst listened with quiet satisfaction. Most especially was he interested in the fate of "Ash-heels," as the Innocent persisted in denominating the "swift-footed Achilles."

So, with small food and much of Homer and the accordion, a week   25 passed over the heads of the outcasts. The sun again forsook them, and again from leaden skies the snowflakes were sifted over the land. Day by day closer around them drew the snowy circle, until at last they looked from their prison over drifted walls of dazzling white that towered twenty feet above their heads. It became more and more difficult to replenish their fires, even from the fallen trees beside them, now half hidden drifts. And yet no one complained. The lovers turned from the dreary prospect and looked into each other's eyes, and were happy. Mr. Oakhurst settled himself coolly to the losing game before him. The Duchess, more cheerful than she had been, assumed the care of Piney. Only Mother Shipton—once the strongest of the party—seemed to sicken and fade. At midnight on the tenth day she called Oakhurst to her side. "I'm going," she said, in a voice of querulous weakness, "but don't say anything about it. Don't waken the kids. Take the bundle from under my head, and open it." Mr. Oakhurst did so. It contained Mother Shipton's rations for the last week, untouched. "Give 'em to the child," she said, pointing to the sleeping Piney. "You've starved yourself," said the gambler. "That's what they call it," said the woman querulously, as she lay down again, and turning her face to the wall, passed quietly away.

The accordion and the bones were put aside that day, and Homer was forgotten. When the body of Mother Shipton had been committed to the snow, Mr. Oakhurst took the Innocent aside, and showed him a pair of snow-shoes, which he had fashioned from the old pack-saddle. "There's one chance in a hundred to save her yet," he said, pointing to Piney; "but it's there," he added, pointing toward Poker Flat. "If you can reach there in two days she's safe." "And you?" asked Tom Simson. "I'll stay here," was the curt reply.

The lovers parted with a long embrace. "You are not going, too?" said the Duchess, as she saw Mr. Oakhurst apparently waiting to accompany him. "As far as the canyon," he replied. He turned suddenly and kissed the Duchess, leaving her pallid face aflame, and her trembling limbs rigid with amazement.

Night came, but not Mr. Oakhurst. It brought the storm again and the whirling snow. Then the Duchess, feeding the fire, found that someone had quietly piled beside the hut enough fuel to last a few days longer. The tears rose to her eyes, but she hid them from Piney.

The women slept but little. In the morning, looking into each other's faces, they read their fate. Neither spoke, but Piney, accepting the position of the stronger, drew near and placed her arm around Duchess's waist. They kept this attitude for the rest of the day. That night the storm reached its greatest fury, and rending asunder the protecting vines, invaded the very hut.

Toward morning they found themselves unable to feed the fire, which 30 gradually died away. As the embers slowly blackened, the Duchess crept closer to Piney, and broke the silence of many hours: "Piney, can you pray?" "No, dear," said Piney simply. The Duchess, without knowing exactly why, felt relieved, and putting her head upon Piney's shoulder, spoke no more. And so reclining, the younger and purer pillowing the head of her soiled sister upon her virgin breast, they fell asleep.

The wind lulled as if it feared to waken them. Feathery drifts of snow, shaken from the long pine boughs, flew like white winged birds, and settled about them as they slept. The moon through the rifted clouds looked down upon what had been the camp. But all human stain, all trace of earthly travail, was hidden beneath the spotless mantle mercifully flung from above.

They slept all that day and the next, nor did they waken when voices and footsteps broke the silence of the camp. And when pitying fingers brushed the snow from their wan faces, you could scarcely have told from the equal peace that dwelt upon them which was she that had sinned. Even the law of Poker Flat recognized this, and turned away, leaving them still locked in each other's arms.

But at the head of the gulch, on one of the largest pine trees, they found the deuce of clubs pinned to the bark with a bowie knife. It bore the following, written in pencil in a firm hand:

†

BENEATH THIS TREE

LIES THE BODY

OF

JOHN OAKHURST,

WHO STRUCK A STREAK OF BAD LUCK

ON THE 23D OF NOVEMBER, 1850,

AND HANDED IN HIS CHECKS ON THE 7TH DECEMBER, 1850.

And pulseless and cold, with a derringer by his side and a bullet in his heart, though still calm as in life, beneath the snow lay he who was at once the strongest and yet the weakest of the outcasts of Poker Flat.

Sarah Orne Jewett   *(1849–1909)*

INVITATION TO READING: Sarah Orne Jewett was a New England writer who believed that literature did not have to deal with grand subjects but could faithfully honor the familiar ordinary life of the community. Like the great British novelist George Eliot (Marian Evans), she believed in the "beauty of the commonplace." The following story takes us to a rural setting that is only a distant memory for most Americans, but the story raises an issue that is a vital commitment for many of them in today's world. When the colonists first came to the North American continent, vast swarms of birds—millions of passenger pigeons, huge numbers of pink flamingoes—were part of the wildlife. However, the white heron in Jewett's story is already a lone endangered survivor. Is the farm setting of the story only a distant nostalgic memory for you or others of your generation? Is the clash of the two opposing attitudes toward the endangered wildlife in this story similar to conflicts or confrontations we see today? Or is it different?

A White Heron   *1886*

I

The woods were already filled with shadows one June evening, just before eight o'clock, though a bright sunset still glimmered faintly among the trunks of the trees. A little girl was driving home her cow, a plodding, dilatory, provoking creature in her behavior, but a valued companion for all that. They were going away from whatever light there was, and striking deep into the woods, but their feet were familiar with the path, and it was no matter whether their eyes could see it or not.

There was hardly a night the summer through when the old cow could be found waiting at the pasture bars; on the contrary, it was her greatest pleasure to hide herself away among the huckleberry bushes, and though she wore a loud bell she had made the discovery that if one stood perfectly still it would not ring. So Sylvia had to hunt for her until she found her, and call Co'! Co'! with never an answering Moo, until her childish patience was quite spent. If the creature had not given good milk and plenty of it, the case would have seemed very different to her owners. Besides, Sylvia had all the time there was, and very little use to make of it. Sometimes in pleasant weather it was a consolation to look upon the cow's pranks as an intelligent attempt to play hide and seek, and as the child had no playmates she lent herself to this amusement with a good deal of zest. Though this chase had been so long that the wary animal herself had given an unusual signal of her whereabouts, Sylvia had only laughed when she came upon Mistress Moolly at the swampside, and urged her affectionately homeward with a twig of birch leaves. The old cow was not inclined to wander farther, she even turned in the right direction for once as they left the pasture, and stepped along the road at a good pace. She was quite ready to be milked now, and seldom stopped to browse. Sylvia wondered what her grandmother would say because they were so late. It was a great while since she had left home at half-past five o'clock, but everybody knew the difficulty of making this errand a short one. Mrs. Tilley had chased the horned torment too many summer evenings herself to blame any one else for lingering, and was only thankful as she waited that she had Sylvia, nowadays, to give such valuable assistance. The good woman suspected that Sylvia loitered occasionally on her own account; there never was such a child for straying about out-of-doors since the world was made! Everybody said that it was a good change for a little maid who had tried to grow for eight years in a crowded manufacturing town, but as for Sylvia herself, it seemed as if she never had been alive at all before she came to live at the farm. She thought often with wistful compassion of a wretched geranium that belonged to a town neighbor.

" 'Afraid of folks,' " old Mrs. Tilley said to herself, with a smile, after she had made the unlikely choice of Sylvia from her daughter's houseful of children, and was returning to the farm. " 'Afraid of folks,' they said! I guess she won't be troubled no great with 'em up to the old place!" When they reached the door of the lonely house and stopped to unlock it, and the cat came to purr loudly, and rub against them, a deserted pussy, indeed, but fat with young robins, Sylvia whispered that this was a beautiful place to live in, and she never should wish to go home.

The companions followed the shady woodroad, the cow taking slow steps and the child very fast ones. The cow stopped long at the brook to drink, as if the pasture were not half a swamp, and Sylvia stood still and waited, letting her bare feet cool themselves in the shoal water, while the great twilight moths struck softly against her. She waded on through the brook as the cow moved away, and listened to the thrushes with a heart that beat fast with pleasure. There was a stirring in the great boughs overhead. They were full of little birds and beasts that seemed to be wide awake, and going about their world, or else saying goodnight to each other in sleepy twitters. Sylvia herself felt sleepy as she walked along. However, it was not much farther to the house, and the air was soft and sweet. She was not often in the woods so late as this, and it made her feel as if she were a part of the gray shadows and the moving leaves. She was just thinking how long it seemed since she first came to the farm a year ago, and wondering if everything went on in the noisy town just the same as when she was there; the thought of the great red-faced boy who used to chase and frighten her made her hurry along the path to escape from the shadow of the trees.

Suddenly this little woods-girl is horror-stricken to hear a clear whistle not   5
very far away. Not a bird's-whistle, which would have a sort of friendliness, but a boy's whistle, determined, and somewhat aggressive. Sylvia left the cow to whatever sad fate might await her, and stepped discreetly aside into

the brushes, but she was just too late. The enemy had discovered her, and called out in a very cheerful and persuasive tone, "Halloa, little girl, how far is it to the road?" and trembling Sylvia answered almost inaudibly, "A good ways."

She did not dare to look boldly at the tall young man, who carried a gun over his shoulder, but she came out of her bush and again followed the cow, while he walked alongside.

"I have been hunting for some birds," the stranger said kindly, "and I have lost my way, and need a friend very much. Don't be afraid," he added gallantly. "Speak up and tell me what your name is, and whether you think I can spend the night at your house, and go out gunning early in the morning."

Sylvia was more alarmed than before. Would not her grandmother consider her much to blame? But who could have foreseen such an accident as this? It did not seem to be her fault, and she hung her head as if the stem of it were broken, but managed to answer "Sylvy," with much effort when her companion again asked her name.

Mrs. Tilley was standing in the doorway when the trio came into view. The cow gave a loud moo by way of explanation.

"Yes, you'd better speak up for yourself, you old trial! Where'd she tucked herself away this time, Sylvy?" But Sylvia kept an awed silence; she knew by instinct that her grandmother did not comprehend the gravity of the situation. She must be mistaking the stranger for one of the farmer-lads of the region.   10

The young man stood his gun beside the door, and dropped a lumpy game-bag beside it; then he bade Mrs. Tilley good-evening, and repeated his wayfarer's story, and asked if he could have a night's lodging.

"Put me anywhere you like," he said. "I must be off early in the morning, before day; but I am very hungry, indeed. You can give me some milk at any rate, that's plain."

"Dear sakes, yes," responded the hostess, whose long slumbering hospitality seemed to be easily awakened. "You might fare better if you went out to the main road a mile or so, but you're welcome to what we've got. I'll milk right off, and you make yourself at home. You can sleep on husks or feathers," she proffered graciously. "I raised them all myself. There's good pasturing for geese just below here towards the ma'sh. Now step round and set a plate for the gentleman, Sylvy!" And Sylvia promptly stepped. She was glad to have something to do, and she was hungry herself.

It was a surprise to find so clean and comfortable a little dwelling in this New England wilderness. The young man had known the horrors of its most primitive housekeeping, and the dreary squalor of that level of society which does not rebel at the companionship of hens. This was the best thrift of an old-fashioned farmstead, though on such a small scale that it seemed like a hermitage. He listened eagerly to the old woman's quaint talk, he watched Sylvia's pale face and shining gray eyes with ever growing enthusiasm, and insisted that this was the best supper he had eaten for a month, and afterward the new-made friends sat down in the door-way together while the moon came up.

Soon it would be berry-time, and Sylvia was a great help at picking. The   15
cow was a good milker, though a plaguy thing to keep track of, the hostess
gossiped frankly, adding presently that she had buried four children, so
Sylvia's mother, and a son (who might be dead) in California were all the
children she had left. "Dan, my boy, was a great hand to go gunning," she
explained sadly. "I never wanted for pa'tridges or gray squer'ls while he was
to home. He's been a great wand'rer, I expect, and he's no hand to write
letters. There, I don't blame him, I'd ha' seen the world myself if it had been
so I could."

"Sylvy takes after him," the grandmother continued affectionately, after a
minute's pause. "There ain't a foot o'ground she don't know her way over,
and the wild creaturs counts her one o'themselves. Squer'ls she'll tame to
come an' feed right out o'her hands, and all sorts o'birds. Last winter she got
the jaybirds to bangeing here, and I believe she'd 'a' scanted herself of her
own meals to have plenty to throw out amongst 'em, if I hadn't kep' watch.
Anything but crows, I tell her, I'm willin' to help support—though Dan he
had a tamed one o' them that did seem to have reason same as folks. It was
round here a good spell after he went away. Dan an' his father they didn't
hitch,—but he never held up his head ag'in after Dan had dared him an'
gone off."

The guest did not notice this hint of family sorrows in his eager interest
in something else.

"So Sylvy knows all about birds, does she?" he exclaimed, as he looked
round at the little girl who sat, very demure but increasingly sleepy, in the
moonlight. "I am making a collection of birds myself. I have been at it ever
since I was a boy." (Mrs. Tilley smiled.) "There are two or three very rare
ones I have been hunting for these five years. I mean to get them on my
own grounds if they can be found."

"Do you cage 'em up?" asked Mrs. Tilley doubtfully, in response to this
enthusiastic announcement.

"Oh no, they're stuffed and preserved, dozens and dozens of them," said   20
the ornithologist, "and I have shot or snared every one myself. I caught a
glimpse of a white heron a few miles from here on Saturday, and I have followed it in this direction. They have never been found in this district at all.
The little white heron, it is," and he turned again to look at Sylvia with the
hope of discovering that the rare bird was one of her acquaintances.

But Sylvia was watching a hop-toad in the narrow footpath.

"You would know the heron if you saw it," the stranger continued eagerly.
"A queer tall white bird with soft feathers and long thin legs. And it would
have a nest perhaps in the top of a high tree, made of sticks, something like
a hawk's nest."

Sylvia's heart gave a wild beat; she knew that strange white bird, and had
once stolen softly near where it stood in some bright green swamp grass,
away over at the other side of the woods. There was an open place where
the sunshine always seemed strangely yellow and hot, where tall, nodding
rushes grew, and her grandmother had warned her that she might sink in
the soft black mud underneath and never be heard of more. Not far beyond
were the salt marshes just this side the sea itself, which Sylvia wondered and

dreamed much about, but never had seen, whose great voice could sometimes be heard above the noise of the woods on stormy nights.

"I can't think of anything I should like so much as to find that heron's nest," the handsome stranger was saying. "I would give ten dollars to anybody who could show it to me," he added desperately, "and I mean to spend my whole vacation hunting for it if need be. Perhaps it was only migrating, or had been chased out of its own region by some bird of prey."

Mrs. Tilley gave amazed attention to all this, but Sylvia still watched the toad, not divining, as she might have done at some calmer time, that the creature wished to get to its hole under the door-step, and was much hindered by the unusual spectators at that hour of the evening. No amount of thought, that night, could decide how many wished-for treasures the ten dollars, so lightly spoken of, would buy.

The next day the young sportsman hovered about the woods, and Sylvia kept him company, having lost her first fear of the friendly lad, who proved to be most kind and sympathetic. He told her many things about the birds and what they knew and where they lived and what they did with themselves. And he gave her a jack-knife, which she thought as great a treasure as if she were a desert-islander. All day long he did not once make her troubled or afraid except when he brought down some unsuspecting singing creature from its bough. Sylvia would have liked him vastly better without his gun; she could not understand why he killed the very birds he seemed to like so much. But as the day waned, Sylvia still watched the young man with loving admiration. She had never seen anybody so charming and delightful; the woman's heart, asleep in the child, was vaguely thrilled by a dream of love. Some premonition of that great power stirred and swayed these young creatures who traversed the solemn woodlands with soft-footed silent care. They stopped to listen to a bird's song; they pressed forward again eagerly, parting the branches—speaking to each other rarely and in whispers; the young man going first and Sylvia following, fascinated, a few steps behind, with her gray eyes dark with excitement.

She grieved because the longed-for white heron was elusive, but she did not lead the guest, she only followed, and there was no such thing as speaking first. The sound of her own unquestioned voice would have terrified her—it was hard enough to answer yes or no when there was need of that. At last evening began to fall, and they drove the cow home together, and Sylvia smiled with pleasure when they came to the place where she heard the whistle and was afraid only the night before.

II

Half a mile from home, at the farther edge of the woods, where the land was highest, a great pine-tree stood, the last of its generation. Whether it was left for a boundary mark, or for what reason, no one could say; the woodchoppers who had felled its mates were dead and gone long ago, and a whole forest of sturdy trees, pines and oaks and maples, had grown again. But the stately head of this old pine towered above them all and made a landmark for sea and shore miles and miles away. Sylvia knew it well. She had always believed that whoever climbed to the top of it could see the ocean; and the little girl had often laid her hand on the great rough trunk and looked up wistfully at those dark boughs that the wind always stirred, no matter how hot and still the air might be below. Now she thought of the tree with a new excitement, for why, if one climbed it at break of day could not one see all the world, and easily discover from whence the white heron flew, and mark the place, and find the hidden nest?

What a spirit of adventure, what wild ambition! What fancied triumph and delight and glory for the later morning when she could make known the secret! It was almost too real and too great for the childish heart to bear.

All night the door of the little house stood open and the whippoorwills   30 came and sang upon the very step. The young sportsman and his old hostess were sound asleep, but Sylvia's great design kept her broad awake and watching. She forgot to think of sleep. The short summer night seemed as long as the winter darkness, and at last when the whippoorwills ceased, and she was afraid the morning would after all come too soon, she stole out of the house and followed the pasture path through the woods, hastening toward the open ground beyond, listening with a sense of comfort and companionship to the drowsy twitter of a half-awakened bird, whose perch she had jarred in passing. Alas, if the great wave of human interest which flooded for the first time this dull little life should sweep away the satisfactions of an existence heart to heart with nature and the dumb life of the forest!

There was the huge tree asleep yet in the paling moonlight, and small and silly Sylvia began with utmost bravery to mount to the top of it, with tingling, eager blood coursing the channels of her whole frame, with her bare feet and fingers, that pinched and held like bird's claws to the monstrous ladder reaching up, up, almost to the sky itself. First she must mount the white oak tree that grew alongside, where she was almost lost among the dark branches and the green leaves heavy and wet with dew; a bird fluttered off its nest, and a red squirrel ran to and fro and scolded pettishly at the harmless housebreaker. Sylvia felt her way easily. She had often climbed there, and knew that higher still one of the oak's upper branches chafed against the pine trunk, just where its lower boughs were set close together. There, when she made the dangerous pass from one tree to the other, the great enterprise would really begin.

She crept out along the swaying oak limb at last, and took the daring step across into the old pine-tree. The way was harder than she thought; she must reach far and hold fast, the sharp dry twigs caught and held her and scratched her like angry talons, the pitch made her thin little fingers clumsy and stiff as she went round and round the tree's great stem, higher and higher upward. The sparrows and robins in the woods below were beginning to wake and twitter to the dawn, yet it seemed much lighter there aloft in the pine-tree, and the child knew she must hurry if her project were to be of any use.

The tree seemed to lengthen itself out as she went up, and to reach farther and farther upward. It was like a great main-mast to the voyaging earth; it must truly have been amazed that morning through all its ponderous frame as it felt this determined spark of human spirit wending its way from higher branch to branch. Who knows how steadily the least twigs held themselves to advantage this light, weak creature on her way! The old pine must have loved his new dependent. More than all the hawks, and bats, and moths, and even the sweet voiced thrushes, was the brave, beating heart of the solitary gray-eyed child. And the tree stood still and frowned away the winds that June morning while the dawn grew bright in the east.

Sylvia's face was like a pale star, if one had seen it from the ground, when the last thorny bough was past, and she stood trembling and tired but wholly triumphant, high in the treetop. Yes, there was the sea with the dawning sun making a golden dazzle over it, and toward that glorious east flew two hawks with slow-moving pinions. How low they looked in the air from that height when one had only seen them before far up, and dark against the blue sky. Their gray feathers were as soft as moths; they seemed only a little way from the tree, and Sylvia felt as if she too could go flying away among the clouds. Westward, the woodlands and farms reached miles and miles into the distance; here and there were church steeples, and white villages, truly it was a vast and awesome world!

The birds sang louder and louder. At last the sun came up bewilderingly 35 bright. Sylvia could see the white sails of ships out at sea, and the clouds that were purple and rose-colored and yellow at first began to fade away. Where was the white heron's nest in the sea of green branches, and was this wonderful sight and pageant of the world the only reward for having climbed to such a giddy height? Now look down again, Sylvia, where the green marsh is set among the shining birches and dark hemlocks; there where you saw the white heron once you will see him again; look, look! a white spot of him like a single floating feather comes up from the dead hemlock and grows larger, and rises, and comes close at last, and goes by the landmark pine with steady sweep of wing and outstretched slender neck and crested head. And wait! wait! do not move a foot or a finger, little girl, do not send an arrow of light and consciousness from your two eager eyes, for the heron has perched on a pine bough not far beyond yours, and cries back to his mate on the nest and plumes his feathers for the new day!

The child gives a long sigh a minute later when a company of shouting cat-birds comes also to the tree, and vexed by their fluttering and lawlessness the solemn heron goes away. She knows his secret now, the wild, light, slender bird that floats and wavers, and goes back like an arrow presently to his home in the green world beneath. Then Sylvia, well satisfied, makes her perilous way down again, not daring to look far below the branch she stands on, ready to cry sometimes because her fingers ache and her lamed feet slip. Wondering over and over again what the stranger would say to her, and what he would think when she told him how to find his way straight to the heron's nest.

"Sylvy, Sylvy!" called the busy old grandmother again and again, but nobody answered, and the small husk bed was empty and Sylvia had disappeared.

The guest waked from a dream, and remembering his day's pleasure hurried to dress himself that might it sooner begin. He was sure from the way the shy little girl looked once or twice yesterday that she had at least seen the white heron, and now she must really be made to tell. Here she comes now, paler than ever, and her worn old frock is torn and tattered, and smeared with pine pitch. The grandmother and the sportsman stand in the door together and question her, and the splendid moment has come to speak of the dead hemlock-tree by the green marsh.

But Sylvia does not speak after all, though the old grandmother fretfully rebukes her, and the young man's kind, appealing eyes are looking straight in her own. He can make them rich with money; he has promised it, and they are poor now. He is so well worth making happy, and he waits to hear the story she can tell.

No, she must keep silence! What is it that suddenly forbids her and makes   40
her dumb? Has she been nine years growing and now, when the great world for the first time puts out a hand to her, must she thrust it aside for a bird's sake? The murmur of the pine's green branches is in her ears, she remembers how the white heron came flying through the golden air and how they watched the sea and the morning together, and Sylvia cannot speak; she cannot tell the heron's secret and give its life away.

Dear loyalty, that suffered a sharp pang as the guest went away disappointed later in the day, that could have served and followed him and loved him as a dog loves! Many a night Sylvia heard the echo of his whistle haunting the pasture path as she came home with the loitering cow. She forgot even her sorrow at the sharp report of his gun and the sight of thrushes and sparrows dropping silent to the ground, their songs hushed and their pretty feathers stained and wet with blood. Were the birds better friends than their hunter might have been,—who can tell? Whatever treasures were lost to her, woodlands and summer-time, remember! Bring your gifts and graces and tell your secrets to this lonely country child!

Ambrose Bierce   *(1842–1913)*

INVITATION TO READING: Like Mark Twain and Bret Harte, Ambrose Bierce was a widely read nineteenth-century storyteller who made a living as a journalist. He was a master at catering to popular taste of his time: Audiences liked melodramatic flourishes, with a character acting gallant or unflappable in the face of disaster or death. They liked heart-wrenching separations from or reunions with loved ones. At the same time, they liked the hard-nosed wit showing that the author was nobody's fool. The following Civil War story takes place after the Confederate army lost Corinth in Mississippi in 1862. Bierce had risen from drummer boy to staff officer in the Union army. Is it strange that the central character in his story is a spy on the Southern side— "ardently devoted to the Southern cause"? Bierce had witnessed the battle at Shiloh and General Sherman's march through Georgia and to the sea, and the war experience reinforced his pessimistic outlook on life, which explains his nickname, "Bitter Bierce." Bierce knew how to spin a yarn that carried his spellbound readers along. Does Bierce's story make a statement about war? Or is it a masterfully plotted story catering to popular taste?

An Occurrence at Owl Creek Bridge   *1891*

I

A man stood upon a railroad bridge in Northern Alabama, looking down into the swift waters twenty feet below. The man's hands were behind his back, the wrists bound with a cord. A rope loosely encircled his neck. It was attached to a stout cross-timber above his head, and the slack fell to the level of his knees. Some loose boards laid upon the sleepers supporting the metals of the railway supplied a footing for him and his executioners—two private soldiers of the Federal army, directed by a sergeant, who in civil life may have been a deputy sheriff. At a short remove upon the same temporary platform was an officer in the uniform of his rank, armed. He was a captain. A sentinel at each end of the bridge stood with his rifle in the position known as "support," that is to say, vertical in front of the left shoulder, the hammer resting on the forearm thrown straight across the chest—a formal and unnatural position, enforcing an erect carriage of the body. It did not appear to be the duty of these two men to know what was occurring at the centre of the bridge; they merely blockaded the two ends of the foot plank which traversed it.

Beyond one of the sentinels nobody was in sight; the railroad ran straight away into a forest for a hundred yards, then, curving, was lost to view. Doubtless there was an outpost further along. The other bank of the stream was open ground—a gentle acclivity crowned with a stockade of vertical tree trunks, loop-holed for rifles, with a single embrasure through which protruded the muzzle of a brass cannon commanding the bridge. Midway of the slope between bridge and fort were the spectators—a single company of infantry in line, at "parade rest," the butts of the rifles on the ground, the barrels inclining slightly backward against the right shoulder, the hands crossed upon the stock. A lieutenant stood at the right of the line, the point of his sword upon the ground, his left hand resting upon his right. Excepting the group of four at the centre of the bridge not a man moved. The company faced the bridge, staring stonily, motionless. The sentinels, facing the banks of the stream, might have been statues to adorn the bridge. The captain stood with folded arms, silent, observing the work of his subordinates but making no sign. Death is a dignitary who, when he comes announced, is to be received with formal manifestations of respect, even by those most familiar with him. In the code of military etiquette silence and fixity are forms of deference.

The man who was engaged in being hanged was apparently about thirty-five years of age. He was a civilian, if one might judge from his dress, which was that of a planter. His features were good—a straight nose, firm mouth, broad forehead, from which his long, dark hair was combed straight back, falling behind his ears to the collar of his well-fitting frock coat. He wore a moustache and pointed beard, but no whiskers; his eyes were large and dark grey and had a kindly expression which one would hardly have expected in one whose neck was in the hemp. Evidently this was no vulgar assassin. The liberal military code makes provision for hanging many kinds of people, and gentlemen are not excluded.

The preparations being complete, the two private soldiers stepped aside and each drew away the plank upon which he had been standing. The sergeant turned to the captain, saluted and placed himself immediately behind that officer, who in turn moved apart one pace. These movements left the condemned man and the sergeant standing on the two ends of the same plank, which spanned three of the cross-ties of the bridge. The end upon which the civilian stood almost, but not quite, reached a fourth. This plank had been held in place by the weight of the captain; it was now held by that of the sergeant. At a signal from the former, the latter would step aside, the plank would tilt and the condemned man go down between two ties. The arrangement commended itself to his judgment as simple and effective. His face had not been covered nor his eyes bandaged. He looked a moment at his "unsteadfast footing," then let his gaze wander to the swirling water of the stream racing madly beneath his feet. A piece of dancing driftwood caught his attention and his eyes followed it down the current. How slowly it appeared to move! What a sluggish stream!

He closed his eyes in order to fix his last thoughts upon his wife and chil-   5
dren. The water, touched to gold by the early sun, the brooding mists under the banks at some distance down the stream, the fort, the soldiers, the piece of drift—all had distracted him. And now he became conscious of a new disturbance. Striking through the thought of his dear ones was a sound which he could neither ignore nor understand, a sharp, distinct, metallic percussion like the stroke of a blacksmith's hammer upon the anvil; it had the same ringing quality. He wondered what it was, and whether immeasurably distant or near by—it seemed both. Its recurrence was regular, but as slow as the tolling of a death knell. He awaited each stroke with impatience and—he knew not why—apprehension. The intervals of silence grew progressively longer, the delays became maddening. With their greater infrequency the sounds increased in strength and sharpness. They hurt his ear like the thrust of a knife; he feared he would shriek. What he heard was the ticking of his watch.

He unclosed his eyes and saw again the water below him. "If I could free my hands," he thought, "I might throw off the noose and spring into the stream. By diving I could evade the bullets, and, swimming vigorously, reach the bank, take to the woods, and get away home. My home, thank God, is as yet outside their lines; my wife and little ones are still beyond the invader's farthest advance."

As these thoughts, which have here to be set down in words, were flashed into the doomed man's brain rather than evolved from it, the captain nodded to the sergeant. The sergeant stepped aside.

II

Peyton Farquhar was a well-to-do planter, of an old and highly-respected Alabama family. Being a slave owner, and, like other slave owners, a politician, he was naturally an original secessionist and ardently devoted to the Southern cause. Circumstances of an imperious nature which it is unnecessary to relate here, had prevented him from taking service with the gallant army which had fought the disastrous campaigns ending with the fall of

Corinth, and he chafed under the inglorious restraint, longing for the release of his energies, the larger life of the soldier, the opportunity for distinction. That opportunity, he felt, would come, as it comes to all in war time. Meanwhile he did what he could. No service was too humble for him to perform in aid of the South, no adventure too perilous for him to undertake if consistent with the character of a civilian who was at heart a soldier, and who in good faith and without too much qualification assented to at least a part of the frankly villainous dictum that all is fair in love and war.

One evening while Farquhar and his wife were sitting on a rustic bench near the entrance to his grounds, a grey-clad soldier rode up to the gate and asked for a drink of water. Mrs. Farquhar was only too happy to serve him with her own white hands. While she was gone to fetch the water, her husband approached the dusty horseman and inquired eagerly for news from the front.

"The Yanks are repairing the railroads," said the man, "and are getting   10
ready for another advance. They have reached the Owl Creek bridge, put it in order, and built a stockade on the other bank. The commandant has issued an order, which is posted everywhere, declaring that any civilian caught interfering with the railroad, its bridges, tunnels, or trains, will be summarily hanged. I saw the order."

"How far is it to the Owl Creek bridge?" Farquhar asked.

"About thirty miles."

"Is there no force on this side the creek?"

"Only a picket post half a mile out, on the railroad, and a single sentinel at this end of the bridge."

"Suppose a man—a civilian and student of hanging—should elude the   15
picket post and perhaps get the better of the sentinel," said Farquhar, smiling, "what could he accomplish?"

The soldier reflected. "I was there a month ago," he replied. "I observed that the flood of last winter had lodged a great quantity of driftwood against the wooden pier at this end of the bridge. It is now dry and would burn like tow."

The lady had now brought the water, which the soldier drank. He thanked her ceremoniously, bowed to her husband, and rode away. An hour later, after nightfall, he repassed the plantation, going northward in the direction from which he had come. He was a Federal scout.

III

As Peyton Farquhar fell straight downward through the bridge, he lost consciousness and was as one already dead. From this state he was awakened—ages later, it seemed to him—by the pain of a sharp pressure upon his throat, followed by a sense of suffocation. Keen, poignant agonies seemed to shoot from his neck downward through every fibre of his body and limbs. These pains appeared to flash along well-defined lines of ramification, and to beat with an inconceivably rapid periodicity. They seemed like streams of pulsating fire heating him to an intolerable temperature. As to his head, he was conscious of nothing but a feeling of fullness—of congestion. These sensations were unaccompanied by thought. The intellectual part of his nature was already effaced; he had power only to feel, and feeling was torment. He was conscious of motion. Encompassed in a luminous cloud, of which he was now merely the fiery heart, without material substance, he swung through unthinkable arcs of oscillation, like a vast pendulum. Then all at once, with terrible suddenness, the light about him shot upward with the noise of a loud plash; a frightful roaring was in his ears, and all was cold and dark. The power of thought was restored; he knew that the rope had broken and he had fallen into the stream. There was no additional strangulation; the noose about his neck was already suffocating him, and kept the water from his lungs. To die of hanging at the bottom of a river!—the idea seemed to him ludicrous. He opened his eyes in the blackness and saw above him a gleam of light, but how distant, how inaccessible! He was still sinking, for the light became fainter and fainter until it was a mere glimmer. Then it began to grow and brighten, and he knew that he was rising toward the surface—knew it with reluctance, for he was now very comfortable. "To be hanged and drowned," he thought, "that is not so bad; but I do not wish to be shot. No; I will not be shot; that is not fair."

He was not conscious of an effort, but a sharp pain in his wrist apprised him that he was trying to free his hands. He gave the struggle his attention, as an idler might observe the feat of a juggler, without interest in the outcome. What splendid effort!—what magnificent, what superhuman strength! Ah, that was a fine endeavour! Bravo! The cord fell away; his arms parted and floated upward, the hands dimly seen on each side in the growing light. He watched them with a new interest as first one and then the other pounced upon the noose at his neck. They tore it away and thrust it fiercely aside, its undulations resembling those of a water-snake. "Put it back, put it back!" He thought he shouted these words to his hands, for the undoing of the noose had been succeeded by the direst pang which he had yet experienced. His neck ached horribly; his brain was on fire; his heart, which had been fluttering faintly, gave a great leap, trying to force itself out at his mouth. His whole body was racked and wrenched with an insupportable anguish! But his disobedient hands gave no heed to the command. They beat the water vigorously with quick, downward strokes, forcing him to the surface. He felt his head emerge; his eyes were blinded by the sunlight; his chest expanded convulsively, and with a supreme and crowning agony his lungs engulfed a great draught of air, which instantly he expelled in a shriek!

He was now in full possession of his physical senses. They were, indeed, preternaturally keen and alert. Something in the awful disturbance of his organic system had so exalted and refined them that they made record of things never before perceived. He felt the ripples upon his face and heard their separate sounds as they struck. He looked at the forest on the bank of the stream, saw the individual trees, the leaves and the veining of each leaf—the very insects upon them, the locusts, the brilliant-bodied flies, the grey spiders stretching their webs from twig to twig. He noted the prismatic colors in all the dewdrops upon a million blades of grass. The humming of the gnats that danced above the eddies of the stream, the beating of the dragon flies' wings, the strokes of the water spiders' legs, like oars which had lifted their boat—all these made audible music. A fish slid along beneath his eyes and he heard the rush of its body parting the water.

20

He had come to the surface facing down the stream; in a moment the visible world seemed to wheel slowly round, himself the pivotal point, and he saw the bridge, the fort, the soldiers upon the bridge, the captain, the sergeant, the two privates, his executioners. They were in silhouette against the blue sky. They shouted and gesticulated, pointing at him; the captain had drawn his pistol, but did not fire; the others were unarmed. Their movements were grotesque and horrible, their forms gigantic.

Suddenly he heard a sharp report and something struck the water smartly within a few inches of his head, spattering his face with spray. He heard a second report, and saw one of the sentinels with his rifle at his shoulder, a light cloud of blue smoke rising from the muzzle. The man in the water saw the eye of the man on the bridge gazing into his own through the sights of the rifle. He observed that it was a grey eye, and remembered having read that grey eyes were keenest and that all famous marksmen had them. Nevertheless, this one had missed.

A counter swirl had caught Farquhar and turned him half round; he was again looking into the forest on the bank opposite the fort. The sound of a clear, high voice in a monotonous singsong now rang out behind him and came across the water with a distinctness that pierced and subdued all other sounds, even the beating of the ripples in his ears. Although no soldier, he had frequented camps enough to know the dread significance of that deliberate, drawling, aspirated chant; the lieutenant on shore was taking a part in the morning's work. How coldly and pitilessly—with what an even, calm intonation, presaging and enforcing tranquility in the men—with what accurately-measured intervals fell those cruel words:

"Attention, company . . . Shoulder arms . . . Ready . . . Aim . . . Fire."

Farquhar dived—dived as deeply as he could. The water roared in his ears like the voice of Niagara, yet he heard the dulled thunder of the volley, and rising again toward the surface, met shining bits of metal, singularly flattened, oscillating slowly downward. Some of them touched him on the face and hands, then fell away, continuing their descent. One lodged between his collar and neck; it was uncomfortably warm, and he snatched it out.

As he rose to the surface, gasping for breath, he saw that he had been a long time under water; he was perceptibly farther down stream—nearer to safety. The soldiers had almost finished reloading; the metal ramrods flashed all at once in the sunshine as they were drawn from the barrels, turned in the air, and thrust into their sockets. The two sentinels fired again, independently and ineffectually.

The hunted man saw all this over his shoulder; he was now swimming vigorously with the current. His brain was as energetic as his arms and legs; he thought with the rapidity of lightning.

"The officer," he reasoned, "will not make that martinet's error a second time. It is as easy to dodge a volley as a single shot. He has probably already given the command to fire at will. God help me, I cannot dodge them all!"

An appalling plash within two yards of him, followed by a loud rushing sound, *diminuendo,* which seemed to travel back through the air to the fort and died in an explosion which stirred the very river to its deeps! A rising sheet of water, which curved over him, fell down upon him, blinded him, strangled him! The cannon had taken a hand in the game. As he shook his head free from the commotion of the smitten water, he heard the deflected shot humming through the air ahead, and in an instant it was cracking and smashing the branches in the forest beyond.

"They will not do that again," he thought; "the next time they will use a   30
charge of grape. I must keep my eye upon the gun; the smoke will apprise me—the report arrives too late; it lags behind the missile. It is a good gun."

Suddenly he felt himself whirled round and round—spinning like a top. The water, the banks, the forest, the now distant bridge, fort and men—all were commingled and blurred. Objects were represented by their colors only; circular horizontal streaks of color—that was all he saw. He had been caught in a vortex and was being whirled on with a velocity of advance and gyration which made him giddy and sick. In a few moments he was flung upon the gravel at the foot of the left bank of the stream—the southern bank—and behind a projecting point which concealed him from his enemies. The sudden arrest of his motion, the abrasion of one of his hands on the gravel, restored him and he wept with delight. He dug his fingers into the sand, threw it over himself in handfuls and audibly blessed it. It looked like gold, like diamonds, rubies, emeralds; he could think of nothing beautiful which it did not resemble. The trees upon the bank were giant garden plants; he noted a definite order in their arrangement, inhaled the fragrance of their blooms. A strange, roseate light shone through the spaces among their trunks, and the wind made in their branches the music of æolian harps. He had no wish to perfect his escape, was content to remain in that enchanting spot until retaken.

A whizz and rattle of grapeshot among the branches high above his head roused him from his dream. The baffled cannoneer had fired him a random farewell. He sprang to his feet, rushed up the sloping bank, and plunged into the forest.

All that day he travelled, laying his course by the rounding sun. The forest seemed interminable; nowhere did he discover a break in it, not even a woodman's road. He had not known that he lived in so wild a region. There was something uncanny in the revelation.

By nightfall he was fatigued, footsore, famishing. The thought of his wife and children urged him on. At last he found a road which led him in what he knew to be the right direction. It was as wide and straight as a city street, yet it seemed untravelled. No fields bordered it, no dwelling anywhere. Not so much as the barking of a dog suggested human habitation. The black bodies of the great trees formed a straight wall on both sides, terminating on the horizon in a point, like a diagram in a lesson in perspective. Overhead, as he looked up through this rift in the wood, shone great golden stars looking unfamiliar and grouped in strange constellations. He was sure they were arranged in some order which had a secret and malign significance. The wood on either side was full of singular noises, among which—once, twice, and again—he distinctly heard whispers in an unknown tongue.

His neck was in pain, and, lifting his hand to it, he found it horribly   35
swollen. He knew that it had a circle of black where the rope had bruised it. His eyes felt congested; he could no longer close them. His tongue was

swollen with thirst; he relieved its fever by thrusting it forward from between his teeth into the cool air. How softly the turf had carpeted the untravelled avenue! He could no longer feel the roadway beneath his feet!

Doubtless, despite his suffering, he fell asleep while walking, for now he sees another scene—perhaps he has merely recovered from a delirium. He stands at the gate of his own home. All is as he left it, and all bright and beautiful in the morning sunshine. He must have travelled the entire night. As he pushes open the gate and passes up the wide white walk, he sees a flutter of female garments; his wife, looking fresh and cool and sweet, steps down from the verandah to meet him. At the bottom of the steps she stands waiting, with a smile of ineffable joy, an attitude of matchless grace and dignity. Ah, how beautiful she is! He springs forward with extended arms. As he is about to clasp her, he feels a stunning blow upon the back of the neck; a blinding white light blazes all about him, with a sound like the shock of a cannon—then all is darkness and silence!

Peyton Farquhar was dead; his body, with a broken neck, swung gently from side to side beneath the timbers of the Owl Creek bridge.

Joseph Conrad   *(1857–1924)*

INVITATION TO READING: Polish-born Joseph Conrad, who wrote English as a third language, became known as a powerful storyteller, with a following around the globe. Conrad's admirers still consider his novel *The Heart of Darkness* an unsurpassed masterpiece. Conrad had worked much of his life as a sailor and officer on ships plying the trade routes of the nineteenth-century European colonial empires. His tales are set against a background of the dangers of the sea, the lure of exotic places, and the mysteries of threatening, disorienting foreign lands. His greatest tales put his characters in situations where the thin protective layer of civilized routines and conventions has failed or disappeared. We focus on characters put to the test of who they really are as they cope with—and sometimes break under—tremendous stress. Conrad wrote about colonial Africa when many of his contemporaries were still reciting the British poet Rudyard Kipling's poem about the civilizing mission of colonialism and the "white man's burden." The ironic title of Conrad's tale mocks these rationalizations: Whatever this story brings to the lives of both the Africans and the two British colonials, it is not progress. For us as postcolonials today, what does Conrad's story say about the colonial experience? Is the story demeaning or offensive to Africans? to Europeans?

An Outpost of Progress

There were two white men in charge of the trading station. Kayerts, the chief, was short and fat; Carlier, the assistant, was tall, with a large head and a very broad trunk perched upon a long pair of thin legs. The third man on the staff was a Sierra Leone Negro, who maintained that his name was Henry Price. However, for some reason or other, the natives down the river had given him the name of Makola, and it stuck to him through all his wanderings about the country. He spoke English and French with a warbling accent, wrote a beautiful hand, understood bookkeeping, and cherished in his innermost heart the worship of evil spirits. His wife was a negress from Loanda, very large and very noisy. Three children rolled about in sunshine before the door of his low, shed-like dwelling. Makola, taciturn and impenetrable, despised the two white men. He had charge of a small clay storehouse with a dried-grass roof, and pretended to keep a correct account of beads, cotton cloth, red kerchiefs, brass wire, and other trade goods it contained. Besides the storehouse and Makola's hut, there was only one large building in the cleared ground of the station. It was built neatly of reeds, with a veranda on all the four sides. There were three rooms in it.

The one in the middle was the living room, and had two rough tables and a few stools in it. The other two were the bedrooms for the white men. Each had a bedstead and a mosquito net for all furniture. The plank floor was littered with the belongings of the white men; open half-empty boxes, torn wearing apparel, old boots; all the things dirty, and all the things broken, that accumulate mysteriously round untidy men. There was also another dwelling place some distance away from the buildings. In it, under a tall cross much out of the perpendicular, slept the man who had seen the beginning of all this; who had planned and had watched the construction of this outpost of progress. He had been, at home, an unsuccessful painter who, weary of pursuing fame on an empty stomach, had gone out there through high protections. He had been the first chief of that station. Makola had watched the energetic artist die of fever in the just finished house with his usual kind of "I told you so" indifference. Then, for a time, he dwelt alone with his family, his account books, and the Evil Spirit that rules the lands under the equator. He got on very well with his god. Perhaps he had propitiated him by a promise of more white men to play with, by and by. At any rate the director of the Great Trading Company, coming up in a steamer that resembled an enormous sardine box with a flat-roofed shed erected on it, found the station in good order, and Makola as usual quietly diligent. The director had the cross put up over the first agent's grave, and appointed Kayerts to the post. Carlier was told off as second in charge. The director was a man ruthless and efficient, who at times, but very imperceptibly, indulged in grim humor. He made a speech to Kayerts and Carlier, pointing out to them the promising aspect of their station. The nearest trading post was about three hundred miles away. It was an exceptional opportunity for them to distinguish themselves and to earn percentages on the trade. This appointment was a favor done to beginners. Kayerts was moved almost to tears by his director's kindness. He would, he said, by doing his best, try to justify the flattering confidence, etc., etc. Kayerts had been in the Administration of the Telegraphs, and knew how to express himself correctly. Carlier, an ex-noncommissioned officer of cavalry in an army guaranteed from harm by several European powers, was less impressed. If there were commissions to get, so much the better; and, trailing a sulky glance over the river, the forests, the impenetrable bush that seemed to cut off the station from the rest of the world, he muttered between his teeth, "We shall see, very soon."

Next day, some bales of cotton goods and a few cases of provisions having been thrown on shore, the sardine-box steamer went off, not to return for another six months. On the deck the director touched his cap to the two agents, who stood on the bank waving their hats, and turning to an old servant of the Company on his passage to headquarters, said, "Look at those two imbeciles. They must be mad at home to send me such specimens. I told those fellows to plant a vegetable garden, build new storehouses and fences, and construct a landing stage. I bet nothing will be done! They won't know how to begin. I always thought the station on this river useless, and they just fit the station!"

"They will form themselves there," said the old stager with a quiet smile.

"At any rate, I am rid of them for six months," retorted the director.   5

The two men watched the steamer round the bend, then, ascending arm in arm the slope of the bank, returned to the station. They had been in this vast and dark country only a very short time, and as yet always in the midst of other white men, under the eye and guidance of their superiors. And now, dull as they were to the subtle influences of surroundings, they felt themselves very much alone, when suddenly left unassisted to face the wilderness; a wilderness rendered more strange, more incomprehensible by the mysterious glimpses of the vigorous life it contained. They were two perfectly insignificant and incapable individuals, whose existence is only rendered possible through the high organization of civilized crowds. Few men realize that their life, the very essence of their character, their capabilities and their audacities, are only the expression of their belief in the safety of their surroundings. The courage, the composure, the confidence; the emotions and principles; every great and every insignificant thought belongs not to the individual but to the crowd: to the crowd that believes blindly in the irresistible force of its institutions and of its morals, in the power of its police and of its opinion. But the contact with pure unmitigated savagery, with primitive nature and primitive man, brings sudden and profound trouble into the heart. To the sentiment of being alone of one's kind, to the clear perception of the loneliness of one's thoughts, of one's sensations—to the negation of the habitual, which is safe, there is added the affirmation of the unusual, which is dangerous; a suggestion of things vague, uncontrollable, and repulsive, whose discomposing intrusion excites the imagination and tries the civilized nerves of the foolish and the wise alike.

Kayerts and Carlier walked arm in arm, drawing close to one another as children do in the dark, and they had the same, not altogether unpleasant, sense of danger which one half suspects to be imaginary. They chatted persistently in familiar tones. "Our station is prettily situated," said one. The other assented with enthusiasm, enlarging volubly on the beauties of the situation. Then they passed near the grave. "Poor devil!" said Kayerts. "He died of fever, didn't he?" muttered Carlier, stopping short. "Why," retorted Kayerts, with indignation, "I've been told that the fellow exposed himself recklessly to the sun. The climate here, everybody says, is not at all worse than at home, as long as you keep out of the sun. Do you hear that, Carlier? I am chief here, and my orders are that you should not expose yourself to the sun!" He assumed his superiority jocularly, but his meaning was serious. The idea that he would, perhaps, have to bury Carlier and remain alone, gave him an inward shiver. He felt suddenly that this Carlier was more precious to him here, in the center of Africa, than a brother could be anywhere else. Carlier, entering into the spirit of the thing, made a military salute and answered in a brisk tone, "Your orders shall be attended to, chief!" Then he burst out laughing, slapped Kayerts on the back and shouted, "We shall let life run easily here! Just sit still and gather in the ivory those savages will bring. This country has its good points, after all!" They both laughed loudly while Carlier thought: "That poor Kayerts; he is so fat and unhealthy. It would be awful if I had to bury him here. He is a man I respect." . . . Before they reached the veranda of their house they called one another "my dear fellow."

The first day they were very active, pottering about with hammers and nails and red calico, to put up curtains, make their house habitable and pretty; resolved to settle down comfortably to their new life. For them an impossible task. To grapple effectually with even purely material problems requires more serenity of mind and more lofty courage than people generally imagine. No two beings could have been more unfitted for such a struggle. Society, not from any tenderness, but because of its strange needs, had taken care of those two men, forbidding them all independent thought, all initiative, all departure from routine; and forbidding it under pain of death. They could only live on condition of being machines. And now, released from the fostering care of men with pens behind the ears, or of men with gold lace on the sleeves, they were like those life-long prisoners who, liberated after many years, do not know what use to make of their freedom. They did not know what use to make of their faculties, being both, through want of practice, incapable of independent thought.

At the end of two months Kayerts often would say, "If it was not for my Melie, you wouldn't catch me here." Melie was his daughter. He had thrown up his post in the Administration of the Telegraphs, though he had been for seventeen years perfectly happy there, to earn a dowry for his girl. His wife was dead, and the child was being brought up by his sisters. He regretted the streets, the pavements, the cafés, his friends of many years; all the things he used to see, day after day; all the thoughts suggested by familiar things—the thoughts effortless, monotonous, and soothing of a Government clerk; he regretted all the gossip, the small enmities, the mild venom, and the little jokes of Government offices. "If I had had a decent brother-in-law," Carlier would remark, "a fellow with a heart, I would not be here." He had left the army and had made himself so obnoxious to his family by his laziness and impudence, that an exasperated brother-in-law had made superhuman efforts to procure him an appointment in the Company as a second-class agent. Having not a penny in the world he was compelled to accept this means of livelihood as soon as it became quite clear to him that there was nothing more to squeeze out of his relations. He, like Kayerts, regretted his old life. He regretted the clink of saber and spurs on a fine afternoon, the barrack-room witticisms, the girls of garrison towns; but, besides, he had also a sense of grievance. He was evidently a much ill-used man. This made him moody, at times. But the two men got on well together in the fellowship of their stupidity and laziness. Together they did nothing, absolutely nothing, and enjoyed the sense of the idleness for which they were paid. And in time they came to feel something resembling affection for one another.

They lived like blind men in a large room, aware only of what came in   10
contact with them (and of that only imperfectly), but unable to see the general aspect of things. The river, the forest, all the great land throbbing with life, were like a great emptiness. Even the brilliant sunshine disclosed nothing intelligible. Things appeared and disappeared before their eyes in an unconnected and aimless kind of way. The river seemed to come from nowhere and flow nowhither. It flowed through a void. Out of that void, at times, came canoes, and men with spears in their hands would suddenly crowd the yard of the station. They were naked, glossy black, ornamented with snowy shells and glistening brass wire, perfect of limb. They made an uncouth babbling noise when they spoke, moved in a stately manner, and sent quick, wild glances out of their startled, never-resting eyes. Those warriors would squat in long rows, four or more deep, before the veranda, while their chiefs bargained for hours with Makola over an elephant tusk. Kayerts sat on his chair and looked down on the proceedings, understanding nothing. He stared at them with his round blue eyes, called out to Carlier, "Here, look! look at that fellow there—and that other one, to the left. Did you ever see such a face? Oh, the funny brute!"

Carlier, smoking native tobacco in a short wooden pipe, would swagger up twirling his mustaches, and surveying the warriors with haughty indulgence, would say:

"Fine animals. Brought any bone? Yes? It's not any too soon. Look at the muscles of that fellow—third from the end. I wouldn't care to get a punch on the nose from him. Fine arms, but legs no good below the knee. Couldn't make cavalry men of them." And after glancing down complacently at his own shanks, he always concluded, "Pah! Don't they stink! You, Makola! Take that herd over to the fetish" (the storehouse was in every station called the fetish, perhaps because of the spirit of civilization it contained) "and give them up some of the rubbish you keep there. I'd rather see it full of bone than full of rags."

Kayerts approved.

"Yes, yes! Go and finish that palaver over there, Mr. Makola. I will come round when you are ready, to weigh the tusk. We must be careful." Then turning to his companion: "This is the tribe that lives down the river; they are rather aromatic. I remember, they had been once before here. D'ye hear that row? What a fellow has got to put up with in this dog of a country! My head is split."

Such profitable visits were rare. For days the two pioneers of trade and   15
progress would look on their empty courtyard in the vibrating brilliance of vertical sunshine. Below the high bank, the silent river flowed on glittering and steady. On the sands in the middle of the stream, hippos and alligators sunned themselves side by side. And stretching away in all directions, surrounding the insignificant cleared spot of the trading post, immense forests, hiding fateful complications of fantastic life, lay in the eloquent silence of mute greatness. The two men understood nothing, cared for nothing but for

the passage of days that separated them from the steamer's return. Their predecessor had left some torn books. They took up these wrecks of novels, and, as they had never read anything of the kind before, they were surprised and amused. Then during long days there were interminable and silly discussions about plots and personages. In the center of Africa they made acquaintance of Richelieu and of d'Artagnan, of Hawk's Eye and of Father Goriot, and of many other people. All these imaginary personages became subjects for gossip as if they had been living friends. They discounted their virtues, suspected their motives, decried their successes; were scandalized at their duplicity or were doubtful about their courage. The accounts of crimes filled them with indignation, while tender or pathetic passages moved them deeply. Carlier cleared his throat and said in a soldierly voice, "What nonsense!" Kayerts, his round eyes suffused with tears, his fat cheeks quivering, rubbed his bald head, and declared, "This is a splendid book. I had no idea there were such clever fellows in the world." They also found some old copies of a home paper. That print discussed what it was pleased to call "Our Colonial Expansion" in high-flown language. It spoke much of the rights and duties of civilization, of the sacredness of the civilizing work, and extolled the merits of those who went about bringing light, and faith, and commerce to the dark places of the earth. Carlier and Kayerts read, wondered, and began to think better of themselves. Carlier said one evening, waving his hand about, "In a hundred years, there will be perhaps a town here. Quays, and warehouses, and barracks, and—and—billiard rooms. Civilization, my boy, and virtue—and all. And then, chaps will read that two good fellows, Kayerts and Carlier, were the first civilized men to live in this very spot!" Kayerts nodded, "Yes, it is a consolation to think of that." They seemed to forget their dead predecessor; but, early one day, Carlier went out and replanted the cross firmly. "It used to make me squint whenever I walked that way," he explained to Kayerts over the morning coffee. "It made me squint, leaning over so much. So I just planted it upright. And solid, I promise you! I suspended myself with both hands to the cross-piece. Not a move. Oh, I did that properly."

At times Gobila came to see them. Gobila was the chief of the neighboring villages. He was a gray-headed savage, thin and black, with a white cloth round his loins and a mangy panther skin hanging over his back. He came up with long strides of his skeleton legs, swinging a staff as tall as himself, and, entering the common room of the station, would squat on his heels to the left of the door. There he sat, watching Kayerts, and now and then making a speech which the other did not understand. Kayerts, without interrupting his occupation, would from time to time say in a friendly manner: "How goes it, you old image?" and they would smile at one another. The two whites had a liking for that old and incomprehensible creature, and called him Father Gobila. Gobila's manner was paternal, and he seemed really to love all white men. They all appeared to him very young, indistinguishably alike (except for stature), and he knew that they were all brothers, and also immortal. The death of the artist, who was the first white man whom he knew intimately, did not disturb this belief, because he was firmly convinced that the white stranger had pretended to die and got himself buried for some mysterious purpose of his own, into which it was useless to inquire. Perhaps it was his way of going home to his own country? At any rate, these were his brothers, and he transferred his absurd affection to them. They returned it in a way. Carlier slapped him on the back, and recklessly struck off matches for his amusement. Kayerts was always ready to let him have a sniff at the ammonia bottle. In short, they behaved just like that other white creature that had hidden itself in a hole in the ground. Gobila considered them attentively. Perhaps they were the same being with the other—or one of them was. He couldn't decide—clear up that mystery; but he remained always very friendly. In consequence of that friendship the women of Gobila's village walked in single file through the reedy grass, bringing every morning to the station, fowls, and sweet potatoes, and palm wine, and sometimes a goat. The Company never provisions the stations fully, and the agents required those local supplies to live. They had them through the good will of Gobila, and lived well. Now and then one of them had a bout of fever, and the other nursed him with gentle devotion. They did not think much of it. It left them weaker, and their appearance changed for the worse. Carlier was hollow-eyed and irritable. Kayerts showed a drawn, flabby face above the rotundity of his stomach, which gave him a weird aspect. But being constantly together, they did not notice the change that took place gradually in their appearance, and also in their dispositions.

Five months passed in that way.

Then, one morning, as Kayerts and Carlier, lounging in their chairs under the veranda, talked about the approaching visit of the steamer, a knot of armed men came out of the forest and advanced towards the station. They were strangers to that part of the country. They were tall, slight, draped classically from neck to heel in blue fringed cloths, and carried percussion muskets over their bare right shoulders. Makola showed signs of excitement, and ran out of the storehouse (where he spent all his days) to meet these visitors. They came into the courtyard and looked about them with steady, scornful glances. Their leader, a powerful and determined-looking Negro with bloodshot eyes, stood in front of the veranda and made a long speech. He gesticulated much, and ceased very suddenly.

There was something in his intonation, in the sounds of the long sentences he used, that startled the two whites. It was like a reminiscence of something not exactly familiar, and yet resembling the speech of civilized men. It sounded like one of those impossible languages which sometimes we hear in our dreams.

"What lingo is that?" said the amazed Carlier. "In the first moment I fancied the fellow was going to speak French. Anyway, it is a different kind of gibberish to what we ever heard."   20

"Yes," replied Kayerts. "Hey, Makola, what does he say? Where do they come from? Who are they?"

But Makola, who seemed to be standing on hot bricks, answered hurriedly, "I don't know. They come from very far. Perhaps Mrs. Price will understand. They are perhaps bad men."

The leader, after waiting for a while, said something sharply to Makola, who shook his head. Then the man, after looking round, noticed Makola's hut and walked over there. The next moment Mrs. Makola was heard speaking with great volubility. The other strangers—they were six in all—strolled about with an air of ease, put their heads through the door of the storeroom, congregated round the grave, pointed understandingly at the cross, and generally made themselves at home.

"I don't like those chaps—and, I say, Kayerts, they must be from the coast; they've got firearms," observed the sagacious Carlier.

Kayerts also did not like those chaps. They both, for the first time, became aware that they lived in conditions where the unusual may be dangerous, and that there was no power on earth outside of themselves to stand between them and the unusual. They became uneasy, went in and loaded their revolvers. Kayerts said, "We must order Makola to tell them to go away before dark." 25

The strangers left in the afternoon, after eating a meal prepared for them by Mrs. Makola. The immense woman was excited, and talked much with the visitors. She rattled away shrilly, pointing here and there at the forests and at the river. Makola sat apart and watched. At times he got up and whispered to his wife. He accompanied the strangers across the ravine at the back of the station-ground, and returned slowly looking very thoughtful. When questioned by the white men he was very strange, seemed not to understand, seemed to have forgotten French—seemed to have forgotten how to speak altogether. Kayerts and Carlier agreed that the fellow had had too much palm wine.

There was some talk about keeping a watch in turn, but in the evening everything seemed so quiet and peaceful that they retired as usual. All night they were disturbed by a lot of drumming in the villages. A deep, rapid roll near by would be followed by another far off—then all ceased. Soon short appeals would rattle out here and there, then all mingle together, increase become vigorous and sustained, would spread out over the forest, roll through the night, unbroken and ceaseless, near and far, as if the whole land had been one immense drum booming out steadily an appeal to heaven. And through the deep and tremendous noise sudden yells that resembled snatches of songs from a madhouse darted shrill and high in discordant jets of sound which seemed to rush far above the earth and drive all peace from under the stars.

Carlier and Kayerts slept badly. They both thought they had heard shots fired during the night—but they could not agree as to the direction. In the morning Makola was gone somewhere. He returned about noon with one of yesterday's strangers, and eluded all Kayerts' attempts to close with him: had become deaf apparently. Kayerts wondered. Carlier, who had been fishing off the bank, came back and remarked while he showed his catch, "The fellows seem to be in a deuce of a stir; I wonder what's up. I saw about fifteen canoes cross the river during the two hours I was there fishing." Kayerts, worried, said, "Isn't this Makola very queer today?" Carlier advised, "Keep all our men together in case of some trouble."

II

There were ten station men who had been left by the Director. Those fellows, having engaged themselves to the Company for six months (without having any idea of a month in particular and only a very faint notion of time in general), had been serving the cause of progress for upwards of two years. Belonging to a tribe from a very distant part of the land of darkness and sorrow, they did not run away, naturally supposing that as wandering strangers they would be killed by the inhabitants of the country; in which they were right. They lived in straw huts on the slope of a ravine overgrown with reedy grass, just behind the station buildings. They were not happy, regretting the festive incantations, the sorceries, the human sacrifices of their own land; where they also had parents, brothers, sisters, admired chiefs, respected magicians, loved friends, and other ties supposed generally to be human. Besides, the rice rations served out by the Company did not agree with them, being a food unknown to their land, and to which they could not get used. Consequently they were unhealthy and miserable. Had they been of any other tribe they would have made up their minds to die—for nothing is easier to certain savages than suicide—and so have escaped from the puzzling difficulties of existence. But belonging, as they did, to a warlike tribe with filed teeth, they had more grit, and went on stupidly living through disease and sorrow. They did very little work, and had lost their splendid physique. Carlier and Kayerts doctored them assiduously without being able to bring them back into condition again. They were mustered every morning and told off to different tasks—grass-cutting, fence-building, tree-felling, etc., etc., which no power on earth could induce them to execute efficiently. The two whites had practically very little control over them.

In the afternoon Makola came over to the big house and found Kayerts   30
watching three heavy columns of smoke rising above the forests. "What is that?" asked Kayerts. "Some villages burn," answered Makola, who seemed to have regained his wits. Then he said abruptly: "We have got very little ivory; bad six months' trading. Do you like get a little more ivory?"

"Yes," said Kayerts, eagerly. He thought of percentages which were low.

"Those men who came yesterday are traders from Loanda who have got more ivory than they can carry home. Shall I buy? I know their camp."

"Certainly," said Kayerts. "What are those traders?"

"Bad fellows," said Makola, indifferently. "They fight with people, and catch women and children. They are bad men, and got guns. There is a great disturbance in the country. Do you want ivory?"

"Yes," said Kayerts. Makola said nothing for a while. Then: "Those work-   35
men of ours are no good at all," he muttered, looking round. "Station in very bad order, sir. Director will growl. Better get a fine lot of ivory, then he say nothing."

"I can't help it; the men won't work," said Kayerts. "When will you get that ivory?"

"Very soon," said Makola. "Perhaps tonight. You leave it to me, and keep indoors, sir. I think you had better give some palm wine to our men to make a dance this evening. Enjoy themselves. Work better tomorrow. There's plenty palm wine—gone a little sour."

Kayerts said "yes," and Makola, with his own hands, carried big calabashes to the door of his hut. They stood there till the evening, and Mrs. Makola looked into every one. The men got them at sunset. When Kayerts and Carlier retired, a big bonfire was flaring before the men's huts. They could hear their shouts and drumming. Some men from Gobila's village had joined the station hands, and the entertainment was a great success.

In the middle of the night, Carlier waking suddenly, heard a man shout loudly; then a shot was fired. Only one. Carlier ran out and met Kayerts on the veranda. They were both startled. As they went across the yard to call Makola, they saw shadows moving in the night. One of them cried, "Don't shoot! It's me, Price." Then Makola appeared close to them. "Go back, go back, please," he urged, "you spoil all." "There are strange men about," said Carlier. "Never mind; I know," said Makola. Then he whispered, "All right. Bring ivory. Say nothing! I know my business." The two white men reluctantly went back to the house, but did not sleep. They heard footsteps, whispers, some groans. It seemed as if a lot of men came in, dumped heavy things on the ground, squabbled a long time, then went away. They lay on their hard beds and thought: "This Makola is invaluable." In the morning Carlier came out, very sleepy, and pulled at the cord of the big bell. The station hands mustered every morning to the sound of the bell. That morning nobody came. Kayerts turned out also, yawning. Across the yard they saw Makola come out of his hut, a tin basin of soapy water in his hand. Makola, a civilized Negro, was very neat in his person. He threw the soapsuds skillfully over a wretched little yellow cur he had, then turning his face to the agent's house, he shouted from the distance, "All the men gone last night!"

They heard him plainly, but in their surprise they both yelled out together: "What!" Then they stared at one another. "We are in a proper fix now," growled Carlier. "It's incredible!" muttered Kayerts. "I will go to the huts and see," said Carlier, striding off. Makola coming up found Kayerts standing alone.   40

"I can hardly believe it," said Kayerts tearfully. "We took care of them as if they had been our children."

"They went with the coast people," said Makola after a moment of hesitation.

"What do I care with whom they went—the ungrateful brutes!" exclaimed the other. Then with sudden suspicion, and looking hard at Makola, he added: "What do you know about it?"

Makola moved his shoulders, looking down on the ground. "What do I know? I think only. Will you come and look at the ivory I've got there? It is a fine lot. You never saw such."

He moved towards the store. Kayerts followed him mechanically, thinking about the incredible desertion of the men. On the ground before the door of the fetish lay six splendid tusks.   45

"What did you give for it?" asked Kayerts, after surveying the lot with satisfaction.

"No regular trade," said Makola. "They brought the ivory and gave it to me. I told them to take what they most wanted in the station. It is a beautiful lot. No station can show such tusks. Those traders wanted carriers badly, and our men were no good here. No trade, no entry in books; all correct."

Kayerts nearly burst with indignation. "Why!" he shouted, "I believe you have sold our men for these tusks!" Makola stood impassive and silent. "I—I—will—I," stuttered Kayerts. "You fiend!" he yelled out.

"I did the best for you and the Company," said Makola, imperturbably. "Why you shout so much? Look at this tusk."

"I dismiss you! I will report you—I won't look at the tusk. I forbid you to   50
touch them. I order you to throw them into the river. You—you!"

"You very red, Mr. Kayerts. If you are so irritable in the sun, you will get
fever and die—like the first chief!" pronounced Makola impressively.

They stood still, contemplating one another with intense eyes, as if they
had been looking with effort across immense distances. Kayerts shivered.
Makola had meant no more than he said, but his words seemed to Kayerts
full of ominous menace! He turned sharply and went away to the house.
Makola retired into the bosom of his family; and the tusks, left lying before
the store, looked very large and valuable in the sunshine.

Carlier came back on the veranda. "They're all gone, hey?" asked Kayerts
from the far end of the common room in a muffled voice. "You did not find
anybody?"

"Oh, yes," said Carlier, "I found one of Gobila's people lying dead before
the huts—shot through the body. We heard that shot last night."

Kayerts came out quickly. He found his companion staring grimly over   55
the yard at the tusks, away by the store. They both sat in silence for a while.
Then Kayerts related his conversation with Makola. Carlier said nothing. At
the midday meal they ate very little. They hardly exchanged a word that day.
A great silence seemed to lie heavily over the station and press on their lips.
Makola did not open the store; he spent the day playing with his children.
He lay full-length on a mat outside his door, and the youngsters sat on his
chest and clambered all over him. It was a touching picture. Mrs. Makola
was busy cooking all day as usual. The white men made a somewhat better meal in the evening. Afterwards, Carlier smoking his pipe strolled over
to the store; he stood for a long time over the tusks, touched one or two
with his foot, even tried to lift the largest one by its small end. He came back
to his chief, who had not stirred from the veranda, threw himself in the chair
and said:

"I can see it! They were pounced upon while they slept heavily after
drinking all that palm wine you've allowed Makola to give them. A put-up
job! See? The worst is, some of Gobila's people were there, and got carried
off too, no doubt. The least drunk woke up, and got shot for his sobriety.
This is a funny country. What will you do now?"

"We can't touch it, of course," said Kayerts.

"Of course not," assented Carlier.

"Slavery is an awful thing," stammered out Kayerts in an unsteady voice.

"Frightful—the sufferings," grunted Carlier with conviction.   60

They believed their words. Everybody shows a respectful deference to
certain sounds that he and his fellows can make. But about feelings people really know nothing. We talk with indignation or enthusiasm; we talk
about oppression, cruelty, crime, devotion, self-sacrifice, virtue, and we
know nothing real beyond the words. Nobody knows what suffering or
sacrifice mean—except, perhaps, the victims of the mysterious purpose of
these illusions.

Next morning they saw Makola very busy setting up in the yard the
big scales used for weighing ivory. By and by Carlier said: "What's that filthy
scoundrel up to?" and lounged out into the yard. Kayerts followed. They
stood watching. Makola took no notice. When the balance was swung true,

he tried to lift a tusk into the scale. It was too heavy. He looked up helplessly without a word, and for a minute they stood round that balance as
mute and still as three statues. Suddenly Carlier said: "Catch hold of the
other end, Makola—you beast!" and together they swung the tusk up. Kayerts trembled in every limb. He muttered, "I say! O! I say!" and putting his
hand in his pocket found there a dirty bit of paper and the stump of a pencil. He turned his back on the others, as if about to do something tricky, and
noted stealthily the weights which Carlier shouted out to him with unnecessary loudness. When all was over Makola whispered to himself: "The sun's
very strong here for the tusks." Carlier said to Kayerts in a careless tone: "I
say, chief, I might just as well give him a lift with this lot into the store."

As they were going back to the house Kayerts observed with a sigh: "It
had to be done." And Carlier said: "It's deplorable, but, the men being Company's men, the ivory is Company's ivory. We must look after it." "I will report to the Director, of course," said Kayerts. "Of course; let him decide,"
approved Carlier.

At midday they made a hearty meal. Kayerts sighed from time to time.
Whenever they mentioned Makola's name they always added to it an opprobrious epithet. It eased their conscience. Makola gave himself a half-
holiday, and bathed his children in the river. No one from Gobila's villages
came near the station that day. No one came the next day, and the next, nor
for a whole week. Gobila's people might have been dead and buried for
any sign of life they gave. But they were only mourning for those they had
lost by the witchcraft of white men, who had brought wicked people into
their country. The wicked people were gone, but fear remained. Fear always
remains. A man may destroy everything within himself, love and hate and
belief, and even doubt; but as long as he clings to life he cannot destroy
fear: the fear, subtle, indestructible, and terrible, that pervades his being; that
tinges his thoughts; that lurks in his heart; that watches on his lips the struggle of his last breath. In his fear, the mild old Gobila offered extra human
sacrifices to all the Evil Spirits that had taken possession of his white friends.
His heart was heavy. Some warriors spoke about burning and killing,
but the cautious old savage dissuaded them. Who could foresee the woe
those mysterious creatures, if irritated, might bring? They should be left
alone. Perhaps in time they would disappear into the earth as the first one
had disappeared. His people must keep away from them, and hope for the
best.

Kayerts and Carlier did not disappear, but remained above on this earth,   65
that, somehow, they fancied had become bigger and very empty. It was not
the absolute and dumb solitude of the post that impressed them so much
as an inarticulate feeling that something from within them was gone, something that worked for their safety, and had kept the wilderness from interfering with their hearts. The images of home; the memory of people like
them, of men that thought and felt as they used to think and feel, receded
into distances made indistinct by the glare of unclouded sunshine. And out
of the great silence of the surrounding wilderness, its very hopelessness
and savagery seemed to approach them nearer, to draw them gently, to
look upon them, to envelop them with a solicitude irresistible, familiar, and
disgusting.

Days lengthened into weeks, then into months. Gobila's people drummed and yelled to every new moon, as of yore, but kept away from the station. Makola and Carlier tried once in a canoe to open communications, but
were received with a shower of arrows, and had to fly back to the station
for dear life. That attempt set the country up and down the river into an uproar that could be very distinctly heard for days. The steamer was late. At
first they spoke of delay jauntily, then anxiously, then gloomily. The matter
was becoming serious. Stores were running short. Carlier cast his lines off
the bank, but the river was low, and the fish kept out in the stream. They
dared not stroll far away from the station to shoot. Moreover, there was no
game in the impenetrable forest. Once Carlier shot a hippo in the river. They
had no boat to secure it, and it sank. When it floated up it drifted away, and
Gobila's people secured the carcass. It was the occasion for a national holiday, but Carlier had a fit of rage over it and talked about the necessity of
exterminating all the people before the country could be made habitable.
Kayerts mooned about silently; spent hours looking at the portrait of his
Melie. It represented a little girl with long bleached tresses and a rather sour
face. His legs were much swollen, and he could hardly walk. Carlier, undermined by fever, could not swagger any more, but kept tottering about,
still with a devil-may-care air, as became a man who remembered his crack
regiment. He had become hoarse, sarcastic, and inclined to say unpleasant
things. He called it "being frank with you." They had long ago reckoned
their percentages on trade, including in them that last deal of "this infamous
Makola." They had also concluded not to say anything about it. Kayerts hesitated at first—was afraid of the Director.

"He has seen worse things done on the quiet," maintained Carlier, with a
hoarse laugh. "Trust him! He won't thank you if you blab. He is no better
than you or me. Who will talk if we hold our tongues? There is nobody
here."

That was the root of the trouble! There was nobody there; and being left
there alone with their weakness, they became daily more like a pair of accomplices than like a couple of devoted friends. They had heard nothing
from home for eight months. Every evening they said, "Tomorrow we shall
see the steamer." But one of the Company's steamers had been wrecked,
and the Director was busy with the other, relieving very distant and important stations on the main river. He thought that the useless station, and the
useless men, could wait. Meantime Kayerts and Carlier lived on rice boiled
without salt, and cursed the Company, all Africa, and the day they were
born. One must have lived on such diet to discover what ghastly trouble the
necessity of swallowing one's food may become. There was literally nothing else in the station but rice and coffee; they drank the coffee without
sugar. The last fifteen lumps Kayerts had solemnly locked away in his box,
together with a half-bottle of cognac, "in case of sickness," he explained.
Carlier approved. "When one is sick," he said, "any little extra like that is
cheering."

They waited. Rank grass began to sprout over the courtyard. The bell
never rang now. Days passed, silent, exasperating, and slow. When the two
men spoke, they snarled; and their silences were bitter, as if tinged by the
bitterness of their thoughts.

One day after a lunch of boiled rice, Carlier put down his cup untasted,   70
and said: "Hang it all! Let's have a decent cup of coffee for once. Bring out
that sugar, Kayerts!"

"For the sick," muttered Kayerts, without looking up.

"For the sick," mocked Carlier. "Bosh! . . . Well! I am sick."

"You are no more sick than I am, and I go without," said Kayerts in a
peaceful tone.

"Come! Out with that sugar, you stingy old slave dealer."

Kayerts looked up quickly. Carlier was smiling with marked insolence.   75
And suddenly it seemed to Kayerts that he had never seen that man before. Who was he? He knew nothing about him. What was he capable of?
There was a surprising flash of violent emotion within him, as if in the
presence of something undreamt-of, dangerous, and final. But he managed to pronounce with composure:

"That joke is in very bad taste. Don't repeat it."

"Joke!" said Carlier, hitching himself forward on his seat. "I am hungry—
I am sick—I don't joke! I hate hypocrites. You are a hypocrite. You are a
slave dealer. I am a slave dealer. There's nothing but slave dealers in this
cursed country. I mean to have sugar in my coffee today, anyhow!"

"I forbid you to speak to me in that way," said Kayerts with a fair show
of resolution.

"You!—What?" shouted Carlier, jumping up.

Kayerts stood up also. "I am your chief," he began, trying to master the   80
shakiness of his voice.

"What?" yelled the other. "Who's chief? There's no chief here. There's nothing here: there's nothing but you and I. Fetch the sugar—you pot-bellied ass."

"Hold your tongue. Go out of this room," screamed Kayerts. "I dismiss
you—you scoundrel!"

Carlier swung a stool. All at once he looked dangerously in earnest. "You
flabby, good-for-nothing civilian—take that!" he howled.

Kayerts dropped under the table, and the stool struck the grass inner wall
of the room. Then, as Carlier was trying to upset the table, Kayerts in desperation made a blind rush, head low, like a cornered pig would do, and
overturning his friend, bolted along the veranda, and into his room. He
locked the door, snatched his revolver, and stood panting. In less than a
minute Carlier was kicking at the door furiously, howling, "If you don't bring
out that sugar, I will shoot you at sight, like a dog. Now then—one—two—
three. You won't? I will show you who's the master."

Kayerts thought the door would fall in, and scrambled through the square   85
hole that served for a window in his room. There was then the whole
breadth of the house between them. But the other was apparently not strong
enough to break in the door, and Kayerts heard him running round. Then
he also began to run laboriously on his swollen legs. He ran as quickly as he
could, grasping the revolver, and unable yet to understand what was happening to him. He saw in succession Makola's house, the store, the river,
the ravine, and the low bushes; and he saw all those things again as he ran
for the second time round the house. Then again they flashed past him. That
morning he could not have walked a yard without a groan.

And now he ran. He ran fast enough to keep out of sight of the other man.

Then as, weak and desperate, he thought, "Before I finish the next round I shall die," he heard the other man stumble heavily, then stop. He stopped also. He had the back and Carlier the front of the house, as before. He heard him drop into a chair cursing, and suddenly his own legs gave way, and he slid down into a sitting posture with his back to the wall. His mouth was as dry as a cinder, and his face was wet with perspiration—and tears. What was it all about? He thought it must be a horrible illusion; he thought he was dreaming; he thought he was going mad! After a while he collected his senses. What did they quarrel about? That sugar! How absurd! He would give it to him—didn't want it himself. And he began scrambling to his feet with a sudden feeling of security. But before he had fairly stood upright, a common-sense reflection occurred to him and drove him back into despair. He thought: "If I give way now to that brute of a soldier, he will begin this horror again tomorrow—and the day after—every day—raise other pretensions, trample on me, torture me, make me his slave—and I will be lost! Lost! The steamer may not come for days—may never come." He shook so that he had to sit down on the floor again. He shivered forlornly. He felt he could not, would not move any more. He was completely distracted by the sudden perception that the position was without issue—that death and life had in a moment become equally difficult and terrible.

All at once he heard the other push his chair back; and he leaped to his feet with extreme facility. He listened and got confused. Must run again! Right or left? He heard footsteps. He darted to the left, grasping his revolver, and at the very same instant, as it seemed to him, they came into violent collision. Both shouted with surprise. A loud explosion took place between them; a roar of red fire, thick smoke; and Kayerts, deafened and blinded, rushed back thinking: "I am hit—it's all over." He expected the other to come round—to gloat over his agony. He caught hold of an upright of the roof—"All over!" Then he heard a crashing fall on the other side of the house, as if somebody had tumbled headlong over a chair—then silence. Nothing more happened. He did not die. Only his shoulder felt as if it had been badly wrenched, and he had lost his revolver. He was disarmed and helpless! He waited for his fate. The other man made no sound. It was a stratagem. He was stalking him now! Along what side? Perhaps he was taking aim this very minute!

After a few moments of an agony frightful and absurd, he decided to go and meet his doom. He was prepared for every surrender. He turned the corner, steadying himself with one hand on the wall; made a few paces, and nearly swooned. He had seen on the floor, protruding past the other corner, a pair of turned-up feet. A pair of white naked feet in red slippers. He felt deadly sick, and stood for a time in profound darkness. Then Makola appeared before him, saying quietly: "Come along, Mr. Kayerts. He is dead." He burst into tears of gratitude; a loud, sobbing fit of crying. After a time he found himself sitting in a chair and looking at Carlier, who lay stretched on his back. Makola was kneeling over the body.

"Is this your revolver?" asked Makola, getting up.   90

"Yes," said Kayerts; then he added very quickly, "He ran after me to shoot me—you saw!"

"Yes, I saw," said Makola. "There is only one revolver; where's his?"

"Don't know," whispered Kayerts in a voice that had become suddenly very faint.

"I will go and look for it," said the other, gently. He made the round along the veranda, while Kayerts sat still and looked at the corpse. Makola came back empty-handed, stood in deep thought, then stepped quietly into the dead man's room, and came out directly with a revolver, which he held up before Kayerts. Kayerts shut his eyes. Everything was going round. He found life more terrible and difficult than death. He had shot an unarmed man.

After meditating for a while, Makola said softly, pointing at the dead man   95
who lay there with his right eye blown out:

"He died of fever." Kayerts looked at him with a stony stare. "Yes," repeated Makola, thoughtfully, stepping over the corpse, "I think he died of fever. Bury him tomorrow."

And he went away slowly to his expectant wife, leaving the two white men alone on the veranda.

Night came, and Kayerts sat unmoving on his chair. He sat quiet as if he had taken a dose of opium. The violence of the emotions he had passed through produced a feeling of exhausted serenity. He had plumbed in one short afternoon the depths of horror and despair, and now found repose in the conviction that life had no more secrets for him: neither had death! He sat by the corpse thinking; thinking very actively, thinking very new thoughts. He seemed to have broken loose from himself altogether. His old thoughts, convictions, likes and dislikes, things he respected and things he abhorred, appeared in their true light at last! Appeared contemptible and childish, false and ridiculous. He reveled in his new wisdom while he sat by the man he had killed. He argued with himself about all things under heaven with that kind of wrong-headed lucidity which may be observed in some lunatics. Incidentally he reflected that the fellow dead there had been a noxious beast anyway; that men died every day in thousands; perhaps in hundreds of thousands—who could tell?—and that in the number that one death could not possibly make any difference; couldn't have any importance, at least to a thinking creature. He, Kayerts, was a thinking creature. He had been all his life, till that moment, a believer in a lot of nonsense like the rest of mankind—who are fools; but now he thought! He knew! He was at peace; he was familiar with the highest wisdom! Then he tried to imagine himself dead, and Carlier sitting in his chair watching him; and his attempt met with such unexpected success, that in a very few moments he became not at all sure who was dead and who was alive. This extraordinary achievement of his fancy startled him, however, and by a clever and timely effort of mind he saved himself just in time from becoming Carlier. His heart thumped, and he felt hot all over at the thought of that danger. Carlier! What a beastly thing! To compose his now disturbed nerves—and no wonder!—he tried to whistle a little. Then, suddenly, he fell asleep, or thought he had slept; but at any rate there was a fog, and somebody had whistled in the fog.

He stood up. The day had come, and a heavy mist had descended upon the land: the mist penetrating, enveloping, and silent; the morning mist of tropical lands; the mist that clings and kills; the mist white and deadly, immaculate and poisonous. He stood up, saw the body, and threw his arms above his head with a cry like that of a man who, waking from a trance, finds himself immured forever in a tomb. "*Help! . . . My God!*"

A shriek inhuman, vibrating and sudden, pierced like a sharp dart the 100 white shroud of that land of sorrow. Three short, impatient screeches followed, and then, for a time, the fog-wreaths rolled on, undisturbed, through a formidable silence. Then many more shrieks, rapid and piercing, like the yells of some exasperated and ruthless creature, rent the air. Progress was calling to Kayerts from the river. Progress and civilization and all the virtues. Society was calling to its accomplished child to come, to be taken care of, to be instructed, to be judged, to be condemned; it called him to return to that rubbish heap from which he had wandered away, so that justice could be done.

Kayerts heard and understood. He stumbled out of the veranda, leaving the other man quite alone for the first time since they had been thrown there together. He groped his way through the fog, calling in his ignorance upon the invisible heaven to undo its work. Makola flitted by in the mist, shouting as he ran:

"Steamer! Steamer! They can't see. They whistle for the station. I go ring the bell. Go down to the landing, sir. I ring."

He disappeared, Kayerts stood still. He looked upwards; the fog rolled low over his head. He looked round like a man who has lost his way; and he saw a dark smudge, a cross-shaped stain, upon the shifting purity of the mist. As he began to stumble towards it, the station bell rang in a tumultuous peal its answer to the impatient clamor of the steamer.

The Managing Director of the Great Civilizing Company (since we know that civilization follows trade) landed first, and incontinently lost sight of the steamer. The fog down by the river was exceedingly dense; above, at the station, the bell rang unceasing and brazen.

The Director shouted loudly to the steamer: 105

"There is nobody down to meet us; there may be something wrong, though they are ringing. You had better come, too!"

And he began to toil up the steep bank. The captain and the engine-driver of the boat followed behind. As they scrambled up the fog thinned, and they could see their Director a good way ahead. Suddenly they saw him start forward, calling to them over his shoulder: "Run! Run to the house! I've found one of them. Run, look for the other!"

He had found one of them! And even he, the man of varied and startling experience, was somewhat discomposed by the manner of this finding. He stood and fumbled in his pockets (for a knife) while he faced Kayerts, who was hanging by a leather strap from the cross. He had evidently climbed the grave, which was high and narrow, and after tying the end of the strap to the arm, had swung himself off. His toes were only a couple of inches above the ground; his arms hung stiffly down; he seemed to be standing rigidly at attention, but with one purple cheek playfully posed on the shoulder. And, irreverently, he was putting out a swollen tongue at his Managing Director.

Jack London   *(1876–1916)*

INVITATION TO READING: Jack London worked on a ship sailing to Japan and the northern Bering Sea, and he joined in the gold rush to the Klondike in 1898. Some of his best-known stories are set in the frozen North. There, as the following story says, human beings are reminded that on this planet they are "able only to live within certain narrow limits of heat and cold." London's *The Call of the Wild* (1903) has been called "one of the world's great dog stories," and it made him internationally famous. With this book and *The Sea Wolf* (1904), London became known worldwide as an outstanding practitioner of naturalistic fiction. Naturalism meant not idealizing nature as a sentimentalized nurturing presence but instead treating nature or also human society as an arena where the struggle for survival is played out. Charles Darwin and his followers had made *natural selection* and the *survival of the fittest* household words. Do modern readers tend to think of nature as a nurturing, healing presence? Or do they tend to think of it as a powerful challenging force mocking our human efforts at taming or controlling it?

To Build a Fire   1908

Day had broken cold and gray, exceedingly cold and gray, when the man turned aside from the main Yukon trail and climbed the high earth-bank, where a dim and little-travelled trail led eastward through the fat spruce timberland. It was a steep bank, and he paused for breath at the top, excusing the act to himself by looking at his watch. It was nine o'clock. There was no sun nor hint of sun, though there was not a cloud in the sky. It was a clear day, and yet there seemed an intangible pall over the face of things, a subtle gloom that made the day dark, and that was due to the absence of sun. This fact did not worry the man. He was used to the lack of sun. It had been days since he had seen the sun, and he knew that a few more days must pass before that cheerful orb, due south, should just peep above the sky line and dip immediately from view.

The man flung a look back along the way he had come. The Yukon lay a mile wide and hidden under three feet of ice. On top of this ice were as many feet of snow. It was all pure white, rolling in gentle undulations where the ice jams of the freeze-up had formed. North and south, as far as his eye could see, it was unbroken white, save for a dark hairline that curved and twisted from around the spruce-covered island to the south, and that curved and twisted away into the north, where it disappeared behind another spruce-covered island. This dark hairline was the trail—the main trail—that led south five hundred miles to the Chilcoot Pass, Dyea, and salt water, and that led north seventy miles to Dawson, and still on to the north a thousand miles to Nulato, and finally to St. Michael, on Bering Sea, a thousand miles and half a thousand more.

But all this—the mysterious, far-reaching hairline trail, the absence of sun from the sky, the tremendous cold, and the strangeness and weirdness of it all—made no impression on the man. It was not because he was long used to it. He was a newcomer in the land, a *chechaquo,* and this was his first winter. The trouble with him was that he was without imagination. He was quick and alert in the things of life, but only in the things, and not in the significances. Fifty degrees below zero meant eight-odd degrees of frost. Such fact impressed him as being cold and uncomfortable, and that was all. It did not lead him to mediate upon his frailty as a creature of temperature, and upon man's frailty in general, able only to live within certain narrow limits of heat and cold; and from there on it did not lead him to the conjectural field of immortality and man's place in the universe. Fifty degrees below zero stood for a bite of frost that hurt and that must be guarded against by the use of mittens, ear flaps, warm moccasins, and thick socks. Fifty degrees below zero was to him just precisely fifty degrees below zero. That there should be anything more to it than that was a thought that never entered his head.

As he turned to go on, he spat speculatively. There was a sharp, explosive crackle that startled him. He spat again. And again, in the air, before it could fall to the snow, the spittle crackled. He knew that at fifty below spittle crackled on the snow, but this spittle had crackled in the air. Undoubtedly it was colder than fifty below—how much colder he did not know. But the temperature did not matter. He was bound for the old claim on the left fork of Henderson Creek, where the boys were already. They had come over across the divide from the Indian Creek country, while he had come the roundabout way to take a look at the possibilities of getting out logs in the spring from the islands in the Yukon. He would be in to camp by six o'clock; a bit after dark, it was true, but the boys would be there, a fire would be going, and a hot supper would be ready. As for lunch, he pressed his hand against the protruding bundle under his jacket. It was also under his shirt, wrapped up in a handkerchief and lying against the naked skin. It was the only way to keep the biscuits from freezing. He smiled agreeably to himself as he thought of those biscuits, each cut open and sopped in bacon grease, and each enclosing a generous slice of fried bacon.

He plunged in among the big spruce trees. The trail was faint. A foot of   5
snow had fallen since the last sled had passed over, and he was glad he was without a sled, traveling light. In fact, he carried nothing but the lunch wrapped in the handkerchief. He was surprised, however, at the cold. It certainly was cold, he concluded, as he rubbed his numb nose and cheekbones with his mittened hand. He was a warm-whiskered man, but the hair on his face did not protect the high cheekbones and the eager nose that thrust itself aggressively into the frosty air.

At the man's heels trotted a dog, a big native husky, the proper wolf dog, gray-coated and without any visible or temperamental difference from its brother, the wild wolf. The animal was depressed by the tremendous cold.

It knew that it was no time for traveling. Its instinct told it a truer tale than was told to the man by the man's judgment. In reality, it was not merely colder than fifty below zero; it was colder than sixty below, than seventy below. It was seventy-five below zero. Since the freezing point is thirty-two above zero, it meant that one hundred and seven degrees of frost obtained. The dog did not know anything about thermometers. Possibly in its brain there was no sharp consciousness of a condition of very cold such as was in the man's brain. But the brute had its instinct. It experienced a vague but menacing apprehension that subdued it and made it slink along at the man's heels, and that made it question eagerly every unwonted movement of the man as if expecting him to go into camp or to seek shelter somewhere and build a fire. The dog had learned fire, and it wanted fire, or else to burrow under the snow and cuddle its warmth away from the air.

The frozen moisture of its breathing had settled on its fur in a fine powder of frost, and especially were its jowls, muzzle, and eyelashes whitened by its crystalled breath. The man's red beard and mustache were likewise frosted, but more solidly, the deposit taking the form of ice and increasing with every warm, moist breath he exhaled. Also, the man was chewing tobacco, and the muzzle of ice held his lips so rigidly that he was unable to clear his chin when he expelled the juice. The result was that a crystal beard of the color and solidity of amber was increasing its length on his chin. If he fell down it would shatter itself, like glass, into brittle fragments. But he did not mind the appendage. It was the penalty all tobacco chewers paid in that country, and he had been out before in two cold snaps. They had not been so cold as this, he knew, but by the spirit thermometer at Sixty Mile he knew they had been registered at fifty below and at fifty-five.

He held on through the level stretch of woods for several miles, crossed a wide flat . . . , and dropped down a bank to the frozen bed of a small stream. This was Henderson Creek, and he knew he was ten miles from the forks. He looked at his watch. It was ten o'clock. He was making four miles an hour, and he calculated that he would arrive at the forks at half-past twelve. He decided to celebrate that event by eating his lunch there.

The dog dropped in again at his heels, with a tail drooping discouragement, as the man swung along the creek bed. The furrow of the old sled trail was plainly visible, but a dozen inches of snow covered the marks of the last runners. In a month no man had come up or down that silent creek. The man held steadily on. He was not much given to thinking, and just then particularly he had nothing to think about save that he would eat lunch at the forks and that at six o'clock he would be in camp with the boys. There was nobody to talk to; and, had there been, speech would have been impossible because of the ice muzzle on his mouth. So he continued monotonously to chew tobacco and to increase the length of his amber beard.

Once in a while the thought reiterated itself that it was very cold and that   10
he had never experienced such cold. As he walked along he rubbed his cheekbones and nose with the back of his mittened hand. He did this automatically, now and again changing hands. But, rub as he would, the instant he stopped his cheekbones went numb, and the following instant the end of his nose went numb. He was sure to frost his cheeks; he knew that, and experienced a pang of regret that he had not devised a nose strap of

the sort Bud wore in cold snaps. Such a strap passed across the cheeks, as well, and saved them. But it didn't matter much, after all. What were frosted cheeks? A bit painful, that was all; they were never serious.

Empty as the man's mind was of thoughts, he was keenly observant, and he noticed the changes in the creek, the curves and bends and timber jams, and always he sharply noted where he placed his feet. Once, coming around a bend, he shied abruptly, like a startled horse, curved away from the place where he had been walking, and retreated several paces back along the trail. The creek he knew was frozen clear to the bottom—no creek could contain water in that arctic winter—but he knew also that there were springs that bubbled out from the hillsides and ran along under the snow and on top the ice of the creek. He knew that the coldest snaps never froze these springs, and he knew likewise their danger. They were traps. They hid pools of water under the snow that might be three inches deep, or three feet. Sometimes a skin of ice half an inch thick covered them, and in turn was covered by the snow. Sometimes there were alternate layers of water and ice skin, so that when one broke through he kept on breaking through for a while, sometimes wetting himself to the waist.

That was why he had shied in such panic. He had felt the give under his feet and heard the crackle of a snow-hidden ice skin. And to get his feet wet in such a temperature meant trouble and danger. At the very least it meant delay, for he would be forced to stop and build a fire, and under its protection to bare his feet while he dried his socks and moccasins. He stood and studied the creek bed and its banks, and decided that the flow of water came from the right. He reflected awhile, rubbing his nose and cheeks, then skirted to the left, stepping gingerly and testing the footing for each step. Once clear of the danger, he took a fresh chew of tobacco and swung along at his four-mile gait.

In the course of the next two hours he came upon several similar traps. Usually the snow above the hidden pools had a sunken, candied appearance that advertised the danger. Once again, however, he had a close call; and once, suspecting danger, he compelled the dog to go on in front. The dog did not want to go. It hung back until the man shoved it forward, and then it went quickly across the white, unbroken surface. Suddenly it broke through, floundered to one side, and got away to firmer footing. It had wet its forefeet and legs, and almost immediately the water that clung to it turned to ice. It made quick efforts to lick the ice off its legs, then dropped down in the snow and began to bite out the ice that had formed between the toes. This was a matter of instinct. To permit the ice to remain would mean sore feet. It did not know this. It merely obeyed the mysterious prompting that arose from the deep crypts of its being. But the man knew, having achieved a judgment on the subject, and he removed the mitten from his right hand and helped tear out the ice particles. He did not expose his fingers more than a minute, and was astonished at the swift numbness that smote them. It certainly was cold. He pulled on the mitten hastily, and beat the hand savagely across his chest.

At twelve o'clock the day was at its brightest. Yet the sun was too far south on its winter journey to clear the horizon. The bulge of the earth intervened between it and Henderson Creek, where the man walked under a clear sky at noon and cast no shadow. At half-past twelve, to the minute, he arrived at the forks of the creek. He was pleased at the speed he had made. If he kept it up, he would certainly be with the boys by six. He unbuttoned his jacket and shirt and drew forth his lunch. The action consumed no more than a quarter of a minute, yet in that brief moment the numbness laid hold of the exposed fingers. He did not put the mitten on, but, instead, struck the fingers a dozen sharp smashes against his leg. Then he sat down on a snow-covered log to eat. The sting that followed upon the striking of his fingers against his leg ceased so quickly that he was startled. He had had no chance to take a bite of biscuit. He struck the fingers repeatedly and returned them to the mitten, baring the other hand for the purpose of eating. He tried to take a mouthful, but the ice muzzle prevented. He had forgotten to build a fire and thaw out. He chuckled at his foolishness, and as he chuckled he noted the numbness creeping into the exposed fingers. Also, he noted that the stinging which had first come to his toes when he sat down was already passing away. He wondered whether the toes were warm or numb. He moved them inside the moccasins and decided that they were numb.

He pulled the mitten on hurriedly and stood up. He was a bit frightened. 15 He stamped up and down until the stinging returned into the feet. It certainly was cold, was his thought. That man from Sulphur Creek had spoken the truth when telling how cold it sometimes got in the country. And he had laughed at him at the time! That showed one must not be too sure of things. There was no mistake about it, it *was* cold. He strode up and down, stamping his feet and threshing his arms, until reassured by the returning warmth. Then he got out matches and proceeded to make a fire. From the undergrowth, where high water of the previous spring had lodged a supply of seasoned twigs, he got his firewood. Working carefully from a small beginning, he soon had a roaring fire, over which he thawed the ice from his face and in the protection of which he ate his biscuits. For the moment the cold of space was outwitted. The dog took satisfaction in the fire, stretching out close enough for warmth and far enough away to escape being singed.

When the man had finished, he filled his pipe and took his comfortable time over a smoke. Then he pulled on his mittens, settled the ear flaps of his cap firmly about his ears, and took the creek trail up the left fork. The dog was disappointed and yearned back toward the fire. This man did not know cold. Possibly all the generations of his ancestry had been ignorant of cold, of real cold, of cold one hundred and seven degrees below freezing point. But the dog knew; all its ancestry knew, and it had inherited the knowledge. And it knew that it was not good to walk abroad in such fearful cold. It was the time to lie snug in a hole in the snow and wait for a curtain of cloud to be drawn across the face of outer space whence this cold came. On the other hand, there was no keen intimacy between the dog and the man. The one was the toil slave of the other, and the only caresses it had ever received were the caresses of the whip lash and of harsh and menacing throat sounds that threatened the whip lash. So the dog made no effort to communicate its apprehension to the man. It was not concerned in the welfare of the man; it was for its own sake that it yearned back toward the fire. But the man whistled, and spoke to it with the sound of whip lashes, and the dog swung in at the man's heels and followed after.

The man took a chew of tobacco and proceeded to start a new amber beard. Also, his moist breath quickly powdered with white his mustache, eyebrows, and lashes. There did not seem to be so many springs on the left fork of the Henderson, and for half an hour the man saw no signs of any. And then it happened. At a place where there were no signs, where the soft, unbroken snow seemed to advertise solidity beneath, the man broke through. It was not deep. He wet himself halfway to the knees before he floundered out to the firm crust.

He was angry, and cursed his luck aloud. He had hoped to get into camp with the boys at six o'clock, and this would delay him an hour, for he would have to build a fire and dry out his footgear. This was imperative at that low temperature—he knew that much; and he turned aside to the bank, which he climbed. On top, tangled in the underbrush about the trunks of several small spruce trees, was a highwater deposit of dry firewood—sticks and twigs, principally, but also larger portions of seasoned branches and fine dry last year's grasses. He threw down several large pieces on top of the snow. This served for a foundation and prevented the young flame from drowning itself in the snow it otherwise would melt. The flame he got by touching a match to a small shred of birch bark that he took from his pocket. This burned even more readily than paper. Placing it on the foundation, he fed the young flame with wisps of dry grass and with the tiniest dry twigs.

He worked slowly and carefully, keenly aware of his danger. Gradually, as the flame grew stronger, he increased the size of the twigs with which he fed it. He squatted in the snow, pulling the twigs out from their entanglement in the brush and feeding directly to the flame. He knew there must be no failure. When it is seventy-five below zero, a man must not fail in his first attempt to build a fire—that is, if his feet are wet. If his feet are dry, and he fails, he can run along the trail for half a mile and restore his circulation. But the circulation of wet and freezing feet cannot be restored by running when it is seventy-five below. No matter how fast he runs, the wet feet will freeze the harder.

All this the man knew. The old-timer on Sulphur Creek had told him   20
about it the previous fall, and now he was appreciating the advice. Already all sensation had gone out of his feet. To build the fire he had been forced to remove his mittens, and the fingers had quickly gone numb. His pace of four miles an hour had kept his heart pumping blood to the surface of his body and to all the extremities. But the instant he stopped, the action of the pump eased down. The cold of space smote the unprotected tip of the planet, and he, being on that unprotected tip, received the full force of the blow. The blood of his body recoiled before it. The blood was alive, like the dog, and like the dog it wanted to hide away and cover itself up from the fearful cold. So long as he walked four miles an hour, he pumped that blood, willy-nilly, to the surface; but now it ebbed away and sank down into the recesses of his body. The extremities were the first to feel its absence. His wet feet froze the faster, and his exposed fingers numbed the faster, though they had not yet begun to freeze. Nose and cheeks were already freezing, while the skin of all his body chilled as it lost its blood.

But he was safe. Toes and nose and cheeks would be only touched by the frost, for the fire was beginning to burn with strength. He was feeding it with twigs the size of his finger. In another minute he would be able to feed it with branches the size of his wrist, and then he could remove his wet footgear, and, while it dried, he could keep his naked feet warm by the fire, rubbing them at first, of course, with snow. The fire was a success. He was safe. He remembered the advice of the old-timer on Sulphur Creek, and smiled. The old-timer had been very serious in laying down the law that no man must travel alone in the Klondike after fifty below. Well, here he was; he had had the accident; he was alone; and he had saved himself. Those oldtimers were rather womanish, some of them, he thought. All a man had to do was to keep his head, and he was all right. Any man who was a man could travel alone. But it was surprising, the rapidity with which his cheeks and nose were freezing. And he had not thought his fingers could go life-less in so short a time. Lifeless they were, for he could scarcely make them move together to grip a twig, and they seemed remote from his body and from him. When he touched a twig, he had to look and see whether or not he had hold of it. The wires were pretty well down between him and his finger ends.

All of which counted for little. There was the fire, snapping and crackling and promising life with every dancing flame. He started to untie his moc-casins. They were coated with ice; the thick German socks were like sheaths of iron halfway to the knees; and the moccasin strings were like rods of steel all twisted and knotted as by some conflagration. For a moment he tugged with his numb fingers, then, realizing the folly of it, he drew his sheath knife.

But before he could cut the strings, it happened. It was his own fault or, rather, his mistake. He should not have built the fire under the spruce tree. He should have built it in the open. But it had been easier to pull the twigs from the brush and drop them directly on the fire. Now the tree under which he had done this carried a weight of snow on its boughs. No wind had blown for weeks, and each bough was fully freighted. Each time he had pulled a twig he had communicated a slight agitation to the tree—an im-perceptible agitation, so far as he was concerned, but an agitation sufficient to bring about the disaster. High up in the tree one bough capsized its load of snow. This fell on the boughs beneath, capsizing them. This process con-tinued, spreading out and involving the whole tree. It grew like an ava-lanche, and it descended without warning upon the man and the fire, and the fire was blotted out! Where it had burned was a mantle of fresh and dis-ordered snow.

The man was shocked. It was as though he had just heard his own sen-tence of death. For a moment he sat and stared at the spot where the fire had been. Then he grew very calm. Perhaps the old-timer on Sulphur Creek was right. If he had only had a trail mate he would have been in no dan-ger now. The trail mate could have built the fire. Well, it was up to him to build the fire over again, and this second time there must be no failure. Even if he succeeded, he would most likely lose some toes. His feet must be badly frozen by now, and there would be some time before the second fire was ready.

Such were his thoughts, but he did not sit and think them. He was busy   25
all the time they were passing through his mind. He made a new foundation

for a fire, this time in the open, where no treacherous tree could blot it out. Next he gathered dry grasses and tiny twigs from the high-water flotsam. He could not bring his fingers together to pull them out, but he was able to gather them by the handful. In this way he got many rotten twigs and bits of green moss that were undesirable, but it was the best he could do. He worked methodically, even collecting an armful of the larger branches to be used later when the fire gathered strength. And all the while the dog sat and watched him, a certain yearning wistfulness in its eyes, for it looked upon him as the fire provider, and the fire was slow in coming.

When all was ready, the man reached in his pocket for a second piece of birch bark. He knew the bark was there, and, though he could not feel it with his fingers, he could hear its crisp rustling as he fumbled for it. Try as he would, he could not clutch hold of it. And all the time, in his consciousness, was the knowledge that each instant his feet were freezing. This thought tended to put him in a panic, but he fought against it and kept calm. He pulled on his mittens with his teeth, and threshed his arms back and forth, beating his hands with all his might against his sides. He did this sitting down, and he stood up to do it; and all the while the dog sat in the snow, its wolf brush of a tail curled around warmly over its forefeet, its sharp wolf ears pricked forward intently as it watched the man. And the man, as he beat and threshed with his arms and hands, felt a great surge of envy as he regarded the creature that was warm and secure in its natural covering.

After a time he was aware of the first faraway signals of sensation in his beaten fingers. The faint tingling grew stronger till it evolved into a stinging ache that was excruciating, but which the man hailed with satisfaction. He stripped the mitten from his right hand and fetched forth the birch bark. The exposed fingers were quickly going numb again. Next he brought out his bunch of sulphur matches. But the tremendous cold had already driven the life out of his fingers. In his effort to separate one match from the others, the whole bunch fell in the snow. He tried to pick it out of the snow, but failed. The dead fingers could neither touch nor clutch. He was very careful. He drove the thought of his freezing feet, and nose, and cheeks, out of his mind, devoting his whole soul to the matches. He watched, using the sense of vision in place of that of touch, and when he saw his fingers on each side the bunch, he closed them—that is he willed to close them, for the wires were down, and the fingers did not obey. He pulled the mitten on the right hand, and beat it fiercely against his knee. Then, with both mittened hands, he scooped the bunch of matches, along with much snow, into his lap. Yet he was no better off.

After some manipulation he managed to get the bunch between the heels of his mittened hands. In this fashion he carried it to his mouth. The ice crackled and snapped when by a violent effort he opened his mouth. He drew the lower jaw in, curled the upper lip out of the way, scraped the bunch with his upper teeth in order to separate a match. He succeeded in getting one, which he dropped on his lap. He was no better off. He could not pick it up. Then he devised a way. He picked it up in his teeth and scratched in on his leg. Twenty times he scratched before he succeeded in lighting it. As it flamed he held it with his teeth to the birch bark. But the burning brimstone went up his nostrils and into his lungs, causing him to cough spasmodically. The match fell into the snow and went out.

The old-timer on Sulphur Creek was right, he thought in the moment of controlled despair that ensued: after fifty below, a man should travel with a partner. He beat his hands, but failed in exciting any sensation. Suddenly he bared both hands, removing the mittens with his teeth. He caught the whole bunch between the heels of his hands. His arm muscles not being frozen enabled him to press the hand heels tightly against the matches. Then he scratched the bunch along his leg. It flared into flame, seventy sulphur matches at once! There was no wind to blow them out. He kept his head to one side to escape the strangling fumes, and held the blazing bunch to the birch bark. As he so held it, he became aware of sensation in his hand. His flesh was burning. He could smell it. Deep down below the surface he could feel it. The sensation developed into pain that grew acute. And still he endured it, holding the flame of the matches clumsily to the bark that would not light readily because his own burning hands were in the way, absorbing most of the flame.

At last, when he could endure no more, he jerked his hands apart. The blazing matches fell sizzling into the snow, but the birch bark was alight. He began laying dry grasses and the tiniest twigs on the flame. He could not pick and choose, for he had to lift the fuel between the heels of his hands. Small pieces of rotten wood and green moss clung to the twigs, and he bit them off as well as he could with his teeth. He cherished the flame carefully and awkwardly. It meant life, and it must not perish. The withdrawal of blood from the surface of his body now made him begin to shiver, and he grew more awkward. A large piece of green moss fell squarely on the little fire. He tried to poke it out with his fingers, but his shivering frame made him poke too far, and he disrupted the nucleus of the little fire the burning grasses and tiny twigs separating and scattering. He tried to poke them to-gether again, but in spite of the tenseness of the effort, his shivering got away with him, and the twigs were hopelessly scattered. Each twig gushed a puff of smoke and went out. The fire provider had failed. As he looked ap-athetically about him, his eyes chanced on the dog, sitting across the ruins of the fire from him, in the snow, making restless, hunching movements, slightly lifting one forefoot and then the other, shifting its weight back and forth on them with wistful eagerness.

The sight of the dog put a wild idea into his head. He remembered the tale of the man, caught in a blizzard, who killed a steer and crawled inside the carcass, and so was saved. He would kill the dog and bury his hands in the warm body until the numbness went out of them. Then he could build another fire. He spoke to the dog, calling it to him; but in his voice was a strange note of fear that frightened the animal, who had never known the man to speak in such way before. Something was the matter, and its suspicious nature sensed danger—it knew not what danger, but somewhere, somehow, in its brain arose an apprehension of the man. It flattened its ears down at the sound of the man's voice, and its restless, hunching movements and the liftings and shiftings of its forefeet became more pronounced; but it would not come to the man. He got on his hands

30

and knees and crawled toward the dog. This unusual posture again excited suspicion, and the animal sidled mincingly away.

The man sat up in the snow for a moment and struggled for calmness. Then he pulled on his mittens, by means of his teeth, and got upon his feet. He glanced down at first in order to assure himself that he was really standing up, for the absence of sensation in his feet left him unrelated to the earth. His erect position in itself started to drive the webs of suspicion from the dog's mind; and when he spoke peremptorily, with the sound of whip lashes in his voice, the dog rendered its customary allegiance and came to him. As it came within reaching distance the man lost his control. His arms flashed out to the dog, and he experienced genuine surprise when he discovered that his hands could not clutch, that there was neither bend nor feeling in the fingers. He had forgotten for the moment that they were frozen and that they were freezing more and more. All this happened quickly, and before the animal could get away, he encircled its body with his arms. He sat down in the snow, and in this fashion held the dog, while it snarled and whined and struggled.

But it was all he could do, hold its body encircled in his arms and sit there. He realized that he could not kill the dog. There was no way to do it. With his helpless hands he could neither draw nor hold his sheath knife nor throttle the animal. He released it, and it plunged wildly away, with tail between its legs, and still snarling. It halted forty feet away and surveyed him curiously, with ears sharply pricked forward.

The man looked down at his hands in order to locate them, and found them hanging on the ends of his arms. It struck him as curious that one should have to use his eyes in order to find out where his hands were. He began threshing his arms back and forth, beating the mittened hands against his sides. He did this for five minutes, violently, and his heart pumped enough blood up to the surface to put a stop to his shivering. But no sensation was aroused in the hands. He had an impression that they hung like weights on the ends of his arms, but when he tried to run the impression down, he could not find it.

A certain fear of death, dull and oppressive, came to him. This fear   35 quickly became poignant as he realized that it was no longer a mere matter of freezing his fingers and toes, or of losing his hands and feet, but that it was a matter of life and death with the chances against him. This threw him into a panic, and he turned and ran up the creek bed along the old, dim trail. The dog joined in behind and kept up with him. He ran blindly, without intention, in fear such as he had never known in his life. Slowly, as he plowed and floundered through the snow, he began to see things again— the banks of the creek, the old timber jams, the leafless aspens, and the sky. The running made him feel better. He did not shiver. Maybe, if he ran on, his feet would thaw out; and, anyway, if he ran far enough, he would reach camp and the boys. Without doubt he would lose some fingers and toes and some of his face; but the boys would take care of him, and save the rest of him when he got there. And at the same time there was another thought in his mind that said he would never get to the camp and the boys; that it was too many miles away, that the freezing had too great a start on him, and that he would soon be stiff and dead. This thought he kept in the background and refused to consider. Sometimes it pushed itself forward and demanded to be heard, but he thrust it back and strove to think of other things.

It struck him as curious that he could run at all on feet so frozen that he could not feel them when they struck the earth and took the weight of his body. He seemed to himself to skim along above the surface, and to have no connection with the earth. Somewhere he had once seen a winged Mercury, and he wondered if Mercury felt as he felt when skimming over the earth.

His theory of running until he reached camp and the boys had one flaw in it: he lacked the endurance. Several times he stumbled, and finally he tottered, crumpled up, and fell. When he tried to rise, he failed. He must sit and rest, he decided, and next time he would merely walk and keep on going. As he sat and regained his breath, he noted that he was feeling quite warm and comfortable. He was not shivering, and it even seemed that a warm glow had come to his chest and trunk. And yet, when he touched his nose or cheeks, there was no sensation. Running would not thaw them out. Nor would it thaw out his hands and feet. Then the thought came to him that the frozen portions of his body must be extending. He tried to keep this thought down, to forget it, to think of something else; he was aware of the panicky feeling that it caused, and he was afraid of the panic. But the thought asserted itself, and persisted, until it produced a vision of his body totally frozen. This was too much, and he made another wild run along the trail. Once he slowed down to a walk, but the thought of the freezing extending itself made him run again.

And all the time the dog ran with him, at his heels. When he fell down a second time, it curled its tail over its forefeet and sat in front of him, facing him, curiously eager and intent. The warmth and security of the animal angered him, and he cursed it till it flattened down its ears appeasingly. This time the shivering came more quickly upon the man. He was losing in his battle with the frost. It was creeping into his body from all sides. The thought of it drove him on, but he ran no more than a hundred feet, when he staggered and pitched headlong. It was his last panic. When he had recovered his breath and control, he sat up and entertained in his mind the conception of meeting death with dignity. However, the conception did not come to him in such terms. His idea of it was that he had been making a fool of himself, running around like a chicken with its head cut off—such was the simile that occurred to him. Well, he was bound to freeze anyway, and he might as well take it decently. With this new-found peace of mind came the first glimmerings of drowsiness. A good idea, he thought, to sleep off to death. It was like taking an anesthetic. Freezing was not so bad as people thought. There were lots worse ways to die.

He pictured the boys finding his body next day. Suddenly he found himself with them, coming along the trail and looking for himself. And, still with them, he came around a turn in the trail and found himself lying in the snow. He did not belong with himself any more, for even then he was out of himself, standing with the boys and looking at himself in the snow. It certainly was cold, was his thought. When he got back to the States he could tell the folks what real cold was. He drifted on from this to a vision of the old-timer on Sulphur Creek. He could see him quite clearly, warm and comfortable, and smoking a pipe.

"You were right, old hoss; you were right," the man mumbled to the old-   40
timer of Sulphur Creek.

Then the man drowsed off into what seemed to him the most comfortable and satisfying sleep he had ever known. The dog sat facing him and waiting. The brief day drew to a close in a long, slow twilight. There were no signs of a fire to be made, and, besides, never in the dog's experience had it known a man to sit like that in the snow and make no fire. As the twilight drew on, its eager yearning for the fire mastered it, and with a great lifting and shifting of forefeet, it whined softly, then flattened its ears down in anticipation of being chidden by the man. But the man remained silent. Later the dog whined loudly. And still later it crept close to the man and caught the scent of death. This made the animal bristle and back away. A little longer it delayed, howling under the stars that leaped and danced and shone brightly in the cold sky. Then it turned and trotted up the trail in the direction of the camp it knew, where were the other food providers and fire providers.

Willa Cather   *(1873–1947)*

INVITATION TO READING: Willa Cather's novels show her love of her native Nebraska and of the early immigrants who turned an inhospitable forbidding setting into their home. "Paul's Case," her best-known short story, shows her to be an explorer of the unknown and at times frightening regions of our ordinary human minds. For Cather's early readers, as for his teachers, Paul in the following story is likely to have been a puzzle: a problem student and troublemaker. No one really knew what to do with him. Today, teachers and fellow students may recognize in him a familiar contemporary: an alienated student who tunes out the teacher's instruction or annotates it with "humorous remarks," who finds an escape from oppressive everyday reality in an alternative universe of music and the stage, and whose emotional problems may at any time erupt in destructive or self-destroying violence. How much is Paul like today's alienated youth, and how is he different? What have we learned about a case like Paul's since Cather wrote this story?

Paul's Case   1905

It was Paul's afternoon to appear before the faculty of the Pittsburgh High School to account for his various misdemeanors. He had been suspended a week ago, and his father had called at the Principal's office and confessed his perplexity about his son. Paul entered the faculty-room suave and smiling. His clothes were a trifle outgrown, and the tan velvet on the collar of his open overcoat was frayed and worn; but for all that there was something of the dandy about him, and he wore an opal pin in his neatly knotted black four-in-hand, and a red carnation in his buttonhole. This latter adornment the faculty somehow felt was not properly significant of the contrite spirit befitting a boy under the ban of suspension.

Paul was tall for his age and very thin, with high, cramped shoulders and a narrow chest. His eyes were remarkable for a certain hysterical brilliancy, and he continually used them in a conscious, theatrical sort of way, peculiarly offensive in a boy. The pupils were abnormally large, as though he were addicted to belladonna, but there was a glassy glitter about them which that drug does not produce.

When questioned by the Principal as to why he was there, Paul stated, politely enough, that he wanted to come back to school. This was a lie, but Paul was quite accustomed to lying; found it, indeed, indispensable for overcoming friction. His teachers were asked to state their respective charges against him, which they did with such a rancor and aggrievedness as evinced that this was not a usual case. Disorder and impertinence were among the offenses named, yet each of his instructors felt that it was scarcely possible to put into words the real cause of the trouble, which lay in a sort of hysterically defiant manner of the boy's; in the contempt which they all knew he felt for them, and which he seemingly made not the least effort to conceal. Once, when he had been making a synopsis of a paragraph at the blackboard, his English teacher had stepped to his side and attempted to guide his hand. Paul had started back with a shudder and thrust his hands violently behind him. The astonished woman could scarcely have been more hurt and embarrassed had he struck at her. The insult was so involuntary and definitely personal as to be unforgettable. In one way and another, he had made all his teachers, men and women alike, conscious of the same feeling of physical aversion. In one class he habitually sat with his hand shading his eyes; in another he always looked out of the window during the recitation; in another he made a running commentary on the lecture, with humorous intent.

His teachers felt this afternoon that his whole attitude was symbolized by his shrug and his flippantly red carnation flower, and they fell upon him without mercy, his English teacher leading the pack. He stood through it smiling, his pale lips parted over his white teeth. (His lips were continually twitching, and he had a habit of raising his eyebrows that was contemptuous and irritating to the last degree.) Older boys than Paul had broken down and shed tears under that ordeal, but his set smile did not once desert him, and his only sign of discomfort was the nervous trembling of the fingers that toyed with the buttons of his overcoat, and an occasional jerking of the other hand which held his hat. Paul was always smiling, always glancing about him, seeming to feel that people might be watching him and trying to detect something. This conscious expression, since it was as far as possible from boyish mirthfulness, was usually attributed to insolence or "smartness."

As the inquisition proceeded, one of his instructors repeated an impertinent remark of the boy's, and the Principal asked him whether he thought that a courteous speech to make to a woman. Paul shrugged his shoulders slightly and his eyebrows twitched.

5

"I don't know," he replied. "I didn't mean to be polite or impolite, either. I guess it's a sort of way I have, of saying things regardless."

The Principal asked him whether he didn't think that a way it would be well to get rid of. Paul grinned and said he guessed so. When he was told that he could go, he bowed gracefully and went out. His bow was like a repetition of the scandalous red carnation.

His teachers were in despair, and his drawing master voiced the feeling of them all when he declared there was something about the boy which none of them understood. He added: "I don't really believe that smile of his comes altogether from insolence; there's something sort of haunted about it. The boy is not strong, for one thing. There is something wrong about the fellow."

The drawing master had come to realize that, in looking at Paul, one saw only his white teeth and the forced animation of his eyes. One warm afternoon the boy had gone to sleep at his drawing-board, and his master had noted with amazement what a white, blue-veined face it was; drawn and wrinkled like an old man's about the eyes, the lips twitching even in his sleep.

His teachers left the building dissatisfied and unhappy; humiliated to have felt so vindictive towards a mere boy, to have uttered this feeling in cutting terms, and to have set each other on, as it were, in the gruesome game of intemperate reproach. One of them remembered having seen a miserable street cat set at bay by a ring of tormentors. 10

As for Paul, he ran down the hill whistling the Soldiers' Chorus from *Faust,* looking wildly behind him now and then to see whether some of his teachers were not there to witness his light-heartedness. As it was now late in the afternoon and Paul was on duty that evening as usher at Carnegie Hall, he decided that he would not go home to supper.

When he reached the concert hall the doors were not yet open. It was chilly outside, and he decided to go up into the picture gallery—always deserted at this hour—where there were some of Raffelli's gay studies of Paris streets and an airy blue Venetian scene or two that always exhilarated him. He was delighted to find no one in the gallery but the old guard, who sat in the corner, a newspaper on his knee, a black patch over one eye and the other closed. Paul possessed himself of the place and walked confidently up and down, whistling under his breath. After a while he sat down before a blue Rico and lost himself. When he bethought him to look at his watch, it was after seven o'clock, and he rose with a start and ran downstairs, making a face at Augustus Cæsar, peering out from the castroom, and an evil gesture at the Venus of Milo as he passed her on the stairway.

When Paul reached the ushers' dressing-room half-a-dozen boys were there already, and he began excitedly to tumble into his uniform. It was one of the few that at all approached fitting, and Paul thought it very becoming—though he knew the tight, straight coat accentuated his narrow chest, about which he was exceedingly sensitive. He was always excited while he dressed, twanging all over to the tuning of the strings and the preliminary flourishes of the horns in the music-room; but tonight he seemed quite beside himself, and he teased and plagued the boys until, telling him that he was crazy, they put him down on the floor and sat on him.

Somewhat calmed by his suppression, Paul dashed out to the front of the house to seat the early comers. He was a model usher. Gracious and smiling he ran up and down the aisles. Nothing was too much trouble for him; he carried messages and brought programs as though it were his greatest pleasure in life, and all the people in his section thought him a charming boy, feeling that he remembered and admired them. As the house filled, he grew more and more vivacious and animated, and the color came to his cheeks and lips. It was very much as though this were a great reception and Paul were the host. Just as the musicians came out to take their place, his English teacher arrived with checks for the seats which a prominent manufacturer had taken for the season. She betrayed some embarrassment when she handed Paul the tickets, and a *hauteur* which subsequently made her feel very foolish. Paul was startled for a moment, and had the feeling of wanting to put her out; what business had she here among all these fine people and gay colors? He looked her over and decided that she was not appropriately dressed and must be a fool to sit downstairs in such togs. The tickets had probably been sent her out of kindness, he reflected, as he put down a seat for her, and she had about as much right to sit there as he had.

When the symphony began Paul sank into one of the rear seats with a   15 long sigh of relief, and lost himself as he had done before the Rico. It was not that symphonies, as such, meant anything in particular to Paul, but the first sigh of the instruments seemed to free some hilarious spirit within him; something that struggled there like the Genius in the bottle found by the Arab fisherman. He felt a sudden zest of life; the lights danced before his eyes and the concert hall blazed into unimaginable splendor. When the soprano soloist came on, Paul forgot even the nastiness of his teacher's being there, and gave himself up to the peculiar intoxication such personages always had for him. The soloist chanced to be a German woman, by no means in her first youth, and the mother of many children; but she wore a satin gown and a tiara, and she had that indefinable air of achievement, that world-shine upon her, which always blinded Paul to any possible defects.

After a concert was over, Paul was often irritable and wretched until he got to sleep,—and tonight he was even more than usually restless. He had the feeling of not being able to let down; of its being impossible to give up this delicious excitement which was the only thing that could be called living at all. During the last number he withdrew and, after hastily changing his clothes in the dressing-room, slipped out to the side door where the singer's carriage stood. Here he began pacing rapidly up and down the walk, waiting to see her come out.

Over yonder the Schenley, in its vacant stretch, loomed big and square through the fine rain, the windows of its twelve stories glowing like those of a lighted cardboard house under a Christmas tree. All the actors and singers of any importance stayed there when they were in the city, and a number of the big manufacturers of the place lived there in the winter. Paul had often hung about the hotel, watching the people go in and out, longing to enter and leave schoolmasters and dull care behind him forever.

At last the singer came out, accompanied by the conductor, who helped her into her carriage and closed the door with a cordial *auf wiedersehen,*— which set Paul to wondering whether she were not an old sweetheart of his.

Paul followed the carriage over to the hotel, walking so rapidly as not to be far from the entrance when the singer alighted and disappeared behind the swinging glass doors which were opened by a negro in a tall hat and a long coat. In the moment that the door was ajar, it seemed to Paul that he, too, entered. He seemed to feel himself go after her up the steps, into the warm, lighted building, into an exotic, a tropical world of shiny, glistening surfaces and basking ease. He reflected upon the mysterious dishes that were brought into the dining-room, the green bottles in buckets of ice, as he had seen them in the supper party pictures of the Sunday supplement. A quick gust of wind brought the rain down with sudden vehemence, and Paul was startled to find that he was still outside in the slush of the gravel driveway; that his boots were letting in the water and his scanty overcoat was clinging wet about him; that the lights in front of the concert hall were out, and that the rain was driving in sheets between him and the orange glow of the windows above him. There it was, what he wanted—tangibly before him, like the fairy world of a Christmas pantomime; as the rain beat in his face, Paul wondered whether he were destined always to shiver in the black night outside, looking up at it.

He turned and walked reluctantly towards the car tracks. The end had to come sometime; his father in his night-clothes at the top of the stairs, explanations that did not explain, hastily improvised fictions that were forever tripping him up, his upstairs room and its horrible yellow wall-paper, the creaking bureau with the greasy plush collar-box, and over his painted wooden bed the pictures of George Washington and John Calvin, and the framed motto, "Feed my Lambs," which had been worked in red worsted by his mother, whom Paul could not remember.

Half an hour later, Paul alighted from the Negley Avenue car and went 20 slowly down one of the side streets off the main thoroughfare. It was a highly respectable street, where all the houses were exactly alike, and where businessmen of moderate means begot and reared large families of children, all of whom went to Sabbath-school and learned the shorter catechism, and were interested in arithmetic; all of whom were as exactly alike as their homes, and of a piece with the monotony in which they lived. Paul never went up Cordelia Street without a shudder of loathing. His home was next the house of the Cumberland minister. He approached it tonight with the nerveless sense of defeat, the hopeless feeling of sinking back forever into ugliness and commonness that he had always had when he came home. The moment he turned into Cordelia Street he felt the waters close above his head. After each of these orgies of living, he experienced all the physical depression which follows a debauch; the loathing of respectable beds, of common food, of a house permeated by kitchen odors; a shuddering repulsion for the flavorless, colorless mass of everyday existence; a morbid desire for cool things and soft lights and fresh flowers.

The nearer he approached the house, the more absolutely unequal Paul felt to the sight of it all: his ugly sleeping chamber; the cold bathroom with the grimy zinc tub, the cracked mirror, the dripping spigots; his father, at the top of the stairs, his hairy legs sticking out from his nightshirt, his feet thrust into carpet slippers. He was so much later than usual that there would certainly be inquiries and reproaches. Paul stopped short before the door. He felt that he could not be accosted by his father tonight; that he could not toss again on that miserable bed. He would not go in. He would tell his father that he had no carfare, and it was raining so hard he had gone home with one of the boys and stayed all night.

Meanwhile, he was wet and cold. He went around to the back of the house and tried one of the basement windows, found it open, raised it cautiously, and scrambled down the cellar wall to the floor. There he stood, holding his breath, terrified by the noise he had made; but the floor above him was silent, and there was no creak on the stairs. He found a soap-box, and carried it over to the soft ring of light that streamed from the furnace door, and sat down. He was horribly afraid of rats, so he did not try to sleep, but sat looking distrustfully at the dark, still terrified lest he might have awakened his father. In such reactions, after one of the experiences which made days and nights out of the dreary blanks of the calendar, when his senses were deadened, Paul's head was always singularly clear. Suppose his father had heard him getting in at the window and had come down and shot him for a burglar? Then, again, suppose his father had come down, pistol in hand, and he had cried out in time to save himself, and his father had been horrified to think how nearly he had killed him? Then, again, suppose a day should come when his father would remember that night, and wish there had been no warning cry to stay his hand? With this last supposition Paul entertained himself until daybreak.

The following Sunday was fine; the sodden November chill was broken by the last flash of autumnal summer. In the morning Paul had to go to church and Sabbath-school, as always. On seasonable Sunday afternoons the burghers of Cordelia Street usually sat out on their front "stoops," and talked to their neighbors on the next stoop, or called to those across the street in neighborly fashion. The men sat placidly on gay cushions upon the steps that led down to the sidewalk, while the women, in their Sunday "waists," sat in rockers on the cramped porches, pretending to be greatly at their ease. The children played in the streets; there were so many of them that the place resembled the recreation grounds of a kindergarten. The men on the steps—all in their shirt sleeves, their vests unbuttoned—sat with their legs well apart, their stomachs comfortably protruding, and talked of the prices of things, or told anecdotes of the sagacity of their various chiefs and overlords. They occasionally looked over the multitude of squabbling children, listened affectionately to their high-pitched, nasal voices, smiling to see their own proclivities reproduced in their offspring, and interspersed their legends of the iron kings with remarks about their sons' progress at school, their grades in arithmetic, and the amounts they had saved in their toy banks.

On this last Sunday of November, Paul sat all the afternoon on the lowest step of his "stoop," staring into the street, while his sisters, in their rockers, were talking to the minister's daughters next door about how many shirtwaists they had made in the last week, and how many waffles someone had eaten at the last church supper. When the weather was warm, and his father was in a particularly jovial frame of mind, the girls made lemonade, which was always brought out in a red-glass pitcher, ornamented with forget-me-nots in blue enamel. This the girls thought very fine, and the neighbors joked about the suspicious color of the pitcher.

Today Paul's father, on the top step, was talking to a young man who shifted a restless baby from knee to knee. He happened to be the young man who was daily held up to Paul as a model, and after whom it was his father's dearest hope that he would pattern. This young man was of a ruddy complexion, with a compressed, red mouth, and faded, nearsighted eyes, over which he wore thick spectacles, with gold bows that curved about his ears. He was clerk to one of the magnates of a great steel corporation, and was looked upon in Cordelia Street as a young man with a future. There was a story that, some five years ago—he was now barely twenty-six— he had been a trifle "dissipated," but in order to curb his appetites and save the loss of time and strength that a sowing of wild oats might have entailed, he had taken his chief's advice, oft reiterated to his employees, and at twenty-one had married the first woman whom he could persuade to share his fortunes. She happened to be an angular schoolmistress, much older than he, who also wore thick glasses, and who had now borne him four children, all nearsighted, like herself.

The young man was relating how his chief, now cruising in the Mediterranean, kept in touch with all the details of the business, arranging his office hours on his yacht just as though he were at home, and "knocking off work enough to keep two stenographers busy." His father told, in turn, the plan his corporation was considering, of putting in an electric railway plant at Cairo. Paul snapped his teeth; he had an awful apprehension that they might spoil it all before he got there. Yet he rather liked to hear these legends of the iron kings, that were told and retold on Sundays and holidays; these stories of palaces in Venice, yachts on the Mediterranean, and high play at Monte Carlo appealed to his fancy, and he was interested in the triumphs of cash boys who had become famous, though he had no mind for the cash-boy stage.

After supper was over, and he had helped to dry the dishes, Paul nervously asked his father whether he could go to George's to get some help in his geometry, and still more nervously asked for carfare. This latter request he had to repeat, as his father, on principle, did not like to hear requests for money, whether much or little. He asked Paul whether he could not go to some boy who lived nearer, and told him that he ought not to leave his school work until Sunday; but he gave him the dime. He was not a poor man, but he had a worthy ambition to come up in the world. His only reason for allowing Paul to usher was that he thought a boy ought to be earning a little.

Paul bounded upstairs, scrubbed the greasy odor of the dishwater from his hands with the ill-smelling soap he hated, and then shook over his fingers a few drops of violet water from the bottle he kept hidden in his drawer. He left the house with his geometry conspicuously under his arm, and the moment he got out of Cordelia Street and boarded a downtown car, he shook off the lethargy of two deadening days, and began to live again.

The leading juvenile of the permanent stock company which played at one of the downtown theaters was an acquaintance of Paul's, and the boy had been invited to drop in at the Sunday-night rehearsals whenever he could. For more than a year Paul had spent every available moment loitering about Charley Edwards's dressing-room. He had won a place among Edwards's following not only because the young actor, who could not afford to employ a dresser, often found him useful, but because he recognized in Paul something akin to what churchmen term "vocation."

It was at the theater and at Carnegie Hall that Paul really lived; the rest 30 was but a sleep and a forgetting. This was Paul's fairy tale, and it had for him all the allurement of a secret love. The moment he inhaled the gassy, painty, dusty odor behind the scenes, he breathed like a prisoner set free, and felt within him the possibility of doing or saying splendid, brilliant things. The moment the cracked orchestra beat out the overture from *Martha*, or jerked at the serenade from *Rigoletto*, all stupid and ugly things slid from him, and his senses were deliciously, yet delicately fired.

Perhaps it was because, in Paul's world, the natural nearly always wore the guise of ugliness, that a certain element of artificiality seemed to him necessary in beauty. Perhaps it was because his experience of life elsewhere was so full of Sabbath-school picnics, petty economies, wholesome advice as to how to succeed in life, and the unescapable odors of cooking, that he found this existence so alluring, these smartly clad men and women so attractive, that he was so moved by these starry apple orchards that bloomed perennially under the limelight.

It would be difficult to put it strongly enough how convincingly the stage entrance of that theater was for Paul the actual portal of Romance. Certainly none of the company ever suspected it, least of all Charley Edwards. It was very like the old stories that used to float about London of fabulously rich Jews, who had subterranean halls, with palms, and fountains, and soft lamps, and richly appareled women who never saw the disenchanting light of London day. So, in the midst of that smoke-palled city, enamored of figures and grimy toil, Paul had his secret temple, his wishing carpet, his bit of blue-and-white Mediterranean shore bathed in perpetual sunshine.

Several of Paul's teachers had a theory that his imagination had been perverted by garish fiction; but the truth was, he scarcely ever read at all. The books at home were not such as would either tempt or corrupt a youthful mind, and as for reading the novels that some of his friends urged upon him—well, he got what he wanted much more quickly from music; any sort of music, from an orchestra to a barrel organ. He needed only the spark, the indescribable thrill that made his imagination master of his senses, and he could make plots and pictures enough of his own. It was equally true that he was not stage-struck—not, at any rate, in the usual acceptation of that expression. He had no desire to become an actor, any more than he had to become a musician. He felt no necessity to do any of these things; what he wanted was to see, to be in the atmosphere, float on the wave of it, to be carried out, blue league after blue league, away from everything.

After a night behind the scenes, Paul found the schoolroom more than ever repulsive; the bare floors and naked walls; the prosy men who never wore frock coats, or violets in their buttonholes; the women with their dull gowns, shrill voices, and pitiful seriousness about prepositions that govern the dative. He could not bear to have the other pupils think, for a moment, that he took these people seriously; he must convey to them that he considered it all trivial, and was there only by way of a joke, anyway. He had autographed pictures of all the members of the stock company which he showed his classmates, telling them the most incredible stories of his familiarity with these people, of his acquaintance with the soloists who came to Carnegie Hall, his suppers with them and the flowers he sent them. When these stories lost their effect, and his audience grew listless, he would bid all the boys good-by, announcing that he was going to travel for awhile; going to Naples, to California, to Egypt. Then, next Monday, he would slip back, conscious and nervously smiling; his sister was ill, and he would have to defer his voyage until spring.

Matters went steadily worse with Paul at school. In the itch to let his instructors know how heartily he despised them, and how thoroughly he was appreciated elsewhere, he mentioned once or twice that he had no time to fool with theorems; adding—with a twitch of the eyebrows and a touch of that nervous bravado which so perplexed them—that he was helping the people down at the stock company; they were old friends of his.   35

The upshot of the matter was that the Principal went to Paul's father, and Paul was taken out of school and put to work. The manager at Carnegie Hall was told to get another usher in his stead; the doorkeeper at the theater was warned not to admit him to the house; and Charley Edwards remorsefully promised the boy's father not to see him again.

The members of the stock company were vastly amused when some of Paul's stories reached them—especially the women. They were hard-working women, most of them supporting indolent husbands or brothers, and they laughed rather bitterly at having stirred the boy to such fervid and florid inventions. They agreed with the faculty and with his father that Paul's was a bad case.

The east-bound train was plowing through a January snowstorm; the dull dawn was beginning to show grey when the engine whistled a mile out of Newark. Paul started up from the seat where he had lain curled in uneasy slumber, rubbed the breath-misted window glass with his hand, and peered out. The snow was whirling in curling eddies above the white bottom lands, and the drifts lay already deep in the fields and along the fences, while here and there the long dead grass and dried weed stalks protruded black above it. Lights shone from the scattered houses, and a gang of laborers who stood beside the track waved their lanterns.

Paul had slept very little, and he felt grimy and uncomfortable. He had made the all-night journey in a day coach because he was afraid if he took a Pullman he might be seen by some Pittsburgh businessman who had noticed him in Denny & Carson's office. When the whistle woke him, he clutched quickly at his breast pocket, glancing about him with an uncertain smile. But the little, clay-bespattered Italians were still sleeping, the slatternly women across the aisle were in open-mouthed oblivion, and even the crumby, crying babies were for the nonce stilled. Paul settled back to struggle with his impatience as best he could.

When he arrived at the Jersey City station, he hurried through his break-   40
fast, manifestly ill at ease and keeping a sharp eye about him. After he

reached the Twenty-third Street station, he consulted a cabman, and had himself driven to a men's furnishing establishment which was just opening for the day. He spent upward of two hours there, buying with endless re-considering and great care. His new street suit he put on in the fitting-room; the frock coat and dress clothes he had bundled into the cab with his new shirts. Then he drove to a hatter's and a shoe house. His next errand was at Tiffany's, where he selected silver mounted brushes and a scarf-pin. He would not wait to have his silver marked, he said. Lastly, he stopped at a trunk shop on Broadway, and had his purchases packed into various trav-eling bags.

It was a little after one o'clock when he drove up to the Waldorf, and, after settling with the cabman, went into the office. He registered from Washington; said his mother and father had been abroad, and that he had come down to await the arrival of their steamer. He told his story plausibly and had no trouble, since he offered to pay for them in advance, in engag-ing his rooms; a sleeping-room, sitting-room and bath.

Not once, but a hundred times Paul had planned this entry into New York. He had gone over every detail of it with Charley Edwards, and in his scrapbook at home there were pages of description about New York hotels, cut from the Sunday papers.

When he was shown to his sitting-room on the eighth floor, he saw at a glance that everything was as it should be; there was but one detail in his mental picture that the place did not realize, so he rang for the bell boy and sent him down for flowers. He moved about nervously until the boy re-turned, putting away his new linen and fingering it delightedly as he did so. When the flowers came, he put them hastily into water, and then tumbled into a hot bath. Presently he came out of his white bathroom, resplendent in his new silk underwear, and playing with the tassels of his red robe. The snow was whirling so fiercely outside his windows that he could scarcely see across the street; but within, the air was deliciously soft and fragrant. He put the violets and jonquils on the tabouret beside the couch, and threw himself down with a long sigh, covering himself with a Roman blanket. He was thoroughly tired; he had been in such haste, he had stood up to such a strain, covered so much ground in the last twenty-four hours, that he wanted to think how it had all come about. Lulled by the sound of the wind, the warm air, and the cool fragrance of the flowers, he sank into deep, drowsy retrospection.

It had been wonderfully simple; when they had shut him out of the the-ater and concert hall, when they had taken away his bone, the whole thing was virtually determined. The rest was a mere matter of opportunity. The only thing that at all surprised him was his own courage—for he realized well enough that he had always been tormented by fear, a sort of appre-hensive dread that, of late years, as the meshes of the lies he had told closed about him, had been pulling the muscles of his body tighter and tighter. Until now, he could not remember a time when he had not been dreading something. Even when he was a little boy, it was always there—behind him, or before, or on either side. There had always been the shadowed corner, the dark place into which he dared not look, but from which something seemed always to be watching him—and Paul had done things that were not pretty to watch, he knew.

But now he had a curious sense of relief, as though he had at last thrown down the gauntlet to the thing in the corner.

Yet it was but a day since he had been sulking in the traces; but yesterday afternoon that he had been sent to the bank with Denny & Carson's deposit, as usual—but this time he was instructed to leave the book to be balanced. There was above two thousand dollars in checks, and nearly a thousand in the bank notes which he had taken from the book and quietly transferred to his pocket. At the bank he had made out a new deposit slip. His nerves had been steady enough to permit of his returning to the office, where he had finished his work and asked for a full day's holiday tomorrow, Saturday, giving a perfectly reasonable pretext. The bank book, he knew, would not be returned before Monday or Tuesday, and his father would be out of town for the next week. From the time he slipped the bank notes into his pocket until he boarded the night train for New York, he had not known a moment's hesitation.

How astonishingly easy it had all been; here he was, the thing done; and this time there would be no awakening, no figure at the top of the stairs. He watched the snow flakes whirling by his window until he fell asleep.

When he awoke, it was four o'clock in the afternoon. He bounded up with a start; one of his precious days gone already! He spent nearly an hour in dressing, watching every stage of his toilet carefully in the mirror. Everything was quite perfect; he was exactly the kind of boy he had always wanted to be.

When he went downstairs, Paul took a carriage and drove up Fifth Avenue toward the Park. The snow had somewhat abated; carriages and tradesmen's wagons were hurrying soundlessly to and fro in the winter twilight; boys in woollen mufflers were shoveling off the doorsteps; the avenue stages made fine spots of color against the white street. Here and there on the corners whole flower gardens blooming behind glass windows, against which the snow flakes stuck and melted; violets, roses, carnations, lilies of the valley—somehow vastly more lovely and alluring that they blossomed thus unnaturally in the snow. The Park itself was a wonderful stage winter-piece.

When he returned, the pause of the twilight had ceased, and the tune of the streets had changed. The snow was falling faster, lights streamed from the hotels that reared their many stories fearlessly up into the storm, defying the raging Atlantic winds. A long, black stream of carriages poured down the avenue, intersected here and there by other streams, tending horizontally. There were a score of cabs about the entrance of his hotel, and his driver had to wait. Boys in livery were running in and out of the awning stretched across the sidewalk, up and down the red velvet carpet laid from the door to the street. Above, about, within it all, was the rumble and roar, the hurry and toss of thousands of human beings as hot for pleasure as himself, and on every side of him towered the glaring affirmation of the omnipotence of wealth.

The boy set his teeth and drew his shoulders together in a spasm of re-alization; the plot of all dramas, the text of all romances, the nerve-stuff of all sensations was whirling about him like the snow flakes. He burnt like a faggot in a tempest.

When Paul came down to dinner, the music of the orchestra floated up the elevator shaft to greet him. As he stepped into the thronged corridor, he sank back into one of the chairs against the wall to get his breath. The lights, the chatter, the perfumes, the bewildering medley of color—he had, for a moment, the feeling of not being able to stand it. But only for a moment; these were his own people, he told himself. He went slowly about the cor-ridors, through the writing-rooms, smoking-rooms, reception-rooms, as though he were exploring the chambers of an enchanted palace, built and peopled for him alone.

When he reached the dining-room he sat down at a table near a window. The flowers, the white linen, the many-colored wine glasses, the gay toilets of the women, the low popping of corks, the undulating repetitions of the *Blue Danube* from the orchestra, all flooded Paul's dream with bewildering radiance. When the roseate tinge of his champagne was added—that cold, precious, bubbling stuff that creamed and foamed in his glass—Paul won-dered that there were honest men in the world at all. This was what all the world was fighting for, he reflected; this was what all the struggle was about. He doubted the reality of his past. Had he ever known a place called Cordelia Street, a place where fagged-looking businessmen boarded the early car? Mere rivets in a machine they seemed to Paul,—sickening men, with combings of children's hair always hanging to their coats, and the smell of cooking in their clothes. Cordelia Street—Ah, that belonged to another time and country! Had he not always been thus, had he not sat here night after night, from as far back as he could remember, looking pensively over just such shimmering textures, and slowly twirling the stem of a glass like this one between his thumb and middle finger? He rather thought he had.

He was not in the least abashed or lonely. He had no especial desire to meet or to know any of these people; all he demanded was the right to look on and conjecture, to watch the pageant. The mere stage properties were all he contended for. Nor was he lonely later in the evening, in his loge at the Opera. He was entirely rid of his nervous misgivings, of his forced ag-gressiveness, of the imperative desire to show himself different from his sur-roundings. He felt now that his surroundings explained him. Nobody questioned the purple; he had only to wear it passively. He had only to glance down at his dress coat to reassure himself that here it would be im-possible for anyone to humiliate him.

He found it hard to leave his beautiful sitting-room to go to bed that night, and sat long watching the raging storm from his turret window. When he went to sleep, it was with the lights turned on in his bedroom; partly be-cause of his old timidity, and partly so that, if he should wake in the night, there would be no wretched moment of doubt, no horrible suspicion of yel-low wall-paper, or of Washington and Calvin above his bed. 55

On Sunday morning the city was practically snow-bound. Paul break-fasted late, and in the afternoon he fell in with a wild San Francisco boy, a freshman at Yale, who said he had run down for a "little flyer" over Sunday.

The young man offered to show Paul the night side of the town, and the two boys went off together after dinner, not returning to the hotel until seven o'clock the next morning. They had started out in the confiding warmth of a champagne friendship, but their parting in the elevator was singularly cool. The freshman pulled himself together to make his train, and Paul went to bed. He awoke at two o'clock in the afternoon, very thirsty and dizzy, and rang for ice-water, coffee, and the Pittsburgh papers.

On the part of the hotel management, Paul excited no suspicion. There was this to be said for him, that he wore his spoils with dignity and in no way made himself conspicuous. His chief greediness lay in his ears and eyes, and his excesses were not offensive ones. His dearest pleasures were the grey winter twilights in his sitting-room; his quiet enjoyment of his flowers, his clothes, his wide divan, his cigarette and his sense of power. He could not remember a time when he had felt so at peace with himself. The mere release from the necessity of petty lying, lying every day and every day, restored his self-respect. He had never lied for pleasure, even at school; but to make himself noticed and admired, to assert his difference from other Cordelia Street boys; and he felt a good deal more manly, more honest, even, now that he had no need for boastful pretensions, now that he could, as his actor friends used to say, "dress the part." It was characteristic that remorse did not occur to him. His golden days went by without a shadow, and he made each as perfect as he could.

On the eighth day after his arrival in New York, he found the whole affair exploited in the Pittsburgh papers, exploited with a wealth of detail which indicated that local news of a sensational nature was at a low ebb. The firm of Denny & Carson announced that the boy's father had refunded the full amount of his theft, and that they had no intention of prosecuting. The Cumberland minister had been interviewed, and expressed his hope of yet reclaiming the motherless lad, and Paul's Sabbath-school teacher declared that she would spare no effort to that end. The rumor had reached Pitts-burgh that the boy had been seen in a New York hotel, and his father had gone East to find him and bring him home.

Paul had just come in to dress for dinner; he sank into a chair, weak in the knees, and clasped his head in his hands. It was to be worse than jail, even; the tepid waters of Cordelia Street were to close over him finally and forever. The grey monotony stretched before him in hopeless, unrelieved years; Sabbath-school, Young People's Meeting, the yellow-papered room, the damp dish towels; it all rushed back upon him with sickening vividness. He had the old feeling that the orchestra had suddenly stopped, the sinking sensation that the play was over. The sweat broke out on his face, and he sprang to his feet, looked about him with his white, conscious smile, and winked at himself in the mirror. With something of the childish belief in miracles with which he had so often gone to class, all his lessons unlearned, Paul dressed and dashed whistling down the corridor to the elevator.

He had no sooner entered the dining-room and caught the measure of the music, than his remembrance was lightened by his old elastic power of claiming the moment, mounting with it, and finding it all sufficient. The glare and glitter about him, the mere scenic accessories had again, and for the last time, their old potency. He would show himself that he was game, 60 he would finish the thing splendidly. He doubted, more than ever, the existence of Cordelia Street, and for the first time he drank his wine recklessly. Was he not, after all, one of these fortunate beings? Was he not still himself, and in his own place? He drummed a nervous accompaniment to the music and looked about him, telling himself over and over that it had paid.

He reflected drowsily, to the swell of the violin and the chill sweetness of his wine, that he might have done it more wisely. He might have caught an outbound steamer and been well out of their clutches before now. But the other side of the world had seemed too far away and too uncertain then; he could not have waited for it; his need had been too sharp. If he had to choose over again, he would do the same thing tomorrow. He looked affectionately about the dining-room, now gilded with a soft mist. Ah, it had paid indeed!

Paul was awakened next morning by a painful throbbing in his head and feet. He had thrown himself across the bed without undressing, and had slept with his shoes on. His limbs and hands were lead heavy, and his tongue and throat were parched. There came upon him one of those fateful attacks of clear-headedness that never occurred except when he was physically exhausted and his nerves hung loose. He lay still and closed his eyes and let the tide of realities wash over him.

His father was in New York; "stopping at some joint or other," he told himself. The memory of successive summers on the front stoop fell upon him like a weight of black water. He had not a hundred dollars left; and he knew now, more than ever, that money was everything, the wall that stood between all he loathed and all he wanted. The thing was winding itself up; he had thought of that on his first glorious day in New York, and had even provided a way to snap the thread. It lay on his dressing-table now; he had got it out last night when he came blindly up from dinner,—but the shiny metal hurt his eyes, and he disliked the look of it, anyway.

He rose and moved about with a painful effort, succumbing now and again to attacks of nausea. It was the old depression exaggerated; all the world had become Cordelia Street. Yet somehow he was not afraid of anything, was absolutely calm; perhaps because he had looked into the dark corner at last, and knew. It was bad enough, what he saw there; but somehow not so bad as his long fear of it had been. He saw everything clearly now. He had a feeling that he had made the best of it, that he had lived the sort of life he was meant to live, and for half an hour he sat staring at the revolver. But he told himself that was not the way, so he went downstairs and took a cab to the ferry.

When Paul arrived at Newark, he got off the train and took another cab, 65 directing the driver to follow the Pennsylvania tracks out of town. The snow lay heavy on the roadways and had drifted deep in the open fields. Only here and there the dead grass or dried weed stalks projected, singularly black, above it. Once well into the country, Paul dismissed the carriage and walked, floundering along the tracks, his mind a medley of irrelevant things. He seemed to hold in his brain an actual picture of everything he had seen that morning. He remembered every feature of both his drivers, the toothless old woman from whom he had bought the red flowers in his coat, the agent from whom he had got his ticket, and all of his fellow-passengers on the ferry. His mind, unable to cope with vital matters near at hand, worked feverishly and deftly at sorting and grouping these images. They made for him a part of the ugliness of the world, of the ache in his head, and the bitter burning on his tongue. He stooped and put a handful of snow into his mouth as he walked, but that, too, seemed hot. When he reached a little hillside, where the tracks ran through a cut some twenty feet below him, he stopped and sat down.

The carnations in his coat were drooping with the cold, he noticed; all their red glory over. It occurred to him that all the flowers he had seen in the show windows that first night must have gone the same way, long before this. It was only one splendid breath they had, in spite of their brave mockery at the winter outside the glass. It was a losing game in the end, it seemed, this revolt against the homilies by which the world is run. Paul took one of the blossoms carefully from his coat and scooped a little hole in the snow, where he covered it up. Then he dozed awhile, from his weak condition, seeming insensible to the cold.

The sound of an approaching train woke him, and he started to his feet, remembering only his resolution, and afraid lest he should be too late. He stood watching the approaching locomotive, his teeth chattering, his lips drawn away from them in a frightened smile; once or twice he glanced nervously sidewise, as though he were being watched. When the right moment came, he jumped. As he fell, the folly of his haste occurred to him with merciless clearness, the vastness of what he had left undone. There flashed through his brain, clearer than ever before, the blue of Adriatic water, the yellow of Algerian sands.

He felt something strike his chest—his body was being thrown swiftly through the air, on and on, immeasurably far and fast, while his limbs gently relaxed. Then, because the picture-making mechanism was crushed, the disturbing visions flashed into black, and Paul dropped back into the immense design of things.

D.H. Lawrence   *(1885–1930)*

INVITATION TO READING: D.H. Lawrence was fascinated with the strange obsessions and compulsions that drive apparently normal people. He had grown up in poverty as a British coal miner's son, and he struggled with illness most of his life. He wrote at a time when psychologists, writers, and artists were going beyond the conscious surface to probe the repressed emotional turmoil of the subconscious. They explored impulses that are hidden even from our conscious selves and manifest themselves in strange imaginings and tormented dreams. Lawrence's explicit treatment of the powerful sexual drives and conflicted longings of both men and women made him a target of the bigots and prudes for whom vital human passions were lewdness and pornography. A whole edition of one of his books was destroyed by court order. The police raided an exhibition of his paintings. His *Lady Chatterley's Lover* was for many years printed only in a bowdlerized, tamed-down version. In 1959, an American court decision ruling the book not obscene made the publication of the unexpurgated Grove Press edition a major publishing event. In spite of censorship and persecution, Lawrence's *Sons and Lovers* (1913) and *Women in Love* (1920) became milestones of early-twentieth-century literature.

The Horse-Dealer's Daughter   1922

"Well, Mabel, and what are you going to do with yourself?" asked Joe, with foolish flippancy. He felt quite safe himself. Without listening for an answer, he turned aside, worked a grain of tobacco to the tip of his tongue, and spat it out. He did not care about anything, since he felt safe himself.

The three brothers and the sister sat round the desolate breakfast table, attempting some sort of desultory consultation. The morning's post had given the final tap to the family fortunes, and all was over. The dreary dining-room itself, with its heavy mahogany furniture, looked as it were waiting to be done away with.

But the consultation amounted to nothing. There was a strange air of ineffectuality about the three men, as they sprawled at table, smoking and reflecting vaguely on their own condition. The girl was alone, a rather short, sullen-looking young woman of twenty-seven. She did not share the same life as her brothers. She would have been good-looking, save for the impassive fixity of her face, "bulldog," as her brothers called it.

There was a confused tramping of horses' feet outside. The three men all sprawled round in their chairs to watch. Beyond the dark holly-bushes that separated the strip of lawn from the high-road, they could see a cavalcade of shire horses swinging out of their own yard, being taken for exercise. This was the last time. These were the last horses that would go through their hands. The young men watched with critical, callous look. They were all frightened at the collapse of their lives, and the sense of disaster in which they were involved left them no inner freedom.

Yet they were three fine, well-set fellows enough. Joe, the eldest, was a   5
man of thirty-three, broad and handsome in a hot, flushed way. His face was red, he twisted his black moustache over a thick finger, his eyes were shallow and restless. He had a sensual way of uncovering his teeth when he laughed, and his bearing was stupid. Now he watched the horses with a glazed look of helplessness in his eyes, a certain stupor of downfall.

The great draught-horses swung past. They were tied head to tail, four of them, and they heaved along to where a lane branched off from the high-road, planting their great hoofs floutingly in the fine black mud, swinging their great rounded haunches sumptuously, and trotting a few sudden steps as they were led into the lane, round the corner. Every movement showed a massive, slumbrous strength, and a stupidity which held them in subjection. The groom at the head looked back, jerking the leading rope. And the cavalcade moved out of sight up the lane, the tail of the last horse, bobbed up tight and stiff, held out taut from the swinging great haunches as they rocked behind the hedges in a motionlike sleep.

Joe watched with glazed hopeless eyes. The horses were almost like his own body to him. He felt he was done for now. Luckily, he was engaged to a woman as old as himself, and therefore her father, who was steward of a neighbouring estate, would provide him with a job. He would marry and go into harness. His life was over, he would be a subject animal now.

He turned uneasily aside, the retreating steps of the horses echoing in his ears. Then, with foolish restlessness, he reached for the scraps of bacon-rind from the plates, and making a faint whistling sound, flung them to the terrier that lay against the fender. He watched the dog swallow them, and waited till the creature looked into his eyes. Then a faint grin came on his face, and in a high, foolish voice he said:

"You won't get much bacon, shall you, you little b———?"

The dog faintly and dismally wagged its tail, then lowered its haunches, circled round, and lay down again. 10

There was another helpless silence at the table. Joe sprawled uneasily in his seat, not willing to go till the family conclave was dissolved. Fred Henry, the second brother, was erect, clean-limbed, alert. He had watched the passing of the horses with more *sangfroid*. If he was an animal, like Joe, he was an animal which controls, not one which is controlled. He was master of any horse, and he carried himself with a well-tempered air of mastery. But he was not master of the situations of life. He pushed his coarse brown moustache upwards, off his lip, and glanced irritably at his sister, who sat impassive and inscrutable.

"You'll go and stop with Lucy for a bit, shan't you?" he asked. The girl did not answer.

"I don't see what else you can do," persisted Fred Henry.

"Go as a skivvy," Joe interpolated laconically.

The girl did not move a muscle. 15

"If I was her, I should go in for training for a nurse," said Malcolm, the youngest of them all. He was the baby of the family, a young man of twenty-two, with a fresh, jaunty *museau*.

But Mabel did not take any notice of him. They had talked at her and round her for so many years, that she hardly heard them at all.

The marble clock on the mantel-piece softly chimed the half-hour, the dog rose uneasily from the hearthrug and looked at the party at the breakfast table. But still they sat on in ineffectual conclave.

"Oh, all right," said Joe suddenly, *à propos* of nothing. "I'll get a move on."

He pushed back his chair, straddled his knees with a downward jerk, to get them free, in horsey fashion, and went to the fire. Still he did not go out of the room; he was curious to know what the others would do or say. He began to charge his pipe, looking down at the dog and saying, in a high, affected voice: 20

"Going wi' me? Going wi' me are ter? Tha'rt goin' further than tha counts on just now, dost hear?"

The dog faintly wagged its tail, the man stuck out his jaw and covered his pipe with his hands, and puffed intently, losing himself in the tobacco, looking down all the while at the dog, with an absent brown eye. The dog looked up at him in mournful distrust. Joe stood with his knees stuck out, in real horsey fashion.

"Have you had a letter from Lucy?" Fred Henry asked of his sister.

"Last week," came the neutral reply.

"And what does she say?"   25

There was no answer.

"Does she *ask* you to go and stop there?" persisted Fred Henry.

"She says I can if I like."

"Well, then, you'd better. Tell her you'll come on Monday."

This was received in silence.   30

"That's what you'll do then, is it?" said Fred Henry, in some exasperation.

But she made no answer. There was a silence of futility and irritation in the room. Malcolm grinned fatuously.

"You'll have to make up your mind between now and next Wednesday," said Joe loudly, "or else find yourself lodgings on the kerbstone."

The face of the young woman darkened, but she sat on immutable.

"Here's Jack Fergusson!" exclaimed Malcolm, who was looking aimlessly   35 out of the window.

"Where?" exclaimed Joe, loudly.

"Just gone past."

"Coming in?"

Malcolm craned his neck to see the gate.

"Yes," he said.   40

There was a silence. Mabel sat on like one condemned, at the head of the table. Then a whistle was heard from the kitchen. The dog got up and barked sharply. Joe opened the door and shouted:

"Come on."

After a moment, a young man entered. He was muffled up in overcoat and a purple woolen scarf, and his tweed cap, which he did not remove, was pulled down on his head. He was of medium height, his face was rather long and pale, his eyes looked tired.

"Hello, Jack! Well, Jack!" exclaimed Malcolm and Joe. Fred Henry merely said "Jack!"

"What's doing?" asked the newcomer, evidently addressing Fred Henry.   45

"Same. We've got to be out by Wednesday—Got a cold?"

"I have—got it bad, too."

"Why don't you stop in?"

"*Me* stop in? When I can't stand on my legs, perhaps I shall have a chance." The young man spoke huskily. He had a slight Scotch accent.

"It's a knock-out, isn't it," said Joe boisterously, "if a doctor goes round   50 croaking with a cold. Looks bad for the patients, doesn't it?"

The young doctor looked at him slowly.

"Anything the matter with *you,* then?" he asked, sarcastically.

"Not as I know of. Damn your eyes, I hope not. Why?"

"I thought you were very concerned about the patients, wondered if you might be one yourself."

"Damn it, no, I've never been patient to no flaming doctor, and hope I   55 never shall be," returned Joe.

At this point Mabel rose from the table, and they all seemed to become aware of her existence. She began putting the dishes together. The young doctor looked at her, but did not address her. He had not greeted her. She went out of the room with the tray, her face impassive and unchanged.

"When are you off then, all of you?" asked the doctor.

"I'm catching the eleven-forty," replied Malcolm. "Are you goin' down wi' th' trap, Joe?"

"Yes, I've told you I'm going down wi' th' trap, haven't I?"

"We'd better be getting her in then.—So long, Jack, if I don't see you be- 60 fore I go," said Malcolm, shaking hands.

He went out, followed by Joe, who seemed to have his tail between his legs.

"Well, this is the devil's own," exclaimed the doctor, when he was left alone with Fred Henry. "Going before Wednesday, are you?"

"That's the orders," replied the other.

"Where, to Northampton?"

"That's it." 65

"The devil!" exclaimed Fergusson, with quiet chagrin.

And there was silence between the two.

"All settled up, are you?" asked Fergusson.

"About."

There was another pause. 70

"Well, I shall miss yer, Freddy boy," said the young doctor.

"And I shall miss thee, Jack," returned the other.

"Miss you like hell," mused the doctor.

Fred Henry turned aside. There was nothing to say. Mabel came in again, to finish clearing the table.

"What are *you* going to do then, Miss Pervin?" asked Fergusson. "Going 75 to your sister's, are you?"

Mabel looked at him with her steady, dangerous eyes, that always made him uncomfortable, unsettling his superficial ease.

"No," she said.

"Well, what in the name of fortune *are* you going to do? Say what you *mean* to do," cried Fred Henry, with futile intensity.

But she only averted her head, and continued her work. She folded the white table-cloth, and put on the chenille cloth.

"The sulkiest bitch that ever trod!" muttered her brother. 80

But she finished her task with perfectly impassive face, the young doctor watching her interestedly all the while. Then she went out.

Fred Henry stared after her, clenching his lips, his blue eyes fixing in sharp antagonism, as he made a grimace of sour exasperation.

"You could bray her into bits, and that's all you'd get out of her," he said, in a small, narrowed tone.

The doctor smiled faintly.

"What's she *going* to do then?" he asked. 85

"Strike me if *I* know!" returned the other.

There was a pause. Then the doctor stirred.

"I'll be seeing you to-night, shall I?" he said to his friend.

"Ay—where's it to be? Are we going over to Jessdale?"

"I don't know. I've got such a cold on me. I'll come round to the Moon   90
and Stars, anyway."

"Let Lizzie and May miss their night for once, eh?"

"That's it—if I feel as I do now."

"All's one—"

The two young men went through the passage and down to the back
door together. The house was large, but it was servantless now, and desolate. At the back was a small bricked house-yard, and beyond that a big
square, gravelled fine and red, and having stables on two sides. Sloping,
dank, winter-dark fields stretched away on the open sides.

But the stables were empty. Joseph Pervin, the father of the family, had   95
been a man of no education, who had become a fairly large horse dealer.
The stables had been full of horses, there was a great turmoil and come-
and-go of horses and of dealers and grooms. Then the kitchen was full of
servants. But of late things had declined. The old man had married a second time, to retrieve his fortunes. Now he was dead and everything was
gone to the dogs, there was nothing but debt and threatening.

For months, Mabel had been servantless in the big house, keeping the
home together in penury for her ineffectual brothers. She had kept house
for ten years. But previously, it was with unstinted means. Then, however
brutal and coarse everything was, the sense of money had kept her proud,
confident. The men might be foul-mouthed, the women in the kitchen might
have bad reputations, her brothers might have illegitimate children. But so
long as there was money, the girl felt herself established, and brutally proud,
reserved.

No company came to the house, save dealers and coarse men. Mabel had
no associates of her own sex, after her sister went away. But she did not
mind. She went regularly to church, she attended to her father. And she
lived in the memory of her mother, who had died when she was fourteen,
and whom she had loved. She had loved her father, too, in a different way,
depending upon him, and feeling secure in him, until at the age of fifty-four
he married again. And then she had set hard against him. Now he had died
and left them all hopelessly in debt.

She had suffered badly during the period of poverty. Nothing, however,
could shake the curious sullen, animal pride that dominated each member
of the family. Now, for Mabel, the end had come. Still she would not cast
about her. She would follow her own way just the same. She would always
hold the keys of her own situation. Mindless and persistent, she endured
from day to day. Why should she think? Why should she answer anybody?
It was enough that this was the end, and there was no way out. She need
not pass any more darkly along the main street of the small town, avoiding
every eye. She need not demean herself any more, going into the shops and
buying the cheapest food. This was at an end. She thought of nobody, not
even of herself. Mindless and persistent, she seemed in a sort of ecstasy to
be coming nearer to her fulfilment, her own glorification, approaching her
dead mother, who was glorified.

In the afternoon she took a little bag, with shears and sponge and a small
scrubbing brush, and went out. It was a grey, wintry day, with saddened,
dark-green fields and an atmosphere blackened by the smoke of foundries

not far off. She went quickly, darkly along the causeway, heeding nobody, through the town to the churchyard.

There she always felt secure, as if no one could see her, although as a matter of fact she was exposed to the stare of everyone who passed along under the churchyard wall. Nevertheless, once under the shadow of the great looming church, among the graves, she felt immune from the world, reserved within the thick churchyard wall as in another country.

Carefully she clipped the grass from the grave, and arranged the pinky-white, small chrysanthemums in the tin cross. When this was done, she took an empty jar from a neighbouring grave, brought water, and carefully, most scrupulously sponged the marble headstone and the coping-stone.

It gave her sincere satisfaction to do this. She felt in immediate contact with the world of her mother. She took minute pains, went through the park in a state bordering on pure happiness, as if in performing this task she came into a subtle, intimate connection with her mother. For the life she followed here in the world was far less real than the world of death she inherited from her mother.

The doctor's house was just by the church. Fergusson, being a mere hired assistant, was slave to the countryside. As he hurried now to attend to the outpatients in the surgery, glancing across the graveyard with his quick eye, he saw the girl at her task at the grave. She seemed so intent and remote, it was like looking into another world. Some mystical element was touched in him. He slowed down as he walked, watching her as if spell-bound.

She lifted her eyes, feeling him looking. Their eyes met. And each looked again at once, each feeling, in some way, found out by the other. He lifted his cap and passed on down the road. There remained distinct in his consciousness, like a vision, the memory of her face, lifted from the tombstone in the churchyard, and looking at him with slow, large, portentous eyes. It *was* portentous, her face. It seemed to mesmerise him. There was a heavy power in her eyes which laid hold of his whole being, as if he had drunk some powerful drug. He had been feeling weak and done before. Now the life came back into him, he felt delivered from his own fretted, daily self.

He finished his duties at the surgery as quickly as might be, hastily filling up the bottles of the waiting people with cheap drugs. Then, in perpetual haste, he set off again to visit several cases in another part of his round, before teatime. At all times he preferred to walk, if he could, but particularly when he was not well. He fancied the motion restored him.

The afternoon was falling. It was grey, deadened, and wintry, with a slow, moist, heavy coldness sinking in and deadening all the faculties. But why should he think or notice? He hastily climbed the hill and turned across the dark-green fields, following the black cinder-track. In the distance, across a shallow dip in the country, the small town was clustered like smouldering ash, a tower, a spire, a heap of low, raw, extinct houses. And on the nearest fringe of the town, sloping into the dip, was Oldmeadow, the Pervins' house. He could see the stables and the outbuildings distinctly, as they lay towards him on the slope. Well, he would not go there many more times! Another resource would be lost to him, another place gone: the only company he cared for in the alien, ugly little town he was losing. Nothing but work, drudgery, constant hastening from dwelling to dwelling among the colliers and the iron-workers. It wore him out, but at the same time he had a craving for it. It was a stimulant to him to be in the homes of the working people, moving as it were through the innermost body of their life. His nerves were excited and gratified. He could come so near, into the very lives of the rough, inarticulate, powerfully emotional men and women. He grumbled, he said he hated the hellish hole. But as a matter of fact it excited him, the contact with the rough, strongly-feeling people was a stimulant applied direct to his nerves.

Below Oldmeadow, in the green, shallow, soddened hollow of fields, lay a square, deep pond. Roving across the landscape, the doctor's quick eye detected a figure in black passing through the gate of the field, down towards the pond. He looked again. It would be Mabel Pervin. His mind suddenly became alive and attentive.

Why was she going down there? He pulled up on the path on the slope above, and stood staring. He could just make sure of the small black figure moving in the hollow of the failing day. He seemed to see her in the midst of such obscurity, that he was like a clairvoyant, seeing rather with the mind's eye than with ordinary sight. Yet he could see her positively enough, whilst he kept his eye attentive. He felt, if he looked away from her, in the thick, ugly falling dusk, he would lose her altogether.

He followed her minutely as she moved, direct and intent, like something transmitted rather than stirring in voluntary activity, straight down the field towards the pond. There she stood on the bank for a moment. She never raised her head. Then she waded slowly into the water.

He stood motionless as the small black figure walked slowly and delib-   110 erately towards the centre of the pond, very slowly, gradually moving deeper into the motionless water, and still moving forward as the water got up to her breast. Then he could see her no more in the dusk of the dead afternoon.

"There!" he exclaimed. "Would you believe it?"

And he hastened straight down, running over the wet, soddened fields, pushing through the hedges, down into the depression of callous wintry obscurity. It took him several minutes to come to the pond. He stood on the bank, breathing heavily. He could see nothing. His eyes seemed to penetrate the dead water. Yes, perhaps that was the dark shadow of her black clothing beneath the surface of the water.

He slowly ventured into the pond. The bottom was deep, soft clay, he sank in, and the water clasped dead cold round his legs. As he stirred he could smell the cold, rotten clay that fouled up into the water. It was objectionable in his lungs. Still, repelled and yet not heeding, he moved deeper into the pond. The cold water rose over his thighs, over his loins, upon his abdomen. The lower part of his body was all sunk in the hideous cold element. And the bottom was so deeply soft and uncertain, he was afraid of pitching with his mouth underneath. He could not swim, and was afraid.

He crouched a little, spreading his hands under the water and moving them round, trying to feel for her. The dead cold pond swayed upon his chest. He moved again, a little deeper, and again, with his hands underneath, he felt all around under the water. And he touched her clothing. But it evaded his fingers. He made a desperate effort to grasp it.

And so doing he lost his balance and went under, horribly, suffocating in   115
the foul earthy water, struggling madly for a few moments. At last, after what
seemed an eternity, he got his footing, rose again into the air and looked
around. He gasped, and knew he was in the world. Then he looked at the
water. She had risen near him. He grasped her clothing, and drawing her
nearer, turned to take his way to land again.

He went very slowly, carefully, absorbed in the slow progress. He rose
higher, climbing out of the pond. The water was not only about his legs; he
was thankful, full of relief to be out of the clutches of the pond. He lifted
her and staggered on to the bank, out of the horror of wet, grey clay.

He laid her down on the bank. She was quite unconscious and running
with water. He made the water come from her mouth, he worked to restore
her. He did not have to work very long before he could feel the breathing
begin again in her; she was breathing naturally. He worked a little longer.
He could feel her live beneath his hands; she was coming back. He wiped
her face, wrapped her in his overcoat, looked round into the dim, dark-grey
world, then lifted her and staggered down the bank and across the fields.

It seemed an unthinkably long way, and his burden so heavy he felt he
would never get to the house. But at last he was in the stable-yard, and then
in the house-yard. He opened the door and went into the house. In the
kitchen he laid her down on the hearthrug, and called. The house was
empty. But the fire was burning in the grate.

Then again he kneeled to attend to her. She was breathing regularly, her
eyes were wide open as if conscious, but there seemed something missing in
her look. She was conscious in herself, but unconscious of her surroundings.

He ran upstairs, took blankets from a bed, and put them before the fire   120
to warm. Then he removed her saturated, earthy-smelling clothing, rubbed
her dry with a towel, and wrapped her naked in the blankets. Then he went
into the dining-room, to look for spirits. There was a little whiskey. He
drank a gulp himself, and put some into her mouth.

The effect was instantaneous. She looked full into his face, as if she had
been seeing him for some time, and yet had only just become conscious of
him.

"Dr. Fergusson?" she said.

"What?" he answered.

He was divesting himself of his coat, intending to find some dry clothing
upstairs. He could not bear the smell of the dead, clayey water, and he was
mortally afraid for his own health.

"What did I do?" she asked.   125

"Walked into the pond," he replied. He had begun to shudder like one
sick, and could hardly attend to her. Her eyes remained full on him, he
seemed to be going dark in his mind, looking back at her helplessly.
The shuddering became quieter in him, his life came back in him, dark and
unknowing, but strong again.

"Was I out of my mind?" she asked, while her eyes were fixed on him all
the time.

"Maybe, for the moment," he replied. He felt quiet, because his strength
had come back. The strange fretful strain had left him.

"Am I out of my mind now?" she asked.

"Are you?" he reflected a moment. "No," he answered truthfully, "I don't 130
see that you are." He turned his face aside. He was afraid, now, because
he felt dazed, and felt dimly that her power was stronger than his, in this
issue. And she continued to look at him fixedly all the time. "Can you tell
me where I shall find some dry things to put on?" he asked.

"Did you dive into the pond for me?" she asked.

"No," he answered. "I walked in. But I went in overhead as well."

There was silence for a moment. He hesitated. He very much wanted to
go upstairs to get into dry clothing. But there was another desire in him. And
she seemed to hold him. His will seemed to have gone to sleep, and left
him, standing there slack before her. But he felt warm inside himself. He did
not shudder at all, though his clothes were sodden on him.

"Why did you?" she asked.

"Because I didn't want you to do such a foolish thing," he said.   135

"It wasn't foolish," she said, still gazing at him as she lay on the floor, with
a sofa cushion under her head. "It was the right thing to do. *I* knew best,
then."

"I'll go and shift these wet things," he said. But still he had not the power
to move out of her presence, until she sent him. It was as if she had the life
of his body in her hands, and he could not extricate himself. Or perhaps he
did not want to.

Suddenly she sat up. Then she became aware of her own immediate condition. She felt the blankets about her, she knew her own limbs. For a moment it seemed as if her reason were going. She looked round, with wild
eye, as if seeking something. He stood still with fear. She saw her clothing
lying scattered.

"Who undressed me?" she asked, her eyes resting full and inevitable on
his face.

"I did," he replied, "to bring you round."   140

For some moments she sat and gazed at him awfully, her lips parted.

"Do you love me then?" she asked.

He only stood and stared at her, fascinated. His soul seemed to melt.

She shuffled forward on her knees, and put her arms round him, round
his legs, as he stood there, pressing her breasts against his knees and thighs,
clutching him with strange, convulsive certainty, pressing his thighs against
her, drawing him to her face, her throat, as she looked up at him with flaring, humble eyes of transfiguration, triumphant in first possession.

"You love me," she murmured, in strange transport, yearning and tri- 145
umphant and confident. "You love me. I know you love me, I know."

And she was passionately kissing his knees, through the wet clothing,
passionately and indiscriminately kissing his knees, his legs, as if unaware
of everything.

He looked down at the tangled wet hair, the wild, bare, animal shoulders. He was amazed, bewildered, and afraid. He had never thought of loving her. He had never wanted to love her. When he rescued her and
restored her, he was a doctor, and she was a patient. He had had no single personal thought of her. Nay, this introduction of the personal element
was very distasteful to him, a violation of his professional honour. It was

horrible to have her there embracing his knees. It was horrible. He revolted from it, violently. And yet—and yet—he had not the power to break away.

She looked at him again, with the same supplication of powerful love, and that same transcendent, frightening light of triumph. In view of the delicate flame which seemed to come from her face like a light, he was powerless. And yet he had never intended to love her. He had never intended. And something stubborn in him could not give way.

"You love me," she repeated, in a murmur of deep, rhapsodic assurance. "You love me."

Her hands were drawing him, drawing him down to her. He was afraid, 150 even a little horrified. For he had, really, no intention of loving her. Yet her hands were drawing him towards her. He put out his hand quickly to steady himself, and grasped her bare shoulder. A flame seemed to burn the hand that grasped her soft shoulder. He had no intention of loving her: his whole will was against his yielding. It was horrible—And yet wonderful was the touch of her shoulder, beautiful the shining of her face. Was she perhaps mad? He had a horror of yielding to her. Yet something in him ached also.

He had been staring away at the door, away from her. But his hand remained on her shoulder. She had gone suddenly very still. He looked down at her. Her eyes were now wide with fear, with doubt, the light was dying from her face, a shadow of terrible greyness was returning. He could not bear the touch of her eyes' question upon him, and the look of death behind the question.

With an inward groan he gave way, and let his heart yield towards her. A sudden gentle smile came on his face. And her eyes, which never left his face, slowly, slowly filled with tears. He watched the strange water rise in her eyes, like some slow fountain coming up. And his heart seemed to burn and melt away in his breast.

He could not bear to look at her any more. He dropped on his knees and caught her head with his arms and pressed her face against his throat. She was very still. His heart, which seemed to have broken, was burning with a kind of agony in his breast. And he felt her slow, hot tears wetting his throat. But he could not move.

He felt the hot tears wet his neck and the hollows of his neck, and he remained motionless, suspended through one of man's eternities. Only now it had become indispensable to him to have her face pressed close to him; he could never let her go again. He could never let her head go away from the close clutch of his arm. He wanted to remain like that for ever, with his heart hurting him in a pain that was also life to him. Without knowing, he was looking down on her damp, soft brown hair.

Then, as it were suddenly, he smelt the horrid stagnant smell of the 155 water. And at the same moment she drew away from him and looked at him. Her eyes were wistful and unfathomable. He was afraid of them, and he fell to kissing her, not knowing what he was doing. He wanted her eyes not to have that terrible, wistful, unfathomable look.

When she turned her face to him again, a faint delicate flush was glowing, and there was again dawning that terrible shining of joy in her eyes, which really terrified him, and yet which he now wanted to see, because he feared the look of doubt still more.

"You love me?" she said, rather faltering.

"Yes." The word cost him a painful effort. Not because it wasn't true. But because it was too newly true, the *saying* seemed to tear open again his newly-torn heart. And he hardly wanted it to be true, even now.

She lifted her face to him, and he bent forward and kissed her on the mouth gently, with the one kiss that is an eternal pledge. And as he kissed her his heart strained again in his breast. He never intended to love her. But now it was over. He had crossed over the gulf to her, and all that he had left behind had shrivelled and become void.

After the kiss, her eyes again slowly filled with tears. She sat still, away 160 from him, with her face drooped aside, and her hands folded in her lap. The tears fell very slowly. There was complete silence. He too sat there motionless and silent on the hearthrug. The strange pain of his heart that was broken seemed to consume him. That he should love her? That this was love! That he should be ripped open in this way!—Him, a doctor!—How they would all jeer if they knew!—It was agony to him to think they might know.

In the curious naked pain of the thought he looked again to her. She was sitting there drooped into a muse. He saw a tear fall, and his heart flared hot. He saw for the first time that one of her shoulders was quite uncovered, one arm bare, he could see one of her small breasts; dimly, because it had become almost dark in the room.

"Why are you crying?" he asked, in an altered voice.

She looked up at him, and behind her tears the consciousness of her situation for the first time brought a dark look of shame to her eyes.

"I'm not crying, really," she said, watching him half frightened.

He reached his hand, and softly closed it on her bare arm.   165

"I love you! I love you!" he said in a soft, low vibrating voice, unlike himself.

She shrank, and dropped her head. The soft, penetrating grip of his hand on her arm distressed her. She looked up at him.

"I want to go," she said. "I want to go and get you some dry things."

"Why?" he said. "I'm all right."

"But I want to go," she said. "And I want you to change your things."   170

He released her arm, and she wrapped herself in the blanket, looking at him rather frightened. And still she did not rise.

"Kiss me," she said wistfully.

He kissed her, but briefly, half in anger.

Then, after a second, she rose nervously, all mixed up in the blanket. He watched her in her confusion, as she tried to extricate herself and wrap herself up so that she could walk. He watched her relentlessly, as she knew.

And as she went, the blanket trailing, and as he saw a glimpse of her feet 175 and her white leg, he tried to remember her as she was when he had wrapped her in the blanket. But then he didn't want to remember, because she had been nothing to him then, and his nature revolted from remembering her as she was when she was nothing to him.

A tumbling muffled noise from within the dark house startled him. Then he heard her voice:—"There are clothes." He rose and went to the foot of the stairs, and gathered up the garments she had thrown down. Then he came back to the fire, to rub himself down and dress. He grinned at his own appearance, when he had finished.

The fire was sinking, so he put on coal. The house was now quite dark, save for the light of a street-lamp that shone in faintly from beyond the holly trees. He lit the gas with matches he found on the mantel-piece. Then he emptied the pockets of his own clothes, and threw all his wet things in a heap into the scullery. After which he gathered up her sodden clothes, gently, and put them in a separate heap on the copper-top in the scullery.

It was six o'clock on the clock. His own watch had stopped. He ought to be back to the surgery. He waited, and still she did not come down. So he went to the foot of the stairs and called:

"I shall have to go."

Almost immediately he heard her coming down. She had on her best 180 dress of black voile, and her hair was tidy, but still damp. She looked at him—and in spite of herself, smiled.

"I don't like you in those clothes," she said.

"Do I look a sight?" he answered.

They were shy of one another.

"I'll make you some tea," she said.

"No, I must go."   185

"Must you?" And she looked at him again with the wide, strained, doubtful eyes. And again, from the pain of his breast, he knew how he loved her. He went and bent to kiss her, gently, passionately, with his heart's painful kiss.

"And my hair smells so horrible," she murmured in distraction. "And I'm so awful, I'm so awful! Oh, no, I'm too awful." And she broke into bitter, heartbroken sobbing. "You can't want to love me, I'm horrible."

"Don't be silly, don't be silly," he said, trying to comfort her, kissing her, holding her in his arms. "I want you, I want to marry you, we're going to be married, quickly, quickly—to-morrow if I can."

But she only sobbed terribly, and cried.

"I feel awful. I feel awful. I feel I'm horrible to you."   190

"No, I want you, I want you," was all he answered blindly, with that terrible intonation which frightened her almost more than her horror lest he should *not* want her.

Edith Wharton   *(1862–1937)*

INVITATION TO READING: Feminist critics have focused renewed interest on Edith Wharton's patient psychological studies of the tedious lives of fashionable well-educated wealthy women of a patriarchal society. Wharton grew up in a wealthy upper-class setting in New York City, and she held up the mirror to a society of privilege in her widely read novels *The House of Mirth* (1905) and *The Age of Innocence* (1920). As a child, she lived in a world of governesses and tutors and of stays in additional family homes in Paris and Rhode Island. She spent much of her later life in Paris at a time when "well-cared-for" society women filled their days with social functions and travel abroad, with the Baedeker guidebook directing them to suitable accommodations. Her "Roman Fever" story probes the hidden resentments, long-standing rivalries, and venomous jealousies lurking under the polished civilized surface. The setting is Rome, the city of the Seven Hills (one of them mentioned in the story is the Palatine). What final satirical touch does the traditional surprise ending add to the story?

Roman Fever   *1936*

I

From the table at which they had been lunching two American ladies of ripe but well-cared-for middle age moved across the lofty terrace of the Roman restaurant and, leaning on its parapet, looked first at each other, and then down on the outspread glories of the Palatine and the Forum, with the same expression of vague but benevolent approval.

As they leaned there a girlish voice echoed up gaily from the stairs leading to the court below. "Well, come along, then," it cried, not to them but to an invisible companion, "and let's leave the young things to their knitting" and a voice as fresh laughed back: "Oh, look here, Babs, not actually *knitting*—" "Well, I mean figuratively," rejoined the first. "After all, we haven't left our poor parents much else to do . . . " and at that point the turn of the stairs engulfed the dialogue.

The two ladies looked at each other again, this time with a tinge of smiling embarrassment, and the smaller and paler one shook her head and colored slightly.

"Barbara!" she murmured, sending an unheard rebuke after the mocking voice in the stairway.

The other lady, who was fuller, and higher in color, with a small determined nose supported by vigorous black eyebrows, gave a good-humored laugh. "That's what our daughters think of us!"   5

Her companion replied by a deprecating gesture. "Not of us individually. We must remember that. It's just the collective modern idea of Mothers. And you see—" Half guiltily she drew from her handsomely mounted black hand-bag a twist of crimson silk run through by two fine knitting needles. "One never knows," she murmured. "The new system has certainly given us a good deal of time to kill; and sometimes I get tired just looking—even at this." Her gesture was now addressed to the stupendous scene at their feet.

The dark lady laughed again, and they both relapsed upon the view, contemplating it in silence, with a sort of diffused serenity which might have been borrowed from the spring effulgence of the Roman skies. The luncheon-hour was long past, and the two had their end of the vast terrace to themselves. At its opposite extremity a few groups, detained by a lingering look at the outspread city, were gathering up guide-books and fumbling for tips. The last of them scattered, and the two ladies were alone on the air-washed height.

"Well, I don't see why we shouldn't just stay here," said Mrs. Slade, the lady of the high color and energetic brows. Two derelict basket-chairs stood near, and she pushed them into the angle of the parapet, and settled herself in one, her gaze upon the Palatine. "After all, it's still the most beautiful view in the world."

"It always will be, to me," assented her friend Mrs. Ansley, with so slight a stress on the "me" that Mrs. Slade, though she noticed it, wondered if it were not merely accidental, like the random underlinings of old-fashioned letter-writers.

"Grace Ansley was always old-fashioned," she thought; and added aloud, 10 with a retrospective smile: "It's a view we've both been familiar with for a good many years. When we first met here we were younger than our girls are now. You remember?"

"Oh, yes, I remember," murmured Mrs. Ansley, with the same undefinable stress—"There's that head-waiter wondering," she interpolated. She was evidently far less sure than her companion of herself and of her rights in the world.

"I'll cure him of wondering," said Mrs. Slade, stretching her hand toward a bag as discreetly opulent-looking as Mrs. Ansley's. Signing to the head-waiter, she explained that she and her friend were old lovers of Rome, and would like to spend the end of the afternoon looking down on the view—that is, if it did not disturb the service? The head-waiter, bowing over her gratuity, assured her that the ladies were most welcome, and would be still more so if they would condescend to remain for dinner. A full moon night, they would remember . . .

Mrs. Slade's black brows drew together, as though references to the moon were out-of-place and even unwelcome. But she smiled away her frown as the head-waiter retreated. "Well, why not? We might do worse. There's no knowing, I suppose, when the girls will be back. Do you even know back from *where*? I don't!"

Mrs. Ansley again colored slightly. "I think those young Italian aviators we met at the Embassy invited them to fly to Tarquinia for tea. I suppose they'll want to wait and fly back by moonlight."

"Moonlight—moonlight! What a part it still plays. Do you suppose they're 15 as sentimental as we were?"

"I've come to the conclusion that I don't in the least know what they are," said Mrs. Ansley. "And perhaps we didn't know much more about each other."

"No; perhaps we didn't."

Her friend gave her a shy glance. "I never should have supposed you were sentimental, Alida."

"Well, perhaps I wasn't." Mrs. Slade drew her lids together in retrospect; and for a few moments the two ladies, who had been intimate since childhood, reflected how little they knew each other. Each one, of course, had a label ready to attach to the other's name; Mrs. Delphin Slade, for instance, would have told herself, or any one who asked her, that Mrs. Horace Ansley, twenty-five years ago, had been exquisitely lovely—no, you wouldn't believe it, would you? . . . though, of course, still charming, distinguished . . . Well, as a girl she had been exquisite; far more beautiful than her daughter

Barbara, though certainly Babs, according to the new standards at any rate, was more effective—had more *edge,* as they say. Funny where she got it, with those two nullities as parents. Yes; Horace Ansley was—well, just the duplicate of his wife. Museum specimens of old New York. Good-looking, irreproachable, exemplary. Mrs. Slade and Mrs. Ansley had lived opposite each other—actually as well as figuratively—for years. When the drawing-room curtains in No. 20 East 73rd Street were renewed, No. 23, across the way, was always aware of it. And of all the movings, buyings, travels, anniversaries, illnesses—the tame chronicle of an estimable pair. Little of it escaped Mrs. Slade. But she had grown bored with it by the time her husband made his big *coup* in Wall Street, and when they bought in upper Park Avenue had already begun to think: "I'd rather live opposite a speak-easy for a change; at least one might see it raided." The idea of seeing Grace raided was so amusing that (before the move) she launched it at a woman's lunch. It made a hit, and went the rounds—she sometimes wondered if it had crossed the street, and reached Mrs. Ansley. She hoped not, but didn't much mind. Those were the days when respectability was at a discount, and it did the irreproachable no harm to laugh at them a little.

A few years later, and not many months apart, both ladies lost their husbands. There was an appropriate exchange of wreaths and condolences, and a brief renewal of intimacy in the half-shadow of their mourning; and now, after another interval, they had run across each other in Rome, at the same hotel, each of them the modest appendage of a salient daughter. The similarity of their lot had again drawn them together, lending itself to mild jokes, and the mutual confession that, if in old days it must have been tiring to "keep up" with daughters, it was now, at times, a little dull not to. [20]

No doubt, Mrs. Slade reflected, she felt her unemployment more than poor Grace ever would. It was a big drop from being the wife of Delphin Slade to being his widow. She had always regarded herself (with a certain conjugal pride) as his equal in social gifts, as contributing her full share to the making of the exceptional couple they were: but the difference after his death was irremediable. As the wife of the famous corporation lawyer, always with an international case or two on hand, every day brought its exciting and unexpected obligation: the impromptu entertaining of eminent colleagues from abroad, the hurried dashes on legal business to London, Paris or Rome, where the entertaining was so handsomely reciprocated; the amusement of hearing in her wake: "What, that handsome woman with the good clothes and the eyes is Mrs. Slade—*the* Slade's wife? Really? Generally the wives of celebrities are such frumps."

Yes; being *the* Slade's widow was a dullish business after that. In living up to such a husband all her faculties had been engaged; now she had only her daughter to live up to, for the son who seemed to have inherited his father's gifts had died suddenly in boyhood. She had fought through that agony because her husband was there, to be helped and to help; now, after the father's death, the thought of the boy had become unbearable. There was nothing left but to mother her daughter; and dear Jenny was such a perfect daughter that she needed no excessive mothering. "Now with Babs Ansley I don't know that I *should* be so quiet," Mrs. Slade sometimes half-enviously reflected; but Jenny, who was younger than her brilliant friend, was that rare accident, an extremely pretty girl who somehow made youth and prettiness seem as safe as their absence. It was all perplexing—and to Mrs. Slade a little boring. She wished that Jenny would fall in love—with the wrong man, even; that she might have to be watched, out-manœuvred, rescued. And instead, it was Jenny who watched her mother, kept her out of draughts, made sure that she had taken her tonic. . .

Mrs. Ansley was much less articulate than her friend, and her mental portrait of Mrs. Slade was slighter, and drawn with fainter touches. "Alida Slade's awfully brilliant; but not as brilliant as she thinks," would have summed it up; though she would have added, for the enlightenment of strangers, that Mrs. Slade had been an extremely dashing girl; much more so than her daughter, who was pretty, of course, and clever in a way, but had none of her mother's—well, "vividness," some one had once called it. Mrs. Ansley would take up current words like this, and cite them in quotation marks, as unheard-of audacities. No; Jenny was not like her mother. Sometimes Mrs. Ansley thought Alida Slade was disappointed; on the whole she had had a sad life. Full of failures and mistakes; Mrs. Ansley had always been rather sorry for her . . .

So these two ladies visualized each other, each through the wrong end of her little telescope.

II

For a long time they continued to sit side by side without speaking. It seemed as though, to both, there was a relief in laying down their somewhat futile activities in the presence of the vast Memento Mori which faced them. Mrs. Slade sat quite still, her eyes fixed on the golden slope of the Palace of the Caesars, and after a while Mrs. Ansley ceased to fidget with her bag, and she too sank into meditation. Like many intimate friends, the two ladies had never before had occasion to be silent together, and Mrs. Ansley was slightly embarrassed by what seemed, after so many years, a new stage in their intimacy, and one with which she did not yet know how to deal.

Suddenly the air was full of that deep clangor of bells which periodically covers Rome with a roof of silver. Mrs. Slade glanced at her wristwatch. "Five o'clock already," she said, as though surprised.

Mrs. Ansley suggested interrogatively: "There's bridge at the Embassy at five." For a long time Mrs. Slade did not answer. She appeared to be lost in contemplation, and Mrs. Ansley thought the remark had escaped her. But after a while she said, as if speaking out of a dream: "Bridge, did you say? Not unless you want to . . . But I don't think I will, you know."

"Oh, no," Mrs. Ansley hastened to assure her. "I don't care to at all. It's so lovely here; and so full of old memories, as you say." She settled herself in her chair, and almost furtively drew forth her knitting. Mrs. Slade took sideway note of this activity, but her own beautifully cared for hands remained motionless on her knee.

"I was just thinking," she said slowly, "what different things Rome stands for to each generation of travelers. To our grandmothers, Roman fever; to

25

our mothers, sentimental danger—how we used to be guarded!—to our daughters, no more dangers than the middle of Main Street. They don't know it—but how much they're missing!"

The long golden light was beginning to pale, and Mrs. Ansley lifted her   30 knitting a little closer to her eyes. "Yes; how we were guarded!"

"I always used to think," Mrs. Slade continued, "that our mothers had a much more difficult job than our grandmothers. When Roman fever stalked the streets it must have been comparatively easy to gather in the girls at the danger hour; but when you and I were young, with such beauty calling us, and the spice of disobedience thrown in, and no worse risk than catching cold during the cool hour after sunset, the mothers used to be put to it to keep us in—didn't they?"

She turned again toward Mrs. Ansley, but the latter had reached a delicate point in her knitting. "One, two, three—slip two; yes, they must have been," she assented, without looking up.

Mrs. Slade's eyes rested on her with a deepened attention. "She can knit—in the face of *this!* How like her . . ."

Mrs. Slade leaned back, brooding, her eyes ranging from the ruins which faced her to the long green hollow of the Forum, the fading glow of the church fronts beyond it, and the outlying immensity of the Colosseum. Suddenly she thought: "It's all very well to say that our girls have done away with sentiment and moonlight. But if Babs Ansley isn't out to catch that young aviator—the one who's a Marchese—then I don't know anything. And Jenny has no chance beside her. I know that too. I wonder if that's why Grace Ansley likes the two girls to go everywhere together? My poor Jenny as a foil—!" Mrs. Slade gave a hardly audible laugh, and at the sound Mrs. Ansley dropped her knitting.

"Yes—?"   35

"I—oh, nothing. I was only thinking how your Babs carries everything before her. That Campolieri boy is one of the best matches in Rome. Don't look so innocent, my dear—you know he is. And I was wondering, ever so respectfully, you understand . . . wondering how two such exemplary characters as you and Horace had managed to produce anything quite so dynamic." Mrs. Slade laughed again, with a touch of asperity.

Mrs. Ansley's hands lay inert across her needles. She looked straight out at the great accumulated wreckage of passion and splendor at her feet. But her small profile was almost expressionless. At length she said: "I think you overrate Babs, my dear."

Mrs. Slade's tone grew easier. "No; I don't. I appreciate her. And perhaps envy you. Oh, my girl's perfect; if I were a chronic invalid I'd—well, I think I'd rather be in Jenny's hands. There must be times . . . but there! I always wanted a brilliant daughter . . . and never quite understood why I got an angel instead."

Mrs. Ansley echoed her laugh in a faint murmur. "Babs is an angel too."

"Of course—of course! But she's got rainbow wings. Well, they're wan-   40 dering by the sea with their young men; and here we sit . . . and it all brings back the past a little too acutely."

Mrs. Ansley had resumed her knitting. One might almost have imagined (if one had known her less well, Mrs. Slade reflected) that, for her also, too many memories rose from the lengthening shadows of those august ruins. But no; she was simply absorbed in her work. What was there for her to worry about? She knew that Babs would almost certainly come back engaged to the extremely eligible Campolieri. "And she'll sell the New York house, and settle down near them in Rome, and never be in their way . . . she's much too tactful. But she'll have an excellent cook, and just the right people in for bridge and cocktails . . . and a perfectly peaceful old age among her grandchildren."

Mrs. Slade broke off this prophetic flight with a recoil of self-disgust. There was no one of whom she had less right to think unkindly than of Grace Ansley. Would she never cure herself of envying her? Perhaps she had begun too long ago.

She stood up and leaned against the parapet, filling her troubled eyes with the tranquilizing magic of the hour. But instead of tranquilizing her the sight seemed to increase her exasperation. Her gaze turned toward the Colosseum. Already its golden flank was drowned in purple shadow, and above it the sky curved crystal clear, without light or color. It was the moment when afternoon and evening hang balanced in mid-heaven.

Mrs. Slade turned back and laid her hand on her friend's arm. The gesture was so abrupt that Mrs. Ansley looked up, startled.

"The sun's set. You're not afraid, my dear?"   45

"Afraid—?"

"Of Roman fever or pneumonia? I remember how ill you were that winter. As a girl you had a very delicate throat, hadn't you?"

"Oh, we're all right up here. Down below, in the Forum, it does get deathly cold, all of a sudden . . . but not here."

"Ah, of course you know because you had to be so careful." Mrs. Slade turned back to the parapet. She thought: "I must make one more effort not to hate her." Aloud she said: "Whenever I look at the Forum from up here I remember that story about a great-aunt of yours, wasn't she? A dreadfully wicked great-aunt?"

"Oh yes; Great-aunt Harriet. The one who was supposed to have sent her   50 young sister out to the Forum after sunset to gather a night-blooming flower for her album. All our great-aunts and grandmothers used to have albums of dried flowers."

Mrs. Slade nodded. "But she really sent her because they were in love with the same man—"

"Well, that was the family tradition. They said Aunt Harriet confessed it years afterward. At any rate, the poor little sister caught the fever and died. Mother used to frighten us with the story when we were children."

"And you frightened *me* with it, that winter when you and I were here as girls. The winter I was engaged to Delphin."

Mrs. Ansley gave a faint laugh. "Oh, did I? Really frightened you? I don't believe you're easily frightened."

"Not often; but I was then. I was easily frightened because I was too   55 happy. I wonder if you know what that means?"

"I—yes . . . " Mrs. Ansley faltered.

"Well, I suppose that was why the story of your wicked aunt made such an impression on me. And I thought: 'There's no more Roman fever, but the

Forum is deathly cold after sunset—especially after a hot day. And the Colosseum's even colder and damper.' "

"The Colosseum—?"

"Yes. It wasn't easy to get in, after the gates were locked for the night. Far from easy. Still, in those days it could be managed; it was managed, often. Lovers met there who couldn't meet elsewhere. You knew that?"

"I—I daresay. I don't remember."   60

"You don't remember? You don't remember going to visit some ruins or other one evening, just after dark, and catching a bad chill? You were supposed to have gone to see the moon rise. People always said that expedition was what caused your illness."

There was a moment's silence; then Mrs. Ansley rejoined: "Did they? It was all so long ago."

"Yes. And you got well again—so it didn't matter. But I suppose it struck your friend—the reason given for your illness, I mean—because everybody knew you were so prudent on account of your throat, and your mother took such care of you . . . You *had* been out late sight-seeing, hadn't you, that night?"

"Perhaps I had. The most prudent girls aren't always prudent. What made you think of it now?"

Mrs. Slade seemed to have no answer ready. But after a moment she   65
broke out: "Because I simply can't bear it any longer—!"

Mrs. Ansley lifted her head quickly. Her eyes were wide and very pale. "Can't bear what?"

"Why—your not knowing that I've always known why you went."

"Why I went—?"

"Yes. You think I'm bluffing, don't you? Well, you went to meet the man I was engaged to—and I can repeat every word of the letter that took you there."

While Mrs. Slade spoke Mrs. Ansley had risen unsteadily to her feet. Her   70
bag, her knitting and gloves, slid in a panic-stricken heap to the ground. She looked at Mrs. Slade as though she were looking at a ghost.

"No, no—don't," she faltered out.

"Why not? Listen, if you don't believe me. 'My one darling, things can't go on like this. I must see you alone. Come to the Colosseum immediately after dark tomorrow. There will be somebody to let you in. No one whom you need fear will suspect'—but perhaps you've forgotten what the letter said?"

Mrs. Ansley met the challenge with an unexpected composure. Steadying herself against the chair she looked at her friend, and replied: "No; I know it by heart too."

"And the signature? 'Only *your* D.S.' Was that it? I'm right, am I? That was the letter that took you out that evening after dark?"

Mrs. Ansley was still looking at her. It seemed to Mrs. Slade that a slow   75
struggle was going on behind the voluntarily controlled mask of her small quiet face. "I shouldn't have thought she had herself so well in hand," Mrs. Slade reflected, almost resentfully. But at this moment Mrs. Ansley spoke, "I don't know how you knew. I burnt that letter at once."

"Yes; you would, naturally—you're so prudent!" The sneer was open now. "And if you burnt the letter you're wondering how on earth I know what was in it. That's it, isn't it?"

Mrs. Slade waited, but Mrs. Ansley did not speak.

"Well, my dear, I know what was in that letter because I wrote it!"

"You wrote it?"

"Yes."　　　　　　　　　　　　　　　　　　　　　　　　　　　　　80

The two women stood for a minute staring at each other in the last golden light. Then Mrs. Ansley dropped back into her chair. "Oh," she murmured, and covered her face with her hands.

Mrs. Slade waited nervously for another word or movement. None came, and at length she broke out: "I horrify you."

Mrs. Ansley's hands dropped to her knee. The face they uncovered was streaked with tears. "I wasn't thinking of you. I was thinking—it was the only letter I ever had from him!"

"And I wrote it. Yes; I wrote it! But I was the girl he was engaged to. Did you happen to remember that?"

Mrs. Ansley's head dropped again. "I'm not trying to excuse myself . . . I　85 remembered . . . "

"And still you went?"

"Still I went."

Mrs. Slade stood looking down on the small bowed figure at her side. The flame of her wrath had already sunk, and she wondered why she had ever thought there would be any satisfaction in inflicting so purposeless a wound on her friend. But she had to justify herself.

"You do understand? I'd found out—and I hated you, hated you. I knew you were in love with Delphin—and I was afraid; afraid of you, of your quiet ways, your sweetness . . . your . . . well, I wanted you out of the way, that's all. Just for a few weeks; just till I was sure of him. So in a blind fury I wrote that letter . . . I don't know why I'm telling you now."

"I suppose," said Mrs. Ansley slowly, "it's because you've always gone on　90 hating me."

"Perhaps. Or because I wanted to get the whole thing off my mind." She paused. "I'm glad you destroyed the letter. Of course I never thought you'd die."

Mrs. Ansley relapsed into silence, and Mrs. Slade, leaning above her, was conscious of a strange sense of isolation, of being cut off from the warm current of human communion. "You think me a monster!"

"I don't know . . . It was the only letter I had, and you say he didn't write it?"

"Ah, how you care for him still!"

"I cared for that memory," said Mrs. Ansley.　　　　　　　　　　95

Mrs. Slade continued to look down on her. She seemed physically reduced by the blow—as if, when she got up, the wind might scatter her like a puff of dust. Mrs. Slade's jealousy suddenly leapt up again at the sight. All these years the woman had been living on that letter. How she must have loved him, to treasure the mere memory of its ashes! The letter of the man her friend was engaged to. Wasn't it she who was the monster?

"You tried your best to get him away from me, didn't you? But you failed; and I kept him. That's all."

"Yes. That's all."

"I wish now I hadn't told you. I'd no idea you'd feel about it as you do; I thought you'd be amused. It all happened so long ago, as you say; and you must do me the justice to remember that I had no reason to think you'd ever taken it seriously. How could I, when you were married to Horace Ansley two months afterward? As soon as you could get out of bed your mother rushed you off to Florence and married you. People were rather surprised—they wondered at its being done so quickly; but I thought I knew. I had an idea you did it out of *pique*—to be able to say you'd got ahead of Delphin and me. Girls have such silly reasons for doing the most serious things. And your marrying so soon convinced me that you'd never really cared."

"Yes, I suppose it would," Mrs. Ansley assented.   100

The clear heaven overhead was emptied of all its gold. Dusk spread over it, abruptly darkening the Seven Hills. Here and there lights began to twinkle through the foliage at their feet. Steps were coming and going on the deserted terrace—waiters looking out of the doorway at the head of the stairs, then reappearing with trays and napkins and flasks of wine. Tables were moved, chairs straightened. A feeble string of electric lights flickered out. Some vases of faded flowers were carried away, and brought back replenished. A stout lady in a dust-coat suddenly appeared, asking in broken Italian if any one had seen the elastic band which held together her tattered Baedeker. She poked with her stick under the table at which she had lunched, the waiters assisting.

The corner where Mrs. Slade and Mrs. Ansley sat was still shadowy and deserted. For a long time neither of them spoke. At length Mrs. Slade began again: "I suppose I did it as a sort of joke—"

"A joke?"

"Well, girls are ferocious sometimes, you know. Girls in love especially. And I remember laughing to myself all that evening at the idea that you were waiting around there in the dark, dodging out of sight, listening for every sound, trying to get in—Of course I was upset when I heard you were so ill afterward."

Mrs. Ansley had not moved for a long time. But now she turned slowly 105 toward her companion. "But I didn't wait. He'd arranged everything. He was there. We were let in at once," she said.

Mrs. Slade sprang up from her leaning position. "Delphin there? They let you in?—Ah, now you're lying!" she burst out with violence.

Mrs. Ansley's voice grew clearer, and full of surprise. "But of course he was there. Naturally he came—"

"Came? How did he know he'd find you there? You must be raving!"

Mrs. Ansley hesitated, as though reflecting. "But I answered the letter. I told him I'd be there. So he came."

Mrs. Slade flung her hands up to her face. "Oh, God—you answered! I 110 never thought of your answering . . . "

"It's odd you never thought of it, if you wrote the letter."

"Yes. I was blind with rage."

much English, he seems to have done well. Once upon a time he worked for the railways in Chengdu, Szechwan Province, and during the Wuchang Uprising, he was shot at. When I'm down, when I'm lonely for my husband, when I think of our son, or when I need to be held, I think of Charity's uncle. If I hadn't left home, I'd never have heard of the Wuchang Uprising. I've broadened my horizons.

Very late that night my husband calls me from Ahmadabad, a town of textile mills north of Bombay. My husband is a vice president at Lakshmi Cotton Mills. Lakshmi is the goddess of wealth, but LCM (Priv.), Ltd., is doing poorly. Lockouts, strikes, rock-throwings. My husband lives on digitalis, which he calls the food for our *yuga* of discontent.

"We had a bad mishap at the mill today." Then he says nothing for 　50
seconds.

The operator comes on. "Do you have the right party, sir? We're trying to reach Mrs. Butt."

"Bhatt," I insist. "*B* for Bombay, *H* for Haryana, *A* for Ahmadabad, double *T* for Tamil Nadu." It's a litany. "This is she."

"One of our lorries was firebombed today. Resulting in three deaths. The driver, old Karamchand, and his two children."

I know how my husband's eyes look this minute, how the eye rims sag and the yellow corneas shine and bulge with pain. He is not an emotional man—the Ahmadabad Institute of Management has trained him to cut losses, to look on the bright side of economic catastrophes—but tonight he's feeling low. I try to remember a driver named Karamchand, but can't. That part of my life is over, the way *trucks* have replaced *lorries* in my vocabulary, the way Charity Chin and her lurid love life have replaced inherited notions of marital duty. Tomorrow he'll come out of it. Soon he'll be eating again. He'll sleep like a baby. He's been trained to believe in turnovers. Every morning he rubs his scalp with cantharidine oil so his hair will grow back again.

"It could be your car next." Affection, love. Who can tell the difference 　55
in a traditional marriage in which a wife still doesn't call her husband by his first name?

"No. They know I'm a flunky, just like them. Well paid, maybe. No need for undue anxiety, please."

Then his voice breaks. He says he needs me, he misses me, he wants me to come to him damp from my evening shower, smelling of sandalwood soap, my braid decorated with jasmines.

"I need you too."

"Not to worry, please," he says. "I am coming in a fortnight's time. I have already made arrangements."

Outside my window, fire trucks whine, up Eighth Avenue. I wonder if he 　60
can hear them, what he thinks of a life like mine, led amid disorder.

"I am thinking it'll be like a honeymoon. More or less."

When I was in college, waiting to be married, I imagined honeymoons were only for the more fashionable girls, the girls who came from slightly racy families, smoked Sobranies in the dorm lavatories and put up posters of Kabir Bedi, who was supposed to have made it as a big star in the West.

My husband wants us to go to Niagara. I'm not to worry about foreign exchange. He's arranged for extra dollars through the Gujarati Network, with a cousin in San Jose. And he's bought four hundred more on the black market. "Tell me you need me. Panna, please tell me again."

I change out of the cotton pants and shirt I've been wearing all day and put on a sari to meet my husband at JFK. I don't forget the jewelry; the marriage necklace of *mangalsutra,* gold drop earrings, heavy gold bangles. I don't wear them every day. In this borough of vice and greed, who knows when, or whom, desire will overwhelm.

My husband spots me in the crowd and waves. He has lost weight, and changed his glasses. The arm, uplifted in a cheery wave, is bony, frail, almost opalescent.

In the Carey Coach, we hold hands. He strokes my fingers one by one.   65
"How come you aren't wearing my mother's ring?"

"Because muggers know about Indian women," I say. They know with us it's 24-karat. His mother's ring is showy, in ghastly taste anywhere but India: a blood-red Burma ruby set in a gold frame of floral sprays. My mother-in-law got her guru to bless the ring before I left for the States.

He looks disconcerted. He's used to a different role. He's the knowing, suspicious one in the family. He seems to be sulking, and finally he comes out with it. "You've said nothing about my new glasses." I compliment him on the glasses, how chic and Western-executive they make him look. But I can't help the other things, necessities until he learns the ropes. I handle the money, buy the tickets. I don't know if this makes me unhappy.

Charity drives her Nissan upstate, so for two weeks we are to have the apartment to ourselves. This is more privacy than we ever had in India. No parents, no servants, to keep us modest. We play at housekeeping. Imre has lent us a hibachi, and I grill saffron chicken breasts. My husband marvels at the size of the Perdue hens. "They're big like peacocks, no? These Americans, they're really something!" He tries out pizzas, burgers, McNuggets. He chews. He explores. He judges. He loves it all, fears nothing, feels at home in the summer odors, the clutter of Manhattan streets. Since he thinks that the American palate is bland, he carries a bottle of red peppers in his pocket. I wheel a shopping cart down the aisles of the neighborhood Grand Union, and he follows, swiftly, greedily. He picks up hair rinses and high-protein diet powders. There's so much I already take for granted.

One night, Imre stops by. He wants us to go with him to a movie. In his work shirt and red leather tie, he looks arty or strung out. It's only been a week, but I feel as though I am really seeing him for the first time. The yellow hair worn very short at the sides, the wide, narrow lips. He's a good-looking man, but self-conscious, almost arrogant. He's picked the movie we should see. He always tells me what to see, what to read. He buys the *Voice.* He's a natural avant-gardist. For tonight he's chosen *Numéro Deux.*

"Is it a musical?" my husband asks. The Radio City Music Hall is on his   70
list of sights to see. He's read up on the history of the Rockettes. He doesn't catch Imre's sympathetic wink.

Guilt, shame, loyalty. I long to be ungracious, not ingratiate myself with both men.

That night my husband calculates in rupees the money we've wasted on Godard. "That refugee fellow, Nagy, must have a screw loose in his head. I paid very steep price for dollars on the black market."

Some afternoons we go shopping. Back home we hated shopping; but now it is a lovers' project. My husband's shopping list startles me. I feel I am just getting to know him. Maybe, like Imre, freed from the dignities of old-world culture, he too could get drunk and squirt Cheez Whiz on a guest. I watch him dart into stores in his gleaming leather shoes. Jockey shorts on sale in outdoor bins on Broadway entrance him. White tube socks with different bands of color delight him. He looks for microcassettes, for anything small and electronic and smuggleable. He needs a garment bag. He calls it a "wardrobe," and I have to translate.

"All of New York is having sales, no?"

My heart speeds watching him this happy. It's the third week in August,   75
almost the end of summer, and the city smells ripe, it cannot bear more heat, more money, more energy.

"This is so smashing! The prices are so excellent!" Recklessly, my prudent husband signs away traveller's checks. How he intends to smuggle it all back I don't dare ask. With a microwave, he calculates, we could get rid of our cook.

This has to be love, I think. Charity, Eric, Phil: they may be experts on sex. My husband doesn't chase me around the sofa, but he pushes me down on Charity's battered cushions, and the man who has never entered the kitchen of our Ahmadabad house now comes toward me with a dish tub of steamy water to massage away the pavement heat.

Ten days into his vacation my husband checks out brochures for sight-seeing tours. Shortline, Grayline, Crossroads: his new vinyl briefcase is full of schedules and pamphlets. While I make pancakes out of a mix, he comparison-shops. Tour number one costs $10.95 and will give us the World Trade Center, Chinatown, and the United Nations. Tour number three would take us both uptown *and* downtown for $14.95, but my husband is absolutely sure he doesn't want to see Harlem. We settle for tour number four: Downtown and the Dame. It's offered by a new tour company with a small, dirty office at Eighth and Forty-eighth.

The sidewalk outside the office is colorful with tourists. My husband sends me in to buy the tickets because he has come to feel Americans don't understand his accent.

The dark man, Lebanese probably, behind the counter comes on too   80
friendly. "Come on, doll, make my day!" He won't say which tour is his. "Number four? Honey, no! Look, you've wrecked me! Say you'll change your mind." He takes two twenties and gives back change. He holds the tickets, forcing me to pull. He leans closer. "I'm off after lunch."

My husband must have been watching me from the sidewalk. "What was the chap saying?" he demands. "I told you not to wear pants. He thinks you are Puerto Rican. He thinks he can treat you with disrespect."

The bus is crowded and we have to sit across the aisle from each other. The tour guide begins his patter on Forty-sixth. He looks like an actor, his hair bleached and blow-dried. Up close he must look middle-aged, but from where I sit his skin is smooth and his cheeks faintly red.

"Welcome to the Big Apple, folks." The guide uses a microphone. "Big Apple. That's what we native Manhattan degenerates call our city. Today we have guests from fifteen foreign countries and six states from this U. S. of A. That makes the Tourist Bureau real happy. And let me assure you that while we may be the richest city in the richest country in the world, it's okay to tip your charming and talented attendant." He laughs. Then he swings his hip out into the aisle and sings a song.

"And it's mighty fancy on old Delancey Street, you know . . . "

My husband looks irritable. The guide is, as expected, a good singer.   85
"The bloody man should be giving us histories of buildings we are passing, no?" I pat his hand, the mood passes. He cranes his neck. Our window seats have both gone to Japanese. It's the tour of his life. Next to this, the quick business trips to Manchester and Glasgow pale.

"And tell me what street compares to Mott Street, in July . . . "

The guide wants applause. He manages a derisive laugh from the Americans up front. He's working the aisles now. "I coulda been somebody, right? I coulda been a star!" Two or three of us smile, those of us who recognize the parody. He catches my smile. The sun is on his harsh, bleached hair. "Right, your highness? Look, we gotta maharani with us! Couldn't I have been a star?"

"Right!" I say, my voice coming out a squeal. I've been trained to adapt; what else can I say?

We drive through traffic past landmark office buildings and churches. The guide flips his hands. "Art deco," he keeps saying. I hear him confide to one of the Americans: "Beats me. I went to a cheap guide's school." My husband wants to know more about this Art Deco, but the guide sings another song.

"We made a foolish choice," my husband grumbles. "We are sitting in the   90
bus only. We're not going into famous buildings." He scrutinizes the pamphlets in his jacket pocket. I think, at least it's air-conditioned in here. I could sit here in the cool shadows of the city forever.

Only five of us appear to have opted for the "Downtown and the Dame" tour. The others will ride back uptown past the United Nations after we've been dropped off at the pier for the ferry to the Statue of Liberty.

An elderly European pulls a camera out of his wife's designer tote bag. He takes pictures of the boats in the harbor, the Japanese in kimonos eating popcorn, scavenging pigeons, me. Then, pushing his wife ahead of him, he climbs back on the bus and waves to us. For a second I feel terribly lost. I wish we were on the bus going back to the apartment. I know I'll not be able to describe any of this to Charity, or to Imre. I'm too proud to admit I went on a guided tour.

The view of the city from the Circle Line ferry is seductive, unreal. The skyline wavers out of reach, but never quite vanishes. The summer sun pushes through fluffy clouds and dapples the glass of office towers. My husband looks thrilled, even more than he had on the shopping trips down Broadway. Tourists and dreamers, we have spent our life's savings to see this skyline, this statue.

"Quick, take a picture of me!" my husband yells as he moves toward a gap of railings. A Japanese matron has given up her position in order to change film. "Before the Twin Towers disappear!"

I focus, I wait for a large Oriental family to walk out of my range. My   95 husband holds his pose tight against the railing. He wants to look relaxed, an international businessman at home in all the financial markets.

A bearded man slides across the bench toward me. "Like this," he says and helps me get my husband in focus. "You want me to take the photo for you?" His name, he says, Is Goran. He is Goran from Yugoslavia, as though that were enough for tracking him down. Imre from Hungary. Panna from India. He pulls the old Leica out of my hand, signaling the Orientals to beat it, and clicks away. "I'm a photographer," he says. He could have been a camera thief. That's what my husband would have assumed. Somehow, I trusted. "Get you a beer?" he asks.

"I don't. Drink, I mean. Thank you very much." I say those last words very loud, for everyone's benefit. The odd bottles of Soave with Imre don't count.

"Too bad." Goran gives back the camera.

"Take one more!" my husband shouts from the railing. "Just to be sure!"

The island itself disappoints. The Lady has brutal scaffolding holding her   100 in. The museum is closed. The snack bar is dirty and expensive. My husband reads out the prices to me. He orders two french fries and two Cokes. We sit at picnic tables and wait for the ferry to take us back.

"What was that hippie chap saying?"

As if I could say. A day-care center has brought its kids, at least forty of them, to the island for the day. The kids, all wearing name tags, run around us. I can't help noticing how many are Indian. Even a Patel, probably a Bhatt if I looked hard enough. They toss hamburger bits at pigeons. They kick styrofoam cups. The pigeons are slow, greedy, persistent. I have to shoo one off the table top. I don't think my husband thinks about our son.

"What hippie?"

"The one on the boat. With the beard and the hair."

My husband doesn't look at me. He shakes out his paper napkin and tries   105 to protect his french fries from pigeon feathers.

"Oh, him. He said he was from Dubrovnik." It isn't true, but I don't want trouble.

"What did he say about Dubrovnik?"

I know enough about Dubrovnik to get by. Imre's told me about it. And about Mostar and Zagreb. In Mostar white Muslims sing the call to prayer. I would like to see that before I die: white Muslims. Whole peoples have moved before me; they've adapted. The night Imre told me about Mostar was also the night I saw my first snow in Manhattan. We'd walked down to Chelsea from Columbia. We'd walked and talked and I hadn't felt tired at all.

"You're too innocent," my husband says. He reaches for my hand. "Panna," he cries with pain in his voice, and I am brought back from perfect, floating memories of snow, "I've come to take you back. I have seen how men watch you."

"What?"   110

"Come back, now. I have tickets. We have all the things we will ever need. I can't live without you."

A little girl with wiry braids kicks a bottle cap at his shoes. The pigeons wheel and scuttle around us. My husband covers his fries with spread-out fingers. "No kicking," he tells the girl. Her name, Beulah, is printed in green ink on a heart-shaped name tag. He forces a smile, and Beulah smiles back. Then she starts to flap her arms. She flaps, she hops. The pigeons go crazy for fries and scraps.

"Special ed. course is two years," I remind him. "I can't go back."

My husband picks up our trays and throws them into the garbage before I can stop him. He's carried disposability a little too far. "We've been taken," he says, moving toward the dock, though the ferry will not arrive for another twenty minutes. "The ferry costs only two dollars round-trip per person. We should have chosen tour number one for $10.95 instead of tour number four for $14.95."

With my Lebanese friend, I think. "But this way we don't have to worry 115 about cabs. The bus will pick us up at the pier and take us back to midtown. Then we can walk home."

"New York is full of cheats and whatnot. Just like Bombay." He is not accusing me of infidelity. I feel dread all the same.

That night, after we've gone to bed, the phone rings. My husband listens, then hands the phone to me. "What is this woman saying?" He turns on the pink Macy's lamp by the bed. "I am not understanding these Negro people's accents."

The operator repeats the message. It's a cable from one of the directors of Lakshmi Cotton Mills. "Massive violent labor confrontation anticipated. Stop. Return posthaste. Stop. Cable flight details. Signed Kantilal Shah."

"It's not your factory," I say. "You're supposed to be on vacation."

"So, you are worrying about me? Yes? You reject my heartfelt wishes but 120 you worry about me?" He pulls me close, slips the straps of my nightdress off my shoulder. "Wait a minute."

I wait, unclothed, for my husband to come back to me. The water is running in the bathroom. In the ten days he has been here he has learned American rites: deodorants, fragrances. Tomorrow morning he'll call Air India; tomorrow evening he'll be on his way back to Bombay. Tonight I should make up to him for my years away, the gutted trucks, the degree I'll never use in India. I want to pretend with him that nothing has changed.

In the mirror that hangs on the bathroom door, I watch my naked body turn, the breasts, the thighs glow. The body's beauty amazes. I stand here shameless, in ways he has never seen me. I am free, afloat, watching somebody else.

Leslie Marmon Silko   *(born 1948)*

Leslie Marmon Silko grew up on the Laguna Pueblo reservation near Albuquerque, New Mexico. As with other Americans of the Southwest, Native American, Mexican, and Anglo strands meet in her ethnic heritage. She became a college teacher and widely known author, becoming known especially for her novel *Ceremony* (1977). In the spiritual lives of Silko's characters, Native American traditions and the white man's religion blend in strange and contradictory ways. Characters from the ghost stories and spirit world of traditional storytelling, like the *ka'tsina* in the following story, come into the world of today's reservation life, with its paved roads, trucks, and ranchers eyeing their Native American neighbors with suspicion. In *Storyteller* (1981), Silko brought together a rich collection of folktales, autobiographical anecdotes, and her own poems and stories.

Yellow Woman   *1974*

I

My thigh clung to his with dampness, and I watched the sun rising up through the tamaracks and willows. The small brown water birds came to the river and hopped across the mud, leaving brown scratches in the alkali-white crust. They bathed in the river silently. I could hear the water, almost at our feet where the narrow fast channel bubbled and washed green ragged moss and fern leaves. I looked at him beside me, rolled in the red blanket on the white river sand. I cleaned the sand out of the cracks between my toes, squinting because the sun was above the willow trees. I looked at him for the last time, sleeping on the white river sand.

I felt hungry and followed the river south the way we had come the afternoon before, following our footprints that were already blurred by the lizard tracks and bug trails. The horses were still lying down, and the black one whinnied when he saw me but he did not get up—maybe it was because the corral was made out of thick cedar branches and the horses had not yet felt the sun like I had. I tried to look beyond the pale red mesas to the pueblo. I knew it was there, even if I could not see it, on the sand rock hill above the river, the same river that moved past me now and had reflected the moon last night.

The horse felt warm underneath me. He shook his head and pawed the sand. The bay whinnied and leaned against the gate trying to follow, and I remembered him asleep in the red blanket beside the river. I slid off the horse and tied him close to the other horse. I walked north with the river again, and the white sand broke loose in footprints over footprints.

"Wake up."

He moved in the blanket and turned his face to me with his eyes still   5
closed. I knelt down to touch him.

"I'm leaving."

He smiled now, eyes still closed. "You are coming with me, remember?" He sat up now with his bare dark chest and belly in the sun.

"Where?"

"To my place."

"And will I come back?"   10

He pulled his pants on. I walked away from him, feeling him behind me and smelling the willows.

"Yellow Woman," he said.

I turned to face him. "Who are you?" I asked.

He laughed and knelt on the low, sandy bank, washing his face in the river. "Last night you guessed my name, and you knew why I had come."

I stared past him at the shallow moving water and tried to remember the   15
night, but I could only see the moon in the water and remember his warmth around me.

"But I only said that you were him and that I was Yellow Woman—I'm not really her—I have my own name and I come from the pueblo on the other side of the mesa. Your name is Silva and you are a stranger I met by the river yesterday afternoon."

He laughed softly. "What happened yesterday has nothing to do with what you will do today, Yellow Woman."

"I know—that's what I'm saying—the old stories about the ka'tsina spirit and Yellow Woman can't mean us."

My old grandpa liked to tell those stories best. There is one about Badger and Coyote who went hunting and were gone all day, and when the sun was going down they found a house. There was a girl living there alone, and she had light hair and eyes and she told them that they could sleep with her. Coyote wanted to be with her all night so he sent Badger into a prairie-dog hole, telling him he thought he saw something in it. As soon as Badger crawled in, Coyote blocked up the entrance with rocks and hurried back to Yellow Woman.

"Come here," he said gently.   20

He touched my neck and I moved close to him to feel his breathing and to hear his heart. I was wondering if Yellow Woman had known who she was—if she knew that she would become part of the stories. Maybe she'd had another name that her husband and relatives called her so that only the ka'tsina from the north and the storytellers would know her as Yellow Woman. But I didn't go on; I felt him all around me, pushing me down into the white river sand.

Yellow Woman went away with the spirit from the north and lived with him and his relatives. She was gone for a long time, but then one day she came back and she brought twin boys.

"Do you know the story?"

"What story? He smiled and pulled me close to him as he said this. I was afraid lying there on the red blanket. All I could know was the way he felt, warm, damp, his body beside me. This is the way it happens in the stories, I was thinking, with no thought beyond the moment she meets the ka'tsina spirit and they go.

"I don't have to go. What they tell in stories was real only then, back in   25
time immemorial, like they say."

He stood up and pointed at my clothes tangled in the blanket. "Let's go,"
he said.

I walked beside him, breathing hard because he walked fast, his hand
around my wrist. I had stopped trying to pull away from him, because his
hand felt cool and the sun was high, drying the river bed into alkali. I will
see someone, eventually I will see someone, and then I will be certain that
he is only a man—some man from nearby—and I will be sure that I am not
Yellow Woman. Because she is from out of time past and I live now and
I've been to school and there are highways and pickup trucks that Yellow
Woman never saw.

It was an easy ride north on horseback. I watched the change from the cottonwood trees along the river to the junipers that brushed past us in the foothills, and finally there were only piñons, and when I looked up at the rim
of the mountain plateau I could see pine trees growing on the edge. Once
I stopped to look down, but the pale sandstone had disappeared and the
river was gone and the dark lava hills were all around. He touched my hand,
not speaking, but always singing softly a mountain song and looking into
my eyes.

I felt hungry and wondered what they were doing at home now—my
mother, my grandmother, my husband, and the baby. Cooking breakfast,
saying, "Where did she go?—maybe kidnapped," and Al going to the tribal
police with the details: "She went walking along the river."

The house was made with black lava rock and red mud. It was high   30
above the spreading miles of arroyos and long mesas. I smelled a mountain
smell of pitch and buck brush. I stood there beside the black horse, looking down on the small, dim country we had passed, and I shivered.

"Yellow Woman, come inside where's it's warm."

II

He lit a fire in the stove. It was an old stove with a round belly and an
enamel coffeepot on top. There was only the stove, some faded Navajo
blankets, and a bedroll and cardboard box. The floor was made of smooth
adobe plaster, and there was one small window facing east. He pointed at
the box.

"There's some potatoes and the frying pan." He sat on the floor with his
arms around his knees pulling them close to his chest and he watched me
fry the potatoes. I didn't mind him watching me because he was always
watching me—he had been watching me since I came upon him sitting on
the river bank trimming leaves from a willow twig with his knife. We ate
from the pan and he wiped the grease from his fingers on his Levis.

"Have you brought women here before?" He smiled and kept chewing,
so I said, "Do you always use the same tricks?"

"What tricks?" He looked at me like he didn't understand.   35

"The story about being a ka'tsina from the mountains. The story about
Yellow Woman."

Silva was silent; his face was calm.

"I don't believe it. Those stories couldn't happen now," I said.

He shook his head and said softly, "But someday they will talk about us, and they will say, 'Those two lived long ago when things like that happened.' "

He stood up and went out. I ate the rest of the potatoes and thought about things—about the noise the stove was making and the sound of the mountain wind outside. I remembered yesterday and the day before, and then I went outside. 40

I walked past the corral to the edge where the narrow trail cut through the black rim rock. I was standing in the sky with nothing around me but the wind that came down from the blue mountain peak behind me. I could see faint mountain images in the distance miles across the vast spread of mesas and valleys and plains. I wondered who was over there to feel the mountain wind on those sheer blue edges—who walks on the pine needles in those blue mountains.

"Can you see the pueblo?" Silva was standing behind me.

I shook my head. "We're too far away."

"From here I can see the world." He stepped out on the edge. "The Navajo reservation begins over there." He pointed to the east. "The Pueblo boundaries are over here." He looked below us to the south, where the narrow trail seemed to come from. "The Texans have their ranches over there, starting with that valley, the Concho Valley. The Mexicans run some cattle over there too."

"Do you ever work for them?" 45

"I steal from them," Silva answered. The sun was dropping behind us and shadows were filling the land below. I turned away from the edge that dropped forever into the valleys below.

"I'm cold," I said; "I'm going inside," I started wondering about this man who could speak the Pueblo language so well but who lived on a mountain and rustled cattle. I decided that this man Silva must be Navajo, because Pueblo men didn't do things like that.

"You must be a Navajo."

Silva shook his head gently. "Little Yellow Woman," he said, "you never give up, do you? I have told you who I am. The Navajo people know me, too." He knelt down and unrolled the bedroll and spread the extra blankets out on a piece of canvas. The sun was down, and the only light in the house came from outside—the dim orange light from sundown.

I stood there and waited for him to crawl under the blankets. 50

"What are you waiting for?" he said, and I lay down beside him. He undressed me slowly like the night before beside the river—kissing my face gently and running his hands up and down my belly and legs. He took off my pants and then he laughed.

"Why are you laughing?"

"You are breathing so hard."

I pulled away from him and turned my back to him.

He pulled me around and pinned me down with his arms and chest. 55 "You don't understand, do you, little Yellow Woman? You will do what I want."

And again he was all around me with his skin slippery against mine, and I was afraid because I understood that his strength could hurt me. I lay underneath him and I knew that he could destroy me. But later, while he slept beside me, I touched his face and I had a feeling—the kind of feeling for him that overcame me that morning along the river. I kissed him on the forehead and he reached out for me.

When I woke up in the morning he was gone. It gave me a strange feeling because for a long time I sat there on the blankets and looked around the little house for some object of his—some proof that he had been there or maybe that he was coming back. Only the blankets and the cardboard box remained. The .30-30 that had been leaning in the corner was gone, and so was the knife I had used the night before. He was gone, and I had my chance to go now. But first I had to eat, because I knew it would be a long walk home.

I found some dried apricots in the cardboard box, and I sat down on a rock at the edge of the plateau rim. There was no wind and the sun warmed me. I was surrounded by silence. I drowsed with apricots in my mouth, and I didn't believe that there were highways or railroads or cattle to steal.

When I woke up, I stared down at my feet in the black mountain dirt. Little black ants were swarming over the pine needles around my foot. They must have smelled the apricots. I thought about my family far below me. They would be wondering about me, because this had never happened to me before. The tribal police would file a report. But if old Grandpa weren't dead he would tell them what happened—he would laugh and say, "Stolen by a ka'tsina, a mountain spirit. She'll come home—they usually do." There are enough of them to handle things. My mother and grandmother will raise the baby like they raised me. Al will find someone else, and they will go on like before, except that there will be a story about the day I disappeared while I was walking along the rver. Silva had come for me; he said he had. I did not decide to go. I just went. Moonflowers blossom in the sand hills before dawn, just as I followed him. That's what I was thinking as I wandered along the trail through the pine trees.

It was noon when I got back. When I saw the stone house I remembered   60
that I had meant to go home. But that didn't seem important any more, maybe because there were little blue flowers growing in the meadow behind the stone house and the gray squirrels were playing in the pines next to the house. The horses were standing in the corral, and there was a beef carcass hanging on the shady side of a big pine in front of the house. Flies buzzed around the clotted blood that hung from the carcass. Silva was washing his hands in a bucket full of water. He must have heard me coming because he spoke to me without turning to face me.

"I've been waiting for you."

"I went walking in the big pine trees."

I looked into the bucket full of bloody water with brown-and-white animal hairs floating in it. Silva stood there letting his hand drip, examining me intently.

"Are you coming with me?"

"Where?" I asked him.   65

"To sell the meat in Marquez."

"If you're sure it's O.K."

"I wouldn't ask you if it wasn't," he answered.

He sloshed the water around in the bucket before he dumped it out and set the bucket upside down near the door. I followed him to the corral and watched him saddle the horses. Even beside the horses he looked tall, and I asked him again if he wasn't Navajo. He didn't say anything; he just shook his head and kept cinching up the saddle.

"But Navajos are tall."   70

"Get on the horse," he said, "and let's go."

The last thing he did before we started down the steep trail was to grab the .30-30 from the corner. He slid the rifle into the scabbard that hung from his saddle.

"Do they ever try to catch you?" I asked

"They don't know who I am."

"Then why did you bring the rifle?"   75

"Because we are going to Marquez where the Mexicans live."

III

The trail leveled out on a narrow ridge that was steep on both sides like an animal spine. On one side I could see where the trail went around the rocky gray hills and disappeared into the southeast where the pale sandrock mesas stood in the distance near my home. On the other side was a trail that went west, and as I looked far into the distance. I thought I saw the little town. But Silva said no, that I was looking in the wrong place, that I just thought I saw houses. After that I quit looking off into the distance; it was hot and the wildflowers were closing up their deep-yellow petals. Only the waxy cactus flowers bloomed in the bright sun, and I saw every color that a cactus blossom can be; the white ones and the red ones were still buds, but the purple and the yellow were blossoms, open full and the most beautiful of all.

Silva saw him before I did. The white man was riding a big gray horse, coming up the trail toward us. He was traveling fast and the gray horse's feet sent rocks rolling off the trail into the dry tumbleweeds. Silva motioned for me to stop and we watched the white man. He didn't see us right away, but finally his horse whinnied at our horses and he stopped. He looked at us briefly before he loped the gray horse across the three hundred yards that separated us. He stopped his horse in front of Silva, and his young fat face was shadowed by the brim of his hat. He didn't look mad, but his small, pale eyes moved from the blood-soaked gunny sacks hanging from my saddle to Silva's face and then back to my face.

"Where did you get the fresh meat?" the white man asked.

"I've been hunting," Silva said, and when he shifted his weight in the saddle the leather creaked.   80

"The hell you have, Indian. You've been rustling cattle. We've been looking for the thief for a long time."

The rancher was fat, and sweat began to soak through his white cowboy shirt and the wet cloth stuck to the thick rolls of belly fat. He almost seemed to be panting from the exertion of talking, and he smelled rancid, maybe because Silva scared him.

Silva turned to me and smiled. "Go back up the mountain, Yellow Woman."

The white man got angry when he heard Silva speak in a language he couldn't understand. "Don't try anything, Indian. Just keep riding to Marquez. We'll call the state police from there."

The rancher must have been unarmed because he was very frightened and if he had a gun he would have pulled it out then. I turned my horse around and the rancher yelled, "Stop!" I looked at Silva for an instant and there was something ancient and dark—something I could feel in my stomach—in his eyes, and when I glanced at his hand I saw his finger on the trigger of the .30–30 that was still in the saddle scabbard. I slapped my horse across the flank and the sacks of raw meat swung against my knees as the horse leaped up the trail. It was hard to keep my balance, and once I thought I felt the saddle slipping backward; it was because of this that I could not look back.

I didn't stop until I reached the ridge where the trail forked. The horse was breathing deep gasps and there was a dark film of sweat on its neck. I looked down in the direction I had come from, but I couldn't see the place. I waited. The wind came up and pushed warm air past me. I looked up at the sky, pale blue and full of thin clouds and fading vapor trails left by jets.

I think four shots were fired—I remember hearing four hollow explosions that reminded me of deer hunting. There could have been more shots after that, but I couldn't have heard them because my horse was running again and the loose rocks were making too much noise as they scattered around his feet.

Horses have a hard time running downhill, but I went that way instead of uphill to the mountain because I thought it was safer. I felt better with the horse running southeast past the round gray hills that were covered with cedar trees and black lava rock. When I got to the plain in the distance I could seen the dark green patches of tamaracks that grew along the river; and beyond the river I could see the beginning of the pale sandrock mesas. I stopped the horse and looked back to see if anyone was coming; then I got off the horse and turned the horse around, wondering if it would go back to its corral under the pines on the mountain. It looked back at me for a moment and then plucked a mouthful of green tumbleweeds before it trotted back up the trail with its ears pointed forward, carrying its head daintily to one side to avoid stepping on the dragging reins. When the horse disappeared over the last hill, the gunny sacks full of meat were still swinging and bouncing.

IV

I walked toward the river on a wood-hauler's road that I knew would eventually lead to the paved road. I was thinking about waiting beside the road for someone to drive by, but by the time I got to the pavement I had decided it wasn't very far to walk if I followed the river back the way Silva and I had come.

The river water tasted good, and I sat in the shade under a cluster of sil-   90
very willows. I thought about Silva, and I felt sad at leaving him; still, there
was something strange about him, and I tried to figure it out all the way
back home.

I came back to the place on the river bank where he had been sitting the
first time I saw him. The green willow leaves that he had trimmed from the
branch were still lying there, wilted in the sand. I saw the leaves and I
wanted to go back to him—to kiss him and to touch him—but the mountains were too far away now. And I told myself, because I believe it, he will
come back sometime and be waiting again by the river.

I followed the path up from the river into the village. The sun was getting low, and I could smell supper cooking when I got to the screen door
of my house. I could hear their voices inside—my mother was telling my
grandmother how to fix the Jell-o and my husband, Al, was playing with the
baby. I decided to tell them that some Navajo had kidnapped me, but I was
sorry that old Grandpa wasn't alive to hear my story because it was the
Yellow Woman stories he liked to tell best.

Amy Tan   *(born 1952)*

In 1993, the movie based on Amy Tan's novel *The Joy Luck Club*
helped make her one of the country's best-known Asian American writers. Born in Oakland, California, she writes about California's immigrant
Chinese—their journey between the values and traumas of the Chinese
past and the challenges of the American future. Her novel *The Kitchen
God's Wife* (1991) continued to explore the role that ties to the mainland
culture and the interlocking relationships of the large traditional family
play in the lives of Chinese Americans. Her novel *The Hundred Secret
Senses* was published in 1995.

Two Kinds   1989

My mother believed you could be anything you wanted to be in America. You could open a restaurant. You could work for the government and
get good retirement. You could buy a house with almost no money down.
You could become rich. You could become instantly famous.

"Of course you can be prodigy, too," my mother told me when I was
nine. "You can be best anything. What does Auntie Lindo know? Her daughter, she is only best tricky."

America was where all my mother's hopes lay. She had come here in
1949 after losing everything in China: her mother and father, her family
home, her first husband, and two daughters, twin baby girls. But she never
looked back with regret. There were so many ways for things to get better.

We didn't immediately pick the right kind of prodigy. At first my mother
thought I could be a Chinese Shirley Temple. We'd watch Shirley's old
movies on TV as though they were training films. My mother would poke

my arm and say, "*Ni kan*"—You watch. And I would see Shirley tapping her feet, or singing a sailor song, or pursing her lips into a very round O while saying, "Oh my goodness."

"*Ni kan*," said my mother as Shirley's eyes flooded with tears. "You al-   5
ready know how. Don't need talent for crying!"

Soon after my mother got this idea about Shirley Temple, she took me to a beauty training school in the Mission district and put me in the hands of a student who could barely hold the scissors without shaking. Instead of getting big fat curls, I emerged with an uneven mass of crinkly black fuzz. My mother dragged me off to the bathroom and tried to wet down my hair.

"You look like Negro Chinese," she lamented, as if I had done this on purpose.

The instructor of the beauty training school had to lop off these soggy clumps to make my hair even again. "Peter Pan is very popular these days," the instructor assured my mother. I now had hair the length of a boy's, with straight-across bangs that hung at a slant two inches above my eyebrows. I liked the haircut and it made me actually look forward to my future fame.

In fact, in the beginning, I was just as excited as my mother, maybe even more so. I pictured this prodigy part of me as many different images, trying each one on for size. I was a dainty ballerina girl standing by the curtains, waiting to hear the right music that would send me floating on my tiptoes. I was like the Christ child lifted out of the straw manger, crying with holy indignity. I was Cinderella stepping from her pumpkin carriage with sparkly cartoon music filling the air.

In all of my imaginings, I was filled with a sense that I would soon be-   10
come *perfect*. My mother and father would adore me. I would be beyond reproach. I would never feel the need to sulk for anything.

But sometimes the prodigy in me became impatient. "If you don't hurry up and get me out of here, I'm disappearing for good," it warned. "And then you'll always be nothing."

Every night after dinner, my mother and I would sit at the Formica kitchen table. She would present new tests, taking her examples from stories of amazing children she had read in *Ripley's Believe It or Not*, or *Good Housekeeping, Reader's Digest*, and a dozen other magazines she kept in a pile in our bathroom. My mother got these magazines from people whose houses she cleaned. And since she cleaned many houses each week, we had a great assortment. She would look through them all, searching for stories about remarkable children.

The first night she brought out a story about a three-year-old boy who knew the capitals of all the states and even most of the European countries. A teacher was quoted as saying the little boy could also pronounce the names of the foreign cities correctly.

"What's the capital of Finland?" my mother asked me, looking at the magazine story.

All I knew was the capital of California, because Sacramento was the   15
name of the street we lived on in Chinatown. "Nairobi!" I guessed, saying the most foreign word I could think of. She checked to see if that was possibly one way to pronounce "Helsinki" before showing me the answer.

The tests got harder—multiplying numbers in my head, finding the queen of hearts in a deck of cards, trying to stand on my head without using my hands, predicting the daily temperatures in Los Angeles, New York, and London.

One night I had to look at a page from the Bible for three minutes and then report everything I could remember. "Now Jehoshaphat had riches and honor in abundance and . . . that's all I remember, Ma," I said.

And after seeing my mother's disappointed face once again, something inside of me began to die. I hated the tests, the raised hopes and failed expectations. Before going to bed that night, I looked in the mirror above the bathroom sink and when I saw only my face staring back—and that it would always be this ordinary face—I began to cry. Such a sad, ugly girl! I made high-pitched noises like a crazed animal, trying to scratch out the face in the mirror.

And then I saw what seemed to be the prodigy side of me—because I had never seen that face before. I looked at my reflection, blinking so I could see more clearly. The girl staring back at me was angry, powerful. This girl and I were the same. I had new thoughts, willful thoughts, or rather thoughts filled with lots of won'ts. I won't let her change me, I promised myself. I won't be what I'm not.

So now on nights when my mother presented her tests, I performed list-   20
lessly, my head propped on one arm. I pretended to be bored. And I was. I got so bored I started counting the bellows of the foghorns out on the bay while my mother drilled me in other areas. The sound was comforting and reminded me of the cow jumping over the moon. And the next day, I played a game with myself, seeing if my mother would give up on me before eight bellows. After a while I usually counted only one, maybe two bellows at most. At last she was beginning to give up hope.

Two or three months had gone by without any mention of my being a prodigy again. And then one day my mother was watching *The Ed Sullivan Show* on TV. The TV was old and the sound kept shorting out. Every time my mother got halfway up from the sofa to adjust the set, the sound would go back on and Ed would be talking. As soon as she sat down, Ed would go silent again. She got up, the TV broke into loud piano music. She sat down. Silence. Up and down, back and forth, quiet and loud. It was like a stiff embraceless dance between her and the TV set. Finally she stood by the set with her hand on the sound dial.

She seemed entranced by the music, a little frenzied piano piece with this mesmerizing quality, sort of quick passages and then teasing lilting ones before it returned to the quick playful parts.

"*Ni kan,*" my mother said, calling me over with hurried hand gestures. "Look here."

I could see why my mother was fascinated by the music. It was being pounded out by a little Chinese girl, about nine years old, with a Peter Pan haircut. The girl had the sauciness of a Shirley Temple. She was proudly modest like a proper Chinese child. And she also did this fancy sweep of a curtsy, so that the fluffy skirt of her white dress cascaded slowly to the floor like the petals of a large carnation.

In spite of these warning signs, I wasn't worried. Our family had no piano 25
and we couldn't afford to buy one, let alone reams of sheet music and piano
lessons. So I could be generous in my comments when my mother bad-
mouthed the little girl on TV.

"Play note right, but doesn't sound good! No singing sound," complained
my mother.

"What are you picking on her for?" I said carelessly.

"She's pretty good. Maybe she's not the best, but she's trying hard." I
knew almost immediately I would be sorry I said that.

"Just like you," she said. "Not the best. Because you not trying." She gave
a little huff as she let go of the sound dial and sat down on the sofa.

The little Chinese girl sat down also to play an encore of "Anitra's 30
Dance" by Grieg. I remember the song, because later on I had to learn how
to play it.

Three days after watching *The Ed Sullivan Show,* my mother told me what
my schedule would be for piano lessons and piano practice. She had talked
to Mr. Chong, who lived on the first floor of our apartment building. Mr.
Chong was a retired piano teacher and my mother had traded houseclean-
ing services for weekly lessons and a piano for me to practice on every day,
two hours a day, from four until six.

When my mother told me this, I felt as though I had been sent to hell. I
whined and then kicked my foot a little when I couldn't stand it anymore.

"Why don't you like me the way I am? I'm *not* a genius! I can't play the
piano. And even if I could, I wouldn't go on TV if you paid me a million
dollars!" I cried.

My mother slapped me. "Who ask you be genius?" she shouted. "Only
ask you be your best. For you sake. You think I want you be genius? Hnnh!
What for! Who ask you!"

"So ungrateful," I heard her mutter in Chinese. "If she had as much tal- 35
ent as she has temper, she would be famous now."

Mr. Chong, whom I secretly nicknamed Old Chong, was very strange, always tapping his fingers to the silent music of an invisible orchestra. He
looked ancient in my eyes. He had lost most of the hair on top of his head
and he wore thick glasses and had eyes that always looked tired and sleepy.
But he must have been younger than I thought, since he lived with his
mother and was not yet married.

I met Old Lady Chong once and that was enough. She had this peculiar
smell like a baby that had done something in its pants. And her fingers felt
like a dead person's, like an old peach I once found in the back of the refrigerator; the skin just slid off the meat when I picked it up.

I soon found out why Old Chong had retired from teaching piano. He
was deaf. "Like Beethoven!" he shouted to me. "We're both listening only in
our head!" And he would start to conduct his frantic silent sonatas.

Our lessons went like this. He would open the book and point to different things, explaining their purpose: "Key! Treble! Bass! No sharps or flats!
So this is C major! Listen now and play after me!"

And then he would play the C scale a few times, a simple chord, and 40
then, as if inspired by an old, unreachable itch, he gradually added more

notes and running trills and a pounding bass until the music was really something quite grand.

I would play after him, the simple scale, the simple chord, and then I just played some nonsense that sounded like a cat running up and down on top of garbage cans. Old Chong smiled and applauded and then said, "Very good! But now you must learn to keep time!"

So that's how I discovered that Old Chong's eyes were too slow to keep up with the wrong notes I was playing. He went through the motions in half-time. To help me keep rhythm, he stood behind me, pushing down on my right shoulder for every beat. He balanced pennies on top of my wrists so I would keep them still as I slowly played scales and arpeggios. He had me curve my hand around an apple and keep that shape when playing chords. He marched stiffly to show me how to make each finger dance up and down, staccato like an obedient little soldier.

He taught me all these things, and that was how I also learned I could be lazy and get away with mistakes, lots of mistakes. If I hit the wrong notes because I hadn't practiced enough, I never corrected myself. I just kept playing in rhythm. And Old Chong kept conducting his own private reverie.

So maybe I never really gave myself a fair chance. I did pick up the basics pretty quickly, and I might have become a good pianist at that young age. But I was so determined not to try, not to be anybody different that I learned to play only the most earsplitting preludes, the most discordant hymns.

Over the next year, I practiced like this, dutifully in my own way. And then one day I heard my mother and her friend Lindo Jong both talking in a loud bragging tone of voice so others could hear. It was after church, and I was leaning against the brick wall wearing a dress with stiff white petticoats. Auntie Lindo's daughter, Waverly, who was about my age, was standing farther down the wall about five feet away. We had grown up together and shared all the closeness of two sisters squabbling over crayons and dolls. In other words, for the most part, we hated each other. I thought she was snotty. Waverly Jong had gained a certain amount of fame as "Chinatown's Littlest Chinese Chess Champion." 45

"She bring home too many trophy," lamented Auntie Lindo that Sunday. "All day she play chess. All day I have no time do nothing but dust off her winnings." She threw a scolding look at Waverly, who pretended not to see her.

"You lucky you don't have this problem," said Auntie Lindo with a sigh to my mother.

And my mother squared her shoulders and bragged: "Our problem worser than yours. If we ask Jing-mei wash dish, she hear nothing but music. It's like you can't stop this natural talent."

And right then, I was determined to put a stop to her foolish pride.

* * *

A few weeks later, Old Chong and my mother conspired to have me play in a talent show which would be held in the church hall. By then, my parents had saved up enough to buy me a secondhand piano, a black Wurlitzer spinet with a scarred bench. It was the showpiece of our living room. 50

For the talent show, I was to play a piece called "Pleading Child" from Schumann's *Scenes from Childhood.* It was a simple, moody piece that sounded more difficult than it was. I was supposed to memorize the whole thing, playing the repeat parts twice to make the piece sound longer. But I dawdled over it, playing a few bars and then cheating, looking up to see what notes followed, I never really listened to what I was playing. I daydreamed about being somewhere else, about being someone else.

The part I liked to practice best was the fancy curtsy: right foot out, touch the rose on the carpet with a pointed foot, sweep to the side, left leg bends, look up and smile.

My parents invited all the couples from the Joy Luck Club to witness my debut. Auntie Lindo and Uncle Tin were there. Waverly and her two older brothers had also come. The first two rows were filled with children both younger and older than I was. The littlest ones got to go first. They recited simple nursery rhymes, squawked out tunes on miniature violins, twirled Hula Hoops, pranced in pink ballet tutus, and when they bowed or curtsied, the audience would sigh in unison, "Awww," and then clap enthusiastically.

When my turn came, I was very confident. I remember my childish excitement. It was as if I knew, without a doubt, that the prodigy side of me really did exist. I had no fear whatsoever, no nervousness. I remember thinking to myself, This is it! This is it! I looked out over the audience, at my mother's blank face, my father's yawn, Auntie Lindo's stiff-lipped smile, Waverly's sulky expression. I had on a white dress layered with sheets of lace, and a pink bow in my Peter Pan haircut. As I sat down I envisioned people jumping to their feet and Ed Sullivan rushing up to introduce me to everyone on TV.

And I started to play. It was so beautiful. I was so caught up in how   55 lovely I looked that at first I didn't worry how I would sound: So it was a surprise to me when I hit the first wrong note and I realized something didn't sound quite right. And then I hit another and another followed that. A chill started at the top of my head and began to trickle down. Yet I couldn't stop playing, as though my hands were bewitched. I kept thinking my fingers would adjust themselves back, like a train switching to the right track. I played this strange jumble through two repeats, the sour notes staying with me all the way to the end.

When I stood up, I discovered my legs were shaking. Maybe I had just been nervous and the audience, like Old Chong, had seen me go through the right motions and had not heard anything wrong at all. I swept my right foot out, went down on my knee, looked up and smiled. The room was quiet, except for Old Chong, who was beaming and shouting, "Bravo! Bravo! Well done!" But then I saw my mother's face, her stricken face. The audience clapped weakly, and as I walked back to my chair, with my whole face quivering as I tried not to cry, I heard a little boy whisper loudly to his mother, "That was awful," and the mother whispered back, "Well, she certainly tried."

And now I realized how many people were in the audience, the whole world it seemed. I was aware of eyes burning into my back. I felt the shame of my mother and father as they sat stiffly throughout the rest of the show.

We could have escaped during intermission. Pride and some strange sense of honor must have anchored my parents to their chairs. And so we watched it all: the eighteen-year-old boy with a fake mustache who did a magic show and juggled flaming hoops while riding a unicycle. The breasted girl with white makeup who sang from *Madama Butterfly* and got honorable mention. And the eleven-year-old boy who won first prize playing a tricky violin song that sounded like a busy bee.

After the show, the Hsus, the Jongs, and the St. Clairs from the Joy Luck Club came up to my mother and father.

"Lots of talented kids," Auntie Lindo said vaguely, smiling broadly.   60

"That was somethin' else," said my father, and I wondered if he was referring to me in a humorous way, or whether he even remembered what I had done.

Waverly looked at me and shrugged her shoulders. "You aren't a genius like me," she said matter-of-factly. And if I hadn't felt so bad, I would have pulled her braids and punched her stomach.

But my mother's expression was what devastated me: a quiet, blank look that said she had lost everything. I felt the same way, and it seemed as if everybody were now coming up, like gawkers at the scene of an accident, to see what parts were actually missing. When we got on the bus to go home, my father was humming the busy-bee tune and my mother was silent. I kept thinking she wanted to wait until we got home before shouting at me. But when my father unlocked the door to our apartment, my mother walked in and then went to the back, into the bedroom. No accusations. No blame. And in a way, I felt disappointed. I had been waiting for her to start shouting, so I could shout back and cry and blame her for all my misery.

I assumed my talent-show fiasco meant I never had to play the piano again. But two days later, after school, my mother came out of the kitchen and saw me watching TV.

"Four clock," she reminded me as if it were any other day. I was stunned,   65 as though she were asking me to go through the talent-show torture again. I wedged myself more tightly in front of the TV.

"Turn off TV," she called from the kitchen five minutes later.

I didn't budge. And then I decided. I didn't have to do what my mother said anymore. I wasn't her slave. This wasn't China. I had listened to her before and look what happened. She was the stupid one.

She came out from the kitchen and stood in the arched entryway of the living room. "Four clock," she said once again, louder.

"I'm not going to play anymore," I said nonchalantly. "Why should I? I'm not a genius."

She walked over and stood in front of the TV. I saw her chest was heav-   70 ing up and down in an angry way.

"No!" I said, and I now felt stronger, as if my true self had finally emerged. So this was what had been inside me all along.

"No! I won't!" I screamed.

She yanked me by the arm, pulled me off the floor, snapped off the TV. She was frighteningly strong, half pulling, half carrying me toward the piano as I kicked the throw rugs under my feet. She lifted me up and onto the hard bench. I was sobbing by now, looking at her bitterly. Her chest was heaving even more and her mouth was open, smiling crazily as if she were pleased I was crying.

"You want me to be someone that I'm not!" I sobbed. "I'll never be the kind of daughter you want me to be!"

"Only two kinds of daughters," she shouted in Chinese. "Those who are obedient and those who follow their own mind! Only one kind of daughter can live in this house. Obedient daughter!"

"Then I wish I wasn't your daughter. I wish you weren't my mother," I shouted. As I said these things I got scared. I felt like worms and toads and slimy things were crawling out of my chest, but it also felt good, as if this awful side of me had surfaced, at last.

"Too late change this," said my mother shrilly.

And I could sense her anger rising to its breaking point. I wanted to see it spill over. And that's when I remembered the babies she had lost in China, the ones we never talked about. "Then I wish I'd never been born!" I shouted. "I wish I were dead! Like them."

It was as if I had said the magic words. Alakazam!—and her face went blank, her mouth closed, her arms went slack, and she backed out of the room, stunned, as if she were blowing away like a small brown leaf, thin, brittle, lifeless.

It was not the only disappointment my mother felt in me. In the years that followed, I failed her so many times, each time asserting my own will, my right to fall short of expectations. I didn't get straight As. I didn't become class president. I didn't get into Stanford. I dropped out of college.

For unlike my mother, I did not believe I could be anything I wanted to be. I could only be me.

And for all those years, we never talked about the disaster at the recital or my terrible accusations afterward at the piano bench. All that remained unchecked, like a betrayal that was now unspeakable. So I never found a way to ask her why she had hoped for something so large that failure was inevitable.

And even worse, I never asked her what frightened me the most: Why had she given up hope?

For after our struggle at the piano, she never mentioned my playing again. The lessons stopped. The lid to the piano was closed, shutting out the dust, my misery, and her dreams.

So she surprised me. A few years ago, she offered to give me the piano, for my thirtieth birthday. I had not played in all those years. I saw the offer as a sign of forgiveness, a tremendous burden removed.

"Are you sure?" I asked shyly. "I mean, won't you and Dad miss it?"

"No, this is your piano," she said firmly. "Always your piano. You only one can play."

"Well, I probably can't play anymore," I said. "It's been years."

"You pick up fast," said my mother, as if she knew this was certain. "You have natural talent. You could been genius if you want to."

"No I couldn't."   90

"You just not trying," said my mother. And she was neither angry nor sad. She said it as if to announce a fact that could never be disproved. "Take it," she said.

But I didn't at first. It was enough that she had offered it to me. And after that, every time I saw it in my parents' living room, standing in front of the bay windows, it made me feel proud, as if it were a shiny trophy I had won back.

Last week I sent a tuner over to my parents' apartment and had the piano reconditioned, for purely sentimental reasons. My mother had died a few months before and I had been getting things in order for my father, a little bit at a time. I put the jewelry in special silk pouches. The sweaters she had knitted in yellow, pink, bright orange—all the colors I hated—I put those in moth-proof boxes. I found some old Chinese silk dresses, the kind with little slits up the sides. I rubbed the old silk against my skin, then wrapped them in tissue and decided to take them home with me.

After I had the piano tuned, I opened the lid and touched the keys. It sounded even richer than I remembered. Really, it was a very good piano. Inside the bench were the same exercise notes with handwritten scales, the same secondhand music books with their covers held together with yellow tape.

I opened up the Schumann book to the dark little piece I had played 195 at the recital. It was on the left-hand side of the page, "Pleading Child." It looked more difficult than I remembered. I played a few bars, surprised at how easily the notes came back to me.

And for the first time, or so it seemed, I noticed the piece on the right-hand side. It was called "Perfectly Contented." I tried to play this one as well. It had a lighter melody but the same flowing rhythm and turned out to be quite easy. "Pleading Child" was shorter but slower; "Perfectly Contented" was longer but faster. And after I played them both a few times, I realized they were two halves of the same song.

Anne Tyler   *(born 1941)*   ◉

Anne Tyler is a widely published modern novelist who has lived and worked in places including North Carolina, Montreal in Canada, and Baltimore, Maryland. One editor traced as a connecting thread in her work her sympathy for characters who "want more from life than ever comes to them." Like all of us, they "travel paths we do not choose." They may try to "connect with a past in another place or a present where they do not fit." They feel, as one of Tyler's character says, that a simple error of judgment should not have "such far-reaching effects. You would think that life could be a little more forgiving." The following story is part of a groundswell modern movement to help us break through the crust of prejudice and neglect and ask us to see and accept the retarded or intellectually disabled as fellow human beings.

The author chronicles faithfully the concerns and apprehensions of the mother in this story, without preaching or complaint. What is the subtext? What are the true deep-down feelings of the mother?

Average Waves in Unprotected Waters   1977

As soon as it got light, Bet woke him and dressed him, and then she walked him over to the table and tried to make him eat a little cereal. He wouldn't, though. He could tell something was up. She pressed the edge of the spoon against his lips till she heard it click on his teeth, but he just looked off at a corner of the ceiling—a knobby child with great glassy eyes and her own fair hair. Like any other nine-year-old, he wore a striped shirt and jeans, but the shirt was too neat and the jeans too blue, unpatched and unfaded, and would stay that way till he outgrew them. And his face was elderly—pinched, strained, tired—though it should have looked as unused as his jeans. He hardly ever changed his expression.

She left him in his chair and went to make the beds. Then she raised the yellowed shade, rinsed a few spoons in the bathroom sink, picked up some bits of magazines he'd torn the night before. This was a rented room in an ancient, crumbling house, and nothing you could do to it would lighten its cluttered look. There was always that feeling of too many lives layered over other lives, like the layers of brownish wallpaper her child had peeled away in the corner by his bed.

She slipped her feet into flat-heeled loafers and absently patted the front of her dress, a worn beige knit she usually saved for Sundays. Maybe she should take it in a little; it hung from her shoulders like a sack. She felt too slight and frail, too wispy for all she had to do today. But she reached for her coat anyhow, and put it on and tied a blue kerchief under her chin. Then she went over to the table and slowly spun, modelling the coat. "See, Arnold?" she said. "We're going out."

Arnold went on looking at the ceiling, but his gaze turned wild and she knew he'd heard.

She fetched his jacket from the closet—brown corduroy, with a hood. It   15 had set her back half a week's salary. But Arnold didn't like it; he always wanted his old one, a little red duffel coat he'd long ago outgrown. When she came toward him, he started moaning and rocking and shaking his head. She had to struggle to stuff his arms in the sleeves. Small though he was, he was strong, wiry; he was getting to be too much for her. He shook free of her hands and ran over to his bed. The jacket was on, though. It wasn't buttoned, the collar was askew, but never mind; that just made him look more real. She always felt bad at how he stood inside his clothes, separate from them, passive, unaware of all the buttons and snaps she'd fastened as carefully as she would a doll's.

She gave a last look around the room, checked to make sure the hot plate was off, and then picked up her purse and Arnold's suitcase. "Come along, Arnold," she said.

He came, dragging out every step. He looked at the suitcase suspiciously, but only because it was new. It didn't have any meaning for him. "See?" she said. "It's yours. It's Arnold's. It's going on the train with us."

But her voice was all wrong. He would pick it up, for sure. She paused in the middle of locking the door and glanced over at him fearfully. Anything could set him off nowadays. He hadn't noticed, though. He was too busy staring around the hallway, goggling at a freckled, walnut-framed mirror as if he'd never seen it before. She touched his shoulder. "Come, Arnold," she said.

They went down the stairs slowly, both of them clinging to the sticky mahogany railing. The suitcase banged against her shins. In the entrance hall, old Mrs. Puckett stood waiting outside her door—a huge, soft lady in a black crêpe dress and orthopedic shoes. She was holding a plastic bag of peanut-butter cookies, Arnold's favorites. There were tears in her eyes. "Here, Arnold," she said, quavering. Maybe she felt to blame that he was going. But she'd done the best she could: babysat him all these years and only given up when he'd grown too strong and wild to manage. Bet wished Arnold would give the old lady some sign—hug her, make his little crowing noise, just take the cookies, even. But he was too excited. He raced on out the front door, and it was Bet who had to take them. "Well, thank you, Mrs. Puckett," she said. "I know he'll enjoy them later."

"Oh, no . . . " said Mrs. Puckett, and she flapped her large hands and   10
gave up, sobbing.

They were lucky and caught a bus first thing. Arnold sat by the window. He must have thought he was going to work with her; when they passed the red-and-gold Kresge's sign, he jabbered and tried to stand up. "No, honey," she said, and took hold of his arm. He settled down then and let his hand stay curled in hers awhile. He had very small, cool fingers, and nails as smooth as thumbtack heads.

At the train station, she bought the tickets and then a pack of Wrigley's spearmint gum. Arnold stood gaping at the vaulted ceiling, with his head flopped back and his arms hanging limp at his sides. People stared at him. She would have liked to push their faces in. "Over here, honey," she said, and she nudged him toward the gate, straightening his collar as they walked.

He hadn't been on a train before and acted a little nervous, bouncing up and down in his seat and flipping the lid of his ashtray and craning forward to see the man ahead of them. When the train started moving, he crowed and pulled at her sleeve. "That's right, Arnold. Train. We're taking a trip," Bet said, She unwrapped a stick of chewing gum and gave it to him. He loved gum. If she didn't watch him closely, he sometimes swallowed it— which worried her a little because she'd heard it clogged your kidneys; but at least it would keep him busy. She looked down at the top of his head. Through the blond prickles of his hair, cut short for practical reasons, she could see his skull bones moving as he chewed. He was so thin-skinned, almost transparent; sometimes she imagined she could see the blood travelling in his veins.

When the train reached a steady speed, he grew calmer, and after a while he nodded over against her and let his hands sag on his knees. She watched his eyelashes slowly drooping—two colorless, fringed crescents, heavier and heavier, every now and then flying up as he tried to fight off sleep. He had never slept well, not ever, not even as a baby. Even before they'd noticed anything wrong, they'd wondered at his jittery, jerky catnaps, his tiny hands clutching tight and springing open, his strange single wail sailing out while he went right on sleeping. Avery said it gave him the chills. And after the doctor talked to them Avery wouldn't have anything to do with Arnold anymore—just walked in wide circles around the crib, looking stunned and sick. A few weeks later, he left. She wasn't surprised. She even knew how he felt, more or less. Halfway, he blamed her; halfway, he blamed himself. You can't believe a thing like this will just fall on you out of nowhere.

She'd had moments herself of picturing some kind of evil gene in her   15
husband's ordinary, stocky body—a dark little egg like a black jelly bean, she imagined it. All his fault. But other times she was sure the gene was hers. It seemed so natural; she never could do anything as well as most people. And then other times she blamed their marriage. They'd married too young, against her parents' wishes. All she'd wanted was to get away from home. Now she couldn't remember why. What was wrong with home? She thought of her parents' humped green trailer, perched on cinder blocks near a forest of masts in Salt Spray, Maryland. At this distance (parents dead, trailer rusted to bits, even Salt Spray changed past recognition), it seemed to her that her old life had been beautifully free and spacious. She closed her eyes and saw wide gray skies. Everything had been ruled by the sea. Her father (who'd run a fishing boat for tourists) couldn't arrange his day till he'd heard the marine forecast—the wind, the tides, the small-craft warnings, the height of average waves in unprotected waters. He loved to fish, offshore and on, and he swam every chance he could get. He'd tried to teach her to bodysurf, but it hadn't worked out. There was something about the breakers: she just gritted her teeth and stood staunch and let them slam into her. As if standing staunch were a virtue, really. She couldn't explain it. Her father thought she was scared, but it wasn't that at all.

She'd married Avery against their wishes and been sorry ever since—sorry to move so far from home, sorrier when her parents died within a year of each other, sorriest of all when the marriage turned grim and cranky. But she never would have thought of leaving him. It was Avery who left; she would have stayed forever. In fact, she did stay on in their apartment for months after he'd gone, though the rent was far too high. It wasn't that she expected him back. She just took some comfort from enduring.

Arnold's head snapped up. He looked around him and made a gurgling sound. His chewing gum fell onto the front of his jacket. "Here, honey," she told him. She put the gum in her ashtray. "Look out the window. See the cows?"

He wouldn't look. He began bouncing in his seat, rubbing his hands together rapidly.

"Arnold? Want a cookie?"

If only she'd brought a picture book. She'd meant to and then forgot. She   20
wondered if the train people sold magazines. If she let him get too bored, he'd go into one of his tantrums, and then she wouldn't be able to handle him. The doctor had given her pills just in case, but she was always afraid that while he was screaming he would choke on them. She looked around

the car. "Arnold," she said, "see the . . . see the hat with feathers on? Isn't it pretty? See the red suitcase? See the, um . . . ."

The car door opened with a rush of clattering wheels and the conductor burst in, singing "Girl of my dreams, I love you." He lurched down the aisle, plucking pink tickets from the back of each seat. Just across from Bet and Arnold, he stopped. He was looking down at a tiny black lady in a purple coat, with a fox fur piece biting its own tail around her neck. "You!" he said.

The lady stared straight ahead.

"You, I saw you. You're the one in the washroom."

A little muscle twitched in her cheek.

"You got on this train in Beulah, didn't you. Snuck in the washroom.   25
Darted back like you thought you could put something over on me. I saw that bit of purple! Where's your ticket gone to?"

She started fumbling in a blue cloth purse. The fumbling went on and on. The conductor shifted his weight.

"Why!" she said finally. "I must've left it back in my other seat."

"What other seat?"

"Oh, the one back . . . ." She waved a spidery hand.

The conductor sighed. "Lady," he said, "you owe me money."   30

"I do no such thing!" she said. "Viper! Monger! Hitler!" Her voice screeched up all at once; she sounded like a parrot. Bet winced and felt herself flushing, as if *she* were the one. But then at her shoulder she heard a sudden, rusty clang, and she turned and saw that Arnold was laughing. He had his mouth wide open and his tongue curled, the way he did when he watched "Sesame Street." Even after the scene had worn itself out, and the lady had paid and the conductor had moved on, Arnold went on chortling and la-laing, and Bet looked gratefully at the little black lady, who was settling her fur piece fussily and muttering under her breath.

From the Parkinsville Railroad Station, which they seemed to be tearing down or else remodelling—she couldn't tell which—they took a taxicab to Parkins State Hospital. "Oh, I been out there many and many a time," said the driver. "Went out there just the other—"

But she couldn't stop herself; she had to tell him before she forgot. "Listen," she said, "I want you to wait for me right in the driveway. I don't want you to go on away."

"Well, fine," he said.

"Can you do that? I want you to be sitting right by the porch or the steps   35
or whatever, right where I come out of, ready to take me back to the station. Don't just go off and—"

"I *got* you, I got you," he said.

She sank back. She hoped he understood.

Arnold wanted a peanut-butter cookie. He was reaching and whimpering. She didn't know what to do. She wanted to give him anything he asked for, anything; but he'd get it all over his face and arrive not looking his best. She couldn't stand it if they thought he was just ordinary and unattractive. She wanted them to see how small and neat he was, how somebody cherished him. But it would be awful if he went into one of his rages. She broke off a little piece of cookie from the bag. "Here," she told him. "Don't mess, now."

He flung himself back in the corner and ate it, keeping one hand flattened across his mouth while he chewed.

The hospital looked like someone's great pillared mansion, with square   40
brick buildings all around it. "Here we are," the driver said.

"Thank you," she said. "Now you wait here, please. Just wait till I get—"

"*Lady,*" he said. "I'll wait."

She opened the door and nudged Arnold out ahead of her. Lugging the suitcase, she started toward the steps. "Come on, Arnold," she said.

He hung back.

"Arnold?"   45

Maybe he wouldn't allow it, and they would go on home and never think of this again.

But he came, finally, climbing the steps in his little hobbled way. His face was clean, but there were a few cookie crumbs on his jacket. She set down the suitcase to brush them off. Then she buttoned all his buttons and smoothed his shirt collar over his jacket collar before she pushed open the door.

In the admitting office, a lady behind a wooden counter showed her what papers to sign. Secretaries were clacketing typewriters all around. Bet thought Arnold might like that, but instead he got lost in the lights—chilly, hanging ice-cube-tray lights with a little flicker to them. He gazed upward, looking astonished. Finally a flat-fronted nurse came in and touched his elbow. "Come along, Arnold. Come, Mommy. We'll show you where Arnold is staying," she said.

They walked back across the entrance hall, then up wide marble steps with hollows worn in them. Arnold clung to the bannister. There was a smell Bet hated, pine-oil disinfectant, but Arnold didn't seem to notice. You never knew, sometimes smells could just put him in a state.

The nurse unlocked a double door that had chicken-wired windows.   50
They walked through a corridor, passing several fat, ugly women in shapeless gray dresses and ankle socks. "Ha!" one of the women said, and fell giggling into the arms of a friend. The nurse said, "*Here* we are." She led them into an enormous hallway lined with little white cots. Nobody else was in it; there wasn't a sign that children lived here except for a tiny cardboard clown picture hanging on one vacant wall. "This one is your bed, Arnold," said the nurse. Bet laid the suitcase on it. It was made up so neatly, the sheets might have been painted on. A steely-gray blanket was folded across the foot. She looked over at Arnold, but he was pivoting back and forth to hear how his new sneakers squeaked on the linoleum.

"Usually," said the nurse, "we like to give new residents six months before the family visits. That way they settle in quicker, don't you see." She turned away and adjusted the clown picture, though as far as Bet could tell it was fine the way it was. Over her shoulder, the nurse said, "You can tell him goodbye now, if you like."

"Oh," Bet said. "All right." She set her hands on Arnold's shoulders. Then she laid her face against his hair, which felt warm and fuzzy. "Honey," she said. But he went on pivoting. She straightened and told the nurse, "I brought his special blanket."

"Oh, fine," said the nurse, turning toward her again. "We'll see that he gets it."

"He always likes to sleep with it; he has ever since he was little."

"All right."   55

"Don't wash it. He hates if you wash it."

"Yes. Say goodbye to Mommy now, Arnold."

"A lot of times he'll surprise you. I mean there's a whole lot to him. He's not just—"

"We'll take very good care of him, Mrs. Blevins, don't worry."

"Well," she said. "'Bye, Arnold."   60

She left the ward with the nurse and went down the corridor. As the nurse was unlocking the doors for her, she heard a single, terrible scream, but the nurse only patted her shoulder and pushed her gently on through.

In the taxi, Bet said, "Now, I've just got fifteen minutes to get to the station. I wonder if you could hurry?"

"Sure thing," the driver said.

She folded her hands and looked straight ahead. Tears seemed to be coming down her face in sheets.

Once she'd reached the station, she went to the ticket window. "Am I in   65
time for the twelve-thirty-two?" she asked.

"Easily," said the man. "It's twenty minutes late."

"What?"

"Got held up in Norton somehow."

"But you can't!" she said. The man looked startled. She must be a sight, all swollen-eyed and wet-cheeked. "Look," she said, in a lower voice. "I figured this on purpose. I chose the one train from Beulah that would let me catch another one back without waiting. I do not want to sit and wait in this station."

"Twenty *minutes,* lady. That's all it is."   70

"What am I going to do?" she asked him.

He turned back to his ledgers.

She went over to a bench and sat down. Ladders and scaffolding towered above her, and only ten or twelve passengers were dotted through the rest of the station. The place looked bombed out—nothing but a shell. "Twenty minutes!" she said aloud. "What am I going to do?"

Through the double glass doors at the far end of the station, a procession of gray-suited men arrived with briefcases. More men came behind them, dressed in work clothes, carrying folding chairs, black trunklike boxes with silver hinges, microphones, a wooden lectern, and an armload of bunting. They set the lectern down in the center of the floor, not six feet from Bet. They draped the bunting across it—an arc of red, white, and blue. Wires were connected, floodlights were lit. A microphone screeched. One of the workmen said, "Try her, Mayor." He held the microphone out to a fat man in a suit, who cleared his throat and said, "Ladies and gentlemen, on the occasion of the expansion of this fine old railway station—"

"Sure do get an echo here," the workman said. "Keep on going."   75
The Mayor cleared his throat again. "If I may," he said, "I'd like to take about twenty minutes of your time, friends."

He straightened his tie. Bet blew her nose, and then she wiped her eyes and smiled. They had come just for her sake, you might think. They were putting on a sort of private play. From now on, all the world was going to be like that—just something on a stage, for her to sit back and watch.

Guadalupe Valdés   *(born 1941)*

Guadalupe Valdés is a Chicana who was born in El Paso but grew up in Chihuahua, Mexico. She became a Spanish teacher at New Mexico State University in Las Cruces and has worked and published widely in the area of language teaching and language learning. Her articles have appeared in publications like *Hispania, Colorado Quarterly,* and *Revista Chicano-Riqueña.* The title of the following story is a Spanish word for remembering.

Recuerdo   *1976*

It was noon. It was dusty. And the sun, blinding in its brightness, shone unmercifully on the narrow dirty street.

It was empty. And to Rosa, walking slowly past the bars and the shops and the curio stands, it seemed as if they all were peering out at her, curiously watching what she did.

She walked on . . . toward the river, toward the narrow, muddy strip of land that was the dry Rio Grande; and she wished suddenly that it were night and that the tourists had come across, making the street noisy and gay and full of life.

But it was noon. And there were no happy or laughing Americanos; no eager girls painted and perfumed and waiting for customers; no blaring horns or booming bongos . . . only here and there a hungry dog, a crippled beggar, or a drunk, thirsty and broke from the night before.

She was almost there. She could see the narrow door and the splintered   5
wooden steps. And instinctively she stopped. Afraid suddenly, feeling the hollow emptiness again, and the tightness when she swallowed.

And yet, it was not as if she did not know why he had wanted her to come, why he had sent for her. It was not as though she were a child. Her reflection in a smudged and dirty window told her that she was no longer even a girl.

And still, it was not as if she were old, she told herself, it was only that her body was rounded and full, and her eyes in the dark smooth face were hard and knowing, mirroring the pain and the disappointment and the tears of thirty-five years . . .

She walked to the narrow door slowly, and up the stairs . . . thumping softly on the creaking swollen wood. At the top, across a dingy hallway, she knocked softly at a door. It was ajar, and Rosa could see the worn chairs and the torn linoleum and the paper-littered desk. But she did not go in. Not until the man came to the door and looked out at her impatiently.

He saw her feet first and the tattered sandals. Then her dress clean but faded, a best dress obviously, because it was not patched. Finally, after what seemed to Rosa an eternity, he looked at her face, at her dark black hair knotted neatly on top of her head; and at last, into her eyes.

"Come in, Rosa," he said slowly, "I am glad that you could come."   10

"Buenas tardes Don Lorenzo." Rosa said meekly, looking up uneasily at the bulky smelly man. "I am sorry I am late."

"Yes," he said mockingly; and turning, he walked back into the small and dirty room.

Rosa followed him, studying him, while he could not see her, seeing the wrinkled trousers, the sweat stained shirt, and the overgrown greasy hair on the back of his pudgy neck.

He turned suddenly, his beady eyes surveying his domain smugly; then deliberately, he walked to the window and straightened the sign that said:

DIVORCES . . . LORENZO PEREZ SAUZA . . . ATTORNEY AT LAW

It was not as important as the neon blinking sign, of course, but sometimes people came from the side street, and it was good to be prepared.

"Well, Rosa," he said, looking at her again, "and where is Maruca?"   15

"She is sick, señor."

"Sick?"

"Yes, she has had headaches and she is not well . . . she . . . "

"Has she seen a doctor, Rosa?" The question was mocking again.

"No . . . she . . . it will pass, señor. . . . It's only that now . . . I do not   20
think that she should come to work."

"Oh?" He was looking out of the window distractedly, ignoring her.

"I am sorry, I should have come before," she continued meekly . . .

"Maruca is very pretty, Rosa," Don Lorenzo said suddenly.

"Thank you, señor, you are very kind." She was calmer now . . .

"She will make a man very happy, someday," he continued.   25

"Yes."

"Do you think she will marry soon then?" he asked her, watching her closely.

"No," she hesitated, "that is, I don't know, she . . . there isn't anyone yet."

"Ah!" It was said quietly but somehow triumphantly . . .

And Rosa waited, wondering what he wanted, sensing something and   30
suddenly suspicious.

"Do you think she likes me, Rosa," he asked her deliberately, baiting her.

And she remembered Maruca's face, tear-stained, embarrassed telling her: "I can't go back, Mama. He does not want me to help in his work. He touches me, Mother . . . and smiles. And today, he put his large sweaty hand on my breast, and held it, smiling, like a cow. Ugly!"

"Why, yes, Don Lorenzo," she lied quickly. "She thinks you are very nice." Her heart was racing now, hoping and yet not daring to—

"I am much of a man, Rosa," he went on slowly, "and the girl is pretty. . . . I would take care of her . . . if she let me."

"Take care of her?" Rosa was praying now, her fingers crossed behind her   35
back.

"Yes, take care of her," he repeated. "I would be good to her, you would have money. And then, perhaps, if there is a child . . . she would need a house . . . "

"A house." Rosa repeated dully. A house for Maruca. That it might be. That it might be, really, was unbelievable. To think of the security, of the happy future frightened her suddenly, and she could only stare at the fat man, her eyes round and very black.

"Think about it, Rosita," he said smiling benevolently . . . "You know me . . . ." And Rosa looked at him angrily, remembering, and suddenly feeling very much like being sick.

The walk home was long; and in the heat Rosa grew tired. She wished that she might come to a tree, so that she could sit in the shade and think. But the hills were bare and dry, and there were no trees. There were only shacks surrounded by hungry crying children.

And Rosa thought about her own, about the little ones. The ones that still   40
depended on her even for something to eat. And she felt it again, the strange despair of wanting to cry out: "Don't, don't depend on me! I can hardly depend on myself."

But they had no one else; and until they could beg or steal a piece of bread and a bowl of beans, they would turn to her, only to her, not ever to Pablo.

And it wasn't because he was drunk and lazy, or even because only the last two children belonged to him. He was kind enough to all of them. It was, though, as if they sensed that he was only temporary.

And still it was not that Pablo was bad. He was better actually than the others. He did not beat her when he drank, or steal food from the children. He was not even too demanding. And it gave them a man, after all, a man to protect them. . . . It was enough, really.

True, he had begun to look at Maruca, and it had bothered Rosa. But perhaps it WAS really time for Maruca to leave. For the little ones, particularly. Because men are men, she said to herself, and if there is a temptation . . .

But she was not fooling anyone, and when at last she saw the tin and   45
cardboard shack against the side of the hill, with its cluttered front and screaming children, she wanted to turn back.

Maruca saw her first.

"There's Mama," she told the others triumphantly, and at once they took up the shout: "Mama! Mama! Mama!"

The other girl, standing with Maruca, turned to leave as Rosa came closer.

"Buenas tardes," she said uncomfortably, sensing the dislike and wanting to hurry away.

"What did Petra want?" Rosa asked Maruca angrily, even before Petra was   50
out of earshot.

"Mama, por favor, she'll hear you."

"I told you I did not want her in this house."

"We were only talking, Mama. She was telling me about her friends."

"Her friends!" Rosa cut in sharply, "as if we did not know that she goes with the first American that looks at her. Always by the river that one, with one soldier and another, her friends indeed!"

"But she says she has fun, Mama, and they take her to dance and buy   55
her pretty things."

"Yes, yes, and tomorrow, they will give her a baby. . . . And where is the fun then . . . eh? She is in the streets . . . no?"

Rosa was shaking with anger. "Is that what you want? Do you?"

"No, Mama," Maruca said meekly, "I was just listening to her talk."

"Well, remember it," Rosa snapped furiously, but then seeing Maruca's face, she stopped suddenly. "There, there, it's alright," she said softly. "We will talk about it later."

And Rosa watched her, then, herding the children into the house gently,   60
gracefully; slim and small, angular still, with something perhaps a little doltish in the way she held herself, impatient, and yet distrusting, not quite daring to go forward.

And she thought of Don Lorenzo, and for a moment, she wished that he were not so fat, or so ugly, and especially, so sweaty.

But it was an irrecoverable chance! Old men with money did not often come into their world, and never to stay.

To Rosa, they had been merely far away gods at whose houses she had worked as a maid or as a cook; faultless beings who were to be obeyed without question; powerful creatures who had commanded her to come when they needed variety or adventure . . .

But only that.

She had never been clever enough, or even pretty enough to make it be   65
more.

But Maruca! Maruca could have the world.

No need for her to marry a poor young bum who could not even get a job. No need for her to have ten children all hungry and crying. No need for her to dread, even, that the bum might leave her. No need at all.

"Maruca," Rose said decidedly, turning to where she sat playing with the baby, "I went to see Don Lorenzo."

"Oh?" There was fear in the bright brown eyes.

"And he wants to take care of you," Rosa continued softly. "He thinks   70
you're pretty, and he likes you."

"Take care of me?" It was more of a statement than a question.

"He wants to make an arrangement with you, Maruca." Rosa too was afraid now. "He would come to see you . . . and . . . well . . . if there is a baby, there might very well be a house."

"A baby?" The face was pale now, the eyes surprised and angry. "You want me to go to bed with Don Lorenzo? You want me to let him put his greasy hands all over me, and make love to me? You want that? Is that how much better I can do than Petra?"

"Don't you see, I want you to be happy, to be safe. I want you to have pretty things and not to be afraid. I want you to love your babies when you have them, to hear them laugh with full fat stomachs . . . I want you to love life, to be glad that you were born."

"To be happy?" Maruca repeated slowly, as if it had never occurred to her 75
that she was not.

"Yes, to be happy."

"And sleeping with Don Lorenzo," Maruca asked uncertainly, "will that
make me glad that I was born?"

And Rosa looked at her, saw her waiting for an answer, depending on it . . .

And she wanted to scream out. "No, no! You will hate it probably, and
you will dread his touch on you and his breath smelling of garlic. But it isn't
HE, that will make you happy. It's the rest of it. Don't you see, can't you understand how important HE is?"

But the brown eyes stared at her pleadingly, filling with tears, like a 80
child's, and Rosa said quietly: "Yes, Maruca, it will make you happy."

But then suddenly, unexpectedly, she felt alone and very very tired.

"Go on to church now," she said slowly, "it's time for benediction and
you have the novena to complete." And Rosa watched her go, prayer book
clutched tightly in one hand, hopeful still, trusting still, and so very, very
young still. And she wondered if she would change much, really, after Don
Lorenzo, and the baby and the house. She wondered if she would still be
gay and proud and impatient.

But then suddenly Maruca was out of sight, and Rosa turned to the others, kissing one, patting another's head, and hurrying to have the beans hot
and the house tidy for the time that Pablo would come home.

Eudora Welty   *(1909–2001)*

Eudora Welty was born and spent most of her life in Mississippi. Both
as a writer and as a friendly critic of other writers' work, she helped
make the modern short story a prominent genre of twentieth-century
literature. Major themes in her work have been her love of the South,
the pain of growing up, and the agony of loneliness. Her novels include
The Optimist's Daughter, for which she received the Pulitzer Prize in 1973.
Welty helped set the tone for much modern fiction by her refusal to indulge in "false dreams" and sentimental hopes. Another master of the
modern short story said of Welty that she had "an eye and ear sharp,
shrewd, true as a tuning fork" (Katherine Anne Porter).

A Visit of Charity   *1941*

It was mid-morning—a very cold, bright day. Holding a potted plant before her, a girl of fourteen jumped off the bus in front of the Old Ladies'
Home, on the outskirts of town. She wore a red coat, and her straight yellow hair was hanging down loose from the pointed white cap all the little
girls were wearing that year. She stopped for a moment beside one of the
prickly dark shrubs with which the city had beautified the Home, and then

proceeded slowly toward the building, which was of whitewashed brick and reflected the winter sunlight like a block of ice. As she walked vaguely up the steps she shifted the small pot from hand to hand; then she had to set it down and remove her mittens before she could open the heavy door.

"I'm a Campfire Girl. . . . I have to pay a visit to some old lady," she told the nurse at the desk. This was a woman in a white uniform who looked as if she were cold; she had close-cut hair which stood up on the very top of her head exactly like a sea wave. Marian, the little girl, did not tell her that this visit would give her a minimum of only three points in her score.

"Acquainted with any of our residents?" asked the nurse. She lifted one eyebrow and spoke like a man.

"With any old ladies? No—but—that is, any of them will do," Marian stammered. With her free hand she pushed her hair behind her ears, as she did when it was time to study Science.

The nurse shrugged and rose. "You have a nice *multiflora cineraria*   5 there," she remarked as she walked ahead down the hall of closed doors to pick out an old lady.

There was loose, bulging linoleum on the floor. Marian felt as if she were walking on the waves, but the nurse paid no attention to it. There was a smell in the hall like the interior of a clock. Everything was silent until, behind one of the doors, an old lady of some kind cleared her throat like a sheep bleating. This decided the nurse. Stopping in her tracks, she first extended her arm, bent her elbow, and leaned forward from the hips—all to examine the watch strapped to her wrist; then she gave a loud double-rap on the door.

"There are two in each room," the nurse remarked over her shoulder.

"Two what?" asked Marian without thinking. The sound like a sheep's bleating almost made her turn around and run back.

One old woman was pulling the door open in short, gradual jerks, and when she saw the nurse a strange smile forced her old face dangerously awry. Marian, suddenly propelled by the strong, impatient arm of the nurse, saw next the side-face of another old woman, even older, who was lying flat in bed with a cap on and a counterpane drawn up to her chin.

"Visitor," said the nurse, and after one more shove she was off up the   10 hall.

Marian stood tongue-tied; both hands held the potted plant. The old woman, still with that terrible, square smile (which was a smile of welcome) stamped on her bony face, was waiting. . . . Perhaps she said something. The old woman in bed said nothing at all, and she did not look around.

Suddenly Marian saw a hand, quick as a bird claw, reach up in the air and pluck the white cap off her head. At the same time, another claw to match drew her all the way into the room and the next moment the door closed behind her.

"My, my, my," said the old lady at her side.

Marian stood enclosed by a bed, a washstand and a chair; the tiny room had altogether too much furniture. Everything smelled wet—even the bare floor. She held onto the back of the chair, which was wicker and felt soft and damp. Her heart beat more and more slowly, her hands got colder and colder, and she could not hear whether the old women were saying anything or not. She could not see them very clearly. How dark it was! The window shade was down, and the only door was shut. Marian looked at the ceiling. . . . It was like being caught in a robber's cave, just before one was murdered.

"Did you come to be our little girl for awhile?" the first robber asked.   15

Then something was snatched from Marian's hand—the little potted plant.

"Flowers!" screamed the old woman. She stood holding the pot in an undecided way. "Pretty flowers," she added.

Then the old woman in bed cleared her throat and spoke. "They are not pretty," she said, still without looking around, but very distinctly.

Marian suddenly pitched against the chair and sat down in it.

"Pretty flowers," the first old woman insisted. "Pretty—pretty. . . ."   20

Marian wished she had the little pot back for just a moment—she had forgotten to look at the plant herself before giving it away. What did it look like?

"Stinkweeds," said the other old woman sharply. She had a bunchy white forehead and red eyes like a sheep. Now she turned them toward Marian. The fogginess seemed to rise in her throat again, and she bleated, "Who—are—you?"

To her surprise, Marian could not remember her name. "I'm a Campfire Girl," she said finally.

"Watch out for the germs," said the old woman like a sheep, not addressing anyone.

"One came out last month to see us," said the first old woman.   25

A sheep or a germ? wondered Marian dreamily, holding onto the chair.

"Did not!" cried the other old woman.

"Did so! Read to us out of the Bible, and we enjoyed it!" screamed the first.

"Who enjoyed it!" said the woman in bed. Her mouth was unexpectedly small and sorrowful, like a pet's.

"We enjoyed it," insisted the other. "You enjoyed it—I enjoyed it."   30

"We all enjoyed it," said Marian, without realizing that she had said a word.

The first old woman had just finished putting the potted plant high, high on the top of the wardrobe, where it could hardly be seen from below. Marian wondered how she had ever succeeded in placing it there, how she could ever have reached so high.

"You mustn't pay any attention to old Addie," she now said to the little girl. "She's ailing today."

"Will you shut your mouth?" said the woman in bed. "I am not."

"You're a story."   35

"I can't stay but a minute—really, I can't," said Marian suddenly. She looked down at the wet floor and thought that if she were sick in here they would have to let her go.

With much to-do the first old woman sat down in a rocking chair—still another piece of furniture!—and began to rock. With the fingers on one hand she touched a very dirty cameo pin on her chest. "What do you do at school?" she asked.

"I don't know. . ." said Marian. She tried to think but she could not.

"Oh, but the flowers are beautiful," the old woman whispered. She seemed to rock faster and faster; Marian did not see how anyone could rock so fast.

"Ugly," said the woman in bed.   40

"If we bring flowers—" Marian began, and then fell silent. She had almost said that if Campfire Girls brought flowers to the Old Ladies' Home, the visit would count one extra point, and if they took a Bible with them on the bus and read it to the old ladies, it counted double. But the old woman had not listened, anyway; she was rocking and watching the other one, who watched back from the bed.

"Poor Addie is ailing. She has to take medicine—see?" she said, pointing a horny finger at a row of bottles on the table, and rocking so high that her black comfort shoes lifted off the floor like a little child's.

"I am no more sick than you are," said the woman in bed.

"Oh yes you are!"

"I just got more sense than you have, that's all," said the other old   45
woman, nodding her head.

"That's only the contrary way she talks when *you all* come," said the first old lady with sudden intimacy. She stopped the rocker with a neat pat of her feet and leaned toward Marian. Her hand reached over—it felt like a petunia leaf, clinging and just a little sticky.

"Will you hush! Will you hush!" cried the other one.

Marian leaned back rigidly in her chair.

"When I was a little girl like you, I went to school and all," said the old woman in the same intimate, menacing voice. "Not here—another town. . . ."

"Hush!" said the sick woman. "You never went to school. You never came   50
and you never went. You never were anywhere—only here. You never were born! You don't know anything. Your head is empty, your heart and hands and your old black purse are all empty, even that little old box that you brought with you you brought empty—you showed it to me. And yet you talk, talk, talk, talk, talk all the time until I think I'm losing my mind. Who are you? You're a stranger—a perfect stranger! Don't you know you're a stranger? Is it possible that they have actually done a thing like this to any-one—sent them in a stranger to talk, and rock, and tell away her whole long rigmarole? Do they seriously suppose that I'll be able to keep it up, day in, day out, night in, night out, living in the same room with a terrible old woman—forever?"

Marian saw the old woman's eyes grow bright and turn toward her. This old woman was looking at her with despair and calculation in her face. Her small lips suddenly dropped apart, and exposed a half circle of false teeth with tan gums.

"Come here, I want to tell you something," she whispered. "Come here!"

Marian was trembling, and her heart nearly stopped beating altogether for a moment.

"Now, now, Addie," said the first old woman. "That's not polite. Do you know what's really the matter with old Addie today?" She, too, looked at Marian; one of her eyelids drooped low.

"The matter?" the child repeated stupidly. "What's the matter with her?"   55

"Why, she's mad because it's her birthday!" said the first old woman, beginning to rock again and giving a little crow as though she had answered her own riddle.

"It is not, it is not!" screamed the old woman in bed. "It is not my birthday, no one knows when that is but myself, and will you please be quiet and say nothing more, or I'll go straight out of my mind!" She turned her eyes toward Marian again, and presently she said in the soft, foggy voice, "When the worst comes to the worst, I ring this bell, and the nurse comes." One of her hands was drawn out from under the patched counterpane—a thin little hand with enormous black freckles. With a finger which would not hold still she pointed to a little bell on the table among the bottles.

"How old are you?" Marian breathed. Now she could see the old woman in bed very closely and plainly, and very abruptly, from all sides, as in dreams. She wondered about her—she wondered for a moment as though there was nothing else in the world to wonder about. It was the first time such a thing had happened to Marian.

"I won't tell!"

The old face on the pillow, where Marian was bending over it, slowly   60
gathered and collapsed. Soft whimpers came out of the small open mouth. It was a sheep that she sounded like—a little lamb. Marian's face drew very close, the yellow hair hung forward.

"She's crying!" She turned a bright, burning face up to the first old woman.

"That's Addie for you," the old woman said spitefully.

Marian jumped up and moved toward the door. For the second time, the claw almost touched her hair, but it was not quick enough. The little girl put her cap on.

"Well, it was a real visit," said the old woman, following Marian through the doorway and all the way out into the hall. Then from behind she suddenly clutched the child with her sharp little fingers. In an affected, high-pitched whine she cried, "Oh, little girl, have you a penny to spare for a poor old woman that's not got anything of her own? We don't have a thing in the world—not a penny for candy—not a thing! Little girl, just a nickel—a penny—"

Marian pulled violently against the old hands for a moment before she   65
was free. Then she ran down the hall, without looking behind her and without looking at the nurse, who was reading *Field & Stream* at her desk. The nurse, after another triple motion to consult her wrist watch, asked automatically the question put to all visitors in all institutions: "Won't you stay and have dinner with us?"

Marian never replied. She pushed the heavy door open into the cold air and ran down the steps.

Under the prickly shrub she stooped and quickly, without being seen, retrieved a red apple she had hidden there.

Her yellow hair under the white cap, her scarlet coat, her bare knees all flashed in the sunlight as she ran to meet the big bus rocketing through the street.

"Wait for me!" she shouted. As though at an imperial command, the bus ground to a stop.

She jumped on and took a big bite out of the apple.   70

Poetry

When I began to read nursery rhymes for myself,
and, later, to read other verses and ballads, I
knew I had discovered the most important things
that could be ever. There they were, seemingly
lifeless, made only of black and white, but out
of them, out of their own being, came love and
terror and pity and pain and wonder and all
the other vague abstractions that made our
ephemeral lives dangerous, great, and bearable.

DYLAN THOMAS

12 PREVIEW

The Voice of Poetry

Courtesy Richard B. Ressman

*The poet, lacking the impediment of speech with
which the rest of us are afflicted, gazes, records,
diagnoses, and prophesies.*

RICHARD SELZER

Sei que canto. E a canção é tudo.
Tem sangue eterno e asa ritmada.
E um dia sei que estarei mudo:
—mais nada.

*I know that I sing. And song is all for me.
Its heart beats forever as it flies on rhythmic wing.
And I also know that one day my voice will fall
    silent—
Never to be heard again.*

CECÍLIA MEIRELES

FOCUS ON POETRY

Poets are in love with words. The gift of language makes us human,
and poets make the fullest use of it. We might call poetry language at its
best: Poets use its full potential, using more of it and using it to better
advantage than we usually do. They often seem to write with a heightened sense of awareness, with a special intensity—"in a fine frenzy," in
Shakespeare's words. Poetry mobilizes the image-making capacity of
language. It delights the ear and stirs our emotions. It has the potential,
if we let it, of making us more thoughtful human beings.

Listen to the human voice speaking in a poem. That voice may be
speaking about anything within the realm of human experience, real or
imagined. Here is a modern American poet speaking to you about the
pain of separation.

W. S. Merwin   *(born 1927)*

Separation   *1963*

Your absence has gone through me
Like thread through a needle.
Everything I do is stitched with its color.

What makes this a poem rather than ordinary prose?

✗ Out of the confusing flow of experience, the poet has brought something into *focus*. For a moment, we stop hurrying to whatever we were doing next. We stop to pay attention. We linger for a while—to contemplate, to take something in.

✗ What we take in is not just talk. We are helped to *imagine* what separation is like. The poem gives us something to visualize, to take in with the mind's eye. It is as if our days, like a piece of embroidery, were stitched through with a continuing thread—of missing the other person. A sewing needle does not jab the fabric once and then think about something else. It does its work by making one stitch after the other, stitching in the thread that will hold the fabric together or that will shape a pattern in a piece of embroidered material.

✗ The poem does not just give us information to feed into a data bank. We are not expected to record the message with no more emotion than a fax machine. The poet assumes that we are capable of caring one way or the other. We are capable of entering imaginatively into the poet's *feelings,* of sharing his sense of loss.

✗ Finally, the poem is printed as lines of verse. These measure out or mark off units of thought. They lay out the message in a satisfying *pattern* (that we can take in at a glance). When we finish reading, we have the satisfying sense of having taken in a complete whole.

Poetry is one of our oldest heirlooms as human beings. Civilization began when artists first painted bison on the walls of caves and when poets first chanted songs about the exploits of the tribe or the creation of all living things. In many early cultures, a dominant form, or genre, was the **epic,** a long poem that spoke to its listeners in an elevated style and embodied their values, aspirations, and traumas. Often, the traditional epic focused on a high point in the history of a people, the way Homer in the *Iliad* sang the Greek expedition to besiege and destroy the fabled city of Troy:

> As the many tribes of winged birds—
> The geese, the cranes, and the long-throated swans—
> Make their flight this way and that
> And then settle in fluttering swarms
> While a vast field echoes with their cries,
> So these many tribes poured out from their ships
> Onto the plain of Troy.

When we talk about poetry today, we usually think of a more personal kind of writing. We think of a fairly short poem that communicates personal observations, feelings, and thoughts. We call such a short poem the **lyric,** named after the lyre, or small harp, that the poets of ancient Greece played as they recited their verses.

A FESTIVAL OF NATURE POETRY

FIRST READING

Poets have often looked at the natural world with awe and wonder. They focus on something in the natural world so we can truly look at it and become fully aware of it. A poem may ask us to stop and marvel at the startling beauty of birds or at the power of the shark or the whale. Poets remind us of our kinship with other living creatures, making us aware of our roots in the natural world. They teach us to rejoice in or to fear the vital energies around us. They can make us feel that human beings cut off from their natural roots are not fully alive.

Working with a group, you may want to prepare a **poetry reading** focused on the following nature poems. Your group may want to script a brief introduction to a poem and then one or more personal responses to each poem.

David Wagoner   *(born 1926)*

Lost   *1976*

Stand still. The trees ahead and the bushes beside you
Are not lost. Wherever you are is called Here,
And you must treat it as a powerful stranger,
Must ask permission to know it and be known.
The forest breathes. Listen. It answers,   5
I have made this place around you.
If you leave it, you may come back again, saying Here.
No two trees are the same to Raven.
No two branches are the same to Wren.
If what a tree or a bush does is lost on you,   10
You are surely lost. Stand still. The forest knows
Where you are. You must let it find you.

The Receptive Reader

To you, is the forest alive? Is it "breathing"? How well do you think birds know their way around in their natural environment? Do you really think that for birds no two trees or two branches are alike? Why does the poet make the point that we as human beings may be lost in a natural setting—but the plant life and wildlife are not lost? (Why does the word *lost* provide the title? And why does it echo several times in the poem?) Are you a person on whom what a tree or a bush does is lost? Does this poem help you think of the natural world not as "inanimate" matter but as full of mysterious life? Why, or why not?

Denise Levertov   *(born 1923)*

Come into Animal Presence   *1963*

Come into animal presence.
No man is so guileless as
the serpent. The lonely white
rabbit on the roof is a star
twitching its ears at the rain.   5
The llama intricately
folding its hind legs to be seated
not disdains but mildly
disregards human approval.
What joy when the insouciant   10
armadillo glances at us and doesn't
quicken his trotting
across the track into the palm brush.

What is this joy? That no animal
falters, but knows what it must do?   15
That the snake has no blemish,
that the rabbit inspects his strange surroundings
in white star-silence? The llama
rests in dignity, the armadillo
has some intention to pursue in the palm-forest.   20
Those who were sacred have remained so,
holiness does not dissolve, it is a presence
of bronze, only the sight that saw it
faltered and turned from it.
An old joy returns in holy presence.   25

The Receptive Reader

Isn't the serpent a symbol of guile and deceit? Why is it "guileless" in this poem? How could a tiny rabbit have something in common with the stars? What do all the animals in this poem have in common? Why bring in the serpent, the llama, and the "insouciant" (carefree or unbothered) armadillo rather than more familiar and less exotic animals? The poet harks back to a time when animals were sacred or represented holy energies in nature. Why did human beings once see animals as holy? (Do you remember examples from your study of history or religion?) And then what changed? Do you believe that some of the ancient awe humans felt when faced with the animal kingdom still survives today?

W.S. Merwin   *(born 1927)*

For a Coming Extinction   1967

Gray whale
Now that we are sending you to The End
That great god
Tell him
That we who follow you invented forgiveness   5
And forgive nothing

I write as though you could understand
And I could say it
One must always pretend something
Among the dying   10
When you have left the seas nodding on their stalks
Empty of you
Tell him that we were made
On another day

The bewilderment will diminish like an echo   15
Winding along your inner mountains
Unheard by us
And find its way out
Leaving behind it the future
Dead   20
And ours

When you will not see again
The whale calves trying the light
Consider what you will find in the black garden
And its court   25
The sea cows the Great Auks the gorillas
The irreplaceable hosts ranged countless
And fore-ordained as stars
Our sacrifices
Join your word to theirs   30
Tell him
That it is we who are important

The Receptive Reader

Merwin is a poet who knows how to make us take a startled new look at things we thought we knew and understood. (For instance, human beings talk much about mercy and forgiveness. Why does the poet say that we "invented forgiveness / And forgive nothing"?) Why does the threat of extinction facing the gray whale stand out for us among the threats to other endangered wildlife? Is it just a question of size? Do you think religions should make us imagine our fellow creatures of the natural world as assembling for a final reckoning at the end of time? We often think of endangered species as isolated and half extinct. How does the poet's vision of the "irreplaceable hosts ranged countless" change that perspective? What fellow creatures does the poet actually ask us to visualize or imagine? What guided his choice? What creatures would *you* have chosen to represent the animal world?

Bruce Weigl   *(born 1949)*

Snowy Egret   *1985*

My neighbor's boy has lifted his father's shotgun and stolen
Down to the backwaters of the Elizabeth
And in the moon he's blasted a snowy egret
From the shallows it stalked for small fish.

Midnight. My wife wakes me. He's in the backyard   5
With a shovel so I go down half-drunk with pills
That let me sleep to see what I can see and if it's safe.
The boy doesn't hear me come across the dewy grass.
He says through tears he has to bury it,
He says his father will kill him   10
And he digs until the hole is deep enough and gathers
The egret carefully into his arms
As if not to harm the blood-spattered wings
Gleaming in the flashlight beam.

His man's muscled shoulders   15
Shake with the weight of what he can't set right no matter what,
But one last time he tries to stay a child, sobbing
Please don't tell. . . .
He says he only meant to flush it from the shadows,
He only meant to watch it fly   20
But the shot spread too far
Ripping into the white wings
Spanned awkwardly for a moment
Until it glided into brackish death.

I want to grab his shoulders,   25
Shake the lies loose from his lips but he hurts enough,
he burns with shame for what he's done,
With fear for his hard father's
Fists I've seen crash down on him for so much less.
I don't know what to do but hold him.   30
If I let go he'll fly to pieces before me.
What a time we share, that can make a good boy steal away,
Wiping out from the blue face of the pond

What he hadn't even known he loved, blasting
Such beauty into nothing.   35

The Receptive Reader

   Dictionaries describe the egret as a long-legged wading bird with white
showy plumage. Where in the poem do you come to see or visualize the bird?
What image or images does it leave in your mind? The poet calls the boy's excuses "lies"—what were the lies? What does the poet think was the truth? Is the
boy in this poem callous and irresponsible? (How does he a last time try "to
stay a child"?) How would you describe the mixed emotions of the boy? Although he is never at the scene, the father comes into the poem several times.
What is his role? To the poet, this was not an "isolated incident." What does it
say to him about the "time we share"? Where are you in this poem? Do you
identify with the poet? the father? the boy? Would the poem still make its point
if the bird had not been so beautiful?

Margaret Atwood   *(born 1939)*

Elegy for the Giant Tortoises   1976

Let others pray for the passenger pigeon,
the dodo, the whooping crane, the Eskimo:
everyone must specialize

I will confine myself to a meditation
upon the giant tortoises   5
withering finally on a remote island.

I concentrate in subway stations,
in parks, I can't quite see them,
they move to the peripheries of my eyes

but on the last day they will be there;   10
already the event
like a wave traveling shapes vision:

on the road where I stand they will materialize,
plodding past me in a straggling line
awkward without water   15

their small heads pondering
from side to side, their useless armor
sadder than tanks and history,

in their closed gaze ocean and sunlight paralyzed,
lumbering up the steps, under the archways   20
toward the square glass altars

where the brittle gods are kept,

the relics of what we have destroyed,
our holy and obsolete symbols.

The Receptive Reader

Can you and fellow students pool what you know about the passenger pigeon, the dodo, and the whooping crane? (Would anyone "pray" for them?) Why does the poet mention the Eskimo in the same breath? While in subway stations or parks, the poet "concentrates" to try to see the far distant tortoises with the mind's eye. What kind of creatures does she see? What details in the poem do most to make the creatures real for you? This poet again imagines a time when animals were living holy symbols that are now becoming obsolete— totally a thing of the past—or are now mere relics. To judge from your reading of these nature poems, what is the connection between poetry and religion?

Mary Oliver   *(born 1935)*

Wild Geese   *1986*

You do not have to be good.
You do not have to walk on your knees
for a hundred miles through the desert, repenting.
You only have to let the soft animal of your body love what it loves.
Tell me about despair, yours, and I will tell you mine.   5
Meanwhile the world goes on.
Meanwhile the sun and the clear pebbles of the rain
are moving across the landscapes,
over the prairies and the deep trees,
the mountains and the rivers.   10
Meanwhile the wild geese, high in the clean blue air,
are heading home again.
Whoever you are, no matter how lonely,
the world offers itself to your imagination,
calls to you like the wild geese, harsh and exciting—   15
over and over announcing your place
in the family of things.

The Receptive Reader

This poem sounds an affirmative note that contrasts with doomsday scenarios for our endangered wildlife. What is this poet's answer to despair? Why does she make a point of telling us that we "do not have to be good"? For you, are the sun and the rain or the prairies, trees, or rivers merely soulless material features of our universe? Or do you have an emotional or spiritual relationship with any of them? With which of them and why? The wild geese become a central symbol in this poem. What kind of birds are they? Are they beautiful? What do they symbolize or stand for? What is their message—what are they "announcing"?

Audre Lorde   *(1934–1992)*

Coping   *1968*

It has rained for five days
running
the world is
a round puddle
of sunless water   5
where small islands
are only beginning
to cope
a young boy
in my garden   10
is bailing out water
from his flower patch
when I ask him why
he tells me
young seeds that have not seen sun   15
forget
and drown easily.

The Receptive Reader

Poetry at times takes you to strange and exciting places. However, often the poet invites you to take a fresh look at something familiar—something close to home. After five days of rain, the poet's world has become a different world. What is ordinary about the situation described in this poem? What is different from the ordinary about the way this poet looks at the rain? What gives the seeds a significance beyond their ordinary literal meaning? What is their symbolic meaning? What is the central word in this poem? How does the poet highlight it? What is its full meaning?

The Personal Response

The following passage is a student writer's personal response to David Wagoner's "Lost." Which of the nature poems you have read had a special personal meaning for you? Did you identify with the speaker or relate to the situation? Write a journal entry about the thoughts and feelings inspired by the poem.

After I read the poem, a recent trip came to mind, where I spent weeks in the woods living in a tent. When I first arrived at my camp in the woods, I must admit that I felt incredibly lost. The vast and seemingly endless forest was initially very intimidating. I couldn't help feeling alone and somewhat vulnerable in the depths of the great Alaskan wilderness. As Wagoner accurately describes it, I saw the woods as a "powerful stranger." However, after days of solitude, I began to realize a change in my perspective. I was starting to feel comfortable in my new home. I was soon noticing aspects of the forest that I had overlooked at my first arrival. Lying in my tent in the early morning hours initially seemed so quiet that I felt as if I was surrounded by utter emptiness. However, as the length of my visit increased, I began to notice more and more about the woods. I began to hear the voices of the forest: the distant chirping of birds, the drops of moisture from the leaves of the overhanging trees, the hum of the air as it circulates through the valleys. I realized that the forest was indeed "breathing" and full of life. Not only was it full of life, unlike a city it was full of "natural life," created by the hands of God alone. I realized that I was in a whole different world, a world run by plants and wild animals—with no cars, no pollution, and no unnatural noise. I would watch the squirrels move about the treetops with no fear of the fifty-foot fall that lay below. I would quietly notice how the moose could move through the brush and thickets. However, I realized that I was out of my element in these surroundings. I was the stranger, not the woods. Maybe 10,000 years ago, people could once roam in harmony with nature. But those times have long since changed. What the trees and bushes did was indeed lost on me.

THE POET'S LANGUAGE

I dwell in Possibility—
A fairer House than Prose—
More numerous of Windows—
Superior—for Doors—

EMILY DICKINSON

Poems demand your attention. They use a language richer in meaning than ordinary talk. As you read and study poems, you become more sensitive to recurrent features of the poet's language:

Image *How does the poem appeal to the eye and your other senses?* Poets think in images. The **images** in a poem bring an experience to life by appealing to your senses—by making you see, hear, smell, taste, and touch. A dictionary might define *presentiment* as a sudden fleeting feeling of anxiety—a sudden, passing sense of foreboding; a premonition that something hurtful is going to happen. Unlike a dictionary definition, the following poem does not *state* this idea; it brings it to life. It gives you something to see, to visualize.

Emily Dickinson   *(1830–1886)*

Presentiment   1863

Presentiment—is that long Shadow—on the Lawn—
Indicative that Suns go down—
The Notice to the startled Grass
That Darkness—is about to pass—

The poem starts with a striking image: On a sunny day, we all of a sudden notice the dark shadow on the lawn that announces (or is an indication of) the coming of evening. Like the grass, we may be startled, afraid of darkness. We may share in a shuddery feeling. We are reminded that "suns go down"; like them, sunny parts of our lives must sooner or later alternate with darkness. Although there are feelings and thoughts in this poem, they come to us through the poet's use of vivid imagery.

Metaphor   *How does the language of the poem make imaginative connections?* The images in a poem often carry meanings beyond their literal surface impact. The most basic device poets use to convey meanings beyond those of ordinary literal speech is the **metaphor.** It "carries us beyond" literal meanings to something else. Metaphors are imaginative comparisons carrying meanings that might remain pale or incomplete when spelled out in literal terms. The poet Gregory Orr says, "Like any other man / I was born with a knife / in one hand / and a wound in the other." He does not mean that literally at birth he had a knife and a wound. He means that he, like all of us, was born with the ability and perhaps genetic inclination to kill. At the same time, he, like all of us, was born capable of being harmed, of becoming in turn a victim.

A poet may trace a metaphor into its various ramifications, following up related similarities. Look at the **extended metaphor** in the following poem:

Donald Justice   *(born 1925)*

Time and the Weather   *1967*

Time and the weather wear away
The houses that our fathers built.
Their ghostly furniture remains—
All the sad sofas we have stained
With tears of boredom and of guilt,   5

The fraying mottoes, the stopped clocks. . .
And still sometimes these tired shapes
Haunt the damp parlors of the heart.
What Sunday prisons they recall!
And what miraculous escapes!   10

In this poem, the poet remembers actual literal houses that have since disappeared with the passage of time. These houses turn into an extended metaphor that develops throughout the poem. The word *weather* is already metaphorical: It is *as if* heavy weather had over the years washed the houses away under the onslaught of rain and wind. The once literal furniture now "haunts" us—*as if* the sofas and clocks were ghosts come back from the past. It is *as if* our minds had "parlors" in which the furnishings could continue their ghostly existence. It is *as if* the Sundays when young people had to stay home had been a prison from which the inmates at times staged "miraculous escapes."

Symbol *What in the poem has a meaning beyond itself?* A **symbol** carries a literal meaning and yet at the same time has a larger significance. A poet may show you a person carrying a real gun. For many readers, guns will have symbolic associations—of manliness for some, of murderous violence for others. A poem may take you to the site of a nuclear plant. In the early part of the poem, the plant may be seen through the eyes of an earlier generation as a symbol of technological progress— of a future without backbreaking toil and fuel shortages. Later in the poem, the plant may be seen through the eyes of a later generation as the symbol of the arrogant pride of an overreaching technology heedless of its disastrous side effects.

The following poem, one of the best loved and most often discussed in the English language, is often read for its symbolic meaning.

Robert Frost   *(1874–1963)*

Stopping by Woods on a Snowy Evening   *1923*

Whose woods these are I think I know.
His house is in the village, though;
He will not see me stopping here
To watch his woods fill up with snow.

My little horse must think it queer   5
To stop without a farmhouse near
Between the woods and frozen lake
The darkest evening of the year.

He gives his harness bells a shake
To ask if there is some mistake.   10
The only other sound's the sweep
Of easy wind and downy flake.

The woods are lovely, dark and deep.
But I have promises to keep,
And miles to go before I sleep,   15
And miles to go before I sleep.

In this poem, we find ourselves on a deserted rural road in the winter, away from the nearest village or farmhouse, with the driver of the horse-drawn vehicle stopping to look at the woods filling up with snow. It is cold enough for the lake to have frozen over, and the evening is getting very dark, so the normal thing would be to hurry on home. (The horse certainly seems to think so, wondering "if there is some mistake.")

But something strange happens in this poem: It is very quiet; the wind is an "easy wind." The snowflakes are "downy"—soft like the feathers in a down-filled pillow beckoning toward rest. The snow-covered woods look "lovely." It would be tempting not to go on—to go to sleep in the soft snow. It would be restful to push out of mind whatever cares, responsibilities, or pressures are waiting in the village. While ordinarily we would be afraid to die in the freezing cold, to a harried person, death could begin to seem restful and beautiful. In the end, tempting as the thought may be of dropping out, of going to "sleep," the speaker in the poem is kept going by the thought of "promises to keep." There are still "miles to go," as the speaker says twice, "miles to go."

If we read the woods in Frost's poems not as a place for a temporary rest but as a beckoning toward the final long rest of death, we are reading them as a symbol. A symbol has a literal reality and at the same time a larger meaning. The woods in the Frost poem are literally there; we may choose to give them a larger symbolic significance.

The Receptive Reader

1. What kind of "promises" do you think the speaker had in mind?

2. Critics have argued over whether or not the dark woods in this poem are a symbol of death. What would be your answer, and how would you support it?

3. What is the effect of the poet's repeating the last line?

Rhyme   *Does the poem use the echo effect of rhyme?* Rhyme and meter are formal features of much traditional poetry, but they became more and more optional during the twentieth century. **Rhyme** is an echo effect produced when a poet repeats the same sounds at the end of the final syllables (sometimes whole final words) of two or more lines:

The grizzly bear whose potent HUG
Was feared by all is now a RUG.

ARTHUR GUITERMAN

Rhyme keeps alive the delight in repetition, in finding recurrent patterns, that children experience when they recite "Hickory-dickory-DOCK / The mouse ran up the CLOCK." At the same time, rhyme helps a poet create patterns by marking off regular intervals, by measuring off lines of verse. Rhyme can help a poet give shape to a **stanza,** a set of related lines with a pattern that may be repeated in other such stanzas in the same poem. In the following opening stanza of a song from a Shakespeare play, we see an interlaced rhyme scheme: The first and third lines rhyme (*sun/done*). So do the second and fourth, as well as the fifth and sixth (giving us a pattern of *ababcc*):

Fear no more the heat of the SUN,   a
Nor the furious winter's RAGES;   b
Thou thy worldly task hast DONE,   a
Home art gone, and taken thy WAGES.   b
Golden lads and girls all MUST,   c
As chimney-sweepers, come to DUST.   c

The following poem is by an eighteenth-century English poet who uses rhyme extensively. Lines and stanzas are neatly marked off and packaged.

William Cowper   *(1731–1800)*

The Snail   *before 1800*

Give but his horns the slightest touch,
His self-collective power is such,
He shrinks into his house with much
    Displeasure.

Wherever he dwells, he dwells alone,   5
Except himself, has chattels° none,
Well satisfied to be his own   *goods*
    Whole treasure.

Thus hermit-like his life he leads,
Nor partner of his banquet needs,°
And if he meets one, only feeds   *nor does he need*   10
    The faster.

Who seeks him must be worse than blind
—He and his house are so combined—
If finding it, he fails to find   15
    Its master.

The Receptive Reader

1. What in the outward form of this poem mirrors the shrinking of the snail as it withdraws into the shell?

2. How does this poet go beyond the simplest use of rhyme—two consecutive lines that rhyme? Can you read this poem out loud so as to do justice to the echo effect of rhyme and to the spilling over of the sense (or the sentence) from the third into the fourth line of each stanza?

3. In how many ways does this poem compare the snail to a human being? With what effect? How are we reminded in the poem that the animal is *different* from a human being?

4. What is witty about this poem? Does it have a serious point?

Most poets of our century (and some earlier ones) have done *without* rhyme. They have moved from traditional form, with consistent use of rhyme and an underlying regular beat, or meter, toward more open form. They lay out their poems and give shape to them by other means.

Meter   *Does the poem have a strong regular rhythm, or meter?* In much traditional poetry, rhyme and meter go hand in hand. **Meter** regulates the free-flowing, irregular rhythms of ordinary speech. It sets up a regular underlying beat—the kind that in music you could accentuate by a drumbeat, by tapping your toes, or by clapping your hands. (Meter provides only the underlying beat, not the music.) Strongly metrical poetry, rhymed or unrhymed, was the norm till well into the nineteenth century. Much modern poetry has moved toward freer, more irregular rhythms—hard to chart, or scan, as a regular beat.

Meter has an enticing (and something hypnotic) effect. It mirrors basic rhythms of life: the lub-DUB, lub-DUB, lub-DUB of the heart; the one-two, one-two of walking or running; the in-and-out of deep breathing. The following lines from the poem by Robert Frost that you read earlier have an exceptionally regular beat. Each second syllable has a stronger stress than the first—with the exception of the fourth word in the first and second lines and the second word in the third line. These variations keep the basic four-beat line from becoming monotonous, like the tick-tack of a metronome:

> Whose WOODS these <u>are</u> I THINK I KNOW.
> His HOUSE is <u>in</u> the VILLAGE THOUGH;
> He <u>will</u> not SEE me STOPPING HERE
> To WATCH his WOODS fill UP with SNOW.

To chart the basic meter, we can cut up the line into four pairs of syllables, each with an *unstressed* or weak syllable first and a *stressed* or emphasized syllable second:

> To WATCH | his WOODS | fill UP | with SNOW.

Each of these four segments is called a **foot.** A foot with only two syllables and the stress last is an **iambic** foot, and the "DETROIT—DETROIT—DETROIT" meter it sets up is called iambic meter. The following poem is by Alfred, Lord Tennyson, poet-sage of the Victorian Age (roughly the mid–nineteenth century). Read the poem out loud, or hear it read out loud. Which lines come closest to a regular four-beat iambic meter? What makes the second and third lines different?

Alfred, Lord Tennyson   *(1809–1892)*

The Eagle   *1851*

He clasps the crag with crooked hands;
Close to the sun in lonely lands,

Ringed with the azure° world, he stands.   *deep sky-blue*
The wrinkled sea beneath him crawls;
He watches from his mountain walls,   5
And like a thunderbolt he falls.

The first line of the poem, like the fourth, has a very regular beat:

He CLASPS | the CRAG | with CROOK | ed HANDS

But at the beginning of the second line (and also of the third), the
stress pattern is reversed. This reversal, or inversion, sets up the kind of
counterrhythm that keeps meter from becoming too mechanical:

CLOSE to | the SUN | in LONE | ly LANDS

The Receptive Reader

1. How should this poem sound when read aloud? Listen as several classmates read the poem. Which of them comes closest to the right balance—making the reader sense the underlying rhythm without making it mechanical or
obtrusive?

2. Although almost extinct, the eagle is everywhere in traditional lore and
public symbols. What images, ideas, or associations does the eagle bring to
mind? Are any of them echoed in Tennyson's poem? Is there anything new or
different about the way Tennyson asks us to imagine the eagle in this poem?

Rhythm   *How does the poem use the natural rhythms of language?*
Even in Tennyson's time, poets were experimenting with less regular
rhythms. Here is an example of **free verse** by the American poet Walt
Whitman, the "poet of democracy." Whitman's free verse has a strong
rhythm, but it does not have an easily charted regular beat. Some lines
are short, but others go on and on. Whitman saw himself as the prophet
of a new national consciousness and a new spirituality, and his lines
have the flow and sweep of a prophet's inspirations. We can imagine
that we are hearing the poet chant these lines. In the words of one student reader, "The almost chanting, yet not mesmerizingly regular rhythm
elevates the tone of the poem and gives it almost oracular power."

Walt Whitman   *(1819–1892)*

A Noiseless Patient Spider   *1881*

A noiseless patient spider
I marked where on a little promontory° it stood isolated,   *outcropping*
Marked how to explore the vacant vast surrounding
It launched forth filament, filament, filament out of itself,

Ever unreeling them, ever tirelessly speeding them.   5
And you O my soul where you stand,
Surrounded, detached, in measureless oceans of space,
Ceaselessly musing, venturing, throwing, seeking the spheres
    to connect them,
Till the bridge you will need be formed, till the ductile° anchor   *easily bent*
    hold,
Till the gossamer thread you fling catch somewhere, O my soul.   10

    This poem revolves around the parallel between "the noiseless patient spider" and the human soul. The spider stands "isolated" as if on a cliff jutting out into the sea, encircled by the "vacant vast surrounding." Similarly, the soul finds itself "detached, in measureless oceans of space"— in the vast spaces our thoughts can travel. The spider with tireless repetition spins and launches forth "filament, filament, filament," hoping they will catch at points beyond the empty space to allow it to anchor its net. Similarly, the human soul, "ceaselessly musing, venturing, throwing, seeking," launches forth the thoughts that will allow it to connect with what gives meaning to our lives. The slow, solemn rhythm of the lines suits the elevated subject. Here is how you might mark the stresses that account for the rhythm of the first three lines.

    A NOISEless PATIENT SPIDer
    I MARKED where on a LITTLE PROMONtory it STOOD Isolated,
    MARKED how to EXPLORE the VACANt VAST surROUNDing

The Receptive Reader

    1. How well do you respond to the *rhythm* of Whitman's verse? Can you chart the major stressed syllables in the rest of the poem? Do you and your classmates agree on the rhythmic patterns of the lines?

    2. What ideas or associations do spiders usually bring to mind? What is *different* about the way Whitman looks at the spider in this poem?

    3. What is the connection between the spider and the poet's *soul?* What is the "bridge" the soul will need? What is the "gossamer thread" the soul flings in this poem?

    4. Why does the poet start with the *image* of the patient spider—rather than with the central idea of the poem? What does the poet lose or gain by not letting us know till halfway through the poem that it is addressed to his soul?

    Open Form   *What gives the poem its unique shape?* Much later poetry has a less strong, less chanting rhythm than Whitman's poems. Modern poets have used the full range of **open form,** which allows them to give each poem its own individual shape and rhythm. What gives the following poem its unique shape? Gwendolyn Brooks is best known for eloquent poems about the injustices suffered by black Americans, although many of her poems are loving portraits of people she cherished.

Gwendolyn Brooks   *(1917–2000)*

Truth   *1949*

And if sun comes
How shall we greet him?
Shall we not dread him,
Shall we not fear him
After so lengthy a   5
Session with shade?

Though we have wept for him,
Though we have prayed
All through the night-years—
What if we wake one shimmering morning to   10
Hear the fierce hammering
Of his firm knuckles
Hard on the door?

Shall we not shudder?—
Shall we not flee   15
Into the shelter, the dear thick shelter
Of the familiar
Propitious° haze?   *promising good fortune*

Sweet is it, sweet is it
To sleep in the coolness   20
Of snug unawareness.

The dark hangs heavily
Over the eyes.

The Receptive Reader

1. This poem does not use traditional rhyme and meter. What guides you in reading the poem with the right rhythm? Point out examples of the poet's repeating phrases or sentence frames. Can you show how this repetition sets up patterns that help make the poem a unified whole? What is the effect of the frequent repetition or echoing on you as the reader?

2. Traditional guidelines for rhyme ruled out the repetition of identical words at the end of lines. It occurs in contemporary poetry—where does it occur in this poem? Pairs of words that do not rhyme but more distantly sound alike are **half-rhymes** or **slant rhymes.** Where do you find these in the poem?

3. How are the images and feelings associated with the sun in this poem different from more familiar or predictable ones? How are the images and feelings associated with the dark, its opposite, different from what we might expect?

4. What "fierce" and feared or dreaded truths do you think the poet had in mind? What kind of "night-years" may the poet have been thinking about?

Theme   *Does the poem as a whole make a statement?* Poems do not usually hand on ideas ready-made. A poem may imply or suggest ideas;

it may play them off or act them out. When we look for the statement made by a poem as a whole, we are looking for its **theme.** The theme is the answer the poem as a whole seems to give to the questions it raises.

The following poem is exceptionally direct in the message it addresses to its readers. A Spanish scholar, playwright, and poet who has been called "the first poetic figure of the New World" here takes up a theme to which she repeatedly returned in her poems. She wrote at a time when conventions of courtship required the male lover to pursue or "importune" the lady, who was expected to be reluctant or disdainful, and who was then blamed for being cruel and cold.

Juana Inés de la Cruz   *(1651–1695)*

From "A Satirical Romance"   *1692*

TRANSLATED BY JUDITH THURMAN

Ignorant men, who disclaim
women with no reason,
you do not see you are the reason
for what you blame.

Importuning her disdain   5
with such pressing desire,
why is it goodness you then require,
who have caused her shame?

What humour° can be so rare   *state of mind*
that carelessly will blur   10
a mirror, and then aver°   *claim*
that it's not clear?

Critics: In your sight
no woman can win:
keep you out, and she's too tight;   15
she's too loose if you get in.

The Receptive Reader

1. How does this poem lead up to its central message? What makes the mirror image effective?

2. Do you think this message by a seventeenth-century poet has lost its timeliness? Or does it still speak to the modern reader? Do you think the poet's indictment of men is justified?

3. Do you think women today speak this frankly to men?

4. Do you think this poem is addressed only to men—or also to women?

5. Write a journal entry as a reply to or comment on this poem.

Making Connections—For Discussion or Writing

Which of the poems in this group speaks to you most directly as a reader? Which is least meaningful for you? Which lives up best to what you expect poetry to be?

CLOSE READING AND THE PERSONAL RESPONSE

The poem must provoke its readers: force
them to hear—to hear themselves.

OCTAVIO PAZ

The purpose of poetry is to remind us how
difficult it is to remain just one person, for our
house is open, there are no keys in the doors,
and invisible guests come in and out at will.

CZESLAW MILOSZ, "THE POETIC VOICE IN US"

May God us keep
From single vision.

WILLIAM BLAKE

What is your role as the reader? A poem is not like an art object in a glass case in a museum, with a sign that says "Do not touch the artifacts." A successful poem does something for you as the reader: It may open a new perspective. It may shake you up; it may move you to laughter or to tears. The poem ceases to be just words on a page when it triggers this kind of interaction between the poet and you as the reader.

Some readers get much out of even a fairly short or simple poem. It is as if their antennas were especially well equipped to pick up the signals the poem sends. To make the most of your reading, consider guidelines like the following:

✗ *Give the poem a close reading.* Take in as much as you can; be open to whatever the poem has to offer. Many readers start with a quick reading of the whole poem to get an overall impression. But then they go back to take in important details. They linger over a key line. They weigh the impact of a key image. They puzzle over apparent contradictions.

✗ *Get your bearings.* Who is speaking in the poem? What is the situation or occasion? What seems to be the agenda? For instance, are we looking at a scene from the world of nature? Are we witnessing a confrontation between parent and child? Is a lover talking to the beloved?

✗ *Respond to the poem as a whole.* Try to get a sense of its overall pattern. Look for key words or phrases that echo in the poem. Look at how the poem as a whole takes shape. For instance, does it move from now to then (and then perhaps back again to now)? Does it play off two different ways of looking at our world? Does it set up polarities—for instance, does it move from innocence to experience? Does it travel between city life and nature?

✗ *Get into the spirit of the poem.* We are disappointed when someone reading a poem aloud reads without expression, without feeling. We want the reader's face, gestures, and body language to act out the mood, the rhythm, or the overall shape of the poem. Even when reading silently, a receptive reader may show by nods and frowns and gestures that the poem is being experienced, acted out, in the reader's mind.

✗ *Be ready for a personal response.* We do not read poetry in order to analyze poems that leave us cold. Writing poetry is an act of faith assuming that the poet's observations and experiences will find an echo in the experience of the reader. A poem that is reprinted and reread time and again has touched a chord in many different readers. To be moved by a poem about the loss of a father, we need not have lost a father ourselves, but the poem may remind us of the loss of somebody or something dear to us.

Give the following short poem a careful, patient, line-by-line reading. Then look at one student reader's close reading of the poem. What did you miss that the student reader noticed? What in turn did you notice that she apparently missed?

Linda Pastan   *(born 1932)*

Sometimes in Winter   1991

when I look into
the fragile faces
of those I love,

I long to be
one of those people who skate   5
over the surface

of their lives, scoring
the ice with patterns
of their own making,

people who have   10
no children,
who are attached

to earth only by
silver blades moving
at high speed,   15

who have learned to use
the medium of the cold
to dance in.

Compare the reading in the following sample student paper with your own reading of the poem:

Sample Student Paper

Dancing in the Medium of the Cold

In the poem "Sometimes in Winter," we are asked to explore the relationship between life and ice-skating. Taken out of context, the metaphor of life as skating over ice might not appear to be entirely serious. But the images that are used in this poem make us think seriously about the comparison. The comparison is followed up in a chain of related words and images: winter, cold, a surface that can be scored but not penetrated, patterns sketched in the ice, silver blades speeding across the ice.

On the surface, the sight of the "silver blades moving / at high speed" across the ice is very appealing. The skaters score "the ice with patterns / of their own making." They seem in charge, in control, deciding for themselves whether they want to score in the ice a figure 8 or some other kind of graceful loop. What a relief it would be to be a free-floating skater and not to have to worry about the needs and demands of others who depend on us.

However, the person speaking to us in the poem cannot be like an ice-skater skimming over the surface of life. For her, love means attachment. Looking into the "fragile" faces of those she loves, she sees how vulnerable they are. The speaker implies that love for children holds her to the earth when she says that people who have no children are attached to the earth only by "silver blades moving / at high speed." Is this connection enough to hold a person to the earth for very long? What happens to the ice-skater when this tenuous connection is severed? Does she fly off the earth? Does she cease to exist? That is what the metaphor implies. People who are not attached to loved ones are not fully participating in life; they only glide over the surface. They dance on top of life, but they do not enter into it.

The speaker in the poem says that she longs to be one of the people who skate over the surface of life, but the metaphor she uses belies or contradicts that claim. She may be attracted to the speed and flash of the ice-skater, but the images we see make us realize that the flash is all on the surface. The skaters are adapting to the medium in which they live; they are surrounded by the cold, so they have learned to dance (live) in it. If they were allowed to choose all over again, might they not say that they long to be attached to the earth by something more than silver blades moving at high speed?

Bickering, emergency phone calls, and disrupted schedules make life in close contact with others very different from skating gracefully over the ice. But could we stand "the medium of the cold" if we severed our ties?

The Receptive Reader

Does this reading explain why there are so much ice and cold in this poem? What do the "silver blades" make you see or feel? Were you surprised by the use of the word *fragile* at the beginning of the poem? (Does the student writer do enough to explain how it makes us feel?) How do you explain that the skaters are "dancing"?

To judge from this student paper, our personal response to this poem will depend at least in part on how we feel about living in a close web of personal relationships as against the free-floating loneliness of the skater. But the student writer's own personal answer is only implied. (One reader started a more personal response to this poem by saying, "Not just sometimes in winter but several times a day I muse how I might be better off on my own.")

The two responses that follow the next poem (by an Irish poet) are by the same reader. The first response is again the kind of close reading that tries to do justice to the poem in front of us on the page. The second response, however, goes a step further. The reader asked: What does this poem mean to me personally? Is there any personal connection between this poem and something in my own life? Study the two different dimensions of this reader's response. How are they different? How are they related?

Seamus Heaney   *(born 1939)*

Valediction   *1966*

Lady with the frilled blouse
And simple tartan skirt,
Since you have left the house
Its emptiness has hurt
All thought. In your presence   5
Time rode easy, anchored
On a smile; but absence
Rocked love's balance, unmoored
The days. They buck and bound
Across the calendar   10
Pitched from the quiet sound
Of your flower-tender
Voice. Need breaks on my strand;°   *beach, shore*
You've gone, I am at sea.
Until you resume command   15
Self is in mutiny.

Look at the way the following reading pulls out and interprets significant details in the poem:

CLOSE READING: The poem "Valediction" describes the emotional experience of a man whose female companion (probably his wife) has left him. The poet uses a central metaphor to explain the speaker's emotional state, a metaphor he develops in a variety of ways, to describe exactly how the man in the poem is affected by her absence.

The metaphor in the poem is that of a boat on a lake or an ocean. When the "lady with the frilled blouse / And simple tartan skirt" was present, the boat was "anchored" secure in its mooring. "Time rode easy," suggesting the placid setting and the speaker's previously peaceful state of mind. With her absence, however, the calmness is lost: "love's balance," which existed in her presence, is "rocked," and the days "unmoored." Time is no longer safe at anchor but cast off, wild. The days now "buck" and "bound" as the boat pitches in the water; there is nothing smooth about the man's existence any more.

Meanwhile, the waves have started to break on the beach. The waves are the man's "need," the beach his "strand." With the lady gone, the speaker is truly "at sea." He can only visualize calm in his life once more if she will return to "command" the boat that is the speaker himself. Until that time the boat is doomed to be "in mutiny," that is, beyond his control, at the mercy of time and the waves.

The Receptive Reader

What details in the poem follow up the contrast between the calm before and the turmoil after the woman's departure? Were you surprised by the phrase "resume command"? What do you think it shows about the relationship between the two people? Did this reader miss any significant details in this poem?

Look at the way the following response by the same reader relates the poem to the reader's own experience. A paper anchored in close reading but going on to the personal connection would answer both basic questions: What does this poem mean—to perhaps a majority of perceptive readers? And what does the poem mean to me?

PERSONAL RESPONSE: It is easy to identify with a poem that carries such an obvious central metaphor. It uses the boat rocked by waves as the metaphor for an event disturbing the equilibrium of someone's life. While I have never experienced what it is like to have the most important person in my life walk out on me, curiously enough, I dreamed about this happening to me just a few nights ago. In my dream I was in college, and J. had just left me. (As is common with dreams, there was no obvious reason for this occurrence.)

I experienced total and utter despair. Although several close friends and family were with me, they were unable, even unwilling, to help me through the experience. I was truly "at sea." I started out into the streets, attempting to find my way "home" to J. A wind started to roar towards me, hindering my steps, and the flat road suddenly became a hill. My last impression before awaking involved a clear realization that I never would succeed in reaching the crest of the hill and passing over to the other side.

Thinking about this dream, I have become aware that I fear greatly this absence that Heaney describes in his poem. I find myself believing that I would act like the man he describes and like the person I appeared to be in my dream. Fortunately for me, I have the warning ahead of time—never to take your loved ones for granted.

The Receptive Reader

How do you explain this reader's dream? What is the connection between the dream and the poem? Did this poem bring any personal associations or memories to your mind? How did you personally react to the poem?

Read the following poem carefully, paying special attention to details that might seem difficult or unexpected on first reading. Present your own close reading of the poem in such a way that it could lead a fellow reader to a fuller understanding and appreciation of the poem. Then present your personal response to the poem, explaining your personal reaction or showing why the poem has a special meaning for you as a reader.

Alice Walker   *(born 1944)*

New Face   *1972*

I have learned not to worry about love;
but to honor its coming
with all my heart.
To examine the dark mysteries
of the blood   5
with headless heed and
swirl,
to know the rush of feelings
swift and flowing
as water.   10
The source appears to be
some inexhaustible
spring
within our twin and triple
selves;   15
the new face I turn up
to you
no one else on earth
has ever
seen.   20

The Receptive Reader

1. What is the focus of this poem? What sets it in motion?

2. Although this poem addresses a large recurrent question in our lives, it translates the poet's feelings and ideas into strong graphic images. What are striking examples? What gives them special force?

3. This poem comes to a close with a beautiful fresh image. What is its meaning?

THE CREATIVE DIMENSION

Talking becomes poetry as walking becomes dancing.

JOSEPHINE MILES

Anyone who breathes is in the rhythm business.

WILLIAM STAFFORD

One way of "getting into" a poem is to allow it to trigger a creative response, to bring your own creativity into play. When a poem moves you in a special way, it may trigger a creative effort of your own—a poem, a prose passage, a drawing, a photograph. Such a creative response or **re-creation** may sum up a personal impression. It may pursue a train of thought set in motion by something in the original poem. It may focus on a haunting image or take off from a provocative phrase. It may talk back to the original poem. One basic function of poetry is to keep alive the poet in each of us. We are not likely to become good readers of poetry if we seldom use our own imagination.

One way to get into the spirit of a poem is to write a similar poem of your own. This way you get to know the poem "from the inside"—the way a person playing an instrument or acting a part in amateur performance ceases to be a passive spectator. The following is a poem that invites imitation—not a dutiful copying but a playing with the same basic format and tone:

Wallace Stevens   *(1879–1955)*

Disillusionment of Ten O'Clock   *1923*

The houses are haunted
By white night-gowns.
None are green,
Or purple with green rings,
Or green with yellow rings,

5

Or yellow with blue rings.
None of them are strange,
With socks of lace
And beaded ceintures.°   *fancy sashes*
People are not going   10
To dream of baboons and periwinkles.°   *cone-shaped snails*
Only, here and there, an old sailor,
Drunk and asleep in his boots,
Catches tigers
In red weather.   15

The Receptive Reader

1. Why is this poet "disillusioned"? About what?

2. What is funny about the idea of these houses being "haunted"? Why does the color of people's nightgowns matter in this poem? The critic Irving Howe said that the nightgowns are the "uniform of ordinariness and sober nights." What did he mean?

3. Why do *dreams* matter in this poem? What do the people's dreams and their nightgowns have in common?

4. Does the poet share the conventional attitude toward *drunks?* Howe said that the sailor is the one person in this poem who "stands outside the perimeter of busy dullness." What did he mean?

The Creative Dimension

We know that a student has understood and appreciated the Wallace Stevens poem when we see the following student-written re-creation. How or how well does the student poem capture the mood and intention of the original? How close is it to the original in pattern or form? Try your hand at a similar creative effort, inspired by this or another poem you have read.

Disenchantment at the Dance
The dance is crowded
With blue denim.
There are no dresses
Of shiny, red satin
Or shimmering silk.
No bright feathered hats
No rhinestone buttons.
People aren't dancing
The foxtrot or cha cha.
Only, once in a while,
A few underclassmen
In T-shirts and jeans
Clap their hands
Shuffle their feet.

The Range of Interpretation

In the following excerpt, a widely read modern critic puts Stevens' poem in the larger context of the poet's work. How does this added perspective confirm or change your own reading of the poem?

Irving Howe

Reading "Disillusionment of Ten O'Clock"

How shall we live with and then perhaps beyond the crisis of belief? It is to confront this question that Stevens keeps returning to the theme of reality and imagination . . . because his main concern is with discovering and, through his poetry, enacting the possibilities for human self-renewal in an impersonal and recalcitrant age.

How recalcitrant that age can be, Stevens knew very well. The fragmentation of personality, the loss of the self in its social roles, the problem of discovering one's identity amid a din of public claims—all this so obsessively rehearsed in modern literature, is the premise from which Stevens moves to poetry. When Stevens does write directly about such topics, it is often with lightness and humor, taking easily on a tangent what other writers can hardly bear to face. An early little poem, "Disillusionment of Ten O'Clock" is about houses that are haunted by "white night-gowns," for Stevens the uniform of ordinariness and sober nights.

> None are green,
> Or purple with green rings,
> Or green with yellow rings,
> None of them are strange,
> With socks of lace
> And beaded ceintures.

In this flat world "People are not going / To dream of baboons and periwinkles." Only here and there an old sailor, one who by age and trade stands outside the perimeter of busy dullness . . .

> Drunk and asleep in his boots,
> Catches tigers
> In red weather.

I hope it will not seem frivolous if I suggest that this drunken sailor embodies a central intention of Stevens' mind, and that when Stevens in his later poems turns to such formidable matters as inquiries into the nature of reality or the relation between the perceiving eye and the perceived object, he still keeps before him the figure of that old sailor dreaming in red weather.

In Axelrod and Deese, *Critical Essays on Wallace Stevens,* 1988

In the following unrhymed modern poem, the layout of the lines on the page guides us in setting up the pauses that shape the rhythm of the poem as a whole. Have you ever felt like leaving a message that might begin "This is just to say"?

William Carlos Williams   *(1883–1963)*

This Is Just to Say   *1934*

I have eaten
the plums
that were in
the icebox

and which
you were probably
saving
for breakfast

Forgive me
they were delicious
so sweet
and so cold

The Creative Dimension

Look at the following student-written response to the Williams poem. How or how well did the student reader get into the spirit of the original poem? Then write a "This is just to say" message of your own.

This is just to say

I used
the last of
the gas
in your car

you will probably be in
a rush tomorrow
and won't have
time
to refill the
tank

I'm sorry
but I had
no money
and I so
detest the

smell of gas
on my
hands

Successful poets develop their own style, their own voice. However, often that personal style shows the influence of other poets who inspired the writer. That influence may be only a distant echo. At times, however, the connection shows more directly, as it does in the following pair of poems. How closely does the second poem follow the pattern of the first? How close an imitation or re-creation is it of the first?

Donald Justice   *(born 1925)*

Men at Forty   1966

Men at forty
Learn to close softly
The doors to rooms they will not be
Coming back to.

At rest on a stair landing,   5
They feel it
Moving beneath them now like the deck of a ship,
Though the swell is gentle.

And deep in mirrors
They rediscover   10
The face of the boy as he practices tying
His father's tie there in secret

And the face of that father,
Still warm with the mystery of lather.
They are more fathers than sons themselves now.   15
Something is filling them, something

That is like the twilight sound
Of the crickets, immense,
Filling the woods at the foot of the slope
Behind their mortgaged houses.   20

The Receptive Reader

1. The doors, the stair landing, the mirror, and the crickets in this poem all have a meaning beyond what meets the eye. What is their role in the poem?

2. Is there a keynote or a connecting thread in the poet's vision of men at forty?

Maurya Simon   *(born 1950)*

Women at Thirty   *1986*

After a poem by Donald Justice

Women at thirty
Learn to swing slightly
In the hinges of their steps
As they ascend.

At ease on the carpeting   5
They feel it gliding
Beneath them now like an air-borne sail,
Though its speed is slowed down.

And deep in mirrors
They recover   10
The face of the girl as she tries on
Her mother's smile and kisses

The face of that mother
Still warmed by the mystery of father.
They are more and more women now.   15
Something is touching them, something

That is like the sun's brush
Of white light, minute,
Unfurling the ferns at the base of the yard
Beyond their children's windows.   20

The Receptive Reader

1. What role do the steps, the carpeting, the mirrors, the sun, and the ferns play in this poem?

2. Do you think this poet's vision of women at thirty is more positive than Justice's vision of men at forty? Why or why not?

The Creative Dimension

Choose your own variation of the title—such as "Boys at Eighteen," "Men at Sixty," "Young Women at Twenty-Five"—and write your own passage or poem.

JUXTAPOSITIONS

Reading and Writing Haiku

As we know from the Japanese experience of the haiku, as well as the experience of many brief poems in the Western tradition, poetry can be

present in fifteen words, or in ten words. Length
or meter or rhyme have nothing to do with it.
ROBERT BLY

Boy with dollar cries
Sign in poetry shop reads:
"No haiku today"
STUDENT HAIKU

Several traditional kinds of Japanese poetry work on the principle of "much in little." They give you snapshots (or **vignettes**) of three lines or five lines each—very short poems that focus your attention on something that is worth looking at but that busy, harried people might overlook. Reading and re-creating these short poems can help you move from passive to more active and appreciative reading.

The best known of these centuries-old short forms is the three-liner, or **haiku.** It fixes a sight or observation in a beautifully crafted form, the way amber encases and preserves an insect caught in the sap of a tree. (One early translator said that haiku about dragonflies are almost as numerous as the dragonflies themselves in the early autumn.)

> A giant firefly
> that way, this way, that way, this—
> and it passes by.

In its strict traditional form, the haiku arranges exactly seventeen syllables in three lines of five, seven, and five syllables. Count the syllables in the following example. (The *m* in the last line counts as a separate syllable.)

Kumonosu no	5	Ah! Unsuspecting	5
Atari ni asobu	7	the whir of the dragonfly	7
To-m-bo kana	5	Near the spider's net	5

The most famous haiku poet is Bashō and his most famous haiku, often translated, is the following:

Bashō   *(1644–1694)*

Furuike ya	5	An old quiet pond—	5
kawazu tobikomu	7	Frog splashes into water,	7
mizu no oto	5	Breaking the silence	5

Most modern re-creations keep the basic three-line format but do not observe the strict syllable count. The following translations preserve the short-long-short of the haiku without the strict five-seven-five pattern.

Both originals were written by women, who "dominated the early years of the literary tradition in Japan not only in numbers, but in formal, aesthetic terms as well" (Rob Swigart).

Ukihashi   *(17th century)*

TRANSLATED BY KENNETH REXROTH AND IKUKO ATSUMI

Whether I sit or lie
My empty mosquito net
Is too large.

Kawai Chigetsu-Ni   *(1632–1736)*

TRANSLATED BY KENNETH REXROTH AND IKUKO ATSUMI

Grasshoppers
Chirping in the sleeves
Of a scarecrow.

Study the following student-written examples of modernized haiku. Then try your hand at some of your own. Note that the focus in the poems themselves is on what we see—although we as readers may take the poem as a starting point for thoughts and feelings. Note the focus on thought-provoking specifics—the absence of blank-check words like *beautiful, sweet, innocent.* The first two examples are formal haiku observing the 5-7-5 pattern:

FORMAL:	A seed yearning for the dark warm earth to moisten must practice patience.	Husband's warm body, Comforting hum of furnace— I drift back to sleep.
INFORMAL:	An old woman looking at granddaughter reminisces	Bright yellow cranes, Old building standing Condemned to die.
	Tranquil is the garden of Eden before the inevitable intrusion Of the stealthy reptile	

A related Japanese form, fixing a moment in time, is the five-liner (or **tanka**). In the strict traditional form, it adds two seven-syllable lines, giving the poet a little more elbowroom. (Historically, the haiku is actually an abbreviated tanka, first written by poets who considered the five-liner too wordy.) The following translation does not observe the strict syllable count:

Lady Horikawa   *(12th century)*

TRANSLATED BY KENNETH REXROTH AND IKUKO ATSUMI

How long will it last?
I do not know
his heart.
This morning my thoughts are tangled
as my black hair.

The following student-written tanka does rise to the challenge of the traditional 5-7-5-7-7 pattern:

On the bottom shelf	5
the cheese from three months ago	7
has grown pale-blue fur	5
and I think I heard it growl	7
I'm pretty sure it was cheese.	7

The following student-written five-liners vary the traditional pattern. Try writing some five-line poems of your own.

Batman	Honey
flits across my rooftop,	Comb, the Queen Bee,
sits on my TV antenna	Reigns with trifling, stoic
and pretends	Elegance, keeping her left eye
he's a 200-pound pigeon.	Droneward.

WRITING ABOUT LITERATURE

12 Keeping a Poetry Journal
     WRITING FOCUS: First Responses to Poems

Cover done by MAC
Inside done by IBM
Each word is a joy

"WORD PROCESSING HAIKU," STUDENT JOURNAL

The Writing Workshop   Keeping a poetry journal helps you become a more responsive, more thoughtful reader. Your journal can also be the place where you do much of the **prewriting** for more structured formal papers. In writing a paper, you will be able to turn to your journal for tentative ideas, relevant evidence, and background information.

✗ Your journal gives you a chance to formulate your *overall impres-sion* of a poem. You may start with first impressions, trying to organize them into some preliminary pattern. You may try to get down and or-ganize some of the free-floating associations and reactions that the poem activates on first reading. Keeping a journal will get you into the habit of thinking about the significance, shape, and tone of a poem as a whole.

✗ Your journal enables you to keep a rough record of what you take in as you read. You may want to use part of your journal for a *running commentary,* highlighting striking passages, key images, or notes struck more than once in a poem. In your journal, you can focus on a ques-tion that bothers you or on puzzling details. Your journal then serves as the record of your close reading of a poem, as you get involved in the way it takes shape and as you try to do justice to nuances and shades of meaning.

✗ Your journal gives you a chance to formulate your *personal re-sponse.* Some poems move us strongly. They strike a powerful chord. We seem to be listening to a kindred spirit. Other poems are impressive or thought-provoking, but we read them from a respectful distance. Still other poems we fight, because they seem to be looking at our world through the wrong end of the telescope. Or they may make us confront topics or issues we have been trying to avoid. In your journal, you can begin to explain and justify to yourself your own personal interaction with a poem.

The following sample entries from student journals illustrate possible topics and formats for your own journal. Note that the entries show ev-idence of careful firsthand reading—weaving into the text quoted words and phrases, half lines and whole lines, from the poems being discussed.

Focus on Words   A large part of careful close reading is trying to de-code fully the shades of meaning, the overtones, and the associations of the poet's words. In a short poem, each word counts. (It has been esti-mated that the weight-per-word is five to ten times in a poem what it would be in ordinary casual prose.) The author of the following journal entry "read out" of the poet's choice of words considerably more than their bare dictionary meaning:

William Carlos Williams in "The Dance" makes us see the peasants making merry in a painting by Breughel, a sixteenth-century Flemish painter of peasant life. Right away we see that the people in the painting are big, beefy, corpulent, solid peasant types. The poet uses the word *round* several times ("the dancers go round, they go round and / around"). The poet compares their bellies to the "thick-sided glasses whose wash they impound."

Williams uses words like *squeal* and *blare* and *tweedle* to describe the music of the bagpipes. These words are not normally used to describe music; in fact, they have connotations of being really annoying sounds. *Squeal* brings to mind pictures of stuck pigs, angry children, or the air being let out of tires. *Blare* makes us hear the horns of frustrated drivers, the sound a donkey makes, unwelcome stereos at 3 A.M., or a charging elephant. *Tweedle* to me is an annoying, monotonous sound that alternates between two high-pitched notes, back and forth, back and forth. The choice of these words gives us an idea that the dancers are not a noble bunch. These are people whose children probably don't wear shoes; these dancers dance to loud music and drink and belch and don't give a second thought. Just from these word choices, I see big bellies that shirts don't quite cover. I see women with enormous hips. Food in enormous quantities is being eaten, perhaps without utensils or even plates. Faces are being wiped on sleeves, not napkins or towels. These people are hard workers, and they celebrate hard, with great happiness.

Focus on Metaphor Often a poem comes into focus for us as we begin to see the full meaning of a central metaphor or organizing symbol. The following journal entry traces in detail the possible ramifications of a haunting central image:

Spiders usually bring associations of haunted, spooky places inhabited by ghosts, witches, and skeletons. Spiders are often thought of as cruel beings who suck the blood out of poor trapped helpless bugs. On the other hand, spiders also bring visions of beautiful, sparkling, intricate webs. In his poem "A Noiseless Patient Spider," Walt Whitman takes us way beyond the ordinary associations. He sees the spider sympathetically as it noiselessly and patiently performs the simple life-supporting function of sending out its web in search of its needs. So Whitman can easily slip into the parallel search of each person (not just poets!). "Ceaselessly musing, venturing, throwing," we search for the ideas, beliefs, values, or mission that can be the anchor of our lives. The "gossamer threads" that the soul flings are the searching thoughts, the trial and error, the seeking that each person performs to find a happy or at least bearable environment in which the mind and heart can live. The bridge each soul seeks to build will take it to a meaning that imposes order on the universe, which without it remains an incomprehensible, dangerous place.

The Reader's Background A poem is a transaction between the poet and the reader. A poem is not sufficient unto itself. It activates and shapes what the reader brings to the poem—in the way of memories, associations, overtones of words, shared values, or cultural heritage. The student author of the following entry was able to get into the spirit of a poem because it stimulated a range of relevant associations. She was able to make the right connections:

In his poem "Pied Beauty," G. M. Hopkins writes about beauty that is not smooth and boring but instead dappled, freckled, "counter, original, spare, strange." The poem cites as an example different occupations or trades with their "gear and tackle and trim." I thought right away of a friend who was a rock climber—he had a fascinating variety of ropes, clips, wedges, "helpers," with the ropes and slings in bright, varied colors. I also thought of painters or roofers, with their trucks loaded down with various gear—ladders, paint cans with paint dripping down the sides, plastic coverings, drop cloths spattered with paint. Hopkins looked with wonder and delight at asymmetrical things that to him became a symbol of the color and variety of God's creation.

The student who wrote the following entry felt he had a special way into a poem because of his regional background:

An image is the picture that is worth a thousand words. But do images communicate equally effectively with different readers? If the reader does not have the background that a poet assumes, does the significance of the poem suffer? I cannot help feeling that something is lost if people are not aware of what it takes to rise on a bitter cold winter morning as "imaged" in Robert Hayden's poem "Those Winter Sundays." In the "blueblack cold," the father, with cracked hands that ached from his weekday labor, made the "banked fires blaze"—but "no one ever thanked him" for this labor of love. As an Easterner transplanted to Southern California, I know it is difficult to explain bitter cold, or the glory of thunderstorms, or the bite of the air on a crisp autumn day. Here there is no weather. Spirits cannot be brought down by yearning for a weekend that is then rained out—two months in a row. Spirits cannot be raised by the first sight of buds on the trees, the first call of spring birds. There are no major mood swings.

The Personal Response   How we as readers experience a poem depends on our private agendas, emotional needs, and moral values. A poem can have a powerful impact on us if it gives voice and direction to what we already strongly feel:

In his poem "London," William Blake takes us to an eighteenth-century city where we hear the "infant's cry of fear," "the hapless soldier's sigh," and the "youthful harlot's curse" among soot-blackened churches and castles whose walls are figuratively covered with blood. Every day my own point of view toward today's cities comes closer to Blake's. Cities today are filled with poverty, violence, and hunger. I cannot walk to school without seeing the lines of people in the naturalization offices, the children waiting in line at the rescue mission, or the homeless and mentally challenged sleeping on the grass outside Grace Baptist Church. I honestly don't know why I get so upset about all the poverty in the city. I guess I feel so guilty because of all the advantages I have had. And when I see the children lining up to get at least one real meal, the guilt sets in.

The Creative Dimension   A poem may serve as a stimulus or catalyst for a creative effort of your own that spins off from the original. The student author of the following entry had read Thomas Hardy's end-of-the-century poem "The Darkling Thrush" (Chapter 13)—the century being the nineteenth century. She wrote the following farewell poem for the twentieth century:

An Epitaph for the Twentieth Century by 438-11-7322
Nine digits we're linked to
from birth
A number that stays with us
till our last day on earth

Without a number
You can have no card

Without a card
All business retards

Whether you're a king, queen, or jack
Hinges on where your card fits into the stack

In the future they'll remark:
Humankind gave the digit a high place
and did much to erase
Fingerprint and face.

How to Cite Poetry   In writing your journal entries, practice the conventions that you will have to observe in more formal papers.

✖ Put the title of the poem in quotation marks; *italicize* (underscore on an old-fashioned typewriter) the book or collection in which it appears.

Judy Grahn's poem "Paris and Helen" appears in her collection *The Queen of Wands.*

✖ When you run in lines of poetry as part of your own text, use a **slash** (with a space on either side) to show line breaks in the original poem:

Asked to let anger out of its cage, the speaker in the poem says that anger, once loose, "may / turn on me, maul / my face, draw blood."

✖ Normally, set off three or more lines of verse as a **block quotation**—indent and center on page, *no* quotation marks. (You may choose to set off even a single line or two lines to make them stand out.)

The rose plays a somewhat unusual role in the opening lines of Gwendolyn Brooks' poem "A Song in the Front Yard":

I've stayed in the front yard all my life.
I want to peek at the back
Where it's rough and untended and hungry weeds grow.
A girl gets sick of a rose.

✖ Use double quotation marks for ordinary quotations; use **single quotation marks** for a quote-within-a-quote:

In her introduction to Janet Lewis' *Poems Old and New: 1918–1978,* Helen Trimpi says that Lewis' poetry has a drive "toward balance—to 'bind despair and joy / into a stable whole'—in life as well as in music and art."

13 PATTERN

The Whole Poem

Courtesy Richard B. Ressman

The person who writes out of an inner need is trying to order his corner of the universe; very often the meaning of an experience or an emotion becomes clear only in this way.

MAXINE KUMIN

When I was young, to make something in language, a poem that was all of a piece, a poem that could stand for what I was at the time—that seemed to be the most miraculous thing in the world.

THEODORE ROETHKE

FOCUS ON PATTERN

Poetry, like its sister arts, springs from our impulse to give shape to experience. A poem opens, moves forward, and comes to a close. It has an overall pattern; it has a design. When we read attentively, we sense how the poem takes shape. As we read and reread, we begin to see how details work in **context**—in a web of meanings. Parts that seemed puzzling at first may slowly fall into place. They become part of the whole.

Each poem is different. However, organizing strategies like the following may help a poet shape a poem as a whole:

✗ *A poem may ask a question and then work out an answer.* That answer may not be the last word on the issue. It will not suit everyone. But it can give us a sense that the poet finished what he or she started.

✗ *A poem may play off opposites.* When we see clearly defined polar opposites, we call them **polarities**. Polarities help us organize our thoughts; they help us draw our mental maps. They are built into the texture of our lives: man and woman, night and day, land and sea, arrival and departure, storm and calm. We chart our course between opposite poles: work and play, success and failure, dependence and independence. The following passage from the King James Bible (Ecclesiastes 3:1–8) rehearses age-old polarities that are constants in human experience. Which of these opposed pairs from biblical times still play a major role in our lives? For those that seem dated or obsolete, what would be a modern counterpart?

Ecclesiastes 3:1–8

To every thing there is a season, and a time to every purpose under the
    heaven:

A time to be born, and a time to die; a time to plant, and a time to pluck
  up that which is planted;
A time to kill, and a time to heal; a time to break down, and a time to
  build up;
A time to weep, and a time to laugh; a time to mourn, and a time to
  dance;
A time to cast away stones, and a time to gather stones together; a time to   5
  embrace, and a time to refrain from embracing;
A time to get, and a time to lose; a time to keep, and a time to cast away;
A time to rend, and a time to sew; a time to keep silence, and a time to
  speak;
A time to love, and a time to hate; a time of war, and a time of peace.

✕ *A poem may play off contrasting points of view.* In some early
poems about love, the pleas of the male lover alternate with the doubts
and misgivings expressed by the woman. A poem may juxtapose one
person's feelings about another at the beginning and at the end of a
relationship.

✕ *A poem may build to a high point.* To build up to a **climax,**
we often start slowly and in a low key. Then we gradually pile up
strong and stronger details until we reach the high point. How does
Archibald MacLeish in his poem "The Genius" follow this pattern? How
does the poet give extra force to the high point? (Sleepers in rural communities used to be awakened by the bugling, blaring cockadoodledoo
of the rooster, stretching its neck and throwing back its head to greet
the morning.)

Archibald MacLeish   *(1892–1982)*

The Genius   1933

Waked by the pale pink
Intimation° to the eastward,   *first hint*
  Cock, the prey of every beast,
  Takes breath upon the hen-house rafter,
Leans above the fiery brink   5
And shrieks in brazen obscene burst
On burst of uncontrollable derisive° laughter: *contemptuous*
Cock has seen the sun! He first! He first!

A poem may move from the present back to the past or onward to the
future. It may move between dream and waking, or between surface appearance and underlying reality. When a poem has reached its destination, when it has had its say, we feel a satisfying sense of completeness.

We say that the poem has achieved **closure.** Something worth our attention has been accomplished or completed.

FIRST READING

The Sense of Completion

The following is a poem that many readers have found beautifully finished, complete in itself. When they finish reading it, the poem has satisfied the expectations it has created. The poet takes us on a journey of the mind—a journey from one state of mind to another. The poem focuses on a need. The poem as a whole then fills that need. What images or ideas about nature do you bring to this poem? What images or associations does the word *nature* bring to mind?

Wendell Berry   *(born 1934)*

The Peace of Wild Things   1968

When the despair of the world grows in me
and I wake in the night at the least sound
in fear of what my life and my children's life may
    be,
I go and lie down where the wood drake°   *male duck with brilliant plumage*
rests in his beauty on the water, and the great   5
    heron feeds.
I come into the peace of wild things
who do not tax their lives with forethought
of grief. I come into the presence of still water.
And I feel above me the day-blind stars
waiting with their light. For a time   10
I rest in the grace of the world, and am free.

The Receptive Reader

1. What is the need the speaker in the poem feels while lying awake in the dark of night? How does the poem provide the needed antidote?

2. For you, what are the key contrasts between the speaker's human world and the world of the "wild things" of nature? What does the speaker mean by "forethought of grief"?

3. How are the stars "day-blind"? For the speaker, do you think the stars were comforting or distant and cold?

4. The word *grace* has several possible meanings, from "gracefulness" to "divine grace." What does the word mean in the context of the last line?

The Personal Response

What do you think are the fears that keep the speaker in the poem awake at night? Do you think people can find ways to escape from "forethought" or worry about the future?

THE POWER OF ATTENTION

A poem is a momentary stay against confusion.
                                                    ROBERT FROST

How do poems organize the flow of experience? First of all, poems focus our attention. Too often we are hurried, unable to pay undivided attention to any one thing. The poet asks us to slow down, to stop for a closer look. The poem, for a time, brings part of our human reality into **focus.** For instance, it may ask us to focus on a place, a person, or an event in order to fix a moment in time. The following poem is like a freeze-frame capturing a picture that, though mute, has something to say to us. What does the poem invite you to see? What does it make you feel? Does it make you think?

William Carlos Williams   *(1883–1963)*

Between Walls   1934

the back wings
of the

hospital where
nothing

will grow lie   5
cinders

in which shine
the broken

pieces of a green
bottle   10

The Receptive Reader

1. Why do you think the poet bypassed the rest of the building and the hospital grounds to focus your attention where he does?

2. Some of the key words in this poem are *hospital, nothing,* and *cinders.* Why are they key words? How does the poem make them stand out?

3. What is the lone touch of *color* in these lines? What does it make you feel or think?

4. This poem uses bare-minimum lines, with no chance for lush rhythms to develop. Why?

The following poem is by a poet who became well known in the eighties. What do you see in the frame the poet sets up in the poem? Is there a movement or a mental journey to give a pattern to the poem as a whole?

Sharon Olds   *(born 1942)*

The Possessive   *1980*

My daughter—as if I
owned her—that girl with the
hair wispy as a frayed bellpull

has been to the barber, that knife grinder,
and had the edge of her hair sharpened.   5

Each strand now cuts
both ways. The blade of new bangs
hangs over her red-brown eyes
like carbon steel.

       All the little   10
spliced ropes are sliced. The curtain of
dark paper-cuts veils the face that
started from next to nothing in my body—

My body. My daughter. I'll have to find
another word. In her bright helmet   15
she looks at me as if across a
great distance. Distant fires can be
glimpsed in the resin light of her eyes:

the watch fires of an enemy, a while before
the war starts.   20

This poem focuses on a crucial stage in the relationship between mother and daughter: The distance seems to be growing between mother and child.

We come in at a turning point when the daughter is moving from a non-threatening wispy-hair or curly-hair stage to a new helmet-like hairdo, with bangs that remind the mother of sharpened blades, hinting at future hostility and aggressiveness. The poem leaves us with the uneasy sense of a coming confrontation. Parent and child are headed for a future where they will be like two armies, each waiting around its campfires on the evening before battle.

The Receptive Reader

1. How does hair become an issue in this poem? (What exactly did the barber do to the girl's hair?)

2. How many words in the poem remind you of *weapons* used to fend off or hurt an enemy?

3. Possessive pronouns show where or to whom something belongs: *my* daughter, *your* son, *her* briefcase. Where and how does a possessive pronoun become an issue in this poem?

The Personal Response

Long hair, bald heads, ethnic hairstyles—why or how does hair become an issue in the confrontation between the generations? Do adults overreact to the hairstyles of the young?

The Creative Dimension

Often what lingers in the mind after we read a poem is something that appeals strongly to the visual imagination—a central image or a key metaphor (or a web of related metaphors). What did the student-author of the following re-creation carry away from the poem? Do a similar brief re-creation of a central image or metaphor in this or in an earlier poem in this chapter.

> My daughter has pulled on a helmet
> as protection from sharp words.
> She hears nothing but feels
> >   all.
> Her eyes look out from behind the blades
> of her new bangs.
> Behind their curtain
> she prepares for battle.

The following poem again focuses on a significant moment. A poet from the Southwest, who published a book of poems called *Hijo del Pueblo*—Son of the Pueblo—remembers an encounter that acquires a new meaning in retrospect. What is that meaning?

Leroy V. Quintana   *(born 1944)*

Legacy II   *1976*

Grandfather never went to school
spoke only a few words of English,
a quiet man; when he talked
talked about simple things

planting corn or about the weather   5
sometimes about herding sheep as a child.
One day pointed to the four directions
taught me their names

El Norte

Poniente   Oriente   10

El Sur

He spoke their names as if they were
one of only a handful of things
a man needed to know

Now I look back   15
only two generations removed
realize I am nothing but a poor fool
who went to college

trying to find my way back
to the center of the world   20
where Grandfather stood
that day

The Receptive Reader

1. *El Norte* and *El Sur* are Spanish for north and south; *Poniente* means west ("where the sun sets") and *Oriente* means east ("where the sun rises"). Poems that use the physical arrangement of words on a page to mirror meaning are often called **concrete poetry**. How does the arrangement of the Spanish names on the page help the poet make the main point of the poem?

2. How are we supposed to feel about or toward the grandfather who is at the center of this poem?

3. How does the treatment of the grandfather-grandson relationship compare with the treatment of the mother-daughter relationship in the poem by Sharon Olds?

The Personal Response

A central issue in our growing up is how we accept or reject the heritage of family tradition, regional ties, or ethnic roots. Write about your relation to one major part of your own legacy.

The two following poems observe a similar pattern: Both focus on a scene from the natural world. This scene then inspires feelings and reflections. Thomas Hardy, an English poet and novelist who had become well known by the 1880s and 1890s, wrote the first of the two poems on the last day of the nineteenth century. During the preceding decades, there had been much questioning of traditional religious faith. What was the poet's end-of-century mood? (The thrush is a small bird known as an excellent singer.)

Thomas Hardy   *(1840–1928)*

The Darkling Thrush   1900

I leant upon a coppice° gate   grove of small trees
    When Frost was specter-gray,
And Winter's dregs made desolate
    The weakening eye of day.
The tangled bine-stems° scored the sky   shoots of climbers   5
    Like strings of broken lyres,°   small (poets') harps
And all mankind that haunted nigh°   near
    Had sought their household fires.

The land's sharp features seemed to be
    The Century's corpse outleant,   10
His crypt the cloudy canopy,°   raised cloth covering
    The wind his death-lament.
The ancient pulse of germ and birth
    Was shrunken hard and dry,
And every spirit upon earth   15
    Seemed fervorless° as I.   without passion

At once a voice arose among
    The bleak twigs overhead
In a full-hearted evensong°   sung evening prayer
    Of joy illimited;°   unlimited   20
An aged thrush, frail, gaunt, and small,
    In blast-beruffled plume,°   feathers, plumage
Had chosen thus to fling his soul
    Upon the growing gloom.

So little cause for carolings   25
    Of such ecstatic sounds
Was written on terrestrial° things   earthly
    Afar or nigh around,
That I could think there trembled through
    His happy good-night air   30
Some blessed Hope, whereof he knew
    And I was unaware.

The Receptive Reader

1. Take a close look at the poet's *language:* What is "the weakening eye of day"? What is the "cloudy canopy"? What is the "ancient pulse of germ and birth"? How was the bird's plumage "blast-beruffled"?

2. Where did you expect this poem to lead you as the reader? What details help make the *setting* unpromising for what happens later in the poem?

3. Where does this poem leave you? What makes the thrush in this poem a good *symbol* for hope?

4. Which words in the poem have religious overtones or *connotations?* Do you think the poet is religious?

The Creative Dimension

Assume today is the last day of another century, a hundred years after Hardy wrote his poem. Write your own epitaph for the *twentieth* century.

Compare the following poem with the poem by Hardy. Compare and contrast the natural scenes the two poets bring into focus, the emotions they invite you to share, and the thoughts they inspire.

Sylvia Plath   *(1932–1963)*

Frog Autumn   1959

Summer grows old, cold-blooded mother.
The insects are scant, skinny.
In these palustral° homes we only   *swampy*
Croak and wither.

Mornings dissipate in somnolence.°   *sleepiness*   5
The sun brightens tardily
Among the pithless° reeds. Flies fail us.   *weak-stemmed*
The fen° sickens.   *bog, swamp*

Frost drops even the spider. Clearly
The genius of plenitude°   *bountifulness*   10
Houses himself elsewhere. Our folk thin
Lamentably.

The Receptive Reader

1. Who is speaking in this poem? To whom? How does the choice of speaker change our usual *perspective* on life in the bog? What details make us imagine real creatures of the fen or swamp?

2. Some of the sentences in this poem are very sparse yet charged with meaning. What are some striking examples? (Why is a sparse, bare-bones sentence style appropriate to this poem?)

3. The word *lamentably* points to something to be lamented, to be mourned and deplored. How does the poet make the word stand out? How does the rest of the poem lead up to it?

The Personal Response

Do you consider the poem complete? Do you want it to go on—for instance, to find out what happens to the bog-dwellers? Why or why not?

Making Connections—For Discussion or Writing

Many poets have turned to nature as an oracle, listening intently for its message. In this chapter, three poets—Berry, Hardy, and Plath—look in the mirror of nature and each see a different face. Compare and contrast the poets' relationship to nature in these three poems.

THE SHAPE OF THE POEM

To know one thing, you must know its opposite
just as much; else you don't know that one thing.

HENRY MOORE

Each poem has its own unique shape. There is no standard formula to guide the poet's creative imagination. Nevertheless, when we look at a finished poem, we often see shaping forces at work that we recognize. The ability to focus, to concentrate, takes us a first big step toward bringing order into miscellaneous experience. A second organizing strategy that poets employ is intentional, purposeful **repetition**. Repetition can be thoughtless or mechanical; it then grates on our ears. Repetition is purposeful when used to highlight, to emphasize. It can line up like and like or confront like and unlike. In the following poem, the poet repeats exactly the way each set of lines, or stanza, is laid out on the page. What are the uses of repetition in the poem?

Dorothy Parker   *(1893–1967)*

Solace   1931

There was a rose that faded young;
I saw its shattered beauty hung
    Upon a broken stem.

I heard them say, "What need to care
With roses budding everywhere?"   5
    I did not answer them.

There was a bird, brought down to die;
They said, "A hundred fill the sky—
    What reason to be sad?"
There was a girl, whose lover fled;   10
I did not wait, the while they said:
    "There's many another lad."

This poem, like much poetry traditional in form, uses repetition at the most basic level to create sound patterns pleasing to the ear. End rhymes, in an interlaced rhyme scheme, mark off lines of similar length and help punctuate the poet's words. Lines with a recurrent underlying iambic meter (there WAS a ROSE that FADed YOUNG) alternate with a three-beat line (UPON a BROken STEM). These formal features serve to reinforce a pattern of repetition that helps guide our thoughts and feelings in the poem as a whole. The same sentence frame—"*There was a* rose"; "*There was a* bird"; "*There was a* girl"—introduces each of the three parts of the poem. These sentences are **parallel** in grammatical form—a signal to the reader that the three scenarios they introduce might also be parallel in content or in meaning.

The Receptive Reader

1. What is the same basic story that is repeated in the three parts of the poem? What is the reaction of the speaker in the poem?

2. Can you trace the close similarity in the way each parallel mini-event is patterned beyond the first half of the opening lines?

The Personal Response

Are you inclined to side with the "I" or the "they" of the poem?

Repetition sets up the routine of our lives. It helps us identify the constants that enable us to chart our course. Other basic patternings are similarly rooted in common human experience. For instance, we often see a sequence of events built up to a climactic high point. Clouds slowly darken the sky until a climactic thunderstorm releases crashing thunder and pouring rain. Tensions in a marriage slowly build up until they explode in a divorce. Much of what we plan and do is **cumulative**—we build on what has gone before until we reach a destination. In the following poem, repetition and climactic order combine with a further organizing strategy: The poem hinges on a pivotal *but* that provides the turning point. We go from point to **counterpoint**, from statement to counterstatement.

William Meredith   *(born 1919)*

A Major Work   1958

Poems are hard to read
Pictures are hard to see
Music is hard to hear
And people are hard to love

But whether from brute need   5
Or divine energy
At last mind eye and ear
And the great sloth heart will move.

In the first four lines, the basic sentence frame ("——— are hard to ———") is repeated four times. We sense that all four grammatically parallel statements are part of the same pattern. They are parallel not only in structure but also in *meaning:* Our minds are slow to grapple with a serious poem. Our eyes only slowly take in the rich texture in the painting of an old master (or puzzle over the strange shapes in the work of a modern). The untrained ear resists Beethoven. And finally, people—no less complicated than a sonnet or a sonata—are also hard to read and love.

Here, however, we come to the reversal or counterpoint: As we again look at mind, eye, ear, and heart in the same parallel order, we see them overcome resistance or inertia. When we come to the inertia-ridden and slothful "great sloth heart," we realize that the order of the four test cases was not accidental but cumulative. It is the slowness of the human heart to be moved to love that most concerns the poet. The last line is climactic; the poem as a whole has led up to this weighty, emphatically stressed line: "And the GREAT / SLOTH / HEART / WILL / MOVE."

The Receptive Reader

1. What does the phrase "from brute need / Or divine energy" mean?

2. If the poet were asked to spell out how, why, where, or when the "great sloth heart will move," what do you think he would say?

Look for the uses of repetition and the play of point and counterpoint in the following lines from a longer poem by New England's first poet.

Anne Bradstreet   *(about 1612–1672)*

From "The Vanity of All Worldly Things"   1650

As he said "vanity!" so "vain!" say I,
"Oh! vanity, O vain all under sky."
Where is the man can say,° "Lo, I have found   *who can say*
On brittle earth a consolation sound"?

What is 't in honor to be set on high?°   *raised to high station*   5
No, they like beasts and sons of men shall die,
And whilst they live, how oft doth turn their fate;
He's now a captive that was king of late.°   *only recently*
What is 't in wealth great treasures to obtain?
No, that's but labor, anxious care, and pain.   10
He heaps up riches, and he heaps up sorrow,
It's his today, but who's his heir tomorrow?
What then? Content in pleasure canst thou find?
More vain than all, that's but to grasp the wind.
The sensual senses for a time they please,   15
Meanwhile the conscience rage, who shall appease?
What is 't in beauty? No, that's but a snare,
They're foul° enough today that once were fair.   *ugly*
What is 't in flowering youth or manly age?
The first is prone to vice, the last to rage.   20
Where is it then, in wisdom, learning, arts?
Sure, if on earth, it must be in those parts;
Yet these the wisest man of men did find
But vanity, vexation of mind.

The Receptive Reader

1. The poet's first line takes up the words of the preacher who repeated the biblical "Vanity of vanities; all is vanity." Can you show that the parts making up this excerpt are *parallel* both in wording and in meaning?

2. What examples of *point and counterpoint* can you find in these lines?

3. Religion in Bradstreet's time was often more demanding than in ours. How much of her outlook is strange and how much is familiar to you as a modern reader?

The Creative Dimension

We call a heightened and compressed playing off of opposites an **antithesis.** (*Thesis* and *antithesis* are the original Greek words for statement and counterstatement.) Study the following examples of antithesis. For each, write one or more imitations (close or approximate) of your own.

1. To err is human; to forgive, divine. (Alexander Pope)
   SAMPLE IMITATION: To whine is childish; to ask, adult.

2. There are a thousand hacking at the branches of evil to one who is striking at the root. (Henry David Thoreau)
   SAMPLE IMITATION: There are a thousand correcting with red ink to one who writes an encouraging word.

3. It is a miserable state of mind to have few things to desire and many things to fear. (Sir Francis Bacon)

At times, the patterning that gives shape to a poem seems to be directly inspired by the patterns of nature or of ordinary human life. The following poem reminds us of the cycle of the seasons, but it uses thoughts about the falling leaves of October as a springboard for reflections on the similar cycle of youth and age. Autumn with the falling of leaves is a major waystation of the passing year, just as the realization of approaching age is a major waystation in human life. The sumac mentioned in the poem is a shrub whose leaves turn a brilliant dark red in the fall.

Kay Boyle　　*(1903–1992)*

October 1954　　　　　　　　　　　　　　　　*1954*

Now the time of year has come for the leaves to be burning.
October, and the months fill me with grief
For the girl who used to run with the black dogs through them,
Singing, before they burned. Light as a leaf
Her heart, and her mouth red as the sumac turning.　　　　　　5

Oh, girl, come back to tell them with your bell-like singing
That you are this figure who stands alone, watching the dead leaves burn.
(The wind is high in the trees, and the clang of bluejay voices ringing
Turns the air to metal. This is not a month for anyone who grieves.)
For they would say that a witch had passed in fury if I should turn,　　10
Gray-haired and brooding, and run now as once I ran through the leaves.

The Receptive Reader

1. How does the poet focus our attention on the burning leaves? What do they stand for as a central symbol in the poem? How does the poet use *repetition* to make the key words echo through the poem?

2. How many details help develop the *polarity* of youth and age?

3. Why is October "not a month for anyone who grieves"?

The Personal Response

To some people, the cycle of the changing seasons has come to mean very little. What does it mean in your own life?

JUXTAPOSITIONS

The Daily Cycle

Both of the following poems follow the ever-recurring daily cycle from dawn through noon to dusk and night. One makes us trace it in wonder and awe, as if we were the first people on earth. The other plays variations on it that are part serious, part tongue in cheek. The first poem is by a poet of Kiowa ancestry who grew up in Oklahoma and often in his poems draws on the legends and ways of the tribal life of the past.

N. Scott Momaday   *(born 1934)*

New World   *1976*

1.
First Man,
behold:
the earth
glitters
with leaves;   5
the sky
glistens
with rain.   2.
Pollen   At dawn
is borne   eagles   10
on winds   hie and
that low   hover
and lean   above   3.
upon   the plain   At noon
mountains.   where light   turtles   15
Cedars   gathers   enter
blacken   in pools.   slowly
the slopes—   Grasses   into   4.
and pines.   shimmer   the warm   At dusk
                and shine.   dark loam.   the gray   20
                Shadows   Bees hold   foxes
                withdraw   the swarm.   stiffen
                and lie   Meadows   in cold;
                away   recede   blackbirds
                like smoke.   through planes are fixed   25
                                of heat   in the
                                and pure   branches.
                                distance.   Rivers
                                                follow
                                                the moon,   30
                                                the long
                                                white track
                                                of the
                                                full moon.

The Receptive Reader

1. For people living closer to nature than we do, each stage of the day (like each stage in the cycle of the seasons) had its own characteristic feel or atmosphere. What is the morning feeling in this poem? How do the details

selected by the poet conjure up the feeling of high noon? What is striking about the visual images that bring up dusk?

2. How does the sense of an immemorial cycle that gives shape to this poem affect you as a reader? What feelings are you left with as you finish the poem?

The Creative Dimension

What are the three (four? five?) stages of the day in your own present-day world? Bring them to life for your reader in a poem or prose passage.

The second poem is by an English poet of the early seventeenth century who rewrote conventions and crossed established boundaries. He was one of the **metaphysical** poets of his time, passionate, but at the same time forever analyzing and rationalizing their emotions. What use does the poet make of the familiar stages of the daily cycle? How does he impose his own perspective and priorities?

John Donne   *(1572–1631)*

A Lecture upon the Shadow   *1635*

Stand still, and I will read to thee
A lecture, love, in Love's philosophy.
    These three hours that we have spent
    Walking here, two shadows went
Along with us, which we ourselves produced;   5
But, now° the sun is just above our head,   *now that*
    We do those shadows° tread,   *on those shadows*
    And to brave clearness all things are reduced.
So, whilst our infant loves did grow,
Disguises did and shadows flow   10
From us and our cares,° but now 't is not so.   *our fears*

That love hath not attained the highest degree
Which is still diligent lest others° see   *so others won't*

Except° our loves at this noon stay,   *Unless*
We shall new shadows make the other way.   15
    As the first were made to blind
    Others, these which come behind
Will work upon ourselves, and blind our eyes,
If our loves faint and westwardly decline,
    To me thou falsely thine,   20
    And I to thee mine, actions shall disguise.
The morning shadows wear away,
But these grow longer all the day;
But oh, love's day is short, if love decay.

Love is a growing or full constant light,   25
And his first minute after noon is night.

The Receptive Reader

1. The shadow cast by the sun becomes the central *metaphor* in this poem. What were the shadows in the morning? (What were the "cares" and "disguises" of the morning?) What happens to the shadows at high noon? What is the crucial difference between the morning shadows and the shadows after noon?

2. How does this poem ask you to revise your usual sense of the daily cycle? What familiar associations of dawn, noon, and night does the poem preserve? How does it depart from them?

The Personal Response

How do you react to the three student-written responses that follow? Which comes closest to your own response to the poem, and why? Which do you disagree with, and why?

1. John Donne did not write flowery, sickening-sweet love poetry but instead took his images from areas like philosophy, botany, or astronomy. The link between the shadow and love is not a worn-out comparison like spring or a rough road. What could be less permanent or more fleeting and transitory than a shadow? Just as a day ages and changes, so do the lovers age and change, and so does their love. Naturally the sun will not obey the lovers' wants and commands. It follows a cyclical pattern: Love grows, reaches a high point, and then declines and dies. This poem leaves me unsettled. I keep getting the idea that as soon as I fall in love I better steel myself so that I will not be disappointed when the shadows reappear.

2. I like the beginning of this poem much more than the end. As the sun moves through the sky, the shadows cast according to the position of the sun change, just as love in a relationship is different when it is young and when it is tried and true. At first, we hide behind shadows or façades instead of showing our true selves, but after a while we can put our disguises away just as at noon we can walk on our shadows. However, in the afternoon, love might grow weary and turn false, with the afternoon shadows pointing forward to the night and the end of love. The reason I would rather focus on the first half of the poem is that I think love should continue to grow and build on itself. If love grows weary, making "new shadows" the other way, I don't think it was love in the first place. I have never heard a parent say: "I have fallen out of love with my children; I think I will find a more suitable child elsewhere." Would that be true love?

3. This poem takes a very intellectual approach. It fuses "reason" and "love" to create an intellectual's love poetry. The very first sentence commands his lover to "stand still" so that the speaker can give a lecture on "Love's philosophy." This is an unusual way to begin a poem, since the word *lecture* makes us expect to be preached to and given a lesson. Donne seems to say that the sun can be held in check, not physically in the actual universe around us, but spiritually by an effort of our minds that preserves love's "full noon." But his philosophy is an "all-or-nothing" philosophy, since the "first minute after noon" is already night. As we see the lengthening

shadows and observe deceit creeping into our love, we realize our vulnerability. The lecturer sounded very cool and intellectual at the beginning, but he ends by being naked and vulnerable. Having chosen the sun as a symbol of love, what can he do to avoid the evening and night?

Making Connections—For Discussion or Writing

John Donne's "A Lecture upon the Shadow" and Marge Piercy's "Simple Song" (see below), though separated by three centuries, focus on our yearning for full and complete communication with another human being and the obstacles that defeat or thwart us in our quest. Compare and contrast the two poems.

POEMS FOR FURTHER STUDY

In reading the following poems, pay special attention to features that give shape to the poem as a whole. For instance, where does the poem focus your attention? Is there a playing off of opposites? Is there a movement from then to now, or from question to answer? What makes the poem a complete, finished whole?

Marge Piercy   *(born 1936)*

Simple Song   1968

When we are going toward someone we say
You are just like me
your thoughts are my brothers
word matches word
how easy to be together.   5

When we are leaving someone we say
how strange you are
we cannot communicate
we can never agree
how hard, hard and weary to be together.   10

We are not different nor alike
But each strange in his leather body
sealed in skin and reaching out clumsy hands
and loving is an act
that cannot outlive   15
the open hand
the open eye
the door in the chest standing open.

The Receptive Reader

1. What is simple about this "simple song"?

2. What does the poet mean by "your thoughts are my brothers"? (Or by "word matches word"?) What are we supposed to think or feel when we are told that we are in a "leather body" and "sealed in skin"? What is the role or significance of the open hand, the open eye, the open door?

3. How does this poem use *parallelism* to line up opposites and to bond things that are similar?

4. How would you chart the overall *development* or shape of this poem?

The Creative Dimension

Some poems leave an exceptionally clear or compelling pattern imprinted on our minds. Choose one such poem. Can you sum up the pattern as briefly as the student-author did in the following response to the Piercy poem? (Can you do so without oversimplifying?)

When we agree
I like you
we are one.
When we disagree
I don't like you
we are separate.
You are my enemy.

Lisel Mueller   *(born 1924)*

The Story   *1980*

You are telling a story:
How Fire Took Water to Wife

It's always like this, you say,
opposites attract

They want to enter each other,   5
be one,
so he burns her as hard as he can
and she tries to drown him

It's called love at first
and doesn't hurt   10

but after a while she weeps
and says he is killing her,
he shouts that he cannot breathe
underwater—

Make up your own   15
ending, you say to the children,
and they will, they will

The Receptive Reader

1. In how many ways does the poem follow up or develop the central pattern of opposites meeting?

2. The poet says "opposites attract." If you wanted to sum up what really happens in the poem, what would you say?

3. The poem at the end asks the children to make up their own ending. What ending would you write?

4. Compare/contrast the meeting of opposites in Marge Piercy's and in Lisel Mueller's poem.

Arna Bontemps   *(1902–1973)*

A Black Man Talks of Reaping   *1940*

I have sown beside all waters in my day.
I planted deep, within my heart the fear
That wind or fowl would take the grain away.
I planted safe against this stark, lean year.

I scattered seed enough to plant the land   5
In rows from Canada to Mexico,
But for my reaping only what the hand
Can hold at once is all that I can show.

Yet what I sowed and what the orchard yields
My brother's sons are gathering stalk and root,   10
Small wonder then my children glean in fields
They have not sown, and feed on bitter fruit.

The Receptive Reader

1. How is the central claim the speaker in this poem makes reinforced or reiterated by sentences *parallel* in form and meaning?

2. Where does the countermovement start in this poem, and how is it sustained or reinforced? (How is "gleaning" different from "reaping"?)

3. A rhyme word at the end of a line, a group of lines, or the whole poem can highlight a crucial idea and make us pause and ponder its significance. How does the poem as a whole lead up to the phrase "bitter fruit"?

4. The imaginative comparisons around which the poem is built are the harvest metaphor and the family metaphor. What gives them special force? (Do you remember any traditional lore or biblical quotations that involve sowing and reaping?)

Gary Soto   *(born 1952)*

We more and more see the work of **bilingual** poets. Well-known American poets speak English as a second language or are part of the first generation in their family to speak mainly English while another language is still the language of the home. The following poem is by a Chicano poet who grew up in a Mexican American neighborhood in Fresno, California. One listener at one of Soto's poetry readings said that he "was funny, and humble, and touching, and completely terrific."

Oranges   *1985*

The first time I talked
With a girl, I was twelve,
Cold, and weighted down
With two oranges in my jacket.
December. Frost cracking   5
Beneath my steps, my breath
Before me, then gone,
As I walked toward
Her house, the one whose
Porch light burned yellow   10
Night and day, in any weather.
A dog barked at me, until
She came out pulling
At her gloves, face bright
With rouge. I smiled,   15
Touched her shoulder, and led
Her down the street, across
A used car lot and a line
Of newly planted trees,
Until we were breathing   20
Before a drugstore. We
Entered, the tiny bell
Bringing a saleslady
Down a narrow aisle of goods.
I turned to the candies   25
Tiered like bleachers
And asked what she wanted—
Light in her eyes, a smile
Starting at the corners
Of her mouth. I fingered   30
A nickel in my pocket,
And when she lifted a chocolate
That cost a dime,
I didn't say anything.
I took the nickel from   35
My pocket, then an orange,

And set them quietly on
The counter. When I looked up,
The lady's eyes met mine,
And held them, knowing   40
Very well what it was all
About.

      Outside,
A few cars hissing past,
Fog hanging like old   45
Coats between the trees.
I took my girl's hand
In mine for two blocks,
Then released it to let
Her unwrap the chocolate.   50
I peeled my orange
That was so bright against
The grey of December
That, from some distance,
Someone might have thought   55
I was making a fire in my hands.

The Receptive Reader

1. This poet has an uncanny gift for recalling the small revealing details that conjure up scenes from the past. What are striking examples in this poem?

2. How does this poem develop and take shape? What is the overall pattern? What are major stages or high points? What helps the reader experience a sense of completion?

3. Gary Soto is known for poems presenting candid and bittersweet childhood memories in understated and wryly humorous fashion. How does this poem show these qualities?

The Creative Dimension

In a poem, we typically see the world through the eye of the speaker in the poem. The more autobiographical the poem is, the more we are looking at people and events from the poet's point of view. How might the same scene or the same event look from the point of view of an onlooker? How might it look from the point of view of people who are the "other" in the poem—someone spoken to in the poem, or someone playing a role in the scenario recorded by the poet? Use your imagination to put yourself in the place of a person talked to or talked about in a poem—for instance, the young girl in Soto's "Oranges," the daughter in Sharon Olds' "The Possessive," or the dull night-capped sleepers in Wallace Stevens' "Disillusionment of Ten O'Clock." Who is speaking in the following creative response to the Soto poem?

> The first time I saw them
> the day was cold, clear.
> I watched them stop, a dog barking at them.
> They exchanged glances; they laughed.
> They came closer to my shop.

They were so young,
their faces shining,
hers shy—his excited.
Like a knight with his lady, he
held the door and bade her enter.
He gestured for her to choose:
She pointed to a big bar—10 cents
He never paused or frowned.
Carefully he produced a nickel
and a large ripe orange.
Our eyes met.
I understood.
I picked up the orange and
inhaled the scent.

James Laughlin   *(born 1914)*

Junk Mail   *1986*

is a pleasure to at least
one person a dear old man

in our town who is drift-
ing into irreality he

walks each morning to the
post office to dig the   5

treasure from his box he
spreads it out on the lob-

by counter and goes through
it with care and delight.   10

The Receptive Reader

1. A **vignette** is a snapshot (using words or a picture) that captures a moment in time. It makes us focus briefly on something worth attention, or it
makes us look at something from a fresh perspective. Does the above vignette
fit this definition?

2. Is there any movement or development in this poem? From what to what?

Robert Frost   *(1874–1963)*

Fire and Ice   *1923*

Some say the world will end in fire,
Some say in ice.
From what I've tasted of desire
I hold with those who favor fire.

But if I had to perish twice,   5
I think I know enough of hate
To say that for destruction ice
Is also great
And would suffice.

The Receptive Reader

1. How is Frost playing off opposites in this poem? How well do fire and ice fit the emotions for which they serve as symbols in this poem?

2. How does the rhyme scheme in this poem serve to highlight the polar opposites?

The Personal Response

Where have you encountered the destructiveness of desire as a theme in your reading or viewing?

Adrienne Rich   *(born 1929)*

Novella   *1967*

Two people in a room, speaking harshly.
One gets up, goes out to walk.
(That is the man.)
The other goes out into the next room
and washes the dishes, cracking one.   5
(That is the woman.)
It gets dark outside.
The children quarrel in the attic.
She has no blood left in her heart.
The man comes back to a dark house.   10
The only light is in the attic.
He has forgotten his key.
He rings at his own door
and hears sobbing on the stairs.
The lights go on in the house.   15
The door closes behind him.
Outside, separate as minds,
the stars too come alight.

The Receptive Reader

1. From what perspective or vantage point are we watching the scene unfolding in this poem?

2. Many of the sentences in this poem are spare and factual. What are striking examples? Where and how do the powerful emotions involved in what we observe shine through?

3. A **novella** is a story that is shorter and more pointed than a full-length novel. Does the poet expect us to read this poem as the story of two specific individuals? Or are the people in this poem representative or even archetypal—standing for an age-old, often repeated pattern?

4. The final two lines bring the poem to a close by serving as a summing up and last word. How?

WRITING ABOUT LITERATURE

13 The Shape of the Poem
WRITING FOCUS: From Notes to Revision

The Writing Workshop How does a successful paper about a poem take shape? Think of your writing as a process that starts with your first reading of a poem and ends with a revised final draft. Be prepared to take a paper through overlapping stages: careful reading, note taking, thinking about the poem, planning your strategy, preparing a rough first draft, working on a more polished revision, final editing and proofreading. Remember that false starts and blind alleys are part of a writer's day. Be prepared to change direction as necessary. Always go back to the poem itself as your main source of ideas and evidence.

Reading Notes Suppose you are working on a paper about Marge Piercy's "Simple Song." Allow time for the preliminary note-taking stage. Many readers find it useful to jot down a running commentary as they work their way through a poem. Here they note key phrases and striking images, questions that arise in the reader's mind, or possible clues to the poet's intention or the larger meaning of the poem. Your **reading notes** for the poem might look like this:

title: why "Simple Song"? Words in the poem are very simple (none need to be looked up in a dictionary)

(line 5) it's "easy to be together" because they don't really see who's there

second stanza is exactly parallel in layout to the first—but now we exit from the relationship

(line 7) "how strange you are"—the other person was not really known to begin with

(line 10) last lines in first and second stanzas are parallel: "how easy. . ."; "how hard. . ." But the same line in second stanza is longer, more drawn-out ("how hard, hard and weary. . .") to make the point of how hard and weary it is to stay together when love is gone (line 12) "leather body"—leather used as a protection since early times; it's tough, more impenetrable than human skin

(line 17) the "open eye"—we really see others for what they are?

(line 18) "door in the chest standing open"—willingness to let someone in

Reading Journal   A journal entry will often record your interpretation of a poem—the way you make sense of it—and your more personal reaction. It may also note your queries—your attempts to puzzle out difficult passages, your tentative answers to unsolved questions. In your paper, you will then be able to draw on some of the more unstructured and informal material in your journal. A journal entry for the Piercy poem might look as follows:

I felt in reading this poem that most people operate exactly the way the first ten lines of this poem describe. In the early stages of courtship, all is euphoria. People focus on everything they can share and agree on. They say, "how easy to be together." Then they slowly let down their guard. They let their differences come to the surface; they become impatient with each other. They start calling each other weird and "strange." Getting along becomes "hard, hard and weary." Although this poem seems to talk mainly about romantic or sexual relationships, I believe the pattern applies to friendships as well.

Planning the Paper   Even while taking notes and recording tentative reactions, you will be thinking about how to lay out your material in a paper. You will be pushing toward an overall impression or keynote—a key idea or ideas what will make your details add up. You will be sketching out a master plan—the major stages through which you will take your reader. Give special thought to the following way stations in the itinerary to be traveled by your reader:

✘ *Introduction*   What is going to be your lead? How are you going to attract and focus the attention of your reader? You may want to lead your readers into the poem from a biographical fact, such as a revealing detail about the poet's war experience or family history that could serve to illuminate the poem. You may want to start with a striking quote from the poet, illuminating his or her intention. You may want to dramatize the setting or the time, vividly re-creating the context of the poem.

✘ *Overview*   What will be your central focus? If possible, let a graphic, vivid introduction lead your readers directly to your main point. State it as your **thesis** and then devote your paper to developing and supporting it. A thesis sums up in a short, memorable statement what the paper as a whole is trying to prove. (Sometimes, however, you will prefer to raise a question to be pondered by the reader and to be answered by the paper as a whole.) Give the kind of preview or overview here that will point your readers in the right direction. Often a thesis statement broadly hints at the major stages in the writer's master plan. It furnishes the reader with a capsule itinerary for the journey ahead.

✗ *Plan* How are you going to follow up your thesis? For the body of a short paper, try sketching out a three-step or four-point plan. Make sure that you arrive at a clear agenda: first this, next this, then that. Highlight the transitions from one major point or stage to the next, so your readers will not get lost in detail. Signal turning points, crucial objections, clinching arguments. Provide links like "on the other hand"; "readers hostile to easy answers may object. . ."; "however, such objections will carry much less weight when we realize. . ."

Often the way the poem itself takes shape will provide a tentative blueprint for all or part of your paper. The "Simple Song" poem swings from the extreme of euphoria, of being blissfully and uncritically in love, to the opposite extreme of sour disappointment and failure to communicate. We may well look to the third and last part of the poem for some middle ground, or for some lesson to be learned, or for some sort of answer. The paper, like the poem, could go from point to counterpoint and then toward some kind of resolution.

✗ *Follow-up* Whatever your claims or generalizations, each general statement you make is a promise to your readers. You are saying in effect, "This is what I claim, and here is the evidence to support it." Much of your text should show a rich texture of quotation, explication (close careful explanation), and interpretation. Choose brief revealing quotations—but don't rip them out of context, omitting essential ifs and buts. Explain what your quotations say and how they say it; explore their overtones and implications. Relate them to the larger context of the poem: What role do they play in the poem as a whole?

✗ *Conclusion* End on a strong note. Pull together essentials of your argument. Put them in perspective: Place them in the context of today, or of your own experience, or of the readers' lives. Or relate the individual poem to the larger patterns of the poet's work. Aim for a wrap-up or a clincher sentence that your readers will remember.

✗ *Title* Writers are often content with a dull working title while drafting a paper ("Structure in Marge Piercy's 'Simple Song' "). Then, first things last, they hit on the title that is both informative and provocative. An effective title does justice to the topic but also beckons to the reader. A thought-provoking quote can attract the reader's attention. A play on a key word or an allusion to a figure from myth or legend can make a title stand out.

Read the following student paper to see how it lives up to the criteria sketched in these guidelines.

Sample Student Paper

The Real Act of Love

In her introduction to *Circle on the Water,* a book of her selected poems, Marge Piercy writes that a poem should "function for us in the ordinary chaos of our lives." Her intention in writing her poems is to "give voice to something in the experience of life. . . . To find ourselves spoken for in art gives dignity to our pain, our anger, our lust, our losses."

Her poem "Simple Song" achieves these goals for me. The poem asks us to face the most terrifying and difficult of human activities: loving another person and opening ourselves to love in return. The title promises us a "simple song." The simplicity promised in the title is carried out in the three-part structure of the poem and conveyed in its simple language. By focusing on the essentials of a very complex issue, the poem helps us see first the lacking sense of reality and second the inevitable alienation that defeats us when we "reach out" to others. It then takes us to a third stage that explains the dilemma and may offer a way out.

The poem filters out all intermediate stages to focus on the two phases that are like turning points in our lives: "going toward" and "leaving." The first group of five lines makes us feel the sweetness and newness of someone we have just met. This is the state of falling in love when we feel totally in harmony with the other person. We say, "You are just like me / your thoughts are my brothers / word matches word / how easy to be together." We feel we have found the perfect soulmate, who thinks and speaks like us.

However, anyone with experience can already forecast the exact opposite stage. In the next set of five lines, we are leaving. The other person has become "strange": "we cannot communicate / we can never agree / how hard, hard and weary to be together." Here we have a feeling of loss, a feeling of confusion and defeat as for some reason we stop loving. The lines in this second stanza are arranged in parallel fashion to those in the first; they serve as a mirror image to those in the first. "You are just like me" turns into "how strange you are." "Word matches word" turns into "we cannot communicate." These contrasting lines give us a clue that maybe our "going toward" was not a clear-eyed move but at least in part self-deception. It did not make allowance for hard times or unexpected problems. Did we know the person whom we told "your thoughts are my brothers" in any real sense?

The last stanza moves beyond the dilemma that confronts us in the first two stanzas and points toward a possible solution to our confusion and pain. The first three lines of the stanza say, "We are not different nor alike / But each strange in his leather body / sealed in skin and reaching out clumsy hands." Our problem is not that we are different from each other. We are all "strange." We are each in a leather body, which sounds tough, isolated from human touch like an animal. To be "sealed in skin" sounds sterile, like being put in a vacuum plastic pouch. We are impenetrable, isolated human beings, groping for contact with "clumsy hands." But we are too thick-skinned to let in another in order to know the soft-skinned person inside the leather covering.

The last five lines may be pointing to a course between the polar opposites of uncritical acceptance and resentful rejection. The poem says, "loving is an act / that cannot outlive the open hand / the open eye / the door in the chest standing open." The image of the open hand may imply an opening up of our fist to show what's there and let the other person see who we really are. But it may also imply the willingness to accept what the other person has to offer, without illusions that we create about the other person in our minds. The "open eye" implies willingness to see others as they really are, to see that rarely does "word match word" and that it is not "easy to be together" on a continuous basis. We have to risk the open door if we do not want to be satisfied with the less fearful business of having someone fill a temporary need for companionship.

The type of love in the first stanza cannot last because it makes us imagine a perfect merging of people who are really unique and strange. When we exaggerate everything we have in common, we already program ourselves for the disappoint-ment acted out in the second stanza. I read a book recently that talks about a "matching game"—trying to build a relationship on everything that makes two peo-ple alike. The real key is to teach our "clumsy hands" to be more accepting of what makes us different. This way we can be in love with a real person rather than with a creation of our own minds.

Questions for Peer Review

This student paper makes it clear that the poet is giving us a "simple song" about what is really one of the most challenging and difficult pat-terns in human relations.

1. How effectively do title and introduction lead toward the main point of the paper? What makes the *starter quote* from the poet intriguing or thought-provoking? What ideas that might ordinarily be considered contradictory are brought together here?

2. What overview or *preview* does the paper provide—how effectively does it prepare you for what is to come? How clear does the "three-part structure" of the poem become to the reader?

3. The student author's introduction uses the terms *simple* and *simplicity* but also *difficult* and *complex*. How does the student writer bring these apparently contradictory ideas together? A *paradox* is a contradictory statement or situa-tion that begins to make sense on second thought. For you, does the student writer make sense of the paradoxes in the poem?

4. What *transitions* guide the reader through the three phases or stages of the poem? What makes the transitions live or dynamic—moving the reader along—rather than static or routine?

5. What important *details* stand out? Where do the student writer's explana-tions or interpretations help you understand or respond to the poem?

6. What does the *conclusion* do that the rest of the paper has not already done? How does it make clear the personal meaning that the poem had for the student writer?

7. What is your *personal response* to the student writer's message at the end of the paper? Where do you agree and where do you part company with the student writer?

A Checklist for Revision

If at all possible, let your draft lie on
your desk or sit in your computer. Then reread
your draft. To revise and polish your paper, you
will need some distance, some perspective. Ask
yourself questions like the following:

1. Is the introduction too colorless and dutiful?
Does it say things like "In this paper, I will
examine important similarities and differences
between two poems"? When revising, try highlighting one key difference or similarity to give your
readers a foretaste of your paper.

2. Does your paper have a clear focus? Can you
point to a sentence that spells out your main
point or your overall perspective? Does it stand
out as a **thesis statement** early in your paper or
as a well-earned conclusion at the end?

3. Does your preview or overview give your readers a sense of direction? For instance, does it
signal that your paper will be built around a
contrast of then and now, or around a turning
from despair to a renewal of hope?

4. As your paper develops, is your master plan
clear enough to your readers? Smooth out apparent
detours, backtrackings, or leads that lead
nowhere. Can you sum up your strategy in a three-
point or four-point (maybe a five-point) outline?

5. Do you signal major way stations in your
paper clearly enough? Check for lame **transitions**
like "also" or "another point we might mention."
Spell out why the next point is the logical next
step in your paper. For instance, does it introduce clinching evidence for a claim you made
earlier? Does it raise an important objection?

6. Do you use enough striking, revealing quotations? Do you use striking short quotations early in the paper to get the reader into the spirit of the poem (or poems)? For example, in writing about Gwendolyn Brooks' poem "Truth," do you early in the paper make your readers hear "the fierce hammering" of the knuckles of Truth on the door?

7. Do you tie your personal reactions to a detailed reading of the text? Or are you using isolated phrases and images as a launching pad to spin you out on journeys of your own?

8. Have you found the happy medium between a hyperformal and a casual use of words? Make sure the language of a poem, alive with image and rhythm, does not clash with your own stodgy, impersonal style. ("A deep look at the whole poem gives overwhelming reference to the plight of alienation and illuminates the poet's transcendent purpose.") Skirt the opposite extreme of language you might use to ask for pretzels in the pub. ("Wait a minute! I thought this was a poem about a spider!")

9. Does your conclusion bring your paper to a satisfying close? Does it leave your readers with a point, an image, or a question to remember? Revise a conclusion that will seem too interchangeable—saying things that could be said about many different poems. ("This poem asks readers to be more aware of their environment and to be more critical of themselves.")

14 IMAGE

The Open Eye

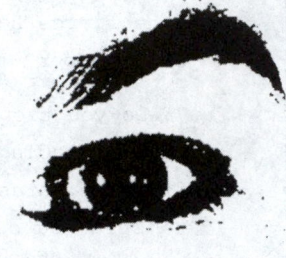

Courtesy Richard B. Ressman

*Great literature, if we read it well, opens us up to
the world. It makes us more sensitive to it, as if
we acquired eyes that could see through things
and ears that could hear smaller sounds.*

DONALD HALL

*It is better to present one image in a lifetime than
to produce voluminous works.*

EZRA POUND

*I am an instrument in the shape of a woman
trying to translate pulsations into images*

ADRIENNE RICH, "PLANETARIUM"

FOCUS ON IMAGE

Poets take you into a world of images. An **image** is a vividly imagined detail that speaks to your sense of sight, hearing, smell, taste, or touch. Poets expect you to read their poems with open eyes and willing ears. They write with a heightened awareness, asking you to take in more of the world around you than people do who see only the stretch of asphalt in front of their cars. Poets ask you to look, to marvel at what you see. It is as if the poet were clearing a fogged-over windshield to help you take a closer look at your world—to take in the textures and shapes of clouds, the looks on faces in the crowd, the dartings and peckings of birds.

Poets tend to have a highly developed visual imagination. ("This morning," Javier Gálvez says, "the sun broke / my window / and came in laughing.") For many poets, insisting on concrete images, anchored in authentic firsthand observation, has been a safeguard against secondhand ideas. They are likely to speak in vivid images even when making a general point about life or about people. They are likely to remind us that the poem and a prose translation, or paraphrase, are not the same. Look at the relation between idea and image in the following lines by the poet Kenneth Rexroth, who became known as a voice of the Beat Generation:

The trout is taken when he
Bites an artificial fly.
Confronted with fraud, keep your
Mouth shut, and don't volunteer.

How is fraud like fishing for trout? What would be lost if this poet had given us only the last two lines? The trout is without guile, going about its legitimate business as nature prompts it. People producing the artificial fly used in trout fishing invest great ingenuity and resourcefulness in producing something to fool an unsuspecting victim. By dramatizing the relationship between the perpetrator and the victim of fraud, the poet makes us "see it feelingly"; we know how it feels to be hooked.

The images we grasp with our senses make poetry **concrete**—they bring our eyes and ears and nerve endings into play. Concrete, sensory details take us into a world of sights, sounds, smells, tastes, and sensations. Concrete details are at the opposite end of the spectrum from **abstract** ideas. Abstract ideas like happiness, freedom, and honor "draw us away" from concrete experience toward large categories and general labels. When they are not anchored to concrete experience, abstractions easily become deceptive. Mere abstract talk about justice or equality may turn out to be an empty promise.

FIRST READING
The Texture of Experience

The following poem is by a poet who revels in the sights and sounds and smells of the apple harvest. Does he succeed in making you share in the experience?

Peter Meinke   *(born 1932)*

Sunday at the Apple Market   1977

Apple-smell everywhere!
Haralson McIntosh Fireside Rome
old ciderpresses weathering in the shed
old ladders tilting at empty branches
boxes and bins of apples by the cartload   5
yellow and green and red
piled crazy in the storehouse barn
miraculous profusion, the crowd
around the testing table laughing rolling
the cool applechunks in their mouths   10
dogs barking at children in the appletrees
couples holding hands, so many people
out in the country carrying bushels
and baskets and bags and boxes of apples
to their cars, the smell of apples   15
making us for one Sunday afternoon free
and happy as people must have been meant to be.

The Receptive Reader

1. Apples are everywhere in this poem. Where in this poem do you see, smell, or taste apples? What are striking realistic details that only an observer who knows the scene well could have noticed? Which images in this poem stay with you after you finish reading?

2. Some poems early strike a *keynote* that sets the tone and recurs through the poem like the tolling of a bell. What is the keynote in this poem, and how does it echo through the poem?

The Personal Response

Why does the apple market become a symbol of happiness for the poet? Are you the kind of person who would have shared in the happy feeling? Why, or why not?

VISUAL AND OTHER IMAGES

Images in verse are not mere decoration, but the very essence of an intuitive language.

T. E. HULME

By *image*, we usually mean a picture we see with the mind's eye. However, we also use the word more generally for any detail that speaks to our senses, whether of sight, hearing, smell, taste, or touch. Most poetic images are visual images—something we can see the way we look in a mirror and see an image of ourselves. However, others are sound images, like the rustling of leaves or the pounding of the surf. Still others are taste images—like the sourness of a lemon that makes the mouth pucker. Still others might be touch images, like the sensation we feel when we run our fingers over the rough bark of a tree. What is it like to look at, hold, touch, bite into, and taste a piece of fruit?

Nan Fry   *(born 1945)*

The Plum   1991

Dark globe that fits easily into the palm,
your skin is speckled with pale galaxies,
an endless scattering.
Everywhere Adam and Eve are leaving
the Garden. You are the fruit we pluck   5
and eat. We need no serpent to urge us,
drawn as we are to your swelling,
your purple shading to rose, your skin
that yields to the touch, to the teeth:
all the world's waters and all its sweetness   10

rolled into fruit that explodes
on the tongue. We eat and drink flesh
the color of garnets, rubies, wounds.
It is bitter just under the skin.

The Receptive Reader

1. What words or phrases in this poem bring the looks, color, and taste of the plum to life for the reader? Which words or phrases are unusual or striking? What details show the poet to be a careful observer?

2. What makes the poet think of Adam and Eve and the serpent?

The following poem centers on a memorable visual image. It asks you to focus on and take in a striking sight. If you let it, the central image in this poem will etch itself on your memory. It will start a chain of association activating disturbing thoughts and feelings. It may come back to haunt you at unexpected moments.

William Stafford   *(1914–1992)*

At the Bomb Testing Site   *1960*

At noon in the desert a panting lizard
waited for history, its elbows tense,
watching the curve of a particular road
as if something might happen.

It was looking for something farther off   5
than people could see, an important scene
acted in stone for little selves
at the flute end of consequences.

There was just a continent without much on it
under a sky that never cared less.   10
Ready for a change, the elbows waited.
The hands gripped hard on the desert.

This poem begins and ends with the sight the poet calls up before our eyes. The panting watchful lizard, its elbows tense, grips the desert floor hard with its hands, surrounded by the empty desert (like a "continent without much on it"), under the empty, uncaring, cloudless sky. This is a striking image, and the poet takes the time to let it sink in. At the same time, there is more to the lizard than meets the eye. Our first hint is that the panting lizard "waited for history." We *are* at a bomb testing site. Something disastrous might happen to the desert life at any moment. The lizard, part of life that has existed on this earth for untold millions of years, might presently perish in the blinding flash of a nuclear holocaust. A chain of associations and forebodings will take each of us to our own personal version of the distant "important scene" at the "flute end of consequences"–where our common history will be channeled as toward the end of a flute, toward its final destination.

The Receptive Reader

1. Does it make any difference to the poem as a whole that the time is noon? that the lizard is watching a curve in the road? Why is the "important scene" in the future acted out for "little selves"?

2. The poem does not preach; the image of the lizard is mute and eloquent at the same time. For you, what is its message?

3. For many people, lizards, like other reptiles, seem alien, remote from human beings in the chain of evolution. For you, does the lizard make a good central image for this poem? Why or why not? (What for you would have been a better choice?)

Vivid and thought-provoking imagery satisfies what for many readers is the test of true poetry: A poem should not verbalize ideas but embed ideas and feelings in graphic images. It should not tell us about an experience but act it out for us. It should not take inventory of feelings but make us share in them. Look for the striking visual images in the following poem. What does the poem invite you to see? What does it make you feel? Does it ask you to think?

Mary Oliver   *(born 1935)*

The Black Snake   *1979*

When the black snake
flashed onto the morning road,
and the truck could not swerve—
death, that is how it happens.

Now he lies looped and useless   5
as an old bicycle tire.
I stop the car
and carry him into the bushes.

He is as cool and gleaming
as a braided whip, he is as beautiful and quiet   10
as a dead brother.
I leave him under the leaves

and drive on, thinking
about *death:* its suddenness,
its terrible weight,   15
its certain coming. Yet under

reason burns a brighter fire, which the bones
have always preferred.
It is the story of endless good fortune.
It says to oblivion: not me!   20

It is the light at the center of every cell.
It is what sent the snake coiling and flowing forward

happily all spring through the green leaves before
he came to the road.

The speaker in this poem is thinking about what keeps us going in face
of the knowledge that disaster may strike. Death may lurk at any turn in
the road. (The one thing sure about death is its "certain coming.") However,
the person speaking does her thinking in vivid images. The poem focuses
on the black snake—which has to become real for us if the poem is to carry
its true weight. We need to imagine the snake as it moves "happily through
the green leaves" until it meets sudden death in the road. Perhaps then we
will be ready to say with the poet: "That's how it happens." The snake apparently is not some alien creature "out there." We are like the snake, moving through life merrily until all of a sudden something terrible overtakes us.
We feel the "terrible weight" of that knowledge.

The Receptive Reader

1. What graphic images make you see the way the snake moved when it
was alive? What images help you see the way it looked after it had been hit?

2. How is what "reason" says in this poem different from what people know
(or prefer to believe) in their "bones"? What striking image helps you visualize
the intense vital energy of that knowledge?

3. What is "the light at the center of every cell"? What do you know about
cells that can help you understand this phrase and its role in the poem?

The Personal Response

As you look back over the poem, are you likely to remember the image of
the dead snake or the image of the live snake moving "happily all spring
through the green leaves"? What for you is stronger in the poem—the experience of death or the affirmation of life?

The Creative Dimension

Some readers get into the spirit of a poem—imagining themselves at the
scene as bystanders or participants. How or how well did the student author of
the following response get "inside the poem"? Write a similar "getting-inside-
the-poem" response to this poem or another poem of your choice.

Forward
    The snake, forward into the road,
always forward, and in the end, curving around, coiling,
beginning to end and back again, this
snake, instinct pushing, pulling it forward,
knowing, not knowing. Straight forward still, to
die, to touch me, to add fuel to the fire inside
of me. Not me, I say. Not me, I announce. The
snake shows it differently. You, says the snake,
you and me. Bending down, I touch the snake,
the whip, the dead coiled line. I stand

in the road, alive, the fire still believing in
my bones, the life still pushing me forward,
straight ahead. Straight and forward, into life,
again and always forward into
                the road.

The American poet Theodore Roethke had a special gift for using the
image-making language of poetry to re-create the rich texture of sensory
experience. In the following poem, Roethke uses visual images, but he
also uses images that speak strongly to other senses. What does the
poem make you see? And how does the poet go *beyond* visual images
to include other kinds of sensory detail? What sensations and feelings
does the boy experience?

Theodore Roethke   *(1908–1963)*

My Papa's Waltz   1948

The whiskey on your breath
Could make a small boy dizzy;
But I hung on like death:
Such waltzing was not easy.

We romped until the pans   5
Slid from the kitchen shelf;
My mother's countenance
Could not unfrown itself.

The hand that held my wrist
Was battered on one knuckle;   10
At every step you missed
My right ear scraped a buckle.

You beat time on my head
With a palm caked hard by dirt,
Then waltzed me off to bed   15
Still clinging to your shirt.

The Receptive Reader

1. What does this poem make you see? What details in the poem bring
senses *other* than sight into play?

2. What helps you put yourself in the boy's place? Where and how do *you*
share in what the boy sensed and felt?

The Range of Interpretation

Many readers find that this poem makes them relive the experience but does
not tell them what to make of it. Whether the boy in the poem felt a sickening
fear or a mad dizzy joy is for our own emotional antennas to pick up. Critics
have read the poem different ways—depending on their negative or positive

reactions to the father. *Romp* is usually an approving word; it makes us think of a happy, boisterous, energetic kind of running or dancing. Do you think the boy liked the romp in this poem? As he looks back, how does the speaker in the poem feel about his father? Is he critical of the father? Or is he expressing feelings of love for him? How do *you* feel about the father?

Philip Schultz   *(born 1945)*

Laughter   *1978*

One night my father yanked a tablecloth
from under my face & plates spun like meteors
as he wrapped it over his shoulders & his bald head lit up
like a pumpkin as he waltzed my mother round our crooked house
& tears soaked my collar & my stomach jumped into my mouth   5
as they flew chair over sofa & the world was a moment so full of us
I think of the Samurai playing with a daisy as he waits for his enemy
& only the daisy & the bright summer sun in his smile & I ask you
if at a time like this you would wonder if there was a beginning or end
with angels gathering on the roof to fear such loud tearing   10
at the fiery curtain of human delight.

The Receptive Reader

1. Is what happens in this poem similar to what happens in "My Papa's Waltz"? In what ways? Is it in some ways different?

2. Are the adults in the two poems similar? Are they in some ways different?

3. What about the kid who is speaking in the poem? What are his feelings? Does he seem akin to the speaker of the other poem to you?

4. The speaker in the Roethke poem is having an imaginary conversation with the father. The speaker in this poem turns to the reader—to say what? How does this change in the person spoken to change the poem as a whole?

IMAGES AND FEELINGS

*If . . . it makes my whole body so cold no fire can
ever warm me, I know that is poetry. If I feel physically as if the top of my head were taken off, I
know that is poetry.*

EMILY DICKINSON

Poetic images have the power to stir our emotions. At times, the poet may seem to adopt the stance of the neutral, unemotional observer. The poet's eye then is the objective camera eye, recording dispassionately what it sees. However, many poems travel without warning from what the poet saw to what the poet felt and thought. The scene we find ourselves reenacting in the following poem has the hallucinatory intensity of a dream. What feeling or feelings does it invite you to share?

Ursula K. Le Guin   *(born 1929)*

The Old Falling Down   *1988*

In the old falling-down
house of my childhood
I go down-
stairs to sleep out-
side on the porch   5
under stars and dream
of trying to go up-
stairs but there are no
stairs so I climb
hand over hand clambering   10
scared and when I get there
to my high room, find
no bed, no chair, bare floor.

The Receptive Reader

1. What for you is the dominant *emotion* in this poem? (Does it make you share in mixed or contradictory emotions?) What haunting images create the emotional effect?

2. What is the difference between "climbing" and "clambering"?

3. Several split or *divided words* in this poem make us move on from the end of a line to the next without the break or rest we would normally expect. Do you see any connection between this extra effort required of the reader and the subject of the poem?

The Creative Dimension

Do you recognize the feeling or feelings pervading this poem? Have you ever had a similar dream? Write a journal entry (poem or prose) about a haunting and perhaps recurrent dream.

Poets vary greatly in how fully they signal their emotions. Often, like Theodore Roethke in "My Papa's Waltz," they let the experience speak for itself. Contrast the Roethke poem with another father-son poem by Robert Hayden, who in other poems has written eloquently about the African American heritage. In this poem, the poet makes us suffer the bitter cold by appealing to our senses of sight and touch. We can visualize the "blueblack cold" and feel the "cracked hands that ached." When the blazing fire drives out the icy cold, our sense of hearing is brought into play: As the blazing wood shifts and splits, we seem to "hear the

cold splintering, breaking." What feelings does the poet express in response to the scenes he dramatizes in this poem? What was his relationship with his father when he was a boy? How does he feel about his
father now?

Robert Hayden   *(1913–1980)*

Those Winter Sundays   1962

Sundays too my father got up early,
and put his clothes on in the blueblack cold,
then with cracked hands that ached
from labor in the weekday weather made
banked fires blaze. No one ever thanked him.   5

I'd wake and hear the cold splintering, breaking.
When the rooms were warm, he'd call,
and slowly I would rise and dress,
fearing the chronic angers of that house.

Speaking indifferently to him,   10
who had driven out the cold
and polished my good shoes as well.
What did I know, what did I know
of love's austere and lonely offices?

The Receptive Reader

1. What do you learn about the boy's family situation as he grew up? As the
poet steers your emotions in this poem, what are your feelings toward the
lonely father?

2. The word *austere* means being self-denying but at the same time being
proud to be so, holding aloof. How does this key word fit into the poem?

3. Why does the poet repeat the question "What did I know?" in the next to
the last line of the poem?

The Creative Dimension

Most of us can think of an occasion or person that we did not appreciate
properly. We remember lost opportunities, occasions for regret. Write a passage
or poem on the theme of "What did I know, what did I know."

Making Connections—For Discussion or Writing

Look at poems that center on parent-child relations, like Sharon Olds' "The
Possessive," Theodore Roethke's "My Papa's Waltz," and Robert Hayden's
"Those Winter Sundays." Are there recurrent concerns? Or do the poems offer
very different perspectives?

Both of the following poems take you to a place to which the poet
has strong emotional ties. What images make the settings real for you?

How do the poets communicate their feelings? Can you share in the feelings expressed in these poems?

William Stafford   *(1914–1992)*

One Home   *1963*

Mine was a Midwest home—you can keep your world.
Plain black hats rode the thoughts that made our code.
We sang hymns in the house; the roof was near God.

The light bulb that hung in the pantry made a wan light,
but we could read by it the names of preserves—   5
outside, the buffalo grass, and the wind in the night.

A wildcat sprang at Grandpa on the Fourth of July
when he was cutting plum bushes for fuel,
before Indians pulled the West over the edge of the sky.

To anyone who looked at us we said, "My friend";   10
liking the cut of a thought, we could say, "Hello."
(But plain black hats rode the thoughts that made our code.)

The sun was over our town; it was like a blade.
Kicking cottonwood leaves we ran toward storms.
Wherever we looked the land would hold us up.   15

The Receptive Reader

1. What striking images put us in the Midwest that was the poet's home? Where do the poet's feelings about the land show? Where do his feelings about the people show? How?

2. The poem is divided into stanzas, or sets of lines that each follow a similar pattern, like the verses of a song. Can you show that each stanza (or almost each stanza) focuses on one dimension or aspect of the Midwestern tradition or mentality that is the subject of this poem?

3. In some songlike poems, the same line comes back in each stanza as a refrain. In this poem, a key line is repeated only once. Why is it important enough for the poet to repeat it?

4. This poem makes some limited, low-key use of rhyme. Where and how? The poem also uses lines of roughly similar length, with a steady underlying beat. Can you find some lines that have a clear five-beat rhythm? Why is it not surprising that this poet would like a style that is low-key but has a steady underlying beat?

The second poem about a favorite place takes us to the now empty and fenced-in lots under a raised freeway in California, with the small houses gone and the fruit trees and vegetable patches running wild. The Hispanic poet talking here about childhood scenes slides from English into Spanish (the language of her childhood) and back, moving easily between two languages like other bilingual Americans.

Lorna Dee Cervantes   *(born 1954)*

Freeway 280   1981

Las casitas° near the gray cannery   *the little houses*
nestled amid wild abrazos° of climbing roses   *hugs*
and man-high red geraniums
are gone now. The freeway conceals it
all beneath a raised scar.   5

But under the fake windsounds of the open lanes,
in the abandoned lots below, new grasses sprout,
wild mustard remembers, old gardens
come back stronger than they were,
trees have been left standing in their yards.   10
Albaricoqueros, cerezos, nogales° . . .   *apricot, cherry, and walnut*
Viejitas° come here with paper bags to gather greens.   *little old women*
Espinaca, verdolagas, yerbabuena° . . .   *spinach, purslane, mint*

I scramble over the wire fence
that would have kept me out.   15
Once, I wanted out, wanted the rigid lanes
to take me to a place without sun,
without the smell of tomatoes burning
on swing shift in the greasy summer air.

Maybe it's here   20
en los campos extranos de esta ciudad°   *in the strange fields of this city*
where I'll find it, that part of me
mown under
like a corpse
or a loose seed.   25

The Receptive Reader

1. What is the "raised scar"? What are the "windsounds," and why are they "fake"? How does the poet feel about the freeway?

2. How did the poet feel about this setting when she grew up there? What role did the cannery play in her childhood or adolescence?

3. What are her feelings as she returns to this setting? What does she mean when she says that "wild mustard remembers"?

4. Students of language use the term *code-switching* for shifting from one language, or linguistic code, to the other. At what points in the poem does the poet shift back to the Spanish of her childhood? Can you speculate why? What might have been lost if she had used the literal English translations here printed in the margin?

The Personal Response

Do you think the part of the poet (or of her past) that was "mown under" will prove a "corpse" or a "seed"? What images of continuing growth earlier in this poem might help you answer this question?

The Creative Dimension

Most people have intense personal associations—positive or negative—with a childhood setting that may haunt them in their dreams. Write a poem or prose passage about a childhood setting or favorite place recalled in vivid memories or revisited in a dream.

JUXTAPOSITIONS

Writing to Commemorate

One of the earliest functions of poetry was to keep alive the memory of the dead. The two following poems take us to the Vietnam War Memorial in Washington, D.C., which records on an unadorned granite wall the names of Americans who died in Vietnam. The wall cuts into a hillside, with sections starting close to the ground and then gradually rising to full height, with name after name after name cut into the black stone. What does each poet see? What thoughts and feelings go through each poet's mind? How are the two poems similar and alike?

Alberto Rios   *(born 1952)*

The Vietnam Wall   *1988*

I
Have seen it
And I like it: The magic,
The way like cutting onions
It brings water out of nowhere.   5
Invisible from one side, a scar
Into the skin of the ground
From the other, a black winding
Appendix line.
       A dig.   10
       An archaeologist can explain.
The walk is slow at first,
Easy, a little black marble wall
Of a dollhouse,
A smoothness, a shine   15
The boys in the street want to give.
One name. And then more
Names, long lines, lines of names until
They are the shape of the U.N. Building
Taller than I am: I have walked   20
Into a grace.

And everything I expect has been taken away, like that, quick:
        The names are not alphabetized.
        They are in the order of dying,
           An alphabet of—somewhere—screaming.   25
I start to walk out. I almost leave
But stop to look up names of friends,
My own name. There is somebody
Severiano Ríos.
Little kids do not make the same noise   30
Here, junior high school boys don't run
Or hold each other in headlocks.
No rules, something just persists
Like pinching on St. Patrick's Day
Every year for no green.   35
            No one knows why.
Flowers are forced
Into the cracks
Between sections.
Men have cried   40
At this wall.
I have
Seen them.

The Receptive Reader

1. What details in the poem are realistic details remembered by an alert observer? How do the details help you reenact the poet's walk past the monument?

2. Where and how does this poet convey the powerful emotional effect the sight of the monument had on him, as it has on many of its observers?

3. The speaker in the poem says, "everything I expect has been taken away." How did what he saw and experienced go counter to ordinary expectations?

4. Many sentences in this poem are short, matter-of-fact: "One knows why." "I have seen them." Why do you think the poem uses this matter-of-fact style in talking about a subject that inspires powerful emotions?

5. What do you think you are most likely to remember when you think of this poem?

What did the author of the following poem see and feel at the memorial? How was his experience similar to or different from that of the other poet?

Jeffrey Harrison   (born 1957)

Reflection on the Vietnam War Memorial   1987

Here it is, the back porch of the dead.
You can see them milling around in there,
    screened in by their own names,
    looking at us in the same

vague and serious way we look at them.   5

An underground house, a roof of grass—
one version of the underworld. It's all
   we know of death, a world
   like our own (but darker, blurred)
inhabited by beings like ourselves.   10

The location of the name you're looking for
can be looked up in a book whose resemblance
   to a phone book seems to claim
   some contact can be made
through the simple act of finding a name.   15

As we touch the name the stone absorbs our grief.
It takes us in—we see ourselves inside it.
   And yet we feel it as a wall
   and realize the dead are all
just names now, the separation final.   20

The Receptive Reader

1. At times in this poem, the wall seems almost transparent; at other times
it becomes a real wall. How are the thoughts and feelings the wall inspires different at the beginning and at the end of the poem?

2. The poet keeps coming back to the names—the names on the wall, the
entries in the book guiding visitors in finding a name. How does each mention
make you see the names in a somewhat different light?

The Personal Response

Do you think your own feelings and attitudes would have resembled those
of the first poet or the second? Or would your reactions have been different
from either? How and why?

POETRY AND PARAPHRASE

I think that the one thing that's been consistently
true about my poetry is this determination to get
authenticity of detail.

MAXINE KUMIN

In a paraphrase, we put someone else's ideas into our own words,
thus making sure we understand the plain literal meaning. At the same
time, we try not to lose too much of what the poem does to involve our
senses, our hearts, and our minds. In reading the following poem, pay
special attention to the images that make the speaker's thoughts and

feelings real for us. What makes the poem different from the paraphrase that follows it?

Edna St. Vincent Millay   *(1892–1950)*

Childhood Is the Kingdom Where Nobody Dies   *1934*

Childhood is not from birth to a certain age and at a certain age
The child is grown, and puts away childish things.
Childhood is the kingdom where nobody dies.

Nobody that matters, that is. Distant relatives of course
Die, whom one never has seen or has seen for an hour,   5
And they gave one candy in a pink-and-green striped bag, or a jack-knife,
And went away, and cannot really be said to have lived at all.

And cats die. They lie on the floor and lash their tails,
And their reticent fur is suddenly all in motion
With fleas that one never knew were there,   10
Polished and brown, knowing all there is to know,
Trekking off into the living world.
You fetch a shoe-box, but it's much too small, because she won't curl up
    now:
So you find a bigger box, and bury her in the yard, and weep.

But you do not wake up a month from then, two months,   15
A year from then, two years, in the middle of the night
And weep, with your knuckles in your mouth, and say Oh, God! Oh, God!
Childhood is the kingdom where nobody dies that matters,— mothers and
    fathers don't die.

And if you have said, "For heaven's sake, must you always be kissing a
    person?"
Or, "I do wish to gracious you'd stop tapping on the window with your   20
    thimble!"
Tomorrow, or even the day after tomorrow if you're busy having fun,
Is plenty of time to say, "I'm sorry, mother."

To be grown up is to sit at the table with people who have died, who nei-
    ther listen nor speak;
Who do not drink their tea, though they always said
Tea was such a comfort.   25

Run down into the cellar and bring up the last jar of raspberries; they are
    not tempted.
Flatter them, ask them what was it they said exactly
That time, to the bishop, or to the overseer, or to Mrs. Mason;
They are not taken in.
Shout at them, get red in the face, rise,   30

The Brooklyn Bridge: Variation on an Old Theme. 1939.
By Joseph Stella (1877–1946).
Oil on canvas, 70 x 42 in. (177.8 x 106.7 cm). Collection of the Whitney Museum of American Art, New York. Photograph © 2000 Jerry L. Thompson

RIVER SONG
Warren Woessner

Crossing late is best.
The bridge strung
over the water
like a huge harp.
Sun caught in the black strings
forms one pure note—
trembling,
falling as we rise,
reach out,
strain to hear
the perfect sound
that must be fading
just above our heads.

The Yellow House. 1888.
By Vincent Van Gogh (1853–1890).
Vincent's house in Arles. Oil on canvas, 28.37 x 36 in. (72 x 91.5 cm). Van Gogh Museum (Vincent Van Gogh Foundation), Amsterdam

THE YELLOW HOUSE
Gerald Locklin

build a yellow house
and they will come.
a yellow building, actually.
but in fact they didn't come.

or they come—gauguin at least—
and leave.

even with the broad street
and a restaurant around the corner.

even with the sky a deeper
blue than the mediterranean.

even after you've painted the
shutters a sherwood green.

even with the fine tile roofs
to match the summer trees.

even with white awnings and
white-bonneted neighbors,

you wait, week after week,
in your warm yellow house.
and no one comes
(or gauguin comes and goes)
until, at last, only
sorrow comes to your door.

Woman Powdering Her Neck.
By Kitagawa Utamaro (1753–1806).
© Reunion des Musées Nationaux/
Art Resource, NY/Musée des Arts
Asiatiques-Guimet, Paris, France

Her hair is black
with hints of red,
the color of seaweed
spread over rocks.

Morning begins the ritual
wheel of the body,
the application of translucent
  skins.
She practices pleasure:
the pressure of three fingertips
applying powder.
Fingertips of pollen
some other hand will trace.

The peach-dyed kimono
patterned with maple leaves
drifting across the silk,
falls from right to left
in a diagonal, revealing
the nape of her neck
and the curve of a shoulder
like the slope of a hill
set deep in snow in a country of
huge white solemn birds.
Her face appears in the mirror,
a reflection in a winter pond,
rising to meet itself.

She dips a corner of her sleeve
Like a brush into water
to wipe mirrors;
she is about to paint herself.

GIRL POWDERING
HER NECK
Cathy Song

The light is the inside
sheen of an oyster shell,
sponged with talc and vapor,
moisture from a bath.

A pair of slippers
are placed outside
the rice paper doors.
She kneels at a low table
in the room,
her legs folded beneath her
as she sits on a buckwheat pillow.

The eyes narrow
in a moment of self-scutiny.
The mouth parts
as if desiring to disturb
the placid plum face:
Break the symmetry of silence.
But the berry-stained lips,
stenciled into the mask of beauty,
do not speak.
Two chrysanthemums
touch in the middle of the lake
  and drift apart.

Young Woman with a Water Jug.
By Johannes Vermeer (Dutch, 1632–1675).
Oil on canvas, H. 18 x 16 in. (45.7 x 40.6 cm). The Metropolitan Museum of Art, Marquand Collection,
Gift of Henry G. Marquand, 1889. (89.15.21). Photograph © 1993 The Metropolitan Museum of Art

VERMEER
Stephen Mitchell

She stands by the table, poised
at the corner of your vision,
with her left hand
just barely on
the pitcher's handle, and her right
lightly touching the windowframe.
Serene as a clear sky, luminous
in her blue dress and many-toned
white cotton wimple, she is looking
nowhere. Upon her lips
is the subtlest and most lovely
of smiles, caught
for an instant
like a snowflake in a warm hand.

How weightless her body feels
as she stands, absorbed, within this
fulfillment that has brought more
than any harbinger could.
She looks down with an infinite
tenderness in her eyes,
as though the light at the window
were a newborn child
and her arms open enough
to hold it on her breast, forever.

Bananas and Grapefruits III. 1972.
By Roy Lichtenstein (American, 1923–1997).
Oil and magna on canvas, 20 x 40 in. (71.1 x 101.6 cm).
© Estate of Roy Lichtenstein

ON BANANAS AND GRAPEFRUIT #3
Deborah Pope

plump slump

slick lick

slug plug

slow flow

broke yolk

squirt shirt

(hello

taste

yellow!)

haste

sealed in

unpeeled skin

gulppulp

gold fold

fruit suit

sweet part

sluice of juices

squeezy teases

eat

swelling lemon

art

jujubeezes

tipped ship

nape shape

goo canoe

peel deal

rind grind

rough slough

Classic Landscape. 1931. By Charles Sheeler (American, 1883–1965).
Oil on canvas, 25 x 32.25 in. (63.5 x 81.9 cm). 2000.39.2./PA. Collection of Mr. and Mrs. Barney A. Ebsworth. Photograph by Lyle Peterzell
© 2002 Board of Trustees, National Gallery of Art

CLASSIC SCENE
William Carlos Williams

A power-house
in the shape of
a red brick chair
90 feet high

on the seat of which
sit the figures
of two metal
stacks—aluminum—
commanding an area
of squalid shacks
side by side—
from one of which

butt smoke
streams while under
a grey sky
the other remains

passive today—

Composition with Red, Yellow, and Blue. 1930.
By Piet Mondrian (1872–1944).
51 x 51 cm. © Giraudon/Art Resource/© 2003 Mondrian/Holtzman Trust, c/o Beeldrecht/Artist Rights Society (ARS), NY/Private Collection, New York, NY

ORGANIZATION
Paula Mangin

Fits together,
picture-perfect,
organized,
and clear.
This is for certain
not
my life. Well, maybe
next year.

Night Snow.
By Hiroshige.
Detail of Japanese woodblock print

KAMBARA
Steve Sano

Gray,
Shades of black.
The lack of color
Is cold.
Only the figures have color,
Only the color has warmth,
Only warmth has life.
The life moves ankle-deep
Through gray powder.
The same powder covers
Living backs,
The mountains, trees
And the thatched roof
Of dark houses.
Look at the sky:
one shade of gray
Except far on the horizon
Where it is black,
One shade of gray
With gray powder falling,
Cold,
Bleak,
Forever
Gray

Drag them up out of their chairs by their stiff shoulders and shake them
    and yell at them;
They are not startled, they are not even embarrassed; they slide back into
    their chairs.

Your tea is cold now.
You drink it standing up,
And leave the house.   35

A short prose paraphrase of the flow of thought in this poem might read
like this:

> Childhood is not a matter of chronology; we leave it behind when we become
> aware of the reality of death. During childhood, death is not real. Death is not real
> when distant relatives die whom we have known only from short visits. Childhood
> pets die and are buried, but they do not cause wild passionate grief that lasts for
> months and years. Our childhood continues as long as our parents are spared and
> there is plenty of time to apologize and make amends after a temporary estrange-
> ment. We know that we have passed from childhood to adulthood when we are
> forced to accept the fact that people who were close to us and part of our lives
> are gone forever. They and their familiar mannerisms may be so vivid in our memo-
> ries that they may seem to be in the room with us, but we are forever cut off from
> communicating with them. We find ourselves alone in an empty house; we have no
> reason to linger there to be with someone close to us.

This paraphrase can serve as a chart to the poet's thoughts, but we must
remember that it is different from the real poem, just as a map of a river is
different from the river. In the paraphrase, the relatives, the pets, the parents, and grief for their loss all remain abstractions, as different from the living currency of thought and feeling as the figures in a checkbook are from
the actual currency we spend.

The Receptive Reader

What striking images make the relatives and childhood perceptions of them
real for the reader? What graphic, unexpected images dramatize the death of
childhood pets? What images make the speaker's grief real when people die
who "matter"? How does the poet dramatize the feeling of being cut off from
human contact with the dead?

The Personal Response

Millay was widely admired in her day but fell from favor when critical trends
encouraged distance and control in the expression of personal emotions. Feminist critics today praise her as women writers increasingly use poetry as a
medium for coming to terms with intensely felt personal experience. How do
you respond to the emotions expressed in this poem?

POEMS FOR FURTHER STUDY

In reading the following poems, pay special attention to imagery that brings a scene or a natural setting to life for the reader. How does it appeal to the senses? What does it do for the reader?

Dana Gioia   *(born 1950)*

California Hills in August   *1982*

I can imagine someone who found
these fields unbearable, who climbed
the hillside in the heat, cursing the dust,
cracking the brittle weeds underfoot,
wishing a few more trees for shade.   5

An Easterner especially, who would scorn
the meagreness of summer, the dry
twisted shapes of black elm,
scrub oak, and chaparral—a landscape
August has already drained of green.   10

One who would hurry over the clinging
thistle, foxtail, golden poppy,
knowing everything was just a weed,
unable to conceive that these trees
And sparse brown bushes were alive.   15

And hate the bright stillness of the noon,
without wind, without motion,
the only other living thing
a hawk, hungry for prey, suspended
in the blinding, sunlit blue.   20

And yet how gentle it seems to someone
raised in a landscape short of rain—
the skyline of a hill broken by no more
trees than one can count, the grass,
the empty sky, the wish for water.   25

The Receptive Reader

1. What is the task the poet set himself in this poem? Why does he make us look at the landscape familiar to his through the eyes of the *outsider?*

2. What images or details make the landscape real for you? Were you surprised when the poem reached its turning point at the beginning of the last stanza?

3. What phrase or phrases would you nominate as the key to the characteristic quality of the landscape in this poem?

4. Do your sympathies lie with the Easterner or the Westerner in this poem?

John Keats   *(1795–1821)*

To Autumn   *1819*

Season of mists and mellow fruitfulness,
    Close bosom friend of the maturing sun;
Conspiring with him how to load and bless
    With fruit the vines that round the thatch eaves° run;   *of thatched roofs*
To bend with apples the mossed cottage trees,   5
    And fill all fruit with ripeness to the core;
        To swell the gourd, and plump the hazel shells
With a sweet kernel; to set budding more,
    And still more, later flowers for the bees,
    Until they think warm days will never cease,   10
        For summer has over-brimmed° their clammy cells. *filled to overflowing*

Who hath not seen thee oft amid thy store?
    Sometimes whoever seeks abroad may find
Thee sitting careless on a granary floor,
    Thy hair soft-lifted by the winnowing wind;   15
Or on a half-reaped furrow sound asleep,
    Drowsed with the fume of poppies, while thy hook
        Spares the next swath and all its twinèd° flowers: *intertwined*
And sometimes like a gleaner thou dost keep
    Steady thy laden head across a brook;   20
    Or by a cider-press with patient look
        Thou watchest the last oozings hours by hours.

Where are the songs of Spring? Aye, where are they?
    Think not of them, thou hast thy music too,—
While barrèd° clouds bloom the soft-dying day,   *streaked* 25
    And touch the stubble-plains with rosy hue;
Then in a wailful choir the small gnats mourn
    Among the river sallows,° borne aloft   *low willow trees*
        Or sinking as the light wind lives or dies;
And full-grown lambs loud bleat from hilly bourn;°   *field* 30
    Hedge crickets sing; and now with treble soft
    The redbreast whistles from a garden-croft;°   *small plot*
        And gathering swallows twitter in the skies.

The Receptive Reader

1. Readers have long turned to Keats' poetry for its rich sensuous imagery. How much of Keats' *harvest imagery* does the modern reader still recognize? (Can you visualize the reaper cutting a swath through the wheat interspersed with flowers; can you visualize the wind winnowing the grain—by blowing the lighter chaff away as the grain is thrown into the air?)

2. What words and images in this poem help create the prevailing *mood*— the rich harvest mood of things coming to fruition, offering a feast to the

senses? (Which images are visual images? Which are sound images? Which involve sensations—touch, taste?) What does Keats' way of looking at the nuts, the bees, or the cider press contribute to the characteristic feeling that pervades the poem?

3. Why are the swallows gathering? Is it a mere coincidence that Keats mentions them last in the poem?

The Personal Response

Keats, like other Romantic poets of the early nineteenth century, saw the healing influence of nature as an antidote to the ills of city civilization. Can you get into the spirit of his nature poetry? Is your own relationship with nature similar or different?

T. S. Eliot   *(1888–1965)*

Preludes   *1917*

I

The winter evening settles down
With smell of steaks in passageways.
Six o'clock.
The burnt-out ends of smoky days.
And now a gusty shower wraps.   5
The grimy scraps
Of withered leaves about your feet
And newspapers from vacant lots;
The showers beat
On broken blinds and chimney-pots,   10
And at the corner of the street
A lonely cab-horse steams and stamps.
And then the lighting of the lamps.

II

The morning comes to consciousness
Of faint stale smells of beer   15
From the sawdust-trampled street
With all its muddy feet that press
To early coffee-stands.
With the other masquerades
That time resumes,   20
One thinks of all the hands
That are raising dingy shades
In a thousand furnished rooms.

III

You tossed a blanket from the bed,
You lay upon your back, and waited;   25
You dozed, and watched the night revealing
The thousand sordid images
Of which your soul was constituted;
They flickered against the ceiling.
And when all the world came back   30
And the light crept up between the shutters
And you heard the sparrows in the gutters,
You had such a vision of the street
As the street hardly understands;
Sitting along the bed's edge, where   35
You curled the papers from your hair,
Or clasped the yellow soles of feet
In the palms of both soiled hands.

IV

His soul stretched tight across the skies
That fade behind a city block,   40
Or trampled by insistent feet
At four and five and six o'clock;
And short square fingers stuffing pipes,
And evening newspapers, and eyes
Assured of certain certainties,   45
The conscience of a blackened street
Impatient to assume the world.

   I am moved by fancies that are curled
   Around these images, and cling:
   The notion of some infinitely gentle   50
   Infinitely suffering thing.

   Wipe your hand across your mouth, and laugh;
   The worlds revolve like ancient women
   Gathering fuel in vacant lots.

The Receptive Reader

1. T. S. Eliot was a leader in the early modern rebellion against the conventionally beautiful or superficially pretty in poetry. How many of the images make this poem head in the opposite direction? Which are most striking or memorable for you, and why?

2. How does the "you" addressed in the poem relate to the "sordid" images shown in this poem? How does the "I" that is speaking? How do you?

The Creative Dimension

Much modern poetry explores negative or mixed emotions about the urban landscape or cityscape in which most of us live. Write a passage or poem packed with images that project your own feelings about the city or about the American small town. How do you react to the following example?

> After the first rain, the city's smells only reek louder and damper: damp wool, wet newspapers, the oily dirty street. The smell of yesterday's meatloaf wafts from the neighboring apartment when I open the window to smell the wet cement. Today will be like yesterday. I open a thousand locks on the front door and lock a thousand behind me.

Ann Darr   *(born 1920)*

Advice I Wish Someone Had Given Me   *1971*

Be strange if it is necessary, be
quiet, kindly as you can without
feeling the heel marks on your head.
Be expert in some way that pleasures
you, story-telling, baking, bed;   5
marvel at the marvelous
in leaves, stones, intercepted light;
put truth and people in their rightful angle in the sun . . . find the shadow,
what it falls upon.   10
Trust everyone a little, no one much.
Care carefully.
Thicken your skin to hints and hurts, be
allergic to the soul scrapers.

The Receptive Reader

1. Explain the striking *visual* images in this poem. How would we put "truth and people in their rightful angle in the sun"? What is the "shadow" that we are asked to find?

2. Which images are visual while at the same time bringing bodily *sensations* into play? What sensations are we made to experience by the "heel marks" (and what caused them)? Who are the "soul scrapers"? What sensations or feelings does the phrase bring into play?

3. What is contradictory or paradoxical about the *play on words* in "Care carefully"? Does this piece of advice make sense to you? Does any of the advice in this poem have a special meaning for you?

4. This poet makes minimal and somewhat unusual use of *rhyme*. How?

JUXTAPOSITIONS: WORD AND IMAGE

Reading Images, Seeing Poems

Poetry is a speaking picture; a painting is silent poetry.

SIMONIDES OF KEOS

The creative imagination works in many media and through many channels. From the beginnings of human history, artists, storytellers, and poets have found ways to fashion shapes that beckon to the eye and patterns that please the ear. They have worked in wood and clay and stone, with colors and with sounds to create a world of feelings. They have made visible and audible the unseen and unheard inner world of human emotions, memories, hopes, and sorrows.

Through much of human history, the sister arts were not isolated, fenced-off specialties. Poetry was sung or chanted by bards, who accompanied themselves on the small harplike Greek lyre or the medieval lute, distant cousin of the modern guitar. Traditional stories were acted out in communal celebrations with drumming, song, and dance.

In the history of human culture, there has been much dynamic interaction between the visual arts and the art of poetry. Both painter and poet are makers of images. Poetry calls forth pictures in the mind. It uses words to conjure up rivers and mountains, blossoming meadows, and mean city streets. It uses language to make us marvel at the vital energies of the endangered wildlife of our planet. Through the magic of the word, we observe as fellow humans act out their fears and longings, or we tag along as they take us with them into the world of their dreams.

In turn, painters and sculptors have often felt the urge to give visible concrete shape to the world created by the word magic of storytellers and poets. The vase paintings of ancient Greece show us the Greek goddess of love rising from the sea. They show us the legendary warriors of the Bronze Age war against Troy in battle and at play. They show us the Greek chieftain Odysseus and his sailors wandering around the island world of the Mediterranean, battling monsters and resisting the song of the Sirens.

The link between word and image has often been a true interaction. Artists of the Middle Ages used the stained glass windows and the vaulted ceilings of the cathedrals to picture the story of the creation, of Adam and Eve seduced by the serpent, of Noah's flood, and of the crucifixion and resurrection. In return, poets have often responded in words to gripping or provocative shapes and images created by architects, sculptors, and painters. Often a powerful or disturbing painting creates a chain of feelings and associations. It calls up memories and echoes from a perhaps buried or half-forgotten past.

The following juxtapositions of image and word invite you to inter-disciplinary or cross-disciplinary explorations, crossing the boundaries between artistic specialties or crafts. (See color Inserts I and IV.)

WORD AND IMAGE:
VIEWING, READING, DISCUSSING, WRITING

Joseph Stella (1877–1946), *The Brooklyn Bridge: Variation on an Old Theme,* **1939   (Insert I i)**

Warren Woessner (born 1944), "River Song," 2001

The Receptive Viewer and Reader

Before the great Brooklyn Bridge was built in New York City, Walt Whitman, the nineteenth-century American "poet of democracy," had already chanted the "innumerable crowds" of Manhattan and its sister borough Brooklyn across the Hudson river: "I loved well those cities, loved well the stately and rapid river." Built as an ambitious project at great cost and at a cost in human lives, the Brooklyn Bridge became an engineering marvel of the industrial age and a symbol of the city that for many has been the true hub of Whitman's "nation of nations." An immigrant from a small village in Italy, Stella had early been car-ried along by Whitman's celebration of the young American democracy and its "great futuristic" vision.

1. Suppose your mind were a computer and you could punch in the term *bridge* for a search of the memory banks or database of your mind. What im-ages, associations, memories, and meanings would come up? Jot down as many of these as you can. Are they all helter-skelter or miscellaneous? Or is there a pattern—connections or a common thread?

2. The basic function of a bridge is practical or utilitarian—it enables peo-ple to get from here to there. Do you think bridges are beautiful? What makes a bridge beautiful? What makes Stella's painting of the Brooklyn Bridge beau-tiful? What features of the bridge did the painters focus on or highlight? What do you notice especially? As you look at the image, can you put your thoughts and feelings into words?

3. For some observers, Stella's painting has seemed to emphasize the geometric angular lines and shapes of the steel construction of a new tech-nological future. What enabled the poet to make the leap from engineering to music? Can you see how or why the bridge is for Woessner "like a huge harp"? How does the poem follow up or build on that simile or imaginative comparison?

4. Do you think factories and other products of the world of engineering have to be ugly? Can you give other examples of something practical or useful that became beautiful to you?

Vincent Van Gogh (1853–1890), *The Yellow House,* 1888 (Insert I ii)

Gerald Locklin, "The Yellow House," 1998

The Receptive Viewer and Reader

Vincent Van Gogh and Paul Gauguin, poor and unrecognized as artists, briefly lived and worked together in 1888 in Arles, France. They painted the same scenes, each with his own vision. They argued violently but admired each other's work. Together they ushered in a new way of painting since their collaboration, however brief, made it difficult not to be influenced by each other. After their last quarrel, Van Gogh cut a piece of his ear off—and lived to paint his self-portrait with a bandaged head. Van Gogh painted *The Yellow House* in 1888, anticipating Gauguin's extended visit.

1. The poet, Gerald Locklin, focuses on the yellow house, piling up image after image: "broad street," "restaurant," "sky a deeper blue," "Sherwood green shutters," "tile roof," "summer trees," "white awnings," and "white-bonneted neighbors." Locklin's focus on each of these images helps us become aware that Van Gogh chose each of these colors, painted each of these details. What other details do you see that Locklin did not include?

2. What feelings do these images and their colors suggest—are they more on the side of cheerful than gloomy? What, then, is suggested by the five-fold repetition of the word "even"? "Even" though he painted this bright house in this sunny, peaceful summer landscape, what does not happen?

3. Locklin tells us that "Gauguin comes and goes." Who might the "they" be? What does Locklin hint at of Van Gogh's career as a painter? What might the "sorrow" be that "comes to you door"? Locklin's use of these bright, intense, detailed images are in stark contrast to "no one comes." What is Locklin implying about genius? About hard work? Are they necessarily recognized? How many artists, writers, or musicians can you name who never achieved recognition in their lifetimes?

4. Doors usually invite us in: we speak of "opening doors" when a positive change comes. According to Locklin, not only does "no one come," but finally "only sorrow comes to your door." Write a journal entry in which you explore "doors" that have opened or closed in your life so far.

Kitagawa Utamaro (1753–1806), *Woman Powdering Her Neck* (Insert I iii)

Cathy Song (born 1955), "Girl Powdering Her Neck," 1983

The Receptive Viewer and Reader

The Japanese printmaker and painter Utamaro produced over two thousand prints and many paintings, and he illustrated a number of books. Late in his career, Utamaro concentrated on making single portraits of women, of which *Woman Powdering Her Neck* is an outstanding example. Utamaro lovingly depicts a daily ritual carried out by millions of women in different parts of the world.

1. In ancient Greek myth, Narcissus looked in the smooth surface of a pond and fell in love with his own beautiful image. How do you think the woman in the painting is looking at herself in the mirror—critically? admiringly? in a businesslike manner? without thinking—just doing a daily chore?

2. Song reads the painting with a poet's eye. What details does the poet trace that a more hurried or superficial viewer might pass over or overlook? What imaginative comparisons does the poet use to make us take a second closer look and help us take in what we should see? How many of the imaginative comparisons are taken from a world of nature? Taken together, what effect do they have on the reader?

3. In the poem, the painted face becomes a mask. What is masklike about the "mask of beauty"? What are the poet's feelings toward the woman? Does the poet judge or condemn the woman for her traditional makeup?

4. For you, is the woman an alien being from a different culture, or can you iedntify with her as a fellow human being?

5. What do you see when you look in the mirror? Are all of us fascinated with seeing our own image? Are some people afraid or distrustful of the mirror? Does the mirror image shape our self-image—does it shape our sense of who we are?

Johannes Vermeer (1632–1675), *Young Woman with a Water Jug, 1645*   (Insert I iv)

Stephen Mitchell (born 1957), "Vermeer"

The Receptive Viewer and Reader

Vermeer takes us to the vanished world of a prosperous middle-class society that flourished in his seventeenth-century Holland. In warm but subdued colors, he re-creates the quiet and calm of clean well-lighted domestic interiors, allowing us to imagine a happy interval of well-ordered protected lives in a century of revolution and religious war.

1. Artists and scientists of Vermeer's time were fascinated with the mystery of light. The woman at the window is bathed in light. Where does the light originate? What does the light highlight? Is there a play of light and shadow in the painting?

2. What makes the woman look prosperous? Some of the wall is bare, but we get a glimpse of the furnishings. What do you see? How would you describe the style or the overall effect? Would you want to live in these surroundings? Why, or why not?

3. The poet starts by simply describing what he sees: The woman "stands by the table," her left hand is just barely touching the pitcher's handle, and her right hand is "lightly touching the windowframe." (What do these details already tell you about the woman?)

4. After focusing our attention on the visual details, the poet goes beyond the visual surface to make us share in what the woman in the painting is thinking and feeling. What key words does Mitchell use to take us into the woman's world of thought and feeling? Which for you sums up best the overall impression the poet is trying to convey?

5. Poets may take an imaginative leap beyond ordinary literal-minded reality. Where does that leap take you in the concluding lines of the poem? Has the poem as a whole prepared you for it? Are you willing to make the connection?

Roy Lichtenstein (1923–1997), *Bananas and Grapefruit III,* 1972 (Insert I v)

Deborah Pope, "On 'Bananas and Grapefruit #3,' " 2001

The Receptive Viewer and Reader

Lichtenstein, a New Yorker, was part of the American Pop Art movement that turned everyday objects and images of contemporary American life into a fantasyland of familiar and yet strange shapes and forms. He used the thick black lines and dot patterns of commercial printing, reproducing comic strip images or adapting the images of other painters.

1. Successive stages in the history of modern art have made traditional critics say: "This is not art!" "This should not be in an art museum!" For you, is Lichtenstein's painting art? Why or why not?

2. Reacting to the painting, the poet pulls the reader along on a roller-coaster ride, following up a chain of associations and impressions. Which of these for you pick up best on elements of the painter's image? (Which seem to be in tune best with the spirit of the painting?) Which seem most like a "stretch"— careening off from the original painting? Do your fellow students agree?

3. Make sure to read the poem out loud or listen to it read out loud. What effect do the continuous short-rhymes (*plump slump/slug plug*) have on the listener? Is there anything in the original painting that has a similar effect?

4. The puzzling ending of the poem says "eat / art." For many literal-minded people, eating and art are two separate areas of life. Does the painting establish a connection between the two for you? Does the poem? Have you observed people for whom dealing with food or preparing food seems to be an art?

5. Lichtenstein was known as the master of the stereotype—playing with objects and images that viewers could instantly recognize as simplified symbols of the contemporary American scene. If he were painting today, what stereotypes of contemporary American life or the current media scene do you think might find their way into his work?

Charles Sheeler (1883–1965), *Classic Landscape,* 1931 (Insert I vi)

William Carlos Williams (1883–1963), "Classic Scene," 1939

The Receptive Viewer and Reader

For many modern artists and poets, the industrial age put an end to an era when artists could conjure up an imaginary world of brooks, birdsong, and flower-strewn meadows. Sheeler was an American painter and photographer who painted the realities of the machine age. He worked for a time for the automobile tycoon Henry Ford, who hired him to make a photographic record of Ford's pioneering mass-production assembly-line automotive plants.

1. What do you usually expect to see in a painting that has the word *landscape* in it? How is this industrial landscape different? What first catches your eye or impresses the viewer? What minor details come slowly into focus, and what do they contribute to the painting?

2. One viewer of this painting said, "The world of nature has been finally concreted over." Is there anything in this industrial world of steel and concrete that reminds the viewer of the world of nature?

3. Modern artists have often found a new harsh kind of beauty in the strong outlines and angles of the industrial world of concrete and steel. Does this painting project the sense of force and power that was part of the cult of progress of the machine age? In "classic" art, we expect to see a carefully worked out design with the interplay of shapes and lines creating a sense of balance and harmony. Is there anything "classic" about the design or composition of this painting?

4. How does the poet respond to the industrial scene? What words and details do most to steer his reader's reactions? Does the poet see any signs of life in this industrial setting? The stanzas of this poem are made up of minimal short lines. Does the form of the poem suit the subject matter? How?

Piet Mondrian, *Composition with Red, Yellow, and Blue*   **(Insert I vii)**

Ando Hiroshige, *Night Snow*   **(Insert I viii)**

The Creative Response

Study the student responses to a traditional Japanese print of a natural scene and to a modern painting constructing a pattern from bare geometric shapes. Ando Hiroshige (1797–1858) produced thousands of prints that revitalized the Japanese tradition of landscape painting. Piet Mondrian (1872–1944) was a Dutch painter who became a member of the New York avant-garde and a leading figure in the movement of abstract art—reducing reality to constructs made from simple lines and colored panes, as in his *Composition with Red, Yellow, and Blue*. Study the two student responses and write a similar personal response to one of the art works in this "Word and Image" section.

WRITING ABOUT LITERATURE

14 Responding to Imagery
WRITING FOCUS: Tracking Key Details

The Writing Workshop   You need to read a poem with an open eye and a willing ear. One of your first questions will be: "What does the poet want me to see and hear? What does the poet want me to visualize, to imagine?" You have to be receptive to the signals that are designed to call up vivid images on your mental screen. In preparing a paper on the imagery of a poem, ask yourself questions like the following:

✘ How does the poet make the *setting* real for you? Where is the poem taking you? What revealing details bring the place, the people, or the situation to life?

✘ What *key images* are striking or revealing? What sights seem to stand out? Why are they important in the poem as a whole? Quote phrases, half-lines, or lines to make your reader see key images and how they come back or find an echo at other points in the poem.

✘ Does the poem appeal to more than your sense of sight? Does it bring *other senses* into play—your hearing, your sense of smell, or your sense of touch? One way to organize your paper might be to sort out the different kinds of imagery.

✘ What *emotions* do the images in the poem stir in the reader? What attitudes do they bring into play? Do they trigger contradictory feelings or mixed emotions? One way to organize your paper might be to look first at images that steer the reader's reactions one way and then at images that point in a different direction.

✘ Is the poem unified by a prevailing *mood?* Or does it move through stages as images shift or as the associations and implications of key images change? One way to organize your paper might be to mark off major stages in the way the poem shapes the reader's thoughts and feelings.

Study the following student paper focused on a poem's imagery. How does the writer set her paper in motion? Is there a preview or hint of her general strategy? Does the paper follow up what you took to be the writer's overall plan? What use does she make of short, apt quotations? How does she wind up her paper?

Sample Student Paper

At Peter Meinke's Apple Market

"Apple-smell everywhere!" So starts Peter Meinke's poem "Sunday at the Apple Market." Apples of all kinds (Haralson, McIntosh, Fireside, Rome), apple smells, and the paraphernalia of the apple harvest are everywhere in this poem—in "miraculous profusion." The poet could simply have said, "The apple market was busy Sunday afternoon with lots of people buying tons of apples of different colors and kinds." Instead, Peter Meinke assaults our senses with a feast of concrete imagery. We can choose to let this poem simply "be," as Archibald MacLeish says— to let it simply exist and speak for itself. Or we can choose to look behind the images to find a larger meaning. Either way, we cannot help relishing the rich sensuous quality of its "being."

Poems often display vivid visual and auditory imagery, and this poem does so in exceptional profusion. We see yellow, green, and red apples "piled crazy in the storehouse barn" (7), apples in "bushels / and baskets and bags and boxes" (13–14), "apples by the cartload" (5). We hear "the crowd / around the testing table laughing" and the "dogs barking at children in the appletrees."

However, this poem appeals to all the senses; indeed, apple smell is everywhere from the beginning to the "smell of apples" at the end (15). We experience taste along with smell as the people around the testing table roll "the cool applechunks in their mouths" (10) or as we recall the juice made by the "old ciderpresses weathering in the shed" (3). We can imagine ourselves holding hands as the couples do in the poem; we carry the weight of bushels, baskets, bags, and boxes.

Why is the crowd laughing; why are the people happy? We see them at the apple market at the time of harvest, of ripeness and fruition. All the previous stages, from winter and pruning of the trees through blossom time, have led up to this stage of fullness and culmination. We can imagine the harvest cycle as parallel to our own journey through life, since all the stages of our own growth are represented: We see the children in the apple trees; we see the couples holding hands; we see the children's parents carrying apples back to their cars. We can enjoy a sense of cycle that leads up to this moment when we enjoy the fruits of our journey through life.

However, the poem does not stop there. Contrasting with the dominating concrete images of the ample harvest are hints of a further stage in the cycle. The "old ciderpress weathering in the shed" (3) suggests fermentation and aging. The "old ladders tilting at the empty branches" (4) foreshadow the end of fertility, with the coming of barrenness and decay—the inevitable continuation of the process we experience at the high point of the cycle in this poem. We see "so many people out in the country" on this Sunday to capture and carry back with them this happy moment of fulfillment that cannot last. For "one Sunday afternoon" these people are "free / and happy as people must have been meant to be" (15–16).

Reading the poem, I was struck by the image of the dogs barking at the children in the apple trees. It brought to mind a time when my grandparents' orchard was for me a "free and happy" world of its own. I remember a Sunday when I was hiding from my cousins in my grandmother's apple tree, stifling giggles on a high branch, my Sunday dress torn on the rough bark. I wrote a brief poem recalling the experience; it ends as follows:

In Sunday black and white like spotted puppies
they sniff and search under apple carts
and behind the stacked up empty wooden crates.
Behind heavy leaves red apples hide.
I hide, too.

Questions for Peer Review

This student paper tries to get the reader into the spirit of the poem—the carefree, intoxicating mood of the apple market that for a happy interval takes people away from the cares and stresses of everyday.

1. How does the student writer set the scene or the tone? How well does she get you into the spirit of the poem? She promises a "feast," a "profusion," a "rich" harvest of *concrete images*. Do her early paragraphs begin to deliver what she promises? Where or how?

2. In this poem, images are not merely visual. How or where does the student paper point out other *sensory images*—showing that the poem "appeals to all the senses"?

3. The student writer says that "we can choose to look behind the images to find a larger meaning." Where and how does this paper begin to do that? How does the writer develop the larger human meaning of the "harvest cycle"? What images does she use to support her *interpretation* of this dimension of the poem?

4. How well does the student writer weave in or integrate *short quotations* from the poem?

5. What does the *personal conclusion* add to this paper?

6. Is your response to the poem similar to or different from that of the student writer? How or why?

15 METAPHOR

Making Connections

Courtesy Richard B. Ressman

*When we attempt to express living experience
with words, logical speech quickly becomes
permeated with symbols and metaphors.*

CHARLES M. JOHNSTON

*To a wholly new experience, one can give
sufficient organization only by relating it to the
already known, by perceiving a relation between
this experience and another experience already
ordered, placed, and incorporated.*

JAMES OLNEY

*Metaphor, in the small sense and the large, is the
main property of poetry.*

RICHARD WILBUR

FOCUS ON METAPHOR

Poets use striking imaginative comparisons to go beyond the resources of literal speech. They take us into a world of vivid visual images, but often there is more to the image than meets the eye. Diane Wakoski says in "Meeting an Astronomer,"

> We drive the same highways
> in the dark, not seeing each other,
>   only the lights.

As we visualize the car lights we encounter when driving at night, we know we are not on a real highway. We could be at home, in a classroom, or in a hallway on the way to work. But it is *as if* the people we encounter were drivers whose faces we cannot see and whose thoughts we cannot read—because the only thing we can see is their lights.

The car lights are examples of **metaphor**, language used imaginatively to carry ideas and feelings that otherwise might be hard to put into words. A metaphor is a brief, compressed comparison that talks about one thing as if it were another. The comparison is implied, not spelled out. It comes into the poem unannounced, without the words *like* or *as* to signal that something is not literally a road but only in some ways like a road. A close cousin of metaphor, which signals the comparison by words such as *like* or *as if,* is called a **simile**. When Shakespeare says, "My reason, the physician to my love," he is using metaphor. When he says, "My love is as a fever, longing still," he is using a simile.

Often several related metaphors work together. In Linda Pastan's "After an Absence," the alien uncharted territory, the beckoning garden in the desert, the life-giving water, and the sand in the parched mouth are all metaphors offering contrasting perspectives on marriage:

I had even forgotten how married love
is a territory more mysterious
the more it is explored, like one of those terrains
you read about, a garden in the desert
where you stoop to drink, never knowing
if your mouth will fill with water or sand.

Poetic metaphors range from the easily accessible to the more challenging. Many of the metaphors of ordinary speech are well established: We turn to a dog-eared page, watch tempers boil, or give someone a fish-eyed stare. Some familiar metaphors may once have been fresh and appealing, but they have become overused, losing their tread like a bald tire, turning into **clichés**: *the tip of the iceberg, the window of opportunity*. By contrast, poetic metaphors are often fresh and thought-provoking. They forge new connections; they discover unexpected, revealing similarities. When the American poet Carl Sandburg asks us to

Remember all paydays of lilacs and songbirds

no familiar connection between paydays and songbirds guides us. We have to work out the implied equation ourselves. It sounds as if the poet had in mind the sense of reward and elation that workers might feel on payday. That elation corresponds to the joy brought by the rich blooms of the lilac and the song of birds.

FIRST READING
Thinking in Metaphors

The following poem does not talk about ideas; it acts them out in vivid images. These images have a meaning beyond what meets the eye. As readers, we have to decode the metaphors.

Linda Pastan   *(born 1932)*

Anger   1985

You tell me
that it's all right
to let it out of its cage,
though it may claw someone,

even bite.   5
You say that letting it out
may tame it somehow.
But loose it may
turn on me, maul
my face, draw blood.   10
Ah, you think you know so much,
you whose anger is a pet dog,
its canines dull with disuse.
But mine is a rabid thing, sharpening its teeth
on my very bones,   15
and I will never let it go.

The Receptive Reader

1. What is the *central metaphor* in this poem? Into how many details can you trace this central metaphor? Which details are especially graphic or concrete?

2. Where and how does the metaphor branch out into two opposite variations?

3. Where do you stand on the question raised by this poem?

The Creative Dimension

How do *you* visualize anger? Write an imaginative response to this poem, using your own central metaphor instead of the one used by the poet. Or do the same for another poem with a striking central metaphor. How do you react to the following student-written sample?

I watch you,
you who say,
"Be emotional; it's all right."
But you sit with the emotion
clamped to your leg
like a steel trap on a rabbit.
You struggle to get free
without chance of success.
I watch you
trying to gnaw it loose
as the rabbit would.

READING FOR METAPHOR

Without metaphor, language would lose its
lifeblood and stiffen into a conventional system
of signs.

ERNST CASSIRER

I love metaphor. It provides two loaves where
there seems to be one. Sometimes it throws in a
load of fish.

BERNARD MALAMUD

The English eighteenth-century poet William Blake says, "The tigers of wrath are wiser than the horses of instruction." We need no nudging to make us realize that these animals are not literally there. They are brought in by way of comparison. Reading such metaphors, we mentally fill in the possible connections: Righteous anger is fiery *like* a tiger and moves us to swift action. Compared with the powerful welling-up of passion, instruction is more plodding, like the horses pulling a brewery wagon. It makes us do what we are told, as horses do what pleases their masters. It is not likely to move us to generous or passionate endeavor.

Both an image on the literal level and a metaphor may appeal strongly to our visual imagination. The difference is that the metaphor makes us visualize something that we could not literally interact with or see. When the poet Adrien Stoutenburg says, "The strawberry's leaves / Are a green hand spread open," we are looking at real leaves but not at a real hand. We are looking at small leaves that together form a kind of hand holding up the ripening strawberry. The psalm says, "The Lord is my shepherd; / I shall not want. / He maketh me to lie down in green pastures: / He leadeth me beside the still waters." When we recite the psalm, the sheep and the caring, protecting shepherd are not literally there as part of our lives. *We* are there, and the psalm is about our relationship to the Lord.

Metaphor (from a Greek word meaning "to carry over") carries us over from the normal surface meaning of a word to something else. It exploits similarities and makes connections between things we might otherwise keep apart. A metaphor may be a single word: Blake uses the single word *tiger* to set up the metaphorical connection between righteous wrath and the fiery, ferocious, threatening animal. The richer the metaphor, the more it challenges our imagination to call up a full range of similarities. For instance, righteous anger is fiery and passionate. It is threatening to evildoers, and it would probably be futile to try to control.

Often, the poet will develop a metaphor beyond a single word. Such an **extended metaphor** traces the ramifications of the implied comparison, following up related similarities. When a single extended metaphor gives shape to a poem as a whole, it becomes an organizing metaphor (it is also called a **controlling metaphor**). More often, however, a poem moves through several related, interacting metaphors. The following poem is built around three related metaphors: the house, the horse, and the dog. Look at the way these metaphors work together. What do they make you see? What feelings do they bring into play? How do they challenge more familiar ways of looking at our bodies?

May Swenson   *(1919–1989)*

Question   *1954*

Body my house
my horse my hound
What will I do
When you are fallen

Where will I sleep   5
How will I ride
What will I hunt

Where can I go without my mount
all eager and quick
How will I know   10
in thicket ahead
is danger or treasure
When Body my good
bright dog is dead

How will it be   15
to lie in the sky
without roof or door
and wind for an eye

with cloud for shift°   *woman's shirt or chemise*
how will I hide?   20

In this poem, three interlocking, meshing metaphors make us re-examine the way we feel about our bodies. To judge from the way the poet develops or follows them up, these metaphors mean something like the following:

✖ The poet calls the body "my house," reminding us that it puts up the roof and walls giving us shelter and the doors barring intruders. It offers us a place to sleep, to hide. The word *house* is likely to make us think of a place that offers refuge and protection.

✖ The poet calls the body "my horse." Apparently we are asked to imagine not a tired nag but a spirited mount—"all eager and quick"—ready to carry us to adventure. We are not rooted like a tree. Life is movement, motion, activity—but only if we can depend on the body to carry us into action.

✖ The poet calls the body "my hound"—a "good bright dog" that like a hunting dog serves its master well. It alerts us to danger (lurking "in thicket ahead") or hunts down "treasure." We depend on our bodies to keep us alert, prepared to deal with the threats and promises of every day.

The Receptive Reader

1. How is the way this poem looks at the body different from other, more familiar ways of looking at our bodies? Do you share the feelings or sympathize with the attitudes that the metaphors in this poem suggest?

2. For you, what is the connecting *thread* that links the three metaphors? What do they have in common?

3. What tone does the *title* set for the poem? What is the poet's "question"? Does the poem suggest an answer?

The Creative Dimension

Explore your own possible metaphors for the body. Complete the line "My body my . . ." in your own way, writing your own body poem or passage about the body. How well does the central metaphor work in the following example?

```
Body
You ship of a fool!
Why do I worry about
     sprung planks
     leaky decks
     spent rigging
     peeling paint?
The rats left a long time ago,
and you're still afloat!
```

What is the central metaphor in the following poem? How does the poet develop it into an extended metaphor? Which of the similarities between hope and "the thing with feathers" seem most fitting? Which seem most strange? Which to you are most thought-provoking or revealing?

Emily Dickinson   *(1830–1886)*

"Hope" is the thing with feathers   *1861*

"Hope" is the thing with feathers—
That perches in the soul—
And sings the tune without the words—
And never stops—at all—

And sweetest—in the Gale—is heard—   5
And sore must be the storm—
That could abash° the little Bird   *subdue and silence*
That kept so many warm—

I've heard it in the chillest land—
And on the strangest Sea—   10
Yet, never, in Extremity,°   *in extreme danger or adversity*
It asked a crumb—of Me.

The Receptive Reader

1. What, to the poet, makes the bird a good metaphor for hope? What related details or ramifications make this *extended metaphor* vivid or real for you?

2. Why would the song be heard "sweetest in the gale"? How does the song keep "so many warm"? What does it say about hope that the bird never "asked a crumb"?

The Creative Dimension

Cluster the word *hope*. What images, memories, or associations does the word call up? In your cluster, how do they branch out from the central stimulus word? What kind of pattern takes shape? Write a passage that pulls together the ideas and associations. How do your own associations with the word compare with those in Dickinson's poem?

Making Connections—For Discussion or Writing

Dickinson's "'Hope' is the thing with feathers" and Hardy's "The Darkling Thrush" are both poems about hope. Explore how one poet uses a bird as an image and the other uses a bird as a metaphor.

Motorists driving through the Midwest see silos rising over the wheat fields—grain elevators "blocks long, a cathedral of high and mighty cylinders of white" (Ursula K. Le Guin). To an observer with a vivid imagination, they suggest comparisons, like those in the following poem.

Rita Dove　　*(born 1952)*

Silos　　1989

Like martial swans in spring paraded against the city sky's
shabby blue, they were always too white and
suddenly there

They were never fingers, never xylophones, although once
a stranger said they put him in mind of Pan's pipes　　5
and all the lost songs of Greece. But to the townspeople
they were like cigarettes, the smell chewy and bitter
like a field shorn of milkweed, or beer brewing, or
a fingernail scorched over a flame.

No, no, exclaimed the children. They're a fresh packet of chalk,　　10
dreading math work.

They were masculine toys. They were tall wishes. They
were the ribs of the modern world.

The Receptive Reader

1. Which of the imaginative comparisons in this poem are to you the most fitting? Which are the most unexpected or far-ranging? (What is a xylophone? What kind of pipes did Pan, the ancient Greek god of shepherds, play?)

2. Is this poem all playful? Does it have a serious point?

FIGURATIVE LANGUAGE: METAPHOR, SIMILE, PERSONIFICATION

Metaphor is one kind of nonliteral language under the larger umbrella heading of **figurative language**. Like a metaphor, a **simile** is a brief, compressed imaginative comparison. Unlike a metaphor, a simile uses the words *as* or *like* or *as if* to advertise that a comparison will follow. These signals alert us to look for the similarities that the poet had in mind: "My love is like a red, red rose"; "My love is like a silken tent." A simile says outright that something is like something else. Sometimes similes are considered merely a special kind of metaphor—a metaphor announced rather than implied.

Love poems through the centuries have used metaphor and simile to express feelings that might otherwise be hard to put into words. A famous simile opens the following poem by the Scottish poet Robert Burns. Look at what the two similes in the opening stanza (group of four related lines) do for the poem as a whole. Note that *fair* in this poem means "beautiful"—as in much early love poetry.

Robert Burns   *(1759–1796)*

A Red, Red Rose   *1796*

O my luve's like a red, red rose
That's newly sprung in June;
O my luve's like the melodie
That's sweetly played in tune.

As fair art thou, my bonny lass,°   *my dear girl*   5
So deep in luve am I;
And I will luve thee still, my dear,
Till a' the seas gang dry°—   *run (go) dry*

Till a'° the seas gang dry, my dear,   *all*
And the rocks melt wi' the sun: 10
O I will luve thee still, my dear,
While the sands o' life shall run.

And fare thee weel, my only luve,
And fare thee weel awhile!

And I will come again, my luve,   15
Though it were a thousand mile.

    The opening simile here draws on the rich traditional associations of the rose: For instance, its rich red color is pleasing to the eye (and it is often associated with passion). People who love roses treasure the delicate petals and the fresh scent on a June morning. The second simile likens the poet's love to a melody "sweetly played in tune"—soothing the nerves frazzled by the jangling noises of every day. The poet then tells his readers what many of them want to hear: A love like the poet's is not a casual, passing encounter. It will last forever, longer than the rocks and the sea. Any separation will be only for "awhile."

The Receptive Reader

    1. How, or how well, do the two opening *similes* work together?

    2. What explains the "sands of life" *metaphor?* Sand (on beaches) does not usually "run." What traditional device used sand to measure time?

    3. Much traditional love poetry used *hyperbole,* or extreme exaggeration—for instance, to praise the beauty of the beloved to the skies. What instances of hyperbole can you find in this poem?

The Personal Response

    To you, does Burns' love poem seem timeless or out of date? Would you consider sending it to someone? If someone sent it to you, what might be your response?

    In the thirties and forties, Langston Hughes came to be considered the "poet laureate" or unofficial voice of black America. Each simile in the following poem sets up a different scenario for what might happen if a dream is deferred or hope denied.

Langston Hughes   *(1902–1967)*

Dream Deferred   *1951*

What happens to a dream deferred?
Does it dry up
Like a raisin in the sun?
Or fester like a sore—
And then run?   5
Does it stink like rotten meat?
Or crust and sugar over—
like a syrupy sweet?

Maybe it just sags
like a heavy load.   10

Or does it explode?

The Receptive Reader

1. Which similes in this poem fit exceptionally well? Which of the alternative scenarios can you most vividly imagine? Which seems to you most likely?

2. How does the poem build up to its ending? What makes it especially dramatic?

The bolder and the more original a poet's similes, the more they are likely to stimulate our imagination. The following poem focuses on the big bird—"the great gull"—that came from the sea. What images and feelings are brought into the poem by two key similes: "like a high priest" and "like a merchant prince"?

Howard Nemerov   *(born 1920)*

The Great Gull   *1951*

Restless, rising at dawn
I saw the great gull come from the mist
To stand upon the lawn.
And there he shook his savage wing
To quiet, and stood like a high priest   5
Bird-masked, mantled in gray.
Before his fierce austerity
My thought bowed down, imagining
The wild sea-lanes he wandered by
And the wild waters where he slept   10
Still as a candle in the crypt.
Noble, and not courteous,
He stared upon my green concerns.
Then, like a merchant prince
Come to some poor province,   15
Who, looking all about, discerns
No spice, no treasure house,
Nothing that can be made
Delightful to his haughty trade,
And so spreads out his sail,   20
Leaving to savage men
Their miserable regimen;°   *rigidly ordered life*
So did he rise, making a gale
About him with his wings,

And fought his huge freight into air
And vanished seaward with a cry—
A strange tongue but the tone clear.

This poem focuses on the large seabird that came out of the ocean fog to stand on the lawn. The speaker in the poem is fascinated by the sight of the bird, from the time it lands and stashes its large wings for an at-rest position until it finally unfolds them again for takeoff. Concrete visual images help us imagine this fascinating bird: First, the bird "shook his savage wing / To quiet"; later, it spread out its wings like a sail, creating a miniature storm like a gale at sea, "fighting" its way into the air to lift the "huge freight" of its body. The poet's carefully trimmed lawn (his "green concerns") must seem petty and tame to this "savage," "fierce," and "haughty" bird from the "wild sea-lanes" and "wild waters."

The poet uses several similes to help us share his feelings about this majestic wild bird. For instance, he compares the bird to a high priest, wearing a bird mask and mantle of gray (like its coat of gray feathers), expecting us to bow down to it as to a priest in a strange pagan ritual. This simile should help us sense the bird's "fierce austerity": The bird is aloof, not wasting time on frivolous diversions; it is "not courteous"—not folksy like someone trying to sell us a used car.

The Receptive Reader

1. The second simile compares the bird to a "merchant prince." How would such a person be different from an ordinary merchant? What would such a merchant prince be looking for, and where? What would be disappointing about the "poor province" the gull actually found? What does this second simile have in common with the first?

2. A third simile makes us imagine the bird sleeping on the waters "Still as a candle in a crypt." What images and feelings does this simile bring into the poem? How is it related to the other two similes?

3. For you, what is the connecting thread that links the three similes? How do they work together; how are they related?

The Personal Response

What animal would *you* choose to represent untamed savage nature? Do you think a sea animal would be a better choice than a land animal? Why?

Personification is a metaphor or a simile that treats something non-human as if it were human. It is figurative language that makes things or animals act human. Personification can make the world around us mirror our own state of mind. When a blues singer sings, "The sky is crying / Look at the tears roll down the street," the whole world seems to share the singer's sadness and loneliness. The metaphors in the following poem make us think of both the frost and the flower as if they were human beings, acting out a grim mini-drama.

Emily Dickinson   *(1830–1886)*

Apparently with no surprise   *1884*

Apparently with no surprise
to any happy Flower
The Frost beheads it at its play—
In accidental power—
The blonde Assassin passes on—   5
The Sun proceeds unmoved
To measure off another Day
For an approving God.

As we read this poem, our first hint that the poet is speaking metaphorically is the word *happy* applied to the flower. Flowers are not literally
happy or unhappy. They have no feelings, just as they do not "play" (any
more than they go about serious business). These metaphors are each an
example of personification. It is *as if* the flower had been happily and innocently at play when it was attacked by the frost. It is *as if* the killer frost
were an executioner who "beheads" the condemned victim. It is *as if* the
frost were an "assassin," thus adding the idea of treachery to the brutality of
the victim's execution.

The Receptive Reader

1. Dickinson's poems often have puzzling, provocative phrases tucked away
in them. Why "accidental power"? Why "blonde Assassin"? Is the scene being
watched by an "approving God"?

2. What contrast does the poem set up between the work of the killer frost
and the sun proceeding on its course?

3. Does this poem stir your feelings? Do you shudder at the swift destruction of the helpless flower? Do you feel a twinge of terror at seeing it destroyed?
Why or why not?

Some poets let their imagination run riot. The author of the following
poem writes to share his feelings of elation about a cloudburst on a hot
summer day after weeks of "dead heat." Do you enjoy his extravagant
imaginative comparisons?

Edward Hirsch   *(born 1950)*

In the Middle of August   *1986*

The dead heat rises for weeks,
Unwanted, unasked for, but suddenly,
Like the answer to a question,
A real summer shower breaks loose
In the middle of August. So think   5

Of trumpets and cymbals, a young girl
In a sparkling tinsel suit leading
A parade down Fifth Avenue, all
The high school drummers in the city
Banging away at once. Think of   10
Bottles shattering against a warehouse,
Or a bowl of apricots spilling
From a tenth-floor window: the bright
Rat-a-tat-tat on the hot pavement,
The squeal of adults scurrying   15
For cover like happy children.
Down the bar, someone says it's like
The night she fell asleep standing
In the bathroom of a dank tavern
And woke up shivering in an orchard   20
Of lemon trees at dawn, surprised
By the sudden omnipotence of yellows.
Someone else says it's like spinning
A huge wheel and winning at roulette,
Or drawing four aces and thinking: 25
"It's true, it's finally happening."
Look, I'm not saying that the pretty
Girl in the fairy tale really does
Let down her golden hair for all
The poor kids in the neighborhood—   30
Though maybe she does. But still
I am saying that a simple cloud
Bursts over the city in mid-August
And suddenly, in your lifetime,
Everyone believes in his own luck.   35

The Receptive Reader

1. The poet draws his imaginative comparisons from a whole range of experience. Which seem most fitting? Which seem most unexpected? Which work best for you?

2. The poet seems to try to make his feelings intelligible in turn to readers from different interests and backgrounds. What are some of the different groups he seems to address?

3. Can you classify some of the suggested comparisons in this poem as metaphors and others as similes?

4. Would the poet's statement in his concluding lines apply to you?

The Personal Response

Some people get a natural high from events that seem ordinary to others. Do you ever get excited about something that might fail to stir others?

JUXTAPOSITIONS

The Range of Metaphor

Poets vary in how boldly they explore new metaphorical connections. Love poems of earlier centuries featured fanciful extended metaphors called **conceits**. These were elaborately developed, setting up an analogy and then tracing it in careful detail. Such conceits were an expected ornament of the love sonnets written by the Italian fourteenth-century poet Petrarch and his many followers. The **sonnet** is an elaborately crafted fourteen-line poem with an interlaced rhyme scheme and iambic meter. In the following example by one of Petrarch's English translators, the lover's "enemy" steering the ship is also called "my lord." Both of these terms early love poets applied to the haughty, disdainful "cruel" lady to whom they addressed their "plaints." What is the central conceit or extended metaphor in the poem? How is it developed?

Thomas Wyatt   *(1503–1542)*

My Galley Charged with Forgetfulness   *before 1540*

My galley charged with forgetfulness
Thorough° sharp seas in winter nights doth pass   *through*
'Tween rock and rock; and eke° mine enemy, alas,   *also*
That is my lord, steereth with cruelness;
And every oar a thought in readiness,   5
As though that death were light in such a case.
An endless wind doth tear the sail apace
Of forced sighs and trusty fearfulness
A rain of tears, a cloud of dark disdain,
Hath done the wearied cords great hinderance;   10
Wreathed with error and eke with ignorance,
The stars be hid° that led me to this pain;   *are hidden*
Drowned is reason that should me consort,°   *stay with me*
And I remain despairing of the port.

The Receptive Reader

1. A conceit often follows the basic metaphor into every conceivable detail. (In this poem, once we are on the ship, we stay on the ship.) Why is it winter and night? What are the oars, the wind, the rain, the cloud, the harbor? Who or what drowned? What are the rocks?

2. What is the *keynote* of this poem? What are the prevailing emotions? Why do you think generations of readers related to this kind of love poetry (and still do)?

In the more conventional kind of conceit, the poet stays on the track prescribed by the dominating metaphor. By contrast, the metaphors in a

Shakespearean sonnet often keep developing and shifting. They may start as elaborate conceits, but then they escalate, following up new and unexpected associations. What are the three key metaphors in the following sonnet? How do they develop; how do they mesh? (Note that the word *choir* in the fourth line stands for the part of a church reserved for the choir.)

William Shakespeare   *(1564–1616)*   👁

Sonnet 73   *before 1598*

That time of year thou mayst in me behold
When yellow leaves, or none, or few, do hang
Upon those boughs which shake against the cold,
Bare ruined choirs, where late the sweet birds sang.
In me thou seest the twilight of such day   5
As after sunset fadeth in the west;
Which by and by° black night doth take away,   *gradually*
Death's second self, that seals up all in rest.
In me thou seest the glowing of such fire
That on the ashes of his youth doth lie,   10
As the deathbed whereon it must expire,
Consumed with that which it was nourished by.
This thou perceivest, which makes thy love more strong,
To love that well which thou must leave ere long.°   *before long*

The much-analyzed first metaphor in this sonnet makes us think of approaching age as the late autumn of the speaker's life, when we see the bare branches of the tree shaken by cold winds, with only a few last withered yellow leaves clinging to the boughs. But the metaphor shifts and develops: The bare wood of the branches apparently makes the poet think of the wooden pews where the choirboys or choristers used to sit in church (where they sang the way the "sweet birds" sang in the tree). Now the church is in ruins (like many of the great abbey churches of England after the Protestant Reformation had shut down the monasteries). Both the tree and the church used to be filled with sweet song, but they are now fitting metaphors for the approaching decay and loneliness of age. They are likely to make us long for the rich growth and sweet birdsong of summers past.

The Receptive Reader

1. What is the *second* major metaphor, developed in the second set of four lines (or quatrain) in the sonnet? What parallels or connections make it especially fitting or expressive? How does it shift to acquire a further dimension? (How is night "Death's second self"?)

2. What is the metaphor in the *third* set of four lines? (What was "Consumed with that which it was nourished by," and how?) Can you see more than one parallel or connection between this third major metaphor and the other two?

3. Many Shakespearean sonnets provide a "turning" in the final couplet, or set of two lines—an answer to a central question, or a *counterpoint* to an earlier assertion. How does this sonnet fit this pattern?

Making Connections—For Discussion or Writing

We are often told that our language today is deficient in the language of the emotions. Look at Gary Soto's "Oranges," Robert Burns' "A Red, Red Rose," and the sonnets by Thomas Wyatt and Shakespeare. Does the language of love in any of these poems have something to teach to today's lovers?

POEMS FOR FURTHER STUDY

Pay special attention to the workings of metaphor, simile, or personification in the following poems.

Rosemary Catacalos   *(born 1944)*

La Casa   *1984*

The house by the acequia,°   *irrigation canal*
its front porch dark and
cool with begonias,
an old house, always there,
always of the same adobe,   5
always full of the same lessons.
We would like to stop.
We know we belonged there once.
Our mothers are inside.
All the mothers are inside,   10
lighting candles, swaying
back and forth on their knees,
begging The Virgin's forgiveness
for having reeled us out
on such very weak string.   15
They are afraid for us.
They know we will not stop.
We will only wave as we pass by.
They will go on praying
that we might be simple again.   20

In this poem by a bilingual Mexican American poet, what is the key metaphor for parents' sending children into the outside world? What are the implications and ramifications of the metaphor? Is the speaker in the poem thinking of a literal house—a real house she remembers from her childhood? How would you sum up the speaker's attitude toward the past?

William Shakespeare   *(1564–1616)*

Sonnet 29   *before 1598*

When, in disgrace with Fortune and men's eyes,
I all alone beweep my outcast state,
And trouble deaf heaven with my bootless° cries,   *useless*
And look upon myself and curse my fate,
Wishing me like to one more rich in hope,   5
Featured like him, like him with friends possessed,
Desiring this man's art and that man's scope,
With what I most enjoy contented least;
Yet in these thoughts myself almost despising,
Haply I think on thee, and then my state°   *condition* 10
(Like to the lark at break of day arising
From sullen earth) sings hymns at heaven's gate;
For thy sweet love remembered such wealth brings
That then I scorn to change my state with kings.

1. In the first eight lines, or *octave,* of this sonnet, what is literal statement; what is metaphor? (What image or associations does the reference to Fortune bring to mind?)

2. Lines 11 and 12 combine simile, metaphor, and personification. How? As Shakespeare's use of figurative language often does, the lark simile seems to escalate, shifting to a further and bolder metaphor in midflight. How, and with what effect on the reader?

3. Sonnets often reach a turning point at the end of the octave; Shakespeare's sonnets especially often lead up to a concluding couplet that leaves us with a thought to remember. How does this sonnet illustrate both of these features?

Sylvia Plath   *(1932–1963)*

Metaphors   *1960*

I'm a riddle in nine syllables,
An elephant, a ponderous° house,   *very weighty*
A melon strolling on two tendrils.

O red fruit, ivory, fine timbers!
This loaf's big with its yeasty rising.   5
Money's new-minted in this fat purse.
I'm a means, a stage, a cow in calf.
I've eaten a bag of green apples,
Boarded the train there's no getting off.

The Receptive Reader

1. Where in your reading of the poem did you first guess at the answer to the riddle? What in the poem did most to confirm your guess?

2. Why "nine syllables"? Why a poem of nine lines of nine syllables each? (The title has nine letters, but this may be just a coincidence.)

3. Why green apples? Which metaphors in the poem seem to be most expressive or to fit the speaker's condition best?

4. What are the speaker's feelings? Which of the metaphors do most to reveal her attitude? Is there humor in the poem, and what kind?

The Personal Response

The situation in which the speaker in this poem finds herself has often inspired mixed emotions or contradictory feelings. Have you observed or perhaps personally shared these? Write about the mixed emotions.

John Donne   *(1572–1631)*

A Valediction: Forbidding Mourning   *1611*

As virtuous men pass mildly away,
And whisper to their souls to go,
Whilst some of their sad friends do say
The breath goes now, and some say no:

So let us melt, and make no noise,   5
No rear floods, nor sigh-tempests move;
'Twere profanation° of our joys   *it would make something sacred common*
To tell the laity our love.

Moving of the earth° brings harms and fears;   *earthquakes*
Men reckon what it did and meant;   10
But trepidation of the spheres,°   *trembling of the heavenly spheres*
Though greater far, is innocent.

Dull sublunary° lovers' love   *below the moon, earthbound*
(Whose soul is sense) cannot admit
Absence, because it doth remove   15
Those things which elemented° it.   *gave it substance*

But we, by a love so much refined
That ourselves know not what it is,
Inter-assured° of the mind,   *mutually sure*

Care less eyes, lips, and hands to miss. 20

Our two souls, therefore, which are one,
Though I must go, endure not yet
A breach, but an expansion,
Like gold° to airy thinness beat. *like gold leaf*

If they be two, they are two so 25
As stiff twin compasses are two:
Thy soul, the fixed foot, makes no show
To move, but doth if the other do.

And though it in the center sit,
Yet when the other far doth roam, 30
It leans and harkens after it,
And grows erect as that comes home.

Such wilt thou be to me, who must,
Like the other foot, obliquely° run; *at a wide angle*
Thy firmness makes my circle just,° *makes it perfect* 35
And makes me end where I begun.

The Receptive Reader

1. According to Izaak Walton, a contemporary biographer, Donne wrote this farewell poem for his wife before leaving on a journey to France. What is the connection between the parting of the spouses and the death scene described in the first stanza? (Why do you think Donne's contemporaries believed that good, virtuous people would have a "mild" or gentle death?)

2. If outsiders are the "laity," what does the implied comparison make the two people in love?

3. Donne's contemporaries believed that the heavens were perfect (reflecting the perfection of God). Everything "sublunary"—below the moon, on this earth—was *im*perfect, subject to decay and death. Furthermore, the planets moving in orbit around the earth in the geocentric, earth-centered Ptolemaic view of the universe were attached to spheres of crystal. At times these moved or shook, accounting for apparent irregularities in the astronomers' calculations. How does Donne draw on these contemporary beliefs in this poem?

4. Probably the best-known example of figurative language in English literature is the comparison of the two people in love to the pair of "twin compasses" used in geometry classes to draw a circle. What does this device look like? How does it work? How does Donne put it to work in this poem?

The Personal Response

Critics (and presumably lovers) have been divided on whether to welcome into love poetry comparisons drawn from areas like astronomy, geometry, and medicine. How would you vote on this issue, and why?

<<<*Find It on the Web*>>>   ***Donne and Early Modern Science***

Modern readers have been fascinated by Donne's use of images and metaphors drawn from the science of his time. Donne and his contemporaries found themselves at the crossroads between the traditional Ptolemaic geocentric world system and revolutionary new developments in astronomy, physics, and geography. The new astronomy had moved the earth from the center of the universe into an orbit around the sun. The exploration of new continents was making traditional maps obsolete. The following is an example of online sources exploring Donne's relation to "old and new ways of imagining the cosmos."

Gorton, Lisa. "John Donne's Use of Space." *Early Modern Literary Studies* 4.2/ Special Issue 3 (Sept. 1998): 9.1-27. 30 May 2001. <http://www.shu.ac.uk/emls/04-2/gortjohn.htm>

WRITING ABOUT LITERATURE

15 Reading for Metaphor
WRITING FOCUS: Tracking Figurative Language

The Writing Workshop In reading a poem, we have to be alert to metaphor and simile. We have to respond to imaginative comparisons that make us see one thing while making us think of another. For instance, in John Donne's "A Valediction: Forbidding Mourning," we are asked to visualize "gold to airy thinness beat"—gold hammered incredibly thin by the goldsmith's art, so that an ounce or less of the metal will yield enough gold leaf to gild a whole column or an altar in a church. But in reading the poem, we are expected to make the connection between the gold leaf we see and the love uniting the speaker in the poem and his wife. Their love (precious like gold) also is infinitely malleable or "stretchable," so that instead of the journey causing a "breach" or break, their love will merely expand (enduring an "expansion") to bridge the distance.

When you prepare a paper that focuses on the workings of metaphor, consider the following guidelines:

✖ Look for imaginative comparisons *spelled out or implied*. Similes are easy to recognize because the *as* or *like* or *as if* is part of the text ("*As* virtuous men pass mildly away . . ."). Metaphors do not carry such a label; the *as if* is merely implied. They are easiest to recognize when something is clearly not literally true. "Tear-floods" and "sigh-tempests" are not literally floods and tempests.

✖ Look for *sustained or extended metaphors* that the poet traces into their ramifications. The poet comparing his love to a ship lost at sea is likely to show more than one way in which being in love is like being on a drifting ship.

✖ Look for organizing *metaphors* that play a central role in the poem as a whole. A poem may be built around the metaphor of the ice skaters, who are like people moving quickly across the surface of their lives, dancing on the ice. (Often a poem builds up to a culminating metaphor that stays with us after we finish reading.)

✖ Respond to the *range of associations* of key metaphors. With most poetic metaphors, there is no simple one-to-one relationship between figurative and literal meaning. Try to do justice to what is left out in a simple prose paraphrase of a metaphorical line. Explore the images it conjures up; respond to the emotions it brings into play.

✖ Look for the *connections* between the metaphors in a poem. For instance, they may be variations on a theme, reinforcing or driving home a central concern of the poet. Or they may reflect polarities that set up the basic tension or challenge in a poem. Or they may be part of an escalating series of metaphors that lead up to a new way of seeing or feeling.

Reading Notes   When writing a paper about a poem rich in metaphor and simile, you may want to start with reading notes that take stock of the imaginative comparisons in the poem. Here are sample reading notes for John Donne's "A Valediction: Forbidding Mourning":

The parting of the lovers is compared to a death: "As virtuous men pass mildly away . . . so let us melt, and make no noise." Virtuous people who are dying have nothing to fear in the afterlife and therefore die in peace. A journey separating the lovers is in some ways like the separation caused by death, but it should be like a virtuous person's death—without fear and emotional upheaval.

The noisy mourning of others is compared to floods ("tear-floods") and tempests ("sigh-tempests").

Telling others of the speaker's intimate, private love (through loud display of grief) would be like priests revealing the mysteries of their faith to "the laity," that is, to lay people—to unappreciative, unprepared outsiders. The lovers would then "profane" the mysteries of their love—desecrating something sacred by taking it down to the level of ordinary reality.

The upheavals in the lives of ordinary lovers are earthquakes ("moving of the earth"). But any disturbance in the more refined loves of the two people in this poem is "a trepidation of the spheres"—it is like the far-off trembling in the crystal spheres of the heavens, which is "innocent" or harmless as far as actual damage in the world around us is concerned.

The "souls" of ordinary clods are not really soul but sense—they stay on the level of sense perception and sensual feeling; they don't really have a "soul."

True love is like gold—it can be stretched incredibly thin like gold leaf without breaking.

The souls of the two lovers are joined like twin compasses. One leg, "the fixed foot," is planted firmly in the center. The other "travels," describing a perfect circle, returning to its point of origin. The farther the moving leg extends from the fixed center, the more the stationary leg needs to incline or lean toward it (it "harkens after it"). But at the same time the stationary leg keeps the moving leg from roaming too far, from going off on a tangent. In fact the firmness of the "fixed foot" (the person who stayed home) makes sure the absent lover comes full circle.

Organizing the Paper How would you organize this material? The metaphors and similes in Donne's poem are each bold and original in their own right. You often need to make the required mental leap from what you see to what it means. At the same time, the metaphors shift rapidly, and you need to be alert if you are not to be left behind. To write a unified paper, you will have to aim at working out an overall framework or perspective. You will have to try to fit the rapidly shifting individual metaphors into an overall pattern.

The student author of the following paper uses the idea of the journey—which is the subject of the poem—as the organizing principle for the paper.

Sample Student Paper

Thou Shalt Not Cry When I Am Gone

In a favorite scene in yesterday's romantic movies, someone is boarding a train, going off to war or to some far-off assignment or tour of duty. The person left behind is fighting back tears as the train slowly pulls out of the station. The traveler is trying to stay calm, forestalling the "tear-floods" and "sigh-tempests" that John Donne dreads in his farewell poem, "A Valediction: Forbidding Mourning." Scheduled to leave on a journey to France, Donne pleads with his wife Anne More to accept his departure in a spirit of calm acceptance, confident that the strength of their love will triumph over their physical separation.

In arguing against mourning and emotional upheaval, Donne takes us on a journey through a sequence of bold unexpected images, each one a metaphor or a simile for the love between him and his wife. Finally we reach the circle drawn by the twin compasses in the final stanzas as the metaphor for a perfect love that will bring him back to the starting point of his journey, making "me end where I begun." The structure of the poem, a progression from one striking metaphor or simile to another, is the more appropriate when we consider that the poem was presented to his wife before he departed on a journey.

The journey begins with an unexpected analogy between the impending separation of the lovers and death. The poet says "So let us melt"—go quietly, like snow that melts in the March sun, making "no noise" (5). The startling comparison is between their parting and the death of "virtuous men," who "pass mildly away / And whisper to their souls to go" (1–2). Virtuous men and their friends have no need to mourn unduly at their passing—after all, their virtue in this life has assured them of glory and reward in the life to come. Similarly, the poet and his love have no need for noise at their separation—"no tear-floods, nor sigh-tempests" (6). There is no need to weep and sigh, since the beauty and strength of their love will survive their separation.

Their love is in fact almost sacred. It would be profaned if it should be made known to others, who could not comprehend love on such a high spiritual plane. Since it is almost holy, the lovers should not cheapen or defile it through such ordinary demonstration of grief as weeping or lamenting. Like priests, they should guard their sacred mysteries from "profanation" by the laity (7–8).

We next move to a larger circle than the temple where love is protected from the uninitiated. Even the earth is not adequate to contain true love. For more common lovers, the earthquake of separation would bring "harms and fears" (9). But the love between the poet and his wife is above the reach of such earthly upheavals. It is as if their love resided in the heavens, among the crystal spheres of the Ptolemaic universe. Even when there is "trepidation" or trembling of the spheres, it is "innocent"—it will cause no harm here below. Donne remains in the Ptolemaic universe for another verse or two; Ordinary earthbound lovers are caught up in the physical presence of the other person, which like all material things in this "sublunary" sphere below the moon is subject to change and decay. Their "soul is sense"; the only outlet for what soul they have is through the five senses. Their love hinges on the physical act of love, which cannot be consummated in the absence of the beloved. More refined lovers don't need the presence of the physical body; they "care less" if they have to miss "eyes, lips, and hands" (13–20).

The love of these two exceptional lovers is like gold—not just because it is precious, but because gold can be beaten into a layer of the thinnest gold leaf that stretches incredibly far—perhaps even from England to France without a "breach" or breaking. However, the culminating metaphor is that of the twin compasses, which "are two" only in the sense that there are two legs joined permanently at the top. The "fixed foot" of the stay-at-home "leans and harkens" after the other that "far doth roam" (25–30). As the foot that actually draws the circle travels around the stationary part, that part must incline at the right angle. (It cannot just forget about the "roaming" part.)

Together, the twin compasses create a circle, to Donne's contemporaries the most perfect shape in the universe. The firmness of the "other foot" enables the poet to come full circle; it makes his journey "end where I begun" (36).

Questions for Peer Review

The student author finds in the poem (and interprets for us) metaphors or similes from a whole range of areas of human experience. These include seasonal change, death, priests guarding temples, traditional astronomers' views of the perfect heavens, the goldsmith's art, and the use of the pair of compasses in geometry. How does the student writer weave these into a meaningful pattern or progression?

1. According to the student writer, on what kind of "journey" does the poem take the reader—or the wife as the intended audience? How does the writer give us a preview of the *circle image* as central to the movement of the whole poem?

2. How does the idea of the "quiet" and almost resigned parting become nevertheless "startling" and provocative? How does it move on, as often in a Donne poem, to a *quasi-religious* level?

3. How does the metaphorical journey move on, as often in Donne's poetry, to images from *astronomy*—as the student writer says, from the Ptolemaic astronomy that was being superseded by the new Copernican view? How

well does the student writer tie in or explain the idea of the traditional "sublunary sphere"?

4. How does the writer explain the significance and impact of the "culminating metaphor" of the *twin compasses?* How does it tie the whole poem together and "circle" back to the beginning?

5. Which of *the imaginative comparisons* in this poem seem to you particularly unexpected or strange? Which metaphors or similes make sense after you look at the student writer's explanations or after you have a chance to think about them?

6. One reader of this poem thought the poem "terribly romantic," because the poet wants the love between him and his wife to be perfect—better than anyone else's. At the opposite end of the spectrum, another reader found the poem romantic on the surface but really insensitive. The poet is lecturing a silent, passive partner about what she should feel and think. Where do *you* stand? Do you tend toward the one view or the other?

16 SYMBOL

A World of Meanings

Courtesy Richard B. Ressman

*Symbols are the bridging language between the
visible and the invisible world.*

ANGELIS ARRIEN

FOCUS ON SYMBOLS

A **symbol** is something that you can see but that has taken on a meaning beyond itself. We all know the language of symbols: The dove of peace prevails when nations sheathe the sword. The daily bread sustains life; it becomes the staff of life. Political posters often speak a symbolic language: The raised fist calls to armed struggle. Hands joined in a handshake proclaim human brotherhood. Chains used to shackle prisoners become a symbol of slavery and oppression. A broken chain, in turn, becomes a symbol of freedom.

Powerful symbols activate a network of associations. A plow was the peasant's basic tool—needed to break the sod and start the planting cycle that would lead to the bounty of the harvest. Over the centuries, the plow became a symbol for the steady toil required to feed humankind. It reminds us to honor the labor that staves off famine. It admonishes the privileged, who squander in thoughtless luxury what the workers in the fields gain toiling from sunup to sundown. As William Langland says in the medieval poem *Piers Plowman,*

> Some were following the plow, with no time for pleasure,
> Sowing the seed, sweating at their labor,
> Winning the wealth that the worthless waste in luxury.

Poets use or adapt traditional symbols, but they will also often give new symbolic significance to objects and events. Rather than bring the meaning of a symbol *into* the poem from the outside, we have to read the meaning of the symbol *out of* the poem.

What is the difference between symbol and metaphor?

✗ A symbol is *literally* there. It is literally there, but it has a meaning beyond itself. The speaker in Paul Goodman's "Haiku" is a person who actually grows roses—which assume a symbolic meaning:

> Sprayed with strong poison
> my roses are crisp this year
> In the crystal vase

In this poem, we are made to visualize actual roses in a crystal vase. They have been sprayed with actual pest killer or fungicide. It is this fact that takes us to a meaning beyond the ordinary reaction of "How nice to have roses." The roses become a symbol of beauty that, like other good things in our lives, is produced at the cost of using potentially lethal agents.

✕ When Laura St. Martin in a poem called "The Ocean" says, "the ocean is a strange / midnight lover," we are asked to imagine a real ocean, but not a literal human lover. The ocean, to the person swimming at night, is in some ways *like* a lover—caressing, passionate, changeable. There is no human lover in this ocean at this time. The lover in this poem is metaphorical.

FIRST READING
A Central Symbol

The Taíno in the following poem were the Caribbean people Columbus encountered when he first reached the New World. He described them as generous and without guile, endowed with acute intelligence. Enslaved by Columbus and the Spaniards in their search for gold, ravaged by the white man's diseases, the Taíno people were decimated and disappeared. How does Espada pay tribute to them in the following poem?

Martín Espada   *(born 1957)*

Colibrí   *1987*

FOR KATHERINE, ONE YEAR LATER

In Jayuya,
the lizards scatter
like a fleet of green canoes
before the invader.
The Spanish conquered   5
with iron and words:
"Taíno" for the people who took life
from the plátanos in the trees,
those multiple green fingers
curling around unseen spears,   10
who left the rock carvings
of eyes and mouths
in perfect circles of amazement.

So the hummingbird
was christened "colibrí,"   15
Now the colibrí

darts and hangs
between the white walls
of the hacienda
a racing Taíno heart   20
frantic as if hearing
the bellowing god of gunpowder
for the first time.

The colibrí
becomes pure stillness,   25
seized in the paralysis
of the prey,
when your hands
cup the bird
and lift him   30
through the red shutters
of the window,
where he disappears
into a paradise of sky,
a nightfall of singing frogs.   35

If only history
were like your hands.

The Receptive Reader

1. In how many ways does the poet allude to the historical facts of the Spanish invasion and conquest?

2. How do the lizards and the rock carvings help the reader share in the feelings of the indigenous peoples?

3. How does the small darting hummingbird, whose whirring wings keep it in place while it sucks the nectar from blooms, become a symbol of the conquered people?

4. How would history be different if it were like the hands of the person addressed in the poem?

THE LANGUAGE OF SYMBOLS

What the bee knows
Tastes in the honey
Sweet and sunny.
O wise bee. O rose.
       JOHN FANDEL, "TRIBUTE"

A poem will often center on a unifying symbol. Often these symbols are rooted in age-old human experience, drawing on a community of shared meanings. For instance, green is a potently symbolic color: Since the dawn of history, the first budding green life of April, after the barrenness and ice of winter, has served as a symbol of rebirth, of the triumph of life over death. In the depth of winter, a sprig of evergreen (or a whole tree) can symbolize our faith that burgeoning life will return to the barren, frozen land. Poets draw on this common fund of symbolic meanings. In reading the following poem, we soon realize that the frogs in the basement of the abandoned house are more than a footnote in the speaker's childhood memories. The "green chorus" of the green frogs, who had "slept in an icy bed" all winter, comes back to life in the spring, "pouring / out of their green throats."

David Wagoner   *(born 1926)*

The Other House   *1983*

As a boy, I haunted an abandoned house
Whose basement was always full of dark-green water
Or dark-green ice in winter,
Where frogs came back to life and sang each spring.

On broken concrete under the skeleton   5
Of a roof, inside ribbed walls, I listened alone
Where the basement stairs went down
Under the water, down into their music.

During storms, our proper house would be flooded too.
The water would spout from drains, through the foundation   10
And climb the basement stairs
But silently, and would go away silently,

As silent as my father and mother were
All day and during dinner and after
And after the radio   15
With hardly a murmur all the way into sleep.

All winter, the frogs slept in an icy bed,
Remembering how to sing when it melted.
If I made a sound, they stopped
And listened to me sing nothing, singing nothing.   20

But gradually, finally April would come pouring
Out of their green throats in a green chorus
To chorus me home toward silence.
Theirs was the only home that sang all night.

The Receptive Reader

1. Would you call the sound the frogs make "music"? What makes the "other house" an unlikely or unpromising setting for songs celebrating the return of spring? Do the frogs and the setting undercut the symbolism of spring and renewal for you?

2. The poet does not take us to the boy's own "proper house" until the third stanza. Why? What is the key to the polar opposition of what the two houses stand for? How is this polarity central to the poem as a whole?

3. Is there anything symbolic about the frogs' falling silent when they heard the boy?

4. Do you think the boy has been permanently influenced by his parents? Do you agree with the following student reaction to the poem?

> There is no renewal in spring-green trees if it does not resonate on the inside. A soul that cannot sing at the melting of the snows is winter-cold, icehard, regardless of the sun's warmth. A dark mysterious center that sings without sunlight breathes more life than this proper emptiness. The coldness of the silent parent is visited upon the son, perhaps for always, so his soul can never vibrate with mysterious yearnings, never feel the spring-green trees.

The Personal Response

In your own growing up, how much "silence" has there been, and how much "song"?

The Creative Dimension

When we read a poem that has a strong impact on us, a haunting image or central symbol may linger in our minds. Look at the way the following student-written passage re-creates the lasting impression the poem left in the student's mind. Then do your own re-creation of a lasting impression left in your mind by this poem or by another poem in this chapter.

> In spring,
> after the ice melts
> and the drains fill
> the concrete cracks
> of the basement floor
> with green water,
> the frogs are born
> to keep me company
> and fill my silent nights
> with songs.

When the language of symbols becomes too conventional, poets—like painters, photographers, or journalists—help it evolve and become fresh again. In today's world, the bulldozer and the oil-drenched seabird have become symbols of the confrontation between technological progress and ecological survival. In a newspaper photograph printed after an oil spill, we do not just see an individual bird, its plumage clotted with black goo. We see a symbol of life endangered by a technology spinning out of control. In the following poem, the poet seizes on a symbolic incident in order to enlist the readers' sympathies. How does the chain saw become a symbol for the machine age in the poem?

Donald Finkel   *(born 1929)*

They   1975

are at the end of our street now cutting down trees
a scream like a seven foot locust
they have cut off another
neatly at the pavement
never again will the pin-oak threaten a taxi   5
will the ash lie in wait to fall on a child

it is a good time for this
the sun is bright
the plane has only just begun
to sprout little shoots from under her fingernails   10
never again will she dance
her terrible saraband° in the tornado   *stately court dance*
the sweet gum trembles
bristling with tiny mines like brown sea urchins
never again will he drop them on the walk   15
to menace the sensible shoes of mailmen

they have brought a machine that eats trees
and shits sawdust
they cut off limbs to feed it
snarling it chews the pale green fingers of the plane   20
the pin-oak's wrinkled elbows and knees
they fill truck after truck with the dust
in the schoolyard now they are cutting down the children
I hear their screams
first at the ankles   25
it is nothing then to sever
their soles from the asphalt
there is no danger their falling
on the school and crushing it

I have invented a machine that shoots words   30
I type faster and faster
I cannot keep up with them
in front of the house now they are cutting the rosebush
vainly she scratches their hands like a drowning kitten
they are cutting the grass   35
scythes in their wheels they race over our lawn
flashing in the sun like the chariots of the barbarians
the grass blades huddle whimpering
there is no place to go
it is spring and the street is alive   40
with the clamor of motors
the laughter of saws

The Receptive Reader

1. Where in the poem do we hear the voices approving of the tree-cutting operation? With what effect does the poet cite them?

2. How many examples can you find of pervasive *personification* in this poem—ascribing quasi-human features to the vegetation? What is the effect on the readers? How does it prepare them for what happens in the schoolyard? (Why is there no stanza break or transition before the schoolyard massacre?) What makes the cutting of the rosebush especially traumatic?

3. How does the chariot *simile* reinforce the prevailing perspective of the poem? Why does the poet keep reminding us that it is spring?

The Personal Response

What makes the machines in this poem frightening symbols of human technology? What side do you take in the confrontation conjured up by this poet?

The following poem focuses our attention on the rose and on water, which are both rich in symbolic overtones and associations. The rose, often a deep red or blood red, has long stood for passion or for beauty. The more arid the country, the more water is likely to be worshiped as the source of life, making the desert bloom, creating an oasis in a wasteland of rock or sand. What are the symbolic meanings of the rose and of water in this poem?

Denise Levertov   *(born 1923)*

To One Steeped in Bitterness   *1964*

Nail the rose
            to your mind's door
like a rat, a thwarted chickenhawk.
Yes, it has had its day.

And the water   5
            poured for you
which you disdain to drink,
yes, throw it away.

Yet the fierce rose
            stole nothing   10
from your cooped heart,
nor plucked your timid eye;

and from inviolate rock
            the liquid light
was drawn, that's dusty now   15
and your lips dry.

In this poem, we see a number of symbolic objects and symbolic gestures. We can imagine someone being offered a rose or a drink of water.

We can also imagine the person turning these down. In the poem, as in real life, both of these gestures invite symbolic interpretation. Both the water and the disdainful gesture that throws it out are likely to mean something beyond themselves. They reveal an attitude, a state of mind. The gesture of pouring the water may mean friendship or hospitality. The gesture of refusing it may symbolize bitterness and hostility.

The Receptive Reader

1. What is likely to be the symbolic meaning of the rose? We are asked to imagine it nailed to the "mind's door" by the bitter, hostile person being addressed in the poem. The person "steeped in bitterness," with a "cooped heart," would nail the rose to the barn door (the way ranchers nail "varmints" they consider their natural enemies). Why?

2. What is likely to be the symbolic meaning of the water? The person steeped in bitterness disdainfully rejects the offered water, which is like "liquid light," and which would bring much-needed liquid to dry, parched lips. What would the parched soul be thirsting for?

The following poem is by a Chinese immigrant who came with his parents from Indonesia. Central to the poem is the meeting of two worlds: One world is symbolized by the scroll paintings that link the father to old-country tradition and by the fruit (the persimmon) that is a touch of home to the poet but a curiosity to his classmates. The other world is represented by the monolingual teacher questioning the intelligence of a student learning to learn in a new language, learning to live in a new culture.

Li-Young Lee   *(born 1957)*

Persimmons   *1986*

In sixth grade Mrs. Walker
slapped the back of my head
and made me stand in the corner
for not knowing the difference
between *persimmon* and *precision*.   5
How to choose

persimmons. This is precision.
Ripe ones are soft and brown-spotted.
Sniff the bottoms. The sweet one
will be fragrant. How to eat: 10
put the knife away, lay down newspaper.
Peel the skin tenderly, not to tear the meat.
Chew on the skin, suck it,
and swallow. Now, eat

the meat of the fruit,   15
so sweet
all of it, to the heart.

Dona undresses, her stomach is white.
In the yard, dewy and shivering
with crickets, we lie naked,   20
face-up, face-down.
I teach her Chinese. Crickets: *chiu chiu*. Dew: I've forgotten.
Naked: I've forgotten.
Ni, wo: you and me.
I part her legs,   25
remember to tell her
she is beautiful as the moon.

Other words
that got me into trouble were
fight and *fright, wren* and *yarn.*   30
Fight was what I did when I was frightened,
fright was what I felt when I was fighting.
Wrens are small, plain birds,
yarn is what one knits with.
Wrens are soft as yarn.   35
My mother made birds out of yarn.
I loved to watch her tie the stuff;
a bird, a rabbit, a wee man.

Mrs. Walker brought a persimmon to class
and cut it up   40
so everyone could taste
a *Chinese apple.* Knowing
it wasn't ripe or sweet, I didn't eat
but watched the other faces.

My mother said every persimmon has a sun   45
inside, something golden, glowing,
warm as my face.

Once, in the cellar, I found two wrapped in newspaper
forgotten and not yet ripe.
I took them and set them both on my bedroom windowsill,   50
where each morning a cardinal
sang. *The sun, the sun.*

Finally understanding
he was going blind,
my father would stay up all one night   55
waiting for a song, a ghost.
I gave him the persimmons,

swelled, heavy as sadness,
and sweet as love.

This year, in the muddy lighting   60
of my parents' cellar, I rummage, looking
for something I lost.
My father sits on the tired, wooden stairs,
black cane between his knees,
hand over hand, gripping the handle.   65

He's so happy that I've come home.
I ask how his eyes are, a stupid question.
All gone, he answers.

Under some blankets, I find a box.
Inside the box I find three scrolls.   70
I sit beside him and untie
three paintings by my father:
Hibiscus leaf and a white flower.
Two cats preening.
Two persimmons, so full they want to drop from the cloth.   75

He raises both hands to touch the cloth,
asks, *Which is this?*

This is persimmons, Father.

Oh, the feel of the wolftail on the silk,
the strength, the tense   80
precision in the wrist.
I painted them hundreds of times
eyes closed. These I painted blind.
Some things never leave a person:
scent of the hair of one you love,   85
the texture of persimmons,
in your palm, the ripe weight.

The Receptive Reader

1. From what angle are you looking at the bilingual student's learning in this poem? How is it different from what you might have expected? (How does the poem turn the tables on the teacher?)

2. The persimmon is first introduced in a casual or humorous way. (How and why?) It becomes a *central symbol,* providing a common strand for the poem as a whole. What different associations and memories cluster around the fruit? What role does it play in the poem as a whole?

3. What other details in this poem have a symbolic significance?

4. How close to or distant from the family's cultural roots is the speaker in the poem?

The Personal Response

What experience have you had with different cultural traditions or bilingual Americans? What have you learned about barriers to communication? Does this poem help you cross the barriers separating different cultures?

The Creative Dimension

Write about a symbolic object or incident that for you calls up memories of home, family, or the older generation. Choose a symbol that best sums up deep-seated feelings or vivid memories.

Making Connections—For Discussion or Writing

Poets have often looked for symbolic significance in the burgeoning life of the natural world that surrounds us. Is there a common strand in the nature symbolism in such poems as David Wagoner's "The Other House," Denise Levertov's "To One Steeped in Bitterness," and Li-Young Lee's "Persimmons"?

The following poem was written by a famous English poet of the Romantic age, an era of both revolution and reaction. The title of the poem names an Egyptian pharaoh who, like other early Egyptian rulers, commissioned colossal statues of himself.

Percy Bysshe Shelley   *(1792–1822)*

Ozymandias   *1818*

I met a traveler from an antique land
Who said: "Two vast and trunkless legs of stone
Stand in the desert . . . Near them on the sand,
Half-sunk, a shattered visage° lies, whose frown,   *face*
And wrinkled lip, and sneer of cold command,   5
Tell that its sculptor well those passions read
Which yet survive, stamped on these lifeless things,
The hand that mocked them, and the heart that fed:
And on the pedestal these words appear:
'My name is Ozymandias, king of kings: 10
Look on my works, ye Mighty, and despair!'
Nothing beside remains. Round the decay
Of that colossal wreck, boundless and bare
The lone and level sands stretch far away."

The Receptive Reader

1. According to the poem, what did the pharaoh want the statue he commissioned to symbolize? What does the statue symbolize for the poet?

2. Shelley, like other Romantics, was a rebel against tyrannical authority. How does this commitment show in the poem?

PUBLIC AND PRIVATE SYMBOLS

*All poems say the same thing, and each poem is
unique.*

OCTAVIO PAZ

Some poets develop a symbolic language of their own that may at first seem private or obscure. However, it gradually becomes meaningful as we learn more about the poet or read several poems by the same poet. We learn the poet's symbolic language; we gradually feel less like strangers in the poet's world of meanings. The English poet William Blake was a precursor of the Romantic movement. For him, all experience was shot through with symbolic meanings—he was able "to see a world in a grain of sand / And a heaven in a wild flower." Breaking with eighteenth-century standards of rationality and restraint, he used bold, unusual symbols to celebrate the divine energies at work in the universe. The following is Blake's most famous poem. What do you think would be the poet's answers to the questions he asks in this poem?

William Blake   *(1757–1827)*

The Tyger   *1794*

Tyger! Tyger! burning bright
In the forests of the night,
What immortal hand or eye
Could frame thy fearful symmetry?

In what distant deeps or skies   5
Burnt the fire of thine eyes?
On what wings dare he aspire?
What the hand, dare° seize the fire?   *hand that dares*

And what shoulder, & what art,
Could twist the sinews of thy heart?   10
And when thy heart began to beat,
What dread hand? & what dread feet?

What the hammer? what the chain?
In what furnace was thy brain?
What the anvil? what dread grasp   15
Dare its deadly terrors clasp?

When the stars threw down their spears,
And watered heaven with their tears,
Did he smile his work to see?
Did he who made the lamb make thee?   20

Tyger! Tyger! burning bright
In the forests of the night,
What immortal hand or eye
Dare frame thy fearful symmetry?

The Receptive Reader

1. How does Blake make us see the tiger as beautiful and terrifying at the same time?

2. How does Blake make us imagine the process of creation? (What associations do the images in the fourth stanza—the anvil, the furnace, the forge—bring into play?) How is his vision of the process different from what we might conventionally expect?

3. How has the lamb traditionally been used as a symbol of goodness? How has the tiger traditionally been used as a symbol of evil? How is Blake's use of these symbols different? Is the tiger evil or sinister in this poem?

4. What is the answer to the questions the poet asks in this poem?

Adrienne Rich has been called "perhaps the leading American feminist poet of her generation" (Eric Mendelsohn). In her poems as in her essays and editorial work, she played a pioneering role in exploring a new language of thought and feeling for women breaking out of a traditional patriarchal mold. What new or different meanings do familiar symbols assume in the following poem?

Adrienne Rich   *(born 1929)*

Aunt Jennifer's Tigers   1951

Aunt Jennifer's tigers prance across a screen,
Bright topaz denizens of a world of green.
They do not fear the men beneath the tree;
They pace in sleek chivalric certainty.

Aunt Jennifer's fingers fluttering through her wool   5
Find even the ivory needle hard to pull.
The massive weight of Uncle's wedding band
Sits heavily upon Aunt Jennifer's hand.

When Aunt is dead, her terrified hands will lie
Still ringed with ordeals she was mastered by.   10
The tigers in the panel that she made
Will go on prancing, proud and unafraid.

The Receptive Reader

1. What do the tigers represent in Aunt Jennifer's world? What does the wedding band represent? How do these two symbols function as *polar opposites* in this poem?

2. What is the range of meaning your dictionary gives for words like *topaz, denizen, chivalric, ordeal?* What do these words mean in the context of this poem?

3. In a later reprinting of this poem, the poet changed the words *prance* (line 1) and *prancing* (line 12) to *stride* and *striding*. What difference does the change make? Why do you think the poet might have wanted to change the words?

4. How have the central symbols in this poem changed from more traditional meanings and associations?

Making Connections—For Discussion or Writing

How are Blake's tiger and Rich's tigers related in their symbolic meanings or associations? In what ways are they similar? In what ways are they different?

The Irish poet William Butler Yeats stands out among poets using a highly individual symbolic language. In his earlier poetry, he had drawn inspiration from the lore of Ireland. In his later years, he repeatedly used symbols from the rich religious art of Byzantium (later Constantinople and now Istanbul), the fabled capital of the eastern part of the Roman Empire during the early Christian era. Byzantine art was famous for precious materials and finely crafted artifice. It was legendary for the ornamental patterns of its mosaics; for its carved ivory, its enamelwork, and the work of its goldsmiths. Shortly before he wrote the following poem, Yeats had seen spectacular examples of Byzantine mosaics depicting saints and prophets (the "sages" mentioned in the third stanza) in a church at Ravenna in Northern Italy.

In the poem, the poet takes us on a symbolic voyage. We travel from a country of the young to "the holy city of Byzantium"—a place more attuned to the spiritual needs of the aging speaker in the poem. What special fascination does the "artifice" of the Greek artists of Byzantium hold for the poet?

William Butler Yeats   *(1865–1939)*

Sailing to Byzantium   1927

1

That is no country for old men. The young
In one another's arms, birds in the trees
—Those dying generations—at their song,
The salmon-falls, the mackerel-crowded seas,

Fish, flesh, or fowl, commend all summer long   5
Whatever is begotten, born, and dies.
Caught in that sensual music all neglect
Monuments of unaging intellect.

2

An aged man is but a paltry thing,
A tattered coat upon a stick, unless   10
Soul clap its hands and sing, and louder sing
For every tatter in its mortal dress,
Nor is there singing school but studying
Monuments of its own magnificence;
And therefore I have sailed the seas and come   15
To the holy city of Byzantium.

3

O sages standing in God's holy fire
As in the gold mosaic of a wall,
Come from the holy fire, perne in a gyre,°   *turn with a spiral motion*
And be the singing masters of my soul.   20
Consume my heart away, sick with desire
And fastened to a dying animal
It knows not what it is; and gather me
Into the artifice of eternity.

4

Once out of nature, I shall never take   25
My bodily form from any natural thing,
But such a form as Grecian goldsmiths make   *Greek*
Of hammered gold and gold enameling
To keep a drowsy Emperor awake;
Or set upon a golden bough to sing   30
To lords and ladies of Byzantium
Of what is past, or passing, or to come.

Much of the early part of the poem revolves around a polar opposition of
youth and age. The speaker in the poem finds himself out of place in a country of the young that is full of "sensual music." To the aging speaker in the
poem, fastened to his decaying body as "to a dying animal" (line 22), there
is no comfort in the surface vitality of a life caught up in the world
of the senses. The second stanza focuses on the central paradox of the poem:
The body decays, leaving the physical person little more than a scarecrow,

"a tattered coat upon a stick." However, the intellect survives; the soul is still capable of song and artistic creation. Here is the answer to the decay of the body: The soul can metaphorically "clap its hands" and create immortal music. The "singing school" for the soul, teaching it to triumph over decay, is the work of artists who have gone before.

The Receptive Reader

1. We are conditioned to think positively of youth and burgeoning nature. What turns the speaker away from them?

2. Much of this poem revolves around related *polarities:* the opposition of youth and age, of intellect and the body, and of nature and art. What striking details help flesh out each of these polarities?

3. Why do the salmon fighting their way up the "salmon-falls" provide the poet with an especially appropriate *symbol* for life in the natural world?

4. What vision of art or "artifice" is developed in the final two stanzas? How will "artifice" provide the answer to age and decay? What makes the artifacts of Byzantine art apt symbols for the poet's way of transcending or overcoming age?

5. In this poem, Yeats uses a finely crafted, interlaced rhyme scheme called **ottava rima** (or "set of eight"). Why is it more appropriate to this poem than free-flowing free verse would be?

The Personal Response

Do you think art should celebrate the vitality of life or help us triumph over its imperfections?

Making Connections—For Discussion or Writing

Another famous exploration of the relation between life and art is John Keats' "Ode on a Grecian Urn" (reprinted in Chapter 22). Compare and contrast the way the two poems deal with a central theme, such as youth and age, change and permanence, or nature and art.

The Russian poet Yevgeny Yevtushenko said, "Poetry is like a bird. It ignores all frontiers." How true is this statement of the language of symbols? How universal are they? Look at the use of a central but multifaceted symbol in the following poem by a Latin American poet. Gabriela Mistral grew up in poverty in Chile and left school at age eleven, but she became a teacher and was for many years the best-known woman writing in Latin America. The first Latin American to win the Nobel Prize (1945), she worked on educational reform in Mexico and later taught in New England and Puerto Rico.

Gabriela Mistral   *(1889–1957)*

To Drink   *1938*

TRANSLATED BY GUNDA KAISER

I remember gestures of infants
and they were gestures of giving me water.

In the valley of Rio Blanco
where the Aconcagua has its beginning,
I came to drink, I rushed to drink   5
in the fountain of a cascade,
which fell long and hard
and broke up rigid and white.
I held my mouth to the boiling spring
and the blessed water burned me,   10
and my mouth bled three days
from that sip from the valley of Aconcagua.

In the fields of Mitla, a day
of harvest flies, of sun, of motion,
I bent down to a well and a native came   15
to hold me over the water,
and my head, like a fruit,
was within his palms.
I drank what he drank,
for his face was with my face,   20
and in a lightning flash I realized
I, too, was of the race of Mitla.

On the island of Puerto Rico,
during the slumber of full blue,
my body calm, the waves wild,   25
and the palms like a hundred mothers,
a child broke through skill
close to my mouth a coconut for water,
and I drank, like a daughter,
water from a mother, water from a palm.   30
And I have not partaken greater sweetness
with my body nor with my soul.

At the house of my childhood
my mother brought me water.
From one sip to another sip   35
I saw her over the jug.
The more her head rose up
the more the jug was lowered.
I still have my valley,
I have my thirst and her vision.   40
This will be eternity
for we still are as we were.

I remember gestures of infants
    and they were gestures of giving me water.

The Receptive Reader

How does water serve as the central symbol in this poem? What are its widening circles of association and symbolic meaning? Which of the symbolic meanings and associations seem universal? Which seem specific to this poem or to this poet's experience?

The Creative Dimension

Water—like sun, earth, light, birth, or death—is one of the great constants of human experience. Cluster one of these. Then write a passage tracing the web of meanings that the term has for you.

JUXTAPOSITIONS

Symbol and Allegory

In an **allegory**, symbols work together in a set pattern. Symbolic figures or objects play their roles like actors in a drama. The author of the first of the following two poems belonged to the Pre-Raphaelites, a group of English painters and writers who turned to medieval art and religion for inspiration. In her poem, the road, the hill, the inn, the darkness at end of day, the traveler, and the other wayfarers all play their assigned roles in the poet's allegorical vision of our spiritual journey to our final destination. In the earlier allegorical poem by the English poet William Blake, what is the meaning of the symbolic details? What role does each play in the allegory?

Christina Rossetti   *(1830–1894)*

Uphill   *1858*

Does the road wind uphill all the way?
    Yes, to the very end.
Will the day's journey take the whole long day?
    From morn to night, my friend.

But is there for the night a resting place?   5
    A roof for when the slow dark hours begin.
May not the darkness hide it from my face?
    You cannot miss that inn.

Shall I meet other wayfarers at night?
    Those who have gone before.   10
Then must I knock, or call when just in sight?
    They will not keep you standing at that door.

Shall I find comfort, travel-sore and weak?
    Of labor you shall find the sum.
Will there be beds for me and all who seek?   15
    Yea, beds for all who come.

The Receptive Reader

Who are the two speakers in this poem? What is the meaning of each of the symbolic details in this allegory? What makes this poem earnest and uplifting in the Victorian nineteenth-century manner?

William Blake   *(1757–1827)*

A Poison Tree   *1794*

I was angry with my friend:
I told my wrath, my wrath did end.
I was angry with my foe:
I told it not, my wrath did grow.

And I watered it in fears,   5
Night and morning with my tears:
And I sunned° it with smiles,   *gave it sunlight*
And with soft deceitful wiles.

And it grew both day and night,
Till it bore an apple bright.   10
And my foe beheld it shine,
And he knew that it was mine.

And into my garden stole
When the night had veiled the pole:
In the morning glad I see   15
My foe outstretched beneath the tree.

The Receptive Reader

1. Much medieval poetry had preached against wrath as one of the seven deadly sins. Is this poem a warning against wrath?

2. What makes this poem simple and almost childlike in its form and its symbolism? Does the simple form undercut the serious question the poem raises?

The Personal Response

Are you aware of any trends in pop psychology that relate to the issue of whether to hold in or release negative emotions?

POEMS FOR FURTHER STUDY

In reading the following poems, pay special attention to objects or figures that may have symbolic significance. How does the poet use or change familiar symbols? What images, emotions, or ideas does the symbol bring into play? What role does a symbol play in the poem as a whole?

Lorna Dee Cervantes   *(born 1954)*

Refugee Ship   *1981*

Like wet cornstarch, I slide
past my grandmother's eyes. Bible
at her side, she removes her glasses.
The pudding thickens.
Mama raised me without language,   5

I'm orphaned from my Spanish name.
The words are foreign, stumbling
on my tongue. I see in the mirror
My reflection: bronzed skin, black hair.

I feel I am a captive   10
aboard the refugee ship.
The ship that will never dock.
El barco que nunca atraca.

The Receptive Reader

1. Do the cornstarch and the Bible in this poem have possible symbolic meanings?

2. How could the speaker in the poem have been raised "without language" and be "orphaned" from her Spanish name?

3. What did the mirror tell her?

4. The last line repeats in Spanish the previous line about the refugee ship "that will never dock." Why are some refugee ships not allowed to dock or their passengers not allowed to reach land? What makes the refugee ship a symbol of the speaker's own journey? What makes it a symbol of the experience of untold millions of refugees in the modern world?

The Creative Dimension

Sometimes a poem is for us like a mirror in which we see our own faces. Look at what one student saw in the mirror of the Cervantes poem. Then write your own response to a poem that seems like a mirror for a part of yourself.

> The refugee ship reminds me of the girl I see in the mirror every day. The speaker feels left out of the culture in which she grew up. In the Hispanic culture, there is a certain pressure from the family to retain one's culture. Maybe the poet is a refugee because she forgot all her tradition. Now she sees the Hispanic only in her appearance, not in her head.

Matthew Arnold   *(1822–1888)*

Dover Beach   *1867*

The sea is calm tonight.
The tide is full, the moon lies fair
Upon the straits; on the French coast the light
Gleams and is gone; the cliffs of England stand,
Glimmering and vast, out in the tranquil bay.   5
Come to the window, sweet is the night-air!
Only, from the long line of spray
Where the sea meets the moon-blanched° land,   *pale under the moon*
Listen! you hear the grating roar
Of pebbles which the waves draw back, and fling,   10
At their return, up the high strand,
Begin, and cease, and then again begin,
With tremulous cadence° slow, and bring   *regular rhythm*
The eternal note of sadness in.

Sophocles° long ago   *Greek playwright*   15
Heard it on the Aegean,° and it brought   *sea circling Greece*
Into his mind the turbid° ebb and flow   *murky*
Of human misery; we
Find also in the sound a thought,
Hearing it by this distant northern sea.   20

The Sea of Faith
Was once, too, at the full, and round° earth's shore   *around*
Lay like the folds of a bright girdle° furled.   *sash circling waist*
But now I only hear
Its melancholy, long, withdrawing roar,   25
Retreating, to the breath
Of the night-wind, down the vast edges drear
And naked shingles° of the world.   *pebble-strewn beaches*

Ah, love, let us be true
To one another! for the world, which seems   30
To lie before us like a land of dreams,
So various, so beautiful, so new,

Hath really neither joy, nor love, nor light,
Nor certitude, nor peace, nor help for pain;
And we are here as on a darkling plain   35
Swept with confused alarms of struggle and flight,
Where ignorant armies clash by night.

The Receptive Reader

Matthew Arnold, influential Victorian lecturer and critic, was part of an idealistic generation beset by religious doubts. What is the *central symbol* in this
poem? What gives it its special power or hold on the imagination? How is it followed up or reinforced in the poem? What is the poet's answer to the religious
soul searching of his time?

John Keats   *(1795–1821)*

Bright Star   *1819*

Bright star, would° I were steadfast as thou art—   *I wish*
    Not in lone splendor hung aloft the night°   *high in night sky*
And watching, with eternal lids apart,
    Like nature's patient, sleepless Eremite,°   *religious hermit*
The moving waters at their priestlike task   5
    Of pure ablution° round earth's human shores,   *cleansing*
Or gazing on the new soft fallen mask
    Of snow upon the mountains and the moors—
No—yet still steadfast, still unchangeable,
    Pillowed upon my fair love's ripening breast,   10
To feel forever its soft fall and swell.
    Awake forever in a sweet unrest,
Still, still to hear her tender-taken breath,
And so live ever—or else swoon to death.

The Receptive Reader

1. Like the other Romantic poets of his generation, Keats intuitively and naturally imbued the physical universe around us with quasi-human life and feeling, at the same time endowing it with divine qualities inspiring religious awe.
How does personification help Keats achieve these ends in this poem? (What
is striking about images like the "eternal lids apart" or ebb and tide attending
to their task of "pure ablution"?)

2. The first eight lines (or octave) of this sonnet develops one set of symbolic associations for the star, and then the next six lines (sestet) *reject* these.
Why? What is the basic symbolic meaning of the star in this poem? Why is it
strange or unexpected when applied to human love?

Lucille Clifton   *(born 1936)*

my mama moved among the days   *1969*

my mama moved among the days
like a dreamwalker in a field;
seemed like what she touched was hers
seemed like what touched her couldn't hold,
she got us almost through the high grass   5
then seemed like she turned around and ran
right back in
right back on in

The Receptive Reader
    What is the symbolic meaning of the high grass? Why does the poet repeat
the last line? How would you sum up the poet's attitude toward her mother?

Octavio Paz   *(born 1914)*   ●

Wind and Water and Stone   *1979*

TRANSLATED BY MARK STRAND

The water hollowed the stone,
the wind dispersed the water,
the stone stopped the wind.
Water and wind and stone.

The wind sculpted the stone,   5
the stone is a cup of water,
the water runs off and is wind.
Stone and wind and water.

The wind sings in its turnings,
the water murmurs as it goes,   10
the motionless stone is quiet.
Wind and water and stone.

One is the other, and is neither:
among their empty names
they pass and disappear,   15
water and stone and wind.

The Receptive Reader
    In this poem, what is the relationship of water, wind, and stone? What is
their possible symbolic significance? Why does the order of the three vary in
the last line of each stanza?

Nighthawks. 1942.
By Edward Hopper (American, 1882–1967).
Oil on canvas, 84.1 x 152.4 cm. Friends of American Art Collection, 1942.51. Photograph © 2002, The Art Institute of Chicago. All rights reserved.

NIGHTHAWKS
From HOPPER'S WOMEN
Sue Standing

She minds her cheap gardenia perfume,
her tight red dress.
The way this reflection goes
she sees only her angular arms
and the drugstore counter,
neon blots out the rest, except for fragments
of her dress mirrored on the coffee urn.
The men can't figure why she comes here
night after night.
They haven't seen her room and won't.
She wonders why she can't leave
the harsh light of this town, wonders
if every town contains only two stories.

DRAGON VASE, 15TH CENTURY, MING DYNASTY
Gerald Locklin

a blue dragon:
how beautiful!

where did the dragons go?
I don't believe the imagination
makes *anything completely* out of nothing.

is there something
like a dragon
that we feared and fought and finally exterminated?

or did we just see dragons
in the flames of
fire out of control,
in the Sargasso,
in the ice-floes,
or in the hallucinations of
starving, freezing dehydration?

whatever it was, we pictured
the dragon as a force that killed us,
a force we had to kill
to survive and to shelter our children,
the way those who still live near
the bear and mountain lion,
—even those who love them—
cannot afford *not* to kill them.

in return we grant them
the immortality of totemic art
and the eternal wilderness.

Poppy. 1927.
By Georgia O'Keeffe (American, 1887–1986).
Oil on canvas, 30 x 36 in. Gift of Charles C. and Margaret Stevenson Henderson in memory of Jeanne Crawford

RED POPPY
Christopher Buckley

I want you to see
what I see of flowers—
the meaning of a word is not
the meaning of a color,
and so this scarlet poppy
doubled and redoubled
with its life,
as flowers are relatively small
and no one has the time,
and seeing takes time.

There is no doubt here;
this effusive flower
draws us with a feeling

as direct as the sun, when,
as a child one bright-hot day,
I held my hand up
to shield my eyes and
saw my fingers glow
red as any flower or star
as the light seeped through them.

There is a dark abstraction
at the heart of it,
an intangible
that only comes clear in paint—
the colors in their lines
are often the most definite form

to say what I mean,
just as where I was born
and how I've lived do not,
when compared to what I've done.
What is of interest
is to love some small thing
and see how it grows within you,
how the petals,
the papery flesh of the flower,
barter with the wind
and carry life outward
as obviously as blood,
and not so unlike us.

Tar Beach. 1988.
By Faith Ringgold.
Acrylic pieced and printed fabric, 74 x 69 in.
Collection: Solomon R. Guggenheim Museum.
© Faith Ringgold Inc.

FROM ABOVE
Angela Johnson

When it is a warm time
    in the evening
and my people are
    laughing
and warm
beside me,
it almost feels like
I can fly
above the city and
    everything
I know.

—And I am happy in
    the coolness
as I am in the warmth,
because I can fly as
free as I feel
and watch my people
with love
from
above.

The Figure 5 in Gold, 1928.
By Charles Henry Demuth (American, 1883–1935).
Oil on composition board, H. 35-1/2 in., W. 30 in. (90.2 x 76.2 cm). The Metropolitan Museum of Art, Alfred Stieglitz Collection, 1949. (49.59.1) Photograph ©1979 The Metropolitan Museum of Art.

THE GREAT FIGURE
William Carlos Williams

Among the rain
and lights
I saw the figure 5
in gold
on a red
firetruck
moving
tense
unheeded
to gong clangs
siren howls
and wheels rumbling
through the dark city.

GIRLS ON THE BRIDGE
Derek Mahon

Audible trout,
Notional midges. Beds,
Lamplight and crisp linen, wait
In the house there for the sedate
Limbs and averted heads
Of the girls out

Late on the bridge.
The dusty road that slopes
Past is perhaps the main road south,
A symbol of world-wondering youth,
Of adolescent hopes
And privileges;

But stops to find
The girls content to gaze
At the unplumbed, reflective lake,
Their plangent conversational quack
Expressive of calm days
And peace of mind.

Grave daughters
Of time, you lightly toss
Your hair as the long shadows grow
And night begins to fall. Although
Your laughter calls across
The dark waters,

A ghastly sun
Watches in pale dismay.
Oh, you may laugh, being as you are
Fair sisters of the evening star,
But wait—if not today
A day will dawn

When the bad dreams
You hardly know will scatter
The punctual increment of your lives.
The road resumes, and where it curves,
A mile from where you chatter,
Somebody screams . . .

Number 1, 1950 (Lavender Mist).
By Jackson Pollock (American, 1912–1956).
Oil, enamel, and aluminum on canvas, 87 x 118 in. (221 x 299.7 cm).
1976.37.1.(2697)/PA. Ailsa Mellon Bruce Fund, Photograph by Richard Carafelli
© 2002 Board of Trustees, National Gallery of Art, Washington, DC

FRENZIED MOVEMENT: JACKSON POLLOCK'S #1
Tom Hauber

I see his movements. He is entranced
by his own creative frenzy.
He swirls his arms over the canvas,
squeezing tubes of pigment, dashing from one
end of the canvas to the other.
The paint oozes, drips, and splashes
onto the white surface below.
Black, then white, then splashes of blue and
yellow, then more long loops of black lines.
The layers pile one, one on top of the other.
I sit still and watch him work.
I wonder what is on his mind.
Is he thinking of his life? A war? The City?
Perhaps traffic? I have no idea.
I see only his movement.
The canvas comes alive with movement.
The painting IS movement.

Under the Wave off Kanagawa.
By Hokusai.

HOW REAL ARE DREAMS?
John Reidy

To examine Hokusai's *The Great Wave* and really suspend yourself in it, is to put yourself in a dream-like state. The painting contains many of the paradoxical qualitites found in a dream.

The whole painting is unreal, yet more real than reality itself. The wave, boats, and men seem to be moving, but at the same time, standing still. The sky gets darker as it gets closer to the horizon with Mount Fujiama in the distance, as if to beckon the dreamer.

The waves and the entire ocean are topped by whitewater which seems to float, as if detached from the water. The wave seems to be a collection of many claws, reaching to grab the fishermen, yet never quite reaching them.

All of these things happening: the wave reaching, the men rowing, Mount Fuji beckoning, seem to work cooperatively in the unfolding of a great destiny. The destiny itself is a paradox: The fishermen following their own will, yet subject to the forces of nature. The ocean and wave, a force which is spontaneous, yet all within the ordered will of God. The mountain, a sign of steadiness amid turmoil, yet too passing away.

Dreams are our own code of life-symbols. When we awaken, we see these same symbols in the real world. Do we really know the difference between dream and reality?

JUXTAPOSITIONS: WORD AND IMAGE

Reading Images, Seeing Poems

In the work of creative artists, we see that much is communicated without words. Painters speak to us using the language of color—for instance, using red to suggest flaming passion or green to suggest budding growth and hope. Shapes may convey feelings and attitudes. Strong angular geometric lines may suggest discipline and control. Snaking or twisted intertwining patterns may suggest churning out-of-control emotions. Sculptors may use the language of gestures to express expectation, deep thought, anger, or dismay.

The *painter's language* of colors and shapes and the *poet's language* of words and ideas may at times seem far apart, but at other times they seem to use different means of expression to achieve similar ends. As an outstanding example, painters and poets both use the language of symbols. They show us images that may be colorful or visually interesting in their own right—but we sense they have a meaning beyond themselves.

Much symbolism is part of the shared visual language of a culture. We know how to read the meaning of eloquent images like hands clasped in prayer, hands joined in brotherhood, or a fist raised in defiance. A painter can trust us to read the meaning of a head bent in sorrow, perhaps with a hand shading the eyes. However, often the symbolic meanings are less direct or obvious but no less powerful. The smooth unadorned granite wall of the Vietnam memorial in Washington, D.C., lines up thousands of names of the dead. It does without empty or inflated words, without frivolous decoration. The powerful implied message is that we should not adorn the stark fact of death and of sacrifice with speech-making or pompous decoration.

Symbols are open-ended—subject to interpretation. Much of their meaning may be in the eye of the beholder. Edward Hopper, a master of American realism, painted stark realistic American settings, often with a dark or unlighted backdrop. However, often his paintings will draw the eye toward a lighted part of the painting. Sometimes we see people looking toward a source of light. There are at least two ways of reading and responding to Hopper's paintings. We may, like the poet in the juxtaposition of painting and poem that follows, feel that Hopper throws a harsh light on the grim realities of ordinary lives. Or we may feel that Hopper looks for the light that will illuminate up our dark world, helping to make it habitable.

Poets, being wordsmiths and magicians of the word, have often felt the urge to put into words, to spell out, what a powerfully emotional or richly symbolic painting says. In the juxtapositions of images and words, do the poets put into words meanings and responses similar to or different from yours? (See color Inserts II and IV.)

WORD AND IMAGE:
VIEWING, READING, DISCUSSING, WRITING

Edward Hopper (1882–1967), *Nighthawks*, 1942   (Insert II i)

Sue Standing, "Nighthawks," from "Hopper's Women"

The Receptive Viewer and Reader

Edward Hopper is a favorite of viewers who distrust what is flashy, noisy, or trendy. He recorded in loving detail the unretouched realities of ordinary American life. In his dark city, there are oases of light. People who may have worked a late shift walk lonely streets to a diner where they join others at a counter with a counterman who shows his respect for his customer by his white outfit and cap and by maintaining well-polished coffee urns. Other paintings also show Hopper looking for light in an often gray world. In a painting by Hopper, light may flood an empty room. Vacationers sit quietly outside their simple habitation looking toward the sun.

1. It has been said of Hopper's canvases that silence pervades them and that this silence lures us into telling a story about what seems to be going on. What would be the answer if you asked one of the people in Hopper's painting: "What is your story?" Choose one and imagine yourself in the person's place. Tell the person's story.

2. Several poets have been moved to write about this famous painting. Sue Standing focuses on the "nighthawk" who is the woman in the painting. How does the poet want us to see her? Why does she comment on the perfume, the dress, the arms? What mental world and life history does the poet construct for the people in the painting?

3. Do you think the people in the painting know one another? For you, does the neon light "blot out" the rest of the diner? What for you explains the poet's negative reading of the nighttime scene?

Unknown, *Covered Dragon Jar*, Taiping period   (Insert II ii)

Gerald Locklin, "Dragon Vase"

The Receptive Viewer and Reader

1. Dragons are said to symbolize the unification of four elements of the ancient Chinese world: air, earth, water, and fire. They reflect the paradox at the heart of human existence: creation and destruction; darkness and light. Beyond these opposites, dragons suggest a primal energy at work in the universe. Where, in the image of a dragon, do you see air, earth, fire, and water?

2. The Welsh flag, with its red dragon, still testifies to its symbolic power. However, in modern times the dragon has increasingly been connected to raw power and the Freudian unconscious. Read Locklin's poem. What is the effect of his opening exclamation? The Sargasso Sea is a calm area of the North Atlantic noted for its abundance of seaweed. In what ways is "seeing dragons" in flames, in ice floes, or in hallucinations similar to seeing them in seaweed?

3. Dragons, Locklin suggests, are symbolic of a danger. The question is, are dragons a figment of the human imagination, or are they the embodiment of something at work in the universe that is "something like a dragon"? What is the poet's stance? What is your stance?

4. The last stanza points to a reciprocal relationship between humans and dragons; that is, human beings "give" back the "immortality of totemic art." A totem is an object with symbolic significance to a family or a clan or a culture. Write a journal entry in which you describe an object of symbolic significance in your life and what it means to you.

Georgia O'Keeffe (1887–1986), *Poppy*, 1927   (Insert II iii)

Christopher Buckley (born 1952), "Red Poppy," 1988

The Receptive Reader and Viewer

Independent and strong-minded Georgia O'Keeffe's personal, expressive charcoal drawings first brought her to the attention of a large public. By the mid-twenties, O'Keeffe had become one of America's most successful artists, painting unusual close-ups of flowers and making glass-and-steel buildings blossom into flowerlike shapes. After the death of her photographer-husband and collaborator Alfred Stieglitz in 1946, O'Keeffe moved to New Mexico, where she painted stark, harshly beautiful desert landscapes.

1. As the poet says, "flowers are relatively small" and no one really has the time to take a long close look at them. Nevertheless, do you think this painting succeeds in creating an intense feeling—how and why? Can flowers be "effusive"? Can you see a connection between the color of the flower and the light of a star or the sun?

2. What do you think the "dark abstraction at the heart of" the red poppy might be? What for you could be the mystery at the heart of the flower?

Faith Ringgold, *Tar Beach*, 1988   (Insert II iv)

Angela Johnson, "From Above," 2001

The Receptive Viewer and Reader

Faith Ringgold, an African American artist who grew up in Harlem, has won two Coretta King awards. Her *Tar Beach* painting is a multimedia work. It is painted on traditional canvas, but the border around it is made of printed, painted, quilted, and pieced-together cloth. For a new generation of African American artists and writers, the traditional quilt, patched together from squares cut from old clothes and from rags, became a symbol of the creative spirit triumphing over poverty and deprivation. Black Americans were long denied the resources of mainstream artists—studios, canvases, marble, or rich patrons. They found an outlet for their creative talents in quilt-making, in their gardens, and in music like the traditional blues, which did not require a symphony hall and orchestra.

1. Many artists today want art to be part of people's lives—part of a living culture—and not a dead artifact preserved as if under glass in a museum or

traded as a commodity at multimillion-dollar auctions. Can you explain to classmates why quilts are an exceptionally good example of art enhancing ordinary life? Can you think of other examples of creative work crossing the traditional boundary between art and ordinary life?

2. The bleak rooftops of tenements in treeless, shrubless poor neighborhoods have often been pictured as evidence of hopelessness. How does the painter overcome and leave behind these familiar associations? In how many ways does the painter turn the tarred rooftop into a scene of warm human life? (*Warm* is a favorite word of the poet writing the poem paired here with the painting—she uses it three times.) How does the tarred surface become a "beach"—a "tar beach"? Which of the details in the painting have for you a possible symbolic meaning?

3. If asked to put yourself in place of one of the people in the painting, which one would you choose? Imagine yourself in the person's place. What is your story? What is is like to be part of this family and part of this scene?

4. The poet feels close to and loving toward those she calls "my people." Is there a group of people—large or small—in your life that you think of as "my people"? What would you include in a journal entry or short paper entitled "My People"?

Charles Demuth (1883–1935), *I Saw the Figure 5 in Gold*, 1928 (Insert II v)

William Carlos Williams (1883–1963), "The Great Figure"

The Receptive Viewer and Reader

Establishment art critic and art historian Robert Hughes called Charles Demuth's *Figure 5* painting "one of the great icons of American modernism." He saw in it a "prediction"—an early example pointing toward the future—of the wave of pop art of the sixties and seventies. Pop art took ordinary objects and sights of the everyday American scene—coke bottles, soup can labels, panels from comic strips—and framed them like works of art. It thus made viewers look at and wonder at what was everywhere around them. Whereas often a painting will inspire a poem, in this case the poem came first: William Carlos Williams' "Great Figure" poem was written by a poet famous for calling up thought-provoking images from our everyday environment in the reader's mind.

1. Children run after fire trucks. Why? What words did the poet use to make a poem—often read silently—call up the noisy confusion of the passing truck? Noise is often unpleasant. Why isn't it unpleasant in this poem?

2. Often a painter will highlight a striking sight through a contrast with its background or setting. Is there such an offsetting contrast in the poem? Is there such an offsetting contrast in the painting?

3. The painter was fascinated with the "figure 5 / in gold / on a red / firetruck" that is at the heart of the poem. He repeats it, as if echoing or mirroring it, several times. In your mind, does the highlighted and repeated figure 5 call up ideas, feelings, or associations? What does it make you think or feel? Is it just a striking shape, or does it have possible symbolic meanings?

Edvard Munch (1863–1944), *White Night*   (Insert II vi)

Derek Mahon, "Girls on the Bridge," 1982

The Receptive Viewer and Reader

Anxiety haunts Norwegian Edvard Munch's art, most famously in his painting "The Scream" in which a person is depicted standing on a bridge, mouth wide open in a silent cry. His existential terror is expressed symbolically through lurid colors leaning to reds and purples. "My art," Munch declared, "is rooted in a single reflection: Why am I not as others are? Why was there a curse on my cradle? Why did I come into the world without any choice?"

1. At first glance, "Girls on the Bridge" renders an idyllic setting of peaceful homes, trimmed trees, quiet lake, and well-dressed and contemplative girls. In the first stanza Derek Mahon sets the stage, imagining the sanctuary of the girls' homes to which they will be returning, imagining their gazing at trout about to break the surface of the still lake, imagining tiny insects in the air surrounding them ("notional midges"). What other details in the rest of the poem support this image of peace?

2. The second stanza speaks of the "main road south" as symbolic. Symbolic of what? Why south and not north?

3. The third stanza tells us that this "road" stops, however. They're not going anywhere yet. Their plaintive sounds suggest no serious talk. Why "quack" and "chatter"? What does the "unplumbed, reflective lake" imply about these girls on this bridge?

4. The symbolism darkens in stanzas four and five. What words and phrases foreshadow problems and issues and disappointments to come?

5. Why do you think Mahon calls the four girls "daughters of time"? What does he know is around the bend? What words and phrases support the mood of darkness, of resignation, of gloom?

6. Name three images depicted by Munch or by the poet that work symbolically and describe how.

7. Write a journal entry in which you write about your own adolescent hopes and dreams. After you write, discuss in small groups whether—and how—those dreams have changed as you have grown older.

Jackson Pollock, *Number 1, 1950 (Lavender Mist)*   (Insert II vii)

Hokusai, *Under the Wave of Kanagawa*   (Insert II viii)

The Creative Response

Study the student responses to two widely known or recognized images of world art. Jackson Pollock (1912–1956) painted his *Number One* (1950) as one of the leading creators and promoters of modern abstract art. Abstract art cut itself loose from the representation or mirroring of recognizable reality. It created shapes and patterns and colors that took the viewer into a world of disembodied sensations and feelings. The Japanese artist Hokusai (1760–1849) created the woodblock print of *The Great Wave* (about 1831) that shows a huge wave apparently ready to overwhelm a small group of fishermen. The sacred Mount

Fuji is seen unperturbed in the distance. Some viewers, like the students who wrote the following responses, are exceptionally good at entering imaginatively into the world of a work of art—getting into the spirit, experiencing the emotions and thoughts called up by the work. Write your own imaginative response to one of the paintings in this section.

WRITING ABOUT LITERATURE

16 Seeing Symbols in Context
WRITING FOCUS: Reviewing Prewriting Techniques

A short poem is like a cricket; it rubs parts of its small body together to produce a sound that is magnified far above that of larger bodies and leaves a loud, chirping sound reverberating in the ears of a listener, saying, "I am small, but I am alive."

STUDENT PAPER

The Writing Workshop   When you write about symbolic meanings, you steer your course between two extremes. Some readers are too literal-minded. To them, water is always just water. A rose is a rose. They need to become more perceptive, more alert to possible symbolic overtones. Water, for instance, may become the symbol of spiritual regeneration in a wasteland of dried-up feeling, where a poet says: "In the desert of the heart / Let the healing fountain start" (W. H. Auden).

At the other extreme, some readers free-associate too freely, leaving the poem behind too soon. Unless you keep an eye on how a symbol works in the poem, anything may come to mean anything else. Look for reinforcement of possible symbolic meanings in the **context** of the poem as a whole. Green, a color that in one poem may symbolize envy, may in another poem be a symbol of growth, standing for the bright un-tamed vitality of nature. Ask yourself:

✘ Does a poem focus on *recurrent* elements with symbolic meanings? In Adrienne Rich's poem, "Aunt Jennifer's Tigers," the proud, unafraid tigers keep prancing and pacing throughout the poem.

✘ Does the poem play off symbolic elements against their *opposites,* the way Rich plays off the untamed tigers against the restraining heavy wedding band symbolizing an oppressive marriage?

✖ Does the poem *build up* to the poet's introduction of a central symbol?

Focus on Prewriting   The following might be part of your prewriting for a paper on Adrienne Rich's "Aunt Jennifer's Tigers."

Reading Notes   Here is a partial record of one student's close attention to key words and phrases:

"Aunt Jennifer's *tigers* prance across a screen"

> Rich uses the tigers to represent Aunt Jennifer's free and true spirit, that part of her which is suppressed by her marriage to Uncle. This symbol is close to Blake's "Tyger," which represents divine energy that animates all creation. In Rich, the tiger represents that same energy within Aunt Jennifer, and ultimately in all women. The tiger is feared but not despised. Its ferocity is tempered because of its feline, catlike grace that makes it seem both beautiful and terrible at the same time.

"Bright *topaz* denizens of a world of green
They pace in sleek *chivalric* certainty."

> The word *topaz* stands for a jewel, implying that the tigers are precious to the aunt. *Denizen* means "native inhabitant." These tigers are in their natural element, just as Aunt Jennifer wishes to be her true self. *Chivalric* seems to imply that like knights in armor the tigers are proud and sure in their role, not afraid of the men in their native territory.

"The *massive* weight of Uncle's *wedding band*
Sits *heavily* upon Aunt Jennifer's hand."

> The wedding ring, traditionally a symbol of love, honor, and protection, is transformed by words like *massive* and *heavily*. We get a mental picture of shackles and chains, not of wedding bells and love tokens.

Clustering   Clustering is a way of exploring the associations and connections of key words or concepts. In the more linear kind of free association, you jot ideas down more or less in the order in which they come to mind. Clustering instead allows you to branch out from a common core, pursuing different lines of association that soon form a web of meaning. Clustering is more suited to sketch possible *connections* than other kinds of brainstorming and prewriting.

Since many related associations tend to cluster around a central symbol, clustering may prove a good way to map the possible range of associations of a symbol that you mean to focus on in a paper. Here is one student's cluster of the key word *green*:

Here is the student's written results of the cluster:

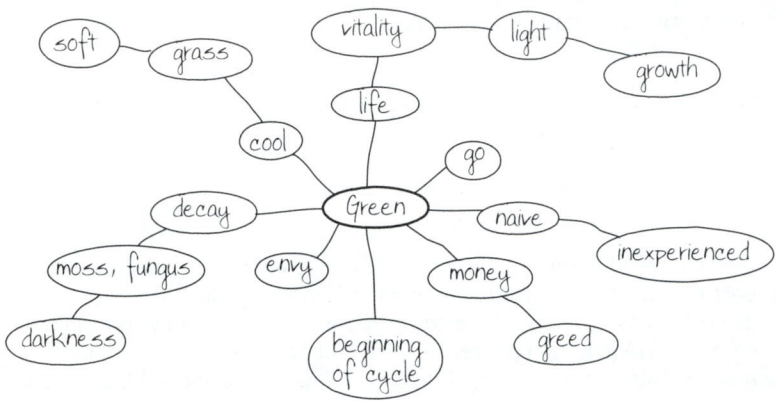

The word *green* has many positive associations; in fact, I listed all of my positive ones before the negative ones. Green makes us think of grass, rich in color, soft to the touch. Green vegetation signifies life—a plant thriving with water and sunlight. Plants are green at the beginning of their life cycle. (They fall into the "sear and yellow leaf" at the end—see *Macbeth*.) With this comes vitality. On the possibly negative side, green represents envy, as well as the greed associated with money. Green can be found in moss and fungus, a note of contrast with the green grass. Green, because of its use with unripe early vegetation, also represents inexperience (one who "just fell off the turnip truck"; one who is not street-smart).

Background Notes   The tiger poem is one of the poet's earlier poems (Rich wrote it while she was a student). She wrote about Aunt Jennifer "with deliberate detachment" as a woman of a different generation, keeping a "cool" distance. In hindsight, she realized that she was weaving into this poem a part of herself she did not yet fully understand or recognize—her own role as a woman in a man's world. One student writer found the following illuminating statement by the poet in a collection of her essays:

> In writing this poem, composed and apparently cool as it is, I thought I was creating a portrait of an imaginary woman. But this woman suffers from the opposition of her imagination, worked out in tapestry, and her life-style, "ringed with ordeals she was mastered by." It was important to me that Aunt Jennifer was a person as distinct from myself as possible—distanced by the formalism of the poem, by its objective, observant tone—even by putting the woman in a different generation.

On Lies, Secrets, and Silence, p. 40

A paper has a good chance of success when the writer at the beginning of the process of shaping and organizing has this kind of prewriting material at hand—a rich array of notes and tentative ideas to sort out and pull into shape.

Sample Student Paper

Tigers and Terrified Hands

"When Aunt is dead, her terrified hands will lie / Still ringed with ordeals she was mastered by. / The tigers in the panel that she made / Will go on prancing, proud and unafraid." So ends the lush and very focused poem "Aunt Jennifer's Tigers" by Adrienne Rich. With memorable symbolism, the poet illuminates the tragedy of a woman who has lived the greater part of her life as the subordinate member in an unbalanced marriage.

The tiger has been symbolically used many times, and readers may assume that the presence of a tiger represents evil or darkness. In this poem, however, the tigers have an entirely different symbolic meaning. Aunt Jennifer's tigers, those "topaz denizens of a world of green" (2) are the brilliant jewel-like embodiments of the faded shadows hiding in their creator's spirit. Their world of green, bursting with life, vitality, regeneration, receives its life-force from the crushed stirrings in Aunt Jennifer's defeated soul. Any shred of hope or victory or joy that somehow remains within her flows unconsciously through her fluttering fingers into the tapestry she so painfully sews. These wonderful tigers do not sidle or sneak or skulk; they stride "proud and unafraid" (12). With the natural confidence of knighthood, they "pace in sleek chivalric certainty" (4). And, perhaps most importantly, they "do not fear the men beneath the tree" (3). Aunt Jennifer stitches her defiance the only way she can, unconscious of her own vision.

Aunt Jennifer is the perfect foil for her creations, the gorgeous tigers. She is so fraught with anxiety, nervous confusion, exhausted resignation, fear, and defeat, that her fingers, which can only "flutter" through her wool (5), "find even the ivory needle hard to pull" (6). This shade of a woman is still weighed down by the "massive weight of Uncle's wedding band," which has doubtlessly drained her of any capacity for joy, celebration of life, or even peace. She is feeble, afraid, and "mastered." Even in death her "terrified hands will lie / Still ringed with ordeals she was mastered by" (9–10). She cannot escape the "ordeals" that were thrust upon her by her partner in marriage; the dominance and oppression that were her lot in marriage will always be part of who she was.

However, she has left a legacy. She has stitched a panel of glittering tigers that will "go on prancing, proud and unafraid" (12). Other women will come after Aunt Jennifer, and they may be inspired by her tigers to hold their heads up proudly and assume their rightful places as equals, rejecting any subordinate or humiliating roles. The tigers, often symbols of vitality, power, pride, fearlessness, here are those and more: They are the irrepressible human spirit and symbols of hope for woman's future.

The readers are not told of the particular ordeals in her marriage that defeated Aunt Jennifer. But they can make guesses and poke around for possibilities. The word *mastered* itself, used to describe Aunt Jennifer's situation, implies a "master." It is not a wild or unlikely conjecture that Aunt Jennifer's husband resembled other males who played the role of "master of the house," such as the poet's own father. Rich has said about her father: "After your death I met you again as the face of patriarchy, could name at last precisely the principle you embodied; there was an ideology at last which let me dispose of you, identify the suffering you caused, hate you righteously as part of a system, the kingdom of the fathers." Aunt Jennifer's husband, in the poet's mind, represents the traditional power of the male. And as one who has stated that "the search for justice and compassion is the great wellspring for poetry in our time," Rich is drawing from that wellspring in her poem "Aunt Jennifer's Tigers."

Questions For Peer Review

1. How does the initial quotation bring the two central interacting symbols in the poem into focus? What sentence in the introduction serves as the *thesis* spelling out the aunt's role in her marriage?

2. The body of the paper has a clear *plan;* it is laid out in accordance with a simple design. We look first at the tigers and their symbolic implications: What, according to this paper, do they symbolize? We then look at the symbolic meaning of the wedding ring: For what does it serve as a symbol? We then *return* to the tigers and look at them as the aunt's legacy: How does it point forward to the life of a future generation?

3. The flow of the paper owes much to *transitions* that point up an organic or dynamic rather than mechanical sequence. (The writer does not start major sections by saying, "The first symbol means . . ." and "The second symbol means . . .") What major links highlight logical connections between key sections of the paper?

4. Major paragraphs of this paper have a rich *texture* of brief quotations interwoven with explanation and interpretation. For instance, how does the writer spell out shades of meanings or overtones and associations when looking at the role key words like *prance* or *chivalric* play in the poem?

5. Having finished the close reading of the poem, the writer addresses a question in the minds of many readers: "What is the connection between this poem and the poet's own life?" How does the *conclusion* of the paper answer this question?

6. Where do you agree and where do you want to take issue with this writer?

17 WORDS

The Web of Language

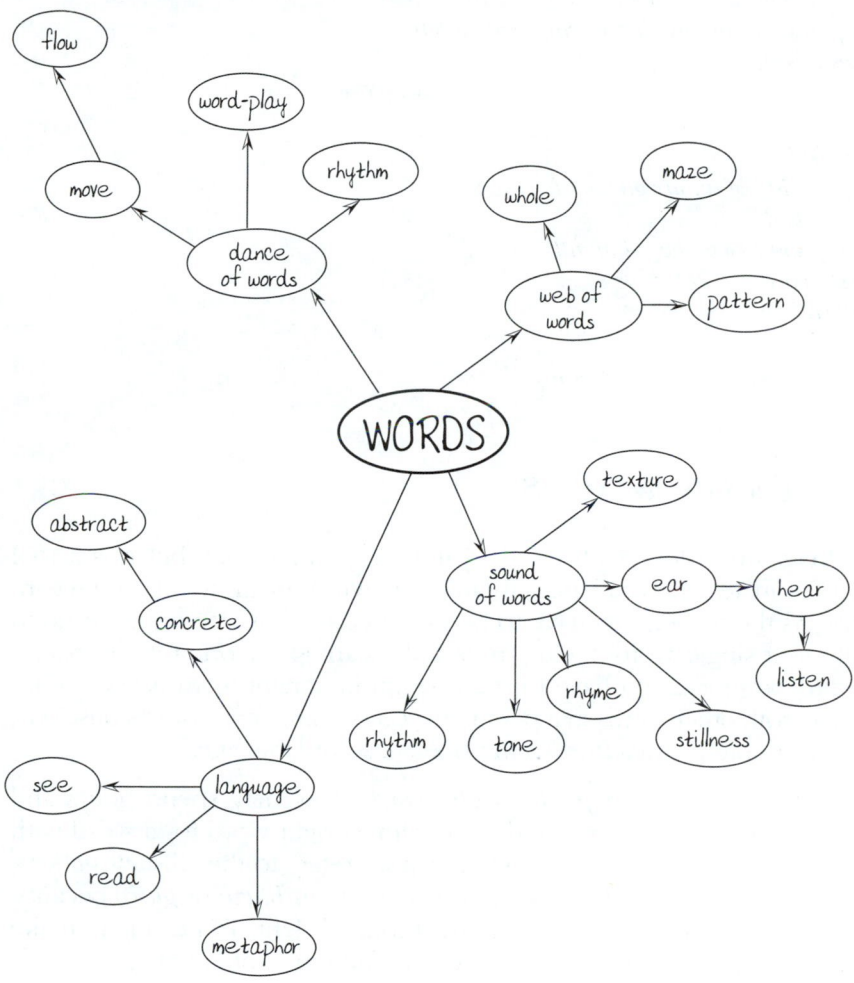

*Humans are animals suspended in webs of
significance they themselves have spun.*
CLIFFORD GEERTZ

*After many years as a writer, I find myself falling
in love with words. Maybe this is strange, like a
carpenter suddenly discovering how much he
likes wood.*
J. RUTH GENDLER

*Stripped
day by day of all my garments,
dry naked tree,
in my solitary withered mouth
fresh words
will still blossom*

ALAÍDE FOPPA, "WORDS"

FOCUS ON WORDS

Poets are in love with words. Language is their tool, but it is a tool that fascinates and challenges them. They wrestle with words and meanings. As the reader, you have to be prepared to slow down and respond fully to a single word, taking in its full meaning, savoring its overtones and associations. You have to see how an important word echoes or interacts with other words in a poem. As you become more word-conscious, you will note key features of the poet's use of language:

▮ *Poets are sticklers for the right word.* They may spend hours and days fine-tuning a poem—trading an almost-right word for a word with the exact shade of meaning. When a poet refers to the "distant glitter / of the January sun," *glitter* is a better word than *blaze* or *glare* because it is colder, more frigid, less blinding, though bright. To be able to make the right choices, poets use more of the full range of language than ordinary talk.

▮ *Poets have a keen ear for the emotional quality of words.* Language is alive with threat, warning, pleading, rejection, and regret. Words do not simply point—they point with pride; they point the finger. A *demagogue* was once literally a "leader of the people," but today we use the word to point the finger at a leader who leads the people by the nose. A *paramour* (a word using the French word for love) is more than an ordinary lover; medieval poets used the word for a lover cherished in defiance of society. We call the emotional overtones and attitudes that words carry the **connotations** of a word. We call the stripped-down, bare-fact meaning of a word its **denotation**. The following lines glow with the magic of words that have pleasing connotations—*slender, roses, music, blooms, flares, candles*—the more so since they are played off against the drab "grey streets":

> When I with you so wholly disappear
> into the mirror of your slender hand
> grey streets of the city grow roses
> and daisies, the music of flowers
> blooms in our voices, the eye of
> the grocer flares like a candle
> > Peter Meinke, "When I with You"

✖ *Poets have a keen ear for differences in tone.* When the opening lines of a poem set the **tone**, they establish the attitude that words suggest toward the subject or toward the reader. Many nineteenth-century poets cultivated a formal, solemn tone. For an elevated effect, they might use **archaic** language—language no longer in common use: *brethren* for *brothers, fain* or *lief* for *gladly,* and *ere* for *before. Thou, thy,* and *thine* were still current in Shakespeare's time, used in exchanges between people who, as we would say today, were on a first-name basis. ("Hamlet, thou hast thy father much offended," says Queen Gertrude to her son.) As these forms became archaic, poets used them to strike a solemn note: "Dust thou art, to dust returnest, / Was not spoken of the soul" (Henry Wadsworth Longfellow). At the other end of the scale, a poet may echo the folk speech of factory, pool hall, or down-home neighborhood. "We real cool" begins a famous poem by Gwendolyn Brooks.

✖ *Poets have a keen ear for the sound of words.* When words seem to sound out the sounds they describe, we call them **onomatopoeic**, or sound-mirroring, words. We hear a sound-mirroring effect in the hisssing of snakes, the buzzzing of bees, the rUMBLing of thunder, and the C-R-A-C-K of a whip. Although sound seldom echoes sense this closely, the right word in a poem is often a word that sounds right. When G. M. Hopkins says that "Generations have TROD, have TROD," we seem to hear the heavy, slow, monotonous tread of successive generations. The same poet asks us to imagine a plowshare being made shiny by the friction of the plowed-up earth as the plodding horse pulls the plow through the furrow: "sheer PLOD makes PLOW down sillion [furrow] / Shine." The repeated initial *pl-* sound (which seems to offer more resistance than a simple *l*), together with the sequence of single syllables that each seem to require almost equal stress, seems to slow down the reader. It attunes the reader's ear to the slow plodding movement the passage describes.

When we look at a poet's choice of words, we focus on the poet's diction. At times, prevailing fashion made poets adopt a special **poetic diction**, more refined or elegant than ordinary speech. Poets went out of their way to widen the distance between common language and the language of poetry. The deer hunted in the forest became the "beasts of chase" and the antlered trophies in the hunter's lodge became the "horny spoils that grace the walls." A phrase that takes the long way around, like *primary residence* for home, is called a **circumlocution**. In the eighteenth century, a fashionable poet might have called finches "members of the feathered tribe" or the plow "the plowman's humble tool." Modern poets tend to think of common language and poetic language as a continuum. The poet uses our common mother tongue, making us hear in poetry the echo of the natural human voice. But the poet makes fuller and better use of it, going beyond the limited register of everyday talk.

FIRST READING
What's in a Word?

When the author of the following poem records his observations of bathtubs, he chooses the right words to help us share in his feelings and reactions. Some words in the poem carry special freight—like the name of Marat, the fiery French revolutionary who was murdered in his bathtub by the counterrevolutionary Charlotte Corday in 1793.

Jeffrey Harrison   *(born 1957)*

Bathtubs, Three Varieties   *1988*

First the old-fashioned kind, standing on paws,
like a domesticated animal—
I once had a whole flock of these
(seven—for good luck? I never asked
the landlord) under a walnut tree   5
in my backyard, like sheep in shade.
They collected walnuts in the fall
then filled up with snow, like thickening wool.

Modern tubs are more like ancient tombs.
And it is a kind of death we ask for   10
in the bath. Nothing theatrical
like Marat with his arm hanging out—
just that the boundary between the body
and the world dissolve, that we forget
ourselves, and that the tub become   15
the sarcophagus of dreams.

My bathtub in Japan was square, and deep.
You sat cross-legged like a Zen
monk in meditation, up to your neck
in water always a little too hot,   20
relaxed and yet attentive to the moment
(relaxation as a discipline)—
staring through a rising cloud of steam
at the blank wall in front of you.

The Receptive Reader

1. When do you use the word *flock,* when the word *herd?*

2. What is the difference between a *tomb* and a *grave?* Is every performance in a theater by definition *theatrical?* What is the difference between a *sarcophagus* and an ordinary coffin? What is the difference between *meditation* and ordinary thinking?

3. Would you consider it weird to think of "relaxation as a discipline"? Why, or why not?

THE WILLING EAR

*I wanted to write poetry in the beginning because
I had fallen in love with words. The first poems I
knew were nursery rhymes, and before I could
read them for myself I had come to love them just
for the words of them, the words alone.*

DYLAN THOMAS

Although poems speak to the heart and the mind, they first of all please the ear. Words have a shape and texture of their own, and they combine in patterns that please (or grate upon) our ears. Children first fall in love with poetry because of its sound. (What is the meaning of "Hickory-dickory-dock / The mouse ran up the clock"?) The following poem makes us see the nighttime setting and share in night thoughts. However, it asks us first of all to relish the words and revel in the way they echo and play off one another in the poem. How should the poem sound when read aloud?

Reuel Denney   *(born 1913)*

Fixer of Midnight   *1961*

He went to fix the awning,
Fix the roping,
In the middle of the night,

On the porch;
He went to fix the awning,   5
In pajamas went to fix it,
Fix the awning,
In the middle of the moonlight,
On the porch;
He went to fix it yawning;   10
The yawning of this awning
In the moonlight
Was his problem of the night;
It was knocking,
And he went to fix its flight.   15
He went to meet the moonlight
In the porch-night
Where the awning was up dreaming
Dark and light.
It was shadowy and seeming;   20
In the night the unfixed awning,
In his nightmare,
Had been knocking dark and bright.
It seemed late
To stop it in its deep careening.   25
The yawner went to meet it,
Meet the awning,
By the noon of middle night,
On his porch;
And he went to fix it right.   30

The sounds in this poem echo and run together without a full stop until
the end. We can listen to the sound the way we can listen to the comings
and goings of the surf as it washes over rocks by the shore. However, even
with this poem, we do not just let the sounds wash over us. We delight in
the interplay of sound and meaning. We can imagine the wide open mouth
of the sleepy "yawner" as the words y-A-A-W-W-n-i-n-g and A-A-W-W-ning
echo through the poem. We can almost hear the "fixer" tip-toeing "in the
middle of the night." We seem to hear the repeated KNOCK-KNOCK-KNOCKING
of the careening awning echoing through the nightmare of the sleeper by
the moon of middle night.

The Receptive Reader

Listen to more than one classmate read this poem aloud. How close do they
come to how you think the poem is meant to sound?

When sound and sense intertwine as they do in "Fixer of Midnight,"
the sound seems to dance out the meaning. Sound echoes sense just as
strongly in the following poem, inspired by a painting by the sixteenth-
century Flemish painter Pieter Breughel. Breughel delighted in painting
down-to-earth scenes of rural life, showing the peasants cavorting at

weddings or at a country fair (the traditional Kermess). Look for the words that help you hear the sounds of the peasant music. Look for the words that help you see the peasants dance.

William Carlos Williams   *(1883–1963)*

The Dance   *1944*

In Breughel's great picture, The Kermess,
the dancers go round, they go round and
around, the squeal and the blare and the
tweedle of bagpipes, a bugle and fiddles
tipping their bellies (round as the thick-   5
sided glasses whose wash they impound)
their hips and their bellies off balance
to turn them. Kicking and rolling about
The Fair Grounds, swinging their butts, those
shanks must be sound to bear up under such   10
rollicking measures, prance as they dance
in Breughel's great picture, The Kermess.

Many of the words here seem exactly right for what they stand for. Blunt words like *bellies* (thick as the thick-sided glasses) and *butts* and *shanks* seem more right than would squeamish words when applied to the anatomy of these very physical, unpolished merrymakers. *Squeal* and *blare* and *tweedle* make us hear the rustic instruments (it's not the New York Philharmonic!). The word *squeal* seems to sound out the penetrating, high-pitched sound that pigs make when in distress; *tweedle* seems to tootle like a bagpipe that forever runs over the same limited range of sounds. The words for movements seem to roll and rollick just as the peasants do. *Prance* is indeed a prancing word, quite different from *slink* or *shuffle* or *slouch*. (To prance, we need room to high-step and half-lift our arms, proud of ourselves, feeling our oats.)

The Receptive Reader

1. Can you read this poem with the right rolling, rollicking rhythm? Can you read it so that your listeners can hear the underlying drumbeat of the peasant music? (Your class may want to audition several readings of this poem and vote for the best rendition.)

2. How would you describe a *blaring* sound? What is the difference between *violins* and *fiddles,* between *belly* and *abdomen?*

3. Where does the poet show that he is not *limited* to blunt down-to-earth language? What does the poet mean when he says the revelers "impound" the wash of their thick-sided glasses?

The Personal Response

What kind of readers would love this poem? What kind of readers might get little out of it?

What makes the following poem appeal to the ear as much as to the eye and the mind?

Al Young   *(born 1939)*

For Poets   *1968*

Stay beautiful
but dont stay down underground too long
Dont turn into a mole
or a worm
or a root   5
or a stone

Come on out into the sunlight
Breathe in trees
Knock out mountains
Commune with snakes   10
& be the very hero of birds

Dont forget to poke your head up
& blink
think
Walk all around   15
Swim upstream

Dont forget to fly

The Receptive Reader

1. How should this poem sound when read aloud? How does this poet use rhyme, repetition, and parallel phrasing? How do you think they should guide the reader?

2. Where does this poem go counter to what is conventional or expected? Where does a counter-rhythm seem to mirror the poet's determination to "swim upstream"?

Making Connections—For Discussion or Writing

Which of the poems in this group do you personally find most pleasing to the ear? Which least? Why?

THE RIGHT WORD

*A poet is, before anything else, a person who is
passionately in love with language.*

W. H. AUDEN

*I try to make each and every word carry its full
measure and not just its meaning defined.*

LUCILLE CLIFTON

*I have a lot to say,
but no words to use.
I have problems to release,
but no release valve.
HELP ME!*

> STUDENT POEM

Poets wrestle with both the sounds of words and their meanings. A short poem is a message that says much in little; the poet knows how to make every word count. Instead of three words that blur the point, a poet may find the one word that has the right shade of meaning. The following poem, though very short, has long been a favorite of readers:

William Carlos Williams   *(1883–1963)*

The Red Wheelbarrow   *1923*

so much depends
upon

a red wheel
barrow

glazed with rain   5
water

beside the white
chickens.

In a poem addressed to Williams and titled "So Much Depends," William Coles, a fellow poet, talked about "so many things / the rest of us would never / have seen except for you." How does rainwater look on a surface like that of the wheelbarrow? If we said the water "coated" the surface, the objection might be that often a coat covers up what is underneath. "*Glazed* with rain / water" is right because it means coated with a shiny, transparent cover not hiding what is underneath.

The Creative Dimension

Write your own "So much depends" passage or poem.

Poets have a range of vocabulary that enables them to make the right choices. The following poem stays close to the tangible details that make up firsthand experience. In much of this poem, the poet's language serves as a mirror of "what was there." Many of the words are specific, accurate words that give a faithful accounting of sights and events. (Others bring in striking imaginative comparisons, like the simile that compares the pink swim-bladder of the fish to a big peony.)

Elizabeth Bishop   *(1911–1979)*

The Fish   *1946*

I caught a tremendous fish
and held him beside the boat
half out of water, with my hook
fast in a corner of his mouth.
He didn't fight.   5
He hadn't fought at all.
He hung a grunting weight,
battered and venerable
and homely. Here and there
his brown skin hung in strips   10
like ancient wall-paper,
and its pattern of darker brown
was like wall-paper:
shapes like full-blown roses
stained and lost through age.   15
He was speckled with barnacles,
fine rosettes of lime,
and infested
with tiny white sea-lice,
and underneath two or three   20
rags of green weed hung down.
While his gills were breathing in
the terrible oxygen
—the frightening gills,
fresh and crisp with blood,   25
that can cut so badly—
I thought of the coarse white flesh
packed in like feathers,
the big bones and the little bones,
the dramatic red and blacks   30
of his shiny entrails,
and the pink swim-bladder

like a big peony.
I looked into his eyes
which were far larger than mine   35
but shallower, and yellowed,
the irises backed and packed
with tarnished tinfoil
seen through the lenses
of old scratched isinglass.°   *fish gelatin*   40
They shifted a little, but not
to return my stare.
—It was more like the tipping
of an object toward the light.
I admired his sullen face,   45
the mechanism of his jaw,
and then I saw
that from his lower lip
—if you would call it a lip—
grim, wet, and weapon-like,   50
hung five old pieces of fish-line,
or four and a wire leader
with the swivel still attached,
with all their five big hooks
grown firmly in his mouth.   55
A green line, frayed at the end
where he broke it, two heavier lines,
and a fine black thread
still crimped from the strain and snap
when it broke and he got away.   60
Like medals with their ribbons
frayed and wavering,
a five-haired beard of wisdom
trailing from his aching jaw.
I stared and stared   65
and victory filled up the little rented boat,
from the pool of bilge
where oil had spread a rainbow
around the rusted engine
to the bailer rusted orange,   70
the sun-cracked thwarts,
the oarlocks on their strings,
the gunnels—until everything
was rainbow, rainbow, rainbow!
And I let the fish go.   75

This poet has the language resources to do justice to the details that call the scene up before your eyes. She uses **specific** words—*barnacles, gills*—to call things by their right names. Many are **concrete** words that bring your senses into play, calling up for you things you can see, hear, or touch. (Can you visualize the fish "speckled with barnacles" and "infested with tiny white sea-lice"? the brown skin that "hung in strips"? Can you feel its "grunt-ing weight" as the fish hangs half out of water with a "hook / fast in the cor-ner of his mouth"?) Without the concrete words and without the striking similes—the "tarnished tinfoil" of the irises, the "beard of wisdom"—the poet could not make her readers share as completely in the experience she relives here.

The Receptive Reader

1. How familiar are you with the *special language* of boaters and anglers? What are thwarts, oarlocks, gunnels?

2. How and where does the speaker in the poem show her *feelings* about the fish? Which details make the fish seem near-human? Which remind you that it is a fish?

3. What was the *rainbow* that the speaker saw spreading in the bilge at the bottom of the boat?

4. Were you ready for the *ending?* Were you prepared for what happened in the last line of the poem? Why or why not?

The wording in a poem may be compressed, with much meaning packed into a compact phrase. For instance, in the following poem, the phrase "Fresh firecoal chestnut-falls" asks us to visualize chestnuts that have freshly fallen from the tree. They have split open their thick green covering on hitting the ground, revealing the intense reddish-brown of their skins. These seem to glow like coals on fire. This poem, in the words of one reader, is about "all the lovely dappled, alternating, changing and shifting things in the world" that come from God (J. R. Watson). The poem is by a nineteenth-century Catholic priest whose in-tense and difficult poetry remained unpublished in his lifetime, but who delighted twentieth-century readers with his bold, unconventional use of language.

Gerard Manley Hopkins   *(1844–1889)*

Pied Beauty   *1877*

Glory be to God for dappled things—
    For skies of couple-color as a brinded° cow;   *streaked, flecked*
        For rose-moles all in stipple upon trout that swim;
Fresh firecoal chestnut-falls; finches' wings;
    Landscape plotted and pieced—fold,° fallow, and plow;   *pasture* 5
        And áll trádes, their gear and tackle and trim.
All things counter, original, spare, strange;
    Whatever is fickle, freckled (who knows how?)
        With swift, slow; sweet, sour; adazzle, dim;
He fathers-forth whose beauty is past change: 10
        Praise him.

The poet draws on a range of words for the "pied beauty" that he loves—and that he prefers to whatever is too smooth, too simple, too much of one piece. The word *pied* itself means showing two or more colors in blotches or splotches, like the hide of a horse. Then we have *dappled, stipple, plotted* (for land laid out in small strips and plots that alternate pasture, land lying fallow, and land under the plow). We have *pieced* (together), *freckled*. All these words work together to show the poet's preference for what goes "counter" to boring smoothness and simplicity. The poet's vocabulary is rooted in common speech: A cow is a cow, and a finch a finch. *Plow, trade, gear,* and *tackle* are all part of our everyday vocabulary. However, the poet's language easily moves *beyond* common speech: With "swift, slow," we might expect "bright, dim" as a parallel pairing of opposites. However, the poet uses "*adazzle,* dim" instead—heightening the contrast, making it more dazzling.

The Receptive Reader

1. What in the *wording* of this poem is most difficult for you? What are skies of "couple-color"? What do you make of the compressed phrase "fathers-forth"?

2. How would the gear and tackle of different trades meet Hopkins' criteria of beauty? Can you give examples of what he might have had in mind? What, for you, would be examples of things "counter, original, spare, strange"?

3. Is it strange that an unchanging God would create beauty that is variable and made up of contradictory elements?

4. How does the language of this poem live up to the poet's own standard of what is beautiful?

The Personal Response

The poet Richard Wilbur calls this poem a "celebration of the rich and quirky particularity of all things whatever." Can you relate to this taste for the "quirky" and irregular, or do you prefer beauty that is smooth and harmonious?

Richard Wilbur

In the following excerpt, a twentieth-century poet probes the workings of Hopkins' rich and complex poem. What does he help you see in the poem that you might have missed in your own reading?

Reading Hopkins' "Pied Beauty"

God is praised first and last; but what lies between is very different. Hopkins does not give us an inventory of the creation; rather, he sets out to celebrate one kind of beauty—pied beauty, the beauty of things that are patchy, particolored, variegated. And in his tally of variegated things there is no hierarchy or other logic: his mind jumps, seemingly at random, from sky to trout to chestnuts to finches, and finally, by way of landscape, to the gear and tackle of the various trades. The poem sets out, then, to give scattered examples of a single class of things; and yet in its final effect this is a poem of universal praise. Why does it work out that way?

It works that way, for one thing, because of the randomness I just pointed out; when a catalogue has a random air, when it seems to have been assembled by chance, it implies a vast reservoir of other things that might just as well have been mentioned. In the second place, Hopkins's poem may begin with dappled things, but when we come to "gear and tackle and trim," the idea of variegation is far less clear, and seems to be yielding to that of character. When, in the next line, Hopkins thanks God for "All things counter, original, spare, strange," we feel the poem opening out toward the celebration of the rich and quirky particularity of all things whatever.

The great tug-of-war in Hopkins's poetry is between his joy in the intense selfhood and whatness of earthly things, and his feeling that all delights must be referred and sacrificed to God.

"Poetry and Happiness," in *Responses, Prose Pieces: 1953–1976,* 1976

In our response to a poem, much depends on the connotations—the feelings and attitudes—we read into key words. The following short poem makes us feel the contradictory emotions of first getting up in the morning:

Charles Simic   *(born 1938)*

Poem   *1971*

Every morning I forget how it is.
I watch the smoke mount
In great strides above the city.
I belong to no one.

Then, I remember my shoes,   5
How I have to put them on,
How, bending over to tie them up,
I will look into the earth.

As many readers read this poem, the central polarity in it opposes the sensation of looking up into the morning sky and feeling free ("I belong to no one") to the feeling of bending over to put on shoes, a move that brings us down to earth. The two key words at the opposite poles of this poem are *strides* and *earth. Stride* is a very different word from *slink, trudge,* or *shuffle* (let alone *crawl* or *creep*). When we stride, we walk with fresh energy and a sense of purpose, ready to meet the opportunities of the new day. *Earth* has the right connotations to convey the opposite feeling. Earth represents what is heavy, tied down, and grubby about our existence. It keeps us from soaring.

The Receptive Reader

1. *Earth* is a richly *connotative* word that has different associations in different contexts. What other connotations could the word have in other contexts? (Cluster the word to explore the personal meanings and associations it has for you.)

2. Some readers see the *polarity* in this poem differently. The first stanza to them has negative connotations. It makes them feel disconnected and lost, like the smoke that rises and dissipates, dooming them "to belong to no one." Could you argue in favor of this alternative reading? And do you think there is a way to read the second stanza positively—finding security and safety in our bonds to the earth?

The Personal Response

How well did the student who wrote the following response get into the spirit of the poem? How do *you* respond to the poem?

> Every morning I wake up like Charles Simic and forget how the city is. I watch the smoke mount in vaporous strides over city roof tops. In the morning, the smoke and I belong to no one. Then I remember that the hard lines of schedules wait for me to put my shoes on and walk those lines. How I hate putting them on; the bending stiffens me. I tie the leather on the stumps of my feet, locking myself to the earth.

JUXTAPOSITIONS

Cityscapes

In the following poems (written within ten years of each other), two English poets look at the city of London. However, they use language to steer the reader's reactions in very different directions. In reading these poems, explore especially the connotations of words—their emotional impact, overtones, and associations.

William Wordsworth   *(1770–1850)*

Composed upon Westminster Bridge, September 3, 1802   *1802*

Earth has not anything to show more fair:°   *more beautiful*
Dull would he be of soul who could pass by
A sight so touching in its majesty;
This City now doth, like a garment, wear
The beauty of the morning; silent, bare,   5
Ships, towers, domes, theaters, and temples lie

Open unto the fields, and to the sky;
All bright and glittering in the smokeless air.
Never did sun more beautifully steep
In his first splendor, valley, rock, or hill;   10
Never saw I, never felt, a calm so deep!
The river glideth at his own sweet will
Dear God! the very houses seem asleep;
And all that mighty heart is lying still!

The Receptive Reader

Explore the associations and overtones of the many connotative words in this poem. What would be missing from the poem if the poet had said, "Dull would he be of brain" rather than "of soul"? What if he had said, "doth, like a coat, wear" instead of "like a garment" wear? What makes the words *domes* and *temples* different from the word *churches?* What if the poet had said "With his first rays" rather than "In his first splendor"? What would be different if the poet had said at the end "that mighty nerve center" rather than "that mighty heart"?

William Blake   *(1757–1827)*

London   1794

I wander through each chartered° street,   *legally set up*
Near where the chartered Thames does flow,
And mark in every face I meet
Marks of weakness, marks of woe.
In every cry of every man,   5
In every Infant's cry of fear,
In every voice, in every ban,°   *announcement*
The mind-forged manacles I hear.

How the chimney-sweeper's cry
Every blackening church appalls;   10
And the hapless soldier's sigh
Runs in blood down Palace walls.

But most through midnight streets I hear
How the youthful Harlot's curse
Blasts the new-born Infant's tear,   15
And blights with plagues the Marriage hearse.

The Receptive Reader

1. What words most directly describe the speaker's *emotions* when contemplating a city with maimed or penniless veterans, young prostitutes, and soot-covered churches? What would be different if the poet had used "mind-made bonds" rather than "mind-forged manacles"? What would be missing in the last line if he had said "damages" rather than "blights"?

2. What gives *metaphors* like "Runs in blood down Palace walls" and the "Marriage hearse" their special force?

3. How would you pinpoint the difference in perspective between this and Wordsworth's poem?

The Personal Response

If you were to write out your feelings about one of today's cities, would your point of view be closer to Wordsworth's or to Blake's?

The Creative Dimension

Try your hand at a modern rewrite or update of one of these poems. How might a modern poet looking at the identical sights describe them—in what language?

THE LIMITS OF LANGUAGE

*The reader must not sit back and expect the poet
to do all the work.*

EDITH SITWELL

*Everything which opens out to us a new world is
bound to appear strange at first.*

EDITH SITWELL

Poets vary greatly in how far they will stretch the limits of language. Difficult but rewarding poets use language in original or intensely personal ways. First of all, the poet's vocabulary may include exotic gleanings brought back from excursions into ancient history, legend, or fabled places. The following poem delights readers who cherish words that, like rare coins, seldom see the light of common day.

John Masefield   *(1878–1967)*

Cargoes   *1902*

Quinquereme of Nineveh from distant Ophir,
Rowing home to haven in sunny Palestine,
With a cargo of ivory,
And apes and peacocks,
Sandalwood, cedarwood, and sweet white wine.   5

Stately Spanish galleon coming from the Isthmus,
Dipping through the Tropics by the palm-green shores,
With a cargo of diamonds,
Emeralds, amethysts,
Topazes, and cinnamon, and gold moidores.   10

Dirty British coaster with a salt-caked smoke-stack,
Butting through the Channel in the mad March days,

With a cargo of Tyne coal,
Road-rails, pig-lead,
Firewood, iron-ware, and cheap tin trays.   15

What is a quinquereme? The context of the poem tells us that it is an ancient ship being rowed to its home harbor, carrying rich exotic cargo. (Some
readers may remember the triremes of ancient Rome, with three banks of
galley slaves plying *three* levels of oars. The legendary ship in this poem then
would have *five* levels of oars.) Nineveh is clearly a city in ancient Palestine,
wealthy enough to outfit magnificent trading ships. (It is mentioned in the
Bible as a great city.) Ophir sounds like a legendary faraway city of great
wealth. (Poets mention it: "More than all of Ophir's gold / does the fleeting
second hold.")

The second of the three ships in this poem—the elaborately ornamented
Spanish galleon carrying rich loot from tropical Central America back to the
Old World—takes us closer to what we know about history and geography.
The "Isthmus" should be the isthmus of Panama—a thin strip of land that
kept ships from reaching the Pacific from the Caribbean until the Panama
Canal was built. We may not own emeralds, amethysts, and topazes, but we
can at least revel in the marvelous exotic names of these priceless gems. If
quinquereme has not sent us to the dictionary, *moidores* will. (The conquis-
tadores melted down the golden artifacts of Aztecs and Incas to make gold
coins—"money of gold" minted in Portugal and Brazil.)

By the third stanza, finally, we are within range of a more everyday vocabulary: The coal is from Newcastle-upon-Tyne. ("Carrying coals to New-
castle" was for a long time the equivalent of shipping hogs to Missouri.)

The Receptive Reader

1. One student reader called this poem a "three-sided prism," with each
stanza reflecting a different view of the cargo ships that since time immemorial
have plied the seas. How would you label the three different cargoes?

2. Which words in this poem are rich in *connotation*—in overtones or personal association—for you? For instance, what ideas or feelings do words like
Palestine, ivory, peacock, galleon, or *emerald* bring to mind?

The Range of Interpretation

Where do you stand on the issue raised in the following excerpt from a student paper about this poem? What in the poem helps you make up your mind
one way or the other?

> The last stanza is particularly intriguing in its contrast with the other two.
> The "dirty British coaster" brings us forward in time to the grimy industrial
> age. The sooty words and leaden cargo describe a harshly realistic working
> vessel, whereas the other two ships were romanticized, idealized, and seen
> through a nostalgic haze. We could easily argue that the harshness of the
> final stanza gives us a negative view of the modern world. We get a glimpse
> here of the sordid materialism of our age.
>
> However, we might easily argue the opposite as well. If the poet had cast
> the same realistic eye on the past as he did on the present, he might have

picked slave ships or cattle boats, quite common in the ancient days, or he might have shown us the chained galley slaves rowing the splendid ancient ship. The dirty British coaster then would not come off so badly after all. In any case, Masefield suggests strength and power and working muscle in his description of the coaster "butting" stubbornly through the English Channel in ugly weather. This ship carries no glittering body from "palm-green shores." It is a workaday mule of the seas. Its cargo represents the everyday needs served by the economy of an industrial nation. We should not look down on it but accept it as part of living everyday reality.

Poets may not only extend the reaches of language but also use language resources in provocative, creative ways. Some of the poets most admired by modern readers test the boundaries of language. They may use words that combine familiar building blocks in strange new patterns. They may employ strange telescopings or foreshortenings. The following poem shows the wordplay and wrenchings of normal word order that we expect to find in the tense religious poetry of Gerard Manley Hopkins. The poem centers on the dove as a familiar symbol of peace. But here the bird is a "wild wooddove," shyly "roaming" around the poet. As a wild bird of the forest, it is hard to entice it to settle down with the speaker in the poem, who would, like a tree, spread for it protective "boughs."

Gerard Manley Hopkins   *(1844–1889)*

Peace   *1887*

When will you ever, Peace, wild wooddove, shy wings shut,
Your round me roaming end, and under be my boughs?
When, when, Peace, will you, Peace? I'll not play hypocrite
To own my heart: I yield° you do come sometimes; but   *I admit*
That piecemeal peace is poor peace. What pure peace allows   5
Alarms of wars, the daunting wars, the death of it?

O surely, reaving° Peace, my Lord should leave in lieu   *taking away*
Some good! And so he does leave Patience exquisite,
That plumes° to Peace thereafter. And when Peace does   *spreads plumage*
    here house
He comes with work to do, he does not come to coo,   10
       He comes to brood and sit.

Where does the text of the poem run counter to what you are prepared to read? What changes does the poet ring on the central word *peace*?

The phrase "Your round me roaming end" would normally be "end your roaming around me." The poet's reordering of the words pulls the key word out for emphasis: "Your ROUND me roaming end" (the bird keeps away, roaming *around* the speaker). At the same time, the reshuffling sets up a strong counter-pull or counter-rhythm (part of what the poet called **sprung rhythm**). The result is a jostling effect in keeping with the restless, "peaceless" feelings of someone whose strong faith has yet left him strangely restless, with only "sometimes" a feeling of inner peace. The poet uses two **puns** to keep the word *peace* ringing in our ears. We use a pun when we play on the different meanings of words that sound or look alike. We want *peace* that is all of a *piece*. Instead, we get *piecemeal* peace that comes in small unsatisfactory pieces. That makes the peace we obtain *poor* peace when what we desire is *pure* peace. As one student reader said, "Hopkins must make his own peace with the piecemeal bits of faith that come to him."

The Receptive Reader

1. Could you argue that the changed *word order* in "under be my boughs" and "To own my heart" also pulls a key word to the front of a phrase?

2. What does the *metaphor* make you visualize when the poet says that patience "plumes to Peace thereafter"?

3. What kind of *work* does the poet seem to have in mind at the end? (What kind of brooding is productive rather than counterproductive?)

In the following poem, the English Romantic poet John Keats moves beyond everyday language to create a rich overlay of associations taking us beyond the ordinary. He compares his awe and excitement at discovering Chapman's sixteenth-century translation of Homer's *Iliad* to the excitement the Spanish conquerors of Mexico must have felt when they first saw the Pacific Ocean from Darien in Panama. Which words are unfamiliar or difficult for you? Which would you have to check in a dictionary?

John Keats   *(1795–1821)*

On First Looking into Chapman's Homer   *1816*

Much have I traveled in the realms of gold,
    And many goodly states and kingdoms seen;
    Round many western islands have I been
Which bards in fealty to Apollo hold.
Oft of one wide expanse had I been told   5
    That deep-browed Homer ruled as his demesne;
    Yet did I never breathe its pure serene
Till I heard Chapman speak out loud and bold:
Then felt I like some watcher of the skies
    When a new planet swims into his ken;   10
Or like stout Cortez when with eagle eyes
    He stared at the Pacific—and all his men
Looked at each other with a wild surmise—
    Silent, upon a peak in Darien.

The Receptive Reader

1. Each of the following is a simpler or more familiar word for a richer, *more connotative* word used by the poet Parentheses enclose the overtones or associations added by the word Keats actually chose in the poem. Which word in the poem matches each of the following? (ancient, venerable) kingdom; (ancient, honored) poets; loyalty (to a feudal medieval overlord); (brilliant, divine) patron of poetry; (a lord's) lands; expanse (of calm, pure sky or sea); (sharply perceived) field of vision.

2. What features make you recognize this poem as a *sonnet?* Where is its turning point? Can you argue that the poem follows a cumulative or climactic order?

Dylan Thomas, a Welsh poet, often seems impatient with plodding ordinary language, leaping ahead instead to make new connections. One reader said of him that he "strips from words their old, dull, used sleepiness, and gives them a refreshed and awakened meaning." Read the following poem the first time without puzzling over difficult phrases. Allow yourself to be carried along by the chanting rhythm. Then go back over the poem, trying to see connections and meanings in his plays on words and in his strange telescopings or juxtapositions. (Fern Hill is the name of a farm that Thomas' uncle and aunt rented as tenant farmers.)

Dylan Thomas   *(1914–1953)*

Fern Hill   *1946*

Now as I was young and easy under the apple boughs
About the lilting house and happy as the grass was green,
    The night above the dingle° starry,   *wooded valley*
      Time let me hail and climb
    Golden in the heydays of his eyes,   5
And honored among wagons I was prince of the apple towns
And once below a time I lordly had the trees and leaves
      Trail with daisies and barley
    Down the rivers of the windfall light.

And as I was green and carefree, famous among the barns   10
About the happy yard and singing as the farm was home,
    In the sun that is young once only,
      Time let me play and be
    Golden in the mercy of his means,
And green and golden I was huntsman and herdsman, the calves   15
Sang to my horn, the foxes on the hills barked clear and cold,
      And the sabbath rang slowly
    In the pebbles of the holy streams.

All the sun long it was running, it was lovely, the hay
Fields high as the house, the tunes from the chimneys, it was air   20
    And playing, lovely and watery

      And fire green as grass
   And nightly under the simple stars
As I rode to sleep the owls were bearing the farm away,
All the moon long I heard, blessed among stables, the night-jars°   *night birds*   25
      Flying with the ricks,° and the horses   *haystacks*
         Flashing into the dark.

And then to awake, and the farm, like a wanderer white
With the dew, come back, the cock on his shoulder: it was all
      Shining, it was Adam and maiden,   30
            The sky gathered again
      And the sun grew round that very day.
So it must have been after the birth of the simple light
In the first, spinning place, the spellbound horses walking warm
      Out of the whinnying green stable   35
         On to the fields of praise.

And honored among foxes and pheasants by the gay house
Under the new made clouds and happy as the heart was long,
      In the sun born over and over,
            I ran my heedless ways,   40
      My wishes raced through the house high hay
And nothing I cared, at my sky blue trades, that time allows
In all his tuneful turning so few and such morning songs
      Before the children green and golden
            Follow him out of grace,   45

Nothing I cared, in the lamb white days, that time would take me
Up to the swallow thronged loft by the shadow of my hand,
      In the moon that is always rising,
            Nor that riding to sleep
      I should hear him fly with the high fields   50
And wake to the farm forever fled from the childless land,
Oh as I was young and easy in the mercy of his means,
            Time held me green and dying
      Though I sang in my chains like the sea.

The Receptive Reader

1. Try to puzzle out possible connections that explain telescoped phrases or strange juxtapositions in the early stanzas. For instance, what could have been "lilting" about the house? How did the child "hail and climb golden" in the heydays of Time? How was he "prince of the apple towns"? What is the connection between light and "rivers" and a "windfall"? Why in this poem is the sun "young once only"?

2. What is the *symbolic* meaning of the colors "green and golden," whose names echo through this poem?

3. What are key *images* and prevailing feelings in the poet's account of the first days after Creation? What is borrowed from and what is different from the account in Genesis?

4. What are the "chains" at the conclusion of the poem? Assuming the words are not meant literally, in what sense did Time hold the child "green and dying"?

Making Connections—For Discussion or Writing

Gerard Manley Hopkins' "Pied Beauty," William Wordsworth's "Composed upon Westminster Bridge," and Dylan Thomas' "Fern Hill" each project a vision of what is beautiful in the world in which we live. What is different or unique in each poet's vision? Is there a common thread?

For a time, observers of language habits assumed that radio, television, and cheap paperbacks would average out regional differences. However, recent years have seen a renewed pride in traditional **dialects**, which help their speakers assert a regional identity separate from that promoted by a central government and official national language. Dialects are regional variations of a common language that are still mutually intelligible—but some are actually on the borderline of becoming separate languages. How much do you understand of the Scots, or Scottish dialect, in the following lines?

Hugh MacDiarmid   *(1892–1978)*

Weep and Wail No More   *1948*

Stop killin' the deid. Gi'e owre
Your weepin' and wailin'.
   You maun keep quiet
If you want to hear them still
And no' blur their image in your mind.   5

For they've only a faint wee whisperin' voice
Makin' nae mair noise ava'
Than the growin' of the grass
That flourishes whaur naebody walks.

POEMS FOR FURTHER STUDY

In reading the following poems, pay special attention to the poet's word choice, or diction. Which poems seem especially pleasing to the ear? Where does the sound of words seem to mirror sense? Which words seem particularly accurate or fitting? Which seem to have just the right connotations, overtones, or associations? Where does the poet seem to stretch the limits of language?

Mark Strand   *(born 1934)*

The End   1990

Not every man knows what he shall sing at the end,
Watching the pier as the ship sails away, or what it will seem like
When he's held by the sea's roar, motionless, there at the end,
Or what he shall hope for once it is clear that he'll never go back.

When the time has passed to prune the rose or caress the cat,   5
When the sunset torching the lawn and the full moon icing it down
No longer appear, not every man knows what he'll discover instead.
When the weight of the past leans against nothing, and the sky

Is no more than remembered light, and the stories of cirrus
And cumulus come to a close, and all the birds are suspended in flight,   10
Not every man knows what is waiting for him, or what he shall sing
When the ship he is on slips into darkness, there at the end.

The Receptive Reader

1. What repetitions of words and patterns help set up the rhythm of this poem? Is repetition in this poem merely pleasing to the ear, or does it serve to highlight or to emphasize?

2. What are the metaphorical meanings of the song, the ship, and the sea in this poem? (Would you have used different metaphors for a similar situation?)

The Creative Dimension

In looking back over life, why did the poet select the details that become most vivid in this poem? What details would *you* have selected? Write a poem or prose passage featuring sights and sounds you are likely to remember "at the end."

Margaret Atwood   *(born 1939)*

Dreams of the Animals   1970

Mostly the animals dream
of other animals   each
according to its kind

       (though certain mice and small rodents
        have nightmares of a huge pink   5
       shape with five claws descending)

: moles dream of darkness and delicate
mole smells

frogs dream of green and golden
frogs   10
sparkling like wet suns
among the lilies

red and black
striped fish, their eyes open
have red and black striped
dreams   defense, attack, meaningful   15
patterns

birds dream of territories
enclosed by singing.

Sometimes the animals dream of evil   20
in the form of soap and metal
but mostly the animals dream
of other animals.

There are exceptions:

    the silver fox in the roadside zoo   25
    dreams of digging out
    and of baby foxes, their necks bitten

    the caged armadillo
    near the train
    station, which runs   30
    all day in figure eights
    its piglet feet pattering,
    no longer dreams
    but is insane when waking;

    the iguana   35
    in the petshop window on St. Catherine Street
    crested, royal-eyed, ruling
    its kingdom of water-dish and sawdust

    dreams of sawdust

The Receptive Reader

1. What are the usual associations of the animals in this poem? How does the poem transform these associations or leave them behind? Look at the words that cluster around the names of the animals here. Which of the words have positive connotations, showing the poet's empathy or fellow-feeling? (Which of these words are especially *unusual* or unexpected?)

2. In this poem, what is the difference between the animals in the wild and those in captivity? What words especially drive home the contrast between the animals in the wild and their caged cousins?

The Personal Response

Disney cartoons have often made animals seem cute, harmless, and lovable. Disney wildlife films, however, have often taken an uncompromisingly honest look at life in the wild. Does Atwood make animals seem too lovable and human?

Gerard Manley Hopkins   *(1844–1889)*

The Windhover   *1877*

To Christ Our Lord

I caught this morning morning's minion,° king-   *beloved*
    dom of daylight's dauphin,° dapple-dawn-drawn   *crown prince*
      Falcon, in his riding
    Of the rolling level underneath him steady air, and striding
High there, how he rung upon the rein of a wimpling° wing.   *rippling*
In his ecstasy! then off, off forth on swing,   5
    As a skate's heel sweeps smooth on a bow-bend: the hurl
      and gliding
    Rebuffed the big wind. My heart in hiding
Stirred for a bird,—the achieve of, the mastery of the thing!

Brute beauty and valor and act, oh, air, pride, plume here
    Buckle! AND the fire that breaks from thee then, a billion   10
Times told lovelier, more dangerous, O my chevalier!°.   *knight*

    No wonder of it: shéer plód makes plow down sillion°   *furrow*
Shine, and black-blue embers, ah my dear,
    Fall, gall themselves, and gash gold-vermilion.

The Receptive Reader

1. Several of the words Hopkins applies to the falcon and to Christ suggest the glamor and pageantry of chivalry: a *minion* is a cherished, beloved court favorite; the *Dauphin* was the crown prince of medieval France; a *chevalier* is a knight who represents the chivalric virtues (*chevalier* and *chivalry* come from the same root). Where in the poem does Hopkins spell out the *connotations* that these words suggest?

2. When the poet celebrates the masterful, ecstatic flight of the falcon, what do *concrete* words like *riding, striding, sweep, hurl,* and *gliding* add to the meaning of the generic term *fly?* (What does each make you visualize? What associations or feelings does it carry with it?) What makes *rebuff* different from *resist?*

3. In the pivotal word *buckle,* not only do the inspiring qualities of the falcon "come together" or are welded together (as the two ends of a belt are buckled or fastened). The two parts of the poem also meet: the splendor of God's creation and the billionfold "lovelier, more dangerous" splendor of "Our Lord." How do the two concluding images in the last three lines of the poem mirror the relationship between the "brute" creature and its creator?

4. In addition to the end rhyme that is traditional in a sonnet like this one, Hopkins uses **alliteration**—the repetition of the same sound at the beginning of several words in the same line ("this MORNing MORNing's MINion"). The telescoped phrase "dapple-dawn-drawn" allows the poet to complete the alliteration started by "DAylight's DAUphin." How would you spell out the meaning of the telescoped phrase in more ordinary language?

The Range of Interpretation

According to a recent introduction to Hopkins' poetry, some critics "have seen the poem as one of frustration and sadness." The poem is "concerned with the unbridgeable distance between the hawk, flying so freely and beautifully, and the poet, whose heart is 'in hiding'; the heart is hidden away as if afraid, locked up by the severe discipline of the priesthood and the demands of self-sacrifice which it makes." To other readers, the poem "does not seem to be a poem of frustration so much as a poem of enthusiasm and exultation. . . . The excitement is conveyed in the way in which the heart, while it may have been 'in hiding,' that is inactive, now 'Stirred for a bird'; as if the heart moved and leaped at the sight of the hawk" (J. R. Watson, *The Poetry of Gerard Manley Hopkins*). Which of these two interpretations would you be inclined to support? (What do *you* make of the phrase "my heart in hiding"?)

Wole Soyinka   *(born 1934)*

Nobel Prize winner Wole Soyinka—playwright, poet, and novelist—is one of the African writers best known in the West. After the end of British colonial rule, his native Nigeria went through a phase of tribal conflict, with an unsuccessful war of secession fought by the Ibo. Soyinka, a Yoruba, wrote some of his poems while imprisoned during the civil war. He has written with biting satire about discrimination based on color and about the political maneuverings of leaders, whether in the Western imperialist, the Eastern socialist, or the Third World camp.

Lost Tribe   1988

Ants disturbed by every passing tread,
The wandering tribe still scurries round
In search of lost community. Love by rote,
Care by inscription. Incantations without magic.
Straws outstretched to suck at every passing broth,   5
Incessant tongues pretend to a way of thought—
Where language mints are private franchise,
The coins prove counterfeit on open markets.

Hard-sell pharmacies dispense all social pills:
"Have a nice day now." "Touch someone."   10
There's premium on the verb imperative—some
Instant fame psychologist pronounced it on TV—
He's now forgotten like tomorrow's guru,
Instant cult, disposable as paper diaper—
Firm commands denote sincerity;   15
The wish is wishy-washy, lacks "contact
Positive." The waiter barks: "Enjoy your meal,"
Or crisper still "Enjoy!" You feel you'd better!
Buses, subway, park seats push the gospel,
Slogans like tickertapes emblazon foreheads—   20

"Talk it over with someone—now, not later!"
"Take down fences, not mend them."
"Give a nice smile to someone." But, a tear-duct
Variant: "Have you hugged your child today?"

The Receptive Reader

1. Soyinka has a marvelous quick ear for how language reveals (or betrays) who we are. How does this poem show him to be a good listener?

2. What has happened to the magic of language according to this poem? Who or what is to blame?

3. This poem is rich in provocative metaphor. What are the figurative meanings of the ants, the straws, the coins, the pharmacies, the paper diaper? Look at the lines referring to the tickertapes and to the tear ducts. Can you translate what they say into more ordinary language? What is the difference between the ordinary-language version and the poet's use of language?

4. To judge from the poet's examples, what is the imperative form of a verb? What kind of question concludes the poem?

5. In what sense were the original lost tribes of Israel lost, and what use does the poem make of this biblical allusion?

The Personal Response

Do you share the poet's allergy to the kind of language he focuses on in this poem? Can you think of other examples? Is there something to be said in defense of this kind of language?

John Heaviside

A Gathering of Deafs   1989

By the turnstiles
in the station
where the L train greets
the downtown six
a congregation of deafs   5
passes forth
jive wild
and purely physical
in a world dislocated
from the subway howling   10
hard sole shoe stampede
punk rock blasted radio
screaming, pounding, honking
they gather in community
engaging   15
in a dexterous conversation

An Old Women
of her dead husband tells

caressing the air
wrinkled fingers   20
the story
delicate, mellifluous motion
she places gentle configurations
before the faces of the group

A young Puerto Rican   25
describes a fight with his mother
emphasizing each word
abrupt, staccato movements
jerking his elbows
and twisting his wrists
teeth clenched   30
lips pressed
the story concludes
a fist into his palm

By the news stand   35
two lovers
stroke the air
syllables
graceful and slow
their joining   40
the flow
of fingertips

The Receptive Reader

1. In this student-written poem, what is right about words like *congregation, jive, community, dexterous, configuration?* How effective or expressive are the words setting up the contrast between the punk rock and the silent conversation of the deaf?

2. What is the difference between *mellifluous* and *staccato?* What words clustering around each of these help a reader unfamiliar with them?

3. What statement is the student poet making about the sign language of the deaf?

WRITING ABOUT LITERATURE

17 Reading for Connotations
WRITING FOCUS: Marshaling the Evidence

The Writing Workshop   When studying a poem rich in connotative language, you will be paying special attention to emotional overtones and implied attitudes. How do emotionally charged words steer the reactions of the reader? (Remember that dictionaries tend to concentrate on the denotations of words, though they may include hints on possible connotations.)

✗ *You may want to start by defining your key term.* You may want to get the subject of connotative language clearly into focus, using brief, striking illustrations.

✗ *Show that you have read carefully for implications.* Show that you have gone through the poem line by line, paying special attention to key words or to recurrent words that echo in the poem.

The following are connotative words from John Heaviside's "A Gathering of Deafs." They don't just describe or point—they suggest attitudes and feelings:

CONGREGATION: A congregation might just technically mean a group of parishioners assembling for services and supporting their local church. But it often means more than that—a group united by feelings of fellowship and perhaps loyalty to or support for their spiritual leader or shepherd of the flock.

COMMUNITY: Newspapers might call anything from a neighborhood to a small town a community—a group of people living together sharing public services. But people invoking the spirit of community often mean something more—people united by an emotional attachment and a sense of responsibility, striving together for a better life. The word is often used as an inspirational term, not just a sociological term.

FINGERTIPS: Anatomically, these are just literally the tips of the fingers. But they connote the ability to touch something not crudely or aggressively but with sensitivity—just with the tips of the fingers as if to explore it or so as not to hurt it.

✗ *Do not take words out of context.* Is a word part of a network of similar or related terms? Are its associations or implications reinforced by what goes with it in the poem? Or are unusual associations negated or overruled by other words that strongly affect the tone or emotional quality of the poem?

✗ *Work out a clear overall plan.* For instance, you may want to follow the overall pattern of the poem. (Is there perhaps an initial set of words with very similar connotations but then a turning, with the poem moving in a different or opposed direction?) Or you may sort out different kinds of connotative language or different effects of connotative language on the reader.

Study the model student paper examining connotative language in a poem. How carefully has the writer read the poem? What use does she make of evidence from the poem? Are any of the connotations she traces private or personal rather than widely shared associations? How convincing are her conclusions?

Sample Student Paper

Connotative Language: Harrison's Three Bathtubs

Dictionary meanings are usually denotative meanings; they give us exact, objective, limited definitions. When words take us beyond objective labeling to expand our associations, when they carry an overlay of emotional association, they have connotative meaning. For example, the word *house* denotes a structure with walls, floors, ceilings, and doors, and including bedrooms and a kitchen; *house* does not have the emotional overlay that the word *home* suggests. *Home* may recall the warmth of a featherbed in winter or the smell of newly mown grass in summer. It suggests a place that provides security and protection, an anchor in an uncertain world.

Connotative meanings may be personal and private. Abigail may be a beautiful name to many, but if we have known an Abigail who was cross and domineering, the word will have unpleasant associations for us. To work for the poet, a word must usually have more broadly shared layers of meaning. When Romeo calls Juliet's balcony the east and Juliet the sun, we know he is suggesting that, like the rising sun, Juliet is new, fresh, bright, warm, and central in his life.

In Jeffrey Harrison's "Bathtubs, Three Varieties," the poet relies on both the denotative and connotative meanings of words. In three stanzas, he describes three kinds of bathtubs: "an old-fashioned kind," "modern tubs," and his "bathtub in Japan." He does not flatly state his preference for one kind of bathtub over another, but if we focus on his word choices and the connotations of certain words, we may conclude that he does indeed have a preference.

In the first stanza, the speaker in the poem surprises us with not one but seven old-fashioned tubs under a walnut tree in his backyard. Parenthetically, he adds that he has not asked his landlord why they are there, but he associates seven with "good luck." Interior decorators call old-fashioned tubs claw-footed or lion-footed, but the speaker chooses to see this kind of tub as standing on "paws, / like a domesticated animal." Unlike lions' claws, paws are nonthreatening and connote the softness of a cat's paws. Another reference to a domesticated animal, tame and trusting, reinforces this kind of feeling: Seven of these tubs make a "whole flock" of "sheep in shade"; the connotation here is of a gathering of domesticated animals in a pleasant, pastoral scene. When cold weather comes, the tubs fill with snow—normally cold and forbidding, but here compared to the thickening wool of the sheep; thus the snow sounds paradoxically warm and protecting. Earlier, the tubs were collecting walnuts, reminding us of the rich bounty of harvest time.

The second stanza, on modern tubs, presents a startling contrast. Here we have tubs "like ancient tombs," a bath that is a "kind of death," and a tub that becomes a "sarcophagus," or massive stone coffin. Our tub death is not even "theatrical," like the dramatic death in the French painter David's portrait of Marat, the French revolutionary hero stabbed in his bath.

In the third stanza, we find ourselves in a Japanese tub described as "square"—without the welcoming comfort of a circular or oval shape. We do not stretch out in this tub but sit "cross-legged like a Zen monk in meditation." We sit up to our necks in deep water "always a little too hot." We hear an echo here of the expressions "up to our necks in something" and "being in hot water," both of which have negative implications. This is a strange mixture of relaxation with "discipline," as we find ourselves staring "at the blank wall." This tub sounds uninviting for any but those stoic people who like a strenuous life.

For me, at least, the tubs in the first stanza suggest memories of peaceful contentment. There is something bleak and forbidding about the modern tomblike tub. And it would probably take special training in Zen to maintain the half-relaxed, half-disciplined attitude proper to the over-hot, steamy Japanese variety.

Questions for Peer Review

The student author of this paper did a careful "word-for-word" reading of the poem. Did the paper make you see associations and connotations that you missed or overlooked?

1. How and how successfully does the student writer explain the difference between shared or *public* as against personal or *private* connotations?

2. Where or how does the writer show that the poet's use of language can change or go counter to *familiar* associations?

3. Where or how does the student writer show that *clusters* of words with similar or related associations may help steer our feelings or attitudes in the direction intended by the poet?

4. Which of the connotations the student writer traces seem widely shared and convincing to you? Do any seem *doubtful* or very personal—bringing in private associations of the writer?

5. Would you personally react to the three bathtubs in the same way or differently? Do you *agree* with the three different kinds of outlook or emotional environment the student writer set up? Or would you modify the overall scheme? How or why? Would your preference be similar or different?

6. Have you found yourself in different settings or living arrangements where just the style of your surroundings put you in a different frame of mind or made you feel like a different person?

18 FORM

Rhyme, Meter, and Stanza

Courtesy Richard B. Ressman

*Remember: Our deepest perceptions are a waste
if we have no sense of form.*

THEODORE ROETHKE

*Let chaos storm!
Let cloud shapes swarm!
I wait for form.*

ROBERT FROST, "PERTINAX"

FOCUS ON FORM

Poetry today moves between the poles of traditional form and the **open form** that became second nature to many modern poets. Traditional form is shaped by features like rhyme, meter, and stanza. Open form in varying degrees modifies or abandons these, allowing the poet to give each poem its own unique pattern and rhythm. Poets long wrote strongly metrical lines of verse, regularizing the natural rhythms of language: "With HOW / sad STEPS / O MOON / thou CLIMB'ST / the SKIES" (Sir Philip Sidney). Often such lines were linked by rhyme: SKIES/TRIES. Poems were often arranged in stanzas, or sets of lines, of similar shape. When handled mechanically, these traditional formal features make a poem jingle, lulling us to sleep rather than sharpening our attention. However, for first-rate poets, traditional form has been a challenge, stimulating their imagination and creative abilities.

To read with an alert eye and attentive ear, you need to respond to formal features like the following:

❚ *Poets exploit our delight in the echo effects of language.* In the following poem, Ogden Nash, the heavyweight of light verse, uses traditional **end rhyme:** BLIND/KIND. He adds some internal rhyme (rhyme words in the *same* line) for good measure: PLUCK and LUCK. Traditionally, rhyme helps mark off lines. However, it also has a bonding effect by linking two or more lines in a poem.

Ogden Nash   *(1902–1971)*

The Hunter   1949

The hunter crouches in his BLIND
'Neath camouflage of every KIND,
And conjures up a quacking NOISE
To lend allure to his decOYS.
This grown-up man, with PLUCK and LUCK,   5
Is hoping to outwit a DUCK.

✕ *Poets build on the natural rhythms of language.* Some syllables are stressed or accentuated in ordinary speech: deᴘᴀʀᴛ, ᴀᴄᴄident, interroɢᴀtion. By laying words and phrases with the same stress pattern end to end, poets set up the drumbeat of **meter**. Meter is exceptionally regular in the following opening lines of a Shakespeare sonnet:

That tíme | of yéar | thou máyst | in mé | behóld
When yél|low léaves, | or nóne, | or féw, | do háng
Upón | those bóughs | which sháke | agáinst | the cóld.

Remember that meter provides the *underlying* beat, over which the actual lines may play variations:

Lét me nót | to the márriage | of trúe mínds
Admít impédiments.

✕ *Poets appeal to our delight in recurrent patterns.* Traditionally, poets have often broken up a poem into **stanzas**—sets of lines following a similar pattern. Sometimes, each stanza replicates, or repeats, an elaborate rhyme scheme, with perhaps the same alternation of shorter and longer lines. Even in the following lighthearted example, each stanza uses rhyme the same way. In the first two stanzas, there is a similar alternation of a two-beat and a three-beat line.

Gwendolyn Brooks   *(1917–2000)*

Old Mary   1960

My last defense
Is the present tense.

It little hurts me to know
I shall not go

Cathedral-hunting in Spain   5
Nor cherrying in Michigan or Maine.

FIRST READING
Song and Poem

At one time, most poetry was sung or chanted. Song and poem had not yet parted company. We can still see rhyme, meter, and stanza at work in song lyrics and in poems that have a songlike quality. What role do they play in the following song lyrics?

American Folk Song   *(Anonymous)*

Black Is the Color   traditional

Black, black, black is the color of my true love's hair.
His lips are something wond'rous fair,
The purest eyes and the fairest hands,
I love the ground whereon he stands.
Black, black, black is the color of my true love's hair.   5

I love my love and well he knows
I love the ground whereon he goes.
And if my love no more I see,
My life would quickly fade away.
Black, black, black is the color of my true love's hair.   10

The Receptive Reader

1. What is haunting or appealing about the opening line that comes back twice as the refrain in this poem? What other line is repeated in slightly different form? (Why isn't this other line repeated exactly?)

2. There is much repetition in this poem. Does the poem nevertheless move on or go forward? From what to what?

3. In our culture, do you expect love lyrics to be written and sung by the male rather than the female lover? Does this folk song seem different in this respect? Why or why not?

The Creative Dimension

Some traditional cultures have open-ended songs that allow members of a group to improvise additional verses. You and your classmates may want to make up additional stanzas for this folk song. How close can you come to the rhythm and rhyme scheme of the original?

RHYME, ALLITERATION, FREE VERSE

Like meter, rhyme is a highly formal device. It is a
signal that language is going to be used in an
unusual, often a serious and memorable,
way. . . . Because it is out of the ordinary, rhyme
attracts our attention and prepares us for a
completely organized and unusually expressive
language.

KARL SHAPIRO

Why **rhyme?** Rhyme bonds two or more lines by final syllables that start out differently but end alike. Children—and adults who have kept children's gift for enjoying elementary pleasures—delight in the echo effects of rhyme: "Celery, RAW / Develops the JAW / But celery, STEWED / Is more quietly CHEWED" (Ogden Nash). Beyond this simple pleasure, as elementary as the pleasure of hopping and skipping, rhyme serves as the most visible sign that the poem we are reading has a shape, a pattern. It is going to be more patterned, more ordered, than ordinary disjointed experience.

Rhyme helps the poet measure off lengths of verse; it sets up recurrent points of rest. It thus helps set up a basic rhythm, as different from disjointed chatter as purposeful walking is from scurrying hither and yon. At the same time, rhyme has a bonding effect, giving a sense of continuity, of meaningful forward movement. This effect of pulling things together or keeping them headed in the same direction is especially strong with **multiple rhymes**—more than two lines rhyming—as in the following opening lines of a Bob Dylan song:

Darkness at the break of noon	a
Shadows even the silver spoon	a
The handmade blade, the child's balloon	a
Eclipses both the sun and moon	a
To understand you know too soon,	a
There is no sense in trying.	b

Bob Dylan, "It's Alright Ma (I'm Only Bleeding)"

Rhymes that are too predictable (*love/dove*) make a poem sound slight and pat. At the opposite extreme, far-fetched or forced rhymes can have a humorous effect—sometimes unintentional but often, as in the last two lines of the following excerpt, intentional:

I shall be sweet and crafty, soft and sly;
You will not catch me reading any more:
I shall be called a wife to pattern by;
And some day when you knock and push the door,
Some sane day, not too bright and not too stormy,
I shall be gone, and you may whistle for me.

Edna St. Vincent Millay, "Oh, Oh, You Will Be Sorry for That Word!"

In the eighteenth century, when prevailing fashion encouraged the tidy packaging of ideas, rhyme helped seal off sets of two rhyming lines in self-contained **closed couplets**. In the following poem, rhyme helps the poet frame snapshots of city sights in two neatly boxed lines. Most of the couplets give us a capsule portrait of one of the city people—from the apprentice cleaning up the employer's premises to the prison turnkey letting out his jailbirds at night for most irregular purposes.

Jonathan Swift   *(1667–1745)*

A Description of the Morning   *1709*

Now hardly here and there a hackney-coach	a
Appearing, showed the ruddy morn's approach.	a
Now Betty from her master's bed had flown,	b
And softly stole to discompose her own;	b
The slip-shod 'prentice from his master's door	c 5
Had pared the dirt and sprinkled round the floor.	c
Now Moll had whirled her mop with dexterous airs,	d
Prepared to scrub the entry and the stairs.	d
The youth with broomy stumps began to trace	e
The kennel-edge, where wheels had worn the place.	e 10
The small-coal man was heard with cadence deep,	f
Till drowned in shriller notes of chimney-sweep:	f
Duns at his lordship's gate began to meet;	g
And brickdust Moll had screamed through half the street.	g
The turnkey now his flock returning sees,	h 15
Duly let out a-nights to steal for fees:	h
The watchful bailiffs take their silent stand,	i
And schoolboys lag with satchels in their hands.	i

The Receptive Reader

1. Which of the *couplets* strike you as exceptionally neatly packaged?

2. Swift had a sharp *satirical* eye. What are some of the seedier sights you see in this poem? (What are duns, and why is their appearance at the lord's gate one of Swift's satirical touches?) Do the more positive elements in this "description of the morning" counterbalance the negative ones?

The Creative Dimension

Eighteenth-century writers delighted in using the closed couplet to sum up a striking thought in pointed, quotable form. You are likely to appreciate the polish and sparkle of these couplets more if you have tried your hand at a few of them. See how close you can come to the form and spirit of the original couplets.

ORIGINAL: Good nature and good sense must ever join;
To err is human; to forgive, divine.
Alexander Pope, "Essay on Criticism"

SAMPLE IMITATION: Use witty sayings once, and then no more—
First time, it's wit; the second time, a bore.

Later poets moved away from neatly packaged rhymed couplets. We see fewer boxed-in lines where rhyme signals "end of a sentence, end of a line." Instead, we see spillovers where the unfinished sense pulls us over into the next line. Then the sentence may end halfway through the next line, causing a strong break *within* rather than *between* lines. Critics call the spillover from one line to the next **enjambment**. They call the strong break *within* a line a **caesura** (literally, a "cut" that divides the line). The straddling effect of enjambment partly counteracts the segmenting effect of rhyme. It sometimes helps weave a long series of lines into a kind of verse paragraph. In the following lines by the English Romantic poet Percy Bysshe Shelley, notice the spillover at the ends of the second and third lines and the strong break in the third:

> We are as clouds that veil the midnight moon;
> How restlessly they speed, and gleam, and quiver, →
> Streaking the darkness radiantly! | | Yet soon →
> Night closes round, and they are lost forever.
>
> > "Mutability"

Like songbirds, rhymes are easier to listen to and enjoy than to classify. Rhyme-watchers note variations from the simple *love/dove, moon/soon* pattern:

✖ Most rhymes are **end rhymes**, marking off a line of verse. **Internal rhymes** multiply the echo effect of rhyme *within* a line:

> All is SEARED with trade; BLEARED, SMEARED with toil.
> > Gerard Manley Hopkins, "God's Grandeur"

✖ Most common are **single** (or **masculine**) **rhymes**—single-syllable rhymes. Only the opening consonant (or consonant cluster) varies, while the rest of the syllable stays the same: *high/sky, leave/grieve, stone/own.* **Double (feminine) rhymes** match two-syllable words (or parts of words), with the first syllable stressed and the second unstressed: *ocean/motion, started/parted, (re)peated/(de)feated.* More unusual are **triple rhymes**—three-syllable rhymes, with stress on the first of the three (*beautiful/dutiful*). The following stanza uses all three kinds of rhyme:

Now Donna Inez had, with all her merit,	a	double
A great opinion of her own good qualities;	b	triple
Neglect, indeed, requires a saint to bear it,	a	double
And such, indeed, she was in her moralities;	b	triple
But then she had a devil of a spirit,	a	double
And sometimes mixed up fancies with realities,	b	triple
And let few opportunities escape	c	single
Of getting her liege lord into a scrape.	c	single

> > Lord Byron, "Don Juan"

✘ In the stanza from "Don Juan," the double rhymes are actually only **half-rhymes**, since the vowel sounds in the first syllables of *merit—bear it—spirit* are only similar, not alike. Byron here uses them tongue-in-cheek. However, for poets who found traditional rhyme too predictable, such **slant rhymes** were a step toward a greater range of choice. In the following poem, which rhymes are slant rhymes?

Emily Dickinson   *(1830–1886)*

The Soul selects her own Society   *about 1862*

The Soul selects her own Society—
Then—shuts the Door—
To her divine Majority—
Present no more—

Unmoved—she notes the Chariots—pausing   5
At her low Gate—
Unmoved—an Emperor be kneeling
Upon her Mat—

I've known her—from an ample nation—
Choose One—   10
Then—close the Valves of her attention—
Like Stone—

The Receptive Reader

1. Which are conventional *full* rhymes? Which are slant rhymes?
2. A literal *paraphrase* of this poem might run like this:

The human soul chooses friends or soulmates carefully and then shuts out any others, allowing no one else to join in. It will not be moved by others humbly asking to be admitted. I have known her to select only one from a large group and then pay absolutely no attention to anyone else.

How do the metaphors in the poem go beyond this bare-bones paraphrase? What do they make you see? What do they make you feel? What do they make you think?

✘ When only the internal vowel sounds of final syllables are similar or alike, the result is **assonance**, again a more distant echo than full rhyme. Assonance is a partial sound echo, as in *break/fade* or *mice/fight*.

✘ **Alliteration**, an echo effect that was once a key feature of poetry, is still active in popular speech: "safe and sound," "spick and span," "kit and caboodle." Alliteration was the precursor and the opposite of end rhyme. Traditionally, three or more stressed syllables in a line *started* with the same sound: "A wonder on the wave—water turned bone" (from a riddle whose answer is "ice"). The words that alliterated started either with the same consonant or else with any vowel. The earliest recorded poems in English used an alliterating four-beat line, approximated in the following modernized passage:

> Leave ṢORROW aṢIDE / for it ṢEEMS more WISE
> To ḞIGHT for a ḞRIEND / than to ḞRET and MOURN.
> We ᴀLL in the ᴇND / go ᴏUT of this WORLD.
> Let us ḎO great ḎEEDS / before ḎEATH TAKES us.
> That is ᴮEST for the ᴮRAVE / who are ᴮORN to DIE.
>   From *Beowulf*

In later times, partial alliteration—not following a regular pattern and perhaps stretching over more than a line—has enriched the texture of both rhymed and unrhymed verse. Shakespeare at times uses alliteration to accentuate the highly individualized rhythm of his sonnets. Look for the repetition of initial consonants in the following example:

William Shakespeare   *(1564–1616)*

Sonnet 30   *before 1598*

When to the sessions of sweet silent thought		
I summon up remembrance of things past,		
I sigh the lack of many a thing I sought,		
And with old woes new wail° my dear time's waste:	*newly mourn*	
Then can I drown an eye (unused to flow)		5
For precious friends hid in death's dateless° night,	*endless*	
And weep afresh love's long since canceled woe,		
And moan the expense° of many a vanished sight,	*the loss*	
Then can I grieve at grievances foregone,°	*griefs long past*	
And heavily from woe to woe tell o'er°	*tell over again*	10
The sad account of fore-bemoaned moan,		
Which I new pay as if not paid before.		
But if the while I think on thee, dear friend,		
All losses are restored and sorrows end.		

The Receptive Reader

1. Look at the repetition of the initial *s* in the first three lines. In reading the poem aloud, how much would you make the alliterating syllables stand out?

WHEN to | the <u>SESS</u> | ions of | <u>SWEET SI</u> | lent THOUGHT

I <u>SUMM</u> | on UP | reMEM | brance of | things PAST,

I <u>SIGH</u> | the LACK | of MAN | y a THING | I <u>SOUGHT</u>.

2. How many other examples of repeated initial consonants can you find? How important are the alliterating words in the poem?

3. Where is the *turning point* in this sonnet? How does the poem lead up to it?

During the last century, rhyme became increasingly optional. Today, some poets rely on rhyme; many more don't. Some use it when it suits their purpose. Instead of making every line, or every second line, rhyme, they may use rhyme, if at all, at irregular intervals. The decline of rhyme, together with the appeal of rhythms freer and more variable than traditional meter, made possible the rise of **free verse**—poetry less governed by formal conventions—as the dominant mode of poetry.

JUXTAPOSITIONS

The Role of Rhyme

Do you find yourself shifting gears, so to speak, when reading the following three passages aloud? Point out any examples of full rhyme, single and double rhyme, half-rhyme, internal rhyme, assonance, or alliteration.

1. Durable bird pulls interminable worm,
   Coiled in subterranean caverns;
   Feeds on fossils of ferns and monsters.

       Beatrice Janosco, "To a Tidelands Oil Pump"

2. Last night I saw the savage world
   And heard the blood beat up the stair;
   The fox's bark, the owl's shrewd pounce,
   The crying creatures—all were there,
   And men in bed with love and fear.

       Elizabeth Jennings, "Song for a Birth or a Death"

3. I bring fresh showers for the thirsting flowers,
   From the seas and the streams;
   I bear light shade for the leaves when laid
   In their noonday dreams.
   From my wings are shaken the dews that waken
   The sweet buds every one,
   When rocked to rest on their mother's breast,
   As she dances about the sun.

       Percy Bysshe Shelley, "The Cloud"

RHYTHM AND METER

*Poetry is oral; it is not words, but words
performed. . . . the "real" poem is not the
scratches on the paper, but the sounds those
scratches stand for.*

JUDSON JEROME

*In a poem, the words charm the ear as much as
what is said charms the mind.*

WILLIAM J. MARTZ

*The line will have the more charm for not being
mechanically straight. We enjoy the straight
crookedness of a good walking stick.*

ROBERT FROST

Poetry is rhythmic, like breathing, walking, dancing. When the rhythm of successive lines is regular enough to become predictable, we call it meter. **Meter** regularizes the natural rhythms of speech. The poet enters into a metrical contract with the reader, setting up an underlying recurring beat over which the actual poem plays variations. The meter is the steadying beat of the metronome over which longer and shorter notes dance out the actual music of the verse.

In natural speech, **stress** (or accent) makes us raise our voices slightly and makes us seem to linger over the accented syllable. Stress makes one syllable stand out in words like reMAIN and dePART; or LISten and SUMMon; or PEDigree and destiNATion. It makes words (or stressed parts of words) stand out in phrases like "in the WOODS," "under the SUN," or "have to aGREE." In poems employing traditional meter, the stressed syllables set up a regular beat, as in the opening lines of the Beatles song:

PICture yourSELF on a BOAT in a RIVer,
With TANgerine TREES and MARmalade SKIES,
SOMEbody CALLS you, you ANSwer quite SLOWly,
A GIRL with kaLEIdoscope EYES.

"Lucy in the Sky with Diamonds"

Meter is rhythm regular enough to be charted, or *scanned*. Scanning charts the underlying beat and its variations, the way a cardiogram charts the heartbeat and any irregularities. In the actual poem, of course, meter is not noted or transcribed as part of the written text; we need to listen for it with the inner ear. To make meter visible, we can use a special notation for stressed and unstressed syllables: a sharp accent (ˊ) for strong stress; a flat accent (ˋ) for weaker stress; no mark (or often a small half-circle resting on its curved side) for an unstressed syllable.

Read the following short poem first with exaggerated emphasis on the underlying beat ("The WAY a CROW / Shook DOWN on ME"). Then try to read it with enough variation in the *degree* of stress to bring your reading closer to the natural rhythms of speech. Note weaker or secondary stress alternating with strong stress in the first two lines:

Robert Frost   *(1874–1963)*

Dust of Snow   *1923*

The wày a crów
Shook dówn on mè
The dúst of snów
From a hémlock trée

                                                                                              5

Has gíven my héart
A chánge of móod
And sáved some párt
Of a dáy I had rúed.°   *viewed with regret*

The basic unit of our metrical currency is the **foot**—one stressed syllable with one or more unstressed ones. Several feet together make up a line of verse. The Frost poem uses an unusually short line with only two feet: the dúst | of snów. The traditional line of verse most commonly used is a four-beat or five-beat line; in other words, it is made up of four or five feet:

Wórds are | like léaves; | and whére | they móst | abóund,
Much frúit | of sénse | benéath | is ráre | ly fóund.

                                    Alexander Pope, "Essay on Criticism"

Different stress patterns account for different kinds of meter:

iambic | Detroit—Detroit—Detroit
trochaic | boston—boston—boston
anapestic | New Rochelle—New Rochelle—New Rochelle
dactylic | baltimore—baltimore—baltimore

✘ The most common meter of English poetry has been **iambic**—a "one-TWO | one-TWO | one-TWO" rhythm akin to the rhythm of walking. The iamb is a foot made up of two syllables, with the stressed one last: Detroit—Detroit—Detroit—Detroit. (The Greek name originally labeled a lame-footed person, whose gimpy gait made one foot come down harder than the other.) The following lines set up a prevailing iambic beat. Notice that words spill over from one foot to the next, preventing the meter from cutting the lines mechanically like slices of cheese:

I képt | my áns | wers smáll | and képt | them néar;
Big qués | tions brúised | my mínd | but stíll | I lét

Small áns | wers bé | a búl | wark tò | my féar.

Elizabeth Jennings, "Answers"

✖ The first line in the Pope couplet shows a common reversal (or **inversion**): "WORDS are | like leaves . . . " The stress has shifted to the first syllable; the result is a **trochaic** foot, or trochee, on the "BOSTON— BOSTON—BOSTON" model. A line of trochaic feet changes the metrical pattern from "clip-CLOP | clip-CLOP | clip-CLOP" to "CLIP-clop | CLIP-clop | CLIP-clop." Poems with an underlying trochaic beat throughout are rare. The most common assignment of the trochaic foot is to bring variation into a prevailing iambic pattern. A trochaic foot, starting out strong, can serve as an attention-getter. (Is it only an accident that in Pope's couplet the most important word—namely *Words*—is pulled to the front of the first line by trochaic inversion?)

Here is an example of a predominantly trochaic poem. In reading this poem aloud, can you make the listener aware of the trochaic pattern—without making it sound mechanical?

Percy Bysshe Shelley   *(1792–1822)*

To ———   *1824*

Músic, | whèn soft | vóices | díe,	trochaic
Víbrates | in the | mémo | rý.	trochaic
Ódors, | whèn sweet | víolets | sícken,	trochaic
Líve with | ìn the | sénse they | quícken.	trochaic
Róse leaves, | whèn the | róse is | déad,	trochaic
Are héaped | fòr the | belóv | ed's béd.	iambic
And só | thy thóughts, | when thóu | art góne,	iambic
Lóve it | sélf shall | slúmber | ón.	trochaic

✖ A third kind of foot may also serve as a bit player introducing variation into an iambic line. The **anapest** doubles up two unstressed syllables to lead up to the third and stressed syllable, on the "New ROCHELLE— New ROCHELLE—New ROCHELLE" model. The added unstressed syllable can have a "hurry UP—hurry UP—hurry UP" effect. A predominantly anapestic line would look like this:

But his wíngs | *will not* rést | *and his* féet | *will not* stáy | for us.

Algernon Charles Swinburne, "At Parting"

More common is anapestic variation in an otherwise iambic line:

The wóods | *are pre*pár | *ing to* waít | out wínter.
Gusts blów | *with an* éarn | *est of* áll | there ís | *to be* dóne

Charles Tomlinson, "The View"

❖ A fourth kind of foot, reversing the pattern of the anapest, is nearly extinct in English. The **dactyl** doubles up two unstressed syllables after a stressed one, on the "BALtimore—BALtimore—BALtimore" model. A hundred years ago, a large popular audience read dactylic verse like the following. Listen for the doubling up of the unstressed syllables in Longfellow's six-beat line:

Thís *is the* | fórest *prim* | éval; *but* | whére *are the* | héarts *that*
  be | néath it
Léaped *like the* | róe, *when he* | héars *in the* | wóodland *the* | vóice
  of the | húntsman?

Henry Wadsworth Longfellow, "Evangeline"

❖ The **spondee** is a variation that can strongly emphasize *part* of a line. It is *all* emphasis—it juxtaposes *two* stressed syllables, slowing down the reader. (This is the way many people pronounce HONG KONG.) A spondee often follows or comes before a set of two *un*stressed syllables, so that the total number of beats in a line need not change. The following are the opening lines of a sonnet John Milton wrote in 1655 about his blindness. The spondee in the second line propels us into the world of darkness in which he already lived when he dictated his most ambitious poems:

When I | consíd | er hòw | my líght | is spént
Ere hálf | my dáys | *in this* | DARK WORLD | and wíde . . .

Even in verse that is alive with variations and pauses, exceptionally regular lines may help maintain the underlying beat. Meter is the combined product of the chosen kind of foot multiplied by the *number* of feet per line. To label kinds of meter, we identify the kind of foot (iambic or trochaic, for instance) and then show the number of feet (for instance, pentameter—a five-beat line). Here are the Greek names we still use for lines of different length:

five-beat line	pentameter
four-beat line	tetrameter
three-beat line	trimeter
six-beat line	hexameter

❖ The five-beat line is by far the most common, whether rhymed as in the sonnet, or unrhymed as in the **blank verse** of Shakespeare's plays. As the pentagon is a building with five sides, so **pentameter** is a meter with five stressed syllables to the line. A five-foot line using predominantly iambic feet is in iambic pentameter. The iambic pentameter line often sounds natural and unforced; it seems to stay close to the natural speech patterns of English:

By dáy the bát is cóusin tò the móuse.
He líkes the áttic òf an áging hóuse.

Theodore Roethke

▮ Three-beat or four-beat lines make up many songs and songlike poems. As a trilogy is a set of three books (or plays), so **trimeter** is meter with three stressed syllables to the line. **Tetrameter** is meter with four stressed syllables to the line. In folk song and ballad, tetrameter and trimeter often alternate in a four-line stanza:

They líghted dówn to táke a drínk	tetrameter
Of the spríng that rán so cléar,	trimeter
And dówn the spríng ran his góod heart's blóod,	tetrameter
And sóre she begán to féar.	trimeter
"Hold úp, hold úp, Lord Wílliam," she sáys,	tetrameter
"For I féar that yòu are sláin."	trimeter
"'Tis nóthing but the shádow of my scárlet clóak,	tetrameter
That shínes in the wáter so pláin."	trimeter

Anonymous, "The Douglas Tragedy"

▮ A six-beat line, or **hexameter**, was the line of Homer's epics. In the following lines, as often with hexameter, a slight break, marked here by a slash, divides the long lines into half-lines. How would you read these lines?

I would that we were, my beloved, / white birds on the foam of the
    sea!
We tire of the flame of the meteor, / before it can fade and flee;
And the flame of the blue star of twilight, / hung low on the rim of
    the sky,
Has awaked in our hearts, my beloved, / a sadness that may not die.

William Butler Yeats, "The White Birds"

When poetry started to break loose from traditional meter, poets like Walt Whitman for a time wrote poems with irregular length of line and with a harder-to-chart but nevertheless strongly felt rhythm. In most of the free-flowing, irregular **free verse** of the twentieth century, the rhythmic beat was less pronounced. Commenting on long-prevailing critical trends, one recent observer said, "the cooler the voice, the warmer the reception" (Alicia Ostriker). The following poem is in its own way insistent and cumulative, but its beat does not become chanting. (The opening lines allude to the beginning of a sonnet by William Wordsworth: "The world is too much with us.")

Denise Levertov   *(born 1923)*

O Taste and See   1962

The world is
not with us enough.
O taste and see

the subway Bible poster said,
meaning The Lord, meaning   5
if anything all that lives
to the imagination's tongue,

grief, mercy, language,
tangerine, weather, to
breathe them, bite,   10
savor, chew, swallow, transform
into our flesh our
deaths, crossing the street, plum, quince,
living in the orchard and being

hungry, and plucking   15
the fruit.

The Receptive Reader

1. How noticeable should the *line breaks* be when the poem is read aloud?

2. This poem owes its insistent rhythm in part to its repeated use of a *series*—several items of the same kind, separated by commas and juxtaposed in a sequence that allows us to dwell briefly on each. Which series can you identify? Which string together items that are clearly related? Which contain items that seem oddly matched?

3. How is what the speaker in the poem says about the imagination analogous to what the Bible poster said about God?

4. How does the poem as a whole lead up to the last few lines?

JUXTAPOSITIONS

The Matter of Meter

In reading the following passages aloud, how do you have to shift gears to do justice to the different kinds of meter? What is the dominant meter in each of the passages as a whole or in individual lines? What variations are there?

1. Double, double, toil and trouble;
   Fire burn and cauldron bubble.

   Shakespeare, *Macbeth*

2. My wife and I lived all alone,
   contention was our only bone.
   I fought with her, she fought with me,
   and things went on right merrily.

   > Robert Creeley, "Ballad of the
   > Despairing Husband"

3. It was many and many a year ago,
   In a kingdom by the sea,
   That a maiden there lived whom you may know
   By the name of Annabel Lee.

   > Edgar Allan Poe, "Annabel Lee"

4. But yesterday the word of Caesar might
   Have stood against the world. Now lies he here,
   And none so poor to do him reverence.

   > Shakespeare, *Julius Caesar*

5. Poplars are standing there still as death.

   > Arna Bontemps, "Southern Mansion"

TRADITIONAL STANZA FORM

Scorn not the sonnet: Critic, you have frowned
Mindless of its just honors; with this key
Shakespeare unlocked his heart.

WILLIAM WORDSWORTH

Much traditional poetry is laid out in **stanzas**—sets of lines similar in shape. Traditional stanzas may repeat the same rhyme scheme, as if programmed to make lines rhyme according to the same formula. They may show the same alternation of longer and shorter lines, making lines expand or contract in the same sequence. As each stanza leads us through the familiar established pattern, we experience the pleasure of recognition.

Familiar stanza form harks back to a time when the history of song and poem was still one. We expect a songlike poem to have stanzas the way we expect a song to have successive verses, all sung to the same melody. Some of the golden moments in Shakespeare's comedies come when the jester and assorted revelers take time out to sing haunting, bitter-sweet songs of innocent young love, simple country life, or cruel death. Look at the rhyme scheme that is shared by both stanzas in each of the following songs. Look at how the final lines of the stanza come back as a **refrain** in the second song:

William Shakespeare   *(1564–1616)*

O Mistress Mine   1602

O mistress mine, where are you roaming?	a
O, stay and hear; your true love's coming	a
That can sing both high and low.	b
Trip no further, pretty sweeting,	c
Journeys end in lovers meeting,	c 5
Every wise man's son doth know.	b

What is love? 'Tis not hereafter;
Present mirth hath present laughter;
What's to come is still unsure.
In delay there lies no plenty;   10
Then come kiss me, sweet and twenty,
Youth's a stuff will not endure.

Under the Greenwood Tree   1599

Under the greenwood tree	a
Who loves to lie with me,	a
And turn his merry note	b
Unto the sweet bird's throat,	b
Come hither, come hither, come hither!	c 5
Here shall he see	a
No enemy	a
But winter and rough weather.	c

Who doth ambition shun,
And loves to live in the sun,   10
Seeking the food he eats,
And pleased with what he gets,
Come hither, come hither, come hither!
Here shall he see
No enemy   15
But winter and rough weather.

                     From *As You Like It*

The Receptive Reader

The repetition of an interlaced, intertwining rhyme scheme and variation in sentence length help make the two stanzas in each song parallel. In each song, what is the pattern of the stanza?

Making Connections—For Discussion or Writing

Do you know any current popular songs that are in form and content in some way similar to these Shakespearean songs? Do you know any that are strikingly different? Compare or contrast the lyrics of one or several current favorites with these Shakespeare lyrics.

Refrains come back and drive home a prevailing mood or idea in other songlike poems—the **popular ballads**. These anonymous folk ballads (many of them going back to the Middle Ages) were originally sung to record a notable exploit or calamity, often presented in stark outline, hitting home without frivolous embellishment. Some of the best-known early ballads follow a question-and-answer format in a pattern of **cumulative** repetition. The questioner persists in asking questions until the horrible truth is revealed. "Why does your sword so drip with blood?" the mother keeps asking her son in one of the best-known Scottish ballads. "I have killed my hawk," answers the son; and then, "I have killed my steed"; and finally, "I have killed my father" at the end of the third.

Poets of later ages have often re-created the ballad style. The following **literary ballad** picks up the question-and-answer style of earlier ballads. Once we become attuned to the pattern, we wait for the next question—and the next answer, as the poem builds up to its grim conclusion. Make sure you read this poem—or hear the poem read—aloud.

Melvin Walker La Follette   *(born 1930)*

The Ballad of Red Fox   *1959*

Yellow sun yellow
Sun yellow sun,
When, oh, when
Will red fox run?
When the hollow horn shall sound,   5
When the hunter lifts his gun
And liberates the wicked hound,
Then, oh, then shall red fox run.

Yellow sun yellow
Sun yellow sun, Where, oh, where   10
Will red fox run?

Through meadows hot as sulphur,
Through forests cool as clay,
Through hedges crisp as morning
And grasses limp as day.   15

Yellow sky yellow
Sky yellow sky,
How, oh, how
Will red fox die?

With a bullet in his belly,   20
A dagger in his eye,
And blood upon his red red brush
Shall red fox die.

The Receptive Reader

1. The questions in this poem provide a variable rather than completely identical *refrain*. How does it change?

2. To what extent do the answers in this poem follow the *rhyme* scheme of the traditional ballad stanza—a four-liner (or quatrain) rhyming *abcb*? A rhyming pattern can place special emphasis on key words in a poem. What rhymes make key words echo throughout this poem?

3. What do you think accounts for the continuing appeal of the old ballad style?

The Personal Response

In the battle between the hunter and the hunted, on which side is the poet? On which side are you?

Many traditional stanza patterns go back to the love poetry of the Middle Ages and the Renaissance. The word *artificial* then did not yet mean unnatural or insincere. Rather, it meant artfully done, finely crafted, pleasing to the eye and ear. One such artfully crafted form is the **villanelle** (originally a song in a country setting). Intermeshing rhymes link the three-line stanzas (or **tercets**) until the poem slows down and comes to a stop in the final four-line stanza (or **quatrain**). Rhymes and whole lines keep coming back. What is the pattern?

Elizabeth Bishop   *(1911–1979)*

One Art   *1976*

The art of losing isn't hard to master;
so many things seem filled with the intent
to be lost that their loss is no disaster.

Lose something every day. Accept the fluster
of lost door keys, the hour badly spent.   5
The art of losing isn't hard to master.

Then practice losing farther, losing faster:
places, and names, and where it was you meant
to travel. None of these will bring disaster.

I lost my mother's watch. And look! my last, or   10
next-to-last, of three loved houses went.
The art of losing isn't hard to master.

I lost two cities, lovely ones. And, vaster,
some realms I owned, two rivers, a continent.
I miss them, but it wasn't a disaster.   15

—Even losing you (the joking voice, a gesture
I love) I shan't have lied. It's evident

the art of losing's not too hard to master
though it may look like (Write it!) like disaster.

The Receptive Reader

1. What is the *rhyme* scheme of this villanelle? Where does the poet stretch it by slant rhyme or by a playful forced rhyme?

2. The villanelle uses a double *refrain*. How does it work?

3. The highly patterned villanelle can be half playful and half serious. What are the serious and the playful parts in this poem?

The best-known and most widely practiced traditional stanza form is the **sonnet**. The sonnet is a single stanza of fourteen lines, although the early sonneteers repeated the same form again and again in sonnet sequences of over a hundred poems. During the height of the sonneteering vogue in the sixteenth century, most sonnets were poems of unrequited love, with the mournful, humble lover forever replaying his "plaint" to the cruel, disdainful lady. Soon, however, poets extended the form to other subjects.

Traditionally, the sonnet works with a five-beat iambic line; it therefore often has ten or eleven syllables to the line. When following the model of the Italian poet Petrarch, sonneteers rhyme the first eight lines (the **octave**) in an interlaced pattern: *abbaabba*. The remaining six lines (the **sestet**) may rhyme *cdcdee* or *cdecde*. Sonneteers imitating the Shakespearean sonnet group the fourteen lines somewhat differently: They have alternating rhymes in the first three **quatrains**, or groups of four (*abab/cdcd/efef*), followed by a concluding couplet (*gg*).

In a Petrarchan sonnet, a turning in the flow of thought may start at or near the break after the first eight lines. The remaining six lines then represent a kind of countertide. (Robert Frost said that "a true sonnet goes eight lines and then takes a turn for better or worse.") Where is the turn in the flow of ideas in John Milton's poem on his blindness?

John Milton   *(1608–1674)*

When I Consider How My Light Is Spent   1655

When I consider how my light is spent	
Ere° half my days, in this dark world and wide,	*before*
And that one talent which is death to hide	
Lodged with me useless, though my soul more bent	
To serve therewith my Maker, and present	5
My true account, lest he° returning chide;	*so he won't*
"Doth God exact day-labor, light denied?"°	*with sight denied*
I fondly° ask; but Patience to prevent	*foolishly*
That murmur, soon replies, "God doth not need	
Either man's work or his own gifts; who best	10

Bear his mild yoke, they serve him best. His state
Is kingly. Thousands at his bidding speed
And post° over land and ocean without rest: carry messages
They also serve who only stand and wait."

In Milton's sonnet, the magnificent long first sentence runs through all but
the last three lines of the fourteen-line poem. The underlying pattern is
"When I think about my blindness . . . I ask a foolish, rebellious question
(does God expect a blind poet to continue his work?) . . . but Patience
replies that God does not depend on any one person's labor or gifts." This
long elaborate sentence puts the poet's whole situation—both the question
it raises and the answer the poet has reached—before us. But after the first
period, which comes almost at the end of the eleventh line, we stop short
at a sentence that goes to the opposite extreme. It has four words. It makes
us take in and ponder the essence of the lesson the poet has learned: the
majesty of God. "His state / Is kingly." His glory does not depend on our
praise or service, however dedicated.

The Receptive Reader

1. What *rhyme* words fill in the typical Petrarchan rhyme scheme?

2. What lines come closest to perfect *iambic pentameter?* Where do you see
clear examples of trochaic inversion at the beginning of a line?

3. What are some striking examples of *enjambment,* with the sense spilling
over into the next line to give the poem a characteristically Miltonic sense of
flow—of long, rich sentences moving forward regardless of line boundaries?
(Where does a subsequent *caesura,* or cut within a line, help to set up a syn-
copating counter-rhythm?)

4. How does the poem as a whole lead up to its famous last line?

Conventionally, sonnets looked at love from the perspective of the
lover yearning for a love that often seemed unattainable. How does the
author of the following sonnet depart from this convention?

Edna St. Vincent Millay   *(1892–1950)*

I, Being Born a Woman and Distressed   1923

I, being born a woman and distressed
By all the needs and notions of my kind,
Am urged by your propinquity° to find   nearness
Your person fair, and feel a certain zest
To bear your body's weight upon my breast: 5
So subtly is the fume of life designed
To clarify the pulse and cloud the mind,
And leave me once again undone, possessed.
Think not for this, however, the poor treason
Of my stout blood against my staggering brain,   10
I shall remember you with love, or season

My scorn with pity,—let me make it plain:
I find this frenzy insufficient reason
For conversation when we meet again.

The Receptive Reader

1. What *formal* features of the traditional sonnet does this poem illustrate? What is the rhyme scheme?

2. What basic *polarities* help organize this poem? Where in this sonnet is there a turning or counter-tide, and what makes it central to the poem as a whole?

The Personal Response

Millay has been called "very much a revolutionary in all her sympathies, and a whole-hearted Feminist" (Floyd Dell). In most of the sonnet tradition, the woman was the silent audience and the silent partner in the love relationship. How do you react as the woman in this poem speaks up and talks back?

Making Connections—For Discussion or Writing

Compare and contrast the perspective on love in this sonnet with the perspective on love in sonnets in the Petrarchan tradition—sonnets by Wyatt (Chapter 15), Petrarch (Chapter 20), and Shakespeare (Chapters 15 and 20).

TRADITIONAL FORM AND OPEN FORM

*Of all the possible distinctions between verse and
prose, the simplest, and most objective, is that
verse uses the line as a unit. Prose goes right
on . . . Verse turns.*

JUDSON JEROME

For a time, champions of modernism did battle with defenders of tradition, who scorned poets playing "tennis with the net down" (Robert Frost). The objection to traditional form is that it may become a straitjacket. A poet might feel hemmed in by the requirements of traditional meter and rhyme. Defenders of traditional form would say that traditional form allows much creative freedom.

The following poem is a traditional sonnet, written by a leading poet of the English Romantic movement. The poem has fourteen lines and an interlaced rhyme scheme: "free—Nun—sun—(tranquili)ty; Sea—(a)wake—make—(everlasting)ly" (*abbaacca*). It has the traditional underlying five-beat meter (iambic pentameter): "The HO|ly TIME | is QUI|et AS | a NUN." However, its pattern, rhythm, and tone make it memorable and unique. It is different from any other sonnet. Look at the interplay of traditional form and creative freedom in this poem. Like several other Wordsworth poems, this poem addresses a younger sister, who lived with him and shared his love of nature.

William Wordsworth   *(1770–1850)*

It Is a Beauteous Evening   1807

It is a beauteous° evening, calm and free,   *beautiful*
The holy time is quiet as a Nun
Breathless with adoration; the broad sun
Is sinking down in its tranquility;
The gentleness of heaven broods over the Sea: 5
Listen! the Mighty Being is awake,
And doth with his eternal motion make
A sound like thunder—everlastingly.
Dear Child! dear Girl! that walkest with me here,
If thou appear untouched by solemn thought,   10
Thy nature is not therefore less divine:
Thou liest in Abraham's bosom all the year,
And worshipst at the Temple's inner shrine,
God being with thee when we know it not.

This poem has a strong metrical pattern, but it is not monotonous. At key points, the poem reverses the iambic (DETROIT—DETROIT) pattern to stress the first syllable of a line: "BREATHless with adoration"; "LISTEN! the Mighty Being is awake." This variation emphasizes key words; it sets off key stages in the poem as a whole. Rhyme words do not neatly mark off sentences. At the end of the second line, we are pulled over into the third with only a minor pause. But then we come to a major break *within* the line, setting up a strong counter-rhythm: "The holy time is quiet as a Nun / Breathless with adoration; | | the broad sun . . . "

The Receptive Reader

1. Where else in this poem do strong breaks vary the rhythm? With what effect?

2. How should this poem *sound* when read aloud? How much should the reading make the listener aware of the meter—and of the line breaks following the rhyme words?

As rhyme, meter, and stanza became optional, a basic definition of poetic form remained: Poetry is lines of verse, laid out in a pattern on a page. The individual lines slow down the hasty reader. They encourage full attention to the individual image and to each phase in the flow of thought. This laying out of the text signals that even modern **open form** is not formless. It still uses patterns of repetition; the echoing of sounds and of words; the playing off of opposites; the interplay of sound and meaning. Widely admired contemporary poets have written poems in either vein—some poems with a stricter traditional pattern, and some in a more open, modern style. Study the following two examples by poets who move easily between traditional formal discipline and modern creative freedom. What can traditional form do that might be hard to achieve

in a more open format? What is possible with open form that traditional form might make it hard for the poet to do?

Anne Sexton   *(1928–1974)*

Her Kind   *1960*

I have gone out, a possessed witch,
haunting the black air, braver at night;
dreaming evil, I have done my hitch
over the plain houses, light by light:
lonely thing, twelve-fingered, out of mind.   5
A woman like that is not a woman, quite.
I have been her kind.

I have found the warm caves in the woods,
filled them with skillets, carvings, shelves,
closets, silks, innumerable goods;   10
fixed the suppers for the worms and the elves:
whining, rearranging the disaligned.
A woman like that is misunderstood.
I have been her kind.

I have ridden in your cart, driver,   15
waved my nude arms at villages going by,
learning the last bright routes, survivor
where your flames still bite my thigh
and my ribs crack where your wheels wind.
A woman like that is not ashamed to die.   20
I have been her kind.

How do the formal features of this poem serve the poet's purpose? The poem is intense, concentrated, deliberate. It is like an incantation—the poem puts a spell (or a hex, as it were) on the reader. The poem is divided into three stanzas of identical shape, each laid out according to the same plan. Each stanza frames a striking, haunting picture. Within each stanza, the interlacing rhyme scheme knits the material together, as if all distracting detail had been left out. The threefold repetition of the stanza form makes us expect that each of the three will be part of the same story. This expectation is reinforced by **parallelism**, that is, closely similar sentence structure or wording. The opening lines are parallel in sentence pattern: "I have gone . . . "; "I have found . . . "; "I have ridden . . . ". So is the last-but-one line in each stanza ("A woman like that is . . . "). We sense that the perspective will remain the same: The speaker will continue to look at the witch not from the point of view of her persecutors but of someone who identifies with the outcast: "I have been her kind."

The Receptive Reader

1. How does the *rhyme scheme* bond the two weighty final lines of each stanza to the earlier lines? How does the rhyme scheme link stanza to stanza?

2. What *details* give this poem the intensity of a nightmare?

3. What role does the refrain play in this poem? What makes its repetition cumulative—how does the poem build up to a climax?

4. Women accused of being witches were for centuries the target of persecution and lynch justice. How does the poet want you to think of the women behind the caricatures and stereotypes?

The Creative Dimension

Have you ever identified with the outcast, the outsider, the underdog? Write a journal entry (poem or prose) in which the refrain might be "I have been her (his) kind."

In the following poem, what gives shape to the poem as a whole—in the absence of such traditional features as rhyme, meter, and stanza?

Sharon Olds   *(born 1942)*

I Go Back to May 1937   1987

I see them standing at the formal gates of their colleges,
I see my father strolling out
under the ochre sandstone arch, the
red tiles glinting like bent
plates of blood behind his head, I   5
see my mother with a few light books at her hip
standing at the pillar made of tiny bricks with the
wrought-iron gate still open behind her, its
sword-tips black in the May air,
they are about to graduate, they are about to get married,   10
they are kids, they are dumb, all they know is they are
innocent, they would never hurt anybody.
I want to go up to them and say Stop,
don't do it—she's the wrong woman,
he's the wrong man, you are going to do things   15
you cannot imagine you would ever do,
you are going to do bad things to children,
you are going to suffer in ways you never heard of,
you are going to want to die. I want to go
up to them there in the late May sunlight and say it,   20
her hungry pretty blank face turning to me,
her pitiful beautiful untouched body,
his arrogant handsome blind face turning to me,
his pitiful beautiful untouched body,
but I don't do it. I   25

want to live. I take them up like the male and female
paper dolls and bang them together
at the hips like chips of flint as if to
strike sparks from them. I say
Do what you are going to do, and I will tell about it.   30

What makes this poem an example of open form? There is no rhyme (although there are some echo effects like "at the *hips* like *chips*"). The lines are of irregular length, and the line breaks often come at strange points in the middle of a phrase (the / red tiles). There is no steady underlying drumbeat of meter. No stanzas segment the poem. Compared with the Sexton poem, this poem seems more open-ended. The story of the speaker's parents, and her attempt to come to terms with it, are still in progress. We can still share in the impulse to tell her parents No! but then resolve to let human nature take its course. Key phrases like "I want to live" are not set off; they appear as natural stages in the flow of thought. Parallelism in this poem sets up open frames allowing the poet to multiply striking lifelike details (or urgent warnings). Open-ended parallel structure ("I see . . . "; "I see . . . "; "I see . . . ") allows the poet to build up the details that make the campus scene come hauntingly to life, from the sandstone arch and glinting red tiles to the "few light books" at the mother's hip and the black "sword-tips" of the wrought-iron gate.

The Receptive Reader

1. What *line breaks* come at an unexpected place in a sentence or in the middle of a phrase, partly counteracting the pause traditionally signaled by the end of a line?

2. How does *parallel structure* serve for emphasis in the lines making us look at the faces and bodies of the parents? How do these lines sum up the mixed emotions of the speaker?

3. How does this poem achieve *closure,* leaving us with a satisfying sense of completeness?

The Personal Response

In recent years, the concern of (grown) children with the quality of the parenting they received has become a major focus in the media and in popular psychology. How would you sum up the attitude of the speaker in this poem toward her parents? How does it compare with your own attitudes?

In much modern poetry, the traditional line of separation between poetry and prose has become thin. The division of the poem into lines may be our main clue that we are reading a poem. What other features of the following poem make it poetry?

Kathleen Lynch   *(born 1943)*

How to Build an Owl   1985

1. Decide you must.

2. Develop deep respect
   for feather, bone, claw.

3. Place your trembling thumb
   where the heart will be: 5
   for one hundred hours watch
   so you will know
   where to put the first feather.

4. Stay awake forever.
   When the bird takes shape   10
   gently pry open its beak
   and whisper into it: *mouse*

5. Let it go.

The Creative Dimension

Write similar instructions for creating an animal or plant you know well.

A **prose poem** does not have rhyme, meter, stanzas, or even a pattern of lines laid out on a page. It is, however, likely to share other features with poems less close to the border between poetry and prose. For instance, it may have striking images, a strong appeal to the reader's emotions, and the unified impact that results from the poet's concentrating on a central concern. What central concern comes into focus in the following prose poem?

Edward Wolf

Comfort Food   1995

Somewhere I'd heard that expression before—"comfort food"—but I'd never really thought about it. And I'm no cook—but it turns out I can dish up comfort food. Know what that is? French toast, rice pudding, cupcakes; something soft, warm, sweet. Of course I'm trying to be clever with this too, clever enough to get him to eat, eat anything. I could never have   5
imagined what a 106 pound man would look like. Studying the anatomy of my 44 year old friend, everything on the surface. The skin so stretched out—for the first time I really see where leather comes from. And bones.

The wrist is so big, the cheek is so delicate. Large pots of soup and an an-   10
gel food cake. Anything. Anything he wants. I dragged an old upholstered
chair into the garden and covered it with tarps at night. When he can, he
sits in it in the morning light and drinks hot chocolate (I made it from
scratch) and drifts in and out. The garden is full of nasturtiums this year
and I suddenly remember a salad we had once in a restaurant in North
Beach. Someone had put a handful of orange nasturtiums in it. A salad of   15
flowers. Now I'm wondering what else I could make that will work.

The Receptive Reader

1. What gives the beginning of this prose poem a casual, chatty tone? Where
and how does it turn serious?

2. What kind of person is speaking in the poem? What is the relationship
between the two people?

3. What images from this poem are likely to linger in your mind?

4. What is the prevailing attitude here toward the sickness that is at the center of this poem? What is the dominant feeling?

5. What makes the title rich in meaning and overtones?

Making Connections—For Discussion or Writing

Poets and their readers are still taking sides in the debate over the merits of
traditional form and modern open form. Select a favorite poem as your key example in a defense of one of these options.

JUXTAPOSITIONS

Close and Free Translation

*Translation is not an art for the soft-hearted: for
every nuance translated, ten are left behind.*

MEG BOGIN

Many translations use a more open form than the original poet did. It
is hard to be faithful to the original meaning while at the same time reproducing features of poetic form, such as meter and rhyme. Study the
following translations of a much-translated poem by a widely translated
German poet. The first translation hews close to the regular iambic pentameter and the end rhymes of the original stanzas. (In the original, the
first and third lines of each stanza also rhyme.) The second translation
aims at getting close to the spirit of the original while abandoning traditional formal features.

Rainer Maria Rilke   *(1875–1926)*

The Panther   1927

Jardin des Plantes, Paris

TRANSLATED BY HANS P. GUTH

From pacing past the barriers of his cage
His tired gaze no longer seems to see.
All that exists: a thousand iron bars.
The world beyond the bars has ceased to be.

The supple tread of sinuous steps revolves   5
In circles of benumbing narrowness,
Like power dancing round a pedestal
Where a majestic will stands powerless.

And yet, at times, the veil that blunts his eye
Moves stealthily aside—an image enters,   10
Glides through the silence of his tautened limbs—
And ceases where his being centers.

    Many translators of poetry are poets in their own right. They bring to the translator's task a special empathy, a special ability to get into the spirit of a fellow poet. This affinity shows when Robert Bly translates and comments on the same Rilke poem:

From seeing and seeing the seeing has become so exhausted
it no longer sees anything anymore.
The world is made of bars, a hundred thousand
bars, and behind the bars, nothing.

The lithe swinging of that rhythmical easy stride   5
that slowly circles down to a single point
is like a dance of energy around a hub,
in which a great will stands stunned and numbed.

At times the curtains of the eye lift
without a sound—then a shape enters,   10
slips through the tightened silence of the shoulders,
reaches the heart and dies.

    The poet translator said about this much-reprinted poem:

Rilke . . . watched a panther at the zoo, and his German lines, in rhythm and sound, embody movingly the repetitive, desperate walk of the panther. By the end of the poem he is somehow inside the panther's body. Each time the panther glimpses a shape, say a dog or a child, the image goes to the body's center, the place from which a leap begins; but no leap can take place. A leap can't take place, and so the image "reaches the heart, and dies."

The Receptive Reader

Where do the two translations seem very close, reflecting the common original? Where do they diverge, and with what effect? What difference does the difference in form make to your response? What do you think is the key to the fascination this poem has had for readers and translators around the world?

POEMS FOR FURTHER STUDY

In reading the following poems, pay special attention to the way they use or modify traditional formal features, such as rhyme, meter, and stanza form.

Popular Ballad   *(Anonymous)*

Lord Randal   *traditional*

"O where have you been, Lord Randal, my son?
And where have you been, my handsome young man?"
"I have been at the greenwood; mother, make my bed soon,
For I'm wearied with hunting, and fain° would lie down."   *gladly*

"And who met you there, Lord Randal, my son?   5
And who met you there, my handsome young man?"
"O I met with my true-love; mother, make my bed soon,
For I'm wearied with hunting, and fain would lie down."

"And what did she give you, Lord Randal, my son?
And what did she give you, my handsome young man?"   10
"Eels fried in a pan; mother, make my bed soon,
For I'm wearied with hunting, and fain would lie down."

"And who got your leavings, Lord Randal, my son?
And what became of them, my handsome young man?"
"My hawks and my hounds; mother, make my bed soon,   15
For I'm wearied with hunting, and fain would lie down."

"And what became of them, Lord Randal, my son?
And what became of them, my handsome young man?"
"They stretched their legs out and died; mother, make my bed soon,
For I'm wearied with hunting, and fain would lie down."   20

"O I fear you are poisoned, Lord Randal, my son!
I fear you are poisoned, my handsome young man!"
"O yes, I am poisoned; mother, make my bed soon,
For I'm sick at heart, and fain would lie down."

"What d' you leave to your mother, Lord Randal, my son?   25
What d' you leave to your mother, my handsome young man?"
"Four and twenty milk kine;° mother, make my bed soon,   *cattle*
For I'm sick at heart, and fain would lie down."

"What d' you leave to your sister, Lord Randal, my son?
What d' you leave to your sister, my handsome young man?"   30
"My gold and my silver; mother, make my bed soon,
For I'm sick at heart, and fain would lie down."

"What d' you leave to your brother, Lord Randal, my son?
What d' you leave to your brother, my handsome young man?"
"My houses and my lands; mother, make my bed soon,   35
For I'm sick at heart, and fain would lie down."

"What d' you leave to your true-love, Lord Randal, my son?
What d' you leave to your true-love, my handsome young man?"
"I leave her hell and fire; mother, make my bed soon,
For I'm sick at heart, and fain would lie down."   40

The Receptive Reader

When does the often-repeated *refrain* first turn ominous? How does this ballad use the pattern of *cumulative repetition* twice? How does the ballad strip
the story down to *essentials*? What do you think made this story survive through
the centuries?

Christine de Pisan   *(1363–1430)*

Marriage Is a Lovely Thing   *before 1400*

TRANSLATED BY JOANNA BANKIER

Marriage is a lovely thing
—my own example proves it—
for her whose husband is as kind
as he whom God has found for me.
Since day by day he has sustained me,   5
praised be He who guards his life
and keeps him safe for me,
          and surely my gentle one loves me well.

On the night of our union,
the first time we slept together   10
I could see how kind he was.
Nothing did that could have hurt me
and before the rising sun
had kissed me, oh a hundred times
but never urged against my will,   15
          and surely my gentle one loves me well.

And how sweet the words he spoke;
"Dearest Friend, God led me to you
to serve you courteously and well
as if he wished to raise me up."   20

Thus he mused all through the night
and his manner never faltered
but stayed the same, unwaveringly,
            and surely my gentle one loves me well.

O Prince, his love can drive me to distraction   25
when he assures me he's all mine
and of sweetness makes me burst.

The Receptive Reader

1. Like many other love poems of the Middle Ages, this poem has a *refrain* and a "send-off" (or *envoi*) of three lines. (The modern translator has not attempted to reproduce the rhymes of the original French poem.) What gives the refrain in this poem its special appeal or special force? How does the poem as a whole lead up to the send-off?

2. Christine de Pisan, a native of Italy living in France, was happily married for a few short years. After her husband's death, she became one of the first women in Europe to support herself by her writing. How is the treatment of love in this poem different from that in other early love lyrics you have read?

William Wordsworth   *(1770–1850)*

I Wandered Lonely as a Cloud   *1807*

I wandered lonely as a cloud
    That floats on high o'er vales and hills,
When all at once I saw a crowd,
    A host,° of golden daffodils;   *massed ranks*
Beside the lake, beneath the trees,   5
Fluttering and dancing in the breeze.

Continuous as the stars that shine
    And twinkle on the milky way,
They stretched in never-ending line
    Along the margin of a bay: 10
Ten thousand saw I at a glance,
Tossing their heads in sprightly dance.

The waves beside them danced; but they
    Outdid the sparkling waves in glee;
A poet could not but be gay,   15
    In such a jocund° company;   *joyful*
I gazed—and gazed—but little thought
What wealth the show to me had brought:

For oft, when on my couch I lie
    In vacant or in pensive° mood,   *thoughtful*   20
They flash upon that inward eye
    Which is the bliss of solitude;

And then my heart with pleasure fills,
And dances with the daffodils.

The Receptive Reader

How does the poet use rhyme, meter, stanza form? Does the poet make the experience reenacted in this poem come to life for you as the reader? Can you follow, and sympathize with, the train of thought in the last stanza?

Making Connections—For Discussion or Writing

During the years when Wordsworth wrote his best-known nature poetry, his sister Dorothy kept her *Journals,* in which she recorded many of the activities they shared: their long nature walks, their observation of the rapidly changing moods of nature, their observation of the country people at work in the fields or on the road in search of work or a place to live. The following is Dorothy Wordsworth's journal account of the same (or same kind of) experience that inspired her brother's poem. What are the major differences in the way the prose and the poem affect the reader? What does the poem do that the prose journal does not? What does the journal have that the poem does not?

> The wind seized our breath; the lake was rough. There was a boat by itself floating in the middle of the bay below Water Millock. . . . When we were in the woods beyond Gowbarrow park we saw a few daffodils close to the waterside. We fancied that the lake had floated the seeds ashore and that a little colony had sprung up. But as we went along, there were more and yet more; and at last under the boughs of the trees, we saw that there was a long belt of them along the shore, about the breadth of a country turnpike road. I never saw daffodils so beautiful. They grew among the mossy stones and about them, some rested their heads upon these stones as on a pillow for weariness, and the rest tossed and reeled and danced and seemed as if they verily laughed. The wind blew upon them over the lake; they looked so gay ever glancing ever changing.

Thomas Nashe   *(1567–1601)*

A Litany in Time of Plague   *1592*

Adieu, farewell, earth's bliss;
This world uncertain is;
Fond° are life's lustful joys;   *foolish*
Death proves them all but toys;
None from his darts can fly;   5
I am sick; I must die.
             Lord, have mercy on us!

Rich men, trust not in wealth,
Gold cannot buy you health:
Physic° himself must fade;   *the physician's art* 10
All things to end are made;

The plague full swift goes by.
I am sick, I must die.
            Lord, have mercy on us!

Beauty is but a flower   15
Which wrinkles will devour;
Brightness falls from the air;
Queens have died young and fair;
Dust hath closed Helen's° eye.   *Helen of Troy*
I am sick, I must die.   20
            Lord, have mercy on us!

Strength stoops unto the grave,
Worms feed on Hector° brave;   *Trojan prince*
Swords may not fight with fate;
Earth still holds open her gate;   25
Come, come, the bells do cry.
I am sick, I must die.
            Lord, have mercy on us!

Wit with his wantonness
Tastes death's bitterness;   30
Hell's executioner
Hath no ears for to hear
What vain art can reply.
I am sick, I must die.
            Lord, have mercy on us!   35

Haste, therefore, each degree,°   *rank*
To welcome destiny;
Heaven is our heritage,
Earth but a player's stage;
Mount we° unto the sky;   *let us mount*   40
I am sick, I must die.
            Lord, have mercy on us!

The Receptive Reader

1. A litany is a chantlike prayer with much *repetition*. What use does this prayer make of outright repetition? What use does it make of parallel structure?

2. What is the *rhyme scheme?* How does rhyme carry over from one stanza to the next? What is the central word to which the carryover rhyme directs attention?

3. What is the underlying *meter* in the first five lines of each stanza? In what lines does it show most clearly? What is the major recurrent variation on this metrical pattern? How does the meter change in the refrain? How does the change in meter affect your reading of the poem?

The Personal Response

How remote or how understandable are the sentiments expressed in this poem for you as a modern reader?

Theodore Roethke   (1908–1963)

The Waking   1953

I wake to sleep, and take my waking slow.
I feel my fate in what I cannot fear.
I learn by going where I have to go.

We think by feeling. What is there to know?
I hear my being dance from ear to ear.   5
I wake to sleep, and take my waking slow.

Of those so close beside me, which are you?
God bless the ground! I shall walk softly there,
And learn by going where I have to go.

Light takes the Tree; but who can tell us how?   10
The lowly worm climbs up a winding stair;
I wake to sleep, and take my waking slow.

Great Nature has another thing to do
To you and me; so take the lively air,
And, lovely, learn by going where to go.   15

This shaking keeps me steady. I should know
What falls away is always. And is near.
I wake to sleep, and take my waking slow.
I learn by going where I have to go.

The Receptive Reader

1. How does this poem illustrate the traditional formal features of the *villanelle?* Where does it modify the traditional rhyme scheme by the use of half-rhymes?

2. What is the meaning of some of the *recurrent phrases* to which the circular pattern of the villanelle keeps returning? How does the poem as a whole lead up to the two concluding lines?

Quincy Troupe   (born 1943)

Impressions/of Chicago; For Howlin' Wolf   1972

1

the wind/blade cutting in
& out swinging in over the lake
slicing white foam from the tips
of delicate fingers
that danced & weaved   5
under the sunken light/night;
this wind/blade was so sharp & cold

it'd cut a four-legged mosquito into fours
while a hungry lion slept on the wings of some chittlins
slept within the blues of a poem that was forming   10

we came in the sulphuric night drinkin' old crow
while a buzzard licked its beak atop the head of richard nixon
while gluttonous daly ate hundreds of pigs that were his ego
while daddy-o played bop on the box
came to the bituminous breath of chicago   15
howling with three million voices of pain

& this is the music;
the kids of chicago have eyes that are older than the deepest pain in the
    world
& they run with feet bared over south/side streets
shimmering with a billion shivers of glass   20
razors that never seem to cut their feet;
they dance in & out of the traffic,
the friday night smells of fish
the scoobedoo sounds
of bo diddley   25

2

these streets belong to the dues payers
to the blues players drinkin whiskey on satdaynight
muddy waters & the wolfman howlin smokestack lightnin
how many more years down in the bottom
no place to go moanin' for my baby   30
a spoonful of evil
back door man
all night long how many more years
down in the bottom built for comfort

The Receptive Reader

1. In this example of free verse, there are only a few rhymes, and even these are not traditional end rhymes. How many can you find?

2. Do you think the references to the world of jazz and blues—Bo Diddley, Muddy Waters, the Wolfman—still mean anything to the current generation? How does the poem re-create some of the world of thought and feeling of the blues?

3. What details in this poem seem like a realistic reflection of the Chicago scene? (For a generation of Chicagoans, Mayor Daly embodied the traditional white power structure.) How is the scene transformed by a zany, surreal imagination?

4. Which lines best sum up for you the unifying theme or overall point of the poem?

WRITING ABOUT LITERATURE

18 Connecting Form and Meaning
   WRITING FOCUS: From First to Second Draft

The Writing Workshop   Much writing about poetry aims at showing the connection between form and meaning. It traces the relationship between technical formal features and what the poem as a whole does for the reader. As you write about form and meaning, you may be focusing on how traditional formal features work in a poem. You may be focusing on how formal features are modified or replaced in much modern poetry. Remember the following guidelines:

✘ *See what use the poem makes of rhyme.* Does it use traditional full rhymes throughout? part of the time? in strategic places? Is there an alternating rhyme scheme or other pattern that bonds a series of lines? Does the poem make use of half-rhymes or internal rhymes? Does rhyme serve to highlight important words? Does it help to segment the poem neatly into lines, or does the sense of a line frequently spill over into the next line (enjambment)?

✘ *Check if the poem sets up a strong underlying beat, or meter.* (Be sure to read lines aloud.) Does it use the common iambic pentameter line? How regular are the lines? Is there much variation—with what effect? Is variation used for emphasis, or to speed up or slow down a line? If the poem uses free verse, is it strongly rhythmic—and does the rhythm give the lines an eloquent or hypnotic effect? Or is the rhythm of the lines closer to the casual pattern of ordinary speech? Is the poet's treatment of the subject or attitude toward the reader also casual?

✘ *Check whether the poem is divided into stanzas.* Does the poet use a traditional stanza such as the four-line ballad stanza or the fourteen-line sonnet? If the first, does the poem have a songlike quality? Does it keep commentary out, ballad-style? Does it use a refrain—with what effect? If the second, does the poem have the ceremonial, carefully crafted quality of the traditional sonnet?

✘ *In a poem using open form, look for features that help give shape to the poem.* Look for deliberate repetition for emphasis; parallel sentence structure tying together closely related parts of the poem; the echoing of words or phrases; the playing off of opposites.

The following are key sections from the first draft of a student paper that focuses on form and meaning. The comments are feedback from an instructor; they are designed to guide the writer in revising and strengthening the paper. Study the comments, and then see how the student writer has responded to them in the second draft of the paper.

First Draft

New England Discipline

COMMENT: Title too dry or uninformative? Use a title that conveys the spirit of the poem in more dramatic fashion?

In his sonnet "New England," Edwin Arlington Robinson skillfully employs the powers of form and sound to intensify the meaning of the poem. Robinson fittingly uses the most demanding of poetic forms, the Petrarchan or Italian sonnet, to frame his objection to the New England tradition of emphasizing discipline and self-denial at the expense of love and joy. Robinson himself observes the strict discipline of the traditional fourteen lines, subdivided into octet (first eight lines) and sestet (remaining six lines) . . .

COMMENT: Excellent focus on the central concern of the poem and on its overall intention. To introduce your thesis more effectively, replace the somewhat interchangeable first sentence (it could fit many different poems)? Perhaps start with a striking quotation instead?

The first word of the poem appropriately forms an inversion of the iambic rhythm, a trochee: "Here's where the wind is always north-northeast," focusing the reader's attention quite forcibly on cold New England. The "always north-northeast" wind and the children in the next line who "learn to walk on frozen toes" start out the poem on a distinctly chilly note. New England is cold in more ways than one. Here it is so cold that "Joy shivers in the corner where she knits." Note that in this line the word *joy* forms a spondee with the following word, *shivers,* adding emphasis . . .

COMMENT: Good here and later on how formal features emphasize or highlight meaning. Try to explain more—and demonstrate the workings of the technical features a little more graphically?

Lines three to eight introduce a major contrast. They are like a simmering stew of lush, hothouse words that describe the opposite of traditional New England values—"those / Who boil elsewhere with such a lyric yeast / Of love that you will hear them at a feast / Where demons would appeal for some repose, / Still clamoring where the chalice overflows / And crying wildest who have drunk the least." Here all the bars are down—the words rush by and knock down the structure that contained them. The reader is flooded with a rush of passionate warmth and feeling, which the New Englander can only regard with "wonder [that] begets envy." Robinson has used enjambment to create this effect . . .

COMMENT: A good paragraph. Set off the group of five lines as a block quotation for easier reading (and for added emphasis). Use partial quotes to avoid awkward use of square brackets?

At the end of line eight, the sonnet takes its traditional turn in direction. The excursion into passion ends. The sestet, or concluding six lines, sums up the poet's rebellion against the traditional New England attitude toward life: "Passion here is a soilure of the wits, / We're told, and Love a cross for them to bear," it begins . . .

Edwin Arlington Robinson, himself a New Englander with deep roots in the Puritan tradition, has written a memorable poem that utilized traditional form very effectively to deepen its message.

COMMENT: Your conclusion, like your introduction, seems too perfunctory and interchangeable. Develop the key point about the poet's own New England roots?

Second Draft

Shivering Joy, Comfortable Conscience

"Joy shivers in the corner where she knits / And conscience always has the rocking chair" (11–12). With such vivid images, Edwin Arlington Robinson in his sonnet "New England" explores the New England values of hard work, moral uprightness, and distrust of emotion. Robinson skillfully employs form and sound to enhance the meaning of the poem.

Fittingly, he uses the most highly disciplined and demanding of poetic forms, the sonnet, to explore and question the New England tradition of rigorous discipline and self-denial at the expense of human passions such as love and joy. Robinson's sonnet observes the traditional discipline of fourteen lines, a variation of the traditional Petrarchan rhyme scheme (*abba/abba/cdcdcd*), and the traditional iambic pentameter. Ironically, however, the traditional sonnet form here becomes a vehicle for questioning traditional attitudes that restrict the free development of the human spirit.

The very first word of the poem causes an inversion of the iambic rhythm, shifting the stress from the second syllable of the line to the first (a trochee). The first line reads: "*Here's* where | the wind | is al | ways north- | north-east," focusing the reader's attention forcibly on cold New England. The "always north-north-east" wind and the children in the next line who "learn to walk on frozen toes" start out the poem on a distinctly chilly note. The poet's native New England is cold in more ways than one, we are soon to learn. Here it is so cold that "Joy shivers in the corner where she knits" (11). In this line, the word *Joy,* stressed at the beginning of the line, forms a spondee with what would normally be the second and accented syllable of the first iambic foot: "*Joy shiv* |ers in | the cor |ner where |she knits.*" Several words in that line—*shivers, in, knits*—have the short *i* sound, suggesting smallness or diminution, which is apparently what the strict New Englanders, apprehensive that joy might get out of hand, would desire. And even joy must not sit idly wasting time—she sits in her designated cold corner, knitting, probably warm mittens or woolen socks needed for survival in the chill outdoors.

And now for the polar opposite: Lines 3 to 8 are a simmering stew of lush, hothouse words, describing those

> Who boil elsewhere with such a lyric yeast
> Of love that you will hear them at a feast
> Where demons would appeal for some repose,
> Still clamoring where the chalice overflows
> And crying wildest who have drunk the least. (4–8)

Here all the bars are down: The words rush unrestrainedly, seemingly of their own volition, and knock down the structure that has been carefully erected to contain them. The lines spill over (enjambment), as in "the lyric yeast / Of love" (4–5). The reader is flooded with a rush of passionate warmth and feeling, which the New Englander can only regard with wonder that "begets an envy" (3).

At the end of line 8, however, the sonnet takes the traditional turn in direction. The excursion into passion ends. The sestet, or concluding six lines, reaffirms the dominance of a more restrictive view of life. "Passion here is a soilure of the wits, / We're told, and Love a cross for them to bear" (9–10). The key word at the beginning of these lines again is emphasized by trochaic inversion: "*Passion* | here is." In these final six lines, everything is again under control, with the thoughts arranged in neat rhyming couplets. Here we see Joy shivering in her corner, while the mistress of the house, Conscience, "always has the rocking chair." Conscience is perversely "cheerful"—note again the emphasis on this unexpected word through trochaic inversion: "*Cheer*ful | as when . . . " (13). She was apparently equally cheerful when she caused the first cat to be killed, not, as in the familiar saying, by curiosity but, New England style, by too much worry and care.

Edwin Arlington Robinson was himself a New Englander with deep roots in the Puritan tradition. He was related through his mother to Anne Bradstreet, Puritan New England's first poet. In this poem, he uses the traditional sonnet form effectively to explore the New England tradition of stressing discipline and distrusting emotion.

Questions for Peer Review

The student writer of this paper set out to show that in a successful poem form is not imposed on content or ideas from the outside, like clothes put on a body. How well does the writer show that they intermesh?

1. How does the rewritten *introduction* dramatize the key point of the paper? According to the writer, how are form and meaning in this poem organically related? What is "fitting" about using the traditional sonnet form for a poem about the New England setting?

2. What *technical features* of the sonnet form does the student writer explain and demonstrate? What do you learn about rhyme schemes, inversion, and other technical features?

3. Slowly throughout the paper the student writer fills in the key features or *historical stereotypes* associated with the New England tradition that he sees at the center of this poem. What are the key features pinpointed in this paper?

4. Where or how does this paper go beyond technical analysis of formal features? Where and how does the student writer show examples of outward form serving as a "*mirror to the sense*"?

5. In the end, although the form of the poem was at first shown to be "fitting," the student writer says that seen from a different angle it is also "ironic." What is questioning or skeptical about the poet's attitude that could be setting up an ironic modern *counterpoint* to the New England tradition?

6. Readers of the poem disagree whether the poet was truly being critical of the New England tradition or whether he was mocking people perpetuating negative stereotypes. When confronted with the *polarity* explored in this paper, to what side would you personally incline?

19 PERSONA

Masks and Faces

Courtesy Richard B. Ressman

All writing is the assumption of a mask,
a persona, an implied author.

DAVID W. SMIT

This is my daily mask
daughter, sister
wife, mother
poet, teacher
grandmother.

My mask is control
concealment
endurance
my mask is escape
from my
self

MITSUYE YAMADA,
"MASKS OF WOMAN"

FOCUS ON PERSONA

The **persona** is the voice speaking to you in a poem. This voice may be different from that of the poet as a person. In reading a poem, you may need to ask: "Who is speaking? And to whom?" You may need to distinguish between the poet as a biographical person (whom you could interview and question about the poem) and the "I" addressing you in the poem—the persona. The distance between the poet and the persona speaking in the poem varies greatly from poem to poem:

✗ *A poet may share with you real-life experiences and personal feelings.* You hear the voice of the poet speaking to you as a person, taking you into his or her confidence, the way you might talk to someone you trust in a frank personal letter. A poem may be the poet's way of working through painful experiences or personal traumas. It may reveal a side of the poet's personality that others might hide from public view. (Highly personal poems taking you into the poet's confidence are sometimes called **confessional** poetry.)

✗ *A poem may present a guarded or edited version of the human being behind the poem.* The poet may be revealing to you only one part of his or her personality. Or else the voice speaking in the poem may be an idealized version of the poet-as-a-person. The poet may be speaking to you in a public role, living up to a public image or speaking to you as the voice of a group or a movement. The persona speaking in the poem may be a disguise, a mask—designed to shield the real poet from prying eyes.

✕ *A poet may adopt the stance of the detached observer.* Many twentieth-century critics have encouraged poets to keep a distance from their material, to maintain an intellectual perspective. They have warned the poet not to be swept away by raw personal emotions.

✕ *The persona may be an imaginary character very different from the poet.* In the opening lines of a poem by C. K. Williams titled "Hood," a bully speaks to the person he used to bully. Most readers would assume that the poet is identifying not with the booted bully who made teachers and students cringe but with the victim:

Remember me? I was the one
In high school you were always afraid of.
I kept cigarettes in my sleeve, wore
engineer's boots, long hair, my collar
up in back and there were always
girls with me in the hallways.
You were nothing. I had it in for you—
when I peeled rubber at the lights
you cringed like a teacher.

In the concluding lines, the poem enacts the comeuppance of the bully that is a favorite daydream of the people abused:

And when I crashed and broke both lungs
on the wheel, you were so relieved
that you stroked the hard Ford paint
And your hands shook.

If we remember being bullied ourselves, we are likely to sympathize with the bully's victim. We are likely to share the cringing—and the guilty feeling of relief when the bully crashed. Where is the poet in this poem? Maybe the poet is somewhat of a bully, but more likely the bully is a persona, an assumed identity.

FIRST READING

An Earlier Self

A poem may take us back to an earlier self. The following poem takes us to a childhood world of thought and feeling.

Rita Dove   *(born 1952)*

Flash Cards   1989

In math I was the whiz kid, keeper
of oranges and apples. *What you don't understand,*
master, my father said; the faster
I answered, the faster they came.

I could see one bud on the teacher's geranium,   5
one clear bee sputtering at the wet pane.
The tulip trees always dragged after heavy rain
so I tucked my head as my boots slapped home.

My father put up his feet after work
and relaxed with a highball and *The Life of Lincoln.*   10
After supper we drilled and I climbed the dark
before sleep, before a thin voice hissed
numbers as I spun on a wheel. I had to guess.
Ten, I kept saying, *I'm only ten.*

The Receptive Reader

1. Do you think this poem is based on the poet's real-life experience? Why or why not?

2. What lifelike details make the speaker's childhood experience real for you as the reader?

3. Why or how does the speaker in the poem spin "on a wheel" in her sleep? What gives a special twist to the number she keeps saying in her sleep?

4. Do you consider the experience that this poem reenacts a positive or a negative experience?

5. What kind of person do you think the poet is?

THE AUTOBIOGRAPHICAL "I"

A real poet can make everything into poetry,
including his or her own life.
                    DIANE WAKOSKI

I hadn't found the courage yet to do without
authorities, or even to use the pronoun "I."
                    ADRIENNE RICH

I am not a metaphor or symbol.
This you hear is not the wind in the trees,
Nor a cat being maimed in the street.
It is I being maimed in the street.
        CALVIN C. HERNTON, "THE DISTANT DRUM"

Poets using the **autobiographical "I"** share with us their personal experiences and feelings. The poet takes us into his or her confidence, revealing part of the self that may normally be hidden behind a noncommittal facade. We are privileged to look beyond the outer shell that shields people from prying or ridicule. The more autobiographical the poem, the more the person speaking in the poem and the poet who wrote the poem become identical in the reader's mind.

Some poems are occasioned by actual events in the poet's life. A poet-playwright and contemporary of Shakespeare wrote the following poem about an actual son who was named Benjamin (literally "child of the right hand") and who died at age seven.

Ben Jonson   *(1572–1637)*

On My First Son   1616

Farewell, thou child of my right hand, and joy;
My sin was too much hope of thee, loved boy:
Seven years thou wert lent to me, and thee I pay,°   *pay back*
Exacted° by thy fate, on the just day.   *when billed*
O could I lose all father° now! For why   *fatherly thoughts*   5
Will man lament the state he should envy—
To have so soon escaped world's and flesh's rage
And, if no other misery, yet age?
Rest in soft peace and, asked,° say, "Here doth lie   *when asked*
Ben Jonson his° best piece of poetry."   *Jonson's*   10
For whose sake henceforth all° his vows be such   *may all*
As what he loves may never° like too much.   *may be never*

The Receptive Reader

1. The father's feelings in this poem are in keeping with traditional religious attitudes toward death. How? Are these attitudes still meaningful to the modern reader? Why or why not?

2. Where in the poem do you think the father's personal feelings show most strongly? Where do his thoughts and feelings seem different or unexpected to you?

Poets take a risk when they remove the mask that hides private feelings from the outside world. However, they also set up a special human contact with the sympathetic reader. Poetry in the "I" mode often records a part of the poet's spiritual history. We embark with the poet on an exploration of inner space, which may take us to childhood scenes or to waystations in the poet's later life. We watch a fellow human being fitting together the pieces of the puzzle that together make up a person. How well do you come to know or understand the persons behind the two following poems?

Maxine Kumin   *(born 1925)*

Nurture   *1976*

From a documentary on marsupials I learn
that a pillowcase makes a fine
substitute pouch for an orphaned kangaroo.

I am drawn to such dramas of animal rescue.
They are warm in the throat. I suffer, the critic proclaims,   5
from an overabundance of maternal genes.

Bring me your fallen fledgling, your bummer lamb,
lead the abused, the starvelings, into my barn.
Advise the hunted deer to leap into my corn.

And had there been a wild child—   10
filthy and fierce as a ferret, he is called
in one nineteenth-century account—

a wild child to love, it is safe to assume,
given my fireside inked with paw prints,
there would have been room.   15

Think of the language we two, same and not-same,
Might have constructed from sign,
scratch, grimace, grunt, vowel:

Laughter our first noun, and our long verb, howl.

The Receptive Reader

1. What *tone* does the poet set by her opening reference to kangaroos and other marsupials?

2. What in this poem strikes you as autobiographical fact and what as imaginative *what if?*

3. What is the special fascination of stories about abandoned children growing up wild without human nurture or language? What is the special fascination of such stories for the poet?

4. What is the perspective on *language* in this poem? What poet's-eye view does the poem give you of the origin or basic functions of language?

5. What kind of *person* would you expect the poet to be? Where would you expect to encounter her? What would you expect her to do?

The Personal Response

Is a nurturing, caring attitude toward life a gender-specific quality? Is nurturing the special province of women? What are some practical or political implications of the debate—what difference does it make? What side would you take?

In classical Greece, the Nine Muses were quasi-divine beings who inspired poets, musicians, historians, and followers of the other arts and sciences. The philosopher Plato called Sappho "the tenth Muse," and many

Greeks considered her their most outstanding lyric poet. She lived on the island of Lesbos and is thought to have run a school for women there. Book burners of a later age destroyed most of her poems (but not her legendary reputation). A few whole poems and fragments of others survive. Gay women still call themselves lesbians in her honor.

Sappho   *(about 620–550 B.C.)*

Letter to Anaktoria   *6th Century* B.C.

TRANSLATED BY RICHMOND LATTIMORE

Like the very gods in my sight is he who
sits where he can look in your eyes, who listens
close to you, to hear the soft voice, its sweetness
    murmur in love and

laughter, all for him. But it breaks my spirit;   5
underneath my breath all the heart is shaken.
Let me only glance where you are, the voice dies,
    I can say nothing,

but my lips are stricken to silence, under-
neath my skin the tenuous flame suffuses;   10
nothing shows in front of my eyes, my ears are
    muted in thunder.

And the sweat running upon me, fever
shakes my body, paler I turn than grass is;
I can feel that I have been changed, I feel that   15
    death has come near me.

The Receptive Reader

What kind of person is speaking in this poem? What is the situation? What are the mixed emotions the speaker feels toward the two people in this poem? Do her feelings seem strange or familiar? How would you expect to react to a poem written 2,500 years ago? How do you react to this poem?

The Creative Dimension

Write a poem or prose passage that re-creates what for you is the dominant emotion in this poem.

Intensely personal poetry often seems like a catharsis—a cleansing or purifying of painful memories and passionate grievances. In recent decades, minority authors have made the majority listen to the voices of those that Martin Luther King, Jr., called the "unheard." The following poem speaks for young Native Americans taken from their families to be made over in the white man's image. Of German and Chippewa heritage, the poet relives her experience with the forced assimilation of young people denied pride in their own past.

Louise Erdrich   *(born 1954)*

Indian Boarding School: The Runaways   *1984*

Home's the place we head for in our sleep.
Boxcars stumbling north in dreams
don't wait for us. We catch them on the run.
The rails, old lacerations that we love,
soot parallel across the face and break   5
just under Turtle Mountains. Riding scars
you can't get lost. Home is the place they cross.

The lame guard strikes a match and makes the dark
less tolerant. We watch through cracks in boards
as the land starts rolling, rolling till it hurts   10
to be here, cold in regulation clothes.
We know the sheriff's waiting at midrun
to take us back. His car is dumb and warm.
The highway doesn't rock, it only hums
like a wing of long insults. The worn-down welts   15
of ancient punishments lead back and forth.

All runaways wear dresses, long green ones,
the color you would think shame was. We scrub
the sidewalks down because it's shameful work.
Our brushes cut the stone in watered arcs   20
and in the soak frail outlines shiver clear
a moment, things us kids pressed on the dark
face before it hardened, pale, remembering
delicate old injuries, the spines of names and leaves.

The Receptive Reader

1. To you, does the poem seem like intensely felt *personal experience* or like an imaginary situation vividly imagined? If pressed to explain your answer, what would you say?

2. What *assumptions* about reservation life and Indian schools do you bring to this poem? How does this poem change or challenge them?

3. What is the *situation* of the runaways? What do they think, feel, and remember?

4. In this poem, much of what you see—the railroad tracks, the highway, work, a color—takes on *symbolic* significance. Where and how?

The Personal Response

When you read this poem, are you looking at the young runaways from the outside? Do you identify with the "we" speaking in the poem? Why or why not?

The speaker in the following poem shared the experience of young Japanese Americans who were confined with their parents in the Tule Lake relocation camp during World War II.

Janice Mirikitani   *(born 1938)*

For My Father   *1976*

He came over the ocean
carrying Mt. Fuji on
his back/Tule Lake on his chest
hacked through the brush
of deserts   5
and made them grow
strawberries

    we stole berries
    from the stem
    we could not afford them   10
    for breakfast

his eyes held
nothing
as he whipped us
for stealing.   15

the desert had dried
his soul.

wordless
he sold
the rich,   20
full berries
to hakujin°   *white people*
whose children
pointed at our eyes

    they ate fresh   25
    strawberries
    on corn flakes.

Father,
i wanted to scream
at your silence.   30
Your strength
was a stranger
i could never touch.

iron
in your eyes   35
to shield
the pain
to shield desert-like wind
from patches
of strawberries   40
grown

from

tears.

The Receptive Reader

1. What details in the poem remind you of the poet's Japanese American ancestry?

2. What is the story of the poet's father? What are the daughter's feelings about him? Do you come to understand him?

3. How do the strawberries serve as a central *symbol* in this poem?

Making Connections—For Discussion or Writing

Sharon Olds' "I Go Back to May 1937," Ben Jonson's "On My First Son," and Janice Mirikitani's "For My Father" offer a range of perspectives on parent-child relationships. How do these perspectives differ? Is there a common thread?

JUXTAPOSITIONS

Variations of "I"

Even when using the autobiographical "I," poets differ widely in how completely they bare their souls. (Mitsuye Yamada has said that to discover our real selves we have to peel away our masks "like the used skin / of a growing reptile.") In much nineteenth-century poetry, even personal emotions went dressed in a high-minded vocabulary, with anything low or disturbing locked away in the private recesses of the mind. In the twentieth century, candor gradually drove out Victorian uplift and decorum. Compare the two following examples. The first is one of a series of sonnets that Elizabeth Barrett addressed to the poet Robert Browning when they were about to be married. The second was written more than a hundred years later in a more modern vein.

Elizabeth Barrett Browning   *(1806–1861)*

How Do I Love Thee? Let Me Count the Ways   *1845*

How do I love thee? Let me count the ways.
I love thee to the depth and breadth and height
My soul can reach, when feeling out of sight
For the ends of Being and ideal Grace.
I love thee to the level of every day's   5
Most quiet need, by sun and candle-light.
I love thee freely, as men strive for right;
I love thee purely, as they turn from Praise.

I love thee with the passion put to use
In my old griefs, and with my childhood's faith.   10
I love thee with a love I seemed to lose
With my lost saints—I love thee with the breath,
Smiles, tears, of all my life!—and, if God choose,
I shall but love thee better after death.

The Receptive Reader

1. What kind of person is speaking in this poem? What kind of voice do you hear? Do you think of the person speaking as the poet herself or as a public *persona?*

2. What feelings voiced in this sonnet seem *old-fashioned* to you? How do you explain that this poem still appears in almost every major collection of favorite poems? What about it might still speak strongly to a modern reader?

3. How does the poet use a pattern of insistent *repetition* building up to a climactic ending?

What part of the poet's personality is uppermost in the following poem?

Gwendolyn Brooks   *(1917–2000)*

A Song in the Front Yard   *1945*

I've stayed in the front yard all my life.
I want to peek at the back
Where it's rough and untended and hungry weeds grow.
A girl gets sick of a rose.
I want to go in the back yard now   5
And maybe down the alley,
To where the charity children play.
I want a good time today.

They do some wonderful things.
They have some wonderful fun.   10
My mother sneers, but I say it's fine
How they don't have to go in at quarter to nine.
My mother, she tells me that Johnnie Mae
Will grow up to be a bad woman.
That George will be taken to Jail soon or late   15
(On account of last winter he sold our back gate).

But I say it's fine. Honest, I do.
And I'd like to be a bad woman, too,
And wear the black stockings of night-black lace
And strut down the street with paint on my face.   20

The Receptive Reader

1. What is the *symbolic* meaning of the front yard, the back yard, the alley, and the street? Does it matter that the song is about the back yard but is sung in the front yard?

2. Brooks published this poem when she was an adult. What *identity* is she assuming in this poem? (What is the persona?) What kind of voice are you hearing? What kind of person does it make you imagine? (How is the person talking?)

3. Often a single *metaphor* carries much meaning, with various implications and associations. What is the full meaning of the line "A girl gets sick of a rose"? (Does it make a difference that this is one of the shortest lines in a poem of longer lines?)

The Personal Response

How well do the following student reactions get into the spirit of the poem? Write your own personal response to the poem.

1. I've always been a good boy. I've done what my parents say. I want to see how the others live. I want to throw a rock through a window and get chased by the cops. I want to knock on a door and run and hide. I want to be bad, just for a day.

2. How can a girl get sick of a rose? A rose has everything. It has beauty and ugliness; it grows and dies. A rose is well-balanced: If you are sick of a rose, try its thorns.

Making Connections—For Discussion or Writing

Which of the two poets do you think you come to know better as a person, and why? Which style of voicing personal emotions appeals to you more, and why?

THE PUBLIC PERSONA

The age
requires this task:
create
a different image;
re-animate
the mask.

DUDLEY RANDALL

The "I" we hear in a poem may be speaking to us as the voice of a group, a commitment, or a cause. The plural *we* (like the editorial *we* or the royal *we*) may replace the singular *I*. It is as if the poet were speaking to us in an official capacity, assuming a public persona. Dylan Thomas was a Welsh poet whose chanting voice and powerful cryptic poems converted a generation of listeners and readers to the cause of poetry. In the following poem, he speaks of his mission as a poet with a grand sweep, without diffidence or self-doubt. The persona he assumes in the poem is that of the charismatic bard, dramatizing and glorifying the poet's calling.

Dylan Thomas   *(1914–1953)*

In My Craft or Sullen Art   *1946*

In my craft or sullen art
Exercised in the still night
When only the moon rages
And the lovers lie abed
With all their griefs in their arms,   5
I labor by singing light
Not for ambition or bread
Or the strut and trade of charms
On the ivory stages
But for the common wages   10
Of their most secret heart.

Not for the proud man apart
From the raging moon I write
On these spindrift° pages   *sea spray*
Nor for the towering dead   15
With their nightingales and psalms
But for the lovers, their arms
Round the griefs of the ages,
Who pay no praise or wages
Nor heed my craft or art.   20

The Receptive Reader

1. Dylan Thomas' poetry was shot through with bold, provocative *metaphors*. Why or how could his art be "sullen," and what could he mean by "singing light"? How does he use metaphorically *bread, strut, ivory, common wages, spindrift pages, towering dead?*

2. Where and how often does the central word *art* appear in the poem, and with what effect? What other key word rhymes with it, and where in the poem? Why is *wages* also a key word in the poem? Where does it appear, and how many rhymes help it echo through the poem?

3. What is the *symbolic* role of the moon in this poem?

4. With what *tone* should this poem be read? What kind of person do you imagine the poet to be?

Among poets who have seen themselves as the conscience of their time, Walt Whitman created for himself a persona as the voice of a new continent and a new nation. In many of his poems, he is speaking to us as the prophet of the new American democracy. The following poem, a part of his *Song of Myself,* shows the kind of **empathy**—sharing the feelings of others—that could make him say, "I am the hounded slave," and "I do not ask the wounded person how he feels; I myself become the wounded person."

Walt Whitman   *(1819–1892)*

I Understand the Large Hearts of Heroes   1855

I understand the large hearts of heroes.
The courage of present times and all times,
How the skipper saw the crowded and rudderless wreck of the steamship,
    and Death chasing it up and down the storm,
How he knuckled tight and gave not back an inch, and was faithful of
    days and faithful of nights,
And chalked in large letters on a board, "Be of good cheer, we will not   5
    desert you";
How he followed with them and tacked with them three days and would
    not give it up,
How he saved the drifting company at last,
How the lank loose-gowned women looked when boated from the side of
    their prepared graves,
How the silent old-faced infants and the lifted sick, and the sharp-lipped
    unshaved men;
All this I swallow, it tastes good, I like it well, it becomes mine,   10
I am the man, I suffered, I was there.

The Receptive Reader

1. Whitman was fascinated with *people*—how they looked and talked and moved, whether in developing the continent or in the agonies of civil war. What striking, revealing details make this account of shipwreck and rescue come to life for the reader?

2. What kind of *person* is speaking to you in this poem? Whitman has at times been accused of striking heroic poses. Do you think he is sincere in this poem? Why or why not?

The Personal Response

How do you react to the following *journal entry* by a fellow student?

"All this I swallow, it tastes good, I like it well, it becomes mine, / I am the man, I suffered, I was there." Whitman here boldly proclaims the glorious things that common people only sense in a confused, ambiguous way while thinking to themselves. At achieving this grand persona, few have matched the grandeur of Whitman. In this poem, Whitman rises to the level of a great and heroic event. The sea captain is the kind of person who will not deviate from a cause once the course is set. With absolute determination, "he knuckled tight and gave not back an inch, and was faithful of days and . . . nights." Whitman makes himself the spokesperson that commemorates and celebrates this courage and heroism: "I understand the large hearts of heroes / The courage of present times and all times." Today, a poet might view the state of our nation as slipping into chaos one notch at a time. Every time an oil tanker spills its load or someone is gunned down in the streets, America loses another piece of its soul. In Whitman's time, this country was taking gigantic leaps forward. He had ample subject matter for such heart-swelling subjects as this.

Today, eloquent voices speak to us in the name of a larger group. They help formulate a changed consciousness, a new sense of group identity. They may speak for women in search of a new self-image. They may speak for minority groups proud of their heritage. The following poem is by an American poet of West Indian descent who has said that she speaks not only for the woman who inhabits her physical self but "for all those feisty incorrigible black women who insist on standing up and saying, 'I *am* and you cannot wipe me out, no matter how irritating I am, how much you fear what I might represent.' "

Audre Lorde   *(1934–1992)*

Coal   *1976*

I
is the total black, being spoken
from the earth's inside.
There are many kinds of open
how a diamond comes into a knot of flame   5
how sound comes into a word, colored
by who pays what for speaking.
Some words are open like a diamond
on glass windows
singing out within the passing crash of sun.   10
Then there are words like stapled wagers
in a perforated book,—buy and sign and tear apart—
and come whatever wills all chances
the stub remains
an ill-pulled tooth with a ragged edge.   15
Some words live in my throat
breeding like adders. Others know sun
seeking like gypsies over my tongue
to explode through my lips
like young sparrows bursting from shell.   20
Some words
bedevil me.

Love is a word, another kind of open.
As the diamond comes into a knot of flame
I am Black because I come from the earth's inside   25
now take my word for jewel in the open light.

The Receptive Reader

1. Look at the bold, provocative *metaphors* and *similes* in this poem. What is their meaning? What role do they play in the poem?

2. The word *open* becomes a key word in this poem. What role does it play? What meanings and associations cluster around it?

3. Some earlier black poets used a formal literary language, avoiding all echoes of *Black English*. How is this poem different? What is the effect on the reader?

4. Who is the collective *I* speaking in this poem? What kind of collective self-image takes shape in this poem?

Making Connections—For Discussion or Writing

Compare and contrast the two poems by Whitman and Lorde. How do the two poets compare as voices of social awareness? How do they shape our self-image as members of society, as socially responsible beings?

IMAGINED SELVES

Aye! I am a poet and upon my tomb
Shall maidens scatter rose leaves
And men myrtles, ere the night
Slays day with her dark sword.

EZRA POUND

Sometimes the voice speaking in a poem is clearly distant or separate from the poet's autobiographical self. The "I" speaking may be an imaginary or historical character who has a special fascination for the poet. We may sense a special affinity or attraction, as we do in the following poem about Cassandra, the mad Trojan princess and priestess, who in the ancient Greek poems and plays about the siege of Troy speaks as the voice of impending doom. In her prophetic visions, Cassandra saw her native city in flames, with its towers crashing down. She also prophesied that Agamemnon, the Greek commander who carried her off as part of the spoils of war, would be murdered on his return to Greece by his wife and her lover.

Louise Bogan   *(1897–1970)*

Cassandra   *1968*

To me, one silly task is like another.
I bare the shambling tricks of lust and pride.
This flesh will never give a child its mother—
Song, like a wing, tears through my breast, my side,
And madness chooses out my voice again,   5
Again. I am the chosen no hand saves:
The shrieking heaven lifted over men,
Not the dumb earth, wherein they set their graves.

The Receptive Reader

1. What do you think is the special attraction the character of Cassandra had for the author as a woman and as a poet? What might make the legendary character a kind of *alter ego* for her—a "second self" or counterpart?

2. Why is it strange or contradictory that this poem should have a neat, regular rhyme scheme and underlying iambic meter? Is it a coincidence that the word *again,* repeated at the beginning of the sixth line, breaks up the pattern of neatly marked-off lines as it pulls us over into the new line?

What is the role the poet imagines for herself in the following poem? When Hitler drove many German artists and writers into exile, others, including this poet, went through a period of "emigration to the interior"—staying in Germany while trying to live intellectually and spiritually outside the mentality of the Nazi era. She was much honored by the West German literary establishment after the war. The following poem shows her affinity with an active women's movement in Germany.

Marie Luise Kaschnitz   *(1901–1974)*

Women's Program   *1972*

TRANSLATED BY LISEL MÜLLER

I give a talk on the radio
Toward morning when no one is listening
I offer my recipes
Pour milk into the telephone
Let your cats sleep   5
In the dishwashers
Smash the clocks in your washing machines
Leave your shoes behind

Season your peaches with paprika
And your soup meat with honey   10

Teach your children the alphabet of foxes
Turn the leaves in your gardens silver side up
Take the advice of the owl

When summer arrives put on your furs
Go meet the ones with the bagpipes   15
Who come from inside the mountains
Leave your shoes behind

Don't be too sure
Evening will come
Don't be too sure   20
That God loves you.

The Receptive Reader

1. What kind of person is speaking in this poem? (How close do you think the poet's personality is to the *persona* in the poem?)

2. What is the point and the motivation of the subversive advice given in this poem? (Does any of it seem particularly strange or particularly sensible?)

3. Where and how does the poet *allude* to the story of the Pied Piper of Hamlin? How does her use of the story depart from what you might expect?

In some poems, we listen to a **dramatic monologue**, or lengthy first-person speech, as it might be delivered by a character in a play. The best-known author of dramatic monologues is the English nineteenth-century poet Robert Browning, who lived for a time in Italy after eloping with his fellow poet Elizabeth Barrett, the semi-invalid daughter of a domineering father. In many of his monologues, we listen as artists, scholars, church dignitaries, or aristocrats of the Italian Renaissance reveal to us their ambitions and aspirations—or, as in the following poem, their passions and hidden motives. In the poem that follows, we listen to a sixteenth-century duke of Ferrara whose last duchess died young and who is now talking to a representative of another aristocratic family about a second marriage.

Robert Browning   *(1812–1889)*

My Last Duchess   *1842*

Ferrara

That's my last duchess painted on the wall,
Looking as if she were alive. I call
That piece a wonder, now: Frà Pandolf's° hands   *Brother Pandolf's (a monk or friar)*
Worked busily a day, and there she stands.
Will 't please you sit and look at her? I said   5
"Frà Pandolf" by design,° for never read   *on purpose*
Strangers like you that pictured countenance,°   *face*
The depth and passion of its earnest glance,

But to myself they turned (since none puts by
The curtain I have drawn for you, but I)   10
And seemed as they would ask me, if they durst,°   *dared*
How such a glance came there; so, not the first
Are you to turn and ask thus. Sir, 't was not
Her husband's presence only, called° that spot   *that called*
Of joy into the Duchess' cheek: perhaps   15
Frà Pandolf chanced to say "Her mantle laps
Over my lady's wrist too much," or "Paint
Must never hope to reproduce the faint
Half-flush that dies along her throat": such stuff
Was courtesy, she thought, and cause enough   20
For calling up that spot of joy. She had
A heart—how shall I say?— too soon made glad,
Too easily impressed; she liked whate'er
She looked on, and her looks went everywhere.
Sir, 't was all one! My favor° at her breast,   *love token*   25
The dropping of the daylight in the west,
The bough of cherries some officious° fool   *eager to serve*
Broke in the orchard for her, the white mule
She rode with round the terrace—all and each
Would draw from her alike the approving speech,   30
Or blush, at least. She thanked men—good!
          but thanked
Somehow—I know not how—as if she ranked
My gift of a nine-hundred-years-old name
With anybody's gift. Who'd stoop to blame
This sort of trifling? Even had you° skill   *if you had*   35
In speech—which I have not—to make your will
Quite clear to such an one, and say, "Just this
Or that in you disgusts me; here you miss,
Or there exceed the mark"—and if she let
Herself be lessoned so, nor plainly set   40
Her wit to yours, forsooth,° and made excuse   *in truth*
—Even then would be some stooping; and I choose
Never to stoop. Oh sir, she smiled, no doubt,
Whenever I passed her, but who passed without
Much the same smile? This grew; I gave commands;   45
Then all smiles stopped together. There she stands
As if alive. Will 't please you rise? We'll meet
The company below, then. I repeat,
The Count your master's known munificence°   *generosity*
Is ample warrant° that no just pretense°   *guarantee*   50
                                                                 demand
Of mine for dowry will be disallowed;
Though his fair daughter's self, as I avowed
At starting, is my object. Nay, we'll go
Together down, sir. Notice Neptune, though,
Taming a sea-horse, thought a rarity,   55
Which Claus of Innsbruck cast in bronze for me.

The Receptive Reader

1. What is the *situation?* Where in the poem did you first suspect what happened to the duchess? When were you sure?

2. To judge from this monologue by her husband, what was the duchess like as a *person?* What was her offense? Do you consider her a frivolous or superficial person?

3. What is the key to the *persona* created by Browning in this poem? What is the duke's problem? Why didn't he explain how he felt to the duchess?

4. What is strange about the duke's speaking in a relaxed, polite conversational *tone?* Is it in keeping with his character? Many of his sentences start in the middle of a line and spill over into the next. (The technical term for this effect is *enjambment*—from the French word for "straddling.") How does the straddling effect contribute to the conversational tone?

5. What public persona has the duke created for himself—what *image* does he present to the world? (The Italian Renaissance was a golden age of the creative arts. What is the role of art in this poem?)

The Personal Response

Has the duke's mentality become extinct with the passing of the aristocratic society of his time? Do you think there could be any modern parallels to his mind-set and behavior?

POEMS FOR FURTHER STUDY

In reading the following poems, pay special attention to questions like the following: Who is speaking? What kind of voice do you hear in the poem? What is the persona or assumed identity? How much distance do you think there is between the persona and the person behind the poem?

Yusef Komunyakaa   *(born 1947)*

My Father's Love Letters   1993

On Fridays he'd open a can of Jax
After coming home from the mill,
& ask me to write a letter to my mother
Who sent postcards of desert flowers
Taller than men. He would beg,   5
Promising to never beat her
Again. Somehow I was happy
She had gone, & sometimes wanted
To slip in a reminder, how Mary Lou
Williams' "Polka Dots & Moonbeams"   10
Never made the swelling go down.
His carpenter's apron always bulged
With old nails, a claw hammer

Looped at his side & extension cords
Coiled around his feet.   15
Words rolled from under the pressure
Of my ballpoint: Love,
Baby, Honey, Please.
We sat in the quiet brutality
Of voltage meters & pipe threaders,   20
Lost between sentences . . .
The gleam of a five-pound wedge
On the concrete floor
Pulled a sunset
Through the doorway of his toolshed.   25
I wondered if she laughed
& held them over a gas burner.
My father could only sign
His name, but he'd look at blueprints
& say how many bricks   30
Formed each wall. This man,
Who stole rose & hyacinth
For his yard, would stand there
With eyes closed & fists balled,
Laboring over a simple word, almost   35
Redeemed by what he tried to say.

The Receptive Reader

1. What is the portrait of the father that emerges from this poem? What is his history? What is his problem, or what are his problems?

2. What are the son's mixed feelings or contradictory emotions about the father? Are the son's memories of the father completely negative?

Denise Levertov   *(born 1923)*

In Mind   *1964*

There's in my mind a woman
of innocence, unadorned but

fair-featured, and smelling of
apples or grass. She wears

a utopian smock or shift, her hair   5
is light brown and smooth, and she

is kind and very clean without
ostentation—
              but she has
no imagination.   10
              And there's a
turbulent moon-ridden girl

or old woman or both
dressed in opals and rags, feathers

and torn taffeta.   15
and who knows strange songs—

but she is not kind.

The Receptive Reader

Do you recognize the two different personalities in this poem? What are
their virtues and shortcomings? (Are they polar opposites?) Do you think two
such different personalities could dwell in the same mind?

Making Connections—For Discussion or Writing

Compare the treatment of two sides of the same personality in this poem
and in Gwendolyn Brooks' "A Song in the Front Yard" earlier in this chapter.

Sylvia Plath   *(1932–1963)*

Mirror   *1961*

I am silver and exact. I have no preconceptions.
Whatever I see I swallow immediately
Just as it is, unmisted by love or dislike.
I am not cruel, only truthful—
The eye of a little god, four-cornered.   5
Most of the time I meditate on the opposite wall.
It is pink, with speckles. I have looked at it so long
I think it is a part of my heart. But it flickers.
Faces and darkness separate us over and over.

Now I am a lake. A woman bends over me,   10
Searching my reaches for what she really is.
Then she turns to those liars, the candles or the moon.
I see her back, and reflect it faithfully.
She rewards me with tears and an agitation of hands.
I am important to her. She comes and goes.   15
Each morning it is her face that replaces the darkness.
In me she has drowned a young girl, and in me an old woman
Rises toward her like a terrible fish.

The Receptive Reader

1. What touches early in the poem might make the mirror sound like a curious observer—with a limited or even naive perspective and no evil intentions?
(How is the mirror like the eye of a god—and why of "a little god"?)

2. How does the lake metaphor make the mirror seem more knowing and
more threatening? Why or how would "candles or the moon" be more likely to
prove liars than the mirror?

3. Do you think the mirror is cruel? Do you think the poet is being cruel? Where is the poet in this poem?

The Creative Dimension

What story would your own mirror tell if it could speak?

Making Connections—For Discussion or Writing

Several poems in this chapter (as well as in other parts of this book) are the record of a poet exploring her identity as a woman or embarked on the search of self. Study several such poems, looking for shared themes, recurrent issues, or similar perspectives.

WRITING ABOUT LITERATURE

19 Playing Roles / Assuming Identities
  WRITING FOCUS: Creative Imitation and Re-Creation

The Writing Workshop   Many poets passed through phases where they idolized a mentor or role model, and often the experience strongly influenced their attempts to find a style of their own. They often learned their craft by conscious **imitation** of what was famous, fashionable, or new. Adrienne Rich has said that at age sixteen she spent months memorizing and writing imitations of the sonnets of Edna St. Vincent Millay; "in notebooks of that period I find what are obviously attempts to imitate Dickinson's metrics and verbal compression."

Creative Imitation   As readers, we can learn as much from creative imitation as practicing poets do. Imitation or re-creation (like translation from another language) makes us enter into a poet's world of imagination more fully than a passive reading can. It alerts us to distinctive features of the poet's style, making us look at them from the performer's rather than the spectator's point of view.

Study the following attempts to re-create the persona of a poem in this chapter, and then try your hand at a similar imitation or re-creation of a poem of your choice. The first poem quoted in this chapter is C. K. Williams' "Hood." The student who wrote the following personal recreation of the passages from the "Hood" poem tried to create a similar persona. Compare the original and this student's response. How successful was the student poet?

Bully
Remember me?
I'm the one who calls you Chinaman.
I laugh at you all the time
and throw balls at you
when you don't know how to play.
I play jokes around you with my friends.
I took your lunch money in the restroom.
I'm the one you hate and fear the most.
When Teacher yelled at me,
you felt good.
When I am absent,
you feel safe.

The Tradition of Parody　Poets with an especially unmistakable style seem to invite imitation. Their poems seem to cry out for **parody**—an imitation that lovingly or mockingly exaggerates characteristic traits. The poetry of Robert Browning has been much imitated and much parodied. What features of the original did the student capture who wrote the following dramatic monologue?

My Last Essay
That's my last essay pinned up on the wall,
Looking as if it's not survived. I call
That piece a wonder, now! Jim Bello's hand
Worked busily an hour, and thus its state.
Will 't please you stay and read of it? I said
"Jim Bello" by design, for never saw
Strangers like you such tattered manuscript
But to myself they turned in stunned surprise
And seemed as they would ask me, if they durst,
How such red marks came there; so not the first
Are you to turn and ask thus. Nay, 't was not
Just split infinitives that roused his ire—
"Support unclear," he muttered through his teeth
In reference to my cherished prose. He had
A mind—how shall I say?— too soon made mad,
Too easily overcome; he slashed what words
He looked on, and his looks went everywhere!
Yes, 't was all one. My pronoun reference fault,
Verb disagreement, too—and "Comma splice!"
So, friend you see my tattered work displayed,
Defiled with red disgracefully, I know.
But I retyped it, and the ms sold
To Murdoch's tabloid for an even thou'.
You caught that issue? Thanks!

A parody is a close imitation with a humorous twist, achieving comic effects by exaggerating characteristic features of the original. A parody may be affectionate, gently spoofing mannerisms that are like quirks of someone we love. But a parody may also be cruel, holding up to ridicule what is overdone or outdated in its target.

To parody something well takes time and careful attention. Poets who write successful parody need a quick ear and a gift for patient observation. The following stanza is from a flip poem (written in 1601) by a would-be lover eager to dispense with the tedious preliminaries of courtship. The next stanza is from a student-written parody written almost four hundred years later.

> I care not for these ladies,
> That must be wooed and prayed:
> Give me kind Amaryllis,
> The wanton country maid.
>   Her when we court and kiss,
>   She cries, "Forsooth, let go!"
>   But when we come where comfort is,
>   She never will say no.
>
>   Thomas Campion

The student who wrote the following rejoinder had a good ear, and she gets well into the spirit of the original poem:

> They care not for us ladies
> That want to be loved and pursued.
> They care for Amaryllis
> Who is impure and crude.
>   'Cause when men seek a kiss,
>   Her cries have just begun.
>   No longer can she resist;
>   She pleads for more than one.
>
>   Sharee Pearson, "Ladies"

20 TONE

The Language of the Emotions

Courtesy Richard B. Ressman

Poetry is the revelation of a feeling that the poet
believes to be interior and personal but which the
readers recognize as their own.

SALVATORE QUASIMODO

The poet sheds his blood in the ring and calls the
pools poems.

GEORGE BARKER

this is important enough:
to get your feelings down.
it is better than shaving
or cooking beans with garlic.

CHARLES BUKOWSKI,
"COOKING BEANS WITH GARLIC"

FOCUS ON TONE

Reading poetry can be an education in the language of the emotions.
In the poet's language, as in ordinary language, much of the message
is in the **tone.** Live language has a human coloring that conveys the
feelings, attitudes, and intentions of the speaker. "It's you again!" may
be said in a tone of welcome ("it's you again—how wonderful"). But it
may also be said in a tone of disappointment ("it's you again—of all
people").

Facing a speaker, you read the speaker's body language. You respond
to the knowing wink or defiant gesture. You may flinch at the raised volume; you may perk up your ears at a whispered aside. When looking at
a poem on the printed page, you have to read for tone the way an actor
reads a script for clues to gesture and movement. The poet's words convey tone without the raised eyebrows, the shrug of the shoulders, or the
raised decibels. To respond to tone, you need to become sensitive to
tender or harsh or angry words. You need to respond to how a poet lets
passion build up—or plays down an emotion-charged situation. You
need to sense when the poet is being serious and when speaking
tongue-in-cheek.

Tone in poetry runs the gamut of human attitudes and emotions. The
poet may set a mournful tone, as Walt Whitman does in the opening
lines of his great elegy on the death of President Lincoln:

When lilacs last in the dooryard bloomed,
And the great star early drooped in the western sky in the night,
I mourned, and yet shall mourn with ever-returning spring.

The poet may speak in a tone of religious awe, as the seventeenth-century poet Henry Vaughan does in the opening lines of his poem "The World":

> I saw eternity the other night
> Like a great ring of pure and endless light,
>   All calm as it was bright;
> And round beneath it, Time, in hours, days, years,
>   Driven by the spheres,
> Like a vast shadow moved, in which the world
>   And all her train were hurled.

Toward the other end of the spectrum, the tone of a poem may be irreverent, as in these rebellious lines from Maxine Kumin's "Address to the Angels":

> Angels, where were you when
> my best friend did herself in?
> Were you lunching beside us
> that final noon, did you catch
> some nuance that went past my ear?
> Did you ease my father out
> of his cardiac arrest that wet
> fall day I sat at the high crib bed
> holding his hand? And when
> my black-eyed susan-child ran
> off with her European lover
> and has been ever since an unbelonger,
> were you whirligiging over
> the suitcases

Much of the best-known modern poetry has an ironic tone. Whenever something seems too beautiful to be true, we seem prepared for the ironic counterpoint. We seem ready for the revenge of reality on rosy projections. The following concluding stanza from a poem by Sylvia Plath is well attuned to the modern temper:

> Droll, vegetarian, the water rat
> Saws down a reed and swims from his limber grove,
> While the students stroll or sit,
> Hands laced, in a moony indolence° of love—   *carefree laziness*
> Black-gowned, but unaware
> How in such mild air
> The owl shall stoop from his turret,° the rat cry out.   *small tower jutting from a castle*

The first few words of this stanza already hint at an unusual perspective: The water rat (which we might expect to be repulsive) is described as "droll"—amusing in a harmless eccentric way—and "vegetarian," as if watching its health like a fellow human. The rat provides an ironic underside to the idyllic college setting where students stroll lazily in the "mild air," absorbed in moony thoughts of young love. They are ironically unaware of the life-and-death drama played out as the owl swoops down on the harmless-seeming amusing rat. When we least suspect it, evil lurks, ready to strike and make us "cry out."

To become sensitive to tone, remember that in reading a poem you are listening to a human voice. The printed poem on the page is to experiencing the poem as the sheet music is to Beethoven's "Moonlight Sonata." Reading aloud and hearing others read aloud is insurance against proving tone deaf to the living human voice speaking to you in a poem.

FIRST READING
Reading for Tone

What is the prevailing tone in the following poem? How overt is the poem in expressing the poet's attitudes and emotions? Where or what do you have to read between the lines? What kind of voice do you hear in the poem?

Robert Hass   *(born 1941)*

Song   *1973*

Afternoon cooking in the fall sun—
who is more naked
                    than the man
yelling, "Hey, I'm home!"
            to an empty house?   5
thinking because the bay is clear,
the hills in yellow heat,
& scrub oak red in gullies
        that great crowds of family
should tumble from the rooms   10
            to throw their bodies on the Papa-body,
                I-am-loved.

Cat sleeps in the windowgleam,
            dust motes.
        On the oak table   15
    filets of sole

stewing in the juice of tangerines,
  slices of green pepper
    on a bone-white dish.

The Receptive Reader

1. What is the *situation* that the poet remembers or imagines in this poem?
What is happening (or not happening)?

2. What is the *underlying emotion* in this poem? For you, what images or
phrases come closest to bringing it to the surface?

3. Would you call the poem as a whole emotional or *understated?*

4. Are the filets of sole and the bone-white dish in the poem by accident?
How do the many short lines or half lines affect the tone of the poem?

The Personal Response

Can you imagine yourself in the shoes of the person in the poem? Why, or
why not?

THE REGISTER OF EMOTIONS

Forgive me that I pitch your praise too low.
Such reticence my reverence demands.
For silence falls with laying on of hands.
Forgive me that my words come thin and slow.

JOHN WAIN, "APOLOGY FOR UNDERSTATEMENT"

the voice of your eyes is deeper than all roses)
nobody, not even the rain, has such small hands

E. E. CUMMINGS, "SOMEWHERE I HAVE NEVER TRAVELLED"

Poems vary greatly in emotional intensity. Traditionally, poetry has
been the voice of passion: the joy of mutual love and the sorrow of separation. Homer's warriors wept for their dead comrades. Religious poetry
through the ages has sung the grandeur of God. Much contemporary poetry has been more sparing in its expression of emotions. It has often
opted for dry wit or ironic detachment rather than for an outpouring of
passion. Poets have tended to understate rather than to overstate their
feelings.

The following poem about a dream recalls more violent emotions
than we encounter in much other modern poetry.

Louise Bogan   *(1897–1970)*

The Dream   *1941*

O God, in the dream the terrible horse began
To paw at the air, and make for me with his blows.
Fear kept for thirty-five years poured through his mane,
And retribution equally old, or nearly, breathed through
    his nose.   5

Coward complete, I lay and wept on the ground
When some strong creature appeared, and leapt for the rein.
Another woman, as I lay half in a swound°   *fainting fit*
Leapt in the air, and clutched at the leather and chain.

Give him, she said, something of yours as a charm.   10
Throw him, she said, some poor thing you alone claim.
No, no, I cried, he hates me; he's out for harm,
And whether I yield or not, it is all the same.

But, like a lion in a legend, when I flung the glove
Pulled from my sweating, my cold right hand,   15
The terrible beast, that no one may understand,
Came to my side, and put down his head in love.

The Receptive Reader

1. What is the *prevailing tone* in this poem? What kind of a dream are you asked to share? What words and phrases openly label emotion? What images help project it? How many words refer to violent motion?

2. How is this poem like a legend or *fairy tale?*

3. How did you expect the poem to *end?* How did you react to the ending?

4. Do you think that in our dreams emotions surface that we tend to subdue or suppress in our waking life?

The Personal Response

What nightmares, if any, do you have? Have they changed over the years?

In much traditional love poetry, the poet's emotional thermostat is set high, with the poem giving voice to yearning, ecstasy, or despair. Romantic love celebrates love as an overwhelming passion, promising fulfillment, giving meaning to otherwise meaningless lives. Poets in this tradition were given to **hyperbole**—frank overstatement, praising the angelic beauty of the beloved, idealizing the devotion of the lover. Many of Shakespeare's sonnets use the heightened, exalted language of idealized love.

William Shakespeare   *(1564–1616)*

Sonnet 18   *before 1598*

Shall I compare thee to a summer's day?
Thou art more lovely and more temperate:
Rough winds do shake the darling buds of May,
And summer's lease hath all too short a date:°   *time span*
Sometimes too hot the eye of heaven shines,   5
And often is his gold complexion dimmed;
And every fair° from fair sometimes declines,   *everything lovely*
By chance or nature's changing course untrimmed;°   *undone*
But thy eternal summer shall not fade,
Nor lose possession of that fair thou owst;°   *you own* 10
Nor shall death brag thou wanderst in his shade,
When in eternal lines° to time thou growst: *lines of verse*
So long as men can breathe, or eyes can see,
So long lives this, and this gives life to thee.

The Receptive Reader

1. How does this sonnet employ *hyperbole?* (How, in fact, does it go hyperbole one better?) Normally, to compare the beloved to the days of early summer or to the dazzling beauty of the glorious sun would be considered high praise. Why does the poet consider these comparisons inadequate?

2. Sometimes the final six lines (the **sestet**) and sometimes the final couplet provide a major "turning" in a sonnet. Which is it here? What answer does this poem give to the questions raised earlier?

Early in the twentieth century, the richer chords of much traditional poetry began to give way to the sparer, understated tone that became the modern idiom. **Understatement** makes the poet play down personal feelings, letting the images of a poem speak for themselves. This does not mean that the poem is devoid of feeling. It often means that the poet trusts images and incidents faithfully rendered to call up the emotions and attitudes in the reader. The following is an understated modern poem that lets a thought-provoking, disturbing incident speak for itself.

William Stafford   *(1914–1992)*

Traveling through the Dark   *1960*

Traveling through the dark I found a deer
dead on the edge of the Wilson River road.
It is usually best to roll them into the canyon:
that road is narrow; to swerve might make more dead.

By glow of the tail-light I stumbled back of the car   5
and stood by the heap, a doe, a recent killing;

she had stiffened already, almost cold.
I dragged her off; she was large in the belly.

My fingers touching the side brought me the reason—
her side was warm; her fawn lay there waiting,   10
alive, still, never to be born.
Beside that mountain road I hesitated.

The car aimed ahead its lowered parking lights;
under the hood purred the steady engine.
I stood in the glare of the warm exhaust turning red;   15
around our group I could hear the wilderness listen.

I thought hard for us all—my only swerving—
then pushed her over the edge into the river.

This poem starts on a dry, matter-of-fact note: The deer is dead; the road is narrow; best "to roll them into the canyon" to prevent further accidents. The speaker in the poem unceremoniously calls the dead deer a "heap"; he notes that it is "a recent killing." But he soon makes it hard for us as readers to maintain a matter-of-fact attitude: The side of the killed deer is still warm; she is large with a fawn, "alive, still, never to be born." The speaker in the poem hesitates, but only for a time. Then he does the right thing.

What are the poet's feelings? Maybe the poet is sick at heart at the thought of a mindless machine barreling down the highway to destroy one of God's creatures. However, the poem does not say. We can "hear the wilderness listen," and we also listen. But we hear no expressions of protest or grief; the only sound we hear is the motor of the automobile "purring" steadily in the background. Whatever he may feel, the speaker in the poem does the practical and necessary thing. He does not wave his arms or shout "I hate you!" at the universe. We know he "thought hard for us all." As one student reader said, "for a brief moment, he makes us think of the impossible task of saving the fawn." He hesitates for a time—that was his "only swerving" from acting businesslike and sensible. We as readers are left to wrestle with the traumatic event.

The Receptive Reader

1. Some readers have found the title of the poem to have more than a simple descriptive or factual significance. What could be its *symbolic* meaning?

2. What details or phrases for you do most to *set the tone* of the poem?

3. Do you think the poet felt emotions that the poem does not express? Do you think he *should have* expressed them?

The Personal Response

Do you think different readers would react differently to this poem? How much depends on the reader's experience with similar situations and on the reader's mind-set or personality?

Poems may reflect a mood of fatalistic acceptance but also a mood of rebellion or defiance. Departing from the prevailing mode of wry understatement, the Welsh poet Dylan Thomas found a large audience for chanting, intensely emotional poems like the following:

Dylan Thomas   *(1914–1953)*

Do Not Go Gentle into That Good Night   1952

Do not go gentle into that good night,
Old age should burn and rave at close of day;
Rage, rage against the dying of the light.

Though wise men at their end know dark is right,
Because their words had forked no lightning they   5
Do not go gentle into that good night.

Good men, the last wave by, crying how bright
Their frail deeds might have danced in a green bay,
Rage, rage against the dying of the light.

Wild men who caught and sang the sun in flight,   10
And learn too late, they grieved it on its way,
Do not go gentle into that good night.

Grave men, near death, who see with blinding sight
Blind eyes could blaze like meteors and be gay,
Rage, rage against the dying of the light.   15

And you, my father, there on the sad height,
Curse, bless, me now with your fierce tears, I pray.
Do not go gentle into that good night.
Rage, rage against the dying of the light.

The Receptive Reader

1. How is the tone in this poem *different* from what you might expect in a poem about death?

2. The speaker in the poem does not address his own father directly until the *last stanza* of the poem. How does this last stanza affect your response to the poem? (How do you think your response to the poem might have been different if the father had been brought into the poem at the beginning?)

3. Thomas attracted a large following in the thirties and forties by writing with passionate intensity about the experiences of *ordinary people.* In this poem, what are striking examples of his writing about ordinary experience in heightened, intensely emotional language? How much of the heightened, passionate quality of his verse results from the playing off of extreme *opposites?*

4. This poem uses the traditional form of the *villanelle,* a set of three-line stanzas repeating the same rhyme scheme (*aba*), which is further reinforced by

a fourth line added to the concluding stanza (rhyming *abaa*). What are the two opposed key words in the poem that the rhyme scheme keeps driving home? Two final lines alternate in the stanzas till they are juxtaposed in the concluding couplet. Why is this kind of insistent *repetition* more appropriate to Thomas' poem than it would be to a poem written in a more understated style?

The Personal Response

If wise men know that in the end "dark is right," is the "rage" the poet calls up futile? (Is it impious?)

Some of the earliest known poems are **elegies**, or poems of mourning and lamentation. Like the following modern poem of mourning, traditional elegies do not always maintain the same note of bitterness to the end. They often work their way through bitter grief to calm acceptance or to the joyful certainty of resurrection. How does the following poem come to terms with loss?

N. Scott Momaday   *(born 1934)*

Earth and I Gave You Turquoise   *1974*

Earth and I gave you turquoise
   when you walked singing
We lived laughing in my house
   and told old stories
You grew ill when the owl cried   5
We will meet on Black Mountain

I will bring corn for planting
   and we will make fire
Children will come to your breast
   You will heal my heart   10
I speak your name many times
The wild cane remembers you

My young brother's house is filled
   I go there to sing
We have not spoken of you   15
   but our songs are sad
When Moon Woman goes to you
I will follow her white way

Tonight they dance near Chinle
   by the seven elms   20
There your loom whispered beauty
   They will eat mutton
and drink coffee till morning
You and I will not be there

I saw a crow by Red Rock   25
    standing on one leg
It was the black of your hair
    The years are heavy
I will ride the swiftest horse
You will hear the drumming hooves   30

The Receptive Reader

Although Momaday places his poem in the setting of the tribal past, it speaks
a language that transcends time and place. Which of the images and statements
in the poem do most to help you share the speaker's emotions? Which do most
to help you place yourself in the speaker's place? How does the speaker deal
with his grief?

The Creative Dimension

The following re-creation captures the elegiac tone of Momaday's poem. For
this or another poem in this chapter, do a similar re-creation that captures the
tone of the original.

> We walked the earth together
> In my house we danced and drank coffee till morning
> I planted corn
> You wanted children
> But you became ill
> I thought love could heal you
> The years drag
> I'll dance no more
> But one day I'll speak your name
> And you'll come on a swift horse

Making Connections—For Discussion or Writing

William Stafford's "Traveling through the Dark," Dylan Thomas' "Do Not Go
Gentle into That Good Night," and N. Scott Momaday's "Earth and I Gave You
Turquoise" all confront the readers with emotions inspired by the thought of
death. Which of these poems seems to you most eloquent or truest to emotions
you yourself might feel in a similar situation? Which seems less so, and why?

THE USES OF IRONY

Snowy egrets stand
graceful, majestic, serene
among the beer cans
        STUDENT HAIKU

Some poets filter out what is ugly or disappointing in life. Filtered
poetry is like a portrait photographer who airbrushes blemishes,
frowns, and signs of age. We are flattered by the retouched picture, but
we know it tells only part of the truth. Many modern poets take naturally to irony and paradox as ways of doing justice to the undercurrents

and countercurrents of life. Modern poets have often been fascinated by the crosscurrents and subtexts that complicate conventionally expected feelings. Irony and paradox are the poet's way of bringing in a neglected or ignored part of the story:

✗ **Irony** produces a wry humorous effect by bringing in a part of the truth that we might have preferred to hide. Irony knows that the idol has feet of clay, and it may tell us so with glee. It often has the last word, undercutting the more flattering or idealizing hypothesis.

✗ A **paradox** is an apparent contradiction that begins to make sense on second thought. Something at first does not seem true, but when we think about it we see how it might be. Like irony, paradox is aware of the discrepancy between the rest of the idol and its feet, but it is more likely to make us try to resolve the contradiction. We may begin to see the point of it: Life itself is neither all clay or all gold. What is beautiful in our world is rooted in common clay.

What is the irony in the following poem? One of his readers said of this Latino poet (North American of Puerto Rican ancestry) that he "brings to life his love for his people while etching haunting pictures that create lasting images" for his readers. What contradictory thoughts or mixed feelings do you think were in the poet's mind in front of the pawnshop window?

Martín Espada   *(born 1957)*

Latin Night at the Pawnshop   *1987*

Chelsea, Massachusetts
Christmas, 1987

The apparition of a salsa band
gleaming in the Liberty Loan
pawnshop window:

Golden trumpet,
silver trombone,
congas, maracas, tambourine,   5
all with price tags dangling
like the city morgue ticket
on a dead man's toe.

The Receptive Reader

1. What is sad and ironic about the name of the pawnshop? What is ironic about the time of year?

2. What for you is the central irony in this poem? How does the poet heighten it or drive it home?

3. What are the emotions created by the concluding simile?

Illness provides an ironic counterpoint to our hopes for a happy and fulfilled life. The author of the following poem, admired by fellow poets and fiercely loyal readers, struggled with and was finally defeated by mental illness.

Anne Sexton   *(1928–1975)*

Ringing the Bells   1960

And this is the way they ring
the bells in Bedlam
and this is the bell-lady
who comes each Tuesday morning
to give us a music lesson   5
and because the attendants make you go
and because we mind by instinct,
like bees caught in the wrong hive,
we are the circle of the crazy ladies
who sit in the lounge of the mental house   10
and smile at the smiling woman
who passes us each a bell,
who points at my hand
that holds my bell, E flat,
and this is the gray dress next to me   15
who grumbles as if it were special
to be old, to be old,
and this is the small hunched squirrel girl
on the other side of me
who picks at the hair over her lip,   20
who picks at the hairs over her lip all day,
and this is how the bells really sound,
as untroubled and clean
as a workable kitchen,
and this is always my bell responding   25
to my hand that responds to the lady
who points at me, E flat;
and although we are no better for it,
they tell you to go. And you do.

The Receptive Reader

1. Bedlam (originally Bethlehem) was the name of a notorious London insane asylum. In the dark ages of mental health care, people came there to gawk at the antics of the inmates. What is the irony in the poet's use of this name?

2. What is ironic about the music therapy she describes? What is ironic about the smiles in this poem? What is ironic about the sound of the bells? (How are the patients like "bees caught in the wrong hive"?)

3. Why is there so much repetition, with everything running together without proper punctuation?

The following bitterly ironic poem looks at the exploitation of the Indian past as a tourist attraction from the point of view of a Native American poet. nila northSun was born in Nevada and is of Shoshone-Chippewa heritage. What is the irony in this poem?

nila northSun   *(born 1951)*

Moving Camp Too Far   *1984*

i can't speak of
    many moons
    moving camp on travois
i can't tell of
    the last great battle   5
    counting coup or
    taking scalp
i don't know what it
    was to hunt buffalo
    or do the ghost dance   10
but
i can see an eagle
    almost extinct
    on slurpee plastic cups
i can travel to powwows   15
    in campers & winnebagos
i can eat buffalo meat
    at the tourist burger stand
i can dance to indian music
    rock-n-roll hey-a-hey-o   20
i can
    & unfortunately
    i do

The Receptive Reader

1. What's the meaning of *travois* and *counting coup?* What does the title mean?

2. An editor reprinting this poem said, "This poem is a mourning song, as it is one of a stunted and trivialized vision made to fit a pop-culture conception of the Indian. . . . it highlights some of the more enraging aspects of American culture" as they can appear only to Native Americans. What did she mean?

Making Connections—For Discussion or Writing

What in the poems by Louise Erdrich (Chapter 19), N. Scott Momaday, and nila northSun seems to you specific to the Native American experience? What has parallels in your own experience or in the experience of other people you know? Have you ever experienced feelings similar to those expressed in these poems?

We use the term *irony* in two major ways. A contrast between what we expect and what really happens makes for **irony of situation**. When the ocean liner *Titanic,* touted as unsinkable, went down on its maiden voyage with a terrible loss of life, the English poet Thomas Hardy pondered the ironic contrast between human "vaingloriousness" and the ship's inglorious end. A contrast between what we say and what we really mean makes for **verbal irony**—intentional irony in our use of language. The following poem, by a British-born poet who became an American citizen, is an extended exercise in verbal irony, starting with the title. Monuments to the Unknown Soldier commemorated the heroic war dead by honoring the remains of an unidentified soldier killed in action. As we read the following poem, we find that there is nothing heroic about the "unknown citizen," and it is not the poet's intention to honor him. What *is* the poet's intention?

W. H. Auden   *(1907–1973)*

The Unknown Citizen   *1940*

(To JS/07/M/378
This Marble Monument
Is Erected by the State)

He was found by the Bureau of Statistics to be
One against whom there was no official complaint,
And all the reports of his conduct agree
That in the modern sense of an old-fashioned word, he was
     a saint,
For in everything he did he served the Greater Community.   5
Except for the War till the day he retired
He worked in a factory and never got fired,
But satisfied his employers, Fudge Motors Inc.
Yet he wasn't a scab° or odd in his views,   *strike breaker*
For his Union reports that he paid his dues,   10
(Our report on his Union shows it was sound)
And our Social Psychology workers found
That he was popular with his mates° and liked a drink.   *his friends*
The Press are convinced that he bought a paper every day
And that his reactions to advertisements were normal in every   15
     way.
Policies taken out in his name prove that he was fully insured,
And his Health-card shows he was once in a hospital but left it
     cured.

Both Producers Research and High-Grade Living declare
He was fully sensible to the advantages of the Installment Plan
And had everything necessary to the Modern Man,   20
A phonograph, a radio, a car and a frigidaire.
Our researchers into Public Opinion are content
That he held the proper opinions for the time of year;
When there was peace, he was for peace; when there was war
  he went.
He was married and added five children to the population,   25
Which our Eugenist° says was the right number for a   *population planner*
  parent of his generation,
And our teachers report that he never interfered with their
  education.
Was he free? Was he happy? The question is absurd:
Had anything been wrong, we should certainly have heard.

The Receptive Reader

1. The Unknown Soldier was anonymous because the remains could not be identified. Why does Auden give his Unknown Citizen no name but only a number?

2. What clues in the poem remind us that the poet is speaking ironically? For instance, what is wrong with holding "the proper opinions for the time of year"? What is ironic about the citizen's attitude toward war? Why is what the teachers say about him a left-handed compliment? (Can you find other examples of mock compliments that are examples of verbal irony?)

3. Many of the institutions keeping tab on the citizenry apparently regarded JS/07/M/378 as a model citizen, if not a "saint." What is the poet's basic criticism of him? (What is the poet's basic criticism of the state?)

The Creative Dimension

Auden wrote this poem in 1940. What would you include in an updated portrait of the Unknown Citizen or the Unknown Consumer? Write your own ironic portrait of today's Unknown Citizen.

A poet with a strong sense of irony may play off popular stereotypes against the poet's perception of the truth. How does the following poem by Walt Whitman go counter to stereotypes current in periods of gay-bashing or homophobia?

Walt Whitman   *(1819–1892)*

A Glimpse

A glimpse through an interstice caught,
Of a crowd of workmen and drivers in a bar-room around the stove late
  of a winter night, and I unremarked seated in a corner,
Of a youth who loves me and whom I love, silently approaching and
  seating himself near, that he may hold me by the hand,

A long while amid the noises of coming and going, of drinking and oath
 and smutty jest,
There we two, content, happy in being together, speaking little, perhaps   5
 not a word.

The Receptive Reader

1. Who are the other people in the barroom? What ironic contrast does the
poet set up between them and the two lovers?

2. The two people at the center of this poem spoke little, "perhaps not a
word." How important is the spoken word in a love relationship?

JUXTAPOSITIONS
Modern Parables

A man said to the universe:
"Sir, I exist!"
"However," replied the universe,
"The fact has not created in me
A sense of obligation."

STEPHEN CRANE

A **parable** is a brief story with a weighty meaning, which the listeners or readers are left to ponder and make out for themselves. Study the
workings of irony in the following examples. Is there a common thread
or a shared underlying attitude?

Stephen Crane   *(1871–1900)*

The Wayfarer   *1895*

The wayfarer,
Perceiving the pathway to truth,
Was struck with astonishment.
It was thickly grown with weeds.
"Ha," he said,   5
"I see that none has passed here
In a long time."
Later he saw that each weed was a singular knife.
"Well," he mumbled at last,
"Doubtless there are other roads."   10

The Receptive Reader
What is Crane's ironic comment on the pursuit of truth?

Bruce Bennett   *(born 1940)*

Leader   *1984*

A man shot himself
in the foot.

    "ow!" he howled,
hopping this way and
that. "Do something!
Do something!"   5
    "We are! We are!"
shouted those around
him. "We're hopping!
We're hopping!"

The Receptive Reader

How closely does this poem follow the pattern of Stephen Crane's "A-man-did-such-and-such" poems? What is the poet's ironic comment on leaders and followers?

The Creative Dimension

Write your own updated "A-person-did-such-and-such" poem.

THE USES OF PARADOX

Although life is an affair of light and shadow, we
never accept it as such. We are always reaching
toward the light. From childhood we are given
values which correspond only to an ideal world.
The shadowy side of real life is ignored. Thus, we
are unable to deal with the mixture of light and
shadow of which life really consists.

MIGUEL SERRAN

Life is bounded by wonder on one side and terror
on the other.

SAM KEEN

A **paradox** is a seeming contradiction that begins to make sense on second thought. Like irony, a paradox challenges us to keep more than one idea in mind at the same time. We are confronted with a paradox when we are told that many feel lonely in a crowd. They are alone in the midst of our crowded, congested cities. This apparent contradiction makes sense on second thought: The physical presence of others is not enough; we need to be with people who understand and who care. Irony and paradox both bring in a part of the truth that simpleminded people might ignore. But irony tends to undercut the simpler or more optimistic assumption. A paradox asks us to puzzle over the apparent contradiction and to balance off the conflicting points of view. We may have to live with the paradox.

Poets have found love a paradoxical emotion, fraught with attraction and rejection, joy and pain, hope and despair. What makes the following poem about love paradoxical?

Nelle Fertig   *(born 1919)*

I Have Come to the Conclusion   *1974*

I have come to the conclusion
    she said
that when we fall in love
we really fall in love with ourselves—
that we choose particular people   5
because they provide
the particular mirrors
in which we wish to see.

And when did you discover
this surprising bit of knowledge?   10
he asked.

After I had broken a few
very fine mirrors
she said.

What the woman in this poem says is paradoxical because at first glance it doesn't seem to be true. Supposedly, when we fall in love, we go beyond our usual self-love to make someone else more important than we are to ourselves. Isn't the beauty of love that it makes us care for somebody else? On second thought, we may begin to see the point: We may be prone to fall in love with people who think that we are in some way special or wonderful. We are moved when we ask the mirror on the wall "Who's the fairest of them all?" and the mirror replies: "You are."

The Receptive Reader

1. Cluster the word *mirror*. What images, associations, or memories does the word bring to mind? Are any of them related to the role mirrors play in Fertig's poem?

2. How do you recognize the ironic tone of the second speaker in the poem?

3. How do you think the mirrors got broken?

Love poetry in the Western world long followed the lead of the Italian fourteenth-century poet Petrarch. In the Petrarchan tradition, love was a paradoxical mixture of joy and sorrow. Love was a source of much joy, but it was often disappointed and therefore also the cause of much suffering. The following is a modern translation of a sonnet by Petrarch. (Trace the interlaced rhyme scheme of the traditional fourteen-line poem, and listen for the underlying iambic meter.) What makes this poem paradoxical? How much of it makes sense on second thought?

Francesco Petrarca   *(1304–1374)*

Or Che 'l Ciel e la Terra e 'l Vento Tace   1369

TRANSLATED BY HANS P. GUTH

Calm now are heaven and earth, and the winds asleep.
No birds now stir; wild beasts in slumber lie.
Night guides her chariot across the starry sky.
No wave now moves the waters of the deep.
I only keep vigil—I think, I burn, I weep.   5
She who destroys me dazzles my mind's eye.
At war with myself, raging and grieving, I
Long for the peace that's hers to give or keep.
From the same single fountain of life
Rise the bitter and sweet that feed my soul.   10
I am caressed and slashed by the same hand.
A martyr in a world of ceaseless strife,
I have died and risen a thousandfold.
So far am I from reaching the promised land.

The Receptive Reader

1. What is fitting, and what is *paradoxical,* about the nighttime setting?

2. What examples can you find of *opposed* concepts, clashing images, and mixed emotions?

3. Poets who made love into a religion often used the vocabulary of religious devotion. Where and how does this poem use *religious imagery?* What makes the religious images paradoxical?

In the following Shakespeare sonnet, a central paradox sets up many of the apparent contradictions in the poem. At first, the time of year seems to be winter—freezing, bare, and barren. A loved person is away, and everything seems dark and empty. But here is the paradox: It's actually summer, the season of birdsong and abundance. Why then is the speaker in the poem shivering and freezing? The answer is that it is summer outside but winter in the poet's soul.

Shakespeare   (1564–1616)

97   before 1598

like a winter hath my absence been
n thee, the pleasure of the fleeting° year!   *quickly passing*
.hat freezings have I felt, what dark days seen!
What old December's bareness everywhere!
And yet this time removed° was summer's time   *with you absent*   5
The teeming° autumn, big with rich increase,   *full of new life*
Bearing the wanton burthen of the prime,°   *giving birth to spring's*
Like widowed wombs after their lords' decease: *luxurious offspring*
Yet this abundant issue seemed to me
But hope of orphans and unfathered fruit;   10
For summer and his pleasures wait on thee,
And, thou away,° the very birds are mute.   *with you away*
Or, if they sing, 'tis° with so dull a cheer   *it is*
That leaves look pale, dreading the winter's near.

The Receptive Reader

1. As one student reader said, "In this poem, summer comes only when the loved person is there." In how many different ways is this *central paradox* followed up or echoed in this poem?

2. Where and how does the central metaphor shift from autumn to widowhood? What is the connection? What paradoxical emotions does the orphan metaphor bring into the poem?

3. How do the leaves in the last line illustrate *personification*—reading human qualities into the inanimate world? Where else does the poem show the power of personification to turn the world around us into a mirror of our emotions?

The following is a poem of mourning that does not focus on the sadness of the bereaved. What are the memories and paradoxical emotions in the mourners' minds?

John Crowe Ransom   (1888–1974)

Bells for John Whiteside's Daughter   1924

There was such speed in her little body,
And such lightness in her footfall,
It is no wonder her brown study
Astonishes us all.

Her wars were bruited° in our high window,   *were heard of*   5
We looked among orchard trees and beyond
Where she took arms against her shadow,
Or harried unto the pond

The lazy geese like a snow cloud
Dripping their snow on the green grass,   10
Tricking and stopping, sleepy and proud,
Who cried in goose, Alas,

For the tireless heart within the little
Lady with rod that made them rise
From their apple-dreams and scuttle   15
Goose-fashion under the skies!

But now go the bells, and we are ready,
In one house we are sternly stopped
To say we are vexed at her brown study,
Lying so primly propped.   20

In this understated modern poem, the speaker does not pour forth his grief at the untimely death of a child. Instead, much of the poem helps us relive the speaker's delight in the remembered quickness and light footfall of the young girl. We flash back to the girl who used to play tirelessly in the orchard, conducting shadow wars with her own shadow or harrying the lazy, sleepy geese, driving them toward the pond. Now, as the bells call the mourners to pay their last respects to the body, they are "astonished" to see the child, who used to be so full of life, at rest as if in a "brown study"—as if she were absorbed in deciphering a difficult passage in a book. They are "vexed" or annoyed to see her once so speedy little body "lying so primly propped."

The Receptive Reader

1. Is there any hint of the mourners' emotions beyond their being "vexed"?
2. What is witty about the geese crying out "in goose"?
3. Do you feel mixed emotions in reading this poem?

The Range of Interpretation

Critics have interpreted this poem in very different ways. Which of the two following ways of reading this poem seems more persuasive to you?

1. In this poem, the remembered delight in a child full of innocent life and the bitter disappointment at her death make us experience mixed emotions. The poet's feelings are ambivalent (from a Latin word meaning "marching in two directions at once"). For a parent or friend of the family, the loss of a young innocent child, full of life, is a shattering blow. But it is as if the vivid memory of the "tireless" child, carrying on her mock "wars" with the geese, and our "astonishment" at her transformation could for a time fend off the bitter irony of her death. We protect ourselves against the harsh, merciless reality of death by dwelling on our memory of the living child and by pretending to be "astonished" and not fully understand what has happened to her.

2. The speakers in the poem (the "we" in the poem) can recall the child's vitality in astonishment because it is not their child; it is "John Whiteside's

Daughter." The speakers have watched the girl from their "high window,"
suggesting that the girl without a name of her own is a servant's child.
(Ransom was a Southern poet.) The poem is not one of grief or bereave-
ment as much as it is a poem of shock, of vexation. The speakers are not
weeping or mourning; they are "sternly stopped." They are troubled more
by the unpredictability of death's indifference to youth and vitality than
they are grieving, as parents would.

The **metaphysical** poets of the early seventeenth century love paradox. They are fond of yoking together things from widely different areas
of experience. In their religious poetry, they translate the mysteries of
faith into language borrowed from science, medicine, mechanics, or war.
They deal with the central paradoxes of religious doctrine: the certainty
of death but yet the belief in life after death; our yearning for God's love
and yet our stubborn attachment to sin. The following poem focuses on a
key paradox of Christian doctrine: Central to the believer's religious
awakening is the realization of mortality, the fear of death. But ultimately
the hope of resurrection makes death lose its sting. Death has no reason
to "swell" with pride.

John Donne   *(1572–1631)*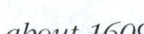

Holy Sonnet 10   *about 1609*

Death, be not proud, though some have callèd thee
Mighty and dreadful, for thou art not so;
For those whom thou thinkst thou dost overthrow
Die not, poor Death, nor yet canst thou kill me.
From rest and sleep, which but thy pictures be,°   *are your look-alikes*   5
Much pleasure—then from thee much more must flow,
And soonest our best men with thee do go,
Rest of their bones, and soul's delivery.°   *release of their souls*
Thou art slave to fate, chance, kings, and desperate men,
And dost with poison, war, and sickness dwell,   10
And poppy or charm can make us sleep as well
And better than thy stroke; why swellst thou then?
One short sleep past, we wake eternally
And death shall be no more; Death, thou shalt die.

The Receptive Reader

1. In his religious poems, as in his earlier love poetry, Donne projects his
personal feelings onto a large screen. He acts out his personal soul-searching
on a large cosmic stage. What makes this poem a striking example?

2. How is death a "slave" to "fate, chance, kings, and desperate men"? How would he do their bidding? The poet refers to sleep once literally and once figuratively—where and how?

3. Donne often structures his poem like a set of arguments—the *rhetoric* of a lawyer pleading a case in front of a jury, for instance. Can you outline the arguments he uses to devalue "poor Death"?

4. What is the meaning of the *play on words* in the last half of the last line? How has the poem as a whole led up to it?

JUXTAPOSITIONS
Convention and Originality

Gather ye rosebuds while ye may
Old time is still a-flying
And this same flower that smiles today
Tomorrow will be dying.

ROBERT HERRICK,
"TO THE VIRGINS, TO MAKE MUCH OF TIME"

Readers of seventeenth-century poetry recognize the plea of the lover to a reluctant partner: "Seize the day; make use of the passing day" (**carpe diem** in the original Latin). The too-soon fading rose "smiles today," but if we do not enjoy it now, it will have wilted by tomorrow. Therefore, "gather ye rosebuds while ye may." The two poems that follow depart from this convention, each in its own way. The first one, in the metaphysical vein, is Andrew Marvell's "To His Coy Mistress" (meaning "To His Reluctant Lady," without the current connotations of *mistress*). This poem has no rosebuds, no songbirds, and no conventional springtime setting in the English countryside. Then read a poem by the Countess of Dia, a French poet of the twelfth century, who looks at love and courtship from a female rather than the conventional male perspective.

In Marvell's poem, bold and paradoxical images roam from the Humber River in northern England to the river Ganges in India (then famous for its jewels and spices) and from there to "deserts of vast eternity." The poem ranges over vast stretches of time, from Noah's flood to the "conversion of the Jews," then not expected till the end of time. Paradoxically, the metaphors and similes in this poem are drawn from geography, biblical history, and botany—areas not conventionally associated with love.

Andrew Marvell   *(1621–1678)*

To His Coy Mistress   *before 1678*

Had we but world enough, and time,
This coyness, lady, were° no crime.   *would be*
We would sit down and think which way
To walk and pass our long love's day.
Thou by the Indian Ganges' side   5
Shouldst rubies find; I by the tide
Of Humber would complain.° I would   *write plaintive love songs*
Love you ten years before the flood,
And you should, if you please, refuse
Till the conversion of the Jews.   10
My vegetable love should grow
Vaster than empires and more slow;
An hundred years should go to praise
Thine eyes and on thy forehead gaze,
Two hundred to adore each breast,   15
But thirty thousand to the rest,
An age at least to every part,
And the last age should show your heart.
For, lady, you deserve this state,°   *this high station*
Nor would I love at lower rate.   20
    But at my back I always hear
Time's wingèd chariot hurrying near,
And yonder all before us lie
Deserts of vast eternity.
Thy beauty shall no more be found,   25
Nor, in thy marble vault, shall sound
My echoing song; then worms shall try
That long-preserved virginity,
And your quaint honor° turn to dust,   *deliberate virtue*
And into ashes all my lust.   30
The grave's a fine and private place,
But none, I think, do there embrace.
    Now therefore, while the youthful hue
Sits on thy skin like morning dew,
And while thy willing soul transpires°   *breathes forth* 35
At every pore with instant fires,
Now let us sport us while we may,
And now, like amorous birds of prey,
Rather at once our time devour
Than languish in his slow-chapped° power.   *chewing with slow-moving jaws* 40
Let us roll all our strength and all
Our sweetness up into one ball,
And tear our pleasures with rough strife
Through the iron gates of life.

Thus, though we cannot make our sun   45
Stand still, yet we will make him run.

The Receptive Reader

1. Where and how does Marvell carry *hyperbole,* or poetic exaggeration, to new extremes?

2. What is paradoxical about a "vegetable love" growing slowly to vast size like a giant cabbage? On second thought, what might be desirable or welcome about the idea?

3. What images and associations do time and eternity usually bring to your mind? How are the metaphors Marvell uses different? (What were the original uses of a chariot?)

4. What is the effect of the poet's bringing graveyard imagery into a love poem? (Can you find a good example of *verbal irony* in this passage?)

5. When Marvell replaces the conventional songbirds with birds of prey, what is the effect on the way we think about love and lovers? How do these birds help him turn the tables on all-devouring time? Why does he make us imagine "the iron gates of life" rather than a meadow with spring flowers?

6. Why would lovers want to make the sun "stand still"? How would they make the sun "run" to keep up with them?

The Creative Dimension

A student poet wrote in her "Reply of Your Coy Mistress":

We have the world, and we have the time;
To wait a while longer would be no crime.

Write your own personal reply or response to Marvell.

We tend to think of the early love poets, or troubadours, of southern France as male. However, the poems of several women troubadours have come down to us. How does the following poem depart from the conventions of much male-oriented love poetry?

Countess of Dia   *(born about 1140)*

I Sing of That Which I Would Rather Hide   *before 1200*

TRANSLATED BY HANS P. GUTH

I sing of that which I would rather hide:
Where is the one who should be at my side
And whom I dearly love, come ebb or tide?
My kindness and sweet grace he has denied,
My beauty and good sense and goodly show.   5
I am betrayed, deceived, my love defied,
As if I were the lowest of the low.

Yet I take heart: I never brought you shame
Nor ever did the least to hurt your name.
My love surpasses loves of greater fame,   10
And I am pleased I beat you at love's game—
Outscored you when devotion was the test.
Your cold words and your slights all speak the same—
And yet you play the charmer with the rest.

The Receptive Reader

1. How is the *perspective* of the speaker in this poem different from that in traditional male-oriented poems of love and courtship? How much of this poem seems to belong to a different time, a different world? How much seems relevant or intelligible in our own time?

2. Modern translators of the southern French, or Provençal, poetry of the early Middle Ages often do not attempt to reproduce the finely crafted *stanza forms* and the intricate rhyme scheme of the originals. How do you think the rhyme scheme and the stanza form re-created here affect the reader's reactions to the poem?

Making Connections—For Discussion or Writing

In traditional *carpe diem* poetry, the woman who is admonished to make the most of time remains silent. What she thinks while the speaker in the poem makes his plea is not recorded. For an indication of possible unconventional responses, compare the Countess of Dia's poem with a modern poem like Edna St. Vincent Millay's "I, Being Born a Woman and Distressed" (Chapter 18).

POEMS FOR FURTHER STUDY

When reading the following poems, pay special attention to tone. What is the prevailing tone in each poem? What kind of voice is speaking to you in the poem? If the poem uses irony, is it gentle and teasing or bitter and sarcastic? If the poem uses paradox, what is the basic contradiction?

Sir John Suckling   *(1609–1642)*

Song   *1638*

Why so pale and wan, fond° lover?   *foolish*
    Prithee,° why so pale?   *Please*
Will, when looking well can't move her,
    Looking ill prevail?
    Prithee, why so pale?   5

Why so dull and mute, young sinner?
    Prithee, why so mute?
Will, when speaking well can't win her,
    Saying nothing do 't?

Quit, quit, for shame; this will not move,°   *persuade* 10
    This cannot take her.
If of herself she will not love,
    Nothing can make her:
    The devil take her!

Richard Lovelace   *(1618–1658)*

To Lucasta, Going to the Wars   *1649*

Tell me not, sweet, I am unkind
That from the nunnery
Of thy chaste breast and quiet mind,
To war and arms I fly.°   *hurry*

True, a new mistress now I chase,   5
The first foe in the field;
And with a stronger faith embrace
A sword, a horse, a shield.

Yet this inconstancy is such
As you too shall adore;   10
I could not love thee, dear, so much,
Loved I° not honor more.   *if I did not love*

The Receptive Reader

    What is the central metaphor the poet chooses for going away to war? What makes it playful or humorous? How does the poet play on words in the final two lines?

Sharon Olds   *(born 1942)*

Quake Theory   *1980*

When two plates of earth scrape along each other
like a mother and daughter
it is called a fault.

There are faults that slip smoothly past each other
an inch a year, with just a faint rasp   5
like a man running his hand over his chin,
that man between us,

and there are faults that get stuck at a bend for twenty years.
The ridge bulges up like a father's sarcastic forehead
and the whole thing freezes in place, the man between us.   10

When this happens, there will be heavy damage
to industrial areas and leisure residence
when the deep plates
finally jerk past
the terrible pressure of their contact.   15
                              The earth cracks
and innocent people slip gently in like swimmers.

The Receptive Reader

How does the earthquake metaphor affect the tone of this poem? In developing the implications of this central metaphor, how does the poet start in a low key and build up to a climax? (Where is the high point? How does the poet make it stand out?) What is the speaker's attitude toward the daughter? What is the speaker's attitude toward the father? Who are the "innocent people"?

Joy Harjo   *(born 1951)*

Leaving   *1983*

Four o'clock this morning there was a call.
She talked Indian, so it was probably her mother.
It was. Something not too drastic, tone of voice,
no deaths or car wrecks. But something. I was
out of the sheets, unwrapped from the blankets,   5
fighting to stay in sleep. Slipped in and out of her
voice, her voice on the line.
She came back to me. Lit cigarette blurred in the dark.
All lights off but that. Laid
down next to me, empty, these final hours   10
before my leaving.

Her sister was running away from her boyfriend and
was stranded in Calgary, Alberta. Needed money
and comfort for the long return back home.

I dreamed of a Canadian plain, and warm arms around me,   15
the soft skin of the body's landscape. And I dreamed
of bear, and a thousand mile escape homeward.

The Receptive Reader

1. What is the situation in this poem by a Native American poet? What is happening? What clues are there in the poem?

2. What is the prevailing tone in this poem about parting? What are the speaker's emotions? Are they what you would expect in this situation?

William Shakespeare   *(1564–1616)*

Sonnet 130   before 1598

My mistress' eyes are nothing like the sun;
Coral is far more red than her lips' red;
If snow be white, why then her breasts are dun;°   *grayish brown*
If hairs be wires, black wires grow on her head.
I have seen roses damasked,° red and white,   *multicolored*   5
But no such roses see I in her cheeks;
And in some perfumes there is more delight
Than in the breath that from my mistress reeks.
I love to hear her speak, yet well I know
That music hath a far more pleasing sound;   10
I grant I never saw a goddess go;
My mistress, when she walks, treads on the ground.
And yet, by heaven, I think my love as rare°   *marvelous*
As any she belied° with false compare.   *any woman misrepresented*

The Receptive Reader

1. How does this poem illustrate the idea that irony is the revenge of reality on poetic exaggeration?

2. Readers hostile to irony accuse it of undercutting our capacity for sincere emotion. Do you think it does so in this sonnet?

Pablo Neruda   *(1904–1973)*

The Fickle One   1972

TRANSLATED BY DONALD D. WALSH

My eyes went away from me
Following a dark girl
who went by.

She was made of black mother-of-pearl,
Made of dark-purple grapes,   5
and she lashed my blood
with her tail of fire.

After them all
I go.

A pale blonde went by   10
like a golden plant
swaying her gifts.
And my mouth went
like a wave
discharging on her breast   15
lightning bolts of blood.

After them all
I go.

But to you, without my moving,
without seeing you, distant you,   20
go my blood and my kisses,
my dark one and my fair one,
my tall one and my little one,
my broad one and my slender one,
my ugly one, my beauty,   25
made of all the gold
and of all the silver,
made of all the wheat
and of all the earth,
made of all the water   30
of the sea waves,
made for my arms,
made for my kisses,
made for my soul.

The Receptive Reader

1. What is strange or paradoxical about the imagery in the early parts of the poem? How do you explain the yoking of contraries in the last part of the poem?

2. Do you think the speaker in the poem can be sincere in the last part of the poem after what he said in the earlier parts?

3. What is your personal reaction to the poem?

WRITING ABOUT LITERATURE

20 Listening for Tone
WRITING FOCUS: Reading the Clues

The Writing Workshop   When you write about tone, you need to read between the lines. You need to have your antenna out for the emotional quality of a poem. For instance, you might expect a poem about a funeral to be sad and solemn. However, you cannot take the tone for granted. The poem may have been written in a tone of stern moralizing about the shortcomings of the deceased. Or it may dwell on bittersweet memories of happier hours.

Make your paper show that you have read for clues to the attitudes and feelings that seem built into a poem:

✗ *Pay special attention to the connotations of words.* Words like *vexed, angry,* and *furious* mark different points on a continuing scale. They go from a low-key state of annoyance and perplexity (or "vexation") through ordinary anger to furious, uncontrolled rage. Look for a network of related words that might help set the tone of a poem. A poet might create a careless, joyful mood by the repeated use of synonyms or near-synonyms like *mirth, merry, jocund, revelry, good cheer, fiesta, frolic, joyous.* (A poem in which words like these echo is not likely to be a solemn ode in praise of the Puritan work ethic.)

✗ *Listen to the rhythm of the poem as it is read out loud.* Is the poem slow-moving, deliberate, earnest? Is it skipping and cheerful? Is it urgent, insistent, driven by passionate indignation?

✗ *Look at the attitude the poem adopts toward the reader or listener.* Is the tone defiant, challenging? Does the poem take you into the speaker's confidence as if in a conspiratorial whisper? Does it treat you like a boon companion?

✗ *Try to become sensitive to nuances.* Unconditional love or hate or admiration is rare. A poet may admire something "this side idolatry" (as Ben Jonson did his fellow poet and playwright William Shakespeare).

✗ *Look for signs of humorous intention or irreverent wit.* When Lord Byron says about the high-toned philosophical speculations of a fellow poet, "I wish he would explain his explanations," we know that Byron's attitude will be less than worshipful. Watch especially for irreverent slangy expressions that undercut serious pretensions ("thus Milton's universe *went to smash*").

✗ *Look for shifts in tone that help shape a poem as a whole.* A poem may move from a tone of bitterness and indignation to a more understanding and forgiving tone. An elegy may start with notes of deep mourning but is likely to work its way to the joyful certainty of resurrection.

In John Milton's *Lycidas,* probably the most famous elegy in the English language, the speaker in the poem mourns the early death of a beloved friend. In a beautiful rural setting, he calls on a pageant of mythological figures to help him pay tribute to the deceased. But toward the end, he starts saying "Weep no more, woeful shepherds, weep no more." He begins to imagine the dead friend "in the blest kingdoms meek of joy and love," singing the glory of the Creator. In the last few lines, the speaker in the poem moves on to a new beginning,

Tomorrow to fresh woods, and pastures new.

How does the following student paper read the clues that help the poet set the tone?

Sample Student Paper

"Quake Theory," or Whose Fault Is It?

There is nothing quite as much fun as a punning wit. To utilize one word to mean two different things creates an effect like those optical illusions where we can see an old woman or a young girl . . . or again an old woman—this tickles the brain. And, tickled, we smile until, as in Sharon Olds' poem "Quake Theory," the serious message sinks in, and we realize this isn't fun anymore.

An initial metaphor is developed in the first stanza; it also sets up the pun: "When two plates of earth scrape along each other / like a mother and daughter / it is called a fault." The word *fault* does double-time here as a description of a fracture in the earth and as a key word to alert us to the distance between a mother and her daughter. That distance can best be summed up in the question: "Whose fault is it?" What is the *it* that isn't working?

The poem does not enlighten us immediately. Instead it sounds for a moment as though it might drone along in a professorial manner, informing us of two different kinds of fault in two stanzas. ("There are faults that slip smoothly past each other / an inch a year.") We read along, smiling in anticipation of further developments in what may prove an extended joke. The tone is dry, almost too dry, but we have been trained by generations of deadpan comedians to expect lurking underneath the surface dryness the levity of a joke. Sharon Olds lures us in but then abruptly shifts gears to refer to "that man between us."

Just who is this man? The man, as Sharon Olds intended, is a discordant note in this poem. Not only does his introduction into the poem upset the flow of the poem, but he himself is an upsetting influence in the relationship between mother and daughter.

We read in the second stanza that a fault can be trouble-free with only a bit of friction—friction likened to what results when a man rubs his five-o'clock shadow (not just any man, but "that man between us"). However, in the third stanza, we read that a fault may also be blocked and build up tension "like a father's sarcastic forehead," and "the whole thing freezes in place, the man between us." With this ominous note, the poem no longer seems to point toward a humorous conclusion. The repeated references to "that man," ending each of the two stanzas, remind us that the central metaphor in this poem is the earthquake.

The point of view is that of the mother speaking to the daughter (or perhaps vice versa). The speaker is trying to describe their relationship, which remains in constant motion, "scraping" at times, building up tension at others. But there is also a third dynamic, "that man," the father. He is there benignly or as an active threat. But he is certainly there.

What is the result when the tension builds up between the two locked bodies? "There will be heavy damage . . . when the deep plates / finally jerk past / the terrible pressure of their contact." In keeping with the metaphor of the earthquake, the poem itself fractures at this point, skips a line, and then resumes:

The earth cracks
and innocent people slip gently in like swimmers.

What an odd analogy! We may assume that in a clash of wills or land masses, some who are bystanders will suffer, perhaps even be swallowed, but this image seems both deadly and harmless at the same time. To "slip gently in like swimmers" seems to belie the violence just described. But this is perhaps as it should be: In any family upset there are not necessarily bleeding victims left lying around afterwards. People are sucked under without a surface struggle or disturbance.

In this poem, we are carried along at first amused, then puzzled or disturbed, and then saddened at the end. We sense that things might have been different; there is regret here. But whose "fault" is it? It is neither the mother's nor the daughter's but, as in plate tectonics, the fault of the rift between them, the father.

Questions for Peer Review

This student paper carefully traces the shifts in the tone of the poem from half-amused, first to "puzzling or disturbed," and then to sadness or regret.

1. The pun is a kind of *word play* that is irresistible to some but is not amusing or attractive to others. Do you respond to puns, and do you know punsters? (Can you provide some examples of puns, good or bad?) Would you have caught the double meaning of *fault* in this poem the way the student writer does? For you, is the playing with the double meaning funny? Why or why not?

2. Into how many details does the student writer trace the meaning and the continuing applications of the *key metaphor* of the shifting plates that cause an earthquake? Most readers would associate the idea of the earthquake with death and destruction. How does the student writer explain the shift in tone as the victims "slip in gently like swimmers"?

3. Where does the student writer find a striking illustration of a close connection between *form and meaning,* or between "sound and sense"?

4. Do you agree when the student writer makes what happened between the mother and daughter the father's "*fault*"?

5. Have you ever seen a joke turn *serious,* or have you ever watched a happy mood slowly turn to sadness and regret?

21 THEME
The Making of Meaning

Courtesy Richard B. Ressman

For me the real issues of our time are the issues of
every time—the hurt and wonder of loving;
making in all its forms, children, loaves of bread,
paintings, building; and the conservation of life
of all people and all places, the jeopardizing of
which no abstract doubletalk of "peace" or
"implacable foes" can excuse.

SYLVIA PLATH

A goal I think you can find in all my poems is to
plead with the world, with the reader, with the
person the poem is addressed to, to be kinder,
more compassionate, more understanding, more
intelligent. My poems are often about the pain I
feel and they are a plea to the world to relieve it.

DIANE WAKOSKI

When I landed in the republic of conscience
it was so noiseless when the engines stopped
I could hear a curlew high above the runway.

SEAMUS HEANEY,
"FROM THE REPUBLIC OF CONSCIENCE"

FOCUS ON THEME

Poetry helps us find meanings in the bewildering flow of experience. Poems make us think: Often a poem invites us to look at a familiar idea in a new light, challenging familiar rutted ways of thinking. It may nudge us into trying a new route to the solution of a familiar problem. When we focus on the **theme** of a poem, we try to sum up its meaning. We try to put into words what makes the poem thought-provoking: We look at the issues a poem seems to raise and the possible answers it suggests. We try to formulate the idea or insights that the poem as a whole seems to leave us with, for us to ponder and remember.

Some poets leave larger meanings implied, hinted at, suggested only. Most contemporary poets have been wary of large abstractions: happiness, alienation, patriotism, love. **Abstractions** are labels for large areas of human experience. In themselves, they are neither good nor bad. However, they do abstract—they "draw us away," from specifics and individuals. They extrapolate the larger patterns that help us chart our way. Many modern poets have steered clear of them, afraid they might become *mere* abstractions, mere labels that remove us from flesh-and-blood realities.

Other poets are less shy about spelling out key ideas in so many words. Poets of earlier ages, and some in our own time, draw explicit conclusions; they formulate their insights. Even so, you have to remember an important caution: Ideas in poetry are live ideas—anchored to what you can see and hear and feel. You cannot take them out of a poem the way you take candy out of a wrapper. The poet's ideas take shape before your eyes—embedded in graphic images, acted out in scenes and events that stir your emotions.

FIRST READING

Focusing on Meaning

What statement does the following poem make about what immigrants to this country think and feel about their children?

Pat Mora   *(born 1942)*

The Immigrants   *1991*

wrap their babies in the American flag,
feed them mashed hot dogs and apple pie,
name them Bill and Daisy,
buy them blonde dolls that blink blue
eyes or a football and tiny cleats   5
before the baby can even walk,
speak to them in thick English,
hallo, babee, hallo,
whisper in Spanish or Polish
when the babies sleep, whisper   10
in a dark parent bed, that dark
parent fear, "Will they like
our boy, our girl, our fine american
boy, our fine american girl?"

The Receptive Reader

1. What items would you select for a list of six items as American as apple pie? Would any of the items from Mora's list be on yours?

2. How would you sum up the thoughts and feelings of the immigrant parents in plain prose? What makes the experience of reading the poem different from reading a prose statement of the ideas embedded in it?

3. Do you think the poet is right about the majority of immigrant parents? Do you think she is too critical of them?

IDEA AND IMAGE

*Poems are like dreams; in them you put what you
don't know you know.*

ADRIENNE RICH

*Poetry doesn't just come from the mind. Art is not
just a thing of the intellect, but of the spirit.*

LUCILLE CLIFTON

Poets and critics use the word *theme* in two different but related ways:
Sometimes the term simply points to the general subject, to an area of
concern. A collection may sort poems out under thematic headings like
Love, Family, Identity, Alienation, and Dissent. Such themes are large
umbrella headings, under which individual poems will offer different
perspectives. Under the heading of Family, one poem might be mourning the lost golden world of childhood. Another poem might focus on
the need for breaking the fetters the family clamps on the individual.
However, often the term *theme* stands for the statement that a poem as
a whole makes *about* a subject. The theme then is what the poem as a
whole says about identity, alienation, or dissent. The theme is the recurrent message, insistent plea, or fresh insight that stays with us as we
leave the poem behind.

Poets vary greatly in how explicitly they verbalize the ideas implied
in or acted out in their poems. Some poets largely let their images speak
for themselves. Other poets speak for their images, serving as guides or
interpreters, spelling out more or less fully the message embedded in
metaphor or symbol. In the following poem, what is the relation between idea and image? How does the poet take a large abstraction to the
level of firsthand experience?

William Stafford   *(1914–1992)*

Freedom   *1969*

Freedom is not following a river.
Freedom is following a river
     though, if you want to.
It is deciding now by what happens now.
It is knowing that luck makes a difference.   5

No leader is free; no follower is free—
     the rest of us can often be free.
Most of the world are living by
creeds too odd, chancy, and habit-forming
     to be worth arguing about by reason.   10

If you are oppressed, wake up about
four in the morning; most places
you can usually be free some of the time
    if you wake up before other people.

What does this poem say about freedom? Much in our lives *restricts* our freedom. Apparently, being a leader and being a follower are both incompatible with making free choices. (Both leader and follower march with the main body of troops.) To be caught up in habitual creeds, to make today's decisions bound by yesterday's precedents, to be oppressed—all these limit the sphere of free choice. Nevertheless, there is a margin of freedom—if only in the margins of our existence—such as in the early morning hours, before the mechanisms that constrain us kick in.

The Receptive Reader

1. What do you make of the concrete *images* in this poem? When or how would someone want to follow a river? What does freedom have to do with following or not following it? What does freedom have to do with getting up early?

2. Why do you think the speaker claims that part of freedom is "deciding now by what happens now"? What makes the speaker in the poem say that neither a "leader" nor a "follower" can be free? What is "habit-forming" about "creeds" (and how do they limit your freedom)?

3. Does the poem provide any hints or guidelines on how to enlarge your margin of freedom?

4. How would you sum up in a sentence or two the *theme* of this poem—the statement the poem as a whole makes about freedom?

The Personal Response

How does the statement about freedom that the poem makes as a whole compare with the ideas you yourself associate with the word?

The following is a famous poetic manifesto embodying the modern distrust of mere words. Its title, meaning "A Guide to the Art of Poetry," is borrowed from a work by the Roman poet Horace, who lived from 65 to 8 B.C. (One of the familiar catchphrases from Horace's treatise is the admonition that poetry should both "teach and delight.")

Archibald MacLeish   *(1892–1982)*

Ars Poetica   1926

A poem should be palpable and mute
As a globed fruit,

Dumb
As old medallions to the thumb

Silent as the sleeve-worn stone   5
Of casement ledges where the moss has grown—

A poem should be wordless
As the flight of birds.
                    *

A poem should be motionless in time
As the moon climbs,   10

Leaving, as the moon releases
Twig by twig the night-entangled trees,

Leaving, as the moon behind the winter leaves,
Memory by memory the mind—

A poem should be motionless in time   15
As the moon climbs.
                    *

A poem should be equal to:
Not true.

For all the history of grief
An empty doorway and a maple leaf.   20

For love,
The leaning grasses and two lights above the sea—

A poem should not mean
But be.

The subtext, or implied message, of this poem is that poets should not use words lightly. There should be no showy displays of grief, no gushing about love. Since language is the poet's medium, what explains MacLeish's paradoxical preference for silence? The poet wrote when the horrors of World War I had alienated many poets and artists from the oratory of flag-waving politicians. To MacLeish's generation, speeches eulogizing the "grateful dead" who had died in the trenches seemed impious. What was real was the grass growing over the graves in the military cemeteries, the bones in the sandy soil, and the wind and rain. Better to remain silent than to use words dishonestly.

But of course poems, including this one, are not literally silent. They are not literally "mute," "dumb," or "wordless." They use words, but, according to the speaker in this poem, they should use words to create images that speak for themselves. They should create for us something we can touch (something that is "palpable"), like the "globed fruit" over whose curved outline we can run our fingers, reading its texture and shape. Poems should give us something concrete to see and contemplate, like the "flight of birds" or the "empty doorway." A central paradox of the poem is that "silent" sights can be more eloquent than preachings or editorializings. The grief of separation sinks in as we contemplate the "empty doorway" where friends or lovers used to linger while bidding each other good night.

The Receptive Reader

1. Why do people finger (or thumb) "old medallions"? What emotions do you think you would feel when contemplating a "casement ledge" or windowsill worn smooth by people's sleeves resting on it but now overgrown with moss?

2. Why does the moon seem "motionless" while yet it is climbing at the same time? If we prefer poems without much overt motion (apparently preferring the still frames capturing the moon rising slowly behind the bare twigs of the wintery trees), what kinds of poetry would we seem to rule out?

3. Is it paradoxical that MacLeish himself spelled out the central idea of his poem in his concluding lines?

The Personal Response

Are you resistant or allergic to preaching, editorializing, lecturing?

Poets before and after MacLeish have often opted intuitively for concrete images over theory and explicit assertion. The following poem by the American poet Walt Whitman clearly "makes a statement" about the speaker's alienation from coldly analytical science, but it does so without verbalizing the poet's implied attitude. What is the poet's statement?

Walt Whitman   *(1819–1892)*

When I Heard the Learned Astronomer   1865

When I heard the learned astronomer,
When the proofs, the figures, were ranged in columns before me,
When I was shown the charts and diagrams, to add, divide, and measure
    them,
When I sitting heard the astronomer where he lectured with much
    applause in the lecture room,
How soon unaccountable I became tired and sick,   5
Till rising and gliding out I wandered off by myself,
In the mystical moist night air, and from time to time,
Looked up in perfect silence at the stars.

What is the theme of Whitman's poem? The poem does not make an explicit assertion about the scientific temperament. But we can infer the poet's attitude from the brief scenario we see acted out. The speaker in the poem attended an astronomy lecture that showed modern science at its most analytical—with its toolbox of charts, diagrams, logical proofs, and mathematical calculations. Feeling "tired and sick," the speaker wandered off by himself. Once outside, he found the antidote: Instead of feeling stifled by figures and charts, he could commune "in perfect silence" with the stars, soothed by the "mystical moist night air." The poem as a whole points to a unifying central idea: Paradoxically, astronomy, when taught in a dryly analytical mode, does not help us find wonder and inspiration in the stars.

The Personal Response

Do you sympathize with the poet's response to the astronomy lecture? Do you feel there is something to be said on the other side?

The title of the following religious poem refers not to altars or incense but to a mechanical device made of wheels, blocks, and rope. A pulley was used to multiply human strength and lift heavy weights in the days before steam-powered or electricity-driven winches. One of Herbert's editors has said that the secret of Herbert's poetry is "the recovery of fresh feeling" from old formulas. What is different or unexpected about the relationship between God and humanity in the poem? What is the central paradox in this poem?

George Herbert　　*(1593–1633)*

The Pulley　　　　　　　　　　　　　　*1633*

When God at first made man,
Having a glass of blessings standing by,
"Let us," he said, "pour on him all we can:
Let the world's riches, which dispersèd° lie,　　　　*lie scattered*
　　Contract into a span."°　　　　　　　　　　　*short space*　5

　　So strength first made a way;
Then beauty flowed, then wisdom, honor, pleasure.
When almost all was out, God made a stay,°　　　　*paused*
Perceiving that, alone of all his treasure,
　　Rest in the bottom lay.　　　　　　　　　　　　　　　10

　　"For if I should," said he,
"Bestow° this jewel also on my creature,　　　　*pass on to*
He would adore my gifts instead of me,
And rest in Nature, not the God of Nature;
　　So both should losers be.　　　　　　　　　　　　　15

　　"Yet let him keep the rest,
But keep them with repining° restlessness:　　　　*yearning*
Let him be rich and weary, that at least,
If goodness lead him not, yet weariness
　　May toss him to my breast."　　　　　　　　　　　20

The Receptive Reader

1. Admirers have praised Herbert and the other metaphysical poets for their *wit*—in the more general sense of a quick mind or intellectual alertness. Part of this mental quickness is their willingness to use a play on words, or *pun*, even when writing about solemn subjects. What does the word *rest* mean when "*Rest* in the bottom lay"? (*Restlessness* later appears as its opposite.) What does the word mean when God's creature is likely to "*rest* in Nature, not the God of Nature"? How does the poet pun, or play on the word, when God decides to

let us "keep the *rest*"—everything except *rest?* (How does the poet make this key word stand out in the poem?)

2. What is paradoxical about richly blessed creatures suffering from "repining restlessness"? Do you think it is true?

3. One student wrote that in this poem humanity is "deprived rather than depraved." What did she mean?

John Donne's *Holy Sonnets* centered on the basic doctrines of traditional faith. However, Donne, like other metaphysical poets, did not simply restate traditional beliefs. His poems are not **didactic** in the sense of teaching ideas already accepted and approved. Instead, the poet asks basic questions and then works his way toward the answers. How does the following poem reveal the poet's own religious temperament and the workings of the poet's imagination?

John Donne   *(1573–1631)*

Holy Sonnet 5   *1635*

I am a little world made cunningly°   *made skillfully*
Of elements and an angelic sprite,°   *angel-like spirit*
But black sin hath betrayed to endless night
My world's both parts, and O, both parts must die.
You which° beyond that heaven which was most high   *You who*   5
Have found new spheres and of new lands can write,
Pour new seas in mine eyes, that so I might
Drown my world with my weeping earnestly,
Or wash it if it must be drowned no more.°   *(God's promise to Noah)*
But O, it must be burnt! Alas, the fire   10
Of lust and envy have burnt it heretofore,
And made it fouler; let their flames retire,
And burn me, O Lord, with a fiery zeal
Of Thee and Thy house, which doth in eating heal.

The Receptive Reader

1. The poet starts from a basic shared assumption: the duality of body and soul. Where and how does this idea enter into the poem? What other *polarities* help organize this poem?

2. One familiar feature of Donne's poetry is the *paradoxical* intermingling of scientific and biblical lore. Where or how do science and faith meet in this poem?

3. Donne's *metaphors,* like Shakespeare's, are not static; they develop and shift in unexpected ways as the poem takes shape. How do both water and fire change their significance in the course of the poem?

The Personal Response

The following is one student's record of a close reading of the poem. How familiar or strange are Donne's religious ideas to a reader of your generation?

Water and Fire

Donne's Holy Sonnet 5 deals with the basic theme of sin and redemption. However, this poem is not a dry lecture on the subject of salvation. The poet is "weeping earnestly" for his sins and looking forward to redemption with "fiery zeal." In his search for his soul's salvation, he ranges from the waters that drowned the earth during Noah's flood to the reaches of outer space discovered by the new astronomy. His tears of repentance must be like oceans; or, alternatively, his repentance must be like a fire that cleanses and heals as it consumes the sins it feeds on.

What are the basic doctrines assumed by the poem? The poet tells us that he is a world cunningly, skillfully made of two parts: body and soul. This "little world" or microcosm, like the larger universe that it mirrors, houses both matter and spirit. The body is made up of the elements of the world of matter (such as earth and water). The soul is the "angelic sprite," a spirit made of the same substance as the angels.

The crucial "But" comes at the beginning of the third line of the sonnet: As the serpent entered the Garden of Eden, so sin has entered "my world's both parts" and "betrayed" them. As a result, both parts must die and face the "endless night" of damnation.

What is the answer? Donne, ranging far beyond our everyday world, turns to the astronomers who in his time were beginning to find new worlds beyond our own solar system. (These are the "new spheres" beyond the traditional heaven.) He invokes the explorers who, traveling across the uncharted oceans, were finding "new lands" or new continents. Between them, can the stargazers and navigators find new oceans to replenish his tears, so that his weeping can drown out his sinful world with a flood of tears? Or, since God promised after Noah's flood that he would drown humanity no more, the poet's tears could wash him clean of sin.

He feels that if he repents for his sins, he will be saved. Actually, however, the world will end not by water but by fire, as flames consume the world on the Day of Judgment. Before then, the flames of lust and envy (which turn the world foul) have to die out, and the flames of a "fiery" religious zeal have to cleanse the sinner. The poet knows he has to repent in time, because he knows what will happen if his heart is not with God at the point of death.

THE COMMITTED POET

The galleries are full of music, the pianist is
storming the keys,
the great cellist is crucified over his instrument,
That none may hear the ejaculations of the
sentinels,
Nor the sighs of the most numerous and the most
poor;
the thud of their falling bodies.

W. H. AUDEN

I am a poet
who yearns to dance on rooftops,
to whisper delicate lines about joy
and the blessings of human understanding.
I try. I go to my land, my tower of words and
bolt the door, but the typewriter doesn't fade out
the sounds of blasting and muffled outrage.

LORNA DEE CERVANTES,
"POEM FOR THE YOUNG WHITE MAN"

Should poems take sides? When we explore the ideas embedded in poems, we face the question of the poet's engagement or commitment. Should poets take a stand on the social and political issues of their time? Can they afford to testify on behalf of causes? Can poets serve party, ideology, or country?

Poets have often been warned to speak for neither their class nor their kind nor their trade: "Wrap the bard in a flag or a school and they'll jimmy his / door down and be thick in his bed—for a month" (Archibald MacLeish). When art becomes propaganda, when poets write poems "for daily political use," their art becomes disposable, fading like the campaign posters of yesteryear. When poets follow a party line, they may seem to cease speaking to us in their own right as one human being to another. Nevertheless, poets from William Shakespeare and John Milton to Gwendolyn Brooks and Adrienne Rich have found it hard to stay aloof from the political and ideological struggles of their time. When the British suppressed the Easter Rebellion in Ireland in 1916 and executed the leading rebels, William Butler Yeats, who was to become a leading poet of the Irish Renaissance, wrote:

We know their dream; enough
To know they dreamed and are dead . . .

I write it out in a verse—
MacDonagh and MacBride
And Connolly and Pearse
Now and in time to be,
Wherever green is worn,
Are changed, changed utterly:
A terrible beauty is born.

"Easter 1916"

Two world wars, the rise of fascism and communism, the struggle against colonialism, the Vietnam War—these made it hard for poets to stay on the fence. Many found they could not remain as Rapunzel in the tower, never letting her hair down to ground level to help the real world climb in. Much modern poetry has been poetry of protest and of warning. At the same time, a poet's keeping *silent* about the political issues of the time has also often been seen as a political statement. By not confronting the issues, a poem might seem to be signaling acceptance of, or at least resignation to, oppression or abuses.

Much contemporary poetry has focused on the ironic contrast between official war propaganda and the horrible realities of war. The following poem is by Wilfred Owen, a British officer who wrote about the "sorrowful dark hell" of the Great War—World War I—and who was killed on the western front a week before the armistice ended the war in 1918. The motto he quotes in the title of the poem (and again at the end) is a quotation from the Roman poet Horace. It was known to every British schoolboy of Owen's generation: *Dulce et decorum est pro patria mori*—"How sweet and fitting it is to die for one's country." Owen once said, "My subject is war and the pity of war. The poetry is in the pity."

Wilfred Owen   *(1893–1918)*

Dulce et Decorum Est   1918

Bent double, like old beggars under sacks,
Knock-kneed, coughing like hags, we cursed through sludge,
Till on the haunting flares we turned our backs
And toward our distant rest began to trudge.
Men marched asleep. Many had lost their boots   5
But limped on, blood-shod. All went lame; all blind;
Drunk with fatigue; deaf even to the hoots
Of tired, outstripped Five-Nines° that dropped behind.   *gas shells*

Gas! Gas! Quick, boys!—An ecstasy of fumbling,
Fitting the clumsy helmets just in time;   10
But someone still was yelling out and stumbling,
And floundering like a man in fire or lime . . .
Dim through the misty panes and thick green light,
As under a green sea, I saw him drowning.
In all my dreams, before my helpless sight,   15
He plunges at me, guttering, choking, drowning.

If in some smothering dreams you too could pace
Behind the wagon that we flung him in,
And watch the white eyes writhing in his face,
His hanging face, like a devil's sick of sin;   20
If you could hear, at every jolt, the blood
Come gargling from his froth-corrupted lungs,
Obscene as cancer, bitter as the cud
Of vile, incurable sores on innocent tongues—
My friend, you would not tell with such high zest   25
To children ardent for some desperate glory,
The old Lie: Dulce et decorum est
Pro patria mori.

The Receptive Reader

1. How does the picture the first stanza paints of the troops being withdrawn from the front lines for "rest" differ from the one you would expect to encounter on propaganda posters or in patriotic speeches? Why is there a bitter irony in the *timing* of the gas attack in this poem?

2. Many people have read about the use of poison gas by the belligerents in World War I. How does Owen drive the realities of chemical warfare home? From what *perspectives*—when and how—do you see the victim? What is the effect on you as the reader?

3. How and with what effect is the word *drowning* repeated in this poem? What gives the word *innocent* toward the end of the poem its special power? Who is guilty in this poem?

4. This poem owes its eloquence in part to the insistent piling on of related words and similar, *parallel* structures. Where, and how?

5. What is the basic irony in this poem?

The Personal Response

Are we today too removed from the realities of war to share feelings like those expressed in this poem? Are our feelings too blunted from overexposure? How does the treatment of war in the media affect our feelings about war?

The following poem by an African American writer pays tribute to Frederick Douglass, who in his autobiography told the story of his rebellion against and escape from slavery. As a journalist and public speaker, Douglass became a leader of the antislavery movement in the United States. What makes the following poem in his honor eloquent?

Robert Hayden   *(1913–1980)*

Frederick Douglass   *1966*

When it is finally ours, this freedom, this liberty, this beautiful
and terrible thing, needful to man as air,
usable as earth; when it belongs at last to all,
when it is truly instinct, brain matter, diastole, systole,°   *phases of the heartbeat*
reflex action; when it is finally won, when it is more   5
than the gaudy mumbo jumbo of politicians:
this man, this Douglass, this former slave, this Negro
beaten to his knees, exiled, visioning a world
where none is lonely, none hunted, alien,
this man, superb in love and logic, this man   10
shall be remembered. Oh, not with statues' rhetoric,
nor with legends and poems and wreaths of bronze alone,
but with the lives grown out of his life, the lives
fleshing his dream of the beautiful, needful thing.

The Receptive Reader

1. What in this poem is different from the "gaudy mumbo jumbo of politicians" and conventional rhetoric in praise of liberty? What is strange or unexpected in the poet's description of freedom?

2. Is the poet speaking for a limited group? Is he speaking to a limited group? Do you think the poem would speak eloquently to a white audience? Why, or why not?

The Personal Response

We are often told that modern audiences have few heroes. Write a tribute (poem or prose passage) to someone you admire, trying to make it convincing for the skeptical modern reader.

Poetry can be timely and timeless at the same time if readers sense that the poet's long-range solidarity with suffering and deluded humanity is as strong as the commitment to the current struggle. Does the following poem takes sides? Whose?

Denise Levertov   *(born 1923)*

What Were They Like?   *1966*

1) Did the people of Vietnam
   use lanterns of stone?
2) Did they hold ceremonies
   to reverence the opening of buds?
3) Were they inclined to quiet laughter?   5
4) Did they use bone and ivory,
   jade and silver, for ornament?
5) Had they an epic poem?
6) Did they distinguish between speech and singing?

1) Sir, their light hearts turned to stone.   10
   It is not remembered whether in gardens
   stone lanterns illumined pleasant ways.
2) Perhaps they gathered once to delight in blossom,
   but after the children were killed
   there were no more buds.   15
3) Sir, laughter is bitter to the burned mouth.
4) A dream ago, perhaps. Ornament is for joy.
   All the bones were charred.
5) It is not remembered. Remember,
   most were peasants; their life   20
   was in rice and bamboo.
   When peaceful clouds were reflected in the paddies
   and the water buffalo stepped surely along terraces,
   maybe fathers told their sons old tales.
   When bombs smashed those mirrors   25
   there was time only to scream.

6) There is an echo yet
    of their speech which was like a song.
    It was reported their singing resembled
    the flight of moths in moonlight.   30
    Who can say? It is silent now.

The Receptive Reader

1. Who are the two speakers in this poem? What is the difference in their *points of view?* What kind of person is asking the questions? What kind of person is giving the answers?

2. Why do you think the poet used a *question-and-answer* format? What effect does it have on the reader?

3. The poem shifts easily from the factual questionnaire mode to the metaphorical language of the poet. What are memorable *metaphors,* and what role do they play in the poem?

The Personal Response

What for you is the message of this poem? What is your personal response to this poem?

The Polish poet Czeslaw Milosz resigned from the post–World War II communist Polish government in protest against political repression. He is an eloquent voice of human solidarity, of shared values crossing the borders of race, sex, and creed. What is the central idea or dominant theme in the following poem? How does the interplay of large abstractions and striking images give shape to the poem?

Czeslaw Milosz   *(born 1911)*

Incantation   *1968*

TRANSLATED BY ROBERT PINSKY AND CZESLAW MILOSZ

Human reason is beautiful and invincible.
No bars, no barbed wire, no pulping of books,
No sentence of banishment can prevail against it.
It establishes the universal ideas in language,
And guides our hand so we write Truth and Justice   5
With capital letters, lie and oppression with small.
It puts what should be above things as they are,
Is an enemy of despair and a friend of hope.
It does not know Jew from Greek or slave from master,
Giving us the estate of the world to manage.   10
It saves austere and transparent phrases
From the filthy discord of tortured words.
It says that everything is new under the sun,

Opens the congealed fist of the past
Beautiful and very young are Philo-Sophia   15
And poetry, her ally in the service of the good.
As late as yesterday Nature celebrated their birth,
The news was brought to the mountains by a unicorn and an echo.
Their friendship will be glorious; their time has no limit.
Their enemies have delivered themselves to destruction.   20

By modern standards, this poem has a high abstraction count. It invokes (with capital letters) ideas like Truth, Justice, and Nature. These abstractions are easy to abuse ("Go in fear of abstractions," said the American poet Ezra Pound). But the concern with the abuse of abstractions turns out to be exactly the impetus behind this poem. The poet's agenda is to cleanse "austere and transparent" words like *reason* and *justice* of the verbal pollution they have suffered. The agenda is to rescue them from dishonest use by time-servers, party hacks, and oppressors.

This work of renewal and reconstruction Milosz accomplishes with the tools of the poet. He employs the eloquent image: the undesirable books being pulled off the shelves to be shredded and reduced to pulp. He uses the potent metaphor: Reason is "guiding our hand" as we write *Truth* and *Justice;* reason is helping us "open the congealed fist of the past." He uses words with a witty twist, as when he starts *oppression* with a lowercase letter, while capitalizing *Truth* and *Justice.* Finally, he restores jaded words to their full meaning (such as philosophy—"Philo-Sophia"—the "love of wisdom"). The unicorn bringing the good news to the mountains is a lovely symbol for the triumph of the imagination over its literal-minded enemies.

The Receptive Reader

1. Where is the theme or central idea that animates this poem most directly spelled out? How would you state it in your own words or in language your peers or your generation would understand?

2. Why is it witty that the poem starts *oppression* with a lowercase letter? What familiar saying does the poet play on when he says "everything is new under the sun"? What does he mean?

3. In your own words, what does this poem say about the large abstractions—Reason, Truth, and Justice? What does it say about the abuse of language? What is this poet's perspective on oppression?

4. When a poet's political agenda becomes overt, poetry shades over into political advocacy and finally into political propaganda. How overt is the poet's political agenda in this poem? Where would you place this poem on a spectrum ranging from disinterested poetry cutting across party lines, through strong political commitment, to political propaganda?

The Personal Response

Are any lines or phrases especially eloquent for you? Do any of them raise questions in your mind? In what ways does this poem connect with your own experience?

Making Connections—For Discussion or Writing

W. H. Auden's "The Unknown Citizen" (Chapter 20), William Stafford's "Freedom," and Czeslaw Milosz' "Incantation" are among poems that offer or imply a political message. What differing perspectives do they offer on society? Are there recurrent themes or a recurrent note? Are the poems too preachy or abstract for you as the reader?

JUXTAPOSITIONS

Poems of War

Much modern poetry has dealt with the subject of war. From what point of view are you asked to look at war in each of the following poems? Does the poet spell out the ideas or attitudes implied or embedded in the poem? What does the poem as a whole say about war?

Henry Reed   *(born 1914)*

Naming of Parts   *1946*

Today we have naming of parts. Yesterday,
We had daily cleaning. And tomorrow morning,
We shall have what to do after firing. But today,
Today we have naming of parts. Japonica
Glistens like coral in all of the neighboring gardens,   5
          And today we have naming of parts.

This is the lower sling swivel. And this
Is the upper sling swivel, whose use you will see,
When you are given your slings. And this is the piling swivel,
Which in your case you have not got. The branches   10
Hold in the gardens their silent, eloquent gestures,
          Which in our case we have not got.

This is the safety-catch, which is always released
With an easy flick of the thumb. And please do not let me
See anyone using his finger. You can do it quite easy   15
If you have any strength in your thumb. The blossoms
Are fragile and motionless, never letting anyone see
          Any of them using their finger.

And this you can see is the bolt. The purpose of this
Is to open the breech, as you see. We can slide it   20
Rapidly backwards and forwards: we call this
Easing the spring. And rapidly backwards and forwards

The early bees are assaulting and fumbling the flowers:
       They call it easing the Spring.

They call it easing the Spring: it is perfectly easy   25
If you have any strength in your thumb: like the bolt,
And the breech, and the cocking-piece, and the point of balance,
Which in our case we have not got; and the almond-blossom
Silent in all of the gardens and the bees going backwards and forwards,
       For today we have naming of parts.   30

The Receptive Reader

1. Much of the talking in this poem is done by the drill instructor. Is what he says a **caricature**—a comic distortion exaggerating key traits to make them ridiculous? Or does it sound to you like a fairly accurate rendering of what an instructor might say?

2. The technology of war and the world of nature provide a steady play of *point and counterpoint* in this poem. How? With what effect? What does the poem as a whole say about technology and nature?

3. What is this poet's attitude toward war?

Richard Eberhart   *(born 1904)*

The Fury of Aerial Bombardment   *1947*

You would think the fury of aerial bombardment
Would rouse God to relent; the infinite spaces
Are still silent. He looks on shock-pried faces.
History, even, does not know what is meant.

You would feel that after so many centuries   5
God would give man to repent; yet he can kill
As Cain could, but with multitudinous will,
No farther advanced than in his ancient furies.

Was man made stupid to see his own stupidity?
Is God by definition indifferent, beyond us all?   10
Is the eternal truth man's fighting soul
Wherein the Beast ravens° in its own avidity?   *prowls*

Of Van Wettering I speak, and Averill,
Names on a list, whose faces I do not recall
But they are gone to early death, who late in school   15
Distinguished the belt feed lever from the belt holding pawl.

The Receptive Reader

1. What questions does this poem raise about God's intentions? What questions does it raise about our human responsibilities? Why does the poet bring the *allusion* to Cain into the poem?

2. Like Reed's poem, this poem takes us to the school rooms of military training. (Eberhart himself was for a time an aerial gunnery instructor in World War II.) How is Eberhart's use of the training experience similar to or different from Reed's?

3. Does this poem answer the questions it raises?

POEMS FOR FURTHER STUDY

In reading the following poems, pay special attention to theme. What ideas or attitudes are expressed or implied in the poem? What statement does the poem as a whole have for the reader? Does the poem spell it out in so many words? How does the poem as a whole carry its message?

Bethlyn Madison Webster   *(born 1964)*

Stamps   *1995*

I'm watching the woman
who is watching my groceries
rolling along the conveyor belt.
She stands Cheerio-mouthed
in a pink and white dress   5
sporting a crisp, curled hairdo
and staring as much as she pleases
while I stand behind my husband,
hiding behind him and the baby.
She has seen him produce   10
a book of foodstamps
from his pocket, and I think she wants
to see how her tax dollars
are being wasted today.
Eggs, milk, peanut butter, bread   15
root beer and a bag of store brand
chocolate chips. She looks
at those the longest.
I want to tell her that we work
for ten cents above minimum.   20
I want to explain
that it's Friday, we're tired,
and our chocolate is none of her business.
Somehow, we're on display
along with the tabloids and gum.   25
With long pink-nailed fingertips,
she puts her stuff up now:
a big red rib-eye steak
a head of green lettuce,
the leafy kind, and a bottle of merlot.   30

Our total is rung
and my husband pays.
The checker lays the coupons upside-down,
like a blackjack hand,   35
and pounds them with a rubber stamp.

The Receptive Reader

1. What is the point of this poem? What are key phrases? What are telling
or revealing details? Does the ending have a possible symbolic meaning?

2. Does the poet expect you to take sides? What side are you on in reading
this poem?

Philip Larkin   *(1922–1985)*

Born Yesterday   *1955*

Tightly folded bud,
I have wished you something
None of the others would:
Not the usual stuff
About being beautiful,   5
Or running off a spring
Of innocence or love—
They all wish you that.
And should it prove possible,
Well, you're a lucky girl.   10

But if it shouldn't, then
May you be ordinary;
Have like other women
An average of talents:
Not ugly, not good-looking,   15
Nothing uncustomary
To pull you off your balance,
That, unworkable in itself,
Stops all the rest from working.
In fact, may you be dull—   20
If that is what a skilled,
Vigilant, flexible,
Unemphasized, enthralled
Catching of happiness is called.

The Receptive Reader

1. What is the meaning and effect of the *metaphor* in the first line?

2. One of the oldest temptations is for the older generation to make wishes
or chart directions for the next. How does this poet try to steer clear of the
"usual stuff"? What are his best wishes for the child's future?

The Personal Response

How would you react if someone told you "May you be ordinary" and "May you be dull"?

Denise Levertov   *(born 1923)*

The Mutes   *1966*

Those groans men use
passing a woman on the street
or on the steps of the subway
to tell her she is a female
and their flesh knows it,   5

are they a sort of tune,
an ugly enough song, sung
by a bird with a slit tongue

but meant for music?

Or are they the muffled roaring   10
of deafmutes trapped in a building that
is slowly filling with smoke?

Perhaps both.

Such men most often
look as if groan were all they could do,   15
yet a woman, in spite of herself,

knows it's a tribute:
if she were lacking all grace
they'd pass her in silence:

so it's not only to say she's   20
a warm hole. It's a word

in grief-language, nothing to do with
primitive, not an ur-language;°   *earliest human language*
language stricken, sickened, cast down

in decrepitude.° She wants to   *deterioration*   25
throw the tribute away, disgusted,
and can't,

it goes on buzzing in her ear,
it changes the pace of her walk,
the torn posters in echoing corridors   30

spell it out, it
quakes and gnashes as the train comes in.
Her pulse sullenly

had picked up speed,

but the cars slow down and   35
jar to a stop while her understanding
keeps on translating:
"Life after life after life goes by
without poetry
without seemliness   40
without love."

The Receptive Reader

1. What is the role in the poem of the bird metaphor? Why is the deafmute metaphor central to the poem? What kind of counterpoint does the subway provide in the poem?

2. What, in your own words, is the theme the poet spells out in the last stanza? How does the poem as a whole lead up to it?

3. Does this poem express hostility toward men?

The Personal Response

What attitudes about sexual harassment are widespread among women? What reactions to current concerns about sexual harassment are widespread among men? How does the poem relate to either?

Alice Walker   *(born 1944)*

Women   *1970*

They were women then
My mamma's generation
Husky of voice—Stout of
Step
With fists as well as   5
Hands
How they battered down
Doors
And ironed
Starched white   10
Shirts
How they led
Armies
Headragged Generals
Across mined   15
Fields
Booby-trapped

Ditches
To discover books
Desks   20
A place for us
How they knew what we
Must know
Without knowing a page
Of it   25
Themselves.

The Receptive Reader

1. What is the role of the *military metaphor* in this poem? (Why "Head-ragged" generals?) What was the campaign in which the women of the mother's generation participated? (What clue is provided by the shirts?)

2. What is the paradox that concludes the poem?

3. What, for you, is the prevailing *mood* or emotion in this poem?

Claude McKay   *(1890–1948)*

If We Must Die   *1919*

If we must die, let it not be like hogs
Hunted and penned in an inglorious spot,
While round us bark the mad and hungry dogs,
Making their mock at our accursèd lot.
If we must die, O let us nobly die,   5
So that our precious blood may not be shed
In vain; then even the monsters we defy
Shall be constrained to honor us though dead!
O kinsmen we must meet the common foe!
Though far outnumbered let us show us brave,   10
And for their thousand blows deal one deathblow!
What though before us lies the open grave?
Like men we'll face the murderous, cowardly pack
Pressed to the wall, dying, but fighting back!

The Receptive Reader

1. How should this poem be read? What is the *stance* of the speaker in the poem? What words and images most strongly convey his feelings?

2. The language of protest and of race relations has changed since McKay's day. If you had been a contemporary of the poet, do you think you would have been moved by McKay's defiant rhetoric? Why, or why not?

WRITING ABOUT LITERATURE

21 Finding the Common Theme
WRITING FOCUS: Juxtaposing Poems for Comparison

The Writing Workshop   Comparison is a good teacher. It can alert us to what otherwise might go unnoticed; it can make us take a fresh look at what we took for granted. We value what we have when we look at what might take its place. We question what we have come to accept when someone shows us a viable alternative.

A **comparison-and-contrast paper** presents a special challenge to your ability to organize material. You will have to develop a strategy for laying out your material in such a way that your reader can see the points of comparison. The reader has to see important connections—whether unsuspected similarities or striking differences setting apart things that seem similar on the surface. Consider some familiar strategies for organizing a comparison and contrast of two poems:

✗ *You may want to develop a* **point-by-point comparison.** For instance, you may want to begin by showing how two poets share a distrust of "big words." This idea then provides the starting point both for your paper and for their poetic technique. You may go on to show how both poets rely on startling, thought-provoking images. Here you come to the heart of both your paper and of their way of writing poetry. You may conclude by showing how both nevertheless in the end spell out the kind of thought that serves as an *earned* conclusion, a generalization that the poem as a whole has worked out. Simplified, the scheme for such a point-by-point comparison might look like this:

> Point 1—poem A and then B
> Point 2—poem A and then B
> Point 3—poem A and then B

✗ *You may want to develop a* **parallel-order comparison.** You show first the distrust of abstractions, then the bold, provocative images, and finally the poet's spelling out of the theme in poem A. You then take these three points up again in the same, or parallel, order for poem B. This way you may be able to give your reader a better sense of how each poem works on its own terms, as a self-contained whole. However, you will have to make a special effort to remind your readers of what in the second poem is parallel to or different from what you showed in the first.

✗ *You may want to start from a common base.* You may want to emphasize similarities first. You may then want to go on to the significant differences. You might vary this strategy by starting with surface similarities that might deceive the casual observer. You then go on to essential distinctions.

How does the following student paper use or adapt these organizing strategies?

Sample Student Paper

Today We Have Naming of Parts

Disillusioned by the experience of World War II, Henry Reed in "Naming of Parts" and Richard Eberhart in "The Fury of Aerial Bombardment" condemn and reject the horror of war. Both poems condemn our failure to see war as it is, attack our indifference, and reflect postwar anti-war feeling. We shall see that Eberhart's poem takes the attack on indifference one step further than Reed's poem does.

Henry Reed's "Naming of Parts" satirically attacks the callousness of the military. By using impersonal, neutral words and phrases ("Today we have naming of parts. Yesterday / we had daily cleaning"), the speaker satirizes how precise and impersonal these lessons are. The trainee learns a process, without being taught or made aware of how terrible and ugly practicing that process is. References to "the lower sling swivel," "the upper sling swivel," and the "slings" describe machinery. Such references to mechanical parts evoke neutral or even positive feelings, since most machines are used for the good of humanity. This technical language conceals the horror of using this particular machinery. Saying that "you can do it quite easy / If you have any strength in your thumb" obscures the possibility that it might be difficult emotionally to gun down a fellow human being.

Reed uses a comparison to nature at the end of each stanza. Jumping from the mechanics of the gun to the beauty of the garden in consecutive sentences presents a contrast between the gun and the flower, the one a symbol of death and the other a symbol of life. The references in the first two stanzas stress the innocence of nature. "Japonica / glistens like coral in all of the neighboring gardens" evokes an image of serenity and peace. The branches with "their silent, eloquent gestures" paint another image of bliss. The sterile descriptions of the gun and the beautiful descriptions of nature proceed in a point-counterpoint fashion.

Richard Eberhart's "The Fury of Aerial Bombardment" shares the theme of "Naming of Parts" in that both poems attack indifference to violence and suffering. By saying that "History, even, does not know what is meant," the poet seems to lament that even painful experience does not teach us to prevent the senselessness of war. We are "no farther advanced," making the poet ask: "Was man made stupid?" Here again, as in Reed's poem, technical, impersonal references to the "belt feed lever" and the "belt holding pawl" imply a criticism of the callousness with which people handle the subject of war. A lesson about a belt feed lever might be more instructive if the part were named the genocide lever, for instance.

However, "The Fury of Aerial Bombardment" contrasts with "Naming of Parts" because Eberhart goes beyond attacking human indifference by attacking divine indifference to the horrors of war. The poet questions why God has not intervened to stop the aerial bombardment. The answer, that "the infinite spaces / Are still silent," is a criticism of God's looking passively upon "shock-pried faces." These are the faces of the people who have witnessed the horror of the bombing but to whom God offers no respite. The poet seems to expect a thinking, feeling entity to intervene, but no such intervention takes place. Men still kill with "multitudinous will." In the third stanza, the poet asks: "Is God by definition indifferent, beyond us all?"

Both of these poems were written half a century ago, yet their relevance remains undiminished today. In an age when we read daily of war and death, indifference is commonplace. The way in which a news reporter casually reads death tolls from current conflicts is reminiscent of the cold, sterile wording of "Naming of Parts." The casual and callous projections of the cost in human lives of "winning" a nuclear war are another example of what is under attack in these poems. And people who ponder such atrocities as Auschwitz and Hiroshima have cause to question divine indifference, for the earth is long on suffering.

Questions for Peer Review

The student writer traces a carefully developed comparison and contrast between two poems dealing with the same or a similar theme.

1. The student emphasizes Reed's attack on the *technical* "impersonal" nature of military training. How well does he document it? What are striking examples? What is wrong with making training in the technical dimensions of warfare technical?

2. How effectively does the *counterpoint* of the outside natural world emerge from the student paper?

3. How well does the student writer trace the similarities between the two poems? What are striking *parallels*?

4. How, according to the student writer, does the second poem go *beyond* the first?

5. Have these poems become *dated*? Has the development of the high-tech weaponry of and logistics of modern warfare made these poems obsolete?

6. In recent history, public sentiment has moved between calls for building up military strength to periods of distrust of or antagonism toward a military mentality. Do you think these two poems are out of step with the *national mood* today?

22 MYTH AND ALLUSION
Recovered Memories

Courtesy Richard B. Ressman

The capacity to personify, mythologize, imagine,
harmonize, improvise, is one of the great mercies
granted in human life.

STEPHEN NACHMANOVITCH

Myths are public dreams; dreams are private
myths. Myths are vehicles of communication
between the conscious and the unconscious just
as dreams are.

JOSEPH CAMPBELL

The mythic journey is as ancient as the human
race itself.

JOHN A. ALLEN

FOCUS ON MYTH

Myths (from *mythos,* the Greek word for tale) are stories about gods, godlike heroes, and monstrous adversaries. Myths are rooted in prehistoric oral tradition. People heard them in a spirit of religious awe, listening for clues to the nature of the mysterious universe in which they lived. Creation myths celebrated genesis—the creation of the earth, of man and woman, of sun and moon. In the dark of winter, myths of rebirth kept alive the faith in renewal, in the return of spring. Many early cultures had myths about the titanic struggle between good and evil. Often myths were embedded in **rituals** that acted out a mythical story or celebrated a godlike champion or redeemer.

Our world has rediscovered myth as a mirror—often obscure and tantalizing—of deep-seated human needs and feelings. What fascinates modern scholars is that many ancient myths have parallels in diverse cultures. It is as if recurrent mythical patterns were part of our collective consciousness, wired into the collective memory of the human species. Many myths focus on **archetypal** experiences and needs that are constants in the lives of people from different times and places. The American poet Stanley Kunitz said, "Old myths, old gods, old heroes have never died. They are only sleeping at the bottom of our minds, waiting for our call." Some of the myths "sleeping at the bottom of our minds" have had a special fascination for moderns:

✗ In traditions from many sources, we see a mythical god-king undergo a ritual of death and mourning, followed by rebirth or resurrection. We witness a cycle of defeat, death, and triumphant return. In the words of Joseph Campbell, we see different incarnations of "a hero with a thousand faces."

✴ Students of myth, from nineteenth-century anthropologists to today's feminist scholars, have reconstructed myths about the earth goddess that echo in the earliest lore of the Middle East, cradle of Western civilization. These myths give a voice to the need for bonding and nurturing essential for human survival. The Babylonian Ishtar and the Greek Demeter, goddess of the harvest, may hark back to a phase of human culture centered on the worship of a life-giving and life-preserving feminine principle.

✴ Many cultures have myths about the fire-bringer—who brings the fire that symbolizes warmth, the hearth, survival, permanence, the light of knowledge. The fire-bringer in Greek mythology was Prometheus, who defied the king of gods by returning to humanity the fire that Zeus had meant to deny them. To poets and artists of later generations, Prometheus became a symbol of aspiration, of rebellion, of determination "to defy power, which seems omnipotent" (Percy Bysshe Shelley, *Prometheus Unbound*). We still call people Promethean who are willing to test the boundaries, to reach for what was thought unattainable.

Poets and artists discovered in myth and legend rich sources of symbol and allusion. An **allusion** is a brief mention that calls up a whole story, rich in overtones and associations. A single word, a single name, may activate a whole network of memories. When a poet alludes to Cassandra, we see with the mind's eye the Trojan princess to whom the god Apollo had given the gift of foreseeing the future—and the curse of not being believed. In her mad ravings, she foresaw the death of Hector, the Trojan champion; she saw Troy in flames, the towers falling down, the men killed, the women sold into slavery. But no one believed her. As Robinson Jeffers says in his poem "Cassandra," people truly "hate the truth"; they would sooner

> Meet a tiger on the road.
> Therefore the poets honey their truth with lying.

FIRST READING
Catching the Allusion

The following example shows the central role allusion can play in a poem. The central figure is a balloon vendor who is literally lame. But the poet calls him "goat-footed"—a hint that we may be watching a half-human, half-animal mythic creature.

E. E. Cummings   *(1894–1962)*

in Just-   1923

in Just-
spring   when the world is mud-
luscious the little
lame balloonman

whistles   far   and wee   5

and eddieandbill come
running from marbles and
piracies and it's
spring

when the world is puddle-wonderful   10

the queer
old balloonman whistles
far   and   wee
and bettyandisbel come dancing

from hop-scotch and jump-rope and   15

it's
spring
and
   the

      goat-footed   20

balloonMan   whistles
far
and
wee

   Who has goat's feet and whistles? Pan, Greek god of flocks and shepherds, often appears in works of art as a sensual being with horns, a snub nose, and goat's feet. He is often shown dancing or playing the shepherd's flute, which he had invented. Often, he is leading the dances of the nymphs, or female woodland creatures. Pan is one of the many lesser semidivine beings who, in Greek mythology, populate nature. They turn it from an alien, savage place into a world full of breathing, sensitive life. For Cummings, the goat-footed balloonman (Pan in a modern disguise) becomes a fitting symbol of spring—of the spirit of joy, mirth, frolic, holiday, or fiesta.

The Receptive Reader

1. What is "luscious" about mud or "wonderful" about puddles?

2. How should the poem *sound* when read aloud? Spring here is a time of children dancing and skipping—as the poem itself skips over the printed page. How does it "dance out" the dancing and skipping it describes?

3. How does the poet use *repetition* and pauses to highlight, to focus our attention?

4. In ancient Greek times, Pan played his flute for grown-up beings. Why aren't there any adults in this modern poem?

5. Do you think this poem would work for readers who have never heard of Pan? Why or why not?

THE RANGE OF ALLUSION

People do gossip
And they say about
Leda, that she
Once found an egg
hidden under
wild hyacinths
SAPPHO

Allusion is a kind of shorthand. What does a writer mean when saying, "We are all Custer?" The short, cryptic statement encloses layers of meaning that we can peel away like the layers of an onion. George Armstrong Custer was an American general in command of the U.S. Seventh Cavalry. He attacked a large encampment of the Sioux, or Lakota, on the Little Big Horn in 1876. He was killed with most of his men in the last desperate battle the Lakota fought against the invaders. The allusion here, however, says more: As Americans, it suggests, we are all implicated in a history that pitted the U.S. Cavalry against the Native American tribes, ravaged by the starvation and disease the white settlers had brought. We share the guilt for the massacre at Wounded Knee, where men, women, and children were gunned down.

Richly allusive poetry assumes a shared cultural tradition that allows the poet to play on a common knowledge of myth, legend, and history. The language of allusion is as much a shared language as the language of the computer age—and it similarly challenges the uninitiated. One large source of allusion is **Greek mythology**—the body of myths and legends poets inherited from the civilization of ancient, classical Greece. What kind of cultural literacy does the poet assume in the following poem? What is the poet's range of allusion?

William Butler Yeats   *(1865–1939)*

Leda and the Swan   *1923*

A sudden blow: the great wings beating still
Above the staggering girl, her thighs caressed
By the dark webs, her nape caught in his bill,
He holds her helpless breast upon his breast.

How can those terrified vague fingers push   5
The feathered glory from her loosening thighs?
And how can body, laid in that white rush,
But feel the strange heart beating where it lies?

A shudder in the loins engenders there
The broken wall, the burning roof and tower   10
And Agamemnon dead.
                              Being so caught up,

So mastered by the brute blood of the air,
Did she put on his knowledge with his power
Before the indifferent beak could let her drop?   15

The terrifying swan is a mythic creature: Zeus, the king of the Olympian
gods (the Greek gods, residing on Mount Olympus) has assumed the shape
of an animal. The offspring of his union with Leda is going to be Helen,
whose abduction by the Trojan prince Paris will launch the "thousand ships"
of the Greek war against Troy. The "broken wall, the burning roof and
tower" call up before our eyes the city of Troy being reduced to rubble and
ashes in defeat. In the aftermath of the war, Agamemnon, the leader of the
Greek forces, will return home after years of absence, to be murdered by
his wife Clytemnestra and her lover Aegisthus.

The Receptive Reader

1. In the world of Greek myth, animals often do not have derogatory connotations. What are the connotations of the animals in Yeats' poem? Is the swan
mostly beast? human? divine?

2. Greek art and literature were more explicit about sex than later civilizations. What would you say to readers who may find this poem offensive?

Helen of Troy—the daughter of Zeus, who had made love to Leda in
the shape of a swan—was often blamed for the bloody conflict between
Greece and Troy. Helen had married Menelaus, king of Sparta, and she
incurred the hatred of her fellow Greeks when she allowed the "fire-
brand" Trojan prince Paris to carry her away to Troy, thus causing the
bloody Trojan War. What two different ways of viewing Helen contend
in the following poem?

H. D. (Hilda Doolittle)   *(1886–1961)*

Helen   *1924*

All Greece hates
the still eyes in the white face,
the luster as of olives
where she stands,
And the white hands.   5

All Greece reviles
the wan face when she smiles,
hating it deeper still
when it grows wan and white,
remembering past enchantments   10
And past ills.

Greece sees unmoved,
God's daughter, born of love,
the beauty of cool feet
and slenderest knees,   15
could love indeed the maid,
only if she were laid,
white ash amid funereal cypresses.

The Receptive Reader

1. How does the poet emphasize and drive home the unrelenting hate felt for Helen by her countrymen and countrywomen?

2. What labels applied here to Helen and what descriptive details *counteract* these powerful negative feelings, and how? Explore the connotations—associations, implications—of words like *luster, enchantments, maid,* and of phrases like "God's daughter, born of love" and "beauty of cool feet/and slenderest knees."

3. Is the poet herself taking sides? As you read the poem, are you?

JUXTAPOSITIONS

The Sacrifice of Isaac

For many centuries, allusions to the Bible have been woven into the language of poets and artists. Old Testament themes like Cain's fratricide, Noah's flood, or David slaying Goliath are part of our collective memory bank of archetypes and symbols. New Testament parables like those of the Good Samaritan help shape our thinking on subjects like charity and anti-welfare reform. The sacrifice of Isaac as the Lord's test of Abraham's obedience has long been a favorite subject for artists. Compare the Old Testament story with its use by a twentieth-century poet.

Genesis 22:1–13

And it came to pass after these things that God did tempt Abraham and said unto him, Abraham: and he said, Behold, here I am.

And he said, Take now thy son, thine only son Isaac, whom thou lovest, and get thee into the land of Moriah; and offer him there for a burnt offering upon one of the mountains which I will tell thee of.

And Abraham rose up early in the morning, and saddled his ass, and took two of his young men with him, and Isaac his son, and clave the wood for the burnt offering, and rose up, and went unto the place of which God had told him.

Then on the third day Abraham lifted up his eyes, and saw the place afar off.

And Abraham said unto his young men, Abide ye here with the ass; and I and the lad will go yonder and worship, and come again to you.

And Abraham took the wood of the burnt offering, and laid it upon Isaac his son; and he took the fire in his hand, and a knife; and they went both of them together.

And Isaac spake unto Abraham his father, and said, My father: and he said, Here am I, my son. And he said, Behold the fire and the wood: but where is the lamb for a burnt offering?

And Abraham said, My son, God will provide himself a lamb for the burnt offering: so they went both of them together.

And they came to the place which God had told him of; and Abraham built an altar there, and laid the wood in order, and bound Isaac his son, and laid him on the altar upon the wood.

And Abraham stretch forth his hand, and took the knife to slay his son.

And the angel of the Lord called unto him out of heaven, and said, Abraham, Abraham: and he said, Here am I.

And he said, Lay not thine hand upon the lad, neither do thou anything unto him: for now I know that thou fearest God, seeing thou hast not withheld thy son, thine only son from me.

And Abraham lifted up his eyes, and looked, and behold behind him a ram caught in a thicket by his horns: and Abraham went and took the ram, and offered him up for a burnt offering in the stead of his son.

Wilfred Owen wrote his adaptation of the biblical story during the years of trench warfare in World War I, when Britain, France, and Germany were sacrificing the lives of hundreds of thousands of young men. How far and how closely does the poet follow the biblical story? When do you first realize that Owen has transposed the story from its ancient setting? How does he change the climactic ending of the story?

Wilfred Owen   *(1893–1918)*

The Parable of the Old Men and the Young   1918

So Abram rose, and clave° the wood, and went,   *split*
And took the fire with him, and a knife.
And as they journeyed both of them together,
Isaac the first-born spake and said, My Father,
Behold the preparations, fire and iron,   5
But where the lamb for this burnt-offering?
Then Abram bound the youth with belts and straps,
And builded parapets° and trenches there,   *earthworks*
And stretched forth the knife to slay his son.
When lo! an angel called him out of heaven,   10
Saying, Lay not thy hand upon the lad,
Neither do anything to him. Behold,
A ram caught in a thicket by its horns;
Offer the Ram of Pride instead of him.
But the old man would not so, but slew° his son—   *killed*   15
And half the seed° of Europe, one by one.   *offspring*

The Receptive Reader

1. What are the *common* elements in both versions of the story?

2. How has the poet *changed* the meaning of the test undergone by Abraham? What does the "Ram of Pride" stand for? Who or what is the target of Owen's indictment?

3. What biblical *parables* do you know? How is the poem like a parable? Why does the poet's use of the biblical story give his indictment special force?

THE LANGUAGE OF MYTH

. . . still the heart doth need a language, still
Doth the old instinct bring back the old names.
          SAMUEL TAYLOR COLERIDGE

Man today, stripped of myth, stands famished
among all his pasts and must dig frantically for
roots, even if among the most remote antiquities.
          FRIEDRICH NIETZSCHE

To many modern readers, myths have seemed, in the words of the psychoanalyst Carl Jung, "still fresh and living" in the hidden recesses of their minds. Anthropologists and psychoanalysts have probed recurrent **archetypes**—symbolic embodiments of vital forces and life cycles that we encounter in many disguises and variations. The earliest religions may have centered on mother goddesses associated with the development of agriculture and worshiped in fertility cults. Such earth goddesses were Ishtar of Mesopotamia (now Iraq) or Cybele of Asia Minor (now Turkey). To some contemporary feminist poets, they symbolize the human need for bonding and for living in harmony with the generative forces in nature. In Greek myth, the earth mother or "grain mother" is Demeter, the goddess of the harvest, who sustains and nourishes all that lives on land, in the sea, and in the air.

Judy Grahn   *(born 1940)*

They Say She Is Veiled   *1982*

They say she is veiled
and a mystery. That is
one way of looking.
Another
is that she is where   5
she has always been,
exactly in place,
and it is we,
we who are mystified,
we who are veiled   10
and without faces.

The Receptive Reader

How does the poet play on the words *mystery* and *mystified?* What are the two ways "of looking" in this poem?

At times, poets have turned to Greek myth as a world more attuned to the heart's desire than inadequate reality. English Romantic poets like John Keats take us to classical Greece (of the sixth or fifth century B.C.) as the ideal homeland of the artistic imagination. In his "Ode on a Grecian Urn," Keats calls up before our eyes scenes he may have seen as vase paintings on ancient Greek amphoras (literally, vases with two handles). A Greek **ode** has elaborate stanzas first for solemn subjects. As we read the stanzas of the ode, Keats makes us see the scenes pictured on the urn as we slowly turn it. We see young men (or gods?) pursuing young women in a forest setting. We see a musician playing a shepherd's flute in a springtime setting of fresh leaves and flowers. We see a religious procession leading an animal to the altar for sacrifice. In this mythical world, gods and mortals intermingle, music resounds in forest glades, and the rich ceremonial of a religious holiday satisfies our yearning for dignity, grace, and beauty.

Like other poems taking us to the world of Greek mythology, the poem assumes a reader steeped in classical tradition. The setting is Greek: *Tempe* is a beautiful valley in Greece; *Arcady* (or Arcadia) is a Greek mountain region symbolic of idyllic, carefree country life. An *Attic* shape is from Attica, the region around Athens. Keats calls the urn a cold (not moving or breathing) *pastoral* because, like traditional pastoral poetry, it takes us to fields and meadows, where *pastors,* or shepherds, tend their sheep. The *pipes* and *timbrels* are the simple flutes and small drums of early Greek times.

John Keats   *(1795–1821)*   👁

Ode on a Grecian Urn   *1819*

1

Thou still unravished bride of quietness,
    Thou foster-child of silence and slow time,
Sylvan° historian, who canst thus express   *of the woods*
    A flowery tale more sweetly than our rhyme:
What leaf-fringed legend haunts about thy shape   5
    Of deities or mortals, or of both,
        In Tempe or the dales° of Arcady?   *valleys*
    What men or gods are these? What maidens loth?°   *unwilling*
What mad pursuit? What struggle to escape?
        What pipes and timbrels? What wild ecstasy?   10

2

Heard melodies are sweet, but those unheard
    Are sweeter; therefore, ye soft pipes, play on;
Not to the sensual ear, but, more endeared,
    Pipe to the spirit ditties° of no tone: *songs*
Fair youth, beneath the trees, thou canst not leave   15
    Thy song, nor ever can those trees be bare;
        Bold Lover, never, never canst thou kiss,
Though winning near the goal—yet, do not grieve;
        She cannot fade, though thou hast not thy bliss,
    For ever wilt thou° love, and she be fair!   *will you* 20

3

Ah, happy, happy boughs! that cannot shed
    Your leaves, nor ever bid the Spring adieu;°   *farewell*
And, happy melodist,° unwearied,   *musician*
    For ever piping songs for ever new;
More happy love! more happy, happy love!   25
    For ever warm and still to be enjoyed,
        For ever panting, and for ever young;
All breathing human passion far above,
    That leaves a heart high-sorrowful and cloyed,
        A burning forehead, and a parching tongue.   30

4

Who are these coming to the sacrifice?
    To what green altar, O mysterious priest,
Leadst thou that heifer° lowing at the skies,   *young cow*
    And all her silken flanks with garlands dressed?
What little town by river or sea shore,   35
    Or mountain-built which peaceful citadel,°   *fortress*
        Is emptied of this folk, this pious morn?
And, little town, thy streets for evermore
    Will silent be; and not a soul to tell
        Why thou art desolate, can ever return.   40

5

O Attic shape! Fair attitude! with brede°   *interwoven pattern*
    Of marble men and maidens overwrought,
With forest branches and the trodden weed;
    Thou, silent form, dost tease us out of thought
As doth eternity: Cold Pastoral!   45
    When old age shall this generation waste,
        Thou shalt remain, in midst of other woe
    Than ours, a friend to man, to whom thou sayst,°   *you say*
"Beauty is truth, truth beauty,"—that is all
        Ye know on earth, and all ye° need to know.   *you* 50

The Receptive Reader

1. In this poem, the language of myth provides the medium for the Romantic rebellion against the ordinary. The silent shape of the urn is able to "tease us out of" our ordinary dejected thoughts. How are the scenes you see here different from ordinary living?

2. The lovers are not flesh and blood; the music ("the spirit ditties of no tone") remains "unheard." We might ordinarily think cold, frozen images inferior to warm breathing life. Why does the poet think that they are really superior? Why are the "unheard" melodies of the vase sweeter than heard ones? What is the advantage that art has over nature?

The Personal Response

The poem culminates in the credo of the poet starved for beauty and passion in an unimaginative society: "Beauty is truth, truth beauty." That is all we need to know. (Keats said in one of his letters, "What the imagination seizes as beauty must be truth.") This conclusion gives trouble to skeptical readers: Beauty is only skin deep, they say. Surface beauty may be a thin varnish covering ugly truths. As you see it, is the truth ever beautiful? Or is it more likely to be ugly? Does the phrase "Beauty is truth" in some way have meaning for you?

The Creative Dimension

Museum-goers and gallery-goers (and readers of art books) experience thoughts and feelings that they often do not put into words. Verbalize the thoughts and feelings passing through your mind as you look at a work of art (or architecture) that your readers might recognize. For instance, write about the *Mona Lisa,* a Chagall painting, Michelangelo's *Creation of Adam* from the Sistine Chapel, the Lincoln Memorial, or the Guggenheim Museum in New York.

JUXTAPOSITIONS

The Icarus Myth

According to a universally known Greek myth, Daedalus fashioned wings for himself and his son Icarus, but as Icarus flew too close to the sun, the wax gluing the feathers in his wings melted and he perished in the sea. The myth is part of a web of stories taking place on the island of Crete, where Pasiphaë, the queen of King Minos, had been consumed by tormented longing for a beautiful white bull and given birth to a monstrous offspring, half man, half bull—the Minotaur. Daedalus was the Athenian inventor employed by King Minos to build the maze, or labyrinth, designed to pen in the Minotaur. Afterward, when Minos refused Daedalus' request to let him and his son return to Athens, Daedalus constructed wings from feathers and wax so that father and son could make their escape through the air. The Roman poet Ovid (43 B.C.–A.D. 18) concludes his retelling of the myth as follows:

When the boy, too bold, too young, too ambitious in daring,
    Forced his way too high, leaving his father below,
So the bonds of the wings were loosened, the fastenings melted,
    Nor could the moving arms hold in the desert of air. . . .
All of the wax was gone: his arms were bare as he struggled
    Beating the void of the air, unsupported, unstayed.
"Father!" he cried as he fell, "Oh, father, father, I'm falling!"
    Till the green of the wave closed on the agonized cry,
While the father, alas, a father no longer, was calling,
    "Icarus, where do you fly, Icarus, where in the sky?
Icarus!" he would call—and saw the wings on the water.
    Now earth covers his bones; now that sea has his name.

Translated by Rolfe Humphries

Different readers have used the traditional story as a prompt to construct their own private myths. Here are some of the readings:

✗ The myth acts out the age-old archetypes of impetuous, headstrong, ambitious youth and cautious, prudent, shell-shocked age.

✗ The myth focuses on the theme of overreaching, of overambitious, heedless pride that goes before a fall. In the words of a student reader, "each time we dare, we taunt the gods a little." The Greeks called arrogant human pride *hubris,* and they expected it to provoke the wrath of the gods.

✗ The myth glorifies the human capacity for aspiration, for "testing the boundaries." Flight has long been a symbol for our human capacity to struggle up from the mud and clay, even at the risk of failure.

✗ The myth focuses on the strongest kind of human love—the love of a parent for a child.

Look at the treatment of the Icarus myth in the following modern poems. What is the meaning of the myth for each poet?

Anne Sexton   *(1928–1974)*

To a Friend Whose Work Has Come to Triumph   *1962*

Consider Icarus, pasting those sticky wings on,
testing that strange little tug at his shoulder blade,
and think of that first flawless moment over the lawn
of the labyrinth. Think of the difference it made!
There below are the trees, as awkward as camels;   5
and here are the shocked starlings pumping past
and think of innocent Icarus who is doing quite well;
larger than a sail, over the fog and blast
of the plushy ocean he goes. Admire his wings!
Feel the fire at his neck and see how casually   10
he glances up and is caught, wondrously tunneling
into that hot eye. Who cares that he fell back into the sea?
See him acclaiming the sun and come plunging down
while his sensible daddy goes straight into town.

The Receptive Reader

1. Traditionally, people have listened to myths with grave attention. What details and imaginative comparisons give this poem a more irreverent or *ironic* modern twist?

2. What in the poem could lead a reader to conclude that nevertheless the myth has a serious meaning for the modern poet? What is the *theme* of this poem?

3. Both form and content of this poem play modern variations on traditional patterns. How does this fourteen-line poem live up to the requirements of the traditional *sonnet?* How does it depart from them?

The following poem gives us a retelling that takes us "down to earth" in its search for the reality behind the mythical tradition. The poem thus becomes a modern countermyth in which the ancient story becomes de-mythologized and the original heroes become modern antiheroes. The tone is irreverent toward both gods and human beings. How much does the poem preserve of the spirit or appeal of the original myth?

David Wagoner   *(born 1926)*

The Return of Icarus   *1958*

He showed up decades later, crook-necked and hip-sprung,
Not looking for work but cadging food and wine as artfully
As a king, while our dogs barked themselves inside out
At the sight of his hump and a whiff of his goatskin.

We told him Daedalus was dead, worn out with honors   5
(Some of them fabulous), but especially for making
Wings for the two of them and getting them off the ground.
He said he remembered that time, but being too young a mooncalf,

He hadn't cared about those labyrinthine double-dealings
Except for the scary parts, the snorting and bellowing.   10
He'd simply let the wax be smeared over his arms
And suffered handfuls of half-stuck second-hand chicken feathers

And flapped and flapped, getting the heft of them, and taken
Off (to both their amazements), listening for his father's
Endless, garbled, and finally inaudible instructions   15
From further and further below, and then swooping

And banking and trying to hover without a tail and stalling
While the old man, a slow learner, got the hang of it.
At last, with the weight of his years and his genius,
Daedalus thrashed aloft and was gawkily airborne.   20

And they went zigzagging crosswing and downwind over
        the water,
Half-baked by the sirocco,° with Daedalus explaining   *hot wind*
Everything now: which way was up, how to keep your mouth
Shut for the purpose of breathing and listening,

How to fly low (having no choice himself) in case of Harpies,° *monstrous birds* 25
And how to keep Helios,° beaming at a comfortable distance   *the sun*
By going no higher than the absolute dangling minimum
To avoid kicking Poseidon,° the old salt, square in the froth.   *god of the sea*

But Icarus saw the wax at his skinny quill-tips sagging,
And he couldn't get a word in edgewise or otherwise,   30
So he strained even higher, searching for ships or landfalls
While he still had time to enjoy his share of the view,

And in the bright, high-spirited silence, he took comfort
From his father's lack of advice, and Helios turned

Cool, not hot as Icarus rose, joining a wedge of geese   35
For an embarrassing, exhilarating moment northward,

And then he grew cold till the wax turned brittle as marble,
Stiffening his elbows and suddenly breaking
Away, leaving him wingless, clawing at nothing, then falling
Headfirst with a panoramic, panchromatic vista   40

Of the indifferent sun, the indifferent ocean, and a blurred
Father passing sideways, still chugging and flailing away
With rows of eagle feathers. When Icarus hit the water,
He took its salt as deeply as his own.

He didn't tell us how he'd paddled ashore or where   45
He'd been keeping himself or what in the world he'd been doing
For a living, yet he didn't seem bitter. "Too bad
You weren't around," we said, "there'd have been something in it

For you, probably—an apartment straddling an aqueduct,   *crowds (as in*
Orchards, invitations, hecatombs° of women."   *communal tombs)*   50
"No hard feelings," he said. "Wings weren't my idea."
And he told odd crooked stories to children for hours

About what lived under water, what lived under the earth,
And what still lived in the air, and why. A few days later
He slouched off on his game leg and didn't come back.   55
He didn't steal any chickens or girls' hearts

Or ask after his father's grave or his father's money
Or even kick the dogs. But he showed us calluses
Thicker than hooves on his soles and palms, and told us
That's how he'd stay in touch, keeping his feet on the ground.   60

The Receptive Reader

1. How does the first stanza signal that the ancient story is again being re-told with a modern twist? How does it realign your perspective?

2. How does this retelling redraw the portrait of the father? How does it change your image of the father and your image of the young son? How does it reinterpret or refashion the relationship between father and son?

3. In the retelling of the flight, which parts of it are *humorous;* which seem serious?

4. For you, does the last line of the poem spell out the *theme* of the poem? Does it point to a moral? Does it strike the keynote for the poem as a whole?

5. What is witty about the *allusion* in the father's "labyrinthine double-dealings" and the "snorting and bellowing"? What other references remind you that we are in the world of Greek mythology?

The Personal Response

Do this poet's changes in the story make the myth more believable or less?

The following modern sonnet strips the Icarus myth of many of its traditional trappings. There is no literal flight in this poem—no flying with false feathers like the original Icarus, nor flying in a metal bird that shears the clouds and becomes a menace to real birds. The flights here are "imaged" flights, journeys of the mind. Although our bodies are earthbound, our minds are capable of tremendous flights of the imagination, making us outsoar the highest reaches of heaven and making us plummet to deepest hell.

Vassar Miller   *(born 1924)*

The New Icarus   *1956*

Slip off the husk of gravity to lie
Bedded with wind; float on a whimsy, lift
Upon a wish: your bow's own arrow, rift
Newton's decorum—only when you fly.
But naked. No false-feathered fool, you try   5
Dalliance with heights, nor, plumed with metal, shift
And shear the clouds, imperiling lark and swift
And all birds bridal-bowered in the sky.

Your wreck of bone, barred their delight's dominions,
Lacking their formula for flight, holds imaged   10
Those alps of air no eagle's wing can quell.
With arms flung crosswise, pinioned to wooden pinions,
You in one motion, plucked and crimson-plumaged,
Outsoar all Heaven, plummeting all Hell.

The Receptive Reader

1. Examine the poet's graphic *metaphors*. What is exceptionally appropriate or fitting about the image she creates by the phrase "Slip off the husk of gravity"?

2. Look at the *paradoxical* metaphors—metaphors that at first glance seem contradictory or physically impossible: How could the person addressed be told to be "your bow's own arrow"? (We propel our imaginary selves on the imagined voyage with the force of our own will and desire; these serve as the bow shooting forth ourselves as the arrow.) What do you make of the paradoxical "plumed with metal" or "alps of air"? What sense do they make on second thought?

3. The *allusion* to Newton, another physicist and mathematician of the eighteenth century, makes us think of Newtonian science. We are expected to think of a mechanistic model of the universe, where everything behaves according to the strict laws of physics—as if in accordance with strict etiquette or "decorum." How would the new Icarus "rift/Newton's decorum"?

4. The *pun* in the phrase "pinioned (fastened, shackled) to wooden pinions (wings)" makes us imagine a person with arms flung wide and fastened to the wooden wings as to a cross. Are you prepared to agree with the student who wrote the following passage about the possible religious implications of the poem?

The new Icarus is Christ, whose "wreck of bone" finds salvation through suffering. Christ "pinioned to wooden pinons" and "crimson plumaged" reaches heights of love that ancient humanity (Icarus) or modern humanity, "plumed with metal" of modern airplanes, will never outsoar. Living the life of the spirit incurs a great risk, since it can bring suffering, a "plummeting" to "all Hell." However, although Christ lacks the birds' "formula for flight," he can go the eagle one better. He can rise from his "plucked" "wreck of bone" to "those alps of air no eagle's wing can quell." Despite being nailed to the cross, "pinioned to wooden pinions," he can "in one motion . . . outsoar all Heaven."

The following poem is one of several commenting on the painting *The Fall of Icarus* by the Flemish painter Pieter Breughel (about 1525–1569). How does the poem put the mythical story in perspective?

William Carlos Williams   *(1883–1963)*

Landscape with the Fall of Icarus   1960

According to Breughel
when Icarus fell
it was spring

a farmer was plowing
his field   5
the whole pageantry

of the year was
awake tingling
near

the edge of the sea   10
concerned with itself
sweating in the sun
that melted the wings' wax

unsignificantly
off the coast   15
there was

a splash quite unnoticed
this was
Icarus drowning

Making Connections—For Discussion or Writing

Explore the versions of the Icarus myth found in these poems. What do they show about the perennial or universal appeal of the myth? What do they show about the difference between more traditional and more modern perspectives? Which of the poems do you find most congenial or personally appealing and why?

The Creative Dimension

Write your own personal version of the Icarus myth or of another myth that you have known for some time.

MODERN MYTHS

goddess of the silver screen
the only original American queen
                    JUDY GRAHN, "HELEN IN HOLLYWOOD"

Although many myths are age-old, we see the mythmaking faculty at work in our own time. The lone rider of the frontier assumed mythical proportions in the cowboy myth that is at the heart of American popular culture. Its central figure, like mythical heroes of the past, appears in countless permutations, from Buffalo Bill to space-age cowboys like *Star Trek*'s Captain Kirk. To city dwellers hemmed in by city life, the cowboy seems to stimulate a collective memory of wide open spaces, of depending on oneself, of being able to move on.

The Hollywood dream factory created mythical sex goddesses. Norma Jean Baker was turned into Marilyn Monroe, who became the daydream of every immature male: "Marilyn, who was every man's love affair . . . who was blonde and beautiful and had a little rinky-dink of a voice . . . which carried such ripe overtones of erotic excitement and yet was the voice of a little child" (Norman Mailer, *Marilyn*). After her death, admirers and defenders created the countermyth of the actress rebelling against the stereotype of the dumb blonde that denied her her own humanity—Marilyn "who tried, I believe, to help us see that beauty has a mind of its own" (Judy Grahn).

Sharon Olds   *(born 1942)*

The Death of Marilyn Monroe   1983

The ambulance men touched her cold
body, lifted it, heavy as iron,
onto the stretcher, tried to close the
mouth, closed the eyes, tied the
arms to the sides, moved a caught
strand of hair, as if it mattered,
saw the shape of her breasts, flattened by
gravity, under the sheet,

5

carried her, as if it were she,
down the steps.   10

These men were never the same. They went out
afterwards, as they always did,
for a drink or two, but they could not meet
each other's eyes.

             Their lives took   15
a turn—one had nightmares, strange
pains, impotence, depression. One did not
like his work, his wife looked
different, his kids. Even death
seemed different to him—a place where she   20
would be waiting,

And one found himself standing at night
in the doorway to a room of sleep, listening to
a woman breathing, just an ordinary
woman   25
breathing.

The Receptive Reader

1. What was the cause of Marilyn Monroe's death?

2. Why were the men in the poem "never the same"? What is the *mythic* or symbolic significance of Monroe in this poem?

3. Has popular entertainment left the *stereotype* of the Hollywood blonde behind?

4. Is the Marilyn Monroe myth alive?

The Creative Dimension

What is the keynote of this poem to you? What lasting impression does it leave in your mind? Look at the following re-creation by a fellow student, and then write your own.

    Those ambulance men
    shocked into recognition of death and tenuous life
    shifted the body
    prepared her for the journey
    The body wasn't going anywhere special
    they were
    One to nightmares, strangeness
    Another to dislike, to fear
    The last to listening.

How does the following poem rewrite the cowboy myth?

E. E. Cummings   *(1894–1962)*

Buffalo Bill's   1923

Buffalo Bill's
defunct
            who used to
            ride a watersmooth-silver
                                        stallion   5
and break onetwothreefourfive pigeonsjustlikethat
                                        Jesus

he was a handsome man
                            and what i want to know is
how do you like your blueeyed boy   10
Mister Death

The Receptive Reader

Who was Buffalo Bill? What was his claim to fame? In what ways is he a
symbol of his period in American history? What is the attitude toward him in
this poem?

The Creative Dimension

A student wrote the "Portrait II" tribute shortly after E. E. Cummings had
died. How well did the student writer get into the spirit of the original? Another
student wrote the "Portrait III" imitation of this poem upon the death of Jerry
Garcia, the lead singer of the Grateful Dead, whom a generation of "dead-
heads" had followed from concert to concert. (Do you catch any allusions in
this re-creation?) Try your hand at a similar portrait of someone more recently
defunct.

Portrait II
e. e. someone
buried by busy ones,
            used to
            wish yes aprils with a you
                            and a me
and write onetwothreefourfive poemsjustlikethat
                            by dong and ding
he was a perceptive man
                            and what i want to know is
where is he now when we need him
Mister Death

Portrait III
Jerry Garcia's
            dead
                    who used to

<pre>
                play a custom rosewood
                        guitar
    chubby   fingers   onetwothreefourfive
            winding just like that
            up the fretboard
  he was a weathered man
        and what I want to know is
    is the fat man finally grateful
    Mr. Death
</pre>

Many myths of ancient Greece centered on a miraculous transformation, or **metamorphosis**. For instance, when Daphne was pursued by the god Apollo, she prayed for deliverance and was miraculously transformed into a laurel tree. The Greek gods were able to assume the shape of animals or human beings. The following poem tells the story of a more recent change of identity.

Alison Hawthorne Deming   *(born 1946)*

The Man Who Became a Deer   1994

for Dick Nelson

What little I know
about the man who
became a deer is this—
his feet did not cleave
into hooves, his head   5
never sprouted antlers,
and the parts that mean
manhood did not thicken
with pelt. Once he wanted
to become an Eskimo,   10
so he ate raw, rancid meat
and slept on the ground.
But he did not change.
This time he hunted
with a dog who could hear   15
the gesture of a silent
command and the meat he ate
was dark and fresh
as water from a deep well.
The muscle, the blood,   20
the hair and the skin
replaced themselves
cell by cell—each one
incorporating the molecules
of deer which he ate   25
three times a day. And

the deer remained hidden,
disguised as a man
in the perfect camouflage
of his body. Sometimes   30
in his face his friends
would see a quickness,
in his legs a jitter,
a tensing to leap—
his patience became that   35
of a browser, his heart
that of a hart, and his brain
which only loses, day after day,
never gains cells, woke up
one winter morning to   40
the heat of the blood of deer
running through its
pipes like antifreeze.
That's all I know about the man who became a deer—
and that when he loved a woman   45
she tasted the forest on his lips.

The Receptive Reader

1. What is really happening in this poem to the man who became a deer?

2. Many of the Greek transformation myths or metamorphoses involved a transaction between human beings and nature. Does this poet reflect a yearning for a closer union with nature?

3. Is this poem about a male fantasy or about a female fantasy?

POEMS FOR FURTHER STUDY

In reading the following poems, pay special attention to the poet's use of myth and allusion. What knowledge of myth, legend, or history does the poet assume? What is the role of an allusion in a poem as a whole?

Maurya Simon   (born 1950)

King Midas's Daughter   1989

She retires to the tower, her only haven
away from the artless glare of gold.
Weighted down with plums and a melon
not yet hardened by her father's hold,
she mounts the stone stairs, her steps fierce,   5
her long red hair uncoiling from its spiral.
From the window the far waves break in tiers;
he will not touch them, he is too fearful

Sacrifice of Isaac. 1455.
By Khatchatur.
The Walters Art Museum, Baltimore

THE PARABLE OF OLD MEN AND THE YOUNG
Wilfred Owen

So Abram rose, and clave the wood, and went,
And took the fire with him, and a knife.
And as they journeyed both of them together,
Isaac the first-born spake and said, My Father,
Behold the preparations, fire and iron,
But where the lamb for this burnt-offering?
Then Abram bound the youth with belts and straps,
And builded parapets and trenches there,
And stretched forth the knife to slay his son.
When lo! an angel called him out of heaven,
Saying, Lay not thy hand upon the lad,
Neither do anything to him. Behold,
A ram caught in a thicket by its horns;
Offer the Ram of Pride instead of him.
But the old man would not so, but slew his son—
And half the seed of Europe, one by one.

The Birth of Venus.
By Sandro Botticelli (1444–1510).
© Scala/ Art Resource, NY/Uffizi, Florence, Italy

TESTIMONY
Lisel Mueller

You forget I was in the sea
a long time, breathing through gills,
before I surfaced on that shell,
the "glorious moment" you speak of.
Nor did you notice my folded lungs
fight for that first deep draft of air.
Telling the story, you omit
that in the beginning my hair was green
seaweed, before it turned
into the yellow silk you admire.
You paint me floating ashore
with rose-tipped breasts lifting
toward the sun, and the sun avid,
and you say I stepped into heated shoes
of glittering white sand.
What poor eyewitnesses you are.
I remember it was a cloudy day;
a starved dog ran along the shore,
the rocks and shells cut into my feet.
No one was there. I was cold and lost.
The straggly leaves all pointed
in one direction, toward the interior.
I had no other place to go.

Landscape with the Fall of Icarus.
By Pieter the Elder Brueghel (1525–1569).
© Scala/Art Resource, NY

MUSÉE DES BEAUX ARTS
W. H. Auden

About suffering they were never wrong,
The old Masters: how well they understood
Its human position; how it takes place
While someone else is eating or opening a window or just walking
    dully along;
How, when the aged are reverently, passionately waiting
For the miraculous birth, there always must be
Children who did not specially want it to happen, skating
On a pond at the edge of the wood:
They never forgot
That even dreadful martyrdom must run its course
Anyhow in a corner, some untidy spot
Where the dogs go on with their doggy life and the torturer's horse
Scratches its innocent behind on a tree.

In Brueghel's *Icarus*, for instance: how everything turns away
Quite leisurely from the disaster; the ploughman may
Have heard the splash, the forsaken cry,
But for him it was not an important failure; the sun shone
As it had to on the white legs disappearing into the green
Water; and the expensive delicate ship that must have seen
Something amazing, a boy falling out of the sky,
Had somewhere to get to and sailed calmly on.

THE MISSING FATHER
Lou Lipsitz

*"About suffering they were never wrong,
The Old Masters . . ."*

Never wrong because as their
paintings demonstrate, suffering
occurs while others fail to notice,
or care. People close their windows
while the girl screams in the alley.
They drive past the strange man
staggering alongside the road.

Brueghel's *Landscape with the Fall
of Icarus* gives Auden his example.
Icarus has just plummeted into the sea.
In the painting, only his legs and
a tiny splash are still visible. Yet,
the ploughman in the foreground
goes on ploughing. And the "expensive,
delicate ship" whose passengers may
have seen Icarus fall had, as Auden writes,
"somewhere to get to, and sailed calmly on."

And so here's my question: where is
the father in this painting? Where
is Daedalus, who conceived and created
the wings and planned their escape
from the island prison; who carefully
instructed his son on the dangers
of flight and then, magically, sprang
into the air with him? Why did Brueghel
and Auden not see him scanning
the waters for a sign of his foolish
elated boy; and not finding Icarus,
then search through every island;
and finally, realizing what must
have happened, pull up to the spot,
run down into the ditch, choke back
his tears, frantically try to pry open
the door of the crushed vehicle?

Icarus, from Jazz.
By Henri Matisse (1869–1954).
© New York Public Library/Art Resource, NY/Musée d'Art Ancien, Brussels, Belgium. Paris, 1947 Astor, Lenox, and Tilden Foundation. © 2003 Succession H. Matisse, Paris/ARS, NY. The Spencer Collection

EL ICARO
Salvador Jacinto Polo de Medina

Por mares de esplendor navegas luces
con blandos remos, Icaro atrevido,
a perderte en el sol vas, mariposa;
mas una ola furiosa
te despeña encendido,
penacho, destrozado por las nubes,

porque al dorado oceano te subes;
y en veloz precipio vuelves luego,
y con alas de fuego
pretendes en el humedo elemento
los vientos de cristal volar sediento
pero dan las espumas
blando sepulcro a tus flamantes plumas.

Through a splendid sea of light
    you navigate
with feathered wings, bold Icarus,
soaring—small lunar moth—
only to lose yourself in the sun.
Ardent, inflamed, you are sent tumbling,
and a furious wave rises up
to strip you of your arrogant plumage.

Through gilded oceans of sky
you ascended
only to plummet toward moist clouds
into rapid ruin,
screaming for an end to the burning.
Fiery wings daring crystalline winds,
your fall was sudden, violent.
The foaming froth caught your
    luminous fire,
and you perished, the watery waste
a muffled tomb
for your flaming feathers.

(translated by Stephanie Rico)

Lullaby. 1947.
By Robert Gwathmey.
Private Collection. © 2002 Estate of Robert Gwathmey/Licensed by VAGA.
New York, NY/ Superstock, NY.

NOW THAT I AM
FOREVER WITH CHILD
Audre Lorde

How the days went while you
    were blooming within me
I remember each upon each—
the swelling changed planes of
    my body
and how you first fluttered,
    then jumped
and I thought it was my heart.

How the days wound down
and the turning of winter
I recall, with you growing heavy
against the wind. I thought
now her hands
are formed, and her hair
has started to curl
now her teeth are done
now she sneezes.
Then the seed opened
I bore you one morning just
    before spring
My head rang like a fiery piston
my legs were towers
    between which
A new world was passing.

Since then
I can only distinguish
one thread within running hours
You, flowing through selves
toward You.

to leave his glowing world, his golden throne.
Against the curved blade of the horizon,   10
she sees a ship with fluttering sails blown
dangerously close to the harbor: *Don't come,*
she silently commands it, and it goes.

She is like a plant calling for water.
She is like a fist pounding a pillow.   15
She's forgotten the taste of her own laughter,
and the sound of a mockingbird in the willow.
She sees him below in a garden among statues
that are grotesque, familiar, golden.
And he's calling up to her now: *Come choose*   20
a flower, any flower! And his foolish exuberance
makes her jump from her chair and rush to him,
wanting to shake this curse from his shoulders,
wanting to hug his thinning body, unloosen
its cold grief, its sorrow of greed, however   25
he scolds her, or dazzles her into silence.

The Receptive Reader

What is the story of Midas? How has the modern poet changed the perspective and the impact of the traditional story? What is the meaning of the myth for you as a modern reader?

William Wordsworth   *(1770–1850)*

The World Is Too Much with Us   *1807*

The world is too much with us; late and soon,
Getting and spending, we lay waste our powers;
Little we see in nature that is ours;
We have given our hearts away, a sordid boon.
This sea that bares her bosom to the moon,   5
The winds that will be howling at all hours,
And are up-gathered now like sleeping flowers,
For this, for everything, we are out of tune;
It moves us not.—Great God! I'd rather be
A pagan suckled in a creed outworn;   10
So might I, standing on this pleasant lea,°   *grassland*
Have glimpses that would make me less forlorn;
Have sight of Proteus rising from the sea;
Or hear old Triton blow his wreathèd horn.

The Receptive Reader

From a dictionary or other reference work, what can you find out about Proteus and Triton? What role do they play in the poem? What does the world of Greek myth mean to the speaker in this sonnet?

Edna St. Vincent Millay   *(1892–1950)*

An Ancient Gesture   1931

I thought, as I wiped my eyes on the corner of my apron:
Penelope did this too.
And more than once: you can't keep weaving all day
And undoing it all through the night;
Your arms get tired, and the back of your neck gets tight;   5
And along towards morning, when you think it will never be light,
And your husband has been gone, and you don't know where, for years,
Suddenly you burst into tears;
There is simply nothing else to do.

And I thought, as I wiped my eyes on the corner of my apron: 10
This is an ancient gesture, authentic, antique,
In the very best tradition, classic, Greek;
Ulysses did this too.
But only as a gesture,—a gesture which implied
To the assembled throng that he was much too moved to speak.   15
He learned it from Penelope. . .
Penelope, who really cried.

The Receptive Reader

1. What is the story of the roaming Ulysses, hero of Homer's *Odyssey,* and
his stay-at-home wife Penelope? Why did she "keep weaving all day / And undoing it all through the night"?

2. In Homer's epic poems, men weep over their slain comrades. What
makes this poet suspicious of Ulysses' tears? (Does a "gesture" always have to
be insincere?)

The Creative Dimension

In ancient Greek myth, women are often seen through the eyes of their men
or of male gods. Can you imagine yourself as speaking for one of these
women? In the following example, what variation does the student writer play
on Penelope's story?

Tonight I hang my apron
on the peg of the antique cupboard
for the last time.
The apron has grown tight,
the nights have grown long,
the weaving is finished.
The Greek bands of blue
are the color of the Mediterranean.
The white linen threads
tell the story of loss.

Donald Finkel   *(born 1929)*

The Sirens   1959

The news lapped at us out of all
Horizons: the ticking night full
Of gods; sensed, heard the tactile

Sea turn in his bed, prickling
Among derelicts. When the song   5
Was clear enough, we spread our hair,

Caught it. Under the comb the strands
Whipped into fresh harmonies, untangled
Again. The wind took it, and he heard.

The droll ship swung leeward;   10
Caught sight of him (rather, could
Have seen, busy with the fugue)

Yanking his bonds, the strings of his wide
Neck drawn like shrouds, his scream
Caught in the sail.   15
    Now in a sea

Of wheat he rows, reconstructing.
In his ridiculous, lovely mouth the strains
Tumble into place. Do you think
Wax could have stopped us, or chains?   20

The Receptive Reader

1. The sirens were mythical women whose song was so irresistible that
mariners would steer their ships into the rocks of the sirens' island and perish.
This poem alludes to the story of a famous traveler who passed by the island
during his far-flung voyages. What is the story of Ulysses and the sirens? How
does this poem reverse the usual perspective from which we see this story—
and with what effect?

JUXTAPOSITIONS: WORD AND IMAGE

Reading Images, Seeing Poems

In early cultures, the mythmaking imagination peopled the natural
world with spiritual forces. Rivers and forests might have presiding or in-
dwelling divine or semidivine beings. In communal rituals, the spirits of
the ancestors or of tribal heroes returned to awe or inspire the populace.
During the late eighteenth and early nineteenth centuries, Romantic
poets began to warn that in the literal-minded modern industrial world
the mythmaking faculty was beginning to atrophy. However, modern

psychologists and anthropologists claim that the mythmaking imagination is still creating new modern myths. We can observe it as it creates celebrities adored by multitudes. It transforms artists or thinkers into cultural icons. It stages transgalactic combat between good and evil.

In many early cultures, word, image, song, and dance worked together to give visible and audible form to the visions created by the mythmaking imagination. Rituals employing masks, totems, or ritual combat acted out or danced out myths anchored in deep-seated allegiances, fears, or aspirations. In the plays of ancient Greece that are still performed on modern stages, we can hear echoes of prayers to the gods and magic incantations, of mythical heroes and monsters.

Through the ages, painters and poets have kept alive the myths that have come down to us from prehistoric times. They have often retold them their own way, reinterpreting them for their own times or seeing them through their own personal lens. Ancient poems retelling the myths of Greek and Roman antiquity have inspired generations of artists. Juxtapositions of image and word invite you to interdisciplinary or cross-disciplinary explorations of the world of myth. (See color Insert III.)

WORD AND IMAGE:
VIEWING, READING, DISCUSSING, WRITING

Khatchatur, *Sacrifice of Isaac*, 1455   (Insert III i)

Wilfred Owen (1893–1918), "The Parable of the Old Men and the Young"

The Receptive Viewer and Reader

In the biblical story, God tested Abraham's faith by asking him to offer up his fifteen-year-old son as a human sacrifice. Abraham traveled to the appointed place, built an altar, bound his son, and laid him upon the wood he had brought to burn the offering. At the last moment, an angel stayed the father's hand, pointing toward a ram caught in the thicket and telling the father to offer the animal up as a sacrifice instead. The ancient Armenian manuscript faithfully reproduces the elements of the biblical story: kneeling father with the knife, bound boy, gesturing angel, and animal caught in the thicket.

1. What do you know about sacrifices—human or animal—in early stages of religion? What was the purpose or rationale? What were some of the rituals? Where have you read or heard about them?

2. Wilfred Owen was a British officer who wrote bitter antiwar poetry during the fratricidal carnage of World War I. He was killed shortly before the end of the war at age twenty-five. He rewrote the story of Abraham and Isaac—how and why? In the context of the "Great War," who is Isaac? Who is Abraham? What's the equivalent of Abraham's preparation for the sacrifice?

3. The biblical story focuses on the issue of unconditional human submission to God's will. Owen's poem focuses on the issue of pride. Whose pride? Why was the drawn-out conflict of World War I a consequence of pride?

Sandro Botticelli (1444–1510), *The Birth of Venus,* 1485 (Insert III ii)

Lisel Mueller (born 1924), "Testimony," 1980

The Receptive Viewer and Reader

Botticelli painted during the European Renaissance of the late fifteenth and the early sixteenth centuries. Artists and writers in Italy were developing a new way of looking at and thinking about the world. After centuries of medieval otherworldliness, artists were rediscovering the beauty of the human body and of the human face. Often the Renaissance artists turned to the art and myth-making of ancient Greece for inspiration. In keeping with the Renaissance philosophy of his time, Botticelli made the human soul shine through the outer surface beauty.

1. In one of the world's most famous paintings, Botticelli is celebrating the coming of love and beauty into the world. Aphrodite, the Greek goddess of love called Venus by the Romans, arrives full grown on the seashell as the west wind blows and spring is ready to enfold her in a flowered satin cape. Why do you think she is coming from the sea in the ancient story? Is the shell just decoration or might it have some symbolic meaning? What is the role of leaves and vegetation in the painting? Why is the wind blowing?

2. Poet Lisel Mueller, living in a modern world that no longer believes in goddesses or the dawn of a new age of love and beauty, tells a different story. In this poet's version, what does the goddess tell us about her previous life in the sea and why? Does the color of the hair matter? Why bring the dog in? How do the leaves in this poem differ from those you saw in the painting?

3. Some observers like to divide people into yeasayers and naysayers. Yeasayers believe that even in our anxiety-ridden violent world awesome beautiful inspiring things can emerge from the sea (or happen in some other way). Naysayers, watching this painting in the midst of thousands of admiring tourists in its Florence museum, might ignore the welcoming gentle breezes and imagine the goddess turning into a stranger walking lost toward town, probably mugged on the road. Which side do you incline toward?

Pieter Brueghel the Elder (1525–1569), *Landscape with the Fall of Icarus*   (Insert III iii)

W.H. Auden (1907–1973), "Musée des Beaux Arts," 1940

The Receptive Viewer and Reader

The story of Daedalus and Icarus is one of the most widely visualized and explored by painters and writers in the vast repertory of ancient Greek myth and legend. To return home against the wishes of his employer, the Greek architect and inventor Daedalus plotted his escape by designing wings made of feathers and wax for himself and his son Icarus. The son flew too close to the sun, and the wax in his wings melted, causing him to perish in the sea.

Brueghel was a painter of the Northern European Renaissance who often painted scenes of ordinary peasant life, re-creating with zest both the pleasures and the foolishness of ordinary human beings.

1. The poet calls the key event "something amazing" but makes a point of ordinary life going on all around. What seems ordinary in the painting? What are the activities going on? What helps make what we see a peaceful beautiful scene?

2. To people who are drawn into a great personal tragedy the experience can be shattering. Why remind us that ordinary life is going on and that people are going about their business? Is the poet callous or oblivious to human suffering? Is the painter?

3. What are the other outstanding miraculous or dreadful events the poet selects to support his point? Does he change the way you would normally think of them? (How are his three key examples related?)

4. Auden asks us to imagine ourselves as tourists viewing Brueghel's painting in the Museum of the Fine Arts in Belgium—in a part of Europe not far from where the painter lived and worked. Why do you think Auden makes a point of the painting being in a museum? Does the museum experience tend to isolate us from the human meaning of art? Or do the art works in the great art museum bring to life for us truths about human life we might ignore in the course of our ordinary lives?

Marc Chagall (1887–1985), *Fall Of Icarus,* 1973   (Insert III iv)

Lou Lipsitz (born 1939), "The Missing Father"

The Receptive Viewer and Reader

Chagall was a Russian Jewish painter who early left the village life of his childhood but carried with him the scenes of rural work and play and religious ritual that he wove into colorful free-floating dreamlike paintings that became known and instantly recogizable around the globe.

1. What do you see in Chagall's painting? What makes the flaming fall of Chagall's Icarus dramatic? What do the colors contribute? What is the role of the people in this painting? (Why are there so many?)

2. How does Chagall's painting reverse the perspective of Brueghel's painting and of Auden's poem? According to Chagall's vision of the event, were the "old masters" wrong about suffering after all?

3. Like other modern poets, Lou Lipsitz transposes the ancient myth into a modern setting. In how many ways does he do that and with what effect?

4. Like Chagall, Lipsitz also does a rereading of the Brueghel painting and of the Auden poem, although he seems to go along with them for the early part of his poem. However, in the second half of the poem, Lipsitz focuses on the father who planned and executed the escape. How do you explain that he was left out of the other visual or poetic retellings of the myth? How do you explain that Lipsitz makes the father the focus of our attention?

Henri Matisse (1869–1954), *Icarus, from Jazz*   (Insert III v)

Salvador Jacinto Polo de Medina (1603–1676), "El Icaro"

The Receptive Viewer and Reader

Untold art lovers around the world have let the French painter Matisse take them into a bright airy world of color and light. He delighted in the hues and and multifarious shapes of flowers, in the simple outlines of the human face and the human form, in the print patterns of women's dresses, and in the simple decorative patterns of wallpapers and tablecloths. It was as if again and again he used his art to tell us: "You don't need to go to exotic islands in search of color and life—look around you and see everywhere lines and shapes and colors pleasing to the eye!" In his later years, when illness began to keep him from conventional painting and sculpting, he used scissors and bright paper to create cut-outs, of which his *Icarus* is a famous example.

1. Matisse's cut-out of Icarus is reduced to four strong colors: a black body with a red heart falling through a night-blue background, surrounded by exploding yellow stars. What feeling does the shape of Icarus suggest? Does he seem to be in control or not? How do you know? What is the effect of the red heart on us, the viewers? The effect of the yellow stars? In what ways do they also suggest the volatility of fire?

2. Translation from one language to another is a complex, delicate process, yielding a transmutation of the original in the new language. De Medina's poem, written in the seventeenth century, rhymes. The translation does not. Rather than being literally faithful to the original, it attempts to capture de Medina's passionate description of flight and fall, his images of sky and sea, of water and air. What are some words and phrases in the English that refer to sky? To sea?

3. If you have watched moths at night, what do they tend to do? How does the flight of moths parallel the flight of Icarus?

4. How does the "ardent" flight of Icarus result in his fall? Why do you think he might be "ardent" about his journey? Why do you think his plumage is "arrogant"?

Robert Gwathmey (1903–1988), *Lullaby,* 1947   (Insert III vi)

Audre Lorde (born 1934), "Now That I Am Forever with Child"

The Receptive Viewer and Reader

From Richmond, Virginia, Gwathmey focused his art on the lives of African Americans and their struggle to be recognized in American society. Asked if he was a "social artist," he replied, "I'm a social being, and I don't see how you can be an artist and be separate."

1. One of the oldest continuing themes in Western art is the bond between mother and child. What images—traditional or modern—do you remember of the Madonna and the child? How were the mother and child shown? Does this painting remind you of traditional renderings of the Madonna and the child? Apart from the religious tradition, have you seen other paintings or photographs that focused on the mother-and-child relationship?

2. How does the title of the painting set the tone for the painting? Does the child seem protected or sheltered in its mother's lap? Do the angular lines and shapes of the mother's body or clothing keep her figure from being maternal? Why do you think the artist did not give the mother a more conventional motherly shape or features? What is added to the painting by the background that is barely sketched in?

3. How or why is the poet "forever with child"? Have you ever had someone walk you through the stages of pregnancy and birth the way this poet does? What for her were key phases or key stages? What powerful imaginative comparisons dramatize the culminating event of the birth? How would a child be "flowing through selves / toward You"?

WRITING ABOUT LITERATURE

22 Mythmaking in the Modern World
WRITING FOCUS: Feedback and Peer Review

The Writing Workshop   Writers don't write in a vacuum. They live with feedback from friends, family, colleagues, editors, reviewers—or just plain readers. In a classroom, you can simulate such input by having your peers react to your writing as individuals or in a group. Such feedback helps make you more audience-conscious; it strengthens your sense of what happens when your writing reaches the reader.

In turn, when you act as a peer reviewer for others, you help alert other writers to the reader's needs. You help them see their writing through the reader's eyes. Remember that critics and reviewers easily lapse into a fault-finding mode. Although it is important to identify weaknesses and mistakes, it is just as important to help writers develop what is promising and to help them build on their strengths. Try to balance negative criticism with constructive suggestions. The key question in your mind should be: What can the writer do to improve, to make the writing more instructive, more effective?

Here are sample passages with comments that might help a writer develop the full potential of a paper:

Ovid, David Wagoner, and Vassar Miller offer vastly different interpretations of the classic myth. However, we are also able to see a few similarities.

COMMENT: What *are* these differences and similarities? Give us a hint to keep us interested? Give us more of a preview?

In the biblical account, Abraham "bound Isaac his son, and laid him upon the altar upon the wood." Owen's poem says that "Abram bound the youth with belts and straps, / And builded parapets and trenches." Belts and straps, parapets and trenches are surely alien to people of biblical times who herded sheep for a living. These words denote the military.

COMMENT: Follow up and explain? Why does the poet use these "military" references? What kind of warfare and what war does he have in mind?

The first thing that must be taken into consideration about this poem is its basis in the traditional biblical story. . . . Once the element of war and sacrifice has been introduced, the whole concept of sacrifice is looked at in respect to the ones that do the sacrificing as well as the ones being sacrificed. . . . Owen has successfully conveyed the personalities and situations involved with war and sacrifice.

COMMENT: Rewrite to avoid the wooden, impersonal passive? "The element of war and sacrifice *has been introduced*"—by whom? Try "Once the poet *has introduced* . . . he *looks* at this theme. . ."? Cut down on jargony words like *basis, element, concept, situation?* Rewrite chunky passages like "looked at in respect to the ones that"?

Student Paper for Peer Review

Monroe: Quest of Beauty

Marilyn Monroe became something more than human even before her suicide in the early 60s. Her image—celluloid clips, photo stills—keeps appearing in sometimes unlikely places. Sometimes her image reappears in another embodiment, such as Madonna, and the casual observer will still think "Monroe" before recognition sets in. We know who she is, or was. Or at least we think we do.

Norman Mailer in <u>Marilyn</u>, one of a never-ending stream of books about the "goddess of the silver screen," said, "She was not the dark contract of the passionate brunette depths that speak of blood, vows taken for life, and the furies of vengeance . . . no, Marilyn suggested sex might be difficult or dangerous with others, but ice cream with her." Mailer said, "we think of Marilyn who was every man's love affair" and whose "little rinky-dink voice" carried "ripe overtones of erotic excitement and yet was the voice of a little child."

In her poem, "The Death of Marilyn Monroe," Sharon Olds describes the impact that Marilyn's death had on the ambulance attendants who carried "her cold body" to the ambulance. "These men were never the same." One had nightmares, became impotent, suffered depression. One did not "like his work, his wife / looked different, his kids." Death became a place "where she would be waiting." Another

found himself standing at night
in the doorway to a room of sleep, listening to
a woman breathing, just an ordinary
woman
breathing.

For these men, and all men and women, the death of Marilyn meant far more than the tragedy of an individual; it was the death of a modern goddess, of a mythical being.

To Judy Grahn, a feminist poet, Monroe, like Harlow, Holliday, or Taylor, represents an older myth, that of Helen of Troy. In her poem, "Helen in Hollywood," she says, "'That's the one,' we say in instant recognition, / because our breath is taken away by her beauty, / or what we call her beauty." Helen herself, to Judy Grahn, is merely the human incarnation of a deity humanity has almost forgotten. This deity goes by many names and lives in many cultures and is represented in our world by the Hollywood star who

> writes in red red lipstick
> on the window of her body,
> long for me, oh need me!

We, her fans, crowd around her to share on her "luminescent glow," and we may destroy her in the process:

> We adore her. we imitate and rob her
> adulate   envy
> admire   neglect
> scorn.   leave alone
> invade, fill
> ourselves with her.
> we love her, we say
> and if she isn't careful
> we may even kill her.

She is our "leaping, laughing leading lady," who "sweeps eternally / down the steps / in her long round gown." But it is also she "who lies strangled / in the bell-tower"; it is she "who is monumentally drunk and suicidal." It is she who when "locked waiting in the hightower . . . leaps from her blue window."

For years after Marilyn's death, men would say (and women, too): "If only she had met me, I could have saved her!" Something in her flawed beauty, in her vulnerability, made her personal to millions of people. She became the best celluloid representation of the goddess of beauty, approachable and accepting of everyone's gifts. She taught us the power of sexual awareness, the power of our sexual selves. Everyone was welcome at her well. To Sharon Olds, not to have Marilyn as a symbol in our lives is the price the ambulance crew paid. It is not to have connection; it is not to have sexual, social, or family bonds. It is to stand alone in the dark, doubting and seeking reaffirmation of the reality of a loved person in our lives, "listening to / a woman breathing, just an ordinary / woman breathing."

Questions for Peer Review

The student writer brings into focus a basic question about the role myth has played in human culture. Myth or mythical themes have often had a powerful attraction that we do not really understand. They engage us at a deeper level than simple intellectual explanations. As a result, we often see artists and writers read and interpret and reread mythical material in their own personal way.

1. Should the writer have brought out her *thesis* earlier or more clearly in the paper? What would you suggest as a possible thesis statement early in the paper? Compare your suggestions with those of your classmates.

2. Could the relation among Mailer, Olds, and Grahn have been clarified more to make the overall *pattern* or drift of the paper clearer to the reader? What is the connection? What is the overall pattern?

3. Do you feel anywhere in the essay a need for additional *explanation* or discussion of the quoted passages?

4. Do you need additional *quotations?* Do you need more of a sense of the overall *intention* and pattern of a source? Where or why?

5. Do you have suggestions for strengthening *beginning and end*—title, introduction, conclusion?

6. What is your personal *reaction* to this writer's interpretation of the Monroe myth? Does it need more explanation or justification? How do you think other readers will react?

7. "Helen in Hollywood" appears in Judy Grahn's *Queen of Wands,* along with other Helen poems. Does this paper make you want to read the whole poem by Judy Grahn or more of her poetry? Why or why not?

23 THREE POETS IN DEPTH

Dickinson, Frost, Brooks

*In our age, and typically in a large, mobile
industrial society . . . people tend to become
indifferent about their ability to think or feel for
themselves . . . the poet's voice is needed now
more than ever before—that voice which
celebrates the difficult, joyous, imaginative
process by which the individual discovers and
enacts selfhood.*

                                    EDWIN HONIG

*Experiment escorts us last—
His pungent company
Will not allow an Axiom
An Opportunity*

          EMILY DICKINSON

FOCUS ON THE POET

Reading a poet like Emily Dickinson, Robert Frost, or Gwendolyn Brooks, we treasure the poet's personal voice. We recognize it with pleasure, the way we welcome a cherished face. We do not usually read an anonymous poem and then discover it is by Walt Whitman. As we read, we are already attuned to the poet's way of looking at the world. Our previous reading of the poet shapes our expectations—although of course a poem by a favorite poet may take a puzzling turn.

In the poet's work, the individual poem is part of a larger whole. We call a poet's accumulated work the **canon** when it is formidable enough to be inventoried by critics and scholars. Moving from one poem to the next, we recognize favorite themes. One poem helps us understand another. We interpret a difficult passage by way of cross-reference to a similar passage elsewhere. In addition, we may test our interpretation against statements made by the poet or by people in the poet's confidence.

Looking at three poets in depth, this chapter will ask you to focus in turn on three kinds of investigation that can enhance your understanding of an individual poem.

The Poet's Voice   The best-loved poets have an unmistakable personal idiom or **style**. They have an inimitable, personal way of looking at the world and sharing with us what they see. We do not mistake Emily Dickinson for E. E. Cummings, or Sylvia Plath for Adrienne Rich.

Author Biography   Ever since Samuel Johnson wrote his *Lives of the Poets* (1779–1781), **author biography** has been practiced by writers who agree with him that "the biographical part of literature is what I love most." Who is the biographical person behind the persona speaking in a poem? Who is the person behind the masks and disguises particular poems may create? How does a poem become more meaningful when we see it in the context of the poet's life? With a poet like Robert Frost, the legend of the poet-sage—the struggle for recognition, the impact of adversity, the vicissitudes of success—looms large.

The Poet's Commitment   In the work of an **engaged**, politically committed poet, individual poems may be bulletins from an ongoing struggle. To relate to recurrent themes, we may have to understand the poet's sense of mission. We may have to understand the poet's social conscience, class consciousness, or solidarity with the oppressed. It would be hard to read poems by Gwendolyn Brooks while disregarding her involvement in the struggle of African Americans to achieve a place in the sun, her fierce loyalty to her people.

EMILY DICKINSON: THE POET'S VOICE

In Amherst Emily lived on
though the world forgot
moving with calm coiled hair through tidy days.
Her face shrank to a locket. She explored
miniaturized worlds known only to moths and
*   angels*
walked to the far side of a raindrop—
trespassed
on Infinity.

                    OLGA CABRAL

Maybe that is one of the most valuable things
about the poetry of Emily Dickinson: to teach that
there is something in poetry that cannot be
handled, cannot be studied scientifically.

                    LINDA GREGG

Surgeons must be very careful
When they take the knife!
Underneath their fine incisions
Stirs the culprit,—Life!

          EMILY DICKINSON

Emily Dickinson (1830–1886) is the outstanding example of a poet with a distinctive voice—a voice that seemed willfully strange to her contemporaries but that gradually came to be cherished by lovers of poetry everywhere. She led a withdrawn life and found practically no recognition in her day. She thought about success and fame ("Fame is a bee. / It has a song— / It has a sting— / Ah, too it has a wing"), but she ultimately had to settle for "fame of my mind"—recognition in her own mind. It was for posterity to discover her

> sheer sanity
> of vision, the serious mischief
> language, the economy of pain.
> > Linda Pastan, "Emily Dickinson"

Although she submitted over a hundred poems for publication, only a handful found their way into print in her lifetime. To editors, the bold experimental features of her poetry seemed "technical imperfections." Her work, like the work of other great innovators, was considered uncontrolled and eccentric. When they did publish her poems, editors conventionalized them. They changed bold metaphorical words to dull ones; they changed her dashes to commas and periods; they made her off-rhymes and half-rhymes rhyme. A collection of over a hundred poems published shortly after Dickinson's death astonished her publishers by running through eleven editions in two years. Almost two thousand of her poems have since been found and published. Today, with her poems everywhere anthologized and "with feminist considerations of her work abounding" (Leslie Camhi), she is widely recognized as America's greatest poet.

Much ink has flowed to create, embroider, and question the legend of Emily Dickinson as the mysterious lady in white living secluded in her father's house, embarked on her own private "journey into the interior." Who was the biographical person behind the persona—which she called the "supposed person"—that speaks to us in her poetry?

Dickinson "was born into a family that did everything for her but understand her" (Richard B. Sewall). Her father—a lawyer, judge, and member of Congress—practiced a stern Puritanical religion in the New England tradition. He led morning prayers for family and servants, reading Scripture in what his daughter Emily called a "militant accent." At a time when questioning even minor points of doctrine was scandalous, Dickinson developed serious doubts about original sin. She stopped going to church by the time she was thirty. She decided to keep the sabbath at home, where, in her words, a "noted clergyman" (namely God) preached better and shorter sermons.

Suspicious of books that "joggle the mind," her father banned novels, which young Emily and her brother Austin had to smuggle into the house while the father was "too busy with his briefs to notice what we do." She read and admired the great woman writers of her day, from the Brontë sisters to Elizabeth Barrett Browning. In addition to the Bible, Shakespeare, and theological works, her reading included Charlotte Brontë's *Jane Eyre* and George Eliot's *Middlemarch,* each the record of the spiritual pilgrimage of a woman in search of an identity other than the role expected of her by society. In a poem she wrote after Charlotte Brontë's death, the poet said:

> Soft fall the sounds of Eden
> Upon her puzzled ear—
> Oh what an afternoon for Heaven,
> When "Bronte" entered there!

Dickinson attended Amherst Academy and for a year Mount Holyoke Female Seminary, one of the first women's colleges. Letters she wrote as a student show a young woman in love with exuberant word play and fired by youthful enthusiasm. Her quick wit and lively sense of irony never deserted her—in a poem written many years later, she said about a pompous fraud that "He preached upon 'Breadth' till it argued him narrow." However, she gradually withdrew from the outside world. One of her best-known poems begins "The Soul selects her own Society/Then—shuts the door—/To her divine Majority—/Present no more."

She stayed in touch by letter with the few people who provided her with feedback for her poetry, including her sister-in-law Susan Gilbert Dickinson and Thomas Wentworth Higginson, the *Atlantic Monthly* editor whom she addressed as her mentor, or "preceptor." Although Higginson had advanced ideas for his time, he was unable to come to terms with the strange and "wayward" poems she sent him. She in turn could not conform to the demands of the literary marketplace—to auction off "the Mind of Man" and to merchandise "Heavenly Grace" and the "Human Spirit."

Much literary detective work has probed possible psychological, social, or medical reasons for her increasing isolation. In poems and letters, she alludes to intense emotional attachments that ended in anguish and disappointment. Passionate, yearning letters to an unknown recipient survive, possibly addressed to a married minister. Feminist critics have focused on poems like the following, which hints at love and loss in a passionate relationship with another woman. (Numbers of poems refer to the numbering in Thomas H. Johnson's *The Collected Poems of Emily Dickinson*.)

Ourselves were wed one summer—dear   *about 1862*

J.631

Ourselves were wed one summer—dear—
Your Vision—was in June—
And when Your little Lifetime failed,
I wearied—too—of mine—

And overtaken in the Dark—   5
Where You had put me down—
By Some one carrying a Light—
I—too—received the Sign.

'Tis true—Our Futures different lay—
Your cottage—faced the sun—   10
While Oceans—and the North must be—
On every side of mine

'Tis true, Your Garden led the Bloom,
For mine—in Frosts—was sown—
And yet, one Summer, we were Queens—   15
But You—were crowned in June—

Outlets for the creative energies of a fiercely independent woman
were limited if not nonexistent in Dickinson's day. Thwarted in early visions of fame, she was forced into resignation. Alternatively, psychoanalysts have searched her relationship with an authoritarian father, an
invalid mother, or an uncomprehending brother and sister for clues to
the intense, disturbed emotions in some of her poems. She may have
suffered from agoraphobia, a debilitating fear of public places. What is
certain is that she found in everyday household routines and in the enclosed natural life of her garden plot the food for far-flung questionings
and explorations. Her work, in the words of poet Amy Clampitt, is "studded with allusions to places she had never seen." As one of her recent
editors says,

> From a life narrow by conventional standards, and from the house-
> hold tasks that women have performed silently for generations, Dick-
> inson drew the material for metaphysical speculation. Baking,
> sweeping, caring for the ill, mourning the dead, and observing the
> quiet nature of a garden were the occasions for sudden myster-
> ies. . . . Ambivalent religious attitudes, together with the themes of
> death, immortality, and eternity, permeate her work. The Puritan
> sense of spiritual mystery inhabiting the circumstances of everyday
> life informs her minute observations of nature. Her meter is adapted
> from eighteenth-century hymns. But hers was "that religion/That
> doubts as fervently as it believes" (poem 1144).
>
> > Leslie Camhi, "Emily Dickinson," in Marian Arkin and
> > Barbara Shollar, eds., *Longman Anthology of World
> > Literature by Women, 1875–1975.*

What is the distinctive voice that makes her poems unmistakably hers?
First of all, her poems remain fresh because of their intensely personal,
often startling *perspective*. Her poems typically make us look at the
world from an unexpected angle, thus forcing us to see something anew
as if for the first time. She summed up her poetic credo in the following
poem.

Tell all the Truth but tell it slant   *about 1868*

J.1129

Tell all the Truth but tell it slant—
Success in circuit lies
Too bright for our infirm Delight
The Truth's superb surprise

As Lightning to the Children eased   5
With explanation kind
The truth must dazzle gradually
Or every man be blind—

The truth is a "superb surprise," and it is too bright and dazzling for our
infirm and weak capacity to absorb it. It must be presented "in circuit"—in
a roundabout way. It must be allowed to dazzle and delight us "gradually."
The way to tell the truth therefore is to tell it "slant"—not directly but aslant,
so that it can approach us not head-on but from a slanted, nonthreatening
angle.

Making Connections—For Discussion or Writing

What is the connection between this poem and Gwendolyn Brooks' poem
"Truth" (Chapter 12)?

The way Dickinson tells the truth "slant" is not to preach at us but to
speak to us through startling graphic *images* and eye-opening
metaphors. She looks at the world with a special alertness, marveling at
what she finds, keeping alive in us the art of wondering. For people who
notice birds only in passing, the following poem presents a series of
striking visual images designed to surprise them into paying attention:

A Bird came down the Walk   *about 1862*

J.328

A Bird came down the Walk—
He did not know I saw—
He bit an Angleworm in halves
And ate the fellow, raw,

And then he drank a Dew   5
From a convenient Grass—
And then hopped sidewise to the Wall
To let a Beetle pass—

He glanced with rapid eyes
That hurried all around—   10
They looked like frightened Beads, I thought—
He stirred his Velvet Head

Like one in danger. Cautious,
I offered him a Crumb
And he unrolled his feathers   15
And rowed him softer home—

Than Oars divide the Ocean,
Too silver for a seam—
Or Butterflies, off Banks of Noon
Leap, plashless° as they swim.   *without a splash*   20

The opening lines give us a startling close-up view of the visitor that has come down from the air to go about essential bird business: We see the angleworm being bitten "in halves," then eaten raw, and washed down with dew drunk from a conveniently close blade of grass. We keep watching as the bird hops sidewise to get out of the way of a beetle. We get a glimpse of the beadlike eyes that are forever hurriedly glancing and shifting, looking for danger. At the approach of the human observer (who means no harm and offers a crumb), the bird returns to its natural airborne habitat, where he "rows him softer home" than an oar-propelled boat does in the ocean. We watch the striking transition from the comically hopping, restless and anxious earthbound bird to the bird at home in the seamless air where it effortlessly glides. Does the transformation of the bird from its awkwardly hopping, frightened grounded state to its serenely floating skyborne state have a symbolic meaning? Are our bodies stumbling awkwardly through life in our present earthbound existence? Will our souls float serenely upward, returning to their spiritual home, during a future state? The poem does not say. If this is the larger truth hinted at in the poem, the poet tells it "slant."

The Receptive Reader

1. Dickinson's *wording* is often cryptic—compressing or telescoping meaning into short, puzzling phrases. When she talks about the "ocean" of air, what is the meaning of "too silver for a seam"? What is it about silver that keeps us from expecting to see seams? How would butterflies leap "off banks of noon"?

2. Many people lay out money for photographs, paintings, or figurines of pretty birds. Is the bird in this poem pretty? Why or why not?

3. What words and images in this poem make the natural creatures seem almost human? Which remind us that they are not? One student said after reading this poem, "We like to humanize animals, but we cannot communicate with them. Sometimes we feel kinship with animals, and at other times we don't." How would you sum up the poet's perspective on the animal world in this poem?

Dickinson's *metaphors* are often startling and thought-provoking because they connect mundane details of every day with the most troubling questions about life, death, and immortality. In the following poem, household chores become a solemn metaphor for the housekeeping of the heart:

The Bustle in a House   *about 1866*

J.1078

The Bustle in a House
The Morning after Death
Is solemnest of industries°   chores
Enacted upon Earth—

The Sweeping up the Heart   5
And putting Love away
We shall not want to use again
Until Eternity.

The poem focuses on the bustling of activity in the house after some-one beloved has died. Literally, the diligent or industrious activity (the "solemnest of industries") involves tidying up—sweeping the house and putting things away that with the deceased gone may not be used again for a long time, if ever. But metaphorically these commonplace activities come to stand for the wrenching adjustments we have to make in our hearts. We try to purge our hearts of cluttered, destructive emotions; we try to put everything in order. We realize we can no longer put our love to its accustomed daily uses; we can only keep it on a back shelf until the distant day of resurrection.

A third feature of Dickinson's poetry is the deceptive *simplicity* of her style. Her basic line is a sparse irregular three-beat or four-beat line. Lines are usually held loosely together by slant rhyme or half-rhyme in a four-line stanza, reminding us of simple popular forms like hymns and ballads. The absence of extraneous adornment highlights the importance of the individual word, the individual metaphor. In one of her last letters, she wrote, "I hesitate which word to take, as I can take but a few and each must be the chiefest."

What features of the following poem seem to illustrate the distinctive Dickinson style? For instance, does it show her way of looking at the world from a startling new perspective? Does it show her way of giving concrete shape to abstract ideas? Does it seem simple on the surface?

Because I could not stop for Death   *about 1863*

J.712

Because I could not stop for Death—
He kindly stopped for me—
The Carriage held but just Ourselves—
And Immortality.

We slowly drove—He knew no haste   5
And I had put away
My labor and my leisure too,
For His Civility—

We passed the School, where Children strove
At Recess—in the Ring—   10
We passed the Fields of Gazing Grain—
We passed the Setting Sun—

Or rather—He passed Us—
The Dews drew quivering and chill—
For only Gossamer, my Gown—   15
My Tippet—only Tulle°—   *scarf of lacelike material*

We paused before a House that seemed
A Swelling of the Ground—
The Roof was scarcely visible—
The Cornice°—in the Ground—   *ornamental strip, usually high up*   20

Since then—'tis Centuries—and yet
Feels shorter than the Day
I first surmised the Horses' Heads
Were toward Eternity—

The Receptive Reader

1. What is strange or different about the *attitude toward death* reflected in this poem? Can you sympathize with or relate to the feelings that seem to be mirrored in this poem?

2. What is the *symbolism* of the school, the fields, the setting sun, the house "that seemed/A Swelling of the Ground"?

Dickinson was an intensely personal poet, looking at the world from a highly individual perspective. In turn, critics have looked at her poetry from highly individual points of view. Study the following poem and the range of readers' responses in the quotations that follow it.

I heard a Fly buzz—when I died   *about 1862*

J.465

I heard a Fly buzz—when I died—
The Stillness in the Room
Was like the Stillness in the Air—
Between the Heaves of Storm—

The Eyes around—had wrung them dry—   5
And Breaths were gathering firm
For that last Onset—when the King
Be witnessed—in the Room—

I willed my Keepsakes—Signed away
What portion of me be   10
Assignable°—and then it was   *transferable*
There interposed a Fly—

With Blue—uncertain stumbling Buzz—
Between the light—and me—

And then the Windows failed—and then   15
I could not see to see—

The Range of Interpretation

Study the range of responses in the following quotations. How do you react
to them? Which do you tend to agree with and why?

1. The buzzing fly, so familiar a part of the natural order of persistent household discomfort, is brought in at the last to give the touch of petty irritabilities
that are concomitant with living—and indeed with dying. (Thomas Johnson)

2. The dying person does in fact not merely suffer an unwelcome external
interruption of an otherwise resolute expectancy but falls from a higher consciousness, from liberating insight, from faith, into an intensely skeptical
mood. . . . To the dying person, the buzzing fly would thus become a timely,
untimely reminder of man's final, cadaverous condition and putrefaction. (Ger-
hard Friedrich)

3. I understand that fly to be the last kiss of the world. . . . think of the fly
not as a distraction taking Emily's thoughts from glory and blocking the divine
light . . . but a last dear sound from the world as the light of consciousness
sank from her. (John Ciardi)

4. The only sound of heavenly music, or of wings taking flight, was the
"Blue—uncertain stumbling Buzz" of a fly that filled her dying ear. Instead of
a final vision of the hereafter, this world simply faded from her eyes. (Ruth
Miller)

5. And what kind of fly? A fly "With Blue—uncertain stumbling Buzz"—a
blowfly. . . . She was a practical housewife, and every housewife abhors a
blowfly. It pollutes everything it touches. Its eggs are maggots. . . . What we
know of Emily Dickinson gives us assurance that just as she would abhor the
blowfly she would abhor the deathbed scene. (Caroline Hogue)

Making Connections—For Discussion or Writing

Other poems by Emily Dickinson included earlier in this volume are "Apparently with no surprise" (Chapter 15), "'Hope' is the thing with feathers"
(Chapter 15), and "The Soul selects her own Society" (Chapter 18). Do these
poems illustrate such characteristic features as a startling different perspective,
bold metaphors, or a deceptive simplicity?

POEMS FOR FURTHER STUDY

The following selection includes many of the most widely read of
Dickinson's poems. What in each poem helps you recognize her personal voice? What are themes she returns to again and again? What is
her characteristic way of treating them?

J.67

about 1859

Success is counted sweetest
By those who ne'er succeed
To comprehend a nectar°   *drink of the gods*
Requires sorest need.

Not one of all the purple Host   5
Who took the Flag today
Can tell the definition
So clear of Victory

As he defeated—dying—
On whose forbidden ear   10
The distant strains of triumph
Burst agonized and clear!

J.84

about 1859

Her breast is fit for pearls,
But I was not a "Diver"—
Her brow is fit for thrones
But I have not a crest.°   *aristocrat's logo*
Her heart is fit for *home*—   5
I—a Sparrow—build there
Sweet of twigs and twine
My perennial nest.

J.249

about 1861

Wild Nights—Wild Nights!
Were I with thee
Wild Nights should be
Our luxury!

Futile—the Winds—   5
To a Heart in port—
Done with the Compass—
Done with the Chart!

Rowing in Eden—
Ah, the Sea!   10
Might I but moor—Tonight—
In Thee!

J.258

about 1861

There's a certain Slant of light,
Winter Afternoons—
That oppresses, like the Heft
Of Cathedral Tunes—

Heavenly Hurt, it gives us—   5
We can find no scar,
But internal difference,
Where the Meanings, are—

None may teach it—Any—
'Tis the Seal Despair—   10
An imperial affliction
Sent us of the Air—

When it comes, the Landscape listens—
Shadows—hold their breath—
When it goes, 'tis like the Distance   15
On the look of Death—

J.288   *about 1861*

I'm Nobody! Who are you?
Are you—Nobody—Too?
Then there's a pair of us?
Don't tell! They'd advertise—you know!

How dreary—to be—Somebody!   5
How public—like a Frog—
To tell one's name—the livelong June—
To an admiring Bog!

J.341   *about 1862*

After great pain, a formal feeling comes—
The Nerves sit ceremonious, like Tombs—
The stiff Heart questions was it He, that bore,
And Yesterday, or Centuries before?

The Feet, mechanical, go round—   5
Of Ground, or Air, or Ought°—   *anything*
A Wooden way
Regardless grown,
A Quartz contentment, like a stone—

This is the Hour of Lead—   10
Remembered, if outlived,
As Freezing persons, recollect the Snow—
First—Chill—then Stupor—then the letting go—

J.435   *about 1862*

Much Madness is divinest Sense—
To a discerning Eye—
Much Sense—the starkest Madness—
'Tis the Majority
In this, as All, prevail—   5

Assent—and you are sane—
Demur°—you're straightway dangerous—   *disagree*
And handled with a Chain—

J.449   *about 1862*

I died for Beauty—but was scarce
Adjusted in the Tomb
When One who died for Truth, was lain
In an adjoining Room—

He questioned softly "Why I failed?"   5
"For Beauty," I replied—
"And I—for Truth—Themself Are One—
We Brethren, are," He said—

And so, as Kinsmen, met a Night—
We talked between the Rooms—   10
Until the Moss had reached our lips—
And covered up—our names—

J.518   *about 1862*

Her sweet Weight on my Heart a Night
Had scarcely deigned to lie—
When, stirring, for Belief's delight,
My Bride had slipped away—

If 'twas a Dream—made solid—just   5
The Heaven to confirm—
Or if myself were dreamed of Her—
The power to presume—

With Him remain—who unto Me—
Gave—even as to All—   10
A Fiction superseding Faith—
By so much—as 'twas real—

J.526   *about 1862*

To hear an Oriole sing
May be a common thing—
Or only a divine.

It is not of the Bird
Who sings the same, unheard,   5
As unto Crowd—

The Fashion of the Ear
Attireth that it hear
In Dun,° or fair—   *unpleasing*

So whether it be Rune,°   *weighty writing*   10
Or whether it be none
Is of within.

The "Tune is in the Tree—"
The Skeptic—showeth me—
"No Sir! In Thee!"   15

J.579   *about 1862*

I had been hungry, all the Years—
My Noon had Come—to dine—
I trembling drew the Table near—
And touched the Curious Wine—

'Twas this on Tables I had seen—   5
When turning, hungry, Home
I looked in Windows, for the Wealth
I could not hope—for Mine—

I did not know the ample Bread—
'Twas so unlike the Crumb   10
The Birds and I, had often shared
In Nature's—Dining Room—

The Plenty hurt me—'twas so new—
Myself felt ill—and odd—
As Berry—of a Mountain Bush—   15
Transplanted—to the Road—

Nor was I hungry—so I found
That Hunger—was a way
Of Persons outside Windows—
The Entering—takes away—   20

J.986   *about 1865*

A narrow fellow in the Grass
Occasionally rides—
You may have met him—did you not
His notice sudden is—

The grass divides as with a Comb—   5
A spotted shaft is seen—
And then it closes at your feet
And opens further on—

He likes a Boggy Acre°—   *swampy ground*
A Floor too cool for Corn—   10
Yet when a Boy, and Barefoot—
I more than once at Noon

Have passed, I thought, a Whiplash
Unbraiding in the Sun
When stooping to secure it   15
It wrinkled, and was gone—

Several of Nature's People
I know, and they know me—
I feel for them a transport°   *sudden impulsive feeling*
Of cordiality—   20

But never met this Fellow
Attended, or alone
Without a tighter breathing
And Zero at the bone—

J.1052   *about 1865*

I never saw a Moor—
I never saw the Sea—
Yet know I how the Heather looks
And what a Billow° be.   *large wave*

I never spoke with God   5
Nor visited in Heaven—
Yet certain am I of the spot
As if the Checks were given—

J.1263   *about 1873*

There is no Frigate° like a Book   *fast sailing ship*
To take us Lands away
Nor any Coursers° like a Page   *swift horses*
Of prancing Poetry—
This Traverse may the poorest take   5
Without oppress of Toll—
How frugal is the Chariot
That bears the Human soul.

J.1732   *about 1896*

My life closed twice before its close—
It yet remains to see
If Immortality unveil
A third event to me

So huge, so hopeless to conceive   5
As these that twice befell
Parting is all we know of heaven,
And all we need of hell.

The Creative Dimension

From the poems by Dickinson you have read, choose a haunting image or a striking, puzzling detail that left a lasting impression. Write a passage in which you re-create the image or impression and follow the train of associations—of images, thoughts, or feelings—that it sets in motion in your mind.

Making Connections—For Discussion and Writing

For a library research project, search for books and articles that would provide material for a treatment of one of the following topics:

✘ a range of critical interpretations of the same Dickinson poem. How does the same poem look when read by different readers? Are there major areas of agreement? What are major differences in interpretation, and what might explain them?

✘ several critics' treatment of a recurrent theme in Dickinson's poetry. What do different critics say about the poet's treatment of a central recurrent theme like death, nature, love, faith, or immortality?

✘ several critics' discussion of a key feature of her style or personal voice.

Numberless discussions of Dickinson's poetry have appeared in periodicals ranging from the *Explicator* to *New Literary History*. Book-length sources you may be able to consult include the following:

Charles R. Anderson, *Emily Dickinson's Poetry: Stairway to Surprise* (1960)
Richard B. Sewall, ed., *Emily Dickinson: A Collection of Critical Essays* (1963)
Albert Gelpi, *Emily Dickinson: The Mind of the Poet* (1965)
Ruth Miller, *The Poetry of Emily Dickinson* (1974)
Richard B. Sewall, *The Life of Emily Dickinson* (1974)
Robert Weisbuch, *Emily Dickinson's Poetry* (1975)
Sharon Cameron, *Lyric Time: Dickinson and the Limits of Genre* (1980)
Joanne F. Diehl, *Dickinson and the Romantic Imagination* (1981)
David Porter, *Dickinson: The Modern Idiom* (1981)
Antonina Clarke Mossberg, *Emily Dickinson: When a Writer Is a Daughter* (1982)
Suzanne Juhasz, *The Undiscovered Continent: Emily Dickinson and the Space of the Mind* (1983)
Suzanne Juhasz, ed., *Feminist Critics Read Emily Dickinson* (1983)
Jerome Loving, *Emily Dickinson: The Poet on the Second Story* (1986)
Helen McNeil, *Emily Dickinson* (1986)
Cynthia Griffin Wolff, *Emily Dickinson* (1986)
Christanne Miller, *Emily Dickinson: A Poet's Grammar* (1987)
Jamie Fuller, *The Diary of Emily Dickinson* (1993)
Suzanne Juhasz, *Comic Power in Emily Dickinson* (1993)

ROBERT FROST: POET AND PERSONA

If Robert Frost was much honored in his lifetime,
it was because a good many preferred to ignore
his darker truths.

JOHN F. KENNEDY

Robert Frost (1874–1963) became a living legend—the closest that twentieth-century America came to having a national poet. As with other legendary literary figures, biographers and critics have searched for the real-life person behind the legend. They have probed the paradoxical relationship between the public persona of the adored poet-sage and the private demons of the poet's life.

In the early years, Frost struggled to make a living for himself and his family—as a farmer, a part-time teacher, a poet. Although he is commonly associated with the New England setting, he was born in San Francisco and spent his boyhood years in California. Frost's father, a Southerner who had named the boy Robert Lee, died when Frost was eleven years old. His Scottish mother then took him to New England, where she had relatives. Frost attended Lawrence High School in Massachusetts, where the curriculum was heavy on Greek and Roman history and literature. He later married Elinor White, who had been his co-valedictorian there. He attended first Dartmouth and then Harvard, but, as he put it later, he walked out of both of them, deciding to learn not from teachers but from "writers who had written before me."

With help from his grandfather, Frost bought a farm in New Hampshire, the setting of many of his early poems. Unable to make a living as a farmer and part-time teacher, unable to get more than a few poems accepted for publication, Frost and his wife took their growing family to England, where he made friends with other aspiring young poets. He was first recognized as a poet while in England, where he published two volumes: *A Boy's Will* (1913) and *North of Boston* (1914). When he returned to the United States, he was almost forty years old. Magazines started to print his poems, and he gradually became widely known as a poet and lecturer. Honors multiplied: four Pulitzer Prizes, honorary degrees from Oxford and Cambridge, travel abroad as a government-sponsored ambassador of goodwill. Prestigious teaching appointments included stints as "poet in residence" at Amherst College and later at the University of Michigan in Ann Arbor. He returned to Ann Arbor late in his life for the kind of poetry reading where he was adored and lionized by thousands of students.

As a poet, performer, and public figure, Frost played the role of the New England sage. He appeared "wide-shouldered, craggy, tough in texture, solid as New Hampshire granite" (Louis Untermeyer). He spoke as the voice of homely truths, distrusting science, progress, and professors. He maintained the image of someone staying close to the grass roots, keeping in touch with the simple realities of rural living, distancing himself from movements and trends. ("I never dared be radical when young/For fear it would make me conservative when old.")

In the following poem, Frost assumes the stance of the country sage: Something ordinary happens, related to the familiar chores of the country dweller. Some small happening raises a question in the poet's mind. Two different ways of looking at the issue suggest themselves. The speaker in the poem weighs simple alternatives, thinking the matter through. On reflection, what seemed a simple matter has a bearing on how we think of ourselves or shape our lives. There is no waving of arms, no getting up on a soapbox to make a speech. The tone is one of New England **understatement**. There is something here worth thinking about, without getting all bothered and excited.

The Tuft of Flowers   1906

I went to turn the grass once after one
Who mowed it in the dew before the sun.

The dew was gone that made his blade so keen
Before I came to view the leveled scene.

I looked for him behind an isle of trees;   5
I listened for his whetstone on the breeze.

But he had gone his way, the grass all mown,
And I must be, as he had been—alone.

"As all must be," I said within my heart,
"Whether they work together or apart."   10

But as I said it, swift there passed me by
On noiseless wing a bewildered butterfly,

Seeking with memories grown dim o'er night
Some resting flower of yesterday's delight.

And once I marked his flight go round and round,   15
As where some flower lay withering on the ground.

And then he flew as far as eye could see,
And then on tremulous wing came back to me.

I thought of questions that have no reply,
And would have turned to toss the grass to dry;   20

But he turned first, and led my eye to look
At a tall tuft of flowers beside a brook,

A leaping tongue of bloom the scythe had spared
Beside a reedy brook the scythe had bared.

The mower in the dew had loved them thus,   25
By leaving them to flourish, not for us,

Nor yet to draw one thought of ours to him,
But from sheer morning gladness at the brim.

The butterfly and I had lit upon,
Nevertheless, a message from the dawn,   30

That made me hear the wakening birds around,
And hear his long scythe whispering to the ground,

And feel a spirit kindred to my own;
So that henceforth I worked no more alone,

But glad with him, I worked as with his aid,   35
And weary, sought at noon with him the shade;

And dreaming, as it were, held brotherly speech
With one whose thought I had not hoped to reach.

"Men work together," I told him from the heart,
"Whether they work together or apart."   40

This poem has an almost childlike simplicity. Most of the stanzas are self-contained couplets in iambic pentameter, with little metrical variation. (Early and again in the last stanza, initial inversion—"WHETHER / they WORK"—alerts us to the key issue.) The stanzas tell the story step by step in simple "and-then" fashion. The speaker in the poem sees the grass that had been mown before and that is to be turned so it will dry in the sun. The mower is nowhere to be seen. The speaker in the poem thinks about the lonely fellow worker's morning labor, concluding that all workers work essentially alone, doing their jobs whether recognized by others or not. But the fluttering butterfly appears at the right time to guide us to the counter-evidence: the tall tuft of flowers, the "leaping tongue of bloom," that the mower has left standing.

The Receptive Reader

How does noticing the tuft of flowers change the speaker's thinking? How and where does the poet line up the two contrasting points of view in parallel form?

Although Frost's best-loved poems are simple on the surface, they may turn out to be puzzlers; they remain open-ended. Frost once said that he liked to write poems that seem "altogether obvious" to the casual reader but that turn out to be subtle in unexpected ways. They disturb our set ways of thinking, making us ponder first one way of looking at things, then another. Some of Frost's most famous poems have been interpreted in radically different ways. For instance, different readers have read diametrically opposed meanings into the poem "Mending

Wall." Is it true that "Good fences make good neighbors"? Or is this kind of territorial thinking the product of an obsolete Stone Age mentality?

Mending Wall   *1914*

Something there is that doesn't love a wall,
That sends the frozen-ground-swell under it
And spills the upper boulders in the sun,
And makes gaps even two can pass abreast.
The work of hunters is another thing: 5
I have come after them and made repair
Where they have left not one stone on a stone,
But they would have the rabbit out of hiding,
To please the yelping dogs. The gaps I mean,
No one has seen them made or heard them made,   10
But at spring mending-time we find them there.
I let my neighbor know beyond the hill;
And on a day we meet to walk the line
And set the wall between us once again.
We keep the wall between us as we go.   15
To each the boulders that have fallen to each.
And some are loaves and some so nearly balls
We have to use a spell to make them balance:
"Stay where you are until our backs are turned!"
We wear our fingers rough with handling them.   20
Oh, just another kind of outdoor game,
One on a side. It comes to little more:
There where it is we do not need the wall:
He is all pine and I am apple orchard.
My apple trees will never get across   25
And eat the cones under his pines, I tell him.
He only says, "Good fences make good neighbors."
Spring is the mischief in me, and I wonder
If I could put a notion in his head:
"Why do they make good neighbors? Isn't it   30
Where there are cows? But here there are no cows.
Before I built a wall I'd ask to know
What I was walling in or walling out,
And to whom I was like to give offense.
Something there is that doesn't love a wall,   35
That wants it down." I could say "Elves" to him,
But it's not elves exactly, and I'd rather
He said if for himself. I see him there,
Bringing a stone grasped firmly by the top
In each hand, like an old-stone savage armed.   40
He moves in darkness as it seems to me,
Not of woods only and the shade of trees.
He will not go behind his father's saying,

And he likes having thought of it so well
He says again, "Good fences make good neighbors."   45

The Range of Interpretation

The two critical excerpts that follow continue the dialogue between the speaker in the poem and his neighbor. What side does the first reader take and why? How does he support his interpretation of the poem? What assumptions does the second reader bring to the poem? What evidence leads him to a very different conclusion? Which of the two readings do you agree with and why? Which of the two competing attitudes toward walls do you sympathize with and why?

1. Much of the public knows Frost by the phrase "Good fences make good neighbors." But the speaker in "Mending Wall" is saying just the opposite: that there is some mysterious force at work to break down barriers between human beings. "Elves," he calls it, in contrast to the matter-of-fact damage done by hunters (lines 5–11). But this is only a hint of what each person must discover for himself—companionship, respect, love, or the mystical togetherness of men who work.

The speaker's description of his neighbor makes the point even clearer (lines 38–42). The man and his ideas still belong to stone-age savagery. The darkness which surrounds him is not simply the natural darkness of the woods, but the primordial destructiveness in the heart of man. There is darkness also in the conventional mentality that makes a man repeat "Good fences make good neighbors" simply because his father said it (lines 43–44), when it does not fit the new situation at all (lines 30–31).

The poem, however, illustrates the difficulty of making a definite statement about any of Frost's ideas. The speaker does not agree with his neighbor in theory (lines 23–36); but, in the fact of his labor, he is doing the same thing his neighbor is doing.

From David A. Sohn and Richard H. Tyre, *Frost: The Poet
and His Poetry,* 1967

2. Many general readers—and doubtless some stray sophisticated ones too—still see the poem as an argument against walls of all sorts, be they literal or metaphorical. To them walls are the divisive creations of selfish or shortsighted men who erect barriers to keep other people away. If only you will do away with useless, outmoded walls, they say, you will bring about a closer bond of fellowship—a deeper sense of community— among neighbors, in society at large, even among nations.

Generally, however, careful readers regard such views as hostile to the themes and attitudes they characteristically find in Frost. To them "Mending Wall" is Frost's finest expression of concern that in a world which doesn't seem to love a wall the individual may somehow get lost. To them the Yankee farmer, despite the scoffing questions that he puts to his neighbor, is the symbol of all those who love their privacy and their independence, and are resentful of those people—individuals or social planners—who would intrude upon that privacy. Or he is any individual who resents the levelers who would destroy walls and thus let others, even if friend or neighbor, infringe upon his right to be alone and to think his own thoughts after his own fashion. In short, despite the obvious warm appeal of the good neighborliness that wants walls down—even for the Yankee individualist resentful of intrusions—walls are nonetheless the essential barriers that must exist between man and man if the individual is to preserve his own soul, and mutual understanding and respect are to survive and flourish. . . .

A wall is something more than the means for walling something visible in or out. If apple trees and pine cones were the only concern, then good fences would scarcely be worth the trouble it takes to keep them repaired. But in spite of all his scoffing the narrator knows that this is the least of the purposes that are served by good fences. This is why each spring it is he who takes the initiative and lets his neighbor know beyond the hill that once again it's time for mending wall. Good fences make good neighbors.

From William S. Ward, "Lifted Pot Lids and Unmended Walls," College English, February 1966

Frost took his readers from the neuroses of city living to a simpler rural world. In the words of Babette Deutsch in *Poetry in Our Time,* he wrote about the commonplace subjects of country life: "the steady caring for crops and creatures"; the "homely details of barn and farmhouse, orchard, pasture and wood lot"; apple-picking, haymaking, repairing orchard walls of loosely piled stones. He celebrated "the jeweled vision of blueberries in rain-wet leaves"; no one wrote "more tenderly of the young life on and about the farm, be it a runaway colt, a young orchard threatened by false spring, a nestful of fledglings exposed by the cultivator."

Frost did not ignore the harsher side of farm life: the "drudgery and isolation"; ghastly accidents caused by machinery. However, only rarely do his best-known poems show the poet's darker and more pessimistic side. Donald Hall adored the older man when Hall himself was an aspiring young poet and befriended the aging poet toward the end of his career. Hall wrote about the anguish and sense of guilt that lay behind the public image of the "twinkling Yankee" of the Frost legend:

To him—I learned over the years—his family background seemed precarious, dangerous; and his adult life cursed with tragedy, for which he took responsibility. His father was a sometime drunk, dead at an early age; his mother endured a bad marriage, was widowed young, and failed as a schoolteacher when she returned to her native Massachusetts; yet she was a fond mother, kind to her children—and she wrote poems. Her son felt dangerously close to her, and followed that fondness into devotion to one young woman, Elinor White, whom he courted extravagantly, romantically, and doggedly. Apparently losing her, he considered suicide; at least, he later dropped hints to friends that he had considered suicide. When Elinor and Robert finally married, they settled in Derry, New Hampshire, and lived in poverty, enduring an extraordinary series of family misfortunes.

From *Remembering Poets: Reminiscences and Opinions,* 1977

Frost lost four of his children to fatal illness, insanity, death in childbirth, or suicide. His surviving daughter Lesley turned against him. The following late sonnet is the best known of the poems in which Frost confronted "the anguish of existence and the presence of the malign" (Babette Deutsch).

Design   *1922*

I found a dimpled spider, fat and white,
On a white heal-all, holding up a moth
Like a white piece of rigid satin cloth—
Assorted characters of death and blight
Mixed ready to begin the morning right,   5
Like the ingredients of a witches' broth—
A snow-drop spider, a flower like a froth,
And dead wings carried like a paper kite.

What had that flower to do with being white,
The wayside blue and innocent heal-all?   10
What brought the kindred spider to that height,
Then steered the white moth thither in the night?
What but design of darkness to appall?—
If design govern in a thing so small.

This poem is a finely crafted sonnet, with an underlying iambic pentameter beat, and with the interlaced rhyme scheme in the Petrarchan manner. The almost casual and at times playful tone sets up an ironic contrast with the miniature scene of death and blight:

> Frost achieves utter horror in this poem, which many consider his most terrifying work, by juxtaposing pleasant images with disgusting ones: the fat spider is "dimpled" and "white" like a baby; "dead wings" become a "paper kite": "death and blight" are cheerfully "mixed ready to begin the morning right," as in an ad for breakfast food. An air of abnormality pervades the entire poem. The flower, ironically called the "heal-all," is usually blue, but this is a mutant. The spider is at a height where it would not normally be found. Moths are ordinarily attracted by light, but this one has been "steered" to its death in the night. And all the "characters of death" share the same ghastly whiteness.

Can we escape the conclusion that a dark design in nature plotted against the moth? The last line may not offer the ray of light its tone suggests. What would be better—that darkness terrorize by design, or that all the little evils in the world operate without design?

From David A. Sohn and Richard H. Tyre, *Frost: The Poet and His Poetry,* 1967

The Receptive Reader

Do you agree with these two editors on the "utter horror" and on the "air of abnormality" that they say pervades the poem? Do you tend to answer the final question raised by the poem the same way they do?

Robert Frost was admired by critics and fellow poets while at the same time reaching a large popular audience. Critics and poets acclaimed him even though he was at odds with poetic fashions in the first half of the twentieth century. The most widely imitated poets of his time were poets like T. S. Eliot and Ezra Pound. They wrote difficult poems, filled with shifting images and obscure allusions, that made Frost's more accessible poems seem unsophisticated by comparison. Furthermore, Frost made himself the advocate of traditional form when the modern tendency was to reject traditional meter and rhyme as artificial, confining, or extraneous. He said on the role of form in our lives and in the world,

Any psychiatrist will tell you that making a basket, or making a horseshoe, or giving anything form gives you a confidence in the universe . . . that it has form, see. When you talk about your troubles and go to somebody about them, you're just a fool. The best way to settle them is to make something that has form, because all you want to do is get a sense of form.

JUXTAPOSITIONS

Variations on a Theme

What makes the two following poems seem like variations on a theme? What makes the second poem read like a tribute to the earlier poet? Compare the two poems on points such as the use of nature imagery, simplicity of theme, and use of traditional form. What images are common to both poems? How does each poet use them? What is similar or alike in the poets' perspectives on the passing of time? Are there nevertheless major differences between the two poems?

Robert Frost

Nothing Gold Can Stay   *1923*

Nature's first green is gold,
Her hardest hue to hold.
Her early leaf's a flower;
But only so an hour.
Then leaf subsides to leaf.   5
So Eden sank to grief,
So dawn goes down to day.
Nothing gold can stay.

Linda Pastan   *(born 1932)*

Posterity   *1991*

For every newborn child
We planted one live tree,
A green posterity,
So death could be beguiled°   *deluded or diverted*
By root and branch and flower   5
To abdicate° some power.   *give up*
And we were reconciled.

Now we must move away
Leaving the trees behind
For anyone to climb.   10
The gold-rimmed sky goes gray.
Snow, as we turn our backs
Obliterates our tracks.
Not even leaves can stay.

Making Connections—For Discussion or Writing

✗ Other poems by Robert Frost printed earlier in this volume include "Stopping by Woods" (Chapter 12) and "Fire and Ice" (Chapter 13). Do they illustrate some of the features characteristic of the poems you have just read?

✗ Compare and contrast Frost's "Design" with Whitman's "A Noiseless Patient Spider" (Chapter 12)—another poem in which a spider serves as the central symbol.

POEMS FOR FURTHER STUDY

In reading these poems by Robert Frost, keep in mind questions like the following: Does the poem conform to the pattern of making a natural scene or an event real for you and then making you share in the reflections it inspires? Does the poem play off two different ways of looking at things? Which prevails, and how? Is the poem in the "cool" New England voice? Or do you hear a more bitter, passionate, or questioning voice in the poem?

After Apple-Picking   *1914*

My long two-pointed ladder's sticking through a tree
Toward heaven still,
And there's a barrel that I didn't fill
Beside it, and there may be two or three
Apples I didn't pick upon some bough.   5
But I am done with apple-picking now.
Essence of winter sleep is on the night,
The scent of apples: I am drowsing off.
I cannot rub the strangeness from my sight
I got from looking through a pane of glass   10
I skimmed this morning from the drinking trough
And held against the world of hoary grass.
It melted, and I let it fall and break.
But I was well
Upon my way to sleep before it fell,   15
And I could tell
What form my dreaming was about to take.
Magnified apples appear and disappear,
Stem end and blossom end,
And every fleck of russet showing clear.   20
My instep arch not only keeps the ache,
It keeps the pressure of a ladder-round.
I feel the ladder sway as the boughs bend.
And I keep hearing from the cellar bin
The rumbling sound   25
Of load on load of apples coming in.
For I have had too much
Of apple-picking: I am overtired
Of the great harvest I myself desired.
There were ten thousand thousand fruit to touch,   30
Cherish in hand, lift down, and not let fall.
For all
That struck the earth,
No matter if not bruised or spiked with stubble,
Went surely to the cider-apple heap   35
As of no worth.

One can see what will trouble
This sleep of mine, whatever sleep it is.
Were he not gone,
The woodchuck could say whether it's like his   40
Long sleep, as I describe its coming on,
Or just some human sleep.

The Road Not Taken   1915

Two roads diverged in a yellow wood,
And sorry I could not travel both
And be one traveler, long I stood
And looked down one as far as I could
To where it bent in the undergrowth;   5

Then took the other, as just as fair,
And having perhaps the better claim,
Because it was grassy and wanted wear;
Though as for that, the passing there
Had worn them really about the same,   10

And both that morning equally lay
In leaves no step had trodden black.
Oh, I kept the first for another day!
Yet knowing how way leads on to way,
I doubted if I should ever come back.   15

I shall be telling this with a sigh
Somewhere ages and ages hence:
Two roads diverged in a wood, and I—
I took the one less traveled by,
And that has made all the difference.   20

The Oven Bird   1916

There is a singer everyone has heard,
Loud, a mid-summer and a mid-wood bird,
Who makes the solid tree trunks sound again.
He says that leaves are old and that for flowers
Mid-summer is to spring as one to ten.   5
He says the early petal-fall is past,
When pear and cherry bloom went down in showers
On sunny days a moment overcast;
And comes that other fall we name the fall.
He says the highway dust is over all.   10
The birds would cease and be as other birds
But that he knows in singing not to sing.
The question that he frames in all but words
Is what to make of a diminished thing.

Once by the Pacific   *1928*

The shattered water made a misty din.
Great waves looked over others coming in,
And thought of doing something to the shore
That water never did to land before.
The clouds were low and hairy in the skies,   5
Like locks blown forward in the gleam of eyes.
You could not tell, and yet it looked as if
The shore was lucky in being backed by cliff,
The cliff in being backed by continent;
It looked as if a night of dark intent   10
Was coming, and not only a night, an age.
Someone had better be prepared for rage.
There would be more than ocean-water broken
Before God's last *Put out the Light* was spoken.

Acquainted with the Night   *1928*

I have been one acquainted with the night.
I have walked out in rain—and back in rain.
I have outwalked the furthest city light.

I have looked down the saddest city lane.
I have passed by the watchman on his beat   5
And dropped my eyes, unwilling to explain.

I have stood still and stopped the sound of feet
When far away an interrupted cry
Came over houses from another street,

But not to call me back or say good-by;   10
And further still at an unearthly height,
One luminary clock against the sky
Proclaimed the time was neither wrong nor right.
I have been one acquainted with the night.

Neither Out Far Nor In Deep   *1936*

The people along the sand
All turn and look one way.
They turn their back on the land.
They look at the sea all day.

As long as it takes to pass   5
A ship keeps raising its hull;

The wetter ground like glass
Reflects a standing gull.

The land may vary more;
But wherever the truth may be—   10
The water comes ashore,
And the people look at the sea.

They cannot look out far.
They cannot look in deep.
But when was that ever a bar   15
To any watch they keep?

The Silken Tent   *1939*

She is as in a field a silken tent
At midday when a sunny summer breeze
Has dried the dew and all its ropes relent,
So that in guys it gently sways at ease,
And its supporting central cedar pole,   5
That is its pinnacle to heavenward
And signifies the sureness of the soul,
Seems to owe naught to any single cord,
But strictly held by none, is loosely bound
By countless silken ties of love and thought   10
To everything on earth the compass round,
And only by one's going slightly taut
In the capriciousness of summer air
Is of the slightest bondage made aware.

One Step Backward Taken   *1947*

Not only sands and gravels
Were once more on their travels,
But gulping muddy gallons
Great boulders off their balance
Bumped heads together dully   5
And started down the gully.
Whole capes caked off in slices.
I felt my standpoint shaken
In the universal crisis.
But with one step backward taken   10
I saved myself from going.
A world torn loose went by me.
Then the rain stopped and the blowing
And the sun came out to dry me.

The Night Light   1947

She always had to burn a light
Beside her attic bed at night.
It gave bad dreams and broken sleep,
But helped the Lord her soul to keep.
Good gloom on her was thrown away.   5
It is on me by night or day,
Who have, as I suppose, ahead
The darkest of it still to dread.

On Being Idolized   1947

The wave sucks back and with the last of water
It wraps a wisp of seaweed round my legs,
And with the swift rush of its sandy dregs
So undermines my barefoot stand I totter
And did I not take steps would be tipped over   5
Like the ideal of some mistaken lover.

Making Connections—For Discussion or Writing

For a library research project, search for books and articles that would provide material for the treatment of one of the following topics:

� several critical discussions of the same poem by Robert Frost. How does
the poem look from different critical perspectives? How much common ground
is there? What are significant differences, and how do you explain them?

✘ several different perspectives on the private person behind the public legend. Books and articles have been written to defend Frost against what friends
and biographers considered unjustified attacks on the poet. What was involved
in these controversies?

Books you may be able to consult include the following:

Reuben Brower, *The Poetry of Robert Frost* (1963)
Radcliffe Squires, *The Major Themes of Robert Frost* (1963)
J. F. Lynan, *The Pastoral Art of Robert Frost* (1964)
Philip L. Gerber, *Robert Frost* (1966)
Reginald L. Cook, *Robert Frost: A Living Voice* (1975)
Richard Poirier, *Robert Frost: The Work of Knowing* (1977)
John C. Kemp, *Robert Frost and New England: The Poet as Regionalist* (1979)
James L. Potter, *The Robert Frost Handbook* (1980)
William Pritchard, *Frost: A Literary Life Reconsidered* (1984)
John Evangelist Walsh, *Into My Own: The English Years of Robert Frost* (1988)
Judith Osper, *Toward Robert Frost the Reader and the Poet* (1992)
Katherine Kearns, *Robert Frost and a Poetics of Appetite* (1994)
Earl J. Wilcox, ed., *His Incalculable Influence on Others: Essays on Robert
    Frost in Our Time* (1994)
Jeffrey Myers, *Robert Frost: A Biography* (1996)

```
<<<Find It on the Web>>>

   For poets who have become icons of American culture, you may find a
range of online materials providing background material on the poet's life,
personal philosophy, or outreach to a large public. You may want to check
out the following and similar updated sites for background material on
Robert Frost.


Calhoun, Richard. Interview with Robert Frost. 1974. 5 Sept 2001.
   <http://www. libarts.sfasu.edu/Frost/Calhoun34.html>


The Popularity of Robert Frost. Selected critical excerpts. 5 Sept 2001.
   <http://www.libarts.sfasu.edu/Frost/Popularity.html>


Frost: Images of the Poet, Family, and Work. Electronic exhibit. 5 Sept 2001.
   <http://www.lib.virginia.edu/exhibits/frost/home.html>


Rector and Visitors of the U of Virginia. A Frost Bouquet. 1996. 24 Sept.
   2001.
   <http://www.lib.virginia.edu/exhibits/frost/home.html>


"Robert Frost." Great Books Online Website. 1997. 20 Oct. 2001.
   <http://www.bartleby.com/frost/>
```

GWENDOLYN BROOKS:
COMMITMENT AND UNIVERSALITY

*Gwendolyn Brooks has never denied her
engagement in the contemporary situation or
been over-obsessed by it.*

HARVEY CURTIS WEBSTER

*Art hurts. Art urges voyages—
and it is easier to stay at home,
the nice beer ready.*

GWENDOLYN BROOKS, "THE CHICAGO PICASSO"

*I am absolutely free of what any white critic
might say because I feel that it's going to be
amazing if any of them understand the true
significance of the struggle that's going on.*

GWENDOLYN BROOKS

Gwendolyn Brooks (1917–2000) was the most powerful and most
widely respected of contemporary African American poets. Many of her
poems deal uncompromisingly with the bleak realities of poverty and

racism. At the same time, they often bring tremendous empathy to representative lives and people in the black community, especially the old and the very young. (She has written many poems for or about children.) In the late sixties and early seventies, she became part of the movement that explored sources of strength in the black heritage and in solidarity with fellow artists exploring the African past. During an age of passionate but often short-lived rhetoric, she has written poems of understated eloquence and harsh beauty.

Gwendolyn Brooks was born in Topeka, Kansas, but she lived most of her life in Chicago, and she became Poet Laureate of the State of Illinois. She grew up in a closely knit, loving traditional family ("no child abuse, no prostitution, no Mafia membership," she said in a 1984 self-interview). The Brooks' house was filled with poetry, story, music, and song; she grew up in a "family-oriented" world with much visiting by and of relatives, traditional holiday feasts, family and church picnics. Her parents, she says, "subscribed to duty, decency, dignity, industry—*kindness.*" Her first poem was published in a children's magazine when she was ten; when in high school, she published several poems in the *Defender,* an African American newspaper in Chicago. She received a Pulitzer Prize for poetry in 1950, the first and only black woman to receive the award until Alice Walker won a Pulitzer for *The Color Purple* in 1983. In 1987, Brooks was the first black woman to be elected an honorary fellow of the Modern Language Association. She spent much of her time working with young people in colleges and schools and promoting workshops and awards for young poets.

The constant in Brooks' poetry was her loyalty to characters who find themselves trapped in an environment scarred by racial discrimination, poverty, and violence. She populated the imaginary community of Bronzeville with a haunting array of the human beings behind the stereotypes and government statistics. She chronicled their gray daily lives, their disillusionment and self-doubts, their defiance and futile rebellions. She observed with icy scorn the charitable rich who, from winters in Palm Beach and their world of "hostess gowns, and sunburst clocks,/Turtle soup, Chippendale" venture forth in search of the "worthy poor," only to be appalled by the squalor of the slums. Her most famous poem is a poem of doomed youth—jaunty, defiant, lost:

We Real Cool   *1960*

The Pool Players.
Seven at the Golden Shovel.

We real cool. We
Left school. We

Lurk late. We
Strike straight. We

Sing sin. We   5
Thin gin. We

Jazz June. We
Die soon.

This poem, with its broken, syncopated, beboppy counter-rhythm ("We real cool. We/Left school"), is an anthem for doomed youth who act "cool" as a defensive armor. They have dropped out and find themselves in the slow lane to a dead end. They jazz up, or live up, June and will be dead soon after.

The Receptive Reader

Do you think you recognize the young people in the poem? What do you think is the poet's attitude toward them? How does she relate to them? How do you?

Brooks writes with special affection of young people who rebel against the narrow boundaries of their lives, adopting a stance of defiance or escaping into an intensely imagined fantasy world. The sense of being trapped and intensely imagined dreams of escape become recurrent themes in poems like "Hunchback Girl":

Hunchback Girl: She Thinks of Heaven   1945

My Father, it is surely a blue place
And straight. Right. Regular. Where I shall find
No need for scholarly nonchalance or looks
A little to the left or guards upon the
Heart to halt love that runs without crookedness   5
Along its crooked corridors. My Father,
It is a planned place surely. Out of coils,
Unscrewed, released, no more to be marvelous,
I shall walk straightly through most proper halls
Proper myself, princess of properness.   10

The poem is in the form of a passionate prayer, with the girl addressing "My Father" twice. The hunchbacked girl thinks of a future state where her burden will be lifted. In heaven ("surely a blue place/and straight"), she will no longer be stared or marveled at ("no more to be marvelous"). Everything that is crooked or coiled will there be straightened out, made right and regular and proper. She will walk "straightly through most proper halls," a very "princess of properness." She will no longer have to try hard to look nonchalant when being stared at; she will no longer have to avoid people's eyes. So desperately needed is this release, so insistently wished for and imagined, so firmly believed in, that no one, inside the poem or out, could have the heart to call it merely a dream.

The Receptive Reader

1. To judge from the poem, what is the girl's usual way of coping with her disability?

2. Some critics have noted the *ambiguity* of the words *marvel* and *marvelous*. These words may refer to something to be stared at in fear but also to something arousing wonder or to be contemplated in awe. Does the poem bring into play either or both of these meanings?

3. Is it *paradoxical* that in the girl's heart love runs "without crookedness"— but that the corridors of the heart (hers? ours?) are themselves crooked? What did the poet have in mind? How do you explain the paradox?

4. One reader said that the irony underlying this poem is that "nothing in life is without its crookedness." What did she mean?

The Personal Response

Would *you* call the feelings expressed in this poem a mere dream? Have you or has someone you know well ever experienced similar feelings?

Brooks seems to speak most directly in her personal voice in poems of buried emotion, of humanity defeated by harsh reality. In the following sonnet, the "glory" of the pianist's music and the feeling of "proud delight" it calls up prevail for a time until they are drowned out by the unheard phantom cries of bitter men killed in war.

Piano after War   *1945*

On a snug evening I shall watch her fingers,
Cleverly ringed, declining to clever pink,
Beg glory from the willing keys. Old hungers
Will break their coffins, rise to eat and thank.
And music, warily, like the golden rose   5
That sometimes after sunset warms the west,
Will warm that room, persuasively suffuse
That room and me, rejuvenate a past.
But suddenly, across my climbing fever
Of proud delight—a multiplying cry.   10
A cry of bitter dead men who will never
Attend a gentle maker of musical joy.
Then my thawed eye will go again to ice.
And stone will shove the softness from my face.

The music in this poem unfolds like a "golden rose," wakening long since buried capacities for joy. "Old hungers" break their coffins. The glow thaws the icy heart—but only for a time. Suddenly, the memory of the dead undercuts the feeling of gentleness and joy; their fate makes the glories of culture an unkept promise. However tempting, the blessings of traditional culture cannot really soften the bitterness left behind by disappointed hopes.

The Receptive Reader

1. What do you think are the "old hungers" aroused from "their coffins" in this poem?

2. How does this sonnet follow the traditional pattern of a *turning point* in the middle of a poem and of a concluding *couplet* that leaves the reader with a strong final impression?

3. Were you *surprised* by the turn the poem takes? Does the poem early strike a note of wariness, of ironic detachment?

Brooks writes with special empathy and understated tenderness about children, like the two girls in the following poem from *Bronzeville Boys and Girls:*

Mexie and Bridie   *1945*

A tiny tea-party
Is happening today.
Pink cakes, and nuts and bon-bons on
A tiny, shiny tray.

It's out within the weather,   5
Beneath the clouds and sun.
And pausing ants have peeked upon,
As birds and gods have done.

Mexie's in her white dress,
And Bridie's in her brown.   10
There are no finer ladies
Tea-ing in the town.

In the words of Gary Smith, the children in Brooks' poems confront the essential dilemma of "how to find meaning and purpose in a world that denies their very existence." They live in a world of enclosed space—"alleyways, front and back yards, vacant lots, and back rooms"—symbolizing the restrictions that prevent their physical and mental growth. "Although trees, flowers, and grass poke through the concrete blocks of the urban environment, they are only reminders of a forbidden Eden." Not surprisingly,

the overwhelming desire for many of her children is the need to escape, to flee, the various forms of socioeconomic and psychological oppression that thwart self-fulfillment and threaten to destroy their lives. Because it is to a world free of adults where most of her children wish to escape, their unique ability to imagine this world—albeit on the wings of fantasy—distinguishes them from adults and creates some sense of hope.

> From Gary Smith, "Paradise Regained: The Children of
> Gwendolyn Brooks' *Bronzeville*," in Marie Mootry and
> Gary Smith, eds., *A Life Distilled: Gwendolyn Brooks,*
> *Her Poetry and Fiction*

Many of Brooks' poems were milestones in the spiritual journey of the black community from the goal of assimilation to the defiant acceptance of one's own identity. For her, as for many other black artists and writers, the years from 1967 to 1972 were years of awakening as the movement toward black pride and self-respect, in her words, "italicized black identity, solidarity, self-possession" and "vitally acknowledged African roots." In these years of "hot-breathing hope," when "the air was heavy with logic, illogic, zeal, construction," she read books about the black experience from W. E. Burghardt Du Bois' *The Souls of Black Folk* to the novels of Zora Neale Hurston. She exchanged views with black writers from James Baldwin to Don L. Lee. As she said later, "we talked, we walked, we read our work in taverns and churches and jail." She started to organize workshops for young poets and future teachers.

During these years, Brooks found her way to the self-affirmation and positive self-image needed to break the hold of negative stereotypes on one's own mind. She said,

Black woman . . . must remember that her personhood precedes her femalehood; that sweet as sex may be, she cannot endlessly brood on Black man's blondes, blues, blunders. She is a person in the world— with wrongs to right, stupidities to outwit, with her man if possible, on her own when not. And she is also here to enjoy. She will be here, like any other, once only. Therefore she must, in the midst of tragedy and hatred and neglect, in the midst of her own efforts to purify, mightily enjoy the readily available: sunshine and pets and children and conversation and games and travel (tiny or large) and books and walks and chocolate cake.

From *Report from Part One,* 1972

During the years of the civil rights movement, Brooks' work, like the work of many black writers and artists, became more committed and more political. In her poems on major events in the struggle, she speaks both as a "seer and sayer" for the black experience and as the voice of conscience for the larger community. One of her best-known poems takes stock of a reporter's foray to Little Rock, Arkansas, during the desegregation battle fought over the admission of the first nine black students to Central High. Backed by the Supreme Court's *Brown* decision outlawing segregated public schools, protected by federal troops called in by President Eisenhower, the students prevailed against the governor of the state, spitting and jeering mobs, and harassment and abuse from fellow students. For a year, in a last-ditch stand, the governor closed all public schools.

The Chicago Defender Sends a Man to Little Rock   1960

Fall, 1957

In Little Rock the people bear
Babes, and comb and part their hair
And watch the want ads, put repair
To roof and latch. While wheat toast burns
A woman waters multiferns.   5
Time upholds or overturns
The many, tight, and small concerns.

In Little Rock the people sing
Sunday hymns like anything,
Through Sunday pomp and polishing.   10

And after testament and tunes,
Some soften Sunday afternoons
With lemon tea and Lorna Doones.

I forecast
And I believe   15
Come Christmas Little Rock will cleave
To Christmas tree and trifle, weave,
From laugh and tinsel, texture fast.

In Little Rock is baseball; Barcarolle.
That hotness in July . . . the uniformed figures raw and implacable   20
And not intellectual,
Batting the hotness or clawing the suffering dust.
The Open Air Concert, on the special twilight green. . . .
When Beethoven is brutal or whispers to lady-like air.
Blanket-sitters are solemn, as Johann troubles to lean   25
To tell them what to mean. . . .

There is love, too, in Little Rock. Soft women softly
Opening themselves in kindness,
Or, pitying one's blindness,
Awaiting one's pleasure   30
In azure
Glory with anguished rose at the root. . . .
To wash away old semi-discomfitures.
They re-teach purple and unsullen blue.
The wispy soils go. And uncertain   35
Half-havings have they clarified to sures.

In Little Rock they know
Not answering the telephone is a way of rejecting life,
That it is our business to be bothered, is our business
To cherish bores or boredom, be polite   40
To lies and love and many-faceted fuzziness.

I scratch my head, massage the hate-I-had.
I blink across my prim and pencilled pad.
The saga I was sent for is not down.   45
Because there is a puzzle in this town.
The biggest News I do not dare
Telegraph to the Editor's chair:
"They are like people everywhere."
The angry Editor would reply   50
In hundred harryings of Why.

And true, they are hurling spittle, rock,
Garbage and fruit in Little Rock.
And I saw coiling storm a-writhe
On bright madonnas. And a scythe   55
Of men harassing brownish girls.
(The bows and barrettes in the curls
And braids declined away from joy.)

I saw a bleeding brownish boy. . . .

The lariat lynch-wish I deplored.
                                                        60
The loveliest lynchee was our Lord.

The people in this poem attend to their many large and small concerns—giving birth, baking, grooming, watering, tinkering, answering the telephone. They listen to operatic favorites (Offenbach's "Barcarolle") and Beethoven. Sitting on blankets, they solemnly listen at the open-air concert to Johann (Sebastian Bach). They sing Sunday hymns "like anything," and come Christmas they will do it justice, tree and tinsel and all. They are capable of love, politeness, and boredom. The problem is that all this ordinariness is not what the editor of the *Defender* sent the reporter to Little Rock to find.

The dramatic discovery in this poem is what the German Jewish writer Hannah Arendt has called the "banality of evil." The reporter from the *Chicago Defender* was ready to hate and revile melodramatic villains. But the "biggest news" is: Evil here is committed in a city of everyday people. The rock-throwing, spittle-hurling mob disperses to return to everyday homes. This discovery makes us rethink our usual assumption that people who do evil are monstrous creatures very different from ourselves. The people throwing the rocks and spitting on the "bright madonnas" are someone's Uncle Joe or Cousin Roy. Jesus was crucified in a city full of ordinary people.

The Receptive Reader

1. How do you think the people trying to block desegregation were seen by the civil rights workers at the time? How do you think the segregationists saw themselves? How is the poet's perspective different from either?

2. What use does she make of *religious* references at the end of the poem? With what effect?

3. Do you think the stand the poet took on the events of the time was too strong or not strong enough?

4. Are racial terrorism and racial violence in this country a thing of the past?

Making Connections—For Discussion or Writing

Other poems by Gwendolyn Brooks included earlier in this volume are "Truth" (Chapter 12) and "A Song in the Front Yard" (Chapter 19). Do you recognize in them the poet's characteristic voice or way of looking at the world?

POEMS FOR FURTHER STUDY

An editor and fellow poet said about Gwendolyn Brooks that she was "a woman who cannot live without her art, but who has never put her art above or before the people she writes about." In reading the following poems, pay special attention to the relation between content and form, between the poet's subject matter and her use of language.

When You Have Forgotten Sunday: The Love Story   1945

————And when you have forgotten the bright bedclothes on a Wednes-
    day and a Saturday,
And most especially when you have forgotten Sunday—
When you have forgotten Sunday halves in bed,
Or me sitting on the front-room radiator in the limping afternoon
Looking off down the long street   5
To nowhere,
Hugged by my plain old wrapper of no-expectation
And nothing-I-have-to-do and I'm-happy-why?
And if-Monday-never-had-to-come—
When you have forgotten that, I say,   10
And how you swore, if somebody beeped the bell,
And how my heart played hopscotch if the telephone rang;
And how we finally went in to Sunday dinner,
That is to say, went across the front-room floor to the ink-spotted table in
    the southwest corner
To Sunday dinner, which was always chicken and noodles   15
Or chicken and rice
And salad and rye bread and tea
And chocolate chips cookies—
I say, when you have forgotten that,
When you have forgotten my little presentiment   20
That the war would be over before they got to you;
And how we finally undressed and whipped out the light and flowed into
    bed,
And lay loose-limbed for a moment in the week-end
Bright bedclothes,
Then gently folded into each other—   25

When you have, I say, forgotten all that,
Then you may tell,
Then I may believe
You have forgotten me well.

The Chicago Picasso, August 15, 1967   *1967*

Mayor Daley tugged a white ribbon, loosing the
blue percale wrap. A hearty cheer went up as the
covering slipped off the big steel sculpture that
looks at once like a bird and a woman.

CHICAGO SUN-TIMES

(Seiji Ozawa leads the Symphony.
The Mayor smiles.
And 50,000 See.)

Does man love Art? Man visits Art, but squirms.
Art hurts. Art urges voyages—
and it is easier to stay at home,
the nice beer ready.
    In commonrooms   5
we belch, or sniff, or scratch.
Are raw.

But we must cook ourselves and style ourselves for Art, who
is a requiring courtesan.
We squirm.   10
We do not hug the Mona Lisa.
We
may touch or tolerate
an astounding fountain, or a horse-and-rider.
At most, another Lion.   15

Observe the tall cold of a Flower
which is as innocent and as guilty,
as meaningful and as meaningless as any
other flower in the western field.

The Preacher Ruminates behind the Sermon   *1945*

I think it must be lonely to be God.
Nobody loves a master. No. Despite
the bright hosannas, bright dear-Lords, and bright
Determined reverence of Sunday eyes.

Picture Jehovah striding through the hall   5
Of His importance, creatures running out
From servant-corners to acclaim, to shout
Appreciation of his merit's glare.

But who walks with Him?—dares to take His arm,

To slap him on the shoulder, tweak His ear,   10
Buy Him a Coca-Cola or a beer,
Pooh-pooh his politics, call Him a fool?

Perhaps—who knows?—He tires of looking down.
Those eyes are never lifted. Never straight.
Perhaps sometimes he tires of being great   15
In solitude. Without a hand to hold.

The Ballad of the Light-Eyed Little Girl   *1949*

Sweet Sally took a cardboard box,
And in went pigeon poor.
Whom she had starved to death but not
For lack of love, be sure.

The wind it harped as twenty men.   5
The wind it harped like hate.
It whipped our light-eyed little girl,
It made her wince and wait.

It screeched a hundred elegies
As it punished her light eyes   10
(Though only kindness covered these)
And it made her eyebrows rise.

"Now bury your bird," the wind it bawled,
"And bury him down and down
Who had to put his trust in one   15
So light-eyed and so brown.

"So light-eyed and so villainous,
Who whooped and who could hum
But could not find the time to toss
Confederate his crumb."   20

She has taken her passive pigeon poor,
She has buried him down and down.
He never shall sally to Sally
Nor soil any roofs of the town.

She has sprinkled nail polish on dead dandelions.   25
And children have gathered around
Funeral for him whose epitaph
Is "PIGEON—Under the ground."

The Bean Eaters   *1960*

They eat beans mostly, this old yellow pair.
Dinner is a casual affair.
Plain chipware on a plain and creaking wood,
Tin flatware.

Two who are Mostly Good.   5
Two who have lived their day,
But keep on putting on their clothes
And putting things away.

And remembering . . .
Remembering, with twinklings and twinges,   10
As they lean over the beans in their rented back room that is full of beads
        and receipts and dolls and cloths, tobacco crumbs, vases and fringes.

The Boy Died in My Alley   *1975*

Without my having known.
Policeman said, next morning,
"Apparently died Alone."
"You heard a shot?" Policeman said.
Shots I hear and Shots I hear.   5
I never see the dead.

The Shot that killed him yes I heard
as I heard the Thousand shots before;
careening tinnily down the nights
across my years and arteries.   10

Policeman pounded on my door.
"Who is it?" "POLICE!" Policeman yelled.
"A boy was dying in your alley.
A boy is dead, and in your alley.

And have you known this Boy before?"   15
I have known this Boy before.
I have known this Boy before, who
ornaments my alley.
I never saw his face at all.
I never saw his futurefall.   20
But I have known this Boy.

I have always heard him deal with death.
I have always heard the shout, the volley.
I have closed my heart-ears late and early.
And I have killed him ever.   25

I joined the Wild and killed him
with knowledgeable unknowing.
I saw where he was going.
I saw him Crossed. And seeing,
I did not take him down.   30

He cried not only "Father!"
but "Mother!
Sister!
Brother!"
The cry climbed up the alley.   35

It went up to the wind.
It hung upon the heaven
for a long
stretch-strain of Moment.

The red floor of my alley   40
is a special speech to me.

The Creative Dimension

In the following poem, a fellow poet pays tribute to Gwendolyn Brooks.
Write a similar poem or a prose passage paying tribute to a writer, leader, or
role model you admire.

Margaret Walker   *(born 1915)*

For Gwen—1969   *1969*

The slender, shy, and sensitive young girl
is woman now
her words a power in the Ebon land.
Outside her window on the street
a mass of life move by.   5
Chicago is her city.
Her heart flowers with its flame—
old stock years, new beaches
all the little store-front churches
and the bar on the corner.   10
Dreamer and seer of tales
She witnesses rebellion,
struggle and sweat.
The people are her heartbeat—
In their footsteps pulsate daily   15
all her black words of fire and blood.

Making Connections—For Discussion or Writing

For a library research project, search for books and articles that would provide material on one of the following topics:

✗ Gwendolyn Brooks' view of the social responsibility of the writer. What is
the relationship between protest and poetry in her work? What are her views
on the political responsibilities of the poet?

✗ Gwendolyn Brooks' relationship with or influence on other African American writers. What writer or writers did most to help shape her poetry or her
views? What has been her influence on other black poets?

✗ What was the treatment of black men in her poetry? Did it change over
the years?

Books you may be able to consult include the following:

Harry B. Shaw, *Gwendolyn Brooks* (1980)

Claudia Tate, *Black Women Writers at Work* (1983)

Mari Evans, ed., *Black Women Writers (1950–80): A Critical Evaluation* (1984)

R. Baxter Miller, ed., *Black American Poets between Worlds, 1940–60* (1986)

Haki Madhubuti, *Say That the River Turns: The Impact of Gwendolyn Brooks* (1987)

D. H. Melhem, *Gwendolyn Brooks: Poetry and the Heroic Voice* (1987)

Marie Mootry and Gary Smith, eds., *A Life Distilled: Gwendolyn Brooks, Her Poetry and Fiction* (1987)

George E. Kent, *A Life of Gwendolyn Brooks* (1990)

Stephen C. Wright, ed., *On Gwendolyn Brooks: Reliant Contemplation* (1995)

<<<Find It On The Web>>>

Critics and scholars based at universities and colleges maintain websites with information, scholarly material, and reader responses on a range of modern poets. You may decide to check out material on Gwendolyn Brooks or other modern poets that is archived or indexed at sites like the following:

Tongier, Brian, and Emily C. Jacobson. "Gwendolyn Brooks, " 'We Real Cool.' " <u>Voices from the Gaps: Women Writers of Color</u>. U of Minnesota. 5 Sept. 2001. 6 Nov. 2001.
<http://www.voices.la.umn.edu/gwendolynbrooks.html>

Nelson, Cary Nelson. "Gwendolyn Brooks." <u>MAPS: Modern American Poetry</u>. U of Illinois at Urbana-Champaign. 1999. 6 Nov. 2001.
<http://www.english.uiuc.edu/maps/index.htm>

WRITING ABOUT LITERATURE

23 Critical Re-evaluations of a Poet
WRITING FOCUS: The Documented Paper

The Writing Workshop   For the projects outlined earlier in this chapter, you will have to develop your own productive way of using library resources. Your finished paper will differ from other papers you have written in two major ways: You will be *integrating* material from a range of different sources. (Make sure that your paper will not appear to be made up of large chunks of undigested quotation.) You will be *documenting* your sources, giving full information about the books and articles you have used.

Finding Promising Leads   To work up material for your paper, begin by checking in electronic or printed indexes for books, collections of critical articles, and individual articles in periodicals. For a writer like Dickinson, Frost, or Brooks, most college libraries will have a wide range of critical and scholarly sources. Often critical studies will include bibliographies alerting you to other promising leads.

Taking Notes   During your exploratory reading, you need to look sources over quickly, deciding whether they will be helpful. But you also have to slow down and close in when you hit upon promising materials. Remember:

✗ *Be a stickler for accuracy.* Copy direct quotations accurately, word for word. Enclose all quoted material in quotation marks to show material copied verbatim. (Include the *closing* quotation mark to show where the quotation ends.)

✗ *Tag your notes.* Start your notes with a tag or descriptor. (Indicate the subtopic or section of your paper where a quotation or piece of information will be useful.)

✗ *Record publishing information.* On your first entry for any one source (or in a separate bibliography entry), record all data you will need later when you identify your source in a documented paper. Include exact page numbers for your quotations. (Also record inclusive page numbers for a whole article or story.) Sample notes might look like this:

Self-contained quotation

Dickinson—Sexual Imagery
"Like her nature poetry, her use of female sexual imagery suggests . . . not the 'subversion' of an existing male tradition, nor the 'theft' of male power—but rather the assertion of a concept of female sexuality and female creativity."

Paula Bennett, Emily Dickinson: Woman Poet (Iowa City: U of Iowa P, 1990) 180.

Paraphrase with partial direct quotation

Dickinson—Freudian Perspective
The prime motive in D.'s life and poetry was fear created by a "bad child-parent relationship," specifically with her "cold and forbidding father." This relationship shaped her view of men, love, marriage, and religion. She viewed God as a forbidding father-figure who spurned her.

Clark Griffith, The Long Shadow: Emily Dickinson's Tragic Poetry (Princeton: Princeton UP, 1964) 78.

Distinguish clearly between paraphrase and direct quotation. When you paraphrase, you put someone else's ideas in your own words, highlighting what seems most important and condensing other parts. Even when you paraphrase, be sure to use quotation marks for striking phrases that you keep in the exact wording of the author.

Note finer points: Use **single quotation marks** for a phrase that appears as a quote-within-a-quote. Use the **ellipsis**—three spaced periods—to show an omission (see Bennett quotation above). Use four periods when the periods include the period at the end of a sentence. **Square brackets** show that you have inserted material into the original quotation: "In this poem, based on the Emmett Till murder [1955], Brooks creates a surreal aura of hysteria and violence underlying an ostensibly calm domestic scene."

Pushing toward a Thesis   Early in your note taking, begin to follow up tentative patterns and promising connections that you discover in your reading. Start looking for a unifying thread. Avoid a stitched-together pattern that goes from "one critic said this" to "another critic said that." Look for recurrent issues; look for a note that in your materials is struck again and again.

Suppose you are moving toward a paper showing how different critics have answered the question of Emily Dickinson's religious faith. The following might be a tentative thesis:

> TRIAL THESIS: Emily Dickinson was not a believer or a skeptic but a poet always in search of the truth.

Using a Working Outline   To give direction to your reading and writing, sketch out a working outline as soon as you have a rough idea how your material is shaping up. At first, your plan might be very tentative. A working outline is not a final blueprint; its purpose is to help you visualize a possible pattern and to help you refine it as you go along. At an early stage, your working outline for the paper about Dickinson's faith might look like this:

> WORKING OUTLINE: —poems of faith
> —poems of despair
> —poems of alienation
> —poems of rebellion

Drafting and Revising   In your first draft, you are likely to concentrate on feeding into your paper the evidence you have collected. As always, feel free to work on later sections of the paper first—perhaps concentrating on key segments and filling in the connecting threads later. In your first draft, quotations are likely to be chunky, to be woven into the paper more tightly or more smoothly during revision. Often you will need to read a first draft back to yourself to see where major changes in strategy would be advisable. A reordering of major sections might be necessary to correct awkward backtrackings. You might need to strengthen the evidence for major points and play down material that tends to distract from your major arguments.

Documenting the Paper   When you draw on a range of sources—for instance, a range of critical interpretations of a poem—you may be asked to provide **documentation.** Remember that in a documented paper, you fully identify your sources, furnishing complete publishing information and exact page numbers. Accurate documentation shows that your readers are welcome to go to the sources you have drawn on—to check your use of them and to get further information from them if they wish. As with other documented papers, follow the current style of the Modern Language Association (MLA) unless instructed otherwise. This current style no longer uses footnotes (though it still allows for **explanatory notes** at the end of a paper).

Remember three key features of the MLA style:

✗ *Identify your sources briefly in your text.* Generally, introduce a quotation by saying something like the following:

In her article "Puns and Accordions: Emily Dickinson and the Unsaid," Mary Jo Salter says that Dickinson "has inspired a massive critical industry rivaling that devoted to Shakespeare and Milton."

✗ *Give page references in parentheses in your text.* Usually, they will go at the end of the sentence and before the final period, for instance (89) or (89–90). If you have not mentioned the author, give his or her last name (Salter 192–93). If you are using more than one source by the same author, you may also have to specify briefly which one (Salter, "Puns" 192–93). Remember to tag author or title in parentheses only if you have *not* already given the information in your running text.

✗ *Describe each source fully in a final alphabetical listing of Works Cited.* Originally a bibliography (literally the "book list"), it now often includes *nonprint* sources—interviews, lectures, PBS broadcasts, videotapes, and online material. Here is a typical entry for an article in a critical journal. This entry includes *volume number* (a volume usually covers all issues for one year), the *year,* and the complete *page numbers* for the whole article (not just the material you have quoted):

Morris, Timothy. "The Development of Dickinson's Style." American Literature 60 (1988): 26–42.

Study sample entries for your alphabetical listing of Works Cited. Observe the following guidelines:

A Checklist for Listing Sources   **MLA Style**

As advised by your instructor, use *italics* or <u>underlining</u> for the title of a *whole publication*—whether a book-length study, a collection or anthology of poems or essays, a periodical that prints critical articles, or a newspaper that prints reviews. (The MLA style requires underlining—<u>underscoring</u>—for manuscripts that go to a printer for type-marking. Italics are required if your manuscript is to be scanned or reproduced "as is" for publication.)

Use quotation marks for titles of poems or critical articles that are *part* of a collection or larger publication.

Indent the second and following lines of each entry one half inch or five typewriter spaces.

Leave *one* space after periods marking off *blocks of data* in the entry.

Use appropriate *abbreviations:* ed. for editor; trans. for a translator. Abbreviate the names of publishing houses (Prentice for Prentice Hall, Inc; Southern Illinois UP for Southern Illinois University Press). Abbreviate the names of the months: Dec., Apr., Mar. Abbreviate the names of states when needed to locate a little-known place of publication: CA, NY, NJ.

Primary sources: listing of poems, lectures, interviews

Lipsitz, Lou. <u>Seeking the Hook: New and Selected Poems</u>. Chapel Hill, NC: Signal, 1997.
   [A book of poems by a contemporary poet, with title and subtitle]

Brooks, Gwendolyn. <u>The World of Gwendolyn Brooks</u>. New York; Harper, 1971.
   [Collected poems of the author]

Hammons, Laura. "Ambulance Ride." <u>TYCA-Southeast Journal</u> (Spring 2001):30.
   [A poem published in a regional professional periodical, with date and page number]

Colman, Cathy. "After Swimming in the Pacific." <u>New Poets: Women</u>. Ed. Terri Whetherby. Millbrae, CA: Les Femmes, 1976. 13.
   [A poem printed in an anthology, with editor's name and with page number for the poem]

Johnson, Thomas H., ed. <u>The Complete Poems of Emily Dickinson</u>. Boston: Little, Brown, 1960.
   [Editor's name first when editor's contribution is important]

Lorde, Audre. Interview. <u>Black Women Writers at Work</u>. Ed. Claudia Tate. Harpenden, Herts.: Oldcastle, 1985. 100–16.
   [An interview with the poet, published in a collection of interviews]

Juarez, Juanita. Lecture. Distinguished Visiting Poets Series. San Jose. 3 Oct. 2002.

[Talk by a poet as part of a lecture series]

Olsen, Tillie. Foreword. Black Women Writers at Work. Ed. Claudia Tate. Harpenden, Herts.: Oldcastle, 1985. ix-xxvi.

[Foreword by other than editor, with page numbers in small Roman numerals for introductory material]

Secondary Sources: listing of critical studies, articles, or reviews

Birenbaum, Harvey. The Happy Critic. Mountain View, CA: Mayfield, 1997.

[Introduction to literary study, with standard publishing data for a book]

Johnson, Thomas H. Emily Dickinson: An Interpretive Biography. Cambridge: Harvard UP, 1966.

[Biography with subtitle, published by a university press]

Rich, Adrienne. On Lies, Secrets, and Silence: Selected Prose 1966–1978. New York: Norton, 1975.

[Book with subtitle, with critical essays by the author]

Foucault, Michel. The History of Sexuality: Vol. 1: An Introduction. Trans. Robert Hurley. New York: Vintage, 1990.

[One volume of a work published as several volumes, with translator's name]

Spillers, Hortense J. "Gwendolyn the Terrible: Propositions on Eleven Poems." A Life Distilled: Gwendolyn Brooks, Her Poetry and Fiction. Eds. Maria K. Mootry and Gary Smith. Urbana: U of Illinois P, 1987. 224–35.

[Article in a collection, with inclusive page numbers. Note "Ed." for the editors who assembled the collection.]

Morris, Timothy. "The Development of Dickinson's Style." American Literature 60 (1988): 26–42.

[Journal article, with volume number and inclusive page numbers. Note quotation marks for title of article; underlining for title of publication]

Monteiro, George. "Dickinson's 'We Thirst at First.' " The Explicator 48 (1990): 193–94.

[Title of poem (with single quotation marks) is cited in title of article (with double quotation marks)]

Jones, Rowena Revis. " 'A Royal Seal': Emily Dickinson's Rite of Baptism." Religion and Literature 18.3 (1986): 29–51.

[Periodical with number of volume and issue. Number of issue may be needed when pages are not numbered consecutively throughout a single volume.]

Montgomery, Karen. "Today's Minimalist Poets." New York Times 22 Feb. 1992, late ed., sec. 2: 1+.

[Newspaper article, with edition and section specified. Article starts on page 1 and continues not on the next page but later in the newspaper.]

Rev. of The Penguin Book of Women Poets, ed. Carol Cosman, Joan Keefe, and Kathleen Weaver. Arts and Books Forum May 1990: 17–19.

[Untitled, unsigned review of a poetry collection]

Bakhtin, M.M. The Dialogic Imagination. Trans. Terence Irwin. Indianopolis: Hackett, 1985.

[Influential theoretical study with translator's name]

Poets of Revolution. Narr. Sybil Aptos. Writ. and prod. Amos Cervantes. KSBM, Los Angeles. 12 Feb. 2002.

[A television program with names of narrator and writer-producer. To be listed alphabetically under "Poets"]

<<<Find It On The Web>>>   *Listing Internet Sources*

Guidelines for citing material from the Internet are still evolving, and you may encounter instructions slightly different from those given here. For electronic sources, include available publishing data or site addresses. Include the date the material was posted (if available) and also the date you accessed the material. Enclose the Internet address or URL in angled brackets. Here are sample entries:

Elder, John. "The Poetry of Experience." <u>New Literary History</u> 1999. 24 Sept. 2001.
    <http://muse.jhu.edu//journals/new_literary_history/v030/30.3elder.html>
    [Article in a critical journal available online]

Quinn, G. "Frost's Synecdochic Allusions." <u>Resources for American Literary Study</u>. 1999. 24 Sept. 2001.
    <http://muse.jhu.edu/demo/resources_for_american_literary_study/25.2quinn.html>
    [Article archived or available in a databank]

Horn, Jason Gary. Rev. of <u>Robert Frost and Feminine Literary Tradition. American Literature</u> Sept 2000. 24 Sept. 2001.
    <http://muse.jhu.edu//journals/american_literature/v072/72.3horn.html>
    [Review of a new book about a major poet, available online]

<u>The Emily Dickinson Journal</u>. U of Colorado Dept. of English, 1998. 24 Sept. 2001.
    <http://www.colorado.edu/EDIS;journal/index.html>
    [Web address of a critical journal devoted to a major poet]

Emily Dickinson International Society. Case Western Reserve U, 1998. 24 Sept. 2001.
    <http://www.cwru.edu/affil/edis/edisindex.html>
    [Website of an organization devoted to the study of a major poet]

Study the following example of a documented paper. How well does the paper bring its subject into focus? How well does it support its main points? How clear and effective is its use of quotations from the poet and from the critics? Study the use of parenthetical documentation and the entries in the Works Cited. Pay special attention to unusual situations or entries.

Reviewing Research Paper Format

Format your paper according to the instructions in the *MLA Handbook for Writers of Research Papers*, Fifth Edition (1999).

✗ **Doublespace** your typescript throughout, including your title and your final list of Works Cited.

✗ Leave *standard margins*—an inch on each side, half an inch at the top and bottom.

✗ Use *running heads* (your last name and page number) at the top of each page, flush right.

✗ Use half an inch for paragraph indentation. Use an additional half inch for *block quotations*.

Sample Documented Paper

Emily Dickinson's Strange Irreverence

Joyce Carol Oates has called Emily Dickinson "our poet of the soul: our most endlessly fascinating American poet." As her contemporary Walt Whitman "so powerfully addresses the exterior of American life," so Dickinson addresses "its unknowable interior." In what Oates calls Dickinson's "riddlesome, obsessive, haunting" poetic quest, the poet's exploration or questioning of her religious feelings plays a central role (2).

Religion in one guise or another pervades many of Dickinson's poems. It appears in the form of tender and not so tender prayers, skeptical questionings, and bitter confrontations. Critics have constructed a whole range of interpretations designed to provide a key to her changing, ambivalent religious attitudes. Some have cast her in the role of the rebel, rescuing her readers from the harshness of a rigid, constricted religious tradition, erecting for them a "citadel of art" and cultivating "the ego or consciousness" (Burbick 62). Others, however, see her as a "lone pilgrim" in the tradition of Puritan austerity and asceticism. She could not "allow herself the long luxury" of the evangelical movement of her own day, which was turning away from earlier, harsher versions of the Christian faith and promoting a sentimental attitude toward God as a "creature of caring, even motherly generosity" (Wolff 260).

Still others attribute Dickinson's ambivalent, shifting religious attitudes to her need to keep her friends, to her "preoccupation with attachment" (Burbick 65). Some of Dickinson's dearest friends, to whom she wrote about her cherished hope for "one unbroken company in heaven," had experienced a religious conversion at Mt. Holyoke Seminary, and she felt she had to follow their example so the bonds of friendship that were so precious to her would not be dissolved.

Perhaps the closest to a connecting thread is Denis Donoghue's discussion of her as a truth-seeker, who in life as in poetry was looking for the truth. As Donoghue says, "In a blunt paraphrase, many of her poems would contradict one another; but her answers are always provisional." Her answers are tentative; "only her questions are definitive" (13). Although there are in her poems many references to the Old and New Testaments, "nothing is necessarily believed" but may be entertained only as a poetic or symbolic truth (17).

Because of the elusive, ambivalent nature of Dickinson's relation to religion, each poem must be interpreted individually in the quest to plumb her heart. Several of her poems are direct affirmations of her faith in Christ. In poem 698 in the Johnson edition ("Life—is what we make it"), she calls Christ a "tender pioneer," who blazed the trail of life and death for his "little Fellowmen":

> He—would trust no stranger—
> Others—could betray—
> Just his own endorsement—
> That—sufficeth me.
>
> All the other Distance
> He hath traversed first—
> No new mile remaineth—
> Far as Paradise—
>
> His sure foot preceding—
> Tender Pioneer—
> Base must be the Coward—
> Dare not venture—now—(333–34)

In other poems, however, the faith that is supposed to provide a bridge to the hereafter proves a bridge with "mouldering" or "brittle" piers. In a famous poem, "I heard a Funeral in my Brain" (280 in the Johnson edition), the promise of faith seems unable to counteract the sense of the nothingness at the end of life. The Christian teachings of resurrection and an afterlife here do not seem to avail against the "plunge" into despair:

> And then I heard them lift a Box
> And creak across my Soul
> With those same Boots of Lead, again,
> Then Space—began to toll,
>
> As all the Heavens were a Bell,
> And Being, but an Ear,
> And I, and Silence, some strange Race
> Wrecked, solitary, here—
>
> And then a Plank in Reason, broke,
> And I dropped down, and down—
> And hit a World, at every plunge,
> And Finished knowing—then (128–29)

Other poems seem to protest against the "ambiguous silence maintained by God" (Griffith 273). The following are the opening lines of poem 376 in Johnson's edition:

> Of course—I prayed-
> And did God Care?
> He cared as much as on the Air
> A Bird—had stamped her foot—
> And cried "Give Me"—(179)

Many of her poems seem to mourn the absence of God, as does the following stanza from poem 502 in Johnson:

Thou settest Earthquake in the South—
And Maelstrom, In the Sea—
Say, Jesus Christ of Nazareth—
Hast thou no Arm for Me? (244)

In her most rebellious poems, she openly expresses defiance. She protests against the "tyranny" of God that forced Abraham to consent to offer his own son Isaac in sacrifice (Johnson 571). She rebels against commandments that keep us within a "magic prison," a limited and "constricted life," while we are within sight of the feast of happiness that is earthly pleasure—as if God were jealous of "the heaven on earth that is human happiness" (McNeil 60).

A lifelong reader of Dickinson has said that in one of the poems about death "each dash is a stopped heartbeat," as we try to cross divides that cannot be bridged (Spires 228). To read Emily Dickinson's poems is to see a poet's struggle for finding a meaning in her existence, rebelling at times against blind faith but also shrinking from complete doubt. Dickinson looked for evidence of the divine not in traditional revealed faith but in our earthly human existence. In a letter written several years before her death, she wrote: "To be human is more than to be divine . . . when Christ was divine he was uncontented until he had been human" (qtd. in Wolff 519).

Works Cited

Burbick, Joan. "'One Unbroken Company': Religion and Emily Dickinson." New England Quarterly 53 (1980): 62–75.

Donoghue, Denis. Emily Dickinson. U of Minnesota Pamphlets on American Writers. No. 81. 1969.

Griffith, Clark. The Long Shadow: Emily Dickinson's Tragic Poetry. Princeton: Princeton UP, 1964.

Johnson, Thomas H., ed. The Complete Poems of Emily Dickinson. Boston: Little, Brown, 1960.

McNeil, Helen. Emily Dickinson. New York: Pantheon, 1986.

Oates, Joyce Carol. "'Soul at the White Heat': The Romance of Emily Dickinson's Poetry." Critical Inquiry (Summer 1987). 4 June 2001. <http://storm.usfca.edu/~southerr/romance.html>

Spires, Elizabeth. Memoir. First Loves. Ed. Carmela Ciuraru. New York: Scribner, 2000.

Wolff, Cynthia Griffin. Emily Dickinson. Menlo Park, CA: Addison, 1988.

Questions for Peer Review

The student writer focuses on one major dimension of the ongoing critical explorations of Dickinson's poetry. How close was the poet in spirit to modern readers who look for spiritual meaning in their lives without affiliating with traditional organized religion?

1. How does the *introduction* set the scene or set the tone for the rest of the essay? For you, how successfully does it set up an overall perspective?

2. What major directions does the student writer sketch in the summary of major *critical approaches* to her topic? What quotations seem especially helpful or revealing?

3. Does the writer provide a *thesis* or overview for her paper? Where or how? What key term or key concept helps sum up her point of view for you?

4. What are the major waystations in her overall *plan*? What are major transitions, and how clearly are they signaled?

5. How convincing are the major points the writer makes? At what points in the paper would you have liked more *explanation* or support?

6. How effective is the writer's selection of *sample poems*? Are any especially effective or thought-provoking?

7. Does the *conclusion* merely restate points already made? Or does it go a step beyond the rest of the paper? How or why?

8. Does the writer use a *range* of sources? Do her parenthetical documentation and her list of Works Cited show variations from standard entries?

24 PERSPECTIVES

The Age of Theory

Courtesy Richard B. Ressman

*Until we understand the assumptions in which
we are drenched we cannot know ourselves.*

ADRIENNE RICH

*We are all toadies to the fashionable metaphor of
the hour. Great is he who imposes the metaphor.*

ROBERT FROST

FOCUS ON CRITICAL PERSPECTIVES

Poets are influenced by ideas about poetry. They may be part of a major movement, like the Romantic nature poetry of the early nineteenth century. In an increasingly industrialized and urban society, poets then reminded city dwellers of the awesome beauties and healing powers of the natural world. As they did during the Romantic period, poets with shared interests and commitments may exchange ideas, collaborate on manifestos, and contribute to collections publishing the work of their friends. Poets then become trend makers, helping shape movements and countermovements. Great poets—from Samuel Taylor Coleridge to T. S. Eliot and Adrienne Rich—have often been poet-critics, publishing programmatic statements that chart new directions.

At the same time, poets have long coexisted in an uneasy relationship with critics—those who write about, interpret, and evaluate the poetry of their time. Critics may set standards that poets may try to meet—or that they may rebel against as too artificial or too confining. A critical establishment may help establish trends or fashions that turn poets marching to a different drummer into mavericks or outsiders.

Today much criticism and scholarship dealing with poetry is published in book review sections of major newspapers and periodicals, in critical and scholarly journals, and in books by both university presses and commercial publishers. The following are active areas of critical and scholarly activity:

POET BIOGRAPHY

There is a large specialized public for new explorations of major poet's lives. Today's biographers may at times seem obsessed with exposing the disreputable or seamy side of poet's private lives to public view. Joyce Carol Oates called studies seemingly preoccupied with the pathological not biography but pathography. At the same time, attacks may call forth rebuttals or tributes from admirers.

For example, agressive reevaluations of Robert Frost's work and stature continue. Critics explore the contradictions they see in Frost's character and public persona, with critical and admiring biographers waging what has been called "a war of biographies." With his wry humor, Frost would very likely have enjoyed the continuing critical controversies. He once said, "No sweeter music can come to my ears than the clash of arms over my dead body when I am down." A tentative source list of recent studies and collections might include titles like the following:

Richardson, Mark. *The Ordeal of Robert Frost.* Chicago: U of Illinois, Chicago P. 1997.
Parini, Jay. *Robert Frost: A Life.* New York: Henry Holt, 1999.
Wilcox, Earl J. and Jonathan Barron, eds. *Roads Not Taken: ReReading Robert Frost.* Columbia: U of Missouri P. 2000.

TRENDS IN CRITICISM

Reputations of major poets may undergo ups and downs as critical fashions and public preferences change. Nineteenth-century poets like the British Tennyson and the American Longfellow were once hugely popular. Today they are little read, and they are treated condescendingly by modern critics who fault them for their easy rhymes, stilted solemn language, and predictable uplifting sentiments.

In the twentieth century, a poet like Edna St. Vincent Millay could undergo successive revaluations. She was widely popular during the twenties as a poet of the Jazz Age. A post–World War I generation was challenging conventions and experimenting with heavy new sexual freedoms. In the forties and fifties, her poetry fell from favor with critics who were looking for more impersonal, more intellectually challenging poetry. They favored a more technically sophisticated kind of poetry, requiring a close reading of metaphor, symbol, and allusion. Millay's candid emotionalism came to seem dated in an age of irony and "aesthetic distance." Then, in the eighties and nineties, feminist readers and critics rediscovered Millay as they looked for poetry with a strong dimension of personal candor and revelation. They found in her poems a reflection of the challenges and emotions of women's lives.

A tentative source list for a study of the poet's changing reputation might include titles like the following:

Nancy Milford. *Savage Beauty.* New York: Random, 2001.
Epstein, Daniel Mark. *What My Lips Have Kissed: The Loves and Love Poems of Edna St. Vincent Millay.* New York: Henry Holt, 2001.
Thesing, William B., ed. *Critical Essays on Edna St. Vincent Millay.* New York: G. K. Hall, 1993.
Walker, Cheryl. *Masks, Outrageous and Austere: Culture, Psyche, and Personality in Modern Women Poets.* Bloomington: Indiana UP, 1991.
Newcomb, John Timberman. "The Woman as Political Poet: Edna St. Vincent Millay and the Mid-Century Canon." *Criticism* 37.2 (Spring 1995): 261.
< http://library.northernlight.comSL19970923040011553.html>

REDEFINING THE CANON

Scholars and critics have often defined the *canon*—an established widely agreed-upon list of major poets. They have enshrined major poets and important works that educated people had to know to attain true cultural literacy. Much recent scholarly and critical work has been devoted to expanding and rethinking the traditional canon to reflect the true range and diversity of poetry written in English.

Starting with the poets of the Harlem Renaissance and honoring pioneering African American poets like Langston Hughes and Arna Bontemps, critics have worked to include an increasing number of poets from minority backgrounds in the pantheon of American poetry. Henry Louis Gates, Jr., as W. E. B. Du Bois Professor of Humanities and chair of the department of Afro-American Studies at Harvard, is a scholar-teacher who has broadened critical horizons. He has edited a widely acclaimed, anthology of African American literature as well as two multi-volume series devoted to nineteenth-century and early-twentieth-century black women writers.

In 1985, the feminist scholars Sandra M. Gilbert and Susan Gubar published a widely studied anthology of literature by women writing in English. They included poets from England's Queen Elizabeth and the colonial American Ann Bradstreet to the the twentieth-century lesbian poet Judy Grahn. Anthologies of modern poetry began to include authors like the Hispanic (or Latina) poet Lorna Dee Cervantes, the Native American poet Diane Burns, and the Japanese American poet Mitsuye Yamada. Increasingly, the study and teaching of poetry began to do justice to the rich multicultural life of Walt Whitman's "nation of nations."

MAJOR DIRECTIONS IN CRITICISM

The twentieth century was an age of criticism. It has been called the Age of Theory and the Age of Analysis. In the latter half of the century especially, poets, like writers of fiction, were becoming increasingly self-aware. They were becoming "self-reflective"—conscious of their assumptions and self-conscious about their use of language.

Major critical schools of thought continue to influence the way critics and scholars read and interpret poetry. Here are major perspectives that influence the perceptions of critical readers:

Biographical Criticism   Much critical analysis ties in discussion of the poet's work with biographical data—the poet's marital history, or the poet's alienation from materialistic American society. In the poem by

E. E. Cummings, who is the anyone who "lived in a pretty how town" where "he sang his didn't he danced his did"? A student of the poet's biography might answer this question as follows:

> A translation . . . might be, "The poet lived year by year in an ordinary town, where he sang his negations and danced his affirmations" . . . Later in the same poem, when he says that "noone loved him more by more," it is obvious that "noone" is the poet's wife. After his second divorce, Cummings was happily married for nearly thirty years, a fact attested by some of his finest poems.
>
> Malcolm Cowley, "Cummings: One Man Alone"

Intensely personal poetry reveals, disguises, and transforms the poet's personal experience. Much critical discussion, for instance, has focused on the relationship between Anne Sexton's poetry and the personal demons that bedeviled and finally destroyed her life.

Katha Pollitt

Anne Sexton: The Death Is Not the Life

It seems oddly apt that Diane Wood Middlebrook's "Anne Sexton: A Biography," the first full-scale life of the poet, should already have attracted some of the same kind of scandalized attention as did Sexton herself. Most readers will be aware of the debate surrounding the decision of Sexton's first long-term psychiatrist, Dr. Martin T. Orne, to give Ms. Middlebrook (a professor of English at Stanford University and herself a poet and literary critic) access to tapes of his therapy sessions with Sexton—tapes that Ms. Middlebrook, with the permission of Linda Gray Sexton, the poet's daughter and literary executor, extensively quotes. (Actually, debate is the wrong word, since nobody but the parties to the use of the tapes has risen to defend it. Thunderous condemnation is more like it.)

In view of the uproar, it seems important to say right up front that Ms. Middlebrook has written a wonderful book: just, balanced, insightful, complex in its sympathies and in its judgment of Sexton both as a person and as a writer. While she spares no detail of Sexton's pathology, her book is not, in any sense, what Joyce Carol Oates has called "a pathography." It is, rather, a deeply moving account of how one young woman—badly educated, marooned in the Boston suburbs and hampered at every turn by mental illness—managed to become, for a while, a poet of distinctive and original gifts.

When Sexton began seeing Dr. Orne in 1956, after the first of what would be many breakdowns and suicide attempts, she was almost 28 years old, a finishing-school dropout and, in her own view, a total failure as a wife to her businessman husband, Alfred Muller Sexton 2d (nicknamed Kayo), and as a mother to her two small daughters—who, indeed, spent much of their toddlerhood living with Kayo's mother. Sexton was obsessed with childhood traumas—her mother was cold and vain, her father rigid, alcoholic and abusive; her great-aunt Nana, who alone in the family had given her the affection she craved, had gone mad and died in a nursing home. When Dr. Orne asked her if there was anything she felt she could do well, the only answer she came up with was prostitution. He suggested writing instead: perhaps she could be of help to others who were suffering from mental illness.

Two years after writing her first sonnet—sparked by a program on educational television—Sexton had written the poems that were collected in her first book, "To Bedlam and Part Way Back," which was published in 1960. Within 10 years she was one of the most honored poets in America: a Pulitzer Prize winner, a fellow of the Royal Society of Literature, the first female member of the Harvard chapter of Phi Beta Kappa, the subject of a television documentary.

To Sexton's many fans—and with nearly half a million copies of her books sold in the United States alone, she has a huge audience among people who read little other poetry—her appeal, like that of Sylvia Plath, lies partly in her life and early death, with its inescapable feminist drama, and partly in the apparent candor of her self-presentation. Ms. Middlebrook carefully shows how simplistic this picture is.

Like other so-called confessional poets, Sexton reworked her life to suit artistic purposes. "I use the personal when I am applying a mask to my face," she wrote, "like a rubber mask that the robber wears." As her friend the British poet George MacBeth astutely noted, "She saw sincerity as a *technique,* the style that happened to fit what she wanted to say." Sexton made her debut, after all, as a formalist, with poems relentlessly pushed through 20 and 30 drafts and shaped by criticism in workshops with Robert Lowell and John Holmes—sessions attended by Plath, George Starbuck and Maxine Kumin, who became her lifelong friend and closest reader. Had Sexton merely been versifying her autobiography, she wouldn't have lasted two minutes in that crowd.

"How did a mad housewife become a star?" Ms. Middlebrook asks in her preface. Sexton's rise is a quintessential American success story, in which talent, ambition and staggering amounts of work (plus career smarts and a thoroughgoing refusal of domestic labor) triumph over seemingly insuperable obstacles: lack of formal education and family encouragement; treatment with mind-numbing drugs like Thorazine, which was first prescribed in 1964 and whose side effects she struggled against for the next eight years; an inability to go anywhere alone, even a bookstore or a supermarket.

Reading about how Sexton compensated for these disabilities (for she never overcame them) is a bit like reading about how an amputee became an Olympic athlete. She threw herself at teachers and mentors—including James Wright and W. D. Snodgrass—and became a "gaga student" of literature. She went off Thorazine to write (the drug, she joked, was "supposed to make the rhymer go away"), then endured the consequent mania. She enlisted friends, paid companions—and, at one point, even a prospective bi-ographer—to travel with her when she had to give poetry readings. Cer-tainly she was exploitative, narcissistic, impossibly demanding. But one is struck by how many people speak warmly of her in these pages: former lovers, neighbors, even her daughters, despite their hair-raising childhoods. "Annie gave as good as she got," Maxine Kumin told Ms. Middlebrook, and one feels she really did.

Unfortunately, Sexton's particularly American success led to a particularly American downfall—an urgent need for ever more attention and esteem, and an inability to reckon the cost. By the end of the 1960's, alcohol and pills were impairing her creativity, and the quest for fame had become an end in itself. When she started writing, Sexton had wanted to reach her fel-low sufferers, but also what Maxine Kumin called the "vertical audience" of her poet peers and literary history. "In the field I have chosen, to be halfway is to be nothing," she told Dr. Orne. But increasingly she craved a kind of celebrity that can hardly ever be achieved in our time by words alone. . . .

How well do Sexton's poems hold up today? Rereading her work for this review, I was struck by the freshness, pathos and brio of many of her poems from the late 1950's and early 60's: "Music Swims Back to Me," "The Dou-ble Image" (her long and complex exploration of mothers and daughters), "The Starry Night," "The Touch." As Ms. Middlebrook points out, Sexton was writing for an audience that did not yet exist, for readers who wanted to hear women speaking in their own voices about their own lives. And in her strongest poems one can still feel the excitement of a writer who knows she is bringing into literature a range of human experience previously thought to be beneath its attention.

From the *New York Times Book Review,* 1991

The Receptive Reader

Why was the biographer's use of the psychiatrist's tapes controversial? (Do you have strong feelings about the point at issue?) What role does the American dream of success (or style of success) play in this discussion? What light does the reviewer shed on the relationship between the poet's struggle against ill-ness and her writing?

Historical Criticism   Literary historians have charted the movements and countermovements marking off major stages in the history of literary sensibility. For instance, literary historians recognized the Romantic rebel-lion against the neoclassical tradition of the eighteenth century as a water-shed in the history of poetic style. Outstanding among **neoclassical** poet-critics, Alexander Pope wrote his *Essay on Criticism* (1711) in pol-ished closed couplets at the age of twenty-three. The Age of Enlighten-ment was enshrining human reason as "one clear, unchanged, and universal light," stressing the need for rational control over our impulses and emotions. Sound judgment should guide and restrain the poetic imagination. The poet should prune, correct, and revise first rough efforts. Pope saw poetic language and form as the vehicle for the poet's ideas—frequently ideas that were already part of the thinking of well-informed people:

> 'Tis more to guide than spur the Muse's steed;
> Restrain his fury, than provoke his speed.

> True wit is nature to advantage dressed,
> What oft was thought, but ne'er so well expressed;

> Something, whose truth convinced at sight we find,
> That gives us back the image of our mind.

> Expression is the dress of thought, and still
> Appears more decent, as more suitable.

The **Romantics** rebelled against the neoclassical emphasis on the analytical intellect and artificial restraint. Celebrating the creative imagination, Romantic writers and artists exalted passion over reason, vital energy over static control. English Romantic poets called the reasoning intellect "the false secondary power"; they were afraid that the analytical intellect would dry up the wellsprings of intuition, emotion, and inspiration that are the sources of the poet's art. They believed that original genius could not be confined within the limits of rules and conventions. They turned to the healing influence of nature as the antidote to the neuroses of the technological Industrial Age. Like other Romantic poets, the English poet John Keats (1795–1821) believed that what we feel deeply and sincerely cannot be wrong. In the following excerpt from a letter written in 1817, he champions the passions and sensation, or sense experience, as against "consecutive reasoning."

> I am certain of nothing but of the holiness of the Heart's affections and the truth of Imagination—What the Imagination seizes as Beauty must be truth—whether it existed before or not—for I have the same Idea of all our Passions as of Love: they are all in their sublime creative of essential Beauty. . . . I am the more zealous in this affair because I have never yet been able to perceive how anything can be known for truth by consecutive reasoning—and yet it must be—Can it be that even the greatest Philosopher ever arrived at his goal without putting aside numerous objections—However it may be, O for a Life of Sensations rather than of Thoughts!

A critic applying the categories of traditional literary history may think in terms of the major literary **periods** or period styles. For instance, critics have seen the Welsh poet Dylan Thomas as a latter-day Romantic—"very close to Wordsworth and his religion of nature, and perhaps closer still to Whitman (whom he very much admired) and his belief in a World Soul" (Oliver Evans). (In one of Thomas' poems, the speaker wanders on the seashore, seeing everywhere signs of "blessed, unborn God and his Ghost, / And every soul his priest.") Critics linking Thomas to the Romantic sensibility have pointed to Thomas' rich sensuous language ("In My Craft and Sullen Art"), his love of nature and glorification of a rural childhood ("Fern Hill"), and his preoccupation with death ("Do Not Go Gentle into That Good Night"). In the following excerpt, a critic discusses Thomas' ambivalent relationship to the Romantic tradition:

Alfred Kazin

Dylan Thomas and Romanticism

All of Thomas' poetry shows the profound romantic need to intensify existence, to make it all come alive as it is in personal consciousness. But where so many great poets—Blake, Wordsworth, Keats, even Whitman— have recognized that their task is not to love their new vision of the commonplace world but to explain and to unite it to human existence, Thomas felt absurd and histrionic, acted like a man who in his heart thought himself a fake.

He was too humble. It is a strange thing to remember of anyone whose gift was so personal and sweeping, but he regarded his own gift as slightly absurd; he sheltered it, wouldn't have his poems discussed, because he couldn't admit that poetry is thought, and that what he said in his poems many of his contemporaries really believed and were most deeply grateful to a poet for saying again. He was left with his fantastic linguistic gift as if it were something to read from, to entertain with, but not, in the artistic sense, to practice as a criticism of life.

From "The Posthumous Life of Dylan Thomas," *The Atlantic,* 1957

Formalist Criticism   Much twentieth-century discussion of poets and poems reacted against a Victorian nineteenth-century poetry of uplift and ennobling sentiment, of "the best that has been thought and said" (Matthew Arnold). Early moderns like Ezra Pound and T. S. Eliot insisted that poetry was not meant to be versified prose. It had its own language, its own challenging way of seeing. Criticism in the **New Critical,** or **formalist,** mode, modeled its standards on the practice of the seventeenth-century metaphysical poets: John Donne, Andrew Marvell, and George Herbert in England; Edward Taylor in America. The metaphysicals married intellect and emotion; they built into their poems multilayered tensions and complexities that challenge the reader.

The early modern tradition of close reading and detailed formal analysis has shaped the expectations of many readers:

✗ Modern readers have looked in poetry for freshness of language. They have looked for phrases that make us pay attention, that recharge our power of vision, that startle us into taking a new look.

✗ Modern readers have looked in poetry for more than raw experience. They have looked for the shaping or control needed to keep poetry from being a mere "turning loose of emotion" (T. S. Eliot). They have looked for evidence of the sifting and shaping that take a poem beyond the expression of raw emotion. They expect poets to put some distance between themselves and whatever pain or grievance or joy might have been the original impetus of a poem.

✗ Modern readers have looked in poetry for a challenge, for complexity. Poetry that is too regular, too smooth has seemed to them undemanding and simple-minded. Whatever ordering or shaping takes place should make us sense that jostling reality has been brought under control. Modern critics have looked for the tensions, the paradoxes, or the ironies that enable poets to do justice to mixed emotions and divided loyalties. They have looked for attempts to face and resolve ambiguities. They look for the inversions and breaks or counter-rhythms that break up the tedúm-tedúm-tedúm patterns of "jingle-poets." Complexity of form became for the modern critic one manifestation of a poem's "maturity or sophistication or richness or depth, and hence its value" (W. K. Wimsatt).

✗ Modern readers expect emotion to be appropriate to the subject or justified by the context. Modern critics have been wary of overindulgence in emotion. They disapprove of **sentimentality,** which allows readers to bask in a glow of self-approving emotions. It does not challenge them to examine their thoughts and actions.

The following poem, "God's Grandeur" (1877) by Gerard Manley Hopkins, is one of the great poems of English literature. Its richness and complexity invite the kind of close reading that became a hallmark of formalistic analysis in the New Critical tradition.

The world is charged with the grandeur of God.
    It will flame out, like shining from shook foil;
    It gathers to a greatness, like the ooze of oil
Crushed. Why do men then now not reck his rod?
Generations have trod, have trod, have trod;
    And all is seared with trade; bleared, smeared with toil
    And wears man's smudge and shares man's smell: the soil
Is bare now, nor can foot feel, being shod.

And for all this, nature is never spent;
    There lives the dearest freshness deep down things;
And though the last lights off the black West went
    Oh, morning, at the brown brink eastward, springs—

Because the Holy Ghost over the bent
    World broods with warm breast and with ah! bright wings.

Does the following explication, or line-by-line explanation by an experienced reader, help you respond more fully to the richness of the poem?

J. R. Watson

A Close Reading of G. M. Hopkins' "God's Grandeur"

The world is charged with the grandeur of God.

As a first line this is uncompromising. Its rhythm is confident and assured, and the full stop at the end of the line seems to emphasize the completeness and finality of the statement. The world is charged with God's grandeur, and that is that. Hopkins was so careful with line-endings and rhythms that this sentence within a line is evidently there for a purpose, to make the claim as strongly as possible. It does so especially because of the emphatic word "charged," which usefully has two meanings: "loaded," and "full of electricity" as a battery is when it has been charged. The world is therefore electric with God's grandeur, and loaded with it (which suggests that the grandeur is heavy and substantial): the image of electricity is carried on in the second line, when he senses that the grandeur of God will "flame out, like shining from shook foil." As foil, when shaken, gives off shining light, so the world, when looked at carefully, is full of the shining light of God Himself, leaping out like flames or sparks. Hopkins described it to Bridges as "I mean foil in its sense of leaf or tinsel, . . . Shaken gold foil gives off broad glares like sheet lightning, and this is true of nothing else, owing to its zigzag dints and creasings and network of small many-cornered facets, a sort of fork lightning too" (L B 169). Its fullness is indicated by the next image

    It gathers to a greatness, like the ooze of oil
Crushed.

Hopkins is here thinking of an olive press, with the oil oozing from the pressed fruit. It oozes from every part of the press, in a fine film, and then the trickles gather together to form a jar of oil. In the same way the grandeur of God is found everywhere, trickling from every simple thing in the created universe and accumulating to form a greatness, a grandeur that is perceived by the discerning mind of the Christian and poet. This is made clear in the lines that follow, which are a lament for the neglect and indifference shown by mankind. Once again the poetry is dense with metaphors: instead of saying "why do men take no notice?" Hopkins writes

Why do men then now not reck his rod?

The rhythms and sounds are themselves awkward, like the question: "men then," "now not" and "reck his rod" (care for his rule: "reck" means "heed," occurring in ordinary speech in the word "reckless"). And these sounds continue, as if Hopkins is using the vocabulary and rhythms of his verse to act out, as well as describe, the situation:

> Generations have trod, have trod, have trod;
>   And all is seared with trade; bleared, smeared with toil;
>   And wears man's smudge and shares man's smell: the soil
> Is bare now, nor can foot feel, being shod.

Here the mechanical forces are captured in verse by the heavy accents. What is sometimes called the "daily grind" is a repetitive thump in which the feet of generations march on; and the "trod . . . trod . . . trod" sets up the three-beat rhythm of the next line: "seared . . . bleared . . . smeared." The verbs themselves sprawl across the line, preventing any delicacy of feeling or perception. "Seared," for instance, means "dried up" or it can mean "rendered incapable of feeling": it is accomplished by "bleared" (blurred in inflammation of the eyes) and "smeared" (rubbed over with dirt). When we think of the minute attention to detail of Hopkins' drawings, these adjectives take on yet more force: they are part of the process of treading down, smudging, and generally spoiling nature. Because of this the soil is barren, and feet, being both shod with boots, cannot feel it. For Hopkins, the "foot feel" is but a part of the whole process of insensitivity: as a man's feet are encased in boots, so his whole soul is bound up, unfree. . . .

It is then that the sestet throws into the equation another mysterious force, the feeling of freshness and growth of nature that causes it to live on, to survive against all the neglect and exploitation of man. Its nature is in this way to be itself: to go on growing each year with its own process of generation and renewed life, so that against the unfeeling energies of man there is placed something greater, the inexhaustible forces of nature. Its spirit of growth is everywhere: it is as natural and inevitable as the coming of morning after nightfall. It is the "dearest freshness" deep down in things which ensures that "nature is never spent"; and in the final lines this inexhaustible quality is associated with the working of the Holy Ghost, the spirit of God who created all things and sustains them:

> Because the Holy Ghost over the bent
>   World broods with warm breast and with ah! bright wings.

From The Poetry of Gerard Manley Hopkins, 1987

The Receptive Reader

How does the critic show that the word *charged* is charged with meaning? What inside information does he use from the poet himself? Where and how does the critic show the meshing of content and form? What difficulties does this reading clear up for you? How does this excerpt change your understanding of and response to the poem?

Psychoanalytic Criticism   Critics indebted to the tradition of Freudian psychoanalysis focus on the creative power of the unconscious mind. They insist that we need more than intellectual analysis to respond fully to a poem. They treat the intellectual content of much poetry as surface rationalizations that mask but also indirectly reveal the basic psychic conflicts and needs of the individual. Freud himself, who wrote extensively about art and literature, had applied to poetry such basic psychoanalytic categories as repressed desire and the conflict between rebellious instinctual energies and control by the conscious rational mind—the conflict between the id and the ego. He inspired critics to look for fantasies of wish fulfillment or for instances of sublimation—channeling sexual energy away from forbidden objects of desire into socially approved intellectual or artistic pursuits.

In richly symbolic poems by poets like William Blake or W. B. Yeats, critics schooled in Freudian psychology find much sexually charged imagery and the symbolic acting out of personal conflicts and confusions. In the following excerpt, two students of early modern critical crosscurrents give an admittedly simplified account of Freudian readings of Yeats' "The Second Coming." Earlier in the same chapter of their *The Muse of Fire,* they discuss Yeats' "long romance" with Maud Gonne, "whom he loved deeply and long," but who instead married John MacBride, a hero of the Irish nationalists who was executed in 1916. He alludes to her in poems speaking from his "embittered heart" to a soul enslaved by "fanaticism and hate." Rejected by her again, he found himself in love with Maud Gonne's adopted daughter Iseult but eventually married another woman. Here are the opening lines of Yeats' "The Second Coming" (see Chapter 25 for the complete poem).

> Turning and turning in the widening gyre°   *spiral*
> The falcon cannot hear the falconer;
> Things fall apart; the center cannot hold;
> Mere anarchy is loosed upon the world,
> The blood-dimmed tide is loosed, and everywhere
> The ceremony of innocence is drowned;
> The best lack all conviction, while the worst
> Are full of passionate intensity.

H. Edward Richardson and Frederick B. Shroyer

Freudian Analysis and Yeats' "Second Coming"

Yeats' feverish quest for marriage may suggest, on a broad level, a search for some kind of stability, or for love and wisdom, but its frantic circumstances indicate a desperate grasping for order within a life of chaos. In psychological terms, this would indicate a loss of ego control and an anarchy of the libido, which must have always been especially strong in Yeats.

If we accept Freud's thesis of an event of the present making "a strong impression on the writer," it would seem that Maud Gonne's "second coming" into Yeats' life would have been a sufficient causal agent to have "stirred up a memory of an earlier experience." If Yeats had indeed retreated far enough into his old memories, he may have stirred up a sexual fantasy for the Maud Gonne about whom, projecting his ego outward, he had often dreamed, and he may have then transmitted those dreams into poetry.

Within such a Freudian context, several images in "The Second Coming" take on sexual overtones. For example, the title may indicate, on one level, a significant "second" meeting, or on another, sexual orgasm; line 1, possibly, sexual intercourse; line 2, the lack of personal control or mastery of the ego over powerful unconscious desires; lines 3–5, a freely associated identity with the disintegrating world of order and propriety; line 6, a conscious awareness of guilt, the source of which may still be disguised, representing either the "ceremony" of his recent marriage, or his child about to be born, or both; lines 7–8, castigation of himself as "the best," perhaps a condemnation of Madame MacBride in the role of temptress as "the worst," although she still exudes for him her typical "passionate intensity.". . .

If we pursue the approach further, the final wish-fulfillment may be easy to explain in psychological terms, if one can imagine that Yeats' guilt and disillusionment in himself and in Madame MacBride were deep enough. The "rocking cradle" (perhaps the as-yet-unborn and innocent child) is an antipode to the probable consequences of this loss of control, this trammeling on innocence, this identity with disorder, chaos, and Dionysian revelry, and finally, to the ultimate destruction of the world. Why would Yeats choose such an antithetical image within the context of such annihilative violence? The answer may indicate Yeats' Protestant fear of breaking the Mosaic law— a real fear, deep in his unconscious, but functioning in such a way as to dominate his ego. Only the traditional summoning to judgment at the end of the world can lift the burden of what the ego can interpret only as tormenting shame. At this point, then, libido gives way to mortido, and life to death.

From *Muse of Fire: Approaches to Poetry*, 1971

The Receptive Reader

Many have read the opening lines of Yeats' poem as a prophetic vision of a modern world threatened by political and moral chaos. In how many ways does this account find possible personal meanings in these same lines? How does this account show the parallel between the traditional opposition of order and anarchy and the Freudian opposition of the ego and the id? (What is the role of the falcon image in these lines?)

Political Criticism   Politically engaged critics insist on raising the question of the poet's social responsibility. Much traditional art or literature seems to them a retreat into a private sphere of aesthetic gratification—

of art or beauty for its own sake. For critics indebted to **Marxist** thought, for instance, the key question has been: Does the poet collaborate in or oppose oppression by the state? In studying a Romantic poet like Samuel Taylor Coleridge or Percy Bysshe Shelley, they are likely to stress the poet's political engagement, the fight against tyranny, against "state repression." Much academic criticism today assumes it to be the poet's task "to promote an ideal republicanism" (Terence Diggory)—a utopian society where oppression and exploitation of the strong by the weak has been superseded.

Marxist critics use contemporary political events and recent history as a test of the poet's and the critic's political commitments. For instance, they fault poets and teachers of poetry for dealing not at all or only indirectly with the horrors of the Vietnam War and the role of American "corporate power" in the struggle of a Third World country against the legacy of colonialism. Even when a poet like Robert Bly sympathizes with the anticolonial struggle, he is likely to be criticized: He sees the "oriental other" through the lens of Western think schemes and formal categories, and he depicts the Vietnamese as victims rather than as "formidable foes of white America" (Michael Bibby).

Even when not committed to a specific ideology, politically engaged poets and critics have seen poetry as a means for awakening the reader's social conscience and sense of injustice. The following poem is Jane Flanders' "The House That Fear Built: Warsaw 1943." The form of the poem is borrowed from a children's rhyme: "This is the house that Jack built." But the subject of the poem is far removed from child's play. The poem reminds readers of a haunting photograph taken during World War II: As the Nazi occupiers crush the Jewish resistance during the desperate uprising in the Warsaw ghetto, a group of Jewish civilians is led away by German soldiers. In the critical discussion that follows the poem, an editor who chose the poem for publication tries to explain why he was powerfully affected by the way this poem conveyed its message.

The purpose of poetry is to remind us
how difficult it is to remain just one person,
for our house is open, there are no keys in the
doors. . .

    CZESLAW MILOSZ, FROM "ARS POETICA"

I am the boy with his hands raised over his head
in Warsaw.

I am the soldier whose rifle is trained
on the boy with his hands raised over his head
in Warsaw.

I am the woman with lowered gaze
who fears the soldier whose rifle is trained
on the boy with his hands raised over his head
in Warsaw.

I am the man in the overcoat
who loves the woman with lowered gaze
who fears the soldier whose rifle is trained
on the boy with his hands raised over his head
in Warsaw.

I am the stranger who photographs
the man in the overcoat
who loves the woman with lowered gaze
who fears the soldier whose rifle is trained
on the boy with his hands raised over his head
in Warsaw.

The crowd, of which I am each part, moves on
beneath my window, for I am the crone too
who shakes her sheets
over every street in the world
muttering
What's this? What's this?

Richard Foerster

Message and Means in Jane Flanders' "The House That Fear Built"

I remember enjoying initially the sound of this poem, the way it evoked not only "The House That Jack Built," an eighteenth-century nursery rhyme that some scholars believe is based on a sixteenth-century Hebrew chant, but also Elizabeth Bishop's "Visits to St. Elizabeths." The incremental repetition of such poems has its roots in medieval ballads, in the plainspeak and melodies of communal entertainment, and I found myself responding to this ancient aural technique and the haunting mood it generated in counterpoint to the poem's World War II setting.

I was moved also by the poem's other sound effects, though I can't say I was conscious of them on first hearing. The labels come with hindsight. Now I detect an almost Anglo-Saxon use of alliteration and caesura to enhance the syntactic balance of many of the lines, such as:

who loves the woman   with lowered gaze
who fears the soldier   whose rifle is trained

Assonance and approximate rhymes thread through the stanzas, stitching together images and ideas:

| stranger | gaze | trained | raised |

and

| beneath | sheets | streets |

"The sound must seem an echo to the sense" is one Popean truism I find ignored by too many poets today. Flanders makes her sounds serve sense in a striking way. Like Eliot before her in "The Hollow Men" ("This is the way the world ends") and—to my mind—like Ravel in "La Valse," she uses traditional rhythms to overthrow tradition, to give us a glimpse of the deterioration of order. Against the ironic counterpoint of the innocent children's rhyme, Flanders unfolds a widening perspective of the horrors of twentieth-century war. Her rhythms and incremental repetitions undermine our initial expectations. The skipping rhythm introduced in the first stanza leads us to believe that the boy's arms might be raised in play. By the poem's end, however, we realize he is part of a gruesome, complex tableau of the Warsaw Ghetto Uprising of the spring of 1943. . . .

The progression of the poem's images and ideas seemed to me both surprising and inevitable; appropriately for a poem based on a photograph, they moved cinematically, from close-up to panorama, from boy to crowd to "every street in the world."

Seeing the typescript made clear for me the relationship between the epigraph and both the title and the subject of the poem. "Our house" I understood not only as Parnassus and the poet's ability to assume masks but also as the entire modern world, which seems increasingly invaded and controlled by fear. The poet/spectator of this drama is helpless to prevent herself from identifying with each of her characters. Unable "to remain just one person," as Milosz says, the poet becomes a part of each of them, shares in their fears, love, brutality, and indifference, and imparts these to us through craft. Reading the poem, I, too, found myself becoming each of the characters: boy/victim, soldier/victimizer, resigned woman, compassionate but equally helpless man, one of the crowd that "moves on," and finally the on-looking crone, who in traditional nursery rhymes shakes out the world's woes from her bedding. In Flanders' modern version, however, the crone cannot absolve herself of complicity by pretending not to understand the nature of the tragedy occurring beneath her window.

I also enjoyed the double-edged words that add to the poem's depth: *Warsaw* became in my mind a "war saw"; the soldier's rifle significantly is not aimed but *trained,* suggesting the political indoctrination that made young German men into instruments of the Nazi Reich, tools of the Final Solution; and finally the crone and her sheets. I imagine her not only attending to her domestic chores but also hiding behind the sheets of a

newspaper, the way we overlook the world from our armchairs while muttering "What's this?" when certain headlines catch our eye.

From *Spreading the Word: Editors on Poetry,* 1990

The Receptive Reader

According to Foerster, why did the poet borrow the form of the children's
rhyme? How does it serve as a "counterpoint" to the subject of the poem? What
effect does it supposedly have on the reader? In reading this poem by Jane
Flanders, were you too "helpless" to prevent yourself "from identifying with
each of her characters"? (Why or why not?) What, according to the critic, is the
role of "the crone and her sheets"?

Making Connections—For Discussion or Writing

Another poem that treats a weighty, complex subject in strangely, deceptively simple language is Denise Levertov's "What Were They Like?" Examine
the relationship between "message" and "means" in the poems by Flanders and
Levertov.

Feminist Criticism Successive waves of critical theory—including
myth criticism and Freudian psychoanalysis—have challenged the dominance of the New Critical model of close textual analysis. Feminist writers have questioned formal complexity as an end in itself, and they have
privileged the powerful expression of personal emotions. They have encouraged the poet to come out from behind the poetic persona, rehabil-
itating what has been called **confessional poetry,** devoted to personal
revelation.

Feminist readings of poetry refocus attention on how poetic form and
poetic language serve the human meaning of literature. For example,
they can make us more sensitive to how Emily Dickinson "forced language into a new pattern and created a combination of paradox and
physical acuteness of imagery" nearly unparalleled. At the same time,
however, they can make us see how Dickinson used her language "as a
scalpel," laying "bare the finest nerves of love." They can help us see
how her "difficult, awesome poems express a radical syntax of the heart"
(Stephen Coote).

Feminist critics have paid special attention to the struggles of women
to reconcile their mission as poets with traditional societal roles, as
when Sylvia Plath says, "If I want to keep on being a triple-threat
woman: wife, writer, and teacher . . . I can't be a drudge." They have sym-
pathized with the struggle for self-realization and self-fulfillment, about
which Plath said, "I am making a self, in great pain, often, as for a birth,
but it is right that it should be so" and "By reforging my soul, I am a
woman now the like of which I could never have dreamed" (*Letters
Home*).

The following article is excerpted from a collection of feminist reevaluations of the life and work of Emily Dickinson, "the greatest woman

poet in the English language" (Suzanne Juhasz). Feminist critics have revised a traditional view of Emily Dickinson as eccentric or quaint, showing her instead as a woman of genius in rebellion against "the nineteenth-century corseting of women's bodies, choices, and sexuality." From a feminist perspective, Dickinson's life was neither a flight from reality nor a sacrifice nor a substitution, but a strategy for creating the kind of person she was; "it was a life deliberately organized on her terms" (Adrienne Rich). The following article reopens the much debated issue of Dickinson's emotional attachments to men or women.

Adelaide Morris

I see the better in the Dark—
I do not need a light—
The Love of Thee—a Prism be—
Excelling Violet

EMILY DICKINSON

A Feminist Reading of Emily Dickinson

The list of Dickinson's possible attachments is long, and our confusion is augmented by the fact that many of her letters and no doubt many of her poems have been lost to us, both through carelessness and through deliberate destruction. Two significant sets of writing to those she loved remain, however. The letters to the man she called "Master" are, as Richard Sewall points out, "among the most intense and fervent love letters she ever wrote," and they are supplemented by dozens of poems with similar vocabulary, rhythm, imagery, and symbolic pattern. The other group, addressed to her friend, sister-in-law, and next-door neighbor, Susan Gilbert Dickinson, consists of 154 extant notes and letters and 276 identifiable poems and poem fragments, probably a mere fraction of a lifetime's whole. The biographical details are gone: we don't know who her "Master" was, we know almost nothing of her sensual experience, we don't even know if those she loved loved her back. A plentitude of verbal detail remains, however, to allow us to compare the two prisms these loves formed and the very different spectrums they cast.

The rhetoric that describes the two relationships is surprisingly, even suspiciously similar, as if Dickinson were writing to the Master and Sue out of some peculiarly elliptic book of pattern letters. Both correspondences are highly compressed and heavily revised: the Master letters exist in drafts that hesitate over each choice of diction, syntax, and symbol, and rough drafts remain for even the most casual of notes sent across the lawn to Sue. In both cases, the revisions make continuous minute adjustments between advance and evasion, excitement and control. Urgent and edgy, her writing teases, pleads, chides, jests, and sighs. The rhythms are by turns abrupt and sustained, gnomic and rhapsodic.

Both the Master and Sue evoke her passion; both are passionately solicited, courted with imagery chosen to convey their magnetic pull. Again and again she describes herself as bewitched, overwhelmed. The most revealing recurrence, however, is the linked imagery of sun, storms, volcanoes, and wounds that she uses in both sets of letters and poems. Sue is "an Avalanche of Sun!," a woman of "torrid Noons"; the Master becomes her "man of noon . . . *mightier* than the morning." When the element of disturbance joins this imagery of huge heat and height, we have the thunderstorms described in so many poems sent to Sue. The setting is explosive, even volcanic: a sky sealed with "A Cap of Lead" (1649), wind rocking the grass (824), thunder piling and crumbling (1247), while

> Through fissures in
> Volcanic cloud
> The yellow lightning shone—
>
> [1694]

When explosion is withheld, Dickinson's image shifts from the thunderstorm to the silent, suppressed volcano vividly present in both sets of material. "Vesuvius dont talk—Etna—dont—," Dickinson reminds the Master, but so intense is the repressed force, she continues, "one of them—said a syllable—a thousand years ago, and Pompeii heard it, and hid forever." This is the dangerous "Vesuvius at Home" (1705), the deceptively domestic surface she describes in a poem sent to Sue:

> On my volcano grows the Grass
> A meditative spot—
> An acre for a Bird to choose
> Would be the General thought—
>
> How red the Fire rocks below
> How insecure the sod
> Did I disclose
> Would populate with awe my solitude.
>
> [1677]

The red, rocking, inner fire of this poem is unreleased passion, passion that endangers everything around it. The heat, intensity, and destructively deep interiority this image stresses connect it with the last of the series: the image of the profound inner wound. This is the hurt Dickinson describes to Sue as a sting (156), a stab (238), the gash that "wantoned with a Bone" (479), and to the Master as a stab, the "bullet" which "hit a Bird," the "Tomahawk in my side.". . .

This is an intense—and intensely familiar—discourse. Sun, storms, volcanoes, wounds, rescue, redemption: all emerge from that catalogue of romantic generalities Adrienne Rich calls "the language of love-letters, of suicide notes." This language seems to fit so easily into both sets of letters and poems that we might suppose it signifies a mode of loving Dickinson solicited from men and women both. Such a suspicion is bolstered by the existence of love poems with alternate sets of pronouns: in a particularly apt example, one variant of poem 494 begins "Going to Him! Happy letter!" while the other starts, "Going—to—Her!/Happy—Letter!" We would be wrong, however, to conclude that similar rhetoric describes a similar sort of love. The kind of love Dickinson desires and develops with a woman is very different from the love she desires and develops with a man. The similarities in rhetoric mask deep dissimilarities of structure.

Romantic rhetoric permits only one set of relations, the paradigm of disturbance and idolatry that is everywhere consonant with the structures of her love for Sue. Western traditions offer no developed discourse for love between women and thus, in need of a precedent, Dickinson may have used conventional romantic rhetoric in the letters and poems to Sue as a linguistic formula signifying an intensity (love) rather than a structure (dominance/submission). The most intriguing aspect of the writing to Sue is the consistency with which the clichés of romantic love are undermined by a revolutionary revision of love's possibilities.

The differences in structure are coded into the names Dickinson assigned her lovers: a "Master" can exist only in a world of difference and hierarchy; a "Sister," on the other hand, inhabits a world of similarity and equality. The structures of the Master's world are predominantly vertical and its dramas are largely dramas of positioning: the prostration of the woman, the exaltation of the man. She is forever "a tiny courtier" as the pageant of his tremendous glory (151). By contrast, the structures of the sisters' world are horizontal, not a universe but a neighborhood. Its dramas detail the flexible push and pull, the coming and going of those who live day to day, side by side. Against the abstract dignity of stasis in the Master material, the two figures in the poems and letters to Sue demonstrate a scrappy spontaneity: they are alternately large and small, far and near, magisterial and coy.

In Suzanne Juhasz, ed., *Feminist Critics Read Emily Dickinson*, 1983

The Receptive Reader

How much does Morris rely on biographical data, how much on Dickinson's letters, how much on her poems? How, according to Morris, is Dickinson's rhetoric of love for men and for women "surprisingly, even suspiciously similar"? What difference in the two kinds of relationships is masked by this similarity?

Deconstructionism   In recent years, poststructuralist and deconstructionist critics have read familiar classics (Milton, Wordsworth) from a radically new perspective. The following much-anthologized poem by a leader of the English Romantic movement is accompanied by a deconstructionist reading that clears away much of the apparent surface meaning of the poem. The critic then discovers a new and different dimension of meaning as the language used by the poet dances out its own significance.

The poem, as the critic says, is "a kind of epitaph," being part of the "Lucy poems," which commemorate a country girl who had died young.

A "meta-epitaphic" poem would in some way go *beyond* the familiar conventions of an epitaph. Other words that are part of the critic's vocabulary here are *laconic* (very brief, using the fewest possible words) and *mimetic* (imitating or mirroring). The German word *aufgehoben,* used by the critic at a key point, means literally "taken up, lifted" but figuratively also "put up, preserved" and "taken off, canceled." Here is William Wordsworth's "A Slumber Did My Spirit Seal" (1800), followed by Geoffrey Hartman's critical reading:

A slumber did my spirit seal;
   I had no human fears:
She seemed a thing that could not feel
   The touch of earthly years.

No motion has she now, no force;
   She neither hears nor sees;
Rolled round in earth's diurnal course,°   *daily*
   With rocks, and stones, and trees.

Geoffrey Hartman

Deconstructing Wordsworth's "A Slumber Did My Spirit Seal"

It does not matter whether you interpret the second stanza (especially its last line) as tending toward affirmation, or resignation, or a grief verging on bitterness. . . .

That [the poem] is a kind of epitaph is relevant, of course. We recognize, even if genre is not insisted on, that Wordsworth's style is laconic, even lapidary. There may be a mimetic or formal motive related to the ideal of epitaphic poetry. But the motive may also be, in a precise way, meta-epitaphic. The poem, first of all, marks the closure of a life that has never opened up: Lucy is likened in other poems to a hidden flower or the evening star. Setting overshadows rising, and her mode of existence is inherently inward, westering. I will suppose then, that Wordsworth was at some level giving expression to the traditional epitaphic wish: Let the earth rest lightly on the deceased. If so, his conversion of this epitaphic formula is so complete that to trace the process of conversion might seem gratuitous. The formula, a trite if deeply grounded figure of speech, has been catalyzed out of existence. Here it is formula itself, or better, the adjusted words of the mourner that lie lightly on the girl and everyone who is a mourner.

I come back, then, to the "aesthetic" sense of a burden lifted, rather than denied. A heavy element is made lighter. One may still feel that the term "elation" is inappropriate in this context; yet elation is, as a mood, the very subject of the first stanza. For the mood described is love or desire when it *eternizes* the loved person, when it makes her a star-like being that "could not feel / The touch of earthly years." This *naïve* elation, this spontaneous movement of the spirit upward, is reversed in the downturn or cata-strophe of the second stanza. Yet this stanza does not close out the illusion; it preserves it within the elegiac form. The illusion is elated, in our use of the word: *aufgehoben* seems the proper term. For the girl is still, and all the more, what she seemed to be: beyond touch, like a star, if the earth in its daily motion is a planetary and erring rather than a fixed star, and if all on this star of earth must partake of its sublunar, mortal, temporal nature. . . .

To sum up: In Wordsworth's lyric the specific gravity of words is weighed in the balance of each stanza; and this balance is as much a judgment on speech in the context of our mortality as it is a meaningful response to the individual death. At the limit of the medium of words, and close to silence, what has been purged is not concreteness, or the empirical sphere of the emotions—shock, disillusion, trauma, recognition, grief, atonement—what has been purged is a series of flashy schematisms and false or partial mediations: artificial plot, inflated consolatory rhetoric, the coercive absolutes of logic or faith.

From "Elation in Hegel and Wordsworth,"
The Unremarkable Wordsworth, 1987

The Receptive Reader

What for you is the "surface meaning" of the poem? For you, does the poem as a whole tend "toward affirmation, or resignation, or grief verging on bitterness"? How or why does Hartman feel that the words of the poem have a lightening effect, producing a sense of a burden lifted? What, according to Hartman, has been "purged" by the poem?

Reader Response "Central to the reading of every literary work is the interaction between its structure and its recipient," says Wolfgang Iser, leading exponent of **reader response** theory. The printed text is to our live response as the script of a play is to a live performance—in fact, to a live performance in which director and actors put their own strong personal imprint on the play.

How much of the reader's response is shaped and controlled by the poem? How much depends on what we as readers bring to the poem? In recent years, critics have become more willing to admit that we see a poem through the lens of our own experience, our own preoccupations and preferences. One reader may say of a poem about a kid on a merry-go-round: "It brings back a sensitivity of my youth. It is the excitement and wonder and mouth-gaping curiosity found at a carnival. It is wild imagination bounded by mother's pessimism and the authority of the traffic cop" (Tom E. Knowlton). Another reader may be allergic to Sousa music used for "colorful nostalgia" and find that the poem "never gets past cuteness" (Stanley Cooperman). Nevertheless, unless they are merely using the poem as a jumping off point, both readers are responding to the same poem, with the actual lived experience of the poem residing in the dynamic interchange between the objective text and the subjectivity of the reader.

Reader response theory thus provides a larger theoretical framework for the critical practice of others. When a psychoanalytic critic, a Marxist critic, and a deconstructionist respond to the same poem, the poem stays the same. The difference is in the perspective and commitments of the reader; it is in the eye of the beholder.

JUXTAPOSITIONS
The Range of Interpretation

*I am learning and mastering new words each
day, and drunker than Dylan, harder than
Hopkins, younger than Yeats in my saying.*
                    SYLVIA PLATH

Sylvia Plath's life and work have been a challenge to critics. The pessimism or alienation seemingly pervading many of her poems, her problematic marriage to fellow poet Ted Hughes, and her eventual suicide have triggered contradictory responses and explanations. In her novel *The Bell Jar,* Plath traced the odyssey of a young woman through a sterile suburban childhood, the deceptive glamor of a stint as an apprentice editor in the big city, bouts with mental illness, and attempted suicide. Before looking at the following sampling of critical responses to Plath, you may want to read or reread "Frog Autumn" (in Chapter 13), "Metaphors" (in Chapter 15), and "Mirror" (in Chapter 19).

Margaret Dickie

Sylvia Plath and Pregnancy

It is true that [Sylvia Plath's] poems generally lack the acerbic force of her attack in *The Bell Jar* on male-dominated marriage and cow-like pregnancy, but they can jab at the lust of the empty-headed man for a mechanical doll-wife or reduce the pregnant woman to a comic "melon strolling on two tendrils." Still these particular poems reveal not so much a scorn for domesticity or pregnancy as an attack on the conventions or a playful regard for the grotesque quality of pregnancy. When she treats these subjects directly in her poems, Plath displays a kind of knowing humor.

From "Sylvia Plath's Narrative Strategies," in *Iowa Review,* 1983

Peter Porter

On Sylvia Plath's "Mirror"

Crossing the Water is the second posthumous collection of poems. . . full of perfectly realized works. . . . Once more death has all the best parts, but his disguises and metamorphoses are doubly audacious. In "Mirror," for example, the little, four-cornered god denies it has any preconceptions, but when a woman bends over it she sees not only her own agitation but the fate which awaits her:

> In me she has drowned a young girl, and in me an old woman
> Rises toward her day after day, like a terrible fish.

In this period of Plath's poetry, objects come towards the reader like frightening Greek messengers. The gifts are not even ambiguous; they are seen wearing their proud colors of destruction.

From "Collecting Her Strength," *New Statesman,* 1971

Damian Grant

Sylvia Plath's Mirror Image

Winter Trees is the slimmest as well as the last of Sylvia Plath's collections; there are nineteen poems here on forty printed pages. But there is ample further evidence of her endless imaginative resource in the restatement of her familiar themes: all proceeding, ultimately, from the "divided self," the self which is alienated, oppressed, disembodied, dissolved. We meet again the familiar images, particularly the (characteristically schizoid) image of the mirror, which appears in all but two of these poems and seems to haunt them with its inevitability and its destructiveness:

> Mirrors can kill and talk, they are terrible rooms
> in which a torture goes on one can only watch.

From "Winter Trees," *Critical Quarterly,* 1972

Laurence Lerner

Plath's Mirror

This is a witty poem in the best sense, not only in the precision of the details, and the verbal sprightliness, but in the amusing self-importance given to the mirror. . . . Is the woman who bends over the mirror, for instance, to be seen as the author? We cannot say, but if she is, there is an extra irony in knowing that she is not yet 30 when she sees an old woman rising towards her; and the obsessive concern with itself given to the mirror takes on an extra resonance if it echoes the similar obsession in the author of the poem.

From "Sylvia Plath," *Encounter,* 1982

Katha Pollitt

Plath and the Critics

Literary evaluations of Sylvia Plath have a way of turning into sermons, in which critics forsake close reading in favor of moral pronouncements on whatever issues strike them as pertinent to her case. Is life worth living? Most critics think it is. Is madness admirable? Most agree it is not. Are men the enemy? A chorus of cheers from feminists. Can one justifiably connect one's small, private, middle-class life with fascism, war, and the Holocaust? Yes, claims A. Alvarez, for whom Plath is the ultimate literary risk-taker. No, argues Irving Howe, who is not only outraged by Plath's appropriation of the death camps to her personal situation but does not understand what, exactly, she was so upset about, anyway. The very fact that Plath was a woman has dazed many a strong mind. For Stephen Spender she is "a priestess cultivating her hysteria"; for Robert Lowell she is "hardly a person at all, or a woman," but Dido, Phaedra, Medea. George Steiner sees her poems as propelled by "the need of a superbly intelligent, highly literate young woman to cry out about her especial being, about the tyrannies of blood and gland, of nervous spasm and sweating skin, the rankness of sex and childbirth in which a woman is still compelled to be wholly of her organic condition." And you thought men sweated too.

From the *Nation,* 1982

Sandra M. Gilbert

Plath and the Divided Literary Tradition

Because Plath is usually seen as either a sort of neurasthenic sorceress of syntax—a witty, wily, willful witch of words—or a diligent devotee of *Roget's Thesaurus*—a docile and decorous ephebe [recruit] of 'fifties elegance—she isn't often understood to be what she really was: an extraordinarily conscious and at least semi-self-conscious student of the peculiarly new literary tradition in which she quite pivotally participated. . . . Plath was exactly what many of her most expert readers are: a sophisticated student of a twentieth-century literary tradition that was constituted out of an implicit if not explicit battle between highly cultured intellectual men (Pound, Eliot, Joyce, Lawrence) and their female counterparts . . . a cultured . . . even presumptuous group (H. D., Stein, Woolf, Moore).

From "In Yeats' House: The Death and Resurrection of Sylvia Plath," in Linda W. Wagner, ed., *Critical Essays on Sylvia Plath,* 1984

What are recurrent themes or issues in these critical excerpts? Are there major differences in perspective? Do you see the issues treated here reflected in the poems by Plath that you have read?

POETS ON POETRY

*A poet writes always of his personal life, in his
finest work out of its tragedy, whatever it be,
remorse, lost love, or mere loneliness.*

WILLIAM BUTLER YEATS

*I was early in life sick to my very pit with order
that cuts off the crab's feelers to make it fit into
the box.*

WILLIAM CARLOS WILLIAMS

Poets have often written *about* poetry—explaining their work, defending their art, or revisiting waystations in their poetic careers. Poets vary greatly in their writing habits and in how they explain their motives and procedures in writing poetry. They offer a range of perspectives on the relation between poetry and critical theory, poetry and politics, or poetry and the larger culture.

Dylan Thomas

Dylan Thomas became a poet because he "had fallen in love with words." Thomas was a Welsh poet who knew how to make his readers and listeners sense the sheer inspired exuberance of the creative act. The following excerpt is from "Notes on the Art of Poetry" that he wrote in response to a student's questions. A crowd-pleasing performer, he insisted that "a poem on a page is only half a poem," with the actual shared reading of a poem serving as the culminating acting out and interpretation of the written text.

Notes on the Art of Poetry

I wanted to write poetry in the beginning because I had fallen in love with words. The first poems I knew were nursery rhymes, and before I could read them for myself I had come to love just the words of them, the words alone. What the words stand for, symbolized, or meant was of very secondary importance. What mattered was the sound of them as I heard them for the first time on the lips of the remote and incomprehensible grown-ups who seemed, for some reason, to be living in my world. And

these words were, to me, as the notes of bells, the sounds of musical instruments, the noises of wind, sea, and rain, the rattle of milkcarts, the clop-
ping of hooves on cobbles, the fingering of branches on a window pane,
might be to someone, deaf from birth, who has miraculously found his hearing. I did not care what the words said, overmuch, nor what happened to
Jack and Jill and the Mother Goose rest of them; I cared for the shapes of
sound that their names, and the words describing their actions, made in my
ears; I cared for the colors the words cast on my eyes. I realize that I
may be, as I think all that way, romanticizing my reactions to the simple and
beautiful words of those pure poems; but that is all I can honestly remember, however much time might have falsified my memory. I fell in love—
that is the only expression I can think of—at once, and am still at the mercy
of words, though sometimes now, knowing a little of their behavior very
well, I think I can influence them slightly and have even learned to beat
them now and then, which they appear to enjoy. I tumbled for words at
once. And, when I began to read the nursery rhymes for myself, and, later,
to read other verses and ballads, I knew that I had discovered the most important thing to me, that could be ever. There they were, seemingly lifeless,
made only of black and white, but out of them, out of their own being,
came love and terror and pity and pain and wonder and all the other vague
abstractions that make our ephemeral lives dangerous, great, and bearable.
Out of them came the gusts and grunts and hiccups and heehaws of common fun on the earth; and though what the words meant was, in its own
way, often deliciously funny enough, so much funnier seemed to me, at that
almost forgotten time, the shape and shade and size and noise of the words
as they hummed, strummed, jugged and galloped along.

In James Scully, ed., *Modern Poetics*

The Receptive Reader

How would you describe this poet's relationship with words? In this selection, what are striking examples of Thomas' own wildly imaginative use of
words?

Making Connections—For Discussion or Writing

Poems by Dylan Thomas reprinted in this volume include "In My Craft
or Sullen Art" (Chapter 19), "Do Not Go Gentle into That Good Night" (Chapter 20), and "Fern Hill" (Chapter 17). How do they show the poet's love of
language?

Richard Wilbur

*I have never been one to write by rule, even by
my own rules.*

T. S. ELIOT

Modern poets have debated whether or not the demands of traditional form are artificial and have a constraining effect on poetic expression. Richard Wilbur has written about how a poem might start with a

close-up look at his herb patch, which reminded him of miniature Japanese gardens, which in turn reminded him of the mini-stanzas of the Japanese haiku. In the following excerpt, he explains how in his work a poem finds its form without the poet bringing ready-made formal patterns to the poem from without. Early in this excerpt, he pays tribute to the nineteenth-century American poet and essayist Ralph Waldo Emerson, who championed individualism and authentic self-expression.

Letting a Poem Find Its Form

One thing I know is that I have never deliberately set about to "write heroic couplets" or "write a sonnet." Poetry is both art and craft, but I abominate formal exercises and am stuck with the Emersonian feeling that a poem is something which finds out what it has to say, and in the process discovers the form which will best stress its tone and meaning. It may seem improbable to some poets of the last thirty years that such a process could result in, let us say, a rondeau [repeating only two rhymes, with the opening words coming back as a refrain]; but that is because such poets are free-verse practitioners who lack my generation's instinctive sense—got both by reading and writing—of the capabilities of certain traditional forms.

Though I commonly work in meters, my way of going about a poem is very like the free-verse writer's; that is, I begin by letting the words find what line lengths seem right to them. Often this will result in a stanza of some sort, which (though the ensuing stanzas keep the metrical pattern) will still be flexible enough to permit the argument to move and speak as it likes. All of my poems, therefore, are formally *ad hoc;* quite a few are, so far as I know, without formal precedent, and none set out to fulfill the "rules" of some standard form.

In David Lehman, ed., *Ecstatic Occasions, Expedient Forms,* 1987

The Receptive Reader

How does Wilbur challenge the familiar assumption that poets using traditional forms fit content into ready-made patterns? What does Wilbur mean when he says that his poems are "formally *ad hoc*" and often "without formal precedent"?

Audre Lorde

A new generation of women poets is already
working out of the psychic energy released when
women begin to move out toward what the
feminist philosopher Mary Daly has described as
the "new space" in the boundaries of patriarchy.
Women are speaking to and of women in these

poems, out of a newly released courage to name,
to love each other, to share risk and grief and
celebration.

ADRIENNE RICH

For many women who are part of the women's movement, poetry has become a means of self-definition and self-assertion. Audre Lorde is an African American poet of West Indian heritage. What does she mean when she says that "poems are not luxuries"?

Poems Are Not Luxuries

For each of us as women, there is a dark place within where hidden and growing our true spirit rises, "Beautiful and tough as chestnut / Stanchions against our nightmare of weakness" and of impotence. These places of possibility within ourselves are dark because they are ancient and hidden; they have survived and grown strong through darkness. Within these deep places, each one of us holds an incredible reserve of creativity and power, storehouse of unexamined and unrecorded emotion and feeling. The woman's place of power within each of us is neither white nor surface; it is dark, it is ancient, and it is deep.

When we view living, in the european mode, only as a problem to be solved, we rely solely upon our ideas to make us free, for these were what the white fathers told us were precious. But as we become more in touch with our own ancient, black, noneuropean view of living as a situation to be experienced and interacted with, we learn more and more to cherish our feelings, to respect those hidden sources of our power from where true knowledge and therefore lasting action comes. At this point in time, I believe that women carry within ourselves the possibility for fusion of these two approaches as a keystone for survival, and we come closest to this combination in our poetry. I speak here of poetry as the revelation or distillation of experience, not the sterile word play that, too often, the white fathers distorted the word *poetry* to mean—in order to cover their desperate wish for imagination without insight.

For women, then, poetry is not a luxury. It is a vital necessity of our existence. It forms the quality of the light within which we predicate our hopes and dreams toward survival and change, first made into language, then into idea, then into more tangible action. Poetry is the way we help give name to the nameless so it can be thought. The farthest external horizons of our hopes and fears are cobbled by our poems, carved from the rock experiences of our daily lives.

As they become known and accepted to ourselves, our feelings, and the honest exploration of them, become sanctuaries and fortresses and spawning ground for the most radical and daring of ideas, the house of difference so necessary to change and the conceptualization of any meaningful action. Right now, I could name at least ten ideas I would once have found intolerable or incomprehensible and frightening, except as they came after dreams and poems. This is not idle fantasy, but the true meaning of "It feels right to me." We can train ourselves to respect our feelings and to discipline (transpose) them into a language that catches those feelings so they can be shared.

In Donald Hall, ed., Claims for Poetry, 1982

The Receptive Reader

According to this poet, what is the role of poetry in women's struggle for change and survival? What is the difference between the European and the non-European mode?

Making Connections—For Discussion or Writing

Audre Lorde's poem "Coal" appears in Chapter 19 of this volume. How does it live up to the program sketched out in this selection?

In the following selections, two poets speak with exceptional candor about what makes them write. What inspired or motivated them as poets?

Diane Wakoski

On Experience and Imagination

It has always been a premise of mine in writing poetry that the poet has the same experiences everybody else does, but the technical challenge is to invent some imaginative way of talking about these problems, these realities, so that they can be taken seriously. It does not really seem like a big deal to anyone else when you say a man or woman you loved betrayed you. So what? Everyone sometimes feels betrayed. However, that's precisely why it is so important for the poet to find a way to say it. I believe in the use of extravagant surrealist imagery, like the girl riding naked on a zebra wearing only diamonds, as a way of making the reader accept the specialness of the feelings of the speaker in the poem.

I write in the first person because I have always wanted to make my life more interesting than it was. So I created a Diane whose real experiences were dramatized and exaggerated, were presented as surrealist experiences or metaphysical ones, who involved herself with imaginary people who often had the characteristics of real people but were more interesting and mysterious. Perhaps I have always been the isolated lonely person living around dull or sad people, and the poems were a way of inventing myself into a new life. I do feel a strange connection with the worlds I have created and the people in them, though I do not feel they are me or my world. It had been my obsession to try to see and understand the world truly, but that means seeing it over and over again, with all its changes, its attendant contradictions. I am never satisfied with anything I see but must keep inventing and reinventing ways to understand it.

From the introduction to *Trilogy*, 1974

The Receptive Reader

What, for Wakoski, is the relationship between common shared experience and imaginative creation? What, for her, is the relationship between "realism" and "surrealism"? What do you learn about the **persona** in those of her poems she likes best?

Pablo Neruda

Childhood and Poetry

One time, investigating in the backyard of our house in Temuco the tiny objects and minuscule beings of my world, I came upon a hole in one of the boards of the fence. I looked through the hole and saw a landscape like that behind our house, uncared for, and wild. I moved back a few steps, because I sensed vaguely that something was about to happen. All of a sudden a hand appeared—a tiny hand of a boy about my own age. By the time I came close again, the hand was gone, and in its place there was a marvelous white sheep.

The sheep's wool was faded. Its wheels had escaped. All of this only made it more authentic. I had never seen such a wonderful sheep. I looked back through the hole but the boy had disappeared. I went into the house and brought out a treasure of my own: a pinecone, opened, full of odor and resin, which I adored. I set it down in the same spot and went off with the sheep.

I never saw either the hand or the boy again. And I have never again seen a sheep like that either. The toy I lost finally in a fire. But even now, in 1954, almost fifty years old, whenever I pass a toy shop, I look furtively into the window, but it's no use. They don't make sheep like that anymore.

I have been a lucky man. To feel the intimacy of brothers is a marvelous thing in life. To feel the love of people whom we love is a fire that feeds our life. But to feel the affection that comes from those whom we do not know, from those unknown to us, who are watching over our sleep and solitude, over our dangers and our weaknesses—that is something still greater and more beautiful because it widens out the boundaries of our being, and unites all living things.

That exchange brought home to me for the first time a precious idea: that all of humanity is somehow together. That experience came to me again much later; this time it stood out strikingly against a background of trouble and persecution.

It won't surprise you then that I attempted to give something resiny, earthlike, and fragrant in exchange for human brotherhood. Just as I once left the pinecone by the fence, I have since left my words on the door of so many people who were unknown to me, people in prison, or hunted, or alone.

From Robert Bly, ed., *Neruda and Vallejo: Selected Poems,* 1962

The Receptive Reader

What was the significance of the childhood incident for the poet? In what way did it become a motivating force for his poetry?

WRITING ABOUT LITERATURE

24 *Preparing for Essay Exams*
WRITING FOCUS: Testing Your Reading Skills

The Writing Workshop   When you write about poetry as part of an essay exam, you need to be a quick, alert reader, and you need to think on your feet. Common types of essay questions will ask you to

✗ interpret a poem without detailed questions to guide you. You are on your own, applying the critical skills you have learned.

✗ do a close reading of a poem, responding to detailed questions focused on the formal features of the poem.

✗ compare and contrast two poems, mapping similarities but also striking differences in areas such as form, theme, or point of view.

✗ respond to the thematic implications of a poem. You may, for instance, be asked to compare the way a common theme is treated in a poem and in a related prose passage.

Study the following sample exam. How would you answer the questions? Compare your answers with the student responses that follow the questions.

Instructions   Study the following poem, one of John Donne's *Holy Sonnets* (Number 5). Then answer the questions that follow it.

I am a little world made cunningly°	*skillfully*	
Of elements and an angelic sprite;°	*spirit*	
But black sin hath betrayed to endless night		
My world's both parts, and O, both parts must die.		
You which beyond that heaven which was most high°	*You who*	5
Have found new spheres and of new lands can write,		
Pour new seas in mine eyes, that so I might		
Drown my world with my weeping earnestly,		
Or wash it if it must be drowned no more.		

But O, it must be burned! Alas, the fire   10
Of lust and envy have burnt it heretofore
And made it fouler; let their flames retire,
And burn me, O Lord, with a fiery zeal
Of thee and thy house, which doth in eating heal.

Questions for Peer Review

1. What is the sustained or organizing metaphor in the first four lines?

2. By Donne's time, the new science of astronomy had made people think of new reaches of space beyond the traditional heavenly spheres. Explorers and navigators like Columbus had discovered new worlds. What use does Donne make of these developments in this poem?

3. After Noah's flood, God had promised not ever to send floods again to drown sinful humanity. Where and how does the poet allude to this promise?

4. Sonnets often reach a turning point at or near the division between the opening octet and the concluding sestet. Does this sonnet follow this pattern?

5. The final lines of the poem make us imagine three different kinds of fire or flame. What are they?

6. What is paradoxical about the concluding couplet?

7. What is the prevailing tone of this sonnet? What are the dominant emotions? What kind of speaker does it make you imagine?

8. How does the poem as a whole develop or take shape? What is the overall movement or pattern that gives shape to the poem as a whole?

Compare your own answers with the following sample student responses:

Sample Student Responses

1. The sustained opening metaphor compares the speaker in the poem to the larger universe in which we live. A human being is a "little world" (a microcosm) made by the same creator that created the larger world outside. A human being is composed of earthly elements and an angelic, heavenly soul, just as the universe is composed of the earth and the heavens, inhabited by spirits or angels. Both the "little world" of the individual and the larger world (the macrocosm) will eventually be destroyed—the one at the end of our natural lives, the other on the eve of eternity.

2. Donne seems fascinated with geography, astronomy, and the other sciences. The opening up of new vistas in geography and astronomy gave his hyperbolical mind new areas in which to wander. In lines 5 and 6, he is turning to the new astronomers (who "have found new spheres") and to the discoverers of new continents (who can write "of new lands"). He asks them hyperbolically about newly discovered oceans that might replenish the reservoir of tears he has shed in weeping for his sins.

3. The speaker in the poem wants to "drown" his sinful "little world" with weeping, submerging it in tears. But God had promised Noah that He would not again allow humanity to be drowned; therefore, the speaker will use his tears merely to "wash" and cleanse rather than to drown (line 9).

4. There is a turning signaled by the word *but,* not exactly at the end of the octave but at the beginning of line 10. The tears of repentance alone will not be enough; the whole world will have to be destroyed by fire before we can enter into communion with God (no more floods—"the fire next time").

5. The first kind of fire is the physical fire that will destroy the world at the end. The second is the "fire of lust and envy" that leaves everything "foul" or scorched and besmirched. The third is the "fiery zeal" that cleanses us of sin.

6. It is paradoxical that Donne asks to be destroyed in order to be saved. The idea of a healing fire is paradoxical because the fire eats or devours what it consumes. But this fire "heals" by consuming only the infected part—it burns out sin.

7. The tone is paradoxical. The poem is somber and full of passionate remorse and despair, but it ends on a note of reaffirming the poet's faith. The speaker is a very intense person, passionately introspective, constantly dramatizing his own emotions.

8. The poem develops beautifully by first making us admire God's handiwork (the little world of the human body, "made cunningly" by God). But the poet almost immediately mourns its desperate condition after it has been "betrayed" by sin. The poet then asks for cleansing by water, then corrects himself in a rush of passion by asking for all-consuming fire. The poem proceeds by playing off polar opposites: the angelic spirit and the dark night of sin, water and fire.

25 OTHER VOICES/ OTHER VISIONS

A Gathering of Poets

Anonymous

Edward   *(traditional Scottish ballad)*

1

"Why does your brand sae drap wi' bluid,°   *sword so drip with blood*
    Edward, Edward,
Why does your brand sae drap wi' bluid,
    And why sae sad gang ye,° O?"   *so sadly go*
"O I ha'e killed my hawk sae guid,°   *good*   5
    Mither, mither,
O I ha'e killed my hawk sae guid,
    And I had nae mair° but he, O."   *no more*

2

"Your hawke's bluid was never sae reid,°   *red*
    Edward, Edward,   10
Your hawke's bluid was never sae reid,
    My dear son I tell thee, O."
"O I ha'e killed my reid-roan steed,
    Mither, mither,
O I ha'e killed my reid-roan steed,   15
    That erst was° sae fair and free, O."   *that once was*

3

"Your steed was auld, and ye ha'e gat mair,°   *more*
    Edward, Edward,
Your steed was auld, and ye ha'e gat mair,
    Some other dule ye drie,° O."   *other grief you suffer*   20
"O I ha'e killed my fader dear,
    Mither, mither,
O I ha'e killed my fader dear,
    Alas, and wae° is me, O!"   *woe*

4

"And whatten° penance wul ye drie for that,   *what sort of*   25
    Edward, Edward?
And whatten penance wul ye drie for that,
    My dear son, now tell me, O?"
"I'll set my feet in yonder boat,
    Mither, mither,   30
I'll set my feet in yonder boat,
    And I'll fare over the sea, O."

5

"And what wul ye do wi' your towers and your ha',°   *ball*
    Edward, Edward?
And what wul ye do wi' your towers and your ha',   35

That were sae fair to see, O?"
"I'll let them stand tul they down fa',°   *fall*
    Mither, mither,
I'll let them stand tul they down fa',
    For here never mair maun° I be, O."   *never more must*   40

6

"And what wul ye leave to your bairns° and your wife,   *children*
    Edward, Edward?
And what wul ye leave to your bairns and your wife,
    Whan ye gang over the sea, O?"
"The warlde's° room, let them beg thrae° life,   *world's / through* 45
    Mither, mither,
The warlde's room, let them beg thrae life,
    For them never mair wul I see, O."

7

"And what wul ye leave to your ain mither dear,
    Edward, Edward?   50
And what wul ye leave to your ain mither dear,
    My dear son, now tell me, O?"
"The curse of hell frae me sall° ye bear,   *from me shall*
    Mither, mither,
The curse of hell frae me sall ye bear,   55
    Sic° counsels ye gave to me, O."   *such*

Anonymous

Sir Patrick Spens   *thirteenth century*

1

The king sits in Dumferling town,
    Drinking the blude-reid° wine: *blood-red*
"O whar will I get guid° sailor,   *good*
    To sail this ship of mine?"

2

Up and spak an eldern knicht,°   *spoke an elderly knight*   5
    Sat at the king's richt° knee: *right*
"Sir Patrick Spens is the best sailor
    That sails upon the sea."

3

The king has written a braid° letter   *broad*
    And signed it wi' his hand,   10
And sent it to Sir Patrick Spens,
    Was walking on the sand.

4

The first line that Sir Patrick read,
    A loud lauch° lauched he;   *laugh*
The next line that Sir Patrick read,   15
    The tear blinded his ee.°   *eye*

5

"O wha is this has done this deed,
    This ill deed done to me,
To send me out this time o' the year,
    To sail upon the sea?   20

6

"Mak haste, mak haste, my mirry men all,
    Our guid ship sails the morn."
"O say na sae,° my master dear,   *not so*
    For I fear a deadly storm.

7

"Late, late yestre'en I saw the new moon   25
    Wi' the auld moon in hir arm,
And I fear, I fear, my dear master,
    That we will come to harm."

8

O our Scots nobles were richt laith°   *loath*
    To weet their cork-heeled shoon,°   *wet their cork-heeled shoes* 30
But lang or° a' the play were played   *before*
    Their hats they swam aboon.°   *above*

9

O lang, lang may their ladies sit,
    Wi' their fans into their hand,
Or ere they see Sir Patrick Spens   35
    Come sailing to the land.

10

O lang, lang may the ladies stand
    Wi' their gold kems° in their hair,   *combs*
Waiting for their ain° dear lords,   *own*
    For they'll see them na mair.   40

11

Half o'er, half o'er to Aberdour
    It's fifty fadom deep,
And there lies guid Sir Patrick Spens
    Wi' the Scots lords at his feet.

John Ashbery   *(born 1927)*

At North Farm   1984

Somewhere someone is traveling furiously toward you,
At incredible speed, traveling day and night,
Through blizzards and desert heat, across torrents, through narrow passes.
But will he know where to find you,
Recognize you when he sees you,   5
Give you the thing he has for you?

Hardly anything grows here,
Yet the granaries are bursting with meal,
The sacks of meal piled to the rafters.
The streams run with sweetness, fattening fish;   10
Birds darken the sky. Is it enough
That the dish of milk is set out at night,
That we think of him sometimes,
Sometimes and always, with mixed feelings?

Aphra Behn   *(1640–1689)*

Song   1676

Love in fantastic triumph° sat,   *celebration of victory*
Whilst bleeding hearts around him flowed,
For whom fresh pains he did create,
And strange tyrannic power he showed.
From thy bright eyes he took his fire,   5
Which round about, in sport he hurled;
But 't was from mine he took desire,
Enough to undo the amorous° world.   *filled with love*

From me he took his sighs and tears,
From thee his pride and cruelty;   10
From me his languishments and fears,
And every killing dart from thee.
Thus thou and I, the god have armed,
And set him up a deity;°   *as a deity*
But my poor heart alone is harmed,   15
Whilst thine the victor is, and free.

John Berryman   *(1914–1972)*

Dream Song 14   1964

Life, friends, is boring. We must not say so.
After all, the sky flashes, the great sea yearns,
we ourselves flash and yearn,
and moreover my mother told me as a boy
(repeatingly) "Ever to confess you're bored   5
means you have no

Inner Resources." I conclude now I have no
inner resources, because I am heavy bored.
Peoples bore me,
literature bores me, especially great literature,   10
Henry bores me, with his plights & gripes
as bad as achilles,°   *mythical Greek warrior*
                                  invulnerable except in the heel

who loves people and valiant art, which bores me.
And the tranquil hills, & gin, look like a drag
and somehow a dog   15
has taken itself & its tail considerably away
into mountains or sea or sky, leaving
behind: me, wag.

William Blake   *(1757–1827)*

The Chimney Sweeper   1789

When my mother died I was very young,
And my father sold me while yet my tongue
Could scarcely cry weep weep weep weep.°   *child's pronunciation of*
So your chimneys I sweep & in soot I sleep.   *"sweep sweep"?*

There's little Tom Dacre, who cried when his head   5
That curled like a lamb's back, was shaved, so I said
Hush Tom never mind it, for when your head's bare,
You know that the soot cannot spoil your white hair.

And so he was quiet, & that very night,
As Tom was a sleeping he had such a sight,   10
That thousands of sweepers Dick, Joe, Ned & Jack
Were all of them locked up in coffins of black°   *due to lung diseases*

And by came an Angel who had a bright key,
And he opened the coffins & set them all free.
Then down a green plain leaping laughing they run   15
And wash in a river and shine in the Sun.

Then naked & white, all their bags left behind,
They rise upon clouds, and sport in the wind.
And the Angel told Tom if he'd be a good boy,
He'd have God for his father & never want° joy.   *lack*   20

And so Tom awoke and we rose in the dark
And got with our bags & our brushes to work.
Though the morning was cold, Tom was happy & warm,
So if all do their duty, they need not fear harm.

William Blake   *(1757–1827)*

The Lamb   *1789*

    Little Lamb, who made thee?
    Dost thou know who made thee?
Gave thee life & bid thee feed,
By the stream & o'er the mead;°   *meadow*
Gave thee clothing of delight,   5
Softest clothing wooly bright;
Gave thee such a tender voice,
Making all the vales° rejoice!   *valleys*
    Little Lamb who made thee?
    Dost thou know who made thee?   10

    Little Lamb I'll tell thee,
    Little Lamb I'll tell thee!
He is callèd by thy name,
For he calls himself a Lamb:
He is meek & he is mild,   15
He became a little child:
I a child & thou a lamb,
We are callèd by his name.
    Little Lamb God bless thee.
    Little Lamb God bless thee.   20

Louise Bogan   *(1897–1970)*

Women   *1923*

Women have no wilderness in them,
They are provident° instead,   *frugal*
Content in the tight hot cell of their hearts
To eat dusty bread.

They do not see cattle cropping red winter grass,   5
They do not hear
Snow water going down under culverts
Shallow and clear.

They wait, when they should turn to journeys,
They stiffen, when they should bend.   10
They use against themselves that benevolence°   *good will*
To which no man is friend.

They cannot think of so many crops to a field
Or of clean wood cleft by° an axe.   *split by*
Their love is an eager meaninglessness   15
Too tense, or too lax.

They hear in every whisper that speaks to them
A shout and a cry.
As like as not, when they take life over their door-sills
They should let it go by.   20

Judith Ortiz Cofer   *(born 1952)*

The Other   *1993*

A sloe-eyed dark woman shadows me.
In the morning she sings
Spanish love songs in a high
falsetto filling my shower stall
with echoes.   5
She is by my side
in front of the mirror as I slip
into my tailored skirt and she
into her red cotton dress.
She shakes out her black mane as I   10
run a comb through my close-cropped cap.
Her mouth is like a red bull's eye
daring me.
Everywhere I go I must
make room for her; she crowds me   15
in elevators where others wonder
at all the space I need.
At night her weight tips my bed, and
it is her wild dreams that run rampant
through my head exhausting me. Her heartbeats   20
like dozens of spiders carrying the poison
of her restlessness over the small
distance that separates us,

drag their countless legs
over my bare flesh.   25

Samuel Taylor Coleridge   *(1772–1834)*

Kubla Khan   *1798*

or a vision in a dream, a fragment

In Xanadu did Kubla Khan°   *13th-century Chinese ruler*
A stately pleasure dome decree:
Where Alph, the sacred river, ran
Through caverns measureless to man
      Down to a sunless sea.   5
So twice five miles of fertile ground
With walls and towers were girdled round:
And there were gardens bright with sinuous rills,°   *winding brooks*
Where blossomed many an incense-bearing tree;
And here were forests ancient as the hills,   10
Enfolding sunny spots of greenery.

But oh! that deep romantic chasm which slanted
Down the green hill athwart° a cedarn cover!   *across*
A savage place! as holy and enchanted
As ever beneath a waning moon was haunted   15
By woman wailing for her demon lover!
And from this chasm, with ceaseless turmoil seething,
As if this earth in fast thick pants were breathing,
A mighty fountain momently° was forced: *moment by moment*
Amid whose swift half-intermitted burst   20
Huge fragments vaulted like rebounding hail,
Or chaffy grain beneath the thresher's flail:
And 'mid these dancing rocks at once and ever
It flung up momently the sacred river.
Five miles meandering with a mazy motion   25
Through wood and dale° the sacred river ran,   *valley*
Then reached the caverns measureless to man,
And sank in tumult to a lifeless ocean:
And 'mid this tumult Kubla heard from far
Ancestral voices prophesying war!   30
      The shadow of the dome of pleasure
      Floated midway on the waves;
      Where was heard the mingled measure
      From the fountain and the caves.
It was a miracle of rare device,   35
A sunny pleasure dome with caves of ice!

      A damsel with a dulcimer°   *a stringed musical instrument*
      In a vision once I saw:

It was an Abyssinian° maid,   *Ethiopian*
And on her dulcimer she played,   40
Singing of Mount Abora.
Could I revive within me
Her symphony and song,
To such a deep delight 'twould win me,
That with music loud and long,   45
I would build that dome in air,
That sunny dome! those caves of ice!
And all who heard should see them there,
And all should cry, Beware! Beware!
His flashing eyes, his floating hair!   50
Weave a circle round him thrice,
And close your eyes with holy dread,
For he on honey-dew hath fed,
And drunk the milk of Paradise.

Robert Creeley   *(born 1926)*

Fathers   *1986*

Scattered, aslant
faded faces a column
a rise of the packed
peculiar place to a
modest height makes   5
a view of common lots
in winter then, a ground
of battered snow crusted
at the edges under
it all, there under   10
my fathers their
faded women, friends,
the family all echoed,
names trees more tangible
physical place more tangible   15
the air of this place the road
going past to Watertown
or down to my mother's
grave, my father's grave, not
now this resonance of   20
each other one was his, his
survival only, his curious
reticence, his dead state,
his emptiness, his acerbic
edge cuts the hands to   25
hold him, hold on, wants
the ground, *wants* this frozen ground.

E. E. Cummings   *(1894–1962)*

my sweet old etcetera   1926

my sweet old etcetera
aunt lucy during the recent

war could and what
is more did tell you just
what everybody was fighting   5

for,
my sister

isabel created hundreds
(and
hundreds) of socks not to   10
mention shirts fleaproof earwarmers

etcetera wristers etcetera, my

mother hoped that

i would die etcetera
bravely of course my father used   15
to become hoarse talking about how it was
a privilege and if only he
could meanwhile my

self etcetera lay quietly
in the deep mud et   20

cetera
(dreaming,
et
   cetera, of
Your smile   25
eyes knees and of your Etcetera)

Alison Hawthorne Deming   *(born 1946)*

The Woman Painting Crates   1983

*All structure is a manifestation of underlying
process.*
                                       FRITJOF CAPRA

The day after the physicist speaks
I paint crates frosty berry blue
as if to confirm they are solid

or else to admire their masterful
illusion—there is no solid stuff   5

in these structures made of particles

no one can touch or stop
from spinning at fierce velocities.
I am mostly empty space

and for an instant the terror   10
of flying apart rushes through me
like a close call on the interstate.

Even this body, good paint,
which I am finally comfortable riding
is made of nothing but process,   15

is no different from the crate
or the atoms of hydrogen in this brush.
Once all things could be understood

if broken into smaller pieces.
Now, the physicist tells me, matter   20
disappears into haloes

of transforming unexpected
connectedness. I am more than
that accidental assembly—

but to say it, is like trying   25
to copy the curved face of Earth
on a flat map. If I could know

that process of energy in myself
I could know what continues.
But knowing is what I try   30
to train myself out of,
painting these crates a new color
closer to a certain blue.

Chitra Divakaruni   *(born 1956)*

The Quilt   *1991*

The parrot flies to the custard-apple tree.
The bees are among the pomegranates.
I call and call you, little bride.
Why do you not speak?
                    BENGALI FOLK SONG

Blue and sudden as beginning,
a quilt at the bottom
of the small mahogany chest
which holds her things.

She died in childbirth,   5
this grandmother whose name
no one can tell me.

He married again,
a strong woman this time,
straight backed, wide-hipped   10
for boy-children.
In the portrait downstairs
she wears the family diamonds
and holds her fourth son.

There are no pictures   15
of the wife who failed.

Her quilt leaves on my fingers
satin dust
as from a butterfly wing.

I spread it against   20
the floor's darkness, see her fingers
working it into the world-design,
the *gul-mohur* tree
bright yellow against the blue,
the river winding through rice fields   25
into a horizon where men with swords
march to a war
or a wedding.

As the baby grew she stitched in
a drifting afternoon boat   30
with a peacock sail.
In the foreground, young grass.
A woman with a deer.
She is left unfinished,
no eyes, no mouth,   35
her face a smooth blankness
tilted up at birds
that fall like flames from the sky.

John Donne   *(1572–1631)*

The Good-Morrow   *1633*

I wonder, by my troth,° what thou and I   truthfully
Did, till we loved? were we not weaned till then?
But sucked on country pleasures, childishly?
Or snorted° we in the Seven Sleepers'° den?   snored / they slept 230 years in a cave
'Twas so; but this,° all pleasures fancies be.   except for this   5
If ever any beauty I did see,
Which I desired, and got, 'twas but a dream of thee.

And now good-morrow to our waking souls,
Which watch not one another out of fear;
For love, all love of other sights controls, 10
And makes one little room an everywhere.
Let sea-discoverers to new worlds have gone,
Let maps° to others, worlds on worlds have shown,   *maps of the heavens*
Let us possess our world, each hath one, and is one.

My face in thine eye, thine in mine appears, 15
And true plain hearts do in the faces rest;
Where can we find two better hemispheres,
Without sharp north, without declining west?
Whatever dies was not mixed equally;°   *dies as a result of bodily imbalance*
If our two loves be one, or, thou and I 20
Love so alike that none do slacken, none can die.

John Donne   *(1572–1631)*

Holy Sonnet 14   *1633*

Batter my heart, three-personed God; for You
As yet but knock, breathe, shine, and seek to mend;
That I may rise and stand, overthrow me, and bend
Your force to break, blow, burn, and make me new.
I, like an usurped town, to another due, 5
Labor to admit You, but Oh, to no end.
Reason, Your viceroy in me, me should defend,
But is captived, and proves weak or untrué.
Yet dearly I love You, and would be loved fain,°   *gladly*
But am betrothed unto Your enemy: 10
Divorce me, untie or break that knot again,
Take me to You, imprison me, for I,
Except You enthrall me,° never shall be free,   *unless you enslave me*
Nor ever chaste, except You ravish me.

T. S. Eliot   *(1888–1965)*   👁

The Love Song of J. Alfred Prufrock   *1917*

S'io credesse che mia risposta fosse
A persona che mai tornasse al mondo,
Questa fiamma staria senza piu scosse.
Ma perciocche giammai di questo fondo
Non torno vivo alcun, s'i'odo il vero,
Senza tema d'infamia ti rispondo.

[From Dante's *Inferno:* "If I thought my answer were given / to anyone who would ever return to the world, / this flame would stand still
without moving any further. / But since never from this abyss has
anyone ever returned alive, if what I hear is true, / without fear of infamy I answer thee."]

Let us go then, you and I,
When the evening is spread out against the sky
Like a patient etherized upon a table;
Let us go, through certain half-deserted streets,
The muttering retreats   5
Of restless nights in one-night cheap hotels
And sawdust restaurants with oyster-shells:
Streets that follow like a tedious argument
Of insidious intent
To lead you to an overwhelming question . . .   10
Oh, do not ask, "What is it?"
Let us go and make our visit.

In the room the women come and go
Talking of Michelangelo.

The yellow fog that rubs its back upon the window-panes   15
The yellow smoke that rubs its muzzle on the window-panes
Licked its tongue into the corners of the evening,
Lingered upon the pools that stand in drains,
Let fall upon its back the soot that falls from chimneys,
Slipped by the terrace, made a sudden leap,   20
And seeing that it was a soft October night,
Curled once about the house, and fell asleep.

And indeed there will be time
For the yellow smoke that slides along the street,
Rubbing its back upon the window-panes;   25
There will be time, there will be time
To prepare a face to meet the faces that you meet;
There will be time to murder and create,
And time for all the works and days of hands
That lift and drop a question on your plate;   30
Time for you and time for me,
And time yet for a hundred indecisions,
And for a hundred visions and revisions,
Before the taking of a toast and tea.

In the room the women come and go   35
Talking of Michelangelo.

And indeed there will be time
To wonder, "Do I dare?" and, "Do I dare?"
Time to turn back and descend the stair,
With a bald spot in the middle of my hair—   40
(They will say: "How his hair is growing thin!")

My morning coat, my collar mounting firmly to the chin,
My necktie rich and modest, but asserted by a simple pin—
(They will say: "But how his arms and legs are thin!")
Do I dare   45
Disturb the universe?
In a minute there is time
For decisions and revisions which a minute will reverse.

For I have known them all already, known them all:
Have known the evenings, mornings, afternoons,   50
I have measured out my life with coffee spoons;
I know the voices dying with a dying fall
Beneath the music from a farther room.
    So how should I presume?

And I have known the eyes already, known them all—   55
The eyes that fix you in a formulated phrase,
And when I am formulated, sprawling on a pin,
When I am pinned and wriggling on the wall,
Then how should I begin
To spit out all the butt-ends of my days and ways?   60
    And how should I presume?

And I have known the arms already, known them all—
Arms that are braceleted and white and bare
(But in the lamplight, downed with light brown hair!)
Is it perfume from a dress   65
That makes me so digress?
Arms that lie along a table, or wrap about a shawl.
    And should I then presume?
    And how should I begin?

     . . . . .

Shall I say, I have gone at dusk through narrow streets   70
And watched the smoke that rises from the pipes
Of lonely men in shirt-sleeves, leaning out of windows? . . .

I should have been a pair of ragged claws
Scuttling across the floors of silent seas.

     . . . . .

And the afternoon, the evening, sleeps so peacefully!   75
Smoothed by long fingers,
Asleep . . . tired . . . or it malingers,
Stretched on the floor, here beside you and me.
Should I, after tea and cakes and ices,
Have the strength to force the moment to its crisis?   80
But though I have wept and fasted, wept and prayed,
Though I have seen my head (grown slightly bald) brought in upon a
    platter,
I am no prophet—and here's no great matter;

I have seen the moment of my greatness flicker,
And I have seen the eternal Footman hold my coat, and snicker,   85
And in short, I was afraid.

And would it have been worth it, after all,
After the cups, the marmalade, the tea,
Among the porcelain, among some talk of you and me,
Would it have been worth while,   90
To have bitten off the matter with a smile,
To have squeezed the universe into a ball
To roll it toward some overwhelming question,
To say: "I am Lazarus,° come from the dead,   *whom Jesus raised from the dead*
Come back to tell you all, I shall tell you all"—   95
If one, settling a pillow by her head,
        Should say: "That is not what I meant at all.
        That is not it, at all."

And would it have been worth it, after all,
Would it have been worth while,   100
After the sunsets and the dooryards and the sprinkled streets,
After the novels, after the teacups, after the skirts that trail along the
        floor—
And this, and so much more?—
It is impossible to say just what I mean!
But as if a magic lantern threw the nerves in patterns on a screen: 105
Would it have been worth while
If one, settling a pillow or throwing off a shawl,
And turning toward the window, should say:
        "That is not it at all,
        That is not what I meant, at all."   110

                    . . . . .

No! I am not Prince Hamlet, nor was meant to be;
Am an attendant lord, one that will do
To swell a progress, start a scene or two,
Advise the prince; no doubt, an easy tool,
Deferential, glad to be of use,   115
Politic, cautious, and meticulous;
Full of high sentence, but a bit obtuse;
At times, indeed, almost ridiculous—
Almost, at times, the Fool.

I grow old . . . I grow old . . .   120
I shall wear the bottoms of my trousers rolled.

Shall I part my hair behind? Do I dare to eat a peach?
I shall wear white flannel trousers, and walk upon the beach.
I have heard the mermaids singing, each to each.

I do not think that they will sing to me.   125

I have seen them riding seaward on the waves
Combining the white hair of the waves blown back
When the wind blows the water white and black.

We have lingered in the chambers of the sea
By sea-girls wreathed with seaweed red and brown   130
Till human voices wake us, and we drown.

Lawrence Ferlinghetti   *(born 1919)*

Constantly Risking Absurdity   *1958*

    Constantly risking absurdity
               and death
        whenever he performs
               above the heads
                  of his audience   5
   the poet like an acrobat
           climbs on rime
              to a high wire of his own making
and balancing on eyebeams
              above a sea of faces   10
        paces his way
             to the other side of day
     performing *entrechats*°
             and sleight-of-foot tricks   *ballet leaps*
and other high theatrics   15
        and all without mistaking
    any thing
        for what it may not be
   For he's the super realist
           who must perforce perceive   20
     taut truth
           before the taking of each stance or step
  in his supposed advance
           toward that still higher perch
where Beauty stands and waits   25
        with gravity
           to start her death-defying leap
   And he
     a little charleychaplin man
          who may or may not catch   30

her fair eternal form
                    spreadeagled in the empty air
    of existence

Allen Ginsberg   *(1926–1997)*

A Supermarket in California   1956

What thoughts I have of you tonight, Walt Whitman, for I walked down the sidestreets under the trees with a headache self-conscious looking at the full moon.

In my hungry fatigue, and shopping for images, I went into the neon fruit supermarket, dreaming of your enumerations!°   *cataloging of data*

What peaches and what penumbras!° Whole families shopping at night! Aisles full of husbands! Wives in the avocados, babies in the tomatoes—and you, Garcia Lorca,° what were you doing down by the watermelons?   *partial shadows*

spanish poet

I saw you, Walt Whitman, childless, lonely old grubber, poking among the meats in the refrigerator and eyeing the grocery boys.

I heard you asking questions of each: Who killed the pork chops? What price bananas? Are you my Angel?   5

I wandered in and out of the brilliant stacks of cans following you, and followed in my imagination by the store detective.

We strode down the open corridors together in our solitary fancy tasting artichokes, possessing every frozen delicacy, and never passing the cashier.

Where are we going, Walt Whitman? The doors close in an hour. Which way does your beard point tonight?

(I touch your book and dream of our odyssey in the supermarket and feel absurd.)

Will we walk all night through solitary streets? The trees add shade to shade, lights out in the houses, we'll both be lonely.   10

Will we stroll dreaming of the lost America of love past blue automobiles in driveways, home to our silent cottage?

Ah, dear father, graybeard, lonely old courage-teacher, what America did you have when Charon° quit poling his ferry and you got out on a smoking bank and stood watching the boat disappear on the black waters of Lethe?°

*mythical ferryman
conveying souls across River
Styx to Hades*

*mythical underworld river
of forgetfulness*

Louise Glück   *(born 1943)*

Gratitude   1975

Do not think I am not grateful for your small
kindness to me.
I like small kindnesses.
In fact I actually prefer them to the more
substantial kindness, that is always eyeing you,   5
like a large animal on a rug,
until your whole life reduces
to nothing but waking up morning after morning
cramped, and the bright sun shining on its tusks.

Donald Hall   *(born 1928)*

My Son My Executioner   1955

My son, my executioner,
    I take you in my arms,
Quiet and small and just astir,
    And whom my body warms.

Sweet death, small son, our instrument
    Of immortality,   5
Your cries and hungers document
    Our bodily decay.

We twenty-five and twenty-two,
    Who seemed to live forever,
Observe enduring life in you   10
    And start to die together.

Thomas Hardy   *(1840–1928)*

In Time of "The Breaking of Nations"   1915

Only a man harrowing clods°   *breaking up lumps (thrown up by the plow)*
In a slow silent walk
With an old horse that stumbles and nods
Half asleep as they stalk.

Only thin smoke without flame   5
From the heaps of couch-grass;°   *creeping grassy weed*
Yet this will go onward the same
Though dynasties pass.

Yonder a maid and her wight°   *young male*
Come whispering by: 10

War's annals will cloud into night
Ere° their story die.   *before*

Seamus Heaney   *(born 1939)*

The Forge   *1969*

All I know is a door into the dark.
Outside, old axles and iron hoops rusting;
Inside, the hammered anvil's short-pitched ring,
The unpredictable fantail of sparks
Or hiss when a new shoe toughens in water.   5
The anvil must be somewhere in the center.
Horned as a unicorn, at one end square,
Set there immovable: an altar
Where he expends himself in shape and music.
Sometimes, leather-aproned, hairs in his nose,   10
He leans out on the jamb, recalls a clatter
Of hoofs where traffic is flashing in rows;
Then grunts and goes in, with a slam and flick
To beat real iron out, to work the bellows.

George Herbert   *(1593–1633)*

The Collar   *1633*

I struck the board° and cried, "No more;   *table*
    I will abroad!
What? shall I ever sigh and pine?
My lines and life are free, free as the road,
    Loose as the wind, as large as store.°   *abundance*   5
        Shall I be still in suit?°   *begging favors*
    Have I no harvest but a thorn
    To let me blood, and not restore
What I have lost with cordial° fruit?   *life-giving*
        Sure there was wine   10
    Before my sighs did dry it; there was corn
    Before my tears did drown it.
Is the year only lost to me?
    Have I no bays° to crown it,   *laurel wreaths symbolizing honor*
No flowers, no garlands gay? All blasted?   15
        All wasted?
    Not so, my heart; but there is fruit,
        And thou hast hands.
    Recover all thy sigh-blown age
On double pleasures: leave thy cold dispute   20
Of what is fit and not. Forsake thy cage,

Thy rope of sands,
Which petty thoughts have made, and made to thee
Good cable, to enforce and draw,
And be thy law,   25
While thou didst wink and wouldst not see.
Away! take heed;
I will abroad.
Call in thy death's-head° there; tie up thy fears.   *skull*
He that forbears   30
To suit and serve his need,
Deserves his load."
But as I raved and grew more fierce and wild
At every word,
Methought I heard one calling, *Child!*   35
And I replied, *My Lord.*

Robert Herrick   *(1591–1674)*

To the Virgins, to Make Much of Time   *1648*

Gather ye rosebuds while ye may,
   Old time is still a-flying;
And this same flower that smiles today
   Tomorrow will be dying.

The glorious lamp of heaven, the sun,   5
   The higher he's a-getting,
The sooner will his race be run,
   And nearer he's to setting.

That age is best which is the first,
   When youth and blood are warmer;   10
But being spent, the worse, and worst
   Times still succeed the former.

Then be not coy, but use your time,
   And, while ye may, go marry;
For, having lost but once your prime,   15
   You may forever tarry.

A. E. Housman   *(1859–1936)*

Is My Team Plowing   *1896*

"Is my team plowing
   That I was used to drive
And hear the harness jingle
   When I was man alive?"

Ay, the horses trample,   5
   The harness jingles now;
No change though you lie under
   The land you used to plow.

"Is football playing
   Along the river shore,   10
With lads to chase the leather,
   Now I stand up no more?"

Ay, the ball is flying,
   The lads play heart and soul;
The goal stands up, the keeper   15
   Stands up to keep the goal.

"Is my girl happy,
   That I thought hard to leave,
And has she tired of weeping
   As she lies down at eve?"   20

Ay, she lies down lightly,
   She lies not down to weep:
Your girl is well contented.
   Be still, my lad, and sleep.

"Is my friend hearty,   25
   Now I am thin and pine,
And has he found to sleep in
   A better bed than mine?"

Yes, lad, I lie easy,
   I lie as lads would choose;   30
I cheer a dead man's sweetheart,
   Never ask me whose.

A. E. Housman   *(1859–1936)*

Be Still, My Soul, Be Still   *1896*

Be still, my soul, be still; the arms you bear are brittle,
   Earth and high heaven are fixt of old and founded strong.
Think rather,—call to thought, if now you grieve a little,
   The days when we had rest, O soul, for they were long.

Men loved unkindness then, but lightless in the quarry   5
   I slept and saw not; tears fell down, I did not mourn;
Sweat ran and blood sprang out and I was never sorry:
   Then it was well with me, in days ere I was born.

Now, and I muse for why and never find the reason,
    I pace the earth, and drink the air, and feel the sun.   10
Be still, be still, my soul; it is but for a season:
    Let us endure an hour and see injustice done.

Ay, look: high heaven and earth ail from the prime
        foundation;
    All thoughts to rive° the heart are here, and all are vain: *tear*   15
Horror and scorn and hate and fear and indignation—
    Oh why did I awake? when shall I sleep again?

A. E. Housman   *(1859–1936)*

To an Athlete Dying Young   *1896*

The time you won your town the race
We chaired you through the market-place;
Man and boy stood cheering by,
And home we brought you shoulder-high.

Today, the road all runners come,   5
Shoulder-high we bring you home,
And set you at your threshold down,
Townsman of a stiller town.

Smart lad, to slip betimes° away   *early*
From fields where glory does not stay   10
And early though the laurel grows
It withers quicker than the rose.

Eyes the shady night has shut
Cannot see the record cut,
And silence sounds no worse than cheers   15
After earth has stopped the ears:

Now you will not swell the rout
Of lads that wore their honors out,
Runners whom renown outran
And the name died before the man.   20

So set, before its echoes fade,
The fleet° foot on the sill of shade,   *speedy*
And hold to the low lintel° up   *low beam*
The still-defended challenge-cup.

And round that early-laureled head   25
Will flock to gaze the strengthless dead,

And find unwithered on its curls
The garland briefer than a girl's.

Langston Hughes   *(1902–1967)*

Ballad of the Landlord   1940

Landlord, landlord,
My roof has sprung a leak.
Don't you 'member I told you about it
Way last week?

Landlord, landlord,   5
These steps is broken down.
When you come up yourself
It's a wonder you don't fall down.

Ten Bucks you say I owe you?
Ten Bucks you say is due?   10
Well, that's Ten Bucks more'n I'll pay you
Till you fix this house up new.

What? You gonna get eviction orders?
You gonna cut off my heat?
You gonna take my furniture and   15
Throw it in the street?

Um-huh! You talking high and mighty.
Talk on—till you get through.
You ain't gonna be able to say a word
If I land my fist on you.   20

Police! Police!
Come and get this man!
He's trying to ruin the government
And overturn the land!

Copper's whistle!   25
Patrol bell!
Arrest.

Precinct Station.
Iron cell.
Headlines in press: 30

MAN THREATENS LANDLORD
TENANT HELD NO BAIL
JUDGE GIVES NEGRO 90 DAYS IN COUNTY JAIL

Langston Hughes   *(1902–1967)*

End   *1959*

There are
No clocks on the wall,
And no time,
No shadows that move
From dawn to dusk   5
Across the floor.

There is neither light
Nor dark
Outside the door.

There is no door!   10

Ted Hughes   *(born 1930)*

Hawk Roosting   *1959*

I sit in the top of the wood, my eyes closed.
Inaction, no falsifying dream
Between my hooked head and hooked feet:
Or in sleep rehearse perfect kills and eat.

The convenience of the high trees!   5
The air's buoyancy and the sun's ray
Are of advantage to me;
And the earth's face upward for my inspection.

My feet are locked upon the rough bark.
It took the whole of Creation   10
To produce my foot, my each feather:
Now I hold Creation in my foot
Or fly up, and revolve it all slowly—
I kill where I please because it is all mine.

There is no sophistry° in my body: *plausible but fallacious argument*   15
My manners are tearing off heads—

The allotment of death.
For the one path of my flight is direct
Through the bones of the living.
No arguments assert my right: 20

The sun is behind me.
Nothing has changed since I began.
My eye has permitted no change.
I am going to keep things like this.

Vicente Huidobro   *(1892–1948)*

Ars Poetica   *1963*

TRANSLATED BY DAVID M. GUSS

Let poetry be like a key
Opening a thousand doors.
A leaf falls; something flies by;
Let all the eye sees be created
And the soul of the listener tremble.   5

Invent new worlds and watch your word;
The adjective, when it doesn't give life, kills it.

We are in the age of nerves.
The muscle hangs,
Like a memory, in museums;   10
But we are not the weaker for it:
True vigor
Resides in the head.

Oh Poets, why sing of roses!
Let them flower in your poems;   15
For us alone
Do all things live beneath the Sun.

The poet is a little God.

Ben Jonson   *(1572–1637)*

Song: To Celia   *1616*

Drink to me only with thine eyes,
And I will pledge with mine;
Or leave a kiss but in the cup,
And I'll not look for wine.
The thirst that from the soul doth rise,   5
Doth ask a drink divine:
But might I of Jove's° nectar sup,   *Roman name of Zeus*
I would not change for thine.

I sent thee late° a rosy wreath,   *recently*
Not so much honoring thee,   10
As giving it a hope, that there
It could not withered be.
But thou thereon didst only breathe,
And sentst it back to me;
Since when it grows and smells, I swear,   15
Not of itself, but thee.

John Keats   *(1795–1821)*

A Thing of Beauty Is a Joy for Ever   *1820*

from Endymion

A thing of beauty is a joy for ever:
Its loveliness increases; it will never
Pass into nothingness; but still will keep
A bower° quiet for us, and a sleep   *a quiet, protected arbor*
Full of sweet dreams, and health, and quiet breathing.   5
Therefore, on every morrow, are we wreathing
A flowery band to bind us to the earth,
Spite of despondence,° of the inhuman dearth   *in spite of despair*
Of noble natures, of the gloomy days,
Of all the unhealthy and o'er-darkened ways   10
Made for our searching: yes, in spite of all,
Some shape of beauty moves away the pall°   *the dark cloud*
From our dark spirits. Such the sun, the moon,
Trees old and young, sprouting a shady boon°   *a welcome shade*
For simple sheep; and such are daffodils   15
With the green world they live in; and clear rills
That for themselves a cooling covert make
'Gainst the hot season; the mid-forest brake,°   *the thicket in the middle of*
Rich with a sprinkling of fair musk-rose blooms: *the fores of the tragic fatest*
And such too is the grandeur of the dooms   20
We have imagined for the mighty dead;
All lovely tales that we have heard or read:
An endless fountain of immortal drink,
Pouring unto us from the heaven's brink.
Nor do we merely feel these essences   25
For one short hour; no, even as the trees
That whisper round a temple become soon
Dear as the temple's self, so does the moon,
The passion poesy,° glories infinite,   *our passionate feeling for poetry*
Haunt us till they become a cheering light   30
Unto our souls, and bound to us so fast,
That, whether there be shine, or gloom o'ercast,
They always must be with us, or we die.

John Keats   *(1795–1821)*

La Belle Dame sans Merci   *1819*

O what can ail thee, Knight at arms,
    Alone and palely loitering?
The sedge has withered from the Lake
    And no birds sing!

O what can ail thee, Knight at arms,   5
    So haggard, and so woebegone?
The squirrel's granary is full
    And the harvest's done.

I see a lily on thy brow
    With anguish moist and fever dew,   10
And on thy cheeks a fading rose
    Fast withereth too.

I met a Lady in the Meads,
    Full beautiful, a faery's child,
Her hair was long, her foot was light   15
    And her eyes were wild.

I made a Garland for her head,
    And bracelets too, and fragrant Zone;°   *sash*
She looked at me as she did love
    And made sweet moan.   20

I set her on my pacing steed
    And nothing else saw all day long,
For sidelong would she bend and sing
    A faery's song.

She found me roots of relish sweet,   25
    And honey wild, and manna dew,
And sure in language strange she said
    "I love thee true."

She took me to her elfin grot°   *grotto*
    And there she wept and sighed full sore,   30
And there I shut her wild wild eyes
    With kisses four.

And there she lulléd me asleep,
    And there I dreamed, Ah Woe betide!
The latest dream I ever dreamt   35
    On the cold hill side.

I saw pale Kings, and Princes too,
    Pale warriors, death-pale were they all;
They cried, "La belle dame sans merci°   *the cruel lady for*
    Thee hath in thrall!"   40

I saw their starved lips in the gloam
    With horrid warning gapéd wide,
And I awoke, and found me here
    On the cold hill's side.

And this is why I sojourn here,   45
    Alone and palely loitering;
Though the sedge is withered from the Lake
    And no birds sing.

John Keats   (1795–1821)

Ode to a Nightingale   1820

1

My heart aches, and a drowsy numbness pains
    My sense, as though of hemlock° I had drunk,   *poison*
Or emptied some dull opiate to the drains
    One minute past, and Lethe-wards° had sunk: *toward Lethe, mythical under-*
'Tis not through envy of thy happy lot,   *world river of forgetfulness*   5
    But being too happy in thine happiness—
        That thou, light-wingèd Dryad° of the trees,   *wood nymph*
        In some melodious plot
Of beechen green, and shadows numberless,
    Singest of summer in full-throated ease.   10

2

O, for a draught of vintage!° that hath been   *drink of wine*
    Cooled a long age in the deep-delvèd° earth,   *dug out deep*
Tasting of Flora° and the country green,   *Roman goddess of flowers*
    Dance, and Provençal song,° and sunburnt mirth!   *songs of Provence, in*
O for a beaker full of the warm South,   *southern France*   15
    Full of the true, the blushful Hippocrene,°   *foundation of the Muses in Greece*
        With beaded bubbles winking at the brim,
        And purple-stainèd mouth;
That I might drink, and leave the world unseen,
    And with thee fade away into the forest dim: 20

3

Fade far away, dissolve, and quite forget
    What thou among the leaves hast never known,
The weariness, the fever, and the fret
    Here, where men sit and hear each other groan;
Where palsy shakes a few, sad, last gray hairs,   25
    Where youth grows pale, and specter-thin, and dies,
        Where but to think is to be full of sorrow
        And leaden-eyed despairs,
Where Beauty cannot keep her lustrous° eyes,   *shining*
    Or new Love pine at them beyond tomorrow.   30

4

Away! away! for I will fly to thee,
    Not charioted by Bacchus and his pards,°   *god of wine and his leopards*
But on the viewless° wings of Poesy,   *invisible*
    Though the dull brain perplexes and retards:
Already with thee! tender is the night,   35
    And haply the Queen-Moon is on her throne,
        Clustered around by all her starry Fays;°   *fairies*

But here there is no light,
            Save what from heaven is with the breezes blown
                  Through verdurous° glooms and winding   *filled with green vegetation*   40
                  mossy ways.

5

I cannot see what flowers are at my feet,
            Nor what soft incense hangs upon the boughs,
But, in embalmed° darkness, guess each sweet   *perfumed*
            Wherewith the seasonable month endows
The grass, the thicket, and the fruit tree wild;   45
            White hawthorn, and the pastoral eglantine;°   *wood roses*
                  Fast fading violets covered up in leaves;
                        And mid-May's eldest child,
            The coming musk-rose, full of dewy wine,
                  The murmurous haunt of flies on summer eves.   50

6

Darkling° I listen; and for many a time   *in darkness*
            I have been half in love with easeful Death,
Called him soft names in many a musèd rhyme,
            To take into the air my quiet breath;
Now more than ever seems it rich to die,   55
            To cease upon the midnight with no pain,
                  While thou art pouring forth thy soul abroad
                        In such an ecstasy!
            Still wouldst thou sing, and I have ears in vain—
                  To thy high requiem become a sod.   60

7

Thou wast not born for death, immortal Bird!
            No hungry generations tread thee down;
The voice I hear this passing night was heard
            In ancient days by emperor and clown:°   *peasant*
Perhaps the selfsame song that found a path   65
            Through the sad heart of Ruth,° when, sick for home,   *of the biblical*
                  She stood in tears amid the alien corn;   *Book of Ruth*
                        The same that ofttimes hath
            Charmed magic casements, opening on the foam
                  Of perilous seas, in faery lands forlorn.   70

8

Forlorn! the very word is like a bell
            To toll me back from thee to my sole self!
Adieu! the fancy cannot cheat so well
            As she is famed to do, deceiving elf.
Adieu! adieu! thy plaintive anthem fades   75
            Past the near meadows, over the still stream,
                  Up the hill side; and now 'tis buried deep

In the next valley-glades:
Was it a vision, or a waking dream?
Fled is that music.—Do I wake or sleep?   80

John Keats   *(1795–1821)*

When I Have Fears   *1818*

When I have fears that I may cease to be
   Before my pen has gleaned my teeming° brain,   *fertile*
Before high-pilèd books, in charactery,°   *written symbols*
   Hold like rich garners° the full-ripened grain;   *granaries*
When I behold, upon the night's starred face,   5
   Huge cloudy symbols of a high romance,
And think that I may never live to trace
   Their shadows, with the magic hand of chance;
And when I feel, fair creature of an hour,
   That I shall never look upon thee more,   10
Never have relish in the faery° power   *magical*
   Of unreflecting love!—then on the shore
Of the wide world I stand alone, and think
Till Love and Fame to nothingness do sink.

Galway Kinnell   *(born 1927)*

Wait   *1980*

Wait, for now.
Distrust everything if you have to.
But trust the hours. Haven't they
carried you everywhere, up to now?
Personal events will become interesting again.   5
Hair will become interesting.
Pain will become interesting.
Buds that open out of season will become interesting.
Second-hand gloves will become lovely again;
their memories are what give them   10
the need for other hands. And the desolation
of lovers is the same: that enormous emptiness
carved out of such tiny beings as we are
asks to be filled; the need
for the new love is faithfulness to the old.   15

Wait.
Don't go too early.
You're tired. But everyone's tired.
But no one is tired enough.

Only wait a little and listen: 20
music of hair,
music of pain,
music of looms weaving all our loves again.
Be there to hear it, it will be the only time,
most of all to hear   25
the flute of your whole existence,
rehearsed by the sorrows,
play itself into total exhaustion.

Etheridge Knight   *(born 1933)*

He Sees through Stone   1968

He sees through stone
he has the secret
eyes this old black one
who under prison skies
sits pressed by the sun   5
against the western wall
his pipe between purple gums
the years fall
like overripe plums
bursting red flesh   10
on the dark earth

his time is not my time
but I have known him
in a time gone

he led me trembling cold   15
into the dark forest
taught me the secret rites
to take a woman
to be true to my brothers
to make my spear drink   20
the blood
of my enemies

now black cats circle him
flash white teeth
snarl at the air   25
mashing green grass beneath
shining muscles
ears peeling his words
he smiles
he knows   30
the hunt the enemy
he has the secret eyes
he sees through stone

Maxine Kumin   *(born 1925)*   👁

Woodchucks   *1971*

Gassing the woodchucks didn't turn out right.
The knockout bomb from the Feed and Grain Exchange
was featured as merciful, quick at the bone
and the case we had against them was airtight,
both exits shoehorned shut with puddingstone,   5
but they had a sub-sub-basement out of range.

Next morning they turned up again, no worse
for the cyanide than we for our cigarettes
and state-store Scotch, all of us up to scratch.
They brought down the marigolds as a matter of course   10
and then took over the vegetable patch
nipping the broccoli shoots, beheading the carrots.

The food from our mouths, I said, righteously thrilling
to the feel of the .22, the bullets' neat noses.
I, a lapsed pacifist fallen from grace   15
puffed with Darwinian pieties for killing,
now drew a bead on the littlest woodchuck's face.
He died down in the everbearing roses.

Ten minutes later I dropped the mother. She
flipflopped in the air and fell, her needle teeth   20
still hooked in a leaf of early Swiss chard.
Another baby next. O one-two-three
the murderer inside me rose up hard,
the hawkeye killer came on stage forthwith.

There's one chuck left. Old wily fellow, he keeps   25
me cocked and ready day after day after day.

D. H. Lawrence   *(1885–1930)*

Snake   *1923*

A snake came to my water trough
On a hot, hot day, and I in pajamas for the heat,
To drink there.

In the deep, strange-scented shade of the great dark
    carob tree
I came down the steps with my pitcher   5
And must wait, must stand and wait, for there he was
    at the trough before me.

He reached down from a fissure in the earth-wall in the
    gloom   10

And trailed his yellow-brown slackness soft-bellied
      down, over the edge of the stone trough
And rested his throat upon the stone bottom,
And where the water had dripped from the tap, in a
      small clearness,   15
He sipped with his straight mouth,
Softly drank through his straight gums, into his slack
      long body,
Silently.

Someone was before me at my water trough,   20
And I, like a second comer, waiting.

He lifted his head from his drinking, as cattle do,
And looked at me vaguely, as drinking cattle do,
And flickered his two-forked tongue from his lips, and
      mused a moment,   25
And stooped and drank a little more,
Being earth brown, earth golden from the burning burning
      bowels of the earth
On the day of Sicilian July, with Etna smoking.

The voice of my education said to me   30
He must be killed,
For in Sicily the black, black snakes are innocent, the
      gold are venomous.

And voices in me said, If you were a man
You would take a stick and break him now, and finish   35
      him off.

But I must confess how I liked him,
How glad I was he had come like a guest in quiet, to
      drink at my water trough
And depart peaceful, pacified, and thankless,   40
Into the burning bowels of this earth.

Was it cowardice, that I dared not kill him?
Was it perversity, that I longed to talk to him?
Was it humility, to feel so honored?
I felt so honored.   45

And yet those voices:
If you were not afraid, you would kill him!

And truly I was afraid, I was most afraid
But even so, honored still more
That he should seek my hospitality   50
From out the dark door of the secret earth.

He drank enough
And lifted his head, dreamily, as one who has drunken,
And flickered his tongue like a forked night on the air,
      so black,   55

Seeming to lick his lips,
And looked around like a god, unseeing, into the air,
And slowly turned his head,
And slowly, very slowly, as if thrice adream,
Proceeded to draw his slow length curving round   60
And climb again the broken bank of my wall-face.

And as he put his head into that dreadful hole,
And as he slowly drew up, snake-easing his shoulders, and entered farther
A sort of horror, a sort of protest against his withdrawing into that horrid
    black hole,   65
Deliberately going into the blackness, and slowly drawing himself after,
Overcame me now his back was turned.

I looked around, I put down my pitcher,
I picked up a clumsy log
And threw it at the water trough with a clatter.   70

I think I did not hit him,
But suddenly that part of him that was left behind convulsed in
    undignified haste,
Writhed like lightning, and was gone
Into the black hole, the earth-lipped fissure in the wall-front,   75
At which, in the intense still noon, I stared with fascination.

And immediately I regretted it.
I thought how paltry, how vulgar, what a mean act!
I despised myself and the voices of my accursed human education.
And I thought of the albatross,   80
And I wished he would come back, my snake.

For he seemed to me again like a king,
Like a king in exile, uncrowned in the underworld,
Now due to be crowned again.

And so, I missed my chance with one of the lords   85
Of life.
And I have something to expiate;
A pettiness.

Audre Lorde   *(1934–1992)*

Conversation in Crisis   *1985*

I speak to you as a friend speaks
or a true lover
not out of friendship or love
but for a clear meeting
of self upon self   5

in sight of our hearth
but without fire.

I cherish your words that ring
like late summer thunders
to sing without octave   10
and fade, having spoken the season.
But I hear the false heat of this voice
as it dries up the sides of your words
coaxing melodies from your tongue
and this curled music is treason.   15

Must I die in your fever—
or, as the flames was, take cover
in your heart's culverts
crouched like a stranger
under the scorched leaves of your other burnt loves   20
until the storm passes over?

Robert Lowell   *(1917–1977)*

Skunk Hour   *1959*

(for Elizabeth Bishop)

Nautilus Island's° hermit   *in Castine, Maine*
heiress still lives through winter in her Spartan cottage;
her sheep still graze above the sea.
Her son's a bishop. Her farmer
is first selectman° in our village;   *elected official*   5
she's in her dotage.°   *second childhood*

Thirsting for
the hierarchic privacy
of Queen Victoria's century,
she buys up all   10
the eyesores facing her shore,
and lets them fall.

The season's ill—
we've lost our summer millionaire,
who seemed to leap from an L. L. Bean°   *sporting goods company*   15
catalogue. His nine-knot yawl°   *boat*
was auctioned off to lobstermen.
A red fox stain covers Blue Hill.

And now our fairy
decorator brightens his shop for fall;   20
his fishnet's filled with orange cork,
orange, his cobbler's bench and awl;
there is no money in his work,

he'd rather marry.

One dark night,   25
my Tudor Ford climbed the hill's skull;
I watched for love-cars. Lights turned down,
they lay together, hull to hull,
Where the graveyard shelves on the town. . . .
My mind's not right.   30

A car radio bleats,
"Love, O careless Love. . . ." I hear
my ill-spirit sob in each blood cell,
as if my hand were at its throat. . . .
I myself am hell;   35
nobody's here—

only skunks, that search
in the moonlight for a bite to eat.
They march on their soles up Main Street:
white stripes, moonstruck eyes' red fire   40
under the chalk-dry and spar spire°   *pole used as a mast*
of the Trinitarian Church.

I stand on top
of our back steps and breathe the rich air—
a mother skunk with her column of kittens swills the garbage pail.   45
She jabs her wedge-head in a cup
of sour cream, drops her ostrich tail,
and will not scare.

Christopher Marlowe   *(1564–1593)*

The Passionate Shepherd to His Love   *1599*

Come live with me and be my love,
And we will all the pleasures prove°   *try*
That valleys, groves, hills, and fields,
Woods, or steepy mountain yields.

And we will sit upon the rocks,   5
Seeing the shepherds feed their flocks,
By shallow rivers to whose falls
Melodious birds sing madrigals.°   *harmonic songs*

And I will make thee beds of roses
And a thousand fragrant posies,°   *bouquets* 10
A cap of flowers, and a kirtle°   *skirt*
Embroidered all with leaves of myrtle;

A gown made of the finest wool
Which from our pretty lambs we pull;

Fair lined slippers for the cold,   15
With buckles of the purest gold;

A belt of straw and ivy buds,
With coral clasps and amber studs:
And if these pleasures may thee move,
Come live with me, and be my love.   20

The shepherds' swains° shall dance and sing   *lowers*
For thy delight each May morning:
If these delights thy mind may move,
Then live with me and be my love.

Andrew Marvell   *(1621–1678)*

The Definition of Love   *before 1678*

My Love is of a birth as rare
As 'tis, for object, strange and high;
It was begotten by Despair
Upon Impossibility.

Magnanimous Despair alone   5
Could show me so divine a thing,
Where feeble Hope could never have flown
But vainly flapped its tinsel wing.

And yet I quickly might arrive
Where my extended soul is fixed;   10
But Fate does iron wedges drive,
And always crowds itself betwixt.°   *between*

For Fate with jealous eye does see
Two perfect loves, nor lets them close;°   *write*
Their union would her ruin be,   15
And her tyrannic power depose.

And therefore her decrees of steel
Us as the distant poles have placed
(Though Love's whole world on us doth wheel),
Not by themselves to be embraced,   20

Unless the giddy heaven fall,
And earth some new convulsion tear,°   *be torn by a new upheaval*
And, us to join, the world should all
Be cramped into a planisphere.°   *sphere projected on a plane surface*

As lines, so loves oblique may well   25
Themselves in every angle greet;°   *may converge*
But ours, so truly parallel,
Though infinite, can never meet.

Therefore the love which us doth bind,
But Fate so enviously debars,°   *prevents*   30
Is the conjunction of the mind,
And opposition of the stars.

James Merrill   *(1926–1995)*

Charles on Fire   *1966*

Another evening we sprawled about discussing
Appearances. And it was the consensus
That while uncommon physical good looks
Continued to launch one, as before, in life
(Among its vaporous eddies and false calms),   5
Still, as one of us said into his beard,
"Without your intellectual and spiritual
Values, man, you are sunk." No one but squared
The shoulders of his own unloveliness.
Long-suffering Charles, having cooked and served the meal,   10
Now brought out little tumblers finely etched
He filled with amber liquor and then passed.
"Say," said the same young man, "in Paris, France,
They do it this way"—bounding to his feet
And touching a lit match to our host's full glass.   15
A blue flame, gentle, beautiful, came, went
Above the surface. In a hush that fell
We heard the vessel crack. The contents drained
As who should step down from a crystal coach.
Steward of spirits, Charles's glistening hand   20
All at once gloved itself in eeriness.
The moment passed. He made two quick sweeps and
Was flesh again. "It couldn't matter less,"
He said, but with a shocked, unconscious glance
Into the mirror. Finding nothing changed,   25
He filled a fresh glass and sank down among us.

W. S. Merwin   *(born 1927)*

For the Anniversary of My Death   *1967*

Every year without knowing it I have passed the day
When the last fires will wave to me
And the silence will set out
Tireless traveler
Like the beam of a lightless star   5

Then I will no longer
Find myself in life as in a strange garment

Surprised at the earth
And the love of one woman
And the shamelessness of men   10
As today writing after three days of rain
Hearing the wren sing and the falling cease
And bowing not knowing to what

Edna St. Vincent Millay   *(1892–1950)*

Pity Me Not Because the Light of Day   *1923*

Pity me not because the light of day
At close of day no longer walks the sky;
Pity me not for beauties passed away
From field and thicket as the years go by;
Pity me not the waning of the moon,   5
Nor that the ebbing tide goes out to sea,
Nor that man's desire is hushed so soon,
And you no longer look with love on me.
This have I known always: Love is no more
Than the wide blossom which the wind assails,   10
Than the great tide that treads the shifting shore,
Strewing fresh wreckage gathered in the gales:
Pity me that the heart is slow to learn
What the swift mind beholds at every turn.

John Milton   *(1608–1674)*

How Soon Hath Time   *1631*

How soon hath Time, the subtle thief of youth,
    Stoln on his wing my three and twentieth year!
    My hasting days fly on with full career,°   *full speed*
    But my late spring no bud or blossom shewth.°   *shows*
Perhaps my semblance° might deceive the truth,   *appearance*   5
    That I to manhood am arrived so near,
    And inward ripeness doth much less appear,
    That some more timely-happy spirits enduth.°   *endows*
Yet be it less or more, or soon or slow,
    It shall be still in strictest measure even   10
    To that same lot, however mean or high,
Toward which Time leads me, and the will of Heaven;
    All is, if I have grace to use it so,
    As ever in my great Taskmaster's eye.

Wilfred Owen   *(1893–1918)*

Anthem for Doomed Youth   1920

What passing-bells for these who die as cattle?
    Only the monstrous anger of the guns.
    Only the stuttering rifles' rapid rattle
Can patter out their hasty orisons.°   *prayers*
No mockeries now for them; no prayers nor bells,   5
    Nor any voice of mourning save the choirs—
The shrill, demented choirs of wailing shells;
    And bugles calling for them from sad shires.°   *shire horses*

What candles may be held to speed them all?
    Not in the hands of boys, but in their eyes   10
Shall shine the holy glimmers of good-byes.
    The pallor of girls' brows shall be their pall;
Their flowers the tenderness of patient minds,
And each slow dusk a drawing-down of blinds.

Ezra Pound   *(1885–1972)*

In a Station of the Metro   1916

The apparition of these faces in the crowd;
Petals on a wet, black bough.

Ezra Pound   *(1885–1972)*

The River-Merchant's Wife: A Letter   1915

(after Rihaku)°   *Japanese name for Li Po,*
                              an 81b-century Chinese poet

While my hair was still cut straight across my forehead
I played about the front gate, pulling flowers.
You came by on bamboo stilts, playing horse,
You walked about my seat, playing with blue plums.
And we went on living in the village of Chokan: 5
Two small people, without dislike or suspicion.

At fourteen I married My Lord you.
I never laughed, being bashful.
Lowering my head, I looked at the wall.
Called to, a thousand times, I never looked back.   10

At fifteen I stopped scowling,
I desired my dust to be mingled with yours
For ever and for ever and for ever.
Why should I climb the look out?

At sixteen you departed,
You went into far Ku-to-yen, by the river of swirling eddies,   15
And you have been gone five months.
The monkeys make sorrowful noise overhead.

You dragged your feet when you went out.
By the gate now, the moss is grown, the different mosses,
Too deep to clear them away!
The leaves fall early this autumn, in wind.   20
The paired butterflies are already yellow with August
Over the grass in the West garden;
They hurt me. I grow older,
If you are coming down through the narrows of the river Kiang,
Please let me know beforehand,   25
And I will come out to meet you
    As far as Cho-fu-Sa.

Sir Walter Raleigh   *(1552–1618)*

The Nymph's Reply to the Shepherd   *1600*

(A reply to Marlowe's "The Passionate Shepherd to His Love")

If all the world and love were young,
And truth in every shepherd's tongue,
These pretty pleasures might me move
To live with thee and be thy love.

Time drives the flocks from field to fold   5
When rivers rage and rocks grow cold,
And Philomel° becometh dumb;   *the nightingale*
The rest complains of cares to come.

The flowers do fade, and wanton fields
To wayward winter reckoning yields;   10
A honey tongue, a heart of gall,°   *bitter heart*
Is fancy's spring, but sorrow's fall.

Thy gowns, thy shoes, thy beds of roses,
Thy cap, thy kirtle,° and thy posies   *dress*
Soon break, soon wither, soon forgotten—   15
In folly ripe, in reason rotten.

Thy belt of straw and ivy buds,
Thy coral clasps and amber studs,
All these in me no means can move
To come to thee and be thy love.   20

But could youth last and love still breed,
Had joys no date° nor age no need,   *no end*

Then these delights my mind might move
To live with thee and be thy love.

Dudley Randall   *(born 1914)*

Ballad of Birmingham   1969

(On the bombing of a church in Birmingham, Alabama, 1963)

"Mother dear, may I go downtown
Instead of out to play,
And march the streets of Birmingham
In a Freedom March today?"

"No, baby, no, you may not go,   5
For the dogs are fierce and wild,
And clubs and hoses, guns and jails
Aren't good for a little child."

"But, mother, I won't be alone.
Other children will go with me,   10
And march the streets of Birmingham
To make our country free."

"No, baby, no, you may not go,
For I fear those guns will fire.
But you may go to church instead   15
And sing in the children's choir."

She has combed and brushed her night-dark hair,
And bathed rose petal sweet.
And drawn white gloves on her small brown hands,
And white shoes on her feet.   20

The mother smiled to know her child
Was in the sacred place,
But that smile was the last smile
To come upon her face.

For when she heard the explosion,   25
Her eyes grew wet and wild.
She raced through the streets of Birmingham
Calling for her child.

She clawed through bits of glass and brick,
Then lifted out a shoe.   30
"Oh, here's the shoe my baby wore,
But, baby, where are you?"

Edwin Arlington Robinson   *(1869–1935)*

Eros Turannos°   *Tyrannical Eros (god of love)*   1916

She fears him, and will always ask
   What fated her to choose him;
She meets in his engaging mask
   All reasons to refuse him;
But what she meets and what she fears   5
Are less than are the downward years,
Drawn slowly to the foamless weirs
   Of age, were she to lose him.

Between a blurred sagacity
   That once had power to sound him,   10
And Love, that will not let him be
   The Judas that she found him,
Her pride assuages her almost,
As if it were alone the cost—
He sees that he will not be lost,   15
   And waits and looks around him.

A sense of ocean and old trees
   Envelops and allures him;
Tradition, touching all he sees,
   Beguiles and reassures him;   20
And all her doubts of what he says
Are dimmed with what she knows of days—
Till even prejudice delays
   And fades, and she secures him.

The falling leaf inaugurates   25
   The reign of her confusion;
The pounding wave reverberates
   The dirge of her illusion;
And home, where passion lived and died,
Becomes a place where she can hide,   30
While all the town and harbor side
   Vibrate with her seclusion.

We tell you, tapping on our brows,
   The story as it should be—
As if the story of a house   35
   Were told or ever could be;
We'll have no kindly veil between
Her visions and those we have seen—
As if we guessed what hers have been,
   Or what they are or would be.   40

Meanwhile we do no harm; for they
  That with a god have striven,
Not hearing much of what we say,
  Take what the god has given;
Though like waves breaking it may be,   45
Or like a changed familiar tree,
Or like a stairway to the sea
  Where down the blind are driven.

Theodore Roethke   *(1908–1963)*

I Knew a Woman   *1958*

I knew a woman, lovely in her bones,
When small birds sighed, she would sigh back at them;
Ah, when she moved, she moved more ways than one:
The shapes a bright container can contain!
Of her choice virtues only gods should speak,   5
Or English poets who grew up on Greek
(I'd have them sing in chorus, cheek to cheek).

How well her wishes went! She stroked my chin,
She taught me Turn, and Counter-turn,
     and Stand;°   *dance moves of chorus in Greek plays*
She taught me Touch, that undulant° white skin;   *wavy*   10
I nibbled meekly from her proffered hand;
She was the sickle; I, poor I, the rake,
Coming behind her for her pretty sake
(But what prodigious mowing we did make).

Love likes a gander, and adores a goose: 15
Her full lips pursed, the errant° note to seize;   *straying*
She played it quick, she played it light and loose,
My eyes, they dazzled at her flowing knees;
Her several parts could keep a pure repose,
Or one hip quiver with a mobile nose   20
(She moved in circles, and those circles moved).

Let seed be grass, and grass turn into hay:
I'm martyr to a motion not my own;
What's freedom for? To know eternity.
I swear she cast a shadow white as stone.   25
But who would count eternity in days?
These old bones live to learn her wanton ways:
(I measure time by how a body sways).

Wendy Rose   *(born 1948)*

I Expected My Skin and My Blood to Ripen   1977

*"When the blizzard subsided four days later
(after the massacre), a burial party was sent to
Wounded Knee. A long trench was dug. Many of
the bodies were stripped by whites who went out
in order to get the ghost shirts and other accou-
trements the Indians wore . . . the frozen bodies
were thrown into the trench stiff and naked . . .
only a handful of items remain in private hands
. . . exposure to snow has stiffened the leggings
and moccasins and all the objects show the
effects of age and long use. . . ." There follows:
moccasins at $140, hide scraper at $350, buckskin shirt at $1200, woman's leggings at $275,
bone breastplate at $1000.*

PLAINS INDIAN ART SALES CATALOG
BY KENNETH CANFIELD

I expected my skin and my blood
to ripen
not be ripped from my bones;
like green fruit I am peeled
tasted, discarded; my seeds are stepped on   5
and crushed
as if there were no future. Now
there has been
no past.
My own body gave up the beads   10
my own arms handed the babies away
to be strung on bayonets, to be counted
one by one like rosary stones and then
to be tossed to each side of life
as if the pain of their borning   15
had never been.
My feet were frozen to the leather,
pried apart, left behind—bits of flesh
on the moccasins, bits of papery deerhide
on the bones. My back was stripped   20
of its cover, its quilling intact; was torn,
was taken away, was restored.
My leggings were taken like in a rape
and shriveled to the size of stick figures
like they had never felt   25
the push of my strong woman's body
walking in the hills.

It was my own baby whose cradleboard I held.
would've put her in my mouth
like a snake   30
if I could, would've turned her
into a bush or old rock
if there'd been enough magic
to work such changes. Not enough magic
even to stop the bullets.   35
Not enough magic
to stop the scientists.
Not enough magic
to stop the collectors.

Anne Sexton   *(1928–1974)*

The Truth the Dead Know   *1961*

*For my mother, born March 1902, died March 1959 and my father, born
February 1900, died June 1959*

Gone, I say and walk from church,
refusing the stiff procession to the grave,
letting the dead ride alone in the hearse.
It is June. I am tired of being brave.

We drive to the Cape. I cultivate   5
myself where the sun gutters from the sky,
where the sea swings in like an iron gate
and we touch. In another country people die.

My darling, the wind falls in like stones
from the whitehearted water and when we touch   10
we enter touch entirely. No one's alone.
Men kill for this, or for as much.

And what of the dead? They lie without shoes
in their stone boats. They are more like stone
than the sea would be if it stopped. They refuse   15
to be blessed, throat, eye and knucklebone.

William Shakespeare   *(1564–1616)*

Sonnet 116   *1609*

Let me not to the marriage of true minds
Admit impediments. Love is not love
Which alters when it alteration finds,°   *when it encounters change*
Or bends with the remover to remove:°   *responds to inconstancy*
Oh, no! it is an ever-fixèd mark,   *with inconstancy*   5

That looks on tempests and is never shaken;
It is the star to every wandering bark,°   boat
Whose worth's unknown, although his height be taken.°   *although its elevation can*
Love's not Time's fool, though rosy lips and cheeks   *be measured*
Within his bending sickle's compass come;   10
Love alters not with his brief hours and weeks,
But bears it out even to the edge of doom.°   *Day of Judgment*
If this be error and upon me proved,
I never writ,° nor no man ever loved.   *wrote*

Percy Bysshe Shelley   *(1792–1822)*

To a Skylark   *1820*

  Hail to thee, blithe Spirit!
    Bird thou never wert,
  That from Heaven, or near it,
    Pourest thy full heart
In profuse strains° of unpremeditated art.   *melodies*   5

  Higher still and higher
    From the earth thou springest
  Like a cloud of fire;
    The blue deep thou wingest,
And singing still dost soar, and soaring ever singest.   10

  In the golden lightning
    Of the sunken sun,
  O'er which clouds are brightening,
    Thou dost float and run;
Like an unbodied joy whose race is just begun.   15

  The pale purple even
    Melts around thy flight;
  Like a star of Heaven,
    In the broad daylight
Thou are unseen, but yet I hear thy shrill delight,   20

  Keen as are the arrows
    Of that silver sphere,°   *star*
  Whose intense lamp narrows
    In the white dawn clear
Until we hardly see—we feel that it is there.   25

  All the earth and air
    With thy voice is loud,
  As, when night is bare,
    From one lonely cloud
The moon rains out her beams, and Heaven is overflowed.   30

What thou art we know not;
　　What is most like thee?
From rainbow clouds there flow not
　　Drops so bright to see
As from thy presence showers a rain of melody.　　　　　　　　　35

Like a Poet hidden
　　In the light of thought,
Singing hymns unbidden,
　　Till the world is wrought°　　　　　　　　　*moved*
To sympathy with hopes and fears it heeded not:　　　　　　　40

Like a high-born maiden
　　In a palace tower,
Soothing her love-laden
　　Soul in secret hour
With music sweet as love, which overflows her bower:°　　*private chamber*　45

Like a glowworm golden
　　In a dell° of dew,　　　　　　　　　*hideaway*
Scattering unbeholden
　　Its aërial hue
Among the flowers and grass, which screen it from the view!　　50

Like a rose embowered
　　In its own green leaves,
By warm winds deflowered,
　　Till the scent it gives
Makes faint with too much sweet those heavy-wingèd thieves:　　55

Sound of vernal° showers　　　　　　　　　*spring*
　　On the twinkling grass,
Rain-awakened flowers,
　　All that ever was
Joyous, and clear, and fresh, thy music doth surpass:　　　　　60

Teach us, Sprite° or Bird,　　　　　　　　　*spirit*
　　What sweet thoughts are thine:
I have never heard
　　Praise of love or wine
That panted forth a flood of rapture so divine.　　　　　　　65

Chorus Hymeneal°　　　　　　　　　*as for a wedding*
　　Or triumphal chant,
Matched with thine would be all
　　But an empty vaunt,°　　　　　　　　　*boast*
A thing wherein we feel there is some hidden want.　　　　　　70

What objects are the fountains
　　Of thy happy strain?
What fields, or waves, or mountains?
　　What shapes of sky or plain?
What love of thine own kind? what ignorance of pain?　　　　　75

With thy clear keen joyance°   *joyful song*
    Languor° cannot be: *sluggishness*
Shadow of annoyance
    Never came near thee:
Thou lovest—but never knew love's sad satiety.   80

Waking or asleep,
    Thou of death must deem
Things more true and deep
    Than we mortals dream,
Or how could thy notes flow in such a crystal stream?   85

We look before and after,
    And pine° for what is not: *yearn*
Our sincerest laughter
    With some pain is fraught;°   *burdened*
Our sweetest songs are those that tell of saddest thought.   90

Yet if we could scorn
    Hate, and pride, and fear;
If we were things born
    Not to shed a tear,
I know not how thy joy we ever should come near.   95

Better than all measures
    Of delightful sound,
Better than all treasures
    That in books are found,
Thy skill to poet were, thou scorner of the ground!   100

Teach me half the gladness
    That thy brain must know,
Such harmonious madness
    From my lips would flow
The world should listen then—as I am listening now.   105

Gary Snyder *(born 1930)*

After Work   *1959*

The shack and a few trees
float in the blowing fog

I pull out your blouse,
warm my cold hands
    on your breasts.   5
you laugh and shudder
peeling garlic by the
    hot iron stove.
bring in the axe, the rake,
the wood   10

we'll lean on the wall
against each other
stew simmering on the fire
as it grows dark
        drinking wine.   15

Cathy Song   *(born 1955)*

Lost Sister   *1983*

1

In China,
even the peasants
named their first daughters
Jade—
the stone that in the far fields   5
could moisten the dry season,
could make men move mountains
for the healing green of the inner hills
glistening like slices of winter melon.

And the daughters were grateful: 10
They never left home.
To move freely was a luxury
stolen from them at birth.
Instead, they gathered patience;
learning to walk in shoes   15
the size of teacups,
without breaking—
the arc of their movements
as dormant as the rooted willow,
as redundant as the farmyard hens.   20
But they traveled far
in surviving,
learning to stretch the family rice,
to quiet the demons,
the noisy stomachs.   25

2

There is a sister
across the ocean,
who relinquished her name,
diluting jade green
with the blue of the Pacific.   30
Rising with a tide of locusts,
she swarmed with others
to inundate another shore.
In America,

there are many roads   35
and women can stride along with men.

But in another wilderness,
the possibilities,
the loneliness,
can strangulate like jungle vines.   40
The meager provisions and sentiments
of once belonging—
fermented roots, Mah-Jong° tiles and firecrackers—set but   *Chinese game*
a flimsy household
in a forest of nightless cities.   45
A giant snake rattles above,
spewing black clouds into your kitchen.
Dough-faced landlords
slip in and out of your keyholes,
making claims you don't understand,   50
tapping into your communication systems
of laundry lines and restaurant chains.

You find you need China:
your one fragile identification,
a jade link   55
handcuffed to your wrist.
You remember your mother
who walked for centuries,
footless—
and like her,   60
you have left no footprints,
but only because
there is an ocean in between,
the unremitting space of your rebellion.

Wallace Stevens   *(1879–1955)*

Anecdote of the Jar   *1923*

I placed a jar in Tennessee,
And round it was, upon a hill.
It made the slovenly wilderness
Surround that hill.

The wilderness rose up to it,   5
And sprawled around, no longer wild.
The jar was round upon the ground
And tall and of a port in air.

It took dominion everywhere.
The jar was gray and bare.   10
It did not give of bird or bush,
Like nothing else in Tennessee.

Wallace Stevens   *(1879–1955)*

Thirteen Ways of Looking at a Blackbird   *1923*

1

Among twenty snowy mountains,
The only moving thing
Was the eye of the blackbird.

2

I was of three minds,
Like a tree   5
In which there are three blackbirds.

3

The blackbird whirled in the autumn winds.
It was a small part of the pantomime.

4

A man and a woman
Are one.
A man and a woman and a blackbird   10
Are one.

5

I do not know which to prefer,
The beauty of inflections
Or the beauty of innuendoes,   15
The blackbird whistling
Or just after.

6

Icicles filled the long window
With barbaric glass.
The shadow of the blackbird   20
Crossed it, to and fro.
The mood
Traced in the shadow
An indecipherable cause.

7

O thin men of Haddam,°   *an industrial Connecticut* 25
Why do you imagine golden birds?   *town*
Do you not see how the blackbird
Walks around the feet
Of the women about you?

8

I know noble accents   30
And lucid,° inescapable rhythms;   *clear*
But I know, too,
That the blackbird is involved
In what I know.

9

When the blackbird flew out of sight,   35
It marked the edge
Of one of many circles.

10

At the sight of blackbirds
Flying in a green light,
Even the bawds of euphony°   *those who prostitute themselves to beautiful sounds*   40
Would cry out sharply.

11

He rode over Connecticut
In a glass coach.
Once, a fear pierced him,
In that he mistook   45
The shadow of his equipage°   *carriage*
For blackbirds.

12

The river is moving.
The blackbird must be flying.

13

It was evening all afternoon.   50
It was snowing.
And it was going to snow.
The blackbird sat
In the cedar-limbs.

Mark Strand   *(born 1934)*

Eating Poetry   *1967*

Ink runs from the corners of my mouth.
There is no happiness like mine.
I have been eating poetry.

The librarian does not believe what she sees.
Her eyes are sad   5
and she walks with her hands in her dress.

The poems are gone.
The light is dim.
The dogs are on the basement stairs and coming up.

Their eyeballs roll,   10
their blond legs burn like brush.
The poor librarian begins to stamp her feet and weep.

She does not understand.
When I get on my knees and lick her hand,
she screams.   15

I am a new man.
I snarl at her and bark.
I romp with joy in the bookish dark.

Edward Taylor   *(1645–1729)*

The Golden Key   *1682*

Earth once was Paradise of Heaven below,
Till ink-faced sin had it with poison stocked
And chased this Paradise away into
Heaven's upmost loft, and it in Glory locked.
But thou, sweet Lord, hast with thy golden key
unlocked the door, and made a golden day.

•   5

Hell's spider gets
His entrails spun to whipcords thus
And woven to nets
and sets.

To tangle Adam's race   10
In his stratagems
To their destruction, spoiled, made base
By venom things—
Damned sins.

But, mighty, gracious Lord,   15
Communicate
Thy grace to break the cord, afford
Us Glory's gate
and state.

•   20

Who blew the bellows of His furnace vast?
Or held the mold wherein the world was cast?
Who laid its cornerstone? Or whose command?
Where stand the pillars upon which it stands?
Who spread its canopy, or curtains spun?   25
Who in this bowling alley bowled the sun?

Alfred, Lord Tennyson   *(1809–1892)*

Ulysses   1833

It little profits° that an idle king,   *it is little use*
By this still hearth, among these barren crags,
Matched with an agéd wife, I mete and dole°   *measure out*
Unequal laws unto a savage race,
That hoard, and sleep, and feed, and know not me.   5
I cannot rest from travel; I will drain
Life to the lees.° All times I have enjoyed   *dregs*
Greatly, have suffered greatly, both with those
That love me, and alone; on shore, and when
Through scudding drifts the rainy Hyades   10
Vexed the dim sea. I am become a name;
For always roaming with a hungry heart
Much have I seen and known—cities of men
And manners, climates, councils, governments,
Myself not least, but honored of them all—   15
And drunk delight of battle with my peers,
Far on the ringing plains of windy Troy.
I am a part of all that I have met;
Yet all experience is an arch wherethrough
Gleams that untraveled world whose margin fades   20
For ever and for ever when I move.
How dull it is to pause, to make an end,
To rust unburnished,° not to shine in use!   *unpolished*
As though to breathe were life! Life piled on life
Were all too little, and of one to me   25
Little remains; but every hour is saved
From that eternal silence, something more,
A bringer of new things; and vile it were°   *would be*
For some three suns to store and hoard myself,
And this gray spirit yearning in desire   30
To follow knowledge like a sinking star,
Beyond the utmost bound of human thought.
        This is my son, mine own Telemachus,
To whom I leave the scepter and the isle,—
Well-loved of me, discerning to fulfill   35
This labor, by slow prudence to make mild
A rugged people, and through soft degrees
Subdue them to the useful and the good.
Most blameless is he, centered in the sphere
Of common duties, decent not to fail   40
In offices of tenderness, and pay
Meet adoration to my household gods,
When I am gone. He works his work, I mine.
        There lies the port; the vessel puffs her sail;
There gloom the dark, broad seas. My mariners,   45

Souls that have toiled, and wrought, and thought with me,—
That ever with a frolic° welcome took   *cheerful*
The thunder and the sunshine, and opposed
Free hearts, free foreheads—you and I are old;
Old age hath yet his honor and his toil.   50
Death closes all; but something ere° the end,   *before*
Some work of noble note, may yet be done,
Not unbecoming men that strove with Gods.
The lights begin to twinkle from the rocks;
The long day wanes; the slow moon climbs; the deep   55
Moans round with many voices. Come, friends,
'Tis not too late to seek a newer world.
Push off, and sitting well in order smite°   *strike*
The sounding furrows; for my purpose holds
To sail beyond the sunset, and the baths   60
Of all the western stars, until I die.
It may be that the gulfs will wash us down;
It may be we shall touch the Happy Isles,
And see the great Achilles, whom we knew.
Though much is taken, much abides;° and though   *remains* 65
We are not now that strength which in old days
Moved earth and heaven, that which we are, we are,—
One equal temper of heroic hearts,
Made weak by time and fate, but strong in will
To strive, to seek, to find, and not to yield.   70

Dylan Thomas   *(1914–1953)*

The Force That through the Green Fuse Drives the Flower   *1934*

The force that through the green fuse drives the flower
Drives my green age; that blasts the roots of trees
Is my destroyer.
And I am dumb to tell the crooked rose°   *I have no way of telling the*
My youth is bent by the same wintry fever.   *rose*   5

The force that drives the water through the rocks
Drives my red blood; that dries the mouthing streams
Turns mine to wax.
And I am dumb to mouth unto my veins
How at the mountain spring the same mouth sucks.   10

The hand that whirls the water in the pool
Stirs the quicksand; that ropes the blowing wind
Hauls my shroud sail.
And I am dumb to tell the hanging man
How of my clay is made the hangman's lime.°   *hangman's tree*   15

The lips of time leech to the fountain head;
Love drips and gathers, but the fallen blood
Shall calm her sores.
And I am dumb to tell a weather's wind
How time has ticked a heaven round the stars.   20

And I am dumb to tell the lover's tomb
How at my sheet goes the same crooked worm.

Edmund Waller   *(1606–1687)*

Go, Lovely Rose   *1645*

    Go, lovely rose,
Tell her that wastes her time and me
    That now she knows,
When I resemble° her to thee,   *compare*
    How sweet and fair she seems to be.   5

    Tell her that's young,
And shuns to have her graces spied,°   *observed*
    That hadst thou sprung
In deserts, where no men abide,°   *dwell*
    Thou must have uncommended died.   10

    Small is the worth
Of beauty from the light retired;
    Bid her come forth,
Suffer herself to be desired,
    And not blush so to be admired.   15

    Then die, that she
The common fate of all things rare
    May read in thee:
How small a part of time they share,
    That are so wondrous sweet and fair.   20

Walt Whitman   *(1819–1892)*

There Was a Child Went Forth   *1855*

There was a child went forth every day,
And the first object he looked upon, that object he
    became,
And that object became part of him for the day or a
    certain part of the day,
Or for many years or stretching cycles of years.

The early lilacs became part of this child,   5

And grass and white and red morning-glories, and
    white and red clover, and the song of the
    phoebe-bird,
And the Third-month° lambs and the sow's pink-   *March*
    faint litter, and the mare's foal and the cow's
    calf,
And the noisy brood of the barnyard or by the mire
    of the pond-side,
And the fish suspending themselves so curiously below there,
    and the beautiful curious liquid,
And the water-plants with their graceful flat heads,   10
    all became part of him.

The field-sprouts of Fourth-month and Fifth-month
    became part of him,
Winter-grain sprouts and those of the light-yellow
    corn, and the esculent° roots of the garden,   *edible*
And the apple-trees covered with blossoms and the
    fruit afterward, and wood-berries, and the commonest
    weeds by the road,
And the old drunkard staggering home from the outhouse
    of the tavern whence he had lately risen,
And the schoolmistress that passed on her way to   15
    the school,
And the friendly boys that passed, and the quarrel-
    some boys,
And the tidy and fresh-cheeked girls, and the bare-
    foot negro boy and girl,
And all the changes of city and country wherever he
    went.

His own parents, he that had fathered him and she
    that had conceived him in her womb and
    birthed him,
They gave this child more of themselves than that,   20
They gave him afterward every day, they became
    part of him.

The mother at home quietly placing the dishes on
    the supper-table,
The mother with mild words, clean her cap and
    gown, a wholesome odor falling off her person
    and clothes as she walks by,
The father, strong, self-sufficient, manly, mean, angered,
    unjust,
The blow, the quick loud word, the tight bargain, the crafty lure,   25
The family usages, the language, the company, the
    furniture, the yearning and swelling heart,
Affection that will not be gainsayed,° the sense of   *denied*
    what is real, the thought if after all it should
    prove unreal,

The doubts of day-time and the doubts of night-
    time, the curious whether and how,
Whether that which appears so is so, or is it all
    flashes and specks?
Men and women crowding fast in the streets, if they   30
    are not flashes and specks what are they?
The streets themselves and the façades of houses,
    and goods in the windows,
Vehicles, teams, the heavy-planked wharves, the
    huge crossing at the ferries,
The village on the highland seen from afar at sunset,
    the river between,
Shadows, aureola° and mist, the light falling   *bands of light*
    on roofs and gables of white or brown two miles off,
The schooner near by sleepily dropping down the   35
    tide, the little boat slack-towed astern,
The hurrying tumbling waves, quick-broken crests,
    slapping,
The strata of colored clouds, the long bar of maroon-
    tint away solitary by itself, the spread of
    purity it lies motionless in,
The horizon's edge, the flying sea-crow, the fragrance
    of salt marsh and shore mud,
These became part of that child who went forth
    every day, and who now goes, and will always
    go forth every day.

Walt Whitman   *(1819–1892)*

A March in the Ranks Hard-Pressed   *1865*

A march in the ranks hard-pressed, and the road unknown,
A route through the heavy wood with muffled steps in the darkness,
Our army foiled with loss severe, and the sullen remnant retreating,
Till after midnight glimmer upon us the lights of a dim-lighted building.
We come to an open space in the woods, and halt by the dim-lighted   5
    building,
'Tis a large old church at the crossing roads, now an impromptu hospital,
Entering but for a minute I see a sight beyond all the pictures and poems
    ever made,
Shadows of deepest, deepest black, just lit by moving candles and lamps,
And by one great pitchy torch stationary with wild red flame and clouds
    of smoke,
By these, crowds, groups of forms vaguely I see on the floor, some in the   10
    pews laid down,
At my feet more distinctly a soldier, a mere lad, in danger of bleeding
    to death
    (he is shot in the abdomen),

I stanch the blood temporarily (the youngster's face is white as a lily),
Then before I depart I sweep my eyes over the scene fain to absorb it all,
Faces, varieties, postures beyond description, most in obscurity, some of
    them dead,
Surgeons operating, attendants holding lights, the smell of ether, the odor   15
    of blood,
The crowd, O the crowd of the bloody forms, the yard outside also filled,
Some on the bare ground, some on planks or stretchers, some in the
    death spasm sweating,
An occasional scream or cry, the doctor's shouted orders or calls,
The glisten of the little steel instruments catching the glint of the torches,
These I resume as I chant, I see again the forms, I smell the odor,   20
Then hear outside the orders given, Fall in, my men, fall in;
But first I bend to the dying lad, his eyes open, a half-smile gives he me,
Then the eyes close, calmly close, and I speed forth to the darkness,
Resuming, marching, ever in darkness marching, on in the ranks,
The unknown road still marching.   25

Richard Wilbur   *(born 1921)*

The Writer   *1976*

In her room at the prow of the house
Where light breaks, and the windows are tossed
    with linden,°   *shade trees with heart-shaped leaves*
My daughter is writing a story.

I pause in the stairwell, hearing
From her shut door a commotion of typewriter-keys   5
Like a chain hauled over a gunwale.°   *boat's rail*

Young as she is, the stuff
Of her life is a great cargo, and some of it heavy:
I wish her a lucky passage.

But now it is she who pauses,   10
As if to reject my thought and its easy figure.
A stillness greatens, in which

The whole house seems to be thinking,
And then she is at it again with a bunched clamor
Of strokes, and again is silent.   15

I remember the dazed starling°   *common bird*
Which was trapped in that very room, two years ago,
How we stole in, lifted a sash

And retreated, not to affright° it;   *frighten*
And how for a helpless hour, through the crack of the door,   20
We watched the sleek, wild, dark

nt° creature   *brilliantly colored*
t the brilliance, drop like a glove
loor, or the desk-top,

...wait then, humped and bloody,   25
For the wits to try it again; and how our spirits
Rose when, suddenly sure,

It lifted off from a chair-back,
Beating a smooth course for the right window
And clearing the sill of the world.   30

It is always a matter, my darling,
Of life or death, as I had forgotten. I wish
What I wished you before, but harder.

Miller Williams   *(born 1930)*

Thinking about Bill, Dead of AIDS   1989

We did not know the first thing about
how blood surrenders to even the smallest threat
when old allergies turn inside out,

the body rescinding all its normal orders
to all defenders of flesh, betraying the head,   5
pulling its guards back from all its borders.

Thinking of friends afraid to shake your hand,
we think of your hand shaking, your mouth set,
your eyes drained of any reprimand.

Loving, we kissed you, partly to persuade   10
both you and us, seeing what eyes had said,
that we were loving and were not afraid.

If we had had more, we would have given more.
As it was we stood next to your bed,
stopping, though, to set our smiles at the door.   15

Not because we were less sure at the last.
Only because, not knowing anything yet,
we didn't know what look would hurt you least.

William Carlos Williams   *(1883–1963)*

Spring and All   1923

By the road to the contagious hospital
under the surge of the blue
mottled clouds driven from the

northeast—a cold wind. Beyond, the
waste of broad, muddy fields   5
brown with dried weeds, standing and fallen

patches of standing water
the scattering of tall trees

All along the road the reddish
purplish, forked, upstanding, twiggy   10
stuff of bushes and small trees
with dead, brown leaves under them
leafless vines—

Lifeless in appearance, sluggish
dazed spring approaches—   15

They enter the new world naked,
cold, uncertain of all
save that they enter. All about them
the cold, familiar wind—

Now the grass, tomorrow   20
the stiff curl of wildcarrot leaf
One by one objects are defined—
It quickens: clarity, outline of leaf

But now the stark dignity of
entrance—Still, the profound change   25
has come upon them: rooted, they
grip down and begin to awaken

William Wordsworth   *(1770–1850)*

Lines Composed a Few Miles above Tintern Abbey *(1798)*

[In 1798, Wordsworth revisited the banks of the river Wye, which he
had not seen for five years. The ruins of Tintern Abbey, a beautiful medieval abbey church, are located in the river valley. His sister Dorothy
was with him on this walking tour to the river, and the last part of the
poem is directly addressed to her.]

1

Five years have passed; five summers, with the length
Of five long winters! and again I hear
These waters, rolling from their mountain-springs
With a soft inland murmur. Once again
Do I behold these steep and lofty cliffs,   5
That on a wild secluded scene impress
Thoughts of more deep seclusion, and connect
The landscape with the quiet of the sky.
The day is come when I again repose

Here, under this dark sycamore, and view   10
These plots of cottage ground, these orchard tufts,
Which at this season, with their unripe fruits,
Are clad in one green hue, and lose themselves
'Mid groves and copses.° Once again I see   *among small stands of trees*
These hedgerows, hardly hedgerows, little lines   15
Of sportive wood run wild;° these pastoral farms,   *of playful shrubs that have*
Green to the very door; and wreaths of smoke   *grown wild*
Sent up, in silence, from among the trees—
With some uncertain notice, as might seem
Of vagrant dwellers° in the houseless woods,   *of drifters making a home*   20
Or of some hermit's cave, where by his fire   *in . . .*
The hermit sits alone.

2

                            These beauteous forms,
Through a long absence, have not been to me
As is a landscape to a blind man's eye;
But oft, in lonely rooms, and 'mid the din   25
Of towns and cities, I have owed to them,
In hours of weariness, sensations sweet,
Felt in the blood, and felt along the heart;
And passing even into my purer mind,
With tranquil restoration°—feelings too   *with calm healing power*   30
Of unremembered pleasure; such, perhaps,
As have no slight or trivial influence
On that best portion of a good man's life,
His little, nameless, unremembered, acts
Of kindness and of love. Nor less, I trust,   35
To them I may have owed another gift,
Of aspect more sublime:° that blessed mood,   *of a more sublime kind the*
In which the burthen° of the mystery,   *burden*
In which the heavy and the weary weight
Of all this unintelligible world,   40
Is lightened—that serene and blessed mood,
In which the affections gently lead us on—
Until, the breath of this corporeal frame°   *of our bodily frame*
And even the motion of our human blood
Almost suspended, we are laid asleep   45
In body, and become a living soul;
While with an eye made quiet by the power
Of harmony, and the deep power of joy,
We see into the life of things.
                            If this
Be but a vain belief, yet, oh! how oft—   50
In darkness and amid the many shapes
Of joyless daylight; when the fretful stir°   *the restless, useless activity*
Unprofitable, and the fever of the world,
Have hung upon the beatings of my heart—

How oft, in spirit, have I turned to thee,   55
O sylvan Wye!° Thou wanderer through the woods,   *° river of the forest*
How often has my spirit turned to thee!

3

And now, with gleams of half-extinguished thought,
With many recognitions dim and faint,
And somewhat of a sad perplexity,   60
The picture of the mind revives again;
While here I stand, not only with the sense
Of present pleasure, but with pleasing thoughts
That in this moment there is life and food
For future years. And so I dare to hope,   65
Though changed, no doubt, from what I was when first
I came among these hills; when like a roe
I bounded o'er the mountains, by the sides
Of the deep rivers, and the lonely streams,
Wherever nature led—more like a man   70
Flying from something that he dreads than one
Who sought the thing he loved. For nature then
(The coarser pleasures of my boyish days,
And their glad animal movements all gone by)
To me was all in all. I cannot paint   75
What then I was. The sounding cataract
Haunted me like a passion; the tall rock,
The mountain, and the deep and gloomy wood,
Their colors and their forms, were then to me
An appetite; a feeling and a love,   80
That had no need of a remoter charm,
By thought supplied, nor any interest
Unborrowed from the eye.   That time is past,
And all its aching joys are now no more,
And all its dizzy raptures. Not for this   85
Faint I,° nor mourn nor murmur. Other gifts   *do I lose heart*
Have followed—for such loss, I would believe,
Abundant recompense.° For I have learned   *more than enough*
To look on nature, not as in the hour   *compensation*
Of thoughtless youth; but hearing oftentimes   90
The still, sad music of humanity,
Nor harsh nor grating, though of ample power
To chasten and subdue. And I have felt
A presence that disturbs me with the joy
Of elevated thoughts: a sense sublime   95
Of something far more deeply interfused,°   *deeply blended*
Whose dwelling is the light of setting suns,
And the round ocean and the living air,
And the blue sky, and in the mind of man—
A motion and a spirit that impels°   *that gives life to* 100

All thinking things, all objects of all thought,
And rolls through all things. Therefore am I still
A lover of the meadows and the woods
And mountains; and of all that we behold
From this green earth; of all the mighty world   105
Of eye and ear—both what they half create,
And what perceive; well pleased to recognize
In nature and the language of the sense°   *language of our senses*
The anchor of my purest thoughts, the nurse,
The guide, the guardian of my heart, and soul   110
Of all my moral being.

4

                    Nor perchance,
If I were not thus taught, should I the more
Suffer my genial spirits to decay.°   *allow the powers of my soul*
For thou art with me here upon the banks   *to weaken*
Of this fair river; thou my dearest friend,   115
My dear, dear friend; and in thy voice I catch
The language of my former heart, and read
My former pleasures in the shooting lights
Of thy wild eyes. Oh! yet a little while
May I behold in thee what I was once,   120
My dear, dear sister! And this prayer I make,
Knowing that Nature never did betray
The heart that loved her. 'Tis her privilege,
Through all the years of this our life, to lead
From joy to joy: for she can so inform°   *can so shape* 125
The mind that is within us, so impress
With quietness and beauty, and so feed
With lofty thoughts, that neither evil tongues,
Rash judgments, nor the sneers of selfish men,
Nor greetings where no kindness is, nor all   130
The dreary intercourse of daily life,
Shall e'er prevail against us, or disturb
Our cheerful faith, that all which we behold
Is full of blessings.
                    Therefore let the moon   135
Shine on thee in thy solitary walk;
And let the misty mountain winds be free
To blow against thee; and, in after years,
When these wild ecstasies shall be matured
Into a sober pleasure; when thy mind   140
Shall be a mansion for all lovely forms,
Thy memory be as a dwelling place
For all sweet sounds and harmonies; oh! then,
If solitude, or fear, or pain, or grief
Should be thy portion, with what healing thoughts   145

Of tender joy wilt thou remember me,
And these my exhortations!° Nor, perchance—   *my passionate, heartfelt advice*
If I should be where I no more can hear
Thy voice, nor catch from thy wild eyes these gleams
Of past existence—wilt thou then forget   150
That on the banks of this delightful stream
We stood together; and that I, so long
A worshiper of Nature, hither came
Unwearied in that service; rather say
With warmer love—oh! with far deeper zeal   155
Of holier love. Nor wilt thou then forget,
That after many wanderings, many years
Of absence, these steep woods and lofty cliffs,
And this green pastoral landscape, were to me
More dear, both for themselves and for thy sake!   160

William Wordsworth   *(1770–1850)*

She Dwelled among the Untrodden Ways   *1798*

She dwelled among the untrodden ways
  Beside the springs of Dove,°   *a river in the north of England*
A Maid whom there were none to praise
  And very few to love;

A violet by a mossy stone   5
  Half hidden from the eye!
—Fair as a star, when only one
  Is shining in the sky.

She lived unknown, and few could know
  When Lucy ceased to be;   10
But she is in her grave, and, oh,
  The difference to me!

William Wordsworth   *(1770–1850)*   👁

The Solitary Reaper   *1807*

Behold her, single in the field,
  Yon solitary highland lass!
Reaping and singing by herself;
  Stop here, or gently pass!
Alone she cuts and binds the grain,   5
And sings a melancholy strain;
O listen! for the vale° profound   *valley*
Is overflowing with the sound.

No nightingale did ever chant
     More welcome notes to weary bands   10
Of travelers in some shady haunt,
     Among Arabian sands:
A voice so thrilling never was heard
In spring-time from the cuckoo-bird,
Breaking the silence of the seas   15
Among the farthest Hebrides.°   *distant northern islands*

Will no one tell me what she sings?
     Perhaps the plaintive numbers° flow   *mournful verses*
For old, unhappy, far-off things,
     And battles long ago: 20
Or is it some more humble lay,°   *song*
Familiar matter of today?
Some natural sorrow, loss, or pain,
That has been, and may be again?

Whatever the theme, the Maiden sang   25
     As if her song could have no ending;
I saw her singing at her work,
     And over the sickle bending—
I listened, motionless and still;
And, as I mounted up the hill,   30
The music in my heart I bore,
Long after it was heard no more.

Sir Thomas Wyatt   (1503–1542)

They Flee from Me   *1557*

They flee from me, that sometime did me seek,
With naked foot stalking in my chamber.
I have seen them, gentle, tame, and meek,
That now are wild, and do not remember
That sometime they put themselves in danger   5
To take bread at my hand; and now they range,
Busily seeking with a continual change.

Thanked be Fortune it hath been otherwise,
Twenty times better; but once in special,
In thin array, after a pleasant guise,°   *in a pleasing way* 10
When her loose gown from her shoulders did fall,
And she me caught in her arms long and small,°   *slender*
And therewith all sweetly did me kiss
And softly said, "Dear heart, how like you this?"

It was no dream, I lay broad waking.   15
But all is turned, through my gentleness,
Into a strange fashion of forsaking;

And I have leave to go, of her goodness,
And she also to use newfangleness.°   *try something new*
But since that I so kindely° am served,   *according to her nature*   20
I fain° would know what she hath deserved.   *gladly*

Mitsuye Yamada   *(born 1923)*

A Bedtime Story   *1976*

Once upon a time,
an old Japanese legend
goes as told
by Papa,
an old woman traveled through   5
many small villages
seeking refuge
for the night.
Each door opened
a sliver   10
in answer to her knock
then closed.
Unable to walk
any further
she wearily climbed a hill   15
found a clearing
and there lay down to rest
a few moments to catch
her breath.

The village town below   20
lay asleep except
for a few starlike lights.
Suddenly the clouds opened
and a full moon came into view
over the town.   25

The old woman sat up
turned toward
the village town
and in supplication
called out   30
Thank you people
of the village,
If it had not been for your
kindness
in refusing me a bed   35
for the night
these humble eyes would never
have seen this
memorable sight.

Papa paused, I waited.   40
In the comfort of our
hilltop home in Seattle
overlooking the valley,
I shouted
"That's the *end?*"   45

William Butler Yeats   *(1865–1939)*

The Second Coming   *1921*

Turning and turning in the widening gyre°   spiral
The falcon cannot hear the falconer;
Things fall apart; the center cannot hold;
Mere anarchy is loosed upon the world,
The blood-dimmed tide is loosed, and everywhere   5
The ceremony of innocence is drowned;
The best lack all conviction, while the worst
Are full of passionate intensity.

Surely some revelation is at hand;
Surely the Second Coming° is at hand;   coming of Christ   10
The Second Coming! Hardly are those words out
When a vast image out of *Spiritus Mundi*°   spirit of the World
Troubles my sight: somewhere in sands of the desert
A shape with lion body and the head of a man,°   sphinx
A gaze blank and pitiless as the sun,   15
Is moving its slow thighs, while all about it
Reel shadows of the indignant desert birds.
The darkness drops again; but now I know
That twenty centuries of stony sleep
Were vexed to nightmare by a rocking cradle,   20
And what rough beast, its hour come round at last,
Slouches towards Bethlehem to be born?

Al Young   *(born 1939)*

Birthday Poem   *1966*

First light of day in Mississippi
son of laborer & of house wife
it says so on the official photostat
not son of fisherman & child fugitive
from cottonfields & potato patches   5
from sugarcane chickens & well-water
from kerosene lamps & watermelons
mules named jack or jenny & wagonwheels,

years of meaningless farm work
work Work WORK WORK WORK—   10
"Papa pull you outta school bout March
to stay on the place & work the crop"
—her own earliest knowledge
of human hopelessness & waste

She carried me around nine months   15
inside her fifteen year old self
before here I sit numbering it all

How I got from then to now
is the mystery that could fill a whole library
much less an arbitrary stanza   20

But of course you already know about that
from your own random suffering
& sudden inexplicable bliss

Drama

*There is a hunger to see the human presence
acted out. As long as that need remains, people
will find a way to do theater.*

ZELDA FICHANDLER

26 PREVIEW

The Heart of Drama

Courtesy Richard B. Ressman

*On the stage is always now; the personages are
standing on that razor edge between the past
and the future that is the essential character of
conscious beings.*

ANATOLE BROYARD

*We live in what is, but we find a thousand ways
not to face it. Great theater strengthens our
faculty to face it.*

THORNTON WILDER

FOCUS ON THEATER

What is the magic of live theater? The magic of the stage makes us witness a live performance. The actors, handed the play as words on a page, bring it to life. We see their faces, hear their voices. We respond to the language of gestures, to the actors' body language. A successful performance draws us in; it carries us along. We participate in other lives. These may be more magnificent or drearier than our own. Or they may be so close to our own world that we experience the shock of recognition, making us say: "That is exactly the way it is."

A stage production is a collaboration. The playwright furnishes the script—often the result of much revision. Many contemporary dramatists revise their plays after tryouts and initial reviews. A director (or perhaps a directorial committee) charts directions or develops a concept. For instance, a director might highlight the youthfulness of Shakespeare's Romeo and Juliet—their eagerness, their refusal to wait, their moving from heavenly joy to deadly despair in the course of a day. Strong directors, as strong conductors do with music, reinterpret traditional plays for their time and audience. An experimental director might teleport Shakespeare's *Hamlet* from its original setting in Denmark to the antebellum mansion of a Southern senator named Claudius, whose wife is a Southern belle named Gertrude, and whose financial adviser is a talkative old man named Polonius. Claudius' stepson (Hamlet), as in the original play, will be a young man alienated from his corrupt elders.

The performers, in turn, take their cue (and sometimes dictatorial instructions) from the director. However, they may be as stubbornly independent as directors can be, and at any rate they bring a part to life in their own way. In a BBC production available on videotape in many college libraries, Ron Cook plays Shakespeare's evil Richard III less as the traditional sniggering and gloating hunchback and more like a conniving, corrupt bank vice president. This change makes the character more deadly and the threat more real, since audiences cannot simply laugh at him as a stage villain. The actor's conception of the character takes murderous intent and brilliant deceit out of the world of stage melo-drama and puts it into the real world.

Not all the action in the theater is on the stage. A major silent partic-ipant in the performance is you—the spectator. Without your collabora-tion, the stage will not work its magic. In the theater, you become part of a community embarked on a common venture. There is something contagious about the enthusiasm or laughter of a live audience. As a group, the members of the audience "act out" their reactions to the play: They sigh and gasp; they may watch in stunned silence; they express re-lief in a burst of happy laughter. When the chemistry is right, there is a special interaction between performers and spectators. Performers re-spond to a receptive audience, creating for the performance the height-ened mood of a festive event.

THE ELEMENTS OF DRAMA

Any theater's special limitations are part of what
gives it its special intensity. The curtain rising
behind the proscenium arch says, "Fix your
whole attention on this little space: Everything
will happen here. For these three hours, there is
nothing outside it."

AMLIN GRAY

Reading a printed play, you translate the words on the page into ac-tion and dialogue the way directors and actors do. The difference is that you are enacting the drama in the theater of the mind. How do the ele-ments of a play—situation, character, dialogue, plot, style—work together to bring the play to life?

Situation   *Where do we as spectators come in?* The early scenes of a play answer basic questions in the spectators' minds: Where are we? What is the issue or the problem? What past history explains the current situation? The early scenes of a play may give you important details of a family history, hints about skeletons in the family closet, or signs of quar-rels of long standing. Sometimes, **flashbacks** to earlier days will help you understand the characters' current predicaments. Be prepared to see a situation develop that carries the seeds of conflict.

Tina Howe   *(born 1937)*

The following excerpt is the opening scene from Tina Howe's play *Mus-eum* (1989), which takes you to an avant-garde art museum. One of the ex-hibits is a clothesline with a basket of round-headed clothespins under it;

another is a picture of a businessman with one shoe. What is going on in this opening scene? What kind of play does this opening scene make you expect?

Museum   1989

It's morning, several minutes before the museum opens. The gallery is in darkness. Nothing happens; then faraway sounds of footsteps and clanging doors are heard.

THE GUARD *walks briskly into the room and turns on the lights. First the Agnes Vaags are illuminated with pinpricks of light, then the Moes are revealed, and finally the clothesline. As* THE GUARD *brings everything to life, a voice sounding something like a combination of God and a newscaster announces:*

VOICE: Sandro Botticelli's priceless masterpiece *The Birth of Venus* was attacked and virtually destroyed yesterday afternoon by a hooded man armed with a handgun who opened fire on the painting while screaming, "Cursed is the ground for thy sake." Before he was finally overcome by three guards and numerous bystanders, the heavily built assailant pumped more than eighteen bullets into the nude Venus figure, literally shooting her off the face of the canvas. The Acting Director of the Uffizi Gallery, which houses the masterpiece, said in an interview last night that it was the most violent attack ever made against a Renaissance painting. Restoration will be impossible.

THE GUARD *stores this information along with everything else he knows and begins his daily process of becoming watchful yet as unobtrusive as possible. He rocks on his heels, sucks his breakfast out from between his teeth, picks fuzz off his uniform, hoists up his underwear, and waits.*

MICHAEL WALL *enters carrying an arsenal of photographic equipment including a camera attached to a tripod. He looks around the room, finds the Zachery Moes, and sets his gear down in front of* Landscape I. *He walks up to it, backs away, walks up close again, and takes out his light meter for a reading. He adjusts his camera and prepares to shoot, all with enormous concentration, energy, and flair.* THE GUARD *is mesmerized by him. After several moments,* WALL *poises his finger on the shutter release.*

THE GUARD: It's against museum regulations to photograph the artworks.
MICHAEL WALL (*whirling around, furious*): You're kidding!
THE GUARD: It's against museum regulations to photograph the artworks.
MICHAEL WALL: Thanks a lot for waiting to tell me until I was all set up . . .
THE GUARD: I'm surprised they even let you in with all that stuff . . .
MICHAEL WALL (*shaking his head*): Too much!
THE GUARD: The attendant downstairs is supposed to see that all photographic equipment is left in the Checkroom . . .
MICHAEL WALL: I don't believe this . . .
THE GUARD: . . . and that includes binoculars, telescopes, folding—
MICHAEL WALL: You wait until I'm all set up, tripod locked, camera attached, f-stop set—

THE GUARD: I've seen the attendant downstairs refuse visitors admittance who were just carrying . . . film!

MICHAEL WALL: —AND WHEN ALL OF THAT IS DONE, THEN YOU TELL ME IT'S AGAINST MUSEUM REGULATIONS TO PHOTOGRAPH THE ARTWORKS!

THE GUARD: And not just film either, but radios, tape recorders, typewriters, and sandwiches . . .

MICHAEL WALL: Who do I see to get permission?

THE GUARD: I've seen the attendant downstairs stop visitors who had bulging pockets.

MICHAEL WALL (*detaching his camera from the tripod*): The Head of Public Relations? The Administrative Assistant?

THE GUARD: The public has no respect for *place* anymore.

MICHAEL WALL: The Curator? The Chairman of the Board?

THE GUARD: They wear tennis shorts to church. They drink soda at the opera. They bring flash cameras to museums . . .

MICHAEL WALL, *his camera in hand, walks up to* THE GUARD *and starts snapping his picture.*

MICHAEL WALL: Come on, who do I see for permission to photograph the artworks? (*taking a picture with each guess*) The Cinematic Representative? The Acting President of the Exhibition? The Liaison for Public Information? (*pause*) You have an interesting profile.

The Receptive Reader

What is the connection between the action in the announcement heard at the beginning and the interaction between the guard and Michael Wall? What is going on between these two people? What is the contrast between the two personalities? Where do you think this play might be headed?

Character   *Who are these people?* Dramatists create characters and set them in motion. Much of a playwright's task early in the play is **characterization**—feeding you the information that makes the characters come to life.

✗ You will learn much about the characters from what they say and do. They may take you into their confidence in brief **asides** shared only with the audience. Or they might confide in you in lengthy solo speeches—**soliloquies**. Sometimes a **confidant**—a close friend or trusted servant—may serve as a substitute or surrogate for the audience. Much of what makes a character in a play a living person is in revealing gestures and remarks made as if in passing.

✗ Often what truly defines major characters is their behavior in test situations—what they say and do when a major confrontation or challenge puts them to the test. When threatened by an unexpected turn of events, a character who seemed calmly in control may reveal a capacity for sudden anger and for lashing out at those perceived as enemies. Another character may reveal a tendency to shift blame or to abandon friends in need. A character who seemed weak may show fortitude or generosity.

❭ In addition, you will do well to listen to what *others* say about a central figure—this is often a major function of minor characters. Often a supporting character serves as a **foil** who highlights by contrast a key quality in a major figure.

The characters in true drama are not stereotypical or one-dimensional, but **complex.** For instance, a play may show us the contrast between a public mask and the private self. A character may present a surface of conformity and yet harbor smouldering rebellion. Furthermore, live characters change and grow. The movement of a play may be a journey toward **recognition,** in the sense of insight or self-realization.

ntozake shange   *(born 1948)*

The following excerpt is from ntozake shange's *for colored girls who have considered suicide / when the rainbow is enuf.* The playwright works mainly with extended **monologues** punctuated by short exchanges among the characters. Seven black women take turns telling us about their personal histories and their views of the world. In this short sample monologue, the "lady in red" in the play talks about a terminated relationship. What does this monologue tell you about the character?

lady in red   *1976*

without any assistance or guidance from you
i have loved you assiduously for 8 months 2 wks & a day
i have been stood up four times
i've left 7 packages on yr doorstep
forty poems 2 plants & 3 handmade notecards i left   5
town so i cd send to you have been no help to me
on my job
you call at 3:00 in the mornin on weekdays
so i cd drive 27 1/2 miles cross the bay before i go to work
charmin charmin   10
but you are of no assistance
i want you to know
this waz an experiment
to see how selfish i cd be
if i wd really carry on to snare a possible lover   15
if i waz capable of debasin my self for the love of another
if i cd stand not being wanted
when i wanted to be wanted
& i cannot
so   20

with no further assistance & no guidance from you
i am endin this affair

this note is attached to a plant
i've been waterin since the day i met you
you may water it   25
yr damn self

The Receptive Reader

What kind of person takes shape in this monologue? What details are especially telling or revealing? What ideas are familiar, which different? How do you react to or relate to the character?

Dialogue   *How much of the interaction takes place through words?* Shakespeare's plays were acted on a wooden stage with little scenery and few props. He relied on the power of words to conjure up throne rooms, battlefields, the queen's bedroom, or a fog-shrouded heath. He asked of his audiences, "Think when we talk of horses that you see them / Printing their proud hooves in the receiving earth." However, the chief function of **dialogue,** the verbal give-and-take between the characters, is to serve as the medium of human interaction in the play. Dialogue becomes **monologue** when one person for a time does all or most of the talking. When there is not even a silent listener serving as captive audience, a monologue becomes a **soliloquy**—a character's extended conversation with himself or herself. Soliloquies give the audience a chance to listen in on thoughts and feelings usually hidden behind the polite social facade.

Many successful playwrights have an uncanny ear for how people talk. The characters in a play speak in a characteristic **idiom**—a register of language, a way of talking. In Arthur Miller's *Death of a Salesman,* Willy Loman is a master of the trite, folksy, shirtsleeve English of the white lower middle class, peppered with small-town Chamber of Commerce clichés ("Well, I figure, what the hell, life is short, a couple of jokes"). In Tennessee Williams' *The Glass Menagerie,* the mother speaks in a refined, genteel Southern lady style that hides harsh realities behind euphemistic talk: "You just have a little defect . . . when people have a slight disadvantage like that, they cultivate other things to make up for it." Her alienated son talks back to her in the rough language of his street buddies: "Every time you come in yelling that God damn 'Rise and Shine!' 'Rise and Shine!' I say to myself, 'How lucky dead people are!'"

The following is a "slice of life" selection of dialogue of the kind theatergoers often hear on the stage. Nothing happens—there is no action. The action is in the dialogue. What impression do you form of the two speakers as you listen to them? What kind of people are they? What is on their minds? For you, are they, as the title promises, from "the middle of ordinary life"?

Don DeLillo   *(born 1936)*

The Mystery at the Middle of Ordinary Life   *2001*

CHARACTERS

WOMAN
MAN

A MAN *and a* WOMAN *in a room.*

WOMAN: I was thinking how strange it is.

MAN: What?

WOMAN: That people are able to live together. Days and nights and years. Five years go by. How do they do it? Ten, eleven, twelve years. Two people making one life. Sharing ten thousand meals. Talking to each other face to face, open face, like hot sandwiches. All the words that fill the house. What do people say over a lifetime? Trapped in each other's syntax. The same voice. The droning tonal repetition. I'll tell you something.

MAN: You'll tell me something.

WOMAN: There's a mystery here. The people behind the walls of the brown house next door. What do they say and how do they survive it? All that idle dialogue. The nasality. The banality. I was thinking how strange it is. How do they do it, night after night, all those nights, those words, those few who do it and survive?

MAN: They make love. They make salads.

WOMAN: But sooner or later they have to speak. This is what shatters the world. I mean isn't it gradually shattering to sit and listen to the same person all the time, without reason or rhyme. Words that trail away. The pauses. The clauses. How many thousands of times can you look at the same drained face and watch the mouth begin to open? Everything's been fine up to now. It is when they open their mouths. It is when they speak.

[Pause.]

MAN: I'm still not over this cold of mine.

WOMAN: Take those things you take.

MAN: The tablets.

WOMAN: The caplets.

[Pause.]

MAN: Long day.

WOMAN: Long day.

MAN: A good night's sleep.

WOMAN: Long slow day.

[Lights slowly down.]

Curtain

The Receptive Reader

1. Do you think these are "ordinary people"? Does anything they say remind you of things you have heard before?

2. Is the issue the woman raises a live issue for you? What kind of audience do you think would sympathize with or respond to her concern? What would you say in response to her?

The Personal Response

Are you a good listener? Do you find this conversation interesting? Or do you find it boring? Are you one of the people who can listen to ordinary people and be fascinated? Or do you tend to tune them out?

The Creative Response

You may want to team up with one or more other students to stage a conversation from the middle of ordinary life.

Plot   *How are the events related?* The **plot** of a play is the thread that leads us from initial tensions or problems, through complications, to climactic confrontations or turning points, and to the windup or final **resolution** of a conflict.

✗ Plays differ greatly in what drives the plot and leads to the final resolution. Often, in a gripping drama, we see what happens when people make fateful choices. In some of the great tragedies of ancient Greece, we see admirable outstanding individuals embark on a course that the audience begins to realize will lead to disaster. In a Shakespearean history play, rebels with legitimate grievances may take up arms against a corrupt weak king but find in the end they cannot muster the forces to prevail against established authority marching under the banner of national unity.

✗ Often the central conflict takes shape between strong-willed individuals. A clash of values may put major characters on a collision course. In plays by the Norwegian playwright Henrik Ibsen, a strong-willed self-righteous father and an alienated idealistic son meet in a fateful contest. Or a strong-willed woman in a conventional wifely role may in the end challenge the traditional authority of the husband.

✗ Even in a play with much external action, the central conflict may be an **internal conflict.** It may be staged in the mind of the central character. Shakespeare's *Macbeth* is a play with much external action: Macbeth murders his king, destroys people who are in his way, and is finally defeated by an army raised by the dead king's son. However, much of the time we focus on the internal conflict within a central figure with a mind divided against itself. With one part of his mind, he yields to the siren song of ambition that makes him plot the assassination of King Duncan. But in another part of his mind, Macbeth is deeply troubled by his violated loyalty to his king, who is also a kinsman. Macbeth has a conscience; his religion teaches the abhorrence of murder. This inner conflict makes him a reluctant murderer, a hesitant assassin.

Playwrights vary greatly in how they develop the basic plot line and lead it to its conclusion. Some writers and their audiences like sudden reversals or turns in the road, unexpected complications, and surprise endings. Others like to see a play march purposefully forward to what comes to seem a logical foregone conclusion. Some plays build to a **climax,** preparing the audience for a high point or culminating event.

In some of Shakespeare's plays, the tide metaphor well describes the overall movement of the plot. In *Macbeth,* the rebel and usurper at first hesitates but then becomes hardened in his evil purpose as he eliminates potential threats to his power. We see the rising tide of tyranny drive out upright individuals. The tyrant eliminates people threatening his power; he becomes bloodier, more isolated, and more desperate as he moves on. But slowly the tide turns, and the forces of justice and retribution gather strength. In the end, the avenging armies corner the despot in his lair.

The resolution may be happy (as in comedy), unhappy (as in tragedy), or open-ended (as in many modern plays). The playwright may respond to the spectators' yearning for good news, for a happy end, if only as the result of a lucky coincidence. The ancient Greek theater had a contraption for lowering a god or goddess—the **deus ex machina**—onto the stage to work last-minute surprises. In some plays, parallel conflicts or **subplots** reinforce the central theme of a play.

Susan Glaspell   *(1876–1948)*

Glaspell was among the first writers to realize that it was not enough to present women at the center of the stage. If there were to be a radical break with plays of the past, women would have to exist in a world tailored to their persons and speak a language not borrowed from men.

ENOCH BRATER

Susan Glaspell devoted much of her life to the theater. Educated at Drake University in Des Moines, Iowa, she worked for a time as a newspaper reporter and drew on her experiences as a journalist in her short stories, novels, and plays. She was a cofounder of the Provincetown Players, who performed many of the American playwright Eugene O'Neill's one-act plays and who performed her own one-act play *Trifles.* She acted and directed; she wrote a dozen plays; and she won the Pulitzer Prize for drama in 1931. As head of the Chicago bureau of a federal theater project, she reviewed hundreds of plays and helped in the production of important works by black playwrights. Although she did much of her work in the East, she said, "Almost everything I write has its roots in the Middle West; I suppose because my own are there." She was a spiritual descendant of her pioneer ancestors who left "comfortable homes for unknown places." Many of her characters struggle against "fixity and stagnation," trying to move, as their pioneer forebears did, "into a new sphere, if not of place then of spirit" (Enoch Brater).

Glaspell's work was rediscovered by feminist critics who found in her plays a "woman's version" of events, created at a time when the theater was heavily dominated by male dramatists. Like her British contemporary Virginia Woolf, she has become an inspiration to women whose goal is "control over their own bodies and a voice with which to speak about it" (Susan Rubin Suleiman).

Although her play *Trifles* involves violent death, it is not a drama of violence or of physical action. Instead, the plot focuses on the unraveling of motives and on the loyalties of the survivors. As in Greek tragedy, we witness none of the violent events directly—we merely hear about them. The real drama is in what goes on in the minds of the characters as they *react* to the events—as they think through their responsibilities, bring their memories to bear, come to understand what happened, and take sides.

Trifles   1916

CHARACTERS

GEORGE HENDERSON, county attorney
HENRY PETERS, sheriff
LEWIS HALE, a neighboring farmer
MRS. PETERS
MRS. HALE

THE SETTING: *The kitchen in the now abandoned farmhouse of* JOHN WRIGHT.

SCENE: *The kitchen in the now abandoned farmhouse of* JOHN WRIGHT, *a gloomy kitchen, and left without having been put in order—unwashed pans under the sink, a loaf of bread outside the breadbox, a dish towel on the table—other signs of incompleted work. At the rear the outer door opens and the* SHERIFF *comes in followed by the* COUNTY ATTORNEY *and* HALE. *The* SHERIFF *and* HALE *are men in middle life, the* COUNTY ATTORNEY *is a young man; all are much bundled up and go at once to the stove. They are followed by the two women—the* SHERIFF'S *wife first; she is a slight wiry woman, a thin nervous face.* MRS. HALE *is larger and would ordinarily be called more comfortable looking, but she is disturbed now and looks fearfully about as she enters. The women have come in slowly, and stand close together near the door.*

COUNTY ATTORNEY (*rubbing his hands*): This feels good. Come up to the fire, ladies.

MRS. PETERS (*after taking a step forward*): I'm not—cold.

SHERIFF (*unbuttoning his overcoat and stepping away from the stove as if to mark the beginning of official business*): Now, Mr. Hale, before we move things about, you explain to Mr. Henderson just what you saw when you came here yesterday morning.

COUNTY ATTORNEY: By the way, has anything been moved? Are things just as you left them yesterday?

SHERIFF (*looking about*): It's just the same. When it dropped below zero last night I thought I'd better send Frank out this morning to make a fire for us—no use getting pneumonia with a big case on, but I told him not to touch anything except the stove—and you know Frank.

COUNTY ATTORNEY: Somebody should have been left here yesterday.

SHERIFF: Oh—yesterday. When I had to send Frank to Morris Center for that man who went crazy—I want you to know I had my hands full yesterday, I knew you could get back from Omaha by today and as long as I went over everything here myself—

COUNTY ATTORNEY: Well, Mr. Hale, tell just what happened when you came here yesterday morning.

HALE: Harry and I had started to town with a load of potatoes. We came along the road from my place and as I got here I said, "I'm going to see if I can't get John Wright to go in with me on a party telephone." I spoke to Wright about it once before and he put me off, saying folks talked too much anyway, and all he asked was peace and quiet—I guess you know about how much he talked himself; but I thought maybe if I went to the house and talked about it before his wife, though I said to Harry that I didn't know as what his wife wanted made much difference to John—

COUNTY ATTORNEY: Let's talk about that later, Mr. Hale. I do want to talk about that, but tell now just what happened when you got to the house.

HALE: I didn't hear or see anything; I knocked at the door, and still it was all quiet inside. I knew they must be up, it was past eight o'clock. So I knocked again, and I thought I heard somebody say, "Come in." I wasn't sure, I'm not sure yet, but I opened the door—this door (*indicating the door by which the two women are still standing*) and there in that rocker—(*pointing to it*) sat Mrs. Wright.

They all look at the rocker.

COUNTY ATTORNEY: What—was she doing?

HALE: She was rockin' back and forth. She had her apron in her hand and was kind of—pleating it.

COUNTY ATTORNEY: And how did she—look?

HALE: Well, she looked queer.

COUNTY ATTORNEY: How do you mean—queer?

HALE: Well, as if she didn't know what she was going to do next. And kind of done up.

COUNTY ATTORNEY: How did she seem to feel about your coming?

HALE: Why, I don't think she minded—one way or other. She didn't pay much attention. I said, "How do, Mrs. Wright, it's cold, ain't it?" And she said, "Is it?"—and went on kind of pleating at her apron. Well, I was surprised; she didn't ask me to come up to the stove, or to set down, but just sat there, not even looking at me, so I said, "I want to see John." And then she—laughed. I guess you would call it a laugh. I thought of Harry and the team outside, so I said a little sharp: "Can't I see John?" "No," she says, kind o' dull like. "Ain't he home?" says I. "Yes," says she, "he's home." "Then why can't I see him?" I asked her, out of patience. "'Cause he's dead," says she. *"Dead?"* says I. She just nodded her head, not getting a bit excited, but rockin' back and forth. "Why—where is he?" says I, not knowing what to say. She just pointed upstairs—like that (*himself pointing to the room above*). I got up, with the idea of going up there. I walked from there to here—then I says, "Why, what did he die of?" "He died of a rope round his neck," says she, and just went on pleatin' at her apron. Well, I went out and called Harry. I thought I might—need help. We went upstairs and there he was lyin'—

COUNTY ATTORNEY: I think I'd rather have you go into that upstairs, where you can point it all out. Just go on now with the rest of the story.

HALE: Well, my first thought was to get that rope off. It looked . . . (*stops, his face twitches*) . . . but Harry, he went up to him, and he said, "No, he's dead all right, and we'd better not touch anything." So we went back down stairs. She was still sitting that same way. "Has anybody been notified?" I asked. "No," says she, unconcerned. "Who did this, Mrs. Wright?" said Harry. He said it businesslike—and she stopped pleatin' of her apron. "I don't know," she says. "You don't *know?*" says Harry. "No," says she. "Weren't you sleepin' in the bed with him?" says Harry. "Yes," says she, "but I was on the inside." "Somebody slipped a rope round his neck and strangled him and you didn't wake up?" says Harry. "I didn't wake up," she said after him. We must 'a looked as if we didn't see how that could be, for after a minute she said, "I sleep sound." Harry was going to ask her more questions but I said maybe we ought to let her tell her story first to the coroner, or the sheriff, so Harry went fast as he could to Rivers' place, where there's a telephone.

COUNTY ATTORNEY: And what did Mrs. Wright do when she knew that you had gone for the coroner?

HALE: She moved from that chair to this one over here (*pointing to a small chair in the corner*) and just sat there with her hands held together and looking down. I got a feeling that I ought to make some conversation, so I said I had come in to see if John wanted to put in a telephone, and at that she started to laugh, and then she stopped and looked at me— scared. (*The* COUNTY ATTORNEY, *who has had his notebook out, makes a note.*) I dunno, maybe it wasn't scared. I wouldn't like to say it was. Soon Harry got back, and then Dr. Lloyd came, and you, Mr. Peters, and so I guess that's all I know that you don't.

COUNTY ATTORNEY (*looking around*): I guess we'll go upstairs first—and then out to the barn and around there. (*to the* SHERIFF) You're convinced that there was nothing important here—nothing that would point to any motive.

SHERIFF: Nothing here but kitchen things.

The COUNTY ATTORNEY, *after again looking around the kitchen, opens the door of a cupboard closet. He gets up on a chair and looks on a shelf. Pulls his hand away, sticky.*

COUNTY ATTORNEY: Here's a nice mess.

The women draw nearer.

MRS. PETERS (*to the other woman*): Oh, her fruit; it did freeze. (*to the* COUNTY ATTORNEY) She worried about that when it turned so cold. She said the fire'd go out and her jars would break.

SHERIFF: Well, can you beat the women! Held for murder and worryin' about her preserves.

COUNTY ATTORNEY: I guess before we're through she may have something more serious than preserves to worry about.

HALE: Well, women are used to worrying over trifles.

The two women move a little closer together.

COUNTY ATTORNEY (*with the gallantry of a young politician*): And yet, for all their worries, what would we do without the ladies? (*The women do not unbend. He goes to the sink, takes a dipperful of water from the pail and pouring it into a basin, washes his hands. Starts to wipe them on the roller towel, turns it for a cleaner place.*) Dirty towels! (*kicks his foot against the pans under the sink*) Not much of a housekeeper, would you say, ladies?

MRS. HALE (*stiffly*): There's a great deal of work to be done on a farm.

COUNTY ATTORNEY: To be sure. And yet (*with a little bow to her*) I know there are some Dickson county farmhouses which do not have such roller towels.

He gives it a pull to expose its full length again.

MRS. HALE: Those towels get dirty awful quick. Men's hands aren't always as clean as they might be.

COUNTY ATTORNEY: Ah, loyal to your sex, I see. But you and Mrs. Wright were neighbors. I suppose you were friends, too.

MRS. HALE (*shaking her head*): I've not seen much of her of late years. I've not been in this house—it's more than a year.

COUNTY ATTORNEY: And why was that? You didn't like her?

MRS. HALE: I liked her all well enough. Farmers' wives have their hands full, Mr. Henderson. And then—

COUNTY ATTORNEY: Yes—?

MRS. HALE (*looking about*): It never seemed a very cheerful place.

COUNTY ATTORNEY: No—it's not cheerful. I shouldn't say she had the home-making instinct.

MRS. HALE: Well, I don't know as Wright had, either.

COUNTY ATTORNEY: You mean that they didn't get on very well?

MRS. HALE: No, I don't mean anything. But I don't think a place'd be any cheerfuller for John Wright's being in it.

COUNTY ATTORNEY: I'd like to talk more of that a little later. I want to get the lay of things upstairs now.

He goes to the left, where three steps lead to a stair door.

SHERIFF: I suppose anything Mrs. Peters does'll be all right. She was to take in some clothes for her, you know, and a few little things. We left in such a hurry yesterday.

COUNTY ATTORNEY: Yes, but I would like to see what you take, Mrs. Peters, and keep an eye out for anything that might be of use to us.

MRS. PETERS: Yes, Mr. Henderson.

The women listen to the men's steps on the stairs, then look about the kitchen.

MRS. HALE: I'd hate to have men coming into my kitchen, snooping around and criticizing.

She arranges the pans under sink which the COUNTY ATTORNEY *had shoved out of place.*

MRS. PETERS: Of course it's no more than their duty.

MRS. HALE: Duty's all right, but I guess that deputy sheriff that came out to make the fire might have got a little of this on. (*gives the roller towel a pull*) Wish I'd thought of that sooner. Seems mean to talk about her for not having things slicked up when she had to come away in such a hurry.

MRS. PETERS (*who has gone to a small table in the left rear corner of the room, and lifted one end of a towel that covers a pan*): She had bread set.

Stands still.

MRS. HALE (*Eyes fixed on a loaf of bread beside the breadbox, which is on a low shelf at the other side of the room. Moves slowly toward it.*): She was going to put this in there. (*Picks up loaf, then abruptly drops it. In a manner of returning to familiar things.*) It's a shame about her fruit. I wonder if it's all gone. (*gets up on the chair and looks*) I think there's some here that's all right, Mrs. Peters. Yes—here; (*holding it toward the window*) this is cherries, too. (*looking again*) I declare I believe that's the only one. (*Gets down, bottle in her hand. Goes to the sink and wipes it off on the outside.*) She'll feel awful bad after all her hard work in the hot weather. I remember the afternoon I put my cherries last summer.

She puts the bottle on the big kitchen table, center of the room. With a sigh, is about to sit down in the rocking-chair. Before she is seated realizes what chair it is; with a slow look at it, steps back. The chair which she has touched rocks back and forth.

MRS. PETERS: Well, I must get those things from the front room closet. (*She goes to the door at the right, but after looking into the other room, steps back.*) You coming with me, Mrs. Hale? You could help me carry them.

They go in the other room; reappear, MRS. PETERS *carrying a dress and skirt,* MRS. HALE *following with a pair of shoes.*

MRS. PETERS: My, it's cold in there.

She puts the clothes on the big table, and hurries to the stove.

MRS. HALE (*examining the skirt*): Wright was close. I think maybe that's why she kept so much to herself. She didn't even belong to the Ladies Aid. I suppose she felt she couldn't do her part, and then you don't enjoy things when you feel shabby. She used to wear pretty clothes and be lively, when she was Minnie Foster, one of the town girls singing in the choir. But that—oh, that was thirty years ago. This all you was to take in?

MRS. PETERS: She said she wanted an apron. Funny thing to want, for there isn't much to get you dirty in jail, goodness knows. But I suppose just to make her feel more natural. She said they was in the top drawer in this cupboard. Yes, here. And then her little shawl that always hung behind the door. (*opens stair door and looks*) Yes, here it is.

Quickly shuts door leading upstairs.

MRS. HALE (*abruptly moving toward her*): Mrs. Peters?

MRS. PETERS: Yes, Mrs. Hale?

MRS. HALE: Do you think she did it?

MRS. PETERS (*in a frightened voice*): Oh, I don't know.

MRS. HALE: Well, I don't think she did. Asking for an apron and her little shawl. Worrying about her fruit.

MRS. PETERS (*Starts to speak, glances up, where footsteps are heard in the room above. In a low voice.*): Mr. Peters says it looks bad for her. Mr. Henderson is awful sarcastic in a speech and he'll make fun of her sayin' she didn't wake up.

MRS. HALE: Well, I guess John Wright didn't wake when they was slipping that rope under his neck.

MRS. PETERS: No, it's strange. It must have been done awful crafty and still. They say it was such a—funny way to kill a man, rigging it all up like that.

MRS. HALE: That's just what Mr. Hale said. There was a gun in the house. He says that's what he can't understand.

MRS. PETERS: Mr. Henderson said coming out that what was needed for the case was a motive; something to show anger, or—sudden feeling.

MRS. HALE (*who is standing by the table*): Well, I don't see any signs of anger around here. (*She puts her hand on the dish towel which lies on the table, stands looking down at table, one half of which is clean, the other half messy.*) It's wiped to here. (*Makes a move as if to finish work, then turns and looks at loaf of bread outside the breadbox. Drops towel. In that voice of coming back to familiar things.*) Wonder how they are finding things upstairs. I hope she had it a little more red-up up there. You know, it seems kind of *sneaking*. Locking her up in town and then coming out here and trying to get her own house to turn against her!

MRS. PETERS: But Mrs. Hale, the law is the law.

MRS. HALE: I s'pose 'tis. (*unbuttoning her coat*) Better loosen up your things, Mrs. Peters. You won't feel them when you go out.

MRS. PETERS *takes off her fur tippet, goes to hang it on hook at back of room, stands looking at the under part of the small corner table.*

MRS. PETERS: She was piecing a quilt.

She brings the large sewing basket and they look at the bright pieces.

MRS. HALE: It's log cabin pattern. Pretty, isn't it? I wonder if she was goin' to quilt it or just knot it?

Footsteps have been heard coming down the stairs. The SHERIFF *enters followed by* HALE *and the* COUNTY ATTORNEY.

SHERIFF: They wonder if she was going to quilt it or just knot it!

The men laugh; the women look abashed.

COUNTY ATTORNEY (*rubbing his hands over the stove*): Frank's fire didn't do much up there, did it? Well, let's go out to the barn and get that cleared up.

The men go outside.

MRS. HALE (*resentfully*): I don't know a's there's anything so strange, our takin' up our time with little things while we're waiting for them to get the evidence. (*She sits down at the big table smoothing out a block with decision.*) I don't see as it's anything to laugh about.

MRS. PETERS (*apologetically*): Of course they've got awful important things on their minds.

Pulls up a chair and joins MRS. HALE *at the table.*

MRS. HALE (*examining another block*): Mrs. Peters, look at this one. Here, this is the one she was working on, and look at the sewing! All the rest of it has been so nice and even. And look at this! It's all over the place! Why, it looks as if she didn't know what she was about! (*After she has said this they look at each other, then start to glance back at the door. After an instant* MRS. HALE *has pulled at a knot and ripped the sewing.*)

MRS. PETERS: Oh, what are you doing, Mrs. Hale?

MRS. HALE (*mildly*): Just pulling out a stitch or two that's not sewed very good. (*threading a needle*) Bad sewing always made me fidgety.

MRS. PETERS (*nervously*): I don't think we ought to touch things.

MRS. HALE: I'll just finish up this end. (*suddenly stopping and leaning forward*) Mrs. Peters?

MRS. PETERS: Yes, Mrs. Hale?

MRS. HALE: What do you suppose she was so nervous about?

MRS. PETERS: Oh—I don't know. I don't know as she was nervous. I sometimes sew awful queer when I'm just tired. (MRS. HALE *starts to say something, looks at* MRS. PETERS, *then goes on sewing.*) Well, I must get these things wrapped up. They may be through sooner than we think. (*putting apron and other things together*) I wonder where I can find a piece of paper, and string.

MRS. HALE: In that cupboard, maybe.

MRS. PETERS (*looking in cupboard*): Why, here's a birdcage. (*holds it up*) Did she have a bird, Mrs. Hale?

MRS. HALE: Why, I don't know whether she did or not—I've not been here for so long. There was a man around last year selling canaries cheap, but I don't know as she took one; maybe she did. She used to sing real pretty herself.

MRS. PETERS (*glancing around*): Seems funny to think of a bird here. But she must have had one, or why would she have a cage? I wonder what happened to it.

MRS. HALE: I s'pose maybe the cat got it.

MRS. PETERS: No, she didn't have a cat. She's got that feeling some people have about cats—being afraid of them. My cat got in her room and she was real upset and asked me to take it out.

MRS. HALE: My sister Bessie was like that. Queer, ain't it?

MRS. PETERS (*examining the cage*): Why, look at this door. It's broke. One hinge is pulled apart.

MRS. HALE (*looking too*): Looks as if someone must have been rough with it.

MRS. PETERS: Why, yes.

She brings the cage forward and puts it on the table.

MRS. HALE: I wish if they're going to find any evidence they'd be about it. I don't like this place.

MRS. PETERS: But I'm awful glad you came with me, Mrs. Hale. It would be lonesome for me sitting here alone.

MRS. HALE: It would, wouldn't it? (*dropping her sewing*) But I tell you what I do wish, Mrs. Peters. I wish I had come over sometimes when *she* was here. I—(*looking around the room*)—wish I had.

MRS. PETERS: But of course you were awful busy, Mrs. Hale—your house and your children.

MRS. HALE: I could've come. I stayed away because it weren't cheerful—and that's why I ought to have come. I—I've never liked this place. Maybe because it's down in a hollow and you don't see the road. I dunno what it is, but it's a lonesome place and always was. I wish I had come over to see Minnie Foster sometimes. I can see now—

Shakes her head.

MRS. PETERS: Well, you mustn't reproach yourself, Mrs. Hale. Somehow we just don't see how it is with other folks until—something comes up.

MRS. HALE: Not having children makes less work—but it makes a quiet house, and Wright out to work all day, and no company when he did come in. Did you know John Wright, Mrs. Peters?

MRS. PETERS: Not to know him; I've seen him in town. They say he was a good man.

MRS. HALE: Yes—good; he didn't drink, and kept his word as well as most, I guess, and paid his debts. But he was a hard man, Mrs. Peters. Just to pass the time of day with him—(*shivers*). Like a raw wind that gets to the bone. (*pauses, her eye falling on the cage*) I should think she would 'a wanted a bird. But what do you suppose went with it?

MRS. PETERS: I don't know, unless it got sick and died.

She reaches over and swings the broken door, swings it again. Both women watch it.

MRS. HALE: You weren't raised 'round here, were you? (MRS. PETERS *shakes her head*.) You didn't know—her?

MRS. PETERS: Not till they brought her yesterday.

MRS. HALE: She—come to think of it, she was kind of like a bird herself—real sweet and pretty, but kind of timid and—fluttery. How—she—did—change. (*silence; then as if struck by a happy thought and relieved to get back to everyday things*) Tell you what, Mrs. Peters, why don't you take the quilt in with you? It might take up her mind.

MRS. PETERS: Why, I think that's a real nice idea, Mrs. Hale. There couldn't possibly be any objection to it, could there? Now, just what would I take? I wonder if her patches are in here—and her things.

They look in the sewing basket.

MRS. HALE: Here's some red. I expect this has got sewing things in it. (*brings out a fancy box*) What a pretty box. Looks like something somebody would give you. Maybe her scissors are in here. (*Opens box. Suddenly puts her hand to her nose.*) Why—(MRS. PETERS *bends nearer, then turns her face away.*) There's something wrapped up in this piece of silk.

MRS. PETERS: Why, this isn't her scissors.

MRS. HALE (*lifting the silk*): Oh, Mrs. Peters—it's—

MRS. PETERS *bends closer.*

MRS. PETERS: It's the bird.

MRS. HALE (*jumping up*): But, Mrs. Peters—look at it! Its neck! Look at its neck! It's all—other side *to.*

MRS. PETERS: Somebody—wrung—its—neck.

Their eyes meet. A look of growing comprehension, of horror. Steps are heard outside. MRS. HALE *slips box under quilt pieces, and sinks into her chair. Enter* SHERIFF *and* COUNTY ATTORNEY. MRS. PETERS *rises.*

COUNTY ATTORNEY (*as one turning from serious things to little pleasantries*): Well, ladies, have you decided whether she was going to quilt it or knot it?

MRS. PETERS: We think she was going to—knot it.

COUNTY ATTORNEY: Well, that's interesting, I'm sure. (*seeing the birdcage*) Has the bird flown?

MRS. HALE (*putting more quilt pieces over the box*): We think the—cat got it.

COUNTY ATTORNEY (*preoccupied*): Is there a cat?

MRS. HALE *glances in a quick covert way at* MRS. PETERS.

MRS. PETERS: Well, not *now.* They're superstitious, you know. They leave.

COUNTY ATTORNEY (*to* SHERIFF PETERS, *continuing an interrupted conversation*): No sign at all of anyone having come from the outside. Their own rope. Now let's go up again and go over it piece by piece. (*They start upstairs.*) It would have to have been someone who knew just the—

MRS. PETERS *sits down. The two women sit there not looking at one another, but as if peering into something and at the same time holding back. When they talk now it is in the manner of feeling their way over strange ground, as if afraid of what they are saying, but as if they cannot help saying it.*

MRS. HALE: She liked the bird. She was going to bury it in that pretty box.

MRS. PETERS (*in a whisper*): When I was a girl—my kitten—there was a boy took a hatchet, and before my eyes—and before I could get there—(*covers her face an instant*) If they hadn't held me back I would have—(*catches herself, looks upstairs where steps are heard, falters weakly*)—hurt him.

MRS. HALE (*with a slow look around her*): I wonder how it would seem never to have had any children around. (*pause*) No, Wright wouldn't like the bird—a thing that sang. She used to sing. He killed that, too.

MRS. PETERS (*moving uneasily*): We don't know who killed the bird.

MRS. HALE: I knew John Wright.

MRS. PETERS: It was an awful thing was done in this house that night, Mrs. Hale. Killing a man while he slept, slipping a rope around his neck that choked the life out of him.

MRS. HALE: His neck. Choked the life out of him.

Her hand goes out and rests on the birdcage.

MRS. PETERS (*with rising voice*): We don't know who killed him. We don't *know*.

MRS. HALE (*her own feeling not interrupted*): If there'd been years and years of nothing, then a bird to sing to you, it would be awful—still, after the bird was still.

MRS. PETERS (*something within her speaking*): I know what stillness is. When we homesteaded in Dakota, and my first baby died—after he was two years old, and me with no other then—

MRS. HALE (*moving*): How soon do you suppose they'll be through, looking for the evidence?

MRS. PETERS: I know what stillness is. (*pulling herself back*) The law has got to punish crime, Mrs. Hale.

MRS. HALE (*not as if answering that*): I wish you'd seen Minnie Foster when she wore a white dress with blue ribbons and stood up there in the choir and sang. (*a look around the room*) Oh, I *wish* I'd come over here once in a while! That was a crime! That was a crime! Who's going to punish that?

MRS. PETERS (*looking upstairs*): We mustn't—take on.

MRS. HALE: I might have known she needed help! I know how things can be—for women. I tell you, it's queer, Mrs. Peters. We live close together and we live far apart. We all go through the same things—it's all just a different kind of the same thing. (*brushes her eyes; noticing the bottle of fruit, reaches out for it*) If I was you I wouldn't tell her her fruit was gone. Tell her it *ain't*. Tell her it's all right. Take this in to prove it to her. She—she may never know whether it was broke or not.

MRS. PETERS (*Takes the bottle, looks about for something to wrap it in; takes petticoat from the clothes brought from the other room, very nervously begins winding this around the bottle. In a false voice.*): My, it's a good thing the men couldn't hear us. Wouldn't they just laugh! Getting all stirred up over a little thing like a—dead canary. As if that could have anything to do with—with—wouldn't they *laugh!*

The men are heard coming down stairs.

MRS. HALE (*under her breath*): Maybe they would—maybe they wouldn't.

COUNTY ATTORNEY: No, Peters, it's all perfectly clear except a reason for doing it. But you know juries when it comes to women. If there was some definite thing. Something to show—something to make a story about—a thing that would connect up with this strange way of doing it—

The women's eyes meet for an instant. Enter HALE *from outer door.*

HALE: Well, I've got the team around. Pretty cold out there.

COUNTY ATTORNEY: I'm going to stay here a while by myself. (*to the* SHERIFF) You can send Frank out for me, can't you? I want to go over everything. I'm not satisfied that we can't do better.

SHERIFF: Do you want to see what Mrs. Peters is going to take in?

The COUNTY ATTORNEY *goes to the table, picks up the apron, laughs.*

COUNTY ATTORNEY: Oh, I guess they're not very dangerous things the ladies have picked out. (*Moves a few things about, disturbing the quilt pieces which cover the box. Steps back.*) No, Mrs. Peters doesn't need supervising. For that matter, a sheriff's wife is married to the law. Ever think of it that way, Mrs. Peters?

MRS. PETERS: Not—just that way.

SHERIFF (*chuckling*): Married to the law. (*moves toward the other room*) I just want you to come in here a minute, George. We ought to take a look at these windows.

COUNTY ATTORNEY (*scoffingly*): Oh, windows!

SHERIFF: We'll be right out, Mr. Hale.

HALE *goes outside. The* SHERIFF *follows the* COUNTY ATTORNEY *into the other room. Then* MRS. HALE *rises, hands tight together, looking intensely at* MRS. PETERS, *whose eyes make a slow turn, finally meeting* MRS. HALE'S. *A moment* MRS. HALE *holds her, then her own eyes point the way to where the box is concealed. Suddenly* MRS. PETERS *throws back quilt pieces and tries to put the box in the bag she is wearing. It is too big. She opens box, starts to take bird out, cannot touch it, goes to pieces, stands there helpless. Sound of a knob turning in the other room.* MRS. HALE *snatches the box and puts it in the pocket of her big coat. Enter* COUNTY ATTORNEY *and* SHERIFF.

COUNTY ATTORNEY (*facetiously*): Well, Henry, at least we found out that she was not going to quilt it. She was going to—what is it you call it, ladies?

MRS. HALE (*her hand against her pocket*): We call it—knot it, Mr. Henderson.

Curtain.

The Receptive Reader

1. Very early in the first scene, Hale, the neighbor, says in passing, "I didn't know as what his wife wanted made much difference to John." How does this statement give you a first hint of the major *conflict* underlying the play?

2. Why does the playwright have the characters talk about the preserves? To wind up this discussion, Hale says, "Well, women are used to worrying over trifles." How does this statement point forward to a major *theme* of the play? What makes the use of the word here and in the title of the play ironic? How is the theme of the "little things" that matter to women taken up again in the discussion of the quilt?

3. How do you first gather that Mrs. Hale does not share the men's views but instead has a feeling of solidarity with Mrs. Wright? How do you begin to

realize that in much of this you will be looking at events and issues from the women's *point of view*?

4. The men representing the law are asking about a *motive*—"something to show anger, or—sudden feeling." What are some of the first clues that point toward the answer the play gives to this question?

5. What clues and comments help you piece together your view of John Wright's *character* as the women talk mostly about other things? What is ironic about his being described as "a good man"?

6. What makes the bird a central *symbol* in this play? What makes you first realize that the women are going to close ranks behind Mrs. Wright? What are some of the things the playwright does to help you understand and sympathize with their decision?

7. What is the *irony* in Mrs. Peters' being "married to the law"?

8. The events of this play might have provided the material for a traditional detective story or an episode in a crime show. How is the treatment of the story in this play different from what you might expect in a more conventional format?

The Creative Dimension

A major player in the events leading up to the events of the play—John, the husband—is no longer present to testify. What do you think he might say if, like Hamlet's father's ghost, he could come back among the living for a time to tell his side of the story? Or, what do you think he might have said in a letter he left for a friend to be read after an untimely death?

Style   *How does the playwright use language?* The style of drama ranges from the ceremonial through the realistic to the surreal. Much traditional drama is in verse. In ancient Greek tragedy, the ceremonial chants of the chorus were written in elaborately crafted stanzas, or **odes.** Much eighteenth-century drama was written in **rhymed couplets,** as in Molière's *The Misanthrope.* The couplet—two self-contained lines—is a perfect medium for the neatly packaged, emphatic pronouncements Molière's characters love:

> To accept wholesale friendship I firmly decline;
> Who befriends one and all is no friend of mine.

Much modern drama is in prose. It approximates the freely moving rhythms of everyday speech—if only to mock them, as the British playwright Harold Pinter does in the following passage from *The Homecoming*:

> She's a great help to me over there. She's a wonderful wife and mother. She's a very popular woman. She's got lots of friends. It's a great life, at the University . . . you know . . . it's a very good life. We've got a lovely house . . . we've got all . . . we've got everything we want. It's a very stimulating environment.

The language of the people in a play may be as empty of poetry as the emotional lives of Pinter's characters. Or it may be alive with the soaring poetry of Shakespeare's Hamlet, to whom the star-spangled heavens are alternately "this majestical roof fretted with golden fire" and "a foul and pestilent congregation of vapors." Playwrights vary greatly in how much they supplement the language of words with the language of gestures and the language of **symbols.** In an Ibsen play, props of fateful significance—a wounded wild duck nursed back to health in an attic, an incriminating letter waiting in a mailbox—may serve to focus the attention and nurture the suspense of the audience.

August Wilson   *(born 1945)*

August Wilson is an African American playwright whose endlessly talkative and articulate characters speak black English. What features of it do you recognize? How would you react to it as a theatergoer or reader? The following excerpt is from Wilson's *The Piano Lesson,* a play first staged by the Yale Repertory Theatre in 1988. Bill Moyers, interviewing Wilson, asked, "I was going to ask you, don't you grow weary of thinking black, writing black, being asked questions about being black?" Wilson replied, "How could one grow weary of that? Whites don't get tired of thinking white or being who they are. I'm just who I am. You never transcend who you are. Black is not limiting. There's no idea in the world that is not contained by black life. I could write forever about the black experience in America."

How Avery Got to Be a Preacher   1987

BOY WILLIE: How you get to be a preacher, Avery? I might want to be a preacher one day. Have everybody call me Reverend Boy Willie.
AVERY: It come to me in a dream. God called me and told me he wanted me to be a shepherd for his flock. That's what I'm gonna call my church . . . The Good Shepherd Church of God in Christ.
DOAKER: Tell him what you told me. Tell him about the three hobos.
AVERY: Boy Willie don't want to hear all that.
LYMON: I do. Lots a people say your dreams can come true.
AVERY: Naw. You don't want to hear all that.
DOAKER: Go on. I told him you was a preacher. He didn't want to believe me. Tell him about the three hobos.
AVERY: Well, it come to me in a dream. See . . . I was sitting out in this railroad yard watching the trains go by. The train stopped and these three hobos got off. They told me they had come from Nazareth and was on their way to Jerusalem. They had three candles. They gave me one and told me to light it . . . but to be careful that it didn't go out. Next thing I knew I was standing in front of this house. Something told me to go knock on the door. This old woman opened the door and said they had

been waiting on me. Then she led me into this room. It was a big room and it was full of all kinds of different people. They looked like anybody else except they all had sheep heads and was making noise like sheep make. I heard somebody call my name. I looked around and there was these same three hobos. They told me to take off my clothes and they give me a blue robe with gold thread. They washed my feet and combed my hair. Then they showed me these three doors and told me to pick one.

I went through one of them doors and that flame leapt off that candle and it seemed like my whole head caught fire. I looked around and there was four or five other men standing there with these same blue robes on. Then we heard a voice tell us to look out across this valley. We looked out and saw the valley was full of wolves. The voice told us that these sheep people that I had seen in the other room had to go over to the other side of this valley and somebody had to take them. Then I heard another voice say, "Who shall I send?" Next thing I knew I said, "Here I am. Send me." That's when I met Jesus. He say, "If you go, I'll go with you." Something told me to say, "Come on. Let's go." That's when I woke up. My head still felt like it was on fire . . . but I had a peace about myself that was hard to explain. I knew right then that I had been filled with the Holy Ghost and called to be a servant of the Lord. It took me a while before I could accept that. But then a lot of little ways God showed me that it was true. So I became a preacher.

LYMON: I see why you gonna call it the Good Shepherd Church. You dreaming about them sheep people. I can see that easy.

(Act One, Scene 1)

The Receptive Reader

1. A reviewer in the *New York Times* said about *The Piano Lesson* that "the play's real music is in the language." What did he mean?

2. In the past, regional or cultural varieties of English have often been ridiculed. Do you think college audiences of your generation are ready to accept the use of language in this play? Why or why not?

3. What role do language differences—for example, Southern speech, British accents, street language—play in American popular culture today? Do you think their role has changed over the years?

Making Connections—For Discussion or Writing

Compare and contrast the way people talk in the selections by Oscar Wilde, Susan Glaspell, ntozake shange, and August Wilson. What is the relationship between language and the characters' view of the world?

CONFLICT: THE HEART OF DRAMA

Sometimes a play seems to march single-mindedly to a foregone conclusion. But in a truly dramatic play, the issue may be in doubt until close to the end. We experience the pull of divided loyalties as first the one side and then the other scores points. We are drawn into the **dialectic** of the play, the playing off of differing or opposite points of view. We share in the play of point and counterpoint. The Irish playwright George Bernard Shaw said about the characters in his plays that all of them were right *from their own point of view*—and that those who could not understand this vital point could not understand drama (and indeed life).

Henrik Ibsen   *(1828–1906)*

Ibsen brings to the test of his ideal the society of his own times, observing it pitilessly, exactly, and at close range, studying the immediate and the particular in terms of the universal and the continuing.

UNA ELLIS-FERMOR

Everything I have written is intimately connected with what I have lived through, even if I have not lived it myself. Every new work has served me as emancipation and catharsis; for none of us can escape the guilt of the society to which we belong.

HENRIK IBSEN

The Norwegian playwright Henrik Ibsen has been described as "in love with a future that will redeem the past." His great plays—*A Doll's House, The Wild Duck, Hedda Gabler, Ghosts*—continue to remind theatergoers of his gift for asking questions to which they are still seeking the answers.

Ibsen was a master at setting up and playing out the conflicts that are the heart of drama. His central characters are often in rebellion against the dominant middle-class morality of his time. He knew well the prosperous middle class of shopkeepers, industrialists, bank managers, and doctors who in the cities and small towns were *The Pillars of the Community* (the title of an Ibsen play). He attacked their self-righteousness: their belief that they stood for morality and law and order. In his plays, present prosperity more often than not had its roots in shady business deals or the betrayal of friends. For all its genteel trappings, the bourgeois society of the time was shown as ruthlessly competitive, with the strong prospering and the weak going under. On the fringe of proper, well-to-do society were poor relations, business failures, and misfits who lived in genteel poverty, embittered by their lot.

Ibsen was one of the first great truth-tellers in the modern vein. He put on the stage businessmen who were unable to relate emotionally to their families, alienated from wife and children. They compensated for the sexual inhibitions of their time by furtive affairs with maids and prostitutes.

In a world without modern birth control, these often left in their wake a legacy of disowned illegitimate children, venereal disease, and dysfunctional marriages. In *Ghosts* (1881), the sins of the father are visited on a son whose life is being destroyed by the syphilis he has inherited from his father.

Ibsen's most memorable characters were women—Nora Helmer in *A Doll's House* (1879), Hedda in *Hedda Gabler* (1892)—who were in rebellion against the role reserved for them in this late-nineteenth-century Scandinavian version of a man's world. They talked back to the domineering men in their lives; they rebelled against the stereotype of the woman whose duty was to husband and family. They refused to be the "little woman" who was humored and condescended to and never entrusted with real responsibility.

The truths that Ibsen told and that often outraged his early audiences were rooted in his own experience. His father, a lavish spender, went bankrupt when Henrik was six. Ibsen was at odds with his brothers and alienated from his father, and in later years he had contacts only with his sister Hedwig. Instead of studying to be a physician, as he had hoped, he spent miserable years as a pharmacist's apprentice. He had a child out of wedlock with an older servant and paid child support for many years. Determined to be a playwright, Ibsen eventually found a small job with a theater. He managed to have plays printed and performed, but none were commercial successes, and he lived in what one of his translators calls "wretched poverty" for many years with his wife and son. (He recalled eating well for a few days when unsold copies of an early play were sold to a grocer for wrapping paper.) Assisted by a government grant, Ibsen eventually left Norway to live for many years in self-imposed exile, writing many of his best-known plays abroad in Germany and Italy.

Among these plays, which later became known as **problem plays,** *A Doll's House* (1879) was the most spectacular and provocative. The play questioned the institution of marriage during an age when marriage was for life. The play was eventually performed in Germany, and in an adaptation, in England, creating much scandal and controversy, and it made Ibsen's reputation. He once said, "My enemies have been a great help to me—their attacks have been so vicious that people come flocking to see what all the shouting is about."

A Doll's House   *1879*

TRANSLATED BY PETER WATTS

The legal subordination of one sex to the other is wrong in itself and now one of the chief hindrances to human improvement.

JOHN STUART MILL

I thought the time had come when a few
boundaries ought to be moved.

HENRIK IBSEN

CHARACTERS

TORVALD HELMER, a lawyer
NORA, his wife
DR. RANK
NILS KROGSTAD, a barrister
MRS. LINDE
HELMER's three small children
ANNA-MARIA, the nurse
A HOUSEMAID
A PORTER

The action takes place in HELMER's *flat.*

Act One

A comfortable room, furnished inexpensively, but with taste. In the back wall there are two doors; that to the right leads out to a hall, the other, to the left, leads to HELMER's *study. Between them stands a piano.*

In the middle of the left-hand wall is a door, with a window on its nearer side. Near the window is a round table with armchairs and a small sofa.

In the wall on the right-hand side, rather to the back, is a door, and farther forward on this wall there is a tiled stove with a couple of easy chairs and a rocking-chair in front of it. Between the door and the stove stands a little table.

There are etchings on the walls, and there is a cabinet with china ornaments and other bric-à-brac, and a small bookcase with handsomely bound books. There is a carpet on the floor, and the stove is lit. It is a winter day.

A bell rings in the hall outside, and a moment later the door is heard to open. NORA *comes into the room, humming happily. She is in outdoor clothes, and is carrying an armful of parcels which she puts down on the table to the right. Through the hall door, which she has left open, can be seen a* PORTER; *he is holding a Christmas tree and a hamper, and he gives them to the* MAID *who has opened the front door.*

NORA: Hide the Christmas tree properly, Helena. The children mustn't see it till this evening, when it's been decorated (*to the* PORTER, *taking out her purse*) How much is that?

PORTER: Fifty cents.

NORA: There's a crown. No, keep the change.

The PORTER *thanks her and goes.* NORA *shuts the door, and takes off her outdoor clothes, laughing quietly and happily to herself. Taking a bag of macaroons from her pocket, she eats one or two, then goes cautiously to her husband's door and listens.*

Yes, he's in. (*She starts humming again as she goes over to the table on the right.*)

HELMER (*from his study*): Is that my little skylark twittering out there?

NORA (*busy opening the parcels*): It is.

HELMER: Scampering about like a little squirrel?

NORA: Yes.

HELMER: When did the squirrel get home?

NORA: Just this minute. (*She slips the bag of macaroons in her pocket and wipes her mouth.*) Come in here, Torvald, and you can see what I've bought.

HELMER: I'm busy! (*A moment later he opens the door and looks out, pen in hand.*) Did you say "bought"? What, all that? Has my little featherbrain been out wasting money again?

NORA: But, Torvald, surely this year we can let ourselves go just a little bit? It's the first Christmas that we haven't had to economize.

HELMER: Still, we mustn't waste money, you know.

NORA: Oh, Torvald, surely we can waste a little now—just the teeniest bit? Now that you're going to earn a big salary, you'll have lots and lots of money.

HELMER: After New Year's Day, yes—but there'll be a whole quarter before I get paid.

NORA: Pooh, we can always borrow till then.

HELMER: Nora! (*He goes to her and takes her playfully by the ear.*) The same little scatterbrain. Just suppose I borrowed a thousand crowns today and you went and spent it all by Christmas, and then on New Year's Eve a tile fell on my head, and there I lay—

NORA (*putting a hand over his mouth*): Sh! Don't say such horrid things!

HELMER: But suppose something of the sort were to happen. . . .

NORA: If anything as horrid as that were to happen, I don't expect I should care whether I owed money or not.

HELMER: But what about the people I'd borrowed from?

NORA: Them? Who bothers about them? They're just strangers.

HELMER: Nora, Nora! Just like a woman! But seriously, Nora, you know what I think about that sort of thing. No debts, no borrowing. There's something constrained, something ugly even, about a home that's founded on borrowing and debt. You and I have managed to keep clear up till now, and we shall still do so for the little time that is left.

NORA (*going over to the stove*): Very well, Torvald, if you say so.

HELMER (*following her*): Now, now, my little songbird mustn't be so crestfallen. Well? Is the squirrel sulking? (*taking out his wallet*) Nora . . . guess what I have here!

NORA (*turning quickly*): Money!

HELMER: There! (*He hands her some notes.*) Good heavens, I know what a lot has to go on housekeeping at Christmas time.

NORA (*counting*): Ten—twenty—thirty—forty! Oh, thank you, Torvald, thank you! This'll keep me going for a long time!

HELMER: Well, you must see that it does.

NORA: Oh yes, of course I will. But now come and see all the things I've bought—so cheaply, too. Look, here's a new suit for Ivar, and a sword too. Here's a horse and a trumpet for Bob; and here's a doll and a doll's bed for Emmy. They're rather plain, but she'll soon smash them to bits anyway. And these are dress-lengths and handkerchiefs for the maids. . . . Old Nanny really ought to have something more. . . .

HELMER: And what's in *that* parcel?

NORA (*squealing*): No, Torvald! You're not to see that till this evening!

HELMER: Aha! And now, little prodigal, what do you think you want for yourself?

NORA: Oh, me? I don't want anything at all.

HELMER: Ah, but you must. Now tell me anything—within reason—that you feel you'd like.

NORA: No . . . I really can't think of anything. Unless . . . Torvald . . .

HELMER: Well?

NORA (*not looking at him—playing with his waistcoat buttons*): If you *really* want to give me something, you could—well, you could . . .

HELMER: Come along—out with it!

NORA (*in a rush*): You could give me money, Torvald. Only what you think you could spare—and then one of these days I'll buy something with it.

HELMER: But, Nora—

NORA: Oh, *do,* Torvald . . . please, please do! Then I'll wrap it in pretty gold paper and hang it on the Christmas tree. Wouldn't that be fun?

HELMER: What do they call little birds who are always making money fly?

NORA: Yes, I know—ducks-and-drakes! But let's do what I said, Torvald, and then I'll have time to think of something that I really want. Now, that's very sensible, isn't it?

HELMER (*smiling*): Oh, very. That is, it would be if you really kept the money I give you, and actually bought something for yourself with it. But if it goes in with the housekeeping, and gets spent on all sorts of useless things, then I only have to pay out again.

NORA: Oh, but, Torvald—

HELMER: You can't deny it, little Nora, now can you? (*putting an arm round her waist*) It's a sweet little bird, but it gets through a terrible amount of money. You wouldn't believe how much it costs a man when he's got a little songbird like you!

NORA: Oh, how *can* you say that? I really do save all I can.

HELMER (*laughing*): Yes, that's very true—"all you can." But the thing is, you can't!

NORA (*nodding and smiling happily*): Ah, if you only knew what expenses we skylarks and squirrels have, Torvald.

HELMER: What a funny little one you are! Just like your father—always on the look-out for all the money you can get, but the moment you have it, it seems to slip through your fingers and you never know what becomes of it. Well, I must take you as you are—it's in your blood. Oh yes, Nora, these things are hereditary.

NORA: I wish I'd inherited more of Papa's good qualities.

HELMER: And I wouldn't want you to be any different from what you are— just my sweet little songbird. But now I come to think of it, you look rather—rather—how shall I put it—rather as if you've been up to mischief today.

NORA: Do I?

HELMER: Yes, you certainly do. Look me straight in the face.

NORA (*looking at him*): Well?

HELMER (*wagging a finger at her*): Surely your sweet tooth didn't get the better of you in town today?

NORA: No . . . how could you think that?

HELMER: Didn't Little Sweet-Tooth just look in at the confectioner's?

NORA: No, honestly, Torvald.

HELMER: Not to taste one little sweet?

NORA: No, of course not.

HELMER: Not even to nibble a macaroon or two?

NORA: No, Torvald, really; I promise you.

HELMER: There, there, of course I was only joking.

NORA (*going to the table on the right*): I wouldn't do anything that you don't like.

HELMER: No, I know you wouldn't—besides, you've given me your word. (*going over to her*) Well, you keep your little Christmas secrets to yourself, Nora darling; I dare say I shall know them all this evening when the Christmas tree's lighted up.

NORA: Did you remember to invite Dr. Rank?

HELMER: No, but there's no need to—it's an understood thing that he dines with us. Still, I'll ask him when he looks in before lunch. I've ordered an excellent wine. . . . Oh, Nora, you can't imagine how much I'm looking forward to this evening.

NORA: So am I, Torvald—and how the children will love it.

HELMER: Oh, it's certainly wonderful to think that one has a good safe post and ample means. It's a very comforting thought, isn't it?

NORA: Oh, it's wonderful!

HELMER: Do you remember last Christmas? For three whole weeks beforehand you shut yourself up every evening till long after midnight, making flowers for the Christmas tree, and all the other wonderful surprises for us. Ugh, those were the most boring three weeks I've ever had to live through.

NORA: It wasn't the least bit boring for me.

HELMER (*smiling*): But there was so little to show for it, Nora!

NORA: Now, you mustn't tease me about that again. How could I help it if the cat got in and tore everything to bits?

HELMER: Poor little Nora—of course you couldn't. You did your best to please us—that's the main thing. But it's certainly good that the hard times are over.

NORA: Oh, it's really wonderful!

HELMER: Now I needn't sit here by myself and be bored, and you needn't tire your pretty eyes or your sweet little fingers—

NORA (*clapping her hands*): No, I needn't, need I? Not any more. Oh, it's really wonderful to know that. (*taking his arm*) Now I'll tell you how I've been thinking we ought to arrange things, Torvald. As soon as Christmas is over—

A bell rings in the hall.

Oh, that's the door! (*She tidies the room a little.*) It must be someone to see us—oh, that *is* tiresome!

HELMER: I'm not at home to callers, remember.

MAID (*at the door*): There's a lady to see you, Madam.

NORA: Well, show her in.

MAID (*to* HELMER): And the Doctor's here as well, sir.

HELMER: Has he gone straight to my study?

MAID: Yes, sir.

> HELMER *goes to his study. The* MAID *shows in* MRS. LINDE, *who is in travelling clothes, and shuts the door after her.*

MRS. LINDE (*subdued and rather hesitant*): How do you do, Nora?

NORA (*doubtfully*): How do you do . . .

MRS. LINDE: You don't remember me.

NORA: No, I'm afraid I—Wait a minute . . . surely it's—(*impulsively*) Kristina! Is it really you?

MRS. LINDE: Yes, it really is.

NORA: Kristina! And to think I didn't know you! But how could *I*? (*more gently*) You *have* changed, Kristina.

MRS. LINDE: Yes, I have . . . nine years—nearly ten—it's a long time.

NORA: Is it really as long as that since we saw each other? Yes, I suppose it is. But you know, I've been so happy these last eight years! And now you've come to town too? How brave of you to travel all that way in the middle of winter.

MRS. LINDE: I arrived by steamer this morning.

NORA: In time to have a lovely Christmas. Oh, this is wonderful! We'll have a splendid time. But do take your things off—aren't you absolutely frozen? (*helping her*) There! Now come and sit by the stove where it's cosy. No, you have the armchair, I'll sit in the rocking-chair. (*taking her hands*) Yes, now you look like your old self again—it was just the first moment. . . . But you're paler, Kristina, and a little thinner, perhaps. . . .

MRS. LINDE: And a lot older, Nora.

NORA: A little older, perhaps—just a teeny bit—but certainly not a lot. (*suddenly checking herself and speaking seriously*) Oh, how thoughtless of me! Here I am, chattering away . . . dear sweet Kristina, can you ever forgive me?

MRS. LINDE: What do you mean, Nora?

NORA: Poor Kristina, you're a widow now.

MRS. LINDE: Yes . . . three years ago.

NORA: Yes, I know; I saw it in the papers. Oh, Kristina, I kept meaning to write to you, honestly I did, but something always cropped up and I put it off . . .

MRS. LINDE: Dear Nora, I do understand.

NORA: No, it was horrid of me. Oh, poor Kristina, what you must have gone through! And he didn't leave you anything to live on?

MRS. LINDE: No.

NORA: And no children?

MRS. LINDE: No.

NORA: Nothing at all?

MRS. LINDE: Not even any regrets to break my heart over.

NORA (*looking at her incredulously*): Oh, but Kristina, that can't be true.

MRS. LINDE (*stroking* NORA'S *hair with a sad smile*): It happens like that sometimes, Nora.

NORA: But to be so completely alone—that must be terribly sad for you. *I* have three lovely children; you can't see them just now, they're out with their Nanny. . . . But now you must tell me all about it.

MRS. LINDE: No, no, I want to hear about you.

NORA: No, you first—I mustn't be selfish today—I'm not going to think about anything but your troubles. I must just tell you one thing, though. Do you know, we've just had the most wonderful stroke of luck—only the other day.

MRS. LINDE: Oh? What was it?

NORA: Just think—my husband's been made Manager of the Savings Bank.

MRS. LINDE: Your husband? But that's wonderful.

NORA: Yes, it's magnificent! A barrister's life is such an uncertain one—especially when he won't touch any case that isn't absolutely respectable. Of course Torvald never would—and I quite agree with him. Well, you can imagine how delighted we are. He's to start at the Bank on New Year's Day, and he'll have a big salary and lots of commission. Oh, we shall be able to live quite differently from now on—to live as we'd like to. Oh, Kristina, I'm so happy! It'll be really wonderful to have lots of money, and never need to worry, won't it?

MRS. LINDE: Yes, it must be pleasant to have everything you need.

NORA: Oh, not just what we need! Heaps and heaps of money!

MRS. LINDE (*with a smile*): Nora, Nora! Haven't you learned sense yet? Even at school you were a terrible spendthrift.

NORA (*laughing quietly*): Yes, Torvald says I still am. (*wagging her finger*) But "Nora, Nora" isn't as silly as you think. We simply hadn't the money for me to waste; we both had to work.

MRS. LINDE: You as well?

NORA: Yes, with odds and ends of needlework—crochet and embroidery and so on. (*casually*) And in other ways too. You see, when we married, Torvald gave up his government post—there wasn't any hope of promotion in his department, and of course he had to earn more money than before. But he overworked dreadfully that first year; you see, he had to take on all sorts of extra jobs, and he worked from morning till night. He couldn't stand it; he was dreadfully ill, and the doctors said he'd simply *have* to go to the south.

MRS. LINDE: Oh yes, you went to Italy for a whole year, didn't you?

NORA: Yes, we did. It wasn't easy to manage, I can tell you. It was just after Ivar was born, but of course we had to go. Oh, it was a wonderful trip—beautiful! And it saved Torvald's life. But it cost a terrible lot of money, Kristina!

MRS. LINDE: I'm sure it did.

NORA: Twelve hundred dollars—four thousand eight hundred crowns. That's a lot of money.

MRS. LINDE: Yes, at times like that, it's very lucky to have money.

NORA: Well, you see, we got it from Papa.

MRS. LINDE: Oh? Yes, I remember, your father died just about then.

NORA: Yes, just then. And just think, Kristina, I couldn't go and nurse him. I was expecting Ivar to arrive any day, and there was my poor Torvald, dreadfully ill, to look after. Dear, kind Papa—I never saw him again— that was the hardest thing I've had to bear in all my married life, Kristina.

MRS. LINDE: I know how fond of him you were. . . . And so you went to Italy?

NORA: Yes, we left a month later. We had the money then, and the doctors said there was no time to lose.

MRS. LINDE: And when you came back your husband was cured?

NORA: Fit as a fiddle!

MRS. LINDE: But the doctor . . . ?

NORA: What doctor?

MRS. LINDE: That man who arrived at the same time as I did—I thought your maid said he was the doctor?

NORA: Ah, that was Dr. Rank—but he doesn't come here professionally, he's our best friend, he always looks in at least once a day. No, Torvald's never had a day's illness since. And the children are well and strong, and so am I. (*jumping up and clapping her hands*) Oh Lord, Kristina, it's wonderful to be alive and happy! Oh, but how awful of me, I've just gone on talking about myself! (*She sits on a footstool beside* KRISTINA *and puts her arms on her knees.*) Now, you mustn't be angry with me. Tell me, is it really true that you didn't love your husband? Why did you marry him, then?

MRS. LINDE: My mother was still alive; she was bedridden and helpless, and I had my two younger brothers to look after—I didn't feel I *could* refuse his offer.

NORA: No, no, I suppose you couldn't. And he was rich in those days?

MRS. LINDE: I believe he was quite well off; but his business wasn't sound, and when he died it went to pieces and there wasn't anything left.

NORA: And you . . . ?

MRS. LINDE: Well, I just had to struggle along—I ran a little shop, then a small school, and anything else I could turn my hand to. These last three years I never seem to have stopped working. Still, that's all over now, Nora— poor Mother's gone, she doesn't need me any longer. Nor do the boys— they're working, and they can look after themselves.

NORA: How relieved you must feel.

MRS. LINDE: No . . . just unspeakably empty—I've no one to live for any more. (*She gets up restlessly.*) That's why I couldn't bear to stay in that little backwater any longer. It must be easier to find some sort of work here that'll keep me busy and take my mind off things. If only I could be lucky enough to find some office work . . .

NORA: But, Kristina, that's terribly tiring, and you look worn out already. It'd be much better for you to go for a holiday.

MRS. LINDE (*going over to the window*): I haven't a father to pay my fare, Nora.

NORA (*rising*): Oh, don't be angry with me.

MRS. LINDE (*going to her*): No, Nora, it's you who mustn't be angry with me. That's the worst of my sort of life—it makes you so bitter. There's no one to work for, yet you can never relax. You must live, so you become self-centered. Why, do you know, when you told me the news of your good fortune, I wasn't nearly so glad for your sake as for my own!

NORA: But . . . Oh, I see what you mean—you think perhaps Torvald might be able to do something for you.

MRS. LINDE: Yes, I thought he might.

NORA: Oh, he will, Kristina; just leave it to me. I'll bring the subject up very cleverly. . . . I'll think of some wonderful way to put him in a good mood. . . . Oh, I should so like to help you.

MRS. LINDE: It *is* kind of you, Nora, to want to do this for me . . . especially when *you* know so little about the troubles and hardships of life.

NORA: I? So little?

MRS. LINDE (*smiling*): Well, good Heavens, a little bit of sewing and that sort of thing! You're only a baby, Nora!

NORA (*crossing the room with a toss of her head*): Don't be so superior.

MRS. LINDE: No?

NORA: You're like all the others—you none of you think I could do anything worthwhile. . . .

MRS. LINDE: Well?

NORA: And you think I've had an easy life, with nothing to contend with.

MRS. LINDE: But, Nora dear, you've just told me all your troubles.

NORA: Pooh, they were nothing. (*dropping her voice*) I haven't told you the really important thing.

MRS. LINDE: The important thing? What was that?

NORA: I expect you look down on me, Kristina, but you've no right to. You're proud because you worked so hard for your mother all those years.

MRS. LINDE: I don't look down on anyone; but of course I'm proud—and glad—to know that I was able to make Mother's last days a little easier.

NORA: And you're proud of what you did for your brothers.

MRS. LINDE: I think I have every right to be.

NORA: I quite agree. But now let me tell you something, Kristina; I've got something to be proud of, too.

MRS. LINDE: I'm sure you have; what is it?

NORA: Not so loud—suppose Torvald were to hear! I wouldn't have him find out for the world. No one must know about it—no one but you, Kristina.

MRS. LINDE: But what is it?

NORA: Come over here. (*pulling her down on the sofa beside her*) Oh yes, I've something to be proud of. It was I who saved Torvald's life.

MRS. LINDE: Saved his life? But how?

NORA: I told you about our trip to Italy. Torvald would never have got better if we hadn't gone there.

MRS. LINDE: Yes, but your father gave you the money you needed.

NORA (*smiling*): That's what Torvald thinks—and so does everyone else—but . . .

MRS. LINDE: Well?

NORA: Papa never gave us a penny. It was I who raised the money.

MRS. LINDE: You? All that money?

NORA: Twelve hundred dollars—four thousand eight hundred crowns. What do you think of that?

MRS. LINDE: But how could you, Nora? Did you win it in a lottery?

NORA (*contemptuously*): A lottery! (*with a snort*) Pooh—where would be the glory in that?

MRS. LINDE: Where did you get it then?

NORA (*with an enigmatic smile*): Aha! (*humming*) Tra-la-la!

MRS. LINDE: Because you certainly couldn't have borrowed it.

NORA: Oh? Why not?

MRS. LINDE: Because a wife can't borrow without her husband's consent.

NORA (*with a toss of her head*): Ah, yes she can—when it's a wife with a little flair for business—a wife who knows how to set about it . . .

MRS. LINDE: But, Nora, I don't see how—

NORA: There's no reason why you should. Besides, I never said anything about *borrowing* the money. There are all sorts of ways I might have got it. (*lying back on the sofa*) I might have got it from some admirer or other—after all, I'm quite attractive . . .

MRS. LINDE: Don't be so silly!

NORA: You know, you're simply dying of curiosity, Kristina!

MRS. LINDE: Now, Nora dear, listen to me—you haven't done anything rash, have you?

NORA (*sitting up*): Is it rash to save your husband's life?

MRS. LINDE: I think it's rash to do something without his knowing . . .

NORA: But I couldn't possibly let him know. Good heavens, don't you see?—it would never have done for him to realize how ill he was. It was to *me* that the doctors came; they said that his life was in danger and that the only way to save him was to take him to the south. Do you think I didn't try to wheedle him into it first? I told him how nice it would be for me to have a holiday abroad like all the other young wives. I tried tears and entreaties—I told him that he really ought to think about my condition—that he must be a dear and do what I asked. I hinted that he could easily borrow the money. But then, Kristina, he nearly lost his temper, he told me I was frivolous, and that it was his duty as a husband not to give in to what I believe he called my "whims and fancies." "All right," I thought, "but your life must be saved somehow." And then I thought of a way . . .

MRS. LINDE: But surely your father must have told him that the money didn't come from him?

NORA: No—it was just then that Papa died. I'd always meant to tell him about it and ask him not to give me away, but he was so ill . . . and I'm afraid in the end there was no need.

MRS. LINDE: And *you've* never told your husband?

NORA: Good heavens no, how could I? When he's so strict about that sort of thing. . . . Besides, Torvald has his pride—most men have—he'd be terribly hurt and humiliated if he thought he owed anything to me. It'd spoil everything between us, and our lovely happy home would never be the same again.

MRS. LINDE: Aren't you ever going to tell him?

NORA (*thoughtfully, with a little smile*): Well—one day, perhaps. But not for a long time. When I'm not pretty any more. No, you mustn't laugh. What I mean, of course, is when Torvald isn't as fond of me as he is now—when my dancing and dressing up and reciting don't amuse him any longer. It might be a good thing, then, to have something up my sleeve . . . (*breaking off*). But that's nonsense—that time'll never come. Well, Kristina, what do you think of my great secret? Am I still no use? What's more, you can take my word for it that it's all been a great worry to me—it hasn't been at all easy to meet all my obligations punctually. In business, you know, there are things called "quarterly payments" and "installments," and they're always dreadfully hard to meet, so you see, I've had to scrape together a little bit here and a little bit there, whenever I could. I couldn't save much out of the housekeeping money, because Torvald has to live properly, and I couldn't have the children looking shabby. I didn't feel I could touch the money that I had for my little darlings.

MRS. LINDE: So it all had to come out of your own pocket-money? Poor Nora.

NORA: Of course. After all, it was my own doing. So whenever Torvald gave me money for new dresses and things, I never spent more than half of it—I always bought the simplest, cheapest things. Thank goodness anything looks well on me, so Torvald never noticed. But, oh Kristina, it hasn't been at all easy, because it's so nice to be beautifully dressed, isn't it?

MRS. LINDE: It certainly is.

NORA: Then I've found other ways of earning money too. Last winter I was lucky enough to get a lot of copying to do, so I locked myself in and sat writing—often till after midnight. Oh, I was so tired sometimes . . . so tired. Still, it was really tremendous fun sitting there working and earning money. It was almost like being a man.

MRS. LINDE: But how much have you been able to pay off?

NORA: Well, I don't really know exactly. You see, with a thing like that, it's very difficult to keep accounts. All I know is that I've paid out every penny that I've been able to scrape together. Often I've been at my wits' end. . . . (*smiling*) Then I used to sit here and imagine that a rich old gentleman had fallen in love with me—

MRS. LINDE: Oh? Who was it?

NORA: Wait a minute—and that he died, and when they read his will, there it was, as large as life: "All my money is to go to the lovely Mrs. Nora Helmer—cash down."

MRS. LINDE: But, Nora dear, who was he?

NORA: Oh, good heavens, don't you see? There wasn't really any old gentleman, it was just something that I used to sit here and imagine—often and often—when I simply didn't know which way to turn for the money. But that's all over now; the silly old gentleman can stay where he is for all I care—I've finished with him and his will, my troubles are all over! (*jumping up*) Oh, goodness, Kristina, just think of it! No more worries! To be able to have no more worries at all! To be able to romp with the children, and to have all the lovely up-to-date things about the house that

Torvald likes so much. . . . And then it'll soon be spring, and the sky'll be so blue, and perhaps we'll be able to go away for a bit. Perhaps I shall see the sea again. Oh, isn't it wonderful to be alive and happy?

The doorbell is heard from the hall.

MRS. LINDE (*getting up*): There's someone at the door—perhaps I'd better go.

NORA: No, stay. It'll be someone for Torvald, they won't come in here.

MAID (*at the hall door*): Excuse me, Madam, there's a gentleman to see the Lawyer—

NORA: The Bank Manager, you mean.

MAID: Yes, the Bank Manager. But I didn't know—seeing the Doctor's with him—

NORA: Who is it?

KROGSTAD (*in the doorway*): It's me, Mrs. Helmer.

MRS. LINDE *gives a start, then, collecting herself, turns away to the window.*

NORA (*tensely and in a low voice, taking a step toward him*): You? What is it? Why do you want to see my husband?

KROGSTAD: Bank business—in a way. I have a small post at the Savings Bank, and I hear your husband is to be our new Manager—

NORA: So it's only—

KROGSTAD: Only dull official business, Mrs. Helmer; nothing else whatever.

NORA: Well, you'll find him in his study. (*She bows perfunctorily and shuts the hall door. Then she goes over and attends to the stove.*)

MRS. LINDE: Nora . . . who was that man?

NORA: He's a lawyer named Krogstad.

MRS. LINDE: So it was really he . . .

NORA: Do you know him?

MRS. LINDE: I used to know him—years ago. He was once in a lawyer's office back at home.

NORA: Yes, so he was.

MRS. LINDE: How he's changed!

NORA: He's had a very unhappy married life.

MRS. LINDE: And now he's a widower?

NORA: With lots of children. There, that should burn up now.

She shuts the door of the stove and pushes the rocking-chair a little to one side.

MRS. LINDE: He has a finger in all sorts of business, they say.

NORA: Really? Well, they may be right, I don't know anything about. . . . But don't let's talk about business—it's so boring.

DR. RANK *comes out of* HELMER'S *room.*

RANK (*in the doorway*): No no, my dear fellow, I don't want to be in the way. Besides, I'd like to see your wife for a bit. (*As he shuts the door he notices* MRS. LINDE.) Oh, I'm sorry—I'm in the way here, too.

NORA: Not in the least. (*introducing them*) This is Dr. Rank—Mrs. Linde.

RANK: Ah, now that's a name that I'm constantly hearing in this house. I think I passed you on the stairs as I came up.

MRS. LINDE: Yes, I don't like stairs—I have to take them very slowly.

RANK: Ah, some little internal weakness?

MRS. LINDE: Only overwork, I think.

RANK: Is that all? So you've come to town for a rest—at all the parties?

MRS. LINDE: I've come here to look for work.

RANK: Is that a wise remedy for overwork?

MRS. LINDE: One must live, Doctor.

RANK: Yes, there seems to be a general impression that it's necessary.

NORA: Now, Dr. Rank, you know you want to live, too.

RANK: Yes, indeed I do. However wretched I may be, I always want to prolong the agony as long as possible. All my patients have the same idea. And it's the same with people whose sickness is moral, too. At this very moment there's a moral invalid in there with Helmer, and—

MRS. LINDE (*softly*): Ah.

NORA: Whom do you mean?

RANK: Oh, you wouldn't know him—it's a lawyer named Krogstad. He's rotten to the core, but the first thing he said—as if it were something really important—was that he must live.

NORA: Oh. What did he want to see Torvald about?

RANK: I don't really know; all I heard was that it was something to do with the Bank.

NORA: I didn't know that Krog—that this lawyer had anything to do with the Bank.

RANK: Yes, he has some sort of post there. (*to* MRS. LINDE) I don't know if it's the same where you live, but here there are people who grub around sniffing out moral corruption, and when they've found it they put it in a good job somewhere where they can keep an eye on it. The honest man probably finds himself left out in the cold.

MRS. LINDE: Well, I suppose the sick need looking after.

RANK (*shrugging his shoulders*): There you are! That's the sort of theory that's turning the community into a regular hospital!

NORA, *deep in her own thoughts, suddenly gives a quiet laugh and claps her hands.*

RANK: Why do you laugh at that? Do you really know what the community is?

NORA: What do I care for your dreary old community? I was laughing at something quite different—something frightfully funny. Tell me, Dr. Rank, do all the people who work at the Bank depend on Torvald now?

RANK: Is that what you found so "frightfully funny"?

NORA (*smiling and humming*): Ah, that's my business—that's my business! (*pacing around the room*) Yes, it really is frightfully funny to think that we—that Torvald has all that power over so many people. (*taking a bag from her pocket*) Won't you have a macaroon, Dr. Rank?

RANK: Macaroons? Now, now! I thought they were forbidden here!

NORA: Yes, but these are some that Kristina gave me.

MRS. LINDE: What? But I . . . ?

NORA: No, no, don't be frightened; you weren't to know that Torvald had forbidden them. The thing is, he's afraid I shall spoil my teeth with them.

But pooh—just this once! That's right, isn't it, Dr. Rank? Here! (*She pops a macaroon into his mouth.*) And now you, Kristina. And I'll have one as well—just a little one. Or two at the most. (*pacing about again*) Oh, I'm really terribly happy! Now there's just one thing in the world that I want terribly badly.

RANK: Oh? What is it?

NORA: It's something that I've been wanting terribly to say in front of Torvald.

RANK: Then why can't you say it?

NORA: Oh, I daren't—it's very bad.

MRS. LINDE: Bad?

RANK: Then you'd better not say it. Though surely to *us* . . . What is it that you want so much to say in front of Torvald?

NORA: I terribly want to say—"Well I'm damned!"

RANK: You must be mad!

MRS. LINDE: But, good gracious, Nora—

RANK: Well, here he comes. Say it.

NORA (*hiding the macaroons*): Sh! Sh!

HELMER *comes out of his room with a coat over his arm and a hat in his hand.*

NORA (*going to him*): Well, so you got rid of him, Torvald dear?

HELMER: Yes, he's just gone.

NORA: Let me introduce you: this is Kristina—she's come to town.

HELMER: Kristina . . . ? I'm sorry, I'm afraid I don't—

NORA: Mrs. Linde, Torvald dear! Kristina Linde.

HELMER: Oh yes—surely you and my wife were girls together?

MRS. LINDE: Yes, we knew each other in the old days.

NORA: And just think, she's come all this way to see you!

HELMER: To see *me?*

NORA: Kristina's frightfully clever at office work, and she wants terribly to work under a really able man so that she can learn more still. . . .

HELMER: That's very wise of you, Mrs. Linde.

NORA: So when she heard that you'd been made a Bank Manager—they had a telegram about it—she came down here as quickly as she could. You'll be able to do something for her, Torvald, won't you? Just to please me?

HELMER: Well, it's not impossible. . . . I take it that you're a widow, Mrs. Linde?

MRS. LINDE: Yes.

HELMER: And you've had commercial experience?

MRS. LINDE: A certain amount, yes.

HELMER: Ah, then it's highly probable that I shall be able to find a post for you.

NORA (*clapping her hands*): There you are! You see!

HELMER: You've come at just the right moment, Mrs. Linde . . .

MRS. LINDE: I can't tell you how grateful I am.

HELMER: Oh, there's no need . . . (*putting on his overcoat*) But now you must excuse me. . . .

RANK: Wait, I'll come with you. (*He gets his fur coat from the hall and warms it at the stove.*)

NORA: Don't be long, Torvald dear.

HELMER: I shan't be more than about an hour.

NORA: Are you going too, Kristina?

MRS. LINDE (*putting on her outdoor things*): Yes, I must go and look for a room.

HELMER: Then perhaps we can all go down the street together.

NORA (*helping her*): How tiresome that we're so short of room here—we couldn't possibly—

MRS. LINDE: Oh no, you mustn't think of it. Good-bye, Nora dear—and thank you.

NORA: Good-bye for the present—you'll come back this evening, won't you? And you, too, Dr. Rank. What? "If you feel up to it"? Of course you will. Wrap up well, now!

They go out into the hall still talking: the CHILDREN'S *voices are heard on the stairs.*

NORA: Here they are! Here they are!

She runs out and opens the door; the nurse, ANNA-MARIA, *comes in with the* CHILDREN.

Come in, come in! (*She stoops down and kisses them.*) Oh, my little darlings! Look at them, Kristina, aren't they sweet?

RANK: Don't stand there chattering in the draught!

HELMER: Come along, Mrs. Linde, this is no place for anyone but a mother!

He and DR. RANK *and* MRS. LINDE *go down the stairs. The* NURSE *comes into the room with the* CHILDREN, *and* NORA *follows, shutting the hall door.*

NORA: How nice and healthy you look! Oh, what pink cheeks—like apples and roses!

The CHILDREN *keep chattering to her during the following:*

Did you enjoy yourselves? That's good. And so you gave Emmy and Bob a ride on your sledge? Both together? Well, fancy that! What a big boy you are, Ivar. Oh, let me take her for a minute, Nanny—my little baby dolly! (*She takes the youngest from the* NURSE *and dances with her.*) Yes, yes, Mummy'll dance with Bob too! What? You've been snowballing? Oh, I wish I'd been there. No, leave them, Nanny, I'll take their things off. Yes, let me do it, it's such fun. You look frozen—there's some hot coffee for you on the stove in the next room.

The NURSE *goes into the room on the left.* NORA *takes off the* CHILDREN'S *outdoor things, throwing them down anywhere, while the* CHILDREN *all talk at once.*

NORA: Well! So a great big dog ran after you? But he didn't bite you? No, dogs don't bite dear little baby dollies! No, don't look inside those parcels, Ivar. What's in them? Ah, wouldn't you like to know? No, no, it isn't anything nice at all! What, you want a game? What shall we play? Hide and seek? Yes, let's play hide and seek. Bob, you hide first. Me? All right, I'll hide first.

She and the CHILDREN *play, laughing and shouting, both in this room and the room on the right. At last,* NORA *hides under the table. The* CHILDREN *come rushing in to look for her but they can't find her. Then, hearing her smothered laughter, they run to the table, lift the cloth, and see her. Loud shouts. She comes out on all fours as if to frighten them. Fresh shouts. Meanwhile there has been knocking on the front door, but no one has noticed it. Now the door half opens, revealing* KROGSTAD. *He waits a little as the game continues.*

KROGSTAD: Excuse me, Mrs. Helmer . . .

NORA (*with a stifled cry she turns and half rises*): Oh! What do you want?

KROGSTAD: I'm sorry; the front door was open. Somebody must have forgotten to shut it.

NORA (*getting up*): My husband is out, Mr. Krogstad.

KROGSTAD: Yes, I know.

NORA: Then . . . what do you want here?

KROGSTAD: A word with you.

NORA: With . . . ?(*quietly, to the* CHILDREN) Go to Nanny. What? No, the strange man isn't going to hurt Mummy—directly he's gone, we'll go on with our game. (*She takes the* CHILDREN *out to the room on the left, shutting the door after them. Then, tense and wary.*) You want to see me?

KROGSTAD: Yes, I do.

NORA: Today? But it isn't the first of the month yet. . . .

KROGSTAD: No, it's Christmas Eve. It all depends on you whether you have a happy Christmas or not.

NORA: What do you want? I can't manage any today—

KROGSTAD: We'll talk about that later; this is something different. Can you spare a moment?

NORA: Well, yes . . . I can, but—

KROGSTAD: Good. I was sitting in Olsen's restaurant, and I saw your husband go down the street—

NORA: Well?

KROGSTAD: —with a lady.

NORA: What of it?

KROGSTAD: May I be so bold as to ask if the lady was a Mrs. Linde?

NORA: She was.

KROGSTAD: She's just arrived in town?

NORA: Today, yes.

KROGSTAD: She's a great friend of yours?

NORA: Yes, she is. But I don't see—

KROGSTAD: I knew her once, too.

NORA: Yes, I know.

KROGSTAD: Oh? So you know about it? I thought so. All right, then I can ask you straight out: is Mrs. Linde to have a post at the Bank?

NORA: How dare you question me, Mr. Krogstad—one of my husband's subordinates. But since you ask, I'll tell you. Yes, Mrs. Linde is to have a post, and it was I who recommended her, Mr. Krogstad. So now you know.

KROGSTAD: Yes, I guessed as much.

NORA (*walking up and down*): So it looks as if one has a *little* influence—just because one's a woman, it doesn't necessarily mean that—and people in subordinate positions, Mr. Krogstad, should be careful not to offend anyone who—well—

KROGSTAD: . . . who has influence?

NORA: Exactly.

KROGSTAD (*changing his tone*): Mrs. Helmer . . . would you please be good enough to use your influence on my behalf?

NORA: How? What do you mean?

KROGSTAD: Would you be so kind as to see that I keep my subordinate position at the Bank?

NORA: What do you mean? Who's trying to take it away?

KROGSTAD: Oh, you needn't pretend to *me* that you don't know. I can quite see that it wouldn't be pleasant for your friend to have to keep running into me. What's more, I know now whom I shall have to thank for getting me dismissed.

NORA: But I assure you—

KROGSTAD: Oh, of course, of course. But don't let's beat about the bush—I advise you, while there's still time, to use your influence to prevent it.

NORA: But, Mr. Krogstad, I haven't any influence.

KROGSTAD: No? I thought you said just now—

NORA: I didn't mean it like that, of course. I? How do you think I could influence my husband in that sort of thing?

KROGSTAD: Well . . . I've known your husband since his student days—I don't think our noble Bank Manager is more inflexible than any other husband.

NORA: If you speak disrespectfully of my husband I shall show you the door!

KROGSTAD: How brave of you!

NORA: I'm not afraid of you any more. After the New Year I shall very quickly be free of the whole thing.

KROGSTAD (*controlling himself*): Listen to me, Mrs. Helmer. If need be, I shall fight to keep my little post at the Bank as I'd fight for my life.

NORA: So it seems.

KROGSTAD: It's not just for the money—that's the least important thing about it. No, there's something else . . . Well, I might as well tell you—it's this: of course you know—everyone does—that I got into trouble a few years ago.

NORA: I believe I heard something of the sort.

KROGSTAD: It never came to court, but since then it's been as if every way was closed to me—that's why I took to the business that you know about. I had to live somehow, and I think I can claim that I haven't been as bad as some. But now I want to give up all that sort of thing. My sons are growing up, and in fairness to them I must try to win back as much respect as I can in the town. This post at the Bank was the first step for me—and now your husband's going to kick me off the ladder again, back into the mud.

NORA: But honestly, Mr. Krogstad, there's nothing that I can do to help you.

KROGSTAD: That's because you don't want to. But I have ways of making you.

NORA: You won't tell my husband that I owe you money?

KROGSTAD: Ah . . . suppose I did?

NORA: That would be a vile thing to do. (*with tears in her voice*) I've been so proud of my secret; I couldn't bear to have him hear it like that—brutally and clumsily—and from *you*. It would put me in a most unpleasant position.

KROGSTAD: Only unpleasant?

NORA (*impetuously*): All right, then—tell him! But it'll be the worse for you, because my husband will see what a brute you are, and then you'll certainly lose your post.

KROGSTAD: I asked you if it was only domestic unpleasantness that you were afraid of?

NORA: If my husband finds out, naturally he'll pay you whatever I still owe, and then we'll have nothing more to do with you.

KROGSTAD (*taking a step toward her*): Listen, Mrs. Helmer; either my memory isn't very good, or you don't know much about business. I shall have to make things a little clearer to you.

NORA: How?

KROGSTAD: When your husband was ill you came to me to borrow twelve hundred dollars.

NORA: I didn't know where else to go.

KROGSTAD: I promised to find you the money—

NORA: And you did find it.

KROGSTAD: I promised to find you the money on certain conditions. At the time you were so worried about your husband's illness, and so anxious to get the money for your journey, that I don't think you paid much attention to the details—so it won't be out of place if I remind you of them. Well . . . I promised to find you the money against a note of hand which I drew up.

NORA: Yes, and which I signed.

KROGSTAD: Exactly. But below that I'd added a few lines making your father surety for the money. Your father was to sign this clause.

NORA: Was to? But he did sign.

KROGSTAD: I'd left the date blank—that's to say, your father was to fill in the date when he signed the paper. Do you remember?

NORA: Yes, I think so . . .

KROGSTAD: Then I gave you the document so that you could post it to your father. Is that correct?

NORA: Yes.

KROGSTAD: And of course you sent it at once, because only five or six days later you brought it back to me with your father's signature . . . and I handed over the money.

NORA: Well? Haven't I paid it off regularly?

KROGSTAD: Yes, fairly regularly. But—to get back to the point—you were going through a trying time just then, Mrs. Helmer?

NORA: I certainly was.

KROGSTAD: Your father was ill, I believe?

NORA: He was dying.

KROGSTAD: He died soon afterwards?

NORA: Yes.

KROGSTAD: Tell me, Mrs. Helmer, do you happen to remember the day he died? The day of the month, I mean?

NORA: Papa died on the twenty-ninth of September.

KROGSTAD: That is correct—I've confirmed that for myself. And that brings us to a curious thing (*producing a paper*) which I'm quite unable to explain.

NORA: What curious thing? I don't know of any—

KROGSTAD: The curious thing, Mrs. Helmer, is that your father signed this note of hand three days after his death.

NORA: How? I don't understand.

KROGSTAD: Your father died on the twenty-ninth of September. But look at this—your father has dated his signature the second of October. Isn't that a curious thing, Mrs. Helmer?

NORA *is silent.*

Can you explain it?

NORA *is still silent.*

It's odd, too, that the words October the second and the year aren't in your father's handwriting, but in a writing that I think I know. Well, of course, that could be explained—your father might have forgotten to date his signature, and someone else might have guessed at the date before they knew of his death. There's nothing wrong in that. It's the signature that really matters. That *is* genuine, isn't it, Mrs. Helmer? It really was your father himself who wrote his name there?

NORA (*after a moment's pause, throwing her head back and looking defiantly at him*): No, it was not. *I* wrote Papa's name.

KROGSTAD: Look, Mrs. Helmer, you know that that's a very dangerous admission?

NORA: Why? You'll soon get your money.

KROGSTAD: May I ask you something? Why didn't you send the paper to your father?

NORA: I couldn't; he was far too ill. If I'd asked him for his signature, I should have had to tell him what the money was for—and when he was so ill himself, I couldn't tell him that my husband's life was in danger— I couldn't possibly.

KROGSTAD: Then it would have been better for you if you'd given up your trip abroad.

NORA: I couldn't do that. The journey was to save my husband's life—how could I give it up?

KROGSTAD: But didn't it occur to you that you were tricking me?

NORA: I couldn't worry about that—I wasn't thinking about you at all. I couldn't bear the way you were so cold-blooded—the way you made difficulties although you knew how desperately ill my husband was.

KROGSTAD: Mrs. Helmer, you obviously don't realize what you've been guilty of; but let me tell you that the thing that I once did that ruined my reputation was nothing more—and nothing worse—than that.

NORA: You? Are you trying to tell me that you would have done a brave deed to save your wife's life?

KROGSTAD: The law is not concerned with motives.

NORA: Then it must be a very stupid law.

KROGSTAD: Stupid or not, it's the law that you'll be judged by if I produce this paper in court.

NORA: I simply don't believe that. Hasn't a daughter the right to protect her dying father from worry and anxiety? Hasn't a wife the right to save her husband's life? I don't know much about the law, but I'm quite certain that it must say somewhere that things like that are allowed. Don't you, a lawyer, know that? You must be a very stupid lawyer, Mr. Krogstad.

KROGSTAD: Possibly. But you'll admit that I do understand business—the sort of business that you and I have been engaged in? Very well, you do as you please. But I tell you this—if I'm to be flung out for the second time, you'll keep me company! (*He bows and goes out through the hall.*)

NORA (*after a moment's thought, with a toss of her head*): What nonsense! Trying to frighten me like that! I'm not as silly as all that. (*She starts to busy herself by tidying the children's clothes, but soon stops.*) But . . . No, it isn't possible . . . I did it for love!

CHILDREN (*at the door to the left*): Mamma, the strange man's just gone out of the front door.

NORA: Yes . . . yes, I know. Now, you're not to tell anyone about the strange man, do you hear? Not even Papa.

CHILDREN: No, Mamma. Will you come and play with us again now?

NORA: No—not just now.

CHILDREN: But, Mamma, you promised!

NORA: Yes, but now I can't. Run along. I'm busy—run along, there's good children. (*She pushes them gently into the other room and shuts the door after them. She sits on the sofa and, picking up her needlework, she does a stitch or two but soon stops.*) No! (*She throws down the work and, rising, goes to the hall door and calls.*) Helena—bring me the tree, please. (*Going to the table on the left, she opens the drawer, then pauses again.*) No! It's simply not possible!

MAID (*with the Christmas tree*): Where shall I put it, Madam?

NORA: Here, in the middle of the room.

MAID: Is there anything else you want?

NORA: No, thank you, I've got all I want.

The MAID, *having put the tree down, goes out.*

NORA (*busily decorating the tree*): A candle here . . . and flowers here. . . . That horrible man! It's all nonsense . . . nonsense, there's nothing in it! We shall have a lovely tree—I'll do all the things you like, Torvald, I'll sing and dance—

HELMER *comes in with a bundle of papers under his arm.*

NORA: Oh, are you back already?

HELMER: Yes. Has there been anyone here?

NORA: Here? No.

HELMER: That's odd; I saw Krogstad coming out of the gate.

NORA: Did you? Oh yes, that's right; Krogstad *was* here for a moment.

HELMER: Nora, I can see by your face that he's been here begging you to put in a good word for him.

NORA: Yes.

HELMER: And you were to make it look as if it was your own idea. You weren't to let me know that he'd been here. That was what he asked, wasn't it?

NORA: Yes, Torvald, but—

HELMER: Nora, Nora, would you lend yourself to that sort of thing? Talking to a man like that—making him promises? And, worst of all, telling me a lie!

NORA: A lie?

HELMER: Didn't you say that no one had been here? (*shaking a finger at her*) My little songbird mustn't ever do that again. A songbird must have a clear voice to sing with—no false notes. (*putting his arm around her*) That's true, isn't it? Yes, I knew it was. (*letting her go*) Now we won't say any more about it. (*sitting by the stove*) Ah, this is nice and comfortable! (*He glances through his papers.*)

NORA (*after working at the Christmas tree for a little*): Torvald?

HELMER: Yes?

NORA: I'm terribly looking forward to the day after tomorrow—the fancy-dress party at the Stenborgs.

HELMER: And I'm "terribly" curious to see what surprise you're planning for me.

NORA: Oh, it's so silly . . .

HELMER: What is?

NORA: I can't think of anything that'll do. Everything seems so stupid and pointless.

HELMER: So little Nora's realized that?

NORA (*behind his chair, with her arms on the chair-back*): Are you very busy, Torvald?

HELMER: Well . . .

NORA: What are all those papers?

HELMER: Bank business.

NORA: Already?

HELMER: I've asked the retiring Manager to give me full authority to make some necessary changes in the staff, and the working arrangements—that'll take me all Christmas week. I want to have everything ready by New Year's Day.

NORA: So that was why poor Krogstad—

HELMER: Hm!

NORA (*still leaning over the chair-back, and gently stroking his hair*): If you hadn't been so busy, Torvald, I'd have asked you a terribly great favor. . . .

HELMER: Well, what is it? Tell me.

NORA: No one has such good taste as you have, and I do so want to look nice at the fancy-dress party. Torvald, couldn't you take me in hand and decide what I'm to go as—what my costume's to be?

HELMER: Aha! So my little obstinate one's out of her depth, and wants someone to rescue her?

NORA: Yes, Torvald, I can't do anything without you to help me.

HELMER: Well, well . . . I'll think about it. We'll find something.

NORA: Oh, that *is* nice of you! (*She goes to the Christmas tree again. Pause.*) How pretty these red flowers look. . . . Tell me about this Krogstad—was it really so bad, what he did?

HELMER: He forged a signature. Have you any idea what that means?

NORA: Mightn't he have done it from dire necessity?

HELMER: Possibly—or, like so many others, from sheer foolhardiness. Oh, I'm not so hard-hearted that I'd condemn a man outright for just a single slip.

NORA: No, you wouldn't, would you, Torvald?

HELMER: Many a man can redeem his character if he freely confesses his guilt and takes his punishment.

NORA: Punishment . . . ?

HELMER: But Krogstad did nothing of the sort—he tried to wriggle out of it with tricks and subterfuges. That's what has corrupted him.

NORA: Do you think that would . . . ?

HELMER: Just think how a guilty man like that must have to lie and cheat and play the hypocrite with everyone. How he must wear a mask even with those nearest and dearest to him—yes, even with his own wife and children. Yes, even with his children—that's the most dreadful thing, Nora.

NORA: Why?

HELMER: Because an atmosphere of lies like that infects and poisons the whole life of a home. In a house like that, every breath that the children take is filled with the germs of evil.

NORA (*closer behind him*): Are you certain of that?

HELMER: Oh, my dear, as a lawyer I've seen it so often; nearly all young men who go to the bad have had lying mothers.

NORA: Why only mothers?

HELMER: It's generally the fault of the mother, though of course a father can have the same effect—as every lawyer very well knows. And certainly for years this fellow Krogstad has been going home and poisoning his own children with lies and deceit. That's why I call him a moral outcast. (*holding out his hands to her*) So my darling little Nora must promise me not to plead his cause. Let's shake hands on that. Now then, what's this? Give me your hand. . . . That's better; now it's a bargain. I tell you, it'd be quite impossible for me to work with him; when I'm near people like that, I actually feel physically ill.

NORA (*withdrawing her hand and going over to the far side of the Christmas tree*): How hot it is in here! And I have so much to see to.

HELMER (*rising and collecting his papers*): Yes, and I must try to look through a few of these before dinner. And I'll think about your fancy-dress, too. And perhaps I'll have something in gold paper to hang on the

Christmas tree. (*taking her head in his hands*) My darling little songbird! (*He goes to his room, shutting the door behind him.*)

NORA (*in a hushed voice, after a moment*): Oh no! It can't be true. . . . No, it's not possible. It *can't* be possible!

NURSE (*at the door on the left*): The children want to come in to Mamma—they're asking so prettily.

NORA: No! No! Don't let them come near me! Keep them with you, Nanny.

NURSE: Yes Ma'am. (*She shuts the door.*)

NORA (*white with fear*): Corrupt my little children—poison my home? (*She pauses, then throws up her head.*) That's not true! It could never, never be true.

Act Two

The same room. In the corner by the piano stands the Christmas tree; it is stripped and dishevelled, with the stumps of burnt-out candles. NORA'S *outdoor clothes are on the sofa.*

NORA, *alone in the room, walks about restlessly. Eventually she stops by the sofa and picks up her cloak.*

NORA (*letting the cloak fall again*): Someone's coming! (*She goes to the door to listen.*) No—there's no one there. Of course no one would come today—not on Christmas Day. Nor tomorrow either. But perhaps . . . (*She opens the door and looks out.*) No, there's nothing in the letter-box—it's quite empty. (*coming back into the room*) What nonsense—he can't really have meant it. A thing like that *couldn't* happen. It isn't possible—I have three little children!

The NURSE *comes in from the room on the left, with a huge cardboard box.*

NURSE: I've found the box with the fancy-dress at last.

NORA: Thank you; put it on the table.

NURSE (*doing so*): But it's in a terrible state.

NORA: I should like to tear it all to pieces.

NURSE: Heaven forbid! It can soon be put right—it only needs a little patience.

NORA: Yes, I'll go and get Mrs. Linde to help me.

NURSE: You're not going out again—in this awful weather? You'll catch your death of cold, Miss Nora, Ma'am!

NORA: Well, there are worse things than that. How are the children?

NURSE: The poor little mites are playing with their presents, but—

NORA: Do they ask for me much?

NURSE: You see, they're so used to having their Mamma with them.

NORA: But, Nanny, I *can't* be with them like I used to.

NURSE: Oh well, young children'll get used to anything.

NORA: Do you think so? Do you think they'd forget their Mamma if she went away altogether?

NURSE: Went away altogether? But bless my soul . . . !

NORA: Tell me, Nanny . . . I've often wondered, how did you ever have the heart to hand over your child to strangers?

NURSE: But I had to, so that I could come and be Nanny to my little Nora.

NORA: Yes, but how could you *want* to?

NURSE: When I had the chance of such a good place? Any poor girl who'd got into trouble would be glad to. And that blackguard of a man never did a thing for me.

NORA: I suppose your daughter's quite forgotten you?

NURSE: No, indeed she hasn't. She wrote to me when she was confirmed, and again when she got married.

NORA (*putting her arms round her*): Dear old Nanny, you were a wonderful mother to me when I was little.

NURSE: Poor little Nora—she hadn't any other mother but me.

NORA: And if *my* babies hadn't any other mother, I know you'd . . . Oh, I'm talking nonsense. (*opening the box*) Go to them now; I must just—You'll see how fine I shall look tomorrow.

NURSE: I'm sure there won't be anyone in all the party as fine as you, Miss Nora, Ma'am. (*She goes out to the room on the left.*)

NORA (*starting to unpack the box, but soon pushing it away*): Oh, if only I dared go out! If I could be sure that no one would come—that nothing would happen here in the meantime. . . . Don't be so silly—no one will come. I just mustn't think about it. I'll brush the muff. Pretty, pretty gloves! Don't think about it—don't think! One . . . two . . . three . . . four . . . five . . . six—(*She screams.*) Ah, they're coming!

She starts for the door, but stands irresolute. MRS. LINDE *comes in from the hall, where she has left her street clothes.*

NORA: Oh, it's you, Kristina! There isn't anyone else out there? Oh, it was good of you to come!

MRS. LINDE: They told me you'd been over to ask for me.

NORA: Yes, I was just passing. Actually, there's something you could help me with. Come and sit on the sofa. Look, the people upstairs, the Stenborgs, are having a fancy-dress party tomorrow night, and Torvald wants me to go as a Neopolitan fisher-girl and dance the tarantella that I learned in Capri.

MRS. LINDE: I see, you're going to give a real performance?

NORA: Yes, Torvald says I ought to. Look, here's the costume—Torvald had it made for me when we were out there, but it's so torn now—I really don't know—

MRS. LINDE: Oh, we can easily put that right—it's just that some of the trimming's come undone in places. Have you got a needle and cotton? There, that's all we want.

NORA: Oh, this *is* kind of you.

MRS. LINDE (*as she sews*): So tomorrow you'll be all dressed up? I tell you what, Nora, I'll drop in for a moment and see you in all your finery. But I'm quite forgetting to thank you for a lovely evening yesterday.

NORA (*getting up and crossing the room*): Oh, yesterday . . . I didn't think it was as nice as usual. I wish you'd come up to town earlier, Kristina. Yes, Torvald certainly knows how to make a house attractive and comfortable.

MRS. LINDE: And so do you, if you ask *me*, or you wouldn't be your father's daughter. But tell me, is Dr. Rank always as depressed as he was last night?

NORA: No, it was worse than usual last night. But he's really very ill, poor man, he has consumption of the spine. The fact is, his father was a horrible man who had mistresses and that sort of thing, so, you see, the son's been delicate all his life.

MRS. LINDE (*putting down her sewing*): But, dearest Nora, how do you come to know about things like that?

NORA (*walking about*): Pooh—when you've had three children, you get visits from—from women with a certain amount of medical knowledge—and they gossip about these things.

MRS. LINDE (*after a short silence—sewing again*): Does Dr. Rank come here every day?

NORA: Oh yes, he and Torvald have been friends all their lives, and he's a great friend of mine too. Why, Dr. Rank's almost one of the family.

MRS. LINDE: But tell me, is he quite sincere? I mean doesn't he rather like saying things to please people?

NORA: Not in the least. Whatever makes you think that?

MRS. LINDE: Well, when you introduced us yesterday, he said he'd often heard my name in this house, but I noticed later that your husband had no idea who I was. So how could Dr. Rank . . . ?

NORA: Yes, that's quite right, Kristina. You see, Torvald's so incredibly fond of me that he wants to keep me all to himself, as he says. In the early days he used to get quite jealous if I even mentioned people I'd liked back at home, so of course I gave it up. But I often talk to Dr. Rank, because, you see, he likes to hear about them.

MRS. LINDE: Look, Nora, in lots of things you're still a child. I'm older than you in many ways and I've had a little more experience. There's something I'd like to say to you: you ought to stop all this with Dr. Rank.

NORA: What ought I to stop?

MRS. LINDE: Well . . . two things, I think. Yesterday you were talking about a rich admirer who was going to bring you money—

NORA: Yes, but he doesn't exist—unfortunately. But what about it?

MRS. LINDE: Is Dr. Rank rich?

NORA: Oh yes.

MRS. LINDE: And has no one to provide for?

NORA: No one; but—

MRS. LINDE: And he comes to the house every day?

NORA: Yes, I just said so.

MRS. LINDE: How can a man of his breeding be so tactless?

NORA: I simply don't know what you mean.

MRS. LINDE: Don't pretend, Nora. Do you think I don't know whom you borrowed that twelve hundred dollars from?

NORA: Have you gone completely mad? How could you think a thing like that? From a friend who comes here every single day? That would have been an absolutely impossible situation.

MRS. LINDE: It really wasn't him?

NORA: No, I promise you. Why, it would never have entered my head for a moment. Besides, in those days he hadn't the money to lend—he came into it later.

MRS. LINDE: Well, Nora dear, I think that was lucky for you.

NORA: No, it would never have entered my head to ask Dr. Rank. Though I'm quite sure that if I *were* to ask him . . .

MRS. LINDE: But of course you wouldn't.

NORA: Of course not. I can't imagine that there'd ever be any need. But I'm quite sure that if I told Dr. Rank—

MRS. LINDE: Behind your husband's back?

NORA: I must get clear of this other thing—that's behind his back too. I must get clear of that.

MRS. LINDE: Yes, that's what I was saying yesterday, but—

NORA (*pacing up and down*): A man can straighten out these things so much better than a woman . . .

MRS. LINDE: Her husband, yes.

NORA: Nonsense. (*coming to a halt*) When you've paid off everything you owe, you do get your bond back, don't you?

MRS. LINDE: Of course.

NORA: And you can tear it into little pieces and burn it—the horrid filthy thing?

MRS. LINDE (*giving her a penetrating look, she puts down her sewing and rises slowly*): Nora, you're hiding something from me.

NORA: Is it as obvious as all that?

MRS. LINDE: Something's happened to you since yesterday morning. Nora, what is it?

NORA (*going to her*): Kristina—(*listening*) Sh! Here's Torvald coming back. Look, go in and sit with the children for a bit—Torvald can't bear to see dressmaking. Let Nanny help you.

MRS. LINDE (*picking up a pile of things*): All right then; but I'm not going away till we've talked the whole thing over.

She goes out to the left as HELMER *comes in from the hall.*

NORA (*going to him*): Oh, Torvald dear, I've been so longing for you to come back.

HELMER: Was that the dressmaker?

NORA: No, it was Kristina—she's helping me to mend my costume. You know, I'm going to look so nice. . . .

HELMER: Now wasn't that a good idea of mine?

NORA: Splendid. But wasn't it nice of me to do as you said?

HELMER (*lifting her chin*): Nice? To do what your husband says? All right, little scatterbrain, I know you didn't mean it like that. But don't let me interrupt you—I know you'll be wanting to try it on.

NORA: I suppose you've got work to do?

HELMER: Yes (*showing her a bundle of papers*); look, I've been down to the Bank. (*He starts to go to his study.*)

NORA: Torvald . . .

HELMER (*stopping*): Yes?

NORA: If your little squirrel were to ask you very prettily for something . . .

HELMER: Well?

NORA: Would you do it?

HELMER: Well, naturally I should have to know what it is, first.

NORA: Your squirrel will scamper about and do all her tricks, if you'll be nice and do what she asks.

HELMER: Out with it, then.

NORA: Your skylark'll sing all over the house—up and down the scale . . .

HELMER: Oh well, my skylark does that anyhow!

NORA: I'll be a fairy and dance on a moonbeam for you, Torvald.

HELMER: Nora, you surely don't mean that matter you mentioned this morning?

NORA (*nearer*): Yes, Torvald, I really do beg you—

HELMER: I'm surprised at your bringing that up again.

NORA: Oh, but you must do as I ask—you must let Krogstad keep his place at the Bank.

HELMER: My dear Nora, it's his place that I'm giving to Mrs. Linde.

NORA: Yes, that's terribly nice of you. But you could dismiss some other clerk instead of Krogstad.

HELMER: Now, you're just being extremely obstinate. Because you're irresponsible enough to go and promise to put in a word for him, you expect me to—

NORA: No, it isn't that, Torvald—it's for your own sake. The man writes for the most scurrilous newspapers—you told me so yourself—there's no knowing what harm he could do you. I'm simply frightened to death of him. . . .

HELMER: Ah, now I understand; you remember what happened before, and that frightens you.

NORA: What do you mean?

HELMER: You're obviously thinking of your father.

NORA: Yes—yes, that's it. Just remember the wicked things they put in the papers about Papa—how cruelly they slandered him. I believe they'd have had him dismissed if the Ministry hadn't sent you to look into it, and if you hadn't been so kind and helpful to him.

HELMER: Dear little Nora, there's a considerable difference between your father and me. Your father's reputation as an official was not above suspicion—mine is, and I hope it will continue to be as long as I hold this position.

NORA: But you never know what harm people can do. We could live so happily and peacefully now, you and I and the children, Torvald, without a care in the world in our comfortable home. That's why I do implore you—

HELMER: But it's precisely by pleading for him that you make it impossible for me to keep him. They know already at the Bank that I mean to dismiss Krogstad; suppose it were to get about that the new Manager had let himself be influenced by his wife. . . .

NORA: Well, would that matter?

HELMER: No, of course not! So long as an obstinate little woman got her own way! So I'm to make a laughingstock of myself before the whole staff—

with everybody saying that I can be swayed by all sorts of outside influences? I should soon have to face the consequences, I can tell you. Besides, there's one thing which makes it quite impossible for Krogstad to stay at the Bank so long as I'm Manager.

NORA: What?

HELMER: Perhaps at a pinch I might have overlooked his moral failings—

NORA: Yes, Torvald, couldn't you?

HELMER: And I hear that he's quite a good worker, too. But he was at school with me—it was one of those unfortunate friendships that one so often comes to regret later in life. I may as well tell you frankly that we were on Christian-name terms, and he's tactless enough to keep it up still—in front of everyone! In fact, he seems to think he has a *right* to be familiar with me, and out he comes with "Torvald this" and "Torvald that" all the time. I tell you, it's most unpleasant for me—he'll make my position in the Bank quite intolerable.

NORA: You surely can't mean that, Torvald!

HELMER: Oh? Why not?

NORA: Well—that's such a petty reason.

HELMER: What do you mean? Petty? Do you think I'm petty?

NORA: No, Torvald dear—far from it; that's just why—

HELMER: Never mind! You said my motives were petty, so I must be petty too. Petty! Very well, we'll settle this matter once and for all. (*He goes to the hall door and calls.*) Helena!

NORA: What are you going to do?

HELMER (*searching among his papers*): Settle things.

The MAID *comes in.*

Here, take this letter downstairs at once, find a messenger, and get him to deliver it. Immediately, mind. The address is on it. Wait—here's the money.

MAID: Yes, sir. (*She goes with the letter.*)

HELMER (*collecting his papers*): There, little Miss Stubborn!

NORA (*breathless*): Torvald . . . what was in that letter?

HELMER: Krogstad's notice.

NORA: Call it back, Torvald—there's still time. Oh Torvald, call it back, for my sake—for your own sake—for the children's sake. Listen, Torvald, you don't know what that letter can do to us all.

HELMER: It's too late.

NORA: Yes . . . it's too late.

HELMER: My dear Nora, I can forgive your anxiety—though actually it's rather insulting to me. Oh yes, it is. Isn't it insulting to believe that I could be afraid of some wretched scribbler's revenge? Still, it's a very touching proof of your love for me, so I forgive you. (*He takes her in his arms.*) Now, my own darling Nora, that's all settled. Whatever happens, when it comes to the point you can be quite sure that I shall have the necessary courage and strength. You'll see that I'm man enough to take it all on myself.

NORA (*horror-struck*): What do you mean?

HELMER: Exactly what I say.

NORA (*recovering*): You shall never never have to do that.

HELMER: Very well, Nora, then we shall share it as man and wife; that's what we'll do. (*caressing her*) Are you happy now? There—there—there—don't look like a little frightened dove—the whole thing's just sheer imagination. Now you must rehearse your tarantella—with the tambourine. I'll go and sit in the inner room and shut the doors, so you can make all the noise you like—I shan't hear a thing. (*turning in the doorway*) And when Dr. Rank comes, tell him where I am. (*Taking his papers, he gives her a nod and goes into his room, shutting the door behind him.*)

NORA (*half crazy with fear, she stands as if rooted to the spot and whispers*): He'd really do it—he'd do it! He'd do it in spite of everything. No—never in the world! Anything rather than that! There must be some way out—some help.

There is a ring at the door.

Dr. Rank! Yes, anything rather than that—anything—whatever it is.

Passing her hands over her face, she pulls herself together and goes and opens the hall door. DR. RANK *is standing there hanging up his fur coat. During the following scene it begins to grow dark.*

NORA: Good afternoon, Dr. Rank—I recognized your ring. But you mustn't go in to Torvald now, I think he's got some work to finish.

RANK: What about you?

NORA (*shutting the door after him as he comes into the room*): Oh, I always have time for you—you know that.

RANK: Thank you. I shall take advantage of that for as long as I'm able.

NORA: What do you mean by that? As long as you're able?

RANK: Yes . . . does that alarm you?

NORA: It seemed such an odd way to put it. Is anything going to happen?

RANK: Yes . . . something that I've been expecting for a long time—though I never really thought it'd come quite so soon.

NORA (*clutching his arm*): What have you just learned? Dr. Rank, you must tell me!

RANK (*sitting by the stove*): The sands are running out for me. . . . There's nothing to be done about it.

NORA (*with a sigh of relief*): Then it's *you* . . . !

RANK: Who else? There's no point in deceiving myself—I'm the most wretched of all my patients, Mrs. Helmer. These last few days I've been holding an audit of my internal economy. Bankrupt! In less than a month, perhaps, I shall lie rotting in the churchyard.

NORA: Oh no—that's a horrible thing to say.

RANK: The thing itself is damnably horrible. But worst of all is the horror that must be gone through first. There's still one more test to make, and when I've finished *that* I shall know pretty well when the final disintegration will begin. But there's something I want to say to you; Helmer's too sensitive to be able to face anything ugly—I won't have him in my sick-room.

NORA: But, Dr. Rank—

RANK: I won't have him there—not on any account. I shall lock the door against him. As soon as I'm quite certain that the worst has come, I shall send you my card with a black cross on it and then you'll know that my disgusting end has begun.

NORA: No, you're really being absurd today—and just when I so wanted you to be in a particularly good mood.

RANK: What, with death just round the corner? And when it's to pay for someone else's sins! Where's the justice in that? Yet in one way or another there isn't a single family where some such inexorable retribution isn't being exacted.

NORA (*stopping her ears*): Nonsense! Cheer up—cheer up!

RANK: Yes, indeed, the whole thing's nothing but a joke! My poor innocent spine must pay for my father's amusements as a gay young subaltern.

NORA (*by the table on the left*): He was too fond of asparagus and *foie gras*—isn't that it?

RANK: Yes, and truffles.

NORA: Truffles, yes. And oysters, too, I suppose?

RANK: Oysters? Oh yes, certainly oysters.

NORA: And then all that port and champagne. What a shame that all those nice things should attack the bones.

RANK: Especially when the unfortunate bones that they attack never had the least enjoyment out of them.

NORA: Yes, that's the saddest part of all.

RANK (*with a searching look at her*): Hm! . . .

NORA (*after a moment*): Why did you smile?

RANK: No, it's you who were laughing.

NORA: No, you smiled, Dr. Rank.

RANK (*getting up*): You're more of a rascal than I thought.

NORA: I'm in a ridiculous mood today.

RANK: So it seems.

NORA (*putting both hands on his shoulders*): Dear, dear Dr. Rank, you mustn't die and leave Torvald and me.

RANK: Oh, you'd soon get over it—those who go away are quickly forgotten.

NORA (*looking at him anxiously*): Do you believe that?

RANK: People make new friends, and then . . .

NORA: Who makes new friends?

RANK: You and Torvald will, when I'm gone. It looks to me as if *you're* starting already. What was that Mrs. Linde doing here last night?

NORA: Oh, surely you're not jealous of poor Kristina.

RANK: Yes, I am. She'll take my place in this house. After I've gone, I expect that woman will—

NORA: Sh! Not so loud—she's in there!

RANK: There you are! She's here again today.

NORA: Only to mend my dress. Good gracious, you *are* being absurd. (*sitting on the sofa*) Now be nice, Dr. Rank, and tomorrow you'll see how beautifully I shall dance, and you can tell yourself that it's all for you—and for Torvald too, of course. (*taking various things out of the box*) Come and sit here, Dr. Rank, and I'll show you something.

RANK: What is it?

NORA: Look here. Look.

RANK: Silk stockings.

NORA: Flesh colored—aren't they lovely? The light's bad in here now, but tomorrow . . . No, no, no, you must only look at the feet. Oh well, you may see the rest, too.

RANK: Hm . . .

NORA: Why are you looking so critical? Don't you think they'll fit?

RANK: I can't possibly give you an opinion on that.

NORA (*looking at him for a moment*): You ought to be ashamed of yourself! (*She flips him lightly on the cheek with the stockings.*) Take that! (*She rolls them up again.*)

RANK: What other pretty things have you to show me?

NORA: You shan't see another thing—you've been very naughty. (*She hums a little as she rummages among her things.*)

RANK (*after a short pause*): When I sit here like this talking to you so intimately, I can't imagine—no, I really can't—what would have become of me if I hadn't had this house to come to.

NORA (*smiling*): I believe you really do feel at home with us.

RANK (*more quietly, looking straight in front of him*): And to have to leave it all!

NORA: Nonsense, you're not going to leave us.

RANK (*as before*): Not to be able to leave behind even the smallest token of gratitude—hardly even a passing regret. Nothing but an empty place that the next person to come along will fill just as well.

NORA: Suppose I were to ask you for a . . . No . . .

RANK: For a what?

NORA: For a great proof of your friendship.

RANK: Yes.

NORA: No, I mean a terribly great favor.

RANK: I should be very happy if—just for once—you'd give me the chance.

NORA: Ah, but you don't know what it is.

RANK: Tell me, then.

NORA: No, Dr. Rank, I can't. It's something really enormous—not just advice or help, but a really great favor.

RANK: The greater the better. I can't think what it can be, so tell me. Don't you trust me?

NORA: There's no one else I'd trust more than you. I know you're my best, most faithful friend, so I'll tell you. . . . Well, Dr. Rank—it's something you must help me to stave off. You know how much—how incredibly deeply—Torvald loves me. He wouldn't hesitate for a moment to give his life for me.

RANK (*leaning nearer to her*): Nora . . . Do you think he's the only one?

NORA (*with a slight start*): The only one . . . ?

RANK: Who'd gladly give his life for you?

NORA (*sadly*): Ah . . .

RANK: I promised myself that I'd tell you before I went away, and I could never have a better opportunity. Well, Nora, now you know. And you know, too, that you can trust me—more than anyone else.

NORA (*calmly and evenly; rising*): I must go.

RANK (*making way for her, but still sitting*): Nora . . .

NORA (*in the hall doorway*): Helena, bring the lamp. (*going to the stove*) Oh, dear Dr. Rank, that was really horrid of you.

RANK (*rising*): To have loved you as deeply as anyone else—was that horrid?

NORA: No . . . but to go and tell me so. There was really no need to do that.

RANK: What do you mean? Did you know?

The MAID *brings in the lamp, puts it on the table, and goes again.*

RANK: Nora—Mrs. Helmer—I ask you: did you know?

NORA: Oh, how can I say if I knew or didn't know? I've really no idea. How could you be so clumsy, Dr. Rank? When everything was going so well. . . .

RANK: Well, at any rate you know that I'm at your service—body and soul. So won't you say what it is?

NORA (*looking at him*): After what's happened?

RANK: Please—please tell me what it is.

NORA: I can never tell you now.

RANK: Please. You mustn't punish me like this. If you'll let me, I promise to do anything for you that a man can.

NORA: There's nothing you can do for me now. Besides, I certainly don't need any help—it was all my imagination, really it was. Honestly. (*smiling*) You're a fine one, Dr. Rank! Aren't you ashamed of yourself, now that the lamp's come on?

RANK: No . . . not really. But perhaps I ought to go—for good.

NORA: No. You certainly mustn't do that—of course you must come here just as usual. You know Torvald couldn't get on without you.

RANK: But what about you?

NORA: Oh, I'm always tremendously glad to see you.

RANK: That's just what misled me. You're a mystery to me. . . . I've sometimes thought you'd as soon be with me as with Helmer.

NORA: You see, there are some people that one loves, and others that perhaps one would rather be with.

RANK: Yes, there's something in that.

NORA: When I lived at home, naturally I loved Papa best, but I always found it terribly amusing to slip into the servants' hall, because they always talked about such interesting things, and they never lectured me at all.

RANK: Ah, and now I've taken their place?

NORA (*jumping up and going over to him*): Oh, dear kind Dr. Rank, that isn't what I meant at all. But I'm sure you can see that being with Torvald is very like being with Papa.

The MAID *comes in from the hall.*

MAID: Excuse me, Madam. . . . (*She whispers to* NORA *as she hands her a card.*)

NORA (*glancing at the card*): Oh! (*She puts it in her pocket.*)

RANK: Is there anything wrong?

NORA: No, no, not in the least. It's only something . . . it's my new dress.

RANK: But . . . ? Surely your dress is out there?

NORA: Ah, that one, yes. But this is another one that I've ordered—I don't want Torvald to know. . . .

RANK: Aha! So *that's* your great secret?

NORA: Yes, of course. Go in to Torvald—he's in the inner room—keep him there till . . .

RANK: Don't worry, I shan't let him escape. (*He goes into* HELMER's *room.*)

NORA (*to the* MAID): Is he waiting in the kitchen?

MAID: Yes, Madam, he came up the back stairs.

NORA: But didn't you tell him there was someone here?

MAID: Yes, but it wasn't any good.

NORA: He wouldn't go away?

MAID: No, he won't go till he's seen you, Madam.

NORA: Oh, all right, let him come in. Quietly, though. Helena, you mustn't mention this to anyone—it's a surprise for my husband.

MAID: Yes, I understand. (*She goes.*)

NORA: Oh, this is dreadful—it's going to happen after all. No, no, no, it *can't*—I won't let it!

> *She goes and pushes the bolt home on* HELMER's *door. The* MAID *opens the hall door to let* KROGSTAD *in, and shuts it after him. He is wearing travelling clothes, high boots, and a fur cap.*

NORA (*going to him*): Keep your voice down—my husband's at home.

KROGSTAD: What of it?

NORA: What do you want?

KROGSTAD: To find out something.

NORA: Be quick, then; what is it?

KROGSTAD: You know that I've been dismissed?

NORA: I couldn't stop it, Mr. Krogstad. I did absolutely everything I could for you, but it was no good.

KROGSTAD: Your husband can't love you very much, can he? He knows that I can expose you, and yet he dares to—

NORA: You surely don't imagine that he knows about it?

KROGSTAD: Well, no—I didn't really think so; it wouldn't be at all like our worthy Torvald Helmer to have so much courage.

NORA: Kindly show some respect for my husband, Mr. Krogstad.

KROGSTAD: But of course—all the respect he deserves. As you seem so anxious to keep things secret, I presume that you have a rather clearer idea than you had yesterday of what it is that you've actually done.

NORA: Clearer than you could ever make it.

KROGSTAD: Oh yes, I'm such a stupid lawyer!

NORA: What do you want?

KROGSTAD: Only to see how things stood with you, Mrs. Helmer. I've been thinking about you all day. Even a mere cashier, a scribbler, a—well, a man like me, has a certain amount of what is called "feeling," you know.

NORA: Then show it. Think of my little children.

KROGSTAD: Have you or your husband ever thought of mine? But never mind that; I only wanted to tell you that you needn't take all this too seriously—I shan't make any accusation for the present.

NORA: No, of course not—I didn't think you would.

KROGSTAD: It can all be settled quite amicably. Nothing need come out—it can just be arranged between us three.

NORA: My husband must never know anything about it.

KROGSTAD: How can you stop it? Unless, perhaps, you can pay off the rest of the debt.

NORA: Well, not at the moment.

KROGSTAD: Then perhaps you've found some way to raise the money within the next day or two.

NORA: No way that I'd use.

KROGSTAD: Well, it wouldn't have helped you, anyhow. Even if you were to stand there with a mint of money in your hand, you wouldn't get your bond back from me.

NORA: What are you going to do with it? Tell me.

KROGSTAD: Just keep it—have it in my possession. No one who isn't concerned need know anything about it. So if you have any desperate plan—

NORA: I have.

KROGSTAD: —If you've thought of running away from your home—

NORA: I have.

KROGSTAD: —or of anything worse—

NORA: How did you know?

KROGSTAD: —you'd better give up the idea.

NORA: How did you know that I'd thought of *that?*

KROGSTAD: Most of us think of that at first. I thought of it, too—only I hadn't the courage.

NORA (*dully*): Nor had I.

KROGSTAD (*relieved*): No, you haven't the courage either, have you?

NORA: No, I haven't—I haven't.

KROGSTAD: Besides, it would have been a very stupid thing to do. You've only got just one domestic storm to go through, then . . . I have a letter to your husband in my pocket.

NORA: Telling him everything?

KROGSTAD: In the gentlest possible way.

NORA (*quickly*): He must never see it. Tear it up. I'll get the money somehow.

KROGSTAD: Excuse me, Mrs. Helmer, but I believed I told you just now—

NORA: Oh, I don't mean the money I owe you. Tell me how much you're asking from my husband, and I'll get it.

KROGSTAD: I'm not asking your husband for any money.

NORA: What are you asking, then?

KROGSTAD: I'll tell you. I want to get back my standing in the world, Mrs. Helmer; I want to get on, and that's where your husband's going to help me. For the last eighteen months I haven't touched anything dishonest, and all that time I've been struggling against the most difficult conditions. I was prepared to work my way up step by step. Now I'm being thrown down again, and it's not going to be good enough for me to be taken back as a favor. I want to get on, I tell you; I want to get back into the Bank—and in a better job. Your husband must make one for me.

NORA: He'll never do that.

KROGSTAD: I know him—he'll do it! He daren't so much as murmur. And once I'm in there with him, then you'll see! Inside a year, I shall be the Manager's right-hand man. It'll be Nils Krogstad who runs the Bank, not Torvald Helmer.

NORA: That'll never happen as long as you live.

KROGSTAD: Do you mean that you'll—

NORA: Yes, I have the courage now.

KROGSTAD: Oh, you can't frighten me! A fine pampered lady like you—

NORA: You'll see—you'll see!

KROGSTAD: Under the ice, perhaps? Down into the cold black water? And then in the spring you'd float up to the top, ugly, hairless, unrecognizable—

NORA: You can't frighten me.

KROGSTAD: Nor can you frighten me. People don't do such things, Mrs. Helmer. And what good would it be, anyhow? I'd still have the letter in my pocket!

NORA: Still? Even if I weren't . . .

KROGSTAD: You forget that *then* your reputation would be in my hands.

NORA *stands speechless, looking at him.*

KROGSTAD: Yes, now you've been warned, so don't do anything stupid. I shall expect to hear from Helmer as soon as he gets my letter. And re-member, it's your husband who's forced me to do this sort of thing again. I shall never forgive him for that. Good-bye, Mrs. Helmer. (*He goes out into the hall.*)

NORA (*going to the hall door and opening it a little to listen*): He's going! He hasn't left the letter. No, no, it couldn't happen! (*She opens the door inch by inch.*) Listen—he's standing just outside—he's not going down the stairs. . . . Has he changed his mind? Is he . . . ?

A letter falls into the box. KROGSTAD'S *footsteps are heard fading away down the staircase.*

NORA (*With a stifled cry, runs over to the sofa table. A short pause.*): It's in the letter-box! (*creeping stealthily back to the hall door*) Yes, it's there. Oh, Torvald . . . Torvald—there's no hope for us now!

MRS. LINDE (*coming in from the left with the dress*): There—I don't think there's anything else that wants mending. Let's try it on.

NORA (*in a hoarse whisper*): Kristina, come here.

MRS. LINDE (*throwing the dress on the sofa*): What's the matter? What's upset you so?

NORA: Come here. Do you see that letter? There, look—through the glass of the letter-box.

MRS. LINDE: I can see it—Well?

NORA: That letter's from Krogstad.

MRS. LINDE: Nora . . . it was Krogstad who lent you the money!

NORA: Yes. And now Torvald'll find out everything.

MRS. LINDE: But, Nora, believe me, that'll be best for both of you.

NORA: There's something that you don't know. I forged a signature.

MRS. LINDE: Good heavens . . . !

NORA: There's just one thing I want to say, Kristina, and you shall be my witness.

MRS. LINDE: Witness? But what am I to—

NORA: If I were to go mad—as I easily might—

MRS. LINDE: Nora!

NORA: Or if anything else were to happen to me, so that I shouldn't be here—

MRS. LINDE: Nora, Nora, you must be out of your senses!

NORA: And in case there was someone else who tried to take it all on himself—all the blame, you understand—

MRS. LINDE: Yes . . . but how can you think . . . ?

NORA: —then, Kristina, you must bear witness that it isn't true. I'm perfectly sane, and I know exactly what I'm doing now, and I tell you this: no one else knew anything about it—I did it all by myself. Remember that.

MRS. LINDE: Of course I will. But I don't understand.

NORA: How could you understand this? We're going to see—a miracle.

MRS. LINDE: A miracle?

NORA: Yes, a miracle. But it's so dreadful. Kristina, it *mustn't* happen—not for anything in the world.

MRS. LINDE: I'm going straight round to talk to Krogstad.

NORA: No, don't go to him, he might do you some harm.

MRS. LINDE: There was a time when he would gladly have done anything for me.

NORA: Krogstad?

MRS. LINDE: Where does he live?

NORA: How should I know? Wait—(*feeling in her pocket*)—here's his card. But the letter—the letter . . . !

HELMER (*from inside his room, knocking on the door*): Nora!

NORA (*with a frightened cry*): What is it? What do you want?

HELMER (*off*): All right, there's nothing to be frightened of; we're not coming in. You've locked the door—are you trying on your dress?

NORA: Yes, I'm trying it on. I look so nice in it, Helmer.

MRS. LINDE (*having read the card*): He lives only just round the corner.

NORA: Yes, but it's no good; there's no hope for us now—the letter's in the box.

MRS. LINDE: And your husband has the key!

NORA: He always keeps it.

MRS. LINDE: Krogstad must ask for his letter back—unopened. He must find some excuse.

NORA: But this is just the time when Torvald always—

MRS. LINDE: Put him off. I'll be back as soon as I can. Go in to him now. (*She hurries out through the hall.*)

NORA (*going to* HELMER's *door, unlocking it, and peeping in*): Torvald.

HELMER (*from the inner room*): Well, am I allowed in my own room again? Come along, Rank, now we're going to see—(*at the door*) But what's all this?

NORA: What, Torvald dear?

HELMER: Rank led me to expect a great transformation scene.

RANK (*at the door*): I certainly thought so—I must have been wrong.

NORA: No one's allowed to admire me in all my finery till tomorrow.

HELMER: But, Nora dear, you look tired out—have you been rehearsing too much?

NORA: No, I haven't rehearsed at all.

HELMER: Oh, but you should have.

NORA: Yes, I know I should have, but I can't do anything unless you help me, Torvald. I've forgotten absolutely everything.

HELMER: Oh, we'll soon polish it up again.

NORA: Yes, do take me in hand, Torvald—promise you will. I'm so nervous—all those people . . . You must give up the whole evening to me; you mustn't do a scrap of business—not even pick up a pen! You'll do that, won't you, dear Torvald?

HELMER: I promise. This evening I'll be wholly and entirely at your service— you poor helpless little creature! Ah, but first, while I think of it, I must just—(*going toward the hall door*).

NORA: What do you want out there?

HELMER: I'm just seeing if the post's come.

NORA: No, no, Torvald—don't do that.

HELMER: Why not?

NORA: Please don't Torvald—there's nothing there.

HELMER: I'll just look. (*He starts to go.*)

NORA, *at the piano, plays the opening bars of the tarantella.*

HELMER (*stopping in the doorway*): Aha!

NORA: I shan't be able to dance tomorrow if I don't go over it with you.

HELMER (*going to her*): Nora dear, are you really so worried about it?

NORA: Yes, terribly worried. Let me rehearse it now—there's still time before dinner. Sit down and play for me, Torvald dear; criticize me, and show me where I'm wrong, the way you always do.

HELMER: I'd like to, if that's what you want. (*He sits at the piano.*)

NORA *pulls a tambourine out of the box, then a long particolored shawl which she quickly drapes round herself. Then, with a bound, she takes up her position in the middle of the floor, and calls:*

NORA: Now play for me, and I'll dance!

HELMER *plays and* NORA *dances.* DR. RANK *stands behind* HELMER *at the piano and looks on.*

HELMER (*as he plays*): Slower—slower!

NORA: I can only do it this way.

HELMER: Not so violently, Nora!

NORA: This is how it should go.

HELMER (*stops playing*): No, no, that's all wrong.

NORA (*laughing and brandishing her tambourine*): There! Didn't I tell you?

RANK: Let me play for her.

HELMER (*rising*): Yes, do; then I can show her better.

RANK *sits at the piano and plays.* NORA *dances more and more wildly.* HELMER, *taking up a position by the stove, gives her frequent directions as she dances. She seems not to hear them, her hair comes down and falls*

over her shoulders, but she goes on dancing without taking any notice.
MRS. LINDE *comes in.*

MRS. LINDE (*stopping spellbound in the doorway*): Ah!
NORA (*as she dances*): Oh, this is fun, Kristina!
HELMER: But, Nora darling, you're dancing as if your life depended on it!
NORA: So it does.
HELMER: Stop, Rank. This is sheer madness—stop, I tell you!

RANK *stops playing, and* NORA *comes to an abrupt halt.*

HELMER (*going to her*): I'd never have believed it—you've forgotten every-
    thing I taught you.
NORA (*throwing the tambourine aside*): There! You see.
HELMER: Well, you'll certainly need a lot of coaching.
NORA: Yes, you see how much I need. You must coach me up to the last
    minute—promise me you will, Torvald?
HELMER: You can rely on me.
NORA: All today and all tomorrow, you mustn't think of anything else but
    me. You mustn't open any letters—you mustn't even open the letter-box.
HELMER: Ah, you're still afraid of that man.
NORA: Oh yes, that as well.
HELMER: Nora, I can see by your face that there's a letter from him already.
NORA: There may be—I don't know. But you mustn't read anything like that
    now; we won't let anything horrid come between us till this is all over.
RANK (*quietly to* HELMER): You'd better not upset her.
HELMER (*putting his arm round her*): My baby shall have her own way. But
    tomorrow night, after you've danced—
NORA: Then you'll be free.
MAID (*at the door on the right*): Dinner is served, Madam.
NORA: We'll have champagne, Helena.
MAID: Very good, Madam. (*She goes.*)
HELMER: Well, well—so we're having a banquet!
NORA: A champagne supper—lasting till dawn. (*calling*) And some maca-
    roons, Helena—lots and lots, just for once.
HELMER (*taking her hands*): Now, now, now! You mustn't be so wild and
    excitable. Be my own little skylark again.
NORA: Oh yes, I will. But go into the dining-room now—and you too, Dr.
    Rank. Kristina, you must help me put my hair straight.
RANK (*quietly as they go*): There isn't anything . . . ? I mean, she's not
    expecting . . . ?
HELMER: Oh no, my dear fellow. I've told you—she gets over-excited, like a
    child.

They go out to the right.

NORA: Well?
MRS. LINDE: He's gone out of town.
NORA: I saw it in your face.
MRS. LINDE: He'll be back tomorrow night; I left a note for him.
NORA: You should have let things alone—not tried to stop them. After all,
    it's a wonderful thing to be waiting for a miracle.

MRS. LINDE: What is it you're expecting?

NORA: You wouldn't understand. Go in and join the others—I'll come in a minute.

MRS. LINDE *goes into the dining-room.*

NORA (*standing for a moment as if to collect herself, then looking at her watch*): Seven hours till midnight. Then twenty-four hours till midnight tomorrow. Then the tarantella will be over. Twenty-four and seven . . . thirty-one hours to live.

HELMER (*at the door on the right*): But where's my little skylark?

NORA (*going to him with arms outstretched*): Here she is!

Act Three

The same scene. The table and chairs round it have been moved to the middle of the room; a lamp is alight on the table. The hall door is open and music for dancing can be heard from the flat above.

MRS. LINDE is sitting at the table, idly turning the pages of a book. She tries to read, but seems unable to concentrate. Once or twice she listens anxiously for the outer door.

MRS. LINDE (*looking at her watch*): Not here yet! There's not much more time—I do hope he hasn't—(*listening again*) Ah, here he is.

She goes out to the hall and carefully opens the front door. Soft footsteps are heard on the stairs. She whispers:

Come in—there's no one here.

KROGSTAD (*in the doorway*): I found a note from you at home. What's this about?

MRS. LINDE: I had to have a talk with you.

KROGSTAD: Oh? And did you have to have it in this house?

MRS. LINDE: I couldn't see you at the place where I'm staying—there's no separate entrance to my room. Come in, we're quite alone; the maid's asleep, and the Helmers are upstairs at the dance.

KROGSTAD (*coming into the room*): What? The Helmers at a dance tonight? Really?

MRS. LINDE: Yes. Why not?

KROGSTAD: True—why not?

MRS. LINDE: Well, Nils, let us have a talk.

KROGSTAD: Have you and I got anything more to talk about?

MRS. LINDE: A great deal.

KROGSTAD: I shouldn't have thought so.

MRS. LINDE: Well, you never really understood me.

KROGSTAD: Was there anything to understand—except what was so obvious to the whole world: a heartless woman throwing a man over when someone richer turns up?

MRS. LINDE: Do you really think I'm as heartless as all that? And do you think it was easy to break with you?

KROGSTAD: Wasn't it?

MRS. LINDE: Nils, did you really think that?

KROGSTAD: If it wasn't true, why did you write to me as you did at the time?

MRS. LINDE: What else could I do? I had to break with you, so it was up to me to kill any feeling that you might have had for me.

KROGSTAD (*clenching his hands*): So that was it? You did it—all of it—for the sake of the money?

MRS. LINDE: You mustn't forget that my mother was quite helpless, and that I had two small brothers. We couldn't wait for you, Nils—especially as you had no prospects in those days.

KROGSTAD: Even so, you had no right to throw me over for someone else.

MRS. LINDE: I've often asked myself if I had the right . . . I really don't know.

KROGSTAD (*softly*): When I lost you, it was just as if the very ground had given way under my feet. Look at me now—a shipwrecked man clinging to a spar.

MRS. LINDE: Help could be near.

KROGSTAD: It *was* near—until you came and got in the way.

MRS. LINDE: Without knowing it, Nils. I found out today that it's *your* place that I'm to have at the Bank.

KROGSTAD: I'll believe you if you say so. But now that you do know, aren't you going to give it up?

MRS. LINDE: No. You see, that wouldn't benefit you in the least.

KROGSTAD: "Benefit—benefit!" *I* would have done it.

MRS. LINDE: I've learned to think before I act. Life and bitter necessity have taught me that.

KROGSTAD: Life has taught me not to believe in fine speeches.

MRS. LINDE: Then life has taught you something valuable. But you must believe in deeds?

KROGSTAD: What do you mean by that?

MRS. LINDE: You said you were like a shipwrecked man clinging to a spar.

KROGSTAD: I had good reason to say so.

MRS. LINDE: I'm like a shipwrecked woman clinging to a spar—no one to cry over, and no one to care for.

KROGSTAD: It was your own choice.

MRS. LINDE: There was no other choice at the time.

KROGSTAD: Well?

MRS. LINDE: Nils . . . suppose we two shipwrecked people could join forces?

KROGSTAD: What do you mean?

MRS. LINDE: Two on one spar would be better off than each of us alone.

KROGSTAD: Kristina!

MRS. LINDE: Why do you suppose I came to town?

KROGSTAD: Were you really thinking of me?

MRS. LINDE: I must work or life isn't bearable. All my life, as long as I can remember, I've worked—that's been my one great joy. But now that I'm alone in the world I feel completely lost and empty. There's no joy in working for oneself. Nils . . . let me have something—and someone—to work for.

KROGSTAD: I don't trust that. It's nothing but a woman's exaggerated sense of nobility prompting her to sacrifice herself.

MRS. LINDE: Have you ever noticed anything exaggerated in me?

KROGSTAD: Could you really do it? Tell me, do you know all about my past?

MRS. LINDE: Yes.

KROGSTAD: And do you know my reputation here?

MRS. LINDE: You suggested just now that with me you might have been a different man.

KROGSTAD: I'm certain of it.

MRS. LINDE: Couldn't that still happen?

KROGSTAD: Kristina—have you really thought about what you're saying? Yes, you have—I see it in your face. And you really have the courage?

MRS. LINDE: I need someone to be a mother to, and your children need a mother. You and I need each other. I have faith in you—the real you— Nils, with you I could dare anything.

KROGSTAD (*grasping her hands*): Thank you—thank you, Kristina. Now I shall be able to set myself right in the eyes of the world too. Oh, but I'm forgetting—

MRS. LINDE (*listening*): Sh! The tarantella! Go—quickly.

KROGSTAD: Why? What is it?

MRS. LINDE: Don't you hear the dancing up there? As soon as this is over, they'll be coming back.

KROGSTAD: Yes—I'll go. But all this will come to nothing . . . you see, you don't know what I've done against the Helmers.

MRS. LINDE: Yes, Nils, I know about it.

KROGSTAD: And you still have the courage . . . ?

MRS. LINDE: I know only too well how far despair can drive a man like you.

KROGSTAD: Oh, if only I could undo it!

MRS. LINDE: You can—your letter's still in the box.

KROGSTAD: Are you sure?

MRS. LINDE: Quite sure—but . . .

KROGSTAD (*with a searching look at her*): You want to save your friend at any price—is that it? Tell me frankly—is it?

MRS. LINDE: Nils, when you've sold yourself once for the sake of others, you don't do it a second time.

KROGSTAD: I shall ask for my letter back.

MRS. LINDE: No, no!

KROGSTAD: But of course. I'll wait here till Helmer comes down, and I'll tell him that he must give me my letter back—that it's only about my dismissal, and that he's not to read it.

MRS. LINDE: No, Nils, you mustn't ask for your letter back.

KROGSTAD: But surely that was the very reason why you asked me to come here?

MRS. LINDE: Yes—in my first moment of panic. But now, a whole day's gone by and I've witnessed things in this house that I could hardly believe. Helmer must know the whole story. This wretched secret must be brought into the open so that there's complete understanding between them. That'd be impossible while there's so much concealment and subterfuge.

KROGSTAD: Very well—if you'll take the risk. . . . But there's one thing I can do—and it shall be done at once—

MRS. LINDE (*listening*): Go—quickly! The dance is over—we can't stay here a moment longer.

KROGSTAD: I'll wait for you downstairs.

MRS. LINDE: Yes, do. You must see me home.

KROGSTAD: Kristina, this is the most marvellous thing that's ever happened to me.

He goes out by the front door. The door between the room and the hall remains open.

MRS. LINDE (*tidying the room a little, and putting her hat and cape ready*): What a difference—what a difference! Someone to work for—and live for. A home to look after—and oh, I'll make it so comfortable. Oh, if they'd only hurry up and come! (*listening*) Ah, here they are—I'll put my things on.

She picks up her hat and cape. HELMER'S *and* NORA'S *voices are heard outside. A key turns, and* HELMER *pulls* NORA *almost forcibly into the room. She is in Italian costume with a great black shawl round herself; he is in a black domino which opens to show his evening dress underneath.*

NORA (*still in the doorway, struggling with him*): No, no, I don't want to go in—I want to go back upstairs. It's far too early to leave.

HELMER: But, my darling Nora—

NORA: Oh, please, Torvald—I do beg you. . . . Just one more hour!

HELMER: Not a single minute, Nora dear—you know what we agreed. Now come along in, you'll catch cold out here.

In spite of her resistance he brings her gently into the room.

MRS. LINDE: Good evening.

. NORA: Kristina!

HELMER: Why, Mrs. Linde—here so late?

MRS. LINDE: Yes, forgive me, but I did want to see Nora in her costume.

NORA: Have you been sitting here waiting for me?

MRS. LINDE: Yes, I'm afraid I didn't get here in time—you'd already gone upstairs—and I felt I really couldn't go away without seeing you.

HELMER (*taking* NORA'S *shawl off*): Yes, just look at her! She's worth seeing, if you ask *me!* Isn't she lovely, Mrs. Linde?

MRS. LINDE: She certainly is.

HELMER: Remarkably lovely, isn't she? And that's what everybody at the dance thought, too. But this sweet little thing's dreadfully obstinate. What are we to do with her? You'd hardly believe it, but I practically had to use force to get her away.

NORA: You'll be very sorry you didn't let me stay, Torvald—even for just half an hour longer.

HELMER: Just listen to her, Mrs. Linde! She danced her tarantella; it was a huge success—and rightly so, even if it *was,* perhaps, a trifle too realistic—I mean, a little more so than was, strictly speaking, artistically necessary. . . . But never mind, it was a success—a huge success. Could I let her stay after that, and spoil the effect? No thank you; I put my arm round my lovely little Capri girl—I might almost say my *capricious* little Capri girl—we made a quick turn of the room, a bow all round, and then, as they say in the novels, the beautiful vision was gone! An exit should always be well-timed, Mrs. Linde; but that's something I simply cannot get Nora to see! Phew, it's warm in here. (*He throws his domino on a chair and opens the door to his room.*) Hullo, it's all dark! Oh yes, of course. . . . Excuse me—(*He goes in and lights the candles.*)

NORA (*in a rapid and breathless whisper*): Well?

MRS. LINDE (*softly*): I've had a talk with him.

NORA: Yes?

MRS. LINDE: Nora, you must tell your husband everything.

NORA (*dully*): I knew it.

MRS. LINDE: You've nothing to fear from Krogstad. But you *must* tell your husband.

NORA: I'll never tell him.

MRS. LINDE: Then the letter will.

NORA: Thank you, Kristina; now I know what I must do. . . . Sh!

HELMER (*coming in again*): Well, Mrs. Linde, you have been admiring her?

MRS. LINDE: Yes, indeed . . . and now I must say good night.

HELMER: What, already? Is this yours, this knitting?

MRS. LINDE (*taking it*): Oh yes, thank you—I nearly forgot it.

HELMER: So you knit?

MRS. LINDE: Oh yes.

HELMER: You know, it'd be much better if you did embroidery.

MRS. LINDE: Oh? Why?

HELMER: It's so much more graceful. I'll show you. You hold embroidery like this, in your left hand, and you work the needle with your right—in long easy sweeps. Isn't that so?

MRS. LINDE: Yes, I suppose so.

HELMER: But knitting's quite another matter—it can't help being ungraceful. Look here—arms held tightly in, needles going up and down—it has an almost Chinese effect. . . . That really was an excellent champagne they gave us tonight. . . .

MRS. LINDE: Well, good night. And Nora—don't be obstinate any longer.

HELMER: That's quite right, Mrs. Linde.

MRS. LINDE: Good night, Mr. Helmer.

HELMER (*seeing her to the door*): Good night—good night. I hope you get home safely. I'd be very glad to . . . but then you haven't far to go, have you? Good night—good night.

She goes. He shuts the door after her and comes back.

Well, I thought she'd never go—she's a terrible bore, that woman.

NORA: Aren't you tired out, Torvald?

HELMER: No, not in the least.

NORA: Not sleepy?

HELMER: Not a bit—in fact, I feel particularly lively. What about you? Yes, you do look tired out—why, you're half asleep.

NORA: Yes, I'm very tired—I could fall asleep here and now.

HELMER: There you are—there you are! You see how right I was not to let you stay any longer.

NORA: You're always right, Torvald, whatever you do.

HELMER (*kissing her on the forehead*): Now my little skylark's talking like a reasonable being. Did you notice how cheerful Rank was this evening?

NORA: Oh, was he? I didn't get a chance to talk to him.

HELMER: I hardly did; but I haven't seen him in such good spirits for a long time. (*He looks at* NORA *for a moment, then goes to her.*) Ah, it's wonderful to be back home again, all alone with you. . . . How fascinating you are, you lovely little thing.

NORA: Don't look at me like that, Torvald.

HELMER: Mayn't I look at my dearest treasure? At all the beauty that belongs to no one but me—that's all my very own?

NORA (*going round to the other side of the table*): You mustn't say things like that tonight.

HELMER (*following her*): I see you still have the tarantella in your blood—it makes you more enchanting than ever. Listen—the party's beginning to break up. (*softly*) Nora—soon the whole house'll be quiet . . .

NORA: Yes, I hope so.

HELMER: Yes, you do, don't you, my own darling Nora? I'll tell you something: when I'm out with you at a party, do you know why I hardly talk to you—don't come near you—and only steal a glance at you every now and then . . . do you know why? It's because I pretend that we're secretly in love—engaged in secret—and that no one dreams that there's anything between us.

NORA: Oh yes, yes, I know that you're always thinking of me.

HELMER: And when it's time to go, and I'm putting your shawl over your lovely young shoulders—round your exquisite neck—then I imagine that you're my little bride, that we've just come from the wedding, and that I'm bringing you back to my home for the first time—that for the first time I shall be alone with you—all alone with your young trembling loveliness. All the evening I've been longing for nothing but you. While I watched you swaying and beckoning in the tarantella, it set my blood on fire till I couldn't bear it any longer. That's why I brought you home so early—

NORA: No, Torvald, go away. Leave me alone—I don't want—

HELMER: What's all this? So my little Nora's playing with me! "Don't want"? I'm your husband, aren't I?

There is a knock on the front door.

NORA (*startled*): Listen!

HELMER (*going to the hall*): Who is it?

RANK (*outside*): It's I—may I come in for a moment?

HELMER (*angrily, under his breath*): Oh, what does he want now? (*aloud*) Wait a minute. (*He goes and opens the door.*) Ah, it's nice of you not to pass our door without looking in.

RANK: I thought I heard you talking, and I felt I'd like to see you. (*He lets his eye roam quickly round the room.*) Ah yes, this dear familiar place; you two must be very happy and comfortable here.

HELMER: It looked as if you were pretty happy upstairs, too.

RANK: Wonderfully—why not? Why shouldn't one enjoy everything the world has to offer—at any rate, as much as one can—and for as long as one can? The wine was superb!

HELMER: Especially the champagne.

RANK: You thought so too, did you? It's quite incredible the amount I managed to put away!

NORA: Torvald drank a good deal of champagne tonight, too.

RANK: Oh?

NORA: Yes, and that always puts him in high spirits.

RANK: Well, why shouldn't a man have a pleasant evening after a good day's work?

HELMER: A good day's work? I'm afraid I can't claim that.

RANK (*slapping him on the back*): Ah, but *I* can!

NORA: Dr. Rank . . . then you must have been working on a scientific test today?

RANK: Exactly.

HELMER: Well, well! Little Nora talking about scientific tests!

NORA: And am I to congratulate you on the result?

RANK: You may indeed.

NORA: It was good, then?

RANK: The best possible result—for doctor *and* patient. . . . Certainty.

NORA (*quickly, probing*): Certainty?

RANK: Complete certainty. So why shouldn't I give myself a jolly evening after that?

NORA: Yes, of course you must, Dr. Rank.

HELMER: I quite agree—as long as you don't have to pay for it the next morning.

RANK: Ah well, you don't get anything for nothing in this life.

NORA: Dr. Rank—you like fancy-dress parties, don't you?

RANK: Yes, when there are lots of pretty costumes.

NORA: Then tell me—what are you and I going to wear at our next?

HELMER: Little scatterbrain—thinking about the next dance already!

RANK: You and I? Yes, I can tell you—you shall be a mascot.

HELMER: Ah, but what costume would suggest that?

RANK: Your wife could go in what she wears every day . . .

HELMER: Very charmingly put. But don't you know what you'll wear?

RANK: Oh yes, my dear fellow, I'm quite certain about that.

HELMER: Well?

RANK: At the next fancy-dress party, I shall be invisible.

HELMER: What an odd idea!

RANK: There's a big black hat—you've heard of the Invisible Hat?—you put it on, and then no one can see you.

HELMER (*hiding a smile*): Well, perhaps you're right.

RANK: But I'm quite forgetting what I came for. Give me a cigar, Helmer—one of the black Havanas.

HELMER: With the greatest pleasure (*offering him the case*).

RANK (*taking one and cutting the end*): Thanks.

NORA (*striking a match*). Let me give you a light.

RANK: Thank you.

She holds the match while he lights the cigar.

And now—good-bye.

HELMER: Good-bye—good-bye, my dear fellow.

NORA: Sleep well, Dr. Rank.

RANK: Thank you for that wish.

NORA: Wish me the same.

RANK: You? Well, if you want me to. . . . Sleep well. And—thank you for the light. . . . (*With a nod to them both, he goes.*)

HELMER (*subdued*): He's had too much to drink.

NORA (*absently*): Perhaps.

HELMER, *taking his keys from his pocket, goes out to the hall.*

NORA: Torvald—what do you want out there?

HELMER: I must empty the letter-box, it's almost full; there won't be room for tomorrow's paper.

NORA: Are you going to work tonight?

HELMER: You know perfectly well I'm not. Here, what's this? Someone's been at the lock!

NORA: At the lock?

HELMER: Yes, they certainly have. What can this mean? I shouldn't have thought that the maid—Here's a broken hairpin—Nora, it's one of yours!

NORA (*quickly*): Perhaps the children . . .

HELMER: Then you must break them of that sort of thing. Ugh—ugh—There, I've got it open all the same. (*emptying the letter-box and calling into the kitchen*) Helena? Helena, put out the lamp at the front door. (*He shuts the front door and comes into the room with the letters in his hand.*) Look—just look what a lot there are! (*looking through them*) Whatever's this?

NORA (*at the window*): The letter! No, Torvald, no!

HELMER: Two visiting-cards—from Rank.

NORA: From Dr. Rank?

HELMER (*looking at them*): "S. Rank, M.D." They were on top—he must have put them in as he left.

NORA: Is there anything on them?

HELMER: There's a black cross over the name . . . look. What a gruesome idea—it's just as if he were announcing his own death.

NORA: That's what he's doing.

HELMER: What? Do you know about it? Has he told you something?

NORA: Yes, when these cards came, it would be to say good-bye to us; he's going to shut himself up to die.

HELMER: My poor old friend. Of course I knew that he wouldn't be with me much longer—but so soon . . . . ! And to go away and hide, like a wounded animal . . .

NORA: If it *must* be, then it's best to go without a word, isn't it, Torvald?

HELMER (*pacing up and down*): He'd come to be so much a part of our lives. I can't realize that he's gone. With all his loneliness and suffering, he seemed like a background of clouds that set off the sunshine of our happiness. Well, perhaps it's all for the best—for him, at any rate. (*coming to a halt*) And maybe for us too, Nora, now that you and I have no one but each other. (*putting an arm round her*) Oh, my darling, I feel as if I can't hold you close enough. You know, Nora, I've often wished that you could be threatened by some imminent danger so that I could risk everything I had—even my life itself—to save you.

NORA (*freeing herself, and speaking firmly and purposefully*): Now you must read your letters, Torvald.

HELMER: No, no, not tonight. I want to be with my darling wife.

NORA: When your friend's dying . . . ?

HELMER: Yes, you're right—it's upset us both. Something ugly has come between us—the thought of death and decay. We must try to shake it off. . . . And until we do, let us keep apart.

NORA (*putting her arms round his neck*): Good night, Torvald—good night.

HELMER (*kissing her on the forehead*): Good night, Nora—sleep well, my little songbird. Now I'll go and read my letters. (*He takes the bundle into his room, shutting the door behind him.*)

NORA (*Wild-eyed, groping round her she seizes* HELMER's *domino and pulls it round herself. She speaks in hoarse, rapid, broken whispers.*): I shall never see him again! Never—never—never! (*She throws the shawl over her head.*) And never see the children again either—never, never again. The water's black, and cold as ice—and deep . . . so deep. . . . Oh, if only it were all over! He has it now—he's reading it. . . . Oh no, no— not yet! Good-bye, Torvald—good-bye, my children—

She is about to rush out through the hall, when HELMER *flings his door open and stands there with the open letter in his hand.*

HELMER: Nora!

NORA (*with a loud cry*): Ah . . . !

HELMER: What is all this? Do you know what's in this letter?

NORA: Yes, I know. Let me go—let me out!

HELMER (*holding her back*): Where are you going?

NORA (*struggling to free herself*): You shan't save me, Torvald!

HELMER (*taken aback*): It's true! So what it says here is true? How terrible! No, no, it's not possible—it *can't* be true.

NORA: It *is* true. I've loved you more than anything in the world.

HELMER: Now don't let's have any silly excuses.

NORA (*taking a step toward him*): Torvald . . . !

HELMER: You wretched woman—what have you done?

NORA: Let me go. You *shan't* take the blame—I won't let you suffer for me.

HELMER: We won't have any melodrama. (*locking the front door*) Here you shall stay until you've explained yourself. Do you realize what you've done? Answer me—do you realize?

NORA (*looking fixedly at him, her expression hardening as she speaks*): Yes, now I'm beginning to realize everything.

HELMER (*pacing about the room*): What a terrible awakening! For these last eight years you've been my joy and my pride—and now I find that you're a liar, a hypocrite—even worse—a criminal! Oh, the unspeakable ugliness of it all! Ugh!

NORA *looks fixedly at him without speaking. He stops in front of her.*

I might have known that something of this sort would happen—I should have foreseen it. All your father's shiftless character—Be quiet!—all your father's shiftless character has come out in you. No religion, no morality, no sense of duty . . . So this is what I get for condoning his fault! I did it for your sake, and this is how you repay me!

NORA: Yes—like this.

HELMER: You've completely wrecked my happiness, you've ruined my whole future! Oh, it doesn't bear thinking of. I'm in the power of a man without scruples; he can do what he likes with me—ask what he wants of me—order me about as he pleases, and I dare not refuse. And I'm brought so pitifully low all because of a shiftless woman!

NORA: Once I'm out of the way, you'll be free.

HELMER: No rhetoric, please! Your father was always ready with fine phrases too. How would it help me if you were "out of the way," as you call it? Not in the least! He can still see that the thing gets about, and once he does, I may very well be suspected of having been involved in your crooked dealings. They may well think that I was behind it—that I put you up to it. And it's you that I have to thank for all this—and after I've cherished you all through our married life. *Now* do you realize what you've done to me?

NORA (*calm and cold*): Yes.

HELMER: It's so incredible that I can't grasp it. But we must try to come to some understanding. Take off that shawl—take it off, I tell you. Somehow or other I must try to appease him—the thing must be hushed up at all costs. As for ourselves—we must seem to go on just as before . . . but only in the eyes of the world of course. You will remain here in my house—that goes without saying—but I shall not allow you to bring up the children . . . I shouldn't dare trust you with them. Oh, to think that I should have to say this to someone I've loved so much—someone I still . . . Well, that's all over—it must be; from now on, there'll be no question of happiness, but only of saving the ruin of it—the fragments—the mere facade . . .

There is a ring at the front door.

HELMER (*collecting himself*): What's that—at this hour? Can the worst have—Could he . . . ? Keep out of sight, Nora—say that you're ill.

NORA *remains motionless.* HELMER *goes and opens the hall door.*

MAID (*at the door, half-dressed*): There's a letter for the Mistress.

HELMER: Give it to me. (*He takes the letter and shuts the door.*) Yes, it's from him. You're not to have it—I shall read it myself.

NORA: Yes, read it.

HELMER (*by the lamp*): I hardly dare—it may mean ruin for both of us. No, I *must* know! (*Tearing open the letter, he runs his eye over a few lines, looks at a paper that is enclosed, then gives a shout of joy.*) Nora!

She looks at him inquiringly.

Nora! Wait, I must just read it again. . . . Yes, it's true; I'm saved! Nora, I'm saved!

NORA: And I?

HELMER: You too, of course. We're both saved—both you and I. Look, he's sent you back your bond. He says that he regrets . . . and apologizes . . . a fortunate change in his life. . . . Oh, never mind what he says—we're saved, Nora, no one can touch you now. Oh Nora, Nora—Wait, first let me destroy the whole detestable business. (*casting his eye over the bond*) No, I won't even look at it—I shall treat the whole thing as nothing but a bad dream. (*Tearing the bond and the two letters in pieces, he throws them on the stove, and watches them burn.*) There! Now it's all gone. He said in his letter that since Christmas Eve you'd . . . Oh, Nora, these three days must have been terrible for you.

NORA: They've been a hard struggle, these three days.

HELMER: How you must have suffered—seeing no way out except . . . No, we'll put all those hateful things out of our minds. Now we can shout for joy, again and again: "It's all over—it's all over!" Listen, Nora—you don't seem to realize—it's all over. What the matter? Such a grim face? Poor little Nora, I see what it is: you simply can't believe that I've forgiven you. But I have, Nora, I swear it—I've forgiven you everything. I know now that what you did was all for love of me.

NORA: That is true.

HELMER: You loved me as a wife *should* love her husband. It was just that you hadn't the experience to realize what you were doing. But do you imagine that you're any less dear to me for not knowing how to act on your own? No, no, you must simply rely on me—I shall advise you and guide you. I shouldn't be a proper man if your feminine helplessness didn't make you twice as attractive to me. You must forget all the hard things that I said to you in that first dreadful moment when it seemed as if the whole world was falling about my ears. I've forgiven you, Nora, I swear it—I've forgiven you.

NORA: Thank you for your forgiveness. (*She goes out through the door to the right.*)

HELMER: No, don't go. (*He looks in.*) What are you doing out there?

NORA (*off*): Taking off my fancy-dress.

HELMER (*at the open door*): Yes, do. Try to calm down and set your mind at peace, my frightened little songbird. You can rest safely, and my great wings will protect you. (*He paces up and down by the door.*) Oh, Nora, how warm and cosy our home is; it's your refuge, where I shall protect you like a hunted dove that I've saved from the talons of a hawk. Little by little, I shall calm your poor fluttering heart, Nora, take my word for it. In the morning you'll look on all this quite differently, and soon everything will be just as it used to be. There'll be no more need for me to tell you that I've forgiven you—you'll feel in your heart that I have. How can you imagine that I could ever think of rejecting—or even reproaching—you? Ah, you don't know what a real man's heart is like, Nora. There's something indescribably sweet and satisfying for a man to know deep down that he has forgiven his wife—completely forgiven her, with all his heart. It's as if that made her doubly his—as if he had brought her into the world afresh! In a sense, she has become both his wife and his child. So from now on, that's what you shall be to me, you poor, frightened, helpless, little darling. You mustn't worry about anything, Nora—only be absolutely frank with me, and I'll be both your will and your conscience. . . . Why, what's this? Not in bed? You've changed your clothes!

NORA *(in her everyday things)*: Yes, Torvald, I've changed my clothes.

HELMER: But why? At *this* hour!

NORA: I shan't sleep tonight.

HELMER: But, my dear Nora—

NORA *(looking at her watch)*: It's not so very late. Sit down here, Torvald— you and I have a lot to talk over. *(She sits down at one side of the table.)*

HELMER: Nora—what is all this? Why do you look so stern?

NORA: Sit down—this'll take some time. I have a lot to talk to you about.

HELMER *(sitting across the table from her)*: Nora, you frighten me—I don't understand you.

NORA: No, that's just it—you don't understand me. And I've never understood you—until tonight. No, you mustn't interrupt—just listen to what I have to say. Torvald, this is a reckoning.

HELMER: What do you mean by that?

NORA *(after a short pause)*: Doesn't it strike you that there's something strange about the way we're sitting here?

HELMER: No . . . what?

NORA: We've been married for eight years now. Don't you realize that this is the first time that we two—you and I, man and wife—have had a serious talk together?

HELMER: Serious? What do you mean by that?

NORA: For eight whole years—no, longer than that—ever since we first met, we've never exchanged a serious word on any serious subject.

HELMER: Was I to keep forever involving you in worries that you couldn't possibly help me with?

NORA: I'm not talking about worries; what I'm saying is that we've never sat down in earnest together to get to the bottom of a single thing.

HELMER: But, Nora dearest, what good would that have been to you?

NORA: That's just the point—you've never understood me. I've been dreadfully wronged, Torvald—first by Papa, and then by you.

HELMER: What? By your father and me? The two people who loved you more than anyone else in the world.

NORA *(shaking her head)*: You've never loved me, you've only found it pleasant to be in love with me.

HELMER: Nora—what are you saying?

NORA: It's true, Torvald. When I lived at home with Papa, he used to tell me his opinion about everything, and so I had the same opinion. If I thought differently, I had to hide it from him, or he wouldn't have liked it. He called me his little doll, and he used to play with me just as I played with my dolls. Then I came to live in your house—

HELMER: That's no way to talk about our marriage!

NORA (*undisturbed*): I mean when I passed out of Papa's hands into yours. You arranged everything to suit your own tastes, and so I came to have the same tastes as yours . . . or I pretended to. I'm not quite sure which . . . perhaps it was a bit of both—sometimes one and sometimes the other. Now that I come to look at it, I've lived here like a pauper—simply from hand to mouth. I've lived by performing tricks for you, Torvald. That was how you wanted it. You and Papa have committed a grievous sin against me: it's your fault that I've made nothing of my life.

HELMER: That's unreasonable, Nora—and ungrateful. Haven't you been happy here?

NORA: No, that's something I've never been. I thought I had, but really I've never been happy.

HELMER: Never . . . happy?

NORA: No, only gay. And you've always been so kind to me. But our home has been nothing but a play-room. I've been your doll-wife here, just as at home I was Papa's doll-child. And the children have been my dolls in their turn. I liked it when you came and played with me, just as they liked it when I came and played with them. That's what our marriage has been, Torvald.

HELMER: There is some truth in what you say, though you've exaggerated and overstated it. But from now on, things will be different. Play-time's over, now comes lesson-time.

NORA: Whose lessons? Mine or the children's?

HELMER: Both yours and the children's, Nora darling.

NORA: Ah, Torvald, you're not the man to teach me to be a real wife to you—

HELMER: How can you say that?

NORA: —and how am I fitted to bring up the children?

HELMER: Nora!

NORA: Didn't you say yourself, a little while ago, that you daren't trust them to me?

HELMER: That was in a moment of anger—you mustn't pay any attention to that.

NORA: But you were perfectly right—I'm not fit for it. There's another task that I must finish first—I must try to educate myself. And you're not the man to help me with that; I must do it alone. That's why I'm leaving you.

HELMER (*leaping to his feet*): What's that you say?

NORA: I must stand on my own feet if I'm to get to know myself and the world outside. That's why I can't stay here with you any longer.

HELMER: Nora—Nora . . . !

NORA: I want to go at once. I'm sure Kristina will take me in for the night.

HELMER: You're out of your mind. I won't let you—I forbid it.

NORA: It's no good your forbidding me anything any longer. I shall take the things that belong to me, but I'll take nothing from you—now or later.

HELMER: But this is madness . . .

NORA: Tomorrow I shall go home—to my old home, I mean—it'll be easier for me to find something to do there.

HELMER: Oh, you blind, inexperienced creature . . . !

NORA: I must try to *get* some experience, Torvald.

HELMER: But to leave your home—your husband and your children. . . . You haven't thought of what people will say.

NORA: I can't consider that. All I know is that this is necessary for me.

HELMER: But this is disgraceful. Is this the way you neglect your most sacred duties?

NORA: What do you consider is my most sacred duty?

HELMER: Do I have to tell you that? Isn't it your duty to your husband and children?

NORA: I have another duty, just as sacred.

HELMER: You can't have. What duty do you mean?

NORA: My duty to myself.

HELMER: Before everything else, you're a wife and a mother.

NORA: I don't believe that any longer. I believe that before everything else I'm a human being—just as much as you are . . . or at any rate I shall try to become one. I know quite well that most people would agree with you, Torvald, and that you have warrant for it in books; but I can't be satisfied any longer with what most people say, and with what's in books. I must think things out for myself and try to understand them.

HELMER: Shouldn't you first understand your place in your own home? Haven't you an infallible guide in such matters—your religion?

NORA: Ah, Torvald, I don't really know what religion is.

HELMER: What's that you say?

NORA: I only know what Pastor Hansen taught me when I was confirmed. He told me that religion was this, that, and the other. When I get away from all this, and am on my own, I want to look into that too. I want to see if what Pastor Hansen told me was right—or at least, if it is right for me.

HELMER: This is unheard-of from a young girl like you. But if religion can't guide you, then let me rouse your conscience. You must have *some* moral sense. Or am I wrong? Perhaps you haven't.

NORA: Well, Torvald, it's hard to say; I don't really know—I'm so bewildered about it all. All I know is that I think quite differently from you about things; and now I find that the law is quite different from what I thought, and I simply can't convince myself that the law is right. That a woman shouldn't have the right to spare her old father on his deathbed, or to save her husband's life! I can't believe things like that.

HELMER: You're talking like a child; you don't understand the world you live in.

NORA: No, I don't. But now I mean to go into that, too. I must find out which is right—the world or I.

HELMER: You're ill, Nora—you're feverish. I almost believe you're out of your senses.

NORA: I've never seen things so clearly and certainly as I do tonight.

HELMER: Clearly and certainly enough to forsake your husband and your children?

NORA: Yes.

HELMER: Then there's only one possible explanation . . .

NORA: What?

HELMER: You don't love me any more.

NORA: No, that's just it.

HELMER: Nora! How can you say that?

NORA: I can hardly bear to, Torvald, because you've always been so kind to me—but I can't help it. I don't love you any more.

HELMER (*with forced self-control*): And are you clear and certain about that, too?

NORA: Yes, absolutely clear and certain. That's why I won't stay here any longer.

HELMER: And will you also be able to explain how I've forfeited your love?

NORA: Yes, I can indeed. It was this evening, when the miracle didn't happen—because then I saw that you weren't the man I'd always thought you.

HELMER: I don't understand that. Explain it.

NORA: For eight years I'd waited so patiently—for, goodness knows, I realized that miracles don't happen every day. Then this disaster overtook me, and I was completely certain that now the miracle would happen. When Krogstad's letter was lying out there, I never imagined for a moment that you would submit to his conditions. I was completely certain that you would say to him "Go and publish it to the whole world!" And when that was done . . .

HELMER: Well, what then? When I'd exposed my own wife to shame and disgrace?

NORA: When that was done, I thought—I was completely certain—that you would come forward and take all the blame—that you'd say "*I'm* the guilty one."

HELMER: Nora!

NORA: You think that I should never have accepted a sacrifice like that from you? No, of course I shouldn't. But who would have taken my word against yours? That was the miracle I hoped for . . . and dreaded. It was to prevent *that* that I was ready to kill myself.

HELMER: Nora, I'd gladly work night and day for you, and endure poverty and sorrow for your sake. But no man would sacrifice his *honor* for the one he loves.

NORA: Thousands of women have.

HELMER: Oh, you're talking and thinking like a stupid child.

NORA: Perhaps . . . But you don't talk or think like the man I could bind myself to. When your first panic was over—not about what threatened me, but about what might happen to *you*—and when there was no more danger, then, as far as you were concerned, it was just as if nothing had happened at all. I was simply your little songbird, your doll, and from now on you would handle it more gently than ever because it was so delicate and fragile. (*rising*) At that moment, Torvald, I realized that for eight years I'd been living here with a strange man, and that I'd borne him three children. Oh, I can't bear to think of it—I could tear myself to little pieces!

HELMER (*sadly*): Yes. I see—I see. There truly is a gulf between us. . . . Oh, but Nora, couldn't we somehow bridge it?

NORA: As I am now, I'm not the wife for you.

HELMER: I could change . . .

NORA: Perhaps—if your doll is taken away from you.

HELMER: But to lose you—to lose you, Nora! No, no, I can't even imagine it . . .

NORA (*going out to the right*): That's just why it *must* happen.

She returns with her outdoor clothes, and a little bag which she puts on a chair by the table.

HELMER: Nora! Not now, Nora—wait till morning.

NORA (*putting on her coat*): I couldn't spend the night in a strange man's house.

HELMER: But couldn't we live here as brother and sister?

NORA (*putting her hat on*): You know quite well that that wouldn't last. (*She pulls her shawl round her.*) Good-bye, Torvald. I won't see my children—I'm sure they're in better hands than mine. As I am now, I'm no good to them.

HELMER: But some day, Nora—some day . . . ?

NORA: How can I say? I've no idea what will become of me.

HELMER: But you're my wife—now, and whatever becomes of you.

NORA: Listen, Torvald: I've heard that when a wife leaves her husband's house as I'm doing now, he's legally freed from all his obligations to her. Anyhow, *I* set you free from them. You're not to feel yourself bound in any way, and nor shall I. We must both be perfectly free. Look, here's your ring back—give me mine.

HELMER: Even that?

NORA: Even that.

HELMER: Here it is.

NORA: There. Now it's all over. Here are your keys. The servants know all about running the house—better than I did. Tomorrow, when I've gone, Kristina will come and pack my things that I brought from home; I'll have them sent after me.

HELMER: Over! All over! Nora, won't you ever think of me again?

NORA: I know I shall often think of you—and the children, and this house.

HELMER: May I write to you, Nora?

NORA: No . . . you must never do that.

HELMER: But surely I can send you—

NORA: Nothing—nothing.

HELMER: —or help you, if ever you need it?

NORA: No, I tell you, I couldn't take anything from a stranger.

HELMER: Nora—can't I ever be anything more than a stranger to you?

NORA (*picking up her bag*): Oh, Torvald—there would have to be the greatest miracle of all . . .

HELMER: What would that be—the greatest miracle of all?

NORA: Both of us would have to be so changed that—Oh, Torvald, I don't believe in miracles any longer.

HELMER: But I'll believe. Tell me: "so changed that . . . "?

NORA: That our life together could be a real marriage. Good-bye. (*She goes out through the hall.*)

HELMER (*sinking down on a chair by the door and burying his face in his hands*): Nora! Nora! (*He rises and looks round.*) Empty! She's not here any more! (*with a glimmer of hope*) "The greatest miracle of all . . . "?

From below comes the noise of a door slamming.

The Receptive Reader

1. In the early acts, Torvald Helmer holds forth on the role of the husband, standards of honesty or probity for dealing with money. Above all, in his talk and in many little ways, he demonstrates the role he has assigned to Nora in their household. What are revealing things he says and does? What portrait of him as a *major character* emerges in Acts 1 and 2? How do you react to him?

2. In what ways does Nora live up to the stereotype of the "little woman"? How does she conform to her husband's conception of her? What are telling details or patterns of behavior that make her the weaker partner in their marriage? What are revealing things she says or does in the early acts of the play?

3. When do you see the first signs that there might be another side to Nora's personality? When do you see signs that she might be a *complex* rather than a simple character? What are the first hints that Torvald and Nora are going to come into conflict?

4. In Acts 1 and 2, how does Mrs. Linde serve as a *foil* to Nora? How does Ibsen use her to remind the audience of the harsh economic realities facing women on the fringes of middle-class society? (What light do the comments of the Nurse throw on the role of lower-class women?)

5. Among the other *supporting characters,* what is the role of Dr. Rank, the physician? What role does he play in Nora's life? From what perspective does Rank see the major characters? How does Ibsen use him to throw added light on Nora and Torvald and their society?

6. What is Krogstad's central role in the *plot* of the play? How does he bring out into the open Helmer's (and his society's) standards about money, credit, and respectability? Why is the fact that at one time the two men were schoolmates an embarrassment to Helmer? What is the role of the relationship between Krogstad and Mrs. Linde in the play as a whole?

7. Krogstad at one point tells Nora that even "a man like me has a certain amount of what is called feeling." How do you react to him? Is he a stage villain—someone all bad, whom the audience can hiss and despise?

8. What is the nature of Nora's dealings with Krogstad? How do they test her character and her view of the world? How do they make her change or grow? How do the revelations about the hushed-up events of the past change your view of Nora?

9. At the *climax,* or high point, of the play, Torvald fails Nora—he fails to live up to her expectations. Why and how? What does she expect of him? How and why does she judge him? Do you concur in her judgment? In these climactic scenes in Act 3, what does Ibsen try to show about the workings of Torvald's kind of bourgeois morality? about Torvald's kind of person?

10. What questions does Nora raise about the nature of marriage in the final scenes? What answers does the play suggest? What is the meaning of Nora's concept of the "duty to myself"? What is her idea of a "real marriage"?

The Creative Dimension

To get his play performed in Germany, with opportunities for fame and fortune far beyond those of his native Norway, Ibsen rewrote the ending to make it more acceptable to the outraged forces of middle-class respectability. Gritting his teeth, he wrote a final scene in which Torvald makes Nora take a last look at her sleeping children:

TORVALD: Tomorrow, when they wake up and call for their mother, they will be . . . motherless!
NORA (*trembling*): Motherless!
TORVALD: As you once were.
NORA: Motherless! (*After an inner struggle, she lets her bag fall, and says*) Ah, though it is a sin against myself, I cannot leave them!

Choose one: Pretend you are a drama critic in Ibsen's time. Attack or defend the changed ending. Or, do your own rewrite of the final page or pages for a current adaptation of the play—for instance, for a Hollywood movie or for an avant-garde production.

JUXTAPOSITIONS

The Range of Interpretation

Ibsen's *A Doll's House* inspired furious denunciation by its enemies and spirited defense by its admirers. Many people read it in a printed version even when they did not see it on the stage. In the 1880s and 1890s, this play and other Ibsen plays contributed to the heady intellectual ferment that was calling many conventional middle-class assumptions into question. The following selections relate Ibsen's drama to the ideological cross-currents of his time.

Joan Templeton

Ibsen admired women who fought the battle for women's right to vote. Calling their female contemporaries "morally disabled," they advanced the ideal of an independent, educated New Woman taking her place in the world of work and politics. In 1884, Ibsen joined with the president of the

Norwegian Women's Rights League and with fellow writers in signing a petition supporting a proposed law establishing property rights for married women. He advised legislators against consulting men on this topic: "To consult men in such a matter is like asking wolves if they desire better protection for the sheep."

Ibsen and Feminism

Ibsen's contemporaries, the sophisticated as well as the crude, recognized *A Doll's House* as the clearest and most substantial expression of the "woman question" that had yet appeared. In Europe and America, from the 1880's on, the articles poured forth: "Der Noratypus" [The Nora Type], "Ibsen und die Frauenfragen" [Ibsen and the Women's Questions], "Ibsen et la femme," "La Représentation féministe et sociale d'Ibsen," "A Prophet of the New Womanhood," "Ibsen as a Pioneer of the Woman Movement." These are a small sampling of titles from scholars and journalists who agreed with their more famous contemporaries Lou Andréas Salomé, Alla Nazimova, Georg Brandes, and August Strindberg, along with every other writer on Ibsen, whether in the important dailies and weeklies or in the highbrow and lowbrow reviews, that the theme of *A Doll's House* was the subjection of women by men.

Havelock Ellis, filled with a young man's dreams and inspired by Nora, proclaimed that she held out nothing less than "the promise of a new social order." In 1890, eleven years after Betty Hennings as Nora first slammed the shaky backdrop door in Copenhagen's Royal Theatre, he summarized what *A Doll's House* meant to the progressives of Ibsen's time:

> The great wave of emancipation which is now sweeping across the civilized world means nominally nothing more than that women should have the right to education, freedom to work, and political enfranchisement—nothing in short but the bare ordinary rights of an adult human creature in a civilized state.

Profoundly disturbing in its day, *A Doll's House* remains so still because, in James Huneker's succinct analysis, it is "the plea for woman as a human being, neither more nor less than man, which the dramatist made." . . .

A Doll's House is a natural development of the play Ibsen had just written, the unabashedly feminist *Pillars of Society;* both plays reflect Ibsen's extremely privileged feminist education, which he shared with few other nineteenth-century male authors and which he owed to a trio of extraordinary women: Suzannah Thoresen Ibsen, his wife; Magdalen Thoresen, his colleague at the Norwegian National Theatre in Bergen, who was Suzannah's stepmother and former governess; and Camilla Wergeland Collett, Ibsen's literary colleague, valued friend, and the founder of Norwegian feminism.

Magdalen Thoresen wrote novels and plays and translated the French plays Ibsen put on as a young stage manager at the Bergen theater. She was probably the first "New Woman" he had ever met. She pitied the insolvent young writer, took him under her wing, and brought him home. She had passed her strong feminist principles on to her charge, the outspoken and irrepressible Suzannah, who adored her strong-minded stepmother and whose favorite author was George Sand [pen name of Lucile Dudevant]. The second time Ibsen met Suzannah he asked her to marry him. Hjordis, the fierce shield-maiden of *The Vikings at Helgeland,* the play of their engagement, and Svanhild, the strong-willed heroine of *Love's Comedy,* the play that followed, owe much to Suzannah Thoresen Ibsen. Later, Nora's way of speaking would remind people of Suzannah's.

The third and perhaps most important feminist in Ibsen's life was his friend Camilla Collett, one of the most active feminists in nineteenth-century Europe and founder of the modern Norwegian novel. Fifteen years before Mill's *Subjection of Women,* Collett wrote *Amtmandens Døttre (The Governor's Daughters).* Faced with the choice of a masculine *nom de plume* [pen name] or no name at all on the title page, Collett brought out her novel anonymously in two parts in 1854 and 1855, but she nonetheless became widely known as the author. Its main argument, based on the general feminist claim that women's feelings matter, is that women should have the right to educate themselves and to marry whom they please. In the world of the governor's daughters, it is masculine success that matters. Brought up to be ornaments and mothers, women marry suitable men and devote their lives to their husbands' careers and to their children. The novel, a cause célèbre, made Collett famous overnight.

Collett regularly visited the Ibsens in their years of exile in Germany, and she and Suzannah took every occasion to urge Ibsen to take up the feminist cause. They had long, lively discussions in the years preceding *A Doll's House,* when feminism had become a strong movement and the topic of the day in Scandinavia. Collett was in Munich in 1877, when Ibsen was hard at work on *Pillars of Society,* and Ibsen's biographer Koht speculates that Ibsen may have deliberately prodded her to talk about the women's movement in order to get material for his dialogue. . . .

It is foolish to apply the formalist notion that art is never sullied by argument to Ibsen's middle-period plays, written at a time when he was an outspoken and direct fighter in what he called the "mortal combat between two epochs." . . . While it is true that Ibsen never reduced life to "ideas," it is equally true that he was passionately interested in the events and ideas of his day. He was as deeply anchored his time as any writer has been before or since.

From "The *Doll House* Backlash: Criticism, Feminism, and Ibsen," 1989

The Receptive Reader

One school of critics has seen Nora's search for her own true self as transcending sex roles. The play is "a metaphor for individual freedom" generally (Robert Brustein). Nora is Everyman trying to find himself or herself. However, feminist critics have stressed Nora's identity as a "nineteenth-century married woman." *A Doll's House* "is not about Everybody's struggle to find himself or herself" but "about Everywoman's struggle against Everyman" (Joan Templeton). Which of these two views is closer to your own reading of the play?

Errol Durbach

Ibsen wrote at the time of the first stirrings of socialism and communism that foreshadowed the revolutionary upheavals of the twentieth century. He helped turn drama into a political force, inspiring disciples like the Irish playwright George Bernard Shaw, whose plays were manifestos and at the same time highly successful drama. American admirers drew the parallel between Ibsen's provincial bourgeois society and small-town American middle-class life, seeing him as a champion of the "victories of self-assertion over the oppression of society, and of naked truth over conventional shams" (Edwin Slosson). The following selection focuses on the impact Ibsen had on avant-garde intellectuals in England.

Ibsen and Marxism

For the English Ibsenites, the Norwegian Master was full of ideological fervor, a champion of political causes from Marxism and Fabianism to secularism, hedonism, and atheism. Eleanor Marx played Nora to Aveling's Torvald, roles that they acted with the utter conviction that the "miracle" had already taken place in their pleasant house in Great Russell Street. The couple had just published an article called "The Woman Question: From a Socialist Point of View" in which they argued that when the revolution came—and Eleanor believed that *A Doll's House* was its harbinger—men and women would be joined in free contract, mind to mind, as a whole and completed entity. For Marxists, *A Doll's House* envisioned the emancipation of men and women from the capitalist system with the abolition of class rule serving as a prerequisite for the abolition of sex rule, and because, for Eleanor Marx, the status of women in society was directly analogous to that of the proletariat, she submerged all interest in sectarian feminism into the larger issues of social change through revolutionary action. For her, Nora's predicament was a metaphor for the oppression and exploitation of the working classes, and marriage in Ibsen's play symbolized the last bastion of serfdom recognized by law. The resounding door slam was viewed as the first rumble of momentous social rebellion, and if Ibsen's play ends on a note of tenuous possibility that some secular "miracle" might transform Christmas into a celebration of cultural renewal, for Eleanor Marx that "miracle" was socialism, which would bring economic and intellectual emancipation for women and workers alike.

From *A Doll's House: Ibsen's Myth of Transformation*, 1991

The Receptive Reader

Can you see why for socialist readers of Ibsen's play "the status of women in society was directly analogous to that of the proletariat"? Would you use the term *oppression* for Nora's situation in the play? Why or why not?

WRITING ABOUT LITERATURE

26 *Keeping a Drama Journal*
WRITING FOCUS: Options for Writing

The Writing Workshop   In reading or watching a play, you will ideally be carried along by the action that develops. Later, as you sort out your impressions, you will find it useful to keep a drama journal that allows you to record both your scene-by-scene reactions and your first thoughts about the play as a whole. Different journal entries might explore topics like the following: Where does the play take us—what setting or context does it create? How do the characters come into focus? How do major issues shape up? Does a central conflict begin to give shape to the play as a whole? Does a major theme begin to echo in key passages? What means does the dramatist use to steer the reactions of the audience or to create dramatic effects?

In form, your journal entries may vary greatly, ranging from reading notes (or viewing notes) to finished paragraphs and mini-essays. Study the following sample entries:

Running Commentary   Many readers find it useful to keep a **running commentary** on key developments and key passages in a play. Look at the way the following sample entries start recording queries and important evidence on key points in the opening scenes of Ibsen's *A Doll's House*. Note the amount of direct quotation for possible later use in a more formal paper:

Torvald constantly uses what he thinks are terms of endearment that actually belittle Nora: "Is that my little skylark twittering out there?" "Scampering about like a little squirrel?" "Has my little featherbrain been out wasting money again?" "My little songbird mustn't be so crestfallen."

Torvald gives lectures on not getting into debt: "No debts, no borrowing. There's something constrained, something ugly even about a home that's founded on borrowing and debt." He calls Nora a "prodigal" who spends money "on all sorts of useless things."

Nora's "sweet tooth" becomes an issue. She is treated like a child?

Focusing on Character   You may want to devote an entry to a major character, pulling together impressions that at first might have seemed contradictory or inconclusive. The following sample entry is a **character portrait** of a major character in the ancient Greek playwright Euripides' *The Women of Troy*. He wrote the play toward the end of the fifth century B.C., when his native Athens was reaching the end of a disastrous long drawn-out war. In the words of one student reader, the play "draws portraits of strong, independent, capable individuals, gathered together in the hours after the fall of Troy to the Greeks to mourn their dead and say good-bye to their homeland and to one another." Although the women are about to be taken into slavery, they speak up with great dignity and passion. A major source of strength to the other women is Hecabe, the newly widowed wife of King Priam, who with many of his sons and warriors has been killed in the fall of Troy.

Euripides' women each have a unique personality, each dealing with her terrible fate as best she can. Hecabe, former wife of King Priam of Troy, is a truly pitiable tragic character of impressive stature. Early in the play, she says, "Lift your neck from the dust; up with your head! This is not Troy." She maintains this royal bearing and pride throughout the play, even when, "maddened and sick with horror," she awaits her fate. She bemoans aloud her fate of having to be a slave in Greece where she is likely to be a keeper of keys and answerer of doors, sleeping on the floor and wearing rags. The audience can share in her anguish when she finds that her daughter Polyxena has been offered as a human sacrifice at the grave of the Greek champion Achilles. She is also an extremely sympathetic character when she buries her little grandson Astyanax, killed by the Greeks to keep the boy from growing up to seek vengeance for the death of his father, Hector. However, Hecabe shows a vengeful or vindictive streak when she denounces Helen, whom she blames for much of what has befallen her city, in front of Helen's husband Menelaus. At a time when Helen is trying to save her life in the presence of the husband she had betrayed, Hecabe shows her thirst for vengeance and her unforgiving hatred of her enemies.

Focusing on Plot   Preparing a **plot summary** (of the play as a whole or perhaps of one climactic act) can give you a better sense of the flow of a play. When debating the larger questions about a play, you will often find it useful to go back to exactly what happens in an act or a scene. A caution to observe: You may not learn much if your summary turns into a perfunctory stock-taking of events on the "and-then" model ("And then Willy's sons take him to a restaurant"). Instead, ask yourself: Why are these plot developments important? For instance, your summary might trace major developments building up to a major turning point or to the final catastrophe. The following sample entry summarizes the action in the final scenes of Arthur Miller's *Death of a Salesman*. Willy Loman is losing his already weak grip on reality; his relationship with his alienated son Biff is coming to a head; Willy is hatching the scheme that will make up for his and Biff's lifetimes of failures:

After leaving Willy "babbling in a toilet" at the restaurant, the boys go out on the town with their dates only to come home to be thoroughly castigated by their mother: "There isn't a stranger you would do that to!" Linda shouts. Meanwhile, Willy, retreating into his world of illusion, is planting vegetable seeds in the garden—in the middle of the night—while carrying on a conversation with the legendary Uncle Ben (who walked into the jungle and came back rich). At this point, we learn of Willy's plan to commit suicide, leaving the proceeds of his life insurance to Biff. "God, he'll be great yet," Willy explains to Ben. "And now with twenty-five thousand behind him." "It sounds like an interesting proposition, William," Ben concurs.

After Linda's bitter lecture to the boys, Biff tells his mother that he is no good and that he is leaving, never to return. He goes into the garden to bring his father into the kitchen where the climactic scene occurs. When Willy learns Biff is leaving, he is furious and denounces Biff for wasting his life. "Spite!" Willy screams. "Spite is the word of your undoing!" Ultimately, Biff breaks down, crying, "Let me go. Can't you see that I'm just no good? There's not spite in it anymore! I am just what I am." Willy, too, is overcome, although he still cannot let go of his illusion: "God, he'll be great yet."

Once everyone retires—Biff is to leave the following morning—Willy proceeds with his plan. But this is not the end of the play. We are in for yet another sad irony. The final scene is the funeral. Throughout the play, Willy prided himself on his popularity gained during all his years of selling; he had believed he was "well-liked." No one comes to his funeral—a bitter and tragic ending for one consumed by the "American Dream."

Focusing on Technique   The dramatist's means—the tools of the playwright's trade—are most effective when we are not aware of them. They help the playwright create the illusion of reality. It may not be until we try to understand the effect or the workings of a play that we become consciously aware of the means. The following journal entry focuses on a device Arthur Miller uses repeatedly to alert the audience to the sad and laughable mixture of daydream and reality in Willy Loman's talk:

Already in the first scene we become acutely aware of Willy's tendency to drift in and out of reality. His words are filled with contradictions as he evades the truth only to face it a moment later full of self-pity. His sales estimates change in the same breath from boasting ("I'm vital in New England!") to pitiful excuses (three of the stores were half-closed). He says "Biff is a lazy bum!" and a few lines later resolutely talks himself into believing the opposite: "And such a hard worker! There's one thing about Biff—he's not lazy." The rapid shifting from sad recognition of the truth—that, for Willy, it is all over—to sudden outbursts of illusion and false hope, characterizes Willy throughout the play. Miller does a superlative job with dialogue as Willy contradicts himself continuously, particularly in scenes with Linda. For example, when Linda is explaining what they owe for the month, she mentions the payment due on the refrigerator. Willy remarks, "I hope we didn't get stuck on that machine." Linda replies, "But it has the best advertisements." Willy responds, "Oh, I know, it's a fine machine."

Focusing on an Issue   An entry may explore a major theme or issue in a play. It may look at pros and cons, presenting a **trial thesis** that could be argued more fully in a formal paper. The following entry takes on a key question raised by Ibsen's *A Doll's House*: Did Nora make the right decision at the end of the play?

"I am going to see if I can make out who is right, the world or I," Nora Helmer says near the end of Act 3 of *A Doll's House*. I know my reaction is based on hindsight, but a woman today might well urge Nora to be cautious in pitting herself against the world. In leaving her husband and children, she violates a social order larger and more powerful than herself. People like Torvald more often than not close ranks against the rebel who threatens the status quo and jealously guard their advantage. Women will not befriend her except for those who are themselves outside the order. Kristina, who is respectable as a widow, may or may not stand by her.

As it happens, the world is bigger, meaner, colder, and more ruthless than a single, isolated person such as Nora is likely to be. She should not refuse Torvald's help nor should she walk out taking only what she brought as a bride. Nora is likely to find that the world is manned by Torvalds. She is likely to be drawn to them and they to her, for it has been a lifetime pattern already deeply instilled. She has the natural gift to delight and charm men, and she has worked this gift down to a science as Ibsen shows us in the first two acts. It has been her vocation to be the perfect wife—charming and diverting on the surface and ruthlessly practical behind the scenes in arranging the loan and paying it back all these years.

Torvald's self-preoccupation, rage, and condemnation of her when he learns about the loan shatter Nora's illusion of him. Nora moves very quickly from focusing on what has happened in her relationship with Torvald—his selfishness and knee-jerk condemnation of her worth as a human being—to going into the world to find out who is right or wrong. The risks and variables of surviving in the world alone are large. She will need money and friends, and she may have neither because of her defiance of conventional, accepted behavior for women. She may not want to live a celibate life, either. Permanent relationships may offer the same kind of traps she is in with Torvald—maybe worse, temporary ones are fraught with danger, disease, unwanted pregnancy, further loss of status in the community.

In today's terms, Nora has no job skills, no money, no connections other than Kristina and Krogstad. Today's feminists might urge her to see an attorney and get as much information as she can before she departs. Life may be rough at home, but it can be even worse alone and friendless in the cold, hard world.

The Personal Connection   A play will move us most strongly if it strikes a chord somewhere in our own experience, if at some level it relates to something we have strongly felt. In reading or watching a play, have you ever felt the kind of personal connection that is the subject of the following journal entry?

Shakespeare has a way of making the agony of a play intensely personal. Hamlet's anguish, I feel, is caused mainly by external difficulties, by people other than himself. He finds himself in a situation not of his own making, a situation over which he has no control. He says, "The world is out of joint. O cursed spite that I was born to set it right." Perhaps I relate to him strongly because I have had a traumatic experience of being at the mercy of other people's initiatives, with my own role being that of experiencing reactions rather than taking action. My parents each remarried shortly after their divorce ("O wicked speed"). I know what it feels like to be avoided, to be in the way. My father did not tell me that he got married until three weeks after the wedding. Of course, Hamlet's grievance was much stronger because he was a prince who had expected to follow his father to the crown. He struggled with the obligation to avenge his father. Today, instead of striking back, we are expected to work our way through the psychological upheaval. We are expected to "cope."

A Drama Review   Drama is one of the oldest of the performance arts. Write a critical review of a live performance or of a videotape of a theatrical production. If you can, attend a performance of a play at your college theater, at a community theater, or at a roadshow performance of a national company. Play the role of a theater critic for a local or national publication. Theater reviews often include the following elements:

✘ overall estimate of the success of the performance;

✘ capsule description of the play, perhaps showing its significance or contemporary relevance;

✘ discussion of the director's conception of the play or the special emphasis given the play in the current production;

✘ a look at outstanding contributions of both major and supporting actors;

✘ evaluation of the role of scenery or special effects;

✘ discussion of shortcomings or unresolved problems;

✘ discussion of audience reaction or community reception of the play or performance.

The following sample journal entry was written by a student as part of her preparation for a paper on the role of women in ancient Greek tragedy.

The performance of *Trojan Women* at the Mayer Theater was truly captivating, and if you are a lover of Greek tragedy, then it is strongly advised that you go see this play. *Trojan Women* truly displayed theatrical drama at its best, breathing life into issues like the inherent suffering that one undergoes in merciless times of war. The women in the play undoubtedly portrayed this, with Heccuba taking center stage for the most pained woman in Thebes. There were times throughout the performance when the women would moan and unleash terrible wailing at the same time. As a spectator, I could honestly say that moments like those truly brought me to a catharsis—I remember feeling something pulling at my stomach when I heard the moans of all these women. It was as if I knew what they were feeling, yet I was dumbfounded at the same time. The repercussions of the actresses were truly felt by the audience—you could see it in people's reactions. This alone makes the play an excellent production. After all, it is not the purpose of Greek tragedy to move its audience?

There was also a big "shift" in time that brought the theme of the play together. The play begins in modern-day times, where two people are excavating in the ruins of the city of Thebes. They are excited to make such a discovery, and it is the discovery of Hector's shield that commences the play. This shield becomes a major part of the play, as it represents the terror of war, and the inherent pain that follows it. As the play develops, the spectator is able to see how war ravages the women and children of a "once great" city. The hands of the gods in these affairs also play an important role in conveying this message to the spectators. The actors/actresses did a good job of portraying how the gods can themselves be merciless and unjust where the trials of war are concerned. Notions of injustice also seem to pervade the play, and the spectator is able to feel this through the strong performance of the actors/actresses on stage. There is an overwhelming feeling of irony at the end of the play, which also ends with a scene from modern-day times. Just after watching the city of Thebes go down in flames, in all its greatness, it dawns on the spectator that the loss of the city truly symbolizes the tragedy of lost glory. The excavators continue to sift through the remains of the once great city, and part of the sadness of the play lies in their ignorance. For they do not know the emotions and the history of the horrifying and glorious events that took place there—only the spectators know.

✗ Compare and contrast Ibsen's Nora and Sophocles' Antigone as strong independent self-willed women in a male-dominated patriarchal society.

Claire Bloom and Anthony Hopkins as Nora and Torvald Helmer in *A Doll's House* (courtesy of Photofest)

27 GREEK TRAGEDY:

The Embattled Protagonist

Many awesome things walk the earth,
but nothing more awesome than humankind.

SOPHOCLES, *ANTIGONE*

The structure of a play is always the story of how
the birds come home to roost.

ARTHUR MILLER

Everyone is alone on the core of the earth
pierced by a ray of sunlight;
and suddenly it's evening.

QUASIMODO UNGARETTI

FOCUS ON GREEK DRAMA

The golden age of Greek drama takes us back 2,500 years to the Athens of the fifth century B.C. Greek drama was "formed at the center of the culture of its time, and at the center of the life and awareness of the community" (Francis Fergusson). But the great plays—*Antigone, Oedipus Rex, The Trojan Women*—are still gripping drama today. In Sophocles' *Antigone,* the characters speak to us across the gulf of time in terms we understand. In the first scene, Antigone speaks to an issue that has confronted many in our time: The powers that command her to be loyal to the state—to honor her allegiance to the larger community. However, what she is asked to do goes against her conscience. What the law requires offends her sense of what is right. The question is: Is there a higher law that the individual should obey? Can the individual defy the state? If the individual chooses to defy authority, will friends and family desert the rebel in order to save themselves?

In the Greek plays, we witness the appearance of recognizable human beings that give voice to the hopes and fears, the dreams and nightmares, of our common humanity. True, the characters that occupy center stage are members of a privileged class: tribal chieftains or warlords and their spouses and the clans they represent. But their thoughts and feelings, their ambitions and disappointments, as well as the calamities that overtake them, often mirror our own, although projected onto a larger screen. When they talk about their gods and myths and taboos, we may need a scholar or a cultural historian to annotate references that have lost their meaning. However, when they talk about their loyalties and jealousies, we often do not need an interpreter. We see a strong individual—man or woman—center stage, engaged in a fateful conflict. Sometimes the conflict is with other human beings. Sometimes it is a conflict with the gods.

✖ Greek drama—from the Greek for "doings" or "things done"—grew out of springtime festivals in honor of the god Dionysos. (To the Romans, he later became known as Bacchus, the god of wine and revelry.) A statue of the god was close to the stage. A priest of Dionysos had a special front-row seat. The word *tragedy* originally meant "goat-song," from the goat that was offered to the god as a ritual sacrifice. Like the earlier religious rituals, the theater performances were part of a community festival, with as many as fifteen thousand people in attendance. During the drama festivals, multitudes of spectators crowded a large semicircular outdoor theater, carved into the side of a hill, with steeply rising tiered stone seats.

✖ Plays were chosen during elaborately organized drama contests. The plays were usually performed in groups of three, with the three playwrights competing for first prize. The major plays were **tragedies**, focused on famous calamities that had befallen the mighty. The basic fare of three serious plays was spiced with a satyr play (named after the goat-footed, oversexed satyrs of Greek mythology). This early kind of **comedy** featured coarse, suggestive humor and satirical jabs at greedy contemporaries and obtuse leaders.

✖ Actors spoke through masks with exaggerated features—so that spectators on the periphery could see who was king, queen, servant, or priest. The masks are also assumed to have helped the actors project their voices to the distant highest seats. With the spectators unable to read emotions in the face, the actors were likely to have used large sweeping gestures to express fear, hostility, defiance, and rage. In later periods, the actors wore high-soled boots (a kind of elevator shoe) that amplified their stature. As on Shakespeare's stage and in the Japanese Kabuki theater, male actors played female roles.

The following are some of the conventions, or customary ways of doing theater, of classical Greek drama:

Actors and the Chorus   Greek drama evolved from religious rituals using song and dance. As in the earlier rituals, the **chorus**, a group of performers, made solemn ceremonial entrances and exits. Led by the *choragos,* the chorus chanted and danced at regular intervals in the dramatic action. Before there were individual actors, the chorus, in song and dance, told the whole story. Gradually, individual actors (or soloists) began to act out the high points. Sophocles took an important step by having more than two actors interacting on the stage at one time. In his plays, the chorus reacts to and comments on the action. The chorus verbalizes for us what the reactions of a group of contemporary onlookers might have been. The alternation of scenes featuring spirited dialogue by the actors with the solemn ritualistic chants of the chorus sets up the basic rhythm of the classic Greek play.

Offstage Action   Greek drama stays in one place, such as the steps and open area in front of the king's palace. A familiar walk-on part in Greek tragedy is that of the **messenger**: News of key events comes to the central location through messages or eyewitness reports. As a result, there is little external action. The plays do not act out the violence found in the ancient stories. Assassinations, suicides, parricides (slayings of parents), fatal quarrels, the abandonment or exposure of infants—these are reported rather than enacted on the stage. The result is that the plays focus on *psychological action*—the characters' motives, loyalties, decisions, uncertainties—rather than on sensational physical violence.

Unity of Impact   Greek drama concentrates in single-minded fashion on the main action. There are no subplots, no comic interludes. A crisis or fateful conflict comes into focus; we are absorbed in how it came about and what will come of it. The concentrated effect comes from the celebrated three unities: unity of place, unity of time (a single day or at most a day and a half), unity of action.

The best-known Greek tragedies were traditional stories of terrible deeds among persons linked by close kinship. Later generations have brought to the tragedies expectations shaped by centuries of discussion of tragedy as a **genre**, or literary form. To this day, our definition of tragedy harks back to the Greek philosopher Aristotle, who included guidelines for the ideal tragedy in his discussion of imaginative literature, the *Poetics* (330 B.C.).

Plot   To Aristotle, the "life and soul" of tragedy was the plot, which had to be more than simply a sequence of disjointed episodes. He said, "The plot should be framed in such a way that even without seeing the events take place, someone simply hearing the story should be moved to fear and pity." Aristotle distinguished two major phases: first, setting up a problem, or **complication**; and then setting in motion the **denouement** (or unraveling) that resolves the issue. To Aristotle, the most powerful part of the plot was a sudden turn in the fortunes of the main character. This reversal (or **peripety**) was often brought on by an unexpected discovery. The turning point of the play might be the discovery of the true identity of the hero, or it might be the revelation of a long-forgotten incident from the past.

Character   Aristotle said that it was in the nature of tragedy to "arouse pity and fear." The purpose was to bring about a cleansing or purging, or **catharsis**, of these feelings. To arouse these tragic emotions, the playwright needed a tragic hero neither totally good nor totally bad. To see an outstandingly good person overtaken by undeserved calamity would arouse not fear but indignation—rebellion against unjust punishment. To see a villain come to a well-deserved end would arouse not pity but satisfaction. The ideal character would be an "intermediate" kind of person—great or admirable in some way but in other ways more like us. The character's misfortune would be brought on by an "error of judgment" or an imbalance in the character's personality. Taking their cue from Aristotle, critics have looked in the personality of the hero for the **tragic flaw**—for instance, anger, self-righteousness, or indecision. In ancient Greek religion, the tragic flaw of arrogant humans was **hubris**— the overreaching pride that makes them forget their human limitations and makes them challenge the gods.

Self-Realization   In our time, critics have looked in true tragedy for evidence of growth in the tragic hero. They look for some kind of maturing or spiritual development. You might think of the experience of tragedy as a spiritual journey. You come in at one point in the character's moral or spiritual development and come out at another. The central heroic figure should not just be a victim who is ground into the dust and learns nothing from the experience. The mere passive experience of pain and misery would represent not tragedy but **pathos** (from the Greek word for "suffering").

SOPHOCLES AND THE GREEK STAGE

Fate leads the willing, drags the unwilling.
                    CLEANTHES

Quisque suos patimur.
We each suffer our own destinies.
                    VIRGIL

Sophocles wrote over a hundred plays for the drama festivals of ancient Athens. His *Antigone* (about 441 B.C.) is the first of three plays he based on the traditional story of Oedipus, king of Thebes, and his family. The doomed king had tried in vain to escape the fate marked out for him by the oracle of Apollo—

> that I should lie with my own mother, breed
> Children from whom all men would turn their eyes;
> And that I should be my father's murderer.

Forewarned by the oracle, the parents of Oedipus—King Laios and Queen Jocasta of Thebes—had their newborn son exposed on a mountain to die, but the child was rescued by a shepherd and raised by the

King of Corinth as his own son. When Oedipus was a young man, the oracle again sounded its prophecy of incest and parricide. In a vain attempt to thwart the oracle, Oedipus left his foster parents—whom he assumed to be his real parents. On a mountain highway, he became involved in a fatal quarrel and killed another traveler—unknown to him, this traveler was Laios, his real father. He cleared the Theban countryside of the rule of the monstrous Sphinx by solving her deadly riddle, and the grateful citizens of Thebes made him their king. He married their widowed queen Jocasta—unknown to him, his real mother. In Sophocles' play known as *Oedipus Rex*—"King Oedipus"—Oedipus discovers his true identity and comes face to face with the unspeakable horror of incest.

In the earlier *Antigone* play, Sophocles tells the story of the four children from Oedipus' incestuous union with Jocasta. Their father has died in exile, and their uncle Creon is now king of Thebes. Antigone is the more strong-willed and Ismene the more cautious of the two sisters. The two sons of Oedipus had quarreled over their arrangement for ruling over Thebes. One of the brothers, Eteocles, stayed in Thebes and has died fighting on the side of his native city. Polyneices, the other brother, crossed over to the side of the enemy in a war with neighboring Argos. The two brothers met in battle and have been killed fighting each other. Creon declares Polyneices a traitor and decrees that his corpse be denied burial and be left to be devoured by dogs.

Creon's decree sets up the basic **conflict** of the play. Modern cultural historians remind us that this conflict was not simply a clash of good and evil:

✱ On the one hand, loyalty to country—to the city-state (or *polis*)— was then as strong a force as patriotism, with the demands of the state for allegiance, is today. The Greek city-states had their gods who embodied the spirit of solidarity and loyalty of the community—like the goddess Athena, who was the patron and protector of Athens.

✱ However, as in other early civilizations, burial customs and funeral rites were a cornerstone of Greek religion. Honoring its dead was a central duty of every family. In Homer's *Iliad*, the Greek champion Achilles at first dishonors the body of his slain Trojan adversary Hector, tying the corpse to his horse, dragging it around the battlefield. However, he finally has the corpse washed and anointed and hands it over to Hector's father, for a great burial ceremony honoring the Trojan hero.

Antigone is caught between these two conflicting loyalties. Should she obey the law of the gods and perform at least a symbolic burial for her dishonored brother? Her central role makes her the tragic **protagonist** in the play. Originally, *protagonist* meant the "first competitor," or first actor, initiating the action. However, today the term stands for a major force or principle of action in the play. Antigone is a powerfully motivated character who sets a fateful chain of events in motion. She is pitted against a worthy opponent, Creon, who is the **antagonist**. He is the counterforce that makes for a clash of powerful opposites.

Sophocles   *(496–406/5 B.C.)*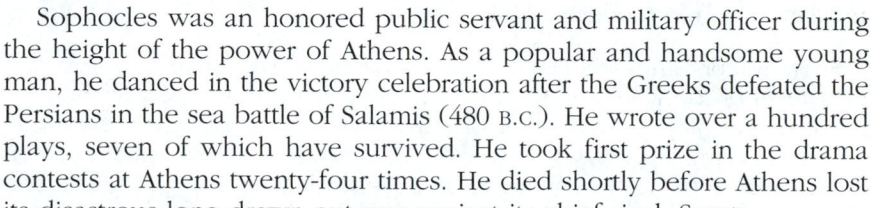

Sophocles was an honored public servant and military officer during the height of the power of Athens. As a popular and handsome young man, he danced in the victory celebration after the Greeks defeated the Persians in the sea battle of Salamis (480 B.C.). He wrote over a hundred plays, seven of which have survived. He took first prize in the drama contests at Athens twenty-four times. He died shortly before Athens lost its disastrous long drawn-out war against its chief rival, Sparta.

Keep the following advice in mind while reading the Antigone play:

✗ Try to visualize the clash between protagonist and antagonist as they act out their fateful confrontation. (If you can, try to view all or part of the play on videotape). Antigone and Creon are often face to face, trading pointed scornful remarks in the quick-fire exchanges the Greeks called *stichomythy.*

✗ Listen carefully to the supporting characters who are caught between the two mighty opposites. Ismene, Antigone's sister, provides a **foil** to Antigone by voicing the more cautious view. Haemon, Antigone's fiancé, is caught between his headstrong father and his strong-willed intended bride.

✗ Although he is at first belittled and scorned, the priest Teiresias is likely to play a central role. As in the later *Oedipus* play, the blind priest and prophet is a voice of warning heeded too late.

✗ Listen to the views expressed by the chorus—and be alert to any change in their sentiments or perspective. The chorus makes the play interactive: Its members are concerned citizens who are not just passive spectators to the action. They are allowed to offer their commentary—as if the audience had its own representatives on the stage.

Help for the Modern Reader   The characters in this play, and especially the chorus, use **allusions** to myths and legends familiar to Sophocles' audience.

✗ The chorus honors Dionysos, "god of many names." He is variously called Dionysos, Iacchos, and Bacchus. He was the offspring of Zeus' union with a mortal, Semele.

✗ Other gods are mentioned: Aphrodite, goddess of love; Ares, god of war; and Demeter, goddess of the harvest.

✗ Antigone alludes to Niobe, who wept after losing all her numerous children and who was in the end turned to stone.

✗ The chorus compares Antigone's fate to that of Danaë, another mortal lover of Zeus, and to the fate of Lycurgus, a king who was punished for trying to suppress the cult of Dionysos.

A Note on the Translation   The story of Antigone has fascinated playwrights. The Irish poet and playwright William Butler Yeats, the French playwright Jean Anouilh, and the German poet-playwright Bertolt Brecht all prepared their own versions of the play, ranging from close faithful translation to free modern adaptation.

✗ Translators and scholars studying ancient Greek have long debated what level of formality and solemnity audiences should expect in the language of the play. One admirer of Sophocles commented on the natural vigor of his language, "with no words wasted and no words poured on for effect"; plainspoken "when plainness is appropriate"; and not "elevated" except by its force of natural eloquence.

The language used in Athenian tragedy ranges from the solemn chants of the chorus to the vigorous, spirited exchanges between the major characters. On the one hand, Greek tragedy was a solemn, highly structured kind of drama. It was rooted in religious ritual. Solemn entrances, dances, and exits by the chorus set up the rhythm of the performance. The odes chanted by the chorus at the end of each scene were highly stylized, carefully patterned poems.

On the other hand, the plays spoke not to a small select audience but to large crowds of theatergoers in their current language. Both King Creon and his challenger Antigone plead their case eloquently while addressing the chorus of citizens and the larger audience. Much of the connecting dialogue is animated and fast-moving. Antigone talks freely and confidentially to her sister, out of hearing of others. When Creon is angry, he blusters and denounces first the sentry and then the priest, as king and prophet accuse each other mutually of being corrupt and greedy. The king engages with both Antigone and the priest in the spirited, quick-witted exchange of one-liners that was a favorite of playwrights and spectators. When his son turns against him, Creon denounces him in the hot language of a parent whose anger is spilling over.

✗ Translators differ on how fully to spell out *allusions*—traditional stories called to mind only by brief summaries or sometimes just hints that seem roundabout to modern listeners. Greek storytellers and playwrights liked to refer to gods and heroes not directly by their most common name but by alternate names, by hints of family origin or home base, or by honorific titles. The original Greek audiences easily recognized the many different names they used to honor their gods. For instance, Iacchos and Bacchus, "Child of Semele and the god of thunder," and "Prince of the Maenads" all stand for the same god: Dionysos, the patron of the tragic theater.

The original audiences easily recognized allusions to traditional myths, the way we fill in associations called up by names like Valley Forge or General Custer or Gettysburg. The translators of the current version of the play have made a special effort to make riddling references to traditional stories meaningful to today's readers. The Greeks, like the people of other early cultures, had a special fondness for puzzles and riddles.

✗ Translators who have immersed themselves in the world of a play often make suggestions for *staging*, adapting the conventions of the Greek theater. They may give advice on whether and how to use masks, or on how to make them more lifelike, less cumbersome than the original masks of the Greek theater. The translators of the version you will be reading recommended that the odes originally chanted in unison by the chorus should be recited by alternating single voices from the chorus, to help a modern audience follow and understand the meaning of the verses. The translators approved of such special modern touches as having Creon remove his tragic mask at the end of the play to show the crushed, defeated human being underneath.

The authors of the following translation knew many of the surviving Greek plays intimately as translators, editors, and critics. They aimed at being true to the sense and emotional quality of every passage in the play. They made it their goal to show that the Greek plays, "however remote from us in time, can yet speak to us with the immediacy and truth that it had for its original audience." They agreed with Yeats that translators should not try to achieve an artificial solemnity by using words "unfitted for living speech" or used out of their "natural order."

Antigone   *about 441 B.C.*

Come out of the twilight
and walk before us a while
friendly, with the light step
of one whose mind is fully made up.
BERTOLT BRECHT, *ANTIGONE*

AN ENGLISH VERSION BY DUDLEY FITTS AND ROBERT FITZGERALD

CHARACTERS

ANTIGONE, daughter of Oedipus and Jocasta
ISMENE, sister of Antigone
CREON, king of Thebes and uncle of Antigone and Ismene
EURYDICE, wife of Creon
HAIMON, son of Creon and Eurydice, fiancé of Antigone
TEIRESIAS, a blind prophet
A chorus of leading older citizens of Thebes, led by the choragos
A sentry and a messenger

TIME

> *It is early morning in front of the royal palace of Creon, king of Thebes.*
> *The army of Argos has been driven back from the city. Fighting on oppo-*
> *site sides, Antigone's brothers, Eteocles and Polyneices, have killed each*
> *other in combat.*

SETTING

> *We see the front of the palace, with a central double door and two side*
> *doors. A platform extends the length of the front of the building, and*
> *from this platform, three steps lead down to the orchestra, or dancing*
> *ground of the chorus.*

Prologue

[ANTIGONE *and* ISMENE *enter from the central door of the Palace.*]

ANTIGONE: Ismene, dear sister,
   You would think that we had already suffered enough
   For the curse on Oedipus:
   I cannot imagine any grief
   That you and I have not gone through. And now—
   Have they told you of the new decree of our King Creon?
ISMENE: I have heard nothing: I know
   That two sisters lost two brothers, a double death
   In a single hour; and I know that the Argive army
   Fled in the night; but beyond this, nothing.
ANTIGONE: I thought so. And that is why I wanted you
   To come out here with me. There is something we must do.
ISMENE: Why do you speak so strangely?
ANTIGONE: Listen, Ismene:
   Creon buried our brother Eteocles
   With military honors, gave him a soldier's funeral,
   And it was right that he should; but Polyneices,
   Who fought as bravely and died as miserably,—
   They say that Creon has sworn
   No one shall bury him, no one mourn for him,
   But his body must lie in the fields, a sweet treasure
   For carrion birds to find as they search for food.
   That is what they say, and our good Creon is coming here
   To announce it publicly; and the penalty—
   Stoning to death in the public square!
                              There it is,
   And now you can prove what you are:
   A true sister, or a traitor to your family.
ISMENE: Antigone, you are mad! What could I possibly do?
ANTIGONE: You must decide whether you will help me or not.
ISMENE: I do not understand you. Help you in what?
ANTIGONE: Ismene, I am going to bury him. Will you come?

ISMENE: Bury him! You have just said the new law forbids it.

ANTIGONE: He is my brother. And he is your brother, too.

ISMENE: But think of the danger! Think what Creon will do!

ANTIGONE: Creon is not strong enough to stand in my way.

ISMENE: Ah sister!
    Oedipus died, everyone hating him
    For what his own search brought to light, his eyes
    Ripped out by his own hand; and Iocaste died,
    His mother and wife at once: she twisted the cords
    That strangled her life; and our two brothers died,
    Each killed by the other's sword. And we are left:
    But oh, Antigone,
    Think how much more terrible than these
    Our own death would be if we should go against Creon
    And do what he has forbidden! We are only women,
    We cannot fight with men, Antigone!
    The law is strong, we must give in to the law
    In this thing, and in worse. I beg the Dead
    To forgive me, but I am helpless: I must yield
    To those in authority. And I think it is dangerous business
    To be always meddling.

ANTIGONE: If that is what you think,
    I should not want you, even if you asked to come.
    You have made your choice, you can be what you want to be.
    But I will bury him; and if I must die,
    I say that this crime is holy: I shall lie down
    With him in death, and I shall be as dear
    To him as he to me.
              It is the dead,
    Not the living, who make the longest demands:
    We die for ever . . .
              You may do as you like,
    Since apparently the laws of the gods mean nothing to you.

ISMENE: They mean a great deal to me; but I have no strength
    To break laws that were made for the public good.

ANTIGONE: That must be your excuse, I suppose. But as for me,
    I will bury the brother I love.

ISMENE: Antigone,
    I am so afraid for you!

ANTIGONE: You need not be
    You have yourself to consider, after all.

ISMENE: But no one must hear of this, you must tell no one!
    I will keep it a secret, I promise!

ANTIGONE: Oh tell it! Tell everyone!
    Think how they'll hate you when it all comes out
    If they learn that you knew about it all the time!

ISMENE: So fiery! You should be cold with fear.

ANTIGONE: Perhaps. But I am doing only what I must.

ISMENE: But can you do it? I say that you cannot.

ANTIGONE: Very well: when my strength gives out, I shall do no more.
ISMENE: Impossible things should not be tried at all.
ANTIGONE: Go away, Ismene:
    I shall be hating you soon, and the dead will too,
    For your words are hateful. Leave me my foolish plan:
    I am not afraid of the danger; if it means death,
    It will not be the worst of deaths—death without honor.
ISMENE: Go then, if you feel that you must.
    You are unwise,
    But a loyal friend indeed to those who love you.

[*Exit into the Palace.* ANTIGONE *goes off, L. Enter the* CHORUS.]

Parodos [*Song in Praise of Victorious Thebes*]

[*Strophe 1*]

CHORUS: Now the long blade of the sun, lying
    Level east to west, touches with glory
    Thebes of the Seven Gates. Open, unlidded
    Eye of golden day! O marching light
    Across the eddy and rush of Dirce's stream,
    Striking the white shields of the enemy
    Thrown headlong backward from the blaze of morning!
CHORAGOS: Polyneices their commander
    Roused them with windy phrases,
    He the wild eagle screaming
    Insults above our land,
    His wings their shields of snow,
    His crest their marshalled helms.

[*Antistrophe 1*]

CHORUS: Against our seven gates in a yawning ring
    The famished spears came onward in the night;
    But before his jaws were sated with our blood,
    Or pinefire took the garland of our towers,
    He was thrown back; and as he turned, great Thebes—
    No tender victim for his noisy power—
    Rose like a dragon behind him, shouting war.
CHORAGOS: For God hates utterly
    The bray of bragging tongues;
    And when he beheld their smiling,
    Their swagger of golden helms,
    The frown of his thunder blasted
    Their first man from our walls.

[*Strophe 2*]

CHORUS: We heard his shout of triumph high in the air
    Turn to a scream; far out in a flaming are
    He fell with his windy torch, and the earth struck him.
    And others storming in fury no less than his
    Found shock of death in the dusty joy of battle.

CHORAGOS: Seven captains at seven gates
   Yielded their clanging arms to the god
   That bends the battle-line and breaks it.
   These two only, brothers in blood,
   Face to face in matchless rage,
   Mirroring each the other's death,
   Clashed in long combat.

CHORUS: But now in the beautiful morning of victory   *[Antistrophe 2]*
   Let Thebes of the many chariots sing for joy!
   With hearts for dancing we'll take leave of war:
   Our temples shall be sweet with hymns of praise,
   And the long night shall echo with our chorus.

Scene 1

CHORAGOS: But now at last our new King is coming:
   Creon of Thebes, Menoikeus' son.
   In this auspicious dawn of his reign
   What are the new complexities
   That shifting Fate has woven for him?
   What is his counsel? Why has he summoned
   The old men to hear him?

[*Enter* CREON *from the Palace, C. He addresses the* CHORUS *from the top step.*]

CREON: Gentlemen: I have the honor to inform you that our Ship of State, which recent storms have threatened to destroy, has come safely to harbor at last, guided by the merciful wisdom of Heaven. I have summoned you here this morning because I know that I can depend upon you: your devotion to King Laios was absolute; you never hesitated in your duty to our late ruler Oedipus; and when Oedipus died, your loyalty was transferred to his children. Unfortunately, as you know, his two sons, the princes Eteocles and Polyneices, have killed each other in battle; and I, as the next in blood, have succeeded to the full power of the throne.

   I am aware, of course, that no Ruler can expect complete loyalty from his subjects until he has been tested in office. Nevertheless, I say to you at the very outset that I have nothing but contempt for the kind of Governor who is afraid, for whatever reason, to follow the course that he knows is best for the State; and as for the man who sets private friendship above the public welfare,—I have no use for him, either. I call God to witness that if I saw my country headed for ruin, I should not be afraid to speak out plainly; and I need hardly remind you that I would never have any dealings with an enemy of the people. No one values friendship more highly than I; but we must remember that friends made at the risk of wrecking our Ship are not real friends at all.

   These are my principles, at any rate, and that is why I have made the following decision concerning the sons of Oedipus: Eteocles, who died as a man should die, fighting for his country, is to be buried with full

military honors, with all the ceremony that is usual when the greatest heroes die; but his brother Polyneices, who broke his exile to come back
with fire and sword against his native city and the shrines of his fathers'
gods, whose one idea was to spill the blood of his blood and sell his
own people into slavery—Polyneices, I say, is to have no burial: no man
is to touch him or say the least prayer for him; he shall lie on the plain,
unburied; and the birds and the scavenging dogs can do with him whatever they like.

    This is my command, and you can see the wisdom behind it. As long
as I am King, no traitor is going to be honored with the loyal man. But
whoever shows by word and deed that he is on the side of the State,—
he shall have my respect while he is living, and my reverence when he
is dead.

CHORAGOS: If that is your will, Creon son of Menoikeus,
    You have the right to enforce it: we are yours.
CREON: That is my will. Take care that you do your part.
CHORAGOS: We are old men: let the younger ones carry it out.
CREON: I do not mean that: the sentries have been appointed.
CHORAGOS: Then what is it that you would have us do?
CREON: You will give no support to whoever breaks this law.
CHORAGOS: Only a crazy man is in love with death!
CREON: And death it is; yet money talks and the wisest
    Have sometimes been known to count a few coins too many.

    [*Enter* SENTRY *from L.*]

SENTRY: I'll not say that I'm out of breath from running, King, because every
    time I stopped to think about what I have to tell you, I felt like going
    back. And all the time a voice kept saying, "You fool, don't you know
    you're walking straight into trouble?"; and then another voice: "Yes, but
    if you let somebody else get the news to Creon first, it will be even
    worse than that for you!" But good sense won out, at least I hope it was
    good sense, and here I am with a story that makes no sense at all; but
    I'll tell it anyhow, because, as they say, what's going to happen's going
    to happen, and—
CREON: Come to the point. What have you to say?
SENTRY: I did not do it. I did not see who did it. You must not punish me
    for what someone else has done.
CREON: A comprehensive defense! More effective, perhaps,
    If I knew its purpose. Come: what is it?
SENTRY: A dreadful thing. . .I don't know how to put it—
CREON: Out with it!
SENTRY: Well, then;
    The dead man—
               Polyneices—

[*Pause. The* SENTRY *is overcome, fumbles for words.* CREON *waits impassively.*]

                    out there—
                         someone,—
New dust on the slimy flesh!

[*Pause. No sign from* CREON]

Someone has given it burial that way, and
Gone. . .

[*Long pause.* CREON *finally speaks with deadly control.*]

CREON: And the man who dared do this?
SENTRY: I swear I
  Do not know! You must believe me!
                                        Listen:
  The ground was dry, not a sign of digging, no,
  Not a wheeltrack in the dust, no trace of anyone.
  It was when they relieved us this morning: and one of them,
  The corporal, pointed to it.
                             There it was,
  The strangest—
                Look:
  The body, just mounded over with light dust: you see?
  Not buried really, but as if they'd covered it
  Just enough for the ghost's peace. And no sign
  Of dogs or any wild animal that had been there.
  And then what a scene there was! Every man of us
  Accusing the other: we all proved the other man did it,
  We all had proof that we could not have done it.
  We were ready to take hot iron in our hands,
  Walk through fire, swear by all the gods,
  It was not I!
  I do not know who it was, but it was not I!

[CREON'*s rage has been mounting steadily, but the* SENTRY *is too intent upon his story to notice it.*]

And then, when this came to nothing, someone said
  A thing that silenced us and made us stare
  Down at the ground: you had to be told the news,
  And one of us had to do it! We threw the dice,
  And the bad luck fell to me. So here I am,
  No happier to be here than you are to have me:
  Nobody likes the man who brings bad news.
CHORAGOS: I have been wondering, King: can it be that the gods have
  done this?
CREON [*furiously*]. Stop!
  Must you doddering wrecks
  Go out of your heads entirely? "The gods!"
  Intolerable!
  The gods favor this corpse? Why? How had he served them?
  Tried to loot their temples, burn their images,
  Yes, and the whole State, and its laws with it!
  Is it your senile opinion that the gods love to honor bad men?
  A pious thought!—
                 No, from the very beginning

There have been those who have whispered together,
Stiff-necked anarchists, putting their heads together,
Scheming against me in alleys. These are the men,
And they have bribed my own guard to do this thing.
Money!
[*Sententiously*] There's nothing in the world so demoralizing as money.
Down go your cities,
Homes gone, men gone, honest hearts corrupted,
Crookedness of all kinds, and all for money!
[*To* SENTRY]   But you—!
I swear by God and by the throne of God,
The man who has done this thing shall pay for it!
Find that man, bring him here to me, or your death
Will be the least of your problems: I'll string you up
Alive, and there will be certain ways to make you
Discover your employer before you die;
And the process may teach you a lesson you seem to have missed:
The dearest profit is sometimes all too dear:
That depends on the source. Do you understand me?
A fortune won is often misfortune.

SENTRY: King, may I speak?

CREON: Your very voice distresses me.

SENTRY: Are you sure that it is my voice, and not your conscience?

CREON: By God, he wants to analyze me now!

SENTRY: It is not what I say, but what has been done, that hurts you.

CREON: You talk too much.

SENTRY: Maybe; but I've done nothing.

CREON: Sold your soul for some silver: that's all you've done.

SENTRY: How dreadful it is when the right judge judges wrong!

CREON: Your figures of speech
May entertain you now; but unless you bring me the man,
You will get little profit from them in the end.

[*Exit* CREON *into the Palace.*]

SENTRY: "Bring me the man"—!
I'd like nothing better than bringing him the man!
But bring him or not, you have seen the last of me here.
At any rate, I am safe!

[*Exit* SENTRY.]

Ode 1 [*Song in Praise of Humankind*]

[*Strophe 1*]

CHORUS: Numberless are the world's wonders, but none
More wonderful than man; the stormgray sea
Yields to his prows, the huge crests bear him high;
Earth, holy and inexhaustible, is graven
With shining furrows where his plows have gone
Year after year, the timeless labor of stallions.

The lightboned birds and beasts that cling to cover,   [*Antistrophe 1*]
The lithe fish lighting their reaches of dim water,
All are taken, tamed in the net of his mind;
The lion on the hill, the wild horse windy-maned,
Resign to him; and his blunt yoke has broken
The sultry shoulders of the mountain bull.

     [*Strophe 2*]

Words also, and thought as rapid as air,
He fashions to his good use; statecraft is his,
And his the skill that deflects the arrows of snow,
The spears of winter rain: from every wind
He has made himself secure—from all but one:
In the late wind of death he cannot stand.

     [*Antistrophe 2*]

O clear intelligence, force beyond all measure!
O fate of man, working both good and evil!
When the laws are kept, how proudly his city stands!
When the laws are broken, what of his city then?
Never may the anarchic man find rest at my hearth,
Never be it said that my thoughts are his thoughts.

Scene 2

[*Re-enter* SENTRY *leading* ANTIGONE.]

CHORAGOS: What does this mean? Surely this captive woman
     Is the Princess, Antigone. Why should she be taken?
SENTRY: Here is the one who did it! We caught her
     In the very act of burying him.—Where is Creon?
CHORAGOS: Just coming from the house.

[*Enter* CREON, *C.*]

CREON: What has happened?
     Why have you come back so soon?
SENTRY [*expansively*].   O King,
     A man should never be too sure of anything:
     I would have sworn
     That you'd not see me here again: your anger
     Frightened me so, and the things you threatened me with;
     But how could I tell then
     That I'd be able to solve the case so soon?

No dice-throwing this time: I was only too glad to come!

Here is this woman. She is the guilty one:
We found her trying to bury him.
Take her, then; question her; judge her as you will.
     I am through with the whole thing now, and glad of it.
CREON: But this is Antigone! Why have you brought her here?
SENTRY: She was burying him, I tell you!
CREON [*severely*].   Is this the truth?
SENTRY: I saw her with my own eyes. Can I say more?

CREON: The details: come, tell me quickly!

SENTRY: It was like this:
   After those terrible threats of yours, King,
   We went back and brushed the dust away from the body.
   The flesh was soft by now, and stinking,
   So we sat on a hill to windward and kept guard.
   No napping this time! We kept each other awake.
   But nothing happened until the white round sun
   Whirled in the center of the round sky over us:
   Then, suddenly,
   A storm of dust roared up from the earth, and the sky
   Went out, the plain vanished with all its trees
   In the stinging dark. We closed our eyes and endured it.
   The whirlwind lasted a long time, but it passed;
   And then we looked, and there was Antigone!
   I have seen
   A mother bird come back to a stripped nest, heard
   Her crying bitterly a broken note or two
   For the young ones stolen. Just so, when this girl
   Found the bare corpse, and all her love's work wasted,
   She wept, and cried on heaven to damn the hands
   That had done this thing.
                   And then she brought more dust
   And sprinkled wine three times for her brother's ghost.
   We ran and took her at once. She was not afraid,
   Not even when we charged her with what she had done.
   She denied nothing.
              And this was a comfort to me,
   And some uneasiness: for it is a good thing
   To escape from death, but it is no great pleasure
   To bring death to a friend.
                  Yet I always say
   There is nothing so comfortable as your own safe skin!

CREON [*slowly, dangerously*]. And you, Antigone,
   You with your head hanging,—do you confess this thing?

ANTIGONE: I do. I deny nothing.

CREON [*to* SENTRY].   You may go. [*Exit* SENTRY.]
   [*To* ANTIGONE] Tell me, tell me briefly:
   Had you heard my proclamation touching this matter?

ANTIGONE: It was public. Could I help hearing it?

CREON: And yet you dared defy the law.

ANTIGONE: I dared.
   It was not God's proclamation. That final Justice
   That rules the world below makes no such laws.
   Your edict, King, was strong,
   But all your strength is weakness itself against
   The immortal unrecorded laws of God.
   They are not merely now: they were, and shall be,
   Operative for ever, beyond man utterly.

I knew I must die, even without your decree:
I am only mortal. And if I must die
Now, before it is my time to die,
Surely this is no hardship: can anyone
Living, as I live, with evil all about me,
Think Death less than a friend? This death of mine
Is of no importance; but if I had left my brother
Lying in death unburied, I should have suffered.
Now I do not.
                    You smile at me. Ah Creon,
Think me a fool, if you like; but it may well be
That a fool convicts me of folly.

CHORAGOS: Like father, like daughter: both headstrong, deaf to reason!
    She has never learned to yield.

CREON: She has much to learn.
    The inflexible heart breaks first, the toughest iron
    Cracks first, and the wildest horses bend their necks
    At the pull of the smallest curb.
                                            Pride? In a slave?
    This girl is guilty of a double insolence,
    Breaking the given laws and boasting of it.
    Who is the man here,
    She or I, if this crime goes unpunished?
    Sister's child, or more than sister's child,
    Or closer yet in blood—she and her sister
    Win bitter death for this!
    [*To servants*]   Go, some of you,
    Arrest Ismene. I accuse her equally.
    Bring her: you will find her sniffling in the house there.

    Her mind's a traitor: crimes kept in the dark
    Cry for light, and the guardian brain shudders;
    But how much worse than this
    Is brazen boasting of barefaced anarchy!

ANTIGONE: Creon, what more do you want than my death?

CREON: Nothing.
    That gives me everything.

ANTIGONE: Then I beg you: kill me.
    This talking is a great weariness: your words
    Are distasteful to me, and I am sure that mine
    Seem so to you. And yet they should not seem so:
    I should have praise and honor for what I have done.
    All these men here would praise me
    Were their lips not frozen shut with fear of you.
    [*Bitterly*] Ah the good fortune of kings,
    Licensed to say and do whatever they please!

CREON: You are alone here in that opinion.

ANTIGONE: No, they are with me. But they keep their tongues in leash.

CREON: Maybe. But you are guilty, and they are not.

ANTIGONE: There is no guilt in reverence for the dead.

CREON: But Eteocles—was he not your brother too?

ANTIGONE: My brother too.

CREON: And you insult his memory?

ANTIGONE [*softly*]. The dead man would not say that I insult it.

CREON: He would: for you honor a traitor as much as him.

ANTIGONE: His own brother, traitor or not, and equal in blood.

CREON: He made war on his country. Eteocles defended it.

ANTIGONE: Nevertheless, there are honors due all the dead.

CREON: But not the same for the wicked as for the just.

ANTIGONE: Ah Creon, Creon,
    Which of us can say what the gods hold wicked?

CREON: An enemy is an enemy, even dead.

ANTIGONE: It is my nature to join in love, not hate.

CREON [*finally losing patience*]. Go join them, then; if you must have your love,
    Find it in hell!

CHORAGOS: But see, Ismene comes:

[*Enter* ISMENE, *guarded.*]

    Those tears are sisterly, the cloud
    That shadows her eyes rains down gentle sorrow.

CREON: You too, Ismene,
    Snake in my ordered house, sucking my blood
    Stealthily—and all the time I never knew
    That these two sisters were aiming at my throne!
                                        Ismene,
    Do you confess your share in this crime, or deny it?
    Answer me.

ISMENE: Yes, if she will let me say so. I am guilty.

ANTIGONE [*coldly*]. No, Ismene. You have no right to say so.
    You would not help me, and I will not have you help me.

ISMENE: But now I know what you meant; and I am here
    To join you, to take my share of punishment.

ANTIGONE: The dead man and the gods who rule the dead
    Know whose act this was. Words are not friends.

ISMENE: Do you refuse me, Antigone? I want to die with you:
    I too have a duty that I must discharge to the dead.

ANTIGONE: You shall not lessen my death by sharing it.

ISMENE: What do I care for life when you are dead?

ANTIGONE: Ask Creon. You're always hanging on his opinions.

ISMENE: You are laughing at me. Why, Antigone?

ANTIGONE: It's a joyless laughter, Ismene.

ISMENE: But can I do nothing?

ANTIGONE: Yes. Save yourself. I shall not envy you.
    There are those who will praise you; I shall have honor, too.

ISMENE: But we are equally guilty!

ANTIGONE: No more, Ismene.
    You are alive, but I belong to Death.

CREON [*to the* CHORUS]. Gentlemen, I beg you to observe these girls:
   One has just now lost her mind; the other,
   It seems, has never had a mind at all.
ISMENE: Grief teaches the steadiest minds to waver, King.
CREON: Yours certainly did, when you assumed guilt with the guilty!
ISMENE: But how could I go on living without her?
CREON: You are.
   She is already dead.
ISMENE: But your own son's bride!
CREON: There are places enough for him to push his plow.
   I want no wicked women for my sons!
ISMENE: O dearest Haimon, how your father wrongs you!
CREON: I've had enough of your childish talk of marriage!
CHORAGOS: Do you really intend to steal this girl from your son?
CREON: No; Death will do that for me.
CHORAGOS: Then she must die?
CREON [*ironically*]. You dazzle me.
                         —But enough of this talk!
   [*To* GUARDS] You, there, take them away and guard them well:
   For they are but women, and even brave men run
   When they see Death coming.

[*Exeunt* ISMENE, ANTIGONE, *and* GUARDS.]

Ode 2 [On Divine Power and Human Pride]

[*Strophe 1*]

CHORUS: Fortunate is the man who has never tasted God's vengeance!
   Where once the anger of heaven has struck, that house is shaken
   For ever: damnation rises behind each child
   Like a wave cresting out of the black northeast,
   When the long darkness under sea roars up
   And bursts drumming death upon the windwhipped sand.

[*Antistrophe 1*]

   I have seen this gathering sorrow from time long past
   Loom upon Oedipus' children: generation from generation
   Takes the compulsive rage of the enemy god.
   So lately this last flower of Oedipus' line
   Drank the sunlight! but now a passionate word
   And a handful of dust have closed up all its beauty.

[*Strophe 2*]

      What mortal arrogance
      Transcends the wrath of Zeus?
   Sleep cannot lull him, nor the effortless long months
   Of the timeless gods: but he is young for ever,
      And his house is the shining day of high Olympos.
      All that is and shall be,
      And all the past, is his.
   No pride on earth is free of the curse of heaven.

    The straying dreams of men
      May bring them ghosts of joy:
But as they drowse, the waking embers burn them;
Or they walk with fixed eyes, as blind men walk.
But the ancient wisdom speaks for our own time:
      Fate works most for woe
      With Folly's fairest show.
Man's little pleasure is the spring of sorrow.

Scene 3

CHORAGOS: But here is Haimon, King, the last of all your sons.
    Is it grief for Antigone that brings him here,
    And bitterness at being robbed of his bride?

[*Enter* HAIMON.]

CREON: We shall soon see, and no need of diviners.°   *soothsayers, prophets*
                                —Son,
    You have heard my final judgment on that girl:
    Have you come here hating me, or have you come
    With deference and with love, whatever I do?
HAIMON: I am your son, father. You are my guide.
    You make things clear for me, and I obey you.
    No marriage means more to me than your continuing wisdom.
CREON: Good. That is the way to behave: subordinate
    Everything else, my son, to your father's will.
    This is what a man prays for, that he may get
    Sons attentive and dutiful in his house,
    Each one hating his father's enemies,
    Honoring his father's friends. But if his sons
    Fail him, if they turn out unprofitably,
    What has he fathered but trouble for himself
    And amusement for the malicious?
                         So you are right
    Not to lose your head over this woman.
    Your pleasure with her would soon grow cold, Haimon,
    And then you'd have a hellcat in bed and elsewhere.
    Let her find her husband in Hell!
    Of all the people in this city, only she
    Has had contempt for my law and broken it.

    Do you want me to show myself weak before the people?
    Or to break my sworn word? No, and I will not.
    The woman dies.
    I suppose she'll plead "family ties." Well, let her.
    If I permit my own family to rebel,
    How shall I earn the world's obedience?
    Show me the man who keeps his house in hand,
    He's fit for public authority.

                    I'll have no dealings
With law-breakers, critics of the government:
Whoever is chosen to govern should be obeyed—
Must be obeyed, in all things, great and small,
Just and unjust! O Haimon,
The man who knows how to obey, and that man only,
Knows how to give commands when the time comes.
You can depend on him, no matter how fast
The spears come: he's a good soldier, he'll stick it out.

Anarchy, anarchy! Show me a greater evil!
This is why cities tumble and the great houses rain down,
This is what scatters armies!

No, no: good lives are made so by discipline.
We keep the laws then, and the lawmakers,
And no woman shall seduce us. If we must lose,
Let's lose to a man, at least! Is a woman stronger than we?
CHORAGOS: Unless time has rusted my wits,
     What you say, King, is said with point and dignity.
HAIMON [*earnest*]. Father:
     Reason is God's crowning gift to man, and you are right
     To warn me against losing mine. I cannot say—
     I hope that I shall never want to say!—that you
     Have reasoned badly. Yet there are other men
     Who can reason, too; and their opinions might be helpful.
     You are not in a position to know everything
     That people say or do, or what they feel:
     Your temper terrifies them—everyone
     Will tell you only what you like to hear.
     But I, at any rate, can listen; and I have heard them
     Muttering and whispering in the dark about this girl.
     They say no woman has ever, so unreasonably,
     Died so shameful a death for a generous act:
     "She covered her brother's body. Is this indecent?
     She kept him from dogs and vultures. Is this a crime?
     Death?—She should have all the honor that we can give her!"

This is the way they talk out there in the city.
You must believe me:
Nothing is closer to me than your happiness.
What could be closer? Must not any son
Value his father's fortune as his father does his?
I beg you, do not be unchangeable:
Do not believe that you alone can be right.
The man who thinks that,
The man who maintains that only he has the power
To reason correctly, the gift to speak, the soul—
A man like that, when you know him, turns out empty.

It is not reason never to yield to reason!

In flood time you can see how some trees bend,
And because they bend, even their twigs are safe,
While stubborn trees are torn up, roots and all.
And the same thing happens in sailing:
Make your sheet fast, never slacken,—and over you go,
Head over heels and under: and there's your voyage.

Forget you are angry! Let yourself be moved!
I know I am young; but please let me say this:
The ideal condition
Would be, I admit, that men should be right by instinct;
But since we are all too likely to go astray,
The reasonable thing is to learn from those who can teach.

CHORAGOS: You will do well to listen to him, King,
If what he says is sensible. And you, Haimon,
Must listen to your father.—Both speak well.

CREON: You consider it right for a man of my years and experience
To go to school to a boy?

HAIMON: It is not right
If I am wrong. But if I am young, and right,
What does my age matter?

CREON: You think it right to stand up for an anarchist?

HAIMON: Not at all. I pay no respect to criminals.

CREON: Then she is not a criminal?

HAIMON: The City would deny it, to a man.

CREON: And the City proposes to teach me how to rule?

HAIMON: Ah. Who is it that's talking like a boy now?

CREON: My voice is the one voice giving orders in this City!

HAIMON: It is no City if it takes orders from one voice.

CREON: The State is the King!

HAIMON: Yes, if the State is a desert.

[Pause.]

CREON: This boy, it seems, has sold out to a woman.

HAIMON: If you are a woman: my concern is only for you.

CREON: So? Your "concern"! In a public brawl with your father!

HAIMON: How about you, in a public brawl with justice?

CREON: With justice, when all that I do is within my rights?

HAIMON: You have no right to trample on God's right.

CREON [completely out of control]. Fool, adolescent fool! Taken in by a
woman!

HAIMON: You'll never see me taken in by anything vile.

CREON: Every word you say is for her!

HAIMON [quietly, darkly].   And for you.
And for me. And for the gods under the earth.

CREON: You'll never marry her while she lives.

HAIMON: Then she must die.—But her death will cause another.

CREON: Another?
Have you lost your senses? Is this an open threat?

HAIMON: There is no threat in speaking to emptiness.

CREON: I swear you'll regret this superior tone of yours!
  You are the empty one!
HAIMON: If you were not my father,
  I'd say you were perverse.
CREON: You girlstruck fool, don't play at words with me!
HAIMON: I am sorry. You prefer silence.
CREON: Now, by God—!
  I swear, by all the gods in heaven above us,
  You'll watch it, I swear you shall!
                    [*To the* SERVANTS] Bring her out!
  Bring the woman out! Let her die before his eyes!
  Here, this instant, with her bridegroom beside her!
HAIMON: Not here, no; she will not die here, King.
  And you will never see my face again.
  Go on raving as long as you've a friend to endure you.
  [*Exit* HAIMON.]
CHORAGOS: Gone, gone.
  Creon, a young man in a rage is dangerous!
CREON: Let him do, or dream to do, more than a man can.
  He shall not save these girls from death.
CHORAGOS: These girls?
  You have sentenced them both?
CREON: No, you are right.
  I will not kill the one whose hands are clean.
CHORAGOS: But Antigone?
CREON [*somberly*].   I will carry her far away
  Out there in the wilderness, and lock her
  Living in a vault of stone. She shall have food,
  As the custom is, to absolve the State of her death.
  And there let her pray to the gods of hell:
  They are her only gods:
  Perhaps they will show her an escape from death,
  Or she may learn,
                    though late,
  That piety shown the dead is pity in vain.
  [*Exit* CREON.]

Ode 3 [*To Aphrodite, Goddess of Love*]

[Strophe]

CHORUS: Love, unconquerable
  Waster of rich men, keeper
  Of warm lights and all-night vigil
  In the soft face of a girl:
  Sea-wanderer, forest-visitor!
  Even the pure Immortals cannot escape you,
  And mortal man, in his one day's dusk,
  Trembles before your glory.

[*Antistrophe*]

Surely you swerve upon ruin
The just man's consenting heart,
As here you have made bright anger
Strike between father and son—
And none has conquered but Love!
A girl's glance working the will of heaven:
Pleasure to her alone who mocks us,
Merciless Aphrodite.

Scene IV

CHORAGOS [*as* ANTIGONE *enters guarded*]. But I can no longer stand in awe
    of this,
    Nor, seeing what I see, keep back my tears.
    Here is Antigone, passing to that chamber
    Where all find sleep at last.

[*Strophe 1*]

ANTIGONE: Look upon me, friends, and pity me
    Turning back at the night's edge to say
    Good-by to the sun that shines for me no longer;
    Now sleepy Death
    Summons me down to Acheron, that cold shore:
    There is no bridesong there, nor any music.
CHORUS: Yet not unpraised, not without a kind of honor,
    You walk at last into the underworld;
    Untouched by sickness, broken by no sword.
    What woman has ever found your way to death?

[*Antistrophe 1*]

ANTIGONE: How often I have heard the story of Niobe,
    Tantalos' wretched daughter, how the stone
    Clung fast about her, ivy-close: and they say
    The rain falls endlessly
    And sifting soft snow; her tears are never done.
    I feel the loneliness of her death in mine.
CHORUS: But she was born of heaven, and you
    Are woman, woman-born. If her death is yours,
    A mortal woman's, is this not for you
    Glory in our world and in the world beyond?

[*Strophe 2*]

ANTIGONE: You laugh at me. Ah, friends, friends,
    Can you not wait until I am dead? O Thebes,
    O men many-charioted, in love with Fortune,
    Dear springs of Dirce, sacred Theban grove,
    Be witnesses for me, denied all pity,
    Unjustly judged! and think a word of love
    For her whose path turns
    Under dark earth, where there are no more tears.
CHORUS: You have passed beyond human daring and come at last
    Into a place of stone where Justice sits.

I cannot tell
What shape of your father's guilt appears in this.

[Antistrophe 2]

ANTIGONE: You have touched it at last: that bridal bed
   Unspeakable, horror of son and mother mingling:
   Their crime, infection of all our family!
   O Oedipus, father and brother!
   Your marriage strikes from the grave to murder mine.
   I have been a stranger here in my own land:
   All my life
   The blasphemy of my birth has followed me.
CHORUS: Reverence is a virtue, but strength
   Lives in established law: that must prevail.
   You have made your choice,
   Your death is the doing of your conscious hand.

[Epode]

ANTIGONE: Then let me go, since all your words are bitter,
   And the very light of the sun is cold to me.
   Lead me to my vigil, where I must have
   Neither love nor lamentation; no song, but silence.
   [CREON *interrupts impatiently.*]
CREON: If dirges and planned lamentations could put off death,
   Men would be singing for ever.
                [*To the* SERVANTS] Take her, go!
   You know your orders: take her to the vault
   And leave her alone there. And if she lives or dies,
   That's her affair, not ours: our hands are clean.
ANTIGONE: O tomb, vaulted bride-bed in eternal rock,
   Soon I shall be with my own again
   Where Persephone welcomes the thin ghosts underground:
   And I shall see my father again, and you, mother,
   And dearest Polyneices—
                        dearest indeed
   To me, since it was my hand
   That washed him clean and poured the ritual wine:
   And my reward is death before my time!
   And yet, as men's hearts know, I have done no wrong.
   [Not for my children, if I had lived to be a mother,
   and not for a husband who might have died,
      lying rotting before me,
   would I have thus defined the law—
   if my husband had died, I could have wedded another;
   If I had lost a child, I could have had another child;
   But with my mother and father
   Both gone to the world below,
   I will never have another brother.]*

I have not sinned before God. Or if I have,

* passage in the original that is omitted in this translation

I shall know the truth in death. But if the guilt
Lies upon Creon who judged me, then, I pray,
May his punishment equal my own.
CHORAGOS: O passionate heart,
Unyielding, tormented still by the same winds!
CREON: Her guards shall have good cause to regret their delaying.
ANTIGONE: Ah! That voice is like the voice of death!
CREON: I can give you no reason to think you are mistaken.
ANTIGONE: Thebes, and you my fathers' gods,
And rulers of Thebes, you see me now, the last
Unhappy daughter of a line of kings,
Your kings, led away to death. You will remember
What things I suffer, and at what men's hands,
Because I would not transgress the laws of heaven.

[*To the* GUARDS, *simply*] Come: let us wait no longer.

[*Exit* ANTIGONE, *L., guarded.*]

Ode 4 [*On the Power of Fate*]

[*Strophe 1*]

CHORUS: All Danae's beauty was locked away
In a brazen cell where the sunlight could not come:
A small room, still as any grave, enclosed her.
Yet she was a princess too,
And Zeus in a rain of gold poured love upon her.
O child, child,
No power in wealth or war
Or tough sea-blackened ships
Can prevail against untiring Destiny!

[*Antistrophe 1*]

And Dryas, son also, that furious king,
Bore the god's prisoning anger for his pride:
Sealed up by Dionysos in deaf stone,
His madness died among echoes.
So at the last he learned what dreadful power
His tongue had mocked:
For he had profaned the revels,
And fired the wrath of the nine,
Implacable Sisters that love the sound of the flute.

[*Strophe 2*]

And old men tell a half-remembered tale
Of horror done where a dark ledge splits the sea
And a double surf beats on the gray shores:
How a king's new woman, sick
With hatred for the queen he had imprisoned,
Ripped out his two sons' eyes with her bloody hands
While grinning Ares watched the shuttle plunge
Four times: four blind wounds crying for revenge,

Crying, tears and blood mingled.—Piteously born,
Those sons whose mother was of heavenly birth!
Her father was the god of the North Wind
And she was cradled by gales,
She raced with young colts on the glittering hills
And walked untrammeled in the open light:
But in her marriage deathless Fate found means
To build a tomb like yours for all her joy.

Scene 5

[*Enter blind* TEIRESIAS, *led by a boy. The opening speeches of* TEIRESIAS
should be in singsong contrast to the realistic lines of CREON.]

TEIRESIAS: This is the way the blind man comes, Princes, Princes,
   Lock-step, two heads lit by the eyes of one.
CREON: What new thing have you to tell us, old Teiresias?
TEIRESIAS: I have much to tell you: listen to the prophet, Creon.
CREON: I am not aware that I have ever failed to listen.
TEIRESIAS: Then you have done wisely, King, and ruled well.
CREON: I admit my debt to you. But what have you to say?
TEIRESIAS: This, Creon: you stand once more on the edge of fate.
CREON: What do you mean? Your words are a kind of dread.
TEIRESIAS: Listen, Creon:
   I was sitting in my chair of augury, at the place
   Where the birds gather about me. They were all a-chatter,
   As is their habit, when suddenly I heard
   A strange note in their jangling, a scream, a
   Whirring fury; I knew that they were fighting,
   Tearing each other, dying
   In a whirlwind of wings clashing. And I was afraid.
   I began the rites of burnt-offering at the altar,
   But Hephaistos failed me: instead of bright flame,
   There was only the sputtering slime of the fat thigh-flesh
   Melting: the entrails dissolved in gray smoke,
   The bare bone burst from the welter. And no blaze!
   This was a sign from heaven. My boy described it,
   Seeing for me as I see for others.

   I tell you, Creon, you yourself have brought
   This new calamity upon us. Our hearth and altars
   Are stained with the corruption of dogs and carrion birds
   That glut themselves on the corpse of Oedipus' son.
   The gods are deaf when we pray to them, their fire
   Recoils from our offering, their birds of omen
   Have no cry of comfort, for they are gorged
   With the thick blood of the dead.
                                    O my son,
   These are no trifles! Think: all men make mistakes,
   But a good man yields when he knows his course is wrong,

And repairs the evil. The only crime is pride.

Give in to the dead man, then: do not fight with a corpse—
What glory is it to kill a man who is dead?
Think, I beg you:
It is for your own good that I speak as I do.
You should be able to yield for your own good.

CREON: It seems that prophets have made me their especial province.
All my life long
I have been a kind of butt for the dull arrows
Of doddering fortune-tellers!

                    No, Teiresias:
If your birds—if the great eagles of God himself
Should carry him stinking bit by bit to heaven,
I would not yield. I am not afraid of pollution:
No man can defile the gods.

                    Do what you will,
Go into business, make money, speculate
In India gold or that synthetic gold from Sardis,
Get rich otherwise than by my consent to bury him.
Teiresias, it is a sorry thing when a wise man
Sells his wisdom, lets out his words for hire!

TEIRESIAS: Ah Creon! Is there no man left in the world—
CREON: To do what?—Come, let's have the aphorism!
TEIRESIAS: No man who knows that wisdom outweighs any wealth?
CREON: As surely as bribes are baser than any baseness.
TEIRESIAS: You are sick, Creon! You are deathly sick!
CREON: As you say: it is not my place to challenge a prophet.
TEIRESIAS: Yet you have said my prophecy is for sale.
CREON: The generation of prophets has always loved gold.
TEIRESIAS: The generation of kings has always loved brass.
CREON: You forget yourself! You are speaking to your King.
TEIRESIAS: I know it. You are a king because of me.
CREON: You have a certain skill; but you have sold out.
TEIRESIAS: King, you will drive me to words that—
CREON: Say them, say them!
Only remember: I will not pay you for them.
TEIRESIAS: No, you will find them too costly.
CREON: No doubt. Speak:
Whatever you say, you will not change my will.
TEIRESIAS: Then take this, and take it to heart!
The time is not far off when you shall pay back
Corpse for corpse, flesh of your own flesh.
You have thrust the child of this world into living night,
You have kept from the gods below the child that is theirs:
The one in a grave before her death, the other,
Dead, denied the grave. This is your crime:
And the Furies and the dark gods of Hell
Are swift with terrible punishment for you.
Do you want to buy me now, Creon?

Not many days,
And your house will be full of men and women weeping,
And curses will be hurled at you from far
Cities grieving for sons unburied, left to rot
Before the walls of Thebes.
These are my arrows, Creon: they are all for you.
[*To* BOY] But come, child: lead me home.
Let him waste his fine anger upon younger men.
Maybe he will learn at last
To control a wiser tongue in a better head. [*Exit* TEIRESIAS.]

CHORAGOS: The old man has gone, King, but his words
Remain to plague us. I am old, too,
But I cannot remember that he was ever false.

CREON: That is true. . . . It troubles me.
Oh it is hard to give in! but it is worse
To risk everything for stubborn pride.

CHORAGOS: Creon: take my advice.

CREON: What shall I do?

CHORAGOS: Go quickly: free Antigone from her vault
And build a tomb for the body of Polyneices.

CREON: You would have me do this?

CHORAGOS: Creon, yes!
And it must be done at once: God moves
Swiftly to cancel the folly of stubborn men.

CREON: It is hard to deny the heart! But I
Will do it: I will not fight with destiny.

CHORAGOS: You must go yourself, you cannot leave it to others.

CREON: I will go.
            —Bring axes, servants:
Come with me to the tomb. I buried her, I
Will set her free.
            Oh quickly!
My mind misgives—
The laws of the gods are mighty, and a man must serve them
To the last day of his life!

[*Exit* CREON.]

Pæan [*Hymn of Praise to Iacchos/Dionysos, God of Many Names*]

[*Strophe 1*]

CHORAGOS: God of many names

CHORUS: O Iacchos
                          son
of Kadmeian Semele
            O born of the Thunder!
Guardian of the West
                  Regent°   *ruler*
of Eleusis' plain

O Prince of maenad Thebes
and the Dragon Field by rippling Ismenos:

[Antistrophe 1]

CHORAGOS: God of many names
CHORUS: the flame of torches
   flares on our hills
                          the nymphs of Iacchos
   dance at the spring of Castalia:
   from the vine-close mountain
                              come ah come in ivy:
   Evohe evohe! sings through the streets of Thebes

[Strophe 2]

CHORAGOS: God of many names
CHORUS: Iacchos of Thebes
   heavenly Child
                          of Semele bride of the Thunderer!
   The shadow of plague is upon us:
                                    come
   with clement feet
                          oh come from Parnasos
   down the long slopes
                          across the lamenting water

[Antistrophe 2]

CHORAGOS: Io Fire! Chorister of the throbbing stars!
   O purest among the voices of the night!
   Thou son of God, blaze for us!
CHORUS: Come with choric rapture of circling Maenads
   Who cry
                     God of many names!

Scene 6

[*Enter* MESSENGER, *L.*]

MESSENGER: Men of the line of Kadmos, you who live
   Near Amphion's citadel:
                          I cannot say
Of any condition of human life "This is fixed,
This is clearly good, or bad." Fate raises up,
And Fate casts down the happy and unhappy alike:
No man can foretell his Fate.
                              Take the case of Creon:
Creon was happy once, as I count happiness:
Victorious in battle, sole governor of the land,
Fortunate father of children nobly born.
And now it has all gone from him! Who can say
That a man is still alive when his life's joy fails?
He is a walking dead man. Grant him rich,
Let him live like a king in his great house:
If his pleasure is gone, I would not give

So much as the shadow of smoke for all he owns.
CHORAGOS: Your words hint at sorrow: what is your news for us?
MESSENGER: They are dead. The living are guilty of their death.
CHORAGOS: Who is guilty? Who is dead? Speak!
MESSENGER: Haimon.
Haimon is dead; and the hand that killed him
Is his own hand.
CHORAGOS: His father's? or his own?
MESSENGER: His own, driven mad by the murder his father had done.
CHORAGOS: Teiresias, Teiresias, how clearly you saw it all!
MESSENGER: This is my news: you must draw what conclusions you can
    from it.
CHORAGOS: But look: Eurydice, our Queen:
Has she overheard us?

[*Enter* EURYDICE *from the Palace, C.*]

EURYDICE: I have heard something, friends:
As I was unlocking the gate of Pallas' shrine,
For I needed her help today, I heard a voice
Telling of some new sorrow. And I fainted
There at the temple with all my maidens about me.
But speak again: whatever it is, I can bear it:
Grief and I are no strangers.
MESSENGER: Dearest Lady,
I will tell you plainly all that I have seen.
I shall not try to comfort you: what is the use,
Since comfort could lie only in what is not true?
The truth is always best.
                                    I went with Creon
To the outer plain where Polyneices was lying,
No friend to pity him, his body shredded by dogs.
We made our prayers in that place to Hecate
And Pluto, that they would be merciful. And we bathed
The corpse with holy water, and we brought
Fresh-broken branches to burn what was left of it,
And upon the urn we heaped up a towering barrow
Of the earth of his own land.
                                    When we were done, we ran
To the vault where Antigone lay on her couch of stone.
One of the servants had gone ahead,
And while he was yet far off he heard a voice
Grieving within the chamber, and he came back
And told Creon. And as the King went closer,
The air was full of wailing, the words lost,
And he begged us to make all haste. "Am I a prophet?"
He said, weeping, "And must I walk this road,
The saddest of all that I have gone before?
My son's voice calls me on. Oh quickly, quickly!
Look through the crevice there, and tell me

If it is Haimon, or some deception of the gods!"
We obeyed; and in the cavern's farthest corner
We saw her lying:
She had made a noose of her fine linen veil
And hanged herself. Haimon lay beside her,
His arms about her waist, lamenting her,
His love lost under ground, crying out
That his father had stolen her away from him.
When Creon saw him the tears rushed to his eyes
And he called to him: "What have you done, child? Speak to me.
What are you thinking that makes your eyes so strange?
O my son, my son, I come to you on my knees!"
But Haimon spat in his face. He said not a word,
Staring—
           And suddenly drew his sword
And lunged. Creon shrank back, the blade missed; and the boy,
Desperate against himself, drove it half its length
Into his own side, and fell. And as he died
He gathered Antigone close in his arms again.
Choking, his blood bright red on her white cheek.
And now he lies dead with the dead, and she is his
At last, his bride in the houses of the dead.

[*Exit* EURYDICE *into the Palace.*]

CHORAGOS: She has left us without a word. What can this mean?
MESSENGER: It troubles me, too; yet she knows what is best,
Her grief is too great for public lamentation,
And doubtless she has gone to her chamber to weep
For her dead son, leading her maidens in his dirge.
CHORAGOS: It may be so: but I fear this deep silence.

[*Pause.*]

MESSENGER: I will see what she is doing. I will go in.

[*Exit* MESSENGER *into the Palace.*]

[*Enter* CREON *with attendants, bearing* HAIMON'S *body.*]

CHORAGOS: But here is the King himself: oh look at him,
Bearing his own damnation in his arms.
CREON: Nothing you say can touch me any more.
My own blind heart has brought me
From darkness to final darkness. Here you see
The father murdering, the murdered son—
And all my civic wisdom!
Haimon, my son, so young, so young to die,
I was the fool, not you; and you died for me.
CHORAGOS: That is the truth; but you were late in learning it.
CREON: This truth is hard to bear. Surely a god
Has crushed me beneath the hugest weight of heaven,
And driven me headlong a barbaric way

To trample out the thing I held most dear.
The pains that men will take to come to pain!

[*Enter* MESSENGER *from the Palace.*]

MESSENGER: The burden you carry in your hands is heavy,
  But it is not all: you will find more in your house.
CREON: What burden worse than this shall I find there?
MESSENGER: The Queen is dead.
CREON: O port of death, deaf world,
  Is there no pity for me? And you, Angel of evil,
  I was dead, and your words are death again.
  Is it true, boy? Can it be true?
  Is my wife dead? Has death bred death?
MESSENGER: You can see for yourself.

[*The doors are opened, and the body of* EURYDICE *is disclosed within.*]

CREON: Oh pity!
  All true, all true, and more than I can bear!
  O my wife, my son!
MESSENGER: She stood before the altar, and her heart
  Welcomed the knife her own hand guided,
  And a great cry burst from her lips for Megareus dead,
  And for Haimon dead, her sons; and her last breath
  Was a curse for their father, the murderer of her sons.
  And she fell, and the dark flowed in through her closing eyes.
CREON: O God, I am sick with fear.
  Are there no swords here? Has no one a blow for me?
MESSENGER: Her curse is upon you for the deaths of both.
CREON: It is right that it should be. I alone am guilty.
  I know it, and I say it. Lead me in,
  Quickly, friends.
  I have neither life nor substance. Lead me in.
CHORAGOS: You are right, if there can be right in so much wrong.
  The briefest way is best in a world of sorrow.
CREON: Let it come,
  Let death come quickly, and be kind to me.
  I would not ever see the sun again.
CHORAGOS: All that will come when it will; but we, meanwhile,
  Have much to do. Leave the future to itself.
CREON: All my heart was in that prayer!
CHORAGOS: Then do not pray any more: the sky is deaf.
CREON: Lead me away. I have been rash and foolish.
  I have killed my son and my wife.
  I look for comfort; my comfort lies here dead.
  Whatever my hands have touched has come to nothing.
  Fate has brought all my pride to a thought of dust.

[*As* CREON *is being led into the house, the* CHORAGOS *advances and speaks
directly to the audience.*]

CHORAGOS: There is no happiness where there is no wisdom;
   No wisdom but in submission to the gods.
   Big words are always punished,
   And proud men in old age learn to be wise.

The Receptive Reader

Greek drama had continuous action with no formal division into acts and scenes. In this reprinting of the play, the scenes are numbered for the convenience of the reader. The rhythm of the play is set up by the alternation of the dramatic episodes with the chants (or **odes**) of the chorus. The following questions should help you respond to the flow of the play as the central conflict works itself out and proceeds to its seemingly inevitable conclusion.

1. (Prologue) How does the playwright set up the situation? How does he fill you in on the necessary background? What is your first impression of Antigone? Where does she most forcefully state her convictions? What is the relationship between the two sisters? Can you understand Ismene's position? In the first appearance of the chorus, what subject does it talk about and what is its stance? How does its perspective on the recent warlike events differ from that of Antigone?

2. (Scene 1) What is your first impression of Creon? Does he seem an effective ruler? Or does he seem stubborn and wrong-headed to you? How does he deal with defiance or dissent? What stand does the chorus take as the challenge to Creon's authority unfolds?

3. (Scene 2) How does the contest of wills between protagonist and antagonist take shape in this scene? Where are the two polar opposites most clearly defined? Is there any common ground? Are you surprised by the stand Ismene takes in this scene?

4. (Scene 3) How would you describe Haimon's initial stance toward his father? What is his strategy in trying to deal with his father? How does it work out and why? For you, which are the strongest arguments used by Creon and Haimon in this scene? What are striking examples of the rapid-fire trading of one-liners, or *stichomythy?* Does this scene change or confirm your estimate of Creon's character?

5. (Scene 4) What is the final impression you retain of Antigone in this last scene in which you see her? Antigone said about the chorus in Scene 2:

All these men here would praise me
Were their lips not frozen shut with fear of you.

Was she right? In Scene 3, what side does the chorus seem to take in the confrontation between Creon and his son? What is the role and position of the chorus in Scene 4?

6. (Scene 5) The appearance of Teiresias, the blind prophet, signals the turning point, or **peripety**, of the play. What is the blind seer's intention and message? What causes Teiresias to reveal his horrible prophecy? What is Creon's reaction? How does the playwright guide your reactions to the seer's prediction?

7. (Scene 6) Greek tragedy often appeals to our sense of *irony* as we witness with a bitter smile the contrast between people's hopes and their actual fate. In what ways is Creon the victim or target of irony? The play concludes with orthodox warnings against **hubris**, the sin of arrogant pride. How does the play as a whole lead up to this conclusion?

The Creative Response

Traditional drama reviews and theater criticism have tended to focus on the main actor or actors, played by lionized star performers. In recent years, however, critics have often also paid serious attention to minor or supporting characters. They have looked at them, for instance, for the light they throw on prevailing attitudes or cultural patterns of the playwright's time or of the time of the play. For a journal entry or brief oral presentation, script a speech in which you enter into the point of view of one of the characters in Sophocles' *Antigone*. Choose a character whose motives and arguments you sympathize with or feel you understand. Write in the first person, starting your presentation with one of the following:

✗ "I, Antigone, daughter of Oedipus, . . ."

✗ "I, Ismene, sister of Antigone, . . ."

✗ "I, Creon, king of Thebes, . . ."

✗ "I, Haimon, son of Creon, . . ."

✗ "I, Teiresias, prophet, . . ."

✗ "I, member of the Chorus and citizen of Thebes, . . ."

Sample Student Response

I, Teiresias the prophet am blind, yet I see. I see that death and destruction follow on the heels of prideful arrogance. Creon, a man intoxicated with the strong drink of power, ignored the decrees of the gods, holding his own firm resolve in higher esteem. Yet I saw without seeing his self-righteousness lead him down the path of no return. His blood lust turned triumph into a sorrowful river overflowing with the blood of those he held most dear, a fate too terrible to bear and yet he shall bear it, for by his own voice, he declared death and dishonor for those whose only crime was to love. I stood ridiculed as my prophecies touched his ears. Now they burn his heart and there is no escape, for his vengeance sent out has gathered force and has not returned unto him void.

The Whole Play—For Discussion or Writing

1. In Greek tragedy, we are often told that a person's *fate* was decreed by the gods. However, we also see strong-willed individuals making fateful choices. To become great or admirable, the characters must not be mere pawns of fate but show evidence of strength of will. To what extent do both the major and the supporting characters in this play exercise **free will**—showing evidence of deliberate choice or independent judgment? To what extent do they seem to you victims of fate?

2. Recent studies have reexamined the role of women in ancient Greek society and in other early cultures. What attitude toward *women* does Creon reveal in his denunciation of Antigone? Is his attitude shared by others in the play? Do you think it is shared by the playwright? Do you think the playwright expected the audience to share it?

3. George Steiner, in a book on the influence of *Antigone* on Western culture, has said that the drama brings into play all five major sources of *conflict* inherent in the human condition:

- the confrontation of men and women
- the conflict between youth and age
- the conflicting demands of society and the individual
- the respect due the the living and the dead
- the conflict between the desires of human beings and the will of the gods.

Can you show that each kind of conflict plays a role in the drama? How important is each in the play as a whole?

The Range Of Interpretation

Creon says at the end, "The guilt is all mine." Do you agree? What is your final judgment of Antigone as the tragic heroine? One translator of this play questioned Antigone's "total indifference to the rights of the city" to protect itself against treason. He claimed that no one in the play really praises her, with the exception of her fiancé. She herself says that if the gods allowed her to suffer death for her stand she would know she was wrong. Was she wrong? In your opinion, what in this play could or should have been done differently, and by whom?

The Creative Dimension

Much research has gone into reconstructing the original staging of the Greek plays. Scholars have studied the use of masks, tried to reconstruct the dance movements and gesture language of the chorus, and debated the nature of Greek music. Recordings of reconstructed early Greek music are available. Your class may want to initiate a research project leading to a mini-production of selected or adapted scenes from *Antigone*. The project should attempt to give your classmates a sense of the visual and auditory effects and of the overall impact of Greek drama.

Making Connections—For Discussion or Writing

In Sophocles' *Antigone*, rival loyalties compete for the character's allegiance: loyalty to family, loyalty to country or state, loyalty to the laws of religion. Compare and contrast Sophocles' tragic heroine with Ibsen's Nora as heroines faced with divided loyalties. What is the nature of the conflict in each case? How does the heroine resolve it? What are important parallels or key differences?

✗ A recent popular bestseller was built on the thesis that men and women are from different planets in their attitudes toward life, their use of language, and the expectations they bring to relationships. Compare and contrast Sophocles' *Antigone* and Ibsen's *A Doll's House* as plays centered on a conflict between a man and a woman.

WRITING ABOUT LITERATURE

27 Tracing a Central Conflict
WRITING FOCUS: Focusing Your Paper

The Writing Workshop   A well-focused paper may target the central conflict in a play. Is an embattled protagonist locked in a struggle with a worthy antagonist? Is there a clash between two opposed forces or points of view? Does a central confrontation help shape the play as a whole? Here are some possibilities you might consider for a paper focused on a central conflict:

✗ For many in the audience, the heart of Ibsen's *A Doll's House* is the conflict between Torvald's paternalistic attitude toward women and Nora's need to be respected for her own decisions, right or wrong.

✗ The heart of Sophocles' *Antigone* is the conflict between Creon's insistence on loyalty to the state and Antigone's stubborn insistence on obeying the laws of the gods.

✗ In the plays by Arthur Miller, Lorraine Hansberry, or Tennessee Williams later in this book, you might focus on the conflict between the generations.

In working up material for your paper, you will soon want to push beyond the kind of open, exploratory note taking you might do in a journal. Early in your thinking and writing, try to bring the central conflict into focus. You can then start the purposeful note taking that will give you ample evidence to draw on as you trace basic opposites and their ramifications.

Focused Note Taking   Look for details and quotations that help you line up the two sides in the central conflict. For instance, in Shakespeare's *Macbeth,* Lady Macbeth is committed to having her husband become king of Scotland through the murder of King Duncan. She early starts to prod and criticize her reluctant, hesitating partner in crime. She preaches the need for moving ahead swiftly and without scruples. (She knows that dwelling on the horror of the deed will drive them mad.)

Reading notes like the following will give you the ammunition needed to drive home the contrast in your paper:

✗ At the beginning of the play, the two partners seem to have a kind of tacit understanding. Lady Macbeth makes the expected Renaissance choice, to become his "dearest partner in greatness." Today, we would criticize her for not creating a life of her own, for her ruthless ethics, and for following the party line, buying into "what greatness is promised thee" (1.5.14).

✗ The key difference between the two shows is their different way of looking at ambition. To Macbeth, "o'ervaulting ambition" gives him pause (it leaps and falls on the other side); ambition represents his "deep and dark desires." Lady Macbeth early points to his problem: He is not ruthless enough; he wants to win the prize by honest means. She perceives him as ambitious but too sensitive, too kind:

> Yet do I fear thy nature;
> It is too full of the milk of human kindness
> To catch the nearest way (1.5.17–19)

✗ When he falters, she shames her husband: "Art thou afeard / To be the same in thine own act and valor / As thou art in desire?" (1.7.39–41).

✗ She finds she has to attend to much of the actual preparation of the deed, relieving Macbeth of petty planning details. She attends to their alibi: "I have drugged their possets, / That death and nature do contend about them, / Whether they live or die" (2.2.6–8) and plants the tools "I laid their daggers ready" (2.2.11).

✗ As Macbeth is conscience-stricken over his "deed," she keeps him focused and attends to the grisly coverup:

> Infirm of purpose!
> Give me the daggers. The sleeping and the dead
> Are but as pictures. 'Tis the eye of childhood
> That fears a painted devil. If he do bleed,
> I'll gild the faces of the grooms withal,
> For it must seem their guilt. (2.2.51–56)

> My hands are of your color, but I shame
> To wear a heart so white. . . . Retire we to our chamber
> A little water clears us of this deed:
> How easy is it then! Your constancy
> Hath left you unattended. (2.3.63–68)

✗ Understanding that Duncan's murder is only the beginning, Macbeth is perturbed by setbacks: "We have scorched the snake, not killed it" (3.2.13). Lady Macbeth thinks that "Things without all remedy / Should be without regard: what's done is done" (3.2.11–12).

Clustering   Cluster a key character or key idea. Let associations and details branch out from a central core as they come to mind. Let your cluster help you map important associations and help you see them as part of a pattern. The sample cluster on the following page brings into focus a range of ideas that will help you define one pole in the play of opposites in *Macbeth*.

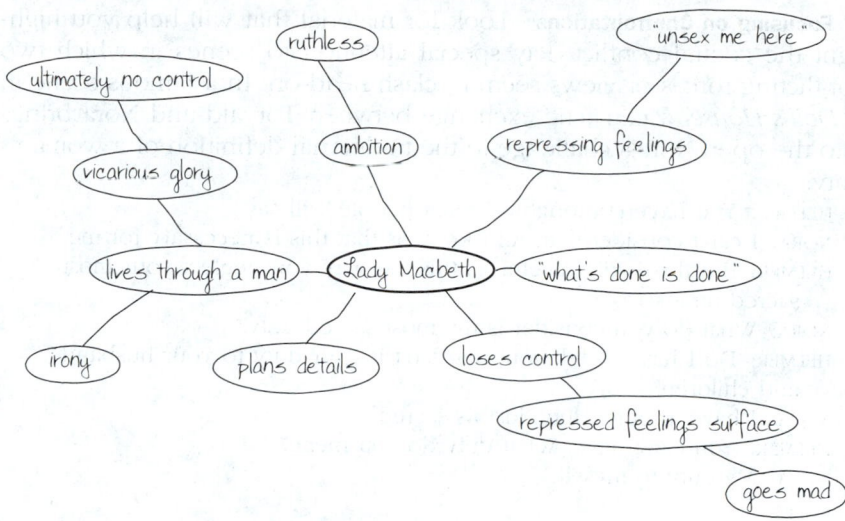

Here is the *capsule portrait* of Lady Macbeth that grew out of this cluster:

Early in the play, Lady Macbeth seems to be the stronger of the two partners. She eggs on her husband and plans or supervises the details of the murder. She appears ruthless and bold, driven by overriding ambition. She represses any natural feelings of remorse or pity ("Unsex me here"). But the only way she has of realizing her ambitions is through her husband. She shares vicariously in his glory, and she has no control over an independent destiny. Her statement that "what's done is done" is ironic, because what she and her husband have done will destroy them both. The fears she had repressed or pushed down rise to the surface to destroy her, and she goes mad.

Summing Up the Contrast As your paper begins to take shape in your mind, clarify or sharpen the overall pattern, the overall strategy. Push toward a summing up; line up the conflicting positions or agendas. Sharpen the contrast so that the basic conflict comes clearly into focus:

LADY MACBETH: Lady Macbeth holds the view, much echoed in later centuries, that power goes to the strong and ruthless. Traditional values like meekness, loyalty, and pity are designed to "hold the strong in awe." They are a handicap for those who are truly ambitious. Conscience and fear of divine retribution are creations of our own guilty imaginations; they are like tales told to frighten children.

MACBETH: Macbeth is torn between ambition and his guilty conscience, "the scorpions of the mind." When he talks to the murderers, he talks as if manliness meant being strong and tough, like the strongest and swiftest predators in the animal kingdom. But at other times he talks as if being a man meant being more than an animal—honoring ties of kinship, of gratitude, of friendship. Even when he has intellectually accepted the arguments of his wife, "horrible imaginings" rise from his subconscious.

Focusing on Confrontations   Look for material that will help you high-light the central conflict. Pay special attention to scenes in which two conflicting forces or views seem to clash head-on. In a famous scene in *A Doll's House,* a climactic exchange between Torvald and Nora brings into the open Nora's challenge to the traditional definition of a woman's duty:

HELMER: You haven't thought of what people will say.

NORA: I can't consider that. All I know is that this is necessary for me.

HELMER: But this is disgraceful. Is this the way you neglect your most sacred duties?

NORA: What do you consider is my most sacred duty?

HELMER: Do I have to tell you that? Isn't it your duty to your husband and children?

NORA: I have another duty, just as sacred.

HELMER: You can't have. What duty do you mean?

NORA: My duty to myself.

Focusing on Parallels   Often supporting characters or subplots echo and reinforce the major concerns of a play. Try to work into your paper exchanges that parallel in some way the major confrontations between protagonist and antagonist. For instance, in the initial exchange in *Antigone,* the heroine tests the loyalty of her sister Ismene, who has no wish "to dishonor the laws that the gods hold in honor" but who says: "Defy the city? I have no strength for that." The sisters' disagreement anticipates the later clashes between Antigone and Creon over the demands of religious law and the conflicting demands of the state. Later, the exchange between Creon and his son Haimon again focuses on the central question: Does Creon's need for loyalty and obedience give him the right "to trample down the honor of the gods"?

Focusing on the Resolution   How is the conflict resolved? In Shakespeare's *Macbeth,* Macbeth himself seems for a time the weaker partner. But in the end, Lady Macbeth crumbles, her mind diseased by "that perilous stuff / Which weighs upon the heart." The guilt feelings she has belittled or repressed surface and drive her insane. Macbeth, by contrast, is terribly lucid at the end. He finds that by denying all human ties and feelings, he has isolated himself from all human contact. Wanting to be first, he has wound up alone:

> All that which should accompany old age,
> As honor, love, obedience, troops of friends,
> I must not look to have; but in their stead,
> Curses, not loud but deep, mouth-honor, breath,
> Which the poor heart would fain deny and dare not. (5.3.25–29)

Study the following sample student paper. How well does it bring the central conflict of the play into focus? How well does it trace the conflict into its ramifications? Does the writer adopt an independent view? Does the writer succeed in showing the appeal of the play to the modern audience?

Sample Student Paper

Antigone: A Contest of Wills

All ways of thinking contain their own blindnesses.

Marilyn French

In his tragedy Antigone, Sophocles sets up a classic conflict between two characters who are neither entirely in the right nor entirely in the wrong. Instead, both are sincere in their beliefs. Both are proud and self-righteous. The difference is that one turns out to be right in putting the law of the gods above human laws.

When Antigone's brother Polyneices dies a traitor, King Creon orders that his body remain unburied. He wants the corpse to be "carrion for the birds and dogs to tear, / an obscenity for the citizens to behold." Creon's decree serves a double purpose: it continues to punish Polyneices even after death (his soul cannot go to heaven if he is not properly buried), and it is a reminder to the citizens of Thebes that the king's will is law. Anyone who defies the king defies the state, and is therefore a traitor. From Creon's point of view, there is no more deadly peril than disobedience. Even though Creon has declared that the penalty for defying his order is death, Antigone decides that the gods' law supersedes Creon's edict, and she buries her brother.

The striking feature of this play is that we see two strong-willed characters locked in battle. The trait that both Antigone and Creon have in common is their stubbornness—their unshakable conviction that they are right, their inability to change their minds until it is too late. However, American readers tend to view Antigone as the "righter" of the two characters, although perhaps for somewhat different reasons than the original Greek audience. We tend to rank the voice of the individual above that of society or the state. We tend to agree with Henry David Thoreau that a person who is in the right is in a majority of one already. As a result, we are predisposed to agree with Antigone when she says, "It wasn't Zeus, not in the least, / who made this proclamation." For her, "Justice, dwelling with the gods," has more force than the edict of "a mere mortal."

On the other hand, Antigone is totally unyielding, and her tremendous faith in her own righteousness can be seen as a flaw that helps bring disaster down on her and her lover and betrothed. She is totally contemptuous of her sister Ismene, who at first opts to take the practical, reasonable course: "to obey the ones who stand in power." Ismene says, in the words of a modern translation,

> we must be sensible. Remember we are women.
> We're not born to contend with men. Then too,
> we're underlings, ruled by much stronger hands.
> So we must submit in this, and things still worse.

The word "submit" is not in Antigone's vocabulary; she vows to reject Ismene's help "even if you should have a change of heart."

Creon speaks up for the safety of the "ship of state," and at first the chorus seems to honor his claim. The leader of the chorus says about Antigone: "Like father, like daughter, / passionate, wild . . . / she hasn't learned to bend before adversity." Later, the chorus tells Antigone, "attacks on power never go unchecked."

However, Creon doesn't get any more sympathy from a modern audience than he received from his advisers his family, or, finally, his subjects. To us, he really does not seem to aim at serving his people; he does not profess to serve a higher power; he only serves himself. His image as a man is at stake: "There's no room for pride, not in a slave, / not with the lord and master standing by." Several characters try to point out to Creon that he is suffering from an excess of egotism, willfulness, and pride. But he's too self-absorbed to accept any of this criticism. His son provides us with an accurate sketch of Creon's character when he observes,

> Whoever thinks that he alone possesses intelligence,
> the gift of eloquence, he and no one else,
> and character too . . . such men, I tell you,
> spread them open—you will find them empty.

This self-righteousness, coupled with Creon's refusal to acknowledge the laws of heaven, leads him down the dark path of tragedy. It takes the death of his wife and son to convince him that he has been mistaken.

In the contest of wills, it is Antigone who stays the course. In the end, Antigone remains true to her principles; she chooses to die rather than acquiesce in an unjust civil law. It is Creon who capitulates (too late to save anyone but himself). It is Creon who changes his mind and admits, "it's best to keep the established laws / to the very day we die." In the contest of wills, Antigone has perished, but her principles have prevailed.

Creon tried to coerce his subjects into being loyal by making the penalty for disobedience as severe as he could. He failed to take into account the fact that loyalty cannot be commanded into existence—or coerced into being. It must be given freely, or it can no longer be called loyalty; it becomes subjugation.

Questions for Peer Review

1. What is the *thesis* of this paper? How does the writer lead up to it? Does it offer you a new or different perspective on the play? Do you agree with it, or would you take issue with it?

2. Where is the *central conflict* best summed up or described? Does the writer trace it into its ramifications? Does she look at the role of supporting characters?

3. What is the general *plan* or strategy of the paper? Is it easy or hard to outline?

4. Does the writer use sufficient *evidence*? What use does the writer make of firsthand quotation? Are any quotations especially telling or effective?

5. Does the paper leave you with any unanswered questions or loose ends?

6. Do you agree with the writer on the way a contemporary audience is likely to respond to the play?

7. What does Marilyn French mean when she says, "All ways of thinking contain their own blindnesses"? Why did the student writer use this statement as a motto or starter quotation for this paper?

28 SHAKESPEAREAN TRAGEDY

The Inner Conflict

*Shakespeare's plays are not in the rigorous and
critical sense either tragedies or comedies, but
compositions of a distinct kind—exhibiting the
real state of sublunary nature, which partakes of
good and evil, joy and sorrow . . . and
expressing the course of the world, in which the
loss of one is the gain of another; in which, at
the same time, the reveler is hastening to his
wine, and the mourner burying his friend.*

SAMUEL JOHNSON, *PREFACE TO SHAKESPEARE,* 1765

*Shakespeare himself was an actor, and the
art of acting is at the very root of his whole
playwrighting art.*

FRANCIS FERGUSSON

FOCUS ON SHAKESPEARE'S STAGE

Shakespeare's insight into human motives often makes spectators feel that the playwright knows them better than they know themselves. They hear characters on his stage voice their own secret thoughts and feelings. Crossing cultural boundaries, plays like *Romeo and Juliet, As You Like It, Hamlet, Macbeth, Othello,* or *King Lear* act out for spectators the drama of human contact and interaction. Juliet and her Romeo, Portia and Shylock from *The Merchant of Venice,* young Hamlet, and Lady Macbeth people the imagination of theater goers around the world.

Nevertheless, Shakespeare's plays were part of a thriving contemporary culture and have deep roots in the politics and beliefs of his time. They were part of a great flowering of the theater during the Elizabethan age. Under Queen Elizabeth I of the house of Tudor, England had come to enjoy a measure of prosperity, self-confidence, and national unity. The golden age of the English stage lasted from the 1580s to the time the Puritans, hostile to worldly entertainment, closed the theaters in 1642.

Remember the contemporary setting as you read a Shakespeare play:

A Mirror of English History   Shakespeare's first successes dramatized recent English history. Under Elizabeth and the Tudor monarchy, England was leaving behind the fratricidal civil wars of the feudal Middle Ages. Feudalism had been a system of splintered authority. Powerful local warlords owed allegiance and military service to the king, but often they were his rivals for power. Shakespeare's history plays show a nation trying to emerge from the "civic broils" that pitted brother against brother, "blood against blood, Self against Self" (*Richard III,* 2.4.62–64). A recurrent theme in these plays is the yearning for stable, legitimate government, legitimized by true religion and "true descent." However, the plays are set in the feudal world: Like Shakespeare's *Hamlet,* many of the plays center on the quarrels of the succession. An older relative tries to head off a young heir's rise to power. A person with a dubious claim takes on a vulnerable incumbent. Powerful individuals challenge traditional authority, and often the rebels have good lines.

A Popular Theater   Shakespeare's audiences came to the theater for a spectacle with a large cast and a sprawling plot—often with the future of a kingdom at stake, with astonishing instances of loyalty and treachery, and with moments of high drama in climactic confrontations. Often the central issue was settled in the ordeal of the final battle. The task of playwright was to fill a commercial theater—"large, cheap, and popular"— several times a week (G. E. Bentley). Plays were at first performed in the courtyards of inns, which saw such popular entertainments as bear-baitings and cockfights on other occasions. They gradually moved to specially constructed wooden open-roofed theaters holding several thousand spectators. There were special seats in "galleries," or roofed balconies, for the wealthy; there was standing room in the "yard" (surrounding the stage) for those Hamlet calls the "groundlings." Shakespeare's own theatrical company enjoyed the patronage of the court, but the clergy and civil authorities suspected the theaters of breeding immorality. The Globe Theatre, most famous of the Elizabethan theaters, was built in 1599 on the other (south) side of the Thames River, beyond the reach of the restrictive city ordinances of London magistrates.

The repertory changed with popular taste—with some plays, as Hamlet says to the players visiting his court, performed "not above once." Others enjoyed long runs. The plays, like Hollywood scripts, were often the result of collaboration. They were further adapted and modified by actors. Clowns, especially, as Hamlet says, were apt to speak "more than was set down for them" to get cheap laughs from a "quantity of barren spectators." When the plays were printed, the printer might use imperfect actors' copies. Modern editors have tried to reconstruct authentic texts of Shakespeare's plays by comparing early printings—the *quartos*—with the *folio*—texts collected and printed in 1623, seven years after the playwright's death. (The smaller quartos and the large folio are named after the size of the page.)

Modern directors have restored key features of the Elizabethan stage. Boy actors, it is true, no longer play the women's roles. But we often see Shakespeare performed, as in his time, on an open stage, with free-flowing action and no curtain coming down between acts or scenes. (These were edited in by later editors.) There may be two levels, with a balcony as in *Romeo and Juliet*. The action moves rapidly from place to place.

The Apprentice Playwright   The great successes of the early Elizabethan stage show what audiences came to see when Shakespeare arrived in

London from his hometown, Stratford-on-Avon, to make his way as an actor and apprentice playwright. One spectacular success was Thomas Kyd's *The Spanish Tragedy,* a play of **intrigue,** of plotting and counter-plotting, first written and acted about 1585. When Shakespeare wrote *Hamlet,* it was not the first time his audiences had seen a **revenge tragedy:** a play that starts with the ghost of the victim clamoring for revenge for a foul murder and ends with the avenger triumphing over his adversaries, taking them down with him to bloody death. Another popular long-running play was Christopher Marlowe's *Tamburlane the Great,* first performed in 1587. It was the spectacular story of an obscure Middle Eastern shepherd who by sheer force of ambition made himself emperor of the known world. Tamburlane is the **colossal protagonist,** a larger-than-life central figure dominating the stage. He is the Renaissance superman, subduing his enemies by ruthless terror. At the same time, he has whole armies and their generals crossing over to his side, dazzled by his charismatic personality and his soaring eloquence.

Blank Verse   Marlowe wrote *Tamburlane* in **blank verse**—the un-rhymed iambic pentameter line that was to become the dominant medium of Shakespeare's serious plays. In the following sample passage, some lines are regular five-beat lines, with stress always on the second syllable of each foot: "UnTIL | we REACH | the RIP|est FRUIT | of ALL." Others play familiar variations on the underlying iambic beat. The next line starts with trochaic inversion, and it also has an unstressed or weakly stressed second syllable in the third foot: "NAture | that FRAMED | us of | four EL|eMENTS." (Notice how the departure from the regular beat makes the key word—*nature*—seem to stand out.) As later in Shakespeare, lines tend to combine in a verse paragraph that develops its own soaring rhythm:

> Nature that framed us of four elements
> Warring within our breasts for regiment,
> Doth teach us all to have aspiring minds:
> Our souls whose faculties can comprehend
> The wondrous architecture of the world
> And measure every wandering planet's course. . .
> Wills us to wear ourselves and never rest
> Until we reach the ripest fruit of all. . .
> The sweet fruition of an earthly crown.

Religion and Mythology   Religion and religious doctrine play more of a role in the language of Shakespeare's plays than they do in the language and thinking of many moderns. Playwright and audience shared religious beliefs, beliefs about ghosts, and popular superstitions—whether believed wholeheartedly or viewed more skeptically. Hamlet's good friend Horatio says about some of the spirit lore, "So have I heard and do in part believe it" (1.1.165).

At the same time, the Elizabethan age was part of the European Renaissance, a time of revived interest in ancient Greek and Roman art and literature. Shakespeare is steeped in Greek legend and **mythology.** As a young man, he wrote *Venus and Adonis*—a long poem about Venus, the goddess of love, and her mortal lover. The dialogue of a Shakespeare play is shot through with allusions to playful Cupid, aiming his darts or arrows at lovers; or "plated Mars"—the armor-plated god of war. When Hamlet asks the itinerant player to recite a favorite speech about the death of King Priam, the playwright expects the audience to know the story of the Trojan War, the siege and fall of Troy. The player proceeds to raise a storm of passion over Queen Hecuba's witnessing the slaying of Priam, her husband and father of the Trojan hero Hector.

Language   The language of Shakespeare's time was in transition from medieval English (or Middle English) to modern speech:

✗ There still were special pronouns (and matching verb forms) for talking to one rather than several persons: *thou art, thou wilt, thou canst;* and also *may it please thee* and *take what is thine.* Use of this familiar *thou* instead of the more formal *you* corresponded roughly to being on a first-name basis. *Methinks* and *methought* were still used for *I think* and *I thought.* Many of our modern auxiliaries or helping verbs are still missing: *Ride you tonight?* for *do you ride?; prepare we* for *let us prepare.*

✗ Word order often differs from ours. In modern English, "We will *our kingdom* give" has become "We will give *our kingdom.*" "Hamlet, thou hast *thy father* much offended" today would be "Hamlet, you have much offended *your father.*" (Objects now generally follow the complete verb.)

✗ Listeners and readers soon get used to frequently used words like *prithee* (please), *forsooth* (in truth), *anon* (presently, very soon), *aught* (anything), *ere* (before). *Would* is often used in the sense of *wish* or *want* ("*Would* it were true" for "*I wish* it were true").

In the following edition of *Hamlet,* prepared for this book, footnotes have been replaced by marginal glosses to help you read and study the play. These glosses give you suggested modern meanings close at hand and in the context of the line. Where the text is obscure or imperfect, these meanings represent the educated guesses of editors and scholars. As in other modern editions aimed at the general reader, spellings and sometimes word forms have been cautiously modernized.

THE ENIGMA OF HAMLET

Since Hamlet *touches the complete alphabet of
human experience, every actor feels he is born to
play it. The bold extrovert will dazzle and play
with the word power, the scenes of vengeance,
and blast Ophelia and Gertrude off the stage.
The introvert will see every line pointed at him,
the outsider, the loner, the watcher, he with his
one trusting friend, and a quick answer for
everything lest it be a barb. The wit will play
for laughs and the lunatic for madness. The
romantic for ideals. So you cannot be miscast
for Hamlet.*

STEVEN BERKOFF

To many critics, *Hamlet* has been Shakespeare's most searching comment on life and human nature. "It is *we* who are Hamlet," said the Romantic critic William Hazlitt. Directors and actors have made the play their Mount Everest. As the actor-director Steven Berkoff says in *I Am Hamlet,* "in every actor is a Hamlet struggling to get out." Yet at the same time, *Hamlet* has proved Shakespeare's most challenging and mysterious play. A library of critical volumes has been written on the contest of wills between Prince Hamlet and his murderous stepfather Claudius; on Hamlet's relationship with his doting mother, Queen Gertrude (who "lives by his looks"); on his harsh treatment of Ophelia (whom he tells, "I loved you once"); and on his long-delayed revenge on Claudius, the "king of shreds and patches," who killed his father and married his mother.

Although Hamlet is often accused of inaction, the play itself is a fast-moving spectacle, with much **stage business**—encounters with a ghost, a quarrel at a graveside, a climactic duel. Many scenes have long been audience favorites: Hamlet taunts the king's talky and slow-witted counselor (and Ophelia's father) Polonius. Hamlet talks with a group of itinerant traveling players about his love of the theater. Hamlet plays cat and mouse with the king's spies, his former schoolmates Rosencrantz and Guildenstern. However, audiences and critics rivet their attention especially on the great **soliloquies** in which Hamlet bares his soul: "To be or not to be"; "O that this too too sullied flesh would melt."

The dying Hamlet asks his friend Horatio "to tell my story"—to clear his reputation, to clear his "wounded name" of false accusations and evil rumors. Then Hamlet casts his vote for young Fortinbras, son of the King of Norway, to be the next king. Order will be restored and continuity assured. However, audiences and critics have not been content to let the matter rest there. They have found Hamlet a rich, complex, paradoxical character. As you read the play, keep in mind questions that audiences and critics have asked about Hamlet and his role in the play:

✗ How trustworthy is the ghost? Is the ghost of Hamlet's father, who spurs Hamlet on to revenge, a good or an evil spirit? Is he a "spirit of health or goblin damned"? Hamlet concludes that he is seeing and talking to an "honest ghost," and he reluctantly responds to the ghost's call for vengeance. But at least one modern critic has argued that, according to the spirit lore of Shakespeare's time, the ghost must have been an evil spirit, luring Hamlet on to damnation (as the witches did to Macbeth).

✗ What explains the delay? Why does it take Hamlet so long to accomplish his revenge, his "almost blunted purpose"? Are the reasons Hamlet gives for delaying his revenge merely pretexts? Is he temperamentally averse to decisive action? Is he too much the intellectual, forever debating, forever finding scruples and complications? Does he suffer from paralysis of the will, as the Romantic critics claimed?

✗ What are the true sources of Hamlet's melancholy? Is he melancholy by temperament, illustrating one of the character types of the psychology of Shakespeare's time? (According to the psychology of "humors," excess of one such humor or bodily fluid would tilt a person toward melancholy, chronic anger, or cheerfulness.)

✗ How mad is Hamlet? He feigns madness to gain time to prepare his revenge. How close is the turmoil in his soul to driving him truly mad—instead of his just pretending to be insane to disorient the king?

✗ What is Hamlet's true relationship with his mother? Why is he so obsessed with lurid images of physical intimacy between her and the uncle? What evidence is there for or against his having Oedipal feelings toward his mother? (In some modern productions, these are acted out graphically in the bedroom scene.)

William Shakespeare   *(1564–1616)*

Hamlet   *1600–1601*

Hamlet must be the best known of all characters in the theater of the world.

BERNARD LOTT

CHARACTERS

CLAUDIUS, King of Denmark
HAMLET, nephew to the King
GERTRUDE, Queen of Denmark, mother to HAMLET
GHOST of HAMLET's father
POLONIUS, counselor to the King
LAERTES, son to POLONIUS
OPHELIA, daughter to POLONIUS
HORATIO, friend to HAMLET

And also:

VOLTEMAND ⎤
CORNELIUS │
ROSENCRANTZ │
GUILDENSTERN ├ courtiers,
OSRIC │
A gentleman ⎦
MARCELLUS ⎤
BERNARDO ⎬ soldiers
FRANCISCO ⎦
REYNALDO, servant to POLONIUS
FORTINBRAS, Prince of Norway
PLAYERS
Two CLOWNS, gravediggers
A Norwegian CAPTAIN
English Ambassadors
Lords, Ladies, Priests, Officers, Soldiers, Sailors, Messengers, Attendants

Act One

SCENE 1. Elsinore Castle. The platform of the guard.

[*Enter* BERNARDO *and* FRANCISCO, *two sentinels from opposite directions.*]

BERNARDO: Who's there?
FRANCISCO: Nay, answer me. Stand and unfold° yourself.   *identify*
BERNARDO: Long live the King!
FRANCISCO: Bernardo?
BERNARDO: He.   5
FRANCISCO: You come most carefully upon your hour.°   *at the exact time*
BERNARDO: 'Tis now struck twelve. Get thee to bed,
     Francisco.
FRANCISCO: For this relief much thanks. 'Tis bitter cold,
     And I am sick at heart.
BERNARDO: Have you had quiet guard?
FRANCISCO: Not a mouse   10
     stirring.
BERNARDO: Well, good night.
     If you do meet Horatio and Marcellus,
     The rivals° of my watch, bid them make haste.   *partners*

[*Enter* HORATIO *and* MARCELLUS.]

FRANCISCO: I think I hear them. Stand! Who's there?
HORATIO: Friends to this ground.
MARCELLUS: And liegemen to the Dane.°   *loyal Danish*   15
                                                                                subjects
FRANCISCO: Give you good night.
MARCELLUS: O, farewell, honest soldier.
     Who hath relieved you?

FRANCISCO: Bernardo hath my place.
  Give you good night.

                              [*He leaves.*]

MARCELLUS: Holla, Bernardo!
BERNARDO: Say—
  What, is Horatio there?
HORATIO: A piece of him.
BERNARDO: Welcome, Horatio. Welcome, good Marcellus.   20
MARCELLUS: What, has this thing appeared again tonight?
BERNARDO: I have seen nothing.
MARCELLUS: Horatio says 'tis but our fantasy,
  And will not let belief take hold of him
  Touching this dreaded sight, twice seen of us.   25
  Therefore I have entreated him along,
  With us to watch the minutes of this night,
  That, if again this apparition come,
  He may approve our eyes° and speak to it.   confirm what we saw
HORATIO: Tush, tush, 'twill not appear.
BERNARDO: Sit down awhile,   30
  And let us once again assail your ears,
  That are so fortified against our story,
  What we two nights have seen.
HORATIO: Well, sit we down,
  And let us hear Bernardo speak of this.
BERNARDO: Last night of all,   35
  When yond same star that's westward from the pole
  Had made his° course to illume that part of heaven   its
  Where now it burns, Marcellus and myself,
  The bell then beating one—

  [*Enter* GHOST.]

MARCELLUS: Peace! break thee off! Look where it comes
  again!   40
BERNARDO: In the same figure,° like the King that's dead.   looking the same as
MARCELLUS: Thou art a scholar; speak to it, Horatio.
BERNARDO: Looks it not like the King? Mark it, Horatio.
HORATIO: Most like. It harrows me with fear and wonder.
BERNARDO: It would be spoke to.
MARCELLUS: Question it, Horatio.   45
HORATIO: What art thou that usurpest this time of night
  Together with that fair and warlike form
  In which the majesty of buried Denmark°   the buried Danish king
  Did sometimes march? By heaven I charge thee speak!
MARCELLUS: It is offended.
BERNARDO: See, it stalks away!   50
HORATIO: Stay! Speak, speak! I charge thee speak!

                      [GHOST *leaves.*]

MARCELLUS: 'Tis gone and will not answer.

BERNARDO: How now, Horatio? You tremble and look
  pale. Is not this something more than fantasy?
  What think you on't?°   *do you think of it*   55

HORATIO: Before my God, I might not this believe
  Without the sensible and true avouch°   *concrete testimony*
  Of mine own eyes.

MARCELLUS: Is it not like the King?

HORATIO: As thou art to thyself.
  Such was the very armor he had on   60
  When he the ambitious Norway° combated;   *(king of Norway)*
  So frowned he once when, in an angry parle,°   *parley*
  He smote the sledded Polacks° on the ice.   *Poles in sleds*
  'Tis strange.

MARCELLUS: Thus twice before, and jump° at this dead hour,   *exactly*   65
  With martial stalk hath he gone by our watch.

HORATIO: In what particular thought to work I know not;
  But, in the gross and scope of my opinion,°   *in my general opinion*
  This bodes some strange eruption° to our state. *means some strange upheaval*

MARCELLUS: Good now, sit down and tell me, he that
  knows,   70
  Why this same strict and most observant watch
  So nightly toils the subject of the land,°   *makes our citizens toil*
  And why such daily cast of brazen cannon
  And foreign mart° for implements of war;   *shopping abroad*
  Why such impress° of shipwrights, whose sore task   *rushed hiring*   75
  Does not divide the Sunday from the week;
  What might be toward,° that this sweaty haste   *be in store*
  Doth make the night joint-laborer with the day?
  Who is't that can inform me?

HORATIO: That can I.
  At least, the whisper goes so. Our last King,   80
  Whose image even but now appeared to us,
  Was, as you know, by Fortinbras of Norway,
  Thereto pricked on by a most emulate° pride,   *envious*
  Dared to the combat; in which our valiant Hamlet° *(Hamlet senior, the*
  (For so this side of our known world esteemed him)   *dead king)*   85
  Did slay this Fortinbras; who, by a sealed compact,° *solemnly sealed treaty*
  Well ratified by law and heraldry,
  Did forfeit, with his life, all those his lands
  Which he stood seized of,° to the conqueror;   *which he held*
  Against the which a moiety competent°   *similar pledge*   90
  Was gaged by our King; which had° returned   *would have*
  To the inheritance of Fortinbras,
  Had he° been vanquisher, as, by the same comart°   *if he had/agreement*
  And carriage of the article designed,°   *meaning of the stipulated article*
  His fell to Hamlet. Now, sir, young Fortinbras,   95
  Of unimproved mettle° hot and full,   *untested spirit*

Hath in the skirts° of Norway, here and there,   *outskirts*
Sharked up° a list of lawless resolutes,°   *drummed up/adventurers*
For food and diet to some enterprise
That hath a stomach in't;° which is no other,   *that takes courage* 100
As it doth well appear unto our state,
But to recover of us, by strong hand
And terms compulsatory,° those foresaid lands   *(threatening terms)*
So by his father lost; and this, I take it,
Is the main motive of our preparations,   105
The source of this our watch, and the chief head°   *main well-spring*
Of this post-haste and romage° in the land.   *commotion and turmoil*
BERNARDO: I think it be no other but e'en so.
Well may it sort° that this portentous figure   *it fits well*
Comes armed through our watch, so like the King   110
That was and is the question° of these wars.   *cause*
HORATIO: A mote° it is to trouble the mind's eye.   *speck of dust*
In the most high and palmy state of Rome,
A little ere the mightiest Julius fell,°   *before Julius Caesar was killed*
The graves stood tenantless,° and the sheeted dead *without their occupants* 115
Did squeak and gibber in the Roman streets;
As stars with trains of fire,° and dews of blood,   *(meteors or comets)*
Disasters in the sun; and the moist star°   *the moon (governing the tides)*
Upon whose influence Neptune's empire stands
Was sick almost to doomsday with eclipse.   120
And even the like precurse° of fierce events,   *forerunners*
As harbingers° preceding still the fates   *messengers*
And prologue to the omen coming on,
Have heaven and earth together demonstrated
Unto our climatures° and countrymen.   *area* 125

[*Enter* GHOST *again.*]

But soft! behold! Lo, where it comes again!
I'll cross it,° though it blast me—Stay, illusion!   *cross its path*
If thou hast any sound, or use of voice,
Speak to me.
If there be any good thing to be done,   130
That may to thee do ease, and grace to me,
Speak to me.
If thou art privy to° thy country's fate,   *if you have secret knowledge of*
Which happily foreknowing may avoid,
O, speak!   135
Or if thou hast uphoarded in thy life
Extorted treasure in the womb of earth
(For which, they say, you spirits oft walk in death),

[*The cock crows.*]

Speak of it! Stay, and speak!—Stop it, Marcellus!
MARCELLUS: Shall I strike at it with my partisan?°   *weapon* 140

HORATIO: Do, if it will not stand.
BERNARDO: 'Tis here!
HORATIO: 'Tis here!
MARCELLUS: 'Tis gone!

[GHOST *leaves.*]

We do it wrong, being so majestical,
To offer it the show of violence;
For it is as the air, invulnerable,   145
And our vain blows malicious mockery.
BERNARDO: It was about to speak, when the cock crew.
HORATIO: And then it started, like a guilty thing
Upon a fearful summons. I have heard
The cock, that is the trumpet to the morn,   150
Doth with his lofty and shrill-sounding throat
Awake the god of day; and at his warning,
Whether in sea or fire, in earth or air,
The extravagant and erring spirit hies°   *hurries back*
To his confine;° and of the truth herein   *prison* 155
This present object made probation.°   *showed proof*
MARCELLUS: It faded on the crowing of the cock.
Some say that ever 'gainst that season comes
Wherein our Savior's birth is celebrated,
The bird of dawning singeth all night long;   160
And then, they say, no spirit dare stir abroad,
The nights are wholesome, then no planets strike,°   *no evil influences of planets*
No fairy takes, nor witch hath power to charm,
So hallowed° and so gracious is the time.   *sacred*
HORATIO: So have I heard and do in part believe it.   165
But look, the morn, in russet mantle clad,°   *in a reddish coat*
Walks over the dew of yon high eastern hill.
Break we our watch up;° and by my advice   *let us break up our watch*
Let us impart what we have seen tonight
Unto young Hamlet; for, upon my life,   170
This spirit, dumb to us, will speak to him.
Do you consent we shall acquaint him with it,
As needful in our loves, fitting our duty?
MARCELLUS: Let's do't, I pray; and I this morning know
Where we shall find him most conveniently.   175

[*They leave.*]

SCENE 2. Elsinore Castle. An audience chamber.

[*Flourish of trumpets. Enter* CLAUDIUS, *King of Denmark,* GERTRUDE *the Queen,* HAMLET, POLONIUS, LAERTES
and his sister OPHELIA, *and attending lords.*]

KING: Though yet of Hamlet our dear brother's death
The memory be green,° and that it us befitted   *is very recent*
To bear our hearts in grief, and our whole kingdom

To be contracted in one brow of woe,
Yet so far hath discretion fought with nature   5
That we with wisest sorrow think on him
Together with remembrance of ourselves.
Therefore our sometime sister,° now our queen,   *former sister-in-law*
The imperial jointress° to this warlike state,   *partner*
Have we, as 'twere with a defeated joy,   10
With an auspicious,° and a dropping eye,   *happy*
With mirth in funeral, and with dirge in marriage,
In equal scale weighing delight and dole,°   *grief*
Taken to wife; nor have we herein barred
Your better wisdoms,° which have freely gone   *wise advice* 15
With this affair along. For all, our thanks.
Now follows, that you know, young Fortinbras,
Holding a weak supposal° of our worth,   *estimate*
Or thinking by our late dear brother's death
Our state to be disjoint° and out of frame,   *weakened* 20
Colleagued with° this dream of his advantage,   *joined to*
He hath not failed to pester us with message
Importing° the surrender of those lands   *asking for*
Lost by his father, with all bands of law,°   *due formalities*
To our most valiant brother. So much for him.   25

[*Enter* VOLTEMAND *and* CORNELIUS.]

Now for ourself and for this time of meeting.
Thus much the business is: we have here writ°   *written*
To Norway,° uncle of young Fortinbras—   *(the king of Norway)*
Who, impotent and bedrid,° scarcely hears   *bedridden*
Of this his nephew's purpose—to suppress°   *stop* 30
His further gait herein, in that the levies,°   *proceedings*
The lists, and full proportions are all made
Out of his subject;° and we here dispatch   *from among his subjects*
You, good Cornelius, and you, Voltemand,
For bearers of this greeting to old Norway,   35
Giving to you no further personal power
To business° with the King, more than the scope   *to do business*
Of these dilated articles° allow.   *detailed points*

[*Gives a paper.*]

Farewell, and let your haste commend your° duty.   *show your sense of*
CORNELIUS, VOLTEMAND: In that, and all things, will we
        show our duty.   40
KING: We doubt it nothing.° Heartily farewell.   *not at all*

[VOLTEMAND *and* CORNELIUS *leave.*]

And now, Laertes, what's the news with you?
You told us of some suit.° What is't, Laertes?   *request*
You cannot speak of reason to the Dane°   *(the Danish king)*
And lose your voice.° What wouldst thou beg, Laertes,   *speak in vain* 45

That shall not be my offer, not thy asking?
The head is not more native° to the heart,   *akin*
The hand more instrumental to the mouth,
Than is the throne of Denmark to thy father.
What wouldst thou have, Laertes?

LAERTES: My dread lord,   50
　Your leave° and favor to return to France,   *permission*
　From whence° though willingly I came to Denmark   *from where*
　To show my duty in your coronation,
　Yet now I must confess, that duty done,
　My thoughts and wishes bend again toward France   55
　And bow them to your gracious leave and pardon.°   *submit to your permission*

KING: Have you your father's leave? What says Polonius?

POLONIUS: He hath, my lord, wrung from me my slow
　　leave°   *reluctant approval*
　By laborsome petition, and at last
　Upon his will I sealed my hard consent.   60
　I do beseech you give him leave to go.

KING: Take thy fair hour,° Laertes. Time be thine,   *use the favorable hour*
　And thy best graces spend it at thy will!
　But now, my cousin Hamlet, and my son—

HAMLET [*aside*]: A little more than kin, and less than   65
　　kind!°   *(a play on "one's kind"*
                                                   and "being kind")

KING: How is it that the clouds still hang on you?

HAMLET: Not so, my lord. I am too much in the sun.

QUEEN: Good Hamlet, cast thy nighted color off,
　And let thine eye look like a friend on Denmark.°   *(the king of Denmark)*
　Do not for ever with thy vailèd° lids   *lowered* 70
　Seek for thy noble father in the dust.
　Thou know'st 'tis common,° all that lives must die,   *common experience*
　Passing through nature to eternity.

HAMLET: Ay, madam, it is common.

QUEEN: If it be,
　Why seems it so particular with thee?   75

HAMLET: Seems, madam? Nay, it is. I know not "seems."
　'Tis not alone my inky° cloak, good mother,   *ink-black*
　Nor customary suits of solemn black,
　Nor windy suspiration° of forced breath,   *heavy sighs*
　No, nor the fruitful river in the eye,   80
　Nor the dejected havior of the visage,°   *behavior of the face*
　Together with all forms, moods, shapes of grief,
　That can denote me truly. These indeed seem,
　For they are actions that a man might play;
　But I have that within which passeth show—   85
　These but the trappings and the suits of woe.

KING: 'Tis sweet and commendable in your nature,
　　Hamlet,
　To give these mourning duties to your father;
　But you must know, your father lost a father;

That father lost, lost his, and the survivor bound   90
In filial obligation for some term
To do obsequious sorrow.° But to persever   *to show downcast grief*
In obstinate condolement° is a course   *stubborn grieving*
Of impious stubbornness. 'Tis unmanly grief;
It shows a will most incorrect° to heaven,   *rebellious* 95
A heart unfortified, a mind impatient,
An understanding simple and unschooled;
For what we know must be, and is as common
As any the most vulgar° thing to sense,   *ordinary*
Why should we in our peevish opposition   100
Take it to heart? Fie! 'tis a fault to heaven,
A fault against the dead, a fault to nature,
To reason most absurd, whose common theme
Is death of fathers, and who still° hath cried,   *which always*
From the first corse° till he that died today,   *corpse* 105
"This must be so." We pray you throw to earth
This unprevailing woe, and think of us
As of a father; for let the world take note
You are the most immediate° to our throne,   *next in line*
And with no less nobility of love   110
Than that which dearest father bears his son
Do I impart toward you. For your intent
In going back to school in Wittenberg,
It is most retrograde to our desire;°   *the opposite of our wish*
And we beseech you, bend you to remain   115
Here in the cheer and comfort of our eye,
Our chiefest courtier, cousin, and our son.
QUEEN: Let not thy mother lose her prayers, Hamlet:
I pray thee° stay with us, go not to Wittenberg.   *I ask you to*
HAMLET: I shall in all my best obey you, madam.   120
KING: Why, 'tis a loving and a fair reply.
Be as ourself in Denmark. Madam, come.
This gentle and unforced accord° of Hamlet   *consent*
Sits smiling to my heart; in grace whereof,°   *in honor of which*
No jocund health° that Denmark drinks today   *joyful toast* 125
But the great cannon to the clouds shall tell,
And the King's rouse the heaven shall bruit again,°   *the sky shall echo the*
Respeaking earthly thunder. Come away.   *king's celebration*

     [Flourish of trumpets. All leave except HAMLET.]

HAMLET: O that this too too sullied flesh would melt,
Thaw, and resolve° itself into a dew!   *dissolve* 130
Or that the Everlasting had not fixed
His canon° 'gainst self-slaughter! O God! God!   *law*
How weary, stale, flat, and unprofitable
Seem to me all the uses of this world!
Fie on't! ah, fie!° 'Tis an unweeded garden   *for shame* 135
That grows to seed; things rank and gross in nature

Possess it merely.° That it should come to this!   *have taken it over*
But two months dead—nay, not so much, not two!
So excellent a king, that was to this
Hyperion to a satyr;° so loving to my mother   *like a god compared to a being half goat* 140
That he might not beteem° the winds of heaven   *allow*
Visit her face too roughly. Heaven and earth!
Must I remember? Why, she would hang on him
As if increase of appetite had grown
By what it fed on; and yet, within a month—   145
Let me not think on't! Frailty, thy name is woman!—
A little month, or ere° those shoes were old   *before*
With which she followed my poor father's body
Like Niobe, all tears—why she, even she
(O God! a beast that wants discourse of reason°   *lacks reasoning power* 150
Would have mourned longer) married with my uncle;
My father's brother, but no more like my father
Than I to Hercules. Within a month,
Ere yet the salt of most unrighteous tears
Had left the flushing of her gallèd eyes,°   *stopped reddening her inflamed eyes* 155
She married. O, most wicked speed, to post°   *hurry*
With such dexterity° to incestuous sheets!   *agility*
It is not, nor it cannot come to good.
But break my heart, for I must hold my tongue!

[*Enter* HORATIO, MARCELLUS, *and* BERNARDO.]

HORATIO: Hail to your lordship!
HAMLET: I am glad to see you well.   160
     Horatio—or I do forget myself!
HORATIO: The same, my lord, and your poor servant ever.
HAMLET: Sir, my good friend—I'll change that name with
     you.
     And what make you from° Wittenberg, Horatio?   *are you doing away from*
     Marcellus?   165
MARCELLUS: My good lord!
HAMLET: I am very glad to see you.—[*to* BERNARDO] Good
     even, sir.—
     But what, in faith, make you from Wittenberg?
HORATIO: A truant disposition, good my lord.
HAMLET: I would not hear your enemy say so,   170
     Nor shall you do my ear that violence
     To make it truster of° your own report   *to make it trust*
     Against yourself. I know you are no truant.
     But what is your affair in Elsinore?
     We'll teach you to drink deep ere° you depart.   *before* 175
HORATIO: My lord, I came to see your father's funeral.
HAMLET: I prithee do not mock me, fellow student,
     I think it was to see my mother's wedding.
HORATIO: Indeed, my lord, it followed hard upon.°   *closely after*
HAMLET: Thrift, thrift, Horatio! The funeral baked meats   180

Did coldly furnish forth° the marriage tables.　　　　　　*served as cold cuts for*
Would I° had met my dearest foe in heaven　　　　　　　　　*I wish I had*
Or ever° I had seen that day, Horatio!　　　　　　　　　　*before*
My father—methinks I see my father.
HORATIO: O, where, my lord?
HAMLET:　　　　　　　　　　　In my mind's eye, Horatio.　　　　　　　　185
HORATIO: I saw him once. He was a goodly king.
HAMLET: He was a man, take him for all in all.
　I shall not look upon his like again.
HORATIO: My lord, I think I saw him yesternight.
HAMLET: Saw? who?　　　　　　　　　　　　　　　　　　　　　190
HORATIO: My lord, the King your father.
HAMLET:　　　　　　　　　　　　　　　The King my father?
HORATIO: Season your admiration° for a while　　　　　*control your amazement*
　With an attent° ear, till I may deliver,　　　　　　　　*attentive*
　Upon the witness of these gentlemen,
　This marvel to you.
HAMLET:　　　　　　　　　For God's love let me hear!　　　　　　　195
HORATIO: Two nights together had these gentlemen
　(Marcellus and Bernardo) on their watch
　In the dead vast° and middle of the night　　　　　　　*vast emptiness*
　Been thus encountered. A figure like your father,
　Armed at point exactly, cap-a-pe,°　　　　　　　　　*head to foot* 200
　Appears before them and with solemn march
　Goes slow and stately by them. Thrice he walked
　By their oppressed and fear-surprisèd eyes,
　Within his truncheon's length; whilst they, distilled°　　　　*changed*
　Almost to jelly with the act of fear,　　　　　　　　　　205
　Stand dumb and speak not to him. This to me
　In dreadful secrecy impart they did,°　　　　　　　　*they told*
　And I with them the third night kept the watch;
　Where, as they had delivered,° both in time,　　　　*reported*
　Form of the thing, each word made true and good,　　　　210
　The apparition comes. I knew your father:
　These hands are not more like.
HAMLET:　　　　　　　　　　　But where was this?
MARCELLUS: My lord, upon the platform where we watched.
HAMLET: Did you not speak to it?
HORATIO:　　　　　　　　　　　My lord, I did;
　But answer made it none. Yet once methought　　　　　215
　It lifted up its head and did address
　Itself to motion,° like as it would speak;　　　　　　*prepared to move*
　But even then the morning cock crew° loud,　　　　　*crowed*
　And at the sound it shrunk in haste away
　And vanished from our sight.
HAMLET:　　　　　　　　　　'Tis very strange.　　　　　　　220
HORATIO: As I do live, my honored lord, 'tis true;
　And we did think it writ down in our duty
　To let you know of it.

HAMLET: Indeed, indeed, sirs, but this troubles me.
    Hold you the watch tonight?   225
BOTH [MARCELLUS *and* BERNARDO]: We do, my lord.
HAMLET: Armed, say you?
BOTH: Armed, my lord.
HAMLET: From top to toe?
BOTH: My lord, from head to foot.
HAMLET: Then saw you not his face?   230
HORATIO: O, yes, my lord! He wore his beaver° up.   *the face cover of his helmet*
HAMLET: What, looked he frowningly?
HORATIO: A countenance more in sorrow than in anger.
HAMLET: Pale or red?
HORATIO: Nay, very pale.
HAMLET: And fixed his eyes upon you?   235
HORATIO: Most constantly.
HAMLET: I would I had° been there.   *wish I could have*
HORATIO: It would have much amazed you.
HAMLET: Very like,° very like. Stayed it long?   *very likely*
HORATIO: While one with moderate haste might tell a
    hundred.   240
BOTH: Longer, longer.
HORATIO: Not when I saw't.
HAMLET: His beard was grizzled—no?
HORATIO: It was, as I have seen it in his life,
    A sable silvered.°   *black with silver touches*
HAMLET: I will watch tonight.
    Perchance° 'twill walk again.   *perhaps*
HORATIO: I warrant it will.
HAMLET: If it assume my noble father's person,   245
    I'll speak to it, though hell itself should gape
    And bid me hold my peace.° I pray you all,   *tell me to be quiet*
    If you have hitherto concealed this sight,
    Let it be tenable in your silence still;°   *go on keeping it silent*
    And whatsoever else shall hap° tonight,   *happen* 250
    Give it an understanding but no tongue.°   *think but do not speak about it*
    I will requite° your loves. So, fare you well.   *reward*
    Upon the platform, 'twixt° eleven and twelve,   *between*
    I'll visit you.
ALL: Our duty to your honor.
HAMLET: Your loves, as mine to you. Farewell.   255

[*All but* HAMLET *leave.*]

My father's spirit—in arms? All is not well.
I doubt° some foul play. Would the night were come!   *suspect*
Till then sit still, my soul. Foul deeds will rise,
Though all the earth overwhelm them, to men's eyes.

[*He leaves.*]

SCENE 3. Elsinore. POLONIUS' house.

[*Enter* LAERTES *and* OPHELIA.]

LAERTES: My necessaries are embarked.° Farewell.   luggage is on board
  And, sister, as the winds give benefit
  And convoy is assistant,° do not sleep,   ships are available
  But let me hear from you.
OPHELIA: Do you doubt that?
LAERTES: For Hamlet, and the trifling of his favor,   5
  Hold it a fashion, and a toy in blood;°   think of it as a fad and whim
  A violet in the youth of primy nature,°   nature at springtime
  Forward,° not permanent; sweet, not lasting;   fleeting
  The perfume and suppliance° of a minute;   aroma and pastime
  No more.
OPHELIA: No more but so?
LAERTES: Think it no more.   10
  For nature crescent° does not grow alone   a maturing person
  In thews and bulk, but as this temple waxes,°   not only in body, but as it grows
  The inward service of the mind and soul
  Grows wide withal.° Perhaps he loves you now,   along with it
  And now no soil nor cautel° doth besmirch   no stain or deceit   15
  The virtue of his will; but you must fear,
  His greatness weighed,° his will is not his own,   when his status is weighed
  For he himself is subject to his birth.°   the role he was born into
  He may not, as unvalued persons do,
  Carve for himself, for on his choice depends   20
  The safety and health of his whole state,
  And therefore must his choice be circumscribed°   limited
  Unto the voice and yielding of that body
  Whereof he is the head. Then if he says he loves you,
  It fits your wisdom so far to believe it   25
  As he in his particular act and place
  May give his saying deed,° which is no further   follow word with deed
  Than the main voice of Denmark goes withal.°   public opinion permits
  Then weigh what loss your honor may sustain
  If with too credent ear you list° his songs,   too willing ear you listen to   30
  Or lose your heart, or your chaste treasure open
  To his unmastered importunity.°   uncontrolled urging
  Fear it, Ophelia, fear it, my dear sister,
  And keep you in the rear of your affection,
  Out of the shot° and danger of desire.   out of firing range   35
  The chariest° maid is prodigal° enough   most careful / loose
  If she unmask her beauty to the moon.
  Virtue itself scapes° not calumnious strokes.   escapes
  The canker galls the infants of the spring°   worm ruins spring flowers
  Too oft before their buttons be° disclosed,   their buds are   40
  And in the morn and liquid dew of youth
  Contagious blastments are most imminent.

Be wary then; best safety lies in fear.
Youth to itself° rebels, though none else near.   *by itself*
OPHELIA: I shall the effect of this good lesson keep   45
  As watchman to my heart. But, good my brother,
  Do not as some ungracious pastors° do,   *faithless priests*
  Show me the steep and thorny way to heaven,
  Whiles, like a puffed and reckless libertine,°   *pleasure lover*
  Himself the primrose path of dalliance treads   50
  And recks not his own rede.°   *disregards his own counsel*
LAERTES: O, fear me not!°   *do not worry about me*

[*Enter* POLONIUS.]

  I stay too long. But here my father comes.
  A double blessing is a double grace;
  Occasion smiles upon a second leave.°   *leave-taking*
POLONIUS: Yet here, Laertes? Aboard, aboard, for shame!   55
  The wind sits in the shoulder of your sail,°   *wind is favorable*
  And you are stayed for.° There—my blessing with thee!   *waited for*
  And these few precepts in thy memory
  Look thou character.° Give thy thoughts no tongue,   *make sure to record*
  Nor any unproportioned thought his act.°   *its action*   60
  Be thou familiar,° but by no means vulgar: *mingling with all*
  Those friends thou hast, and their adoption tried,°   *after testing them*
  Grapple them to thy soul with hoops of steel;
  But do not dull thy palm° with entertainment   *wear out your hand*
  Of each new-hatched, unfledged comrade. Beware   65
  Of entrance to a quarrel; but being in,
  Bear't that the opposed° may beware of thee.   *act so that the opponent*
  Give every man thine ear, but few thy voice;
  Take each man's censure, but reserve thy judgment.
  Costly thy habit as thy purse can buy,°   *buy clothes you can afford* 70
  But not expressed in fancy; rich, not gaudy;
  For the apparel oft proclaims the man,
  And they in France of the best rank and station
  Are most select and generous, chief in that.
  Neither a borrower nor a lender be;   75
  For loan oft loses both itself and friend,
  And borrowing dulls the edge of husbandry.°   *undermines good management*
  This above all: to thine own self be true,
  And it must follow, as the night the day,
  Thou canst not then be false to any man.   80
  Farewell. My blessing season this in thee!
LAERTES: Most humbly do I take my leave, my lord.
POLONIUS: The time invites you. Go, your servants tend.°   *wait*
LAERTES: Farewell, Ophelia, and remember well
  What I have said to you.
OPHELIA: 'Tis in my memory locked,   85
  And you yourself shall keep the key of it.
LAERTES: Farewell.

[*He leaves.*]

POLONIUS: What is't, Ophelia, he hath said to you?

OPHELIA: So please you, something touching the Lord
    Hamlet.

POLONIUS: Marry, well bethought!°   *good thinking*   90
    'Tis told me he hath very oft of late
    Given private time to you, and you yourself
    Have of your audience been most free and
        bounteous.°   *have been freely available*
    If it be so—as so 'tis put on me,°   *as I've been told*
    And that in way of caution—I must tell you   95
    You do not understand yourself so clearly
    As it behooves° my daughter and your honor.   *as is required of*
    What is between you? Give me up the truth.

OPHELIA: He hath, my lord, of late made many tenders°   *given many signs*
    Of his affection to me.   100

POLONIUS: Affection? Pooh! You speak like a green girl,
    Unsifted° in such perilous circumstance.   *inexperienced*
    Do you believe his tenders, as you call them?

OPHELIA: I do not know, my lord, what I should think.

POLONIUS: Marry, I will teach you! Think yourself a baby   105
    That you have taken these tenders for true pay,
    Which are not sterling.° Tender yourself more dearly,   *not true currency*
    Or (not to crack the wind of the poor phrase,
    Running it thus) you'll tender me° a fool.   *make me (or you) seem*

OPHELIA: My lord, he hath importuned me with love   110
    In honorable fashion.

POLONIUS: Ay, fashion you may call it. Go to, go to!

OPHELIA: And hath given countenance to his speech, my lord,
    With almost all the holy vows of heaven.

POLONIUS: Ay, springes to catch woodcocks!° I do know,   *traps for birds* 115
    When the blood burns, how prodigal the soul
    Lends the tongue vows. These blazes, daughter,
    Giving more light than heat, extinct° in both   *ready to go out*
    Even in their promise, as it is a-making,
    You must not take for fire. From this time   120
    Be somewhat scanter of your maiden presence.°   *make yourself scarcer*
    Set your entreatments at a higher rate
    Than a command to parley.° For Lord Hamlet,   *a mere summons to talk*
    Believe so much in him, that he is young,
    And with a larger tether may he walk   125
    Than may be given you. In few,° Ophelia,   *in short*
    Do not believe his vows; for they are brokers,
    Not of that dye which their investments° show,   *appearances*
    But mere implorators of unholy suits,°   *instigators of dishonest proposals*
    Breathing like sanctified and pious bawds,°   *pimps* 130
    The better to beguile. This is for all:
    I would not, in plain terms, from this time forth
    Have you so slander any moment° leisure   *so misuse any moment's*

As to give words or talk with the Lord Hamlet.
Look to't, I charge you. Come your ways.   135
OPHELIA: I shall obey, my lord.

[*They leave.*]

SCENE 4. Elsinore Castle. The platform of the guard.

[*Enter* HAMLET, HORATIO, *and* MARCELLUS.]

HAMLET: The air bites shrewdly; it is very cold.
HORATIO: It is a nipping and an eager air.
HAMLET: What hour now?
HORATIO: I think it lacks of° twelve.   *It's not quite*
MARCELLUS: No, it is struck.
HORATIO: Indeed? I heard it not. It then draws near the season°   *near the time*   5
Wherein the spirit held his wont to walk.°   *used to walk*

[*A flourish of trumpets, and two cannons go off.*]

What does this mean, my lord?
HAMLET: The King doth wake tonight and takes his rouse,°   *stays up to carouse*
Keeps wassail, and the swaggering upspring reels,°   *drinks and dances*
And, as he drains his draughts of Rhenish° down,   *Rhine wine*   10
The kettledrum and trumpet thus bray out
The triumph of his pledge.
HORATIO: Is it a custom?
HAMLET: Ay, marry, is't;
But to my mind, though I am native here
And to the manner born, it is a custom   15
More honored in the breach° than the observance.   *in disregarding it*
This heavy-headed revel east and west
Makes us traduced and taxed of° other nations;   *defamed and blamed by*
They call us drunkards and with swinish phrase
Soil our addition;° and indeed it takes   *stain our reputation*   20
From our achievements, though performed at height,
The pith and marrow of our attribute.°   *the core of our good name*
So oft it chances in particular men
That for some vicious mole of nature in them,
As in their birth—wherein they are not guilty,   25
Since nature cannot choose his origin—
By their overgrowth of some complexion,°   *some exaggerated trait*
Oft breaking down the pales and forts° of reason,   *defenses*
Or by some habit that too much overleavens
The form of plausive° manners, that these men   *acceptable*   30
Carrying, I say, the stamp of one defect,
Being nature's livery,° or fortune's star—   *which nature has dressed them in*
Their virtues else (be they as pure as grace,
As infinite as man may undergo)
Shall in the general censure take corruption°   *in everyone's opinion be tarnished*   35
From that particular fault. The dram° of evil   *drop*

Doth all the noble substance often dout°   *drive out*
To his own scandal.°   *its complete disgrace*

[*Enter* GHOST.]

HORATIO: Look, my lord, it comes!
HAMLET: Angels and ministers of grace defend us!
    Be thou° a spirit of health or goblin damned,   *whether you are*   40
    Bring with thee airs from heaven or blasts from hell,
    Be thy intents wicked or charitable,
    Thou com'st in such a questionable shape
    That I will speak to thee. I'll call thee Hamlet,
    King, father, royal Dane. O, answer me!   45
    Let me not burst in ignorance, but tell
    Why thy canonized° bones, hearsed in death,   *sanctified and duly buried*
    Have burst their cerements;° why the sepulchre   *left their burial shroud*
    Wherein we saw thee quietly inurned,
    Hath oped his° ponderous and marble jaws   *opened its*   50
    To cast thee up again. What may this mean
    That thou, dead corpse, again in complete steel,°   *in full armor*
    Revisits thus the glimpses of the moon,
    Making night hideous, and we fools of nature
    So horridly to shake our disposition°   *upset our reason*   55
    With thoughts beyond the reaches of our souls?
    Say, why is this? wherefore? What should we do?

[GHOST *beckons* HAMLET.]

HORATIO: It beckons you to go away with it,
    As if it some impartment° did desire   *communication*
    To you alone.
MARCELLUS: Look with what courteous action   60
    It waves you to a more removed ground.
    But do not go with it!
HORATIO: No, by no means!
HAMLET: It will not speak. Then will I follow it.
HORATIO: Do not, my Lord!
HAMLET: Why, what should be the fear?
    I do not set my life at a pin's fee;°   *the price of a pin*   65
    And for my soul, what can it do to that,
    Being a thing immortal as itself?
    It waves me forth again. I'll follow it.
HORATIO: What if it tempt you toward the flood, my lord,
    Or to the dreadful summit of the cliff   70
    That beetles° over his base into the sea,   *juts out*
    And there assume some other, horrible form
    Which might deprive your sovereignty of reason°   *overthrow your sovereign reason*
    And draw you into madness? Think of it.
    The very place puts toys of desperation,°   *desperate thoughts*   75
    Without more motive, into every brain

That looks so many fathoms to the sea
And hears it roar beneath.
HAMLET: It waves me still.
   Go on, I'll follow thee.
MARCELLUS: You shall not go, my lord.
HAMLET: Hold off your hands!   80
HORATIO: Be ruled, you shall not go.
HAMLET: My fate cries out
   And makes each petty artery in this body
   As hardy as the Nemean lion's nerve.°   *lion's sinews*

[GHOST *beckons*.]

Still am I called. Unhand me, gentlemen—
By heaven, I'll make a Ghost of him that lets° me!   *stops* 85
I say, away!—Go on, I'll follow thee.

[GHOST *and* HAMLET *leave*.]

HORATIO: He waxes° desperate with imagination.   *grows*
MARCELLUS: Let's follow; 'tis not fit thus to obey him.
HORATIO: Have after.° To what issue will this come?   *let's go after him*
MARCELLUS: Something is rotten in the state of Denmark.   90
HORATIO: Heaven will direct it.
MARCELLUS: Nay, let's follow him.

[*They leave*.]

SCENE 5. Same. Another part of the ramparts.

[*Enter* GHOST *and* HAMLET.]

HAMLET: Wither° wilt thou lead me? Speak, I'll go no further.   *where*
GHOST: Mark me.°   *listen carefully*
HAMLET: I will.
GHOST: My hour is almost come,
   When I to sulphurous and tormenting flames
   Must render up myself.
HAMLET: Alas, poor ghost!
GHOST: Pity me not, but lend thy serious hearing   5
   To what I shall unfold.
HAMLET: Speak, I am bound to hear.
GHOST: So art thou to revenge, when thou shalt hear.
HAMLET: What?
GHOST: I am thy father's spirit,
   Doomed for a certain term to walk the night,   10
   And for the day confined to fast in fires,
   Till the foul crimes done in my days of nature
   Are burnt and purged away. But that I am forbid
   To tell the secrets of my prison house,
   I could a tale unfold whose lightest word   15
   Would harrow up thy soul, freeze thy young blood,
   Make thy two eyes, like stars, start from their spheres,

Thy knotted and combined locks to part,
And each particular hair to stand on end
Like quills upon the fretful porpentine.°   *angry porcupine*   20
But this eternal blazon° must not be   *this news of the supernatural world*
To ears of flesh and blood. List, list, O, list!
If thou didst ever thy dear father love—
HAMLET: O God!
GHOST: Revenge his foul and most unnatural murder.   25
HAMLET: Murder?
GHOST: Murder most foul, as in the best it is;
But this most foul, strange, and unnatural.
HAMLET: Hast me to know't, that I, with wings as swift
As meditation or the thoughts of love,   30
May sweep to my revenge.
GHOST: I find thee apt;
And duller shouldst thou be than the fat weed
That rots itself in ease on Lethe° wharf,   *river of oblivion*
Wouldst thou not stir° in this. Now, Hamlet, hear: *take action*
'Tis given out that, sleeping in my orchard,   35
A serpent stung me; so the whole ear of Denmark
Is by a forgèd process° of my death   *false account*
Rankly abused; but know, thou noble youth,
The serpent that did sting thy father's life
Now wears his crown.
HAMLET: O my prophetic soul!   40
My uncle?
GHOST: Ay, that incestuous, that adulterate beast,
With witchcraft of his wit, with traitorous gifts—
O wicked wit and gifts, that have the power
So to seduce!—won to his shameful lust   45
The will of my most seeming-virtuous queen.
O Hamlet, what a falling-off was there,
From me, whose love was of that dignity
That it went hand in hand even with the vow
I made to her in marriage, and to decline°   *to lower herself*   50
Upon a wretch whose natural gifts were poor
To those of mine!
But virtue, as it never will be moved,
Though lewdness court it in a shape of heaven,
So lust, though to a radiant angel linked,   55
Will sate itself° in a celestial bed   *will grow bored*
And prey on garbage.
But soft! methinks I scent the morning air.
Brief let me be. Sleeping within my orchard,
My custom always of the afternoon,   60
Upon my secure° hour thy uncle stole,   *thought to be safe*
With juice of cursed hebenon° in a vial,   *poison plant*
And in the porches of my ears did pour
The leperous distilment,° whose effect   *deadly liquid*

Holds such an enmity with° blood of man   *is so at war with*   65
That swift as quicksilver it courses° through   *runs*
The natural gates and alleys of the body,
And with a sudden vigor it doth posset°   *curdle*
And curd, like eager droppings° into milk,   *acid drops*
The thin and wholesome blood; so did it mine,   70
And a most instant tetter barked about,°   *sudden rash covered*
Most lazar-like,° with vile and loathsome crust   *like a leper*
All my smooth body.
Thus was I, sleeping, by a brother's hand
Of life, of crown, of queen, at once dispatched;   75
Cut off even in the blossoms of my sin,°   *with my sins in full flower*
Unhouseled, disappointed, unaneled,°   *without sacrament or*
No reckoning made, but sent to my account   *forgiveness of sins*
With all my imperfections on my head.
HAMLET: O, horrible! O, horrible! most horrible!   80
GHOST: If thou hast nature in thee, bear it not.
    Let not the royal bed of Denmark be
    A couch for luxury° and damnèd incest.   *bed for licentiousness*
    But, howsoever thou pursuest this act,
    Taint not thy mind, nor let thy soul contrive   85
    Against thy mother aught.° Leave her to heaven,   *anything against your mother*
    And to those thorns that in her bosom lodge
    To prick and sting her. Fare thee well at once,
    The glowworm shows the matin° to be near   *morning*
    And gins to pale his uneffectual fire.°   *begins to make it seem pale*   90
    Adieu, adieu, adieu! Remember me.

                                    [He leaves.]

HAMLET: O all you host of heaven! O earth! What else?
    And shall I couple hell?° O fie! Hold, hold, my heart!   *shall I add hell*
    And you, my sinews, grow not instant old,
    But bear me stiffly up. Remember thee?   95
    Ay, thou poor ghost, while memory holds a seat
    In this distracted globe.° Remember thee?   *perturbed (globelike) head*
    Yea, from the table° of my memory   *record*
    I'll wipe away all trivial fond records,°   *foolish entries*
    All saws° of books, all forms, all pressures past   *wise sayings*   100
    That youth and observation copied there,
    And thy commandment all alone shall live
    Within the book and volume of my brain,
    Unmixed with baser matter. Yes, by heaven!
    O most pernicious woman!   105
    O villain, villain, smiling, damnèd villain!
    My tables, my tables!° Meet it is° I set it down   *note-keeping slates/it's right*
    That one may smile, and smile, and be a villain;
    At least I'm sure it may be so in Denmark.

    [Writes.]

So, uncle, there you are. Now to my word: 110
  It is "Adieu, adieu! Remember me."
  I have sworn't.
HORATIO [*within*]: My lord, my lord!

[*Enter* HORATIO *and* MARCELLUS.]

MARCELLUS: Lord Hamlet!
HORATIO: Heaven secure
  him!°   *keep him safe*
HAMLET: So be it!
MARCELLUS: Illo, ho, ho, my lord!°   *(falconer's call)* 115
HAMLET: Hillo, ho, ho, boy! Come, bird, come.
MARCELLUS: How is't, my noble lord?
HORATIO: What news, my lord?
HAMLET: O, wonderful!
HORATIO: Good my lord, tell it.
HAMLET: No, you'll reveal it.
HORATIO: Not I, my lord, by heaven!
MARCELLUS: Nor I, my lord.   120
HAMLET: How say you then? Would heart of man once
  think it?
  But you'll be secret?
BOTH: Ay, by heaven, my lord.
HAMLET: There's never a villain dwelling in all Denmark
  But he's an arrant knave.°   *utter scoundrel*
HORATIO: There needs no ghost, my lord, come from the grave   125
  To tell us this.
HAMLET: Why, right! You are in the right!
  And so, without more circumstance° at all,   *ceremony*
  I hold it fit that we shake hands and part;
  You, as your business and desires shall point you,
  For every man hath business and desire,
  Such as it is; and for my own poor part,   130
  Look you, I'll go pray.
HORATIO: These are but wild and whirling words, my lord.
HAMLET: I am sorry they offend you, heartily;
  Yes, faith, heartily.
HORATIO: There's no offense, my lord.   135
HAMLET: Yes, by Saint Patrick, but there is, Horatio,
  And much offense too. Touching this vision here,
  It is an honest ghost,° that let me tell you.   *(not an evil spirit)*
  For° your desire to know what is between us,   *as for*
  O'ermaster't° as you may. And now, good friends,   *overcome it* 140
  As you are friends, scholars, and soldiers,
  Give° me one poor request.   *grant*
HORATIO: What is't, my lord? We will.
HAMLET: Never make known what you have seen tonight.
BOTH: My lord, we will not.
HAMLET: Nay, but swear't.

HORATIO: In faith,   145
  My lord, not I.

MARCELLUS: Nor I, my lord—in faith.

HAMLET: Upon my sword.

MARCELLUS: We have sworn, my lord, already.

HAMLET: Indeed, upon my sword, indeed.

  [GHOST *cries under the stage*.]

GHOST: Swear.

HAMLET: Aha boy, say'st thou so? Art thou there, true-penny?   150
  Come on! You hear this fellow in the cellarage.
  Consent to swear.

HORATIO: Propose the oath, my lord.

HAMLET: Never to speak of this that you have seen.
  Swear by my sword.

GHOST [*beneath*]: Swear.   155

HAMLET: Hic et ubique?° Then we'll shift our ground.   *(Latin) here and everywhere*
  Come hither, gentlemen,
  And lay your hands again upon my sword.
  Never to speak of this that you have heard:
  Swear by my sword.   160

GHOST [*beneath*]: Swear by his sword.

HAMLET: Well said, old mole! Canst work in the earth so fast?
  A worthy pioner!° Once more remove, good friends.   *miner*

HORATIO: O day and night, but this is wondrous strange!

HAMLET: And therefore as a stranger give it welcome.   165
  There are more things in heaven and earth, Horatio,
  Than are dreamt of in your philosophy.
  But come!
  Here, as before, never, so help you mercy,
  How strange or odd soever° I bear myself   *however strange or odd*   170
  (As I perchance hereafter shall think meet°   *perhaps will think it right*
  To put an antic disposition on),°   *to act very strange*
  That you, at such times seeing me, never shall,
  With arms encumbered° thus, or this head-shake,   *folded*
  Or by pronouncing of some doubtful phrase,   175
  As "Well, well, we know," or "We could, an if we
    would,"
  Or "If we list° to speak," or "There be, an if they might,"   *if we wanted*
  Or such ambiguous giving out, to note
  That you know aught of me—this not to do,
  So grace and mercy at your most need help you,   180
  Swear.

GHOST [*beneath*]: Swear.

  [*They swear.*]

HAMLET: Rest, rest, perturbèd spirit! So, gentlemen,
  With all my love I do commend me to you;
  And what so poor a man as Hamlet is   185

May do to express his love and friending° to you,   *friendship*
God willing, shall not lack. Let us go in together;
And still° your fingers on your lips, I pray.   *always*
The time is out of joint. O cursèd spite
That ever I was born to set it right!   190
Nay, come, let's go together.

[*They leave.*]

The Receptive Reader

1. (Act One, Scene 1) Shakespeare treats the sighting of the ghost in care-fully worked-out detail. Why do you think the playwright shows us that the guards are punctual for the changing of the watch? What picture do we get of Horatio here? What are his credentials; what is his attitude? Is he superstitious? How much of contemporary spirit lore can we reconstruct from this scene? (Why do you think the playwright kept Hamlet out of these first encounters with the ghost of his murdered father?)

2. (Act One, Scene 2) In this scene, what first impression do you form of Hamlet as the central character and *protagonist?* What different sides of his per-sonality do you see in his interaction with the king and queen, in his solilo-quies and asides, and in his interaction with Horatio? How does Hamlet react to his friends' reports of the ghost?

3. (Act One, Scene 3) What first impressions do you form of Polonius, Laertes, and Ophelia as major *supporting characters* in the play? How do Polo-nius and Laertes treat Ophelia, and how does she respond?

4. (Act One, Scenes 4 and 5) What are the major elements in the ghost's in-dictment of Claudius and Queen Gertrude? (How implicated or guilty do you think she is?) How do Hamlet's behavior and mood change as he first encoun-ters the ghost, after he listens to the ghost's charges, and again when his asso-ciates rejoin him? How do you explain his irreverent behavior toward the ghost at the end of the scene? What does Hamlet say about the pretended madness that becomes a major strand in the play? How does he begin to act out his "antic disposition"?

The Personal Dimension

Do you recognize any of the people in this play? Can you identify with or re-late to any of them? Do you begin to understand their situation, their concerns, their motives?

Act Two

SCENE 1. Elsinore. POLONIUS' house.

[*Enter* POLONIUS *and* REYNALDO.]

POLONIUS: Give him this money and these notes, Reynaldo.
REYNALDO: I will, my lord.
POLONIUS: You shall do marvelous wisely, good Reynaldo,

Before you visit him, to make inquire
Of his behavior.

REYNALDO: My lord, I did intend it.   5

POLONIUS: Marry, well said, very well said. Look you, sir,
Inquire me first what Danskers° are in Paris;   *Danish visitors*
And how, and who, what means, and where they keep,
What company, at what expense; and finding
By this encompassment and drift of question°   *roundabout questioning*   10
That they do know my son, come you more nearer
Than your particular demands will touch it.
Take you,° as 'twere, some distant knowledge of him;   *pretend*
As thus, "I know his father and his friends,
And in part him." Do you mark this, Reynaldo?   15

REYNALDO: Ay, very well, my lord.

POLONIUS: "And in part, him, but," you may say, "not well.
But if't be he I mean, he's very wild,
Addicted so and so"; and there put on him
What forgeries° you please; marry,° none so rank   *falsehoods/truly*   20
As may dishonor him—take heed of that;
But, sir, such wanton, wild, and usual slips
As are companions noted and most known
To youth and liberty.

REYNALDO: As gaming, my lord.

POLONIUS: Ay, or drinking, fencing, swearing, quarrelling,   25
Drabbing.° You may go so far.   *running after loose women*

REYNALDO: My lord, that would dishonor him.

POLONIUS: Faith, no, as you may season it in the charge.°   *word it mildly*
You must not put another scandal on him,
That he is open to incontinency.°   *loose living*   30
That's not my meaning. But breathe his faults so quaintly°   *carefully*
That they may seem the taints of liberty,
The flash and outbreak of a fiery mind,
A savageness in unreclaimèd blood,
Of general assault.°   *commonly befalling young people*   35

REYNALDO: But, my good lord—

POLONIUS: Wherefore should you do this?

REYNALDO: Ay, my lord,
I would know that.

POLONIUS: Marry, sir, here's my drift,
And I believe it is a fetch of warrant.°   *permissible ploy*
You laying these slight sullies on my son
As 'twere a thing a little soiled in the working,   40
Mark you,
Your party in converse,° him you would sound,   *conversation*
Having ever seen in the prenominate° crimes   *before-named*
The youth you breathe of guilty, be assured
He closes with you in this consequence:°   *chimes in in this conclusion*   45
"Good sir," or so, or "friend," or "gentleman"—

According to the phrase or the addition°   *proper way to address*
Of man and country—
REYNALDO: Very good, my lord.
POLONIUS: And then, sir, does he this—he does—What was I
     about to say? By the mass, I was about to say   50
     something! Where did I leave?
REYNALDO: At "closes in the consequence," at "friend or so,"
     and "gentleman."
POLONIUS: At "closes in the consequence"—Ay, marry!
     He closes thus: "I know the gentleman.   55
     I saw him yesterday, or the other day,
     Or then, or then, with such or such; and, as you say,
     There was he gaming; there o'ertook in 's rouse;°   *overcome in his carousing*
     There falling out at tennis"; or perchance,
     "I saw him enter such a house of sale,"   60
     Videlicet,° a brothel, or so forth.   *namely*
     See you now—
     Your bait of falsehood takes this carp of truth;
     And thus do we of wisdom and of reach,
     With windlasses and with assays of bias,°   *approaching it sideways* 65
     By indirections find directions out.
     So, by my former lecture and advice,
     Shall you my son. You have° me, have you not?   *understand*
REYNALDO: My lord, I have.
POLONIUS: God be wi' you, fare you well!
REYNALDO: Good my lord!   70
POLONIUS: Observe his inclination in yourself.°   *for yourself*
REYNALDO: I shall, my lord.
POLONIUS: And let him ply his music.°   *do not interfere*
REYNALDO: Well, my lord.
POLONIUS: Farewell!

                    [REYNALDO *leaves*.]

[*Enter* OPHELIA.]

                    How now, Ophelia? What's the matter?
OPHELIA: O my lord, my lord, I have been so affrighted!°   *frightened* 75
POLONIUS: With what, in the name of God?
OPHELIA: My lord, as I was sewing in my closet,°   *private room*
     Lord Hamlet, with his doublet all unbraced,°   *jacket all loosened*
     No hat upon his head, his stockings fouled,°   *twisted*
     Ungartered, and down-gyvèd° to his ankle;   *coiled down* 80
     Pale as his shirt, his knees knocking each other,
     And with a look so piteous in purport°   *meaning*
     As if he had been loosèd out of hell
     To speak of horrors—he comes before me.
POLONIUS: Mad for thy love?
OPHELIA: My lord, I do not know,
     But truly I do fear it.   85

POLONIUS: What said he?
OPHELIA: He took me by the wrist and held me hard;
   Then goes he to the length of all his arm,
   And, with his other hand thus over his brow,
   He falls to such perusal° of my face   *study*   90
   As° he would draw it. Long stayed he so.   *as if*
   At last, a little shaking of mine arm,
   And thrice his head thus waving up and down,
   He raised a sigh so piteous and profound
   As it did seem to shatter all his bulk   95
   And end his being. That done, he lets me go,
   And with his head over his shoulder turned
   He seemed to find his way without his eyes,
   For out of doors he went without their help
   And to the last bended their light on me.   100
POLONIUS: Come, go with me. I will go seek the King.
   This is the very ecstasy° of love,   *the true madness*
   Whose violent property° fordoes itself   *quality*
   And leads the will to desperate undertakings
   As oft as any passion under heaven   105
   That does afflict our natures. I am sorry.
   What, have you given him any hard words of late?
OPHELIA: No, my good lord; but, as you did command,
   I did repel° his letters and denied   *reject*
   His access to me.
POLONIUS: That hath made him mad.   110
   I am sorry that with better heed and judgment
   I had not quoted° him. I feared he did but trifle   *observed*
   And meant to wrack° thee; but beshrew° my jealousy!   *ruin/curse*
   By heaven, it is as proper to our age
   To cast beyond ourselves in our opinions   115
   As it is common for the younger sort
   To lack discretion. Come, go we to the King.
   This must be known; which, being kept close,° might   *if kept secret*
      move
   More grief to hide than hate to utter love.°   *cause more grief to hide love than*
   Come.   *it would cause hate to reveal it*   120

                              [*They leave.*]

SCENE 2. Elsinore. A room in the Castle.

   [*Flourish of trumpets. Enter* KING *and* QUEEN, ROSENCRANTZ,
   and GUILDENSTERN, *and others.*]

KING: Welcome, dear Rosencrantz and Guildenstern.
   Moreover° that we much did long to see you,   *besides*
   The need we have to use you did provoke
   Our hasty sending. Something have you heard
   Of Hamlet's transformation. So I call it,   5

Sith° nor the exterior nor the inward man   *since*
Resembles that it was. What it should be,
More than his father's death, that thus hath put him
So much from the understanding of himself,
I cannot dream of. I entreat you both   10
That, being of so young days° brought up with him,   *from your youngest days*
And since so neighbored° to his youth and havior,   *so close*
That you vouchsafe your rest° here in our court   *consent to stay*
Some little time; so by your companies
To draw him on to pleasures, and to gather   15
So much as from occasion you may glean,
Whether aught to us unknown afflicts him thus
That, opened,° lies within our remedy.   *when known*
QUEEN: Good gentlemen, he hath much talked of you,
  And sure I am two men there are not living   20
  To whom he more adheres.° If it will please you   *feels closer*
  To show us so much gentry° and good will   *courtesy*
  As to expend your time with us awhile
  For the supply and profit of our hope,°   *so we may gain what we hope for*
  Your visitation shall receive such thanks   25
  As fits a king's remembrance.
ROSENCRANTZ: Both your Majesties
  Might, by the sovereign power you have of us,
  Put your dread pleasures° more into command   *wishes that we must treat with awe*
  Than to entreaty.°   *polite request*
GUILDENSTERN: But we both obey,
  And here give up ourselves, in the full bent,°   *to the fullest* 30
  To lay our service freely at your feet,
  To be commanded.
KING: Thanks, Rosencrantz and gentle Guildenstern.
QUEEN: Thanks, Guildenstern and gentle Rosencrantz.
  And I beseech you instantly to visit   35
  My too much changed son.—Go, some of you,
  And bring these gentlemen where Hamlet is.
GUILDENSTERN: Heavens make our presence and our
     practices
  Pleasant and helpful to him!
QUEEN: Ay, amen!

[ROSENCRANTZ *and* GUILDENSTERN *leave, with some attendants.*]

[*Enter* POLONIUS.]

POLONIUS: The ambassadors from Norway, my good lord,   40
  Are joyfully returned.
KING: Thou still hast° been the father of good news.   *you always have*
POLONIUS: Have I, my lord? Assure you, my good liege,°   *overlord*
  I hold my duty as I hold my soul,
  Both to my God and to my gracious king;   45
  And I do think—or else this brain of mine

Hunts not the trail of policy° so sure   *statecraft*
As it hath used to do—that I have found
The very cause of Hamlet's lunacy.
KING: O, speak of that! That do I long to hear.   50
POLONIUS: Give first admittance to the ambassadors,
    My news shall be the fruit° to that great feast.   *come as dessert*
KING: Thyself do grace to them, and bring them in.

                                    [POLONIUS *leaves.*]

He tells me, my dear Gertrude, he hath found
    The head and source of all your son's distemper.°   *disturbed mind*   55
QUEEN: I doubt° it is no other but the main,°   *suspect/chief cause*
    His father's death and our overhasty marriage.
KING: Well, we shall sift° him.   *examine*

[*Enter* POLONIUS, VOLTEMAND, *and* CORNELIUS.]

                                    Welcome, my good friends.
    Say, Voltemand, what from our brother Norway?
VOLTEMAND: Most fair return of greetings and desires.   60
    Upon our first, he sent out to suppress
    His nephew's levies,° which to him appeared   *warlike preparations*
    To be a preparation 'gainst the Polack,°   *against the Poles*
    But better looked into,° he truly found   *when he looked into it*
    It was against your Highness; whereat grieved,   65
    That so his sickness, age, and impotence°   *infirmity*
    Was falsely borne in hand,° sends out arrests°   *deceived/commands*
    On Fortinbras; which he, in brief, obeys,
    Receives rebuke from Norway, and, in fine,°   *finally*
    Makes vow before his uncle never more   70
    To give the assay of arms° against your Majesty.   *make war*
    Whereon old Norway, overcome with joy,
    Gives him three thousand crowns in annual fee°   *payment*
    And his commission to employ those soldiers,
    So levied as before, against the Polack;   75
    With an entreaty, herein further shown,

[*Gives a paper.*]

    That it might please you to give quiet pass°   *grant the right to pass*
    Through your dominions for this enterprise,
    On such regards° of safety and allowance   *with such assurances*
    As therein are set down.
KING: It likes us well;°   *we like it*   80
    And at our more considered time we'll read,
    Answer, and think upon this business.
    Meantime we thank you for your well-took labor.
    Go to your rest; at night we'll feast together.
    Most welcome home!

                                    [*Ambassadors leave.*]

POLONIUS: This business is well ended.   85
　　My liege, and madam, to expostulate
　　What majesty should be, what duty is,
　　Why day is day, night night, and time is time,
　　Were nothing but to waste night, day, and time.
　　Therefore, since brevity is the soul of wit,°   *intelligence*   90
　　And tediousness the limbs and outward flourishes,
　　I will be brief. Your noble son is mad.
　　Mad call I it; for, to define true madness,
　　What is't but to be nothing else but mad?
　　But let that go.
QUEEN: More matter,° with less art.   *substance*   95
POLONIUS: Madam, I swear I use no art at all.
　　That he is mad, 'tis true: 'tis true 'tis pity;
　　And pity 'tis 'tis true. A foolish figure!°   *figure of speech*
　　But farewell it, for I will use no art.
　　Mad let us grant him then. And now remains   100
　　That we find out the cause of this effect—
　　Or rather say, the cause of this defect,
　　For this effect defective comes by cause.
　　Thus it remains, and the remainder thus.
　　Perpend:°   *listen carefully* 105
　　I have a daughter (have while she is mine),
　　Who in her duty and obedience, mark,
　　Hath given me this. Now gather, and surmise.

[*Reads the letter.*]

　　　　To the celestial, and my soul's idol, the most beautified
　　　　　Ophelia,—   110
　　That's an ill phrase, a vile phrase; "beautified" is a vile
　　　　phrase.
　　But you shall hear. Thus:

[*Reads.*]

　　　　In her excellent white bosom, these, etc.
QUEEN: Came this from Hamlet to her?
POLONIUS: Good madam, stay awhile. I will be faithful.°   *patient*   115

[*Reads.*]

　　　　Doubt thou the stars are fire;
　　　　　Doubt that the sun doth move;
　　　　Doubt truth to be a liar;
　　　　　But never doubt I love.

　　　　O dear Ophelia, I am ill at these numbers;° I have   *not good at verse* 120
　　not art to reckon my groans; but that I love thee best,
　　O most best, believe it. Adieu.
　　　　　Thine evermore, most dear lady, whilst this
　　　　　　machine° is to him, HAMLET.   *body*

This, in obedience, hath my daughter shown me;°   *has reported to me* 125
And more above, hath his solicitings,°   *pleas*
As they fell out by time, by means, and place,
All given to mine ear.
KING: But how hath she
    Received his love?
POLONIUS: What do you think of me?
    KING: As of a man faithful and honorable.   130
POLONIUS: I would fain° prove so. But what might you think,   *gladly*
    When I had seen this hot love on the wing
    (As I perceived it, I must tell you that,
    Before my daughter told me), what might you,
    Or my dear Majesty your queen here, think,   135
    If I had played the desk or table book,°   *mere passive recorder*
    Or given my heart a winking, mute and dumb,
    Or looked upon this love with idle sight?
    What might you think? No, I went round to work
    And my young mistress thus I did bespeak:°   *lecture* 140
    "Lord Hamlet is a prince, out of thy star.°   *outside your sphere*
    This must not be." And then I precepts gave her,
    That she should lock herself from his resort,°   *company*
    Admit no messengers, receive no tokens.
    Which done, she took the fruits of my advice,   145
    And he, repulsed, a short tale to make,
    Fell into a sadness, then into a fast,
    Thence to a watch, thence into a weakness,
    Thence to a lightness, and, by this declension,°   *downward progression*
    Into the madness wherein now he raves,   150
    And all we mourn for.
    KING: Do you think 'tis this?
QUEEN: It may be, very like.°   *very likely*
POLONIUS: Hath there been such a time—I would fain
        know that—
    That I have positively said "'Tis so,"
    When it proved otherwise?
    KING: Not that I know.   155
POLONIUS [*points to his head and shoulder*]: Take this from
        this, if this be otherwise.
    If circumstances lead me, I will find
    Where truth is hid, though it were hid indeed
    Within the center
    KING: How may we try° it further?   *check* 160
POLONIUS: You know sometimes he walks four hours
        together
    Here in the lobby.
    QUEEN: So he does indeed.
POLONIUS: At such a time I'll loose° my daughter to him.   *release*
    Be you and I behind an arras° then.   *tapestry curtain*

Mark the encounter. If he love her not,   165
And be not from his reason fallen° thereon,   *gone out of his mind*
Let me be no assistant for a state,°   *councilor of state*
But keep a farm and carters.°   *drivers of carts*
KING: We will try it.

[*Enter* HAMLET, *reading a book.*]

QUEEN: But look where sadly the poor wretch comes
    reading.
POLONIUS: Away, I do beseech you, both away!   170
    I'll board° him presently. O, give me leave.   *approach*

[KING *and* QUEEN *leave, with attendants.*]

    How does my good Lord Hamlet?
HAMLET: Well, God-a-mercy.
POLONIUS: Do you know me, my lord?
HAMLET: Excellent well. You are a fishmonger.   175
POLONIUS: Not I, my lord.
HAMLET: Then I would you were so honest a man.
POLONIUS: Honest, my lord?
HAMLET: Ay, sir. To be honest, as this world goes, is
    to be one man picked out of ten thousand.   180
POLONIUS: That's very true, my lord.
HAMLET: For if the sun breed maggots in a dead dog,
    being a god kissing carrion—Have you a daughter?
POLONIUS: I have, my lord.
HAMLET: Let her not walk in the sun. Conception is a   185
    blessing, but not as your daughter may conceive.
    Friend, look to't.
POLONIUS [*aside*]: How say you by that? Still harping
    on my daughter. Yet he knew me not at first. He
    said I was a fishmonger. He is far gone, far gone!   190
    And truly in my youth I suffered much extremity
    for love—very near this. I'll speak to him again.—
    What do you read, my lord?
HAMLET: Words, words, words.
POLONIUS: What is the matter, my lord?   195
HAMLET: Between who?
POLONIUS: I mean, the matter that you read, my lord.
HAMLET: Slanders, sir; for the satirical rogue says here
    that old men have grey beards; that their faces are
    wrinkled; their eyes purging° thick amber and   *dripping* 200
    plum-tree gum; and that they have a plentiful lack
    of wit, together with most weak hams. All which,
    sir, though I most powerfully and potently be-
    lieve, yet I hold it not honesty° to have it thus set   *good manners*
    down; for you yourself, sir, should be old as I am   205
    if, like a crab, you could go backward.

POLONIUS [*aside*]: Though this be madness, yet there
   is method in't.—Will you walk out of the air, my
   lord?

HAMLET: Into my grave?   210

POLONIUS: Indeed, that is out of the air. [*aside*] How
   pregnant° sometimes his replies are! a happiness   *meaningful*
   that often madness hits on, which reason and san-
   ity could not so prosperously be delivered of. I
   will leave him and suddenly contrive the means of   215
   meeting between him and my daughter.—My
   honorable lord, I will most humbly take my leave
   of you.

HAMLET: You cannot, sir, take from me anything that
   I will more willingly part withal°—except my life,   *part with* 220
   except my life, except my life.

[*Enter* ROSENCRANTZ *and* GUILDENSTERN.]

POLONIUS: Fare you well, my lord.

HAMLET: These tedious old fools!

POLONIUS: You go to seek the Lord Hamlet. There he
   is.   225

ROSENCRANTZ [*to* POLONIUS]: God save you, sir!

[POLONIUS *leaves.*]

GUILDENSTERN: My honored lord!

ROSENCRANTZ: My most dear lord!

HAMLET: My excellent good friends! How dost thou,
   Guildenstern? Ah, Rosencrantz! Good lads, how   230
   do ye both?

ROSENCRANTZ: As the indifferent° children of the earth.   *ordinary*

GUILDENSTERN: Happy in that we are not over-happy.
   On Fortune's cap we are not the very button.°   *top*

HAMLET: Nor the soles of her shoe?   235

ROSENCRANTZ: Neither, my lord.

HAMLET: Then you live about her waist, or in the middle of her favors?

GUILDENSTERN: Faith, her privates° we.   *intimate friends*

HAMLET: In the secret parts of Fortune? O, most true!   240
   she is a strumpet. What news?

ROSENCRANTZ: None, my lord, but that the world's
   grown honest.

HAMLET: Then is doomsday near! But your news is
   not true. Let me question more in particular. What   245
   have you, my good friends, deserved at the hands
   of Fortune that she sends you to prison hither?

GUILDENSTERN: Prison, my lord?

HAMLET: Denmark's a prison.

ROSENCRANTZ: Then is the world one.   250

HAMLET: A goodly one; in which there are many con-
fines,° wards, and dungeons, Denmark being one   *cells*
of the worst.

ROSENCRANTZ: We think not so, my lord.

HAMLET: Why, then 'tis none to you, for there is noth-   255
ing either good or bad but thinking makes it so.
To me it is a prison.

ROSENCRANTZ: Why, then your ambition makes it one.
'Tis too narrow for your mind.

HAMLET: O God, I could be bounded in a nutshell   260
and count myself a king of infinite space, were it
not that I have bad dreams.

GUILDENSTERN: Which dreams indeed are ambition;
for the very substance of the ambitious is merely
the shadow of a dream.   265

HAMLET: A dream itself is but a shadow.

ROSENCRANTZ: Truly, and I hold ambition of so airy
and light a quality that it is but a shadow's
shadow.

HAMLET: Then are our beggars bodies, and our mon-   270
archs and outstretched heroes the beggars' shad-
ows. Shall we to the court? for, by my fay,° I   *faith*
cannot reason.

BOTH: We'll wait upon you.

HAMLET: No such matter! I will not sort° you with the   *class* 275
rest of my servants; for, to speak to you like an
honest man, I am most dreadfully attended.° But   *very poorly served*
in the beaten way of friendship, what make you at
Elsinore?

ROSENCRANTZ: To visit you, my lord; no other occasion.   280

HAMLET: Beggar that I am, I am even poor in thanks;
but I thank you; and sure, dear friends, my thanks
are too dear° a halfpenny. Were you not sent for?   *too dear at (or by)*
Is it your own inclining? Is it a free visitation?
Come, deal justly with me. Come, come! Nay,   285
speak.

GUILDENSTERN: What should we say, my lord?

HAMLET: Why, anything, but to the purpose.°You   *point*
were sent for, and there is a kind of confession in
your looks, which your modesties have not craft   290
enough to color.° I know the good King and   *not skill enough to disguise*
Queen have sent for you.

ROSENCRANTZ: To what end, my lord?

HAMLET: That you must teach me. But let me conjure
you° by the rights of our fellowship, by the con-   *plead with you* 295
sonancy° of our youth, by the obligation of our   *harmony*
ever-preserved love, and by what more dear a
better proposer° could charge you withal, be even   *talker*

and direct with me, whether you were sent for or
no.   300

ROSENCRANTZ [*aside to* GUILDENSTERN]: What say you?

HAMLET [*aside*]: Nay then, I have an eye of you.° If   *I am on to you*
you love me, hold not off.

GUILDENSTERN: My lord, we were sent for.   305

HAMLET: I will tell you why, so shall my anticipation
prevent your discovery,° and your secrecy to the   *your giving yourself away*
King and Queen moult no feather.° I have of   *not be damaged*
late—but wherefore I know not—lost all my
mirth, forgone all custom of exercises;° and in-   *all ordinary activities* 310
deed, it goes so heavily with my disposition that
this goodly frame, the earth, seems to me a sterile
promontory;° this most excellent canopy, the air,   *barren outcropping*
look you, this brave overhanging firmament, this
majestical roof fretted° with golden fire—why, it   *ornamented* 315
appeareth no other thing to me than a foul and
pestilent congregation of vapors. What a piece of
work is a man! how noble in reason! how infinite
in faculties! in form and moving how express° and   *well made*
admirable! in action how like an angel! in appre-   320
hension° how like a god! the beauty of the world,   *understanding*
the paragon of animals! And yet to me what is this
quintessence° of dust? Man delights not me—no,   *ultimate essence*
nor woman neither, though by your smiling you
seem to say so.   325

ROSENCRANTZ: My lord, there was no such stuff in my
thoughts.

HAMLET: Why did you laugh then, when I said "Man
delights not me"?

ROSENCRANTZ: To think, my lord, if you delight not in   330
man, what lenten entertainment° the players shall   *meager treatment*
receive from you. We coted° them on the way,   *passed*
and hither are they coming to offer you service.

HAMLET: He that plays the king shall be welcome—
his Majesty shall have tribute of me; the adventur-   335
ous knight shall use his foil and target;° the lover   *sword and shield*
shall not sigh gratis; the humorous man shall end
his part in peace; the clown shall make those laugh
whose lungs are tickle o' the sere;° and the lady   *quick on the trigger*
shall say her mind freely, or the blank verse shall   340
halt° for't. What players are they?   *stumble*

ROSENCRANTZ: Even those you were wont to° take   *you used to*
such delight in, the tragedians of the city.

HAMLET: How chances it they travel? Their residence,
both in reputation and profit, was better both   345
ways.

ROSENCRANTZ: I think their inhibition° comes by the   *their being kept out*
means of the late innovation.°   *recent fad*

HAMLET: Do they hold the same estimation they did
    when I was in the city? Are they so followed?   350
ROSENCRANTZ: No indeed are they not.
HAMLET: How comes it? Do they grow rusty?
ROSENCRANTZ: Nay, their endeavor keeps in the
    wonted° pace; but there is, sir, an eyrie of children   *accustomed*
    little eyases,° that cry out on the top of question   *bird's brood of shrill little hawks* 355
    and are most tyrannically clapped° for't. These are   *wildly applauded*
    now the fashion, and so berattle the common
    stages° (so they call them) that many wearing   *put down ordinary theaters*
    rapiers are afraid of goosequills° and dare scarce   *fear the playwright's pen*
    come thither.   360
HAMLET: What, are they children? Who maintains
    them? How are they escoted?° Will they pursue the   *supported*
    quality° no longer than they can sing? Will they not   *play this role*
    say afterwards, if they should grow themselves to
    common players (as it is most like, if their means   365
    are no better), their writers do them wrong to
    make them exclaim against their own succession?°   *future roles*
ROSENCRANTZ: Faith, there has been much to do on
    both sides; and the nation holds it no sin to tarre
    them° to controversy. There was, for a while, no   *egg them on* 370
    money bid for argument° unless the poet and the   *for a new play*
    player went to cuffs in the question.°   *on this topic*
HAMLET: Is't possible?
GUILDENSTERN: O, there has been much throwing
    about of brains.   375
HAMLET: Do the boys carry it away?
ROSENCRANTZ: Ay, that they do, my lord—Hercules
    and his load° too.   *Hercules carrying the globe*
                                                                (as on the Globe theater sign)
HAMLET: It is not very strange; for my uncle is King of
    Denmark, and those that would make mows° at   *faces* 380
    him while my father lived give twenty, forty, fifty,
    a hundred ducats apiece for his picture in little.°   *miniature portrait*
    'Sblood,° there is some thing in this more than   *by God's blood*
    natural, if philosophy could find it out.

    [*Flourish of trumpets for the* PLAYERS.]

GUILDENSTERN: There are the players.   385
HAMLET: Gentlemen, you are welcome to Elsinore.
    Your hands, come! The appurtenance° of wel-   *usual expression*
    come is fashion and ceremony. Let me comply
    with you in this garb,° lest my extent° to the play-   *treat you in this fashion/*
    ers (which I tell you must show fairly outwards)   *welcome*
    should more appear like entertainment than   390
    yours. You are welcome. But my uncle-father and
    aunt-mother are deceived.
GUILDENSTERN: In what, my dear lord?

HAMLET: I am but mad north-north-west. When the   395
wind is southerly I know a hawk from a handsaw.

[*Enter* POLONIUS.]

POLONIUS: Well be with you, gentlemen!
HAMLET: Hark you, Guildenstern—and you too—at
each ear a hearer! That great baby you see there
is not yet out of his swaddling clouts.°   *diapers* 400
ROSENCRANTZ: Happily he's the second time come to
them; for they say an old man is twice a child.
HAMLET: I will prophesy he comes to tell me of the
players. Mark it.—You say right, sir; a Monday
morning; 'twas so indeed.   405
POLONIUS: My lord, I have news to tell you.
HAMLET: My lord, I have news to tell you: when
Roscius was an actor in Rome—
POLONIUS: The actors are come hither, my lord.
HAMLET: Buzz, buzz!   410
POLONIUS: Upon my honor—
HAMLET: Then came each actor on his ass—
POLONIUS: The best actors in the world, either for trag-
edy, comedy, history, pastoral, pastoral-comical,
historical-pastoral, tragical-historical, tragical-comical-   415
historical-pastoral; scene individable, or poem un-
limited.° Seneca cannot be too heavy, nor Plautus°   *plays classical or irregular*
too light. For the law of writ and the liberty, these   *(Roman playwrights)*
are the only men.
HAMLET: O Jephthah,° judge of Israel, what a treasure   *(a biblical figure)* 420
hadst thou!
POLONIUS: What a treasure had he, my lord?
HAMLET: Why,

>   *One fair daughter, and no more,*
>   *The which he loved passing well.*   425

POLONIUS [*aside*]: Still on my daughter.
HAMLET: Am I not in the right, old Jephthah?
POLONIUS: If you call me Jephthah, my lord, I have a
daughter that I love passing well.
HAMLET: Nay, that follows not.   430
POLONIUS: What follows then, my lord?
HAMLET: Why,

>   *As by lot, God wot,*

and then, you know,

>   *It came to pass, as most like it was.*   435

The first row° of the pious chanson will show you   *stanza*
more; for look where my abridgement° comes.   *interruption*

[*Enter four or five* PLAYERS.]

You are welcome, masters; welcome all.—I am
glad to see thee well.—Welcome, good friends.—
O, my old friend? Why, thy face is valanced° since   *fringed* 440
I saw thee last. Com'st thou to beard me in Den-
mark? —What, my young lady and mistress? By'r
Lady,° your ladyship is nearer to heaven than when   *by Our Lady*
I saw you last by the altitude of a chopine.° Pray   *the length of high heels*
God your voice, like a piece of uncurrent gold,° be   *defective coin* 445
not cracked° within the ring.—Masters, you are all   *do not crack (or change)*
welcome. We'll even to't° like French falconers, fly   *we'll go to it*
at anything we see. We'll have a speech straight.
Come, give us a taste of your quality.° Come, a   *talent*
passionate speech.   450

1. PLAYER: What speech, my good lord?

HAMLET: I heard thee speak me a speech once, but it
was never acted; or if it was, not above once; for
the play, I remember, pleased not the million,
'twas caviary to the general;° but it was (as I re-   *too choice for the many* 455
ceived it, and others, whose judgments in such
matters cried in the top of mine)° an excellent   *outweighed mine*
play, well digested° in the scenes, set down with   *arranged*
as much modesty as cunning.° I remember one   *moderation as skill*
said there were no sallets° in the lines to make the   *coarse jokes* 460
matter savory, nor no matter in the phrase that
might indict the author of affectation; but called it
an honest method, as wholesome as sweet, and
by very much more handsome than fine. One
speech in it I chiefly loved. 'Twas Æneas' tale to   465
Dido, and thereabout of it especially where he
speaks of Priam's slaughter. If it live in your memory, begin at this line—let me see, let me see:

The rugged Pyrrhus, like the Hyrcanian beast°—   *Asian tiger*

'Tis not so; it begins with Pyrrhus: 470

The rugged Pyrrhus, he whose sable arms,°   *black-hued armor*
Black as his purpose, did the night resemble
When he lay crouched in the ominous horse,°   *hidden in the wooden*
Hath now this dread and black complexion smeared   *Trojan horse*
With heraldry more dismal. Head to foot   475
Now is he total gules,° *horridly tricked*   *heraldic red*
With blood of fathers, mothers, daughters, sons,
Baked and impasted with the parching° *streets,*   *fire-parched*
That lend a tyrannous and a damned light
To their lord's murder. Roasted in wrath and fire,   480
And thus oversized with coagulate gore,°   *smeared with clotted gore*
With eyes like carbuncles,° *the hellish Pyrrhus*   *fiery-red stones*
Old grandsire Priam seeks.

So, proceed you.

POLONIUS: Fore God, my lord, well spoken, with   485
   good accent and good discretion.

1. PLAYER: *Anon he finds him,*
   Striking too short at Greeks. His antique sword,
   Rebellious to his arm, lies where it falls,
   Repugnant to command.° *Unequal matched,*   *refusing obedience* 490
   Pyrrhus at Priam drives, in rage strikes wide;
   But with the whiff and wind of his fell° *sword*   *deadly*
   The unnerved father falls. Then senseless Ilium,°   *the unfeeling city*
   Seeming to feel this blow, with flaming top°   *with a tower on fire*
   Stoops to his base,° *and with a hideous crash*   *crashes to its base* 495
   Takes prisoner° *Pyrrhus' ear. For lo! his sword,*   *distracts*
   Which was declining on the milky° *head*   *milk-white*
   Of reverend Priam, seemed in the air to stick.
   So, as a painted tyrant, Pyrrhus stood,
   And, like a neutral to° *his will and matter,*   *as if detached from* 500
   Did nothing.
   But, as we often see, against some storm,
   A silence in the heavens, the rack° *stand still,*   *threatening clouds*
   The bold winds speechless, and the orb below
   As hush as death—anon the dreadful thunder   505
   Doth rend the region; so, after Pyrrhus' pause,
   Aroused vengeance sets him new awork;
   And never did the Cyclops' hammers fall
   On Mars's armor, forged for proof eterne,°   *made to last forever*
   With less remorse than Pyrrhus' bleeding sword   510
   Now falls on Priam.
   Out, out, thou strumpet Fortune! All you gods,
   In general synod° *take away her power;*   *council*
   Break all the spokes and fellies° *from her wheel,*   *outer rim*
   And bowl the round nave° *down the hill of heaven,*   *hub* 515
   As low as to the fiends!

POLONIUS: This is too long.

HAMLET: It shall to the barber's, with your beard.—
   Prithee say on. He's for a jig or a tale of bawdry,
   or he sleeps.° Say on; come to Hecuba.   *or else he falls asleep* 520

1. PLAYER: *But who, O who, had seen the mobled*° *queen—*   *veiled*

HAMLET: "The mobled queen"?

POLONIUS: That's good! "Mobled queen" is good.

1. PLAYER: *Run barefoot up and down, threatening the flames*
   With bisson rheum;° *a clout*° *upon that head*   *blinding tears/rag* 525
   Where late the diadem stood, and for a robe,
   About her lank and all overteemed° *loins,*   *worn out from childbirth*
   A blanket, in the alarm of fear caught up—
   Who this had seen, with tongue in venom steeped
   'Gainst Fortune's state would treason have
      pronounced.   530
   But if the gods themselves did see her then,
   When she saw Pyrrhus make malicious sport

In mincing with his sword her husband's limbs,
The instant burst of clamor that she made
(Unless things mortal move them not at all)   535
Would have made milch°°° the burning eyes of   moist with the milk of tears
    heaven
And passion in the gods.

POLONIUS: Look, whether he has not turned his color,
    and has tears in his eyes. Prithee no more!

HAMLET: 'Tis well. I'll have thee speak out the rest of   540
    this soon.—Good my lord, will you see the play-
    ers well bestowed?° Do you hear? Let them be well   accommodated
    used; for they are the abstract° and brief chronicles   summary
    of the time. After your death you were better have
    a bad epitaph than their ill report while you live.   545

POLONIUS: My lord, I will use them according to their
    desert.

HAMLET: God's bodykins, man, much better! Use
    every man after his desert, and who should scape
    whipping? Use them after your own honor and   550
    dignity. The less they deserve, the more merit is in
    your bounty.° Take them in.   generosity

POLONIUS: Come, sirs.

HAMLET: Follow him, friends. We'll hear a play
    tomorrow.   555

[POLONIUS *and* PLAYERS *(except the first) leave.*]

Dost thou hear me, old friend? Can you play "The
    Murder of Gonzago"?

1. PLAYER: Ay, my lord.

HAMLET: We'll have it tomorrow night. You could, for
    a need, study a speech of some dozen or sixteen   560
    lines which I would set down and insert in it,
    could you not?

1. PLAYER: Ay, my lord.

HAMLET: Very well. Follow that lord—and look you
    mock him not. [*First* PLAYER *leaves. To* ROSENCRANTZ.]   565
    My good friends, I'll leave you till night. You are
    welcome to Elsinore.

ROSENCRANTZ: Good my lord!

HAMLET: Ay, so, Good bye to you.

[ROSENCRANTZ *and* GUILDENSTERN *leave.*]

Now I am alone.
O, what a rogue and peasant slave am I!   570
Is it not monstrous that this player here,
But in a fiction, in a dream of passion,
Could force his soul so to his own conceit°   imagination
That, from her working, all his visage wanned,°   his face paled
Tears in his eyes, distraction in's aspect,°   in his looks 575

A broken voice, and his whole function suiting
With forms to his conceit? And all for nothing!
For Hecuba!
What's Hecuba to him, or he to Hecuba,
That he should weep for her? What would he do,   580
Had he the motive and the cue for passion
That I have? He would drown the stage with tears
And cleave the general ear° with horrid speech;   *split everyone's ear*
Make mad the guilty and appal the free,°   *innocent*
Confound the ignorant, and amaze indeed   585
The very faculties of eyes and ears.
Yet I,
A dull and muddy-mettled° rascal, peak°   *weak-souled/mope*
Like John-a-dreams, unpregnant of° my cause,   *unmoved by*
And can say nothing! No, not for a king,   590
Upon whose property and most dear life
A damned defeat was made.° Am I a coward?   *inflicted*
Who calls me villain? breaks my pate across?°   *cudgels my head*
Plucks off my beard and blows it in my face?
Tweaks me by the nose? gives me the lie in the throat°   *calls me a liar* 595
As deep as to the lungs? Who does me this, ha?
'Swounds,° I should take it! for it cannot be   *by God's wounds*
But I am pigeon-livered and lack gall
To make oppression bitter, or ere this°   *before now*
I should have fatted all the region kites°   *the vultures in the air* 600
With this slave's offal.° Bloody, bawdy, villain!   *rotting scraps*
Remorseless, treacherous, lecherous, kindless° villain!   *unnatural*
O, vengeance!
Why, what an ass am I! This is most brave,
That I, the son of a dear father murdered,   605
Prompted to my revenge by heaven and hell,
Must (like a whore) unpack my heart with words
And fall a-cursing like a very drab,°   *a true harlot*
A scullion!°   *kitchen wench*
Fie upon't! foh! About, my brain! I have heard   610
That guilty creatures, sitting at a play,
Have by the very cunning° of the scene   *ingenious arrangement*
Been struck so to the soul that presently
They have proclaimed their malefactions;°   *crimes*
For murder, though it have no tongue, will speak   615
With most miraculous organ. I'll have these players
Play something like the murder of my father
Before mine uncle. I'll observe his looks,
I'll tent° him to the quick; if he but blench,°   *test/turn pale*
I know my course. The spirit that I have seen   620
May be a devil; and the devil hath power
To assume a pleasing shape; yea, and perhaps
Out of my weakness and my melancholy,
As he is very potent with such spirits,°   *knows how to exploit such traits*

Abuses° me to damn me. I'll have grounds   *deceives* 625
More relative° than this. The play's the thing   *relevant*
Wherein I'll catch the conscience of the King.

[*He leaves.*]

The Receptive Reader

1. (Acts One and Two) One reviewer described the Claudius in a new production as a king "who is disturbed, dishonest, and yet an ordinary respectable and sensual stuffed-shirt politician" (Harold Clurman). What in Claudius' talk and behavior in the first two acts lives up to this billing? What image do you get of him in his dealings with Laertes, Polonius, Hamlet? How formidable an *antagonist* does he present for Hamlet?

2. (Act Two, Scene 1) Here and earlier, how silly or pompous does Polonius seem to you? Is he worthy of at least some respect? What kind of father is he for Laertes and Ophelia? How weak and submissive is Ophelia? Does she have any good lines?

3. (Act Two, Scene 2) In this scene, Hamlet starts his fencing and sparring with those in the service of the king. Is there a pattern in Hamlet's baiting of Polonius? (What makes Polonius say, "Though this be madness, yet there's method in't"?) How does Hamlet deal with Rosencrantz and Guildenstern? (Of what does he accuse them?) What side of Hamlet's character does his relationship with the actors bring out? (What do we learn here and in Act Three, Scene 2, indirectly about Shakespeare's views about the theater?)

4. Hamlet's "I have of late" speech is seen by many as a major *thematic passage.* What are the polarities that help structure the speech? What is the keynote?

5. The concluding "O what a rogue and peasant slave" *soliloquy* is prime evidence for critics debating the question of Hamlet's delay or hesitation in pursuing his revenge. What occasions this speech? What is the keynote or prevailing tone? Does it lead anywhere?

Act Three

SCENE 1. Elsinore. A room in the Castle.

[*Enter* KING, QUEEN, POLONIUS, OPHELIA, ROSENCRANTZ, GUILDENSTERN, *and lords.*]

KING: And can you by no drift of circumstance°   *roundabout talk*
    Get from him why he puts on this confusion,°   *acts in this disturbed fashion*
    Grating so harshly all his days of quiet
    With turbulent and dangerous lunacy?
ROSENCRANTZ: He does confess he feels himself distracted,   5
    But from what cause he will by no means speak.
GUILDENSTERN: Nor do we find him forward to be sounded,°   *willing to be*
    But with a crafty madness keeps aloof   *found out*
    When we would bring him on to some confession
    Of his true state.

QUEEN: Did he receive you well?   10
ROSENCRANTZ: Most like a gentleman.
GUILDENSTERN: But with much forcing of his disposition.°   *strained politeness*
ROSENCRANTZ: Niggard of question,° but of our demands   *asking few questions*
  Most free in his reply.°   *answering freely*
QUEEN: Did you assay° him   *invite*
  To any pastime?   15
ROSENCRANTZ: Madam, it so fell out that certain players
  We overraught° on the way. Of these we told him,   *overtook*
  And there did seem in him a kind of joy
  To hear of it. They are here about the court,
  And, as I think, they have already order   20
  This night to play before him.
POLONIUS: 'Tis most true;
  And he beseeched me to entreat your Majesties
  To hear and see the matter.
KING: With all my heart, and it doth much content me
  To hear him so inclined.   25
  Good gentlemen, give him a further edge
  And drive his purpose on to these delights.
ROSENCRANTZ: We shall, my lord.

[ROSENCRANTZ *and* GUILDENSTERN *leave*.]

KING: Sweet Gertrude, leave us too;
  For we have closely sent for Hamlet hither,
  That he, as 'twere by accident, may here   30
  Affront° Ophelia.   *encounter*
  Her father and myself (lawful espials)°   *spies in a good cause*
  Will so bestow ourselves that, seeing unseen,
  We may of their encounter frankly judge
  And gather° by him, as he is behaved,   *make up our minds* 35
  If't be the affliction of his love, or no,
  That thus he suffers for.
QUEEN: I shall obey you;
  And for your part, Ophelia, I do wish
  That your good beauties be the happy cause
  Of Hamlet's wildness. So shall I hope your virtues   40
  Will bring him to his wonted way° again,   *normal state*
  To both your honors.
OPHELIA: Madam, I wish it may.

[QUEEN *leaves*.]

POLONIUS: Ophelia, walk you here.—Gracious, so please
  you, We will bestow ourselves.°—[*To* OPHELIA.] Read   *take up our posts*
  on this book,
  That show of such an exercise may color°   *may serve as an excuse for* 45
  Your loneliness.—We are oft to blame in this,
  'Tis too much proved, that with devotion's visage°   *with the facade of religion*

And pious action we do sugar over
The devil himself.
KING [*aside*]:   O, 'tis too true!
How smart a lash that speech doth give my conscience!   50
The harlot's cheek, beautied with plastering art,
Is not more ugly to the thing that helps it
Than is my deed to my most painted word.
O heavy burden!
POLONIUS: I hear him coming. Let's withdraw, my lord.   55

[KING *and* POLONIUS *leave*.]

[*Enter* HAMLET.]

HAMLET: To be, or not to be, that is the question:
Whether 'tis nobler in the mind to suffer
The slings and arrows of outrageous fortune
Or to take arms against a sea of troubles,
And by opposing end them.° To die—to sleep—   *end them by fighting them*   60
No more; and by a sleep to say we end
The heartache, and the thousand natural shocks
That flesh is heir to. 'Tis a consummation°   *crowning end result*
Devoutly to be wished. To die—to sleep.
To sleep—perchance to dream: ay, there's the rub!°   *that's what stops us*   65
For in that sleep of death what dreams may come
When we have shuffled off this mortal coil,°   *shell*
Must give us pause. There's the respect
That makes calamity of so long life.°   *makes misery so long-lived*
For who would bear the whips and scorns of time,   70
The oppressor's wrong, the proud man's contumely,°   *contempt*
The pangs of despised love, the law's delay,
The insolence of office, and the spurns°   *abuses*
That patient merit of the unworthy takes,
When he himself might his quietus° make   *ending for good*   75
With a bare bodkin?° Who would fardels° bear,   *dagger/burdens*
To grunt and sweat under a weary life,
But that the dread of something after death—
The undiscovered country, from whose bourn°   *border*
No traveler returns—puzzles the will,   80
And makes us rather bear those ills° we have   *evils*
Than fly to others that we know not of?
Thus conscience does make cowards of us all,
And thus the native hue of resolution
Is sicklied over° with the pale cast of thought,   *made to look sick*   85
And enterprises of great pitch and moment°   *great force and impact*
With this regard° their currents turn awry   *because of this*
And lose the name of action.—Soft you now!°   *now let me be quiet*
The fair Ophelia!—Nymph, in thy orisons°   *prayers*
Be all my sins remembered.

OPHELIA: Good my lord,   90
  How does your honor for this many a day?
HAMLET: I humbly thank you; well, well, well.
OPHELIA: My lord, I have remembrances of yours°   *souvenirs from you*
  That I have longed to redeliver.
  I pray you, now receive them.
HAMLET: No, not I!   95
  I never gave you aught.°   *anything*
OPHELIA: My honored lord, you know right well you did,
  And with them words of so sweet breath composed
  As made the things more rich. Their perfume lost,
  Take these again; for to the noble mind   100
  Rich gifts wax poor when givers prove unkind.°   *turn cheap*
  There, my lord.
HAMLET: Ha, ha! Are you honest?°   *virtuous*
OPHELIA: My lord?
HAMLET: Are you fair?°   *beautiful* 105
OPHELIA: What means your lordship?
HAMLET: That if you be honest and fair, your honesty
  should admit no discourse to° your beauty.   *should not talk to*
OPHELIA: Could beauty, my lord, have better com-
  merce than with honesty?   110
HAMLET: Ay, truly; for the power of beauty will sooner
  transform honesty from what it is to a bawd° than   *turn virtue into vice*
  the force of honesty can translate beauty into his
  likeness. This was sometime a paradox, but now
  the time gives it proof. I did love you once.   115
OPHELIA: Indeed, my lord, you made me believe so.
HAMLET: You should not have believed me; for virtue
  cannot so inoculate our old stock but we shall rel-
  ish of it.° I loved you not.   *so change our sinful nature*
OPHELIA: I was the more deceived.   *that we no longer show it* 120
HAMLET: Get thee to a nunnery! Why wouldst thou be
  a breeder of sinners? I am myself indifferent hon-
  est,° but yet I could accuse me of such things that   *fairly virtuous*
  it were better my mother had not borne me. I am
  very proud, revengeful, ambitious; with more of-   125
  fenses at my beck than I have thoughts to put
  them in, imagination to give them shape, or time
  to act them in. What should such fellows as I do,
  crawling between earth and heaven? We are arrant
  knaves° all; believe none of us. Go thy ways to a   *utter villains* 130
  nunnery. Where's your father?
OPHELIA: At home, my lord.
HAMLET: Let the doors be shut upon him, that he may
  play the fool nowhere but in's own house. Farewell.
OPHELIA: O, help him, you sweet heavens!   135
HAMLET: If thou dost marry, I'll give thee this plague°   *curse*
  for thy dowry: be thou as chaste as ice, as pure as

snow, thou shalt not escape calumny. Get thee to
a nunnery. Go, farewell. Or if thou wilt needs°   *if you absolutely want to*
marry, marry a fool; for wise men know well   140
enough what monsters you make of them. To a
nunnery, go; and quickly too. Farewell.

OPHELIA: O heavenly powers, restore him!

HAMLET: I have heard of your paintings° too, well   *makeup*
enough. God hath given you one face, and you   145
make yourselves another. You jig, you amble, and
you lisp; you nickname° God's creatures and   *give fancy names to*
make your wantonness your ignorance.° Go to, I'll   *pretend you act wanton*
                                                          from ignorance
no more on't! it hath made me mad. I say, we will
have no more marriages. Those that are married   150
already—all but one—shall live; the rest shall
keep as they are. To a nunnery, go.

[*He leaves.*]

OPHELIA: O, what a noble mind is here o'erthrown!
The courtier's, soldier's, scholar's, eye, tongue, sword,
The expectancy° and rose of the fair state,   *hope* 155
The glass of fashion and the mould of form,
The observed of all observers—quite, quite down!
And I, of ladies most deject° and wretched,   *dejected*
That sucked the honey of his music vows,
Now see that noble and most sovereign reason,   160
Like sweet bells jangled, out of tune and harsh;
That unmatched form and feature of blown youth°   *youth in full bloom*
Blasted with ecstasy.° O, woe is me   *ruined by madness*
To have seen what I have seen, see what I see!

[*Enter* KING *and* POLONIUS.]

KING: Love? his affections do not that way tend;   165
Nor what he spoke, though it lacked form a little,
Was not like madness. There's something in his soul
Over which his melancholy sits on brood°   *brooding*
And I do doubt the hatch and the disclose°   *I fear the hatching and disclosure*
                                                          (of what was inside) 170
Will be some danger, which for to prevent,
I have in quick determination
Thus set it down: he shall with speed to England
For the demand of our neglected tribute.°   *tribute due but in arrears*
Haply° the seas, and countries different,   *perhaps*
With variable objects, shall expel   175
This something°-settled matter in his heart,   *somewhat*
Whereon his brains still beating puts him thus
From fashion of himself.° What think you on't?   *beside himself*

POLONIUS: It shall do well. But yet do I believe
The origin and commencement of his grief   180
Sprung from neglected love. How now, Ophelia?
You need not tell us ~~~at Lord Hamlet said,

We heard it all. My lord, do as you please;
But if you hold it fit, after the play
Let his queen mother all alone entreat him   185
To show his grief. Let her be round° with him;   open
And I'll be placed, so please you, in the ear°   within earshot
Of all their conference.° If she find him not,°   talk/not find out about him
To England send him; or confine him where
Your wisdom best shall think.

KING: It shall be so.   190
    Madness in great ones must not unwatched go.

                              [*They leave.*]

SCENE 2. Elsinore. A hall in the Castle.

[*Enter* HAMLET *and three of the* PLAYERS.]

HAMLET: Speak the speech, I pray you, as I pronounced
    it to you, trippingly on the tongue. But if you mouth
    it, as many of our players do, I had as lief° the town   as soon
    crier spoke my lines. Nor do not saw the air too
    much with your hand, thus, but use all gently; for   5
    in the very torrent, tempest, and (as I may say)
    whirlwind of your passion, you must acquire and
    beget a temperance that may give it smoothness.
    O, it offends me to the soul to hear a robustious
    periwig-pated° fellow tear a passion to tatters, to   boisterous, bewigged   10
    very rags, to split the ears of the groundlings, who
    (for the most part) are capable of° nothing but in-   who can take in
    explicable dumb shows° and noise. I would have   mimed action
    such a fellow whipped for overdoing Termagant. It
    out-herods Herod.° Pray you avoid it.   (bombastic stage characters)   15

PLAYER: I warrant your honor.°   I promise it

HAMLET: Be not too tame neither; but let your own
    discretion be your tutor. Suit the action to the
    word, the word to the action; with this special ob-
    servance,° that you o'erstep not the modesty of na-   rule   20
    ture: for anything so overdone is from the purpose
    of playing, whose end, both at the first and now,
    was and is, to hold, as 'twere, the mirror up to na-
    ture; to show virtue her own feature, scorn her
    own image, and the very age and body of the time   25
    his form and pressure. Now this overdone, or
    come tardy off,° though it make the unskilful°   be badly done/uneducated
    laugh, cannot but make the judicious grieve; the
    censure of the which one must in your allowance°   judgment
    overweigh a whole theater of others. O, there be   30
    players that I have seen play, and heard others
    praise, and that highly (not to speak it profanely),°   speaking without offense
    that, neither having the accent of Christians nor the
    gait of Christian, pagan, nor man, have s

and bellowed that I have thought some of Nature's 　　　　　　　　　　35
journeymen° had made men, and not made them 　　　　　*day laborers*
well, they imitated humanity so abominably.

PLAYER: I hope we have reformed that indifferently° 　　　　　*fairly well*
with us, sir.

HAMLET: Oh, reform it altogether! And let those that 　　　　40
play your clowns speak no more than is set down
for them. For there be of them that will themselves laugh, to set on some quantity of barren
spectators to laugh too, though in the mean time
some necessary question of the play be then to be 　　　　45
considered. That's villainous and shows a most
pitiful ambition in the fool that uses it. Go make
you ready.

[*The* PLAYERS *leave.*]

[*Enter* POLONIUS, ROSENCRANTZ, *and* GUILDENSTERN.]

How now, my lord? Will the King hear this piece
of work? 　　　　　　　　　　　　　　　　　50

POLONIUS: And the Queen too, and that presently.

HAMLET: Bid the players make haste. [POLONIUS *leaves.*]
Will you two help to hasten them?

BOTH: We will, my lord.

[*Both leave.*]

HAMLET: What, ho, Horatio! 　　　　　　　　　　55

[*Enter* HORATIO.]

HORATIO: Here, sweet lord, at your service.

HAMLET: Horatio, thou art even° as just a man 　　　　*you are indeed*
As ever my conversation coped withal.° 　　　　　*as I have ever met*

HORATIO: O, my dear lord!

HAMLET: 　　　　　　　　Nay, do not think I flatter;
For what advancement may I hope from thee, 　　　　60
That no revenue° hast but thy good spirits 　　　　　　*income*
To feed and clothe thee? Why should the poor be flattered?
No, let the candied tongue lick absurd pomp,
And crook the pregnant° hinges of the knee 　　　　*bend the willing*
Where thrift may follow° fawning. Dost thou hear? 　*profit may result from*　65
Since my dear soul was mistress of her choice
And could of men distinguish, her election° 　　　　　　*choice*
Hath sealed thee for herself.° For thou hast been 　　*has singled you out*
As one, in suffering all, that suffers nothing;
A man that Fortune's buffets° and rewards 　　　　　　*blows*　70
Hast taken with equal thanks; and blest are those
Whose blood and judgment° are so well commingled 　*passion and reason*
That they are not a pipe for Fortune's finger
To sound what stop she please.° Give me that man 　　*(as on a flute)*
That is not passion's slave, and I will wear him 　　　　75

In my heart's core, ay, in my heart of heart,
As I do thee. Something too much of this.
There is a play tonight before the King.
One scene of it comes near the circumstance,°   *parallels the details*
Which I have told thee, of my father's death.   80
I prithee, when thou seest that act afoot,
Even with the very comment of thy soul
Observe my uncle. If his occulted° guilt   *hidden*
Do not itself unkennel in° one speech,   *reveal itself during*
It is a damnèd ghost that we have seen,   85
And my imaginations are as foul°   *dark and dirty*
As Vulcan's stithy.° Give him heedful note;   *the divine blacksmith's workshop*
For I mine eyes will rivet to his face,
And after we will both our judgments join
In censure of his seeming.°   *to judge his behavior*
HORATIO: Well, my lord.   90
If he steal aught the whilst this play is playing,
And scape detecting, I will pay the theft.°   *pay for the stolen item*

[*Flourish of trumpets. Trumpets and kettledrums play
a Danish march. Enter* KING, QUEEN, POLONIUS, OPHELIA,
ROSENCRANTZ, GUILDENSTERN, *and other lords, with the*
KING'S *guard carrying torches.*]

HAMLET: They are coming to the play: I must be idle.°   *play the fool*
    Get you a place.
KING: How fares our cousin Hamlet?   95
HAMLET: Excellent, in faith, of the chameleon's dish:°   *food*
    I eat the air, promise-crammed. You cannot feed
    capons so.
KING: I have nothing with this answer, Hamlet. These
    words are not mine.   100
HAMLET: No, nor mine now. [*to* POLONIUS] My lord,
    you played once i' the university, you say?
POLONIUS: That did I, my lord, and was accounted a
    good actor.
HAMLET: What did you enact?   105
POLONIUS: I did enact Julius Caesar; I was killed in the
    Capitol; Brutus killed me.
HAMLET: It was a brute part of him to kill so capital°   *outstanding*
    a calf there. Be the players ready?
ROSENCRANTZ: Ay, my lord. They stay upon your   110
    patience.°   *await your permission*
QUEEN: Come hither, my dear Hamlet, sit by me.
HAMLET: No, good mother, here's metal more
    attractive.°   *magnetic*
POLONIUS [*aside to the* KING]: O, ho! do you mark that?   115
HAMLET [*to* OPHELIA]: Lady, shall I lie in your lap?
OPHELIA: No, my lord.

HAMLET: I mean, my head upon your lap?

OPHELIA: Ay, my lord.

HAMLET: Do you think I meant country matters?°   *rustic horseplay* 120

OPHELIA: I think nothing, my lord.

HAMLET: That's a fair thought to lie between maids'
   legs.

OPHELIA: What is, my lord?

HAMLET: Nothing.   125

OPHELIA: You are merry, my lord.

HAMLET: Who, I?

OPHELIA: Ay, my lord.

HAMLET: O God, your only jig-maker! What should a
   man do but be merry? For look you how cheer-   130
   fully my mother looks, and my father died within's
   two hours.°   *no more than two hours ago*

OPHELIA: Nay, 'tis twice two months, my lord.

HAMLET: So long? Nay then, let the devil wear black,
   for I'll have a suit of sables.° O heavens! die two   *of rich dark cloth and fur* 135
   months ago, and not forgotten yet? Then there's
   hope a great man's memory may outlive his life
   half a year. But, by'r Lady, he must build churches
   then; or else shall he suffer not thinking on,° with   *not being remembered*
   the hobby-horse, whose epitaph is "For O, for   140
   O, the hobby-horse is forgot!"

*[Oboes play. The dumb show enters: Enter a King
and a Queen very lovingly; the Queen embracing
him. She kneels, and makes show of protestation
unto him. He takes her up, and declines his head
upon her neck. He lays him down upon a bank of
flowers. She, seeing him asleep, leaves him. Anon
comes in a fellow, takes off his crown, kisses it,
pours poison in the King's ears, and exits. The
Queen returns, finds the King dead, and makes
passionate action. The Poisoner, with some two or
three Mutes, comes in again, seeming to lament
with her. The dead body is carried away. The Poisoner woos the Queen with gifts; she seems loath
and unwilling awhile, but in the end accepts his
love.]*

[They leave.]

OPHELIA: What means this, my lord?

HAMLET: Marry, this is miching malicho;° it means   *bad trouble*
   mischief.

OPHELIA: Belike° this show imports the argument° of   *probably/summarizes the action* 145
   the play.

[Enter PROLOGUE.]

HAMLET: We shall know by this fellow.° The players   *from what he says*
cannot keep counsel; they'll tell all.

OPHELIA: Will he tell us what this show meant?

HAMLET: Ay, or any show that you'll show him. Be not   150
you ashamed to show, he'll not shame to tell you
what it means.

OPHELIA: You are naught,° you are naught! I'll mark°   *wicked/pay attention to*
the play.

PROLOGUE: *For us, and for our tragedy,*   155
  Here stooping to your clemency,
  We beg your hearing patiently.

                              [*Leaves.*]

HAMLET: Is this a prologue, or the posy° of a ring?   *inscription*

OPHELIA: 'Tis brief, my lord.

HAMLET: As woman's love.   160

[*Enter two* PLAYERS *as King and Queen.*]

PLAYER KING: *Full thirty times hath Phoebus' cart gone round*
  Neptune's salt wash and Tellus' orbed ground,°   *the ocean and*
  And thirty dozen moons with borrowed sheen   *the round earth*
  About the world have times twelve thirties been,
  Since love our hearts, and Hymen° did our hands,   *(god of marriage)* 165
  Unite comutual° in most sacred bands.   *mutually*

PLAYER QUEEN: *So many journeys may the sun and moon*
  Make us again count over ere love be done!
  But woe is me! you are so sick of late,
  So far from cheer and from your former state,   170
  That I distrust you.° Yet, though I distrust,   *I fear for you*
  Discomfort you, my lord, it nothing must;
  For women's fear and love holds quantity,°   *go together*
  In neither aught, or in extremity.°   *either nonexistent or extreme*
  Now what my love is, proof hath made you know;   175
  And as my love is sized, my fear is so.
  Where love is great, the littlest doubts are fear;
  Where little fears grow great, great love grows there.

PLAYER KING: *Faith, I must leave thee, love, and shortly too;*
  My operant° powers their functions leave to do.°   *vital/cease to do* 180
  And thou shalt live in this fair world behind,
  Honored, beloved, and haply one as kind
  For husband shalt thou—

PLAYER QUEEN: *O, confound the rest!*
  Such love must needs be treason in my breast.
  In second husband let me be accurst!   185
  None wed the second but who killed the first.

HAMLET [*aside*]: Wormwood, wormwood!°   *a bitter potion*

PLAYER QUEEN: *The instances that second marriage move°*   *the motives for marrying again*
  Are base respects of thrift,° but none of love.   *thoughts of property*

A second time I kill my husband dead   190
When second husband kisses me in bed.
PLAYER KING: *I do believe you think what now you speak;*
   But what we do determine oft we break.
   Purpose is but the slave to memory,
   Of violent birth, but poor validity;   195
   Which now, like fruit unripe, sticks on the tree,
   But fall unshaken when they mellow be.
   Most necessary 'tis that we forget
   To pay ourselves what to ourselves is debt.
   What to ourselves in passion we propose,   200
   The passion ending, doth the purpose lose.
   The violence of either grief or joy
   Their own enactures° with themselves destroy.   *acts*
   Where joy most revels, grief doth most lament;
   Grief joys, joy grieves, on slender accident.   205
   This world is not for aye,° nor 'tis not strange   *forever*
   That even our loves should with our fortunes change;
   For 'tis a question left us yet to prove,
   Whether love lead fortune, or else fortune love.
   The great man down, you mark his favorite flies,°   *his protégé abandons him* 210
   The poor advanced makes° friends of enemies;   *when the poor succeed, they make*
   And hitherto doth love on fortune tend,
   For who not needs° shall never lack a friend,   *who is not in need*
   And who in want a hollow friend doth try,
   Directly seasons° him his enemy.   *immediately makes* 215
   But, orderly to end where I begun,
   Our wills and fates do so contrary run
   That our devices° still are overthrown;   *plans*
   Our thoughts are ours, their ends none of our own.
   So think thou wilt no second husband wed;   220
   But die thy thoughts° when thy first lord is dead.   *your intentions will change*
PLAYER QUEEN: *Nor earth° to me give food, nor heaven light,*   *let the earth not . . .*
   Sport and repose lock from me day and night,
   To desperation turn my trust and hope,
   An anchor's cheer in prison be my scope,°   *let a hermit's fare be my portion* 225
   Each opposite that blanks the face of joy
   Meet what I would have well, and it destroy,
   Both here and hence pursue me lasting strife,
   If, once a widow, ever I be wife!
HAMLET: If she should break it now!   230
PLAYER KING: *'Tis deeply sworn. Sweet, leave me here awhile.*
   My spirits grow dull, and fain I would beguile
   The tedious day with sleep.
PLAYER QUEEN: *Sleep rock thy brain,*

   [*He sleeps.*]

And never come mischance between us twain!

               [*She leaves.*]

HAMLET: Madam, how like you this play?   235
QUEEN: The lady doth protest° too much, methinks.   *advertise her feelings*
HAMLET: O, but she'll keep her word.
KING: Have you heard the argument?° Is there no of-   *plot*
    fense in it?
HAMLET: No, no! They do but jest, poison in jest; no   240
    offense in the world.
KING: What do you call the play?
HAMLET: "The Mousetrap." Marry, how? Tropically.°   *metaphorically*
    This play is the image of a murder done in Vienna.
    Gonzago is the duke's name: his wife, Baptista.   245
    You shall see anon. 'Tis a knavish° piece of work;   *villainous*
    but what of that? Your Majesty, and we that have
    free souls,° it touches us not. Let the galled jade°   *who are innocent/sore horse*
    wince; our withers are unwrung.°   *our own necks are untouched*

[*Enter* LUCIANUS.]

This is one Lucianus, nephew to the King.   250
OPHELIA: You are as good as a chorus, my lord.
HAMLET: I could interpret between° you and your   *speak for*
    love, if I could see the puppets dallying.°   *(as in a puppet show)*
OPHELIA: You are keen,° my lord, you are keen.   *sharp*
HAMLET: It would cost you a groaning to take off my   255
    edge.
OPHELIA: Still better, and worse.
HAMLET: So you must take your husbands. Begin,
    murderer. Pox,° leave thy damnable faces, and   *a plague on it*
    begin! Come, the croaking raven doth bellow for   260
    revenge.
LUCIANUS: *Thoughts black, hands apt, drugs fit, and*
    time agreeing;
    Confederate season,° else no creature seeing;   *with the occasion conspiring*
    Thou mixture rank, of midnight weeds collected,   265
    With Hecate's ban thrice blasted, thrice infected,
    Thy natural magic and dire property
    On wholesome life usurp° immediately.   *inflict*

[*Pours the poison in his ears.*]

HAMLET: He poisons him in the garden for his estate;
    his name's Gonzago. The story is extant,° and   *exists* 270
    writ° in choice Italian. You shall see anon how the   *written*
    murderer gets the love of Gonzago's wife.
OPHELIA: The King rises.
HAMLET: What, frighted with false fire?°   *gunfire without bullets*
QUEEN: How fares my lord?   275
POLONIUS: Give over° the play.   *stop*
KING: Give me some light! Away!
ALL: Lights, lights, lights!

[*All leave but* HAMLET *and* HORATIO.]

HAMLET: Why, let the strucken deer go weep,
     The hart ungallèd° play;   *uninjured deer* 280
For some must watch, while some must sleep:
     Thus runs the world away.
Would not this, sir, and a forest of feathers—if the
rest of my fortunes turn Turk° with me—with two   *take a bad turn*
Provincial roses on my razed shoes, get me a fel-   285
lowship in a cry of° players, sir?   *a group of*
HORATIO: Half a share.
HAMLET: A whole one I!
For thou dost know, O Damon dear,°   *(a faithful friend)*
     This realm dismantled was   290
Of Jove himself; and now reigns here
     A very, very—pajock.°   *(repulsive) peacock*
HORATIO: You might have rhymed.
HAMLET: O good Horatio, I'll take the ghost's word for
a thousand pound! Didst perceive?   295
HORATIO: Very well, my lord.
HAMLET: Upon the talk of the poisoning?
HORATIO: I did very well note him.
HAMLET: Aha! Come, some music! Come, the recorders!
For if the King like not the comedy,   300
Why then, belike he likes it not, perdy.
Come, some music!

[*Enter* ROSENCRANTZ *and* GUILDENSTERN.]

GUILDENSTERN: Good my lord, vouchsafe me a word
with you.
HAMLET: Sir, a whole history.   305
GUILDENSTERN: The King, sir—
HAMLET: Ay, sir, what of him?
GUILDENSTERN: Is in his retirement,° marvellous   *private rooms*
distempered.°   *upset*
HAMLET: With drink, sir?   310
GUILDENSTERN: No, my lord; rather with choler.°   *anger*
HAMLET: Your wisdom should show itself more richer
to signify this to his doctor; for, for me to put him
to his purgation would perhaps plunge him into
far more choler.   315
GUILDENSTERN: Good my lord, put your discourse into
some frame, and start not so wildly from my affair.
HAMLET: I am tame, sir; pronounce.
GUILDENSTERN: The Queen, your mother, in most great
affliction of spirit hath sent me to you.   320
HAMLET: You are welcome.
GUILDENSTERN: Nay, good my lord, this courtesy is not
of the right breed. If it shall please you to make
me a wholesome° answer, I will do your mother's   *right kind of*
commandment; if not, your pardon and my return   325
shall be the end of my business.

HAMLET: Sir, I cannot.

GUILDENSTERN: What, my lord?

HAMLET: Make you a wholesome answer; my wit's
diseased. But, sir, such answer as I can make, you   330
shall command; or rather, as you say, my mother.
Therefore no more, but to the matter! My mother,
you say—

ROSENCRANTZ: Then thus she says: your behavior hath
struck her into amazement and admiration.°   *wonder* 335

HAMLET: O wonderful son, that can so astonish a
mother! But is there no sequel at the heels of this
mother's admiration? Impart.°   *let me know*

ROSENCRANTZ: She desires to speak with you in her
closet° ere you go to bed.   *private room* 340

HAMLET: We shall obey, were she° ten times our   *even if she were*
mother. Have you any further trade with us?

ROSENCRANTZ: My lord, you once did love me.

HAMLET: And do still, by these pickers and stealers!°   *thieving hands*

ROSENCRANTZ: Good my lord, what is your cause of dis-   345
temper? You do surely bar the door upon your own
liberty,° if you deny your griefs to your friend.   *liberation from grief*

HAMLET: Sir, I lack advancement.

ROSENCRANTZ: How can that be, when you have the
voice of the King himself for your succession in   350
Denmark?

HAMLET: Ay, sir, but "while the grass grows"°—the   *("... the horse starves")*
proverb is something musty.

[*Enter the* MUSICIANS *with recorders.*]

O, the recorders! Let me see one. To withdraw with
you—why do you go about to recover the wind of°   *to be downwind from* 355
me, as if you would drive me into a toil?°   *trap*

GUILDENSTERN: O my lord, if my duty be too bold, my
love is too unmannerly.°   *makes me forget good manners*

HAMLET: I do not well understand that. Will you play
upon this pipe?°   *recorder* 360

GUILDENSTERN: My lord, I cannot.

HAMLET: I pray you.

GUILDENSTERN: Believe me, I cannot.

HAMLET: I do beseech you.

GUILDENSTERN: I know no touch of it, my lord.   365

HAMLET: It is as easy as lying. Govern these ventages°   *control these openings*
with your finger and thumb, give it breath with
your mouth, and it will discourse° most eloquent   *make*
music. Look you, these are the stops.

GUILDENSTERN: But these cannot I command to any ut-   370
terance of harmony. I have not the skill.

HAMLET: Why, look you now, how unworthy a thing
you make of me! You would play upon me; you

would seem to know my stops; you would pluck
out the heart of my mystery; you would sound me   375
from my lowest note to the top of my compass;°   *range*
and there is much music, excellent voice, in this little organ,° yet cannot you make it speak. 'Sblood,   *instrument*
do you think I am easier to be played on than a
pipe? Call me what instrument you will, though   380
you can fret° me, you cannot play upon me.   *annoy (pun on preparing*
                                                      an instrument)

[*Enter* POLONIUS.]

God bless you, sir!
POLONIUS: My lord, the Queen would° speak with   *wants to* 385
   you, and presently.
HAMLET: Do you see yonder cloud that's almost in
   shape of a camel?
POLONIUS: By the mass, and 'tis like a camel indeed.
HAMLET: Methinks° it is like a weasel.   *I think*
POLONIUS: It is backed like a weasel.
HAMLET: Or like a whale.   390
POLONIUS: Very like a whale.
HAMLET: Then will I come to my mother by-and-by.
   They fool me° to the top of my bent. I will come   *make me play the fool*
   by-and-by.
POLONIUS: I will say so.   395

[*He leaves.*]

HAMLET: "By-and-by" is easily said. Leave me, friends.

[*All but* HAMLET *leave.*]

'Tis now the very witching time of night,
When churchyards yawn, and hell itself breathes out
Contagion to this world. Now could I drink hot blood
And do such bitter business as the day   400
Would quake to look on. Soft! now to my mother!
O heart, lose not thy nature;° let not ever   *let me not be unnatural*
The soul of Nero° enter this firm bosom.   *(the bloody Roman emperor)*
Let me be cruel, not unnatural;
I will speak daggers to her, but use none.   405
My tongue and soul in this be hypocrites—
How in my words soever she be shent,°   *shamed*
To give them seals° never, my soul, consent!   *seal them with actions*

[*He leaves.*]

SCENE 3. A room in the Castle.

[*Enter* KING, ROSENCRANTZ, *and* GUILDENSTERN.]

KING: I like him not, nor stands it safe with us
   To let his madness range. Therefore prepare you;
   I your commission will forthwith dispatch,°   *right away draw up your orders*

And he to England shall along° with you.   *shall travel*
The terms of our estate° may not endure   *my position*   5
Hazard° so near us as doth hourly grow   *extreme danger*
Out of his lunacies.
GUILDENSTERN: We will ourselves provide.°   *will get ready*
Most holy and religious fear it is
To keep those many many bodies safe
That live and feed upon your Majesty   10
ROSENCRANTZ: The single and peculiar° life is bound   *private*
With all the strength and armor of the mind
To keep itself from noyance;° but much more   *harm*
That spirit upon whose weal° depends and rests   *welfare*
The lives of many. The cease of majesty°   *death of a king*   15
Dies not alone, but like a gulf° doth draw   *whirlpool*
What's near it with it. It is a massy wheel,
Fixed on the summit of the highest mount,
To whose huge spokes ten thousand lesser things
Are mortised° and adjoined; which when it falls,   *attached*   20
Each small annexment,° petty consequence,   *minor attachment*
Attends° the boisterous ruin. Never alone   *shares in*
Did the king sigh, but with a general groan.°   *sorrow for all the people*
KING: Arm you,° I pray you, to this speedy voyage;   *prepare yourselves*
For we will fetters put upon° this fear,   *will chain up*   25
Which now goes too free-footed.
BOTH: We will haste us.

                        [*They leave.*]

[*Enter* POLONIUS.]

POLONIUS: My lord, he's going to his mother's closet.
Behind the arras° I'll convey myself   *wall hanging*
To hear the process. I'll warrant she'll tax him home;°   *rebuke him sharply*
And, as you said, and wisely was it said,   30
'Tis meet° that some more audience than a mother,   *it's right*
Since nature makes them partial, should overhear
The speech, of vantage.° Fare you well, my liege.   *from a vantage point*
I'll call upon you ere you go to bed
And tell you what I know.
KING: Thanks, dear my lord.   35

                        [POLONIUS *leaves.*]

O, my offense is rank, it smells to heaven;
It hath the primal eldest° curse upon't,   *first and oldest*
A brother's murder! Pray can I not,
Though inclination be as sharp as will.
My stronger guilt defeats my strong intent,   40
And, like a man to double business bound,°   *who has to do two things*
I stand in pause° where I shall first begin,   *hesitate*
And both neglect. What if this cursèd hand
Were thicker than itself with brother's blood,

Is there not rain enough in the sweet heavens   45
To wash it white as snow? Whereto serves mercy
But to confront the visage of offense?°   *to battle with the face of guilt*
And what's in prayer but this twofold force,
To be forestalled ere we° come to fall,   *before we*
Or pardoned being down?° Then I'll look up;   *when we have fallen* 50
My fault is past. But, O, what form of prayer
Can serve my turn? "Forgive me my foul murder"?
That cannot be; since I am still possessed
Of those effects for which I did the murder—
My crown, mine own ambition, and my queen.   55
May one be pardoned and retain the offense?°   *the fruits of the crime*
In the corrupted currents of this world
Offense's gilded hand may shove by° justice,   *push aside*
And oft 'tis seen the wicked prize itself
Buys out the law; but 'tis not so above.   60
There is no shuffling;° there the action lies°   *no cheating/appears*
In his° true nature, and we ourselves compelled,   *its*
Even to the teeth and forehead of our faults,
To give in evidence. What then? What rests?
Try what repentance can. What can it not?   65
Yet what can it when one cannot repent?
O wretched state! O bosom black as death!
O limèd° soul, that, struggling to be free,   *trapped*
Art more engaged!° Help, angels! Make assay.   *becomes more entangled*
Bow, stubborn knees; and heart with strings of steel,   70
Be soft as sinews of the new-born babe!
All may be well.

[*He kneels.*]

[*Enter* HAMLET.]

HAMLET: Now might I do it pat, now he is praying;
    And now I'll do't. And so he goes to heaven,
    And so am I revenged. That would be scanned.°   *should be examined* 75
    A villain kills my father; and for that,
    I, his sole son, do this same villain send
    To heaven.
    Why, this is hire° and salary, not revenge!   *reward*
    He took my father grossly, full of bread,°   *after a heavy meal* 80
    With all his crimes broad blown,° as flush as May;   *in full bloom*
    And how his audit stands, who knows save heaven?
    But in our circumstance and course of thought,°   *according to common opinion*
    'Tis heavy with him;° and am I then revenged,   *he is in deep trouble*
    To take him in the purging° of his soul,   *cleansing* 85
    When he is fit and seasoned for his passage?
    No.
    Up, sword, and know thou a more horrid hent.°   *be ready for more horrible use*
    When he is drunk asleep; or in his rage;
    Or in the incestuous pleasure of his bed;   90

At gaming, swearing, or about some act
That has no relish of salvation in't—
Then trip him, that his heels may kick at heaven,
And that his soul may be as damned and black
As hell, whereto it goes. My mother stays.°   *waits*   95
This physic° but prolongs thy sickly days.   *medicine*

[*He leaves.*]

KING [*rises*]: My words fly up, my thoughts remain below;
Words without thoughts never to heaven go.

[*He leaves.*]

SCENE 4. The QUEEN's private chamber.

[*Enter* QUEEN *and* POLONIUS.]

POLONIUS: He will come straight. Look you lay home to him.°   *see that you*
Tell him his pranks have been too broad to bear with,   *speak frankly*
And that your Grace hath screened and stood between
Much heat and him. I'll silence me even here.°   *I'll say no more*
Pray you be round° with him.   *outspoken*   5
HAMLET [*within*]: Mother, mother, mother!
QUEEN: I'll warrant° you; fear me not. Withdraw;   *I promise*
I hear him coming.

[POLONIUS *hides behind the arras.*]

[*Enter* HAMLET.]

HAMLET: Now, mother, what's the matter?
QUEEN: Hamlet, thou hast thy father much offended.   10
HAMLET: Mother, you have my father much offended.
QUEEN: Come, come, you answer with an idle tongue.
HAMLET: Go, go, you question with a wicked tongue.
QUEEN: Why, how now, Hamlet?
HAMLET: What's the matter now?
QUEEN: Have you forgot me?
HAMLET: No, by the rood,° not so!   *by the Cross*   15
You are the Queen, your husband's brother's wife,
And—would it were° not so—you are my mother.   *I wish it were*
QUEEN: Nay, then I'll set those to you° that can speak.   *I'll make you talk to those*
HAMLET: Come, come, and sit you down, you shall not
budge!
You go not till I set you up a glass°   *mirror*   20
Where you may see the inmost part of you.
QUEEN: What wilt thou do? Thou wilt not murder me?
Help, help, ho!
POLONIUS [*behind the arras*]: What, ho! help, help, help!
HAMLET [*draws his sword*]: How now? a rat? Dead for
a ducat,° dead!   *(a gold coin)*   25

[*Stabs through the arras and kills* POLONIUS.]

POLONIUS: O, I am slain!
QUEEN: O me, what hast thou done?
HAMLET: Nay, I know not. Is it the King?
QUEEN: O, what a rash and bloody deed is this!
HAMLET: A bloody deed—almost as bad, good mother,
  As kill a king, and marry with his brother.   30
QUEEN: As kill a king?
HAMLET: Ay, lady, 'twas my word.

[*Pulls aside arras and sees* POLONIUS.]

Thou wretched, rash, intruding fool, farewell!
I took thee for thy better.° Take thy fortune.   *mistook you for your king*
Thou find'st to be too busy is some danger.
[*to his mother*] Leave° wringing of your hands.   *stop* 35
  Peace! sit you down
And let me wring your heart; for so I shall
If it be made of penetrable° stuff;   *that can be penetrated*
If damnèd custom have not brazed it so°   *force of habit has not made it so brazen*
That it is proof and bulwark against sense.°   *feeling* 40
QUEEN: What have I done that thou dar'st wag thy tongue
  In noise so rude against me?
HAMLET: Such an act
That blurs the grace and blush of modesty;
Calls virtue hypocrite; takes off the rose
From the fair forehead of an innocent love,   45
And sets a blister° there; makes marriage vows   *brand of shame*
As false as dicers'° oaths. O, such a deed   *gamblers'*
As from the body of contraction° plucks   *marriage contract*
The very soul, and sweet religion makes
A rhapsody° of words! Heaven's face doth glow;°   *garbled string/blush* 50
Yea, this solidity and compound mass,°   *this solid earth*
With tristful visage,° as against the doom,°   *mournful face/on the eve of doom*
Is thought-sick at the act.
QUEEN: Ay me, what act,
That roars so loud and thunders in the index?°   *in your listing*
HAMLET: Look here upon this picture, and on this,   55
The counterfeit presentment° of two brothers.   *painted likeness*
See what a grace was seated on this brow;
Hyperion's° curls; the front of Jove himself;   *(beautiful divine being)*
An eye like Mars,° to threaten and command;   *(god of war)*
A station° like the herald Mercury°   *bearing/(messenger of the gods)* 60
New lighted° on a heaven-kissing hill: *having just landed*
A combination and a form indeed
Where every god did seem to set his seal
To give the world assurance of a man.
This was your husband. Look you now what follows.   65
Here is your husband, like a mildewed ear°   *an infected ear of corn*
Blasting° his wholesome brother. Have you eyes?   *spreading infection to*
Could you on this fair mountain leave to feed,

And batten on this moor?° Ha! have you eyes?   *feed greedily on a swamp*
You cannot call it love; for at your age   70
The heyday in the blood° is tame, it's humble,   *of physical passion*
And waits upon the judgment;° and what judgment   *is guided by reason*
Would step from this to this? Sense° sure you have,   *sensations*
Else could you not have motion; but sure that sense
Is apoplexed;° for madness would not err,   *paralyzed* 75
Nor sense to ecstasy was never so thralled°   *was never such a slave*
But it reserved some quantity of choice   *to madness*
To serve in such a difference. What devil was't
That thus hath cozened you at hoodman-blind?°   *cheated you at blindman's bluff*
Eyes without feeling, feeling without sight,   *(game with blindfolded player)* 80
Ears without hands or eyes, smelling sans° all,   *without*
Or but a sickly part of one true sense
Could not so mope.°   *blunder*
O shame! where is thy blush? Rebellious hell,
If thou canst mutiny in a matron's bones,   85
To flaming youth let virtue be as wax
And melt in her own fire. Proclaim no shame
When the compulsive ardor gives the charge,°   *passion leads the attack*
Since frost itself as actively doth burn,
And reason panders will.°   *panders to desire*
QUEEN: O Hamlet, speak no more!   90
Thou turn'st mine eyes into my very soul,
And there I see such black and grainèd° spots   *ingrained*
As will not leave their tinct.°   *lose their color*
HAMLET: Nay, but to live
In the rank sweat of an enseamed° bed,   *greasy*
Stewed in corruption, honeying and making love   95
Over the nasty sty!
QUEEN: O, speak to me no more!
These words like daggers enter in mine ears.
No more, sweet Hamlet!
HAMLET: A murderer and a villain!
A slave that is not twentieth part the tithe°   *tenth share*
Of your precedent° lord; a vice° of kings;   *former/parody* 100
A cutpurse° of the empire and the rule,   *purse snatcher*
That from a shelf the precious diadem stole
And put it in his pocket!
QUEEN: No more!

[*Enter* GHOST.]

HAMLET: A king of shreds and patches—
Save me and hover over me with your wings,   105
You heavenly guards! What would your gracious figure?
QUEEN: Alas, he's mad!
HAMLET: Do you not come your tardy son to chide,
That, lapsed° in time and passion, lets go by   *negligent*

The important acting of your dread command?   110
O, say!

GHOST: Do not forget. This visitation
Is but to whet thy almost blunted purpose.
But look, amazement on thy mother sits.
O, step between her and her fighting soul!   115
Conceit° in weakest bodies strongest works.   *imagination*
Speak to her, Hamlet.

HAMLET: How is it with you, lady?

QUEEN: Alas, how is't with you,
That you do bend your eye on vacancy,°   *vacant space*
And with the incorporal° air do hold discourse?   *bodiless* 120
Forth at your eyes your spirits wildly peep;
And, as the sleeping soldiers in the alarm,
Your bedded hairs, like life in excrements,°   *inert outgrowths*
Start up and stand on end. O gentle son,
Upon the heat and flame of thy distemper°   *your disturbed mind* 125
Sprinkle cool patience! Whereon do you look?

HAMLET: On him, on him! Look you how pale he glares!
His form and cause conjoined, preaching to stones,
Would make them capable°—Do not look upon me,   *enable them to feel*
Lest with this piteous action you convert   130
My stern effects.° Then what I have to do   *my stern deeds*
Will want° true color—tears perchance for blood.   *lack*

QUEEN: To whom do you speak this?

HAMLET: Do you see nothing
there?

QUEEN: Nothing at all; yet all that is I see.

HAMLET: Nor did you nothing hear?

QUEEN: No, nothing but ourselves.   135

HAMLET: Why, look you there! Look how it steals away!
My father, in his habit° as he lived!   *garment*
Look where he goes even now out at the portal!

[GHOST *leaves.*]

QUEEN: This is the very coinage of your brain.
This bodiless creation ecstasy°   *madness* 140
Is very cunning in.°   *is very good at*

HAMLET: Ecstasy?
My pulse as yours doth temperately keep time
And makes as healthful music. It is not madness
That I have uttered. Bring me to the test,
And I the matter will reword, which madness   145
Would gambol from.° Mother, for love of grace,   *shy away from*
Lay not that flattering unction° to your soul,   *soothing ointment*
That not your trespass but my madness speaks.
It will but skin and film° the ulcerous place,   *cover up*
Whilst rank corruption, mining° all within,   *undermining* 150

Infects unseen. Confess yourself to heaven;
Repent what's past; avoid what is to come;
And do not spread the compost on the weeds
To make them ranker.° Forgive me this my virtue;   *grow wilder*
For in the fatness of these pursy° times   *bloated* 155
Virtue itself of vice must pardon beg—
Yea, curb and woo for leave° to do him good.   *bow for permission*
QUEEN: O Hamlet, thou has cleft° my heart in twain.   *you have split*
HAMLET: O, throw away the worser part of it,
   And live the purer with the other half.   160
   Good night—but go not to my uncle's bed.
   Assume a virtue,° if you have it not.   *pretend to be virtuous*
   That monster, custom,° who all sense doth eat   *habit*
   Of habits evil, is angel yet in this,
   That to the use of actions fair and good   165
   He likewise gives a frock or livery,°   *an outward appearance*
   That aptly is put on. Refrain tonight,
   And that shall lend a kind of easiness
   To the next abstinence; the next more easy;
   For use° almost can change the stamp of nature,   *force of habit* 170
   And either master the devil, or throw him out
   With wondrous potency. Once more, good night;
   And when you are desirous to be blest,
   I'll blessing beg of you.—For this same lord,
   I do repent; but heaven hath pleased it so,   175
   To punish me with this, and this with me,
   That I must be their scourge and minister.
   I will bestow him,° and will answer well   *dispose of him*
   The death° I gave him. So again, good night.   *for the death*
   I must be cruel, only to be kind;   180
   Thus bad begins, and worse remains behind.°   *is yet to come*
   One word more, good lady.
QUEEN: What shall I do?
HAMLET: Not this, by no means, that I bid you do:
   Let the bloat King tempt you again to bed;
   Pinch wanton on your cheek; call you his mouse;   185
   And let him, for a pair of reechy° kisses,   *reeking*
   Or paddling in your neck with his damned fingers,
   Make you to ravel all this matter out,
   That I essentially am not in madness,
   But mad in craft.° 'Twere good you let him know;   *on purpose* 190
   For who that's but a queen, fair, sober, wise,
   Would from a paddock,° from a bat, a gib,°   *toad/tomcat*
   Such dear concernings hide? Who would do so?
   No, in despite of sense and secrecy,
   Unpeg° the basket on the house's top,   *unfasten* 195
   Let the birds fly, and like the famous ape,
   To try conclusions,° in the basket creep   *make an experiment*
   And break your own neck down.°   *fall down (while trying to fly)*

QUEEN: Be thou assured, if words be made of breath,
   And breath of life, I have no life to breathe°   *reveal* 200
   What thou hast said to me.
HAMLET: I must to England; you know that?
QUEEN: Alack,°   *alas*
   I had forgot! 'Tis so concluded on.°   *so decided*
HAMLET: There's letters sealed; and my two schoolfellows,
   Whom I will trust as I will adders fanged,   205
   They bear the mandate;° they must sweep my way   *carry the instructions*
   And marshal me to knavery. Let it work;
   For 'tis the sport to have the enginer°   *engineer*
   Hoist with his own petar;° and 't shall go hard   *blown up by his own bomb*
   But I will delve° one yard below their mines   *dig* 210
   And blow them at the moon. O 'tis most sweet
   When in one line two crafts directly meet.°   *two plots converge*
   This man shall set me packing:
   I'll lug the guts into the neighbor room.
   Mother, good night. Indeed, this counsellor   215
   Is now most still, most secret, and most grave,
   Who was in life a foolish prating knave.
   Come, sir, to draw toward an end with you.
   Good night, mother.

[*Both leave, with* HAMLET *dragging* POLONIUS.]

The Receptive Reader

1. (Act Three, Scene 1) By the end of this scene, how aware is the audience of a plot of *intrigue?* How much has it seen of plotting and counterplotting on the part of two major opposed parties?

2. The "To be or not to be" soliloquy is usually seen as Hamlet's debating the pros and cons of suicide. (Some critics read the speech as a debate on "To act or not to act"—whether to take decisive action against Claudius.) What are the pros and cons? Does he seem to you to be in a highly disturbed or suicidal frame of mind? How does this speech round out your understanding of Hamlet's character?

3. In his encounter with Ophelia, why does Hamlet deny having loved her or having given her tokens of affection? What is the point of Hamlet's *satirical* commentary on beauty, marriage, and offspring? Why does he direct it at Ophelia? Does Ophelia hold her own or is she the passive victim?

4. (Act Three, Scene 2) What does Hamlet's relationship with Horatio show about his character? When Hamlet praises his friend, what are to him the ideal qualities of an admirable person?

5. What is the tone or direction of Hamlet's running commentary during the play-within-the-play? What is the upshot of Hamlet's "mousetrap" scheme? What is Hamlet's frame of mind by the end of this scene?

6. What is sarcastic about remarks like "We will obey, were she ten times our mother"? What other examples of Hamlet's *sarcastic tone* can you cite?

7. (Act Three, Scene 3) How does the prayer scene change your view of Claudius as the villain of the play?

8. (Act Three, Scene 4) The killing of Polonius can be seen as a major turning point in the **plot** of the play. How and why? How does Hamlet explain his killing of Polonius? What is his reaction; how does he treat the dead body?

9. What are the major themes in Hamlet's denunciation of his mother? What picture does he paint of his dead father, of Claudius (his "father-uncle"), of his mother? Is he in full control of his sense, as he claims, or profoundly disturbed? How does Queen Gertrude act in this *climactic* scene? What do you conclude about her guilt—her implication in the murder? (What does the reappearance of the ghost add to this climactic scene?)

The Range of Interpretation

Hamlet's role in the prayer scene has been much debated. He refuses to kill the king at prayer because in the state of repentance Claudius might be forgiven his sin, with his soul going to heaven. To make the revenge complete, Claudius should be sent to hell—killed when caught in some sinful act without a chance of repentance. Some critics have found this attitude too brutal and un-Christian to fit with their understanding of Hamlet's character. Is he more harsh and brutal in this thirst for revenge than you would expect? Or is his attitude here in keeping with his character as you understand it? Or is Hamlet perhaps using the king's praying as a pretext, as an excuse for further delaying his task? Or is the playwright perhaps signaling to the audience that Hamlet is not as admirable and virtuous as we might think—he himself is also infected by the moral corruption of his time?

Act Four

SCENE 1. Elsinore. A room in the Castle.

[*Enter* KING *and* QUEEN, *with* ROSENCRANTZ *and* GUILDENSTERN.]

KING: There's matter in these sighs. These profound heaves
You must translate; 'tis fit we understand them.
Where is your son?
QUEEN: Bestow this place on us° a little while.   *leave us alone*

[ROSENCRANTZ *and* GUILDENSTERN *leave*.]

Ah, mine own lord, what have I seen tonight!   5
KING: What, Gertrude? How does Hamlet?
QUEEN: Mad as the sea and wind when both contend
Which is the mightier. In his lawless fit,
Behind the arras hearing something stir,
Whips out his rapier, cries "A rat, a rat!"   10
And in this brainish apprehension° kills   *brainsick fit*
The unseen good old man.
KING: O heavy deed!
It had been so with us,° had we been there.   *this would have happened to me*

His liberty is full of threats to all—
To you yourself, to us, to every one.   15
Alas, how shall this bloody deed be answered?
It will be laid to us,° whose providence   *we will be blamed*
Should have kept short, restrained, and out of haunt°   *away from people*
This mad young man. But so much was our love
We would not understand what was most fit,   20
But, like the owner of a foul disease,
To keep it from divulging,° let it feed   *from being known*
Even on the pith° of life. Where is he gone?   *essence*
QUEEN: To draw apart the body he hath killed,
Over whom his very madness, like some ore°   *a more valuable vein*   25
Among a mineral of metals base,
Shows itself pure. He weeps for what is done.
KING: O Gertrude, come away!
The sun no sooner shall the mountains touch
But we will ship him hence; and this vile deed   30
We must with all our majesty and skill
Both countenance° and excuse. Ho, Guildenstern!   *sanction*

[*Enter* ROSENCRANTZ *and* GUILDENSTERN.]

Friends both, go join you with some further aid.
Hamlet in madness hath Polonius slain,
And from his mother's closet hath he dragged him.   35
Go seek him out; speak fair,° and bring the body   *talk to him politely*
Into the chapel. I pray you haste in this.

[ROSENCRANTZ *and* GUILDENSTERN *leave.*]

Come, Gertrude, we'll call up our wisest friends
And let them know both what we mean to do
And what's untimely done. So haply° slander   *perhaps*   40
Whose whisper over the world's diameter,
As level as the cannon to his blank,°   *straight . . . to its target*
Transports his poisoned shot—may miss our name
And hit the woundless° air.—O, come away!   *which cannot be wounded*
My soul is full of discord and dismay.   45

[*They leave.*]

SCENE 2. The same. A passage in the Castle.

[*Enter* HAMLET.]

HAMLET: Safely stowed.°   *hidden*
GENTLEMEN (*within*): Hamlet! Lord Hamlet!
HAMLET: But soft! What noise? Who calls on Hamlet?
O, here they come.

[*Enter* ROSENCRANTZ *and* GUILDENSTERN.]

ROSENCRANTZ: What have you done, my lord, with the
dead body?   5

HAMLET: Compounded° it with dust, whereto 'tis kin.   *mingled*
ROSENCRANTZ: Tell us where 'tis, that we may take it
   thence. And bear it to the chapel.
HAMLET: Do not believe it.   10
ROSENCRANTZ: Believe what?
HAMLET: That I can keep your counsel,° and not mine   *secret*
   own. Besides, to be demanded of° a sponge, what   *when questioned by*
   replication° should be made by the son of a king?   *answer*
ROSENCRANTZ: Take you me for a sponge, my lord?   15
HAMLET: Ay, sir, that soaks up the King's counte-
   nance,° his rewards, his authorities.° But such of-   *looks*
                                                                                       appointments
   ficers do the King best service in the end. He
   keeps them, like an ape, in the corner of his jaw;
   first mouthed, to be last swallowed.° When he   *(like saving unswallowed*   20
   needs what you have gleaned, it is but squeezing   *food in one's cheeks)*
   you and, sponge, you shall be dry again.
ROSENCRANTZ: I understand you not, my lord.
HAMLET: I am glad of it: a knavish° speech sleeps in   *wicked*
   a foolish ear.   25
ROSENCRANTZ: My lord, you must tell us where the
   body is and go with us to the King.
HAMLET: The body is with the King, but the King is
   not with the body. The King is a thing—
GUILDENSTERN: A thing, my lord?   30
HAMLET: Of nothing. Bring me to him. Hide fox, and
   all after.

                                 [They leave.]

SCENE 3. The same. A room as before.

   [Enter KING.*]*

KING: I have sent to seek him and to find the body.
   How dangerous is it that this man goes loose!
   Yet must not we put the strong law on him.
   He's loved of the distracted multitude,°   *by the fickle crowds*
   Who like not in their judgment,° but their eyes;   *not by good judgment*   5
   And where 'tis so, the offender's scourge is weighed,°   *the penalty is questioned*
   But never the offense. To bear all° smooth and even,   *to make all seem*
   This sudden sending him away must seem
   Deliberate pause.° Diseases desperate grown   *like a well-weighed plan*
   By desperate appliance° are relieved,   *remedies*   10
   Or not at all.

   [Enter ROSENCRANTZ.*]*

           How now? What hath befallen?
ROSENCRANTZ: Where the dead body is bestowed, my lord,
   We cannot get from him.
KING: But where is he?
ROSENCRANTZ: Without,° my lord; guarded, to know   *outside*
   your pleasure.

KING: Bring him before us.   15

ROSENCRANTZ: Ho, Guildenstern! Bring in my lord.

[*Enter* HAMLET *and* GUILDENSTERN *with attendants.*]

KING: Now, Hamlet, where's Polonius?

HAMLET: At supper.

KING: At supper? Where?

HAMLET: Not where he eats, but where he is eaten. A   20
  certain convocation of politic° worms are even at   *assembly of politically minded*
  him. Your worm is your only emperor for diet. We
  fat° all creatures else to fat us, and we fat ourselves   *fatten*
  for maggots. Your fat king and your lean beggar is
  but variable service—two dishes, but to one table.   25
  That's the end.

KING: Alas, alas!

HAMLET: A man may fish with the worm that hath eat
  of a king, and eat of the fish that hath fed of that
  worm.   30

KING: What dost thou mean by this?

HAMLET: Nothing but to show you how a king may go
  a progress° through the guts of a beggar.   *make his way*

KING: Where is Polonius?

HAMLET: In heaven. Send thither to see. If your mes-   35
  senger find him not there, seek him in the other
  place yourself. But indeed, if you find him not
  within this month, you shall nose° him as you go   *smell*
  up the stairs into the lobby.

KING [*to attendants*]: Go seek him there.   40

HAMLET: He will stay till you come.

[*Attendants leave.*]

KING: Hamlet, this deed, for thine especial safety—
  Which we do tender° as we dearly grieve   *cherish*
  For that which thou hast done—must send thee hence
  With fiery quickness. Therefore prepare thyself.   45
  The bark is ready and the wind at help,
  The associates tend,° and everything is bent   *your companions are waiting*
  For England.

HAMLET: For England?

KING: Ay, Hamlet.

HAMLET: Good.

KING: So is it, if thou knew'st our purposes.

HAMLET: I see a cherub° that sees them. But come, for   *an all-knowing angel* 50
  England! Farewell, dear mother.

KING: Thy° loving father, Hamlet.   *I am your*

HAMLET: My mother! Father and mother is man and
  wife; man and wife is one flesh; and so, my
  mother. Come, for England!   55

[He leaves.]

KING: Follow him at foot; tempt° him with speed   *urge*
    aboard;
  Delay it not, I'll have him hence° tonight.   *away from here*
  Away! for everything is sealed and done
  That else leans on° the affair. Pray you make haste.   *relates to*

[ROSENCRANTZ and GUILDENSTERN leave.]

  And, England, if my love thou hold'st at aught°—   *value my love at all* 60
  As my great power thereof may give thee sense,°   *may impress it on you*
  Since yet thy cicatrice° looks raw and red   *scar*
  After the Danish sword, and thy free awe°   *you willingly out of fear*
  Pays homage to us—thou mayst not coldly set°   *set aside*
  Our sovereign process,° which imports at full,   *royal command* 65
  By letters congruing to° that effect,   *pointing to*
  They present° death of Hamlet. Do it, England;   *immediate*
  For like the hectic° in my blood he rages,   *severe fever*
  And thou must cure me. Till I know 'tis done,
  However my haps,° my joys were never begun.   *whatever my fortunes* 70

[Leaves.]

SCENE 4. Near Elsinore Castle.

[Enter FORTINBRAS with his army, marching across the stage.]

FORTINBRAS: Go, Captain, from me greet the Danish king.
  Tell him that by his license° Fortinbras   *permission*
  Craves the conveyance° of a promised march   *requests safe conduct*
  Over° his kingdom. You know the rendezvous.   *through*
  If that his Majesty would aught with us,°   *wants to see us* 5
  We shall express our duty in his eye;
  And let him know so.
CAPTAIN: I will do't, my lord.
FORTINBRAS: Go softly on.

[All but the CAPTAIN leave.]

[Enter HAMLET, ROSENCRANTZ, GUILDENSTERN, and others.]

HAMLET: Good sir, whose powers° are these?   *forces*
CAPTAIN: They are of Norway, sir.   10
HAMLET: How purposed,° sir, I pray you?   *with what destination*
CAPTAIN: Against some part of Poland.
HAMLET: Who commands them, sir?
CAPTAIN: The nephew to old Norway, Fortinbras.
HAMLET: Goes it against the main° of Poland, sir,   *the central part* 15
  Or for some frontier?
CAPTAIN: Truly to speak, and with no addition,
  We go to gain a little patch of ground
  That hath in it no profit° but the name.   *value*
  To pay five ducats, five, I would not farm it;   20

Nor will it yield to Norway or the Pole
   A ranker rate, should it be sold in fee.°   *a higher rate if sold outright*
HAMLET: Why, then the Polack never will defend it.
CAPTAIN: Yes, it is already garrisoned.
HAMLET: Two thousand soul and twenty thousand ducats   25
   Will not debate the question of° this straw.   *settle the argument over*
   This is the imposthume° of much wealth and peace,   *malignant growth*
   That inward breaks, and shows no cause without°   *external cause*
   Why the man dies—I humbly thank you, sir.
CAPTAIN: God be wi' you, sir.

                         [*He leaves.*]

ROSENCRANTZ: Will't please you go, my lord?   30
HAMLET: I'll be with you straight. Go a little before.

               [*All but* HAMLET *leave.*]

How all occasions do inform against me°   *accuse me*
And spur my dull revenge! What is a man,
If his chief good and market of his time
Be but to sleep and feed? A beast, no more.   35
Sure he that made us with such large discourse,°   *far-ranging reasoning*
Looking before and after, gave us not
That capability and godlike reason
To fust° in us unused. Now, whether it be   *spoil*
Bestial oblivion, or some craven scruple°   40
Of thinking too precisely on the event,—   *beastlike apathy or*
                                      cowardly hesitation
A thought which, quartered,° hath but one part wisdom *when divided in four*
And ever three parts coward—I do not know
Why yet I live to say "This thing's to do,"
Sith° I have cause, and will, and strength, and means   *since* 45
To do't. Examples gross as° earth exhort me.   *as plain as*
Witness this army of such mass and charge,°   *and cost*
Led by a delicate and tender prince,
Whose spirit, with divine ambition puffed,
Makes mouths at the invisible event,°   *makes light of the outcome* 50
Exposing what is mortal and unsure
To all that fortune, death, and danger dare,
Even for an eggshell. Rightly to be great
Is not to stir without great argument,°   *take action without a great cause*
But greatly to find quarrel in a straw   55
When honor's at the stake. How stand I then,
That have a father killed, a mother stained,
Excitements° of my reason and my blood,   *incentives*
And let all sleep, while to my shame I see
The imminent death of twenty thousand men   60
That for a fantasy and trick of fame
Go to their graves like beds, fight for a plot
Whereon the numbers cannot try the cause,°   *decide the conflict*
Which is not tomb enough and continent°   *container*

To hide the slain? O, from this time forth,   65
My thoughts be bloody, or be nothing worth!

                                [He leaves.]

SCENE 5. Elsinore. A room in the Castle.

[Enter QUEEN, HORATIO, *and a* GENTLEMAN.]

QUEEN: I will not speak with her.
GENTLEMAN: She is importunate,° indeed distract;°   *insistent/distracted*
   Her mood will needs be° pitied.   *must be*
QUEEN: What would she have?°   *what is her wish*
GENTLEMAN: She speaks much of her father; says she hears
   There's tricks in the world, and hems, and beats her
      heart;   5
   Spurns enviously° at straws; speaks things in doubt,   *strikes out angrily*
   That carry but half sense. Her speech is nothing,
   Yet the unshaped use of it doth move
   The hearers to collection;° they aim at it,   *attention*
   And botch the words up fit to their own thoughts;   10
   Which, as her winks and nods and gestures yield them,
   Indeed would make one think there might be thought,
   Though nothing sure, yet much unhappily.°   *much that is sad*
HORATIO: 'Twere good she were spoken with; for she
      may strew
   Dangerous conjectures in ill-breeding° minds.   *thriving on bad news*   15
QUEEN: Let her come in.

                          [GENTLEMAN *leaves.]*

   [aside] To my sick soul (as sin's true nature is)
   Each toy° seems prologue to some great amiss.   *trifle*
   So full of artless jealousy° is guilt   *clumsy suspicion*
   It spills° itself in fearing to be spilt.   *reveals*   20

   [Enter OPHELIA *distracted.]*

OPHELIA: Where is the beauteous Majesty of Denmark?
QUEEN: How now, Ophelia?
OPHELIA *[sings]*:

   How should I your true-love know
      From another one?
   By his cockle hat° and staff   *pilgrim's hat (with a cockle shell)*   25
      And his sandal shoon.°   *shoes*

QUEEN: Alas, sweet lady, what imports° this song?   *what is the meaning of*
OPHELIA: Say you? Nay, pray you mark.°   *please listen*

   [sings] He is dead and gone, lady,
      He is dead and gone;   30
   At his head a grass-green turf,
      At his heels a stone.

   O, ho!

QUEEN: Nay, but Ophelia—
OPHELIA: Pray you mark.   35

    [*sings*] *White his shroud as the mountain snow—*

    [*Enter* KING.]

QUEEN: Alas, look here, my lord!
OPHELIA [*sings*]:

> *Larded all with° sweet flowers;*   *garnished with*
> *Which bewept to the grave did not go*
>   *With true-love showers.°*   *showers of tears* 40

KING: How do you, pretty lady?
OPHELIA: Well, God 'ild you!° They say the owl was a   *God shield you*
   baker's daughter. Lord, we know what we are, but
   know not what we may be. God be at your table!
KING: Conceit upon° her father.   *she is thinking about* 45
OPHELIA: Pray let's have no words of this; but when
   they ask you what it means, say you this:

> [*sings*] *Tomorrow is Saint Valentine's day,*
>   *All in the morning betime,°*   *early*
> *And I a maid at your window,*   50
>   *To be your Valentine.*

> *Then up he rose and donned his clothes*
>   *And dupped° the chamber door,*   *opened*
> *Let in the maid, that out a maid°*   *as a virgin*
>   *Never departed more.*   55

KING: Pretty Ophelia!
OPHELIA: Indeed, la, without an oath, I'll make an end on't!

> [*sings*] *By Gis° and by Saint Charity,*   *(by Jesus)*
>   *Alack, and fie for shame!*   60
> *Young men will do't if they come to't.*
>   *By Cock,° they are to blame.*   *weaker swearword for "by God"*

> *Quoth she, "Before you tumbled me,*
>   *You promised me to wed."*

He answers: 65

> *"So would I have done, by yonder sun,*
>   *And thou hadst not° come to my bed."*   *if you had not*

KING: How long hath she been thus?
OPHELIA: I hope all will be well. We must be patient;
   but I cannot choose but weep to think they would   70
   lay him in the cold ground. My brother shall know
   of it; and so I thank you for your good counsel.
   Come, my coach! Good night, ladies. Good night,
   sweet ladies. Good night, good night.

[*She leaves.*]

KING: Follow her close; give her good watch, I pray you.   75

[HORATIO *leaves.*]

O, this is the poison of deep grief; it springs
All from her father's death. O Gertrude, Gertrude,
When sorrows come, they come not single spies,°   *not as single advance scouts*
But in battalions! First, her father slain;
Next, your son gone, and he most violent author   80
Of his own just remove;° the people muddied,   *deserved exile*
Thick and unwholesome in their thoughts and
     whispers
For good Polonius' death, and we have done but
     greenly°   *acted unthinkingly*
In hugger-mugger to inter° him; poor Ophelia   *in secrecy and disorder to bury*
Divided from herself and her fair judgment,   85
Without the which we are pictures or mere beasts;
Last, and as much containing as all these,
Her brother is in secret come from France;
Feeds on his wonder, keeps himself in clouds,
And wants not buzzers to infect his ear°   *does not lack talebearers*   90
With pestilent speeches of his father's death,
Wherein necessity, of matter beggared,°   *void of true substance*
Will nothing stick° our person to arraign   *will not hesitate*
In ear and ear.° O my dear Gertrude, this,   *in people's ears*
Like to a murdering piece,° in many places   *a cannon with scattered shot*   95
Gives me superfluous death.

[*A noise outside.*]

QUEEN: Alack, what noise is this?
KING: Where are my Switzers?° Let them guard the door.   *Swiss bodyguards*

[*Enter a* MESSENGER.]

What is the matter?
MESSENGER: Save yourself, my lord:
The ocean, overpeering of his list,°   *rising over its borders*
Eats not the flats° with more impetuous haste   *coastal flatlands*   100
Than young Laertes, in a riotous head,°   *heading a mob*
Overbears your officers. The rabble call him lord;
And, as the world were now but to begin,
Antiquity forgot,° custom not known,   *as if tradition were forgotten*
The ratifiers and props of every word,°   *pledge*   105
They cry "Choose we, Laertes shall be king!"
Caps, hands, and tongues applaud it to the clouds,
"Laertes shall be king! Laertes king!"

[*A noise outside.*]

QUEEN: How cheerfully on the false trail they cry!
    O, this is counter,° you false Danish dogs!   *on the wrong trail* 110
KING: The doors are broke.°   *forced open*

[*Enter* LAERTES *with others.*]

LAERTES: Where is this king?—Sirs, stand you all without.
ALL: No, let's come in!
LAERTES: I pray you give me leave.
ALL: We will, we will!
LAERTES: I thank you. Keep the door.   115

[*His followers leave.*]

    O thou vile king,
    Give me my father!
QUEEN: Calmly, good Laertes.
LAERTES: That drop of blood that's calm proclaims
    me bastard;°   *shows I am not my father's true son*
    Cries cuckold to my father; brands the harlot   *(making the mother a whore)*
    Even here between the chaste unsmirched brows   120
    Of my true mother.
KING: What is the cause, Laertes,
    That thy rebellion looks so giantlike?
    Let him go, Gertrude. Do not fear our person.°   *don't be afraid on my behalf*
    There's such divinity doth hedge° a king   *such divine sanction that protects*
    That treason can but peep to what it would,°   *at its goal* 125
    Acts little of his will.° Tell me, Laertes,   *acts out little of what it intends*
    Why thou art thus incensed. Let him go, Gertrude.
    Speak, man.
LAERTES: Where is my father?
KING: Dead.
QUEEN: But not by him!
KING: Let him demand his fill.°   *question freely* 130
LAERTES: How came he dead?° I'll not be juggled with: *how did he die*
    To hell, allegiance! vows, to the blackest devil!
    Conscience and grace, to the profoundest pit!
    I dare damnation. To this point I stand,
    That both the worlds I give to negligence,°   *write off both earth and heaven* 135
    Let come what comes; only I'll be revenged
    Most thoroughly for my father.
KING: Who shall stay° you?   *hinder*
LAERTES: My will,° not all the world.   *if I have my will*
    And for my means, I'll husband° them so well   *use*
    They shall go far with little.
KING: Good Laertes,   140
    If you desire to know the certainty°   *actual facts*
    Of your dear father's death, is't writ in your revenge
    That swoopstake° you will draw both friend and foe,   *like a reckless gambler*
    Winner and loser?

LAERTES: None but his enemies.

KING: Will you know them then?   145

LAERTES: To his good friends thus wide I'll open my arms
    And, like the kind life-rendering pelican,
    Repast them with my blood.°   *feed them with my own blood*
                                                          (as the pelican was thought to
KING: Why, now you speak   *feed its young)*
    Like a good child and a true gentleman.
    That I am guiltless of your father's death,   150
    And am most sensibly° in grief for it,   *feelingly*
    It shall as level to your judgment appear°
    As day does to your eye.   *strike your reason as directly*

[*A noise outside: "Let her come in."*]

LAERTES: How now? What noise is that?

[*Enter* OPHELIA.]

    O heat, dry up my brains! Tears seven times salt   155
    Burn out the sense and virtue° of mine eye!   *faculty*
    By heaven, thy madness shall be paid by weight
    Till our scale turn the beam.° O rose of May!   *till the retribution outweighs*
    Dear maid, kind sister, sweet Ophelia!   *the offense on the scale*
    O heavens! is't possible a young maid's wits   160
    Should be as mortal as an old man's life?
    Nature is fine in love, and where 'tis fine,
    It sends some precious instance of itself
    After the thing it loves.

OPHELIA [*sings*]:

    They bore him barefaced on the bier   165
        (Hey non nony, nony, hey nony)
    And in his grave rained many a tear.

    Fare you well, my dove!

LAERTES: Hadst thou thy wits, and didst persuade re-   170
    venge, it could not move thus.°   *not incite me the same way*

OPHELIA: You must sing "A-down, a-down," and you,
    "Call him a-down-a." O, how the wheel becomes
    it! It is the false steward, that stole his master's
    daughter.

LAERTES: This nothing's more than matter.°   *these ramblings have more* 175
                                                 meaning than sane talk
OPHELIA: There's rosemary, that's for remembrance.
    Pray you, love, remember. And there is pansies,
    that's for thoughts.

LAERTES: A document° in madness! Thoughts and re-   *lesson*
    membrance fitted.   180

OPHELIA: There's fennel for you, and columbines.
    There's rue for you, and here's some for me. We
    may call it herb of grace o' Sundays. O, you must
    wear your rue with a difference! There's a daisy. I

would give you some violets, but they withered   185
all when my father died. They say he made a
good end.

[sings] For bonny sweet Robin is all my joy.

LAERTES: Thought and affliction, passion, hell itself,
    She turns to favor° and to prettiness.   *charm*
OPHELIA [*sings*]:

  And will he not come again?   190
  And will he not come again?
    No, no, he is dead;
    Go to thy deathbed;
  He never will come again.

  His beard was as white as snow,   195
  All flaxen was his poll.°   *head*
    He is gone, he is gone,
    And we cast away moan.
  God have mercy on his soul!

  And of all Christian souls, I pray God. God be wi' you.   200

                             [Leaves.]

LAERTES: Do you see this, O God?
KING: Laertes, I must commune with your grief,°   *talk to you in your grief*
  Or you deny me right.° Go but apart,   *what is my right*
  Make choice of whom your wisest friends you will,
  And they shall hear and judge 'twixt you and me.   205
  If by direct or by collateral° hand   *indirect*
  They find us touched,° we will our kingdom give,   *implicated*
  Our crown, our life, and all that we call ours,
  To you in satisfaction; but if not,
  Be you content to lend your patience to us,   210
  And we shall jointly labor with your soul
  To give it due content.
LAERTES: Let this be so.
  His means of death,° his obscure funeral—   *the way he died*
  No trophy, sword, nor hatchment° o'er his bones,   *coat of arms*
  No noble rite nor formal ostentation°—   *display* 215
  Cry to be heard, as 'twere from heaven to earth,
  That I must call't in question.°   *must raise questions*
KING: So you shall;
  And where the offense is let the great axe fall.
  I pray you go with me.

                      [They leave.]

SCENE 6. The same. Another room in the Castle.

[*Enter* HORATIO *with an* ATTENDANT.]

HORATIO: What are they that would speak° with me?   *want to speak*
SERVANT: Sailors, sir. They say they have letters for you.
HORATIO: Let them come in.

[ATTENDANT *leaves.*]

I do not know from what part of the world
I should be greeted, if not from Lord Hamlet.   5

[*Enter* SAILORS.]

SAILOR: God bless you, sir.
HORATIO: Let him bless thee too.
SAILOR: He shall, sir, an't please him.° There's a letter   *if it pleases him*
   for you, sir—it comes from the ambassador that
   was bound for° England—if your name be Hora-   *headed for*   10
   tio, as I am let to know it is.
HORATIO [*reads the letter*]: *Horatio, when thou shalt
   have overlooked this,°* give these fellows some   *looked this over*
   means° to the King. They have letters for him. Ere   *means of access*
   we were two days old at sea, a pirate of very war-
   like appointment° gave us chase. Finding ourselves   *equipment*
   too slow of sail, we put on a compelled valor, and
   in the grapple I boarded them. On the instant they
   got clear of our ship; so I alone became their pris-
   oner. They have dealt with me like thieves of mercy;   20
   but they knew what they did: I am to do a good
   turn for them. Let the King have the letters I have
   sent, and repair thou to me° with as much speed   *join me*
   as thou wouldst fly° death. I have words to speak in   *flee from*
   thine ear will make thee dumb; yet are they much   25
   too light for the bore° of the matter. These good fel-   *caliber*
   lows will bring thee where I am. Rosencrantz and
   Guildenstern hold their course for England. Of
   them I have much to tell thee. Farewell.
         He that thou knowest thine,° HAMLET.   *be who you know is yours*   30

Come, I will give you way° for these your letters,   *provide a channel*
And do it the speedier that you may direct me
To him from whom you brought them.

[*They leave.*]

SCENE 7. Another room in the Castle.

[*Enter* KING *and* LAERTES.]

KING: Now must your conscience my acquittance seal,°   *confirm my acquittal*
   And you must put me in your heart for friend,
   Sith° you have heard, and with a knowing ear,   *since*
   That he which hath your noble father slain
   Pursued my life.

LAERTES: It well appears. But tell me   5
    Why you proceeded not against these feats°   *deeds*
    So crimeful and so capital in nature,°   *so criminal and deserving death*
    As by your safety, wisdom, all things else,
    You mainly were stirred up.°   *were mightily impelled*
KING: O, for two special reasons,
    Which may to you, perhaps, seem much unsinewed,°   *very weak*   10
    But yet to me they are strong. The Queen his mother
    Lives almost by his looks; and for myself—
    My virtue or my plague, be it either which—
    She's so conjunctive° to my life and soul   *so closely joined*
    That, as the star moves not but in his sphere,   15
    I could not but by her. The other motive
    Why to a public count° I might not go   *accounting*
    Is the great love the general gender° bear him,   *common people*
    Who, dipping all his faults in their affection,
    Would, like the spring that turneth wood to stone,   20
    Convert his gyves° to graces; so that my arrows,   *prison chains*
    Too slightly timbered° for so loud a wind,   *made of too flimsy wood*
    Would have reverted to my bow again,
    And not where I had aimed them.
LAERTES: And so have I a noble father lost;   25
    A sister driven into desperate terms,°   *conditions*
    Whose worth, if praises may go back again,°   *may go back to the past*
    Stood challenger on mount of all the age°   *could challenge all rivals*
    For her perfections. But my revenge will come.
KING: Break not your sleeps° for that. You must not think   *do not lose sleep*   30
    That we are made of stuff so flat and dull
    That we can let our beard be shook with danger,
    And think it pastime. You shortly shall hear more.
    I loved your father, and we love ourself,
    And that, I hope, will teach you to imagine—   35

[*Enter a* MESSENGER *with letters.*]

    How now? What news?
MESSENGER: Letters, my lord, from Hamlet:
    This to your Majesty; this to the Queen.
KING: From Hamlet? Who brought them?
MESSENGER: Sailors, my lord, they say; I saw them not.
    They were given me by Claudio; he received them   40
    Of him that brought them.
KING: Laertes, you shall hear them.
    Leave us.

[MESSENGER *leaves.*]

[*reads*] *High and Mighty—You shall know I am set*
naked° *on your kingdom. Tomorrow shall I beg*   *stripped of everything*
leave to see your kingly eyes; when I shall (first   45

asking your pardon thereunto) recount the occa-
sion of my sudden and more strange return.

HAMLET.
What should this mean? Are all the rest come back?
Or is it some abuse,° and no such thing?   deception   50
LAERTES: Know you the hand?°   handwriting
KING: 'Tis Hamlet's character.
"Naked!"
And in a postscript here, he says "alone."
Can you advise me?
LAERTES: I am lost in it, my lord. But let him come!   55
It warms the very sickness in my heart
That I shall live and tell him to his teeth,
"Thus did'st thou."
KING: If it be so, Laertes
(As how should it be so? how otherwise?),
Will you be ruled by me?
LAERTES: Ay, my lord,   60
So you will not overrule me to a peace.
KING: To thine own peace. If he be now returned,
As checking at° his voyage, and that he means   abandoning
No more to undertake it, I will work him
To an exploit now ripe in my device,°   now fully plotted by me   65
Under the which he shall not choose but fall;
And for his death no wind of blame shall breathe,
But even his mother shall uncharge the practice°   not allege wrongdoing
And call it accident.
LAERTES: My lord, I will be ruled;
The rather, if you could devise it so   70
That I might be the organ.°   instrument
KING: It falls right.
You have been talked of since your travel much,
And that in Hamlet's hearing, for a quality
Wherein they say you shine. Your sum of parts°   good qualities
Did not together pluck such envy from him   75
As did that one; and that, in my regard,
Of the unworthiest siege.°   of least importance
LAERTES: What part is that, my lord?
KING: A very riband° in the cap of youth—   a mere adornment
Yet needful too; for youth no less becomes°   no less fits
The light and careless livery° that it wears   clothing   80
Than settled age his sables and his weeds,°   its rich formal garments
Importing° health and graveness.° Two months since   showing/seriousness
Here was a gentleman of Normandy.
I have seen myself, and serve against, the French,
And they can well° on horseback; but this gallant   do well   85
Had witchcraft in it. He grew unto his seat,
And to such wondrous doing brought his horse
As had he been incorpsed and demi-natured°   made one body and
                                                      half of its nature

With the brave beast. So far he topped my thought
That I, in forgery of° shapes and tricks,   *even in inventing*   90
Come short of what he did.
LAERTES: A Norman was't?
KING: A Norman.
LAERTES: Upon my life, Lamound.
KING: The very same.
LAERTES: I know him well. He is the brooch° indeed   *chief ornament*
And gem of all the nation.   95
KING: He made confession of you;°   *conceded your superior talent*
And gave you such a masterly report
For art and exercise in your defense,
And for your rapier most especially,
That he cried out 'twould be a sight indeed   100
If one could match you. The scrimers° of their nation   *fencers*
He swore had neither motion, guard, nor eye,
If you opposed them. Sir, this report of his
Did Hamlet so envenom with his envy
That he could nothing do but wish and beg   105
Your sudden coming over to play° with him.   *fence*
Now, out of this—
LAERTES: What out of this, my lord?
KING: Laertes, was your father dear to you?
Or are you like the painting of a sorrow,
A face without a heart?
LAERTES: Why ask you this?   110
KING: Not that I think you did not love your father,
But that I know love is begun by time,
And that I see, in passages of proof,°   *by relevant examples*
Time qualifies the spark and fire of it.
There lives within the very flame of love   115
A kind of wick or snuff that will abate it,°   *will put it out*
And nothing is at a like goodness still;
For goodness, growing to a plurisy,°   *malignant swelling*
Dies in his own too-much. That we would do,
We should do when we would;° for this "would"   *when we want to*
   changes,   120
And hath abatements° and delays as many   *has obstacles*
As there are tongues, are hands, are accidents;
And then this "should" is like a spendthrift sigh,
That hurts by easing. But to the quick of the ulcer!
Hamlet comes back. What would you undertake   125
To show yourself your father's son in deed
More than in words?
LAERTES: To cut his throat in the church!
KING: No place indeed should murder sanctuarize;°   *give sanctuary to murder*
Revenge should have no bounds.° But, good Laertes,   *know no boundaries*
Will you do this? Keep close° within your chamber.   *stay inside*   130
Hamlet, returned, shall know you are come home.

We'll put on those shall praise° your excellence   *instigate people to praise*
And set a double varnish on the fame
The Frenchman gave you; bring you in fine° together   *at last*
And wager on your heads. He, being remiss,°   *unsuspecting* 135
Most generous, and free from all contriving,
Will not peruse the foils;° so that with ease,   *check the weapons*
Or with a little shuffling, you may choose
A sword unbated,° and, in a pass of practice,°   *not blunted/treachery*
Requite him° for your father.   *pay him back*

LAERTES: I will do't!   140
And for that purpose I'll anoint my sword.
I bought an unction of a mountebank,°   *lotion from a quack*
So mortal° that, but dip a knife in it,   *lethal*
Where it draws blood no cataplasm° so rare,   *antidote*
Collected from all simples° that have virtue   *medicinal herbs* 145
Under the moon, can save the thing from death
That is but scratched withal.° I'll touch my point   *with it*
With this contagion,° that, if I gall° him slightly,   *poison/scratch*
It may be death.

KING: Let's further think of this,
Weigh what convenience both of time and means   150
May fit us to our shape. If this should fail,
And that our drift look° through our bad   *that our plan should show*
    performance,
'Twere better not assayed.° Therefore this project   *tried*
Should have a back° for second, that might hold   *backup*
If this did blast in proof.° Soft! let me see.   *fail when put to the test* 155
We'll make a solemn wager on your cunnings°—   *skills*
I have it!
When in your motion you are hot and dry—
As made your bouts more violent to that end—
And that he calls for drink, I'll have prepared him   160
A chalice for the nonce;° whereon but sipping,   *cup for that occasion*
If he by chance escape your venomed stuck,°   *thrust*
Our purpose may hold° there.—But stay, what noise?   *may still prevail*

[*Enter* QUEEN.]

How now, sweet queen?
QUEEN: One woe doth tread upon another's heel,   165
  So fast they follow. Your sister's drowned, Laertes.
LAERTES: Drowned! O, where?
QUEEN: There is a willow grows aslant a brook,
  That shows his hoar° leaves in the glassy stream.   *silvery-grey*
  There with fantastic garlands did she come   170
  Of crowflowers, nettles, daisies, and long purples,
  That liberal° shepherds give a grosser° name,   *outspoken/coarser*
  But our cold maids° do dead men's fingers call them.   *chaste maidens*
  There on the pendent boughs° her coronet weeds   *hanging branches*
  Clambering to hang, an envious sliver° broke,   *spiteful small branch* 175

When down her weedy trophies and herself
Fell in the weeping brook. Her clothes spread wide
And, mermaid-like, awhile they bore her up;
Which time she chanted snatches of old tunes,
As one incapable of° her own distress,   *unaware of* 180
Or like a creature native and indued°   *born there and used*
Unto that element; but long it could not be
Till that her garments, heavy with their drink,
Pulled the poor wretch from her melodious lay°   *song*
To muddy death.
LAERTES: Alas, then she is drowned?   185
QUEEN: Drowned, drowned.
LAERTES: Too much of water hast thou, poor Ophelia,
And therefore I forbid my tears; but yet
It is our trick;° nature her custom holds,   *natural trait*
Let shame say what it will. When these are gone,   190
The woman will be out.° Adieu, my lord.   *the woman in me will disappear*
I have a speech of fire, that fain° would blaze   *gladly*
But that this folly douts it.°   *puts it out*

[*He leaves.*]

KING: Let's follow, Gertrude.
How much I had to do to calm his rage!
Now fear I this will give it start again;   195
Therefore let's follow.

[*They leave.*]

The Receptive Reader

1. (Act Four, Scenes 1–3) In these scenes, the plot thickens. What are the key developments here?

2. (Act Four, Scene 4) How does Fortinbras' expedition against Poland become for Hamlet an occasion "to spur my dull revenge"? Hamlet's *soliloquy* here is key evidence for critics debating Hamlet's delay in executing the ghost's command. What does Hamlet say about the delay? What is the tone of the soliloquy? What is Hamlet's train of thought? What is his definition of "greatness"? What is the conclusion or upshot of the soliloquy?

3. (Act Four, Scene 5) How does Ophelia's madness change the course of the play? Is it dramatically a digression or detour? Is Hamlet implicated in Ophelia's madness? How does it help make Laertes a major player in the final acts? Critics have listened to Ophelia's disjointed talk and songs for clues to a repressed or hidden personality. What kinds of clues do you think they might have found?

4. (Act Four, Scenes 6 and 7) What role does *chance* or sheer accident begin to play in the plot here? What impression do you get of Laertes as the King enlists his help in the King's plot? How does the King sway him?

The Creative Dimension

By the end of Act Four, some of the supporting characters—Polonius, Ophelia—have made their exit. Rosencrantz and Guildenstern will not return from their voyage to England; we will not see them again. Assume the role of one of the supporting characters in the play. Tell the story of your involvement in the events, looking at people and events from your own limited point of view. (You might want to start your story "I, Polonius, . . . " or "I, Ophelia, . . . ")

Act Five

SCENE 1. Elsinore. A churchyard.

[*Enter two* CLOWNS, *with spades and pickaxes*.]

CLOWN: Is she to be buried in Christian burial that wilfully seeks her own salvation?

OTHER: I tell thee she is; therefore make her grave straight. The crowner hath sat on her,° and finds it Christian burial.   *coroner has examined her case*   5

CLOWN: How can that be, unless she drowned herself in her own defense?

OTHER: Why, 'tis found so.

CLOWN: It must be *se offendendo;*° it cannot be else. For here lies the point: if I drown myself wittingly, it argues an act; and an act hath three branches— it is to act, to do, and to perform; argal,° she drowned herself wittingly.   *"doing violence to herself"*   10 *(garbled for* ergo, *"therefore")*

OTHER: Nay, but hear you, Goodman Delver!

CLOWN: Give me leave. Here lies the water; good.   15 Here stands the man; good. If the man go to this water and drown himself, it is, will he, nill he, he goes—mark you that. But if the water come to him and drown him, he drowns not himself. Argal, he that is not guilty of his own death shortens not his   20 own life.

OTHER: But is this law?

CLOWN: Ay, marry,° is't—crowner's quest° law.   *yes indeed/inquest*

OTHER: Will you have the truth on't? If this had not been a gentlewoman, she should have been   25 buried out o' Christian burial.°   *without religious rites*

CLOWN: Why, there thou say'st! And the more pity that great folk should have countenance° in this   *more right* world to drown or hang themselves more than their even-Christian.° Come, my spade! There is   *ordinary Christians* 30 no ancient gentlemen but gardeners, ditches, and grave-makers. They hold up° Adam's profession.   *uphold*

OTHER: Was he a gentleman?

CLOWN: He was the first that ever bore arms.°   *(pun on arms and weapons)*

OTHER: Why, he had none.   35

CLOWN: What, art a heathen? How dost thou understand the Scripture? The Scripture says Adam
digged. Could he dig without arms? I'll put another question to thee. If thou answerest me not
to the purpose,° confess thyself—   *not to the point*   40
OTHER: Go to!
CLOWN: What is he that builds stronger than either
the mason, the shipwright, or the carpenter?
OTHER: The gallows-maker; for that frame outlives a
thousand tenants.   45
CLOWN: I like thy wit well, in good faith. The gallows
does well. But how does it well? It does well to
those that do ill. Now, thou dost ill to say the gal-
lows is built stronger than the church. Argal, the
gallows may do well to thee. To't again, come!   50
OTHER: Who builds stronger than a mason, a ship-
wright, or a carpenter?
CLOWN: Ay, tell me that, and unyoke.°   *quit for the day*
OTHER: Marry, now I can tell.
CLOWN: To't.   55
OTHER: Mass,° I cannot tell.   *by the Holy Mass*

[*Enter* HAMLET *and* HORATIO *afar off.*]

CLOWN: Cudgel thy brains no more about it, for your
dull ass° will not mend his pace with beating; and   *dim-witted donkey*
when you are asked this question next, say "a
grave-maker." The houses he makes lasts till   60
doomsday. Go, get thee to Yaughan; fetch me a
stoup° of liquor.   *cup*

[SECOND CLOWN *leaves.*]

[CLOWN *digs and sings.*]

In youth when I did love, did love,
    Methought it was very sweet;
To contract°—*O—the time for—a—my behove,*°   *to shorten/my benefit*   65
    O, methought there—a—was nothing—a—
meet.

HAMLET: Has this fellow no feeling of his business,
that he sings at grave-making?
HORATIO: Custom hath made it in him a property of
easiness.°   *habit has made it natural*   70
HAMLET: 'Tis e'en so. The hand of little employment
hath the daintier sense.°   *the little-used hand has the*
CLOWN [*sings*]:   *more sensitive touch*

But age with his stealing steps
    Hath clawed me in his clutch,
And hath shipped me intil the land,°   *put me in the ground*   75
    As if I had never been such.

[*Digs up a skull.*]

HAMLET: That skull had a tongue in it, and could sing
    once. How the knave jowls° it to the ground, as if   *hurls*
    'twere Cain's jawbone, that did the first murder!
    This might be the pate of a politician, which this   80
    ass now overreaches;° one that would circumvent°   *gets the better of/outwit*
    God, might it not?
HORATIO: It might, my lord.
HAMLET: Or of a courtier, which could say "Good
    morrow, sweet lord! How dost thou, good lord?"   85
    This might be my Lord Such-a-one, that praised
    my Lord Such-a-one's horse when he meant to
    beg it°—might it not?   *beg for it*
HORATIO: Ay, my lord.
HAMLET: Why, even so! and now my Lady Worm's,   90
    chapless,° and knocked about the mazzard° with   *jawless/head*
    a sexton's spade. Here's fine revolution, if we had
    the trick to see't. Did these bones cost no more
    the breeding but to play at loggets with them?°   *to throw them around*
    Mine ache to think on't.   *like sticks* 95
CLOWN [*sings*]:

A pickaxe and a spade, a spade,
    For and a shrouding sheet;
O, a pit of clay for to be made
    For such a guest is meet.

[*Digs up another skull.*]

HAMLET: There's another. Why may not that be the   100
    skull of a lawyer? Where be his quiddities now,
    his quillets,° his cases, his tenures, and his tricks?   *quibbles and hair-splittings*
    Why does he suffer this rude knave now to knock
    him about the sconce° with a dirty shovel, and   *head*
    will not tell him of his action of battery? Hum! This   105
    fellow might be in's time a great buyer of land,
    with his statutes, his recognizances, his fines, his
    double vouchers, his recoveries. Is this the fine of
    his fines,° and the recovery of his recoveries, to   *the final end of his fines*
    have his fine pate full of fine dirt? Will his vouch-   110
    ers vouch him no more of his purchases, and dou-
    ble ones too, than the length and breadth of a pair
    of indentures?° The very conveyances of his lands   *contracts*
    will scarcely lie in this box; and must the inheritor
    himself have no more, ha?   115
HORATIO: Not a jot more, my lord.
HAMLET: Is not parchment made of sheepskins?
HORATIO: Ay, my lord, and of calveskins too.

HAMLET: They are sheep and calves which seek out
assurance in that. I will speak to this fellow.
Whose grave's this, sirrah?   120
CLOWN: Mine, sir.

[*sings*] *O, a pit of clay for to be made*
     For such a guest is meet.°   *just right*

HAMLET: I think it be thine indeed, for thou liest in't.   125
CLOWN: You lie out on't, sir, and therefore 'tis not
yours. For my part, I do not lie in't, yet it is mine.
HAMLET: Thou dost lie in't, to be in't and say it is
thine. 'Tis for the dead, not for the quick;° there-   *the living*
fore thou liest.   130
CLOWN: 'Tis a quick lie, sir; 'twill away again from me
to you.
HAMLET: What man dost thou dig it for?
CLOWN: For no man, sir.
HAMLET: What woman then?   135
CLOWN: For none neither.
HAMLET: Who is to be buried in't?
CLOWN: One that was a woman, sir; but, rest her soul,
she's dead.
HAMLET: How absolute° the knave is! We must speak   *what a stickler* 140
by the card,° or equivocation° will undo us. By the   *exactly/double meanings*
Lord, Horatio, this three years I have taken note of
it, the age is grown so picked° that the toe of the   *has become so sophisticated*
peasant comes so near the heel of the courtier he
galls his kibe.°—How long hast thou been a   *rubs his sore heel* 145
gravemaker?
CLOWN: Of all the days in the year, I came to't that
day that our last king Hamlet overcame Fortinbras.
HAMLET: How long is that since?
CLOWN: Cannot you tell that? Every fool can tell that.   150
It was the very day that young Hamlet was born—
he that is mad, and sent into England.
HAMLET: Ay, marry, why was he sent into England?
CLOWN: Why, because he was mad. He shall recover
his wits there; or, if he do not, 'tis no great matter°   *does not matter much* 155
there.
HAMLET: Why?
CLOWN: 'Twill not be seen in him there. There the
men are as mad as he.
HAMLET: How came he mad?   160
CLOWN: Very strangely, they say.
HAMLET: How strangely?
CLOWN: Faith, even with losing his wits.
HAMLET: Upon what ground?

CLOWN: Why, here in Denmark. I have been sexton   165
    here, man and boy, thirty years.

HAMLET: How long will a man lie in the earth ere° he   *before*
    rot?

CLOWN: Faith, if he be not rotten before he die (as we
    have many pocky corses° now-a-days that will   *pox-riddled corpses* 170
    scarce hold the laying in),° he will last you some   *last till the burial*
    eight year or nine year. A tanner° will last you nine   *leather worker*
    year.   *(preparing hides)*

HAMLET: Why he more than another?

CLOWN: Why, sir, his hide is so tanned with his trade   175
    that he will keep out water a great while; and
    your water is a sore decayer of your whoreson
    dead body. Here's a skull now: this skull hath lain
    in the earth three-and-twenty years.

HAMLET: Whose was it?   180

CLOWN: A whoreson mad fellow's it was. Whose do
    you think it was?

HAMLET: Nay, I know not.

CLOWN: A pestilence on him for a mad rogue! He
    poured a flagon of Rhenish° on my head once. This   *a pitcher of wine* 185
    same skull, sir, was Yorick's skull, the King's jester.

HAMLET: This?

CLOWN: Even that.

HAMLET: Let me see. [*takes the skull*] Alas, poor Yorick!
    I knew him, Horatio. A fellow of infinite jest, of   190
    most excellent fancy. He hath borne me on his
    back a thousand times. And now how abhorred in
    my imagination it is! My gorge rises at it. Here
    hung those lips that I have kissed I know not how
    oft. Where be your gibes° now? your gambols?   *barbs* 195
    your songs? your flashes of merriment that were
    wont to set the table on a roar?° Not one now, to   *used to make the guests roar*
    mock your own grinning? Quite chapfallen?° Now   *down in the mouth*
    get you to my lady's chamber, and tell her, let her
    paint an inch thick, to this favor° she must come.   *look* 200
    Make her laugh at that. Prithee, Horatio, tell me
    one thing.

HORATIO: What's that, my lord?

HAMLET: Dost thou think Alexander° looked of this   *(Alexander the Great)*
    fashion in the earth?   205

HORATIO: Even so.

HAMLET: And smelt so? Pah!

[*Puts down the skull.*]

HORATIO: Even so, my lord.

HAMLET: To what base uses we may return, Horatio!
    Why may not imagination trace the noble dust of   210
    Alexander till he find it stopping a bunghole?°   *tap hole of a barrel*

HORATIO: 'Twere to consider too curiously, to consider so.

HAMLET: No, faith, not a jot; but to follow him thither
with modesty enough, and likelihood to lead it; as   215
thus: Alexander died, Alexander was buried,
Alexander returneth into dust; the dust is earth; of
earth we make loam; and why of that loam
(whereto he was converted) might they not stop a
beer barrel?

> Imperious Caesar, dead and turned to clay,   220
> Might stop a hole to keep the wind away.
> O, that that earth which kept the world in awe
> Should patch a wall t' expel° the winter's flaw!   *to keep out*

But soft! but soft! aside! Here comes the King—

[*Enter* KING, QUEEN, LAERTES, *and a coffin, with priests and lords.*]

The Queen, the courtiers. Who is this they follow?   225
And with such maimèd rites?° This doth betoken   *minimal ceremony*
The corpse they follow did with desperate hand
Fordo its own life. 'Twas of some estate.°   *of fairly high rank*
Couch we awhile,° and mark.   *let us lie low*

[*Retires with* HORATIO.]

LAERTES: What ceremony else?°   *additional ceremony*
HAMLET: That is Laertes,   230
A very noble youth. Mark.
LAERTES: What ceremony else?
PRIEST: Her obsequies° have been as far enlarged   *funeral rites*
As we have warranty. Her death was doubtful;°   *suspicious*
And, but that° great command oversways the order,   *except that* 235
She should in ground unsanctified have
lodged°   *have been buried outside the churchyard*
Till the last trumpet. For° charitable prayers,   *instead of*
Shards, flints, and pebbles should be thrown on her.
Yet here she is allowed her virgin crants,°   *garlands*
Her maiden strewments,° and the bringing home   *strewn flowers* 240
Of bell and burial.
LAERTES: Must there no more be done?
PRIEST: No more be done.
We should profane the service of the dead
To sing a requiem and such rest to her
As to peace-parted souls.°   *those who died at peace*
LAERTES: Lay her i' the earth,   245
And from her fair and unpolluted flesh
May violets spring! I tell thee, churlish priest,
A ministering angel shall my sister be
When thou liest howling.°   *in hell*
HAMLET: What, the fair Ophelia?

QUEEN: Sweets to the sweet! Farewell.   250

[*Scatters flowers.*]

I hoped thou shouldst have been my Hamlet's wife;
I thought thy bride-bed to have decked,° sweet maid,   *strewn with flowers*
And not have strewed thy grave.
LAERTES: O, treble woe°   *three times woe*
Fall ten times treble on that cursèd head
Whose wicked deed thy most ingenious sense   255
Deprived thee of!° Hold off the earth awhile,   *deprived you of your fine mind*
Till I have caught° her once more in mine arms.   *taken*

[*Leaps in the grave.*]

Now pile your dust upon the quick° and dead   *the living*
Till of this flat a mountain you have made
To over top old Pelion or the skyish head   260
Of blue Olympus.°   *to be higher than the*
HAMLET [*advancing*]: What is he whose grief   *legendary Greek mountains*
Bears such an emphasis?° whose phrase of sorrow   *cries out so loud*
Conjures the wandering stars,° and makes them stand   *puts a spell on the planets*
Like wonder-wounded hearers? This is I,   265
Hamlet the Dane.

[*Leaps in after* LAERTES.]

LAERTES: The devil take thy soul!

[*Grappling with him.*]

HAMLET: Thou pray'st not well.
I prithee take thy fingers from my throat;
For, though I am not splenitive° and rash,   *bad-tempered*
Yet have I in me something dangerous,   270
Which let thy wisdom fear. Hold off thy hand!
KING: Pluck them asunder.
QUEEN: Hamlet, Hamlet!
ALL: Gentlemen!
HORATIO: Good my lord, be quiet.

[*Attendants part them, and they leave the grave.*]

HAMLET: Why, I will fight with him upon this theme°   *for this cause*
Until my eyelids will no longer wag.   275
QUEEN: O my son, what theme?
HAMLET: I loved Ophelia. Forty thousand brothers
Could not (with all their quantity of love)
Make up my sum. What wilt thou do for her?
KING: O, he is mad, Laertes.   280
QUEEN: For love of God, forbear him!
HAMLET: 'Swounds, show me what thou't do.
Woo't° weep? woo't fight? woo't fast? woo't tear thyself?   *will you*
Woo't drink up eisell?° eat a crocodile?   *vinegar*
I'll do't. Dost thou come here to whine?   285

To outface me with leaping in her grave?
Be buried quick° with her, and so will I.   *alive*
And if thou prate of mountains, let them throw
Millions of acres on us, till our ground,
Singeing his pate against the burning zone,°   *its top burned by the sun*   290
Make Ossa° like a wart! Nay, an thou'lt mouth,   *(a huge Greek mountain)*
I'll rant as well as thou.
QUEEN: This is mere madness;
And thus a while the fit will work on him.
Anon,° as patient as the female dove   *soon*
When that her golden couplets° are disclosed,   *the twin yellow hatchlings* 295
His silence will sit drooping.
HAMLET: Hear you, sir!
What is the reason that you use° me thus?   *treat*
I loved you ever. But it is no matter.
Let Hercules° himself do what he may,   *(legendary mighty Greek hero)*
The cat will mew, and dog will have his day.   300

> [*He leaves.*]

KING: I pray thee, good Horatio, wait upon him.

> [HORATIO *leaves.*]

[*to* LAERTES] Strengthen your patience in our° last   *remembering our*
    night's speech.
We'll put the matter to the present push.°   *immediate test*
Good Gertrude, set some watch° over your son.   *guard*
This grave shall have a living° monument.   *lasting*   305
An hour of quiet shortly shall we see;
Till then in patience our proceeding be.

> [*They leave.*]

SCENE 2. A hall in the Castle.

[*Enter* HAMLET *and* HORATIO.]

HAMLET: So much for this, sir; now shall you see the other.
    You do remember all the circumstance?
HORATIO: Remember it, my lord!
HAMLET: Sir, in my heart there was a kind of fighting
    That would not let me sleep. Methought° I lay   *I thought*   5
    Worse than the mutines in the bilboes.° Rashly—   *than shackled mutineers*
    (And praised be rashness for it) let us know,
    Our indiscretion sometime serves us well
    When our deep plots do pall.° And that should learn° us   *falter/teach*
    There's a divinity that shapes our ends,°   *that guides our path*   10
    Rough-hew them how we will°—   *no matter how roughly*
HORATIO: That is most certain.   *we sketch it out*
HAMLET: Up from my cabin,
    My sea-gown scarfed about me,° in the dark   *wrapped in sailor's gown*
    Groped I to find out them, had my desire,
    Fingered° their packet, and in fine withdrew   *stole*   15

To mine own room again, making so bold°   *becoming so bold as*
(My fears forgetting manners) to unseal
Their grand commission, where I found, Horatio
(O royal knavery!), an exact command,
Larded° with many several sorts of reasons,   *embellished*   20
Importing° Denmark's health, and England's too,   *related to*
With, ho! such bugs and goblins° in my life—   *such terrible deeds*
That, on the supervise,° no leisure bated,°   *upon the reading/allowed*
No, not to stay° the grinding of the axe,   *to wait for*
My head should be struck off.
HORATIO: Is't possible?   25
HAMLET: Here's the commission;° read it at more leisure. *instructions*
But wilt thou hear me how I did proceed?
HORATIO: I beseech you.
HAMLET: Being thus benetted round° with villainies,   *trapped*
Ere° I could make a prologue to my brains,   *before*   30
They had begun the play. I sat me down;
Devised a new commission; wrote it fair.
I once did hold it, as our statists° do,   *officials*
A baseness to write fair, and labored much
How to forget that learning; but, sir, now   35
It did me yeoman's service. Wilt thou know
The effect of what I wrote?
HORATIO: Ay, good my lord.
HAMLET: An earnest conjuration° from the King,   *plea*
As England was his faithful tributary,°   *payer of tribute*
As love between them like the palm might flourish,   40
As peace should still her wheaten garland wear
And stand a comma° 'tween their amities,°   *as a link/friendships*
And many such-like as's of great charge,
That, on the view and knowing of these contents,
Without debatement further, more or less,   45
He should the bearers° put to sudden death,   *bearers of these papers*
Not shriving time° allowed.   *no time for confession of sins*
HORATIO: How was this sealed?
HAMLET: Why, even in that was heaven ordinant.°   *heaven took charge*
I had my father's signet° in my purse,   *signet ring*
Which was the model of that Danish seal;   50
Folded the writ° up in the form of the other,   *document*
Subscribed it, gave't the impression, placed it safely,
The changeling° never known. Now, the next day   *substitution*
Was our sea-fight; and what to this was sequent°   *what followed*
Thou know'st already.   55
HORATIO: So Guildenstern and Rosencrantz go to't.
HAMLET: Why, man, they did make love to this employment.° *pursued it eagerly*
They are not near my conscience;° their defeat   *on my conscience*
Does by their own insinuation grow.°   *results from their meddling*
'Tis dangerous when the baser nature comes   60

Between the pass and fell° incensèd points   *thrust and cruel*
Of mighty opposites.
HORATIO: Why, what a king is this!
HAMLET: Does it not, think'st thee, stand me now upon°—   *become my task*
He that hath killed my king, and whored my mother,
Popped in between the election° and my hopes,   *election to the throne*   65
Thrown out his angle° for my proper life,   *his fishhook*
And with such cozenage°—is't not perfect conscience   *trickery*
To quit him° with this arm? And is't not to be damned   *pay him back*
To let this canker° of our nature come   *blight*
In further evil?   70
HORATIO: It must be shortly known to him from England
What is the issue of the business there.
HAMLET: It will be short; the interim is mine,
And a man's life's no more than to say "one."
But I am very sorry, good Horatio,   75
That to Laertes I forgot myself;
For by the image of my cause I see
The portraiture of his. I'll court his favors.
But sure the bravery° of his grief did put me   *showy display*
Into a towering passion.
HORATIO: Peace!° Who comes here?   *quiet*   80

[*Enter young* OSRIC, *a courtier.*]

OSRIC: Your lordship is right welcome back to
    Denmark.
HAMLET: I humbly thank you, sir. [*aside to* HORATIO]
    Dost know this waterfly?
HORATIO [*aside to* HAMLET]: No, my good lord.
HAMLET [*aside to* HORATIO]: Thy state is the more gra-   85
    cious;° for 'tis a vice to know him. He hath much   *soul is closer to grace*
    land, and fertile. Let a beast be lord of beasts, and
    his crib° shall stand at the king's mess. 'Tis a   *trough*
    chough;° but, as I say, spacious in the possession   *chattering bird*
    of dirt.   90
OSRIC: Sweet lord, if your lordship were at leisure, I
    should impart a thing to you from his Majesty.
HAMLET: I will receive it, sir, with all diligence of spirit.
    Put your bonnet to his right use, 'tis for the head.
OSRIC: I thank your lordship, it is very hot.   95
HAMLET: No, believe me, 'tis very cold; the wind is
    northerly.
OSRIC: It is indifferent cold,° my lord, indeed.   *fairly cold*
HAMLET: But yet methinks it is very sultry and hot for
    my complexion.   100
OSRIC: Exceedingly, my lord; it is very sultry, as
    'twere—I cannot tell how. But, my lord, his

Majesty bade me signify to you that he has laid a
great wager on your head. Sir, this is the matter—

HAMLET: I beseech you remember.   105

[HAMLET *moves him to put on his hat.*]

OSRIC: Nay, good my lord; for mine ease, in good
faith. Sir, here is newly come to court Laertes; believe me, an absolute gentleman, full of most excellent differences, of very soft society and great
showing. Indeed, to speak feelingly of him, he is   110
the card or calendar° of gentry; for you shall find   *guide and index*
in him the continent° of what part a gentleman   *sum*
would see.

HAMLET: Sir, his definement suffers no perdition in
you;° though, I know, to divide him inventorially   *(Hamlet is aping Osric's* 115
would dozy the arithmetic of memory, and yet but   *precious and hyper-*
yaw neither in respect of his quick sail. But, in the   *refined diction)*
verity of extolment, I take him to be a soul of great
article, and his infusion of such dearth and rareness
as, to make true diction of him, his semblable is his   120
mirror, and who else would trace him, his um-
brage,° nothing more.   *shadow*

OSRIC: Your lordship speaks most infallibly of him.

HAMLET: The concernancy,° sir? Why do we wrap the   *point*
gentleman in our more rawer breath?   125

OSRIC: Sir?

HORATIO [*aside to* HAMLET]: Is't not possible to understand in another tongue? You will do't, sir, really.

HAMLET: What imports the nomination of° this   *why do you name*
gentleman?   130

OSRIC: Of Laertes?

HORATIO [*aside*]: His purse is empty already; all's
golden words are spent.

HAMLET: Of him, sir.

OSRIC: I know you are not ignorant—   135

HAMLET: I would you did, sir; yet, in faith, if you did,
it would not much approve me. Well, sir?

OSRIC: You are not ignorant of what excellence
Laertes is—

HAMLET: I dare not confess that, lest I should compare   140
with him in excellence; but to know a man well
were to know himself.

OSRIC: I mean, sir, for his weapon; but in the impu-
tation° laid on him by them, in his meed he's   *reputation*
unfellowed.°   *his merit is unequaled* 145

HAMLET: What's his weapon?

OSRIC: Rapier and dagger.

HAMLET: That's two of his weapons—but well.

OSRIC: The King, sir, hath wagered with him six Barbary horses; against the which he has impawned,° *staked* 150
as I take it, six French rapiers and poniards,° with *daggers*
their assigns,° as girdle, hangers,° and so. Three of *with their gear/carrying straps*
the carriages, in faith, are very dear to fancy, very
responsive to the hilts, most delicate carriages,
and of very liberal conceit.° *of rich design* 155

HAMLET: What call you the carriages?

HORATIO [*aside to* HAMLET]: I knew you must be edi-
fied by the margent° ere you had done. *helped by notes in the margin*
(like readers of this text)

OSRIC: The carriages, sir, are the hangers.

HAMLET: The phrase would be more germane° to the *suitable* 160
matter if we could carry cannon by our sides. I
would it might be hangers till then. But on! Six
Barbary horses against six French swords, their assigns, and three liberal-conceited carriages: that's
the French bet against the Danish. Why is this all 165
impawned, as you call it?

OSRIC: The King, sir, hath laid° that, in a dozen passes° *has bet/bouts*
between yourself and him, he shall not exceed you
three hits; he hath laid on twelve for nine, and it
would come to immediate trial° if your lordship *test* 170
would vouchsafe the answer.° *agree to respond*

HAMLET: How if I answer no?

OSRIC: I mean, my lord, the opposition of your per-
son° in trial. *appearing in person*

HAMLET: Sir, I will walk here in the hall. If it please his 175
Majesty, it is the breathing time° of day with me. *exercise time*
Let the foils° be brought, the gentleman willing, *blunt fencing weapons*
and the King hold his purpose,° I will win for him *sticks to his intention*
if I can; if not, I will gain nothing but my shame
and the odd hits. 180

OSRIC: Shall I redeliver you° even so? *bring back your answer*

HAMLET: To this effect, sir, after what flourish your nature will.

OSRIC: I commend my duty to your lordship.

HAMLET: Yours, yours. [OSRIC *leaves*.] He does well to 185
commend it himself; there are no tongues else
for's turn.° *to serve his turn*

HORATIO: This lapwing runs away with the shell on
his head.° *newly hatched bird*

HAMLET: He did comply with his dug° before he *spoke politely to the nipple* 190
sucked it. Thus has he, and many more of the
same bevy that I know the drossy° age dotes on, *silly*
only got the tune of the time and outward habit of
encounter—a kind of yeasty° collection, which *frothy*
carries them through and through the most fanned 195
and winnowed opinions; and do but blow them
to their trial°—the bubbles are out. *if you blow on them*
to test them

[*Enter a* LORD.]

LORD: My lord, his Majesty commended him to you
    by° young Osric, who brings back to him that you   *sent you greetings by*
    attend him in the hall. He sends to know if your   200
    pleasure hold to play° with Laertes, or that you   *fence*
    will take longer time.
HAMLET: I am constant to my purposes; they follow
    the King's pleasure. If his fitness speaks, mine is
    ready; now or whensoever, provided I be so able
    as now.   205
LORD: The King and Queen and all are coming
    down.
HAMLET: In happy time.°   *at the right time*
LORD: The Queen desires you to use some gentle en-
    tertainment° to Laertes before you fall to play.   *to speak courteously*
HAMLET: She well instructs me.   210

                      [LORD *leaves.*]

HORATIO: You will lose this wager, my lord.
HAMLET: I do not think so. Since he went into France
    I have been in continual practice; I shall win at the
    odds. But thou wouldst not think how ill all's here
    about my heart. But it is no matter.   215
HORATIO: Nay, good my lord—
HAMLET: It is but foolery, but it is such a kind of gain-
    giving° as would perhaps trouble a woman.   *misgiving*
HORATIO: If your mind dislike anything, obey it. I will
    forestall their repair° hither and say you are not fit.   *prevent their coming* 220
HAMLET: Not a whit, we defy augury;° there's a spe-   *let us ignore evil omens*
    cial providence in the fall of a sparrow. If it be
    now, 'tis not to come; if it be not to come, it will
    be now; if it be not now, yet it will come. The
    readiness is all. Since no man has aught of what   225
    he leaves,° what is't to leave betimes?° Let be.   *profits from what he*
                                                             leaves behind/early

[*Enter* KING, QUEEN, LAERTES, OSRIC, *and lords, with
other attendants with foils and daggers. A table
and cups of wine on it.*]

KING: Come, Hamlet, come, and take this hand from
    me.

[*He puts* LAERTES' *hand into* HAMLET'S.]

HAMLET: Give me your pardon, sir. I have done you wrong;
    But pardon't, as you are a gentleman.   230
    This presence° knows,   *assembled company*
    And you must needs have heard, how I am punished
    With sore distraction.° What I have done   *a severely disturbed mind*

That might your nature, honor, and exception°   *disapproval*
Roughly awake, I here proclaim was madness.   235
Was't Hamlet wronged Laertes? Never Hamlet.
If Hamlet from himself be taken away,
And when he's not himself does wrong Laertes,
Then Hamlet does it not. Hamlet denies it.
Who does it, then? His madness. If't be so,   240
Hamlet is of the faction that is wronged;
His madness is poor Hamlet's enemy.
Sir, in this audience,
Let my disclaiming from a purposed evil°   *any evil done on purpose*
Free me so far in your most generous thoughts   245
That I have shot my arrow o'er the house
And hurt my brother.

LAERTES: I am satisfied in nature,°   *my personal feelings*
Whose motive in this case should stir me most
To my revenge. But in my terms of honor
I stand aloof,° and will no reconcilement   *I have to hold off* 250
Till by some elder masters of known honor
I have a voice and precedent° of peace   *confirmation of precedent*
To keep my name ungored. But till that time   *for making peace*
I do receive your offered love like love,
And will not wrong it.

HAMLET: I embrace it freely,   255
And will this brother's wager frankly play.°   *enter fully into the contest*
Give us the foils. Come on.

LAERTES: Come, one for me.

HAMLET: I'll be your foil,° Laertes. In mine ignorance   *contrast setting off*
Your skill shall, like a star in the darkest night,   *something precious*
Stick fiery off indeed.°   *show fiery by contrast*

LAERTES: You mock me, sir.   260

HAMLET: No, by this hand.

KING: Give them the foils, young Osric. Cousin Hamlet,
You know the wager?

HAMLET: Very well, my lord.
Your Grace has laid the odds on the weaker side.

KING: I do not fear it,° I have seen you both;   *I am not worried* 265
But since he is bettered,° we have therefore odds.   *has improved*

LAERTES: This is too heavy; let me see another.

HAMLET: This likes me well. These foils have all a length?

[*They prepare to fence.*]

OSRIC: Ay, my good lord.

KING: Set me the stoups° of wine upon that table.   *cups* 270
If Hamlet give the first or second hit,
Or quit° in answer of the third exchange,   *hit back*
Let all the battlements their ordnance° fire;   *cannon*
The King shall drink to Hamlet's better breath,
And in the cup an union° shall he throw   *a pearl* 275

Richer than that which four successive kings
In Denmark's crown have worn. Give me the cups;
And let the kettle° to the trumpet speak,   *the kettledrum*
The trumpet to the cannoneer without,
The cannons to the heavens, the heaven to earth,   280
"Now the King drinks to Hamlet." Come, begin.
And you the judges, bear a wary eye.
HAMLET: Come on, sir.
LAERTES: Come, my lord.

  [*They fence.*]

HAMLET: One.
LAERTES: No.
HAMLET: Judgment!
OSRIC: A hit, a very palpable hit.
LAERTES: Well, again!
KING: Stay,° give me drink. Hamlet, this pearl is thine;   *wait* 285
  Here's to thy health.

  [*Drum; trumpets sound; a cannon goes off outside.*]

                    Give him the cup.
HAMLET: I'll play this bout first; set it by awhile.
  Come. [*They fight.*] Another hit. What say you?
LAERTES: A touch, a touch; I do confess.
KING: Our son shall win.
QUEEN: He's fat,° and scant of breath.   *sweaty* 290
  Here, Hamlet, take my napkin,° rub thy brows.   *handkerchief*
  The Queen carouses to thy fortune, Hamlet.
HAMLET: Good madam!
KING: Gertrude, do not drink.
QUEEN: I will, my lord; I pray you pardon me.

  [*She drinks.*]

KING [*aside*]: It is the poisoned cup; it is too late.   295
HAMLET: I dare not drink yet, madam; by-and-by.
QUEEN: Come, let me wipe thy face.
LAERTES: My lord, I'll hit him now.
KING: I do not think't.
LAERTES [*aside*]: And yet it is almost against my
    conscience.
HAMLET: Come for the third, Laertes! You but dally;   300
  I pray you pass with your best violence;
  I am afeard you make a wanton of me.°   *treat me like a child*
LAERTES: Say you so? Come on.

  [*They fence.*]

OSRIC: Nothing neither way.
LAERTES: Have at you now!

[LAERTES *wounds* HAMLET*; then, in scuffling, they change rapiers, and* HAMLET *wounds* LAERTES.]

KING: Part them! They are incensed.°   *enraged* 305
HAMLET: Nay come! again!

[*The* QUEEN *falls.*]

OSRIC: Look to the Queen there, ho!
HORATIO: They bleed on both sides. How is it, my lord?
OSRIC: How is't, Laertes?
LAERTES: Why, as a woodcock to mine own springe,°   *like a (decoy) bird*
    Osric.   *caught in my own trap*
    I am justly killed with mine own treachery.   310
HAMLET: How does the Queen?
KING: She swoons to see them bleed.
QUEEN: No, no! the drink, the drink! O my dear Hamlet!
    The drink, the drink! I am poisoned.

[*She dies.*]

HAMLET: O villainy! Ho! let the door be locked.
    Treachery! Seek it out.   315

[LAERTES *falls.*]

LAERTES: It is here, Hamlet. Hamlet, thou art slain;
    No medicine in the world can do thee good.
    In thee there is not half an hour of life.
    The treacherous instrument is in thy hand,
    Unbated° and envenomed. The foul practice°   *unchecked/vicious scheme* 320
    Hath turned itself on me. Lo, here I lie,
    Never to rise again. Thy mother's poisoned.
    I can no more. The King, the King's to blame.
HAMLET: The point envenomed too?
    Then, venom, to thy work.   325

[*Hurts the* KING.]

ALL: Treason! treason!
KING: O, yet defend me, friends! I am but hurt.
HAMLET: Here, thou incestuous, murderous, damned
        Dane,
    Drink off this potion! Is thy union here?°   *is this what you meant by a pearl*
    Follow my mother.

[KING *dies.*]

LAERTES: He is justly served.   330
    It is a poison tempered by° himself.   *prepared by*
    Exchange forgiveness with me, noble Hamlet.
    Mine and my father's death come not upon thee,°   *you are not guilty of*
    Nor thine on me!

[*Dies.*]

HAMLET: Heaven make thee free° of it! I follow thee.   *may heaven clear you*   335
 I am dead, Horatio. Wretched queen, adieu!
 You that look pale and tremble at this chance,°   *mischance*
 That are but mutes° or audience to this act,   *silent spectators*
 Had I but time (as this fell sergeant,° Death,   *this cruel law officer*
 Is strict in his arrest) O, I could tell you—   340
 But let it be. Horatio, I am dead;
 Thou liv'st; report me and my cause aright
 To the unsatisfied.°   *those who do not know the truth*
HORATIO: Never believe it.
 I am more an antique Roman° than a Dane.   *(like a Roman believing in*
 Here's yet some liquor left.   *honorable suicide)*
HAMLET: As th'art a man,   345
 Give me the cup. Let go! By heaven, I'll have't.
 O good Horatio, what a wounded name
 (Things standing thus unknown) shall live behind me!
 If thou didst ever hold me in thy heart,
 Absent thee from felicity° awhile,   *turn your back on ultimate*   350
 And in this harsh world draw thy breath in pain,   *happiness*
 To tell my story.

[March afar off, and sound of cannon.]

 What warlike noise is this?
OSRIC: Young Fortinbras, with conquest° come from   *after his conquest*
  Poland,
 To the ambassadors of England gives
 This warlike volley.
HAMLET: O, I die, Horatio!   355
 The potent poison quite overcrows° my spirit.   *overpowers (like a cock in*
 I cannot live to hear the news from England,   *a cockfight)*
 But I do prophesy the election lights
 On° Fortinbras. He has my dying voice.   *choice of a new king goes to*
 So tell him, with the occurrents,° more and less,   *events*   360
 Which have solicited°—the rest is silence.   *incited me*

[Dies.]

HORATIO: Now cracks a noble heart. Good night, sweet
  prince,
 And flights of angels sing thee to thy rest!

[Sound of marching outside.]

 Why does the drum come hither?

[Enter FORTINBRAS and English ambassadors, with drum,
flags, and attendants.]

FORTINBRAS: Where is this sight?
HORATIO: What is it you would see?   365
 If aught° of woe or wonder, cease your search.   *anything*
FORTINBRAS: This quarry cries on havoc.° O proud   *these bodies call out for*
  Death,   *vengeance*

What feast is toward° in thine eternal cell   *ahead*
That thou so many princes at a shot
So bloodily hast struck?
AMBASSADOR: The sight is dismal;   370
And our affairs° from England come too late.   *news of our business*
The ears are senseless° that should give us hearing   *without life*
To tell him his commandment is fulfilled,
That Rosencrantz and Guildenstern are dead.
Where should we have our thanks?
HORATIO: Not from his° mouth,   *(Claudius')* 375
Had it the ability of life to thank you.
He never gave commandment for their death.
But since, so jump upon this bloody question,°   *right at the moment of*
You from the Polack wars, and you from England,   *bloodshed*
Are here arrived, give order that these bodies   380
High on a stage be placed to the view;
And let me speak to the yet unknowing world
How these things came about. So shall you hear
Of carnal, bloody, and unnatural acts;
Of accidental judgments, casual slaughters;°   *accidental killings* 385
Of deaths put on by cunning and forced cause;
And, in this upshot, purposes mistook°
Fallen on the inventors' heads. All this can I   *intentions badly carried out*
Truly deliver.
FORTINBRAS: Let us haste to hear it,
And call the noblest to the audience.   390
For me, with sorrow I embrace my fortune.
I have some rights of memory° in this kingdom,   *remembered claims*
Which now to claim my vantage° doth invite me.   *opportunity*
HORATIO: Of that I shall have also cause to speak,
And from his mouth whose voice will draw on more.   395
But let this same be presently performed,
Even while men's minds are wild, lest more mischance
On plots and errors happen.
FORTINBRAS: Let four captains
Bear Hamlet like a soldier to the stage;°   *platform*
For he was likely, had he been put on,°   *if he had been made king* 400
To have proved most royally; and for his passage
The soldiers' music and the rites of war
Speak loudly for him.
Take up the bodies. Such a sight as this
Becomes the field, but here shows much amiss.   405
Go, bid the soldiers shoot.

[*They leave marching, after which cannons are fired.*]

The Receptive Reader

1. (Act Five, Scene 1) The gravediggers' scene is an outstanding example of
the **dark humor** Elizabethan audiences apparently expected and loved. What

is the content and mode of the jests? Is the grim or macabre humor here mere comic relief or interlude, or is it related to the overall development of the play? (What kind of *foreshadowing* is going on here?)

2. How do Laertes and Hamlet behave at Ophelia's funeral? What side of either character comes to the fore here? What stance toward Ophelia's death is adopted by the church? by the other characters? Was her death suicide?

3. (Act Five, Scene 2) Hamlet's final exchanges with his *confidant* Horatio give the audience a glimpse of his frame of mind as he approaches the tragic conclusion (or *denouement*) of the play. What are his last words on life, on fate, on human nature? In Hamlet's return from the voyage, what was the role of his own initiative; what was the role of Providence? How does Hamlet react to the deaths of Rosencrantz and Guildenstern?

4. The precious Osric gives Hamlet a last opportunity to display his satirical wit. What makes Osric a prime target?

5. In preparing for the fencing contest, Hamlet treats Laertes with extreme courtesy. How and why? (How do you reconcile his behavior here with his extreme lack of courtesy in other situations?) Is the ending or denouement an example of happenstance—of confused accidental happenings that make a mockery of human planning? Is the ending an example of poetic justice, with the plotters finally getting their just deserts? Is the ending a triumph of *irony,* with the plot backfiring on the plotters, and with the "enginer hoist with his own petar"?

The Creative Dimension

Working with a group, make plans for a *mini-production* that would focus on a major issue in the play, throw light on one of its puzzles, or look at part of it from a new or different perspective. Help the group with developing a concept and a script. You might want to transpose a scene or scenes to a modern setting, or you might want to rewrite a scene or scenes as seen through the eyes of a minor character. (In working with Shakespeare's *Macbeth,* one group of students staged "The Trial of Macbeth"—for killing King Duncan; another staged a mini-production called "Ms. Beth," in which Lady Macbeth had become transformed into a ruthless corporation vice president plotting to take over the job of President Duncan.)

The Whole Play—For Discussion or Writing

1. Laertes' final verdict is, "The King, the King's to blame." Does guilt in this play rest mainly on a single individual? Is Claudius a *stereotypical villain?* What are the sources or what is the root cause of evil in this play?

2. Until recently, most critics did not question the validity of the *revenge ethic* preached by the ghost (an eye for an eye; a tooth for a tooth; a life for a life). Yet critics have also puzzled endlessly over Hamlet's apparent hesitation or delay in carrying out his dead father's command. How do you explain this paradox? Is Hamlet fully committed to the (pre-Christian) tradition of revenge or not?

3. Is Hamlet temperamentally unsuited for the task assigned him by the ghost? Did Shakespeare create a character too *introspective,* sensitive, or poetic for the initiative and effective action needed?

4. Is Hamlet a *tragic hero?* Does he have a tragic flaw? Does he progress toward self-realization—a fuller understanding of himself and his situation?

5. Is Hamlet's treatment of Ophelia and his mother harsh and unreasonable? Is it part of a pattern of misogyny deeply engrained in the culture he represents?

6. The English critic J. Dover Wilson has said that "there is a savage side" to Hamlet's character (shown for instance in his ruthless treatment of Rosencrantz and Guildenstern or of Polonius), but that it is not meant to "detract from our general sense of the nobility and greatness" of Hamlet. Do you agree?

7. Rebecca West said that "Hamlet was disgusted by his own kind." How profound or complete is Hamlet's *disillusionment* with humankind?

8. Some critics have seen poison as the master metaphor in this play. What is its role, literally and figuratively, in the play? For you, does it sum up a central theme?

JUXTAPOSITIONS

The Range of Interpretation

Some mystery should be left in the revelation
of character in a play, just as a great deal of
mystery is always left in the revelation of
character in life, even in one's own character
to himself.

TENNESSEE WILLIAMS

Different schools of thought focus on different dimensions of Hamlet's multifaceted, complex character. In the words of C. S. Lewis, the fact that the critics "can never leave *Hamlet* alone" is strong evidence that "we have here something of inestimable importance." The following is a brief sampling of critical perspectives on Hamlet and his role in the play. Which of these seem most attuned to your own reading of and reaction to the play?

Samuel Taylor Coleridge   *(1772–1834)*

The **Romantic** poets revered Shakespeare, initiating the modern Shakespeare cult. The Romantics rejected the eighteenth-century view of Shakespeare as an untutored natural genius, who wrote irregular, uneven plays with flashes of brilliance. To Samuel Taylor Coleridge and other Romantics, Shakespeare's work showed the creative imagination at its most sublime. Every detail in a play was subordinated to an overriding purpose that gave "organic unity" to the whole. For Coleridge and other Romantic poets and critics, that overriding purpose in *Hamlet* was to explore a temperament akin to their own. The Romantic Hamlet is the melancholy, solitary, introspective Hamlet. He is forever musing; his "powers of action have been eaten up by thought." Coleridge, who said "I have a smack of Hamlet myself," frequently returned to the topic of Hamlet's character in his lecture notes and critical essays.

The Romantic Hamlet

In Hamlet, [Shakespeare] seems to have wished to exemplify the moral necessity of a due balance between our attention to the objects of our senses and our meditations on the working of our minds—an *equilibrium* between the real and imaginary worlds. In Hamlet, this balance is disturbed: his thoughts, and the images of his fancy, are far more vivid than his actual perceptions, and his very perceptions, instantly passing through the medium of his contemplations, acquire, as they pass, a form and a color not naturally their own. Hence, we see a great, an almost enormous, intellectual activity, and a proportionate aversion to real action. . . . This character Shakespeare places in circumstances under which it is obliged to act on the spur of the moment: Hamlet is brave and careless of death; but he vacillates from sensibility, and procrastinates from thought, and loses the power of action in the energy of resolve. Thus it is that this tragedy presents a direct contrast to that of Macbeth; the one proceeds with the utmost slowness, the other with a crowded and breathless rapidity.

The effect of the overbalance of the imaginative power is beautifully illustrated in the everlasting broodings and superfluous activities of Hamlet's mind, which, unseated from its healthy relation, is constantly occupied with the world within and abstracted from the world without—giving substance to shadows and throwing a mist over all commonplace actualities.

The Receptive Reader

1. What scenes in the play best bear out the Romantic conception of the solitary, melancholy Hamlet, "sicklied o'er by the pale cast of thought"?

2. Coleridge said that Hamlet "delays action till action is of no use and dies the victim of mere circumstance and accident." Is this view borne out by your reading of the final scenes of the play?

Elmer Edgar Stoll

Literary history keeps us from taking a play out of its original time frame and seeing it from an anachronistic, modern point of view. In the historical context of the author's time, Hamlet is a Renaissance prince—"a lord of the Renaissance, and loves name and fame" (E. E. Stoll). In Ophelia's words, he is a courtier, a soldier, and a scholar. Fortinbras says at the end that Hamlet would have made a truly kingly ruler: "he was likely, had he been put on, / To have proved most royal." The Renaissance ideal was not a solitary, withdrawn individual but a person functioning easily and competently in society. Hamlet is a trusting friend to Horatio; he is a courteous, generous host to the wandering players; he is fully in control when playing cat and mouse with Polonius or the king's spies. Elmer Edgar Stoll tries to show that Hamlet's self-image, and the image of him mirrored in the words of other characters, is very different from that of the indecisive, hesitating Romantic Hamlet.

The Renaissance Hamlet

By his tone and bearing, likewise, and a conduct that is (if we be not cavilling) irreproachable, and a reputation that is stainless, is Hamlet to be judged. Even early in the play—as, in the soliloquy "O what a rogue," he looks forward to the Mousetrap—the tone is exactly the same that we notice when he is looking forward to the fencing match:

I'll tent him to the quick; if he but blench,
I know my course.

Such accents (unless I be utterly blind to the finer shades of expression, and deaf to the differences in rhythm of verse and speech) are not meant for those of irresolution or shiftiness, apathy, or frailty . . .

In the form and fashion of Hamlet's speech, there is no trace of uncertainty or fatuity, as there is no trace of suspiciousness or childishness, before he falls into the human devils' clutches, in Othello. And after one's ear (for are we not at the theater?) one's simple wits. In this case [the killing of Polonius], as at the fencing match and on the trip to England, and in the same way, he makes his previous words good; for he kills the man he thinks to be the king. What is plainer still, he thus makes good the words he had uttered as he withheld his hand from the fratricide [of the king at prayer] a minute or so before. Here, indeed, is the "more horrid hent"—to "trip him as his heels may kick at heaven," as he catches the murderer spying on him. And these plain and tangible things, this record of promise and fulfillment, the audience would notice, and were meant to notice; and if a few of them stopped to think that in keeping the great deed to the last he was like the heroes of all revenge tragedies they knew of, they were used to that, and would instinctively approve of it. It is both the traditional form and the natural procedure; obviously, the deed done, the tragedy is over.

From *Art and Artifice in Shakespeare,* 1933

The Receptive Reader

1. Can you find and cite other passages in which Hamlet sounds determined or resolute?

2. For critics in the Romantic tradition, scenes like Hamlet's deciding not to kill the king at prayer are mere *pretexts* or excuses for continued inaction. What side do you incline to after rereading the scene?

3. Do you think both the sensitive, meditative side of Hamlet's character stressed by the Romantics and the aggressive, determined side stressed by Stoll could be parts of the same character?

Ernest Jones

Psychoanalytic criticism focuses on Hamlet's inner turmoil as evidence of a profoundly disturbed, "unhinged" mind. What explains his misogyny—his harsh abusive treatment of the innocent Ophelia and his hateful comments about women in general? Psychoanalysts, trained to trace severe maladjustments to the workings of sexual repression, looked for buried, unacknowledged desires as the source of Hamlet's "near madness." Ernest Jones, a British follower of Freud, tried to show in the play detailed evidence of the Oedipus complex: intense jealousy and resentment directed at the mother (seen as having betrayed the son's love); hatred of the mother's husband (Claudius) as the successful rival for the mother's affection; inability to overcome the fixation on the mother and transfer love or sexual desire to a younger woman (Ophelia). Jones saw in Hamlet's idealized picture of his dead father the result of the conscious mind adopting the teachings of society. These teachings cause the overlay of dutiful respect and filial piety covering up the repressed resentment and sexual jealousy against the father that still lurk in the subconscious.

The Psychoanalytic Hamlet

His [Hamlet's] resentment against women is still further inflamed by the hypocritical prudishness with which Ophelia follows her father and brother in seeing evil in his natural affection, an attitude which poisons his love in exactly the same way that the love of his childhood, like that of all children, must have been poisoned. He can forgive a woman neither her rejection of his sexual advances nor, still less, her alliance with another man. Most intolerable of all to him, as Bradley well remarks, is the sight of sensuality in a quarter from which he had trained himself ever since infancy vigorously to exclude it. The total reaction culminates in the bitter misogyny of his outburst against Ophelia, who is devastated at having to bear a reaction so wholly out of proportion to her own offense and has no idea that in reviling her Hamlet is really expressing his bitter resentment against his mother. The identification is further demonstrated in the course of the play by Hamlet's killing the men who stand between him and his mother and Ophelia (Claudius and Polonius). On only one occasion does he for a moment escape from the sordid implication with which his love has been impregnated and achieve a healthier attitude toward Ophelia, namely at the open grave when in remorse he breaks out at Laertes for presuming to pretend that his feeling for her could ever equal that of her lover.

The intensity of Hamlet's repulsion against women in general, and Ophelia in particular, is a measure of the powerful repression to which his sexual feelings are being subjected. The outlet for those feelings in the direction of his mother has always been firmly dammed, and now that the narrower channel in Ophelia's direction has also been closed the increase in the original direction consequent on the awakening of early memories tasks all his energy to maintain the repression. His pent up feelings find a partial vent in other directions. The petulant irascibility and explosive outbursts called forth by his vexation at the hands of Guildenstern and Rosencrantz, and especially of Polonius, are evidently to be interpreted in this way, as also is in part the burning nature of his reproaches to his mother. Indeed toward the end of his interview with his mother the thought of her misconduct expresses itself in that almost physical disgust which is so characteristic a manifestation of intensely repressed sexual feeling.

> Let the bloat king tempt you again to bed;
> Pinch wanton on your cheek; call you his mouse;
> And let him, for a pair of reechy kisses,
> Or paddling in your neck with his damned fingers,
> Make you to ravel all this matter out . . . (III.iv)
>   From the introduction to *Hamlet, Prince of Denmark,* 1947

The Receptive Reader

For you, does this excerpt throw new light on Hamlet's anger and hostility? What scenes or details from the play does Jones make you reconsider? How persuasive is Jones' explanation of Hamlet's misogyny? What are other possible explanations?

Sandra K. Fischer

Some **feminist criticism** has focused on those of Shakespeare's female characters who exhibit in varying degrees "independence, self-control, and, frequently, defiance": "By creating confident, attractive, independent women whom we like, he questions the wisdom of a power structure that insists they relinquish personal freedom" (Irene G. Dash). Other feminists have focused on those of Shakespeare's women who seem defeated by a patriarchal society. The author of the following excerpt said that the two essential steps toward a feminist approach to the play were (1) to notice how much in *Hamlet* is "based on a stereotyped judgment of women as *others,*" and (2) "to read female characters in as real and serious a fashion as the males—as grappling with their identities, needing outlets for their conflicts, and trying to articulate their truths" when denied full voice. In the following excerpt, the author tries to hear one of the "quieter and less powerful voices" almost drowned out by Hamlet's assertive rhetoric.

The Feminist Hamlet: Hearing Ophelia

Ophelia's debut is with Laertes, who bids her farewell by solidifying her role as object and by squelching any effort on her part for mutual perspective and adult interchange. Polonius and Laertes, father and son, both treat her like a child who lacks self-knowledge and apprehension about the ways of the world. As Polonius speaks his truisms to Laertes, so Laertes gives his platitudinous wisdom to Ophelia, establishing a chain of cultural dissemination and control. Remarkably missing in this scene is an outside audience or any sense of commentary on the action. In contradistinction, Hamlet's entrance reveals "the privileges of the Self . . . attributed to the masculine hero. The hero is, to begin with, *concerned* with himself; the first privilege of the Self is to have an *extra* Self who comments on or is simply aware of the original one. The tragic hero explains and justifies himself, he finds fault with himself, he insists on himself, he struggles to be true to himself" (Linda Bamber). In Ophelia's discourse, these functions are completely externalized: she finds herself explained, faulted, and struggled over by rival authorities outside herself.

Ophelia's language is an index to her enforced silence and circumscribed self. With Laertes, her familiar, she is allowed mostly half-lines and questions that are codes of acquiescence without the gesture of assent. They actually invite further commands: "Do you doubt that? . . . No more but so?" (I.iii.4, 9). Her allowed discourse with Polonius is even more frightening. First, in the course of thirteen lines she breaks her promise of secrecy to Laertes by relating to her father the gist of their conversation. Moreover, her speeches here are marked by phrases of self-effacing obeisance: "So please you . . . my lord . . . I do not know, my lord, what I should think. . . . I shall obey, my lord" (89–136).

In his intervening scene, I.iv, Hamlet again is afforded the medium of intimate and leisurely dialogue that establishes and cements his sense of self. Here is the camaraderie of the watch and the comforting mirror of Horatio; here as well is discourse with the ghost, which is remarkably similar to soliloquy. Ophelia's link with Hamlet's mission from the ghost is to be the recipient of his first attempt at an antic disposition. The prologue to her description of his madness is in her usual tentative form—"O my lord, my lord, I have been so affrighted. . . . My lord, I do not know, / But truly I do fear it" (II.i.75,85–86). As she describes to Polonius what she has witnessed, she depicts herself throughout as the passive object of Hamlet's actions: he holds her wrist; stares at her face; shakes her arm; nods, sighs; leaves while staring at her still. To obedience, acquiescence, and obeisance is now added negative objectification. The cause of this treatment has not been Ophelia's self, but rather her absence: "No, my good lord, but as you did command, / I did repel his letters and denied / His access to me" (II.i.108–10). Ophelia's closet scene is remarkable for acting as a discursive pivot. Here the characters embarked on parallel tragic courses are alone together, yet the chance for dialogue is missed, and each begins a path toward a stunning isolation. Ophelia loses all interlocutors as Polonius objectifies her further, "loosing" her (in the sense of unlocking or offering for mating) to probe the depths of Hamlet's self. Hamlet, meanwhile, complains of his isolation, yet he is constantly allowed confrontations that permit him to shape his changing sense of identity: with Polonius, with Rosencrantz and Guildenstern, and with the Players. As Belsey notes, "since meaning is plural, to be able to speak is to be able to take part in the contest for meaning which issues in the production of new subject-positions, new determinations of what it is possible to be." These exchanges result in Hamlet's second soliloquy, beginning "Now I am alone" (II.ii.569). Yet it is Ophelia whose linguistic isolation is the most profound, and she is offered no means to vent her confusion. Her confrontation with Hamlet in III.i, with Polonius and Claudius as silent observers, is a mistimed parody of what might have ensued in the closet scene. Both are aware of their audience. Ophelia tries her usual speech forms, half-lines, and questions, in addition to cautious and polite assertions of a changed reality, but Hamlet refuses to communicate, judging her the bait in the trap of his selfhood.

From *Renaissance and Reformation* 26, 1990

The Receptive Reader

This article focuses on functions of language other than merely communicating information. What are some of these functions? What is their meaning or symbolic significance? What are striking illustrations from the play? Do they alert you to striking differences between the roles of Hamlet and Ophelia? How does this article change your thinking about sex roles or gender roles in the play?

Steven Berkoff

Modern **experimental theater** has often taken literary monuments down from their pedestal. Steven Berkoff is an experimental actor-director who staged a modern-dress *Hamlet* with all the actors remaining on stage all the time "as if they were witnesses at a trial." Berkoff had the gravedigger in the graveyard sing "My old man's a dustman, he wears a dustman's hat" during his labors. Given "the most awful battering" by the English press, the production went on to a successful two-year tour of the European continent. In the following excerpt from his book *I Am Hamlet* (1989), Berkoff explores a biblical parallel as "one of the many backgrounds against which the play can be viewed."

The Experimental Hamlet

Many of Hamlet's lines have a biblical quality to them which gives Hamlet a Messianic fervour at times. Certainly a man of great moral fiber, and one through whom we test the corruption of the times: "If thine eye offend thee, pluck it out" could be *throw away the worser part of it.* He could be a preacher advising us and exhorting us to respect the sanctity of life. Hamlet the Messiah—for so the play seems as we tour Europe with our twelve disciples, armed with our play of Christian and humanistic ethics—an adventure story carefully concealing a profound, moving philosophy. A human being is pitted against the pursy corruption of his times and sacrificed like Jesus for daring to speak and fight against it. Betrayed by Judas/Laertes.

On our last tour to Europe there was a rumor that the Messiah was about to appear. It was his time to come and someone claimed to have seen him in the east end of London! One day on the train, idly letting my mind go its own way, I discovered that in our cast or company were exactly thirteen people including myself: nine actors, one musician, and three stage-managers, a magic number. Then, playing around with the idea more fully, Laertes was a Judas, Claudius a Pilate, and Polonius the Fisherman. The Ghost was a spirit of God instructing me and sending me down to do his will. Gertrude was the Virgin Mary, and Ophelia, Mary Magdalene. The players were the children that Jesus loved, and Hamlet's soliloquies were sermons to the people. Hamlet was certainly a Jesus figure—someone who must be sacrificed from time to time to remind the world when it strays from the path of virtue or excellence; as if the world throws up these "purer specimens" that it worships and adores but somehow has to destroy, since the constant light is too much, but then can mourn the loss later.

Now the strange thing is that one found reflections of this within the group. As people got into their characters they tended to sleep in them. Hamlet was betrayed by Laertes who, like Judas, was once his ally, and Horatio was always his ally in a way like John the Baptist. In any great work one sees the struggle between two forces of light and darkness, if you like, and the shades of grey between; the audience or reader is gathered somehow from his slumbers in the nether region and encouraged to climb the top and see the view. The members of the audience are almost like floating voters who wish to be inspired and delivered from themselves into a collective force. In the struggle of the forces the martyr arises who is born of the struggle and who then guides it until his eventual destruction. He is invariably destroyed since, once he is discovered, he is then "claimed"—so the same struggle that would forge Jesus would forge Hamlet. Both are in a sense shaped by the very hostility around them. They become a mould which the forces of the world try to crush.

From *I Am Hamlet,* 1989

The Receptive Reader

Does the biblical parallel seem far-fetched, or is it thought-provoking? What features of the play does it make you rethink or reexamine?

WRITING ABOUT LITERATURE

28 Studying Character
WRITING FOCUS: Reading for Clues

O brave new world that has such people in it!
SHAKESPEARE, *THE TEMPEST*

The Writing Workshop   The theater creates characters who often assume a life of their own, beyond the duration of the two-hour or three-hour play. As spectator or reader, you enter imaginatively into how other human beings think and feel. A play may bring into focus human motives that you may have only imperfectly understood. A play may make you wonder at the fixed ideas and maddening contradictions that make a character human.

Writing a paper about a central character or about several key characters in a play gives you a chance to sum up what you see in the mirror the play holds up to human nature. Is there a single clue or dominant trait that will help the audience understand the character? Or are there perhaps several major related traits, and do they form an understandable pattern? Can you perhaps clear up puzzling questions about one limited but important trait? Can you take a close look at apparent contradictions in the character to see if they can be resolved? No matter what the exact focus on your paper, will you help your readers understand the character's thoughts, feelings, and actions?

When you write about a central character or the key characters in a play, consider the following general guidelines:

✗ *Be a patient listener.* Quote revealing things a character says. In the theater, as in real life, language in many ways reveals (and sometimes betrays) people's thoughts. Look for clues to a character in what he or she says at key points—for instance, when confiding in a friend, when defiantly talking back to an adversary, or when uttering last words.

✗ *Listen to the testimony of others.* However, remember who is talking. Consider the source. (People who love and those who hate a character are likely to give conflicting accounts.) Pay special attention when a consensus develops among different supporting characters. In Sophocles' *Antigone,* Creon is convicted of stubborn, unreasonable pride out of the mouth not only of the hostile prophet but also of his own son.

✗ *Pay special attention to test situations.* What happens when a character is forced to make a decision or take a stand? In the *Antigone* play, for instance, what happens when Ismene is forced to take a stand or when Haemon faces his father?

✗ *Look at the character's behavior in revealing incidents.* Events that are apparent digressions may provide a challenge or a test. Hamlet's encounter with the players shows something about his large-mindedness or magnanimity, his liberality. "Treat them after your own honor and dignity," he tells Polonius—make sure your treatment of them reflects your own stature. Don't go strictly by what is their due, as people do who niggle and haggle (splitting a luncheon check down to the last decimal).

✗ *Pay attention to nonverbal as well as verbal language.* Look for meaning in gesture, revealing incidents, or recurrent symbols. What does the frantic tarantella symbolize that Nora dances at a climactic point in the Ibsen play?

✗ *Try to understand before you judge.* When you are angry enough at a character, you may be tempted to oversimplify, to stereotype. When you intensely dislike someone, it is easy to trace everything the person does to one single disreputable motive. Make allowance for ambivalent feelings on the part of the author—for a mixture of admirable and less admirable traits, for a mingling of lovable and hateful features.

Be prepared to watch for clues to a character at key points in a play:

✗ Watch for preliminary *capsule descriptions* of the character. Claudius says early in *Hamlet*:

There's something in his soul o'er which his melancholy sits on brood.

✗ Listen to the *self-revelations* of the character in **soliloquies** and confidential **asides;** in exchanges with **confidants**—trusted friends or associates:

Give me that man that is not passion's slave
And I'll wear him in my heart of hearts.

✗ Listen to *climactic confrontations* that bring to the surface thoughts and feelings that until then may have been hidden under polite or cautious disguises. Hamlet had earlier said: "O break my heart, for I must hold my tongue." Now, at a **climax** or high point of the play, he is ready to indict his mother. When she reproaches him for having offended his (new) father, or stepfather, he charges her with her offense against his (real) father, her murdered husband. He reveals his righteous anger:

QUEEN: Hamlet, thou hast thy father much offended.
HAMLET: Mother, you have my father much offended.
QUEEN: Come, come, you answer with an idle tongue.
HAMLET: Go, go, you question with a wicked tongue. (3.4.10–13)

Remember especially: Try not to build generalizations about character on a single quote, a single incident. Look for what is part of a *pattern*:

✗ Look for evidence of *recurrent traits*. For instance, Hamlet's harsher side shows in his baiting of Polonius and unceremonious treatment of Polonius' corpse; his passionate extended denunciation of his mother; his coolly sending his former schoolmates Rosencrantz and Guildenstern to their deaths. ("They are not near my conscience.")

✗ Bring together relevant evidence from *different parts* of the play. What evidence can you bring together on Hamlet's true feelings about Ophelia? In spite of his harsh treatment of her, was he capable of love for her? To answer this question, you would have to look at a range of contradictory evidence. For instance, Ophelia says, looking back: "And I, of ladies most deject and wretched / That sucked the honey of his music vows . . ." (3.1.158–59).

Hamlet, fending her off, alternately affirms and denies his love for her:

HAMLET: I did love you once.

OPHELIA: Indeed, my lord, you made me believe so.

HAMLET: You should not have believed me, for virtue cannot so inoculate our old stock but we shall relish of it. I loved you not. (3.1.115–19)

Hamlet aggressively vaunts his love for her at her grave, in his altercation with Laertes:

I loved Ophelia. Forty thousand brothers
Could not with all their quantity of love
Make up my sum. What wilt thou do for her? (5.1.277–79)

The following student paper is focused on one aspect of Hamlet's multifaceted character.

Sample Student Paper

Playing for Time

Though this be madness, there is method in't.
Hamlet, Prince of Denmark: "unhinged mind" or master of intrigue? That this question continues to be asked after nearly four hundred years is testimony to the intriguing complexity of Hamlet's character. Samuel Taylor Coleridge, in *The Lectures of 1811–1812* (Lecture XII), regards Hamlet as

> an admirable and consistent character, deeply acquainted with his own feelings, painting them with such wonderful power and accuracy . . . Such a mind as Hamlet's is near akin to madness.

How near? Most of the evidence points to the conclusion that Hamlet was fully in possession of his faculties. His behavior, while sometimes erratic or unpredictable, always has a rational motive behind it. It is true that he faces tremendous pressures. He is a victim of hostile circumstance. To Horatio he exclaims,

The time is out of joint. O cursèd spite,
That ever I was born to set it right! (1.5.189–90)

However, throughout the play, Hamlet shows himself to be a perceptive, cogent observer of human nature and of his own inner being. He sees his mother's pretended grief. He recognizes Polonius' dishonesty. He sees through the hypocritical friendliness of Rosencrantz and Guildenstern. ("You were sent for, and there is a kind of confession in your looks" 2.2.290–91.) The father's ghost reveals that he was murdered by his own brother and, although Hamlet questions the validity of the apparition, he gradually accepts the evidence of foul play. ("It is an honest ghost, that let me tell you" 1.5.138.) With only a few exceptions, Hamlet conducts himself not as a madman, but as a man weighed down with the task of avenging his father's death, his own grief and anger, and his princely duties. As Laertes says to Ophelia,

his will is not his own.
For he himself is subject to his birth. (1.3.17–18)

This statement speaks of obligations and knowledge beyond the grasp or experience of common humanity. Neither Hamlet nor his actions can be judged within the limited understanding that ordinary vision affords.

Hamlet himself consistently maintains that he is "mad in craft." In other words, he pretends to have an unhinged mind in order to be able to observe and thwart his enemies while confusing and disorienting them. For this purpose he warns his friends that he might see fit "to put an antic disposition on" (1.5.172). As he says later,

> I am but mad north-northwest: when the wind is southerly I know a hawk from a handsaw. (2.2.395–96)

His mother calls the ghost who speaks to him again in her bedroom "the very coinage of your brain" ("Alas, he's mad!" 3.4.107). Hamlet answers,

> My pulse as yours doth temperately keep time
> And makes as healthful music. It is not madness
> That I have uttered. . . .
> Lay not that flattering unction to your soul
> That not your trespass but my madness speaks. (3.4.142–48)

In assessing Hamlet's condition, we should remember that most of the discussion of his mental state comes from others' perceptions of his behavior. Ophelia, describing an encounter with Hamlet, tells her father that he came before her "as if he had been loosèd out of hell" (2.1.83). Polonius, prime target of Hamlet's "wild and whirling words" (1.5.133), prides himself on having found "the very cause of Hamlet's lunacy" (2.2.49). In Act 4, as he returns from England, Hamlet hears the gravediggers talking about "Hamlet . . . he that is mad."

Modern psychoanalysts, like the Romantic poets before them, see Hamlet as flirting with the idea of suicide ("To be or not to be . . ."). Even in his morbid or depressed state, however, Hamlet manages to develop a brilliant strategy. No madman could have so fine-tuned his revenge as Hamlet does when he instructs the players in how to show the utmost restraint in playing the scene that he hopes will unhinge his mother and murderous uncle. He tells the players,

> in the very torrent, tempest and (as I may say) whirlwind of your passion, you must acquire and beget a temperance that may give it smoothness. (3.2.6–9)

Here Hamlet displays a keen grasp of situation and moment; he also invokes a treasured Renaissance ideal: temperance. Temperance is the opposite of the loss of control in a deranged mind. Hamlet shows this ideal in action as the play races toward its tragic conclusion. In the scene just before the duel between Laertes and Hamlet, both men enter into a refined, gentlemanly discourse, an amends-making, that could not have been executed by a man bereft of reason. His understanding of the harm he has done and his obvious remorse comes through when he tells Laertes,

> Let my disclaiming from a purposed evil
> Free me so far in your most generous thoughts
> That I have shot my arrow o'er the house
> And hurt my brother. (5.2.244–47)

Considering all that Hamlet faces and endures, much of which he abides with disarming grace, it hardly seems likely he was mad. That he would have known any other outcome is also unlikely, given the treachery and duplicity surrounding him. He is an extraordinary person in extraordinary circumstances. To judge him by conventional standards is to reduce the complexity of his character and situation to a trivial stature.

Questions for Peer Review

This paper raises a central question about Hamlet's state of mind that has been answered in different ways by critics—with the differing answers steering critical interpretations as well as stage productions of the play into at times very different directions.

1. How and how effectively does the writer raise the central issue that is the focus of the paper? Where does the writer first sum up the answer that the paper as a whole is going to give to the question it raises? Where does the writer restate again the key point that serves as the thesis of this paper?

2. What are the key points in the writer's supporting arguments? What are the key facets of Hamlet's personality that the paper covers in building its case? (Which to you seem most important or convincing?) What are key examples the paper offers as evidence? How convincing are they?

3. Where and how does the writer deal with arguments or viewpoints that point toward a different answer to the central question raised in this paper? Does the paper do a good job of anticipating and defusing objections?

4. In many current discussions and performances of the play, Hamlet's relationship with his mother plays a central role. Do you agree that Queen Gertrude's grief is a "pretended grief"? What parallels does the writer see in the roles played by Gertrude, Polonius, and Rosenkrantz and Guildenstern?

5. How and how well does the conclusion restate the central thesis of the paper? What does the writer do to give the paper a strong send-off?

6. Does this paper change your own reading or interpretation of the play? How or why? Does the paper leave questions unanswered in your mind? What would you say in a peer response or e-mail to the author?

29 AMERICAN DRAMA
The Mirror of Reality

Courtesy Richard B. Ressman

*I am simply asking for a theater in which adults
who want to live can find plays that will heighten
their awareness of what living in our time
involves.*

ARTHUR MILLER

*In my plays I want to look at life—at the
commonplace of existence—as if we had just
turned a corner and run into it for the first time.*

CHRISTOPHER FRY

FOCUS ON MODERN AMERICAN DRAMA

The modern American theater has given theatergoers a wide range of choices: commercial and experimental, traditional and avant-garde, Broadway and off-Broadway and off-off-Broadway. One major strand in modern drama by American playwrights has been the tradition of realistic drama, which harks back to the problem plays of Henrik Ibsen. This tradition has produced such slice-of-life plays as Arthur Miller's *All My Sons* and *Death of a Salesman,* Tennessee Williams' *The Glass Menagerie* and *A Streetcar Named Desire,* and Lorraine Hansberry's *A Raisin in the Sun.*

Part of the definition of **realism** is the *ordinariness* of many of the characters. They are not people of heroic caliber. They are not outstanding either in dedication and courage or in grandiose plans for evil. They are likely to be the modern antihero—vacillating between bravado and cowardice, capable of pettiness and vindictiveness. Critics therefore question whether true tragedy is still possible in the modern world. Can the modern stage still present great characters worthy of our admiration? Much of the time, we may witness not the fall of the mighty but the slow slide of the lowly. We may, however, still feel pity and fear.

A modern play often scales down the single dominant character. The characters are often part of a web of human relationships. They define themselves through their interaction with others. A recurrent theme in much modern American drama is invisible walls: the environment that hems the characters in. They are caught in a web of social and family ties that may become a trap. They are snared in patterns of social interaction that defeat them. What they can do may be in large part determined by how and where they live. Even so, characters like Miller's salesman or Hansberry's Mama—the black matriarch who is a tower of strength for her family—loom large.

Realism in these plays means more than the surface realism of lives in tenement buildings or once-prosperous Southern mansions; of jobs as sales reps and assistant managers and truck drivers. The plays do not stay nailed down to the prosaic facts. Modern audiences expect **psychological realism**. We deal with the characters' *perception* of reality—their world made up of their personal memories, prejudices, and resentments. Furthermore, a character like Arthur Miller's Willy Loman in *Death of a Salesman* drifts easily from his perception of reality (such as it is) to his daydreams. He lives in a world made up of his grievances, obsessions, and ambitions. In the enormously successful plays of Tennessee Williams—*The Glass Menagerie, A Streetcar Named Desire, Cat on a Hot Tin Roof* among the best known—the suppressed desires and frustrations smouldering under the surface break through, derailing safe established patterns of living and thinking.

IN SEARCH OF THE AMERICAN DREAM

Both Arthur Miller's *Death of a Salesman* and Lorraine Hansberry's *A Raisin in the Sun* appeal to their audiences' belief in the American dream: People have the right to a decent place to live, to a fair reward for hard work, to a recognition of their worth as human beings. The two plays probe the same basic question: Has the American dream become for many an unkept promise? Has it always been a mirage?

Arthur Miller   *(born 1915)*

I understand Willy Loman's longing for immortality. . . . Willy's writing his name in a cake of ice on a hot day but he wishes he were writing in stone.

ARTHUR MILLER

Arthur Miller has been called "essentially a moralist" and "a moral force speaking for the conscience of America." He was born in New York City as the son of middle-class Jewish parents. His mother taught, and his father was a garment manufacturer. Miller started to write plays at the University of Michigan, and several of his plays became American classics as stage productions, movies, or television plays. He was married for a time to Marilyn Monroe, writing the screenplay for her movie *The Misfits* (1961) and later writing *After the Fall* (1964), a play about the breakup of their marriage. In the nineties, a new play by Arthur Miller, *The Ride down Mt. Morgan,* was a big hit on the London stage.

Miller's best-known plays—*All My Sons, Death of a Salesman, The Crucible*—are classics of the modern American stage. *Death of a Salesman* was first performed in 1949 with Elia Kazan as the director; it ran for 742 performances. In the fifties, like other writers and artists, Miller tussled with the House Un-American Activities Committee over earlier communist ties. Senator Joe McCarthy was using the press as a media circus, ferreting out alleged reds—making professors, university presidents, and politicians tremble. Out of this experience grew Miller's *The Crucible* (1953), the play in which he used the Salem witchcraft trials as a parable for the witchhunts, purges, and censorship binges of the twentieth century.

From its legendary first production with Lee J. Cobb, to its spectacular revivals with Dustin Hoffman in 1984 and Brian Dennehy in 1998, *Death of a Salesman* has been the classic probing of the American dream. Willy Loman became the archetypal disciple of the American gospel of success—of popularity, of easy money for those who know how to make the system work and are "well liked." For theatergoers around the world, Willy became the symbol of the "drummer"—the traveling sales rep, carrying his sample cases in search of the next sale, traveling on a shoeshine and a smile. Willy's credo was that those who command the easy smile, the glad hand, and the corny joke shall not want.

The sad and funny part of Willy Loman's story is that with one part of his mind he knows better. While he is trying hard to believe in his own cheerful clichés, he has lucid intervals. He knows deep down that stubborn reality does not conform to his optimistic bromides. The truth is that he is falling behind in the rat race. The facts—about his age, his dwindling sales, and his alienated family—are catching up with him. Willy Loman is not a great heroic figure. He is not a good husband or a model parent or a leader in community affairs. But does this mean that Arthur Miller wanted us to think of him as a fool or buffoon?

Death of a Salesman   1949

Certain Private Conversations in Two Acts and a Requiem

CHARACTERS

WILLY LOMAN
LINDA
BIFF
HAPPY
BERNARD
THE WOMAN
CHARLEY
UNCLE BEN
HOWARD WAGNER
JENNY
STANLEY
MISS FORSYTHE
LETTA

The action takes place in WILLY LOMAN'S *house and yard and in various places he visits the New York and Boston of today.*

Throughout the play, in the stage directions, left and right mean stage left and stage right.

Act One

(AN OVERTURE)

A melody is heard, played upon a flute. It is small and fine, telling of grass and trees and the horizon. The curtain rises.

Before us is the Salesman's house. We are aware of towering, angular shapes behind it, surrounding it on all sides. Only the blue light of the sky falls upon the house and forestage; the surrounding area shows an angry glow of orange. As more light appears, we see a solid vault of apartment houses around the small, fragile-seeming home. An air of the dream clings to the place, a dream rising out of reality. The kitchen at center seems actual enough, for there is a kitchen table with three chairs, and a refrigerator. But no other fixtures are seen. At the back of the kitchen there is a draped entrance, which leads to the living room. To the right of the kitchen, on a level raised two feet, is a bedroom furnished only with a brass bedstead and a straight chair. On a shelf over the bed a silver athletic trophy stands. A window opens onto the apartment house at the side.

Behind the kitchen, on a level raised six and a half feet, is the boys' bedroom, at present barely visible. Two beds are dimly seen, and at the back of the room a dormer window. (This bedroom is above the unseen living room.) At the left a stairway curves up to it from the kitchen.

The entire setting is wholly or, in some places, partially transparent. The roof-line of the house is one-dimensional; under and over it we see the apartment buildings. Before the house lies an apron, curving beyond the forestage into the orchestra. This forward area serves as the back yard as well as the locale of all Willy's imaginings and of his city scenes. Whenever the action is in the present the actors observe the imaginary wall-lines, entering the house only through its door at the left. But in the scenes of the past these boundaries are broken, and characters enter or leave a room by stepping "through" a wall onto the forestage.

From the right, WILLY LOMAN, *the Salesman, enters, carrying two large sample cases. The flute plays on. He hears but is not aware of it. He is past sixty years of age, dressed quietly. Even as he crosses the stage to the doorway of the house, his exhaustion is apparent. He unlocks the door, comes into the kitchen, and thankfully lets his burden down, feeling the soreness of his palms. A word-sigh escapes his lips—it might be "Oh, boy, oh, boy." He closes the door, then carries his cases out into the living room, through the draped kitchen doorway.*

LINDA, *his wife, has stirred in her bed at the right. She gets out and puts on a robe, listening. Most often jovial, she has developed an iron repression of her exceptions to* WILLY'S *behavior—she more than loves him, she admires him, as though his mercurial nature, his temper, his massive dreams and*

*little cruelties, served her only as sharp reminders of the turbulent longings
within him, longings which she shares but lacks the temperament to utter
and follow to their end.*

LINDA (*hearing* WILLY *outside the bedroom, calls with some trepidation*): Willy!
WILLY: It's all right. I came back.
LINDA: Why? What happened? (*slight pause*) Did something happen, Willy?
WILLY: No, nothing happened.
LINDA: You didn't smash the car, did you?
WILLY (*with casual irritation*): I said nothing happened. Didn't you hear me?
LINDA: Don't you feel well?
WILLY: I'm tired to the death. (*The flute has faded away. He sits on the bed
beside her, a little numb.*) I couldn't make it. I just couldn't make it, Linda.
LINDA (*very carefully, delicately*): Where were you all day? You look terrible.
WILLY: I got as far as a little above Yonkers. I stopped for a cup of coffee.
Maybe it was the coffee.
LINDA: What?
WILLY (*after a pause*): I suddenly couldn't drive any more. The car kept going
off onto the shoulder, y'know?
LINDA (*helpfully*): Oh. Maybe it was the steering again. I don't think Angelo
knows the Studebaker.
WILLY: No, it's me, it's me. Suddenly I realize I'm goin' sixty miles an hour
and I don't remember the last five minutes. I'm—I can't seem to—keep
my mind to it.
LINDA: Maybe it's your glasses. You never went for your new glasses.
WILLY: No, I see everything. I came back ten miles an hour. It took me nearly
four hours from Yonkers.
LINDA (*resigned*): Well, you'll just have to take a rest, Willy, you can't con-
tinue this way.
WILLY: I just got back from Florida.
LINDA: But you didn't rest your mind. Your mind is overactive, and the mind
is what counts, dear.
WILLY: I'll start out in the morning. Maybe I'll feel better in the morning. (*She
is taking off his shoes.*) These goddam arch supports are killing me.
LINDA: Take an aspirin. Should I get you an aspirin? It'll soothe you.
WILLY (*with wonder*): I was driving along, you understand? And I was fine.
I was even observing the scenery. You can imagine, me looking at
scenery, on the road every week of my life. But it's so beautiful up there,
Linda, the trees are so thick, and the sun is warm. I opened the wind-
shield and just let the warm air bathe over me. And then all of a sudden
I'm goin' off the road! I'm tellin' ya, I absolutely forgot I was driving. If
I'd've gone the other way over the white line I might've killed somebody.
So I went on again—and five minutes later I'm dreamin' again, and I
nearly—(*He presses two fingers against his eyes.*) I have such thoughts,
I have such strange thoughts.
LINDA: Willy, dear. Talk to them again. There's no reason why you can't
work in New York.
WILLY: They don't need me in New York. I'm the New England man. I'm vital
in New England.

LINDA: But you're sixty years old. They can't expect you to keep traveling every week.

WILLY: I'll have to send a wire to Portland. I'm supposed to see Brown and Morrison tomorrow morning at ten o'clock to show the line. Goddammit, I could sell them! (*He starts putting on his jacket.*)

LINDA (*taking the jacket from him*): Why don't you go down to the place tomorrow and tell Howard you've simply got to work in New York? You're too accommodating, dear.

WILLY: If old man Wagner was alive I'd a been in charge of New York now! That man was a prince, he was a masterful man. But that boy of his, that Howard, he don't appreciate. When I went north the first time, the Wagner Company didn't know where New England was!

LINDA: Why don't you tell those things to Howard, dear?

WILLY (*encouraged*): I will, I definitely will. Is there any cheese?

LINDA: I'll make you a sandwich.

WILLY: No, go to sleep. I'll take some milk. I'll be up right away. The boys in?

LINDA: They're sleeping. Happy took Biff on a date tonight.

WILLY (*interested*): That so?

LINDA: It was so nice to see them shaving together, one behind the other, in the bathroom. And going out together. You notice? The whole house smells of shaving lotion.

WILLY: Figure it out. Work a lifetime to pay off a house. You finally own it, and there's nobody to live in it.

LINDA: Well, dear, life is a casting off. It's always that way.

WILLY: No, no, some people—some people accomplish something. Did Biff say anything after I went this morning?

LINDA: You shouldn't have criticized him, Willy, especially after he just got off the train. You mustn't lose your temper with him.

WILLY: When the hell did I lose my temper? I simply asked him if he was making any money. Is that a criticism?

LINDA: But, dear, how could he make any money?

WILLY (*worried and angered*): There's such an undercurrent in him. He became a moody man. Did he apologize when I left this morning?

LINDA: He was crestfallen, Willy. You know how he admires you. I think if he finds himself, then you'll both be happier and not fight any more.

WILLY: How can he find himself on a farm? Is that a life? A farmhand? In the beginning, when he was young, I thought, well, a young man, it's good for him to tramp around, take a lot of different jobs. But it's more than ten years now and he has yet to make thirty-five dollars a week!

LINDA: He's finding himself, Willy.

WILLY: Not finding yourself at the age of thirty-four is a disgrace!

LINDA: Shh!

WILLY: The trouble is he's lazy, goddammit!

LINDA: Willy, please!

WILLY: Biff is a lazy bum!

LINDA: They're sleeping. Get something to eat. Go on down.

WILLY: Why did he come home? I would like to know what brought him home.

LINDA: I don't know. I think he's still lost, Willy. I think he's very lost.

WILLY: Biff Loman is lost. In the greatest country in the world a young man with such—personal attractiveness, gets lost. And such a hard worker. There's one thing about Biff—he's not lazy.

LINDA: Never.

WILLY (*with pity and resolve*): I'll see him in the morning; I'll have a nice talk with him. I'll get him a job selling. He could be big in no time. My God! Remember how they used to follow him around in high school? When he smiled at one of them their faces lit up. When he walked down the street . . . (*He loses himself in reminiscences.*)

LINDA (*trying to bring him out of it*): Willy, dear, I got a new kind of American-type cheese today. It's whipped.

WILLY: Why do you get American when I like Swiss?

LINDA: I just thought you'd like a change—

WILLY: I don't want a change! I want Swiss cheese. Why am I always being contradicted?

LINDA (*with a covering laugh*): I thought it would be a surprise.

WILLY: Why don't you open a window in here, for God's sake?

LINDA (*with infinite patience*): They're all open, dear.

WILLY: The way they boxed us in here. Bricks and windows, windows and bricks.

LINDA: We should've bought the land next door.

WILLY: The street is lined with cars. There's not a breath of fresh air in the neighborhood. The grass don't grow any more, you can't raise a carrot in the back yard. They should've had a law against apartment houses. Remember those two beautiful elm trees out there? When I and Biff hung the swing between them?

LINDA: Yeah, like being a million miles from the city.

WILLY: They should've arrested the builder for cutting those down. They massacred the neighborhood. *Lost:* More and more I think of those days, Linda. This time of year it was lilac and wisteria. And then the peonies would come out, and the daffodils. What fragrance in this room!

LINDA: Well, after all, people had to move somewhere.

WILLY: No, there's more people now.

LINDA: I don't think there's more people. I think—

WILLY: There's more people! That's what's ruining this country! Population is getting out of control. The competition is maddening! Smell the stink from that apartment house! And another one on the other side . . . How can they whip cheese?

On WILLY'S *last line,* BIFF *and* HAPPY *raise themselves up in their beds, listening.*

LINDA: Go down, try it. And be quiet.

WILLY (*turning to* LINDA, *guiltily*): You're not worried about me, are you, sweetheart?

BIFF: What's the matter?

HAPPY: Listen!

LINDA: You've got too much on the ball to worry about.

WILLY: You're my foundation and my support, Linda.

LINDA: Just try to relax, dear. You make mountains out of molehills.

WILLY: I won't fight with him any more. If he wants to go back to Texas, let him go.

LINDA: He'll find his way.

WILLY: Sure. Certain men just don't get started till later in life. Like Thomas Edison, I think. Or B. F. Goodrich. One of them was deaf. (*He starts for the bedroom doorway.*) I'll put my money on Biff.

LINDA: And Willy—if it's warm Sunday we'll drive in the country. And we'll open the windshield, and take lunch.

WILLY: No, the windshields don't open on the new cars.

LINDA: But you opened it today.

WILLY: Me? I didn't. (*He stops.*) Now isn't that peculiar! Isn't that a remarkable—(*He breaks off in amazement and fright as the flute is heard distantly.*)

LINDA: What, darling?

WILLY: That is the most remarkable thing.

LINDA: What, dear?

WILLY: I was thinking of the Chevy. (*slight pause*) Nineteen twenty-eight . . . when I had that red Chevy—(*breaks off*) That funny? I coulda sworn I was driving that Chevy today.

LINDA: Well, that's nothing. Something must've reminded you.

WILLY: Remarkable. Ts. Remember those days? The way Biff used to simonize that car? The dealer refused to believe there was eighty thousand miles on it. (*He shakes his head.*) Heh! (*to* LINDA) Close your eyes, I'll be right up. (*He walks out of the bedroom.*)

HAPPY (*to* BIFF): Jesus, maybe he smashed up the car again!

LINDA (*calling after* WILLY): Be careful on the stairs, dear! The cheese is on the middle shelf! (*She turns, goes over to the bed, takes his jacket, and goes out of the bedroom.*)

Light has risen on the boys' room. Unseen, WILLY *is heard talking to himself, "Eighty thousand miles," and a little laugh.* BIFF *gets out of bed, comes downstage a bit, and stands attentively.* BIFF *is two years older than his brother* HAPPY, *well built, but in these days bears a worn air and seems less self-assured. He has succeeded less, and his dreams are stronger and less acceptable than* HAPPY'S. HAPPY *is tall, powerfully made. Sexuality is like a visible color on him, or a scent that many women have discovered. He, like his brother, is lost, but in a different way, for he has never allowed himself to turn his face toward defeat and is thus more confused and hard-skinned, although seemingly more content.*

HAPPY (*getting out of bed*): He's going to get his license taken away if he keeps that up. I'm getting nervous about him, y'know, Biff?

BIFF: His eyes are going.

HAPPY: No, I've driven with him. He sees all right. He just doesn't keep his mind on it. I drove into the city with him last week. He stops at a green light and then it turns red and he goes. (*He laughs.*)

BIFF: Maybe he's color-blind.

HAPPY: Pop? Why, he's got the finest eye for color in the business. You know that.

BIFF (*sitting down on his bed*): I'm going to sleep.

HAPPY: You're not still sour on Dad, are you, Biff?

BIFF: He's all right, I guess.

WILLY (*underneath them, in the living room*): Yes, sir, eighty thousand miles—eighty-two thousand!

BIFF: You smoking?

HAPPY (*holding out a pack of cigarettes*): Want one?

BIFF (*taking a cigarette*): I can never sleep when I smell it.

WILLY: What a simonizing job, heh!

HAPPY (*with deep sentiment*): Funny, Biff, y'know? Us sleeping in here again? The old beds. (*He pats his bed affectionately.*) All the talk that went across those two beds, huh? Our whole lives.

BIFF: Yeah. Lotta dreams and plans.

HAPPY (*with a deep and masculine laugh*): About five hundred women would like to know what was said in this room.

They share a soft laugh.

BIFF: Remember that big Betsy something—what the hell was her name—over on Bushwick Avenue?

HAPPY (*combing his hair*): With the collie dog!

BIFF: That's the one. I got you in there, remember?

HAPPY: Yeah, that was my first time—I think. Boy, there was a pig! (*They laugh, almost crudely.*) You taught me everything I know about women. Don't forget that.

BIFF: I bet you forgot how bashful you used to be. Especially with girls.

HAPPY: Oh, I still am, Biff.

BIFF: Oh, go on.

HAPPY: I just control it, that's all. I think I got less bashful and you got more so. What happened, Biff? Where's the old humor, the old confidence? (*He shakes* BIFF'S *knee.* BIFF *gets up and moves restlessly about the room.*) What's the matter?

BIFF: Why does Dad mock me all the time?

HAPPY: He's not mocking you, he—

BIFF: Everything I say there's a twist of mockery on his face. I can't get near him.

HAPPY: He just wants you to make good, that's all. I wanted to talk to you about Dad for a long time, Biff. Something's—happening to him. He—talks to himself.

BIFF: I noticed that this morning. But he always mumbled.

HAPPY: But not so noticeable. It got so embarrassing I sent him to Florida. And you know something? Most of the time he's talking to you.

BIFF: What's he say about me?

HAPPY: I can't make it out.

BIFF: What's he say about me?

HAPPY: I think the fact that you're not settled, that you're still kind of up in the air . . .

BIFF: There's one or two other things depressing him, Happy.

HAPPY: What do you mean?

BIFF: Never mind. Just don't lay it all to me.

HAPPY: But I think if you just got started—I mean—is there any future for you out there?

BIFF: I tell ya, Hap, I don't know what the future is. I don't know—what I'm supposed to want.

HAPPY: What do you mean?

BIFF: Well, I spent six or seven years after high school trying to work myself up. Shipping clerk, salesman, business of one kind or another. And it's a measly manner of existence. To get on that subway on the hot mornings in summer. To devote your whole life to keeping stock, or making phone calls, or selling or buying. To suffer fifty weeks of the year for the sake of a two-week vacation, when all you really desire is to be outdoors, with your shirt off. And always to have to get ahead of the next fella. And still—that's how you build a future.

HAPPY: Well, you really enjoy it on a farm? Are you content out there?

BIFF (*with rising agitation*): Hap, I've had twenty or thirty different kinds of jobs since I left home before the war, and it always turns out the same. I just realized it lately. In Nebraska when I herded cattle, and the Dakotas, and Arizona, and now in Texas. It's why I came home now, I guess, because I realized it. This farm I work on, it's spring there now, see? And they've got about fifteen new colts. There's nothing more inspiring or— beautiful than the sight of a mare and a new colt. And it's cool there now, see? Texas is cool now, and it's spring. And whenever spring comes to where I am, I suddenly get the feeling, my God, I'm not gettin' anywhere! What the hell am I doing, playing around with horses, twenty-eight dollars a week! I'm thirty-four years old, I oughta be makin' my future. That's when I come running home. And now, I get here, and I don't know what to do with myself. (*after a pause*) I've always made a point of not wasting my life, and every time I come back here I know that all I've done is to waste my life.

HAPPY: You're a poet, you know that, Biff? You're a—you're an idealist!

BIFF: No, I'm mixed up very bad. Maybe I oughta get married. Maybe I oughta get stuck into something. Maybe that's my trouble. I'm like a boy. I'm not married, I'm not in business, I just—I'm like a boy. Are you content, Hap? You're a success, aren't you? Are you content?

HAPPY: Hell, no!

BIFF: Why? You're making money, aren't you?

HAPPY (*moving about with energy, expressiveness*): All I can do now is wait for the merchandise manager to die. And suppose I get to be merchandise manager? He's a good friend of mine, and he just built a terrific estate on Long Island. And he lived there about two months and sold it, and now he's building another one. He can't enjoy it once it's finished. And I know that's just what I would do. I don't know what the hell I'm workin' for. Sometimes I sit in my apartment—all alone. And I think of the rent I'm paying. And it's crazy. But then, it's what I always wanted. My own apartment, a car, and plenty of women. And still, goddammit, I'm lonely.

BIFF (*with enthusiasm*): Listen, why don't you come out West with me?

HAPPY: You and I, heh?

BIFF: Sure, maybe we could buy a ranch. Raise cattle, use our muscles. Men built like we are should be working out in the open.

HAPPY (*avidly*): The Loman Brothers, heh?

BIFF (*with vast affection*): Sure, we'd be known all over the counties!

HAPPY (*enthralled*): That's what I dream about, Biff. Sometimes I want to just rip my clothes off in the middle of the store and outbox that goddam merchandise manager. I mean I can outbox, outrun, and outlift anybody in that store, and I have to take orders from those common, petty sons-of-bitches till I can't stand it any more.

BIFF: I'm tellin' you, kid, if you were with me I'd be happy out there.

HAPPY (*enthused*): See, Biff, everybody around me is so false that I'm constantly lowering my ideals . . .

BIFF: Baby, together we'd stand up for one another, we'd have someone to trust.

HAPPY: If I were around you—

BIFF: Hap, the trouble is we weren't brought up to grub for money. I don't know how to do it.

HAPPY: Neither can I!

BIFF: Then let's go!

HAPPY: The only thing is—what can you make out there?

BIFF: But look at your friend. Builds an estate and then hasn't the peace of mind to live in it.

HAPPY: Yeah, but when he walks into the store the waves part in front of him. That's fifty-two thousand dollars a year coming through the revolving door, and I got more in my pinky finger than he's got in his head.

BIFF: Yeah, but you just said—

HAPPY: I gotta show some of those pompous, self-important executives over there that Hap Loman can make the grade. I want to walk into the store the way he walks in. Then I'll go with you, Biff. We'll be together yet, I swear. But take those two we had tonight. Now weren't they gorgeous creatures?

BIFF: Yeah, yeah, most gorgeous I've had in years.

HAPPY: I get that any time I want, Biff. Whenever I feel disgusted. The only trouble is, it gets like bowling or something. I just keep knockin' them over and it doesn't mean anything. You still run around a lot?

BIFF: Naa. I'd like to find a girl—steady, somebody with substance.

HAPPY: That's what I long for.

BIFF: Go on! You'd never come home.

HAPPY: I would! Somebody with character, with resistance! Like Mom, y' know? You're gonna call me a bastard when I tell you this. That girl Charlotte I was with tonight is engaged to be married in five weeks. (*He tries on his new hat.*)

BIFF: No kiddin'!

HAPPY: Sure, the guy's in line for the vice-presidency of the store. I don't know what gets into me, maybe I just have an overdeveloped sense of competition or something, but I went and ruined her, and furthermore I can't get rid of her. And he's the third executive I've done that to. Isn't that a crummy characteristic? And to top it all, I go to their weddings! (*indignantly, but laughing*) Like I'm not supposed to take bribes. Manufacturers offer me a hundred-dollar bill now and then to throw an order their way. You know how honest I am, but it's like this girl, see. I hate myself for it. Because I don't want the girl, and, still, I take it and—I love it!

BIFF: Let's go to sleep.

HAPPY: I guess we didn't settle anything, heh?

BIFF: I just got one idea that I think I'm going to try.

HAPPY: What's that?

BIFF: Remember Bill Oliver?

HAPPY: Sure, Oliver is very big now. You want to work for him again?

BIFF: No, but when I quit he said something to me. He put his arm on my shoulder, and he said, "Biff, if you ever need anything, come to me."

HAPPY: I remember that. That sounds good.

BIFF: I think I'll go to see him. If I could get ten thousand or even seven or eight thousand dollars I could buy a beautiful ranch.

HAPPY: I bet he'd back you. 'Cause he thought highly of you, Biff. I mean, they all do. You're well liked, Biff. That's why I say to come back here, and we both have the apartment. And I'm tellin' you, Biff, any babe you want . . .

BIFF: No, with a ranch I could do the work I like and still be something. I just wonder though. I wonder if Oliver still thinks I stole that carton of basketballs.

HAPPY: Oh, he probably forgot that long ago. It's almost ten years. You're too sensitive. Anyway, he didn't really fire you.

BIFF: Well, I think he was going to. I think that's why I quit. I was never sure whether he knew or not. I know he thought the world of me, though. I was the only one he'd let lock up the place.

WILLY (below): You gonna wash the engine, Biff?

HAPPY: Shh!

BIFF *looks at* HAPPY, *who is gazing down, listening.* WILLY *is mumbling in the parlor.*

HAPPY: You hear that?

They listen. WILLY *laughs warmly.*

BIFF (*growing angry*): Doesn't he know Mom can hear that?

WILLY: Don't get your sweater dirty, Biff!

A look of pain crosses BIFF'S *face.*

HAPPY: Isn't that terrible? Don't leave again, will you? You'll find a job here. You gotta stick around. I don't know what to do about him, it's getting embarrassing.

WILLY: What a simonizing job!

BIFF: Mom's hearing that!

WILLY: No kiddin', Biff, you got a date? Wonderful!

HAPPY: Go on to sleep. But talk to him in the morning, will you?

BIFF (*reluctantly getting into bed*): With her in the house. Brother!

HAPPY (*getting into bed*): I wish you'd have a good talk with him.

The light on their room begins to fade.

BIFF (*to himself in bed*): That selfish, stupid . . .

HAPPY: Sh . . . Sleep, Biff.

Their light is out. Well before they have finished speaking, WILLY'S *form is dimly seen below in the darkened kitchen. He opens the refrigerator, searches in there, and takes out a bottle of milk. The apartment houses are fading out, and the entire house and surroundings become covered with leaves. Music insinuates itself as the leaves appear.*

WILLY: Just wanna be careful with those girls, Biff, that's all. Don't make any promises. No promises of any kind. Because a girl, y'know, they always believe what you tell 'em, and you're very young, Biff, you're too young to be talking seriously to girls.

Light rises on the kitchen. WILLY, *talking, shuts the refrigerator door and comes downstage to the kitchen table. He pours milk into a glass. He is totally immersed in himself, smiling faintly.*

WILLY: Too young entirely, Biff. You want to watch your schooling first. Then when you're all set, there'll be plenty of girls for a boy like you. (*He smiles broadly at a kitchen chair.*) That so? The girls pay for you? (*He laughs.*) Boy, you must really be makin' a hit.

WILLY *is gradually addressing—physically—a point offstage, speaking through the wall of the kitchen, and his voice has been rising in volume to that of a normal conversation.*

WILLY: I been wondering why you polish the car so careful. Ha! Don't leave the hubcaps, boys. Get the chamois to the hubcaps. Happy, use newspaper on the windows, it's the easiest thing. Show him how to do it, Biff! You see, Happy? Pad it up, use it like a pad. That's it, that's it, good work. You're doin' all right, Hap. (*He pauses, then nods in approbation for a few seconds, then looks upward.*) Biff, first thing we gotta do when we get time is clip that big branch over the house. Afraid it's gonna fall in a storm and hit the roof. Tell you what. We get a rope and sling her around, and then we climb up there with a couple of saws and take her down. Soon as you finish the car, boys, I wanna see ya. I got a surprise for you, boys.

BIFF (*offstage*): Whatta ya got, Dad?

WILLY: No, you finish first. Never leave a job till you're finished—remember that. (*looking toward the "big trees"*) Biff, up in Albany I saw a beautiful hammock. I think I'll buy it next trip, and we'll hang it right between those two elms. Wouldn't that be something? Just swingin' there under those branches. Boy, that would be . . .

YOUNG BIFF *and* YOUNG HAPPY *appear from the direction* WILLY *was addressing.* HAPPY *carries rags and a pail of water.* BIFF, *wearing a sweater with a block "S," carries a football.*

BIFF (*pointing in the direction of the car offstage*): How's that, Pop, professional?

WILLY: Terrific. Terrific job, boys. Good work, Biff.

HAPPY: Where's the surprise, Pop?

WILLY: In the back seat of the car.

HAPPY: Boy! (*He runs off.*)

BIFF: What is it, Dad? Tell me, what'd you buy?

WILLY (*laughing, cuffs him*): Never mind, something I want you to have.

BIFF (*turns and starts off*): What is it, Hap?

HAPPY (*offstage*): It's a punching bag!

BIFF: Oh, Pop!

WILLY: It's got Gene Tunney's signature on it!

HAPPY *runs onstage with a punching bag.*

BIFF: Gee, how'd you know we wanted a punching bag?

WILLY: Well, it's the finest thing for the timing.

HAPPY (*lying down on his back and pedaling with his feet*): I'm losing weight, you notice, Pop?

WILLY (*to* HAPPY): Jumping rope is good too.

BIFF: Did you see the new football I got?

WILLY (*examining the ball*): Where'd you get a new ball?

BIFF: The coach told me to practice my passing.

WILLY: That so? And he gave you the ball, heh?

BIFF: Well, I borrowed it from the locker room. (*He laughs confidentially.*)

WILLY (*laughing with him at the theft*): I want you to return that.

HAPPY: I told you he wouldn't like it!

BIFF (*angrily*): Well, I'm bringing it back!

WILLY (*stopping the incipient argument, to* HAPPY): Sure, he's gotta practice with a regulation ball, doesn't he? (*to* BIFF) Coach'll probably congratulate you on your initiative!

BIFF: Oh, he keeps congratulating my initiative all the time, Pop.

WILLY: That's because he likes you. If somebody else took that ball there'd be an uproar. So what's the report, boys, what's the report?

BIFF: Where'd you go this time, Dad? Gee we were lonesome for you.

WILLY (*pleased, puts an arm around each boy and they come down to the apron*): Lonesome, heh?

BIFF: Missed you every minute.

WILLY: Don't say? Tell you a secret, boys. Don't breathe it to a soul. Someday I'll have my own business, and I'll never have to leave home any more.

WILLY: Hey, looka Bernard. What're you lookin' so anemic about, Bernard?

BERNARD: He's gotta study, Uncle Willy. He's got Regents next week.

HAPPY (*tauntingly, spinning* BERNARD *around*): Let's box, Bernard!

BERNARD: Biff! (*He gets away from* HAPPY.) Listen, Biff, I heard Mr. Birnbaum say that if you don't start studyin' math he's gonna flunk you, and you won't graduate. I heard him!

WILLY: You better study with him, Biff. Go ahead now.

BERNARD: I heard him!

BIFF: Oh, Pop, you didn't see my sneakers! (*He holds up a foot for* WILLY *to look at.*)

WILLY: Hey, that's a beautiful job of printing!

BERNARD (*wiping his glasses*): Just because he printed University of Virginia on his sneakers doesn't mean they've got to graduate him, Uncle Willy!

WILLY (*angrily*): What're you talking about? With scholarships to three universities they're gonna flunk him?

BERNARD: But I heard Mr. Birnbaum say—

WILLY: Don't be a pest, Bernard! (*to his boys*) What an anemic!

BERNARD: Okay, I'm waiting for you in my house, Biff.

BERNARD *goes off. The Lomans laugh.*

WILLY: Bernard is not well liked, is he?

BIFF: He's liked, but he's not well liked.

HAPPY: That's right, Pop.

WILLY: That's just what I mean. Bernard can get the best marks in school, y'understand, but when he gets out in the business world, y'understand, you are going to be five times ahead of him. That's why I thank Almighty God you're both built like Adonises. Because the man who makes an appearance in the business world, the man who creates personal interest, is the man who gets ahead. Be liked and you will never want. You take me, for instance. I never have to wait in line to see a buyer. "Willy Loman is here!" That's all they have to know, and I go right through.

BIFF: Did you knock them dead, Pop?

WILLY: Knocked 'em cold in Providence, slaughtered 'em in Boston.

HAPPY (*on his back, pedaling again*): I'm losing weight, you notice, Pop?

LINDA *enters, as of old, a ribbon in her hair, carrying a basket of washing.*

LINDA (*with youthful energy*): Hello, dear!

WILLY: Sweetheart!

LINDA: How'd the Chevy run?

WILLY: Chevrolet, Linda, is the greatest car ever built. (*to the boys*) Since when do you let your mother carry wash up the stairs?

BIFF: Grab hold there, boy!

HAPPY: Where to, Mom?

LINDA: Hang them up on the line. And you better go down to your friends, Biff. The cellar is full of boys. They don't know what to do with themselves.

BIFF: Ah, when Pop comes home they can wait!

WILLY (*laughing appreciatively*): You better go down and tell them what to do, Biff.

BIFF: I think I'll have them sweep out the furnace room.

WILLY: Good work, Biff.

BIFF (*He goes through wall-line of kitchen to doorway at back and calls down.*): Fellas! Everybody sweep out the furnace room! I'll be right down!

VOICES: All right! Okay, Biff.

BIFF: George and Sam and Frank, come out back! We're hangin' up the wash! Come on, Hap, on the double! (*He and* HAPPY *carry out the basket.*)

LINDA: The way they obey him!

WILLY: Well, that's training, the training. I'm tellin' you, I was sellin' thousands and thousands, but I had to come home.

LINDA: Oh, the whole block'll be at that game. Did you sell anything?

WILLY: I did five hundred gross in Providence and seven hundred gross in Boston.

LINDA: No! Wait a minute, I've got a pencil. (*She pulls pencil and paper out of her apron pocket.*) That makes your commission . . . Two hundred— my God! Two hundred and twelve dollars!

WILLY: Well, I didn't figure it yet, but . . .

LINDA: How much did you do?

WILLY: Well, I—I did—about a hundred and eighty gross in Providence. Well, no—it came to—roughly two hundred gross on the whole trip.

LINDA (*without hesitation*): Two hundred gross. That's . . . (*She figures.*)

WILLY: The trouble was that three of the stores were half closed for inventory in Boston. Otherwise I woulda broke records.

LINDA: Well, it makes seventy dollars and some pennies. That's very good.

WILLY: What do we owe?

LINDA: Well, on the first there's sixteen dollars on the refrigerator—

WILLY: Why sixteen?

LINDA: Well, the fan belt broke, so it was a dollar eighty.

WILLY: But it's brand new.

LINDA: Well, the man said that's the way it is. Till they work themselves in, y'know.

They move through the wall-line into the kitchen.

WILLY: I hope we didn't get stuck on that machine.

LINDA: They got the biggest ads of any of them!

WILLY: I know, it's a fine machine. What else?

LINDA: Well, there's nine-sixty for the washing machine. And for the vacuum cleaner there's three and a half due on the fifteenth. Then the roof, you got twenty-one dollars remaining.

WILLY: It don't leak, does it?

LINDA: No, they did a wonderful job. Then you owe Frank for the carburetor.

WILLY: I'm not going to pay that man! That goddam Chevrolet, they ought to prohibit the manufacture of that car!

LINDA: Well, you owe him three and a half. And odds and ends, comes to around a hundred and twenty dollars by the fifteenth.

WILLY: A hundred and twenty dollars! My God, if business don't pick up I don't know what I'm gonna do!

LINDA: Well, next week you'll do better.

WILLY: Oh, I'll knock 'em dead next week. I'll go to Hartford. I'm very well liked in Hartford. You know, the trouble is, Linda, people don't seem to take to me.

They move onto the forestage.

LINDA: Oh, don't be foolish.

WILLY: I know it when I walk in. They seem to laugh at me.

LINDA: Why? Why would they laugh at you? Don't talk that way, Willy.

WILLY *moves to the edge of the stage.* LINDA *goes into the kitchen and starts to darn stockings.*

WILLY: I don't know the reason for it, but they just pass me by. I'm not noticed.

LINDA: But you're doing wonderful, dear. You're making seventy to a hundred dollars a week.

WILLY: But I gotta be at it ten, twelve hours a day. Other men—I don't know—they do it easier. I don't know why—I can't stop myself—I talk too much. A man oughta come in with a few words. One thing about Charley. He's a man of few words, and they respect him.

LINDA: You don't talk too much, you're just lively.

WILLY (*smiling*): Well, I figure, what the hell, life is short, a couple of jokes. (*to himself*) I joke too much! (*The smile goes.*)

LINDA: Why? You're—

WILLY: I'm fat. I'm very—foolish to look at, Linda. I didn't tell you, but Christmas time I happened to be calling on F. H. Stewarts, and a salesman I know, as I was going in to see the buyer I heard him say something about—walrus. And I—I cracked him right across the face. I won't take that. I simply will not take that. But they do laugh at me. I know that.

LINDA: Darling . . .

WILLY: I gotta overcome it. I know I gotta overcome it. I'm not dressing to advantage, maybe.

LINDA: Willy, darling, you're the handsomest man in the world—

WILLY: Oh, no, Linda.

LINDA: To me you are. (*slight pause*) The handsomest.

From the darkness is heard the laughter of a woman. WILLY *doesn't turn to it, but it continues through* LINDA'S *lines.*

LINDA: And the boys, Willy. Few men are idolized by their children the way you are.

Music is heard as behind a scrim, to the left of the house, THE WOMAN, *dimly seen, is dressing.*

WILLY (*with great feeling*): You're the best there is, Linda, you're a pal, you know that? On the road—on the road I want to grab you sometimes and just kiss the life outa you.

The laughter is loud now, and he moves into a brightening area at the left, where THE WOMAN *has come from behind the scrim and is standing, putting on her hat, looking into a "mirror" and laughing.*

WILLY: 'Cause I get so lonely—especially when business is bad and there's nobody to talk to. I get the feeling that I'll never sell anything again, that I won't make a living for you, or a business, a business for the boys. (*He talks through* THE WOMAN'S *subsiding laughter;* THE WOMAN *primps at the "mirror."*) There's so much I want to make for—

THE WOMAN: Me? You didn't make me, Willy. I picked you.

WILLY (*pleased*): You picked me?

THE WOMAN (*who is quite proper-looking,* WILLY'S *age*): I did. I've been sitting at that desk watching all the salesmen go by, day in, day out. But you've got such a sense of humor, and we do have such a good time together, don't we?

WILLY: Sure, sure. (*He takes her in his arms.*) Why do you have to go now?

THE WOMAN: It's two o'clock . . .

WILLY: No, come on in! (*He pulls her.*)

THE WOMAN: . . . my sisters'll be scandalized. When'll you be back?

WILLY: Oh, two weeks about. Will you come up again?

THE WOMAN: Sure thing. You do make me laugh. It's good for me. (*She squeezes his arm, kisses him.*) And I think you're a wonderful man.

WILLY: You picked me, heh?

THE WOMAN: Sure. Because you're so sweet. And such a kidder.

WILLY: Well, I'll see you next time I'm in Boston.

THE WOMAN: I'll put you right through to the buyers.

WILLY (*slapping her bottom*): Right. Well, bottoms up!

THE WOMAN (*She slaps him gently and laughs.*): You just kill me, Willy. (*He suddenly grabs her and kisses her roughly.*) You kill me. And thanks for the stockings. I love a lot of stockings. Well, good night.

WILLY: Good night. And keep your pores open!

THE WOMAN: Oh, Willy!

> THE WOMAN *bursts out laughing, and* LINDA'S *laughter blends in.* THE WOMAN *disappears into the dark. Now the area at the kitchen table brightens.* LINDA *is sitting where she was at the kitchen table, but now is mending a pair of her silk stockings.*

LINDA: You are, Willy. The handsomest man. You've got no reason to feel that—

WILLY (*coming out of* THE WOMAN'*s dimming area and going over to* LINDA): I'll make it all up to you, Linda, I'll—

LINDA: There's nothing to make up, dear. You're doing fine, better than—

WILLY (*noticing her mending*): What's that?

LINDA: Just mending my stockings. They're so expensive—

WILLY (*angrily, taking them from her*): I won't have you mending stockings in this house! Now throw them out!

> LINDA *puts the stockings in her pocket.*

BERNARD (*entering on the run*): Where is he? If he doesn't study!

WILLY (*moving to the forestage, with great agitation*): You'll give him the answers!

BERNARD: I do, but I can't on a Regents! That's a state exam! They're liable to arrest me!

WILLY: Where is he? I'll whip him, I'll whip him!

LINDA: And he'd better give back that football, Willy, it's not nice.

WILLY: Biff! Where is he? Why is he taking everything?

LINDA: He's too rough with the girls, Willy. All the mothers are afraid of him!

WILLY: I'll whip him!

BERNARD: He's driving the car without a license!

> THE WOMAN'S *laugh is heard.*

WILLY: Shut up!

LINDA: All the mothers—

WILLY: Shut up!

BERNARD (*backing quietly away and out*): Mr. Birnbaum says he's stuck up.

WILLY: Get outa here!

BERNARD: If he doesn't buckle down he'll flunk math! (*He goes off.*)

LINDA: He's right, Willy, you've gotta—

WILLY (*exploding at her*): There's nothing the matter with him! You want him to be a worm like Bernard? He's got spirit, personality . . .

As he speaks, LINDA, *almost in tears, exits into the living room.* WILLY *is alone in the kitchen, wilting and staring. The leaves are gone. It is night again, and the apartment houses look down from behind.*

WILLY: Loaded with it. Loaded! What is he stealing? He's giving it back, isn't he? Why is he stealing? What did I tell him? I never in my life told him anything but decent things.

HAPPY *in pajamas has come down the stairs;* WILLY *suddenly becomes aware of* HAPPY'S *presence.*

HAPPY: Let's go now, come on.

WILLY (*sitting down at the kitchen table*): Huh! Why did she have to wax the floors herself? Everytime she waxes the floors she keels over. She knows that!

HAPPY: Shh! Take it easy. What brought you back tonight?

WILLY: I got an awful scare. Nearly hit a kid in Yonkers. God! Why didn't I go to Alaska with my brother Ben that time! Ben! That man was a genius, that man was success incarnate! What a mistake! He begged me to go.

HAPPY: Well, there's no use in—

WILLY: You guys! There was a man started with the clothes on his back and ended up with diamond mines!

HAPPY: Boy, someday I'd like to know how he did it.

WILLY: What's the mystery? The man knew what he wanted and went out and got it! Walked into a jungle, and comes out, the age of twenty-one, and he's rich! The world is an oyster, but you don't crack it open on a mattress!

HAPPY: Pop, I told you I'm gonna retire you for life.

WILLY: You'll retire me for life on seventy goddam dollars a week? And your women and your car and your apartment, and you'll retire me for life! Christ's sake, I couldn't get past Yonkers today! Where are you guys, where are you? The woods are burning! I can't drive a car!

CHARLEY *has appeared in the doorway. He is a large man, slow of speech, laconic, immovable. In all he says, despite what he says, there is pity, and, now, trepidation. He has a robe over pajamas, slippers on his feet. He enters the kitchen.*

CHARLEY: Everything all right?

HAPPY: Yeah, Charley, everything's . . .

WILLY: What's the matter?

CHARLEY: I heard some noise. I thought something happened. Can't we do something about the walls? You sneeze in here, and in my house hats blow off.

HAPPY: Let's go to bed, Dad. Come on.

CHARLEY *signals to* HAPPY *to go.*

WILLY: You go ahead, I'm not tired at the moment.

HAPPY (*to* WILLY): Take it easy, huh? (*He exits.*)

WILLY: What're you doin' up?

CHARLEY (*sitting down at the kitchen table opposite* WILLY): Couldn't sleep good. I had a heartburn.

WILLY: Well, you don't know how to eat.

CHARLEY: I eat with my mouth.

WILLY: No, you're ignorant. You gotta know about vitamins and things like that.

CHARLEY: Come on, let's shoot. Tire you out a little.

WILLY (*hesitantly*): All right. You got cards?

CHARLEY (*taking a deck from his pocket*): Yeah, I got them. Some place. What is it with those vitamins?

WILLY (*dealing*): They build up your bones. Chemistry.

CHARLEY: Yeah, but there's no bones in a heartburn.

WILLY: What are you talkin' about? Do you know the first thing about it?

CHARLEY: Don't get insulted.

WILLY: Don't talk about something you don't know anything about.

They are playing. Pause.

CHARLEY: What're you doin' home?

WILLY: A little trouble with the car.

CHARLEY: Oh. (*pause*) I'd like to take a trip to California.

WILLY: Don't say.

CHARLEY: You want a job?

WILLY: I got a job, I told you that. (*after a slight pause*) What the hell are you offering me a job for?

CHARLEY: Don't get insulted.

WILLY: Don't insult me.

CHARLEY: I don't see no sense in it. You don't have to go on this way.

WILLY: I got a good job. (*slight pause*) What do you keep comin' in here for?

CHARLEY: You want me to go?

WILLY (*after a pause, withering*): I can't understand it. He's going back to Texas again. What the hell is that?

CHARLEY: Let him go.

WILLY: I got nothin' to give him, Charley, I'm clean, I'm clean.

CHARLEY: He won't starve. None a them starve. Forget about him.

WILLY: Then what have I got to remember?

CHARLEY: You take it too hard. To hell with it. When a deposit bottle is broken you don't get your nickel back.

WILLY: That's easy enough for you to say.

CHARLEY: That ain't easy for me to say.

WILLY: Did you see the ceiling I put up in the living room?

CHARLEY: Yeah, that's a piece of work. To put up a ceiling is a mystery to me. How do you do it?

WILLY: What's the difference?

CHARLEY: Well, talk about it.

WILLY: You gonna put up a ceiling?

CHARLEY: How could I put up a ceiling?

WILLY: Then what the hell are you bothering me for?

CHARLEY: You're insulted again.

WILLY: A man who can't handle tools is not a man. You're disgusting.

CHARLEY: Don't call me disgusting, Willy.

> UNCLE BEN, *carrying a valise and an umbrella, enters the forestage from around the right corner of the house. He is a stolid man, in his sixties, with a mustache and an authoritative air. He is utterly certain of his destiny, and there is an aura of far places about him. He enters exactly as* WILLY *speaks.*

WILLY: I'm getting awfully tired, Ben.

> BEN'S *music is heard.* BEN *looks around at everything.*

CHARLEY: Good, keep playing; you'll sleep better. Did you call me Ben?

> BEN *looks at his watch.*

WILLY: That's funny. For a second there you reminded me of my brother Ben.

BEN: I only have a few minutes. (*He strolls, inspecting the place.* WILLY *and* CHARLEY *continue playing.*)

CHARLEY: You never heard from him again, heh? Since that time?

WILLY: Didn't Linda tell you? Couple of weeks ago we got a letter from his wife in Africa. He died.

CHARLEY: That so.

BEN (*chuckling*): So this is Brooklyn, eh?

CHARLEY: Maybe you're in for some of his money.

WILLY: Naa, he had seven sons. There's just one opportunity I had with that man . . .

BEN: I must take a train, William. There are several properties I'm looking at in Alaska.

WILLY: Sure, sure! If I'd gone with him to Alaska that time, everything would've been totally different.

CHARLEY: Go on, you'd froze to death up there.

WILLY: What're you talking about?

BEN: Opportunity is tremendous in Alaska, William. Surprised you're not up there.

WILLY: Sure, tremendous.

CHARLEY: Heh?

WILLY: There was the only man I ever met who knew the answers.

CHARLEY: Who?

BEN: How are you all?

WILLY (*taking a pot, smiling*): Fine, fine.

CHARLEY: Pretty sharp tonight.

BEN: Is Mother living with you?

WILLY: No, she died a long time ago.

CHARLEY: Who?

BEN: That's too bad. Fine specimen of a lady, Mother.

WILLY (*to* CHARLEY): Hey?

BEN: I'd hoped to see the old girl.

CHARLEY: Who died?

BEN: Heard anything from Father, have you?

WILLY (*unnerved*): What do you mean, who died?

CHARLEY (*taking a pot*): What're you talkin' about?

BEN (*looking at his watch*): William, it's half-past eight!

WILLY (*As though to dispel his confusion he angrily stops* CHARLEY's *hand.*): That's my build!

CHARLEY: I put the ace—

WILLY: If you don't know how to play the game I'm not gonna throw my money away on you!

CHARLEY (*rising*): It was my ace, for God's sake!

WILLY: I'm through, I'm through!

BEN: When did Mother die?

WILLY: Long ago. Since the beginning you never knew how to play cards.

CHARLEY (*picks up the cards and goes to the door*): All right! Next time I'll bring a deck with five aces.

WILLY: I don't play that kind of game!

CHARLEY (*turning to him*): You ought to be ashamed of yourself!

WILLY: Yeah?

CHARLEY: Yeah! (*He goes out.*)

WILLY (*slamming the door after him*): Ignoramus!

BEN (*as* WILLY *comes toward him through the wall-line of the kitchen*): So you're William.

WILLY (*shaking* BEN's *hand*): Ben! I've been waiting for you so long! What's the answer? How did you do it?

BEN: Oh, there's a story in that.

LINDA *enters the forestage, as of old, carrying the wash basket.*

LINDA: Is this Ben?

BEN (*gallantly*): How do you do, my dear.

LINDA: Where've you been all these years? Willy's always wondered why you—

WILLY (*pulling* BEN *away from her impatiently*): Where is Dad? Didn't you follow him? How did you get started?

BEN: Well, I don't know how much you remember.

WILLY: Well, I was just a baby, of course, only three or four years old—

BEN: Three years and eleven months.

WILLY: What a memory, Ben!

BEN: I have many enterprises, William, and I have never kept books.

WILLY: I remember I was sitting under the wagon in—was it Nebraska?

BEN: It was South Dakota, and I gave you a bunch of wild flowers.

WILLY: I remember you walking away down some open road.

BEN (*laughing*): I was going to find Father in Alaska.

WILLY: Where is he?

BEN: At that age I had a very faulty view of geography, William. I discovered after a few days that I was heading due south, so instead of Alaska, I ended up in Africa.

LINDA: Africa!

WILLY: The Gold Coast!

BEN: Principally diamond mines.

LINDA: Diamond mines!

BEN: Yes, my dear. But I've only a few minutes—

WILLY: No! Boys! Boys! (YOUNG BIFF *and* HAPPY *appear.*) Listen to this. This is your Uncle Ben, a great man! Tell my boys, Ben!

BEN: Why, boys, when I was seventeen I walked into the jungle, and when I was twenty-one I walked out. (*He laughs.*) And by God I was rich.

WILLY (*to the boys*): You see what I been talking about? The greatest things can happen!

BEN (*glancing at his watch*): I have an appointment in Ketchikan Tuesday week.

WILLY: No, Ben! Please tell about Dad. I want my boys to hear. I want them to know the kind of stock they spring from. All I remember is a man with a big beard, and I was in Mamma's lap, sitting around a fire, and some kind of high music.

BEN: His flute. He played the flute.

WILLY: Sure, the flute, that's right!

New music is heard, a high, rollicking tune.

BEN: Father was a very great and a very wild-hearted man. We would start in Boston, and he'd toss the whole family into the wagon, and then he'd drive the team right across the country; through Ohio, and Indiana, Michigan, Illinois, and all the Western states. And we'd stop in the towns and sell the flutes that he'd made on the way. Great inventor, Father. With one gadget he made more in a week than a man like you could make in a lifetime.

WILLY: That's just the way I'm bringing them up, Ben—rugged, well liked, all-around.

BEN: Yeah? (*to* BIFF) Hit that, boy—hard as you can. (*He pounds his stomach.*)

BIFF: Oh, no, sir!

BEN (*taking boxing stance*): Come on, get to me! (*He laughs.*)

WILLY: Go to it, Biff! Go ahead, show him!

BIFF: Okay! (*He cocks his fists and starts in.*)

LINDA (*to* WILLY): Why must he fight, dear?

BEN (*sparring with Biff*): Good boy! Good boy!

WILLY: How's that, Ben, heh?

HAPPY: Give him the left, Biff!

LINDA: Why are you fighting?

BEN: Good boy! (*Suddenly he comes in, trips Biff, and stands over him, the point of his umbrella poised over* BIFF'S *eye.*)

LINDA: Look out, Biff!

BIFF: Gee!

BEN (*patting* BIFF'S *knee*): Never fight fair with a stranger, boy. You'll never get out of the jungle that way. (*taking* LINDA'S *hand and bowing*) It was an honor and a pleasure to meet you, Linda.

LINDA (*withdrawing her hand coldly, frightened*): Have a nice—trip.

BEN (*to* WILLY): And good luck with your—what do you do?

WILLY: Selling.

BEN: Yes. Well . . . (*He raises his hand in farewell to all.*)

WILLY: No, Ben, I don't want you to think . . . (*He takes Ben's arm to show him.*) It's Brooklyn, I know, but we hunt too.

BEN: Really, now.

WILLY: Oh, sure, there's snakes and rabbits and—that's why I moved out here. Why, Biff can fell any one of these trees in no time! Boys! Go right over to where they're building the apartment house and get some sand. We're gonna rebuild the entire front stoop right now! Watch this, Ben!

BIFF: Yes, sir! On the double, Hap!

HAPPY (*as he and* BIFF *run off*): I lost weight, Pop, you notice?

CHARLEY *enters in knickers, even before the boys are gone.*

CHARLEY: Listen, if they steal any more from that building the watchman'll put the cops on them!

LINDA (*to* WILLY): Don't let Biff . . .

BEN *laughs lustily.*

WILLY: You shoulda seen the lumber they brought home last week. At least a dozen six-by-tens worth all kinds a money.

CHARLEY: Listen, if that watchman—

WILLY: I gave them hell, understand. But I got a couple of fearless characters there.

CHARLEY: Willy, the jails are full of fearless characters.

BEN (*clapping* WILLY *on the back, with a laugh at* CHARLEY): And the stock exchange, friend!

WILLY (*joining in* BEN'S *laughter*): Where are the rest of your pants?

CHARLEY: My wife bought them.

WILLY: Now all you need is a golf club and you can go upstairs and go to sleep. (*to* BEN) Great athlete! Between him and his son Bernard they can't hammer a nail!

BERNARD (*rushing in*): The watchman's chasing Biff!

WILLY (*angrily*): Shut up! He's not stealing anything!

LINDA (*alarmed, hurrying off left*): Where is he? Biff, dear! (*She exits.*)

WILLY (*moving toward the left, away from* BEN): There's nothing wrong. What's the matter with you?

BEN: Nervy boy. Good!

WILLY (*laughing*): Oh, nerves of iron, that Biff!

CHARLEY: Don't know what it is. My New England man comes back and he's bleedin', they murdered him up there.

WILLY: It's contacts, Charley, I got important contacts!

CHARLEY (*sarcastically*): Glad to hear it, Willy. Come in later, we'll shoot a little casino. I'll take some of your Portland money. (*He laughs at* WILLY *and exits.*)

WILLY (*turning to* BEN): Business is bad, it's murderous. But not for me, of course.

BEN: I'll stop by on my way back to Africa.

WILLY (*longingly*): Can't you stay a few days? You're just what I need, Ben, because I—I have a fine position here, but I—well, Dad left when I was such a baby and I never had a chance to talk to him and I still feel—kind of temporary about myself.

BEN: I'll be late for my train.

They are at opposite ends of the stage.

WILLY: Ben, my boys—can't we talk? They'd go into the jaws of hell for me, see, but I—

BEN: William, you're being first-rate with your boys. Outstanding, manly chaps!

WILLY (*hanging on his words*): Oh, Ben, that's good to hear! Because sometimes I'm afraid that I'm not teaching them the right kind of—Ben, how should I teach them?

BEN (*giving great weight to each word, and with a certain vicious audacity*): William, when I walked into the jungle, I was seventeen. When I walked out I was twenty-one. And, by God, I was rich! (*He goes off into darkness around the right corner of the house.*)

WILLY: . . . was rich! That's just the spirit I want to imbue them with! To walk into a jungle! I was right! I was right! I was right!

BEN *is gone, but* WILLY *is still speaking to him as* LINDA, *in nightgown and robe, enters the kitchen, glances around for* WILLY, *then goes to the door of the house, looks out and sees him. Comes down to his left. He looks at her.*

LINDA: Willy, dear? Willy?

WILLY: I was right!

LINDA: Did you have some cheese? (*He can't answer.*) It's very late, darling. Come to bed, heh?

WILLY (*looking straight up*): Gotta break your neck to see a star in this yard.

LINDA: You coming in?

WILLY: Whatever happened to that diamond watch fob? Remember? When Ben came from Africa that time? Didn't he give me a watch fob with a diamond in it?

LINDA: You pawned it, dear. Twelve, thirteen years ago. For Biff's radio correspondence course.

WILLY: Gee, that was a beautiful thing. I'll take a walk.

LINDA: But you're in your slippers.

WILLY (*starting to go around the house at the left*): I was right! I was! (*half to Linda, as he goes, shaking his head*) What a man! There was a man worth talking to. I was right!

LINDA (*calling after* WILLY): But in your slippers, Willy!

WILLY *is almost gone when* BIFF, *in his pajamas, comes down the stairs and enters the kitchen.*

BIFF: What is he doing out there?

LINDA: Sh!

BIFF: God Almighty, Mom, how long has he been doing this?

LINDA: Don't, he'll hear you.

BIFF: What the hell is the matter with him?

LINDA: It'll pass by morning.

BIFF: Shouldn't we do anything?

LINDA: Oh, my dear, you should do a lot of things, but there's nothing to do, so go to sleep.

HAPPY *comes down the stairs and sits on the steps.*

HAPPY: I never heard him so loud, Mom.

LINDA: Well, come around more often; you'll hear him. (*She sits down at the table and mends the lining of* WILLY'S *jacket.*)

BIFF: Why didn't you ever write me about this, Mom?

LINDA: How would I write to you? For over three months you had no address.

BIFF: I was on the move. But you know I thought of you all the time. You know that, don't you, pal?

LINDA: I know, dear, I know. But he likes to have a letter. Just to know that there's still a possibility for better things.

BIFF: He's not like this all the time, is he?

LINDA: It's when you come home he's always the worst.

BIFF: When I come home?

LINDA: When you write you're coming, he's all smiles, and talks about the future, and—he's just wonderful. And then the closer you seem to come, the more shaky he gets, and then, by the time you get here, he's arguing, and he seems angry at you. I think it's just that maybe he can't bring himself to—to open up to you. Why are you so hateful to each other? Why is that?

BIFF (*evasively*): I'm not hateful, Mom.

LINDA: But you no sooner come in the door than you're fighting!

BIFF: I don't know why. I mean to change. I'm tryin', Mom, you understand?

LINDA: Are you home to stay now?

BIFF: I don't know. I want to look around, see what's doin'.

LINDA: Biff, you can't look around all your life, can you?

BIFF: I just can't take hold, Mom. I can't take hold of some kind of a life.

LINDA: Biff, a man is not a bird, to come and go with the springtime.

BIFF: Your hair . . . (*He touches her hair.*) Your hair got so gray.

LINDA: Oh, it's been gray since you were in high school. I just stopped dyeing it, that's all.

BIFF: Dye it again, will ya? I don't want my pal looking old. (*He smiles.*)

LINDA: You're such a boy! You think you can go away for a year and . . . You've got to get it into your head now that one day you'll knock on this door and there'll be strange people here—

BIFF: What are you talking about? You're not even sixty, Mom.

LINDA: But what about your father?

BIFF (*lamely*): Well, I meant him too.

HAPPY: He admires Pop.

LINDA: Biff, dear, if you don't have any feeling for him, then you can't have any feeling for me.

BIFF: Sure I can, Mom.

LINDA: No. You can't just come to see me, because I love him. (*with a threat, but only a threat, of tears*) He's the dearest man in the world to me, and I won't have anyone making him feel unwanted and low and blue.

You've got to make up your mind now, darling, there's no leeway any more. Either he's your father and you pay him that respect, or else you're not to come here. I know he's not easy to get along with—nobody knows that better than me—but . . .

WILLY (*from the left, with a laugh*): Hey, hey, Biffo!

BIFF (*starting to go out after* WILLY): What the hell is the matter with him? (*Happy stops him.*)

LINDA: Don't—don't go near him!

BIFF: Stop making excuses for him! He always, always wiped the floor with you. Never had an ounce of respect for you.

HAPPY: He's always had respect for—

BIFF: What the hell do you know about it?

HAPPY (*surlily*): Just don't call him crazy!

BIFF: He's got no character—Charley wouldn't do this. Not in his own house—spewing out that vomit from his mind.

HAPPY: Charley never had to cope with what he's got to.

BIFF: People are worse off than Willy Loman. Believe me, I've seen them!

LINDA: Then make Charley your father, Biff. You can't do that, can you? I don't say he's a great man. Willy Loman never made a lot of money. His name was never in the paper. He's not the finest character that ever lived. But he's a human being, and a terrible thing is happening to him. So attention must be paid. He's not to be allowed to fall into his grave like an old dog. Attention, attention must be finally paid to such a person. You called him crazy—

BIFF: I didn't mean—

LINDA: No, a lot of people think he's lost his—balance. But you don't have to be very smart to know what his trouble is. The man is exhausted.

HAPPY: Sure!

LINDA: A small man can be just as exhausted as a great man. He works for a company thirty-six years this March, opens up unheard-of-territories to their trademark, and now in his old age they take his salary away.

HAPPY (*indignantly*): I didn't know that, Mom.

LINDA: You never asked, my dear! Now that you get your spending money someplace else you don't trouble your mind with him.

HAPPY: But I gave you money last—

LINDA: Christmas time, fifty dollars! To fix the hot water it cost ninety-seven fifty! For five weeks he's been on straight commission, like a beginner, an unknown!

BIFF: Those ungrateful bastards!

LINDA: Are they any worse than his sons? When he brought them business, when he was young, they were glad to see him. But now his old friends, the old buyers that loved him so and always found some order to hand him in a pinch—they're all dead, retired. He used to be able to make six, seven calls a day in Boston. Now he takes his valises out of the car and puts them back and takes them out again and he's exhausted. Instead of walking he talks now. He drives seven hundred miles, and when he gets there no one knows him any more, no one welcomes him. And what goes through a man's mind, driving seven hundred miles home without having earned a cent? Why shouldn't he talk to himself? Why? When he has to go to Charley and borrow fifty dollars a week and pretend to me that it's his pay? How long can that go on? How long? You see what I'm sitting here and waiting for? And you tell me he has no character? The man who never worked a day but for your benefit? When does he get the medal for that? Is this his reward—to turn around at the age of sixty-three and find his sons, who he loved better than his life, one a philandering bum—

HAPPY: Mom!

LINDA: That's all you are, my baby! (*to* BIFF) And you! What happened to the love you had for him? You were such pals! How you used to talk to him on the phone every night! How lonely he was till he could come home to you!

BIFF: All right, Mom. I'll live here in my room, and I'll get a job. I'll keep away from him, that's all.

LINDA: No, Biff. You can't stay here and fight all the time.

BIFF: He threw me out of this house, remember that.

LINDA: Why did he do that? I never knew why.

BIFF: Because I know he's a fake and he doesn't like anybody around who knows!

LINDA: Why a fake? In what way? What do you mean?

BIFF: Just don't lay it all at my feet. It's between me and him—that's all I have to say. I'll chip in from now on. He'll settle for half my pay check. He'll be all right. I'm going to bed. (*He starts for the stairs.*)

LINDA: He won't be all right.

BIFF (*turning on the stairs, furiously*): I hate this city and I'll stay here. Now what do you want?

LINDA: He's dying, Biff.

HAPPY *turns quickly to her, shocked.*

BIFF (*after a pause*): Why is he dying?

LINDA: He's been trying to kill himself.

BIFF (*with great horror*): How?

LINDA: I live from day to day.

BIFF: What're you talking about?

LINDA: Remember I wrote you that he smashed up the car again? In February?

BIFF: Well?

LINDA: The insurance inspector came. He said that they have evidence. That all these accidents in the last year—weren't—weren't—accidents.

HAPPY: How can they tell that? That's a lie.

LINDA: It seems there's a woman . . . (*she takes a breath as*)

BIFF (*sharply but contained*): What woman?

LINDA (*simultaneously*): . . . and this woman . . .

LINDA: What?

BIFF: Nothing. Go ahead.

LINDA: What did you say?

BIFF: Nothing. I just said what woman?

HAPPY: What about her?

LINDA: Well, it seems she was walking down the road and saw his car. She says that he wasn't driving fast at all, and that he didn't skid. She says he came to that little bridge, and then deliberately smashed into the railing, and it was only the shallowness of the water that saved him.

BIFF: Oh, no, he probably just fell asleep again.

LINDA: I don't think he fell asleep.

BIFF: Why not?

LINDA: Last month . . . (*with great difficulty*) Oh, boys, it's so hard to say a thing like this! He's just a big stupid man to you, but I tell you there's more good in him than in many other people. (*She chokes, wipes her eyes.*) I was looking for a fuse. The lights blew out, and I went down the cellar. And behind the fuse box—it happened to fall out—was a length of rubber pipe—just short.

HAPPY: No kidding?

LINDA: There's a little attachment on the end of it. I knew right away. And sure enough, on the bottom of the water heater there's a new little nipple on the gas pipe.

HAPPY (*angrily*): That—jerk.

BIFF: Did you have it taken off?

LINDA: I'm—I'm ashamed to. How can I mention it to him? Every day I go down and take away that little rubber pipe. But, when he comes home, I put it back where it was. How can I insult him that way? I don't know what to do. I live from day to day, boys. I tell you, I know every thought in his mind. It sounds so old-fashioned and silly, but I tell you he put his whole life into you and you've turned your backs on him. (*She is bent over in the chair, weeping, her face in her hands.*) Biff, I swear to God! Biff, his life is in your hands!

HAPPY (*to* BIFF): How do you like that damned fool!

BIFF (*kissing her*): All right, pal, all right. It's all settled now. I've been remiss. I know that, Mom. But now I'll stay, and I swear to you, I'll apply myself. (*kneeling in front of her, in a fever of self-reproach*) It's just—you see, Mom, I don't fit in business. Not that I won't try. I'll try, and I'll make good.

HAPPY: Sure you will. The trouble with you in business was you never tried to please people.

BIFF: I know, I—

HAPPY: Like when you worked for Harrison's. Bob Harrison said you were tops, and then you go and do some damn fool thing like whistling whole songs in the elevator like a comedian.

BIFF (*against* HAPPY): So what? I like to whistle sometimes.

HAPPY: You don't raise a guy to a responsible job who whistles in the elevator!

LINDA: Well, don't argue about it now.

HAPPY: Like when you'd go off and swim in the middle of the day instead of taking the line around.

BIFF (*his resentment rising*): Well, don't you run off? You take off sometimes, don't you? On a nice summer day?

HAPPY: Yeah, but I cover myself!

LINDA: Boys!

HAPPY: If I'm going to take a fade the boss can call any number where I'm supposed to be and they'll swear to him that I just left. I'll tell you something that I hate to say, Biff, but in the business world some of them think you're crazy.

BIFF (*angered*): Screw the business world!

HAPPY: All right, screw it! Great, but cover yourself!

LINDA: Hap, Hap!

BIFF: I don't care what they think! They've laughed at Dad for years, and you know why? Because we don't belong in this nuthouse of a city! We should be mixing cement on some open plain, or—or carpenters. A carpenter is allowed to whistle!

WILLY *walks in from the entrance of the house, at left.*

WILLY: Even your grandfather was better than a carpenter. (*Pause. They watch him.*) You never grew up. Bernard does not whistle in the elevator, I assure you.

BIFF (*as though to laugh* WILLY *out of it*): Yeah, but you do, Pop.

WILLY: I never in my life whistled in an elevator! And who in the business worlds thinks I'm crazy?

BIFF: I didn't mean it like that, Pop. Now don't make a whole thing out of it, will ya?

WILLY: Go back to the West! Be a carpenter, a cowboy, enjoy yourself!

LINDA: Willy, he was just saying—

WILLY: I heard what he said!

HAPPY (*trying to quiet* WILLY): Hey, Pop, come on now . . .

WILLY (*continuing over* HAPPY's *line*): They laugh at me, heh? Go to Filene's, go to the Hub, go to Slattery's, Boston. Call out the name Willy Loman and see what happens! Big shot!

BIFF: All right, Pop.

WILLY: Big!

BIFF: All right!

WILLY: Why do you always insult me?

BIFF: I didn't say a word. (*to* LINDA) Did I say a word?

LINDA: He didn't say anything, Willy.

WILLY (*going to the doorway of the living room*): All right, good night, good night.

LINDA: Willy, dear, he just decided . . .

WILLY (*to* BIFF): If you get tired hanging around tomorrow, paint the ceiling I put up in the living room.

BIFF: I'm leaving early tomorrow.

HAPPY: He's going to see Bill Oliver, Pop.

WILLY (*interestedly*): Oliver? For what?

BIFF (*with reserve, but trying, trying*): He always said he'd stake me. I'd like to go into business, so maybe I can take him up on it.

LINDA: Isn't that wonderful?

WILLY: Don't interrupt. What's wonderful about it? There's fifty men in the City of New York who'd stake him. (*to* BIFF) Sporting goods?

BIFF: I guess so. I know something about it and—

WILLY: He knows something about it! You know sporting goods better than Spalding, for God's sake! How much is he giving you?

BIFF: I don't know, I didn't even see him yet, but—

WILLY: Then what're you talkin' about?

BIFF (*getting angry*): Well, all I said was I'm gonna see him, that's all!

WILLY (*turning away*): Ah, you're counting your chickens again.

BIFF (*starting left for the stairs*): Oh, Jesus, I'm going to sleep!

WILLY (*calling after him*): Don't curse in this house!

BIFF (*turning*): Since when did you get so clean?

HAPPY (*trying to stop them*): Wait a . . .

WILLY: Don't use that language to me! I won't have it!

HAPPY (*grabbing* BIFF, *shouts*): Wait a minute! I got an idea. I got a feasible idea. Come here, Biff, let's talk this over now, let's talk some sense here. When I was down in Florida last time, I thought of a great idea to sell sporting goods. It just came back to me. You and I, Biff—we have a line, the Loman Line. We train a couple of weeks, and put on a couple of exhibitions, see?

WILLY: That's an idea!

HAPPY: Wait! We form two basketball teams, see? Two water-polo teams. We play each other. It's a million dollars' worth of publicity. Two brothers, see? The Loman Brothers. Displays in the Royal Palms—all the hotels. And banners over the ring and the basketball court: "Loman Brothers." Baby, we could sell sporting goods!

WILLY: That is a one-million-dollar idea!

LINDA: Marvelous!

BIFF: I'm in great shape as far as that's concerned.

HAPPY: And the beauty of it is, Biff, it wouldn't be like a business. We'd be out playin' ball again . . .

BIFF (*enthused*): Yeah, that's . . .

WILLY: Million-dollar . . .

HAPPY: And you wouldn't get fed up with it, Biff. It'd be the family again. There'd be the old honor, and comradeship, and if you wanted to go off for a swim or somethin'—well, you'd do it! Without some smart cooky gettin' up ahead of you!

WILLY: Lick the world! You guys together could absolutely lick the civilized world.

BIFF: I'll see Oliver tomorrow. Hap, if we could work that out . . .

LINDA: Maybe things are beginning to—

WILLY (*wildly enthused, to* LINDA): Stop interrupting! (*to* BIFF) But don't wear sport jacket and slacks when you see Oliver.

BIFF: No, I'll—

WILLY: A business suit, and talk as little as possible, and don't crack any jokes.

BIFF: He did like me. Always liked me.

LINDA: He loved you!

WILLY (*to* LINDA): Will you stop! (*to* BIFF) Walk in very serious. You are not applying for a boy's job. Money is to pass. Be quiet, fine, and serious. Everybody likes a kidder, but nobody lends him money.

HAPPY: I'll try to get some myself, Biff. I'm sure I can.

WILLY: I see great things for you kids, I think your troubles are over. But remember, start big and you'll end big. Ask for fifteen. How much you
gonna ask for?

BIFF: Gee, I don't know—

WILLY: And don't say "Gee." "Gee" is a boy's word. A man walking in for fifteen thousand dollars does not say "Gee!"

BIFF: Ten, I think, would be top though.

WILLY: Don't be so modest. You always started too low. Walk in with a big
laugh. Don't look worried. Start off with a couple of your good stories to
lighten things up. It's not what you say, it's how you say it—because personality always wins the day.

LINDA: Oliver always thought the highest of him—

WILLY: Will you let me talk?

BIFF: Don't yell at her, Pop, will ya?

WILLY (*angrily*): I was talking, wasn't I?

BIFF: I don't like you yelling at her all the time, and I'm tellin' you, that's all.

WILLY: What're you, takin' over this house?

LINDA: Willy—

WILLY (*turning on her*): Don't take his side all the time, goddammit!

BIFF (*furiously*): Stop yelling at her!

WILLY (*suddenly pulling on his cheek, beaten down, guilt-ridden*): Give my
best to Bill Oliver—he may remember me. (*He exits through the living-
room doorway.*)

LINDA (*her voice subdued*): What'd you have to start that for? (BIFF *turns
away.*) You see how sweet he was as soon as you talked hopefully? (*She
goes over to* BIFF.) Come up and say good night to him. Don't let him go
to bed that way.

HAPPY: Come on, Biff, let's buck him up.

LINDA: Please, dear. Just say good night. It takes so little to make him happy.
Come. (*She goes through the living-room doorway, calling upstairs from
within the living room.*) Your pajamas are hanging in the bathroom, Willy!

HAPPY (*looking toward where* LINDA *went out*): What a woman! They broke
the mold when they made her. You know that, Biff?

BIFF: He's off salary. My God, working on commission!

HAPPY: Well, let's face it: he's no hot-shot selling man. Except that sometimes, you have to admit, he's a sweet personality.

BIFF (*deciding*): Lend me ten bucks, will ya? I want to buy some new ties.

HAPPY: I'll take you to a place I know. Beautiful stuff. Wear one of my
striped shirts tomorrow.

BIFF: She got gray. Mom got awful old. Gee, I'm gonna go in to Oliver
tomorrow and knock him for a—

HAPPY: Come on up. Tell that to Dad. Let's give him a whirl. Come on.

BIFF (*steamed up*): You know, with ten thousand bucks, boy!

HAPPY (*as they go into the living room*): That's the talk, Biff, that's the first
time I've heard the old confidence out of you! (*from within the living
room, fading off*) You're gonna live with me, kid, and any babe you
want just say the word . . . (*The last lines are hardly heard. They are
mounting the stairs to their parents' bedroom.*)

LINDA (*Entering her bedroom and addressing* WILLY, *who is in the bathroom. She is straightening the bed for him.*): Can you do anything about the shower? It drips.

WILLY (*from the bathroom*): All of a sudden everything falls to pieces! God-dam plumbing, oughta be sued, those people. I hardly finished putting it in and the thing . . . (*His words rumble off.*)

LINDA: I'm just wondering if Oliver will remember him. You think he might?

WILLY (*coming out of the bathroom in his pajamas*): Remember him? What's the matter with you, you crazy? If he'd've stayed with Oliver he'd be on top by now! Wait'll Oliver gets a look at him. You don't know the average caliber any more. The average young man today—(*He is getting into bed.*)—is got a caliber of zero. Greatest thing in the world for him was to bum around.

BIFF *and* HAPPY *enter the bedroom. Slight pause.*

WILLY (*stops short, looking at* BIFF): Glad to hear it, boy.

HAPPY: He wanted to say good night to you, sport.

WILLY (*to* BIFF): Yeah. Knock him dead, boy. What'd you want to tell me?

BIFF: Just take it easy, Pop. Good night. (*He turns to go.*)

WILLY (*unable to resist*): And if anything falls off the desk while you're talking to him—like a package or something—don't you pick it up. They have office boys for that.

LINDA: I'll make a big breakfast—

WILLY: Will you let me finish? (*to* BIFF) Tell him you were in the business in the West. Not farm work.

BIFF: All right, Dad.

LINDA: I think everything—

WILLY (*going right through her speech*): And don't undersell yourself. No less than fifteen thousand dollars.

BIFF (*unable to bear him*): Okay. Good night, Mom. (*He starts moving.*)

WILLY: Because you got a greatness in you, Biff, remember that. You got all kinds a greatness . . . (*He lies back, exhausted.* BIFF *walks out.*)

LINDA (*calling after* BIFF): Sleep well, darling!

HAPPY: I'm gonna get married, Mom. I wanted to tell you.

LINDA: Go to sleep, dear.

HAPPY (*going*): I just wanted to tell you.

WILLY: Keep up the good work. (HAPPY *exits.*) God . . . remember that Ebbets Field game? The championship of the city?

LINDA: Just rest. Should I sing to you?

WILLY: Yeah. Sing to me. (LINDA *hums a soft lullaby.*) When that team came out—he was the tallest, remember?

LINDA: Oh, yes. And in gold.

BIFF *enters the darkened kitchen, takes a cigarette, and leaves the house. He comes downstage into a golden pool of light. He smokes, staring at the night.*

WILLY: Like a young god. Hercules—something like that. And the sun, the sun all around him. Remember how he waved to me? Right up from the field, with the representatives of three colleges standing by? And the buyers I brought, and the cheers when he came out—Loman, Loman, Loman! God Almighty, he'll be great yet. A star like that, magnificent, can never really fade away!

The light on WILLY *is fading. The gas heater begins to glow through the kitchen wall, near the stairs, a blue flame beneath red coils.*

LINDA (*timidly*): Willy dear, what has he got against you?
WILLY: I'm so tired. Don't talk any more.

BIFF *slowly returns to the kitchen. He stops, stares toward the heater.*

LINDA: Will you ask Howard to let you work in New York?
WILLY: First thing in the morning. Everything'll be all right.

BIFF *reaches behind the heater and draws out a length of rubber tubing. He is horrified and turns his head toward* WILLY'S *room, still dimly lit, from which the strains of* LINDA'S *desperate but monotonous humming rise.*

WILLY (*staring through the window into the moonlight*): Gee, look at the moon moving between the buildings!

BIFF *wraps the tubing around his hand and quickly goes up the stairs.*
Curtain.

Act Two

Music is heard, gay and bright. The curtain rises as the music fades away. WILLY, *in shirt sleeves, is sitting at the kitchen table, sipping coffee, his hat in his lap.* LINDA *is filling his cup when she can.*

WILLY: Wonderful coffee. Meal in itself.
LINDA: Can I make you some eggs?
WILLY: No. Take a breath.
LINDA: You look so rested, dear.
WILLY: I slept like a dead one. First time in months. Imagine, sleeping till ten on a Tuesday morning. Boys left nice and early, heh?
LINDA: They were out of here by eight o'clock.
WILLY: Good work!
LINDA: It was so thrilling to see them leaving together. I can't get over the shaving lotion in this house!
WILLY (*smiling*): Mmm—
LINDA: Biff was very changed this morning. His whole attitude seemed to be hopeful. He couldn't wait to get downtown to see Oliver.
WILLY: He's head for a change. There's no question, there simply are certain men that take longer to get—solidified. How did he dress?
LINDA: His blue suit. He's so handsome in that suit. He could be a—anything in that suit!

WILLY *gets up from the table.* LINDA *holds his jacket for him.*

WILLY: There's no question, no question at all. Gee, on the way home tonight I'd like to buy some seeds.

LINDA (*laughing*): That'd be wonderful. But not enough sun gets back there. Nothing'll grow any more.

WILLY: You wait, kid, before it's all over we're gonna get a little place out in the country, and I'll raise some vegetables, a couple of chickens . . .

LINDA: You'll do it yet, dear.

WILLY *walks out of his jacket.* LINDA *follows him.*

WILLY: And they'll get married, and come for a weekend. I'll build a little guest house. 'Cause I got so many fine tools, all I'd need would be a little lumber and some peace of mind.

LINDA (*joyfully*): I sewed the lining . . .

WILLY: I could build two guest houses, so they'd both come. Did he decide how much he's going to ask Oliver for?

LINDA (*getting him into the jacket*): He didn't mention it, but I imagine ten or fifteen thousand. You going to talk to Howard today?

WILLY: Yeah. I'll put it to him straight and simple. He'll just have to take me off the road.

LINDA: And Willy, don't forget to ask for a little advance, because we've got the insurance premium. It's the grace period now.

WILLY: That's a hundred . . . ?

LINDA: A hundred and eight, sixty-eight. Because we're a little short again.

WILLY: Why are we short?

LINDA: Well, you had the motor job on the car . . .

WILLY: That goddam Studebaker!

LINDA: And you got one more payment on the refrigerator . . .

WILLY: But it just broke again!

LINDA: Well, it's old, dear.

WILLY: I told you we should've bought a well-advertised machine. Charley bought a General Electric and it's twenty years old and it's still good, that son-of-a-bitch.

LINDA: But, Willy—

WILLY: Whoever heard of a Hastings refrigerator? Once in my life I would like to own something outright before it's broken! I'm always in a race with the junkyard! I just finished paying for the car and it's on its last legs. The refrigerator consumes belts like a goddam maniac. They time those things. They time them so when you finally paid for them, they're used up.

LINDA (*buttoning up his jacket as he unbuttons it*): All told, about two hundred dollars would carry us, dear. But that includes the last payment on the mortgage. After this payment, Willy, the house belongs to us.

WILLY: It's twenty-five years!

LINDA: Biff was nine years old when we bought it.

WILLY: Well, that's a great thing. To weather a twenty-five-year mortgage is—

LINDA: It's an accomplishment.

WILLY: All the cement, the lumber, the reconstruction I put in this house! There ain't a crack to be found in it any more.

LINDA: Well, it served its purpose.

WILLY: What purpose? Some stranger'll come along, move in, and that's that. If only Biff would take this house, and raise a family . . . (*He starts to go.*) Good-by, I'm late.

LINDA (*suddenly remembering*): Oh, I forgot! You're supposed to meet them for dinner.

WILLY: Me?

LINDA: At Frank's Chop House on Forty-eighth near Sixth Avenue.

WILLY: Is that so! How about you?

LINDA: No, just the three of you. They're gonna blow you to a big meal!

WILLY: Don't say! Who thought of that?

LINDA: Biff came to me this morning, Willy, and he said, "Tell Dad, we want to blow him to a big meal." Be there six o'clock. You and your two boys are going to have dinner.

WILLY: Gee whiz! That's really somethin'. I'm gonna knock Howard for a loop, kid. I'll get an advance, and I'll come home with a New York job. Goddammit, now I'm gonna do it!

LINDA: Oh, that's the spirit, Willy!

WILLY: I will never get behind a wheel the rest of my life!

LINDA: It's changing, Willy, I can feel it changing!

WILLY: Beyond a question. G'by, I'm late. (*He starts to go again.*)

LINDA (*calling after him as she runs to the kitchen table for a handkerchief*): You got your glasses?

WILLY (*He feels for them, then comes back in.*):—Yeah, yeah, got my glasses.

LINDA (*giving him the handkerchief*): And a handkerchief.

WILLY: Yeah, handkerchief.

LINDA: And your saccharine?

WILLY: Yeah, my saccharine.

LINDA: Be careful on the subway stairs.

She kisses him, and a silk stocking is seen hanging from her hand. WILLY *notices it.*

WILLY: Will you stop mending stockings? At least while I'm in the house. It gets me nervous. I can't tell you. Please.

LINDA *hides the stocking in her hand as she follows* WILLY *across the forestage in front of the house.*

LINDA: Remember, Frank's Chop House.

WILLY (*passing the apron*): Maybe beets would grow out there.

LINDA (*laughing*): But you tried so many times.

WILLY: Yeah. Well, don't work hard today. (*He disappears around the right corner of the house.*)

LINDA: Be careful!

As WILLY *vanishes,* LINDA *waves to him. Suddenly the phone rings. She runs across the stage and into the kitchen and lifts it.*

LINDA: Hello? Oh, Biff! I'm so glad you called, I just . . . Yes, sure, I just told him. Yes, he'll be there for dinner at six o'clock, I didn't forget. Listen, I was just dying to tell you. You know that little rubber pipe I told you about? That he connected to the gas heater? I finally decided to go down the cellar this morning and take it away and destroy it. But it's gone! Imagine? He took it away himself, it isn't there! (*She listens.*) When? Oh, then you took it. Oh—nothing, it's just that I'd hoped he'd taken it away himself. Oh, I'm not worried, darling, because this morning he left in such high spirits, it was like the old days! I'm not afraid any more. Did Mr. Oliver see you? . . . Well, you wait there then. And make a nice impression on him, darling. Just don't perspire too much before you see him. And have a nice time with Dad. He may have big news too! . . . That's right, a New York job. And be sweet to him tonight, dear. Be loving to him. Because he's only a little boat looking for a harbor. (*She is trembling with sorrow and joy.*) Oh, that's wonderful, Biff, you'll save his life. Thanks, darling. Just put your arm around him when he comes into the restaurant. Give him a smile. That's the boy . . . Good-by, dear . . . You got your comb? . . . That's fine. Good-by, Biff dear.

In the middle of her speech, HOWARD WAGNER, *thirty-six, wheels in a small typewriter table on which is a wire-recording machine and proceeds to plug it in. This is on the left forestage. Light slowly fades on* LINDA *as it rises on* HOWARD. HOWARD *is intent on threading the machine and only glances over his shoulder as* WILLY *appears.*

WILLY: Pst! Pst!

HOWARD: Hello, Willy, come in.

WILLY: Like to have a little talk with you, Howard.

HOWARD: Sorry to keep you waiting. I'll be with you in a minute.

WILLY: What's that, Howard?

HOWARD: Didn't you ever see one of these? Wire recorder.

WILLY: Oh. Can we talk a minute?

HOWARD: Records things. Just got delivery yesterday. Been driving me crazy, the most terrific machine I ever saw in my life. I was up all night with it.

WILLY: What do you do with it?

HOWARD: I bought it for dictation, but you can do anything with it. Listen to this. I had it home last night. Listen to what I picked up. The first one is my daughter. Get this. (*He flicks the switch and "Roll out the Barrel" is heard being whistled.*) Listen to that kid whistle.

WILLY: That is lifelike, isn't it?

HOWARD: Seven years old. Get that tone.

WILLY: Ts, ts. Like to ask a little favor if you . . .

The whistling breaks off, and the voice of HOWARD'S *daughter is heard.*

HIS DAUGHTER: "Now you, Daddy."

HOWARD: She's crazy for me! (*Again the same song is whistled.*) That's me! Ha! (*He winks.*)

WILLY: You're very good!

The whistling breaks off again. The machine runs silent for a moment.

HOWARD: Sh! Get this now, this is my son.

HIS SON: "The capital of Alabama is Montgomery; the capital of Arizona is Phoenix; the capital of Arkansas is Little Rock; the capital of California is Sacramento . . ." (*and on, and on*)

HOWARD (*holding up five fingers*): Five years old, Willy!

WILLY: He'll make an announcer some day!

HIS SON (*continuing*): "The capital . . ."

HOWARD: Get that—alphabetical order! (*The machine breaks off suddenly.*) Wait a minute. The maid kicked the plug out.

WILLY: It certainly is a—

HOWARD: Sh, for God's sake!

HIS SON: "It's nine o'clock, Bulova watch time. So I have to go to sleep."

WILLY: That really is—

HOWARD: Wait a minute! The next is my wife.

They wait.

HOWARD'S VOICE: "Go on, say something." (*pause*) "Well, you gonna talk?"

HIS WIFE: "I can't think of anything."

HOWARD'S VOICE: "Well, talk—it's turning."

HIS WIFE (*shyly, beaten*): "Hello." (*silence*) "Oh, Howard, I can't talk into this . . ."

HOWARD (*snapping the machine off*): That was my wife.

WILLY: That is a wonderful machine. Can we—

HOWARD: I tell you, Willy, I'm gonna take my camera, and my bandsaw, and all my hobbies, and out they go. This is the most fascinating relaxation I ever found.

WILLY: I think I'll get one myself.

HOWARD: Sure, they're only a hundred and a half. You can't do without it. Supposing you wanna hear Jack Benny, see? But you can't be at home at that hour. So you tell the maid to turn the radio on when Jack Benny comes on, and this automatically goes on with the radio . . .

WILLY: And when you come home you . . .

HOWARD: You can come home twelve o'clock, one o'clock, any time you like, and you get yourself a Coke and sit yourself down, throw the switch, and there's Jack Benny's program in the middle of the night!

WILLY: I'm definitely going to get one. Because lots of time I'm on the road, and I think to myself, what I must be missing on the radio!

HOWARD: Don't you have a radio in the car?

WILLY: Well, yeah, but who ever thinks of turning it on?

HOWARD: Say, aren't you supposed to be in Boston?

WILLY: That's what I want to talk to you about, Howard. You got a minute? (*He draws a chair in from the wing.*)

HOWARD: What happened? What're you doing here?

WILLY: Well . . .

HOWARD: You didn't crack up again, did you?

WILLY: Oh, no. No . . .

HOWARD: Geez, you had me worried there for a minute. What's the trouble?

WILLY: Well, tell you the truth, Howard. I've come to the decision that I'd rather not travel any more.

HOWARD: Not travel! Well, what'll you do?

WILLY: Remember, Christmas time, when you had the party here? You said you'd try to think of some spot for me here in town.

HOWARD: With us?

WILLY: Well, sure.

HOWARD: Oh, yeah, yeah. I remember. Well, I couldn't think of anything for you, Willy.

WILLY: I tell ya, Howard. The kids are all grown up, y'know. I don't need much any more. If I could take home—well, sixty-five dollars a week, I could swing it.

HOWARD: Yeah, but Willy, see I—

WILLY: I tell ya why, Howard. Speaking frankly and between the two of us, y'know—I'm just a little tired.

HOWARD: Oh, I could understand that, Willy. But you're a road man, Willy, and we do a road business. We've only got a half-dozen salesmen on the floor here.

WILLY: God knows, Howard, I never asked a favor of any man. But I was with the firm when your father used to carry you in here in his arms.

HOWARD: I know that, Willy, but—

WILLY: Your father came to me the day you were born and asked me what I thought of the name of Howard, may he rest in peace.

HOWARD: I appreciate that, Willy, but there just is no spot here for you. If I had a spot I'd slam you right in, but I just don't have a single solitary spot.

He looks for his lighter. WILLY *has picked it up and gives it to him. Pause.*

WILLY (*with increasing anger*): Howard, all I need to set my table is fifty dollars a week.

HOWARD: But where am I going to put you, kid?

WILLY: Look, it isn't a question of whether I can sell merchandise, is it?

HOWARD: No, but it's a business, kid, and everybody's gotta pull his own weight.

WILLY (*desperately*): Just let me tell you a story, Howard—

HOWARD: 'Cause you gotta admit, business is business.

WILLY (*angrily*): Business is definitely business, but just listen for a minute. You don't understand this. When I was a boy—eighteen, nineteen—I was already on the road. And there was a question in my mind as to whether selling had a future for me. Because in those days I had a yearning to go to Alaska. See, there were three gold strikes in one month in Alaska, and I felt like going out. Just for the ride, you might say.

HOWARD (*barely interested*): Don't say.

WILLY: Oh, yeah, my father lived many years in Alaska. He was an adventurous man. We've got quite a little streak of self-reliance in our family. I thought I'd go out with my older brother and try to locate him, and maybe settle in the North with the old man. And I was almost decided to go, when I met a salesman in the Parker House. His name was Dave Singleman. And he was eighty-four years old, and he'd drummed merchandise in thirty-one states. And old Dave, he'd go up to his room, y'understand, put on his green velvet slippers—I'll never forget—and pick up his phone and call the buyers, and without ever leaving his room, at the age of eighty-four, he made his living. And when I saw that, I realized that selling was the greatest career a man could want. 'Cause what could be more satisfying than to be able to go, at the age of eighty-four, into twenty or thirty different cities, and pick up a phone, and be remembered and loved and helped by so many different people? Do you know? when he died—and by the way he died the death of a salesman, in his green velvet slippers in the smoker of the New York, New Haven and Hartford, going into Boston—when he died, hundreds of salesmen and buyers were at his funeral. Things were sad on a lotta trains for months after that. (*He stands up.* HOWARD *has not looked at him.*) In those days there was personality in it, Howard. There was respect, and comradeship, and gratitude in it. Today, it's all cut and dried, and there's no chance for bringing friendship to bear—or personality. You see what I mean? They don't know me any more.

HOWARD (*moving away, to the right*): That's just the thing, Willy.

WILLY: If I had forty dollars a week—that's all I'd need. Forty dollars, Howard.

HOWARD: Kid, I can't take blood from a stone, I—

WILLY (*desperation is on him now*): Howard, the year Al Smith was nominated, your father came to me and—

HOWARD (*starting to go off*): I've got to see some people, kid.

WILLY (*stopping him*): I'm talking about your father! There were promises made across this desk! You mustn't tell me you've got people to see—I put thirty-four years into this firm, Howard, and now I can't pay my insurance! You can't eat the orange and throw the peel away—a man is not a piece of fruit! (*after a pause*) Now pay attention. Your father—in 1928 I had a big year. I averaged a hundred and seventy dollars a week in commissions.

HOWARD (*impatiently*): Now, Willy, you never averaged—

WILLY (*banging his hand on the desk*): I averaged a hundred and seventy dollars a week in the year of 1928! And your father came to me—or rather, I was in the office here—it was right over this desk—and he put his hand on my shoulder—

HOWARD (*getting up*): You'll have to excuse me, Willy, I gotta see some people. Pull yourself together. (*going out*) I'll be back in a little while.

On HOWARD's *exit, the light on his chair grows very bright and strange.*

WILLY: Pull myself together! What the hell did I say to him? My God, I was yelling at him! How could I! (WILLY *breaks off, staring at the light, which occupies the chair, animating it. He approaches this chair, standing across the desk from it.*) Frank, Frank, don't you remember what you told me that time? How you put your hand on my shoulder, and Frank . . . (*he leans on the desk and as he speaks the dead man's name he accidentally switches on the recorder, and instantly*)

HOWARD'S SON: " . . . of New York is Albany. The capital of Ohio is Cincinnati, the capital of Rhode Island is . . ." (*The recitation continues.*)

WILLY (*leaping away with fright, shouting*): Ha! Howard! Howard! Howard!

HOWARD (*rushing in*): What happened?

WILLY (*pointing at the machine, which continues nasally, childishly, with the capital cities*): Shut it off! Shut it off!

HOWARD (*pulling the plug out*): Look, Willy . . .

WILLY (*pressing his hands to his eyes*): I gotta get myself some coffee. I'll get some coffee . . .

WILLY *starts to walk out.* HOWARD *stops him.*

HOWARD (*rolling up the cord*): Willy, look . . .

WILLY: I'll go to Boston.

HOWARD: Willy, you can't go to Boston for us.

WILLY: Why can't I go?

HOWARD: I don't want you to represent us. I've been meaning to tell you for a long time now.

WILLY: Howard, are you firing me?

HOWARD: I think you need a good long rest, Willy.

WILLY: Howard—

HOWARD: And when you feel better, come back, and we'll see if we can work something out.

WILLY: But I gotta earn money, Howard. I'm in no position to—

HOWARD: Where are your sons? Why don't your sons give you a hand?

WILLY: They're working on a very big deal.

HOWARD: This is no time for false pride, Willy. You go to your sons and you tell them that you're tired. You've got two great boys, haven't you?

WILLY: Oh, no question, no question, but in the meantime . . .

HOWARD: Then that's that, heh?

WILLY: All right, I'll go to Boston tomorrow.

HOWARD: No, no.

WILLY: I can't throw myself on my sons. I'm not a cripple!

HOWARD: Look, kid, I'm busy this morning.

WILLY (*grasping* HOWARD'S *arm*): Howard, you've got to let me go to Boston!

HOWARD (*hard, keeping himself under control*): I've got a line of people to see this morning. Sit down, take five minutes, and pull yourself together, and then go home, will ya? I need the office, Willy. (*He starts to go; turns, remembering the recorder, starts to push off the table holding the recorder.*) Oh, yeah. Whenever you can this week, stop by and drop off the samples. You'll feel better, Willy, and then come back and we'll talk. Pull yourself together, kid, there's people outside.

HOWARD *exits, pushing the table off left.* WILLY *stares into space, exhausted. Now the music is heard—*BEN'S *music—first distantly, then closer, closer. As* WILLY *speaks,* BEN *enters from the right. He carries valise and umbrella.*

WILLY: Oh, Ben, how did you do it? What is the answer? Did you wind up the Alaska deal already?

BEN: Doesn't take much time if you know what you're doing. Just a short business trip. Boarding ship in an hour. Wanted to say good-by.

WILLY: Ben, I've got to talk to you.

BEN (*glancing at his watch*): Haven't the time, William.

WILLY (*crossing the apron to* BEN): Ben, nothing's working out. I don't know what to do.

BEN: Now, look here, William. I've bought timberland in Alaska and I need a man to look after things for me.

WILLY: God, timberland! Me and my boys in those grand outdoors!

BEN: You've a new continent at your doorstep, William. Get out of these cities, they're full of talk and time payments and courts of law. Screw on your fists and you can fight for a fortune up there.

WILLY: Yes, yes! Linda, Linda!

LINDA *enters as of old, with the wash.*

LINDA: Oh, you're back?

BEN: I haven't much time.

WILLY: No, wait! Linda, he's got a proposition for me in Alaska.

LINDA: But you've got—(*to* BEN) He's got a beautiful job here.

WILLY: But in Alaska, kid, I could—

LINDA: You're doing well enough, Willy!

BEN (*to* LINDA): Enough for what, my dear?

LINDA (*frightened of* BEN *and angry at him*): Don't say those things to him! Enough to be happy right here, right now. (*to* WILLY, *while* BEN *laughs*) Why must everybody conquer the world? You're well liked, and the boys love you, and someday—(*to* BEN)—why, old man Wagner told him just the other day that if he keeps it up he'll be a member of the firm, didn't he, Willy?

WILLY: Sure, sure. I am building something with this firm, Ben, and if a man is building something he must be on the right track, mustn't he?

BEN: What are you building? Lay your hand on it. Where is it?

WILLY (*hesitantly*): That's true, Linda, there's nothing.

LINDA: Why? (*to* BEN) There's a man eighty-four years old—

WILLY: That's right, Ben, that's right. When I look at that man I say, what is there to worry about?

BEN: Bah!

WILLY: It's true, Ben. All he has to do is go into any city, pick up the phone, and he's making his living and you know why?

BEN (*picking up his valise*): I've got to go.

WILLY (*holding* BEN *back*): Look at this boy!

BIFF, *in his high school sweater, enters carrying suitcase.* HAPPY *carries* BIFF's *shoulder guards, gold helmet, and football pants.*

WILLY: Without a penny to his name, three great universities are begging for him, and from there the sky's the limit, because it's not what you do, Ben. It's who you know and the smile on your face! It's contacts, Ben, contacts! The whole wealth of Alaska passes over the lunch table at the Commodore Hotel, and that's the wonder, the wonder of this country, that a man can end with diamonds here on the basis of being liked! (*He turns to* BIFF.) And that's why when you get out on that field today it's important. Because thousands of people will be rooting for you and loving you. (*to* BEN, *who has again begun to leave*) And Ben! when he walks into a business office his name will sound out like a bell and all the doors will open to him! I've seen it, Ben, I've seen it a thousand times! You can't feel it with your hand like timber, but it's there!

BEN: Good-by, William.

WILLY: Ben, am I right? Don't you think I'm right? I value your advice.

BEN: There's a new continent at your doorstep, William. You could walk out rich. Rich! (*He is gone.*)

WILLY: We'll do it here, Ben! You hear me? We're gonna do it here!

YOUNG BERNARD *rushes in. The gay music of the Boys is heard.*

BERNARD: Oh, gee, I was afraid you left already!

WILLY: Why? What time is it?

BERNARD: It's half-past one!

WILLY: Well, come on, everybody! Ebbets Field next stop! Where's the pennants? (*He rushes through the wall-line of the kitchen and out into the living room.*)

LINDA (*to* BIFF): Did you pack fresh underwear?

BIFF (*who has been limbering up*): I want to go!

BERNARD: Biff, I'm carrying your helmet, ain't I?

HAPPY: No, I'm carrying the helmet.

BERNARD: Oh, Biff, you promised me.

HAPPY: I'm carrying the helmet.

BERNARD: How am I going to get in the locker room?

LINDA: Let him carry the shoulder guards. (*She puts her coat and hat on in the kitchen.*)

BERNARD: Can I, Biff? 'Cause I told everybody I'm going to be in the locker room.

HAPPY: In Ebbets Field it's the clubhouse.

BERNARD: I meant the clubhouse. Biff!

HAPPY: Biff!

BIFF (*grandly, after a slight pause*): Let him carry the shoulder guards.

HAPPY (*as he gives* BERNARD *the shoulder guards*): Stay close to us now.

WILLY *rushes in with the pennants.*

WILLY (*handing them out*): Everybody wave when Biff comes out on the field. (HAPPY *and* BERNARD *run off.*) You set now, boy?

The music has died away.

BIFF: Ready to go, Pop. Every muscle is ready.

WILLY (*at the edge of the apron*): You realize what this means?

BIFF: That's right, Pop.

WILLY (*feeling* BIFF'S *muscles*): You're comin' home this afternoon captain of the All-Scholastic Championship Team of the City of New York.

BIFF: I got it, Pop. And remember, pal, when I take off my helmet, that touchdown is for you.

WILLY: Let's go! (*He is starting out, with his arms around* BIFF, *when* CHARLEY *enters, as of old, in knickers.*) I got no room for you, Charley.

CHARLEY: Room? For what?

WILLY: In the car.

CHARLEY: You goin' for a ride? I wanted to shoot some casino.

WILLY (*furiously*): Casino! (*incredulously*) Don't you realize what today is?

LINDA: Oh, he knows, Willy. He's just kidding you.

WILLY: That's nothing to kid about!

CHARLEY: No, Linda, what's goin' on?

LINDA: He's playing in Ebbets Field.

CHARLEY: Baseball in this weather?

WILLY: Don't talk to him. Come on, come on! (*He is pushing them out.*)

CHARLEY: Wait a minute, didn't you hear the news?

WILLY: What?

CHARLEY: Don't you listen to the radio? Ebbets Field just blew up.

WILLY: You go to hell! (CHARLEY *laughs. Pushing them out.*) Come on, come on! We're late.

CHARLEY (*as they go*): Knock a homer, Biff, knock a homer!

WILLY (*the last to leave, turning to* CHARLEY): I don't think that was funny, Charley. This is the greatest day of his life.

CHARLEY: Willy, when are you going to grow up?

WILLY: Yeah, heh? When this game is over, Charley, you'll be laughing out of the other side of your face. They'll be calling him another Red Grange. Twenty-five thousand a year.

CHARLEY (*kidding*): Is that so?

WILLY: Yeah, that's so.

CHARLEY: Well, then, I'm sorry, Willy. But tell me something.

WILLY: What?

CHARLEY: Who is Red Grange?

WILLY: Put up your hands. Goddam you, put up your hands!

> CHARLEY, *chuckling, shakes his head and walks away, around the left corner of the stage.* WILLY *follows him. The music rises to a mocking frenzy.*

WILLY: Who the hell do you think you are, better than everybody else? You don't know everything, you big, ignorant, stupid . . . Put up your hands!

Light rises, on the right side of the forestage, on a small table in the reception room of CHARLEY'S *office. Traffic sounds are heard.* BERNARD, *now mature, sits whistling to himself. A pair of tennis rackets and an overnight bag are on the floor beside him.*

WILLY (*offstage*): What are you walking away for? Don't walk away! If you're going to say something say it to my face! I know you laugh at me behind my back. You'll laugh out of the other side of your goddam face after this game. Touchdown! Touchdown! Eighty thousand people! Touchdown! Right between the goal posts.

> BERNARD *is a quiet, earnest, but self-assured young man.* WILLY'S *voice is coming from right upstage now.* BERNARD *lowers his feet off the table and listens.* JENNY, *his father's secretary, enters.*

JENNY (*distressed*): Say, Bernard, will you go out in the hall?

BERNARD: What is that noise? Who is it?

JENNY: Mr. Loman. He just got off the elevator.

BERNARD (*getting up*): Who's he arguing with?

JENNY: Nobody. There's nobody with him. I can't deal with him any more, and your father gets all upset everytime he comes. I've got a lot of typing to do, and your father's waiting to sign it. Will you see him?

WILLY (*entering*): Touchdown! Touch—(*He sees* JENNY.) Jenny, Jenny, good to see you. How're ya? Workin'? Or still honest?

JENNY: Fine. How've you been feeling?

WILLY: Not much any more, Jenny. Ha, ha! (*He is surprised to see the rackets.*)

BERNARD: Hello, Uncle Willy.

WILLY (*almost shocked*): Bernard! Well, look who's here! (*He comes quickly, guiltily, to* BERNARD *and warmly shakes his hand.*)

BERNARD: How are you? Good to see you.

WILLY: What are you doing here?

BERNARD: Oh, just stopped by to see Pop. Get off my feet till my train leaves. I'm going to Washington in a few minutes.

WILLY: Is he in?

BERNARD: Yes, he's in his office with the accountant. Sit down.

WILLY (*sitting down*): What're you going to do in Washington?

BERNARD: Oh, just a case I've got there, Willy.

WILLY: That so? (*indicating the rackets*) You going to play tennis there?

BERNARD: I'm staying with a friend who's got a court.

WILLY: Don't say. His own tennis court. Must be fine people, I bet.

BERNARD: They are, very nice. Dad tells me Biff's in town.

WILLY (*with a big smile*): Yeah, Biff's in. Working on a very big deal, Bernard.

BERNARD: What's Biff doing?

WILLY: Well, he's been doing very big things in the West. But he decided to establish himself here. Very big. We're having dinner. Did I hear your wife had a boy?

BERNARD: That's right. Our second.

WILLY: Two boys! What do you know!

BERNARD: What kind of a deal has Biff got?

WILLY: Well, Bill Oliver—very big sporting-goods man—he wants Biff very badly. Called him in from the West. Long distance, carte blanche, special deliveries. Your friends have their own private tennis court?

BERNARD: You still with the old firm, Willy?

WILLY (*after a pause*): I'm—I'm overjoyed to see how you made the grade, Bernard, overjoyed. It's an encouraging thing to see a young man really—really—Looks very good for Biff—very—(*he breaks off, then*) Bernard—(*He is so full of emotion, he breaks off again.*)

BERNARD: What is it, Willy?

WILLY (*small and alone*): What—what's the secret?

BERNARD: What secret?

WILLY: How—how did you? Why didn't he ever catch on?

BERNARD: I wouldn't know that, Willy.

WILLY (*confidentially, desperately*): You were his friend, his boyhood friend. There's something I don't understand about it. His life ended after that Ebbets Field game. From the age of seventeen nothing good ever happened to him.

BERNARD: He never trained himself for anything.

WILLY: But he did, he did. After high school he took so many correspondence courses. Radio mechanics; television; God knows what, and never made the slightest mark.

BERNARD (*taking off his glasses*): Willy, do you want to talk candidly?

WILLY (*rising, faces* BERNARD): I regard you as a very brilliant man, Bernard. I value your advice.

BERNARD: Oh, the hell with the advice, Willy. I couldn't advise you. There's just one thing I've always wanted to ask you. When he was supposed to graduate, and the math teacher flunked him—

WILLY: Oh, that son-of-a-bitch ruined his life.

BERNARD: Yeah, but, Willy, all he had to do was go to summer school and make up that subject.

WILLY: That's right, that's right.

BERNARD: Did you tell him not to go to summer school?

WILLY: Me? I begged him to go. I ordered him to go!

BERNARD: Then why wouldn't he go?

WILLY: Why? Why! Bernard, that question has been trailing me like a ghost for the last fifteen years. He flunked the subject, and laid down and died like a hammer hit him!

BERNARD: Take it easy, kid.

WILLY: Let me talk to you—I got nobody to talk to. Bernard, Bernard, was it my fault? Y'see? It keeps going around in my mind, maybe I did something to him. I got nothing to give him.

BERNARD: Don't take it so hard.

WILLY: Why did he lay down? What is the story there? You were his friend!

BERNARD: Willy, I remember, it was June, and our grades came out. And he'd flunked math.

WILLY: That son-of-a-bitch!

BERNARD: No, it wasn't right then. Biff just got very angry, I remember, and he was ready to enroll in summer school.

WILLY (surprised): He was?

BERNARD: He wasn't beaten by it at all. But then, Willy, he disappeared from the block for almost a month. And I got the idea that he'd gone up to New England to see you. Did he have a talk with you then?

WILLY stares in silence.

BERNARD: Willy?

WILLY (with a strong edge of resentment in his voice): Yeah, he came to Boston. What about it?

BERNARD: Well, just that when he came back—I'll never forget this, it always mystifies me. Because I'd thought so well of Biff, even though he'd always taken advantage of me. I loved him, Willy, y'know? And he came back after that month and took his sneakers—remember those sneakers with "University of Virginia" printed on them? He was so proud of those, wore them every day. And he took them down in the cellar, and burned them up in the furnace. We had a fist fight. It lasted at least half an hour. Just the two of us, punching each other down the cellar, and crying right through it. I've often thought of how strange it was that I knew he'd given up his life. What happened in Boston, Willy?

WILLY looks at him as at an intruder.

BERNARD: I just bring it up because you asked me.

WILLY (angrily): Nothing. What do you mean, "What happened?" What's that got to do with anything?

BERNARD: Well, don't get sore.

WILLY: What are you trying to do, blame it on me? If a boy lays down is that my fault?

BERNARD: Now, Willy, don't get—

WILLY: Well, don't—don't talk to me that way! What does that mean, "What happened?"

CHARLEY *enters. He is in his vest, and he carries a bottle of bourbon.*

CHARLEY: Hey, you're going to miss that train. (*He waves the bottle.*)

BERNARD: Yeah, I'm going. (*He takes the bottle.*) Thanks, Pop. (*He picks up his rackets and bag.*) Good-by, Willy, and don't worry about it. You know, "If at first you don't succeed . . ."

WILLY: Yes, I believe in that.

BERNARD: But sometimes, Willy, it's better for a man just to walk away.

WILLY: Walk away?

BERNARD: That's right.

WILLY: But if you can't walk away?

BERNARD (*after a slight pause*): I guess that's when it's tough. (*extending his hand*) Good-by, Willy.

WILLY (*shaking* BERNARD'S *hand*): Good-by, boy.

CHARLEY (*an arm on* BERNARD'S *shoulder*): How do you like this kid? Gonna argue a case in front of the Supreme Court.

BERNARD (*protesting*): Pop!

WILLY (*genuinely shocked, pained, and happy*): No! The Supreme Court!

BERNARD: I gotta run. 'By, Dad!

CHARLEY: Knock 'em dead, Bernard!

BERNARD *goes off.*

WILLY (*as* CHARLEY *takes out his wallet*): The Supreme Court! And he didn't even mention it!

CHARLEY (*counting out money on the desk*): He don't have to—he's gonna do it.

WILLY: And you never told him what to do, did you? You never took any interest in him.

CHARLEY: My salvation is that I never took any interest in anything. There's some money—fifty dollars. I got an accountant inside.

WILLY: Charley, look . . . (*with difficulty*) I got my insurance to pay. If you can manage it—I need a hundred and ten dollars.

CHARLEY *doesn't reply for a moment; merely stops moving.*

WILLY: I'd draw it from my bank but Linda would know, and I . . .

CHARLEY: Sit down, Willy.

WILLY (*moving toward the chair*): I'm keeping an account of everything, remember. I'll pay every penny back. (*He sits.*)

CHARLEY: Now listen to me, Willy.

WILLY: I want you to know I appreciate . . .

CHARLEY (*sitting down on the table*): Willy, what're you doin'? What the hell is goin' on in your head?

WILLY: Why? I'm simply . . .

CHARLEY: I offered you a job. You can make fifty dollars a week. And I won't send you on the road.

WILLY: I've got a job.

CHARLEY: Without pay? What kind of a job is a job without pay? (*He rises.*) Now, look, kid, enough is enough. I'm no genius but I know when I'm being insulted.

WILLY: Insulted!

CHARLEY: Why don't you want to work for me?

WILLY: What's the matter with you? I've got a job.

CHARLEY: Then what're you walkin' in here every week for?

WILLY (*getting up*): Well, if you don't want me to walk in here—

CHARLEY: I am offering you a job.

WILLY: I don't want your goddam job!

CHARLEY: When the hell are you going to grow up?

WILLY (*furiously*): You big ignoramus, if you say that to me again I'll rap you one! I don't care how big you are! (*He's ready to fight.*)

Pause.

CHARLEY (*kindly, going to him*): How much do you need, Willy?

WILLY: Charley, I'm strapped, I'm strapped. I don't know what to do. I was just fired.

CHARLEY: Howard fired you?

WILLY: That snotnose. Imagine that? I named him. I named him Howard.

CHARLEY: Willy, when're you gonna realize that them things don't mean anything? You named him Howard, but you can't sell that. The only thing you got in this world is what you can sell. And the funny thing is that you're a salesman, and you don't know that.

WILLY: I've always tried to think otherwise, I guess. I always felt that if a man was impressive, and well liked, that nothing—

CHARLEY: Why must everybody like you? Who liked J. P. Morgan? Was he impressive? In a Turkish bath he'd look like a butcher. But with his pockets on he was very well liked. Now listen, Willy, I know you don't like me, and nobody can say I'm in love with you, but I'll give you a job because—just for the hell of it, put it that way. Now what do you say?

WILLY: I—I just can't work for you, Charley.

CHARLEY: What're you, jealous of me?

WILLY: I can't work for you, that's all, don't ask me why.

CHARLEY (*angered, taking out more bills*): You been jealous of me all your life, you damned fool! Here, pay your insurance. (*He puts the money in* WILLY'S *hand.*)

WILLY: I'm keeping strict accounts.

CHARLEY: I've got some work to do. Take care of yourself. And pay your insurance.

WILLY (*moving to the right*): Funny, y'know? After all the highways, and the trains, and the appointments, and the years, you end up worth more dead than alive.

CHARLEY: Willy, nobody's worth nothin' dead. (*after a slight pause*) Did you hear what I said?

WILLY *stands still, dreaming.*

CHARLEY: Willy!

WILLY: Apologize to Bernard for me when you see him. I didn't mean to argue with him. He's a fine boy. They're all fine boys, and they'll end up big—all of them. Someday they'll all play tennis together. Wish me luck, Charley. He saw Bill Oliver today.

CHARLEY: Good luck.

WILLY (*on the verge of tears*): Charley, you're the only friend I got. Isn't that a remarkable thing? (*He goes out.*)

CHARLEY: Jesus!

CHARLEY *stares after him a moment and follows. All light blacks out. Suddenly raucous music is heard, and a red glow rises behind the screen at right.* STANLEY, *a young waiter, appears, carrying a table, followed by* HAPPY, *who is carrying two chairs.*

STANLEY (*putting the table down*): That's all right, Mr. Loman, I can handle it myself. (*He turns and takes the chairs from* HAPPY *and places them at the table.*)

HAPPY (*glancing around*): Oh, this is better.

STANLEY: Sure, in the front there you're in the middle of all kinds of noise. Whenever you got a party, Mr. Loman, you just tell me and I'll put you back here. Y'know, there's a lotta people they don't like it private, because when they go out they like to see a lotta action around them because they're sick and tired to stay in the house by theirself. But I know you, you ain't from Hackensack. You know what I mean?

HAPPY (*sitting down*): So how's it coming, Stanley?

STANLEY: Ah, it's a dog's life. I only wish during the war they'd a took me in the Army. I coulda been dead by now.

HAPPY: My brother's back, Stanley.

STANLEY: Oh, he come back, heh? From the Far West.

HAPPY: Yeah, big cattle man, my brother, so treat him right. And my father's coming too.

STANLEY: Oh, your father too!

HAPPY: You got a couple of nice lobsters?

STANLEY: Hundred per cent, big.

HAPPY: I want them with the claws.

STANLEY: Don't worry, I don't give you no mice. (HAPPY *laughs.*) How about some wine? It'll put a head on the meal.

HAPPY: No. You remember, Stanley, that recipe I brought you from overseas? With the champagne in it?

STANLEY: Oh, yeah, sure. I still got it tacked up yet in the kitchen. But that'll have to cost a buck apiece anyways.

HAPPY: That's all right.

STANLEY: What'd you, hit a number or somethin'?

HAPPY: No, it's a little celebration. My brother is—I think he pulled off a big deal today. I think we're going into business together.

STANLEY: Great! That's the best for you. Because a family business, you know what I mean?—that's the best.

HAPPY: That's what I think.

STANLEY: 'Cause what's the difference? Somebody steals? It's in the family. Know what I mean? (*sotto voce*) Like this bartender here. The boss is goin' crazy what kinda leak he's got in the cash register. You put it in but it don't come out.

HAPPY (*raising his head*): Sh!

STANLEY: What?

HAPPY: You notice I wasn't lookin' right or left, was I?

STANLEY: No.

HAPPY: And my eyes are closed.

STANLEY: So what's the—?

HAPPY: Strudel's comin'.

STANLEY (*catching on, looks around*): Ah, no, there's no—

He breaks off as a furred, lavishly dressed girl enters and sits at the next table. Both follow her with their eyes.

STANLEY: Geez, how'd ya know?

HAPPY: I got radar or something. (*staring directly at her profile*) Oooooooo . . . Stanley.

STANLEY: I think that's for you, Mr. Loman.

HAPPY: Look at that mouth. Oh, God. And the binoculars.

STANLEY: Geez, you got a life, Mr. Loman.

HAPPY: Wait on her.

STANLEY (*going to the girl's table*): Would you like a menu, ma'am?

GIRL: I'm expecting someone, but I'd like a—

HAPPY: Why don't you bring her—excuse me, miss, do you mind? I sell champagne, and I'd like you to try my brand. Bring her a champagne, Stanley.

GIRL: That's awfully nice of you.

HAPPY: Don't mention it. It's all company money. (*He laughs.*)

GIRL: That's a charming product to be selling, isn't it?

HAPPY: Oh, gets to be like everything else. Selling is selling, y'know.

GIRL: I suppose.

HAPPY: You don't happen to sell, do you?

GIRL: No, I don't sell.

HAPPY: Would you object to a compliment from a stranger? You ought to be on a magazine cover.

GIRL (*looking at him a little archly*): I have been.

STANLEY *comes in with a glass of champagne.*

HAPPY: What'd I say before, Stanley? You see? She's a cover girl.

STANLEY: Oh, I could see, I could see.

HAPPY (*to the girl*): What magazine?

GIRL: Oh, a lot of them. (*She takes the drink.*) Thank you.

HAPPY: You know what they say in France, don't you? "Champagne is the drink of the complexion"—Hiya, Biff!

BIFF *has entered and sits with* HAPPY.

BIFF: Hello, kid. Sorry I'm late.

HAPPY: I just got here. Uh, Miss—?

GIRL: Forsythe.

HAPPY: Miss Forsythe, this is my brother.

BIFF: Is Dad here?

HAPPY: His name is Biff. You might've heard of him. Great football player.

GIRL: Really? What team?

HAPPY: Are you familiar with football?

GIRL: No, I'm afraid I'm not.

HAPPY: Biff is quarterback with the New York Giants.

GIRL: Well, that is nice, isn't it? (*She drinks.*)

HAPPY: Good health.

GIRL: I'm happy to meet you.

HAPPY: That's my name. Hap. It's really Harold, but at West Point they called me Happy.

GIRL (*now really impressed*): Oh, I see. How do you do? (*She turns her profile.*)

BIFF: Isn't Dad coming?

HAPPY: You want her?

BIFF: Oh, I could never make that.

HAPPY: I remember the time that idea would never come into your head. Where's the old confidence, Biff?

BIFF: I just saw Oliver—

HAPPY: Wait a minute. I've got to see that old confidence again. Do you want her? She's on call.

BIFF: Oh, no. (*He turns to look at the girl.*)

HAPPY: I'm telling you. Watch this. (*turning to the girl*) Honey? (*She turns to him.*) Are you busy?

GIRL: Well, I am . . . but I could make a phone call.

HAPPY: Do that, will you, honey? And see if you can get a friend. We'll be here for a while. Biff is one of the greatest football players in the country.

GIRL (*standing up*): Well, I'm certainly happy to meet you.

HAPPY: Come back soon.

GIRL: I'll try.

HAPPY: Don't try, honey, try hard.

The girl exits. STANLEY *follows, shaking his head in bewildered admiration.*

HAPPY: Isn't that a shame now? A beautiful girl like that? That's why I can't get married. There's not a good woman in a thousand. New York is loaded with them, kid!

BIFF: Hap, look—

HAPPY: I told you she was on call!

BIFF (*strangely unnerved*): Cut it out, will ya? I want to say something to you.

HAPPY: Did you see Oliver?

BIFF: I saw him all right. Now look, I want to tell Dad a couple of things and I want you to help me.

HAPPY: What? Is he going to back you?

BIFF: Are you crazy? You're out of your goddam head, you know that?

HAPPY: Why? What happened?

BIFF (*breathlessly*): I did a terrible thing today, Hap. It's been the strangest day I ever went through. I'm all numb, I swear.

HAPPY: You mean he wouldn't see you?

BIFF: Well, I waited six hours for him, see? All day. Kept sending my name in. Even tried to date his secretary so she'd get me to him, but no soap.

HAPPY: Because you're not showin' the old confidence, Biff. He remembered you, didn't he?

BIFF (*stopping* HAPPY *with a gesture*): Finally, about five o'clock, he comes out. Didn't remember who I was or anything. I felt like such an idiot, Hap.

HAPPY: Did you tell him my Florida idea?

BIFF: He walked away. I saw him for one minute. I got so mad I could've torn the walls down! How the hell did I ever get the idea I was a salesman there? I even believed myself that I'd been a salesman for him! And then he gave me one look and—I realized what a ridiculous lie my whole life has been! We've been talking in a dream for fifteen years. I was a shipping clerk.

HAPPY: What'd you do?

BIFF (*with great tension and wonder*): Well, he left, see. And the secretary went out. I was all alone in the waiting room. I don't know what came over me, Hap. The next thing I know I'm in his office—paneled walls, everything. I can't explain it. I—Hap, I took his fountain pen.

HAPPY: Geez, did he catch you?

BIFF: I ran out. I ran down all eleven flights. I ran and ran and ran.

HAPPY: That was an awful dumb—what'd you do that for?

BIFF (*agonized*): I don't know, I just—wanted to take something, I don't know. You gotta help me, Hap, I'm gonna tell Pop.

HAPPY: You crazy? What for?

BIFF: Hap, he's got to understand that I'm not the man somebody lends that kind of money to. He thinks I've been spiting him all these years and it's eating him up.

HAPPY: That's just it. You tell him something nice.

BIFF: I can't.

HAPPY: Say you got a lunch date with Oliver tomorrow.

BIFF: So what do I do tomorrow?

HAPPY: You leave the house tomorrow and come back at night and say Oliver is thinking it over. And he thinks it over for a couple of weeks, and gradually it fades away and nobody's the worse.

BIFF: But it'll go on forever!

HAPPY: Dad is never so happy as when he's looking forward to something!

WILLY *enters.*

HAPPY: Hello, scout!

WILLY: Gee, I haven't been here in years!

STANLEY *has followed* WILLY *in and sets a chair for him.* STANLEY *starts off but* HAPPY *stops him.*

HAPPY: Stanley!

STANLEY *stands by, waiting for an order.*

BIFF (*going to* WILLY *with guilt, as to an invalid*): Sit down, Pop. You want a drink?

WILLY: Sure, I don't mind.

BIFF: Let's get a load on.

WILLY: You look worried.

BIFF: N-no. (*to* STANLEY) Scotch all around. Make it doubles.

STANLEY: Doubles, right. (*He goes.*)

WILLY: You had a couple already, didn't you?

BIFF: Just a couple, yeah.

WILLY: Well, what happened, boy? (*nodding affirmatively, with a smile*) Everything go all right?

BIFF (*takes a breath, then reaches out and grasps* WILLY's *hand*): Pal . . . (*He is smiling bravely, and* WILLY *is smiling too.*) I had an experience today.

HAPPY: Terrific, Pop.

WILLY: That so? What happened?

BIFF (*high, slightly alcoholic, above the earth*): I'm going to tell you everything from first to last. It's been a strange day. (*Silence. He looks around, composes himself as best he can, but his breath keeps breaking the rhythm of his voice.*) I had to wait quite a while for him, and—

WILLY: Oliver?

BIFF: Yeah, Oliver. All day, as a matter of cold fact. And a lot of—instances—facts, Pop, facts about my life came back to me. Who was it, Pop? Who ever said I was a salesman with Oliver?

WILLY: Well, you were.

BIFF: No, Dad, I was a shipping clerk.

WILLY: But you were practically—

BIFF (*with determination*): Dad, I don't know who said it first, but I was never a salesman for Bill Oliver.

WILLY: What're you talking about?

BIFF: Let's hold on to the facts tonight, Pop. We're not going to get anywhere bullin' around. I was a shipping clerk.

WILLY (*angrily*): All right, now listen to me—

BIFF: Why don't you let me finish?

WILLY: I'm not interested in stories about the past or any crap of that kind because the woods are burning, boys, you understand? There's a big blaze going on all around. I was fired today.

BIFF (*shocked*): How could you be?

WILLY: I was fired, and I'm looking for a little good news to tell your mother, because the woman has waited and the woman has suffered. The gist of it is that I haven't got a story left in my head, Biff. So don't give me a lecture about facts and aspects. I am not interested. Now what've you got to say to me?

STANLEY *enters with three drinks. They wait until he leaves.*

WILLY: Did you see Oliver?

BIFF: Jesus, Dad!

WILLY: You mean you didn't go up there?

HAPPY: Sure he went up there.

BIFF: I did. I—saw him. How could they fire you?

WILLY (*on the edge of his chair*): What kind of a welcome did he give you?

BIFF: He won't even let you work on commission?

WILLY: I'm out! (*driving*) So tell me, he gave you a warm welcome?

HAPPY: Sure, Pop, sure!

BIFF (*driven*): Well, it was kind of—

WILLY: I was wondering if he'd remember you. (*to* HAPPY) Imagine, man doesn't see him for ten, twelve years and gives him that kind of a welcome!

HAPPY: Damn right!

BIFF (*trying to return to the offensive*): Pop, look—

WILLY: You know why he remembered you, don't you? Because you impressed him in those days.

BIFF: Let's talk quietly and get this down to the facts, huh?

WILLY (*as though* BIFF *had been interrupting*): Well, what happened? It's great news, Biff. Did he take you into his office or'd you talk in the waiting room?

BIFF: Well, he came in, see, and—

WILLY (*with a big smile*): What'd he say? Betcha he threw his arm around you.

BIFF: Well, he kinda—

WILLY: He's a fine man. (*to* HAPPY) Very hard man to see, y'know.

HAPPY (*agreeing*): Oh, I know.

WILLY (*to* BIFF): Is that where you had the drinks?

BIFF: Yeah, he gave me a couple of—no, no!

HAPPY (*cutting in*): He told him my Florida idea.

WILLY: Don't interrupt. (*to* BIFF) How'd he react to the Florida idea?

BIFF: Dad, will you give me a minute to explain?

WILLY: I've been waiting for you to explain since I sat down here! What happened? He took you into his office and what?

BIFF: Well—I talked. And—and he listened, see.

WILLY: Famous for the way he listens, y'know. What was his answer?

BIFF: His answer was—(*He breaks off, suddenly angry.*) Dad, you're not letting me tell you what I want to tell you!

WILLY (*accusing, angered*): You didn't see him, did you?

BIFF: I did see him!

WILLY: What'd you insult him or something? You insulted him, didn't you?

BIFF: Listen, will you let me out of it, will you just let me out of it!

HAPPY: What the hell!

WILLY: Tell me what happened!

BIFF (*to* HAPPY): I can't talk to him!

A single trumpet note jars the ear. The light of green leaves stains the house, which holds the air of night and a dream. YOUNG BERNARD *enters and knocks on the door of the house.*

YOUNG BERNARD (*frantically*): Mrs. Loman, Mrs. Loman!

HAPPY: Tell him what happened!

BIFF (*to* HAPPY): Shut up and leave me alone!

WILLY: No, no! You had to go and flunk math!

BIFF: What math? What're you talking about?

YOUNG BERNARD: Mrs. Loman, Mrs. Loman!

LINDA *appears in the house, as of old.*

WILLY (*wildly*): Math, math, math!

BIFF: Take it easy, Pop!

YOUNG BERNARD: Mrs. Loman!

WILLY (*furiously*): If you hadn't flunked you'd've been set by now!

BIFF: Now, look, I'm gonna tell you what happened, and you're going to listen to me.

YOUNG BERNARD: Mrs. Loman!

BIFF: I waited six hours—

HAPPY: What the hell are you saying?

BIFF: I kept sending in my name but he wouldn't see me. So finally he . . . (*He continues unheard as light fades low on the restaurant.*)

YOUNG BERNARD: Biff flunked math!

LINDA: No!

YOUNG BERNARD: Birnbaum flunked him! They won't graduate him!

LINDA: But they have to. He's gotta go to the university. Where is he? Biff! Biff!

YOUNG BERNARD: No, he left. He went to Grand Central.

LINDA: Grand—You mean he went to Boston!

YOUNG BERNARD: Is Uncle Willy in Boston?

LINDA: Oh, maybe Willy can talk to the teacher. Oh, the poor, poor boy!

Light on house area snaps out.

BIFF (*at the table, now audible, holding up a gold fountain pen*): . . . so I'm washed up with Oliver, you understand? Are you listening to me?

WILLY (*at a loss*): Yeah, sure. If you hadn't flunked—

BIFF: Flunked what? What're you talking about?

WILLY: Don't blame everything on me! I didn't flunk math—you did! What pen?

HAPPY: That was awful dumb, Biff, a pen like that is worth—

WILLY (*seeing the pen for the first time*): You took Oliver's pen?

BIFF (*weakening*): Dad, I just explained it to you.

WILLY: You stole Bill Oliver's fountain pen!

BIFF: I didn't exactly steal it! That's just what I've been explaining to you!

HAPPY: He had it in his hand and just then Oliver walked in, so he got nervous and stuck it in his pocket!

WILLY: My God, Biff!

BIFF: I never intended to do it, Dad!

OPERATOR'S VOICE: Standish Arms, good evening!

WILLY (*shouting*): I'm not in my room!

BIFF (*frightened*): Dad, what's the matter? (*He and* HAPPY *stand up.*)

OPERATOR: Ringing Mr. Loman for you!

WILLY: I'm not there, stop it!

BIFF (*horrified, gets down on one knee before* WILLY): Dad, I'll make good, I'll make good. (WILLY *tries to get to his feet.* BIFF *holds him down.*) Sit down now.

WILLY: No, you're no good, you're no good for anything.

BIFF: I am, Dad, I'll find something else, you understand? Now don't worry about anything. (*He holds up* WILLY's *face.*) Talk to me, Dad.

OPERATOR: Mr. Loman does not answer. Shall I page him?

WILLY (*attempting to stand, as though to rush and silence the* OPERATOR): No, no, no!

HAPPY: He'll strike something, Pop.

WILLY: No, no . . .

BIFF (*desperately, standing over* WILLY): Pop, listen! Listen to me! I'm telling you something good. Oliver talked to his partner about the Florida idea. You listening? He—he talked to his partner, and he came to me . . . I'm going to be all right, you hear? Dad, listen to me, he said it was just a question of the amount!

WILLY: Then you . . . got it?

HAPPY: He's gonna be terrific, Pop!

WILLY (*trying to stand*): Then you got it, haven't you? You got it! You got it!

BIFF (*agonized, holds* WILLY *down*): No, no. Look, Pop. I'm supposed to have lunch with them tomorrow. I'm just telling you this so you'll know that I can still make an impression, Pop. And I'll make good somewhere, but I can't go tomorrow, see?

WILLY: Why not? You simply—

BIFF: But the pen, Pop!

WILLY: You give it to him and tell him it was an oversight!

HAPPY: Sure, have lunch tomorrow!

BIFF: I can't say that—

WILLY: You were doing a crossword puzzle and accidentally used his pen!

BIFF: Listen, kid, I took those balls years ago, now I walk in with his fountain pen? That clinches it, don't you see? I can't face him like that! I'll try elsewhere.

PAGE'S VOICE: Paging Mr. Loman!

WILLY: Don't you want to be anything?

BIFF: Pop, how can I go back?

WILLY: You don't want to be anything, is that what's behind it?

BIFF (*now angry at* WILLY *for not crediting his sympathy*): Don't take it that way! You think it was easy walking into that office after what I'd done to him? A team of horses couldn't have dragged me back to Bill Oliver!

WILLY: Then why'd you go?

BIFF: Why did I go? Why did I go! Look at you! Look at what's become of you!

Off left, THE WOMAN *laughs.*

WILLY: Biff, you're going to go to that lunch tomorrow, or—

BIFF: I can't go. I've got no appointment!

HAPPY: Biff, for . . . !

WILLY: Are you spiting me?

BIFF: Don't take it that way! Goddammit!

WILLY (*He strikes* BIFF *and falters away from the table.*): You rotten little louse! Are you spiting me?

THE WOMAN: Someone's at the door, Willy!

BIFF: I'm no good, can't you see what I am?

HAPPY (*separating them*): Hey, you're in a restaurant! Now cut it out, both of you! (*The girls enter.*) Hello, girls, sit down.

THE WOMAN *laughs, off left.*

MISS FORSYTHE: I guess we might as well. This is Letta.

THE WOMAN: Willy, are you going to wake up?

BIFF (*ignoring* WILLY): How're ya, miss, sit down. What do you drink?

MISS FORSYTHE: Letta might not be able to stay long.

LETTA: I gotta get up very early tomorrow. I got jury duty. I'm so excited! Were you fellows ever on a jury?

BIFF: No, but I been in front of them! (*The girls laugh.*) This is my father.

LETTA: Isn't he cute? Sit down with us, Pop.

HAPPY: Sit him down, Biff!

BIFF (*going to him*): Come on, slugger, drink us under the table. To hell with it! Come on, sit down, pal.

On BIFF'S *last insistence,* WILLY *is about to sit.*

THE WOMAN (*now urgently*): Willy, are you going to answer the door!

THE WOMAN'S *call pulls* WILLY *back. He starts right, befuddled.*

BIFF: Hey, where are you going?

WILLY: Open the door.

BIFF: The door?

WILLY: The washroom . . . the door . . . where's the door?

BIFF (*leading* WILLY *to the left*): Just go straight down.

WILLY *moves left.*

THE WOMAN: Willy, Willy, are you going to get up, get up, get up, get up?

WILLY *exits left.*

LETTA: I think it's sweet you bring your daddy along.

MISS FORSYTHE: Oh, he isn't really your father!

BIFF (*at left, turning to her resentfully*): Miss Forsythe, you've just seen a prince walk by. A fine, troubled prince. A hard-working, unappreciated prince. A pal, you understand? A good companion. Always for his boys.

LETTA: That's so sweet.

HAPPY: Well, girls, what's the program? We're wasting time. Come on, Biff. Gather round. Where would you like to go?

BIFF: Why don't you do something for him?

HAPPY: Me!

BIFF: Don't you give a damn for him, Hap?

HAPPY: What're you talking about? I'm the one who—

BIFF: I sense it, you don't give a good goddam about him. (*He takes the rolled-up hose from his pocket and puts it on the table in front of* HAPPY.) Look what I found in the cellar, for Christ's sake. How can you bear to let it go on?

HAPPY: Me? Who goes away? Who runs off and—

BIFF: Yeah, but he doesn't mean anything to you. You could help him—I can't! Don't you understand what I'm talking about? He's going to kill himself, don't you know that?

HAPPY: Don't I know it! Me!

BIFF: Hap, help him! Jesus . . . help him . . . Help me, help me, I can't bear to look at his face! (*Ready to weep, he hurries out, up right.*)

HAPPY (*starting after him*): Where are you going?

MISS FORSYTHE: What's he so mad about?

HAPPY: Come on girls, we'll catch up with him.

MISS FORSYTHE (*as* HAPPY *pushes her out*): Say, I don't like that temper of his!

HAPPY: He's just a little overstrung, he'll be all right!

WILLY (*off left, as* THE WOMAN *laughs*): Don't answer! Don't answer!

LETTA: Don't you want to tell your father—

HAPPY: No, that's not my father. He's just a guy. Come on, we'll catch Biff, and, honey, we're going to paint this town! Stanley, where's the check! Hey, Stanley!

They exit. STANLEY *looks toward left.*

STANLEY (*calling to* HAPPY *indignantly*): Mr. Loman! Mr. Loman!

STANLEY *picks up a chair and follows them off. Knocking is heard off left.* THE WOMAN *enters, laughing.* WILLY *follows her. She is in a black slip; he is buttoning his shirt. Raw, sensuous music accompanies their speech.*

WILLY: Will you stop laughing? Will you stop?

THE WOMAN: Aren't you going to answer the door? He'll wake the whole hotel.

WILLY: I'm not expecting anybody.

THE WOMAN: Whyn't you have another drink, honey, and stop being so damn self-centered?

WILLY: I'm so lonely.

THE WOMAN: You know you ruined me, Willy? From now on, whenever you come to the office, I'll see that you go right through to the buyers. No waiting at my desk any more, Willy. You ruined me.

WILLY: That's nice of you to say that.

THE WOMAN: Gee, you are self-centered! Why so sad? You are the saddest, self-centeredest soul I ever did see-saw. (*She laughs. He kisses her.*) Come on inside, drummer boy. It's silly to be dressing in the middle of the night. (*as knocking is heard*) Aren't you going to answer the door?

WILLY: They're knocking on the wrong door.

THE WOMAN: But I felt the knocking. And he heard us talking in here. Maybe the hotel's on fire!

WILLY (*his terror rising*): It's a mistake.

THE WOMAN: Then tell him to go away!

WILLY: There's nobody there.

THE WOMAN: It's getting on my nerves, Willy. There's somebody standing out there and it's getting on my nerves!

WILLY (*pushing her away from him*): All right, stay in the bathroom here, and don't come out. I think there's a law in Massachusetts about it, so don't come out. It may be that new room clerk. He looked very mean. So don't come out. It's a mistake, there's no fire.

The knocking is heard again. He takes a few steps away from her, and she vanishes into the wing. The light follows him, and now he is facing YOUNG BIFF, *who carries a suitcase.* BIFF *steps toward him. The music is gone.*

BIFF: Why didn't you answer?

WILLY: Biff! What are you doing in Boston?

BIFF: Why didn't you answer? I've been knocking for five minutes, I called you on the phone—

WILLY: I just heard you. I was in the bathroom and had the door shut. Did anything happen home?

BIFF: Dad—I let you down.

WILLY: What do you mean?

BIFF: Dad . . .

WILLY: Biffo, what's this about? (*putting his arm around* BIFF) Come on, let's go downstairs and get you a malted.

BIFF: Dad, I flunked math.

WILLY: Not for the term?

BIFF: The term. I haven't got enough credits to graduate.

WILLY: You mean to say Bernard wouldn't give you the answers?

BIFF: He did, he tried, but I only got a sixty-one.

WILLY: And they wouldn't give you four points?

BIFF: Birnbaum refused absolutely. I begged him, Pop, but he won't give me those points. You gotta talk to him before they close the school. Because if he saw the kind of man you are, and you just talked to him in your way, I'm sure he'd come through for me. The class came right before practice, see, and I didn't go enough. Would you talk to him? He'd like you, Pop. You know the way you could talk.

WILLY: You're on. We'll drive right back.

BIFF: Oh, Dad, good work! I'm sure he'll change it for you!

WILLY: Go downstairs and tell the clerk I'm checkin' out. Go right down.

BIFF: Yes, sir! See, the reason he hates me, Pop—one day he was late for class so I got up at the blackboard and imitated him. I crossed my eyes and talked with a lithp.

WILLY (*laughing*): You did? The kids like it?

BIFF: They nearly died laughing!

WILLY: Yeah? What'd you do?

BIFF: The thquare root of thixthy twee is . . . (WILLY *bursts out laughing;* BIFF *joins him.*) And in the middle of it he walked in!

WILLY *laughs, and* THE WOMAN *joins in offstage.*

WILLY (*without hesitation*): Hurry downstairs and—

BIFF: Somebody in there?

WILLY: No, that was next door.

THE WOMAN *laughs offstage.*

BIFF: Somebody got in your bathroom!

WILLY: No, it's the next room, there's a party—

THE WOMAN (*Enters, laughing. She lisps this.*): Can I come in? There's something in the bathtub, Willy, and it's moving!

WILLY *looks at* BIFF, *who is staring open-mouthed and horrified at* THE WOMAN.

WILLY: Ah—you better go back to your room. They must be finished painting by now. They're painting her room so I let her take a shower here. Go back, go back . . . (*He pushes her.*)

THE WOMAN (*resisting*): But I've got to get dressed, Willy, I can't—

WILLY: Get out of here! Go back, go back . . . (*suddenly striving for the ordinary*) This is Miss Francis, Biff, she's a buyer. They're painting her room. Go back, Miss Francis, go back . . .

THE WOMAN: But my clothes, I can't go out naked in the hall!

WILLY (*pushing her offstage*): Get outa here! Go back, go back!

BIFF *slowly sits down on his suitcase as the argument continues offstage.*

THE WOMAN: Where's my stockings? You promised me stockings, Willy!

WILLY: I have no stockings here!

THE WOMAN: You had two boxes of size nine sheers for me, and I want them!

WILLY: Here, for God's sake, will you get outa here!

THE WOMAN (*entering, holding a box of stockings*): I just hope there's nobody in the hall. That's all I hope. (*to* BIFF) Are you football or baseball?

BIFF: Football.

THE WOMAN (*angry, humiliated*): That's me too. G'night. (*She snatches her clothes from* WILLY, *and walks out.*)

WILLY (*after a pause*): Well, better get going. I want to get to the school first thing in the morning. Get my suits out of the closet. I'll get my valise. (BIFF *doesn't move.*) What's the matter? (BIFF *remains motionless, tears falling.*) She's a buyer. Buys for J. H. Simmons. She lives down the hall—they're painting. You don't imagine—(*He breaks off. After a pause.*) Now listen, pal, she's just a buyer. She sees merchandise in her room and they have to keep it looking just so . . . (*Pause. Assuming command.*) All right, get my suits. (BIFF *doesn't move.*) Now stop crying and do as I say. I gave you an order. Biff, I gave you an order! Is that what you do when I give you an order? How dare you cry! (*putting his arm around* BIFF) Now look, Biff, when you grow up you'll understand about these things. You mustn't—you mustn't overemphasize a thing like this. I'll see Birnbaum first thing in the morning.

BIFF: Never mind.

WILLY (*getting down beside* BIFF): Never mind! He's going to give you those points. I'll see to it.

BIFF: He wouldn't listen to you.

WILLY: He certainly will listen to me. You need those points for the U. of Virginia.

BIFF: I'm not going there.

WILLY: Heh? If I can't get him to change that mark you'll make it up in summer school. You've got all summer to—

BIFF (*his weeping breaking from him*): Dad . . .

WILLY (*infected by it*): Oh, my boy . . .

BIFF: Dad . . .

WILLY: She's nothing to me, Biff. I was lonely, I was terribly lonely.

BIFF: You—you gave her Mama's stockings! (*His tears break through and he rises to go.*)

WILLY (*grabbing for* BIFF): I gave you an order!

BIFF: Don't touch me, you—liar!

WILLY: Apologize for that!

BIFF: You fake! You phony little fake! You fake! (*Overcome, he turns quickly and weeping fully goes out with his suitcase.* WILLY *is left on the floor on his knees.*)

WILLY: I gave you an order! Biff, come back here or I'll beat you! Come back here! I'll whip you!

STANLEY *comes quickly in from the right and stands in front of* WILLY.

WILLY (*shouting at* STANLEY): I gave you an order . . .

STANLEY: Hey, let's pick it up, pick it up, Mr. Loman. (*He helps* WILLY *to his feet.*) Your boys left with the chippies. They said they'll see you home.

A second waiter watches some distance away.

WILLY: But we were supposed to have dinner together.

Music is heard, WILLY'S *theme.*

STANLEY: Can you make it?

WILLY: I'll—sure, I can make it. (*suddenly concerned about his clothes*) Do I—I look all right?

STANLEY: Sure, you look all right. (*He flicks a speck off* WILLY'S *lapel.*)

WILLY: Here—here's a dollar.

STANLEY: Oh, your son paid me. It's all right.

WILLY (*putting it in* STANLEY'S *hand*): No, take it. You're a good boy.

STANLEY: Oh, no, you don't have to . . .

WILLY: Here—here's some more, I don't need it any more. (*after a slight pause*) Tell me—is there a seed store in the neighborhood?

STANLEY: Seeds? You mean like to plant?

As WILLY *turns,* STANLEY *slips the money back into his jacket pocket.*

WILLY: Yes. Carrots, peas . . .

STANLEY: Well, there's hardware stores on Sixth Avenue, but it may be too late now.

WILLY (*anxiously*): Oh, I'd better hurry. I've got to get some seeds. (*He starts off to the right.*) I've got to get some seeds, right away. Nothing's planted. I don't have a thing in the ground.

WILLY *hurries out as the light goes down.* STANLEY *moves over to the right after him, watches him off. The other waiter has been staring at* WILLY.

STANLEY (*to the waiter*): Well, whatta you looking at?

The waiter picks up the chairs and moves off right. STANLEY *takes the table and follows him. The light fades on this area. There is a long pause, the sound of the flute coming over. The light gradually rises on the kitchen, which is empty.* HAPPY *appears at the door of the house, followed by* BIFF. HAPPY *is carrying a large bunch of long-stemmed roses. He enters the kitchen, looks around for* LINDA. *Not seeing her, he turns to* BIFF, *who is just outside the house door, and makes a gesture with his hands, indicating "Not here, I guess." He looks into the living room and freezes. Inside,*

LINDA, *unseen, is seated,* WILLY'S *coat on her lap. She rises ominously and quietly and moves toward* HAPPY, *who backs up into the kitchen, afraid.*

HAPPY: Hey, what're you doing up? (LINDA *says nothing but moves toward him implacably.*) Where's Pop? (*He keeps backing to the right, and now* LINDA *is in full view in the doorway to the living room.*) Is he sleeping?

LINDA: Where were you?

HAPPY (*trying to laugh it off*): We met two girls, Mom, very fine types. Here, we brought you some flowers. (*offering them to her*) Put them in your room, Ma.

She knocks them to the floor at BIFF'S *feet. He has now come inside and closed the door behind him. She stares at* BIFF, *silent.*

HAPPY: Now what'd you do that for? Mom, I want you to have some flowers—

LINDA (*cutting* HAPPY *off, violently to* BIFF): Don't you care whether he lives or dies?

HAPPY (*going to the stairs*): Come upstairs, Biff.

BIFF (*with a flare of disgust, to* HAPPY): Go away from me! (*to* LINDA) What do you mean, lives or dies? Nobody's dying around here, pal.

LINDA: Get out of my sight! Get out of here!

BIFF: I wanna see the boss.

LINDA: You're not going near him!

BIFF: Where is he? (*He moves into the living room and* LINDA *follows.*)

LINDA (*shouting after* BIFF): You invite him for dinner. He looks forward to it all day—(BIFF *appears in his parents' bedroom, looks around, and exits.*)—and then you desert him there. There's no stranger you'd do that to!

HAPPY: Why? He had a swell time with us. Listen, when I—(LINDA *comes back into the kitchen.*)—desert him I hope I don't outlive the day!

LINDA: Get out of here!

HAPPY: Now look, Mom . . .

LINDA: Did you have to go to women tonight? You and your lousy rotten whores!

BIFF *reenters the kitchen.*

HAPPY: Mom, all we did was follow Biff around trying to cheer him up! (*to* BIFF) Boy, what a night you gave me!

LINDA: Get out of here, both of you, and don't come back! I don't want you tormenting him any more. Go on now, get your things together! (*to* BIFF) You can sleep in his apartment. (*She starts to pick up the flowers and stops herself.*) Pick up this stuff, I'm not your maid any more. Pick it up, you bum, you!

HAPPY *turns his back to her in refusal.* BIFF *slowly moves over and gets down on his knees, picking up the flowers.*

LINDA: You're a pair of animals! Not one, not another living soul would have had the cruelty to walk out on that man in a restaurant!

BIFF (*not looking at her*): Is that what he said?

LINDA: He didn't have to say anything. He was so humiliated he nearly limped when he came in.

HAPPY: But, Mom, he had a great time with us—

BIFF (*cutting him off violently*): Shut up!

Without another word, HAPPY *goes upstairs.*

LINDA: You! You didn't even go in to see if he was all right!

BIFF (*still on the floor in front of* LINDA, *the flowers in his hand; with self-loathing*): No. Didn't. Didn't do a damned thing. How do you like that, heh? Left him babbling in a toilet.

LINDA: You louse. You . . .

BIFF: Now you hit it on the nose! (*He gets up, throws the flowers in the waste-basket.*) The scum of the earth, and you're looking at him!

LINDA: Get out of here!

BIFF: I gotta talk to the boss, Mom. Where is he?

LINDA: You're not going near him. Get out of this house!

BIFF (*with absolute assurance, determination*): No. We're gonna have an abrupt conversation, him and me.

LINDA: You're not talking to him!

Hammering is heard from outside the house, off right. BIFF *turns toward the noise.*

LINDA (*suddenly pleading*): Will you please leave him alone?

BIFF: What's he doing out there?

LINDA: He's planting the garden!

BIFF (*quietly*): Now? Oh, my God!

BIFF *moves outside,* LINDA *following. The light dies down on them and comes up on the center of the apron as* WILLY *walks into it. He is carrying a flashlight, a hoe, and a handful of seed packets. He raps the top of the hoe sharply to fix it firmly, and then moves to the left, measuring off the distance with his foot. He holds the flashlight to look at the seed packets, reading off the instructions. He is in the blue of night.*

WILLY: Carrots . . . quarter-inch apart. Rows . . . one-foot rows. (*He measures it off.*) One foot. (*He puts down a package and measures off.*) Beets. (*He puts down another package and measures again.*) Lettuce. (*He reads the package, puts it down.*) One foot—(*He breaks off as* BEN *appears at the right and moves slowly down to him.*) What a proposition, ts, ts. Terrific, terrific. 'Cause she's suffered, Ben, the woman has suffered. You understand me? A man can't go out the way he came in, Ben, a man has got to add up to something. You can't, you can't—(BEN *moves toward him as though to interrupt.*) You gotta consider, now. Don't answer so quick. Remember, it's a guaranteed twenty-thousand-dollar proposition. Now look, Ben, I want you to go through the ins and outs of this thing with me. I've got nobody to talk to, Ben, and the woman has suffered, you hear me?

BEN (*standing still, considering*): What's the proposition?

WILLY: It's twenty thousand dollars on the barrelhead. Guaranteed, gilt-edged, you understand?

BEN: You don't want to make a fool of yourself. They might not honor the policy.

WILLY: How can they dare refuse? Didn't I work like a coolie to meet every premium on the nose? And now they don't pay off? Impossible!

BEN: It's called a cowardly thing, William.

WILLY: Why? Does it take more guts to stand here the rest of my life ringing up a zero?

BEN (*yielding*): That's a point, William. (*He moves, thinking, turns.*) And twenty thousand—that *is* something one can feel with the hand, it is there.

WILLY (*now assured, with rising power*): Oh, Ben, that's the whole beauty of it! I see it like a diamond, shining in the dark, hard and rough, that I can pick up and touch in my hand. Not like—like an appointment! This would not be another damned-fool appointment, Ben, and it changes all the aspects. Because he thinks I'm nothing, see, and so he spites me. But the funeral—(*straightening up*) Ben, that funeral will be massive! They'll come from Maine, Massachusetts, Vermont, New Hampshire! All the old-timers with the strange license plates—that boy will be thunderstruck, Ben, because he never realized—I am known! Rhode Island, New York, New Jersey—I am known, Ben, and he'll see it with his eyes once and for all. He'll see what I am, Ben! He's in for a shock, that boy!

BEN (*coming down to the edge of the garden*): He'll call you a coward.

WILLY (*suddenly fearful*): No, that would be terrible.

BEN: Yes. And a damned fool.

WILLY: No, no, he mustn't, I won't have that! (*He is broken and desperate.*)

BEN: He'll hate you, William.

The gay music of the Boys is heard.

WILLY: Oh, Ben, how do we get back to all the great times? Used to be so full of light, and comradeship, the sleigh-riding in winter, and the ruddiness on his cheeks. And always some kind of good news coming up, always something nice coming up ahead. And never even let me carry the valises in the house, and simonizing, simonizing that little red car! Why, why can't I give him something and not have him hate me?

BEN: Let me think about it. (*He glances at his watch.*) I still have a little time. Remarkable proposition, but you've got to be sure you're not making a fool of yourself.

BEN *drifts off upstage and goes out of sight.* BIFF *comes down from the left.*

WILLY (*suddenly conscious of* BIFF, *turns and looks up at him, then begins picking up the packages of seeds in confusion*): Where the hell is that seed? (*indignantly*) You can't see nothing out here! They boxed in the whole goddam neighborhood!

BIFF: There are people all around here. Don't you realize that?

WILLY: I'm busy. Don't bother me.

BIFF (*taking the hoe from* WILLY): I'm saying good-by to you, Pop. (WILLY *looks at him, silent, unable to move.*) I'm not coming back any more.

WILLY: You're not going to see Oliver tomorrow?

BIFF: I've got no appointment, Dad.

WILLY: He put his arm around you, and you've got no appointment?

BIFF: Pop, get this now, will you? Every time I've left it's been a fight that sent me out of here. Today I realized something about myself and I tried to explain it to you and I—I think I'm just not smart enough to make any sense out of it for you. To hell with whose fault it is or anything like that. (*He takes* WILLY's *arm.*) Let's just wrap it up, heh? Come on in, we'll tell Mom. (*He gently tries to pull* WILLY *to left.*)

WILLY (*frozen, immobile, with guilt in his voice*): No, I don't want to see her.

BIFF: Come on! (*He pulls again, and* WILLY *tries to pull away.*)

WILLY (*highly nervous*): No, no, I don't want to see her.

BIFF (*trying to look into* WILLY's *face, as if to find the answer there*): Why don't you want to see her?

WILLY (*more harshly now*): Don't bother me, will you?

BIFF: What do you mean, you don't want to see her? You don't want them calling you yellow, do you? This isn't your fault; it's me, I'm a bum. Now come inside! (WILLY *strains to get away.*) Did you hear what I said to you?

WILLY *pulls away and quickly goes by himself into the house.* BIFF *follows.*

LINDA (*to* WILLY): Did you plant, dear?

BIFF (*at the door, to* LINDA): All right, we had it out. I'm going and I'm not writing any more.

LINDA (*going to* WILLY *in the kitchen*): I think that's the best way, dear. 'Cause there's no use drawing it out, you'll just never get along.

WILLY *doesn't respond.*

BIFF: People ask where I am and what I'm doing, you don't know, and you don't care. That way it'll be off your mind and you can start brightening up again. All right? That clears it, doesn't it? (WILLY *is silent, and* BIFF *goes to him.*) You gonna wish me luck, scout? (*He extends his hand.*) What do you say?

LINDA: Shake his hand, Willy.

WILLY (*turning to her, seething with hurt*): There's no necessity to mention the pen at all, y'know.

BIFF (*gently*): I've got no appointment, Dad.

WILLY (*erupting fiercely*): He put his arm around . . . ?

BIFF: Dad, you're never going to see what I am, so what's the use of arguing? If I strike oil I'll send you a check. Meantime forget I'm alive.

WILLY (*to* LINDA): Spite, see?

BIFF: Shake hands, Dad.

WILLY: Not my hand.

BIFF: I was hoping not to go this way.

WILLY: Well, this is the way you're going. Good-by.

BIFF *looks at him a moment, then turns sharply and goes to the stairs.*

WILLY (*stops him with*): May you rot in hell if you leave this house!

BIFF (*turning*): Exactly what is it that you want from me?

WILLY: I want you to know, on the train, in the mountains, in the valleys, wherever you go, that you cut down your life for spite!

BIFF: No, no.

WILLY: Spite, spite, is the word of your undoing! And when you're down and out, remember what did it. When you're rotting somewhere beside the railroad tracks, remember, and don't you dare blame it on me!

BIFF: I'm not blaming it on you!

WILLY: I won't take the rap for this, you hear?

HAPPY *comes down the stairs and stands on the bottom step, watching.*

BIFF: That's just what I'm telling you!

WILLY (*sinking into a chair at the table, with full accusation*): You're trying to put a knife in me—don't think I don't know what you're doing!

BIFF: All right, phony! Then let's lay it on the line. (*He whips the rubber tube out of his pocket and puts it on the table.*)

HAPPY: You crazy—

LINDA: Biff! (*She moves to grab the hose, but* BIFF *holds it down with his hand.*)

BIFF: Leave it there! Don't move it!

WILLY (*not looking at it*): What is that?

BIFF: You know goddam well what that is.

WILLY (*caged, wanting to escape*): I never saw that.

BIFF: You saw it. The mice didn't bring it into the cellar! What is this supposed to do, make a hero out of you? This supposed to make me sorry for you?

WILLY: Never heard of it.

BIFF: There'll be no pity for you, you hear it? No pity!

WILLY (*to* LINDA): You hear the spite!

BIFF: No, you're going to hear the truth—what you are and what I am!

LINDA: Stop it!

WILLY: Spite!

HAPPY (*coming down toward* BIFF): You cut it now!

BIFF (*to* HAPPY): The man don't know who we are! The man is gonna know! (*to* WILLY) We never told the truth for ten minutes in this house!

HAPPY: We always told the truth!

BIFF (*turning on him*): You big blow, are you the assistant buyer? You're one of the two assistants to the assistant, aren't you?

HAPPY: Well, I'm practically—

BIFF: You're practically full of it! We all are! And I'm through with it. (*to* WILLY) Now hear this, Willy, this is me.

WILLY: I know you!

BIFF: You know why I had no address for three months? I stole a suit in Kansas City and I was in jail. (*to* LINDA, *who is sobbing*) Stop crying. I'm through with it.

LINDA *turns away from them, her hands covering her face.*

WILLY: I suppose that's my fault!

BIFF: I stole myself out of every good job since high school!

WILLY: And whose fault is that?

BIFF: And I never got anywhere because you blew me so full of hot air I could never stand taking orders from anybody! That's whose fault it is!

WILLY: I hear that!

LINDA: Don't, Biff!

BIFF: It's goddam time you heard that! I had to be boss big shot in two weeks, and I'm through with it!

WILLY: Then hang yourself! For spite, hang yourself!

BIFF: No! Nobody's hanging himself, Willy! I ran down eleven flights with a pen in my hand today. And suddenly I stopped, you hear me? And in the middle of that office building, do you hear this? I stopped in the middle of that building and I saw—the sky. I saw the things that I love in this world. The work and the food and time to sit and smoke. And I looked at the pen and said to myself, what the hell am I grabbing this for? Why am I trying to become what I don't want to be? What am I doing in an office, making a contemptuous, begging fool of myself, when all I want is out there, waiting for me the minute I say I know who I am! Why can't I say that, Willy? (*He tries to make* WILLY *face him, but* WILLY *pulls away and moves to the left.*)

WILLY (*with hatred, threateningly*): The door of your life is wide open!

BIFF: Pop! I'm a dime a dozen, and so are you!

WILLY (*turning on him now in an uncontrolled outburst*): I am not a dime a dozen! I am Willy Loman, and you are Biff Loman!

BIFF *starts for* WILLY, *but is blocked by* HAPPY. *In his fury,* BIFF *seems on the verge of attacking his father.*

BIFF: I am not a leader of men, Willy, and neither are you. You were never anything but a hard-working drummer who landed in the ash can like all the rest of them! I'm one dollar an hour, Willy! I tried seven states and couldn't raise it. A buck an hour! Do you gather my meaning? I'm not bringing home any prizes any more, and you're going to stop waiting for me to bring them home!

WILLY (*directly to* BIFF): You vengeful, spiteful mut!

BIFF *breaks from* HAPPY. WILLY, *in fright, starts up the stairs.* BIFF *grabs him.*

BIFF (*at the peak of his fury*): Pop, I'm nothing! I'm nothing, Pop. Can't you understand that? There's no spite in it any more. I'm just what I am, that's all.

BIFF'S *fury has spent itself, and he breaks down, sobbing, holding on to* WILLY, *who dumbly fumbles for* BIFF'S *face.*

WILLY (*astonished*): What're you doing? What're you doing? (*to* LINDA) Why is he crying?

BIFF (*crying, broken*): Will you let me go, for Christ's sake? Will you take that phony dream and burn it before something happens? (*Struggling to contain himself, he pulls away and moves to the stairs.*) I'll go in the morning. Put him—put him to bed. (*Exhausted,* BIFF *moves up the stairs to his room.*)

WILLY (*after a long pause, astonished, elevated*): Isn't that—isn't that remarkable? Biff—he likes me!

LINDA: He loves you, Willy!

HAPPY (*deeply moved*): Always did, Pop.

WILLY: Oh, Biff! (*staring wildly*) He cried! Cried to me. (*He is choking with his love, and now cries out his promise.*) That boy—that boy is going to be magnificent!

BEN *appears in the light just outside the kitchen.*

BEN: Yes, outstanding, with twenty thousand behind him.

LINDA (*sensing the racing of his mind, fearfully, carefully*): Now come to bed, Willy. It's all settled now.

WILLY (*finding it difficult not to rush out of the house*): Yes, we'll sleep. Come on. Go to sleep, Hap.

BEN: And it does take a great kind of a man to crack the jungle.

In accents of dread, BEN'S *idyllic music starts up.*

HAPPY (*his arm around* LINDA): I'm getting married, Pop, don't forget it. I'm changing everything. I'm gonna run that department before the year is up. You'll see, Mom. (*He kisses her.*)

BEN: The jungle is dark but full of diamonds, Willy.

WILLY *turns, moves, listening to* BEN.

LINDA: Be good. You're both good boys, just act that way, that's all.

HAPPY: 'Night, Pop. (*He goes upstairs.*)

LINDA (*to* WILLY): Come, dear.

BEN (*with greater force*): One must go in to fetch a diamond out.

WILLY (*to* LINDA, *as he moves slowly along the edge of the kitchen, toward the door*): I just want to get settled down, Linda. Let me sit alone for a little.

LINDA (*almost uttering her fear*): I want you upstairs.

WILLY (*taking her in his arms*): In a few minutes, Linda. I couldn't sleep right now. Go on, you look awful tired. (*He kisses her.*)

BEN: Not like an appointment at all. A diamond is rough and hard to the touch.

WILLY: Go on now. I'll be right up.

LINDA: I think this is the only way, Willy.

WILLY: Sure, it's the best thing.

BEN: Best thing!

WILLY: The only way. Everything is gonna be—go on, kid, get to bed. You look so tired.

LINDA: Come right up.

WILLY: Two minutes.

LINDA *goes into the living room, then reappears in her bedroom.* WILLY *moves just outside the kitchen door.*

WILLY: Loves me. (*wonderingly*) Always loved me. Isn't that a remarkable thing? Ben, he'll worship me for it!

BEN (*with promise*): It's dark there, but full of diamonds.

WILLY: Can you imagine that magnificence with twenty thousand dollars in his pocket?

LINDA (*calling from her room*): Willy! Come up!

WILLY (*calling into the kitchen*): Yes! Yes. Coming! It's very smart, you realize that, don't you, sweetheart? Even Ben sees it. I gotta go, baby. 'By! 'By! (*going over to* BEN, *almost dancing*) Imagine? When the mail comes he'll be ahead of Bernard again!

BEN: A perfect proposition all around.

WILLY: Did you see how he cried to me? Oh, if I could kiss him, Ben!

BEN: Time, William, time!

WILLY: Oh, Ben, I always knew one way or another we were gonna make it, Biff and I!

BEN (*looking at his watch*): The boat. We'll be late. (*He moves slowly off into the darkness.*)

WILLY (*elegiacally, turning to the house*): Now when you kick off, boy, I want a seventy-yard boot, and get right down the field under the ball, and when you hit, hit low and hit hard, because it's important, boy. (*He swings around and faces the audience.*) There's all kinds of important people in the stands, and the first thing you know . . . (*suddenly realizing he is alone*) Ben! Ben, where do I . . . ? (*He makes a sudden movement of search.*) Ben, how do I . . . ?

LINDA (*calling*): Willy, you coming up?

WILLY (*uttering a gasp of fear, whirling about as if to quiet her*): Sh! (*He turns around as if to find his way; sounds, faces, voices, seem to be swarming in upon him and he flicks at them, crying.*) Sh! Sh! (*Suddenly music, faint and high, stops him. It rises in intensity, almost to an unbearable scream. He goes up and down on his toes, and rushes off around the house.*) Shhh!

LINDA: Willy?

There is no answer. LINDA *waits.* BIFF *gets up off his bed. He is still in his clothes.* HAPPY *sits up.* BIFF *stands listening.*

LINDA (*with real fear*): Willy, answer me! Willy!

There is the sound of a car starting and moving away at full speed.

LINDA: No!

BIFF (*rushing down the stairs*): Pop!

As the car speeds off, the music crashes down in a frenzy of sound, which becomes the soft pulsation of a single cello string. BIFF *slowly returns to his bedroom. He and* HAPPY *gravely don their jackets.* LINDA *slowly walks out of her room. The music has developed into a dead march. The leaves of day are appearing over everything.* CHARLEY *and* BERNARD, *somberly dressed, appear and knock on the kitchen door.* BIFF *and* HAPPY *slowly descend the stairs to the kitchen as* CHARLEY *and* BERNARD *enter. All stop a moment when* LINDA, *in clothes of mourning, bearing a little bunch of roses, comes through the draped doorway into the kitchen. She goes to* CHARLEY *and takes his arm. Now all move toward the audience, through the wall-line of the kitchen. At the limit of the apron,* LINDA *lays down the flowers, kneels, and sits back on her heels. All stare down at the grave.*

Requiem

CHARLEY: It's getting dark, Linda.

LINDA *doesn't react. She stares at the grave.*

BIFF: How about it, Mom? Better get some rest, heh? They'll be closing the gate soon.

LINDA *makes no move. Pause.*

HAPPY (*deeply angered*): He had no right to do that. There was no necessity for it. We would've helped him.

CHARLEY (*grunting*): Hmmm.

BIFF: Come along, Mom.

LINDA: Why didn't anybody come?

CHARLEY: It was a very nice funeral.

LINDA: But where are all the people he knew? Maybe they blame him.

CHARLEY: Naaa. It's a rough world, Linda. They wouldn't blame him.

LINDA: I can't understand it. At this time especially. First time in thirty-five years we were just about free and clear. He only needed a little salary. He was even finished with the dentist.

CHARLEY: No man only needs a little salary.

LINDA: I can't understand it.

BIFF: There were a lot of nice days. When he'd come home from a trip; or on Sundays, making the stoop; finishing the cellar; putting on the new porch; when he built the extra bathroom; and put up the garage. You know something, Charley, there's more of him in that front stoop than in all the sales he ever made.

CHARLEY: Yeah. He was a happy man with a batch of cement.

LINDA: He was so wonderful with his hands.

BIFF: He had the wrong dreams. All, all, wrong.

HAPPY (*almost ready to fight* BIFF): Don't say that!

BIFF: He never knew who he was.

CHARLEY (*Stopping* HAPPY'S *movement and reply. To* BIFF.): Nobody dast blame this man. You don't understand: Willy was a salesman. And for a salesman, there is no rock bottom to the life. He don't put a bolt to a nut, he don't tell you the law or give you medicine. He's a man way out there in the blue, riding on a smile and a shoeshine. And when they start not smiling back—that's an earthquake. And then you get yourself a couple of spots on your hat, and you're finished. Nobody dast blame this man. A salesman is got to dream, boy. It comes with the territory.

BIFF: Charley, the man didn't know who he was.

HAPPY (*infuriated*): Don't say that!

BIFF: Why don't you come with me, Happy?

HAPPY: I'm not licked that easily. I'm staying right in this city, and I'm gonna beat this racket! (*He looks at* BIFF, *his chin set.*) The Loman Brothers!

BIFF: I know who I am, kid.

HAPPY: All right, boy. I'm gonna show you and everybody else that Willy Loman did not die in vain. He had a good dream. It's the only dream you can have—to come out number-one man. He fought it out here, and this is where I'm gonna win it for him.

BIFF (*With a hopeless glance at* HAPPY, *he bends toward his mother.*): Let's go, Mom.

LINDA: I'll be with you in a minute. Go on, Charley. (*He hesitates.*) I want to, just for a minute. I never had a chance to say good-by.

CHARLEY *moves away, followed by* HAPPY. BIFF *remains a slight distance up and left of* LINDA. *She sits there, summoning herself. The flute begins, not far away, playing behind her speech.*

LINDA: Forgive me, dear. I can't cry. I don't know what it is, but I can't cry. I don't understand it. Why did you ever do that? Help me, Willy, I can't cry. It seems to me that you're just on another trip. I keep expecting you. Willy, dear, I can't cry. Why did you do it? I search and search and I search, and I can't understand it, Willy. I made the last payment on the house today. Today, dear. And there'll be nobody home. (*A sob rises in her throat.*) We're free and clear. (*sobbing more fully, released*) We're free. (BIFF *comes slowly toward her.*) We're free . . . We're free . . .

BIFF *lifts her to her feet and moves out upright with her in his arms.* LINDA *sobs quietly.* BERNARD *and* CHARLEY *come together and follow them, followed by* HAPPY. *Only the music of the flute is left on the darkening stage as over the house the hard towers of the apartment buildings rise into sharp focus, and*

The curtain falls.

The Receptive Reader

Like other classics, *Death of a Salesman* is a play that different spectators see in their own personal light. Much of your own reaction is likely to be determined by how you react to the different *characters* and their interplay in Miller's drama. How would you answer questions like the following?

1. How and where in the play do you come to know and understand Willy Loman? What are revealing things he says and does? At times, Willy will say in the same breath the opposite of what he just said. What are striking contradictions in the way he talks about himself, others, business, life? Is there an explanation for some of these contradictions?

2. Who or what is to blame for Willy's disastrous relationship with Biff, his oldest son? How central is Biff's traumatic discovery of the father's infidelity? How are we supposed to feel about Happy, the younger brother?

3. Is Uncle Ben, who went to Alaska and came back rich, just another vehicle for one of Willy's pipe dreams? (Or is he meant to be a symbol of predatory business practices destroying the environment?)

4. How does Uncle Charley serve as a **foil** for Willy? How do you react to his sayings? How do you react to Bernard, who serves as a foil to Biff?

5. Linda, Willy's downtrodden wife, is loyal to Willy to the end and is one of the last people to speak up in his defense. What does she say? Why do you think some critics have taken the comments she makes on Willy Loman toward the end as the **theme** of the play? At the same time, however, Linda has been blamed for encouraging or at least tolerating Willy's "self-deceit and lies" or, alternatively, for prodding and nagging him to his destruction. What is her role in Willy's life and in the play as a whole?

6. As feminist critics point out, in this play from the fifties women serve in stereotypically subordinate roles. What are striking examples? How much do the men in the play conform to familiar patterns: idolizing the mother but bragging about their conquests of the other sex, using sports for male bonding, thinking of business as an arena in which males compete?

7. Freud and his disciples popularized the Oedipus situation, in which the son competes with the father for the love of the mother and—actually or symbolically—destroys his rival. Many critics have seen the relationship between Biff and his father as the core of the play. For Biff, the father who was to serve

him as role model has failed him. What were Willy's dreams and hopes for his son? What defeated them? What do we learn from the flashbacks, from the mutual accusations and recriminations?

The Personal Response

✘ What to you is the verdict of the play as a whole on Willy Loman? Is Willy simply a creature of his time and of his circumstances? Was he the wrong man for his job? Was he a product and a victim of the system? Did he ever have a real chance to make his life take a different turn? How?

✘ In this play, do you sympathize with the younger or with the older generation?

✘ How much has the business environment changed—or failed to change—since the days when Miller created Willy Loman?

Making Connections—For Discussion or Writing

Both Ibsen and Miller shone a searching light on the ethics and self-image of a middle-class business society. Are there points where their analyses converge? Does their criticism of middle-class society have a common base? On the other hand, are there important differences between Nora Helmer's nineteenth-century Europe and Willy Loman's twentieth-century America?

JUXTAPOSITIONS

Miller's *Salesman* at Fifty

This is Death of a Salesman *for the millennium.*
DONALD LYONS, *NEW YORK POST*

The turn of the century saw the fiftieth anniversary of the first Broadway production of Miller's *Death of a Salesman,* first performed at the Morosco Theater on Broadway on February 10, 1949. A spectacular new production with Brian Dennehy was sweeping the Tony Awards with awards for Best Revival of a Play, Best Direction of a Play Award to Robert Falls, Best Actor Award for Dennehy, and Best Featured Actress Award for Elizabeth Franz.

Seeing the massive Dennehy play Willy Loman nearing the end of his salesman's journey reminded critics and theatergoers that the play has nothing to do with whether Willy is heavyset or slight, New York Jewish, or Tokyo lower middle class. Millions around the world have at some level and in some way agreed with the reviewer who first said, "We are all Willy Loman."

The universal appeal of the play has outlasted the negative criticism of doubters:

✕ Some critics at first found the **flashbacks** of the play distracting; they doubted that reality-minded audiences would relate to this "expressionist" experimental feature. Today audiences around the world have no problem with drifting with Willy in and out of present reality into memories of the past and worries about the future, as they all do in their own minds. As Miller told a Chinese audience about Willy, "He cannot bear reality, and since he cannot do much to change it, he keeps changing his ideas of it." In the words of a theater critic,

> Willy, who is unraveling emotionally, is often simultaneously in the present and the past, remembering a significant yesterday while suffering an unendurable today.

> Helen Dudar, "A Modern Tragedy's Road to Maturity," *New York Times*

✕ At a time when Cold War tensions were building up, the play was for a time caught in the crossfire between political camps. Attacks from the right critized the author for contributing to a "salesman as scumbag" genre and unfairly criticizing the capitalist system. Attacks from the left took the author to task for its feeble sentimental criticism of the capitalist system, not politically correct enough by prevailing Marxist terms.

What light do the following selections throw on the staying power of Miller's play as a classic of the modern stage?

Elyse Sommers

Curtain Up is an online magazine of theater reviews and listings, tracking not only Broadway and Off-Broadway productions but also theater in sites from London to Los Angeles. You may want to visit its home page at <http://www.curtainup.com>

Second Thoughts about Death of a Salesman   1999

Willy Loman has become a character as familiar as some of Shakespeare's most famous tragic figures like Hamlet and Macbeth and King Lear. Willy, unlike the Bard's doomed anti-heroes, is a common man from that vast spectrum of the upwardly striving lower middle class to which audiences can immediately relate. And, like the Shakespeare characters, you keep revisiting new productions to see what new light has been cast on Willy's character as well as that of his family members.

If you count the movie, I've visited with Willy and his family so many times I've lost count. His name has entered my lexicon as an every day allusion for a self-deluded boaster and striver, as has Linda Loman's famous "Attention, attention must be paid." Its melodramatic excesses notwithstanding, *Death of a Salesman* remains one of the most enduring plays in my theatrical memory book. Each new Willy brings something different. Each viewing of the play prompts thoughts of people who though unlike Willy nevertheless seem to contain bits and pieces of him. (The same is true of Linda, Biff, Happy and Charley.)

In 1984 Dustin Hoffman brought Willy's physical size in line with the smallness of the man's character and stature in the larger scheme of things Now, coinciding with the play's fiftieth anniversary, director Robert Fall has once again brought us a physical giant of a Willy by casting Brian Dennehy, an actor of gigantic talent. He has also married him to Elizabeth Franz, who introduces a fascinating aggressiveness into loyal Linda Loman's traditional passivity.

These terrific actors and the fine supporting cast alone make this Chicago originated production a welcome addition to Broadway. Like Michael Rodman who directed the 1984 revival with Dustin Hoffman, Mr. Fall has focused on the father and son relationship. (Kevin Anderson is a convincing Biff.) He has also done for *Death of a Salesman* what director Michael Mayer recently did for Miller's *A View From the Bridge*. There's a kitchen sink, but it's just barely visible here. What we have is a set that is now more of a piece with the expressionistic dream scenes that the playwright projected into the social realism of his story and dialogue. Thus Mark Wendland's turntable set is furnished with minimum props, with black shadows surrounding and spotlighting the actors cinematically. The introductory music—described in Miller's stage description as "a melody . . . played on a flute"—has been replaced by dissonant city noises made by horns and drums.

Unlike some longtime Miller watchers who may find this starkly expressionistic staging distracting, I found it exciting and extremely effective. The only distraction comes from seeing a play for the umpteenth time and tending to catch yourself waiting for the most often quoted lines. It made me almost envious of the mostly twenty-five to forty-ish audience that packed the house at the Wednesday night performances I attended. They're unlikely to have seen the play often enough to be able to lipsycnch along with Linda's "Attention must be paid . . ." and Willy's "You can't eat the orange and throw the peel away—a man is not a piece of fruit!"

And yet, expected or not, coming from Franz and Dennehy the words still do demand attention, as does this play. That's because [it] is as much a tribute to fully realized human beings as it is an indictment of false values. It hasn't weathered fifty years—with productions in many languages—without reason. It would be nice to think that members of The Drama Desk, which also celebrated its fiftieth birthday this week, will soon have a chance to review a new play that will endure midway into the coming millennium, when a new production of *Death of a Salesman* is more than likely to be playing on one stage or another.

The Receptive Reader

What would you include in a capsule portrait of this writer as a drama fan and aficionado and as a longtime follower and admirer of Miller's play? What is the mix of topics in her feature: theater lore, personal history, production review, comment on the staying power of the play? Does anything surprise you about her interests, her insider's knowledge, or her enthusiasm?

Arthur Miller

Miller has written and talked to audiences many times about his own personal history, about the origin of the play, about its major themes, about the directors and actors who brought it to life, and the audiences who loved it.

"Salesman" at 50   1999

As far as I know, nobody has figured out time. Not chronological time, of course—that's merely what the calendar tells—but real time, the kind that baffles the human mind when it confronts, as mine does now, the apparent number of months, weeks, and years that have elapsed since 1948, when I sat down to write a play about a salesman. I say "apparent" because I cannot find a means of absorbing the idea of half a century rolling away beneath my feet. Half a century is a very long time, yet I must already have been grown up way back then, indeed I must have been a few years past thirty, if my calculations are correct, and this fact I find indigestible.

A few words about the theatrical era that *Death of a Salesman* emerged from. The only theatre available to a playwright in the late forties was Broadway, the most ruthlessly commercialized theatre in the world, with the off-Broadway evolution still a decade away. That theatre had one single audience, not two or three, as is the case today, catering to very different levels of age, culture, education, and intellectual sophistication. Its critics were more than likely to be ex-sports reporters or general journalists rather than scholars or specialists university-trained in criticism. So a play worked or it didn't, made them laugh or cry or left them bored. (It really isn't all that different today except that the reasoning is perhaps more elevated.) That unified audience was the same for musicals, farce, O'Neill's tragedies, or some imported British, French, or Middle European lament. Whatever its limitations, it was an audience that loved theatre, and many of its members thought theatregoing not quite a luxury but an absolute necessity for a civilized life.

For playwriting, what I believe was important about that unified audience was that a writer with ambitions reaching beyond realistic, made-for-entertainment plays could not expect the support of a coterie of like-minded folk who would overlook his artistic lapses so long as his philosophical agenda tended to justify their own. That unified audience had come in from the rain to be entertained, and even instructed, if need be, provided the instruction was entertaining. But the writer had to keep in mind that his proofs, so to speak, had to be accessible both to the lawyers in the audience and to the plumbers, to the doctors and the housewives, to the college students and the kids at the Saturday matinee. One result of this mix was the ideal, if not the frequent fulfillment, of a kind of play that would be complete rather than fragmentary, an emotional rather than an intellectual experience, a play basically of heart with its ulterior moral gesture integrated with action rather than rhetoric. In fact, it was a Shakespearean ideal, a theatre for anyone with an understanding of English and perhaps some common sense.

Some of the initial readers of the *Death of a Salesman* script were not at all sure that the audience of 1949 was going to follow its manipulations of time, for one thing. Josh Logan, a leading stage and film director of numerous hits, *Mr. Roberts* and *South Pacific* among them, had greeted *All My Sons* two years earlier with great warmth, and invested a thousand dollars in *Salesman*, but when he read the script he apologetically withdrew five hundred. No audience, he felt, would follow the story, and no one would ever be sure whether Willy was imagining or really living through one or another scene in the play. Some thirty years later I would hear the same kind of reaction from the theatre people in the Beijing People's Art Theatre, where I had been invited to stage the play, which, in the view of many there, was not a play at all but a poem. It was only when they saw it played that its real dramatic nature came through.

In the 1949 Broadway audience there was more to worry about than their following the story. In one of his letters, O'Neill had referred to that theatre as a "showshop," a crude place where a very uncultivated, materialistic public cut off from its own spirituality gathered for a laugh or a tear. Clifford Odets, with his first successes surely the most hotly acclaimed playwright in Broadway history, would also end in bitter alienation from the whole system of Broadway production. The problem, in a word, was seriousness. There wasn't very much of it in the audience, and it was resented when it threatened to appear on the stage.

So it seemed. But *All My Sons* had all but convinced me that if one totally integrated a play's conceptual life with its emotional one so that there was no perceptible dividing line between the two, such a play could reach such an audience. In short, the play had to move forward not by following a narrow, discreet line, but as a phalanx, all of its elements moving together simultaneously. There was no model I could adapt for this play, no past history for the kind of work I felt it could become. What I had before me was the way the mind—at least my mind—actually worked. One asks a policeman for directions; as one listens, the hairs sticking out of his nose become important, reminding one of a father, brother, son with the same feature, and one's conflicts with him or one's friendship come to mind, and this all over a period of seconds while objectively taking note of how to get to where one wants to go. Initially based, as I explained in *Timebends,* my autobiography, on an uncle of mine, Willy rapidly took over my imagination and became something that had never existed before, a salesman with his feet on the subway stairs and his head in the stars.

His language and that of the Loman family were liberative from any enslavement to "the way people speak." There are some people who simply don't speak the way people speak. The Lomans, like their models in life, are not content with who and what they are, but want to be other, wealthier, more cultivated perhaps, closer to power. "I've been remiss," Biff says to Linda about his neglect of his father, and there would be many who seized on this usage as proof of the playwright's tin ear or some inauthenticity in the play. But it is in Biff's mouth precisely because it is indeed an echo, a slightly misunderstood signal from above, from the more serious and cultivated part of society, a signal indicating that he is now to be taken with utmost seriousness, even remorseful of his past neglect. "Be liked and you will never want" is also not quite from Brooklyn, but Willy needs aphoristic authority at this point, and again, there is an echo of a—for want of a better word—Victorian authority to back him up.

These folk are the innocent receivers of what they imagine as a more elegant past, a time "finer" than theirs. As Jews light-years away from religion or a community that might have fostered Jewish identity, they exist in a spot that probably most Americans feel they inhabit—on the sidewalk side of the glass looking in at a well-lighted place.

As it turned out, this play seems to have shown that most of the world shares something similar to that condition. Having seen it in five or six countries, and directed it in China and Sweden, neither of whose languages I know, it was both mystifying and gratifying to note that people everywhere react pretty much the same in the same places of the play. When I arrived in China to begin rehearsals the people in the American embassy, with two exceptions, were sure the Chinese were too culturally remote from the play to ever understand it. The American ambassador and the political officer thought otherwise, the first because he had been born and raised in China, and the second, I supposed, because it was his job to understand how the Chinese thought about life. And what they were thinking turned out to be more or less what they were thinking in New York or London or Paris, namely that being human—a father, mother, son—is something most of us fail at most of the time, and a little mercy is eminently in order, given the societies we live in, which purport to be stable and sound as mountains when, in fact, they are all trembling in a fast wind, blowing mindlessly around the earth.

The Receptive Reader

1. The audiences of ancient Greek drama and of Shakespeare's Elizabethan stage came from a broad cross section of the community. How is the "single audience" or "unified audience" that Miller describes for the original Broadway production similar? What was the range of people he envisioned in the audience? How were the drama critics of the time also more representative of a "populist" popular culture than of an "elitist" sophisticates' culture?

2. How does Miller define the audience expectations that theatergoers were bringing to the theater? What does he say on such criteria as entertainment vs. instruction, intellect vs. emotion, action vs. rhetoric?

3. Miller mentions outstanding playwrights who became alienated from the commercial Broadway stage. How does he describe or explain their attitude? Like these fellow playwrights, Miller was also critical of the crass callous commercialism of society. How do you explain that instead of becoming alienated from the commercial theater and the larger society he became a major leading figure in both?

4. At various times and with varying emphasis, Miller has talked about what the Lomans and their models in real life stand for. How does he describe their role and central motivation in this retrospective article?

Joyce Carol Oates

Joyce Carol Oates is a widely published much-admired and much-criticized writer of fiction who has also written extensively about the self-image and motivation of writers and their role in modern society.

Arthur Miller's Death of a Salesman: A Celebration

He's a man way out there in the blue, riding on
a smile and a shoeshine. And when they start
not smiling back—that's an earthquake. And
then you get yourself a couple of spots on your
hat, and you're finished. Nobody dast blame this
man. A salesman is got to dream, boy. It comes
with the territory.

DEATH OF A SALESMAN

Was it our comforting belief that Willy Loman was "only" a salesman? That *Death of a Salesman* was about—well, an American salesman? And not about all of us?

When I first read this play at the age of fourteen or fifteen, I may have thought that Willy Loman was sufficiently "other"—"old." He hardly resembled the men in my family, my father or grandfathers, for he was "in sales" and not a factory worker or small-time farmer, he wasn't a manual laborer but a man of words, speech—what his son Biff bluntly calls "hot air." His occupation, for all its adversities, was "white collar," and his class not the one into which I'd been born; I could not recognize anyone I knew intimately in him, and certainly I could not have recognized myself, nor foreseen a time decades later when it would strike me forcibly that, for all his delusions and intellectual limitations, about which Arthur Miller is unromantically clear-eyed, Willy Loman is all of us. Or, rather, we are Willy Loman, particularly those of us who are writers, poets, dreamers; the yearning soul "way out there in the blue." Dreaming is required of us, even if our dreams are very possibly self-willed delusions. And we recognize our desperate child's voice assuring us, like Willy Loman pep-talking himself at the edge of a lighted stage as at the edge of eternity—"God Almighty, [I'll] be great yet! A star like that, magnificent, can never really fade away!"

Except of course, it can.

It would have been in the early 1950s that I first read *Death of a Salesman,* a few years after its Broadway premiere and enormous critical and popular success. I would have read it in an anthology of *Best Plays of the Year.* As a young teenager I'd begun avidly devouring drama; apart from Shakespeare, no plays were taught in the schools I attended in upstate New York (in the small city of Lockport and the Village of Williamsville, a suburb of Buffalo), and so I read plays with no sense of chronology, in no historic context, no doubt often without much comprehension. Reading late at night when the rest of the household was asleep was an intense activity for me, imbued with mystery, and reading drama was far more enigmatic than reading prose fiction. It seemed to me a challenge that so little was explained in the stage directions; there was no helpful narrative voice; you were obliged to visualize, to "see" the stage in your imagination, the play's characters always in present tense, vividly alive. In drama, people presented themselves primarily in speech, as they do in life. Yet there was an eerie, dreamlike melding of past and present in Arthur Miller's *Death of a Salesman,* Willy Loman's "present-action" dialogue and his conversations with the ghosts of his past like his revered brother Ben; there was a melting of the barriers between inner and outer worlds that gave to the play its disturbing, poetic quality. (Years later I would learn that Arthur Miller had originally conceived of the play as a monodrama with the title *The Inside of His Head.*)

In the intervening years, Willy Loman has become our quintessential American tragic hero, our domestic Lear, spiraling toward suicide as toward an act of selfless grace, his mad scene on the heath a frantic seed-planting episode by flashlight in the midst of which the once-proud, now disintegrating man confesses, "I've got nobody to talk to." His salesmanship, his family relations, his very life—all have been talk, optimistic and inflated sales rhetoric; yet, suddenly, in this powerful scene, Willy Loman realizes he has nobody to talk *to;* nobody to *listen.* Perhaps the most memorable single remark in the play is the quiet observation that Willy Loman is "liked . . . but not well-liked." In America, this is not enough.

Nearly fifty years after its composition, *Death of a Salesman* strikes us as the most achingly contemporary of our classic American plays. It has proved to have been a brilliant strategy on the part of the thirty-four-year-old playwright to temper his gifts for social realism with the Expressionistic techniques of experimental drama like Eugene O'Neill's *Strange Interlude* and *The Hairy Ape,* Elmer Rice's *The Adding Machine,* Thornton Wilder's *Our Town,* work by Chekhov, the later Ibsen, Strindberg, and Pirandello, for by these methods Willy Loman is raised from the parameters of regionalism and ethnic specificity to the level of the more purely, symbolically "American." Even the claustrophobia of his private familial and sexual obsessions has a universal quality, in the plaintive-poetic language Miller has chosen for him. As we near the twenty-first century, it seems evident that America has become an ever more frantic, self-mesmerized world of salesmanship, image without substance, empty advertising rhetoric, and that peculiar product of our consumer culture "public relations"—a synonym for hypocrisy, deceit, fraud. Where Willy Loman is a salesman, his son Biff is a thief. Yet these are fellow Americans to whom "attention must be paid." Arthur Miller has written the tragedy that illuminates the dark side of American success—which is to say, the dark side of us.

The Receptive Reader

1. Can you describe and explain the different phases or layers in Oates' relation to the play? How and why did she first come to know it? What at first made it dificult for her to relate to the people or the world of the play? Then how and why did she come to identify with Willy Loman—generally as a human being but also particularly as a writer?

2. What in retrospect makes Willy Loman for Oates' the "quintessential American tragic hero"? Why does she claim that instead of becoming dated, the play today more strongly than before illuminates the "dark side of American success"?

Kay Stanton

You're my foundation and my support, Linda.
      WILLY LOMAN, IN *DEATH OF A SALESMAN*

In current reexaminations of Miller's play, readers have paid special attention to the role of Linda Loman, Willy's wife. In the first of the following excerpts, a feminist critic examines gender roles in the play, looking closely at Linda Loman's second-class status yet essential role in the Loman household. Second, a critic indebted to the Marxist emphasis on economic relations and realities looks at Linda's role in the economics of Willy Loman's world. What do these critics alert you to that you might have missed in your own reading? Where do you tend to agree or disagree with them?

Women and the American Dream 1989

The Loman men are all less than they hold themselves to be, but Linda is more than she is credited to be. She is indeed the foundation that has allowed the Loman men to build themselves up, if only in dreams, and she is the support that enables them to continue despite their failures. Linda is the one element holding the façade of the family together. Yet even Miller, her creator, seems not to have fully understood her character. Linda is described in the opening stage directions as follows: "Most often jovial, she has developed an iron repression of her exceptions to Willy's behavior—she more than loves him, she admires him, as though his mercurial nature, his temper, his massive dreams and little cruelties, served her only as sharp reminders of the turbulent longings . . . which she shares but lacks the temperament to utter and follow to their end." She thus seems inferior to Willy; yet she demonstrates a level of education superior to his in terms of grammatical and mathematical ability, and she is definitely more gifted in diplomatic and psychological acumen. In her management of Willy, she embodies the American Dream ideal of the model post–World War II wife, infinitely supportive of her man. She makes no mistakes, has no flaws in wifely perfection. But the perfect American wife is not enough for American Dreamers like Willy. He has been unfaithful to her, and he rudely interrupts and silences her, even when she is merely expressing support for him. She can be the foundation of the house; he must rebuild the façade.

If the Loman house represents the Loman family, with Linda as the steady foundation and support, the façade is constructed with stolen goods. The enemy apartment buildings that so anger Willy have provided the materials that he and his sons used in such projects as rebuilding the front stoop. Linda knows that they need not have been "boxed in" by the apartment buildings; she says, "We should've bought the land next door." Possibly she

had suggested the idea at the appropriate time but was ignored. But Willy prefers to transfer the blame for the diminishment of his Green World: "They should've had a law against apartment houses. Remember those two beautiful elm trees out there? . . . They should've arrested the builder for cutting those down." Of course, there is a law against stealing property, which Willy thought nothing of disobeying when he encouraged the boys to steal from the construction site, calling them "fearless characters." Laws are for lesser men to follow, not the Loman men. In the realm of the Home, Willy and his sons are associated with rebuilding through theft, and Linda is associated with cleaning, mending, and repair.

In Willy's flashback sequences, Linda habitually appears with the laundry, suggesting that it is her responsibility to clean up the males' dirtiness, on all levels. In both past and present, she is shown mending, not only her own stockings but also Willy's jacket. Often when Linda speaks, she discusses repairs, which she oversees; she must mend the male machinery. Willy is "sold" by other salesmen or advertisements on the quality of products and fails to recognize that even the "best" breaks down from daily wear and tear—including Willy himself. Although Linda's functions of cleaning, mending, and overseeing repairs are traditionally "feminine," they are significant because they are the ones maintained when other traditionally "feminine" elements are appropriated by Willy. It is not Linda but Willy who asserts the importance of physical attractiveness, who prefers a fantasy life of glamor to the reality of daily toil, who suffers from the "empty nest syndrome," and who insists on having the most significant role in child-rearing.

Willy works hard at preventing Linda from having any substantive impact on shaping the boys' characters; he tries continually to make them his alone, just as he had implied that they had sprung from his "stock" alone. After thanking God for Adonis-like looks in his sons, Willy confesses to Linda that he himself is "not noticed," "fat," "foolish to look at," and had been called a "walrus." Evidently, the physical attractiveness, strength, and resilience of the boys derive from Linda rather than Willy, but "God," not she, is given credit. Although Linda is the continual presence in the boys' lives at home, as Mother Loman had been for Willy, Willy undermines Linda's authority when he returns from the road. In a flashback sequence, Linda disapproves of various manifestations of Biff's bad behavior and runs from the scene almost in tears after Willy refuses to support her. She represents human dignity and values: cooperative, moral, humane behavior as opposed to lawless assertion of self over all others through assumed superiority. . . . in the home, Woman through Linda as submerged element, is the measure of human dignity and the accountant of worth.

From "Women and the American Dream," *Feminist Readings of Modern American Drama,* ed. June Schlueter, 1989

The Receptive Reader

Where does this critic most effectively anchor her interpretation to the text of the play? In her discussion, what elements of the play assume unexpected symbolic value or significance? What are the key elements in her reevaluation of Linda's role in the play?

Beverly Hume

Linda Loman as "The Woman"   1985

It has never been acknowledged by critics of Miller's *Death of a Salesman* that in Linda Loman, one finds traces of an intense materialism which not only estranges her from her husband, Willy, but places her in league with "the Woman" who haunts Willy's memory and, along with the ghostly Ben, helps drive him toward suicide. Linda's materialistic attitude partially exists because, as family bookkeeper, she is aware of their financial problems; but it primarily exists because of her absorption in Willy's success dream, an absorption which proves malignant, fatal.

In his stage directions, Miller characterizes Linda Loman as a woman with an "iron repression of her exceptions to Willy's behavior," as a woman who not only loves Willy, but "admires him, as though his mercurial nature, his temper, his massive dreams and little cruelties served only as sharp reminders of the turbulent longings within him, longings which she shares but lacks the temperament to utter and follow to their end." Linda, then, is a woman who is at once passive and possessed by intense (perhaps unconscious) longings; and in *Salesman,* her "iron repression" often combines with these longings to make her presence painful to Willy.

In the memory sequences of the play, for example, Willy frequently recalls how Linda's materialism increases his sense of failure. Just before "the Woman" first enters, Willy and Linda engage in this economic exchange:

LINDA: . . . Did you sell anything?

WILLY: I did five hundred gross in Providence and seven hundred gross in Boston.

LINDA: No! Wait a minute, I've got a pencil. (*She pulls pencil and paper out of her apron pocket.*) That makes your commission . . . Two hundred—my God! Two hundred and twelve dollars!

WILLY: Well, I didn't figure it yet, but . . .

LINDA: How much did you do?

WILLY: Well, I—I did—about a hundred and eighty gross in Providence. Well, no—it came to—roughly two hundred gross on the whole trip.

LINDA (*without hesitation*): Two hundred gross. That's . . . (*She figures.*)

WILLY: The trouble was that three of the stores were half closed for inventory in Boston. Otherwise I woulda broke records.

LINDA: Well, it makes seventy dollars and some pennies. That's very good.

First, Linda asks the tentative (and, for her, typical) question. Then, encouraged by Willy's response, she grows excited at the amount of money, but when she sees Willy falter, she retreats back to another tentative question. He fumbles, answers her question, and then, "without hesitating," she calculates (exactly) how well he's done, finally offering the patronizing sentiment, "Well, it makes seventy dollars and some pennies. That's very good." One finds Linda repeating this pattern of meekness, materialistic excitement, more meekness, pragmatic calculation, and, finally, patronizing compassion throughout the play. Indeed, it is not surprising that "the Woman" enters Willy's memory shortly after this particular dialogue—directly, in fact, after his reflection that he fears "that I'll never sell anything again, that I won't make a living for you [Linda], or a business . . . for the boys." With mocking laughter, "the Woman" disrupts Willy's understandable anxiety about failing to meet Linda's contradictory demands; "the Woman" disrupts his statement to flatter him and tell him he need not worry about failing her. And Willy responds quickly to the deception.

"The Woman" and audience know that she is lying, that she is manipulating Willy only for money (or stockings); but her manipulations strangely mirror the deceptions Linda practices on Willy, and it cannot be a coincidence that Miller early has Linda's laughter "blend" with "the Woman's." For both women contribute, through their material longings, to Willy's final destruction—"the Woman" mockingly, maliciously by her betrayal of Willy before Biff; Linda unwittingly, in her repressed need to realize Willy's materialistic success dream. Like "the Woman," Linda constantly lies to Willy to build him up, constantly insists that she doesn't want anything from him (even though she does), constantly tells him that she thinks him potent, lively (even when it is clear that he is depressed).

From *Notes on Modern American Literature,* 1985

The Receptive Reader

What are some of the identical elements in the play that both of these critics examine? How and why do they differ in their interpretations? What details examined by Hume make you rethink your reaction to the play? Overall, which of the two views of Linda is closer to your own? Which of the views seems to carry more weight, is more convincing?

Lorraine Hansberry   *(1930–1965)*

One cannot live with sighted eyes and a feeling heart and not know and react to the miseries which afflict this world.

LORRAINE HANSBERRY

Lorraine Hansberry was the first African American woman to have a play performed on Broadway (after she had raised the money for the out-of-town tryouts herself). Her *A Raisin in the Sun,* a "milestone in the American theater" (Leonard Ashley), opened in New York in 1959 and ran for nineteen months. It was made into a movie with Sidney Poitier, Claudia McNeil, and Ruby Dee. Today, with the race issue in this country unresolved, Hansberry's play remains a powerful study of the invisible walls that keep America's minorities from achieving their place in the sun.

Working as a journalist for a progressive paper, Hansberry met leading African American intellectuals and artists like Paul Robeson, W. E. B. Du Bois, and Langston Hughes, and she was friends with James Baldwin, author of *Notes of a Native Son* and *The Fire Next Time*. After watching her play in 1959, James Baldwin said, "it will demand a far less guilty and constricted people than the present-day Americans to be able to assess it. . . . I had never in my life seen so many black people in the theater. And the reason was that never before, in the entire history of the American theater, had so much of the truth of black people's lives been seen on the stage." Hansberry championed the work of the French feminist Simone de Beauvoir, author of *The Second Sex*. She quoted with admiration a speech made in 1879 by Susan B. Anthony, the early American feminist, who challenged the denial of a woman's right to vote as the denial of her "right of consent as one of the governed" and who called on "every man and woman in whose veins coursed a drop of human sympathy" to break the law that forbade offering a cup of water or a night's shelter to a fugitive slave.

Hansberry's *A Raisin in the Sun* is about what it means to be black in white America. Whether to hold on to the American dream or abandon it in disillusionment becomes a major issue in her play. Hansberry had witnessed the struggle against racial segregation firsthand. She was eight when her family moved into affluent and segregated Hyde Park in Chicago, where she encountered the curses, spitting, and brick-throwing of "hellishly hostile" white neighbors. Her family was evicted from the house; her father, a real-estate broker, worked with NAACP lawyers to carry his case all the way to the Supreme Court, which ruled in favor of the Hansberry family. Hansberry attributed her father's early death to this bitter struggle.

A Raisin in the Sun was part of the search for a new black identity and a new definition of the black role in society. Hansberry looked at the movement back to African roots and the challenge it presented to the traditional ideal of assimilation. She dramatized the role of the strong maternal female, or matriarch, in the black family, with the corresponding marginalization of the young black male. She shone a probing light into the workings of prejudice and tried to help people gain the spiritual strength to deal with it. Hansberry died young of cancer shortly after her second play, *The Sign in Sidney Brustein's Window,* opened on Broadway in 1964. After her death, her husband, Robert Nemiroff, edited and published several of her unpublished plays. In 1969, a dramatic adaptation of a biography drawing on her letters, journals, and plays was produced posthumously under the title *To Be Young, Gifted, and Black.*

It became a long-running off-Broadway play and toured hundreds of college campuses.

A Raisin in the Sun   *1959*

What happens to a dream deferred?
Does it dry up
Like a raisin in the sun?
Or fester like a sore—
And then run?
Does it stink like rotten meat?
Or crust and sugar over—
Like a syrupy sweet?

Maybe it just sags
Like a heavy load.
Or does it explode?

LANGSTON HUGHES

CHARACTERS

RUTH YOUNGER
TRAVIS YOUNGER
WALTER LEE YOUNGER (BROTHER)
BENEATHA YOUNGER
LENA YOUNGER (MAMA)
JOSEPH ASAGAI
GEORGE MURCHISON
KARL LINDNER
BOBO
MOVING MEN

The action of the play is set in Chicago's Southside, sometime between World War II and the present.

Act One
SCENE 1: *Friday morning.*
SCENE 2: *The following morning.*

Act Two
SCENE 1: *Later, the same day.*
SCENE 2: *Friday night, a few weeks later.*
SCENE 3: *Moving day, one week later.*

Act Three
An hour later.

Act One

SCENE 1

The YOUNGER *living room would be a comfortable and well-ordered room if it were not for a number of indestructible contradictions to this state of being. Its furnishings are typical and undistinguished and their primary feature now is that they have clearly had to accommodate the living of too many people for too many years—and they are tired. Still, we can see that at some time, a time probably no longer remembered by the family (except perhaps for* MAMA*), the furnishings of this room were actually selected with care and love and even hope—and brought to this apartment and arranged with taste and pride.*

That was a long time ago. Now the once loved pattern of the couch upholstery has to fight to show itself from under acres of crocheted doilies and couch covers which have themselves finally come to be more important than the upholstery. And here a table or a chair has been moved to disguise the worn places in the carpet; but the carpet has fought back by showing its weariness, with depressing uniformity, elsewhere on its surface.

Weariness has, in fact, won in this room. Everything has been polished, washed, sat on, used, scrubbed too often. All pretenses but living itself have long since vanished from the very atmosphere of this room.

Moreover, a section of this room, for it is not really a room unto itself, though the landlord's lease would make it seem so, slopes backward to provide a small kitchen area, where the family prepares the meals that are eaten in the living room proper, which must also serve as dining room. The single window that has been provided for these "two" rooms is located in this kitchen area. The sole natural light the family may enjoy in the course of a day is only that which fights its way through this little window.

At left, a door leads to a bedroom which is shared by MAMA *and her daughter,* BENEATHA. *At right, opposite, is a second room (which in the beginning of the life of this apartment was probably a breakfast room) which serves as a bedroom for* WALTER *and his wife,* RUTH.

TIME: *Sometime between World War II and the present.*

PLACE: *Chicago's Southside.*

AT RISE: *It is morning dark in the living room.* TRAVIS *is asleep on the makedown bed at center. An alarm clock sounds from within the bedroom at right, and presently* RUTH *enters from that room and closes the door behind her. She crosses sleepily toward the window. As she passes her sleeping son she reaches down and shakes him a little. At the window she raises the shade and a dusky Southside morning light comes in feebly. She fills a pot with water and puts it on to boil. She calls to the boy, between yawns, in a slightly muffled voice.*

RUTH *is about thirty. We can see that she was a pretty girl, even exceptionally so, but now it is apparent that life has been little that she expected, and disappointment has already begun to hang in her face. In a few years, before thirty-five even, she will be known among her people as a "settled woman."*

She crosses to her son and gives him a good, final, rousing shake.

RUTH: Come on now, boy, it's seven thirty! (*Her son sits up at last, in a stupor of sleepiness.*) I say hurry up, Travis! You ain't the only person in the world got to use a bathroom! (*The child, a sturdy, handsome little boy of ten or eleven, drags himself out of the bed and almost blindly takes his towels and "today's clothes" from drawers and a closet and goes out to the bathroom, which is in an outside hall and which is shared by another family or families on the same floor.* RUTH *crosses to the bedroom door at right and opens it and calls in to her husband.*) Walter Lee! . . . It's after seven thirty! Lemme see you do some waking up in there now! (*She waits.*) You better get up from there, man! It's after seven thirty I tell you. (*She waits again.*) All right, you just go ahead and lay there and next thing you know Travis be finished and Mr. Johnson'll be in there and you'll be fussing and cussing round here like a madman! And be late too! (*She waits, at the end of patience.*) Walter Lee—it's time for you to GET UP!

She waits another second and then starts to go into the bedroom, but is apparently satisfied that her husband has begun to get up. She stops, pulls the door to, and returns to the kitchen area. She wipes her face with a moist cloth and runs her fingers through her sleep-disheveled hair in a vain effort and ties an apron around her housecoat. The bedroom door at right opens and her husband stands in the doorway in his pajamas, which are rumpled and mismated. He is a lean, intense young man in his middle thirties, inclined to quick nervous movements and erratic speech habits—and always in his voice there is a quality of indictment.

WALTER: Is he out yet?

RUTH: What you mean *out?* He ain't hardly got in there good yet.

WALTER (*wandering in, still more oriented to sleep than to a new day*): Well, what was you doing all that yelling for if I can't even get in there yet? (*stopping and thinking*) Check coming today?

RUTH: They *said* Saturday and this is just Friday and I hopes to God you ain't going to get up here first thing this morning and start talking to me 'bout no money—'cause I 'bout don't want to hear it.

WALTER: Something the matter with you this morning?

RUTH: No—I'm just sleepy as the devil. What kind of eggs you want?

WALTER: Not scrambled. (RUTH *starts to scramble eggs.*) Paper come? (RUTH *points impatiently to the rolled up Tribune on the table, and he gets it and spreads it out and vaguely reads the front page.*) Set off another bomb yesterday.

RUTH (*maximum indifference*): Did they?

WALTER (*looking up*): What's the matter with you?

RUTH: Ain't nothing the matter with me. And don't keep asking me that this morning.

WALTER: Ain't nobody bothering you. (*reading the news of the day absently again*) Say Colonel McCormick is sick.

RUTH (*affecting tea-party interest*): Is he now? Poor thing.

WALTER (*sighing and looking at his watch*): Oh, me. (*He waits.*) Now what is that boy doing in that bathroom all this time? He just going to have to start getting up earlier. I can't be being late to work on account of him fooling around in there.

RUTH (*turning on him*): Oh, no he ain't going to be getting up no earlier no such thing! It ain't his fault that he can't get to bed no earlier nights 'cause he got a bunch of crazy good-for-nothing clowns sitting up running their mouths in what is supposed to be his bedroom after ten o'clock at night . . .

WALTER: That's what you mad about, ain't it? The things I want to talk about with my friends just couldn't be important in your mind, could they?

He rises and finds a cigarette in her handbag on the table and crosses to the little window and looks out, smoking and deeply enjoying this first one.

RUTH (*almost matter of factly, a complaint too automatic to deserve emphasis*): Why you always got to smoke before you eat in the morning?

WALTER (*at the window*): Just look at 'em down there . . . Running and racing to work . . . (*he turns and faces his wife and watches her a moment at the stove, and then, suddenly*) You look young this morning, baby.

RUTH (*indifferently*): Yeah?

WALTER: Just for a second—stirring them eggs. Just for a second it was—you looked real young again. (*He reaches for her; she crosses away. Then, drily.*) It's gone now—you look like yourself again!

RUTH: Man, if you don't shut up and leave me alone.

WALTER (*looking out to the street again*): First thing a man ought to learn in life is not to make love to no colored woman first thing in the morning. You all some eeeevil people at eight o'clock in the morning.

TRAVIS *appears in the hall doorway, almost fully dressed and quite wide awake now, his towels and pajamas across his shoulders. He opens the door and signals for his father to make the bathroom in a hurry.*

TRAVIS (*watching the bathroom*): Daddy, come on!

WALTER *gets his bathroom utensils and flies out to the bathroom.*

RUTH: Sit down and have your breakfast, Travis.

TRAVIS: Mama, this is Friday. (*gleefully*) Check coming tomorrow, huh?

RUTH: You get your mind off money and eat your breakfast.

TRAVIS (*eating*): This is the morning we supposed to bring the fifty cents to school.

RUTH: Well, I ain't got no fifty cents this morning.

TRAVIS: Teacher say we have to.

RUTH: I don't care what teacher say. I ain't got it. Eat your breakfast, Travis.

TRAVIS: I *am* eating.

RUTH: Hush up now and just eat!

The boy gives her an exasperated look for her lack of understanding, and eats grudgingly.

TRAVIS: You think Grandmama would have it?

RUTH: No! And I want you to stop asking your grandmother for money, you hear me?

TRAVIS (*outraged*): Gaaaleee! I don't ask her, she just gimme it sometimes!

RUTH: Travis Willard Younger—I got too much on me this morning to be—

TRAVIS: Maybe Daddy—

RUTH: Travis!

The boy hushes abruptly. They are both quiet and tense for several seconds.

TRAVIS (*presently*): Could I maybe go carry some groceries in front of the supermarket for a little while after school then?

RUTH: Just hush, I said. (*Travis jabs his spoon into his cereal bowl viciously, and rests his head in anger upon his fists.*) If you through eating, you can get over there and make up your bed.

The boy obeys stiffly and crosses the room, almost mechanically, to the bed and more or less folds the bedding into a heap, then angrily gets his books and cap.

TRAVIS (*sulking and standing apart from her unnaturally*): I'm gone.

RUTH (*looking up from the stove to inspect him automatically*): Come here. (*He crosses to her and she studies his head.*) If you don't take this comb and fix this here head, you better! (TRAVIS *puts down his books with a great sigh of oppression, and crosses to the mirror. His mother mutters under her breath about his "stubbornness."*) 'Bout to march out of here with that head looking just like chickens slept in it! I just don't know where you get your stubborn ways . . . And get your jacket, too. Looks chilly out this morning.

TRAVIS (*with conspicuously brushed hair and jacket*): I'm gone.

RUTH: Get carfare and milk money—(*waving one finger*)—and not a single penny for no caps, you hear me?

TRAVIS (*with sullen politeness*): Yes'm.

He turns in outrage to leave. His mother watches after him as in his frustration he approaches the door almost comically. When she speaks to him, her voice has become a very gentle tease.

RUTH (*mocking; as she thinks he would say it*): Oh, Mama makes me so mad sometimes, I don't know what to do! (*She waits and continues to his back as he stands stock-still in front of the door.*) I wouldn't kiss that woman good-bye for nothing in this world this morning! (*The boy finally turns around and rolls his eyes at her, knowing the mood has changed and he is vindicated; he does not, however, move toward her yet.*) Not for nothing in this world! (*She finally laughs aloud at him and holds out her arms to him and we see that it is a way between them, very old and practiced. He crosses to her and allows her to embrace him warmly but keeps his face fixed with masculine rigidity. She holds him back from her presently and looks at him and runs her fingers over the features of his face. With utter gentleness.*) Now—whose little old angry man are you?

TRAVIS (*The masculinity and gruffness start to fade at last.*): Aw gaalee—Mama . . .

RUTH (*mimicking*): Aw—gaaaaalleeeee, Mama! (*She pushes him, with rough playfulness and finality, toward the door.*) Get on out of here or you going to be late.

TRAVIS (*in the face of love, new aggressiveness*): Mama, could I *please* go carry groceries?

RUTH: Honey, it's starting to get so cold evenings.

WALTER (*coming in from the bathroom and drawing a make-believe gun from a make-believe holster and shooting at his son*): What is it he wants to do?

RUTH: Go carry groceries after school at the supermarket.

WALTER: Well, let him go . . .

TRAVIS (*quickly, to the ally*): I *have* to—she won't gimme the fifty cents . . .

WALTER (*to his wife only*): Why not?

RUTH (*simply, and with flavor*): 'Cause we don't have it.

WALTER (*to RUTH only*): What you tell the boy things like that for? (*reaching down into his pants with a rather important gesture*) Here, son—

He hands the boy the coin, but his eyes are directed to his wife's. TRAVIS *takes the money happily.*

TRAVIS: Thanks, Daddy.

He starts out. RUTH *watches both of them with murder in her eyes.* WALTER *stands and stares back at her with defiance, and suddenly reaches into his pocket again on an afterthought.*

WALTER (*without even looking at his son, still staring hard at his wife*): In fact, here's another fifty cents . . . Buy yourself some fruit today—or take a taxicab to school or something!

TRAVIS: Whoopee—

He leaps up and clasps his father around the middle with his legs, and they face each other in mutual appreciation; slowly WALTER LEE *peeks around the boy to catch the violent rays from his wife's eyes and draws his head back as if shot.*

WALTER: You better get down now—and get to school, man.

TRAVIS (*at the door*): O.K. Good-bye.

He exits.

WALTER (*after him, pointing with pride*): That's *my* boy. (*She looks at him in disgust and turns back to her work.*) You know what I was thinking 'bout in the bathroom this morning?

RUTH: No.

WALTER: How come you always try to be so pleasant!

RUTH: What is there to be pleasant 'bout!

WALTER: You want to know what I was thinking 'bout in the bathroom or not!

RUTH: I know what you thinking 'bout.

WALTER (*ignoring her*): 'Bout what me and Willy Harris was talking about last night.

RUTH (*immediately—a refrain*): Willy Harris is a good-for-nothing loud-mouth.

WALTER: Anybody who talks to me has got to be a good-for-nothing loud-mouth, ain't he? And what you know about who is just a good for-nothing loudmouth? Charlie Atkins was just a "good-for-nothing loud-mouth" too, wasn't he! When he wanted me to go in the dry-cleaning business with him. And now—he's grossing a hundred thousand a year. A hundred thousand dollars a year! You still call *him* a loudmouth!

RUTH (*bitterly*): Oh, Walter Lee . . .

She folds her head on her arms over the table.

WALTER (*rising and coming to her and standing over her*): You tired, ain't you? Tired of everything. Me, the boy, the way we live—this beat-up hole—everything. Ain't you? (*She doesn't look up, doesn't answer.*) So tired—moaning and groaning all the time, but you wouldn't do nothing to help, would you? You couldn't be on my side that long for nothing, could you?

RUTH: Walter, please leave me alone.

WALTER: A man needs for a woman to back him up . . .

RUTH: Walter—

WALTER: Mama would listen to you. You know she listen to you more than she do me and Bennie. She think more of you. All you have to do is just sit down with her when you drinking your coffee one morning and talk-ing 'bout things like you do and—(*He sits down beside her and demon-strates graphically what he thinks her methods and tone should be.*)—you just sip your coffee, see, and say easy like that you been thinking 'bout that deal Walter Lee is so interested in, 'bout the store and all, and sip some more coffee, like what you saying ain't really that important to you—And the next thing you know, she be listening good and asking you questions and when I come home—I can tell her the details. This ain't no fly-by-night proposition, baby. I mean we figured it out, me and Willy and Bobo.

RUTH (*with a frown*): Bobo?

WALTER: Yeah. You see, this little liquor store we got in mind cost seventy-five thousand and we figured the initial investment on the place be 'bout thirty thousand, see. That be ten thousand each. Course, there's a couple of hundred you got to pay so's you don't spend your life just waiting for them clowns to let your license get approved—

RUTH: You mean graft?

WALTER (*frowning impatiently*): Don't call it that. See there, that just goes to show you what women understand about the world. Baby, don't *nothing* happen for you in this world 'less you pay *somebody* off!

RUTH: Walter, leave me alone! (*she raises her head and stares at him vigor-ously—then says, more quietly*) Eat your eggs, they gonna be cold.

WALTER (*straightening up from her and looking off*): That's it. There you are. Man say to his woman: I got me a dream. His woman say: Eat your eggs. (*sadly, but gaining in power*) Man say: I got to take hold of this here world, baby! And a woman will say: Eat your eggs and go to work. (*passionately now*) Man say: I got to change my life, I'm choking to death, baby! And his woman say—(*in utter anguish as he brings his fists down on his thighs*)—Your eggs is getting cold!

RUTH (*softly*): Walter, that ain't none of our money.

WALTER (*not listening at all or even looking at her*): This morning, I was lookin' in the mirror and thinking about it . . . I'm thirty-five years old; I been married eleven years and I got a boy who sleeps in the living room—(*very, very quietly*)—and all I got to give him is stories about how rich white people live . . .

RUTH: Eat your eggs, Walter.

WALTER (*slams the table and jumps up*): DAMN MY EGGS—DAMN ALL THE EGGS THAT EVER WAS!

RUTH: Then go to work.

WALTER (*looking up at her*): See—I'm trying to talk to you 'bout myself—(*shaking his head with the repetition*)—and all you can say is eat them eggs and go to work.

RUTH (*wearily*): Honey, you never say nothing new. I listen to you every day, every night and every morning, and you never say nothing new. (*shrugging*) So you would rather *be* Mr. Arnold than be his chauffeur. So—I would *rather* be living in Buckingham Palace.

WALTER: That is just what is wrong with the colored woman in this world . . . Don't understand about building their men up and making 'em feel like they somebody. Like they can do something.

RUTH (*drily, but to hurt*): There *are* colored men who do things.

WALTER: No thanks to the colored woman.

RUTH: Well, being a colored woman, I guess I can't help myself none.

She rises and gets the ironing board and sets it up and attacks a huge pile of rough-dried clothes, sprinkling them in preparation for the ironing and then rolling them into tight fat balls.

WALTER (*mumbling*): We one group of men tied to a race of women with small minds!

His sister BENEATHA enters. She is about twenty, as slim and intense as her brother. She is not as pretty as her sister-in-law, but her lean, almost intellectual face has a handsomeness of its own. She wears a bright-red flannel nightie, and her thick hair stands wildly about her head. Her speech is a mixture of many things; it is different from the rest of the family's insofar as education has permeated her sense of English—and perhaps the Midwest rather than the South has finally—at last—won out in her inflection; but not altogether, because over all of it is a soft slurring and transformed use of vowels which is the decided influence of the Southside. She passes through the room without looking at either RUTH or WALTER and goes to the outside door and looks, a little blindly, out to the bathroom. She sees that it has been lost to the Johnsons. She closes the door with a sleepy vengeance and crosses to the table and sits down a little defeated.

BENEATHA: I am going to start timing those people.

WALTER: You should get up earlier.

BENEATHA (*Her face in her hands. She is still fighting the urge to go back to bed.*): Really—would you suggest dawn? Where's the paper?

WALTER (*pushing the paper across the table to her as he studies her almost clinically, as though he has never seen her before*): You a horrible-looking chick at this hour.

BENEATHA (*drily*): Good morning, everybody.

WALTER (*senselessly*): How is school coming?

BENEATHA (*in the same spirit*): Lovely. Lovely. And you know, biology is the greatest. (*looking up at him*) I dissected something that looked just like you yesterday.

WALTER: I just wondered if you've made up your mind and everything.

BENEATHA (*gaining in sharpness and impatience*): And what did I answer yesterday morning—and the day before that?

RUTH (*from the ironing board, like someone disinterested and old*): Don't be so nasty, Bennie.

BENEATHA (*still to her brother*): And the day before that and the day before that!

WALTER (*defensively*): I'm interested in you. Something wrong with that? Ain't many girls who decide—

WALTER AND BENEATHA (*in unison*): —"to be a doctor."

Silence.

WALTER: Have we figured out yet just exactly how much medical school is going to cost?

RUTH: Walter Lee, why don't you leave that girl alone and get out of here to work?

BENEATHA (*exits to the bathroom and bangs on the door*): Come on out of there, please!

She comes back into the room.

WALTER (*looking at his sister intently*): You know the check is coming tomorrow.

BENEATHA (*turning on him with a sharpness all her own*): That money belongs to Mama, Walter, and it's for her to decide how she wants to use it. I don't care if she wants to buy a house or a rocket ship or just nail it up somewhere and look at it. It's hers. Not ours—*hers*.

WALTER (*bitterly*): Now ain't that fine! You just got your mother's interest at heart, ain't you, girl? You such a nice girl—but if Mama got that money she can always take a few thousand and help you through school too—can't she?

BENEATHA: I have never asked anyone around here to do anything for me!

WALTER: No! And the line between asking and just accepting when the time comes is big and wide—ain't it!

BENEATHA (*with fury*): What do you want from me, Brother—that I quit school or just drop dead, which!

WALTER: I don't want nothing but for you to stop acting holy 'round here. Me and Ruth done made some sacrifices for you—why can't you do something for the family?

RUTH: Walter, don't be dragging me in it.

WALTER: You are in it—Don't you get up and go work in somebody's kitchen for the last three years to help put clothes on her back?

RUTH: Oh, Walter—that's not fair . . .

WALTER: It ain't that nobody expects you to get on your knees and say thank you, Brother; thank you, Ruth; thank you, Mama—and thank you, Travis, for wearing the same pair of shoes for two semesters—

BENEATHA (*dropping to her knees*): Well—I *do*—all right?—thank everybody! And forgive me for ever wanting to be anything at all! (*pursuing him on her knees across the floor*) FORGIVE ME, FORGIVE ME, FORGIVE ME!

RUTH: Please stop it! Your mama'll hear you.

WALTER: Who the hell told you you had to be a doctor? If you so crazy 'bout messing 'round with sick people—then go be a nurse like other women— or just get married and be quiet . . .

BENEATHA: Well—you finally got it said . . . It took you three years but you finally got it said. Walter, give up; leave me alone—it's Mama's money.

WALTER: He was my father, too!

BENEATHA: So what? He was mine, too—and Travis' grandfather—but the insurance money belongs to Mama. Picking on me is not going to make her give it to you to invest in any liquor stores—(*underbreath, dropping into a chair*)—and I for one say, God bless Mama for that!

WALTER (*to* RUTH): See—did you hear? Did you hear!

RUTH: Honey, please go to work.

WALTER: Nobody in this house is ever going to understand me.

BENEATHA: Because you're a nut.

WALTER: Who's a nut?

BENEATHA: You—you are a nut. Thee is mad, boy.

WALTER (*looking at his wife and his sister from the door, very sadly*): The world's most backward race of people, and that's a fact.

BENEATHA (*turning slowly in her chair*): And then there are all those prophets who would lead us out of the wilderness—(WALTER *slams out of the house.*)—into the swamps!

RUTH: Bennie, why you always gotta be pickin' on your brother? Can't you be a little sweeter sometimes? (*Door opens.* WALTER *walks in. He fumbles with his cap, starts to speak, clears throat, looks everywhere but at* RUTH. *Finally.*)

WALTER (*to* RUTH): I need some money for carfare.

RUTH (*looks at him, then warms; teasing, but tenderly*): Fifty cents? (*She goes to her bag and gets money.*) Here—take a taxi!

WALTER *exits.* MAMA *enters. She is a woman in her early sixties, full-bodied and strong. She is one of those women of a certain grace and beauty who wear it so unobtrusively that it takes a while to notice. Her dark-brown face is surrounded by the total whiteness of her hair, and, being a woman who has adjusted to many things in life and overcome many more, her face is full of strength. She has, we can see, wit and faith of a kind that keep her eyes lit and full of interest and expectancy. She is, in a word, a beautiful woman. Her bearing is perhaps most like the noble bearing of the women of the Hereros of Southwest Africa—rather as if she imagines that as she walks she still bears a basket or a vessel upon her head. Her speech, on the other hand, is as careless as her carriage is precise—she is inclined to slur everything—but her voice is perhaps not so much quiet as simply soft.*

MAMA: Who that 'round here slamming doors at this hour?

She crosses through the room, goes to the window, opens it, and brings in a feeble little plant growing doggedly in a small pot on the window sill. She feels the dirt and puts it back out.

RUTH: That was Walter Lee. He and Bennie was at it again.

MAMA: My children and they tempers. Lord, if this little old plant don't get more sun than it's been getting it ain't never going to see spring again. (*She turns from the window.*) What's the matter with you this morning, Ruth? You looks right peaked. You aiming to iron all them things? Leave some for me. I'll get to 'em this afternoon. Bennie honey, it's too drafty for you to be sitting 'round half dressed. Where's your robe?

BENEATHA: In the cleaners.

MAMA: Well, go get mine and put it on.

BENEATHA: I'm not cold, Mama, honest.

MAMA: I know—but you so thin . . .

BENEATHA (*irritably*): Mama, I'm not cold.

MAMA (*seeing the make-down bed as* TRAVIS *has left it*): Lord have mercy, look at that poor bed. Bless his heart—he tries, don't he?

She moves to the bed TRAVIS *has sloppily made up.*

RUTH: No—he don't half try at all 'cause he knows you going to come along behind him and fix everything. That's just how come he don't know how to do nothing right now—you done spoiled that boy so.

MAMA (*folding bedding*): Well—he's a little boy. Ain't supposed to know 'bout housekeeping. My baby, that's what he is. What you fix for his breakfast this morning?

RUTH (*angrily*): I feed my son, Lena!

MAMA: I ain't meddling—(*underbreath; busy-bodyish*) I just noticed all last week he had cold cereal, and when it starts getting this chilly in the fall a child ought to have some hot grits or something when he goes out in the cold—

RUTH (*furious*): I gave him hot oats—is that all right!

MAMA: I ain't meddling. (*pause*) Put a lot of nice butter on it? (RUTH *shoots her an angry look and does not reply.*) He likes lots of butter.

RUTH (*exasperated*): Lena—

MAMA (*To* BENEATHA. MAMA *is inclined to wander conversationally sometimes.*): What was you and your brother fussing 'bout this morning?

BENEATHA: It's not important, Mama.

She gets up and goes to look out at the bathroom, which is apparently free, and she picks up her towels and rushes out.

MAMA: What was they fighting about?

RUTH: Now you know as well as I do.

MAMA (*shaking her head*): Brother still worrying hisself sick about that money?

RUTH: You know he is.

MAMA: You had breakfast?

RUTH: Some coffee.

MAMA: Girl, you better start eating and looking after yourself better. You almost thin as Travis.

RUTH: Lena—

MAMA: Un-hunh?

RUTH: What are you going to do with it?

MAMA: Now don't you start, child. It's too early in the morning to be talking about money. It ain't Christian.

RUTH: It's just that he got his heart set on that store—

MAMA: You mean that liquor store that Willy Harris want him to invest in?

RUTH: Yes—

MAMA: We ain't no business people, Ruth. We just plain working folks.

RUTH: Ain't nobody business people till they go into business. Walter Lee say colored people ain't never going to start getting ahead till they start gambling on some different kinds of things in the world—investments and things.

MAMA: What done got into you, girl? Walter Lee done finally sold you on investing.

RUTH: No. Mama, something is happening between Walter and me. I don't know what it is—but he needs something—something I can't give him any more. He needs this chance, Lena.

MAMA (*frowning deeply*): But liquor, honey—

RUTH: Well—like Walter says—I spec people going to always be drinking themselves some liquor.

MAMA: Well—whether they drinks it or not ain't none of my business. But whether I go into business selling it to 'em *is,* and I don't want that on my ledger this late in life. (*stopping suddenly and studying her daughter-in-law*) Ruth Younger, what's the matter with you today? You look like you could fall over right there.

RUTH: I'm tired.

MAMA: Then you better stay home from work today.

RUTH: I can't stay home. She'd be calling up the agency and screaming at them, "My girl didn't come in today—send me somebody! My girl didn't come in!" Oh, she just have a fit . . .

MAMA: Well, let her have it. I'll just call her up and say you got the flu—

RUTH (*laughing*): Why the flu?

MAMA: 'Cause it sounds respectable to 'em. Something white people get, too. They know 'bout the flu. Otherwise they think you been cut up or something when you tell 'em you sick.

RUTH: I got to go in. We need the money.

MAMA: Somebody would of thought my children done all but starved to death the way they talk about money here late. Child, we got a great big old check coming tomorrow.

RUTH (*sincerely, but also self-righteously*): Now that's your money. It ain't got nothing to do with me. We all feel like that—Walter and Bennie and me—even Travis.

MAMA (*thoughtfully, and suddenly very far away*): Ten thousand dollars—

RUTH: Sure is wonderful.

MAMA: Ten thousand dollars.

RUTH: You know what you should do, Miss Lena? You should take yourself a trip somewhere. To Europe or South America or someplace—

MAMA (*throwing up her hands at the thought*): Oh, child!

RUTH: I'm serious. Just pack up and leave! Go on away and enjoy yourself some. Forget about the family and have yourself a ball for once in your life—

MAMA (*drily*): You sound like I'm just about ready to die. Who'd go with me? What I look like wandering 'round Europe by myself?

RUTH: Shoot—these here rich white women do it all the time. They don't think nothing of packing up they suitcases and piling on one of them big steamships and—swoosh!—they gone, child.

MAMA: Something always told me I wasn't no rich white woman.

RUTH: Well—what are you going to do with it then?

MAMA: I ain't rightly decided. (*Thinking. She speaks now with emphasis.*) Some of it got to be put away for Beneatha and her schoolin'—and ain't nothing going to touch that part of it. Nothing. (*She waits several seconds, trying to make up her mind about something, and looks at* RUTH *a little tentatively before going on.*) Been thinking that we maybe could meet the notes on a little old two-story somewhere, with a yard where Travis could play in the summertime, if we use part of the insurance for a down payment and everybody kind of pitch in. I could maybe take on a little day work again, few days a week—

RUTH (*studying her mother-in-law furtively and concentrating on her ironing, anxious to encourage without seeming to*): Well, Lord knows, we've put enough rent into this here rat trap to pay for four houses by now . . .

MAMA (*looking up at the words "rat trap" and then looking around and leaning back and sighing—in a suddenly reflective mood*): "Rat trap"—yes, that's all it is. (*smiling*) I remember just as well the day me and Big Walter moved in here. Hadn't been married but two weeks and wasn't planning on living here no more than a year. (*She shakes her head at the dissolved dream.*) We was going to set away, little by little, don't you know, and buy a little place out in Morgan Park. We had even picked out the house. (*chuckling a little*) Looks right dumpy today. But Lord, child, you should know all the dreams I had 'bout buying that house and fixing it up and making me a little garden in the back—(*She waits and stops smiling.*) And didn't none of it happen.

Dropping her hands in a futile gesture.

RUTH (*keeps her head down, ironing*): Yes, life can be a barrel of disappointments, sometimes.

MAMA: Honey, Big Walter would come in here some nights back then and slump down on that couch there and just look at the rug, and look at me and look at the rug and then back at me—and I'd know he was down then . . . really down. (*After a second very long and thoughtful pause; she is seeing back to times that only she can see.*) And then, Lord, when I lost that baby—little Claude—I almost thought I was going to lose Big Walter too. Oh, that man grieved hisself! He was one man to love his children.

RUTH: Ain't nothin' can tear at you like losin' your baby.

MAMA: I guess that's how come that man finally worked hisself to death like he done. Like he was fighting his own war with this here world that took his baby from him.

RUTH: He sure was a fine man, all right. I always liked Mr. Younger.

MAMA: Crazy 'bout his children! God knows there was plenty wrong with Walter Younger—hard-headed, mean, kind of wild with women—plenty wrong with him. But he sure loved his children. Always wanted them to have something—be something. That's where Brother gets all these notions, I reckon. Big Walter used to say, he'd get right wet in the eyes sometimes, lean his head back with the water standing in his eyes and say, "Seem like God didn't see fit to give the black man nothing but dreams—but He did give us children to make them dreams seem worth while." (*She smiles.*) He could talk like that, don't you know.

RUTH: Yes, he sure could. He was a good man, Mr. Younger.

MAMA: Yes, a fine man—just couldn't never catch up with his dreams, that's all.

BENEATHA *comes in, brushing her hair and looking up to the ceiling, where the sound of a vacuum cleaner has started up.*

BENEATHA: What could be so dirty on that woman's rugs that she has to vacuum them every single day?

RUTH: I wish certain young women 'round here who I could name would take inspiration about certain rugs in a certain apartment I could also mention.

BENEATHA (*shrugging*): How much cleaning can a house need, for Christ's sakes.

MAMA (*not liking the Lord's name used thus*): Bennie!

RUTH: Just listen to her—just listen!

BENEATHA: Oh, God!

MAMA: If you use the Lord's name just one more time—

BENEATHA (*a bit of a whine*): Oh, Mama—

RUTH: Fresh—just fresh as salt, this girl!

BENEATHA (*drily*): Well—if the salt loses its savor—

MAMA: Now that will do. I just ain't going to have you 'round here reciting the scriptures in vain—you hear me?

BENEATHA: How did I manage to get on everybody's wrong side by just walking into a room?

RUTH: If you weren't so fresh—

BENEATHA: Ruth, I'm twenty years old.

MAMA: What time you be home from school today?

BENEATHA: Kind of late. (*with enthusiasm*) Madeline is going to start my guitar lessons today.

MAMA *and* RUTH *look up with the same expression.*

MAMA: Your *what* kind of lessons?

BENEATHA: Guitar.

RUTH: Oh, Father!

MAMA: How come you done taken it in your mind to learn to play the guitar?

BENEATHA: I just want to, that's all.

MAMA (*smiling*): Lord, child, don't you know what to do with yourself? How long it going to be before you get tired of this now—like you got tired of that little play-acting group you joined last year? (*looking at* RUTH) And what was it the year before that?

RUTH: The horseback-riding club for which she bought that fifty-five-dollar riding habit that's been hanging in the closet ever since!

MAMA (*to* BENEATHA): Why you got to flit so from one thing to another, baby?

BENEATHA (*sharply*): I just want to learn to play the guitar. Is there anything wrong with that?

MAMA: Ain't nobody trying to stop you. I just wonders sometimes why you has to flit so from one thing to another all the time. You ain't never done nothing with all that camera equipment you brought home—

BENEATHA: I don't flit! I—I experiment with different forms of expression—

RUTH: Like riding a horse?

BENEATHA: —People have to express themselves one way or another.

MAMA: What is it you want to express?

BENEATHA (*angrily*): Me! (MAMA *and* RUTH *look at each other and burst into raucous laughter.*) Don't worry—I don't expect you to understand.

MAMA (*to change the subject*): Who you going out with tomorrow night?

BENEATHA (*with displeasure*): George Murchison again.

MAMA (*pleased*): Oh—you getting a little sweet on him?

RUTH: You ask me, this child ain't sweet on nobody but herself— (*underbreath*) Express herself!

They laugh.

BENEATHA: Oh—I like George all right, Mama. I mean I like him enough to go out with him and stuff, but—

RUTH (*for devilment*): What does *and stuff* mean?

BENEATHA: Mind your own business.

MAMA: Stop picking at her now, Ruth. (*She chuckles—then a suspicious sudden look at her daughter as she turns in her chair for emphasis.*) What DOES it mean?

BENEATHA (*wearily*): Oh, I just mean I couldn't ever really be serious about George. He's—he's so shallow.

RUTH: Shallow—what do you mean he's shallow? He's *Rich!*

MAMA: Hush, Ruth.

BENEATHA: I know he's rich. He knows he's rich, too.

RUTH: Well—what other qualities a man got to have to satisfy you, little girl?

BENEATHA: You wouldn't even begin to understand. Anybody who married Walter could not possibly understand.

MAMA (*outraged*): What kind of way is that to talk about your brother?

BENEATHA: Brother is a flip—let's face it.

MAMA (*to* RUTH, *helplessly*): What's a flip?

RUTH (*glad to add kindling*): She's saying he's crazy.

BENEATHA: Not crazy. Brother isn't really crazy yet—he—he's an elaborate neurotic.

MAMA: Hush your mouth!

BENEATHA: As for George. Well. George looks good—he's got a beautiful car and he takes me to nice places and, as my sister-in-law says, he is probably the richest boy I will ever get to know and I even like him sometimes—but if the Youngers are sitting around waiting to see if their little Bennie is going to tie up the family with the Murchisons, they are wasting their time.

RUTH: You mean you wouldn't marry George Murchison if he asked you someday? That pretty, rich thing? Honey, I knew you was odd—

BENEATHA: No I would not marry him if all I felt for him was what I feel now. Besides, George's family wouldn't really like it.

MAMA: Why not?

BENEATHA: Oh, Mama—The Murchisons are honest-to-God-real-*live*-rich colored people, and the only people in the world who are more snobbish than rich white people are rich colored people. I thought everybody knew that. I've met Mrs. Murchison. She's a scene!

MAMA: You must not dislike people 'cause they well off, honey.

BENEATHA: Why not? It makes just as much sense as disliking people 'cause they are poor, and lots of people do that.

RUTH (*A wisdom-of-the-ages manner. To* MAMA.): Well, she'll get over some of this—

BENEATHA: Get over it? What are you talking about, Ruth? Listen, I'm going to be a doctor. I'm not worried about who I'm going to marry yet—if I ever get married.

MAMA *and* RUTH: *If!*

MAMA: Now, Bennie—

BENEATHA: Oh, I probably will . . . but first I'm going to be a doctor, and George, for one, still thinks that's pretty funny. I couldn't be bothered with that. I am going to be a doctor and everybody around here better understand that!

MAMA (*kindly*): 'Course you going to be a doctor, honey, God willing.

BENEATHA (*drily*): God hasn't got a thing to do with it.

MAMA: Beneatha—that just wasn't necessary.

BENEATHA: Well—neither is God. I get sick of hearing about God.

MAMA: Beneatha!

BENEATHA: I mean it! I'm just tired of hearing about God all the time. What has He got to do with anything? Does He pay tuition?

MAMA: You 'bout to get your fresh little jaw slapped!

RUTH: That's just what she needs, all right!

BENEATHA: Why? Why can't I say what I want to around here, like everybody else?

MAMA: It don't sound nice for a young girl to say things like that—you wasn't brought up that way. Me and your father went to trouble to get you and Brother to church every Sunday.

BENEATHA: Mama, you don't understand. It's all a matter of ideas, and God is just one idea I don't accept. It's not important. I am not going out and be immoral or commit crimes because I don't believe in God. I don't even think about it. It's just that I get tired of Him getting credit for all the things the human race achieves through its own stubborn effort.

There simply is no blasted God—there is only man and it is *he* who makes miracles!

MAMA *absorbs this speech, studies her daughter and rises slowly and crosses to* BENEATHA *and slaps her powerfully across the face. After, there is only silence and the daughter drops her eyes from her mother's face, and* MAMA *is very tall before her.*

MAMA: Now—you say after me, in my mother's house there is still God. (*There is a long pause and* BENEATHA *stares at the floor wordlessly.* MAMA *repeats the phrase with precision and cool emotion.*) In my mother's house there is still God.

BENEATHA: In my mother's house there is still God.

A long pause.

MAMA (*Walking away from* BENEATHA, *too disturbed for triumphant posture. Stopping and turning back to her daughter.*): There are some ideas we ain't going to have in this house. Not long as I am at the head of this family.

BENEATHA: Yes, ma'am.

MAMA *walks out of the room.*

RUTH (*almost gently, with profound understanding*): You think you a woman, Bennie—but you still a little girl. What you did was childish— so you got treated like a child.

BENEATHA: I see. (*quietly*) I also see that everybody thinks it's all right for Mama to be a tyrant. But all the tyranny in the world will never put a God in the heavens!

She picks up her books and goes out. Pause.

RUTH (*goes to* MAMA'S *door*): She said she was sorry.

MAMA (*coming out, going to her plant*): They frightens me, Ruth. My children.

RUTH: You got good children, Lena. They just a little off sometimes—but they're good.

MAMA: No—there's something come down between me and them that don't let us understand each other and I don't know what it is. One done almost lost his mind thinking 'bout money all the time and the other done commence to talk about things I can't seem to understand in no form or fashion. What is it that's changing, Ruth.

RUTH (*soothingly, older than her years*): Now . . . you taking it all too seriously. You just got strong-willed children and it takes a strong woman like you to keep 'em in hand.

MAMA (*looking at her plant and sprinkling a little water on it*): They spirited all right, my children. Got to admit they got spirit—Bennie and Walter. Like this little old plant that ain't never had enough sunshine or nothing—and look at it . . .

She has her back to RUTH, *who has had to stop ironing and lean against something and put the back of her hand to her forehead.*

RUTH (*trying to keep* MAMA *from noticing*): You . . . sure . . . loves that little old thing, don't you? . . .

MAMA: Well, I always wanted me a garden like I used to see sometimes at the back of the houses down home. This plant is close as I ever got to having one. (*She looks out of the window as she replaces the plant.*) Lord, ain't nothing as dreary as the view from this window on a dreary day, is there? Why ain't you singing this morning, Ruth? Sing that "No Ways Tired." That song always lifts me up so—(*She turns at last to see that* RUTH *has slipped quietly to the floor, in a state of semiconsciousness.*) Ruth! Ruth honey—what's the matter with you . . . Ruth!

Curtain.

SCENE 2

It is the following morning; a Saturday morning, and house cleaning is in progress at the YOUNGERS. *Furniture has been shoved hither and yon and* MAMA *is giving the kitchen-area walls a washing down.* BENEATHA, *in dungarees, with a handkerchief tied around her face, is spraying insecticide into the cracks in the walls. As they work, the radio is on and a Southside disk-jockey program is inappropriately filling the house with a rather exotic saxophone blues.* TRAVIS, *the sole idle one, is leaning on his arms, looking out of the window.*

TRAVIS: Grandmama, that stuff Bennie is using smells awful. Can I go downstairs, please?

MAMA: Did you get all them chores done already? I ain't seen you doing much.

TRAVIS: Yes'm—finished early. Where did Mama go this morning?

MAMA (*looking at* BENEATHA): She had to go on a little errand.

The phone rings. BENEATHA *runs to answer it and reaches it before* WALTER, *who has entered from bedroom.*

TRAVIS: Where?

MAMA: To tend to her business.

BENEATHA: Haylo . . . (*disappointed*) Yes, he is. (*She tosses the phone to* WALTER, *who barely catches it.*) It's Willie Harris again.

WALTER (*as privately as possible under* MAMA'S *gaze*): Hello, Willie. Did you get the papers from the lawyer? . . . No, not yet. I told you the mailman doesn't get here till ten-thirty . . . No, I'll come there . . . Yeah! Right away. (*He hangs up and goes for his coat.*)

BENEATHA: Brother, where did Ruth go?

WALTER (*as he exits*): How should I know!

TRAVIS: Aw come on, Grandma. Can I go outside?

MAMA: Oh, I guess so. You stay right in front of the house, though, and keep a good lookout for the postman.

TRAVIS: Yes'm. (*He darts into bedroom for stickball and bat, reenters, and sees* BENEATHA *on her knees spraying under sofa with behind upraised. He edges closer to the target, takes aim, and lets her have it. She screams.*) Leave them poor little cockroaches alone, they ain't bothering you none!

(*He runs as she swings the spraygun at him viciously and playfully.*) Grandma! Grandma!

MAMA: Look out there, girl, before you be spilling some of that stuff on that child!

TRAVIS (*safely behind the bastion of* MAMA): That's right—look out, now! (*He exits.*)

BENEATHA (*drily*): I can't imagine that it would hurt him—it has never hurt the roaches.

MAMA: Well, little boys' hides ain't as tough as Southside roaches. You better get over there behind the bureau. I seen one marching out of there like Napoleon yesterday.

BENEATHA: There's really only one way to get rid of them, Mama—

MAMA: How?

BENEATHA: Set fire to this building! Mama, where did Ruth go?

MAMA (*looking at her with meaning*): To the doctor, I think.

BENEATHA: The doctor? What's the matter? (*They exchange glances.*) You don't think—

MAMA (*with her sense of drama*): Now I ain't saying what I think. But I ain't never been wrong 'bout a woman neither.

The phone rings.

BENEATHA (*at the phone*): Hay-lo . . . (*pause, and a moment of recognition*) Well—when did you get back! . . . And how was it? . . . Of course I've missed you—in my way . . . This morning? No . . . house cleaning and all that and Mama hates it if I let people come over when the house is like this . . . You *have?* Well, that's different . . . What is it—Oh, what the hell, come on over . . . Right, see you then. *Arrividerci.*

She hangs up.

MAMA (*who has listened vigorously, as is her habit*): Who is that you inviting over here with this house looking like this? You ain't got the pride you was born with!

BENEATHA: Asagai doesn't care how houses look, Mama—he's an intellectual.

MAMA: Who?

BENEATHA: Asagai—Joseph Asagai. He's an African boy I met on campus. He's been studying in Canada all summer.

MAMA: What's his name?

BENEATHA: Asagai, Joseph. Ah-sah-guy . . . He's from Nigeria.

MAMA: Oh, that's the little country that was founded by slaves way back . . .

BENEATHA: No, Mama—that's Liberia.

MAMA: I don't think I never met no African before.

BENEATHA: Well, do me a favor and don't ask him a whole lot of ignorant questions about Africans. I mean, do they wear clothes and all that—

MAMA: Well, now, I guess if you think we so ignorant 'round here maybe you shouldn't bring your friends here—

BENEATHA: It's just that people ask such crazy things. All anyone seems to know about when it comes to Africa is Tarzan—

MAMA (*indignantly*): Why should I know anything about Africa?

BENEATHA: Why do you give money at church for the missionary work?

MAMA: Well, that's to help save people.

BENEATHA: You mean save them from *heathenism*—

MAMA (*innocently*): Yes.

BENEATHA: I'm afraid they need more salvation from the British and the French.

RUTH comes in forlornly and pulls off her coat with dejection. They both turn to look at her.

RUTH (*dispiritedly*): Well, I guess from all the happy faces—everybody knows.

BENEATHA: You pregnant?

MAMA: Lord have mercy, I sure hope it's a little old girl. Travis ought to have a sister.

BENEATHA and RUTH give her a hopeless look for this grandmotherly enthusiasm.

BENEATHA: How far along are you?

RUTH: Two months.

BENEATHA: Did you mean to? I mean did you plan it or was it an accident?

MAMA: What do you know about planning or not planning?

BENEATHA: Oh, Mama.

RUTH (*wearily*): She's twenty years old, Lena.

BENEATHA: Did you plan it, Ruth?

RUTH: Mind your own business.

BENEATHA: It is my business—where is he going to live, on the *roof*? (*There is silence following the remark as the three women react to the sense of it.*) Gee—I didn't mean that, Ruth, honest. Gee, I don't feel like that at all. I—I think it is wonderful.

RUTH (*dully*): Wonderful.

BENEATHA: Yes—really. (*There is a sudden commotion from the street and she goes to the window to look out.*) What on earth is going on out there? These kids. (*There are, as she throws open the window, the shouts of children rising up from the street. She sticks her head out to see better and calls out.*) TRAVIS! TRAVIS! . . . WHAT ARE YOU DOING DOWN THERE? (*She sees.*) Oh Lord, they're chasing a rat!

RUTH covers her face with hands and turns away.

MAMA (*angrily*): Tell that youngun to get himself up here, at once!

BENEATHA: TRAVIS . . . YOU COME UPSTAIRS . . . AT ONCE!

RUTH (*her face twisted*): Chasing a rat . . .

MAMA (*looking at RUTH, worried*): Doctor say everything going to be all right?

RUTH (*far away*): Yes—she says everything is going to be fine . . .

MAMA (*immediately suspicious*): "She"—What doctor you went to?

RUTH just looks at MAMA meaningfully and MAMA opens her mouth to speak as TRAVIS bursts in.

TRAVIS (*excited and full of narrative, coming directly to his mother*): Mama, you should of seen the rat . . . Big as a cat, honest! (*He shows an exaggerated size with his hands.*) Gaaleee, that rat was really cuttin' and Bubber caught him with his heel and the janitor, Mr. Barnett, got him with a stick—and then they got him in a corner and—BAM! BAM! BAM!—and he was still jumping around and bleeding like everything too   there's rat blood all over the street—

RUTH *reaches out suddenly and grabs her son without even looking at him and clamps her hand over his mouth and holds him to her.* MAMA *crosses to them rapidly and takes the boy from her.*

MAMA: You hush up now . . . talking all that terrible stuff . . . (TRAVIS *is staring at his mother with a stunned expression.* BENEATHA *comes quickly and takes him away from his grandmother and ushers him to the door.*)

BENEATHA: You go back outside and play . . . but not with any rats. (*She pushes him gently out the door with the boy straining to see what is wrong with his mother.*)

MAMA (*worriedly hovering over* RUTH): Ruth honey—what's the matter with you—you sick?

RUTH *has her fists clenched on her thighs and is fighting hard to suppress a scream that seems to be rising in her.*

BENEATHA: What's the matter with her, Mama?

MAMA (*working her fingers in* RUTH'S *shoulders to relax her*): She be all right. Women gets right depressed sometimes when they get her way. (*speaking softly, expertly, rapidly*) Now you just relax. That's right . . . just lean back, don't think 'bout nothing at all . . . nothing at all—

RUTH: I'm all right . . .

The glassy-eyed look melts and then she collapses into a fit of heavy sobbing. The bell rings.

BENEATHA: Oh, my God—that must be Asagai.

MAMA (*to* RUTH): Come on now, honey. You need to lie down and rest awhile . . . then have some nice hot food.

They exit, RUTH'S *weight on her mother-in-law.* BENEATHA, *herself profoundly disturbed, opens the door to admit a rather dramatic-looking young man with a large package.*

ASAGAI: Hello, Alaiyo—

BENEATHA (*holding the door open and regarding him with pleasure*): Hello . . . (*long pause*) Well—come in. And please excuse everything. My mother was very upset about my letting anyone come here with the place like this.

ASAGAI (*coming into the room*): You look disturbed too . . . Is something wrong?

BENEATHA (*still at the door, absently*): Yes . . . we've all got acute ghetto-itus. (*She smiles and comes toward him, finding a cigarette and sitting.*) So—sit down! No! Wait! (*She whips the spraygun off sofa where she had left it and puts the cushions back. At last perches on arm of sofa. He sits.*) So, how was Canada?

ASAGAI (*a sophisticate*): Canadian.

BENEATHA (*looking at him*): Asagai, I'm very glad you are back.

ASAGAI (*looking back at her in turn*): Are you really?

BENEATHA: Yes—very.

ASAGAI: Why?—you were quite glad when I went away. What happened?

BENEATHA: You went away.

ASAGAI: Ahhhhhhhh.

BENEATHA: Before—you wanted to be so serious before there was time.

ASAGAI: How much time must there be before one knows what one feels?

BENEATHA (*Stalling this particular conversation. Her hands pressed together, in a deliberately childish gesture.*): What did you bring me?

ASAGAI (*handing her the package*): Open it and see.

BENEATHA (*eagerly opening the package and drawing out some records and the colorful robes of a Nigerian woman*): Oh, Asagai! . . . You got them for me! . . . How beautiful . . . and the records too! (*She lifts out the robes and runs to the mirror with them and holds the drapery up in front of herself.*)

ASAGAI (*coming to her at the mirror*): I shall have to teach you how to drape it properly. (*He flings the material about her for the moment and stands back to look at her.*) Ah—Oh-pay-gay-day, oh-gbah-mu-shay. (*a Yoruba exclamation for admiration*) You wear it well . . . very well . . . muti-lated hair and all.

BENEATHA (*turning suddenly*): My hair—what's wrong with my hair?

ASAGAI (*shrugging*): Were you born with it like that?

BENEATHA (*reaching up to touch it*): No . . . of course not.

She looks back to the mirror, disturbed.

ASAGAI (*smiling*): How then?

BENEATHA: You know perfectly well how . . . as crinkly as yours . . . that's how.

ASAGAI: And it is ugly to you that way?

BENEATHA (*quickly*): Oh, no—not ugly . . . (*more slowly, apologetically*) But it's so hard to manage when it's, well—raw.

ASAGAI: And so to accommodate that—you mutilate it every week?

BENEATHA: It's not mutilation!

ASAGAI (*laughing aloud at her seriousness*): Oh . . . please! I am only teas-ing you because you are so very serious about these things. (*He stands back from her and folds his arms across his chest as he watches her pulling at her hair and frowning in the mirror.*) Do you remember the first time you met me at school? . . . (*He laughs.*) You came up to me and you said—and I thought you were the most serious little thing I had ever seen—you said: (*He imitates her.*) "Mr. Asagai—I want very much to talk with you. About Africa. You see, Mr. Asagai, I am looking for my identity!"

He laughs.

BENEATHA (*turning to him, not laughing*): Yes—

Her face is quizzical, profoundly disturbed.

ASAGAI (*still teasing and reaching out and taking her face in his hands and turning her profile to him*): Well . . . it is true that this is not so much a profile of a Hollywood queen as perhaps a queen of the Nile—(*a mock dismissal of the importance of the question*) But what does it matter? Assimilationism is so popular in your country.

BENEATHA (*wheeling, passionately, sharply*): I am not an assimilationist!

ASAGAI (*The protest hangs in the room for a moment and* ASAGAI *studies her, his laughter fading.*): Such a serious one. (*There is a pause.*) So—you like the robes? You must take excellent care of them—they are from my sister's personal wardrobe.

BENEATHA (*with incredulity*): You—you sent all the way home—for me?

ASAGAI (*with charm*): For you—I would do much more . . . Well, that is what I came for. I must go.

BENEATHA: Will you call me Monday?

ASAGAI: Yes . . . We have a great deal to talk about. I mean about identity and time and all that.

BENEATHA: Time?

ASAGAI: Yes. About how much time one needs to know what one feels.

BENEATHA: You see! You never understood that there is more than one kind of feeling which can exist between a man and a woman—or, at least, there should be.

ASAGAI (*shaking his head negatively but gently*): No. Between a man and a woman there need be only one kind of feeling. I have that for you . . . Now even . . . right this moment . . .

BENEATHA: I know—and by itself—it won't do. I can find that anywhere.

ASAGAI: For a woman it should be enough.

BENEATHA: I know—because that's what it says in all the novels that men write. But it isn't. Go ahead and laugh—but I'm not interested in being someone's little episode in America or—(*with feminine vengeance*)—one of them! (ASAGAI *has burst into laughter again.*) That's funny as hell, huh!

ASAGAI: It's just that every American girl I have known has said that to me. White—black—in this you are all the same. And the same speech, too!

BENEATHA (*angrily*): Yuk, yuk, yuk!

ASAGAI: It's how you can be sure that the world's most liberated women are not liberated at all. You all talk about it too much!

MAMA *enters and is immediately all social charm because of the presence of a guest.*

BENEATHA: Oh—Mama—this is Mr. Asagai.

MAMA: How do you do?

ASAGAI (*total politeness to an elder*): How do you do, Mrs. Younger. Please forgive me for coming at such an outrageous hour on a Saturday.

MAMA: Well, you are quite welcome. I just hope you understand that our house don't always look like this. (*chatterish*) You must come again. I would love to hear all about—(*not sure of the name*)—your country. I think it's so sad the way our American Negroes don't know nothing about Africa 'cept Tarzan and all that. And all that money they pour into these churches when they ought to be helping you people over there drive out them French and Englishmen done taken away your land.

The mother flashes a slightly superior look at her daughter upon completion of the recitation.

ASAGAI (*taken aback by this sudden and acutely unrelated expression of sympathy*): Yes . . . yes . . .

MAMA (*smiling at him suddenly and relaxing and looking him over*): How many miles is it from here to where you come from?

ASAGAI: Many thousands.

MAMA (*looking at him as she would* WALTER): I bet you don't half look after yourself, being away from your mama either. I spec you better come 'round here from time to time to get yourself some decent homecooked meals . . .

ASAGAI (*moved*): Thank you. Thank you very much. (*they are all quiet, then*) Well . . . I must go. I will call you Monday, Alaiyo.

MAMA: What's that he call you?

ASAGAI: Oh—"Alaiyo." I hope you don't mind. It is what you would call a nickname, I think. It is a Yoruba word. I am a Yoruba.

MAMA (*looking at* BENEATHA): I—I thought he was from—(*uncertain*)

ASAGAI (*understanding*): Nigeria is my country. Yoruba is my tribal origin—

BENEATHA: You didn't tell us what Alaiyo means . . . for all I know, you might be calling me Little Idiot or something . . .

ASAGAI: Well . . . let me see . . . I do not know how just to explain it . . . The sense of a thing can be so different when it changes languages.

BENEATHA: You're evading.

ASAGAI: No—really it is difficult . . . (*thinking*) It means . . . it means One for Whom Bread—Food—Is Not Enough. (*He looks at her.*) Is that all right?

BENEATHA (*understanding, softly*): Thank you.

MAMA (*looking from one to the other and not understanding any of it*): Well . . . that's nice . . . You must come see us again—Mr.—

ASAGAI: Ah-sah-guy . . .

MAMA: Yes . . . Do come again.

ASAGAI: Good-bye.

He exits.

MAMA (*after him*): Lord, that's a pretty thing just went out here! (*insinuatingly, to her daughter*) Yes, I guess I see why we done commence to get so interested in Africa 'round here. Missionaries my aunt Jenny!

She exits.

BENEATHA: Oh, Mama! . . .

She picks up the Nigerian dress and holds it up to her in front of the mirror again. She sets the headdress on haphazardly and then notices her hair again and clutches at it and then replaces the headdress and frowns at herself. Then she starts to wriggle in front of the mirror as she thinks a Nigerian woman might. TRAVIS *enters and stands regarding her.*

TRAVIS: What's the matter, girl, you cracking up?

BENEATHA: Shut up.

She pulls the headdress off and looks at herself in the mirror and clutches at her hair again and squinches her eyes as if trying to imagine something. Then, suddenly, she gets her raincoat and kerchief and hurriedly prepares for going out.

MAMA (*coming back into the room*): She's resting now. Travis, baby, run next door and ask Miss Johnson to please let me have a little kitchen cleanser. This here can is empty as Jacob's kettle.

TRAVIS: I just came in.

MAMA: Do as you told. (*He exits and she looks at her daughter.*) Where you going?

BENEATHA (*halting at the door*): To become a queen of the Nile!

She exits in a breathless blaze of glory. RUTH *appears in the bedroom doorway.*

MAMA: Who told you to get up?

RUTH: Ain't nothing wrong with me to be lying in no bed for. Where did Bennie go?

MAMA (*drumming her fingers*): Far as I could make out—to Egypt. (RUTH *just looks at her.*) What time is it getting to?

RUTH: Ten twenty. And the mailman going to ring that bell this morning just like he done every morning for the last umpteen years.

TRAVIS *comes in with the cleanser can.*

TRAVIS: She say to tell you that she don't have much.

MAMA (*angrily*): Lord, some people I could name sure is tight-fisted! (*directing her grandson*) Mark two cans of cleanser down on the list there. If she that hard up for kitchen cleanser, I sure don't want to forget to get her none!

RUTH: Lena—maybe the woman is just short on cleanser—

MAMA (*not listening*): Much baking powder as she done borrowed from me all these years, she could of done gone into the baking business!

The bell sounds suddenly and sharply and all three are stunned—serious and silent—mid-speech. In spite of all the other conversations and distractions of the morning, this is what they have been waiting for, even TRAVIS, *who looks helplessly from his mother to his grandmother.* RUTH *is the first to come to life again.*

RUTH (*to* TRAVIS): *Get down them steps, boy!*

TRAVIS *snaps to life and flies out to get the mail.*

MAMA (*her eyes wide, her hand to her breast*): You mean it done really come?

RUTH (*excited*): Oh, Miss Lena!

MAMA (*collecting herself*): Well . . . I don't know what we all so excited about 'round here for. We known it was coming for months.

RUTH: That's a whole lot different from having it come and being able to hold it in your hands . . . a piece of paper worth ten thousand dollars . . . (TRAVIS *bursts back into the room. He holds the envelope high above his head, like a little dancer, his face is radiant and he is breathless. He moves to his grandmother with sudden slow ceremony and puts the envelope into her hands. She accepts it, and then merely holds it and looks at it.*) Come on! Open it . . . Lord have mercy, I wish Walter Lee was here!

TRAVIS: Open it, Grandmama!

MAMA (*staring at it*): Now you all be quiet. It's just a check.

RUTH: Open it . . .

MAMA (*still staring at it*): Now don't act silly . . . We ain't never been no people to act silly 'bout no money—

RUTH (*swiftly*): We ain't never had none before—OPEN IT!

MAMA *finally makes a good strong tear and pulls out the thin blue slice of paper and inspects it closely. The boy and his mother study it raptly over* MAMA'S *shoulders.*

MAMA: Travis! (*She is counting off with doubt.*) Is that the right number of zeros?

TRAVIS: Yes'm . . . ten thousand dollars. Gaalee, Grandmama, you rich.

MAMA (*She holds the check away from her, still looking at it. Slowly her face sobers into a mask of unhappiness.*): Ten thousand dollars. (*She hands it to* RUTH.) Put it away somewhere, Ruth. (*She does not look at* RUTH; *her eyes seem to be seeing something somewhere very far off.*) Ten thousand dollars they give you. Ten thousand dollars.

TRAVIS (*to his mother, sincerely*): What's the matter with Grandmama—don't she want to be rich?

RUTH (*distractedly*): You go on out and play now, baby. (TRAVIS *exits.* MAMA *starts wiping dishes absently, humming intently to herself.* RUTH *turns to her, with kind exasperation.*) You've gone and got yourself upset.

MAMA (*not looking at her*): I spec if it wasn't for you all . . . I would just put that money away or give it to the church or something.

RUTH: Now what kind of talk is that. Mr. Younger would just be plain mad if he could hear you talking foolish like that.

MAMA (*stopping and staring off*): Yes . . . he sure would. (*sighing*) We got enough to do with that money, all right. (*She halts then, and turns and looks at her daughter-in-law hard;* RUTH *avoids her eyes and* MAMA *wipes her hands with finality and starts to speak firmly to* RUTH.) Where did you go today, girl?

RUTH: To the doctor.

MAMA (*impatiently*): Now, Ruth . . . you know better than that. Old Doctor Jones is strange enough in his way but there ain't nothing 'bout him make somebody slip and call him "she"—like you done this morning.

RUTH: Well, that's what happened—my tongue slipped.

MAMA: You went to see that woman, didn't you?

RUTH (*defensively, giving herself away*): What woman you talking about?

MAMA (*angrily*): That woman who—

WALTER *enters in great excitement.*

WALTER: Did it come?

MAMA (*quietly*): Can't you give people a Christian greeting before you start asking about money?

WALTER (*to* RUTH): Did it come? (RUTH *unfolds the check and lays it quietly before him, watching him intently with thoughts of her own.* WALTER *sits down and grasps it close and counts off the zeros.*) Ten thousand dollars—(*He turns suddenly, frantically to his mother and draws some papers out of his breast pocket.*) Mama—look. Old Willy Harris put everything on paper—

MAMA: Son—I think you ought to talk to your wife . . . I'll go on out and leave you alone if you want—

WALTER: I can talk to her later—Mama, look—

MAMA: Son—

WALTER: WILL SOMEBODY PLEASE LISTEN TO ME TODAY!

MAMA (*quietly*): I don't 'low no yellin' in this house, Walter Lee, and you know it—(WALTER *stares at them in frustration and starts to speak several times.*) And there ain't going to be no investing in no liquor stores.

WALTER: But, Mama, you ain't even looked at it.

MAMA: I don't aim to have to speak on that again.

A long pause.

WALTER: You ain't looked at it and you don't aim to have to speak on that again? You ain't even looked at it and *you* have decided—(*crumpling his papers*) Well, *you* tell that to my boy tonight when you put him to sleep on the living-room couch . . . (*turning to* MAMA *and speaking directly to her*) Yeah—and tell it to my wife, Mama, tomorrow when she has to go out of here to look after somebody else's kids. And tell it to *me*, Mama, every time we need a new pair of curtains and I have to watch *you* go out and work in somebody's kitchen. Yeah, you tell me then!

WALTER *starts out.*

RUTH: Where you going?

WALTER: I'm going out!

RUTH: Where?

WALTER: Just out of this house somewhere—

RUTH (*getting her coat*): I'll come too.

WALTER: I don't want you to come!

RUTH: I got something to talk to you about, Walter.

WALTER: That's too bad.

MAMA (*still quietly*): Walter Lee—(*She waits and he finally turns and looks at her.*) Sit down.

WALTER: I'm a grown man, Mama.

MAMA: Ain't nobody said you wasn't grown. But you still in my house and my presence. And as long as you are—you'll talk to your wife civil. Now sit down.

RUTH (*suddenly*): Oh, let him go on out and drink himself to death! He makes me sick to my stomach! (*She flings her coat against him and exits to bedroom.*)

WALTER (*violently flinging the coat after her*): And you turn mine too, baby! (*The door slams behind her.*) That was my biggest mistake—

MAMA (*still quietly*): Walter, what is the matter with you?

WALTER: Matter with me? Ain't nothing the matter with *me!*

MAMA: Yes there is. Something eating you up like a crazy man. Something more than me not giving you this money. The past few years I been watching it happen to you. You get all nervous acting and kind of wild in the eyes—(WALTER *jumps up impatiently at her words.*) I said sit there now, I'm talking to you!

WALTER: Mama—I don't need no nagging at me today.

MAMA: Seem like you getting to a place where you always tied up in some kind of knot about something. But if anybody ask you 'bout it you just yell at 'em and bust out the house and go out and drink somewheres. Walter Lee, people can't live with that. Ruth's a good, patient girl in her way—but you getting to be too much. Boy, don't make the mistake of driving that girl away from you.

WALTER: Why—what she do for me?

MAMA: She loves you.

WALTER: Mama—I'm going out. I want to go off somewhere and be by my-self for a while.

MAMA: I'm sorry 'bout your liquor store, son. It just wasn't the thing for us to do. That's what I want to tell you about—

WALTER: I got to go out, Mama—

He rises.

MAMA: It's dangerous, son.

WALTER: What's dangerous?

MAMA: When a man goes outside his home to look for peace.

WALTER (*beseechingly*): Then why can't there never be no peace in this house then?

MAMA: You done found it in some other house?

WALTER: No—there ain't no woman! Why do women always think there's a woman somewhere when a man gets restless. (*picks up the check*) Do you know what this money means to me? Do you know what this money can do for us? (*puts it back*) Mama—Mama—I want so many things . . .

MAMA: Yes, son—

WALTER: I want so many things that they are driving me kind of crazy . . . Mama—look at me.

MAMA: I'm looking at you. You a good-looking boy. You got a job, a nice wife, a fine boy and—

WALTER: A job. (*looks at her*) Mama, a job? I open and close car doors all day long. I drive a man around in his limousine and I say, "Yes, sir; no, sir; very good, sir; shall I take the Drive, sir?" Mama, that ain't no kind of job . . . that ain't nothing at all. (*very quietly*) Mama, I don't know if I can make you understand.

MAMA: Understand what, baby?

WALTER (*quietly*): Sometimes it's like I can see the future stretched out in front of me—just plain as day. The future, Mama. Hanging over there at the edge of my days. Just waiting for me—a big, looming blank space—full of *nothing*. Just waiting for *me*. But it don't have to be. (*Pause. Kneeling beside her chair.*) Mama—sometimes when I'm down-town and I pass them cool, quiet-looking restaurants where them white boys are sitting back and talking 'bout things . . . sitting there turning deals worth millions of dollars . . . sometimes I see guys don't look much older than me—

MAMA: Son—how come you talk so much 'bout money?

WALTER (*with immense passion*): Because it is life, Mama!

MAMA (*quietly*): Oh—(*very quietly*) So now it's life. Money is life. Once upon a time freedom used to be life—now it's money. I guess the world really do change . . .

WALTER: No—it was always money, Mama. We just didn't know about it.

MAMA: No . . . something has changed. (*She looks at him.*) You something new, boy. In my time we was worried about not being lynched and getting to the North if we could and how to stay alive and still have a pinch of dignity too . . . Now here come you and Beneatha—talking 'bout things we ain't never even thought about hardly, me and your daddy. You ain't satisfied or proud of nothing we done. I mean that you had a home; that we kept you out of trouble till you was grown; that you don't have to ride to work on the back of nobody's streetcar—You my children—but how different we done become.

WALTER (*A long beat. He pats her hand and gets up.*): You just don't understand, Mama, you just don't understand.

MAMA: Son—do you know your wife is expecting another baby? (WALTER *stands, stunned, and absorbs what his mother has said.*) That's what she wanted to talk to you about. (WALTER *sinks down into a chair.*) This ain't for me to be telling—but you ought to know. (*She waits.*) I think Ruth is thinking 'bout getting rid of that child.

WALTER (*slowly understanding*): No—no—Ruth wouldn't do that.

MAMA: When the world gets ugly enough—a woman will do anything for her family. *The part that's already living.*

WALTER: You don't know Ruth, Mama, if you think she would do that.

RUTH *opens the bedroom door and stands there a little limp.*

RUTH (*beaten*): Yes I would too, Walter. (*pause*) I gave her a five-dollar down payment.

There is total silence as the man stares at his wife and the mother stares at her son.

MAMA (*presently*): Well—(*tightly*) Well—son, I'm waiting to hear you say something . . . (*She waits.*) I'm waiting to hear how you be your father's son. Be the man he was . . . (*Pause. The silence shouts.*) Your wife say she going to destroy your child. And I'm waiting to hear you talk like him and say we a people who give children life, not who destroys them— (*She rises*). I'm waiting to see you stand up and look like your daddy and say we done give up one baby to poverty and that we ain't going to give up nary another one . . . I'm waiting.

WALTER: Ruth—(*He can say nothing.*)

MAMA: If you a son of mine, tell her! (WALTER *picks up his keys and his coat and walks out. She continues, bitterly.*) You . . . you are a disgrace to your father's memory. Somebody get me my hat!

Curtain.

Act Two

SCENE 1

TIME: *Later the same day.*

AT RISE: RUTH *is ironing again. She has the radio going. Presently* BENEATHA'S *bedroom door opens and* RUTH'S *mouth falls and she puts down the iron in fascination.*

RUTH: What have we got on tonight!

BENEATHA (*emerging grandly from the doorway so that we can see her thoroughly robed in the costume Asagai brought*): You are looking at what a well-dressed Nigerian woman wears—(*She parades for* RUTH, *her hair completely hidden by the headdress; she is coquettishly fanning herself with an ornate oriental fan, mistakenly more like Butterfly than any Nigerian that ever was.*) Isn't it beautiful? (*She promenades to the radio and, with an arrogant flourish, turns off the good loud blues that is playing.*) Enough of this assimilationist junk! (RUTH *follows her with her eyes as she goes to the phonograph and puts on a record and turns and waits ceremoniously for the music to come up. Then, with a shout—*) OCOMOGOSIAY!

RUTH *jumps. The music comes up, a lovely Nigerian melody.* BENEATHA *listens, enraptured, her eyes far away—"back to the past." She begins to dance.* RUTH *is dumfounded.*

RUTH: What kind of dance is that?

BENEATHA: A folk dance.

RUTH (*Pearl Bailey*): What kind of folks do that, honey?

BENEATHA: It's from Nigeria. It's a dance of welcome.

RUTH: Who you welcoming?

BENEATHA: The men back to the village.

RUTH: Where they been?

BENEATHA: How should I know—out hunting or something. Anyway, they are coming back now . . .

RUTH: Well, that's good.

BENEATHA (*with the record*):
Alundi, alundi
Alundi alunya
Jop pu a jeepua
Ang gu sooooooooooo

Ai yai yae . . .
Ayehaye—alundi . . .

WALTER *comes in during this performance; he has obviously been drinking. He leans against the door heavily and watches his sister, at first with distaste. Then his eyes look off—"back to the past"—as he lifts both his fists to the roof, screaming.*

WALTER: YEAH . . . AND ETHIOPIA STRETCH FORTH HER HANDS AGAIN! . . .

RUTH (*drily, looking at him*): Yes—and Africa sure is claiming her own tonight. (*She gives them both up and starts ironing again.*)

WALTER (*all in a drunken, dramatic shout*): Shut up! . . . I'm digging them drums . . . them drums move me! . . . (*He makes his weaving way to his wife's face and leans in close to her.*) In my *heart of hearts*—(*He thumps his chest.*)—I am much warrior!

RUTH (*without even looking up*): In your heart of hearts you are much drunkard.

WALTER (*coming away from her and starting to wander around the room, shouting*): Me and Jomo . . . (*Intently, in his sister's face. She has stopped dancing to watch him in this unknown mood.*) That's my man, Kenyatta. (*shouting and thumping his chest* FLAMING SPEAR! HOT DAMN! (*He is suddenly in possession of an imaginary spear and actively spearing enemies all over the room.*) OCOMOGOSIAY . . .

BENEATHA (*to encourage* WALTER, *thoroughly caught up with this side of him*): OCOMOGOSIAY, FLAMING SPEAR!

WALTER: THE LION IS WAKING . . . OWIMOWEH! (*He pulls his shirt open and leaps up on the table and gestures with his spear.*)

BENEATHA: OWIMOWEH!

WALTER (*On the table, very far gone, his eyes pure glass sheets. He sees what we cannot, that he is a leader of his people, a great chief, a descendant of Chaka, and that the hour to march has come.*): Listen, my black brothers—

BENEATHA: OCOMOGOSIAY!

WALTER: —Do you hear the waters rushing against the shores of the coastlands—

BENEATHA: OCOMOGOSIAY!

WALTER: —Do you hear the screeching of the cocks in yonder hills beyond where the chiefs meet in council for the coming of the mighty war—

BENEATHA: OCOMOGOSIAY!

And now the lighting shifts subtly to suggest the world of WALTER'S *imagination, and the mood shifts from pure comedy. It is the inner* WALTER *speaking: the Southside chauffeur has assumed an unexpected majesty.*

WALTER: —Do you hear the beating of the wings of the birds flying low over the mountains and the low places of our land—

BENEATHA: OCOMOGOSIAY!

WALTER: —Do you hear the singing of the women, singing the war songs of our fathers to the babies in the great houses? Singing the sweet war songs! (*The doorbell rings.*) OH, DO YOU HEAR, MY *BLACK* BROTHERS!

BENEATHA (*completely gone*): We hear you, Flaming Spear—

RUTH *shuts off the phonograph and opens the door.* GEORGE MURCHISON *enters.*

WALTER: Telling us to prepare for the GREATNESS OF THE TIME! (*Lights back to normal. He turns and sees* GEORGE.) Black Brother!

He extends his hand for the fraternal clasp.

GEORGE: Black Brother, hell!

RUTH (*having had enough, and embarrassed for the family*): Beneatha, you got company—what's the matter with you? Walter Lee Younger, get down off that table and stop acting like a fool . . .

WALTER *comes down off the table suddenly and makes a quick exit to the bathroom.*

RUTH: He's had a little to drink . . . I don't know what her excuse is.

GEORGE (*to* BENEATHA): Look honey, we're going *to* the theatre—we're not going to be *in* it . . . so go change, huh?

BENEATHA *looks at him and slowly, ceremoniously, lifts her hands and pulls off the headdress. Her hair is close-cropped and unstraightened.* GEORGE *freezes mid-sentence and* RUTH'S *eyes all but fall out of her head.*

GEORGE: What in the name of—

RUTH (touching BENEATHA'S hair): Girl, you done lost your natural mind!? Look at your head!

GEORGE: What have you done to your head—I mean your hair!

BENEATHA: Nothing—except cut it off.

RUTH: Now that's the truth—it's what ain't been done to it! You expect this boy to go out with you with your head all nappy like that?

BENEATHA (looking at GEORGE): That's up to George. If he's ashamed of his heritage—

GEORGE: Oh, don't be so proud of yourself, Bennie—just because you look eccentric.

BENEATHA: How can something that's natural be eccentric?

GEORGE: That's what being eccentric means—being natural. Get dressed.

BENEATHA: I don't like that, George.

RUTH: Why must you and your brother make an argument out of everything people say?

BENEATHA: Because I hate assimilationist Negroes!

RUTH: Will somebody please tell me what assimila-who-ever means!

GEORGE: Oh, it's just a college girl's way of calling people Uncle Toms—but that isn't what it means at all.

RUTH: Well, what does it mean?

BENEATHA (cutting GEORGE off and staring at him as she replies to RUTH): It means someone who is willing to give up his own culture and submerge himself completely in the dominant, and in this case oppressive culture!

GEORGE: Oh, dear, dear, dear! Here we go! A lecture on the African past! On our Great West African Heritage! In one second we will hear all about the great Ashanti empires; the great Songhay civilizations; and the great sculpture of Bénin—and then some poetry in the Bantu—and the whole monologue will end with the word heritage! (nastily) Let's face it, baby, your heritage is nothing but a bunch of raggedy-assed spirituals and some grass huts!

BENEATHA: GRASS HUTS! (RUTH *crosses to her and forcibly pushes her toward the bedroom.*) See there . . . you are standing there in your splendid ignorance talking about people who were the first to smelt iron on the face of the earth! (RUTH *is pushing her through the door.*) The Ashanti were performing surgical operations when the English—(RUTH *pulls the door to, with* BENEATHA *on the other side, and smiles graciously at* GEORGE. BENEATHA *opens the door and shouts the end of the sentence defiantly at* GEORGE.)— were still tatooing themselves with blue dragons! (She goes back inside.)

RUTH: Have a seat, George. (*They both sit.* RUTH *folds her hands rather primly on her lap, determined to demonstrate the civilization of the family.*) Warm, ain't it? I mean for September. (*pause*) Just like they always say about Chicago weather: If it's too hot or cold for you, just wait a minute and it'll change. (*She smiles happily at this cliché of clichés.*) Everybody say it's got to do with them bombs and things they keep setting off. (*pause*) Would you like a nice cold beer?

GEORGE: No, thank you. I don't care for beer. (*He looks at his watch.*) I hope she hurries up.

RUTH: What time is the show?

GEORGE: It's an eight-thirty curtain. That's just Chicago, though. In New York standard curtain time is eight forty.

He is rather proud of this knowledge.

RUTH (*properly appreciating it*): You get to New York a lot?

GEORGE (*offhand*): Few times a year.

RUTH: Oh—that's nice. I've never been to New York.

WALTER *enters. We feel he has relieved himself, but the edge of unreality is still with him.*

WALTER: New York ain't got nothing Chicago ain't. Just a bunch of hustling people all squeezed up together—being "Eastern."

He turns his face into a screw of displeasure.

GEORGE: Oh—you've been?

WALTER: *Plenty* of times.

RUTH (*shocked at the lie*): Walter Lee Younger!

WALTER (*staring her down*): Plenty! (*pause*) What we got to drink in this house? Why don't you offer this man some refreshment. (*to* GEORGE) They don't know how to entertain people in this house, man.

GEORGE: Thank you—I don't really care for anything.

WALTER (*feeling his head; sobriety coming*): Where's Mama?

RUTH: She ain't come back yet.

WALTER (*looking* MURCHISON *over from head to toe, scrutinizing his carefully casual tweed sports jacket over cashmere V-neck sweater over soft eyelet shirt and tie, and soft slacks, finished off with white buckskin shoes*): Why all you college boys wear them faggoty-looking white shoes?

RUTH: Walter Lee!

GEORGE MURCHISON *ignores the remark.*

WALTER (*to* RUTH): Well, they look crazy as hell—white shoes, cold as it is.

RUTH (*crushed*): You have to excuse him—

WALTER: No he don't! Excuse me for what? What you always excusing me for! I'll excuse myself when I needs to be excused! (*a pause*) They look as funny as them black knee socks Beneatha wears out of here all the time.

RUTH: It's the college *style,* Walter.

WALTER: Style, hell. She looks like she got burnt legs or something!

RUTH: Oh, Walter—

WALTER (*an irritable mimic*): Oh, Walter! Oh, Walter! (*to* MURCHISON) How's your old man making out? I understand you all going to buy that big hotel on the Drive? (*He finds a beer in the refrigerator, wanders over to* MURCHISON, *sipping and wiping his lips with the back of his hand, and straddling a chair backwards to talk to the other man.*) Shrewd move. Your old man is all right, man. (*tapping his head and half winking for emphasis*) I mean he knows how to operate. I mean he thinks *big,* you know what I mean, I mean for a *home,* you know? But I think he's kind of running out of ideas now. I'd like to talk to him. Listen, man, I got some plans that could turn this city upside down. I mean think like he does. *Big.* Invest big, gamble big, hell, lose *big* if you have to, you know what I mean. It's hard to find a man on this whole Southside who understands my kind of thinking—you dig? (*He scrutinizes* MURCHISON *again, drinks his beer, squints his eyes and leans in close, confidential, man to man.*) Me and you ought to sit down and talk sometimes, man. Man, I got me some ideas . . .

MURCHISON (*with boredom*): Yeah—sometimes we'll have to do that, Walter.

WALTER (*understanding the indifference, and offended*): Yeah—well, when you get the time, man. I know you a busy little boy.

RUTH: Walter, please—

WALTER (*bitterly, hurt*): I know ain't nothing in this world as busy as you colored college boys with your fraternity pins and white shoes . . .

RUTH (*covering her face with humiliation*): Oh, Walter Lee—

WALTER: I see you all the time—with the books tucked under your arms—going to your (*British A—a mimic*) "clahsses." And for what! What the hell you learning over there? Filling up your heads—(*counting off on his fingers*)—with the sociology and the psychology—but they teaching you how to be a man? How to take over and run the world? They teaching you how to run a rubber plantation or a steel mill? Naw—just to talk proper and read books and wear them faggoty-looking white shoes . . .

GEORGE (*looking at him with distaste, a little above it all*): You're all wacked up with bitterness, man.

WALTER (*intently, almost quietly, between the teeth, glaring at the boy*): And you—ain't you bitter, man? Ain't you just about had it yet? Don't you see no stars gleaming that you can't reach out and grab? You happy?—You contented son-of-a-bitch—you happy? You got it made? Bitter? Man, I'm a volcano. Bitter? Here I am a giant—surrounded by ants! Ants who can't even understand what it is the giant is talking about.

RUTH (*passionately and suddenly*): Oh, Walter—ain't you with nobody!

WALTER (*violently*): No! 'Cause ain't nobody with me! Not even my own mother!

RUTH: Walter, that's a terrible thing to say!

BENEATHA *enters, dressed for the evening in a cocktail dress and earrings, hair natural.*

GEORGE: Well—hey—(*crosses to* BENEATHA; *thoughtful, with emphasis, since this is a reversal*) You look great!

WALTER (*seeing his sister's hair for the first time*): What's the matter with your head?

BENEATHA (*tired of the jokes now*): I cut it off, Brother.

WALTER (*coming close to inspect it and walking around her*): Well, I'll be damned. So that's what they mean by the African bush . . .

BENEATHA: Ha ha. Let's go, George.

GEORGE (*looking at her*): You know something? I like it. It's sharp. I mean it really is. (*helps her into her wrap*)

RUTH: Yes—I think so, too. (*She goes to the mirror and starts to clutch at her hair.*)

WALTER: Oh no! You leave yours alone, baby. You might turn out to have a pin-shaped head or something!

BENEATHA: See you all later.

RUTH: Have a nice time.

GEORGE: Thanks. Good night. (*Half out the door, he reopens it. To* WALTER.) Good night, Prometheus!

BENEATHA and GEORGE exit.

WALTER (*to* RUTH): Who is Prometheus?

RUTH: I don't know. Don't worry about it.

WALTER (*in fury, pointing after* GEORGE): See there—they get to a point where they can't insult you man to man—they got to go talk about something ain't nobody never heard of!

RUTH: How do you know it was an insult? (*to humor him*) Maybe Prometheus is a nice fellow.

WALTER: Prometheus! I bet there ain't even no such thing! I bet that simple-minded clown—

RUTH: Walter—

She stops what she is doing and looks at him.

WALTER (*yelling*): Don't start!

RUTH: Start what?

WALTER: Your nagging! Where was I? Who was I with? How much money did I spend?

RUTH (*plaintively*): Walter Lee—why don't we just try to talk about it . . .

WALTER (*not listening*): I been out talking with people who understand me. People who care about the things I got on my mind.

RUTH (*wearily*): I guess that means people like Willy Harris.

WALTER: Yes, people like Willy Harris.

RUTH (*with a sudden flash of impatience*): Why don't you all just hurry up and go into the banking business and stop talking about it!

WALTER: Why? You want to know why? 'Cause we all tied up in a race of people that don't know how to do nothing but moan, pray and have babies!

The line is too bitter even for him and he looks at her and sits down.

RUTH: Oh, Walter . . . (*softly*) Honey, why can't you stop fighting me?

WALTER (*without thinking*): Who's fighting you? Who even cares about you?

This line begins the retardation of his mood.

RUTH: Well—(*She waits a long time, and then with resignation starts to put away her things.*) I guess I might as well go on to bed . . . (*more or less to herself*) I don't know where we lost it . . . but we have . . . (*then, to him*) I—I'm sorry about this new baby, Walter. I guess maybe I better go on and do what I started . . . I guess I just didn't realize how bad things was with us . . . I guess I just didn't realize—(*She starts out to the bedroom and stops.*) You want some hot milk?

WALTER: Hot milk?

RUTH: Yes—hot milk.

WALTER: Why hot milk?

RUTH: 'Cause after all that liquor you come home with you ought to have something hot in your stomach.

WALTER: I don't want no milk.

RUTH: You want some coffee then?

WALTER: No, I don't want no coffee. I don't want nothing hot to drink. (*almost plaintively*) Why you always trying to give me something to eat?

RUTH (*standing and looking at him helplessly*): What *else* can I give you, Walter Lee Younger?

She stands and looks at him and presently turns to go out again. He lifts his head and watches her going away from him in a new mood which began to emerge when he asked her "Who cares about you?"

WALTER: It's been rough, ain't it, baby? (*She hears and stops but does not turn around and he continues to her back.*) I guess between two people there ain't never as much understood as folks generally thinks there is. I mean like between me and you—(*She turns to face him.*) How we gets to the place where we scared to talk softness to each other. (*He waits, thinking hard himself.*) Why you think it got to be like that? (*He is thoughtful, almost as a child would be.*) Ruth, what is it gets into people ought to be close?

RUTH: I don't know, honey. I think about it a lot.

WALTER: On account of you and me, you mean? The way things are with us. The way something done come down between us.

RUTH: There ain't so much between us, Walter . . . Not when you come to me and try to talk to me. Try to be with me . . . a little even.

WALTER (*total honesty*): Sometimes . . . sometimes . . . I don't even know how to try.

RUTH: Walter—

WALTER: Yes?

RUTH (*coming to him, gently and with misgiving, but coming to him*): Honey . . . life don't have to be like this. I mean sometimes people can do things so that things are better . . . You remember how we used to talk when Travis was born . . . about the way we were going to live . . . the kind of house . . . (*She is stroking his head.*) Well, it's all starting to slip away from us . . .

He turns her to him and they look at each other and kiss, tenderly and hungrily. The door opens and MAMA *enters—*WALTER *breaks away and jumps up. A beat.*

WALTER: Mama, where have you been?

MAMA: My—them steps is longer than they used to be. Whew! (*She sits down and ignores him.*) How you feeling this evening, Ruth?

RUTH *shrugs, disturbed at having been interrupted and watching her husband knowingly.*

WALTER: Mama, where have you been all day?

MAMA (*still ignoring him and leaning on the table and changing to more comfortable shoes*): Where's Travis?

RUTH: I let him go out earlier and he ain't come back yet. Boy, is he going to get it!

WALTER: Mama!

MAMA (*as if she has heard him for the first time*): Yes, son?

WALTER: Where did you go this afternoon?

MAMA: I went downtown to tend to some business that I had to tend to.

WALTER: What kind of business?

MAMA: You know better than to question me like a child, Brother.

WALTER (*rising and bending over the table*): Where were you, Mama? (*bringing his fists down and shouting*) Mama, you didn't go do something with that insurance money, something crazy?

The front door opens slowly, interrupting him, and TRAVIS *peeks his head in, less than hopefully.*

TRAVIS (*to his mother*): Mama, I—

RUTH: "Mama I" nothing! You're going to get it, boy! Get on in that bedroom and get yourself ready!

TRAVIS: But I—

MAMA: Why don't you all never let the child explain hisself.

RUTH: Keep out of it now, Lena.

MAMA *clamps her lips together, and* RUTH *advances toward her son menacingly.*

RUTH: A thousand times I have told you not to go off like that—

MAMA (*holding out her arms to her grandson*): Well—at least let me tell him something. I want him to be the first one to hear . . . Come here, Travis. (*The boy obeys, gladly.*) Travis—(*She takes him by the shoulder and looks into his face.*)—you know that money we got in the mail this morning?

TRAVIS: Yes'm—

MAMA: Well—what you think your grandmama gone and done with that money?

TRAVIS: I don't know, Grandmama.

MAMA (*putting her finger on his nose for emphasis*): She went out and she bought you a house! (*The explosion comes from* WALTER *at the end of the revelation and he jumps up and turns away from all of them in a fury.* MAMA *continues, to* TRAVIS.) You glad about the house? It's going to be yours when you get to be a man.

TRAVIS: Yeah—I always wanted to live in a house.

MAMA: All right, gimme some sugar then—(TRAVIS *puts his arms around her neck as she watches her son over the boy's shoulder. Then, to* TRAVIS, *after the embrace.*) Now when you say your prayers tonight, you thank God and your grandfather—'cause it was him who give you the house—in his way.

RUTH (*taking the boy from* MAMA *and pushing him toward the bedroom*): Now you get out of here and get ready for your beating.

TRAVIS: Aw, Mama—

RUTH: Get on in there—(*closing the door behind him and turning radiantly to her mother-in-law*) So you went and did it!

MAMA (*quietly, looking at her son with pain*): Yes, I did.

RUTH (*raising both arms classically*): PRAISE GOD! (*Looks at* WALTER *a moment, who says nothing. She crosses rapidly to her husband.*) Please, honey— let me be glad . . . you be glad too. (*She has laid her hands on his shoulders, but he shakes himself free of her roughly, without turning to face her.*) Oh, Walter . . . a home . . . *a home.* (*She comes back to* MAMA.) Well—where is it? How big is it? How much it going to cost?

MAMA: Well—

RUTH: When we moving?

MAMA (*smiling at her*): First of the month.

RUTH (*throwing back her head with jubilance*): *Praise God!*

MAMA (*tentatively, still looking at her son's back turned against her and* RUTH): It's—it's a nice house too . . . (*She cannot help speaking directly to him. An imploring quality in her voice, her manner, makes her almost like a girl now.*) Three bedrooms—nice big one for you and Ruth . . . Me and Beneatha still have to share our room, but Travis have one of his own— and (*with difficulty*) I figure if the—new baby—is a boy, we could get one of them double-decker outfits . . . And there's a yard with a little patch of dirt where I could maybe get to grow me a few flowers . . . And a nice big basement . . .

RUTH: Walter honey, be glad—

MAMA (*still to his back, fingering things on the table*): 'Course I don't want to make it sound fancier than it is . . . It's just a plain little old house—but it's made good and solid—and it will be *ours.* Walter Lee—it makes a difference in a man when he can walk on floors that belong to *him* . . .

RUTH: Where is it?

MAMA (*frightened at this telling*): Well—well—it's out there in Clybourne Park—

RUTH's *radiance fades abruptly, and* WALTER *finally turns slowly to face his mother with incredulity and hostility.*

RUTH: Where?

MAMA (*matter-of-factly*): Four o six Clybourne Street, Clybourne Park.

RUTH: Clybourne Park? Mama, there ain't no colored people living in Clybourne Park.

MAMA (*almost idiotically*): Well, I guess there's going to be some now.

WALTER (*bitterly*): So that's the peace and comfort you went out and bought for us today!

MAMA (*raising her eyes to meet his finally*): Son—I just tried to find the nicest place for the least amount of money for my family.

RUTH (*trying to recover from the shock*): Well—well—'course I ain't one never been 'fraid of no crackers, mind you—but—well, wasn't there no other houses nowhere?

MAMA: Them houses they put up for colored in them areas way out all seem to cost twice as much as other houses. I did the best I could.

RUTH (*Struck senseless with the news, in its various degrees of goodness and trouble, she sits a moment, her fists propping her chin in thought, and then she starts to rise, bringing her fists down with vigor, the radiance spreading from cheek to cheek again.*): Well—well!—All I can say is—if this is my time in life—MY TIME—to say good-bye—(*And she builds with momentum as she starts to circle the room with an exuberant, almost tearfully happy release.*)—to these Goddamned cracking walls!—(*She pounds the walls.*)—and these marching roaches!—(*She wipes at an imaginary army of marching roaches.*)—and this cramped little closet which ain't now or never was no kitchen! . . . then I say it loud and good, HALLELUJAH! AND GOOD-BYE MISERY . . . I DON'T NEVER WANT TO SEE YOUR UGLY FACE AGAIN! (*She laughs joyously, having practically destroyed the apartment, and flings her arms up and lets them come down happily, slowly, reflectively, over her abdomen, aware for the first time perhaps that the life therein pulses with happiness and not despair.*) Lena?

MAMA (*moved, watching her happiness*): Yes, honey?

RUTH (*looking off*): Is there—is there a whole lot of sunlight?

MAMA (*understanding*): Yes, child, there's a whole lot of sunlight.

Long pause.

RUTH (*collecting herself and going to the door of the room* TRAVIS *is in*): Well—I guess I better see 'bout Travis. (*to* MAMA) Lord, I sure don't feel like whipping nobody today!

She exits.

MAMA (*The mother and son are left alone now and the mother waits a long time, considering deeply, before she speaks.*): Son—you—you understand what I done, don't you? (WALTER *is silent and sullen.*) I—I just seen my family falling apart today . . . just falling to pieces in front of my eyes . . . We couldn't of gone on like we was today. We was going backwards 'stead of forwards—talking 'bout killing babies and wishing each other was dead . . . When it gets like that in life—you just got to do something different, push on out and do something bigger . . . (*She waits.*) I wish you say something, son . . . I wish you'd say how deep inside you think I done the right thing—

WALTER (*crossing slowly to his bedroom door and finally turning there and speaking measuredly*): What you need me to say you done right for? *You* the head of this family. You run our lives like you want to. It was your money and you did what you wanted with it. So what you need for me to say it was all right for? (*bitterly, to hurt her as deeply as he knows is possible*) So you butchered up a dream of mine—you—who always talking 'bout your children's dreams . . .

MAMA: Walter Lee—

He just closes the door behind him. MAMA *sits alone, thinking heavily.*

Curtain.

SCENE 2

TIME: *Friday night. A few weeks later.*

AT RISE: *Packing crates mark the intention of the family to move.* BENEATHA *and* GEORGE *come in, presumably from an evening out again.*

GEORGE: O.K. . . . O.K., whatever you say . . . (*They both sit on the couch. He tries to kiss her. She moves away.*) Look, we've had a nice evening; let's not spoil it, huh? . . .

He again turns her head and tries to nuzzle in and she turns away from him, not with distaste but with momentary lack of interest; in a mood to pursue what they were talking about.

BENEATHA: I'm *trying* to talk to you.

GEORGE: We always talk.

BENEATHA: Yes—and I love to talk.

GEORGE (*exasperated; rising*): I know it and I don't mind it sometimes . . . I want you to cut it out, see—The moody stuff, I mean. I don't like it. You're a nice-looking girl . . . all over. That's all you need, honey, forget the atmosphere. Guys aren't going to go for the atmosphere—they're going to go for what they see. Be glad for that. Drop the Garbo routine. It doesn't go with you. As for myself, I want a nice—(*groping*)—simple (*thoughtfully*)—sophisticated girl . . . not a poet—O.K.?

He starts to kiss her, she rebuffs him again and he jumps up.

BENEATHA: Why are you angry, George?

GEORGE: Because this is stupid! I don't go out with you to discuss the nature of "quiet desperation" or to hear all about your thoughts—because the world will go on thinking what it thinks regardless—

BENEATHA: Then why read books? Why go to school?

GEORGE (*with artificial patience, counting on his fingers*): It's simple. You read books—to learn facts—to get grades—to pass the course—to get a degree. That's all—it has nothing to do with thoughts.

A long pause.

BENEATHA: I see. (*He starts to sit.*) Good night, George.

GEORGE *looks at her a little oddly, and starts to exit. He meets* MAMA *coming in.*

GEORGE: Oh—hello, Mrs. Younger.

MAMA: Hello, George, how you feeling?

GEORGE: Fine—fine, how are you?

MAMA: Oh, a little tired. You know them steps can get you after a day's work. You all have a nice time tonight?

GEORGE: Yes—a fine time. A fine time.

MAMA: Well, good night.

GEORGE: Good night. (*He exits.* MAMA *closes the door behind her.*) Hello, honey. What you sitting like that for?

BENEATHA: I'm just sitting.

MAMA: Didn't you have a nice time?

BENEATHA: No.

MAMA: No? What's the matter?

BENEATHA: Mama, George is a fool—honest. (*She rises.*)

MAMA (*Hustling around unloading the packages she has entered with. She stops.*): Is he, baby?

BENEATHA: Yes.

BENEATHA *makes up* TRAVIS' *bed as she talks.*

MAMA: You sure?

BENEATHA: Yes.

MAMA: Well—I guess you better not waste your time with no fools.

BENEATHA *looks up at her mother, watching her put groceries in the refrigerator. Finally she gathers up her things and starts into the bedroom. At the door she stops and looks back at her mother.*

BENEATHA: Mama—

MAMA: Yes, baby—

BENEATHA: Thank you.

MAMA: For what?

BENEATHA: For understanding me this time.

She exits quickly and the mother stands, smiling a little, looking at the place where BENEATHA *just stood.* RUTH *enters.*

RUTH: Now don't you fool with any of this stuff, Lena—

MAMA: Oh, I just thought I'd sort a few things out. Is Brother here?

RUTH: Yes.

MAMA (*with concern*): Is he—

RUTH (*reading her eyes*): Yes.

MAMA *is silent and someone knocks on the door.* MAMA *and* RUTH *exchange weary and knowing glances and* RUTH *opens it to admit the neighbor,* MRS. JOHNSON,* *who is a rather squeaky wide-eyed lady of no particular age, with a newspaper under her arm.*

MAMA (*changing her expression to acute delight and a ringing cheerful greeting*): Oh—hello, there, Johnson.

JOHNSON (*This is a woman who decided long ago to be enthusiastic about* EVERYTHING *in life and she is inclined to wave her wrist vigorously at the height of her exclamatory comments.*): Hello there, yourself! H'you this evening, Ruth?

RUTH (*not much of a deceptive type*): Fine, Mis' Johnson, h'you?

---

*This character and the scene of her visit were cut from the original production and early editions of the play.

JOHNSON: Fine. (*reaching out quickly, playfully, and patting* RUTH's *stomach*) Ain't you starting to poke out none yet! (*She mugs with delight at the overfamiliar remark and her eyes dart around looking at the crates and packing preparation;* MAMA's *face is a cold sheet of endurance.*) Oh, ain't we getting ready round here, though! Yessir! Lookathere! I'm telling you the Youngers is really getting ready to "move on up a little higher!"—Bless God!

MAMA (*a little drily, doubting the total sincerity of the Blesser*): Bless God.

JOHNSON: He's good, ain't He?

MAMA: Oh yes, He's good.

JOHNSON: I mean sometimes He works in mysterious ways . . . but He works, don't He!

MAMA (*the same*): Yes, He does.

JOHNSON: I'm just soooooo happy for y'all. And this here child—(*about* RUTH) looks like she could just pop open with happiness, don't she. Where's all the rest of the family?

MAMA: Bennie's gone to bed—

JOHNSON: Ain't no . . . (*The implication is pregnancy.*) sickness done hit you—I hope . . . ?

MAMA: No—she just tired. She was out this evening.

JOHNSON (*All is a coo, an emphatic coo.*): Aw—ain't that lovely. She still going out with the little Murchison boy?

MAMA (*drily*): Ummmm huh.

JOHNSON: That's lovely. You sure got lovely children, Younger. Me and Isaiah talks all the time 'bout what fine children you was blessed with. We sure do.

MAMA: Ruth, give Mis' Johnson a piece of sweet potato pie and some milk.

JOHNSON: Oh honey, I can't stay hardly a minute—I just dropped in to see if there was anything I could do. (*accepting the food easily*) I guess y'all seen the news what's all over the colored paper this week . . .

MAMA: No—didn't get mine yet this week.

JOHNSON (*lifting her head and blinking with the spirit of catastrophe*): You mean you ain't read 'bout them colored people that was bombed out their place out there?

RUTH *straightens with concern and takes the paper and reads it.* JOHNSON *notices her and feeds commentary.*

JOHNSON: Ain't it something how bad these here white folks is getting here in Chicago! Lord, getting so you think you right down in Mississippi! (*with a tremendous and rather insincere sense of melodrama*) 'Course I thinks it's wonderful how our folks keeps on pushing out. You hear some of these Negroes round here talking 'bout how they don't go where they ain't wanted and all that—but not me, honey! (*This is a lie.*) Wilhemenia Othella Johnson goes anywhere, any time she feels like it! (*with head movement for emphasis*) Yes I do! Why if we left it up to these here crackers, the poor niggers wouldn't have nothing—(*She clasps her hand over her mouth.*) Oh, I always forgets you don't 'low that word in your house.

MAMA (*quietly, looking at her*): No—I don't 'low it.

JOHNSON (*vigorously again*): Me neither! I was just telling Isaiah yesterday when he come using it in front of me—I said, "Isaiah, it's just like Mis' Younger says all the time—"

MAMA: Don't you want some more pie?

JOHNSON: No—no thank you; this was lovely. I got to get on over home and have my midnight coffee. I hear some people say it don't let them sleep but I finds I can't close my eyes right lessen I done had that laaaast cup of coffee . . . (*She waits. A beat. Undaunted.*) My Goodnight coffee, I calls it!

MAMA (*with much eye-rolling and communication between herself and* RUTH): Ruth, why don't you give Mis' Johnson some coffee.

RUTH *gives* MAMA *an unpleasant look for her kindness.*

JOHNSON (*accepting the coffee*): Where's Brother tonight?

MAMA: He's lying down.

JOHNSON: MMmmmmm, he sure gets his beauty rest, don't he? Good-looking man. Sure is a good-looking man! (*reaching out to pat* RUTH*'s stomach again*) I guess that's how come we keep on having babies around here. (*She winks at* MAMA.) One thing 'bout Brother, he always know how to have a *good* time. And soooooo ambitious! I bet it was his idea y'all moving out to Clybourne Park. Lord—I bet this time next month y'all's names will have been in the papers plenty—(*holding up her hands to mark off each word of the headline she can see in front of her*) "NEGROES INVADE CLYBOURNE PARK—BOMBED!"

MAMA (*She and* RUTH *look at the woman in amazement.*): We ain't exactly moving out there to get bombed.

JOHNSON: Oh, honey—you know I'm praying to God every day that don't nothing like that happen! But you have to think of life like it is—and these here Chicago peckerwoods is some baaaad peckerwoods.

MAMA (*wearily*): We done thought about all that Mis' Johnson.

BENEATHA *comes out of the bedroom in her robe and passes through to the bathroom.* MRS. JOHNSON *turns.*

JOHNSON: Hello there, Bennie!

BENEATHA (*crisply*): Hello, Mrs. Johnson.

JOHNSON: How is school?

BENEATHA (*crisply*): Fine, thank you. (*She goes out.*)

JOHNSON (*insulted*): Getting so she don't have much to say to nobody.

MAMA: The child was on her way to the bathroom.

JOHNSON: I know—but sometimes she act like ain't got time to pass the time of day with nobody ain't been to college. Oh—I ain't criticizing her none. It's just—you know how some of our young people gets when they get a little education. (MAMA *and* RUTH *say nothing, just look at her.*) Yes—well. Well, I guess I better get on home. (*unmoving*) 'Course I can understand how she must be proud and everything—being the only one in the family to make something of herself. I know just being a chauffeur ain't never satisfied Brother none. He shouldn't feel like that, though. Ain't nothing wrong with being a chauffeur.

MAMA: There's plenty wrong with it.

JOHNSON: What?

MAMA: Plenty. My husband always said being any kind of a servant wasn't a fit thing for a man to have to be. He always said a man's hands was made to make things, or to turn the earth with—not to drive nobody's car for 'em—or—(*She looks at her own hands.*) carry they slop jars. And my boy is just like him—he wasn't meant to wait on nobody.

JOHNSON (*rising, somewhat offended*): Mmmmmmmmmm. The Youngers is too much for me! (*She looks around.*) You sure one proud-acting bunch of colored folks. Well—I always thinks like Booker T. Washington said that time—"Education has spoiled many a good plow hand"—

MAMA: Is that what old Booker T. said?

JOHNSON: He sure did.

MAMA: Well, it sounds just like him. The fool.

JOHNSON (*indignantly*): Well—he was one of our great men.

MAMA: Who said so?

JOHNSON (*nonplussed*): You know, me and you ain't never agreed about some things, Lena Younger. I guess I better be going—

RUTH (*quickly*): Good night.

JOHNSON: Good night. Oh—(*thrusting it at her*) You can keep the paper! (*with a trill*) 'Night.

MAMA: Good night, Mis' Johnson.

MRS. JOHNSON *exits.*

RUTH: If ignorance was gold . . .

MAMA: Shush. Don't talk about folks behind their backs.

RUTH: You do.

MAMA: I'm old and corrupted. (BENEATHA *enters.*) You was rude to Mis' Johnson, Beneatha, and I don't like it at all.

BENEATHA (*at her door*): Mama, if there are two things we, as a people, have got to overcome, one is the Ku Klux Klan—and the other is Mrs. Johnson. (*She exits.*)

MAMA: Smart aleck.

The phone rings.

RUTH: I'll get it.

MAMA: Lord, ain't this a popular place tonight.

RUTH (*at the phone*): Hello—Just a minute. (*goes to door*) Walter, it's Mrs. Arnold. (*Waits. Goes back to the phone. Tense.*) Hello. Yes, this is his wife speaking . . . He's lying down now. Yes . . . well, he'll be in tomorrow. He's been very sick. Yes—I know we should have called, but we were so sure he'd be able to come in today. Yes—yes, I'm very sorry. Yes . . . Thank you very much. (*She hangs up.* WALTER *is standing in the doorway of the bedroom behind her.*) That was Mrs. Arnold.

WALTER (*indifferently*): Was it?

RUTH: She said if you don't come in tomorrow that they are getting a new man . . .

WALTER: Ain't that sad—ain't that crying sad.

RUTH: She said Mr. Arnold has had to take a cab for three days . . . Walter, you ain't been to work for three days! (*This is a revelation to her.*) Where you been, Walter Lee Younger? (WALTER *looks at her and starts to laugh.*) You're going to lose your job.

WALTER: That's right . . . (*He turns on the radio.*)

RUTH: Oh, Walter, and with your mother working like a dog every day—

A steamy, deep blues pours into the room.

WALTER: That's sad too—Everything is sad.

MAMA: What you been doing for these three days, son?

WALTER: Mama—you don't know all the things a man what got leisure can find to do in this city . . . What's this—Friday night? Well—Wednesday I borrowed Willy Harris' car and I went for a drive . . . just me and myself and I drove and drove . . . Way out . . . way past South Chicago, and I parked the car and I sat and looked at the steel mills all day long. I just sat in the car and looked at them big black chimneys for hours. Then I drove back and I went to the Green Hat. (*pause*) And Thursday—Thursday I borrowed the car again and I got in it and I pointed it the other way and I drove the other way—for hours—way, way up to Wisconsin, and I looked at the farms. I just drove and looked at the farms. Then I drove back and I went to the Green Hat. (*pause*) And today—today I didn't get the car. Today I just walked. All over the Southside. And I looked at the Negroes and they looked at me and finally I just sat down on the curb at Thirty-ninth and South Parkway and I just sat there and watched the Negroes go by. And then I went to the Green Hat. You all sad? You all depressed? And you know where I am going right now—

RUTH *goes out quietly.*

MAMA: Oh, Big Walter, is this the harvest of our days?

WALTER: You know what I like about the Green Hat? I like this little cat they got there who blows a sax . . . He blows. He talks to me. He ain't but 'bout five feet tall and he's got a conked head and his eyes is always closed and he's all music—

MAMA (*rising and getting some papers out of her handbag*): Walter—

WALTER: And there's this other guy who plays the piano . . . and they got a sound. I mean they can work on some music . . . They got the best little combo in the world in the Green Hat . . . You can just sit there and drink and listen to them three men play and you realize that don't nothing matter worth a damn, but just being there—

MAMA: I've helped do it to you, haven't I, son? Walter I been wrong.

WALTER: Naw—you ain't never been wrong about nothing, Mama.

MAMA: Listen to me, now. I say I been wrong, son. That I been doing to you what the rest of the world been doing to you. (*She turns off the radio.*) Walter—(*She stops and he looks up slowly at her and she meets his eyes pleadingly.*) What you ain't never understood is that I ain't got nothing, don't own nothing, ain't never really wanted nothing that wasn't for you. There ain't nothing as precious to me . . . There ain't nothing worth holding on to, money, dreams, nothing else—if it means—if it means it's going to destroy my boy. (*She takes an envelope out of her handbag and puts it in front of him and he watches her without speaking or moving.*) I paid the man thirty-five hundred dollars down on the house. That leaves sixty-five hundred dollars. Monday morning I want you to take this money and take three thousand dollars and put it in a savings account for Beneatha's medical schooling. The rest you put in a checking account—with your name on it. And from now on any penny that come out of it or that go in it is for you to look after. For you to decide. (*She drops her hands a little helplessly.*) It ain't much, but it's all I got in the world and I'm putting it in your hands. I'm telling you to be the head of this family from now on like you supposed to be.

WALTER (*stares at the money*): You trust me like that, Mama?

MAMA: I ain't never stop trusting you. Like I ain't never stop loving you.

She goes out, and WALTER *sits looking at the money on the table. Finally, in a decisive gesture, he gets up, and, in mingled joy and desperation, picks up the money. At the same moment,* TRAVIS *enters for bed.*

TRAVIS: What's the matter, Daddy? You drunk?

WALTER (*sweetly, more sweetly than we have ever known him*): No, Daddy ain't drunk. Daddy ain't going to never be drunk again . . .

TRAVIS: Well, good night, Daddy.

The FATHER *has come from behind the couch and leans over, embracing his son.*

WALTER: Son, I feel like talking to you tonight.

TRAVIS: About what?

WALTER: Oh, about a lot of things. About you and what kind of man you going to be when you grow up . . . Son—son, what do you want to be when you grow up?

TRAVIS: A bus driver.

WALTER (*laughing a little*): A what? Man, that ain't nothing to want to be!

TRAVIS: Why not?

WALTER: 'Cause, man—it ain't big enough—you know what I mean.

TRAVIS: I don't know then. I can't make up my mind. Sometimes Mama asks me that too. And sometimes when I tell her I just want to be like you— she says she don't want me to be like that and sometimes she says she does . . .

WALTER (*gathering him up in his arms*): You know what, Travis? In seven years you going to be seventeen years old. And things is going to be very different with us in seven years, Travis . . . One day when you are seventeen I'll come home—home from my office downtown somewhere—

TRAVIS: You don't work in no office, Daddy.

WALTER: No—but after tonight. After what your daddy gonna do tonight, there's going to be offices—a whole lot of offices . . .

TRAVIS: What you gonna do tonight, Daddy?

WALTER: You wouldn't understand yet, son, but your daddy's gonna make a transaction . . . a business transaction that's going to change our lives . . . That's how come one day when you 'bout seventeen years old I'll come home and I'll be pretty tired, you know what I mean, after a day of conferences and secretaries getting things wrong the way they do . . . 'cause an executive's life is hell, man—(*The more he talks the farther away he gets.*) And I'll pull the car up on the driveway . . . just a plain black Chrysler, I think, with white walls—no—black tires. More elegant. Rich people don't have to be flashy . . . though I'll have to get something a little sportier for Ruth—maybe a Cadillac convertible to do her shopping in . . . And I'll come up the steps to the house and the gardener will be clipping away at the hedges and he'll say, "Good evening, Mr. Younger." And I'll say, "Hello, Jefferson, how are you this evening?" And I'll go inside and Ruth will come downstairs and meet me at the door and we'll kiss each other and she'll take my arm and we'll go up to your room to see you sitting on the floor with the catalogues of all the great schools in America around you . . . All the great schools in the world! And—and I'll say, all right son—it's your seventeenth birthday, what is it you've decided? . . . Just tell me where you want to go to school and you'll *go.* Just tell me, what it is you want to be—and you'll *be* it . . . Whatever you want to be—Yessir! (*He holds his arms open for* TRAVIS.) You just name it, son . . . (TRAVIS *leaps into them.*) and I hand you the world!

WALTER'S *voice has risen in pitch and hysterical promise and on the last line he lifts* TRAVIS *high.*

(Blackout)

SCENE 3

TIME*: Saturday, moving day, one week later.*

Before the curtain rises, RUTH'S *voice, a strident, dramatic church alto, cuts through the silence.*

It is, in the darkness, a triumphant surge, a penetrating statement of expectation: "Oh, Lord, I don't feel no ways tired! Children, oh, glory hallelujah!"

As the curtain rises we see that RUTH *is alone in the living room, finishing up the family's packing. It is moving day. She is nailing crates and tying cartons.* BENEATHA *enters, carrying a guitar case, and watches her exuberant sister-in-law.*

RUTH: Hey!

BENEATHA (*putting away the case*): Hi.

RUTH (*pointing at a package*): Honey—look in that package there and see what I found on sale this morning at the South Center. (RUTH *gets up and moves to the package and draws out some curtains.*) Lookahere—hand-turned hems!

BENEATHA: How do you know the window size out there?

RUTH (*who hadn't thought of that*): Oh—Well, they bound to fit something in the whole house. Anyhow, they was too good a bargain to pass up. (RUTH *slaps her head, suddenly remembering something.*) Oh, Bennie—I meant to put a special note on that carton over there. That's your mama's good china and she wants 'em to be very careful with it.

BENEATHA: I'll do it.

BENEATHA *finds a piece of paper and starts to draw large letters on it.*

RUTH: You know what I'm going to do soon as I get in that new house?

BENEATHA: What?

RUTH: Honey—I'm going to run me a tub of water up to here . . . (*with her fingers practically up to her nostrils*) And I'm going to get in it—and I am going to sit . . . and sit . . . and sit in that hot water and the first person who knocks to tell *me* to hurry up and come out—

BENEATHA: Gets shot at sunrise.

RUTH (*laughing happily*): You said it, sister! (*noticing how large* BENEATHA *is absent-mindedly making the note*) Honey, they ain't going to read that from no airplane.

BENEATHA (*laughing herself*): I guess I always think things have more emphasis if they are big, somehow.

RUTH (*looking up at her and smiling*): You and your brother seem to have that as a philosophy of life. Lord, that man—done changed so 'round here. You know—you know what we did last night? Me and Walter Lee?

BENEATHA: What?

RUTH (*smiling to herself*): We went to the movies. (*looking at* BENEATHA *to see if she understands*) We went to the movies. You know the last time me and Walter went to the movies together?

BENEATHA: No.

RUTH: Me neither. That's how long it been. (*smiling again*) But we went last night. The picture wasn't much good, but that didn't seem to matter. We went—and we held hands.

BENEATHA: Oh, Lord!

RUTH: We held hands—and you know what?

BENEATHA: What?

RUTH: When we come out of the show it was late and dark and all the stores and things was closed up . . . and it was kind of chilly and there wasn't many people on the streets . . . and we was still holding hands, me and Walter.

BENEATHA: You're killing me.

> WALTER *enters with a large package. His happiness is deep in him; he cannot keep still with his new-found exuberance. He is singing and wiggling and snapping his fingers. He puts his package in a corner and puts a phonograph record, which he has brought in with him, on the record player. As the music, soulful and sensuous, comes up he dances over to* RUTH *and tries to get her to dance with him. She gives in at last to his raunchiness and in a fit of giggling allows herself to be drawn into his mood. They dip and she melts into his arms in a classic, body-melding "slow drag."*

BENEATHA (*regarding them a long time as they dance, then drawing in her breath for a deeply exaggerated comment which she does not particularly mean*): Talk about—oldddddddddd-fashionedddddddd—Negroes!

WALTER (*stopping momentarily*): What kind of Negroes?

> *He says this is fun. He is not angry with her today, nor with anyone. He starts to dance with his wife again.*

BENEATHA: Old-fashioned.

WALTER (*as he dances with* RUTH): You know, when these *New Negroes* have their convention—(*pointing at his sister*)—that is going to be the chairman of the Committee on Unending Agitation. (*He goes on dancing, then stops.*) Race, race, race! . . . Girl, I do believe you are the first person in the history of the entire human race to successfully brainwash yourself. (BENEATHA *breaks up and he goes on dancing. He stops again, enjoying his tease.*) Damn, even the N double A C P takes a holiday sometimes! (BENEATHA *and* RUTH *laugh. He dances with* RUTH *some more and starts to laugh and stops and pantomimes someone over an operating table.*) I can just see that chick someday looking down at some poor cat on an operating table and before she starts to slice him, she says . . . (*pulling his sleeves back maliciously*) "By the way, what are your views on civil rights down there? . . ."

He laughs at her again and starts to dance happily. The bell sounds.

BENEATHA: Sticks and stones may break my bones but . . . words will never hurt me!

BENEATHA *goes to the door and opens it as* WALTER *and* RUTH *go on with the clowning.* BENEATHA *is somewhat surprised to see a quiet-looking middle-aged white man in a business suit holding his hat and a briefcase in his hand and consulting a small piece of paper.*

MAN: Uh—how do you do, miss. I am looking for a Mrs.—(*He looks at the slip of paper.*) Mrs. Lena Younger? (*He stops short, struck dumb at the sight of the oblivious* WALTER *and* RUTH.)

BENEATHA (*smoothing her hair with slight embarrassment*): Oh—yes, that's my mother. Excuse me. (*She closes the door and turns to quiet the other two.*) Ruth! Brother! (*Enunciating precisely but soundlessly: "There's a white man at the door!" They stop dancing,* RUTH *cuts off the phonograph,* BENEATHA *opens the door. The man casts a curious quick glance at all of them.*) Uh—come in please.

MAN (*coming in*): Thank you.

BENEATHA: My mother isn't here just now. Is it business?

MAN: Yes . . . well, of a sort.

WALTER (*freely, the Man of the House*): Have a seat. I'm Mrs. Younger's son. I look after most of her business matters.

RUTH *and* BENEATHA *exchange amused glances.*

MAN (*regarding* WALTER, *and sitting*): Well—My name is Karl Lindner . . .

WALTER (*stretching out his hand*): Walter Younger. This is my wife—(RUTH *nods politely.*)—and my sister.

LINDNER: How do you do.

WALTER (*amiably, as he sits himself easily on a chair, leaning forward on his knees with interest and looking expectantly into the newcomer's face*): What can we do for you, Mr. Lindner!

LINDNER (*some minor shuffling of the hat and briefcase on his knees*): Well— I am a representative of the Clybourne Park Improvement Association—

WALTER (*pointing*): Why don't you sit your things on the floor?

LINDNER: Oh—yes. Thank you. (*He slides the briefcase and hat under the chair.*) And as I was saying—I am from the Clybourne Park Improvement

Association and we have had it brought to our attention at the last meeting that you people—or at least your mother—has bought a piece of residential property at—(*He digs for the slip of paper again.*)—four o six Clybourne Street . . .

WALTER: That's right. Care for something to drink? Ruth, get Mr. Lindner a beer.

LINDNER (*upset for some reason*): Oh—no, really. I mean thank you very much, but no thank you.

RUTH (*innocently*): Some coffee?

LINDNER: Thank you, nothing at all.

BENEATHA *is watching the man carefully.*

LINDNER: Well, I don't know how much you folks know about our organization. (*He is a gentle man; thoughtful and somewhat labored in his manner.*) It is one of these community organizations set up to look after—oh, you know, things like block upkeep and special projects and we also have what we call our New Neighbors Orientation Committee . . .

BENEATHA (*drily*): Yes—and what do they do?

LINDNER (*turning a little to her and then returning the main force to* WALTER): Well—it's what you might call a sort of welcoming committee, I guess. I mean they, we—I'm the chairman of the committee—go around and see the new people who move into the neighborhood and sort of give them the lowdown on the way we do things out in Clybourne Park.

BENEATHA (*with appreciation of the two meanings, which escape* RUTH *and* WALTER): Uh-huh.

LINDNER: And we also have the category of what the association calls—(*He looks elsewhere.*)—uh—special community problems . . .

BENEATHA: Yes—and what are some of those?

WALTER: Girl, let the man talk.

LINDNER (*with understated relief*): Thank you. I would sort of like to explain this thing in my own way. I mean I want to explain to you in a certain way.

WALTER: Go ahead.

LINDNER: Yes. Well. I'm going to try to get right to the point. I'm sure we'll all appreciate that in the long run.

BENEATHA: Yes.

WALTER: Be still now!

LINDNER: Well—

RUTH (*still innocently*): Would you like another chair—you don't look comfortable.

LINDNER (*more frustrated than annoyed*): No, thank you very much. Please. Well—to get right to the point I—(*A great breath, and he is off at last.*) I am sure you people must be aware of some of the incidents which have happened in various parts of the city when colored people have moved into certain areas—(BENEATHA *exhales heavily and starts tossing a piece of fruit up and down in the air.*) Well—because we have what I think is going to be a unique type of organization in American community life—not only do we deplore that kind of thing—but we are trying to do something about it. (BENEATHA *stops tossing and turns with a new and quizzical interest to the man.*) We feel—(*gaining confidence in his mission because of the interest in the faces of the people he is talking to*)— we feel that most of the trouble in this world, when you come right down to it—(*He hits his knee for emphasis.*)—most of the trouble exists because people just don't sit down and talk to each other.

RUTH (*nodding as she might in church, pleased with the remark*): You can say that again, mister.

LINDNER (*more encouraged by such affirmation*): That we don't try hard enough in this world to understand the other fellow's problem. The other guy's point of view.

RUTH: Now that's right.

BENEATHA *and* WALTER *merely watch and listen with genuine interest.*

LINDNER: Yes—that's the way we feel out in Clybourne Park. And that's why I was elected to come here this afternoon and talk to you people. Friendly like, you know, the way people should talk to each other and see if we couldn't find some way to work this thing out. As I say, the whole business is a matter of *caring* about the other fellow. Anybody can see that you are a nice family of folks, hard working and honest I'm sure. (BENEATHA *frowns slightly, quizzically, her head tilted regarding him.*) Today everybody knows what it means to be on the outside of *something.* And of course, there is always somebody who is out to take advantage of people who don't always understand.

WALTER: What do you mean?

LINDNER: Well—you see our community is made up of people who've worked hard as the dickens for years to build up that little community. They're not rich and fancy people; just hard-working, honest people who don't really have much but those little homes and a dream of the kind of community they want to raise their children in. Now, I don't say we are perfect and there is a lot wrong in some of the things they want. But you've got to admit that a man, right or wrong, has the right to want to have the neighborhood he lives in a certain kind of way. And at the moment the overwhelming majority of our people out there feel that people get along better, take more of a common interest in the life of the community, when they share a common background. I want you to believe me when I tell you that race prejudice simply doesn't enter into it. It is a matter of the people of Clybourne Park believing, rightly or wrongly, as I say, that for the happiness of all concerned that our Negro families are happier when they live in their *own* communities.

BENEATHA (*with a grand and bitter gesture*): This, friends, is the Welcoming Committee!

WALTER (*dumfounded, looking at* LINDNER): Is this what you came marching all the way over here to tell us?

LINDNER: Well, now we've been having a fine conversation. I hope you'll hear me all the way through.

WALTER (*tightly*): Go ahead, man.

LINDNER: You see—in the face of all the things I have said, we are prepared to make your family a very generous offer . . .

BENEATHA: Thirty pieces and not a coin less!

WALTER: Yeah?

LINDNER (*putting on his glasses and drawing a form out of the briefcase*): Our association is prepared, through the collective effort of our people, to buy the house from you at a financial gain to your family.

RUTH: Lord have mercy, ain't this the living gall!

WALTER: All right, you through?

LINDNER: Well, I want to give you the exact terms of the financial arrangement—

WALTER: We don't want to hear no exact terms of no arrangements. I want to know if you got any more to tell us 'bout getting together?

LINDER (*taking off his glasses*): Well—I don't suppose that you feel . . .

WALTER: Never mind how I feel—you got any more to say 'bout how people ought to sit down and talk to each other? . . . Get out of my house, man.

He turns his back and walks to the door.

LINDNER (*looking around at the hostile faces and reaching and assembling his hat and briefcase*): Well—I don't understand why you people are reacting this way. What do you think you are going to gain by moving into a neighborhood where you just aren't wanted and where some elements—well—people can get awful worked up when they feel that their whole way of life and everything they've ever worked for is threatened.

WALTER: Get out.

LINDER (*at the door, holding a small card*): Well—I'm sorry it went like this.

WALTER: Get out.

LINDNER (*almost sadly regarding* WALTER): You just can't force people to change their hearts, son.

He turns and put his card on a table and exits. WALTER *pushes the door to with stinging hatred, and stands looking at it.* RUTH *just sits and* BENEATHA *just stands. They say nothing.* MAMA *and* TRAVIS *enter.*

MAMA: Well—this all the packing got done since I left out of here this morning. I testify before God that my children got all the energy of the *dead!* What time the moving men due?

BENEATHA: Four o'clock. You had a caller, Mama.

She is smiling, teasingly.

MAMA: Sure enough—who?

BENEATHA (*her arms folded saucily*): The Welcoming Committee.

WALTER *and* RUTH *giggle.*

MAMA (*innocently*): Who?

BENEATHA: The Welcoming Committee. They said they're sure going to be glad to see you when you get there.

WALTER (*devilishly*): Yeah, they said they can't hardly wait to see your face.

Laughter.

MAMA (*sensing their facetiousness*): What's the matter with you all?

WALTER: Ain't nothing the matter with us. We just telling you 'bout the gentleman who came to see you this afternoon. From the Clybourne Park Improvement Association.

MAMA: What he want?

RUTH (*in the same mood as* BENEATHA *and* WALTER): To welcome you, honey.

WALTER: He said they can't hardly wait. He said the one thing they don't have, that they just *dying* to have out there is a fine family of fine colored people! (*to* RUTH *and* BENEATHA) Ain't that right!

RUTH (*mockingly*): Yeah! He left his card—

BENEATHA (*handing card to* MAMA): In case.

MAMA *reads and throws it on the floor—understanding and looking off as she draws her chair up to the table on which she has put her plant and some sticks and some cord.*

MAMA: Father, give us strength. (*knowingly—and without fun*) Did he threaten us?

BENEATHA: Oh—Mama—they don't do it like that any more. He talked Brotherhood. He said everybody ought to learn how to sit down and hate each other with good Christian fellowship.

She and WALTER *shake hands to ridicule the remark.*

MAMA (*sadly*): Lord, protect us . . .

RUTH: You should hear the money those folks raised to buy the house from us. All we paid and then some.

BENEATHA: What they think we going to do—eat 'em?

RUTH: No, honey, marry 'em.

MAMA (*shaking her head*): Lord, Lord, Lord . . .

RUTH: Well—that's the way the crackers crumble. (*a beat*) Joke.

BENEATHA (*laughingly noticing what her mother is doing*): Mama, what are you doing?

MAMA: Fixing my plant so it won't get hurt none on the way . . .

BENEATHA: Mama, you going to take *that* to the new house?

MAMA: Un-huh—

BENEATHA: That raggedy-looking old thing?

MAMA (*stopping and looking at her*): It expresses ME!

RUTH (*with delight, to* BENEATHA): So there, Miss Thing!

WALTER *comes to* MAMA *suddenly and bends down behind her and squeezes her in his arms with all his strength. She is overwhelmed by the suddenness of it and, though delighted, her manner is like that of* RUTH *and* TRAVIS.

MAMA: Look out now, boy! You make me mess up my thing here!

WALTER (*His face lit, he slips down on his knees beside her, his arms still about her.*): Mama . . . you know what it means to climb up in the chariot?

MAMA (*gruffly, very happy*): Get on away from me now . . .

RUTH (*near the gift-wrapped package, trying to catch* WALTER'S *eye*): Psst—

WALTER: What the old song say, Mama . . .

RUTH: Walter—Now?

She is pointing at the package.

WALTER (*speaking the lines, sweetly, playfully, in his mother's face*): I got wings . . . you got wings . . . All God's Children got wings . . .

MAMA: Boy—get out of my face and do some work . . .

WALTER: *When I get to heaven gonna put on my wings, Gonna fly all over God's heaven . . .*

BENEATHA (*teasingly, from across the room*): Everybody talking 'bout heaven ain't going there!

WALTER (*to* RUTH, *who is carrying the box across to them*): I don't know, you think we ought to give her that . . . Seems to me she ain't been very appreciative around here.

MAMA (*eyeing the box, which is obviously a gift*): What is that?

WALTER (*taking it from* RUTH *and putting it on the table in front of* MAMA): Well—what you all think? Should we give it to her?

RUTH: Oh—she was pretty good today.

MAMA: I'll good you—

She turns her eyes to the box again.

BENEATHA: Open it, Mama.

She stands up, looks at it, turns and looks at all of them, and then presses her hands together and does not open the package.

WALTER (*sweetly*): Open it, Mama. It's for you. (MAMA *looks in his eyes. It is the first present in her life without its being Christmas. Slowly she opens her package and lifts out, one by one, a brand-new sparkling set of gardening tools.* WALTER *continues, prodding.*) Ruth made up the note—read it . . .

MAMA (*picking up the card and adjusting her glasses*): "To our own Mrs. Miniver—Love from Brother, Ruth and Beneatha." Ain't that lovely . . .

TRAVIS (*tugging at his father's sleeve*): Daddy, can I give her mine now?

WALTER: All right, son. (TRAVIS *flies to get his gift.*)

MAMA: Now I don't have to use my knives and forks no more . . .

WALTER: Travis didn't want to go in with the rest of us, Mama. He got his own. (*somewhat amused*) We don't know what it is . . .

TRAVIS (*racing back in the room with a large hatbox and putting it in front of his grandmother*): Here!

MAMA: Lord have mercy, baby. You done gone and bought your grandmother a hat?

TRAVIS (*very proud*): Open it!

She does and lifts out an elaborate, but very elaborate, wide gardening hat, and all the adults break up at the sight of it.

RUTH: Travis, honey, what is that?

TRAVIS (*who thinks it is beautiful and appropriate*): It's a gardening hat! Like the ladies always have on in the magazines when they work in their gardens.

BENEATHA (*giggling fiercely*): Travis—we were trying to make Mama Mrs. Miniver—not Scarlett O'Hara!

MAMA (*indignantly*): What's the matter with you all! This here is a beautiful hat! (*absurdly*) I always wanted me one just like it!

She pops it on her head to prove it to her grandson, and the hat is ludi-crous and considerably oversized.

RUTH: Hot dog! Go, Mama!

WALTER (*doubled over with laughter*): I'm sorry, Mama—but you look like you ready to go out and chop you some cotton sure enough!

They all laugh except MAMA, *out of deference to* TRAVIS' *feelings.*

MAMA (*gathering the boy up to her*): Bless your heart—this is the prettiest hat I ever owned—(WALTER, RUTH *and* BENEATHA *chime in—noisily, festively and insincerely congratulating* TRAVIS *on his gift.*) What are we all stand-ing around here for? We ain't finished packin' yet. Bennie, you ain't packed one book.

The bell rings.

BENEATHA: That couldn't be the movers . . . it's not hardly two good yet—

BENEATHA *goes into her room.* MAMA *starts for door.*

WALTER (*turning, stiffening*): Wait—wait—I'll get it.

He stands and looks at the door.

MAMA: You expecting company, son?

WALTER (*just looking at the door*): Yeah—yeah . . .

MAMA *looks at* RUTH, *and they exchange innocent and unfrightened glances.*

MAMA (*not understanding*): Well, let them in, son.

BENEATHA (*from her room*): We need some more string.

MAMA: Travis—you run to the hardware and get me some string cord.

MAMA *goes out and* WALTER *turns and looks at* RUTH. TRAVIS *goes to a dish for money.*

RUTH: Why don't you answer the door, man?

WALTER (*suddenly bounding across the floor to embrace her*): 'Cause some-times it hard to let the future begin! (*stooping down in her face*)

> I got wings! You got wings!
> All God's children got wings!

He crosses to the door and throws it open. Standing there is a very slight little man in a not too prosperous business suit and with haunted fright-ened eyes and a hat pulled down tightly, brim up, around his forehead. TRAVIS *passes between the men and exits.* WALTER *leans deep in the man's face, still in his jubilance.*

> When I get to heaven gonna put on my wings,
> Gonna fly all over God's heaven . . .

The little man just stares at him.

Heaven—

*Suddenly he stops and looks past the little
man into the empty hallway.*

Where's Willy, man?

BOBO: He ain't with me.

WALTER (*not disturbed*): Oh—come on in. You know my wife.

BOBO (*dumbly, taking off his hat*): Yes—h'you, Miss Ruth.

RUTH (*quietly, a mood apart from her husband already, seeing* BOBO): Hello,
Bobo.

WALTER: You right on time today . . . Right on time. That's the way! (*He slaps*
BOBO *on his back.*) Sit down . . . lemme hear.

RUTH *stands stiffly and quietly in back of them, as though somehow she
senses death, her eyes fixed on her husband.*

BOBO (*his frightened eyes on the floor, his hat in his hands*): Could I please
get a drink of water, before I tell you about it, Walter Lee?

WALTER *does not take his eyes off the man.* RUTH *goes blindly to the tap and
gets a glass of water and brings it to* BOBO.

WALTER: There ain't nothing wrong, is there?

BOBO: Lemme tell you—

WALTER: Man—didn't nothing go wrong?

BOBO: Lemme tell you—Walter Lee. (*looking at* RUTH *and talking to her more
than to* WALTER) You know how it was. I got to tell you how it was. I mean
first I got to tell you how it was all the way . . . I mean about the money
I put in, Walter Lee . . .

WALTER (*with taut agitation now*): What about the money you put in?

BOBO: Well—it wasn't much as we told you—me and Willy—(*He stops.*) I'm
sorry, Walter. I got a bad feeling about it. I got a real bad feeling about
it . . .

WALTER: Man, what you telling me about all this for? . . . Tell me what happened in Springfield . . .

BOBO: Springfield.

RUTH (*like a dead woman*): What was supposed to happen in Springfield?

BOBO (*to her*): This deal that me and Walter went into with Willy—Me and
Willy was going to go down to Springfield and spread some money
'round so's we wouldn't have to wait so long for the liquor license . . .
That's what we were going to do. Everybody said that was the way you
had to do, you understand, Miss Ruth?

WALTER: Man—what happened down there?

BOBO (*a pitiful man, near tears*): I'm trying to tell you, Walter.

WALTER (*screaming at him suddenly*): THEN TELL ME, GODDAMMIT . . . WHAT'S THE
MATTER WITH YOU?

BOBO: Man . . . I didn't go to no Springfield, yesterday.

WALTER (*halted, life hanging in the moment*): Why not?

BOBO (*the long way, the hard way to tell*): 'Cause I didn't have no reasons
to . . .

WALTER: Man, what are you talking about!

BOBO: I'm talking about the fact that when I got to the train station yesterday morning—eight o'clock like we planned . . . Man—*Willy didn't never show up.*

WALTER: Why . . . where was he . . . where is he?

BOBO: That's what I'm trying to tell you . . . I don't know . . . I waited six hours . . . I called his house . . . and I waited . . . six hours . . . I waited in that train station six hours . . . (*breaking into tears*) That was all the extra money I had in the world . . . (*looking up at* WALTER *with tears running down his face*) Man, *Willy is gone.*

WALTER: Gone, what you mean Willy is gone? Gone where? You mean he went by himself. You mean he went off to Springfield by himself—to take care of getting the license—(*turns and looks anxiously at* RUTH) You mean maybe he didn't want too many people in on the business down there? (*looks to* RUTH *again, as before*) You know Willy got his own ways. (*looks back to* BOBO) Maybe you was late yesterday and he just went on down there without you. Maybe—maybe—he's been callin' you at home tryin' to tell you what happened or something. Maybe—maybe—he just got sick. He's somewhere—he's got to be somewhere. We just got to find him—me and you got to find him. (*grabs* BOBO *senselessly by the collar and starts to shake him*) We got to!

BOBO (*in sudden angry, frightened agony*): What's the matter with you, Walter! *When a cat take off with your money he don't leave you no road maps!*

WALTER (*turning madly, as though he is looking for* WILLY *in every room*): Willy! . . . Willy . . . don't do it . . . Please don't do it . . . Man, not with that money . . . Man, please, not with that money . . . Oh, God . . . Don't let it be true . . . (*He is wandering around, crying out for* WILLY *and looking for him or perhaps for help from God.*) Man . . . I trusted you . . . Man, I put my life in your hands . . . (*He starts to crumple down on the floor as* RUTH *just covers her face in horror.* MAMA *opens the door and comes into the room, with* BENEATHA *behind her.*) Man . . . (*He starts to pound the floor with his fists, sobbing wildly.*) THAT MONEY IS MADE OUT OF MY FATHER'S FLESH—

BOBO (*standing over him helplessly*): I'm sorry, Walter . . . (*Only* WALTER'S *sobs reply.* BOBO *puts on his hat.*) I had my life staked on this deal, too . . .

He exits.

MAMA (*to* WALTER): Son—(*She goes to him, bends down to him, talks to his bent head.*) Son . . . Is it gone? Son, I gave you sixty-five hundred dollars. Is it gone? All of it? Beneatha's money too?

WALTER (*lifting his head slowly*): Mama . . . I never . . . went to the bank at all . . .

MAMA (*not wanting to believe him*): You mean . . . Your sister's school money . . . you used that too . . . Walter? . . .

WALTER: Yessss! All of it . . . It's all gone . . .

There is total silence. RUTH *stands with her face covered with her hands;* BENEATHA *leans forlornly against a wall, fingering a piece of red ribbon from the mother's gift.* MAMA *stops and looks at her son without recognition and then, quite without thinking about it, starts to beat him senselessly in the face.* BENEATHA *goes to them and stops it.*

BENEATHA: Mama!

MAMA *stops and looks at both of her children and rises slowly and wanders vaguely, aimlessly away from them.*

MAMA: I seen . . . him . . . night after night . . . come in . . . and look at that rug . . . and then look at me . . . the red showing in his eyes . . . the veins moving in his head . . . I seen him grow thin and old before he was forty . . . working and working and working like somebody's old horse . . . killing himself . . . and you—you give it all away in a day—(*She raises her arms to strike him again.*)

BENEATHA: Mama—

MAMA: Oh, God . . . (*She looks up to Him.*) Look down here—and show me the strength.

BENEATHA: Mama—

MAMA (*folding over*): Strength . . .

BENEATHA (*plaintively*): Mama . . .

MAMA: Strength!

Curtain.

Act Three

TIME: *An hour later.*

At curtain, there is a sullen light of gloom in the living room, gray light not unlike that which began the first scene of Act One. At left we can see WALTER *within his room, alone with himself. He is stretched out on the bed, his shirt out and open, his arms under his head. He does not smoke, he does not cry out, he merely lies there, looking up at the ceiling, much as if he were alone in the world.*

In the living room BENEATHA *sits at the table, still surrounded by the now almost ominous packing crates. She sits looking off. We feel that this is a mood struck perhaps an hour before, and it lingers now, full of the empty sound of profound disappointment. We see on a line from her brother's bedroom the sameness of their attitudes. Presently the bell rings and* BENEATHA *rises without ambition or interest in answering. It is* ASAGAI, *smiling broadly, striding into the room with energy and happy expectation and conversation.*

ASAGAI: I came over . . . I had some free time. I thought I might help with the packing. Ah, I like the look of packing crates! A household in preparation for a journey! It depresses some people . . . but for me . . . it is another feeling. Something full of the flow of life, do you understand? Movement, progress . . . It makes me think of Africa.

BENEATHA: Africa!

ASAGAI: What kind of a mood is this? Have I told you how deeply you move me?

BENEATHA: He gave away the money, Asagai . . .

ASAGAI: Who gave away what money?

BENEATHA: The insurance money. My brother gave it away.

ASAGAI: Gave it away?

BENEATHA: He made an investment! With a man even Travis wouldn't have trusted with his most worn-out marbles.

ASAGAI: And it's gone?

BENEATHA: Gone!

ASAGAI: I'm very sorry . . . And you, now?

BENEATHA: Me? . . . Me? . . . Me, I'm nothing . . . Me. When I was very small . . . We used to take our sleds out in the wintertime and the only hills we had were the ice-covered stone steps of some houses down the street. And we used to fill them in with snow and make them smooth and slide down them all day . . . and it was very dangerous, you know . . . far too steep . . . and sure enough one day a kid named Rufus came down too fast and hit the sidewalk and we saw his face just split open right there in front of us . . . And I remember standing there looking at his bloody open face thinking that was the end of Rufus. But the ambulance came and they took him to the hospital and they fixed the broken bones and they sewed it all up . . . and the next time I saw Rufus he just had a little line down the middle of his face . . . I never got over that . . .

ASAGAI: What?

BENEATHA: That that was what one person could do for another, fix him up— sew up the problem, make him all right again. That was the most marvelous thing in the world . . . I wanted to do that. I always thought it was the one concrete thing in the world that a human being could do. Fix up the sick, you know—and make them whole again. This was truly being God . . .

ASAGAI: You wanted to be God?

BENEATHA: No—I wanted to cure. It used to be so important to me. I wanted to cure. It used to matter. I used to care. I mean about people and how their bodies hurt . . .

ASAGAI: And you've stopped caring?

BENEATHA: Yes—I think so.

ASAGAI: Why?

BENEATHA (*bitterly*): Because it doesn't seem deep enough, close enough to what ails mankind! It was a child's way of seeing things—or an idealist's.

ASAGAI: Children see things very well sometimes—and idealists even better.

BENEATHA: I know that's what you think. Because you are still where I left off. You with all your talk and dreams about Africa! You still think you can patch up the world. Cure the Great Sore of Colonialism—(*loftily, mocking it*) with the Penicillin of Independence—!

ASAGAI: Yes!

BENEATHA: Independence *and then what?* What about all the crooks and thieves and just plain idiots who will come into power and steal and plunder the same as before—only now they will be black and do it in the name of the new Independence—WHAT ABOUT THEM?!

ASAGAI: That will be the problem for another time. First we must get there.

BENEATHA: And where does it end?

ASAGAI: End? Who even spoke of an end? To life? To living?

BENEATHA: An end to misery! To stupidity! Don't you see there isn't any real progress, Asagai, there is only one large circle that we march in, around and around, each of us with our own little picture in front of us—our own little mirage that we think is the future.

ASAGAI: That is the mistake.

BENEATHA: What?

ASAGAI: What you just said—about the circle. It isn't a circle—it is simply a long line—as in geometry, you know, one that reaches into infinity. And because we cannot see the end—we also cannot see how it changes. And it is very odd but those who see the changes—who dream, who will not give up—are called idealists . . . and those who see only the circle—we call *them* the "realists"!

BENEATHA: Asagai, while I was sleeping in that bed in there, people went out and took the future right out of my hands! And nobody asked me, nobody consulted me—they just went out and changed my life!

ASAGAI: Was it your money?

BENEATHA: What?

ASAGAI: Was it your money he gave away?

BENEATHA: It belonged to all of us.

ASAGAI: But did you earn it? Would you have had it at all if your father had not died?

BENEATHA: No.

ASAGAI: Then isn't there something wrong in a house—in a world—where all dreams, good or bad, must depend on the death of a man? I never thought to see *you* like this, Alaiyo. You! Your brother made a mistake and you are grateful to him so that now you can give up the ailing human race on account of it! You talk about what good is struggle, what good is anything! Where are we all going and why are we bothering!

BENEATHA: AND YOU CANNOT ANSWER IT!

ASAGAI (*shouting over her*): I LIVE THE ANSWER! (*pause*) In my village at home it is the exceptional man who can even read a newspaper . . . or who ever sees a book at all. I will go home and much of what I will have to say will seem strange to the people of my village. But I will teach and work and things will happen, slowly and swiftly. At times it will seem that nothing changes at all . . . and then again the sudden dramatic events which make history leap into the future. And then quiet again. Retrogression even. Guns, murder, revolution. And I even will have moments when I wonder if the quiet was not better than all that death and hatred. But I look about my village at the illiteracy and disease and ignorance and I will not wonder long. And perhaps . . . perhaps I will be a great man . . . I mean perhaps I will hold on to the substance of truth and find my way always with the right course . . . and perhaps for it I will be butchered in my bed some night by the servants of empire . . .

BENEATHA: *The martyr!*

ASAGAI (*He smiles.*): . . . or perhaps I shall live to be a very old man, respected and esteemed in my new nation . . . And perhaps I shall hold office and this is what I'm trying to tell you, Alaiyo: Perhaps the things

I believe now for my country will be wrong and outmoded, and I will not understand and do terrible things to have things my way or merely to keep my power. Don't you see that there will be young men and women—not British soldiers then, but my own black countrymen—to step out of the shadows some evening and slit my then useless have a Don't you see they have always been there . . . can work . . . And that such a thing as too high all the time—

might kill me ever . . . *to* MAMA *fast—the words pouring out with urgency*
BENEATHA *(operation)*: Lena—I'll work . . . I'll work twenty hours a day in all
ASA kitchens in Chicago . . . I'll strap my baby on my back if I have to and scrub all the floors in America and wash all the sheets in America if I have to—but we got to MOVE! We got to get OUT OF HERE!!

MAMA *reaches out absently and pats* RUTH'S *hand.*

MAMA: No—I sees things differently now. Been thinking 'bout some of the things we could do to fix this place up some. I seen a second-hand bureau over on Maxwell Street just the other day that could fit right there. *(She points to where the new furniture might go.* RUTH *wanders away from her.)* Would need some new handles on it and then a little varnish and it look like something brand-new. And—we can put up them new curtains in the kitchen . . . Why this place be looking fine. Cheer us all up so that we forget trouble ever come . . . *(to* RUTH*)* And you could get some nice screens to put up in your room round the baby's bassinet . . . *(She looks at both of them, pleadingly.)* Sometimes you just got to know when to give up some things . . . and hold on to what you got . . .

WALTER *enters from the outside, looking spent and leaning against the door, his coat hanging from him.*

MAMA: Where you been, son?
WALTER *(breathing hard)*: Made a call.
MAMA: To who, son?
WALTER: To The Man. *(He heads for his room.)*
MAMA: What man, baby?
WALTER *(stops in the door)*: The Man, Mama. Don't you know who The Man is?
RUTH: Walter Lee?
WALTER: *The Man.* Like the guys in the streets say—The Man. Captain Boss—Mistuh Charley . . . Old Cap'n Please Mr. Bossman . . .
BENEATHA *(suddenly)*: Lindner!
WALTER: That's right! That's good. I told him to come right over.
BENEATHA *(fiercely, understanding)*: For what? What do you want to see him for!
WALTER *(looking at his sister)*: We going to do business with him.
MAMA: What you talking 'bout, son?
WALTER: Talking 'bout life, Mama. You all always telling me to see life like it is. Well—I laid in there on my back today . . . and I figured it out. Life just like it is. Who gets and who don't get. *(He sits down with his coat on and laughs.)* Mama, you know it's all divided up. Life is. Sure enough.

Between the takers and the "tooken." (*He laughs.*) I've figured it out finally. (*He looks around at them.*) Yeah. Some of us always getting "tooken." (*He laughs.*) People like Willy Harris, they don't never get "tooken." And you know why the rest of us do? 'Cause we all mixed up. Mixed up bad. We get to looking 'round for the right and the wrong; and we worry about it and cry about it and stay up nights trying to figure out 'bout the wrong and the right of things all the time . . . And all the time, man, them takers is out there operating, just taking and taking. Willy Harris? Shoot—Willy Harris don't even count. He don't even count in the big scheme of things. But I'll say one thing for old Willy Harris . . . he's taught me something. He's taught me to keep my eye on what counts in this world. Yeah—(*shouting out a little*) Thanks, Willy!

RUTH: What did you call that man for, Walter Lee?

WALTER: Called him to tell him to come on over to the show. Gonna put on a show for the man. Just what he wants to see. You see, Mama, the man came here today and he told us that them people out there where you want us to move—well they so upset they willing to pay us *not* to move! (*He laughs again.*) And—and oh, Mama—you would of been proud of the way me and Ruth and Bennie acted. We told him to get out . . . Lord have mercy! We told the man to get out! Oh, we was some proud folks this afternoon, yeah. (*He lights a cigarette.*) We were still full of that old-time stuff . . .

RUTH (*coming toward him slowly*): You talking 'bout taking them people's money to keep us from moving in that house?

WALTER: I ain't just talking 'bout it, baby—I'm telling you that's what's going to happen!

BENEATHA: Oh, God! Where is the bottom! Where is the real honest-to-God bottom so he can't go any farther!

WALTER: See—that's the old stuff. You and that boy that was here today. You all want everybody to carry a flag and a spear and sing some marching songs, huh? You wanna spend your life looking into things and trying to find the right and the wrong part, huh? Yeah. You know what's going to happen to that boy someday—he'll find himself sitting in a dungeon, locked in forever—and the takers will have the key! Forget it, baby! There ain't no causes—there ain't nothing but taking in this world, and he who takes most is smartest—and it don't make a damn bit of difference *how*.

MAMA: You making something inside me cry, son. Some awful pain inside me.

WALTER: Don't cry, Mama. Understand. That white man is going to walk in that door able to write checks for more money than we ever had. It's important to him and I'm going to help him . . . I'm going to put on the show, Mama.

MAMA: Son—I come from five generations of people who was slaves and sharecroppers—but ain't nobody in my family never let nobody pay 'em no money that was a way of telling us we wasn't fit to walk the earth. We ain't never been that poor. (*raising her eyes and looking at him*) We ain't never been that—dead inside.

BENEATHA: Well—we are dead now. All the talk about dreams and sunlight that goes on in this house. It's all dead now.

WALTER: What's the matter with you all! I didn't make this world! It was give to me this way! Hell, yes, I want me some yachts someday! Yes, I want to hang some real pearls 'round my wife's neck. Ain't she supposed to wear no pearls? Somebody tell me—tell me, who decides which women is suppose to wear pearls in this world. I tell you I am a *man*—and I think my wife should wear some pearls in this world!

This last line hangs a good while and WALTER *begins to move about the room. The word "Man" has penetrated his consciousness; he mumbles it to himself repeatedly between strange agitated pauses as he moves about.*

MAMA: Baby, how you going to feel on the inside?

WALTER: Fine! . . . Going to feel fine . . . a man . . .

MAMA: You won't have nothing left then, Walter Lee.

WALTER (*coming to her*): I'm going to feel fine, Mama. I'm going to look that son-of-a-bitch in the eyes and say—(*He falters.*)—and say, "All right, Mr. Lindner—(*He falters even more.*)—that's *your* neighborhood out there! You got the right to keep it like you want! You got the right to have it like you want! Just write the check and—the house is yours." And—and I am going to say—(*His voice almost breaks.*) "And you—you people just put the money in my hand and you won't have to live next to this bunch of stinking niggers! . . ." (*He straightens up and moves away from his mother, walking around the room.*) And maybe—maybe I'll just get down on my black knees . . . (*He does so;* RUTH *and* BENNIE *and* MAMA *watch him in frozen horror.*) "Captain, Mistuh, Bossman—(*groveling and grinning and wringing his hands in profoundly anguished imitation of the slow-witted movie stereotype*) A-hee-hee-hee! Oh, yassuh boss! Yasssssuh! Great white—(*Voice breaking, he forces himself to go on.*)— Father, just gi' ussen de money, fo' God's sake, and we's—we's ain't gwine come out deh and dirty up yo' white folks neighborhood . . ." (*He breaks down completely.*) And I'll feel fine! Fine! FINE! (*He gets up and goes into the bedroom.*)

BENEATHA: That is not a man. That is nothing but a toothless rat.

MAMA: Yes—death done come in this here house. (*She is nodding, slowly, reflectively.*) Done come walking in my house on the lips of my children. You what supposed to be my beginning again. You—what supposed to be my harvest. (*to* BENEATHA) You—you mourning your brother?

BENEATHA: He's no brother of mine.

MAMA: What you say?

BENEATHA: I said that that individual in that room is no brother of mine.

MAMA: That's what I thought you said. You feeling like you better than he is today? (BENEATHA *does not answer.*) Yes? What you tell him a minute ago? That he wasn't a man? Yes? You give him up for me? You done wrote his epitaph too—like the rest of the world? Well, who give you the privilege?

BENEATHA: Be on my side for once! You saw what he just did, Mama! You saw him—down on his knees. Wasn't it you who taught me to despise any man who would do that? Do what he's going to do?

MAMA: Yes—I taught you that. Me and your daddy. But I thought I taught you something else too . . . I thought I taught you to love him.

BENEATHA: Love him? There is nothing left to love.

MAMA: There is *always* something left to love. And if you ain't learned that, you ain't learned nothing. (*looking at her*) Have you cried for that boy today? I don't mean for yourself and for the family 'cause we lost the money. I mean for him: what he been through and what it done to him. Child, when do you think is the time to love somebody the most? When they done good and made things easy for everybody? Well then, you ain't through learning—because that ain't the time at all. It's when he's at his lowest and can't believe in hisself 'cause the world done whipped him so! When you starts measuring somebody, measure him right, child, measure him right. Make sure you done taken into account what hills and valleys he come through before he got to wherever he is.

TRAVIS *bursts into the room at the end of the speech, leaving the door open.*

TRAVIS: Grandmama—the moving men are downstairs! The truck just pulled up.

MAMA (*turning and looking at him*): Are they, baby? They downstairs?

She sighs and sits. LINDNER *appears in the doorway. He peers in and knocks lightly, to gain attention, and comes in. All turn to look at him.*

LINDNER (*hat and briefcase in hand*): Uh-hello . . .

RUTH *crosses mechanically to the bedroom door and opens it and lets it swing open freely and slowly as the lights come up on* WALTER *within, still in his coat, sitting at the far corner of the room. He looks up and out through the room to* LINDNER.

RUTH: He's here.

A long minute passes and WALTER *slowly gets up.*

LINDNER (*coming to the table with efficiency, putting his briefcase on the table and starting to unfold papers and unscrew fountain pens*): Well, I certainly was glad to hear from you people. (WALTER *has begun the trek out of the room, slowly and awkwardly, rather like a small boy, passing the back of his sleeve across his mouth from time to time.*) Life can really be so much simpler than people let it be most of the time. Well—with whom do I negotiate? You, Mrs. Younger, or your son here? (MAMA *sits with her hands folded on her lap and her eyes closed as* WALTER *advances.* TRAVIS *goes closer to* LINDNER *and looks at the papers curiously.*) Just some official papers, sonny.

RUTH: Travis, you go downstairs—

MAMA (*opening her eyes and looking into* WALTER'S): No. Travis, you stay right here. And you make him understand what you doing, Walter Lee. You teach him good. Like Willy Harris taught you. You show where our five generations done come to. (WALTER *looks from her to the boy, who grins at him innocently.*) Go ahead, son—(*She folds her hands and closes her eyes.*) Go ahead.

WALTER (*at last crosses to* LINDNER, *who is reviewing the contract*): Well, Mr. Lindner. (BENEATHA *turns away.*) We called you—(*There is a profound, simple groping quality in his speech.*)—because, well, me and my family (*He looks around and shifts from one foot to the other.*) Well—we are very plain people . . .

LINDNER: Yes—

WALTER: I mean—I have worked as a chauffeur most of my life—and my wife here, she does domestic work in people's kitchens. So does my mother. I mean—we are plain people . . .

LINDNER: Yes, Mr. Younger—

WALTER (*really like a small boy, looking down at his shoes and then up at the man*): And—uh—well, my father, well, he was a laborer most of his life . . .

LINDNER (*absolutely confused*): Uh, yes—yes, I understand. (*He turns back to the contract.*)

WALTER (*a beat; staring at him*): And my father—(*with sudden intensity*) My father almost *beat a man to death* once because this man called him a bad name or something, you know what I mean?

LINDNER (*looking up, frozen*): No, no, I'm afraid I don't—

WALTER (*A beat. The tension hangs; then* WALTER *steps back from it.*): Yeah. Well—what I mean is that we come from people who had a lot of *pride.* I mean—we are very proud people. And that's my sister over there and she's going to be a doctor—and we are very proud—

LINDNER: Well—I am sure that is very nice, but—

WALTER: What I am telling you is that we called you over here to tell you that we are very proud and that this—(*signaling to* TRAVIS) Travis, come here. (TRAVIS *crosses and* WALTER *draws him before him facing the man.*) This is my son, and he makes the sixth generation of our family in this country. And we have all thought about your offer—

LINDNER: Well, good . . . good—

WALTER: And we have decided to move into our house because my father— my father—he earned it for us brick by brick. (MAMA *has her eyes closed and is rocking back and forth as though she were in church, with her head nodding the Amen yes.*) We don't want to make no trouble for no-body or fight no causes, and we will try to be good neighbors. And that's *all* we got to say about that. (*He looks the man absolutely in the eyes.*) We don't want your money. (*He turns and walks away.*)

LINDNER (*looking around at all of them*): I take it then—that you have de-cided to occupy . . .

BENEATHA: That's what the man said.

LINDNER (*to* MAMA *in her reverie*): Then I would like to appeal to you, Mrs. Younger. You are older and wiser and understand things better I am sure . . .

MAMA: I am afraid you don't understand. My son said we was going to move and there ain't nothing left for me to say. (*briskly*) You know how these young folks is nowadays, mister. Can't do a thing with 'em! (*As he opens his mouth, she rises.*) Good-bye.

LINDER (*folding up his materials*): Well—if you are that final about it . . . there is nothing left for me to say. (*He finishes, almost ignored by the family, who are concentrating on* WALTER LEE. *At the door* LINDNER *halts and looks around.*) I sure hope you people know what you're getting into.

He shakes his head and exits.

RUTH (*looking around and coming to life*): Well, for God's sake—if the moving men are here—LET'S GET THE HELL OUT OF HERE!

MAMA (*into action*): Ain't it the truth! Look at all this here mess. Ruth, put Travis' good jacket on him . . . Walter Lee, fix your tie and tuck your shirt in, you look like somebody's hoodlum! Lord have mercy, where is my plant? (*She flies to get it amid the general bustling of the family, who are deliberately trying to ignore the nobility of the past moment.*) You all start on down . . . Travis child, don't go empty-handed . . . Ruth, where did I put that box with my skillets in it? I want to be in charge of it myself . . . I'm going to make us the biggest dinner we ever ate tonight . . . Beneatha, what's the matter with them stockings? Pull them things up, girl . . .

The family starts to file out as two moving men appear and begin to carry out the heavier pieces of furniture, bumping into the family as they move about.

BENEATHA: Mama, Asagai asked me to marry him today and go to Africa—

MAMA (*in the middle of her getting-ready activity*): He did? You ain't old enough to marry nobody—(*seeing the moving men lifting one of her chairs precariously*) Darling, that ain't no bale of cotton, please handle it so we can sit in it again! I had that chair twenty-five years . . .

The movers sigh with exasperation and go on with their work.

BENEATHA (*girlishly and unreasonably trying to pursue the conversation*): To go to Africa, Mama—be a doctor in Africa . . .

MAMA (*distracted*): Yes, baby—

WALTER: *Africa!* What he want you to go to Africa for?

BENEATHA: To practice there . . .

WALTER: Girl, if you don't get all them silly ideas out your head! You better marry yourself a man with some loot . . .

BENEATHA (*angrily, precisely as in the first scene of the play*): What have you got to do with who I marry!

WALTER: Plenty. Now I think George Murchison—

BENEATHA: *George Murchison!* I wouldn't marry him if he was Adam and I was Eve!

WALTER and BENEATHA go out yelling at each other vigorously and the anger is loud and real till their voices diminish. RUTH stands at the door and turns to MAMA and smiles knowingly.

MAMA (*fixing her hat at last*): Yeah—they something all right, my children . . .

RUTH: Yeah—they're something. Let's go, Lena.

MAMA (*stalling, starting to look around at the house*): Yes—I'm coming. Ruth—

RUTH: Yes?

MAMA (*quietly, woman to woman*): He finally come into his manhood today, didn't he? Kind of like a rainbow after the rain . . .

RUTH (*biting her lip lest her own pride explode in front of MAMA*): Yes, Lena.

WALTER'S *voice calls for them raucously.*

WALTER (*off stage*): Y'all come on! These people charges by the hour, you know!

MAMA (*waving* RUTH *out vaguely*): All right, honey—go on down. I be down directly.

> RUTH *hesitates, then exits.* MAMA *stands, at last alone in the living room, her plant on the table before her as the lights start to come down. She looks around at all the walls and ceilings and suddenly, despite herself, while the children call below, a great heaving thing rises in her and she puts her fist to her mouth to stifle it, takes a final desperate look, pulls her coat about her, pats her hat and goes out. The lights dim down. The door opens and she comes back in, grabs her plant, and goes out for the last time.*

Curtain.

The Receptive Reader

1. How much does the playwright steer the director's and actors' interpretation of the characters in the *stage directions?* Prepare a capsule portrait of one or more of the characters as she sketches them out in these introductory descriptions.

2. What does Mama tell the younger generation about the history of her people and the history of her family? What makes Mama the strong *central character* in the play? What for you are the crucial confrontations where her strength is tested?

3. Would you agree that, among the characters in this play, Walter is the rebel? What are the sources of his hostility and rebellion? Where in the play do you most clearly see and understand his bitterness? How are Walter and his actions central to the *plot* of the play? (Some critics have asked how believable or plausible some of the key plot developments are in this play. Do you find them believable? Why or why not?)

4. What is the role of Ruth in the play? Does the confrontation between Walter and his mother make her a *minor character?* What is her relationship with her mother-in-law? What is her relationship with Walter?

5. What roles do the supporting characters play? What role does Murchison play? How does the playwright sketch the rejection by Beneatha and Asagai of the "melting pot" ideal of assimilation? How does Beneatha see the future? How does Asagai? (How does Beneatha provide a *foil* for Walter?)

6. Always in the background of the play is the world of "the Man." What role does it have in the play as a whole? What does Mr. Lindner as its emissary reveal about the working of prejudice or of segregation?

7. Does the play have a "happy ending"? Do you consider the play as a whole optimistic, pessimistic, or neither? What vision of the future does the play as a whole present for African Americans?

The Personal Response

✗ Do you see yourself anywhere in this play? Is there a character with whom you closely identify? Is there a character toward whom you feel strong antagonism? (With which of the characters do you think the author identified most closely?)

✗ Some critics have questioned Hansberry's treatment of the black matriarch as stereotyped or sentimental. Does Mama seem to you overidealized? Or does she seem a believable strong character to you?

✗ Do you think the author is too harsh toward or biased against Walter as the young black male in the family?

The Creative Dimension

As an exercise in **role playing**, prepare a brief monologue in which you assume the role of one of the characters in the play. Bring the character to life for your audience by talking about yourself in this assumed role: your background, your ties with other people, your hopes and aspirations.

Making Connections—For Discussion or Writing

✗ In both *Death of a Salesman* and *A Raisin in the Sun,* the extended family provides the world in which much of the characters' lives is played out. Compare and contrast the web of interpersonal relations in Miller's and in Hansberry's plays.

✗ Critics have asked whether Ibsen's *A Doll's House* speaks to men and women alike or whether it pits men and women against one another. Similarly, some critics have stressed Hansberry's commitment to the struggle of the black community, but it has also been fashionable to claim that Hansberry's play speaks to our "common humanity." Reexamine one of these plays (or both) to decide if you see the play as a polarizing or a unifying force.

WRITING ABOUT LITERATURE

29 *The Play and the Critics*
WRITING FOCUS: The Documented Paper

The Writing Workshop   The critical reception of a major play or of a challenging new playwright makes a good topic for a research paper paper on a literary subject. How sensitive or responsive were the critics? How did early audiences respond, and why? Such a paper allows you to explore questions that fascinate people who love the theater.

✗ What makes a play a success or failure?

✘ How much depends on the playwright, the director, or star performers?

✘ Why are some plays underrated when they first appear?

✘ Why do some plays seem hits at the time but slowly fade from view?

✘ What makes a play a *succès d'estime*—treated with respect (or esteem) by the critics and reviewers, although audiences don't warm to it?

✘ What makes a major new play or playwright controversial?

✘ How do critics react when a prominent director or cast launches a major new production of a classic?

Finding Promising Leads   To work up material for your paper, you are likely to begin by checking in electronic or printed indexes of periodical literature for reviews and critical appraisals in the year of the original production and in the years immediately following. Sometimes, a survey article or an appraisal of the playwright published years later may prove a valuable guide to the original and later reviews. For instance, you might be investigating the critical reception of Lorraine Hansberry's *Raisin in the Sun*. You might come up with leads like the following:

Reviews of the original production:

Atkinson, Brooks. "The Theater: *Raisin in the Sun.*" *New York Times* 12 Mar. 1959. Reprinted in *New York Theatre Critics' Reviews,* 1959, p. 345.

Driver, Tom F. "Theater: *A Raisin in the Sun.*" *The New Republic* 140 (13 Apr. 1959): 21.

Weales, Gerald. "Thoughts on *A Raisin in the Sun.*" *Commentary* 27 no.6 (June 1959) 527–30.

Lewis, Theophilus. "Social Protest in *A Raisin in the Sun.*" *Catholic World* 190 (Oct. 1959): 31–35.

Reviews of the 1961 Columbia Pictures motion picture in *Commonweal* 74 (7 Apr. 1961); *Ebony* 16 (Apr. 1961: 53–56, *The New Republic,* 20 Mar. 1961, p. 19; *New York Times,* 30 Mar. 1961, p. 24; *The New Yorker* 8 Apr. 1961, p. 164; *Newsweek,* 10 Apr. 1961, p. 103.

Later assessments:

Brown-Guillory, Elizabeth. *Their Place on the Stage: Black Women Playwrights in America.* Westport: Greenwood P, 1988.

Ashley, Leonard R.N. "Lorraine Hansberry and the Great Black Way." June Schlueter ed. *Modern American Drama: The Female Canon.* Cranbury, NJ: Assoc. University Presses, 1990.

<<<Find It on the Web>>>

The American playwright David Mamet has in recent years been widely performed, writing plays and screenplays that have stirred bitter controversy and made him one of the most successful dramatists of our time. Nicholas de Jongh, a reviewer for the *London Evening Standard,* said about Mamet's play *The Old Neighborhood:*

> As in the world beyond the theatre, information is fragmented, elusive, and allusive [about] the mingled sweetness and vitriol of memory, the pain of love lost, betrayed, or absent from the cradle, and a nagging dread that modern, urban life is wrong, somehow, not sane or worthwhile enough to nourish the spirit. A play of riveting disquiet.

The following is a sampling of online sources tracked by a student documenting the controversies swirling around one of Mamet's plays:

Faires, Robert. "<u>Oleanna</u>: In a Nightmare Duet." <u>Austin Chronicle</u>. 4 May 2001. 13 Nov. 2001.
   <http://www.austinchronicle.com/issues/dispatch/2001-05-04/arts_exhibitionism.html>

Ebert, Roger. Review of <u>Oleanna</u>. <u>Chicago Sun-Times</u>. 4 Nov. 1994. 13 Nov. 2001.
   <http://www.suntimes.com/ebert/ebert reviews/1994/11/949107.html>

Sheffield, Skip. "Performances First-Rate in Harassment Drama." <u>Boca Raton News</u>. 13 Nov. 2001.
   <http://www.counterforcextc.com/review.oleanna.htm>

Nielson, James. "On Mamet's <u>Oleanna</u>." Letter to the Editor. 9 Oct. 1994. 13 Nov. 2001.
   <http://www.jimnielson.com/eviews/oleanna.html>

Taking Notes In exploratory reading, you need to look a source over quickly, but you also need to slow down and close in when promising materials surface. Be alert for possibly useful material. For instance, with the Hansberry materials, you may find evidence of the reluctance of white producers to put on a play by an unknown black dramatist. However, you may also find evidence of the compensating eagerness of others to support a black woman playwright.

Look for recurrent issues and questions that come up again and again. For example, there has been much discussion of the physical appearance of the actors playing Arthur Miller's Willy Loman. Many reviews of the *Death of a Salesman* revival with Dustin Hoffman talked at length about the contrast between Cobb and Hoffman. Miller made Cobb say,

"I look like a walrus," but for Hoffman he changed the line back to the original "I look like a shrimp." Size or bulk of the lead actor again became an issue in a spectacular more recent revival of the play with the the hefty Brian Dennehy in the title role.

Remember note-takers' guidelines like the following:

✘ *Copy direct quotations exactly, word for word*. Put all the quoted material in **quotation marks** to show material copied verbatim. Make sure to include the closing quotation mark to show where the quotation ends.

✘ *Include all the publishing data you will need later*. Copy exactly all information you will need when you identify your sources in a documented paper. Include exact page numbers. A sample note might look like this:

> ### Reluctance of white producers
> "*To Be Young, Gifted, and Black* was originally conceived not in its present form, but as a work for the stage. As had been the case with *A Raisin in the Sun,* however (and every other black play that I have ever heard of), established producers evinced skepticism—in this case that sufficient public interest would exist in the life of a deceased playwright whose entire reputation rested on two plays."
> Robert Nemiroff. Postscript to *To Be Young, Gifted and Black: Lorraine Hansberry in Her Own Words,* adapted by Robert Nemiroff (Englewoods Cliffs: Prentice, 1969), p. 263.

✘ *Distinguish clearly between paraphrase and direct first-hand quotation*. When you **paraphrase**, you put someone else's ideas in your own words. You can thus highlight what seems most important to you and condense other parts. Even when you paraphrase, be sure to use quotation marks for striking phrases that you keep in the exact wording of the author. The following note might be your summing up of comments on the original casting of *Death of a Salesman* that Arthur Miller made in an article in *Theater Week* in 1991. It combines paraphrase and **partial quotation**:

> Miller admits he believes in typecasting, choosing the actor who looks right for the role, since no director really wants to make over an actor into something he or she isn't. But although Miller wrote the part of Willy Loman originally with a "small, feisty man" in mind, the original Willy Loman turned out to be Lee Cobb, "the closest thing in Equity to a hippo."

✘ *Indicate clearly any omissions or additions*. Have you deleted something or added something to a quotation? Here are related notes from a review by Lloyd Roe, titled "Lost in America," in the *Atlantic* magazine. Note the use of the **ellipsis**—three spaced periods to show an omission, or four when the periods include the period at the end of a sentence. Note the use of **square brackets** to show that material has been inserted into the original quotation. Note finer points like **single**

quotation marks for the phrase "common man" that appears as a quote-within-a-quote.

> "Big and slow-moving, with a suffering dignity in his thick face," Cobb "gave the lie to Miller's view of Willy as a 'common man.' Cobb's pain was outsized. He was like a huge, wounded animal dying from a bullet he never heard coming, and he was as private as an animal—the real source of his agony was hidden and mute. Cobb rendered irrelevant the question of Willy's responsibility for his own defeat by making his sorrow too deep for the circumstances of his life."

> "Coming to the play from a different generation and a different tradition, Hoffman, though he can't ignore Cobb, hardly labors in his shadow. Hoffman couldn't be more different from Cobb, both physically and technically, but he doesn't try for contrasts. . . . His Willy is freshly conceived—the characterization feels new, and there's a sense of discovery in it."

> "Hoffman's Willy is collapsed in on himself, as if he were shrinking . . . Hoffman makes [the Willy in his forties in the flashbacks] optimistic, and then demonstrates how this never-say-die quality, orginally a source for strength, is corrupted by time and hardship. Willy's self-delusions, which may impress a reader of the play as stupid or psychotic, are in Hoffman's performance the end of the optimism of his youth; they're what optimism has to become as life gets smaller."

Pushing Toward a Thesis   Your notetaking becomes truly productive when you begin to follow up tentative patterns and promising connections that you discover in your reading. Even during your exploratory reading and note taking, you will be looking for a possible unifying thread. Avoid a pattern that goes from "one person said this" to "another person said something else." Look for recurrent issues. Look for a note that in your materials is sounded again and again.

In studying the contemporary reaction to Ibsen's plays, for instance, you are likely to be struck by their tendency to polarize the audience. On the one hand, fervent defenders celebrated him as one of the pioneers of modern emancipated thinking. On the other hand, outraged champions of public morality targeted him as an enemy of decency and Western civilization. This recurrent pattern points toward a possible unifying **thesis**: Ibsen, in the words of an English director, "split the English theater in two." The following might be your tentative thesis:

TRIAL THESIS: Ibsen's plays were denounced as immoral by his outraged enemies and at the same time championed as ushering in a new morality.

In reading recent reviews of revivals of Ibsen plays, you may have been struck by reviewers' emphasis on how leading actresses today play

Ibsen's women with a new intensity. Instead of playing his female protagonists as neurotic or gloomy beings, they may portray his strong women as in turn "spirited, sardonic, passionate." One reviewer called Janet McTeer's lead character in a 1997 Broadway revival of *A Doll's House* a "majestic Nora." The following may be your trial thesis for a paper following up these and similar leads:

TRIAL THESIS: Although Ibsen's society tended to cast women in subordinate roles, in his plays women are often revealed as more honest, more realistic, and more determined than their men.

From Working Outline to Draft   As you push forward toward writing your first draft, the different phases of your research and writing are likely to intermesh. Gathering material, bringing it into focus, and shaping your organizing strategy will begin to go hand in hand.

To give direction to your reading and writing, sketch out a **working outline** as soon as you have a rough idea how your material is shaping up. At first, your plan might be very tentative. The whole point of a working outline is to help you visualize a possible pattern. It then helps you refine your strategy as you go along. At an intermediate stage in the Ibsen paper, working outline might look like this:

WORKING OUTLINE: Messenger of Unwelcome Truths
—Polarizing effect of Ibsen's plays
    the "new" morality in his plays
    the "old" morality of his contemporaries
—The attack on Ibsen
    Scott's denunciation
    Archer's collection of criticism
—Shaw's defense of the plays
—Ibsen's getting back at his critics
    portrait of the moralist in his plays
    Ibsen's letters

Remember that writers work out their own system for writing a first draft. Some follow the line of least difficulty—of least resistance. They draft first those sections of the paper for which their notes are most nearly complete or where the material has already very much fallen into place. They then tackle some of the more difficult parts. They check out details or do further research as needed. They are likely to attend to introduction, conclusion, and title last.

Other writers start at the beginning. They systematically fill in the sections and subsections in their working outline, adjusting or refining the outline as needed as they go along. They often make a point of moving on and ahead when they encounter difficult parts of the paper. This way they will not lose the momentum and spend too much time on an issue that should be resolved in revision at a later stage.

Opportunity and time for revision and extent and nature of feedback will vary. Remember three priorities for revision:

✘ *Update your thesis.* Adjust and refine your thesis in the light of what your investigation as a whole has found and what your paper as a whole is trying to show.

✘ *Highlight your organizing strategy.* Clarify your overall plan for your readers so that they can follow from one stage or major phase of your paper to the next. Fill in missing links to signal turning points in the argument or a play of pro and con.

✘ *Consistently support key points.* Look for additional examples, evidence, or expert testimony for sections of your paper where generalizations are not backed up or where the supporting material is uneven.

Criteria for Success   **A Final Evaluation**

The following is the instructor's final evaluation of a paper on the role of illusion and reality in Miller's *Death of a Salesman* and Ibsen's *A Doll's House.* The evaluation applies key criteria for a successful paper to the student's work.

> You bring the central issue into focus well in your introduction: In both Miller's *Death of a Salesman* and Ibsen's *A Doll's House,* major characters create a flattering self-image that will tragically clash with reality. I like your starter quote from Centola's article about the anguish of "being torn away" from our chosen self-image. You give a good authoritative introductory definition of illusion as your key term. Then your thesis brings Arthur Miller's play and Henrik Ibsen's play together and establishes an overall perspective that your paper develops and and follows through—helping the reader stay on track.
>
> With the help of perceptive and sympathetic critics, you trace well Willy Loman's "search for financial success, but also, perhaps more so" his search for "respect and love." Several of your sources do a good of job of helping readers understand why Willy, a "loser" by the standards of many people today, is nevertheless a favorite of millions around the world.
>
> You do a good job of keeping your paper from breaking apart in the middle and turning into two separate mini-essays. You tie the two parts of your paper together effectively by using cross references that keep the connection between Torvald and Willy clearly before the reader. You are especially good at showing how in both plays the rebels against the prevailing world of make-believe and flattering self-image (Biff, Nora) struggle against the fog of self-delusion and finally break free. This is especially true of Nora, although you do not show it quite as convincingly for Biff. Overall, this emphasis in your conclusion gives your paper a bracing "liberating" overall perspective.

Documenting Your Paper   Most serious research requires full source information. When you draw on a range of sources—for instance, reviews that took initiative and perseverance to track down—you are likely to be asked to provide full **documentation**. Documentation identifies your sources, complete with publishing information and exact page numbers. Remember that it should enable your readers to verify your sources and to get further information from them if they wish.

Unless told differently by your instructor or editor, follow the style of documentation of the Modern Language Association (MLA). You use **parenthetical documentation** in the running text of your paper. You use it mainly to provide page numbers in parentheses, but you also use it to tag author and title as needed. Then you give complete information about each source in a final alphabetical listing of **Works Cited**. This was once the **bibliography**, or "book list," but it may now include non-print sources like online material, videocassettes, radio and television programs, or CD-ROMS

Parenthetical documentation does away with the footnotes still used in some other documentation styles. (Numbered explanatory notes may still follow a paper or article as **end notes**.)

✘ If you have said that Susan Sontag in *Against Interpretation* speaks of the "volleying back and forth of clichés" in a long-running play by the Roumanian playwright Ionesco, all you need is the page number or page numbers in parentheses **(119).**

✘ If you have merely said that a prominent critic used that phrase, include her name, so that the reader can find the source in the Works Cited **(Sontag 119).**

✘ If you plan to quote another book or article by Sontag, tag the first source using a shortened version of the title—if possible without interfering with alphabetical ordering later (**Sontag,** *Against Interpretation* **119**). Remember to tag author or title in parentheses only if you have not already given the information in your running text.

✘ For classics available in many different editions, show act, scene, and line in arabic numerals instead of page numbers (3.2.46–49). Some writers prefer the traditional large and small roman numerals for act and scene (III.ii.46–49).

Study sample entries for your alphabetical listing of Works Cited.

A Checklist For Listing Sources   **MLA Style**

✘ As advised by your instructor, use <u>underlining</u> or *italics* for the title of a **whole publication**—whether a book-length study, a collection or anthology of stories or essays, a periodical that prints critical articles, or a newspaper that prints reviews. (The MLA style requires underlining—<u>underscoring</u>—for manuscripts that go to a printer for typemarking. Italics are required if your manuscript is to be scanned or reproduced "as is" for publication.)

✗ Use quotation marks for titles of plays or critical articles that are **part** of a collection or larger publication.

✗ **Indent** the second and following lines of each entry one half inch or five typewriter spaces.

✗ Leave *one* space after periods marking off **blocks of data** in the entry.

✗ Use appropriate **abbreviations:** ed. for editor; trans. for a translator. Abbreviate the names of publishing houses (Prentice for Prentice-Hall, Inc; Southern Illinois UP for Southern Illinois University Press). Abbreviate the names of the months: Dec., Apr., Mar. Abbreviate the names of states when needed to locate a little-known place of publication: CA, NY, NJ.

Listing of Plays

Wilson, August. <u>The Piano Lesson</u>. New York: Plume-NAL, 1990.
[Plume is an imprint, or special line of books, of New American Library.]

Beckett, Samuel. <u>Waiting for Godot: Tragicomedy in 2 Acts</u>. New York: Grove, 1954.
[Play with subtitle]

Shakespeare, William. <u>The Tragedy of Hamlet</u>. Ed. Eward Hubler. New York: NAL: 1963.
[Special edition of a play with editor's name]

Hubler, Edward, ed. <u>The Tragedy of Hamlet</u>. By William Shakespeare. New York: NAL, 1963.
[Editor's name first when editor's work is important]

Nemirov, Robert, ed. <u>Les Blancs: The Collected Last Plays of Lorraine Hansberry</u>. New York: Vintage, 1994.
[Collection of plays with editor's name first]

Hansberry, Lorraine. <u>A Raisin in the Sun</u>. <u>Black Theater: A Twentieth-Century Collection of the Work of Its Best Playwrights</u>. Ed. Lindsay Patterson. New York: Dodd, 1971. 221–76.
[Play in a collection, with complete page numbers for the play]

Aristophanes. <u>Lysistrata</u>. Trans. Donald Sutherland. <u>Classical Comedy Greek and Roman</u>. Ed. Robert W. Corrigan. New York: Applause, 1987. 11–68.
[Play in a collection with translator's name and complete page numbers]

Beaty, Jerome, and J. Paul Hunter. <u>New Worlds of Literature</u>. New York: W.W. Norton, 1989.

[Co-authors of a collection, with last name first only for first author]

Gilman, Richard. Introduction. <u>Seven Plays</u>. By Sam Shepard. New York: Bantam, 1984. xi-xxvii.

[Introductory material with small roman page numbers]

Listing of a Critical Studies or Reviews

Butler, Judith. <u>Antigone's Claim</u>. New York: Columbia UP, 2000.

[Book-length study published by a university press]

Green, Richard, and Eric Handley. <u>Images of the Greek Theater</u>. London: British Museum P, 1995.

Abramovitz, Janet N., et. al. <u>State of the World</u>. New York: London, 1999.

[Co-authored works with only first author's last name first. For more than three authors, you may list only the first author and then put et al. (for "and others")]

Greeley, Andrew. "Today's Morality Play: The Sitcom." <u>New York Times</u> 17 May 1987, late ed., sec. 2: 1+.

[Newspaper article with edition and section specified. Article starts on page 1 and continues later in the newspaper.]

Driver, Tom F. Rev. of <u>A Raisin in the Sun</u>, by Lorraine Hansberry. <u>The New Republic</u> 140 (13 Apr. 1959): 21.

[Untitled review]

LaSalle, Mick. "Plot Muddles Mamet's <u>Heist</u>." Rev. of <u>Heist</u>, by David Mamet. <u>San Francisco Chronicle</u> 9 Nov. 2001: D3.

[Review with title]

Jelinek, Elfriede. "A Doll's House." <u>Modern Drama</u> 41 (1998): 134–40.

[Journal article with volume number]

Davis, Ossie. "The Significance of Lorraine Hansberry." <u>Freedomways</u> 5.3 (1965): 396–402.

[Journal article with number of volume and issue]

Goodman, Charlotte. "The Fox's Cubs: Lillian Hellman, Arthur Miller, and Tennessee Williams." <u>Modern American Drama: The Female Canon</u>. Ed. June Schlueter. New York: Associated UP, 1990. 189–223.

[Article in a collection]

Showalter, Elaine. "Representing Ophelia: Women, Madness, and the Responsibilities of Feminist Contemporary Criticism." <u>William Shakespeare: Hamlet</u>. Ed. Susanne L. Wofford. Case Studies in Contemporary Criticism. Boston: St. Martin's, 1994. 220–38.

[Article in a collection that is part of a series]

"New Scottish Theater: A Frightening Ride." <u>Theater Arts Forum</u> 22 Feb. 2002.
19–20.
[Unsigned article to be listed alphabetically by first word of title
(not counting *A, An,* or *The*)]

Documenting Online Sources

Remember that guidelines for documenting online sources are still
evolving. You may encounter variations from the current MLA style
shown in the following sample entries. These sample entries show you
how you to feed publishing data on online material into your alphabetical list of Works Cited. Include any of the conventional publishing data
that are available. Two dates for an item show first the date it was posted
and then the day you accessed or consulted it. The **URL** or retrieval code
for online material appears in **angled brackets**. Remember not to add
extra spaces or change punctuation in a URL. Keep it on a single line or
break it only at a slash.

Atkinson, Brooks. "Arthur Miller's Tragedy of an Ordinary Man." Rev. of <u>Death of
a Salesman</u>. <u>New York Times</u> 20 Feb. 1949. 3 Mar. 2002.
<http://www.deathofasalesman.com/rev-49_nytimes2.htm>
Watts, Richard, Jr. "<u>Death of a Salesman</u>: A Powerful Drama." <u>New York Post</u>
11 Feb. 1949. 3 Mar. 2002.
<http://www.deathofasalesman.com/rev-49_nypost.htm>
[Archived reviews from major publications]

Corliss, Richard. "The Gamut of Mamet." <u>Time</u> 6 Apr. 1998. 20 Mar. 2002.
[Archived magazine article]

Johnson, Patricia J. "Woman's Third Face: A Psychosocial Reconsideration of
Sophocles' <u>Antigone</u>." <u>Arethusa</u> 30 (1996). 1 Nov. 2001.
<http://www.jhu.edu/journals/arethusa/toc/arev030.html>
[Article from a scholarly journal with volume number]

<u>Shakespeare's Globe</u>. University of Reading, UK. Updated 5 Sept. 2001. 20
Jan. 2002. <http://www.red.ac.ul/globe/>
[Website devoted to Shakespeare's Globe playhouse]

<u>PAL: Perspectives in American Literature</u>. A Research and Reference Guide for
American Playwrights. Paul P. Reuben. California State U, Stanislaus. 2 July
1995. Updated 31 Oct. 2001. 2 Jan. 2002.
<http://www.csustan.ed/english/reuben/home.htm>
[Specialized database for research in American literature]

"Ibsen." <u>Britannica Online</u>. Vers. 97.1.1. Mar. 1997. Encyclopaedia Britannica.
17 Oct. 2001.<http://www.eb.com/>
[Reference work online, with version number and date]

Tollini, Frederick P., SJ. "Directing <u>Lysystrata</u>." E-mail to the author. 10 Nov.
2001.
[E-mail communication to author of the research paper]

Study the following an example of a documented paper. How well does the student writer show the continuing relevance of the topic today? How successful was the student author in finding contemporary sources? How well does the paper support its main points? Study the use of parenthetical documentation and the entries in the Works Cited. Are there unusual situations or entries?

Sample Student Paper

The Furor over Ibsen

What did Henrik Ibsen do? According to Granville-Barker, "he split the English theater in two" (24). Indeed, "as everyone knows, the introduction of Ibsen into England was not a peaceful one. In its wake came one of those great outbursts of critical frenzy and inflamed controversy which at regular intervals enliven literary history" ("Retrospective" 199). In England, as in the rest of Europe, the public was split into two factions: those who placed Ibsen on the blacklist as "immoral"; and those who saw him as the champion of a new morality. A hundred years later, Ibsen continues to stir the conscience of a later generation. In a recent study, Naomi Lebowitz quotes a leading European intellectual on "the shame that overcomes the descendant in the face of an earlier possibility that he has neglected to bring to fruition" (Theodor Adorno, qtd. in Lebowitz 2).

Ibsen's plays aroused both indignation and enthusiasm because he fought against maintaining appearances at the expense of happiness, or what he termed hypocrisy. Una Ellis-Fermor, a translator and lifelong student of Ibsen, said that he "took upon himself the task of exposing the makeshift morality of his contemporaries in private and public life":

> In The Pillars of the Community he examines the lie in public life, the tragic struggle of Karsten Bernick to hide his sin and preserve his reputation at the expense of another man's good name. . . . In A Doll's House and Ghosts the subject is the lie in domestic life; the first shows the destruction of a marriage by an unreal and insincere relationship between husband and wife, and the second the destruction of the lives and souls of the characters by the oppressive tyranny of convention. (Ibsen, Three Plays 9–11)

In Ghosts, a dutiful and unloving wife keeps up an elaborate façade of respectability for a profligate husband. She finds herself defeated when her cherished son returns home suffering incurably from the syphilis he has inherited from his father. According to Bernard Shaw, the play was "an uncompromising and outspoken attack on marriage as a useless sacrifice," the story of a woman who had wasted her life in manufacturing a "monstrous fabric of lies and false appearances" (86, 88).

Against the tyranny of middle-class standards, Ibsen pitted his own concept of individual integrity. He felt, according to Georg Brandes, that "the individuality of the human being is to be preserved for its own sake, not for the sake of higher powers; and since beyond all else the individual should remain free and whole, all concessions made to the world represent to Ibsen the foul fiend, the evil principle" (373). One of the main ideas fused into Ibsen's plays, according to a representative

admiring article in the Encyclopaedia Britannica, is "the supreme importance of individual character, of personality: in the development and enrichment of the individual he saw the only hope for a really cultured and enlightened society" ("Drama" 65).

A Doll's House was particularly loaded with the "first duty to oneself" theme.
Nora, in the last act, wakes to the fact that she is not worthy to be a good mother
and wife because she has been merely a submissive servant and foil first for her
father and then for her husband; she has been so protected and guided by them
that she has no individual conception of life and its complexities. Nora realized that
she did not know enough about the world and her place in it to be really "a reasonable human being," and she felt a duty to become one (Ibsen, Four Plays 65).
Her life all at once seemed so artificial and meaningless to her that she felt like a
doll living in a doll's house. Nora left her husband and children to try to gain an understanding of real life, and when she "banged the door of A Doll's House, the
echo of that violence was heard across the continent" ("Drama" 600).

Ibsen wrote these plays at a time when people felt a general ferment, a "spirit
of the age" or a "movement of the century" that had introduced everywhere a tendency toward change. Voices heralding the modern age referred to the "new phase
into which humanity is passing" and expressed the conviction that "society must
undergo a transformation or perish" (Goodwin 124, 122). But the voices resisting
the clamor for "innovations" were equally strong. Their watchword was devotion to
duty—toward God, country, one's family and husband. Self-denial for the sake of
greater forces was the commendable action. The churches taught it was sinful to
assert one's own wishes and desires. The people, especially the dominated wife
with whom Ibsen frequently deals, were exhorted to live for the good of everyone
but themselves. Advocates of the emancipation of women were told in the public
press that "men are men and women women"; that "sex is a fact-no Act of Parliament can eliminate it"; and that "where two ride on a horse, one must needs ride
behind" (Goodwin 103, 109). They were told that in women's hands "rests the
keeping of a pure tone in society, of a high standard in morality, of a lofty devotion
to duty in political life." If she were to enter openly into political conflict, she would
"debase her sex" and "lower the ideal of womanhood amongst men" (Goodwin
103-4).

The old-fashioned moralists were shocked by the "Ibsenist" view that self-
fulfillment is more important than the sanctity of mariage, one's duty to others,
and even business success. According to Arthur Bingham Walkley, drama critic for
the London Times. "Ibsen became a bogey to many worthy people who had never
read or seen a single one of his plays." To these people, "Ibsenism was supposed
vaguely to connote 'Woman's Rights,' Free Love, a new and fearful kind of wildfowl
called 'Norwegian Socialism,' and generally, every manifestation of discontent with
the existing order of things" (790). Clement Scott, a prominent drama critic, led
such formidable opposition against Ibsen's dramas, especially A Doll's House and
Ghosts, that they were actually banned for a time from English stages. "Ibsen
fails," Scott says, "because he is, I suppose, an atheist, and has not realized what
the great backbone of religion means to the English race." Scott continues, "He
fails because his plays are nasty, dirty, impure, clever if you like, but foul to the
last degree; and healthy-minded English people don't like to stand and sniff over
an ash-pit" (qtd. in Granville-Barker 24).

Many of the people causing the uproar against Ibsen used similar language.
William Archer, the first English translator of Ibsen, collected some of the attacks
appearing in the English press when Ghosts was first produced. The play was
called "disgusting," "loathsome," "gross," and "revoltingly suggestive and blasphemous." It was compared to "a dirty act done publicly" and was called "a piece

to bring the stage into disrepute and dishonour with every right-thinking man and woman" (qtd. in Shaw 91-3).

Those who defended Ibsen—Shaw, Archer, Walkley—blamed his unpleasant reception in England on both his revolutionary themes and his new dramatic technique. I shall steer away from Ibsen's new dramatic technique and instead discuss the defense of Ibsenism as a new moral philosophy. Shaw himself has been called one of the men "who summon their generation to act by a new and higher standard." He made Ibsen his hero because Ibsen championed the view that Shaw made the basis for many of his own plays:

> By "morals" (or "ideals") Shaw means conventional, current standards. Because these standards are universal and inherited from the past, they often do not fit particular situations and present-day societies. Therefore good men—like some of Ibsen's characters—often choose to act "immorally," contrary to accepted morality. (Brower 687)

To Shaw, Ibsen became the first of the two types of pioneers classified by Shaw in The Quintessence of Ibsenism. This type of pioneer asserts "that it is right to do something hitherto regarded as infamous." Ibsen felt that it was right to think first of building himself and secondly of building the institutions of society. To Shaw, this change explained the unkindly reception of Ibsen's new thoughts in England: "So much easier is it to declare the right wrong than the wrong right. . . . a guilty society can more readily be persuaded that any apparently innocent act is guilty than that any apparently guilty act is innocent" (23–25). Shaw seems to feel that Ibsen would have had more success telling people it was wrong to work on Monday than he would have had saying it was right to work on Sunday. People could not accept the idea that the obligation of self-sacrifice could be removed from them—that it would be all right for them to consider a duty toward themselves first.

Shaw complained of the difficulty of finding "accurate terms" for Ibsen's new "realist morality." To Shaw, it was Ibsen's thesis that "the real slavery of today is slavery to ideals of goodness" (146–149). Ibsen had devoted himself to showing that "the spirit of man is constantly outgrowing the ideals," and the "thoughless conformity" to them is constantly producing tragic results (152). Among those "ridden by current ideals," Ibsen's plays were bound to be denounced as immoral. But, Shaw concluded, there can be no question as to the effect likely to be produced on an individual by his conversion from the ordinary acceptance of current ideals as safe standards of conduct, to the vigilant open-mindedness of Ibsen. It must at once greatly deepen the sense of moral responsibility (154).

Ibsen himself knew well and satirized in his plays the moralists who inveighed against "the undermining of family life" and the "defiance of the most solemn truths." In Ghosts Pastor Manders, who represents a timid regard for convention, warns people against books that he vaguely associates with "intellectual progress"—and that he has not read. Rörlund, the schoolmaster in The Pillars of the Community, sums up the position of the guardians of conventional morality when he says: "Our business is to keep society pure . . . to keep out all these experimental notions that an impatient age wants to force on us (Ibsen, Three Plays 27–28) Ironically, Rörlund provides a moral façade for "practical men of affairs" like the shipowner Bernick. Bernick, who talks about his "deep-rooted sense of decency," has abandoned the woman he loved in order to marry a wealthy girl and save the family business. He has abandoned to need and shame a married woman with whom he has had a secret affair. He has saved his own reputation in the community at the expense of having a younger friend blackened as a libertine and a thief. Bernick's defense of his conduct is that he lives in a community in which "a youthful indiscretion is never wiped out." The "community itself forces us into crooked ways" (97–98). But Ibsen's heroes are people who rebel against the "tyranny of custom and convention"; who hold that "the spirit of truth and the spirit of freedom" are the "true pillars of the community" (116, 137).

Ibsen was not intimidated by the controversy caused by his plays. In a letter to a friend he wrote in 1881, he said: "Ghosts will probably cause alarm in some circles. . . . If it didn't do that, there would have been no need to write it." In a letter written a year later, he said: "That my new play would produce a howl from the camp of those "men of stagnation' was something I was quite prepared for" (Ghosts 126). Shortly afterward, he summed up his faith in the future in a letter that said in part:

> In time, and not before very long at that, the good people up home will get into their heads some understanding of Ghosts. But all those desic-cated, decrepit individuals who pounced on this work, they will come in for devastating criticism in the literary histories of the future. People will be able to sniff out the nameless snipers and thugs who directed their dirty missiles at me from their ambush in Professor Goos's mouldy rag and other simlar places. My book holds the future. Yon crowd that roared about it haven't even any proper contact with their own genuinely vital age. (Ghosts 129–30)

It was Ibsen's assertion of the duty to oneself, against the tradition of con-formity to custom and convention, that was the main grounds of the controversy over Ibsen's works. Over a century later, Ibsen's plays have not lost their power to challenge established think schemes and familiar attitudes.

Modern essays on Ibsen's A Doll's House may still trap us into seeing her through her husband's Torvald's eyes "as a silly childlike figure" with "frivolous" ideas (Essays). However, recent reviews of revivals of Ibsen plays stress how lead-ing actresses today play Ibsen's women with a new feminist awareness. Rather than seeing Nora through her husband's eyes as a childlike and unreliable, today's productions may make us see her "as an accomplished actress in sustaining her fiction of youthfulness and irresponsiblity," acting a "prettifying, self-deluding fic-tion of innocence" for her husband (Jelinek 134). Instead of playing Ibsen's female protagonists as neurotic or gloomy beings, today's performers may portray his strong women as in turn "spirited, sardonic, passionate." One reviewer called Janet McTeer's lead character in a 1997 Broadway revival of A Doll's House a "ma-jestic Nora" (Rocamora 34).

Works Cited

Brandes, Georg. Creative Spirits of the Nineteenth Century. Trans. Rasmus B. Anderson. New York: Crowell, 1923.

Brower, Reuben A. "George Bernard Shaw." Major British Writers. Ed. G. B. Harrison. Vol 2. New York: Harcourt, 1959. 687. 2 vols.

"Drama." Encyclopaedia Britannica. 1958.

Essays on A Doll's House. Geocities. 20 Aug. 1998. 12 Jan. 2002.
    <http://www.geocities.com/lesleycody_1998/dollesa.html>

Goodwin, Michael, ed. Nineteenth-Century Opinion: An Anthology (1877–1901). Hammondsworth, Middlesex: Penguin, 1951.

Granville-Barker, Harley "When Ibsen Split the English Stage in Two." Literary Digest 28 (1928): 24–25.

Ibsen, Henrik. Ghosts. Trans. Kai Jurgensen and Robert Schenkkan. New York: Avon, 1965.

---. Three Plays. Trans. Una Ellis-Fermor. Hammondsworth, Middlesex: Penguin, 1950.

Jelinek, Elfriede. "A Doll's House." Modern Drama 41 (1998): 134–40.

"Ibsen, Henrik Johan." Encyclopaedia Britannica. 1958.

"Inside Views of Ibsen in the Nineties." Literary Digest 12 (1928): 24.

Lebowitz, Naomi. Ibsen and the Great World. Baton Rouge: Louisiana State UP, 1990.

"A Retrospective Eye on Ibsen." Theatre Arts Monthly 12 (1928): 199–211.

Rocamora, Carol. "Northern Lights." Nation 19 Nov. 2001: 33–36.

Shaw, Bernard. The Quintessence of Ibsenism. 3rd ed. New York: Hill, 1957.

Walkley, A. B. "Ibsen in England." Living Age 12 (1901): 790.

Questions for Peer Review

Recent spectacular revivals of Ibsen's plays have made modern audiences see in them parallels to or anticipations of the themes of today's culture wars.

1. Does the student writer succeed in drawing you into the controversy? Where does the writer first sum up the conflict between the two opposing camps? How does the conflict between the diametrically opposed views of Ibsen organize the paper as a whole?

2. Early in the paper, the writer gives a brief introductory survey of the major issues or themes treated in Ibsen's plays. Which of these do you recognize or feel prepared for after your own reading of an Ibsen play? How would you sum up in your own words the common thread or the major direction of Ibsen's social criticism? Which of the supporting quotations are for you most instructive, most memorable, or most controversial?

3. Integrity and individualism have for many modern readers become self-approving clichés invoked in too many speeches. However, they were still fighting words in Ibsen's time, and they still are in statements quoted in this paper. To judge from this paper, what were the key points in Ibsen's mission for his supporters? What were the most "revolutionary" parts of his Ibsenite program? For you, which of the supporting quotations still seem strong or quotable today?

4. Are you surprised by the language and passion of the opposing camp? Do you think they have parallels today? Or are our own culture wars more polite or sudued? Which of the ideas or views that Ibsen's opponents attacked are still "bogeys" today? Which may be taking a different form?

5. How well does the paper explain or document the difficulty of finding a new strong and persuasive vocabulary for a new set of values or a new morality? Do you think this difficulty still confronts dissenters from established morality today?

6. What kind of person emerges from the extended quotations, including the block quotation, in the concluding part of the paper? Do the quotations still ring with conviction, or do they seem a voice from the past?

7. Do you think Ibsen's readers today could refer to our own time as a "genuinely vital age"? Why or why not?

Questions for Self-Evaluation

Write a brief self-evaluation of your own research paper project. What did you learn from the project? What challenges did you encounter, or what problems did you solve? Answer questions like the following.

✗ Why did you choose your topic? Did it have a personal meaning for you? Did it present a special challenge?

✗ What tentative focus or key question guided you in your investigation?

✗ What useful background or preparation did you bring to the project?

✗ Where or how did you start your exploration of the subject?

✗ Where or how did you discover promising sources? What obstacles or problems did you encounter in your search for material?

✗ How soon did you develop a trial thesis? Did you modify or adjust it later? How would you sum up the main point or the findings of your paper as a whole?

✗ What organizing strategy or overall plan did you develop? Did you have to reconsider and adjust it? How would you outline the major stages or sections of your paper?

✗ What was your final mix of sources? Which were most helpful, which least?

✗ Who would be your ideal reader? When envisioning your audience, did you consider special needs or possible objections? How did you deal with them?

✗ What advice would you give fellow researchers working on a similar project?

30 COMEDY

A Time for Laughter

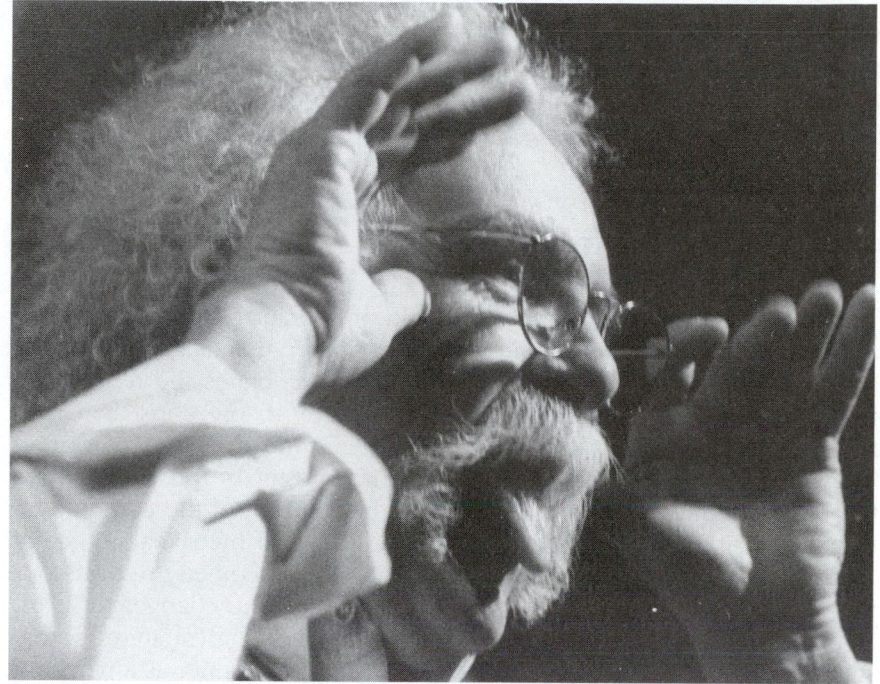

Courtesy Richard B. Ressman

*Characters in a play don't always have to be
bigger fools than in everyday life.*
                                        EUGÈNE IONESCO

*Humor is born in dark places of the soul,
masking anguish with a tilt toward absurdity.*
                                        AL MARTINEZ

*My grandfather used to make home movies and
edit out the joy.*
                                        ANONYMOUS

FOCUS ON COMEDY

Comedy takes us into a golden world of liberating laughter. Tragedy makes us face our limits. It brings men and women up against the boundaries of human hope and endeavor. Comedy celebrates the renewal of hope. Scholars have traced the roots of comedy to pre-Christian Easter festivals that celebrated the return of the sun after the dead of winter. They have looked for its origins in marriage festivals and fertility rites that celebrated the bonding of love and the renewal of the community. Comedy helps us preserve the spirit of holiday—of merrymaking, celebration, fiesta, festival, carnival, revelry. At its best, comedy restores our faith in good fortune, in young love, in generosity and changes of heart.

Comedy intersects with reality when it makes us laugh at attitudes that stand in the way of a more humane world. Wielding humor as a weapon, the comic playwright uses **satire** to do battle against callousness, stinginess, or hypocrisy. Comedy satirizes traits that narrow life, forces that shut off possibility. It mocks bullies and pompous idiots. The miser, the hypochondriac, and the malcontent—forever dissatisfied with everything—have long been **stock characters** that audiences delight in seeing on the stage again and again. We stay in the world of comedy when negative forces are threatening but do not become overpowering. We know that we can best them. At any rate, we can best our own inclinations toward narrowness, intolerance, and tunnel vision.

In ancient Greece, the same audiences who watched with awe as the oracle of Apollo trapped Oedipus watched with happy laughter as the women in Aristophanes' *Lysistrata* (411 B.C.) staged a sex strike to stop their men from dragging out a senseless war. No peace, no sex! No more swaggering among the beans and greens of the marketplace in full military regalia! "Stay away from me," they tell their husbands and lovers, "or you will never eat garlic and black beans again!" Aristophanes established the tradition of irreverence that serves as the comic antidote to solemnity and self-importance. He set a high standard for audacity in insults "against political figures; in obscenity; in mockery of gods, philosophers, and the latest literature; in hilarious spoofs of political and military science—even of economics itself" (Donald Sutherland).

The alternative to tragedy and comedy as separate forms is to mix laughter and tears, as they mix in real life. Shakespeare wrote tragedies and comedies, but even a Shakespearean tragedy may have a licenced jester who tells bitter truths. Shakespeare wrote other plays that represent **tragicomedy**—a mixed genre in which the tragic and the comic visions contend.

What makes audiences laugh? Humor may seem a marvelous gift, but critics have found it puzzling and paradoxical.

✗ Critics early made a distinction between two different kinds of laughter. The first kind of laughter makes us respond to things that are congenial, desirable, agreeable. We laugh (or more often smile) when something delightful happens. The most basic plot of traditional comedy has young people fall in love. They then meet obstacles—greedy parents, lusting elders—but they overcome these in the end. The second kind of laughter is the laughter of ridicule; it makes us laugh *at the opposite* of what is desirable or agreeable to human nature.

✗ The French critic Henri Bergson defined the comic as the opposite of what is natural or organic in human life. We laugh at what is rigid, mechanical, unnatural. People who dance as if they were counting "one-two-three" in their heads; people who follow a totally rigid regimen of diet, exercise, or hygiene (becoming health fanatics or fitness freaks); people who are unbending in their religious or ideological views—these are comic, to others if not to themselves.

✗ A more hard-nosed theory holds that we laugh at shortcomings that make us feel superior to others. People who are hamstrung by their failings are no competition for us. We don't have to take them seriously, and we laugh with relief. Thus, we laugh at bumblers, clumsy lovers, waiters who drop heavy trays, and foreigners who wrestle with the English language.

✗ A more defensive theory looks at humor as a shield, as a kind of armor. It is a mask we may put on to fend off prying or pity. A character may always be wisecracking so as not to let people see the hurt inside. The playwright Wendy Wasserstein has said that "a lot of comedy is a deflection." She said about a character in one of her plays that "she is *always* funny, so as not to say what she feels."

The soul of comedy is often quick, witty dialogue. Audiences delight in the **chase of wit**, with characters trading quick pointed remarks. (Older man: "I had advanced ideas before you were born!" Younger man: "I knew it was a long time ago.") Often comic dialogue is laced with **word play** or verbal humor. Shakespeare's audiences loved **puns**—they delighted in seeing a word put through its paces in a quickly moving exchange:

DUKE (*offering money to the jester who has just finished a song*):
    There's for thy pains.
JESTER: No pains, sir. I take pleasure in singing, sir.
DUKE: I'll pay thy pleasure then.
CLOWN: Truly, sir, and pleasure will be paid one time or another.
                                        Shakespeare, *Twelfth Night*

Audiences delight in **parody**, which apes distinctive or eccentric traits for comic effect. At its most visceral (closest to gut level), comedy becomes **farce**, frowned on by critics but beloved by the multitude. Farce means pratfalls, horseplay, insults, crude jokes. Elderly lovers try to climb to the balcony and fall into the rain barrel; lovers surprised by a spouse with a shotgun flee in their underwear.

Humor is not always a laughing matter. It can serve as a means of in-grouping and outgrouping, of establishing group identity. For satire to work, it must in some way activate shared standards of what is acceptable and what is ridiculous. (Lily Tomlin described the group experience of humor as "sharing for the sharing-impaired.") As a result, while comedy draws us into its charmed circle, it may also leave others out. We are aware of the outgrouping effect of humor when people laugh at us behind our backs—because we are white or black, tall or short, old or young, overdressed or underdressed. Feminist critics look askance at female comedians who perpetuate the comic stereotypes of the goofy housewife or the shrewish spouse.

FIRST READING

The Comedy of Everyday

Wendy Wasserstein is a contemporary American playwright in whose comic sketches every satirical detail counts (and hurts). She was born in Brooklyn, studied creative writing at CCNY (City College of New York), and has done much of her writing in a Greenwich Village apartment. (After her senior year in college, she went west to look for work writing for television and discovered that she "loathed" California.) Several of her plays were successful off-Broadway. Her *Heidi Chronicles* (1988) moved on to Broadway and won a Pulitzer Prize, a Tony Award, and the prize of the New York Critics' Circle. She has written screenplays for television; she published a collection called *Bachelor Girls* in 1990. The characters in her plays are often young, urban, and professional (in short, yuppies). Before she is through with them, the playwright has dissected their dating rituals, their attitudes toward their jobs, their food fetishes, their dependence on their psychiatrists or psychologists. Above all, she mimics the trendy way they talk—about places to be seen, about clothes with snob appeal, about food that is not ordinary, and about schools that are not public schools.

In the following one-act play, Wasserstein looks at the difficulties of communication between parent and offspring. What is sad and funny about this conversation between the father and his daughter?

Wendy Wasserstein   *(born 1950)*

Tender Offer   *1983*

SETTING: *A girl of around nine is alone in a dance studio. She is dressed in traditional leotards and tights. She begins singing to herself, "Nothing Could Be Finer Than to Be in Carolina." She maps out a dance routine, including parts for the chorus. She builds to a finale. A man,* PAUL, *around thirty-five, walks in. He has a sweet, though distant, demeanor. As he walks in,* LISA *notices him and stops.*

PAUL: You don't have to stop, sweetheart.

LISA: That's okay.

PAUL: Looked very good.

LISA: Thanks.

PAUL: Don't I get a kiss hello?

LISA: Sure.

PAUL: (*Embraces her.*) Hi, Tiger.

LISA: Hi, Dad.

PAUL: I'm sorry I'm late.

LISA: That's okay.

PAUL: How'd it go?

LISA: Good.

PAUL: Just good?

LISA: Pretty good.

PAUL: "Pretty good." You mean you got a lot of applause or "pretty good" you could have done better.

LISA: Well, Courtney Palumbo's mother thought I was pretty good. But you know the part in the middle when everybody's supposed to freeze and the big girl comes out. Well, I think I moved a little bit.

PAUL: I thought what you were doing looked very good.

LISA: Daddy, that's not what I was doing. That was tap-dancing. I made that up.

PAUL: Oh. Well it looked good. Kind of sexy.

LISA: Yuch!

PAUL: What do you mean "yuch?"

LISA: Just yuch!

PAUL: You don't want to be sexy?

LISA: I don't care.

PAUL: Let's go, Tiger. I promised your mother I'd get you home in time for dinner.

LISA: I can't find my leg warmers.

PAUL: You can't find your what?

LISA: Leg warmers. I can't go home till I find my leg warmers.

PAUL: I don't see you looking for them.

LISA: I was waiting for you.

PAUL: Oh.

LISA: Daddy.

PAUL: What?

LISA: Nothing.

PAUL: Where do you think you left them?

LISA: Somewhere around here. I can't remember.

PAUL: Well, try to remember, Lisa. We don't have all night.

LISA: I told you. I think somewhere around here.

PAUL: I don't see them. Let's go home now. You'll call the dancing school tomorrow.

LISA: Daddy, I can't go home till I find them. Miss Judy says it's not professional to leave things.

PAUL: Who's Miss Judy?

LISA: She's my ballet teacher. She once danced the lead in *Swan Lake*, and she was a June Taylor dancer.

PAUL: Well, then, I'm sure she'll understand about the leg warmers.

LISA: Daddy, Miss Judy wanted to know why you were late today.

PAUL: Hmmmmmmmmm?

LISA: Why were you late?

PAUL: I was in a meeting. Business. I'm sorry.

LISA: Why did you tell Mommy you'd come instead of her if you knew you had business?

PAUL: Honey, something just came up. I thought I'd be able to be here. I was looking forward to it.

LISA: I wish you wouldn't make appointments to see me.

PAUL: Hmmmmmmm.

LISA: You shouldn't make appointments to see me unless you know you're going to come.

PAUL: Of course I'm going to come.

LISA: No, you're not. Talia Robbins told me she's much happier living without her father in the house. Her father used to come home late and go to sleep early.

PAUL: Lisa, stop it. Let's go.

LISA: I can't find my leg warmers.

PAUL: Forget your leg warmers.

LISA: Daddy.

PAUL: What is it?

LISA: I saw this show on television, I think it was WPIX Channel 11. Well, the father was crying about his daughter.

PAUL: Why was he crying? Was she sick?

LISA: No. She was at school. And he was at business. And he just missed her, so he started to cry.

PAUL: What was the name of this show?

LISA: I don't know. I came in in the middle.

PAUL: Well, Lisa, I certainly would cry if you were sick or far away, but I know that you're well and you're home. So no reason to get maudlin.

LISA: What's maudlin?

PAUL: Sentimental, soppy. Frequently used by children who make things up to get attention.

LISA: I am sick! I am sick! I have Hodgkin's disease and a bad itch on my leg.

PAUL: What do you mean you have Hodgkin's disease? Don't say things like that.

LISA: Swoosie Kurtz, she had Hodgkin's disease on a TV movie last year, but she got better and now she's on *Love Sidney*.

PAUL: Who is Swoosie Kurtz?

LISA: She's an actress named after an airplane. I saw her on *Live at Five*.

PAUL: You watch too much television; you should do your homework. Now, put your coat on.

LISA: Daddy, I really do have a bad itch on my leg. Would you scratch it?

PAUL: Lisa, you're procrastinating.

LISA: Why do you use words I don't understand? I hate it. You're like Daria Feldman's mother. She always talks in Yiddish to her husband so Daria won't understand.

PAUL: Procrastinating is not Yiddish.

LISA: Well, I don't know what it is.

PAUL: Procrastinating means you don't want to go about your business.

LISA: I don't go to business. I go to school.

PAUL: What I mean is you want to hang around here until you and I are late for dinner and your mother's angry and it's too late for you to do your homework.

LISA: I do not.

PAUL: Well, it sure looks that way. Now put your coat on and let's go.

LISA: Daddy.

PAUL: Honey, I'm tired. Really, later.

LISA: Why don't you want to talk to me?

PAUL: I do want to talk to you. I promise when we get home we'll have a nice talk.

LISA: No, we won't. You'll read the paper and fall asleep in front of the news.

PAUL: Honey, we'll talk on the weekend, I promise. Aren't I taking you to the theater this weekend? Let me look. (*He takes out appointment book.*) Yes. Sunday. *Joseph and the Amazing Technicolor Raincoat* with Lisa. Okay, Tiger?

LISA: Sure. It's Dreamcoat.

PAUL: What?

LISA: Nothing. I think I see my leg warmers. (*She goes to pick them up, and an odd-looking trophy.*)

PAUL: What's that?

LISA: It's stupid. I was second best at the dance recital, so they gave me this thing. It's stupid.

PAUL: Lisa.

LISA: What?

PAUL: What did you want to talk about?

LISA: Nothing.

PAUL: Was it about my missing your recital? I'm really sorry, Tiger. I would have liked to have been here.

LISA: That's okay.

PAUL: Honest?

LISA: Daddy, you're prostrastinating.

PAUL: I'm procrastinating. Sit down. Let's talk. So. How's school?

LISA: Fine.

PAUL: You like it?

LISA: Yup.

PAUL: You looking forward to camp this summer?

LISA: Yup.

PAUL: Is Daria Feldman going back?

LISA: Nope.

PAUL: Why not?

LISA: I don't know. We can go home now. Honest, my foot doesn't itch anymore.

PAUL: Lisa, you know what you do in business when it seems like there's nothing left to say? That's when you really start talking. Put a bid on the table.

LISA: What's a bid?

PAUL: You tell me what you want and I'll tell you what I've got to offer. Like Monopoly. You want Boardwalk, but I'm only willing to give you the Railroads. Now, because you are my daughter I'd throw in Water Works and Electricity. Understand, Tiger?

LISA: No. I don't like board games. You know, Daddy, we could get Space Invaders for our home for thirty-five dollars. In fact, we could get an Osborne System for two thousand. Daria Feldman's parents . . .

PAUL: Daria Feldman's parents refuse to talk to Daria, so they bought a computer to keep Daria busy so they won't have to speak in Yiddish. Daria will probably grow up to be a homicidal maniac lesbian prostitute.

LISA: I know what that word *prostitute* means.

PAUL: Good. (*Pause.*) You still haven't told me about school. Do you still like your teacher?

LISA: She's okay.

PAUL: Lisa, if we're talking try to answer me.

LISA: I am answering you. Can we go home now, please?

PAUL: Damn it, Lisa, if you want to talk to me . . . Talk to me!

LISA: I can't wait till I'm old enough so I can make my own money and never have to see you again. Maybe I'll become a prostitute.

PAUL: Young lady, that's enough.

LISA: I hate you, Daddy! I hate you! (*She throws her trophy into the trash bin.*)

PAUL: What'd you do that for?

LISA: It's stupid.

PAUL: Maybe I wanted it.

LISA: What for?

PAUL: Maybe I wanted to put it where I keep your dinosaur and the picture you made of Mrs. Kimbel with the chicken pox.

LISA: You got mad at me when I made that picture. You told me I had to respect Mrs. Kimbel because she was my teacher.

PAUL: That's true. But she wasn't my teacher. I liked her better with the chicken pox. (*Pause.*) Lisa, I'm sorry. I was very wrong to miss your recital, and you don't have to become a prostitute. That's not the type of profession Miss Judy has in mind for you.

LISA: (*Mumbles.*) No.

PAUL: No. (*Pause.*) So Talia Robbins is really happy her father moved out?

LISA: Talia Robbins picks open the eighth-grade lockers during gym period. But she did that before her father moved out.

PAUL: You can't always judge someone by what they do or what they don't do. Sometimes you come home from dancing school and run upstairs and shut the door, and when I finally get to talk to you, everything is "okay" or "fine." Yup or nope?

LISA: Yup.

PAUL: Sometimes, a lot of times, I come home and fall asleep in front of the television. So you and I spend a lot of time being a little scared of each other. Maybe?

LISA: Maybe.

PAUL: Tell you what. I'll make you a tender offer.

LISA: What?

PAUL: I'll make you a tender offer. That's when one company publishes in the newspaper that they want to buy another company. And the company that publishes is called the Black Knight because they want to gobble up the poor little company. So the poor little company needs to be rescued. And then a White Knight comes along and makes a bigger and better offer so the shareholders won't have to tender shares to the Big Black Knight. You with me?

LISA: Sort of.

PAUL: I'll make you a tender offer like the White Knight. But I don't want to own you. I just want to make a much better offer. Okay?

LISA: (*Sort of understanding.*) Okay. (*Pause. They sit for a moment.*) Sort of. Daddy, what do you think about? I mean, like when you're quiet what do you think about?

PAUL: Oh, business usually. If I think I made a mistake or if I think I'm doing okay. Sometimes I think about what I'll be doing five years from now and if it's what I hoped it would be five years ago. Sometimes I think about what your life will be like, if Mount Saint Helen's will erupt again. What you'll become if you'll study penmanship or word processing. If you'll speak kindly of me to your psychiatrist when you are in graduate school. And how the hell I'll pay for your graduate school. And sometimes I try and think what it was I thought about when I was your age.

LISA: Do you ever look out your window at the clouds and try to see which kinds of shapes they are? Like one time, honest, I saw the head of Walter Cronkite in a flower vase. Really! Like look don't those kinda look like if you turn it upside down, two big elbows or two elephant trunks dancing?

4. In real life, scenes like this one can easily end on a note of conflict, bitterness, or estrangement. What makes the difference here? How does the playwright give the events a happy turn?

The Personal Response

From what perspective do you see the people in this play? With whom do you identify? (*At* whom are you laughing and *with* whom?)

The Creative Dimension

Wasserstein's plays often touch on topics of concern to feminist scholars and critics. Could this scene have been played out in a similar way if the two characters had been mother and son instead? Working with a group, you may want to help with a rewrite of the play along different gender lines.

THE HIGH-WIRE ACT OF WIT

In a series of brilliant plays, including *Lady Windermere's Fan* and *The Importance of Being Earnest,* the Irish playwright Oscar Wilde moved admiring audiences beyond the proverbial earnestness of their Victorian parents. Queen Victoria, who reigned from 1837 to 1901, came to symbolize a period in British history when respect for privilege and status, prim and proper demeanor, and a somewhat pompous humorlessness were expected as evidence of good breeding. Aunt Augusta in the scene that follows is Wilde's inspired caricature or satirical portrait of the stereotypical Victorian upper-class type.

Wilde was born and educated in Dublin before being transplanted to Oxford and becoming a source of amusement and scandal to the British public. His mannerisms and flamboyant lifestyle made him notorious. Wits still quote his zinging one-liners, like "Being natural is such a difficult pose to keep up."

The Importance of Being Earnest (1895) is a bravura piece still brilliantly performed by modern theater companies. At a time when society put the premium on serious effort, Wilde put on the stage frivolous young people finding excuses for trips to the country (or the city). At a time when society prized respectability and the family name, one of his heroes was a young man who at birth had been abandoned in a handbag left at a railroad station. In the following scene from *The Importance of Being Earnest,* Jack Worthing is caught in a subterfuge of his own making: His excuse for sneaking away to the city is that he claims to have a younger brother there named Ernest, who needs supervision. Then, when he gets to the city, Jack pretends to be Ernest. The following exchange between Jack and Gwendolen, the young woman he adores, illustrates the witty comeback, the unexpected twist on a cliché, and the parody of pomposity that were hallmarks of Wilde's style.

Oscar Wilde eventually became the victim of homophobia after he sued the influential aristocrat whose son was Wilde's lover for defamation. The accused and the courts turned the tables on him, and he was tried for "gross indecency" and eventually sentenced to jail. A recent play written by Moises Kaufman dramatized the trials that resulted in Wilde's undoing. It brought to life in "stimulating, unsettling, ruthlessly funny" productions the self-righteousness of the frightening stubborn bigoted father, the biting wit and wounded humanity of the cornered poet-playwright, and the scandal-mongering sensational press feeding then as now the prurient appetites of the public.

Oscar Wilde   *(1854–1900)*

A Proposal of Marriage   1895

From The Importance of Being Earnest

CHARACTERS

GWENDOLEN FAIRFAX
JACK WORTHING, known to GWENDOLEN as Ernest
LADY BRACKNELL, GWENDOLEN'S mother

SCENE: *Algernon's apartment in London*

JACK: Charming day it has been, Miss Fairfax.

GWENDOLEN: Pray don't talk to me about the weather, Mr. Worthing. Whenever people talk to me about the weather, I always feel quite certain that they mean something else. And that makes me so nervous.

JACK: I do mean something else.

GWENDOLEN: I thought so. In fact, I am never wrong.

JACK: And I would like to be allowed to take advantage of Lady Bracknell's temporary absence . . . .

GWENDOLEN: I would certainly advise you to do so. Mama has a way of coming back suddenly into a room that I have often had to speak to her about.

JACK (*nervously*): Miss Fairfax, ever since I met you I have admired you more than any girl . . . I have ever met since . . . I met you.

GWENDOLEN: Yes, I am quite aware of the fact. And I often wish that in public, at any rate, you had been more demonstrative. For me you have always had an irresistible fascination. Even before I met you I was far from indifferent to you. (*Jack looks at her in amazement.*) We live, as I hope you know, Mr. Worthing, in an age of ideals. The fact is constantly mentioned in the more expensive monthly magazines, and has reached the provincial pulpits, I am told; and my ideal has always been to love someone of the name of Ernest. There is something in that name that inspires absolute confidence. The moment Algernon first mentioned to me that he had a friend called Ernest, I knew I was destined to love you.

JACK: You really love me, Gwendolen?

GWENDOLEN: Passionately!

JACK: Darling! You don't know how happy you've made me.

GWENDOLEN: My own Ernest!

JACK: But you don't really mean to say that you couldn't love me if my name wasn't Ernest?

GWENDOLEN: But your name is Ernest.

JACK: Yes, I know it is. But supposing it was something else? Do you mean to say you couldn't love me then? Personally, darling, to speak quite candidly, I don't much care about the name of Ernest . . . I don't think the name suits me at all.

GWENDOLEN: It suits you perfectly. It is a divine name. It has a music of its own. It produces vibrations.

JACK: Well, really, Gwendolen, I must say that I think there are lots of other much nicer names. I think Jack, for instance, a charming name.

GWENDOLEN: Jack? . . .No, there is very little music in the name Jack, if any at all, indeed. It does not thrill. It produces absolutely no vibrations . . . . I have known several Jacks, and they all, without exception, were more than usually plain. Besides, Jack is a notorious domesticity for John! And I pity any woman who is married to a man called John. She would probably never be allowed to know the entrancing pleasure of a single moment's solitude. The only really safe name is Ernest.

JACK: Gwendolen, I must get christened at once—I mean we must get married at once. There is no time to be lost.

GWENDOLEN: Married, Mr. Worthing?

JACK (*astounded*): Well . . . surely. You know that I love you, and you led me to believe, Miss Fairfax, that you were not absolutely indifferent to me.

GWENDOLEN: I adore you. But you haven't proposed to me yet. Nothing has been said at all about marriage. The subject has not even been touched on.

JACK: Well . . . may I propose to you now?

GWENDOLEN: I think it would be an admirable opportunity. And to spare you any possible disappointment, Mr. Worthing, I think it only fair to tell you quite frankly beforehand that I am fully determined to accept you.

JACK: Gwendolen!

GWENDOLEN: Yes, Mr. Worthing, what have you got to say to me?

JACK: You know what I have got to say to you.

GWENDOLEN: Yes, but you don't say it.

JACK (*goes on his knees*): Gwendolen, will you marry me?

GWENDOLEN: Of course I will, darling. How long you have been about it! I am afraid you have had very little experience in how to propose.

JACK: My own one, I have never loved anyone in the world but you.

GWENDOLEN: Yes, but men often propose for practice. I know my brother Gerald does. All my girl friends tell me so. What wonderfully blue eyes you have, Ernest! I hope you will always look at me just like that, especially when there are other people present. (*Enter* LADY BRACKNELL.)

LADY BRACKNELL: Mr. Worthing! Rise, sir, from this semirecumbent posture. It is most indecorous.

GWENDOLEN: Mama! (*He tries to rise; she restrains him.*) I must beg you to retire. This is no place for you. Besides, Mr. Worthing has not quite finished yet.

LADY BRACKNELL: Finished what, may I ask?

GWENDOLEN: I am engaged to Mr. Worthing, Mama. (*They rise together.*)

LADY BRACKNELL: Pardon me, you are not engaged to anyone. When you do become engaged to someone, I, or your father, should his health permit him, will inform you of the fact. An engagement should come on a young girl as a surprise, pleasant or unpleasant, as the case may be. It is hardly a matter that she could be allowed to arrange for herself . . . . And now I have a few questions to put to you, Mr. Worthing. While I am making these inquiries, you, Gwendolen, will wait for me below in the carriage.

GWENDOLEN (*reproachfully*): Mama!

LADY BRACKNELL: In the carriage, Gwendolen! (GWENDOLEN *goes to the door. She and* JACK *blow kisses to each other behind* LADY BRACKNELL'S *back.* LADY BRACKNELL *looks vaguely about as if she could not understand what the noise was. Finally turns around.*) Gwendolen, the carriage!

GWENDOLEN: Yes, Mama. (*goes out looking back at* JACK)

LADY BRACKNELL (*sitting down*): You can take a seat, Mr. Worthing. (*looks in her pocket for notebook and pencil*)

JACK: Thank you, Lady Bracknell, I prefer standing.

LADY BRACKNELL (*pencil and notebook in hand*): I feel bound to tell you that you are not down on my list of eligible young men. However, I am quite ready to enter your name, should your answers be what a really affectionate mother requires. Do you smoke?

JACK: Well, yes, I must admit I smoke.

LADY BRACKNELL: I am glad to hear it. A man should always have an occupation of some kind. There are far too many idle men in London as it is. How old are you?

JACK: Twenty-nine.

LADY BRACKNELL: A very good age to be married at. I have always been of the opinion that a man who desires to get married should know either everything or nothing. Which do you know?

JACK (*after some hesitation*): I know nothing, Lady Bracknell.

LADY BRACKNELL: I am pleased to hear it. I do not approve of anything that tampers with natural ignorance. Ignorance is like a delicate exotic fruit; touch it and the bloom is gone. The whole theory of modern education is radically unsound. Fortunately in England, at any rate, education produces no effect whatsoever. If it did, it would prove a serious danger to the upper classes. What is your income?

JACK: Between seven and eight thousand pounds a year.

LADY BRACKNELL (*makes a note in her book*): In land or in investments?

JACK: In investments, chiefly.

LADY BRACKNELL: That is satisfactory. What between the duties expected of one during one's lifetime, and the duties exacted from one after one's death, land has ceased to be either a profit or a pleasure. It gives one position and prevents one from keeping it up. That's all that can be said about land.

JACK: I have a country house with some land, of course, attached to it, about fifteen hundred acres, I believe; but I don't depend on that for my real income. In fact, as far as I can make out, the poachers are the only people who make anything out of it.

LADY BRACKNELL: A country house! How many bedrooms? Well, that point can be cleared up afterward. You have a town house, I hope? A girl with a simple, unspoiled nature, like Gwendolen, could hardly be expected to reside in the country.

JACK: Well, I own a house in Belgrave Square.

LADY BRACKNELL: What number in Belgrave Square?

JACK: One hundred and forty nine.

LADY BRACKNELL (*shaking her head*): The unfashionable side. I thought there was something. However, that could easily be altered.

JACK: Do you mean the fashion, or the side?

LADY BRACKNELL (*sternly*): Both, if necessary, I presume. Are your parents living?

JACK: I have lost both my parents.

LADY BRACKNELL: To lose one parent, Mr. Worthing, may be regarded as a misfortune. To lose both looks like carelessness. Who was your father? He was evidently a man of some wealth. Was he born in what the Radical papers call the purple of commerce, or did he rise from the ranks of the aristocracy?

JACK: I am afraid I really don't know. The fact is, Lady Bracknell, I said I had lost my parents. It would be nearer the truth to say that my parents seem to have lost me. . . . I don't actually know who I am by birth. I was . . . well, I was found.

LADY BRACKNELL: Found!

JACK: The late Mr. Thomas Cardew, an old gentleman of a very charitable and kindly disposition, found me and gave me the name of Worthing, because he happened to have a first-class ticket for Worthing in his pocket at the time. Worthing is a place in Sussex. It is a seaside resort.

LADY BRACKNELL: Where did the charitable gentleman who had a first-class ticket for this seaside resort find you?

JACK (*gravely*): In a handbag.

LADY BRACKNELL: A handbag?

JACK (*very seriously*): Yes, Lady Bracknell. I was in a handbag—a somewhat large, black leather handbag, with handles to it—an ordinary handbag in fact.

LADY BRACKNELL: In what locality did this Mr. James, or Thomas, Cardew come across this ordinary handbag?

JACK: In the cloakroom at Victoria Station. It was given to him in mistake for his own.

LADY BRACKNELL: The cloakroom at Victoria Station?

JACK: Yes. The Brighton line.

LADY BRACKNELL: The line is immaterial. Mr. Worthing, I confess I feel somewhat bewildered by what you have just told me. To be born, or at any rate bred, in a handbag, whether it had handles or not, seems to me to display a contempt for the ordinary decencies of family life that reminds one of the worst excesses of the French Revolution. . . . As for the particular locality in which the handbag was found, a cloakroom at a railway station might serve to conceal a social indiscretion—has probably, indeed, been used for that purpose before now—but it could hardly be regarded as an assured basis for a recognized position in good society.

JACK: May I ask you then what you would advise me to do? I need hardly say I would do anything in the world to insure Gwendolen's happiness.

LADY BRACKNELL: I would strongly advise you, Mr. Worthing, to try and acquire some relations as soon as possible, and to make a definite effort to produce at any rate one parent, of either sex, before the season is quite over.

JACK: Well, I don't see how I could possibly manage to do that. I can produce the handbag at any moment. It is in my dressing room at home. I really think that should satisfy you, Lady Bracknell.

LADY BRACKNELL: Me, sir! What has it to do with me? You can hardly imagine that I and Lord Bracknell would dream of allowing our only daughter— a girl brought up with the utmost care—to marry into a cloakroom, and form an alliance with a parcel. Good morning, Mr. Worthing! (LADY BRACKNELL *sweeps out in majestic indignation.*)

The Receptive Reader

1. Wilde's comic characters in this scene are all talk. Describe each of the three characters and each character's way of talking. What makes Jack Worthing comic? What is hilarious about Gwendolen? What made Lady Bracknell immortal?

2. In his time, Wilde was notorious for witty sayings that stood some cliché or platitude on its head. Can you find examples in this scene?

3. What are the targets of Wilde's satire here—what traits or values does he make seem ridiculous? How serious and how effective is his satire?

4. As you look in the mirror the playwright holds up to human nature in this scene, do you see a reflection of yourself or of people you know?

5. Your class may want to have an audition for a Readers' Theater presentation of this scene. What traits and abilities would you look for in candidates for the three roles?

The Personal Response

Is Wilde's humor too frivolous for our day? Is it obsolete? Do we have more important things to worry about? Are we relapsing into the earnestness of the Victorians?

MOLIÈRE AND THE LIMITS OF COMEDY

The austerest of us are at heart all too human.

MOLIÈRE, *THE MISANTHROPE*

Satire is moral outrage transformed into
comic art.

PHILIP ROTH

The great comic genius in European literature is the French seventeenth-century playwright Molièrc (1622–1673). He is part of the French **neo-classical** tradition—the "new classicism" or classical revival—of the reign of Louis XIV, the Sun King. Molière observed the rules of neoclassical **decorum**—of appropriateness to time, occasion, and social class. While contemporary tragedies put on the stage noble Greeks and Romans, Molière put on the stage *The Would-Be Gentleman*—the commoner who yearned to be noble. His Monsieur Jourdain is everyone's newly rich (nouveau riche) neighbor. Yearning to acquire culture, he brings into the neighborhood dancing teachers, music tutors, and fencing masters. He looks like a stuffed canary in the latest sartorial chic.

Molière started his career with a group of traveling actors and became one of the best-known and best-loved names connected with the stage. His comedies—*The Miser, The Imaginary Invalid, The Would-Be Gentleman, The School for Wives, The Misanthrope, Tartuffe*—continue in the standard repertory at the Comédie Française in Paris and at theaters around the world. Born Jean-Baptiste Poquelin (Molière was his stage name), he first knew the royal court as furnisher and attendant, following in the footsteps of his father. However, his ambition was to be an actor, and he eventually became a protégé of Louis XIV, to whose lavish taste and patronage of the arts later generations owe the palace at Versailles, built to reflect the splendor of the Sun King's reign.

Like Shakespeare, Molière was an actor-playwright with a sense of audience sharpened by much firsthand experience. Like other writers with a satirical bent, he made powerful enemies. He was accused of lampooning important persons and religion (when actually his target was religious hypocrisy). He prospered under the protection of his royal patron, but his life was embittered toward the end by an unhappy marriage to a much younger woman, the daughter of a former mistress. Very ill, he insisted on playing his part as the hypochondriac in *The Imaginary Invalid* in early performances of the play; he died after a hemorrhage during a performance.

Molière's plays run the gamut from farcical horseplay to biting satire and wistful laughter. He knew how to do broad popular humor: In *The Doctor in Spite of Himself* (1666), a wife-beating drunkard of a husband gets his comeuppance. His much-abused wife makes him out to be a miracle-working physician—who will however practice his art only after he is beaten into admitting his hidden talents. At the opposite end of the comic spectrum is Molière's *The Misanthrope* (1666)—about a man whose high standards lead him to hate human nature. Although the play has hilarious moments, at times it seems to turn too serious for laughter altogether. Keeping the following in mind will help you enjoy your reading and help you get into the spirit of the play:

✗ Molière lived in an age when elegance in manners, language, and dress was more highly valued than today. A chief goal was not to seem a country bumpkin. However, in this play, elegant manners are not the unquestioned standard; instead, they are the *issue*. Alceste, the misanthropic hero of the play, lives in an upper-class society where surface politeness and flattery are carried to ridiculous extremes in public, while malicious gossip is a favorite pastime in private. Alceste is forever aghast at the two-faced nature of the people around him. However, he is a comic character in a comic play. Different characters in turn have good lines, and the audience is drawn into the play of point and counterpoint on the central question: whether to be honest and rude or hypocritical and polite.

✗ Try to visualize the characters in the quick, pointed exchanges in which Molière's audiences delighted. The translation that follows uses the rapidly moving four-beat line that French audiences hear when they watch the play or listen to it on cassette. Although the lines are slightly longer than Shakespeare's blank verse (averaging twelve to fourteen instead of ten or eleven syllables), they move fast because of a four-beat instead of the familiar five-beat line:

> *Il est* BIEN *des* ENDROITS *où la* PLAINE *franCHISE*
> *DevienDRAIT ridiCULE et seRAIT peu perMISE.*

> *But to* PRACTICE *strict* CANDOR, *you'll* HAVE *to* AGREE,
> *Would quite* OFTEN *be* FOOLish, *and* PAINful *to* SEE.

✗ At the same time, the lines use end rhyme, with a passage often leading up to a neatly packaged **closed couplet** that wraps up a point. Often such a couplet plays off **antitheses**, or neatly balanced opposites, like the "esteem *for all* / esteem *for none*" in the following example:

> Estéem must sélect from the cómmon rún—
> Estéem for áll is estéem for nóne.

A brief pointed remark is called an **epigram**, and Molière's epigrammatic style makes many of his couplets especially quotable. It also allows his characters to score points and gain (often only temporary) advantage.

✗ Molière follows the conventions of his day in having his characters speak an elevated sugary and abstract language of the emotions. The love relationships (at least as we watch them on the stage) are all talk, and the talk is about *ardors, vows, flames, fervors,* and *amorous fires.* Even Alceste, who denounces the sugary, insincere language of bad poetry, is caught up in this elevated **euphemistic** style. (Euphemisms make things sound more beautiful and refined than they really are.) For more pointed, down-to-earth language, we need to turn to the satirical jabs and barbs, as when Célimène skewers the host who ruined a good meal by serving up his table talk as dessert.

   A note on the French names: The names are generally stressed on the final syllable, with the final *e* silent: Alcest(e), Philint(e), Célimèn(e), Oront(e). (The *in* and *on* are nasalized, sounding similar to *eng* and *ong*.) Arsinoé has a stressed final *e,* pronounced closer to *a* than to *ee* (Arsinoé).

Molière   *(1622–1673)*

The Misanthrope   *1666*

TRANSLATED BY HANS P. GUTH

CHARACTERS

ALCESTE, the misanthrope
PHILINTE, until recently ALCESTE's friend
ORONTE, gentleman of rank and part-time poet
CÉLIMÈNE, loved (with certain reservations) by ALCESTE
ÉLIANTE, friend and cousin of CÉLIMÈNE
ACASTE   } men of distinction
CLITANDRE
ARSINOÉ, reputed to be a prude
SERVANTS
AN OFFICER

Act One

SCENE 1 [PHILINTE, ALCESTE]

PHILINTE: How now? What is wrong?
ALCESTE: Please leave me alone.
PHILINTE: But please do explain your abruptness of tone . . .
ALCESTE: Please leave me, I say, and shame on your head.
PHILINTE: At least you should hear me without turning red . . .
ALCESTE: I *want* to turn red, and refuse you my ear.   5
PHILINTE: I don't understand your temper, I fear,
   And though we are friends, I must say at long last . . .
ALCESTE [*rises abruptly*]: Who, I? and your friend? That's a thing of the past.
   Up to now, it is true, to my heart you were dear,
   But the traits that of late in your nature appear   10
   Make me solemnly state that our friendship has ceased.
   From a tainted attachment you see me released.

PHILINTE: I am then, Alceste, to blame in your eyes?
ALCESTE: All standards of honor your conduct defies.
 For what you have done, no excuse can be found.   15
 For remorse you should weep and your tears stain the ground.
 I see how you greet like a dear, long-lost friend
 A man on whose every word you attend;
 You flatter and banter and put him at ease
 And give to his hand the most violent squeeze;   20
 And when I inquire: Who is he? For shame!
 You hardly so much as remember his name!
 As he leaves, your tender affections depart;
 His back turned, your remarks strike a chill to the heart.
 Just heavens! What cowardly, infamous role   25
 To degrade and betray thus one's innermost soul.
 And if, inadvertent, I had done the same,
 I would hang myself straight and blot out my name.
PHILINTE: Myself, I don't think the offense merits hanging,
 And respectfully hope, despite your haranguing,   30
 That, a merciful judge, you will grant a delay
 And let me stay clear of the noose, if I may.
ALCESTE: Your irony, Sir, is badly misplaced.
PHILINTE: How should I repair, then, my lapses of taste?
ALCESTE: Be sincere; by a strict code of honor abide;   35
 Let in all that you say your heart be your guide.
PHILINTE: When someone accosts me in glad-handed ease
 I have to repay him in kind, if you please,
 Respond as seems best to his jovial tirade
 And pay compliments back for each compliment paid.   40
ALCESTE: No, no! I won't stand for this cowardly way
 That with people of your persuasion bears sway,
 And I hate from the heart the false front you describe,
 The hollow routines of a frivolous tribe:
 The cordial conveyors of untruths that flatter,   45
 Obliging dispensers of valueless chatter,
 Who warmly converse while the heart remains cool
 And treat thus alike the sage and the fool.
 What boots it if people receive me with zeal
 And tenderly talk of the friendship they feel   50
 And commend the way I talk and behave
 And then do the same for an errant knave?
 No, no! And no! Such a prostitute smile
 Will never a true man of honor beguile.
 Our friendship turns cheap if we ever intend   55
 To cherish the world at large as our friend.
 Esteem must select from the common run—
 Esteem for all is esteem for none.
 And since you adopt this vice of our age,
 My affections from you I must disengage.   60
 I refuse the promiscuous warmth of a soul

That denies to merit its central role.
To accept wholesale friendship I firmly decline;
Who befriends one and all is no friend of mine.
PHILINTE: But the world expects that we give to our acts   65
    The civil exterior that custom exacts.
ALCESTE: No, no! We should chastise, upon its detection,
    With merciless rigor all bogus affection.
    We should speak man to man, and strive to reveal
    In the words we pronounce the convictions we feel.   70
    The heart should ever be heard; in no case
    Should empty phrases our feelings debase.
PHILINTE: But to practice strict candor, you'll have to agree,
    Would quite often be foolish, and painful to see,
    And at times, whatever strict honor requires,   75
    We must mask the emotions the world inspires.
    Now, would it be fitting, or make people like us,
    To let one and all know just how they strike us?
    And if people merit dislike or disgrace,
    Should we tell them so openly, straight to the face?   80
ALCESTE: Yes, indeed.
PHILINTE: You would want me to tell Colette
    At her age she is foolish to play the coquette?
    That her make-up is shocking beyond belief?
ALCESTE: That's right.
PHILINTE: I would plunge vain Jacques into grief
    And call his accounts, all heard before,   85
    Of his family's glory a crashing bore?
ALCESTE: Just so.
PHILINTE: But, surely you jest.
ALCESTE: I do not.
    I refuse to spare the fool and the sot.
    My eyes are offended; the court and the town
    Are too full of the sights that compel me to frown.   90
    My mood turns black, and my anger mounts
    To hear of men's actions the daily accounts.
    I find vile flattery ever in season—
    Injustice, deceit, selfishness, treason;
    I quiver with rage, and feel strongly inclined   95
    To challenge to battle all humankind.
PHILINTE: Your high indignation is somewhat naïve
    And I smile to see you thus chafe and grieve.
    The world for you will not change its way—
    And since you believe in frankness, today   100
    I'll be frank myself, and thus have you know
    You amuse those you meet, wherever you go;
    And your fiery anger at custom's mild yoke
    Has made you the butt of many a joke.
ALCESTE: Of that I am glad. That tribute I treasure.   105
    It's a very good sign, and gives me great pleasure.

The men of our times are so vile to my eyes
That I would be disturbed if they thought me wise.
PHILINTE: Your displeasure at human nature is great.
ALCESTE: I've developed for it a terrible hate.   110
PHILINTE: And all poor mortals, of every station,
    Must equally share in this condemnation?
    But you surely admit, there are those who call . . .
ALCESTE: I make no exception. I hate them all.
    For some are actively bad and do wrong,   115
    And the others still suffer this poisonous throng
    And treat them with none of that vigorous scorn
    That vice should inspire in the virtuous-born.
    Such tolerance of the most vicious sort
    Extends to the scoundrel I battle in court.   120
    Behind his mask the traitor shines through,
    And everyone knows what the rascal can do;
    His obsequious manner, so clearly contrived,
    Deceives only those who have newly arrived.
    It is known that this crook, who to hell should be hurled,   125
    Through sleazy employment moved up in the world,
    That his fortune, now grown so tall and so lush,
    Causes merit to groan and virtue to blush.
    Whatever opprobrious names he is called
    Hardly anyone seems by his presence appalled!   130
    Call him criminal, coward, rogue, and thief
    And no one will register disbelief—
    Yet his leer is welcomed without dismay;
    Into every circle he worms his way.
    The reward that should be some honest man's prize   135
    Through intrigue he will snatch from under his eyes.
    God help and protect us! I'm hurt to the quick
    When people condone the shady and slick.
    And at times the desire for being alone
    Makes me yearn for a desert where man is unknown.   140
PHILINTE: O dear! Let us cease to mourn the world's plight
    And see human nature in friendlier light;
    As the rigorous critic its workings dissects
    Let him make some allowance for venial defects.
    A flexible virtue is what the world needs: 145
    Strict wisdom too often due measure exceeds.
    Good sense shuns extravagance even in honor
    And bids us *love* virtue, not dote upon her.
    A code so austere and unforgiven
    Is at odds with the mores of modern living;   150
    It asks too much of mere mortal man.
    We must follow the times as best we can.
    Only foolish presumption would start a movement
    To impose on the world a scheme for improvement.
    Like yours, any day my eyes notice much   155

That could have been this way or might have been such;
But in spite of what daily thus crosses my way,
I do not (as would you) ever anger display.
I simply take men as they are; unlike you,
I accustom my soul to accept what they do.   160
Philosophical calm I aim to acquire
While you must breathe forth philosophical ire.
ALCESTE: But this calm, dear Sir, who argue so well,
    Will it never allow your anger to swell?
    If a bosom friend to be false is shown,   165
    If one schemes to despoil you of all that you own,
    If one spreads ugly rumors to murder your name—
    Will your equable temper stay ever the same?
PHILINTE: I regard the defects of which you've complained
    As vices in human nature ingrained,   170
    And am no more incensed at the cold-blooded look
    Of a self-seeking person, a rogue, or a crook
    Than at vultures I see in their natural shapes,
    Or ferocious wolves, or malicious apes.
ALCESTE: I must then submit to be cheated and sold   175
    Without that I should . . . but the views that you hold
    Are so lax they leave me speechless with rage.
PHILINTE: Indeed, to speak less you would be most sage.
    To discuss your opponent in public forbear
    And devote to your lawsuit all possible care.   180
ALCESTE: I shall devote nothing; that much should be clear.
PHILINTE: But to argue your case, who's been asked to appear?
ALCESTE: Only Justice and Reason—no venal drudge.
PHILINTE: So you will not arrange to have lunch with the judge?
ALCESTE: No. Why? Is my case maybe doubtful or wrong?   185
PHILINTE: Not at all. But the schemer's resources are strong,
    And . . .
ALCESTE: No. I am firmly resolved to stand pat.
    I am right, or I'm wrong.
PHILINTE: Don't trust in that.
ALCESTE: I won't stir.
PHILINTE: But your foe is cunning; prepare
    To see him maneuver and plot . . .
ALCESTE: I don't care.   190
PHILINTE: You're deceived.
ALCESTE: Maybe so. I'll do as I choose.
PHILINTE: And yet . . .
ALCESTE: I would rather be right and lose.
PHILINTE: But at least . . .
ALCESTE: No more. I shall learn through this case
    If it's true that men are criminal, base,
    Perverse, and corrupt to such a degree   195
    As to treat me unjustly for all to see.
PHILINTE: What a man!

ALCESTE: I'd prefer, no matter the cost
   To have proved my point, though the suit was lost.
PHILINTE: Ah, people would snigger and laugh with disdain
   If they could but hear you hold forth in this vein.   200
ALCESTE: The worse for the scoffers.
PHILINTE: But tell me, Alceste.
   The standard that passes your rigorous test—
   That unflinching honor to which you aspire—
   Is it found in the woman you love and admire?
   I'm astonished, for one, that although it seems   205
   You denounce mankind, its customs and schemes,
   Though you claim it is steeped in all you decry,
   You have found in its ranks what charms your eye.
   And one thing surprises me even more:
   Your remarkable choice of a girl to adore.   210
   Sincere Éliante has a weakness for you;
   Arsinoé, the prude, but waits for her cue:
   Your heart receives them with frigid reserve
   While Célimène makes it her private preserve—
   Whose malicious wit and coquettish play   215
   Are much in accord with the trends of the day.
   If you hate our age, does your lady fair
   Of your vehement censure receive her share?
   Do these faults lose their taint in a shape so sweet?
   Are you blind as a lover, or merely discreet?   220
ALCESTE: No. The love this young widow inspires me to feel
   Has not blinded my eyes to the faults you reveal.
   I am, whatever my heart objects,
   The first one to see and condemn her defects.
   But I love her regardless, as everyone sees.   225
   I confess my weakness: she knows how to please.
   I may notice in her what is worthy of blame,
   But in spite of her faults to my heart she lays claim.
   Her appeal is too strong, and my love will cast out
   These faults of the times from her heart I don't doubt.   230
PHILINTE: If in that you succeed, you'll be famed among men.—
   She returns your love, I may take it then?
ALCESTE: Of course, or else I would not be here.
PHILINTE: But if she has shown whom she clearly prefers,
   Why then do your rivals annoy you so much?   235
ALCESTE: A true loving heart can share nothing with such.
   And my coming here today is designed
   To allow me to tell her this weighs on my mind.
PHILINTE: As for me, if I yearned for love's sweet prize,
   I'd address to Éliante, her cousin, my sighs.   240
   Her heart (which esteems you) is loyal and true;
   Such a choice would be happy and fitting for you.
ALCESTE: You are right. And my reason agrees every day.
   But then reason in love holds but little sway.

PHILINTE: I'm disturbed, and fear for the hope you show.   245

SCENE 2 [ORONTE, ALCESTE, PHILINTE]

ORONTE: When I asked for them, I was told below
　　That Éliante is out, and Célimène too;
　　But since I was told I would still find you,
　　I've come up to express with sincerest zeal
　　The enormous esteem that for you I feel.   5
　　I have always hoped you would in the end
　　Know my ardent desire to become your friend.
　　My heart is eager to recognize worth
　　And would trade for your friendship all else on this earth;
　　And you, I am sure without condition   10
　　Will accept a friend of my position.

[*During* ORONTE'S *speech,* ALCESTE *seems absent-minded and acts as if he
does not realize he is being addressed. He takes notice only when* ORONTE
says to him]

　　It is you, if you please, who are thus addressed.
ALCESTE: I, Sir?
ORONTE: Yes, you. You are not distressed?
ALCESTE: Not at all. But I'm struck by surprise, I must say,
　　And I did not expect to be honored this way.   15
ORONTE: You should not be surprised at the love you inspire;
　　In your presence, the world cannot help but admire.
ALCESTE: Dear Sir . . .
ORONTE:　　　　　　　　You surpass in merit, I claim,
　　The bearer of many a famous name.
ALCESTE: Dear Sir . . .
ORONTE:　　　　　　　　Yes, indeed. To me you're endeared   20
　　As much as the finest the country has reared.
ALCESTE: Dear Sir . . .
ORONTE:　　　　　　　　I really mean every word.
　　Allow me to show you how deeply I'm stirred,
　　To clasp to my bosom a long-cherished friend
　　And ask you forever on me to depend.   25
　　Take my hand, I beg you. May I, with respect
　　Call you brother and friend?
ALCESTE:　　　　　　　　　　　　Dear Sir . . .
ORONTE:　　　　　　　　　　　　　　　　You object?
ALCESTE: To accept such generous praise I am loath;
　　And friendship requires a more gradual growth—
　　One surely profanes its most holy name   30
　　When friend and acquaintance are one and the same.
　　Such knots should be tied with forethought and care;
　　To get better acquainted we ought to prepare:
　　We might differ so widely in standards or taste
　　As to make us too late repent of our haste.   35

ORONTE: How well you just put it! How wise and true!
    Your words but increase my regard for you.
    Let us leave it to time then to strengthen our bond;
    But meanwhile I'm yours, and hope you'll respond
    By leaving to me your concerns in high places. 40
    As you know, I enjoy the King's good graces.
    He listens to me, and indeed, I must say
    Is most kind to me in every way.
    In short, I am yours with all my might;
    And because you will judge profoundly and right, 45
    I am going to show you, to strengthen our ties,
    A sonnet I've written, and as you advise
    It shall perish or see the light of day.
ALCESTE: Dear Sir, I am hardly the man to say.
    Please excuse me.
ORONTE: But why?
ALCESTE: I have the defect 50
    To be somewhat franker than people expect.
ORONTE: That is just what I want. And I would complain
    If when asked for your candid response you should feign
    Approval or pleasure, just to be kind.
ALCESTE: If such is your wish, I shall speak my mind. 55
ORONTE: "A Sonnet . . ." (it's a sonnet). "To Hope . . ." (I allude
    To hope inspired by a lady I wooed).
    "To Hope . . ." These verses aren't meant to be grand
    But tender and sweet, you will understand.
ALCESTE: We shall see.
ORONTE: "To Hope . . ." I'm afraid that the style 60
    By its awkward spots might cause you to smile,
    And I hope you will find the thoughts well phrased.
ALCESTE: We shall shortly know.
ORONTE: I was much amazed
    It took but a quarter hour, I recall.
ALCESTE: The time is not the issue at all. 65
ORONTE [reads]: Hope, it is true, gives solace
    And beguiles a few moments with laughter,
    But Phyllis, what unhappy comfort,
    If nothing follows thereafter!
PHILINTE: Ah, how these verses charm and delight! 70
ALCESTE [aside to PHILINTE]: Can you shamelessly tolerate stuff so trite?
ORONTE: At first you were gracious to me,
    But why did you thus incline
    If it was your cruel will
    With mere hope to let me repine? 75
PHILINTE: How elegantly these phrases are turned!
ALCESTE [aside to PHILINTE]: Great God! Vile dissembler! Such stuff should be
    burned.
ORONTE: If such eternal waiting
    Should push my zeal to extremes

To expire I calmly prepare.   80
　　Your concern would be unavailing:
　　Such desperate hope, it seems,
　　Dear Phyllis, makes hope despair.
PHILINTE: The close is tender and not at all lame.
ALCESTE [*aside*]: A plague on your close, in the devil's name!   85
　　I wish you were safely confined and enclosed!
PHILINTE: I've never heard verses so well composed.
ALCESTE [*aside*]: The nerve!
ORONTE [*to* PHILINTE]:　　　　You flatter, and if I may say . . .
PHILINTE: I do not.
ALCESTE [*aside*]:　　Yes, you do! and cheat and betray.
ORONTE [*to* ALCESTE]: But you, Sir, remember to what you agreed.   90
　　Tell us frankly, I pray, what your taste has decreed.
ALCESTE: Here indeed a delicate question is raised.
　　Creative talents desire to be praised.
　　But once to a person (whose name I won't mention)
　　I said when his verses came to my attention   95
　　That a man must be armed against the bite
　　Of the sudden passion he feels to write;
　　That he must control the importunate urge
　　In the flood of his verses his friends to submerge;
　　That the would-be author in quest of his goal   100
　　Runs the risk of playing an unfitting role.
ORONTE: Are you trying to say that the verses I read
　　Would have better remained . . .
ALCESTE:　　　　　　　　　　That's not what I said.
　　Him I told: frigid writing is cold-blooded crime,
　　And just this one fault is enough in our time   105
　　To lower the worthiest man in all eyes—
　　It is just such defects that the world decries.
ORONTE: Do you find that my verses are not for these times?
ALCESTE: That's not what I said. But, to help stop his rhymes,
　　I reminded him strongly that now and then   110
　　Such thirst for glory has spoiled able men.
ORONTE: Are my verses then bad? Do you class me with these?
ALCESTE: That's not what I said. *Him* I asked: If you please,
　　What brings to your eye the ominous glint,
　　What devil compels you to break into print?   115
　　The only bad authors who find us forgiving
　　Are unfortunate wretches who write for a living.
　　So take my advice: resist the temptation;
　　Don't expose yourself to such recrimination;
　　And do not exchange so rashly your claim   120
　　To solid repute and an honest name
　　For the title some publishers gladly purvey
　　Of a poor foolish author sans praise and sans pay.
　　This was what I tried to make him see.
ORONTE: Very well. You indeed are candid with me.   125

But if you were asked how my poem would rank . . .
ALCESTE: I would quietly file it, to be quite frank.
    You have followed bad models, as authors are prone,
    And your phrases quite lack any natural tone.
    For what do you mean: "beguiles with laughter,"   130
    Or what about this: "Nothing follows thereafter."
       [*mimics*] To expire I calmly prepare.
         Such desperate hope, it seems,
         Dear Phyllis, makes hope despair.
    This flowery style of which people are fond   135
    Is far from true feeling and nature's bond.
    You are playing with words; it's quite insincere,
    And nature knows no such affected leer.
    The awful taste of our time gives one pause;
    Our parents more wisely bestowed their applause,   140
    And I prize much less what all now admire
    Than an old-fashioned song I learned from my sire:
       If the king were to say,
       "Take Paris; it's thine"
       And asked me to leave   145
       My sweetheart behind,
       I would say, "Sir King,
       Not for me your bequest;
       My girl I love best, heigh ho!
       My girl I love best."   150
    The rhyme is defective, the style somewhat old,
    But surely it's better, a hundredfold,
    Than these trivial rhymes where good sense is asleep,
    And surely here feeling is pure and deep?
       [*hums or sings sotto voce*]
       If the king were to say,   155
       "Take Paris; it's thine"
       And asked me to leave
       My sweetheart behind,
       I would say, "Sir King,
       Not for me your bequest;   160
       My girl I love best, heigh ho!
       My girl I love best."
    Yes, such is the language that comes from the heart.
    [*to* PHILINTE, *who is smiling*] You sophisticates laugh at its lack of art.
    Yet I treasure these simple lines much more   165
    Than the glittering trifles that you all adore.
ORONTE: As for me, I maintain that my verses are fine.
ALCESTE: For good cause you no doubt to this verdict incline.
    But for other good cause, which I hope you'll respect
    Such a flattering judgment you see me reject.   170
ORONTE: While others do praise them, I'm pleased with my lot.
ALCESTE: They know how to flatter, and I do not.
ORONTE: You pride yourself on your agile wit.

ALCESTE: To find cause for praise, I'd need plenty of it.

ORONTE: I can do quite well *without* your acclaim.   175

ALCESTE: You will have to, because I won't furnish the same.

ORONTE: What verses could you, if faced with the task,
    Produce on this theme, I should like to ask.

ALCESTE: I could, if I would, write lines just as poor,
    Though I would not expose them to view, I am sure.   180

ORONTE: You're most self-assured; your superior tone . . .

ALCESTE: Let others adore you; leave *me* alone.

ORONTE: But, my dear little man, come off your high horse.

ALCESTE: I'll stay on, my big boy, and pursue my own course.

PHILINTE [*comes between them*]: But please, my dear Sirs, that's enough for
    today.   185

ORONTE: I am leaving right now. I did wrong to stay.
    Please accept, dear Sir, my most humble respect.

ALCESTE: And receive, dear Sir, my regards most abject.

                              [ORONTE *leaves*.]

SCENE 3 [PHILINTE, ALCESTE]

PHILINTE: There you have it! Be franker than men can bear
    And at once you're embroiled in a tedious affair.
    The vanity of Oronte is such . . .

ALCESTE: Don't say any more.

PHILINTE: But . . .

ALCESTE: I've had too much.

PHILINTE: But indeed . . .

ALCESTE: Please leave me.

PHILINTE: But let . . .

ALCESTE: No talk.   5

PHILINTE: But at least . . .

ALCESTE: I won't listen.

PHILINTE: The way you balk . . .

ALCESTE: Don't follow me. Go! Stop pulling my sleeve.

PHILINTE: You are not yourself. I refuse to leave.

Act Two

SCENE 1 [ALCESTE, CÉLIMÈNE]

ALCESTE: You must, dear friend, give me leave to complain.
    The way you behave gives me reason for pain:
    Too often your thoughtlessness raises my gall;
    Someday we shall separate once and for all.
    I shall not deceive you with sugared pretense—   5
    I feel I'll be forced with your love to dispense,
    And in spite of all promises you would have heard
    I might not be able to honor my word.

CÉLIMÈNE: It's to quarrel with me, I note with dismay,
    That you've wanted to come and see me today.   10
ALCESTE: I don't quarrel at all. But your generous soul
    To all comers, dear Madam, presents itself whole.
    Too many suitors beleaguer your door;
    I won't share you with every officious bore.
CÉLIMÈNE: Why should I be blamed for the suitors you see?   15
    Can I stop all these people from taking to me?
    And if someone pleads for a share of my time
    Should I reach for a stick to punish his crime?
ALCESTE: A stick, my dear Madam, is not what you need
    But a heart from too facile a tenderness freed.   20
    Your charms do go with you wherever you walk,
    But those lured by your looks are egged on by your talk;
    And your kindly reception (of those I despise)
    Completes the conquest begun by your eyes.
    The radiant smile that you offer to each   25
    Gives hope to every diligent leech.
    If you were to appear more discreetly wise
    You would soon extinguish their amorous sighs.
    But at least, dear Madam, do tell in what way
    Your Clitandre so pleases and charms you, I pray.   30
    On what solid foundation of worth and of skill
    Do you build the esteem you are granting him still?
    Is his letting his graceful fingernails grow
    The cause of the signal fondness you show?
    Have you joined those victims of fashion's cant   35
    Whom the dazzling charms of his wig enchant?
    Does his dandyish garb assure him of grace?
    Does he conquer with masses of ribbon and lace?
    Has he earned by the elegant cut of his pants
    That servitude sweet that a woman grants?   40
    Have his oily smile, his falsetto voice
    Been attractive enough to determine your choice?
CÉLIMÈNE: How unjustly you censure the course I pursue!
    Why I humor the man is no secret to you;
    For he and his friends will lend me support   45
    To help win the case I have pending in court.
ALCESTE: It were better to lose, if it came to the test,
    Than to humor a rival I must detest.
CÉLIMÈNE: The whole world now attracts your jealous abuse!
    The whole world shares alike in your kindness profuse.   50
CÉLIMÈNE: Just that point should appease your tempestuous soul
    Since my tender regard goes to none as a whole.
    You would have juster cause for all this ado
    If I spread it less widely than now I do.
ALCESTE: But I, whom excessively jealous you call,   55
    What is mine, may I ask, that's not shared by them all?
CÉLIMÈNE: The bliss of knowing my love for you.

ALCESTE: How can I convince my heart it is true?
CÉLIMÈNE: I think if I say as much to your face
My word should be more than enough in this case.   60
ALCESTE: But how do I know that as part of the game
   All others might not have been told the same?
CÉLIMÈNE: Your style as a lover is sweet indeed!
   And how highly you think of the life that I lead!
   Well then! just to grant you relief from your care   65
   I deny the esteem I've been rash to declare;
   Now none will deceive you but you alone.
   Good luck!
ALCESTE: Oh, if only my heart were of stone!
   If only my soul could regain its ease
   I would thank and bless the gods on my knees.   70
   I admit it freely: I ever try
   To set myself free from this terrible tie,
   But my strongest efforts are all in vain;
   For my sins, I am sure, I thus groan and complain.
CÉLIMÈNE: Your ardor, indeed, is an unequaled one.   75
ALCESTE: Yes, it is. On this point I will yield to none.
   For no one can fathom my love for you,
   And never has anyone loved as I do.
   Your method is startling and new, I agree,
   For it seems that you court me to quarrel with me.   80
   Your love takes the form of tantrum and whim
   And never before was passion so grim.
ALCESTE: But it is in your power to stop all my grief.
CÉLIMÈNE: Let us bury right now our disputes; and in brief
   Let us open our hearts, and at once let's begin. . . .   85

SCENE 2 [CÉLIMÈNE, ALCESTE, SERVANT]

CÉLIMÈNE: What is it?
SERVANT: Acaste is below.
CÉLIMÈNE: Show him in.

SCENE 3 [CÉLIMÈNE, ALCESTE]

ALCESTE: Indeed! Are we ever alone at all?
   Forever you're ready to see those who call.
   For this once, it seems you might change your routine
   And inform your Acaste you're not to be seen.
CÉLIMÈNE: nd affront him by having him sent away?   5
ALCESTE: Your concern is as usual aimed the wrong way.
CÉLIMÈNE: He's a man who would never forgive me the slight
   Of my having denied myself to his sight.
ALCESTE: But why should you care about what he may feel . . .
CÉLIMÈNE: Why indeed! His good will is worth a great deal.   10
   He is one of those who—I don't know how or why—
   Count for much in the King's and the public's eye.

Their constant meddling I watch with alarm;
They do us no good, but they *can* do us harm.
And no matter what other support we may find,   15
We should never offend loud-mouthed men of his kind.
ALCESTE: Well and good. As I only too well recall
    You find reasons to suffer the presence of all;
    And your pretexts, albeit transparently thin . . .

SCENE 4 [ALCESTE, CÉLIMÈNE, SERVANT]

SERVANT: Clitandre has come, if you please.
CÉLIMÈNE: Show him in.
    [*to* ALCESTE, *who is leaving*] You are off?
ALCESTE: Yes indeed.
CÉLIMÈNE: Please remain.
ALCESTE: But why?
CÉLIMÈNE: Please stay.
ALCESTE: But I can't.
CÉLIMÈNE: I insist.
ALCESTE: I won't try.
    You are set for a long conversational bout.
    It's unfair to require me to sweat it out.   5
CÉLIMÈNE: I insist, I insist!
ALCESTE: I'll be bored to tears.
CÉLIMÈNE: All right, leave! You must have it your way, it appears.

SCENE 5 [ÉLIANTE, PHILINTE, ACASTE, ALCESTE, CLITANDRE, CÉLIMÈNE, SERVANT]

ÉLIANTE [*to* CÉLIMÈNE]:
    I have brought two distinguished friends, as you see.
    But you knew we were here.
CÉLIMÈNE: Yes, indeed. [*to* SERVANT] Chairs for three.
    [*to* ALCESTE] Still not gone?
ALCESTE: No, not yet. I shall leave on condition
    That for them or for me you announce your decision.
CÉLIMÈNE: Oh, be still.
ALCESTE: Today you'll announce who will lose.   5
CÉLIMÈNE: You are out of your mind.
ALCESTE: Not at all. You shall choose.
CÉLIMÈNE: Indeed!
ALCESTE: You'll declare to whom you belong.
CÉLIMÈNE: You are joking, I'm sure.
ALCESTE: I've been patient too long.
CLITANDRE: I have just seen Cléonte, no sage as a rule,
    In full view of the King act the absolute fool.   10
    Let us hope a kind friend will one of these days
    Point out to the man his impossible ways.
CÉLIMÈNE: t is true, his manners amaze and amuse;
    And his bumbling behavior is hard to excuse.
    And the passage of time, it is to be feared,   15
    Far from mellowing him only makes him more weird.

ACASTE: Good grief! Since we're speaking of men who appall,
   I have just shaken off the most tiresome of all:
   Damon, the great talker, an hour or more
   Made me roast in the sun at my carriage door.   20
CÉLIMÈNE: A strange creature, who always crosses one's way
   And though making great speeches has nothing to say!
   His weighty pronouncements lack meaning; and hence
   One hears all the noise but misses the sense.
ÉLIANTE [*to* PHILINTE]: Not bad for a start; in this gay little chat   25
   One's neighbors are treated as mice by the cat.
CLITANDRE: Timante, dear Madam, is also quite queer.
CÉLIMÈNE: The desire for importance has spoiled him, poor dear.
   With preoccupied air he strides into view
   And acts always most busy—with nothing to do.   30
   Whatever he says, he looks solemn and grave,
   Frowns and hems fit to kill—what a way to behave!—
   Forever butts in to confide something awful
   (What's a scandal to him as a rule is quite lawful).
   He makes secrets of trifles and will by and by   35
   Confidentially whisper "hello" and "good-by."
ACASTE: And Gerald, dear Madam?
CÉLIMÈNE: What teller of tales!
   He has always just dined with the Prince of Wales.
   In his talk, he frequents the great of this earth;
   If one isn't a duchess, one has little worth.   40
   He is charmed by a title, and talks without end
   Of the horses and dogs of some blue-blooded friend.
   The most noble and rich are "Dear Marge" and "Old Jim";
   As if "Sir" and "Mylady" were noxious to him.
CLITANDRE: With Bélise, it is said, he gets along well.   45
CÉLIMÈNE: Oh, how lacking in wit and how tongue-tied a belle!
   Her calls are ordeals for whose passing I pray.
   In cold sweat one searches for something to say;
   Her lack of the powers of communication
   Effectively stifles all conversation.   50
   Her silence is solid, and, dumb as a wall,
   She resists all clichés that the mind can recall.
   The sun, the rain, or the wintry blast—
   One tries hard to make their discussion last,
   But her visit, which calls for all of one's strength,   55
   Stretches out to the most unbearable length.
   One yawns like a person about to expire,
   And yet like a log she stays put by the fire.
ACASTE: And what of Adraste?
CÉLIMÈNE: Presumption extreme!
   He's a person inflated with self-esteem.   60
   He forever claims virtues the world fails to see
   And reviles for their blindness the powers that be.
   No matter what post someone else obtains

He claims he was slighted and mopes and complains.
CLITANDRE: And what of Cleon, at whose house you may meet   65
    All the people who count—don't you think he is sweet?
CÉLIMÈNE: He has hired a new cook who's unusually able,
    And the people who visit him visit his table.
ÉLIANTE: He *does* provide most magnificent food.
CÉLIMÈNE: But the last course of all quite ruins the mood: 70
    The host bends one's ear as if one were deaf—
    Thus spoiling the pleasures conferred by the chef.
PHILINTE: On his uncle Damis a man can depend.
    What of him?
CÉLIMÈNE: I have always esteemed him my friend.
PHILINTE: He seems wise and enjoys universal respect.   75
CÉLIMÈNE: He tries hard to seem witty—which is a defect.
    In the absence of any genuine spark
    He labors and strains for the clever remark.
    He decided that brilliance through scorn best is shown
    And his every word turned sardonic in tone.   80
    With all that he reads, he finds fault; I believe
    He assumes that to praise is passé and naïve,
    That one proves one's wit by withering looks,
    That only a fool would *enjoy* reading books,
    And that by sophisticates he is preferred   85
    Who looks down on what pleases the common herd.
    Yes, even mere chit-chat incurs his disdain;
    One's passing remarks he finds banal and vain;
    And crossing his arms, his answers most terse,
    With infinite pity he lets one converse.   90
ACASTE: I'll be damned. That's him! That's the man to a *T!*
CLITANDRE [*to* CÉLIMÈNE]: How precisely you paint the people you see!
ALCESTE: That's it, my dear friends! Strike again! Twist the knife!
    Let everyone join; and spare no one's life.
    Yet as soon as your victim but shows his face,   95
    You hasten to offer your cordial embrace;
    And pumping his arm, you swear and protest
    How you love and prefer him to all the rest.
CLITANDRE: Why blame *us*? If these lively portraits offend
    You should aim your complaint at your charming friend.   100
ALCESTE: No, it's you that I blame. Your gleeful assent
    Draws her out and confirms her satirical bent.
    Her malicious tongue grows more agile and pert
    As you cheer whatever she's pleased to assert.
    In her acid critiques she'd be certain to pause   105
    If for once she should notice a dearth of applause.
    Those who flatter, like you, are always to blame
    For the vices that earn us dishonor and shame.
PHILINTE: But why take the side of the people we mention,
    Who fare worse when they come to *your* attention?   110

CÉLIMÈNE: Very true! How forever he must contradict!
　　Where all are agreed he states views that conflict;
　　He must always give voice to that obstinate pride
　　That at once makes him champion the opposite side.
　　The ideas of others are bound to displease;　　　　　　　　　115
　　Dissent is with him a chronic disease.
　　He assumes that the world would value him less
　　If he ever should falter and simply say "yes."
　　He loves contradiction as misers their pelf
　　And will often in fact contradict himself.　　　　　　　　　120
　　He will charge at his own opinions with force
　　If ever he hears them when others discourse.
ALCESTE: As always the scoffers applaud what you say.
　　You are pleased to taunt me, and well you may.
PHILINTE: However, it's true, you are quick to slap down　　125
　　Whatever one says; and you equally frown
　　At whatever one showers with ample applause
　　And whatever one censures, though both with good cause.
ALCESTE: But men will not ever base judgments on reason:
　　One's anger against them is always in season.　　　　　　　130
　　To whatever profession or trade they belong,
　　Their praise and their censure are equally wrong.
CÉLIMÈNE: But . . .
ALCESTE:　　　　　　No, dear Madam, and come what may,
　　You amuse yourself in a blameable way;
　　And it's wrong to encourage in you with glee　　　　　　　135
　　Those deplorable flaws that all can see.
CLITANDRE: I don't know about that—and indeed I object
　　That to me, for one, she's without a defect.
ACASTE: I can see she is blessed with charm and with grace;
　　If she has any flaws, they don't show in her face.　　　　　140
ALCESTE: They show clearly enough. And rather than hide them
　　The more that I love her, the more I must chide them.
　　A suitor does wrong to be meek as a dove:
　　To chastise is truly a labor of love.
　　And I'd spurn any lover—as everyone ought—　　　　　　　145
　　Who'd officiously echo my every thought,
　　Who would always appease me, and flatter, and coo,
　　And praise to the skies whatever I do.
CÉLIMÈNE: In effect, if to change us but lay in your power,
　　We would in true love turn all sweet into sour,　　　　　　150
　　And to show tender passion it would be quite right
　　To insult those we love, with all our might.
ÉLIANTE: As a rule, true love takes a different course.
　　From praising their choice, our lovers turn hoarse.
　　Their passion affects their vision, it seems,　　　　　　　　155
　　And all is most fair in the girl of their dreams.
　　Her very defects are transformed in this game

And often assume a most flattering name.
The pale one is "white as a lily"; and yet
The swarthy one is "an attractive brunette,"   160
The skinny one "slender" or "girlish of figure,"
The fat one "majestic" (the more so the bigger).
The one that is void of what stimulates passion
Is a girl whose "beauty departs from the fashion."
The tall one looks down with a goddess's face;   165
The short one looks up with most delicate grace.
The insolent one has a "noble mind";
The rogue is "vivacious"; the stupid one "kind."
The gossipy one shows "a sociable heart";
The tongue-tied one's "modesty" sets her apart.   170
And thus our lovers, their ardor extreme,
Love us not as we are but such as we seem.

ALCESTE: And yet . . .
CÉLIMÈNE: Why persist in this line of thought?
  Shall we move and look at some pictures I bought?
  You're not going, my friends?
CLITANDRE AND ACASTE: Oh, no. We shall stay.   175
ALCESTE (*to* CÉLIMÈNE):You're terribly worried they'll leave, I must say.
  [*to the others*] Whatever your plans, I should like you to know
  That *I* shall remain until after you go.
ACASTE: Unless I should be in our hostess's way
  It so happens, dear friend, that I have all day.   180
CLITANDRE: Except to attend on the King tonight
  I don't think I've a single appointment in sight.
CÉLIMÈNE [*to* ALCESTE]: You're being facetious.
ALCESTE: Of those you receive
  We shall find if it's me that you'd like to see leave.

SCENE 6 [ALCESTE, CÉLIMÈNE, ÉLIANTE, ACASTE, PHILINTE, CLITANDRE, SERVANT]

SERVANT: Someone asked for you, Sir, and insists you must know
  What his message is before you go.
ALCESTE: Reply that I'm busy; his message can wait.
SERVANT: His uniform's splendid with tassel and plait,
  And his badge shines like gold.
CÉLIMÈNE [*to* ALCESTE]:   You had better go see.   5
  Or let him come in.

SCENE 7 [ALCESTE, CÉLIMÈNE, ÉLIANTE, ACASTE, PHILINTE, CLITANDRE, A UNIFORMED
  OFFICER]

ALCESTE [*to the* OFFICER]: You are looking for me?
OFFICER: Let us step aside, if you will be so kind.
ALCESTE: Please speak up and inform me of what's on your mind.
OFFICER: Well, then; you will see that my summons is clear:
  In front of the Marshal you'll have to appear,   5
  Dear sir.

ALCESTE: Who me?

OFFICER: That's correct.

ALCESTE: To what end?

PHILINTE: It's the quarrel you had with your poet-friend.

CÉLIMÈNE [*to* PHILINTE]: What's that?

PHILINTE: He insulted Oronte when distraught
  By some trivial verses the latter had brought.
  If now settled, their feud won't come to a head.   10

ALCESTE: I shall not retract one word that I said.

PHILINTE: But you'll have to appear; you had better go.

ALCESTE: What is there to settle, I'd like to know?
  And shall I be made, by official constraint,
  To admire the poem that caused this complaint?   15
  On this point I have not at all changed my mind;
  It is thoroughly bad.

PHILINTE: You could try to be kind . . .

ALCESTE: I refuse to retreat. The lines were absurd.

PHILINTE: You'll express your regret and admit that you erred.
  Come along.

ALCESTE: I shall go, but no words you might waste   20
  Can make me recant.

PHILINTE: We had better make haste.

ALCESTE: Unless a royal decree is proclaimed
  To make me approve of the verses I blamed,
  I'll maintain, so help me! they're void of all worth
  And that poets so bad should be wiped off the earth.   25
  [*to* CLITANDRE *and* ACASTE, *who are laughing*] The devil! What laughter,
  my friends, and what sport
  At my humble expense.

CÉLIMÈNE: Be off, and report
  Where you must.

ALCESTE: I am going there now. After that
  I'll return, so we two can finish our chat.

Act Three

SCENE 1 [CLITANDRE, ACASTE]

CLITANDRE: Dear Marquis, old man, you appear well at ease;
  All strive to amuse you, and none to displease.
  But tell me at once, wishful thinking aside,
  Do you have real grounds for your joy and your pride?

ACASTE: God knows, I don't see when I look at my fate   5
  The slightest occasion for grumbling or hate.
  I am rich, I am young, and descend, as you know,
  From a house whose rank is indeed far from low;
  And my family's name is such that with ease
  I could aim at whatever position I please.   10
  As for stoutness of heart—which all must admire—

I am hardly deficient in generous fire.
I have shown, I may say, if it comes to the test
I can manfully shoot it out with the best.
I have wit and good taste, so much so indeed   15
I discuss and condemn even books I don't read.
A new play makes me haunt foyer and backstage,
Where I shine in my role of critic and sage.
In a beautiful passage when actors excel
I will clap and shout bravo! to help break the spell.   20
I am clever, look handsome; my smile is heartfelt,
My teeth brilliant white, my hips strong but svelte.
In matters of dress, I can say without fear
You'd be challenged indeed to discover my peer.
That I'm highly esteemed by all you can tell: 25
The women pursue me; the King likes me well.
With such traits, I believe, dear Marquis, old man,
One can live in content one's allotted span.

CLITANDRE: Hm—but sure elsewhere of all women's applause,
Why expend your sighs here, in a hopeless cause?   30

ACASTE: I—hopeless? Well, well! I assure you I don't
Breathe passionate love if I'm sure that *she* won't.
No, a man of mean talents and meaner fame
May in anguish adore a disdainful dame,
Go down on his knees when his suit is delayed,   35
Draw on tears and on amorous sighs for aid,
And attempt to obtain through a siege long drawn out
What at first was denied the presumptuous lout,
But the man of distinction has far too much sense
To present his love free and bear all the expense.   40
No matter how dazzling a beauty may be,
I believe that, thank God! I'm as precious as she.
And if she is destined to conquer my heart,
It appears only fair that she should do her part;
And at least, to conform to the rules of fair play,   45
She had better be ready to meet me halfway.

CLITANDRE: And you think Célimène will be glad to conform?

ACASTE: I've no reason to think she departs from the norm.

CLITANDRE: To see you so wrong I'm sincerely aggrieved.
You are blind to the truth and are badly deceived.   50

ACASTE: It is true, I'm deceived, and I'm blind, as you say.

CLITANDRE: Let me ask what has bolstered your hopes, if I may.

ACASTE: I'm deceived.

CLITANDRE: What inspires this exuberant mood?

ACASTE: I am blind.

CLITANDRE: Have you proofs of how well you have wooed?

ACASTE: As I say, I'm a fool.

CLITANDRE: What did she reveal?   55
Has she told you in secret just how she may feel?

ACASTE: She maltreats me.

CLITANDRE: Be frank to a friend true and tried.
ACASTE: I'm forever repulsed.
CLITANDRE: All joking aside:
   Let me know at once what mine you have struck.
ACASTE: I'm the desolate one, and you are in luck.   60
   Her aversion for me is indeed without measure,
   And someday I shall hang myself just for her pleasure.
CLITANDRE: Well, well. But, my friend, befall what may,
   Let us settle this matter the amiable way:
   Whoever can show certain proof on his part   65
   That he's clearly preferred in Célimène's heart,
   Let the other make way; let it be understood
   He'll remove himself from the contest for good.
ACASTE: Ah, well put! You speak with the voice of true love.
   I agree to the terms as listed above.   70
   But quiet!

SCENE 2 [CÉLIMÈNE, ACASTE, CLITANDRE]

CÉLIMÈNE: Still here?
CLITANDRE: Love forbids us to go.
CÉLIMÈNE: I think I just heard a carriage below.
   Who is it?
CLITANDRE: Who knows?

SCENE 3 [CÉLIMÈNE, ACASTE, CLITANDRE, SERVANT]

SERVANT: Arsinoé would fain
   Have a word with you.
CÉLIMÈNE: That woman again?
SERVANT: Éliante below entertains your guest.
CÉLIMÈNE: What on earth does she want? What attracted this pest?
ACASTE: She's renowned as a terrible prude, you know,   5
   And her high moral zeal . . .
CÉLIMÈNE: Yes, indeed—all for show!
   In her heart she is worldly; her greatest desire
   Is to hook some poor man, though her schemes all misfire.
   When another of numerous lovers makes light,
   She can't help turning green with sheer envious spite.   10
   That her pitiful person's ignored by the world
   Is the clue to the angry indictments she's hurled;
   And in vain with the prude's censorious speech
   Does she cover the fact she's avoided by each.
   To protect her poor person from slighting attacks   15
   She denounces as vile the appeal that she lacks;
   And yet she would welcome a lover with zest
   And has even been known to make eyes at Alceste.
   The fact that he loves me annoys her no end,
   And she feels I have stolen her predestined friend.   20
   Her jealous dislike, which she hides very ill,
   Shows in many a token of spite and ill-will;

And where I am concerned, she turns stupid with rage.
Her impertinent tricks would fill many a page,
And . . .   25

SCENE 4 [ARSINOÉ, CÉLIMÈNE, CLITANDRE, ACASTE]

CÉLIMÈNE: How nice you could come! If only you knew
    How warmly I often have thought of you.
ARSINOÉ : I've come over to tell you some things you should hear.
CÉLIMÈNE: What a genuine pleasure to see you appear!

[CLITANDRE *and* ACASTE *walk off, laughing.*]

SCENE 5 [ARSINOÉ, CÉLIMÈNE]

ARSINOÉ : Their leaving just now is most opportune.
CÉLIMÈNE: Please sit down.
ARSINOÉ :   No thanks, I'll be going quite soon.
    Dear Madam, our friendship, if earnest and great,
    Must show in the things that carry most weight.
    And because no need could be more acute   5
    Than to safeguard one's honor and good repute,
    I shall mention your own reputation to you
    As a service I feel as a friend is your due;
    For among some very fine people last night
    Your person by chance did some comment incite.   10
    And your conduct, dear Madam—the splash that you make—
    Was regrettably thought to be quite a mistake.
    The crowd that seems never for long to depart,
    Your constant flirtations, the rumors they start—
    All these found their critics, by virtue inspired,   15
    And rather more strict than I could have desired.
    As you well can imagine, I felt dismayed
    And did all that I could to come to your aid.
    I protested that all your intentions were pure,
    That we all of your goodness of heart could be sure;   20
    Even so, you admit, there are things in our lives
    That are hard to excuse, though one earnestly strives;
    And I found myself forced to make the concession
    That your conduct creates a—dubious impression.
    It appears to all in unfortunate light,   25
    And one hears the unpleasantest stories recite;
    And if ever your sober judgment prevails
    You will give less occasion to bearers of tales.
    I am sure there is nothing unethical—No!
    May heaven protect me from wronging you so!   30
    But it's easy to think of one's neighbor as vicious;
    Private virtue is wasted when all are suspicious.
    Dear Madam, I know you're too just and too kind

view this advice with an equable mind,
ribe it to aught but the fervor and zeal
iend whose devotion is such as I feel.
Though just censure may irk an ungrateful mind,	85
ot quite expect a reply of this kind.
learly, dear friend, in your bitter tirade,
been hurt to the quick by the points I just made.
The reverse is the truth, dear Madam, the fact is
d make these exchanges a permanent practice.	90
ld thus destroy and make utterly perish
lusions concerning ourselves that we cherish.
were of my mind, with commendable zeal
ld loyally aim to unmask and reveal,
ntiously gather and store for review	95
things we might hear, you of me, I of you.
Ah, dear friend! Who would censure *your* innocent life?
e that faults and defects are rife.
Praise and blame are capricious like sunshine and rain,
r age helps decide what we like and disdain.	100
a season in life for love and flirtations
ther that's fitted for prudish orations.
ectly wise to subscribe to the latter
last one's mirror refuses to flatter.
e puts a good front on defeat. I don't claim	105
he unpleasant day I won't do just the same.
ourse, time runs out; but right now I have plenty—
oon to turn prude for a woman of twenty.
ut indeed, my dear friend, how you harp on your age!
in one's birthday would hardly seem sage.	110
dam, what little we differ in years
ly seem reason for joy or for tears;
I do not see why you go to such length
home an attack so deficient in strength.
d I, for my part, do not see why you aim	115
r you go to destroy my good name.
t you work off your frustrations on *me?*
o it if *you* make men falter and flee?
hance to kindle in men ardent passion,
gued with attentions of every fashion,	120
vals you wish should be lavished elsewhere—
earth can I do to assure you your share?
ggle, all women are comrades-in-arms;
ng to thwart the effect of your charms.
w sad if you think that one longs night and day	125
orous crowd you so proudly display!
le weren't able to judge with great ease
ice one can readily garner all these.
claim that the men who pursue you in shoals
d who admire our beautiful souls?	130

Not to view this advice with an equable mir
To ascribe it to aught but the diligent zeal
Of a friend whose devotion is such as I feel
CÉLIMÈNE: My dear Madam, I'm heartily grateful
And so far from my taking your warning an
I shall hasten to show my sincere appreciat
And in turn shall discuss with you *your* rep
Since you show your devotion by saving e
Of the rumors about me you chance to ha
Let me follow your thoughtful example. I,
Hear such tales—I'll repeat what they say
A few days ago, for a visit, I went
To a house that the very best people freq
They discussed what manner of life is the
And your name, as it happened, was dro
But none of those present, alas! seemed t
Of your noisy crusades the inherent appe
The grave airs you put on, and the tedio
In which of our low moral tone you con
The finicky taste by which you are spur
To find vaguely suggestive an innocent
Your complacent belief that *you* pass ea
And those looks full of pity you cast on
Your continual lectures, the faults that y
In what's harmless and pure to the well
Dear Madam, all these, if I may be so c
Were censured more strictly than justice
What's the point (so they said) of that
That's belied by the deeds we recall to
What's the point of appearing in churc
When she's beating her maids and der
By her pious harangues she wears me
But she's coated with rouge and is ea
She's the fig-leaf's best friend, and wil
To ban nudes from the arts (though s
As you well can imagine, I came to y
And attacked the malicious charges th
But they all with one voice rejected r
And concluded by saying how good
If you'd leave the concerns of your r
And invest the time saved in mindin
One should contemplate well one's
Before one would rashly condemn a
The full weight of a blameless life is
So that men can by words *and* by d
And in fact, it is wisest to leave insp
To the men who have made it their
My dear friend, I'm convinced you'

Not to
To asc
Of a fi
ARSINOÉ :
I did
I see c
You've
CÉLIMÈNE:
I woul
We co
The de
If you
We wo
Consci
All the
ARSINOÉ :
It's in
CÉLIMÈNE:
And ou
There's
And an
It is per
When a
Thus on
That sor
In due
It's too s
ARSINOÉ : B
To exult
Dear Ma
Can har
And I st
To drive
CÉLIMÈNE: A
Whereve
Why mus
Can I hel
And if *I*
If I'm pla
With avo
What on
In this str
I do noth
ARSINOÉ : Ho
For the ar
As if peop
At what p
Would yo
Are the ki

That they burn with the fire of honest devotion?
That the fame of your virtues explains this commotion?
Few are quite *that* naïve; and the world, though reputed
To nod, is not blind; there are women well suited
To kindle the flame of true love in men's minds   135
Who yet are not followed by males of all kinds.
From all this it is easy to draw the conclusion:
Platonic devotion remains an illusion;
And it's certain it's not our beautiful eyes
That these lovers will yearn for with amorous sighs.   140
Is this then the glory with which you're inflated?
Your triumphs indeed seem much overrated.
To vaunt your attractions you're too much inclined—
You've no cause to look down on the rest of mankind.
If one envied the conquests that fill you with pride   145
One would easily top your success if one tried
And attract, with more tangible signs of esteem,
As many pursuers as you, it would seem.
CÉLIMÈNE: I hope you will try, and report to me then
The results of this secret of how to please men.   150
And without . . .
ARSINOÉ: Let's break off this fruitless debate.
It might strain both our tempers until it's too late.
I'd have left your apartments some minutes ago
If my carriage had only arrived below.
CÉLIMÈNE: As long as you wish please feel free to remain;   155
Let no hurry disturb the poise you maintain.
Not to tire you with more than politeness demands
I shall leave you, I hope, in congenial hands.
And our friend here, whom chance has just caused to come by,
Will, I'm sure, entertain you much better than I.   160

SCENE 6 [ALCESTE, CÉLIMÈNE, ARSINOÉ]

CÉLIMÈNE: Alceste, I must finish a letter today
That it would be most awkward and rude to delay.
Please stay with our friend. My regrets most sincere
To you, my dear Madam, for leaving you here.

SCENE 7 [ALCESTE, ARSINOÉ]

ARSINOÉ: By her wish, as you see, we'll converse while I wait,
Dearest friend, for my carriage to come to the gate.
I admit that of all the kindness she shows
I'm most charmed by the pleasure this meeting bestows.
How true that a man of moral perfection   5
Can command of us all both respect and affection!
Your merit, I'm sure, has some secret charm
That is ever at work to persuade and disarm.
I am sure if at court one were of my mind,

To your virtue one would be a little less blind.   10
You have cause for complaint; and I note with dismay
How seldom due praise or reward comes your way.

ALCESTE: Comes *my* way, dear Madam? What claim could I enter?
What service to country has made me the center
Of public regard? And in what respect   15
Could I justly complain at court of neglect?

ARSINOÉ: A man that is worthy of royal reward
Need not to such eminent heights have soared;
If occasion is wanting, with virtue imbued,
He shows a potential rectitude.   20
Your merit . . .

ALCESTE: But please, leave my merit aside;
For the court wouldn't know if I cheated and lied.
What a tedious job, what a task to inherit,
To unearth one's subjects' potential merit!   25

ARSINOÉ: True merit, believe me, unearths itself;
And the world won't let yours gather dust on the shelf.
In circles the most select, to be frank,
I have heard you commended by people of rank.

ALCESTE: Ah, Madam, today one commends left and right
And praises whatever appears to one's sight.   30
When the merit of all is extolled beyond measure.
To be recognized ceases to cause one much pleasure.
My grocer was knighted, and soon, I would guess,
My chambermaid's name will appear in the press.

ARSINOÉ: Yet I wish that to give to your talents free scope   35
You would fix on some post of distinction your hope.
Though little you now seem to covet the role,
There are means of smoothing your way to this goal.
I've connections I'd use in promoting your case
Who could have you advanced at the most rapid pace.   40

ALCESTE: And then, dear Madam, what am I to do?
How little I'm suited for public view!
When first I was born, though otherwise whole,
One thing that I lacked was a courtier's soul.
I don't have whatever it takes to succeed   45
In a cold-blooded world of ambition and greed.
Being frank to a fault is a weakness of mine;
For to polish the apple I firmly decline.
And whoever is weak in this versatile art
Cannot play in this world a conspicuous part.   50
Thus removed from the public's eye, it is true,
He lacks titles and pensions him otherwise due;
But the loss of these benefits leaves me quite cool
If it saves me the trouble of playing the fool:
I escape disappointments that sour one's kindness   55
And the tedium of chatter that's empty and mindless,

The compulsion to flatter society belles
Or hear verses against which my stomach rebels.
ARSINOÉ: I see you're determined. Before I depart,
   Let me touch one more subject that's close to my heart.   60
   How my feelings take part in your troubled affection—
   If your love could but take a propitious direction!
   You deserve to fare better by far than you do,
   And the person you love is unworthy of you.
ALCESTE: But whatever kind office to me you intend,   65
   You recall that the person you mean is your friend?
ARSINOÉ: Yes, I do. But my conscience has suffered too long
   To pass over in silence such palpable wrong.
   To see you thus slighted I'm hurt and dismayed,
   And I feel you should know that your love is betrayed.   70
ALCESTE: Your remarks show a very considerate trend,
   And such news obliges a lover no end.
ARSINOÉ: Be she three times my friend, she is, I repeat,
   Unworthy to have a true man at her feet;
   And she has only lukewarm affection for you.   75
ALCESTE: It could be—since our hearts are hidden from view;
   But your role, I must say, would have been much more kind
   Not to plant such a thought in a lover's mind.
ARSINOÉ: If you willingly let yourself be deluded,
   Your friends must be still—I regret I intruded.   80
ALCESTE: On this subject, dear Madam, it must be plain
   It's one's doubts that cause one the greatest pain;
   And therefore a friend should remain aloof
   Until he can furnish convincing proof.
ARSINOÉ: Very well! Fair enough. On this point you shall find   85
   The evidence ample and clearly defined.
   I want you to see there is cause for alarm.
   If you will be so kind as to give me your arm
   I'll be glad to produce the proof you desire
   Of the faithless heart of the one you admire—   90
   And to offer instead, if thus you should choose
   What could amply console you for what you will lose.

Act Four

SCENE 1 [ÉLIANTE, PHILINTE]

PHILINTE: Was ever a soul so hardened in virtue
   Or retraction so strained that just watching it hurt you?
   No matter what argument we would invent
   In his righteous disdain we made hardly a dent;
   And never a quarrel so weird in its kind   5
   Arose to disturb the juridical mind.
   "No, Your Honor," he said, "I am glad to retract

Whatever you wish, except obvious fact.
What was my offense? And what is his complaint?
Is one's honor at stake if one's wit is but faint?   10
My opinion hurts neither his name nor his purse:
One can live like a saint and write damnable verse.
It is not his good name that is touched, I am sure:
I am glad to pronounce his motives most pure
And proclaim his merit to all who would know it;   15
He is noble of soul—but a pitiful poet.
I will praise, if you wish, his large house and expenses,
The way he rides horses and dances and fences;
But to praise his verse I politely refuse
And maintain that a person unkissed by the muse   20
Should restrain his impulse to rhyme and compose
To escape the just censure of friends and of foes."
At last, the extreme of sweetness and light
To which he would bend his pursuit of the right
Was to say in a tone of but ill-feigned ease,   25
"Dear Sir, I regret I am hard to please.
For your sake, I could wish, from the depth of my heart,
To have found you more skilled in the poet's art."
And with this much concession and saving of face
One there made them shake hands and dismissed the case.   30
ÉLIANTE: It is true that his manner departs from the norm;
    Yet I cherish his failure to bend and conform.
    That frankness and candor he prizes so much
    Has a noble and truly heroic touch.
    In our time, these his virtues are far too rare;   35
    I would wish to encounter them everywhere.
PHILINTE: The more that I know him, the more above all
    I'm surprised by the passion that holds him in thrall.
    When a man is endowed with his frame of mind,
    I don't see how his heart could to love have inclined;   40
    And I grasp even less how your cousin became
    The person who kindled this amorous flame.
ÉLIANTE: This merely confirms that love doesn't wait
    To select for itself a compatible mate;
    And what love to congenial souls is imputed   45
    In this instance at least is amply refuted.
PHILINTE: Is he loved in return, from what you can see?
ÉLIANTE: To judge in this case is not easy for me.
    How decide if she'll render his passion in kind?
    In these matters it's rare that she knows her own mind.   50
    She will love and not know it unless she is told,
    Or else *think* she's in love when her heart is quite cold.
PHILINTE: Our friend with this cousin of yours, I believe,
    Will find ample occasion to suffer and grieve.
    If I were in his place—to bare you my soul—   55
    I should fasten my eyes on a different goal,

And with juster discernment I should take my clue
To respond to the kindness long proffered by you.
ÉLIANTE: On this point, I won't speak with a feigned modest air:
    Above all in this matter, I want to be fair.   60
    In no way would I meddle to dampen his zeal,
    But rather I share in all he must feel.
    As far as the outcome depends on my view,
    To unite them, I gladly do all I can do.
    However, if things turn from bad to still worse   65
    And his love should encounter a serious reverse,
    If another must serve to respond to his passion,
    I would hardly object in too vigorous fashion.
    The refusal that severed his previous ties
    Would not lower the man at all in my eyes.   70
PHILINTE: In my turn, I, dear Madam, from meddling desist
    To let you be patient and kind as you list.
    He himself, if he wishes it, may let you hear
    What I have on this point taken care to make clear.
    But if at long last, through their being united,   75
    Your love should be caused to remain unrequited,
    For that favor extreme I should fervently pray
    That your heart now bestows in such one-sided way.
ÉLIANTE: You are speaking in jest.
PHILINTE: I'm in earnest as never.
    At this juncture I have no desire to be clever.   80
    I am ready to offer myself to you whole,
    And I yearn for that moment with all of my soul.

SCENE 2 [ALCESTE, ÉLIANTE, PHILINTE]

ALCESTE: Ah, Madam, I hurry to you to obtain
    Redress for an evil I cannot sustain.
ÉLIANTE: What has happened? What could have excited you so?
ALCESTE: I fear I have suffered a fatal blow.
    I'd be less overwhelmed, I assure you, dear friend,   5
    If in chaos all nature had come to its end.
    All is over . . . .My love . . . .It's too awful to say.
ÉLIANTE: But please steady yourself and be calm, I pray.
ALCESTE: Just heavens! Why send us such odious vice
    In a package that seems all sugar and spice?   10
ÉLIANTE: But, dear Sir, what event . . .
ALCESTE: All is lost . . . beyond aid.
    I am hurt unto death—I am lost and betrayed!
    Célimène . . . (could such terrible news be believed?)
    Célimène is unfaithful, and I am deceived.
ÉLIANTE: And you have just support for this grave supposition?   15
PHILINTE: Perhaps this is merely a passing suspicion;
    And your jealous temper at times makes you see . . .

ALCESTE: Please be silent; you've nothing to do with me.
  [*to* ÉLIANTE] The written proof of her treacherous spite
  Is right here in my pocket in black and white.   20
  Yes, a letter she wrote to Oronte—of all men—
  Shows my shame and her guilt in the strokes of her pen.
  Oronte—whom I thought she for sure would despise,
  Who most harmless a rival appeared to my eyes!
PHILINTE: At first glance by a letter we may be misled;   25
  It may seem less conclusive when later reread.
ALCESTE: Please withhold the advice to which you are prone
  And expend your concern on affairs of your own.
ÉLIANTE: But restrain your emotions; be calm, I ask . . .
ALCESTE: It is you who will have to perform this task;   30
  It's to you that I turn in this hour of smart
  To help me set free a suffering heart.
  Help punish your faithless, ungrateful relation,
  Who rewards with betrayal a man's dedication.
  Help avenge what makes weep the angels above.   35
ÉLIANTE: Avenge? But how?
ALCESTE: By accepting my love.
  Accept the heart that I snatch from her hand,
  And avenge thus an act that bears treason's brand.
  I shall punish her by the sincere devotion,
  The passionate ardor, the urgent emotion,   40
  The respectful attention, and dutiful care
  Which will hallow the love that for you I declare.
ÉLIANTE: I share, I am sure, in the pain that you feel
  And disdain not at all the love you reveal;
  But perhaps on reflection the evil might shrink   45
  And your need for revenge be less clear than you think.
  When one's injured by someone so full of attractions,
  Quite often one's plans are not followed by actions;
  One may threaten and show all the anger you feel,
  Yet the verdict of guilt is reversed on appeal.   50
  Indignation will pass like a shower in May—
  And such quarrels of lovers one sees every day.
ALCESTE: No, Madam. No, no. Her offense is too rank.
  There's no prospect of peace; I must tell her point-blank.
  To abandon the course that I take would be sin;   55
  I would hate myself now if I were to give in.
  Here she is. My just anger revives at her sight.
  I shall strongly denounce her corruption and spite,
  Confound and destroy her, and offer you then
  A heart disengaged from this temptress of men.   60

SCENE 3 [CÉLIMÈNE, ALCESTE]

ALCESTE [*aside*]: O heavens! How can I control my rage?

CÉLIMÈNE: O my dear! What is this performance you stage?
    What disaster explains these mournful sighs?
    And what causes this somber look in your eyes?
ALCESTE: The lowest betrayal a soul can embrace—   5
    Your behavior the most disloyal and base;
    An evil more rank than could ever produce
    A malicious fiend or an angry Zeus.
CÉLIMÈNE: As ever, my tender and loving Alceste.
ALCESTE: Do not laugh. This is hardly the time for jest.   10
    To blush and to weep you have every reason;
    I have certain proofs of your horrible treason.
    Here's the fruit of forebodings my mind would have curbed;
    For it wasn't in vain that my heart was disturbed.
    My frequent suspicions, at which you had snorted,   15
    Have at last shown themselves to be amply supported;
    For in spite of your skill and deceitful charm
    I could read in my stars I had cause for alarm.
    But please, don't assume I'll allow this crime
    To go unrevenged and be mellowed by time.   20
    I know well that affection cannot be constrained,
    That as nature commands one is loved or disdained,
    That one does not invade someone's heart by force,
    That each soul in love must pursue its own course.
    And thus I'd have judged it but fair enough   25
    If I had at your hands had an open rebuff.
    If at first you'd extinguished my passionate flame,
    I would only have had my own fate to blame.
    But to nourish that flame with deceitful smile
    Is most treacherous and perfidious guile.   30
    No punishment ever could be too severe;
    I shall shrink from nothing, I make it quite clear.
    Be warned, and prepare for the worst, if you're sage—
    For I'm not myself; I'm distilled into rage.
    The mortal blow that has pierced my defenses   35
    Has made reason surrender its rule of my senses.
    I abandon myself to my wrath; I warn all:
    I declare I won't answer for what may befall.
CÉLIMÈNE: To what cause should this furious tirade be assigned?
    At long last, if you please, are you out of your mind?   40
ALCESTE: I was out of my mind when I suffered your face
    To entice me to court contempt and disgrace,
    When I thought that the line of your waist and your bust
    Was sufficient as proof of a heart I could trust.
CÉLIMÈNE: And what is this treason of which you complain?   45
ALCESTE: Ah, how well you dissemble, how glibly you feign!
    But to counter your wiles I am fully prepared.
    Please look at this note: here your baseness is bared.
    Behold here a proof that you cannot refute;
    Face to face with this witness you'll have to stand mute.   50

CÉLIMÈNE: Is this then the object you find so exciting?
ALCESTE: Can you bear without blushing to look at your writing?
CÉLIMÈNE: And what is there for me to blush about?
ALCESTE: Will you be then so bold as to brazen it out,
    To disown it because it's an unsigned note?   55
CÉLIMÈNE: But why should I disown a letter I wrote?
ALCESTE: And yet you can see it without any shame
    For the crime against me that its phrases proclaim?
CÉLIMÈNE: It must be admitted: You're one of a kind.
ALCESTE: You defy then a proof to convince the most blind?   60
    The regard for Oronte that you show as you write
    Should not make me indignant nor you contrite?
CÉLIMÈNE: Oronte! And who says it's to him it was sent?
ALCESTE: The people I had it from knew where it went.
    But suppose it was meant for another—What then?   65
    Should I pardon the faults revealed by your pen?
    In what way would this fact serve to lessen your shame?
CÉLIMÈNE: But suppose the address was a *woman's* name—
    Then why should you be hurt, and where is my crime?
ALCESTE: Ah, how clever! You thought of this ruse just in time!   70
    I admit, this gambit I did not expect,
    And you see me at once convinced and checked.
    Do you mean to rely on deception so crude?
    Do you think me so easy to gull and delude?
    Let us see in what way, by what means you would try   75
    To maintain and support such a palpable lie,
    And how, for a female recipient, you fashion
    The words of a note so torrid with passion.
    Now twist, if you please to conform to your aims
    What I'm going to read . . .
CÉLIMÈNE: I refuse to play games.   80
    I am tired of your ludicrous bullying ways
    And the arrogant temper your conduct displays.
ALCESTE: Let us not get excited—please look at this note
    And explain then the phrases I'm going to quote.
CÉLIMÈNE: No, thanks. And I'm sure that in any event   85
    I could hardly care less what you think that it meant.
ALCESTE: But please, convince me, to put me to rest,
    How this note could have been to a woman addressed.
CÉLIMÈNE: It was meant for Oronte—You were perfectly right.
    I receive his attentions with joy and delight;   90
    His talk I admire and his smile I imbibe
    And confess to whatever crimes you describe.
    Now do as you please, ignore all restraints,
    Just stop setting my teeth on edge with complaints!
ALCESTE [*aside*]: O God! Was more cruel a creature created?   95
    Was ever a heart so abused and berated?
    By righteous anger my fury is fed;
    I come to complain, and am nagged instead!

Instead of abating my sorrows and fears,
She confirms all my charges, and does so with sneers!   100
Yet my heart is so weak I endeavor in vain
To break loose from so galling and shameful a chain,
To forswear in anger all further devotion
To the unworthy object of futile emotion.
[*to* CÉLIMÈNE] Perfidious woman, how always you seem   105
To employ against me my weakness extreme,
And exploit for your ends the prodigious excess
Of the fatal love that for you I profess.
Deny at least the charges I brought;
Cease pretending you give to your guilt any thought.   110
Just show that this note is free of all blame,
And I'm urged by my passion to clear your name.
Try to act the faithful lover's part
And I'll try to believe you with all my heart.
CÉLIMÈNE: Go on, you are mad in your jealous delusions.   115
And you do not deserve a lover's effusions.
I would like to find out how you could have concluded
I would stoop to deception to keep you deluded.
Why on earth, if my heart had inclined as you say,
Would I fail to admit it the very same day?   120
Does the open assurance of tender esteem
Fail to counter suspicions as vague as a dream?
When compared with such candor, what weight do they bear?
Why insult me by even admitting they're there?
Since we stretch our good will to its utmost span   125
In deciding to own our love for a man—
Since a woman's honor, that bridle to feeling,
Is opposed to admissions so frankly revealing—
Dare the lover, for whom these risks are incurred,
Contest unpunished the oracle's word?   130
He's to blame if he's not completely consoled
By what after much struggle he's finally told.
Your suspicions well merit my high indignation,
And you've lost all your title to consideration.
It is stupid of me, and simple of mind,   135
To continue to be even partially kind;
I should save my regard for a different face
And make sure your complaints have a solid base.
ALCESTE: Ah, temptress! My weakness for you is absurd.
You deceive me, no doubt, with each sugared word.   140
But no matter, I'll have to submit to my fate;
My heart is yours to love or to hate.
I shall see in the end what you really feel
And what treason or steadfastness time will reveal.
CÉLIMÈNE: I must say that your loving defies every rule.   145
ALCESTE: But compared with my ardor all passion is cool.
In my wish to make known to all its strength

You will see I have gone to unusual length,
For I'm wishing that no one would think you fair,
That you'd suffered a fate the most meager and bare,   150
That at birth you'd been placed in the poorest condition,
Deprived of your wealth, without rank or position,
So that then by my love and most generous trust
I could start to repair a fate so unjust
And rejoice and give thanks to the powers above   155
To see you owe all to the man that you love.
CÉLIMÈNE: Your good will, I must say, takes the strangest form,
And I hope I'll be spared the chance to conform. . . .
But here is your servant, in strange disguise.

SCENE 4 [CÉLIMÈNE, ALCESTE, DUBOIS]

ALCESTE: What's this masquerade? Why these rolling eyes?
    What ails you?
DUBOIS: Dear Sir . . .
ALCESTE: What's your news?
DUBOIS: I can't tell.
ALCESTE: What on earth . . .
DUBOIS: Believe me, Sir, all is not well.
ALCESTE: Why? and how?
DUBOIS: Can I talk?
ALCESTE: Yes—right now, if you please.
DUBOIS: Will nobody hear?
ALCESTE: How this fellow will tease!   5
    Speak up!
DUBOIS: Well, Sir, we must beat a retreat.
ALCESTE: What's this?
DUBOIS: It is time to be quick on our feet.
ALCESTE: But why?
DUBOIS: As I say, we will have to depart.
ALCESTE: For what cause?
DUBOIS: There's no time for goodbys; we must start.
ALCESTE: But *why*, I still ask, do you talk this way?   10
DUBOIS: Because we must pack and depart today.
ALCESTE: I shall cudgel your obstinate head, you lout,
    If you will not explain what all this is about.
DUBOIS: A person in black and gloomy of face
    Has come to present to you at your place   15
    A paper so crowded with legal "whereases"
    That to read it the devil would call for his glasses.
    It's to do with your lawsuit, that much I can tell,
    Though to read it would baffle a fiend out of hell.
ALCESTE: What has that got to do, kindly tell without stumbling,   20
    With this hurried departure of which you were mumbling?
DUBOIS: Some time later, a man—if you'll let me explain—
    Who's your guest quite often in times of less strain
    Arrived at your house in the greatest hurry,

And since you were gone, with an air of great worry   25
  He asked me (a trust loyal service can claim)
  To inform you—now wait, what *is* the man's name?
ALCESTE: Be damned to the name! What is it he said?
DUBOIS: Well, he's one of your friends—why trouble my head?
  To see urgent reason for flight he professed;   30
  You are threatened, he said, with immediate arrest.
ALCESTE: He did! He explained in detail, I should think?
DUBOIS: He did ask, it is true, for some paper and ink
  And has written a note which, I'm sure, will declare
  In all points what's behind this mysterious affair.   35
ALCESTE: Hand it over at once!
CÉLIMÈNE: What can all this mean?
ALCESTE: I don't know, but the truth shall shortly be seen.
  Will it take you all day, in the devil's name?
DUBOIS [*after taking a long time to search for the note*]: On my word, I left
  it at home when I came.
ALCESTE: I don't know what restrains me . . .
CÉLIMÈNE: Be calm, I pray,   40
  And be off to clear up what caused this affray.
ALCESTE: My fate, it appears, whatever I do
  Has vowed to prevent me from talking to you;
  But permit your suitor to thwart its spite,
  And return to you, Madam, before tonight.   45

Act Five

SCENE 1 [ALCESTE, PHILINTE]

ALCESTE: As I stated before, I am firmly resolved.
PHILINTE: But must you, whatever the hardship involved . . .
ALCESTE: However you may insist or upbraid me,
  From what I have said you shall never dissuade me.
  This our age has become iniquity's den,   5
  And I mean to retire from the commerce of men.
  My foe saw arraigned against him and his cause
  Integrity, decency, shame, and the laws;
  The strength of my case all were quick to cite;
  I was calm in the knowledge I was in the right—   10
  And yet all my hopes bear most bitter fruit:
  I've the right on my side, but I lose my suit.
  Yes, a scoundrel, with well-known unsavory past,
  Scores a triumph that leaves honest men aghast!
  His guile thwarts good faith, and, instead of resistance,   15
  In cutting my throat he gains legal assistance!
  His crafty eye, whose mere glance corrodes,
  Overturns plainest justice and time-honored codes!
  One rewards his offense by judicial decree!
  Not content yet with what he has done to me,   20

He refers to a book of most scurrilous type,
Consisting of mere pornographical tripe
That makes one regret that the laws are not tighter—
And whispers to all that I am the writer!
And Oronte his devious malice now shows   25
By spreading this slander wherever he goes!
Oronte, a man of repute and of rank
Whom I've injured by being sincere and frank,
Who comes to me, full of most urgent zeal,
To read me his verses and ask what I feel;   30
And since I respond with unblinking eye
And refuse to deceive him by telling a lie,
He repays me by stooping to slander, and so
Now my would-be friend is my bitterest foe!
And it seems that no pardon could ever be had   35
For just once pointing out that his sonnet was bad.
Are these the high aims that people pursue?
Do these acts represent the things that they do?
Here indeed good faith and a virtuous course
And justice and honor are shown in full force.   40
Too severe are the wounds that the heart here receives;
Let us leave then this den of cutthroats and thieves;
Since you men to be wolf among wolves are proud,
I shall gladly secede from your treacherous crowd.
PHILINTE: For so rash a decision you would be to blame;   45
And all evils are not so intense as you claim.
Your foe, in spreading a lie so abject,
Has yet to produce any serious effect.
His libelous charges fall back on his head;
In the end he will suffer for what he has said.   50
ALCESTE: You think so? Such slanders are greatly in vogue:
He has license to be a most unabashed rogue;
And this caper, so far from destroying his name,
Is bound to procure him still wider acclaim.
PHILINTE: At least, it remains little heed has been paid   55
To the spiteful rumor by which you're dismayed;
And in this respect you have nothing to fear.
In your lawsuit, whose issue I'm sorry to hear,
The decree of the court should be promptly appealed.
The verdict . . .
ALCESTE: No thanks. I shall readily yield.   60
The injustice here done is such obvious fact
I refuse to allow them a chance to retract.
Too clearly it shows how right is ignored,
And in future ages it shall be abhorred
As a famous milestone, a signal mark   65
Of the evils that render our times so dark.
It is true that the cost may well bleed me white,
But it is not too high if it gives me the right

To expose and denounce the injustice of man
And to hate human nature as hard as I can.   70
PHILINTE: But consider . . .
ALCESTE: Consider your efforts as wasted.
   What can sweeten the bitter defeats I have tasted?
   Can you be so brash as intend to my face
   To belittle man's vice and gloss over disgrace?
PHILINTE: Not at all. Your judgment agrees with mine.   75
   All moves through intrigue and ulterior design.
   Only schemers succeed, and it's easy to see
   That man is quite other than what he should be.
   But should their so patient iniquity then
   Make us want to retire from the haunts of men?   80
   All these human defects but give us a chance
   To develop a more philosophical stance—
   And this exercise shows us all at our best;
   For if all were with equal integrity blessed,
   And if all were as honest and just as they should,   85
   Where would be the distinction of those who are good?
   Their most notable mark is a temper that smothers
   Their chafing resentment at wrongs done by others.
   And just as a heart of virtue profound . . .
ALCESTE: How well you talk. Your speeches abound   90
   With impeccable logic and graces sublime.
   Yet, Sir, you are wasting your breath and your time,
   For my safety, my reason enjoins my retreat.
   My tongue has not learned to be smooth and discreet;
   I can't vouch for my words, since I say what I think,   95
   And the feuds I might cause make me shudder and shrink.
   I shall see Célimène, and when she arrives
   She will have to agree to my plan for our lives.
   I shall see if her passion for me is sincere;
   Her reply will at once make all doubt disappear.   100
PHILINTE: Let us go upstairs, and wait for her there.
ALCESTE: No, my soul is too restless and troubled by care.
   Please go first and leave me; and I shall remain
   Alone with the bleakness of heart that's my bane.
PHILINTE: I wish you had company less apt to chill.   105
   I shall ask Éliante to come down, if she will.

SCENE 2 [CÉLIMÈNE, ORONTE, ACASTE]

ORONTE: Yes, Madam, you'll have to decide if it's true
   That so tender a union will tie me to you.
   The assurance I want you should quickly dispense;
   For a lover is irked to be kept in suspense.
   If my passion has wakened responsive chords,   5
   Do not grudge me the pleasure the knowledge affords.
   As your proof (need for proof was never acuter)

You must cease to acknowledge Alceste as your suitor.
This tangible token of love I exact;
I insist you refuse to receive him, in fact.   10

CÉLIMÈNE: But what is the reason you suddenly flout him
After all the to-do you at first made about him?

ORONTE: I'm afraid it's not *my* turn for interrogation.
It is *you* whose behavior needs clarification.
You shall choose which one you prefer of us two;   15
And once *you* are resolved, I shall shortly be too.

ALCESTE [*emerging from his corner*]: Yes, for once he is right. You will have
to decide.
By the sentence we crave we agree to abide.
Like him, I insist you shall not stay aloof;
For my love now demands unmistakable proof.   20
This affair has moved far too slow from the start,
And right now is the time to lay bare your whole heart.

ORONTE: I am sorry with passion so inopportune
To disturb, Sir, your chance to obtain such a boon.

ALCESTE: I am sorry to share with you, jealous or not,   25
To the slightest extent, Sir, what heart she has got.

ORONTE: If your love she to mine should turn out to prefer . . .

ALCESTE: If the least in your favor her judgment should err . . .

ORONTE: I here swear to extinguish all amorous fire.

ALCESTE: I here swear to be cured from all loving desire.   30

ORONTE: Dear Madam, be frank; it is your turn to speak.

ALCESTE: Dear Madam, deliver the verdict we seek.

ORONTE: Let us know whom you choose for your love; please begin.

ALCESTE: Put an end to suspense; may the better man win.

ORONTE: Can you question with whom you long since should have sided?   35

ALCESTE: Can it be that you falter? You seem undecided!

CÉLIMÈNE: My word! How unwelcome the choice you exact,
And how little you show of good sense or of tact!
I am sure of my stand on the question you raise,
And it's not that my heart is lost in a maze.   40
The case is too clear to perplex or confuse,
It's no problem for me to know how to choose.
However, it's terribly awkward, I find,
To announce to you two a choice of this kind.
Whenever we have something painful to broach,   45
We should surely employ a more subtle approach.
There are less drastic methods of communication
Than to shout from the rooftops the heart's inclination.
In short, there are pleasanter means to explain
To a dutiful lover he's burning in vain.   50

ORONTE: Not at all. For frankness is just what we need.
At this point, we should find it most welcome.

ALCESTE: Agreed.
It's exactly this drastic effect I desire;
Of your tactful maneuvers I easily tire.

To please all mankind is your driving ambition;   55
But let's have no more trifling—pronounce your decision.
You must openly state and reveal your affection,
Or I'll see in your silence a tacit rejection.
I would know how to take your refusal to speak
And would thus see confirmed premonitions most bleak.   60
ORONTE: I'm sincerely obliged to your firmness, dear Sir;
And in what you have said I most gladly concur.

SCENE 3 [ÉLIANTE, PHILINTE, CÉLIMÈNE, ORONTE, ALCESTE]

CÉLIMÈNE: Dear cousin, I'm treated extremely ungently
By two men who've conspired to tease and torment me.
In turn, each insists at the top of his voice
That at once to them both I should publish my choice,
That I ask one of them, in effect, to his face   5
His affection for me to subdue and erase.
Please confess: Is it thus that such things should be done?
ÉLIANTE: To provide such advice I am hardly the one.
You have chosen your arbiter rashly, I fear;
I prefer that one's words should be candid and clear.   10
ORONTE: No avenue, Madam, remains for retreat.
ALCESTE: Your evasions, dear Madam, are doomed to defeat.
ORONTE: You must open your heart; you must cast the dice.
ALCESTE: And if not, your silence alone will suffice.
ORONTE: But a single word will unravel the knot.   15
ALCESTE: By your failure to speak I shall know my lot.

SCENE 4 [ARSINOÉ, CÉLIMÈNE, ÉLIANTE, ALCESTE, PHILINTE, ACASTE, CLITANDRE, ORONTE]

ACASTE [*to* CÉLIMÈNE]: We have come here because we both felt we should mention
A little affair that deserves your attention.
CLITANDRE [*to* ORONTE *and* ALCESTE]: It is fortunate that we encounter you here,
For you both are involved, as will shortly appear.
ARSINOÉ [*to* CÉLIMÈNE]: To see me, dear friend, your surprise may be keen,   5
But these gentlemen asked me to witness this scene.
They both came to my house to voice their complaints
Of a trait that would weary the patience of saints.
Your esteemed elevation of soul is a pledge
You can *not* have committed the crime they allege.   10
On their proofs I bestowed the most searching attention,
And, my friendship forgetting our little—dissension,
I accompanied them in the hope, by and large,
To see you deny such a slanderous charge.

ACASTE: Yes, Madam, let's see with an open mind,   15
   What you say to these comments by you undersigned.
   To Clitandre, from you, this letter was sent.
CLITANDRE: And this sweet little note for Acaste was meant.
ACASTE [*to* ORONTE *and* ALCESTE]: You will find that the hand is familiar, I
   trust;
   For, polite as she is, I am sure that she must   20
   On many occasions have written to you.
   But to read her own words—it's no more than her due:
   "It is ironical that you should condemn my ways and allege that I
   never enjoy myself as much as when you are away. You are most un-
   just; and if you don't appear shortly to demand my pardon, I may de-   25
   cide never to forgive you for your offense. Hulking Tom the Count . . ."
   He ought to be here.
   "Hulking Tom the Count, who heads your list of undesirable rivals, is
   not even in the running; and since I have seen him spend three quarters of an hour spitting into a puddle in order to make circles in the   30
   water, he has suffered somewhat in my esteem. As for our little marquis . . ."
   That's me, I'm afraid.
   "As for our little marquis, who insists on holding my hand for hours
   on end, he is the most diminutive person I ever saw, and his appear-   35
   ance owes as much to his tailor as to his creator. As for my morose
   friend . . ."
[*to* ALCESTE] Your turn, Sir.
   "As for my morose friend, I am at times amused by his abrupt and uncouth behavior, but as a rule he bores me to distraction. As for the   40
   maker of sonnets . . ."
[*to* ORONTE] You have not been overlooked.
   "As for the maker of sonnets, who trembles with the urge to create and
   defies humankind to call him author, it is asking too much of me to
   make me listen to what he is saying; and I find his prose as boring as   45
   his verse. Please admit the thought into your head that I don't always
   enjoy myself as much as you think, that I miss you—more than I care
   to admit—at the parties to which I am dragged, and that the true sea-
   soning of life's enjoyments is the presence of those one loves."
CLITANDRE: And here is a relevant excerpt from the other: 50
   "Your Clitandre, who seems to annoy you by his saccharine allusions,
   would be the last man on earth to attract my regard. He is badly mis-
   taken to hope for my love—just as you are badly mistaken to *lack*
   hope. To come closer to the truth, you two should trade expectations.
   Come to see me as often as you can, to help me alleviate the affliction   55
   of his continual presence."
   Revealing bequests of a notable mind—
   And a label that fits would be easy to find.
   Enough. We are leaving. Wherever you go
   We shall publish the traits that these documents show.   60
ACASTE: I have plenty to tell you, and if I refrain
   It's because I must think you beneath my disdain.

And I'll show you that people as little as I
Can find solace in worthiest hearts, if they try.

SCENE 5 [CÉLIMÈNE, ÉLIANTE, ARSINOÉ, ALCESTE, ORONTE, PHILINTE]

ORONTE: So this is how you use your fangs on your betters,
　　After all the sweet phrases you put in *my* letters!
　　And your heart, which so coyly pretended to yearn,
　　To all the male sex is promised in turn!
　　I have acted the fool, but I'm tired of the role;　　　　　　5
　　You have done me a favor in baring your soul.
　　I retrieve here the heart you so lightly regard,
　　And I'm amply revenged now that thence you are barred.
　　[*to* ALCESTE] I shall cease, Sir, to stand in the way of your passion;
　　I am sure she'll respond in most ladylike fashion.　　　　　10

SCENE 6 [CÉLIMÈNE, ÉLIANTE, ARSINOÉ, ALCESTE, PHILINTE]

ARSINOÉ [*to* CÉLIMÈNE]: Without doubt, your behavior is vicious and low;
　　Indignation compels me to label it so.
　　Was ever like course by a woman pursued?
　　I say nothing of others to whom you were rude.
　　[*points to* ALCESTE] But this man, who aspired to make you his wife,　　5
　　A true pillar of honor and upright life,
　　Who worshipped you with an idolatrous zeal,
　　Must he bear . . .
ALCESTE:　　　　　　But excuse me, dear Madam, I feel
　　I myself should handle my own affairs.
　　Why thus charge yourself with superfluous cares?　　　　10
　　Though so warmly you are to my side inclined,
　　I'll, alas! be unable to repay you in kind.
　　It's not *you* I shall call on with passionate voice
　　If I look for redress in a different choice.
ARSINOÉ : Do you think I am yearning for such a match?　　　15
　　You must feel, Sir, you are a most precious catch.
　　How inflated your spirit must be, and how vain,
　　If such are the thoughts that you entertain!
　　What our friend here leaves over is hardly a prize
　　Of a kind to be yearned for with passionate sighs.　　　　20
　　Please be undeceived, and revise your pretensions.
　　On a woman like me you would waste your attentions.
　　Sigh for *her*, as before, till your love is requited;
　　I can't wait to behold you content and united.

SCENE 7 [CÉLIMÈNE, ÉLIANTE, ALCESTE, PHILINTE]

ALCESTE [*to* CÉLIMÈNE]: I've been silent, you see, despite what occurred.
　　I have calmly stood by until all have been heard.
　　Have I curbed my temper enough then today?
　　May I now . . .

CÉLIMÈNE: . . . I agree with all you can say.
  You are quite in your rights to heap scorn on my action;   5
  I shall patiently bear all blame and detraction.
  I've done wrong, I admit it. Contrition and shame
  Would make my excuses seem vapid and lame.
  I have scorned the anger the others have shown;
  But my crime toward you I am ready to own.   10
  I have shown all the traits that you justly despise,
  And I know just how guilty I seem in your eyes.
  In your charge of betrayal all proofs bear you out;
  And you have every reason to hate me, no doubt.
  Go ahead, vent your ire.
ALCESTE: I wish that I could!   15
  I am forced by my love to neglect my own good.
  Though my reason decided to hate and detest,
  Would my heart be prepared to obey its request?
  [to ÉLIANTE *and* PHILINTE] Here you see what an unworthy passion can do.
  You have witnessed what weakness has made me go through,   20
  But the terrible truth is, you haven't seen all:
  You shall watch me play still more abjectly her thrall.
  We're too rashly called sage—that my fate will illumine;
  The austerest of us are at heart all too human.
  [*to* CÉLIMÈNE] Yes, then; I'm prepared to forgive you; and hence   25
  I shall try to excuse and forget your offense;
  I shall call it a weakness to which your young mind
  By corrupting examples was led and inclined—
  Provided you give your wholehearted consent
  To the break with mankind upon which I am bent   30
  And determine to follow me to the retreat
  Where I've sworn I shall live in seclusion complete.
  This heroic decision no doubt in all eyes
  Soon will clear you of spite and malicious lies;
  And thus cleared of a scandal that causes me pain   35
  You'll be worthy again of a love without strain.
CÉLIMÈNE: To renounce the world at my age! Must your wife
  Be buried alive far from civilized life?
ALCESTE: If your love finds its longed-for object in mine,
  Why on earth should you ever for others repine?   40
  Can't we find in each other contentment in plenty?
CÉLIMÈNE: Yes, but solitude frightens a woman of twenty.
  I don't feel I can marshal the grandeur of soul
  That would make me resolve to pursue such a goal.
  If a love sealed in marriage can make you content,   45
  I could muster the courage to give my consent;
  And our union will . . .
ALCESTE: No! You are all I detest.
  This refusal alone is far worse than the rest.
  In effect, since you will not, throughout wedded life,
  Let your husband be all (as *I* would my wife),   50

I here spurn and reject you. This offer you scorn
At long last makes me break the chains I have worn.

SCENE 8 [ÉLIANTE, ALCESTE, PHILINTE]

ALCESTE [*to* ÉLIANTE]:
Your virtues set off your external graces;
You've got, Madam, that candor that nothing replaces.
You have long inspired admiration extreme;
But allow me to hold you thus still in esteem
And consent that my heart, bruised by scorn and defiance,   5
Should no more court the honor of closer alliance.
Too unworthy I feel; and my reason suspects
As a lover I suffer from innate defects.
Too, the courtship you merit should not be a sequel
To the wooing of one who's in no way your equal.   10
In effect . . .
ÉLIANTE: Please do what your feelings command,
Since I'm not at a loss where to grant my hand;
And here is your friend, who in case of need,
To accept such an offer has kindly agreed.
PHILINTE: Ah! That honor, dear Madam, is all that I sigh for,   15
And a prize I am eager to live and to die for.
ALCESTE: May you both find the bliss that will banish dejection
And forever preserve an untarnished affection!
For myself—deeply wronged, maligned, and betrayed—
I shall leave the abyss where all vices parade;   20
I shall search for a place remote from the crowd
Where a life full of honor is still allowed.
PHILINTE: Let us try, dear Madam, let's do all we can
To dissuade from such steps this remarkable man.

The Receptive Reader

1. Do you find yourself taking sides between Alceste and Philinte? What are the most telling points either makes? (What are especially striking epigrammatic couplets?) Is there something to be said on both sides?

2. What makes Alceste's run-in with the would-be poet an example of delightful comedy? Can you see the difference between Oronte's sonnet and Alceste's folk song? Do you think Alceste is absolutely right—or at least in part wrong-headed? Where does Philinte stand in this exchange?

3. Alceste criticizes Célimène's delight in malicious gossip. Compare and contrast Alceste's satirical jabs at Philinte and Oronte with Célimène's attack on Arsinoé and with Célimène's satirical portraits. Are the ways the two use satire similar or basically different? Is Philinte right in saying that the people satirized by Célimène would fare worse if judged by Alceste?

4. In plays modeled on those of Molière, the hypocritical prude became a **stock character**. What makes Arsinoé a good example of the type? Is Célimène's treatment of Arsinoé cruel or malicious?

5. How would you describe Alceste's relationship with Célimène? Is he infatuated? condescending? judgmental? Is Célimène serious about Alceste? Does Alceste's love for Célimène make you question his judgment on the major issues of the play?

6. Molière often uses the comic device of "the worm turns"—a character at first abused or ridiculed gets a chance to strike back. How do the minor characters such as Oronte, Acaste, and Clitandre fit this pattern?

7. Critics have pointed out that the ending may disappoint audiences used to the traditional *happy ending* of comedy. Were you surprised or disappointed? What role does the final exposure of Célimène have in the play? Does it vindicate her archenemy, Arsinoé? How does Alceste react to it—does he seem to be acting in character?

8. What has been settled by the end of the play? Does the play as a whole suggest an answer to the question it raises? How would you formulate the play's unifying *theme?*

9. Molière wrote at the beginning of the Age of Reason, when common sense was invoked as the guide to the good life. In the tradition of the **comedy of manners** that he initiated, a balanced and commonsensical character often serves as the voice of reason. Who qualifies for this role in this play, and why? Does Philinte? Does Éliante?

10. It has been said that in this play Molière reaches the limits of comedy: Because of its serious overtones, the play as a whole becomes too dark or somber, verging toward the end on *tragedy*. Do you agree with this view? Why or why not?

11. Many observers have commented on the deterioration of public manners in America, with loutishness and callousness becoming the order of the day. In this respect, do Molière's characters live on a different planet? Or does the play have something relevant to say to those concerned about public manners today?

The Personal Response

Which of the traits mirrored in this play do you relate to most strongly or understand best? a gusto for malicious gossip? an inclination to brutal honesty? the tendency to compromise? jealousy of more popular or more successful rivals? an author's or artist's vanity? Show the connection between your own personality and the treatment of your chosen trait in the play.

The Creative Dimension

At the end of the play, Philinte asks Éliante to help him talk Alceste out of withdrawing from society. Write a scene (in prose or verse) in which one of these two characters or both present a final plea to Alceste.

Making Connections—For Discussion or Writing

✕ Compare and contrast Alceste with Ibsen's Nora or Sophocles' Antigone as advocates of uncompromising honesty. Are they similar in their temperaments or in their motives? Are we supposed to identify with them?

✗ Is Célimène in this play seen from a male point of view? Compare her with another major female character in a predominantly male world, such as Nora in Ibsen's *A Doll's House*.

WRITING ABOUT LITERATURE

30 *The Language of Comedy*
WRITING FOCUS: Responding to Verbal Humor

The Writing Workshop   The dramatist's, like the poet's, medium is words. Much critical study of imaginative literature takes a close look at the writer's language. In the comedies of writers from Shakespeare and Molière to Wilde and Wasserstein, spectators delight in the verbal fireworks. They respond to word play and verbal humor. They delight in the spirited trading off of barbed comments and quick-witted answers, or repartee.

✗ Verbal humor in a play ranges from clever word play to laughable verbal accidents and misadventures to delightful and witty comebacks:

PUN:	a play on the double meaning of a word
	(Mercutio after being fatally hurt in *Romeo and Juliet*): "Ask for me tomorrow and you will find me a *grave* man" (a man of solemn demeanor—and a man fit for the grave)
MALAPROPISM:	a word used with the wrong meaning
	The constantly misspoken Constable Elbow in a Shakespeare comedy boasts he will arrest the "benefactors" (he means malefactors)
REPARTEE:	the quick-witted reply
	(father to disrespectful son): "I had advanced ideas forty years ago!" (son): "I know it was a long time ago."
PARODY:	exaggerating a laughable trait
	In his *Hamlet,* Shakespeare has the long-winded Polonius explain at length that brevity is the soul of wit.

✗ Some kinds of verbal humor depend much on the dramatic context—on the situation in a play where they occur:

IRONIC ASIDE:	true feelings revealed out of hearing of a deceived or flattered person
	(Philinte to the would-be poet): "Ah, how these verses charm and delight!"

(Alceste aside to Philinte):
"Can you shamelessly tolerate stuff so trite?"

IRONIC UNDERSTATEMENT: weakening a statement until it is laughably inadequate
(The harshly outspoken Alceste "puts it mildly"):
                                        I have the defect
To be somewhat franker than people expect.

POMPOUS DICTION: earnest solemn language used in a ridiculous situation
(Aunt Augusta to the hapless Ernest when his humble origin is revealed): "To be born, or at any rate bred, in a handbag, whether it had handles or not, seems to me to display a contempt for the ordinary decencies of family life that reminds one of the worst excesses of the French Revolution!"

The following student paper takes a close look at the fast-moving language of a Shakespeare comedy reprinted in the concluding chapter of this book. Study the way the student writer identifies major varieties of verbal humor. How successful is the paper in showing the role they play in the comedy as a whole?

Sample Student Paper

"Tragic Mirth": The Language of Comedy in *A Midsummer Night's Dream*

Love as infatuation is the foundation for the comedy of Shakespeare's *A Midsummer Night's Dream*. We laugh at the rash actions of the lovers as their affections change at a dizzy pace during an evening in the midsummer forest. We laugh at the way Puck, the mischievous sprite, manipulates the lovers. We laugh at the play the workmen perform, the "tragedy" of Pyramus and Thisby. But the humor in Shakespeare's play is derived from more than the play's plot, the characters' actions. Weaving witty responses, puns, repartee, and malapropisms through the play's plot, Shakespeare creates a humorous, clever world made of language.

This verbal universe makes us laugh and reveals the characters' personalities and social status. The group of craftsmen, for instance, represent low social standing. Thus, their verbal humor is of a "lower" form, such as vile puns and malapropisms—humorous misuse of words. Those of higher social standing—the lovers—also humorously play with words, but they do so intentionally. They make love the subject of clever remarks, often making it sound more like an intellectual game than a physical attraction or emotional bond. Shakespeare further sets apart the two types of humor by having the workmen speak in prose and the lovers speak in verse. The two groups are brought together in the final act, in which both forms of humor meet.

The lovers—Hermia, Lysander, Helena, and Demetrius—delight in the play of opposites that makes for clever, fast-moving love talk throughout the play. They play off diametrically opposed words by way of repartee—the spirited comebacks that require a quick wit. Hermia and Helena, for instance, have an exchange in rhymed couplets about Demetrius. He loves Hermia—and is rejected by her; he rejects Helena, who loves him.

> Hermia: I frown upon him, yet he loves me still.
> Helena: O that your frowns would teach my smiles such skill!
> Hermia: I give him curses, yet he gives me love.
> Helena: O that my prayers could such affection move!
> Hermia: The more I hate, the more he follows me.
> Helena: The more I love, the more he hateth me. (1.1.194–99)

These characters are prone to punning, another form of verbal humor. In the dialogue, the same word often echoes again and again, often changing its meaning in the process. Hermia greets Helena, calling her beautiful ("fair") Helena: "God speed, fair Helena, whither away?" Helena responds: "Call you me fair? That fair again unsay. / Demetrius loves you fair. O happy fair!" (1.1.180–82). This kind of playing on a repeated word becomes outright punning when Lysander attempts to snuggle up to his love, Hermia. She says, "Nay, good Lysander, for my sake, my dear, / Lie further off, do not lie so near." Lysander assures her that his intentions are honorable; he is not a lying, deceiving seducer: "For lying so, Hermia, I do not lie" (2.2.43–52).

As Helena, obsessed with her love for Demetrius, follows him around, he harshly swears, "I am sick when I do look on thee." Helena responds, "And I am sick when I look not on you" (2.1.212–213). This harsh repudiation of Helena by Demetrius and her unflagging devotion are examples of the lovers' extreme statements occurring throughout the play. Much of the verbal humor results from the lovers' use of extremely exaggerated love talk that parodies the love poems of Shakespeare's time.

The hyperbolical, exaggerated language is especially hilarious when a lover swears undying passion after just having totally turned around, abandoning one love for another under the mischievous Puck's spell. We laugh at Lysander when his consummate love for Hermia suddenly becomes consummate love for Helena. In rhyming couplets he dramatically swears, "I do repent / The tedious minutes I with her [Hermia] have spent. / Not Hermia but Helena I love. / Who will not change a raven for a dove?" (2.2.111–14).

Demetrius, too, uses extreme flowery exaggeration after falling under the spell of the woods and swearing his love for the same Helena. She is perfect, a goddess. Compared with her, crystal is like mud:

> Oh Helen, goddess, nymph, perfect, divine!
> To what, my love, shall I compare thine eyne?
> Crystal is muddy. O, how ripe in show
> Thy lips, those kissing cherries, tempting grow! (3.2.137–41)

Because both men have so suddenly flip-flopped their affections, Helena is certain they, along with Hermia, are playing her for a fool. She calls Hermia a "counterfeit" and a "puppet." Hermia calls Helena a "juggler" and a "cankerblossom." Lysander swears at Hermia, calling her "thou cat, thou burr" and "you dwarf!" All this name-calling releases resentment and frustration that are usually bottled up in accordance with the requirement to be polite and mature. The exchange of insults in Act 3, Scene 2 creates a manic, humorous scene, leading Puck to exclaim, "Lord what fools these mortals be!"

The other mortals upon whom Puck eavesdrops and whom he manipulates are the honest but ignorant Athenian workmen, the characters of low comedy and low social class. These men, together in the forest on the same night as the lovers, are preparing a play to perform at the royal wedding. In prose, the workmen's verbal humor mainly focuses on malapropism—humorous misuses of words. We laugh at the unintentional blunders of these characters. For example, Quince intends to praise his friend Bottom by calling him a "paragon," a model. Instead, however, Quince says "paramour," a lover, and often an illicit or adulterous one.

Bottom constantly stumbles into the same kind of ridiculous verbal errors. Usually Bottom's mistakes stem from his desire to sound sophisticated, but his limited vocabulary leads him to unintentional humorous remarks. For example, after the craftsmen agree to meet in the woods, Bottom says, "We will meet, and there we may rehearse most obscenely and courageously." Later, instead of saying "to the same effect," he says, "to the same defect."

Often with his blunders, Bottom uses a word of opposite meaning or connotation to what he intends. Instead of "odorous [scented] savors sweet," Bottom says "odious [hateful] savors sweet." We laugh, but Bottom is not in on the joke. Also at his own expense are his puns: Like the lovers, he puns, but not intentionally or wittily. When the mischievous fairy Puck transforms Bottom's head into an ass's head, for example, he declares that his friends are making "an ass of him."

When Bottom and his entourage come together with the lovers and the royal couple at the end of the play, the low and high strands of comedy meet. Theseus, the duke, reads the description of the workmen's play:

> "A tedious brief scene of young Pyramus
> And his love Thisby; very tragical mirth." (5.1.56–57)

Here the "low" comics have created an oxymoronic, self-canceling description of their play, unaware of its absurd quality. The duke shows the absurdity with a witty retort:

> Merry and tragical? Tedious and brief?
> That is, hot ice and wondrous strange snow.
> How shall we find the concord of this discord? (5.1.58–60)

Throughout the workmen's production, the aristocrats and lovers make clever punning remarks, at the expense of the "actors." When Quince errs in the prologue with punctuation blunders, Theseus says, "This fellow doth not stand upon points," which has a double meaning: Quince does not heed niceties, nor does he pay attention to punctuation in his reading. Lysander adds, "He hath rid his prologue like a rough colt; / he knows not the stop." The "stop" has two meanings: the stopping of a colt by reining it in, and the full stop, a period as a punctuation mark.

At first glance, one might assume that only the workmen are being ridiculed in this scene. Certainly they are inept and blundering, performing a play that the critic David Bevington has called "an absurdly bad play, full of lame epithets, bombastic alliteration, and bathos." But the bathos and exaggerated laments of the workmen's "lovers" sound suspiciously like the exchanges between the Athenian lovers:

> O night, O night! Alack, alack, alack,
> I fear my Thisby's promise is forgot.
> And thou, O wall, O sweet, O lovely wall,
> That stand'st between her father's ground and mine . . . (5.1.170–73)

Here Shakespeare invites us, the audience, to acknowledge that the exaggerated love talk invites parody. Just as the audience of Pyramus and Thisby laugh at the workmen, we laugh at *A Midsummer Night's Dream*. Who, then, may be laughing at us?

Questions for Peer Review

It has often been said that when a joke has to be explained it is already dead. Modern audiences often laugh heartily during performances of Shakespeare's comedies when in spite of the difficulties of language actors bring jokes to life with broad hints and significant gestures. However, readers have to do without the help of body language or similar nudges. Does the student writer succeed in bringing the verbal humor of the Shakespeare comedy to life for the reader?

1. Some of the puns discussed in this paper, like the *lie/lie* pun, still work today. (Mark Twain said in response to "Let sleeping dogs lie" that it was better to let the newspaper do the lying.) What other jokes or examples of word play make sense to you after the student writer explains them? Which do you think are most difficult or inaccessible for the modern spectator or reader? For which of these can classmates or others offer help?

2. The rich clever love talk of the poetry of Shakespeare's time has in later periods often been criticized as artificial or insincere. Where does the student writer first acknowledge this issue? Where in the paper do you see detailed evidence? What are the giveaway indicators of an overly artificial style? (When does imitation become parody?)

3. According to this paper, what are key differences between the sophisticated upper-class humor on the one hand and the verbal humor in the scenes with the lower-class menials or yokels on the other? What is the difference in the use of puns, for instance? To judge from this paper, does the humor at the expense of the uneducated seem mean-spirited to you?

4. Do you hear clever quick-witted talk? Where? From people with what kind of background? In what situations? Can you give some recent examples?

5. Do you observe humor making fun of low-class people or uneducated people? Where? Initiated by what kind of person and aimed at whom? Did you or others consider it objectionable? Is it all right to make fun of ignorance? Why, or why not?

6. What kind of love talk would you or your friends judge sincere?

31 NEW DIRECTIONS
Crossing the Boundaries

Courtesy Richard B. Ressman

1622

*My characters have nothing. I'm working with
impotence, ignorance, that whole zone of
being that has always been set aside by artists
as something unusable—something by definition
incompatible with art.*

SAMUEL BECKETT

FOCUS ON NEW DIRECTIONS

Much contemporary drama, like much modern art, has been in rebellion against convention. Audiences have learned to expect experiment and innovation. Playwrights from George Bernard Shaw to Harold Pinter and Caryl Churchill have delighted in bourgeois-baiting, shocking the people in the good seats. Yet, after initial controversy, their plays have often become part of the established repertory.

Some major movements have broken with the past more radically than others:

The Theater of the Absurd   The **theater of the absurd** surfaced in the fifties to challenge the tradition of issue-oriented realistic plays and turn theater upside down. Eugène Ionesco's *The Bald Soprano* opened in Paris in 1950 to the derisive laughter of an incredulous audience. For many of them, the play was like a "Japanese movie without subtitles." It has since run in Paris without interruption for as long as anyone can remember. In 1954, Samuel Beckett, an Irish author living in Paris and writing mostly in French, wrote *Waiting for Godot,* one of the classics of the modern stage. It is a play about two homeless people waiting for Godot—a personage who never comes and who, it appears, does not exist. The theater of the absurd mirrored the conviction that the "reality" acted out in most stage plays is artificial. It does not show the world in which most people live. Most people lead disjointed lives. They don't have grand plans. They don't have major crises; they stumble from one trivial crisis to another. They don't discuss the issues; instead they talk as if they were on automatic pilot, with language furnishing them a sheer endless supply of ready-made sayings and banalities.

Epic Theater   Disciples of Bertolt Brecht used the label **epic theater** for his ideologically inspired plays that became a major influence on critics, directors, and performers. Brecht was a German communist dramatist, driven into exile from Nazi Germany, who was one of the great proletarian writers of the century. His plays discarded customary theatrical tricks and conventions for a ballad-like storytelling, with the author often painting the ideological moral. The hero of his *The Life of Galileo* is a sensual, life-loving Renaissance astronomer who believes in the mission of science to lead suffering humanity out of ignorance and poverty but who in the end, like many in Brecht's own generation, finds himself knuckling under to the forces of repression and censorship. The heroine of *Mother Courage and Her Children* survives by selling supplies as a camp follower of the marauding armies of the Thirty Years' War while trying in vain to keep her children from being devoured by the war's carnage. (As one of the characters in the play says, "He who wants to dine with the devil needs a long spoon.")

Psychological Realism   For several decades, a major force on American and European stages has been drama that superficially could be classified as realistic theater. However, it probes deeper into the psychic hurts and existential frustrations of its characters, seemingly responding to some deep-seated need of the audience for catharsis, for pumping out the psychological bilge that poisons lives. Audiences witness searing confrontations that bring to the surface buried hostilities. Verbal slugfests and lacerating self-revelations often leave the characters and the audience emotionally drained. The borderline between sordid everyday reality and the sadistic or masochistic fantasies of the characters is often blurred. Harold Pinter was born and raised in a working-class neighborhood near London's East End. In his *Homecoming* (1965), an American college professor returning to visit his British family is sucked back into a lower-class world of philanderers, pimps, and prostitutes from which for a time he had made his escape to respectability. Edward Albee is an American pioneer of this tradition of naturalistic, slice-of-life psychodrama. His blockbusting success *Who's Afraid of Virginia Woolf?* (1962) shows two married people destroying themselves in a relentless outpouring of recrimination and abuse. David Mamet—*Glengarry Glen Ross* (1983), *Oleanna* (1992), and a score of other plays—is the past master of the theater of confrontation, indictment, and self-laceration.

Feminist Playwrights and Critics   In the last few decades, a major challenge to tradition has been the emergence of female playwrights challenging the domination of the theater by male dramatists. Audiences have witnessed a major effort to redefine and broaden the traditional canon of plays written by predominantly male writers. Feminist critics have reassessed the work and influence of playwrights like Susan Glaspell (*Trifles*), Lillian Hellman (*The Children's Hour,* 1934), and Clare Boothe Luce (*The Women,* 1937). Feminist critics have championed the work of women like ntozake shange, who wrote *for colored girls who have considered suicide/when the rainbow is enuf* (performed on Broadway in 1976) and who spoke of the "struggle to become all that is forbidden by our environment, forfeited by our gender, all that we have forgotten."

Audiences are increasingly watching plays like Beth Henley's *The Wake of Jamey Foster* or *Crimes of the Heart* that reexamine human relationships from a woman's point of view (or women's points of view).

Wendy Wasserstein, in her comedy *Uncommon Women and Others* (1977), explored new directions in a world in which "women's roles have become ambiguous and confusing" (Susan L. Carson). Caryl Churchill's *Top Girls* (1982) explored the obstacles outstanding women face and the price they pay for success. Tina Howe has written comedies of life in the American nuclear family (*Birth and After Birth,* 1974; *Approaching Zanzibar,* 1988). She has said that her ambition is "to get a thousand people in a dark room laughing themselves nearly to death, drenched in tears, rolling in the aisles, ambulances rushing to theater doors." But she has also said:

> As a mother, you experience moments of excruciating tenderness and love, but there is also a great savagery—family life has been overromanticized; the savagery has not been seen enough in the theater and in the movies.

Multicultural Perspectives   Plays from outside the white mainstream have made their way into the established canon from minority sources and from other cultures. Luis Valdez' *The Shrunken Head of Pancho Villa* and other plays made their way into anthologies. In his *Los Vendidos,* white politicians shop for token representatives of minorities the way others shop for used cars. The American playwright August Wilson is making audiences rethink their stereotypes about black people. In *The Piano Lesson* (1990), he is teaching us to listen to authentic folk dialect as the natural expression of the exuberance and humanity of his characters rather than as the badge of poverty and illiteracy. (Willie to his sister, whom he has gotten out of bed at five in the morning: "You ain't had to come down if you didn't want to. I come eighteen hundred miles to see my sister I figure she might want to get up and say hi. Other than that you can go back upstairs.")

Among world authors writing in English, the Nigerian playwright Wole Soyinka stands out. Intimately acquainted with the literary traditions of the West, he yet has remained rooted in and loyal to the culture of his own people. In his *Death and the King's Horseman,* he pays tribute to a tribal culture and tribal traditions that have survived centuries of colonialism and cultural myopia.

FIRST READING

The Terrors of Childhood

David Mamet was born in Chicago. In his autobiographical *Memoir,* he writes about growing up in a loveless, harshly punitive family setting. He went on to become a wizard of the contemporary stage, turning out a succession of searing and immensely successful plays that at times seem bent on tearing the last shred of pretense from their characters. Plays like *Sexual Perversity in Chicago* (1974), *American Buffalo* (1975), and *Speed the Plow* (1988) made him a major force in today's American theater. His *Glengarry Glen Ross* (1983), a play about desperate down-at-heels real estate agents, makes *Death of a Salesman* read like a tribute to an idyllic Golden Age of salesmanship. In *Oleanna* (1992), a female student who at first seems confused and in need of help slowly turns into the Avenger of women who have been belittled, condescended to, and denied access to the privileged upper layers of the academic world. Mamet has written screenplays for films including *Homicide, House of Games,* and *The Verdict.*

The Cryptogram was first produced in 1994. His most personal play, it takes the audience back to the archetypal nightmare fears of childhood. The play's title contains the Greek root *crypto-* meaning "hidden" or "secret"; thus a cryptogram is message written in code. Part of the loneliness and terror of childhood results from the discovery that the grownups are speaking in code, a code that the child may not be able to break. Like other Mamet plays, *The Cryptogram* starts with apparently aimless routine conversation—in this play, involving a mother, a family friend, and a ten-year-old son. Gradually something disturbing or ominous comes into focus. For a time, the characters seem to be talking at cross purposes, having different agendas. We begin to sense that we are in for shattering revelations, watching a human tragedy unfold that we are helpless to head off.

David Mamet   *(born 1947)*

The Cryptogram   1994

This play is dedicated to Gregory Mosher

Last night when you were all in bed
Mrs. O'Leary left a lantern in her shed
                              CAMPING SONG

CHARACTERS

DONNY, a woman in her late thirties
DEL, a man of the same age
JOHN, Donny's son, around ten

> *The action takes place in Donny's*
> *living room in 1959.*

ACT ONE: *One evening*

ACT TWO: *The next night*

ACT THREE: *Evening, one month later*

Act One

A living room. One door leading off to the kitchen, one staircase leading up to the second floor. Evening. DEL *is seated on the couch.* JOHN *comes downstairs dressed in his pajamas.*

JOHN: I couldn't find 'em.

DEL: . . . couldn't find 'em.

JOHN: No.

DEL: What?

JOHN: Slippers.

DEL: Yes?

JOHN: They're packed.

DEL: . . . slippers are packed.

JOHN: Yes.

DEL: Why did you pack them?

JOHN: Take them along.

DEL: How are you going to use your slippers in the woods.

JOHN: To keep my feet warm.

DEL: Mmm.

JOHN: I shouldn't of packed them?

DEL: Well, put something on your feet.

JOHN: What?

DEL: Socks.

JOHN: Put something on my feet now.

DEL: Yes.

JOHN: "As long as I'm warm."

DEL: That's correct.

JOHN: I have 'em. (*Produces socks. Starts putting them on.*)

DEL: That's good. Think ahead.

JOHN: Why did you say "why did you pack them?"

DEL: I wondered that you'd taken them with.

JOHN: Why?

DEL: Out in the Woods?

JOHN: No, but to wear in the Cabin.

DEL: . . . that's right.

JOHN: Don't you think?

DEL: I do.

JOHN: I know I couldn't wear them in the woods.

DEL: No. No. That's right. Where were we?

JOHN: Issues of sleep.

DEL: . . . is . . .

JOHN: Issues of sleep.

DEL: No. I'm sorry. You were quite correct. To take your slippers. I spoke too quickly.

JOHN: That's alright.

DEL: Thank you. (*Pause.*) Where were we? Issues of Sleep.

JOHN: And last night either.

DEL: Mm . . . ?

JOHN: . . . I couldn't sleep.

DEL: So I'm told. (*Pause.*)

JOHN: Last night, either.

DEL: Fine. What does it mean "I could not sleep"?

JOHN: . . . what does it mean?

DEL: Yes. It means nothing other than the meaning you choose to assign to it.

JOHN: I don't get you.

DEL: I'm going to explain myself.

JOHN: Good.

DEL: A "Trip," for example, you've been looking forward to.

JOHN: A trip. Yes. Oh, yes.

DEL: . . . absolutely right.

JOHN: . . . that I'm excited.

DEL: . . . who wouldn't be?

JOHN: *Anyone* would be.

DEL: That's right.

JOHN: . . . to go in the *Woods* . . . ?

DEL: Well. You see? You've answered your own question.

JOHN: Yes. That I'm excited.

DEL: I can't blame you.

JOHN: You can't.

DEL: No. Do you see?

JOHN: That it's natural.

DEL: I think it is.

JOHN: Is it?

DEL: I think it absolutely is. To go with your *father* . . . ?

JOHN: Why isn't he home?

DEL: We don't know.

JOHN: . . . because it's something. To go out there.

DEL: I should say.

JOHN: In the Woods . . . ?

DEL: . . . I hope to tell you.

JOHN: Well, you *know* it is.

DEL: That I do.
    And I will tell you: older people, too. Grown people.
    You know what they do?
    The night before a trip?

JOHN: What do they do?

DEL: Well, many times *they* cannot sleep. *They* will stay up that night.

JOHN: They will?

DEL: Oh yes.

JOHN: Why?

DEL: They can't sleep. No. Why?
    Because their minds, you see, are full of thoughts.

JOHN: What are their thoughts of?

DEL: Their thoughts are of two things.

JOHN: Yes?

DEL: Of what they're *leaving*.

JOHN: . . . yes?

DEL: And what they're going *toward*. (*Pause.*) Just like you.

JOHN: . . . of what they're leaving . . .

DEL: . . . mmm . . . (*Pause.*)

JOHN: How do you know that?

DEL: Well, you know, they say we live and learn.

JOHN: They do?

DEL: That's what they say. And I'll tell you *another* thing . . .

(*A crash is heard offstage.*) (*Pause.*)

DONNY (*offstage*): . . . I'm alright . . .

DEL: . . . what?

DONNY (*offstage*): I'm alright . . .

DEL: . . . did . . .

DONNY (*offstage*): What? Did I what?

DEL: Are you . . . . . .

DONNY (*offstage*): What?

    I've spilt the tea.

DEL: What?

DONNY (*offstage*): I spilled the tea.

DEL: Do you want help?

DONNY (*offstage*): What?

JOHN: Do you want help he said.

DONNY (*offstage*): No.

DEL: You don't? (*To* JOHN.) Go help your mother.

DONNY (*offstage*) (*simultaneous with* "mother"): . . . I'm alright. I'm alright.
    (*To self.*) Oh, hell . . .

DEL: What did you do?

DONNY (*offstage*): What?

DEL: . . . what did you do . . . . . .

DONNY: I broke the pot, I broke the teapot. I'm alright. I broke the teapot.
    (*Pause.*)

DEL (*to* JOHN): Well, there you go . . . a human *being* . . .

JOHN: . . . . . . yes?

DEL: . . . cannot conceal himself.

JOHN: That's an example?

DEL: Well, hell, look at it: anything. When it is *disordered,* any, um,
    "Change," do you see . . . ?

JOHN: What is the change?

DEL: The trip.

JOHN: She ain't going.

DEL: No of course she's not. But *you* are. And your father is. It's an upheaval.

JOHN: It's a minor one.

DEL: Who is to say? (*Pause.*)

JOHN: But did *you* feel that?

DEL: Did I . . . ?

JOHN: Yes.

DEL: Feel what?

JOHN: Last week.

DEL: Feel. Last week.

JOHN: Thoughts on a trip.

DEL: . . . Did I . . . ?

JOHN: When you took *your* trip.

DONNY (*offstage*): It's going to be a minute.

JOHN: . . . when you took your trip.

DONNY (*offstage*): . . . hello . . . . . . ?

DEL: We're alright.

DONNY (*offstage*): The tea is going to be a minute.

JOHN: We're alright in here.

DONNY (*entering*): I've put the . . . . . why aren't you asleep.

DEL: . . . did I feel "pressure"?

DONNY: . . . John . . . ?

JOHN: Yes.

DONNY: Why aren't you asleep?

DEL: Before my trip. No.

JOHN: No. Why?

DEL: Because, and this is important. Because people differ.

DONNY: What are you doing down here?

DEL: We're talking.

JOHN: . . . . . . I came down.

DEL (*to* DONNY): I'm sorry. Are you alright?

DONNY: What? I dropped the teapot. What are you *doing* down . . .

JOHN: We're talking.

DEL: He came down, and I began a conversation.

DONNY: Alright, if you began it.

DEL: I did.

DONNY (*sighs*): We're going to have tea, and then you go upst . . . Where are your slippers?

JOHN: Packed.

DONNY: They're packed.

JOHN: For the trip.

DONNY: And then you go upstairs and you go to sleep.

JOHN: I want to wait till my father comes home.

DONNY: Well, yes, I'm sure you do. But you need your sleep. And if you don't get it, you're not going on the trip.

JOHN: Will he be home soon?

DONNY: Yes. He will.

JOHN: Where is he?

DONNY: I don't know. Yes, I do, yes. He's at the Office. And he'll be home soon.

JOHN: Why is he working late?

DONNY: I don't know. We'll find out when he comes home, John. Must we do this every night?

JOHN: I only want . . .

DEL: Do you know what?

JOHN: I didn't want to upset you, I only . . .

DEL: . . . could I . . . ?

JOHN: I only . . .

DEL (*simultaneous with* "only"): Could I make a suggestion? (*To* JOHN.) Why don't you busy yourself?

DONNY: He has to sleep.

DEL: . . . but he's not *going* to sleep. He's . . .

JOHN: That's right.

DONNY: . . . one moment.

JOHN: . . . If I had something to *do* . . .

DONNY (*simultaneous with* "do"): No. You're absolutely right.

JOHN: . . . something to do. If I had *that* . . .

DONNY: Alright.

DEL: Are you packed?

JOHN: I'm all packed.

DEL: . . . well . . .

JOHN: I, I My *Father* isn't packed, his . . .

DONNY: No . . .

JOHN: . . . I could pack *his* stuff.

DONNY: No, no, I'll tell you what you could do.

JOHN: What?

DONNY: Close up the attic.

JOHN: . . . close it up?

DONNY: Neaten it up. Yes.

JOHN: Is it disturbed?

DONNY: Mmm.

JOHN: Why?

DONNY: . . . after my "rummaging."

JOHN: Alright.

DONNY: . . . and . . .

JOHN: . . . alright.

DONNY: See if you find any things up there.

JOHN: Things.

DONNY: . . . you might need to take.

JOHN: . . . things I might need to take up.

DONNY: Mm.

JOHN: Or that *he* might need.

DONNY: That's right.

JOHN: . . . or that you forgot.

DONNY: Yes.

JOHN: To pack.

DONNY: Yes. Would you do that?

JOHN: Of course.

DONNY: Thank you, John.

DEL: Thank you.

DONNY: And perhaps you'd put on some clothing.

JOHN: Good.

DONNY: Very good. Off you go then.

JOHN: I will.

DEL: "My blessings on your House."

JOHN: That's what the Wizard said.

DEL: That's right.

JOHN: "And mine on yours."

DEL: "Until the whale shall speak."

JOHN: "Until the Moon shall Weep." Mother?

DONNY: I don't remember it . . . (*Pause.*)

JOHN: You don't remember it? (*Pause.*)

DEL: Well then, John. Alright then. Off you go to work.

JOHN (*exiting*): I will.

DEL: Off you go. (*Pause.*)

DONNY: No. I don't understand it.

DEL: Well . . .

DONNY: No.

DEL: He has trouble sleeping.

DONNY: Mm. No.

DEL: That's his nature.

DONNY: Is it?

DEL: Children . . .

DONNY: No. You see. It's grown into this minuet. Every night . . .

DEL: Well, yes. But this is *special,* he . . .

DONNY: No, No. He always has a reason. Some . . . every night . . .

DEL: Yes. Granted. But a Trip to the Woods . . .

DONNY: . . . he . . .

DEL: . . . with his Dad . . . ? It's an *event.* I think. What do I know? But, as his *friend* . . .

DONNY: . . . yes . . .

DEL: . . . as his *friend* . . .

DONNY: Yes. Yes. He Always has a Reason.

DEL: Yes, but I'm saying, in *spite* of . . . *I* don't know. I don't mean to intrude . . . but good. But *Good.* One sends him up to the Attic . . .

DONNY: Oh.

DEL: And that's "it." That's the solution.

DONNY: Oh. Oh . . .

DEL: To, um . . . to, um, what is the word . . . ?

DONNY: Look what I found.

DEL: To um . . . not "portray" . . . to um . . .

DONNY: Look what I found.

DEL: "Participate." That's the word. Is that the word? No. To, um . . .

DONNY: Del. Shut up.

DEL: To um . . .

DONNY (*simultaneous with* "To"): Shut up. Look what I found up in the attic.

(*She goes to a side table and brings back a small framed photograph and hands it to* DEL.)

DEL: (*Pause.*) When was this taken . . .

DONNY (*simultaneous with* "taken"): When I was packing for the trip.

DEL (*simultaneous with* "trip"): Mmm . . . No. When was this taken?

DONNY: Isn't it funny? Though? The things you find? (*Pause.*)

DEL: Huh . . .

DONNY: What?

DEL: I don't understand this photograph. (*Pause.*)

DONNY: What do you mean?

(JOHN *comes down onto the landing.*)

JOHN: Which coat? That's what I forgot. To pack my coat.

DONNY (*to* DEL): Which coat?

JOHN: That's what was on my mind.

DEL: Which coat should he take?

DEL (*looking up from the photograph*): Mm? When were you up there?

DONNY: Where?

DEL: Up in the attic?

DONNY (*simultaneous with* "attic"): In the attic today, cleaning up.

DEL (*of photo*) (*simultaneous with* "up"): . . . this is the damnedest thing . . .

DONNY: *Isn't* it . . . ?

DEL: When, when could this have been taken?

DONNY: And I found that old *Lap* robe.

DEL: The lap robe . . .

DONNY: The *stadium* blanket we . . .

JOHN: Which coat?

DONNY: Which?

JOHN: How cold is it up there yet?

DEL: . . . a lap robe . . .

DONNY: The *stadium* blanket.

JOHN: How cold was it last week? Del?

DONNY: Just bring your regular coat.

JOHN: My blue coat?

DONNY: The melton coat?

JOHN: What's melton?

DONNY: The blue coat. Your fabric coat.

JOHN: The *wool* one?

DONNY (*to* DEL): Is it too cold for that?

DEL: No.

DONNY: Then take it.

JOHN: My *blue* coat.

DONNY: Yes.

JOHN: Do I have any sweaters left?

DONNY: Up there?

JOHN: Yes.

DEL: I think so.

DONNY: I'm sure that you do.

JOHN: You think so?

DEL: They'd be in your bureau.

JOHN: And, the fishing stuff. Is it there?

DONNY: The fishing stuff. They brought back. Last week, John. It's all . . .

JOHN: . . . they brought it back.

DONNY: Yes. It's up in the attic . . .

JOHN (*simultaneous with* "attic"): You should have left it at the Cabin.

DONNY: It's in the attic. You'll see it up there.

DEL: . . . we were afraid . . .

DONNY: . . . they didn't want it to Get Stolen.

JOHN: And the fishing line. Do we have that good line?

DEL (*simultaneous with* "line"): . . . we were afraid it would get taken.

JOHN: . . . that good heavy line . . . ?

DONNY: . . . I'm sorry, John . . . ?

JOHN: The fishing line.

DONNY: I'm sure you. Yes. Fishing line. In the same box.

JOHN: Green? The green one?

DONNY: . . . I . . .

JOHN: The green line? In the Tackle Box? Because if not, we have to stop on the way, and . . .

DONNY: . . . I'm . . .

JOHN: Dad said that the Green line . . .

DEL: What's special about it?

DONNY: Open the box.

JOHN: . . . because if not . . .

DONNY: Find the box.

DEL: What's special about it?

JOHN: It's very strong.

DONNY: Find the box, open it, and check it out.

JOHN: Because that's how we'll know.

DONNY: That's what I'm telling you. (JOHN *exits, up the stairs.*)

DEL: Port out, starboard home.

DONNY: And put some clothing on. (*Pause.*)

DEL (*of photo*): . . . when was this taken?

DONNY: I swear. He's . . .

DEL: What? Well, he's having difficulty sleeping.

DONNY: It's all such a mystery.

DEL: Do you think?

DONNY: Yes. All our good intentions . . .

DEL: Big thing. Going in the Woods. Your Father . . .

DONNY: . . . mmm.

DEL: . . . big thing.

DONNY: Is it?

DEL: Hope to tell you.

DONNY: (*Pause.*) It goes so quickly.

DEL: Certain things remain.

DONNY: Yes?

DEL: (*Pause.*) *Friendship* . . . (*Pause.*) Certain habits.

DONNY: It goes so quickly . . . (*Pause.*)

DEL: Does it?

DONNY: Sometimes I wish I was a Monk.

DEL: Mmm . . . what's that?

DONNY: I wish I were a monk.

DEL: How would that go?

DONNY: An old man for example . . .

DEL: . . . mmm . . .

DONNY: (*Pause.*) . . . and all his sons are gone.

DEL: . . . an Oriental Fantasy.

DONNY: That's right.

DEL: "Mist" . . . "Mountains" . . . So on.

DONNY: . . . mmm . . .

DEL: And what does this man do?

DONNY: The monk.

DEL: Yes.

DONNY: Nothing. (*Pause.*) He sits; and gazes out at his . . .

DEL: Mm. Well, that's a form of meditation . . .

DONNY: Gazes out at his domain.

DEL: Well, I'm sure you'd be very good at it.

DONNY: You're very kind.

DEL: What? I'm very kind, yes. (*Pause.*) For *it's*. A *form*. Of meditation. (*Pause.*) As are they all.

DONNY: Mm.

DEL: The thing about photography is that it is very seductive.

DONNY: Because sometimes it seems the older I get, the less that I know.

DEL: Well, it's a mystery. The whole goddamned thing.

DONNY: Isn't it . . . ?

DEL: I think so. (*Pause.*) Goes fast. Goes quickly.

DONNY: Mmm.

DEL: . . . and then it is gone. (*Pause.*)

DONNY: No, I need a rest.

DEL (*of photograph*): Well, if we look here we see that the *tree* is gone. When would that have been?

DONNY (*to herself*): A fantasy of rest . . . (*Pause.*)

DEL: . . . Oh, oh, oh what are you doing this weekend . . . ?

DONNY: This weekend?

DEL: Yes.

DONNY: Well. I don't know.

DEL: You don't know what you're doing this weekend.

DONNY: I'm going to sit.

DEL: To sit here.

DONNY: Yes.

DEL: Do you want company?

(JOHN *reenters, wrapped in a plaid blanket.*)

DONNY: No. That's not clothing.

JOHN: . . . I . . .

DONNY: You put some clothing on right now. (*Pause.*) What? (*Pause.*)

JOHN: I tore it.

DONNY: You tore what?

JOHN: I tore the blanket. I'm sorry.

DONNY: You tore it?

JOHN (*simultaneous with* "tore"): I was opening the box. I think there was a nail sticking out. I heard something rip . . .

(*He shows the tear.*)

DONNY: You're saying you tore *that* blanket?

JOHN: I heard some . . .

DONNY: John . . .

JOHN: I was doing it too quickly. I know I heard.

DONNY (*simultaneous with* "heard"): John, that was torn so long ago.

JOHN: I heard it rip.

DONNY: No, it was torn years ago.

JOHN (*simultaneous with* "ago"): I didn't tear it?

DONNY: No.

JOHN: I heard it rip.

DEL: You may have heard it in your mind . . .

JOHN: . . . but . . .

DONNY: No we tore that long ago.

DEL: I think your mind is racing.

DONNY: It's alright, John. It's alright. Go upstairs. And you put on some clothing . . . (*Pause.*)

JOHN: It's tied with twine.

DONNY: I don't understand you.

JOHN: The *Tackle* box.

DONNY: Box . . .

JOHN: . . . with the fishing line . . .

DONNY: . . . well, *untie* it. And . . .

JOHN: I can't untie it. That's what I'm saying. I tried to pull the twine off, but . . .

DEL (*Takes out knife. Of knife.*): This'll do it.

JOHN: I can't . . .

DEL: . . . is it alright . . . ?

DONNY: . . . If you don't get some rest, before . . .

DEL (*to* DONNY): Is it alright?

DONNY: What?

DEL: Can he have the knife?

DONNY: . . . to have the knife . . .

DEL: . . . to use. To cut the twine . . .

DONNY (*simultaneous with* "twine"): What would your father say?

JOHN: It's alright.

DONNY: He would?

JOHN: Yes.

DONNY: It's alright for you . . .

JOHN: . . . yes. Oh, yes.

DONNY: . . . to have the knife.

JOHN: Yes.

DONNY (*simultaneous with* "Yes"): I hardly think so.

JOHN: No he *would*.

DEL: Then there you go. (*Hands* JOHN *the knife.*)

JOHN: Where did you get the knife, though?

DONNY: Good *Lord,* John . . . calm *down* tonight.

JOHN: No.

DONNY: What?

JOHN: I can't.

DONNY: . . . why not?

JOHN: The Tea, the Blanket . . . ?

DONNY: I don't understand.

JOHN: I'm *waiting* for it.

DEL: You're waiting for what?

JOHN: "The Third Misfortune."

DEL: "The Third Misfortune."

DONNY: Third . . . ?

JOHN: I'm waiting to see "What is the Third Misfortune?" (*Pause.*)

DONNY: What does he mean?

JOHN: It's in the book.

DEL: Misfortunes come in threes.

DONNY: Where *is* that book, by the way?

JOHN: Misfortunes come in threes.

DONNY: The third misfortune. I remember. Yes.

JOHN: It's in the book.

DONNY: Wait. How long since we've seen that book?

JOHN: A long time.

DONNY: Ha. And you remembered it?

JOHN: Of course I remember it.

DONNY: Isn't that odd?

JOHN: "When we think of sickness, sickness is approaching," said the Wizard.

DEL: . . . That's what the Wizard said.

DONNY: Where *is* that book?

DEL: It will turn up someday.

DONNY: No, did we leave it at the lake?

JOHN: Misfortunes come in threes.

DONNY: Alright, what are the three misfortunes?

JOHN: The Lance, and the Chalice; The Lance was broken by the Lord of
   Night, the Chalice was burnt . . .

DONNY: Yes. No. Not in the book, here.

JOHN: What are the others here?

DONNY: The Three Misfortunes.

JOHN: *Here.*

DONNY: Yes.

JOHN: Alright. One: The Pot, The Teapot broke.

DONNY: That's one, yes. And?

JOHN: The blanket.

DEL: . . . the blanket.

DONNY: What about it?

JOHN: . . . torn . . .

DONNY: No, but it *wasn't* torn. That happened long ago.

JOHN: I *thought* I tore it now.

   (*Sound of teakettle,* DONNY *exits.*)

DONNY (*offstage*): It was torn long ago. You can absolve yourself.

JOHN: . . . I *thought* that I tore it.

DEL: But, you see, in reality, things unfold . . . independent of our fears of
   them.

JOHN: I don't know what you mean.

DEL: Because we *think* a thing is one way does not mean that this is the way
   that this thing must be.

JOHN: The blanket was torn long ago?

DEL: That's what your mother said.

JOHN: How?

DEL: Well . . .

JOHN: Did you see my hat?

DEL: . . . did?

JOHN: At the Cabin?

DEL: Which hat is that?

JOHN: The grey cap.

DEL: Like mine, except grey?

JOHN: Yes.

DEL: I don't remember.

JOHN: Not like yours, actually, it's . . .

DEL: I don't remember.

JOHN: No, it's not actually like yours, it's . . .

DEL: How is it different?

JOHN: It's. I steered you wrong. It's not like yours at all.

DEL: Then I don't know which one you mean.

JOHN: My *Grey* hat. It was on the peg.

DEL: The peg . . .

JOHN: . . . Near the door. At the cabin.

DEL: I don't remember.

JOHN: You don't? Why?

DEL: Because I wasn't looking for it. (*Pause.*) Do you know. I'm going to tell
  you a game.

JOHN: A game?

DEL: A game you can play.
  You and your father. Up there. Eh?
  To "sharpen your skills." (*Pause.*) To "aid your camping."

JOHN: Me and my father.

DEL: Yes.

JOHN: Does he know this game?

DEL: I think that he may.

JOHN: Did he teach it to you?

DEL: No. I learned it independently.

JOHN: Um.

DEL: And. If he does not know it, you can teach it to *him*.

JOHN: Good.

DEL: Yes? You think so?

JOHN: Well, I think so. You have to tell me the game.

DEL: Here it is: . . . you write down . . .

JOHN: ". . . to sharpen our skills . . ."

DEL: You write down your *recollections*.
  Of the things you've seen. During the day.
  Then you compare them.

JOHN: I don't understand.

DEL: To see who has observed the best.
  You observe things during the day. Then, at night you write them down.
  To test your observation. (*Pause.*) Things in the Cabin, for instance. Or

the woods. And, then, you see whose recollection was more accurate. (*Pause.*) You see?

JOHN: See who was more accurate.

DEL: That's correct. (*Pause.*)

JOHN: And why is this game useful?

DEL: If you were lost it could assist you to orient yourself.

JOHN: Would it be things which we *decided before* to observe? Or things . . .

DEL: . . . it could be both.

JOHN: . . . both things we *decided* to observe, and things we decided, later on, we should remember.

DEL: That's right.

JOHN: But something could have been the Third Misfortune, even though it had happened quite long ago. (*Pause.*)

DEL: How could that be?

JOHN: It could be if the "Third Misfortune" happened long ago. If, when it *happened,* no one *noticed,* or . . .

DEL: "at the *time* . . ."

JOHN: Yes, or neglected to *count* it . . .

DEL: . . . I . . .

JOHN: . . . until we recognized it *now* . . . And also, what could we pick. To observe, beside the Cabin?

DEL: What? *Anything.* The *pond,* the . . .

JOHN: . . . where did you get the knife?

DEL: The knife.

JOHN: Yes.

DEL: I told you. Your father gave it to me.

JOHN: He gave you his war knife.

DEL: Yes.

JOHN: His *pilot's* knife . . . ?

DEL: Yes. (*Pause.*)

JOHN: But we couldn't choose the pond.

DEL: Why not?

JOHN: Because it's changing. (*Pause.*) When?

DEL: . . . when what?

JOHN: Did he give it to you?

DEL: Aha.

JOHN: When?

DEL: Last week. When we went camping.

JOHN: Oh.

DEL: Does that upset you?

JOHN: No.

DEL: Aha.

JOHN: What do you mean?

DEL: Nothing.

JOHN: Why did you say "aha."

DEL: Something occurred to me.

JOHN: What?

DEL: Something. (*Pause.*)

JOHN: We couldn't choose the pond.

DEL: The pond?

JOHN: To observe.

DEL: No? Why not?

JOHN: Because it's changing. (DONNY *reenters with tea mugs.*)

DEL: Well, then you choose something else.

JOHN: What should I choose?

DEL: Something that doesn't change. (*Of photo.*) Who, who, what *is* this?

DONNY: It's the Lake.

DEL: No, please, I know where it is, I just don't . . .

DONNY: . . . what?

DEL: . . . I don't remember it.

DONNY: . . . you've seen that photo so . . .

DEL: . . . Well. I don't remember it.

JOHN: You have a strange expression on your face. *Mother:* doesn't . . .

DONNY: Calm down. John.

DEL: . . . I do?

JOHN: You're grinning. (*To* DONNY.) I am calm.

DEL: . . . when was this taken? (DONNY *looks at photo.*)

DONNY: Well, the boathouse is still up . . .

DEL (*to* JOHN): It's strange I'm grinning?

DONNY: . . . so it's . . .

JOHN: It looks unlike you.

DONNY (*of photo, to* DEL): You don't remember this?

DEL: No.

DONNY: *Truly?*

DEL: No. When was it taken?

DONNY (*simultaneous with* "taken"): Well, alright: the boathouse is up, so, I can tell you what *year* it is: The boathouse is up, but the birch is down, so: it's before the War . . .

DEL: . . . it would have to be before the War . . .

DONNY (*simultaneous with* "war"): Wait a moment . . . (JOHN *yawns. Sits on the couch.*) Oh, John; are you getting sleepy?

JOHN: When is Dad coming home?

DONNY: He'll be here when he gets here, I think.

JOHN: . . . I want to tell him this game.

DEL (*of photograph*): I remember the shirt.

DONNY: . . . he'll be home soon, John.

DEL: . . . is this Robert's shirt?

DONNY: What?

DEL: That I'm wearing.

DONNY: In the photo . . .

DEL: Yes . . .

DONNY: . . . I . . . (*Pause.*)

DEL: Do you see my problem? (*Pause.*)

DONNY: Alright.

DEL: Because I remember neither the occasion nor the photograph.

DONNY: . . . Do you have his *shirt* on . . .

DEL: Yes.

DONNY: Why *would* you?

DEL: Well, that's what I'm saying.

DONNY: Can you make the pattern out?

DEL: He's asleep.

DONNY: *Finally. (Pause.)* He thought that he tore the blanket.

DEL: I believe that this Trip has a "meaning" for him.

DONNY: Del, he's always had this problem.

DEL: No, I've had a "clue."

DONNY: No, you're ten years too late. You know, Robert always said: we disagreed about it. From the first. And his theory was "let the child cry."

DEL: . . . let him cry . . .

DONNY: To teach him to . . .

DEL: No, this trip . . .

DONNY: Del, He Always Has a Reason . . .

DEL: He's a sensitive kid . . . ?

DONNY: . . . whatever that means.

DEL: I think it means . . . Well, in *this* case he *told* me, in effect.

DONNY: . . . yes?

DEL: In *this* case it means he's *jealous*.

DONNY: Jealous.

DEL: Of my trip. Last week with Robert.

DONNY: He was jealous?

DEL: That's right.

DONNY: But why does that come out *now*?

And I'll tell you one other thing.

Let him be jealous. What if he was? Yes. I think he needs to spend more time with his father; and, yes, I think that he has to learn the world does not revolve around him. *(Pause.)*

Oh, Lord. I'll tell you. No. You're right. It's guilt.

It's guilt. I'm guilty. I get to spend one weekend on my own. And I'm consumed with guilt.

DEL *(of photo):* Who took this picture? *(Pause.* DONNY *looks at it.)*

DONNY: I don't know.

DEL: Eh? Who could have taken it?

DONNY: Huh. *(Pause.)* I don't . . .

DEL: Do you see? If we're all in it? *(Pause.)*

That's why I don't remember it.

DONNY: I . . . *(Pause.)* Isn't that funny . . . ?

DEL: That's why I don't remember it. *(Pause.)* I knew there was a reason. *(Pause.)*

DONNY: Lord, I found so much *stuff* up there.

DEL: . . . up . . . ?

DONNY: In the attic. The *stadium* blanket, the . . .

DEL: I recognized that.

DONNY: The blanket. Well I hope so.

DEL: How could he think he tore it?

DONNY: . . . I . . .

DEL: He'd seen it for years.

DONNY: . . . so long ago . . .

DEL: Isn't it . . . ? (*Pause.*)

Do you know, at the Hotel. I collect things. I'm amazed. I clean my room out. Every few months. I'm amazed. I always think I've kept it *bare*. But when I clean it out. I find this mass of *things* I have accumulated.

DONNY: They, what are they, mostly?

DEL: Papers. (*Pause.*)

DONNY: I went to the Point.

DEL: You did?

DONNY: I walked down there. Yes.

DEL: Recently?

DONNY: Yes. (*Pause.*)

And I remembered. When the Three of us would go.

Late at night. Before the war.

DEL: I remember.

DONNY: And *Robert* and I. Would make love under a blanket. And I wondered. After all this time, why it never occurred to me. I don't know. But I wondered. Did you *hear* us; and, if you did. If it upset you. (*Pause.*)

DEL: And you've thought about it all this time.

DONNY: That's right.

DEL: Oh, Donny.

DONNY: Did it upset you?

DEL: Aren't you sweet . . . aren't you sweet to worry.

DONNY: Did it?

DEL: Well. I . . .

JOHN (*waking*): What did they say? What?

DONNY: Go to sleep, John.

JOHN: I was going there. But you said to bring the, bring . . . (*Pause.*) Bring them the . . . (*Pause.*)

DONNY: John:

JOHN: . . . huh . . .

DONNY: It's alright.

JOHN: What did they talk about?

DONNY: John . . .

JOHN: I don't like it. I don't like it. No.

DONNY: John . . .

JOHN: I . . . What? No. No. I don't want to. (*Pause.*) Is my father back yet?

DONNY: No. Why don't you go and get in bed . . .

JOHN: When is he coming back?

DONNY: Very soon, I think.

JOHN: He is?

DONNY: Yes. Is that alright?

JOHN (*of photograph*): You asked if the shirt you're wearing is his shirt.

DEL: What?

JOHN: . . . in the photograph.

DEL: Is that His Shirt.

JOHN: You asked that.

DEL: Yes.

JOHN: Well, does it *look* like his shirt?

DEL: It's hard to tell. The picture is old . . .

JOHN (*to* DONNY): I didn't tear the blanket?

DONNY: No.

JOHN: You're certain.

DONNY: We've had it for years.

JOHN: I don't remember it.

DONNY: Yes. You would. If you thought about it.

JOHN: What was it?

DONNY: What? Go to sleep.

JOHN: What did you use it for?

DONNY: What did I use it for?
   A coverlet.

JOHN: To keep you warm.

DONNY: That's right.

JOHN: A coverlet.

DONNY: Yes.

JOHN: Where did it come from? The blanket.

DONNY: Where? In England.

JOHN: England.

DONNY: Yes. From an Arcade.

JOHN: Arcade . . .

DONNY: With stores on either side.

JOHN: Did you buy it together?

DONNY: No. I bought it when he was away.

JOHN: Away.

DONNY: Yes. One day.

JOHN: Away in the War.

DONNY: That's right. (*Pause.*)

JOHN: Did you miss him when he was gone?

DONNY: Yes, I did.

JOHN: What did you think about?

DONNY: (*Pause.*) Many things.

JOHN: What things did you think of?

DONNY: I don't know. *Many* things.

JOHN: Were you frightened for him?

DONNY: Yes. I was.

JOHN: Did you tell him?

DONNY: We used to go out. To the Country, you know . . .

JOHN: Is it wool . . .

DONNY: When he'd come back. Walk in a *field,* or . . .

JOHN: Is it wool?

DONNY: I'm sorry?

JOHN: Is it wool. The blanket.

DONNY: Do you know. When you were small. *You* slept in it. All of the time.
   We covered you.

JOHN: Why did you stop using it.

DONNY: We put it away.

JOHN: Why?

DONNY: It was torn. (*Pause.*) And now you go to sleep.

JOHN: Mother—Do you ever think you hear singing?

DONNY: I don't know what you mean.

JOHN: *Singing.*

DONNY: I don't know what you mean, John.

JOHN: At night. When you are asleep. Before you go to sleep.

DONNY: I don't know.

JOHN: . . . and you hear . . .

DONNY: . . . it's time for bed, now . . .

JOHN: . . . or you think you hear a *radio . . .*

DONNY: . . . a radio . . .

JOHN: Playing *music.* And you think. "Yes. I know. That's a radio." And you listen. But then, you say: "It's just in my head." But you can *listen* to it. It goes on. (*Pause.*) Or *voices.*

DONNY: You hear voices?

JOHN: Just before you go to sleep. Do you ever do that? (*Pause.*) I hear them. Outside my room.

DONNY: What are they saying?

JOHN: Do you ever do that?

DONNY: I don't know.

DEL: What are your voices saying?

JOHN (*simultaneous with* "saying"): Tell me how the blanket was torn.

DONNY: You go to sleep now, John.

JOHN: I want to see my father.

DONNY: Yes. But now you go to sleep.

JOHN: It's time to go to sleep.

DONNY: That's right.

JOHN: Is that right?

DONNY: You have a big . . .

JOHN: *Tomorrow.*

DONNY: Yes.

JOHN: I'm going, you know, I'm going to do that thing.

DONNY: What thing is that?

JOHN: The Game.

DONNY: . . . the Game.

JOHN: To remember. With him.

DONNY: The game. Yes. (JOHN *starts upstairs.*) You take the blanket.

JOHN: To observe.

DONNY: Mmm . . .

JOHN: . . . but it would have to be some thing that would surprise us.

DONNY: That's right.

JOHN: When we look around.

(*He continues up the stairs. Stops to lean over the landing. Looking down at the mantelpiece.*)

So, I'll ask my Dad. First thing. "You tell me the name of an *object.*" Or a "*collection* of things" . . . you know what I mean . . .

DEL: . . . that's right.

JOHN: "As we approach the Cabin."

DONNY: Mm . . .

JOHN: "To test our skills."

DONNY: . . . mm.

JOHN: But it doesn't have to be the Cabin.

DEL: No . . .

JOHN: It could be *anywhere* . . .

DEL: That's right.

JOHN: It could be anywhere at all.

DEL: That's right. As long as it's some *thing.* You have determined to observe.

JOHN: Yes. It could be right here . . .

DEL: That's absolutely right.

DONNY (*goes to him with the blanket*) (*simultaneous with* "and"): . . . and take the blanket . . .

DEL: Goodnight. John.

> (JOHN *picks up white envelope.*)

DONNY (*of envelope*): What have you got?

JOHN: Goodnight.

DONNY: . . . what is that?

JOHN: It's a letter . . . It's a note for you. (*She takes it, opens it.*) And it could be something right here, anything that, that, it would have to be something *new* . . . something that would . . .

DONNY: . . . that's right . . .

JOHN: . . . *surprise* us.

DONNY: . . . when did this get here . . . ?

JOHN: . . . you see?

DONNY: John. Go to bed. Now. Yes.

JOHN: Do you see?

DONNY: Go to bed.

JOHN: Alright. I understand. I'm going.

DEL: Goodnight, John. (JOHN *exits.*)

DEL: What is it?

DONNY: It's a letter to me. (*Pause.*)

DEL: A letter. (*Pause.*) What does it say?

DONNY: My husband's leaving me.

DEL: He's leaving you. (*Pause.*) Why would he want to do that . . . ?

Act Two

The next night.

JOHN, *in his bathrobe, and* DONNY.

JOHN: I thought that maybe there was nothing there. (*Pause.*) I thought that nothing was *there.* Then I was looking at my *book.* I thought "Maybe there's nothing *in* my book." It talked about the *buildings.* Maybe there's nothing *in* the buildings. And . . . or on my *globe.* You know my globe? You know my globe?

DONNY: Yes.

JOHN: Maybe there's nothing on the thing that it is of. We don't know what's there. *We* don't know that those things are there.

DONNY: I've been there. To many of them.

JOHN: Or in *buildings* we have not been in. Or in *history*. In the *history* of things. Or *thought*. (*Pause.*) I was *lying* there, and maybe there is no such thing as *thought*. Who *says* there is? Or human beings. And we are a dream. Who knows we are here? No one knows we are. We are a dream. We are just *dreaming*. I *know* we are. Or else . . . or else . . . . (*Pause.*) . . . and how do we *know* the things we know? We don't know what's real. And all we do is *say* things. (*Pause.*) Where do we *get* them from? And, or that things, go on forever. (*Pause.*) Or that we're *born*. Or that dead people moan. Or that, or that there's *hell*. And maybe we are there. Maybe there are people who've *been* there. Or, or else why should we *think* it? That's what I don't know. And maybe *everything* is true. Maybe it's true that I'm *sitting* here . . .

DONNY: Johnnie.

JOHN: What. . . ?

DONNY: I think . . .

JOHN: . . . don't you think?

DONNY: . . . you have to . . .

JOHN: No, I don't.

DONNY: Please, please do, though.

JOHN: I don't want to, though. (DEL *enters*.) (*Of* DEL.) That's what I mean. I don't want to . . . didn't you, mother. Mother . . .

DONNY (*to* DEL): Did you . . .

DEL (*simultaneous with* "you"): No.

DONNY: Did you find him?

DEL (*to* JOHN): How are you? (*To* DONNY.) No.

JOHN: I'm fine.

DONNY: Where did you look?

DEL: The *Windemere*, and then I stopped at Jimmy's.

DONNY: Did you try The Eagle?

DEL: No. (*Unpacking his paper bag.*) How has he . . .

DONNY: Why *not*? Why *not*?

DEL: I'm sorry . . . why not what?

DONNY (*simultaneous with* "what"): Why didn't you go to the . . .

DEL: . . . I thought you were going to call them.

DONNY: Why should I call them, if they'll say he wasn't *there*? Even if he *is* there . . . ?

DEL (*simultaneous with* "there"): I thought you were going to call them.

DONNY (*simultaneous with* "call"): No. I never said that.

DEL: Well, then, I made a mistake. (*He is preparing syrup from medicine bottle.*)

DONNY: How much was it?

DEL: I told them to charge it to you. (*Holding spoon.*) (*To* JOHN.) Open your mouth.

JOHN: I don't want to take that stuff.

DONNY: You're going to take it and you're going to *sleep*.

JOHN: No. I'm not sleepy.

DONNY: Take the medicine. Did you *hear* me? You're *sick*, and you're going to *bed*.

JOHN: I can't *sleep.*

DEL: . . . that's why . . .

JOHN: Every time I go to sleep I *see* things . . .

DONNY: You must . . .

DEL: That's, that's why you have to take the medicine, John.

JOHN (*simultaneous with* "John"): No. I'm not tired.

DONNY: Do you want to go to the Hospital?

JOHN: No.

DONNY: No? Did you hear what The Doctor said?

JOHN: No.

DEL: . . . what did he say?

DONNY: I want you to go to bed *now.*

DEL: You heard your mother.

JOHN: No. No.

DONNY: Johnnie . . .

JOHN: No one understands. You think that I'm *in* something . . . You don't know what I'm feeling.

DEL: What are you feeling? (*Pause.*) Are you afraid to go to bed?

JOHN: Yes.

DONNY: Why?

DEL: What are you afraid of in there?

JOHN: I don't know.

DONNY: I . . . I . . . I know it *frightens* you . . .

JOHN: I don't want to go to sleep.

DEL: Alright, alright, I'm going to *promise* you . . . look at me. John. I'm going to *promise* you if you take this and . . . you take this and go upstairs then you won't be afraid. I promise. (*Pause.*) I promise you. (*Pause.*)

JOHN: I sweat through the sheets . . .

DEL: We'll change . . .

JOHN: . . . the *bed* is wet.

DEL: We'll change, we'll change the sheets, you don't have to worry.

DONNY: You go lie down in my bed.

DEL: . . . you lie down in your mother's bed. (*Pause.*) You go lie down there.

JOHN: I'm going to sweat them.

DEL: That's alright. Do you hear what I'm telling you . . . ? (*Pause.*)

JOHN: Maybe I'll just . . . maybe I'll just go there . . . maybe I'll just go there and lie down.

DONNY: Yes. You go and lie down now. You take this, now. (DEL *gives* JOHN *his medicine.*)

JOHN: Do you know why I took it, 'cause I'm tired.

DEL: I'm sure you are.

JOHN: . . . 'cause I've been *up* all day . . .

DEL: I know you have. And I know how that feels.

JOHN: I . . . I . . .

DONNY: . . . you go to bed now.

DEL: John? "My blessings on this house. . .," the Wizard said.

JOHN: When is my father coming for me . . . ?

DONNY: Shhhh.

JOHN: . . . No. I don't understand.

DONNY: Shh. It's alright.

JOHN: What's happening to me . . . ?

DONNY (*embracing him*): It's alright. Hush. You go to bed. It's alright. John. Shh. You've only got a fever. Shhh . . .

DEL: . . . you're fine . . .

DONNY: You go upstairs now. Shhh. You go upstairs now, John . . . (*She starts him upstairs. Comes down.*)

DEL: . . . I looked every place I thought that he would *be* . . .

DONNY: I'm sorry.

DEL: But I couldn't find him. (*Pause.*) Do you want a drink?

DONNY: No. (*Pause.*)

DEL: I'm sorry that I couldn't find him. (*Pause.*) Would you like me to go out again?

DONNY: No. (*Pause.*)

DEL: Would you like to play Casino?

DONNY: No.

DEL: No, you're right, that's stupid. Oh God, oh God, that's *stupid*. (*Pause.*) Would you like to play Gin?

DONNY: Del . . .

DEL: Yeah. Do you see what I mean when I talk about myself? (*Pause.*) But would you like to?

DONNY: Let's have a drink.

DEL: Well. I know I know I'm limited.

(DEL *goes to the liquor cabinet, examines bottles.*)

There's only a new one.

DONNY: That's alright, open it. Enough. Enough for one day. I don't care. (*Pause.*) I don't care anymore. I swear to God.

(DEL *takes out bottle, takes out his knife, opens it.*)

DEL (*of bottle*): I think that this is good for you. (*Pause.*) You know why . . . ? Because it's a ceremony. To, to *delimit* umm . . .

DONNY: A ceremony.

DEL: Of . . . of what? Of, of *inebriation,* certainly, of, of of well, of *together-ness* . . . I don't know. (*He goes to the kitchen, comes out with two glasses and the bottle.*) (*Pours two glasses.*)

DONNY: Thank you.

DEL: Uh . . . Days May Come and Days May Go . . . (*Pause.*) Well, *that's* true enough.

DONNY: Isn't it?

DEL: I think so. (*Pause.*) Days May Come and Go.

DONNY: And May we Always be as . . .

DEL: Yes.

DONNY: As . . .

DEL: Unified . . .

DONNY: Well, let's pick something more moving than that.

DEL: Alright . . . be . be . be . be-*nighted?* No, that's not the word I want to use . . . be-*trothed* . . . ? No.

DONNY: Close . . .

DEL: Yes.

DONNY: Close to each other.

DEL: As we happen to be right now. (*Pause.*)

DONNY: Fine.

DEL: (*Pause.*) And . . . May the Spirit of Friendship . . . (*Pause.*) oh, the hell with it. I mean, can't people just have a drink . . . for the love of God? (*They drink.*) Bec, because I swear, because I think there's just too much. In *trial* . . . in *adversity* . . . (*Pause*) and you can't, you can't go always look . . .

DONNY: Go Looking for *answers* . . .

DEL: No.

DONNY: . . . you're absolutely right . . .

DEL: In introspection. (*Pause.*)
You know, at times of *trial* . . .

DONNY: hmm . . .

DEL: Do you hear what I'm telling you?

DONNY: Yes.

DEL: . . . and they come for us all.

DONNY: . . . Oh, Lord.

DEL: Yes. They do. Then many times the answer comes. In reaching out. Or, do you know what? In getting drunk.

DONNY: . . . in drinking.

DEL: Be. Because, you know? Then you forget. (*Pause.*) And I don't *give* a damn. (*Pause.*) In this *shithole.* (*Pause.*) Well. I'm not going to *dwell* upon it. (*Pause.*) You drink, and then, when you *remember* again—this is the good part—when you *remember* again . . . (*Pause.*) It's later on. And time has dulled your, your . . . you know, for whatever portion of time that, that you for*got.* (*Pause.*)

DONNY: "You should get married."

DEL: "It would have to be someone nice."

DONNY: "We'll find them for you."

DEL: "Would you?" (*Pause.*) Although we joke about it. (*Sighs.*) Do you want me to go and look at John?

DONNY: He's going to be alright.

DEL: Are *you* alright, though?

DONNY: Yes.

DEL: I'm sorry that I didn't find Robert.

DONNY (*simultaneous with* "find"): . . . That's

DEL: I *looked* for him, but . . .

DONNY: That's al . . .

DEL: I Didn't find him. I suppose I thought that—in, you know, in addition to the things I said—that it wasn't a good *idea* to have him come here. But what business is that of *mine?* (*Pause.*) None. None, really.

DONNY: That's alright.

DEL: None at all. But I *looked* for him. (*Pause.*)

DONNY: (*Long pause.*) Well . . .

DEL: Worse things have happened, I suppose. (*Pause.*)

DONNY: . . . mmm.

DEL: It's such a shock.

DONNY: However much we . . .

DEL: What?

DONNY: I'm sorry?

DEL: However much . . . ?

DONNY: We could have anticipated it.

DEL: How could we?

DONNY: He tried to tell you.

DEL: What do you mean?

DONNY: He gave you the knife.

DEL: I don't understand.

DONNY: The Odd Gesture. (*Pause.*) Isn't it.

DEL: I don't understand.

DONNY: You don't understand the Gesture?

DEL: No.

DONNY: It was his going-away present. (*Pause.*) Going away. (*Pause.*) Big German knife. His war memento. Do you know the Meaning of it?

DEL: . . . meaning . . .

DONNY: You know what it's for.

DEL: The knife.

DONNY: Yes.

DEL: (*Pause.*) To cut things.

DONNY: I mean the specific . . .

DEL: The specific *purpose?* No. No. I mean, *no.*

DONNY: It's a *pilot's* knife . . .

DEL: . . . yes. I know that . . .

DONNY: If he was forced to *parachute* . . .

DEL: Yes.

DONNY: The pilot would use it to cut the *cords.* If his parachute snagged.

DEL: Huh. If it snagged. On, on what?

DONNY: On a tree.

DEL: Oh, you mean when he landed.

DONNY: Yes.

DEL: Huh. (*Pause.*)

DONNY: And that's the meaning. (*Pause.*)

DEL: . . . yes . . .

DONNY: When he was forced to abandon . . .

DEL: Yes. (*Pause.*) When he was forced to *abandon* his . . . (*Pause.*) He looked for *safety,* and the knife, it cut . . . It "released" him.

DONNY: Yes. That's right.

DEL: . . . as *any* tool . . .

DONNY: And he gave it to you.

DEL: He can be very generous. Is that alright? To . . .

DONNY: Yes. No. He can. (*Pause.*)
  . . . what am I going to do? You tell me. Yes. He could be generous. *I* don't know.

DEL: . . . he was opening a can. With it. And I said . . . actually, he saw me looking at the knife. And he wiped it. And gave it to me. (*Pause.*)

DONNY: When you were at the Camp. Last week.

DEL: That's right—(*Pause.*)

DONNY: Tell me what you talked about.

DEL: What we talked about. In the Woods.

DONNY: Yes.

DEL: We talked about you.

DONNY: About *me* . . . ?

DEL: Yes. (*Pause.*)

DONNY: What did he say?

DEL: How happy he had been.

DONNY: Really.

DEL: That's what he said.

DONNY: How can you understand that. (*Pause.*) How in the world . . .

DEL: I'm so sorry.

DONNY: Did you know he was leaving me?

DEL: No.

DONNY: Did you think that he was?

DEL: No.

DONNY: No? You didn't?

DEL: How could I?

DONNY: . . . he didn't . . . ?

DEL: No. He didn't what . . . ?

DONNY: Give you a sign . . . ?

DEL: A sign. No.

DONNY: How can we understand . . . how . . . *men,* you know. How . . .
men . . .

DEL: I'm going to *tell* you something.
It's funny for two grown men to go camping anyway. (*Pause.*) I don't
care. (*Pause.*) Huh. I was born a *city* boy. (*Pause.*) (*He displays knife.*)
And now I'm a Forester. (*Pause.*) I'm a Ranger . . . did you know there's
a Fraternal Group called the Catholic Order of Foresters?

DONNY: Yes.

DEL: You knew that?

DONNY: Yes. Sure.

DEL: I wonder what they do. (*Pause.*)

DONNY: Did you say he gave that knife to you when you went camping?

DEL: Yes. (*Pause.*)

DONNY: When the two of you went camping. Last . . .

DEL: Last week. That's right. (*Pause.*)

DONNY: He gave the knife to you.

DEL: Yes. He was opening a can of . . . (*Pause.*) Why? (*Pause.*) Why did you
ask?

DONNY: I saw it in the attic. When I went up there. To put the things away.

DEL: (*Pause.*) What things?

DONNY: When I took the camping things up. Last week. (*Pause.*) After your
trip. When you came back.

DEL: I don't understand.

DONNY: When you came back, last week, Robert and you.

DEL: . . . yes . . .

DONNY: From your Trip.

I went up. To put his things away. And the knife was up there. (*Pause.*) It was already in the attic.

DEL: Well, maybe he went up there first, to put it back.

DONNY: . . . What?

DEL: I'm saying, maybe Robert went there first to put it back. When we came back. When we came back from *camping*. (*Pause.*) I'm sure that's what occurred. (*Pause.*)

DONNY: You're saying that he went upstairs to put it back.

DEL: Yes. Because it was precious to him.

DONNY: I don't understand.

DEL: It was a *war* memento. I'm saying that it was so *precious* to him that he went, and *left* the stuff . . . for *you* to put away, but went upstairs and put the *knife* into the trunk himself. (*Pause.*)

DONNY: Then how did *you* get it? (*Pause.*)

DEL: What?

DONNY: How did you get the knife?

DEL: He gave it to me.

DONNY: I don't understand.

DEL: He gave it to me.

DONNY: How could he give it to you?

DEL: What?

DONNY: You said he gave it to you when you were camping. (*Pause.*) How could he give it to you when you were *camping,* when it was here in the trunk when you both came back? (*Pause.*)

DEL: There must be two knives. (*Pause.*)

DONNY: I . . . I don't understand.

DEL: There must be two knives.

DONNY: What?

DEL: I bet if you went in the trunk to look right now you'd see. There was another knife.

DONNY: Yes. No. Wait . . . When did Robert give the knife to you?

DEL: I *thought* . . . isn't it funny? I was sure he gave the knife to me while we were camping. I guess I'm mistaken. (*Pause.*) Huh. (*Pause.*) Unless, no . . . Huh! . . .I . . . I don't know. (*Pause.*) It's a mystery to me. Unless . . .

DONNY: *Wait!*

DEL: What?

DONNY: He came upstairs. He came up. To the attic!

DEL: Who?

DONNY: I was putting the things away. He said. Yes. "Leave the trunk open." (*Pause.*) He *got* it from the trunk. When you came back. He didn't *put* it there. He went up there to *get* it. (*Pause.*)

DEL: That could happen.

DONNY: What do you mean?

DEL: Well, that, that's not so unusual.

DONNY: What isn't.

DEL: . . . for someone to do that. (*Pause.*)

DONNY: Did he do that?

DEL: It's possible. I think he did. Yes. I think *that's*. Um, that's *exactly* what he did. I *think. (Pause.)*

DONNY: Why did you lie to me?

DEL: I didn't lie. It was a slip of memory.

DONNY: Why did you lie?

DEL: If I did I *assure* you, it was, um, *you* know . . .

DONNY: What?

DEL: It was . . .

DONNY: You didn't go camping.

DEL: Who?

DONNY: You and Robert.

DEL: That's ridiculous!

DONNY: You never went.

DEL: That's . . .

DONNY: . . . Yes . . . ?

DEL: Be, because, be . . . what are you *saying* to me? Am, am I to be *accused* of this!

DONNY: Of what?

DEL: Well, that's my point.

DONNY: What did you do?

DEL: I. Why do you say *that?* For god*sake!*

DONNY: What did you do? I'll ask Robert.

DEL: You can't find him!

DONNY: What do you mean?

DEL: He won't tell you. *(Pause.)* Alright. *(Pause.)* But: I want to *tell* you something: I knew that I should not take that knife.

DONNY: Why did you take it?

DEL: Be, because he *gave* it to me.

DONNY: Why? *(Pause.)*

DEL: Huh. Well, that's the *question. (Pause.) That's* what you'd like to *know. (Pause.) Isn't* it? Yes. So you could say, "Old Del, who we thought was so Loyal" . . . I know what you mean. Be*lieve* me. *(Pause.)* Believe me.

DONNY: Why did he give the knife to you?

DEL: You don't want to know.

DONNY: I do.

DEL: *Believe* me, you don't. *(Pause.)* To shut me up. Alright? There. Are you *happy?* I told you you wouldn't be.

DONNY: To shut you up about what? *(Pause.)*

DEL: Because we didn't go.

DONNY: What?

DEL: We didn't *go!* Do I have to *shout* it for you . . . ? We stayed *home.* What do you *think?* He'd traipse off in the *wilds* . . . with *me* . . . ? To talk about *life?* Are you *stupid?* Are you *blind?* He wouldn't spend a *moment* with me. Some poor geek . . . "Here's my Old Friend Del . . ." You're *nuts,* you're *stupid* if you think that's what went on. *(Pause.)* He used my *room,* alright? He said, "Del, can I Use Your Room?" Is that so weird? There. Now I've told you. Now you can sleep easier. I *told* you not to ask. Don't tell me I didn't tell you. *(Pause.)*

DONNY: He used your room.

DEL: That's absolutely right.

DONNY: Why? (*Pause.*)

DEL: To go there with a woman. (*Pause.*) And now, and now you know the truth, How weak I am. How "Evil" I am. He said, "I have some things to do," "I want it to seem like I'm gone." *I* spent the week, *I* slept in the, in my, my nook in the *library*. In *fishing* clothes . . . and don't you think *that* looked stupid! (*Pause.*) I . . . I, actually, I've been waiting for this. I knew that I should tell you. This is the only bad thing I have ever done to you. I'm sorry that it came out like this. Indeed I am. (*Pause.*) But we can't always choose the, um . . . (*Pause.*)

DONNY: Get out. (*Pause.*) Get out.

(DEL *exits.*) (*Pause.*)

(DONNY *starts to cry.*)

DONNY: (*Pause.*) Bobby. Bobby. Bobby. (JOHN *appears in bathrobe.*) (*Pause.*)

JOHN: Are you dead?

DONNY: What?

JOHN: Are you dead? (*Pause.*)

DONNY: Why do you say that?

JOHN (*simultaneous with* "that"): I heard you calling.

DONNY: Go back to bed, John.

JOHN: I heard voices . . .

DONNY: . . . you should go back to bed.

JOHN: . . . and I thought they were you. (*Pause.*)

DONNY: It was me.

JOHN: And so I said, ". . . there's someone troubled." And I walked around. Did you hear walking?

DONNY: No.

JOHN: . . . and so I went outside. I saw a candle. In the dark.

DONNY: Where was this?

JOHN: In my room. It was burning there. I said, "I'm perfectly alone." This is what I was saying to myself: "I'm perfectly alone." And I think I was saying it a long time. 'Cause I didn't have a pen. Did that ever happen to you?

DONNY: I don't know, John.

JOHN: So I came downstairs to write it down. I know that there *are* pens up there. But I don't want to look for them.

(DONNY *goes to him and cradles him.*)

Do you think that was right?

DONNY: Shhh.

JOHN: Do you think that I was right?

DONNY: Go to bed.

JOHN: Mother? (*Pause.*)

DONNY: What?

JOHN: Do you think that I was right.

DONNY: I don't know, John.

JOHN: I saw a candle in my room.

Act Three

Evening. One month later.

The room is denuded. Various packing boxes are seen. JOHN *is sitting on one of them.* DONNY *comes downstairs carrying a box. She puts it down and starts for the kitchen.*

JOHN: Where were you?

DONNY: I'll put the kettle on.

JOHN (*simultaneous with* "on"): Where were you?

DONNY: I went up for your bag.

JOHN: The movers will take it.

DONNY: There were some things I thought that you might like to have.

JOHN: What things?

DONNY: For the first few nights.

   (*Pause.*) Until the boxes come. (*She starts into the kitchen.*)

JOHN: Mother.

DONNY (*offstage*): . . . yes . . .

JOHN: Do you ever think things? (*Pause.*) Mother . . . ?

DONNY (*offstage, simultaneous with* "mother"): What? (*Pause.*) What, John? (DONNY *reenters.*) What did you say?

JOHN: I asked you. Do you think things.

DONNY: What things, John? (*Pause.*)

JOHN: Do you ever wish that you could die? (*Pause.*)

DONNY: . . . do I wish I could die?

JOHN: Yes. (*Pause.*)

DONNY: I don't know.

JOHN: Yes, you do.

DONNY: No, I don't know, John.

JOHN: Yes you do. You can tell me. (*Pause.*)
   It's not such a bad feeling. (*Pause.*) Is it?

DONNY: I don't know.

JOHN: Yes. You do. (*Pause.*) I think you do.

DONNY: John: Things occur. In our lives. And the meaning of them . . . the *meaning* of them . . . is not clear.

JOHN: . . . the meaning of them . . .

DONNY: That's correct. At the time. But we assume they have a meaning. We must. And we don't know what it is.

JOHN: Do you ever wish you could die?
   (*Pause.*) Would you tell me?

DONNY: Do I wish that I could die?

JOHN: You can tell me. You won't frighten me.

DONNY: (*Pause.*) How can I *help* you? Do you see? (*Pause.*) Do you see?

JOHN: No.

DONNY: At some point . . . there are things that have occurred I cannot help you with . . . that . . .

JOHN: I can't sleep.

DONNY: Well. It's an unsettling time.

JOHN: . . . I want . . .

DONNY: Yes?

JOHN: I would like to go to the Cabin.

DONNY: . . . well . . .

JOHN: I want to go to the Lake.

DONNY: Well, no, John, we can't. You know we can't.

JOHN: I don't know that.

DONNY: No. We can't.

JOHN: That's why I can't sleep.

DONNY: What do you want me to do? John? I am not God. I don't control the World. If you could think what it is I could do for you . . . If I could help you . . . (*Sound of kettle, offstage.*)

JOHN: Do you ever wish you could die? (*Pause.*)
It's not such a bad feeling. Is it?

DONNY: I know that you're frightened. I know you are. But at some point, do you see . . . ? (*Pause. Exits.*) (*Offstage.*) John, everyone has a story. Did you know that? In their lives. This is yours. (DEL *enters.*) And finally . . . finally . . . you are going to have to learn how you will deal with it. You understand? I'm going to speak to you as an adult: At some point . . . At some point, we have to learn to face ourselves . . . what kind of tea . . .

DEL: Hello.

JOHN: Hello.

DEL: How are you today?

JOHN: I'm fine.

DONNY (*offstage*): What kind of tea?

DEL: That's good.

DONNY (*offstage*): John?

JOHN: What did my mother say?

DEL: I came to talk to you.

JOHN (*simultaneous with* "you"): . . . what did my mother say?

DEL (*simultaneous with* "say"): She wanted to know what kind of tea . . .

DONNY (*offstage*): John . . . ?

DEL: . . . what sort of tea you wanted. What sort of tea *do* you want? (JOHN *rises to exit.*)

JOHN: I don't know.

DEL: I'd like to talk to you, John.

JOHN: About what?

DEL: Several things.

JOHN: When is my father coming?

DEL: I have something that I'd like to say.

JOHN: I have to go upstairs.

DEL: Could you wait a moment?

(JOHN *exits.*)

DEL: John . . .

DONNY (*offstage*): Do you see? One has to go on. That's all we can say. I'm speaking to you as an adult.

(*She enters, with a tea tray. Pause.*)

DONNY: Where's my son?

DEL: I don't know. He went upstairs. (*Pause.*)

DONNY: Mm.

DEL: That's right.

DONNY: How is my husband.

DEL: I don't see him.

DONNY: No . . . ?

DEL: I came to talk to you. And to the boy.

DONNY: Well, it seems that he's gone upstairs.

DEL: Aha.

DONNY: What do you need to say? (*Pause.*)

DEL: I'm sorry what I did. (*Pause.*) Aren't we a funny race? The things we do. (*Pause.*) And then what we say about them. You'd think, if there were a "Deity" we would all burn. (*Pause.*) Swine that we are. But we go on. (*Pause.*) I brought something for you.

DONNY: You did?

DEL: (*Produces book.*) As you see.

DONNY: And that's supposed to put you back in my good graces?

DEL: What would do that?

DONNY: Nothing you've brought.

DEL: Well. (*Pause.*) Here is a book. It's your book, by the way. I've kept it. All these years. Perhaps that's what rotted my soul. Do you know, they say: it is not the sins we commit that destroy us, but how we act after we've committed them. Is that a useful bit of lore? (*Pause.*) I've found it so. (*Pause.*) And here is the German Pilot's Knife. I was obsessed to bring it. I thought, "But why would she want it?" But, of course, it's not for you. It's a propitiation. To the boy.

DONNY: To the boy . . .

DEL: Yes. Well, he should have it. Shouldn't he?

DONNY: Should he?

DEL: Yes.

DONNY: Why?

DEL: Because I've wronged him.

DONNY: You've wronged him.

DEL: I have.

DONNY: Haven't you wronged me?

DEL: What was I going to bring you, Flowers?

DONNY: But you brought the boy the knife.

DEL: That's right.

DONNY: No, you puzzle me.

DEL: *I* don't deserve it. It's his father's, um, what do they call it? "War" memento. A "combat" trophy. I brought you the bbb . . .

DONNY: . . . it's not a "combat" . . .

DEL: I brought you the *book* . . .

DONNY: It's not a combat trophy.

DEL: Well, well, it's a *War* memen . . .

DONNY: It's not a Combat Trophy.

DEL: *Whatever* it is.

DONNY: It's not . . .

DEL: Alright. He won it in the War. I didn't want to deprive the boy of . . .

DONNY: He didn't win it in the war.

DEL: *Really.*

DONNY: No.

DEL: No. The German Knife.

DONNY: No.

DEL: Well, of *course* he did.

DONNY: Not in the "fighting."

DEL: Oh. He didn't . . . ?

DONNY: No. Not in the "fighting." No.

DEL: He didn't get it in the fighting.

DONNY: No.

DEL: Well, yes, he did.

DONNY: How could he?

DEL: Well, you tell me. How could he *not?* It's a *war* mem . . .

DONNY: He was a flier. Do you see?

DEL: No.

DONNY: He was a flier.

DEL: I don't see.

DONNY: He was in the *air.* Could he capture the knife in the Air?

DEL: I don't understand.

DONNY: Could he get it in the Air? You "fairy"? Could he capture the knife
    from the other man in the Air? You fool.

DEL: (*Pause.*) Then how did he obtain it?

DONNY: How do you think?

DEL: I don't know.

DONNY: But how do you think?

DEL: I don't know. That's why I ask.

DONNY: He bought it.

DEL: He bought the knife.

DONNY: That's right.

DEL: The Combat knife.

DONNY: Mm.

DEL: . . . he gave me.

DONNY: Yes.

DEL: Where?

DONNY: From a man. On the street. In London.

DEL: Huh. (*Pause.*) You're saying he bought the knife. And you thought that
    would hurt me. (*Pause.*) And you're right of course.

DONNY: . . . to hurt you.

DEL: Well, you knew it would.

DONNY: Why would that hurt you?

DEL: Oh, you didn't know that.

DONNY: No.

DEL: Then why did you say it?

DONNY: I . . .

DEL: Why did you say it, then? Excuse me, that the souvenir that he gave me, as a War Memento, with "associations," that it had no meaning for him. And what would *I* know about the war? I live in a *Hotel*. (*Pause.*)

DONNY: I didn't mean to hurt you.

DEL: Oh, if we could speak the truth, do you see, for one instant. Then we would be free. (*Pause.*) I should have chucked it anyway. (*Pause.*)

How could a knife be a suitable gift for a child? No, but we know it can't. We bring our . . . our little "gifts." And take your book. It's your goddam book. I've had it at the hotel. All these years. I borrowed it and never brought it back. How about that. Eh? Years ago. That's how long I've had it. Was ever anyone so false? Take it. I hate it. I hate the whole fucking progression. Here. Take the cursed thing. (*Hands her the book.*)

DONNY: It's your copy.

DEL: It is?

DONNY: Yes.

DEL: How do you know?

DONNY: It's got your name in it. (*Pause.*)

DEL: Where? (*She shows him.*) (*Of book.*) This *is* my copy . . . isn't that funny? (*Pause.*) Because I'd *wondered* what I'd done with it. Do you know how long I've been *looking* for this? (*Pause.*) (*Reads.*) "May you always be as . . ."

DONNY: Aren't you funny.

DEL: I'm pathetic. I know that. You don't have to tell me. The life that I lead is trash. I hate myself. Oh well. (*Pause.*) But I would like to talk to you. (*Pause.*) If I might. (*Pause.*) In spite of . . .

DONNY: In spite of . . .

DEL: What has occurred. (*Pause.*)

DONNY: Why?

DEL: Because there are things. I have been longing to say. To, um . . . "say," for a long . . . And perhaps this is what it takes. Isn't it funny? If you'd permit me. Alright. Thank you. For a long while . . .

(JOHN *appears on the stairs.*)

DONNY: (*Pause.*) Yes? Yes, John . . . ?

JOHN: I'm cold. I'm sorry. (*Pause.*) I'm cold.

My *mind* is racing. I . . .

DONNY: You what? (*Pause.*)

JOHN: . . . I think . . .

DONNY: . . . what can I do about it?

JOHN: I . . .

DONNY: What can I *do* about it, John?

JOHN: I don't know.

DONNY: What do you expect me to do?

JOHN: I don't know.

DONNY: Well.

DEL: . . . may I speak to him?

JOHN: I don't, I'm afraid. I know that I should not *think* about certain things, but . . .

DEL (*to* DONNY): May . . . ?

JOHN: . . . but I . . .

DONNY: John: John: I'd like to help you; now: you have to go to sleep. You must go to sleep.

   If you do *not* sleep, *lay* there. Lay in bed. What you think about there is your concern. No one can help you. Do you understand? *Finally, each* of us.

JOHN: Where is the blanket?

DONNY: I . . . *Each* of us . . .

JOHN: . . . I want the blanket.

DONNY: Is alone.

JOHN: . . . the *stadium* blanket.

DONNY (*simultaneous with* "stadium"): I've put it away.

JOHN: No: Mother . . .

DEL: May I speak to him?

JOHN: I want it.

DONNY: I've put it away, John.

JOHN: I'm cold. Could I have it, please.

DONNY: It's packed away.

JOHN: Where?

DONNY: A box. Up in the attic, I believe . . .

DEL (*simultaneous with* "believe"): It's in the attic, John.

JOHN: I need it. I'm cold.

DONNY: John . . . Alright, now.

JOHN: I . . .

DEL (*to* DONNY): Perhaps he . . .

DONNY: It's packed in a box.

DEL: But couldn't he get it, though?

DONNY: No. It's waiting for the *movers*.

DEL: But might he have it?

DONNY: It's wrapped up.

JOHN: I could undo it.

DONNY: Fine. Then it's in the attic. In the large brown box.

DEL: You see?

JOHN: Yes.

DONNY: With the new address on it.

JOHN: And I can open it. The box?

DONNY: If you will go to sleep. You must go to sleep. Do you hear me?

DEL: That is the point, do you see? John?

DONNY: You can unwrap it if you go to sleep.

DEL: . . . that's right.

DONNY: But you must . . .

DEL: We're talking to you like a man.

DONNY: But you must promise . . .

JOHN: . . . I promise.

DONNY: . . . Because . . .

JOHN: I understand. I promise. (*Pause.*) I promise.

DONNY: Do you understand?

JOHN: Yes. Yes. I promise.

DEL: Good, then, John. Goodnight.

DONNY: Goodnight. (JOHN *exits*.) (*Pause*.) Lucky boy. To have a protector. (*Pause*.)

DEL: Well . . .

DONNY: Don't you think?

DEL: Donny, I . . .

DONNY: Do you know. If I could find one man in my life. Who would not betray me. (*Pause*.)

DEL: I'm sorry.

DONNY: That's what I mean.

DEL: I'm sorry I betrayed you.

DONNY: Isn't that sweet. Aren't you sweet. How could one be miffed with you? The problem must be *mine*.

DEL: I'm sorry I betrayed you.

DONNY: Just like the rest of them. All of you are.

DEL: I'm sorry.

DONNY: Can you explain it to me, though? Why? (*Pause*.) You see? That's what baffles me. I try to say "human nature" . . .

DEL: . . . I know . . .

DONNY: I don't know what our nature is. If I do, then it's bad.

DEL: . . . I know . . .

DONNY: If I do, then it's filthy. No, you don't know. You have no idea. All the men I ever met . . .

DEL: And I'm so sorry. To have added one *iota*, in my stupid . . .

DONNY: . . . in this cesspool.

DEL: Could I . . .

DONNY: (*Pause*.) No. I don't care anymore.

DEL: Could I talk to you? Who am I? Some poor Queen. Lives in a hotel. Some silly old Soul Who loves you.

DONNY: Oh, please.

DEL: No—I need you to forgive me.

DONNY: Why would I do that?

DEL: You should do that if it would make you happy.

DONNY: No, look here: don't tell me I'm going to make a sacrifice for you, and it's for my own good.
Do you see? Because every man I ever met in this shithole . . . Don't you dare come in my house and do that. You faggot. Every man I ever met in my life . . .

DEL: *Well, why does it happen?*

DONNY: Excuse me . . . ?

DEL: Why does it happen? Is it chance? Do you think it's some mystery? What you encounter? What you provoke . . . ?

DONNY: What I *provoke* . . . ?

DEL: That's right.

DONNY: What are you saying?

DEL: Well . . .

DONNY: You might as well say it.

DEL: Are you sure?

DONNY: Oh. Don't "tease" me . . . mmm? For God's sake: don't "tease" me, lad . . .

DEL: . . . No.

DONNY: You came to say your little piece—go on.

DEL: Alright. For some time, for quite a long time I've watched you.

DONNY: *Have* you?

DEL: I have . . .

DONNY: You've *watched* me.

DEL: . . . and I've thought about you. And the boy. Quite a long time.

DONNY: Well . . .

DEL: Alright. Here is what I think: (*Pause.*)

(JOHN *appears at the head of the stairs.*) (*Pause.*)

DONNY: Yes. Yes, John, What?

JOHN: I . . .

DONNY: What? What? You promised. Did you promise?

JOHN: . . . I . . .

DONNY: . . . It's not a small *thing.* You . . .

JOHN: I only . . .

DONNY: Yes, *What? What?* "You Only . . ." You prom. . .

JOHN: . . . I only . . .

DONNY: I DON'T CARE. Do You Know What It Means To Give . . .

JOHN: . . . I . . .

DONNY: . . . to give your word? I DON'T CARE.

JOHN: I . . .

DONNY: I don't care. Do you hear? I don't care. You *promised* me that you would stay upstairs.

JOHN: . . . I . . .

DONNY: I don't care. Go away. You lied.

DEL: Donny . . .

DONNY: I love you, but I can't like you.

DEL: Donny . . .

DONNY: Do you know why? You lied.

DEL: Let me . . . Let me . . . John: Here. Go to bed. Take the book. This is the book, John. We were talking about. It was my copy. It's yours now. "That's what the Wizard said." It's yours. Off you go. If you can't sleep . . .

JOHN: . . . I . . .

DEL: F'you can't sleep, you read it. It's alright now. You go to bed. S'alright. Off you go.

(*Pause.*)

JOHN: I have to cut the twine.

DONNY: The twine.

JOHN: On the box.

DONNY: I don't understand.

JOHN: To get to the blanket. It's tied.

DEL: Alright, go to the kitchen, take, no, they're packed. Are they packed? They're put away, John. The knives are put away. (*Pause.*)

JOHN: You said I could have the blanket.

DEL: Well,

JOHN: You said that.

DEL: Well, you'll have to do without. But you'll be fine, I promise you. We'll . . .

DONNY: Goodnight, John.

DEL: You understand. You'll be fine. Goodnight, now.

JOHN: You said I could have the blanket.

DEL: Goodnight, Jjjj . . .

(JOHN *starts to exit.*)

DONNY: John? Del said "goodnight" to you. (*Pause.*) Did you hear him?

DEL: It's alright.

DONNY: John . . . ?

DEL: It's alr . . .

DONNY: No. It isn't alright. I'm speaking to you. Come back here. John? The man said goodnight to you. Come back down and tell the man you're sorry.

DEL: It's alright, Donny.

DONNY: John? I'm *speaking* to you. What must I do?

DEL: Donn . . .

DONNY: What must I do that you treat me like an animal?

DEL: It's . . .

DONNY: Don't you tell me it's alright, for the love of God. Don't you *dare* to dispute me.

DEL: The child . . .

DONNY: Don't you *dare* to dispute me in my home. Now, I'm *speaking* to you, John. Don't stand there so innocently. I've asked you a question. Do you want me to go mad? Is that what you want? Is that what you want?

DEL: Your mother's speaking to you, John.

DONNY: Is that what you want?

DEL: She asked you a question.

DONNY: Can't you see that I need comfort? Are you blind? For the love of God . . .

JOHN: I hear voices.

DEL: John: Your mother's waiting for you to . . .

JOHN: Before I go to sleep.

DEL: Your mother's waiting, John. What does she want to hear?

JOHN: . . . before I go to sleep.

DEL: What does she want to hear you say?

JOHN: I don't know.

DEL: I think that you do. (*Pause.*) What does she want to hear you say. (*Pause.*)

JOHN: "I'm sorry."

DEL: What?

JOHN: I'm sorry.

DEL: Alright, then.
JOHN: You told me I could have the blanket.
DONNY: Goodnight, John.
JOHN: You told me I could have the blanket.
DEL: Yes. You can.
JOHN: It's wrapped up.
DEL: Take the knife. When you're done . . . (*Hands the boy the knife.*)
JOHN: I can't fall asleep.
DEL: That's up to you, now.
JOHN: I hear voices. They're calling to me. (*Pause.*)
DONNY: Yes I'm sure they are.
JOHN: They're calling me.
DEL: Take the knife and go.
JOHN: They're calling my name. (*Pause.*) Mother. They're calling my name.

The Receptive Reader

1. As you listen to the characters in the opening scene or scenes, what do you learn about the situation? Who are the characters, and how do they relate? When do you first sense that something is wrong?

2. People reacting to this play disagree on whether John is a convincing ten-year-old. Do you understand who and what he is? Why is his inability or unwillingness to sleep such an issue in the play?

3. In this play, the stereotypical emotionally absent father is literally absent. How does he gradually become more central as the play develops?

4. The ripped blanket, the broken teakettle, and the knife are all darkly symbolic. What is their symbolic meaning? What is their role in the play?

5. What is Del's role in the play? When or how do you learn that Del is gay? Does it make any difference to his role in the play?

6. Betrayal becomes a powerful central theme as the play approaches its end. Who betrays whom? Which of the betrayals is the most basic or the most shattering?

7. John is waiting for the "Third Misfortune," having read in a book that misfortunes come in threes. What was the first? What was the second? What is the third? Which of the misfortunes is most ominous? What do they all have in common?

The Personal Response

Who are you in this play? With which of the characters can you identify most directly or most strongly? Why?

The Creative Dimension

Psychiatrist Sheldon Kopp wrote that "childhood is a nightmare." This observation contradicts a common belief that childhood is the best time of life, free from trouble. In a small group or with the class as a whole, discuss which view of childhood you believe to be more nearly true. Turning to your own childhood memories, write a vignette, or snapshot, of some dramatic or traumatic scene that bears out your perspective on childhood. Your class may decide to collect these autobiographical vignettes for a class publication.

THE SEARCH FOR ROOTS

*I discovered that you have no respect for what
you do not understand.*

WOLE SOYINKA,
DEATH AND THE KING'S HORSEMAN

Conservative critics have used the term *multiculturalism* as a divisive slogan. They have seen multiculturalism as an onslaught on the Western cultural heritage by people without Ivy League degrees. Advocates of a multicultural perspective, on the other hand, see a recognition and acceptance of diversity as the essential clue to an understanding of American history and American culture. They see it as the only hope for a world threatened by a relapse into tribalism, "ethnic cleansing," and paranoid, xenophobic nationalism. American literature has always been richer and more vital than a myopic focus on the New England tradition would suggest, important as it is. In a world with a global economy and a worldwide youth culture, the theater can serve its ancient function as a moral force by helping us cross narrow traditional boundaries.

David Henry Hwang   *(born 1957)*   ☜

David Henry Hwang, a Chinese American playwright, explores the lives of Asian Americans, who had seldom been seen on the American stage. He made a dramatic bid for recognition with his *M. Butterfly* (1988), which mocked the stereotype of the meek, submissive, self-sacrificing Asian woman immortalized in Puccini's opera *Madame Butterfly*. The Italian composer had set to lush music the story of the geisha girl who is abandoned by the American naval officer she loved. She hands their love child over to the officer's wife, and then commits suicide. Hwang's Madame Butterfly is a male Chinese opera singer playing women's roles and working for the Chinese government as a spy.

The short play that follows is a dialogue between two of the immigrants who came from starving villages in China to build the transcontinental railroad. One of the characters is a familiar type in Hwang's plays—the FOB, the immigrant "fresh off the boat," who still believes much of what Americans or earlier immigrants tell him. The other is keeping alive his ties with a thousand-year-old Chinese tradition of opera and dance. Hwang sets his play at the time of the Chinese railroad workers' strike of 1867. He says, "So often 'coolie' laborers have been characterized in America as passive and subservient, two stereotypes often attached to Asians. The strike is important because it reminds us that in historical fact these were assertive men who stood up for their rights in the face of great adversity."

The Dance and the Railroad   *1981*

CHARACTERS

LONE, twenty years old, ChinaMan railroad worker.
MA, eighteen years old, ChinaMan railroad worker.

> PLACE: *A mountaintop near the transcontinental railroad.*

> TIME: *June, 1867.*

SYNOPSIS OF SCENES

SCENE 1: *Afternoon.*

SCENE 2: *Afternoon, a day later.*

SCENE 3: *Late afternoon, four days later.*

SCENE 4: *Late that night.*

SCENE 5: *Just before the following dawn.*

Scene 1

> *A mountaintop.* LONE *is practicing opera steps. He swings his pigtail around like a fan.* MA *enters, cautiously, watches from a hidden spot.* MA *approaches* LONE.

LONE: So, there are insects hiding in the bushes.
MA: Hey, listen, we haven't met, but—
LONE: I don't spend time with insects.

> (LONE *whips his hair into* MA's *face;* MA *backs off;* LONE *pursues him, swiping at* MA *with his hair*)

MA: What the—? Cut it out!

> (MA *pushes* LONE *away*)

LONE: Don't push me.
MA: What was that for?
LONE: Don't ever push me again.
MA: You mess like that, you're gonna get pushed.
LONE: Don't push me.
MA: You started it. I just wanted to watch.
LONE: You "just wanted to watch." Did you ask my permission?
MA: What?
LONE: Did you?
MA: C'mon.
LONE: You can't expect to get in for free.
MA: Listen. I got some stuff you'll wanna hear.
LONE: You think so?
MA: Yeah. Some advice.
LONE: Advice? How old are you, anyway?

MA: Eighteen.

LONE: A child.

MA: Yeah. Right. A child. But listen—

LONE: A child who tries to advise a grown man—

MA: Listen, you got this kind of attitude.

LONE: —is a child who will never grow up.

MA: You know, the ChinaMen down at camp, they can't stand it.

LONE: Oh?

MA: Yeah. You gotta watch yourself. You know what they say? They call you "Prince of the Mountain." Like you're too good to spend time with them.

LONE: Perceptive of them.

MA: After all, you never sing songs, never tell stories. They say you act like your spit is too clean for them, and they got ways to fix that.

LONE: Is that so?

MA: Like they're gonna bury you in the shit buckets, so you'll have more to clean than your nails.

LONE: But I don't shit.

MA: Or they're gonna cut out your tongue, since you never speak to them.

LONE: There's no one here worth talking to.

MA: Cut it out, Lone. Look, I'm trying to help you, all right? I got a solution.

LONE: So young yet so clever.

MA: That stuff you're doing—it's beautiful. Why don't you do it for the guys at camp? Help us celebrate?

LONE: What will "this stuff" help celebrate?

MA: C'mon. The strike of course. Guys on a railroad gang, we gotta stick together, you know.

LONE: This is something to celebrate?

MA: Yeah. Yesterday, the weak-kneed ChinaMen, they were running around like chickens without a head: "The white devils are sending their soldiers! Shoot us all!" But now, look—day four, see? Still in one piece. Those soldiers—we've never seen a gun or a bullet.

LONE: So you're all warrior-spirits, huh?

MA: They're scared of us, Lone—that's what it means.

LONE: I appreciate your advice. Tell you what—you go down—

MA: Yeah?

LONE: Down to the camp—

MA: Okay.

LONE: To where the men are—

MA: Yeah?

LONE: Sit there—

MA: Yeah?

LONE: And wait for me.

MA: Okay. (*Pause*) That's it? What do you think I am?

LONE: I think you're an insect interrupting my practice. So fly away. Go home.

MA: Look, I didn't come here to get laughed at.

LONE: No, I suppose you didn't.

MA: So just stay up here. By yourself. You deserve it.

LONE: I do.

MA: And don't expect any more help from me.

LONE: I haven't gotten any yet.

MA: If one day, you wake up and your head is buried in the shit can—

LONE: Yes?

MA: You can't find your body, your tongue is cut out—

LONE: Yes.

MA: Don't worry, 'cuz I'll be there.

LONE: Oh.

MA: To make sure your mother's head is sitting right next to yours.

(MA *exits.*)

LONE: His head is too big for this mountain.

(*Returns to practicing*)

Scene 2

Mountaintop. Next day. LONE *is practicing.* MA *enters.*

MA: Hey.

LONE: You? Again?

MA: I forgive you.

LONE: You . . . what?

MA: For making fun of me yesterday. I forgive you.

LONE: You can't—

MA: No. Don't thank me.

LONE: You can't forgive me.

MA: No. Don't mention it.

LONE: You—! I never asked for your forgiveness.

MA: I know. That's just the kinda guy I am.

LONE: This is ridiculous. Why don't you leave? Go down to your friends and play soldiers, sing songs, tell stories.

MA: Ah! See? That's just it. I got other ways I wanna spend my time. Will you teach me the opera?

LONE: What?

MA: I wanna learn it. I dreamt about it all last night.

LONE: No.

MA: The dance, the opera—I can do it.

LONE: You think so?

MA: Yeah. When I get outa here, I wanna go back to China and perform.

LONE: You want to become an actor?

MA: Well, I wanna perform.

LONE: Don't you remember the story about the three sons whose parents send them away to learn a trade? After three years, they return. The first one says, "I have become a coppersmith." The parents say, "Good. Second son, what have you become?" "I've become a silversmith." "Good— and youngest son, what about you?" "I have become an actor." When the parents hear that their son has become only an actor, they are very sad. The mother beats her head against the ground until the ground, out of pity, opens up and swallows her. The father is so angry he can't even speak, and the anger builds up inside him until it blows his body to pieces—little bits of his skin are found hanging from trees days later. You don't know how you endanger your relatives by becoming an actor.

MA: Well, I don't wanna become an "actor." That sounds terrible. I just wanna perform. Look, I'll be rich by the time I get out of here, right?

LONE: Oh?

MA: Sure. By the time I go back to China, I'll ride in gold sedan chairs, with twenty wives fanning me all around.

LONE: Twenty wives? This boy is ambitious.

MA: I'll give out pigs on New Year's and keep a stable of small birds to give to any woman who pleases me. And in my spare time, I'll perform.

LONE: Between your twenty wives and your birds, where will you find a free moment?

MA: I'll play Gwan Gung and tell stories of what life was like on the Gold Mountain.

LONE: Ma, just how long have you been in "America"?

MA: Huh? About four weeks.

LONE: You are a big dreamer.

MA: Well, all us ChinaMen here are—right? Men with little dreams—have little brains to match. They walk with their eyes down, trying to find extra grains of rice on the ground.

LONE: So, you know all about "America"? Tell me, what kind of stories will you tell?

MA: I'll say, "We laid tracks like soldiers. Mountains? We hung from cliffs in baskets and the winds blew us like birds. Snow? We lived underground like moles for days at a time. Deserts? We—"

LONE: Wait. Wait. How do you know these things after only four weeks?

MA: They told me—the other ChinaMen on the gang. We've been telling stories ever since the strike began.

LONE: They make it sound like it's very enjoyable.

MA: They said it is.

LONE: Oh? And you believe them?

MA: They're my friends. Living underground in winter—sounds exciting, huh?

LONE: Did they say anything about the cold?

MA: Oh, I already know about that. They told me about the mild winters and the warm snow.

LONE: Warm snow?

MA: When I go home, I'll bring some back to show my brothers.

LONE: Bring some—? On the boat?

MA: They'll be shocked—they never seen American snow before.

LONE: You can't. By the time you get snow to the boat, it'll have melted, evaporated, and returned as rain already.

MA: No.

LONE: No?

MA: Stupid.

LONE: Me?

MA: You been here awhile, haven't you?

LONE: Yes. Two years.

MA: Then how come you're so stupid? This is the Gold Mountain. The snow here doesn't melt. It's not wet.

LONE: That's what they told you?

MA: Yeah. It's true.

LONE: Did anyone show you any of this snow?

MA: No. It's not winter.

LONE: So where does it go?

MA: Huh?

LONE: Where does it go, if it doesn't melt? What happens to it?

MA: The snow? I dunno. I guess it just stays around.

LONE: So where is it? Do you see any?

MA: Here? Well, no, but . . . (*Pause*) This is probably one of those places where it doesn't snow—even in winter.

LONE: Oh.

MA: Anyway, what's the use of me telling you what you already know? Hey, c'mon—teach me some of that stuff. Look—I've been practicing the walk—how's this? (*Demonstrates*)

LONE: You look like a duck in heat.

MA: Hey—it's a start, isn't it?

LONE: Tell you what—you want to play some *die siu?*

MA: *Die siu?* Sure.

LONE: You know, I'm pretty good.

MA: Hey, I play with the guys at camp. You can't be any better than Lee—he's really got it down.

(LONE *pulls out a case with two dice*)

LONE: I used to play till morning.

MA: Hey, us too. We see the sun start to rise, and say, "Hey, if we got to sleep now, we'll never get up for work." So we just keep playing.

LONE (*holding out dice*): *Die* or *siu?*

MA: *Siu.*

LONE: You sure?

MA: Yeah!

LONE: All right. (*He rolls.*) *Die!*

MA: *Siu!*

(*They see the result*)

MA: Not bad.

(*They continue taking turns rolling through the following section;* MA *always loses*)

LONE: I haven't touched these in two years.

MA: I gotta practice more.

LONE: Have you lost much money?

MA: Huh? So what?

LONE: Oh, you have gold hidden in all your shirt linings, huh?

MA: Here in "America"—losing is no problem. You know—End of the Year Bonus?

LONE: Oh, right.

MA: After I get that, I'll laugh at what I lost.

LONE: Lee told you there was a bonus, right?

MA: How'd you know?

LONE: When I arrived here, Lee told me there was a bonus, too.

MA: Lee teach you how to play?

LONE: Him? He talked to me a lot.

MA: Look, why don't you come down and start playing with the guys again?

LONE: "The guys."

MA: Before we start playing, Lee uses a stick to write "Kill!" in the dirt.

LONE: You seem to live for your nights with "the guys."

MA: What's life without friends, huh?

LONE: Well, why do *you* think I stopped playing?

MA: Hey, maybe you were the one getting killed, huh?

LONE: What?

MA: Hey, just kidding.

LONE: Who's getting killed here?

MA: Just a joke.

LONE: That's not a joke, it's blasphemy.

MA: Look, obviously you stopped playing 'cause you wanted to practice the opera.

LONE: Do you understand that discipline?

MA: But, I mean, you don't have to overdo it either. You don't have to treat 'em like dirt. I mean, who are you trying to impress?

(*Pause.* LONE *throws dice into the bushes*)

LONE: Oooops. Better go see who won.

MA: Hey! C'mon! Help me look!

LONE: If you find them, they are yours.

MA: You serious?

LONE: Yes.

MA: Here.

(*Finds the dice*)

LONE: Who won?

MA: I didn't check.

LONE: Well, no matter. Keep the dice. Take them and go play with your friends.

MA: Here. (*He offers them to* LONE) A present.

LONE: A present? This isn't a present!

MA: They're mine, aren't they? You gave them to me, right?

LONE: Well, yes, but—

MA: So now I'm giving them to you.

LONE: You can't give me a present. I don't want them.

MA: You wanted them enough to keep them two years.

LONE: I'd forgotten I had them.

MA: See, I know, Lone. You wanna get rid of me. But you can't. I'm paying for lessons.

LONE: With my dice.

MA: Mine now. (*He offers them again*) Here.

(*Pause.* LONE *runs* MA's *hand across his forehead*)

LONE: Feel this.

MA: Hey!

LONE: Pretty wet, huh?

MA: Big deal.

LONE: Well, it's not from playing *die siu.*

MA: I know how to sweat. I wouldn't be here if I didn't.

LONE: Yes, but are you willing to sweat after you've finished sweating? Are you willing to come up after you've spent the whole day chipping half an inch off a rock, and punish your body some more?

MA: Yeah. Even after work, I still—

LONE: No, you don't. You want to gamble, and tell dirty stories, and dress up like women to do shows.

MA: Hey, I never did that.

LONE: You've only been here a month. (*Pause*) And what about "the guys"? They're not going to treat you so well once you stop playing with them. Are you willing to work all day listening to them whisper, "That one— let's put spiders in his soup"?

MA: They won't do that to me. With you, it's different.

LONE: Is it?

MA: You don't have to act that way.

LONE: What way?

MA: Like you're so much better than them.

LONE: No. You haven't even begun to understand. To practice every day, you must have a fear to force you up here.

MA: A fear? No—it's 'cause what you're doing is beautiful.

LONE: No.

MA: I've seen it.

LONE: It's ugly to practice when the mountain has turned your muscles to ice. When my body hurts too much to come here, I look at the other Chi-naMen and think, "They are dead. Their muscles work only because the white man forces them. I live because I can still force my muscles to work for me." Say it. "They are dead."

MA: No. They're my friends.

LONE: Well, then, take your dice down to your friends.

MA: But I want to learn—

LONE: This is your first lesson.

MA: Look, it shouldn't matter—

LONE: It does.

MA: It shouldn't matter what I think.

LONE: Attitude is everything.

MA: But as long as I come up, do the exercises—

LONE: I'm not going to waste time on a quitter.

MA: I'm not!

LONE: Then say it.—"They are dead men."

MA: I can't.

LONE: Then you will never have the dedication.

MA: That doesn't prove anything.

LONE: I will not teach a dead man.

MA: What?

LONE: If you can't see it, then you're dead too.

MA: Don't start pinning—

LONE: Say it!

MA: All right.

LONE: What?

MA: All right. I'm one of them. I'm a dead man too.

(*Pause*)

LONE: I thought as much. So, go. You have your friends.

MA: But I don't have a teacher.

LONE: I don't think you need both.

MA: Are you sure?

LONE: I'm being questioned by a child.

(LONE *returns to practicing. Silence*)

MA: Look, Lone, I'll come up here every night—after work—I'll spend my time practicing, okay? (*Pause*) But I'm not gonna say that they're dead. Look at them. They're on strike; dead men don't go on strike, Lone. The white devils—they try and stick us with a ten-hour day. We want a return to eight hours and also a fourteen-dollar-a-month raise. I learned the demon English—listen: "Eight hour a day good for white man, all same good for ChinaMan." These are the demands of live ChinaMen, Lone. Dead men don't complain.

LONE: All right, this is something new. No one can judge the ChinaMen till after the strike.

MA: They say we'll hold out for months if we have to. The smart men will live on what we've hoarded.

LONE: A ChinaMan's mouth can swallow the earth. (*He takes the dice*) While the strike is on, I'll teach you.

MA: And afterwards?

LONE: Afterwards—we'll decide then whether these are dead or live men.

MA: When can we start?

LONE: We've already begun. Give me your hand.

Scene 3

LONE *and* MA *are doing physical exercises.*

MA: How long will it be before I can play Gwan Gung?

LONE: How long before a dog can play the violin?

MA: Old Ah Hong—have you heard him play the violin?

LONE: Yes. Now, he should take his violin and give it to a dog.

MA: I think he sounds okay.

LONE: I think he caused that avalanche last winter.

MA: He used to play for weddings back home.

LONE: Ah Hong?

MA: That's what he said.

LONE: You probably heard wrong.

MA: No.

LONE: He probably said he played for funerals.

MA: He's been playing for the guys down at camp.

LONE: He should play for the white devils—that will end this stupid strike.

MA: Yang told me for sure—it'll be over by tomorrow.

LONE: Eight days already. And Yang doesn't know anything.

MA: He said they're already down to an eight-hour day and five-dollar raise at the bargaining sessions.

LONE: Yang eats too much opium.

MA: That doesn't mean he's wrong about this.

LONE: You can't trust him. One time—last year—he went around camp looking in everybody's eyes and saying, "Your nails are too long. They're hurting my eyes." This went on for a week. Finally, all the men clipped their nails, made a big pile, which they wrapped in leaves and gave to him. Yang used the nails to season his food—he put it in his soup, sprinkled it on his rice, and never said a word about it again. Now tell me—are you going to trust a man who eats other men's fingernails?

MA: Well, all I know is we won't go back to work until they meet all our demands. Listen, teach me some Gwan Gung steps.

LONE: I should have expected this. A boy who wants to have twenty wives is the type who demands more than he can handle.

MA: Just a few.

LONE: It takes years before an actor can play Gwan Gung.

MA: I can do it. I spend a lot of time watching the opera when it comes around. Every time I see Gwan Gung, I say, "Yeah. That's me. The god of fighters. The god of adventurers. We have the same kind of spirit."

LONE: I tell you, if you work very hard, when you return to China, you can perhaps be the Second Clown.

MA: Second Clown?

LONE: If you work hard.

MA: What's the Second Clown?

LONE: You can play the *p'i p'a,* and dance and jump all over.

MA: I'll buy them.

LONE: Excuse me?

MA: I'm going to be rich, remember? I'll buy a troupe and force them to let me play Gwan Gung.

LONE: I hope you have enough money, then, to pay audiences to sit through your show.

MA: You mean, I'm going to have to practice here every night—and in return, all I can play is the Second Clown?

LONE: If you work hard.

MA: Am I that bad? Maybe I shouldn't even try to do this. Maybe I should just go down.

LONE: It's not you. Everyone must earn the right to play Gwan Gung. I entered opera school when I was ten years old. My parents decided to sell me for ten years to this opera company. I lived with eighty other boys and we slept in bunks four beds high and hid our candy and rice cakes from each other. After eight years, I was studying to play Gwan Gung.

MA: Eight years?

LONE: I was one of the best in my class. One day, I was summoned by my master, who told me I was to go home for two days because my mother had fallen very ill and was dying. When I arrived home, Mother was standing at the door waiting, not sick at all. Her first words to me, the son away for eight years, were, "You've been playing while your village has starved. You must go to the Gold Mountain and work."

MA: And you never returned to school?

LONE: I went from a room with eighty boys to a ship with three hundred men. So, you see, it does not come easily to play Gwan Gung.

MA: Did you want to play Gwan Gung?

LONE: What a foolish question!

MA: Well, you're better off this way.

LONE: What?

MA: Actors—they don't make much money. Here, you make a bundle, then go back and be an actor again. Best of both worlds.

LONE: "Best of both worlds."

MA: Yeah!

(LONE *drops to the ground, begins imitating a duck, waddling and quacking*)

MA: Lone? What are you doing? (LONE *quacks*) You're a duck? (LONE *quacks*) I can see that. (LONE *quacks*) Is this an exercise? Am I supposed to do this? (LONE *quacks*) This is dumb. I never seen Gwan Gung waddle. (LONE *quacks*) Okay. All right. I'll do it. (MA *and* LONE *quack and waddle*) You know, I never realized before how uncomfortable a duck's life is. And you have to listen to yourself quacking all day. Go crazy! (LONE *stands up straight*) Now, what was that all about?

LONE: No, no. Stay down there, duck.

MA: What's the—

LONE (*prompting*): Quack, quack, quack.

MA: I don't—

LONE: Act your species!

MA: I'm not a duck!

LONE: Nothing worse than a duck that doesn't know his place.

MA: All right. (*Mechanically*) Quack, quack.

LONE: More.

MA: Quack.

LONE: More!

MA: Quack, quack, quack!

(MA *now continues quacking, as* LONE *gives commands*)

LONE: Louder! It's your mating call! Think of your twenty duck wives! Good! Louder! Project! More! Don't slow down! Put your tail feathers into it! They can't hear you!

(MA *is now quacking up a storm.* LONE *exits, unnoticed by* MA)

MA: Quack! Quack! Quack! Quack. Quack . . . quack. (*He looks around*) Quack . . . quack . . . Lone? . . .Lone? (*He waddles around the stage looking*) Lone, where are you? Where'd you go? (*He stops, scratches his left leg with his right foot*) C'mon—stop playing around. What is this? (LONE *enters as a tiger, unseen by* MA) Look, let's call it a day, okay? I'm getting hungry. (MA *turns around, notices* LONE *right before* LONE *is to bite him*) Aaaaah! Quack, quack, quack!

(*They face off, in character as animals. Duck-*MA *is terrified*)

LONE: Grrrr!

MA (*as a cry for help*): Quack, quack, quack!

(LONE *pounces on* MA. *They struggle, in character.* MA *is quacking madly, eyes tightly closed.* LONE *stands up straight.* MA *continues to quack*)

LONE: Stand up.

MA (*eyes still closed*): Quack, quack, quack!

LONE (*louder*): Stand up!

MA (*opening his eyes*): Oh.

LONE: What are you?

MA: Huh?

LONE: A ChinaMan or a duck?

MA: Huh? Gimme a second to remember.

LONE: You like being a duck?

MA: My feet fell asleep.

LONE: You change forms so easily.

MA: You said to.

LONE: What else could you turn into?

MA: Well, you scared me—sneaking up like that.

LONE: Perhaps a rock. That would be useful. When the men need to rest, they can sit on you.

MA: I got carried away.

LONE: Let's try . . . a locust. Can you become a locust?

MA: No. Let's cut this, okay?

LONE: Here. It's easy. You just have to know how to hop.

MA: You're not gonna get me—

LONE: Like this.

(*He demonstrates*)

MA: Forget it, Lone.

LONE: I'm a locust.

(*He begins jumping toward* MA)

MA: Hey! Get away!

LONE: I devour whole fields.

MA: Stop it.

LONE: I starve babies before they are born.

MA: Hey, look, stop it!

LONE: I cause famines and destroy villages.

MA: I'm warning you! Get away!

LONE: What are you going to do? You can't kill a locust.

MA: You're not a locust.

LONE: You kill one, and another sits on your hand.

MA: Stop following me.

LONE: Locusts always trouble people. If not, we'd feel useless. Now, if you became a locust, too . . .

MA: I'm not going to become a locust.

LONE: Just stick your teeth out!

MA: I'm not gonna be a bug! It's stupid!

LONE: No man who's just been a duck has the right to call anything stupid.

MA: I thought you were trying to teach me something.

LONE: I am. Go ahead.

MA: All right. There. That look right?

LONE: Your legs should be a little lower. Lower! There. That's adequate. So how does it feel to be a locust?

(LONE *gets up*)

MA: I dunno. How long do I have to do this?

LONE: Could you do it for three years?

MA: Three years? Don't be—

LONE: You couldn't, could you? Could you be a duck for that long?

MA: Look, I wasn't born to be either of those.

LONE: Exactly. Well, I wasn't born to work on a railroad, either. "Best of both worlds." How can you be such an insect!

(*Pause*)

MA: Lone . . .

LONE: Stay down there! Don't move! I've never told anyone my story—the story of my parents' kidnapping me from school. All the time we were crossing the ocean, the last two years here—I've kept my mouth shut. To you, I finally tell it. And all you can say is, "Best of both worlds." You're a bug to me, a locust. You think you understand the dedication one must have to be in the opera? You think it's the same as working on a railroad.

MA: Lone, all I was saying is that you'll go back too, and—

LONE: You're no longer a student of mine.

MA: What?

LONE: You have no dedication.

MA: Lone, I'm sorry.

LONE: Get up.

MA: I'm honored that you told me that.

LONE: Get up.

MA: No.

LONE: No?

MA: I don't want to. I want to talk.

LONE: Well, I've learned from the past. You're stubborn. You don't go. All right. Stay there. If you want to prove to me that you're dedicated, be a locust till morning. I'll go.

MA: Lone, I'm really honored that you told me.

LONE: I'll return in the morning.

(*Exits*)

MA: Lone? Lone, that's ridiculous. You think I'm gonna stay like this? If you do, you're crazy. Lone? Come back here.

Scene 4

Night. MA, *alone, as a locust.*

MA: Locusts travel in huge swarms, so large that when they cross the sky, they block out the sun, like a storm. Second Uncle—back home—when he was a young man, his whole crop got wiped out by locusts one year. In the famine that followed, Second Uncle lost his eldest son and his second wife—the one he married for love. Even to this day, we look around before saying the word "locust," to make sure Second Uncle is out of hearing range. About eight years ago, my brother and I discovered Second Uncle's cave in back of the stream near our house. We saw him come out of it one day around noon. Later, just before the sun went down, we sneaked in. We only looked once. Inside, there must have been hundreds—maybe five hundred or more—grasshoppers in huge bamboo cages—and around them—stacks of grasshopper legs, grasshopper heads, grasshopper antennae, grasshoppers with one leg, still trying to hop but toppling like trees coughing, grasshoppers wrapped around sharp branches rolling from side to side, grasshoppers legs cut off grasshopper bodies, then tied around grasshoppers and tightened till grasshoppers died. Every conceivable kind of grasshopper in every conceivable stage of life and death, subject to every conceivable grasshopper torture. We ran out quickly, my brother and I—we knew an evil place by the thickness of the air. Now, I think of Second Uncle. How sad that the locusts forced him to take out his agony on innocent grasshoppers. What if Second Uncle could see me now? Would he cut off my legs? He might as well. I can barely feel them. But then again, Second Uncle never tortured actual locusts, just weak grasshoppers.

Scene 5

Night. MA *still as a locust.*

LONE: (*Off, singing*)
Hit your hardest
Pound out your tears
The more you try
The more you'll cry
At how little I've moved
And how large I loom
By the time the sun goes down
MA: You look rested.
LONE: Me?
MA: Well, you sound rested.

LONE: No, not at all.

MA: Maybe I'm just comparing you to me.

LONE: I didn't even close my eyes all last night.

MA: Aw, Lone, you didn't have to stay up for me. You coulda just come up here and—

LONE: For you?

MA: —apologized and everything woulda been—

LONE: I didn't stay up for you.

MA: Huh? You didn't?

LONE: No.

MA: Oh. You sure?

LONE: Positive. I was thinking, that's all.

MA: About me?

LONE: Well . . .

MA: Even a little?

LONE: I was thinking about the ChinaMen—and you. Get up, Ma.

MA: Aw, do I have to? I've gotten to know these grasshoppers real well.

LONE: Get up. I have a lot to tell you.

MA: What'll they think? They take me in, even though I'm a little large, then they find out I'm a human being. I stepped on their kids. No trust. Gimme a hand, will you? (LONE *helps* MA *up, but* MA*'s legs can't support him*) Aw, shit. My legs are coming off.

(*He lies down and tries to straighten them out*)

LONE: I have many surprises. First, you will play Gwan Gung.

MA: My legs will be sent home without me. What'll my family think? Come to port to meet me and all they get is two legs.

LONE: Did you hear me?

MA: Hold on. I can't be in agony and listen to Chinese at the same time.

LONE: Did you hear my first surprise?

MA: No. I'm too busy screaming.

LONE: I said, you'll play Gwan Gung.

MA: Gwan Gung?

LONE: Yes.

MA: Me?

LONE: Yes.

MA: Without legs?

LONE: What?

MA: That might be good.

LONE: Stop that!

MA: I'll become a legend. Like the blind man who defended Amoy.

LONE: Did you hear?

MA: "The legless man who played Gwan Gung."

LONE: Isn't this what you want? To play Gwan Gung?

MA: No, I just wanna sleep.

LONE: No, you don't. Look. Here. I brought you something.

MA: Food?

LONE: Here. Some rice.

MA: Thanks, Lone. And duck?

LONE: Just a little.

MA: Where'd you get the duck?

LONE: Just bones and skin.

MA: We don't have duck. And the white devils have been blockading the food.

LONE: Sing—he had some left over.

MA: Sing? That thief?

LONE: And something to go with it.

MA: What? Lone, where did you find whiskey?

LONE: You know, Sing—he has almost anything.

MA: Yeah. For a price.

LONE: Once, even some thousand-day-old eggs.

MA: He's a thief. That's what they told me.

LONE: Not if you're his friend.

MA: Sing don't have any real friends. Everyone talks about him bein' tied in to the head of the klan in San Francisco. Lone, you didn't have to do this. Here. Have some.

LONE: I had plenty.

MA: Don't gimme that. This cost you plenty, Lone.

LONE: Well, I thought if we were going to celebrate, we should do it as well as we would at home.

MA: Celebrate? What for? Wait.

LONE: Ma, the strike is over.

MA: Shit, I knew it. And we won, right?

LONE: Yes, the ChinaMen have won. They can do more than just talk.

MA: I told you. Didn't I tell you?

LONE: Yes. Yes, you did.

MA: Yang told me it was gonna be done. He said—

LONE: Yes, I remember.

MA: Didn't I tell you? Huh?

LONE: Ma, eat your duck.

MA: Nine days, we civilized the white devils. I knew it. I knew we'd hold out till their ears started twitching. So that's where you got the duck, right? At the celebration?

LONE: No, there wasn't a celebration.

MA: Huh? You sure? ChinaMen—they look for any excuse to party.

LONE: But I thought *we* should celebrate.

MA: Well, that's for sure.

LONE: So you will play Gwan Gung.

MA: God, nine days. Shit, it's finally done. Well, we'll show them how to party. Make noise. Jump off rocks. Make the mountain shake.

LONE: We'll wash your body, to prepare you for the role.

MA: What role?

LONE: Gwan Gung. I've been telling you.

MA: I don't wanna play Gwan Gung.

LONE: You've shown the dedication required to become my student, so—

MA: Lone, you think I stayed up last night 'cause I wanted to play Gwan Gung?

LONE: You said you were like him.

MA: I am. Gwan Gung stayed up all night once to prove his loyalty. Well, now I have too. Lone, I'm honored that you told me your story.

LONE: Yes . . . That is like Gwan Gung.

MA: Good. So let's do an opera about *me*.

LONE: What?

MA: You wanna party or what?

LONE: About you?

MA: You said I was like Gwan Gung, didn't you?

LONE: Yes, but—

MA: Well, look at the operas he's got. I ain't even got one.

LONE: Still, you can't—

MA: You tell me, is that fair?

LONE: You can't do an opera about yourself.

MA: I just won a victory, didn't I? I deserve an opera in my honor.

LONE: But it's not traditional.

MA: Traditional? Lone, you gotta figure any way I could do Gwan Gung wasn't gonna be traditional anyway. I may be as good a guy as him, but he's a better dancer. (*Sings*)

Old Gwan Gung, just sits about
Till the dime-store fighters have had it out
Then he pitches his peach pit
Combs his beard
Draws his sword
And they scatter in fear

LONE: What are you talking about?

MA: I just won a great victory. I get—whatcha call it?—poetic license. C'mon. Hit the gongs. I'll immortalize my story.

LONE: I refuse. This goes against all my training. I try and give you your wish and—

MA: Do it. Gimme my wish. Hit the gongs.

LONE: I never—I can't.

MA: Can't what? Don't think I'm worth an opera? No, I guess not. I forgot— you think I'm just one of those dead men.

(*Silence.* LONE *pulls out a gong.* MA *gets into position.* LONE *hits the gong. They do the following in a mock-Chinese-opera style*)

MA: I am Ma. Yesterday, I was kicked out of my house by my three elder brothers, calling me the lazy dreamer of the family. I am sitting here in front of the temple trying to decide how I will avenge this indignity. Here comes the poorest beggar in this village. (*He cues* LONE) He is called Fleaman because his body is the most popular meeting place for fleas from around the province.

LONE: (*Singing*)

Fleas in love,
Find your happiness
In the gray scraps of my suit

MA: Hello, Flea—
LONE: (*Continuing*)

> Fleas in need,
> Shield your families
> In the gray hairs of my beard

MA: Hello, Flea—

(LONE *cuts* MA *off, continues an extended improvised aria*)

MA: Hello, Fleaman.
LONE: Hello, Ma. Are you interested in providing a home for these fleas?
MA: No!
LONE: This couple here—seeking to start a new home. Housing today is so hard to find. How about your left arm?
MA: I may have plenty of my own fleas in time. I have been thrown out by my elder brothers.
LONE: Are you seeking revenge? A flea epidemic on your house? (*To a flea*) Get back there. You should be asleep. Your mother will worry.
MA: Nothing would make my brothers angrier than seeing me rich.
LONE: Rich? After the bad crops of the last three years, even the fleas are thinking of moving north.
MA: I heard a white devil talk yesterday.
LONE: Oh—with hair the color of a sick chicken and eyes round as eggs? The fleas and I call him Chicken-Laying-an-Egg.
MA: He said we can make our fortunes on the Gold Mountain, where work is play and the sun scares off snow.
LONE: Don't listen to chicken-brains.
MA: Why not? He said gold grows like weeds.
LONE: I have heard that it is slavery.
MA: Slavery? What do you know, Fleaman? Who told you? The fleas? Yes, I will go to Gold Mountain.

(*Gongs.* MA *strikes a submissive pose to* LONE)

LONE: "The one hundred twenty-five dollars passage money is to be paid to the said head of said Hong, who will make arrangements with the coolies, that their wages shall be deducted until the debt is absorbed."

(MA *bows to* LONE. *Gongs. They pick up fighting sticks and do a water-crossing dance. Dance ends. They stoop next to each other and rock*)

MA: I have been in the bottom of this boat for thirty-six days now. Tang, how many have died?
LONE: Not me. I'll live through this ride.
MA: I didn't ask how you are.
LONE: But why's the Gold Mountain so far?
MA: We left with three hundred and three.
LONE: My family's depending on me.
MA: So tell me, how many have died?
LONE: I'll be the last one alive.

MA: That's not what I wanted to know.
LONE: I'll find some fresh air in this hole.
MA: I asked, how many have died.
LONE: Is that a crack in the side?
MA: Are you listening to me?
LONE: If I had some air—
MA: I asked, don't you see—?
LONE: The crack—over there—
MA: Will you answer me, please?
LONE: I need to get out.
MA: The rest here agree—
LONE: I can't stand the smell.
MA: That a hundred eighty—
LONE: I can't see the air—
MA: Of us will not see—
LONE: And I can't die.
MA: Our Gold Mountain dream.

(LONE/TANG *dies;* MA *throws his body overboard. The boat docks.* MA *exits, walks through the streets. He picks up one of the fighting sticks, while* LONE *becomes the mountain*)

MA: I have been given my pickax. Now I will attack the mountain.

(MA *does a dance of labor.* LONE *sings*)

LONE:

Hit your hardest
Pound out your tears
The more you try
The more you'll cry
At how little I've moved
And how large I loom
By the time the sun goes down.

(*Dance stops*)

MA: This mountain is clever. But why shouldn't it be? It's fighting for its life, like we fight for ours.

(*The* MOUNTAIN *picks up a stick.* MA *and the* MOUNTAIN *do a battle dance. Dance ends*)

MA: This mountain not only defends itself—it also attacks. It turns our strength against us.

(LONE *does* MA*'s labor dance, while* MA *plants explosives in midair. Dance ends*)

MA: This mountain has survived for millions of years. Its wisdom is immense.

(LONE *and* MA *begin a second battle dance. This one ends with them working the battle sticks together.* LONE *breaks away, does a warrior strut*)

LONE: I am a white devil! Listen to my stupid language. "Wha che doo doo blah blah." Look at my wide eyes—like I have drunk seventy-two pots of tea. Look at my funny hair—twisting, turning, like a snake telling lies. (*To* MA) Bla bla doo doo tee tee.

MA: We don't understand English.

LONE (*angry*): Bla bla doo doo tee tee!

MA (*with chinese accent*): Please you-ah speak-ah Chinese?

LONE: Oh. Work—uh—one—two—more—work—two—

MA: Two hours more? Stupid demons. As confused as your hair. We will strike!

(*Gongs.* MA *is on strike*)

MA (*in broken English*): Eight hours day good for white man, all same good for ChinaMan.

LONE: The strike is over! We've won!

MA: I knew we would.

LONE: We forced the white devil to act civilized.

MA: Tamed the Barbarians!

LONE: Did you think—

MA: Who woulda thought?

LONE: —it could be done?

MA: Who?

LONE: But who?

MA: Who could tame them?

MA *and* LONE: Only a ChinaMan!

(*They laugh*)

LONE: Well, c'mon.

MA: Let's celebrate!

LONE: We have.

MA: Oh.

LONE: Back to work.

MA: But we've won the strike.

LONE: I know. Congratulations! And now—

MA: —back to work?

LONE: Right.

MA: No.

LONE: But the strike is over.

(LONE *tosses* MA *a stick. They resume their stick battle as before, but* MA *is heard over* LONE*'s singing*)

LONE:	MA:
Hit your hardest	Wait.
Pound out your tears	I'm tired of this!
The more you try	How do we end it?
The more you'll cry	Let's stop now, all right?
At how little I've moved	Look, I said enough!
And how large I loom	
By the time the sun goes down	

(MA *tosses his stick away, but* LONE *is already aiming a blow toward it, so that* LONE *hits* MA *instead and knocks him down*)

MA: Oh! Shit . . .

LONE: I'm sorry! Are you all right?

MA: Yeah. I guess.

LONE: Why'd you let go? You can't just do that.

MA: I'm bleeding.

LONE: That was stupid—where?

MA: Here.

LONE: No.

MA: Ow!

LONE: There will probably be a bump.

MA: I dunno.

LONE: What?

MA: I dunno why I let go.

LONE: It was stupid.

MA: But how were we going to end the opera?

LONE: Here. (*He applies whiskey to* MA*'s bruise*) I don't know.

MA: Why didn't we just end it with the celebration? Ow! Careful.

LONE: Sorry. But Ma, the celebration's not the end. We're returning to work. Today. At dawn.

MA: What?

LONE: We've already lost nine days of work. But we got eight hours.

MA: Today? That's terrible.

LONE: What do you think we're here for? But they listened to our demands. We're getting a raise.

MA: Right. Fourteen dollars.

LONE: No. Eight.

MA: What?

LONE: We had to compromise. We got an eight-dollar raise.

MA: But we wanted fourteen. Why didn't we get fourteen?

LONE: It was the best deal they could get. Congratulations.

MA: Congratulations? Look, Lone, I'm sick of you making fun of the ChinaMen.

LONE: Ma, I'm not. For the first time. I was wrong. We got eight dollars.

MA: We wanted fourteen.

LONE: But we got eight hours.

MA: We'll go back on strike.

LONE: Why?

MA: We could hold out for months.

LONE: And lose all that work?

MA: But we just gave in.

LONE: You're being ridiculous. We got eight hours. Besides, it's already been decided.

MA: I didn't decide. I wasn't there. You made me stay up here.

LONE: The heads of the gangs decide.

MA: And that's it?

LONE: It's done.

MA: Back to work? That's what they decided? Lone, I don't want to go back to work.

LONE: Who does?

MA: I forgot what it's like.

LONE: You'll pick up the technique again soon enough.

MA: I mean, what it's like to have them telling you what to do all the time. Using up your strength.

LONE: I thought you said even after work, you still feel good.

MA: Some days. But others . . . (*Pause*) I get so frustrated sometimes. At the rock. The rock doesn't give in. It's not human. I wanna claw it with my fingers, but that would just rip them up. I wanna throw myself head first onto it, but it'd just knock my skull open. The rock would knock my skull open, then just sit there, still, like nothing had happened, like a faceless Buddha. (*Pause*) Lone, when do I get out of here?

LONE: Well, the railroad may get finished—

MA: It'll never get finished.

LONE: —or you may get rich.

MA: Rich. Right. This is the Gold Mountain. (*Pause*) Lone, has anyone ever gone home rich from here?

LONE: Yes. Some.

MA: But most?

LONE: Most . . . do go home.

MA: Do you still have the fear?

LONE: The fear?

MA: That you'll become like them—dead men?

LONE: Maybe I was wrong about them.

MA: Well, I do. You wanted me to say it before. I can say it now: "They are dead men." Their greatest accomplishment was to win a strike that's gotten us nothing.

LONE: They're sending money home.

MA: No.

LONE: It's not much, I know, but it's something.

MA: Lone, I'm not even doing that. If I don't get rich here, I might as well die here. Let my brothers laugh in peace.

LONE: Ma, you're too soft to get rich here, naïve—you believed the snow was warm.

MA: I've got to change myself. Toughen up. Take no shit. Count my change. Learn to gamble. Learn to win. Learn to stare. Learn to deny. Learn to look at men with opaque eyes.

LONE: You want to do that?

MA: I will. 'Cause I've got the fear. You've given it to me.

(*Pause*)

LONE: Will I see you here tonight?

MA: Tonight?

LONE: I just thought I'd ask.

MA: I'm sorry, Lone. I haven't got time to be the Second Clown.

LONE: I thought you might not.

MA: Sorry.

LONE: You could have been a . . . fair actor.

MA: You coming down? I gotta get ready for work. This is gonna be a terrible day. My legs are sore and my arms are outa practice.

LONE: You go first. I'm going to practice some before work. There's still time.

MA: Practice? But you said you lost your fear. And you said that's what brings you up here.

LONE: I guess I was wrong about that, too. Today, I am dancing for no reason at all.

MA: Do whatever you want. See you down at camp.

LONE: Could you do me a favor?

MA: A favor?

LONE: Could you take this down so I don't have to take it all?

(LONE *points to a pile of props*)

MA: Well, okay. (*Pause*) But this is the last time.

LONE: Of course, Ma. (MA *exits*) See you soon. The last time. I suppose so.

(LONE *resumes practicing. He twirls his hair around as in the beginning of the play. The sun begins to rise. It continues rising until* LONE *is moving and seen only in shadow*)

Curtain

The Receptive Reader

1. How do the two *characters* take shape in the early scenes? What kind of person is each character? What clues does the playwright provide in the way they talk and act?

2. How do the two characters *interact?* Is one a foil to the other? Does their relationship change or evolve?

3. Do you see any *connection* between the workers' strike and Lone's devotion to his art?

4. Why can the phrase "best of both worlds" be seen as a *key phrase* in this play? Who uses it and who echoes it, and with what effect?

The Personal Response

Do you think a spectator would have to be Asian or be a member of a minority group to get fully into the spirit of this play?

The Creative Dimension

With a group, you may want to work on a presentation designed to *pantomime*—act out without words—some of the action and especially the animal characters in this play.

JUXTAPOSITIONS

A Modern Everyman

It is always ourselves that we see upon the stage.
                    WILLIAM BUTLER YEATS

Some plays focus on the outstanding heroic individual, others on the Everyman or Everywoman that represents our common humanity. The church of the Middle Ages taught that all were equal in the sight of God and that Death was no respecter of persons. Whether peasant, beggar, merchant, emperor, or pope, all would be summoned to a final reckoning. ("People, in the beginning / Look well ahead to the ending" says the Messenger at the beginning of the *Everyman* play.) The struggle in the soul of Everyman and Everywoman mirrored the struggle between the forces of good and evil in the larger world. The basic conflict in each individual was the battle between sin and righteousness, with the outcome determining salvation or perdition. The two selections that follow ask you to compare the medieval conception of Everyman with a more modern Everyman—a Chicano G.I. being sent to Vietnam in a play by the Mexican American playwright Luis Valdez.

In the European Middle Ages, **morality plays** acted out basic teachings of the church, putting on the stage personified virtues and vices as part of a religious **allegory.** The best-known (and in its time most widely acted) is the anonymous *Everyman* play, written about 1485. A modern adaptation by the Austrian playwright Hugo von Hoffmansthal is still performed each year in front of Salzburg Cathedral. Like much of the teaching literature of the Middle Ages, *Everyman* translates the theology of the church into simple teachings for the common people. In a classroom reading or in a mini-production, the play can still make the modern audience shudder at the sudden summons of incorruptible Death experienced by medieval Christians.

Everyman   *1485*

A Modern Abridgment

TRANSLATED BY HANS P. GUTH

Scene 1

MESSENGER: I ask you all in the audience
        To hear our play with reverence:
        The Summoning of Everyman it is called
        It shows our lives and how they end,
        And how quickly our time passes on this earth.   5
        The topic of our play is most serious,

But the lesson is more precious
And sweet to carry away.
The story says: People, in the beginning
Look well ahead to the ending—   10
No matter how carefree you are.
Sin in the beginning seems most sweet,
But in the end it causes the soul to weep,
When the body has returned to dust.
Here you shall see how Fellowship and Jollity,   15
And Strength, Pleasure, and Beauty,
Will fade away like a flower in May.
And you will hear how our heavenly King
Will call Everyman to a general reckoning.
Now listen to what he will say.   20

The MESSENGER *leaves and* GOD *speaks to the audience.*

GOD: I see here in my majesty
How people forget the love they owe me.
They live without fear in worldly prosperity
And worldly riches is all they think about.
They do not fear the sharp rod of my righteousness.   25
Pride, greed, and every other deadly sin
Have become acceptable in the world.
People think only of their own pleasure.
The more I show them kindness,
The more they live in wickedness.   30
They have forgotten the meaning of charity.
Therefore, I will in all haste
Have a reckoning of Everyman's conduct.
I offered the people great riches of mercy,
But there are few who sincerely seek it.   35
The time has come to pronounce justice
On Everyman living without fear.
Where are you, Death, my mighty messenger?

DEATH *enters.*

DEATH: Almighty God, I am here at your bidding
To fulfill your every commandment.   40
GOD: Go now to Everyman,
And tell him, in my name,
That he must go on a pilgrimage
Which he may in no way avoid,
And tell him to bring a sure accounting   45
Without excuse or any delay.
DEATH: Lord, I will go forth into the world
And search out cruelly both great and small.

GOD *leaves.*

Scene 2

DEATH: I will find Everyman who lives like a beast,
 Ignoring God's laws, and sunk in folly.
 I will strike down those who love riches,
 To dwell in hell for time without end,
 Unless Good Deeds prove their friend.   5
 Lo, yonder I see Everyman walking—
 No way does he expect my coming!
 His mind is on the joys of the flesh and treasure,
 And great pain it shall cause him to endure
 Before the Lord, Heaven's king.   10

 EVERYMAN *enters.*

 Everyman, stand still! Where are you going
 So merrily? Have you forgotten your Maker?
EVERYMAN: Why do you ask?
 Who wants to know?
DEATH: That I will tell you: 15
 In great haste I am sent
 From God in His Majesty.
EVERYMAN: What! Sent to me?
DEATH: Most certainly.
 Though you have forgotten Him here,   20
 He thinks of you in His heavenly sphere,
 As, before we depart, you shall know.
EVERYMAN: What does God want from me?
DEATH: That I will tell you:
 He must have a speedy reckoning   25
 Without any delay.
EVERYMAN: To make a reckoning, I'll need more time.
 This sudden summons catches me unprepared.
DEATH: The time has come to take a long journey.
 And be sure to bring your book of accounts,   30
 For there is no way you could go back for it.
 And be sure your reckoning is straight and true—
 Showing much bad, and good deeds but a few;
 How you have spent your life, in what wise
 Before the Chief Lord of Paradise.   35
 Make yourself ready to take that road,
 For you can send none in your place.
EVERYMAN: Who are you to ask me for this accounting?
DEATH: I am Death, and I fear no one.
 I summon all and spare no creature,   40
 For God has decreed
 That all must obey my call.
EVERYMAN: O Death, you come when I least expected you.
 You have the power to save me—
 If you spare me, I will give you great reward;   45

Yea, a thousand pounds will be yours
If you put off this matter till another day!
DEATH: Everyman, it cannot be.
  I care nothing for gold, silver, or riches,
  Or for pope, emperor, king, duke, or princes,   50
  For if I were to accept gifts,
  I could have all the treasure of this world.
  But such is quite contrary to my custom.
  I brook no delay. Make ready to depart!
EVERYMAN: Alas! Is there no escape?   55
  I may say Death gives no warning.
  To think about you makes me sick at the heart,
  For my book of accounts is not ready at all.
  If I could have just a dozen more years,
  I would clear my accounts in such a way   60
  That a reckoning would not frighten me.
DEATH: In vain it is to cry, weep, or pray—
  In all haste you must go on your journey.
  Now you can put your friends to the test!
  For, know well, time waits for no one,   65
  And every living creature in the world
  Must pay the price of death for the sin of Adam.
EVERYMAN: O gracious God, have mercy on me in my need!
  And may I have any company as I leave this earth,
  And have my acquaintance lead the way?   70
DEATH: Yes—if any be so bold
  To go with you and share your voyage.
  Too long you have thought your life and treasure were yours.
EVERYMAN: I thought so indeed!
DEATH: No, no—these were merely lent for a time!   75
  For as soon as you are gone,
  Another will have them for a while, and then
  Leave them behind, even as you have done.
  Everyman, how foolish you are! You have your five wits,
  But you did not use them to better your life—   80
  For suddenly I come.
EVERYMAN: O wretch that I am! How can I flee
  And escape from endless sorrow?
  Now, kind Death, spare me till tomorrow,
  And give me time to think.   85
DEATH: No, I cannot agree,
  Nor grant a delay to any.
  But I strike suddenly to the heart
  Without warning.
  And now I will leave you for a time—   90
  See that you be ready shortly,
  For this is the appointed day
  That no living person can escape.

  DEATH *leaves*.

Scene 3

EVERYMAN: Alas! I may well weep with deep sighs:
    Now I have no kind of company
    To help me and comfort me in my journey.
    And also my reckoning is quite unready.
    What shall I say to excuse me?   5
    The time passes—God help me, that made all!
    It does me no good to grieve,
    For the day passes and is almost gone.
    To whom can I tell my troubles?
    What if I talked to Fellowship   10
    And told him this sudden news?
    For he is quite in my confidence.
    We have in the world on many a day
    Been good friends in sport and play.
    I see him yonder, certainly.   15
    I trust that he will keep me company.
    Therefore I will speak to him to ease my sorrow.

FELLOWSHIP *enters*.

    Well met, good Fellowship, and good morrow!
FELLOWSHIP: Everyman, good morrow, and good day!
    Why, friend, do you look so distraught?   20
    If anything is amiss, you will let me know
    So that I may help bring the remedy.
EVERYMAN: Good Fellowship, I am in great danger.
FELLOWSHIP: My true friend, tell me what is on your mind.
    I will not forsake you to my life's end   25
    And provide you good company.
EVERYMAN: That was well spoken, and lovingly!
FELLOWSHIP: Sir, I must know the cause of your sorrow.
    I feel pity to see you in any distress.
    If any have wronged you, we shall have revenge,   30
    Though it should cost me my life.
EVERYMAN: I thank you most sincerely, Fellowship!
FELLOWSHIP: Ah—do not worry about thanking me:
    Tell me what is wrong and say no more.
EVERYMAN: But if I should open my heart to you,   35
    And you then turn away from my grief
    And offer me no comfort when I speak,
    Then should I be ten times more sorry.
FELLOWSHIP: Sir, I will do as I say, indeed.
EVERYMAN: Then you are a good friend in time of need,   40
    As I have found you a true friend before.
FELLOWSHIP: And so we shall be forevermore.
    For truly, if you were headed for hell,
    I would not let you go alone on your way.
EVERYMAN: You speak like a good friend, and I believe you.   45
    I will prove worthy of your friendship, you may be sure.

FELLOWSHIP: No need to prove anything between us two!
    For those who will promise and not keep their word
    Do not deserve to live in good company.
    Therefore tell me the sorrow in your mind   50
    As to a friend most loving and kind.
EVERYMAN: I shall show you how it is:
    I am commanded to go on a journey—
    A long way, hard and dangerous—
    And to render strict accounts, without delay,   55
    Before the highest judge of all.
    Therefore I beg of you to keep me company,
    As you have promised, on this journey.
FELLOWSHIP: Here is trouble indeed! A promise is a promise,
    But if I should set out on such a voyage,   60
    I know well it would cause me great grief,
    And I feel fear in my heart.
    Let us consider this matter most carefully,
    For your words would frighten the strongest man.
EVERYMAN: But you said that in my need   65
    You would never forsake me, dead or alive—
    Yes, even on the road to hell!
FELLOWSHIP: So I said, certainly.
    But this is no time for pleasant talk!
    If we took such a journey,   70
    When would we come back again?
EVERYMAN: Truly, never again, till the day of doom!
FELLOWSHIP: By my faith, then I will not go there.
    Who brought you this evil news?
EVERYMAN: It was Death, indeed, who came to see me.   75
FELLOWSHIP: Now by God that redeemed us all,
    If Death was the messenger,
    I will not go on that hated journey
    For any man living today—
    Not for the father that raised me from a child!   80
EVERYMAN: You promised otherwise, that's certain.
FELLOWSHIP: Of that I am well aware.
    And yet, if you wanted to eat, drink, and be merry,
    Or spend the pleasant hours in women's company,
    I would stay with you the livelong day—   85
    For that you may trust me!
EVERYMAN: Yes indeed—then you would be ready!
    Your mind is set on mirth, pleasure, and play,
    And you would sooner attend to such folly
    Than keep me company in my long journey.   90
FELLOWSHIP: I cannot go—that is the truth.
EVERYMAN: Dear Friend, help me in my hour of need.
    Loyal love has long linked us—
    And now, sweet Fellowship, remember me!
FELLOWSHIP: Love or no love, I cannot go!   95

EVERYMAN: But at least do this much for me:
    In the name of charity, see me off at the city gate
    As I set out on the highway!
FELLOWSHIP: For love or money, I will not budge!
    If you could stay—then I would be your friend!   100
    But as it is, good luck in your journey!
    And now I must take my leave.
EVERYMAN: Don't leave me, Fellowship! Will you abandon me?
FELLOWSHIP: I must go. And may God look after you!

    FELLOWSHIP *leaves.*

EVERYMAN: Farewell, sweet Fellowship! Is this the end,   105
    Never to meet again?
    And not a word of comfort at the parting?
    Now where can I turn?
    Friends crowd around us in prosperity
    That will prove faithless in adversity.   110
    Now I must turn to family and kin,
    Asking them for help in my dire need.
    For your kin will befriend you when others shut their door.
    Yonder I see them walking—
    Now I will try their loyalty.   115

    KINSHIP *and* COUSIN *come in.*

Scene 4

KINSHIP: Here we are, at your service.
    Tell us everything that is on your mind,
    And hold nothing back.
COUSIN: Yes, Everyman, and let us know
    What your errand is or your goal,   5
    For, as you know, we will live and die together.
KINSHIP: We will be with you in good luck and bad,
    For no one may turn down his kinfolk in need.
EVERYMAN: Many thanks, my kind friends.
    Now I shall tell you what grieves me.   10
    I received orders from a messenger
    That is the chief officer of a high king:
    He bade me start out on a pilgrimage, without fail,
    From which I know I shall never return.
    I must bring a strict accounting.   15
    And along the way, the great enemy of our souls
    Lies in wait to do me fatal harm.
    Therefore I ask you to be by my side
    And help me in the name of holy charity.
COUSIN: We should be by your side—is that what you ask?   20
    No, Everyman, I would rather fast
    And live on bread and water for five years!

KINSHIP: I hope you do not take it amiss,
    But as for me, you shall go alone!
EVERYMAN: Alas, that ever I was born!   25
    Cousin, will you not come with me?
COUSIN: No, by our Lady! I have a cramp in my toe.
    Do not rely on me, for, so help me,
    You are deceived!
KINSHIP: There is no way you can sway us—   30
    But I have a maid who loves to travel,
    To dance and go to feasts and gad about:
    I will give her leave to go with you on that journey,
    If you and she can agree.
EVERYMAN: Now tell me truly: 35
    Will you go with me or stay behind?
KINSHIP: Stay behind? Yes, that I will and shall!
    Therefore farewell until another day.

    KINSHIP *leaves.*

EVERYMAN: This makes me sad:
    People flatter me with fair promises,   40
    But they forsake me when I need them most.
COUSIN: Cousin Everyman, I bid you farewell,
    For truly I will not go with you.
    It troubles me to think of my own accounting—
    Therefore I will stay and make ready my own reckoning.   45

    COUSIN *leaves.*

Scene 5

EVERYMAN: Is this what I have come to?
    Those who trust fair words are fools.
    Kinship like Fellowship flees from me,
    And all their promises were empty words.
    Where now do I turn for a helping hand?   5
    One thing I do remember:
    All my life I have loved riches.
    If my Worldly Goods could now help me,
    It would set my mind at ease.
    Where are you, my Worldly Goods and riches of this world?   10

The voice of WORLDLY GOODS *is heard from inside.*

WORLDLY GOODS: Who calls me? Everyman? What is your hurry?
    I lie here inside, trussed and piled so high,
    And locked securely in strong chests,
    Or packed into bags—I cannot stir,
    As you may see with your own eye.   15
EVERYMAN: Come here, Worldly Goods, and make haste,
    For I need your advice.

WORLDLY GOODS *enters*.

WORLDLY GOODS: Sir, for any sorrow or adversity in this world,
    I can provide a speedy remedy.

EVERYMAN: My troubles are not of this world.   20
    I must go quite another way
    And give a strick reckoning
    Before the highest judge of all.
    All my life, you have been my pleasure and my joy.
    Therefore, I ask you to come with me,   25
    For it might be that before God Almighty
    You could help me balance my accounts.
    Certainly you have heard it said
    That money can set right many a wrong.

WORLDLY GOODS: No, Everyman—I sing a different song: 30
    I never follow anyone on such an errand.
    For, if I went along,
    You would fare much the worse for my presence.
    Because you always had me in mind,
    Your account is weighed down with many debts   35
    That will count heavily in the balance.
    For your love of me you will have to pay dearly.

EVERYMAN: Alas, I have loved you truly and had great pleasure
    All my life in worldly goods and treasure.

WORLDLY GOODS: That was your downfall—I tell no lie.   40
    For the love of me is contrary to Love Everlasting.
    But if you had loved me with moderation
    And given part of me to the poor,
    Then you would not be in this sorrowful state.

EVERYMAN: False friend that you are,   45
    And traitor to God, you have deceived me
    And caught me in a deadly snare!

WORLDLY GOODS: You have only yourself to blame.
    Your sorrows make me laugh—
    Why should I be sad?   50

EVERYMAN: I gave you all that should have been the Lord's.
    Now will you not come with me, indeed?
    Tell me the truth!

WORLDLY GOODS: I will not follow you, by God!
    Therefore farewell.   55

    WORLDLY GOODS *leaves*.

Scene 6

EVERYMAN: Oh, whom now can I trust
    To go with me on that fearful journey?
    First, Fellowship promised to go with me;
    His words were pleasing and sweet,

But afterward he deserted me.   5
Then I turned to my Kin in despair;
They also answered with words most fair—
But they too forsook me in the end.
Then I turned to my Worldly Goods that I loved,
Hoping to find comfort; but it was not to be—   10
He told me in sharp words
That he has delivered many unto hell.
Now do I feel remorse and shame;
I know I am worthy of blame.
Who is left to counsel me?   15
I think I shall fare badly
Unless I visit my Good Deeds—
But alas! she is most weak;
She can neither walk nor speak.
And yet I must ask her for help.   20
My Good Deeds, where are you?

GOOD DEEDS *speaks, huddled on the ground.*

GOOD DEEDS: Here I lie, on the cold ground.
    Your sins have left me so weak
    That I cannot stir.
EVERYMAN: O Good Deeds, I am sore afraid.   25
    You must counsel me,
    For now help would be most welcome.
GOOD DEEDS: Everyman, I understand
    You have been summoned to a reckoning
    Before the King of the Heavenly Jerusalem.   30
    If you heed my words, I will share in your journey.
EVERYMAN: That indeed was my hope—
    That you would keep me company.
GOOD DEEDS: I most gladly would go, though I can hardly stand.
EVERYMAN: Why, has anything hurt you?   35
GOOD DEEDS: Yes—your heedless neglect!
    Here look at the record of your deeds.

She shows him a book of accounts.

Here is a sorry reckoning, all blotted and defaced,
That spells eternal danger to your soul!
EVERYMAN: Good Deeds, I pray for your help,   40
    Or else I am damned forever!
    Therefore help me with my reckoning
    Before the King that is and was and ever will be.
GOOD DEEDS: Everyman, I pity you in your plight,
    And will help you as much as I can.   45
    And though my feet might not carry me farther,
    I have a sister who will also go with you:
    True Knowledge she is called, to keep with you
    And help you face that dreaded judgment.

TRUE KNOWLEDGE *enters.*

TRUE KNOWLEDGE: Everyman, I will go with you and be your guide,   50
    In your hour of need to stay by your side.
EVERYMAN: Now do my fortunes mend,
    For which I thank my Creator.
GOOD DEEDS: She will bring you to the place
    Where you will be healed of your grief.   55
EVERYMAN: I thank you from my heart, Good Deeds!
    Your sweet words make me glad.
TRUE KNOWLEDGE: Now let us go together lovingly
    To Confession, that cleansing river.

    TRUE KNOWLEDGE *leads* EVERYMAN *to* CONFESSION.

Scene 7

TRUE KNOWLEDGE: Here, this is Confession: kneel down and ask for mercy.
    For his counsel is well esteemed by God Almighty.

    EVERYMAN *kneels.*

EVERYMAN: O glorious fountain that washes away all uncleanness,
    Clear me of the spots of unclean vices.
    I come with True Knowledge for my redemption,   5
    Sorry from the heart for my sins.
CONFESSION: I know your sorrow well, Everyman.
    Because you have come to me with True Knowledge,
    I will comfort you as well as I can.
    And I will give you a precious jewel   10
    Called Penance, that wards off misfortune.
    Through it, your body will be chastised
    With abstinence and perseverance in God's service.
    Here you shall receive this scourge from me,
    As a sign of harsh penance that you must endure,   15
    To remind you that your Savior was lashed for your sake
    With sharp scourges, and suffered patiently.
    So in turn you must suffer patiently to save your soul.
    And if you stay on the right road,
    Your Good Deeds will be with you,   20
    And you will be sure of mercy.

[In a section of the play left out in this adaptation, EVERYMAN *punishes his body for the sins of the flesh and puts on the garment of sorrow. He then takes leave of* BEAUTY, STRENGTH, DISCRETION, *and* THE FIVE WITS *as he readies himself for the final stage of his journey.* GOOD DEEDS *stays with him to the end.]*

Scene 8

EVERYMAN: Alas! I must be on my way
   To present my reckoning and pay my debts,
   For all the time that I had is now spent.
   Remember well, all you who followed my story,
   How they that I loved best abandoned me,   5
   And only Good Deeds stayed with me to the end.
GOOD DEEDS: All the things of this earth are mere vanity.
   Beauty, Strength, and Discretion fade away.
   Foolish friends and heedless next of kin—
   All flee from you, except Good Deeds.   10
EVERYMAN: Have mercy on me, Almighty God!
GOOD DEEDS: Do not fear, I will speak for you.

   EVERYMAN *and* GOOD DEEDS *descend into the grave.*

TRUE KNOWLEDGE: Now he has suffered what we must all endure.
   Good Deeds will offer him safe conduct.
   Now that the end has come   15
   I hear angels singing with great joy
   Bidding welcome to the soul of Everyman.
   Remember: After death no one can make amends,
   And mercy and pity then do not avail.
   If the final reckoning is faulty,   20
   The sinner will burn in everlasting fire.
   But if your accounting is whole and sound,
   You will be crowned high in heaven.

The Receptive Reader

1. How does this play make audiences think or feel about death? How does the perspective on death compare with more modern perspectives?

2. Purposeful insistent repetition, or **reiteration,** was a favorite teaching technique in medieval didactic literature. Is there a recurrent pattern in Everyman's encounters with the different allegorical characters? Are there other examples of repetition?

3. *Allegory* is sometimes described as lifeless or mechanical. Do the characters become human for you? Did the author have a sense of humor?

4. A familiar problem with didactic literature is that the good characters sometimes seem lifeless compared with the bad. Is that true in this play?

The Personal Response

Does the spectator have to be religious to respond to this play? What, to you, is the central message of the play? How do you relate to it as a modern reader?

The Creative Dimension

This translation and abridgment of the play is suitable for a *readers' theater* presentation (where different readers read their parts) or other kind of classroom adaptation. One group of students rewrote the play for a mini-production with *Everywoman* as the updated title. Work with a group of fellow students to prepare a mini-production or adaptation of the play.

Luis Valdez   *(born 1940)*

*If you can sing, dance, walk, march, hold a
picket sign, play a guitar or harmonica or any
other instrument, you can participate! No acting
experience required.*

FROM A RECRUITING LEAFLET FOR THE
TEATRO CAMPESINO

Luis Valdez is the founder of the Teatro Campesino, which has performed and been honored throughout the United States and in Europe. He is a prolific writer, organizer, director, teacher, and promoter of Chicano drama. The dialogue in his plays, like the speech of many Mexican Americans, shifts easily from English to Spanish and back. The Teatro he founded in 1965 began by performing *actos*—short one-act plays—in community centers, church halls, and in the fields in California. The plays were designed to raise the political consciousness of field-workers struggling to make a living and preserve their dignity in a system rigged against them. (A *campesino* is someone who works in the fields.) Valdez has a lively sense of the tragedy and comedy of the lives of ordinary people. He also has a gift for cutting satire: At the beginning of his play *Los Vendidos* (*The Sellouts,* 1967), a secretary from the governor's office comes to Honest Sancho's Used Mexican Lot to look for a not-too-dark Chicano to become a token Mexican American at social functions in the state capital.

Valdez himself started to work in the fields at age six, with the much-interrupted schooling of the children of America's migrant workers. He eventually accepted a scholarship at San Jose State University and graduated with a B.A. in English in 1964. Much of his early experience in the theater was with the San Francisco Mime Troupe, which practiced improvisational theater. Under his leadership, the Teatro Campesino explored the lives of urban Chicano youth, Mexican Indian legend and mythology, and materials from Third World sources. In 1987, Valdez wrote and directed the movie *La Bamba,* a biography of the Chicano rock 'n' roll singer Ritchie Valens. His PBS production of *Corridos: Tales of Passion and Revolution,* with Linda Ronstadt, won the Peabody Award.

Soldado Razo, or *The Buck Private,* was first performed by the Teatro Campesino in 1971. What makes the private a modern Everyman?

The Buck Private

From Soldado Razo

CHARACTERS

JOHNNY
THE FATHER
DEATH
THE MOTHER
CECILIA
THE BROTHER

DEATH (*enters singing*): I'm taking off as a private, I'm going to join the ranks . . . along with the courageous young men who leave behind beloved mothers, who leave their girlfriends crying, crying, crying their farewell. Yeah! How lucky for me that there's a war. How goes it, bro? I am death. What else is new? Well, don't get paranoid because I didn't come to take anybody away. I came to tell you a story. Sure, the story of the Buck Private. Maybe you knew him, eh? He was killed not too long ago in Vietnam.

JOHNNY *enters, adjusting his uniform.*

DEATH: This is Johnny, the Buck Private. He's leaving for Vietnam in the morning, but tonight—well, tonight he's going to enjoy himself, right? Look at his face. Know what he's thinking? He's thinking (Johnny *moves his lips.*) "Now, I'm a man!"

THE MOTHER *enters.*

DEATH: This is his mother. Poor thing. She's worried about her son, like all mothers. "Blessed be God," she's thinking; (THE MOTHER *moves her mouth.*) "I hope nothing happens to my son." (THE MOTHER *touches* JOHNNY *on the shoulder.*)
JOHNNY: Is dinner ready, mom?
MOTHER: Yes, son, almost. Why did you dress like that? You're not leaving until tomorrow.
JOHNNY: Well, you know. Cecilia's coming and everything.
MOTHER: Oh, my son. You're always bringing girlfriends to the house but you never think about settling down.
JOHNNY: One of these days I'll give you a surprise, ma. (*He kisses her forehead. Embraces her.*)
DEATH: Oh, my! What a picture of tenderness, no? But, watch the old lady. Listen to what she's thinking. "Now, my son is a man. He looks so handsome in that uniform."
JOHNNY: Well, mom, it's getting late. I'll be back shortly with Cecilia, okay?
MOTHER: Yes, son, hurry back. (*He leaves.*) May God take care of you, mom's pride and joy.

JOHNNY *reenters and begins to talk.*

DEATH: Out in the street, Johnny begins to think about his family, his girl, his neighborhood, his life.

JOHNNY: Poor mom. Tomorrow it will be very difficult for her. For me as well. It was pretty hard when I went to boot camp, but now? Vietnam! It's a killer, man. The old man, too. I'm not going to be here to help him out. I wasn't getting rich doing fieldwork, but it was something. A little help, at least. My little brother can't work yet because he's still in school. I just hope he stays there. And finishes. I never liked that school stuff, but I know my little brother digs it. He's smart too—maybe he'll even go to college. One of us has got to make it in this life. Me—I guess I'll just get married to Cecilia and have a bunch of kids. I remember when I first saw her at the Rainbow Ballroom. I couldn't even dance with her because I had had a few beers. The next week was pretty good, though. Since then. How long ago was that? June . . . no, July. Four months. Now I want to get hitched. Her parents don't like me, I know. They think I'm a good for nothing. Maybe they'll feel different when I come back from Nam. Sure, the War Veteran! Maybe I'll get wounded and come back with tons of medals. I wonder how the dudes around here are going to think about that? Damn neighborhood—I've lived here all my life. Now I'm going to Vietnam. (*taps and drum*) It's going to be a drag, man. I might even get killed. If I do, they'll bring me back here in a box, covered with a flag . . . military funeral like they gave Pete Gomez . . . everybody crying . . . the old lady—(*stops*) What the hell am I thinking, man? Damn fool! (*He freezes.*)

DEATH *powders* JOHNNY'S *face white during the next speech.*

DEATH: Foolish, but not stupid, eh? He knew the kind of funeral he wanted and he got it. Military coffin, lots of flowers, American flag, women crying, and a trumpet playing taps with a rifle salute at the end. Or was it goodbye? It doesn't matter, you know what I mean. It was first class all the way. Oh, by the way, don't get upset about the makeup I'm putting on him, eh? I'm just getting him ready for what's coming. I don't always do things in a hurry, you know. Okay, then, next scene. (JOHNNY *exits.*)

JOHNNY *goes on to* CECILIA'*s and exits.*

DEATH: Back at the house, his old man is just getting home.

THE FATHER *enters.*

FATHER: Hey, old lady, I'm home. Is dinner ready?

THE MOTHER *enters.*

MOTHER: Yes, dear. Just wait till Juan gets home. What did you buy?
FATHER: A sixpack of Coors.
MOTHER: Beer?
FATHER: Well, why not? Look—This is my son's last night.
MOTHER: What do you mean, his last night? Don't speak like that.
FATHER: I mean his last night at home, woman. You understand—hic.
MOTHER: You're drunk, aren't you?

FATHER: And if I am, what's it to you? I just had a few beers with my buddy and that's it. Well, what is this, anyway . . . ? It's all I need, man. My son's going to war and you don't want me to drink. I've got to celebrate, woman!

MOTHER: Celebrate what?

FATHER: That my son is now a man! And quite a man, the twerp. So don't pester me. Bring me some supper.

MOTHER: Wait for Juan to come home.

FATHER: Where is he? He's not here? Is that so-and-so loafing around again? Juan? Juan?

MOTHER: I'm telling you he went to get Cecilia, who's going to have dinner with us. And please don't use any foul language. What will the girl say if she hears you talking like that?

FATHER: To hell with it! Who owns this damn house, anyway? Aren't I the one who pays the rent? The one who buys the food? Don't make me get angry, huh? Or you'll get it. It doesn't matter if you already have a son who's a soldier.

MOTHER: Please. I ask you in your son's name, eh? Calm down. (*She exits.*)

FATHER: Calm down! Just like that she wants me to calm down. And who's going to shut my trap? My son the soldier? My son . . .

DEATH: The old man's thoughts are racing back a dozen years to a warm afternoon in July. Johnny, eight years old, is running toward him between the vines, shouting: "Paaa, I already picked 20 trays, paaapá!"

FATHER: Huh. Twenty trays. Little bugger.

THE BROTHER *enters*.

BROTHER: Pa, is Johnny here?

DEATH: This is Johnny's little brother.

FATHER: And where are you coming from?

BROTHER: I was over at Polo's house. He has a new motor scooter.

FATHER: You just spend all your time playing, don't you?

BROTHER: I didn't do anything.

FATHER: Don't talk back to your father.

BROTHER (*shrugs*): Are we going to eat soon?

FATHER: I don't know. Go ask your mother.

THE BROTHER *exits*.

DEATH: Looking at his younger son, the old man starts thinking about him. His thoughts spin around in the usual hopeless cycle of defeat, undercut by more defeat.

FATHER: That boy should be working. He's already fourteen years old. I don't know why the law forces them to go to school till they're sixteen. He won't amount to anything, anyway. It's better if he starts working with me so that he can help the family.

DEATH: Sure, he gets out of school and in three or four years, I take him the way I took Johnny. Crazy, huh?

JOHNNY *returns with* CECILIA.

JOHNNY: Good evening, pa.

FATHER: Son! Good evening! What's this? You're dressed as a soldier?

JOHNNY: I brought Cecilia over to have dinner with us.

FATHER: Well, have her come in, come in.

CECILIA: Thank you very much.

FATHER: My son looks good, doesn't he?

CECILIA: Yes, sir.

FATHER: Damn right. He's off to be a buck private. (*pause*) Well, let's see . . . uh, son, would you like a beer?!

JOHNNY: Yes, sir, but couldn't we get a chair first? For Cecilia?

FATHER: But, of course. We have all the modern conveniences. Let me bring one. Sweetheart? The company's here! (*He exits.*)

JOHNNY: How you doing?

CECILIA: Okay. I love you.

DEATH: This, of course, is Johnny's girlfriend. Fine, ha? Too bad he'll never get to marry her. Oh, he proposed tonight and everything—and she accepted, but she doesn't know what's ahead. Listen to what she's thinking. (CECILIA *moves her mouth.*) "When we get married I hope Johnny still has his uniform. We'd look so good together. Me in a wedding gown and him like that. I wish we were getting married tomorrow!"

JOHNNY: What are you thinking?

CECILIA: Nothing.

JOHNNY: Come on.

CECILIA: Really.

JOHNNY: Come on, I saw your eyes. Now come on, tell me what you were thinking.

CECILIA: It was nothing.

JOHNNY: Are you scared?

CECILIA: About what?

JOHNNY: My going to Vietnam.

CECILIA: No! I mean . . . yes, in a way, but I wasn't thinking that.

JOHNNY: What was it?

CECILIA (*pause*): I was thinking I wish the wedding was tomorrow.

JOHNNY: Really?

CECILIA: Yes.

JOHNNY: You know what? I wish it was too. (*He embraces her.*)

DEATH: And, of course, now he's thinking too. But it's not what she was thinking. What a world!

THE FATHER *and* THE BROTHER *enter with four chairs.*

FATHER: Here are the chairs. What did I tell you? (*to* THE BROTHER) Hey, you, help me move the table, come on.

JOHNNY: Do you need help, pa?

FATHER: No, son, your brother and I'll move it. (*He and* THE BROTHER *move imaginary table into place.*) There it is. And your mom says you should start sitting down because dinner's ready. She made tamales, can you believe that!

JOHNNY: Tamales?

BROTHER: They're Colonel Sanders, eeehh.

FATHER: You shut your trap! Look . . . don't pay attention to him, Cecilia; this little bugger, uh, this kid is always saying stupid things, uh, silly things. Sit down.

MOTHER (*entering with imaginary bowl*): Here come the tamales! Watch out because the pot's hot, okay? Oh, Cecilia, good evening.

CECILIA: Good evening, ma'am. Can I help you with anything?

MOTHER: No, no, everything's ready. Sit down, please.

JOHNNY: Ma, how come you made tamales? (DEATH *begins to put some more makeup on* JOHNNY's *face.*)

MOTHER: Well, because I know you like them so much, son.

DEATH: A thought flashes across Johnny's mind: "Too much, man. I should go to war every day." Over on this side of the table, the little brother is thinking: "What's so hot about going to war—tamales?"

BROTHER: I like tamales.

FATHER: Who told you to open your mouth? Would you like a beer, son?

JOHNNY (*nods*): Thanks, dad.

FATHER: And you, Cecilia?

CECILIA (*surprised*): No, sir, uh, thanks.

MOTHER: Juan, don't be so thoughtless. Cecilia's not old enough to drink. What are her parents going to say? I made some Kool-Aid, sweetheart; I'll bring the pitcher right out. (*She exits.*)

DEATH: You know what's going through the little brother's mind? He is thinking: "He offered her a beer! She was barely in the eighth grade three years ago. When I'm 17 I'm going to join the service and get really drunk."

FATHER: How old are you, Cecilia?

CECILIA: Eighteen.

DEATH: She lied, of course.

FATHER: Oh, well, what the heck, you're already a woman! Come on son, don't let her get away.

JOHNNY: I'm not.

MOTHER (*reentering*): Here's the Kool-Aid and the beans.

JOHNNY: Ma, I got an announcement to make. Will you please sit down?

MOTHER: What is it?

FATHER (*to* THE BROTHER): Give your chair to your mother.

BROTHER: What about my tamale?

MOTHER: Let him eat his dinner.

FATHER (*to* THE BROTHER): Get up!

JOHNNY: Sit down, Mom.

MOTHER: What is it, son? (*She sits down.*)

DEATH: Funny little games people play, ha? The mother asks, but she already knows what her son is going to say. So does the father. And even little brother. They are all thinking: "He is going to say: Cecilia and I are getting married!"

JOHNNY: Cecilia and I are getting married!

MOTHER: Oh, son!

FATHER: You don't say!

BROTHER: Really?

MOTHER: When, son?

JOHNNY: When I get back from Vietnam.

DEATH: Suddenly a thought is crossing everybody's mind: "What if he doesn't come back?" But they shove it aside.

MOTHER: Oh, darling! (*She hugs* CECILIA.)

FATHER: Congratulations, son. (*He hugs* JOHNNY.)

MOTHER (*hugging* JOHNNY): My boy! (*She cries.*)

JOHNNY: Hey, mom, wait a minute. Save that for tomorrow. That's enough, ma.

FATHER: Daughter. (*He hugs* CECILIA *properly.*)

BROTHER: Heh, Johnny, why don't I go to Vietnam and you stay here for the wedding? I'm not afraid to die.

MOTHER: What makes you say that, child?

BROTHER: It just came out.

FATHER: You've let out too much already, don't you think?

BROTHER: I didn't mean it! (THE BROTHER *exits.*)

JOHNNY: It was an accident, pa.

MOTHER: You're right; it was an accident. Please, sweetheart, let's eat in peace, ha? Juan leaves tomorrow.

DEATH: The rest of the meal goes by without any incidents. They discuss the wedding, the tamales, and the weather. Then it's time to go to the party.

FATHER: Is it true there's going to be a party?

JOHNNY: Just a small dance, over at Sapo's house.

MOTHER: Which Sapo, son?

JOHNNY: Sapo, my friend.

FATHER: Don't get drunk, okay?

JOHNNY: Oh, come on, dad, Cecilia will be with me.

FATHER: Did you ask her parents for permission?

JOHNNY: Yes, sir. She's got to be home by eleven.

FATHER: Okay. (JOHNNY *and* CECILIA *rise.*)

CECILIA: Thank you for the dinner, ma'am.

MOTHER: You're very welcome.

CECILIA: The tamales were really good.

JOHNNY: Yes, ma, they were terrific.

MOTHER: Is that right, son? You liked them?

JOHNNY: They were great. (*He hugs her.*) Thanks, eh?

MOTHER: What do you mean thanks? You're my son. Go then, it's getting late.

FATHER: Do you want to take the truck, son?

JOHNNY: No thanks, pa. I already have Cecilia's car.

CECILIA: Not mine. My parents' car. They loaned it to us for the dance.

FATHER: It seems like you made a good impression, eh?

CECILIA: He sure did. They say he's more responsible now that he's in the service.

DEATH (*to audience*): Did you hear that? Listen to her again.

CECILIA (*repeats sentence, exactly as before*): They say he's more responsible now that he's in the service.

DEATH: That's what I like to hear!

FATHER: That's good. Then all you have to do is go ask for Cecilia's hand, right, sweetheart?

MOTHER: God willing.

JOHNNY: We're going, then.

CECILIA: Good night.

FATHER: Good night.

MOTHER: Be careful on the road, children.

JOHNNY: Don't worry, mom. Be back later.

CECILIA: Bye!

JOHNNY *and* CECILIA *exit.* THE MOTHER *stands at the door.*

FATHER (*sitting down again*): Well, old lady, little Johnny has become a man. The years fly by, don't they?

DEATH: The old man is thinking about the Korean War. Johnny was born about that time. He wishes he had some advice, some hints, to pass on to him about war. But he never went to Korea. The draft skipped him, and somehow, he never got around to enlisting. (THE MOTHER *turns around.*)

MOTHER (*she sees* DEATH): Oh, my God! (*exit*)

DEATH (*ducking down*): Damn, I think she saw me.

FATHER: What's wrong with you? (THE MOTHER *is standing frozen, looking toward the spot where* DEATH *was standing.*) Answer me, what's up? (*pause*) Speak to me! What am I, invisible?

MOTHER (*solemnly*): I just saw Death.

FATHER: Death? You're crazy.

MOTHER: It's true. As soon as Juan left, I turned around and there was Death, standing—smiling! (THE FATHER *moves away from the spot inadvertently.*) Oh, Blessed Virgin Mary, what if something happens to Juan.

FATHER: Don't say that! Don't you know it's bad luck?

They exit. DEATH *reenters.*

The Greyhound Bus Depot.

DEATH: The next day, Johnny goes to the Greyhound Bus Depot. His mother, his father, and his girlfriend go with him to say goodbye. The Bus Depot is full of soldiers and sailors and old men. Here and there, a drunkard is passed out on the benches. Then there's the announcements: THE LOS ANGELES BUS IS NOW RECEIVING PASSENGERS AT GATE TWO, FOR KINGSBURG, TULARE, DELANO, BAKERSFIELD AND LOS ANGELES, CONNECTIONS IN L.A. FOR POINTS EAST AND SOUTH.

JOHNNY, FATHER, MOTHER, *and* CECILIA *enter.* CECILIA *clings to* JOHNNY.

FATHER: It's been several years since I last set foot at the station.

MOTHER: Do you have your ticket, son?

JOHNNY: Oh, no, I have to buy it.

CECILIA: I'll go with you.

FATHER: Do you have money, son?

JOHNNY: Yes, pa, I have it.

JOHNNY *and* CECILIA *walk over to* DEATH.

JOHNNY: One ticket, please.

DEATH: Where to?
JOHNNY: Vietnam. I mean, Oakland.
DEATH: Round trip or one way?
JOHNNY: One way.
DEATH: Right. One way. (*applies more makeup*)

> JOHNNY *gets his ticket and he and* CECILIA *start back toward his parents.*
> JOHNNY *stops abruptly and glances back at* DEATH, *who has already shifted positions.*

CECILIA: What's wrong?
JOHNNY: Nothing. (*They join the parents.*)
DEATH: For half an hour then, they exchange small talk and trivialities, repeating some of the things that have been said several times before. Cecilia promises Johnny she will be true to him and wait until he returns. Then it's time to go: THE OAKLAND-VIETNAM EXPRESS IS NOW RECEIVING PASSENGERS AT GATE NUMBER FOUR. ALL ABOARD PLEASE.
JOHNNY: That's my bus.
MOTHER: Oh, son.
FATHER: Take good care of yourself then, okay, son?
CECILIA: I love you, Johnny. (*She embraces him.*)
DEATH: THE OAKLAND-VIETNAM EXPRESS IS IN THE FINAL BOARDING STAGES. PASSENGERS WITH TICKETS ALL ABOARD PLEASE. AND THANKS FOR GOING GREYHOUND.
JOHNNY: I'm leaving, now.

> *Embraces all around, weeping, last goodbyes, etc.* JOHNNY *exits. Then parents exit.* THE MOTHER *and* CECILIA *are crying.*

DEATH (*sings*):   *Goodbye, Goodbye*
                    Star of my nights
                    A soldier said in front of a window
                    I'm leaving, I'm leaving
                    But don't cry, my angel
                    For tomorrow I'll be back . . .

So Johnny left for Vietnam, never to return. He didn't want to go and yet he did. It never crossed his mind to refuse. How can he refuse the government of the United States? How could he refuse his family? Besides, who wants to go to prison? And there was the chance he'd come back alive . . . wounded maybe, but alive. So he took a chance—and lost. But before he died he saw many things in Vietnam; he had his eyes opened. He wrote his mother about them.

> JOHNNY *and* THE MOTHER *enter at opposite sides of the stage.* JOHNNY *is in full battle gear. His face is now a skull.*

JOHNNY: Dear mom.
MOTHER: Dear son.
JOHNNY: I am writing this letter.
MOTHER: I received your letter.
JOHNNY: To tell you I'm okay.
MOTHER: And I thank the heavens you're all right.
JOHNNY: How's everybody over there?

MOTHER: Here, we're all doing fine, thank God.

JOHNNY: Ma, there's a lot happening here that I didn't know about before. I don't know if I'm allowed to write about it, but I'm going to try. Yesterday we attacked a small village near some rice paddies. We had orders to kill everybody because they were supposed to be v-c's, communists. We entered the small village and my buddies started shooting. I saw one of them kill an old man and an old lady. My sergeant killed a small boy about seven years old, then he shot his mother or some woman that came running up crying. Blood was everywhere. I don't remember what happened after that but my sergeant ordered me to start shooting. I think I did. May God forgive me for what I did, but I never wanted to come over here. They say we have to do it to defend our country.

MOTHER: Son what you are writing to us makes me sad. I talked to your father and he also got very worried, but he says that's what war is like. He reminds you that you're fighting communists. I have a candle lit and every day I ask God to take good care of you wherever you are and that he return you to our arms healthy and in one piece.

JOHNNY: Ma, I had a dream the other night. I dreamed I was breaking into one of the hooches, that's what we call the Vietnamese's houses. I went in firing my M-16 because I knew that the village was controlled by the gooks. I killed three of them right away, but when I looked down it was my pa, my little brother and you, mother. I don't know how much more I can stand. Please tell Sapo and all the dudes how it's like over here. Don't let them . . .

DEATH *fires a gun, shooting* JOHNNY *in the head. He falls.* THE MOTHER *screams without looking at* JOHNNY.

DEATH: Johnny was killed in action November 1965 at Chu Lai. His body lay in the field for two days and then it was taken to the beach and placed in a freezer, a converted portable food locker. Two weeks later he was shipped home for burial.

DEATH *straightens out* JOHNNY's *body. Takes his helmet, rifle, etc.* THE FATHER, THE MOTHER, THE BROTHER, *and* CECILIA *file past and gather around the body. Taps plays.*

The Receptive Reader

1. The central conflict in the medieval *Everyman* was between sin and virtue. What is the central conflict in *The Buck Private?*

2. To judge from this excerpt, does this play have a universal appeal transcending the appeal to a particular ethnic group? In what ways is the buck private a modern Everyman?

3. How does the role of Death compare in the two plays? How does the role of Kinship compare in the two plays?

The Personal Response

What is the central statement this selection makes about the war in Vietnam?

The Creative Dimension

Like the traditional *Everyman,* Valdez' modern Everyman play lends itself well to adaptation for a mini-production designed to help an audience get into the spirit of the play. One class production changed the G.I. in the Valdez play to a young woman in the Desert Storm war against Iraq. You and your classmates may want to stage your own reenactment of the Valdez play.

EXPERIMENTAL MONOLOGUE THEATER

Like other writers and artists in the sister arts, today's playwrights dread being tagged as conventional—merely playing variations on well-used ways to do theater. **Monologue theater** is a new kind of dramatic performance getting much exposure. It does away with conventional character development, with standard dialogue, and with conventional plot lines. Performers take turns presenting their monologues to the audience, offering different perspectives on a common theme, like jazz musicians doing their personal riffs in intervals between ensemble play.

In the seventies, ntozake shange wrote a series of extended monologues, titled *for colored girls who have considered suicide / when the rainbow is enuf.* Seven African American women take turns talking about their often difficult relationships and problems with men.

Early in the new century, playwright Eve Ensler created a sensation with her award-winning *The Vagina Monologues,* performed in over twenty countries and translated into twenty languages. In her ninety-minute play, Ensler distilled the results of two hundred interviews with women—women who night after night told her "the same stories—women being raped as teenagers, in college, as little girls, as elderly women"; women who had finally escaped being beaten by their husbands and others still terrified to leave. In performances around the country and abroad, celebrity actors vied for spots in the sequence of monologues. Ensler's play became the catalyst for her movement to stop violence against women. At one of her V-Day events, her movement brought 16,000 people to New York's Madison Square Garden. It enlisted the support of a roster of celebrity actors including Glenn Close, Meryl Streep, Jane Fonda, Brooke Shields, and Whoopi Goldberg.

In 1981, Sam Shepard and Joseph Chaikin, known for their work in experimental theater, collaborated on a theater piece called *Savage/Love.* Although using the experimental monologue theater form, the play circled back to the most basic dramatic themes. Chaikin said the play presented "common poems of real and imagined moments in the spell of love."

> We each felt that we wanted the piece to be easily and readily identifiable, not esoteric. We felt it should be made up of love moments which were as immediately familiar to most people in the audience as they were

to Sam and me. . . . When we began to talk and work, even though we each had different stories, we found we shared many thoughts about the human experience of love. We talked especially about the difficulty of expressing tenderness, and the dread of being replaced.

WRITING ABOUT LITERATURE

31 Branching Out
WRITING FOCUS: Independent Reading or Viewing

The Writing Workshop   The test of what you have learned about drama comes when you encounter a new play or an unfamiliar classic on your own. As a theater goer, you sooner or later have to start trusting your own judgment (if only to decide where to spend your ticket money).

What made a play like Peter Shaffer's *Equus* or *Amadeus* a huge audience success? Why did Samuel Becket's *Waiting for Godot* run for three hundred consecutive performances in Paris? Why was it translated into Swedish, Japanese, and many other languages and produced around the world? What did audiences see in Beth Henley's *Crimes of the Heart*—the play and the movie? What made a new black playwright like August Wilson—*Joe Turner's Come and Gone* (1988), *The Piano Lesson* (1987), *Seven Guitars* (1994)—a major figure in American drama? What made David Mamet's disturbing, aggressive, abrasive plays and movie scripts—from *Glengarry Glen Ross* to *Oleanna* to *The Heist*—a major presence on stage and screen?

Consider the following guidelines when you write about your independent reading, viewing, or playgoing:

▮ *If possible, give yourself a head start.* For instance, choose a play that was the subject of a much-discussed local production. Or choose a play that was made into a movie with a stellar cast (and perhaps with modifications and adaptations that split the critical community). Or decide to study a modern classic that you have often seen mentioned but never came to know.

▮ *Check out the critics' reactions.* What have knowledgeable people said about this play? How have they reacted? What questions have the critics raised? Remember not to let the critics answer all your questions for you. You are the spectator (or reader).

▮ *If you can, quote insiders or people in the know.* Look at comments by authors, directors, or actors. What perspective or guidance for interpretation do they offer? Draw on their comments to give your paper the insider's touch.

✘ *Give the new and difficult the benefit of the doubt.* Remember that early audiences considered the operas of Wagner a hoax and that Van Gogh sold now-priceless paintings for the price of a lunch.

✘ *Push toward a central question or unifying theme.* For instance, a play from the theater of the absurd may at first sound or read like inspired nonsense. Does it perhaps actually raise serious questions about society? Does it hold the mirror up to human nature after all—even though we might not like the reflection we see?

✘ *Anchor your judgments to the actual text of the play.* Make extensive use of short, apt quotation. Highlight revealing key quotes. Weave a rich tapestry of firsthand references to the play.

The following sample paper was first published in a student literary magazine. What are strong features that may have moved the editors to print the paper?

Sample Student Paper

Karen Traficante

In Defense of *The American Dream*

Robert Brustein, in his attempt to discredit Edward Albee's play *The American Dream,* claimed there was an "absence of any compelling theme, commitment, or sense of life." Are these accusations true? And if so, do they classify the play as a "fumble"? Harold Clurman's review of the play in the *Nation* advised that Albee "stick closer to the facts of life so his plays may remain humanly and socially relevant." How far does Albee stray?

In order for this play to have a "compelling theme, commitment, or sense of life," a struggle or conflict is needed. But no struggle is found. There is no "man against society" here. The conventional Mommy and Daddy are relatively content with their lives. It does not matter to them that they are living conformities. There are no carrots in their family tree of apples. Mommy and Daddy are typical Jonathan apples. And they don't care. They carry their dull lives to an extreme. Everything about them points to their lack of originality. Their apartment shows no personality. The hideous gilded furniture and frames with no pictures point to their lack of individualism. Socially accepted Mrs. Barker is actually a "dreadful woman"; however, realizing that she is a professional woman and that one is expected to like such elite people, Mommy goes on and explains, "But she is chairman of our woman's club, so naturally I'm terribly fond of her." Naturally! No attempts are made to struggle against society and its conformities here either. And thus, with no struggle, no theme. But the play doesn't need a "theme." It is a parable and a parody. It makes its readers question, struggle, and laugh at the absurdity of their human freedoms. It gives its readers a theme to live by: that is, man against society, mechanization, conformity. The play is not a "fumble"; it is a successful defensive play.

Albee's characters and their lives are exaggerated examples of human mass existence and experience. But he does not deviate that far from the truth. Daniel Bell, in an article on the "Theory of Mass Society," said, "The sense of a radical dehumanization of life which has accompanied events of the past several decades has given rise to the theory of 'mass society.'" And this present mass society has lessened the possibility for "persons of achieving a sense of individual self in our mechanized society." There exists a majority of conventional Mommies and Daddies, and their dull lives are common to many. The uninventive apartment of the play is similar to some modern flats of our society: the rugs blend with the walls which in turn fuse with the upholstery which is highlighted by the paintings on the walls. Why do people tend to buy expensive pictures merely because the wood frame matches their fruitwood cocktail table and the artist's pigments match the color scheme of the room? Paintings are not a part of the furniture. They are unique expressions; they are art.

Mommy and Daddy are overjoyed with the arrival of the new "bumble." He is a "Clean-cut midwest farm boy type, almost insultingly good-looking in a typically American way . . ." And don't most parents look for these traits in their own offspring? They not only conform, but expect their child to fit the mold as well. Mommy and Daddy's first bumble would not concede, and so he was chopped up and thrown away. Mommy and Daddy wanted only another Jonathan apple. Realistically, modern Mommies and Daddies do not chop up their undesired youth. They may, however, smother their children's individualism or simply break ties with them. Brabantio abandoned his lovely daughter Desdemona in Shakespeare's *Othello*. Why? Because she deviated from his hopes and from society's ideals as well. And so it is true of our modern Mommies and Daddies; unmarried pregnant daughters are banned from their homes; interracial and interreligious marriages cause conflict or rejection. So Albee is not straying far from the truth when his Mommy and Daddy throw away their stubborn bumble.

A predominant condition which exists in our world is an inability to communicate. Mommy and Daddy, though married, are essentially strangers. Their daily conversations are vacuums filled with clichés, small talk, and trivialities. Daddy avoids really talking to Mommy. He simply responds with "Have they!" or "Yes . . . yes . . . ," barely recognizing what she is saying. Their marriage exists only in custom. There is no love bond established because they lack the communication necessary to understand one another and thus to love.

Mrs. Barker and Mommy also make some fruitless attempts at social intercourse. With their automatic replies, however, they miss the true substance of what seem to be urbanities: "My, what an unattractive apartment you have!" "Yes, but you don't know what a trouble it is."

Without a "compelling theme, commitment, or sense of life," Albee successfully brings his readers' attentions to the paralysis of conformity, the failure of communication, and a vision of a future world. The vision is exaggerated to the point of humor and horror. But by its existence, it points out the urgency for alterations, struggle, and reform.

Questions for Peer Review

What, according to this paper, accounted for the critics' hostility or lack of comprehension? What are the major points in the student writer's defense of the play? How convincing is her interpretation? How well supported is it? What are some of her most telling points? Does she make you want to see this kind of play?

PLAYS FOR INDEPENDENT READING

Edward Albee	*The American Dream, The Zoo Story*
Imamu Amiri Baraka	*The Dutchman*
Samuel Beckett	*Waiting for Godot, Endgame*
Bertolt Brecht	*Mother Courage, Galileo, The Good Woman of Setzuan*
Caryl Churchill	*Top Girls, Objections to Sex and Violence*
Brian Friel	*Translations*
Beth Henley	*Crimes of the Heart*
Eugène Ionesco	*The Bald Soprano, The Chairs, The Lesson*
David Mamet	*American Buffalo, Glengarry Glen Ross, Oleanna*
Sean O'Casey	*Juno and the Paycock, Red Roses for Me*
Harold Pinter	*The Homecoming, The Birthday Party*
Jean-Paul Sartre	*No Exit, Dirty Hands, The Flies*
Peter Shaffer	*Equus, Amadeus*
ntozake shange	*for colored girls who have considered suicide/ when the rainbow is enuf*
Tom Stoppard	*Rosencrantz and Guildenstern Are Dead, The Real Thing, Arcadia*
Luis Valdez	*Zoot Suit, The Shrunken Head of Pancho Villa, Los Vendidos*
Wendy Wasserstein	*The Heidi Chronicles*
August Wilson	*Joe Turner's Come and Gone, The Piano Lesson, Seven Guitars*

Theater Today

The following is one trend watcher's list of plays that have in recent years received critical attention or attracted large audiences.

Castellanos, Rosario *The Eternal Feminine* (tr. Maureen Ahem)
One of Mexico's major literary figures before her untimely death in 1974, Castellanos was a feminist who wrote: "It isn't

enough to discover who we are. We have to invent ourselves." Recently translated by a professor of Spanish at Ohio State. Castellanos' work is coming to the attention of American readers.

Churchill, Caryl, *Far Away* (2000)
Illuminates a nightmarish vision of a world of apocalypse in which characters turn a blind eye until it is too late.

Devere-Smith, Anna, *House Arrest* (2000)
Explores the mythic role of the presidency in American culture. Her successful new form of theater, which earned her a MacArthur fellowship, is a blend of social commentary, theater, and journalism.

Edson, Margaret, *WIT* (1999)
Pulitzer Prize winning play about a scholar of John Donne's poetry who faces cancer and her own arrogance as she struggles with Donne's metaphysical ideas. Has been made into an acclaimed HBO film.

Gilman, Rebecca, *Boy Gets Girl* (2000)
Addresses the complex question of what constitutes "stalking" by an acclaimed new voice in American theater.

Kushner, Tony, *Angels in America* (1993)
Pulitzer Prize winning play explores the sexual, political, and social issues confronting America in the 1980s as AIDS becomes epidemic.

Machado, Eduardo, *Havana Is Waiting* (2001) Gay Cuban playwright.

Mamet, David, *The Old Neighborhood* (2001)
In this trio of interleaved scenes, almost plotless, a middle-aged Jew returns to the Chicago of his youth only to delve into a host of memories.

Vogel, Paula, *How I Learned to Drive* (2000)
Won the Pulitzer Prize for creating a combination of "wild humor and startling honesty." Says Vogel: "Comedy defuses vigilance so in the next moment we are unprepared for the explosion." This play is a delicate, psychological touching on the dark borders of incest.

Wilson, August, *King Hedley II* (1999)
Set in the 1980s, the play tackles the fate—characterized by failure and violence—of black men in America.

32 PERSPECTIVES

Enter Critic

Courtesy Richard B. Ressman

*Just as artists seek to communicate their
experience of life through the use of the raw
materials and the specific means of their art, so
critics, confronting the resultant creation, shed
a new light on it, enhance our understanding of
it, and finally end by making their own sense
of life significant to their readers. At best, the
critic is an artist whose point of departure is
another artist's work.*

HAROLD CLURMAN

FOCUS ON CRITICAL PERSPECTIVES

A successful dramatist lives with critical attention, wanted or not. There are reviews of tryouts, reviews on opening night, and reviews of a play having a successful run. Often plays are revised (or scuttled) in response to influential criticism. There are critical assessments of an established play, critical reassessments on the occasion of new productions, and critical assessments of a playwright's influence on others.

Here are currents and countercurrents of critical theory that strongly influence discussions of drama:

Historical/Biographical Criticism　　Literary historians remind us that a playwright's work has roots in contemporary social arrangements and systems of belief. For example, many of Shakespeare's contemporaries believed in ghosts. (Hamlet tells his friend Horatio: "There are more things in heaven and earth, Horatio, / Than are dreamt of in your philosophy.") The ghost in *Hamlet* is seen and verified by competent, sober observers, so it cannot be, as Queen Gertrude claims, "the very coinage of your brain"—the product of Hamlet's mad imaginings. When Hamlet overhears Claudius at prayer and postpones killing him, many of Shakespeare's contemporaries are likely to have shared the belief that a repentant sinner, praying for forgiveness, had a chance to go to heaven. (That was indeed the point of repentance.) Better wait until the sinner could be caught in the act of sin.

Shakespeare's audiences were likely to take seriously the question whether the ghost was a good spirit or an evil influence—a "spirit of health or goblin damned." One modern literary historian has argued that the ghost is indeed an evil spirit, leading Hamlet to damnation.

Eleanor Prosser

Shakespeare's Audience and Hamlet's Father's Ghost

The ghost fails the test that every member of Shakespeare's audience undoubtedly would have recognized as the crucial one, a failure that scholars have been trying to rationalize for two centuries: its command violates Christian teaching.

Does the ghost, in fact, pass any of the religious tests? Well, it appears as a man, not as a hop-toad, and no one mentions that it smells of sulphur. On every other test, it fails. Is it humble? How is it conceivable, it asks, that Gertrude could "decline / Upon a wretch whose natural gifts were poor / To those of mine." (Characteristically, it draws our attention to the physical.) Is it in a charitable state? It is thoroughly vindictive, seething in its own hatred and aggravating Hamlet's loathing. Is its voice sweet, soft, musical, and soothing, or "terrible and full of reproach"? The actor who intones these lines with melodious grace is deaf to the meanings of words. Does it carefully refrain from charging others with sin? Its mission is to condemn Claudius. Does it beg Hamlet's prayers? It says "remember *me*."

Some critics have tried to explain these unsettling facts as further proof that the ghost is from Purgatory on the grounds that his anger, vindictiveness, and sensuality merely indicate that he has not yet been sufficiently purged. This argument will not do. The purpose of Purgatory is not to reform a sinner but to erase the debt of punishment incurred by past sins that were repented before death. As Thomas More emphasizes, in Purgatory no soul can be angry, for all are in a state of grace.

From *Hamlet and Revenge*, 1967

The Receptive Reader

On what grounds does this critic find the ghost in *Hamlet* to be un-Christian —and therefore likely to be sent by the devil? (If the ghost were humble and meek in spirit, could it incite Hamlet to revenge?) Would you call Hamlet himself a Christian according to Prosser's criteria?

Psychoanalytic Criticism   Psychoanalytic critics have seen a major source of dramatic conflict in the struggle between our overt rational motives and the repressed subconscious impulses revealed in our dreams. Jocasta says to Oedipus in Scene 3 of Sophocles' *Oedipus* play, "Many a man before you, / in his dreams, has shared his mother's bed." Although the skeptical Jocasta dismisses such dreams as mere "shadows," modern depth psychology, or psychoanalysis, has looked in such dreams for clues to deep hidden desires and traumas of human beings. Sigmund Freud (1865–1939), in *The Interpretation of Dreams*, went beyond the surface action of Sophocles' *Oedipus* to probe for a deeper underlying meaning that would explain the hold the play has on the human imagination. Art and literature, to the psychoanalyst, are like dreams in that much of their deeper meaning is repressed, hidden in the subconscious, acted out in disguises to protect them from condemnation by our moral selves. Seen in this light, Oedipus becomes a symbol of one of the oldest patterns in the collective experience of the human race: The son, as a very young child, depends on and responds with all his being to the overpowering mother love that makes the mother the sun of the child's universe. The father, grudging the undivided attention lavished by the mother on the child, becomes the rival for the mother's affection—and, in the Freudian mythology, a deadly enemy. Secretly, unconsciously, the son comes to wish the father dead. Since the conscious, moral, rational self condemns this parricidal desire with horror, the result is a tortured conscience, self-loathing.

The following is a key passage from Freud's discussion of Oedipus:

Sigmund Freud   *(1865–1939)*

The Oedipus Complex

TRANSLATED BY JAMES STRACHEY

Oedipus Rex is what is known as a tragedy of destiny. Its tragic effect is said to lie in the contrast between the supreme will of the gods and the vain attempts of mankind to escape the evil that threatens them. The lesson, which, it is said, the deeply moved spectator should learn from the tragedy, is submission to the divine will and realization of his own impotence. Modern dramatists have accordingly tried to achieve a similar tragic effect by weaving the same contrast into a plot invented by themselves. But the spectators have looked on unmoved while a curse or an oracle was fulfilled in spite of all the efforts of some innocent man: later tragedies of destiny have failed in their effect.

If *Oedipus Rex* moves the modern audience no less than it did the contemporary Greek one, the explanation can only be that its effect does not lie in the contrast between destiny and human will, but is to be looked for in the particular nature of the material on which that contrast is exemplified. There must be something which makes a voice within us ready to recognize the compelling force of destiny in *Oedipus*, while we can dismiss as merely arbitrary such dispositions as are laid down in modern tragedies of destiny. And a factor of this kind is in fact involved in the story of King Oedipus. His destiny moves us only because it might have been ours—because the oracle laid the same curse upon us before our birth as upon him. It is the fate of all of us, perhaps, to direct our first sexual impulse towards our mother and our first hatred and our first murderous wish against our father. Our dreams convince us that this is so.

From *The Interpretation of Dreams*, 1914

The Receptive Reader

Where in your reading (or viewing) have you encountered reflections of the Freudian triangle of mother—son—father? Can you recall examples of the deadly struggle between father and son? Can you recall examples of a strange, powerful bond between mother and son?

Myth Criticism   Greek drama, like later again the drama of the Middle Ages, grew out of religious ritual. Critics tracing the roots of drama in myth and ritual have often called attention to the echoes of mythical significance in later plays. In a passage preceding the following excerpt, Francis Fergusson had linked Greek tragedy generally to the form of ancient ceremonies enacting the ritual sacrifice of a seasonal god. In such rituals, found in many early cultures, the quasi-divine hero-king fights with a rival, is slain and dismembered, but then rises again with the coming of spring. In Sophocles' *Oedipus* play, Oedipus' struggle, his fall, and his final acceptance of his fate roughly parallel this pattern of death and rebirth. As the culprit who is identified as the source of pollution, Oedipus also fits the mythical figure of the scapegoat driven out of the city into the desert, carrying with it the sins and corruptions of the community, bringing about a cleansing or purgation.

Francis Fergusson

Oedipus as Ritual Sacrifice

The figure of Oedipus himself fulfills all the requirements of the scapegoat, the dismembered king or god-figure. The situation in which Thebes is presented at the beginning of the play—in peril of its life; its crops, its herds, its women mysteriously infertile; signs of a mortal disease of the city; and the disfavor of the gods—is like the withering which winter brings, and calls, in the same way, for struggle, dismemberment, death, and renewal. And this tragic sequence is the substance of the play. It is enough to know that myth and ritual are close together in their genesis, two direct imitations of the perennial experience of the race.

But when one considers *Oedipus* as a ritual one understands it in ways which one cannot by thinking of it merely as a dramatization of a story, even that story. Harrison has shown that the Festival of Dionysus, based ultimately upon the yearly vegetation ceremonies, included *rites de passage* [rituals marking the passing from one stage of life to another], like that celebrating the assumption of adulthood—celebrations of the mystery of individual growth and development. At the same time, it was a prayer for the welfare of the whole city; and this welfare was understood not only as material prosperity, but also as the natural order of the family, the ancestors, the present members, and the generations still to come, and, by the same token, obedience to the gods who were jealous, each in his own province, of this natural and divinely sanctioned order and proportion.

We must suppose that Sophocles' audience (the whole population of the city) came early, prepared to spend the day in the bleachers. At their feet was the semicircular dancing-ground for the chorus, and the thrones for the priests, and the altar. Behind that was the raised platform for the principal actors, backed by the all-purpose emblematic façade, which would presently be taken to represent Oedipus' palace in Thebes. The actors were not professionals in our sense, but citizens selected for religious office, and Sophocles himself had trained them and the chorus.

. . . the element which distinguishes this theater, giving it its unique directness, is the *ritual expectancy*, which Sophocles assumed in his audience. The nearest thing we have to this ritual sense of theater is, I suppose, to be found at an Easter performance of the *St. Matthew Passion*. We can also observe something similar in the dances and ritual mummery of the Pueblo Indians.

From *The Idea of a Theater*, 1949

The Receptive Reader

What does Fergusson mean by "the ritual expectancy" that Sophocles assumed in his audience? In how many ways does this writer remind you of the religious roots and the religious dimension of Greek tragedy? What role does the theme of pollution and purgation play in this discussion?

Feminist Criticism   With the theater long dominated by male playwrights, feminist critics have made a special effort to listen to women's voices or to characters who look at the world from a woman's point of view. They have made us look from a new perspective at Ophelia in *Hamlet*, Jocasta in *Oedipus*, or Linda Loman in *Death of a Salesman*.

In *Shakespeare's Division of Experience*, Marilyn French discusses gender principles that she sees as basic to traditional male perceptions of the world. The masculine principle is associated with power, control, purposefulness, ownership, individualism; it "values action over feeling, thought over sensation." The feminine principle is associated with nature, sensuality, nurturing, pleasure. A major turning point in the history of Western culture was reached when the feminine principle was subdivided into two—benign and malign, represented by the images of the madonna and the whore. For French, this schizophrenic view of womanhood explains Hamlet's attitude toward his mother, which leads him to a general indictment of the female sex.

Marilyn French

Hamlet and Female Sexuality

The root of Hamlet's feeling about his mother's sexuality may perhaps be Oedipal jealousy, but it has been transformed into something very different.

The play is full of clues to the source of his outrage as Hamlet feels it: It lies in a sense of humankind as vicious, and of sex as disgusting, loathsome, and bestial, as a giving up of the control necessary to distinguish man from animal. Woman, the link between these two realms, must therefore renounce sexuality, and this act is *absolutely necessary* to purify, sanctify any human claims to humanness, to difference from, transcendence of the beast. A chaste constant woman would not feel desire, would do "but duty," and would firmly corset her man, and guarantee a line of legitimate males.

The placing of so much weight on the state of a vagina is rationally absurd, and charges of insufficient objective correlatives to Hamlet's emotional state are understandable. But chaste constancy is the cornerstone of Shakespeare's moral universe throughout his work. Hamlet's feelings are understandable only in the context of this fact, understandable perhaps only through immersion in the entire canon. For Shakespeare, without chaste constancy, nothing is real except death, because only death endures when women are not constant, and in a world of appearances, only what endures is real.

The central segment of Hamlet opens with the plot and the attack on Ophelia, closes with the attack on Gertrude. Between these is the visit of the players and the performance of "The Mousetrap." The entire spoken portion of the play-within-the-play concerns constancy, and is implicitly a reproach to inconstant women. The King insists constancy is difficult and perhaps impossible; the Queen insists it is possible and swears herself to it. Hamlet comments: "If she should break it now!" (III.ii.224). He arranges for the play to catch the conscience of the King, he says; but that conscience, which is moved to prayer (or its attempt), seems of little interest to him once it is caught. It is rather the conscience of the Queen that Hamlet is fishing for.

From *Shakespeare's Division of Experience*, 1980

The Receptive Reader

What does French mean by the "transcendence of the beast"? Does it seem true to you that Hamlet is more concerned with his mother's infidelity than with Claudius' fratricide?

Deconstructionism Deconstructionists reacted against the traditional assumption of "organic unity" in a successful literary work. Seen from their perspective, a Shakespeare play is not a finished integrated piece where every detail and comma is deliberate and part of the larger whole, informed by an integrating overall intention. The surface text may disguise underlying tensions, with elements in a precarious unstable balance. The surface plot may mask real underlying agendas.

We may need to read "against the grain"; we may have to listen between the lines. The playwright may be sending coded insider's messages going counter to the overt surface meaning. While Hamlet on the literal level seems to accept unquestioningly the need for revenge, his own long delays and "almost blunted purpose" may be intended as a signal that the author is not endorsing the traditional revenge ethic without question.

René Girard

Deconstructing Hamlet

To read Hamlet against revenge is anachronistic, some people say, because it goes against the conventions of the revenge genre. No doubt, but could Shakespeare be playing according to the conventions of the revenge genre on one level and undermining these same rules at another? Has not this ambiguous practice become a commonplace of modern criticism? Is Shakespeare too slow-witted for such a device? Indications abound that in many other plays, he is doing precisely that, still providing the crowd with the spectacle they demand while simultaneously writing, between the lines, for all those who can read, a devastating critique of that same spectacle.

From "Hamlet's Dull Revenge," in *Stanford Literature Review*, 1984

New Historicism   The rewriting of history from a postimperial or postcolonial perspective has brought about a reevaluation of the politics of traditional authors. Critics representing the **New Historicism** put renewed emphasis on an author's social context—the way literature reflects and comments on the assumptions governing contemporary society.

For example, in Shakespeare's play *The Tempest*, we see Europeans in exile or shipwrecked on an exotic island. Caliban, the only remaining native inhabitant, is made to fetch and carry for his white masters. (His name plays on the indigenous word *carib* that survives in *Caribbean* and *cannibal*.) He says, "You taught me language, and my profit on't is I know how to curse." A critic representing the New Historicism may remind us that Shakespeare knew the writings of his French contemporary Montaigne, an early critic of European colonialism. Montaigne denounced the destruction of ancient cultures and the massacres and enslavement of whole populations that followed the European discovery of the New World. Contemporary Spanish sources "presented cases against the enslavement of the Indians and against the claim to imperial possession of the Americas" (Stephen Greenblatt). In this play, as in other Shakespeare plays, readers attuned to Shakespeare's ambivalent attitude toward authority may sense a strange undertow of sympathy for the underdog defying established authority and conventional morality.

Semiotics   The critic may shift the focus from the individual author to the language system in which the author moves (or is trapped). To a large extent, the language, not the author, speaks. Language speaks through us; it in many ways conditions and shapes what we say and think. We learn not just ways of talking but with them ways of thinking and feeling. The way we talk, quite apart from what we say, has human meaning. A play may be a reflection of, or perhaps a commentary on, the limitations of language.

Generally, recent drama criticism, like other discussions of literature, has questioned unchanging, absolute or universal standards. People belong to **discourse communities** or interpretative communities—they speak the language and honor the assumptions of their group. To what extent individuals and groups can move beyond established social and cultural parameters, or to what extent literature can serve that end, remains an open question.

PLAYWRIGHTS AND CRITICS

Some critical assessments become classics in their own right. They serve as programmatic statements providing guidelines for converts and followers. The theory of tragedy that Aristotle formulated in his *Poetics* became a code for future playwrights to honor or to break. Through the centuries, it guided critical reactions and shaped audience expectations in ways that dramatists found hard to ignore. Modern playwrights have often taken an active part in critical controversies swirling around their craft. The Irish playwright George Bernard Shaw published a famous defense of Ibsen's plays in *The Quintessence of Ibsenism*, celebrating the Norwegian playwright's mirroring of the human spirit as it moved beyond the past in quest of new ideals. Playwrights from Arthur Miller to ntozake shange have spoken up to explain and defend their work.

Aristotle   *(384–322 B.C.)*

Aristotle, the encyclopedic philosopher of classical antiquity, wrote his *Poetics* a century after the height of classical Greek drama. His discussion of tragedy is a spectacular example of **critical theory** read as gospel by many. Although Aristotle developed his theories after the fact, based on plays he loved, his followers in later centuries set them up as rules for future playwrights to follow. In times of classical revival, his *Poetics* became the bible for **neoclassical** critics. The following excerpt from Aristotle's theory of tragedy includes his discussion of **hamartia,** or the tragic flaw. A few references to plays lost or little known have been omitted.

On the Perfect Plot

TRANSLATED BY INGRAM BYWATER

We assume that, for the finest form of tragedy, the plot must be not simple but complex; and further, that it must imitate actions arousing fear and pity, since that is the distinctive function of this kind of imitation. It follows, therefore, that there are three forms of plot to be avoided. (1) A good man must not be seen passing from happiness to misery, or (2) a bad man from misery to happiness. The first situation is not fear-inspiring or piteous, but simply odious to us. The second is the most untragic that can be; it has not one of the requisites of tragedy; it does not appeal either to the human feeling in us, or to our pity, or to our fears. Nor, on the other hand, should (3) an extremely bad man be seen falling from happiness into misery. Such a story may arouse the human feeling in us, but it will not move us to either pity or fear; pity is occasioned by undeserved misfortune, and fear by that of one like ourselves; so that there will be nothing either piteous or fear-inspiring in the situation.

There remains, then, the intermediate kind of person, a man not preeminently virtuous and just, whose misfortune, however, is brought upon him not by vice and depravity but by some error of judgment [hamartia], of the number of those in the enjoyment of great reputation and prosperity; for example, Oedipus, Thyestes, and the men of note of similar families. The perfect plot, accordingly, must have a single, and not (as some tell us) a double issue; the change in the hero's fortunes must be not from misery to happiness, but on the contrary from happiness to misery; and the cause of it must lie not in any depravity, but in some great error on his part; the man himself being either such as we have described, or better, not worse, than that. Fact also confirms our theory. Though the poets began by accepting any tragic story that came to hand, in these days the finest tragedies are always on the story of some few houses, on that of Alcmeon, Oedipus, Orestes, Meleager, Tyestes, Telephus, or any others that may have been involved, as either agents or sufferers, in some deed of horror. The theoretically best tragedy, then, has a plot of this description. The critics, therefore, are wrong who blame Euripides for taking this line in his tragedies, and giving many of them an unhappy ending. It is, as we have said, the right line to take. The best proof is this: on the stage, and in the public performances, such plays, properly worked out, are seen to be the most truly tragic; and Euripides, even if his execution be faulty in every other point, is seen to be nevertheless the most tragic certainly of the dramatists.

After this comes the construction of plot which some rank first, one with a double story . . . and an opposite issue for the good and the bad characters. It is ranked as first only through the weakness of the audiences; the poets merely follow their public, writing as its wishes dictate. But the pleasure here is not that of tragedy. It belongs rather to comedy, where the bitterest enemies in the piece . . . walk off good friends at the end, with no slaying of anyone by anyone.

The tragic fear and pity may be aroused by the spectacle; but they may also be aroused by the very structure and incidents of the play—which is the better way and shows the better poet. The plot in fact should be so framed that, even without seeing the things take place, he who simply hears the account of them shall be filled with horror and pity at the incidents; which is just the effect that the mere recital of the story in *Oedipus* would have on one. To produce this same effect by means of the spectacle is less artistic, and requires extraneous aid. Those, however, who make use of the spectacle to put before us that which is merely monstrous and not productive of fear, are wholly out of touch with tragedy; not every kind of pleasure should be required of a tragedy, but only its own proper pleasure.

The tragic pleasure is that of pity and fear, and the poet has to produce it by a work of imitation; it is clear, therefore, that the causes should be included in the incidents of the story. Let us see, then, what kinds of incident strike one as horrible, or rather as piteous. In a deed of this description the parties must necessarily be either friends, or enemies, or indifferent to one another. Now when enemy does it on enemy, there is nothing to move us to pity either in his doing or in his meditating the deed, except so far as the actual pain of the sufferer is concerned; and the same is true when the parties are indifferent to one another. Whenever the tragic deed, however, is done within the family—when the murder or the like is done or meditated by brother on brother, by son on father, by mother on son, or son on mother—these are the situations the poet should seek after. The traditional stories, accordingly, must be kept as they are, for instance, the murder of Clytaemnestra by Orestes. At the same time even with these there is something left to the poet himself; it is for him to devise the right way of treating them.

Let us explain more clearly what we mean by "the right way." The deed of horror may be done by the doer knowingly and consciously, as in the old poets, and in Medea's murder of her children in Euripides. Or he may do it, but in ignorance of his relationship, and discover that afterwards, as does the Oedipus in Sophocles. . . . A third possibility is for one meditating some deadly injury to another, in ignorance of his relationship, to make the discovery in time to draw back. These exhaust the possibilities, since the deed must necessarily be either done or not done, and either knowingly or unknowingly.

The worst situation is when the character is with full knowledge on the point of doing the deed, and leaves it undone. It is odious and also (through the absence of suffering) untragic; hence it is that no one is made to act thus except in some few instances, e.g., Haemon and Creon in *Antigone*. Next after this comes the actual perpetration of the deed meditated. A better situation than that, however, is for the deed to be done in ignorance, and the relationship discovered afterwards, since there is nothing odious in it, and the discovery will serve to astound us. But the best of all is the last; what we have in *Cresphontes*, for example, where Merope, on the point of slaying her son, recognizes him in time, and in *Iphigenia*, where sister and brother are in a like position.

From *Poetics*, 330 B.C.

The Receptive Reader

1. Aristotle throughout focuses on the effect a play has on the *audience*. How does this concern with audience reaction show in his discussion of the ideal tragic hero?

2. Does Aristotle's definition of the *tragic flaw* fit Antigone? Does it fit Oedipus? Does it fit Hamlet?

Esther Cohen

Esther Cohen conducted her interview with Wendy Wasserstein after being challenged by the editor of *Women's Studies* to write an article on women writers and humor in the theater. Cohen had met the playwright while working as a stage manager for a production of one of Wasserstein's plays. In the following excerpts, Cohen elicits responses that sound casual and funny but that also shed light on the challenges facing women writing comedy today.

Uncommon Woman: Interview with Wendy Wasserstein

ESTHER: I guess my first question is, when did you decide you liked to write? When did writing become something that you liked to do?

WENDY: I remember as a child thinking that my family was very funny. I think this was because my mother was somewhat eccentric. And I do remember watching shows like "Make Room for Daddy" and thinking that those kids were pretty boring. And I actually thought, like Rusty Hammer and Angela Cartwright, they are such good kids, and I thought "no one's family is really like this." And actually I thought our family was far more entertaining than that. So I think partially from that, though I didn't really write those things.

I wrote in high school. I went to school in New York City at Calhoun, and I figured out that one of the ways I could get out of gym was if I wrote something called the Mother-Daughter Fashion Show. I know very little about fashion, but they used to have this Mother-Daughter Fashion Show once a year at the Plaza Hotel, and you got to leave school to go to the fashion show. But if you wrote it you didn't have to go to gym for like two or three weeks, it was fantastic. So, I started writing those. . . .

E: Do you find, as you're writing, that your humor comes more out of the situation you're writing about, or are the characters themselves funny?

W: Sometimes the characters are funny. I mean, sometimes I like to do bright colors, and then they can be quite funny. Sometimes, you know—I haven't learned to use a computer, so I still type, and it's such a pain in the neck—sometimes I just retype scenes and start putting in things. I couldn't believe it—I'm writing a play right now about twenty years of people's lives, and this girl is telling this boy how unhappy she is, and for some reason I started writing Yasser Arafat jokes. For no reason. Because it's so boring retyping this stupid thing. But, you know sometimes it's funny to see. I think for myself, I'm slightly shy actually, and sometimes it's fun for me to write some character who's larger than life. Who would say things I would never say but I know they're funny. And I like to do that a lot. And I also think, to get further into humor and women, that a lot of comedy is a deflection. If you look at "Isn't It Romantic?", Janie Blumberg is *always* funny, so as not to say what she feels. And so, I think you use it—you use it to get a laugh, but you use it deliberately too. I mean the best is when you use it deliberately.

E: Do you think that your women characters are more prone to doing it in that way—using their humor as a deflection?
W: Sometimes, yes, the women use it more as a defense, I think.

E: Do you think that—among your friends, people you know—do women use their humor in different ways than the men do?
W: Yes, I think they do. I think sometimes, men sometimes top each other. Women don't do that. Women know how to lay back and have a good time, you know, and the gossip is great. Great! . . .

E: I think that—certainly in my relationships with my women friends—life is just funny between us, and we share those sorts of humorous moments. We're not always telling each other jokes.
W: No, and I don't even know how to tell a joke. But, you know, if you come home from a bad date, or something's happened, you know, and you've been fired—you know, you've just lost your job to some 21-year-old girl who's blond and can't do anything, but the boss . . . You know that if you go home and tell your story to somebody, you will make it funny. And it will release the pain from you of whatever it is. Because you can't take that nonsense seriously. . . .

E: How about writing for a nonperformance medium? Like articles. Do you have a different emotional reaction to writing those than to writing something that's being performed?
W: I've been writing for a magazine called *New York Woman* recently. And it's fun. It's different though. You know what it is? I remember as a kid someone once told me that I had to learn to postpone gratification. And the thing about magazines is it gets published pretty quickly. I mean, a play you can write and two years from then maybe you'll work it out. And I think in a magazine, because it's a shorter form, you can get—like I just wrote an article about manicures. I'd never write a play, a two-hour play about manicures unless you could do it quite artistically I guess with dancing fingers and stuff. . . .

E: Does your humor translate the same way in each of these different media?

W: It depends. I mean, the magazine I wrote for sent me off to meet Philipe de Montebello at the Met. It was pretty funny. But in these magazine things I always use "I," first person, and there's a persona that I elect to use. You know, there's an "I" that's always talking about how I wish I wore leather miniskirts and I hate pantyhose and things like that. I don't do that so much in the plays. I mean, what's fun about plays is you can divide yourself into a lot of characters and hide yourself in different places.

E: Even though you're not on the stage, do you enjoy that audience feedback?

W: I do. I mean, when it works, it's great. When a production goes wrong, it is hell. It's really hell, it's so painful. That's the other thing. I mean, so you write an article and people don't like it. Or you write an article and they never call you again and they don't publish it. It's not the same pain, it's really not. From the word go, from no actors are available to the director doesn't show up, to the show doesn't work and no one's laughing, to you pick up some terrible review—I mean, all of that is devastating. It's just terrible. It's enough to give you a sense of humor. I mean, it's really awful! I'm writing this play here and I can't even think about all that stuff. It's just too awful.

E: Well, it's such a process.

W: It's a real process. And you don't know what's going to happen. You just don't know.

E: It's true, it's not just your input that will make it in the end. There are so many other factors and people involved. . . . Do you think it's hard for women to get started? To get funding, to get. . .

W: You know what's hard? It's hard to keep one's confidence. It's hard to keep yourself in the middle, not to be a nice girl and not to be a tough girl, you know, but somehow to be yourself. That's hard. And as soon as you start playacting in your writing or in your life, there's trouble, a little bit. Especially in your writing. Because what works is going to be whatever's honest to you. So I think in that way, yes, there's somewhat of a problem. But, I mean, I think the most important thing is that decent women write and get those plays out. I think that's very important.

From *Women's Studies*, 1988

The Receptive Reader

1. What does Wasserstein mean when she says much comedy "is a deflection"?

2. What difference does she see between male and female humor? (Have you observed similar differences?) Where else in the interview does Wasserstein see things from a female perspective?

3. What differences does she see between her writing in her magazine pieces and her work as a playwright? What do you learn from this interview about the playwright's relation with her audience?

David D. Cooper

At the end of the following re-examination, David D. Cooper quotes Robert Nemiroff as calling Hansberry's *A Raisin in the Sun* one of the plays that at the deepest level are not about a specific situation but about "the human condition"—so that "in each generation we recognize ourselves in them anew."

Idealism and Fatalism in A Raisin in the Sun

When duty whispers low, "Thou Must"
The youth replies, "I can!"
      RALPH WALDO EMERSON

Few modern American plays better capture the essence of Emerson's claim for moral exuberance that galvanizes youthful idealism than Lorraine Hansberry's *A Raisin in the Sun*. Set against a backdrop of overt racism and pervasive housing discrimination in the 1950s, Hansberry's play manages to recover and sustain ethical idealism amid conditions, personal and societal, that would make fatalistic surrender understandable. It does so without sentimentality and in spite of the unresolved conflicts and uncertainties that are left over at the play's end, which remain Hansberry's legacy to the continuing struggle for racial justice and decency in America. It is a play about distress, futility, and tragedy, but also about hope and pride and what kind of conviction and commitment it takes to bring hope out of hopelessness, courage out of fear, and idealism out of fatalism. Robert Coles speaks of the black family—the Youngers—and their ordeal of trying to move out of a segregated Chicago borough as a "continual tension between hope and despair in people who have had such a rough time and whose prospects are by no means cheerful" (60). Nowhere in the play is that tension more gripping than in the penultimate scene between Asagai and Beneatha Younger, a scene that Robert Nemiroff, who produced and adapted many of Hansberry's works, describes as capturing "the larger statement of the play—and the ongoing struggle it portends" (Hansberry x).

After Beneatha's brother Walter Lee squanders, on an ill-advised investment, the life insurance money set aside for Beneatha's medical education, she gives in to despair, even cynicism, watching her dream of becoming a doctor seemingly go up in smoke. Beneatha had always pinned her personal aspirations and her hopes for a more equitable and compassionate society on the prospect of becoming a doctor, reflecting Hansberry's belief that social idealism—the commitment to a better society—is intimately tied to individual moral obligation: that social justice is the collective expression of idealism deeply felt by individuals. "I always thought," Beneatha says to

Asagai, that being a doctor "was the one concrete thing in the world that a human being could do. Fix up the sick, you know—and make them whole again."

Once the fragile bond of commitment between her aspirations and society's common welfare is broken, however, Beneatha quickly retrenches into cynicism. "I wanted to cure," Beneatha explains to Asagai. "It used to be so important to me. . . . I used to care. I mean about people and how their bodies hurt. . . . " When Asagai asks her to explain why she stopped caring, Beneatha comes of age, so to speak, morally. "Because [doctoring] doesn't seem deep enough, close enough to what ails mankind! It was a child's way of seeing things—or an idealist's."

At just this point, the play pivots delicately on the moral fulcrum that Coles positions between hope and despair or, put in a socioethical idiom, between idealism and fatalism. Asagai, a patriot for an independent Africa, steps forward to defend hope and idealism. "Children," he reminds Beneatha, "see things very well sometimes—and idealists even better." Beneatha counters, bitterly fatalistic: "You with all your talk and dreams about [a free] Africa! You still think you can patch up the world. Cure the Great Sore of Colonialism—with the Penicillin of Independence—! . . . What about all the crooks and thieves and just plain idiots who will come into power and steal and plunder the same as before—only now they will be black . . .—WHAT ABOUT THEM?!"

Hansberry quickly synthesizes the moral dilemma into two very precise images:

> BENEATHA: Don't you see there isn't any real progress, Asagai, there is only one large circle that we march in, around and around, each of us with our own little picture in front of us—our own little mirage that we think is the future.
>
> ASAGAI: It isn't a circle—it is simply a long line—as in geometry, you know, one that reaches into infinity. And because we cannot see the end—we also cannot see how it changes. And it is very odd but those who see the changes—who dream, who will not give up—are called idealists . . . and those who see only the circle—we call *them* the "realists." (134)

How one imagines the shape of the future—whether as another version of the present or as a limitless plain of possibilities for personal and societal change—dictates one's solution to the central problem of moral life and whether one draws upon the resources of idealism or "realism"—as Asagai defines it here—insofar as moral action and ethical commitment are concerned. Hansberry makes her choice. Beneatha decides to become a doctor—in Africa. The Younger family reaches down for the courage to integrate a white neighborhood. Without addressing the important complexities and ambivalence of those decisions, they represent the courage and moral resourcefulness that were both instrumental in, and essential to, the successes of the following decade's Civil Rights struggles. Among white liberals, for example, the Youngers' decision to move becomes the essence of what liberalism stood for during that time, namely, that racial integration was simultaneously the empowerment of black Americans and the salvation of white America. In his commentary on *A Raisin in the Sun*, Robert Nemiroff lifts the play to this higher level of sociomoral analysis.

> For at the deepest level it is not a specific situation but the human condition, human aspiration and human relationship—the persistence of dreams, of the bonds and conflicts between men and women, parents and children, old ways and new, and the endless struggle against human oppression, whatever the forms it may take, and for individual fulfillment, recognition, and liberation—that are at the heart of such plays. It is not surprising therefore that in each generation we recognize ourselves in them anew. (Hansberry xvii–xviii)

The Explicator, 1993

The Receptive Reader
Why does Cooper select Beneatha and Asagai as key characters in the play? How does he trace Beneatha's journey between idealism and cynicism? What is the symbolism of the circle and the line in the key passage that Cooper quotes?

The Personal Response
Who for you is the key or pivotal character in *A Raisin in the Sun?*

ntozake shange

shange has thought and written passionately about the dilemma of the black playwright: On the one hand, African Americans writing for the theater "have been duped by the same artificial aesthetics that plague our white counterparts," leading to plays that from her point of view were shallow and imitative. On the other hand, theatrical productions about black singers or musicians like Mahalia Jackson and Fats Waller (*Ain't Misbehavin'*) left "the lives of millions of black people who don't sing & dance for a living unattended to" in the theater.

Unrecovered Losses/Black Theater Traditions

although i rarely read reviews of my work/ two comments were repeated to me by "friends" for some reason/ & now that i am writing abt my own work/ i am finally finding some use for the appraisals of strangers. one new york critic had accused me of being too self-conscious of being a writer/ the other from the midwest had asserted that i waz so involved with the destruction of the english language/ that my writing approached verbal gymnastics like unto a reverse minstrel show. in reality/ there is an element of truth in both ideas/ but the lady who thought i waz self-conscious of being a writer/ apparently waz never a blk child who knew that no black people conducted themselves like amos n andy/ she waz not a blk child who knew that blk children didnt wear tiger skins n chase lions around trees n then eat pancakes/ she waznt a blk child who spoke an english that had evolved naturally/ only to hear a white man's version of blk speech that waz entirely made up & based on no linguistic system besides the language of racism. the man who thought i wrote with intentions of outdoing the white man in the acrobatic distortions of english waz absolutely correct. i cant count the number of times i have viscerally wanted to attack deform n maim the language that i waz taught to hate myself in/ the language that perpetuates the notions that cause pain to every black child as he/she learns to speak of the world & the "self." yes/ being an afro-american writer is something to be self-conscious abt/ & yes/ in order to think n communicate the thoughts n feelings i want to think n communicate/ i haveta fix my tool to my needs/ i have to take it apart to the bone/ so that the malignancies/ fall away/ leaving us space to literally create our own image.

From *Three Pieces*, 1981

The Receptive Reader

What is shange's general attitude toward reviewers and critics? What charges were brought against her writing? How does she answer the critics? How does she see her mission as a playwright in dealing with the English language?

The Personal Response

Are you "self-conscious" about language? Have you observed or experienced "language that perpetuates the notions that cause pain"?

WRITING ABOUT LITERATURE

32 The Language of Criticism
WRITING FOCUS: Defining a Critical Term

The Writing Workshop   We would find it hard to talk about drama without terms like *tragedy, protagonist, tragicomedy, subplot*, or *theater of the absurd*. Such critical terms focus our attention and guide our expectations. They help us put into words important similarities and differences. They enable us to formulate our standards, to explain our preferences and aversions.

When you define an important critical term, you stake out the territory it covers. You spell out what it covers and what it fences out. In writing a definition paper, try to find a term that *needs* definition. For instance, you might focus on a term with a rich and confusing history and try to clear up basic ambiguities. Or you might zero in on a trendy term whose meaning is still fuzzy in many people's minds. Consider the following when trying to find a topic that fills a need or presents a challenge:

The History of a Term   Important terms may change their meanings as they serve the agendas of different schools of critical thought. Terms that once had negative connotations may become terms of praise and vice versa. For instance, followers of the classical tradition have tended to frown on mixed genres, being suspicious of "mongrel tragicomedy" (Sir Philip Sidney). But tragicomedy has appealed to the modern temper, which welcomes irony and paradox and resists artificial oversimplification. What is it about this genre that has appealed to modern audiences?

Testing the Limits   Definitions are tested when we apply them to living drama. For instance, is modern tragedy possible? Can a character like Willy Loman, who is not a prince or warlord, who never solved the riddle of the Sphinx, be a tragic hero? As for the comic muse, does Molière's *Misanthrope* turn too serious to be a true comedy?

Drawing the Line   It may prove hard to draw a clear line between often-paired terms. Most definitions of comedy sooner or later contrast it with tragedy. They stress the contrast between ordinary or low-life characters and the exalted personages of the tragic muse. Or they show the difference between the marvelous arrival of good fortune in comedy and the tragic defeat of the tragic hero. What are the key differences? Where do the two genres shade over into each other?

Initiating the Reader   You may want to help the reader become more knowledgeable about modern trends. Your paper might set out to define Bertolt Brecht's epic theater; the theater of the absurd as practiced by Ionesco, Beckett, or Albee; existential drama; feminist drama as defined by leading feminist critics or written by leading feminist playwrights; the art of the mime; dramatic happenings.

In working on a definition paper, consider the following guidelines:

✗ *Be aware of traditional or conventional definitions.* Reckon with the received wisdom—what everybody knows or "what oft was thought" (Alexander Pope). Although dictionary definitions can alert you to important dimensions, you will generally do well not to quote them in your actual paper. Dictionary or encyclopedia entries tend to sound too dry and neutral to get your readers involved in the dialectic of living literature. Consider quoting a critic, a playwright, or a reviewer instead.

✗ *Pull together and spell out your own definition.* Writing a definition paper, like writing other worthwhile papers, should be a voyage of discovery. However, try to sum up somewhere in your paper what continent you have found. Often, you will want to present your overall definition as a preview or **thesis** at the end of a short introduction. For instance, let your readers know that your definition of tragedy comes in

three parts. You might want to make it clear that three essential requirements, or criteria, qualify a play as a true tragedy:

CRITERION 1: A true tragedy arouses the tragic emotions of pity and fear.
CRITERION 2: The tragic hero or heroine exhibits a tragic flaw.
CRITERION 3: The play moves toward insight or self-realization.

Using an alternative strategy, you might start with a trial definition
and then proceed to modify it in the light of important evidence. You
will be taking your reader along *in search of* a more adequate definition. (In such an **inductive** paper—which works *toward* a general conclusion—transitions and overall direction need to be especially clear to
keep the reader moving along to the destination.)

✗ *Fortify your definition against exceptions.* For instance, Molière is a
master of traditional comedy, but his *Misanthrope* is on the borderline.
It does not have a happy ending. It does not culminate in a marriage
festival. No avaricious or lustful uncle obstructs Alceste's union with
Célimène. Often a word like *generally* or *typically* can help protect you
against the charge of overgeneralization. Or you can make it clear that
you are talking about "true comedy" or "comedy as here defined" or
"comedy in the modern vein."

✗ *Use ample supporting examples.* Bridge the gap between theory
and practice. Show that your general criteria actually apply to the characters on the stage, to the things they say and do. Definitions easily remain too neat and unrealistic when they remain abstract.

✗ *Use comparison and contrast with related terms.* A term often becomes clearer as you explain what it does *not* mean. Clarify your key
term by marking it off from related terms—whether near-synonyms or
opposites. For instance, a definition of tragedy can become more meaningful when tragedy is clearly distinguished from melodrama or from
pathos—two forms that in the eyes of the critics tend to play the role of
its poor relations.

Study the following sample student paper. How clear and workable is
its definition of the key term?

Sample Student Paper

Death of a Salesman—a Modern Tragedy?

Ever since Willy Loman trudged into his living room and set down his heavy sample satchel in the first stage production of *Death of a Salesman*, critics have been
arguing whether or not Arthur Miller's creation is a tragedy. Some maintain the play
is a tragedy of the ordinary person, with Willy Loman as the tragic hero. The author
himself said in his "Tragedy and the Common Man" that the "common man is as
apt a subject for tragedy in its highest sense as kings were." Others hold that the
play does not fit the requirements of true tragedy and that Willy Loman is incapable

of being a tragic hero—or indeed any other type of hero at all. Ultimately, the truth may be that Willy Loman fails to become a tragic hero, not because he is modern or because he is common, but because of basic and obvious limitations of his character.

Since Aristotle, critics have tended to agree on the first criterion of true tragedy: It should arouse the tragic emotions of pity and fear. Aristotle used the term *catharsis*—a cleansing or purgation—to describe the emotional experience of the audience. The pity the audience feels for the tragic hero is not patronizing or condescending. Instead it implies a sense of equality, a sharing of grief. The word *fear* is not restricted to fright or abject terror but implies anxious concern, awe, reverence, and apprehension.

Critics have with almost equal unanimity emphasized the second criterion: The tragic hero or heroine should have some tragic flaw that shapes the character's action and helps bring about the eventual downfall. We need to assume that the hero has free will; and we look in his or her character for a flaw that begins the chain of events leading to ruin. Some fatal blindness or weakness in an otherwise admirable person helps explain the tragic course of events.

A third criterion is less universally stressed, but it seems to do much to help the hero or heroine achieve true tragic stature. In the agony, humiliation, and suffering of defeat, the hero reaches a point of increased self-awareness. The hero or heroine is able to look back and see the steps leading to disaster. Or at least the hero or heroine shows an understanding of what is happening. Shakespeare's Macbeth, bitter and pessimistic at the end, begins to see with terrifying clarity his total isolation: "honor, love, obedience, troops of friends / I must not look to have" (5.3.25–26). Othello, in his last words, asks the audience to remember him as one "who loved not wisely, but too well" (5.2.344).

How do these criteria apply to Willy Loman? Miller certainly achieves the effects of pity and fear on his audience. Audiences today as much as ever can sympathize with Willy's terrifying underlying insecurity in a dog-eat-dog system. In Willy's world, as in ours, there is for many people no real safety net. Linda appeals to our sympathy when she says, "You cannot eat the fruit and throw the peel away." Her plea for "attention" is the author's plea for pity for a struggling character whom we saw in the process of going under.

Certainly, Willy possesses a tragic flaw, if not several. But this flaw is perhaps not so much a personal characteristic, a failing in an otherwise great and admirable person. It is more a burden put on him by society. Willy believed in the American dream because he was brought up to do so. He seems too gullible, too credulous. He is too much of a victim to be a great but flawed individual. Much of the play seems to illustrate pathos—the helpless suffering of someone victimized—rather than tragedy.

Willy, finally, never seems to progress toward the self-realization that should be part of true tragedy. If the play were tragic, Willy himself would realize in the last act that, as Biff says, "He had the wrong dreams. All, all, wrong." But this conception remained beyond Willy. He died dreaming another daydream, thinking of himself worth more dead than he was alive, fantasizing about the insurance money that none of his family are likely to see. He dies, as he lived, in a world of illusion, dreaming of Biff as finally a success—"Can you imagine that magnificence with twenty-thousand dollars in his pocket?"

Although Miller's play powerfully stirs the tragic emotions of pity and fear, Willy Loman lacks the stature of a tragic hero. The true tragic effect cannot be achieved without the tragic hero's bitter recognition of his true self.

Questions for Peer Review

1. What are the distinctions between a classical Aristotelian and a "modern" tragedy? How does the writer address this distinction in this paper? What three criteria does the writer spell out?

2. What quotations from classical tragedies does the writer use to illustrate "tragic stature"?

3. How does the writer apply these *criteria* to apply to Willy Loman?

4. How successfully does this writer trace the comparison and contrast between classical tragic heroes and Willy Loman?

5. Where do you find the "turning point" in this paper?

6. Do you agree with this writer's conclusion that "Loman lacks the stature of a tragic hero?" What, according to the writer, is missing? Where and why would you take issue with the writer?

7. How do the ideas in the opening paragraph connect with the ideas in the final paragraph?

33 OTHER VOICES/ OTHER VISIONS

The Magic of the Stage

Courtesy Richard B. Ressman

1738

Sophocles   *(496–406/5 B.C.)*

People of Thebes: look upon Oedipus.
This is the king who solved the riddle of the sphinx
And towered, powerful, above the crowd.
The eyes of mortals looked on him with envy.
Yet ruin overtook him in the end.

SOPHOCLES, *OEDIPUS REX*

Over ten years after he wrote *Antigone,* Sophocles returned to the story of the house of Oedipus. His *Oedipus Rex* (*Oedipus the King*) dramatized the story of Antigone's father, who had tried in vain to thwart Apollo's oracle predicting that he would kill his father and marry his own mother. Aristotle used this play as the example of a perfect tragedy. He saw in the fate that overtakes Oedipus the perfect example of a sudden **reversal**—the unexpected change from good fortune to bad fortune of a great personage.

In Oedipus as king of Thebes, this play has a powerful **protagonist**—a great leader who saved the city from the ravages of the monstrous Sphinx, "that chanting Fury." He solved her riddle, which asked what spoke with one voice but had at various times two feet, four feet, or three feet—moving then on most feet when its strength was weakest. (Answer: a human being, walking on two feet when at full strength, but crawling on all fours when a helpless baby, and using a walking stick as a third leg when old.)

However, although Oedipus quarrels with his brother-in-law Creon and the blind seer Teiresias, his real **antagonist** is the god Apollo. Oedipus' natural parents were King Laius of Thebes and his wife Jocasta. The oracle of Apollo at Delphi had warned them before the birth of Oedipus that this child would slay his father, committing the unspeakable crime of parricide, and marry his mother, breaking the most powerful taboo of Greek culture. Laius and Jocasta had tried to thwart the oracle by having the child exposed, its feet bound, on a mountainside, but shepherds saved him from death. (The injury to his feet earned him his name: Oedipus, or "Swellfoot.") Oedipus is raised by a royal couple in Corinth whom he takes to be his real parents. The oracle of Apollo speaks again: He will commit the unspeakable horrors of parricide and incest. He flees Corinth to forestall the oracle, unknowingly setting in motion the chain of events that will make it come true.

Oedipus Rex takes us closer than the *Antigone* play to the roots of Greek tragedy in myth and ritual. At the beginning of the play, the crops are blighted. A plague, like the epidemics that ravaged the population of Athens during the war with Sparta, infects the city. Women are barren. The priests to whom the people turn in their despair identify the cause of the people's misery: The gods are offended, and they must be appeased. Something has polluted the city, and the city must undergo a ritual of cleansing, of purgation. Students of Greek myth have seen in the downfall of Oedipus a sacrifice to Apollo, a ritual cleansing of the infected community.

In the play, Oedipus is determined to track down the source of pollution and cleanse the city. His struggle to escape the oracle and his stubborn pursuit of the truth that will be his undoing make the play a powerful example of **dramatic irony.** The audience knows the terrible truth before Oedipus does, it watches with a grim knowing smile as the characters on the stage, in their terrible ignorance, head for the abyss. As L. R. Lind said in introducing a new translation of the play,

> Oedipus calls Teiresias blind, when he himself is blinder. . .; Oedipus curses Laius' murderer and thus curses himself; Oedipus answers the Sphinx but finds no answer for his own dilemma.

Although politically splintered and often at war among themselves, the Greeks had common traditions like the Olympic games, and they shared many religious beliefs and institutions. One such institution was the oracle of Apollo at Delphi. Its priests or priestesses passed on the god's widely heeded predictions concerning, for instance, victory and defeat in war. Local priests, like Teiresias in this play, practiced various other kinds of prophecy, including *augury*—reading the future in the flight and intestines of birds.

Oedipus the King   *about 430* B.C.

TRANSLATED BY DUDLEY FITTS AND ROBERT FITZGERALD

CHARACTERS

OEDIPUS, king of Thebes, adopted son of Polybos, king of Corinth
JOCASTE (JOCASTA), widow of King Laïos (Laius) of Thebes, now married
   to Oedipus
CREON, brother of Jocaste
TEIREISIAS, the blind priest and seer
A Chorus of citizens of Thebes, led by the Choragos
ANTIGONE and ISMENE, daughters of Oedipus
A priest
A shepherd
Messengers

Setting

> *We see the front of the palace of Oedipus, King of Thebes. A central door and two side doors open onto a platform that runs the length of the front of the palace. On the platform, right and left, are altars. Three steps lead down into the orchestra, or dancing area of the chorus. The steps are crowded with petitioners who have brought branches and head wreaths of olive leaves and who are desperate for relief from the calamities besetting their city.*

Prologue

OEDIPUS: My children, generations of the living
   In the line of Kadmos,° nursed at his ancient hearth: *founder of Thebes*
   Why have you strewn yourself before these altars
   In supplication, with your boughs and garlands?

The breath of incense rises from the city   5
With a sound of prayer and lamentation.
                                   Children,
I would not have you speak through messengers,
And therefore I have come myself to hear you—
I, Oedipus, who bear the famous name.
(*To a Priest.*) You, there, since you are eldest in the company,
Speak for them all, tell me what preys upon you,   10
Whether you come in dread, or crave some blessing:
Tell me, and never doubt that I will help you
In every way I can; I should be heartless
Were I not moved to find you suppliant° here.   *pleading for help*
PRIEST: Great Oedipus, O powerful King of Thebes!   15
You see how all the ages of our people
Cling to your altar steps: here are boys
Who can barely stand alone, and here are priests
By weight of age, as I am a priest of God,
And young men chosen from those yet unmarried;   20
As for the others, all that multitude,
They wait with olive chaplets in the squares,
At the two shrines of Pallas,° and where Apollo   *the goddess Athena*
Speaks in the glowing embers.°   *oracle using glowing ashes*
                          Your own eyes
Must tell you: Thebes is tossed on a murdering sea   25
And can not lift her head from the death surge.
A rust consumes the buds and fruits of the earth;
The herds are sick; children die unborn,
And labor is vain. The god of plague and pyre°   *funeral fire*
Raids like detestable lightning through the city,   30
And all the house of Kadmos is laid waste,
All emptied, and all darkened: Death alone
Battens upon the misery of Thebes.

You are not one of the immortal gods, we know;   35
Yet we have come to you to make our prayer
As to the man surest in mortal ways
And wisest in the ways of God. You saved us
From the Sphinx,° that flinty singer, and the tribute   *riddling hybrid monster*
We paid to her so long; yet you were never   40
Better informed than we, nor could we teach you:
It was some god breathed in you to set us free.

Therefore, O mighty King, we turn to you:
Find us our safety, find us a remedy,
Whether by counsel of the gods or men.   45
A king of wisdom tested in the past
Can act in a time of troubles, and act well.
Noblest of men, restore
Life to your city! Think how all men call you

Liberator for your triumph long ago;
Ah, when your years of kingship are remembered,   50
Let them not say *We rose, but later fell—*
Keep the State from going down in the storm!
Once, years ago, with happy augury,
You brought us fortune; be the same again!
No man questions your power to rule the land: 55
But rule over men, not over a dead city!
Ships are only hulls, citadels are nothing,
When no life moves in the empty passageways.
OEDIPUS: Poor children! You may be sure I know
    All that you longed for in your coming here.   60
    I know that you are deathly sick; and yet,
    Sick as you are, not one is as sick as I.
    Each of you suffers in himself alone
    His anguish, not another's; but my spirit
    Groans for the city, for myself, for you.   65

    I was not sleeping, you are not waking me.
    No, I have been in tears for a long while
    And in my restless thought walked many ways.
    In all my search, I found one helpful course,
    And that I have taken: I have sent Creon,   70
    Son of Menoikeus, brother of the Queen,
    To Delphi, Apollo's place of revelation,°   *site of the god's oracle*
    To learn there, if he can,
    What act or pledge of mine may save the city.
    I have counted the days, and now, this very day,   75
    I am troubled, for he has overstayed his time.
    What is he doing? He has been gone too long.
    Yet whenever he comes back, I should do ill
    To scant whatever duty God reveals.
PRIEST: It is a timely promise. At this instant   80
    They tell me Creon is here.
OEDIPUS: O Lord Apollo!
    May his news be fair as his face is radiant!
PRIEST: It could not be otherwise: he is crowned with bay,
    The chaplet is thick with berries.
OEDIPUS: We shall soon know;
    He is near enough to hear us now.

    Enter CREON.

                                 O Prince: 85
    Brother: son of Menoikeus:
    What answer do you bring us from the god?
CREON: A strong one. I can tell you, great afflictions
    Will turn out well, if they are taken well.
OEDIPUS: What was the oracle? These vague words   90
    Leave me still hanging between hope and fear.

CREON: Is it your pleasure to hear me with all these
    Gathered around us? I am prepared to speak,
    But should we not go in?
OEDIPUS: Let them all hear it
    It is for them I suffer, more than for myself.   95
CREON: Then I will tell you what I heard at Delphi.

    In plain words
    The god commands us to expel from the land of Thebes
    An old defilement we are sheltering.
    It is a deathly thing, beyond cure.   100
    We must not let it feed upon us longer.
OEDIPUS: What defilement? How shall we rid ourselves of it?
CREON: By exile or death, blood for blood. It was
    Murder that brought the plague-wind on the city.
OEDIPUS: Murder of whom? Surely the god has named him?   105
CREON: My lord: long ago Laïos was our king,
    Before you came to govern us.
OEDIPUS: I know;
    I learned of him from others; I never saw him.
CREON: He was murdered; and Apollo commands us now
    To take revenge upon whoever killed him.   110
OEDIPUS: Upon whom? Where are they? Where shall we find a clue
    To solve that crime, after so many years?
CREON: Here in this land, he said.
                        If we make enquiry,
    We may touch things that otherwise escape us.
OEDIPUS: Tell me: Was Laïos murdered in his house,   115
    Or in the fields, or in some foreign country?
CREON: He said he planned to make a pilgrimage.
    He did not come home again.
OEDIPUS: And was there no one,
    No witness, no companion, to tell what happened?
CREON: They were all killed but one, and he got away   120
    So frightened that he could remember one thing only.
OEDIPUS: What was that one thing? One may be the key
    To everything, if we resolve to use it.
CREON: He said that a band of highwaymen attacked them,
    Outnumbered them, and overwhelmed the King.   125
OEDIPUS: Strange, that a highwayman should be so daring—
    Unless some fraction here bribed him to do it.
CREON: We thought of that. But after Laïos' death
    New troubles arose and we had no avenger.
OEDIPUS: What troubles could prevent your hunting down the killers? 130
CREON: The riddling Sphinx's song
    Made us deaf to all mysteries but her own.
OEDIPUS: Then once more I must bring what is dark to light.
    It is most fitting that Apollo shows,
    As you do, this compunction for the dead.   135

You shall see how I stand by you, as I should,
To avenge the city and the city's god,
And not as though it were for some distant friend,
But for my own sake, to be rid of evil.
Whoever killed King Laïos might—who knows?—   140
Decide at any moment to kill me as well.
By avenging the murdered king I protect myself.

Come, then, my children: leave the altar steps,
Lift up your olive boughs!
                              One of you go
And summon the people of Kadmos to gather here.   145
I will do all that I can; you may tell them that.

Exit a Page.

So, with the help of God,
We shall be saved—or else indeed we are lost.
PRIEST: Let us rise, children. It was for this we came,
And now the King has promised it himself.   150
Phoibos° has sent us an oracle; may he descend   *the god Apollo*
Himself to save us and drive out the plague.

Exeunt OEDIPUS *and* CREON *into the palace by the central door. The* PRIEST
and the Suppliants disperse right and left. After a short pause the CHORUS
enters the orchestra.

Parodos [*Opening Chant of the Chorus*]

                                                      Strophe 1

CHORUS: What is God singing in his profound
     Delphi° of gold and shadow?   *site of Apollo's oracle*
     What oracle for Thebes, the sunwhipped city?

Fear unjoints me, the roots of my heart tremble.

Now I remember, O Healer, your power, and wonder: 5
Will you send doom like a sudden cloud, or weave it
Like nightfall of the past?

Speak, speak to us, issue of holy sound:
Dearest to our expectancy: be tender!

                                                      Antistrophe 1

Let me pray to Athenê, the immortal daughter of Zeus,   10
     And to Artemis her sister
Who keeps her famous throne in the market ring,
And to Apollo, bowman at the far butts of heaven—

O gods, descend! Like three streams leap against
The fires of our grief, the fires of darkness;   15
Be swift to bring us rest!

As in the old time from the brilliant house
Of air you stepped to save us, come again!

Strophe 2

Now our afflictions have no end,
Now all our stricken host lies down   20
And no man fights off death with his mind;

The noble plowland bears no grain,
And groaning mothers can not bear—

See, how our lives like birds take wing,
Like sparks that fly when a fire soars,   25
To the shore of the god of evening.

Antistrophe 2

The plague burns on, it is pitiless,
Though pallid children laden with death
Lie unwept in the stony ways,

And old gray women by every path   30
Flock to the strand about the altars

There to strike their breasts and cry
Worship of Phoibos in wailing prayers:
Be kind, God's golden child!

Strophe 3

There are no swords in this attack by fire,   35
No shields, but we are ringed with cries.

Send the besieger plunging from our homes
Into the vast sea-room of the Atlantic
Or into the waves that foam eastward of Thrace—

For the day ravages what the night spares—   40

Destroy our enemy, lord of the thunder!
Let him be riven by lightning from heaven!

Antistrophe 3

Phoibos Apollo, stretch the sun's bowstring,
That golden cord, until it sing for us,

Flashing arrows in heaven!
                     Artemis, Huntress°,   *chaste goddess of the hunt* 45
Race with flaring lights upon our mountains!

O scarlet god, O golden-banded brow,
O Theban Bacchos in a storm of Maenads°,   *ecstatic woman worshipers*
                                                                of Dionysos/Bacchos

Enter OEDIPUS, *center*.

Whirl upon Death, that all the Undying° hate!   *the immortal gods*
Come with blinding torches, come in joy!   50

Scene 1

OEDIPUS: Is this your prayer? It may be answered. Come,
    Listen to me, act as the crisis demands,
    And you shall have relief from all these evils.

    Until now I was a stranger to this tale,
    As I had been a stranger to the crime.   5
    Could I track down the murderer without a clue?

Scene from a Stratford Shakespeare Festival production of King Oedipus
(courtesy Stratford Festival Archives)

But now, friends,
As one who became a citizen after the murder,
I make this proclamation to all Thebans:

If any man knows by whose hand Laïos, son of Labdakos,   10
Met his death, I direct that man to tell me everything,
No matter what he fears for having so long withheld it.
Let it stand as promised that no further trouble
Will come to him, but he may leave the land in safety.

Moreover: If anyone knows the murderer to be foreign,   15
Let him not keep silent: he shall have his reward from me.
However, if he does conceal it; if any man
Fearing for his friend or for himself disobeys this edict,
Hear what I propose to do:

I solemnly forbid the people of this country,   20
Where power and throne are mine, ever to receive that man
Or speak to him, no matter who he is, or let him
Join in sacrifice, lustration°, or in prayer,   *ritual purification*
I decree that he be driven from every house,
Being, as he is, corruption itself to us: the Delphic   25
Voice of Zeus has pronounced this revelation.
Thus I associate myself with the oracle
And take the side of the murdered king.

As for the criminal, I pray to God—
Whether it be a lurking thief, or one of a number—   30
I pray that that man's life be consumed in evil and wretchedness.
And as for me, this curse applies no less
If it should turn out that the culprit is my guest here,
Sharing my hearth.
                    You have heard the penalty.
I lay it on you now to attend to this   35
For my sake, for Apollo's, for the sick
Sterile city that heaven has abandoned.
Suppose the oracle had given you no command:
Should this defilement go uncleansed for ever?
You should have found the murderer: your king,   40
A noble king, had been destroyed!
                  Now I,
Having the power that he held before me,
Having his bed, begetting children there
Upon his wife, as he would have, had he lived—
Their son would have been my children's brother,   45
If Laïos had had luck in fatherhood!
(But surely ill luck rushed upon his reign)—

I say I take the son's part, just as though
I were his son, to press the fight for him
And see it won! I'll find the hand that brought   50
Death to Labdakos' and Polydoros' child,°   *parent and ancestor of Laïos*
Heir of Kadmos' and Agenor's line.
And as for those who fail me,
May the gods deny them the fruit of the earth,
Fruit of the womb, and may they rot utterly!   55
Let them be wretched as we are wretched, and worse!

For you, for loyal Thebans, and for all
Who find my actions right, I pray the favor
Of justice, and of all the immortal gods.
CHORAGOS: Since I am under oath, my lord, I swear   60
I did not do the murder, I can not name
The murderer. Might not the oracle
That has ordained the search tell where to find him?
OEDIPUS: An honest question. But no man in the world
Can make the gods do more than the gods will.   65
CHORAGOS: There is one last expedient—
OEDIPUS: Tell me what it is.
Though it seem slight, you must not hold it back.
CHORAGOS: A lord clairvoyant to the lord Apollo,
As we all know, is the skilled Teiresias.
One might learn much about this from him, Oedipus.   70
OEDIPUS: I am not wasting time:
Creon spoke of this, and I have sent for him—
Twice, in fact; it is strange that he is not here.
CHORAGOS: The other matter—that old report—seems useless.
OEDIPUS: Tell me, I am interested in all reports.   75
CHORAGOS: The King was said to have been killed by highwaymen.
OEDIPUS: I know. But we have no witnesses to that.
CHORAGOS: If the killer can feel a particle of dread,
Your curse will bring him out of hiding!
OEDIPUS: No.
The man who dared that act will fear no curse.   80

Enter the blind seer TEIRESIAS, *led by a Page.*

CHORAGOS: But there is one man who may detect the criminal.
This is Teiresias, this is the holy prophet
In whom, alone of all men, truth was born.
OEDIPUS: Teiresias: seer: student of mysteries,
Of all that's taught and all that no man tells,   85
Secrets of Heaven and secrets of the earth:
Blind though you are, you know the city lies
Sick with plague; and from this plague, my lord,
We find that you alone can guard or save us.

Possibly you did not hear the messengers?   90
Apollo, when we sent to him,
Sent us back word that this great pestilence
Would lift, but only if we established clearly
The identity of those who murdered Laïos.
They must be killed or exiled.
                    Can you use   95
Birdflight or any art of divination°   *uncovering the truth*
To purify yourself, and Thebes, and me
From this contagion? We are in your hands.
There is no fairer duty
Than that of helping others in distress.   100
TEIRESIAS: How dreadful knowledge of the truth can be
  When there's no help in truth! I knew this well,
  But made myself forget. I should not have come.
OEDIPUS: What is troubling you? Why are your eyes so cold?
TEIRESIAS: Let me go home. Bear your own fate, and I'll   105
  Bear mine. It is better so: trust what I say.
OEDIPUS: What you say is ungracious and unhelpful
  To your native country. Do not refuse to speak.
TEIRESIAS: When it comes to speech, your own is neither temperate
  Nor opportune. I wish to be more prudent.   110
OEDIPUS: In God's name, we all beg you—
TEIRESIAS: You are all ignorant.
  No; I will never tell you what I know.
  Now it is my misery; then, it would be yours.
OEDIPUS: What! You do know something, and will not tell us?
  You would betray us all and wreck the State?   115
TEIRESIAS: I do not intend to torture myself, or you.
  Why persist in asking? You will not persuade me.
OEDIPUS: What a wicked old man you are! You'd try a stone's
  Patience! Out with it! Have you no feeling at all?
TEIRESIAS: You call me unfeeling. If you could only see   120
  The nature of your own feelings . . .
OEDIPUS: Why,
  Who would not feel as I do? Who could endure
  Your arrogance toward the city?
TEIRESIAS: What does it matter!
  Whether I speak or not; it is bound to come.
OEDIPUS: Then, if "it" is bound to come, you are bound to tell me.   125
TEIRESIAS: No, I will not go on. Rage as you please.
OEDIPUS: Rage? Why not!
              And I'll tell you what I think:
  You planned it, you had it done, you all but
  Killed him with your own hands: if you had eyes,
  I'd say the crime was yours, and yours alone.   130
TEIRESIAS: So? I charge you, then,
  Abide by the proclamation you have made:
  From this day forth

Never speak again to these men or to me;
   You yourself are the pollution of this country.   135
OEDIPUS: You dare say that! Can you possibly think you have
   Some way of going free, after such insolence?
TEIRESIAS: I have gone free. It is the truth sustains me.
OEDIPUS: Who taught you shamelessness? It was not your craft.
TEIRESIAS: You did. You made me speak. I did not want to.   140
OEDIPUS: Speak what? Let me hear it again more clearly.
TEIRESIAS: Was it not clear before? Are you tempting me?
OEDIPUS: I did not understand it. Say it again.
TEIRESIAS: I say that you are the murderer whom you seek.
OEDIPUS: Now twice you have spat out infamy. You'll pay for it!   145
TEIRESIAS: Would you care for more? Do you wish to be really angry?
OEDIPUS: Say what you will. Whatever you say is worthless.
TEIRESIAS: I say you live in hideous shame with those
   Most dear to you. You can not see the evil.
OEDIPUS: It seems you can go on mouthing like this for ever.   150
TEIRESIAS: I can, if there is power in truth.
OEDIPUS: There is:
   But not for you, not for you,
   You sightless, witless, senseless, mad old man!
TEIRESIAS: You are the madman. There is no one here
   Who will not curse you soon, as you curse me.   155
OEDIPUS: You child of endless night! You can not hurt me
   Or any other man who sees the sun.
TEIRESIAS: True: it is not from me your fate will come.
   That lies within Apollo's competence,
   As it is his concern.
OEDIPUS: Tell me: 160
   Are you speaking for Creon, or for yourself?
TEIRESIAS: Creon is no threat. You weave your own doom.
OEDIPUS: Wealth, power, craft of statesmanship!
   Kingly position, everywhere admired!
   What savage envy is stored up against these,   165
   If Creon, whom I trusted, Creon my friend,
   For this great office which the city once
   Put in my hands unsought—if for this power
   Creon desires in secret to destroy me!

He has brought this decrepit fortune-teller, this   170
   Collector of dirty pennies, this prophet fraud—
   Why, he is no more clairvoyant than I am!
                               Tell us:
   Has your mystic mummery ever approached the truth?
   When that hellcat the Sphinx was performing here,
   What help were you to these people?   175
   Her magic was not for the first man who came along:
   It demanded a real exorcist. Your birds—
   What good were they? or the gods, for the matter of that?

But I came by,
Oedipus, the simple man, who knows nothing—   180
I thought it out for myself, no birds helped me!
And this is the man you think you can destroy,
That you may be close to Creon when he's king!
Well, you and your friend Creon, it seems to me,
Will suffer most. If you were not an old man,   185
You would have paid already for your plot.

CHORAGOS: We can not see that his words or yours
Have been spoken except in anger, Oedipus,
And of anger we have no need. How can God's will
Be accomplished best? That is what most concerns us.   190

TEIRESIAS: You are a king. But where argument's concerned
I am your man, as much a king as you.
I am not your servant, but Apollo's.
I have no need of Creon to speak for me.
Listen to me. You mock my blindness, do you?   195
But I say that you, with both your eyes, are blind:
You can not see the wretchedness of your life,
Nor in whose house you live, no, nor with whom.
Who are your father and mother? Can you tell me?
You do not even know the blind wrongs   200
That you have done them, on earth and in the world below.
But the double lash of your parents' curse will whip you
Out of this land some day, with only night
Upon your precious eyes.
Your cries then—where will they not be heard?   205
What fastness of Kithairon will not echo them?
And that bridal-descant of yours—you'll know it then,
The song they sang when you came here to Thebes
And found your misguided berthing.
All this, and more, that you can not guess at now,   210
Will bring you to yourself among your children.

Be angry, then. Curse Creon. Curse my words.
I tell you, no man that walks upon the earth
Shall be rooted out more horribly than you.

OEDIPUS: Am I to bear this from him?—Damnation   215
Take you! Out of this place! Out of my sight!

TEIRESIAS: I would not have come at all if you had not asked me.

OEDIPUS: Could I have told that you'd talk nonsense, that
You'd come here to make a fool of yourself, and of me?

TEIRESIAS: A fool? Your parents thought me sane enough.   220

OEDIPUS: My parents again!—Wait: who were my parents?

TEIRESIAS: This day will give you a father, and break your heart.

OEDIPUS: Your infantile riddles! Your damned abracadabra!

TEIRESIAS: You were a great man once at solving riddles.

OEDIPUS: Mock me with that if you like; you will find it true.   225

TEIRESIAS: It was true enough. It brought about your ruin.

OEDIPUS: But if it saved this town?
TEIRESIAS *(to the Page)*:   Boy, give me your hand.
OEDIPUS: Yes, boy; lead him away.
                              —While you are here
   We can do nothing. Go; leave us in peace.
TEIRESIAS: I will go when I have said what I have to say.   230
   How can you hurt me? And I tell you again:
   The man you have been looking for all this time,
   The damned man, the murderer of Laïos,
   That man is in Thebes. To your mind he is foreignborn,
   But it will soon be shown that he is a Theban,   235
   A revelation that will fail to please.
                              A blind man,
   Who has his eyes now; a penniless man, who is rich now;
   And he will go tapping the strange earth with his staff;
   To the children with whom he lives now he will be
   Brother and father—the very same; to her   240
   Who bore him, son and husband—the very same
   Who came to his father's bed, wet with his father's blood.

   Enough. Go think that over.
   If later you find error in what I have said,
   You may say that I have no skill in prophecy.   245

Exit TEIRESIAS, *led by his Page.* OEDIPUS *goes into the palace.*

Ode 1 [*Chant of the Chorus*]

                                        Strophe 1

CHORUS: The Delphic stone of prophecies
   Remembers ancient regicide
   And a still bloody hand.
   That killer's hour of flight has come.
   He must be stronger than riderless   5
   Coursers of untiring wind,
   For the son of Zeus° armed with his father's thunder   *the god Apollo*
   Leaps in lightning after him;
   And the Furies° follow him, the sad Furies.   *avenging female spirits*

                                        Antistrophe 1

   Holy Parnassos' peak of snow°   *mountain sacred to Apollo*   10
   Flashes and blinds that secret man,
   That all shall hunt him down:
   Though he may roam the forest shade
   Like a bull gone wild from pasture
   To rage through glooms of stone.   15
   Doom comes down on him; flight will not avail him;
   For the world's heart calls him desolate,
   And the immortal Furies follow, for ever follow.

But now a wilder thing is heard
From the old man skilled at hearing Fate in the wingbeat of a bird.   20
Bewildered as a blown bird, my soul hovers and can not find
Foothold in this debate, or any reason or rest of mind.
But no man ever brought—none can bring
Proof of strife between Thebes' royal house,
Labdakos' line, and the son of Polybos°;   *Oedipus' adoptive father*   25
And never until now has any man brought word
Of Laïos' dark death staining Oedipus the King.

Divine Zeus and Apollo hold
Perfect intelligence° alone of all tales ever told;   *knowledge*
And well though this diviner works, he works in his own night;   30
No man can judge that rough unknown or trust in second sight,
For wisdom changes hands among the wise.
Shall I believe my great lord criminal
At a raging word that a blind old man let fall?
I saw him, when the carrion woman faced him of old,   35
Prove his heroic mind! These evil words are lies.

Scene 2

CREON: Men of Thebes:
I am told that heavy accusations
Have been brought against me by King Oedipus.

I am not the kind of man to bear this tamely.

If in these present difficulties   5
He holds me accountable for any harm to him
Through anything I have said or done—why, then,
I do not value life in this dishonor.

It is not as though this rumor touched upon
Some private indiscretion. The matter is grave.   10
The fact is that I am being called disloyal
To the State, to my fellow citizens, to my friends.
CHORAGOS: He may have spoken in anger, not from his mind.
CREON: But did you not hear him say I was the one
Who seduced the old prophet into lying?   15
CHORAGOS: The thing was said: I do not know how seriously.
CREON: But you were watching him! Were his eyes steady?
Did he look like a man in his right mind?
CHORAGOS: I do not know.
I can not judge the behavior of great men.
But here is the King himself.

Enter OEDIPUS.

OEDIPUS: So you dared come back.   20
   Why? How brazen of you to come to my house,
   You murderer!
             Do you think I do not know
   That you plotted to kill me, plotted to steal my throne?
   Tell me, in God's name: am I coward, a fool,
   That you should dream you could accomplish this?   25
   A fool who could not see your slippery game?
   A coward, not to fight back when I saw it?
   You are the fool, Creon, are you not? hoping
   Without support or friends to get a throne?
   Thrones may be won or bought: you could do neither.   30
CREON: Now listen to me. You have talked; let me talk, too.
   You can not judge unless you know the facts.
OEDIPUS: You speak well: there is one fact; but I find it hard
   To learn from the deadliest enemy I have.
CREON: That above all I must dispute with you.   35
OEDIPUS: That above all I will not hear you deny.
CREON: If you think there is anything good in being stubborn
   Against all reason, then I say you are wrong.
OEDIPUS: If you think a man can sin against his own kind
   And not be punished for it, I say you are mad.   40
CREON: I agree. But tell me: what have I done to you?
OEDIPUS: You advised me to send for that wizard, did you not?
CREON: I did. I should do it again.
OEDIPUS: Very well. Now tell me:
   How long has it been since Laïos—
CREON: What of Laïos?
OEDIPUS: Since he vanished in that onset by the road?   45
CREON: It was long ago, a long time.
OEDIPUS: And this prophet,
   Was he practicing here then?
CREON: He was; and with honor, as now.
OEDIPUS: Did he speak of me at that time?
CREON: He never did;
   At least, not when I was present.
OEDIPUS: But . . . the enquiry?
   I suppose you held one?
CREON: We did, but we learned nothing.   50
OEDIPUS: Why did the prophet not speak against me then?
CREON: I do not know; and I am the kind of man
   Who holds his tongue when he has no facts to go on.
OEDIPUS: There's one fact that you know, and you could tell it.
CREON: What fact is that? If I know it, you shall have it.   55
OEDIPUS: If he were not involved with you, he could not say
   That it was I who murdered Laïos.
CREON: If he says that, you are the one that knows it!—
   But now it is my turn to question you.

OEDIPUS: Put your questions. I am no murderer.   60
CREON: First then: You married my sister?
OEDIPUS: I married your sister.
CREON: And you rule the kingdom equally with her?
OEDIPUS: Everything that she wants she has from me.
CREON: And I am the third, equal to both of you?
OEDIPUS: That is why I call you a bad friend.   65
CREON: No. Reason it out, as I have done.
    Think of this first: Would any sane man prefer
    Power, with all a king's anxieties,
    To that same power and the grace of sleep?
    Certainly not I.   70
    I have never longed for the king's power—only his rights.
    Would any wise man differ from me in this?
    As matters stand, I have my way in everything
    With your consent, and no responsibilities.
    If I were king, I should be a slave to policy.   75

    How could I desire a scepter more
    Than what is now mine—untroubled influence?
    No, I have not gone mad; I need no honors,
    Except those with the perquisites I have now.
    I am welcome everywhere; every man salutes me,   80
    And those who want your favor seek my ear,
    Since I know how to manage what they ask.
    Should I exchange this ease for that anxiety?
    Besides, no sober mind is treasonable.
    I hate anarchy   85
    And never would deal with any man who likes it.

    Test what I have said. Go to the priestess
    At Delphi, ask if I quoted her correctly.
    And as for this other thing: if I am found
    Guilty of treason with Teiresias,   90
    Then sentence me to death! You have my word
    It is a sentence I should cast my vote for—
    But not without evidence!
                                    You do wrong
    When you take good men for bad, bad men for good.
    A true friend thrown aside—why, life itself   95
    Is not more precious!
                                    In time you will know this well:
    For time, and time alone, will show the just man,
    Though scoundrels are discovered in a day.
CHORAGOS: This is well said, and a prudent man would ponder it.
    Judgments too quickly formed are dangerous.   100
OEDIPUS: But is he not quick in his duplicity?
    And shall I not be quick to parry him?

Would you have me stand still, hold my peace, and let
This man win everything, through my inaction?
CREON: And you want—what is it, then? To banish me?   105
OEDIPUS: No, not exile. It is your death I want,
So that all the world may see what treason means.
CREON: You will persist, then? You will not believe me?
OEDIPUS: How can I believe you?
CREON: Then you are a fool.
OEDIPUS: To save myself?
CREON: In justice, think of me.   110
OEDIPUS: You are evil incarnate.
CREON: But suppose that you are wrong?
OEDIPUS: Still I must rule.
CREON: But not if you rule badly.
OEDIPUS: O city, city!
CREON: It is my city, too!
CHORAGOS: Now, my lords, be still. I see the Queen,
Iocastê, coming from her palace chambers;   115
And it is time she came, for the sake of you both.
This dreadful quarrel can·be resolved through her.

Enter IOCASTÊ.

IOCASTÊ: Poor foolish men, what wicked din is this?
With Thebes sick to death, is it not shameful
That you should rake some private quarrel up?   120
(*To* OEDIPUS.) Come into the house.
                                    —And you, Creon, go now:
Let us have no more of this tumult over nothing.
CREON: Nothing? No, sister: what your husband plans for me
Is one of two great evils: exile or death.
OEDIPUS: He is right.
                            Why, woman, I have caught him squarely   125
Plotting against my life.
CREON: No! Let me die
Accurst if ever I have wished you harm!
IOCASTÊ: Ah, believe it, Oedipus!
In the name of the gods, respect this oath of his
For my sake, for the sake of these people here!   130

Strophe 1

CHORAGOS: Open your mind to her, my lord. Be ruled by her, I beg you!
OEDIPUS: What would you have me do?
CHORAGOS: Respect Creon's word. He has never spoken like a fool,
And now he has sworn an oath.
OEDIPUS: You know what you ask?
CHORAGOS: I do.
OEDIPUS: Speak on, then.
CHORAGOS: A friend so sworn should not be baited so,   135
In blind malice, and without final proof.

OEDIPUS: You are aware, I hope, that what you say
 Means death for me, or exile at the least.

Strophe 2

CHORAGOS: No, I swear by Helios, first in Heaven!
  May I die friendless and accurst,   140
 The worst of deaths, if ever I meant that!
  It is the withering fields
   That hurt my sick heart:
  Must we bear all these ills,
   And now your bad blood as well?   145
OEDIPUS: Then let him go. And let me die, if I must,
 Or be driven by him in shame from the land of Thebes.
 It is your unhappiness, and not his talk,
 That touches me.
     As for him—
 Wherever he goes, hatred will follow him.   150
CREON: Ugly in yielding, as you were ugly in rage!
 Natures like yours chiefly torment themselves.
OEDIPUS: Can you not go? Can you not leave me?
CREON: I can.
 You do not know me; but the city knows me,
 And in its eyes I am just, if not in yours.   155

 Exit CREON.

Antistrophe 1

CHORAGOS: Lady Iocastê, did you not ask the King to go to his chambers?
IOCASTÊ: First tell me what has happened.
CHORAGOS: There was suspicion without evidence; yet it rankled
 As even false charges will.
IOCASTÊ: On both sides?
CHORAGOS: On both.
IOCASTÊ: But what was said?
CHORAGOS:
 Oh let it rest, let it be done with!   160
 Have we not suffered enough?
OEDIPUS: You see to what your decency has brought you:
 You have made difficulties where my heart saw none.

Antistrophe 2

CHORAGOS: Oedipus, it is not once only I have told you—
  You must know I should count myself unwise   165
 To the point of madness, should I now forsake you—
  You, under whose hand,
   In the storm of another time,
  Our dear land sailed out free.
   But now stand fast at the helm!   170
IOCASTÊ: In God's name, Oedipus, inform your wife as well:
 Why are you so set in this hard anger?

OEDIPUS: I will tell you, for none of these men deserves
    My confidence as you do. It is Creon's work,
    His treachery, his plotting against me.   175
IOCASTÊ: Go on, if you can make this clear to me.
OEDIPUS: He charges me with the murder of Laïos.
IOCASTÊ: Has he some knowledge? Or does he speak from hearsay?
OEDIPUS: He would not commit himself to such a charge,
    But he has brought in that damnable soothsayer   180
    To tell his story.
IOCASTÊ: Set your mind at rest.
    If it is a question of soothsayers, I tell you
    That you will find no man whose craft gives knowledge
    Of the unknowable.
                Here is my proof:

An oracle was reported to Laïos once   185
(I will not say from Phoibos himself, but from
His appointed ministers, at any rate)
That his doom would be death at the hands of his own son—
His son, born of his flesh and of mine!

Now, you remember the story: Laïos was killed   190
By marauding strangers where three highways meet;
But his child had not been three days in this world
Before the King had pierced the baby's ankles
And left him to die on a lonely mountainside.
Thus, Apollo never caused that child   195
To kill his father, and it was not Laïos' fate
To die at the hands of his son, as he had feared.
This is what prophets and prophecies are worth!
Have no dread of them.
             It is God himself
Who can show us what he wills, in his own way.   200
OEDIPUS: How strange a shadowy memory crossed my mind,
    Just now while you were speaking; it chilled my heart.
IOCASTÊ: What do you mean? What memory do you speak of?
OEDIPUS: If I understand you, Laïos was killed
    At a place where three roads meet.
IOCASTÊ: So it was said;   205
    We have no later story.
OEDIPUS: Where did it happen?
IOCASTÊ: Phokis, it is called: at a place where the Theban Way
    Divides into the roads toward Delphi and Daulia.
OEDIPUS: When?
IOCASTÊ: We had the news not long before you came
    And proved the right to your succession here.   210
OEDIPUS: Ah, what net has God been weaving for me?
IOCASTÊ: Oedipus! Why does this trouble you?

OEDIPUS: Do not ask me yet.
   First, tell me how Laïos looked, and tell me
   How old he was.
IOCASTÊ: He was tall, his hair just touched
   With white; his form was not unlike your own.   215
OEDIPUS: I think that I myself may be accurst
   By my own ignorant edict.
IOCASTÊ: You speak strangely.
   It makes me tremble to look at you, my King.
OEDIPUS: I am not sure that the blind man can not see.
   But I should know better if you were to tell me—   220
IOCASTÊ: Anything—though I dread to hear you ask it.
OEDIPUS: Was the King lightly escorted, or did he ride
   With a large company, as a ruler should?
IOCASTÊ: There were five men with him in all: one was a herald,
   And a single chariot, which he was driving.   225
OEDIPUS: Alas, that makes it plain enough!
                              But who—
   Who told you how it happened?
IOCASTÊ: A household servant,
   The only one to escape.
OEDIPUS: And is he still
   A servant of ours?
IOCASTÊ: No; for when he came back at last
   And found you enthroned in the place of the dead king,   230
   He came to me, touched my hand with his, and begged
   That I would send him away to the frontier district
   Where only the shepherds go—
   As far away from the city as I could send him.
   I granted his prayer; for although the man was a slave,   235
   He had earned more than this favor at my hands.
OEDIPUS: Can he be called back quickly?
IOCASTÊ: Easily.
   But why?
OEDIPUS: I have taken too much upon myself
   Without enquiry; therefore I wish to consult him.
IOCASTÊ: Then he shall come.
                        But am I not one also   240
   To whom you might confide these fears of yours?
OEDIPUS: That is your right; it will not be denied you,
   Now least of all; for I have reached a pitch
   Of wild foreboding. Is there anyone
   To whom I should sooner speak?   245

   Polybos of Corinth is my father.
   My mother is a Dorian: Meropê.
   I grew up chief among the men of Corinth
   Until a strange thing happened—
   Not worth my passion, it may be, but strange.   250

At a feast, a drunken man maundering in his cups
Cries out that I am not my father's son!

I contained myself that night, though I felt anger
And a sinking heart. The next day I visited
My father and mother, and questioned them. They stormed,   255
Calling it all the slanderous rant of a fool;
And this relieved me. Yet the suspicion
Remained always aching in my mind;
I knew there was talk; I could not rest;
And finally, saying nothing to my parents,   260
I went to the shrine at Delphi.
The god dismissed my question without reply;
He spoke of other things.
                              Some were clear,
Full of wretchedness, dreadful, unbearable:
As, that I should lie with my own mother, breed   265
Children from whom all men would turn their eyes;
And that I should be my father's murderer.
I heard all this, and fled. And from that day
Corinth to me was only in the stars
Descending in that quarter of the sky,   270
As I wandered farther and farther on my way
To a land where I should never see the evil
Sung by the oracle. And I came to this country
Where, so you say, King Laïos was killed.

I will tell you all that happened there, my lady.   275

There were three highways
Coming together at a place I passed;
And there a herald came towards me, and a chariot
Drawn by horses, with a man such as you describe
Seated in it. The groom leading the horses   280
Forced me off the road at his lord's command;
But as this charioteer lurched over towards me
I struck him in my rage. The old man saw me
And brought his double goad down upon my head
As I came abreast.
                    He was paid back, and more!   285
Swinging my club in this right hand I knocked him
Out of his car, and he rolled on the ground.
                              I killed him.

I killed them all.
Now if that stranger and Laïos were—kin,
Where is a man more miserable than I?   290

More hated by the gods? Citizen and alien alike
Must never shelter me or speak to me—
I must be shunned by all.
                              And I myself
Pronounced this malediction upon myself!

Think of it: I have touched you with these hands,   295
These hands that killed your husband. What defilement!

Am I all evil, then? It must be so,
Since I must flee from Thebes, yet never again
See my own countrymen, my own country,
For fear of joining my mother in marriage   300
And killing Polybos, my father.
                              Ah,
If I was created so, born to this fate,
Who could deny the savagery of God?

O holy majesty of heavenly powers!
May I never see that day! Never!   305
Rather let me vanish from the race of men
Than know the abomination destined me!
CHORAGOS: We too, my lord, have felt dismay at this.
    But there is hope: you have yet to hear the shepherd.
OEDIPUS: Indeed, I fear no other hope is left me.   310
IOCASTÊ: What do you hope from him when he comes?
OEDIPUS: This much:
    If his account of the murder tallies with yours,
    Then I am cleared.
IOCASTÊ: What was it that I said
    Of such importance?
OEDIPUS: Why, "marauders," you said,
    Killed the King, according to this man's story.   315
    If he maintains that still, if there were several,
    Clearly the guilt is not mine: I was alone.
    But if he says one man, singlehanded, did it,
    Then the evidence all points to me.
IOCASTÊ: You may be sure that he said there were several;   320
    And can he call back that story now? He can not.
    The whole city heard it as plainly as I.
    But suppose he alters some detail of it:
    He can not ever show that Laïos' death
    Fulfilled the oracle: for Apollo said   325
    My child was doomed to kill him; and my child—
    Poor baby!—it was my child that died first.

No. From now on, where oracles are concerned,
I would not waste a second thought on any.

OEDIPUS: You may be right.

But come: let someone go   330
    For the shepherd at once. This matter must be settled.
IOCASTÊ: I will send for him.
    I would not wish to cross you in anything,
    And surely not in this.—Let us go in.

Exeunt into the palace.

Ode 2 [*Chant of the Chorus*]

Strophe 1

CHORUS: Let me be reverent in the ways of right,
    Lowly the paths I journey on;
    Let all my words and actions keep
    The laws of the pure universe
    From highest Heaven handed down.   5
    For Heaven is their bright nurse,
    Those generations of the realms of light;
    Ah, never of mortal kind were they begot,
    Nor are they slaves of memory, lost in sleep:
    Their Father is greater than Time, and ages not.   10

Antistrophe 1

    The tyrant is a child of Pride
    Who drinks from his great sickening cup
    Recklessness and vanity,
    Until from his high crest headlong
    He plummets to the dust of hope.   15
    That strong man is not strong.
    But let no fair ambition be denied;
    May God protect the wrestler for the State
    In government, in comely policy,
    Who will fear God, and on His ordinance wait.   20

Strophe 2

    Haughtiness and the high hand of disdain
    Tempt and outrage God's holy law;
    And any mortal who dares hold
    No immortal Power in awe
    Will be caught up in a net of pain: 25
    The price for which his levity is sold.
    Let each man take due earnings, then,
    And keep his hands from holy things,
    And from blasphemy stand apart—
    Else the crackling blast of heaven   30
    Blows on his head, and on his desperate heart;
    Though fools will honor impious men,
    In their cities no tragic poet sings.

Shall we lose faith in Delphi's obscurities,
We who have heard the world's core   35
Discredited, and the sacred wood
Of Zeus at Elis° praised no more?   *Greek area including Olympia*
The deeds and the strange prophecies
Must make a pattern yet to be understood.
Zeus, if indeed you are lord of all,   40
Throned in light over night and day,
Mirror this in your endless mind:
Our masters call the oracle
Words on the wind, and the Delphic vision blind!
Their hearts no longer know Apollo,   45
And reverence for the gods has died away.

Scene 3

Enter IOCASTÊ.

IOCASTÊ: Princes of Thebes, it has occurred to me
To visit the altars of the gods, bearing
These branches as a suppliant,° and this incense.   *pleading for help*
Our King is not himself: his noble soul
Is overwrought with fantasies of dread,   5
Else he would consider
The new prophecies in the light of the old.
He will listen to any voice that speaks disaster,
And my advice goes for nothing.

She approaches the altar, right.

                              To you, then, Apollo,
Lycean lord,° since you are nearest, I turn in prayer.   *one of the god's titles* 10
Receive these offerings, and grant us deliverance
From defilement. Our hearts are heavy with fear
When we see our leader distracted, as helpless sailors
Are terrified by the confusion of their helmsman.

Enter MESSENGER.

MESSENGER: Friends, no doubt you can direct me: 15
Where shall I find the house of Oedipus,
Or, better still, where is the King himself?
CHORAGOS: It is this very place, stranger; he is inside.
This is his wife and mother of his children.
MESSENGER: I wish her happiness in a happy house,   20
Blest in all the fulfillment of her marriage.

IOCASTÊ: I wish as much for you: your courtesy
   Deserves a like good fortune. But now, tell me:
   Why have you come? What have you to say to us?   25
MESSENGER: Good news, my lady, for your house and your husband.
IOCASTÊ: What news? Who sent you here?
MESSENGER: I am from Corinth.°
   The news I bring ought to mean joy for you,   *Oedipus'*
   Though it may be you will find some grief in it.   *childhood home*
IOCASTÊ: What is it? How can it touch us in both ways?   30
MESSENGER: The word is that the people of the Isthmus
   Intend to call Oedipus to be their king.
IOCASTÊ: But old King Polybos—is he not reigning still?
MESSENGER: No. Death holds him in his sepulchre.
IOCASTÊ: What are you saying? Polybos is dead?   35
MESSENGER: If I am not telling the truth, may I die myself.
IOCASTÊ (*to a Maidservant*): Go in, go quickly; tell this to your master.

   O riddlers of God's will, where are you now!
   This was the man whom Oedipus, long ago,
   Feared so, fled so, in dread of destroying him—   40
   But it was another fate by which he died.

   Enter OEDIPUS, *center.*

OEDIPUS: Dearest Iocastê, why have you sent for me?
IOCASTÊ: Listen to what this man says, and then tell me
   What has become of the solemn prophecies.
OEDIPUS: Who is this man? What is his news for me?
IOCASTÊ: He has come from Corinth to announce your father's death!   45
OEDIPUS: Is it true, stranger? Tell me in your own words.
MESSENGER: I can not say it more clearly: the King is dead.
OEDIPUS: Was it by treason? Or by an attack of illness?
MESSENGER: A little thing brings old men to their rest.
OEDIPUS: It was sickness, then?
MESSENGER: Yes, and his many years.   50
OEDIPUS: Ah!
   Why should a man respect the Pythian hearth,° or   *the oracle at Delphi*
   Give heed to the birds that jangle above his head?
   They prophesied that I should kill Polybos,
   Kill my own father; but he is dead and buried,   55
   And I am here—I never touched him, never,
   Unless he died of grief for my departure,
   And thus, in a sense, through me. No. Polybos
   Has packed the oracles off with him underground.
   They are empty words.
IOCASTÊ: Had I not told you so?   60
OEDIPUS: You had; it was my faint heart that betrayed me.
IOCASTÊ: From now on never think of those things again.
OEDIPUS: And yet—must I not fear my mother's bed?

IOCASTÉ: Why should anyone in this world be afraid,
     Since Fate rules us and nothing can be foreseen?   65
     A man should live only for the present day.

     Have no more fear of sleeping with your mother:
     How many men, in dreams, have lain with their mothers!
     No reasonable man is troubled by such things.
OEDIPUS: That is true; only—
     If only my mother were not still alive!   70
     But she is alive. I can not help my dread.
IOCASTÉ: Yet this news of your father's death is wonderful.
OEDIPUS: Wonderful. But I fear the living woman.
MESSENGER: Tell me, who is this woman that you fear?   75
OEDIPUS: It is Meropê, man; the wife of King Polybos.
MESSENGER: Meropê? Why should you be afraid of her?
OEDIPUS: An oracle of the gods, a dreadful saying.
MESSENGER: Can you tell me about it or are you sworn to silence?
OEDIPUS: I can tell you, and I will.   80
     Apollo said through his prophet that I was the man
     Who should marry his own mother, shed his father's blood
     With his own hands. And so, for all these years
     I have kept clear of Corinth, and no harm has come—
     Though it would have been sweet to see my parents again.   85
MESSENGER: And is this the fear that drove you out of Corinth?
OEDIPUS: Would you have me kill my father?
MESSENGER: As for that
     You must be reassured by the news I gave you.
OEDIPUS: If you could reassure me, I would reward you.
MESSENGER: I had that in mind, I will confess: I thought   90
     I could count on you when you returned to Corinth.
OEDIPUS: No: I will never go near my parents again.
MESSENGER: Ah, son, you still do not know what you are doing—
OEDIPUS: What do you mean? In the name of God tell me!
MESSENGER: —If these are your reasons for not going home.   95
OEDIPUS: I tell you, I fear the oracle may come true.
MESSENGER: And guilt may come upon you through your parents?
OEDIPUS: That is the dread that is always in my heart.
MESSENGER: Can you not see that all your fears are groundless?
OEDIPUS: How can you say that? They are my parents, surely?   100
MESSENGER: Polybos was not your father.
OEDIPUS: Not my father?
MESSENGER: No more your father than the man speaking to you.
OEDIPUS: But you are nothing to me!
MESSENGER: Neither was he.
OEDIPUS: Then why did he call me son?
MESSENGER: I will tell you:
     Long ago he had you from my hands, as a gift.   105
OEDIPUS: Then how could he love me so, if I was not his?

MESSENGER: He had no children, and his heart turned to you.
OEDIPUS: What of you? Did you buy me? Did you find me by chance?
MESSENGER: I came upon you in the crooked pass of Kithairon.°   *Greek*
                                                                  mountain area
OEDIPUS: And what were you doing there?
MESSENGER: Tending my flocks.   110
OEDIPUS: A wandering shepherd?
MESSENGER: But your savior, son, that day.
OEDIPUS: From what did you save me?
MESSENGER: Your ankles should tell you that.
OEDIPUS: Ah, stranger, why do you speak of that childhood pain?
MESSENGER: I cut the bonds that tied your ankles together.
OEDIPUS: I have had the mark as long as I can remember.   115
MESSENGER: That was why you were given the name you bear.
OEDIPUS: God! Was it my father or my mother who did it? Tell me!
MESSENGER: I do not know. The man who gave you to me
    Can tell you better than I.   120
OEDIPUS: It was not you that found me, but another?
MESSENGER: It was another shepherd gave you to me.
OEDIPUS: Who was he? Can you tell me who he was?
MESSENGER: I think he was said to be one of Laïos' people.
OEDIPUS: You mean the Laïos who was king here years ago?   125
MESSENGER: Yes; King Laïos; and the man was one of his herdsmen.
OEDIPUS: Is he still alive? Can I see him?
MESSENGER: These men here
    Know best about such things.
OEDIPUS: Does anyone here
    Know this shepherd that he is talking about?
    Have you seen him in the fields, or in the town?   130
    If you have, tell me. It is time things were made plain.
CHORAGOS: I think the man he means is that same shepherd
    You have already asked to see. Iocastê perhaps
    Could tell you something.
OEDIPUS: Do you know anything
    About him, Lady? Is he the man we have summoned?   135
    Is that the man this shepherd means?
IOCASTÊ: Why think of him?
    Forget this herdsman. Forget it all.
    This talk is a waste of time.
OEDIPUS: How can you say that,
    When the clues to my true birth are in my hands?
IOCASTÊ: For God's love, let us have no more questioning!   140
    Is your life nothing to you?
    My own is pain enough for me to bear.
OEDIPUS: You need not worry. Suppose my mother a slave,
    And born of slaves: no baseness can touch you.
IOCASTÊ: Listen to me, I beg you: do not do this thing!   145
OEDIPUS: I will not listen; the truth must be made known.
IOCASTÊ: Everything that I say is for your own good!

OEDIPUS: My own good
   Snaps my patience, then; I want none of it.
IOCASTÊ: You are fatally wrong! May you never learn who you are!
OEDIPUS: Go, one of you, and bring the shepherd here.   150
   Let us leave this woman to brag of her royal name.
IOCASTÊ: Ah, miserable!
   That is the only word I have for you now.
   That is the only word I can ever have.

Exit into the palace.

CHORAGOS: Why has she left us, Oedipus? Why has she gone   155
   In such a passion of sorrow? I fear this silence:
   Something dreadful may come of it.
OEDIPUS: Let it come!
   However base my birth, I must know about it.
   The Queen, like a woman, is perhaps ashamed
   To think of my low origin. But I   160
   Am a child of Luck; I can not be dishonored.
   Luck is my mother; the passing months, my brothers,
   Have seen me rich and poor.
               If this is so,
   How could I wish that I were someone else?
   How could I not be glad to know my birth?   165

Ode 3 [*Chant of the Chorus*]

Strophe

CHORUS: If ever the coming time were known
   To my heart's pondering,
   Kithairon, now by Heaven I see the torches
   At the festival of the next full moon,
   And see the dance, and hear the choir sing   5
   A grace to your gentle shade:
   Mountain where Oedipus was found,
   O mountain guard of a noble race!
   May the god who heals us lend his aid,
   And let that glory come to pass   10
   For our king's cradling-ground.

Antistrophe

   Of the nymphs that flower beyond the years,
   Who bore you, royal child,
   To Pan° of the hills or the timberline Apollo,   *god of shepherds*
   Cold in delight where the upland clears,   15
   Or Hermês for whom Kyllenê's° heights are piled?   *mountain where the gods'*
   Or flushed as evening cloud,   *messenger was born*
   Great Dionysos, roamer of mountains,

He—was it he who found you there,
And caught you up in his own proud   20
Arms from the sweet god-ravisher
Who laughed by the Muses' fountains?

Scene 4

OEDIPUS: Sirs: though I do not know the man,
  I think I see him coming, this shepherd we want:
  He is old, like our friend here, and the men
  Bringing him seem to be servants of my house.
  But you can tell, if you have ever seen him.   5

  Enter SHEPHERD *escorted by servants.*

CHORAGOS: I know him, he was Laïos' man. You can trust him.
OEDIPUS: Tell me first, you from Corinth: is this the shepherd
  We were discussing?
MESSENGER: This is the very man.
OEDIPUS: (*to* SHEPHERD): Come here. No, look at me. You must answer
  Everything I ask.—You belonged to Laïos?   10
SHEPHERD: Yes: born his slave, brought up in his house.
OEDIPUS: Tell me: what kind of work did you do for him?
SHEPHERD: I was a shepherd of his, most of my life.
OEDIPUS: Where mainly did you go for pasturage?
SHEPHERD: Sometimes Kithairon, sometimes the hills near-by.   15
OEDIPUS: Do you remember ever seeing this man out there?
SHEPHERD: What would he be doing there? This man?
OEDIPUS: This man standing here. Have you ever seen him before?
SHEPHERD: No. At least, not to my recollection.
MESSENGER: And that is not strange, my lord. But I'll refresh   20
  His memory: he must remember when we two
  Spent three whole seasons together, March to September,
  On Kithairon or thereabouts. He had two flocks;
  I had one. Each autumn I'd drive mine home
  And he would go back with his to Laïos' sheepfold.—   25
  Is this not true, just as I have described it?
SHEPHERD: True, yes; but it was all so long ago.
MESSENGER: Well, then: do you remember, back in those days
  That you gave me a baby boy to bring up as my own?
SHEPHERD: What if I did? What are you trying to say?   30
MESSENGER: King Oedipus was once that little child.
SHEPHERD: Damn you, hold your tongue!
OEDIPUS: No more of that!
  It is your tongue needs watching, not this man's.
SHEPHERD: My King, my Master, what is it I have done wrong?
OEDIPUS: You have not answered his question about the boy.   35
SHEPHERD: He does not know . . . He is only making trouble . . .

OEDIPUS: Come, speak plainly, or it will go hard with you.

SHEPHERD: In God's name, do not torture an old man!

OEDIPUS: Come here, one of you; bind his arms behind him.

SHEPHERD: Unhappy king! What more do you wish to learn?   40

OEDIPUS: Did you give this man the child he speaks of?

SHEPHERD: I did.

And I would to God I had died that very day.

OEDIPUS: You will die now unless you speak the truth.

SHEPHERD: Yet if I speak the truth, I am worse than dead.

OEDIPUS: Very well; since you insist upon delaying—   45

SHEPHERD: No! I have told you already that I gave him the boy.

OEDIPUS: Where did you get him? From your house? From somewhere else?

SHEPHERD: Not from mine, no. A man gave him to me.

OEDIPUS: Is that man here? Do you know whose slave he was?

SHEPHERD: For God's love, my King, do not ask me any more!   50

OEDIPUS: You are a dead man if I have to ask you again.

SHEPHERD: Then . . . Then the child was from the palace of Laïos.

OEDIPUS: A slave child? or a child of his own line?

SHEPHERD: Ah, I am on the brink of dreadful speech!

OEDIPUS: And I of dreadful hearing. Yet I must hear.   55

SHEPHERD: If you must be told, then . . .

                                  They said it was Laïos' child;

But it is your wife who can tell you about that.

OEDIPUS: My wife!—Did she give it to you?

SHEPHERD: My lord, she did.

OEDIPUS: Do you know why?

SHEPHERD: I was told to get rid of it.

OEDIPUS: An unspeakable mother!

SHEPHERD: There had been prophecies . . .   60

OEDIPUS: Tell me.

SHEPHERD: It was said that the boy would kill his own father.

OEDIPUS: Then why did you give him over to this old man?

SHEPHERD: I pitied the baby, my King,

And I thought that this man would take him far away

To his own country.

                    He saved him—but for what a fate!   65

For if you are what this man says you are,

No man living is more wretched than Oedipus.

OEDIPUS: Ah God!

It was true!

        All the prophecies!

                    —Now,

O Light, may I look on you for the last time!   70

I, Oedipus,

Oedipus, damned in his birth, in his marriage damned,

Damned in the blood he shed with his own hand!

He rushes into the palace.

Ode 4 [*Chant of the Chorus*]

CHORUS: Alas for the seed of men.

What measure shall I give these generations
That breathe on the void and are void
And exist and do not exist?

Who bears more weight of joy   5
Than mass of sunlight shifting in images,
Or who shall make his thought stay on
That down time drifts away?

Your splendor is all fallen.

                                                                      10
O naked brow of wrath and tears,
O change of Oedipus!
I who saw your days call no man blest—
Your great days like ghosts gone.

That mind was a strong bow.

Deep, how deep you drew it then, hard archer,   15
At a dim fearful range,
And brought dear glory down!

You overcame the stranger—
The virgin with her hooking lion claws—
And though death sang, stood like a tower   20
To make pale Thebes take heart.

Fortress against our sorrow!

Divine king, giver of laws,
Majestic Oedipus!
No prince in Thebes had ever such renown,   25
No prince won such grace of power.

And now of all men ever known
Most pitiful is this man's story:
His fortunes are most changed, his state
Fallen to a low slave's   30
Ground under bitter fate.

O Oedipus, most royal one!
The great door that expelled you to the light
Gave at night—ah, gave night to your glory:
As to the father, to the fathering son.   35

All understood too late.

How could that queen whom Laïos won,
The garden that he harrowed at his height,
Be silent when that act was done?

Antistrophe 2

But all eyes fail before time's eye,   40
All actions come to justice there.
Though never willed, though far down the deep past,
Your bed, your dread sirings,
Are brought to book at last.
Child by Laïos doomed to die,   45
Then doomed to lose that fortunate little death,
Would God you never took breath in this air
That with my wailing lips I take to cry:

For I weep the world's outcast.

I was blind, and now I can tell why: 50
Asleep, for you had given ease of breath
To Thebes, while the false years went by.

Éxodos [*Concluding Scene (Scene 5)*]

Enter, from the palace, SECOND MESSENGER.

SECOND MESSENGER: Elders of Thebes, most honored in this land,
 What horrors are yours to see and hear, what weight
 Of sorrow to be endured, if, true to your birth,
 You venerate the line of Labdakos!
 I think neither Istros nor Phasis, those great rivers,   5
 Could purify this place of the corruption
 It shelters now, or soon must bring to light—
 Evil not done unconsciously, but willed.

 The greatest griefs are those we cause ourselves.
CHORAGOS: Surely, friend, we have grief enough already;   10
 What new sorrow do you mean?
SECOND MESSENGER: The Queen is dead.
CHORAGOS: Iocastê? Dead? But at whose hand?
SECOND MESSENGER: Her own.
 The full horror of what happened, you can not know,
 For you did not see it; but I, who did, will tell you
 As clearly as I can how she met her death.   15

When she had left us,
In passionate silence, passing through the court,
She ran to her apartment in the house,
Her hair clutched by the fingers of both hands.
She closed the doors behind her; then, by that bed   20
Where long ago the fatal son was conceived—
That son who should bring about his father's death—
We heard her call upon Laïos, dead so many years,
And heard her wail for the double fruit of her marriage,
A husband by her husband, children by her child.   25

Exactly how she died I do not know:
For Oedipus burst in moaning and would not let us
Keep vigil to the end: it was by him
As he stormed about the room that our eyes were caught.
From one to another of us he went, begging a sword,   30
Cursing the wife who was not his wife, the mother
Whose womb had carried his own children and himself.
I do not know: it was none of us aided him,
But surely one of the gods was in control!
For with a dreadful cry   35
He hurled his weight, as though wrenched out of himself,
At the twin doors: the bolts gave, and he rushed in.
And there we saw her hanging, her body swaying
From the cruel cord she had noosed about her neck.
A great sob broke from him, heartbreaking to hear,   40
As he loosed the rope and lowered her to the ground.

I would blot out from my mind what happened next!
For the King ripped from her gown the golden brooches
That were her ornament, and raised them, and plunged them down
Straight into his own eyeballs, crying, "No more,   45
No more shall you look on the misery about me,
The horrors of my own doing! Too long you have known
The faces of those whom I should never have seen,
Too long been blind to those for whom I was searching!
From this hour, go in darkness!" And as he spoke,   50
He struck at his eyes—not once, but many times;
And the blood spattered his beard,
Bursting from his ruined sockets like red hail.

So from the unhappiness of two this evil has sprung,
A curse on the man and woman alike. The old   55
Happiness of the house of Labdakos
Was happiness enough: where is it today?
It is all wailing and ruin, disgrace, death—all
The misery of mankind that has a name—
And it is wholly and for ever theirs.   60

CHORAGOS: Is he in agony still? Is there no rest for him?

SECOND MESSENGER: He is calling for someone to lead him to the gates
    So that all the children of Kadmos may look upon
    His father's murderer, his mother's—no,
    I can not say it!
                 And then he will leave Thebes,   65
    Self-exiled, in order that the curse
    Which he himself pronounced may depart from the house.
    He is weak, and there is none to lead him,
    So terrible is his suffering.
                    But you will see:
    Look, the doors are opening; in a moment   70
    You will see a thing that would crush a heart of stone.

The central door is opened: OEDIPUS, *blinded, is led in.*

CHORAGOS: Dreadful indeed for men to see.
    Never have my own eyes
    Looked on a sight so full of fear.

    Oedipus!   75
    What madness came upon you, what daemon
    Leaped on your life with heavier
    Punishment than a mortal man can bear?
    No: I can not even
    Look at you, poor ruined one.   80
    And I would speak, question, ponder,
    If I were able. No.
    You make me shudder.

OEDIPUS: God. God.
    Is there a sorrow greater?   85
    Where shall I find harbor in this world?
    My voice is hurled far on a dark wind.
    What has God done to me?

CHORAGOS: Too terrible to think of, or to see.

Strophe 1

OEDIPUS: O cloud of night,   90
    Never to be turned away: night coming on,
    I can not tell how: night like a shroud!

    My fair winds brought me here.
                    Oh God. Again
    The pain of the spikes where I had sight,
    The flooding pain   95
    Of memory, never to be gouged out.

CHORAGOS: This is not strange.
    You suffer it all twice over, remorse in pain,
    Pain in remorse.

OEDIPUS: Ah dear friend   100
    Are you faithful even yet, you alone?
    Are you still standing near me, will you stay here,
    Patient, to care for the blind?
                            The blind man!
    Yet even blind I know who it is attends me,
    By the voice's tone—   105
    Though my new darkness hide the comforter.
CHORAGOS: Oh fearful act!
    What god was it drove you to rake black
    Night across your eyes?

OEDIPUS: Apollo. Apollo. Dear   110
    Children, the god was Apollo.
    He brought my sick, sick fate upon me.
    But the blinding hand was my own!
    How could I bear to see
    When all my sight was horror everywhere?   115
CHORAGOS: Everywhere; that is true.
OEDIPUS: And now what is left?
    Images? Love? A greeting even,
    Sweet to the senses? Is there anything?
    Ah, no, friends: lead me away.   120
    Lead me away from Thebes.
                        Lead the great wreck
    And hell of Oedipus, whom the gods hate.
CHORAGOS: Your fate is clear, you are not blind to that.
    Would God you had never found it out!

OEDIPUS: Death take the man who unbound   125
    My feet on that hillside
    And delivered me from death to life! What life?
    If only I had died,
    This weight of monstrous doom
    Could not have dragged me and my darlings down.   130
CHORAGOS: I would have wished the same.
OEDIPUS: Oh never to have come here
    With my father's blood upon me! Never
    To have been the man they call his mother's husband!
    Oh accurst! Oh child of evil,   135
    To have entered that wretched bed—
                            the selfsame one!
    More primal than sin itself, this fell to me.
CHORAGOS: I do not know how I can answer you.
    You were better dead than alive and blind.
OEDIPUS: Do not counsel me any more. This punishment   140

That I have laid upon myself is just.
If I had eyes,
I do not know how I could bear the sight
Of my father, when I came to the house of Death,
Or my mother: for I have sinned against them both   145
So vilely that I could not make my peace
By strangling my own life.
            Or do you think my children,
Born as they were born, would be sweet to my eyes?
Ah never, never! Nor this town with its high walls,
Nor the holy images of the gods.
                For I,   150
Thrice miserable!—Oedipus, noblest of all the line
Of Kadmos, have condemned myself to enjoy
These things no more, by my own malediction
Expelling that man whom the gods declared
To be a defilement in the house of Laïos.   155
After exposing the rankness of my own guilt,
How could I look men frankly in the eyes?
No, I swear it,
If I could have stifled my hearing at its source,
I would have done it and made all this body   160
A tight cell of misery, blank to light and sound:
So I should have been safe in a dark agony
Beyond all recollection.
           Ah Kithairon!
Why did you shelter me? When I was cast upon you,
Why did I not die? Then I should never   165
Have shown the world my execrable birth.

Ah Polybos! Corinth, city that I believed
The ancient seat of my ancestors: how fair
I seemed, your child! And all the while this evil
Was cancerous within me!
           For I am sick   170
In my daily life, sick in my origin.

O three roads, dark ravine, woodland and way
Where three roads met: you, drinking my father's blood,
My own blood, spilled by my own hand: can you remember
The unspeakable things I did there, and the things   175
I went on from there to do?
           O marriage, marriage!
The act that engendered me, and again the act
Performed by the son in the same bed—
                Ah, the net
Of incest, mingling fathers, brothers, sons,

With brides, wives, mothers: the last evil   180
That can be known by men: no tongue can say
How evil!
          No. For the love of God, conceal me
Somewhere far from Thebes; or kill me; or hurl me
Into the sea, away from men's eyes for ever.

Come, lead me. You need not fear to touch me.   185
Of all men, I alone can bear this guilt.

Enter CREON.

CHORAGOS: We are not the ones to decide; but Creon here
    May fitly judge of what you ask. He only
    Is left to protect the city in your place.
OEDIPUS: Alas, how can I speak to him? What right have I   190
    To beg his courtesy whom I have deeply wronged?
CREON: I have not come to mock you, Oedipus,
    Or to reproach you, either.
    (*To Attendants.*)   —You, standing there:
    If you have lost all respect for man's dignity,
    At least respect the flame of Lord Helios°:   *the sun god* 195
    Do not allow this pollution to show itself
    Openly here, an affront to the earth
    And Heaven's rain and the light of day. No, take him
    Into the house as quickly as you can.
    For it is proper   200
    That only the close kindred see his grief.
OEDIPUS: I pray you in God's name, since your courtesy
    Ignores my dark expectation, visiting
    With mercy this man of all men most execrable:
    Give me what I ask—for your good, not for mine.   205
CREON: And what is it that you would have me do?
OEDIPUS: Drive me out of this country as quickly as may be
    To a place where no human voice can ever greet me.
CREON: I should have done that before now—only,
    God's will had not been wholly revealed to me.   210
OEDIPUS: But his command is plain: the parricide
    Must be destroyed. I am that evil man.
CREON: That is the sense of it, yes; but as things are,
    We had best discover clearly what is to be done.
OEDIPUS: You would learn more about a man like me?   215
CREON: You are ready now to listen to the god.
OEDIPUS: I will listen. But it is to you
    That I must turn for help. I beg you, hear me.

The woman in there—
Give her whatever funeral you think proper: 220
She is your sister.

—But let me go, Creon!
Let me purge my father's Thebes of the pollution
Of my living here, and go out to the wild hills,
To Kithairon, that has won such fame with me,
The tomb my mother and father appointed for me,   225
And let me die there, as they willed I should.
And yet I know
Death will not ever come to me through sickness
Or in any natural way: I have been preserved
For some unthinkable fate. But let that be.   230

As for my sons, you need not care for them.
They are men, they will find some way to live.
But my poor daughters, who have shared my table,
Who never before have been parted from their father—
Take care of them, Creon; do this for me.   235
And will you let me touch them with my hands
A last time, and let us weep together?
Be kind, my lord,
Great prince, be kind!
                    Could I but touch them,
They would be mine again, as when I had my eyes.   240

Enter ANTIGONE *and* ISMENE, OEDIPUS' *daughters, with attendants*

Ah, God!
Is it my dearest children I hear weeping?
Has Creon pitied me and sent my daughters?
CREON: Yes, Oedipus: I knew that they were dear to you
In the old days, and know you must love them still.   245
OEDIPUS: May God bless you for this—and be a friendlier
Guardian to you than he has been to me!

Children, where are you?
Come quickly to my hands: they are your brother's—
Hands that have brought your father's once clear eyes   250
To this way of seeing—
                    Ah dearest ones,
I had neither sight nor knowledge then, your father
By the woman who was the source of his own life!
And I weep for you—having no strength to see you—,
I weep for you when I think of the bitterness   255
That men will visit upon you all your lives.
What homes, what festivals can you attend
Without being forced to depart again in tears?
And when you come to marriageable age,
Where is the man, my daughters, who would dare   260
Risk the bane that lies on all my children?
Is there any evil wanting? Your father killed

His father; sowed the womb of her who bore him;
Engendered you at the fount of his own existence!
That is what they will say of you.
                                        Then, whom   265
Can you ever marry? There are no bridegrooms for you,
And your lives must wither away in sterile dreaming.

O Creon, son of Menoikeus!
You are the only father my daughters have,
Since we, their parents, are both of us gone for ever.   270
They are your own blood: you will not let them
Fall into beggary and loneliness;
You will keep them from the miseries that are mine!
Take pity on them; see, they are only children,
Friendless except for you. Promise me this,   275
Great Prince, and give me your hand in token of it.

CREON *clasps his right hand.*

Children:
I could say much, if you could understand me,
But as it is, I have only this prayer for you:
Live where you can, be as happy as you can—   280
Happier, please God, than God has made your father!
CREON: Enough. You have wept enough. Now go within.
OEDIPUS: I must; but it is hard.
CREON: Time eases all things.
OEDIPUS: But you must promise—
CREON: Say what you desire.
OEDIPUS: Send me from Thebes!
CREON: God grant that I may!   285
OEDIPUS: But since God hates me . . .
CREON: No, he will grant your wish.
OEDIPUS: You promise?
CREON: I can not speak beyond my knowledge.
OEDIPUS: Then lead me in.
CREON: Come now, and leave your children.
OEDIPUS: No! Do not take them from me!
CREON: Think no longer
That you are in command here, but rather think   290
How, when you were, you served your own destruction.

Exeunt into the house all but the CHORUS; *the* CHORAGOS *chants directly to
the audience.*

CHORAGOS: Men of Thebes: look upon Oedipus.

This is the king who solved the famous riddle
And towered up, most powerful of men.
No mortal eyes but looked on him with envy,   295
Yet in the end ruin swept over him.

Let every man in mankind's frailty
Consider his last day; and let none
Presume on his good fortune until he find
Life, at his death, a memory without pain.   300

The Receptive Reader

1. (Prologue) How much background or context does the prologue provide for you? What kind of a leader is Oedipus in the initial exchange with his people? What is the role of Creon in this scene? What makes the first chant of the *chorus* more than a dutiful invocation of the gods? (Which gods does the chorus invoke?)

2. (Scene 1) What picture of Oedipus as the king do you form during his long speech to the citizens? Does your picture of Oedipus change as he responds to Tiresias' ominous hint of "dreadful secrets"? What traits of his character does Oedipus show in his denunciation of Creon and in his taunts of the blind seer? What role do blindness and riddles play in the rapid trading off of taunts between the king and the prophet? How and how well does Tiresias establish his authority? What is the reaction of the chorus to what happened in this scene?

3. (Scene 2) Is Creon in this scene a worthy *antagonist* for Oedipus? What role does Jocasta play in the conflict between her husband and her brother? What role does the chorus play? (Are you surprised by their reactions?) How does Jocasta in this scene first show her doubts about oracles? By the end of this scene, Oedipus has reached "a pitch of dark foreboding." How much does he already know or suspect?

4. (Scene 3) What essential pieces of the puzzle does the *messenger* in this scene provide? How does Oedipus show that he is still in the dark? Why and how does Jocasta voice her doubts about priests and oracles in this scene? When or how does Jocasta show that she already knows the truth? (What are your feelings as you watch her attempts to head off the worst?)

5. (Scene 4) In this climactic scene, what is ironic about the deadly game of question-and-answer played out between Oedipus and the old *shepherd?* What motives made the shepherds thwart the plans of Oedipus parents to head off the prediction of the oracle? What makes their motivation ironic? Except for the brief summing in the final scene, the chorus here pronounces its final words on the fate of Oedipus. What to them is the meaning of what has happened?

6. (Scene 5) How does Oedipus face the terrible truth? How does he explain what he has done and what he proposes to do? Does he show any remnant of his old pride? What happens when Oedipus asks to meet his two young daughters for the last time? (Does this part of the scene change your view of Oedipus? of Creon?)

The Whole Play—For Discussion or Writing

1. As you look back over the play as a whole, what is your final estimate of Oedipus? Does he have the kind of *tragic flaw* that was required by Aristotle? Is his tragic flaw pride? anger? blindness to the truth? stubborn pursuit of the "truth that kills"? What qualities does he have that might make audiences nevertheless consider him great and admirable?

2. By the time of Sophocles, the belief in *prophecy* and other tenets of traditional religion were coming under attack. How close to a modern skeptic is Jocasta? How diametrically opposed is her attitude toward the "search for truth" from that of her husband? Do you consider her a strong or a weak character?

3. One critic called Creon in this play "the man of spotless reputation who extricates himself from every risk . . . securing himself, intriguing. . . . He is a man who is cheap by an average standard, born to be second in all things." What do you think explains this estimate? Do you agree with it?

4. To what extent does the chorus in the play seem the voice of orthodox Greek religion? To what extent does it seem to reflect reactions and feelings that might be shared by modern spectators?

William Shakespeare   *(1564–1616)*   👁

A Midsummer Night's Dream is the best loved of Shakespeare's **romantic comedies.** This early Shakespeare play transforms the gray world of everyday into a fantasy world of delightful dreams, amorous adventures, and mischievous pranks. The common theme is love, traced through its full range of variations. On the most fanciful level, the play takes us into the dream world of high **romance**—the magic kingdom of Oberon, king of the fairies, and Titania, his fairy queen. The moonlit forest is a spirit world whose inhabitants are not hemmed in by limitations of time and space (or weighed down by material bodies). Spells and magic potions give power to make others do one's bidding. Miraculous transformations (or **metamorphoses**) are commonplace. The quasi-divine spirits, exempt from mortal inhibitions, delight in creating mischief and playing with human fears.

On the intermediate level, the Greek hero Theseus and the Amazon queen Hippolyta, although legendary figures, take us into the world of human desires and limitations. They provide the frame story that sets us up for a traditional **comedy of love.** Theseus has defeated and won the war-like Amazon queen, and we witness preparations for a marriage festival that set the tone of traditional comedy: mirth, merriment, revelry—casting off pale melancholy. The main plot is spun around the obstacles encountered and overcome by young lovers. Egeus, the father of Hermia, is the traditional obstructing elder: He pits tyrannical parental authority against the love of Hermia and Lysander, trying to force Hermia into an unwanted marriage with Demetrius. Demetrius in turn ignores Helena, who yearns for him in the throes of unrequited, unanswered love.

On the lowest rung of the comic ladder is Peter Quince's troop of workingmen, offering their amateur production of the story of Pyramus and Thisby to their prince. In their hands, the tragic story turns into a parody, a "lamentable comedy," as Peter Quince says. This comic play-within-a-play, or **interlude,** "epitomizes many an amateur dramatic presentation, from the choice of a work inappropriate both for the occasion and the sparse talents of the performers, right through disastrous rehearsals with lines forgotten or misread, down to a performance marred by . . .

Kevin Kline and Michelle Pfeiffer in a scene from *A Midsummer Night's Dream* (courtesy Picture Desk, Inc./Kobal /Collection)

misinterpretation, unintentional bawdiness," and "actors stepping out of character to talk with the audience" (Alice Griffin).

However, in the play as a whole, the fanciful, the real, and the farcical intermesh. Puck, the sprite and jester, causes mischief in both the human and the fairy worlds. He gives love potions to the wrong lovers. He makes Bottom stumble through the woods with a human body and the head of an ass. The beings of the fairy world are not totally disembodied spirits. The queen of fairies, tricked by Puck's potion, falls in love with a half-human monster made up of the ignorant Bottom and an ass's head. Beauty and the beast inhabit the same enchanted forest.

Much of the solemn palaver at the court of Theseus is **blank verse**—the unrhymed iambic pentameter (five-beat) line. Sentences may roam over half a dozen or more lines, with sentence breaks often falling in the middle of a line. Note the inversion (stress on first syllable) and the weaker stresses (ˋ). These help the poet play rhythmic variations on the basic iambic (stress-on-second-syllable) pattern:

> Four dáys | will quícklly stéep | themsélves | in níght,
> Four níghts | will quícklly dréam | awáy | the tíme,
> And thén | the móon, | like to | a síllver bów
> Néw-bent | in héalven, shàll | behóld | the night
> Of óur | solémlnities. (1.1.7–11)

However, the dialogue of the lovers and some other passages are more neatly packaged in **closed couplets**—two rhymed lines. These sound more pat, and they seem suitable especially to the lovers' talk, because what the lovers say often seems predictable—"what they all say":

Love looks not with the eyes, but with the MIND,
And therefore is winged Cupid painted BLIND. (1.1.234–35)

In Shakespeare's moonlit midsummer forest, the native English elves and hobgoblins mingle with creatures from classical Greek myth and legend. The playwright expects us to know that the nymph Daphne was pursued by the god Apollo and was turned into a laurel tree to help her escape his unwanted attentions. We are expected to recognize **allusions** to the Furies, the spirits that came from hell to wreak vengeance on evildoers, and to the Fates, the three fatal sisters who spin the thread of life and whose shears cut it short.

The subjects of Theseus move from the daylight world of his court to the magic moonlit world of the forest and then return. What do they experience during their journey? What do they learn from it?

A Midsummer Night's Dream   *1594–1595*

CHARACTERS

Elders and Lovers:
THESEUS, Duke of Athens
HIPPOLYTA, Queen of the Amazons, engaged to THESEUS
EGEUS, father of HERMIA
HERMIA, daughter of EGEUS, in love with LYSANDER
LYSANDER, in love with HERMIA
DEMETRIUS, also in love with HERMIA, and favored by her father
HELENA, in love with DEMETRIUS
PHILOSTRATE, Master of the Revels, in charge of court entertainments
Attendants

Spirits of the Fairy Kingdom:
OBERON, King of the fairies
TITANIA, Queen of the fairies
ROBIN GOODFELLOW, also called PUCK
PEASEBLOSSOM, COBWEB, MOTH (meaning mote or speck), and MUSTARDSEED, fairies
Other fairies

Athenian workingmen putting on the interlude (or play-within-the-play), with their roles during their performance:
PETER QUINCE, a carpenter (PROLOGUE)
NICK BOTTOM, a weaver (PYRAMUS)
FRANCIS FLUTE, a bellows-mender (THISBY)
TOM SNOUT, a tinker (WALL)
SNUG, a joiner (LION)
ROBIN STARVELING, a tailor (MOONSHINE)

[The names of the "mechanicals," or workers, echo symbols of their trades: Quince is named after quoins, or quines—wooden wedges used by carpenters. Bottom is named after the bobbin on which weavers wind yarn. Flute is named after the fluted exterior of the church organs whose bellows he mends. Snout is named after the snout, or spout, of the kettles he repairs as a tinker. Snug is named after the snug fit of the furniture he makes as a joiner. Starveling is thin and half-starved like a stereotypical tailor.]

Act One

SCENE 1. The Palace of Theseus.

[*Enter* THESEUS, HIPPOLYTA, PHILOSTRATE; *with others.*]

THESEUS: Now fair Hippolyta, our nuptial° hour	*wedding*
Draws on apace:° four happy days bring in	*quickly*
Another moon: but O, methinks° how slow	*it seems to me*
This old moon wanes! she lingers° my desires,	*obstructs*
Like to a stepdame° or a dowager,°	*stepmother/rich widow* 5
Long withering out a young man's revenue.°	*using up his inheritance (while both wither)*
HIPPOLYTA: Four days will quickly steep themselves in night:	
Four nights will quickly dream away the time:	
And then the moon, like to a silver bow	
New-bent in heaven, shall behold the night	10
Of our solemnities.°	*solemn ceremonies*
THESEUS: Go Philostrate,	
Stir up the Athenian youth to merriments,	
Awake the pert° and nimble spirit of mirth,	*lively*
Turn melancholy forth to funerals:	
The pale companion is not for our pomp.°	*not fit for our celebration* 15

[PHILOSTRATE *leaves.*]

Hippolyta, I wooed° thee with my sword,°	*courted/in battle*
And won thy love doing thee injuries:	
But I will wed thee in another key,°	*in different fashion*
With pomp, with triumph,° and with revelling.	*victory procession*

[*Enter* EGEUS *and his daughter* HERMIA, LYSANDER, *and* DEMETRIUS.]

EGEUS: Happy be Theseus, our renownèd duke.	20
THESEUS: Thanks good Egeus: what's the news with thee?	
EGEUS: Full of vexation come I, with complaint	
Against my child, my daughter Hermia.	
Stand forth Demetrius. My noble lord,	
This man hath my consent to marry her.	25
Stand forth Lysander. And my gracious duke,	
This man hath bewitched the bosom of my child.	
Thou, thou Lysander, thou hast given her rhymes,	
And interchanged love tokens with my child:	
Thou hast by moonlight at her window sung,	30

With feigning° voice, verses of feigning love,   *deceiving, yearning ("faining")*
And stolen the impression of her fantasy°   *connect her fancy*
With bracelets of thy hair, rings, gauds,° conceits,°   *baubles/love tokens*
Knacks,° trifles, nosegays,° sweetmeats—messengers   *knickknacks/flowers*
Of strong prevailment in unhardened youth.°   *that dazzle the* 35
                                                                                       inexperienced
With cunning hast thou filched my daughter's heart,
Turned her obedience, which is due to me,
To stubborn harshness. And my gracious duke,
Be it so she will not here before your grace
Consent to marry with Demetrius,   40
I beg the ancient privilege of Athens:
As she is mine, I may dispose of her:
Which shall be, either to this gentleman,
Or to her death, according to our law
Immediately provided° in that case.   *clearly spelled out* 45
THESEUS: What say you, Hermia? Be advised, fair maid.
  To you your father should be as a god:
  One that composed° your beauties: yea and one   *gave life to*
  To whom you are but as a form in wax
  By him imprinted, and within his power   50
  To leave the figure, or disfigure° it: *undo*
  Demetrius is a worthy gentleman.
HERMIA: So is Lysander.
THESEUS: In himself he is:
  But in this kind,° wanting° your father's voice,°   *but here/lacking/consent*
  The other must be held the worthier.   55
HERMIA: I would° my father looked but with my eyes.   *wish*
THESEUS: Rather your eyes must with his judgment look.
HERMIA: I do entreat your grace to pardon me.
  I know not by what power I am made bold,
  Nor how it may concern° my modesty,   *relate to* 60
  In such a presence,° here to plead my thoughts: *in the presence of such*
                                                                                       high authority
  But I beseech your grace that I may know
  The worst that may befall me in this case,
  If I refuse to wed Demetrius.
THESEUS: Either to die the death, or to abjure°   *give up* 65
  For ever the society of men.
  Therefore fair Hermia, question your desires,
  Know of° your youth, examine well your blood,°   *think about/passions*
  Whether, if you yield not to your father's choice,
  You can endure the livery° of a nun,   *garment* 70
  For aye° to be in shady cloister mewed,°   *forever/shut up*
  To live a barren sister all your life,
  Chanting faint hymns to the cold fruitless moon.°   *(symbol of chastity)*
  Thrice blessèd they that master so their blood,°   *control their passions so*
  To undergo such maiden pilgrimage: 75
  But earthlier happy° is the rose distilled,°   *happier in earthly fashion/made*
                                                                                       into perfume (and used for a
                                                                                       purpose)
  Than that which, withering on the virgin thorn,

Grows, lives, and dies, in single blessedness.
HERMIA: So will I grow, so live, so die my lord,
    Ere I will yield my virgin patent° up   *privilege of virginity* 80
    Unto his lordship, whose° unwishèd yoke   *to whose*
    My soul consents not to give sovereignty.
THESEUS: Take time to pause, and by the next moon—
    The sealing day° betwixt my love and me   *day of sealing*
    For everlasting bond of fellowship—   *the marriage bond*
                                         85
    Upon that day either prepare to die
    For disobedience to your father's will,
    Or else to wed Demetrius, as he would,°   *as he wishes*
    Or on Diana's° altar to protest   *(the chaste moon goddess)*
    For aye, austerity and single life.°   *to swear abstinence forever* 90
DEMETRIUS: Relent, sweet Hermia, and Lysander,
    yield
    Thy crazèd title° to my certain right.   *your flawed claim*
LYSANDER: You have her father's love, Demetrius:
    Let me have Hermia's: do you marry him.
EGEUS: Scornful Lysander, true, he hath my love: 95
    And what is mine, my love shall render him.
    And she is mine, and all my right of her
    I do estate unto° Demetrius.   *I make over to*
LYSANDER: I am, my lord, as well derived° as he,   *from as good a family*
    As well possessed:° my love is more than his: *with as much property* 100
    My fortunes every way as fairly ranked
    (If not with vantage)° as Demetrius':   *if not above*
    And, which is more than all these boasts can be,
    I am beloved of beauteous Hermia.
    Why should not I then prosecute° my right?   *pursue* 105
    Demetrius, I'll avouch it to his head,°   *charge it to his face*
    Made love to Nedar's daughter, Helena,
    And won her soul: and she, sweet lady, dotes,
    Devoutly dotes, dotes in idolatry,
    Upon this spotted and inconstant man.   110
THESEUS: I must confess that I have heard so much,
    And with Demetrius thought to have spoke thereof:° *meant to speak with him*
    But being over-full of self-affairs,°   *too busy with my own affairs*
    My mind did lose it. But Demetrius come,
    And come Egeus, you shall go with me: 115
    I have some private schooling° for you both.   *instruction*
    For you fair Hermia, look you arm° yourself,   *prepare*
    To fit your fancies° to your father's will;   *bend your desires*
    Or else the law of Athens yields you up
    (Which by no means we may extenuate)°   *which law I can in no way modify* 120
    To death or to a vow of single life.
    Come my Hippolyta, what cheer my love?
    Demetrius and Egeus, go along:
    I must employ you in some business

Against our nuptial,° and confer with you   *related to our wedding* 125
Of something nearly that concerns yourselves.
EGEUS: With duty and desire we follow you.

[*They leave.*]

[LYSANDER *and* HERMIA *walk.*]

LYSANDER: How now my love? Why is your cheek
   so pale?
   How chance the roses there do° fade so fast?   *how do the roses there happen to*
HERMIA: Belike° for want of rain, which I could well   *probably* 130
   Beteem them from° the tempest of my eyes.   *shower them with*
LYSANDER: Ay me, for aught° that I could ever read,   *to judge by anything*
   Could ever hear by tale or history,
   The course of true love never did run smooth;
   But either it was different in blood°—   *separated by social rank* 135
HERMIA: O cross! too high to be enthralled° to low.   *to be made a slave*
LYSANDER: Or else misgraffed in respect of years°—   *mismatched in age*
HERMIA: O spite! too old to be engaged to young.
LYSANDER: Or else it stood upon the choice of friends°—   *needed relatives approval*
HERMIA: O hell! to choose love by another's eyes.   140
LYSANDER: Or if there were a sympathy in choice,
   War, death, or sickness did lay siege to it;
   Making it momentary as a sound,
   Swift as a shadow, short as any dream,
   Brief as the lightning in the collied° night,   *coal-black* 145
   That, in a spleen, unfolds° both heaven and earth;   *in a flash, reveals*
   And ere° a man hath power to say "Behold,"   *before*
   The jaws of darkness do devour it up:
   So quick bright things come to confusion.°   *grief*
HERMIA: If then true lovers have been ever crossed,°   *always been thwarted* 150
   It stands as an edict in destiny:°   *as a law of fate*
   Then let us teach our trial patience,°   *learn to suffer patiently*
   Because it is a customary cross,
   As due to love as thoughts and dreams and sighs,
   Wishes and tears; poor Fancy's followers.°   *attendants on poor Love* 155
LYSANDER: A good persuasion:° therefore hear me,   *good advice*
      Hermia:
   I have a widow aunt, a dowager,
   Of great revenue,° and she hath no child: *with a large income*
   From Athens is her house remote seven leagues,°   *(20 to 30 miles distant)*
   And she respects me as her only son: 160
   There gentle Hermia, may I marry thee,
   And to that place the sharp Athenian law
   Cannot pursue us. If thou lov'st me then,
   Steal forth° thy father's house tomorrow night: *forth from*
   And in the wood, a league without° the town,   *outside* 165
   Where I did meet thee once with Helena
   To do observance to a morn of May,
   There will I stay for thee.°   *wait for you*

HERMIA: My good Lysander,
I swear to thee, by Cupid's strongest bow,
By his best arrow, with the golden head,°   *arrowhead implanting love*   170
By the simplicity of Venus' doves,
By that which knitteth souls and prospers loves,°   *makes love prosper*
And by that fire which burned the Carthage queen,°   *(Queen Dido, left by the*
When the false Trojan under sail was seen,   *Trojan prince Aeneas,*
                                                                      committed suicide by fire)
By all the vows that ever men have broke,   175
(In number more than ever women spoke)
In that same place thou hast appointed me,
Tomorrow truly will I meet with thee.
LYSANDER: Keep promise love: look, here comes Helena.

[*Enter* HELENA.]

HERMIA: God speed° fair Helena: whither away?   *God's blessing on you*   180
HELENA: Call you me fair? That fair again unsay.°   *take back "beautiful"*
Demetrius loves your fair: O happy fair!
Your eyes are lodestars,° and your tongue's sweet air°   *guiding stars/melody*
More tuneable° than lark to shepherd's ear,   *tuneful*
When wheat is green, when hawthorn buds appear.   185
Sickness is catching: O were favor so,°   *if looks were also*
Yours would I° catch, fair Hermia, ere° I go.   *would I like to/before*
My ear should catch your voice, my eye your eye,
My tongue should catch your tongue's sweet
        melody.
Were the world mine, Demetrius being bated,°   *with the exception of Demetrius*   190
The rest I'd give to be to you translated.°   *be changed into you*
O teach me how you look, and with what art
You sway the motion of Demetrius' heart.
HERMIA: I frown upon him; yet he loves me still.
HELENA: O that your frowns would teach my smiles such skill.   195
HERMIA: I give him curses; yet he gives me love.
HELENA: O that my prayers could such affection move.
HERMIA: The more I hate, the more he follows me.
HELENA: The more I love, the more he hateth me.
HERMIA: His folly, Helena, is no fault of mine.   200
HELENA: None but your beauty;° would that fault   *only your beauty's fault*
        were mine.
HERMIA: Take comfort: he no more shall see my face:
Lysander and myself will fly this place.
Before the time I did Lysander see,
Seemed Athens as a paradise to me: 205
O then, what graces in my love do dwell,°   *what magic is in my love*
That he hath turned a heaven unto a hell!
LYSANDER: Helen, to you our minds we will unfold:
Tomorrow night, when Phoebe° doth behold   *(the moon goddess Diana)*
Her silver visage in the watery glass,°   *mirror of the waters*   210
Decking with liquid pearl the bladed grass

(A time that lovers' flights doth still conceal)°   *always hides*
Through Athens gates have we devised to steal.°   *planned to sneak out*
HERMIA: And in the wood, where often you and I
Upon faint primrose beds were wont to° lie,   *used to* 215
Emptying our bosoms of their counsel sweet,°   *sweet talk*
There my Lysander and myself shall meet,
And thence from Athens turn away our eyes,
To seek new friends and stranger companies°   *the company of strangers*
Farewell, sweet playfellow: pray thou for us: 220
And good luck grant thee thy Demetrius.
Keep word Lysander: we must starve our sight
From lovers' food till morrow deep midnight.°   *till midnight tomorrow*
LYSANDER: I will my Hermia.

[HERMIA *leaves.*]

Helena adieu:
As you on him, Demetrius dote° on you.   *may be dote* 225

[LYSANDER *leaves.*]

HELENA: How happy some, over other some,° can be!   *compared with some others*
Through Athens I am thought as fair as she.
But what of that? Demetrius thinks not so:
He will not know what all but he do know.°   *does not want to know*
                                                       what all others know 230
And as he errs, doting on Hermia's eyes,
So I,° admiring of his qualities.   *so I do also err*
Things base and vile, holding no quantity,°   *quite out of shape*
Love can transpose to form and dignity.°   *change to beautiful shape*
Love looks not with the eyes, but with the mind:
And therefore is winged Cupid painted blind.°   *painted as a blind boy* 235
Nor hath Love's mind of any judgment taste:
Wings, and no eyes, figure unheedy haste.°   *symbolize heedless haste*
And therefore is Love said to be a child:
Because in choice he is so oft beguiled.
As waggish boys in game themselves forswear,   240
So the boy Love is perjured everywhere.
For ere° Demetrius looked on Hermia's eyne,°   *before/eyes*
He hailed down oaths that he was only mine.
And when this hail some heat from Hermia felt,
So he dissolved, and showers of oaths did melt.   245
I will go tell him of fair Hermia's flight:
Then to the wood will he tomorrow night
Pursue her: and for this intelligence,°   *information*
If I have thanks, it is a dear expense:°   *an effort gladly invested*
But herein mean I to enrich my pain,   250
To have his sight thither and back again.°   *the sight of him first removed to*
                                                   there but then back

[She *leaves.*]

SCENE 2. QUINCE's house.

[*Enter* QUINCE *the Carpenter; and* SNUG *the Joiner; and* BOTTOM *the Weaver; and* FLUTE *the Bellows- mender; and* SNOUT *the Tinker; and* STARVELING *the Tailor.*]

QUINCE: Is all our company here?

BOTTOM: You were the best to call them generally,° man by man, according to the scrip.°

QUINCE: Here is the scroll of every man's name which is thought fit, through all Athens, to play in our in- terlude° before the duke and the duchess, on his weddingday at night.

BOTTOM: First good Peter Quince, say what the play treats on, then read the names of the actors: and so grow to a point.

QUINCE: Marry,° our play is "The most lamentable comedy,° and most cruel death of Pyramus and Thisby."

BOTTOM: A very good piece of work I assure you, and a merry. Now good Peter Quince, call forth your actors by the scroll. Masters, spread yourselves.

QUINCE: Answer as I call you. Nick Bottom the weaver?

BOTTOM: Ready: name what part I am for, and proceed.

QUINCE: You, Nick Bottom, are set down for Pyramus.

BOTTOM: What is Pyramus? A lover, or a tyrant?

QUINCE: A lover that kills himself, most gallant, for love.

BOTTOM: That will ask some tears in the true per- forming of it. If I do it, let the audience look to their eyes: I will move storms: I will condole° in some measure. To the rest—yet my chief humor° is for a tyrant. I could play Ercles° rarely, or a part to tear a cat in, to make all split.

> The raging rocks
> And shivering shocks,
> Shall break the locks
>   Of prison gates,
> And Phibbus'° car
> Shall shine from far,
> And make and mar
>   The foolish Fates.

This was lofty. Now name the rest of the players. This is Ercles' vein, a tyrant's vein: a lover is more condoling.

QUINCE: Francis Flute, the bellows-mender?

FLUTE: Here Peter Quince.

QUINCE: Flute, you must take Thisby on you,

Marginal glosses:
- *name them collectively (he means individually)* (line 2)
- *list* (scrip)
- *short dramatic entertainment* (interlude, line 5)
- *truly* (Marry)
- *(he means "tragedy")* (comedy)
- *lament* (condole, line 25)
- *inclination* (humor)
- *Hercules* (Ercles)
- *(he means "Phoebus")* (Phibbus', line 34)

Line numbers: 5, 10, 15, 20, 25, 30, 35, 40

FLUTE: What is Thisby? A wandering knight?

QUINCE: It is the lady that Pyramus must love. 45

FLUTE: Nay faith, let not me play a woman: I have a beard coming.

QUINCE: That's all one:° you shall play it in a mask, and you may speak as small as you will.   *that doesn't matter*

BOTTOM: And° I may hide my face, let me play Thisby too: I'll speak in a monstrous little voice; "Thisne, Thisne," "Ah Pyramus, my lover dear, thy Thisby dear, and lady dear."   *if* 50

QUINCE: No, no, you must play Pyramus; and Flute, you Thisby.   55

BOTTOM: Well, proceed.

QUINCE: Robin Starveling, the tailor?

STARVELING: Here Peter Quince.

QUINCE: Robin Starveling, you must play Thisby's mother. Tom Snout, the tinker?   60

SNOUT: Here Peter Quince.

QUINCE: You, Pyramus' father; myself, Thisby's father; Snug the joiner, you the lion's part: and I hope here is a play fitted.°   *well joined together (as if by a carpenter)* 65

SNUG: Have you the lion's part written? Pray you, if it be, give it me, for I am slow of study.°   *slow to memorize*

QUINCE: You may do it extempore,° for it is nothing but roaring.   *ad lib*

BOTTOM: Let me play the lion too. I will roar, that I will do any man's heart good to hear me. I will roar, that I will make the duke say "Let him roar again: let him roar again."   70

QUINCE: And you should° do it too terribly, you would fright the duchess and the ladies, that they would shriek, and that were enough to hang us all.°   *if you would* 75   *to have us sentenced to hang*

ALL: That would hang us, every mother's son.

BOTTOM: I grant you, friends, if you should fright the ladies out of their wits, they would have no more discretion but to hang us, but I will aggravate my voice° so, that I will roar you as gently as any sucking dove: I will roar you and 'twere° any nightingale.   80   *(he means "lighten my voice")*   *as if it were*

QUINCE: You can play no part but Pyramus, for Pyramus is a sweet-faced man; a proper man as one shall see in a summer's day; a most lovely gentle-man-like man: therefore you must needs play Pyramus.   85

BOTTOM: Well, I will undertake it. What beard were I best to play it in?   90

QUINCE: Why, what you will.

BOTTOM: I will discharge it in either your straw-color
   beard, your orange-tawny beard, your purple-in
   grain beard, or your French-crown°-color beard,   *(French gold coin)*
   your perfect yellow.   95
QUINCE: Some of your French crowns have no hair at
   all,° and then you will play barefaced. But, mas-   *(heads bald from syphilis,*
   ters, here are your parts, and I am to entreat you,   *the "French" disease)*
   request you, and desire you to con° them by to-   *learn*
   morrow night; and meet me in the palace wood, a   100
   mile without° the town, by moonlight; there will   *outside*
   we rehearse, for if we meet in the city, we shall be
   dogged with company, and our devices° known.   *plans*
   In the meantime, I will draw a bill of properties,
   such as our play wants.° I pray you fail me not.   *props needed for our play* 105
BOTTOM: We will and there we may rehearse most ob-
   scenely° and courageously. Take pain, be perfect: *(he means "seemly")*
   adieu.
QUINCE: At the duke's oak we meet.
BOTTOM: Enough: hold, or cut bow-strings.°   *hold tight or cut loose* 110

                [*They leave.*]

Act Two

SCENE 1. A wood near Athens.

   [*Enter a* FAIRY *at one door, and* ROBIN GOODFELLOW *(*PUCK*) at another.*]

PUCK: How now spirit, whither° wander you?   *where to*
FAIRY: Over hill, over dale,°   *valley*
           Thorough° bush, thorough brier,   *through*
        Over park, over pale,°   *enclosure*
           Thorough flood, thorough fire,   5
   I do wander everywhere,
   Swifter than the moon's sphere;
   And I serve the Fairy Queen,
   To dew her orbs upon the green.°   *rings of higher or darker grass*
   The cowslips tall her pensioners° be,   *(royal) bodyguards* 10
   In their gold coats, spots you see:
   Those be rubies, fairy favors;°   *gifts*
   In those freckles live their savors.°   *perfumes*
I must go seek some dewdrops here,
And hang a pearl in every cowslips°' ear.   *primrose* 15
Farewell thou lob° of spirits; I'll be gone.   *you lout*
Our queen and all her elves come here anon.°   *shortly*
PUCK: The king doth keep his revels here tonight.
   Take heed the queen come not within his sight.
   For Oberon is passing fell and wrath,°   *most fierce and angry* 20

Because that she, as her attendant, hath
A lovely boy, stolen from an Indian king.
She never had so sweet a changeling.°   *child stolen by fairies*
And jealous Oberon would° have the child   *wants to*
Knight of his train, to trace° the forests wild.   *roam through* 25
But she, perforce,° withholds the lovèd boy,   *determined*
Crowns him with flowers, and makes him all her joy.
And now, they never meet in grove or green,
By fountain clear, or spangled starlight sheen,
But they do square, that° all their elves for fear   *do quarrel, so that* 30
Creep into acorn cups and hide them° there.   *themselves*
FAIRY: Either I mistake your shape and making quite,
    Or else you are that shrewd and knavish sprite°   *mischievous spirit*
    Called Robin Goodfellow. Are not you he
    That frights the maidens of the villagery?   35
    Skim° milk, and sometimes labor in the quern,°   *you skim/grain grinder*
    And bootless make the breathless housewife
        churn,°   *churn the milk without success*
    And sometime make the drink to bear no barm,°   *no foam (leaving it flat)*
    Mislead night wanderers, laughing at their harm?
    Those that Hobgoblin call you, and sweet Puck,   40
    You do their work, and they shall have good luck.
    Are not you he?
PUCK: Thou speakest aright;
    I am that merry wanderer of the night.
    I jest to Oberon, and make him smile,
    When I a fat and bean-fed horse beguile,   45
    Neighing in likeness of a filly foal;
    And sometime lurk I in a gossip's° bowl,   *old woman's*
    In very likeness of a roasted crab,°   *crabapple*
    And when she drinks, against her lips I bob,
    And on her withered dewlap° pour the ale.   *folds of skin* 50
    The wisest aunt,° telling the saddest tale,   *old woman*
    Sometime for three-foot stool mistaketh me;
    Then slip I from her bum, down topples she,
    And "tailor" cries,° and falls into a cough;   *cries "hold thief?"*
    And then the whole quire° hold their hips and laugh   *company* 55
    And waxen in their mirth,° and sneeze, and swear   *get more and more boisterous*
    A merrier hour was never wasted° there.   *spent*
    But room,° fairy: here comes Oberon.   *make room*
FAIRY: And here, my mistress. Would that he were gone.

[*Enter* OBERON, *the King of fairies, at one door with his train of fairies; and the Queen,* TITANIA, *at another, with hers.*]

OBERON: Ill met° by moonlight, proud Titania.   *an unfortunate encounter* 60
TITANIA: What, jealous Oberon? Fairy, skip hence.
    I have forsworn his bed and company.
OBERON: Tarry, rash wanton.° Am not I thy lord?   *wait, loose mischief-making woman*

TITANIA: Then I must be thy lady, but I know
   When thou has stolen away from fairyland,   65
   And in the shape of Corin° sat all day,   *(a shepherd in love)*
   Playing on pipes of corn,° and versing° love   *simple flutes/making verses of*
   To amorous Phillida. Why are thou here
   Come from the farthest steep of India?
   But that, forsooth, the bouncing Amazon,   70
   Your buskined° mistress and your warrior love,°   *booted/warlike lover*
   To Theseus must be wedded; and you come,
   To give their bed joy and prosperity.
OBERON: How canst thou thus, for shame, Titania,
   Glance at my credit° with Hippolyta,   *hint at my record*   75
   Knowing I know thy love to Theseus?
   Didst thou not lead him through the glimmering night,
   From Perigenia, whom he ravishèd?
   And make him with fair Aegles break his faith,
   With Ariadne, and Antiopa?°   *(all four women are former*   80
                                                   loves of Theseus)
TITANIA: These are the forgeries of jealousy:
   And never, since the middle summer's spring,
   Met we on hill, in dale, forest, or mead°   *meadow*
   By pavèd° fountain, or by rushy brook,   *pebble-strewn*
   Or in the beachèd margent° of the sea,   *beach-lined border*   85
   To dance our ringlets° to the whistling wind,   *circle dances*
   But with thy brawls thou hast disturbed our sport.
   Therefore the winds, piping° to us in vain,   *playing music*
   As in revenge, have sucked up from the sea
   Contagious fogs, which falling in the land,   90
   Hath every pelting° river made so proud,   *petty*
   That they have overborne their continents.°   *risen over their banks*
   The ox hath therefore stretched his yoke in vain,
   The plowman lost his sweat, and the green corn
   Hath rotted ere his youth° attained a beard.   *before its young stalks*   95
   The fold° stands empty in the drownèd field,   *enclosure for sheep or cattle*
   And crows are fatted with the murrion flock.°   *fattened with carrion*
   The nine men's morris° is filled up with mud,   *area cleared for games*
   And the quaint mazes in the wanton green,°   *winding paths in the rich grass*
   For lack of tread, are undistinguishable.   100
   The human mortals want their winter° here;   *miss a true winter*
   No night is now with hymn or carol blest.
   Therefore the moon, the governess of floods,°   *(which governs ebb and tide)*
   Pale in her anger, washes all the air,°   *fills the air with moisture*
   That rheumatic° diseases do abound.   *arthritic*   105
   And thorough this distemperature,° we see   *because of this disturbance*
   The seasons alter, hoary-headed frosts
   Fall in the fresh lap of the crimson rose,
   And on old Hiems' thin and icy crown,°   *on Winter's almost hairless head*
   An odorous chaplet° of sweet summer buds   *sweet-smelling wreath*   110
   Is, as in mockery, set. The spring, the summer,

The childing° autumn, angry winter change   *fruitful*
Their wonted liveries,° and the mazèd° world,   *usual appearance/amazed*
By their increase, now knows not which is which;
And this same progeny of evils° comes   *evil offspring*   115
From our debate, from our dissension:
We are their parents and original.°   *root cause*
OBERON: Do you amend it° then: it lies in you   *change it all for the better*
   Why should Titania cross her Oberon?
   I do but beg a little changeling boy,   120
   To be my henchman.°   *attendant*
TITANIA: Set your heart at rest.
   The fairy land buys not° the child of me.   *all fairyland could not buy*
   His mother was a votaress of my order,°   *a follower of my cult*
   And in the spicèd Indian air,° by night,   *(India was famous for spices)*
   Full often hath she gossiped by my side,   125
   And sat with me on Neptune's yellow sands,
   Marking the embarkèd traders° on the flood—   *watching the merchant ships*
   When we have laughed to see the sails conceive
   And grow big-bellied with° the wanton wind,   *as if pregnant with*
   Which she, with pretty and with swimming gait,°   *pretending to float*   130
   Following (her womb then rich with my young squire)
   Would imitate, and sail upon the land,
   To fetch me trifles, and return again,
   As from a voyage, rich with merchandise.
   But she, being mortal, of that boy did die,°   *died in childbirth*   135
   And for her sake, do I rear up her boy,
   And for her sake, I will not part with him.
OBERON: How long within this wood intend you stay?
TITANIA: Perchance° till after Theseus' wedding day.   *perhaps*
   If you will patiently dance in our round,°   *circle dance*   140
   And see our moonlight revels, go with us.
   If not, shun me, and I will spare° your haunts.   *stay away from*
OBERON: Give me that boy, and I will go with thee.
TITANIA: Not for thy fairy kingdom. Fairies away
   We shall chide° downright, if I longer stay.   *argue*   145

                [TITANIA *and her attendants leave*.]

OBERON: Well, go thy way. Thou shalt not from° this grove,   *not leave*
   Till I torment thee for this injury.
   My gentle Puck, come hither: thou rememberest,
   Since once I sat upon a promontory,°   *cliff*
   And heard a mermaid, on a dolphin's back,   150
   Uttering such dulcet° and harmonious breath,   *sweet*
   That the rude sea grew civil° at her song,   *tame*
   And certain stars shot madly from their spheres,
   To hear the sea maid's music.
PUCK: I remember.
OBERON: That very time, I saw (but thou couldst not)   *chaste*   155
   Flying between the cold° moon and the earth,

Cupid, all armed. A certain aim he took
At a fair Vestal° thronèd by the west,   *virgin priestess (Queen*
                                                                                                    Elizabeth?)
And loosed his love-shaft smartly from his bow,
As° it should pierce a hundred thousand hearts,   *as if* 160
But I might see young Cupid's fiery shaft
Quenched in the chaste beams of the watery moon,
And the imperial votaress passed on,
In maiden meditation, fancy-free.°   *free of love's power*
Yet marked I where the bolt of Cupid fell.   165
It fell upon a little western flower,
Before, milk-white, no purple with love's wound,
And maidens call it love-in-idleness.°   *(the pansy)*
Fetch me that flower; the herb I showed thee once.
The juice of it, on sleeping eyelids laid,   170
Will make or man or woman madly dote
Upon the next live creature that it sees.
Fetch me this herb, and be thou here again
Ere the leviathan° can swim a league.   *the whale, sea monster*
PUCK: I'll put a girdle round about° the earth,   *I will circle* 175
In forty minutes.

[He leaves.]

OBERON: Having once this juice,
I'll watch Titania when she is asleep,
And drop the liquor° of it in her eyes: *liquid*
The next thing then she waking looks upon,
(Be it on lion, bear, or wolf, or bull,   180
On meddling monkey, or on busy ape)
She shall pursue it, with the soul of love.
And ere I take this charm from off her sight
(As I can take it with another herb)
I'll make her render up her page° to me.   *attendant* 185
But who comes here? I am invisible,
And I will overhear their conference.

[*Enter* DEMETRIUS, HELENA *following him.*]

DEMETRIUS: I love thee not; therefore pursue me not.
Where is Lysander and fair Hermia?
The one I'll slay; the other slayeth me.   190
Thou told'st me they were stolen unto this wood,
And here am I, and wood° within this wood,   *gone mad*
Because I cannot meet my Hermia.
Hence, get thee gone, and follow me no more.
HELENA: You draw me, you hard-hearted adamant,°   *diamond-hard magnetic stone* 195
But yet you draw not iron, for my heart
Is true as steel. Leave you your power to draw,
And I shall have no power to follow you.
DEMETRIUS: Do I entice you? Do I speak you fair?°   *speak kindly to you*

Or rather do I not in plainest truth   200
Tell you I do not, nor I cannot love you?
HELENA: And even for that, do I love you the more:
    I am your spaniel; and Demetrius,
    The more you beat me, I will fawn on you.
    Use me but as your spaniel, spurn me, strike me,   205
    Neglect me, lose me; only give me leave,
    Unworthy as I am, to follow you.
    What worser place can I beg in your love
    (And yet a place of high respect° with me)   *regard*
    Than to be usèd as you use your dog?   210
DEMETRIUS: Tempt not too much the hatred of my spirit,
    For I am sick, when I do look on thee.
HELENA: And I am sick, when I look not on you.
DEMETRIUS: You do impeach° your modesty too much,   *endanger*
    To leave the city and commit yourself   215
    Into the hands of one that loves you not,
    To trust the opportunity of night
    And the ill counsel of a desert° place   *deserted*
    With the rich worth of your virginity.
HELENA: Your virtue is my privilege.° For that   *your special powers make it right* 220
    It is not night when I do see your face,
    Therefore I think I am not in the night.
    Nor doth this wood lack worlds of company,
    For you, in my respect,° are all the world.   *opinion*
    Then how can it be said I am alone,   225
    When all the world is here to look on me?
DEMETRIUS: I'll run from thee and hide me in the brakes,°   *thick shrubbery*
    And leave thee to the mercy of wild beasts.
HELENA: The wildest hath not such a heart as you.
    Run where you will; the story shall be changed:°   *reversed: the nymph chases* 230
    Apollo flies, and Daphne holds the chase;   *the god; the dove chases the*
    The dove pursues the griffin; the mild hind   *wild beast; the mild doe*
    Makes speed to catch the tiger. Bootless° speed,   *useless*
    When cowardice pursues, and valor flies.
DEMETRIUS: I will not stay thy questions.° Let me go: *wait for more argument* 235
    Or if thou follow me, do not believe
    but I shall° do thee mischief in the wood.   *that I won't*

[DEMETRIUS *leaves.*]

HELENA: Ay, in the temple, in the town, the field,
    You do me mischief. Fie, Demetrius!
    Your wrongs do set a scandal on my sex.°   *put women in a bad light* 240
    We cannot fight for love, as men may do;
    We should be wooed, and were not made to woo.
    I'll follow thee and make a heaven of hell,
    To die upon° the hand I love so well.   *die by*

[*She leaves.*]

OBERON: Fare thee well nymph. Ere he do leave this grove,   245
   Thou shalt fly° him, and he shall seek thy love.   *flee from*

[*Enter* PUCK.]

Hast thou the flower there? Welcome wanderer.
PUCK: Ay, there it is.
OBERON: I pray thee give it me.
   I know a bank where the wild thyme blows,
   Where oxlips and the nodding violet grows,   250
   Quite over-canopied with luscious woodbine,
   With sweet musk-roses, and with eglantine.°   *(names of wildflowers)*
   There sleeps Titania, sometime of the night,
   Lulled in these flowers, with dances and delight;
   And there the snake throws° her enamelled skin,   *casts off* 255
   Weed wide enough to wrap a fairy in.
   And with the juice of this, I'll streak her eyes,
   And make her full of hateful fantasies.
   Take thou some of it, and seek through this grove:
   A sweet Athenian lady is in love   260
   With a disdainful youth; anoint his eyes,
   But do it when the next thing he espies°   *sees*
   May be the lady. Thou shalt know the man
   By the Athenian garments he hath on.
   Effect it with some care, that he may prove   265
   More fond on her,° than she upon her love: *more smitten by her*
   And look thou meet me ere the first cock crow.
PUCK: Fear not my lord: your servant shall do so.

                     [*They leave.*]

SCENE 2. Another part of the wood.

[*Enter* TITANIA, *Queen of fairies, with her attendants.*]

TITANIA: Come, now a roundel° and a fairy song.   *circle dance*
   Then, for the third part of a minute, hence—
   Some to kill cankers° in the musk-rose buds,   *pests*
   Some war with reremice° for their leather wings,   *attack bats*
   To make my small elves coats, and some keep back   5
   The clamorous owl, that nightly hoots and wonders
   At our quaint° spirits. Sing me now asleep: *dainty*
   Then to your offices,° and let me rest.   *duties*

[*Fairies sing.*]

     You spotted snakes with double tongue,
       Thorny hedgehogs be not seen,   10
     Newts and blindworms° do no wrong,   *small snakelike creatures*
       Come not near our Fairy Queen.

       Philomele,° with melody,   *nightingale (in Greek myth)*
       Sing in our sweet lullaby,

Lulla, lulla, lullaby, lulla, lulla, lullaby.   15
   Never harm,
   Nor spell, nor charm,
  Come our lovely lady nigh.°   *may it not come near*
  So good night, with lullaby.

1. FAIRY: Weaving spiders come not here: 20
   Hence you long-legged spinners, hence:
  Beetles black approach not near:
   Worm nor snail do no offence.

   Philomele, with melody . . .

[*They repeat the refrain.* TITANIA *falls asleep.*]

2. FAIRY: Hence away! now all is well.   25
  One aloof stand sentinel.

[*Fairies leave.*]

[*Enter* OBERON *and applies moisture from the flower to*
TITANIA'*s eyelids.*]

OBERON: What thou seest, when thou dost wake,
  Do it for thy true love take:
  Love and languish for his sake.
  Be it ounce,° or cat,° or bear,   *lynx/wildcat* 30
  Pard,° or boar with bristled hair,   *leopard*
  In thy eye that shall appear,
  When thou wak'st, it is thy dear:
  Wake when some vile thing is near.

[*He leaves.*]

[*Enter* LYSANDER *and* HERMIA.]

LYSANDER: Fair love, you faint with wandering in the wood;   35
  And to speak truth I have forgot our way.
  We'll rest us Hermia, if you think it good,
  And tarry for the comfort° of the day.   *wait for the reassuring arrival*
HERMIA: Be't so Lysander: find you out a bed,
  For I upon this bank will rest my head.   40
LYSANDER: One turf shall serve as pillow for us both,
  One heart, one bed, two bosoms, and one troth.°   *one true love*
HERMIA: Nay good Lysander: for my sake, my dear,
  Lie further off yet; do not lie so near.
LYSANDER: O take the sense, sweet, of my   45
   innocence:°   *understand my innocent meaning*
  Love takes° the meaning in love's conference.   *lovers understand*
  I mean that my heart unto yours is knit,
  So that but one heart we can make of it:
  Two bosoms interchainèd with an oath,
  So then two bosoms and a single troth.   50

Then by your side no bed-room me deny,
For lying so, Hermia, I do not lie.
HERMIA: Lysander riddles very prettily.
Now much beshrew° my manners and my pride,   *may ill befall*
If Hermia meant to say Lysander lied.   55
But gentle friend, for love and courtesy,
Lie further off, in human modesty.
Such separation as may well be said
Becomes a virtuous bachelor and a maid,
So far be distant, and good night, sweet friend.   60
Thy love never alter° till thy sweet life end.   *may your love never change*
LYSANDER: Amen, amen, to that fair prayer say I,
And then end life,° when I end loyalty.   *may my life end*
Here is my bed: sleep give thee all his rest!
HERMIA: With half that wish, the wisher's eyes be pressed.   65

[*They sleep.*]

[*Enter* PUCK.]

PUCK: Through the forest have I gone,
                    But Athenian found I none,
                    One whose eyes I might approve°   *test*
                    This flower's force in stirring love.
                    Night and silence. Who is here?   70
                    Weeds° of Athens he doth wear: *garments*
                    This is he° (my master said)   *he who*
                    Despisèd the Athenian maid:
                    And here the maiden, sleeping sound,
                    On the dank and dirty ground.   75
                    Pretty soul, she durst not lie
                    Near this lack-love, this kill-courtesy.
                    Churl, upon the eyes I throw
                    All the power this charm doth owe:°   *possess*
                    When thou wak'st, let love forbid   80
                    Sleep his seat on thy eyelid.°   *keep sleep from your lids*
                    So awake when I am gone,
                    For I must now to Oberon.

[*He leaves.*]

[*Enter* DEMETRIUS *and* HELENA *running.*]

HELENA: Stay, thou kill me, sweet Demetrius.
DEMETRIUS: I charge thee: hence!° And do not haunt me thus.   *away from here* 85
HELENA: O, wilt thou darkling° leave me? Do not so.   *in the dark*
DEMETRIUS: Stay, on thy peril! I alone will go.

[DEMETRIUS *leaves.*]

HELENA: O, I am out of breath in this fond chase:°   *foolish love chase*
The more my prayer, the lesser is my grace.°   *the less mercy is shown*

Happy is Hermia, wheresoever she lies: 90
For she hath blessèd and attractive eyes.
How came her eyes so bright? Not with salt tears:
If so,° my eyes are oftener washed than hers.   *if that were the cause*
No, no, I am as ugly as a bear,
For beasts that meet me run away for fear.   95
Therefore no marvel,° though Demetrius   *it's no surprise*
Do as a monster,° fly my presence thus.   *as from a monster*
What wicked and dissembling glass° of mine,   *mirror (looking glass)*
Made me compare with Hermia's sphery eyne!°   *starry eyes (set in heavenly spheres)*
But who is here? Lysander, on the ground?   100
Dead, or asleep? I see no blood, no wound.
Lysander, if you live, good sir, awake.
LYSANDER [*wakes*]: And run through fire, I will for thy
        sweet sake.
    Transparent° Helena, nature shows art°   *radiant/magic powers*
    That through thy bosom makes me see thy heart.   105
    Where is Demetrius? O how fit a word
    Is that vile name to perish on my sword!
HELENA: Do not say so, Lysander, say not so.
    What though he love your Hermia? Lord, what though?
    Yet Hermia still loves you; then be content.   110
LYSANDER: Content with Hermia? No! I do repent
    The tedious minutes I with her have spent.
    Not Hermia, but Helena I love.
    Who will not change a raven for a dove?
    The will of man is by his reason swayed,   115
    And reason says you are the worthier maid.
    Things growing are not ripe until their season,
    So I, being young, till now ripe not to
        reason.°   *did not reach mature understanding*
    And touching now the point of human skill,°   *the height of human know-how*
    Reason becomes the marshal to my will,   120
    And leads me to your eyes; where I o'erlook°   *gaze upon*
    Love's stories, written in love's richest book.
HELENA: Wherefore was I to this keen mockery born?
    When at your hands did I deserve this scorn?
    Is't not enough, it's not enough, young man,   125
    That I did never, no, nor never can,
    Deserve a sweet look from Demetrius' eye,
    But you must flout my insufficiency?°   *mock my lack of success*
    Good troth,° you do me wrong; good sooth, you do,   *in truth*
    In such disdainful manner me to woo.   130
    But fare you well. Perforce I must° confess,   *I am forced to*
    I thought you lord of more true gentleness.°   *of a more noble spirit*
    O, that a lady, of° one man refused,   *by*
    Should of another, therefore be abused!

                    [*She leaves.*]

LYSANDER: She sees not Hermia. Hermia, sleep thou there,   135
    And never mayst thou come Lysander near.
    For, as a surfeit° of the sweetest things   *excessive eating*
    The deepest loathing to the stomach brings,
    Or as the heresies that men do leave
    Are hated most of° those they did deceive,   *by* 140
    So thou, my surfeit and my heresy,
    Of all be hated but the most, of me;
    And all my powers, address° your love and might   *apply*
    To honor Helen, and to be her knight.

                            [*He leaves.*]

HERMIA [*wakes*]: Help me, Lysander, help me! Do thy best   145
    To pluck this crawling serpent from my breast.
    Ay me, for pity! What a dream was here?
    Lysander, look how I do quake with fear.
    Methought a serpent ate my heart away,
    And you sat smiling at his cruel prey.°   *its cruel preying* 150
    Lysander! What, removed?° Lysander, lord!   *gone away*
    What, out of hearing, gone? No sound, no word?
    Alack, where are you? Speak, and if you hear!
    Speak, of all loves. I swoon almost with fear.
    No? Then I well perceive you are not nigh:°   *not here* 155
    Either death, or you, I'll find immediately.

                            [*She leaves.*]

Act Three

SCENE 1. The wood.

    [*Enter the* CLOWNS: QUINCE, SNUG, BOTTOM, FLUTE,
    SNOUT *and* STARVELING.]

BOTTOM: Are we all met?
QUINCE: Pat, pat;° and here's a marvellous convenient   *right on time*
    place for our rehearsal. This green plot shall be
    our stage, this hawthorn brake° our tiring-house,°   *thicket/dressing room*
    and we will do it in action, as we will do it before   5
    the duke.
BOTTOM: Peter Quince?
QUINCE: What sayest thou, bully Bottom?°   *my good Bottom*
BOTTOM: There are things in this Comedy of Pyramus
    and Thisby that will never please. First, Pyramus   10
    must draw a sword to kill himself; which the ladies
    cannot abide. How answer you that?
SNOUT: By'r lakin,° a parlous° fear.   *by our lady/terrible*
STARVELING: I believe we must leave the killing out,
    when all is done.   15

BOTTOM: Not a whit:° I have a device° to make all   *not at all/plan*
well. Write me a prologue, and let the prologue
seem to say, we will do no harm with our swords,
and that Pyramus is not killed indeed; and for the
more better assurance, tell them that I Pyramus am   20
not Pyramus, but Bottom the weaver. This will put
them out of fear.

QUINCE: Well, we will have such a prologue, and it
shall be written in eight and six.°   *in the old ballad meter (alternating*

BOTTOM: No, make it two more: let it be written in   *8 and 6 syllables)*   25
eight and eight.

SNOUT: Will not the ladies be afraid of the lion?

STARVELING: I fear it, I promise you.

BOTTOM: Masters, you ought to consider with yourselves, to bring in (God shield us) a lion among
ladies, is a most dreadful thing. For there is not a   30
more fearful wild-fowl than your lion living; and
we ought to look to't.

SNOUT: Therefore another prologue must tell he is not
a lion.   35

BOTTOM: Nay, you must name his name, and half his
face must be seen through the lion's neck, and he
himself must speak through, saying thus, or to the
same defect:° "Ladies," or "Fair ladies—I would   *(he means "effect")*
wish you," or "I would request you," or "I would   40
entreat you, not to fear, not to tremble: my life for
yours. If you think I come hither as a lion, it were
pity of my life.° No, I am no such thing: I am a   *I put my life at risk*
man as other men are." And there indeed let him
name his name, and tell them plainly he is Snug   45
the joiner.

QUINCE: Well, it shall be so, but there is two hard
things: that is, to bring the moonlight into a chamber; for, you know, Pyramus and Thisby meet by
moonlight.   50

SNOUT: Doth the moon shine that night we play our
play?

BOTTOM: A calendar, a calendar! Look in the almanac:
find out moonshine, find out moonshine.

QUINCE: Yes, it doth shine that night.   55

BOTTOM: Why, then may you leave a casement° of the   *hinged window frame*
great chamber window, where we play, open; and
the moon may shine in at the casement.

QUINCE: Ay, or else one must come in with a bush of
thorns and a lantern,° and say he comes to disfig-   *(symbols of man in the*   60
ure,° or to present, the person of Moonshine.   *moon)/(he means*
Then, there is another thing; we must have a wall   *"figure," "act out")*
in the great chamber; for Pyramus and Thisby, says
the story, did talk through the chink of a wall.

SNOUT: You can never bring in a wall. What say you,   65
    Bottom?
BOTTOM: Some man or other must present Wall: and
    let him have some plaster, or some loam, or some
    rough-cast° about him, to signify "Wall"; and let   *gravel plaster*
    him hold his fingers thus, and through that cranny   70
    shall Pyramus and Thisby whisper.
QUINCE: If that may be, then all is well. Come, sit
    down every mother's son, and rehearse your parts.
    Pyramus, you begin. When you have spoken your
    speech, enter into that brake, and so every one ac-   75
    cording to his cue.

    [*Enter* PUCK.]

PUCK: What hempen homespuns° have we swaggering   *coarsely clad bumpkins*
    here,
    So near the cradle° of the Fairy Queen?   *(where she is sleeping)*
    What, a play toward?° I'll be an auditor,°   *about to start/listener*
    An actor too perhaps, if I see cause.   80
QUINCE: Speak Pyramus. Thisby stand forth.
PYRAMUS: Thisby, the flowers of odious savors sweet—
QUINCE: "Odorous, odorous."
PYRAMUS: —odors savors sweet,
        So hath thy breath, my dearest Thisby dear.   85
    But hark, a voice: stay thou but here awhile,
        And by and by I will to thee appear.

          [PYRAMUS *leaves.*]

PUCK: A stranger Pyramus than ever played here.

          [*He leaves.*]

THISBY: Must I speak now?
QUINCE: Ay, marry,° must you. For you must   *yes, indeed*   90
    understand he goes but to see a noise that he
    heard, and is to come again.
THISBY: Most radiant Pyramus, most lily-white of hue,
        Of color like the red rose, on triumphant brier,°   *rose bush*
    Most brisky juvenal,° and eke° most lovely Jew,   *lively juvenile/also*   95
        As true as truest horse, that yet would
            never tire,
    I'll meet thee Pyramus, at Ninny's° tomb.   *(he means Ninus of Nineveh)*
QUINCE: "Ninus' tomb," man: why, you must not
    speak that yet. That you answer to Pyramus. You   100
    speak all your part at once, cues and all.
    Pyramus, enter; your cue is past: it is "never tire."
THISBY: O—As true as truest horse, that yet would never tire.

    [*Enter* BOTTOM *with his head changed to an ass's head,*
    followed by PUCK.]

PYRAMUS: If I were fair, Thisby,° I were only thine. *(his script reads "If I were,*
QUINCE: O monstrous! O strange! We are haunted. Pray,   *fair Thisby"?)* 105
 masters! Fly, masters! Help!

        [They all flee.]

PUCK: I'll follow you: I'll lead you about a round,°   *roundabout*
  Through bog, through bush, through bush, through brake,
   through brier.°   *through thicket and shrub*
 Sometime a horse I'll be, sometime a hound,   110
  A hog, a headless bear, sometime a fire,
 And neigh, and bark, and grunt, and roar, and burn,
 Like horse, hound, hog, bear, fire, at every turn.

        [He leaves.]

BOTTOM: Why do they run away? This is a knavery of
 them to make me afraid.   115

[Enter SNOUT.]

SNOUT: O Bottom, thou art changed. What do I see on thee?
BOTTOM: What do you see? You see an ass-head of
 your own, do you?

       [SNOUT runs away.]

[Enter QUINCE.]

QUINCE: Bless thee, Bottom, bless thee! Thou art translated.° *bewitched*

      [He also runs away.]

BOTTOM: I see their knavery. This is to make an ass of   120
 me, to fright me if they could: but I will not stir
 from this place, do what they can. I will walk up
 and down here, and will sing that and will sing
 that they shall hear I am not afraid.

[Sings.]

    The woosel cock,° so black of hue,   *blackbird* 125
     With orange tawny bill,
    The throstle, with his note so true,
     The wren, with little quill.°   *little piping voice*
TITANIA [*awakening*]: What angel wakes me from my
 flowery bed?   130
BOTTOM [*sings*]: The finch, the sparrow, and the lark,
    The plain-song cuckoo° gray, *(who tells cuckolds of their*
    Whose note full many a man doth mark, *unfaithful wives)*
     And dares not answer nay.
 For indeed, who would set his wit to so foolish a bird?   135
 Who would give a bird the lie,° though he cry "cuckoo" *call it a liar*
 never so?
TITANIA: I pray thee, gentle mortal, sing again.
 Mine ear is much enamored of thy note:°   *music*

So is mine eye enthrallèd to° thy shape,   enslaved to 140
And thy fair virtue's force° perforce doth move me   the force of your
On the first view to say, to swear, I love thee.   beautiful personality
BOTTOM: Methinks° mistress, you should have little   I think
reason for that. And yet, to say the truth, reason
and love keep little company together nowadays.   145
The more the pity, that some honest neighbors will
not make them friends. Nay, I can gleek° upon   make satirical remarks
occasion.
TITANIA: Thou art as wise as thou art beautiful.
BOTTOM: Not so neither: but if I had wit enough to get   150
out of this wood, I have enough to serve mine
own turn.
TITANIA: Out of this wood do not desire to go—
Thou shalt remain here, whether thou wilt or no.
I am a spirit of no common rate:°   of no ordinary rank 155
The summer still doth tend upon my state,°   does my royal bidding
And I do love thee; therefore go with me.
I'll give thee fairies to attend on thee;
And they shall fetch thee jewels from the deep,°   ocean
And sing, while thou on pressèd flowers dost sleep: 160
And I will purge thy mortal grossness so,°   strip you of your heavy
That thou shalt like an airy spirit go.   human body
Peaseblossom, Cobweb, Moth, and Mustardseed!

[*Enter four* FAIRIES.]

PEASEBLOSSOM: Ready.
COBWEB: And I.
MOTH: And I.
MUSTARDSEED: And I.
ALL: Where shall we go?   165
TITANIA: Be kind and courteous to this gentleman,
Hop in his walks and gambol in his eyes,°   dance before him
Feed him with apricots and dewberries,
With purple grapes, green figs, and mulberries.
The honey bags steal from the bumblebees,   170
And for night tapers,° crop° their waxen thighs,   candles/clip
And light them at the fiery glowworm's eyes,
To have my love to bed and to arise;
And pluck the wings from painted butterflies,
To fan the moonbeams from his sleeping eyes.   175
Nod to him, elves, and do him courtesies.
PEASEBLOSSOM: Hail, mortal.
COBWEB: Hail.
MOTH: Hail.
MUSTARDSEED: Hail.   180
BOTTOM: I cry your worship's mercy,° heartily; I   I beg your honor's pardon
beseech your worship's name.

COBWEB: Cobweb.

BOTTOM: I shall desire you of more acquaintance,° *I shall use your services*
good Master Cobweb;° if I cut my finger, I shall *(cobwebs were used as* 185
make bold with you. Your name, honest gentleman? *natural bandaids)*

PEASEBLOSSOM: Peaseblossom.

BOTTOM: I pray you commend me to Mistress Squash,° *unripe pea pod*
your mother, and to Master Peascod,° your father. *ripe pea pod*
Good Master Peaseblossom, I shall desire you of 190
more acquaintance, too. Your name, I beseech
you, sir?

MUSTARDSEED: Mustardseed.

BOTTOM: Good Master Mustardseed, I know your pa-
tience well. That same cowardly giant-like ox beef° *(beef was eaten with mustard)* 195
hath devoured many a gentleman of your house. I
promise you, your kindred hath made my eyes
water ere now.° I desire you of more acquain- *(with pity or with the*
tance, good Master Mustardseed. *sharp flavor?)*

TITANIA: Come, wait upon him; lead him to my 200
    bower.° *enclosed leafy shelter*
  The moon methinks looks with a watery
    eye:
And when she weeps, weeps every little flower,
  Lamenting some enforced° chastity. *violated* 205
Tie up my lover's tongue, bring him silently.

                    [*They leave.*]

SCENE 2. Another part of the forest.

[*Enter* OBERON, *King of fairies, alone.*]

OBERON: I wonder if Titania be awaked;
  Then what it was that next came in her eye,
  Which she must dote on in extremity.° *love to distraction*

[*Enter* PUCK.]

  Here comes my messenger. How now, mad spirit?
  What night-rule° now about this haunted grove? *nighttime capers* 5

PUCK: My mistress with a monster is in love.
  Near to her close and consecrated bower,
  While she was in her dull and sleeping hour,
  A crew of patches, rude mechanicals,° *fools (who should wear the fool's*
  That work for bread upon Athenian stalls, *patched, motley garb), crude menials* 10
  Were met together to rehearse a play,
  Intended for great Theseus' nuptial day.
  The shallowest thickskin of that barren sort,° *ignorant crew*
  Who Pyramus presented° in their sport, *represented*
  Forsook° his scene and entered in a brake,° *left/thicket* 15
  When I did him at this advantage take,
  An ass's nole° I fixèd on his head. *noodle (head)*
  Anon° his Thisby must be answerèd, *soon*

And forth my mimic° comes. When they him spy,   *actor*
As wild geese that the creeping fowler eye,°   *spot the stealthy hunter*   20
Or russet-pated choughs,° many in sort,   *gray-headed jackdaws*
Rising and cawing at the gun's report,
Sever themselves and madly sweep the sky,
So at his sight away his fellows fly;
And at our stamp,° here over and over one falls;   *our stamping (stampeding them)*   25
He "murder" cries, and help from Athens calls.
Their sense thus weak, lost with their fears thus strong,
Made senseless things begin to do them wrong.
For briers and thorns at their apparel snatch:
Some sleeves, some hats, from yielders° all things catch.   *from those ready*   30
I led them on in this distracted fear,   *to yield up*
And left sweet Pyramus translated° there:
When in that moment (so it came to pass)   *transformed*
Titania waked, and straightway loved an ass.
OBERON: This falls out better than I could devise.   35
     But hast thou yet latched° the Athenian's eyes   *moistened*
     With the love juice, as I did bid thee do?
PUCK: I took him sleeping (that is finished too)
     And the Athenian woman by his side;
     That when he waked, of force° she must be eyed.   *necessarily*   40

[*Enter* DEMETRIUS *and* HERMIA.]

OBERON: Stand close: this is the same Athenian.
PUCK: This is the woman, but not this the man.
DEMETRIUS: O why rebuke you him that loves you so?
     Lay breath so bitter on your bitter foe.
HERMIA: Now I but chide; but I should use thee worse,   45
     For thou, I fear, hast given me cause to curse.
     If thou hast slain Lysander in his sleep,
     Being over shoes in blood, plunge in the deep,°   *to the full depth*
     And kill me too.
     The sun was not so true unto the day,   50
     As he to me. Would he have stolen away
     From sleeping Hermia? I'll believe as soon
     This whole° earth may be bored,° and that the moon   *solid/drilled through*
     May through the center creep, and so displease
     Her brother's noontide with the Antipodes.°   *the sun at noon for those on*   55
     It cannot be but thou hast murdered him.   *the other side of the earth*
     So should a murderer look; so dead, so grim.
DEMETRIUS: So should the murdered look, and so should I,
     Pierced through the heart with your stern cruelty.
     Yet you, the murderer, look as bright, as clear,   60
     As yonder Venus in her glimmering sphere.
HERMIA: What's this to my Lysander? Where is he?
     Ah good Demetrius, wilt thou give him me?
DEMETRIUS: I had rather give his carcass to my hounds.

HERMIA: Out dog, out cur! Thou driv'st me past the bounds   65
    Of maiden's patience. Hast thou slain him then?
    Henceforth be never numbered among men.
    O, once tell true! Tell true, even for my sake:
    Durst thou have looked° upon him, being awake?   *would you have dared to look*
    And hast thou killed him sleeping? O brave touch!   70
    Could not a worm,° an adder, do so much?   *serpent*
    An adder did it: for with doubler° tongue   *more forked (and false)*
    Than thine, thou serpent, never adder stung.
DEMETRIUS: You spend your passion on a misprised mood:°   *in mistaken anger*
    I am not guilty of Lysander's blood.   75
    Nor is he dead, for aught that I can tell.
HERMIA: I pray thee, tell me then that he is well.
DEMETRIUS: And if I could, what should I get therefore?°   *in return*
HERMIA: A privilege never to see me more.
    And from thy hated presence part I so: 80
    See me no more, whether he be dead or no.

                          [*She leaves.*]

DEMETRIUS: There is no following her in this fierce vein.
    Here therefore for a while I will remain.
    So sorrow's heaviness doth heavier grow
    For° debt that bankrupt° sleep doth sorrow owe: *because of the/delayed*   85
    Which now in some slight measure it will pay,
    If for his tender here I make some stay.°   *if I wait here for payment*

[*He lies down.*]

OBERON: What hast thou done? Thou hast mistaken quite,
    And laid the love-juice on some true-love's sight.
    Of thy misprison° must perforce ensue   *mistake*   90
    Some true love turned,° and not a false turned true.   *turned bad*
PUCK: Then fate overrules, that one man holding troth,°   *staying faithful*
    A million fail, confounding° oath on oath.   *betraying*
OBERON: About the wood, go swifter than the wind,
    And Helena of Athens look thou find.   95
    All fancy-sick° she is, and pale of cheer,°   *lovesick/face*
    With sighs of love that costs the fresh blood dear.°   *depletes young blood*
    By some illusion see thou bring her here:
    I'll charm his eyes against° she do appear.   *until*
PUCK: I go, I go, look how I go.   100
    Swifter than arrow from the Tartar's bow.

                          [*He leaves.*]

OBERON: Flower of this purple dye,
        Hit with Cupid's archery,
        Sink in apple of his eye:
        When his love he doth espy,°   *he sees*   105
        Let her shine as gloriously
        As the Venus of the sky.

When thou wak'st, if she be by,
Beg of her for remedy.

[*Enter* PUCK.]

PUCK: Captain of our fairy band,   110
          Helena is here at hand,
          And the youth, mistook by me,
          Pleading for a lover's fee.°   *reward*
          Shall we their fond° pageant see?   *foolish*
          Lord, what fools these mortals be!   115
OBERON: Stand aside. The noise they make
          Will cause Demetrius to awake.
PUCK: Then will two at once woo one:
          That must needs be sport alone.°   *great entertainment*
          And those things do best please me   120
          That befall preposterously.

[*Enter* LYSANDER *and* HELENA.]

LYSANDER: Why should you think that I should woo in scorn?°   *woo to mock you*
          Scorn and derision never come in tears.
      Look when I vow,° I weep; and vows so born,   *swear oaths of love*
          In their nativity all truth appears.°   *their tear-stained origin* 125
                                                   makes them genuine
          How can these things in me seem scorn to you,
      Bearing the badge of faith to prove them true?
HELENA: You do advance° your cunning more and   *show*
          more.
          When truth kills truth,° O devilish-holy fray! *(a new "true love" kills the old)*
      These vows are Hermia's. Will you give her o'er?°   *give her up* 130
          Weigh oath with oath, and you will nothing weigh.
      Your vows to her and me, put in two scales,
      Will even weigh; and both as light as tales.
LYSANDER: I had no judgment, when to her I swore.
HELENA: Nor none, in my mind, now you give her o'er.   135
LYSANDER: Demetrius loves her: and he loves not you.
DEMETRIUS [*awakes*]: O Helen, goddess, nymph, perfect, divine,
      To what, my love, shall I compare thine eyne!
      Crystal is muddy. O, how ripe in show,
      Thy lips, those kissing cherries, tempting grow!   140
      That pure congealèd white, high Taurus'° snow,   *(Near Eastern mountain)*
      Fanned with the eastern wind, turns to a crow,
      When thou hold'st up thy hand. O let me kiss
      This princess of pure white, this seal of bliss.
HELENA: O spite! O hell! I see you all are bent   145
      To set against me, for your merriment.
      If you were civil and knew courtesy,
      You would not do me thus much injury.
      Can you not hate me, as I know you do,
      But you must join in souls to mock me too?   150
      If you were men, as men you are in show,°   *appearance*

You would not use a gentle lady° so;   treat a well-born lady
  To vow, and swear, and superpraise my parts,
  When I am sure you hate me with your hearts.
  You both are rivals, and love Hermia;   155
  And now both rivals, to mock Helena.
  A trim° exploit, a manly enterprise,   fine
  To conjure tears up in a poor maid's eyes
  With your derision.° None of noble sort   mockery
  Would so offend a virgin, and extort°   wear down 160
  A poor soul's patience, all to make you sport.
LYSANDER: You are unkind, Demetrius: be not so.
  For you love Hermia; this you know I know.
  And here, with all good will, with all my heart,
  In Hermia's love I yield you up my part;   165
  And yours of Helena to me bequeath,
  Whom I do love, and will do to my death.
HELENA: Never did mockers waste more idle breath.
DEMETRIUS: Lysander, keep thy Hermia; I will none.°   none of her
  If ever I loved her, all that love is gone.   170
  My heart to her but as guestwise sojourned,°   stayed with her only as a guest
  And not to Helen is it home returned,
  There to remain.
LYSANDER: Helen, it is not so.
DEMETRIUS: Disparage not the faith thou dost not know,
  Lest to thy peril thou aby it dear.°   pay for it dearly 175
  Look where thy loves comes; yonder is thy dear.

  [*Enter* HERMIA.]

HERMIA: Dark night, that from the eye his function takes,°   makes the eye useless
  The ear more quick of apprehension makes.°   gives the ear sharper hearing
  Wherein it doth impair the seeing sense,
  It pays the hearing double recompense.   180
  Thou art not by mine eye, Lysander, found;
  Mine ear, I thank it, brought me to thy sound.
  But why unkindly didst thou leave me so?
LYSANDER: Why should he stay, whom love doth press° to go?   force
HERMIA: What love would press Lysander from my side?   185
LYSANDER: Lysander's love, what would not let him bide:
  Fair Helena, who more engilds the night
  Than all you fiery oes and eyes° of light.   o's and i's—orbs and eyes
  Why seek'st thou me? Could not this make thee know,
  The hate I bore thee made me leave thee so?   190
HERMIA: You speak not as you think; it cannot be.
HELENA: Lo, she is one of this confederacy!
  Now I perceive they have conjoined all three,
  To fashion this false sport in spite of me.
  Injurious° Hermia, most ungrateful maid,   insulting 195
  Have you conspired,° have you with these contrived   plotted
  To bait me with this foul derision?

Is all the counsel that we two have shared,
The sisters' vows, the hours that we have spent,
When we have chid° the hasty-footed time   *scolded* 200
For parting us; O, is all forgot?
All schooldays' friendship, childhood innocence?
We Hermia, like two artificial° gods,   *skilled in art*
Have with our needles created both one flower,
Both on one sampler, sitting on one cushion,   205
Both warbling of one song, both in one key;
As if our hands, our sides, voices, and minds
Had been incorporate. So we grew together,°   *made one body*
Like to a double cherry, seeming parted,
But yet an union in partition,   210
Two lovely berries molded on one stem:
So with two seeming bodies, but one heart,
Two of the first, like coats in heraldry,°   *a double coat of arms*
Due but to one, and crownèd with one crest.
And will you rent° our ancient love asunder,   *tear apart* 215
To join with men in scorning your poor friend?
It is not friendly, 'tis not maidenly.
Our sex, as well as I, may chide you for it;
Though I alone do feel the injury.
HERMIA: I am amazèd at your passionate words: 220
    I scorn you not. It seems that you scorn me.
HELENA: Have you not set Lysander, as in scorn,
    To follow me, and praise my eyes and face?
    And made your other love, Demetrius
    (Who even but now did spurn me with his foot)   225
    To call me goddess, nymph, divine, and rare,
    Precious, celestial? Wherefore speaks he this
    To her he hates? And wherefore doth Lysander
    Deny your love,° so rich within his soul,   *his love for you*
    And tender me (forsooth)° affection,   *in truth* 230
    But by your setting on, by your consent?
    What though I be not so in grace as you,
    So hung upon with love, so fortunate,
    But miserable most, to love unloved?
    This you should pity, rather than despise.   235
HERMIA: I understand not what you mean by this.
HELENA: Ay, do. Persèver,° counterfeit sad looks: *persevere*
    Make mouths upon° me when I turn my back: *make faces at*
    Wink each at other, hold the sweet jest up.
    This sport well carried, shall be chronicled.° *if well carried out, should* 240
    If you have any pity, grace, or manners,   *be written up*
    You would not make me such an argument.°   *such a target*
    But fare ye well. 'Tis partly my own fault,
    Which death or absence soon shall remedy.
LYSANDER: Stay, gentle Helena; hear my excuse,°   *defense* 245
    My love, my life, my soul, fair Helena.

HELENA: O excellent!

HERMIA: Sweet, do not scorn° her so.   *mock*

DEMETRIUS: If she cannot entreat,° I can compel.   *succeed by entreating*

LYSANDER: Thou canst compel no more than she entreat.

    Thy threats have no more strength than her weak prayers.   250

    Helen, I love thee, by my life I do:

    I swear by that which I will lose° for thee,   *by my life, which I will risk*

    To prove him false that says I love thee not.

DEMETRIUS: I say I love thee more than he can do.

LYSANDER: If thou say so, withdraw° and prove it too.   *draw your sword* 255

DEMETRIUS: Quick, come.

HERMIA: Lysander, whereto tends all this?

LYSANDER: Away, you Ethiope.°   *(he calls her names alluding to*
                                                           her dark hair)

DEMETRIUS: No, no, sir,

    Seem to break loose: take on as you would follow,°   *pretend you'll follow*
                                                                      me (to a duel)

    But yet come not. You are a tame man, go.

LYSANDER: Hang off, thou cat, thou burr! Vile thing, let loose,°   *let go* 260

    Or I will shake thee from me like a serpent.

HERMIA: Why are you grown so rude? What change is this,

    Sweet love?

LYSANDER: Thy love? Out, tawny Tartar, out!

    Out, loathèd medicine! O hated potion, hence!

HERMIA: Do you not jest?

HELENA: Yes, sooth;° and so do you.   *truly* 265

LYSANDER: Demetrius, I will keep my word with thee.

DEMETRIUS: I would I had your bond.° For I perceive   *wish I had it in writing*

    A weak bond holds you. I'll not trust your word.

LYSANDER: What? Should I hurt her, strike her, kill her dead?

    Although I hate her, I'll not harm her so.   270

HERMIA: What? Can you do me greater harm than hate?

    Hate me, wherefore? O me, what news, my love?

    Am not I Hermia? Are not you Lysander?

    I am as fair now, as I was erewhile.°   *a while ago*

    Since night,° you loved me; yet since night, you left me.   *when night fell* 275

    Why then, you left me—O, the gods forbid—

    In earnest, shall I say?

LYSANDER: Ay, by my life!

    And never did desire to see thee more.

    Therefore be out of hope, of question, of doubt:

    Be certain: nothing truer. 'Tis no jest   280

    That I do hate thee, and love Helena.

HERMIA: O me, you juggler, you canker blossom,°   *worm blighting the blossom*

    You thief of love! What, have you come by night,

    And stolen my love's heart from him?

HELENA: Fine, in faith.

    Have you no modesty, no maiden shame,   285

    No touch of bashfulness? What, will you tear

    Impatient answers from my gentle tongue?

    Fie, fie, you counterfeit, you puppet,° you.   *little doll*

HERMIA: Puppet? why so—ay, that way goes the game.
Now I perceive that she hath made compare   290
Between our statures, she hath urged her height,°   *pointed out how tall she is*
And with her personage, her tall personage,
Her height (forsooth) she hath prevailed with him.
And are you grown so high in his esteem,
Because I am so dwarfish and so low?   295
How low am I, thou painted maypole? Speak:
How low am I? I am not yet so low,
But that my nails can reach unto thine eyes.
HELENA: I pray you, though you mock me, gentlemen,
Let her not hurt me. I was never curst;°   *ill-tempered*   300
I have no gift at all in shrewishness;°   *bad temper*
I am a right maid° for my cowardice.   *true to the stereotype*
Let her not strike me. You perhaps may think,
Because she is something lower than myself,
That I can match her.
HERMIA: Lower? Hark again.   305
HELENA: Good Hermia, do not be so bitter with me,
I evermore did love you, Hermia,
Did ever keep your counsels,° never wronged you;   *always kept your secrets*
Save that in love unto Demetrius,
I told him of your stealth° unto this wood.   *secret trip*   310
He followed you; for love I followed him.
But he hath chid me hence, and threatened me
To strike me, spurn me, nay to kill me too;
And now, so° you will let me quiet go,   *if only*
To Athens will I bear my folly back,   315
And follow you no further. Let me go.
You see how simple and how fond° I am.   *silly*
HERMIA: Why, get you gone. Who is't that hinders you?
HELENA: A foolish heart, that I leave here behind.
HERMIA: What, with Lysander?
HELENA: With Demetrius.   320
LYSANDER: Be not afraid. She shall not harm thee, Helena.
DEMETRIUS: No, sir; she shall not, though you take her part.
HELENA: O when she's angry, she is keen and shrewd.°   *sharp-tongued and hostile*
She was a vixen when she went to school;
And though she be but little, she is fierce.   325
HERMIA: "Little" again? nothing but "low" and "little"?
Why will you suffer her to flout me thus?
Let me come to her.
LYSANDER: Get you gone, you dwarf;
You minimus,° of hindering knot-grass° made;   *tiniest thing/growth-stunting weed*
You bead, you acorn!
DEMETRIUS: You are too officious   330
In her behalf that scorns your services.
Let her alone. Speak not of Helena;
Take not her part. For if thou dost intend

Never so little show of love to her,
Thou shalt aby° it.   *pay for*

LYSANDER: Now she holds me not: 335
Now follow, if thou dar'st, to try° whose right,   *test in combat*
Of thine or mine, is most in Helena.

DEMETRIUS: Follow? Nay, I'll go with thee, cheek by jowl.

[LYSANDER *and* DEMETRIUS *leave.*]

HERMIA: You, mistress, all this coil is long of you.°   *this turmoil is because of you*
Nay, go not back.

HELENA: I will not trust you, I,   340
Nor longer stay in your curst company.
Your hands than mine are quicker for a fray;
My legs are longer though, to run away.

HERMIA: I am amazed,° and know not what to say.   *totally confused*

[*They both leave.*]

OBERON: This is thy negligence: still thou mistak'st,°   *you always blunder* 345
Or else commit'st thy knaveries wilfully.

PUCK: Believe me, king of shadows, I mistook.°   *made an honest mistake*
Did not you tell me I should know the man
By the Athenian garments he had on?
And so far blameless proves my enterprise   350
That I've anointed an Athenian's eyes:
And so far am I glad it so did sort,°   *worked out as such*
As this their jangling I esteem a sport.

OBERON: Thou seest these lovers seek a place to fight;
Hie,° therefore, Robin; overcast the night,   *make haste* 355
The starry welkin cover thou° anon   *cover the heavens*
With dropping fog as black as Acheron,°   *(a river bordering Hell)*
And lead these testy° rivals so astray   *angry*
As° one come not within another's way.   *that*
Like to Lysander sometime frame thy tongue;°   *talk like Lysander* 360
Then stir Demetrius up with bitter wrong;°   *insults*
And sometime rail thou like Demetrius—
And from each other look thou lead them thus;
Till over their brows death-counterfeiting sleep
With leaden legs and batty° wings doth creep.   *batlike* 365
Then crush this herb into Lysander's eye,
Whose liquor hath this virtuous property°   *whose liquid has the power*
To take from thence all error with his might,
And make his eyeballs roll with wonted° sight.   *usual*
When they next wake, all this derision°   *frivolity* 370
Shall seem a dream, and fruitless vision,
And back to Athens shall the lovers wend,°   *go*
With league whose date° till death shall never end.   *in a union whose appointed time*
Whiles I in this affair do thee employ,
I'll to my queen and beg° her Indian boy: *beg for* 375

And then I will her charmed° eye release   *bewitched*
From monster's view, and all things shall be peace.
PUCK: My fairy lord, this must be done with haste,
  For night's swift dragons cut the clouds full fast:
  And yonder shines Aurora's harbinger,°   *(the morning star, the* 380
  At whose approach, ghosts wandering here and there   *messenger of dawn)*
  Troop home to churchyards; damnèd spirits all,
  That in crossways and floods have burial,°   *(suicides buried outside*
  Already to their wormy beds are gone.   *churchyards)*
  For fear lest day should look their shames upon,   385
  They wilfully themselves exile from light,
  And must for aye consort° with black-browed night.   *must forever keep company*
OBERON: But we are spirits of another sort.
  I with the morning's love° have oft made sport,
  And like a forester, the groves may tread   *(the love of Aurora—or*
  Even till the eastern gate all fiery red,   *her legendary lover?)* 390
  Opening on Neptune,° with fair blessèd beams,   *(god of the ocean)*
  Turns into yellow gold his salt green streams.
  But notwithstanding, haste, make no delay:
  We may effect his business yet ere day.°   *before daybreak* 395

                          [*He leaves.*]

PUCK: Up and down, up and down,
               I will lead them up and down.
               I am feared in field and town.
               Goblin, lead them up and down.
  Here comes one.   400

[*Enter* LYSANDER.]

LYSANDER: Where art thou, proud Demetrius? Speak thou now.
PUCK: Here villain, drawn° and ready. Where art thou?   *with sword drawn*
LYSANDER: I will be with thee straight.
PUCK: Follow me then
  To plainer° ground.   *more level*

                          [LYSANDER *leaves.*]

[*Enter* DEMETRIUS.]

DEMETRIUS: Lysander, speak again.
  Thou runaway, thou coward, art thou fled?
SPEAK: in some bush? Where dost thou hide thy head?   405
PUCK: Thou coward, art thou bragging to the stars,
  Telling the bushes that thou look'st for wars,
  And wilt not come? Come, recreant,° come, thou child;   *faithless creature*
  I'll whip thee with a rod. He is defiled°   *dishonored* 410
  That draws a sword on thee.
DEMETRIUS: Yea, art thou there?
PUCK: Follow my voice: we'll try no manhood° here.   *will not test our manly courage*

[*They leave.*]

[*Enter* LYSANDER.]

LYSANDER: He goes before me and still dares me on:
When I come where he calls, then he is gone.
The villain is much lighter-heeled than I;   415
I followed fast, but faster he did fly,
That fallen am I in dark uneven way,
And here will rest me. [*lies down*] Come, thou gentle day,
For if but once thou show me thy grey light,
I'll find Demetrius and revenge this spite.   420

[*Sleeps.*]

[*Enter* PUCK, *taunting* DEMETRIUS *in the voice of* LYSANDER.]

PUCK: Ho, ho, ho! Coward, why com'st thou not?
DEMETRIUS: Abide° me, if thou dar'st, for well I wot°   *wait for/I know*
Thou run'st before me, shifting every place,
And dar'st not stand, nor look me in the face.
Where art thou now?
PUCK: Come hither; I am here.   425
DEMETRIUS: Nay then thou mock'st me. Thou shalt buy
     this dear,°   *pay for this dearly*
If ever I thy face by daylight see.
Now go thy way. Faintness constraineth me.
To measure out° my length on this cold bed.   *stretch out*
By day's approach look to be visited.   430

[*Lies down and sleeps.*]

[*Enter* HELENA.]

HELENA: O weary night, O long and tedious night,
          Abate° thy hours; shine comforts° from   *shorten/may comforting*
               the east,   *rays of light shine*
     That I may back to Athens by daylight,
          From these that my poor company detest:
     And sleep, that sometimes shuts up sorrow's eye,   435
     Steal me awhile from mine own company.

[*Sleeps.*]

PUCK: Yet but three? Come one more,
     Two of both kinds makes up four.
     Here she comes, curst° and sad.   *cross*
     Cupid is a knavish lad,   440
     Thus to make poor females mad.

[*Enter* HERMIA.]

HERMIA: Never so weary, never so in woe,
          Bedabbled with the dew, and torn with briers,
     I can no further crawl, no further go:

My legs can keep no pace with my desires.   445
Here will I rest me till the break of day.
Heavens shield Lysander, if they mean a fray.°   *intend to fight*

[*Lies down and sleeps.*]

PUCK: On the ground,
                       Sleep sound:
                       I'll apply   450
                       To your eye,
                       Gentle lover, remedy.

[*Squeezes the love-juice on* LYSANDER's *eyelids.*]

                       When thou wak'st,
                       Thou tak'st
                       True delight   455
                       In the sight
                       Of thy former lady's eye:
                       And the country proverb known,
                       That every man should take his own,
                       In your waking shall be shown.   460
                          Jack shall have Jill
                          Naught shall go ill;
             The man shall have his mare again, and all shall be well.

[*He leaves. The others remain sleeping on the stage through the next act.*]

Act Four

SCENE 1

[*Enter* TITANIA, *Queen of fairies, and* BOTTOM THE
CLOWN, *and fairies, and the King,* OBERON, *behind
them unseen.*]

TITANIA: Come sit thee down upon this flowery bed,
         While I thy amiable cheeks do coy,°   *caress your lovely cheeks*
     And stick musk-roses in thy sleek smooth head,
     And kiss thy fair large ears, my gentle joy.
BOTTOM: Where's Peaseblossom?   5
PEASEBLOSSOM: Ready.
BOTTOM: Scratch my head, Peaseblossom. Where's
     Monsieur Cobweb?
COBWEB: Ready.
BOTTOM: Monsieur Cobweb, good monsieur, get you   10
     your weapons in your hand, and kill me a red-
     hipped humblebee on the top of a thistle; and,
     good monsieur, bring me the honey bag. Do not
     fret° yourself too much in the action, monsieur;   *exert*
     and, good monsieur, have a care the honey bag   15

break not, I would be loath° to have you over- *I would hate*
flowen with a honey bag, signior. Where's Monsieur Mustardseed?

MUSTARDSEED: Ready.

BOTTOM: Give me your neaf,° Monsieur Mustardseed. *hand* 20
Pray you leave your curtsy,° good monsieur. *stop your ceremonious greeting*

MUSTARDSEED: What's your will?

BOTTOM: Nothing, good monsieur, but to help Cav-
alery° Cobweb to scratch. I must to the barber's *(he means "cavalier," knight)*
monsieur, for methinks I am marvellous hairy 25
about the face. And I am such a tender ass, if my
hair do but tickle me, I must scratch.

TITANIA: What, will thou hear some music, my sweet
love?

BOTTOM: I have a reasonable good ear in music. Let's 30
have the tongs and the bones.° *(peasant music made with clanging metal and bone clappers)*

TITANIA: Or say, sweet love, what thou desirest to eat.

BOTTOM: Truly, a peck of provender. I could munch
your good dry oats. Methinks I have a great desire
to a bottle° of hay. Good hay, sweet hay, hath no *bundle* 35
fellow.° *is unmatched (as good food)*

TITANIA: I have a venturous fairy that shall seek
The squirrel's hoard, and fetch thee new nuts.

BOTTOM: I had rather have a handful or two of dried
peas. But I pray you, let none of your people stir 40
me: I have an exposition° of sleep come upon me. *(he means "disposition")*

TITANIA: Sleep thou, and I will wind thee° in my arms. *hold you*
Fairies, be gone, and be all ways away.

[FAIRIES *leave.*]

So doth the woodbine the sweet honeysuckle
Gently entwist; the female ivy so 45
Enrings the barky fingers° of the elm. *like a woman, it embraces the bark-covered branches*
O how I love thee! how I dote on thee!

[*They sleep.*]

[*Enter* ROBIN GOODFELLOW (PUCK).]

OBERON [*advances*]: Welcome, good Robin. Seest thou this
sweet sight?
Her dotage° now I do begin to pity. *infatuation*
For meeting her of late behind the wood, 50
Seeking sweet favors° for this hateful fool, *flowery love tokens*
I did upbraid her and fall out° with her. *berate her and quarrel*
For she his hairy temples then had rounded
With coronet° of fresh and fragrant flowers. *crownlike garland*
And that same dew which sometime on the buds 55
Was wont to swell like round and orient pearls,° *precious pearls from the East*
Stood now within the pretty flowerets' eyes,
Like tears that did their own disgrace bewail.

When I had at my pleasure taunted her,
And she in mild terms begged my patience,   60
I then did ask of her her changeling child,
Which straight she gave me, and her fairy sent
To bear him to my bower in fairy land.
And now I have the boy, I will undo
This hateful imperfection° of her eyes.   *malfunction*   65
And gentle Puck, take this transformèd scalp
From off the head of this Athenian swain;°   *rustic lover*
That he, awaking when the other do,
May all to Athens back again repair,°   *go back*
And think no more of this night's accidents,°   *happenings*   70
But as the fierce vexation of a dream.
But first I will release the Fairy Queen.
        Be as thou wast wont to° be: *as you used to*
        See, as thou wast wont to see.
        Dian's bud° o'er Cupid's flower   *flower dedicated to the*   75
        Hath such force and blessèd power.   *chaste goddess Diana*
Now my Titania, wake you, my sweet queen.
TITANIA: My Oberon, what visions have I seen!
  Methought I was enamored of an ass.
OBERON: There lies your love.
TITANIA: How came these things to pass?   80
  O, how mine eyes do loathe his visage now!
OBERON: Silence awhile. Robin, take off this head.
  Titania, music call, and strike more dead°   *make their senses slumber*
  Than common sleep of all these five the sense.   *in a more deathlike sleep*
TITANIA: Music, ho music! such as charmeth sleep.   85
PUCK: Now, when thou wak'st, with thine own fool's eyes peep.
OBERON: Sound, music! [*music*] Come my queen, take hands with me,
  And rock the ground whereon these sleepers be.

[*Dance.*]

Now thou and I are new in amity,
And will tomorrow midnight solemnly   90
Dance in Duke Theseus' house triumphantly,
And bless it to all fair prosperity.
There shall the pairs of faithful lovers be
Wedded, with Theseus, all in jollity.
PUCK: Fairy King, attend and mark: 95
        I do hear the morning lark.
OBERON: Then my queen, in silence sad,°   *in solemn silence*
        Trip we after the night's shade.
        We the globe can compass° soon,   *can circle the globe*
        Swifter than the wandering moon.   100
TITANIA: Come my lord, and in our flight,
        Tell me how it came this night
        That I sleeping here was found,
        With these mortals on the ground.

[*They leave.*]

[*The sound of horns. Enter* THESEUS, HIPPOLYTA, EGEUS, *and all his train.*]

THESEUS: Go one of you, find out the forester: 105
For now our observation° is performed.   *observance of May Day*
And since we have the vaward° of the day,   *the vanguard (early morning)*
My love shall hear the music of my hounds.
Uncouple° in the western valley, let them go: *unleash them*
Dispatch,° I say, and find the forester.   *hurry* 110

[*An attendant hurries off.*]

We will, fair queen, up to the mountain's top,
And mark the musical confusion
Of hounds and echo in conjunction.
HIPPOLYTA: I was with Hercules and Cadmus° once,   *(legendary Greek monster killers)*
When in a wood of Crete they bayed° the bear,   *cornered (brought it to bay)* 115
With hounds of Sparta; never did I hear
Such gallant chiding.° For besides the groves,   *brave barking*
The skies, the fountains, every region near
Seemed all one mutual cry.° I never heard   *seemed filled by one single*
So musical a discord, such sweet thunder.   *pack of hounds* 120
THESEUS: My hounds are bred out of the Spartan kind:
So flewed, so sanded,° and their heads are hung   *with hanging cheeks and*
With ears that sweep away the morning dew,   *sand colored*
Crook-kneed, and dewlapped° like Thessalian bulls—   *with chin folds*
Slow in pursuit, but matched in mouth° like bells,   *in sound* 125
Each under each. A cry more tuneable°   *a pack more musical*
Was never holloa'd to,° nor cheered with horn,   *greeted by the hunters' call*
In Crete, in Sparta, nor in Thessaly.°   *(sites in Greece)*
Judge when you hear. But soft. What nymphs are these?
EGEUS: My lord, this is my daughter here asleep,   130
And this Lysander, this Demetrius is,
This Helena, old Nedar's Helena.
I wonder of their being here together.
THESEUS: No doubt they rose up early to observe
The rite of May, and, hearing our intent,   135
Came here in grace of our solemnity.°   *to honor our festivities*
But speak Egeus, is not this the day
That Hermia should give answer of her choice?
EGEUS: It is, my lord.
THESEUS: Go bid the huntsmen wake them with their horns.   140

[*Shout within and sound of horns. They all start up.*]

Good morrow, friends. Saint Valentine is past.
Begin these wood-birds° but to couple now?   *(birds supposedly began to mate*
LYSANDER: Pardon, my lord.   *on Valentine's Day)*

[*They kneel.*]

THESEUS: I pray you all, stand up.
   I know you two are rival enemies.
   How comes this gentle concord in the world,   145
   That hatred is so far from jealousy,°   *suspicion*
   To sleep by hate,° and fear no enmity?   *near a hated person*
LYSANDER: My lord, I shall reply amazedly,°   *bewildered*
   Half sleep, half waking. But as yet, I swear,
   I cannot truly say how I came here.   150
   But as I think—for truly would I speak,
   And now I do bethink me, so it is—
   I came with Hermia hither. Our intent
   Was to be gone from Athens, where we might,
   Without the peril of° the Athenian law—   *beyond the threat from* 155
EGEUS: Enough, enough, my lord: you have enough.
   I beg the law, the law, upon his head.
   They would have stolen away, they would, Demetrius,
   Thereby to have defeated° you and me: *defrauded*
   You of your wife, and me of my consent—   160
   Of my consent that she should be your wife.
DEMETRIUS: My lord, fair Helen told me of their stealth,°   *secret flight*
   Of this their purpose hither, to this wood,
   And I in fury hither followed them;
   Fair Helena in fancy° following me.   *driven by love* 165
   But my good lord, I wot not° by what power   *know not*
   (But by some power it is) my love to Hermia,
   Melted as the snow, seems to me now
   As the remembrance of an idle gaud,°   *worthless toy*
   Which in my childhood I did dote upon;   170
   And all the faith, the virtue of my heart,
   The object and the pleasure of mine eye,
   Is only Helena. To her, my lord,
   Was I betrothed ere I saw Hermia:
   But like a sickness,° did I loathe this food.   *as in sickness* 175
   But as in health, come to my natural taste,
   Now I do wish it, love it, long for it,
   And will for evermore be true to it.
THESEUS: Fair lovers, you are fortunately met.
   Of this discourse we more will hear anon.   180
   Egeus, I will overbear° your will: *overrule*
   For in the temple, by and by,° with us,   *soon*
   These couples shall eternally be knit.
   And for the morning now is something worn,°   *in part gone*
   Our purposed° hunting shall be set aside.   *intended* 185
   Away with us to Athens. Three and three,
   We'll hold a feast in great solemnity.
   Come Hippolyta.

[DUKE, HIPPOLYTA, EGEUS, *and lords leave.*]

DEMETRIUS: These things seem small and undistinguishable,
    Like far-off mountains turnèd into clouds.   190
HERMIA: Methinks I see these things with parted° eye,   *unfocused*
    When everything seems double.
HELENA: So methinks:
    And I have found Demetrius, like a jewel,
    Mine own, and not mine own.°   *(because the jewel might have to be*
DEMETRIUS: Are you sure   *returned to whoever lost it)*
    That we are awake? It seems to me,   195
    That yet we sleep, we dream. Do not you think
    The duke was here, and bid us follow him?
HERMIA: Yea, and my father.
HELENA: And Hippolyta.
LYSANDER: And he did bid us follow to the temple.
DEMETRIUS: Why then, we are awake: let's follow him,   200
    And by the way let us recount our dreams.

[The lovers leave.]

BOTTOM [*wakes*]: When my cue comes, call me, and I
    will answer. My next is "Most fair Pyramus." Hey,
    ho! Peter Quince? Flute the bellows-mender? Snout
    the tinker? Starveling? God's my life!° Stol'n hence,   *God bless my life* 205
    and left me asleep? I have had a most rare vision.
    I have had a dream, past the wit of man to say
    what dream it was. Man is but an ass, if he go
    about to expound this dream. Methought° I was—   *I thought*
    there is no man can tell what. Methought I was,   210
    and methought I had—but man is but a patched
    fool,° if he will offer to say what methought I had.   *fool with patched (motley) garb*
    The eye of man hath not heard, the ear of man
    hath not seen, man's hand is not able to taste, his
    tongue to conceive, nor his heart to report, what   215
    my dream was. I will get Peter Quince to write a
    ballad of this dream: it shall be called Bottom's
    Dream, because it hath no bottom; and I will sing
    it in the latter end of our play, before the duke.
    Peradventure,° to make it the more gracious, I   *perhaps* 220
    shall sing it at her death.°   *at the death of Thisby*

[He leaves.]

SCENE 2. Athens. QUINCE'S house.

[Enter QUINCE, FLUTE, SNOUT, *and* STARVELING.]

QUINCE: Have you sent to Bottom's house? Is he come
    home yet?
STARVELING: He cannot be heard of. Out of doubt he
    is transported.°   *carried off by the spirits*
FLUTE: If he come not, then the play is marred. It goes   5
    not forward, doth it?

QUINCE: It is not possible. You have not a man in all
   Athens able to discharge° Pyramus but he.   *portray*
FLUTE: No, he hath simply the best wit of any handi-
   craft man in Athens.   10
QUINCE: Yea, and the best person too, and he is a very
   paramour° for a sweet voice.   *secret lover*
FLUTE: You must say "paragon." A paramour is (God
   bless us) a thing of naught.°   *a wicked thing*

[*Enter* SNUG *the Joiner.*]

SNUG: Masters, the duke is coming from the temple,   15
   and there is two or three lords and ladies more
   married. If our sport had gone forward, we had all
   been made men.°   *our fortunes would*
FLUTE: O sweet bully Bottom. Thus hath he lost six-   *have been made*
   pence a day during his life: he could not have   20
   'scaped sixpence a day.° And the duke had not   *a pension of sixpence*
   given him sixpence a day for playing Pyramus, I'll
   be hanged. He would have deserved it. Sixpence
   a day in Pyramus, or nothing.

[*Enter* BOTTOM.]

BOTTOM: Where are these lads? Where are these hearts?   25
QUINCE: Bottom! O most courageous° day! O most   *(he may mean "auspicious")*
   happy hour!
BOTTOM: Masters, I am to discourse° wonders; but ask   *speak of*
   me not what. For if I tell you, I am not true Athen-
   ian. I will tell you everything, right as it fell out.   30
QUINCE: Let us hear, sweet Bottom.
BOTTOM: Not a word of me. All that I will tell you is,
   that the duke hath dined. Get your apparel together, good strings to your beards, new ribbands
   to your pumps, meet presently at the palace, every   35
   man look over his part; for the short and the long
   is, our play is preferred.° In any case, let Thisby   *accepted for performance*
   have clean linen, and let not him that plays the
   lion pare his nails, for they shall hang out for the
   lion's claws. And most dear actors, eat no onions   40
   nor garlic, for we are to utter sweet breath; and I
   do not doubt but to hear them say it is a sweet
   comedy. No more words: away, go away.

[*They leave.*]

Act Five

SCENE 1. The palace of THESEUS.

[*Enter* THESEUS, HIPPOLYTA, *and* PHILOSTRATE, *and his lords.*]

HIPPOLYTA: 'Tis strange, my Theseus, that these lovers speak of.
THESEUS: More strange than true. I never may believe

These antick fables, nor these fairy toys.°   *strange tales and trifles*
Lovers and madmen have such seething brains,
Such shaping fantasies, that apprehend°   *take in*   5
More than cool reason ever comprehends.
The lunatic, the lover, and the poet
Are of imagination all compact.°   *made of sheer imagination*
One sees more devils than vast hell can hold:
That is the madman. The lover, all as frantic,   10
Sees Helen's beauty in a brow of Egypt.°   *in a gypsy's face*
The poet's eye, in a fine frenzy rolling,
Doth glance from heaven to earth, from earth to heaven.
And as imagination bodies forth
The forms of things unknown, the poet's pen   15
Turns them to shapes, and gives to airy nothing
A local habitation and a name.
Such tricks hath strong imagination,
That if it would but apprehend some joy,
It comprehends° some bringer of that joy.   *imagines*   20
Or in the night, imagining some fear,
How easy is a bush supposed a bear.
HIPPOLYTA: But all the story of the night told over,
And all their minds transfigured so together,
More witnesseth than° fancy's images,   *proves it's more than*   25
And grows to something of great constancy;°   *a very consistent story*
But howsoever,° strange and admirable.°   *nevertheless/wonderful*

[*Enter lovers:* LYSANDER, DEMETRIUS, HERMIA, *and* HELENA.]

THESEUS: Here come the lovers, full of joy and mirth.
Joy, gentle friends, joy and fresh days of love
Accompany° your hearts.   *may they accompany*
LYSANDER: More° than to us   *more of these*   30
Wait° in your royal walks, your board, your bed.   *may they be found*
THESEUS: Come now, what masques,° what dances shall   *richly costumed song-*
    we have,   *and-dance shows*
To wear away this long age of three hours
Between our aftersupper° and bedtime?   *late snack*
Where is our usual manager of mirth?   35
What revels are in hand? Is there no play,
To ease the anguish of a torturing hour?
Call Philostrate.
PHILOSTRATE: Here, mighty Theseus.
THESEUS: Say, what abridgment° have you for this evening?   *pastime*
What masque, what music? How shall we beguile   40
The lazy time, if not with some delight?
PHILOSTRATE: There is a brief how many sports are ripe:°   *list of entertainments*
Make choice of which your highness will see first.   *that are ready*

[*Gives a paper.*]

THESEUS: "The battle with the Centaurs,° to be sung   *(creatures half*
   By an Athenian eunuch to the harp."   *human, half horse)*   45
   We'll none of that. That have I told my love
   In glory of my kinsman Hercules.
   "The riot of the tipsy Bacchanals,°   *(frenzied followers of Bacchus*
   Tearing the Thracian singer in their rage."   *dismembering Orpheus)*
   That is an old device;° and it was played   *play*   50
   When I from Thebes came last a conqueror.
   "The thrice three° Muses mourning for the death   *three times three (= nine)*
   Of Learning, late deceased in beggary."°   *which died as a pauper*
   That is some satire keen and critical,
   Not sorting with a nuptial ceremony.°   *not fitting for a wedding*   55
   "A tedious brief scene of young Pyramus
   And his love Thisby; very tragical mirth."
   Merry and tragical? tedious and brief?
   That is hot ice and wondrous strange snow.
   How shall we find the concord of this discord?   60
PHILOSTRATE: A play there is, my lord, some ten words long,
   Which is as brief as I have known a play:
   But by ten words, my lord, it is too long,
   Which makes it tedious; for in all the play
   There is not one word apt, one player fitted.°   *fit for the role*   65
   And tragical, my noble lord, it is,
   For Pyramus therein doth kill himself.
   Which when I saw rehearsed, I must confess,
   Made mine eyes water; but more merry tears
   The passion° of loud laughter never shed.   *excitement*   70
THESEUS: What are they that do play it?
PHILOSTRATE: Hard-handed men, that work in Athens here,
   Which never labored in their minds till now;
   And now have toiled their unbreathed memories°   *put their untried*   75
   With this same play, against your nuptial.   *memories to work*
THESEUS: And we will hear it.
PHILOSTRATE: No, my noble lord,
   It is not for you. I have heard it over,
   And it is nothing, nothing in the world;
   Unless you can find sport in their intents,°   *good intentions*
   Extremely stretched and conned° with cruel pain,   *memorized*   80
   To do you service.
THESEUS: I will hear that play.
   For never anything can be amiss,
   When simpleness and duty tender it.°   *when honest loyalty offers it*
   Go bring them in, and take your places, ladies.

[PHILOSTRATE *leaves.*]

HIPPOLYTA: I love not to see wretchedness
   overcharged,°   *wretches attempting too much*   85
   And duty in his service perishing.°   *killing itself to do its service*

THESEUS: Why, gentle sweet, you shall see no such thing.
HIPPOLYTA: He says they can do nothing in this kind.°   *of this nature*
THESEUS: The kinder we, to give them thanks for
 nothing.
Our sport shall be to take what they mistake.°   *untangle what they scramble* 90
And what poor duty cannot do, noble respect°   *a generous outlook*
Takes it in might,° not merit.   *according to effort*
Where I have come, great clerks have purposèd°   *scholars have prepared*
To greet me with premeditated welcomes;
Where I have seen them shiver and look pale,   95
Make periods in the midst of sentences,
Throttle their practised accent in their fears,°   *their well-rehearsed speech*
And in conclusion dumbly have broke off,   *because of stage fright*
Not paying me a welcome. Trust me, sweet,
Out of this silence yet I picked a welcome;   100
And in the modesty of fearful duty°   *of scared but loyal subjects*
I read as much as from the rattling tongue
Of saucy and audacious eloquence.
Love, therefore, and tongue-tied simplicity,
In least, speak most, to my capacity.°   *are most eloquent in the* 105
         fewest words, in my opinion

[*Enter* PHILOSTRATE.]

PHILOSTRATE: So please your grace, the Prologue is addressed.°   *ready*
THESEUS: Let him approach.

[*Flourish of trumpets. Enter* QUINCE *as the* PROLOGUE.]

PROLOGUE: If we offend, it is with our good will.°   *(by stopping in the wrong*
 That you should think, we come not to offend,   *places, Quince changes the*
          meaning of the sentences to
But with good will. To show our simple skill,   *their opposites)* 110
 That is the true beginning of our end.
Consider then, we come but in despite.
 We do not come, as minding° to content you,   *having in mind*
Our true intent is. All for your delight,
 We are not here. That you should here repent you,   115
The actors are at hand; and by their show,
You shall know all, that you are like to know.
THESEUS: This fellow doth not stand upon points.°   *worry overly about points*
LYSANDER: He hath rid his prologue like a rough colt: *of etiquette—and of*
he knows not the stop. A good moral my lord: it is   *punctuation* 120
not enough to speak; but to speak true.
HIPPOLYTA: Indeed he hath played on his prologue
like a child on a recorder: a sound, but not in
government.°   *under control*
THESEUS: His speech was like a tangled chain: nothing   125
impaired,° but all disordered. Who is next?   *broken*

[*Enter* PYRAMUS *and* THISBY, WALL, MOONSHINE, *and* LION.]

PROLOGUE: Gentles, perchance you wonder at this show,
 But wonder on, till truth make all things plain.

This man is Pyramus, if you would know;
    This beauteous lady, Thisby is certain.   130
This man, with lime and rough-cast,° doth present   *plaster*
    Wall, that vile wall which did these lovers sunder;°   *separate*
And through Wall's chink, poor souls, they are content
    To whisper. At the which, let no man wonder.
This man, with lantern, dog, and bush of thorn,   135
    Presenteth Moonshine. For if you will know,
By moonshine did these lovers think no scorn
    To meet at Ninus' tomb, there, there to woo.
This grisly beast (which Lion hight° by name)   *is called*
The trusty Thisby, coming first by night,   140
Did scare away, or rather did affright;
And as she fled, her mantle she did fall.°   *she dropped her coat*
    Which Lion vile with bloody mouth did stain.
Anon comes Pyramus, sweet youth and tall,
    And finds his trusty Thisby's mantle slain:°   *as if she were slain* 145
Whereat, with blade, with bloody blameful blade,
    He bravely broached° his boiling bloody breast.   *stabbed (the many b-*
And Thisby, tarrying in mulberry shade,   *words mimic old-*
    His dagger drew, and died. For all the rest,   *fashioned alliteration)*
Let Lion, Moonshine, Wall, and lovers twain,°   *the two lovers* 150
At large discourse,° while here they do remain.   *speak in full detail*
THESEUS: I wonder if the lion be° to speak.   *is going*
DEMETRIUS: No wonder, my lord: one lion may, when many asses do.

    [PROLOGUE, PYRAMUS, LION, THISBY, *and* MOONSHINE *leave.*]

WALL: In this same interlude it doth befall
    That I, one Snout by name, present a wall;   155
And such a wall, as I would have you think,
That had in it a crannied hole or chink,
Through which the lovers, Pyramus and Thisby,
Did whisper often, very secretly.
This loam, this rough-cast, and this stone doth show   160
That I am that same wall; the truth is so.
And this the cranny is, right and sinister,°   *running right and left*
Through which the fearful lovers are to whisper.
THESEUS: Would you desire lime and hair° to speak better? *(ingredients of mortar)*
DEMETRIUS: It is the wittiest° partition that ever I heard   *most intelligent* 165
    discourse, my lord.

    [*Enter* PYRAMUS.]

THESEUS: Pyramus draws near the wall: silence.
PYRAMUS: O grim-looked night, O night with hue so black,
    O night, which ever art when day is not:
O night, O night, alack, alack, alack,   170
    I fear my Thisby's promise is forgot.
And thou O wall, O sweet, O lovely wall,
    That stand'st between her father's ground and mine,

Thou wall, O wall, O sweet and lovely wall,
    Show me thy chink, to blink through with mine eyne.°   *eyes* 175

[WALL *holds up his fingers.*]

Thanks, courteous wall. Jove shield thee well for this.
    But what see I? No Thisby do I see.
O wicked wall, through whom I see no bliss,
    Cursed be thy stones for thus deceiving me.

THESEUS: The wall, methinks, being sensible, should   180
    curse again.°   *being alive,*
                                        should curse back
PYRAMUS: No, in truth, sir, he should not. "Deceiving
me" is Thisby's cue. She is to enter now, and I am
to spy° her through the wall. You shall see it will   *spot*
fall pat as I told you: yonder she comes.   185

[*Enter* THISBY.]

THISBY: O Wall, full often hast thou heard my moans,
    For parting my fair Pyramus and me.
My cherry lips have often kissed thy stones;
    Thy stones with lime and hair° knit up in thee.   *(to make mortar)*
PYRAMUS: I see a voice: now will I to the chink,   190
    To spy an° I can hear my Thisby's face.   *to see if*
Thisby?
THISBY: My love thou art, my love I think.
PYRAMUS: Think what thou wilt, I am thy lover's grace;°   *your gracious lover*
    And, like Limander,° am I trusty still.   *(he means "Leander")* 195
THISBY: And I like Helen, till the Fates me kill.
PYRAMUS: Not Shafalus to Procrus,° was so true.   *(he means "Cephalus and*
THISBY: As Shafalus to Procrus, I to you.   *Procris," legendary lovers)*
PYRAMUS: O kiss me through the hole of this vile wall.
THISBY: I kiss the wall's hole, not your lips at all.   200
PYRAMUS: Wilt thou at Ninny's tomb meet me
    straightway?
HISBY: Tide life, tide death,° I come without delay.   *come what may—life or death*

                   [PYRAMUS *and* THISBY *leave.*]

WALL: Thus have I, Wall, my part dischargèd so;
    And being done, thus Wall away doth go.   205

                       [*He leaves.*]

THESEUS: Now is the mural° down between the two   *wall*
    neighbors.
DEMETRIUS: No remedy, my lord, when walls are so
    wilful to hear° without warning.   *eager to listen*
HIPPOLYTA: This is the silliest stuff that ever I heard.   210
THESEUS: The best in this kind are but shadows; and the
    worst are no worse, if imagination amend them.°   *helps them out*
HIPPOLYTA: It must be your imagination then, and not
    theirs.

THESEUS: If we imagine no worse of them than they of   215
    themselves, they may pass for excellent men. Here
    come two noble beats in, a man and a lion.

[*Enter* LION *and* MOONSHINE.]

LION: You ladies, you, whose gentle hearts do fear
      The smallest monstrous mouse that creeps on floor,
    May now perchance both quake and tremble here,   220
      When lion rough in wildest rage doth roar.
    Then know that I, as Snug the joiner am
    A lion fell,° nor else no lion's dam:°   *fierce/mate*
    For if I should as lion come in strife°   *aggressively*
    Into this place, 'twere pity on my life.°   *my life would be at stake* 225
THESEUS: A very gentle° beast, and of a good conscience.   *noble*
DEMETRIUS: The very best at a beast, my lord, that ever I saw.
LYSANDER: This lion is a very fox for his valor.
THESEUS: True, and a goose for his discretion.°   *caution*
DEMETRIUS: Not so my lord: for his valor cannot carry   230
    his discretion, and the fox carries the goose.
THESEUS: His discretion, I am sure, cannot carry his
    valor; for the goose carries not the fox. It is well:
    leave it to his discretion, and let us listen to the
    moon.   235
MOONSHINE: This lanthorn° doth the hornèd° moon   *lantern/crescent (with two*
    present—   *horn-like points like a*
                                     cuckolded husband)
DEMETRIUS: He should have worn the horns on his
    head.
THESEUS: He is no crescent, and his horns are invisi-   240
    ble within the circumference.
MOONSHINE: This lanthorn doth the hornèd moon pre-
    sent; Myself, the man in the moon do seem to be.
THESEUS: This is the greatest error of all the rest; the
    man should be put into the lanthorn. How is it else   245
    the man in the moon?
DEMETRIUS: He dares not come there for the candle;
    for you see, it is already in snuff.°   *in need of trimming*
HIPPOLYTA: I am aweary of this moon. Would he
    would change.°   *(like the real moon)* 250
THESEUS: It appears, by his small light of discretion,
    that he is in the wane; but yet in courtesy, in all
    reason, we must stay the time.°   *be patient for the*
                                       allowed time
LYSANDER: Proceed, Moon.
MOONSHINE: All that I have to say, is to tell you that the   255
    lanthorn is the moon, I the man in the moon, this
    thornbush my thornbush, and this dog my dog.
DEMETRIUS: Why, all these should be in the lanthorn,
    for all these are in the moon. But silence: here
    comes Thisby.   260

[*Enter* THISBY.]

THISBY: This is old Ninny's tomb. Where is my love?
LION: Oh!

[*The* LION *roars.* THISBY *runs off.*]

DEMETRIUS: Well roared, Lion.
THESEUS: Well run, Thisby.
HIPPOLYTA: Well shone, Moon. Truly, the moon shines   265
   with a good grace.

[*The* LION *shakes* THISBY*'s coat.*]

THESEUS: Well moused,° Lion.   *shaken, as a cat does to a mouse*
DEMETRIUS: And then came Pyramus.

[*Enter* PYRAMUS. *The* LION *leaves.*]

LYSANDER: And so the lion vanished.
PYRAMUS: Sweet moon, I thank thee for thy sunny beams,   270
        I thank thee, moon, for shining now so bright.
     For by thy gracious, golden, glittering gleams,
      I trust to take of truest Thisby sight.
           But stay: O spite!
           But mark, poor knight,
        What dreadful dole° is here?   *sorrow*
          Eyes, do you see!
          How can it be!
      O dainty duck, O dear!
          Thy mantle good,   280
         What, stained with blood?
      Approach, ye Furies° fell!   *(fierce avenging spirits)*
         O Fates!° come, come: *(sisters spinning and*
          Cut thread and thrum,   *cutting the thread of fate)*
       Quail, crush, conclude, and quell.°   *destroy, crush, make* 285
THESEUS: This passion, and the death of a dear friend,   *an end, and kill*
   would go near to° make a man look sad.   *come close to*
HIPPOLYTA: Beshrew° my heart, but I pity the man.   *wish ill to*
PYRAMUS: O wherefore, Nature, didst thou lions frame?°   *create lions*
      Since lion vile hath here deflowered my dear.   290
     Which is—no, no—which was the fairest dame
      That lived, that loved, that liked, that looked with
        cheer.
         Come tears, confound.°   *sweep all away*
          Out sword, and wound
        The pap° of Pyramus;   *breast* 295
         Ay, that left pap,
         Where heart doth hop.

[*Stabs himself.*]

Thus die I, thus, thus, thus.
  Now am I dead,
  Now am I fled,   300
My soul is in the sky.
  Tongue lose thy light,
  Moon take thy flight,

                 [MOONSHINE *leaves.*]

  Now die, die, die, die, die.

[PYRAMUS *dies.*]

DEMETRIUS: No die, but an ace for him.° For he is but *not the whole die, but only* 305
 one.   *a throw of one (at dice)*

LYSANDER: Less than an ace, man. For he is dead, he
 is nothing.

THESEUS: With the help of a surgeon, he might yet recover, and prove an ass.°   *(play on "ace")* 310

HIPPOLYTA: How chance Moonshine is gone before
 Thisby comes back and finds her lover?

[*Enter* THISBY.]

THESEUS: She will find him by starlight. Here she
 comes, and her passion° ends the play.   *grief*

HIPPOLYTA: Methinks she should not use a long one   315
 for such a Pyramus; I hope she will be brief.

DEMETRIUS: A mote will turn the balance,° which Pyra- *speck will tilt the scale*
 mus, which Thisby, is the better: he for a man,
 God warrant° us; she for a woman, God bless us.   *protect*

LYSANDER: She hath spied him already with those   320
 sweet eyes.

DEMETRIUS: And thus she means, videlicet°—   *laments, namely*

THISBY: Asleep my love?
      What, dead, my dove?
    O Pyramus, arise,   325
      Speak, speak. Quite dumb?
      Dead, dead? A tomb
    Must cover thy sweet eyes.
      These lily lips,
      This cherry nose,   330
    These yellow cowslip cheeks,
      Are gone, are gone.
      Lovers, make moan:
    His eyes were green as leeks.
      O Sisters Three,°   *(the three Fates)* 335
      Come, come to me,
    With hands as pale as milk,
      Lay them in gore,

Since you have shore°   *shorn*
With shears his thread of silk.   340
Tongue, not a word:
Come trusty sword,
Come blade, my breast imbrue°—   *cover with blood*

[*Stabs herself.*]

And farewell, friends.
Thus Thisby ends.   345
Adieu, adieu, adieu.

[*She dies.*]

THESEUS: Moonshine and Lion are left to bury the
dead.
DEMETRIUS: Ay, and Wall too.
BOTTOM [*starts up*]: No, I assure you, the wall is down
that parted their fathers. Will it please you to see   350
the Epilogue, or to hear a Bergomask dance° be-   *(Italian peasant dance)*
tween two of our company?
THESEUS: No epilogue, I pray you; for your play needs
no excuse. Never excuse: for when the players are
all dead, there need none to be blamed. Marry, if   355
he that writ it had played Pyramus and hanged
himself in Thisby's garter, it would have been a
fine tragedy; and so it is truly, and very notably
discharged.° But come, your Bergomask: let your   *performed*
Epilogue alone.   360

[*A dance.*]

The iron tongue of midnight hath told° twelve.   *the bell . . . has tolled*
Lovers, to bed, 'tis almost fairy time.
I fear we shall outsleep the coming morn,
As much as we this night have overwatched.
This palpable gross° play hath well beguiled   *brash and crude* 365
The heavy gait° of night. Sweet friends, to bed.   *slow motion*
A fortnight° hold we this solemnity,   *for two weeks*
In nightly revels, and new jollity.

[*They leave.*]

[*Enter* PUCK *with a broom.*]

PUCK: Now the hungry lion roars,
                And the wolf behowls the moon;   370
            Whilst the heavy plowman snores,
                All with weary task fordone.
            Now the wasted brands° do glow,   *burnt-out embers*
                Whilst the screech owl, screeching loud,
            Puts the wretch that lies in woe   375

In remembrance of a shroud.
Now it is the time of night,
    That the graves, all gaping wide,
Every one lets forth his sprite,°   *ghost*
    In the churchway paths to glide.   380
And we fairies, that do run
    By the triple Hecate's° team,   *(moon goddess of three names*
From the presence of the sun,   *Diana-Phoebe-Hecate)*
    Following darkness like a dream,
Now are frolic:° not a mouse   *make merry* 385
Shall disturb this hallowed house.
I am sent with broom before,
To sweep the dust behind the door.°   *(he supposedly helped with*
                                             household chores)

[*Enter King and Queen of fairies, with all their train.*]

OBERON: Through the house give glimmering light,
        By the dead and drowsy fire,   390
    Every elf and fairy sprite,
        Hop as light as bird from brier,
    And this ditty after me,
    Sing, and dance it trippingly.
TITANIA: First rehearse your song by rote,   395
    To each word a warbling note.
    Hand in hand, with fairy grace,
    Will we sing and bless this place.

[*Song and dance.*]

OBERON: Now, until the break of day,
    Through this house each fairy stray.   400
    To the best bride-bed will we,
    Which by us shall blessèd be;
    And the issue there create,°   *the children there created*
    Ever shall be fortunate.
    So shall all the couples three   405
    Ever true in loving be;
    And the blots of Nature's hand
    Shall not in their issue stand.°   *shall not mar their offspring*
    Never mole, harelip, nor scar,
    Nor mark prodigious,° such as are   *frightening birthmark* 410
    Despisèd in nativity,°   *feared in the newborn*
    Shall upon their children be.
    With this field-dew consecrate,°   *consecrated*
    Every fairy take his gait,
    And each several° chamber bless,   *separate* 415
    Through this palace, with sweet peace;
    And the owner of it blest,
    Ever shall in safety rest.
    Trip away; make no stay;
    Meet me all by break of day.   420

[*All but* PUCK *leave.*]

PUCK: If we shadows° have offended,   *players*
           Think but this and all is mended:
           That you have but slumbered here,
           While these visions did appear.
           And this weak and idle° theme,   *foolish* 425
           No more yielding but° a dream,   *producing nothing more than*
           Gentles, do not reprehend.
           If you pardon, we will mend.
           And as I am an honest Puck,
           If we have unearned luck,   430
           Now to scape the serpent's tongue,°   *snakelike hissing of a hostile audience*
           We will make amends, ere long:
           Else the Puck a liar call.
           So, good night unto you all.
           Give me your hands, if we be friends;   435
           And Robin shall restore amends.°   *do better next time*

[*He leaves.*]

The Receptive Reader

1. (Act One, Scene 1) How does the opening set up the **frame story** for
the comedy as a whole? How does the exchange between Theseus and Hippolyta create the dominating mood? What is the dilemma facing Hermia? (Are
you surprised by her defiance?) How do the two young men come off in this
opening scene? What is the role of Helena on the merry-go-round of love?

2. (Act One, Scene 2) What makes the uneducated lower-class characters
such lovable bumblers?

3. (Act Two, Scene 1) Puck becomes a master mind in much of what happens during the play. What is his characteristic stance or attitude? How serious
is the quarrel between Oberon and Titania? How much and what kind of storytelling are woven into their exchanges? How playful or how serious is
Oberon's plan for his revenge? What changes does the relationship between
Demetrius and Helena ring on more usual patterns of courtship? (What hope
do you think there is for her?)

4. (Act Two, Scene 2) In these early scenes, does Titania seem a good or
evil spirit? What kind of couple do Hermia and Lysander make in this scene?
How does Puck in this scene start the comedy of errors that will account for
many of the **plot** developments in the play? Do you think the sudden transformation of Lysander would be unbelievable to a modern audience? (How
does Helena react to the change? How does Hermia?)

5. (Act Three, Scene 1) What are striking examples of the would-be actors'
literal-mindedness and naïveté? What are examples of their tendency toward
malapropism—choosing, for instance, *odious* (hateful) instead of *odorous*

(sweet-smelling)? What keeps Bottom's transformation from being an isolated practical joke? (How does it relate to what comes before it in this scene and what comes after? How does it parallel or help tie together other plot elements?) Should the love scene between Titania (the Fairy Queen) and Bottom be acted as gross *farce?* Does it have any symbolic or thematic overtones?

6. (Act Three, Scene 2) How does this scene follow up or reiterate the *theme* of mortals at cross-purposes? (Where or how was this theme sounded earlier in the play?) How does Puck continue his mischief-making in this scene? How do Oberon and Puck begin to steer the tangled relations of the lovers toward a resolution?

7. (Act Four, Scene 1) How does this scene get the audience ready to return to Athens and daylight from the forest of moonlight and dreams? Do Athens and daylight symbolize reality in the play? Did we leave reality behind when we entered the forest? Does Theseus seem to represent benign power, benevolent authority? Does he play a godlike role?

8. (Act Four, Scenes 1 and 2) How is the playwright going to bring the three strands of the play—the fairies, the lovers with their elders, and the mechanicals—together at the end?

9. (Act Five, Scene 1) How do the "mechanicals" turn the traditional tragic story into a farce? How does their stage audience react or participate? What are the last words of the major figures—Theseus, Oberon, Puck? What light do their final comments cast on the play as a whole?

The Whole Play—For Discussion or Writing

1. Look at the sources of conflict and misunderstanding in this play and at the way they are resolved. How much in the play can you relate to the theme of mortals at cross-purposes—but brought into harmony by the power of love?

2. Modern readers are often wary of the power of humor to hurt and to exclude. In this play, are the same people exclusively the perpetrators and others exclusively the targets of humor? Are there examples of humor cutting both ways? Are any of the characters at times the joker and at other times the butt of the joke?

The Personal Response

How silly or how real do the lovers appear to you?

The Creative Dimension

Two selections from this play lend themselves exceptionally well to performance as *amateur theatricals:* the rehearsal in the woods, with the transformation of Bottom, followed by his encounter with the fairy queen; and the staging of the lamentable comedy of Pyramus and Thisby at the court, with the wisecracking comments of the court audience. You and your classmates may want to stage a mini-production of one or both for a class party or other special occasion.

Tennessee Williams   *(1911–1983)*

*I have found it easier to identify with the
characters who verge upon hysteria, who
were frightened of life, who were desperate
to reach out to another person.*

TENNESSEE WILLIAMS

Much of Tennessee Williams' work shows his fascination with characters facing lonely struggles in emotionally starved environments. Much of his work has biographical roots, harking back to his own family's atmosphere of repression and anger, evoked through characterizations of psychologically vulnerable women and domineering men. Williams began writing in high school; his first short story was published when he was seventeen. During his college years, he wrote one-act plays. The year 1940 saw the production of his first full-length play. In 1945, *The Glass Menagerie* won the Drama Critics' Circle Award. It was also a spectacular commercial success, the beginning of a series of theatrical triumphs including *A Streetcar Named Desire* (1947), *The Rose Tattoo* (1950), *Cat on a Hot Tin Roof* (1955), *Suddenly Last Summer* (1958), and *The Night of the Iguana* (1961). Many of his plays were made into movies, including the classic *Streetcar* with Vivien Leigh as Blanche and Marlon Brando as Kowalski. *Cat on a Hot Tin Roof* starred Elizabeth Taylor and Paul Newman.

In his memoirs, Williams called *The Glass Menagerie,* with its burden of guilt and cruelty, "the big one—close to the marrow of my being." This play, in which Laura retreats to the private world of her glass animals and Tom leaves while carrying with him an obsession with the past, has its roots in Williams' actual relationship with his sister, Rose, whom he felt he failed in her greatest need. He writes: "It's not very pleasant to look back on [1937] and to know that Rose knew she was going mad and to know, also, that I was not too kind to my sister." In a moment of fury, he hissed at her, "I hate the sight of your ugly old face!" He said about this experience, "This is the cruelest thing I have done in my life, I suspect, and one for which I can never properly atone." After he left home, his parents permitted the procedure of a frontal lobotomy on Rose. These traumatic events left the playwright with a deep sense that love leads inevitably to loss and betrayal. Although the play is usually talked of as Tom's exorcism of a traumatic memory, it can also be seen as an obsessive reenactment. "After all, he does not really escape the family trap. . . . And when the play is seen in this way, one must recognize that, besides its gentle sadness and remorse, there is also ruthlessness in Tom's final command, 'Blow out your candles, Laura—and so goodbye . . .' For Williams, in fact, love and betrayal are always two sides of the same emotion . . . his brutal and gentle characters do more than co-exist, they interexist, one creates the other in a vicious circle of disaster" (John Buell).

Tennessee Williams' theater typically takes his audiences to a Southern setting, made intensely real by his command of Southern speech and manners. His poetic and symbolic drama goes beyond the realistic surface of life to probe the complex psychological intermeshings of "love, pity, regret, guilt, self-lacerating ruthlessness, posing, and bravado" (Brian Parker).

The Glass Menagerie   1945

CHARACTERS

AMANDA WINGFIELD, the mother. A little woman of great but confused vitality clinging frantically to another time and place. Her characterization must be carefully created, not copied from type. She is not paranoiac, but her life is paranoia. There is much to admire in AMANDA, and as much to love and pity as there is to laugh at. Certainly she has endurance and a kind of heroism, and though her foolishness makes her unwittingly cruel at times, there is tenderness in her slight person.

LAURA WINGFIELD, her daughter. AMANDA, having failed to establish contact with reality, continues to live vitally in her illusions, but LAURA's situation is even graver. A childhood illness has left her crippled, one leg slightly shorter than the other, and held in a brace. This defect need not be more than suggested on the stage. Stemming from this, LAURA's separation increases till she is like a piece of her own glass collection, too exquisitely fragile to move from the shelf.

TOM WINGFIELD, her son, and the narrator of the play. A poet with a job in a warehouse. His nature is not remorseless, but to escape from a trap he has to act without pity.

JIM O'CONNOR, the gentleman caller. A nice, ordinary, young man.

SCENE: *An alley in St. Louis.*
PART I: *Preparation for a gentleman caller.*
PART II: *The gentleman calls.*
TIME: *Now and the past.*

AUTHOR'S PRODUCTION NOTES

Being a "memory play," *The Glass Menagerie* can be presented with unusual freedom of convention. Because of its considerably delicate or tenuous material, atmospheric touches and subtleties of direction play a particularly important part. Expressionism and all other unconventional techniques in drama have only one valid aim, and that is a closer approach to truth. When a play employs unconventional techniques, it is not, or certainly shouldn't be, trying to escape its responsibility of dealing with reality, or interpreting experience, but is actually or should be attempting to find a closer approach, a more penetrating and vivid expression of things as they are. The straight realistic play with its genuine frigidaire and authentic ice-cubes, its characters

that speak exactly as its audience speaks, corresponds to the academic landscape and has the same virtue of a photographic likeness. Everyone should
know nowadays the unimportance of the photographic in art: that truth, life,
or reality is an organic thing which the poetic imagination can represent or
suggest, in essence, only through transformation, through changing into
other forms than those which were merely present in appearance.

These remarks are not meant as a preface only to this particular play.
They have to do with a conception of a new, plastic theatre which must take
the place of the exhausted theatre of realistic conventions if the theatre is to
resume vitality as a part of our culture.

The Screen Device. There is *only one important difference between the
original and acting version of the play* and that is the *omission* in the latter
of the device which I tentatively included in my *original* script. This device
was the use of a screen on which were projected magic-lantern slides bearing images or titles. I do not regret the omission of this device from the present Broadway production. The extraordinary power of Miss Taylor's
performance made it suitable to have the utmost simplicity in the physical
production. But I think it may be interesting to some readers to see how this
device was conceived. So I am putting it into the published manuscript.
These images and legends, projected from behind, were cast on a section
of wall between the front-room and dining-room areas, which should be in-
distinguishable from the rest when not in use.

The purpose of this will probably be apparent. It is to give accent to certain values in each scene. Each scene contains a particular point (or several)
which is structurally the most important. In an episodic play, such as this,
the basic structure or narrative line may be obscured from the audience; the
effect may seem fragmentary rather than architectural. This may not be the
fault of the play so much as a lack of attention in the audience. The legend
or image upon the screen will strengthen the effect of what is merely allusion in the writing and allow the primary point to be made more simply and
lightly than if the entire responsibility were on the spoken lines. Aside from
this structural value, I think the screen will have a definite emotional appeal,
less definable but just as important. An imaginative producer or director may
invent many other uses for this device than those indicated in the present
script. In fact the possibilities of the device seem much larger to me than the
instance of this play can possibly utilize.

The Music: Another extra-literary accent in this play is provided by the
use of music. A single recurring tune, "The Glass Menagerie," is used to give
emotional emphasis to suitable passages. This tune is like circus music, not
when you are on the grounds or in the immediate vicinity of the parade, but
when you are at some distance and very likely thinking of something else.
It seems under those circumstances to continue almost interminably and it
weaves in and out of your preoccupied consciousness; then it is the lightest, most delicate music in the world and perhaps the saddest. It expresses
the surface vivacity of life with the underlying strain of immutable and in-
expressible sorrow. When you look at a piece of delicately spun glass you
think of two things: how beautiful it is and how easily it can be broken.
Both of those ideas should be woven into the recurring tune, which dips in
and out of the play as if it were carried on a wind that changes. It serves as

a thread of connection and allusion between the narrator with his separate point in time and space and the subject of his story. Between each episode it returns as reference to the emotion, nostalgia, which is the first condition of the play. It is primarily LAURA'S music and therefore comes out most clearly when the play focuses upon her and the lovely fragility of glass which is her image.

The Lighting. The lighting in the play is not realistic. In keeping with the atmosphere of memory, the stage is dim. Shafts of light are focused on selected areas or actors, sometimes in contradistinction to what is the apparent center. For instance, in the quarrel scene between TOM and AMANDA, in which LAURA has no active part, the clearest pool of light is on her figure. This is also true of the supper scene, when her silent figure on the sofa should remain the visual center. The light upon LAURA should be distinct from the others, having a peculiar pristine clarity such as light used in early religious portraits of female saints or madonnas. A certain correspondence to light in religious paintings, such as El Greco's, where the figures are radiant in atmosphere that is relatively dusky, could be effectively used throughout the play. (It will also permit a more effective use of the screen.) A free, imaginative use of light can be of enormous value in giving a mobile, plastic quality to plays of a more or less static nature.

T. W.

Scene 1

The Wingfield apartment is in the rear of the building, one of those vast hive-like conglomerations of cellular living-units that flower as warty growths in overcrowded urban centers of lower middle-class population and are symptomatic of the impulse of this largest and fundamentally enslaved section of American society to avoid fluidity and differentiation and to exist and function as one interfused mass of automatism.

The apartment faces an alley and is entered by a fire-escape, a structure whose name is a touch of accidental poetic truth, for all of these huge buildings are always burning with the slow and implacable fires of human desperation. The fire-escape is included in the set—that is, the landing of it and steps descending from it.

The scene is memory and is therefore nonrealistic. Memory takes a lot of poetic license. It omits some details; others are exaggerated, according to the emotional value of the articles it touches, for memory is seated and predominantly in the heart. The interior is therefore rather dim and poetic.

At the rise of the curtain, the audience is faced with the dark, grim rear wall of the Wingfield tenement. This building, which runs parallel to the footlights, is flanked on both sides by dark, narrow alleys which run into murky canyons of tangled clotheslines, garbage cans and the sinister lattice work of neighboring fire-escapes. It is up and down these side alleys that exterior entrances and exits are made, during the play. At the end of TOM'S *opening commentary, the dark tenement wall slowly reveals (by means of a transparency) the interior of the ground floor Wingfield apartment.*

Downstage is the living room, which also serves as a sleeping room for LAURA, *the sofa unfolding to make her bed. Upstage, center, and divided by a wide arch or second proscenium with transparent faded portieres (or second curtain), is the dining room. In an old-fashioned what-not in the living room are seen scores of transparent glass animals. A blown-up photograph of the father hangs on the wall of the living room, facing the audience, to the left of the archway. It is the face of a very handsome young man in a doughboy's First World War cap. He is gallantly smiling, ineluctably smiling, as if to say, "I will be smiling forever."*

The audience hears and sees the opening scene in the dining room through both the transparent fourth wall of the building and the transparent gauze portieres of the dining-room arch. It is during this revealing scene that the fourth wall slowly ascends, out of sight. This transparent exterior wall is not brought down again until the very end of the play, during TOM'S *final speech.*

The narrator is an undisguised convention of the play. He takes whatever license with dramatic convention as is convenient to his purposes.

TOM *enters dressed as a merchant sailor from alley, stage left, and strolls across the front of the stage to the fire-escape. There he stops and lights a cigarette. He addresses the audience.*

TOM: Yes, I have tricks in my pocket, I have things up my sleeve. But I am the opposite of a stage magician. He gives you illusion that has the appearance of truth. I give you truth in the pleasant disguise of illusion. To begin with, I turn back time. I reverse it to that quaint period, the thirties, when the huge middle class of America was matriculating in a school for the blind. Their eyes had failed them, or they had failed their eyes, and so they were having their fingers pressed forcibly down on the fiery Braille alphabet of a dissolving economy. In Spain there was revolution. Here there was only shouting and confusion. In Spain there was Guernica. Here there were disturbances of labor, sometimes pretty violent, in otherwise peaceful cities such as Chicago, Cleveland, Saint Louis . . . This is the social background of the play.

(Music.)

The play is memory. Being a memory play, it is dimly lighted, it is sentimental, it is not realistic. In memory everything seems to happen to music. That explains the fiddle in the wings. I am the narrator of the play, and also a character in it. The other characters are my mother, Amanda, my sister, Laura, and a gentleman caller who appears in the final scenes. He is the most realistic character in the play, being an emissary from a world of reality that we were somehow set apart from. But since I have a poet's weakness for symbols, I am using this character also as a symbol; he is the long delayed but always expected something that we live for. There is a fifth character in the play who doesn't appear except in this larger-than-life-size photograph over the mantel. This is our father who left us a long time ago. He was a telephone man who fell in love with long distances; he gave up his job with the telephone company and skipped the light fantastic out of town . . . The last we heard of him was a picture post-card from Mazatlan, on the Pacific coast of Mexico, containing a message of two words—"Hello—Good-bye!" and no address. I think the rest of the play will explain itself. . . .

AMANDA's *voice becomes audible through the portieres.*
    (*Legend on screen: "Où sont les neiges."*)
    He divides the portieres and enters the upstage area.
    AMANDA *and* LAURA *are seated at a drop-leaf table. Eating is indicated by gestures without food or utensils.* AMANDA *faces the audience.* TOM *and* LAURA *are seated in profile.*
    The interior has lit up softly and through the scrim we see AMANDA *and* LAURA *seated at the table in the upstage area.*

AMANDA (*calling*): Tom?
TOM: Yes, Mother.
AMANDA: We can't say grace until you come to the table!
TOM: Coming, Mother. (*He bows slightly and withdraws, reappearing a few moments later in his place at the table.*)
AMANDA (*to her son*): Honey, don't *push* with your *fingers*. If you have to push with something, the thing to push with is a crust of bread. And chew—chew! Animals have sections in their stomachs which enable them to digest food without mastication, but human beings are supposed to chew their food before they swallow it down. Eat food leisurely, son, and really enjoy it. A well-cooked meal has lots of delicate flavors that have to be held in the mouth for appreciation. So chew your food and give your salivary glands a chance to function!

TOM *deliberately lays his imaginary fork down and pushes his chair back from the table.*

TOM: I haven't enjoyed one bite of this dinner because of your constant directions on how to eat it. It's you that make me rush through meals with your hawk-like attention to every bite I take: Sickening—spoils my appetite—all this discussion of—animals' secretion—salivary glands—mastication!
AMANDA (*lightly*): Temperament like a Metropolitan star! (*He rises and crosses downstage.*) You're not excused from the table.
TOM: I'm getting a cigarette.
AMANDA: You smoke too much.

LAURA *rises.*

LAURA: I'll bring in the blanc mange.

He remains standing with his cigarette by the portieres during the following.

AMANDA (*rising*): No, sister, no, sister—you be the lady this time and I'll be the darky.
LAURA: I'm already up.
AMANDA: Resume your seat, little sister—I want you to stay fresh and pretty—for gentlemen callers!

Elizabeth Ashley and Anne Dudek in a scene from the Hartford
Stage production of *The Glass Menagerie* (courtesy Jennifer W. Lester)

LAURA: I'm not expecting any gentlemen callers.

AMANDA (*Crossing out to kitchenette. Airily.*): Sometimes they come when they are least expected! Why, I remember one Sunday afternoon in Blue Mountain—(*enters kitchenette*)

TOM: I know what's coming!

LAURA: Yes, But let her tell it.

TOM: Again?

LAURA: She loves to tell it.

AMANDA *returns with bowl of dessert.*

AMANDA: One Sunday afternoon in Blue Mountain—your mother received— *seventeen!*—gentlemen callers! Why, sometimes there weren't chairs enough to accommodate them all. We had to send the nigger over to bring in folding chairs from the parish house.

TOM (*remaining at portieres*): How did you entertain those gentlemen callers?

AMANDA: I understood the art of conversation!

TOM: I bet you could talk.

AMANDA: Girls in those days *knew* how to talk, I can tell you.

TOM: Yes?

(*Image:* AMANDA *as a girl on a porch, greeting callers.*)

AMANDA: They knew how to entertain their gentlemen callers. It wasn't enough for a girl to be possessed of a pretty face and a graceful figure—although I wasn't slighted in either respect. She also needed to have a nimble wit and a tongue to meet all occasions.

TOM: What did you talk about?

AMANDA: Things of importance going on in the world! Never anything coarse or common or vulgar. (*She addresses* TOM *as though he were seated in the vacant chair at the table though he remains by portieres. He plays this scene as though he held the book.*) My callers were gentlemen—all! Among my callers were some of the most prominent young planters of the Mississippi Delta—planters and sons of planters!

> TOM *motions for music and a spot of light on* AMANDA.
> *Her eyes lift, her face glows, her voice becomes rich and elegiac.*
> (*Screen legend: "Où sont les neiges."*)

There was young Champ Laughlin who later became vice-president of the Delta Planters Bank. Hadley Stevenson who was drowned in Moon Lake and left his widow one hundred and fifty thousand in Government bonds. There were the Cutrere brothers, Wesley and Bates. Bates was one of my bright particular beaux! He got in a quarrel with that wild Wainwright boy. They shot it out on the floor of Moon Lake Casino. Bates was shot through the stomach. Died in the ambulance on his way to Memphis. His widow was also well-provided for, came into eight or ten thousand acres, that's all. She married him on the rebound—never loved her—carried my picture on him the night he died! And there was that boy that every girl in the Delta had set her cap for! That beautiful, brilliant young Fitzhugh boy from Greene County!

TOM: What did he leave his widow?

AMANDA: He never married! Gracious, you talk as though all of my old admirers had turned up their toes to the daisies!

TOM: Isn't this the first you've mentioned that still survives?

AMANDA: That Fitzhugh boy went North and made a fortune—came to be known as the Wolf of Wall Street! He had the Midas touch, whatever he touched turned to gold!

    And I could have been Mrs. Duncan J. Fitzhugh, mind you! But—I picked your *father!*

LAURA (*rising*): Mother, let me clear the table.

AMANDA: No, dear, you go in front and study your typewriter chart. Or practice your shorthand a little. Stay fresh and pretty!—It's almost time for our gentlemen callers to start arriving. (*She flounces girlishly toward the kitchenette.*) How many do you suppose we're going to entertain this afternoon?

> TOM *throws down the paper and jumps up with a groan.*

LAURA (*alone in the dining room*): I don't believe we're going to receive any, Mother.

AMANDA (*reappearing, airily*): What? No one—not one? You must be joking!

(LAURA *nervously echoes her laugh. She slips in a fugitive manner through the half-open portieres and draws them gently behind her. A shaft of very clear light is thrown on her face against the faded tapestry of the curtains.*) (*Music: "The Glass Menagerie" under faintly.*) (*lightly*) Not one gentleman caller? It can't be true! There must be a flood, there must have been a tornado!

LAURA: It isn't a flood, it's not a tornado, Mother. I'm just not popular like you were in Blue Mountain. . . . (TOM *utters another groan.* LAURA *glances at him with a faint, apologetic smile. Her voice catching a little.*) Mother's afraid I'm going to be an old maid.

(*The scene dims out with "Glass Menagerie" music.*)

Scene 2

"Laura, Haven't You Ever Liked Some Boy?"

On the dark stage the screen is lighted with the image of blue roses.
    Gradually LAURA's *figure becomes apparent and the screen goes out. The music subsides.*
    LAURA *is seated in the delicate ivory chair at the small claw-foot table.*
    She wears a dress of soft violet material for a kimono—her hair tied back from her forehead with a ribbon.
    She is washing and polishing her collection of glass.
    AMANDA *appears on the fire-escape steps. At the sound of her ascent,* LAURA *catches her breath, thrusts the bowl of ornaments away and seats herself stiffly before the diagram of the typewriter keyboard as though it held her spellbound.*
    Something has happened to AMANDA. *It is written in her face as she climbs to the landing a look that is grim and hopeless and a little absurd.*
    She has on one of those cheap or imitation velvety-looking cloth coats with imitation fur collar. Her hat is five or six years old, one of those dreadful cloche hats that were worn in the late twenties and she is clasping an enormous black patent-leather pocketbook with nickel clasps and initials. This is her full-dress outfit, the one she usually wears to the D.A.R.
    Before entering she looks through the door.
    She purses her lips, opens her eyes very wide, rolls them upward and shakes her head.
    Then she slowly lets herself in the door. Seeing her mother's expression LAURA *touches her lips with a nervous gesture.*

LAURA: Hello, Mother, I was—(*She makes a nervous gesture toward the chart on the wall.* AMANDA *leans against the shut door and stares at* LAURA *with a martyred look.*)

AMANDA: Deception? Deception? (*She slowly removes her hat and gloves, continuing the sweet suffering stare. She lets the hat and gloves fall on the floor—a bit of acting.*)

LAURA (*shakily*): How was the D.A.R. meeting? (AMANDA *slowly opens her purse and removes a dainty white handkerchief which she shakes out delicately and delicately touches to her lips and nostrils.*) Didn't you go to the D.A.R. meeting, Mother?

AMANDA (*faintly, almost inaudibly*): —No.—No. (*then more forcibly*) I did not have the strength—to go to the D.A.R. In fact, I did not have the courage! I wanted to find a hole in the ground and hide myself in it forever! (*She crosses slowly to the wall and removes the diagram of the type-writer keyboard. She holds it in front of her for a second, staring at it sweetly and sorrowfully—then bites her lips and tears it in two pieces.*)

LAURA (*faintly*): Why did you do that, Mother? (AMANDA *repeats the same procedure with the chart of the Gregg Alphabet.*) Why are you—

AMANDA: Why? Why? How old are you, Laura?

LAURA: Mother, you know my age.

AMANDA: I thought that you were an adult; it seems that I was mistaken. (*She crosses slowly to the sofa and sinks down and stares at* LAURA.)

LAURA: Please don't stare at me, Mother.

AMANDA *closes her eyes and lowers her head. Count ten.*

AMANDA: What are we going to do, what is going to become of us, what is the future?

Count ten.

LAURA: Has something happened, Mother? (AMANDA *draws a long breath and takes out the handkerchief again. Dabbing process.*) Mother, has—something happened?

AMANDA: I'll be all right in a minute, I'm just bewildered—(*count five*)—by life. . . .

LAURA: Mother, I wish that you would tell me what's happened!

AMANDA: As you know, I was supposed to be inducted into my office at the D.A.R. this afternoon. (*Image: A swarm of typewriters.*) But I stopped off at Rubicam's business college to speak to your teachers about your having a cold and ask them what progress they thought you were making down there.

LAURA: Oh. . . .

AMANDA: I went to the typing instructor and introduced myself as your mother. She didn't know who you were. Wingfield, she said. We don't have any such student enrolled at the school! I assured her she did, that you had been going to classes since early in January. "I wonder," she said, "if you could be talking about that terribly shy little girl who dropped out of school after only a few days attendance?" "No," I said, "Laura, my daughter, has been going to school every day for the past six weeks!" "Excuse me," she said. She took the attendance book out and there was your name, unmistakably printed, and all the dates you were absent until they decided that you had dropped out of school. I still said, "No, there must have been some mistake! There must have been some mix-up in the records!" And she said, "No—I remember her perfectly now. Her hands shook so that she couldn't hit the right keys! The first time we gave a speed-test, she broke down completely—was sick at the stomach and almost had to be carried into the wash-room! After that morning she never showed up any more. We phoned the house but never got any answer—while I was working at Famous and Barr, I suppose, demonstrating those—Oh!" I felt so weak I could barely keep on my feet! I had to sit down while they got me a glass of water! Fifty dollars' tuition, all of our plans—my hopes and ambitions for you—just gone up the spout, just gone up the spout like that. (LAURA *draws a long breath and gets awkwardly to her feet. She crosses to the victrola and winds it up.*) What are you doing?

LAURA: Oh! (*She releases the handle and returns to her seat.*)

AMANDA: Laura, where have you been going when you've gone out pretending that you were going to business college?

LAURA: I've just been going out walking.

AMANDA: That's not true.

LAURA: It is. I just went walking.

AMANDA: Walking? Walking? In winter? Deliberately courting pneumonia in that light coat? Where did you walk to, Laura?

LAURA: All sorts of places—mostly in the park.

AMANDA: Even after you'd started catching that cold?

LAURA: It was the lesser of two evils, Mother. (*Image: Winter scene in the park.*) I couldn't go back up. I—threw up—on the floor!

AMANDA: From half past seven till after five every day you mean to tell me you walked around in the park, because you wanted to make me think that you were still going to Rubicam's Business College?

LAURA: It wasn't as bad as it sounds. I went inside places to get warmed up.

AMANDA: Inside where?

LAURA: I went in the art museum and the bird-houses at the Zoo. I visited the penguins every day! Sometimes I did without lunch and went to the movies. Lately I've been spending most of my afternoons in the Jewel-box, that big glass house where they raise the tropical flowers.

AMANDA: You did all this to deceive me, just for deception? (LAURA *looks down.*) Why?

LAURA: Mother, when you're disappointed, you get that awful suffering look on your face, like the picture of Jesus' mother in the museum!

AMANDA: Hush!

LAURA: I couldn't face it.

Pause. A whisper of strings.
(Legend: "The Crust of Humility.")

AMANDA (*hopelessly fingering the huge pocketbook*): So what are we going to do the rest of our lives? Stay home and watch the parades go by? Amuse ourselves with the glass menagerie, darling? Eternally play those wornout phonograph records your father left as a painful reminder of him? We won't have a business career—we've given that up because it gave us nervous indigestion! (*laughs wearily*) What is there left but dependency all our lives? I know so well what becomes of unmarried women who aren't prepared to occupy a position. I've seen such pitiful cases in the South—barely tolerated spinsters living upon the grudging patronage of sister's husband or brother's wife!—stuck away in some little mouse-trap of a room—encouraged by one in-law to visit another—little birdlike women without any nest—eating the crust of humility all their life! Is that the future that we've mapped out for ourselves? I swear it's the only alternative I can think of! It isn't a very pleasant alternative, is it? Of course—some girls *do marry*. (LAURA *twists her hands nervously*.) Haven't you ever liked some boy?

LAURA: Yes. I liked one once. (*rises*) I came across his picture a while ago.

AMANDA (*with some interest*): He gave you his picture?

LAURA: No, it's in the year-book.

AMANDA (*disappointed*): Oh—a high-school boy.

(*Screen image:* JIM *as high-school hero bearing a silver cup*.)

LAURA: Yes. His name was Jim. (LAURA *lifts the heavy annual from the claw-foot table*.) Here he is in *The Pirates of Penzance*.

AMANDA (*absently*): The what?

LAURA: The operetta the senior class put on. He had a wonderful voice and we sat across the aisle from each other Mondays, Wednesdays and Fridays in the Aud. Here he is with the silver cup for debating! See his grin?

AMANDA (*absently*): He must have had a jolly disposition.

LAURA: He used to call me—Blue Roses.

(*Image: Blue roses*.)

AMANDA: Why did he call you such a name as that?

LAURA: When I had that attack of pleurosis—he asked me what was the matter when I came back. I said pleurosis—he thought that I said Blue Roses! So that's what he always called me after that. Whenever he saw me, he'd holler, "Hello, Blue Roses!" I didn't care for the girl that he went out with. Emily Meisenbach. Emily was the best-dressed girl at Soldan. She never struck me, though, as being sincere . . . It says in the Personal Section— they're engaged. That's—six years ago! They must be married by now.

AMANDA: Girls that aren't cut out for business careers usually wind up married to some nice man. (*gets up with a spark of revival*) Sister, that's what you'll do!

LAURA *utters a startled, doubtful laugh. She reaches quickly for a piece of glass*.

LAURA: But, Mother—

AMANDA: Yes? (*crossing to photograph*)

LAURA (*in a tone of frightened apology*): I'm—crippled!

(*Image: Screen*.)

AMANDA: Nonsense! Laura, I've told you never, never to use that word. Why, you're not crippled, you just have a little defect—hardly noticeable, even! When people have some slight disadvantage like that, they cultivate other things to make up for it—develop charm—and vivacity—and—*charm!* That's all you have to do! (*She turns again to the photograph*.) One thing your father had *plenty of*—was *charm!*

TOM *motions to the fiddle in the winds*.

(*The scene fades out with music*.)

Scene 3

(Legend on screen: "After the Fiasco—")
TOM *speaks from the fire-escape landing.*

TOM: After the fiasco at Rubicam's Business College, the idea of getting a
gentleman caller for Laura began to play a more and more important part
in Mother's calculations. It became an obsession. Like some archetype of
the universal unconscious, the image of the gentleman caller haunted our
small apartment. . . . *(Image: Young man at door with flowers.)* An
evening at home rarely passed without some allusion to this image, this
spectre, this hope. . . . Even when he wasn't mentioned, his presence
hung in Mother's preoccupied look and in my sister's frightened, apologetic manner—hung like a sentence passed upon the Wingfields! Mother
was a woman of action as well as words. She began to take logical steps
in the planned direction. Late that winter and in the early spring—realizing that extra money would be needed to properly feather the nest and
plume the bird—she conducted a vigorous campaign on the telephone,
roping in subscribers to one of those magazines for matrons called *The
Home-maker's Companion,* the type of journal that features the serialized
sublimations of ladies of letters who think in terms of delicate cup-like
breasts, slim, tapering waists, rich, creamy thighs, eyes like wood-smoke
in autumn, fingers that soothe and caress like strains of music, bodies as
powerful as Etruscan sculpture.

(Screen image: Glamor magazine cover.)
AMANDA *enters with phone on long extension cord. She is spotted in the
dim stage.*

AMANDA: Ida Scott? This is Amanda Wingfield! We *missed* you at the D.A.R.
last Monday! I said to myself: She's probably suffering with that sinus condition! How is that sinus condition? Horrors! Heaven have mercy!—You're
a Christian martyr, yes, that's what you are, a Christian martyr! Well, I just
now happened to notice that your subscription to the *Companion's* about
to expire! Yes, it expires with the next issue, honey!—just when that wonderful new serial by Bessie Mae Hopper is getting off to such an exciting
start. Oh, honey, it's something that you can't miss! You remember how
Gone With the Wind took everybody by storm? You simply couldn't go
out if you hadn't read it. All everybody *talked* was Scarlett O'Hara. Well,
this is a book that critics already compare to *Gone With the Wind.* It's the
Gone With the Wind of the post-World War generation!—What?—Burning?—Oh, honey, don't let them burn, go take a look in the oven and I'll
hold the wire! Heavens—I think she's hung up!

(Dim out.)
*(Legend on screen: "You think I'm in love with continental
shoemakers?")*
Before the stage is lighted, the violent voices of TOM *and* AMANDA *are
heard. They are quarreling behind the portieres. In front of them stands*
LAURA *with clenched hands and panicky expression.*

A clear pool of light on her figure throughout this scene.

TOM: What in Christ's name am I—

AMANDA (*shrilly*): Don't you use that—

TOM: Supposed to do!

AMANDA: Expression! Not in my—

TOM: Ohhh!

AMANDA: Presence! Have you gone out of your senses?

TOM: I have, that's true, *driven* out!

AMANDA: What is the matter with you, you—big—big—IDIOT!

TOM: Look—I've got *no thing,* no single thing—

AMANDA: Lower your voice!

TOM: In my life here that I can call my own! Everything is—

AMANDA: Stop that shouting!

TOM: Yesterday you confiscated my books! You had the nerve to—

AMANDA: I took that horrible novel back to the library—yes! That hideous book by that insane Mr. Lawrence. (TOM *laughs wildly.*) I cannot control the output of diseased minds or people who cater to them—(TOM *laughs still more wildly.*) BUT I WON'T ALLOW SUCH FILTH BROUGHT INTO MY HOUSE! No, no, no, no, no!

TOM: House, house! Who pays rent on it, who makes a slave of himself to—

AMANDA (*fairly screeching*): Don't you DARE to—

TOM: No, no, *I* mustn't say things! *I've* got to just—

AMANDA: Let me tell you—

TOM: I don't want to hear any more! (*He tears the portieres open. The upstage area is lit with a turgid smoky red glow.*)

AMANDA's *hair is in metal curlers and she wears a very old bathrobe, much too large for her slight figure, a relic of the faithless Mr. Wingfield.*
An upright typewriter and a wild disarray of manuscripts is on the drop-leaf table. The quarrel was probably precipitated by AMANDA's *interruption of his creative labor. A chair lying overthrown on the floor.*
Their gesticulating shadows are cast on the ceiling by the fiery glow.

AMANDA: You *will* hear more, you—

TOM: No, I won't hear more, I'm going out!

AMANDA: You come right back in—

TOM: Out, out, out! Because I'm—

AMANDA: Come back here, Tom Wingfield! I'm not through talking to you!

TOM: Oh, go—

LAURA (*desperately*): —Tom!

AMANDA: You're going to listen, and no more insolence from you! I'm at the end of my patience! (*He comes back toward her.*)

TOM: What do you think I'm at? Aren't I supposed to have any patience to reach the end of, Mother? I know, I know. It seems unimportant to you, what I'm *doing*—what I *want* to do—having a little *difference* between them! You don't think that—

AMANDA: I think you've been doing things that you're ashamed of. That's why you act like this. I don't believe that you go every night to the movies. Nobody goes to the movies night after night. Nobody in their right minds goes to the movies as often as you pretend to. People don't go to the movies at nearly midnight, and movies don't let out at two A.M. Come in stumbling. Muttering to yourself like a maniac! You get three hours' sleep and then go to work. Oh, I can picture the way you're doing down there. Moping, doping, because you're in no condition.

TOM (*wildly*): No, I'm in no condition!

AMANDA: What right have you got to jeopardize your job? Jeopardize the security of us all? How do you think we'd manage if you were—

TOM: Listen! You think I'm crazy *about the warehouse? (He bends fiercely toward her slight figure.)* You think I'm in love with the Continental Shoemakers? You think I want to spend fifty-five *years* down there in that—*celotex interior!* with—*fluorescent—tubes!* Look! I'd rather somebody picked up a crowbar and battered out my brains—than go back mornings! I *go!* Every time you come in yelling that God damn *"Rise and Shine!" "Rise and Shine!"* I say to myself, "How *lucky dead* people are!" But I get up. I *go!* For sixty-five dollars a month I give up all that I dream of doing and being *ever!* And you say self—*self's* all I ever think of. Why, listen, if self is what I thought of, Mother, I'd be where he is—GONE! *(pointing to father's picture)* As far as the system of transportation reaches! *(He starts past her. She grabs his arm.)* Don't grab at me, Mother!

AMANDA: Where are you going?

TOM: I'm going to the *movies!*

AMANDA: I don't believe that lie!

TOM (*Crouching toward her, overtowering her tiny figure. She backs away, gasping.*): I'm going to opium dens! Yes, opium dens, dens of vice and criminals' hang-outs, Mother. I've joined the Hogan gang, I'm a hired assassin, I carry a tommy-gun in a violin case! I run a string of cat-houses in the Valley! They call me Killer, Killer Wingfield, I'm leading a double-life, a simple, honest warehouse worker by day, by night a dynamic *czar* of the *underworld, Mother* I go to gambling casinos, I spin away fortunes on the roulette table! I wear a patch over one eye and a false mustache, sometimes I put on green whiskers. On those occasions they call me— *El Diablo!* Oh, I could tell you things to make you sleepless! My enemies plan to dynamite this place. They're going to blow us all sky-high some night! I'll be glad, very happy, and so will you! You'll go up, up on a broomstick, over Blue Mountain with seventeen gentlemen callers! You ugly—babbling old—*witch*. . . . *(He goes through a series of violent, clumsy movements, seizing his overcoat, lunging to the door, pulling it fiercely open. The women watch him, aghast. His arm catches in the sleeve of the coat as he struggles to pull it on. For a moment he is pinioned by the bulky garment. With an outraged groan he tears the coat off again, splitting the shoulder of it, and hurls it across the room. It strikes against the shelf of* LAURA'S *glass collection, there is a tinkle of shattering glass.* LAURA *cries out as if wounded.*)

(Music. Legend: "The Glass Menagerie.")

LAURA (*shrilly*): My glass!—menagerie. . . . *(She covers her face and turns away.)*

But AMANDA *is still stunned and stupefied by the "ugly witch" so that she barely notices this occurrence. Now she recovers her speech.*

AMANDA (*in an awful voice*): I won't speak to you—until you apologize! (*She crosses through portieres and draws them together behind her.* TOM *is left with* LAURA. LAURA *clings weakly to the mantel with her face averted.* TOM *stares at her stupidly for a moment. Then he crosses to shelf. Drops awkwardly on his knees to collect the fallen glass, glancing at* LAURA *as if he would speak but couldn't.*)

"The Glass Menagerie" steals in as

(*The scene dims out.*)

Scene 4

The interior is dark. Faint light in the alley.

A deep-voiced bell in a church is tolling the hour of five as the scene commences.

TOM *appears at the top of the alley. After each solemn boom of the bell in the tower, he shakes a little noise-maker or rattle as if to express the tiny spasm of man in contrast to the sustained power and dignity of the Almighty. This and the unsteadiness of his advance make it evident that he has been drinking.*

As he climbs the few steps to the fire-escape landing light steals up inside. LAURA *appears in night-dress, observing* TOM'S *empty bed in the front room.*

TOM *fishes in his pockets for door-key, removing a motley assortment of articles in the search, including a perfect shower of movie-ticket stubs and an empty bottle. At last he finds the key, but just as he is about to insert it, it slips from his fingers. He strikes a match and crouches below the door.*

TOM (*bitterly*): One crack—and it falls through!

LAURA *opens the door.*

LAURA: Tom! Tom, what are you doing?
TOM: Looking for a door-key.
LAURA: Where have you been all this time?
TOM: I have been to the movies.
LAURA: All this time at the movies?
TOM: There was a very long program. There was a Garbo picture and a Mickey Mouse and a travelogue and a newsreel and a preview of coming attractions. And there was an organ solo and a collection for the milk-fund—simultaneously—which ended up in a terrible fight between a fat lady and an usher!
LAURA (*innocently*): Did you have to stay through everything?
TOM: Of course! And, oh, I forgot! There was a big stage show! The headliner on this stage show was Malvolio the Magician. He performed

wonderful tricks, many of them, such as pouring water back and forth between pitchers. First it turned to wine and then it turned to beer and then it turned to whiskey. I know it was whiskey it finally turned into because he needed somebody to come up out of the audience to help him, and I came up—both shows! It was Kentucky Straight Bourbon. A very generous fellow, he gave souvenirs. (*He pulls from his back pocket a shimmering rainbow-colored scarf.*) He gave me this. This is his magic scarf. You can have it, Laura. You wave it over a canary cage and you get a bowl of gold-fish. You wave it over the gold-fish bowl and they fly away canaries. . . . But the wonderfullest trick of all was the coffin trick. We nailed him into a coffin and he got out of the coffin without removing one nail. (*He has come inside.*) There is a trick that would come in handy for me—get me out of this 2 by 4 situation! (*flops onto bed and starts removing shoes*)

LAURA: Tom—Shhh!

TOM: What're you shushing me for?

LAURA: You'll wake up Mother.

TOM: Goody, goody! Pay 'er back for all those "Rise an' Shines." (*lies down, groaning*) You know it don't take much intelligence to get yourself into a nailed-up coffin, Laura. But who in hell ever got himself out of one without removing one nail?

As if in answer, the father's grinning photograph lights up.
    (*Scene dims out.*)
    Immediately following: The church bell is heard striking six. At the sixth stroke the alarm clock goes off in AMANDA'S *room, and after a few moments we hear her calling: "Rise and Shine! Rise and Shine! Laura, go tell your brother to rise and shine!"*

TOM (*sitting up slowly*): I'll rise—but I won't shine.

The light increases.

AMANDA: Laura, tell your brother his coffee is ready.

LAURA *slips into front room.*

LAURA: Tom!—It's nearly seven. Don't make Mother nervous. (*He stares at her stupidly. Beseechingly.*) Tom, speak to Mother this morning. Make up with her, apologize, speak to her!

TOM: She won't to me. It's her that started not speaking.

LAURA: If you just say you're sorry she'll start speaking.

TOM: Her not speaking—is that such a tragedy?

LAURA: Please—please!

AMANDA (*calling from kitchenette*): Laura, are you going to do what I asked you to do, or do I have to get dressed and go out myself?

LAURA: Going, going—soon as I get on my coat! (*She pulls on a shapeless felt hat with nervous, jerky movement, pleadingly glancing at* TOM. *Rushes awkwardly for coat. The coat is one of* AMANDA'S, *inaccurately made-over, the sleeves too short for* LAURA.) Butter and what else?

AMANDA (*entering upstage*): Just butter. Tell them to charge it.

LAURA: Mother, they make such faces when I do that.

AMANDA: Sticks and stones can break our bones, but the expression on Mr. Garfinkel's face won't harm us! Tell your brother his coffee is getting cold.

LAURA (*at door*): Do what I asked you, will you, will you, Tom?

He looks sullenly away.

AMANDA: Laura, go now or just don't go at all!

LAURA (*rushing out*): Going—going! (*A second later she cries out.* TOM *springs up and crosses to door.* AMANDA *rushes anxiously in.* TOM *opens the door.*)

TOM: Laura?

LAURA: I'm all right. I slipped, but I'm all right.

AMANDA (*peering anxiously after her*): If anyone breaks a leg on those fire-escape steps, the landlord ought to be sued for every cent he possesses! (*She shuts door. Remembers she isn't speaking and returns to other room.*)

As TOM *enters listlessly for his coffee, she turns her back to him and stands rigidly facing the window on the gloomy gray vault of the areaway. Its light on her face with its aged but childish features is cruelly sharp, satirical as a Daumier print.*

(*Music under: "Ave Maria."*)

TOM *glances sheepishly but sullenly at her averted figure and slumps at the table. The coffee is scalding hot; he sips it and gasps and spits it back in the cup. At his gasp,* AMANDA *catches her breath and half turns. Then catches herself and turns back to window.*

TOM *blows on his coffee, glancing sidewise at his mother. She clears her throat.* TOM *clears his. He starts to rise. Sinks back down again, scratches his head, clears his throat again.* AMANDA *coughs.* TOM *raises his cup in both hands to blow on it, his eyes staring over the rim of it at his mother for several moments. Then he slowly sets the cup down and awkwardly and hesitantly rises from the chair.*

TOM (*hoarsely*): Mother. I—I apologize, Mother. (AMANDA *draws a quick, shuddering breath. Her face works grotesquely. She breaks into childlike tears.*) I'm sorry for what I said, for everything that I said, I didn't mean it.

AMANDA (*sobbingly*): My devotion has made me a witch and so I make myself hateful to my children!

TOM: *No, you* don't.

AMANDA: I worry so much, don't sleep, it makes me nervous!

TOM (*gently*): I understand that.

AMANDA: I've had to put up a solitary battle all these years. But you're my right-hand bower! Don't fall down, don't fail!

TOM (*gently*): I try, Mother.

AMANDA (*with great enthusiasm*): Try and you will SUCCEED! (*The notion makes her breathless.*) Why, you—you're just *full* of natural endowments! Both of my children—they're *unusual* children! Don't you think I know it? I'm so—*proud!* Happy and—feel I've—so much to be thankful for but—Promise me one thing, Son!

TOM: What, Mother?

AMANDA: Promise, son, you'll—never be a drunkard!

TOM (*turns to her grinning*): I will never be a drunkard, Mother.

AMANDA: That's what frightened me so, that you'd be drinking! Eat a bowl of Purina!

TOM: Just coffee, Mother.

AMANDA: Shredded wheat biscuit?

TOM: No. No, Mother, just coffee.

AMANDA: You can't put in a day's work on an empty stomach. You've got ten minutes—don't gulp! Drinking too-hot liquids makes cancer of the stomach. . . . Put cream in.

TOM: No, thank you.

AMANDA: To cool it.

TOM: No! No, thank you, I want it black.

AMANDA: I know, but it's not good for you. We have to do all that we can to build ourselves up. In these trying times we live in, all that we have to cling to is—each other. . . . That's why it's so important to—Tom, I—I sent out your sister so I could discuss something with you. If you hadn't spoken I would have spoken to you. (*sits down*)

TOM (*gently*): What is it, Mother, that you want to discuss?

AMANDA: *Laura!*

> TOM *puts his cup down slowly.*
> (*Legend on screen: "Laura."*)
> (*Music: "The Glass Menagerie."*)

TOM: —Oh.—Laura . . .

AMANDA (*touching his sleeve*): You know how Laura is. So quiet but—still water runs deep! She notices things and I think she—broods about them. (TOM *looks up.*) A few days ago I came in and she was crying.

TOM: What about?

AMANDA: You.

TOM: Me?

AMANDA: She has an idea that you're not happy here.

TOM: What gave her that idea?

AMANDA: What gives her any idea? However, you do act strangely. I—I'm not criticizing, understand *that!* I know your ambitions do not lie in the warehouse, that like everybody in the whole wide world—you've had to—make sacrifices, but—Tom—Tom—life's not easy, it calls for—Spartan endurance! There's so many things in my heart that I cannot describe to you! I've never told you but I—*loved* your father. . . .

TOM (*gently*): I know that, Mother.

AMANDA: And you—when I see you taking after his ways! Staying out late—and—well, you *had* been drinking the night you were in that—terrifying condition! Laura says that you hate the apartment and that you go out nights to get away from it! Is that true, Tom?

TOM: No. You say there's so much in your heart that you can't describe to me. That's true of me, too. There's so much in my heart that I can't describe to *you!* So let's respect each other's—

AMANDA: But, why—*why,* Tom—are you always so *restless?* Where do you go to, nights?

TOM: I—go to the movies.

AMANDA: Why do you go to the movies so much, Tom?

TOM: I go to the movies because—I like adventure. Adventure is something I don't have much of at work, so I go to the movies.

AMANDA: But, Tom, you go to the movies *entirely* too much!

TOM: I like a lot of adventure.

> AMANDA *looks baffled, then hurt. As the familiar inquisition resumes he becomes hard and impatient again.* AMANDA *slips back into her querulous attitude toward him.*
> (*Image on screen: Sailing vessel with Jolly Roger.*)

AMANDA: Most young men find adventure in their careers.

TOM: Then most young men are not employed in a warehouse.

AMANDA: The world is full of young men employed in warehouses and offices and factories.

TOM: Do all of them find adventure in their careers?

AMANDA: They do or they do without it! Not everybody has a craze for adventure.

TOM: Man is by instinct a lover, a hunter, a fighter, and none of those instincts are given much play at the warehouse!

AMANDA: Man is by instinct! Don't quote instinct to me! Instinct is something that people have got away from! It belongs to animals! Christian adults don't want it!

TOM: What do Christian adults want, then, Mother?

AMANDA: Superior things! Things of the mind and the spirit! Only animals have to satisfy instincts! Surely your aims are somewhat higher than theirs! Than monkeys—pigs—

TOM: I reckon they're not.

AMANDA: You're joking. However, that isn't what I wanted to discuss.

TOM (*rising*): I haven't much time.

AMANDA (*pushing his shoulders*): Sit down.

TOM: You want me to punch in red at the warehouse, Mother?

AMANDA: You have five minutes. I want to talk about Laura.

(*Legend: "Plans and Provisions."*)

TOM: All right! What about Laura?

AMANDA: We have to be making some plans and provisions for her. She's older than you, two years, and nothing has happened. She just drifts along doing nothing. It frightens me terribly how she just drifts along.

TOM: I guess she's the type that people call home girls.

AMANDA: There's no such type, and if there is, it's a pity! That is unless the home is hers, with a husband!

TOM: What?

AMANDA: Oh, I can see the handwriting on the wall as plain as I see the nose in front of my face! It's terrifying! More and more you remind me of your father! He was out all hours without explanation!—Then *left! Good-bye!* And me with the bag to hold. I saw that letter you got from the Merchant Marine. I know what you're dreaming of. I'm not standing here blindfolded. Very well, then. Then *do* it! But not till there's somebody to take your place.

TOM: What do you mean?

AMANDA: I mean that as soon as Laura has got somebody to take care of her, married, a home of her own, independent—why, then you'll be free to go wherever you please, on land, on sea, whichever way the wind blows you! But until that time you've got to look out for your sister. I don't say me because I'm old and don't matter! I say for your sister because she's young and dependent. I put her in business college—a dismal failure! Frightened her so it made her sick at the stomach. I took her over to the Young People's League at the church. Another fiasco. She spoke to nobody, nobody spoke to her. Now all she does is fool with those pieces of glass and play those worn-out records. What kind of a life is that for a girl to lead?

TOM: What can I do about it?

AMANDA: Overcome selfishness! Self, self, self is all that you ever think of! (TOM *springs up and crosses to get his coat. It is ugly and bulky. He pulls on a cap with earmuffs.*) Where is your muffler? Put your wool muffler on! (*He snatches it angrily from the closet and tosses it around his neck and pulls both ends tight.*) Tom! I haven't said what I had in mind to ask you.

TOM: I'm too late to—

AMANDA (*Catching his arm—very importunately. Then shyly.*): Down at the warehouse, aren't there some—nice young men?

TOM: No!

AMANDA: There *must* be—*some* . . .

TOM: Mother—

Gesture.

AMANDA: Find out one that's clean-living—doesn't drink and—ask him out for sister!

TOM: What?

AMANDA: For *sister!* To *meet!* Get *acquainted!*

TOM (*stamping to door*): Oh, my *go-osh!*

AMANDA: Will you? (*He opens door. Imploringly.*) Will you? (*He starts down.*) Will you? *Will* you, dear?

TOM (*calling back*): YES!

AMANDA *closes the door hesitantly and with a troubled but faintly hopeful expression.*
  (*Screen image:* Glamor *magazine cover.*)
  Spot AMANDA *at phone.*

AMANDA: Ella Cartwright? This is Amanda Wingfield! How are you, honey? How is that kidney condition? *(count five)* Horrors! *(count five)* You're a Christian martyr, yes, honey, that's what you are, a Christian martyr! Well, I just now happened to notice in my little red book that your subscription to the *Companion* has just run out! I knew that you wouldn't want to miss out on the wonderful serial starting in this new issue. It's by Bessie Mae Hopper, the first thing she's written since *Honeymoon for Three*. Wasn't that a strange and interesting story? Well, this one is even lovelier, I believe. It has a sophisticated, society background. It's all about the horsey set on Long Island!

(*Fade out.*)

Scene 5

(*Legend on screen: "Annunciation."*) *Fade with music.*
 It is early dusk of a spring evening. Supper has just been finished in the Wingfield apartment. AMANDA *and* LAURA *in light-colored dresses are removing dishes from the table, in the upstage area, which is shadowy, their movements formalized almost as a dance or ritual, their moving forms as pale and silent as moths.*
 TOM, *in white shirt and trousers, rises from the table and crosses toward the fire-escape.*

AMANDA (*as he passes her*): Son, will you do me a favor?

TOM: What?

AMANDA: Comb your hair! You look so pretty when your hair is combed! (TOM *slouches on sofa with evening paper. Enormous caption "Franco Triumphs."*) There is only one respect in which I would like you to emulate your father.

TOM: What respect is that?

AMANDA: The care he always took of his appearance. He never allowed himself to look untidy. (*He throws down the paper and crosses to fire-escape.*) Where are you going?

TOM: I'm going out to smoke.

AMANDA: You smoke too much. A pack a day at fifteen cents a pack. How much would that amount to in a month? Thirty times fifteen is how much, Tom? Figure it out and you will be astounded at what you could save. Enough to give you a night-school course in accounting at Washington U! Just think what a wonderful thing that would be for you, Son!

TOM *is unmoved by the thought.*

TOM: I'd rather smoke. (*He steps out on landing, letting the screen door slam.*)

AMANDA (*sharply*): I know! That's the tragedy of it. . . .(*Alone, she turns to look at her husband's picture.*)

(*Dance music: "All the world is waiting for the sunrise!"*)

TOM (*to the audience*): Across the alley from us was the Paradise Dance Hall. On evenings in spring the windows and doors were open and the music came outdoors. Sometimes the lights were turned out except for a large glass sphere that hung from the ceiling. It would turn slowly about and filter the dusk with delicate rainbow colors. Then the orchestra played a waltz or a tango, something that had a slow and sensuous rhythm. Couples would come outside, to the relative privacy of the alley. You could see them kissing behind ash-pits and telephone poles. This was the compensation for lives that passed like mine, without any change or adventure. Adventure and change were imminent in this year. They were waiting around the corner for all these kids. Suspended in the mist over Berchtesgaden, caught in the folds of Chamberlain's umbrella—In Spain there was Guernica! But here there was only hot swing music and liquor, dance halls, bars, and movies, and sex that hung in the gloom like a chandelier and flooded the world with brief, deceptive rainbows. . . . All the world was waiting for bombardments!

AMANDA *turns from the picture and comes outside.*

AMANDA (*sighing*): A fire-escape landing's a poor excuse for a porch. (*She spreads a newspaper on a step and sits down, gracefully and demurely as if she were settling into a swing on a Mississippi veranda.*) What are you looking at?

TOM: The moon.

AMANDA: Is there a moon this evening?

TOM: It's rising over Garfinkel's Delicatessen.

AMANDA: So it is! A little silver slipper of a moon. Have you made a wish on it yet?

TOM: Um-hum.

AMANDA: What did you wish for?

TOM: That's a secret.

AMANDA: A secret, huh? Well, I won't tell mine either. I will be just as mysterious as you.

TOM: I bet I can guess what yours is.

AMANDA: Is my head so transparent?

TOM: You're not a sphinx.

AMANDA: No, I don't have secrets. I'll tell you what I wished for on the moon. Success and happiness for my precious children! I wish for that whenever there's a moon, and when there isn't a moon, I wish for it, too.

TOM: I thought perhaps you wished for a gentleman caller.

AMANDA: Why do you say that?

TOM: Don't you remember asking me to fetch one?

AMANDA: I remember suggesting that it would be nice for your sister if you brought home some nice young man from the warehouse. I think that I've made that suggestion more than once.

TOM: Yes, you have made it repeatedly.

AMANDA: Well?

TOM: We are going to have one.

AMANDA: *What?*

TOM: A gentleman caller!

(*The annunciation is celebrated with music.*)
    AMANDA: *rises.*
    (*Image on screen: Caller with bouquet.*)

AMANDA: You mean you have asked some nice young man to come over?

TOM: Yep. I've asked him to dinner.

AMANDA: You really did?

TOM: I did!

AMANDA: You did, and did he—*accept?*

TOM: He did!

AMANDA: Well, well—well, well! That's—lovely!

TOM: I thought that you would be pleased.

AMANDA: It's definite, then?

TOM: Very definite.

AMANDA: Soon?

TOM: Very soon.

AMANDA: For heaven's sake, stop putting on and tell me some things, will you?

TOM: What things do you want me to tell you?

AMANDA: *Naturally* I would like to know when he's *coming!*

TOM: He's coming tomorrow.

AMANDA: *Tomorrow?*

TOM: Yep. Tomorrow.

AMANDA: But, Tom!

TOM: Yes, Mother?

AMANDA: Tomorrow gives me no time!

TOM: Time for what?

AMANDA: Preparations! Why didn't you phone me at once, as soon as you asked him, the minute that he accepted? Then, don't you see, I could have been getting ready!

TOM: You don't have to make any fuss.

AMANDA: Oh, Tom, Tom, Tom, of course I have to make a fuss! I want things nice, not sloppy! Not thrown together. I'll certainly have to do some fast thinking, won't I?

TOM: I don't see why you have to think at all.

AMANDA: You just don't know. We can't have a gentleman caller in a pig-sty! All my wedding silver has to be polished, the monogrammed table linen ought to be laundered! The windows have to be washed and fresh curtains put up. And how about clothes? We have to *wear* something, don't we?

TOM: Mother, this boy is no one to make a fuss over!

AMANDA: Do you realize he's the first young man we've introduced to your sister? It's terrible, dreadful, disgraceful the poor little sister has never received a single gentleman caller! Tom, come inside! (*She opens the screen door.*)

TOM: What for?

AMANDA: I want to ask you some things.

TOM: If you're going to make such a fuss, I'll call it off, I'll tell him not to come!

AMANDA: You certainly won't do anything of the kind. Nothing offends people worse than broken engagements. It simply means I'll have to work like a Turk! We won't be brilliant, but we will pass inspection. Come on inside. (TOM *follows, groaning.*) Sit down.

TOM: Any particular place you would like me to sit?

AMANDA: Thank heavens I've got that new sofa! I'm also making payments on a floor lamp I'll have sent out! And put the chintz covers on, they'll brighten things up! Of course I'd hoped to have these walls re-papered. . . . What is the young man's name?

TOM: His name is O'Connor.

AMANDA: That, of course, means fish—tomorrow is Friday! I'll have that salmon loaf—with Durkee's dressing! What does he do? He works at the warehouse?

TOM: Of course! How else would I—

AMANDA: Tom, he—doesn't drink?

TOM: Why do you ask me that?

AMANDA: Your father *did!*

TOM: Don't get started on that!

AMANDA: He *does* drink, then?

TOM: Not that I know of!

AMANDA: Make sure, be certain! The last thing I want for my daughter's a boy who drinks!

TOM: Aren't you being a little bit premature? Mr. O'Connor has not yet appeared on the scene!

AMANDA: But will tomorrow. To meet your sister, and what do I know about his character? Nothing! Old maids are better off than wives of drunkards!

TOM: Oh, my God!

AMANDA: Be still!

TOM (*leaning forward to whisper*): Lots of fellows meet girls whom they don't marry!

AMANDA: Oh, talk sensibly, Tom—and don't be sarcastic! (*She has gotten a hairbrush.*)

TOM: What are you doing?

AMANDA: I'm brushing that cow-lick down! What is this young man's position at the warehouse?

TOM (*submitting grimly to the brush and the interrogation*): This young man's position is that of a shipping clerk, Mother.

AMANDA: Sounds to me like a fairly responsible job, the sort of a job *you* would be in if you just had more *get-up*. What is his salary? Have you any idea?

TOM: I would judge it to be approximately eighty-five dollars a month.

AMANDA: Well—not princely, but—

TOM: Twenty more than I make.

AMANDA: Yes, how well I know! But for a family man, eighty-five dollars a month is not much more than you can just get by on. . . .

TOM: Yes, but Mr. O'Connor is not a family man.

AMANDA: He might be, mightn't he? Some time in the future?

TOM: I see. Plans and provisions.

AMANDA: You are the only young man that I know of who ignores the fact that the future becomes the present, the present the past, and the past turns into everlasting regret if you don't plan for it!

TOM: I will think that over and see what I can make of it.

AMANDA: Don't be supercilious with your mother! Tell me some more about this—what do you call him?

TOM: James D. O'Connor. The D. is for Delaney.

AMANDA: Irish on *both* sides! *Gracious!* And doesn't drink?

TOM: Shall I call him up and ask him right this minute?

AMANDA: The only way to find out about those things is to make discreet inquiries at the proper moment. When I was a girl in Blue Mountain and it
was suspected that a young man drank, the girl whose attentions he had
been receiving, if any girl *was,* would sometimes speak to the minister of
his church, or rather her father would if her father was living, and sort of
feel him out on the young man's character. That is the way such things
are discreetly handled to keep a young woman from making a tragic
mistake!

TOM: Then how did you happen to make a tragic mistake?

AMANDA: That innocent look of your father's had everyone fooled! He
smiled—the world was *enchanted!* No girl can do worse than put herself
at the mercy of a handsome appearance! I hope that Mr. O'Connor is not
too good-looking.

TOM: No, he's not too good-looking. He's covered with freckles and hasn't
too much of a nose.

AMANDA: He's not right-down homely, though?

TOM: Not right-down homely. Just medium homely, I'd say.

AMANDA: Character's what to look for in a man.

TOM: That's what I've always said, Mother.

AMANDA: You've never said anything of the kind and I suspect you would
never give it a thought.

TOM: Don't be so suspicious of me.

AMANDA: At least I hope he's the type that's up and coming.

TOM: I think he really goes in for self-improvement.

AMANDA: What reason have you to think so?

TOM: He goes to night school.

AMANDA (*beaming*): Splendid! What does he do, I mean study?

TOM: Radio engineering and public speaking!

AMANDA: Then he has visions of being advanced in the world! Any young
man who studies public speaking is aiming to have an executive job
some day! And radio engineering? A thing for the future! Both of these
facts are very illuminating. Those are the sort of things that a mother
should know concerning any young man who comes to call on her
daughter. Seriously or—not.

TOM: One little warning. He doesn't know about Laura. I didn't let on that
we had dark ulterior motives. I just said, why don't you come and have
dinner with us? He said okay and that was the whole conversation.

AMANDA: I bet it was! You're eloquent as an oyster. However, he'll know
about Laura when he gets here. When he sees how lovely and sweet and
pretty she is, he'll thank his lucky stars he was asked to dinner.

TOM: Mother, you mustn't expect too much of Laura.

AMANDA: What do you mean?

TOM: Laura seems all those things to you and me because she's ours and we
love her. We don't even notice she's crippled any more.

AMANDA: Don't say crippled! You know that I never allow that word to be
used!

TOM: But face facts, Mother. She is and—that's not all—

AMANDA: What do you mean "not all"?

TOM: Laura is very different from other girls.

AMANDA: I think the difference is all to her advantage.

TOM: Not quite all—in the eyes of others—strangers—she's terribly shy and lives in a world of her own and those things make her seem a little peculiar to people outside the house.

AMANDA: Don't say peculiar.

TOM: Face the facts. She is.

(*The dance-hall music changes to a tango that has a minor and somewhat ominous tone.*)

AMANDA: In what way is she peculiar—may I ask?

TOM (*gently*): She lives in a world of her own—a world of—little glass ornaments, Mother. . . . (*Gets up.* AMANDA *remains holding brush, looking at him, troubled.*) She plays old phonograph records and—that's about all—(*He glances at himself in the mirror and crosses to door.*)

AMANDA (*sharply*): Where are you going?

TOM: I'm going to the movies. (*out screen door*)

AMANDA: Not to the movies, every night to the movies! (*follows quickly to screen door*) I don't believe you always go to the movies! (*He is gone.* AMANDA *looks worriedly after him for a moment. Then vitality and optimism return and she turns from the door. Crossing to portieres.*) Laura! Laura! (LAURA *answers from kitchenette.*)

LAURA: Yes, Mother.

AMANDA: Let those dishes go and come in front! (LAURA *appears with dish towel. Gaily.*) Laura, come here and make a wish on the moon!

(*Screen image: Moon.*)

LAURA (*entering*): Moon—moon?

AMANDA: A little silver slipper of a moon. Look over your left shoulder, Laura, and make a wish! (LAURA *looks faintly puzzled as if called out of sleep.* AMANDA *seizes her shoulders and turns her at an angle by the door.*) Now! Now, darling, *wish!*

LAURA: What shall I wish for, Mother?

AMANDA (*her voice trembling and her eyes suddenly filling with tears*): Happiness! Good fortune!

(*The violin rises and the stage dims out.*)

Scene 6

(*Image: High school hero.*)

TOM: And so the following evening I brought Jim home to dinner. I had known Jim slightly in high school. In high school Jim was a hero. He had tremendous Irish good nature and vitality with the scrubbed and polished look of white chinaware. He seemed to move in a continual spot-light. He was a star in basketball, captain of the debating club, president of the senior class and the glee club and he sang the male lead in the annual light operas. He was always running or bounding, never just walking. He seemed always at the point of defeating the law of gravity.

He was shooting with such velocity through his adolescence that you would logically expect him to arrive at nothing short of the White House by the time he was thirty. But Jim apparently ran into more interference after his graduation from Soldan. His speed had definitely slowed. Six years after he left high school he was holding a job that wasn't much better than mine.

(*Image: Clerk.*)

He was the only one at the warehouse with whom I was on friendly terms. I was valuable to him as someone who could remember his former glory, who had seen him win basketball games and the silver cup in debating. He knew of my secret practice of retiring to a cabinet of the wash-room to work on poems when business was slack in the warehouse. He called me Shakespeare. And while the other boys in the warehouse regarded me with suspicious hostility, Jim took a humorous attitude toward me. Gradually his attitude affected the others, their hostility wore off and they also began to smile at me as people smile at an oddly fashioned dog who trots across their path at some distance.

I knew that Jim and Laura had known each other at Soldan, and I had heard Laura speak admiringly of his voice. I didn't know if Jim remembered her or not. In high school Laura had been as unobtrusive as Jim had been astonishing. If he did remember Laura, it was not as my sister, for when I asked him to dinner, he grinned and said, "You know, Shakespeare, I never thought of you as having folks!" He was about to discover that I did. . . .

(*Light up stage.*)

(*Legend on screen: "The Accent of a Coming Foot."*)
Friday evening. It is about five o'clock of a late spring evening which comes "scattering poems in the sky."

A delicate lemony light is in the Wingfield apartment.

AMANDA *has worked like a Turk in preparation for the gentleman caller. The results are astonishing. The new floor lamp with its rose-silk shade is in place, a colored paper lantern conceals the broken light fixture in the ceiling, new billowing white curtains are at the windows, chintz covers are on chairs and sofa, a pair of new sofa pillows make their initial appearance.*

Open boxes and tissue paper are scattered on the floor.

LAURA *stands in the middle with lifted arms while* AMANDA *crouches before her, adjusting the hem of the new dress, devout and ritualistic. The dress is colored and designed by memory. The arrangement of* LAURA's *hair is changed; it is softer and more becoming. A fragile, unearthly prettiness has come out in* LAURA: *she is like a piece of translucent glass touched by light, given a momentary radiance, not actual, not lasting.*

AMANDA (*impatiently*): Why are you trembling?
LAURA: Mother, you've made me so nervous!
AMANDA: How have I made you nervous?
LAURA: By all this fuss! You make it seem so important!

AMANDA: I don't understand you, Laura. You couldn't be satisfied with just sitting home, and yet whenever I try to arrange something for you, you seem to resist it.

She gets up.

Now take a look at yourself. No, wait! Wait just a moment—I have an idea!

LAURA: What is it now?

AMANDA *produces two powder puffs which she wraps in handkerchiefs and stuffs in* LAURA'*s bosom.*

LAURA: Mother, what are you doing?

AMANDA: They call them "Gay Deceivers"!

LAURA: I won't wear them!

AMANDA: You will!

LAURA: Why should I?

AMANDA: Because, to be painfully honest, your chest is flat.

LAURA: You make it seem like we were setting a trap.

AMANDA: All pretty girls are a trap, a pretty trap, and men expect them to be. (*Legend: "A Pretty Trap."*) Now look at yourself, young lady. This is the prettiest you will ever be! I've got to fix myself now! You're going to be surprised by your mother's appearance! (*She crosses through portieres, humming gaily.*)

LAURA *moves slowly to the long mirror and stares solemnly at herself.*
    A wind blows the white curtains inward in a slow, graceful motion and with a faint, sorrowful sighing.

AMANDA (*off stage*): It isn't dark enough yet. (*She turns slowly before the mirror with a troubled look.*)

(*Legend on screen: "This Is My Sister: Celebrate Her with Strings!" Music.*)

AMANDA (*laughing, off*): I'm going to show you something. I'm going to make a spectacular appearance!

LAURA: What is it, Mother?

AMANDA: Possess your soul in patience—you will see! Something I've resurrected from that old trunk! Styles haven't changed so terribly much after all. . . . (*She parts the portieres.*) Now just look at your mother! (*She wears a girlish frock of yellowed voile with a blue silk sash. She carries a bunch of jonquils—the legend of her youth is nearly revived. Feverishly.*) This is the dress in which I led the cotillion. Won the cakewalk twice at Sunset Hill, wore one spring to the Governor's ball in Jackson! See how I sashayed around the ballroom, Laura? (*She raises her skirt and does a mincing step around the room.*) I wore it on Sundays for my gentlemen callers! I had it on the day I met your father—I had malaria fever all that spring. The change of climate from East Tennessee to the Delta—weakened resistance—I had a little temperature all the time—not enough to be serious—just enough to make me restless and giddy!—Invitations poured in—parties all over the Delta!—"Stay in bed," said Mother, "you have fever!"—but I just wouldn't.—I took quinine but kept on going, going!—Evenings, dances!—Afternoons, long, long rides! Picnics—lovely!—So lovely, that country in May.—All lacy with dogwood, literally flooded with jonquils!—That was the spring I had the craze for jonquils. Jonquils became an absolute obsession. Mother said, "Honey, there's no more room for jonquils." And still I kept on bringing in more jonquils. Whenever, wherever I saw them, I'd say, "Stop! Stop! I see jonquils!" I made the young men help me gather the jonquils! It was a joke, Amanda and her jonquils! Finally there were no more vases to hold them, every available space was filled with jonquils. No vases to hold them? All right, I'll hold them myself! And then I—(*She stops in front of the picture. Music.*) met your father! Malaria fever and jonquils and then—this—boy. . . . (*She switches on the rose-colored lamp.*) I hope they get here before it starts to rain. (*She crosses upstage and places the jonquils in bowl on table.*) I gave your brother a little extra change so he and Mr. O'Connor could take the service car home.

LAURA (*with altered look*): What did you say his name was?

AMANDA: O'Connor.

LAURA: What is his first name?

AMANDA: I don't remember. Oh, yes, I do. It was—Jim!

LAURA *sways slightly and catches hold of a chair.*
    (*Legend on screen. "Not Jim!"*)

LAURA (*faintly*): Not—Jim!

AMANDA: Yes, that was it, it was Jim! I've never known a Jim that wasn't nice!

(*Music: Ominous.*)

LAURA: Are you sure his name is Jim O'Connor?

AMANDA: Yes. Why?

LAURA: Is he the one that Tom used to know in high school?

AMANDA: He didn't say so. I think he just got to know him at the warehouse.

LAURA: There was a Jim O'Connor we both knew in high school—(*then, with effort*) If that is the one that Tom is bringing to dinner—you'll have to excuse me, I won't come to the table.

AMANDA: What sort of nonsense is this?

LAURA: You asked me once if I'd ever liked a boy. Don't you remember I showed you this boy's picture?

AMANDA: You mean the boy you showed me in the year book?

LAURA: Yes, that boy.

AMANDA: Laura, Laura, were you in love with that boy?

LAURA: I don't know, Mother. All I know is I couldn't sit at the table if it was him!

AMANDA: It won't be him! It isn't the least bit likely. But whether it is or not, you will come to the table. You will not be excused.

LAURA: I'll have to be, Mother.

AMANDA: I don't intend to humor your silliness, Laura. I've had too much from you and your brother, both! So just sit down and compose yourself till they come. Tom has forgotten his key so you'll have to let them in, when they arrive.

LAURA (*panicky*): Oh, Mother—*you* answer the door!

AMANDA (*lightly*): I'll be in the kitchen—busy!

LAURA: Oh, Mother, please answer the door, don't make me do it!

AMANDA (*crossing into kitchenette*): I've got to fix the dressing for the salmon. Fuss, fuss—silliness!—over a gentleman caller!

Door swings shut. LAURA *is left alone.*
   (*Legend:* "Terror!")
   She utters a low moan and turns off the lamp—sits stiffly on the edge of the sofa, knotting her fingers together.
   (*Legend on screen:* "The Opening of a Door!")
TOM *and* JIM *appear on the fire-escape steps and climb to landing. Hearing their approach,* LAURA *rises with a panicky gesture. She retreats to the portieres.*
   The doorbell. LAURA *catches her breath and touches her throat. Low drums.*

AMANDA (*calling*): Laura, sweetheart! The door!

LAURA *stares at it without moving.*

JIM: I think we just beat the rain.
TOM: Uh-huh. (*He rings again, nervously.* JIM *whistles and fishes for a cigarette.*)
AMANDA (*very, very gaily*): Laura, that is your brother and Mr. O'Connor! Will you let them in, darling?

LAURA *crosses toward kitchenette door.*

LAURA (*breathlessly*): Mother—you go to the door!

AMANDA *steps out of kitchenette and stares furiously at* LAURA. *She points imperiously at the door.*

LAURA: Please, please!
AMANDA (*in a fierce whisper*): What is the matter with you, you silly thing?
LAURA (*desperately*): Please, you answer it, *please!*
AMANDA: I told you I wasn't going to humor you, Laura. Why have you chosen this moment to lose your mind?
LAURA: Please, please, please, you go!
AMANDA: You'll have to go to the door because I can't!
LAURA (*despairingly*): I can't either!
AMANDA: *Why?*
LAURA: I'm *sick!*
AMANDA: I'm sick, too—of your nonsense! Why can't you and your brother be normal people? Fantastic whims and behavior! (TOM *gives a long ring.*) Preposterous goings on! Can you give me one reason—(*calls out lyrically*) COMING! JUST ONE SECOND!—why you should be afraid to open a door? Now you answer it, Laura!
LAURA: Oh, oh, oh . . . (*She returns through the portieres. Darts to the victrola and winds it frantically and turns it on.*)
AMANDA: Laura Wingfield, you march right to that door!
LAURA: Yes—yes, Mother!

A faraway, scratchy rendition of "Dardanella" softens the air and gives her strength to move through it. She slips to the door and draws it cautiously open.

TOM *enters with the caller,* JIM O'CONNOR.

TOM: Laura, this is Jim. Jim, this is my sister, Laura.

JIM (*stepping inside*): I didn't know that Shakespeare had a sister!

LAURA (*retreating stiff and trembling from the door*): How—how do you do?

JIM (*heartily extending his hand*): Okay!

LAURA *touches it hesitantly with hers.*

JIM: Your hand's *cold,* Laura!

LAURA: Yes, well—I've been playing the victrola. . . .

JIM: Must have been playing classical music on it! You ought to play a little hot swing music to warm you up!

LAURA: Excuse me—I haven't finished playing the victrola. . . . (*She turns awkwardly and hurries into the front room. She pauses a second by the victrola. Then catches her breath and darts through the portieres like a frightened deer.*)

JIM (*grinning*): What was the matter?

TOM: Oh—with Laura? Laura is—terribly shy.

JIM: Shy, huh? It's unusual to meet a shy girl nowadays. I don't believe you ever mentioned you had a sister.

TOM: Well, now you know. I have one. Here is the *Post Dispatch.* You want a piece of it?

JIM: Uh-huh.

TOM: What piece? The comics?

JIM: Sports! (*glances at it*) Ole Dizzy Dean is on his bad behavior.

TOM (*disinterest*): Yeah? (*lights cigarette and crosses back to fire-escape door*)

JIM: Where are *you* going?

TOM: I'm going out on the terrace.

JIM (*goes after him*): You know, Shakespeare—I'm going to sell you a bill of goods!

TOM: What goods?

JIM: A course I'm taking.

TOM: Huh?

JIM: In public speaking! You and me, we're not the warehouse type.

TOM: Thanks—that's good news. But what has public speaking got to do with it?

JIM: It fits you for—executive positions!

TOM: Awww.

JIM: I tell you it's done a helluva lot for me.

(*Image: Executive at desk.*)

TOM: In what respect?

JIM: In every! Ask yourself what is the difference between you an' me and men in the office down front? Brains?—No!—Ability?—No! Then what? Just one little thing—

TOM: What is that one little thing?

JIM: Primarily it amounts to—social poise! Being able to square up to people and hold your own on any social level!

AMANDA (*off stage*): Tom?
TOM: Yes, Mother?
AMANDA: Is that you and Mr. O'Connor?
TOM: Yes, Mother.
AMANDA: Well, you just make yourselves comfortable in there.
TOM: Yes, Mother.
AMANDA: Ask Mr. O'Connor if he would like to wash his hands.
JIM: Aw, no—no—thank you—I took care of that at the warehouse. Tom—
TOM: Yes?
JIM: Mr. Mendoza was speaking to me about you.
TOM: Favorably?
JIM: What do you think?
TOM: Well—
JIM: You're going to be out of a job if you don't wake up.
TOM: I am waking up—
JIM: You show no signs.
TOM: The signs are interior.

(*Image on screen: The sailing vessel with Jolly Roger again.*)

TOM: I'm planning to change. (*He leans over the rail speaking with quiet exhilaration. The incandescent marquees and signs of the first-run movie houses light his face from across the alley. He looks like a voyager.*) I'm right at the point of committing myself to a future that doesn't include the warehouse and Mr. Mendoza or even a night-school course in public speaking.
JIM: What are you gassing about?
TOM: I'm tired of the movies.
JIM: Movies!
TOM: Yes, movies! Look at them—(*a wave toward the marvels of Grand Avenue*) All of those glamorous people—having adventures—hogging it all, gobbling the whole thing up! You know what happens? People go to the *movies* instead of *moving!* Hollywood characters are supposed to have all the adventures for everybody in America, while everybody in America sits in a dark room and watches them have them! Yes, until there's a war. That's when adventure becomes available to the masses! *Everyone's* dish, not only Gable's! Then the people in the dark room come out of the dark room to have some adventures themselves—Goody, goody!—It's our turn now, to go to the South Sea Island—to make a safari—to be exotic, far-off!—But I'm not patient. I don't want to wait till then. I'm tired of the *movies* and I am *about* to *move!*
JIM (*incredulously*): Move?
TOM: Yes.
JIM: When?
TOM: Soon!
JIM: Where? Where?

(*Theme three music seems to answer the question, while* TOM *thinks it over. He searches among his pockets.*)

TOM: I'm starting to boil inside. I know I seem dreamy, but inside—well, I'm boiling!—Whenever I pick up a shoe, I shudder a little thinking how short life is and what I am doing!—Whatever that means, I know it doesn't mean shoes—except as something to wear on a traveler's feet! (*finds paper*) Look—

JIM: What?

TOM: I'm a member.

JIM (*reading*): The Union of Merchant Seamen.

TOM: I paid my dues this month, instead of the light bill.

JIM: You will regret it when they turn the lights off.

TOM: I won't be here.

JIM: How about your mother?

TOM: I'm like my father. The bastard son of a bastard! See how he grins? And he's been absent going on sixteen years!

JIM: You're just talking, you drip. How does your mother feel about it?

TOM: Shhh!—Here comes Mother! Mother is not acquainted with my plans!

AMANDA (*enters portieres*): Where are you all?

TOM: On the terrace, Mother.

> *They start inside. She advances to them.* TOM *is distinctly shocked at her appearance. Even* JIM *blinks a little. He is making his first contact with girlish Southern vivacity and in spite of the night-school course in public speaking is somewhat thrown off the beam by the unexpected outlay of social charm.*
>
> *Certain responses are attempted by* JIM *but are swept aside by* AMANDA*'s gay laughter and chatter.* TOM *is embarrassed but after the first shock* JIM *reacts very warmly. Grins and chuckles, is altogether won over.*
>
> (*Image:* AMANDA *as a girl.*)

AMANDA (*coyly smiling, shaking her girlish ringlets*): Well, well, well, so this is Mr. O'Connor. Introductions entirely unnecessary. I've heard so much about you from my boy. I finally said to him, Tom—good gracious!—why don't you bring this paragon to supper? I'd like to meet this nice young man at the warehouse!—Instead of just hearing him sing your praises so much! I don't know why my son is so stand-offish—that's not Southern behavior! Let's sit down and—I think we could stand a little more air in here! Tom, leave the door open. I felt a nice fresh breeze a moment ago. Where has it gone to? Mmm, so warm already! And not quite summer, even. We're going to burn up when summer really gets started. However, we're having—we're having a very light supper. I think light things are better fo' this time of year. The same as light clothes are. Light clothes an' light food are what warm weather calls fo'. You know our blood gets so thick during th' winter—it takes a while fo' us to *adjust* ou'selves!—when the season changes . . . It's come so quick this year. I wasn't prepared. All of a sudden—heavens! Already summer!—I ran to the trunk an' pulled out this light dress—Terribly old! Historical almost! But feels so good—so good an' co-ol, y' know. . . .

TOM: Mother—

AMANDA: Yes, honey?

TOM: How about—supper?

AMANDA: Honey, you go ask Sister if supper is ready! You know that Sister is in full charge of supper! Tell her you hungry boys are waiting for it. (*to* JIM) Have you met Laura?

JIM: She—

AMANDA: Let you in? Oh, good, you've met already! It's rare for a girl as sweet an' pretty as Laura to be domestic! But Laura is, thank heavens, not only pretty but also very domestic. I'm not at all. I never was a bit. I never could make a thing but angel-food cake. Well, in the South we had so many servants. Gone, gone, gone. All vestige of gracious living! Gone completely! I wasn't prepared for what the future brought me. All of my gentlemen callers were sons of planters and so of course I assumed that I would be married to one and raise my family on a large piece of land with plenty of servants. But man proposes—and woman accepts the proposal!—To vary that old, old saying a little bit—I married no planter! I married a man who worked for the telephone company!—That gallantly smiling gentleman over there! (*points to the picture*) A telephone man who—fell in love with long-distance!—Now he travels and I don't even know where!—But what am I going on for about my—tribulations? Tell me yours—I hope you don't have any! Tom?

TOM (*returning*): Yes, Mother?

AMANDA: Is supper nearly ready?

TOM: It looks to me like supper is on the table.

AMANDA: Let me look—(*She rises prettily and looks through portieres.*) Oh, lovely!—But where is Sister?

TOM: Laura is not feeling well and she says that she thinks she'd better not come to the table.

AMANDA: What?—Nonsense—Laura? Oh, Laura!

LAURA (*off stage, faintly*): Yes, Mother.

AMANDA: You really must come to the table. We won't be seated until you come to the table! Come in, Mr. O'Connor. You sit over there, and I'll—Laura? Laura Wingfield! You're keeping us waiting, honey! We can't say grace until you come to the table!

The back door is pushed weakly open and LAURA *comes in. She is obviously quite faint, her lips trembling, her eyes wide and staring. She moves unsteadily toward the table.*

(*Legend: "Terror!"*)

Outside a summer storm is coming abruptly. The white curtains billow inward at the windows and there is a sorrowful murmur and deep blue dusk.

LAURA *suddenly stumbles—she catches at a chair with a faint moan.*

TOM: Laura!

AMANDA: Laura! (*There is a clap of thunder.*) (*Legend: "Ah!"*) (*despairingly*) Why, Laura, you *are* sick, darling! Tom, help your sister into the living room, dear! Sit in the living room, Laura—rest on the sofa. Well! (*to the gentleman caller*) Standing over the hot stove made her ill!—I told her that it was just too warm this evening, but—(TOM *comes back in.* LAURA *is on the sofa.*) Is Laura all right now?

TOM: Yes.

AMANDA: What *is* that? Rain? A nice cool rain has come up! (*She gives the gentleman caller a frightened look.*) I think we may—have grace—now . . . (TOM *looks at her stupidly.*) Tom, honey—you say grace!

TOM: Oh . . . "For these and all thy mercies—" (*They bow their heads,* AMANDA *stealing a nervous glance at* JIM. *In the living room* LAURA, *stretched on the sofa, clenches her hand to her lips, to hold back a shuddering sob.*) God's Holy Name be praised—

(*The scene dims out.*)

Scene 7

A Souvenir.

> *Half an hour later. Dinner is just being finished in the upstage area which is concealed by the drawn portieres.*
>
> *As the curtain rises* LAURA *is still huddled upon the sofa, her feet drawn under her, her head resting on a pale blue pillow, her eyes wide and mysteriously watchful. The new floor lamp with its shade of rose-colored silk gives a soft, becoming light to her face, bringing out the fragile, unearthly prettiness which usually escapes attention. There is a steady murmur of rain, but it is slackening and stops soon after the scene begins; the air outside becomes pale and luminous as the moon breaks out.*
>
> *A moment after the curtain rises, the lights in both rooms flicker and go out.*

JIM: Hey, there, Mr. Light Bulb!

> AMANDA *laughs nervously.*
> (*Legend: "Suspension of a Public Service."*)

AMANDA: Where was Moses when the lights went out? Ha-ha. Do you know the answer to that one, Mr. O'Connor?

JIM: No, Ma'am, what's the answer?

AMANDA: In the dark! (JIM *laughs appreciatively.*) Everybody sit still. I'll light the candles. Isn't it lucky we have them on the table? Where's a match? Which of you gentlemen can provide a match?

JIM: Here.

AMANDA: Thank you, sir.

JIM: Not at all, Ma'am!

AMANDA: I guess the fuse has burnt out. Mr. O'Connor, can you tell a burntout fuse? I know I can't and Tom is a total loss when it comes to mechanics. (*Sound: Getting up: Voices recede a little to kitchenette.*) Oh, be careful you don't bump into something. We don't want our gentleman caller to break his neck. Now wouldn't that be a fine howdy-do?

JIM: Ha-ha! Where is the fuse-box?

AMANDA: Right here next to the stove. Can you see anything?

JIM: Just a minute.

AMANDA: Isn't electricity a mysterious thing? Wasn't it Benjamin Franklin who tied a key to a kite? We live in such a mysterious universe, don't we?

Some people say that science clears up all the mysteries for us. In my opinion it only creates more! Have you found it yet?

JIM: No, Ma'am. All these fuses look okay to me.

AMANDA: Tom!

TOM: Yes, Mother?

AMANDA: That light bill I gave you several days ago. The one I told you we got the notices about?

(*Legend: "Ha!"*)

TOM: Oh.—Yeah.

AMANDA: You didn't neglect to pay it by any chance?

TOM: Why, I—

AMANDA: Didn't! I might have known it!

JIM: Shakespeare probably wrote a poem on that light bill, Mrs. Wingfield.

AMANDA: I might have known better than to trust him with it! There's such a high price for negligence in this world!

JIM: Maybe the poem will win a ten-dollar prize.

AMANDA: We'll just have to spend the remainder of the evening in the nineteenth century, before Mr. Edison made the Mazda lamp!

JIM: Candlelight is my favorite kind of light.

AMANDA: That shows you're romantic! But that's no excuse for Tom. Well, we got through dinner. Very considerate of them to let us get through dinner before they plunged us into everlasting darkness, wasn't it, Mr. O'Connor?

JIM: Ha-ha!

AMANDA: Tom, as a penalty for your carelessness you can help me with the dishes.

JIM: Let me give you a hand.

AMANDA: Indeed you will not!

JIM: I ought to be good for something.

AMANDA: Good for something? (*Her tone is rhapsodic.*) *You?* Why, Mr. O'Connor, nobody, *nobody's* given me this much entertainment in years —as you have!

JIM: Aw, now, Mrs. Wingfield!

AMANDA: I'm not exaggerating, not one bit! But Sister is all by her lonesome. You go keep her company in the parlor! I'll give you this lovely old candelabrum that used to be on the altar at the church of the Heavenly Rest. It was melted a little out of shape when the church burnt down. Lightning struck it one spring. Gypsy Jones was holding a revival at the time and he intimated that the church was destroyed because the Episcopalians gave card parties.

JIM: Ha-ha.

AMANDA: And how about you coaxing Sister to drink a little wine? I think it would be good for her! Can you carry both at once?

JIM: Sure. I'm Superman!

AMANDA: Now, Thomas, get into this apron!

The door of kitchenette swings closed on AMANDA'*s gay laughter, the flickering light approaches the portieres.*

LAURA *sits up nervously as he enters. Her speech at first is low and breathless from the almost intolerable strain of being alone with a stranger.*

(*The legend: "I Don't Suppose You Remember Me at All!"*)

In her first speeches in this scene, before JIM'*s warmth overcomes her paralyzing shyness,* LAURA'*s voice is thin and breathless as though she has just run up a steep flight of stairs.*

JIM'*s attitude is gently humorous. In playing this scene it should be stressed that while the incident is apparently unimportant, it is to* LAURA *the climax of her secret life.*

JIM: Hello, there, Laura.

LAURA (*faintly*): Hello. (*She clears her throat.*)

JIM: How are you feeling now? Better?

LAURA: Yes. Yes, thank you.

JIM: This is for you. A little dandelion wine. (*He extends it toward her with extravagant gallantry.*)

LAURA: Thank you.

JIM: Drink it—but don't get drunk! (*He laughs heartily.* LAURA *takes the glass uncertainly; laughs shyly.*) Where shall I set the candles?

LAURA: Oh—oh, anywhere . . .

JIM: How about here on the floor? Any objections?

LAURA: No.

JIM: I'll spread a newspaper under to catch the drippings. I like to sit on the floor. Mind if I do?

LAURA: Oh, no.

JIM: Give me a pillow?

LAURA: What?

JIM: A pillow!

LAURA: Oh . . . (*hands him one quickly*)

JIM: How about you? Don't you like to sit on the floor?

LAURA: Oh—yes.

JIM: Why don't you, then?

LAURA: I—will.

JIM: Take a pillow! (LAURA *does. Sits on the other side of the candelabrum.* JIM *crosses his legs and smiles engagingly at her.*) I can't hardly see you sitting way over there.

LAURA: I can—see you.

JIM: I know, but that's not fair, I'm in the limelight. (LAURA *moves her pillow closer.*) Good! Now I can see you! Comfortable?

LAURA: Yes.

JIM: So am I. Comfortable as a cow! Will you have some gum?

LAURA: No, thank you.

JIM: I think that I will indulge, with your permission. (*musingly unwraps it and holds it up*) Think of the fortune made by the guy that invented the first piece of chewing gum. Amazing, huh? The Wrigley Building is one of the sights of Chicago.—I saw it summer before last when I went up to the Century of Progress. Did you take in the Century of Progress?

LAURA: No, I didn't.

Anne Dudek and Willis Sparks in a scene from the Hartford Stage production of *The Glass Menagerie* (courtesy Jennifer W. Lester)

JIM: Well, it was quite a wonderful exposition. What impressed me most was the Hall of Science. Gives you an idea of what the future will be in America, even more wonderful than the present time is! (*Pause. Smiling at her.*) Your brother tells me you're shy. Is that right, Laura?

LAURA: I—don't know.

JIM: I judge you to be an old-fashioned type of girl. Well, I think that's a pretty good type to be. Hope you don't think I'm being too personal—do you?

LAURA (*hastily, out of embarrassment*): I believe I *will* take a piece of gum, if you—don't mind. (*clearing her throat*) Mr. O'Connor, have you—kept up with your singing?

JIM: Singing? Me?

LAURA: Yes. I remember what a beautiful voice you had.

JIM: When did you hear me sing?

(*Voice off stage in the pause.*)

VOICE (*off stage*): O blow, ye winds, heigh-ho,
A-roving I will go!
I'm off to my love
With a boxing glove—
Ten thousand miles away!

JIM: You say you've heard me sing?

LAURA: Oh, yes! Yes, very often . . . I —don't suppose—you remember me—at all?

JIM (*smiling doubtfully*): You know I have an idea I've seen you before. I had that idea soon as I opened the door. It seemed almost like I was about to remember your name. But the name that I started to call you—wasn't a name! And so I stopped myself before I said it.

LAURA: Wasn't it—Blue Roses?

JIM (*springs up, grinning*): Blue Roses!—My gosh, yes—Blue Roses! That's what I had on my tongue when you opened the door! Isn't it funny what tricks your memory plays? I didn't connect you with high school some-how or other. But that's where it was; it was high school. I didn't even know you were Shakespeare's sister! Gosh, I'm sorry.

LAURA: I didn't expect you to. You—barely knew me!

JIM: But we did have a speaking acquaintance, huh?

LAURA: Yes, we—spoke to each other.

JIM: When did you recognize me?

LAURA: Oh, right away!

JIM: Soon as I came in the door?

LAURA: When I heard your name I thought it was probably you. I knew that Tom used to know you a little in high school. So when you came in the door—Well, then I was—sure.

JIM: Why didn't you *say* something, then?

LAURA (*breathlessly*): I didn't know what to say, I was—too surprised!

JIM: For goodness' sakes! You know, this sure is funny!

LAURA: Yes! Yes, isn't it, though . . .

JIM: Didn't we have a class in something together?

LAURA: Yes, we did.

JIM: What class was that?

LAURA: It was—singing—Chorus!

JIM: Aw.

LAURA: I sat across the aisle from you in the Aud.

JIM: Aw!

LAURA: Mondays, Wednesdays and Fridays.

JIM: Now I remember—you always came in late.

LAURA: Yes, it was so hard for me, getting upstairs. I had that brace on my leg—it clumped so loud!

JIM: I never heard any clumping!

LAURA (*wincing at the recollection*): To me it sounded like—thunder!

JIM: Well, well, well, I never even noticed.

LAURA: And everybody was seated before I came in. I had to walk in front of all those people. My seat was in the back row. I had to go clumping all the way up the aisle with everyone watching!

JIM: You shouldn't have been self-conscious.

LAURA: I know, but I was. It was always such a relief when the singing started.

JIM: Aw, yes, I've placed you now! I used to call you Blue Roses. How was it that I got started calling you that?

LAURA: I was out of school a little while with pleurosis. When I came back you asked me what was the matter. I said I had pleurosis—you thought I said Blue Roses. That's what you always called me after that!

JIM: I hope you didn't mind.

LAURA: Oh, no—I liked it. You see, I wasn't acquainted with many—people. . . .

JIM: As I remember you sort of stuck by yourself.

LAURA: I—I—never have had much luck at—making friends.   5

JIM: I don't see why you wouldn't.

LAURA: Well, I—started out badly.

JIM: You mean being—

LAURA: Yes, it sort of—stood between me—

JIM: You shouldn't have let it!   10

LAURA: I know, but it did, and—

JIM: You were shy with people!

LAURA: I tried not to be but never could—

JIM: Overcome it?

LAURA: No, I—I never could!   15

JIM: I guess being shy is something you have to work out of kind of gradually

LAURA (sorrowfully): Yes—I guess it—

JIM: Takes time!

LAURA: Yes—

JIM: People are not so dreadful when you know them. That's what you have to remember! And everybody has problems, not just you, but practically everybody has got some problems. You think of yourself as having the only problems, as being the only one who is disappointed. But just look around you and you will see lots of people as disappointed as you are. For instance, I hoped when I was going to high school that I would be further along at this time, six years later, than I am now—You remember that wonderful write-up I had in *The Torch?*

LAURA: Yes! (*She rises and crosses to table.*)

JIM: It said I was bound to succeed in anything I went into! (LAURA *returns with the annual.*) Holy Jeez! *The Torch!* (*He accepts it reverently. They smile across it with mutual wonder.* LAURA *crouches beside him and they begin to turn through it.* LAURA's *shyness is dissolving in his warmth.*)

LAURA: Here you are in *The Pirates of Penzance!*

JIM (*wistfully*): I sang the baritone lead in that operetta.

LAURA (*raptly*): So—*beautifully!*

JIM (*protesting*): Aw—

LAURA: Yes, yes—beautifully—beautifully!

JIM: You heard me?

LAURA: All three times!

JIM: No!

LAURA: Yes!

JIM: All three performances?

LAURA (*looking down*): Yes.

JIM: Why?

LAURA: I—wanted to ask you to—autograph my program.

JIM: Why didn't you ask me to?

LAURA: You were always surrounded by your own friends so much that I never had a chance to.

JIM: You should have just—

LAURA: Well, I—thought you might think I was—

JIM: Thought I might think you was—what?

LAURA: Oh—

JIM (*with reflective relish*): I was beleaguered by females in those days.

LAURA: You were terribly popular!

JIM: Yeah—

LAURA: You had such a—friendly way—

JIM: I was spoiled in high school.

LAURA: Everybody—liked you!

JIM: Including you?

LAURA: I—yes, I—I did, too—(*She gently closes the book in her lap.*)

JIM: Well, well, well!—Give me that program, Laura. (*She hands it to him. He signs it with a flourish.*) There you are—better late than never!

LAURA: Oh, I—what a—surprise!

JIM: My signature isn't worth very much right now. But some day—maybe—it will increase in value! Being disappointed is one thing and being discouraged is something else. I am disappointed but I am not discouraged. I'm twenty-three years old. How old are you?

LAURA: I'll be twenty-four in June.

JIM: That's not old age!

LAURA: No, but—

JIM: You finished high school?

LAURA (*with difficulty*): I didn't go back.

JIM: You mean you dropped out?

LAURA: I made bad grades in my final examinations. (*She rises and replaces the book and the program. Her voice strained.*) How is—Emily Meisenbach getting along?

JIM: Oh, that kraut-head!

LAURA: Why do you call her that?

JIM: That's what she was.

LAURA: You're not still—going with her?

JIM: I never see her.

LAURA: It said in the Personal Section that you were—engaged!

JIM: I know, but I wasn't impressed by that—propaganda!

LAURA: It wasn't—the truth?

JIM: Only in Emily's optimistic opinion!

LAURA: Oh—

(*Legend: "What Have You Done Since High School?"*)

JIM *lights a cigarette and leans indolently back on his elbows smiling at* LAURA *with a warmth and charm which lights her inwardly with altar candles. She remains by the table and turns in her hands a piece of glass to cover her tumult.*

JIM (*after several reflective puffs on a cigarette*): What have you done since high school? (*She seems not to hear him.*) Huh? (*LAURA looks up.*) I said what have you done since high school, Laura?

LAURA: Nothing much.

JIM: You must have been doing something these six long years.

LAURA: Yes.

JIM: Well, then, such as what?

LAURA: I took a business course at business college—

JIM: How did that work out?

LAURA: Well, not very—well—I had to drop out, it gave me—indigestion—

   JIM *laughs gently.*

JIM: What are you doing now?

LAURA: I don't do anything—much. Oh, please don't think I sit around doing nothing! My glass collection takes up a good deal of time. Glass is something you have to take good care of.

JIM: What did you say—about glass?

LAURA: Collection I said—I have one—(*She clears her throat and turns away again, acutely shy.*)

JIM (*abruptly*): You know what I judge to be the trouble with you? Inferiority complex! Know what that is? That's what they call it when someone low-rates himself! I understand it because I had it, too. Although my case was not so aggravated as yours seems to be. I had it until I took up public speaking, developed my voice, and learned that I had an aptitude for science. Before that time I never thought of myself as being outstanding in any way whatsoever! Now I've never made a regular study of it, but I have a friend who says I can analyze people better than doctors that make a profession of it. I don't claim that to be necessarily true, but I can sure guess a person's psychology, Laura! (*takes out his gum*) Excuse me, Laura. I always take it out when the flavor is gone. I'll use this scrap of paper to wrap it in. I know how it is to get it stuck on a shoe. Yep—that's what I judge to be your principal trouble. A lack of confidence in yourself as a person. You don't have the proper amount of faith in yourself. I'm basing that fact on a number of your remarks and also on certain observations I've made. For instance that clumping you thought was so awful in high school. You say that you even dreaded to walk into class. You see what you did? You dropped out of school, you gave up an education because of a clump, which as far as I know was practically nonexistent! A little physical defect is what you have. Hardly noticeable even! Magnified thousands of times by imagination! You know what my strong advice to you is? Think of yourself as *superior* in some way!

LAURA: In what way would I think?

JIM: Why, man alive, Laura! Just look about you a little. What do you see? A world full of common people! All of 'em born and all of 'em going to die! Which of them has one-tenth of your good points! Or mine! Or anyone else's, as far as that goes—Gosh! Everybody excels in some one thing. Some in many! (*unconsciously glances at himself in the mirror*) All you've got to do is discover in *what*! Take me, for instance. (*He adjusts his tie at the mirror.*) My interest happens to lie in electrodynamics. I'm taking a

course in radio engineering at night school, Laura, on top of a fairly responsible job at the warehouse. I'm taking that course and studying public speaking.

LAURA: Ohhhh.

JIM: Because I believe in the future of television! (*turning back to her*) I wish
to be ready to go up right along with it. Therefore I'm planning to get in
on the ground floor. In fact I've already made the right connections and
all that remains is for the industry itself to get under way! Full steam—
(*His eyes are starry.*) Knowledge—zzzzzp! Money—zzzzzp!—Power!
That's the cycle democracy is built on! (*His attitude is convincingly dynamic.* LAURA *stares at him, even her shyness eclipsed in her absolute wonder. He suddenly grins.*) I guess you think I think a lot of myself!

LAURA: No—o-o-o, I—

JIM: Now how about you? Isn't there something you take more interest in
than anything else?

LAURA: Well, I do—as I said—have my—glass collection—

A peal of girlish laughter from the kitchen.

JIM: I'm not right sure I know what you're talking about. What kind of glass
is it?

LAURA: Little articles of it, they're ornaments mostly! Most of them are little
animals made out of glass, the tiniest little animals in the world. Mother
calls them a glass menagerie! Here's an example of one, if you'd like to
see it! This one is one of the oldest. It's nearly thirteen. (*Music: "The Glass
Menagerie."*) (*He stretches out his hand.*) Oh, be careful—if you breathe,
it breaks!

JIM: I'd better not take it. I'm pretty clumsy with things.

LAURA: Go on, I trust you with him! (*places it in his palm*) There now—
you're holding him gently! Hold him over the light, he loves the light! You
see how the light shines through him?

JIM: It sure does shine!

LAURA: I shouldn't be partial, but he is my favorite one.

JIM: What kind of a thing is this one supposed to be?

LAURA: Haven't you noticed the single horn on his forehead?

JIM: A unicorn, huh?

LAURA: Mmm-hmmm!

JIM: Unicorns, aren't they extinct in the modern world?

LAURA: I know!

JIM: Poor little fellow, he must feel sort of lonesome.

LAURA (*smiling*): Well, if he does he doesn't complain about it. He stays on
a shelf with some horses that don't have horns and all of them seem to
get along nicely together.

JIM: How do you know?

LAURA (*lightly*): I haven't heard any arguments among them!

JIM (*grinning*): No arguments, huh? Well, that's a pretty good sign! Where
shall I set him?

LAURA: Put him on the table. They all like a change of scenery once in a
while!

JIM (*stretching*): Well, well, well, well—Look how big my shadow is when I stretch!

LAURA: Oh, oh, yes—it stretches across the ceiling!

JIM (*crossing to door*): I think it's stopped raining. (*opens fire-escape door*) Where does the music come from?

LAURA: From the Paradise Dance Hall across the alley.

JIM: How about cutting the rug a little, Miss Wingfield?

LAURA: Oh, I—

JIM: Or is your program filled up? Let me have a look at it. (*grasps imaginary card*) Why, every dance is taken! I'll just have to scratch some out. (*Waltz music: "La Colondrina."*) Ahhh, a waltz! (*He executes some sweeping turns by himself then holds his arms toward* LAURA.)

LAURA (*breathlessly*): I—can't dance!

JIM: There you go, that inferiority stuff!

LAURA: I've never danced in my life!

JIM: Come on, try!

LAURA: Oh, but I'd step on you!

JIM: I'm not made out of glass.

LAURA: How—how—how do we start?

JIM: Just leave it to me. You hold your arms out a little.

LAURA: Like this?

JIM: A little bit higher. Right. Now don't tighten up, that's the main thing about it—relax.

LAURA (*laughing breathlessly*): It's hard not to.

JIM: Okay.

LAURA: I'm afraid you can't budge me.

JIM: What do you bet I can't? (*He swings her into motion.*)

LAURA: Goodness, yes, you can!

JIM: Let yourself go, now, Laura, just let yourself go.

LAURA: I'm—

JIM: Come on!

LAURA: Trying!

JIM: Not so stiff—Easy does it!

LAURA: I know but I'm—

JIM: Loosen th' backbone! There now, that's a lot better.

LAURA: Am I?

JIM: Lots, lots better! (*He moves her about the room in a clumsy waltz.*)

LAURA: Oh, my!

JIM: Ha-ha!

JIM: I hope that it wasn't the little glass horse with the horn!

LAURA: Yes.

JIM: Aw, aw, aw. Is it broken?

LAURA: Now it is just like all the other horses.

JIM: It's lost its—

LAURA: Horn! It doesn't matter. Maybe it's a blessing in disguise.

JIM: You'll never forgive me. I bet that was your favorite piece of glass.

LAURA: I don't have favorites much. It's no tragedy, Freckles. Glass breaks so easily. No matter how careful you are. The traffic jars the shelves and things fall off them.

JIM: Still I'm awfully sorry that I was the cause.

LAURA (*smiling*): I'll just imagine he had an operation. The horn was removed to make him feel less—freakish! (*They both laugh.*) Now he will feel more at home with the other horses, the ones that don't have horns. . . .

JIM: Ha-ha, that's very funny! (*suddenly serious*) I'm glad to see that you have a sense of humor. You know—you're—well—very different! Surprisingly different from anyone else I know! (*His voice becomes soft and hesitant with a genuine feeling.*) Do you mind me telling you that? (LAURA *is abashed beyond speech.*) I mean it in a nice way . . . (LAURA *nods shyly, looking away.*) You make me feel sort of—I don't know how to put it! I'm usually pretty good at expressing things, but—This is something that I don't know how to say! (LAURA *touches her throat and clears it—turns the broken unicorn in her hands.*) (*even softer*) Has anyone ever told you that you were pretty? (*Pause: Music.*) (LAURA *looks up slowly, with wonder, and shakes her head.*) Well, you are! In a very different way from anyone else. And all the nicer because of the difference, too. (*His voice becomes low and husky.* LAURA *turns away, nearly faint with the novelty of her emotions.*) I wish that you were my sister. I'd teach you to have some confidence in yourself. The different people are not like other people, but being different is nothing to be ashamed of. Because other people are not such wonderful people. They're one hundred times one thousand. You're one times one! They walk all over the earth. You just stay here. They're common as—weeds, but—you—well, you're—*Blue Roses!*

> (*Image on screen: Blue roses.*)
> (*Music changes.*)

LAURA: But blue is wrong for—roses . . .

JIM: It's right for you!—You're—pretty!

LAURA: In what respect am I pretty?

JIM: In all respects—believe me! Your eyes—your hair—are pretty! Your hands are pretty! (*He catches hold of her hand.*) You think I'm making this up because I'm invited to dinner and have to be nice. Oh, I could do that I could put on an act for you, Laura, and say lots of things without being very sincere. But this time I am. I'm talking to you sincerely. I happened to notice you had this inferiority complex that keeps you from feeling comfortable with people. Somebody needs to build your confidence up and make you proud instead of shy and turning away and—blushing—Somebody—ought to—Ought to—*kiss* you, Laura! (*His hand slips slowly up her arm to her shoulder.*) (*Music swells tumultuously.*) (*He suddenly turns her about and kisses her on the lips. When he releases her,* LAURA *sinks on the sofa with a bright, dazed look.* JIM *backs away and fishes in his pocket for a cigarette.*) (*Legend on screen: Souvenir."*) Stumble-john! (*He lights the cigarette, avoiding her look. There is a peal of girlish laughter from* AMANDA *in the kitchen.* LAURA *slowly raises and opens her hand. It still contains the little broken glass animal. She looks at it with a tender, bewildered expression.*) Stumble-john! I shouldn't have done that—That was way off the beam. You don't smoke, do you? (*She looks up, smiling, not hearing the question. He sits beside her a little gingerly.*

She looks at him speechlessly—waiting. He coughs decorously and moves a little farther aside as he considers the situation and senses her feelings, dimly, with perturbation.) (gently) Would you—care for a—mint? (She doesn't seem to hear him but her look grows brighter even.) Peppermint— LifeSaver? My pocket's a regular drug store—wherever I go . . . *(He pops a mint in his mouth. Then gulps and decides to make a clean breast of it. He speaks slowly and gingerly.)* Laura, you know, if I had a sister like you, I'd do the same thing as Tom. I'd bring out fellows and—introduce her to them. The right type of boys of a type to—appreciate her. Only— well—he made a mistake about me. Maybe I've got no call to be saying this. That may not have been the idea in having me over. But what if it was? There's nothing wrong about that. The only trouble is that in my case—I'm not in a situation to—do the right thing. I can't take down your number and say I'll phone. I can't call up next week and—ask for a date. I thought I had better explain the situation in case you—misunderstood it and—hurt your feelings. . . . *(pause) (Slowly, very slowly,* LAURA*'s look changes, her eyes returning slowly from his to the ornament in her palm.)* *(*AMANDA *utters another gay laugh in the kitchen.)*

LAURA *(faintly)*: You—won't—call again?

JIM: No, Laura, I can't. *(He rises from the sofa.)* As I was just explaining, I've—got strings on me. Laura, I've—been going steady! I go out all of the time with a girl named Betty. She's a home-girl like you, and Catholic, and Irish, and in a great many ways we—get along fine. I met her last summer on a moonlight boat trip up the river to Alton, on the *Majestic.* Well—right away from the start it was—love! *(Legend: Love!)* *(*LAURA *sways slightly forward and grips the arm of the sofa. He fails to notice, now enrapt in his own comfortable being.)* Being in love has made a new man of me! *(Leaning stiffly forward, clutching the arm of the sofa,* LAURA *struggles visibly with her storm. But* JIM *is oblivious, she is a long way off.)* The power of love is really pretty tremendous! Love is something that—changes the whole world, Laura! *(The storm abates a little and* LAURA *leans back. He notices her again.)* It happened that Betty's aunt took sick, she got a wire and had to go to Centralia. So Tom—when he asked me to dinner—I naturally just accepted the invitation, not knowing that you—that he—that I—*(He stops awkwardly.)* Huh—I'm a stumble-john! *(He flops back on the sofa.)* *(The holy candles in the altar of* LAURA*'s face have been snuffed out. There is a look of almost infinite desolation.)* *(*JIM *glances at her uneasily.)* I wish that you would—say something. *(She bites her lip which was trembling and then bravely smiles. She opens her hand again on the broken glass ornament. Then she gently takes his hand and raises it level with her own. She carefully places the unicorn in the palm of his hand, then pushes his fingers closed upon it.)* What are you—doing that for? You want me to have him?—Laura? *(She nods.)* What for?

LAURA: A—souvenir . . .

She rises unsteadily and crouches beside the victrola to wind it up.
(Legend on screen: "Things Have a Way of Turning Out So Badly!")
(Or image: "Gentleman Caller Waving Good-bye!—Gaily.")

At this moment AMANDA *rushes brightly back in the front room. She bears a pitcher of fruit punch in an old-fashioned cut-glass pitcher and a plate of macaroons. The plate has a gold border and poppies painted on it.*

AMANDA: Well, well, well! Isn't the air delightful after the shower? I've made you children a little liquid refreshment. (*turns gaily to the gentleman caller*) Jim, do you know that song about lemonade?

"Lemonade, lemonade
Made in the shade and stirred with a spade—
Good enough for any old maid!"

JIM (*uneasily*): Ha-ha! No—I never heard it.

AMANDA: Why, Laura! You look so serious!

JIM: We were having a serious conversation.

AMANDA: Good! Now you're better acquainted!

JIM (*uncertainly*): Ha-ha! Yes.

AMANDA: You modern young people are much more serious-minded than my generation. I was so gay as a girl!

JIM: You haven't changed, Mrs. Wingfield.

AMANDA: Tonight I'm rejuvenated! The gaiety of the occasion, Mr. O'Connor! (*She tosses her head with a peal of laughter. Spills lemonade.*) Oooo! I'm baptizing myself!

JIM: Here—let me—

AMANDA (*setting the pitcher down*): There now. I discovered we had some maraschino cherries. I dumped them in, juice and all!

JIM: You shouldn't have gone to that trouble, Mrs. Wingfield.

AMANDA: Trouble, trouble? Why, it was loads of fun! Didn't you hear me cutting up in the kitchen? I bet your ears were burning! I told Tom how outdone with him I was for keeping you to himself so long a time! He should have brought you over much, much sooner! Well, now that you've found your way, I want you to be a very frequent caller! Not just occasional but all the time. Oh, we're going to have a lot of gay times together! I see them coming! Mmm, just breathe that air! So fresh, and the moon's so pretty! I'll skip back out—I know where my place is when young folks are having a—serious conversation!

JIM: Oh, don't go out, Mrs. Wingfield. The fact of the matter is I've got to be going.

AMANDA: Going, now? You're joking! Why, it's only the shank of the evening, Mr. O'Connor!

JIM: Well, you know how it is.

AMANDA: You mean you're a young workingman and have to keep workingmen's hours. We'll let you off early tonight. But only on the condition that next time you stay later. What's the best night for you? Isn't Saturday night the best night for you workingmen?

JIM: I have a couple of time-clocks to punch, Mrs. Wingfield. One at morning, another one at night!

AMANDA: My, but you *are* ambitious! You work at night, too?

JIM: No, Ma'am, not work but—Betty! (*He crosses deliberately to pick up his hat. The band at the Paradise Dance Hall goes into a tender waltz.*)

AMANDA: Betty? Betty? Who's—Betty! (*There is an ominous cracking sound in the sky.*)

JIM: Oh, just a girl. The girl I go steady with! (*He smiles charmingly. The sky falls.*)

(*Legend: "The Sky Falls."*)

AMANDA (*a long-drawn exhalation*): Ohhhh . . . Is it a serious romance, Mr. O'Connor?

JIM: We're going to be married the second Sunday in June.

AMANDA: Ohhhh—how nice! Tom didn't mention that you were engaged to be married.

JIM: The cat's not out of the bag at the warehouse yet. You know how they are. They call you Romeo and stuff like that. (*He stops at the oval mirror to put on his hat. He carefully shapes the brim and the crown to give a discreetly dashing effect.*) It's been a wonderful evening, Mrs. Wingfield. I guess this is what they mean by Southern hospitality.

AMANDA: It really wasn't anything at all.

JIM: I hope it don't seem like I'm rushing off. But I promised Betty I'd pick her up at the Wabash depot, an' by the time I get my jalopy down there her train'll be in. Some women are pretty upset if you keep 'em waiting.

AMANDA: Yes, I know—The tyranny of women! (*extends her hand*) Goodbye, Mr. O'Connor. I wish you luck—and happiness—and success! All three of them, and so does Laura!—Don't you, Laura?

LAURA: Yes!

JIM (*taking her hand*): Good-bye, Laura. I'm certainly going to treasure that souvenir. And don't you forget the good advice I gave you. (*raises his voice to a cheery shout*) So long, Shakespeare! Thanks again, ladies—Good night!

He grins and ducks jauntily out.
    Still bravely grimacing, AMANDA *closes the door on the gentleman caller. Then she turns back to the room with a puzzled expression. She and* LAURA *don't dare to face each other.* LAURA *crouches beside the victrola to wind it.*

AMANDA (*faintly*): Things have a way of turning out so badly. I don't believe that I would play the victrola. Well, well—well—Our gentleman caller was engaged to be married! Tom!

TOM (*from back*): Yes, Mother?

AMANDA: Come in here a minute. I want to tell you something awfully funny.

TOM (*enters with macaroon and a glass of the lemonade*): Has the gentleman caller gotten away already?

AMANDA: The gentleman caller has made an early departure. What a wonderful joke you played on us!

TOM: How do you mean?

AMANDA: You didn't mention that he was engaged to be married.

TOM: Jim? Engaged?

AMANDA: That's what he just informed us.

TOM: I'll be jiggered! I didn't know about that.

AMANDA: That seems very peculiar.

TOM: What's peculiar about it?

AMANDA: Didn't you call him your best friend down at the warehouse?

TOM: He is, but how did I know?

AMANDA: It seems extremely peculiar that you wouldn't know your best friend was going to be married!

TOM: The warehouse is where I work, not where I know things about people!

AMANDA: You don't know things anywhere! You live in a dream; you manufacture illusions! (*He crosses to door.*) Where are you going?

TOM: I'm going to the movies.

AMANDA: That's right, now that you've had us make such fools of ourselves. The effort, the preparations, all the expense! The new floor lamp, the rug, the clothes for Laura! All for what? To entertain some other girl's fiancé! Go to the movies, go! Don't think about us, a mother deserted, an unmarried sister who's crippled and has no job! Don't let anything interfere with your selfish pleasure! Just go, go, go—to the movies!

TOM: All right, I will! The more you shout about my selfishness to me the quicker I'll go, and I won't go to the movies!

AMANDA: Go, then! Then go to the moon—you selfish dreamer!

> TOM *smashes his glass on the floor. He plunges out on the fire-escape, slamming the door.* LAURA *screams—cut by door.*
>
> *Dance-hall music up.* TOM *goes to the rail and grips it desperately, lifting his face in the chill white moonlight penetrating the narrow abyss of the alley.*
>
> (*Legend on screen: "And So Good-bye . . ."*)
>
> (TOM*'s closing speech is timed with the interior pantomime. The interior scene is played as though viewed through soundproof glass.* AMANDA *appears to be making a comforting speech to* LAURA *who is huddled upon the sofa. Now that we cannot hear the mother's speech, her silliness is gone and she has dignity and tragic beauty.* LAURA*'s dark hair hides her face until at the end of the speech she lifts it to smile at her mother.* AMANDA*'s gestures are slow and graceful, almost dancelike, as she comforts the daughter. At the end of her speech she glances a moment at the father's picture—then withdraws through the portieres. At close of* TOM*'s speech,* LAURA *blows out the candles, ending the play.*)

TOM: I didn't go to the moon, I went much further—for time is the longest distance between two places—Not long after that I was fired for writing a poem on the lid of a shoe-box. I left Saint Louis. I descended the steps of this fire-escape for a last time and followed, from then on, in my father's footsteps, attempting to find in motion what was lost in space—I traveled around a great deal. The cities swept about me like dead leaves, leaves that were brightly colored but torn away from the branches. I would have stopped, but I was pursued by something. It always came upon me unawares, taking me altogether by surprise. Perhaps it was a familiar bit of music. Perhaps it was only a piece of transparent glass—Perhaps I am walking along a street at night, in some strange city, before I have found companions. I pass the lighted window of a shop where perfume is sold. The window is filled with pieces of colored glass, tiny transparent bottles in delicate colors, like bits of a shattered rainbow. Then all at once my sister touches my shoulder. I turn around and look into her eyes . . . Oh, Laura, Laura, I tried to leave you behind me, but I am more faithful than I intended to be! I reach for a cigarette, I cross the street, I run into the movies or a bar, I buy a drink, I speak to the nearest stranger—anything that can blow your candles out! (LAURA *bends over the candles.*)—for nowadays the world is lit by lightning! Blow out your candles, Laura—and so goodbye . . . (*She blows the candles out.*)

(*The scene dissolves.*)

The Receptive Reader

1. What is the difference between a stereotype and an archetype? Is Amanda the stereotype of the Southern belle? Is she the archetype of the fading beauty? Is the playwright's portrayal of Amanda cruel?

2. Is Tom an archetypal representative of adolescent rebellion?

3. Symbols are plentiful in this play. What about the typewriter? Could Laura have been taking harpsichord lessons instead of typing lessons? What is significant about the victrola? The glass animals Laura collects? The unicorn and the loss of its horn?

4. The play of light and darkness becomes a recurrent symbolic pattern in the play. (The lights go out because Tom has not paid the electric bill; Amanda "brightens" and darkens; it is a world of "the blind"; Laura "blows the candles out.") Look for other passages that reflect not only literal darkness but also the darkness of extinguished hopes.

5. Tennessee Williams crafted his plays carefully, with much connection between, and echoing of, images, phrases, symbols, and other elements. With a classmate or in a small group, trace one continuing strand that helps braid all or part of the play into a cohesive whole. Share your findings with the class.

6. If Laura's escape is her glass menagerie, what is Tom's escape? What is Amanda's? How successful are they?

7. What is the role of Laura's physical disability in the play? To what extent is it symbolic?

The Whole Play—For Discussion or Writing

Traditionally, critics have used the term **pathos** instead of tragedy when a central character in a play is an example of passive suffering. To you, is Laura a tragic character or merely pathetic?

Marsha Norman   *(born 1947)*   👁

Marsha Norman is best known for her Pulitzer Prize–winning play *'night, mother* (1983). The play focuses on a woman contemplating suicide; it draws the spectators into her world of thought and feeling, trying to make them understand her history and motivations. The play printed here, *Getting Out,* was Norman's first, and was first produced at the Actors Theatre in Louisville, Kentucky, in 1977. It went on to New

York to become an off-Broadway success. Norman taught in Kentucky schools and worked in an Atlanta hospital, and she has an extraordinary empathy for the traumas, ambitions, and despairs of ordinary people—people who are not celebrities or tragic heroes or demonic psychopaths. A Norman play may be a *tour de force*—a spectacular, provocative feat—in terms of theatrical technique. However, in more basic ways it is likely to honor the tradition of American realistic drama as written by Arthur Miller or Lorraine Hansberry. It is likely to ask you to pay attention to people that society has already written off as losers, asking you to respect their worth as human beings.

In *Getting Out,* the central conflict is between Arlene, a still young woman just released from prison, and Arlie—her alienated, rebellious, delinquent former self. You should try to imagine the play performed as if in a split-screen format: We see the present-day Arlene in a shabby apartment center stage. The present-day Arlene is the ex-convict trying to turn over a new leaf, to jump across her own shadow. During the flashbacks to her former self, however, other parts of the stage light up, taking us to the parents' home, the school, and the prison that were waystations in Arlene's past history. Arlie, Arlene's former self, is the problem student, the smartass kid, a holy terror to well-meaning teachers and counselors, a problem prisoner bent on bringing out the worst in the prison system. Many times in this play, past and present intermesh, as they do constantly in our own minds.

The play asks us to search our souls: Have we as individuals and as a society become cynical about "rehabilitation"? When dealing with criminals, are we ready "to lock them up and throw the key away"? Or do we believe in the redemption of sinners? Do we still have some basic faith in human nature—despite much evidence to the contrary?

Getting Out   *1977*

CHARACTERS

ARLENE, a thin, drawn woman in her late twenties, who has just served an eight-year prison term for murder

ARLIE, Arlene at various times earlier in her life

BENNIE, an Alabama prison guard in his fifties

EVANS, a prison guard

DOCTOR, a psychiatrist in a juvenile institution

CALDWELL, a prison guard

MOTHER, Arlene's mother

SCHOOL PRINCIPAL

RONNIE, a teenager in a juvenile institution

CARL, Arlene's former pimp and partner in various crimes, in his late twenties

WARDEN, Superintendent of Pine Ridge Correctional Institute for Women

RUBY, Arlene's upstairs neighbor, a cook in a diner, also an ex-con, in her late thirties

(SCENE: *Both acts are set in a dingy one-room apartment in a run-down section of downtown Louisville, Kentucky. There is a twin bed and one chair. There is a sink, an apartment-size combination stove and refrigerator, and a counter with cabinets above. Dirty curtains conceal the bars on the outside of the single window. There is one closet and a door to the bathroom. The door to the apartment opens into a hall.)*

(A catwalk stretches above the apartment and a prison cell, Stage Right, connects to it by stairways. An apron Downstage and Stage Left completes the enclosure of the apartment in playing areas for the past. The apartment must seem imprisoned.)

Notes

Arlie is the violent kid Arlene was until her last stretch in prison. She may walk through the apartment quite freely, but no one there will acknowledge her presence. Most of her scenes take place in the prison areas.

Arlie, in a sense, is Arlene's memory of herself, called up by fears, needs, and even simple word cues. The memory haunts, attacks, and warns. But mainly, the memory will not go away.

Arlie's life should be as vivid as Arlene's, if not as continuous. There must be hints in both physical type and gesture that Arlie and Arlene are the same person, though seen at different times in her life. They both speak with a country twang, but Arlene is suspicious and guarded, withdrawal always a possibility. Arlie is unpredictable and incorrigible. The change seen in Arlie during the second act represents a movement toward the adult Arlene, but the transition should never be complete. Only in the final scene are they enjoyably aware of each other.

The life in the prison "surround" needs to convince without distracting. The guards do not belong to any specific institution, but rather, to all the places where Arlene has done time.

Over Loudspeaker—Before Act I Curtain

(These announcements will be broadcast beginning 5 minutes before the house lights come down for Act I. A woman's voice is preferred; a droning loudspeaker tone is essential.)

Kitchen workers, all kitchen workers report immediately to the kitchen. Kitchen workers to the kitchen. The library will not be open today. Those scheduled for book check-out should remain in morning work assignments. Kitchen workers to the kitchen. No library hours today. Library hours resume tomorrow as usual. All kitchen workers to the kitchen.

Frances Mills, you have a visitor at the front gate. All residents and staff, all residents and staff . . . Do not, repeat, Do not, walk on the front lawn today or use the picnic tables on the front lawn during your break after lunch or dinner.

Your attention please. The exercise class for Dorm A residents has been cancelled. Mrs. Fischer should be back at work in another month. She thanks you for your cards and wants all her girls to know she had an 8 pound baby girl.

Doris Creech, see Mrs. Adams at the library before lunch. Frances Mills, you have a visitor at the front gate. The Women's Associates' picnic for the beauty school class has been postponed until Friday. As picnic lunches have already been prepared, any beauty school member who so wishes, may pick up a picnic lunch and eat it at her assigned lunch table during the regular lunch period.

Frances Mills, you have a visitor at the front gate. Doris Creech to see Mrs. Adams at the library before lunch. I'm sorry, that's Frankie Hill, you have a visitor at the front gate. Repeat, Frankie Hill, not Frances Mills, you have a visitor at the front gate.

Act I

(*The warden's voice on tape is heard in the blackout.*)

WARDEN'S VOICE: The Alabama State Parole Board hereby grants parole to Holsclaw, Arlene, subject having served eight years at Pine Ridge Correctional Institute for the second degree murder of a cab driver in conjunction with a filling station robbery involving attempted kidnapping of attendant. Crime occurred during escape from Lakewood State Prison where subject Holsclaw was serving three years for forgery and prostitution. Extensive juvenile records from the state of Kentucky appended hereto. (*As* WARDEN *continues, light comes up on* ARLENE, *walking around the cell, waiting to be picked up for the ride home.*)

(ARLIE *is visible, but just barely, downstage center.*)

(WARDEN's *voice, continuing.*) Subject now considered completely rehabilitated is returned to Kentucky under interstate parole agreement in consideration of family residence and appropriate support personnel in the area. Subject will remain under the supervision of Kentucky parole officers for a period of five years. Prospects for successful integration into community rated good. Psychological evaluation, institutional history and health records attached in Appendix C, this document.

BENNIE'S VOICE: Arlie! (ARLENE *leaves the cell.*)

(*Light comes up on* ARLIE, *seated downstage center. She tells this story rather simply. She enjoys it, but its horror is not lost on her. She may be doing some semi-absorbing activity such as painting her toenails.*)

ARLIE: So, there was this little kid, see, this creepy little fucker next door. Had glasses an somethin wrong with his foot. I don't know, seven, maybe. Anyhow, ever time his daddy went fishin, he'd bring this kid back some frogs. They built this little fence around em in the back yard like they was pets or somethin. An we'd try to go over an see em but he'd start screamin to his mother to come out an git rid of us. Real snotty like. So we got sick of him bein such a goody-goody an one night me an June snuck over there an put all his dumb of frogs in this sack. You never heared such a fuss. (*Makes croaking sounds.*) Slimy bastards, frogs. We was plannin to let em go all over the place, but when they started jumpin an all, we just figured they was askin for it. So, we taken em out front to the porch an we throwed em, one at a time, into the street. (*Laughs.*) Some of em hit cars goin by but most of em jus got squashed, you know, runned over? It was great, seein how far we could throw em, over back of our backs an under our legs an God, it was really fun watchin em fly through the air then SPLAT (*claps hands*) all over somebody's car window or somethin. Then the next day, we was waitin and this little kid comes out in his back yard lookin for his stupid frogs and he don't see any an he gets so crazy, cryin and everything. So me an June goes over an tells him we seen this big mess out in the street, an he goes out an sees all them frogs legs and bodies an shit all over the everwhere, an, man, it was so funny. We bout killed ourselves laughin. Then his mother come out and she wouldn't let him go out an pick up all the pieces, so he jus had to stand there watchin all the cars go by smush his little babies right into the street. I's gonna run out an git him a frog's head, but June yellin at me "Arlie, git over here fore some car slips on them frog guts an crashes into you." (*Pause.*) I never had so much fun in one day in my whole life. (ARLIE *will remain seated as* ARLENE *enters the apartment. It is late evening. Two sets of footsteps are heard coming up the stairs.* ARLENE *opens the door and walks into the room. She stands still, surveying the littered apartment.* BENNIE *is heard dragging a heavy trunk up the stairs.* BENNIE *is wearing his guard uniform. He is a heavy man, but obviously used to physical work.*)

BENNIE (*from outside*): Arlie?

ARLENE: Arlene.

BENNIE: Arlene? (*Bringing the trunk just inside the door.*)

ARLENE: Leave it. I'll git it later.

BENNIE: Oh, now, let me bring it in for you. You ain't as strong as you was.

ARLENE: I ain't as mean as I was. I'm strong as ever. You go on now. (*Beginning to walk around the room.*)

ARLIE (*irritated, as though someone is calling her*): Lay off! (*Gets up and walks past* BENNIE.)

BENNIE (*scoots the trunk into the room a little further*): Go on where, Arlie?

ARLENE: I don't know where. How'd I know where you'd be goin?

BENNIE: I can't go til I know you're gonna do all right.

ARLENE: Look, I'm gonna do all right. I done all right before Pine Ridge, an I done all right at Pine Ridge. An I'm gonna do all right here.

BENNIE: But you don't know nobody. I mean, nobody nice.

ARLENE: Lay off.

BENNIE: Nobody to take care of you.

ARLENE (*picking up old newspapers and other trash from the floor*): I kin take care of myself. I been doin it long enough.

BENNIE: Sure you have, an you landed yourself in prison doin it, Arlie girl.

ARLENE (*wheels around, won't this guy ever shut up?*): Arlie girl landed herself in prison. Arlene is out, O.K.?

BENNIE: Hey, now, I know we said we wasn't gonna say nuthin about that, but I been lookin after you for a long time. I been watchin you eat your dinner for eight years now. I got used to it, you know?

ARLENE: Well, you kin jus' git unused to it.

BENNIE: Then why'd you ask me to drive you all the way up here?

ARLENE: I didn't, now. That was all your big idea.

BENNIE: And what were you gonna do? Ride the bus, pick up some soldier, git yourself in another mess of trouble?

> ARLIE (*struts back into the apartment from the closet door, going over as if to a soldier sitting at a bar*): O.K., who's gonna buy me a beer?

ARLENE: You oughta go by Fort Knox on your way home.

> ARLIE: Fuckin soldiers, don't care where they get theirself drunk. (*Stops.*)

ARLENE: You'd like it.

> ARLIE: Well, Arlie girl, take your pick.

ARLENE: They got tanks right out on the grass to look at.

> ARLIE (*now appears to lean on a bar rail*): You git that haircut today, honey?

BENNIE: I just didn't want you given your 20 dollars the warden gave you to the first pusher you come across.

> (*Arlie laughs.*)

ARLENE: That's what you think I been waitin for?

> (*A guard appears and motions for Arlie to follow him.*)

> ARLIE: Yeah! I heard ya. (*The guard "escorts"* ARLIE *to the cell and slams the door.*)

BENNIE: But God Almighty, I hate to think what you'd done to the first ol bugger tried to make you in that bus station. You got grit, Arlie girl. I gotta credit you for that.

> ARLIE (*from the cell, as she dumps a plate of food on the floor*): Officer!

BENNIE: The screamin you'd do. Wake the dead.

ARLENE: Uh-huh.

BENNIE: An there ain't nobody can beat you for throwin plates. (*Proudly.*)

> ARLIE: Are you gonna clean up this shit or do I have to sit here and look at it til I vomit? (*As the guard comes in to clean it up.*)

BENNIE: Listen, ever prison in Alabama's usin' plastic forks now on account of what you done.

ARLENE: You can quit talkin' just any time now.

> ARLIE: Some life you got, fatso. Bringin me my dinner then wipin it off the walls. (*Laughs.*)

BENNIE: Some of them officers was pretty leery of you. Even the chaplain.

ARLENE: No he wasn't either.

BENNIE: Not me, though. You was just wild, that's all.

ARLENE: Animals is wild, not people. That's what he said.

> ARLIE (*mocking*): Good behavior, good behavior. Shit.

BENNIE: Now what could that four-eyes chaplain know about wild? (ARLENE *looks up sharply.*) O.K. Not wild, then . . .

> ARLIE: I kin git outta here anytime I want. (*Leaves the cell.*)

BENNIE: But you got grit, Arlie.

ARLENE: I have said for you to call me Arlene.

BENNIE: O.K. O.K.

ARLENE: Huh?

BENNIE: Don't git riled. You want me to call you Arlene, then Arlene it is. Yes Ma'am. Now, (*slapping the trunk*) where do you want this? (*No response.*) Arlene, I said, where do you want this trunk?

ARLENE: I don't care. (BENNIE *starts to put it at the foot of the bed.* ARLENE *sees him.*) No! (*Then calmer.*) I seen it there too long. (BENNIE, *is understandably irritated.*) Maybe over here. (*Points to a spot near the window.*) I could put a cloth on it and sit an look out the . . . (*She pulls the curtains apart, sees the bars on the window.*) What's these bars doin here?

BENNIE (*stops moving the trunk*): I think they're to keep out burglars, you know. (*Sits on the trunk.*)

ARLENE: Yeah, I know.

> ARLIE (*appearing on the catwalk, as if stopped during a breakin*): We ain't breakin in, cop, we're just admirin this beautiful window.

ARLENE: I don't want them there. Pull them out.

BENNIE: You can't go tearin up the place, Arlene. Landlord wouldn't like it.

> ARLIE (*to the unseen policeman*): Maybe I got a brick in my hand and maybe I don't.

BENNIE: Not one bit.

> ARLIE: An I'm standin on this garbage can because I like to, all right?

ARLENE: I ain't gonna let no landlord tell me what to do. (*Fairly strong, walking back toward him.*)

BENNIE: The landlord owns the building. You gotta do what he says or he'll throw you out right on your pretty little *behind.* (*Gives her a familiar pat.*)

ARLENE (*slaps his hand away*): You watch your mouth. I won't have no dirty talk.

   ARLIE: Just shut the fuck up, cop! Go bust a wino or somethin. (*Returns to the cell.*)

ARLENE: Here, put the trunk over here. (*Points downstage right.*)

BENNIE: What you got in here, anyhow? Rocks? Rocks from the rock pile? (*Carrying the trunk over to the spot she has picked.*)

ARLENE: That ain't funny.

BENNIE: Oh sweetie, I didn't mean nuthin by that.

ARLENE: And I ain't your sweetie.

BENNIE: We really did have us a rock pile, you know, at the old Men's Prison, yes we did. And those boys, time they did nine or ten years carryin' rocks around, they was pret-ty mean, I'm here to tell you. And strong? God.

ARLENE: Well, what did you expect? (*Beginning to unpack the trunk.*)

BENNIE: You're tellin' me. It was dumb, I kept tellin the warden that. They coulda killed us all, easy, any time, that outfit. Except, we did have the guns.

ARLENE: Uh-huh.

BENNIE: One old bastard sailed a throwin-rock at me one day, woulda took my eye out if I hadn't turned around just then. Still got the scar, see? (*Reaches up to the back of his head.*)

ARLENE: You shoot him?

BENNIE: Nope. Somebody else did. I forget who. Hey! (*Walking over to the window.*) These bars won't be so bad. Maybe you could get you some plants so's you don't even see them. Yeah, plants'd do it up just fine. Just fine.

ARLENE (*pulls a cheaply framed picture of Jesus out of the trunk*): Chaplain give me this.

BENNIE: He got it for free, I bet.

ARLENE: Now, look here. That chaplain was good to me, so you can shut up about him.

BENNIE: Fine. Fine. (*Backing down.*)

ARLENE: Here. (*Handing him the picture.*) You might as well be useful 'fore you go.

BENNIE: Where you want it?

ARLENE: Don't matter.

BENNIE: Course it matters. Wouldn't want me puttin it inside the closet, would you? You gotta make decisions now, Arlene. Gotta decide things.

ARLENE: I don't care.

BENNIE (*insisting*): Arlene.

ARLENE: There. (*Pointing to a prominent position on the apartment wall, center.*)

BENNIE: Yeah. Good place. See it first thing when you get up. (ARLENE *lights a cigarette, as*

   ARLIE *retrieves a hidden lighter from the toilet in the cell.*)

   ARLIE: There's ways . . . gettin outta bars . . . (*Appears to light a fire in the cell, catching her blouse on fire too.*)

BENNIE (*as* ARLIE *is lighting the fire*): This ol nail's pretty loose. I'll find something better to hang it with . . . somewhere or other . . .

> ARLIE (*screams and the* DOCTOR *runs toward her, getting the attention of* EVANS, *a guard who has been goofing off on the catwalk*): Let me outta here! There's a fuckin fire in here! (DOCTOR *arrives at the cell, pats his pockets as if looking for the keys.*) Officer!
>
> DOCTOR: Guard! (GUARD *begins his run to the cell.*)
>
> ARLIE: It's burnin me!
>
> DOCTOR: Hurry!
>
> GUARD-EVANS: I'm comin! I'm comin!
>
> DOCTOR: What the hell were you . . .
>
> GUARD-EVANS: Come on, come on. (*Fumbling for the right key.*)
>
> DOCTOR: For Chrissake! (*Urgent.* GUARD *gets the door open, they rush in.* DOCTOR, *wrestling* ARLIE *to the ground, opens his bag.*) Lay still, dammit. (ARLIE *collapses,* DOCTOR *may appear to give an injection.*) Ow! (*Grabbing his hand.*)
>
> GUARD-EVANS (*lifting* ARLIE *up to the bed*): Get bit, Doc?
>
> DOCTOR: You going to let her burn this place down before you start payin attention up there?
>
> GUARD-EVANS: (*walks to the toilet, feels under the rim*): Uh-huh.

BENNIE: There, that what you had in mind?

ARLENE: Yeah, thanks.

> GUARD-EVANS: She musta had them matches hid right here.

BENNIE (*who has hung the picture and is now staring at it*): How you think he kept his beard trimmed all nice?

ARLENE (*preoccupied with unloading the trunk*): Who?

BENNIE (*pointing to the picture*): Jesus.

> DOCTOR (*quite stern*): I'll have to report you for this.

ARLENE: I don't know.

> DOCTOR: That injection should hold her. I'll check back later. (*Leaves.*)
>
> GUARD-EVANS (*walking over to the bed*): Report me, my ass. We got cells don't have potties, Holsclaw. (*Begins to search her and the bed, handling her very roughly.*) So where is it now? Got it up your pookie, I bet. Oh, that'd be good. Doc comin back an me with my fingers up your . . . roll over . . . don't weight hardly nuthin, do you, dollie?

BENNIE: Never seen him without a moustache either.

ARLENE: Huh?

BENNIE: The picture.

> GUARD-EVANS: Aw now . . . (*Finding the lighter under the mattress.*) That wasn't hard at all. Don't you know bout hide an seek, Arlie, girl? Gonna hide somethin, hide it where it's fun to find it. (*Standing up, going to the door.*) Crazy fuckin someday-we-ain't-gonna-come-save-you bitch!

BENNIE: Well, Arlie girl, (GUARD *slams cell door and leaves*) that ol trunk's bout as empty as my belly.

ARLENE: You have been talkin bout your belly ever since we left this mornin.

BENNIE: You hungry? Them hotdogs we had give out around Nashville.

ARLENE: No. Not really.

BENNIE: You gotta eat, Arlene.

ARLENE: Says who?

BENNIE (*laughs; this is a familiar response*): How bout I pick us up some chicken, give you time to clean yourself up. We'll have a nice little dinner, just the two of us.

ARLENE: I git sick if I eat this late. Besides, I'm tired.

BENNIE: You'll feel better soon's you git somethin on your stomach. Like I always said, "Can't plow less'n you feed the mule."

ARLENE: I ain't never heard you say that.

BENNIE: There's lots you don't know about me, Arlene. You been seein me ever day, but you ain't been payin attention. You'll get to like me now we're out.

ARLENE: You . . . was always out.

BENNIE: Yes sir, I'm gonna like bein retired. I kin tell already. An I can take care of you, like I been, only now . . .

ARLENE (*interrupting*): You tol me you was jus takin a vacation.

BENNIE: I was gonna tell you.

ARLENE: You had some time off an nothin to do . . .

BENNIE: Figured you knew already.

ARLENE: You said you ain't never seen Kentucky like you always wanted to. Now you tell me you done quit at the prison? (*Increasingly angry.*)

BENNIE: They wouldn't let me drive you up here if I was still on the payroll, you know. Rules, against the rules. Coulda got me in big trouble doin that.

ARLENE: You ain't goin back to Pine Ridge?

BENNIE: Nope.

ARLENE: An you drove me all the way up here plannin to stay here?

BENNIE: I was thinkin on it.

ARLENE: Well what are you gonna do?

BENNIE (*not positive, just a possibility*): Hardware.

ARLENE: Sell guns?

BENNIE (*laughs and shakes his head "no"*): Nails. Always wanted to. Some little store with bins and barrels full of nails and screws. Count em out. Put em in little sacks.

ARLENE: I don't need nobody hangin around remindin me where I been.

BENNIE: We had us a good time drivin up here, didn't we? You throwin that tomato outta the car . . . hit that No Litterin sign square in the middle. (*Grabs her arm as if to feel the muscle.*) Good arm you got.

ARLENE (*pulling away sharply*): Don't you go grabbin me.

BENNIE: Listen, you take off them clothes and have yourself a nice hot bath. (*Heading for the bathroom.*) See, I'll start the water. And me, I'll go get us some chicken. (*Coming out of the bathroom.*) You like slaw or potato salad?

ARLENE: Don't matter.

BENNIE (*asking her to decide*): Arlene . . .

ARLENE: Slaw.

BENNIE: One big bucket of slaw comin right up. An extra rolls. You have a nice bath, now, you hear? I'll take my time so's you don't have to hurry fixin yourself up.

ARLENE: I ain't gonna do no fixin.

BENNIE (*a knowing smile*): I know how you gals are when you get in the tub. You got any bubbles?

ARLENE: What?

BENNIE: Bubbles. You know, stuff to make bubbles with . . . bubble bath.

ARLENE: I thought you was goin.

BENNIE: Right. Right. Goin right now. (BENNIE *leaves, locking the door behind him. He has left his hat on the bed.* ARLENE *checks the stove and refrigerator, then goes into the bathroom when noted.*)

> GUARD-CALDWELL (*opening the cell door, carrying a plastic dinner carton*): Got your grub, girlie.
>
> ARLIE: Get out!
>
> GUARD-CALDWELL: Can't. Doc says you gotta take the sun today.
>
> ARLIE: You take it! I ain't hungry. (GUARD *and* ARLIE *begin walk to the downstage table area.*)
>
> GUARD-CALDWELL: You gotta eat, Arlie.
>
> ARLIE: Says who?
>
> GUARD-CALDWELL: Says me. Says the Warden. Says the Department of Corrections. Brung you two rolls.
>
> ARLIE: And you know what you can do with your . . .
>
> GUARD-CALDWELL: Stuff em in your bra, why don't you?
>
> ARLIE: Ain't you got somebody to go beat up somewhere?
>
> GUARD-CALDWELL: Gotta see you get fattened up.
>
> ARLIE: What do you care?

(ARLENE *goes into the bathroom.*)

> GUARD-CALDWELL: Oh, we care all right. (*Setting the food down on the table.*) Got us a two-way mirror in the shower room. (*She looks up, hostile.*) And you don't know which one it is, do you? (*He forces her onto the seat.*) Yes Ma'am. Eat. (*Pointing to the food.*) We sure do care if you go gittin too skinny. (*Walks away, folding his arms and standing watching her, her anger building, despite her hunger.*) Yes Mam. We care a hog lickin lot.
>
> ARLIE: Sons-a bitches! (*Throws the whole carton at him.*)

(*Mother's knock is heard on the apartment door.*)

MOTHER: Arlie? Arlie girl you in there? (ARLENE *walks out of the bathroom, stands still, looking at the door.*)

> (ARLIE *hears the knock at the same time and slips into the apartment and over to the bed, putting the pillow between her legs and holding the yellow teddy bear* ARLENE *has unpacked.*)

(*Knocking louder.*) Arlie?

ARLIE (*pulling herself up weakly on one elbow, speaking with the voice of a very young child*): Mama? Mama?

(ARLENE *walks slowly toward the door.*)

MOTHER (*now pulling the doorknob from the outside, angry that the door is locked*): Arlie? I know you're in there.

    ARLIE: I can't git up, Mama. (*Hands between her legs.*) My legs is hurt.

MOTHER: What's takin you so long?

ARLENE (*smoothing out her dress*): Yeah, I'm comin. (*Puts* BENNIE'*s hat out of sight under the bed.*) Hold on.

MOTHER: I brung you some stuff but I ain't gonna stand here all night. (ARLENE *opens the door and stands back.* MOTHER *looks strong but badly worn. She is wearing her cab driver's uniform and is carrying a plastic laundry basket stuffed with cleaning fluids, towels, bug spray, etc.*)

ARLENE: I didn't know if you'd come.

MOTHER: Ain't I always?

ARLENE: How are you? (*Moves as if to hug her.* MOTHER *stands still,* ARLENE *backs off.*)

MOTHER: Bout the same. (*Walking into the room.*)

ARLENE: I'm glad to see you.

MOTHER (*not looking at* ARLENE): You look tired.

ARLENE: It was a long drive.

MOTHER (*putting the laundry basket on the trunk*): Didn't fatten you up none, I see. (*Walks around the room, looking the place over.*) You always was too skinny. (ARLENE *straightens her clothes again.*) Shoulda beat you like your daddy said. Make you eat.

    ARLIE: Nobody done this to me, Mama. (*Protesting, in pain.*) No! No!

MOTHER: He weren't a mean man, though, your daddy.

    ARLIE: Was . . . (*Quickly.*) my bike. My bike hurt me. The seat bumped me.

MOTHER: You remember that black chewing gum he got you when you was sick?

ARLENE: I remember he beat up on you.

MOTHER: Yeah, (*proudly*) and he was real sorry a coupla times. (*Looking in the closet.*) Filthy dirty. Hey! (*Slamming the closet door,* ARLENE *jumps at the noise.*) I brung you all kinda stuff. Just like Candy not leavin you nuthin. (*Walking back to the basket.*) Some kids I got.

    ARLIE (*curling up into a ball*): No, Mama, don't touch it. It'll git well. It git well before.

ARLENE: Where is Candy?

MOTHER: You got her place so what do you care? I got her outta my house so whatta I care? This'll be a good place for you.

ARLENE (*going to the window*): Wish there was a yard, here.

MOTHER (*beginning to empty the basket*): Nice things, see? Bet you ain't had no colored towels where you been.

ARLENE: No.

MOTHER (*putting some things away in cabinets*): No place like home. Got that up on the kitchen wall now.

        ARLIE: I don't want no tea, Mama.

ARLENE: Yeah?

MOTHER (*repeating* ARLENE'*s answers*): No . . . yeah? . . .You forgit how to talk? I ain't gonna be here all that long. Least you can talk to me while I'm here.

ARLENE: You ever git that swing you wanted?

MOTHER: Dish towels, an see here? June sent along this teapot. You drink tea, Arlie?

ARLENE: No.

MOTHER: June's havin another baby. Don't know when to quit, that girl. Course, I ain't one to talk. (*Starting to pick up trash on the floors, etc.*)

ARLENE: Have you seen Joey?

        ARLIE: I'm tellin you the truth.

MOTHER: An Ray . . .

        ARLIE (*pleading*): Daddy didn't do nuthin to me.

MOTHER: Ray ain't had a day of luck in his life.

        ARLIE: Ask him. He saw me fall on my bike.

MOTHER: Least bein locked up now, he'll keep off June til the baby gits here.

ARLENE: Have you seen Joey?

MOTHER: Your daddy ain't doin' too good right now. Man's been dyin for ten years, to hear him tell it. You'd think he'd git tired of it an jus go ahead . . . pass on.

ARLENE: Mother . . . (*Wanting an answer.*)

MOTHER: Yeah, I seen 'im. Bout two years ago. Got your stringy hair.

ARLENE: You got a picture?

MOTHER: You was right to give him up. Foster homes is good for some kids.

        ARLIE: Where's my Joey-bear? Yellow Joey-bear? Mama?

ARLENE: How'd you see him?

MOTHER: I was down at Detention Center pickin up Pete. (*Beginning her serious cleaning now.*)

ARLENE: How is he? (*Less than interested.*)

MOTHER: I could be workin at the Detention Center I been there so much. All I gotta do's have somethin big goin on an I git a call to come after one of you. Can't jus have kids, no, gotta be pickin em up all over town.

ARLENE: You was just tellin me . . .

MOTHER: Pete is taller, that's all.

ARLENE: You was just tellin me how you saw Joey.

MOTHER: I'm comin back in the cab an I seen him waitin for the bus.

ARLENE: What'd he say?

MOTHER: Oh, I didn't stop. (ARLENE *looks up quickly, hurt and angry.*) If the kid don't even know you, Arlie, he sure ain't gonna know who I am.

ARLENE: How come he couldn't stay at Shirley's?

MOTHER: Cause Shirley never was crazy about washin more diapers. She's the only smart kid I got. Anyway, social worker only put him there til she could find him a foster home.

ARLENE: But I coulda seen him.

MOTHER: Thatta been trouble, him bein in the family. Kid wouldn't have known who to listen to, Shirley or you.

ARLENE: But I'm his mother.

MOTHER (*interrupting*): See, now you don't have to be worryin about him. No kids, no worryin.

ARLENE: He just had his birthday, you know.

ARLIE: Don't let daddy come in here, Mama. Just you an me. Mama?

ARLENE: When I git workin, I'll git a nice rug for this place. He could come live here with me.

MOTHER: Fat chance.

ARLENE: I done my time.

MOTHER: You never really got attached to him anyway.

ARLENE: How do you know that? (*Furious.*)

MOTHER: Now don't you go gettin het up. I'm tellin you . . .

ARLENE: But . . .

MOTHER: Kids need rules to go by an he'll get em over there.

ARLIE: No Daddy! I didn't tell her nuthin. I didn't! I didn't! (*Screaming, gets up from the bed, terrified.*)

MOTHER: Here, help me with these sheets. (*Hands* ARLENE *the sheets from the laundry basket.*) Even got you a spread. Kinda goes with them curtains. (ARLENE *is silent.*) You ain't thanked me, Arlie girl.

ARLENE (*going to the other side of the bed*): They don't call me Arlie no more. It's Arlene now. (ARLENE *and* MOTHER *make up the bed.*)

(ARLIE *jumps up, looks around and goes over to* MOTHER*'s purse. She looks through it hurriedly and pulls out the wallet. She takes some money and runs downstage left where she is caught by a* SCHOOL PRINCIPAL.)

PRINCIPAL: Arlie? You're in an awfully big hurry for such a little girl. (*Brushes at* ARLIE*'s hair.*) That is you under all that hair, isn't it? (ARLIE *resists this gesture.*) Now, you can watch where you're going.

ARLIE: Gotta git home.

PRINCIPAL: But school isn't over for another three hours. And there's peanut butter and chili today. (*As if this mattered.*)

ARLIE: Ain't hungry. (*Struggling free.*)

PRINCIPAL (*now sees* ARLIE*'s hands clenched behind her back*): What do we have in our hands, Arlie? (*Sticky sweet over suspicion.*)

ARLIE: Nuthin.

PRINCIPAL: Let me see your hands, Arlie. Open up your hands. (*Expecting the worst.*)

ARLIE (*bringing hands around in front, opening them, showing crumpled dollars*): It's my money. I earned it.

PRINCIPAL (*taking the money*): And how did we earn this money?

ARLIE: Doin things.

PRINCIPAL: What kind of things?

ARLIE: For my daddy.

PRINCIPAL: Well, we'll see about that. You'll have to come with me.

ARLIE: No. (*Resisting as* PRINCIPAL *pulls her.*)

PRINCIPAL: Your mother was right after all. She said put you in a special school. (*Quickly.*) No, what she said was put you away somewhere and I said, No, she's too young, well I was wrong. I have four hundred other children to take care of here and what have I been doing? Breaking up your fights, talking to your truant officer and washing your writing off the bathroom wall. Well, I've had enough. You've made your choice. You *want* out of regular school and you're going to *get* out of regular school.

ARLIE (*becoming more violent*): You can't make me go nowhere, bitch!

PRINCIPAL (*backing off in cold anger*): I'm not making you go. You've earned it. You've worked hard for this, well, they're used to your type over there. They'll know exactly what to do with you. (PRINCIPAL *stalks off, leaving* ARLIE *alone.*)

MOTHER (*smoothing out the spread*): Spread ain't new, but it don't look so bad. Think we got it right after we got you. No, I remember now. I was pregnant with you an been real sick the whole time. (ARLENE *lights a cigarette,* MOTHER *takes one,* ARLENE *retrieves the pack quickly.*) Your daddy brung me home this big bowl of chili an some jelly doughnuts. Some fare from the airport give him a big tip. Anyway, I'd been eatin peanut brittle all day, only thing that tasted any good. Then in he come with this chili an no sooner'n I got in bed I thrown up all over everwhere. Lucky I didn't throw you up, Arlie girl. Anyhow, that's how come us had to get a new spread. This one here. (*Sits on the bed.*)

ARLENE: You drivin the cab any?

MOTHER: Any? Your daddy ain't drove it at all a long time now. Six years, seven maybe.

ARLENE: You meet anybody nice?

MOTHER: Not anymore. Mostly drivin old ladies to get their shoes. Guess it got around the nursin homes I was reliable. (*Sounds funny to her.*) You remember that time I took you drivin with me that night after you been in a fight an that soldier bought us a beer? Shitty place, hole in the wall?

ARLENE: You made me wait in the car.

MOTHER (*standing up*): Think I'd take a child of mine into a dump like that?

ARLENE: You went in.

MOTHER: Weren't no harm in it. (*Walking over for the bug spray.*) I didn't always look so bad, you know.

ARLENE: You was pretty.

MOTHER (*beginning to spray the floors*): You could look better'n you do. Do somethin with your hair. I always thought if you'd looked better you wouldn't have got in so much trouble.

ARLENE (*pleased and curious*): Joey got my hair?

MOTHER: And skinny.

ARLENE: I took some beauty school at Pine Ridge.

MOTHER: Yeah, a beautician?

ARLENE: I don't guess so.

MOTHER: Said you was gonna work.

ARLENE: They got a law here. Ex-cons can't get no license.

MOTHER: Shoulda stayed in Alabama, then. Worked there.

ARLENE: They got a law there, too.

MOTHER: Then why'd they give you the trainin?

ARLENE: I don't know.

MOTHER: Maybe they thought it'd straighten you out.

ARLENE: Yeah.

MOTHER: But you are gonna work, right? (*Doesn't want another burden.*)

ARLENE: Yeah. Cookin maybe. Somethin that pays good.

MOTHER: You? Cook? (*Laughs.*)

ARLENE: I could learn it.

MOTHER: Your daddy ain't never forgive you for that bologna sandwich. (ARLENE *laughs a little, finally enjoying a memory.*) Oh, I wish I'd seen you spreadin' that Colgate on that bread. He'd have smelled that toothpaste if he hadn't been so sloshed. Little snotty-nosed kid tryin to kill her daddy with a bologna sandwich. An him bein so pleased when you brung it to him . . . (*Laughing.*)

ARLENE (*no longer enjoying the memory*): He beat me good.

MOTHER: Well, now, Arlie, you gotta admit you had it comin to you. (*Wiping tears from laughing.*)

ARLENE: I guess.

MOTHER: You got a broom?

ARLENE: No.

MOTHER: Well, I got one in the cab I brung just in case. I can't leave it here, but I'll sweep up fore I go. (*Walking toward the door.*) You jus rest til I git back. Won't find no work lookin the way you do. (MOTHER *leaves.* ARLENE *finds some lipstick and a mirror in her purse. She makes an attempt to look better while* MOTHER *is gone.*)

 ARLIE (*jumps up, as if talking to another kid*): She is not skinny!

ARLENE (*looking at herself in the mirror*): I guess I could . . .

 ARLIE: And she don't have to git them stinky permanents. Her hair just comes outta her head curly.

ARLENE: Some lipstick.

 ARLIE (*serious*): She drives the cab to buy us stuff, cause we don't take no charity from nobody, cause we got money cause she earned it.

ARLENE (*closing the mirror, dejected, afraid mother might be right*): But you're too skinny and you got stringy hair. (*Sitting on the floor.*)

 ARLIE (*more angry*): She drives at night cause people needs rides at night. People goin to see their friends that are sick, or people's cars broken down an they gotta get to work at the . . . nobody calls my Mama a whore!

MOTHER (*coming back in with the broom*): If I'd known you were gonna sweep up with your butt, I wouldn't have got this broom. Get up! (*Sweeps at* ARLENE *to get her to move.*)

            ARLIE: You're gonna take that back or I'm gonna rip out all your ugly hair and stuff it down your ugly throat.

ARLENE (*tugging at her own hair*): You still cut hair?

MOTHER (*noticing some spot on the floor*): Gonna take a razor blade to get out this paint.

ARLENE: Nail polish.

            ARLIE: Wanna know what I know about your Mama? She's dyin. Somethin's eatin up her insides piece by piece, only she don't want you to know it.

MOTHER (*continuing to sweep*): So, you're callin' yourself Arlene, now?

ARLENE: Yes.

MOTHER: Don't want your girlie name no more?

ARLENE: Somethin like that.

MOTHER: They call you Arlene in prison?

ARLENE: Not at first when I was bein hateful. Just my number then.

MOTHER: You always been hateful.

ARLENE: There was this chaplain, he called me Arlene from the first day he come to talk to me. Here, let me help you. (ARLENE *reaches for the broom.*)

MOTHER: I'll do it.

ARLENE: You kin rest.

MOTHER: Since when? (ARLENE *backs off,* MOTHER *sweeping harder now.*) I ain't hateful, how come I got so many hateful kids? Poor dumb as hell Pat, stealin them wigs, Candy screwin since day one, Pete cuttin up ol Mac down at the grocery, June sellin dope like it was Girl Scout cookies, and you . . . thank God I can't remember it all.

ARLENE (*a very serious request*): Maybe I could come out on Sunday for . . . you still make that pot roast?

MOTHER (*now sweeping over by the picture of Jesus*): That your picture?

ARLENE: That chaplain give it to me.

MOTHER: The one give you your "new name."

ARLENE: Yes.

MOTHER: It's crooked. (*Doesn't straighten it.*)

ARLENE: I liked those potatoes with no skins. An that ketchup squirter we had, jus like in a real restaurant.

MOTHER: People that run them institutions now, they jus don't know how to teach kids right. Let em run around an get in more trouble. They should get you up at the crack of dawn an set you to scrubbin the floor. That's what kids need. Trainin. Hard work.

ARLENE (*a clear request*): I'll probably git my Sundays off.

MOTHER: Sunday . . . is my day to clean house now. (ARLENE *gets the message, finally walks over to straighten the picture.* MOTHER *now feels a little bad about this rejection, stops sweeping for a moment.*) I woulda wrote you but I didn't have nuthin to say. An no money to send, so what's the use?

ARLENE: I made out.

MOTHER: They pay you for workin?

ARLENE: Bout three dollars a month.

MOTHER: How'd you make it on three dollars a month? (*Answers her own question.*) You do some favors?

ARLENE (*sitting down in the chair under the picture, a somewhat smug look*): You jus can't make it by yourself.

MOTHER (*pauses, suspicious, then contemptuous*): You play, Arlie?

ARLENE: You don't know nuthin about that.

MOTHER: I hear things. Girls callin each other "mommy" an bringin things back from the canteen for their "husbands." Makes me sick. You got family, Arlie, what you want with that playin? Don't want nobody like that in my house.

ARLENE: You don't know what you're talkin about.

MOTHER: I still got two kids at home. Don't want no bad example. (*Not finishing the sweeping. Has all the dirt in one place, but doesn't get it up off the floor yet.*)

ARLENE: I could tell them some things.

MOTHER: Like about that cab driver. (*Vicious.*)

ARLENE: Look, that was a long time ago. I wanna work, now, make somethin of myself. I learned to knit. People'll buy nice sweaters. Make some extra money.

MOTHER: We sure could use it.

ARLENE: An then if I have money, maybe they'd let me take Joey to the fair, buy him hotdogs an talk to him. Make sure he ain't foolin around.

MOTHER: What makes you think he'd listen to you? Alice, across the street? Her sister took care her kids while she was at Lexington. You think they pay any attention to her now? Ashamed, that's what. One of em told me his mother done died. Gone to see a friend and died there.

ARLENE: Be different with me and Joey.

MOTHER: He don't even know who you are, Arlie.

ARLENE: Arlene. (*She can't respond; this is all she can say.*)

MOTHER: You forgot already what you was like as a kid. At Waverly, tellin them lies about that campin trip we took, sayin your Daddy made you watch while he an me . . . you know. I'd have killed you then if them social workers hadn't been watchin.

ARLENE: Yeah.

MOTHER: Didn't want them thinkin I weren't fit. Well, what do they know? Each time you'd get out of one of them places, you'd be actin worse than ever. Go right back to that junkie, pimp, Carl, selling the stuff he steals, savin his ass from the police. He follow you home this time, too?

ARLENE: He's got four more years at Bricktown.

MOTHER: Glad to hear it. Here . . . (*Handing her a bucket.*) Water. (ARLENE *fills up the bucket and* MOTHER *washes several dirty spots on the walls, floor and furniture.* ARLENE *knows better than to try to help.*)

(*The* DOCTOR *walks downstage to find* ARLIE *for their counseling session.*)

DOCTOR: So you refuse to go to camp?

ARLIE: Now why'd I want to go to your fuckin camp? Camp's for babies. You can go shit in the woods if you want to, but I ain't goin.

DOCTOR: Oh, you're goin.

ARLIE: Wanna bet?

MOTHER: Arlie, I'm waitin. (*For the water.*)

ARLIE: 'Sides, I'm waitin.

DOCTOR: Waiting for what?

ARLIE: For Carl to come git me.

DOCTOR: And who is Carl?

ARLIE: Jus some guy. We're goin to Alabama.

DOCTOR: You don't go till we say you can go.

ARLIE: Carl's got a car.

DOCTOR: Does he have a driver's license to go with it?

ARLIE (*enraged, impatient*): I'm goin now. (*She stalks away, then backs up toward him again. He has information she wants.*)

DOCTOR: Hey!

ARLENE: June picked out a name for the baby?

MOTHER: Clara . . . or Clarence. Got it from this fancy shampoo she bought.

ARLIE: I don't feel good. I'm pregnant, you know.

DOCTOR: The test was negative.

ARLIE: Well, I should know, shouldn't I?

DOCTOR: No. You want to be pregnant, is that it?

ARLIE: I wouldn't mind. Kids need somebody to bring em up right.

DOCTOR: Raising children is a big responsibility, you know.

ARLIE: Yeah, I know it. I ain't dumb. Everybody always thinks I'm so dumb.

DOCTOR: You could learn if you wanted to. That's what the teachers are here for.

ARLIE: Shit.

DOCTOR: Or so they say.

ARLIE: All they teach us is about geography. Why'd I need to know about Africa. Jungles and shit.

DOCTOR: They want you to know about other parts of the world.

ARLIE: Well, I ain't goin there so whatta I care?

DOCTOR: What's this about Cindy?

ARLIE (*hostile*): She told Mr. Dawson some lies about me.

DOCTOR: I bet.

ARLIE: She said I fuck my Daddy for money.

DOCTOR: And what did you do when she said that?

ARLIE: What do you think I did? I beat the shit out of her.

DOCTOR: And that's a good way to work out your problem?

ARLIE: She ain't done it since. (*Proud.*)

DOCTOR: She's been in traction, since.

ARLIE: So, whatta I care? She say it again, I'll do it again. Bitch!

ARLENE (*looking down at the dirt* MOTHER *is gathering on the floor*): I ain't got a can. Just leave it.

MOTHER: And have you sweep it under the bed after I go? (*Wraps the dirt in a piece of newspaper and puts it in her laundry basket.*)

DOCTOR (*looking at his clipboard*): You're on unit clean-up this week.

ARLIE: I done it last week!

DOCTOR: Then you should remember what to do. The session is over. (*Getting up, walking away.*) And stand up straight! And take off that hat! (DOCTOR *and* ARLIE *go offstage as* MOTHER *finds* BENNIE's *hat.*)

MOTHER: This your hat?

ARLENE: No.

MOTHER: Guess Candy left it here.

ARLENE: Candy didn't leave nuthin. (*Then realizes this was a mistake.*)

MOTHER: Then whose is it? (ARLENE *doesn't answer.*) Do you know whose hat this is? (ARLENE *turns away.*) I'm askin you a question and I want an answer. (ARLENE *turns back to* MOTHER.) Whose hat is this? You tell me right now, whose hat is this?

ARLENE: It's Bennie's.

MOTHER: And who's Bennie?

ARLENE: Guy drove me home from Pine Ridge. A guard.

MOTHER (*upset*): I knew it. You been screwin a goddamn guard. (*Throws the hat on the bed.*)

ARLENE: He jus drove me up here, that's all.

MOTHER: Sure.

ARLENE: I git sick on the bus.

MOTHER: You expect me to believe that?

ARLENE: I'm tellin you, he jus . . .

MOTHER: No man alive gonna drive a girl 500 miles for nuthin.

ARLENE: He ain't never seen Kentucky.

MOTHER: It ain't Kentucky he wants to see.

ARLENE: He ain't gettin nuthin from me.

MOTHER: That's what you think.

ARLENE: He done some nice things for me at Pine Ridge. Gum, funny stories.

MOTHER: He'd be tellin stories all right, tellin his buddies where to find you.

ARLENE: He's gettin us some dinner right now.

MOTHER: And how're you gonna pay him? Huh? Tell me that.

ARLENE: I ain't like that no more.

MOTHER: Oh you ain't. I'm your mother. I know what you'll do.

ARLENE: I tell you I ain't.

MOTHER: I knew it. Well, when you got another bastard in you, don't come cryin to me, cause I done told you.

ARLENE: Don't worry.

MOTHER: An I'm gettin myself outta here fore your boyfriend comes back.

ARLENE: He ain't my boyfriend. (*Increasing anger.*)

MOTHER: I been a lotta things, but I ain't dumb, Arlene. ("*Arlene*" *is mocking.*)

ARLENE: I didn't say you was. (*Beginning to know how this is going to turn out.*)

MOTHER: Oh no? You lied to me!

ARLENE: How?

MOTHER: You took my spread without even sayin thank you. (*Not an answer. Just going on with the fury.*) You're hintin at comin to my house for pot

roast just like nuthin ever happened, an all the time you're hidin a goddamn guard under your bed. (*Furious.*) Uh-huh.

ARLENE: Mama? (*Quietly.*)

MOTHER: What? (*Cold, fierce.*)

ARLENE: What kind of meat makes a pot roast?

MOTHER: A roast makes a pot roast. Buy a roast. Shoulder, chuck . . .

ARLENE: Are you comin back?

MOTHER: You ain't got no need for me.

ARLENE: I gotta ask you to come see me?

MOTHER: I come tonight, didn't I, an nobody asked me?

ARLENE: Just forgit it.

MOTHER (*getting her things together now, ready to go*): An if I hadn't told
them about this apartment, you wouldn't be out at all, how bout that!

ARLENE: Forgit it! (*Stronger.*)

MOTHER: Don't you go talkin to me that way. You remember who I am. I'm
the one took you back after all you done all them years. I brung you that
teapot. I scrubbed your place. You remember that when you talk to me.

ARLENE: Sure.

MOTHER: Uh-huh. (*Now goes to the bed, rips off the spread and stuffs it in her
basket.*) I knowed I shouldn't have come. You ain't changed a bit.

ARLENE: Same hateful brat, right? (*Back to* MOTHER.)

MOTHER: Same hateful brat. Right. (*Arms full, heading for the door.*)

ARLENE: (*rushing toward her*): Mama . . .

MOTHER: Don't you touch me. (MOTHER *leaves.* ARLENE *stares out the door,
stunned and hurt; finally, she slams the door and turns back into the
room.*

ARLENE: No! Don't you touch Mama, Arlie.

RONNIE (*a fellow juvenile offender, runs across the catwalk,
waving a necklace and being chased by* ARLIE): Arlie got a
boyfriend, Arlie got a boyfriend. (*Throws the necklace
downstage.*) Whoo!

ARLIE (*chasing him*): Ronnie, you ugly mother, I'll smash your
fuckin . . .

ARLENE: You might steal all . . . (*Getting more angry.*)

RONNIE (*running down the stairs*): Arlie got a boyfriend . . .

ARLIE: Gimme that necklace or I'll . . .

ARLENE: . . . or eat all Mama's precious pot roast . . .

RONNIE (*as they wrestle on the downstage apron*): You'll tell
the Doctor on me? And get your private room back?
(*Laughing.*)

ARLENE (*cold and hostile*): No, don't touch Mama, Arlie. Cause you might slit
Mama's throat. (*Goes into the bathroom.*)

ARLIE: You wanna swallow all them dirty teeth?

RONNIE: Tell me who give it to you.

ARLIE: No, you tell me where it's at.

RONNIE (*breaks away, pushing* ARLIE *in the opposite direction,
runs for the necklace*): It's right here. (*Drops it down his
pants.*) Come an git it.

ARLIE: Oh now, that was really ignorant, you stupid pig.

RONNIE (*backing away, daring her*): Jus reach right in. First come, first served.

ARLIE: Now, how you gonna pee after I throw your weenie over the fence?

RONNIE: You ain't gonna do that, girl. You gonna fall in love. (*She turns vicious, pins him down, attacking. This is no longer play. He screams.* DOCTOR *appears on the catwalk.*)

DOCTOR: Arlie! (*Heads down the stairs to stop this.*)

CARL (*from outside the apartment door*): Arlie!

DOCTOR: Arlie!

ARLIE: Stupid, ugly . . .

RONNIE: Help! (ARLIE *runs off, hides downstage left.*)

DOCTOR: That's three more weeks of isolation, Arlie. (*Bending down to* RONNIE.) You all right? Can you walk?

RONNIE (*looking back to* ARLIE *as he gets up in great pain*): She was tryin to kill me.

DOCTOR: Yeah. Easy now. You shouldn've known, Ronnie.

ARLIE (*yelling at* RONNIE): You'll get yours, crybaby.

CARL: Arlie . . .

ARLIE: Yeah, I'm comin!

CARL: Bad-lookin dude says move your ass an open up this here door, girl. (ARLENE *does not come out of the bathroom.* CARL *twists the door knob violently, then kicks in the door and walks in.* CARL *is thin and cheaply dressed.* CARL'*s walk and manner are imitative of black pimps, but he can't quite carry it off.*) Where you at, Mama?

ARLENE: Carl?

CARL: Who else? You 'spectin' Leroy Brown?

ARLENE: I'm takin a bath!

CARL (*walking toward the bathroom*): I like my ladies clean. Matter of professional pride.

ARLENE: Don't come in here.

CARL (*mocking her tone*): Don't come in here. I seen it all before, girl.

ARLENE: I'm gittin out. Sit down or somethin.

CARL (*talking loud enough for her to hear him through the door*): Ain't got the time. (*Opens her purse, then searches the trunk.*) Jus come by to tell you it's tomorrow. We be takin our feet to the New York street. (*As though she will be pleased.*) No more fuckin around with these jiveass southern turkeys. We're goin to the big city, baby. Get you some red shades and some red shorts an the john's be linin' up fore we hit town. Four tricks a night. How's that sound? No use wearin out that cute ass you got. Way I hear it, only way to git busted up there's be stupid, an I ain't lived this long bein stupid.

ARLENE (*coming out of the bathroom wearing a towel*): That's exactly how you lived your whole life—bein stupid.

CARL: Arlie . . . (*Moving in on her.*) be sweet, sugar.

ARLENE: Still got your curls.

CARL (*trying to hug her*): You're lookin O.K. yourself.

ARLENE: Oh, Carl. (*Noticing the damage to the door, breaking away from any closeness he might try to force.*)

CARL (*amused*): Bent up your door, some.

ARLENE: How come you're out?

CARL: Sweetheart, you done broke out once, been nabbed and sent to Pine Ridge and got yourself paroled since I been in. I got a right to a little free time too, ain't that right?

ARLENE: You escape?

CARL: Am I standin here or am I standin here? They been fuckin with you, I can tell.

ARLENE: They gonna catch you.

CARL (*going to the window*): Not where we're going. Not a chance.

ARLENE: Where you goin they won't git you?

CARL: Remember that green hat you picked out for me down in Birmingham? Well, I ain't ever wore it yet, but I kin wear it in New York cause New York's where you wear whatever you feel like. One guy tol me he saw this dude wearin a whole ring of feathers roun his leg, right here (*grabs his leg above the knee*) an he weren't in no circus nor no Indian neither.

ARLENE: I ain't seen you since Birmingham. How come you think I wanna see you now?

ARLIE (*appearing suddenly, confronts* CARL): Carl, I ain't goin with that dude, he's weird. (*Pointing as if there is a trick waiting.*)

CARL: Cause we gotta go collect the johns' money, that's "how come."

ARLIE: I don't need you pimpin for me.

ARLENE (*very strong*): I'm gonna work.

CARL: Work?

ARLENE: Yeah.

CARL: What's this "work"?

ARLIE: You always sendin me to them ol' droolers . . .

CARL: You kin do two things, girl . . .

ARLIE: They slobberin all over me . . .

CARL: Breakin out an hookin.

ARLIE: They tyin me to the bed!

ARLENE: I mean real work.

ARLIE (*now screaming, gets further away from him*): I could git killed working for you. Some sicko, some crazy drunk . . . (*Goes offstage, guard puts her in the cell sometime before* BENNIE'*s entrance.*)

CARL: You forget, we seen it all on TV in the dayroom, you bustin outta Lakewood like that. Fakin that palsy fit, then beatin that guard half to death with his own key ring. Whoo-ee! Then that spree you went on . . . stoppin at that fillin station for some cash, then kidnappin the old dude pumpin the gas.

ARLENE: Yeah.

CARL: Then that cab driver comes outta the bathroom an tries to mess with you and you shoots him with his own piece. (*Fires an imaginary pistol.*) That there's nice work, Mama. (*Going over to her, putting his arms around her.*)

ARLENE: That gun . . . it went off, Carl.

CARL (*getting more determined with his affection*): That's what guns do, doll. They go off.

BENNIE'S VOICE (*from outside*): Arlene? Arlene?

CARL: Arlene? (*Jumping up.*) Well, la de da. (BENNIE *opens the door, carrying the chicken dinners. He is confused seeing* ARLENE *wearing a towel and talking to* CARL.)

ARLENE: Bennie, this here's Carl.

CARL: You're interruptin, Jack. Me and Arlie got business.

BENNIE: She's callin herself Arlene.

CARL: I call my ladies what I feel like, chicken man, an you call yourself "gone."

BENNIE: I don't take orders from you.

CARL: Well, you been takin orders from somebody, or did you git that outfit at the army surplus store?

ARLENE: Bennie brung me home from Pine Ridge.

CARL (*walking toward him*): Oh, it's a guard now, is it? That chicken break out or what? (*Grabs the chicken.*)

BENNIE: I don't know what you're doin here, but . . .

CARL: What you gonna do about it, huh? Lock me up in the toilet? You an who else, Batman?

BENNIE (*taking the chicken back walking calmly to the counter*): Watch your mouth, punk. (*Condescending. Doesn't want a fight, for* ARLENE*'s sake, but doesn't want to appear threatened either.*)

CARL (*kicks a chair toward* BENNIE): Punk!

ARLENE (*trying to stop this*): I'm hungry.

BENNIE: You heard her, she's hungry.

CARL (*vicious*): Shut up! (*Mocking.*) Ossifer.

BENNIE: Arlene, tell this guy if he knows what's good for him . . .

CARL (*walking to the counter where* BENNIE *has left the chicken*): Why don't you write me a parkin ticket? (*Shoves the chicken on the floor.*) Don't fuck with me, Dad. It ain't healthy.

BENNIE (*pauses, a real standoff. Finally, bends down and picks up the chicken*): You ain't worth dirtyin' my hands. (CARL *walks by him laughing.*)

CARL: Hey, Arlie. I got some dude to see. (*For* BENNIE*'s benefit as he struts to the door.*) What I need with another beat up guard? All that blood, jus ugly up my threads. (*Very sarcastic.*) Bye y'all.

ARLENE: Bye, Carl.

CARL (*turns back quickly at the door, stopping* BENNIE *who was following him*): You really oughta shine them shoes, man. (*Vindictive laugh, slams the door in* BENNIE*'s face.*)

BENNIE (*relieved, trying to change the atmosphere*): Well, how bout if we eat? You'll catch your death dressed like that.

ARLENE: Turn around then. (ARLENE *gets a shabby housecoat from the closet. She puts it on over her towel, buttons it up, then pulls the towel out from under it. This has the look of a prison ritual.*)

BENNIE (*as she is dressing*): Your parole officer's gonna tell you to keep away from guys like that . . . for your own good, you know. Those types, just like the suckers on my tomatoes back home. Take everything right outta you. Gotta pull em off, Arlie, uh, Arlene.

ARLENE: Now, I'm decent now.

BENNIE: You hear what I said?

ARLENE: I told him that. That's exactly what I did tell him. (*Going to the bathroom for her hairbrush.*)

BENNIE: Who was that anyhow? (*Sits down on the bed, opens up the chicken.*)

ARLENE (*from the bathroom*): Long time ago, me an Carl took a trip together.

BENNIE: When you was a kid, you mean?

ARLENE: I was at this place for kids.

BENNIE: And Carl was there?

ARLENE: No, he picked me up an we went to Alabama. There was this wreck an all. I ended up at Lakewood for forgery. It was him that done it. Got me pregnant too.

BENNIE: That was Joey's father?

ARLENE: Yeah, but he don't know that. (*Sits down.*)

BENNIE: Just as well. Guy like that, don't know what they'd do.

ARLENE: Mother was here while ago. Says she's seen Joey. (*Taking a napkin from* BENNIE.)

BENNIE: Wish I had a kid. Life ain't, well, complete, without no kids to play ball with an take fishin. Dorrie, though, she had them backaches an that neuralgia, day I married her to the day she died. Good woman though. No drinkin, no card playin, real sweet voice . . . what was that song she used to sing? . . .Oh, yeah . . .

ARLENE: She says Joey's a real good-lookin kid.

BENNIE: Well, his Mom ain't bad.

ARLENE: At Lakewood, they tried to git me to have an abortion.

BENNIE: They was just thinkin of you, Arlene.

ARLENE: I told em I'd kill myself if they done that. I would have too. (*Matter-of-fact, no self-pity.*)

BENNIE: But they took him away after he was born.

ARLENE: Yeah. (BENNIE *waits, knowing she is about to say more.*) An I guess I went crazy after that. Thought if I could jus git out an find him . . .

BENNIE: I don't remember any of that on the TV.

ARLENE: No.

BENNIE: Just remember you smilin at the cameras, yellin how you tol that cab driver not to touch you.

ARLENE: I never seen his cab. (*Now forces herself to begin to eat.*)

ARLIE (*in the cell, holding a pillow and singing*): Rock-a-bye baby, on the tree top, when the wind blows, the cradle will . . . (*Not remembering.*) cradle will . . . (*now talking*) what you gonna be when you grow up, pretty boy baby? You gonna be a doctor? You gonna give people medicine an take out they . . . no, don't be no doctor . . . be . . . be a preacher . . . sayin Our Father who is in Heaven . . . Heaven, that's where people go when they dies, when doctors can't save em or somebody kills em fore they even git a chance to . . . no, don't be no preacher neither . . . be . . . go to school an learn good (*tone begins to change*) so you kin . . . make everbody else feel so stupid all the time. Best thing you to be is stay a baby cause nobody beats up on babies or puts them . . . (*much more quiet*) that ain't true, baby. People is mean to babies, so you stay right here with me so nobody kin git you an make you cry an they lay one finger on you (*hostile*) an I'll beat the screamin shit right out of em. They even blow on you an I'll kill em.

(BENNIE *and* ARLENE *have finished their dinner.* BENNIE *puts one carton of slaw in the refrigerator, then picks up all the paper, making a garbage bag out of one of the sacks.*)

BENNIE: Ain't got a can, I guess. Jus use this ol sack for now.

ARLENE: I ain't never emptyin another garbage can.

BENNIE: Yeah, I reckon you know how by now. (*Yawns.*) You bout ready for bed?

ARLENE (*stands up*): I spose.

BENNIE (*stretches*): Little tired myself.

ARLENE: Thanks for the chicken. (*Dusting the crumbs off the bed.*)

BENNIE: You're right welcome. You look beat. How bout I rub your back. (*Grabs her shoulders.*)

ARLENE (*pulling away*): No. (*Walking to the sink.*) You go on now.

BENNIE: Oh come on. (*Wiping his hands on his pants.*) I ain't all that tired.

ARLENE: *I'm* tired.

BENNIE: Well, see then, a back rub is just what the doctor ordered.

ARLENE: No. I don't . . . (*Pulling away.*)

BENNIE (*grabs her shoulders and turns her around, sits her down hard on the trunk, starts rubbing her back and neck*): Muscles git real tight like, right in here.

ARLENE: You hurtin me.

BENNIE: Has to hurt a little or it won't do no good.

ARLENE (*jumps; he has hurt her*): Oh, stop it! (*Slips away from him and out into the room. She is frightened.*)

BENNIE (*smiling, coming after her, toward the bed*): Be lot nicer if you was layin down. Wouldn't hurt as much.

ARLENE: Now, I ain't gonna start yellin. I'm jus tellin you to go.

BENNIE (*straightens up as though he's going to cooperate*): O.K. then. I'll jus git my hat. (*He reaches for the hat, then turns quickly, grabs her and throws her down on the bed. He starts rubbing again.*) Now, you just relax. Don't you go bein scared of me.

ARLENE: You ain't gettin nuthin from me.

BENNIE: I don't want nuthin, honey. Jus tryin to help you sleep.

ARLENE (*struggling*): Don't you call me honey.

BENNIE (*stops rubbing, but keeps one hand on her back. Rubs her hair with his free hand*): See? Don't that feel better?

ARLENE: Let me up.

BENNIE: Why, I ain't holdin you down. (*So innocent.*)

ARLENE: Then let me up.

BENNIE (*takes hands off*): O.K. Git up.

ARLENE (*turns over slowly, begins to lift herself up on her elbows.* BENNIE *puts one hand on her leg*): Move your hand.

BENNIE (ARLENE *gets up, moves across the room*): I'd be happy to stay here with you tonight. Make sure you'll be all right. You ain't spent a night by yourself for a long time.

ARLENE: I remember how.

BENNIE: Well how you gonna git up? You got a alarm?

ARLENE: It ain't all that hard.

BENNIE (*puts one hand in his pocket, leers a little*): Oh yeah it is. (*Walks toward her again.*) Gimme a kiss. Then I'll go.

ARLENE: You stay away from me. (*Edging along the counter, seeing she's trapped.*)

BENNIE (*reaches for her, clamping her hands behind her, pressing up against her*): Now what's it going to hurt you to give me a little ol kiss?

ARLENE: Git out! I said git out! (*Struggling.*)

BENNIE: You don't want me to go. You're jus beginning to git interested. Your ol girlie temper's flarin up. I like that in a woman.

ARLENE: Yeah, you'd love it if I'd swat you one. (*Getting away from him.*)

BENNIE: I been hit by you before. I kin take anything you got.

ARLENE: I could mess you up good.

BENNIE: Now, Arlie. You ain't had a man in a long time. And the ones you had been no count.

ARLENE: Git out! (*Slaps him. He returns the slap.*)

BENNIE (*moving in*): Ain't natural goin without it too long. Young thing like you. Git all shriveled up.

ARLENE (ARLIE *turning on, now*): All right, you sunuvabitch, you asked for it! (*Goes into a violent rage, hitting and kicking him.*)

BENNIE (*overpowering her capably, prison guard style*): Little outta practice, ain't you? (*Amused.*)

ARLENE (*screaming*): I'll kill you, you creep!

BENNIE (*struggle continues,* BENNIE *pinning her arms under his legs as he kneels over her on the bed.* ARLENE *is terrified and in pain*): You will? You'll kill ol Bennie . . . kill ol Bennie like you done that cab driver? (*A cruel reminder he employs to stun and mock her.* ARLENE *looks as though she has been hit.* BENNIE *is still fired up; he unzips his pants.*)

ARLENE (*passive, cold and bitter*): This how you got your Dorrie, rapin?

BENNIE (*unbuttoning his shirt*): That what you think this is, rape?

ARLENE: I oughta know.

BENNIE: Uh-huh.

ARLENE: First they unzip their pants. (BENNIE *pulls his shirt out.*) Sometimes they take off their shirt.

BENNIE: They do huh?

ARLENE: But mostly, they just pull it out and stick it in. (BENNIE *stops, one hand goes to his fly, finally hearing what she has been saying. He straightens up, obviously shocked. He puts his arms back in his shirt.*)

BENNIE: Don't you call me no rapist. (*Pause, then insistent.*) No, I ain't no rapist, Arlie. (*Gets up, begins to tuck his shirt back in and zip up his pants.*)

ARLENE: And I ain't Arlie.

BENNIE (ARLENE *remains on the bed as he continues dressing*): No, I guess you ain't.

ARLENE (*quietly and painfully*): Arlie coulda killed you.

Over Loudspeaker—Before Act II Curtain

(*These announcements will be heard during the last 5 minutes of the intermission.*)

Garden workers will, repeat, will, report for work this afternoon. Bring a hat and raincoat and wear boots. All raincoats will be checked at the front gate at the end of work period and returned to you after supper.

Your attention please. A checkerboard was not returned to the recreation area after dinner last night. Anyone with information regarding the black and red checkerboard missing from the recreation area will please contact Mrs. Duvall after lunch. No checkerboards or checkers will be distributed until this board is returned.

Betty Rickey and Mary Alice Wolf report to the laundry. Doris Creech and Arlie Holsclaw report immediately to the superintendent's office. The movie this evening will be "Dirty Harry" starring Clint Eastwood. Doris Creech and Arlie Holsclaw report to the superintendent's office immediately.

The bus from St. Mary's this Sunday will arrive at 1:00 P.M. as usual. Those residents expecting visitors on that bus will gather on the front steps promptly at 1:20 and proceed with the duty officer to the visiting area after it has been confirmed that you have a visitor on the bus.

Attention all residents. Attention all residents. (*Pause.*) Mrs. Helen Carson has taught needlework classes here at Pine Ridge for thirty years. She will be retiring at the end of this month and moving to Florida where her husband has bought a trailer park. The resident council and the Superintendent's staff has decided on a suitable retirement present. We want every resident to participate in this project—which is—a quilt, made from scraps of material collected from the residents and sewn together by residents and staff alike. The procedure will be as follows. A quilting room has been set up in an empty storage area just off the infirmary. Scraps of fabric will be collected as officers do evening count. Those residents who would enjoy cutting up old uniforms and bedding no longer in use should sign up for this detail with your dorm officer. If you would like to sign your name or send Mrs. Carson some special message on your square of fabric, the officers will have tubes of embroidery paint for that purpose. The backing for the quilt has been donated by the Women's Associates as well as the refreshments for the retirement party to be held after lunch on the 30th. Thank you very much for your attention and participation in this worthwhile tribute to someone we are all very fond of here. You may resume work at this time. Doris Creech and Arlie Holsclaw report to the superintendent's office immediately.

Act II

(*The next morning.* ARLENE *is asleep on the bed.*)

(ARLIE *is locked in a maximum security cell. We do not see the officer to whom she speaks.*)

ARLIE: No, I don't have to shut up, neither. You already got me in seg-re-ga-tion, what else you gonna do? I got all day to sleep, while everybody else is out bustin ass in the laundry. (*Laughs.*) Hey! I know . . . you ain't gotta go do no dorm count, I'll just tell you an you jus sit. Huh? You preciate that? Ease them corns you been moanin about . . . yeah . . . O.K. Write this down. (*Pride, mixed with alternating contempt and amusement.*) Startin down by the john on the back side, we got Mary Alice. Sleeps with her pillow stuffed in her mouth. Says her Mom says it'd keep her from grinding down her teeth or somethin. She be suckin that pillow like she gettin paid for it. (*Laughs.*) Next, it's Betty the Frog. Got her legs all opened out like some fuckin . . . (*Makes croaking noises.*) Then it's Doris eatin pork rinds. Thinks somebody gonna grab em outta her mouth if she eats em during the day. Doris ain't dumb. She fat, but she ain't dumb. Hey! You notice how many girls is fat here? Then it be Rhonda, snorin, Marvene, wheezin and Suzanne, coughin. Then Clara an Ellie be still whisperin. Family shit, who's gettin outta line, which girls is gittin a new work 'signment, an who kin git extra desserts an for how much. Them's the two really run this place. My bed right next to Ellie, for sure it's got some of her shit hid in it by now. Crackers or some crap gonna leak out all over my sheets. Last time I found a fuckin grilled cheese in my pillow. Even had two of them little warty pickles. Christ! O.K. Linda and Lucille. They be real quiet, but they ain't sleepin. Prayin, that's them. Linda be sayin them Hell Mary's till you kin just about scream. An Lucille, she tol me once she didn't believe in no God, jus some stupid spirits whooshin aroun everwhere makin people do stuff. Weird. Now, I'm goin back down the other side, there's . . . (*Screams.*) I'd like to see you try it! I been listenin at you for the last three hours. Your husband's gettin laid off an your lettuce is gettin eat by rabbits. Crap City. *You* shut up! Whadda I care if I wake everybody up? I want the nurse . . . I'm gittin sick in here . . . an there's bugs in here!

(The light comes up in the apartment. Faint morning traffic sounds are heard. ARLENE *does not wake up.)*

> *(The* WARDEN *walks across the catwalk. The* GUARD-EVANS *catches up with him near* ARLIE's *cell.* BENNIE *is stationed at the far end of the walk.)*

LOUDSPEAKER: Dorm A may now eat lunch.

GUARD-EVANS: Warden, I thought 456 . . . *(nodding in* ARLIE's *direction)* was leavin here.

WARDEN: Is there some problem?

GUARD-EVANS: Oh, we can take care of her all right. We're just tired of takin her shit, if you'll pardon the expression.

ARLIE *(interrupting)*: You ain't seen nuthin yet, you mother.

WARDEN: Washington will decide on her transfer. Til then, you do your job.

GUARD-EVANS: She don't belong here. Rest of . . .

LOUDSPEAKER *(interrupts him)*: Betty Rickey and Mary Alice Wolf report to the laundry.

GUARD-EVANS: Most of these girls are mostly nice people, go along with things. She needs a cage.

ARLIE *(vicious)*: I need a knife.

WARDEN: Had it occurred to you that we could send the rest of them home and just keep her? *(Very curt. Walks away.)*

LOUDSPEAKER: Dorm A may now eat lunch. A Dorm to lunch.

GUARD-EVANS *(turning around, muttering to himself)*: Oh, that's a swell idea. Let everybody out except bitches like Holsclaw. *(She makes an obscene gesture at him: he turns back toward the catwalk.)* Smartass Warden, thinks he's runnin a hotel.

BENNIE *(having overheard this last interchange)*: Give you some trouble, did she?

GUARD-EVANS: I can wait.

BENNIE: For what?

GUARD-EVANS: For the day she tries gettin out an I'm here by myself. I'll show that screechin slut a thing or . . .

BENNIE: That ain't the way, Evans.

GUARD-EVANS: The hell it ain't. Beat the livin . . .

BENNIE: Outta a little thing like her? Gotta do her like all the rest. You got your shorts washed by givin Betty Rickey *Milky Ways.* You git your chairs fixed givin Frankie Hill extra time in the shower with Lucille Smith. An you git ol Arlie girl to behave herself with a stick of gum. Gotta have her brand, though.

GUARD-EVANS: You screwin that wildcat?

BENNIE *(starts walk to* ARLIE's *cell)*: Watch *(*ARLIE *is silent as he approaches, but is watching intently.)* Now, *(to nobody in particular)* where was that piece of Juicy Fruit I had in this pocket. Gotta be here somewhere. *(Takes a piece of gum out of his pocket and drops it within* ARLIE's *reach.)* Well, (*feigning disappointment*) I guess I already chewed it. (ARLIE *reaches for the gum and gets it.*) Oh, (*looking down at her now*) how's it goin, kid?

ARLIE: O.K. (ARLIE *says nothing, but unwraps the gum and chews it.* BENNIE *leaves the cell area, motioning to the other guard as if to say,* "See, that's how it's done.")

(*A loud siren goes by in the street below the apartment.* ARLENE *bolts up out of bed, then turns back to it quickly, making it up in a frenzied, ritual manner. As she tucks the spread up under the pillow, the siren stops and so does she. For the first time, now, she looks around the room, realizing where she is and the habit she has just played out. A jackhammer noise gets louder. She walks over to the window and looks out. There is a wolf-whistle from a worker below. She shuts the window in a fury, then grabs the bars. She starts to shake them, but then her hand goes limp. She looks around the room, as if trying to remember what she is doing there. She looks at her watch, now aware that it is late and that she has slept in her clothes.*)

ARLENE: People don't sleep in their clothes, Arlene. An people git up fore noon. (ARLENE *makes a still disoriented attempt to pull herself together, changing shoes, combing her hair, washing her face, etc., as guards and other prison life continues on the catwalk.*)

WARDEN (*walking up to* ARLIE, *remaining some distance from her, but talking directly to her, as he appears to check files or papers.*): Good afternoon, Arlie.

ARLIE: Fuck you. (WARDEN *walks away.*) Wait! I wanna talk to you.

WARDEN: I'm listening.

ARLIE: When am I gittin outta here?

WARDEN: That's up to you.

ARLIE: The hell it is.

WARDEN: When you can show that you can be with the other girls, you can get out.

ARLIE: How'm I supposed to prove that bein in here?

WARDEN: And then you can have mail again and visitors.

ARLIE: You're just fuckin with me. You ain't ever gonna let me out. I been in this ad-just-ment room four months, I think.

WARDEN: Arlie, you see the other girls on the dorm walking around, free to do whatever they want? If we felt the way you seem to think we do, everyone would be in lockup. When you get out of segregation, you can go to the records office and have your time explained to you.

ARLIE: It won't make no sense.

WARDEN: They'll go through it all very slowly . . . when you're eligible for parole, how many days of good time you have, how many industrial days you've earned, what constitutes meritorious good time . . . and how many days you're set back for your write-ups and all your time in segregation.

ARLIE: I don't even remember what I done to git this lockup.

WARDEN: Well, I do. And if you ever do it again, or anything like it again, you'll be right back in lockup where you will stay until you forget *how* to do it.

ARLIE: What was it?

WARDEN: You just remember what I said.

ARLENE: Now, then . . . (*Sounds as if she has something in mind to do. Looks as though she doesn't.*)

ARLIE: What was it?

WARDEN: Oh, and Arlie, the prison chaplain will be coming by to visit you today.

ARLIE: I don't want to see no chaplain!

WARDEN: Did I ask you if you wanted to see the chaplain? No, I did not. I said, the chaplain will be coming by to visit you today. Mrs. Roberts, why hasn't this light bulb been replaced? (*To an unseen guard. Walks away.*)

ARLIE (*screaming*): Get out of my hall! (WARDEN *walks away.*)

(ARLENE *walks to the refrigerator and opens it. She picks out a carton of slaw* BENNIE *put there last night. She walks away from the door, then turns around, remembering to close it. She looks at the slaw, as guard comes up to* ARLIE*'s cell with a plate.*)

ARLENE: I ain't never eatin no more scrambled eggs.

GUARD-CALDWELL: Chow time, cutie pie.

ARLIE: These eggs ain't scrambled, they's throwed up! And I want a fork!

(ARLENE *realizes she has no fork, then fishes one out of the garbage sack from last night. She returns to the bed, takes a bite of slaw and gets her wallet out of her purse. She lays the bills out on the bed one at a time.*)

ARLENE: That's for coffee . . . and that's for milk and bread . . . an that's cookies . . . an cheese an crackers . . . an shampoo an soap . . . an bacon an livercheese. No, pickle loaf . . . an ketchup and some onions . . . an peanut butter an jelly . . . an shoe polish. Well, ain't no need gettin everything all at once. Coffee, milk, ketchup, cookies, cheese, onions, jelly. Coffee, milk . . . oh, shampoo . . .

RUBY (*banging on the door, yelling*): Candy, I gotta have my five dollars back.

ARLENE (*quickly stuffing her money back in her wallet*): Candy ain't here!

RUBY: It's Ruby, upstairs. She's got five dollars I loaned her . . . Arlie? That Arlie? Candy told me her sister be . . . (ARLENE *opens the door hesitantly.*) It is Arlie, right?

ARLENE: It's Arlene. (*Does not extend her hand.*)

RUBY: See, I got these shoes in layaway . . . (*Puts her hand back in her pockets.*) she said you been . . . you just got . . . you seen my money?

ARLENE: No.

RUBY: I don't get em out today they go back on the shelf.

ARLENE (*doesn't understand*): They sell your shoes?

RUBY: Yeah. Welcome back.

ARLENE: Thank you. (*Embarrassed, but relieved.*)

RUBY: She coulda put it in my mailbox. (RUBY *starts to leave,* ARLENE *is closing the door behind her, when* RUBY *turns around.*) Uh . . . listen . . . if you need a phone, I got one most of the time.

ARLENE: I do have to make this call.

RUBY: Ain't got a book though . . . well, I got one but it's holdin up my bed. (*Laughs.*)

ARLENE: I got the number.

RUBY: Well, then . . . (*Awkward.*)

ARLENE: Would you . . . wanna come in?

RUBY: You sure I'm not interruptin anything?

ARLENE: I'm sposed to call my parole officer.

RUBY: Good girl. Most of them can't talk but you call em anyway. (ARLENE *does not laugh.*) Candy go back to that creep?

ARLENE: I guess.

RUBY: I's afraid of that. (*Looking around.*) Maybe an envelope with my name on it? Really cleaned out the place, didn't she?

ARLENE: Yeah. Took everything. (*They laugh a little.*)

RUBY: Didn't have much. Didn't do nuthin here cept . . . sleep.

ARLENE: Least the rent's paid til the end of the month. I'll be workin by then.

RUBY: You ain't seen Candy in a while.

ARLENE: No. Think she was in the 7th grade when . . .

RUBY: She's growed up now, you know.

ARLENE: Yeah. I was thinkin she might come by.

RUBY: Honey, she won't be comin by. He keeps all his . . . (*starting over*) his place is pretty far from here. But . . . (*Stops, trying to decide what to say.*)

ARLENE: But what?

RUBY: But she had a lot of friends, you know. *They* might be comin by.

ARLENE: Men, you mean.

RUBY: Yeah. (*Quietly, waiting for* ARLENE*'s reaction.*)

ARLENE (*realizing the truth*): Mother said he was her boyfriend.

RUBY: I shouldn't have said nuthin. I jus didn't want you to be surprised if some john showed up, his tongue hangin out an all. (*Sits down on the bed.*)

ARLENE: It's O.K. I shoulda known anyway. (*Now suddenly angry.*) No, it ain't O.K. Guys got their dirty fingernails all over her. Some pimp's out buyin green pants while she . . . Goddamn her.

RUBY: Hey now, that ain't your problem. (*Moves toward her.* ARLENE *backs away.*)

      ARLIE (*pointing*): You stick your hand in here again Doris an I'll bite it off.

RUBY: She'll figure it out soon enough.

      ARLIE: (*pointing to another person*): An you, you ain't my Mama, so you can cut the Mama crap.

ARLENE: I wasn't gonna cuss no more.

RUBY: Nuthin in the parole rules says you can't git pissed. My first day outta Gilbertsville I done the damn craziest . . . (ARLENE *looks around, surprised to hear* RUBY *has done time.*) Oh yeah, a long time ago, but . . . hell, I heaved a whole gallon of milk right out the window my first day.

ARLENE: (*somewhat cheered*): It hit anybody?

RUBY: It bounced! Make me feel a helluva lot better. I said, "Ruby, if a gallon of milk can bounce back, so kin you."

ARLENE: That's really what you thought?

RUBY: Well, not exactly. I had to keep sayin it for bout a year fore I finally believed it. I's moppin this lady's floor once an she come in an heard me sayin "gallon-a'-milk, gallon-a'-milk," fired me. She did. Thought I was too crazy to mop her floors. (*Laughs, but is still bitter.* ARLENE *wasn't listening.* RUBY *wants to change the subject now.*) Hey! You have a good trip? Candy said you was in Arkansas.

ARLENE: Alabama. It was O.K. This guard, well he used to be a guard, he just quit. He ain't never seen Kentucky, so he drove me. (*Watching for* RUBY'S *response.*)

RUBY: Pine Ridge?

ARLENE: Yeah.

RUBY: It's co-ed now, ain't it?

ARLENE: Yeah. That's dumb, you know. They put you with men so's they can git you if you're seen with em.

RUBY: Sposed to be more natural, I guess.

ARLENE: I guess.

RUBY: Well, I say it sucks. Still a prison. No matter how many pictures they stick up on the walls or how many dirty movies they show, you still gotta be counted 5 times a day. (*Now beginning to worry about* ARLENE'S *silence.*) You don't seem like Candy said.

ARLENE: She tell you I was a killer?

RUBY: More like the meanest bitch that ever walked. I seen lots worse than you.

ARLENE: I been lots worse.

RUBY: Got to you, didn't it? (ARLENE *doesn't respond, but* RUBY *knows she's right.*) Well, you jus gotta git over it. Bein out, you gotta. . .

ARLENE: Don't you start in on me.

RUBY (*realizing her tone*): Right, sorry.

ARLENE: It's O.K.

RUBY: Ex-cons is the worst. I'm sorry.

ARLENE: It's O.K.

RUBY: Done that about a year ago. New waitress we had. Gave my little goin straight speech, "No booze, no men, no buyin on credit," shit like that, she quit that very night. Stole my fuckin raincoat on her way out. Some speech, huh? (*Laughs, no longer resenting this theft.*)

ARLENE: You a waitress?

RUBY: I am the Queen of Grease. Make the finest french fries you ever did see.

ARLENE: You make a lot of money?

RUBY: I sure know how to. But I ain't about to go back inside for doin it. Cookin out's better'n eatin in, I say.

ARLENE: You think up all these things you say?

RUBY: Know what I hate? Makin salads—cuttin up all that stuff'n floppin it in a bowl. Some day . . . some day . . . I'm gonna hear "tossed salad" an

I'm gonna do jus that. Toss out a tomato, toss out a head a' lettuce, toss out a big ol carrot. (*Miming the throwing act and enjoying herself immensely.*)

ARLENE (*laughing*): Be funny seein all that stuff flyin outta the kitchen.

RUBY: Hey Arlene! (*Gives her a friendly pat.*) You had your lunch yet?

ARLENE (*pulling away immediately*): I ain't hungry.

RUBY (*carefully*): I got raisin toast.

ARLENE: No. (*Goes over to the sink, twists knobs as if to stop a leak.*)

ARLIE: Whaddaya mean, what did she do to me? You got eyes or is they broke? You only seein what you feel like seein. I git ready to protect myself from a bunch of weirdos an then you look.

ARLENE: Sink's stopped up. (*Begins to work on it.*)

ARLIE: You ain't seein when they's leavin packs of cigarettes on my bed an then thinking I owe em or somethin.

RUBY: Stopped up, huh? (*Squashing a bug on the floor.*)

ARLIE: You ain't lookin when them kitchen workers lets up their mommies in line nights they know they only baked half enough brownies.

RUBY: Let me try.

ARLIE: You ain't seen all the letters comin in an goin out with visitors. I'll tell you somethin. One of them workmen buries dope for Betty Rickey in little plastic bottles under them sticker bushes at the water tower. You see that? No, you only seein me. Well, you don't see shit.

RUBY (*a quiet attempt*): Gotta git you some Drano if you're gonna stay here.

ARLIE: I'll tell you what she done. Doris brung me some rollers from the beauty school class. Three fuckin pink rollers. Them plastic ones with the little holes. I didn't ask her. She jus done it.

RUBY: Let me give her a try.

ARLENE: I can fix my own sink.

ARLIE: I's stupid. I's thinkin maybe she were different from all them others. Then that night everybody disappears from the john and she's wantin to brush my hair. Sure, brush my hair. How'd I know she was gonna crack her head open on the sink? I jus barely even touched her.

RUBY (*walking to the bed now, digging through her purse*): Want a Chiclet?

ARLIE: You ain't asked what she was gonna do to me. Huh? When you gonna ask that? You don't give a shit about that cause Doris such a good girl.

ARLENE: Don't work. (*Giving up.*)

RUBY: We got a dishwasher quittin this week if you're interested.

ARLENE: I need somethin that pays good.

RUBY: You type?

ARLENE: No.

RUBY: Do any clerk work?

ARLENE: No.

RUBY: Any key punch?

ARLENE: No.

RUBY: Well, then I hate to tell you, but all us old-timers already got all the good cookin and cleanin jobs. (*Smashes another bug, goes to the cabinet to look for the bug spray.*) She even took the can of Raid! Just as well, empty anyway. (ARLENE *doesn't respond.*) She hit the bugs with it. (*Still no response.*) Now, there's that phone call you was talkin about.

ARLENE: Yeah.

RUBY (*walking toward the door*): An I'll git you that number for the dish-washin job, just in case. (ARLENE *backs off.*) How bout cards? You play any cards? Course you do. I get sick of beatin myself all the time at solitaire. Damn borin bein so good at it.

ARLENE (*goes for her purse*): Maybe I'll jus walk to the corner an make my call from there.

RUBY: It's always broke.

ARLENE: What?

RUBY: The phone . . . at the corner. Only it ain't at the corner. It's inside the A & P.

ARLENE: Maybe it'll be fixed.

RUBY: Look, I ain't gonna force you to play cards with me. It's time for my programs anyway.

ARLENE: I gotta git some pickle loaf an . . . things.

RUBY: Suit yourself. I'll be there if you change your mind.

ARLENE: I have some things I gotta do here first.

RUBY (*trying to leave on a friendly basis*): Look, I'll charge you a dime if it'll make you feel better.

ARLENE (*takes her seriously*): O.K.

RUBY (*laughs, then realizes* ARLENE *is serious*): Mine's the one with the little picture of Johnny Cash on the door. (*Walks to the door and leaves.* BENNIE*'s singing begins almost immediately, as* ARLENE *walks toward the closet. She is delaying going to the store, but is determined to go. She checks little things in the room, remembers to get a scarf, change shoes, checks her wallet, finally, as she is walking out, she stops and looks at the picture of Jesus, then moves closer, having noticed a dirty spot. She goes back into the bathroom for a tissue, wets it in her mouth, then dabs at the offending spot. She puts the tissue in her purse then leaves the room when noted.*)

> BENNIE (*to the tune of "I'll Toe The Line," walks across the cat-walk carrying a tray with cups and a pitcher of water*): I keep my pants up with a piece of twine. I keep my eyes wide open all the time, Da da da da-da da da da da da. (*Doesn't know this line.*) If you'll be mine, please pull the twine.
>
> ARLIE: You can't sing for shit.
>
> BENNIE (*starts down the stairs toward* ARLIE*'s cell*): You know what elephants got between their toes?
>
> ARLIE: I don't care.
>
> BENNIE: Slow natives. (*Laughs.*)

ARLIE: That ain't funny.

GUARD-EVANS (*as* BENNIE *opens* ARLIE*'s door*): Hey, Davis.

BENNIE: Conversation is rehabilitatin, Evans. Want some water?

ARLIE: O.K.

BENNIE: How bout some Kool-Aid to go in it? (*Gives her a glass of water.*)

ARLIE: When does the chaplain come?

BENNIE: Want some gum?

ARLIE: Is it today?

BENNIE: Kool-Aid's gone up, you know. 15¢ and tax. You get out, you'll learn all about that.

ARLIE: Does the chaplain come today?

BENNIE (*going back up the catwalk*): Income tax, sales tax, property tax, gas and electric, water, rent . . .

ARLIE: Hey!

BENNIE: Yeah, he's comin, so don't mess up.

ARLIE: I ain't.

BENNIE: What's he tell you anyway, get you so starry-eyed?

ARLIE: He jus talks to me.

BENNIE: I talk to you.

ARLIE: Where's Frankie Hill?

BENNIE: Gone.

ARLIE: Out?

BENNIE: Pretty soon.

ARLIE: When.

BENNIE: Miss her don't you? Ain't got nobody to bullshit with. Stories you gals tell . . . whoo-ee!

ARLIE: Get to cut that grass now, Frankie, honey.

BENNIE: Huh?

ARLIE: Stupidest thing she said. (*Gently.*) Said first thing she was gonna do when she got out . . .

(ARLENE *leaves the apartment.*)

BENNIE: Get laid.

ARLIE: Shut up. First thing was gonna be going to the garage. Said it always smelled like car grease an turpur . . . somethin.

BENNIE: Turpentine.

ARLIE: Yeah, an gasoline, wet. An she'll bend down an squirt oil in the lawnmower, red can with a long pointy spout. Then cut the grass in the back yard, up an back, up an back. They got this grass catcher on it. Says she likes scoopin up that cut grass an spreadin it out under the trees. Says it makes her real hungry for some lunch. (*A quiet curiosity about all this.*)

BENNIE: I got a power mower, myself.

ARLIE: They done somethin to her. Took out her nerves or somethin. She . . .

BENNIE: She jus got better, that's all.

ARLIE: Hah, know what else? They give her a fork to eat with last week. A fork. A fuckin fork. Now how long's it been since I had a fork to eat with?

BENNIE (*getting ready to leave the cell*): Wish I could help you with that, honey.

ARLIE (*loud*): Don't call me honey.

BENNIE (*locks the door behind him*): That's my girl.

ARLIE: I ain't your girl.

BENNIE (*on his way back up the stairs*): Screechin wildcat.

ARLIE: What time is it? (*Very quiet.*)

(ARLENE *walks back into the apartment. She is out of breath and has some trouble getting the door open. She is carrying a big sack of groceries. As she sets the bag on the counter, it breaks open, spilling cans and packages all over the floor. She just stands and looks at the mess. She takes off her scarf and sets down her purse, still looking at the spilled groceries. Finally, she bends down and picks up the package of pickle loaf. She starts to put it on the counter, then turns suddenly and throws it at the door. She stares at it as it falls.*)

ARLENE: Bounce? (*In disgust.*) Shit. (ARLENE *sinks to the floor. She tears open the package of pickle loaf and eats a piece of it, tearing off the bites in her mouth. She is still angry, but is completely unable to do anything about her anger.*)

ARLIE: Who's out there? Is anybody out there? (*Reading.*) Depart from evil and do good. (*Yelling.*) Now, you pay attention out there cause this is right out of the Lord's mouth. (*Reading.*) And dwell, that means live, dwell for-ever-more. (*Speaking.*) That's like for longer than I've been in here or longer than . . . this Bible the chaplain give me's got my name right in the front of it. Hey! Somebody's sposed to be out there watchin me. Wanna hear some more? (*Reading.*) For the Lord for . . . (*The word is "forsaketh."*) I can't read in here, you turn on my light, you hear me? Or let me out and I'll go read it in the TV room. Please let me out. I won't scream or nuthin. I'll just go right to sleep, O.K.? Somebody! I'll go right to sleep. O.K.? You won't even know I'm there. Hey! Goddammit, somebody let me out of here, I can't stand it in here anymore. Somebody! (*Her spirit finally broken.*)

ARLENE (*she draws her knees up, wraps her arms around them and rests her head on her arms*): Jus gotta git a job an make some money an everything will be all right. You hear me, Arlene? You git yourself up an go find a job. (*Continues to sit.*) An you kin start by cleanin up this mess you made cause food don't belong on the floor. (*Still sitting.* CARL *appears in the doorway of the apartment. When he sees* ARLENE *on the floor, he goes into a fit of vicious, sadistic laughter.*)

CARL: What's happenin, Mama? You havin lunch with the bugs?

ARLENE (*quietly*): Fuck off.

CARL (*threatening*): What'd you say?

ARLENE (*reconsidering*): Go away.

CARL: You watch your mouth or I'll close it up for you.

ARLENE (*stands up now. CARL goes to the window and looks out as if checking for someone*): They after you, ain't they? (CARL *sniffs, scratches at his arm.*)

CARL (*finding a plastic bag near the bed, stuffed with brightly colored knitted things. He pulls out baby sweaters, booties and caps*): What the fuck is this?

ARLENE: You leave them be.

CARL: You got a baby hid here somewhere? I foun its little shoes. (*Laughs, dangling them in front of him.*)

ARLENE: Them's mine. (*Chasing him.*)

CARL: Aw sugar, I ain't botherin nuthin. Just lookin. (*Pulls more out of the sack, dropping one or two on the floor, kicking them away with his feet.*)

ARLENE (*picking up what he's dropped*): I ain't tellin you again. Give me them.

CARL (*turns around quickly, walking away with a few of the sweaters*): How much these go for?

ARLENE: I don't know yet.

CARL: I'll jus take care of em for you—a few coins for the trip. You *are* gonna have to pay your share, you know.

ARLENE: You give me them. I ain't goin with you. (*She walks toward him.*)

CARL: You ain't? (*Mocking,* ARLENE *walks up close to him now, taking the bag in her hands. He knocks her away and onto the bed.*) Straighten up, girlie. (*Now kneels over her.*) You done forgot how to behave yourself. (*Moves as if to threaten her, but kisses her on the forehead, then moves out into the room.*)

ARLENE (*sitting up*): I worked hard on them things. They's nice, too, for babies and little kids.

CARL: I bet you fooled them officers good, doin this shit. (*Throws the bag in the sink.*)

ARLENE: I weren't . . .

CARL (*interrupting*): I kin see that scene. They sayin . . . (*puts on a high Southern voice*) "I'd jus love one a' them nice yella sweaters."

ARLENE: They liked them.

CARL: Those turkeys, sure they did. Where else you gonna git your free sweaters an free washin an free step-right-up-git-your-convict-special-shoe-shine. No, don't give me no money, officer. I's jus doing this cause I likes you. (*Uncle Tom talk.*)

ARLENE: They give em for Christmas presents.

CARL (*checks the window again, then peers into the grocery sack*): What you got sweet, Mama? (*Pulls out a box of cookies and begins to eat them.*)

> ARLIE: I'm sweepin, Doris, cause it's like a pigpen in here. So you might like it, but I don't, so if you get some mops, I'll take one of them, too.

ARLENE: You caught another habit, didn't you?

CARL: You turned into a narc or what?

ARLENE: You scratchin an sniffin like crazy.

CARL: I see a man eatin cookies an that's what you see too.

ARLENE: An you was laughin at me sittin on the floor! You got cops lookin for you an you ain't scored yet this morning. You better git yourself back to prison where you can git all you need.

CARL: Since when Carl couldn't find it if he really wanted it?

ARLENE: An I bought them cookies for me.

CARL: An I wouldn't come no closer if I's you.

ARLENE (*stops, then walks to the door*): Then take the cookies an git out.

CARL (*imitating* BENNIE): Oh, please, Miss Arlene, come go with Carl to the big city. We'll jus have us the best time.

ARLENE: I'm gonna stay here an git a job an save up money so's I kin git Joey. (*Opening the door.*) Now, I ain't sposed to see no ex-cons.

CARL (*big laugh*): You don't know nobody else. Huh, Arlie? Who you know ain't a "con-vict"?

ARLENE: I'll meet em.

CARL: And what if they don't wanna meet you? You ain't exactly a nice girl, you know. An you gotta be jivin about that job shit. (*Throws the sack of cookies on the floor.*)

ARLENE: I kin work. (*Retrieving the cookies.*)

CARL: Doin what?

ARLENE: I don't know. Cookin, cleanin, somethin that pays good.

CARL: You got your choice, honey. You can do cookin an cleanin OR you can do somethin that pays good. You ain't gonna git rich workin on your knees. You come with me an you'll have money. You stay here, you won't have shit.

ARLENE: Ruby works an she does O.K.

CARL: You got any Kool-Aid? (*Looking in the cabinets, moving* ARLENE *out of his way.*) Ruby who?

ARLENE: Upstairs. She cooks. Works nights an has all day to do just what she wants.

CARL: And what, exactly, do she do? See flicks take rides in cabs to pick up see-through shoes?

ARLENE: She watches TV, plays cards, you know.

CARL: Yeah, I know. Sounds just like the dayroom in the fuckin joint.

ARLENE: She likes it.

CARL (*exasperated*): All right. Say you stay here an *finally* find yourself some job. (*Grabs the picture of Jesus off the wall.*) This your boyfriend?

ARLENE: The chaplain give it to me.

CARL: Say it's dishwashin, O.K.? (ARLENE *doesn't answer.*) O.K.?

ARLENE: O.K. (*Takes the picture, hangs it back up.*)

CARL: An you git maybe 75 a week. 75 for standin over a sink full of greasy gray water, fishin out blobs of bread an lettuce. People puttin pieces of chewed up meat in their napkins and you gotta pick it out. 8 hours a day, 6 days a week, to make 75 lousy pictures of Big Daddy George. Now, how long it'll take you to make 75 workin for me?

ARLENE: A night. (*Sits on the bed,* CARL *pacing in front of her.*)

CARL: Less than a night. Two hours maybe. Now, it's the same fuckin 75 bills. You can either work all week for it or make it in 2 hours. You work two hours a night for me an how much you got in a week? (ARLENE *looks puzzled by the multiplication required.* CARL *sits down beside her, even more disgusted*.) Two 75's is 150. Three 150's is 450. You stay here you git 75 a week. You come with me an you git 450 a week. Now, 450, Arlie, is *more* than 75. You stay here you gotta work eight hours a day and your hands git wrinkled and your feet swell up. (*Suddenly distracted*.) There was this guy at Bricktown had webby toes like a duck. (*Back now*.) You come home with me you work two hours a night an you kin sleep all mornin an spend the day buyin eyelashes an tryin out perfume. Come home, have some guy openin the door for you sayin, "Good Evenin, Miss Holsclaw, nice night now ain't it? (*Puts his arm around her.*)

ARLENE: It's Joey I'm thinkin about.

CARL: If you was a kid, would you want your Mom to git so dragged out washin dishes she don't have no time for you an no money to spend on you? You come with me, you kin send him big orange bears an Sting-Ray bikes with his name wrote on the fenders. He'll like that. Holsclaw. (*Amused*.) Kinda sounds like coleslaw, don't it? Joey be tellin all his friends bout his Mom livin up in New York City an bein so rich an sendin him stuff all the time.

ARLENE: I want to be with him.

CARL (*now stretches out on the bed, his head in her lap*): So, fly him up to see you. Take him on that boat they got goes roun the island. Take him up to the Empire State Building, let him play King Kong. (*Rubs her hair, unstudied tenderness*.) He be talkin bout that trip his whole life.

ARLENE (*smoothing his hair*): I don't want to go back to prison, Carl.

CARL (*jumps up, moves toward the refrigerator*): There any chocolate milk? (*Distracted again*.) You know they got this motel down in Mexico named after me? Carlsbad Cabins. (*Proudly*.) Who said anything about goin back to prison? (*Slams the refrigerator door, really hostile*.) What do you think I'm gonna be doin? Keepin you out, that's what!

ARLENE (*stands up*): Like last time? Like you gettin drunk? Like you lookin for kid junkies to beat up?

CARL: God, ain't it hot in this dump. You gonna come or not? You wanna wash dishes, I could give a shit. (*Now yelling*.) But you comin with me, you say it right now, lady! (*Grabs her by the arm*.) Huh?

RUBY (*knocks on the door*): Arlene?

CARL: She ain't here! (*Yelling*.)

RUBY (*alarmed*): Arlene! You all right?

ARLENE: That's Ruby I was tellin you about.

CARL (*catches her arm again, very rough*): We ain't through!

RUBY (*opening the door*): Hey! (*Seeing the rough treatment*.) Goin to the store. (*Very firm*.) Thought maybe you forgot somethin.

CARL (*turns* ARLENE *loose*): You this cook I been hearin about?

RUBY: I cook. So what?

CARL: Buys you nice shoes, don't it, cookin? Why don't you hock your watch an have somethin done to your hair? If you got a watch.

RUBY: Why don't you drop by the coffee shop. I'll spit in your eggs.

CARL: They let you bring home the half-eat chili dogs?

RUBY: You . . . you got half-eat chili dogs for brains. (*To* ARLENE.) I'll stop by later. (*Contemptuous look for* CARL.)

ARLENE: No. Stay. (CARL *gets the message.*)

CARL (*goes over to the sink to get a drink of water out of the faucet, then looks down at his watch*): Piece a' shit. (*Thumps it with his finger.*) Shoulda took the dude's hat, jack. Guy preachin about the end of the world ain't gonna own a watch that works.

ARLENE (*walks over to the sink, bends over* CARL): You don't need me. I'm gittin too old for it, anyway.

CARL: I don't discuss my business with strangers in the room. (*Heads for the door.*)

ARLENE: When you leavin?

CARL: Six. You wanna come, meet me at this bar. (*Gives her a brightly colored matchbook.*) I'm havin my wheels delivered. (*With faintly uncertain pride.*)

ARLENE: You stealin a car?

CARL: Take a cab. (*Gives her a dollar.*) You don't come . . . well, I already laid it out for you. I ain't never lied to you, have I girl?

ARLENE: No.

CARL: Then you be there. That's all the words I got. (*Makes an unconscious move toward her.*) I don't beg nobody. (*Backs off.*) Be there. (*Turns abruptly and leaves.* ARLENE *watches him go, folding up the money in the matchbook. The door remains open.*)

ARLIE (*reading, or trying to, from a small testament*): For the Lord forsaketh not his Saints, but the seed of the wicked shall be cut off.

RUBY (*walks over to the counter, starts to pick up some of the groceries lying on the floor, then stops*): I 'magine you'll want to be puttin these up yourself. (ARLENE *continues to stare out the door.*) He do this?

ARLENE: No.

RUBY: Can't trust these sacks. I seen bag boys punchin holes in em at the store.

ARLENE: Can't trust anybody. (*Finally turning around.*)

RUBY: Well, you don't want to trust him, that's for sure.

ARLENE: We spent a lot of time together, me an Carl.

RUBY: He live here?

ARLENE: No, he jus broke outta Bricktown near where I was. I got word there sayin he'd meet me. I didn't believe it then, but he don't lie, Carl don't.

RUBY: You thinkin of goin with him?

ARLENE: They'll catch him. I told him but he don't listen.

RUBY: Funny ain't it, the number a' men come without ears.

ARLENE: How much that dishwashin job pay?

RUBY: I don't know. Maybe 75.

ARLENE: That's what he said.

RUBY: He tell you you was gonna wear out your hands and knees grubbin for nuthin, git old an be broke an never have a nice dress to wear? (*Sitting down.*)

ARLENE: Yeah.

RUBY: He tell you nobody's gonna wanna be with you cause you done time?

ARLENE: Yeah.

RUBY: He tell you your kid gonna be ashamed of you an nobody's gonna believe you if you tell em you changed?

ARLENE: Yeah.

RUBY: Then he was right. (*Pauses.*) But when you make your two nickels, you can keep both of em.

ARLENE (*shattered by these words*): Well, I can't do that.

RUBY: Can't do what?

ARLENE: Live like that. Be like bein dead.

RUBY: You kin always call in sick . . . stay home, send out for pizza an watch your Johnny Carson on TV . . . or git a bus way out Preston Street an go bowlin . . .

ARLENE (*anger building*): What am I gonna do? I can't git no work that will pay good cause I can't do nuthin. It'll be years fore I have a nice rug for this place. I'll never even have some ol Ford to drive around, I'll never take Joey to no fair. I won't be invited home for pot roast and I'll have to wear this fuckin dress for the rest of my life. What kind of life is that?

RUBY: It's outside.

ARLENE: Outside? Honey I'll either be *inside* this apartment or *inside* some kitchen sweatin over the sink. Outside's where you get to do what you want, not where you gotta do some shit job jus so's you can eat worse than you did in prison. That ain't why I quit bein so hateful, so I could come back and rot in some slum.

RUBY (*word "slum" hits hard*): Well, you can wash dishes to pay the rent on your "slum," or you can spread your legs for any shit that's got the ten dollars. (*With obvious contempt.*)

ARLENE (*not hostile*): An I don't need you agitatin me.

RUBY: An I don't live in no slum.

ARLENE (*sensing* RUBY's *hurt*): Well, I'm sorry . . . it's just . . . I thought . . . (*Increasingly upset.*)

RUBY (*finishing her sentence to her*): . . . it was gonna be different. Well, it ain't. And the sooner you believe it, the better off you'll be.

(*A guard enters* ARLIE's *cell.*)

ARLIE: Where's the chaplain? I got somethin to tell him.

ARLENE: They said I's . . .

GUARD-CALDWELL: He ain't comin.

ARLENE: . . . he tol me if . . . I thought once Arlie . . .

ARLIE: It's Tuesday. He comes to see me on Tuesday.

GUARD-CALDWELL: Chaplain's been transferred, dollie. Gone. Bye-bye. You know.

ARLENE: He said the meek, meek, them that's quiet and good . . . the meek . . . as soon as Arlie . . .

RUBY: What, Arlene? Who said what?

ARLIE: He's not comin back?

ARLENE: At Pine Ridge there was . . .

ARLIE: He woulda told me if he couldn't come back.

ARLENE: I was . . .

GUARD-CALDWELL: He left this for you.

ARLENE: I was . . .

GUARD-CALDWELL: Picture of Jesus, looks like.

ARLENE: This chaplain . . .

RUBY: Arlene . . . (*Trying to call her back from this hysteria.*)

ARLIE (*hysterical*): I need to talk to him.

ARLENE: This chaplain . . .

ARLIE: You tell him to come back and see me.

ARLENE: I was in lockup . . .

ARLIE (*a final, anguished plea*): I want the chaplain!

ARLENE: I don't know . . . years . . .

RUBY: And . . .

ARLENE: This chaplain said I had . . . said Arlie was my hateful self and she was hurtin me and God would find some way to take her away . . . and it was God's will so I could be the meek . . . the meek, them that's quiet and good an git whatever they want . . . I forgit that word . . . they git the Earth.

RUBY: Inherit.

ARLENE: Yeah. And that's why I done it.

RUBY: Done what?

ARLENE: What I done. Cause the chaplain he said . . . I'd sit up nights waitin for him to come talk to me.

RUBY: Arlene, what did you do? What are you talkin about?

ARLENE: They tol me . . . after I's out an it was all over . . . they said after the chaplain got transferred . . . I didn't know why he didn't come no more til after . . . they said it was three whole nights at first, me screamin to God to come git Arlie an kill her. They give me this medicine an thought I's better . . . then that night it happened, the officer was in the dorm doin count . . . an they didn't hear nuthin but they come back out where I was an I'm standin there tellin em to come see, real quiet I'm tellin em, but there's all this blood all over my shirt an I got this fork I'm holdin real tight in my hand . . . (*clenches one hand now, the other hand fumbling with the buttons as if she's going to show*) RUBY this fork, they said Doris stole it from the kitchen an give it to me so I'd kill myself and shut up botherin her . . . an there's all these holes all over me where I been stabbin myself an I'm sayin Arlie is dead for what she done to me, Arlie is dead an it's God's will . . . I didn't scream it, I was jus sayin it over and over . . . Arlie is dead, Arlie is dead . . . they couldn't git that fork outta my hand til . . . I woke up in the infirmary an they said I almost died. They said they's glad I didn't. (*Smiling.*) They said did I feel better now an they was real nice, bringing me chocolate puddin . . .

RUBY: I'm sorry, Arlene. (*Reaches out for her, but* ARLENE *pulls away sharply.*)

ARLENE: I'd be eatin or jus lookin at the ceiling an git a tear in my eye, but it'd jus dry up, you know, it didn't run out or nuthin. An then pretty soon, I's well, an officers was sayin they's seein such a change in me an givin me yarn to knit sweaters an how'd I like to have a new skirt to wear an sometimes lettin me chew gum. They said things ain't never been as clean as when I's doin the housekeepin at the dorm. (*So proud.*) An then I got in the honor cottage an nobody was foolin with me no more or nuthin. An I didn't git mad like before or nuthin. I jus done my work an knit . . . an I don't think about it what happened, cept . . . (*now losing control*) people here keep callin me Arlie an . . . (*has trouble saying "Arlie"*) I didn't mean to do it, what I done . . .

RUBY: Oh, honey . . . (*Trying to help.*)

ARLENE: I did . . . (*This is very difficult.*) I mean, Arlie was a pretty mean kid, but I did . . . (*Very quickly.*) I didn't know what I . . . (*Breaks down completely, screaming, crying, falling, over into* RUBY*'s lap.*) Arlie! (*Grieving for this lost self.*)

RUBY (*rubs her back, her hair, waiting for the calm she knows will come. Finally, but very quietly*): You can still . . . (*now obviously referring to some personal loss of her own*) . . . you can still love people that's gone. (RUBY *continues to hold her tenderly, rocking as with a baby. A terrible crash is heard on the steps outside the apartment.*)

BENNIE'S VOICE: Well, chicken pluckin, hog kickin shit!

RUBY: Don't you move now, it's just somebody out in the hall.

ARLENE: That's . . .

RUBY: It's O.K., Arlene. Everything's gonna be just fine. Nice and quiet now.

ARLENE: That's Bennie that guard I told you about.

RUBY: I'll get it. You stay still now. (*She walks to the door, and looks out into the hall, hands on hips.*) Why you dumpin them flowers on the stairs like that? Won't git no sun at all! (*Turns back to* ARLENE.) Arlene, there's a man plantin a garden out in the hall. You think we should call the police or get him a waterin' can?

BENNIE (*appearing in the doorway, carrying a box of dead looking plants*): I didn't try to fall, you know.

RUBY: Well, when you git ready to *try*, I wanna watch! (*Blocking the door.*)

ARLENE: I thought you's gone.

RUBY (*to* BENNIE): You got a visitin pass?

BENNIE (*coming into the room*): Arlie . . . (*Quickly.*) Arlene. I brung you some plants. You know, plants for your window. Like we talked about, so's you don't see them bars.

RUBY (*picking up one of the plants*): They sure is scraggly lookin things. Next time, git plastic.

BENNIE: I'm sorry I dropped em, Arlene. We kin get em back together an they'll do real good. (*Setting them down on the trunk.*) These ones don't take the sun. I asked just to make sure. Arlene?

RUBY: You up for seein this petunia killer?

ARLENE: It's O.K. Bennie, this is Ruby, upstairs.

BENNIE (*bringing one flower over to show* ARLENE, *stuffing it back into its pot*): See? It ain't dead.

RUBY: Poor little plant. It comes from a broken home.

BENNIE (*walks over to the window, getting the box and holding it up to the window*): That's gonna look real pretty. Cheerful-like.

RUBY: Arlene ain't gettin the picture yet. (*Walking to the window and holding her plant up, too, posing.*) Now. (ARLENE, *looks, but is not amused.*)

BENNIE (*putting the plants back down*): I jus thought, after what I done last night . . . I jus wanted to do somethin nice.

ARLENE (*calmer now*): They is nice. Thanks.

RUBY: Arlene says you're a guard.

BENNIE: I was. I quit. Retired.

ARLENE: Bennie's goin back to Alabama.

BENNIE: Well, I ain't leavin right away. There's this guy at the motel says the bass is hittin pretty good right now. Thought I might fish some first.

ARLENE: Then he's goin back.

BENNIE: (*to* RUBY *as he washes his hands*): I'm real fond of this little girl. I ain't goin til I'm sure she's gonna do O.K. Thought I might help some.

RUBY: Arlene's had about all the help she can stand.

BENNIE: I got a car, Arlene. An money. An . . . (*reaching into his pocket*) I brung you some gum.

ARLENE: That's real nice, too. An I'preciate what you done, bringin me here an all, but . . .

BENNIE: Well, look. Least you can take my number at the motel an give me a ring if you need somethin. (*Gives her a piece of paper.*) Here, I wrote it down for you. (ARLENE *takes the paper.*) Oh, an somethin else, these towel things . . . (*reaching into his pocket, pulling out the packaged towelettes*) they was in the chicken last night. I thought I might be needin em, but they give us new towels every day at that motel.

ARLENE: O.K. then. I got your number.

BENNIE (*backing up toward the door*): Right. Right. Any ol thing, now. Jus any ol thing. You even run outta gum an you call.

RUBY: Careful goin down.

ARLENE: Bye Bennie.

BENNIE: Right. The number now. Don't lose it. You know, in case you need somethin.

ARLENE: No. (BENNIE *leaves,* ARLENE *gets up and picks up the matchbook* CARL *gave her and holds it with* BENNIE*'s piece of paper.*)

RUBY (*watches a moment, sees* ARLENE *trying to make this decision, knowing that what she says now is very important*): We had this waitress put her phone number in matchbooks, give em to guys left her nice tips. Anyway, one night this little ol guy calls her and comes over and says he works at this museum an he don't have any money but he's got this hat belonged to Queen Victoria. An she felt real sorry for him so she screwed him for this little ol lacy hat. Then she takes the hat back the next day to the museum thinkin she'll git a reward or somethin an you know what they done? (*Pause.*) Give her a free membership. Tellin her thanks so much an we're so grateful an wouldn't she like to see this mummy they got downstairs . . . an all the time jus stallin . . . waiting cause they called the police.

ARLENE: You do any time for that?

RUBY (*admitting the story was about her*): County jail.

ARLENE (*quietly, looking at the matchbook*): County jail. (ARLENE *tears up the matchbook and drops it in the sack of trash.*) You got any Old Maids?

RUBY: Huh?

ARLENE: You know.

RUBY: Cards? (*Surprised and pleased.*)

ARLENE (*laughs a little*): It's the only one I know.

RUBY: Old Maid, huh? (*Not her favorite game.*)

ARLENE: I gotta put my food up first.

RUBY: Bout an hour?

ARLENE: I'll come up.

RUBY: Great. (*Stopping by the plants on her way to the door.*) These plants is real ugly. (*Fondly. Exits.* ARLENE *watches her, then turns back to the groceries still on the floor. Slowly, but with great determination, she picks up the items one at a time and puts them away in the cabinet above the counter.*)

(ARLIE *appears on the catwalk, one light on each of them.*)

ARLIE: Hey! You member that time we was playin policeman an June locked me up in Mama's closet an then took off swimmin? An I stood around with them dresses itchin my ears an crashin into that door tryin to git outta there? It was dark in there. So, finally, (*very proud*) I went around an peed in all Mama's shoes. But then she come home an tried to git in the closet only June taken the key so she said, "Who's in there?" an I said, "It's me!" and she said, "What you doin in there?" an I started gigglin an she started pullin on the door an yellin, "Arlie, what you doin in there?" (*Big laugh.*)

ARLIE AND ARLENE (ARLENE *has begun to smile during the story, now they say together, both standing as* MAMA *did, one hand on her hip*): Arlie, what you doin in there?

ARLENE (*still smiling and remembering, stage dark except for one light on her face*): Aw shoot. (*Light dims on her fond smile as* ARLIE *laughs once more.*)

The Receptive Reader

1. What assumptions or expectations about "juvenile delinquents" or "problem kids" do you bring to this play? Does Arlie live up to them? Why, or why not? What do you learn about her character, motivation, or pattern of behavior? Do you think you understand her? What for you are key incidents or revealing details?

2. Recent years have seen much feminist reexamination of the role men play in women's lives. What was Arlie's father like, and what was his role in her life? What was Bennie's role as a prison guard? What is predictable and what is surprising to you about his role in Arlene's present? How would you size up and judge Carl's role in Arlene's past and present? Are the men in this play each different or "all the same"?

3. What is the role of Arlene's mother in the play? What was her marriage like? What is her relation to her children? What has made her what she is? What is happening between Arlene and her mother now—in the scene set in the present?

4. The change from Arlie to Arlene is at the center of this play. What was the role of the prison chaplain in her change? What was the role of her becoming a mother?

5. Arlene encounters Ruby at a crucial stage in Arlene's attempt to chart her future. What do the two have in common? What at first makes their contacts

difficult? What is Ruby's influence on Arlene? Why is her role pivotal in the play?

The Personal Response

1. Do you think Arlene is going to make it? Why, or why not? Do you believe in rehabilitation? Do you believe in second chances? Do you believe in the redemption of sinners?

2. For you, what comment does the play as a whole offer on the prison system? Does the play make you rethink your assumptions about the justice system in general? Why, or why not?

3. One editor asked whether the behavior of Bennie and Carl in the scenes set in the present is "realistic." Do you think their behavior is believable—or does it cater to our sentimental hope that "there is some good in everyone"?

4. *Getting Out* has flashes of humor, as when Ruby says about the plants Bennie has brought and dropped, "Poor little plant. It comes from a broken home." What other examples of humor can you find? What is the role of humor in the play as a whole?

The Creative Dimension

On any given night, spectators for a play on the New York stage are likely to range from hard-boiled to soft-hearted. Working with a group, you may want to collaborate in writing an alternative ending to the play that would act out an attitude or set of expectations different from that of the playwright.

BIOGRAPHIES OF POETS

Julia Alvarez (born 1950) Raised in both the Dominican Republic and New York City, Julia Alvarez's story is one of remarkable triumph. Speaking only Spanish until high school, her talents became apparent when challenged by her high school teacher to write about her experiences of being an outsider in American culture. She has published numerous volumes of poetry and novels.

Maya Angelou (born 1928) is an autobiographer, poet, playwright, composer, screen and stage producer, performer, and singer. She wrote and read the poem "On the Pulse of Morning" at President Bill Clinton's inauguration in 1993. Of her several autobiographies, *I Know Why the Caged Bird Sings* (1969) is her best known. Of Angelou's first collection of poetry, *I Shall Not Be Moved* (1990), Gloria Hull writes: "As I listen, what I hear in her open colloquial poems is racial wit and earthy wisdom, honest black female pain and strength, humor, passion, and rhetorical force."

Matthew Arnold (1822–1888)—English critic, educator, and poet—graduated from Oxford and served as inspector of the British schools for most of his life. As a poet, Arnold was inspired by Greek tragedies, Keats, and Wordsworth. In 1857 he began to teach poetry at Oxford and to publish numerous books on literary criticism. In much of his writing, Arnold took the position of the agnostic unable to accept traditional faith, wishing to replace doctrines that had become doubtful with great literature as a source of inspiration and moral guidance. His prose writings helped define the nineteenth-century ideal of high culture, which he saw as a synthesis of Judeo-Christian ethics and the classical dedication to reason and form.

John Ashbery (born 1927), Pulitzer Prize-winning poet, playwright, translator, and art critic, received degrees from Harvard and Columbia. Ashbery's poetry has been heavily influenced by film and other art forms, particularly modern expressionist art. Jonathan Holden writes that "Ashbery is the first American poet to successfully carry out the possibilities of analogy between poetry and abstract expressionist painting." Critic Helen Vendler observed that Ashbery's style, once considered avant-garde, has since become "so influential that its imitators are legion." One of the most widely honored poets of his generation, Ashbery refuses to impose an artificial order on a world of flux, instead attempting to mirror stream of consciousness by associative rather than logical means.

Margaret Atwood (born 1939) has said, "My life really has been writing since the age of sixteen; all other decisions I made were determined by that fact." Born in Ottawa, Canada, Atwood resides in Toronto but has lived all over Canada as well as in the United States and England. She studied at the University of Toronto and Harvard, and has taught and lectured widely. In addition to two collections of short stories and seven volumes of poetry, Atwood has published six novels, including *The Edible Woman* (1969), *Cat's Eye* (1989), and a chilling portrayal of a nightmarish dystopian future, *The Handmaid's Tale* (1985), which won a *Los Angeles Times* award for best fiction and was made into a movie. Her most recent novel is *The*

Robber Bride (1993). A feminist, Atwood explains that she had confronted issues related to growing up female and sex-role changes long before they were popularized by the women's movement.

W. H. Auden   (1907–1973) was well versed in science, history, politics, philosophy, psychology, art, music, and literature. As a result his poetry "is full of knowledge and wisdom and ideas" (Kenneth Koch). Wystan Hugh Auden believed that "living is always thinking." Born in the ancient city of York, he graduated from Oxford University and became an important voice for the radical criticism of established society by the Marxist left. After serving on the Loyalist side of the Spanish Civil War, he emigrated to America in 1939 and became a U.S. citizen. His first collection of poetry, *Poems,* appeared in 1930. In 1948 he won the Pulitzer Prize for his collection *The Age of Anxiety,* an expression he coined to describe the 1930s. Auden saw poetry "as a game of knowledge, a bringing to consciousness, by naming them, of emotions and their hidden relationships."

Bashō   (1644–1694) was a famous Japanese writer of haiku in the 17th century. His simple, descriptive poems evoke emotions.

Wendell Berry   (born 1934) is a poet, novelist, and essayist who was educated at the University of Kentucky, where he also has taught for many years. Although Berry deals primarily with Kentucky and its people, "one would be hard-pressed to dismiss him as a mere regionalist . . . his work is rooted in the land and in the values of an older America" (Jonathan Yardly). Among his many titles are *The Broken Ground* (1964), *Findings* (1969), *To What Listens* (1975), and *Clearing* (1977). About the archetypal nature of poetry and song, Berry writes: "Song is natural; we have it in common with animals. . . The rhythm of a song or a poem rises, no doubt, in reference to the pulse and breath of the poet. . . [but] it rises also in reference to daily and seasonal—and surely even longer—rhythms in the life of the poet and in the life that surrounds him. . . Song, then, is the testimony of the singer's inescapable relation to the world, to the human community, and also to tradition."

Elizabeth Bishop   (1911–1979), who said, "There's nothing more embarrassing than being a poet," was born in Massachusetts. Only four years old when her father died, she was taken to live with her grandmother after her mother suffered a mental breakdown. After graduating from Vassar, Bishop planned to enter Cornell Medical School, but poet Marianne Moore persuaded her to become a writer. She served as a poetry consultant to the Library of Congress (1949–1950) and taught poetry writing at Harvard. She received numerous awards, including a Pulitzer Prize (1956). Bishop's poetry has been called "both precise and suggestive . . . fantastic yet fanciful" (Louis Untermeyer).

William Blake   (1757–1827), a forerunner of the English Romantic movement, "could transmit his basic consciousness and communicate it to somebody else after he was dead—in other words, build a time machine," said poet Allen Ginsberg. Born in London, Blake was apprenticed at the age of fourteen to an engraver; his engravings illustrated many popular books of his day as well as his own poems. He began to write his richly symbolic, mystical poetry in his youth, and with the financial assistance of his friends published his first collection of poems, *Poetical Sketches,* in 1783. However, efforts to find a publisher for his second manuscript, *Songs of Innocence,* were unsuccessful. The last twenty-five years of his life were marked by extreme poverty; it remained for later audiences to appreciate the complex symbolism of his mystical, enigmatic poetry.

Louise Bogan   (1897–1970), born in Livermore Falls, Maine, was educated at Boston University. She served as consultant in poetry to the Library of Congress, taught at a number of universities in the United States and Austria, and served for over twenty years as a poetry critic for the *New Yorker.* Her books of poetry include

Body of This Death (1923), *Dark Summer, The Blue Estuaries,* and *Collected Poems, 1923–1953* (1954), which won the Bollingen Prize in poetry.

Arna Bontemps   (1902–1973) –American poet, novelist, editor, and biographer— was born in Alexandria, Louisiana, and raised in California. A 1923 graduate of Pacific Union College, Bontemps first published his poetry in *Crisis* magazine in 1924. He turned to the novel, publishing *God Sends Sunday* in 1931, *Black Estuaries* in 1936, and *Drums at Dusk* in 1939. His *Story of the Negro* received the Jane Adams Children's Book Award in 1956. In *Anyplace but Here* he gathered brief biographies of outstanding black Americans. He published a much-read biography of Frederick Douglass in 1959 and an anthology of poetry written by African Americans in 1963.

Kay Boyle   (1903–1992), a native of St. Paul, Minnesota, lived much of her life in France, Austria, Germany, and England. Being in Europe at the beginning of World War II led her to write three books that described the unfolding war: *Primer for Combat, Avalanche,* and *1939.* Her novel *Generation without Farewell* deals with conditions in postwar Germany. An English professor at San Francisco State University, Boyle's recurrent theme was that of youth faced with death or disease.

Anne Bradstreet   (about 1612–1672), author of the first volume of original poetry written in the British colonies of North America, had sailed for America from her native England after marrying at the age of sixteen. Her father, Thomas Dudley, became a governor of the Massachusetts Bay Colony, as did her husband, Simon Bradstreet. The mother of eight children, Bradstreet also wrote an autobiography entitled *Religious Experiences.*

Gwendolyn Brooks   (1917–2000) was the first African American woman to achieve widespread critical acclaim as a poet. Brooks began writing poetry as a child in Chicago and had her first poem published at age ten in a children's magazine. In high school, she saw several of her poems published in *Defender,* a Chicago newspaper. In the early 1940s she won prizes for her poetry and published her first poetry collection in 1945. The first African American woman to be so honored, Brooks won a Pulitzer Prize for poetry in 1950 for her second collection, *Annie Allen.* Other works include *The Bean Eaters* (1960), *In the Mecca* (1968), and *To Disembark* (1981). Not only a major force in the movement to define black identity and to foster black pride, she has also been poet laureate for the state of Illinois and poetry consultant to the Library of Congress. In 1989 she received the National Endowment for the Arts Lifetime Achievement Award, and in 1990 became the only American to receive, from the University of Thessaloniki, Greece, the Society for Literature Award.

Elizabeth Barrett Browning   (1806–1861), who wrote that "grief may be joy misunderstood," had a difficult young life. Born into a well-to-do family in Durham, England, as the oldest of eleven children, Barrett was reading Greek at the age of eight and writing poems that imitated her favorite authors. At fifteen she suffered a spinal injury when she fell from a pony and was a partial invalid when she met the poet Robert Browning in 1845. The two fell in love immediately, but she had to elope to escape from her obsessively jealous father. Because of her health, the couple went to live in Italy. Her most famous collection, *Sonnets from the Portuguese,* love poems written to her husband, was published in 1850.

Robert Browning   (1812–1889) was born in Camberwall, England. He decided to become a poet at age seventeen and after setbacks became one of the best known and most influential poet-sages of Victorian England. He was still receiving financial support from his family when in 1845 he met and fell in love with Elizabeth Barrett, one of the leading poets of the day. *The Ring and the Book,* a series of dramatic monologues based on a seventeenth-century murder, appeared in 1869 and finally brought him popular acclaim. His metrically rough and intellectually challenging poetry secured him a following of dedicated admirers; Browning Societies survive to this day.

Christopher Buckley (born 1948) A professor in the Creative Writing Department at the University of California, Riverside, Buckley has published multiple books of poetry, including *Dust Light* and *Blossoms & Bones,* the last, poems on the life and work of Georgia O'Keeffe. During the 1970s Buckley became fascinated by O'Keeffe's work, explaining, "The vitality she found in everything—from bones in the desert to skyscrapers in Manhattan—suggests . . . a practical cast that cherishes the earth and praises the strength of the human spirit as it endures here." Poet Carol Muske notes that Buckley's poems are not mere documentation or interpretation but "inspired trances: eerie, faceted, gem-clear."

Robert Burns (1759–1796)—born in a small cottage in Alloway, Scotland, to a family of poor tenant farmers—knew poverty and exploitation firsthand. He was steeped in the traditional ballads and songs of his country, and he became for the Romantic poets the embodiment of untutored, spontaneous, original genius throwing off artificial conventions. After years of trying unsuccessfully to earn a living as a farmer, he was offered a job as an overseer in Jamaica. To pay for his passage, he published in 1786 a collection of poems and songs entitled *Poems Chiefly in the Scottish Dialect.* Because of its tremendous success, he was able to give up his Jamaica project. Like the Romantic poets after him, he was fired with generous enthusiasm for the aims of the French Revolution, envisioning a world in which the aristocracy would be swept away and brotherhood and human dignity would prevail.

Rosemary Catacalos (born 1944) is a bilingual Hispanic poet whose work has been reprinted in recent anthologies stressing multicultural themes. She was born in St. Petersburg, Florida, and grew up and attended a two-year college in San Antonio, Texas. She has conducted poetry workshops in schools throughout Texas and has published more than thirty chapbooks, or pamphlets, of students' work. Her collection *Again for the First Time* received the Texas Institute of Letters Poetry Award in 1985.

Lorna Dee Cervantes (born 1954) discovered the world of books in the homes that her mother cleaned. "We were so poor . . . We were brilliant at wishing," she wrote in her poem "To My Brother." Born in San Francisco of Mexican descent, Cervantes published her first poetry collection, *Emplumada,* in 1981. Educated at San José State University, she is the founder of Mango Publications, a small press that publishes books and a literary magazine.

Salvador Jacinto Polo de Medina (1603–1676) "El Icaro" We know only that Polo de Medina was baptized on August 15, 1603. He studied in the College Seminary of San Fulgencio in Murcia, Spain. A man who loved classical myth, he told many of these stories in poetry, such as "Apollo and Daphne." Many of his poems were set to music.

Kawai Chigetsu-Ni (1632–1736) was a Japanese woman writer of the seventeenth century.

Lucille Clifton (born 1936) has said, "I am a Black woman poet, and I sound like one." Born in Depew, New York, and educated at Howard University, Clifton has taught at several colleges, worked as a claims clerk in the New York State Division of Employment, and was a literature assistant in the Office of Education in Washington, D.C. Her first collection of poetry, *Good Times,* was selected as one of the ten best books of 1969 by the *New York Times.* Among her awards are the University of Massachusetts Press Juniper Prize for Poetry, an Emmy Award, and creative writing fellowships from the National Endowment for the Arts. In 1979 she was named Maryland's poet laureate.

Judith Ortiz Cofer (born 1952), who was born in Puerto Rico, illustrates through her work her struggle to create a self out of the cultural ambiguity of a childhood spent traveling between countries. Feminist in perspective, she also explores relationships with parents and grandparents, focusing on the differing expectations for female and male in Hispanic and Anglo-American cultures. To that end, she published a book of autobiographical poems and essays, *Silent Dancing: A Remembrance of a Puerto Rican Childhood* (1990). Chronicling the years from the Depression to the 1960s, her novel *The Line of the Sun* (1990) traces her gradual immigration to the United States.

William Cowper   (1731–1800) was bullied as a child in school. As an adult, Cowper suffered from fits of depression aggravated by his obsession with the doctrine of eternal damnation. He found comfort for a time in his association with evangelical Christians (he coauthored the *Olney Hymns* still familiar to Methodists) but struggled with mental illness to the end of his life.

Stephen Crane   (1871–1900), admired for his harsh realism in the tradition of American naturalism, is best known for his imaginative reenacting of the traumas of the Civil War experience in his novel *The Red Badge of Courage.* Crane was born in Newark, New Jersey, and spent most of his youth in upstate New York. After attending college for two years, he moved to New York City to become a freelance journalist. His fame as a writer grew in the same year with the publication of *The Black Riders,* a collection of free verse. "The Open Boat," one of his two most famous short stories, appeared in 1897. The other, "The Blue Hotel," was published the year before his death of a tubercular infection at the age of twenty-nine.

Juana Inés de la Cruz   (1651–1695) was a childhood prodigy, learning to read at age three and primarily educating herself. Renowned for her intelligence, beauty, wit, and learning, she served as a lady-in-waiting at the New Spanish court and later retired to become a nun, insisting that only monastic life gave her the chance to carry on her intellectual pursuits. In addition to writing poetry she studied literature, history, music, science, and theology. She became known as the Tenth Muse. She wrote a letter considered "a defining work in feminist literature" when authorities of the Catholic Church disapproved of her studies, and she pleaded for equal educational opportunities for women.

E. E. Cummings   (1894–1962) believed that "poetry is being, not doing." One of the most provocative and unconventional of modern poets, Cummings was born in Cambridge, Massachusetts, and educated at Harvard. During World War I, he served as a volunteer ambulance driver and was held briefly as a prisoner of war. After the war he spent several years in Paris, studying art. A talented painter, he often exhibited his artwork. His first volume of poetry, *Tulips and Chimneys* (1923), was both criticized and praised for its unusual use of language and punctuation. "The effect of this experimentation is not to take the meaning away but to add or emphasize a certain kind of meaning. His way of writing seems to call attention to the sense of each word, so that each word counts and is important in the poem" (Kenneth Koch). The centennial edition of his *Complete Poems: 1904–1962* (1994) is part of an ongoing reassessment of Cummings' contribution to literature. Writes George J. Firmage, "Combining Thoreau's controlled belligerence with the brash abandon of an uninhibited Bohemian, Cummings, together with Pound, Eliot, and William Carlos Williams, helped bring about the twentieth-century revolution in literary expression." Richard Kostelanetz considers him "the major American poet of the middle-twentieth century."

Ann Darr   (born 1920) has said, "If I could write the way I want to, my writing would be a cross between that of Woody Allen and Pablo Neruda. I want the poems to be honest and alive, as immediate as I can make them." In addition to writing poetry, Darr has worked as a radio writer and actress for NBC and ABC in New York and as poet-in-residence at several universities. During World War II, she served as an air force pilot. "My dominant metaphor has been flight in all of its meanings," she said.

Alison Hawthorne Deming   (born 1946) came to writing after fifteen years in the field of women's health care. She is now the director of the University of Arizona Poetry Center in Tucson. She has won several prizes with her work, among them the Pablo Neruda Prize, a Wallace Stegner fellowship from Stanford University, and the Walt Whitman Award for *Science and Other Poems* (1993).

Reuel Denney   (born 1913) has said, "When I learned to write, I chalked criticisms of the household on the tile entry of the house. For example, slogans taken from fairy tales such as the Little Tailor's lampoon against the castle holding him prison: 'Too much potatoes and not enuff meat.' Instead of being told that some children somewhere in the world didn't even have potatoes . . . I was praised for my literacy. This was the start of my writing, but I was not published until later, at sixteen or so." Born in New York, Denney was educated at Dartmouth. He lives in Honolulu, Hawaii, where he writes "for three to fifteen hours a week."

Countess of Dia   (born about 1140) was one of the women troubadours of the Provençal courts in southern France, who provided counterpoint to the usually male-oriented tradition of courtly love.

William Dickey   (1928–1994) was called "a national treasure" by critic Brown Miller, who also added that "Dickey writes a rare and enviable sort of poem, truly humorous and truly serious at once." Educated at Harvard and Oxford universities, Dickey taught at Cornell, San Francisco State, and the University of Hawaii. His award-winning work has appeared widely in periodicals such as the *New Yorker, Harper's,* and the *Atlantic.*

Emily Dickinson   (1830–1886) is now considered one of the greatest American poets, but only a few of her poems were published—and those in edited and conventionalized versions—in her lifetime. After attending Amherst Academy and spending a year in a female seminary, she spent her life and died in the same house in Amherst, Massachusetts. In 1862, she wrote to Thomas Wentworth Higginson, editor of the *Atlantic* magazine, enclosing some poems and asking his opinion. Unable to deal with her strange, provocative poetry, he encouraged her to make her poetry more "regular." After her death 1,775 poems were discovered in a dresser drawer in her bedroom. "She did in her poetry what she could never have done out loud," writes Louise Bernikow. "She found a voice both original and strange in which to speak with the kind of honesty that exists in no other poet of her time."

Chitra Divakaruni   (born 1956) was born in India and came to the United States when she was nineteen years old. Having received her Ph.D. from Berkeley, she now teaches at Foothill College in northern California. Her two volumes of poetry are *The Reason for Nasturtiums* (1990) and *Black Candle* (1991). She has recently published a book of short stories entitled *Arranged Marriage* (1996). Very involved in women's issues, Divakaruni is one of the founders of MAITRI, a service that helps South Asian women in distress. Of the importance of writing—and reading— she says, "When you open yourself to writing as a writer or a reader, it changes your life."

John Donne   (1572–1631), English poet, preacher, and religious prose writer, was born in London. He enrolled in Oxford; after converting from Roman Catholicism to the Anglican Church, he was ordained into its priesthood in 1614. In 1621 he became dean of St. Paul's Cathedral in London, a position he held as an influential and compelling preacher until his death. When he was very ill in 1623, he wrote a series of essays called *Meditations.* His early love poems were probably written before 1614; his later religious poems were published in *Poems* in 1633. In recent decades, Donne's poetry and that of other metaphysical poets of the seventeenth century have been the object of much critical discussion. His poems appeal strongly to modern readers who prefer the challenging to the conventional, the complex to the superficial, the ironic to the sentimental.

H. D. (1886–1961), pseudonym of Hilda Doolittle, took on the "prophet's mantel in poetry, anticipating the spirit of the current feminist movement by a good half century" (Tom Clark). Born in Bethlehem, Pennsylvania, H. D. attended Bryn Mawr. In 1911 she went to Europe, where she lived most of her life. The publishing of her work began when in 1913 Ezra Pound sent some of her poems to Harriet Monroe, editor of *Poetry* magazine. H. D. soon became known as one of the leaders of the imagist poets. She published six poetry collections, wrote several novels, and translated Greek literature.

Rita Dove (born 1952), the first black U.S. poet laureate, has been described as a quiet leader who, while she does not avoid race issues, does not make them her central focus: "As a black woman I am concerned with race. . . I cannot run from, I won't run from any kind of truth." Critic Helen Vendler observed of the Pulitzer Prize-winning *Thomas and Beulah* (1987), whose main characters are based on Dove's maternal grandparents, that "though the photograph, and the chronology of the lives of Thomas and Beulah might lead one to suspect that Dove is a poet of simple realism [it] is far from the case. Dove has learned how to make a biographical fact the buried bone of an imagined edifice." Critic A. L. Nielson finds that the poems in *Grace Notes* (1989) "abound in unforgettable details of family character. [Dove] is one of those rare poets who approach common experience with the same sincerity with which the objectivist poets of an earlier generation approached the things of our world." Dove published a novel, *Through the Ivory Gate*, in 1992.

Richard Eberhart (born 1904), critically acclaimed American poet, was educated at Cambridge and has worked as a tutor to the son of the king of Siam, a businessman, a naval officer, a cultural adviser, and a professor. His numerous books of poetry include *Gifts of Being* (1968) and *Selected Poems, 1930–1965* (1976).

T. S. Eliot (1888–1965) was a chief architect of modern poetic theory and one of the twentieth century's most influential poets. Born in St. Louis, Missouri, he studied at Harvard and then settled in London in 1915, becoming a British citizen thirteen years later. His poetry departed dramatically from familiar conventions and techniques, notably in "The Love Song of J. Alfred Prufrock" and the epochal *The Waste Land,* which he dedicated to Ezra Pound. Eliot's later works include *Four Quartets* (1943); his plays *Murder in the Cathedral* (1935), and *The Family Reunion* (1939); and poems for cat lovers, which inspired a triumphantly successful musical. He won the Nobel Prize for literature in 1948.

Louise Erdrich (born 1954) writes about American Indian traditions in her novels *The Beet Queen* and *Love Medicine,* as well as in her shorter works. Part Chippewa Indian, Erdrich is intensely involved in Native American land claims and other issues concerning Native Americans. Born in Little Falls, Minnesota, she spent much of her youth on the North Dakota reservation where her father taught school. She was educated at Dartmouth and Johns Hopkins. She has collaborated with her husband, Michael Dorris, on a nonfiction book, *Broken Chord,* about fetal alcohol syndrome among American Indians, from which his adopted son suffered. They also coauthored the novel *The Crown of Columbus* (1991). Erdrich's newest volume of poetry is *Baptism of Desire* (1991).

Martín Espada (born 1957) was raised in a Brooklyn housing project and became an attorney and a poet, using the "power of the word to fight against what I consider to be wrong." He won the 1991 Peterson Poetry Prize for *Rebellion Is the Circle of a Lover's Hands.* Espada's poetry has often been recited or published with the work of his father—photographer Frank Espada. Both have a deep need to document the social and political conditions in the urban United States. Espada not only loves to write poetry, but also loves to perform it, organizing workshops in the Boston area. In his role as lawyer, Espada defends the civil rights of immigrants.

Nelle Fertig (born 1919) is a teacher and poet whose work has appeared in *Amelia, Blue Unicorn, CQ, Descant, Modern Haiku, Poem Poet Lore,* and other publications. Her book *Brittle Distance* (1974) won the book manuscript publication award from the National Federation of State Poetry Societies.

Donald Finkel (born 1929) "is one of the few Americans," says Peter Meinke, "trying to extend poetry past the internal into the external world." Much of Finkel's work has been praised by the critics for its startling images and "comic extravagance." A New York native, Finkel has taught at the University of Iowa, Washington University, and Princeton. His numerous awards include the National Book Award for his 1979 poetry collection *The Garbage Wars.* Joseph Bennet wrote in the *New York Times Book Review* that Finkel is "so gifted he does not need subjects for his poems. . . He has, above all, the gift of wonderment."

Robert Frost (1874–1963), born in San Francisco, moved to New England at age ten upon his father's death, and his poetry is closely linked with rural Vermont and New Hampshire. After briefly attending Dartmouth and Harvard, Frost worked as a shoemaker, schoolteacher, editor, and farmer. Unable to make a living, he took his family to England, where his first poetry collection, *A Boy's Will,* appeared in 1913. By 1914 his reputation had become firmly established through the publication of *North of Boston,* a collection containing what were to become some of his most popular poems, including "Mending Wall" and "The Death of the Hired Man." Frost won Pulitzer Prizes for poetry in 1924, 1931, 1937, and 1943. He developed a legendary reputation as America's best-known poet; he read "The Gift Outright" at John F. Kennedy's inauguration in 1960.

Nan Fry (born 1945) lives in Washington, D.C., and has written one book of poems, entitled *Relearning the Dark* (1991). Her poem "The Plum" appeared in Carol Burke and Molly Best Tinsley's *The Creative Process,* a guide to writing poems. In writing about this poem, the editors focused on the "complex web of emotion and thought [which] hold the web together, in fact weave it into a sort of bridge between poet and readers. The plum gives readers something to grasp, see, taste, and study, something far more enticing and intriguing than an earnest but simplistic commentary on 'modern life,' 'instant gratification,' or the ambiguities of pleasure."

Dana Gioia (born 1950), whose surname is pronounced "Joy ah," was born in Los Angeles to a cab driver and a telephone operator. Educated at Stanford and Harvard universities, Gioia has said, "Though most of my poems use rhyme or meter, they rarely follow 'traditional' patterns. I love traditional forms, but I find them slightly dangerous. Their music can become so seductive that one loses touch with contemporary speech, which is, to my judgment, the basis for all genuine poetry."

Louise Glück (born 1943) was born in New York City and studied at both Sarah Lawrence College and Columbia University. Her books of poems include *Firstborn* (1969), *The House on Marshland* (1975), *Descending Figure* (1980), *The Triumph of Achilles* (1985), and *Ararat* (1990). The common denominator in Glück's poetry, alternately sensuous and spare, is that "to be human is to love, to long, to suffer, and to know you will die" (A. Poulin, Jr.).

Judy Grahn (born 1940), born in Chicago, graduated from San Francisco State University. She has published eight books of poetry, including *The Work of a Common Woman* and *The Queen of Swords,* which was performed in San Francisco. She has also written books about poetry and language, as well as a novel, *Mundane's World.* The winner of several grants and awards, Grahn founded the Women's Press Collective in 1970 and has taught writing and mythology.

Thomas Hardy (1840–1928)—a major British novelist (*Tess of the D'Urbervilles, The Mayor of Casterbridge*)—produced eleven novels and three collections of stories before he finally abandoned prose for his first love, poetry, in his sixtieth year. He produced delicately bittersweet poems until he was almost ninety. Thinking his power had waned, critics did not take his poetry seriously until he published his epic, *The Dynasts* (1903, 1906, 1908), which established his reputation as a poet. The young poet Siegfried Sassoon wrote that Hardy recorded life with "microscopic exactitude . . . and a subtle ironic sense" of the tragic in human existence: "But his despair is mitigated by tenderness and pity for his fellows. With a wistful understanding he surveys the human scene." As an octogenarian, Hardy published *Late Lyrics and Earlier* (1922); his post-humous *Winter Words in Various Moods and Metres* (1928) was arranged by him before his death. Louis Untermeyer observed that, although his syntax was often clumsy, his poetry is "as disciplined as it is original."

Joy Harjo (born 1951) is a major Native American voice who builds on jazz, story, and prayer in her work. About her latest volume of poetry, *The Woman Who Fell from the Sky* (1994), Harjo writes: "I believe the word *poet* is synonymous with the word *truth teller*. So this collection tells a bit of the truth of what I have seen since my coming of age in the late sixties." Harjo was born in Tulsa, Oklahoma and is a member of the Muskogee Tribe. Her other three books are *She Had Some Horses* (1983), *Secrets from the Center of the World* (1989), and *In Mad Love and War* (1990). She not only writes poetry but performs it, in addition to playing saxophone with her band, Poetic Justice. Poet Adrienne Rich has written: "I turn and return to Harjo's poetry for her heartbreaking, complex witness and for her world-remaking language: precise, unsentimental, miraculous." Teacher as well as visionary and spiritual poet, Harjo is a professor at the University of New Mexico.

Jeffrey Harrison (born 1957) Harrison, a Cincinnati native, was educated at Columbia, Stanford, and the University of Iowa. His first poetry collection, *The Singing Underneath* (1988), was selected by James Merrill for the National Poetry Series. Another book of poetry, *Signs of Arrival,* appeared in 1996. His newest book collection, *Feeding the Fire,* appeared in 2001. He has claimed fellowships from both the Guggenheim Foundation and the National Endowment for the Arts.

Robert Hass (born 1941) was born and raised in San Francisco and studied at St. Mary's College in Oakland and Stanford University. He has taught at the State University of New York at Buffalo, St. Mary's College, and Berkeley. His first book, *Field Guide,* won the 1973 Yale Series of Younger Poets Award; he received a MacArthur Foundation award in 1985. Wrote critic Anthony Libby, "Hass believes that poetry is what defines the self, and it is his ability to describe that process that is the heart" of the pleasure his work gives his readers.

Robert Hayden (1913–1980), born in Detroit, Michigan, graduated from Wayne State University in Detroit and did graduate work at the University of Michigan. He later joined the faculty of Fisk University. *Heart-shape in the Dust,* his first poetry collection, appeared in 1940. His 1963 collection, *A Ballad of Remembrance,* received the grand prize at the World Festival of Negro Arts. Hayden called his work "a form of prayer—a prayer of illumination, perfection."

Seamus Heaney (born 1939) was born to a rural Catholic family in Northern Ireland, received a B.A. from Queen's University in Belfast in 1961, and taught in secondary schools and universities. His first published book, *Death of a Naturalist* (1966), set his reputation as a powerful "rural poet," a label he addresses in these lines: "Between my fingers and my thumb / The squat pen rests. / I'll dig with it." Heaney's poetry is steeped in Irish lore and history and noted for its "inventive language and sharp, immediate physical imagery." More than simply portraying the Irish countryside and folklore, however, Heaney is concerned with the poet's political role, seeing poets as "both helpless witnesses and accomplices in the fratricidal battles" of Ireland. Inevitably, Heaney is favorably compared with the great Irish poet William Butler Yeats. Of his own creative process he writes: "One thing I try to avoid ever saying at readings is 'my poem' because that sounds like a presumption. The poem *came, it came*. I didn't go and fetch it. To some extent you can wait for it, you coax it in the door when it gets there. I prefer to think of myself as a host to the thing rather than a big game hunter."

John Heaviside   published his poem in the *Olivetree Review,* a publication devoted to student work and published at Hunter College of the City University of New York.

George Herbert   (1593–1633), a younger son of a wealthy aristocratic English family, began writing religious verse while an undergraduate at Cambridge University. Until the death of King James in 1625, Herbert enjoyed royal favor and participated in the life of the court. Undecided for a time between the uncertain promise of a career in public office and a career as a churchman, he eventually became an Anglican priest. His collected poems were published after his death in a volume entitled *The Temple.* Like other metaphysical poets of his time, Herbert introduced into religious poetry complex imagery and intense personal emotion.

Robert Herrick   (1591–1674) addressed light, conventional poems about love to imaginary Corinnas and Julias while leading a quiet life as a country priest. Born in London, Herrick was apprenticed as a young man to his uncle, a wealthy goldsmith. Later Herrick entered Cambridge, and at some point before 1627 he was ordained an Anglican priest. Two years later the king appointed him to a rural parish in a location he hated at first but grew to love. His *Hesperion,* published in 1648, contains 1,200 poems.

Edward Hirsch   (born 1950), born in Chicago, Illinois, earned his Ph.D. from the University of Pennsylvania in 1979. He is now a professor of English at the University of Houston in Texas. Hirsch has written four books of poetry, among them *The Night Parade* (1985) and *Earthly Measures* (1994), and contributes poems, stories, and reviews to magazines such as the *New Yorker* and the *New Republic.* About the collection *For the Sleepwalkers* (1981), critic Jay Parini wrote, "Hirsch inhabits, poem, by poem, dozens of other skins. He can become Rimbaud, Rilke, Paul Klee, or Matisse." Fellow poet Carolyn Kizer wrote that "Hirsch's great strength lies in his descriptive powers."

Gerard Manley Hopkins   (1844–1889) saw none of his poems published: during his lifetime. Born in London, this English poet earned a degree from Oxford in 1867, one year after he had converted to Roman Catholicism. He then entered the Society of Jesus and was ordained a Jesuit priest. Troubled by what he saw as a conflict between his life as a priest and as a poet, he burned all his poems when he entered the Jesuit order but began to write poetry again in 1875. His complete poetic works were published nineteen years after Hopkins' death by his friend, the poet Robert Bridges. Modern poets and critics soon provided a receptive audience for its complex diction, startling imagery, and intense religious emotion. His poems defied convention and are marked by what one of his editors called "a kind of creative violence."

Lady Horikawa   (12th century) was a woman poet living in Japan.

A. E. Housman   (1859–1936), born in Worcestershire, England, failed his final examinations at Oxford in 1881. Sometime during the previous four years his lively and outgoing manner became strictly reserved and melancholy, a change that culminated in this bitter disappointment. Working as a clerk in the Patent Office, he pursued studies on his own and contributed numerous articles to classical journals. Eventually he was named professor of Latin at Cambridge and published *A Shropshire Lad,* his major collection of poems, in 1896.

Langston Hughes   (1902–1967) was a central figure of the Harlem Renaissance of the 1920s, a movement that examined and celebrated American black life and its African heritage. Hughes focused on what it was like to be black in America, a thread that runs through his work as poet, editor, and biographer. Born in Joplin, Missouri, Hughes attended high school in Cleveland, and his first published poems appeared in the school's literary magazine. He attended New York's Columbia University for a year and graduated from Lincoln University in Pennsylvania. His first poetry collection, *The Weary Blues,* appeared in 1926. In addition to numerous collections of poetry, Hughes wrote novels, short stories, plays, radio and motion picture scripts, and nonfiction. In his frequent lecture appearances at black colleges throughout the South, Hughes encouraged others to write. He also translated into English the poetry of black writers from other parts of the world. His own poetry has been translated into many other languages.

Angela Johnson   (n. d.) Born in Alabama, Angela Johnson moved to Ohio, although her ties to Alabama and her family continue to inspire her work. Author of a collection of poetry and many books for young readers, Johnson has received two Coretta Scott King Awards for excellence.

Ben Jonson   (1572–1637), called by one critic "the most scholarly of all Elizabethan playwrights," worked for a time at bricklaying, his stepfather's trade. Jonson's real love, however, was the theater, and after military service he became attached to a company of actors as player and playwright. His *Every Man in His Humour* was performed in 1598, with Shakespeare in the cast. Jonson also wrote love lyrics and songs for his many plays and masques.

Donald Justice   (born 1925), known as a poet's poet, was born in Miami, Florida. Paying close attention to the precision of language and to poetic technique, Justice is recognized as one of America's most elegant and distinctive contemporary poets. The central theme of much of his poetry is loss, as interested in how we recover memories as in the specific memories themselves. He wrote, "So far as I can psychologize it, one of the motives for writing is surely to recover and hold what would otherwise be lost totally—memory or experience." Justice has written many books of poetry, among them *Night Light* (1967), *Departures* (1973), and *For the Sleepwalkers* (1981).

Marie Luise Kaschnitz   (1902–1974), like many German artists and writers, was censored and driven into exile by Hitler. Born in Karlsruhe, she was honored with some of the most prestigious German literary prizes after the war. In addition to writing short stories, essays, and poetry, Kaschnitz produced several radio plays. Her reflections of an aging woman in *Tage, Tage, Jahre (Days, Days, Years)* "define the high point of her literary achievement" (Marilyn Sibley Fries).

John Keats   (1795–1821) died at age twenty-six from tuberculosis and became for later generations a symbol of the sensitive artist destroyed by a harsh world. Born in London, Keats gave up studying medicine for writing when thirty-three of his poems were published. He produced some of his finest poetry in 1818 and 1819, including "La Belle Dame sans Merci" and "Ode on a Grecian Urn." Admired for the rich sensuous imagery of his poetry, Keats was passionately concerned with the relationship between emotion and knowledge, between beauty and truth. He expressed a conviction shared by many Romantic writers when he wrote, "I am certain of the heart's affections and the truth of imagination—What the imagination seizes as beauty must be truth."

Yusef Komunyakaa   (born 1947), a Pulitzer Prize winner, confesses that he "never really approached [poetry] from the perspective of making a living. It was simply a need." A war correspondent in Vietnam during the conflict, Komunyakaa has written a number of poems on Vietnam. Critic Leonard Moore, in reviewing *Neon Vernacular: New and Selected Poems,* writes, "A master at interweaving memory and history to shape his experiences into narratives, Komunyakaa, an African American, defines a culture with striking imagery that is often misunderstood by mainstream readers." He has published ten books of poems. Even when writing about emotionally wrenching events about his tour of duty in Vietnam or his relationship with his abusive father, Komunyakaa paradoxically evokes feelings of tenderness.

Maxine Kumin   (born 1925) was born in Philadelphia, Pennsylvania. She earned her B.A. and M.A. degrees from Radcliffe and lives on a farm in New Hampshire. She published her first collection of poetry in 1961 and won the Pulitzer Prize in 1974 for her collection of poems entitled *Up Country*. She has written a number of novels and numerous successful children's books, several in collaboration with her friend, poet Anne Sexton. She has lectured at the University of Massachusetts, Columbia, Brandeis, and Princeton. May Swenson has called Kumin's work "large-hearted, articulate, and acute."

Melvin Walker La Follette   (born 1930) "believes in the sensuous body of the world," wrote Richard Eberhart, adding, "He finds his feelings of the greatest richness of life in three areas . . . youth, the love of small animals," and "the devotion to the idea of saints and sainthood." La Follette was born in Evansville, Indiana. He received his B.A. in creative writing at the University of Washington. He taught for many years at colleges in California, Canada, and Oregon. He also spent time in forestry work in various parts of the Pacific Northwest.

Philip Larkin   (1922–1985), a native of Coventry, England, was considered by some critics to be the finest English poet of his generation. Larkin began his studies at Oxford in 1940. After graduating, he became a librarian at the University of Leicester. In 1946 he published his first poetry collection, *The North Ship,* but it wasn't until 1960, with the publication of *The Less Deceived,* that he gained critical recognition. In addition to publishing many poetry collections, he served as editor of the *Oxford Book of Twentieth-Century Verse* and was a recognized expert on jazz. Larkin once said, "Form holds little interest for me. Content is everything."

James Laughlin   (born 1914) has made the writing of love poems and light verse his principal avocation. He is also well known as publisher of New Directions Books. Laughlin was friends with William Carlos Williams and e. e. cummings, and the influence of both poets is clear in his work. City Lights Books published Laughlin's *Selected Poems, 1935–1985*, and his most recent collection is *The Man in the Wall: Poems* (1993).

D.H. Lawrence   (1885–1930) A powerful, provocative British novelist, poet, and culture critic from a working-class background, Lawrence was one of the early moderns challenging the taboos and hypocrisies of the Victorian past. Hounded by the authorities, he spent much of his life in exile with his German-born wife. His novels *Sons and Lovers* and *Women in Love* rank among the great early modern classics. His *Lady Chatterley's Lover* was long available only in an expurgated version but could finally be read in the original after a notable defeat of the forces of censorship.

Li-Young Lee   (born 1957) has said, "I believe the King James Bible to contain some of the greatest poetry in the world and I hope to own some of its glory and mystery in my own writing one day." Lee was born in Jakarta, Indonesia, to Chinese parents "who were classically educated and in the habit of reciting literally hundreds of ancient Chinese poems." His father, jailed by then-dictator Sukarno in a leper colony, escaped, and the family fled to the United States. They settled in Pennsylvania, where his father became a Presbyterian minister. Lee's volume of poems, *Rose,* appeared in 1986.

Ursula K. Le Guin   (born 1929), the daughter of an anthropologist and a folklorist, has been called "the best living writer of fantasy and science fiction." Her novels include *The Left Hand of Darkness, The Dispossessed,* and *Always Coming Home* (1985). In addition to adult fiction, she has published poetry, children's books, and essays about her travels and her political commitments as a strong feminist, environmentalist, and champion of the dispossessed.

Denise Levertov   (born 1923) has said she grew up in "a house full of books and everyone in the family engaged in some literary activity." The family's vast library and the diverse visitors to the house—"Jewish booksellers, German theologians, Russian priests from Paris, and Viennese opera singers"—were her education. Her father, a biblical scholar and Anglican priest, harbored the lifelong hope of the unification of Judaism and Christianity. Born in Essex, England, Levertov was a civilian nurse in London during World War II, then settled in New York in 1948 with her American husband. The influence of the American poet William Carlos Williams helped her to develop "from a British Romantic with almost Victorian background to an American poet of . . . vitality." Her best-known book of poetry, *The Sorrow Dance* (1967), reflects her feelings of rage over the Vietnam War and the death of her older sister. Her most recent books, dealing with loneliness and personal pilgrimage, include *Evening Train* (1992) and *New and Selected Essays* (1992).

Lou Lipsitz   (born 1938) A former professor of political science at the University of North Carolina, Lipsitz took 21 years off from publishing poetry before releasing his third collection, *Seeking the Hook* (1997). His latest book, *Missing the Father,* will be published in 2002. Now a psychotherapist, his poetry often deals with a range of men's issues from male bonding and divorce to father-son relationships. One reviewer of Lipsitz' recent publication wrote, "*Seeking the Hook* is a remarkable comeback from a poet who obviously never went away. It's a book that was well worth the wait."

Audre Lorde   (1934–1992) Poet, essayist, novelist, and teacher, Lorde was born in New York City on February 18, 1934. She grew up in Manhattan where she attended Catholic school. She loved to read poetry, often reciting whole poems or individual lines to communicate with people. When she could no longer find poems that expressed her feelings, she started writing her own poetry. Her volumes of poetry include *The First Cities* (1968), *From a Land Where Other People Live* (1972), *Coal* (1976), and *The Black Unicorn* (1978). Lorde was professor of English at Hunter College in New York.

Richard Lovelace   (1618–1658) was born in Kent, England, and studied at Oxford. An ardent supporter of Charles I, he was held in London as a prisoner during the civil war between the monarchists and the Puritan rebels. When the king was executed, Lovelace lost everything; he spent the remainder of his life in poverty. Most of his poetry was not published in his lifetime, but today he is one of the best remembered of the Cavalier (royalist) poets.

Kathleen Lynch   (born 1943) has published one book of poems, *How to Build an Owl and Other Poems* and has been published in several literary magazines such as *Midwest Quarterly* and *Poetry Northwest.* Her recent fiction appears in *The Next Parish Over,* an anthology of Irish American writing. She lives in Pleasanton, California, and reads her work, both poetry and fiction, at universities and in bookstores in California. Andrea Hollander Budy says of her, "Her commitment is to the language of the heart and to her hunger to understand both her own wildness and her responsibility to the things of the world."

Hugh MacDiarmid   (1892–1978) "effected, almost single-handed, a literary revolution," wrote David Daiches. "He . . . destroyed one Scottish tradition and founded another." In order to identify himself with his Scots heritage, MacDiarmid changed his name from Christopher Grieve, his English name. Setting himself the task of reviving the great Scottish poetic tradition, he wrote the much-admired lyric poetic sequence *A Drunk Man Looks at the Thistle* in 1926.

Claude McKay (1890–1948), who wrote militant poetry attacking the racism he encountered as a black immigrant to the United States, surprised some readers by converting to Roman Catholicism in the 1940s. "To have a religion," he wrote, "is very much like falling in love with a woman. You love her for her beauty, which cannot be defined." Born in Jamaica, McKay was a published poet before coming to the United States at age twenty-three. His 1919 poem "If We Must Die" helped inaugurate the 1920s Harlem Renaissance. His writings include an autobiography entitled *A Long Way from Home,* published in 1927.

Rod McKuen (born 1933) built a business empire consisting of four record labels, three book publishers, two music-publishing companies, a mail-order venture, and a clothing company named Rod McKuen Casuals. A resident of Los Angeles, he has published many collections of poetry, composed musical scores, and written more than a thousand songs.

Archibald MacLeish (1892–1982) was for a time a leading advocate of the role of poetry in contemporary society. Born in Glencoe, Illinois, he served in World War I in 1917–1918. He graduated from Yale in 1915 and received a degree from Harvard Law School in 1919. He grew tired of law practice and turned to the study of literature, reading the works of the great early moderns, T. S. Eliot and Ezra Pound. President Franklin Roosevelt appointed MacLeish librarian of Congress in 1939, and he served as assistant secretary of state during the final two years of World War II. In 1953, his *Collected Poems, 1917–1952* won him his second Pulitzer. MacLeish taught at Harvard and at Amherst College.

Andrew Marvell (1621–1678) was known in his day for satirical commentary on political events; his poetry was not published until after his death. Today his "To His Coy Mistress" is one of the best-known poems in the English language. Twentieth-century critics rediscovered Marvell and other metaphysical poets (John Donne, George Herbert), championing their love of irony and paradox and their blend of intellectual vigor and passionate intensity. Born in Yorkshire, Marvell entered Oxford at the age of twelve. When the civil war broke out, he was appointed assistant to John Milton in the Cromwell government. After the monarchy was restored, he served in Parliament until his death.

John Masefield (1878–1967), a native of Herefordshire, England, was a young boy when his father, a lawyer, died. At age fourteen Masefield was indentured to work on a merchant ship and became a wanderer for a few years. Staying for a time in New York, he took odd jobs before returning to England at age nineteen. After Masefield read Chaucer, he was determined to become a poet. Not until the 1911 publication of *The Everlasting Mercy* did he become famous. In addition to his poetry, he wrote more than a dozen plays, a book on Shakespeare, twelve volumes of essays, books for youths, and adventure novels.

Peter Meinke (born 1932) was born in Brooklyn, New York. He served in the U.S. Army and received a B.A. from Hamilton College, an M.A. from the University of Michigan, and a Ph.D. from the University of Minnesota. Meinke's reviews, poems, and stories have appeared in periodicals such as the *Atlantic,* the *New Yorker,* and the *New Republic.* His collection of short stories, *The Piano Tuner,* won the 1986 Flannery O'Connor Award. *Scars,* published in 1996, is his newest book of poems.

William Meredith (born 1919), a native of New York City, graduated from Princeton in 1940 and served as a naval aviator during World War II. His award-winning poetry has been published in several collections, including *Ships and Other Figures, The Open Sea,* and *Earth Walk: New & Selected Poems.* He taught at Princeton and Carnegie-Mellon, and Connecticut College.

James Merrill   (born 1926), born in New York City to the founder of Merrill Lynch, believed that wealth and standing only made him feel lonelier, as his father married repeatedly and traveled often. His poetry is both technically formal and intensely autobiographical. Merrill writes to give shape to his experience in order to understand it: "We don't know what we feel until we see it distanced by . . . transformation," he wrote, a stance also held by philosopher Susanne Langer, who wrote, "Art is not expressing feelings the artist has, but feelings the artist knows." Critics have compared his allusive and dense style to that of T. S. Eliot or Robert Lowell.

W. S. Merwin   (born 1927), one of the most prolific poets and translators of his generation, was born the son of a Presbyterian minister in New York City. Educated at Princeton, Merwin was influenced by poet Robert Graves, whose son he tutored in Majorca, Spain. Merwin has translated widely from Spanish, Portuguese, Latin, French, and Russian, in both conventional forms and free verse. He has received numerous fellowships and awards, including a Pulitzer Prize in 1971 for his collection *A Carrier of Ladders*. He went to live in Hawaii in 1968.

Edna St. Vincent Millay   (1892–1950) began writing poetry as a child in Camden, Maine, encouraged by her mother, who had left her father when Millay was eight years old. While a rebellious student at Vassar, Millay dared the president to expel her, and he explained that he didn't want a "banished Shelley on my doorstep." She supposedly replied, "On those terms, I think I can continue to live in this hellhole." She graduated in 1917, the same year her first book of poems was published. In 1923 she won a Pulitzer Prize for her poetry collection *The Harp-Weaver*. In addition to over twenty volumes of verse, she published three verse plays, wrote a libretto for an opera, and translated Baudelaire. Neglected for a time by critics who thought her poetry too traditional in form and too frankly emotional, she has recently been rediscovered by feminist critics as an early champion of feminist themes. 2001 saw a Millay Renaissance. Not one, but two, major biographies were published, and both hit the best seller lists: Nancy Milford, *Savage Beauty,* and Daniel Mark Epstein, *What My Lips Have Kissed: The Loves and Love Poetry of Edna St. Vincent Millay*.

Vassar Miller   (born 1924) calls poetry "an act of love." Born in Houston, Texas, Miller was educated at the University of Houston. She has published several poetry collections, including *Wage War on Silence*. Afflicted with cerebral palsy from birth, Miller has dedicated herself to poetry "and has demonstrated . . . that craftsmanship, religious fervor, and personal joy and agony can produce major poetry" (Chad Walsh).

Czeslaw Milosz   (born 1911) "deals in his poetry with the central issues of our time: the impact of history upon moral being, the search for ways to survive spiritual ruin in a ruined world" (Terrence Des Pres). Milosz, a native of Lithuania, published his first book of poetry at age twenty-one. When Poland was invaded by Germany and Soviet Russia in 1939, Milosz worked with the underground resistance in Warsaw, writing and editing several books published secretly. After the war, Milosz became a member of the new Communist government's diplomatic service but left this post in 1951 and defected to the West. He joined the faculty at the University of California at Berkeley in 1960 and won the Nobel Prize for literature in 1980.

John Milton   (1608–1674) was a poet deeply involved in the political and religious turmoil of his time. Born in Cheapside, London, he was steeped in classical literature and wrote some of his early poems in Latin and Italian. After graduating from Cambridge, Milton traveled the Continent, returning to England shortly before the civil war. Milton was an ardent supporter of the Puritan cause. He joined in the vigorous polemics of the time and published aggressive prose tracts on subjects including censorship. After the overthrow of King Charles I, Milton became Latin secretary in charge of diplomatic correspondence under the dictator Cromwell. He escaped death as a traitor to the crown after the restoration of the monarchy, publishing his monumental religious epic *Paradise Lost* in 1667. By this time he was completely blind and living in poverty. "Lycidas," the best known of his shorter poems, appeared in 1637.

Janice Mirikitani   (born 1938), who lives on the West Coast, has been an outspoken poet of political issues. Her images juxtapose the terrors of Vietnam with the indignities of World War II relocation camps. An early proponent of multicultural awareness, Mirikitani insisted that the language of the Third World was "universal, freeing, connective." She co-edited *Third World Women* (1973), *Time to Greez* (1975), and *Ayumi: The Japanese American Anthology* (1979).

Gabriela Mistral   (1889–1956) adopted her pen name from the names of two poets she admired, Gabriele D'Annunzio and Frederic Mistral. Born in Chile, Mistral wrote about her concerns for children, the social conditions of Chilean workers, and the social emancipation of women. Her books include *Sonetos de la muerte* (1914), *Desolación* (1922), and *Ernura and Tala* (1923). In 1945 she was awarded the Nobel Prize for literature.

Henry Stephen Mitchell   (born 1943) Mitchell has produced definitive versions of spiritual writings and poetry throughout his adult life. His works include *The Gospel According to Jesus* and *Tao Te Ching: A New English Version, Parables and Portraits*. He is also editor of *The Enlightened Heart: An Anthology of Sacred Poetry*.

N. Scott Momaday   (born 1934) is a Kiowa whose writing explores the history and culture of his people. Momaday was born in Lawton, Oklahoma. He graduated from the University of New Mexico in 1958 and received master's and doctoral degrees from Stanford. He began his academic career teaching English at the University of California, Santa Barbara, in 1973. He told the story of his rediscovery of his heritage in *The Journey of Tai-me* (1968)—republished with illustrations by his father, Al Momaday, under the title *The Way to Rainy Mountain*. His novel *The House Made of Dawn* won a Pulitzer Prize in 1969.

Pat Mora   (born 1942) is a native of El Paso, Texas. Her work is rooted in place and culture, developing the themes of the desert and the border. Two of her four poetry collections, *Chants* (1984) and *Borders* (1986), won Southwest Book Awards. In addition, she is the successful children's author of *A Birthday Basket for Tia* (1992), *Pablo's Tree* (1993), and *Tomas and the Library Lady* (1993). Today, she calls Cincinnati, Ohio her home.

Lisel Mueller   (born 1924) German-born Lisel Mueller, according to one critic, has a "breathtaking linguistic virtuosity." Another wrote that her poetry is "a testament to the power of language to interpret the world and the lives in it." Mueller has received the Carl Sandburg Award and a National Endowment for the Arts fellowship. Her collection of poetry, *Alive Together,* won the Pulitzer Prize in 1996.

Ogden Nash   (1902–1971) gave pleasure to untold readers with a steady stream of irreverent light verse. Born in Rye, New York, Nash attended Harvard and worked as a teacher, a bond salesperson, and an editor for Doubleday Publishers in New York City. Later he joined the editorial staff of the *New Yorker*. His collected poems, *I Wouldn't Have Missed It,* appeared in 1975.

Thomas Nashe   (1567–1601), the son of a minister, was born in Lowestoft, England. After graduating from Cambridge, Nashe toured France and Italy and by 1588 was a professional writer living in London. Nashe wrote pamphlets to defend the Anglican Church against attacks by the Puritans. He also wrote several plays and in 1594 published an adventure novel, *The Unfortunate Traveler.*

Howard Nemerov   (born 1920), American poet and literary critic, was born and raised in New York City. He graduated from Harvard and served in World War II with a fighter squadron in the British Royal Air Force. He has taught at Bennington College in Vermont and George Washington University in St. Louis. Known for its clarity and simplicity, his poetry sings the praises of nature and the simple life. In 1988 Nemerov became U.S. poet laureate, succeeding Richard Wilbur and later succeeded by Mark Strand in 1989.

Pablo Neruda   (1904–1973) said, "I like the lives of people who are restless and unsatisfied, whether they are artists or criminals." Neruda himself lived a restless, adventure-filled life. Born Neftali Beltran in a small frontier town in southern Chile, Neruda took his pseudonym at a young age out of admiration for a nineteenth-century Czech writer. When Neruda was still a boy, his father, a railroad worker, was killed in a fall from a train. At age nineteen Neruda published a book called *Twenty Poems of Love and One Ode of Desperation,* which is still a beloved favorite in South America. During that period, he said, "Love poems were sprouting out all over my body." In later years much of his poetry became political. He served as consulate in the Far East and Mexico and traveled widely. He became a member of the Chilean Senate, fleeing from dictatorship for a time. During his years of exile, Neruda wrote *Canto general,* which his translator, Robert Bly, called "the greatest long poem written on the American continent since *Leaves of Grass.*"

nila northSun   (born 1951) was born in Schurz, Nevada, of Shoshoni-Chippewa heritage. She coauthored *After the Drying Up of the Water* and *Diet Pepsi and Nacho Cheese.* She has written about the ironies of exchanging reservation life for city life.

Sharon Olds   (born 1942) has said, "One of the hardest tasks as a poet is to believe in oneself—or to act as if we do!" A self-described "late bloomer," Olds says she was thirty before she found her voice, her ability "to embody on the page thinking about an actual self." Born in San Francisco, Olds earned a B.A. from Stanford and a Ph.D. from Columbia. Winner of many awards, she has taught and given numerous readings at colleges and universities. Her poetry books are *Satan Says* (1980), *The Dead and the Living* (1982), *The Gold Cell* (1987), *The Father* (1992), and, most recently, *The Wellspring* (1995). This sequence of poems takes us back to the womb, on to childhood, to sexual awakening, to the drama of childbirth, to the amazements of parenthood, and to mature love. Always she writes with astonishing frankness and authentic emotion about being a child, a woman, and a mother. Michael Ondaatje observed that Sharon Olds' poems "are pure fire in the hands—risky, on the verge of falling, and in the end leaping up. I love the roughness and humor and brag and tenderness and completion in her work as she carries the reader through rooms of passion and loss."

Mary Oliver   (born 1935) was born in Cleveland, Ohio, and attended both Ohio State and Vassar. She worked as a secretary to the sister of poet Edna St. Vincent Millay. Her first collection of poetry, *No Voyage and Other Poems,* appeared in 1963 and then again in 1965 with nineteen additional poems. Her second collection, *The River Styx, Ohio, and Other Poems,* appeared in 1972. In 1991 Oliver won a pair of awards for *House of Light* and, in 1992, the National Book Award for poetry for *New and Selected Poems.* These recent works reflect a shift to self and a pervasive tone of amazement. Susan Reynolds describes her work as having a "Blake-eyed revelatory quality." In the poem "When Death Comes," Oliver writes: "When it's over I want to say: all my life / I was a bride married to amazement."

Wilfred Owen   (1893–1918) wrote powerful antiwar poems during World War I— poems that are a lasting memorial and tribute to a generation destroyed in the trenches of Flanders and northern France. Owen was killed in action at age twenty-five, one week before the armistice. Born in Shropshire, England, into a devout, relatively poor family, Owen was educated at London University and enlisted in military service when England entered the war. In late 1917 he was wounded and sent to a military hospital. There he met the poet Siegfried Sassoon, who edited and published Owen's poems after Owen's death.

Dorothy Parker   (1893–1967) has been called "the quintessential New York wit, known as much for what she said as for what she wrote" Parker often wrote bitter satire and showed empathy toward suffering. "The humorist has never been happy, anyhow," she once said. "Today he's whistling past worse graveyards to worse tunes." In addition to writing for the *New Yorker* and *Vanity Fair,* Parker wrote screenplays for Hollywood.

Linda Pastan   (born 1932) was born in New York City and studied at Brandeis and Radcliffe. Her first poetry collection, *A Perfect Circle of Sun,* appeared in 1971. Other collections include *Five Stages of Grief* (1978), *AM/PM* (1982), *Imperfect Paradise* (1988), and *Heroes in Disguise* (1991). Poet laureate of the state of Maryland, she has been honored with fellowships from the National Endowment for the Arts. The *Washington Post* noted that Pastan "writes with a music of her own—reinforced by overtones of Yeats and Frost."

Octavio Paz   (born 1914), Mexican poet and critic, won the Nobel Prize for literature in 1991. He has lectured to large audiences in the United States and served as Mexico's ambassador to India, a post from which he resigned in 1968 in protest over the bloody repression of student demonstrators before the Olympic Games in Mexico City. He has written much about the dialogue between the North American and Latin American cultures. Collections of his poetry include *Savage Moon* (1933), *Sun Stone* (1957), and *Selected Poems* (1960).

Francesco Petrarca   (1304–1374) was a humanist of the early Italian Renaissance, participating in the rediscovery of the learning and literature of classical antiquity. His *Canzoniere,* a collection of songs (*canzoni*) and sonnets, started the vogue of Petrarchan love poetry that dominated lyric poetry in Europe for centuries.

Robert Phillips   (born 1938) Phillips has edited and written over 30 books, ranging from poetry to short stories and essays. His primary works include *Spinach Days, Breakdown Lane,* and *The Pregnant Man.* Phillips' poetry is characterized by humanity and wit in a variety of poetic styles ranging from formal to narrative.

Marge Piercy   (born 1936) was born in poverty in Detroit during the Depression. She was the first in her family to go to college and "took five years to recover." She has published eight novels, including *Woman on the Edge of Time* (1976), a science fiction work in which she experiments with a "woman's language." She has also written a play, essays, and nine volumes of poetry, including *Available Light* (1988). When she is not giving readings and conducting workshops throughout the country, she writes in her Cape Cod home.

Christine de Pisan   (about 1364–1430), called "France's first woman of letters" by biographer Charity Cannon Willard, lived and wrote at the end of the Middle Ages. Born in Venice, Italy, she moved to Paris, France, at age four. There her family became part of the royal court, for her father, a scientist, was employed by King Charles V. At age fifteen she married but was widowed after ten years. Her first poetry collection, published by 1402, marked the beginning of a long literary career, during which de Pisan wrote lyrical and allegorical poetry, biographies of important political figures (including Charles V), textbooks, and books about women and government. She is also known for her role in a debate over contemporary negative attitudes toward women and for her championing of women's rights.

Sylvia Plath   (1932–1963) was born near Boston, of an Austrian-born father who was an instructor at Boston University and an expert on bees. She began writing early and sold several stories and poems to *Seventeen* magazine. A 1955 summa cum laude graduate in English from Smith, Plath earned an M.A. at Cambridge as a

Fulbright scholar. In 1956 she married English poet Ted Hughes. *The Colossus,* published in 1960, was her only poetry collection to appear before she committed suicide. *The Bell Jar,* a quasi-autobiographical novel, chronicles the struggles of a brilliant young woman radically alienated from her environment who suffers bouts of suicidal depression. Critic David Young says Plath "lived on a knife-edge, in the presence of a tremendous attraction to death and nothingness." Since her death, her powerful and disturbing poetry has been widely discussed and anthologized.

Alexander Pope   (1668–1744) became arbiter of literary taste in the age of reason. Born into the family of a prosperous London merchant, he was educated largely at home. Excluded from universities discriminating against Catholics, Pope quickly demonstrated his ability to overcome obstacles and adverse criticism. His *Essay on Criticism* (1711), a discussion in poetic form of literary taste and style, established its author's reputation. He undertook monumental translations of Homer's *Iliad* and *Odyssey* by public subscription and became financially independent in the process. *An Essay on Man,* a verse compendium of the fashionable optimistic philosophy of his age, appeared in 1733.

Ezra Pound   (1885–1972) was one of the great innovators and nonconformists of early modern poetry. He championed or inspired writers like Marianne Moore, T. S. Eliot, Robert Frost, William Carlos Williams, Ernest Hemingway, and James Joyce. Pound was born in Idaho and educated at Hamilton College and the University of Pennsylvania. Associated with the imagist poets, Pound translated Chinese, Latin, Japanese, German, French, Italian, Greek, Anglo-Saxon, and Provençal (thirteenth-century French) poetry. In 1945 he was arrested for treason because of his radio broadcasts of Fascist propaganda in Italy during World War II. Found unfit for trial by reason of insanity, he was committed to St. Elizabeth's Hospital in Washington, D.C., where he spent over ten years. His most ambitious and complex work is *The Cantos,* a vast, richly allusive collection of poems he worked on in depth while in a prisoner of war camp near Pisa, Italy; he continued to work on them throughout his life, and they were left unfinished at the time of his death.

Leroy V. Quintana   (born 1944) has said, "In many ways, I'm still basically a small-town New Mexico boy carrying on the oral tradition." Born in Albuquerque, Quintana was raised by his grandparents, who told him *cuentos*—traditional Mexican folktales—and stories of life in the Old West. "I seem to be tied to a sense of the past," he said. "My work reflects the 'sense of place' evoked by New Mexico. I hope I am worthy of portraying the land and its people well." Quintana, a graduate of the University of New Mexico, won the American Book Award for poetry in 1982 for *Sangre*. His other titles include *Hijo del Pueblo: New Mexico Poems* (1976) and *The Reason People Don't Like Mexicans* (1984).

John Crowe Ransom   (1888–1974), both as a poet and a critic, shared in the redirection of modern literary taste associated with the rediscovery of the metaphysical poets of the seventeenth century. Born in Pulaski, Tennessee, Ransom was educated at Vanderbilt University and Oxford, where he was a Rhodes scholar. Ransom made a name for himself as both poet and critic in the 1920s and 1930s. He taught at Vanderbilt and then at Kenyon College, where he was a faculty member for almost forty years. At Kenyon he founded and edited the *Kenyon Review*. He became a leader in what was then called the New Criticism, publishing *The World's Body* in 1938 and *The New Criticism* in 1941.

Henry Reed   (1914–1986), poet and playwright, was born in Birmingham, England. After earning a B.A. from the University of Birmingham in 1937, he worked as a teacher and freelance writer. He served a stint in the British army and wrote poetry about his experience in cadet training, as well as about political events of the time. His only collection of poetry, *A Map of Verona,* appeared in 1946. Soon thereafter, he began writing radio plays, including the popular BBC "Hilda Tablet" series, a parody of British society in the 1930s.

Kenneth Rexroth   (born 1905) has been a painter, essayist, radio and television performer, editor, and journalist as well as a poet. Born in Indiana, Rexroth was mostly self-educated. A guru of the Beat Generation, for many years he lived in San Francisco and has written extensively about California's High Sierra. "Some of his mountain poems are the best nature writing we have" (Hayden Carruth). Rexroth has translated literature from six languages and has written three volumes of critical essays.

Adrienne Rich   (born 1929) Rich was educated by her parents in their Baltimore, Maryland, home until fourth grade. A 1951 Phi Beta Kappa graduate of Radcliffe, Rich won the Yale Younger Poets competition that same year for her collection, *A Change of World*. Since then she has been awarded the prestigious Bollingen prize and has published more than half a dozen books of poetry, including *Diving into the Wreck* (1973). An inspiration to feminist poets and critics, Rich collected some of her incisive, thought-provoking prose in *Our Lies, Secrets, and Silence* (1979). Through her poetry Rich has encouraged the questioning of conventional beliefs on issues such as homosexuality, Jewish heritage, and the politics of oppression. In Rich's work, the male of the species is an overwhelming negative: "Men . . . are depicted universally and exclusively as parasitic on women, emotionally threatened by them, brutal . . . and undeserving of pity." Francine du Plessix Gray has written that "it is vexing to see such a dedicated feminist playing the dangerous game of using the oppressor's tactics."

Rainer Maria Rilke   (1875–1926), perhaps the most widely admired and translated of the twentieth-century German poets, was born in Prague to German-speaking parents. In 1898 he went to Russia, where he met Leo Tolstoy, author of *War and Peace*. In 1905 in France, Rilke served as secretary for the famous French sculptor Rodin, and the influence of this experience can be seen in his collection *New Poems* (1907). When World War I broke out, Rilke moved to Switzerland, where he wrote *Sonnets to Orpheus* (1923) and *The Duino Elegies* (1923). Critic Kenneth Koch has said of Rilke's power as a poet: "When Rilke writes about a subject, it is as if nothing were known about it, as if he started from the very beginning in order to understand deeply, for himself, the power or purpose or beauty of it."

Alberto Rios   (born 1952) was born in Arizona to an English mother and a Mexican American father. He is a professor of creative writing and director of the creative writing program at Arizona State University. He has won a number of awards, including the Pushcart Prize IX, the Governor of Arizona Arts Award, and the Walt Whitman Award of the Academy of American Poets (1981). Rios' poetry has appeared in all of the major poetry reviews in the United States, and he has published several books of poetry, among them *Whispering to Fool the Wind* (1982) and *The Lima Orchard Woman* (1990).

Theodore Roethke   (1908–1963) grew up in Saginaw, Michigan, where his father and uncle owned a greenhouse; greenhouses would serve as prominent images in his poetry. He studied at the University of Michigan and Harvard, and he taught and coached tennis at a number of colleges. He sold his first poems for a dollar, but shortly thereafter his poetry appeared in several widely read magazines. He won a Pulitzer Prize in 1954 for *The Waking: Poems 1933–1953*, which was followed by the Bollingen Prize in 1959 for *Words or the Wind* and two National Book Awards. Abrasive in his criticism of contemporary culture and fellow poets, Roethke looked to the world of nature for sources of spiritual renewal.

Wendy Rose   (born 1948) A Hopi-Miwok mixed-blood Indian, Wendy Rose wrote in her autobiographical essay, "Neon Scars": "I have always swung back and forth between alienation and relatedness. . . . I've always thought in terms of being a half-breed because that is the way both sides of the family treated me." In an interview she spoke of her full-blood Hopi father and her Scots and Irish and Miwok mother. Since the lineage is matriarchal, Rose says, "I am someone who is from [Hopi] society in a biological sense, in what I like to think is a spiritual sense, and certainly in an emotional sense, but culturally I would have to say I'm pretty urbanized: an urban, Pan-Indian kind of person." Both poet and painter, Rose studied anthropology at the University of California at Berkeley. She has published more than ten books.

Christina Rossetti (1830–1894), whose father had come to England as a political refugee from his native Italy, was born in London in a poor neighborhood. Rossetti had no formal education but was taught to read by her mother. From her earliest days she loved to write, and her grandfather had a number of her poems privately printed when she was twelve. Her first collection of poetry, *Goblin Market and Other Poems,* appeared in 1862.

Sappho (about 620–550 B.C.), called "the tenth muse" by Plato, lived on the Greek island of Lesbos, where she wrote passionate love poems addressed to younger women she may have taught. She was an aristocrat involved in controversial political activities that led to her being exiled twice. She married a rich merchant and bore a daughter. In A.D. 1073, a large collection of her verse was publicly burned by church dignitaries of Rome and Constantinople. However, some of her writing—as well as her legendary reputation—has remained intact.

Philip Schultz (born 1945) Philip Schultz has published a number of works, most notable among them, *Like Wings: Poems,* published in 1978, followed six years later by *Deep within the Ravine.* The creator of New York City's Writers Studio, Schultz has said about his poetry and its relation to the reader: "When I work with people I try to figure it out: what is their agenda? And I try to get them free of it."

Anne Sexton (1928–1974) encouraged writers to "put your ear close down to your soul and listen hard." Born in Newton, Massachusetts, she studied at Boston University and Brandeis. At age twenty-eight, a suburban housewife, she suffered a nervous breakdown. Her therapist encouraged her to write, and she soon became a successful poet. She claimed that when she began to write she was reborn, for "suicide is the opposite of the poem." She wrote eight books of poetry; *Live or Die* won the 1967 Pulitzer Prize. Sexton lived a troubled life, punctuated by suicide attempts and hospitalizations, until she finally took her life in 1974, mourned by fellow poets who thought of her as one of the great poetic talents of our time. "When I'm writing, I know I'm doing the thing I was born to do," she said. "I guess I listen for my melody. When it comes, I just turn . . . like a little dancer." A 1991 biography of Anne Sexton made the *New York Times* best-seller list.

William Shakespeare (1564–1616) is the foremost English dramatist of the reigns of Queen Elizabeth and King James I. Shakespeare was actor, playwright, and shareholder in a theatrical company at a time when the English stage enjoyed both royal patronage and popular support. He wrote some thirty-five plays for an audience that liked spectacle and was used to keen competition among theatrical companies and to rapid changes in dramatic fashions. A vast literature of comment, analysis, background information, and textual study has grown up around his works. His great tragedies—*Romeo and Juliet, Hamlet, Othello, King Lear, Macbeth*—probe the paradoxes of our human nature and destiny. Little is known about his life: He was born in the small town of Stratford-on-Avon, and his formal studies ended with grammar school. At age eighteen he married Anne Hathaway. He retired to his hometown at the end of his career.

Percy Bysshe Shelley (1792–1822), most iconoclastic of the younger Romantic poets, was born in Sussex, England, the eldest son of a conservative country squire.

He went to Oxford but was expelled for publishing a pamphlet that advocated atheism. This was but the first of many rebellions against convention and established institutions that marked his brief life. Shelley spent most of his adult life in Italy; many of his shorter and more famous lyric poems, such as "To a Skylark" and "Ode to the West Wind," he wrote in Pisa in 1819. One of his last poems is the elegy written to mourn the death of his close friend John Keats. Shelley himself, who had written "How wonderful is Death, / Death and his brother Sleep," died in a boating accident at age thirty.

Charles Simic (born 1938) came to the United States at age eleven from his native Yugoslavia. The son of an engineer and a dress designer, Simic has published twelve poetry collections. Robert Shaw of the *New Republic* said that Simic's poems are "at once weighty and evasive, and describing them is about as easy as picking up blobs of mercury with mittens on." Many critics have commented on the enigmatic quality of Simic's poetry: "I have not yet decided," writes Diane Wakoski in *Poetry,* "whether Charles Simic is America's greatest living surrealist poet, a children's writer, a religious writer, or simple-minded. . . . his poetry is cryptic and fascinating."

Maurya Simon (born 1950) writes poems that have been called "luminous and beautiful" (Susan Ludvigson). Poet Garrett Hongo compares Simon's work to Elizabeth Bishop's and May Swenson's in its lucidity, and accessibility. She has received a number of awards for her work, including a Fulbright fellowship. Her four volumes of poetry are *The Enchanted Room* (1986), *Days of Awe* (1987), *Speaking in Tongues* (1989), and, in 1995, *The Golden Labyrinth,* poems reflecting her extended stay in India. Simon's images reflect what she learned in India, that "each small world transforms itself." Simon teaches creative writing at the University of California, Riverside.

Cathy Song (born 1955) is the author of *Picture Bride* (nominated for a National Book Critics Circle Award), *Frameless Windows, Squares of Light*; and *School Figures.* Her work has been widely anthologized, including in *The Best American Poetry 2000.* Naomi Shihab Nye has written of Song's work, "To read poems as true on the tongue and the eye as these use a deep, transcendent sweetness. I feel transported, restored to gravity-ground, melodious mind." The recipient of numerous awards, Song lives in Honolulu with her husband and three children.

Gary Soto (born 1952), award-winning Mexican American poet, believes that "writing makes the ordinary stand out, thus enabling us to build in some kind of metaphorical meaning." Much of Soto's writing includes the ordinary events of his childhood in Fresno, California. In addition to the prose memoir *Living up the Street,* Soto has published five books of poetry, including *Home Course in Religion* (1991). An alumnus of Fresno State and the University of California, Irvine, he joined the faculty at Berkeley. Soto says that literature "reshapes experience—both real and invented—to help us see ourselves—our foibles, failures, potential, beauty, pettiness. In short, literature helps define the world for us."

Wole Soyinka (born 1934) is associated worldwide with the struggle for justice and freedom in Africa. Born in Nigeria of Yoruban parents, this Nobel laureate writes plays, poems, and novels. He has worked as a teacher and served as secretary general of the Union of African Writers. His plays were first performed in England while he was a student at the University of Leeds. His poetry collection titles include *Idanre and Other Poems* and *A Shuttle in the Crypt,* which contains poems written while he was imprisoned during the Nigerian civil war.

William Stafford (1914–1992) grew up in small towns of central Kansas, hunting, camping, and fishing in the countryside. He earned a doctorate in English from Iowa State. A member of the United Brethren, Stafford became a conscientious objector during World War II. He worked in labor camps, an experience recorded in a prose memoir, *Down in My Heart*. In 1947 his first collection of poems appeared, and the next year he joined the faculty at Lewis and Clark College in Oregon. His third poetry collection, *Traveling through the Dark*, received the National Book Award in 1963. His poems often explore commonplace events; critics note, however, that on closer examination, Stafford proves to be "a very elusive poet with a distinctive private vision that slips through our grasp when we try to identify, summarize, or paraphrase it" (David Young).

Sue Standing   (born 1952) An English professor at Wheaton, Standing is the recipient of several awards and fellowships, including a National Endowment for the Arts grant and a Bunting Fellowship from the Radcliffe Institute. Her collections of poems include *Amphibious Weather* (Zephyr Press, 1981), *Deception Pass* (Alice James Books, 1984), *Gravida* (Four Way Books, 1995), and *False Horizon* (forthcoming from Four Way Books). She has collaborated with visual artist Katherine Kadish on two exhibitions, *Water Works* and *The Cape Split Cycle*. She is the director of the Creative Writing Program at Wheaton College (Norton, Massachusetts), where she also teaches creative writing and African Literature.

Wallace Stevens   (1879–1955), who commanded a large, loyal following among readers dedicated to the cause of poetry, believed "the poem refreshes the world." Born in Reading, Pennsylvania, Stevens attended Harvard University and New York Law School. He began practicing law in 1904 and then joined the legal department of a Connecticut insurance company, retiring as vice president of the firm. His challenging, complex poetry appeared in journals as early as 1914; his first collection, *Harmonium*, appeared in 1923. His second collection, *Ideas of Order*, was published thirteen years later.

Mark Strand   (born 1934), recipient of a MacArthur Foundation fellowship in 1985 and named U.S. poet laureate in 1990, has written nine books of poetry, three children's books, and a book of short stories. According to one critic, Strand's 1990 collection, *The Continuous Life*, showed him "at his absolute peak." As poet laureate, Strand found opportunity to display his comic flair, turning him, according to Larry Kart of Chicago Trade Books, into "the Steve Martin and Woody Allen of modern verse." Jane Candia Coleman summed up Strand's standing: "Mark Strand is not a poet for Everyone. His is not work that will be set to music or sung on the streets. The cursory reader will be bewildered, lost. But the reader who delves, who meets the poet half-way, will be rewarded by glimpses of a different world, that changeable one of dreams and the elusive beauty that haunts us all."

Sir John Suckling   (1609–1642), who has been called "the most skeptical and libertine of the Cavaliers," was born the son of the secretary of state to King James I. Suckling studied at Cambridge and then traveled throughout Europe. A courtier with a reputation of brilliant wit, Suckling wrote four plays and a number of lyric poems. He became embroiled in political intrigue, committing suicide in 1642.

May Swenson   (1919–1989), a child of immigrant Swedish parents, was born in Logan, Utah. After graduating from Utah State University, she came to New York City and worked as an editor. She has received many awards for her poetry, which is noted for its freshness of perspective and experimental form. Some of her poetry collection titles are *Another Animal* (1954), *Iconographs* (1970), and *Poems to Solve* (1966), a volume for children.

Jonathan Swift   (1667–1745), a towering figure in eighteenth-century English literature, was born in Dublin, Ireland, of English parents. His father died shortly before he was born, and his mother gave him over to the care of a nurse. He was a rebellious and angry youth who barely graduated from Trinity College in Dublin. Swift was ordained a priest of the Anglican Church, although he was more interested in politics than in the church. He wrote political tracts for the Whig Party and later for the Tories, becoming editor of the Tory newspaper. He castigated England's unfair treatment of Ireland and became a hero to the Irish. In 1726 he published *Gulliver's Travels,* a satirical masterpiece in an age of satire.

Alfred, Lord Tennyson   (1809–1892), poet laureate of Victorian England, gave voice to characteristic assumptions and aspirations of his contemporaries. Born the son of a clergyman, Tennyson was educated at Cambridge. His first published poems appeared in 1830; in 1842 he published two volumes that included "Morte d'Arthur" and "Ulysses." His *In Memoriam* (1850), written after the death of a close friend, mirrored the religious doubts and earnestness of his time. His "Idylls of the King" (1859) became required for generations of high school students.

Dylan Thomas   (1914–1953) called his poetry a record of his "struggle from darkness toward some measure of light." Born in Wales, Thomas had his only formal education in grammar school. When his first poetry collection appeared in 1932, he was hailed as a leading modern poet. His radio work in England and his numerous poetry readings at American college campuses made him a popular figure on both sides of the Atlantic. His passionate, visionary tone and wild flights of the imagination appealed to readers starved for mysticism and emotion. Alcoholism and lung ailments precipitated his early death. Thomas once said that his poems, "with all their crudities, doubts, and confusions, are written for the love of man and in Praise of God, and I'd be a damn fool if they weren't."

Quincy Troupe   (born 1943) founded the Watts Writers' Movement and has taught creative writing and black literature courses at UCLA and USC. He has also directed the Malcolm X Center in Los Angeles and the John Coltrane Summer Festival. In 1970 Troupe created and began editing *Confrontation. A Journal of Third World Literature.* His latest books of poems are *Weather Reports: New and Selected Poems* (1991) and *Avalanche* (1996). Also coauthor of *Miles: The Autobiography* and editor of *James Baldwin: The Legacy,* Troupe teaches at the University of California, San Diego.

Ukihashi   (17th century) was a Japanese woman poet. Her work has been translated by Kenneth Rexroth and Ikuko Atsumi.

David Wagoner   (born 1926), "a master technician" (Daniel Halpern), was born in Ohio and educated at Penn State and Indiana University. An award-winning poet and novelist, Wagoner taught English at several colleges and made his home in Seattle. He has been praised for his witty and deep perceptions, as well as his "skillful manipulation of language" (Halpern).

Alice Walker   (born 1944) has said, "All of my poems . . . are written when I have successfully pulled myself out of a completely numbing despair, and stand again in the sunlight." Born in the small town of Eatonsville, Georgia, Walker received her bachelor's degree in 1965 from Sarah Lawrence College. After graduating, she taught at several universities and worked for voter registration and welfare rights. Her novel *The Color Purple* (1982) made her the best-known black writer of her generation. In 1983, she published the essay collection *In Search of Our Mothers' Gardens.* Using language as catharsis and potential for growth is essential to Walker, who said, "No person is your friend (or kin) who demands your silence, or denies your right to grow and be perceived as fully blossomed as you were intended. Or who belittles in any fashion the gifts you labor so to bring into the world."

Bethlyn Madison Webster   (born 1964) is an artist, poet, and part-time teacher of English at the college level, working on her M.F.A. at California State University, Fresno. Her poem "Stamps" was recently nominated for a Pushcart Prize.

Bruce Weigl   (n. d.) On the faculty at Penn State, Bruce Weigl has written twelve volumes of poetry, the most recent of which is *Arch of the Circle* (1999). In his work the theme of war is always close at hand. Early on, the poet struggled with childhood abuse, then after the Vietnam war, with substance abuse. Through his poetry Weigl has become a one-man cultural bridge between Vietnam and the United States.

Walt Whitman   (1819–1892), a giant of American and world literature, successfully created a public persona as the poet of democracy and the voice of an expansive vision of America. Son of a carpenter and farmer, he spent much of his life as a journalist in Brooklyn, Manhattan, and Long Island. In 1855, he published the first edition of *Leaves of Grass,* a milestone of nineteenth-century American literature. He celebrated the varied scene of contemporary America: the steamers and railroads and ferries, the carpenters and pilots and farmers, the cities and plains and mountains. He once said, "The United States themselves are essentially the greatest poem." His use of rhythm as a fluid instrument of poetic structure went far beyond the conventional meter of the day. His work has symphonic qualities, based on repeated yet highly suggestive motifs. He dropped conventional poetic figures, drawing on his own experience for new metaphors. A private printing of *Leaves of Grass* was not widely received partly because it was a half-century ahead of its time. Although he remained relatively poor, the last decade of Whitman's life brought him wide recognition. Gay Wilson Allen notes that Whitman's poetry has been translated into every major language and that he had great influence on poets such as William Carlos Williams, Wallace Stevens, and Allen Ginsberg, "who was inspired by Whitman's bold treatment of sexuality."

Richard Wilbur   (born 1921) had won the first of two Pulitzer Prizes by the time he published his third volume of poetry. Born in New York City, he went to Amherst and to Harvard, becoming a professor of English at Wesleyan University. Wilbur has been called the thinking poet, and we cannot read his poems lightly. For him a poem is not just a vehicle for communicating but rather it is a created object having its own life: "The poem," he says, is an effort to express a knowledge imperfectly felt, to articulate relationships not quite seen, to make or discover some pattern in the world." Richard Wilbur respects the strictness of form: "The strength of the genie comes of his being confined in a bottle." Yet at the same time he is known for his play with sound by a daring originality of language. Appointed U.S. poet laureate in 1987, Wilbur also won a Pulitzer Prize for *Things of This World* (1956).

Miller Williams   (born 1930), born in Hoxie, Arkansas, and educated in the sciences, is described as a "poet who has entirely secured his own line and his own idiom. He has a lively eye, wit and analytic intelligence. His style is lean and spare, streamlined to add up a welter of fresh images and impressions at a remarkable velocity" (Laurence Lieberman). Among his numerous books of poems are titles such as *A Circle of Stones* (1964) and *Why God Permits Evil: Poems* (1977). In 1986 Williams published a prose work, *Patterns of Poetry: An Encyclopedia of Forms.* Joel Conarroe calls him "funny as hell. . . a rare phenomenon."

William Carlos Williams   (1883–1963), writer of fiction, essays, and poetry, also had a full-time career as a physician. Born in Rutherford, New Jersey, Williams attended preparatory schools in New York and Switzerland and studied medicine at the University of Pennsylvania, where he met Ezra Pound. With Pound's encouragement, Williams began publishing poetry. Winner of many prestigious awards, including a National Book Award and a Pulitzer Prize Williams worked in New Jersey as both a poet and a doctor until his death. Radically experimental in technique and form, his mature work was influenced by the imagist movement in its rejection of sentimentality and its reliance on the language of common speech, concrete, sensory experience, and emotional restraint.

Warren Woessner   (born 1944) A former R & B and soul music DJ, Woessner is a Minneapolis resident who doubles as a patent attorney in biotechnology as well as a poet. Woessner has published six volumes of poetry, has received a National Endowment for the Arts Fellowship, and has a hand in establishing *Abraxas,* a literary journal.

Edward Wolf   (n.d.) has published his work in a number of journals such as *New Writing from Gay and Lesbian San Francisco* and *Transfer 36.* He is working on *One Life, One Death,* a book about the AIDS epidemic.

William Wordsworth   (1770–1850), in collaboration with his friend Samuel Taylor Coleridge, published the collection *Lyrical Ballads* in 1798. The poems in this volume and its programmatic preface broke with the poetic conventions of the eighteenth century and signaled the beginning of the English Romantic movement. Wordsworth, born in Westmoreland, England, was educated at Cambridge. He for a time was caught up in the revolutionary fervor of the French Revolution but became a voice of conservatism in his later years. He is best remembered for his poems that turn to the healing influence of nature as the antidote to the ills of city civilization.

Sir Thomas Wyatt   (1503–1541) was the first to introduce into England Petrarch's sonnets of frustrated love, which started the sonnet vogue of the Elizabethan age. Born in Kent, England, Wyatt was educated at Cambridge. His father was a joint constable with the father of Anne Boleyn, who was to become the second wife of Henry VIII and the mother of Elizabeth, the future queen. Wyatt was assigned his first diplomatic mission by Henry VIII in 1525 and led a busy life as a courtier and diplomat.

William Butler Yeats   (1865–1939) became known for poems drawing on the heritage of Irish myth and legend and developed a rich symbolic language in his later poetry. Yeats, who won the Nobel Prize for literature in 1923, is widely recognized as one of the most outstanding poets of the English-speaking world. An Irish dramatist and poet, he was born in Dublin. In the 1890s he became involved in the developing revolution against British rule in Ireland. Cofounder of the Irish Literary Theatre, he wrote plays for its stage. From 1922—the year of the Proclamation of the Irish Free State—until 1928 he was a member of the Irish Senate. Poet Seamus Heaney says that "a Yeats poem gives the feeling of being empowered and thrilled."

Al Young   (born 1939) has said, "Long before the printed word and stuffy ideas about literature turned up in my life, and certainly long before I became the willing ward of schoolteachers, I was sleeping with words." His love for language began in his childhood home in Ocean Springs, Mississippi, where "talk was musical. Clusters of people were forever talking with one another, telling stories, sharing experiences, observations, jokes, riddles, conundrums, and swapping lies." Young believes in the Kenyan proverb "Talking with one another is loving one another." Because of his background, he "never outgrew the need for magic or the curative powers of language." Educated at the University of Michigan, Berkeley, and Stanford—where he was a Wallace E. Stegner creative writing fellow—Young has worked as a freelance musician and disc jockey, and has taught at Berkeley, Stanford, and the University of Washington. In 1982 he was named Distinguished Andrew Mellon Professor of Humanities at Rice University in Houston. In 1972 he began editing, with Ishmael Reed, the *Yardbird Reader* and *Quilt Magazine.* Young has published four novels and two plays in addition to four collections of poetry. Commenting on the power of poetry, Young said, "Word by word, line by line, season upon season, poetry keeps teaching me that the only time there is, is now."

GLOSSARY OF LITERARY TERMS

Abstraction A broad, general label or umbrella term for an idea like happiness, freedom, or honor. Abstractions often label important areas of human experience or thought, but they run the danger of becoming mere words if they are not anchored to concrete experience. See *concrete*.

Absurd See *theater of the absurd*.

Alexandrine A twelve-syllable line made up of six iambic feet (iambic hexameter). The Elizabethan poet Edmund Spenser used the alexandrine in his Spenserian stanza, which is composed of eight pentameter lines followed by an alexandrine. See *iamb*.

Allegory A work in which related symbols work together, with characters, events, or settings representing ideas or moral qualities. The characters of an allegory are often *abstractions* personified. Famous allegories include Spenser's *The Faerie Queene* and Bunyan's *The Pilgrim's Progress*.

Alliteration The repetition of the same sound (or similar sound) at the beginning of successive words, as in Tennyson's "He Clasps the Crag with Crooked hands." Alliteration was widely used in the Germanic epic and in Middle English poetry before end rhyme gradually took its place.

Allusion A brief mention that calls a character, event, or idea to the reader's mind. An allusion taps into associations and meanings already in the reader's memory. Poets and playwrights through the ages have used allusions to Greek mythology and to the Bible.

Ambiguity Intentional or unintentional double meanings. Intentional ambiguity can leave a poem or story open-ended. Formalist critics made multiple layers of possible meaning a major criterion of challenging poetry.

Anapest Two unaccented syllables followed by an accented one, as in New ROCHELLE. The following lines from Percy Bysshe Shelley's "The Cloud" are anapestic: "Like a CHILD from the WOMB, like a GHOST from the TOMB / I ARISE and unBUILD it AGAIN."

Antagonist Originally, the second major character in early Greek plays. The antagonist is the worthy opponent or counterforce that sets up a central conflict in a play or story, doing battle with or trying to thwart the *protagonist*.

Antithesis A playing off of opposites or a balancing of one term against another, as in the point/counterpoint statement, "Man proposes, God disposes." *Thesis* and *antithesis* in the original Greek mean "statement" and "counterstatement."

Antonym A word with the opposite or nearly the opposite meaning of another word. *Order* is an antonym of *chaos*. See *synonym*.

Apostrophe A solemn or dignified invocation addressing a divine being or a personified abstraction like Liberty or Justice.

1961

Archaic language   Language that is no longer in common use. Unlike *obsolete language,* archaic words and phrases have survived but have an old-fashioned flavor, as for instance *brethren* and *paramour.* Used intentionally, archaisms can re-create a past style or evoke a vanished era.

Archetype   A recurrent image that brings into play deep-seated associations anchored in universal patterns of experience. The Swiss psychoanalyst Carl Jung saw archetypes as rising from the collective unconscious of the human species; his followers trace the central role of archetypes in myth, religion, dream, and imaginative literature.

Assonance   Repetition of similar internal vowel sounds of final syllables, as in *break/fade, mice/flight, told/woe,* See *consonance.*

Autobiographical "I"   The personal voice through which poets share their personal experiences and feelings. Confessional poets use the autobiographical "I" to make public their private, often painful, experiences and observations. The first person pronoun in poetry or fiction is not always the autobiographical "I." The "I" may be a *persona* or assumed identity. See *confessional poetry, point of view,* and *speaker.*

Author biography   The study of an author's life for clues to the meaning of a literary work or for insight into the creative process. Much modern literary biography probes the traumas or dilemmas behind the public persona.

Ballad   A songlike narrative poem traditionally characterized by a recurring refrain and four-line stanzas rhyming *abcb.* Anonymous folk ballads were originally sung as the record of a notable exploit or calamity. From *balar,* "to dance," ballads are created both by individual composers and through communal activity. See *literary ballad.*

Blank verse   Unrhymed iambic pentameter. Marlowe's "mighty line" and the prevailing metrical form of Shakespeare's greatest plays. Also used for long poems by poets over the ages from Marlowe to Wordsworth to Frost.

Byplay   An action or gesture which takes place apart from the main action of the play, as in an aside, and which can prepare the audience for future conflict.

Caesura   A strong pause or a break within a line of verse, often creating a counter rhythm. From the Latin for "a cutting off."

Caricature   A comic distortion exaggerating key traits to make them ridiculous. From the Italian for "exaggeration," a caricature usually focuses on personal, physical qualities. Although caricature is most often associated with drawing, it can also refer to writing.

Carpe diem   Latin for "seize the day." A poetic convention urging us to make use of the passing day, to live for the moment. This theme was common in sixteenth- and seventeenth-century love lyrics, as in Robert Herrick's lines, "Gather ye rosebuds while ye may / Old Time is still a-flying, / And this same flower that smiles today, / Tomorrow will be dying."

Character   The representation of a person in a play, story, novel, or poem. A character who has a one-track personality, or who represents a stereotype, is often referred to as *flat.* A character who displays a realistically complex combination of traits—including mixed emotions, conflicting motivations, and divided loyalties—is often called *round.*

Characterization   The way in which an author portrays a character for the reader. Characterization can occur through author exposition about a character as well as through the character's actions, speech, and thoughts. In drama a character's thoughts can be revealed through *soliloquy.*

Chorus   In ancient Greek drama, a group of onlookers or citizens that comment on the action and serve as guides or interpreters for the audience. The chorus chants and dances at set intervals in the play. In Elizabethan drama, a single actor sometimes serves as a one-person chorus, reciting the prologue and epilogue and commenting between acts.

Circumlocution   Indirect, roundabout phrasing, such as calling a "home" a "primary residence." A circumlocution "takes the long way around."

Cliché   A term that has lost its freshness through overuse, such as "strong as an ox," "tip of the iceberg," and "American as apple pie." Overused situations or plot elements also can be regarded as clichés.

Climax   The highest point of interest or intensity in a literary work, reached after a series of preparatory steps. The climax is often the point in a story where the fortunes of the protagonist take an important turn.

Closure   A satisfying conclusion or sense of completion at the end of a work.

Comedy   The traditional genre that provides the alternative to the tragic view of life. Audiences for comedy expect happy endings, good fortune, and young love triumphing over obstacles. **High comedy** creates a spirit of mirth and festival; it delights in love talk and love dilemmas; it features high-spirited, quick-witted dialogue. **Low comedy** tends toward horseplay, pratfalls, and bawdry. See *comedy of manners, farce,* and *romantic comedy.*

Comedy of manners   A comedy that satirizes the stylized fashions and manners of sophisticated society. This type of comedy is characterized by jabs at convention and witty dialogue, or repartee. Some typical comedies of manners include Oliver Goldsmith's *She Stoops to Conquer,* Oscar Wilde's *The Importance of Being Earnest,* and Philip Barry's *The Philadelphia Story.* See *comedy.*

Comic relief   A moment of humor in a serious work. Comic relief provides a temporary break from emotional intensity and may, paradoxically, heighten the seriousness of the story. Shakespeare, for example, employed comic relief in the gravedigger scene in *Hamlet* (Act 5, Scene 1).

Conceit   An extended, ingenious imaginative comparison tracing the same metaphor—spring, the garden, the ship—into many related details or applications. Poets from Petrarch to Shakespeare and Donne wrote love poetry using elaborate conceits.

Concrete   Concrete images are vivid, graphic images that appeal strongly to the senses, as opposed to *abstractions.*

Concrete poetry   Poems that use the physical arrangement of words on a page to mirror meaning (for example, a poem about a bell that is bell-shaped). Concrete poetry takes advantage of the visible shapes of letters and words to create a picture.

Confessional poetry   Poetry that employs the *autobiographical "I"* as the poem's speaker for an often painful, public display of personal, private matters. During the 1960s and 1970s, confessional poets such as Anne Sexton, John Berryman, and Sylvia Plath began to provide an alternative to the detached ironic poetry that had long been fashionable. Although confessional poetry is most often associated with contemporary poets, poets over the ages, such as the ancient Greek poet Sappho, for instance, have employed confessional techniques.

Conflict   Conflict creates tension and suspense and is the heart of drama. For instance, a central character may be in conflict with another person, with a system of beliefs or values, with the gods, or with natural forces (**external conflict**). A character may be at war with himself or herself, with divided loyalties or contradictory motives pulling the character in different directions (**internal conflict**).

Connotation   The associations and attitudes called up by a word, as opposed to its *denotation* or straight, literal meaning. For instance, the words *scent* and *odor* both denote smell, but advertisers uses the different connotations of the words to make us buy either perfume or deodorant.

Consonance   Repetition of similar sounds in the final syllables of words, as in *torn/burn, add/read, heaven/given.* See *assonance.*

Context   The phrase, sentence, or passage in which a word occurs; the situation that helps give meaning to actions or behavior. Words, gestures, and actions have different meanings in different contexts.

Convention   The customary or established way of talking, writing, or behaving. Writers may follow the conventions of their time, but they may also give them a strong personal twist or rebel against them altogether.

Counterpoint   A counterstatement or countercurrent. A strong direct rejoinder pushing a trend or argument in the opposite direction. (In music, counterpoint is a countermelody played off against the dominant original melody.)

Couplet   Two rhymed lines of verse. If set aside or self-contained, the two rhymed lines are called a *closed couplet.*

Criticism   The systematic analysis of works of imaginative literature. Contemporary critical theory is an active and diverse field, with *formalist, psychoanalytic, feminist, Marxist,* and *deconstructionist* critics among others advancing rival views of literature.

Cumulative repetition   See *repetition.*

Dactyl   One stressed syllable followed by two unstressed syllables, as in BALtimore.

Dark humor   A paradoxical, sardonic form of humor that makes us see catastrophe, illness, or other events that usually defeat people in a comic light.

Deconstructionism   A fashionable postmodern critical perspective that goes beyond the surface structure or surface meanings of a work, lifting the disguises that may obscure its true dynamics or built-in contradictions.

Denotation   The literal definition of a word; its stripped-down meaning devoid of emotional overtones or *connotations.*

Dénouement   French for "untying," the *dénouement* is the wrapping up of major plot elements at the end of a play. The term implies an ingenious, satisfying outcome—for instance, the solution to a central dilemma.

Deus ex machina   Latin for "god from a machine." In the ancient Greek theater a contraption lowered a god or goddess onto the stage to intervene in the action and to work a last-minute solution. Thus, the phrase refers to any device, character, or event introduced suddenly to resolve a conflict in a literary work.

Dialectic   The playing off of opposing forces or points of view.

Dialects   The regional variations of a common language that are still mutually intelligible, although some actually border on becoming separate languages.

Dialogue   Verbal exchange between two or more people. In a literary work, dialogue may help establish the situation, delineate character, or focus attention on major themes.

Diction   The writer's choice and use of words.

Didacticism   Heavy reliance on ideas meant to instruct or improve the reader. The term is often used for overt or heavy-handed preaching or editorializing in a literary work.

Dramatic irony   Audience awareness of the meaning of words or actions unknown to one or more characters. Dramatic irony occurs when we are "in on" an event a character is not in on. In *Oedipus Rex,* the readers or viewers know that Oedipus has killed his father and married his mother, a situation Oedipus remains unaware of until the last scene.

Dramatic monologue   A lengthy first-person speech which enlightens the reader about the setting, the speaker's identity, and the dramatic situation.

Elegy   A poem of mourning and lamentation. Elegies are most often sustained, formal poems with a meditative, solemn mood. Walt Whitman's "When Lilacs Last in the Dooryard Bloomed" was an elegy on the death of President Lincoln.

Elizabethan Age   The English literary period named after Queen Elizabeth and lasting from 1558 until 1642, the year of the closing of the theaters. This "golden age" saw such literary figures as Shakespeare develop the beginnings of modern drama and saw an outburst of lyric poetry. Other notable names of the period include Sidney, Spenser, Marlowe, Jonson, and Donne.

Empathy   Imaginative sympathy that allows us to identify with the experience, situation, feelings, or motives of another.

End rhyme   The echo effect that makes the last words of two or more lines of poetry rhyme, as in Gwendolyn Brooks' "My last deFENSE / Is the present TENSE." See also *internal rhyme*.

End-stopped line   A line of poetry that ends with a period, colon, or semicolon. See *enjambment*.

Enjambment   The continuation of a sentence in a poem so that it spills over from one line to the next. "How like a winter has my absence been / From thee . . . (Shakespeare, Sonnet 97). See *end-stopped line*.

Epic poem   A long narrative poem that speaks to the listener in an elevated style and often embodies the central values of a civilization. The traditional epic celebrated the exploits of the tribe or nation and often focused on charismatic heroic leaders. Among epics rooted in age-old oral tradition are Homer's *Iliad* and *Odyssey*, the Old English *Beowulf*, the Spanish *El Cid*, and Virgil's *Aeneid*.

Epigram   A concise, cleverly worded remark making a pointed, witty statement. From the Greek for "inscription," an epigram may play off antithetical ideas, as in "Man proposes, God disposes."

Epiphany   A sudden flash of intuitive understanding when the true meaning of things and events is revealed. The term was coined by James Joyce, and epiphanies appear at the end of many of his stories, including "Araby."

Euphemism   From the Greek for "beautiful words." The use of pleasant-sounding language for harsh realities, often with the intention of sounding less offensive or more refined. Examples of euphemisms are calling garbage disposal "waste management" or calling death a "passing away."

Existentialism   An influential, pervasive twentieth-century philosophy that denies the existence of transcendent meanings and places the burden of giving meaning to their lives on individual human beings. French philosopher, playwright, and novelist Jean-Paul Sartre and French novelist Albert Camus were among prominent disseminators of existentialist thought.

Explication   The line-by-line explanation of a literary text. Explication differs from interpretation in that it usually refers to a literal, step-by-step scrutiny of the language of a work, as opposed to a broader, more subjective look at its overall significance.

Exposition   The part of a play or story that establishes setting and situation and that often introduces important characters and themes.

Extended (or sustained) metaphor   A metaphor traced into several related details, often becoming the central metaphor of a poem.

External evidence Evidence outside a piece of literature itself, examined in an attempt to understand a work's meaning. Characteristic themes in the author's other works or information found in the author's letters or interviews are common forms of external evidence.

Farce An exaggerated kind of low comedy that derives its humor from crude jokes, pratfalls and ineptitude, and rambunctious horseplay. See *comedy*.

Feminine (or double) rhyme Two-syllable rhyme, with the first syllable stressed and the second unstressed, as in *ocean/motion, started/parted*. See also *masculine rhyme*.

Feminist criticism Feminist critics have a special interest in how imaginative literature reflects the lives of women. Feminist scholars have rediscovered and reevaluated women writers of the past; they have focused on how women are marginalized or trivialized in much traditional literature written from a male perspective.

Figurative language Language using imaginative comparison rather than literal statement. See *metaphor, simile*.

Flashback A shifting back to events that took place at an earlier time, allowing the writer to break up straight chronological order by playing off memories of the past against the present.

Foil A character who serves as a contrast to a main character, thus highlighting or underscoring distinctive features of the other.

Folklore Traditional material—stories, legends, proverbs, riddles, charms, spells, folk songs, ballads—reflecting the customs and beliefs of a culture. Echoes of prehistoric myths and rituals often survive in the folklore of a people.

Foot The smallest unit of verse, usually made up of one stressed and one or more unstressed syllables. For different types of metric feet, see *iamb, trochee, dactyl, anapest,* and *spondee*.

Foreshadowing A hint pointing forward to a future development. For instance, foreshadowing may take the form of a mood created by the setting, of ominous hints concerning unsolved problems, of a sense of foreboding expressed by a character, or of frequent focus on an object fraught with symbolic meaning.

Formalist criticism Formalism in the tradition of the New Critics of the forties and fifties reacted against extrinsic approaches that shifted attention too routinely from the literary work to author biography, author psychology, or the sociological context. The New Critics insisted on close reading of the work itself, focusing on how features of form—image, metaphor, symbol, point of view, irony, paradox—gave shape to a poem or work of fiction as a whole.

Frame story A narrative which frames the main series of events, often by setting up an occasion for the narrator to tell the main story.

Free verse Poetry freed from the restraints of strong, regular meter and rhyme, developing instead its own individual pattern and free-flowing rhythm.

Freudian criticism See *psychoanalytic criticism*.

Genre A French word for "type" or "kind," used by critics to mark off traditional subdivisions of imaginative literature. Fiction, poetry, and drama are the three major traditional genres; subgenres include the novel, the short story, the epic, the lyric (further subdivided into categories like elegy, satire, or pastoral), tragedy, and comedy. Traditionalists used to set up rules or conventions for each genre; they objected to mixed genres like tragicomedy.

Ghazal A traditional Persian (Iranian) poetic form made up of sequences of five to fifteen related couplets.

Grotesque   A mixed genre combining the frightening and the ridiculous. The grotesque in literature or art caters to a taste for the bizarre, fantastic, and ominous.

Haiku   A widely practiced traditional Japanese poetic form of three lines of five, seven, and five syllables each. The haiku captures a moment in time, allowing a thought or image to linger in the memory. See also *tanka*.

Half-rhymes   Words that do not rhyme but distantly sound alike.

High comedy   See *comedy*.

Hubris   The overreaching pride of humans that leads to their tragic downfall. The word *hubris* comes from the Greek for "insolence" or "outrage." Hubris makes human beings forget their limitations and makes them challenge the gods. Oedipus, for example, challenged the gods by believing he could escape their prophecy.

Hyperbole   Extreme exaggeration, common in the love poetry of earlier centuries and the opposite of modern understatement. From the Greek for "excess." "Ah, she doth teach the torches to burn bright," says Shakespeare's hyperbolical Romeo.

Iamb   A two-syllable foot with the stress on the last syllable, as in DETROIT. Over the centuries, iambic meter with four or five beats to the line (iambic tetrameter and iambic pentameter) became the most common meter in poetry written in English.

Idiom   The characteristic, natural language of a group, or a phrase or way of expressing an idea that is an example of natural speech.

Image   Not just a vivid visual impression but more generally any concrete detail that speaks directly and vividly to our senses of sight, hearing, smell, taste, or touch. See *concrete*.

Incongruity   Things that clash or violate decorum. The metaphysical poets of the seventeenth century yoked incongruous, discordant elements to compel attention—mixing, for instance, the language of love with the technical language of map making. See also *paradox*.

Interlude   A short, humorous performance presented in the intervals between more serious dramatic entertainment.

Internal rhyme   Two or more words rhyming within a line of poetry rather than at the end of lines. Sometimes occur in combination with *end rhyme*.

Interpretation   Moving beyond line-by-line explication of a text to examine its major themes or larger meanings.

Intruding author   The distinctive feature of a narrative style that allows the author or an authorial persona to step into the story to interrupt the narrative and chat with the reader—for instance, to offer explanations, witty asides, or philosophical reflections. Nineteenth-century readers of fiction were used to the friendly presence of the author taking them into his or her confidence.

Inversion   The reversal of normal word order in a sentence ("*that* I will never do") or the reversal of the rhythmic stress in a poem, for instance by starting a line of iambic pentameter with a trochaic foot.

Irony   A wry, humorous effect produced when an overt or surface meaning is negated by a different meaning representing the writer's or speaker's true intention. ("Easier availability of assault weapons is just what this country needs.") *Verbal irony* refers to a deliberate contrast between what is said and what is meant. *Irony of situation* refers to a contrast between what we expected to happen and what really happened, especially when we should have known better. See also *dramatic irony*.

Jungian criticism   See *myth criticism*.

Literary ballad   A poem written by a poet reviving or imitating the style of the traditional anonymous folk ballad.

Low comedy   See *comedy*.

Lyric   Now a general label for a fairly short poem expressing personal thought and emotion, as contrasted with *narrative poetry* or the traditional *epic*.

Malapropism   An inadvertent and often hilarious misuse of a word. The practice is named after Mrs. Malaprop, in Sheridan's play *The Rivals,* who said things like "*illiterate* him . . . from your memory."

Marxist criticism   Marxist and other politically engaged critics focus on how literature reflects the social and political arrangements that shape people's lives. They call attention to how writers show their origin from or allegiance to a social class, to how writers serve or challenge the interests of the power structure, and to how writers ignore or critique patterns of exploitation and oppression.

Masculine (or single) rhyme   A rhyme that makes only the final accented syllables of two or more words rhyme—for instance, *high/sky, leave/grieve, renown/gown*. Different from *feminine rhyme*.

Melodrama   A wildly popular kind of drama or fiction pitting good against evil and employing sensational plot twists and tear-jerking devices. Traditional melodramas present good and evil stock characters, with the audience weeping over the persecution of wronged innocence, hissing dyed-in-the-wool malefactors, and cheering when the villains are brought to justice. See also *sentimentality*.

Metaphor   An imaginative, often bold or thought-provoking comparison treating one thing as if it were another, without the use of *like* or *as,* as in these Emily Dickinson lines: "Hope is the thing with feathers / That perches in the soul." See *extended metaphor, organizing metaphor,* and *simile*.

Metaphysical poets   Poets of the seventeenth century known for their bold imagery, complex demanding form, and abundant reliance on incongruity, paradox, and irony. Metaphysical poets including John Donne, Andrew Marvell, and George Herbert were rediscovered early in the twentieth century by moderns rebelling against jingle poets, Victorian uplift, and versified sentimentality.

Meter   The underlying beat that in much traditional poetry regularizes the natural rhythms of speech. *Trimeter* is meter with three stressed syllables to the line, *tetrameter* has four stressed syllables, *pentameter* has five, and *hexameter* has six.

Metonymy   A figure of speech that makes a term closely related to something serve as its substitute. For instance, the word *sword* by extension means "military career" in the line "He abandoned the sword." See also *synechdoche*.

Minimalism   A contemporary style of writing that tries to eliminate all rhetoric and emotion or at least to reduce these elements to bare essentials. Minimalist writers include Anne Beattie and Raymond Carver.

Modernism   A movement of the early twentieth century that rebelled against self-approving Victorian earnestness in the arts or literature generally and against versified noble sentiments in poetry in particular. In their search for new contemporary modes of expression, the modernists rejected flowery artificial language and began using experimental techniques, including *stream of consciousness* in fiction and *free verse* in poetry. Pioneering early modernists included James Joyce, Ernest Hemingway, Virginia Woolf, Ezra Pound, and T. S. Eliot. See also *postmodernism*.

Monologue   An extended solo speech by a character in a play (or sometimes a poem). A monologue, since it is typically heard by or directed at other characters, may be less of a private revelation of personal thought and feeling than a *soliloquy*.

Mood   A pervasive emotional quality or psychological cast of a work, which may be created by literary devices including *tone, imagery,* and *setting.*

Morality play   A medieval form of religious drama, with personified abstractions such as Shame, Mercy, and Conscience teaching religious and moral lessons. See also *allegory.*

Myth criticism   Myth critics in the tradition of Jung and his followers see imaginative literature as growing out of age-old rituals that acted out the myths or invoked the archetypes wired into the collective unconscious of the human species.

Narrator   The person speaking to us in a story or telling the story. Twentieth-century critics have paid close attention to the role of the narrator in contemporary fiction. See *point of view, reflector,* and *speaker.*

Naturalism   A literary movement in the late nineteenth and early twentieth centuries that went beyond realism to give readers unvarnished portrayals of nature in the raw. Naturalists set out to right the balance by providing frank portrayals of harsh realities; these were glossed over in more genteel or euphemistic literature. Widely read and influential representatives of the naturalistic movement include the French novelist Émile Zola and the Americans Jack London, Stephen Crane, and John Steinbeck.

Neoclassicism   A dominant eighteenth-century style turning to the art and literature of classical Greek and Roman work for models and inspiration. Neoclassical writers preached that sound judgment should guide and restrain the poetic imagination. They prized order, clarity, economic wording, logic, refinement, and decorum. Theirs was an age of rationalism, wit, and satire. High priests of the neoclassical spirit in literature were Alexander Pope and Samuel Johnson.

New Critics   See *formalist criticism.*

Novel   A work of narrative prose fiction, generally considerably longer and more complex than a short story, with a central character or group of characters whose experiences the reader may follow through a lifetime. The novel, often published in installments in magazines, began to build up a large reading audience in the eighteenth and nineteenth centuries, with favorite authors such as Jane Austen and Charles Dickens eventually read by millions around the world.

Novella   A pointed story shorter than a full-length novel but longer than a traditional short story.

Obsolete language   Words, or meanings of words, that are no longer in use, like *fond* in the sense of "foolish."

Octave   A set of eight lines, such as the first eight lines linked by interlacing rhymes in the traditional sonnet.

Ode   An elaborately crafted, stately poem fit for solemn subjects, often written in imitation of ancient Greek models.

Onomatopoeia   The use of words that seem to sound out their meanings, such as *pop, hiss,* or *buzz.*

Open form   A poetic form abandoning the constraints of regular rhyme, meter, line length, or stanza form.

Oral history   A cultural tradition of passing spoken stories from one generation to the next, often combining myth, history, and current events.

Organizing (or controlling) metaphor   A single extended metaphor that gives shape to a poem as a whole.

Ottava rima   From the Italian for "eighth rhyme." A finely crafted stanza consisting of eight iambic pentameter lines with the rhyme pattern *abababcc.*

Pantomime   Acting that relies solely on gestures or body language rather than words to communicate a story.

Paradox   An apparent contradiction that, on second thought, illuminates a truth. See also *incongruity, irony.*

Parallelism   The repetition of similar or identical structures to emphasize connections between related ideas ("I came, I saw, I conquered").

Paraphrase   Restating someone else's ideas in your own words.

Para-rhyme   See *slant rhyme.*

Parody   A humorous, sometimes affectionate and sometimes mocking imitation, exaggerating or aping characteristic features.

Pastoral   A poetic tradition offering harried city dwellers a nostalgic vision of the idealized simplicity and leisure of country life. Pastorals were first written by the Greeks and continue to be written today. Traditional pastorals dwelled on the love games of make-believe shepherds and shepherdesses but often also became a vehicle for social criticism.

Pathos   A quality in literature or art that arouses pity, sympathy, tenderness, or sorrow. From the Greek for "suffering" and "passion," pathos usually applies to a helpless character who suffers passively.

Peripety   A sudden reversal of fortune for a protagonist, brought on for instance by an unexpected discovery of a long hidden or ignored truth. From the Greek for "to change suddenly."

Persona   The assumed identity the writer presents when speaking to us in poetry or fiction. The persona may be close to the real-life personality of the writer, but it may also be far removed from it, serving perhaps as a mask or disguise.

Personification   Figurative language that endows something nonhuman with human qualities, as in "the trees *whispered* in the wind."

Petrarchan sonnet   A dominant Italian form of the sonnet practiced by Petrarch and imitated by his English translators and admirers. The Petrarchan sonnet tends to have a turning point, or turn, after the first two quatrains before the concluding sestet.

Plot   The chain of events in fiction or drama. A plot may be tightly structured, with a chain of cause and effect leading to a seemingly inevitable conclusion. However, it may also keep readers or spectators in suspense or surprise them with unexpected twists and turns. Plots of traditional novels were often leisurely, with the author exploring byways or indulging in detours, following the slow meandering rhythm of life. Twentieth-century writers have often broken up traditional plot structure with flashbacks, free association, or broken-mirror effects. See also *flashback, subplot.*

Poetic diction   Poetic language more elevated and refined than ordinary speech. Often used for an artificial eighteenth-century style tending toward euphemism and circumlocution.

Point of view   The vantage point from which we see the events of a story; the angle from which a story is told. With a **first-person** point of view, one of the characters narrates the story, seeing and knowing only what that individual can observe from his or her limited point of view. With a **third-person omniscient** point of view, the writer may write as an "all-seeing" author, knowing not only the behavior but also the private thoughts and feelings of the characters. With a **third-person limited** point of view, the writer focuses on the actions and thoughts of only some of the characters. With a **third-person objective** point of view, the writer acts as the impartial observer, offering little or no editorial comment.

Polarity   The setting up and playing off of polar opposites as a major organizing element in our perception of reality and in the patterning of imaginative literature.

Postmodernism   An umbrella term for critical approaches that discount surface meaning and look in a literary work for instance for an implied critique of the limitations of language or the writer's craft.

Problem play   A play in the tradition of the Norwegian playwright Henrik Ibsen, making the audience confront contemporary social problems or issues and often challenging conventional thinking and social mores.

Prose poem   A passage printed like prose but using poetic imagery or asking for concentrated attention like a poem.

Protagonist   The lead actor or principal figure in drama or fiction. The confrontation between the protagonist and the antagonist, the second most important character, is often at the heart of the dramatic conflict in a play. See *antagonist*.

Psychoanalytic criticism   Psychoanalytic critics in the tradition of Freud and his followers look in literature for a reflection of deep-seated psychic conflicts, typically resulting from the repression of our instinctual selves. The symbolic action of a poem or play may show the interplay of the id (the anarchic repressed unconscious self), the ego (the overlay of conscious moral rules and inhibitions), and the superego (the society or moral system as a whole).

Pun   A type of word play, exploiting the similar sense or sound of words or sometimes different meanings of the same word, as when a punster calls a congested bridge the "car-strangled spanner."

Quatrain   A set of four lines, like the two sets of four lines that form the opening part of a Petrarchan sonnet.

Reader response   Reader response criticism calls special attention to what readers bring to the reading of a poem, a story, a play. A poem does not exist as dead letters on a page; it comes to life as its readers decode the text, relating it to their own world of experience and meanings.

Realism   A late-nineteenth-century literary movement that reacted against both the Romantic idealizing of nature and Victorian moral uplift. It emphasized instead the faithful rendering of ordinary human experience. Pioneers included the Norwegian playwright Henrik Ibsen and the British novelists George Eliot (Marian Evans) and Thomas Hardy. Playwrights like Arthur Miller continued the tradition of realistic drama.

Recurrence   The reappearance of themes or key elements, serving to echo issues and concerns introduced earlier.

Reflector   A person through whose eyes we see the events of a story. Although this is often the narrator, it can also be a character within the story if important information is communicated through his or her perceptions or thoughts.

Refrain   In much folk song or ballad, a line (or group of lines) that comes back or echoes at intervals in a poem, often at the end of each stanza.

Reiteration   Purposeful, insistent repetition in poetry or prose to reinforce a basic point.

Repartee   The quick exchange of pointed, witty remarks, with characters trading clever quips or barbed personal comments.

Repetition   Recurrence of the same word or phrase used to highlight or emphasize something in a poem or story. Poets often use purposeful cumulative repetition to build up to a climactic effect.

Revenge tragedy   A form of tragedy going back to the Roman playwright Seneca and popular in Shakespeare's time. The play may start with the ghost of a murdered victim clamoring for revenge, lead into a plot of intrigue revolving around plots and counterplots, and end with the avenger taking the perpetrators down with him to bloody death. Shakespeare's *Hamlet* fits key criteria of the traditional revenge tragedy.

Rhetoric   Traditionally, the effective use of language for purposes of persuasion, especially in politics and law. The early Greek philosopher Aristotle published a first major influential treatise on the art of rhetoric, or effective public speech. The term is now used for the study and practice of effective language both spoken and written. The term has acquired a pejorative alternative meaning as the result of the abuse of language by windbags and manipulators.

Rhyme   The echo effect produced when a writer repeats the same sounds at the ends of words: *moon/June, delighted/indicted*. See *end rhyme, feminine rhyme, half-rhyme, internal rhyme, masculine rhyme, sight rhyme, slant rhyme,* and *triple rhyme*.

Romantic comedy   A type of comedy focusing on love as a chief element of the plot. Romantic comedies may play with the obstacles in the path of young love but tend to culminate in easy reconciliations, happy endings, and multiple marriages.

Romanticism   An artistic revolt against the conventions of the fashionable formal, civilized, and refined neoclassicism of the eighteenth century. Whereas Neoclassicism stressed the "order in beauty," Romanticism stresses the "strangeness in beauty" (Walter Pater). The Romantics dropped conventional poetic diction and forms in favor of freer forms and bolder language. They preached a return to nature, elevated sincere feeling over the dry intellect, and often shared in the revolutionary fervor of the late eighteenth century. Blake, Coleridge, Wordsworth, Keats, Shelley, and Byron are prominent in the pantheon of English Romantic poets.

Sarcasm   A bitter or cutting form of verbal irony.

Satire   The use of humor and often sharp biting wit to critique human misconduct or ridicule stupidity, vice, and folly. Offenders are measured against an implied standard of humane behavior.

Scansion   A system for charting the underlying beat, or meter, of a literary work.

Sentimentality   Working on the emotions of an audience, for instance through exploiting sympathy for helpless victims and through self-righteous indignation at dastardly villains. Sentimentality allows people to bask in the warm glow of self-approving emotions.

Sestet   A six-line poetic stanza.

Setting   Place and time, often providing more than a mere backdrop for the action of a story or play.

Shakespearean sonnet   The typical Shakespearean sonnet has three quatrains followed by a concluding couplet. See *sonnet*.

Sight rhyme   Words that coincide in spelling but not in sound, like *come* and *home*.

Simile   An imaginative comparison signaled by such words as *like, as,* or *as if:* "My love is like a red, red rose." Unlike the implied comparison of a metaphor, a simile says outright that something is like something else.

Slang   Extremely, often aggressively informal language suggesting complete disregard for polite conventions.

Slant (or para-) rhyme   The near rhyming of words that distantly sound alike. See *assonance* and *consonance*.

Soliloquy A solo speech a character makes in a drama revealing his or her feelings and inner conflicts. During a soliloquy, a character usually stands alone on stage, talking without addressing another character. See *monologue*.

Sonnet An elaborately crafted fourteen-line poem in iambic pentameter. The Petrarchan sonnet starts with an eight-line segment, or octave, with an interlaced *abbaabba* rhyme scheme, followed by a sestet (six-line segment) of *cdcdee* or proposition that is answered in the sestet. The Shakespearean sonnet generally is arranged as three quatrains (four-line segments) and a couplet (two lines), with the typical rhyme scheme of *abab/cdcd/efef/gg*. The Spenserian sonnet uses three quatrains and a couplet like the Shakespearean sonnet but employs a linking rhyme scheme more similar to the Petrarchan sonnet: *abab/bcbc/cdcd/ee*. See *sonnet sequence*.

Sonnet sequence A group of sonnets exploring related themes, often centering originally on the sorrows of unrequited love. Petrarch, Sidney, Spenser, and Shakespeare are among sonneteers who wrote extended sonnet sequences or "cycles." A once widely read, later sonnet sequence is Elizabeth Barrett Browning's *Sonnets from the Portuguese*.

Speaker The voice speaking in a poem or story, as distinct from the author as a person. Also called "persona."

Spenserian sonnet See *sonnet*.

Spenserian stanza A nine-line stanza used by Edmund Spenser. It follows the rhyming pattern *ababbcbcc;* the first eight lines are pentameter and the last is an alexandrine (iambic with six stresses).

Spondee A rare metrical foot of two stressed syllables, as in one possible pronunciation of HONG KONG.

Sprung rhythm An irregular, syncopated rhythmic pattern developed by Gerard Manley Hopkins, with stressed syllables followed by a varying number of unstressed syllables.

Stanza A grouping of related lines with a characteristic metrical and rhyme scheme to be repeated or varied in subsequent stanzas.

Stress Accent or emphasis that makes one syllable stand out from the others in a word or phrase.

Stream of consciousness A narrative technique mirroring the flow of sensations, thought, and feelings in our minds—a kaleidoscopic mix of fleeting images, bodily sensations, memories, and half-finished trains of thought.

Stock character A conventional, easily recognizable character; a stereotype. Stock characters of traditional comedy include the skinflint, the grouch, the hypochondriac, and the amorous old man. In popular modern plays, stock characters may include the meddling in-laws, the oversolicitous ethnic mother, or the studious "nerd."

Style At its best, an author's unmistakable personal way of using language, looking at the world, and giving shape to a work of literature. (An author's style may however also be imitative, colorless, or impersonal.)

Subplot Secondary story lines or conflicts that run parallel to the main plot. A subplot may reinforce a work's central theme, such as filial ingratitude in Shakespeare's *King Lear*—the betrayal of a loyal parent by disloyal offspring.

Symbol An object or action that has acquired a meaning beyond itself. Traditional symbols carry a range of familiar associations, but writers may develop their own language of private symbols that readers have to respond to and decode.

Synecdoche   A figure of speech that uses the part to stand for the whole, or the whole to stand for the part: *wheels* to mean "car" and *hired hands* to mean "hired people." See also *metonymy*.

Synonym   A word that has the same or nearly the same meaning as another, such as *liberty* and *freedom*. See also *antonym*.

Tanka   A Japanese poetic form that, like haiku, fixes a moment in time, but is five lines long: three lines of five, seven, and five syllables each and two lines of seven syllables.

Tercet   A set of three lines.

Theater of the Absurd   Drama pioneered by playwrights like Eugène Ionesco, Samuel Beckett, and Edward Albee, rejecting the linear, logical surface of realistic plays as artificial. Absurdist plays mirror the tragicomic gropings of moderns doomed to disappointment in the search for meaning. "Conceived in perplexity and spiritual anguish, the theater of the absurd portrays not a series of connected incidents telling a story but a pattern of images presenting people as bewildered beings in an incomprehensible universe" (Hugh Holman).

Theme   A recurring, unifying subject, idea, or motif—like the breakdown of the family, or the alienation of young people from their parents. However, more specifically and pointedly, the term *theme* may stand for the answer that a literary work as a whole seems to give to the questions it raises (what the work as a whole seems to say *about* family, or alienation). Twentieth-century writers have generally been reluctant to spell out a thematic message in so many words, preferring to let readers ponder implied or suggested meanings.

Thesis   In expository prose, a concise, memorable summing up of what a writer is trying to say or setting out to prove. A thesis statement often appears toward the beginning of a paper or article as a preview or program, setting directions and steering the attention of the reader. However, in a more inductive kind of writing the writer may build toward the thesis and present it as a justified conclusion at the end.

Tone   The human quality or emotional coloring that reveals a writer's attitude toward the subject and toward the reader, ranging from lighthearted or frivolous to bitter or gloomy.

Tragedy   One of the two traditional Greek dramatic genres. Growing out of rituals honoring the god Dionysos, ancient Greek tragedy dramatized stories about lethal conflicts, often among persons closely linked by kinship or marriage. The traditional tragedy recounts the fall of heroes or persons of high degree, as in the fall of a king in Sophocles' *Oedipus Rex* and Shakespeare's *Macbeth*. Modern students of tragedy have focused on such topics as the fateful choices faced by tragic protagonists, the journey toward self-awareness, or archetypal patterns of experience acted out by the tragic hero. See also *revenge tragedy* and *tragic flaw*.

Tragic flaw   A fatal flaw or shortcoming in an otherwise admirable tragic hero. Critics following the lead of the early Greek philosopher Aristotle (in his *Poetics*) use the tragic flaw to explain or justify the downfall of an otherwise outstanding individual. This flaw may be anything from impious pride to uncontrollable anger, jealousy, or indecision. See *hubris*.

Tragicomedy   A mixed genre in which the tragic and comedic elements contend. A tragicomedy, for instance, may take the audience to the brink of tragic events but then end happily, like a comedy. It is likely to have noble and lowlife characters mingle, moving from elevated sentiments to coarse humor.

Transition   A link that smoothly moves the reader from one stanza, paragraph, or idea to the next.

Triple rhyme   Rhyme that makes the whole of a three-syllable word (or phrase) rhyme. The rhyming stressed syllable is followed by two unstressed syllables, as in *moralities/realities* or *meticulous/ridiculous*.

Trochee   A two-syllable metrical foot with the stress on the first syllable (BOSTON). The following example of trochaic meter is from Coleridge: "TROchee TRIPS from LONG to SHORT."

Understatement   A deliberate playing down of the significance and emotional impact of events. Many twentieth-century writers, suspicious of arm-waving and emoting, have cultivated an understated, detached, "cool" modern style. See *tone*.

Vignette   A sketch or brief narrative that focuses on a character or event. It may be a separate whole or serve as a sidelight in a larger work.

Villanelle   A highly crafted traditional poem with songlike or balladlike qualities, the villanelle is a nineteen-line poetic form employing only two rhymes, repeated again and again. Two lines recur at set intervals: Line 1 is repeated at lines 6, 12, and 18; line 3 at lines 9, 15, and 19. The first and third lines return as a rhymed couplet at the end. These intermeshing rhymes link five tercets rhymed *aba*. The poem ends with a quatrain rhymed *abaa*.

Word play   Witty or clever use of words. See also *pun*.

CREDITS

Text

Achebe, Chinua. "Why the Tortoise's Shell is not Smooth" from THINGS FALL APART by Chinua Achebe. Reprinted by permission of Heinemann Educational Publishers.

Alvarez, Julia. "Snow" from HOW THE GARCIA GIRLS LOST THEIR ACCENTS. Copyright © 1991 by Julia Alvarez. Published by Plume, an imprint of Dutton Signet, a division of Penguin USA and originally in hardcover by Algonquin Books of Chapel Hill. Reprinted by permission of Susan Bergholz Literary Services, New York. All rights reserved.

Anderson, Sherwood. "Paper Pills" from WINESBURG, OHIO by Sherwood Anderson, copyright 1919 by B. W. Huebsch; copyright 1947 by Eleanor Copenhaver Anderson. Used by permission of Viking Penguin, a division of Penguin Putnam Inc.

Ashbery, John. "At North Farm" from A WAVE by John Ashbery. Copyright © 1981, 1982, 1983, 1984 by John Ashbery. Published by Viking Penguin, 1984. Reprinted by permission of Georges Borchardt, Inc.

Atwood, Margaret. "Dreams of the Animals" from SELECTED POEMS 1966–1984 by Margaret Atwood. Copyright © Margaret Atwood 1990. Reprinted by permission of Oxford University Press Canada. "Dreams of the Animals" from PROCEDURES FOR UNDERGROUND, SELECTED POEMS 1965–1975. Copyright © 1976 by Margaret Atwood. Reprinted by permission of Houghton Mifflin Company. All rights reserved. "Elegy for the Giant Tortoises" from THE ANIMALS IN THAT COUNTRY, SELECTED POEMS 1965–1975 by Margaret Atwood. Copyright © Oxford University Press Canada 1968. Copyright © 1976 by Margaret Atwood. Reprinted by permission of Houghton Mifflin Company and Oxford University Press Canada. All rights reserved. "Bread" is part of the compilation of short fiction GOOD BONES AND SIMPLE MURDERS by Margaret Atwood. Copyright © 1994 by O.W. Toad, Ltd. Published in the U.S. by Doubleday Dell. Reprinted by permission of Phoebe Larmore.

Auden, W. H. "Musée des Beaux Arts", copyright 1940 and renewed 1968 by W. H. Auden, from W. H. AUDEN: THE COLLECTED POEMS by W. H. Auden. Used by permission of Random House, Inc. "The Unknown Citizen" from COLLECTED POEMS by W. H. Auden, edited by Edward Mendelson. Copyright © 1940 and renewed 1968 by W. H. Auden. Reprinted by permission of Random House, Inc. Lines beginning "The galleries are full of music..." from "The Dog Beneath the Skin" in THE ENGLISH AUDEN, edited by Edward Mendelson. Reprinted by permission of Faber & Faber Ltd.

Bambara, Toni Cade. "The Lesson" from GORILLA, MY LOVE by Toni Cade Bambara. Copyright © 1972 by Toni Cade Bambara. Reprinted by permission of Random House, Inc. Excerpt from "Trying to Stay Centered" in BLACK WOMEN WRITERS AT WORK, edited by Claudia Tate. Oldcastle Books, 1985. Reprinted by permission of the Audrey Wolf Literary Agency.

Malamud, Bernard. "The Magic Barrel" from THE MAGIC BARREL by Bernard Malamud. Copyright © 1950, 1958, renewed 1977, 1986 by Bernard Malamud. Reprinted by permission of Farrar, Straus and Giroux, LLC.

Mamet, David. THE CRYPTOGRAM. Copyright © 1995 by David Mamet. Reprinted by permission of Vintage Books, a Division of Random House, Inc.

Masefield, John. "Cargoes" copyright 1912 by The Macmillan Company; renewed © 1940 by John Masefield. Reprinted by permission of The Society of Authors as the literary representative of the Estate of John Masefield.

Mason, Bobbie Ann. "Shiloh" from SHILOH AND OTHER STORIES by Bobbie Ann Mason. Copyright © 1982 by Bobbie Ann Mason. Reprinted by permission of HarperCollins Publishers, Inc. "Shiloh" originally appeared in THE NEW YORKER.

McGlathery, James M. Excerpt from "Desire's Persecutions in Kafka's 'Judgement,' 'Metamorphosis,' and 'A Country Doctor' " in PERSPECTIVES ON CONTEMPORARY LITERATURE. 7 (1981). Reprinted by permission of David Hershberg. University of Louisville.

Meinke, Peter. "Sunday at the Apple Market" from INLET (Virginia Wesleyan College). Reprinted by permission. Lines from "When I with You" from THE NIGHT TRAIN AND THE GOLDEN BIRD by Peter Meinke. Copyright © 1977 by Peter Meinke. Reprinted by permission of the University of Pittsburgh Press.

Meredith, William. "A Major Work" from PARTIAL ACCOUNTS: NEW AND SELECTED POEMS by William Meredith. Copyright © 1987 by William Meredith. Published by Alfred A. Knopf. Inc. Reprinted by permission of the author.

Merrill, James. "Charles on Fire" from SELECTED POEMS: 1946-1985 by James Merrill. Copyright © 1992 by James Merrill. Reprinted by permission of Alfred A. Knopf.

Merwin, W. S. "Separation" from THE MOVING TARGET. Copyright © 1963 by W. S. Merwin. Reprinted by permission of The Wylie Agency. Excerpt from "Introduction" and lines from "Meeting an Astronomer" in TRILOGY by Diane Wakoski. Copyright © 1962, 1966, 1967, 1974 by Diane Wakoski. Reprinted by Doubleday, a division of Bantam Doubleday Dell Publishing Group, Inc.

Millay, Edna St. Vincent. "Childhood is the Kingdom Where Nobody Dies," "I, Being Born a Woman and Distressed," "An Ancient Gesture," "Pity Me Not Because the Light of Day" and sestet from "Oh, Oh, You Will Be Sorry for That Word" from COLLECTED POEMS by Edna St. Vincent Millay. From COLLECTED POEMS, HarperCollins. Copyright © 1923, 1934, 1951, 1954, 1982 by Edna St. Vincent Millay and Norma Millay Ellis. All rights reserved. Reprinted by permission of Elizabeth Barnett, literary executor.

Miller, Arthur. From DEATH OF A SALESMAN by Arthur Miller, copyright 1949, renewed © 1977 by Arthur Miller. Used by permission of Viking Penguin, a division of Penguin Putnam, Inc. "Preface to the 50th Anniversary Edition", copyright © 1999 by Arthur Miller, from DEATH OF A SALESMAN by Arthur Miller. Used by permission of Viking Penguin, a division of Penguin Putnam Inc.

Miller, Vassar. "The New Icarus" from WAGE WAR ON SILENCE. Copyright © 1960 by Vassar Miller. Reprinted by permission of Wesleyan University Press.

Milosz, Czeslaw. "Incantation" from THE SEPARATE NOTEBOOKS by Czeslaw Milosz. Copyright © 1984 by Czeslaw Milosz Inc. Reprinted by permission of HarperCollins Publishers Inc.

Mirikitani, Janice. "For My Father" from SHEDDING SILENCE by Janice Mirikitani. Copyright © 1987 by Janice Mirikitani. Used by permission of Celestial Arts, P.O. Box 7123, Berkeley, CA 94707.

Mishima, Yukio. "Swaddling Clothes" from DEATH IN MIDSUMMER by Yukio Mishima, translated by Ivan Morris, from DEATH IN MIDSUMMER. Copyright ©

Richardson, H. Edward and Shroyer, Frederick B. H. Edward Richardson and Frederick B. Shroyer. Excerpt from MUSE OF FIRE: APPROACHES TO POETRY by H. Edward Richardson and Frederick B. Shroyer. Copyright © 1971 by Alfred A. Knopf, Inc. Reprinted by permission of Alfred A. Knopf, Inc.

Rilke, Rainer Maria. "The Panther" from SELECTED POEMS OF RAINER MARIA RILKE, edited and translated by Robert Bly. Copyright © 1981 by Robert Bly. Reprinted by permission of HarperCollins Publishers, Inc.

Rios, Alberto. "The Vietnam Wall," From THE LIME ORCHARD WOMAN. Copyright © 1988 by Alberto Rios. Reprinted with the permission of Sheep Meadow Press.

Robison, Mary. "Yours" from AN AMATEUR'S GUIDE TO THE NIGHT by Mary Robison. Copyright © 1983 by Mary Robison. Reprinted by permission of Alfred A. Knopf, Inc.

Roethke, Theodore. "My Papa's Waltz", copyright 1942 by Hearst Magazines, Inc., from THE COLLECTED POEMS OF THEODORE ROETHKE by Theodore Roethke. Used by permission of Doubleday, a division of Random House, Inc. "The Bat", copyright 1938 by Theodore Roethke, "The Waking", copyright 1953 by Theodore Roethke, "I Knew a Woman", copyright 1954 by Theodore Roethke, from THE COLLECTED POEMS OF THEODORE ROETHKE by Theodore Roethke. Used by permission of Doubleday, a division of Random House, Inc.

Rose, Wendy. "I Expected My Skin and My Blood to Ripen" (1977). From BONE DANCE: NEW AND SELECTED POEMS 1965–1993. Published by University of Arizona Press. Reprinted by permission of Malki Museum, Banning, CA.

Sappho. "Letter to Anaktoria" excerpt from "Invocation to Aphrodite" from GREEK LYRICS, 2nd ed., translated by Richmond Lattimore. Copyright © 1949, 1955, 1960 by Richard Lattimore. Reprinted by permission of the University of Chicago Press.

Schultz, Philip. "Laughter", from LIKE WINGS by Philip Schultz, copyright © 1972, 1973, 1975, 1976, 1977, 1978 by Philip Schultz. Used by permission of Viking Penguin, a division of Penguin Putnam Inc.

Sexton, Anne. "The Truth the Dead Know" and "To A Friend Whose Work Has Come to Triumph" from ALL MY PRETTY ONES by Anne Sexton. Copyright © 1962 by Anne Sexton, renewed 1990 by Linda G. Sexton. Reprinted by permission of Houghton Mifflin Company. All rights reserved. "The Starry Night", from ALL MY PRETTY ONES by Anne Sexton. Copyright © 1962 by Anne Sexton, renewed 1990 by Linda G. Sexton. Reprinted by permission of Houghton Mifflin Company. All rights reserved. "Her Kind" and "Ringing the Bells", from TO BEDLAM AND PART WAY BACK by Anne Sexton. Copyright © 1960 by Anne Sexton, renewed 1988 by Linda G. Sexton. Reprinted by permission of Houghton Mifflin Company. All rights reserved.

shange, ntozake. Excerpt from "lady in red" is reprinted with the permission of Scribner, a Division of Simon & Schuster, Inc., from COLORED GIRLS WHO HAVE CONSIDERED SUICIDE/WHEN THE RAINBOW IS ENUF by ntozke shange. Copyright © 1975, 1976, 1977 by ntozake shange. Excerpt from "Unrecovered Losses/Black Theater Traditions" in THREE PIECES, pp. xi–xiii. Copyright © 1981 by ntozake shange. Reprinted by permission of St. Martin's Press, Inc., New York, NY.

INDEX OF AUTHORS, TITLES, AND FIRST LINES

FICTION

Chinua Achebe
Aesop
Julia Alvarez
Sherwood Anderson
Margaret Atwood
Toni Cade Bambara
Donald Barthelme
Ann Beattie
Ambrose Bierce
Raymond Carver
Willa Cather
John Cheever
Anton Chekhov
Frank Chin
Kate Chopin
Sandra Cisneros
Joseph Conrad
Stephen Crane
Paul Laurence Dunbar
Ralph Ellison
Louise Erdrich
William Faulkner
Larry Fondation
Charlotte Perkins Gilman
Bret Harte
Nathaniel Hawthorne
Ernest Hemingway
Shirley Jackson
Sarah Orne Jewett
James Joyce
Franz Kafka
David Michael Kaplan
Jamaica Kincaid
D. H. Lawrence
Ursula K. Le Guin
Doris Lessing
Jack London
Bernard Malamud
Gabriel García Márquez
Bobbie Ann Mason
Guy de Maupassant
Yukio Mishima
Toni Morrison
Bharati Mukherjee
Alice Munro

Tim O'Brien
Flannery O'Connor
Joyce Carol Oates
Tillie Olsen
Grace Paley
Dorothy Parker
Edgar Allan Poe
Katherine Anne Porter
Mary Robison
Leslie Marmon Silko
John Steinbeck
Donald Sutherland
Amy Tan
Anne Tyler
Guadalupe Valdés
Luisa Valenzuela
Alice Walker
Eudora Welty
Edith Wharton
Tobias Wolff

POETRY

Matthew Arnold
John Ashbery
Margaret Atwood
W.H. Auden
Basho
Aphra Behn
Bruce Bennett
Wendell Berry
John Berryman
Elizabeth Bishop
William Blake
Louise Bogan
Arna Bontemps
Kay Boyle
Anne Bradstreet
Gwendolyn Brooks
Christopher Buckley
Charles Bukowski
Robert Burns
Olga Cabral
Rosemary Catacalos
Lorna Dee Cervantes
Kawai Chigetsu-Ni
Lucille Clifton

Judith Ortiz Cofer
Samuel Coleridge
William Cowper
Stephen Crane
Robert Creeley
E.E. Cummings
Ann Darr
Juana Inés de la Cruz
Salvador Jacinto Polo de Medina
Christine De Pisan
Alison Hawthorne Deming
Reuel Denney
Countess of Dia
Emily Dickinson
Chitra Divakaruni
John Donne
H.D. Doolittle
Rita Dove
Richard Eberhart
T.S. Eliot
Louise Erdrich
Martín Espada
Lawrence Ferlinghetti
Nelle Fertig
Donald Finkel
Richard Foerster
Robert Frost
Nan Fry
Allen Ginsberg
Dana Gioia
Louise Glück
Judy Grahn
Donald Hall
Thomas Hardy
Joy Harjo
Jeffrey Harrison
Robert Hass
Robert Hayden
Seamus Heaney
John Heaviside
George Herbert
Calvin Hernton
Robert Herrick
Edward Hirsch
Gerard Manley Hopkins
Lady Horikawa
A.E. Housman
Langston Hughes